PRESENTED

TO _____

FROM _____

DATE _____

I will praise the LORD at all times.
    I will constantly speak his praises.
I will boast only in the LORD;
    let all who are helpless take heart.
Come, let us tell of the LORD's greatness;
    let us exalt his name together.

I prayed to the LORD, and he answered me.
    He freed me from all my fears.
Those who look to him for help will be radiant with joy;
    no shadow of shame will darken their faces.

        — *PSALM 34:1-5*

GOD,
GRANT ME
THE SERENITY
TO ACCEPT THE THINGS
I CANNOT CHANGE,
THE COURAGE TO CHANGE
THE THINGS I CAN,
AND THE WISDOM
TO KNOW THE
DIFFERENCE.
AMEN

THE LIFE RECOVERY® BIBLE

New Living Translation®

SECOND EDITION

Tyndale House Publishers, Inc.
Carol Stream, Illinois

Visit Tyndale online at www.newlivingtranslation.com and www.tyndale.com.

The Life Recovery Bible, copyright © 1998 by Tyndale House Publishers, Inc., Carol Stream, Illinois 60188. All rights reserved.

Notes and Bible helps copyright © 1998 by Stephen Arterburn and David Stoop. All rights reserved.

Cover design by Koechel Peterson & Associates. All rights reserved.

Published in association with the literary agency of Alive Communications, Inc., 7680 Goddard Street, Suite 200, Colorado Springs, CO 80920, www.alivecommunications.com.

The Life Recovery Bible is an edition of the *Holy Bible,* New Living Translation.

Holy Bible, New Living Translation, copyright © 1996, 2004, 2007, 2013 by Tyndale House Foundation. All rights reserved.

ISBN 978-1-4143-0962-0 Hardcover
ISBN 978-1-4143-0961-3 Softcover

Printed in the United States of America

18 17 16 15 14 13
13 12 11 10   9   8

Tyndale House Publishers and Wycliffe Bible Translators share the vision for an understandable, accurate translation of the Bible for every person in the world. Each sale of the *Holy Bible,* New Living Translation, benefits Wycliffe Bible Translators. Wycliffe is working with partners around the world to accomplish Vision 2025—an initiative to start a Bible translation program in every language group that needs it by the year 2025.

CONTENTS

THE BOOKS OF THE BIBLE

ALPHABETICAL LISTING OF BIBLE BOOKS

THE BIBLE is the greatest book on recovery ever written. In its pages we see God set out a plan for the recovery of his broken people and creation. We meet numerous individuals whose hurting lives are restored through the wisdom and power of God. We meet the God who is waiting with arms outstretched for all of us to turn back to him, seek his will, and recover the wonderful life he has for each of us.

Many of us are just waking up to the fact that recovery is an essential part of life for everyone. It is the simple but challenging process of daily seeking God's will for our life instead of demanding to go our own way. Recovery is letting God do for us what we cannot do for ourselves while also taking the steps necessary to draw closer to our Creator and Redeemer. It is allowing God to heal our wounded soul so we can help others in the process of healing. All of us need to take part in this process; it is an inherent part of being human.

Let us set out together on the journey toward healing and newfound strength—not strength found within ourselves, but strength found through trusting God and allowing him to direct our decisions and plans. This journey will take us through the Twelve Steps and other materials designed to help us focus on the provisions our powerful God offers for recovery. *The Life Recovery Bible* will enrich our experience and expand our understanding of the God who loves us and sent his Son to die that we might be made whole.

Without God there is no recovery, only disappointing substitutions and repeated failure. We pray that the resources within these pages will help us all better understand who God is and how he wants to heal our brokenness and set us on the path toward wholeness.

It's Not All Your Fault.

When we struggle with any problem, it's easy to think it's our fault. But it's never solely our fault. Things in our families often happen to us because of patterns of behavior in other family members that are beyond our control. Life in a family can get chaotic, even overwhelming. Or sometimes the other people in our families may be so absent from any relationships that we feel we are either unwelcome or invisible to them. We may think there is something wrong with us, or that we have no willpower, or that we don't even want to stop our behaviors. It may be that what started as a way for us to cope with pain has now become the problem.

Sometimes the hurt and pain inside of us become so deep that we feel we need to do something to ease those feelings. Sometimes we try to ease the pain through self-medication. We begin to drink beer, wine, or some hard liquor. At first, we get this mellow feeling that helps us forget what is causing our pain. But eventually it wears off, and we feel the pain again. Or we may try to numb our pain by turning to other behaviors that eventually become destructive.

Here's What You Need to Know:

There are two types of addictions one can develop. One type is called a "chemical addiction." A person takes into his or her body either alcohol or some other drug in order to simply feel different. Not everyone can develop a chemical addiction to alcohol, but other drugs, which can be highly addictive, have the potential to capture everyone who uses them.

If you begin to use alcohol to ease your pain, here are some danger signs—signs that indicate you may be susceptible to becoming addicted to alcohol. People who develop serious alcohol issues are often able to drink a lot without it having much of an effect on them. They seem to be able to handle their drinking. Another danger sign is what is called "binge" drinking. A lot of alcohol is consumed in, say, a weekend or an evening, but then that person doesn't drink again for several weeks. They point to this to prove to themselves they don't have a dependency problem with alcohol, but they do. Another danger sign is that other people in our family are alcoholics. This means there is a much higher probability of us becoming addicted to alcohol. Watch for these signs—they spell trouble.

Becoming addicted to a drug can start innocently. You may use drugs in order to fit in with friends, not knowing how powerfully addictive they are. Sometimes, people get a legitimate prescription for pain medication from a doctor. It helps for a while, but then its effect wears off and soon more and more is needed. Some people may end up actually getting prescription medications on the street, as well as through a doctor. Others try to self-medicate by using illegal drugs. It begins as a way to escape the pain, but the need for more can easily become a compulsion and then an addiction. The user feels trapped and gradually gets loaded down with shame and guilt.

The other type of addiction is called "process addiction." Here one uses less obvious methods to try to handle their emotional pain. These are compulsive behaviors that are related to a process, not to particular substances like drugs or alcohol. These behaviors start out in small ways and are seemingly innocent. Some people may think they are in control of these behaviors, but when they try to stop them, they realize the repetitive behavior controls them.

Gambling or spending money may be a way we try to deal with our problems. We may find that we are always short of money, and are drawn to the excitement of gambling with its random rewards. Even video games may become our escape from a painful reality. Check it out—decide to not play any video games, do any online gambling, or spend any money for thirty days and see how uncomfortable it is. Each of these activities can become a process addiction.

Process addictions involving eating can be a big issue. Eating is one of the few things we think we can always control. But there are three ways eating can be a problem. One is to overeat. People who struggle with overeating look at food as a source of comfort. When they are in emotional pain, they turn to food in order to "feel good" again. Another eating problem is binge eating, and then having to purge what is overeaten. And then there is the very serious eating disorder of those who over-control their eating habits and chronically lose weight, yet still think they are fat. This can lead to serious, life-threatening physical problems.

Using the Internet can become a problem that leads to devastating addictions. It may be that we are always searching the web, which keeps us living in an unreal world. Or our search may involve pornography. Most think that viewing pornography is something limited to men, but it can be just as big of a problem for women. Research says that the age group most commonly looking at pornography on the Internet is young people—as young as eleven years old. When you start to view pornography early, it changes your brain, which in turn has devastating effects on all of your relationships.

You may know of someone who tries to get rid of their emotional pain by inflicting physical pain on themselves. They usually do this by cutting themselves. The reasons for this are complex, but basically it is a way to feel something different—physical instead of emotional pain—and it is a way for them to feel alive. If they bleed a little, they know they are still here—that they are not invisible. This can become a very serious addiction.

These are some of the ways we may attempt to handle life's problems. We can get caught up in one of these chemical or process addictions and then get angry with ourselves because we can't stop. It's not all our fault, but the answer is always to take responsibility for the choices we make. What you do in response to these problems determines the course of your life, whether you know it or not. You are in control of your choices right now. If you don't know your way around this book, start with Step One, on page 25. It's time now to make the bold move to reclaim your life!

THE TWELVE STEPS

1. We admitted that we were powerless over our problems—that our lives had become unmanageable.
2. We came to believe that a Power greater than ourselves could restore us to sanity.
3. We made a decision to turn our wills and our lives over to the care of God.
4. We made a searching and fearless moral inventory of ourselves.
5. We admitted to God, to ourselves, and to another human being the exact nature of our wrongs.
6. We were entirely ready to have God remove all these defects of character.
7. We humbly asked God to remove our shortcomings.
8. We made a list of all persons we had harmed and became willing to make amends to them all.
9. We made direct amends to such people wherever possible, except when to do so would injure them or others.
10. We continued to take personal inventory, and when we were wrong, promptly admitted it.
11. We sought through prayer and meditation to improve our conscious contact with God, praying only for knowledge of His will for us and the power to carry that out.
12. Having had a spiritual awakening as the result of these steps, we tried to carry this message to others and to practice these principles in all our affairs.

The Twelve Steps used in the Twelve Steps devotional reading plan in this Bible have been adapted from the Twelve Steps of Alcoholics Anonymous.

THE TWELVE STEPS OF ALCOHOLICS ANONYMOUS

1. We admitted we were powerless over alcohol—that our lives had become unmanageable.
2. Came to believe that a Power greater than ourselves could restore us to sanity.
3. Made a decision to turn our will and our lives over to the care of God *as we understood Him.*
4. Made a searching and fearless moral inventory of ourselves.
5. Admitted to God, to ourselves and to another human being the exact nature of our wrongs.
6. Were entirely ready to have God remove all these defects of character.
7. Humbly asked Him to remove our shortcomings.
8. Made a list of all persons we had harmed and became willing to make amends to them all.
9. Made direct amends to such people wherever possible, except when to do so would injure them or others.
10. Continued to take personal inventory and when we were wrong promptly admitted it.
11. Sought through prayer and meditation to improve our conscious contact with God, *as we understood Him,* praying only for knowledge of His will for us and the power to carry that out.
12. Having had a spiritual awakening as the result of these steps, we tried to carry this message to alcoholics, and to practice these principles in all our affairs.

The Twelve Steps are reprinted and adapted with permission of Alcoholics Anonymous World Services, Inc. Permission to reprint and adapt the Twelve Steps does not mean that AA has reviewed or approved the contents of this publication, nor that AA agrees with the views expressed herein. AA is a program of recovery from alcoholism—use of the Twelve Steps in connection with programs and activities which are patterned after AA, but which address other problems, does not imply otherwise.

THE TWELVE STEPS AND SCRIPTURE

The 12 Steps have long been of great help to people in recovery. Much of their power comes from the fact that they capture principles clearly revealed in the Bible. The following page lists the 12 Steps and connects them to corresponding Scriptures that support them. This will help readers familiar with the 12 Steps to discover the true source of their wisdom—the very word of God.

STEP 1: We admitted that we were powerless over our dependencies—that our lives had become unmanageable.
"I know that nothing good lives in me. . . . I want to do what is right, but I can't" (Romans 7:18; see also John 8:31-36; Romans 7:14-25).

STEP 2: We came to believe that a Power greater than ourselves could restore us to sanity.
"God is working in you, giving you the desire and the power to do what pleases him" (Philippians 2:13; see also Romans 4:6-8; Ephesians 1:6-8; Colossians 1:21-22; Hebrews 11:1-10).

STEP 3: We made a decision to turn our wills and our lives over to the care of God.
"Dear brothers and sisters, I plead with you to give your bodies to God because of all he has done for you. Let them be a living and holy sacrifice—the kind he will find acceptable" (Romans 12:1; see also Matthew 11:28-30; Mark 10:14-16; James 4:7-10).

STEP 4: We made a searching and fearless moral inventory of ourselves.
"Let us test and examine our ways. Let us turn back to the Lord" (Lamentations 3:40; see also Matthew 7:1-5; 2 Corinthians 7:8-10).

STEP 5: We admitted to God, to ourselves, and to another human being the exact nature of our wrongs.
"Confess your sins to each other and pray for each other so that you may be healed" (James 5:16; see also Psalms 32:1-5; 51:1-3; 1 John 1:2-6).

STEP 6: We were entirely ready to have God remove all these defects of character. *"Humble yourselves before the Lord, and he will lift you up in honor"* (James 4:10; see also Romans 6:5-11; Philippians 3:12-14).

STEP 7: We humbly asked God to remove our shortcomings.
"If we confess our sins to him, he is faithful and just to forgive us our sins and to cleanse us from all wickedness" (1 John 1:9; see also Luke 18:9-14; 1 John 5:13-15).

STEP 8: We made a list of all the persons we had harmed and became willing to make amends to them all.
"Do to others as you would like them to do to you" (Luke 6:31; see also Colossians 3:12-15; 1 John 3:10-20).

STEP 9: We made direct amends to such people wherever possible, except when to do so would injure them or others.
"If you are presenting a sacrifice at the altar and . . . someone has something against you, leave your sacrifice there at the altar. Go and be reconciled to that person. Then come and offer your sacrifice to God" (Matthew 5:23-24; see also Luke 19:1-10; 1 Peter 2:21-25).

STEP 10: We continued to take personal inventory, and when we were wrong, promptly admitted it.
"If you think you are standing strong, be careful not to fall" (1 Corinthians 10:12; see also Romans 5:3-6; 2 Timothy 2:1-7; 1 John 1:8-10).

STEP 11: We sought through prayer and meditation to improve our conscious contact with God, praying only for knowledge of His will for us and the power to carry that out.
"Devote yourselves to prayer with an alert mind and a thankful heart" (Colossians 4:2; see also Isaiah 40:28-31; 1 Timothy 4:7-8).

STEP 12: Having had a spiritual awakening as the result of these steps, we tried to carry this message to others and to practice these principles in all our affairs.
"Dear brothers and sisters, if another believer is overcome by some sin, you who are godly should gently and humbly help that person back onto the right path. And be careful not to fall into the same temptation yourself" (Galatians 6:1; see also Isaiah 61:1-3; Titus 3:3-7; 1 Peter 4:1-5).

THE TWELVE LAWS OF LIFE RECOVERY

These laws highlight irrefutable truths that you will discover in yourself as you experience recovery while following the Twelve Steps. They provide evidence of the progress you have made and highlight places where growth is still needed. As you experience these laws, you will find—perhaps to your surprise—that the laws of life recovery often give back what they initially seemed to take away.

1. Powerlessness will result in STRENGTH.
We struggle with the feeling of powerlessness because it feels so much like we are helpless. But God often works healing in our lives through what to us is weakness. It is paradoxical that as we experience recovery in our lives, we will find there is great strength in recognizing our powerlessness.

"This foolish plan of God is wiser than the wisest of human plans, and God's weakness is stronger than the greatest of human strength." (1 Corinthians 1:25, page 1457)

2. Humility will result in HONOR.
In our journey of life recovery, it is easy to take pride in the positive changes we are making in our lives. But in God's plan, honor is not something we should seek. It is something we receive as we learn to live in humility. Humility is the path to being honored by God and by others.

"Humble yourselves before the Lord, and he will lift you up in honor." (James 4:10, page 1605)

3. Connection will result in LOVE.
We all long to be loved, but we overlook the fact that being loved always takes place in an emotionally connected relationship. Prior to our recovery, we lived in emotional isolation from others. But God designed us for connection—for relationship. That's the only context in which we can experience true love.

"Let us continue to love one another, for love comes from God. Anyone who loves is a child of God and knows God. But anyone who does not love does not know God, for God is love. . . . Dear friends, since God loved us that much, we surely ought to love each other. No one has ever seen God. But if we love each other, God lives in us, and his love is brought to full expression in us." (1 John 4:7-8, 11-12, page 1632)

4. Willingness will result in GROWTH.
There is the childlike part within all of us that wants to say, "I can do it on my own," and "I can do it my way." But true recovery in our lives begins when we are willing to do it God's way. That's not easy, but without a willingness to be open to God's plan, we will limit our growth. It all begins with a willing and open heart.

"Work willingly at whatever you do, as though you were working for the Lord rather than for people." (Colossians 3:23, page 1535)

5. Sacrifice will result in FULFILLMENT.
Before we started on our recovery journey, it was easy to think and act as if fulfillment came from getting, or from what we owned. But again, God's ways are mysterious and not our ways. We learn in our recovery that sacrifice—doing good and sharing with others, not getting—is the true path to fulfillment.

"And don't forget to do good and to share with those in need. These are the sacrifices that please God." (Hebrews 13:16, page 1595)

6. Faith will result in HOPE.
In God's plan for our recovery, problems and trials are a part of the path that leads to a hope that will not disappoint us. It is all in how we handle our problems and trials. When we endure the hard stuff, we build strength of character, which then builds our faith. It is that faith which leads to a hope built on knowing we are loved by God.

"We can rejoice, too, when we run into problems and trials, for we know that they help us develop endurance. And endurance develops strength of character, and character strengthens our confident hope of salvation. And this hope will not lead to disappointment. For we know how dearly God loves us, because he has given us the Holy Spirit to fill our hearts with his love." (Romans 5:3-5, page 1437)

7. Surrender will result in VICTORY.

James describes surrendering as being "willing to yield to others." Here willingness is coupled with surrendering. When we truly surrender ourselves, we are saying to God, "Your will, not mine." And a truly surrendered life is a life lived out as a celebration of our victory.

> "But the wisdom from above is first of all pure. It is also peace loving, gentle at all times, and willing to yield to others. It is full of mercy and the fruit of good deeds. It shows no favoritism and is always sincere." (James 3:17, page 1605)

8. Service will result in REWARD.

Our acts of service are not to be done in order to gain a reward. They are done out of obedience to what we are learning as we are equipped to do the work of ministry. We are God's hands, feet, and mouth. As we are faithful in our service, the reward is the peace and satisfaction that comes as the result of our obedience.

> "Their responsibility is to equip God's people to do his work and build up the church, the body of Christ." (Ephesians 4:12, page 1514)

9. Forgiveness results in FREEDOM.

We are called to be forgiving people. When we hold a grudge, we are in bondage to the person we refuse to forgive. We forget that forgiveness involves only us, and that the person we need to forgive really isn't part of the process. So there is no real excuse for not being obedient and forgiving others as we have been forgiven by God.

> "You were dead because of your sins and because your sinful nature was not yet cut away. Then God made you alive with Christ, for he forgave all our sins. He canceled the record of the charges against us and took it away by nailing it to the cross." (Colossians 2:13-14, page 1533)

10. Confession will result in HEALING.

You may have wondered why it is so important to confess your inventory to another person as part of your recovery. Healing comes as a result of confessing. We experience something powerful when we confess our shortcomings and failures not only to God but also to another person.

> "Confess your sins to each other and pray for each other so that you may be healed. The earnest prayer of a righteous person has great power and produces wonderful results." (James 5:16, page 1607)

11. Restitution will result in CLOSURE.

Not all acts of restitution are financial repayments, although that can be a very effective way in some circumstances to make restitution. But we need also to make restitution for emotional hurts, or for other non-financial issues. Until we explore ways to make all kinds of restitution, we will struggle with moving on and experiencing closure.

> "They must confess their sin and make full restitution for what they have done, adding an additional 20 percent and returning it to the person who was wronged." (Numbers 5:7, page 177)

12. Responsibility will result in SECURITY.

This is one of the most obvious results of our experiencing life recovery. We have not only made restitution; we have also begun to act responsibly in all areas of our lives. Responsibility is living up to our part of life, not blaming or expecting someone else to make up for our lack. We experience a genuine sense of security when we are doing our part—living responsibly in our everyday lives.

> "Then God said to Abraham, 'Your responsibility is to obey the terms of the covenant. You and all your descendants have this continual responsibility. This is the covenant that you and your descendants must keep.'" (Genesis 17:9-10, page 25)

THE TWELVE MISSTEPS OF LIFE RECOVERY

These false thoughts and assumptions have derailed many in their recovery, and some reflect the mistaken thinking of people sincerely trying to do things God's way. Awareness is the first step in avoiding these common pitfalls.

1. "I can quit tomorrow."

Tomorrow has no power or strength to initiate change into your life. Today—right now—is where the power is! Waiting even one more day is a decision to stay on a path that has proven to be destructive.

> "How do you know what your life will be like tomorrow? Your life is like the morning fog—it's here a little while, then it's gone. . . . Remember, it is sin to know what you ought to do and then not do it." (James 4:14, 17, page 1606)

2. "I can handle it by just trying harder or having more willpower."

Under your own strength you have lived a life that has led to disappointment for you and for those who care about you. Under your own strength you have found only momentary victory or short-term progress. Under God's strength you will experience transforming power that will last forever.

> "But those who trust in the LORD will find new strength. They will soar high on wings like eagles. They will run and not grow weary. They will walk and not faint." (Isaiah 40:31, page 892)

3. "Turning my life over to Christ is the only step I need."

Turning your life over to Christ and repenting of your sins is a huge first step. Surrendering to him is the most important step. But it is still just the beginning. It does not instantly build your character or make you mature in your faith. Working through the steps based on God's Word will lead you to a better place of maturity, wisdom, and transformed character.

> "Solid food is for those who are mature, who through training have the skill to recognize the difference between right and wrong. So let us stop going over the basic teachings about Christ again and again. Let us go on instead and become mature in our understanding." (Hebrews 5:14–6:1, page 1582)

4. "Twelve Step groups that don't talk about Jesus aren't worth my time."

A recovery group that focuses on Christ is helpful for anyone's recovery, but a group like that may not exist anywhere near you. And if we segregate ourselves from others who don't know Christ, they will not hear the message of hope and restoration that we have. You can be a light to another who is walking in darkness.

> "I have come as a light to shine in this dark world, so that all who put their trust in me will no longer remain in the dark." (John 12:46, page 1363)

5. "While recovery might be good for some, it just isn't right for me."

If you have made a decision to surrender your life and your problem to God, you have made a very bold move. But your enemy will be the tendency to drift—to move away from surrender and to compromise, jeopardizing the progress you've made. Recovery prevents you from drifting, providing a path to growth and maturity and the support you need to succeed.

> "But you must continue to believe this truth and stand firmly in it. Don't drift away from the assurance you received when you heard the Good News." (Colossians 1:23, page 1532)

6. "If I follow the Bible, I don't really need to work the Twelve Steps."

Working the Twelve Steps is following the Bible. It is a path through the Bible designed specifically for those who used to have a problem but whose problem now has them. It is a path of hope, healing, and restoration based on God's truth that will totally change the way you think.

> "Don't copy the behavior and customs of this world, but let God transform you into a new person by changing the way you think. Then you will learn to know God's will for you, which is good and pleasing and perfect." (Romans 12:2, page 1447)

7. "Since I'm accountable to God, I don't need a sponsor."
You certainly are accountable to God, but God has also instructed us to be in healthy and supportive relationships with others. You will grow much stronger and more quickly if you have someone to guide you, encourage you, and hold you accountable.

> "As iron sharpens iron, so a friend sharpens a friend." (Proverbs 27:17, page 816)

8. "Since God has forgiven me, I don't need to go back to rehash what I've done."
Yes, God has forgiven you if you have confessed and changed your ways. But he clearly instructs us to not stop with him. When we open up to someone else, it connects us, keeps us humble and grounded in reality, and leads to healing.

> "Confess your sins to each other and pray for each other so that you may be healed. The earnest prayer of a righteous person has great power and produces wonderful results." (James 5:16, page 1607)

9. "Since Jesus would want me to help my old friends, I don't need to change where I go or whom I hang out with."
The Bible is clear that we need to run from people and places that would tempt us to fall back into our old ways. Some call it changing playmates and playgrounds. But not only do we need time away from temptations so we can grow, we also need to seek out those who are on the same path. There will be plenty of time to reach out to those who need your help once you have established your own long-term recovery.

> "Run from anything that stimulates youthful lusts. Instead, pursue righteous living, faithfulness, love, and peace. Enjoy the companionship of those who call on the Lord with pure hearts." (2 Timothy 2:22, page 1562)

10. "Though I can forgive most things, some things are just beyond forgiveness."
There are some things that are so damaging that they may seem to be beyond forgiveness. But forgiveness does not excuse what someone has done or minimize its impact. Forgiveness frees you from having to live in the pain any longer. Some say the most dangerous thing we can possess is justifiable resentment. It does nothing to the other person, but it robs you of the life of freedom God wants for you.

> "Get rid of all bitterness, rage, anger, harsh words, and slander, as well as all types of evil behavior. Instead, be kind to each other, tenderhearted, forgiving one another, just as God through Christ has forgiven you." (Ephesians 4:31-32, page 1515)

11. "Since I'm involved in recovery, I don't need additional counseling or medication."
When we fully surrender to God, we become willing to do whatever it takes to recover. You may not think you need additional help, but someone you love may need you to need it. Working through your pride and reaching out for additional help, like starting recovery, is never a sign of weakness, but a sign of the strength found in humility.

> "Pride leads to disgrace, but with humility comes wisdom." (Proverbs 11:2, page 798)

12. "After making good progress in my recovery, I can start using again in moderation."
If you are on a solid recovery path, the last thing you want to do is try to control what has come to control you. The desire to fall back into it and try it again indicates that you need additional step work, meetings, and other support. Don't go back and relive the hurt and pain you experienced earlier in life.

> "As a dog returns to its vomit, so a fool repeats his foolishness." (Proverbs 26:11, page 815)

THE TWELVE GIFTS OF LIFE RECOVERY

These twelve attributes are not just results or outcomes for people in recovery, but truly gifts from God. They show that recovery doesn't merely provide escape from a destructive problem. It also points toward the possibility of a new and exceptional life.

1. Hope—"We can rejoice, too, when we run into problems and trials, for we know that they help us develop endurance. And endurance develops strength of character, and character strengthens our confident hope of salvation. And this hope will not lead to disappointment. For we know how dearly God loves us, because he has given us the Holy Spirit to fill our hearts with his love" (Romans 5:3-5, page 1437).

2. Power—"For I can do everything through Christ, who gives me strength" (Philippians 4:13, page 1526). "For God has not given us a spirit of fear and timidity, but of power, love, and self-discipline" (2 Timothy 1:7, page 1561).

3. Character—"But the Holy Spirit produces this kind of fruit in our lives: love, joy, peace, patience, kindness, goodness, faithfulness, gentleness, and self-control. There is no law against these things!" (Galatians 5:22-23, page 1505).

4. Clarity—"Now we see things imperfectly, like puzzling reflections in a mirror, but then we will see everything with perfect clarity" (1 Corinthians 13:12, page 1472).

5. Security—"Fear of the LORD leads to life, bringing security and protection from harm" (Proverbs 19:23, page 807). "If God is for us, who can ever be against us? Since he did not spare even his own Son but gave him up for us all, won't he also give us everything else?" (Romans 8:31-32, page 1442).

6. Abundance—"And this same God who takes care of me will supply all your needs from his glorious riches, which have been given to us in Christ Jesus" (Philippians 4:19, page 1526).

7. Wisdom—"Fear of the LORD is the foundation of wisdom. Knowledge of the Holy One results in good judgment" (Proverbs 9:10, page 796). "If you need wisdom, ask our generous God, and he will give it to you. He will not rebuke you for asking" (James 1:5, page 1600).

8. Self-Control—"But you are not controlled by your sinful nature. You are controlled by the Spirit if you have the Spirit of God living in you" (Romans 8:9, page 1441). "But the Holy Spirit produces . . . self-control" (Galatians 5:22-23, page 1505).

9. Freedom—"So Christ has truly set us free. Now make sure that you stay free, and don't get tied up again in slavery to the law" (Galatians 5:1, page 1504).

10. Happiness—"Make me walk along the path of your commands, for that is where my happiness is found" (Psalm 119:35, page 764). "The hopes of the godly result in happiness, but the expectations of the wicked come to nothing" (Proverbs 10:2, page 796).

11. Serenity—"I am convinced that nothing can ever separate us from God's love. Neither death nor life, neither angels nor demons, neither our fears for today nor our worries about tomorrow—not even the powers of hell can separate us from God's love" (Romans 8:38, page 1442).

12. Peace—"I am leaving you with a gift—peace of mind and heart. And the peace I give is a gift the world cannot give. So don't be troubled or afraid" (John 14:27, page 1366).

USER'S GUIDE

THE *HOLY BIBLE* is a book about recovery. It records how the world began and how God created it to be good. Then it tells us about the beginning of sin—about the first time people decided to reject God's plan. It spells out the fatal consequences that result from rejecting God's program. But the Bible doesn't leave us in despair. It reveals a plan for recovery and the source of the power to accomplish it. It provides us with the only pathway to wholeness—God's program for reconciliation and healing.

Each feature in *The Life Recovery Bible* leads readers to the powerful resources for recovery found in the Holy Scriptures:

DEVOTIONAL READING PLANS

tyndal.es/lrbusersguide

Each devotional is set near the Scripture it comments on and directs the reader to the next devotional in the reading chain. To get a bird's-eye view of each of these reading plans, turn to the indexes at the back of this Bible.

- The **Twelve Step Devotional Reading Plan** includes eighty-four Bible-based devotionals built around the Twelve Steps. Videos introducing the 12 steps are linked to the MS Tags embedded in the first devotion for each step. A tag reader is available at: http://tag.microsoft.com/consumer/index.aspx
  To begin this reading plan, turn to page 25.
- The **Recovery Principle Devotional Reading Plan** is composed of fifty-six Bible-based devotionals shaped around principles important in the recovery process.
  To begin this reading plan, turn to page 5.
- The **Serenity Prayer Devotional Reading Plan** is made up of twenty-nine Bible-based devotionals related to the Serenity Prayer.
  To begin this reading plan, turn to page 27.

RECOVERY PROFILES

In this feature sixty individuals and relationships are profiled, and important recovery lessons are drawn from their lives. For a quick view of the profiles included, see the Index to Recovery Profiles on page 1716.

INTRODUCTORY MATERIAL FOR BIBLE BOOKS

Each book of the Bible is preceded by a number of helpful features.
- **Book Introductions** present the content and themes from the standpoint of recovery.
- **The Big Picture** gives a panoramic view of the book in outline form.
- **The Bottom Line** provides vital historical information for the book.
- **Recovery Themes** present and discuss important themes for people in recovery.

RECOVERY COMMENTARY NOTES

The Bible text is supported by numerous **Recovery Notes** that pinpoint passages and thoughts important to recovery. The notes appear at the foot of each page and are indexed in the Life Recovery Topical Index beginning on page 1673.
- Additional commentary material is provided in the **Recovery Reflections** that follow many of the Bible books. The notes are arranged topically. The topics discussed in this feature are indexed in the Index to Recovery Reflections on page 1721.

INDEXES

The **Topical Bible Verse Finder** at the front of this Bible lists topics that concern people who are trying to live by God's wisdom and connects those topics to helpful Bible verses. It's a great tool for finding out what God has to say about your everyday concerns.

The **Life Recovery Topical Index** at the back guides the reader to the important notes, profiles, devotionals, and recovery themes related to more than a hundred terms important to issues in the recovery process.
- The **Index to Recovery Profiles** alphabetically lists and locates the sixty Recovery Profiles that appear in this Bible.
- The **Index to Twelve Step Devotionals** lists and locates the eighty-four Twelve Step devotionals.
- The **Index to Recovery Principle Devotionals** lists and locates the fifty-six Recovery Principle devotionals.
- The **Index to Serenity Prayer Devotionals** lists and locates the twenty-nine Serenity Prayer devotionals.
- The **Index to Recovery Reflections** lists and locates the various topics discussed in the Reflections feature of this Bible.

TOPICAL BIBLE VERSE FINDER

ABORTION
God cares for the unborn (Exodus 21:22-25)
. . . page 104

We should protect the helpless (Psalm 82:3-4)
. . . page 738

Children are from God (Psalm 127:3)
. . . page 770

God forms every child (Psalm 139:13-16)
. . . page 775

God plans the future of every child (Jeremiah
1:5) . . . page 930

ABUSE
God cares about minorities (Exodus 22:21)
. . . page 106

God protects those who are helpless (Psalm 12:5)
. . . page 687

Jesus was abused (Matthew 26:67-68)
. . . page 1240

Abuse has no place in healthy families
(Ephesians 5:21–6:4) . . . page 1516

ACCOUNTABILITY
God will judge our work (2 Chronicles 19:5-10)
. . . page 561

Sin has consequences (Ezekiel 18:20)
. . . page 1031

God will hold us accountable for our sin (Ezekiel
18:30) . . . page 1032

We are accountable for every word that we speak
(Matthew 12:36) . . . page 1215

Confronting others should be done in private
(Matthew 18:15) . . . page 1226

We should hold each other accountable (Luke
17:3) . . . page 1320

We are accountable for what we believe (John
3:18) . . . page 1344

God holds Christians accountable (Romans
14:11-12) . . . page 1450

God will reward Christians for their good deeds
(1 Corinthians 3:8) . . . page 1459

God will examine our actions (2 Corinthians
5:10) . . . page 1485

ACCUSATIONS
Satan accuses God's people of doing wrong
(Zechariah 3:1) . . . page 1176

Jesus was falsely accused (Matthew 26:59-60)
. . . page 1239

Christians' sins are forgiven (Colossians 1:22)
. . . page 1532

Accusations must come from more than one
person (1 Timothy 5:19) . . . page 1556

Satan is known as the Accuser (Revelation 12:10)
. . . page 1660

ADOPTION, SPIRITUAL
God helps his children grow (Deuteronomy 8:5)
. . . page 232

God's children should obey him (Deuteronomy
26:18) . . . page 250

God disciplines his children (2 Samuel 7:14)
. . . page 396

Do not despise God's discipline (Proverbs
3:11-12) . . . page 790

God is our Father (Matthew 6:9) . . . page 1204

Christians are God's children (John 1:12)
. . . page 1341

God's Spirit leads his children (Romans 8:14-17)
. . . page 1442

Christians should be separate from the world
(2 Corinthians 6:17-18) . . . page 1487

All of God's children are equal in God's eyes
(Galatians 3:28) . . . page 1502

God's children will receive a spiritual inheritance
(Galatians 4:4-7) . . . page 1503

God chose us to be his children (Ephesians
1:4-5) . . . page 1510

Jesus is our spiritual brother (Hebrews 2:11)
. . . page 1580

ADULTERY
God forbids adultery (Exodus 20:14) . . . page 102

Adultery has consequences (Proverbs 6:26)
. . . page 794

Adultery is foolish (Proverbs 6:32) . . . page 794

Adultery is disgusting to God (Jeremiah 7:9-10)
. . . page 941

God considers lust as sinful as adultery (Matthew
5:27-28) . . . page 1203

Divorce often leads to adultery (Mark 10:11-12)
. . . page 1268

God can forgive the adulterer (John 8:1-11)
. . . page 1353

ADVICE
Leaders should consider the advice of others
(Exodus 18:13-26) . . . page 100

Older people often give wise advice (1 Kings
12:1-11) . . . page 444

Stay away from people who give wicked advice
(Psalm 1:1) . . . page 680

God's advice is best (Psalm 73:24) . . . page 730

Wise people seek advice (Proverbs 1:5)
. . . page 786

Advice helps provide success (Proverbs 11:14)
. . . page 798

Foolish people do not listen to advice (Proverbs
12:15) . . . page 799

Give advice to those in need (1 Thessalonians
5:14) . . . page 1542

ALCOHOL (see also Drinking)

Being controlled by alcohol is foolish (Proverbs 20:1) . . . *page 807*

Becoming drunk is sin (Romans 13:13-14) . . . *page 1450*

God hates drunkenness (Galatians 5:19-21) . . . *page 1505*

Church leaders should not be controlled by alcohol (Titus 1:7) . . . *page 1569*

ANGELS

Angels carry out God's judgment (2 Samuel 24:16-17) . . . *page 421*

Angels serve God (Psalm 103:21) . . . *page 750*

Angels praise God (Psalm 148:2) . . . *page 780*

Angels are messengers (Daniel 4:17) . . . *page 1081*

Angels protect God's people (Daniel 6:22) . . . *page 1085*

Angels do not marry (Matthew 22:30) . . . *page 1232*

Angels do not die (Luke 20:36) . . . *page 1327*

Angels will be judged by people (1 Corinthians 6:3) . . . *page 1462*

Satan disguises himself as an angel of light (2 Corinthians 11:14) . . . *page 1492*

Angels encourage Christians (Hebrews 1:14) . . . *page 1579*

Angels who sinned were thrown into hell (2 Peter 2:4) . . . *page 1624*

Angels are holy (Jude 1:14) . . . *page 1645*

Angels are in the presence of God (Revelation 4:8) . . . *page 1653*

Angels should not be worshiped (Revelation 22:8-9) . . . *page 1670*

ANGER

Anger can lead to murder (Genesis 4:3-8) . . . *page 9*

Anger leads to evil actions (Psalm 37:8) . . . *page 704*

Showing anger is foolish (Proverbs 12:16) . . . *page 799*

Gentle words can soothe anger (Proverbs 15:1) . . . *page 802*

Being quick-tempered is foolish (Ecclesiastes 7:9) . . . *page 830*

God becomes angry when we are ruled by anger (Amos 1:11) . . . *page 1121*

Anger is like murdering someone (Matthew 5:21-22) . . . *page 1202*

Jesus grew angry at sin (John 2:13-17) . . . *page 1343*

Anger can give Satan a place in your life (Ephesians 4:26-27) . . . *page 1514*

Christians should get rid of anger (Colossians 3:8) . . . *page 1534*

Leaders in the church should not be quick-tempered (Titus 1:7) . . . *page 1569*

Be slow to become angry (James 1:19) . . . *page 1601*

APPEARANCE

God is not impressed by someone's appearance (1 Samuel 16:7) . . . *page 365*

Physical beauty fades (Proverbs 31:30) . . . *page 821*

Do not worry about clothes (Matthew 6:25-34) . . . *page 1206*

Appearances can be deceiving (Matthew 23:27) . . . *page 1233*

Christians should care more about spiritual welfare (1 Timothy 2:9-10) . . . *page 1552*

Do not judge others by their appearance (James 2:2-4) . . . *page 1602*

Inner beauty is more important than physical beauty (1 Peter 3:1-6) . . . *page 1614*

ARGUMENTS

Arguments can be avoided by using gentle words (Proverbs 15:1) . . . *page 802*

Loving arguments is a sin (Proverbs 17:19) . . . *page 805*

A fool is quick to argue (Proverbs 20:3) . . . *page 808*

Avoid becoming entangled in others' arguments (Proverbs 26:17) . . . *page 815*

Avoid arguing with a weak Christian (Romans 14:1) . . . *page 1450*

We should avoid arguments (Philippians 2:14) . . . *page 1523*

Arguments between Christians are useless (Titus 3:9) . . . *page 1571*

ARMOR

Armor for physical battle (1 Samuel 17:38) . . . *page 368*

Soldiers need armor (Jeremiah 46:3-4) . . . *page 987*

Weapons cannot stop God's power (Ezekiel 38:4) . . . *page 1056*

Spiritual armor prepares us for life (Romans 13:12) . . . *page 1450*

Righteousness is a spiritual weapon (2 Corinthians 6:7) . . . *page 1486*

God's weapons conquer Satan's strongholds (2 Corinthians 10:4) . . . *page 1490*

Put on the armor of God (Ephesians 6:11-18) . . . *page 1517*

ASSURANCE

God always holds on to his children (Psalm 37:23-24) . . . *page 705*

God will never abandon his people (Psalm 138:8) . . . *page 774*

God's promises last forever (Jeremiah 32:40) . . . *page 976*

False assurance is dangerous (Luke 18:18-30) . . . *page 1323*

We can be assured of eternal life (John 5:24) . . . *page 1348*

God will not refuse any who come to him (John 6:37-40) . . . *page 1350*

Our place in God's family is secure (John 10:27-28) . . . *page 1358*

Christians have peace with God (Romans 5:1-5) . . . *page 1437*

Nothing can separate us from God's love (Romans 8:35-39) . . . *page 1442*

Salvation cannot be canceled (Romans 11:29)
. . . *page 1447*

Accountability should help others (Galatians
6:1) . . . *page 1506*

Our salvation was guaranteed before Creation
(Ephesians 1:4-5) . . . *page 1510*

Assurance comes from faith (Ephesians 3:12)
. . . *page 1513*

God will guard what has been entrusted to him
(2 Timothy 1:12) . . . *page 1561*

ATONEMENT

God required a perfect sacrifice (Exodus 12:5)
. . . *page 92*

God required blood for our atonement (Leviticus
17:11) . . . *page 155*

Jesus paid for all of our sins (Isaiah 53:3-12)
. . . *page 907*

Atonement is good news (Luke 4:18-19)
. . . *page 1295*

Jesus willingly died for our sins (John 10:17)
. . . *page 1358*

Christ secured salvation through his blood (Acts
20:28) . . . *page 1415*

Jesus provided the atonement for sins (Romans
3:23-25) . . . *page 1435*

Jesus' death purchased forgiveness
(1 Corinthians 7:23) . . . *page 1464*

Jesus died for sins (1 Corinthians 15:3)
. . . *page 1473*

Our atonement allows us to know God
(Ephesians 2:13) . . . *page 1512*

Jesus' death rescues us from eternal punishment
(Colossians 1:13) . . . *page 1531*

Christ's death purifies God's people (Titus 2:14)
. . . *page 1570*

Sin requires that a sacrifice be made (Hebrews
9:22) . . . *page 1587*

Jesus' sacrifice was perfect (1 Peter 1:18-19)
. . . *page 1611*

Jesus took our punishment (1 Peter 2:21-24)
. . . *page 1613*

We cannot improve Jesus' sacrifice (1 Peter 3:18)
. . . *page 1615*

ATTITUDE

Bad attitudes hurt our relationship with God
(Genesis 4:6-7) . . . *page 9*

Bad attitudes lead to poor decisions (Numbers
14:1-4) . . . *page 191*

Always trust God for your life (Proverbs 29:25)
. . . *page 818*

Choose a positive attitude (Habakkuk 3:17-19)
. . . *page 1161*

God will reward the meek (Matthew 5:5)
. . . *page 1202*

God gives Christians a new attitude (Philippians
1:20-25) . . . *page 1521*

We should imitate Jesus' attitude (Philippians
2:5) . . . *page 1522*

Christians should always rejoice (Philippians
4:4) . . . *page 1525*

Never be anxious (Philippians 4:6-7)
. . . *page 1525*

AUTHORITY (see also Respect)

God will hold people in authority
accountable for their actions (Daniel 4:31)
. . . *page 1082*

Jesus is the highest authority (Matthew 28:18)
. . . *page 1243*

God gave government its authority (John 19:11)
. . . *page 1372*

Christians should obey the government (Romans
13:1-2) . . . *page 1449*

Parents are authorities to their children
(Ephesians 6:1) . . . *page 1516*

The Bible is our authority (2 Timothy 3:16)
. . . *page 1564*

Church leaders are authoritative (Hebrews 13:17)
. . . *page 1595*

BELIEF (see also Faith)

Believing God makes us righteous (Genesis 15:6)
. . . *page 22*

Belief in God should be accompanied by action
(Deuteronomy 27:10) . . . *page 251*

Belief affects the way we live (Mark 1:15)
. . . *page 1250*

Right beliefs are important for salvation
(Romans 10:9) . . . *page 1445*

Believing is more than acknowledging (James
2:21) . . . *page 1602*

BIBLE

The Bible is perfect (Psalm 18:30) . . . *page 690*

The Bible is true (Psalm 33:4) . . . *page 701*

The Bible will last forever (Psalm 119:89)
. . . *page 766*

The Bible gives us wisdom (Psalm 119:99)
. . . *page 766*

The Bible can be trusted (Psalm 119:138)
. . . *page 767*

The Bible reveals the truth (Acts 18:28)
. . . *page 1412*

The Bible is holy (Romans 1:2) . . . *page 1430*

God's Holy Spirit helps us understand the Bible
(1 Corinthians 2:12-16) . . . *page 1458*

The Bible is authoritative (Galatians 3:10)
. . . *page 1501*

The Bible is a Christian's spiritual weapon
(Ephesians 6:17) . . . *page 1517*

The Bible is inspired by God (2 Timothy 3:16)
. . . *page 1564*

The Bible judges our life (Hebrews 4:12)
. . . *page 1582*

The Bible helps us grow spiritually (1 Peter 2:2)
. . . *page 1612*

BIRTH

God is the Life-Giver (Genesis 2:7) . . . *page 6*

Children are a blessing from God (Psalm
127:3-5) . . . *page 770*

God carefully creates each person (Psalm
139:13-14) . . . *page 775*

God's Son was born (Isaiah 9:6) . . . *page 858*

God plans the lives of people before they are
born (Jeremiah 1:5) . . . *page 930*

Jesus' birth (Luke 2:7) . . . *page 1290*

God's children are reborn spiritually (John 1:12-13) . . . *page 1341*

People must be reborn spiritually to enter heaven (John 3:3) . . . *page 1344*

BLESSING

God blesses those who obey him (Leviticus 26:3-5) . . . *page 165*

God blesses godly people (Psalm 5:12) . . . *page 682*

We are blessed when we worship God (Psalm 24:3-6) . . . *page 694*

Christians bless God through praise (Psalm 103:1) . . . *page 750*

God will bless those who fear him (Psalm 112:1-3) . . . *page 760*

God blesses us when we seek to please him (Matthew 6:33) . . . *page 1206*

Christians should bless their enemies (Luke 6:28) . . . *page 1299*

Salvation is our greatest blessing (Ephesians 1:3) . . . *page 1510*

The Bible brings us blessing (James 1:25) . . . *page 1601*

BLOOD

God hates the shedding of an innocent person's blood (Genesis 4:10) . . . *page 10*

Jesus' blood seals God's relationship with his people (Matthew 26:28) . . . *page 1238*

Jesus' blood allows us to have access to God (Romans 5:8-9) . . . *page 1437*

Christians are redeemed by Jesus' blood (Ephesians 1:5-7) . . . *page 1510*

Blood is required for forgiveness (Hebrews 9:22) . . . *page 1587*

BODY OF CHRIST

The body of Christ has been given many gifts (Romans 12:3-6) . . . *page 1448*

There are many parts, but one body (1 Corinthians 12:12-13) . . . *page 1470*

Christians make up the body of Christ (1 Corinthians 12:27) . . . *page 1471*

Christians of different nationalities form one body (Ephesians 3:6) . . . *page 1512*

There must be unity in the body of Christ (Ephesians 4:3) . . . *page 1514*

Different members of the body help each other grow (Ephesians 4:11-12) . . . *page 1514*

Jesus is the head of the body (Colossians 1:18) . . . *page 1532*

BOOK OF LIFE

God writes our names in his book (Psalm 87:6) . . . *page 741*

The names of Christians are in the Book of Life (Philippians 4:3) . . . *page 1525*

Our names cannot be removed from the Book of Life (Revelation 3:5) . . . *page 1651*

People not recorded will experience God's wrath (Revelation 20:15) . . . *page 1668*

Only those whose names are in God's Book will enter heaven (Revelation 21:27) . . . *page 1670*

BRIDE

God's children should be as pure as a bride (Isaiah 49:18) . . . *page 903*

We should be devoted to God as a bride is to her husband (Jeremiah 2:2) . . . *page 932*

The church is the bride of Christ (2 Corinthians 11:2-3) . . . *page 1491*

The bride of Christ will be presented to Christ (Revelation 19:7) . . . *page 1666*

BUSINESS

God's people should be good workers (Genesis 31:42) . . . *page 46*

Work should not overrun your time with God (Exodus 16:23) . . . *page 98*

God gives you the ability to work (Exodus 35:30-31) . . . *page 122*

Workers should be trustworthy (Proverbs 25:13) . . . *page 814*

Do the best job you can (Ecclesiastes 9:10) . . . *page 832*

Work as though Jesus were your boss (Ephesians 6:6-7) . . . *page 1517*

Christians should do their best at their job (Titus 2:9-10) . . . *page 1570*

CARING

God cares for his people (Deuteronomy 7:9) . . . *page 231*

God cares for underprivileged people (Psalm 68:5) . . . *page 725*

Protect the needy (Psalm 82:3) . . . *page 738*

God's people should help the oppressed (Isaiah 1:17) . . . *page 850*

Care for your enemies (Luke 6:27) . . . *page 1299*

God's people should care for the needy (Luke 14:13-14) . . . *page 1317*

God cares for his children (Romans 1:6-7) . . . *page 1430*

Treat parents with care (Ephesians 6:2) . . . *page 1516*

Treat coworkers with care (Colossians 4:1) . . . *page 1535*

Care for the elderly (1 Timothy 5:1-4) . . . *page 1555*

Christians need to care for the needy (James 1:27) . . . *page 1601*

CHILDREN

God tells children to honor their parents (Exodus 20:12) . . . *page 102*

Parents should teach their children to follow God (Deuteronomy 6:6-7) . . . *page 230*

Christians are children of God (John 1:12) . . . *page 1341*

Children of God should imitate God (Ephesians 5:1) . . . *page 1515*

Parents should nurture their children (Ephesians 6:4) . . . *page 1516*

Children must obey their parents (Colossians 3:20) . . . *page 1534*

CHURCH (see also Worship)

Jesus is the cornerstone of the church (Psalm 118:22) . . . *page 763*

We should have joy going to God's house (Psalm 122:1) . . . *page 769*

Satan works against the church (Matthew 16:18) . . . *page 1223*

Members of the church should take care of each other (Acts 2:44) . . . *page 1383*

The church sends out missionaries (Acts 13:2) . . . *page 1400*

The church is like a body (1 Corinthians 12:12-13) . . . *page 1470*

The church is a family of Christians (Galatians 6:10) . . . *page 1506*

God's children make up the church (Ephesians 2:19-22) . . . *page 1512*

The church should not allow immoral behavior (Ephesians 5:3-4) . . . *page 1515*

Christ is the head of the church (Colossians 1:18) . . . *page 1532*

Many people groups form one universal church (Colossians 3:11) . . . *page 1534*

Church leaders are qualified to lead by their character (Titus 1:6-9) . . . *page 1568*

The church is made up of God's children (1 John 3:1) . . . *page 1631*

The church is the bride of Christ (Revelation 19:7-8) . . . *page 1666*

COMFORT

Friends should comfort each other (Job 2:12-13) . . . *page 639*

God comforts us (Isaiah 40:1-11) . . . *page 890*

God promises to comfort those who mourn (Matthew 5:4) . . . *page 1202*

God's Holy Spirit is our Comforter (John 14:16) . . . *page 1365*

Jesus has overcome the world's troubles (John 16:33) . . . *page 1368*

God comforts those who are hurting (2 Corinthians 1:3-11) . . . *page 1480*

Christians should comfort each other (1 Thessalonians 4:18) . . . *page 1541*

All pain will end (Revelation 21:3-4) . . . *page 1669*

COMPLAINING

Bring your complaints to God (Psalm 142:1-2) . . . *page 777*

Christians should not complain to each other (Philippians 2:14) . . . *page 1523*

People complain because they want their own way (Jude 1:16) . . . *page 1645*

COMPROMISE

Do not compromise your convictions (1 Kings 11:4) . . . *page 443*

Compromise can be wise (Matthew 5:25) . . . *page 1203*

Compromise can divide our loyalty (Matthew 6:24) . . . *page 1205*

Compromise can keep us from doing what is right (Mark 15:15) . . . *page 1278*

Compromise can weaken faith (2 Corinthians 6:14-18) . . . *page 1487*

CONFESSION OF SIN (see also Repentance)

Sin must be confessed (Leviticus 5:5) . . . *page 138*

God will restore those who turn away from evil (2 Chronicles 7:14) . . . *page 549*

Remorse accompanies confessing sin (Ezra 10:1) . . . *page 599*

God forgives confessed sins (Psalm 32:5) . . . *page 700*

Do not try to hide sin (Proverbs 28:13) . . . *page 817*

Confession of sin accompanies a changed lifestyle (2 Timothy 2:19) . . . *page 1562*

God purifies those who confess their sin (1 John 1:9) . . . *page 1629*

CONSCIENCE

Conscience moves us to turn from our mistakes (Proverbs 28:13) . . . *page 817*

We can suppress our conscience (Jonah 1:5) . . . *page 1136*

The Holy Spirit can speak through our conscience (Romans 9:1) . . . *page 1443*

Keep your conscience clear (1 Timothy 1:18-19) . . . *page 1552*

Church leaders must have clear consciences (1 Timothy 3:9) . . . *page 1553*

Consciences can be destroyed (1 Timothy 4:2) . . . *page 1554*

Jesus' forgiveness clears our conscience (Hebrews 9:14) . . . *page 1586*

A clear conscience helps us live a God-honoring life (1 Peter 3:16) . . . *page 1615*

COURAGE

God gives us victory (Psalm 112:8) . . . *page 760*

Jesus' strength gives us courage (John 16:33) . . . *page 1368*

Courage helps us boldly represent Christ (Acts 4:31) . . . *page 1385*

Christians should be courageous (1 Corinthians 16:13) . . . *page 1476*

Pray for courage (Ephesians 6:19-20) . . . *page 1517*

Christians can pray to God with confidence (Hebrews 4:16) . . . *page 1582*

COVENANT

God's promise can be trusted (Genesis 9:17) . . . *page 15*

Jesus established a new covenant (Luke 22:20) . . . *page 1329*

God's covenant brings life (2 Corinthians 3:6) . . . *page 1482*

The new covenant is superior to the old covenant (Hebrews 8:6) . . . *page 1585*

The old covenant foreshadowed the new covenant (Hebrews 10:1) . . . *page 1588*

CREATION

God the Holy Spirit was involved in Creation (Genesis 1:1-2) . . . *page 4*

God created people (Genesis 1:27) . . . *page 6*

God created the world good (Genesis 1:31) . . . *page 6*

God the Father was involved in Creation (Psalm 33:6) . . . *page 701*

God rules over his creation (Psalm 89:11) . . . *page 742*

God created every angel (Psalm 148:2-5) . . . *page 780*

God created everything (Jeremiah 10:16) . . . *page 947*

Creation reveals God's greatness (Amos 4:13) . . . *page 1124*

Jesus was involved in Creation (Colossians 1:16) . . . *page 1531*

God the Creator is worthy of worship (Revelation 4:11) . . . *page 1653*

God will make a new heaven and new earth (Revelation 21:1-4) . . . *page 1668*

CRITICISM

Correct yourself before criticizing others (Matthew 7:3-5) . . . *page 1206*

Criticism should help people grow (Luke 17:3-5) . . . *page 1320*

Criticism should be given with a loving attitude (1 Corinthians 13:4-5) . . . *page 1471*

Harsh criticism can destroy rather than help (Galatians 5:15) . . . *page 1505*

CROSS

Jesus was crucified (Matthew 27:31-35) . . . *page 1241*

Christians should pick up their own crosses (Mark 8:34-38) . . . *page 1265*

Jesus' death was powerful (1 Corinthians 1:17-18) . . . *page 1457*

Jesus' death unified all Christians (Ephesians 2:16) . . . *page 1512*

Jesus' death was a sacrifice (Colossians 1:20-22) . . . *page 1532*

Jesus' death defeated Satan (Colossians 2:14-15) . . . *page 1533*

Jesus' cross is an example for us (Hebrews 12:2) . . . *page 1592*

DARKNESS, SPIRITUAL

God's Word enlightens us (Psalm 119:105) . . . *page 767*

The way of wicked people is darkness (Proverbs 4:19) . . . *page 792*

Jesus brings light to darkened lives (John 1:5) . . . *page 1340*

Living without God is living in spiritual darkness (Acts 26:17-18) . . . *page 1422*

Christians do not live in spiritual darkness (Ephesians 5:8) . . . *page 1515*

God rescued us from eternal darkness (Colossians 1:13) . . . *page 1531*

There is no darkness in Jesus (1 John 1:5) . . . *page 1628*

Sinners' eternal punishment will be in darkness (Jude 1:4-13) . . . *page 1644*

DEATH

Death is a result of sin (Genesis 3:17-19) . . . *page 8*

Life is short (Job 7:6-7) . . . *page 643*

Every person will face death (Psalm 89:48) . . . *page 743*

Death of Christians is precious (Psalm 116:15) . . . *page 762*

Christians enter perfect peace at death (Isaiah 57:1-2) . . . *page 911*

God has power over death (John 14:19) . . . *page 1365*

The death of Christians brings fellowship with Jesus (Acts 7:59) . . . *page 1391*

God provides eternal life (Romans 6:23) . . . *page 1439*

Jesus will raise everyone who has died (1 Corinthians 15:20-23) . . . *page 1474*

Living in heaven is better than living on earth (2 Corinthians 5:6-7) . . . *page 1485*

Death is not the end of a person (1 Thessalonians 4:13-14) . . . *page 1541*

Prepare your spiritual life for death (Hebrews 9:27-28) . . . *page 1588*

We don't know how long we'll live (James 4:13-14) . . . *page 1606*

God will destroy death (Revelation 21:4) . . . *page 1669*

DECISIONS

Pray before making decisions (Nehemiah 1:4) . . . *page 602*

Decide to do things that honor God (Job 1:8) . . . *page 636*

God's Word helps us make decisions (Psalm 119:105) . . . *page 767*

Get good advice before making decisions (Proverbs 18:15) . . . *page 806*

Ask God for wisdom before making decisions (James 1:2-8) . . . *page 1600*

DEMONS (see also Satan)

Worship in false religions honors demons (Psalm 106:37) . . . *page 755*

Demons try to hinder God's plan (Daniel 10:13) . . . *page 1090*

Demons are no match for Jesus (Mark 1:34) . . . *page 1252*

Demons want to destroy people (Mark 5:5) . . . *page 1258*

Demons submit to the name of Jesus (Luke 10:17) . . . *page 1308*

Demons can be driven out by Jesus' followers (Acts 16:16-18) . . . *page 1407*

Demons are powerful (Acts 19:16) . . . *page 1412*

Demons cannot separate people from God's love (Romans 8:38-39) . . . *page 1442*

Demons deceive people (2 Corinthians 11:13-15) . . . *page 1491*

Christians fight against the plans of demons (Ephesians 6:12) . . . *page 1517*

Demons want to mislead people (1 Timothy 4:1-2) . . . *page 1554*

Demons believe in God (James 2:19) . . . *page 1602*

Demons are angels that have sinned (2 Peter 2:4) . . . *page 1624*

God will judge demons (Jude 1:6) . . . *page 1644*

Do not take demons lightly (Jude 1:8-9)
... *page 1645*

Demons can work miracles (Revelation 16:13-14)
... *page 1663*

In the last days, demons will be bound by God
(Revelation 20:1-3) ... *page 1667*

DEPRESSION

Depression can follow exhausting times (Judges
15:18) ... *page 324*

God can encourage hurting people (2 Samuel
22:29-31) ... *page 418*

Depression can follow success (1 Kings 19:3-4)
... *page 456*

God helps those who feel crushed (Psalm 34:18)
... *page 702*

Abraham had hope when there was no reason to
hope (Romans 4:18-22) ... *page 1436*

God will wipe away depression (Revelation 21:4)
... *page 1669*

DESIRES

You should not desire something that belongs to
someone else (Exodus 20:17) ... *page 103*

Wicked people desire evil (Psalm 36:1-4)
... *page 703*

God gives those who fellowship with him what
they desire (Psalm 37:4) ... *page 704*

Desire to know God (Psalm 42:1) ... *page 708*

Desire to worship God (Psalm 84:1-2)
... *page 739*

Desire to honor God (Psalm 86:12) ... *page 740*

Do not desire self-promotion (Psalm 119:36)
... *page 764*

Money doesn't satisfy desires (Ecclesiastes 5:10)
... *page 828*

Christians should not give in to sinful desires
(Ephesians 4:22) ... *page 1514*

Sinful desires should not have a home with
God's children (1 Peter 1:14) ... *page 1611*

Desire to do God's will (1 Peter 4:2)
... *page 1615*

God's children desire to obey God (1 John 2:3-6)
... *page 1629*

DETERMINATION

Be determined to obey God (1 Samuel 7:3)
... *page 352*

Determine not to sin (Job 31:1) ... *page 699*

Determine to stand firm (Isaiah 7:9) ... *page 856*

God helps us be determined (Isaiah 50:7)
... *page 904*

Determine to follow Christ (Mark 8:34-38)
... *page 1265*

DISCERNMENT

The Bible will help you discern bad teaching
(Acts 17:11) ... *page 1409*

God grants discernment (1 Corinthians 12:10)
... *page 1470*

Discern between right and wrong behavior
(Hebrews 5:14) ... *page 1582*

Ask God for help in discerning his will (James
1:5) ... *page 1600*

DISCIPLESHIP

Christians are to make disciples (Matthew
28:19-20) ... *page 1243*

Jesus' followers are known by their love (John
13:35) ... *page 1364*

Christians should help other Christians grow
(Acts 14:21-22) ... *page 1404*

DISCIPLINE

Punishment is a consequence of sinful actions
(Genesis 3:6-19) ... *page 8*

God's punishment does not change his love for
us (Psalm 89:32-33) ... *page 743*

The Lord disciplines those he loves (Proverbs
3:11-12) ... *page 790*

Parents are responsible to discipline their
children (Proverbs 13:24) ... *page 800*

Punishment for sin may be swift and severe
(Acts 5:1-11) ... *page 1386*

Paul commanded punishment for blatant sin
(1 Corinthians 5:1-5) ... *page 1461*

Punishment should lead to repentance
(2 Corinthians 7:8-9) ... *page 1488*

Sometimes God punishes us to bring us back to
himself (Hebrews 12:5-11) ... *page 1592*

DISCRIMINATION

Be fair in your judgment of others (Leviticus
19:15) ... *page 157*

Don't discriminate against someone who is not
powerful (Deuteronomy 1:17) ... *page 223*

Do not oppress the disadvantaged (Malachi 3:5)
... *page 1190*

God does not discriminate among his people
(Acts 10:34) ... *page 1397*

All Christians are equal in God's eyes (Galatians
3:28) ... *page 1502*

God will judge those who discriminate
(Colossians 3:25) ... *page 1535*

Do not discriminate against the poor (James
2:1-9) ... *page 1602*

DISHONESTY

Dishonesty is listed in the Ten Commandments
(Leviticus 19:11) ... *page 156*

Be honest in your business dealings (Leviticus
19:35-36) ... *page 157*

Do not lie for your own gain (Deuteronomy
19:14) ... *page 244*

Dishonest people cannot know God (Psalm
101:7) ... *page 749*

God hates deception (Proverbs 12:22)
... *page 799*

God will punish those who take advantage of
others (1 Thessalonians 4:6) ... *page 1540*

DOUBT

God will help us overcome doubts (Psalm 42:5-6)
... *page 709*

God doesn't leave us during our time of doubt
(Isaiah 40:27-28) ... *page 892*

Help those who have spiritual doubts (Hebrews
3:12) ... *page 1581*

Doubt inhibits our prayers (James 1:5-7)
... *page 1600*

DRINKING

People controlled by alcohol are fools (Proverbs 20:1) . . . *page 807*

Alcohol can cause you to become poor (Proverbs 21:17) . . . *page 809*

Alcohol can destroy you (Proverbs 23:29-35) . . . *page 812*

God will judge those who are controlled by alcohol (Isaiah 5:22) . . . *page 854*

Becoming drunk is dangerous (Luke 21:34) . . . *page 1329*

Drunkenness is not fitting for a Christian (Romans 13:11-14) . . . *page 1450*

Drunkenness can cause immoral behavior (Ephesians 5:18) . . . *page 1516*

EARTH

God created the earth (Genesis 1:1) . . . *page 4*

People are the caretakers of the earth (Genesis 1:28) . . . *page 6*

The earth was cursed because of sin (Genesis 3:17-19) . . . *page 8*

The earth belongs to God (Psalm 89:11) . . . *page 742*

The earth was created for God's glory (Colossians 1:16) . . . *page 1531*

Jesus sustains the earth (Hebrews 1:3) . . . *page 1578*

EMBARRASSMENT

Be careful not to embarrass others (Ruth 2:15) . . . *page 339*

Embarrassment can lead to rash actions (Matthew 14:1-12) . . . *page 1219*

We should not be embarrassed about the gospel (Romans 1:16) . . . *page 1431*

We should not be embarrassed by Jesus (Galatians 1:10) . . . *page 1498*

EMOTIONS

Emotions can lead us to sin (Genesis 4:2-6) . . . *page 9*

Emotions can lead to foolish promises (Judges 11:29-40) . . . *page 319*

Emotions are a part of worship (Ezra 3:1-13) . . . *page 590*

God heals those with broken hearts (Psalm 34:18) . . . *page 702*

Carefully guard your emotions (Proverbs 4:23) . . . *page 792*

Emotions can crush us (Proverbs 15:13) . . . *page 802*

Do not be led by emotions (Proverbs 19:2) . . . *page 806*

Jesus experienced emotions (John 11:35) . . . *page 1359*

Emotions are not reliable guides (Galatians 5:1-17) . . . *page 1504*

Some emotions can be sinful (Ephesians 4:31) . . . *page 1515*

EMPLOYMENT

God's people should be good workers (Genesis 31:42) . . . *page 46*

Work should not overrun your time with God (Exodus 16:23) . . . *page 98*

God gives you the ability to work (Exodus 35:30-31) . . . *page 122*

Workers should be trustworthy (Proverbs 25:13) . . . *page 814*

Do the best job you can (Ecclesiastes 9:10) . . . *page 832*

Work as though Jesus were your boss (Ephesians 6:6-7) . . . *page 1517*

Christians should do their best at their job (Titus 2:9-10) . . . *page 1570*

ENCOURAGEMENT

Encourage the underprivileged (Isaiah 1:17) . . . *page 850*

God encourages us (Isaiah 40:31) . . . *page 892*

The Holy Spirit encourages us (Acts 9:31) . . . *page 1394*

Encourage your neighbor (Romans 15:2) . . . *page 1451*

The Bible encourages us (Romans 15:4) . . . *page 1451*

Our position in Christ encourages us (Philippians 2:1) . . . *page 1522*

We should encourage each other (1 Thessalonians 4:18) . . . *page 1541*

Encourage those who are weak and afraid (1 Thessalonians 5:14) . . . *page 1542*

Encourage elderly people (1 Timothy 5:1-4) . . . *page 1555*

Encourage others not to sin (Hebrews 3:13) . . . *page 1581*

Encourage others to love (Hebrews 10:24) . . . *page 1589*

ENVY (see also Jealousy)

Envy can destroy someone (Job 5:2) . . . *page 641*

Do not envy those who do wrong (Psalm 37:1) . . . *page 704*

Do not envy the prosperity of wicked people (Psalm 73:2-3) . . . *page 729*

Envy steals your peace (Proverbs 14:30) . . . *page 801*

Envy is a powerful enemy (Proverbs 27:4) . . . *page 815*

Being envious is foolish (Ecclesiastes 4:4) . . . *page 827*

Envy can cause you to act rashly (Acts 7:9) . . . *page 1388*

Envy characterizes sinful people (Romans 1:29) . . . *page 1432*

We should not envy other Christians (Galatians 5:26) . . . *page 1505*

Envy has no place in a Christian's life (Titus 3:3) . . . *page 1571*

Do not harbor envy (James 3:14-15) . . . *page 1604*

Get rid of envy (1 Peter 2:1) . . . *page 1612*

ETERNAL LIFE

Eternal life is only for those who do God's will (Matthew 7:21) . . . *page 1207*

The righteous will receive eternal life (Matthew 25:46) . . . *page 1237*

Belief in Jesus is required for eternal life (John 3:15-16) . . . *page 1344*

Evil people will receive eternal punishment
(John 5:28-29) . . . *page 1348*
Jesus came to give life (John 10:10) . . . *page 1358*
Jesus gives eternal life (John 11:25) . . . *page 1359*
Jesus is eternal life (John 14:6) . . . *page 1365*
Eternal life cannot be earned (Ephesians 2:8-9)
. . . *page 1511*
Eternal life comes from God (Titus 1:2)
. . . *page 1568*
Eternal life gives us hope (Titus 3:7) . . . *page 1571*

EVIL

God will destroy evil people (Job 4:8)
. . . *page 640*
God helps keep his people from sin (Psalm
19:13) . . . *page 692*
God hates people who do evil (Psalm 26:5)
. . . *page 696*
God permits evil (Romans 1:24-28) . . . *page 1432*
God cannot coexist with evil (Galatians 5:16-17)
. . . *page 1505*
Christians should put away evil from their lives
(Ephesians 4:22) . . . *page 1514*
There are spiritual forces behind evil (Ephesians
6:12) . . . *page 1517*

FAITH (see also Belief)

Believing God takes faith (Genesis 15:6)
. . . *page 22*
Only a small amount of faith is needed (Luke
17:6) . . . *page 1321*
Faith is needed for salvation (Romans 3:28)
. . . *page 1435*
Faith puts us in a right relationship with God
(Romans 5:1) . . . *page 1437*
Faith comes from hearing the Word of God
(Romans 10:17) . . . *page 1445*
Accept the person who has weak faith (Romans
14:1) . . . *page 1450*
Christianity is the only true faith (Ephesians 4:5)
. . . *page 1514*
Faith is hoping in what is not seen (Hebrews
11:1) . . . *page 1590*
Faith accompanies obedience to God (Hebrews
11:7-12) . . . *page 1590*

FAMILY

The members of a family can teach each other
about God (Deuteronomy 6:4-9) . . . *page 230*
Do not let sin affect your family life (Psalm
101:2) . . . *page 748*
Do not bring trouble to a family (Proverbs 11:29)
. . . *page 798*
Christian faith is of greater importance than
family (Luke 12:51-53) . . . *page 1314*
Christians are members of God's family
(Ephesians 2:19) . . . *page 1512*
Husbands and wives should love each other
(Ephesians 5:21-33) . . . *page 1516*
Children should obey their parents (Ephesians
6:1) . . . *page 1516*
Church leaders must have a good family life
(1 Timothy 3:4-5) . . . *page 1553*
Families should take care of each other
(1 Timothy 5:3-5) . . . *page 1555*

FEAR

God will protect us (Genesis 15:1) . . . *page 22*
God will not forget us (Genesis 46:3)
. . . *page 68*
We should fear God (Psalm 25:12) . . . *page 695*
Christians do not need to fear anyone (Psalm
27:1) . . . *page 696*
God strengthens us (Psalm 46:1-3) . . . *page 711*
We do not need to fear darkness or violence
(Psalm 91:5) . . . *page 744*
We do not need to fear bad news (Psalm 112:7)
. . . *page 760*
Love drives fear away (1 John 4:18) . . . *page 1633*

FOOLISHNESS

Being foolish is lacking discernment (Job 5:2)
. . . *page 641*
Fools do not acknowledge God (Psalm 14:1)
. . . *page 687*
Fools do not know God (Proverbs 1:7)
. . . *page 786*
Fools invite their own destruction (Proverbs
10:14) . . . *page 797*
Fools enjoy evil (Proverbs 10:23) . . . *page 797*
Fools show their annoyance (Proverbs 12:16)
. . . *page 799*
Stay away from foolish people (Proverbs 14:7)
. . . *page 801*
A foolish person rejects discipline (Proverbs
15:5) . . . *page 802*
Fools return to their folly (Proverbs 26:11)
. . . *page 815*
A foolish person gives in to anger (Proverbs
29:11) . . . *page 818*
A foolish person is lazy (Ecclesiastes 4:5)
. . . *page 827*
The foolishness of God is wiser than man's
wisdom (1 Corinthians 1:25) . . . *page 1457*

FORGIVENESS

God forgives our many sins (Psalm 65:3)
. . . *page 723*
God forgives us because he loves us (Psalm 86:5)
. . . *page 740*
God makes us as clean as freshly fallen snow
(Isaiah 1:18) . . . *page 850*
God removes our impurities (Ezekiel 36:25)
. . . *page 1055*
We must forgive others (Matthew 6:14-15)
. . . *page 1205*
Don't keep track of how many times you forgive
(Matthew 18:21-35) . . . *page 1226*
Freely forgive others as God has forgiven you
(Colossians 3:13) . . . *page 1534*
God will forgive our sins if we confess them
(1 John 1:8-9) . . . *page 1629*

FREEDOM

Christians are spiritually free (John 8:36)
. . . *page 1355*
Christians are free from sin's power (Romans
5:21) . . . *page 1438*
Christians are free in order to serve others
(Galatians 5:1) . . . *page 1504*

FRIENDSHIP (see also Relationships)

Friends can cause great pain (Psalm 55:12-14)
 ... *page 717*

Friends love during difficult times (Proverbs
 17:17) ... *page 805*

Faithful friends are not common (Proverbs
 18:24) ... *page 806*

Friends influence you (Proverbs 22:24-25)
 ... *page 811*

Friendship is marked by sacrifice (John 15:13-15)
 ... *page 1366*

We can be friends with God (James 2:23)
 ... *page 1603*

FUTURE

God has plans for our future (Genesis 12:1-4)
 ... *page 19*

God will bless our future if we obey him
 (Deuteronomy 5:29) ... *page 230*

Do not plan your future like evil people do
 (Jeremiah 10:2-3) ... *page 946*

God gives us hope for our future (Jeremiah
 31:17) ... *page 973*

God prepares a future for us (1 Corinthians 2:9)
 ... *page 1458*

GIVING

God is honored by our gifts (Exodus 35:22)
 ... *page 122*

Generous giving honors God (Ezra 2:68-69)
 ... *page 590*

God will reward us for giving to others (Mark
 9:41) ... *page 1267*

Giving helps others live (Acts 2:44-45)
 ... *page 1383*

We should support Christian workers (Acts
 28:10) ... *page 1425*

Wealthy people should give generously
 (1 Timothy 6:17-19) ... *page 1557*

God is pleased with our gifts (Hebrews 13:16)
 ... *page 1595*

Giving reflects God's love (1 John 3:17)
 ... *page 1632*

GOD

God created everything (Genesis 1:1) ... *page 4*

God is a warrior (Exodus 15:3) ... *page 96*

God is one (Deuteronomy 6:4) ... *page 230*

God is trustworthy (Deuteronomy 7:9)
 ... *page 231*

God is too great to be described (1 Kings 8:27)
 ... *page 438*

God is gracious and merciful (Nehemiah 9:31)
 ... *page 614*

God is good (Psalm 34:8) ... *page 702*

God helps his people when they are in trouble
 (Psalm 46:1) ... *page 711*

God is mighty (Psalm 50:1) ... *page 713*

God is our rock (Psalm 62:6) ... *page 722*

God is our hope (Psalm 71:5) ... *page 728*

God is near everyone (Psalm 75:1) ... *page 731*

God is our salvation (Isaiah 12:2) ... *page 862*

God is sovereign (Isaiah 25:8) ... *page 874*

God is holy (Isaiah 29:23) ... *page 879*

Only God is worthy of glory (Isaiah 42:8)
 ... *page 894*

God is our father (Matthew 6:9) ... *page 1204*

God is all-powerful (Luke 1:37) ... *page 1288*

God is spirit (John 4:24) ... *page 1346*

God is all-knowing (Romans 11:33)
 ... *page 1447*

God is knowable (Ephesians 1:17) ... *page 1511*

God is living (1 Timothy 4:10) ... *page 1555*

God is King of kings (1 Timothy 6:15)
 ... *page 1557*

God is approachable (James 4:8) ... *page 1605*

God is judge (James 4:12) ... *page 1606*

God is love (1 John 4:16) ... *page 1633*

God is almighty (Revelation 1:8) ... *page 1649*

GOD'S WILL

God guides us (Psalm 16:7) ... *page 688*

Ask God for guidance (Psalm 25:4-7) ... *page 695*

God will direct you (Psalm 48:14) ... *page 712*

God works everything out for his plan (Proverbs
 16:4) ... *page 804*

God directs events in our life (Acts 16:6-7)
 ... *page 1407*

God gives wisdom for making decisions (James
 1:2-5) ... *page 1600*

GOSSIP

Do not gossip (Exodus 23:1) ... *page 106*

Be careful not to slander (Leviticus 19:16)
 ... *page 157*

Gossiping betrays confidence (Proverbs 11:13)
 ... *page 798*

Gossip separates friends (Proverbs 16:28)
 ... *page 804*

Gossip prolongs tension between people
 (Proverbs 26:20) ... *page 815*

Gossip is attractive (Proverbs 26:22) ... *page 815*

People who gossip are wicked (Romans 1:29)
 ... *page 1432*

Gossip should have no place among Christians
 (1 Timothy 5:13) ... *page 1556*

GRACE

God is full of grace (Exodus 34:6) ... *page 120*

God is slow to become angry (Psalm 86:15)
 ... *page 740*

God's grace makes salvation possible (Ephesians
 1:7-8) ... *page 1510*

God accepts us by his grace (Ephesians 2:8-9)
 ... *page 1511*

God's grace gives us hope (1 Peter 1:13)
 ... *page 1611*

GREED

Greed creates disagreement (Proverbs 28:25)
 ... *page 817*

The Pharisees had greedy hearts (Matthew 23:25)
 ... *page 1233*

Christians should avoid being greedy (Ephesians
 5:3) ... *page 1515*

People full of greed will not enter heaven
 (Ephesians 5:5) ... *page 1515*

Leaders of the church must not be greedy (Titus
 1:7) ... *page 1569*

GRIEF (see also Sorrow)
Friends should comfort each other (Job 2:12-13) . . . *page 639*

God comforts us in our darkest times (Job 35:9-10) . . . *page 669*

God comforts us (Isaiah 40) . . . *page 890*

God promises to comfort those who grieve (Matthew 5:4) . . . *page 1202*

God's Holy Spirit is our Comforter (John 14:16) . . . *page 1364*

Jesus has overcome the world's troubles (John 16:33) . . . *page 1368*

The Holy Spirit comforts us (Acts 9:31) . . . *page 1394*

The Bible comforts us (Romans 15:4) . . . *page 1451*

God comforts those who grieve (2 Corinthians 1:3-11) . . . *page 1456*

All grief will end (Revelation 21:3-4) . . . *page 1669*

GUIDANCE
Ask God to give you guidance (Psalm 25:4-5) . . . *page 695*

God will guide you (Psalm 32:8) . . . *page 700*

The Bible gives us guidance (Psalm 119:133) . . . *page 767*

God directs your path when you trust him (Proverbs 3:5-6) . . . *page 789*

GUILT
Guilt causes us to hide from God (Genesis 3:7-11) . . . *page 8*

Ask God to forgive hidden sins (Psalm 19:12-13) . . . *page 692*

God forgives sins and removes guilt (Psalm 32:5) . . . *page 700*

God can cleanse us from all sin (Psalm 51:2) . . . *page 714*

All people are guilty of sin (Romans 3:9-12) . . . *page 1434*

Jesus Christ takes away all guilt (Romans 3:23-24) . . . *page 1435*

HATRED
Hatred causes trouble (Proverbs 10:12) . . . *page 797*

Followers of Jesus will be hated (Matthew 10:22) . . . *page 1212*

Many in the world hate Jesus (John 15:18) . . . *page 1367*

Christians should hate evil (Romans 12:9) . . . *page 1448*

All people are equal in Christ (Galatians 3:28-29) . . . *page 1502*

Christians need to get rid of their own hatred (Colossians 3:8) . . . *page 1534*

HEART
Love God with all of your heart (Deuteronomy 6:5) . . . *page 230*

Our heart can have confidence (Psalm 27:3) . . . *page 696*

God will not despise a repentant heart (Psalm 51:17) . . . *page 715*

Guard your heart (Proverbs 4:23) . . . *page 792*

Those who have pure hearts will see God (Matthew 5:8) . . . *page 1202*

Words and actions begin in the heart (Luke 6:45) . . . *page 1300*

HEAVEN
Death will not exist in heaven (Isaiah 25:8) . . . *page 874*

Only righteous people will enter heaven (Matthew 5:17-20) . . . *page 1202*

Few people will enter heaven (Matthew 7:13-14) . . . *page 1206*

Jesus is preparing heaven for his followers (John 14:2-3) . . . *page 1364*

Our lives will not be complete until we enter heaven (2 Corinthians 5:2) . . . *page 1485*

Heaven is much better than earth (Philippians 1:23) . . . *page 1522*

Christians should look forward to heaven (Colossians 3:1-5) . . . *page 1534*

Heaven is the home of righteousness (2 Peter 3:13) . . . *page 1625*

God is the focus of attention in heaven (Revelation 7:17) . . . *page 1656*

There will not be any sadness in heaven (Revelation 21:4) . . . *page 1669*

People in heaven will walk with God (Revelation 22:5) . . . *page 1670*

HELL
God will deliver his children from hell (Psalm 86:13) . . . *page 740*

Hell is a place of weeping (Matthew 8:12) . . . *page 1208*

Hell was prepared for Satan and demons (Matthew 25:41) . . . *page 1237*

Wicked people will receive punishment (Romans 1:18-20) . . . *page 1431*

God will punish those who do not turn from their sin (2 Peter 2:4-9) . . . *page 1624*

Hell is a place of eternal fire (Jude 1:7) . . . *page 1644*

God will send to hell those who do not believe in him (Revelation 21:8) . . . *page 1669*

HOLY
God is known for his holiness (Psalm 93:5) . . . *page 745*

God cannot tolerate sin (Isaiah 59:2) . . . *page 914*

God uses his Word to make us holy (John 17:17) . . . *page 1369*

Christians should try to be holy (1 Peter 1:15) . . . *page 1611*

God is worthy of praise because he is holy (Revelation 4:8) . . . *page 1653*

HOLY SPIRIT
The Holy Spirit was involved in Creation (Genesis 1:2) . . . *page 4*

The Holy Spirit empowers leaders (Judges 3:10) . . . *page 305*

The Holy Spirit teaches us (John 14:26) . . . *page 1366*

The Holy Spirit guides us (John 16:13) . . . *page 1368*

The Holy Spirit empowers us to be witnesses (Acts 1:8) . . . *page 1381*

The Holy Spirit lives within us (Romans 8:11) . . . *page 1442*

The Holy Spirit sanctifies us (Romans 15:16) . . . *page 1452*

The Holy Spirit opens our spiritual eyes (1 Corinthians 2:10) . . . *page 1458*

The Holy Spirit is involved in salvation (Titus 3:5) . . . *page 1571*

HONESTY

Honesty is commanded by God (Exodus 20:16) . . . *page 103*

Only honest people can worship God (Psalm 24:3-4) . . . *page 694*

God is truth and desires truth (Psalm 51:6) . . . *page 715*

God hates lies (Proverbs 6:16-17) . . . *page 793*

Be honest (Proverbs 19:1) . . . *page 806*

Christians should be known by their honesty (Matthew 5:37) . . . *page 1204*

Lies make someone unclean before God (Matthew 15:18-20) . . . *page 1221*

Christians should put away dishonesty from their lives (Ephesians 4:25) . . . *page 1514*

HOPE

God gives hope to the needy (Psalm 9:18) . . . *page 685*

Hope gives us confidence (Psalm 25:3) . . . *page 695*

The Bible gives us hope (Psalm 119:43) . . . *page 764*

Christians always have hope (Romans 8:28) . . . *page 1442*

Hope comes from the Holy Spirit (Romans 15:13) . . . *page 1451*

Jesus' resurrection gives us hope (1 Corinthians 6:14) . . . *page 1462*

We have hope in Jesus (1 Corinthians 15:19) . . . *page 1474*

We have confidence of eternal life (Titus 1:1-2) . . . *page 1568*

HOSPITALITY

Christians should take care of those in need (Matthew 25:34-40) . . . *page 1237*

Hospitality brings heavenly reward (Mark 9:41) . . . *page 1267*

Christians should be hospitable (Romans 12:13) . . . *page 1448*

Christians should be hospitable to people they do not know well (Hebrews 13:2) . . . *page 1594*

Be cheerful about being hospitable (1 Peter 4:9-11) . . . *page 1616*

Hospitality reflects God's love (3 John 1:5-8) . . . *page 1640*

HUMILITY

God humbles us for our own good (Deuteronomy 8:16) . . . *page 233*

God hears the prayers of the humble (2 Chronicles 7:14) . . . *page 549*

God saves those who are humble (Psalm 18:27) . . . *page 690*

God preserves the lives of humble people (Psalm 147:6) . . . *page 780*

Those who are humble become wise (Proverbs 11:2) . . . *page 798*

God cares for the humble (Isaiah 66:2) . . . *page 922*

God will exalt the humble (Luke 18:14) . . . *page 1322*

Be humble in dealing with others (Philippians 2:1-11) . . . *page 1522*

Humble yourself before God (James 4:10) . . . *page 1605*

HYPOCRISY

Do not associate with hypocrites (Psalm 26:4) . . . *page 696*

God hates hypocrisy in worship (Isaiah 29:13) . . . *page 878*

Hypocrites pretend to be devoted to God (Ezekiel 33:31-32) . . . *page 1052*

God finds hypocrites repulsive (Matthew 23:27-28) . . . *page 1233*

Beware of hypocrisy in your life (Luke 12:1-2) . . . *page 1312*

God will punish hypocrisy (Luke 20:46-47) . . . *page 1327*

Hypocrites are worthless (Titus 1:16) . . . *page 1569*

Get rid of hypocrisy (1 Peter 2:1) . . . *page 1612*

IDOLATRY

We should have no other gods (Exodus 20:3) . . . *page 102*

Do not be devoted to anyone or anything more than God (Deuteronomy 4:23) . . . *page 228*

Devote your heart to God (Joshua 24:14) . . . *page 296*

Look to God for your security (Judges 10:13-16) . . . *page 318*

We give in to idolatry when we forget God (Psalm 106:19-22) . . . *page 755*

God will not share his glory with anything else (Isaiah 42:8) . . . *page 894*

Christians cannot serve both God and the things of this world (Luke 16:13) . . . *page 1320*

IMMORALITY

Compromises can lead to immorality (Judges 3:1-11) . . . *page 305*

Stay away from immoral Christians (1 Corinthians 5:9-11) . . . *page 1461*

Practicing immorality treats God lightly (1 Corinthians 6:19-20) . . . *page 1463*

Immorality should have no place among Christians (Ephesians 4:17-19) . . . *page 1514*

INTEGRITY

Leaders should have integrity (Psalm 78:72) . . . *page 735*

Integrity takes effort (Psalm 101:3-8) . . . *page 748*

Leaders in the church should be full of integrity (Titus 1:7) . . . *page 1569*

Maintain integrity in teaching others (Titus 2:7) . . . *page 1570*

INTIMIDATION

God can help us overcome intimidation (Genesis 15:1) . . . *page 22*

God does not forget us when we are intimidated (Genesis 46:3) . . . *page 68*

We do not need to fear anyone (Psalm 27:1) . . . *page 696*

God empowers us (Psalm 46:1-3) . . . *page 711*

We do not need to be intimidated (Psalm 112:7-8) . . . *page 760*

Jesus' strength can give us courage (John 16:33) . . . *page 1368*

God will help us be bold (Acts 4:31) . . . *page 1385*

Be on your guard against intimidation (1 Corinthians 16:13) . . . *page 1476*

Pray for courage (Ephesians 6:19-20) . . . *page 1517*

Christians can pray without being intimidated (Hebrews 4:16) . . . *page 1582*

JEALOUSY (see also Envy)

God doesn't want to share our devotion (Deuteronomy 4:24) . . . *page 228*

Jealousy can destroy someone (Job 5:2) . . . *page 641*

Do not envy those who do wrong (Psalm 37:1) . . . *page 704*

Do not be jealous of wicked people (Psalm 73:2-3) . . . *page 729*

Jealousy steals away peace (Proverbs 14:30) . . . *page 801*

Jealousy is a powerful enemy (Proverbs 27:4) . . . *page 815*

Jealousy is foolish (Ecclesiastes 4:4) . . . *page 827*

Jealousy can cause rash behavior (Acts 7:9) . . . *page 1388*

We should not be jealous of other Christians (Galatians 5:26) . . . *page 1505*

Jealousy has no place in a Christian's life (Titus 3:3-5) . . . *page 1571*

JESUS CHRIST

Jesus is all-powerful (Isaiah 9:6) . . . *page 858*

Jesus has authority over demons (Mark 1:27) . . . *page 1252*

Jesus is the Son of God (Luke 1:35) . . . *page 1288*

Jesus is God (John 1:1-5) . . . *page 1340*

Jesus is the Messiah (John 4:25-26) . . . *page 1346*

Jesus is the Judge (John 5:22) . . . *page 1348*

Jesus gives life (John 10:10) . . . *page 1358*

Jesus is the Good Shepherd (John 10:11) . . . *page 1358*

Jesus is the only way to God (John 14:6) . . . *page 1365*

Jesus is the author of life (Acts 3:15) . . . *page 1384*

Jesus is the wisdom of God (1 Corinthians 1:21-24) . . . *page 1457*

Jesus is the head of the church (Ephesians 5:23) . . . *page 1516*

Jesus is the highest authority (Philippians 2:9-10) . . . *page 1522*

Jesus is the Creator (Colossians 1:15-16) . . . *page 1531*

Jesus is faithful (2 Timothy 2:13) . . . *page 1562*

Jesus is coming again (Titus 2:13) . . . *page 1570*

Jesus is sinless (Hebrews 4:15) . . . *page 1582*

Jesus is holy (Hebrews 7:26) . . . *page 1585*

Jesus is the King of the ages (Revelation 15:3) . . . *page 1663*

Jesus is the Lamb of God (Revelation 21:22) . . . *page 1670*

JUDGMENT

God is able to judge (Job 34:23) . . . *page 668*

God is the ultimate authority (Psalm 9:7) . . . *page 685*

God will judge all people (Ecclesiastes 3:17) . . . *page 827*

God will judge people for their actions (Ecclesiastes 11:9) . . . *page 834*

God will judge everything done in secret (Ecclesiastes 12:14) . . . *page 834*

God will rule that wicked people are guilty (Malachi 3:5) . . . *page 1190*

God will judge the words we speak (Matthew 12:36) . . . *page 1215*

God does not judge by appearances (John 7:21-24) . . . *page 1352*

God will judge Christians (Romans 14:10) . . . *page 1450*

God will judge Christians for their actions (2 Corinthians 5:10) . . . *page 1485*

God will judge all people (Hebrews 9:27) . . . *page 1588*

People whose names are in God's Book of Life will enter heaven (Revelation 20:11-15) . . . *page 1668*

JUSTICE

Justice should not be influenced by a crowd (Exodus 23:2) . . . *page 106*

Protect the poor (Exodus 23:6) . . . *page 106*

Do not hold back justice (Deuteronomy 27:19) . . . *page 251*

God loves justice (Psalm 11:7) . . . *page 687*

Jesus' death was justice for sin (Romans 3:25-26) . . . *page 1435*

KINDNESS

Christians should be kind to each other (Ephesians 4:32) . . . *page 1515*

Be kind to people who treat you wrongly (1 Thessalonians 5:15) . . . *page 1542*

Choose to be kind rather than to argue (2 Timothy 2:24) . . . *page 1563*

Being kind takes effort (2 Peter 1:5-7) . . . *page 1622*

LAZINESS

Laziness can ruin you (Proverbs 6:6-11) . . . *page 793*

Laziness can make you poor (Proverbs 10:4-5) . . . *page 796*

Lazy people work for others (Proverbs 12:24) . . . *page 799*

Lazy people make excuses (Proverbs 22:13) . . . *page 810*

Lazy people oversleep (Proverbs 26:14) . . . *page 815*

Encourage lazy people to work (1 Thessalonians 5:14) . . . *page 1542*

Lazy people should not be freeloaders (2 Thessalonians 3:10) . . . *page 1546*

LEADERSHIP

Leaders should be trustworthy (Exodus 18:21) . . . *page 100*

Leaders look out for the people's best interests (Numbers 27:16-17) . . . *page 209*

Leaders should represent God in their decisions (2 Chronicles 19:5-7) . . . *page 561*

Leaders should receive advice (Proverbs 11:14) . . . *page 798*

Leaders must serve others (Matthew 20:26-28) . . . *page 1229*

Leaders should sacrifice for others (John 10:11) . . . *page 1358*

Leaders should be obeyed (Romans 13:1-4) . . . *page 1449*

Leaders give an account to God for their actions (Hebrews 13:17) . . . *page 1595*

LIFE

Life comes from God (Genesis 2:7) . . . *page 6*

God carefully creates each person (Psalm 139:13-14) . . . *page 775*

Life should be enjoyed (Ecclesiastes 9:9) . . . *page 832*

God plans the lives of people before they are born (Jeremiah 1:5) . . . *page 930*

People must be reborn spiritually to enter heaven (John 3:3) . . . *page 1344*

Jesus came to give abundant life (John 10:10) . . . *page 1358*

We should live lives worthy of our Christian calling (Ephesians 4:1) . . . *page 1513*

Christ is the reason for life (Philippians 1:21) . . . *page 1521*

Our lives should honor God (Colossians 3:17) . . . *page 1534*

LIGHT

Light comes from God (Genesis 1:3) . . . *page 4*

God is light (Psalm 27:1) . . . *page 696*

God's Word enlightens our path (Psalm 119:105) . . . *page 767*

God can turn darkness into light (Isaiah 42:16) . . . *page 894*

Christians are the light of the world (Matthew 5:14) . . . *page 1202*

Jesus is the Light of the World (John 8:12) . . . *page 1354*

Light shines in the hearts of Christians (2 Corinthians 4:6) . . . *page 1484*

Christians are children of light (Ephesians 5:8) . . . *page 1515*

LONELINESS

God is concerned about our loneliness (Genesis 2:18) . . . *page 6*

God encourages the lonely (1 Kings 19:14-18) . . . *page 456*

God takes care of lonely people (Psalm 68:6) . . . *page 725*

Friends help in times of loneliness (Ecclesiastes 4:10-11) . . . *page 828*

God remains with us (Matthew 28:20) . . . *page 1243*

LOVE

Love in marriage is strong (Song of Songs 8:6-7) . . . *page 844*

Love your enemies (Matthew 5:43-44) . . . *page 1204*

Loving God is the most important command (Mark 12:29-30) . . . *page 1272*

Christians must love each other (John 13:34) . . . *page 1364*

We cannot be separated from Jesus' love (Romans 8:35-39) . . . *page 1442*

Love must be genuine (Romans 12:9) . . . *page 1448*

Love never quits (1 Corinthians 13:4-8) . . . *page 1471*

God's love for us is beyond our understanding (Ephesians 3:18) . . . *page 1513*

Love helps you look past offenses (1 Peter 4:8) . . . *page 1616*

God is love (1 John 4:16) . . . *page 1633*

We must be known for our love (2 John 1:5) . . . *page 1638*

LOYALTY

Friends are loyal (Proverbs 17:17) . . . *page 805*

We cannot divide our loyalty (Matthew 6:24) . . . *page 1205*

There must be loyalty in marriage (Hebrews 13:4) . . . *page 1594*

LUST

Lustful thoughts are sinful (Matthew 5:28) . . . *page 1203*

Christians should not give in to lust (Colossians 3:5) . . . *page 1534*

Christians should avoid lust (1 Thessalonians 4:3-5) . . . *page 1540*

Godless people enjoy immorality (1 Peter 4:3) . . . *page 1615*

LYING (see Dishonesty)

MARRIAGE

God hates divorce (Malachi 2:16) . . . *page 1190*

Two people become one through marriage (Mark 10:2-12) . . . *page 1267*

Angels do not get married (Mark 12:25) . . . *page 1272*

Married partners should meet each other's needs (1 Corinthians 7:2-5) . . . *page 1463*

Married partners are united to each other for life (1 Corinthians 7:39) . . . *page 1464*

A Christian wife can witness to her husband (1 Peter 3:1-6) . . . *page 1614*

MERCY

God requires that we show mercy (Micah 6:8) . . . *page 1148*

People who show mercy to others will be rewarded (Matthew 5:7) . . . *page 1202*

We should imitate God's mercy (Luke 6:36)
. . . *page 1299*

Jesus is merciful (1 Timothy 1:2) . . . *page 1550*

Mercy is from God (2 Timothy 1:2) . . . *page 1560*

MONEY

Greed brings trouble (Proverbs 15:27)
. . . *page 803*

Do not make money the most important part of
your life (Matthew 6:19) . . . *page 1205*

Money can distract people from God (Mark
10:17-24) . . . *page 1268*

You cannot serve both God and money (Luke
16:13) . . . *page 1320*

Christians should share their resources with
those in need (Acts 2:42-45) . . . *page 1383*

Christians should not be lovers of money
(1 Timothy 3:3) . . . *page 1553*

We should look to God for security, not money
(1 Timothy 6:17-19) . . . *page 1557*

Do not love money (Hebrews 13:5) . . . *page 1594*

Be careful to treat rich and poor equally (James
2:1-9) . . . *page 1602*

MURDER

God has forbidden murder (Deuteronomy 5:17)
. . . *page 229*

Hateful anger is the same in God's eyes as
murder (Matthew 5:21-22) . . . *page 1202*

OBEDIENCE

Obeying is better than saying, "I'm sorry"
(1 Samuel 15:22) . . . *page 364*

People who obey God's Word will be blessed
(Luke 11:28) . . . *page 1311*

Christians should obey the government (Romans
13:1-4) . . . *page 1449*

Children should obey their parents (Ephesians
6:1) . . . *page 1516*

Christians obey God (1 John 2:3) . . . *page 1629*

PAIN

God cares for his people (Deuteronomy 7:9)
. . . *page 231*

Friends should comfort each other (Job 2:12-13)
. . . *page 639*

God comforts us in our darkest times (Job 35:10)
. . . *page 669*

God watches over the weak (Psalm 12:5)
. . . *page 687*

God comforts us (Isaiah 40:9-11) . . . *page 891*

God promises to comfort those who mourn
(Matthew 5:4) . . . *page 1202*

God's Holy Spirit is our Comforter (John 14:16)
. . . *page 1365*

Christians should comfort each other
(1 Thessalonians 4:18) . . . *page 1541*

All pain will end (Revelation 21:3-4) . . . *page 1669*

PARENTS

Parents should teach children to follow God
(Deuteronomy 6:6-7) . . . *page 230*

Parents should nurture their children (Ephesians
6:4) . . . *page 1516*

Children must obey their parents (Colossians
3:20) . . . *page 1534*

PATIENCE

Be patient with God (Psalm 75:2) . . . *page 731*

Patience is valuable (Proverbs 25:15) . . . *page 814*

Patience is better than pride (Ecclesiastes 7:8)
. . . *page 830*

Patience demonstrates love (1 Corinthians 13:4)
. . . *page 1471*

Patience is evidence of the Holy Spirit working
in our lives (Galatians 5:22) . . . *page 1505*

Be patient with each other (Ephesians 4:2)
. . . *page 1513*

PEACE

Be full of peace (Psalm 34:14) . . . *page 702*

Jesus is known as the Prince of Peace (Isaiah
9:6-7) . . . *page 858*

Wicked people will not know peace (Isaiah
48:22) . . . *page 902*

We can have peace with God (Isaiah 53:5)
. . . *page 907*

Make peace with others quickly (Matthew
5:23-26) . . . *page 1203*

The peace Jesus gives is different than the
world's peace (John 14:27) . . . *page 1366*

Jesus gives us peace (Romans 5:1) . . . *page 1437*

Peace is evidence of the Holy Spirit working in
our lives (Galatians 5:22) . . . *page 1505*

We can have peace through prayer (Philippians
4:4-7) . . . *page 1525*

POWER

Christians receive power from the Holy Spirit
(Acts 1:8) . . . *page 1381*

The Bible is a powerful weapon (Ephesians 6:17)
. . . *page 1517*

Jesus is the greatest power (Hebrews 1:1-4)
. . . *page 1578*

Prayer can be powerful (James 5:16)
. . . *page 1607*

Christians have power to overcome the world
(1 John 5:4-5) . . . *page 1633*

PRAISE (see Worship)

PRAYER

Ask God for help (Psalm 40:13) . . . *page 707*

God does not hear our prayers if we are
purposely sinning (Micah 3:4) . . . *page 1144*

Prayer should not be a show (Matthew 6:6)
. . . *page 1204*

Jesus taught his disciples how to pray (Matthew
6:9-13) . . . *page 1204*

Pray with an attitude of humility (Luke 18:9-14)
. . . *page 1322*

Pray in Jesus' name (John 16:23-24)
. . . *page 1368*

Pray all the time (Ephesians 6:18) . . . *page 1517*

Pray without doubting (James 1:6)
. . . *page 1600*

Pray with the right motives (James 4:3)
. . . *page 1605*

Pray according to God's will (1 John 5:14-15)
. . . *page 1634*

PRIDE (see also Self-Esteem)

Pride leads to shame (Proverbs 11:2) . . . *page 798*

Pride leads to arguments (Proverbs 13:10)
. . . *page 800*
Pride will be punished (Proverbs 16:5)
. . . *page 804*
Pride ends in destruction (Proverbs 16:18)
. . . *page 804*
Pride cuts us off from God and others (Luke
18:9-14) . . . *page 1322*
There is no place for proud boasting in the
Christian life (Romans 3:27) . . . *page 1435*
God chose to reveal himself to the humble
(1 Corinthians 1:26-31) . . . *page 1457*
Pride is not compatible with the fruit of the
Spirit (Galatians 5:22-26) . . . *page 1505*
God opposes the proud (James 4:6) . . . *page 1605*

PROBLEMS (see Stress, Suffering, Trials)

PROCRASTINATION
We must not procrastinate in choosing to serve
the Lord (Joshua 24:15) . . . *page 296*
God does not procrastinate (Habakkuk 2:3)
. . . *page 1159*
Those who procrastinate lose out (Luke
14:16-21) . . . *page 1317*
Today is the day to be saved (2 Corinthians 6:2)
. . . *page 1486*
No one can procrastinate forever (Revelation
10:6) . . . *page 1658*

PURITY
Only God can make us pure (Psalm 51:1-10)
. . . *page 714*
We can remain pure by following God's Word
(Psalm 119:1-20) . . . *page 763*
We cannot claim purity apart from God
(Proverbs 20:9) . . . *page 808*
The pure in heart will see God (Matthew 5:8)
. . . *page 1202*
Purity begins in the heart (Matthew 5:27-30)
. . . *page 1203*
Outward purity cannot substitute for inner
purity (Matthew 23:25-28) . . . *page 1233*
Purity comes from God (John 17:17)
. . . *page 1369*
Purity ought to mark believers' lives (Ephesians
5:1-4) . . . *page 1515*
Our minds should think about things that are
pure (Philippians 4:8) . . . *page 1525*
One day our purity will be like Christ's (1 John
3:1-3) . . . *page 1631*

QUESTIONS
God may not always answer our questions (Job
42:1-3) . . . *page 674*
God welcomes our sincere questions (Luke
7:18-23) . . . *page 1301*
We need not be afraid when questionedfaith
(Luke 21:12-15) . . . *page 1328*
We should be ready with answers when
questioned (1 Peter 3:15) . . . *page 1615*

RELATIONSHIPS (see also Friendship, Marriage)
Our relationship with God is through Jesus
Christ (John 14:19-21) . . . *page 1365*

Our relationships should not compromise our
faith (2 Corinthians 6:14-18) . . . *page 1487*
We are unified with all believers in God's family
(Ephesians 2:21-22) . . . *page 1512*
Our relationship with Christ is deep and abiding
(2 Timothy 2:11-13) . . . *page 1562*
Our relationship with Christ makes us children
of God (1 John 3:1-3) . . . *page 1631*

REPENTANCE (see also Confession of Sin)
Repentance opens a relationship with God (Luke
3:7-8) . . . *page 1292*
Unless we repent of our sins, we will perish
(Luke 13:3-5) . . . *page 1315*
Angels rejoice when a sinner repents (Luke 15:7)
. . . *page 1318*
Forgive those who repent of wrongs done to you
(Luke 17:4) . . . *page 1321*
Repentance is essential for the Holy Spirit to
work (Acts 2:38) . . . *page 1383*
God can use difficulties to encourage us to
repent (2 Corinthians 7:9-10) . . . *page 1488*
God would like everyone to repent and believe
(2 Peter 3:9) . . . *page 1625*

REPUTATION
A good reputation can be built by obeying
God's Word (Deuteronomy 4:1-14)
. . . *page 227*
Integrity builds a good reputation (Ruth 2:1-13)
. . . *page 338*
A bad reputation will follow you (Proverbs
25:9-10) . . . *page 814*
The Christians in Rome had a reputation for
obedience (Romans 16:19) . . . *page 1453*
Guard your reputation (2 Corinthians 8:18-24)
. . . *page 1489*
Maintain a good reputation among
non-Christians (Colossians 4:5) . . . *page 1535*

RESPECT (see also Authority)
God is worthy of our respect (Exodus 3:5)
. . . *page 80*
Our parents are worthy of respect (Leviticus
19:3) . . . *page 156*
Those in authority should have our respect
(1 Samuel 24:1-6) . . . *page 376*
Husbands and wives should respect each other
(Ephesians 5:33) . . . *page 1516*
Those in leadership should have respectful
children (1 Timothy 3:4) . . . *page 1553*
Show respect to all people (1 Peter 2:17)
. . . *page 1613*

RESPONSIBILITY
Responsible people admit their wrongs
(1 Chronicles 21:8) . . . *page 530*
Responsible people are faithful with what
they have been given (Matthew 25:14-30)
. . . *page 1236*
People are responsible for their decision about
Christ (John 3:18-19) . . . *page 1344*

Responsible people know their abilities and limitations (Acts 6:1-7) . . . *page 1387*

People are responsible for their own actions (James 1:13-15) . . . *page 1601*

REST

God gave us an example of and a command to rest (Genesis 2:3) . . . *page 6*

Rest is important for worship (Exodus 20:8) . . . *page 102*

God tells us to rest (Exodus 23:12) . . . *page 106*

Jesus promises to give us rest from our burdens (Matthew 11:28-30) . . . *page 1214*

Rest is a gift of God (Hebrews 4:9-11) . . . *page 1581*

Heaven will be a place of rest (Revelation 14:13) . . . *page 1662*

RESURRECTION

Christ's resurrection is a historical fact (Matthew 28:5-10) . . . *page 1243*

All people will be resurrected (John 5:24-30) . . . *page 1348*

Jesus promised to raise his followers (John 6:38-40) . . . *page 1350*

We know we will be resurrected (John 11:24-26) . . . *page 1359*

We will experience resurrection (Romans 6:3-11) . . . *page 1438*

Jesus' resurrection is the foundation of Christianity (1 Corinthians 15:12-21) . . . *page 1474*

Our resurrected bodies will be eternal bodies (1 Corinthians 15:51-53) . . . *page 1475*

REVENGE

God's people should not seek revenge (Leviticus 19:18) . . . *page 157*

Do not pay back evil for evil (Proverbs 24:29) . . . *page 813*

Believers ought to resist revenge (Matthew 5:38-42) . . . *page 1204*

Leave revenge in God's hands (Romans 12:19) . . . *page 1449*

Desire for revenge is not compatible with the Christian life (1 Thessalonians 5:15) . . . *page 1542*

Jesus is our example (1 Peter 2:21-23) . . . *page 1613*

RIGHTEOUS/RIGHTEOUSNESS

God is completely righteous (Isaiah 45:21-24) . . . *page 899*

We cannot attain righteousness on our own (Isaiah 64:6) . . . *page 920*

Human nature is the opposite of righteousness (Romans 3:10-18) . . . *page 1434*

Righteousness is not attained by works (Romans 4:18-25) . . . *page 1436*

Strict legalism cannot make us righteous (Galatians 3:11-21) . . . *page 1501*

Our God-given righteousness is armor against Satan's attacks (Ephesians 6:14) . . . *page 1517*

We become righteous through faith in Christ (Philippians 3:9) . . . *page 1524*

Studying God's Word helps us grow in righteousness (2 Timothy 3:16) . . . *page 1564*

Righteousness ought to characterize each believer's life (1 Peter 2:24) . . . *page 1614*

SADNESS (see Grief, Sorrow)

SALVATION

Those who receive salvation become God's children (John 1:12-13) . . . *page 1341*

Salvation is a work of the Holy Spirit in a person's life (John 3:1-16) . . . *page 1344*

Belief and trust in Jesus Christ are the only way to be saved (John 14:6) . . . *page 1365*

Salvation includes gaining a relationship with God (John 17:1-5) . . . *page 1368*

Receiving salvation means we must turn from our sins (Acts 2:37-38) . . . *page 1383*

Salvation cannot be earned; it is a gift of God (Romans 6:23) . . . *page 1439*

Receiving salvation is simple and personal (Romans 10:8-10) . . . *page 1445*

Salvation is by God's grace alone (Ephesians 2:1-9) . . . *page 1511*

Salvation rescues us from Satan's dominion (Colossians 1:13-14) . . . *page 1531*

Our salvation was obtained by Jesus' blood (1 Peter 1:18-19) . . . *page 1611*

SATAN (see also Demons)

Satan is under God's authority (Job 1:6-12) . . . *page 636*

Satan will tempt Jesus' followers (Matthew 4:1-11) . . . *page 1200*

Satan is completely evil (John 8:44) . . . *page 1355*

Satan is the temporary ruler over this world (Ephesians 2:1-2) . . . *page 1511*

Satan and his demons are spiritual (Ephesians 6:12) . . . *page 1517*

Satan works through an army of demons (1 Timothy 4:1) . . . *page 1554*

Believers have the authority to resist Satan (James 4:1-10) . . . *page 1605*

Satan is an enemy to Christians (1 Peter 5:8) . . . *page 1617*

Jesus destroyed Satan's work with his death on the cross (1 John 3:7-8) . . . *page 1631*

Satan is a defeated enemy (Revelation 20:10) . . . *page 1668*

SELF-ESTEEM (see also Pride)

We are made in God's image (Genesis 1:26-27) . . . *page 5*

We are a little lower than the angels (Psalm 8:3-5) . . . *page 684*

God took special care to create us (Psalm 139:1-18) . . . *page 775*

We have been formed by God's loving hands (Isaiah 64:8) . . . *page 920*

We are of great value to God (Luke 12:4-12) . . . *page 1312*

God gave his Son for us (John 3:16) . . . *page 1344*

Our self-esteem is affected by our relationship with Christ (Romans 12:1-8) . . . *page 1447*

Our self-esteem is based on God's approval
(2 Corinthians 10:12-18) . . . *page 1491*
We should not overestimate ourselves (Galatians
6:3-5) . . . *page 1506*

SEX

Sex is God's gift to married people (Proverbs
5:15-21) . . . *page 792*
Sex outside of marriage is foolish (Proverbs
6:23-35) . . . *page 794*
Sex within marriage is meant to be a delight
(Song of Songs 4:1-16) . . . *page 841*
Sexual sin begins in the mind (Matthew 5:27-30)
. . . *page 1203*
Sex is a powerful bond not meant to be taken
lightly (1 Corinthians 6:13-20) . . . *page 1462*
Sexual immorality has no place among
Christians (Ephesians 5:1-3) . . . *page 1515*
We are to have nothing to do with sexual
immorality (Colossians 3:5) . . . *page 1534*
God wants us to live in holiness, not lustful
passion (1 Thessalonians 4:1-8) . . . *page 1540*
Sex in marriage is honorable and pure (Hebrews
13:4) . . . *page 1594*

SICKNESS

God cares for the sick (Psalm 41:1-13)
. . . *page 708*
A cheerful spirit can act as good medicine
against sickness (Proverbs 17:22) . . . *page 805*
Jesus can heal sickness (Matthew 4:23-25)
. . . *page 1201*
Believers ought to have compassion on the sick
(Matthew 25:34-40) . . . *page 1237*
It is better to be physically crippled than
spiritually crippled (Mark 9:43-48)
. . . *page 1267*
Paul had an infirmity that God would not
remove (2 Corinthians 12:7-10) . . . *page 1493*

SIN

Sin has consequences (Genesis 3:1-19) . . . *page 7*
God must punish sin (Exodus 32:34)
. . . *page 118*
Our consciences can identify sin (2 Samuel
24:10-15) . . . *page 421*
We should humbly confess our sins to God (Ezra
9:5-15) . . . *page 598*
We should ask God to forgive our sins (Psalm
51:1-10) . . . *page 714*
Stay away from people who lead you to sin
(Proverbs 1:10-19) . . . *page 787*
Sin begins in the mind (Matthew 5:27-28)
. . . *page 1203*
All people have sinned (Romans 3:23)
. . . *page 1435*
Sin leads to eternal death (Romans 6:23)
. . . *page 1439*
Jesus takes the penalty of our sin on himself
(Romans 8:1-2) . . . *page 1441*
Sin begins with temptation (James 1:15)
. . . *page 1601*
We can sin by avoiding something we should do
(James 4:17) . . . *page 1606*

God is willing to forgive our sins (1 John 1:8-9)
. . . *page 1629*

SINGLENESS

Some people remain single to work for God's
Kingdom (Matthew 19:12) . . . *page 1227*
Singleness is a gift from God (1 Corinthians
7:7-8) . . . *page 1463*
Single people can serve God (1 Corinthians
7:25-31) . . . *page 1464*
Single people have more time to focus on service
for God (1 Corinthians 7:32-35) . . . *page 1464*

SORROW (see also Grief)

Sorrow is often a necessary part of repentance
(Judges 2:4-5) . . . *page 304*
Weeping will be followed by joy (Psalm 30:5)
. . . *page 698*
Jesus understands sorrow (Isaiah 53:3-9)
. . . *page 907*
God promises comfort to those who experience
sorrow (Matthew 5:4) . . . *page 1202*
God may use sorrow to draw us back to him
(2 Corinthians 7:10-11) . . . *page 1488*
We sorrow over believers who die, but one day
we will meet again (1 Thessalonians 4:13-18)
. . . *page 1541*
Sorrow will not exist in God's Kingdom
(Revelation 21:3-4) . . . *page 1669*

SOUL

People cannot destroy your soul (Matthew
10:28) . . . *page 1212*
We are to love God with our whole being
(Matthew 22:36-40) . . . *page 1232*
It is of no value to gain the world but lose your
soul (Mark 8:34-38) . . . *page 1265*
We can place our soul under Christ's protection
(John 10:27-29) . . . *page 1358*
Believers are assured of immortality
(1 Corinthians 15:46-53) . . . *page 1475*

SPIRITUAL GIFTS

God expects us to use our gifts (Romans 12:3-8)
. . . *page 1448*
God gives us our spiritual gifts (1 Corinthians
12:4-11) . . . *page 1470*
Spiritual gifts build up the body of Christ
(Ephesians 4:11-13) . . . *page 1514*
Spiritual gifts ought not be denied nor
overemphasized (1 Thessalonians 5:19-22)
. . . *page 1542*
God distributes spiritual gifts according to his
will (Hebrews 2:4) . . . *page 1579*

STRESS

Delegating work can alleviate stress (Exodus
18:13-26) . . . *page 100*
God is a refuge in times of stress (Psalm 62:1-8)
. . . *page 721*
Pray to God in times of stress (Psalm 69:1-36)
. . . *page 726*
Wait upon the Lord (Isaiah 40:30-31)
. . . *page 892*
God is always with us (Romans 8:31-39)
. . . *page 1442*

God cares about our stress (2 Corinthians 4:8-12) . . . *page 1484*

Don't let stress cause you to worry (Philippians 4:4-9) . . . *page 1525*

SUBMISSION (see also Obedience)

Christ is our example of submission to the Father's will (Matthew 26:39, 42) . . . *page 1239*

Following Christ requires submission to him (Luke 14:27) . . . *page 1317*

God created lines of authority for harmonious relationships (1 Corinthians 11:2-16) . . . *page 1468*

Marriage calls for mutual submission (Ephesians 5:21-33) . . . *page 1516*

Submit to God (James 4:7-10) . . . *page 1605*

SUFFERING (see also Trials)

Those who suffer need encouragement (Job 16:1-6) . . . *page 652*

Christ's followers will face suffering (Matthew 16:21-26) . . . *page 1223*

Our suffering helps us comfort others who are suffering (2 Corinthians 1:3-7) . . . *page 1480*

Our suffering will end in glory (2 Corinthians 4:17-18) . . . *page 1485*

Jesus can help us through suffering (Hebrews 2:11-18) . . . *page 1580*

Christ showed how to handle suffering (1 Peter 2:21-24) . . . *page 1613*

There will be no suffering in Christ's Kingdom (Revelation 21:4) . . . *page 1669*

TEACHING (see also Witnessing)

Parents must teach their children about the Lord (Deuteronomy 6:4-9) . . . *page 230*

Believers teach each other (2 Timothy 2:2) . . . *page 1561*

Qualities of a good teacher (2 Timothy 2:22-26) . . . *page 1562*

Instruction to those who teach God's Word (Titus 2:1-15) . . . *page 1570*

TELLING OTHERS (see also Witnessing)

We are God's messengers (Isaiah 43:10-11) . . . *page 895*

Christians bring light to a spiritually dark world (Matthew 5:14-16) . . . *page 1202*

Jesus made salvation available to all people (Matthew 9:9-13) . . . *page 1209*

Be bold in telling what God has done for you (Matthew 10:33) . . . *page 1212*

Jesus sent his followers to make disciples (Matthew 28:18-20) . . . *page 1243*

The Holy Spirit gives us power to speak up (Acts 1:8) . . . *page 1381*

TEMPTATION

Temptation comes from Satan (Genesis 3:1-6) . . . *page 7*

How to avoid temptation (Proverbs 7:1-5) . . . *page 794*

How to respond when tempted (Matthew 4:1-11) . . . *page 1200*

God will provide a way of escape (1 Corinthians 10:13) . . . *page 1467*

Run from temptation (2 Timothy 2:22) . . . *page 1562*

Christ can help us, for he, too, has faced temptation (Hebrews 4:15-16) . . . *page 1582*

God never tempts people to sin (James 1:13-15) . . . *page 1601*

THANKFULNESS

Thank the Lord because he is good (Psalm 107:1-3) . . . *page 756*

Be thankful for answers to prayer (Psalm 138:1-5) . . . *page 774*

Be thankful for salvation (Ephesians 2:4-10) . . . *page 1511*

Our prayers should include words of thankfulness (Philippians 4:6) . . . *page 1525*

Our life should be characterized by thankfulness to God (Colossians 3:15-17) . . . *page 1534*

We are called to give thanks in all circumstances (1 Thessalonians 5:16-18) . . . *page 1542*

TRIALS (see also Suffering)

Christ promises us rest from our trials (Matthew 11:28-30) . . . *page 1214*

Jesus understands our struggles (John 15:18) . . . *page 1367*

Have peace in trials (John 16:33) . . . *page 1368*

Trials help us develop patience (Romans 5:1-5) . . . *page 1437*

God knows what he is doing with our life (Romans 8:28) . . . *page 1442*

Believers can expect to suffer for their faith (2 Corinthians 6:3-13) . . . *page 1486*

Present trials fade in comparison to the joy of our relationship with Christ (Philippians 3:7-11) . . . *page 1524*

God expects us to grow through our trials (James 1:2-4) . . . *page 1600*

TRUST (see Faith)

TRUTH

God wants us to be true and righteous (Psalm 51:1-6) . . . *page 714*

Truth never changes (Proverbs 12:19) . . . *page 799*

Truth sets us free (John 8:31-32) . . . *page 1354*

Truth is found in Jesus Christ (John 14:6) . . . *page 1365*

God's Word is truth (John 17:17) . . . *page 1369*

We must not only believe the truth but also live by it (1 John 1:5-7) . . . *page 1628*

UNITY

Unity among believers pleases God (Psalm 133:1) . . . *page 772*

Christians are not supposed to live in isolation (John 17:11) . . . *page 1369*

Unity includes bearing one another's joys and burdens (Romans 12:9-16) . . . *page 1448*

Believers must seek unity in all essentials (1 Corinthians 1:10) . . . *page 1457*

There can be great unity even in great diversity (Ephesians 4:3-13) . . . *page 1514*

The love Christ commanded should create unity
(Philippians 1:3-11) . . . *page 1520*

Unity ought to be a distinctive mark among
Christians (Philippians 2:1-2) . . . *page 1522*

WISDOM

The fear of God is the beginning of wisdom
(Proverbs 1:7) . . . *page 786*

To find wisdom, first find God (Proverbs 2:6-12)
. . . *page 788*

Wise people accept advice (Proverbs 13:10)
. . . *page 800*

Wise people boast not in their wisdom but in
knowing God (Jeremiah 9:23-24) . . . *page 946*

The wise understand God's ways and follow his
guidance (Hosea 14:9) . . . *page 1110*

Wise people build on the solid foundation
of God and his Word (Matthew 7:24-27)
. . . *page 1207*

God's wisdom is different from the world's
wisdom (1 Corinthians 2:1-16) . . . *page 1458*

God will give us wisdom if we ask for it (James
1:5) . . . *page 1600*

WITNESSING (see also Teaching, Telling Others)

Bringing the good news of Christ is a wonderful
privilege (Isaiah 52:7) . . . *page 906*

God's message will accomplish what he desires
(Isaiah 55:10-11) . . . *page 910*

God holds us accountable for avoiding a chance
to witness (Ezekiel 3:18-19) . . . *page 1017*

Let your light shine (Matthew 5:14-16)
. . . *page 1202*

Jesus commanded all believers to witness
(Matthew 28:16-20) . . . *page 1243*

If we acknowledge our faith before people,
Jesus will acknowledge us (Luke 12:8-9)
. . . *page 1313*

Christians are called to spread the gospel across
the world (Acts 1:8) . . . *page 1381*

We plant or water the seed of faith, but only
God makes it grow (1 Corinthians 3:5-9)
. . . *page 1459*

God has entrusted us with the message we need
to share with others (2 Corinthians 5:18-21)
. . . *page 1486*

Always be ready to tell what God has done for
you (1 Peter 3:15) . . . *page 1615*

WORK

Hard work is honored by God (Genesis 31:38-42)
. . . *page 46*

Use your skills to honor God (Exodus 36:1)
. . . *page 122*

Hard work brings rewards (Proverbs 12:14)
. . . *page 799*

Hard work helps supply basic needs (Proverbs
28:19) . . . *page 817*

Our work for God is never wasted (1 Corinthians
15:58) . . . *page 1475*

All work should be done as though working for
God (Ephesians 6:5-9) . . . *page 1517*

WORRY (see Stress)

WORSHIP (see also Church)

Worship is an encounter with the living and
holy God (Exodus 3:1-6) . . . *page 80*

Worship is reserved for God alone (Exodus
34:14) . . . *page 120*

In worship, we ascribe to the Lord the glory due
him (Psalm 29:1-2) . . . *page 698*

We can worship because of Christ's sacrifice on
our behalf (Hebrews 10:1-10) . . . *page 1588*

We should worship with reverence for God
(Hebrews 12:28) . . . *page 1594*

When we draw near to God, he draws near to us
(James 4:8) . . . *page 1605*

A NOTE TO READERS

The *Holy Bible,* New Living Translation, was first published in 1996. It quickly became one of the most popular Bible translations in the English-speaking world. While the NLT's influence was rapidly growing, the Bible Translation Committee determined that an additional investment in scholarly review and text refinement could make it even better. So shortly after its initial publication, the committee began an eight-year process with the purpose of increasing the level of the NLT's precision without sacrificing its easy-to-understand quality. This second-generation text was completed in 2004, with minor changes subsequently introduced in 2007 and 2013.

The goal of any Bible translation is to convey the meaning and content of the ancient Hebrew, Aramaic, and Greek texts as accurately as possible to contemporary readers. The challenge for our translators was to create a text that would communicate as clearly and powerfully to today's readers as the original texts did to readers and listeners in the ancient biblical world. The resulting translation is easy to read and understand, while also accurately communicating the meaning and content of the original biblical texts. The NLT is a general-purpose text especially good for study, devotional reading, and reading aloud in worship services.

We believe that the New Living Translation—which combines the latest biblical scholarship with a clear, dynamic writing style—will communicate God's word powerfully to all who read it. We publish it with the prayer that God will use it to speak his timeless truth to the church and the world in a fresh, new way.

The Publishers
January 2013

INTRODUCTION TO THE
NEW LIVING TRANSLATION

Translation Philosophy and Methodology

English Bible translations tend to be governed by one of two general translation theories. The first theory has been called "formal-equivalence," "literal," or "word-for-word" translation. According to this theory, the translator attempts to render each word of the original language into English and seeks to preserve the original syntax and sentence structure as much as possible in translation. The second theory has been called "dynamic-equivalence," "functional-equivalence," or "thought-for-thought" translation. The goal of this translation theory is to produce in English the closest natural equivalent of the message expressed by the original-language text, both in meaning and in style.

Both of these translation theories have their strengths. A formal-equivalence translation preserves aspects of the original text—including ancient idioms, term consistency, and original-language syntax—that are valuable for scholars and professional study. It allows a reader to trace formal elements of the original-language text through the English translation. A dynamic-equivalence translation, on the other hand, focuses on translating the message of the original-language text. It ensures that the meaning of the text is readily apparent to the contemporary reader. This allows the message to come through with immediacy, without requiring the reader to struggle with foreign idioms and awkward syntax. It also facilitates serious study of the text's message and clarity in both devotional and public reading.

The pure application of either of these translation philosophies would create translations at opposite ends of the translation spectrum. But in reality, all translations contain a mixture of these two philosophies. A purely formal-equivalence translation would be unintelligible in English, and a purely dynamic-equivalence translation would risk being unfaithful to the original. That is why translations shaped by dynamic-equivalence theory are usually quite literal when the original text is relatively clear, and the translations shaped by formal-equivalence theory are sometimes quite dynamic when the original text is obscure.

The translators of the New Living Translation set out to render the message of the original texts of Scripture into clear, contemporary English.

As they did so, they kept the concerns of both formal-equivalence and dynamic-equivalence in mind. On the one hand, they translated as simply and literally as possible when that approach yielded an accurate, clear, and natural English text. Many words and phrases were rendered literally and consistently into English, preserving essential literary and rhetorical devices, ancient metaphors, and word choices that give structure to the text and provide echoes of meaning from one passage to the next.

On the other hand, the translators rendered the message more dynamically when the literal rendering was hard to understand, was misleading, or yielded archaic or foreign wording. They clarified difficult metaphors and terms to aid in the reader's understanding. The translators first struggled with the meaning of the words and phrases in the ancient context; then they rendered the message into clear, natural English. Their goal was to be both faithful to the ancient texts and eminently readable. The result is a translation that is both exegetically accurate and idiomatically powerful.

Translation Process and Team

To produce an accurate translation of the Bible into contemporary English, the translation team needed the skills necessary to enter into the thought patterns of the ancient authors and then to render their ideas, connotations, and effects into clear, contemporary English. To begin this process, qualified biblical scholars were needed to interpret the meaning of the original text and to check it against our base English translation. In order to guard against personal and theological biases, the scholars needed to represent a diverse group of Evangelicals who would employ the best exegetical tools. Then to work alongside the scholars, skilled English stylists were needed to shape the text into clear, contemporary English.

With these concerns in mind, the Bible Translation Committee recruited teams of scholars that represented a broad spectrum of denominations, theological perspectives, and backgrounds within the worldwide Evangelical community. (These scholars are listed at the end of this introduction.) Each book of the Bible was assigned to three different scholars with proven expertise in the book or group of books to be reviewed. Each of these scholars made a thorough review of a base translation and submitted suggested revisions to the appropriate Senior Translator. The Senior Translator then reviewed and summarized these suggestions and proposed a first-draft revision of the base text. This draft served as the basis for several additional phases of exegetical and stylistic committee review. Then the Bible Translation Committee jointly reviewed and approved every verse of the final translation.

Throughout the translation and editing process, the Senior Translators and their scholar teams were given a chance to review the editing done by the team of stylists. This ensured that exegetical errors would not be introduced late in the process and that the entire Bible Translation Committee was happy with the final result. By choosing a team of qualified scholars and skilled stylists and by setting up a process that allowed their interaction throughout the process, the New Living Translation has been refined to preserve the essential formal elements of the original biblical texts, while also creating a clear, understandable English text.

The New Living Translation was first published in 1996. Shortly after its initial publication, the Bible Translation Committee began a process of further committee review and translation refinement. The purpose of this continued revision was to increase the level of precision without sacrificing the text's easy-to-understand quality. This second-edition text was completed in 2004, with minor changes subsequently introduced in 2007 and 2013.

Written to Be Read Aloud
It is evident in Scripture that the biblical documents were written to be read aloud, often in public worship (see Nehemiah 8; Luke 4:16-20; 1 Timothy 4:13; Revelation 1:3). It is still the case today that more people will hear the Bible read aloud in church than are likely to read it for themselves. Therefore, a new translation must communicate with clarity and power when it is read publicly. Clarity was a primary goal for the NLT translators, not only to facilitate private reading and understanding, but also to ensure that it would be excellent for public reading and make an immediate and powerful impact on any listener.

The Texts behind the New Living Translation
The Old Testament translators used the Masoretic Text of the Hebrew Bible as represented in *Biblia Hebraica Stuttgartensia* (1977), with its extensive system of textual notes; this is an update of Rudolf Kittel's *Biblia Hebraica* (Stuttgart, 1937). The translators also further compared the Dead Sea Scrolls, the Septuagint and other Greek manuscripts, the Samaritan Pentateuch, the Syriac Peshitta, the Latin Vulgate, and any other versions or manuscripts that shed light on the meaning of difficult passages.

The New Testament translators used the two standard editions of the Greek New Testament: the *Greek New Testament,* published by the United Bible Societies (UBS, fourth revised edition, 1993), and *Novum Testamentum Graece,* edited by Nestle and Aland (NA, twenty-seventh edition, 1993). These two editions, which have the same text but differ in punctuation and textual notes, represent, for the most part, the best in modern textual scholarship. However, in cases where strong textual or other scholarly evidence supported the decision, the translators sometimes chose to differ from the UBS and NA Greek texts and followed variant readings found in other ancient witnesses. Significant textual variants of this sort are always noted in the textual notes of the New Living Translation.

Translation Issues
The translators have made a conscious effort to provide a text that can be easily understood by the typical reader of modern English. To this end, we sought to use only vocabulary and language structures in common use today. We avoided using language likely to become quickly dated or that reflects only a narrow subdialect of English, with the goal of making the New Living Translation as broadly useful and timeless as possible.

But our concern for readability goes beyond the concerns of vocabulary and sentence structure. We are also concerned about historical and cultural barriers to understanding the Bible, and we have sought to translate terms shrouded in history and culture in ways that can be immediately understood. To this end:

- We have converted ancient weights and measures (for example, "ephah" [a unit of dry volume] or "cubit" [a unit of length]) to modern English (American) equivalents, since the ancient measures are not generally meaningful to today's readers. Then in the textual footnotes we offer the literal Hebrew, Aramaic, or Greek measures, along with modern metric equivalents.
- Instead of translating ancient currency values literally, we have expressed them in common terms that communicate the message. For example, in the Old Testament, "ten shekels of silver" becomes "ten pieces of silver" to convey the intended message. In the New Testament, we have often translated the "denarius" as "the normal daily wage" to facilitate understanding. Then a footnote offers: "Greek *a denarius,* the payment for a full day's wage." In general, we give a clear English rendering and then state the literal Hebrew, Aramaic, or Greek in a textual footnote.

- Since the names of Hebrew months are unknown to most contemporary readers, and since the Hebrew lunar calendar fluctuates from year to year in relation to the solar calendar used today, we have looked for clear ways to communicate the time of year the Hebrew months (such as Abib) refer to. When an expanded or interpretive rendering is given in the text, a textual note gives the literal rendering. Where it is possible to define a specific ancient date in terms of our modern calendar, we use modern dates in the text. A textual footnote then gives the literal Hebrew date and states the rationale for our rendering. For example, Ezra 6:15 pinpoints the date when the postexilic Temple was completed in Jerusalem: "the third day of the month Adar." This was during the sixth year of King Darius's reign (that is, 515 B.C.). We have translated that date as March 12, with a footnote giving the Hebrew and identifying the year as 515 B.C.

- Since ancient references to the time of day differ from our modern methods of denoting time, we have used renderings that are instantly understandable to the modern reader. Accordingly, we have rendered specific times of day by using approximate equivalents in terms of our common "o'clock" system. On occasion, translations such as "at dawn the next morning" or "as the sun was setting" have been used when the biblical reference is more general.

- When the meaning of a proper name (or a wordplay inherent in a proper name) is relevant to the message of the text, its meaning is often illuminated with a textual footnote. For example, in Exodus 2:10 the text reads: "The princess named him Moses, for she explained, 'I lifted him out of the water.'" The accompanying footnote reads: "*Moses* sounds like a Hebrew term that means 'to lift out.'"

- Sometimes, when the actual meaning of a name is clear, that meaning is included in parentheses within the text itself. For example, the text at Genesis 16:11 reads: "You are to name him Ishmael *(which means 'God hears')*, for the LORD has heard your cry of distress." Since the original hearers and readers would have instantly understood the meaning of the name "Ishmael," we have provided modern readers with the same information so they can experience the text in a similar way.

- Many words and phrases carry a great deal of cultural meaning that was obvious to the original readers but needs explanation in our own culture. For example, the phrase "they beat their breasts" (Luke 23:48) in ancient times meant that people were very upset, often in mourning. In our translation we chose to translate this phrase dynamically for clarity: "They went home *in deep sorrow.*" Then we included a footnote with the literal Greek, which reads: "Greek *went home beating their breasts.*" In other similar cases, however, we have sometimes chosen to illuminate the existing literal expression to make it immediately understandable. For example, here we might have expanded the literal Greek phrase to read: "They went home beating their breasts *in sorrow.*" If we had done this, we would not have included a textual footnote, since the literal Greek clearly appears in translation.

- Metaphorical language is sometimes difficult for contemporary readers to understand, so at times we have chosen to translate or illuminate the meaning of a metaphor. For example, the ancient poet writes, "Your neck is *like* the tower of David" (Song of Songs 4:4). We have rendered it "Your neck is *as beautiful as* the tower of David" to clarify the intended positive meaning of the simile. Another example comes in Ecclesiastes 12:3, which can be literally rendered: "Remember him . . . when the grinding women cease because they are few, and the women who look through the windows see dimly." We have rendered it: "Remember him before your teeth—your few remaining servants—stop grinding; and before your eyes—the women looking through the windows—see dimly." We clarified such metaphors only when we believed a typical reader might be confused by the literal text.

- When the content of the original language text is poetic in character, we have rendered it in English poetic form. We sought to break lines in ways that clarify and highlight the relationships between phrases of the text. Hebrew poetry often uses parallelism, a literary form where a second phrase (or in some instances a third or fourth) echoes the initial phrase in some way. In Hebrew parallelism, the subsequent parallel phrases continue, while also furthering and sharpening, the thought expressed in the initial line or phrase. Whenever possible, we sought to represent these parallel phrases in natural poetic English.

- The Greek term *hoi Ioudaioi* is literally translated "the Jews" in many English translations. In the Gospel of John, however, this term doesn't always refer to the Jewish people generally. In some contexts, it refers more particularly to the Jewish religious leaders. We have attempted to capture the meaning in these different contexts by using terms such as "the people" (with a footnote: Greek *the Jewish people*) or "the religious leaders," where appropriate.

- One challenge we faced was how to translate accurately the ancient biblical text that was originally written in a context where male-oriented terms were used to refer to humanity generally. We needed to respect the nature of the ancient context while also trying to make the translation clear to a modern audience that tends to read male-oriented language as applying only to males. Often the original text, though using masculine nouns and pronouns, clearly intends that the message be applied to both men and women. A typical example is found in the New Testament letters, where the believers are called "brothers" (*adelphoi*). Yet it is clear from the content of these letters that they were addressed to all the believers—male and female. Thus, we have usually translated this Greek word as "brothers and sisters" in order to represent the historical situation more accurately.

- We have also been sensitive to passages where the text applies generally to human beings or to the human condition. In some instances we have used plural pronouns (they, them) in place of the masculine singular (he, him). For example, a traditional rendering of Proverbs 22:6 is: "Train up a child in the way he should go, and when he is old he will not turn from it." We have rendered it: "Direct your children onto the right path, and when they are older, they will not leave it." At times, we have also replaced third person pronouns with the second person to ensure clarity. A traditional rendering of Proverbs 26:27 is: "He who digs a pit will fall into it, and he who rolls a stone, it will come back on him." We have rendered it: "If you set a trap for others, you will get caught in it yourself. If you roll a boulder down on others, it will crush you instead."

- We should emphasize, however, that all masculine nouns and pronouns used to represent God (for example, "Father") have been maintained without exception. All decisions of this kind have been driven by the concern to reflect accurately the intended meaning of the original texts of Scripture.

Lexical Consistency in Terminology

For the sake of clarity, we have translated certain original-language terms consistently, especially within synoptic passages and for commonly repeated rhetorical phrases, and within certain word categories such as divine names and non-theological technical terminology (e.g., liturgical, legal, cultural, zoological, and botanical terms). For theological terms, we have allowed a greater semantic range of acceptable English words or phrases for a single Hebrew or Greek word. We have avoided some theological terms that are not readily understood by many modern readers. For example, we avoided using words such as "justification" and "sanctification," which are carryovers from Latin translations. In place of these words, we have provided renderings such as "made right with God" and "made holy."

The Spelling of Proper Names

Many individuals in the Bible, especially the Old Testament, are known by more than one name (e.g., Uzziah/Azariah). For the sake of clarity, we have tried to use a single spelling for any one individual, footnoting the literal spelling whenever we differ from it. This is especially helpful in delineating the kings of Israel and Judah. King Joash/Jehoash of Israel has been consistently called Jehoash, while King Joash/Jehoash of Judah is called Joash. A similar distinction has been used to distinguish between Joram/Jehoram of Israel and Joram/Jehoram of Judah. All such decisions were made with the goal of clarifying the text for the reader. When the ancient biblical writers clearly had a theological purpose in their choice of a variant name (e.g., Esh-baal/Ishbosheth), the different names have been maintained with an explanatory footnote.

For the names Jacob and Israel, which are used interchangeably for both the individual patriarch and the nation, we generally render it "Israel" when it refers to the nation and "Jacob" when it refers to the individual. When our rendering of the name differs from the underlying Hebrew text, we provide a textual footnote, which includes this explanation: "The names 'Jacob' and 'Israel' are often interchanged throughout the Old Testament, referring sometimes to the individual patriarch and sometimes to the nation."

The Rendering of Divine Names

All appearances of *'el, 'elohim,* or *'eloah* have been translated "God," except where the context demands the translation "god(s)." We have generally rendered the tetragrammaton (*YHWH*) consistently as "the LORD," utilizing a form with small capitals that is common among English translations. This will distinguish it from the name *'adonai,* which we render "Lord." When *'adonai* and *YHWH* appear together, we have rendered it "Sovereign LORD." This also distinguishes *'adonai YHWH* from cases where *YHWH* appears with *'elohim,* which is rendered "LORD God." When *YH* (the short form of *YHWH*) and *YHWH* appear together, we have rendered it "LORD GOD." When *YHWH* appears with the term *tseba'oth,* we have rendered it "LORD of Heaven's Armies" to translate the meaning of the name. In a few cases, we have utilized the transliteration, *Yahweh,* when the personal character of the name is being invoked in contrast to another divine name or the name of some other god (for example, see Exodus 3:15; 6:2-3).

In the New Testament, the Greek word *christos* has normally been translated as "Messiah" when the context assumes a Jewish audience. When a Gentile audience can be assumed, *christos* has been translated as "Christ." The Greek word *kurios* is consistently translated "Lord," except that it is translated "LORD" wherever the New Testament text explicitly quotes from the Old Testament, and the text there has it in small capitals.

Textual Footnotes

The New Living Translation provides several kinds of textual footnotes, all designated in the text with an asterisk:

- When for the sake of clarity the NLT renders a difficult or potentially confusing phrase dynamically, we generally give the literal rendering in a textual footnote. This allows the reader to see the literal source of our dynamic rendering and how our translation relates to other more literal translations. These notes are prefaced with "Hebrew," "Aramaic," or "Greek," identifying the language of the underlying source text. For example, in Acts 2:42 we translated the literal "breaking of bread" (from the Greek) as "the Lord's Supper" to clarify that this verse refers to the ceremonial practice of the church rather than just an ordinary meal. Then we attached a footnote to "the Lord's Supper," which reads: "Greek the breaking of bread."

- Textual footnotes are also used to show alternative renderings, prefaced with the word "Or." These normally occur for passages where an aspect of the meaning is debated. On occasion, we also provide notes on words or phrases that represent a departure from long-standing tradition. These notes are prefaced with "Traditionally rendered." For example, the footnote to the translation "serious skin disease" at Leviticus 13:2 says: "Traditionally rendered *leprosy.* The Hebrew word used throughout this passage is used to describe various skin diseases."

- When our translators follow a textual variant that differs significantly from our standard Hebrew or Greek texts (listed earlier), we document that difference with a footnote. We also footnote cases when the NLT excludes a passage that is included in the Greek text known as the *Textus Receptus* (and familiar to readers through its translation in the King James Version). In such cases, we offer a translation of the excluded text in a footnote, even though it is generally recognized as a later addition to the Greek text and not part of the original Greek New Testament.

- All Old Testament passages that are quoted in the New Testament are identified by a textual footnote at the New Testament location. When the New Testament clearly quotes from the Greek translation of the Old Testament, and when it differs significantly in wording from the Hebrew text, we also place a textual footnote at the Old Testament location. This note includes a rendering of the Greek version, along with a cross-reference to the New Testament passage(s) where it is cited (for example, see notes on Psalms 8:2; 53:3; Proverbs 3:12).

- Some textual footnotes provide cultural and historical information on places, things, and people in the Bible that are probably obscure to modern readers. Such notes should aid the reader in understanding the message of the text. For example, in Acts 12:1, "King Herod" is named in this translation as "King Herod Agrippa" and is identified in a footnote as being "the nephew of Herod Antipas and a grandson of Herod the Great."

- When the meaning of a proper name (or a wordplay inherent in a proper name) is relevant to the meaning of the text, it is either illuminated with a textual footnote or included within parentheses in the text itself. For example, the footnote concerning the name "Eve" at Genesis 3:20 reads: "*Eve* sounds like a Hebrew term that means 'to give life.'" This wordplay in the Hebrew illuminates the meaning of the text, which goes on to say that Eve "would be the mother of all who live."

AS WE SUBMIT this translation for publication, we recognize that any translation of the Scriptures is subject to limitations and imperfections. Anyone who has attempted to communicate the richness of God's Word into another language will realize it is impossible to make a perfect translation. Recognizing these limitations, we sought God's guidance and wisdom throughout this project. Now we pray that he will accept our efforts and use this translation for the benefit of the church and of all people.

We pray that the New Living Translation will overcome some of the barriers of history, culture, and language that have kept people from reading and understanding God's Word. We hope that readers unfamiliar with the Bible will find the words clear and easy to understand and that readers well versed in the Scriptures will gain a fresh perspective. We pray that readers will gain insight and wisdom for living, but most of all that they will meet the God of the Bible and be forever changed by knowing him.

The Bible Translation Committee

BIBLE TRANSLATION TEAM

PENTATEUCH
Daniel I. Block, Senior Translator
Wheaton College

GENESIS
Allen Ross, *Beeson Divinity School, Samford University*
Gordon Wenham, *Trinity College, Bristol*

EXODUS
Robert Bergen, *Hannibal-LaGrange College*
Daniel I. Block, *Wheaton College*
Eugene Carpenter, *Bethel College, Mishawaka, Indiana*

LEVITICUS
David Baker, *Ashland Theological Seminary*
Victor Hamilton, *Asbury College*
Kenneth Mathews, *Beeson Divinity School, Samford University*

NUMBERS
Dale A. Brueggemann, *Assemblies of God Division of Foreign Missions*
R. K. Harrison, *Wycliffe College*
Paul R. House, *Beeson Divinity School, Samford University*
Gerald L. Mattingly, *Johnson Bible College*

DEUTERONOMY
J. Gordon McConville, *University of Gloucester*
Eugene H. Merrill, *Dallas Theological Seminary*
John A. Thompson, *University of Melbourne*

HISTORICAL BOOKS
Barry J. Beitzel, Senior Translator
Trinity Evangelical Divinity School

JOSHUA, JUDGES
Carl E. Armerding, *Schloss Mittersill Study Centre*
Barry J. Beitzel, *Trinity Evangelical Divinity School*
Lawson Stone, *Asbury Theological Seminary*

1 & 2 SAMUEL
Robert Gordon, *Cambridge University*
V. Philips Long, *Regent College*
J. Robert Vannoy, *Biblical Theological Seminary*

1 & 2 KINGS
Bill T. Arnold, *Asbury Theological Seminary*
William H. Barnes, *North Central University*
Frederic W. Bush, *Fuller Theological Seminary*

1 & 2 CHRONICLES
Raymond B. Dillard, *Westminster Theological Seminary*
David A. Dorsey, *Evangelical School of Theology*
Terry Eves, *Erskine College*

RUTH, EZRA—ESTHER
William C. Williams, *Vanguard University*
H. G. M. Williamson, *Oxford University*

WISDOM BOOKS
Tremper Longman III, Senior Translator
Westmont College

JOB
August Konkel, *Providence Theological Seminary*
Tremper Longman III, *Westmont College*
Al Wolters, *Redeemer College*

PSALMS 1–75
Mark D. Futato, *Reformed Theological Seminary*
Douglas Green, *Westminster Theological Seminary*
Richard Pratt, *Reformed Theological Seminary*

PSALMS 76–150
David M. Howard Jr., *Bethel Theological Seminary*
Raymond C. Ortlund Jr., *Immanuel Church, Nashville, Tennessee*
Willem VanGemeren, *Trinity Evangelical Divinity School*

PROVERBS
Ted Hildebrandt, *Gordon College*
Richard Schultz, *Wheaton College*
Raymond C. Van Leeuwen, *Eastern College*

ECCLESIASTES, SONG OF SONGS
Daniel C. Fredericks, *Belhaven College*
David Hubbard, *Fuller Theological Seminary*
Tremper Longman III, *Westmont College*

PROPHETS
John N. Oswalt, Senior Translator
Asbury Theological Seminary

ISAIAH
John N. Oswalt, *Asbury Theological Seminary*
Gary Smith, *Union University*
John Walton, *Wheaton College*

JEREMIAH, LAMENTATIONS
G. Herbert Livingston, *Asbury Theological Seminary*
Elmer A. Martens, *Mennonite Brethren Biblical Seminary*

EZEKIEL
Daniel I. Block, *Wheaton College*
David H. Engelhard, *Calvin Theological Seminary*
David Thompson, *Asbury Theological Seminary*

DANIEL, HAGGAI—MALACHI
Joyce Baldwin Caine, *Trinity College, Bristol*
Douglas Gropp, *Catholic University of America*
Roy Hayden, *Oral Roberts School of Theology*
Andrew Hill, *Wheaton College*
Tremper Longman III, *Westmont College*

HOSEA—ZEPHANIAH
Joseph Coleson, *Nazarene Theological Seminary*
Roy Hayden, *Oral Roberts School of Theology*
Andrew Hill, *Wheaton College*
Richard Patterson, *Liberty University*

GOSPELS AND ACTS
Grant R. Osborne, Senior Translator
Trinity Evangelical Divinity School

MATTHEW
Craig Blomberg, *Denver Seminary*
Donald A. Hagner, *Fuller Theological Seminary*
David Turner, *Grand Rapids Baptist Seminary*

MARK
Robert Guelich, *Fuller Theological Seminary*
George Guthrie, *Union University*
Grant R. Osborne, *Trinity Evangelical Divinity School*

LUKE
Darrell Bock, *Dallas Theological Seminary*
Scot McKnight, *North Park University*
Robert Stein, *The Southern Baptist Theological Seminary*

JOHN
Gary M. Burge, *Wheaton College*
Philip W. Comfort, *Coastal Carolina University*
Marianne Meye Thompson, *Fuller Theological Seminary*

ACTS
D. A. Carson, *Trinity Evangelical Divinity School*
William J. Larkin, *Columbia International University*
Roger Mohrlang, *Whitworth University*

LETTERS AND REVELATION
Norman R. Ericson, Senior Translator
Wheaton College

ROMANS, GALATIANS
Gerald Borchert, *Northern Baptist Theological Seminary*
Douglas J. Moo, *Wheaton College*
Thomas R. Schreiner, *The Southern Baptist Theological Seminary*

1 & 2 CORINTHIANS
Joseph Alexanian, *Trinity International University*
Linda Belleville, *Bethel College, Mishawaka, Indiana*
Douglas A. Oss, *Central Bible College*
Robert Sloan, *Houston Baptist University*

EPHESIANS—PHILEMON
Harold W. Hoehner, *Dallas Theological Seminary*
Moises Silva, *Gordon-Conwell Theological Seminary*
Klyne Snodgrass, *North Park Theological Seminary*

HEBREWS, JAMES, 1 & 2 PETER, JUDE
Peter Davids, *St. Stephen's University*
Norman R. Ericson, *Wheaton College*
William Lane, *Seattle Pacific University*
J. Ramsey Michaels, *S. W. Missouri State University*

1–3 JOHN, REVELATION
Greg Beale, *Westminster Theological Seminary*
Robert Mounce, *Whitworth University*
M. Robert Mulholland Jr., *Asbury Theological Seminary*

SPECIAL REVIEWERS
F. F. Bruce, *University of Manchester*
Kenneth N. Taylor, *Translator,* The Living Bible

COORDINATING TEAM
Mark D. Taylor, *Director and Chief Stylist*
Ronald A. Beers, *Executive Director and Stylist*
Mark R. Norton, *Managing Editor and O.T. Coordinating Editor*
Philip W. Comfort, *N.T. Coordinating Editor*
Daniel W. Taylor, *Bethel University, Senior Stylist*
Sean A. Harrison, *Editor and Stylist*
James A. Swanson, *Lexical Reviewer*

OLD TESTAMENT

GENESIS

THE BIG PICTURE

A. GOD SETS THE STAGE (1:1–11:32)
1. Formation of the Universe (1:1–2:25)
   a. God creates matter, energy, and the natural order (1:1–2:3)
   b. God prepares pristine surroundings for the first family (2:4-25)
2. Fall of the Human Race (3:1-24)
   a. Commission of sin (3:1-8)
   b. Curse on sin (3:9-24)
3. Failure of Society (4:1–9:29)
   a. Failure of humankind (4:1–6:22)
   b. Flood of judgment (7:1–9:29)
4. Folly of Rebellion (10:1–11:32)
   a. Dispersal of the people (10:1-32)
   b. Disobedience of the people (11:1-32)

B. GOD CHOOSES THE PLAYERS (12:1–50:26)
1. Abraham (12:1–25:18)
2. Isaac (25:19–27:46)
3. Jacob (28:1–36:43)
4. Joseph (37:1–50:26)

The book of Genesis is a book of beginnings. It records how the world began and how God created it to be good. It tells us about the first people and how God made them to be excellent. But then it tells us about the beginning of sin—about the first time people decided to reject the program God had laid out for them. It records the first days of shame and of covering up. It records the beginning of our separation from God, each other, and the world God gave us.

We will see how people with perfect health, living in a perfect environment, rebelled against God. And we will see the consequences of their rebellion. We are given intimate glimpses of individuals dominated by hatred, drunkenness, lust, unhealthy family relationships, greed, cheating, irresponsibility, dishonesty, jealousy, violence, and other problems.

But the book of Genesis doesn't leave us in despair. It tells us of yet another beginning. It records how God chose a man named Abraham to father a special nation. And through this nation would come the solution for our separation from God, each other, and the world God gave us. Genesis begins the story of how God began his work of healing broken humanity—a healing to be expressed in the laws he would give his people and culminating in the coming of Jesus, the promised Messiah.

The book of Genesis reminds us of where all our problems began. It spells out the fatal consequences of rejecting God's program. But it also begins the agelong story of God's amazing love for the human race. Through this book we will discover that the only pathway to spiritual wholeness is in following God's program.

THE BOTTOM LINE

PURPOSE: To tell us about the beginning of things, including human opportunities and difficulties, and to demonstrate that God's solutions are the only ones that work. AUTHOR: Moses. AUDIENCE: The people of Israel. DATE WRITTEN: Chapters 1–11 deal with the undatable past; the events of chapters 12–50 are to be dated between about 2000 and 1800 B.C. The book was probably written shortly after 1445 B.C. SETTING: Mesopotamia, then Canaan, finally Egypt. KEY VERSE: "And Abram believed the LORD, and the LORD counted him as righteous because of his faith" (15:6). KEY EVENTS: Creation, the Fall, the Flood, the Tower of Babel. KEY PEOPLE: Abraham, Isaac, Jacob, Joseph.

RECOVERY THEMES

A Good Creation: Everything about God's creation was described as being good except the fact that Adam was alone. In fact, Adam's isolation is the only thing in the first two chapters of Genesis that God considered to be a problem. When God created a partner for man, God was pleased with everything in his creation. Because God was pleased with what he created, he stayed involved, even after Adam and Eve disobeyed him. In fact, ever since the Fall, God has been seeking to make things right again. Our sinfulness always leads us away from God and distorts the way God created us to be. But recovery always involves growth toward God's original ideal for the human race. As we progress in recovery, we take part in God's re-creation of our fallen world.

A Ruined World: Adam's and Eve's disobedience affected all of God's creation. The idyllic world of the garden was gone forever, and life became a struggle. Our futile attempts to avoid the realities of a ruined world have led us into all kinds of destructive behaviors. Recovery begins when we squarely face the broken realities of our world—its daily struggles and hardships. Once we have done this, we have started down the road of recovery. We have entered the spiritual arena where battles are fought to regain what has been lost.

Promises of Healing: The book of Genesis presents us with a series of *new beginnings* that come out of the ruin of our sinfulness. In the original Fall, God promised hope and healing for us when he told the serpent that the offspring of the woman would crush his head. When people generally continued to disobey, God sent the Flood as judgment for their sinfulness. After the Flood, God again promised victory and confirmed that promise with a rainbow. Then the people rejected God again, building a great tower as a memorial of their pride. In response, God confused their languages, further fragmenting society. Then God chose a man named Abram and promised to bless all nations of the world through his offspring. Each time human sin brought ruin, God promised victory and recovery in the face of it.

Hope for Reconciliation: As people began to experience the terrible consequences of their disobedience, God didn't leave them to figure out a plan for recovery all alone; nor did he leave a long list of principles or rules to follow that would repair their damaged relationships. Instead, God always worked with people on a very personal level in the recovery process. As we enter into the recovery process, we find it to be relational in nature. It requires us to seek reconciliation with people close to us, and this includes God. In Genesis, God modeled this pattern for us time and again. He chose certain individuals and worked patiently in their lives, reconciling them with himself and the people around them.

CHAPTER 1
The Account of Creation

In the beginning God created the heavens and the earth.* ²The earth was formless and empty, and darkness covered the deep waters. And the Spirit of God was hovering over the surface of the waters.

³Then God said, "Let there be light," and there was light. ⁴And God saw that the light was good. Then he separated the light from the darkness. ⁵God called the light "day" and the darkness "night."

And evening passed and morning came, marking the first day.

⁶Then God said, "Let there be a space between the waters, to separate the waters of the heavens from the waters of the earth." ⁷And that is what happened. God made this space to separate the waters of the earth from the waters of the heavens. ⁸God called the space "sky."

And evening passed and morning came, marking the second day.

⁹Then God said, "Let the waters beneath the sky flow together into one place, so dry ground may appear." And that is what happened. ¹⁰God called the dry ground "land" and the waters "seas." And

1:1 Or *In the beginning when God created the heavens and the earth, . . .* Or *When God began to create the heavens and the earth, . . .*

1:4 God was pleased with his creation. He declared that it was good. God stopped now and then to approve of what he had designed and created (1:4-5, 9-10, 11-12, 18, 21-22, 25, 31). Many of our problems and dependencies result from the misuse of God's good creation. Recovery sometimes involves discovering the good things that we have misused and learning how to enjoy them in the way God intended.

1:24 The phrase "And that is what happened" (also in 1:9-12, 14-15) shows us that God's creative activity was done in complete conformity to the specifications he had originally intended. God accomplishes his will with certainty and precision. It should reassure us to know that God's good desires for us can be accomplished with the same certainty.

God saw that it was good. ¹¹Then God said, "Let the land sprout with vegetation— every sort of seed-bearing plant, and trees that grow seed-bearing fruit. These seeds will then produce the kinds of plants and trees from which they came." And that is what happened. ¹²The land produced vegetation—all sorts of seed-bearing plants, and trees with seed-bearing fruit. Their seeds produced plants and trees of the same kind. And God saw that it was good.

¹³And evening passed and morning came, marking the third day.

¹⁴Then God said, "Let lights appear in the sky to separate the day from the night. Let them be signs to mark the seasons, days, and years. ¹⁵Let these lights in the sky shine down on the earth." And that is what happened. ¹⁶God made two great lights—the larger one to govern the day, and the smaller one to govern the night. He also made the stars. ¹⁷God set these lights in the sky to light the earth, ¹⁸to govern the day and night, and to separate the light from the darkness. And God saw that it was good.

¹⁹And evening passed and morning came, marking the fourth day.

²⁰Then God said, "Let the waters swarm with fish and other life. Let the skies be filled with birds of every kind." ²¹So God created great sea creatures and every living thing that scurries and swarms in the water, and every sort of bird—each producing offspring of the same kind. And God saw that it was good. ²²Then God blessed them, saying, "Be fruitful and multiply. Let the fish fill the seas, and let the birds multiply on the earth."

²³And evening passed and morning came, marking the fifth day.

²⁴Then God said, "Let the earth produce every sort of animal, each producing offspring of the same kind—livestock, small animals that scurry along the ground, and wild animals." And that is what happened. ²⁵God made all sorts of wild animals, livestock, and small animals, each able to produce offspring of the same kind. And God saw that it was good.

²⁶Then God said, "Let us make human beings* in our image, to be like us. They will reign over the fish in the sea, the birds in the sky, the livestock, all the

1:26a Or *man;* Hebrew reads *adam.*

► The recovery principle devotional reading plan begins here.

SELF-PERCEPTION

READ GENESIS 1:26-31

If we have lived in bondage to our compulsive behaviors for a while, we probably see more bad than good inside us. Many of us tend to see life in terms of all or nothing. As a result, we probably think we are all bad. But in recovery, we need a balanced understanding of ourself. We need to see that along with our bad points we have also been gifted with strengths. It's not an either/or proposition. A balanced view of ourself will help us better understand our shortcomings while also giving us greater hope in our potential.

At the end of the fifth day of creation God had made everything except the first people. The Bible tells us that when he looked at what he had made so far, "God saw that it was good." Then God created the first man and woman. " So God created human beings in his own image. In the image of God he created them; . . . Then God blessed them and said, 'Be fruitful and multiply. Fill the earth and govern it. Reign over the fish in the sea, the birds in the sky, and all the animals that scurry along the ground.' . . . Then God looked over all he had made, and he saw that it was very good!" (Genesis 1:25, 27-31).

God distinguished between the human race and the rest of creation. He made us in his very image, with capacities far beyond those of mere animals. God was (and is) excited about us! He gave us abilities and responsibilities to reflect his own nature in all of creation. When he created us, he was proud of what he had made!

Although we have a sinful nature that came as a result of the Fall, we also must remember that we were created in the likeness of God. There are excellence and dignity inherent in being human that should cause us to ponder our potential for good as well as for bad. *Turn to page 31, Genesis 22.*

wild animals on the earth,* and the small animals that scurry along the ground."

²⁷So God created human beings* in his own image.
In the image of God he created them;
male and female he created them.

²⁸Then God blessed them and said, "Be fruitful and multiply. Fill the earth and govern it. Reign over the fish in the sea, the birds in the sky, and all the animals that scurry along the ground."

²⁹Then God said, "Look! I have given you every seed-bearing plant throughout the earth and all the fruit trees for your food. ³⁰And I have given every green plant as food for all the wild animals, the birds in the sky, and the small animals that scurry along the ground—everything that has life." And that is what happened.

³¹Then God looked over all he had made, and he saw that it was very good!
And evening passed and morning came, marking the sixth day.

CHAPTER 2

So the creation of the heavens and the earth and everything in them was completed. ²On the seventh day God had finished his work of creation, so he rested* from all his work. ³And God blessed the seventh day and declared it holy, because it was the day when he rested from all his work of creation.

⁴This is the account of the creation of the heavens and the earth.

The Man and Woman in Eden

When the LORD God made the earth and the heavens, ⁵neither wild plants nor grains were growing on the earth. For the LORD God had not yet sent rain to water the earth, and there were no people to cultivate the soil. ⁶Instead, springs* came up from the ground and watered all the land. ⁷Then the LORD God formed the man from the dust of the ground. He breathed the breath of life into the man's nostrils, and the man became a living person.

⁸Then the LORD God planted a garden in Eden in the east, and there he placed the man he had made. ⁹The LORD God made all sorts of trees grow up from the ground—trees that were beautiful and that produced delicious fruit. In the middle of the garden he placed the tree of life and the tree of the knowledge of good and evil.

¹⁰A river flowed from the land of Eden, watering the garden and then dividing into four branches. ¹¹The first branch, called the Pishon, flowed around the entire land of Havilah, where gold is found. ¹²The gold of that land is exceptionally pure; aromatic resin and onyx stone are also found there. ¹³The second branch, called the Gihon, flowed around the entire land of Cush. ¹⁴The third branch, called the Tigris, flowed east of the land of Asshur. The fourth branch is called the Euphrates.

¹⁵The LORD God placed the man in the Garden of Eden to tend and watch over it. ¹⁶But the LORD God warned him, "You may freely eat the fruit of every tree in the garden—¹⁷except the tree of the knowledge of good and evil. If you eat its fruit, you are sure to die."

¹⁸Then the LORD God said, "It is not good for the man to be alone. I will make a helper who is just right for him." ¹⁹So the LORD God formed from the ground all the wild animals and all the birds of the sky. He brought them to the man* to see what he would call them, and the man chose a name for each one. ²⁰He gave names to all the livestock, all the birds

---

1:26b As in Syriac version; Hebrew reads *all the earth.* 1:27 Or *the man;* Hebrew reads *ha-adam.* 2:2 Or *ceased;* also in 2:3. 2:6 Or *mist.* 2:19 Or *Adam,* and so throughout the chapter.

2:2-3 This is the first mention of Sabbath rest—one day of rest in seven. By his example God encourages us to designate a portion of our life to rest and spiritual rejuvenation. Without proper rest, it is very difficult to deal with the other matters in our life, especially our progress in recovery.
2:8-14 God provided a perfect environment for the first people. We often blame our outward circumstances for our difficulties. It is important to note here that in spite of their ideal surroundings, our first parents fell—they failed. Although the environments we live in can certainly add to our problems, they are never entirely at fault. We need to take responsibility for our own mistakes and failures.
3:1-5 The account here pictures for us the process of temptation. The serpent offered something that had been forbidden by God as a very attractive option. The serpent also caused Eve to doubt God and the truth of his word. During the debate, Eve offered some halfhearted opposition, but her growing doubt in God weakened her resolve. In the end she gave in. Satan strengthened his temptation by weakening Eve's faith in God. Staying close to God and maintaining our faith in him will weaken the power of temptation in our life.

ADAM & EVE

It was an ideal situation: a man and his wife living harmoniously together in a lush, beautiful garden that God had created for their pleasure. They each enjoyed a perfect relationship with God and with each other. But when Adam and Eve gave in to temptation, they overstepped their God-given boundaries and plunged the human race into sin. Harmony was broken. Shame and guilt penetrated their lives and created an invisible barrier between them and God. The consequences of their disobedience and lack of self-control are with us to this day.

Adam and Eve knew that they had gone against God's plan—a plan that was created with their best interests in mind. And the consequences of their sin followed immediately. Right away they became afraid of the God who loved them so much, and they hid from his presence. They also became ashamed of their nakedness and set out to cover themselves. The relationship between Adam and Eve began to show cracks and strains. Accusations were made. Blame was shifted. Neither of them wanted to be held accountable. Both of them refused to admit that they were wrong. Needless to say, their relationship was damaged. Their sin had separated them from each other and from God.

But the story doesn't end there. Adam and Eve stayed together in spite of the shame and guilt they felt. Their lives were marred by sin and scarred by wounds inflicted on one another. However, they faced the reality that life had to go on and began to build a new life together. And by love, commitment, and the grace of God, they persevered through life's trials.

The story of Adam and Eve is found in the opening chapters of Genesis. Adam and/or Eve are also mentioned in 1 Chronicles 1:1; Romans 5:12-19; 1 Corinthians 15:22, 45-49; 2 Corinthians 11:3; and 1 Timothy 2:13-15.

STRENGTHS AND ACCOMPLISHMENTS:
- They were the parents of the entire human race.
- They were committed to each other through the trials they faced.
- Their story provides us with the first illustration of God's grace.

WEAKNESSES AND MISTAKES:
- They were disobedient to the plan that God had revealed to them.
- They were not willing to take responsibility for their sin.
- They made excuses rather than admit the truth.
- Their actions brought sin into the world.

LESSONS FROM THEIR LIVES:
- A good marriage requires love and commitment even through tough times.
- Relationships that accept God's grace and forgiveness persevere through life's difficulties.
- Complacency is a breeding ground for temptation—be on guard against Satan's schemes.
- The mistakes of parents are often passed on to their descendants.

KEY VERSES:
"Then God said, 'Let us make human beings in our image, to be like ourselves. They will reign over the fish in the sea, the birds in the sky, the livestock, all the wild animals on the earth, and the small animals that scurry along the ground.' So God created human beings in his own image. In the image of God he created them; male and female he created them" (Genesis 1:26-27).

---

of the sky, and all the wild animals. But still there was no helper just right for him.

²¹So the LORD God caused the man to fall into a deep sleep. While the man slept, the LORD God took out one of the man's ribs* and closed up the opening. ²²Then the LORD God made a woman from the rib, and he brought her to the man.

²³"At last!" the man exclaimed.

"This one is bone from my bone,
    and flesh from my flesh!
She will be called 'woman,'
    because she was taken from 'man.'"

2:21 Or took a part of the man's side.

²⁴This explains why a man leaves his father and mother and is joined to his wife, and the two are united into one.

²⁵Now the man and his wife were both naked, but they felt no shame.

CHAPTER 3
The Man and Woman Sin
The serpent was the shrewdest of all the wild animals the LORD God had made. One day he asked the woman, "Did God really say you must not eat the fruit from any of the trees in the garden?"

²"Of course we may eat fruit from the

trees in the garden," the woman replied. ³"It's only the fruit from the tree in the middle of the garden that we are not allowed to eat. God said, 'You must not eat it or even touch it; if you do, you will die.'"

⁴"You won't die!" the serpent replied to the woman. ⁵"God knows that your eyes will be opened as soon as you eat it, and you will be like God, knowing both good and evil."

⁶The woman was convinced. She saw that the tree was beautiful and its fruit looked delicious, and she wanted the wisdom it would give her. So she took some of the fruit and ate it. Then she gave some to her husband, who was with her, and he ate it, too. ⁷At that moment their eyes were opened, and they suddenly felt shame at their nakedness. So they sewed fig leaves together to cover themselves.

⁸When the cool evening breezes were blowing, the man* and his wife heard the LORD God walking about in the garden. So they hid from the LORD God among the trees. ⁹Then the LORD God called to the man, "Where are you?"

¹⁰He replied, "I heard you walking in the garden, so I hid. I was afraid because I was naked."

¹¹"Who told you that you were naked?" the LORD God asked. "Have you eaten from the tree whose fruit I commanded you not to eat?"

¹²The man replied, "It was the woman you gave me who gave me the fruit, and I ate it."

¹³Then the LORD God asked the woman, "What have you done?"

"The serpent deceived me," she replied. "That's why I ate it."

¹⁴Then the LORD God said to the serpent,

"Because you have done this, you are cursed
    more than all animals, domestic and
    wild.
You will crawl on your belly,
    groveling in the dust as long as you
    live.
¹⁵And I will cause hostility between you and
    the woman,
    and between your offspring and her
    offspring.
He will strike* your head,
    and you will strike his heel."

¹⁶Then he said to the woman,

"I will sharpen the pain of your
    pregnancy,
    and in pain you will give birth.
And you will desire to control your
    husband,
    but he will rule over you.*"

¹⁷And to the man he said,

"Since you listened to your wife and ate
    from the tree
    whose fruit I commanded you not
    to eat,
the ground is cursed because of you.
    All your life you will struggle to scratch
    a living from it.
¹⁸It will grow thorns and thistles
    for you,
    though you will eat of its grains.
¹⁹By the sweat of your brow
    will you have food to eat

3:8 Or *Adam,* and so throughout the chapter. **3:15** Or *bruise;* also in 3:15b. **3:16** Or *And though you will have desire for your husband, / he will rule over you.*

3:12-13 When Adam was questioned, notice that he blamed the woman for his problem. He even backhandedly blamed God by reminding God that he was the one who had given him the woman in the first place. Then Eve blamed the serpent for the problem. Passing the buck is a standard human response to guilt. But true recovery requires that we take a thorough inventory of our life, accepting responsibility for everything we have done or failed to do.
3:21 The very first death occurred on the same day as Adam's and Eve's sin; it was the death of an animal to provide a covering for their nakedness. God's immediate provision for sin was the slaying of an innocent substitute to provide skins to clothe the guilty couple. The clothing they wore must have served as a reminder—engraving the sight of the dying animal in their minds— a picture of the terrible consequences of their sin. As we recognize the suffering we may have caused others, we also are reminded of the consequences of rejecting God's program for our life.
4:6-7 When God rejected Cain's offering, Cain reacted with dejection and anger. God did not reject Cain for his strong feelings; he offered him an opportunity for a new start. How sad that Cain refused this second chance and instead went out to kill his brother. We need to be careful when we face obstacles to the recovery process. We need to carefully weigh the strong feelings we encounter within ourself before acting on them. If we don't, we may be passing up an excellent opportunity for a fresh start. God is not put off by our strong feelings. Recovery is based on God's grace, which always offers us an opportunity to begin again.

until you return to the ground
    from which you were made.
For you were made from dust,
    and to dust you will return."

Paradise Lost: God's Judgment

²⁰Then the man—Adam—named his wife Eve, because she would be the mother of all who live.* ²¹And the LORD God made clothing from animal skins for Adam and his wife.

²²Then the LORD God said, "Look, the human beings* have become like us, knowing both good and evil. What if they reach out, take fruit from the tree of life, and eat it? Then they will live forever!" ²³So the LORD God banished them from the Garden of Eden, and he sent Adam out to cultivate the ground from which he had been made. ²⁴After sending them out, the LORD God stationed mighty cherubim to the east of the Garden of Eden. And he placed a flaming sword that flashed back and forth to guard the way to the tree of life.

CHAPTER 4
Cain and Abel

Now Adam* had sexual relations with his wife, Eve, and she became pregnant. When she gave birth to Cain, she said, "With the LORD's help, I have produced* a man!" ²Later she gave birth to his brother and named him Abel.

When they grew up, Abel became a shepherd, while Cain cultivated the ground. ³When it was time for the harvest, Cain presented some of his crops as a gift to the LORD. ⁴Abel also brought a gift—the best portions of the firstborn lambs from his flock. The LORD accepted Abel and his gift, ⁵but he did not accept Cain and his gift. This made Cain very angry, and he looked dejected.

⁶"Why are you so angry?" the LORD asked Cain. "Why do you look so dejected? ⁷You will be accepted if you do what is right. But if you refuse to do what is right, then watch out! Sin is crouching at the door, eager to control you. But you must subdue it and be its master."

⁸One day Cain suggested to his brother, "Let's go out into the fields."* And while they were in the field, Cain attacked his brother, Abel, and killed him.

3:20 *Eve* sounds like a Hebrew term that means "to give life." **3:22** Or *the man;* Hebrew reads *ha-adam.* **4:1a** Or *the man;* also in 4:25. **4:1b** Or *I have acquired. Cain* sounds like a Hebrew term that can mean "produce" or "acquire." **4:8** As in Samaritan Pentateuch, Greek and Syriac versions, and Latin Vulgate; Masoretic Text lacks *"Let's go out into the fields."*

STEP 4

Coming Out of Hiding

BIBLE READING: Genesis 3:6-13

We made a searching and fearless moral inventory of ourselves.

Many of us have spent our life in a state of hiding, ashamed of who we are inside. We may hide by living a double life, by using drugs or other addictions to make us feel like someone else, or by self-righteously setting ourselves above others. Step Four involves uncovering the things we have been hiding, even from ourselves.

After Adam and Eve disobeyed God, "they suddenly felt shame at their nakedness. So they sewed fig leaves together to cover themselves. . . . Then the LORD God called to the man, 'Where are you?' He replied, 'I heard you walking in the garden, so I hid. I was afraid because I was naked.'" (Genesis 3:7-10). Human beings have been covering up and hiding ever since!

Jesus consistently confronted the religious leaders about their hypocrisy. The word *hypocrite* describes a person who pretends to have virtues or qualities that he really doesn't have. One time Jesus said to these leaders, "Hypocrites! For you are so careful to clean the outside of the cup and the dish, but inside you are filthy—full of greed and self-indulgence! . . . First wash the inside of the cup and the dish, and then the outside will become clean, too" (Matthew 23:25-26).

When the real person inside us comes out of hiding, we will have to deal with some dirt! Making this inventory is a good way to "wash the inside"; some of that washing may involve bathing our life with tears. It is only by uncovering the hidden parts of ourself that we will be able to change the outer person, including our addictive/compulsive behaviors. *Turn to* *page 611, Nehemiah 8.*

tyndal.es/lrbstep4

⁹Afterward the LORD asked Cain, "Where is your brother? Where is Abel?"

"I don't know," Cain responded. "Am I my brother's guardian?"

¹⁰But the LORD said, "What have you done? Listen! Your brother's blood cries out to me from the ground! ¹¹Now you are cursed and banished from the ground, which has swallowed your brother's blood. ¹²No longer will the ground yield good crops for you, no matter how hard you work! From now on you will be a homeless wanderer on the earth."

¹³Cain replied to the LORD, "My punishment* is too great for me to bear! ¹⁴You have banished me from the land and from your presence; you have made me a homeless wanderer. Anyone who finds me will kill me!"

¹⁵The LORD replied, "No, for I will give a sevenfold punishment to anyone who kills you." Then the LORD put a mark on Cain to warn anyone who might try to kill him. ¹⁶So Cain left the LORD's presence and settled in the land of Nod,* east of Eden.

The Descendants of Cain

¹⁷Cain had sexual relations with his wife, and she became pregnant and gave birth to Enoch. Then Cain founded a city, which he named Enoch, after his son. ¹⁸Enoch had a son named Irad. Irad became the father of* Mehujael. Mehujael became the father of Methushael. Methushael became the father of Lamech.

¹⁹Lamech married two women. The first was named Adah, and the second was Zillah. ²⁰Adah gave birth to Jabal, who was the first of those who raise livestock and live in tents. ²¹His brother's name was Jubal, the first of all who play the harp and flute. ²²Lamech's other wife, Zillah, gave birth to a son named Tubal-cain. He became an expert in forging tools of bronze and iron. Tubal-cain had a sister named Naamah. ²³One day Lamech said to his wives,

"Adah and Zillah, hear my voice;
  listen to me, you wives of Lamech.
I have killed a man who attacked me,
  a young man who wounded me.
²⁴ If someone who kills Cain is punished
    seven times,
  then the one who kills me will be
    punished seventy-seven times!"

The Birth of Seth

²⁵Adam had sexual relations with his wife again, and she gave birth to another son. She named him Seth,* for she said, "God has granted me another son in place of Abel, whom Cain killed." ²⁶When Seth grew up, he had a son and named him Enosh. At that time people first began to worship the LORD by name.

CHAPTER 5
The Descendants of Adam

This is the written account of the descendants of Adam. When God created human beings,* he made them to be like himself. ²He created them male and female, and he blessed them and called them "human."

³When Adam was 130 years old, he became
  the father of a son who was just like
  him—in his very image. He named his
  son Seth. ⁴After the birth of Seth, Adam
  lived another 800 years, and he had other
  sons and daughters. ⁵Adam lived
  930 years, and then he died.
⁶When Seth was 105 years old, he became
  the father of* Enosh. ⁷After the birth of*
  Enosh, Seth lived another 807 years, and
  he had other sons and daughters. ⁸Seth
  lived 912 years, and then he died.

4:13 Or *My sin.* **4:16** *Nod* means "wandering." **4:18** Or *the ancestor of,* and so throughout the verse. **4:25** *Seth* probably means "granted"; the name may also mean "appointed." **5:1** Or *man;* Hebrew reads *adam;* similarly in 5:2. **5:6** Or *the ancestor of;* also in 5:9, 12, 15, 18, 21, 25. **5:7** Or *the birth of this ancestor of;* also in 5:10, 13, 16, 19, 22, 26.

4:15 The "mark on Cain" was not, as some have taught, a badge of guilt. It was a sign that God gave to Cain for his protection. Even after Cain's great failure, God desired to protect him from harm. Many of us look back and marvel at how God protected us before we began the recovery process. He wants us to be restored and often protects us in the midst of evil so that we are not destroyed. Our gracious God desires only our healing and recovery, even after our greatest failures. **5:1-32** This chapter has often been called the obituary column. Its recurring refrain is "He died . . . he died . . . he died." Although physical death did not come to Adam and Eve on the day they sinned, it did eventually come. They had reestablished their relationship with God, but the physical consequences of their sin could not be avoided forever. We may hope that after reestablishing our relationship with God, our troubles will be over. But a relationship with God rarely frees us from the consequences of past sins. The consequences usually catch up with us sooner or later. But if we suffer for past mistakes, we can know that God will be with us each step of the way.

CAIN & ABEL

How often parents of two children have been heard to exclaim, "There have *never* been two children who were more different!" Adam and Eve could well have been the originators of that comment. Cain apparently felt himself to be in direct competition with Abel. This led to a rivalry that was never resolved, resulting in a major tragedy.

Cain became a farmer and Abel a shepherd. It was their offerings, however, not their occupations, that revealed the true nature of their character. Abel did things God's way, following his requirements. He is called "righteous" in Matthew 23:35, and Hebrews 11:4 says his offering was made by faith. Cain, on the other hand, did things his own way. Jude suggests that his "way" was that of rebellion (Jude 1:11). Cain brought an offering of produce from his gardens, while Abel brought the fatty cuts of meat from his best lambs.

Abel's altar must have been ugly, assaulting every sense with the bloody carcasses lying across it. But the blood was a part of God's plan according to Hebrews 12:24. Cain's offering had the potential of being beautiful. Picture fresh produce, just out of the garden—fruits, vegetables, flowers, and grain—probably lovingly and artistically arranged. Perhaps Cain wanted to be accepted by God on the basis of his own merits. He may not have been willing to have a relationship with God based on a bloody sacrifice. When God accepted Abel's offering and rejected Cain's, Cain became angry. But God did not reject him for his anger. Even at that point, God reasoned with him. He offered Cain another opportunity to change his mind and accept divine grace, but still Cain refused. Jealous of Abel, whose offering had been accepted, and raging because God had rejected his own, Cain murdered his brother.

Cain tried to hide his terrible deed, but God was not fooled. God confronted Cain with the murder and assigned the consequence of lifelong exile. Cain spent the rest of his life as an alien, wandering in lands far from his family. But God protected Cain, even when he was in exile; God placed his mark upon Cain to keep him from being killed.

STRENGTHS AND ACCOMPLISHMENTS:
- Abel was obedient to God.
- Abel is the first hero mentioned in the "Gallery of Faith" in Hebrews 11.
- Both sons developed skills and worked hard in the occupations they chose.

WEAKNESSES AND MISTAKES:
- Cain insisted on doing things his own way.
- When rejected, Cain reacted with rage.
- Cain allowed his rage to lead him to commit the first murder.

LESSONS FROM THEIR LIVES:
- Our righteousness is based on our willingness to follow God's program by faith.
- Feeling angry does not separate us from God unless we express it in destructive ways.
- Though we may try to hide our sins for a time, God's justice will prevail.

KEY VERSE:
"It was by faith that Abel brought a more acceptable offering to God than Cain did. Abel's offering gave evidence that he was a righteous man, and God showed his approval of his gifts. Although Abel is long dead, he still speaks to us by his example of faith" (Hebrews 11:4).

The account of Cain and Abel is given in Genesis 4. Both are also mentioned in Hebrews 11:4 and 1 John 3:12. Cain alone is referred to in Jude 1:11; Abel is spoken of in Matthew 23:35; Luke 11:51; and Hebrews 12:24.

---

⁹When Enosh was 90 years old, he became the father of Kenan. ¹⁰After the birth of Kenan, Enosh lived another 815 years, and he had other sons and daughters. ¹¹Enosh lived 905 years, and then he died.

¹²When Kenan was 70 years old, he became the father of Mahalalel. ¹³After the birth of Mahalalel, Kenan lived another 840 years, and he had other sons and daughters. ¹⁴Kenan lived 910 years, and then he died.

¹⁵When Mahalalel was 65 years old, he became the father of Jared. ¹⁶After the birth of Jared, Mahalalel lived another 830 years, and he had other sons and daughters. ¹⁷Mahalalel lived 895 years, and then he died.

¹⁸When Jared was 162 years old, he became the father of Enoch. ¹⁹After the birth of Enoch, Jared lived another 800 years, and he had other sons and

daughters. ²⁰Jared lived 962 years, and then he died.

²¹When Enoch was 65 years old, he became the father of Methuselah. ²²After the birth of Methuselah, Enoch lived in close fellowship with God for another 300 years, and he had other sons and daughters. ²³Enoch lived 365 years, ²⁴walking in close fellowship with God. Then one day he disappeared, because God took him.

²⁵When Methuselah was 187 years old, he became the father of Lamech. ²⁶After the birth of Lamech, Methuselah lived another 782 years, and he had other sons and daughters. ²⁷Methuselah lived 969 years, and then he died.

²⁸When Lamech was 182 years old, he became the father of a son. ²⁹Lamech named his son Noah, for he said, "May he bring us relief* from our work and the painful labor of farming this ground that the LORD has cursed." ³⁰After the birth of Noah, Lamech lived another 595 years, and he had other sons and daughters. ³¹Lamech lived 777 years, and then he died.

³²After Noah was 500 years old, he became the father of Shem, Ham, and Japheth.

CHAPTER 6
A World Gone Wrong

Then the people began to multiply on the earth, and daughters were born to them. ²The sons of God saw the beautiful women* and took any they wanted as their wives. ³Then the LORD said, "My Spirit will not put up with* humans for such a long time, for they are only mortal flesh. In the future, their normal lifespan will be no more than 120 years."

⁴In those days, and for some time after, giant Nephilites lived on the earth, for whenever the sons of God had intercourse with women, they gave birth to children who became the heroes and famous warriors of ancient times.

⁵The LORD observed the extent of human wickedness on the earth, and he saw that everything they thought or imagined was consistently and totally evil. ⁶So the LORD was sorry he had ever made them and put them on the earth. It broke his heart. ⁷And the LORD said, "I will wipe this human race I have created from the face of the earth. Yes, and I will destroy every living thing—all the people, the large animals, the small animals that scurry along the ground, and even the birds of the sky. I am sorry I ever made them." ⁸But Noah found favor with the LORD.

The Story of Noah

⁹This is the account of Noah and his family. Noah was a righteous man, the only blameless person living on earth at the time, and he walked in close fellowship with God. ¹⁰Noah was the father of three sons: Shem, Ham, and Japheth.

¹¹Now God saw that the earth had become corrupt and was filled with violence. ¹²God observed all this corruption in the world, for everyone on earth was corrupt. ¹³So God said to Noah, "I have decided to destroy all living creatures, for they have filled the earth with violence. Yes, I will wipe them all out along with the earth!

¹⁴"Build a large boat* from cypress wood* and waterproof it with tar, inside and out.

5:29 *Noah* sounds like a Hebrew term that can mean "relief" or "comfort." 6:2 Hebrew *daughters of men;* also in 6:4. 6:3 Greek version reads *will not remain in.* 6:14a Traditionally rendered *an ark.* 6:14b Or *gopher wood.*

5:21-24 Little is said about the spiritual state of these patriarchs of the human race. But the account of Enoch's life provides us with a bright spot in this otherwise dismal chapter. Enoch was known for "walking in close fellowship with God." His example should give us hope. Enoch wasn't trapped by the mistakes or apathy of his peers and ancestors. Instead, he made a new start. And he did it by constantly walking with God.

6:1-12 Some people insist that the human race is developing and becoming better and better. But when we compare the condition of the world in these verses to the way things were back in the Garden of Eden, it is obvious that the trend has gone in the opposite direction. Without God's help, we only get worse. It is only by following God's program and receiving his grace that we can hope to escape the natural slide toward pain and destruction.

6:8-10 God did not destroy the righteous with the wicked. These verses are another statement of God's grace. God extended grace to Noah and his family. Noah, like Enoch, lived his life in constant fellowship with God. He broke the mold set by his ancestors and neighbors by drawing close to God. As a result, Noah lived through the Flood and became the second father of the human race.

Then construct decks and stalls throughout its interior. [15]Make the boat 450 feet long, 75 feet wide, and 45 feet high.* [16]Leave an 18-inch opening* below the roof all the way around the boat. Put the door on the side, and build three decks inside the boat—lower, middle, and upper.

[17]"Look! I am about to cover the earth with a flood that will destroy every living thing that breathes. Everything on earth will die. [18]But I will confirm my covenant with you. So enter the boat—you and your wife and your sons and their wives. [19]Bring a pair of every kind of animal—a male and a female— into the boat with you to keep them alive during the flood. [20]Pairs of every kind of bird, and every kind of animal, and every kind of small animal that scurries along the ground, will come to you to be kept alive. [21]And be sure to take on board enough food for your family and for all the animals."

[22]So Noah did everything exactly as God had commanded him.

CHAPTER 7
The Flood Covers the Earth

When everything was ready, the LORD said to Noah, "Go into the boat with all your family, for among all the people of the earth, I can see that you alone are righteous. [2]Take with you seven pairs—male and female—of each animal I have approved for eating and for sacrifice,* and take one pair of each of the others. [3]Also take seven pairs of every kind of bird. There must be a male and a female in each pair to ensure that all life will survive on the earth after the flood. [4]Seven days from now I will make the rains pour down on the earth. And it will rain for forty days and forty nights, until I have wiped from the earth all the living things I have created."

[5]So Noah did everything as the LORD commanded him.

[6]Noah was 600 years old when the flood covered the earth. [7]He went on board the boat to escape the flood—he and his wife and his sons and their wives. [8]With them were all the various kinds of animals—those approved for eating and for sacrifice and those that were not—along with all the birds and the small animals that scurry along the ground. [9]They entered the boat in pairs, male and female, just as God had commanded Noah. [10]After seven days, the waters of the flood came and covered the earth.

[11]When Noah was 600 years old, on the seventeenth day of the second month, all the underground waters erupted from the earth, and the rain fell in mighty torrents from the sky. [12]The rain continued to fall for forty days and forty nights.

[13]That very day Noah had gone into the boat with his wife and his sons—Shem, Ham, and Japheth—and their wives. [14]With them in the boat were pairs of every kind of animal— domestic and wild, large and small— along with birds of every kind. [15]Two by two they came into the boat, representing every living thing that breathes. [16]A male and a female of each kind entered, just as God had commanded Noah. Then the LORD closed the door behind them.

[17]For forty days the floodwaters grew deeper, covering the ground and lifting the boat high above the earth. [18]As the waters rose higher and higher above the ground, the boat floated safely on the surface. [19]Finally, the water covered even the highest mountains on the earth, [20]rising more than twenty-two feet* above the highest peaks. [21]All the living things on earth died— birds, domestic animals, wild animals, small animals that scurry along the ground, and all the people. [22]Everything that breathed and lived on dry land died. [23]God wiped out every living thing on the earth—people, livestock, small animals that scurry along the ground, and the birds of the sky. All were destroyed. The only people who survived were Noah and those with him in the boat. [24]And the floodwaters covered the earth for 150 days.

6:15 Hebrew *300 cubits* [138 meters] *long, 50 cubits* [23 meters] *wide, and 30 cubits* [13.8 meters] *high.* 6:16 Hebrew *an opening of 1 cubit* [46 centimeters]. 7:2 Hebrew *of each clean animal;* similarly in 7:8. 7:20 Hebrew *15 cubits* [6.9 meters].

6:22 One has to wonder whether God's instructions made any sense to Noah. God told him to build a gigantic boat far from the nearest body of navigable water. But here we see that Noah was obedient even though God's instructions were hard to understand. This is one of the secrets of success in any recovery program. We may not understand how everything works, but we must do what God tells us is necessary for a successful recovery. When we step out in faith, as Noah did, God will give us the success we seek.

CHAPTER 8
The Flood Recedes

But God remembered Noah and all the wild animals and livestock with him in the boat. He sent a wind to blow across the earth, and the floodwaters began to recede. ²The underground waters stopped flowing, and the torrential rains from the sky were stopped. ³So the floodwaters gradually receded from the earth. After 150 days, ⁴exactly five months from the time the flood began,* the boat came to rest on the mountains of Ararat. ⁵Two and a half months later,* as the waters continued to go down, other mountain peaks became visible.

⁶After another forty days, Noah opened the window he had made in the boat ⁷and released a raven. The bird flew back and forth until the floodwaters on the earth had dried up. ⁸He also released a dove to see if the water had receded and it could find dry ground. ⁹But the dove could find no place to land because the water still covered the ground. So it returned to the boat, and Noah held out his hand and drew the dove back inside. ¹⁰After waiting another seven days, Noah released the dove again. ¹¹This time the dove returned to him in the evening with a fresh olive leaf in its beak. Then Noah knew that the floodwaters were almost gone. ¹²He waited another seven days and then released the dove again. This time it did not come back.

¹³Noah was now 601 years old. On the first day of the new year, ten and a half months after the flood began,* the floodwaters had almost dried up from the earth. Noah lifted back the covering of the boat and saw that the surface of the ground was drying. ¹⁴Two more months went by,* and at last the earth was dry!

¹⁵Then God said to Noah, ¹⁶"Leave the boat, all of you—you and your wife, and your sons and their wives. ¹⁷Release all the animals—the birds, the livestock, and the small animals that scurry along the ground—so they can be fruitful and multiply throughout the earth."

¹⁸So Noah, his wife, and his sons and their wives left the boat. ¹⁹And all of the large and small animals and birds came out of the boat, pair by pair.

²⁰Then Noah built an altar to the LORD, and there he sacrificed as burnt offerings the animals and birds that had been approved for that purpose.* ²¹And the LORD was pleased with the aroma of the sacrifice and said to himself, "I will never again curse the ground because of the human race, even though everything they think or imagine is bent toward evil from childhood. I will never again destroy all living things. ²²As long as the earth remains, there will be planting and harvest, cold and heat, summer and winter, day and night."

CHAPTER 9
God Confirms His Covenant

Then God blessed Noah and his sons and told them, "Be fruitful and multiply. Fill the earth. ²All the animals of the earth, all the birds of the sky, all the small animals that scurry along the ground, and all the fish in the sea will look on you with fear and terror. I have placed them in your power. ³I have given them to you for food, just as I have given you grain and vegetables. ⁴But you must never eat any meat that still has the lifeblood in it.

⁵"And I will require the blood of anyone who takes another person's life. If a wild animal kills a person, it must die. And anyone who murders a fellow human must die. ⁶If anyone takes a human life, that person's life will also be taken by human hands. For God

---

8:4 Hebrew *on the seventeenth day of the seventh month;* see 7:11. **8:5** Hebrew *On the first day of the tenth month;* see 7:11 and note on 8:4. **8:13** Hebrew *On the first day of the first month;* see 7:11. **8:14** Hebrew *The twenty-seventh day of the second month arrived;* see note on 8:13. **8:20** Hebrew *every clean animal and every clean bird.*

8:1 Noah had listened to God and obeyed all his requests. But now the boat was floating over the earth on the floodwaters—not an ideal situation to be in. But God didn't forget about Noah. It is comforting to know that when we obey God, he will not forget us. He will stand by us until his plans for us are complete.

9:1-17 Noah and his family were the only people left after the Flood. The comforts of civilization had been washed away. They had to start all over again. God gave Noah his special blessing and instituted a program that, if followed, would result in a healthy society. God has given us his Word, which contains the ultimate blueprint for healthy living. And just as God gave the human race a new start with Noah, he can give each of us a new start, too.

9:20-21 Since the Bible talks so much about Noah's righteousness and his fellowship with God, it is surprising to read that he gave in to the excesses of alcohol. The account of Noah's drunkenness and shame comes as a shock to us, but it is a reminder that even in ideal conditions it is easy for us to slip and fall. We can never completely let down our guard or feel as if we have it made, for that is when we become most vulnerable to failure.

NOAH & SONS

Parents often wonder if they can have a positive affect on their children in our corrupt world. Noah leaves us with a good model of what a godly parent should be like. Noah was the only righteous man left in a generation of corrupt individuals. He led his family by example in a world that looked upon Noah as being "out of touch." Society mocked him for his belief in and obedience to God.

The principles of obedience to God, consistency, and patience were taught to Noah's sons and their wives. When judgment came upon the world, Noah, his wife, his sons, and their wives were spared. The Bible tells us that later in his life, after the Flood, Noah became drunk on the wine of his vineyard. Two of his sons (Shem and Japheth) responded to the situation in a godly manner while one (Ham) did not. Noah's drunkenness and Ham's subsequent indiscretion resulted in the suffering of some of Ham's descendants.

As we look at Noah's life, we are reminded that our children learn from our examples. They often receive great blessings from the good things we do, but they also suffer from our mistakes. Like Noah, all of us have made mistakes. But those mistakes can become insignificant through our repentance and obedience to God's Word. We must remember that children become like the adults who surround them.

STRENGTHS AND ACCOMPLISHMENTS:
- Noah was the only follower of God left in his generation.
- Noah was the second father of the human race.
- Noah taught his sons patience, consistency, and obedience to God.

WEAKNESSES AND MISTAKES:
- Noah embarrassed himself by getting drunk in front of his sons.
- Ham acted in an ungodly manner, which resulted in a curse upon some of his descendants.

LESSONS FROM THEIR LIVES:
- God is faithful to those who trust and obey him.
- Obedience to God is a lifelong commitment.
- Good parents teach their children by example.

KEY VERSE:
"So Noah did everything exactly as God had commanded him" (Genesis 6:22).

The story of Noah and his sons is told in Genesis 5:29–10:32. Noah is referred to in 1 Chronicles 1:4; Isaiah 54:9; Ezekiel 14:14, 20; Matthew 24:37-38; Luke 3:36; 17:26-27; Hebrews 11:7; 1 Peter 3:20; and 2 Peter 2:5.

---

made human beings* in his own image. ⁷Now be fruitful and multiply, and repopulate the earth."

⁸Then God told Noah and his sons, ⁹"I hereby confirm my covenant with you and your descendants, ¹⁰and with all the animals that were on the boat with you—the birds, the livestock, and all the wild animals— every living creature on earth. ¹¹Yes, I am confirming my covenant with you. Never again will floodwaters kill all living creatures; never again will a flood destroy the earth."

¹²Then God said, "I am giving you a sign of my covenant with you and with all living creatures, for all generations to come. ¹³I have placed my rainbow in the clouds. It is the sign of my covenant with you and with all the earth. ¹⁴When I send clouds over the earth, the rainbow will appear in the clouds, ¹⁵and I will remember my covenant with you and with all living creatures. Never again will the floodwaters destroy all life. ¹⁶When I see the rainbow

in the clouds, I will remember the eternal covenant between God and every living creature on earth." ¹⁷Then God said to Noah, "Yes, this rainbow is the sign of the covenant I am confirming with all the creatures on earth."

Noah's Sons

¹⁸The sons of Noah who came out of the boat with their father were Shem, Ham, and Japheth. (Ham is the father of Canaan.) ¹⁹From these three sons of Noah came all the people who now populate the earth.

²⁰After the flood, Noah began to cultivate the ground, and he planted a vineyard. ²¹One day he drank some wine he had made, and he became drunk and lay naked inside his tent. ²²Ham, the father of Canaan, saw that his father was naked and went outside and told his brothers. ²³Then Shem and Japheth took a robe, held it over their shoulders, and backed into the tent to cover their

9:6 Or *man*; Hebrew reads *ha-adam*.

father. As they did this, they looked the other way so they would not see him naked.

²⁴When Noah woke up from his stupor, he learned what Ham, his youngest son, had done. ²⁵Then he cursed Canaan, the son of Ham:

"May Canaan be cursed!
May he be the lowest of servants
to his relatives."

²⁶Then Noah said,

"May the LORD, the God of Shem, be
blessed,
and may Canaan be his servant!
²⁷May God expand the territory of Japheth!
May Japheth share the prosperity of Shem,*
and may Canaan be his servant."

²⁸Noah lived another 350 years after the great flood. ²⁹He lived 950 years, and then he died.

CHAPTER 10
This is the account of the families of Shem, Ham, and Japheth, the three sons of Noah. Many children were born to them after the great flood.

Descendants of Japheth
²The descendants of Japheth were Gomer, Magog, Madai, Javan, Tubal, Meshech, and Tiras.
³The descendants of Gomer were Ashkenaz, Riphath, and Togarmah.
⁴The descendants of Javan were Elishah, Tarshish, Kittim, and Rodanim.* ⁵Their descendants became the seafaring peoples that spread out to various lands, each identified by its own language, clan, and national identity.

Descendants of Ham
⁶The descendants of Ham were Cush, Mizraim, Put, and Canaan.
⁷The descendants of Cush were Seba, Havilah, Sabtah, Raamah, and Sabteca. The descendants of Raamah were Sheba and Dedan.
⁸Cush was also the ancestor of Nimrod, who was the first heroic warrior on earth.
⁹Since he was the greatest hunter in the world,* his name became proverbial. People would say, "This man is like Nimrod, the greatest hunter in the world." ¹⁰He built his kingdom in the land of Babylonia,* with the cities of Babylon, Erech, Akkad, and Calneh. ¹¹From there he expanded his territory to Assyria,* building the cities of Nineveh, Rehoboth-ir, Calah, ¹²and Resen (the great city located between Nineveh and Calah).
¹³Mizraim was the ancestor of the Ludites, Anamites, Lehabites, Naphtuhites, ¹⁴Pathrusites, Casluhites, and the Caphtorites, from whom the Philistines came.*
¹⁵Canaan's oldest son was Sidon, the ancestor of the Sidonians. Canaan was also the ancestor of the Hittites,* ¹⁶Jebusites, Amorites, Girgashites, ¹⁷Hivites, Arkites, Sinites, ¹⁸Arvadites, Zemarites, and Hamathites. The Canaanite clans eventually spread out, ¹⁹and the territory of Canaan extended from Sidon in the north to Gerar and Gaza in the south, and east as far as Sodom, Gomorrah, Admah, and Zeboiim, near Lasha.
²⁰These were the descendants of Ham, identified by clan, language, territory, and national identity.

Descendants of Shem
²¹Sons were also born to Shem, the older brother of Japheth.* Shem was the ancestor of all the descendants of Eber.
²²The descendants of Shem were Elam, Asshur, Arphaxad, Lud, and Aram.
²³The descendants of Aram were Uz, Hul, Gether, and Mash.
²⁴Arphaxad was the father of Shelah,* and Shelah was the father of Eber.
²⁵Eber had two sons. The first was named Peleg (which means "division"), for during his lifetime the people of the world were divided into different language groups. His brother's name was Joktan.
²⁶Joktan was the ancestor of Almodad, Sheleph, Hazarmaveth, Jerah, ²⁷Hadoram, Uzal, Diklah, ²⁸Obal, Abimael, Sheba, ²⁹Ophir, Havilah, and Jobab. All these

---

9:27 Hebrew *May he live in the tents of Shem.* 10:4 As in some Hebrew manuscripts and Greek version (see also 1 Chr 1:7); most Hebrew manuscripts read *Dodanim.* 10:9 Hebrew *a great hunter before the LORD;* also in 10:9b. 10:10 Hebrew *Shinar.* 10:11 Or *From that land Assyria went out.* 10:14 Hebrew *Casluhites, from whom the Philistines came, and Caphtorites.* Compare Jer 47:4; Amos 9:7. 10:15 Hebrew *ancestor of Heth.* 10:21 Or *Shem, whose older brother was Japheth.* 10:24 Greek version reads *Arphaxad was the father of Cainan, Cainan was the father of Shelah.* Compare Luke 3:36.

10:1-32 This chapter is often called the Table of Nations. It is refreshing to realize that the God we worship is not a local deity. He is sovereign over all ethnic and language groups, nations, and political entities. The God who holds kings and empires in his hands surely has the power to hold us, too.

ABRAHAM & SARAH

Many give lip service to walking by faith; Abraham and Sarah modeled it. They were imperfect but willing instruments used by God to implement his perfect plan.

Abram, with Sarai, departed by faith from a pagan world for a new life of God's choosing. God promised a land and a nation of descendants, including One through whom all the peoples of the world would be blessed. The covenant defied human logic: Abram was seventy-five; Sarai was ten years younger and infertile. Their hopes of having children had long vanished. Yet Abram believed God's promises.

During their pilgrimage, the pair often strayed from God's will. They succumbed to fear and dishonesty in dealings with Pharaoh and Abimelech. Difficulty in persevering led them to second-guess God. Abram's subsequent union with Hagar resulted in domestic strife. Jealousy naturally erupted, and family relationships became strained. Abram behaved irresponsibly, and Sarai acted with deliberate cruelty. Years later a wiser Abraham would listen to God's instructions for handling the handmaid Hagar and her son.

Abram's and Sarai's failures neither diminished God's love for them nor altered his commitment to his promises. Through turmoil and temptation, the couple's mutual affection and respect for each other survived. Eventually God changed their names. Sarah's faith grew, and a quarter-century after God's promises were first given, she bore a son. They named him Isaac. The delayed gratification must have been sweet! Sarah enjoyed Isaac for many years. After her death she was tenderly mourned by both husband and son.

Worship and obedience were such a part of Abraham's life that when God tested Abraham's faith, he willingly surrendered his son Isaac as a sacrifice. Then God provided a lamb as a burnt offering to take Isaac's place on the altar. God's provision in Abraham's life can bring hope to us even today.

STRENGTHS AND ACCOMPLISHMENTS:
- They voluntarily left comfortable, familiar surroundings in obedience to God's will.
- Scripture heralds both as examples of faithful obedience.
- Abraham's physical descendants include the Jewish nation, from which came Jesus the Messiah.
- Abraham's spiritual descendants include all who have trusted Jesus for salvation.

WEAKNESSES AND MISTAKES:
- They at times presumed to know God's plans before he revealed them and foolishly attempted to assist him.
- When victimized by fear, Abraham was not above protecting himself at the expense of his wife's safety and integrity.
- Both acted intolerably toward Hagar and her son.

LESSONS FROM THEIR LIVES:
- A fresh start is possible at any stage of life.
- The fulfillment of God's promises does not depend upon our performance but upon his grace.
- It is dangerous to move ahead without first seeking God's direction.

KEY VERSES:
"The LORD kept his word and did for Sarah exactly what he had promised. 2She became pregnant, and she gave birth to a son for Abraham in his old age" (Genesis 21:1-2).

The story of Abraham and Sarah is found in Genesis 11–25. Among the many other references to Abraham are Romans 4:1-24; 9:7-9; Galatians 3:6-9, 14, 18; Hebrews 6:13-15; 7:1-2, 4-6; 11:8-12, 17-19; James 2:21-23. Sarah is mentioned in Romans 4:19; 9:9; Hebrews 11:11; and 1 Peter 3:6.

---

were descendants of Joktan. ³⁰The territory they occupied extended from Mesha all the way to Sephar in the eastern mountains.

³¹These were the descendants of Shem, identified by clan, language, territory, and national identity.

Conclusion

³²These are the clans that descended from Noah's sons, arranged by nation according to their lines of descent. All the nations of the earth descended from these clans after the great flood.

CHAPTER 11
The Tower of Babel

At one time all the people of the world spoke the same language and used the same words. ²As the people migrated to the east, they found a plain in the land of Babylonia* and settled there.

³They began saying to each other, "Let's

11:2 Hebrew *Shinar*.

make bricks and harden them with fire." (In this region bricks were used instead of stone, and tar was used for mortar.) [4]Then they said, "Come, let's build a great city for ourselves with a tower that reaches into the sky. This will make us famous and keep us from being scattered all over the world."

[5]But the LORD came down to look at the city and the tower the people were building. [6]"Look!" he said. "The people are united, and they all speak the same language. After this, nothing they set out to do will be impossible for them! [7]Come, let's go down and confuse the people with different languages. Then they won't be able to understand each other."

[8]In that way, the LORD scattered them all over the world, and they stopped building the city. [9]That is why the city was called Babel,* because that is where the LORD confused the people with different languages. In this way he scattered them all over the world.

The Line of Descent from Shem to Abram
[10]This is the account of Shem's family.

Two years after the great flood, when Shem was 100 years old, he became the father of* Arphaxad. [11]After the birth of* Arphaxad, Shem lived another 500 years and had other sons and daughters.
[12]When Arphaxad was 35 years old, he became the father of Shelah. [13]After the birth of Shelah, Arphaxad lived another 403 years and had other sons and daughters.*
[14]When Shelah was 30 years old, he became the father of Eber. [15]After the birth of Eber, Shelah lived another 403 years and had other sons and daughters.
[16]When Eber was 34 years old, he became the father of Peleg. [17]After the birth of Peleg, Eber lived another 430 years and had other sons and daughters.
[18]When Peleg was 30 years old, he became the father of Reu. [19]After the birth of Reu, Peleg lived another 209 years and had other sons and daughters.
[20]When Reu was 32 years old, he became the father of Serug. [21]After the birth of Serug, Reu lived another 207 years and had other sons and daughters.
[22]When Serug was 30 years old, he became the father of Nahor. [23]After the birth of Nahor, Serug lived another 200 years and had other sons and daughters.
[24]When Nahor was 29 years old, he became the father of Terah. [25]After the birth of Terah, Nahor lived another 119 years and had other sons and daughters.
[26]After Terah was 70 years old, he became the father of Abram, Nahor, and Haran.

The Family of Terah
[27]This is the account of Terah's family. Terah was the father of Abram, Nahor, and Haran;

11:9 Or *Babylon. Babel* sounds like a Hebrew term that means "confusion." **11:10** Or *the ancestor of;* also in 11:12, 14, 16, 18, 20, 22, 24. **11:11** Or *the birth of this ancestor of;* also in 11:13, 15, 17, 19, 21, 23, 25. **11:12-13** Greek version reads [12]*When Arphaxad was 135 years old, he became the father of Cainan.* [13]*After the birth of Cainan, Arphaxad lived another 430 years and had other sons and daughters, and then he died. When Cainan was 130 years old, he became the father of Shelah. After the birth of Shelah, Cainan lived another 330 years and had other sons and daughters, and then he died.* Compare Luke 3:35-36.

11:3-4 Whatever else the Tower of Babel might have represented, it was a mighty monument to human pride. It was a symbol of man's rebellion against the revealed will of God. This type of pride is always destructive to human community and to the process of recovery.

11:5-9 The Tower of Babel incident records the progression of broken communication that began back in the Garden of Eden. After sin entered the world, Adam and Eve began to hide the truth. They tried to blame each other and God for their mistakes, which resulted in separation from God and barriers between that first couple. The sinful pride of the people of Babel caused another great rift in human communication. Numerous languages now divided them into various groups, making their cooperation difficult if not impossible. But the story doesn't end there. God is in the business of restoring broken communication. He chose the people of Israel and spoke to them, giving them his laws. His Son was born through this nation, so he could speak to us and walk among us. And when the Holy Spirit came, the diversity of language was no longer a barrier to communication (Acts 2:5-12). God's program is designed to enhance our communication with him and with the people around us.

12:1 A relationship with God is a two-way street. He is there to help us, but he expects us to follow his plan. When God called Abram to leave his country and his people and go to a land that God would show him, God promised to guide him. But Abram had to step out in faith. God has promised to be with us as we seek his help in recovery, but he may also ask something of us. As with Abram, God may call us away from the familiar world that drags us down. And if we want to progress, we will need to follow his plan.

LOT & FAMILY

Many people in this world live for wealth, comfort, and the easy life. And they want to get it as quickly as possible! To make this happen, they often sacrifice the really important things in life. This was true in the life of Abraham's nephew Lot. Looking for the easy road to wealth and comfort, he made decisions that ended up destroying everything he had lived for.

Lot always thought of himself first. He demonstrated this when he chose the rich pastureland of the valleys, leaving Abraham with the rugged hill country. Embracing the easy comforts of the valley's cities and the physical prosperity they offered, he grew blind to the legacy he was leaving his descendants. When the men of Sodom demanded that Lot send his angelic guests out to take part in their sexual practices, Lot offered his daughters as an alternative. His desire to be accepted by the sinful people of his adopted homeland led him to fail to treat his daughters with the respect and protection they deserved.

The result of Lot's selfishness and greed was the loss of his fortune and the ruin of his family. He sacrificed his family and all he had worked for to the gods of comfort and wealth. He witnessed his wife's death as a result of her disobedience to God—something he had modeled for her. His daughters followed Lot's example, too. They used the quickest and easiest means available to overcome their lonely and childless state—drunkenness, seduction, and incest.

Our society places great value on wealth, comfort, and success, calling us all to join the mad rush to get them. This focus is so pervasive that it may be hard for us to see it as bad. Even though living for wealth may not seem such a terrible sin, its destructive effects upon people in our world are widespread. We must learn to put God first. If we put wealth first, we are setting ourselves up to lose all the really important things in life—our family and our relationship with God.

STRENGTHS AND ACCOMPLISHMENTS:
- Lot was successful at generating wealth.
- The apostle Peter referred to him as a just and righteous man.

WEAKNESSES AND MISTAKES:
- Lot often chose the easiest course of action, usually at the expense of doing what was right.
- When faced with making a decision, Lot thought of himself first.
- Lot's daughters used sinful means to meet their needs, instead of seeking God's provision.

LESSONS FROM THEIR LIVES:
- If we live for comfort and wealth, they can come between us and our families.
- We need to take care of our responsibilities to God and people first if we want our lives to be successful.
- Mistakes made by parents usually lead to mistakes made by their children.
- When we put wealth and comfort before obedience to God, the result will be destructive.

KEY VERSE:
"Come, let's get [Lot] drunk with wine, and then we will have sex with him. That way we will preserve our family line through our father" (Genesis 19:32).

The story of Lot and his family is told in Genesis 13 and 19. Lot is also mentioned in Deuteronomy 2:9; Luke 17:28-32; and 2 Peter 2:7-8.

---

and Haran was the father of Lot. ²⁸But Haran died in Ur of the Chaldeans, the land of his birth, while his father, Terah, was still living. ²⁹Meanwhile, Abram and Nahor both married. The name of Abram's wife was Sarai, and the name of Nahor's wife was Milcah. (Milcah and her sister Iscah were daughters of Nahor's brother Haran.) ³⁰But Sarai was unable to become pregnant and had no children.

³¹One day Terah took his son Abram, his daughter-in-law Sarai (his son Abram's wife), and his grandson Lot (his son Haran's child)

and moved away from Ur of the Chaldeans. He was headed for the land of Canaan, but they stopped at Haran and settled there. ³²Terah lived for 205 years* and died while still in Haran.

CHAPTER 12
The Call of Abram

The LORD had said to Abram, "Leave your native country, your relatives, and your father's family, and go to the land that I will show you. ²I will make you into a great

11:32 Some ancient versions read *145 years;* compare 11:26 and 12:4.

nation. I will bless you and make you famous, and you will be a blessing to others. ³I will bless those who bless you and curse those who treat you with contempt. All the families on earth will be blessed through you."

⁴So Abram departed as the LORD had instructed, and Lot went with him. Abram was seventy-five years old when he left Haran. ⁵He took his wife, Sarai, his nephew Lot, and all his wealth—his livestock and all the people he had taken into his household at Haran—and headed for the land of Canaan. When they arrived in Canaan, ⁶Abram traveled through the land as far as Shechem. There he set up camp beside the oak of Moreh. At that time, the area was inhabited by Canaanites.

⁷Then the LORD appeared to Abram and said, "I will give this land to your descendants.*" And Abram built an altar and dedicated it to the LORD, who had appeared to him. ⁸After that, Abram traveled south and set up camp in the hill country, with Bethel to the west and Ai to the east. There he built another altar and dedicated it to the LORD, and he worshiped the LORD. ⁹Then Abram continued traveling south by stages toward the Negev.

Abram and Sarai in Egypt

¹⁰At that time a severe famine struck the land of Canaan, forcing Abram to go down to Egypt, where he lived as a foreigner. ¹¹As he was approaching the border of Egypt, Abram said to his wife, Sarai, "Look, you are a very beautiful woman. ¹²When the Egyptians see you, they will say, 'This is his wife. Let's kill him; then we can have her!' ¹³So please tell them you are my sister. Then they will spare my life and treat me well because of their interest in you."

¹⁴And sure enough, when Abram arrived in Egypt, everyone noticed Sarai's beauty.

12:7 Hebrew *seed.*

¹⁵When the palace officials saw her, they sang her praises to Pharaoh, their king, and Sarai was taken into his palace. ¹⁶Then Pharaoh gave Abram many gifts because of her—sheep, goats, cattle, male and female donkeys, male and female servants, and camels.

¹⁷But the LORD sent terrible plagues upon Pharaoh and his household because of Sarai, Abram's wife. ¹⁸So Pharaoh summoned Abram and accused him sharply. "What have you done to me?" he demanded. "Why didn't you tell me she was your wife? ¹⁹Why did you say, 'She is my sister,' and allow me to take her as my wife? Now then, here is your wife. Take her and get out of here!" ²⁰Pharaoh ordered some of his men to escort them, and he sent Abram out of the country, along with his wife and all his possessions.

CHAPTER 13
Abram and Lot Separate

So Abram left Egypt and traveled north into the Negev, along with his wife and Lot and all that they owned. ²(Abram was very rich in livestock, silver, and gold.) ³From the Negev, they continued traveling by stages toward Bethel, and they pitched their tents between Bethel and Ai, where they had camped before. ⁴This was the same place where Abram had built the altar, and there he worshiped the LORD again.

⁵Lot, who was traveling with Abram, had also become very wealthy with flocks of sheep and goats, herds of cattle, and many tents. ⁶But the land could not support both Abram and Lot with all their flocks and herds living so close together. ⁷So disputes broke out between the herdsmen of Abram and Lot. (At that time Canaanites and Perizzites were also living in the land.)

⁸Finally Abram said to Lot, "Let's not allow this conflict to come between us or our

12:11-20 As Abram and Sarai approached Egypt, Abram began to fear that the Egyptians would kill him so they could take his beautiful wife. So Abram and Sarai spun a lie to "protect" their relationship; they said that they were brother and sister. This was a half-truth—they actually were half siblings. But it should be recognized that a half-truth is a whole lie. And like most lies, this one backfired, almost destroying Abram and Sarai's marriage. Total honesty is an essential part of recovery. We need to be careful to avoid doing what Abram and Sarai did, even though they did it with the best of intentions. Dishonesty never pays—we should never try to rationalize it.

13:5-11 A conflict developed between the families of Abram and Lot over pastureland for their flocks. To ease the strained family relationship, Abram offered Lot first choice of the land. Abram realized that people were more important than possessions, so he sacrificed his own right to the best land to maintain harmony between their families. In recovery, we need to learn this important lesson: Our relationships are more important than the things we own.

herdsmen. After all, we are close relatives! ⁹The whole countryside is open to you. Take your choice of any section of the land you want, and we will separate. If you want the land to the left, then I'll take the land on the right. If you prefer the land on the right, then I'll go to the left."

¹⁰Lot took a long look at the fertile plains of the Jordan Valley in the direction of Zoar. The whole area was well watered everywhere, like the garden of the LORD or the beautiful land of Egypt. (This was before the LORD destroyed Sodom and Gomorrah.) ¹¹Lot chose for himself the whole Jordan Valley to the east of them. He went there with his flocks and servants and parted company with his uncle Abram. ¹²So Abram settled in the land of Canaan, and Lot moved his tents to a place near Sodom and settled among the cities of the plain. ¹³But the people of this area were extremely wicked and constantly sinned against the LORD.

¹⁴After Lot had gone, the LORD said to Abram, "Look as far as you can see in every direction—north and south, east and west. ¹⁵I am giving all this land, as far as you can see, to you and your descendants* as a permanent possession. ¹⁶And I will give you so many descendants that, like the dust of the earth, they cannot be counted! ¹⁷Go and walk through the land in every direction, for I am giving it to you."

¹⁸So Abram moved his camp to Hebron and settled near the oak grove belonging to Mamre. There he built another altar to the LORD.

CHAPTER 14
Abram Rescues Lot

About this time war broke out in the region. King Amraphel of Babylonia,* King Arioch of Ellasar, King Kedorlaomer of Elam, and King Tidal of Goiim ²fought against King Bera of Sodom, King Birsha of Gomorrah, King Shinab of Admah, King Shemeber of Zeboiim, and the king of Bela (also called Zoar).

³This second group of kings joined forces in Siddim Valley (that is, the valley of the Dead Sea*). ⁴For twelve years they had been subject to King Kedorlaomer, but in the thirteenth year they rebelled against him.

⁵One year later Kedorlaomer and his allies arrived and defeated the Rephaites at Ashteroth-karnaim, the Zuzites at Ham, the Emites at Shaveh-kiriathaim, ⁶and the Horites at Mount Seir, as far as El-paran at the edge of the wilderness. ⁷Then they turned back and came to En-mishpat (now called Kadesh) and conquered all the territory of the Amalekites, and also the Amorites living in Hazazon-tamar.

⁸Then the rebel kings of Sodom, Gomorrah, Admah, Zeboiim, and Bela (also called Zoar) prepared for battle in the valley of the Dead Sea.* ⁹They fought against King Kedorlaomer of Elam, King Tidal of Goiim, King Amraphel of Babylonia, and King Arioch of Ellasar—four kings against five. ¹⁰As it happened, the valley of the Dead Sea was filled with tar pits. And as the army of the kings of Sodom and Gomorrah fled, some fell into the tar pits, while the rest escaped into the mountains. ¹¹The victorious invaders then plundered Sodom and Gomorrah and headed for home, taking with them all the spoils of war and the food supplies. ¹²They also captured Lot—Abram's nephew who lived in Sodom—and carried off everything he owned.

¹³But one of Lot's men escaped and reported everything to Abram the Hebrew, who was living near the oak grove belonging to Mamre the Amorite. Mamre and his relatives, Eshcol and Aner, were Abram's allies.

¹⁴When Abram heard that his nephew Lot had been captured, he mobilized the 318 trained men who had been born into his household. Then he pursued Kedorlaomer's army until he caught up with them at Dan.

13:15 Hebrew *seed;* also in 13:16. **14:1** Hebrew *Shinar;* also in 14:9. **14:3** Hebrew *Salt Sea.* **14:8** Hebrew *Siddim Valley* (see 14:3); also in 14:10.

13:11-13 One bad choice often leads to another. The choices Lot made here and in the following chapters led him toward his eventual fall. Here, he selfishly chose the best land and the easy lifestyle that would come with it. In 13:12-13, he chose to move closer to the wicked city of Sodom. In 19:1-18, he chose to become an important man in a wicked place. In 19:30-38, Lot's descent reached its final depths as he had incestuous relations with his daughters. We need to think ahead, reflecting upon the probable consequences of our present decisions.

14:14-16 A number of important character traits emerge as we examine Abram's prompt military action. He proved himself to be a man of courage, always ready to act when the situation demanded it. He was willing to give up certain luxuries in order to follow the program God had laid out for him. These are important characteristics for us to emulate as we continue in the recovery process.

[15]There he divided his men and attacked during the night. Kedorlaomer's army fled, but Abram chased them as far as Hobah, north of Damascus. [16]Abram recovered all the goods that had been taken, and he brought back his nephew Lot with his possessions and all the women and other captives.

Melchizedek Blesses Abram

[17]After Abram returned from his victory over Kedorlaomer and all his allies, the king of Sodom went out to meet him in the valley of Shaveh (that is, the King's Valley).

[18]And Melchizedek, the king of Salem and a priest of God Most High,* brought Abram some bread and wine. [19]Melchizedek blessed Abram with this blessing:

"Blessed be Abram by God Most High,
　　Creator of heaven and earth.
[20]And blessed be God Most High,
　　who has defeated your enemies for you."

Then Abram gave Melchizedek a tenth of all the goods he had recovered.

[21]The king of Sodom said to Abram, "Give back my people who were captured. But you may keep for yourself all the goods you have recovered."

[22]Abram replied to the king of Sodom, "I solemnly swear to the LORD, God Most High, Creator of heaven and earth, [23]that I will not take so much as a single thread or sandal thong from what belongs to you. Otherwise you might say, 'I am the one who made Abram rich.' [24]I will accept only what my young warriors have already eaten, and I request that you give a fair share of the goods to my allies—Aner, Eshcol, and Mamre."

14:18 Hebrew *El-Elyon;* also in 14:19, 20, 22.

CHAPTER 15
The LORD's Covenant Promise to Abram

Some time later, the LORD spoke to Abram in a vision and said to him, "Do not be afraid, Abram, for I will protect you, and your reward will be great."

[2]But Abram replied, "O Sovereign LORD, what good are all your blessings when I don't even have a son? Since you've given me no children, Eliezer of Damascus, a servant in my household, will inherit all my wealth. [3]You have given me no descendants of my own, so one of my servants will be my heir."

[4]Then the LORD said to him, "No, your servant will not be your heir, for you will have a son of your own who will be your heir." [5]Then the LORD took Abram outside and said to him, "Look up into the sky and count the stars if you can. That's how many descendants you will have!"

[6]And Abram believed the LORD, and the LORD counted him as righteous because of his faith.

[7]Then the LORD told him, "I am the LORD who brought you out of Ur of the Chaldeans to give you this land as your possession."

[8]But Abram replied, "O Sovereign LORD, how can I be sure that I will actually possess it?"

[9]The LORD told him, "Bring me a three-year-old heifer, a three-year-old female goat, a three-year-old ram, a turtledove, and a young pigeon." [10]So Abram presented all these to him and killed them. Then he cut each animal down the middle and laid the halves side by side; he did not, however, cut the birds in half. [11]Some vultures swooped down to eat the carcasses, but Abram chased them away.

15:4-5 Because of the disappointment and frustration of seventy-five childless years, God's promise of numerous children must have stretched Abram's faith to the very limit. God's plan for Abram seemed an impossibility—thousands of descendants from an old man and a barren woman! But God's promise did actually come about. God's plans for us may seem beyond belief—even impossible. We may think we are beyond hope. But with God, nothing is impossible!

15:6 This is one of the most important verses in the Old Testament. Abram believed God, and God declared him righteous. In other words, it was Abram's faith, not his works, that made him righteous before God. For us to continue in recovery, we need to trust God more and trust our works less. We are powerless over the pressures of sin, but God will help us through the toughest temptations if we trust him. He will count us righteous because of our trust in him, not because we are perfect.

16:1-4 Since God's promise of a child had been given, about two years had passed without anything happening. Sometimes the hardest part of recovery is the waiting. Here Abram and Sarai show us what *not* to do when things don't progress as quickly as we might hope. Rather than accept God's timing, they took matters into their own hands. They assigned a servant girl, Hagar, to be a surrogate mother for Abram's son. This "solution" has been a source of conflict to this day. Abram's descendants through Hagar are the Arab nations whose conflicts with the Jews keep the Middle East in constant turmoil.

HAGAR & ISHMAEL

Hagar is often overshadowed by the two prominent people in her life—Abraham and Sarah. Her story is woven into the fabric of great events that make up Abraham's life. Yet God chose this "insignificant" woman to bear the son who was destined to be the father of the Arab nations.

When Hagar became pregnant, she gave in to pride and looked down on her mistress, Sarai, who had been unable to bear children. This prompted a great deal of strife in Abraham's family and much suffering for Hagar. The pain and alienation she suffered because of the baby and her wrong attitude could have put considerable strain on the mother-child relationship from the beginning. But Hagar showed no regrets about having her son. She joyfully received him and accepted him despite the complicated and emotionally charged circumstances surrounding his birth.

Hagar and her son, Ishmael, had much in common. They were both rejected by Abraham's household. Together they experienced the torture of the hot, barren desert after Sarai demanded that Abraham send them away. They became nameless outcasts, discarded by those who had once valued them. Under such circumstances, it must have been difficult to maintain a positive self-assessment.

Yet this mother and son persevered through these trials because they had faith in God, who had appeared to them in the wilderness. They knew that they were of great worth in his sight, and they rebuilt their identity upon his promises. To this day their story is used to illustrate God's deep concern for all who have been discarded and rejected. It also shows us that God's assessment of our life is far more important than what other people think.

STRENGTHS AND ACCOMPLISHMENTS:
• Hagar was willing to humbly return to Sarai even though she had been badly mistreated.
• Hagar stood by her son even though he was the source of many of her trials.

WEAKNESSES AND MISTAKES:
• When Hagar became pregnant, she looked down on Sarai with contempt, prompting much of the strife that followed.
• Hagar momentarily abandoned her son in the shade of a bush at the time of his greatest need.

LESSONS FROM THEIR LIVES:
• A loving mother/child relationship is a precious gift from God.
• God is deeply concerned about those who have been abused and rejected.
• God is able to restore a sense of self-worth even in the most trying times.

KEY VERSES:
"The angel of the LORD said to her, 'Return to your mistress and submit to her authority.' Then he added, 'I will give you more descendants than you can count.' And the angel also said, 'You are now pregnant and will give birth to a son. You are to name him Ishmael (which means "God hears"), for the LORD has heard your cry of distress'" (Genesis 16:9-11).

The story of Hagar and Ishmael is told in Genesis 16–21. The apostle Paul briefly discusses them in Galatians 4:21-31.

---

¹²As the sun was going down, Abram fell into a deep sleep, and a terrifying darkness came down over him. ¹³Then the LORD said to Abram, "You can be sure that your descendants will be strangers in a foreign land, where they will be oppressed as slaves for 400 years. ¹⁴But I will punish the nation that enslaves them, and in the end they will come away with great wealth. ¹⁵(As for you, you will die in peace and be buried at a ripe old age.) ¹⁶After four generations your descendants will return here to this land, for the sins of the Amorites do not yet warrant their destruction."

¹⁷After the sun went down and darkness fell, Abram saw a smoking firepot and a flaming torch pass between the halves of the carcasses. ¹⁸So the LORD made a covenant with Abram that day and said, "I have given this land to your descendants, all the way from the border of Egypt* to the great Euphrates River—¹⁹the land now occupied by the Kenites, Kenizzites, Kadmonites, ²⁰Hittites, Perizzites, Rephaites, ²¹Amorites, Canaanites, Girgashites, and Jebusites."

CHAPTER 16
The Birth of Ishmael
Now Sarai, Abram's wife, had not been able to bear children for him. But she had an

15:18 Hebrew *the river of Egypt,* referring either to an eastern branch of the Nile River or to the Brook of Egypt in the Sinai (see Num 34:5).

Egyptian servant named Hagar. ²So Sarai said to Abram, "The LORD has prevented me from having children. Go and sleep with my servant. Perhaps I can have children through her." And Abram agreed with Sarai's proposal. ³So Sarai, Abram's wife, took Hagar the Egyptian servant and gave her to Abram as a wife. (This happened ten years after Abram had settled in the land of Canaan.)

⁴So Abram had sexual relations with Hagar, and she became pregnant. But when Hagar knew she was pregnant, she began to treat her mistress, Sarai, with contempt. ⁵Then Sarai said to Abram, "This is all your fault! I put my servant into your arms, but now that she's pregnant she treats me with contempt. The LORD will show who's wrong—you or me!"

⁶Abram replied, "Look, she is your servant, so deal with her as you see fit." Then Sarai treated Hagar so harshly that she finally ran away.

⁷The angel of the LORD found Hagar beside a spring of water in the wilderness, along the road to Shur. ⁸The angel said to her, "Hagar, Sarai's servant, where have you come from, and where are you going?"

"I'm running away from my mistress, Sarai," she replied.

⁹The angel of the LORD said to her, "Return to your mistress, and submit to her authority." ¹⁰Then he added, "I will give you more descendants than you can count."

¹¹And the angel also said, "You are now pregnant and will give birth to a son. You are to name him Ishmael (which means 'God hears'), for the LORD has heard your cry of distress. ¹²This son of yours will be a wild man, as untamed as a wild donkey! He will raise his fist against everyone, and everyone will be against him. Yes, he will live in open hostility against all his relatives."

¹³Thereafter, Hagar used another name to refer to the LORD, who had spoken to her. She said, "You are the God who sees me."* She also said, "Have I truly seen the One who sees me?" ¹⁴So that well was named Beer-lahai-roi (which means "well of the Living One who sees me"). It can still be found between Kadesh and Bered.

¹⁵So Hagar gave Abram a son, and Abram named him Ishmael. ¹⁶Abram was eighty-six years old when Ishmael was born.

CHAPTER 17
Abram Is Named Abraham
When Abram was ninety-nine years old, the LORD appeared to him and said, "I am El-Shaddai—'God Almighty.' Serve me faithfully and live a blameless life. ²I will make a covenant with you, by which I will guarantee to give you countless descendants."

³At this, Abram fell face down on the ground. Then God said to him, ⁴"This is my covenant with you: I will make you the father of a multitude of nations! ⁵What's more, I am changing your name. It will no longer be Abram. Instead, you will be called Abraham,* for you will be the father of many nations. ⁶I will make you extremely fruitful. Your descendants will become many nations, and kings will be among them!

⁷"I will confirm my covenant with you and your descendants* after you, from generation to generation. This is the everlasting covenant: I will always be your God and the God of your descendants after you. ⁸And I will give the entire land of Canaan, where you now live as a foreigner, to you and your descendants. It will be their possession forever, and I will be their God."

16:13 Hebrew *El-roi*. 17:5 *Abram* means "exalted father"; *Abraham* sounds like a Hebrew term that means "father of many." 17:7 Hebrew *seed*; also in 17:7b, 8, 9, 10, 19.

16:7-13 When Hagar could not help herself and recognized her powerlessness over her situation, the angel of the Lord came and ministered to her. Until we recognize that our situation is hopeless without outside help, God waits and does not help us. But when we are ready to admit our need and cry out to him, he is ready to step in.

17:5-6 Since Abram was childless, his name (meaning "exalted father") must have been a source of embarrassment to him. Here it is changed to "Abraham," which means "father of many." Abraham's name, in a real sense, became his promise from God. It would have been a continual reminder and source of hope that God would come through for him in the end.

17:9-10, 24-27 Most of our significant relationships are symbolized by an outward sign. For example, married people wear rings as a sign of their marriage commitment. Circumcision was a sign of the agreement or covenant between God and Abraham. It was a mark by which Abraham's descendants were set apart as God's special people. Inner changes need to be accompanied by outer signs; beliefs need to be proven by actions. In recovery, as changes begin to take place inside, we need to express these changes outwardly in our actions and lifestyle.

The Mark of the Covenant

⁹Then God said to Abraham, "Your responsibility is to obey the terms of the covenant. You and all your descendants have this continual responsibility. ¹⁰This is the covenant that you and your descendants must keep: Each male among you must be circumcised. ¹¹You must cut off the flesh of your foreskin as a sign of the covenant between me and you. ¹²From generation to generation, every male child must be circumcised on the eighth day after his birth. This applies not only to members of your family but also to the servants born in your household and the foreign-born servants whom you have purchased. ¹³All must be circumcised. Your bodies will bear the mark of my everlasting covenant. ¹⁴Any male who fails to be circumcised will be cut off from the covenant family for breaking the covenant."

Sarai Is Named Sarah

¹⁵Then God said to Abraham, "Regarding Sarai, your wife—her name will no longer be Sarai. From now on her name will be Sarah.* ¹⁶And I will bless her and give you a son from her! Yes, I will bless her richly, and she will become the mother of many nations. Kings of nations will be among her descendants."

¹⁷Then Abraham bowed down to the ground, but he laughed to himself in disbelief. "How could I become a father at the age of 100?" he thought. "And how can Sarah have a baby when she is ninety years old?" ¹⁸So Abraham said to God, "May Ishmael live under your special blessing!"

¹⁹But God replied, "No—Sarah, your wife, will give birth to a son for you. You will name him Isaac,* and I will confirm my covenant with him and his descendants as an everlasting covenant. ²⁰As for Ishmael, I will bless him also, just as you have asked. I will make him extremely fruitful and multiply his descendants. He will become the father of twelve princes, and I will make him a great nation. ²¹But my covenant will be confirmed with Isaac, who will be born to you and Sarah about this time next year." ²²When God had finished speaking, he left Abraham.

²³On that very day Abraham took his son, Ishmael, and every male in his household, including those born there and those he had bought. Then he circumcised them, cutting off their foreskins, just as God had told him. ²⁴Abraham was ninety-nine years old when

---

17:15 *Sarai* and *Sarah* both mean "princess"; the change in spelling may reflect the difference in dialect between Ur and Canaan. 17:19 *Isaac* means "he laughs."

► **The Twelve Step devotional reading plan begins here.**

STEP 1

No-Win Situations

BIBLE READING: Genesis 16:1-15

We admitted that we were powerless over our problems—that our lives had become unmanageable.

Sometimes we are powerless because of our stations in life. We may be in a situation where other people have power over us. We may feel that we are trapped by the demands of others and that there's no way to please them all. It's a double bind: To please one is to disappoint another. Sometimes when we feel stuck and frustrated with our relationships, we look for a measure of control by escaping through our addictive behaviors.

Hagar is a picture of powerlessness. She had no rights. As a girl, she was a slave to Sarai and Abram. When they were upset because Sarai could not bear children, Hagar was given to Abram as a surrogate. When she did become pregnant, as they had wanted, Sarai was so jealous that she beat Hagar, and Hagar ran away. All alone out in the wilderness, she was met by an angel who gave her an amazing message: "'Return to your mistress, and submit to her authority.' Then he added, 'I will give you more descendants than you can count.' And the angel also said, 'You are now pregnant and will give birth to a son. You are to name him Ishmael (which means "God hears"), for the LORD has heard your cry of distress.'" (Genesis 16:9-11).

When we are caught in no-win situations, it's tempting to run away through our addictive/compulsive escape hatches. At times like these God is there, and he is listening to our woes. We need to learn to express our pain to God instead of just trying to escape it. He hears our cries and is willing to give us hope for the future. *Turn to page 325, Judges 16.*

tyndal.es/lrbstep1

he was circumcised, ²⁵and Ishmael, his son, was thirteen. ²⁶Both Abraham and his son, Ishmael, were circumcised on that same day, ²⁷along with all the other men and boys of the household, whether they were born there or bought as servants. All were circumcised with him.

CHAPTER 18
A Son Is Promised to Sarah

The LORD appeared again to Abraham near the oak grove belonging to Mamre. One day Abraham was sitting at the entrance to his tent during the hottest part of the day. ²He looked up and noticed three men standing nearby. When he saw them, he ran to meet them and welcomed them, bowing low to the ground.

³"My lord," he said, "if it pleases you, stop here for a while. ⁴Rest in the shade of this tree while water is brought to wash your feet. ⁵And since you've honored your servant with this visit, let me prepare some food to refresh you before you continue on your journey."

"All right," they said. "Do as you have said."

⁶So Abraham ran back to the tent and said to Sarah, "Hurry! Get three large measures* of your best flour, knead it into dough, and bake some bread." ⁷Then Abraham ran out to the herd and chose a tender calf and gave it to his servant, who quickly prepared it. ⁸When the food was ready, Abraham took some yogurt and milk and the roasted meat, and he served it to the men. As they ate, Abraham waited on them in the shade of the trees.

⁹"Where is Sarah, your wife?" the visitors asked.

"She's inside the tent," Abraham replied.

¹⁰Then one of them said, "I will return to you about this time next year, and your wife, Sarah, will have a son!"

Sarah was listening to this conversation from the tent. ¹¹Abraham and Sarah were both very old by this time, and Sarah was long past the age of having children. ¹²So she laughed silently to herself and said, "How could a worn-out woman like me enjoy such pleasure, especially when my master—my husband—is also so old?"

¹³Then the LORD said to Abraham, "Why did Sarah laugh? Why did she say, 'Can an old woman like me have a baby?' ¹⁴Is anything too hard for the LORD? I will return about this time next year, and Sarah will have a son."

¹⁵Sarah was afraid, so she denied it, saying, "I didn't laugh."

But the LORD said, "No, you did laugh."

Abraham Intercedes for Sodom

¹⁶Then the men got up from their meal and looked out toward Sodom. As they left, Abraham went with them to send them on their way.

¹⁷"Should I hide my plan from Abraham?" the LORD asked. ¹⁸"For Abraham will certainly become a great and mighty nation, and all the nations of the earth will be blessed through him. ¹⁹I have singled him out so that he will direct his sons and their families to keep the way of the LORD by doing what is right and just. Then I will do for Abraham all that I have promised."

²⁰So the LORD told Abraham, "I have heard a great outcry from Sodom and Gomorrah, because their sin is so flagrant. ²¹I am going down to see if their actions are as wicked as I have heard. If not, I want to know."

²²The other men turned and headed toward Sodom, but the LORD remained with Abra-

---

18:6 Hebrew *3 seahs,* about half a bushel or 22 liters.

18:1-6 Hebrews 13:2 urges the practice of hospitality since some have "entertained angels without realizing it!" Abraham's treatment of the three strangers here may have been the background for this verse in Hebrews. Surely this is an example to be followed. As we progress in recovery, one of our goals is to help others discover the new way of life that we have found. What better way than to be hospitable toward others.

18:17-19 Many people wonder why God chose one man and his family out of all the others. Was this fair? These verses show us that God had an important purpose for choosing this one family. God picked Abraham so Abraham could teach his descendants God's ways, for through his ancestral line would come Jesus the Messiah, a source of blessing for all the nations of the earth. God never planned to bless only one family. God chose one family to bring blessings and a means of recovery to all of us.

18:22-32 Often we are urged to pray for others who have problems and difficulties. In these verses, we see Abraham entreating God on behalf of Lot and his family. He is deeply concerned for their welfare and intercedes for them as he speaks with God. This is similar to what we are asked to do in the twelfth step of the recovery process. We are to reach out and help others who are in need. Prayer is a powerful means of doing this.

► **The Serenity Prayer devotional reading plan begins here.**

GOD grant me the serenity to accept the things I cannot change the courage to change the things I can and the wisdom to know the difference

A M E N

We all face difficult situations that involve the people we love. In some of these situations the wise course of action may not be clear. We may feel a heavy burden to act but have no idea what to do.

Abraham found himself in such a situation. The Lord had told Abraham that he intended to destroy the people of Sodom and Gomorrah for their wickedness. Since Abraham's nephew Lot lived among the people of these cities, Abraham was concerned for their welfare. So Abraham approached God and said, "' Will you sweep away both the righteous and the wicked? Suppose you find fifty righteous people living there in the city—will you still sweep it away and not spare it for their sakes? Surely you wouldn't do such a thing, destroying the righteous along with the wicked. . . . Surely you wouldn't do that! Should not the Judge of all the earth do what is right?' And the LORD replied, 'If I find fifty righteous people in Sodom, I will spare the entire city for their sake'" (Genesis 18:23-26). The bargaining went on: Suppose there are only forty-five . . . forty . . . thirty . . . twenty . . . ten? Finally God said, "Then I will not destroy it for the sake of the ten." (18:32).

Abraham wasn't sure what he could do in the situation he faced; he wasn't even sure what was right in this situation. He talked it over with God, reasoning it out, trying to do whatever he could. When we don't know how much of a change we can or even should make, we can start by talking it over with God. Then we can try to do as much as we feel confident doing. *Turn to page 55, Genesis 37.*

ham. ²³Abraham approached him and said, "Will you sweep away both the righteous and the wicked? ²⁴Suppose you find fifty righteous people living there in the city—will you still sweep it away and not spare it for their sakes? ²⁵Surely you wouldn't do such a thing, destroying the righteous along with the wicked. Why, you would be treating the righteous and the wicked exactly the same! Surely you wouldn't do that! Should not the Judge of all the earth do what is right?"

²⁶And the LORD replied, "If I find fifty righteous people in Sodom, I will spare the entire city for their sake."

²⁷Then Abraham spoke again. "Since I have begun, let me speak further to my Lord, even though I am but dust and ashes. ²⁸Suppose there are only forty-five righteous people rather than fifty? Will you destroy the whole city for lack of five?"

And the LORD said, "I will not destroy it if I find forty-five righteous people there."

²⁹Then Abraham pressed his request further. "Suppose there are only forty?"

And the LORD replied, "I will not destroy it for the sake of the forty."

³⁰"Please don't be angry, my Lord," Abraham pleaded. "Let me speak—suppose only thirty righteous people are found?"

And the LORD replied, "I will not destroy it if I find thirty."

³¹Then Abraham said, "Since I have dared to speak to the Lord, let me continue—suppose there are only twenty?"

And the LORD replied, "Then I will not destroy it for the sake of the twenty."

³²Finally, Abraham said, "Lord, please don't be angry with me if I speak one more time. Suppose only ten are found there?"

And the LORD replied, "Then I will not destroy it for the sake of the ten."

³³When the LORD had finished his conversation with Abraham, he went on his way, and Abraham returned to his tent.

CHAPTER 19
Sodom and Gomorrah Destroyed

That evening the two angels came to the entrance of the city of Sodom. Lot was sitting there, and when he saw them, he stood up to meet them. Then he welcomed them and bowed with his face to the ground. ²"My lords," he said, "come to my home to wash your feet, and be my guests for the night. You may then get up early in the morning and be on your way again."

"Oh no," they replied. "We'll just spend the night out here in the city square."

³But Lot insisted, so at last they went home with him. Lot prepared a feast for them, complete with fresh bread made without yeast, and they ate. ⁴But before they retired for the night, all the men of Sodom, young and old, came from all over the city and surrounded the house. ⁵They shouted to Lot, "Where are the men who came to spend the night with you? Bring them out to us so we can have sex with them!"

⁶So Lot stepped outside to talk to them, shutting the door behind him. ⁷"Please, my brothers," he begged, "don't do such a wicked thing. ⁸Look, I have two virgin daughters. Let me bring them out to you, and you can do with them as you wish. But please, leave these men alone, for they are my guests and are under my protection."

⁹"Stand back!" they shouted. "This fellow came to town as an outsider, and now he's acting like our judge! We'll treat you far worse than those other men!" And they lunged toward Lot to break down the door.

¹⁰But the two angels* reached out, pulled Lot into the house, and bolted the door. ¹¹Then they blinded all the men, young and old, who were at the door of the house, so they gave up trying to get inside.

¹²Meanwhile, the angels questioned Lot. "Do you have any other relatives here in the city?" they asked. "Get them out of this place—your sons-in-law, sons, daughters, or anyone else. ¹³For we are about to destroy this city completely. The outcry against this place is so great it has reached the LORD, and he has sent us to destroy it."

¹⁴So Lot rushed out to tell his daughters' fiancés, "Quick, get out of the city! The LORD is about to destroy it." But the young men thought he was only joking.

¹⁵At dawn the next morning the angels became insistent. "Hurry," they said to Lot. "Take your wife and your two daughters who are here. Get out right now, or you will be swept away in the destruction of the city!"

¹⁶When Lot still hesitated, the angels seized his hand and the hands of his wife and two daughters and rushed them to safety outside the city, for the LORD was merciful. ¹⁷When they were safely out of the city, one of the angels ordered, "Run for your lives! And don't look back or stop anywhere in the valley! Escape to the mountains, or you will be swept away!"

¹⁸"Oh no, my lord!" Lot begged. ¹⁹"You have been so gracious to me and saved my life, and you have shown such great kindness. But I cannot go to the mountains. Disaster would catch up to me there, and I would soon die. ²⁰See, there is a small village nearby. Please let me go there instead; don't you see how small it is? Then my life will be saved."

²¹"All right," the angel said, "I will grant your request. I will not destroy the little village. ²²But hurry! Escape to it, for I can do nothing until you arrive there." (This explains why that village was known as Zoar, which means "little place.")

²³Lot reached the village just as the sun was rising over the horizon. ²⁴Then the LORD rained down fire and burning sulfur from the sky on Sodom and Gomorrah. ²⁵He utterly destroyed them, along with the other cities and villages of the plain, wiping out all the people and every bit of vegetation. ²⁶But Lot's wife

19:10 Hebrew *men;* also in 19:12, 16.

19:16 Even after Lot became aware of Sodom's impending doom, he and his family continued to linger there. The angels had to force them to leave. Sometimes, even when we know what course of action is required, we need a push to get us moving. Let us thank God for the "angels" he has provided to help us through times of crisis. Sometimes, as the twelfth step suggests, we may be needed to push others out of situations that are dangerous for them.

19:17-26 As we seek recovery from our problems and dependencies, there can be no looking back, no lingering. Doing so will only result in our destruction. Lot's wife failed to follow the program that the angels had set out for her family. They were to run from Sodom and never look back. Lot's wife did look back, and it spelled her destruction. As we leave the destructive situations in our life, it will be tempting to look back. But this final episode in the life of Lot's wife demonstrates the fatal consequences. We need to run, without looking back.

looked back as she was following behind him, and she turned into a pillar of salt.

²⁷Abraham got up early that morning and hurried out to the place where he had stood in the LORD's presence. ²⁸He looked out across the plain toward Sodom and Gomorrah and watched as columns of smoke rose from the cities like smoke from a furnace.

²⁹But God had listened to Abraham's request and kept Lot safe, removing him from the disaster that engulfed the cities on the plain.

Lot and His Daughters

³⁰Afterward Lot left Zoar because he was afraid of the people there, and he went to live in a cave in the mountains with his two daughters. ³¹One day the older daughter said to her sister, "There are no men left anywhere in this entire area, so we can't get married like everyone else. And our father will soon be too old to have children. ³²Come, let's get him drunk with wine, and then we will have sex with him. That way we will preserve our family line through our father."

³³So that night they got him drunk with wine, and the older daughter went in and had intercourse with her father. He was unaware of her lying down or getting up again.

³⁴The next morning the older daughter said to her younger sister, "I had sex with our father last night. Let's get him drunk with wine again tonight, and you go in and have sex with him. That way we will preserve our family line through our father." ³⁵So that night they got him drunk with wine again, and the younger daughter went in and had intercourse with him. As before, he was unaware of her lying down or getting up again.

³⁶As a result, both of Lot's daughters became pregnant by their own father. ³⁷When the older daughter gave birth to a son, she named him Moab.* He became the ancestor of the nation now known as the Moabites.

³⁸When the younger daughter gave birth to a son, she named him Ben-ammi.* He became the ancestor of the nation now known as the Ammonites.

CHAPTER 20
Abraham Deceives Abimelech

Abraham moved south to the Negev and lived for a while between Kadesh and Shur, and then he moved on to Gerar. While living there as a foreigner, ²Abraham introduced his wife, Sarah, by saying, "She is my sister." So King Abimelech of Gerar sent for Sarah and had her brought to him at his palace.

³But that night God came to Abimelech in a dream and told him, "You are a dead man, for that woman you have taken is already married!"

⁴But Abimelech had not slept with her yet, so he said, "Lord, will you destroy an innocent nation? ⁵Didn't Abraham tell me, 'She is my sister'? And she herself said, 'Yes, he is my brother.' I acted in complete innocence! My hands are clean."

⁶In the dream God responded, "Yes, I know you are innocent. That's why I kept you from sinning against me, and why I did not let you touch her. ⁷Now return the woman to her husband, and he will pray for you, for he is a prophet. Then you will live. But if you don't return her to him, you can be sure that you and all your people will die."

⁸Abimelech got up early the next morning and quickly called all his servants together. When he told them what had happened, his men were terrified. ⁹Then Abimelech called for Abraham. "What have you done to us?" he demanded. "What crime have I committed that deserves treatment like this, making me and my kingdom guilty of this great sin? No one should ever do what you have done! ¹⁰Whatever possessed you to do such a thing?"

19:37 Moab sounds like a Hebrew term that means "from father." 19:38 Ben-ammi means "son of my kinsman."

19:30-38 The incest in Lot's family was a direct consequence of Lot's irresponsible decisions in the past. He had spent his years in a wicked city and had failed to find suitable husbands for his daughters. Their desire for children led to deceit and incest. But there is hope beyond the shocking details of this story. Even though Lot failed in so many ways, many centuries later the apostle Peter used him as a clear example of one whose righteousness came by grace through faith (2 Peter 2:7-8). Lot was an extremely flawed person, but God is a gracious God. There is hope available for each of us, no matter how sordid our past activities may have been.

20:1-18 Why is it so difficult to learn life's most important lessons? To protect himself, Abraham lied, telling Abimelech that his wife, Sarah, was his sister. The sad truth is, Abraham had made this mistake before (12:10-20). He had fallen into a pattern of using lies and deceit to protect himself. But this practice only caused pain to everyone involved. It also displayed how weak Abraham's faith in God was when he was confronted with a difficult situation. Truth is crucial to building healthy relationships. If we stand by the truth, we can trust God to stand by us when things get tough.

¹¹Abraham replied, "I thought, 'This is a godless place. They will want my wife and will kill me to get her.' ¹²And she really is my sister, for we both have the same father, but different mothers. And I married her. ¹³When God called me to leave my father's home and to travel from place to place, I told her, 'Do me a favor. Wherever we go, tell the people that I am your brother.'"

¹⁴Then Abimelech took some of his sheep and goats, cattle, and male and female servants, and he presented them to Abraham. He also returned his wife, Sarah, to him. ¹⁵Then Abimelech said, "Look over my land and choose any place where you would like to live." ¹⁶And he said to Sarah, "Look, I am giving your 'brother' 1,000 pieces of silver* in the presence of all these witnesses. This is to compensate you for any wrong I may have done to you. This will settle any claim against me, and your reputation is cleared."

¹⁷Then Abraham prayed to God, and God healed Abimelech, his wife, and his female servants, so they could have children. ¹⁸For the LORD had caused all the women to be infertile because of what happened with Abraham's wife, Sarah.

CHAPTER 21
The Birth of Isaac

The LORD kept his word and did for Sarah exactly what he had promised. ²She became pregnant, and she gave birth to a son for Abraham in his old age. This happened at just the time God had said it would. ³And Abraham named their son Isaac. ⁴Eight days after Isaac was born, Abraham circumcised him as God had commanded. ⁵Abraham was 100 years old when Isaac was born.

⁶And Sarah declared, "God has brought me laughter.* All who hear about this will laugh with me. ⁷Who would have said to Abraham that Sarah would nurse a baby? Yet I have given Abraham a son in his old age!"

Hagar and Ishmael Are Sent Away

⁸When Isaac grew up and was about to be weaned, Abraham prepared a huge feast to celebrate the occasion. ⁹But Sarah saw Ishmael—the son of Abraham and her Egyptian servant Hagar—making fun of her son, Isaac.* ¹⁰So she turned to Abraham and demanded, "Get rid of that slave woman and her son. He is not going to share the inheritance with my son, Isaac. I won't have it!"

¹¹This upset Abraham very much because Ishmael was his son. ¹²But God told Abraham, "Do not be upset over the boy and your servant. Do whatever Sarah tells you, for Isaac is the son through whom your descendants will be counted. ¹³But I will also make a nation of the descendants of Hagar's son because he is your son, too."

¹⁴So Abraham got up early the next morning, prepared food and a container of water, and strapped them on Hagar's shoulders. Then he sent her away with their son, and she wandered aimlessly in the wilderness of Beersheba.

¹⁵When the water was gone, she put the boy in the shade of a bush. ¹⁶Then she went and sat down by herself about a hundred yards* away. "I don't want to watch the boy die," she said, as she burst into tears.

¹⁷But God heard the boy crying, and the angel of God called to Hagar from heaven, "Hagar, what's wrong? Do not be afraid! God has heard the boy crying as he lies there. ¹⁸Go to him and comfort him, for I will make a great nation from his descendants."

¹⁹Then God opened Hagar's eyes, and she saw a well full of water. She quickly filled her water container and gave the boy a drink.

²⁰And God was with the boy as he grew up in the wilderness. He became a skillful ar-

20:16 Hebrew *1,000 [shekels] of silver,* about 25 pounds or 11.4 kilograms in weight. **21:6** The name *Isaac* means "he laughs." **21:9** As in Greek version and Latin Vulgate; Hebrew lacks *of her son, Isaac.* **21:16** Hebrew *a bowshot.*

21:1-2 God keeps his word. When we claim his promises, we know that our sovereign God is able to fulfill them. Under normal circumstances there was no way that Sarah could have become a mother. But God gave her a child anyway. Sometimes we may feel that complete recovery is just as impossible, but with God, it can be a reality. With him, anything is possible.

22:1-2 God's request that Abraham sacrifice his son was a great test of faith, perhaps the greatest such test in history. Abraham's lifelong dreams were being realized in his beloved son Isaac. Wasn't God's promise of numerous descendants to be fulfilled through this child? But Abraham believed that God had his best in mind—and Abraham was right! He believed that no matter what God required of him, his obedience to God's plan was most important. He trusted that God would still make his promises come true, even without Isaac. Our faith in God's program may be confronted by similar tests. Are we ready to follow through with obedience?

cher, ²¹and he settled in the wilderness of Paran. His mother arranged for him to marry a woman from the land of Egypt.

Abraham's Covenant with Abimelech
²²About this time, Abimelech came with Phicol, his army commander, to visit Abraham. "God is obviously with you, helping you in everything you do," Abimelech said. ²³"Swear to me in God's name that you will never deceive me, my children, or any of my descendants. I have been loyal to you, so now swear that you will be loyal to me and to this country where you are living as a foreigner."

²⁴Abraham replied, "Yes, I swear to it!" ²⁵Then Abraham complained to Abimelech about a well that Abimelech's servants had taken by force from Abraham's servants.

²⁶"This is the first I've heard of it," Abimelech answered. "I have no idea who is responsible. You have never complained about this before."

²⁷Abraham then gave some of his sheep, goats, and cattle to Abimelech, and they made a treaty. ²⁸But Abraham also took seven additional female lambs and set them off by themselves. ²⁹Abimelech asked, "Why have you set these seven apart from the others?"

³⁰Abraham replied, "Please accept these seven lambs to show your agreement that I dug this well." ³¹Then he named the place Beersheba (which means "well of the oath"), because that was where they had sworn the oath.

³²After making their covenant at Beersheba, Abimelech left with Phicol, the commander of his army, and they returned home to the land of the Philistines. ³³Then Abraham planted a tamarisk tree at Beersheba, and there he worshiped the LORD, the Eternal God.* ³⁴And Abraham lived as a foreigner in Philistine country for a long time.

CHAPTER 22
Abraham's Faith Tested
Some time later, God tested Abraham's faith. "Abraham!" God called.

"Yes," he replied. "Here I am."

²"Take your son, your only son—yes, Isaac, whom you love so much—and go to the land of Moriah. Go and sacrifice him as a burnt offering on one of the mountains, which I will show you."

³The next morning Abraham got up early. He saddled his donkey and took two of his servants with him, along with his son, Isaac.

21:33 Hebrew *El-Olam.*

FAITH

READ GENESIS 22:1-19
We demonstrate faith just by the fact that we are involved in a recovery program. If we didn't have faith in the promise of a better future for ourself and our family, we wouldn't put ourself through the hard work and pain involved in recovery. But as time passes, we may grow discouraged at the length of the process. We may have our spirits dampened by the ups and downs along the road, feeling our faith ebb more often than flow. Some people report instant release from their addictions, but for most of us it will take faith and patience to inherit the promise of a new life.

The writer of Hebrews wrote, "You will follow the example of those who are going to inherit God's promises because of their faith and endurance. For example, there was God's promise to Abraham. . . . God took an oath in his own name, saying: 'I will certainly bless you, and I will multiply your descendants beyond number.' Then Abraham waited patiently, and he received what God had promised" (Hebrews 6:12-15). The entire story of Abraham's life can be found in Genesis 11–25.

The key point to consider here is that Abraham waited 25 years to see the promise fulfilled. As he waited, there were times when he showed impatience. At one point he took matters into his own hands, having a son by means of a second wife. At times he probably wondered if he had ever really received the promise at all. He even laughed in disbelief when he was told the promise was soon to come about. But in the end he did receive the promise, and at the end of his life "the LORD had blessed him in every way" (Genesis 24:1). Let's keep holding on! The fact that recovery usually takes time doesn't mean that our faith is in vain. *Turn to page 103, Exodus 20.*

Then he chopped wood for a fire for a burnt offering and set out for the place God had told him about. [4]On the third day of their journey, Abraham looked up and saw the place in the distance. [5]"Stay here with the donkey," Abraham told the servants. "The boy and I will travel a little farther. We will worship there, and then we will come right back."

[6]So Abraham placed the wood for the burnt offering on Isaac's shoulders, while he himself carried the fire and the knife. As the two of them walked on together, [7]Isaac turned to Abraham and said, "Father?"

"Yes, my son?" Abraham replied.

"We have the fire and the wood," the boy said, "but where is the sheep for the burnt offering?"

[8]"God will provide a sheep for the burnt offering, my son," Abraham answered. And they both walked on together.

[9]When they arrived at the place where God had told him to go, Abraham built an altar and arranged the wood on it. Then he tied his son, Isaac, and laid him on the altar on top of the wood. [10]And Abraham picked up the knife to kill his son as a sacrifice. [11]At that moment the angel of the LORD called to him from heaven, "Abraham! Abraham!"

"Yes," Abraham replied. "Here I am!"

[12]"Don't lay a hand on the boy!" the angel said. "Do not hurt him in any way, for now I know that you truly fear God. You have not withheld from me even your son, your only son."

[13]Then Abraham looked up and saw a ram caught by its horns in a thicket. So he took the ram and sacrificed it as a burnt offering in place of his son. [14]Abraham named the place Yahweh-Yireh (which means "the LORD will provide"). To this day, people still use that name as a proverb: "On the mountain of the LORD it will be provided."

[15]Then the angel of the LORD called again to Abraham from heaven. [16]"This is what the LORD says: Because you have obeyed me and have not withheld even your son, your only son, I swear by my own name that [17]I will certainly bless you. I will multiply your descendants* beyond number, like the stars in the sky and the sand on the seashore. Your descendants will conquer the cities of their enemies. [18]And through your descendants all the nations of the earth will be blessed—all because you have obeyed me."

[19]Then they returned to the servants and traveled back to Beersheba, where Abraham continued to live.

[20]Soon after this, Abraham heard that Milcah, his brother Nahor's wife, had borne Nahor eight sons. [21]The oldest was named Uz, the next oldest was Buz, followed by Kemuel (the ancestor of the Arameans), [22]Kesed, Hazo, Pildash, Jidlaph, and Bethuel. [23](Bethuel became the father of Rebekah.) In addition to these eight sons from Milcah, [24]Nahor had four other children from his concubine Reumah. Their names were Tebah, Gaham, Tahash, and Maacah.

CHAPTER 23
The Burial of Sarah

When Sarah was 127 years old, [2]she died at Kiriath-arba (now called Hebron) in the land of Canaan. There Abraham mourned for her and wept for her.

[3]Then, leaving her body, he said to the Hittite elders, [4]"Here I am, a stranger and a foreigner among you. Please sell me a piece of land so I can give my wife a proper burial."

[5]The Hittites replied to Abraham, [6]"Listen, my lord, you are an honored prince among us. Choose the finest of our tombs and bury her there. No one here will refuse to help you in this way."

[7]Then Abraham bowed low before the Hittites [8]and said, "Since you are willing to help me in this way, be so kind as to ask Ephron son of Zohar [9]to let me buy his cave at Machpelah, down at the end of his field. I will pay the full price in the presence of witnesses,

22:17 Hebrew *seed;* also in 22:17b, 18.

22:16-18 The love Abraham must have felt for this long-awaited son! How his heart must have ached at the thought of killing him! How could this have been right? At the end of the story we see that God spared Isaac by providing a ram as his substitute. God has also provided a substitute for all of us—Jesus Christ. God did not spare himself the pain of seeing his Son suffer and die. He suffered so that we might be spared suffering and have a means for recovery from sin and its destructive effects.

23:1 In this chapter we see Abraham mourning for his precious wife, Sarah. His grief was genuine, and he wanted to make proper preparations for paying his last respects. Grief comes into each of our lives, and proper channels for its expression must be found. If we fail to grieve over our personal losses properly, it will be easy to fall into addictions and dependencies to try and hide the pain. If we express our pain constructively, it will be less likely to destroy us.

so I will have a permanent burial place for my family."

¹⁰Ephron was sitting there among the others, and he answered Abraham as the others listened, speaking publicly before all the Hittite elders of the town. ¹¹"No, my lord," he said to Abraham, "please listen to me. I will give you the field and the cave. Here in the presence of my people, I give it to you. Go and bury your dead."

¹²Abraham again bowed low before the citizens of the land, ¹³and he replied to Ephron as everyone listened. "No, listen to me. I will buy it from you. Let me pay the full price for the field so I can bury my dead there."

¹⁴Ephron answered Abraham, ¹⁵"My lord, please listen to me. The land is worth 400 pieces* of silver, but what is that between friends? Go ahead and bury your dead."

¹⁶So Abraham agreed to Ephron's price and paid the amount he had suggested— 400 pieces of silver, weighed according to the market standard. The Hittite elders witnessed the transaction.

¹⁷So Abraham bought the plot of land belonging to Ephron at Machpelah, near Mamre. This included the field itself, the cave that was in it, and all the surrounding trees. ¹⁸It was transferred to Abraham as his permanent possession in the presence of the Hittite elders at the city gate. ¹⁹Then Abraham buried his wife, Sarah, there in Canaan, in the cave of Machpelah, near Mamre (also called Hebron). ²⁰So the field and the cave were transferred from the Hittites to Abraham for use as a permanent burial place.

CHAPTER 24
A Wife for Isaac

Abraham was now a very old man, and the LORD had blessed him in every way. ²One day Abraham said to his oldest servant, the man in charge of his household, "Take an oath by putting your hand under my thigh. ³Swear by the LORD, the God of heaven and earth, that you will not allow my son to marry one of these local Canaanite women. ⁴Go instead to my homeland, to my relatives, and find a wife there for my son Isaac."

⁵The servant asked, "But what if I can't find a young woman who is willing to travel so far from home? Should I then take Isaac there to live among your relatives in the land you came from?"

⁶"No!" Abraham responded. "Be careful never to take my son there. ⁷For the LORD, the

23:15 Hebrew *400 shekels,* about 10 pounds or 4.6 kilograms in weight; also in 23:16.

STEP 6

Taking Time to Grieve

BIBLE READING: Genesis 23:1-4; 35:19-21

We were entirely ready for God to remove all these defects of character.

The pathway to recovery and finding new life also involves the death process. The different means we used to use to help us cope were "defective," but still, they did give us comfort or companionship. Giving them up is often like suffering the death of a loved one.

Abraham and his grandson Jacob both lost loved ones as they traveled to the Promised Land. "Sarah . . . died at Kiriath-arba (now called Hebron) in the land of Canaan. There Abraham mourned and wept for her. Then, leaving her body, he said . . . 'Here I am, a stranger and a foreigner among you. Please sell me a piece of land so I can give my wife a proper burial.' . . . Then Abraham buried his wife, Sarah, there" (Genesis 23:1-4, 19). A generation later, Jacob was given a new name, Israel, and the promise of a great heritage in the Promised Land. On his way there, he, too, lost his beloved wife. She died while giving birth to their son Benjamin. "So Rachel died and was buried on the way to Ephrath (that is, Bethlehem). Jacob set up a stone monument over Rachel's grave, and it can be seen there to this day. Then Jacob traveled on" (Genesis 35:19-21).

As we journey on in our new life, we will necessarily lose some of our defective ways of coping. When this happens, we need to stop and take time to give our losses a proper burial. We need to put them away, cover the shame, and allow ourselves to grieve the loss of something very familiar to us. When the time of grieving is over, we, too, can journey on. *Turn to page 715, Psalm 51.*

tyndal.es/lrbstep6

God of heaven, who took me from my father's house and my native land, solemnly promised to give this land to my descendants.* He will send his angel ahead of you, and he will see to it that you find a wife there for my son. ⁸If she is unwilling to come back with you, then you are free from this oath of mine. But under no circumstances are you to take my son there."

⁹So the servant took an oath by putting his hand under the thigh of his master, Abraham. He swore to follow Abraham's instructions. ¹⁰Then he loaded ten of Abraham's camels with all kinds of expensive gifts from his master, and he traveled to distant Aram-naharaim. There he went to the town where Abraham's brother Nahor had settled. ¹¹He made the camels kneel beside a well just outside the town. It was evening, and the women were coming out to draw water.

¹²"O LORD, God of my master, Abraham," he prayed. "Please give me success today, and show unfailing love to my master, Abraham. ¹³See, I am standing here beside this spring, and the young women of the town are coming out to draw water. ¹⁴This is my request. I will ask one of them, 'Please give me a drink from your jug.' If she says, 'Yes, have a drink, and I will water your camels, too!'—let her be the one you have selected as Isaac's wife. This is how I will know that you have shown unfailing love to my master."

¹⁵Before he had finished praying, he saw a young woman named Rebekah coming out with her water jug on her shoulder. She was the daughter of Bethuel, who was the son of Abraham's brother Nahor and his wife, Milcah. ¹⁶Rebekah was very beautiful and old enough to be married, but she was still a virgin. She went down to the spring, filled her jug, and came up again. ¹⁷Running over to her, the servant said, "Please give me a little drink of water from your jug."

¹⁸"Yes, my lord," she answered, "have a drink." And she quickly lowered her jug from her shoulder and gave him a drink. ¹⁹When she had given him a drink, she said, "I'll draw water for your camels, too, until they have had enough to drink." ²⁰So she quickly emptied her jug into the watering trough and ran back to the well to draw water for all his camels.

²¹The servant watched her in silence, wondering whether or not the LORD had given him success in his mission. ²²Then at last, when the camels had finished drinking, he took out a gold ring for her nose and two large gold bracelets* for her wrists.

²³"Whose daughter are you?" he asked. "And please tell me, would your father have any room to put us up for the night?"

²⁴"I am the daughter of Bethuel," she replied. "My grandparents are Nahor and Milcah. ²⁵Yes, we have plenty of straw and feed for the camels, and we have room for guests."

²⁶The man bowed low and worshiped the LORD. ²⁷"Praise the LORD, the God of my master, Abraham," he said. "The LORD has shown unfailing love and faithfulness to my master, for he has led me straight to my master's relatives."

²⁸The young woman ran home to tell her family everything that had happened. ²⁹Now Rebekah had a brother named Laban, who ran out to meet the man at the spring. ³⁰He had seen the nose-ring and the bracelets on his sister's wrists, and had heard Rebekah tell what the man had said. So he rushed out to the spring, where the man was still standing beside his camels. ³¹Laban said to him, "Come and stay with us, you who are blessed by the LORD! Why are you standing here outside the town when I have a room all ready for you and a place prepared for the camels?"

³²So the man went home with Laban, and Laban unloaded the camels, gave him straw for their bedding, fed them, and provided water for the man and the camel drivers to wash their feet. ³³Then food was served. But Abraham's servant said, "I don't want to eat until I have told you why I have come."

"All right," Laban said, "tell us."

³⁴"I am Abraham's servant," he explained. ³⁵"And the LORD has greatly blessed my master; he has become a wealthy man. The LORD has given him flocks of sheep and goats, herds of cattle, a fortune in silver and gold, and many male and female servants and camels and donkeys.

³⁶"When Sarah, my master's wife, was very old, she gave birth to my master's son, and my master has given him everything he owns. ³⁷And my master made me take an oath. He said, 'Do not allow my son to marry one of these local Canaanite women. ³⁸Go instead to my father's house, to my relatives, and find a wife there for my son.'

³⁹"But I said to my master, 'What if I can't find a young woman who is willing to go back with me?' ⁴⁰He responded, 'The LORD,

---

24:7 Hebrew *seed;* also in 24:60. **24:22** Hebrew *a gold nose-ring weighing a beka* [0.2 ounces or 6 grams] *and two gold bracelets weighing 10* [*shekels*] [4 ounces or 114 grams].

ISAAC & REBEKAH

Deception is extremely harmful in any relationship but even more so in the relationship between a husband and wife. Isaac and Rebekah began their marriage loving and honoring each other. However, as the marriage progressed, so did the deception on both sides. The end result was a family torn apart by strife.

As his parents, Abraham and Sarah, had also done, Isaac lied to Abimelech, claiming that Rebekah was not his wife. He did this to protect himself, fearing that Abimelech would kill him to take his wife. Deception based on the idea that the end justifies the means may at times seem a necessary evil within some families. But in fact it often starts a string of hurtful lies between marriage partners and other family members.

Isaac and Rebekah were blessed with twin sons, Esau and Jacob. Isaac loved Esau the best, while Rebekah favored Jacob. Showing favoritism split this family in two and set the stage for further conflict and deception. When the time came for Isaac to give Esau his blessing, Jacob willingly took part in Rebekah's plan to deceive her husband. Deception had become a natural practice in this dysfunctional family.

This story of deception in a marriage is sad but hardly uncommon. What started out as a loving marriage based on honesty and a desire to serve God soon became filled with deception and distance. It is important to notice, however, that God remained faithful to his promises to Isaac and Rebekah despite their failures.

STRENGTHS AND ACCOMPLISHMENTS:
- They had a caring and loving marriage—at least until their sons were born.
- They were the recipients of God's promises to Abraham.

WEAKNESSES AND MISTAKES:
- Isaac and Rebekah often allowed the end to justify the means.
- In facing difficult situations, Isaac and Rebekah often lied to avoid their problems.
- Both of them alienated each other by playing favorites with their sons.

LESSONS FROM THEIR LIVES:
- God keeps his promises and remains faithful even when we are faithless.
- God's promises and plans are bigger than we can ever ask for or imagine.
- Playing favorites is harmful in a family.
- Deception is destructive in a marriage and other significant relationships.

KEY VERSE:
"And Isaac brought Rebekah into his mother Sarah's tent, and she became his wife. He loved her deeply, and she was a special comfort to him after the death of his mother" (Genesis 24:67).

Isaac and Rebekah's story is told in Genesis 24–28. Both are mentioned in Romans 9:10. Isaac is also referred to in Romans 9:7-8; Hebrews 11:17-20; and James 2:21-24.

---

in whose presence I have lived, will send his angel with you and will make your mission successful. Yes, you must find a wife for my son from among my relatives, from my father's family. [41]Then you will have fulfilled your obligation. But if you go to my relatives and they refuse to let her go with you, you will be free from my oath.'

[42]"So today when I came to the spring, I prayed this prayer: 'O LORD, God of my master, Abraham, please give me success on this mission. [43]See, I am standing here beside this spring. This is my request. When a young woman comes to draw water, I will say to her, "Please give me a little drink of water from your jug." [44]If she says, "Yes, have a drink, and I will draw water for your camels, too," let her be the one you have selected to be the wife of my master's son.'

[45]"Before I had finished praying in my heart, I saw Rebekah coming out with her water jug on her shoulder. She went down to the spring and drew water. So I said to her, 'Please give me a drink.' [46]She quickly lowered her jug from her shoulder and said, 'Yes, have a drink, and I will water your camels, too!' So I drank, and then she watered the camels.

[47]"Then I asked, 'Whose daughter are you?' She replied, 'I am the daughter of Bethuel, and my grandparents are Nahor and Milcah.' So I put the ring on her nose, and the bracelets on her wrists.

[48]"Then I bowed low and worshiped the LORD. I praised the LORD, the God of my master, Abraham, because he had led me straight to my master's niece to be his son's wife. [49]So tell me—will you or won't you show unfailing love and faithfulness to my master? Please tell me yes or no, and then I'll know what to do next."

⁵⁰Then Laban and Bethuel replied, "The LORD has obviously brought you here, so there is nothing we can say. ⁵¹Here is Rebekah; take her and go. Yes, let her be the wife of your master's son, as the LORD has directed."

⁵²When Abraham's servant heard their answer, he bowed down to the ground and worshiped the LORD. ⁵³Then he brought out silver and gold jewelry and clothing and presented them to Rebekah. He also gave expensive presents to her brother and mother. ⁵⁴Then they ate their meal, and the servant and the men with him stayed there overnight.

But early the next morning, Abraham's servant said, "Send me back to my master."

⁵⁵"But we want Rebekah to stay with us at least ten days," her brother and mother said. "Then she can go."

⁵⁶But he said, "Don't delay me. The LORD has made my mission successful; now send me back so I can return to my master."

⁵⁷"Well," they said, "we'll call Rebekah and ask her what she thinks." ⁵⁸So they called Rebekah. "Are you willing to go with this man?" they asked her.

And she replied, "Yes, I will go."

⁵⁹So they said good-bye to Rebekah and sent her away with Abraham's servant and his men. The woman who had been Rebekah's childhood nurse went along with her. ⁶⁰They gave her this blessing as she parted:

"Our sister, may you become
    the mother of many millions!
May your descendants be strong
    and conquer the cities of their enemies."

⁶¹Then Rebekah and her servant girls mounted the camels and followed the man. So Abraham's servant took Rebekah and went on his way.

⁶²Meanwhile, Isaac, whose home was in the Negev, had returned from Beer-lahai-roi. ⁶³One evening as he was walking and meditating in the fields, he looked up and saw the camels coming. ⁶⁴When Rebekah looked up and saw Isaac, she quickly dismounted from her camel. ⁶⁵"Who is that man walking through the fields to meet us?" she asked the servant.

And he replied, "It is my master." So Rebekah covered her face with her veil. ⁶⁶Then the servant told Isaac everything he had done.

⁶⁷And Isaac brought Rebekah into his mother Sarah's tent, and she became his wife. He loved her deeply, and she was a special comfort to him after the death of his mother.

CHAPTER 25
The Death of Abraham

Abraham married another wife, whose name was Keturah. ²She gave birth to Zimran, Jokshan, Medan, Midian, Ishbak, and Shuah. ³Jokshan was the father of Sheba and Dedan. Dedan's descendants were the Asshurites, Letushites, and Leummites. ⁴Midian's sons were Ephah, Epher, Hanoch, Abida, and Eldaah. These were all descendants of Abraham through Keturah.

⁵Abraham gave everything he owned to his son Isaac. ⁶But before he died, he gave gifts to the sons of his concubines and sent them off to a land in the east, away from Isaac.

⁷Abraham lived for 175 years, ⁸and he died at a ripe old age, having lived a long and satisfying life. He breathed his last and joined his ancestors in death. ⁹His sons Isaac and Ishmael buried him in the cave of Machpelah, near Mamre, in the field of Ephron son of Zohar the Hittite. ¹⁰This was the field Abraham had purchased from the Hittites and where he had buried his wife Sarah. ¹¹After Abraham's death, God blessed his son Isaac, who settled near Beer-lahai-roi in the Negev.

Ishmael's Descendants

¹²This is the account of the family of Ishmael, the son of Abraham through Hagar, Sarah's Egyptian servant. ¹³Here is a list, by their names and clans, of Ishmael's descendants: The oldest was Nebaioth, followed by Kedar,

---

24:67 When we lose someone close to us, it is important that we take some time for rebuilding. It is encouraging to notice that, after losing one major family relationship, Isaac found comfort in a new one. As people are taken away from us, God will provide others to give us the support we need to live a healthy and productive life.

25:23 This prenatal prophecy concerning Jacob and Esau portends conflict between the brothers—and it goes beyond just normal sibling rivalry! Unfortunately, the subsequent family history amply bears this out. Sibling rivalry is often very destructive to family relationships and can easily get out of control. Siblings often separate for life, carrying with them years of hard feelings that taint all their other relationships. Reconciliation with those we have hurt is one of the goals of recovery. Let us take steps toward recovering our important relationships.

ESAU & JACOB

Sibling rivalry is a natural, though sometimes difficult, aspect of family relationships. Brothers, especially those close in age, often don't get along well as children or young adults. But the twins, Esau and Jacob, took this natural conflict to another level of intensity altogether. Fortunately, there was reconciliation later in life, though it required considerable emotional and spiritual growth on the part of both men.

The intense rivalry was actually predicted by God even before the twins were born. And the situation wasn't helped any by the parents playing favorites with their sons. Isaac clearly preferred Esau, while Rebekah favored Jacob. Relationships in this family went from bad to worse when Esau sold Jacob his birthright for the momentary gratification of his hungry stomach.

One event finally shattered the already fragile relationship between these brothers. Jacob deceived his almost blind father into giving him the final blessing that was intended for the firstborn, Esau. Jacob's elaborate scheme, masterminded by his mother, so enraged Esau that he vowed to kill his brother after his father's death. The victim of his own lack of honesty, Jacob fled for his life. He settled with his uncle Laban and in time married his two daughters, Leah and Rachel.

While living with Laban's family, Jacob became the victim of his own uncle's deceitful practices. Through this experience, Jacob learned painful lessons regarding the importance of love and honesty. God had been working in Jacob's life, drawing him progressively closer to himself. So with a sure knowledge of God's presence, Jacob became willing to face his past. He set out on the long journey home and, despite his fears, found forgiveness and reconciliation in the embrace of his waiting brother.

STRENGTHS AND ACCOMPLISHMENTS:
- Both were willing to let go of past failures and hurts to find a better future.
- Esau grew to the point of being able to forgive after feeling significant disappointment and anger.
- Jacob matured to the point where he could be honest and humbly seek forgiveness.

WEAKNESSES AND MISTAKES:
- Both were intent on having their own way with little thought of how it might affect others.
- Esau sought instant gratification and suffered great losses as a result.
- Jacob was often dishonest and deceitful in his dealings.

LESSONS FROM THEIR LIVES:
- Parents should never play favorites with their children.
- Forgiveness can take place even when deep hurts have been suffered.
- Even habitually deceitful people can face the past, change, and recover their relationships.

KEY VERSE:
"Then Esau ran to meet [Jacob] and embraced him, threw his arms around his neck, and kissed him. And they both wept" (Genesis 33:4).

The story of Esau and Jacob is told in Genesis 25–33. Both are also mentioned in Malachi 1:2-3; Acts 3:13; Romans 9:10-13; and Hebrews 11:9, 20-21. Esau is referred to in Hebrews 12:16-17, while Jacob is mentioned in Hosea 12:3-5 and Matthew 1:2; 22:32.

Adbeel, Mibsam, [14]Mishma, Dumah, Massa, [15]Hadad, Tema, Jetur, Naphish, and Kedemah. [16]These twelve sons of Ishmael became the founders of twelve tribes named after them, listed according to the places they settled and camped. [17]Ishmael lived for 137 years. Then he breathed his last and joined his ancestors in death. [18]Ishmael's descendants occupied the region from Havilah to Shur, which is east of Egypt in the direction of Asshur. There they lived in open hostility toward all their relatives.*

The Births of Esau and Jacob

[19]This is the account of the family of Isaac, the son of Abraham. [20]When Isaac was forty years old, he married Rebekah, the daughter of Bethuel the Aramean from Paddan-aram and the sister of Laban the Aramean.

[21]Isaac pleaded with the LORD on behalf of his wife, because she was unable to have children. The LORD answered Isaac's prayer, and Rebekah became pregnant with twins. [22]But the two children struggled with each other in her womb. So she went to ask the LORD about it. "Why is this happening to me?" she asked.

[23]And the LORD told her, "The sons in your womb will become two nations. From the very beginning, the two nations will be rivals. One nation will be stronger than the

other; and your older son will serve your younger son."

²⁴And when the time came to give birth, Rebekah discovered that she did indeed have twins! ²⁵The first one was very red at birth and covered with thick hair like a fur coat. So they named him Esau.* ²⁶Then the other twin was born with his hand grasping Esau's heel. So they named him Jacob.* Isaac was sixty years old when the twins were born.

Esau Sells His Birthright

²⁷As the boys grew up, Esau became a skillful hunter. He was an outdoorsman, but Jacob had a quiet temperament, preferring to stay at home. ²⁸Isaac loved Esau because he enjoyed eating the wild game Esau brought home, but Rebekah loved Jacob.

²⁹One day when Jacob was cooking some stew, Esau arrived home from the wilderness exhausted and hungry. ³⁰Esau said to Jacob, "I'm starved! Give me some of that red stew!" (This is how Esau got his other name, Edom, which means "red.")

³¹"All right," Jacob replied, "but trade me your rights as the firstborn son."

³²"Look, I'm dying of starvation!" said Esau. "What good is my birthright to me now?"

³³But Jacob said, "First you must swear that your birthright is mine." So Esau swore an oath, thereby selling all his rights as the firstborn to his brother, Jacob.

³⁴Then Jacob gave Esau some bread and lentil stew. Esau ate the meal, then got up and left. He showed contempt for his rights as the firstborn.

CHAPTER 26
Isaac Deceives Abimelech

A severe famine now struck the land, as had happened before in Abraham's time. So Isaac moved to Gerar, where Abimelech, king of the Philistines, lived.

²The LORD appeared to Isaac and said, "Do not go down to Egypt, but do as I tell you. ³Live here as a foreigner in this land, and I will be with you and bless you. I hereby confirm that I will give all these lands to you and your descendants,* just as I solemnly promised Abraham, your father. ⁴I will cause your descendants to become as numerous as the stars of the sky, and I will give them all these lands. And through your descendants all the nations of the earth will be blessed. ⁵I will do this because Abraham listened to me and obeyed all my requirements, commands, decrees, and instructions." ⁶So Isaac stayed in Gerar.

⁷When the men who lived there asked Isaac about his wife, Rebekah, he said, "She is my sister." He was afraid to say, "She is my wife." He thought, "They will kill me to get her, because she is so beautiful." ⁸But some time later, Abimelech, king of the Philistines, looked out his window and saw Isaac caressing Rebekah.

⁹Immediately, Abimelech called for Isaac and exclaimed, "She is obviously your wife! Why did you say, 'She is my sister'?"

"Because I was afraid someone would kill me to get her from me," Isaac replied.

¹⁰"How could you do this to us?" Abimelech exclaimed. "One of my people might easily have taken your wife and slept with her, and you would have made us guilty of great sin."

¹¹Then Abimelech issued a public proclamation: "Anyone who touches this man or his wife will be put to death!"

Conflict over Water Rights

¹²When Isaac planted his crops that year, he harvested a hundred times more grain than

---

25:25 *Esau* sounds like a Hebrew term that means "hair." 25:26 *Jacob* sounds like the Hebrew words for "heel" and "deceiver." 26:3 Hebrew *seed;* also in 26:4, 24.

25:34 Esau traded his rights as a firstborn son for a bowl of stew to fill his empty stomach. He was indifferent to the things in life that were really important. His primary concern was to satisfy his immediate physical needs, with no thought at all for his future. He hadn't learned how to delay gratification. The lesson Esau needed to learn is very important for all of us in recovery. We need to see things in the long view. If we can picture the positive, long-range results of life in recovery, we will be able to give up the momentary pleasures that keep us from getting there.

26:6-11 Children learn from their parents. Unfortunately, they are not selective about what they learn. They don't learn the good things and ignore the bad. In these verses Isaac demonstrates what he learned from his father, Abraham. Doubtless, he had heard how Abraham had passed Sarah off as his sister to protect himself (12:10-20; 20:1-18). It is amazing how the sinful patterns of our parents are often repeated in our own life. How often family dysfunctions repeat themselves generation after generation! Isaac would have been wise to tell the truth and trust God to protect him. Trust in God is one weapon we have with which to fight against destructive family patterns.

he planted, for the LORD blessed him. [13]He became a very rich man, and his wealth continued to grow. [14]He acquired so many flocks of sheep and goats, herds of cattle, and servants that the Philistines became jealous of him. [15]So the Philistines filled up all of Isaac's wells with dirt. These were the wells that had been dug by the servants of his father, Abraham.

[16]Finally, Abimelech ordered Isaac to leave the country. "Go somewhere else," he said, "for you have become too powerful for us."

[17]So Isaac moved away to the Gerar Valley, where he set up their tents and settled down. [18]He reopened the wells his father had dug, which the Philistines had filled in after Abraham's death. Isaac also restored the names Abraham had given them.

[19]Isaac's servants also dug in the Gerar Valley and discovered a well of fresh water. [20]But then the shepherds from Gerar came and claimed the spring. "This is our water," they said, and they argued over it with Isaac's herdsmen. So Isaac named the well Esek (which means "argument"). [21]Isaac's men then dug another well, but again there was a dispute over it. So Isaac named it Sitnah (which means "hostility"). [22]Abandoning that one, Isaac moved on and dug another well. This time there was no dispute over it, so Isaac named the place Rehoboth (which means "open space"), for he said, "At last the LORD has created enough space for us to prosper in this land."

[23]From there Isaac moved to Beersheba, [24]where the LORD appeared to him on the night of his arrival. "I am the God of your father, Abraham," he said. "Do not be afraid, for I am with you and will bless you. I will multiply your descendants, and they will become a great nation. I will do this because of my promise to Abraham, my servant." [25]Then Isaac built an altar there and worshiped the LORD. He set up his camp at that place, and his servants dug another well.

Isaac's Covenant with Abimelech

[26]One day King Abimelech came from Gerar with his adviser, Ahuzzath, and also Phicol, his army commander. [27]"Why have you come here?" Isaac asked. "You obviously hate me, since you kicked me off your land."

[28]They replied, "We can plainly see that the LORD is with you. So we want to enter into a sworn treaty with you. Let's make a covenant. [29]Swear that you will not harm us, just as we have never troubled you. We have always treated you well, and we sent you away from us in peace. And now look how the LORD has blessed you!"

[30]So Isaac prepared a covenant feast to celebrate the treaty, and they ate and drank together. [31]Early the next morning, they each took a solemn oath not to interfere with each other. Then Isaac sent them home again, and they left him in peace.

[32]That very day Isaac's servants came and told him about a new well they had dug. "We've found water!" they exclaimed. [33]So Isaac named the well Shibah (which means "oath"). And to this day the town that grew up there is called Beersheba (which means "well of the oath").

[34]At the age of forty, Esau married two Hittite wives: Judith, the daughter of Beeri, and Basemath, the daughter of Elon. [35]But Esau's wives made life miserable for Isaac and Rebekah.

CHAPTER 27
Jacob Steals Esau's Blessing

One day when Isaac was old and turning blind, he called for Esau, his older son, and said, "My son."

"Yes, Father?" Esau replied.

[2]"I am an old man now," Isaac said, "and I don't know when I may die. [3]Take your bow and a quiver full of arrows, and go out into the open country to hunt some wild game for me. [4]Prepare my favorite dish, and bring it here for me to eat. Then I will pronounce the

---

26:23-24 Isaac was afraid, and he had good reason to be. He was surrounded by hostile neighbors who greatly outnumbered his household. He didn't have a place to call his own, except the burial site of his parents. He lived in Gerar "by permission," as it were. At this time God came to Isaac with this soothing message, "Do not be afraid." We may feel as if we don't belong anywhere. We may have forfeited our place in society. It may seem as though there are enemies all around us. But even when things are at their worst, we need to be aware that God is with us, whispering, "Do not be afraid."

27:1-29 It is heartbreaking to watch Rebekah and Jacob conspire to deceive Isaac. Notice the great lengths to which they go to fool the old man. They knew that Jacob was the heir to God's promises through Abraham (see 25:23, 29-33), but they were trying to make God's program happen through their deceit. That never works without causing pain or added trouble somewhere else. God is in charge of the timetable of our recovery program. We need to stick with the truth and move at his pace.

blessing that belongs to you, my firstborn son, before I die."

⁵But Rebekah overheard what Isaac had said to his son Esau. So when Esau left to hunt for the wild game, ⁶she said to her son Jacob, "Listen. I overheard your father say to Esau, ⁷'Bring me some wild game and prepare me a delicious meal. Then I will bless you in the LORD's presence before I die.' ⁸Now, my son, listen to me. Do exactly as I tell you. ⁹Go out to the flocks, and bring me two fine young goats. I'll use them to prepare your father's favorite dish. ¹⁰Then take the food to your father so he can eat it and bless you before he dies."

¹¹"But look," Jacob replied to Rebekah, "my brother, Esau, is a hairy man, and my skin is smooth. ¹²What if my father touches me? He'll see that I'm trying to trick him, and then he'll curse me instead of blessing me."

¹³But his mother replied, "Then let the curse fall on me, my son! Just do what I tell you. Go out and get the goats for me!"

¹⁴So Jacob went out and got the young goats for his mother. Rebekah took them and prepared a delicious meal, just the way Isaac liked it. ¹⁵Then she took Esau's favorite clothes, which were there in the house, and gave them to her younger son, Jacob. ¹⁶She covered his arms and the smooth part of his neck with the skin of the young goats. ¹⁷Then she gave Jacob the delicious meal, including freshly baked bread.

¹⁸So Jacob took the food to his father. "My father?" he said.

"Yes, my son," Isaac answered. "Who are you—Esau or Jacob?"

¹⁹Jacob replied, "It's Esau, your firstborn son. I've done as you told me. Here is the wild game. Now sit up and eat it so you can give me your blessing."

²⁰Isaac asked, "How did you find it so quickly, my son?"

"The LORD your God put it in my path!" Jacob replied.

²¹Then Isaac said to Jacob, "Come closer so I can touch you and make sure that you really are Esau." ²²So Jacob went closer to his father, and Isaac touched him. "The voice is Jacob's, but the hands are Esau's," Isaac said. ²³But he

did not recognize Jacob, because Jacob's hands felt hairy just like Esau's. So Isaac prepared to bless Jacob. ²⁴"But are you really my son Esau?" he asked.

"Yes, I am," Jacob replied.

²⁵Then Isaac said, "Now, my son, bring me the wild game. Let me eat it, and then I will give you my blessing." So Jacob took the food to his father, and Isaac ate it. He also drank the wine that Jacob served him. ²⁶Then Isaac said to Jacob, "Please come a little closer and kiss me, my son."

²⁷So Jacob went over and kissed him. And when Isaac caught the smell of his clothes, he was finally convinced, and he blessed his son. He said, "Ah! The smell of my son is like the smell of the outdoors, which the LORD has blessed!

²⁸ "From the dew of heaven
 and the richness of the earth,
may God always give you abundant
   harvests of grain
 and bountiful new wine.
²⁹ May many nations become your
   servants,
 and may they bow down to you.
May you be the master over your brothers,
 and may your mother's sons bow down
   to you.
All who curse you will be cursed,
 and all who bless you will be blessed."

³⁰As soon as Isaac had finished blessing Jacob, and almost before Jacob had left his father, Esau returned from his hunt. ³¹Esau prepared a delicious meal and brought it to his father. Then he said, "Sit up, my father, and eat my wild game so you can give me your blessing."

³²But Isaac asked him, "Who are you?"

Esau replied, "It's your son, your firstborn son, Esau."

³³Isaac began to tremble uncontrollably and said, "Then who just served me wild game? I have already eaten it, and I blessed him just before you came. And yes, that blessing must stand!"

³⁴When Esau heard his father's words, he

27:33 At this point Isaac realized that he had blessed Jacob instead of Esau, but he could not take his blessing back. Jacob would receive the inheritance and blessing of the firstborn son. It became clear that it was God's plan that Jacob should be the recipient of God's promises to Abraham, so Isaac acquiesced to God's will. There are often times when God, through circumstances, will veto our plans. Through grace, he often delivers us from making bad choices and protects us from terrible consequences. As the third step reminds us, we must surrender our will to God if we are to progress in recovery.

let out a loud and bitter cry. "Oh my father, what about me? Bless me, too!" he begged.

³⁵But Isaac said, "Your brother was here, and he tricked me. He has taken away your blessing."

³⁶Esau exclaimed, "No wonder his name is Jacob, for now he has cheated me twice.* First he took my rights as the firstborn, and now he has stolen my blessing. Oh, haven't you saved even one blessing for me?"

³⁷Isaac said to Esau, "I have made Jacob your master and have declared that all his brothers will be his servants. I have guaranteed him an abundance of grain and wine—what is left for me to give you, my son?"

³⁸Esau pleaded, "But do you have only one blessing? Oh my father, bless me, too!" Then Esau broke down and wept.

³⁹Finally, his father, Isaac, said to him,

"You will live away from the richness
        of the earth,
    and away from the dew of the heaven
        above.
⁴⁰ You will live by your sword,
    and you will serve your brother.
But when you decide to break free,
    you will shake his yoke from your
        neck."

Jacob Flees to Paddan-Aram

⁴¹From that time on, Esau hated Jacob because their father had given Jacob the blessing. And Esau began to scheme: "I will soon be mourning my father's death. Then I will kill my brother, Jacob."

⁴²But Rebekah heard about Esau's plans. So she sent for Jacob and told him, "Listen, Esau is consoling himself by plotting to kill you. ⁴³So listen carefully, my son. Get ready and flee to my brother, Laban, in Haran. ⁴⁴Stay there with him until your brother cools off. ⁴⁵When he calms down and forgets what you have done to him, I will send for you to come back. Why should I lose both of you in one day?"

⁴⁶Then Rebekah said to Isaac, "I'm sick and tired of these local Hittite women! I would rather die than see Jacob marry one of them."

CHAPTER 28

So Isaac called for Jacob, blessed him, and said, "You must not marry any of these Canaanite women. ²Instead, go at once to Paddan-aram, to the house of your grandfather Bethuel, and marry one of your uncle Laban's daughters. ³May God Almighty* bless you and give you many children. And may your descendants multiply and become many nations! ⁴May God pass on to you and your descendants* the blessings he promised to Abraham. May you own this land where you are now living as a foreigner, for God gave this land to Abraham."

⁵So Isaac sent Jacob away, and he went to Paddan-aram to stay with his uncle Laban, his mother's brother, the son of Bethuel the Aramean.

⁶Esau knew that his father, Isaac, had blessed Jacob and sent him to Paddan-aram to find a wife, and that he had warned Jacob, "You must not marry a Canaanite woman." ⁷He also knew that Jacob had obeyed his parents and gone to Paddan-aram. ⁸It was now very clear to Esau that his father did not like the local Canaanite women. ⁹So Esau visited his uncle Ishmael's family and married one of Ishmael's daughters, in addition to the wives he already had. His new wife's name was Mahalath. She was the sister of Nebaioth and the daughter of Ishmael, Abraham's son.

Jacob's Dream at Bethel

¹⁰Meanwhile, Jacob left Beersheba and traveled toward Haran. ¹¹At sundown he arrived at a good place to set up camp and stopped there for the night. Jacob found a stone to rest his head against and lay down to sleep. ¹²As he slept, he dreamed of a stairway that reached from the earth up to heaven. And he saw the angels of God going up and down the stairway.

¹³At the top of the stairway stood the LORD, and he said, "I am the LORD, the God of your grandfather Abraham, and the God of your father, Isaac. The ground you are lying on belongs to you. I am giving it to you and your descendants. ¹⁴Your descendants will be as

27:36 *Jacob* sounds like the Hebrew words for "heel" and "deceiver." **28:3** Hebrew *El-Shaddai.* **28:4** Hebrew *seed;* also in 28:13, 14.

27:34-40 Here Esau demonstrates tearful remorse, but according to Hebrews 12:16-17, it was too late. As a young man he had traded his birthright for instant gratification. Now he had to suffer the consequences for not waiting to fill his hungry stomach. Those of us in recovery know what this is like. Time and again we have chosen to give up the things that are really important in our life for immediate satisfaction or for something that will dull the pain we are hiding inside. But even though time has been lost, there is hope for those who are willing to take steps toward recovery.

numerous as the dust of the earth! They will spread out in all directions—to the west and the east, to the north and the south. And all the families of the earth will be blessed through you and your descendants. [15]What's more, I am with you, and I will protect you wherever you go. One day I will bring you back to this land. I will not leave you until I have finished giving you everything I have promised you."

[16]Then Jacob awoke from his sleep and said, "Surely the LORD is in this place, and I wasn't even aware of it!" [17]But he was also afraid and said, "What an awesome place this is! It is none other than the house of God, the very gateway to heaven!"

[18]The next morning Jacob got up very early. He took the stone he had rested his head against, and he set it upright as a memorial pillar. Then he poured olive oil over it. [19]He named that place Bethel (which means "house of God"), although it was previously called Luz.

[20]Then Jacob made this vow: "If God will indeed be with me and protect me on this journey, and if he will provide me with food and clothing, [21]and if I return safely to my father's home, then the LORD will certainly be my God. [22]And this memorial pillar I have set up will become a place for worshiping God, and I will present to God a tenth of everything he gives me."

CHAPTER 29
Jacob Arrives at Paddan-Aram

Then Jacob hurried on, finally arriving in the land of the east. [2]He saw a well in the distance. Three flocks of sheep and goats lay in an open field beside it, waiting to be watered. But a heavy stone covered the mouth of the well.

[3]It was the custom there to wait for all the flocks to arrive before removing the stone and watering the animals. Afterward the stone would be placed back over the mouth of the well. [4]Jacob went over to the shepherds and asked, "Where are you from, my friends?"

"We are from Haran," they answered.

[5]"Do you know a man there named Laban, the grandson of Nahor?" he asked.

"Yes, we do," they replied.

[6]"Is he doing well?" Jacob asked.

"Yes, he's well," they answered. "Look, here comes his daughter Rachel with the flock now."

[7]Jacob said, "Look, it's still broad daylight—too early to round up the animals. Why don't you water the sheep and goats so they can get back out to pasture?"

[8]"We can't water the animals until all the flocks have arrived," they replied. "Then the shepherds move the stone from the mouth of the well, and we water all the sheep and goats."

[9]Jacob was still talking with them when Rachel arrived with her father's flock, for she was a shepherd. [10]And because Rachel was his cousin—the daughter of Laban, his mother's brother—and because the sheep and goats belonged to his uncle Laban, Jacob went over to the well and moved the stone from its mouth and watered his uncle's flock. [11]Then Jacob kissed Rachel, and he wept aloud. [12]He explained to Rachel that he was her cousin on her father's side—the son of her aunt Rebekah. So Rachel quickly ran and told her father, Laban.

[13]As soon as Laban heard that his nephew Jacob had arrived, he ran out to meet him. He embraced and kissed him and brought him home. When Jacob had told him his story, [14]Laban exclaimed, "You really are my own flesh and blood!"

Jacob Marries Leah and Rachel

After Jacob had stayed with Laban for about a month, [15]Laban said to him, "You shouldn't work for me without pay just because we are relatives. Tell me how much your wages should be."

[16]Now Laban had two daughters. The older daughter was named Leah, and the younger one was Rachel. [17]There was no sparkle in Leah's eyes,* but Rachel had a beautiful figure and a lovely face. [18]Since Jacob was in love with Rachel, he told her father, "I'll work for you for seven years if you'll give me Rachel, your younger daughter, as my wife."

[19]"Agreed!" Laban replied. "I'd rather give her to you than to anyone else. Stay and work

---

29:17 Or *Leah had dull eyes,* or *Leah had soft eyes.* The meaning of the Hebrew is uncertain.

28:20-22 Jacob's vow to God here is possibly just another of his schemes—something like a "foxhole" prayer. But even though Jacob was probably trying to "con" God—give him "an offer he couldn't refuse"—God honored and blessed Jacob. God's dealings with Jacob should give us some idea of how gracious God really is. Jacob wasn't exemplary or wise; he didn't know the God of his fathers as he should have. Yet God was still willing to work with him and bless him.

with me." ²⁰So Jacob worked seven years to pay for Rachel. But his love for her was so strong that it seemed to him but a few days.

²¹Finally, the time came for him to marry her. "I have fulfilled my agreement," Jacob said to Laban. "Now give me my wife so I can sleep with her."

²²So Laban invited everyone in the neighborhood and prepared a wedding feast. ²³But that night, when it was dark, Laban took Leah to Jacob, and he slept with her. ²⁴(Laban had given Leah a servant, Zilpah, to be her maid.)

²⁵But when Jacob woke up in the morning—it was Leah! "What have you done to me?" Jacob raged at Laban. "I worked seven years for Rachel! Why have you tricked me?"

²⁶"It's not our custom here to marry off a younger daughter ahead of the firstborn," Laban replied. ²⁷"But wait until the bridal week is over; then we'll give you Rachel, too—provided you promise to work another seven years for me."

²⁸So Jacob agreed to work seven more years. A week after Jacob had married Leah, Laban gave him Rachel, too. ²⁹(Laban gave Rachel a servant, Bilhah, to be her maid.) ³⁰So Jacob slept with Rachel, too, and he loved her much more than Leah. He then stayed and worked for Laban the additional seven years.

Jacob's Many Children

³¹When the LORD saw that Leah was unloved, he enabled her to have children, but Rachel could not conceive. ³²So Leah became pregnant and gave birth to a son. She named him Reuben,* for she said, "The LORD has noticed my misery, and now my husband will love me."

³³She soon became pregnant again and gave birth to another son. She named him Simeon,* for she said, "The LORD heard that I was unloved and has given me another son."

³⁴Then she became pregnant a third time and gave birth to another son. He was named Levi,* for she said, "Surely this time my husband will feel affection for me, since I have given him three sons!"

³⁵Once again Leah became pregnant and gave birth to another son. She named him Judah,* for she said, "Now I will praise the LORD!" And then she stopped having children.

CHAPTER 30

When Rachel saw that she wasn't having any children for Jacob, she became jealous of her sister. She pleaded with Jacob, "Give me children, or I'll die!"

²Then Jacob became furious with Rachel. "Am I God?" he asked. "He's the One who has kept you from having children!"

³Then Rachel told him, "Take my maid, Bilhah, and sleep with her. She will bear children for me,* and through her I can have a family, too." ⁴So Rachel gave her servant, Bilhah, to Jacob as a wife, and he slept with her. ⁵Bilhah became pregnant and presented him with a son. ⁶Rachel named him Dan,* for she said, "God has vindicated me! He has heard my request and given me a son." ⁷Then Bilhah became pregnant again and gave Jacob a second son. ⁸Rachel named him Naphtali,* for she said, "I have struggled hard with my sister, and I'm winning!"

⁹Meanwhile, Leah realized that she wasn't getting pregnant anymore, so she took her servant, Zilpah, and gave her to Jacob as a wife. ¹⁰Soon Zilpah presented him with a son. ¹¹Leah named him Gad,* for she said, "How fortunate I am!" ¹²Then Zilpah gave Jacob a second son. ¹³And Leah named him Asher,* for she said, "What joy is mine! Now the other women will celebrate with me."

¹⁴One day during the wheat harvest, Reuben found some mandrakes growing in a field and brought them to his mother, Leah. Rachel begged Leah, "Please give me some of your son's mandrakes."

¹⁵But Leah angrily replied, "Wasn't it enough that you stole my husband? Now will you steal my son's mandrakes, too?"

Rachel answered, "I will let Jacob sleep with you tonight if you give me some of the mandrakes."

¹⁶So that evening, as Jacob was coming home from the fields, Leah went out to meet him. "You must come and sleep with me tonight!" she said. "I have paid for you with

---

29:32 *Reuben* means "Look, a son!" It also sounds like the Hebrew for "He has seen my misery." 29:33 *Simeon* probably means "one who hears." 29:34 *Levi* sounds like a Hebrew term that means "being attached" or "feeling affection for." 29:35 *Judah* is related to the Hebrew term for "praise." 30:3 Hebrew *bear children on my knees.* 30:6 *Dan* means "he judged" or "he vindicated." 30:8 *Naphtali* means "my struggle." 30:11 *Gad* means "good fortune." 30:13 *Asher* means "happy."

29:25 Jacob's response to Laban's trickery reveals an interesting principle. Nobody resents being cheated more than a cheater. If there is a characteristic in others that we find particularly annoying, we would be wise to examine ourself. It is probably one of our own.

some mandrakes that my son found." So that night he slept with Leah. [17]And God answered Leah's prayers. She became pregnant again and gave birth to a fifth son for Jacob. [18]She named him Issachar,* for she said, "God has rewarded me for giving my servant to my husband as a wife." [19]Then Leah became pregnant again and gave birth to a sixth son for Jacob. [20]She named him Zebulun,* for she said, "God has given me a good reward. Now my husband will treat me with respect, for I have given him six sons." [21]Later she gave birth to a daughter and named her Dinah.

[22]Then God remembered Rachel's plight and answered her prayers by enabling her to have children. [23]She became pregnant and gave birth to a son. "God has removed my disgrace," she said. [24]And she named him Joseph,* for she said, "May the LORD add yet another son to my family."

Jacob's Wealth Increases

[25]Soon after Rachel had given birth to Joseph, Jacob said to Laban, "Please release me so I can go home to my own country. [26]Let me take my wives and children, for I have earned them by serving you, and let me be on my way. You certainly know how hard I have worked for you."

[27]"Please listen to me," Laban replied. "I have become wealthy, for* the LORD has blessed me because of you. [28]Tell me how much I owe you. Whatever it is, I'll pay it."

[29]Jacob replied, "You know how hard I've worked for you, and how your flocks and herds have grown under my care. [30]You had little indeed before I came, but your wealth has increased enormously. The LORD has blessed you through everything I've done. But now, what about me? When can I start providing for my own family?"

[31]"What wages do you want?" Laban asked again.

Jacob replied, "Don't give me anything. Just do this one thing, and I'll continue to tend and watch over your flocks. [32]Let me inspect your flocks today and remove all the sheep and goats that are speckled or spotted, along with all the black sheep. Give these to me as my wages. [33]In the future, when you check on the animals you have given me as my wages, you'll see that I have been honest. If you find in my flock any goats without speckles or spots, or any sheep that are not black, you will know that I have stolen them from you."

[34]"All right," Laban replied. "It will be as you say." [35]But that very day Laban went out and removed the male goats that were streaked and spotted, all the female goats that were speckled and spotted or had white patches, and all the black sheep. He placed them in the care of his own sons, [36]who took them a three-days' journey from where Jacob was. Meanwhile, Jacob stayed and cared for the rest of Laban's flock.

[37]Then Jacob took some fresh branches from poplar, almond, and plane trees and peeled off strips of bark, making white streaks on them. [38]Then he placed these peeled branches in the watering troughs where the flocks came to drink, for that was where they mated. [39]And when they mated in front of the white-streaked branches, they gave birth to young that were streaked, speckled, and spotted. [40]Jacob separated those lambs from Laban's flock. And at mating time he turned the flock to face Laban's animals that were streaked or black. This is how he built his own flock instead of increasing Laban's.

[41]Whenever the stronger females were ready to mate, Jacob would place the peeled

---

30:18 *Issachar* sounds like a Hebrew term that means "reward." 30:20 *Zebulun* probably means "honor."
30:24 *Joseph* means "may he add." 30:27 Or *I have learned by divination that.*

30:25-43 God always treated Jacob in ways far better than he deserved. God blessed him in spite of his trickery and deceit. God works that way with us, too. He is willing to bless us with healing even when we don't really deserve it. None of us really deserves God's love; all of us have failed in many ways. But God still reaches out to help us when we look to him in faith.

31:3 Moving can be a time of major crisis. It is interesting to note that during all the major change points of Jacob's life, God always reestablished contact with him. Here, as Jacob faced a crisis with Laban's family, God gave Jacob instructions concerning his next move. God revealed to Jacob the next step in his divine program as it was needed. God is always there to help us during our moments of crisis. During these times we need to learn to stop and listen to what he has to say.

31:14-15 Leah and Rachel left their father's home willingly. This is not surprising. We have enough evidence to know that Laban's family was highly dysfunctional. At this point, Jacob and his family needed to move on if they were to become the family God intended them to be. Sometimes our homes of origin are sources of much pain and confusion. In such cases, it is important for us to leave those dysfunctional contexts in order to build a new life in a more healthy atmosphere.

branches in the watering troughs in front of them. Then they would mate in front of the branches. [42]But he didn't do this with the weaker ones, so the weaker lambs belonged to Laban, and the stronger ones were Jacob's. [43]As a result, Jacob became very wealthy, with large flocks of sheep and goats, female and male servants, and many camels and donkeys.

CHAPTER 31
Jacob Flees from Laban

But Jacob soon learned that Laban's sons were grumbling about him. "Jacob has robbed our father of everything!" they said. "He has gained all his wealth at our father's expense." [2]And Jacob began to notice a change in Laban's attitude toward him.

[3]Then the LORD said to Jacob, "Return to the land of your father and grandfather and to your relatives there, and I will be with you."

[4]So Jacob called Rachel and Leah out to the field where he was watching his flock. [5]He said to them, "I have noticed that your father's attitude toward me has changed. But the God of my father has been with me. [6]You know how hard I have worked for your father, [7]but he has cheated me, changing my wages ten times. But God has not allowed him to do me any harm. [8]For if he said, 'The speckled animals will be your wages,' the whole flock began to produce speckled young. And when he changed his mind and said, 'The striped animals will be your wages,' then the whole flock produced striped young. [9]In this way, God has taken your father's animals and given them to me.

[10]"One time during the mating season, I had a dream and saw that the male goats mating with the females were streaked, speckled, and spotted. [11]Then in my dream, the angel of God said to me, 'Jacob!' And I replied, 'Yes, here I am.'

[12]"The angel said, 'Look up, and you will see that only the streaked, speckled, and spotted males are mating with the females of your flock. For I have seen how Laban has treated you. [13]I am the God who appeared to you at Bethel,* the place where you anointed the pillar of stone and made your vow to me. Now get ready and leave this country and return to the land of your birth.'"

[14]Rachel and Leah responded, "That's fine with us! We won't inherit any of our father's wealth anyway. [15]He has reduced our rights to

31:13 As in Greek version and an Aramaic Targum; Hebrew reads *the God of Bethel*.

STEP 10

Personal Boundaries
BIBLE READING: Genesis 31:45-55
We continued to take personal inventory and when we were wrong promptly admitted it.
We all have particular weaknesses, and it is often helpful to establish personal boundary lines to support these weaker areas. We may need to clearly define our commitments to others; we may need to agree on certain limitations in order to maintain peace. Once the boundaries have been established, honesty is needed to maintain them. An assessment of our honesty in keeping our commitments needs to be a regular part of our everyday life.

Jacob and his father-in-law, Laban, had some conflicts. As they were working them out, they entered into an agreement by drawing a clearly defined boundary line and setting up a monument to remind them of that commitment. "'May the LORD keep watch between us to make sure that we keep this covenant when we are out of each other's sight. . . . See this pile of stones,' Laban continued, 'and see this monument I have set between us. They stand between us as witnesses of our vows.' . . . So Jacob took an oath before the fearsome God of his father, Isaac, to respect the boundary line" (Genesis 31:49, 51-53).

Restoring trust in our relationships is part of recovery. To do this we should define our expectations and enter cautiously into commitments. We are not merely responsible for what the other person knows about. We are personally responsible for our own honesty before the watchful eyes of God. These relational commitments are not to be entered into lightly. But when we make them, they must be vigilantly maintained. *Turn to page 1441, Romans 5.*

tyndal.es/lrbstep10

45

those of foreign women. And after he sold us, he wasted the money you paid him for us. [16]All the wealth God has given you from our father legally belongs to us and our children. So go ahead and do whatever God has told you."

[17]So Jacob put his wives and children on camels, [18]and he drove all his livestock in front of him. He packed all the belongings he had acquired in Paddan-aram and set out for the land of Canaan, where his father, Isaac, lived. [19]At the time they left, Laban was some distance away, shearing his sheep. Rachel stole her father's household idols and took them with her. [20]Jacob outwitted Laban the Aramean, for they set out secretly and never told Laban they were leaving. [21]So Jacob took all his possessions with him and crossed the Euphrates River,* heading for the hill country of Gilead.

Laban Pursues Jacob

[22]Three days later, Laban was told that Jacob had fled. [23]So he gathered a group of his relatives and set out in hot pursuit. He caught up with Jacob seven days later in the hill country of Gilead. [24]But the previous night God had appeared to Laban the Aramean in a dream and told him, "I'm warning you—leave Jacob alone!"

[25]Laban caught up with Jacob as he was camped in the hill country of Gilead, and he set up his camp not far from Jacob's. [26]"What do you mean by deceiving me like this?" Laban demanded. "How dare you drag my daughters away like prisoners of war? [27]Why did you slip away secretly? Why did you deceive me? And why didn't you say you wanted to leave? I would have given you a farewell feast, with singing and music, accompanied by tambourines and harps. [28]Why didn't you let me kiss my daughters and grandchildren and tell them good-bye? You have acted very foolishly! [29]I could destroy you, but the God of your father appeared to me last night and warned me, 'Leave Jacob alone!' [30]I can understand your feeling that you must go, and your intense longing for your father's home. But why have you stolen my gods?"

[31]"I rushed away because I was afraid," Ja-cob answered. "I thought you would take your daughters from me by force. [32]But as for your gods, see if you can find them, and let the person who has taken them die! And if you find anything else that belongs to you, identify it before all these relatives of ours, and I will give it back!" But Jacob did not know that Rachel had stolen the household idols.

[33]Laban went first into Jacob's tent to search there, then into Leah's, and then the tents of the two servant wives—but he found nothing. Finally, he went into Rachel's tent. [34]But Rachel had taken the household idols and hidden them in her camel saddle, and now she was sitting on them. When Laban had thoroughly searched her tent without finding them, [35]she said to her father, "Please, sir, forgive me if I don't get up for you. I'm having my monthly period." So Laban continued his search, but he could not find the household idols.

[36]Then Jacob became very angry, and he challenged Laban. "What's my crime?" he demanded. "What have I done wrong to make you chase after me as though I were a criminal? [37]You have rummaged through everything I own. Now show me what you found that belongs to you! Set it out here in front of us, before our relatives, for all to see. Let them judge between us!

[38]"For twenty years I have been with you, caring for your flocks. In all that time your sheep and goats never miscarried. In all those years I never used a single ram of yours for food. [39]If any were attacked and killed by wild animals, I never showed you the carcass and asked you to reduce the count of your flock. No, I took the loss myself! You made me pay for every stolen animal, whether it was taken in broad daylight or in the dark of night.

[40]"I worked for you through the scorching heat of the day and through cold and sleepless nights. [41]Yes, for twenty years I slaved in your house! I worked for fourteen years earning your two daughters, and then six more years for your flock. And you changed my wages ten times! [42]In fact, if the God of my father had not been on my side—the God of Abraham and the fearsome God of Isaac*—you would have sent me away empty-

31:21 Hebrew *the river.* 31:42 Or *and the Fear of Isaac.*

31:17-20 Even though God was very active in Jacob's life, the old patterns still persisted. Jacob's recovery from his deceitful youth was an ongoing process. This time he deceived Laban. Most of us are in recovery for a lifetime. Jacob's habits and tendencies certainly didn't go away overnight. Neither will ours. We need to be aware of our weaknesses and look to God for his help at each step along the way.

handed. But God has seen your abuse and my hard work. That is why he appeared to you last night and rebuked you!"

Jacob's Treaty with Laban

⁴³Then Laban replied to Jacob, "These women are my daughters, these children are my grandchildren, and these flocks are my flocks—in fact, everything you see is mine. But what can I do now about my daughters and their children? ⁴⁴So come, let's make a covenant, you and I, and it will be a witness to our commitment."

⁴⁵So Jacob took a stone and set it up as a monument. ⁴⁶Then he told his family members, "Gather some stones." So they gathered stones and piled them in a heap. Then Jacob and Laban sat down beside the pile of stones to eat a covenant meal. ⁴⁷To commemorate the event, Laban called the place Jegar-sahadutha (which means "witness pile" in Aramaic), and Jacob called it Galeed (which means "witness pile" in Hebrew).

⁴⁸Then Laban declared, "This pile of stones will stand as a witness to remind us of the covenant we have made today." This explains why it was called Galeed—"Witness Pile." ⁴⁹But it was also called Mizpah (which means "watchtower"), for Laban said, "May the LORD keep watch between us to make sure that we keep this covenant when we are out of each other's sight. ⁵⁰If you mistreat my daughters or if you marry other wives, God will see it even if no one else does. He is a witness to this covenant between us.

⁵¹"See this pile of stones," Laban continued, "and see this monument I have set between us. ⁵²They stand between us as witnesses of our vows. I will never pass this pile of stones to harm you, and you must never pass these stones or this monument to harm me. ⁵³I call on the God of our ancestors—the God of your grandfather Abraham and the God of my grandfather Nahor—to serve as a judge between us."

So Jacob took an oath before the fearsome God of his father, Isaac,* to respect the boundary line. ⁵⁴Then Jacob offered a sacrifice to God there on the mountain and invited everyone to a covenant feast. After they had eaten, they spent the night on the mountain.

⁵⁵*Laban got up early the next morning, and he kissed his grandchildren and his daughters and blessed them. Then he left and returned home.

CHAPTER 32

¹*As Jacob started on his way again, angels of God came to meet him. ²When Jacob saw them, he exclaimed, "This is God's camp!" So he named the place Mahanaim.*

Jacob Sends Gifts to Esau

³Then Jacob sent messengers ahead to his brother, Esau, who was living in the region of Seir in the land of Edom. ⁴He told them, "Give this message to my master Esau: 'Humble greetings from your servant Jacob. Until now I have been living with Uncle Laban, ⁵and now I own cattle, donkeys, flocks of sheep and goats, and many servants, both men and women. I have sent these messengers to inform my lord of my coming, hoping that you will be friendly to me.'"

⁶After delivering the message, the messengers returned to Jacob and reported, "We met your brother, Esau, and he is already on his way to meet you—with an army of 400 men!" ⁷Jacob was terrified at the news. He divided his household, along with the flocks and herds and camels, into two groups. ⁸He thought, "If Esau meets one group and attacks it, perhaps the other group can escape."

⁹Then Jacob prayed, "O God of my grandfather Abraham, and God of my father, Isaac—O LORD, you told me, 'Return to your own land and to your relatives.' And you promised me, 'I will treat you kindly.' ¹⁰I am not worthy of all the unfailing love and faithfulness you have shown to me, your servant. When I left home and crossed the Jordan River, I owned nothing except a walking

31:53 Or *the Fear of his father, Isaac.* 31:55 Verse 31:55 is numbered 32:1 in Hebrew text. 32:1 Verses 32:1-32 are numbered 32:2-33 in Hebrew text. 32:2 *Mahanaim* means "two camps."

31:49 This verse is often quoted as a sweet benediction, but in actuality it is a very negative wish that becomes almost a threat. It's as if Laban were saying, "I can't watch you anymore, so when you're out of my sight, I pray that God will keep his eye on you, you rascal!"
32:3 Twenty years prior to these events Jacob had run away from Esau, afraid for his life. Jacob had no way of knowing whether his brother, Esau, had experienced healing from the old wounds and resentments. Since he did not know, he had to make elaborate preparations for reestablishing contact. Jacob's example in this chapter gives many helpful hints to those of us seeking reconciliation with people we have hurt in the past.

stick. Now my household fills two large camps! [11]O LORD, please rescue me from the hand of my brother, Esau. I am afraid that he is coming to attack me, along with my wives and children. [12]But you promised me, 'I will surely treat you kindly, and I will multiply your descendants until they become as numerous as the sands along the seashore—too many to count.'"

[13]Jacob stayed where he was for the night. Then he selected these gifts from his possessions to present to his brother, Esau: [14]200 female goats, 20 male goats, 200 ewes, 20 rams, [15]30 female camels with their young, 40 cows, 10 bulls, 20 female donkeys, and 10 male donkeys. [16]He divided these animals into herds and assigned each to different servants. Then he told his servants, "Go ahead of me with the animals, but keep some distance between the herds."

[17]He gave these instructions to the men leading the first group: "When my brother, Esau, meets you, he will ask, 'Whose servants are you? Where are you going? Who owns these animals?' [18]You must reply, 'They belong to your servant Jacob, but they are a gift for his master Esau. Look, he is coming right behind us.'"

[19]Jacob gave the same instructions to the second and third herdsmen and to all who followed behind the herds: "You must say the same thing to Esau when you meet him. [20]And be sure to say, 'Look, your servant Jacob is right behind us.'"

Jacob thought, "I will try to appease him by sending gifts ahead of me. When I see him in person, perhaps he will be friendly to me." [21]So the gifts were sent on ahead, while Jacob himself spent that night in the camp.

Jacob Wrestles with God
[22]During the night Jacob got up and took his two wives, his two servant wives, and his eleven sons and crossed the Jabbok River with them. [23]After taking them to the other side, he sent over all his possessions.

[24]This left Jacob all alone in the camp, and a man came and wrestled with him until the dawn began to break. [25]When the man saw that he would not win the match, he touched Jacob's hip and wrenched it out of its socket. [26]Then the man said, "Let me go, for the dawn is breaking!"

But Jacob said, "I will not let you go unless you bless me."

[27]"What is your name?" the man asked.

He replied, "Jacob."

[28]"Your name will no longer be Jacob," the man told him. "From now on you will be called Israel,* because you have fought with God and with men and have won."

[29]"Please tell me your name," Jacob said.

"Why do you want to know my name?" the man replied. Then he blessed Jacob there.

[30]Jacob named the place Peniel (which means "face of God"), for he said, "I have seen God face to face, yet my life has been spared." [31]The sun was rising as Jacob left Peniel,* and he was limping because of the injury to his hip. [32](Even today the people of Israel don't eat the tendon near the hip socket because of what happened that night when the man strained the tendon of Jacob's hip.)

CHAPTER 33
Jacob and Esau Make Peace
Then Jacob looked up and saw Esau coming with his 400 men. So he divided the children among Leah, Rachel, and his two servant wives. [2]He put the servant wives and their children at the front, Leah and her children next, and Rachel and Joseph last. [3]Then Jacob went on ahead. As he approached his brother, he bowed to the ground seven times before him. [4]Then Esau ran to meet him and embraced him, threw his arms around his neck, and kissed him. And they both wept.

[5]Then Esau looked at the women and children and asked, "Who are these people with you?"

"These are the children God has graciously given to me, your servant," Jacob replied. [6]Then the servant wives came forward

---

32:28 *Jacob* sounds like the Hebrew words for "heel" and "deceiver." *Israel* means "God fights." **32:31** Hebrew *Penuel,* a variant spelling of Peniel.

33:4 Although Esau does seem genuinely delighted to see his long-lost brother, we can only speculate about his true feelings. This happy reunion certainly didn't signal the end of the brothers' feud. Conflict between their families continued throughout Old Testament times. The book of Obadiah records the joy that Esau's descendants, the Edomites, expressed over the Israelites' defeat. Obadiah, an Israelite, also joyfully announced the doom of Edom. Even in the New Testament, the hated family of Herod traced its lineage back to Esau. Some conflicts are not easily resolved, but if they are left unresolved, they can become a burden to generations far into the future.

with their children and bowed before him. ⁷Next came Leah with her children, and they bowed before him. Finally, Joseph and Rachel came forward and bowed before him.

⁸"And what were all the flocks and herds I met as I came?" Esau asked.

Jacob replied, "They are a gift, my lord, to ensure your friendship."

⁹"My brother, I have plenty," Esau answered. "Keep what you have for yourself."

¹⁰But Jacob insisted, "No, if I have found favor with you, please accept this gift from me. And what a relief to see your friendly smile. It is like seeing the face of God! ¹¹Please take this gift I have brought you, for God has been very gracious to me. I have more than enough." And because Jacob insisted, Esau finally accepted the gift.

¹²"Well," Esau said, "let's be going. I will lead the way."

¹³But Jacob replied, "You can see, my lord, that some of the children are very young, and the flocks and herds have their young, too. If they are driven too hard, even for one day, all the animals could die. ¹⁴Please, my lord, go ahead of your servant. We will follow slowly, at a pace that is comfortable for the livestock and the children. I will meet you at Seir."

¹⁵"All right," Esau said, "but at least let me assign some of my men to guide and protect you."

Jacob responded, "That's not necessary. It's enough that you've received me warmly, my lord!"

¹⁶So Esau turned around and started back to Seir that same day. ¹⁷Jacob, on the other hand, traveled on to Succoth. There he built himself a house and made shelters for his livestock. That is why the place was named Succoth (which means "shelters").

¹⁸Later, having traveled all the way from Paddan-aram, Jacob arrived safely at the town of Shechem, in the land of Canaan. There he set up camp outside the town. ¹⁹Jacob bought the plot of land where he camped from the family of Hamor, the father of Shechem, for 100 pieces of silver.* ²⁰And there he built an altar and named it El-Elohe-Israel.*

CHAPTER 34
Revenge against Shechem

One day Dinah, the daughter of Jacob and Leah, went to visit some of the young

33:19 Hebrew *100 kesitahs;* the value or weight of the kesitah is no longer known. 33:20 *El-Elohe-Israel* means "God, the God of Israel."

STEP 9
Long-Awaited Healing

BIBLE READING: Genesis 33:1-11

We made direct amends to such people wherever possible, except when to do so would injure them or others.

Returning to someone we have hurt is a scary thing. The passing years, lack of communication, and memories of anger and hateful emotional exchanges can all create tremendous anxiety. Even though we may make some contact through a third party, there will still be tension until we see that person face to face.

This was the case for Jacob upon returning to see Esau. "Then Jacob looked up and saw Esau coming with his 400 men. . . . Then Jacob went on ahead. . . . Esau ran to meet him and embraced him, threw his arms around his neck, and kissed him. And they both wept." (Genesis 33:1, 3-4) After being introduced to Jacob's family, Esau asked, "'And what were all the flocks and herds I met as I came?' . . . Jacob replied, 'They are a gift, my lord, to ensure your friendship.' 'My brother, I have plenty,' Esau answered. 'Keep what you have for yourself.' But Jacob insisted, 'No, if I have found favor with you, please accept this gift from me. And what a relief to see your friendly smile. It is like seeing the face of God! Please take this gift I have brought you, for God has been very gracious to me. I have more than enough.' And because Jacob insisted, Esau finally accepted the gift." (Genesis 33:8-11).

Jacob's tremendous fear gave way to relief. The last time Jacob had seen Esau, Jacob was in fear for his life. With the passing of time, both of them had changed. When Jacob faced his brother, he found that there was still affection, even though they both remembered the pain. *Turn to page 399, 2 Samuel 9.*

tyndal.es/lrbstep9

women who lived in the area. ²But when the local prince, Shechem son of Hamor the Hivite, saw Dinah, he seized her and raped her. ³But then he fell in love with her, and he tried to win her affection with tender words. ⁴He said to his father, Hamor, "Get me this young girl. I want to marry her."

⁵Soon Jacob heard that Shechem had defiled his daughter, Dinah. But since his sons were out in the fields herding his livestock, he said nothing until they returned. ⁶Hamor, Shechem's father, came to discuss the matter with Jacob. ⁷Meanwhile, Jacob's sons had come in from the field as soon as they heard what had happened. They were shocked and furious that their sister had been raped. Shechem had done a disgraceful thing against Jacob's family,* something that should never be done.

⁸Hamor tried to speak with Jacob and his sons. "My son Shechem is truly in love with your daughter," he said. "Please let him marry her. ⁹In fact, let's arrange other marriages, too. You give us your daughters for our sons, and we will give you our daughters for your sons. ¹⁰And you may live among us; the land is open to you! Settle here and trade with us. And feel free to buy property in the area."

¹¹Then Shechem himself spoke to Dinah's father and brothers. "Please be kind to me, and let me marry her," he begged. "I will give you whatever you ask. ¹²No matter what dowry or gift you demand, I will gladly pay it—just give me the girl as my wife."

¹³But since Shechem had defiled their sister, Dinah, Jacob's sons responded deceitfully to Shechem and his father, Hamor. ¹⁴They said to them, "We couldn't possibly allow this, because you're not circumcised. It would be a disgrace for our sister to marry a man like you! ¹⁵But here is a solution. If every man among you will be circumcised like we are, ¹⁶then we will give you our daughters, and we'll take your daughters for ourselves. We will live among you and become one

people. ¹⁷But if you don't agree to be circumcised, we will take her and be on our way."

¹⁸Hamor and his son Shechem agreed to their proposal. ¹⁹Shechem wasted no time in acting on this request, for he wanted Jacob's daughter desperately. Shechem was a highly respected member of his family, ²⁰and he went with his father, Hamor, to present this proposal to the leaders at the town gate.

²¹"These men are our friends," they said. "Let's invite them to live here among us and trade freely. Look, the land is large enough to hold them. We can take their daughters as wives and let them marry ours. ²²But they will consider staying here and becoming one people with us only if all of our men are circumcised, just as they are. ²³But if we do this, all their livestock and possessions will eventually be ours. Come, let's agree to their terms and let them settle here among us."

²⁴So all the men in the town council agreed with Hamor and Shechem, and every male in the town was circumcised. ²⁵But three days later, when their wounds were still sore, two of Jacob's sons, Simeon and Levi, who were Dinah's full brothers, took their swords and entered the town without opposition. Then they slaughtered every male there, ²⁶including Hamor and his son Shechem. They killed them with their swords, then took Dinah from Shechem's house and returned to their camp.

²⁷Meanwhile, the rest of Jacob's sons arrived. Finding the men slaughtered, they plundered the town because their sister had been defiled there. ²⁸They seized all the flocks and herds and donkeys—everything they could lay their hands on, both inside the town and outside in the fields. ²⁹They looted all their wealth and plundered their houses. They also took all their little children and wives and led them away as captives.

³⁰Afterward Jacob said to Simeon and Levi, "You have ruined me! You've made me stink among all the people of this land—among all

34:7 Hebrew *a disgraceful thing in Israel.*

34:2 The act of rape is always hideous in itself, but the consequences are usually just as heartbreaking. In this occurrence, rape led to deception and ultimately to murder. Dysfunctional patterns and the acts that result from them feed cycles of deepening destruction and hurt. Someone has to choose to break the cycle and begin the process of recovery and healing.

34:20-31 Vengeance belongs to God and when an individual takes revenge—no matter how just the cause may be—there usually are serious consequences. Because of their deception and slaughter of the Hivites, Jacob and his family became extremely unpopular with their neighbors. Because they were a small clan at this point, such a situation put them in grave danger. In recovery, revenge is extremely counterproductive. It only breaks down the reconciliation process that is necessary for personal growth and healthy relationships.

JACOB & SONS

While not the first dysfunctional family in the Bible, Jacob's brood was certainly among the most controversial. Like father, like son, the saying goes. Jacob's own lack of discretion, honesty, patience, and unconditional love negatively impacted his clan.

Jacob had never been his father's favorite, and he played favorites with his own sons with tragic results. Joseph was obviously preferred; Benjamin ran a close second. The rest were far back in the pack and understandably jealous.

The deceptions that Jacob had put over on his father and brother many years earlier were mirrored in the lies his sons told about Joseph's fate. As the brutal massacre of Shechem illustrated, openness and honesty didn't characterize the sons' relationships with outsiders either. Jacob's silence at Dinah's rape perhaps spurred Simeon and Levi to seek vengeance on their own. Certainly their father set no clear boundaries on their behavior until it was much too late.

Jacob's polygamy also influenced his sons. Reuben even slept with his father's concubine Bilhah. Why not? He had grown up watching a marital triangle expand to include two servant concubines. He had even been a party to his mother's and Rachel's rivalry for Jacob's favors. He was not the only one to sin sexually. Judah succumbed to temptation with his disguised daughter-in-law, Tamar.

Jacob and his sons did mature significantly over the years. When famine forced them to visit Egypt, they were no longer the selfish, jealous, deceitful band of earlier years. Instead, they were genuinely concerned about their aging father, protective of young Benjamin, and remorseful when confronted with the truth of what they had done to Joseph. The past reconciled, they could begin an exciting new life in Egypt with the brother they had once abandoned. They were, to a great extent, worthy to become the forefathers of Israel's 12 tribes. Judah would even head the royal line, with its most famous descendant the King of kings, Jesus Christ.

STRENGTHS AND ACCOMPLISHMENTS:
- In later years the brothers honestly cared about their father.
- They were the forefathers of the 12 tribes of Israel.
- They eventually learned the value of loyalty and honesty.

WEAKNESSES AND MISTAKES:
- Jacob modeled favoritism, impatience, and sexual indiscretion for his sons.
- Unbridled passion and intense jealousy motivated the boys, who found it difficult to establish boundaries for their behavior.
- Honesty was a learned response, acquired rather late in life for Jacob and several of his sons.

LESSONS FROM THEIR LIVES:
- The sins of the parents are often reflected in their children.
- Parental favoritism has devastating consequences.
- God can take the evil in our life and use it to accomplish great good.

KEY VERSE:
"Now hurry back to my father and tell him, 'This is what your son Joseph says: God has made me master over all the land of Egypt. So come down to me immediately!'" (Genesis 45:9).

The story of Jacob and his sons is found in Genesis 34–50. Jacob is also mentioned in Hosea 12:3-5; Matthew 1:2; 22:32; Acts 3:13; 7:46; Romans 9:11-13; and Hebrews 11:9, 20-21.

---

the Canaanites and Perizzites. We are so few that they will join forces and crush us. I will be ruined, and my entire household will be wiped out!"

³¹"But why should we let him treat our sister like a prostitute?" they retorted angrily.

CHAPTER 35
Jacob's Return to Bethel
Then God said to Jacob, "Get ready and move to Bethel and settle there. Build an altar there

to the God who appeared to you when you fled from your brother, Esau."

²So Jacob told everyone in his household, "Get rid of all your pagan idols, purify yourselves, and put on clean clothing. ³We are now going to Bethel, where I will build an altar to the God who answered my prayers when I was in distress. He has been with me wherever I have gone."

⁴So they gave Jacob all their pagan idols and earrings, and he buried them under the

great tree near Shechem. ⁵As they set out, a terror from God spread over the people in all the towns of that area, so no one attacked Jacob's family.

⁶Eventually, Jacob and his household arrived at Luz (also called Bethel) in Canaan. ⁷Jacob built an altar there and named the place El-bethel (which means "God of Bethel"), because God had appeared to him there when he was fleeing from his brother, Esau.

⁸Soon after this, Rebekah's old nurse, Deborah, died. She was buried beneath the oak tree in the valley below Bethel. Ever since, the tree has been called Allon-bacuth (which means "oak of weeping").

⁹Now that Jacob had returned from Paddan-aram, God appeared to him again at Bethel. God blessed him, ¹⁰saying, "Your name is Jacob, but you will not be called Jacob any longer. From now on your name will be Israel."* So God renamed him Israel.

¹¹Then God said, "I am El-Shaddai—'God Almighty.' Be fruitful and multiply. You will become a great nation, even many nations. Kings will be among your descendants! ¹²And I will give you the land I once gave to Abraham and Isaac. Yes, I will give it to you and your descendants after you." ¹³Then God went up from the place where he had spoken to Jacob.

¹⁴Jacob set up a stone pillar to mark the place where God had spoken to him. Then he poured wine over it as an offering to God and anointed the pillar with olive oil. ¹⁵And Jacob named the place Bethel (which means "house of God"), because God had spoken to him there.

The Deaths of Rachel and Isaac

¹⁶Leaving Bethel, Jacob and his clan moved on toward Ephrath. But Rachel went into labor while they were still some distance away. Her labor pains were intense. ¹⁷After a very hard delivery, the midwife finally exclaimed, "Don't be afraid—you have another son!" ¹⁸Rachel was about to die, but with her last breath she named the baby Ben-oni (which means "son of my sorrow"). The baby's father, however, called him Benjamin (which means "son of my right hand"). ¹⁹So Rachel died and was buried on the way to Ephrath (that is, Bethlehem). ²⁰Jacob set up a stone monument over Rachel's grave, and it can be seen there to this day.

²¹Then Jacob* traveled on and camped beyond Migdal-eder. ²²While he was living there, Reuben had intercourse with Bilhah, his father's concubine, and Jacob soon heard about it.

These are the names of the twelve sons of Jacob:

²³The sons of Leah were Reuben (Jacob's oldest son), Simeon, Levi, Judah, Issachar, and Zebulun.

²⁴The sons of Rachel were Joseph and Benjamin.

²⁵The sons of Bilhah, Rachel's servant, were Dan and Naphtali.

²⁶The sons of Zilpah, Leah's servant, were Gad and Asher.

These are the names of the sons who were born to Jacob at Paddan-aram.

²⁷So Jacob returned to his father, Isaac, in Mamre, which is near Kiriath-arba (now called Hebron), where Abraham and Isaac had both lived as foreigners. ²⁸Isaac lived for 180 years. ²⁹Then he breathed his last and died at a ripe old age, joining his ancestors in death. And his sons, Esau and Jacob, buried him.

CHAPTER 36
Descendants of Esau

This is the account of the descendants of Esau (also known as Edom). ²Esau married two young women from Canaan: Adah, the daughter of Elon the Hittite; and Oholibamah, the daughter of Anah and granddaughter of Zibeon the Hivite. ³He also married his cousin Basemath, who was the daughter of Ishmael and the sister of Nebaioth. ⁴Adah gave birth to a son named Eliphaz for Esau. Basemath gave birth to a son named Reuel. ⁵Oholibamah gave birth to sons

35:10 *Jacob* sounds like the Hebrew words for "heel" and "deceiver." *Israel* means "God fights." 35:21 Hebrew *Israel*; also in 35:22a. The names "Jacob" and "Israel" are often interchanged throughout the Old Testament, referring sometimes to the individual patriarch and sometimes to the nation.

35:22 The families in the book of Genesis seem to be inordinately dysfunctional. Deceit and lies are often used for the sake of convenience. Communication between family members is poor. The incidence of incest is high. Here we see that Reuben slept with one of his father's wives. This kind of sexual sin reaps a bitter harvest. Reuben's blessing and inheritance as the firstborn son were forfeited because of this single act of sexual gratification (49:4). Reuben should have kept the long-range view in focus. If he had thought about what he might lose, he might have withstood the temptation.

named Jeush, Jalam, and Korah. All these sons were born to Esau in the land of Canaan.

⁶Esau took his wives, his children, and his entire household, along with his livestock and cattle—all the wealth he had acquired in the land of Canaan—and moved away from his brother, Jacob. ⁷There was not enough land to support them both because of all the livestock and possessions they had acquired. ⁸So Esau (also known as Edom) settled in the hill country of Seir.

⁹This is the account of Esau's descendants, the Edomites, who lived in the hill country of Seir.

¹⁰These are the names of Esau's sons:
Eliphaz, the son of Esau's wife Adah; and Reuel, the son of Esau's wife Basemath.
¹¹The descendants of Eliphaz were Teman, Omar, Zepho, Gatam, and Kenaz.
¹²Timna, the concubine of Esau's son Eliphaz, gave birth to a son named Amalek. These are the descendants of Esau's wife Adah.
¹³The descendants of Reuel were Nahath, Zerah, Shammah, and Mizzah. These are the descendants of Esau's wife Basemath.
¹⁴Esau also had sons through Oholibamah, the daughter of Anah and granddaughter of Zibeon. Their names were Jeush, Jalam, and Korah.

¹⁵These are the descendants of Esau who became the leaders of various clans:

The descendants of Esau's oldest son, Eliphaz, became the leaders of the clans of Teman, Omar, Zepho, Kenaz, ¹⁶Korah, Gatam, and Amalek. These are the clan leaders in the land of Edom who descended from Eliphaz. All these were descendants of Esau's wife Adah.

¹⁷The descendants of Esau's son Reuel became the leaders of the clans of Nahath, Zerah, Shammah, and Mizzah. These are the clan leaders in the land of Edom who descended from Reuel. All these were descendants of Esau's wife Basemath.

¹⁸The descendants of Esau and his wife Oholibamah became the leaders of the clans of Jeush, Jalam, and Korah. These are the clan leaders who descended from Esau's wife Oholibamah, the daughter of Anah.

¹⁹These are the clans descended from Esau (also known as Edom), identified by their clan leaders.

Original Peoples of Edom

²⁰These are the names of the tribes that descended from Seir the Horite. They lived in the land of Edom: Lotan, Shobal, Zibeon, Anah, ²¹Dishon, Ezer, and Dishan. These were the Horite clan leaders, the descendants of Seir, who lived in the land of Edom.

²²The descendants of Lotan were Hori and Hemam. Lotan's sister was named Timna.
²³The descendants of Shobal were Alvan, Manahath, Ebal, Shepho, and Onam.
²⁴The descendants of Zibeon were Aiah and Anah. (This is the Anah who discovered the hot springs in the wilderness while he was grazing his father's donkeys.)
²⁵The descendants of Anah were his son, Dishon, and his daughter, Oholibamah.
²⁶The descendants of Dishon* were Hemdan, Eshban, Ithran, and Keran.
²⁷The descendants of Ezer were Bilhan, Zaavan, and Akan.
²⁸The descendants of Dishan were Uz and Aran.
²⁹So these were the leaders of the Horite clans: Lotan, Shobal, Zibeon, Anah, ³⁰Dishon, Ezer, and Dishan. The Horite clans are named after their clan leaders, who lived in the land of Seir.

Rulers of Edom

³¹These are the kings who ruled in the land of Edom before any king ruled over the Israelites*:

³²Bela son of Beor, who ruled in Edom from his city of Dinhabah.
³³When Bela died, Jobab son of Zerah from Bozrah became king in his place.
³⁴When Jobab died, Husham from the land of the Temanites became king in his place.

36:26 Hebrew *Dishan,* a variant spelling of Dishon; compare 36:21, 28. 36:31 Or *before an Israelite king ruled over them.*

36:6-8 Esau and his family could not live in the same area as Jacob and his family. The excuse they gave for moving was the lack of land available. For some families, no amount of room is enough for them to live together. The reconciliation of these brothers was started, but it seems to never have been completed. We need to expect reconciliation to take time. It doesn't happen with one happy reunion. It needs to be worked out over a period of time, in the everyday situations of life.

³⁵When Husham died, Hadad son of Bedad became king in his place and ruled from the city of Avith. He was the one who defeated the Midianites in the land of Moab.

³⁶When Hadad died, Samlah from the city of Masrekah became king in his place.

³⁷When Samlah died, Shaul from the city of Rehoboth-on-the-River became king in his place.

³⁸When Shaul died, Baal-hanan son of Acbor became king in his place.

³⁹When Baal-hanan son of Acbor died, Hadad* became king in his place and ruled from the city of Pau. His wife was Mehetabel, the daughter of Matred and granddaughter of Me-zahab.

⁴⁰These are the names of the leaders of the clans descended from Esau, who lived in the places named for them: Timna, Alvah, Jetheth, ⁴¹Oholibamah, Elah, Pinon, ⁴²Kenaz, Teman, Mibzar, ⁴³Magdiel, and Iram. These are the leaders of the clans of Edom, listed according to their settlements in the land they occupied. They all descended from Esau, the ancestor of the Edomites.

CHAPTER 37
Joseph's Dreams

So Jacob settled again in the land of Canaan, where his father had lived as a foreigner.

²This is the account of Jacob and his family. When Joseph was seventeen years old, he often tended his father's flocks. He worked for his half brothers, the sons of his father's wives Bilhah and Zilpah. But Joseph reported to his father some of the bad things his brothers were doing.

³Jacob* loved Joseph more than any of his other children because Joseph had been born to him in his old age. So one day Jacob had a special gift made for Joseph—a beautiful robe.* ⁴But his brothers hated Joseph because their father loved him more than the rest of them. They couldn't say a kind word to him.

⁵One night Joseph had a dream, and when he told his brothers about it, they hated him more than ever. ⁶"Listen to this dream," he said. ⁷"We were out in the field, tying up bundles of grain. Suddenly my bundle stood up, and your bundles all gathered around and bowed low before mine!"

⁸His brothers responded, "So you think you will be our king, do you? Do you actually think you will reign over us?" And they hated him all the more because of his dreams and the way he talked about them.

⁹Soon Joseph had another dream, and again he told his brothers about it. "Listen, I have had another dream," he said. "The sun, moon, and eleven stars bowed low before me!"

¹⁰This time he told the dream to his father as well as to his brothers, but his father scolded him. "What kind of dream is that?" he asked. "Will your mother and I and your brothers actually come and bow to the ground before you?" ¹¹But while his brothers were jealous of Joseph, his father wondered what the dreams meant.

¹²Soon after this, Joseph's brothers went to pasture their father's flocks at Shechem. ¹³When they had been gone for some time, Jacob said to Joseph, "Your brothers are pasturing the sheep at Shechem. Get ready, and I will send you to them."

"I'm ready to go," Joseph replied.

¹⁴"Go and see how your brothers and the flocks are getting along," Jacob said. "Then come back and bring me a report." So Jacob sent him on his way, and Joseph traveled to Shechem from their home in the valley of Hebron.

¹⁵When he arrived there, a man from the

36:39 As in some Hebrew manuscripts, Samaritan Pentateuch, and Syriac version (see also 1 Chr 1:50); most Hebrew manuscripts read *Hadar*.   37:3a Hebrew *Israel;* also in 37:13. See note on 35:21.   37:3b Traditionally rendered *a coat of many colors*. The exact meaning of the Hebrew is uncertain.

37:3 The biblical account does not hide the fact that Joseph was Jacob's favorite son. Joseph had no choice but to accept the blessings of this distinction, along with its accompanying sufferings. It is interesting to note that the pattern of parental favoritism did not start with Joseph. It had been played out in the lives of his father Jacob and his grandfather Isaac as well. It is never healthy for parents to play favorites among their children, but it is a common pattern in dysfunctional families. It is a pattern that causes untold suffering many generations down the road.

37:19-20 The terrible impact of jealousy is portrayed in this passage. The brothers were now at the point of planning Joseph's murder. They almost followed through on their plan, but Reuben's and Judah's cooler heads prevailed at the last instant. The brothers sold Joseph into slavery and then lied to their father, Jacob. Here we see the tragic, cumulative effects of the dysfunctional patterns of deceit and favoritism in the family context.

GOD grant me the serenity
to accept the things I cannot change
the courage to change the things I can
and the wisdom to know the difference
AMEN

There are times when life just treats us unfairly. We may protest the injustices, fall victim to self-pity, give in to a "poor me" kind of attitude, or sink into depression. During these times when life is unfair, however, what we really need is serenity.

If anyone in history could claim to have been treated unfairly, it was Joseph. He was one of twelve sons, the favorite of his father. In their jealousy, Joseph's ten older brothers staged his death to fool their father and sold him into slavery in Egypt. Once a slave, Joseph devoted himself to serving his master well and was quickly promoted. He was then propositioned by his master's wife, and when Joseph refused her, he was falsely accused of rape. Thrown into prison with no hope of release, he again did his best to serve. He was soon running the administration of the prison. Finally, after many long years, Joseph was freed. He was promoted to the position of prime minister of Egypt. From this position Joseph was able to eventually confront and forgive his brothers, who had sold him into slavery many years before (Genesis 37–45).

It takes serenity, courage, and wisdom to maintain a healthy attitude when life isn't fair. We can't change the fact that our world is imperfect and things are far from the way they should be, but we can choose our attitudes. We need serenity from God to help us change our responses to the injustices of life. We need courage to face with optimism the days when we are treated unfairly. We need wisdom to know whether to fight injustice or to make the best of a bad situation. *Turn to page 267, Joshua 1.*

---

area noticed him wandering around the countryside. "What are you looking for?" he asked.

16"I'm looking for my brothers," Joseph replied. "Do you know where they are pasturing their sheep?"

17"Yes," the man told him. "They have moved on from here, but I heard them say, 'Let's go on to Dothan.' " So Joseph followed his brothers to Dothan and found them there.

Joseph Sold into Slavery
18When Joseph's brothers saw him coming, they recognized him in the distance. As he approached, they made plans to kill him. 19"Here comes the dreamer!" they said. 20"Come on, let's kill him and throw him into one of these cisterns. We can tell our father, 'A wild animal has eaten him.' Then we'll see what becomes of his dreams!"

21But when Reuben heard of their scheme, he came to Joseph's rescue. "Let's not kill him," he said. 22"Why should we shed any blood? Let's just throw him into this empty cistern here in the wilderness. Then he'll die without our laying a hand on him." Reuben was secretly planning to rescue Joseph and return him to his father.

23So when Joseph arrived, his brothers ripped off the beautiful robe he was wearing. 24Then they grabbed him and threw him into the cistern. Now the cistern was empty; there was no water in it. 25Then, just as they were sitting down to eat, they looked up and saw a caravan of camels in the distance coming toward them. It was a group of Ishmaelite traders taking a load of gum, balm, and aromatic resin from Gilead down to Egypt.

26Judah said to his brothers, "What will we gain by killing our brother? We'd have to cover up the crime.* 27Instead of hurting him, let's sell him to those Ishmaelite traders.

37:26 Hebrew *cover his blood.*

55

After all, he is our brother—our own flesh and blood!" And his brothers agreed. [28]So when the Ishmaelites, who were Midianite traders, came by, Joseph's brothers pulled him out of the cistern and sold him to them for twenty pieces* of silver. And the traders took him to Egypt.

[29]Some time later, Reuben returned to get Joseph out of the cistern. When he discovered that Joseph was missing, he tore his clothes in grief. [30]Then he went back to his brothers and lamented, "The boy is gone! What will I do now?"

[31]Then the brothers killed a young goat and dipped Joseph's robe in its blood. [32]They sent the beautiful robe to their father with this message: "Look at what we found. Doesn't this robe belong to your son?"

[33]Their father recognized it immediately. "Yes," he said, "it is my son's robe. A wild animal must have eaten him. Joseph has clearly been torn to pieces!" [34]Then Jacob tore his clothes and dressed himself in burlap. He mourned deeply for his son for a long time. [35]His family all tried to comfort him, but he refused to be comforted. "I will go to my grave* mourning for my son," he would say, and then he would weep.

[36]Meanwhile, the Midianite traders* arrived in Egypt, where they sold Joseph to Potiphar, an officer of Pharaoh, the king of Egypt. Potiphar was captain of the palace guard.

CHAPTER 38
Judah and Tamar

About this time, Judah left home and moved to Adullam, where he stayed with a man named Hirah. [2]There he saw a Canaanite woman, the daughter of Shua, and he married her. When he slept with her, [3]she became pregnant and gave birth to a son, and he named the boy Er. [4]Then she became pregnant again and gave birth to another son, and she named him Onan. [5]And when she gave birth to a third son, she named him Shelah. At the time of Shelah's birth, they were living at Kezib.

[6]In the course of time, Judah arranged for his firstborn son, Er, to marry a young woman named Tamar. [7]But Er was a wicked man in the LORD's sight, so the LORD took his life. [8]Then Judah said to Er's brother Onan, "Go and marry Tamar, as our law requires of the brother of a man who has died. You must produce an heir for your brother."

[9]But Onan was not willing to have a child who would not be his own heir. So whenever he had intercourse with his brother's wife, he spilled the semen on the ground. This prevented her from having a child who would belong to his brother. [10]But the LORD considered it evil for Onan to deny a child to his dead brother. So the LORD took Onan's life, too.

[11]Then Judah said to Tamar, his daughter-

37:28 Hebrew *20 [shekels],* about 8 ounces or 228 grams in weight. 37:35 Hebrew *go down to Sheol.* 37:36 Hebrew *the Medanites.* The relationship between the Midianites and Medanites is unclear, compare 37:28. See also 25:2.

37:31-35 All Jacob's life he had manipulated people and circumstances to serve his own purposes. He was a schemer and a trickster. Here we see the trickster being tricked once again—by his own sons. Again we see a destructive family pattern being passed on to the next generation.

38:1-5 We are told that Judah moved from his family home, married a Canaanite girl, and settled down among the Canaanites. Some of Judah's unsavory activities in this chapter seem out of sync with what we might expect of one of Israel's patriarchs. We cannot help but wonder whether his behavior was not influenced by the people he was living with. The Canaanites were known for their immoral lifestyle. For us to progress in recovery we need to spend time with people who will encourage us to develop a wholesome lifestyle. We may also need to give up the relationships that lead us into destructive activities.

38:1-30 Judah's more sensational sin of propositioning a prostitute often blinds readers to his primary failure. According to the laws practiced at that time, if a husband died before fathering a son, his family was responsible for providing his widow with a husband. This was Judah's responsibility, but when his second son died soon after marrying Tamar, Judah was understandably shaken and delayed giving her his third son. It seems that Judah was hoping he would never be called upon to carry out his duty. His attitude didn't solve the problem but only led to the sordid events that followed. It is easy for us to act like Judah, ignoring our problems or blaming them on our environment or other people. But the first step in solving any problem is admitting we have it. Then we can take responsible steps to solve it.

38:12-26 When Judah failed to deal with Tamar in a responsible way, Tamar decided to take action. Although not everything she did was exemplary, she wisely confronted Judah in a way that caught his attention without alienating him. Very often direct confrontation with people who have wronged us will only deepen the conflict. In such cases, a less direct means of communication may prove helpful, as long as we are careful not to manipulate by our indirect confrontations.

JUDAH & TAMAR

Judah was the fourth son of Leah, Jacob's first wife. Among the patriarch's 12 sons, Judah evidently occupied a position of prominence.
Early in the biblical story, he persuaded his brothers not to kill Joseph.
And when they went to Egypt for food, Judah spoke and acted on his
brothers' behalf. Later, the royal line would come through the descendants of Judah. Tamar was a girl of Canaanite descent, chosen by
Judah to be the wife of Er, his oldest son.

As the story of Judah begins, we are told that he left his childhood
home and moved some distance away from his brothers. He settled in a
Canaanite community and married a Canaanite girl. Judah's wife gave
birth to three sons: Er, Onan, and Shelah. Er was said to be evil in
God's sight, and after he married Tamar, God punished him with death.
Onan, as Tamar's brother-in-law, was expected to give her a son who
could carry on Er's name and receive his inheritance. But Onan refused
to fulfill his responsibility and suffered the same fate as his older
brother.

Now it was left to young Shelah to raise up offspring for Er and Onan.
But Judah was afraid that his last son would also die. So he told Tamar to
return to her father's house until Shelah was older. Judah's intent seemed
clear: Shelah would eventually fulfill his duty as a brother-in-law and
have a son with Tamar. Time passed and Tamar's expectations were not
fulfilled. So she took matters into her own hands, assumed the guise of a
prostitute, and tricked Judah into getting her pregnant.

When Judah heard that Tamar was pregnant, he demanded her
punishment as any self-respecting father-in-law would do. But she
showed Judah the items he had given as a pledge, proving that he was
the father of the child. So Judah acknowledged that he was in the
wrong. Tamar later gave birth to two sons, one of whom is named in
the kingly lineage of David and of Jesus the Messiah.

**STRENGTHS AND
ACCOMPLISHMENTS:**
- After being confronted, Judah
admitted his failures and took
responsibility for them.

WEAKNESSES AND MISTAKES:
- Judah lost close contact with the
patriarchal family, perhaps
weakening his resolve to do right.
- Judah failed to fulfill his paternal
responsibilities toward Tamar.
- Judah let fear dictate his actions,
perhaps indicating his lack of faith.
- Tamar failed to confront Judah
directly, resorting to indirect
manipulation.

LESSONS FROM THEIR LIVES:
- A shallow walk with God can lead to
trouble in family relationships.
- Commitments made to others,
whether stated or implied, must be
kept.
- God's grace can bring future
blessings out of our biggest
mistakes.
- Tactful confrontation is needed when
legitimate expectations have not
been fulfilled.

KEY VERSE:
"Judah . . . said, 'She is more
righteous than I am, because I didn't
arrange for her to marry my son
Shelah.' And Judah never slept with
Tamar again" (Genesis 38:26).

The story of Judah and Tamar is told in
Genesis 38. Judah is mentioned in
Genesis 29–50 and throughout the
Old Testament as one of the fathers of
the twelve tribes. Judah and Tamar are
both mentioned in Jesus' family tree in
Matthew 1.

---

in-law, "Go back to your parents' home and
remain a widow until my son Shelah is old
enough to marry you." (But Judah didn't
really intend to do this because he was afraid
Shelah would also die, like his two brothers.)
So Tamar went back to live in her father's
home.

¹²Some years later Judah's wife died. After the
time of mourning was over, Judah and his friend
Hirah the Adullamite went up to Timnah to su-
pervise the shearing of his sheep. ¹³Someone told
Tamar, "Look, your father-in-law is going up to
Timnah to shear his sheep."

¹⁴Tamar was aware that Shelah had grown
up, but no arrangements had been made for
her to come and marry him. So she changed
out of her widow's clothing and covered
herself with a veil to disguise herself. Then
she sat beside the road at the entrance to the
village of Enaim, which is on the road to
Timnah. ¹⁵Judah noticed her and thought
she was a prostitute, since she had covered
her face. ¹⁶So he stopped and propositioned
her. "Let me have sex with you," he said,
not realizing that she was his own daughter-
in-law.

"How much will you pay to have sex with me?" Tamar asked.

¹⁷"I'll send you a young goat from my flock," Judah promised.

"But what will you give me to guarantee that you will send the goat?" she asked.

¹⁸"What kind of guarantee do you want?" he replied.

She answered, "Leave me your identification seal and its cord and the walking stick you are carrying." So Judah gave them to her. Then he had intercourse with her, and she became pregnant. ¹⁹Afterward she went back home, took off her veil, and put on her widow's clothing as usual.

²⁰Later Judah asked his friend Hirah the Adullamite to take the young goat to the woman and to pick up the things he had given her as his guarantee. But Hirah couldn't find her. ²¹So he asked the men who lived there, "Where can I find the shrine prostitute who was sitting beside the road at the entrance to Enaim?"

"We've never had a shrine prostitute here," they replied.

²²So Hirah returned to Judah and told him, "I couldn't find her anywhere, and the men of the village claim they've never had a shrine prostitute there."

²³"Then let her keep the things I gave her," Judah said. "I sent the young goat as we agreed, but you couldn't find her. We'd be the laughingstock of the village if we went back again to look for her."

²⁴About three months later, Judah was told, "Tamar, your daughter-in-law, has acted like a prostitute. And now, because of this, she's pregnant."

38:29 *Perez* means "breaking out." 38:30 *Zerah* means "scarlet" or "brightness."

"Bring her out, and let her be burned!" Judah demanded.

²⁵But as they were taking her out to kill her, she sent this message to her father-in-law: "The man who owns these things made me pregnant. Look closely. Whose seal and cord and walking stick are these?"

²⁶Judah recognized them immediately and said, "She is more righteous than I am, because I didn't arrange for her to marry my son Shelah." And Judah never slept with Tamar again.

²⁷When the time came for Tamar to give birth, it was discovered that she was carrying twins. ²⁸While she was in labor, one of the babies reached out his hand. The midwife grabbed it and tied a scarlet string around the child's wrist, announcing, "This one came out first." ²⁹But then he pulled back his hand, and out came his brother! "What!" the midwife exclaimed. "How did you break out first?" So he was named Perez.* ³⁰Then the baby with the scarlet string on his wrist was born, and he was named Zerah.*

CHAPTER 39
Joseph in Potiphar's House

When Joseph was taken to Egypt by the Ishmaelite traders, he was purchased by Potiphar, an Egyptian officer. Potiphar was captain of the guard for Pharaoh, the king of Egypt.

²The LORD was with Joseph, so he succeeded in everything he did as he served in the home of his Egyptian master. ³Potiphar noticed this and realized that the LORD was with Joseph, giving him success in everything he did. ⁴This pleased Potiphar, so he

39:2 God blessed Joseph even in the worst of circumstances. Even though Joseph was a slave in a strange household and in a foreign land, God made him a success. It should not be inferred that God will also make us successful. Rather, our chief goal should be to follow Joseph's example of being faithful to God's program, no matter what the circumstances or consequences.

39:7-18 Joseph withstood the temptation of Potiphar's wife even though he was far from home and the temptation continued day after day. This was not a onetime crisis but a constant, wearing temptation. How did he stand up to it? Two things seem to have helped him: Joseph's respect for his master and, even more important, Joseph's respect for God. As we draw closer to God, we will begin to sense his presence in our life. Doing something that runs counter to his program will cause us pain. Walking close to God will provide us with added protection against the temptations we face.

39:19-20 It seems as if the good guys often finish last—the innocent seem to suffer. It looks as though Joseph's faithfulness to God was rewarded with years in prison. This may have discouraged Joseph, but it didn't stop him. Even in prison he continued to live according to God's program. In the end, after a number of setbacks, he was rewarded. We may need to look beyond difficult present circumstances to see that God may have a purpose in our suffering. It may be an important part of the education necessary for our future success.

soon made Joseph his personal attendant. He put him in charge of his entire household and everything he owned. ⁵From the day Joseph was put in charge of his master's household and property, the LORD began to bless Potiphar's household for Joseph's sake. All his household affairs ran smoothly, and his crops and livestock flourished. ⁶So Potiphar gave Joseph complete administrative responsibility over everything he owned. With Joseph there, he didn't worry about a thing— except what kind of food to eat!

Joseph was a very handsome and well-built young man, ⁷and Potiphar's wife soon began to look at him lustfully. "Come and sleep with me," she demanded.

⁸But Joseph refused. "Look," he told her, "my master trusts me with everything in his entire household. ⁹No one here has more authority than I do. He has held back nothing from me except you, because you are his wife. How could I do such a wicked thing? It would be a great sin against God."

¹⁰She kept putting pressure on Joseph day after day, but he refused to sleep with her, and he kept out of her way as much as possible. ¹¹One day, however, no one else was around when he went in to do his work. ¹²She came and grabbed him by his cloak, demanding, "Come on, sleep with me!" Joseph tore himself away, but he left his cloak in her hand as he ran from the house.

¹³When she saw that she was holding his cloak and he had fled, ¹⁴she called out to her servants. Soon all the men came running. "Look!" she said. "My husband has brought this Hebrew slave here to make fools of us! He came into my room to rape me, but I screamed. ¹⁵When he heard me scream, he ran outside and got away, but he left his cloak behind with me."

¹⁶She kept the cloak with her until her husband came home. ¹⁷Then she told him her story. "That Hebrew slave you've brought into our house tried to come in and fool around with me," she said. ¹⁸"But when I screamed, he ran outside, leaving his cloak with me!"

Joseph Put in Prison

¹⁹Potiphar was furious when he heard his wife's story about how Joseph had treated her. ²⁰So he took Joseph and threw him into the prison where the king's prisoners were held, and there he remained. ²¹But the LORD was with Joseph in the prison and showed him his faithful love. And the LORD made

STEP 5

Overcoming Denial

BIBLE READING: Genesis 38:1-30

We admitted to God, to ourselves, and to another human being the exact nature of our wrongs.

Admitting our wrongs to ourself can be the most difficult part of Step Five. Denial can be blinding! How can we be expected to admit to ourself those things we are blind to? Here's a clue that can help us. We will often condemn in others the wrongs most deeply hidden within ourself.

According to ancient Israelite law, a widow was entitled to marry the surviving brother of her husband in order to produce children (this custom is described in detail in Deuteronomy 25:5-10). Tamar had been married successively to two brothers who died without giving her children. Her father-in-law, Judah, promised to give her his youngest son also, but he never did. This left her alone and destitute. In an effort to protect herself, she disguised herself as a prostitute and became pregnant by Judah himself. And she kept his identification seal, which he had given her as a pledge for payment (Genesis 38:1-23).

When Judah heard that Tamar was pregnant and unmarried, he demanded her execution. "But as they were taking her out to kill her, she sent this message to her father-in-law: 'The man who owns these things made me pregnant. Look closely. Whose seal and cord and walking stick are these?' Judah recognized them immediately and said, 'She is more righteous than I am'" (Genesis 38:25-26).

It won't be easy to be honest with yourself. "The human heart is the most deceitful of all things, and desperately wicked." (Jeremiah 17:9). We can look at those things we condemn in others as a clue to what may be lurking within ourself. *Turn to page 1107, Hosea 11.*

tyndal.es/lrbstep5

Joseph a favorite with the prison warden. ²²Before long, the warden put Joseph in charge of all the other prisoners and over everything that happened in the prison. ²³The warden had no more worries, because Joseph took care of everything. The LORD was with him and caused everything he did to succeed.

CHAPTER 40
Joseph Interprets Two Dreams

Some time later, Pharaoh's chief cup-bearer and chief baker offended their royal master. ²Pharaoh became angry with these two officials, ³and he put them in the prison where Joseph was, in the palace of the captain of the guard. ⁴They remained in prison for quite some time, and the captain of the guard assigned them to Joseph, who looked after them.

⁵While they were in prison, Pharaoh's cup- bearer and baker each had a dream one night, and each dream had its own meaning. ⁶When Joseph saw them the next morning, he noticed that they both looked upset. ⁷"Why do you look so worried today?" he asked them.

⁸And they replied, "We both had dreams last night, but no one can tell us what they mean."

"Interpreting dreams is God's business," Joseph replied. "Go ahead and tell me your dreams."

⁹So the chief cup-bearer told Joseph his dream first. "In my dream," he said, "I saw a grapevine in front of me. ¹⁰The vine had three branches that began to bud and blossom, and soon it produced clusters of ripe grapes. ¹¹I was holding Pharaoh's wine cup in my hand, so I took a cluster of grapes and squeezed the juice into the cup. Then I placed the cup in Pharaoh's hand."

¹²"This is what the dream means," Joseph

40:20 Hebrew *He lifted up the head of.*

said. "The three branches represent three days. ¹³Within three days Pharaoh will lift you up and restore you to your position as his chief cup-bearer. ¹⁴And please remember me and do me a favor when things go well for you. Mention me to Pharaoh, so he might let me out of this place. ¹⁵For I was kidnapped from my homeland, the land of the Hebrews, and now I'm here in prison, but I did nothing to deserve it."

¹⁶When the chief baker saw that Joseph had given the first dream such a positive interpretation, he said to Joseph, "I had a dream, too. In my dream there were three baskets of white pastries stacked on my head. ¹⁷The top basket contained all kinds of pastries for Pharaoh, but the birds came and ate them from the basket on my head."

¹⁸"This is what the dream means," Joseph told him. "The three baskets also represent three days. ¹⁹Three days from now Pharaoh will lift you up and impale your body on a pole. Then birds will come and peck away at your flesh."

²⁰Pharaoh's birthday came three days later, and he prepared a banquet for all his officials and staff. He summoned* his chief cup-bearer and chief baker to join the other officials. ²¹He then restored the chief cup-bearer to his former position, so he could again hand Pharaoh his cup. ²²But Pharaoh impaled the chief baker, just as Joseph had predicted when he interpreted his dream. ²³Pharaoh's chief cup-bearer, however, forgot all about Joseph, never giving him another thought.

CHAPTER 41
Pharaoh's Dreams

Two full years later, Pharaoh dreamed that he was standing on the bank of the Nile River. ²In his dream he saw seven fat, healthy

---

40:1-8 Here we see how Joseph's consistency gained the respect and trust of his jailer and his fellow prisoners. One can imagine that the normal prisoner then, as now, was a pretty sullen character. This makes Joseph's acceptance by them even more significant. His behavior in prison clearly exemplifies the first three steps in recovery. Joseph recognized his powerlessness over the situation he was in and committed his situation to God.

40:23 After prophesying correctly about the chief cup-bearer's release, Joseph must have felt disappointed when he was forgotten. But here again, Joseph refused to play the victim. He didn't poison his life by complaining and assigning blame. He didn't give up and grow bitter. Instead, he continued to live a life that was faithful to God and his plan.

41:14 At last Joseph was given the opportunity for freedom. God's perfect timing had come. We may get discouraged by our slow progress, but we must continue to faithfully follow God the best we can. Someday we may find we are truly free of the things that bind us. If we experience such deliverance, we can then rejoice. For many of us, however, our dependencies will haunt us throughout this life. If we find ourself in this situation, we can still rejoice, knowing that through it all we are building a deeper relationship with God.

JOSEPH & BROTHERS

Overconfidence is usually viewed as a negative personality trait. The youthful boasting that Joseph displayed with his brothers was no exception to the rule. His claims that the others would someday bow down to him, coupled with his father's favoritism, led to his brothers' jealousy and broken family relationships. In the end, his brothers sold him into slavery, cutting him off from his family altogether.

Through years of difficulties and suffering, Joseph's overconfidence was transformed by God into a mature self-assurance. In times of personal struggle, this self-assurance, along with his personal knowledge of God, enabled Joseph to ask, "What shall I do now?" instead of "Why me, God?"

Joseph's self-assurance made him capable of tackling and succeeding at jobs that most other people would have run away from. His high personal integrity, refined throughout his life, took him from the bottom of the social ladder to the top. Because of this, Joseph was in a position to help his family and save the young nation of Israel during a time of terrible famine.

Overconfidence without God's perspective will invariably lead us down the pathway to many other personal problems and mistakes. On the other hand, self-assurance linked with a strong faith in God will enable us to overcome the many obstacles we face in life.

STRENGTHS AND ACCOMPLISHMENTS:
* Joseph was elevated from slavery to the position of prime minister.
* He had high personal integrity.
* He was a man of great spiritual sensitivity.
* He enabled a nation to prepare for a seven-year famine.

WEAKNESSES AND MISTAKES:
* When he was a young man, his overconfidence severely damaged his family relationships.

LESSONS FROM THEIR LIVES:
* Our responses to the circumstances we face are more important than the circumstances themselves.
* God can mold our weaknesses into strengths.
* God can cause situations that others intended for evil to be used for good.

KEY VERSE:
"Then Pharaoh said to Joseph, 'Since God has revealed the meaning of the dreams to you, clearly no one else is as intelligent or wise as you are'" (Genesis 41:39).

Joseph's story is told in Genesis 37–50. Joseph is also mentioned in Psalm 105:17-22; Acts 7:9-18; and Hebrews 11:22.

---

cows come up out of the river and begin grazing in the marsh grass. ³Then he saw seven more cows come up behind them from the Nile, but these were scrawny and thin. These cows stood beside the fat cows on the riverbank. ⁴Then the scrawny, thin cows ate the seven healthy, fat cows! At this point in the dream, Pharaoh woke up.

⁵But he fell asleep again and had a second dream. This time he saw seven heads of grain, plump and beautiful, growing on a single stalk. ⁶Then seven more heads of grain appeared, but these were shriveled and withered by the east wind. ⁷And these thin heads swallowed up the seven plump, well-formed heads! Then Pharaoh woke up again and realized it was a dream.

⁸The next morning Pharaoh was very disturbed by the dreams. So he called for all the magicians and wise men of Egypt. When Pharaoh told them his dreams, not one of them could tell him what they meant.

⁹Finally, the king's chief cup-bearer spoke up. "Today I have been reminded of my failure," he told Pharaoh. ¹⁰"Some time ago, you were angry with the chief baker and me, and you imprisoned us in the palace of the captain of the guard. ¹¹One night the chief baker and I each had a dream, and each dream had its own meaning. ¹²There was a young Hebrew man with us in the prison who was a slave of the captain of the guard. We told him our dreams, and he told us what each of our dreams meant. ¹³And everything happened just as he had predicted. I was restored to my position as cupbearer, and the chief baker was executed and impaled on a pole."

¹⁴Pharaoh sent for Joseph at once, and he was quickly brought from the prison. After he shaved and changed his clothes, he went in and stood before Pharaoh. ¹⁵Then Pharaoh said to Joseph, "I had a dream last night, and no one here can tell me what it

means. But I have heard that when you hear about a dream you can interpret it."

[16]"It is beyond my power to do this," Joseph replied. "But God can tell you what it means and set you at ease."

[17]So Pharaoh told Joseph his dream. "In my dream," he said, "I was standing on the bank of the Nile River, [18]and I saw seven fat, healthy cows come up out of the river and begin grazing in the marsh grass. [19]But then I saw seven sick-looking cows, scrawny and thin, come up after them. I've never seen such sorry-looking animals in all the land of Egypt. [20]These thin, scrawny cows ate the seven fat cows. [21]But afterward you wouldn't have known it, for they were still as thin and scrawny as before! Then I woke up.

[22]"In my dream I also saw seven heads of grain, full and beautiful, growing on a single stalk. [23]Then seven more heads of grain appeared, but these were blighted, shriveled, and withered by the east wind. [24]And the shriveled heads swallowed the seven healthy heads. I told these dreams to the magicians, but no one could tell me what they mean."

[25]Joseph responded, "Both of Pharaoh's dreams mean the same thing. God is telling Pharaoh in advance what he is about to do. [26]The seven healthy cows and the seven healthy heads of grain both represent seven years of prosperity. [27]The seven thin, scrawny cows that came up later and the seven thin heads of grain, withered by the east wind, represent seven years of famine.

[28]"This will happen just as I have described it, for God has revealed to Pharaoh in advance what he is about to do. [29]The next seven years will be a period of great prosperity throughout the land of Egypt. [30]But afterward there will be seven years of famine so great that all the prosperity will be forgotten in Egypt. Famine will destroy the land. [31]This famine will be so severe that even the memory of the good years will be erased. [32]As for having two similar dreams, it means that these events have been decreed by God, and he will soon make them happen.

[33]"Therefore, Pharaoh should find an intelligent and wise man and put him in charge of the entire land of Egypt. [34]Then Pharaoh should appoint supervisors over the land and let them collect one-fifth of all the crops during the seven good years. [35]Have them gather all the food produced in the good years that are just ahead and bring it to Pharaoh's storehouses. Store it away, and guard it so there will be food in the cities. [36]That way there will be enough to eat when the seven years of famine come to the land of Egypt. Otherwise this famine will destroy the land."

Joseph Made Ruler of Egypt

[37]Joseph's suggestions were well received by Pharaoh and his officials. [38]So Pharaoh asked his officials, "Can we find anyone else like this man so obviously filled with the spirit of God?" [39]Then Pharaoh said to Joseph, "Since God has revealed the meaning of the dreams to you, clearly no one else is as intelligent or wise as you are. [40]You will be in charge of my court, and all my people will take orders from you. Only I, sitting on my throne, will have a rank higher than yours."

[41]Pharaoh said to Joseph, "I hereby put you in charge of the entire land of Egypt." [42]Then Pharaoh removed his signet ring from his hand and placed it on Joseph's finger. He dressed him in fine linen clothing and hung a gold chain around his neck. [43]Then he had Joseph ride in the chariot reserved for his second-in-command. And wherever Joseph went, the command was shouted, "Kneel down!" So Pharaoh put Joseph in charge of all Egypt. [44]And Pharaoh said to him, "I am Pharaoh, but no one will lift a hand or foot in the entire land of Egypt without your approval."

[45]Then Pharaoh gave Joseph a new Egyptian name, Zaphenath-paneah.* He also gave him a wife, whose name was Asenath. She was the daughter of Potiphera, the priest of On.* So Joseph took charge of the entire land of Egypt. [46]He was thirty years old when he began serving in the court of Pharaoh, the king of Egypt. And when Joseph left Pharaoh's presence, he inspected the entire land of Egypt.

41:45a *Zaphenath-paneah* probably means "God speaks and lives." **41:45b** Greek version reads *of Heliopolis;* also in 41:50.

41:38-40 The primary quality that Pharaoh saw in Joseph was his dependence on God. Pharaoh ignored the fact that Joseph had a questionable past colored by rumors and a long prison term. Pharaoh could see that God's Spirit was in Joseph, making him a very wise young man. This more than made up for any questions Pharaoh might have had about his past. So Pharaoh promoted Joseph to be the prime minister of Egypt! Some of us may believe that the things we have done in the past have destroyed any hope of a prosperous future. But when we give ourself to God, asking for his help, no past is too terrible or too dark to overcome.

⁴⁷As predicted, for seven years the land produced bumper crops. ⁴⁸During those years, Joseph gathered all the crops grown in Egypt and stored the grain from the surrounding fields in the cities. ⁴⁹He piled up huge amounts of grain like sand on the seashore. Finally, he stopped keeping records because there was too much to measure.

⁵⁰During this time, before the first of the famine years, two sons were born to Joseph and his wife, Asenath, the daughter of Potiphera, the priest of On. ⁵¹Joseph named his older son Manasseh,* for he said, "God has made me forget all my troubles and everyone in my father's family." ⁵²Joseph named his second son Ephraim,* for he said, "God has made me fruitful in this land of my grief."

⁵³At last the seven years of bumper crops throughout the land of Egypt came to an end. ⁵⁴Then the seven years of famine began, just as Joseph had predicted. The famine also struck all the surrounding countries, but throughout Egypt there was plenty of food. ⁵⁵Eventually, however, the famine spread throughout the land of Egypt as well. And when the people cried out to Pharaoh for food, he told them, "Go to Joseph, and do whatever he tells you." ⁵⁶So with severe famine everywhere, Joseph opened up the storehouses and distributed grain to the Egyptians, for the famine was severe throughout the land of Egypt. ⁵⁷And people from all around came to Egypt to buy grain from Joseph because the famine was severe throughout the world.

CHAPTER 42
Joseph's Brothers Go to Egypt

When Jacob heard that grain was available in Egypt, he said to his sons, "Why are you standing around looking at one another? ²I have heard there is grain in Egypt. Go down there, and buy enough grain to keep us alive. Otherwise we'll die."

³So Joseph's ten older brothers went down to Egypt to buy grain. ⁴But Jacob wouldn't let Joseph's younger brother, Benjamin, go with them, for fear some harm might come to him. ⁵So Jacob's* sons arrived in Egypt along with others to buy food, for the famine was in Canaan as well.

⁶Since Joseph was governor of all Egypt and in charge of selling grain to all the people, it was to him that his brothers came. When they arrived, they bowed before him with their faces to the ground. ⁷Joseph recognized his brothers instantly, but he pretended to be a stranger and spoke harshly to them. "Where are you from?" he demanded.

"From the land of Canaan," they replied. "We have come to buy food."

⁸Although Joseph recognized his brothers, they didn't recognize him. ⁹And he remembered the dreams he'd had about them many years before. He said to them, "You are spies! You have come to see how vulnerable our land has become."

¹⁰"No, my lord!" they exclaimed. "Your servants have simply come to buy food. ¹¹We are all brothers—members of the same family. We are honest men, sir! We are not spies!"

¹²"Yes, you are!" Joseph insisted. "You have come to see how vulnerable our land has become."

¹³"Sir," they said, "there are actually twelve of us. We, your servants, are all brothers, sons of a man living in the land of Canaan. Our youngest brother is back there with our father right now, and one of our brothers is no longer with us."

¹⁴But Joseph insisted, "As I said, you are spies! ¹⁵This is how I will test your story. I swear by the life of Pharaoh that you will never leave Egypt unless your youngest brother comes here! ¹⁶One of you must go and get your brother. I'll keep the rest of you here in prison. Then we'll find out whether or not your story is true. By the life of Pharaoh, if it turns out that you don't have a younger brother, then I'll know you are spies."

¹⁷So Joseph put them all in prison for three days. ¹⁸On the third day Joseph said to them, "I am a God-fearing man. If you do as I say, you will live. ¹⁹If you really are honest men, choose one of your brothers to remain in prison. The rest of you may go home with grain for your starving families. ²⁰But you

---

41:51 *Manasseh* sounds like a Hebrew term that means "causing to forget." **41:52** *Ephraim* sounds like a Hebrew term that means "fruitful." **42:5** Hebrew *Israel's*. See note on 35:21.

42:7-20 When Joseph recognized his brothers, he took some time to test them. He wanted to discover something of their attitudes before he revealed himself to them. In recovery we are told to work toward reconciliation with the important people in our life. We need wisdom from God to do this in a way that will bring healing to both ourself and the people close to us. Joseph didn't instantly jump back into a relationship with his brothers. He took the time he needed to do it wisely.

must bring your youngest brother back to me. This will prove that you are telling the truth, and you will not die." To this they agreed.

²¹Speaking among themselves, they said, "Clearly we are being punished because of what we did to Joseph long ago. We saw his anguish when he pleaded for his life, but we wouldn't listen. That's why we're in this trouble."

²²"Didn't I tell you not to sin against the boy?" Reuben asked. "But you wouldn't listen. And now we have to answer for his blood!"

²³Of course, they didn't know that Joseph understood them, for he had been speaking to them through an interpreter. ²⁴Now he turned away from them and began to weep. When he regained his composure, he spoke to them again. Then he chose Simeon from among them and had him tied up right before their eyes.

²⁵Joseph then ordered his servants to fill the men's sacks with grain, but he also gave secret instructions to return each brother's payment at the top of his sack. He also gave them supplies for their journey home. ²⁶So the brothers loaded their donkeys with the grain and headed for home.

²⁷But when they stopped for the night and one of them opened his sack to get grain for his donkey, he found his money in the top of his sack. ²⁸"Look!" he exclaimed to his brothers. "My money has been returned; it's here in my sack!" Then their hearts sank. Trembling, they said to each other, "What has God done to us?"

²⁹When the brothers came to their father, Jacob, in the land of Canaan, they told him everything that had happened to them. ³⁰"The man who is governor of the land spoke very harshly to us," they told him. "He accused us of being spies scouting the land. ³¹But we said, 'We are honest men, not spies. ³²We are twelve brothers, sons of one father. One brother is no longer with us, and the youngest is at home with our father in the land of Canaan.'

³³"Then the man who is governor of the land told us, 'This is how I will find out if you are honest men. Leave one of your brothers here with me, and take grain for your starving families and go on home. ³⁴But you must bring your youngest brother back to me. Then I will know you are honest men and not spies. Then I will give you back your brother, and you may trade freely in the land.'"

³⁵As they emptied out their sacks, there in each man's sack was the bag of money he had paid for the grain! The brothers and their father were terrified when they saw the bags of money. ³⁶Jacob exclaimed, "You are robbing me of my children! Joseph is gone! Simeon is gone! And now you want to take Benjamin, too. Everything is going against me!"

³⁷Then Reuben said to his father, "You may kill my two sons if I don't bring Benjamin back to you. I'll be responsible for him, and I promise to bring him back."

³⁸But Jacob replied, "My son will not go down with you. His brother Joseph is dead, and he is all I have left. If anything should happen to him on your journey, you would send this grieving, white-haired man to his grave.*"

CHAPTER 43
The Brothers Return to Egypt

But the famine continued to ravage the land of Canaan. ²When the grain they had brought from Egypt was almost gone, Jacob said to his sons, "Go back and buy us a little more food."

³But Judah said, "The man was serious when he warned us, 'You won't see my face again unless your brother is with you.' ⁴If you send Benjamin with us, we will go down and buy more food. ⁵But if you don't let Benjamin go, we won't go either. Remember, the man said, 'You won't see my face again unless your brother is with you.'"

42:38 Hebrew *to Sheol.*

42:21-22 After these many years Joseph's brothers were still haunted by their guilty consciences. They had sold their brother into slavery in Egypt with no plans of ever seeing him again—and no hope of reconciliation or forgiveness. We may wonder how many times during those years Reuben said, "I told you so." It is clear that this period had been miserable for the brothers. A necessary step in recovery is seeking reconciliation with others we have wronged. Only then can we experience the healing we need to live a healthy and peaceful life.

42:36 How bitter with grief Jacob had become! He had harbored years of resentment and sadness. His relationship with his sons was built on dishonesty. Walls of lies had been built up— layer upon layer. This separated Jacob from close fellowship with his family. He was all alone in his grief, trapped by the fear that he might lose yet another son. But even though Jacob was alone and helpless in his pain, God had a plan for his deliverance. Jacob would soon be set free from many years of bitterness and grief.

⁶"Why were you so cruel to me?" Jacob* moaned. "Why did you tell him you had another brother?"

⁷"The man kept asking us questions about our family," they replied. "He asked, 'Is your father still alive? Do you have another brother?' So we answered his questions. How could we know he would say, 'Bring your brother down here'?"

⁸Judah said to his father, "Send the boy with me, and we will be on our way. Otherwise we will all die of starvation—and not only we, but you and our little ones. ⁹I personally guarantee his safety. You may hold me responsible if I don't bring him back to you. Then let me bear the blame forever. ¹⁰If we hadn't wasted all this time, we could have gone and returned twice by now."

¹¹So their father, Jacob, finally said to them, "If it can't be avoided, then at least do this. Pack your bags with the best products of this land. Take them down to the man as gifts—balm, honey, gum, aromatic resin, pistachio nuts, and almonds. ¹²Also take double the money that was put back in your sacks, as it was probably someone's mistake. ¹³Then take your brother, and go back to the man. ¹⁴May God Almighty* give you mercy as you go before the man, so that he will release Simeon and let Benjamin return. But if I must lose my children, so be it."

¹⁵So the men packed Jacob's gifts and double the money and headed off with Benjamin. They finally arrived in Egypt and presented themselves to Joseph. ¹⁶When Joseph saw Benjamin with them, he said to the manager of his household, "These men will eat with me this noon. Take them inside the palace. Then go slaughter an animal, and prepare a big feast." ¹⁷So the man did as Joseph told him and took them into Joseph's palace.

¹⁸The brothers were terrified when they saw that they were being taken into Joseph's house. "It's because of the money someone put in our sacks last time we were here," they said. "He plans to pretend that we stole it. Then he will seize us, make us slaves, and take our donkeys."

A Feast at Joseph's Palace

¹⁹The brothers approached the manager of Joseph's household and spoke to him at the entrance to the palace. ²⁰"Sir," they said, "we came to Egypt once before to buy food. ²¹But as we were returning home, we stopped for the night and opened our sacks. Then we discovered that each man's money—the exact amount paid—was in the top of his sack! Here it is; we have brought it back with us. ²²We also have additional money to buy more food. We have no idea who put our money in our sacks."

²³"Relax. Don't be afraid," the household manager told them. "Your God, the God of your father, must have put this treasure into your sacks. I know I received your payment." Then he released Simeon and brought him out to them.

²⁴The manager then led the men into Joseph's palace. He gave them water to wash their feet and provided food for their donkeys. ²⁵They were told they would be eating there, so they prepared their gifts for Joseph's arrival at noon.

²⁶When Joseph came home, they gave him the gifts they had brought him, then bowed low to the ground before him. ²⁷After greeting them, he asked, "How is your father, the old man you spoke about? Is he still alive?"

²⁸"Yes," they replied. "Our father, your servant, is alive and well." And they bowed low again.

²⁹Then Joseph looked at his brother Benjamin, the son of his own mother. "Is this your youngest brother, the one you told me about?" Joseph asked. "May God be gracious to you, my son." ³⁰Then Joseph hurried from the room because he was overcome with emotion for his brother. He went into his private room, where he broke down and wept. ³¹After washing his face, he came back out, keeping himself under control. Then he ordered, "Bring out the food!"

³²The waiters served Joseph at his own table, and his brothers were served at a separate table. The Egyptians who ate with Joseph sat at their own table, because Egyptians despise Hebrews and refuse to eat with them. ³³Joseph told each of his brothers where to sit, and to their amazement, he seated them according to age, from oldest to youngest. ³⁴And Joseph filled their plates with food from his own table, giving Benjamin five times as much as he gave the others. So they feasted and drank freely with him.

CHAPTER 44
Joseph's Silver Cup

When his brothers were ready to leave, Joseph gave these instructions to his palace manager: "Fill each of their sacks with as much grain as they can carry, and put each man's money back into his sack. ²Then put my personal silver cup at the top of the youngest brother's

43:6 Hebrew *Israel;* also in 43:11. See note on 35:21. **43:14** Hebrew *El-Shaddai.*

sack, along with the money for his grain." So the manager did as Joseph instructed him.

³The brothers were up at dawn and were sent on their journey with their loaded donkeys. ⁴But when they had gone only a short distance and were barely out of the city, Joseph said to his palace manager, "Chase after them and stop them. When you catch up with them, ask them, 'Why have you repaid my kindness with such evil? ⁵Why have you stolen my master's silver cup,* which he uses to predict the future? What a wicked thing you have done!'"

⁶When the palace manager caught up with the men, he spoke to them as he had been instructed.

⁷"What are you talking about?" the brothers responded. "We are your servants and would never do such a thing! ⁸Didn't we return the money we found in our sacks? We brought it back all the way from the land of Canaan. Why would we steal silver or gold from your master's house? ⁹If you find his cup with any one of us, let that man die. And all the rest of us, my lord, will be your slaves."

¹⁰"That's fair," the man replied. "But only the one who stole the cup will be my slave. The rest of you may go free."

¹¹They all quickly took their sacks from the backs of their donkeys and opened them. ¹²The palace manager searched the brothers' sacks, from the oldest to the youngest. And the cup was found in Benjamin's sack! ¹³When the brothers saw this, they tore their clothing in despair. Then they loaded their donkeys again and returned to the city.

¹⁴Joseph was still in his palace when Judah and his brothers arrived, and they fell to the ground before him. ¹⁵"What have you done?" Joseph demanded. "Don't you know that a man like me can predict the future?"

¹⁶Judah answered, "Oh, my lord, what can we say to you? How can we explain this? How can we prove our innocence? God is punishing us for our sins. My lord, we have all returned to be your slaves—all of us, not just our brother who had your cup in his sack."

¹⁷"No," Joseph said. "I would never do such a thing! Only the man who stole the cup will be my slave. The rest of you may go back to your father in peace."

Judah Speaks for His Brothers

¹⁸Then Judah stepped forward and said, "Please, my lord, let your servant say just one word to you. Please, do not be angry with me, even though you are as powerful as Pharaoh himself.

¹⁹"My lord, previously you asked us, your servants, 'Do you have a father or a brother?' ²⁰And we responded, 'Yes, my lord, we have a father who is an old man, and his youngest son is a child of his old age. His full brother is dead, and he alone is left of his mother's children, and his father loves him very much.'

²¹"And you said to us, 'Bring him here so I can see him with my own eyes.' ²²But we said to you, 'My lord, the boy cannot leave his father, for his father would die.' ²³But you told us, 'Unless your youngest brother comes with you, you will never see my face again.'

²⁴"So we returned to your servant, our father, and told him what you had said. ²⁵Later, when he said, 'Go back again and buy us more food,' ²⁶we replied, 'We can't go unless you let our youngest brother go with us. We'll never get to see the man's face unless our youngest brother is with us.'

²⁷"Then my father said to us, 'As you know, my wife had two sons, ²⁸and one of them went away and never returned. Doubtless he was torn to pieces by some wild animal. I have never seen him since. ²⁹Now if you take his brother away from me, and any harm comes to him, you will send this grieving, white-haired man to his grave.*'

³⁰"And now, my lord, I cannot go back to my father without the boy. Our father's life is bound up in the boy's life. ³¹If he sees that the boy is not with us, our father will die. We, your servants, will indeed be responsible for sending that grieving, white-haired man to his grave. ³²My lord, I guaranteed to my father that I would take care of the boy. I told him, 'If I don't bring him back to you, I will bear the blame forever.'

³³"So please, my lord, let me stay here as a slave instead of the boy, and let the boy re-

---

44:5 As in Greek version; Hebrew lacks this phrase. 44:29 Hebrew to Sheol; also in 44:31.

44:18-34 Judah stepped forward to plead for Benjamin's freedom, fearing what the youngest brother's enslavement would do to Jacob, their father. Many years earlier, the brothers had chosen to sell Joseph into slavery, just for reasons of personal hatred. This had caused their father deep pain. But here, Judah was willing to put himself on the line for his grieving father. Judah and his brothers had grown up a great deal over the years. They had learned from their past mistakes and proved to Joseph that they were ready for reconciliation with their long-lost brother.

turn with his brothers. [34]For how can I return to my father if the boy is not with me? I couldn't bear to see the anguish this would cause my father!"

CHAPTER 45
Joseph Reveals His Identity

Joseph could stand it no longer. There were many people in the room, and he said to his attendants, "Out, all of you!" So he was alone with his brothers when he told them who he was. [2]Then he broke down and wept. He wept so loudly the Egyptians could hear him, and word of it quickly carried to Pharaoh's palace.

[3]"I am Joseph!" he said to his brothers. "Is my father still alive?" But his brothers were speechless! They were stunned to realize that Joseph was standing there in front of them. [4]"Please, come closer," he said to them. So they came closer. And he said again, "I am Joseph, your brother, whom you sold into slavery in Egypt. [5]But don't be upset, and don't be angry with yourselves for selling me to this place. It was God who sent me here ahead of you to preserve your lives. [6]This famine that has ravaged the land for two years will last five more years, and there will be neither plowing nor harvesting. [7]God has sent me ahead of you to keep you and your families alive and to preserve many survivors.* [8]So it was God who sent me here, not you! And he is the One who made me an adviser* to Pharaoh—the manager of his entire palace and the governor of all Egypt.

[9]"Now hurry back to my father and tell him, 'This is what your son Joseph says: God has made me master over all the land of Egypt. So come down to me immediately! [10]You can live in the region of Goshen, where you can be near me with all your children and grandchildren, your flocks and herds, and everything you own. [11]I will take care of you there, for there are still five years of famine ahead of us. Otherwise you, your household, and all your animals will starve.'"

[12]Then Joseph added, "Look! You can see for yourselves, and so can my brother Benjamin, that I really am Joseph! [13]Go tell my father of my honored position here in Egypt. Describe for him everything you have seen, and then bring my father here quickly." [14]Weeping with joy, he embraced Benjamin, and Benjamin did the same. [15]Then Joseph kissed each of his brothers and wept over them, and after that they began talking freely with him.

Pharaoh Invites Jacob to Egypt

[16]The news soon reached Pharaoh's palace: "Joseph's brothers have arrived!" Pharaoh and his officials were all delighted to hear this.

[17]Pharaoh said to Joseph, "Tell your brothers, 'This is what you must do: Load your pack animals, and hurry back to the land of Canaan. [18]Then get your father and all of your families, and return here to me. I will give you the very best land in Egypt, and you will eat from the best that the land produces.'"

[19]Then Pharaoh said to Joseph, "Tell your brothers, 'Take wagons from the land of Egypt to carry your little children and your wives, and bring your father here. [20]Don't worry about your personal belongings, for the best of all the land of Egypt is yours.'"

[21]So the sons of Jacob* did as they were told. Joseph provided them with wagons, as Pharaoh had commanded, and he gave them supplies for the journey. [22]And he gave each of them new clothes—but to Benjamin he gave five changes of clothes and 300 pieces* of silver. [23]He also sent his father ten male

45:7 Or *and to save you with an extraordinary rescue.* The meaning of the Hebrew is uncertain. **45:8** Hebrew *a father.* **45:21** Hebrew *Israel;* also in 45:28. See note on 35:21. **45:22** Hebrew *300 [shekels],* about 7.5 pounds or 3.4 kilograms in weight.

45:1-3 Joseph finally revealed himself to his brothers. For him it was a beautiful reunion, because he had experienced healing by walking with God. But for his brothers, excluding Benjamin, hidden guilt had burdened them for a long time. They were speechless with terror when they recognized Joseph. It is terrifying to open long-hidden guilt to the light, but this is the only road to reconciliation and peace.

45:4-7 Joseph told his brothers to not be angry at themselves for the mistakes they had made in the past. It was now time to rejoice in the present! This was true forgiveness. Joseph was able to see how God had used their mistake to save thousands of lives, including their own. God often turns past disasters into opportunities for great success. When we begin to see that God is working in our life, we will be better able to forgive the people who have wronged us. And if we can see how God has turned around the lives of people we have wronged, we will begin to understand how much God wants our guilt removed and our relationships reconciled.

donkeys loaded with the finest products of Egypt, and ten female donkeys loaded with grain and bread and other supplies he would need on his journey. [24]So Joseph sent his brothers off, and as they left, he called after them, "Don't quarrel about all this along the way!" [25]And they left Egypt and returned to their father, Jacob, in the land of Canaan.

[26]"Joseph is still alive!" they told him. "And he is governor of all the land of Egypt!" Jacob was stunned at the news—he couldn't believe it. [27]But when they repeated to Jacob everything Joseph had told them, and when he saw the wagons Joseph had sent to carry him, their father's spirits revived. [28]Then Jacob exclaimed, "It must be true! My son Joseph is alive! I must go and see him before I die."

CHAPTER 46
Jacob's Journey to Egypt

So Jacob* set out for Egypt with all his possessions. And when he came to Beersheba, he offered sacrifices to the God of his father, Isaac. [2]During the night God spoke to him in a vision. "Jacob! Jacob!" he called.

"Here I am," Jacob replied.

[3]"I am God,* the God of your father," the voice said. "Do not be afraid to go down to Egypt, for there I will make your family into a great nation. [4]I will go with you down to Egypt, and I will bring you back again. You will die in Egypt, but Joseph will be with you to close your eyes."

[5]So Jacob left Beersheba, and his sons took him to Egypt. They carried him and their little ones and their wives in the wagons Pharaoh had provided for them. [6]They also took all their livestock and all the personal belongings they had acquired in the land of Canaan. So Jacob and his entire family went to Egypt—[7]sons and grandsons, daughters and granddaughters—all his descendants.

[8]These are the names of the descendants of Israel—the sons of Jacob—who went to Egypt:

Reuben was Jacob's oldest son. [9]The sons of Reuben were Hanoch, Pallu, Hezron, and Carmi.

[10]The sons of Simeon were Jemuel, Jamin, Ohad, Jakin, Zohar, and Shaul. (Shaul's mother was a Canaanite woman.)

[11]The sons of Levi were Gershon, Kohath, and Merari.

[12]The sons of Judah were Er, Onan, Shelah, Perez, and Zerah (though Er and Onan had died in the land of Canaan). The sons of Perez were Hezron and Hamul.

[13]The sons of Issachar were Tola, Puah,* Jashub,* and Shimron.

[14]The sons of Zebulun were Sered, Elon, and Jahleel.

[15]These were the sons of Leah and Jacob who were born in Paddan-aram, in addition to their daughter, Dinah. The number of Jacob's descendants (male and female) through Leah was thirty-three.

[16]The sons of Gad were Zephon,* Haggi, Shuni, Ezbon, Eri, Arodi, and Areli.

[17]The sons of Asher were Imnah, Ishvah, Ishvi, and Beriah. Their sister was Serah. Beriah's sons were Heber and Malkiel.

[18]These were the sons of Zilpah, the servant given to Leah by her father, Laban. The number of Jacob's descendants through Zilpah was sixteen.

[19]The sons of Jacob's wife Rachel were Joseph and Benjamin.

[20]Joseph's sons, born in the land of Egypt, were Manasseh and Ephraim. Their

---

46:1 Hebrew *Israel*; also in 46:29, 30. See note on 35:21. 46:3 Hebrew *I am El.* 46:13a As in Syriac version and Samaritan Pentateuch (see also 1 Chr 7:1); Hebrew reads *Puvah.* 46:13b As in some Greek manuscripts and Samaritan Pentateuch (see also Num 26:24; 1 Chr 7:1); Hebrew reads *Iob.* 46:16 As in Greek version and Samaritan Pentateuch (see also Num 26:15); Hebrew reads *Ziphion.*

45:24 Joseph knew his brothers so well; he knew they were inclined to argue. Even though Joseph's brothers had matured a great deal since he had last seen them, they still had a long way to go. Deeply ingrained attitudes and habits are hard to get rid of. It all takes time. Joseph's parting shot here shows that he had a sense of humor. But it also reveals that he had accepted his brothers as they were, arguments and all.
46:1-4 Some might think it was wrong for the Hebrews to leave the Promised Land, but God's promise to Jacob here shows that God approved of this family reunion in Egypt. When our life is subject to God's authority, where and when we go are up to him. God often uses surprising means to work his will. Notice that God brought Jacob and his family to Egypt for their preservation and growth.

mother was Asenath, daughter of Potiphera, the priest of On.*

²¹Benjamin's sons were Bela, Beker, Ashbel, Gera, Naaman, Ehi, Rosh, Muppim, Huppim, and Ard.

²²These were the sons of Rachel and Jacob. The number of Jacob's descendants through Rachel was fourteen.

²³The son of Dan was Hushim.

²⁴The sons of Naphtali were Jahzeel, Guni, Jezer, and Shillem.

²⁵These were the sons of Bilhah, the servant given to Rachel by her father, Laban. The number of Jacob's descendants through Bilhah was seven.

²⁶The total number of Jacob's direct descendants who went with him to Egypt, not counting his sons' wives, was sixty-six. ²⁷In addition, Joseph had two sons* who were born in Egypt. So altogether, there were seventy* members of Jacob's family in the land of Egypt.

Jacob's Family Arrives in Goshen

²⁸As they neared their destination, Jacob sent Judah ahead to meet Joseph and get directions to the region of Goshen. And when they finally arrived there, ²⁹Joseph prepared his chariot and traveled to Goshen to meet his father, Jacob. When Joseph arrived, he embraced his father and wept, holding him for a long time. ³⁰Finally, Jacob said to Joseph, "Now I am ready to die, since I have seen your face again and know you are still alive."

³¹And Joseph said to his brothers and to his father's entire family, "I will go to Pharaoh and tell him, 'My brothers and my father's entire family have come to me from the land of Canaan. ³²These men are shepherds, and they raise livestock. They have brought with them their flocks and herds and everything they own.'"

³³Then he said, "When Pharaoh calls for you and asks you about your occupation, ³⁴you must tell him, 'We, your servants, have raised livestock all our lives, as our ancestors

have always done.' When you tell him this, he will let you live here in the region of Goshen, for the Egyptians despise shepherds."

CHAPTER 47
Jacob Blesses Pharaoh

Then Joseph went to see Pharaoh and told him, "My father and my brothers have arrived from the land of Canaan. They have come with all their flocks and herds and possessions, and they are now in the region of Goshen."

²Joseph took five of his brothers with him and presented them to Pharaoh. ³And Pharaoh asked the brothers, "What is your occupation?"

They replied, "We, your servants, are shepherds, just like our ancestors. ⁴We have come to live here in Egypt for a while, for there is no pasture for our flocks in Canaan. The famine is very severe there. So please, we request permission to live in the region of Goshen."

⁵Then Pharaoh said to Joseph, "Now that your father and brothers have joined you here, ⁶choose any place in the entire land of Egypt for them to live. Give them the best land of Egypt. Let them live in the region of Goshen. And if any of them have special skills, put them in charge of my livestock, too."

⁷Then Joseph brought in his father, Jacob, and presented him to Pharaoh. And Jacob blessed Pharaoh.

⁸"How old are you?" Pharaoh asked him.

⁹Jacob replied, "I have traveled this earth for 130 hard years. But my life has been short compared to the lives of my ancestors." ¹⁰Then Jacob blessed Pharaoh again before leaving his court.

¹¹So Joseph assigned the best land of Egypt—the region of Rameses—to his father and his brothers, and he settled them there, just as Pharaoh had commanded. ¹²And Joseph provided food for his father and his brothers in amounts appropriate to the number of their dependents, including the smallest children.

46:20 Greek version reads *of Heliopolis.* 46:27a Greek version reads *nine sons,* probably including Joseph's grandsons through Ephraim and Manasseh (see 1 Chr 7:14-20). 46:27b Greek version reads *seventy-five;* see note on Exod 1:5.

46:29 God approves of the outward expression of emotion. It is an honest display of feelings that draws us closer to others. To hide our feelings is a form of dishonesty. We need to learn to show our feelings in wise and loving ways. Our culture sometimes urges people to hide their feelings; we are expected to be stoic, even in times of extreme sorrow or joy. Jacob and Joseph embraced and wept a long while, openly displaying their emotions for all to see.

Joseph's Leadership in the Famine

[13]Meanwhile, the famine became so severe that all the food was used up, and people were starving throughout the lands of Egypt and Canaan. [14]By selling grain to the people, Joseph eventually collected all the money in Egypt and Canaan, and he put the money in Pharaoh's treasury. [15]When the people of Egypt and Canaan ran out of money, all the Egyptians came to Joseph. "Our money is gone!" they cried. "But please give us food, or we will die before your very eyes!"

[16]Joseph replied, "Since your money is gone, bring me your livestock. I will give you food in exchange for your livestock." [17]So they brought their livestock to Joseph in exchange for food. In exchange for their horses, flocks of sheep and goats, herds of cattle, and donkeys, Joseph provided them with food for another year.

[18]But that year ended, and the next year they came again and said, "We cannot hide the truth from you, my lord. Our money is gone, and all our livestock and cattle are yours. We have nothing left to give but our bodies and our land. [19]Why should we die before your very eyes? Buy us and our land in exchange for food; we offer our land and ourselves as slaves for Pharaoh. Just give us grain so we may live and not die, and so the land does not become empty and desolate."

[20]So Joseph bought all the land of Egypt for Pharaoh. All the Egyptians sold him their fields because the famine was so severe, and soon all the land belonged to Pharaoh. [21]As for the people, he made them all slaves,* from one end of Egypt to the other. [22]The only land he did not buy was the land belonging to the priests. They received an allotment of food directly from Pharaoh, so they didn't need to sell their land.

[23]Then Joseph said to the people, "Look, today I have bought you and your land for Pharaoh. I will provide you with seed so you can plant the fields. [24]Then when you harvest it, one-fifth of your crop will belong to Pharaoh. You may keep the remaining four-fifths as seed for your fields and as food for you, your households, and your little ones."

[25]"You have saved our lives!" they exclaimed. "May it please you, my lord, to let us be Pharaoh's servants." [26]Joseph then issued a decree still in effect in the land of Egypt, that Pharaoh should receive one-fifth of all the crops grown on his land. Only the land belonging to the priests was not given to Pharaoh.

[27]Meanwhile, the people of Israel settled in the region of Goshen in Egypt. There they acquired property, and they were fruitful, and their population grew rapidly. [28]Jacob lived for seventeen years after his arrival in Egypt, so he lived 147 years in all.

[29]As the time of his death drew near, Jacob* called for his son Joseph and said to him, "Please do me this favor. Put your hand under my thigh and swear that you will treat me with unfailing love by honoring this last request: Do not bury me in Egypt. [30]When I die, please take my body out of Egypt and bury me with my ancestors."

So Joseph promised, "I will do as you ask." [31]"Swear that you will do it," Jacob insisted. So Joseph gave his oath, and Jacob bowed humbly at the head of his bed.*

CHAPTER 48
Jacob Blesses Manasseh and Ephraim

One day not long after this, word came to Joseph, "Your father is failing rapidly." So Joseph went to visit his father, and he took with him his two sons, Manasseh and Ephraim.

[2]When Joseph arrived, Jacob was told, "Your son Joseph has come to see you." So Jacob* gathered his strength and sat up in his bed.

[3]Jacob said to Joseph, "God Almighty* appeared to me at Luz in the land of Canaan and blessed me. [4]He said to me, 'I will make you fruitful, and I will multiply your descendants. I will make you a multitude of nations. And I will give this land of Canaan to your descendants* after you as an everlasting possession.'

[5]"Now I am claiming as my own sons these two boys of yours, Ephraim and Manasseh,

---

47:21 As in Greek version and Samaritan Pentateuch; Hebrew reads *he moved them all into the towns.* **47:29** Hebrew *Israel;* also in 47:31b. See note on 35:21. **47:31** Greek version reads *and Israel bowed in worship as he leaned on his staff.* Compare Heb 11:21. **48:2** Hebrew *Israel;* also in 48:8, 10, 11, 13, 14, 21. See note on 35:21. **48:3** Hebrew *El-Shaddai.* **48:4** Hebrew *seed;* also in 48:19.

48:1-9 Before blessing his grandsons Ephraim and Manasseh, Jacob recalled the blessings that God had bestowed upon him. We know that the sins and failures of parents are often passed on to succeeding generations. But here we see that blessings are passed on as well. Abraham had established a relationship with God that he modeled before Isaac, which was then passed on to Jacob, and then to the succeeding generation. Let us establish the kind of relationship with God that will endure in generations that follow. That way we will be able to bless our children with the blessings God has given us.

who were born here in the land of Egypt before I arrived. They will be my sons, just as Reuben and Simeon are. ⁶But any children born to you in the future will be your own, and they will inherit land within the territories of their brothers Ephraim and Manasseh.

⁷"Long ago, as I was returning from Paddan-aram,* Rachel died in the land of Canaan. We were still on the way, some distance from Ephrath (that is, Bethlehem). So with great sorrow I buried her there beside the road to Ephrath."

⁸Then Jacob looked over at the two boys. "Are these your sons?" he asked.

⁹"Yes," Joseph told him, "these are the sons God has given me here in Egypt."

And Jacob said, "Bring them closer to me, so I can bless them."

¹⁰Jacob was half blind because of his age and could hardly see. So Joseph brought the boys close to him, and Jacob kissed and embraced them. ¹¹Then Jacob said to Joseph, "I never thought I would see your face again, but now God has let me see your children, too!"

¹²Joseph moved the boys, who were at their grandfather's knees, and he bowed with his face to the ground. ¹³Then he positioned the boys in front of Jacob. With his right hand he directed Ephraim toward Jacob's left hand, and with his left hand he put Manasseh at Jacob's right hand. ¹⁴But Jacob crossed his arms as he reached out to lay his hands on the boys' heads. He put his right hand on the head of Ephraim, though he was the younger boy, and his left hand on the head of Manasseh, though he was the firstborn. ¹⁵Then he blessed Joseph and said,

"May the God before whom my
　　grandfather Abraham
　and my father, Isaac, walked—
the God who has been my shepherd
　all my life, to this very day,
¹⁶the Angel who has redeemed me from
　　all harm—
　may he bless these boys.
May they preserve my name
　and the names of Abraham and Isaac.

And may their descendants multiply greatly
　throughout the earth."

¹⁷But Joseph was upset when he saw that his father placed his right hand on Ephraim's head. So Joseph lifted it to move it from Ephraim's head to Manasseh's head. ¹⁸"No, my father," he said. "This one is the firstborn. Put your right hand on his head."

¹⁹But his father refused. "I know, my son; I know," he replied. "Manasseh will also become a great people, but his younger brother will become even greater. And his descendants will become a multitude of nations."

²⁰So Jacob blessed the boys that day with this blessing: "The people of Israel will use your names when they give a blessing. They will say, 'May God make you as prosperous as Ephraim and Manasseh.'" In this way, Jacob put Ephraim ahead of Manasseh.

²¹Then Jacob said to Joseph, "Look, I am about to die, but God will be with you and will take you back to Canaan, the land of your ancestors. ²²And beyond what I have given your brothers, I am giving you an extra portion of the land* that I took from the Amorites with my sword and bow."

CHAPTER 49
Jacob's Last Words to His Sons

Then Jacob called together all his sons and said, "Gather around me, and I will tell you what will happen to each of you in the days to come.

²"Come and listen, you sons of Jacob;
　　listen to Israel, your father.

³"Reuben, you are my firstborn, my
　　strength,
　the child of my vigorous youth.
　You are first in rank and first in power.
⁴But you are as unruly as a flood,
　and you will be first no longer.
For you went to bed with my wife;
　you defiled my marriage couch.

⁵"Simeon and Levi are two of a kind;
　their weapons are instruments
　　of violence.

48:7 Hebrew *Paddan*, referring to Paddan-aram; compare Gen 35:9.　48:22 Or *an extra ridge of land*. The meaning of the Hebrew is uncertain.

49:5-7 Simeon and Levi were characterized by violent tempers, and the history of these brothers in Genesis corroborates Jacob's assessment. After their sister Dinah was raped, they took revenge by deceiving and slaughtering all the men of the city where the atrocity had occurred (34:1-31). This tendency needed to be curbed. Many years later, however, when Moses shouted for all who were on the Lord's side to come and join him, the Levites came and vigorously defended God's cause (see Exodus 32:25-29). As a result, they were chosen as God's priests in Israel. Let us look to God to transform our weaknesses into strengths, just as he did with the descendants of Levi.

⁶May I never join in their meetings;
   may I never be a party to their plans.
For in their anger they murdered men,
   and they crippled oxen just for sport.
⁷A curse on their anger, for it is fierce;
   a curse on their wrath, for it is cruel.
I will scatter them among the descendants
   of Jacob;
   I will disperse them throughout Israel.

⁸"Judah, your brothers will praise you.
   You will grasp your enemies by
      the neck.
   All your relatives will bow before you.
⁹Judah, my son, is a young lion
   that has finished eating its prey.
Like a lion he crouches and lies down;
   like a lioness—who dares to rouse
      him?
¹⁰The scepter will not depart from Judah,
   nor the ruler's staff from his
      descendants,*
until the coming of the one to whom it
   belongs,*
   the one whom all nations will honor.
¹¹He ties his foal to a grapevine,
   the colt of his donkey to a choice
      vine.
He washes his clothes in wine,
   his robes in the blood of grapes.
¹²His eyes are darker than wine,
   and his teeth are whiter than milk.

¹³"Zebulun will settle by the seashore
   and will be a harbor for ships;
   his borders will extend to Sidon.

¹⁴"Issachar is a sturdy donkey,
   resting between two saddlepacks.*
¹⁵When he sees how good the
      countryside is
   and how pleasant the land,
he will bend his shoulder to the
      load
   and submit himself to hard labor.

¹⁶"Dan will govern his people,
   like any other tribe in Israel.
¹⁷Dan will be a snake beside the road,
   a poisonous viper along the path
that bites the horse's hooves

so its rider is thrown off.
¹⁸I trust in you for salvation, O LORD!

¹⁹"Gad will be attacked by marauding
      bands,
   but he will attack them when they
      retreat.

²⁰"Asher will dine on rich foods
   and produce food fit for kings.

²¹"Naphtali is a doe set free
   that bears beautiful fawns.

²²"Joseph is the foal of a wild donkey,
   the foal of a wild donkey at a
      spring—
   one of the wild donkeys on the ridge.*
²³Archers attacked him savagely;
   they shot at him and harassed him.
²⁴But his bow remained taut,
   and his arms were strengthened
by the hands of the Mighty One of Jacob,
   by the Shepherd, the Rock of Israel.
²⁵May the God of your father help you;
   may the Almighty bless you
with the blessings of the heavens above,
   and blessings of the watery depths
      below,
   and blessings of the breasts and womb.
²⁶May my fatherly blessings on you
   surpass the blessings of my
      ancestors,*
   reaching to the heights of the eternal
      hills.
May these blessings rest on the head of
      Joseph,
   who is a prince among his brothers.

²⁷"Benjamin is a ravenous wolf,
   devouring his enemies in the morning
   and dividing his plunder in the
      evening."

²⁸These are the twelve tribes of Israel, and
this is what their father said as he told his
sons good-bye. He blessed each one with an
appropriate message.

Jacob's Death and Burial
²⁹Then Jacob instructed them, "Soon I will
die and join my ancestors. Bury me with my

49:10a Hebrew *from between his feet.* **49:10b** Or *until tribute is brought to him and the peoples obey;* traditionally rendered *until Shiloh comes.* **49:14** Or *sheepfolds,* or *hearths.* **49:22** Or *Joseph is a fruitful tree, / a fruitful tree beside a spring. / His branches reach over the wall.* The meaning of the Hebrew is uncertain. **49:26** Or *of the ancient mountains.*

49:13-27 Jacob's remarks concerning each of his sons seem very harsh, but the information he shared should have given helpful direction to each of them. We have a lot to learn from our parents, but often they aren't willing to be honest with us. Or if they are, we aren't really ready to listen. We need to learn both to speak honestly and to listen with respect.

father and grandfather in the cave in the field of Ephron the Hittite. ³⁰This is the cave in the field of Machpelah, near Mamre in Canaan, that Abraham bought from Ephron the Hittite as a permanent burial site. ³¹There Abraham and his wife Sarah are buried. There Isaac and his wife, Rebekah, are buried. And there I buried Leah. ³²It is the plot of land and the cave that my grandfather Abraham bought from the Hittites."

³³When Jacob had finished this charge to his sons, he drew his feet into the bed, breathed his last, and joined his ancestors in death.

CHAPTER 50

Joseph threw himself on his father and wept over him and kissed him. ²Then Joseph told the physicians who served him to embalm his father's body; so Jacob* was embalmed. ³The embalming process took the usual forty days. And the Egyptians mourned his death for seventy days.

⁴When the period of mourning was over, Joseph approached Pharaoh's advisers and said, "Please do me this favor and speak to Pharaoh on my behalf. ⁵Tell him that my father made me swear an oath. He said to me, 'Listen, I am about to die. Take my body back to the land of Canaan, and bury me in the tomb I prepared for myself.' So please allow me to go and bury my father. After his burial, I will return without delay."

⁶Pharaoh agreed to Joseph's request. "Go and bury your father, as he made you promise," he said. ⁷So Joseph went up to bury his father. He was accompanied by all of Pharaoh's officials, all the senior members of Pharaoh's household, and all the senior officers of Egypt. ⁸Joseph also took his entire household and his brothers and their households. But they left their little children and flocks and herds in the land of Goshen. ⁹A great number of chariots and charioteers accompanied Joseph.

¹⁰When they arrived at the threshing floor of Atad, near the Jordan River, they held a very great and solemn memorial service, with a seven-day period of mourning for Joseph's father. ¹¹The local residents, the Canaanites, watched them mourning at the threshing floor of Atad. Then they renamed that place (which is near the Jordan) Abel-mizraim,* for they said, "This is a place of deep mourning for these Egyptians."

¹²So Jacob's sons did as he had commanded them. ¹³They carried his body to the land of Canaan and buried him in the cave in the field of Machpelah, near Mamre. This is the cave that Abraham had bought as a permanent burial site from Ephron the Hittite.

Joseph Reassures His Brothers

¹⁴After burying Jacob, Joseph returned to Egypt with his brothers and all who had accompanied him to his father's burial. ¹⁵But now that their father was dead, Joseph's brothers became fearful. "Now Joseph will show his anger and pay us back for all the wrong we did to him," they said.

¹⁶So they sent this message to Joseph: "Before your father died, he instructed us ¹⁷to say to you: 'Please forgive your brothers for the great wrong they did to you—for their sin in treating you so cruelly.' So we, the servants of the God of your father, beg you to forgive our sin." When Joseph received the message, he broke down and wept. ¹⁸Then his brothers came and threw themselves down before Joseph. "Look, we are your slaves!" they said.

¹⁹But Joseph replied, "Don't be afraid of me. Am I God, that I can punish you? ²⁰You intended to harm me, but God intended it all for good. He brought me to this position so I could save the lives of many people. ²¹No, don't be afraid. I will continue to take care of you and your children." So he reassured them by speaking kindly to them.

The Death of Joseph

²²So Joseph and his brothers and their families continued to live in Egypt. Joseph lived

50:2 Hebrew *Israel*. See note on 35:21. 50:11 *Abel-mizraim* means "mourning of the Egyptians."

50:15-21 When Jacob died, Joseph's brothers feared that he would take revenge for their past differences. They thought Joseph had spared them only for the sake of their father. But they discovered that Joseph's forgiveness was complete, with no ulterior motives. Joseph had already granted his brothers complete forgiveness; his brothers couldn't believe it and thus had not yet received it. They had needlessly lived in fear of a coming punishment. God hands us forgiveness that is just as complete, but we need to believe it and then receive it. Only then can we experience the freedom he offers.

to the age of 110. [23]He lived to see three generations of descendants of his son Ephraim, and he lived to see the birth of the children of Manasseh's son Makir, whom he claimed as his own.*

[24]"Soon I will die," Joseph told his brothers, "but God will surely come to help you and lead you out of this land of Egypt. He will bring you back to the land he solemnly

50:23 Hebrew *who were born on Joseph's knees.*

promised to give to Abraham, to Isaac, and to Jacob."

[25]Then Joseph made the sons of Israel swear an oath, and he said, "When God comes to help you and lead you back, you must take my bones with you." [26]So Joseph died at the age of 110. The Egyptians embalmed him, and his body was placed in a coffin in Egypt.

REFLECTIONS ON **GENESIS**

insights FROM THE NAMES OF GOD

The Hebrew name for God used in **Genesis 1:1** (*Elohim*) demonstrates the enormity of God's power to transform lives. This name for God is in the plural form, signifying his strength and might. It also hints that God is in some sense plural—a community unto himself (see also 1:26; 3:22; 11:7). But though this name is plural, it is treated grammatically as singular, revealing God's unified and personal nature. He is omnipotent in power but personal in his touch. He is able and willing to provide the help we need.

In **Genesis 2:4** a new Hebrew name for God is introduced: "LORD" (*Yahweh* or *Jehovah*). This is the personal name for God; it is his relationship name. It describes the God who chose Abraham and established a covenant with him. It describes the God who chose to relate to the Israelites and make them his people. It is the name that reminds us that God wants to have a relationship with us.

insights FROM GOD'S CREATION

As the source of all things, God is always able to meet our needs. The Hebrew verb translated "create" in **Genesis 1:1** describes an act that only God can do. It is used to describe three things that science cannot explain: the creation of something from nothing (1:1), the creation of living things from inanimate matter (1:21-22), and the creation of man (1:27). A God who can create people and the world we live in can certainly empower a person in the process of recovery.

Genesis 1:2 describes the earth before it was shaped by God's creative hand. It was empty, formless, and dark. These three characteristics forebode nothing but trouble. But then we are told that "the Spirit of God was hovering over the surface of the waters." This fourth characteristic is a source of hope and promises recovery. The presence of the Holy Spirit was a necessary element in the events of all six days of Creation. In the same way, his presence in our life is necessary before any rebuilding and recovery can take place.

In **Genesis 1:3** God said, "Let there be light." The word *let* in this verse is used to introduce one of God's purposes for his creation—that there should be light in the world. This word is used repeatedly in this chapter to introduce the various things that God intended for his creation (see 1:6, 9, 11, 14-15, 20, 24, 26). He had a purpose and a plan for everything. He also has a plan for each of us. And his plan is designed to bring about the best for his creation. As we go through recovery, we need only be willing to turn the process over to his design and plan.

In **Genesis 1:26-27** we see that the first people were created to be like God. Oceans of ink have been spilled attempting to explain what this means. One characteristic that all the writers agree upon is the ability of people to make moral decisions. We have the power of choice, and we are accountable to God and to others for the choices we make. To continue in recovery we must take responsibility for this aspect of God's nature in each of us—our ability to choose.

insights ABOUT TEMPTATION

In **Genesis 2:16-17** God forbade Adam and Eve to eat from one certain tree. Why did he do this? Why didn't God create a world where people couldn't sin? Or why didn't he make people so they couldn't disobey his commands? The answer lies in the very nature of God. God is love and desires to have a loving relationship with his creatures. He wants us to respond to him with love in return. But a loving response is only possible when we have the choice to do otherwise. He wants us to obey because we love him, not because we have no other choice.

In **Genesis 3:1-3** Satan began his temptation of Eve by planting doubt in her mind concerning what God had said. Notice that Eve wasn't very clear on the details of God's command. God had told them not to *eat* fruit from a certain tree (2:17). Eve claimed that God had said they were not to even *touch* the tree. She was making God's requirements more difficult than God himself had done! Her own confusion about what God had said made her even more susceptible to the serpent's wiles. We need a proper understanding of God's truth if we hope to stand against Satan's temptations.

In **Genesis 3:6** notice that Eve quickly succumbed to a visual temptation. Until Eve really *saw* the tree, she was not influenced by the three common elements of all temptation. She saw that the fruit of the tree would be good to eat ("a craving for physical pleasure"), that it looked lovely and fresh ("a craving for everything we see"), and that it was a tree that would make her wise ("pride in our achievements and possessions"). These are still important weapons in Satan's arsenal of temptation (see 1 John 2:16).

insights ABOUT SIN AND ITS CONSEQUENCES

In **Genesis 3:7** Adam and Eve became aware of their nakedness. With their act of disobedience came embarrassment and shame. They did their best to cover themselves; they didn't like what they saw when they looked at themselves. This happens to all of us when we sin and become dependent on cruel addictions. We don't like what we see, so we cover it up with lies and half-truths. We do it to preserve our relationships. But in the end, our intimacy with others is destroyed. We need to be honest with ourself and with others and work at reestablishing our relationships. This is a significant part of our recovery.

In **Genesis 3:10** Adam admitted that he was hiding from God. One of the terrible consequences of sin is the isolation that results. We want to hide from other people; we want to hide from God. Our failures will always make us want to hide. But recovery means that we must bring our sins out into the open; this will then bring us back into our relationships—with others and with God.

In **Genesis 3:15** it becomes obvious that Adam and Eve were powerless to resist sin by themselves. Alone, they could not overwhelm Satan and escape the temptations he offered. In his grace, however, God promised that the offspring of the woman would defeat Satan. He promised that he would take charge of the recovery process and overcome the enemy. This is good news—the first mention of the gospel of grace that would eventually be fulfilled by the coming of Jesus the Messiah.

In **Genesis 3:18-19** we see that after the Fall, even the earth responded differently to its human masters. In the beginning the earth was their constant ally, yielding its fruits easily to their hands. But now, it brought forth thorns and thistles and weeds. Work became an arduous task, frustrating and unfulfilling.

There was no reason for Adam and Eve to expect to live on after their failure. God had clearly stated that the consequences of their sin would be death (see 2:17). Yet in **Genesis 3:20** Adam displayed his faith in our gracious God by naming his wife Eve, which means "to give life." He believed that she would live to be the mother of the human race. Adam's faith in God gave him hope for the future, even when his past gave him little to hope for.

insights FROM CAIN AND ABEL

In **Genesis 4:4** Abel slew an innocent substitute as his offering, and God accepted him. Abel was obedient to God's instructions. Our relationship with God can be established by accepting God's gracious forgiveness and allowing the innocent sacrifice of his Son to stand in our place. Abel's sacrifice of one of his lambs was the second death mentioned in the Bible.

In **Genesis 4:5** we see that God rejected Cain's offering. We may wonder why. We don't have all the details, but we do know that his offering was given in rebellion (see Jude 1:11). Apparently Cain wanted to do things his way; he didn't want to follow the program that God had mapped out for this first human family. Cain responded to the rejection with anger and dejection. He wanted to be accepted by God, but he wanted to earn divine approval by his hard work in the fields. God could not accept his gift of farm produce. Acceptance by God cannot be bought with hard work; we need to admit our need and humbly allow a sacrifice to stand in our place. God has provided us with the perfect sacrifice in the person of Jesus Christ. He stands in our place, paying for all our failures and sins and freeing us to start again.

insights FROM NOAH'S LIFE

After years of waiting, God saw that the human race still refused to live according to his plan. In **Genesis 6:5-6** we see that things were getting worse, not better. This broke God's heart because of the great love he had for his creation. It should encourage us to know that God doesn't punish us in anger. He does it for our good because he loves us.

In **Genesis 6:7** God promises to judge his fallen and sinful creation. Even though God is patient with us and gives us many chances to change our ways, we cannot act with impunity. Because he is righteous, God must act to protect innocent people who are hurt by sin.

God had assigned Noah the monumental task of rebuilding human society on earth. But God didn't just hand Noah the task and walk away. In **Genesis 9:9-13** God promises not to destroy Noah's work with another flood and sets a rainbow in the sky as a seal of his promise. Many of us are rebuilding, too. We can be sure that God will support our recovery with his presence and promises. And we should keep an eye out for the "rainbows" along the way. God often leaves us signs to remind us of his loving presence and care.

insights FROM ABRAHAM'S LIFE

In **Genesis 12:2-3** God gave Abram some special promises. He would make Abram the father of a great nation, he would bless him and make him famous, and he would make Abram a blessing to others. God promised to bless those who blessed Abram and to curse those who cursed him. Notice that God's promises to Abram illustrate Step 12 in recovery. After receiving God's blessing, Abram was to turn around and share it with others.

We may wonder what Abram expected the Promised Land to be like. In **Genesis 12:10** we see that he arrived to find the land ravaged by famine. It probably wasn't what he had expected or hoped for, but it was the place that God had intended for him and his descendants. There will be times in recovery when things are difficult. Sometimes we may need to do things that we are not comfortable doing. But we need to follow God—even when his program doesn't lead us down the paths we had expected or hoped for.

The lie that Abram decided to tell the Egyptians in **Genesis 12:11-13** showed that he lacked faith in God. He didn't believe that God would protect him, so he took things into his own hands. We may feel that a little lie is justified if it is intended to protect something important to us. We may even succeed in getting away with it for a while, but all lies reap long-term consequences. It is best to trust God to protect us as we tell the truth. The God of truth will stand with us as we step out in faith.

In **Genesis 22:8-13** we find Abraham about to sacrifice his son Isaac. Much to the relief of Abraham and Isaac, however, God provided a substitute. We do not know what Abraham had in mind when he told his son that God would provide a sacrifice, but we do know that God has provided a sacrifice for us—not simply a ram caught in a bush but his only Son. Anyone who believes in him will have the means for discovering a new life now and through eternity as well.

insights FROM JOSEPH'S LIFE

Many commentators have noted that nothing bad is ever said about Joseph. That may be true of his adult life, but as a boy he was irritatingly overconfident. In **Genesis 37:2** we see that he was also a tattletale. Joseph's arrogant behavior as a youth, along with his father's favoritism, planted seeds of hatred in his brothers' hearts. Consequently, Joseph suffered years of slavery in Egypt. Joseph was certainly more worthy of praise than his brothers, but he can hardly be given perfect marks.

In **Genesis 39:19-23** we see that God was with Joseph even in prison. We are told that Joseph prospered in everything he did. And through all his trials, Joseph remained faithful to God. It would have been easy for him to start playing the victim and just give up. When we play the victim, we start to blame others and lose our ability to act. We need to stop blaming and start acting, doing our best in the situations in which God places us.

In **Genesis 50:15-21** a clear message emerges: Man proposes, but God disposes. Joseph's brothers intended their actions toward Joseph for evil, but God used those actions for good. It is wonderful that God can veto our foolish plans, transforming our mistakes and failures into the means for his gracious purposes.

EXODUS

THE BIG PICTURE

A. THE EXODUS: PAINFUL PATHWAY TO FREEDOM (1:1–18:27)
   1. Need: Going from Bad to Worse (1:1–2:25)
   2. Provision: God Restores a Fallen Leader (3:1–4:31)
   3. Intervention: Tough Love, Escalating Consequences (5:1–12:36)
   4. Freedom: The Thrill of Victory, the Agony of Defeat (12:37–18:27)
B. THE LAW: ESTABLISHING ACCOUNTABILITY AND BOUNDARIES (19:1–40:38)
   1. Covenant: Faithful Relationship between God and His People (19:1–24:18)
   2. Closeness: Understanding and Drawing Near to God (25:1–31:18)
   3. Covenant Renewal: Blowing It and Being Restored (32:1–34:35)
   4. Construction: Choosing to Glorify God (35:1–40:38)

Exit . . . Leave . . . Escape—these words tell us what the Exodus was all about. At the end of Genesis the sons of Jacob (Israel) had gone to Egypt to avoid famine and had enjoyed favored status there. But as time passed, their comfortable dream turned into a nightmare. A new pharaoh enslaved the Israelites, forcing them to do backbreaking tasks in his building projects. So the Israelites, hopelessly enslaved, turned their faces heavenward and begged for help.

The Exodus from Egypt was God's answer to his people's cries. He acted by calling a man named Moses—an ordinary man—to lead his people out of bondage to a new life. Moses had already made an exodus from Egypt, fleeing for his life after murdering an Egyptian. God found him in the wilderness near Mount Sinai and called him to deliver his people.

Moses was not exactly an eager leader; he initially balked at God's call. But God used Moses greatly despite his weaknesses. Moses did amazing miracles in Egypt to bring about Israel's deliverance. He also spoke with God face to face, receiving God's instructions for healthy, responsible living in the community of Israel. Moses was living proof that God can use anyone who is available to him.

The Exodus is also part of a much bigger deliverance story. It began with Abraham, whom God chose to father a nation that would carry God's healing touch to our world. God preserved the Israelites through slavery in Egypt and led them through the wilderness to the Promised Land. Centuries later, one of its descendants, Jesus the Messiah, gave his life to deliver the human race from sin's destructive grip. Through him, each of us can add a chapter to this story.

THE BOTTOM LINE

PURPOSE: To trace the deliverance of an enslaved people and their growth as a nation related to God. AUTHOR: Moses. AUDIENCE: The people of Israel. DATE WRITTEN: Sometime between 1445 and 1410 B.C., probably shortly after the writing of Genesis. SETTING: Egypt, then the wilderness of Sinai. KEY VERSES: "Then the LORD told him, 'I have certainly seen the oppression of my people in Egypt. I have heard their cries of distress. . . . Now go, for I am sending you to Pharaoh. You must lead my people Israel out of Egypt'" (3:7, 10). KEY PEOPLE AND RELATIONSHIPS: Moses with Pharaoh, Aaron and Miriam, Zipporah and Jethro, Joshua. KEY PLACES: Egypt, Midian, the Red Sea, the wilderness of Sinai.

RECOVERY THEMES

Deliverance Starts with Slavery: We can never really leave problems behind if we deny they exist. Our denial will only cause our problems to live on inside us. If we are to be delivered from slavery, we need to begin by recognizing that we are slaves. As the book of Exodus begins, the Israelites have just begun to realize that they are helplessly enslaved to the Egyptians. Gradually over the years, the glorious days of Joseph's leadership had faded and disappeared. For decades people had probably denied the truth of their situation by remembering the "good old days." But here, there could be no denial; the people of Israel were slaves. And that recognition was the first step toward their deliverance, just as it is with us. We need to acknowledge our own slavery in order to start the process toward deliverance.

God Hears the Helpless: It is likely that the Israelite slaves in Egypt felt as if God were deaf to their cries for help. But the book of Exodus shows us that God listens to the heart cries of the helpless. After their deliverance from Egypt, the Israelites were instructed to teach their children about God's faithfulness by reminding them of how God heard their cries for help (see Deuteronomy 6:20-25). This would encourage them during the tough situations they would soon face. This should also bring us encouragement today—God still hears the cries of the helpless.

God Uses Broken People: God responded to the cries of his people by choosing a man to lead them. He chose someone who had great skills and training but who also had failed greatly. For 40 years Moses was a fugitive shepherd, hiding because he had murdered an Egyptian. He was also a shy, reticent man who resisted God's calling in his life. He resisted to the point that God became angry and appointed Moses' brother, Aaron, to act as his spokesman to the people. God allows us to see all sides of Moses—the good and the bad—to show us that he can do great things through imperfect people. All we need to do is open ourself to his plan for our life.

God's Program: The story of Moses and the deliverance of the Israelites from Egypt is a continuation of God's recovery program that began in Genesis. Once again God used a relationship with a chosen individual—Moses—to work his plan. He gave Moses and the Israelites instructions for living healthy and holy lives in their traveling community. God's recovery program is designed to release us from the bondage of our sinful dependencies—our personal slavery. He has given us instructions to show us how to live, and he is personally involved in each step of our recovery.

CHAPTER 1
The Israelites in Egypt

These are the names of the sons of Israel (that is, Jacob) who moved to Egypt with their father, each with his family: ²Reuben, Simeon, Levi, Judah, ³Issachar, Zebulun, Benjamin, ⁴Dan, Naphtali, Gad, and Asher. ⁵In all, Jacob had seventy* descendants in Egypt, including Joseph, who was already there.

⁶In time, Joseph and all of his brothers died, ending that entire generation. ⁷But their descendants, the Israelites, had many children and grandchildren. In fact, they multiplied so greatly that they became extremely powerful and filled the land.

⁸Eventually, a new king came to power in Egypt who knew nothing about Joseph or what he had done. ⁹He said to his people, "Look, the people of Israel now outnumber us and are stronger than we are. ¹⁰We must make a plan to keep them from growing even more. If we don't, and if war breaks out, they will join our enemies and fight against us. Then they will escape from the country.*"

¹¹So the Egyptians made the Israelites their slaves. They appointed brutal slave drivers over them, hoping to wear them down with crushing labor. They forced them to build the cities of Pithom and Rameses as supply centers for the king. ¹²But the more the Egyptians oppressed them, the more the Israelites multiplied and spread, and the more alarmed the Egyptians became. ¹³So the Egyptians worked the people of Israel without mercy. ¹⁴They

1:5 Dead Sea Scrolls and Greek version read *seventy-five;* see notes on Gen 46:27. 1:10 Or *will take the country.*

1:8-11 The Israelites had not yet come to the point of admitting their helplessness. Even though they were being oppressed with increasing severity, they continued to rise to the occasion. This did not please the persecuting Egyptians. They feared that Israel would rise up against them and that in the event of war, they might join Egypt's enemies or even leave the country (Exodus 1:9-12). It was not until the Israelites discovered their powerlessness and asked God for help that he responded with deliverance.

made their lives bitter, forcing them to mix mortar and make bricks and do all the work in the fields. They were ruthless in all their demands.

¹⁵Then Pharaoh, the king of Egypt, gave this order to the Hebrew midwives, Shiphrah and Puah: ¹⁶"When you help the Hebrew women as they give birth, watch as they deliver.* If the baby is a boy, kill him; if it is a girl, let her live." ¹⁷But because the midwives feared God, they refused to obey the king's orders. They allowed the boys to live, too.

¹⁸So the king of Egypt called for the midwives. "Why have you done this?" he demanded. "Why have you allowed the boys to live?"

¹⁹"The Hebrew women are not like the Egyptian women," the midwives replied. "They are more vigorous and have their babies so quickly that we cannot get there in time."

²⁰So God was good to the midwives, and the Israelites continued to multiply, growing more and more powerful. ²¹And because the midwives feared God, he gave them families of their own.

²²Then Pharaoh gave this order to all his people: "Throw every newborn Hebrew boy into the Nile River. But you may let the girls live."

CHAPTER 2
The Birth of Moses

About this time, a man and woman from the tribe of Levi got married. ²The woman became pregnant and gave birth to a son. She saw that he was a special baby and kept him hidden for three months. ³But when she could no longer hide him, she got a basket made of papyrus reeds and waterproofed it with tar and pitch. She put the baby in the basket and laid it among the reeds along the bank of the Nile River. ⁴The baby's sister then stood at a distance, watching to see what would happen to him.

⁵Soon Pharaoh's daughter came down to bathe in the river, and her attendants walked along the riverbank. When the princess saw the basket among the reeds, she sent her maid to get it for her. ⁶When the princess opened it, she saw the baby. The little boy was crying, and she felt sorry for him. "This must be one of the Hebrew children," she said.

⁷Then the baby's sister approached the princess. "Should I go and find one of the Hebrew women to nurse the baby for you?" she asked.

⁸"Yes, do!" the princess replied. So the girl went and called the baby's mother.

⁹"Take this baby and nurse him for me," the princess told the baby's mother. "I will pay you for your help." So the woman took her baby home and nursed him.

¹⁰Later, when the boy was older, his mother brought him back to Pharaoh's daughter, who adopted him as her own son. The princess named him Moses,* for she explained, "I lifted him out of the water."

Moses Escapes to Midian

¹¹Many years later, when Moses had grown up, he went out to visit his own people, the Hebrews, and he saw how hard they were forced to work. During his visit, he saw an Egyptian beating one of his fellow Hebrews. ¹²After looking in all directions to make sure

---

1:16 Hebrew *look upon the two stones;* perhaps the reference is to a birthstool. 2:10 *Moses* sounds like a Hebrew term that means "to lift out."

1:18-21 In the short term, the Hebrew midwives had to overcome their fears of the Egyptian king. It must have been terrifying to face such a cruel and powerful person, not knowing how he would respond. Their wisdom not only allowed Israel to continue growing (1:20), but the midwives were also blessed by God with families of their own. They had put off any hope of reward from the king, but God's reward for their patience was worth waiting for.

1:22–2:8 Moses' mother had a problem: She knew that she couldn't hide her beloved baby from the Egyptians indefinitely. So she displayed remarkable wisdom and faith by literally obeying Pharaoh's command to put her son into the Nile River (1:22; 2:3). But she did it in a way that preserved his life, trusting God to look after him. We don't know whether Moses' mother hoped that Pharaoh's daughter would find the baby. But after doing all she could for her son, she was willing to leave him in God's hands.

2:11-14 Moses undoubtedly thought that he was helping his fellow Hebrew when he killed this Egyptian taskmaster. However, covering up his violent deed did not help the situation. He couldn't just bury his mistake in the sand or in the past to keep it from being known and rising to haunt him. He needed to responsibly and honestly face what he had done. When we hide our mistakes, they have a way of coming back to haunt us. It is best to face them right away so we can put them to rest, once and for all.

no one was watching, Moses killed the Egyptian and hid the body in the sand.

¹³The next day, when Moses went out to visit his people again, he saw two Hebrew men fighting. "Why are you beating up your friend?" Moses said to the one who had started the fight.

¹⁴The man replied, "Who appointed you to be our prince and judge? Are you going to kill me as you killed that Egyptian yesterday?"

Then Moses was afraid, thinking, "Everyone knows what I did." ¹⁵And sure enough, Pharaoh heard what had happened, and he tried to kill Moses. But Moses fled from Pharaoh and went to live in the land of Midian.

When Moses arrived in Midian, he sat down beside a well. ¹⁶Now the priest of Midian had seven daughters who came as usual to draw water and fill the water troughs for their father's flocks. ¹⁷But some other shepherds came and chased them away. So Moses jumped up and rescued the girls from the shepherds. Then he drew water for their flocks.

¹⁸When the girls returned to Reuel, their father, he asked, "Why are you back so soon today?"

¹⁹"An Egyptian rescued us from the shepherds," they answered. "And then he drew water for us and watered our flocks."

²⁰"Then where is he?" their father asked. "Why did you leave him there? Invite him to come and eat with us."

²¹Moses accepted the invitation, and he settled there with him. In time, Reuel gave Moses his daughter Zipporah to be his wife. ²²Later she gave birth to a son, and Moses named him Gershom,* for he explained, "I have been a foreigner in a foreign land."

²³Years passed, and the king of Egypt died. But the Israelites continued to groan under their burden of slavery. They cried out for help, and their cry rose up to God. ²⁴God heard their groaning, and he remembered his covenant promise to Abraham, Isaac, and Jacob. ²⁵He looked down on the people of Israel and knew it was time to act.*

CHAPTER 3
Moses and the Burning Bush

One day Moses was tending the flock of his father-in-law, Jethro,* the priest of Midian. He led the flock far into the wilderness and came to Sinai,* the mountain of God. ²There the angel of the LORD appeared to him in a blazing fire from the middle of a bush. Moses stared in amazement. Though the bush was engulfed in flames, it didn't burn up. ³"This is amazing," Moses said to himself. "Why isn't that bush burning up? I must go see it."

⁴When the LORD saw Moses coming to take a closer look, God called to him from the middle of the bush, "Moses! Moses!"

"Here I am!" Moses replied.

⁵"Do not come any closer," the LORD warned. "Take off your sandals, for you are standing on holy ground. ⁶I am the God of your father*—the God of Abraham, the God of Isaac, and the God of Jacob." When Moses heard this, he covered his face because he was afraid to look at God.

⁷Then the LORD told him, "I have certainly seen the oppression of my people in Egypt. I have heard their cries of distress because of their harsh slave drivers. Yes, I am aware of their suffering. ⁸So I have come down to rescue them from the power of the Egyptians and lead them out of Egypt into their own fertile and spacious land. It is a land flowing with milk and honey—the land where the Canaanites, Hittites, Amorites, Perizzites, Hivites, and Jebusites now live. ⁹Look! The cry of the people of Israel has reached me, and I have seen how harshly the Egyptians abuse them. ¹⁰Now go, for I am sending you to Pharaoh. You must lead my people Israel out of Egypt."

¹¹But Moses protested to God, "Who am I to appear before Pharaoh? Who am I to lead the people of Israel out of Egypt?"

2:22 *Gershom* sounds like a Hebrew term that means "a foreigner there." **2:25** Or *and acknowledged his obligation to help them.* **3:1a** Moses' father-in-law went by two names, Jethro and Reuel. **3:1b** Hebrew *Horeb,* another name for Sinai. **3:6** Greek version reads *your fathers.*

2:23-25 The Israelites finally hit bottom and admitted to themselves that they were powerless over their circumstances. They turned to God and begged him to deliver them from their slavery. But as we see, God's deliverance didn't come right away. They had to wait patiently for God to change their dismal situation. We need to see that we are helpless and give our situations over to God. But in doing so, we must recognize that we are also giving up control. We must be willing to let God do things his way and according to his timing.

3:10-11 Moses felt totally unqualified to fill the role God was commanding him to assume. He was well educated. Having grown up as the son of the princess, he knew the ways of the royal court of Egypt (2:10). He also had great leadership ability, which he would demonstrate for the

¹²God answered, "I will be with you. And this is your sign that I am the one who has sent you: When you have brought the people out of Egypt, you will worship God at this very mountain."

¹³But Moses protested, "If I go to the people of Israel and tell them, 'The God of your ancestors has sent me to you,' they will ask me, 'What is his name?' Then what should I tell them?"

¹⁴God replied to Moses, "I AM WHO I AM.* Say this to the people of Israel: I AM has sent me to you." ¹⁵God also said to Moses, "Say this to the people of Israel: Yahweh,* the God of your ancestors—the God of Abraham, the God of Isaac, and the God of Jacob—has sent me to you.

This is my eternal name,
my name to remember for all
generations.

¹⁶"Now go and call together all the elders of Israel. Tell them, 'Yahweh, the God of your ancestors—the God of Abraham, Isaac, and Jacob—has appeared to me. He told me, "I have been watching closely, and I see how the Egyptians are treating you. ¹⁷I have promised to rescue you from your oppression in Egypt. I will lead you to a land flowing with milk and honey—the land where the Canaanites, Hittites, Amorites, Perizzites, Hivites, and Jebusites now live."'

¹⁸"The elders of Israel will accept your message. Then you and the elders must go to the king of Egypt and tell him, 'The LORD, the God of the Hebrews, has met with us. So please let us take a three-day journey into the wilderness to offer sacrifices to the LORD, our God.'

¹⁹"But I know that the king of Egypt will not let you go unless a mighty hand forces him.* ²⁰So I will raise my hand and strike the Egyptians, performing all kinds of miracles among them. Then at last he will let you go. ²¹And I will cause the Egyptians to look favorably on you. They will give you gifts when you go so you will not leave empty-handed. ²²Every Israelite woman will ask for articles of silver and gold and fine clothing from her Egyptian neighbors and from the foreign women in their houses. You will dress your sons and daughters with these, stripping the Egyptians of their wealth."

CHAPTER 4
Signs of the LORD's Power

But Moses protested again, "What if they won't believe me or listen to me? What if they say, 'The LORD never appeared to you'?"

²Then the LORD asked him, "What is that in your hand?"

"A shepherd's staff," Moses replied.

³"Throw it down on the ground," the LORD told him. So Moses threw down the staff, and it turned into a snake! Moses jumped back.

⁴Then the LORD told him, "Reach out and grab its tail." So Moses reached out and grabbed it, and it turned back into a shepherd's staff in his hand.

⁵"Perform this sign," the LORD told him. "Then they will believe that the LORD, the God of their ancestors—the God of Abraham, the God of Isaac, and the God of Jacob—really has appeared to you."

⁶Then the LORD said to Moses, "Now put your hand inside your cloak." So Moses put his hand inside his cloak, and when he took it out again, his hand was white as snow with a severe skin disease.* ⁷"Now put your hand back into your cloak," the LORD said. So Moses put his hand back in, and when he took it out again, it was as healthy as the rest of his body.

⁸The LORD said to Moses, "If they do not

3:14 Or *I WILL BE WHAT I WILL BE.* **3:15** *Yahweh* (also in 3:16) is a transliteration of the proper name *YHWH* that is sometimes rendered "Jehovah"; in this translation it is usually rendered "the LORD" (note the use of small capitals). **3:19** As in Greek and Latin versions; Hebrew reads *will not let you go, not by a mighty hand.* **4:6** Or *with leprosy.* The Hebrew word used here can describe various skin diseases.

---

next 40 years. These qualities made him the best man for the job. But Moses was unable to see or accept this reality. He didn't have an accurate sense of who he was. Perhaps he saw himself as a fugitive murderer, worthy of no task greater than shepherding his father-in-law's livestock. Often our past mistakes blind us to our present gifts. We need to see ourself as God sees us and then respond accordingly.

3:16-22 God called Moses to speak to the elders of Israel regarding the new life awaiting them in the Promised Land (Genesis 15:18-21). Along with the hope of entering such wonderful new territory, however, was the reality of dealing with the king of Egypt. The promise was wonderful, but the difficulty of the process could not be underestimated. They had a powerful Egyptian king to confront; they had years of ingrained attitudes of domination to overcome. The process we may face in recovery may also be difficult. But no matter what the pain, it will be worth it if we reach the point of freedom and blessing.

believe you and are not convinced by the first miraculous sign, they will be convinced by the second sign. [9]And if they don't believe you or listen to you even after these two signs, then take some water from the Nile River and pour it out on the dry ground. When you do, the water from the Nile will turn to blood on the ground."

[10]But Moses pleaded with the LORD, "O Lord, I'm not very good with words. I never have been, and I'm not now, even though you have spoken to me. I get tongue-tied, and my words get tangled."

[11]Then the LORD asked Moses, "Who makes a person's mouth? Who decides whether people speak or do not speak, hear or do not hear, see or do not see? Is it not I, the LORD? [12]Now go! I will be with you as you speak, and I will instruct you in what to say."

[13]But Moses again pleaded, "Lord, please! Send anyone else."

[14]Then the LORD became angry with Moses. "All right," he said. "What about your brother, Aaron the Levite? I know he speaks well. And look! He is on his way to meet you now. He will be delighted to see you. [15] Talk to him, and put the words in his mouth. I will be with both of you as you speak, and I will instruct you both in what to do. [16]Aaron will be your spokesman to the people. He will be your mouthpiece, and you will stand in the place of God for him, telling him what to say. [17]And take your shepherd's staff with you, and use it to perform the miraculous signs I have shown you."

Moses Returns to Egypt

[18]So Moses went back home to Jethro, his father-in-law. "Please let me return to my relatives in Egypt," Moses said. "I don't even know if they are still alive."

"Go in peace," Jethro replied.

[19]Before Moses left Midian, the LORD said to him, "Return to Egypt, for all those who wanted to kill you have died."

[20]So Moses took his wife and sons, put them on a donkey, and headed back to the land of Egypt. In his hand he carried the staff of God.

[21]And the LORD told Moses, "When you arrive back in Egypt, go to Pharaoh and perform all the miracles I have empowered you to do. But I will harden his heart so he will refuse to let the people go. [22]Then you will tell him, 'This is what the LORD says: Israel is my firstborn son. [23]I commanded you, "Let my son go, so he can worship me." But since you have refused, I will now kill your firstborn son!'"

[24]On the way to Egypt, at a place where Moses and his family had stopped for the night, the LORD confronted him and was about to kill him. [25]But Moses' wife, Zipporah, took a flint knife and circumcised her son. She touched his feet* with the foreskin and said, "Now you are a bridegroom of blood to me." [26](When she said "a bridegroom of blood," she was referring to the circumcision.) After that, the LORD left him alone.

[27]Now the LORD had said to Aaron, "Go out into the wilderness to meet Moses." So Aaron went and met Moses at the mountain of God, and he embraced him. [28]Moses then told Aaron everything the LORD had commanded him to say. And he told him about the miraculous signs the LORD had commanded him to perform.

[29]Then Moses and Aaron returned to Egypt and called all the elders of Israel together. [30]Aaron told them everything the LORD had told Moses, and Moses performed the miraculous signs as they watched. [31]Then the people of Israel were convinced that the LORD had sent Moses and Aaron. When they heard that the LORD was concerned about them and had seen their misery, they bowed down and worshiped.

4:25 The Hebrew word for "feet" may refer here to the male sex organ.

4:10-12 Moses may have had a speech impediment, but that wasn't a legitimate excuse for not following God's plan. He didn't have an accurate perception of who he could become with God's help. While Moses was engaging in a kind of self-examination, he was doing so with a negative, fearful attitude. He was not yet at the point of letting God change him. Our weaknesses should never be an excuse for us to avoid recovery. With God's help, anything is possible. We need to realize that God can capitalize on our strengths, helping us reach our full potential.

4:18-28 Before Moses could take the mantle of Israel's leadership, there was an unresolved issue he needed to face. Moses had not circumcised his son, which was his responsibility under the covenant God had given to Abraham and his descendants (Genesis 17:9-14). So here God forced the issue so Moses could legitimately lead God's covenant people. We often need to deal with unresolved issues from the past before progressing with God's program for our life.

MOSES

A flaw in an old coin can sometimes enhance its value; a flaw in a gem will cause its value to significantly decrease. The flaws in Moses' life worked both ways. In light of his many flaws, Moses' greatness as a person and leader is truly remarkable. He struggled constantly with besetting weaknesses. His self-doubt plagued him and almost caused him to refuse God's initial call.

Moses often reacted impulsively to the situations around him without thinking or listening to God first. He killed an Egyptian slave driver to protect a Hebrew slave. He jumped in to referee a fight between two Hebrews. He even disobeyed a direct order from God at one point, striking a rock to obtain water when he had been commanded to speak to it and honor God. Moses was impulsive, and it often got him into trouble. Moses also had to learn to set personal boundaries, sharing his leadership role with the people under him. At one point he worked from dawn till dusk just solving the people's disputes.

But weaknesses are just one side of the coin; the other side is stamped with strengths. Moses' self-doubt and personal fears gave God a chance to show his power. God turned a fugitive shepherd into a great national leader. God called him into his very presence! God could never have used a proud, strong person in this way.

God also used Moses' impulsive tendencies for good. When Moses killed an Egyptian to protect a Hebrew slave, he fled to the wilderness on his own personal exodus from Egypt. But through this, God was preparing Moses to lead a nation out of that land. Moses' skill at reacting to crises undoubtedly strengthened him as the leader of a great traveling nation. He was decisive in dealing with conflicts; he knew how to get things done. The positive side of Moses' failure to set personal boundaries was his sacrificial leadership over many years.

Moses persevered through numerous ups and downs. He climbed to many mountaintop experiences—periods of faith and commitment to God that resulted in extraordinary spiritual growth. However, he also had times when his lack of patience and faith or his self-doubt caused him problems. Scripture and God himself claim Moses as one of the greatest people who ever lived. Despite Moses' emotional ups and downs and periods of self-doubt, God was able to use him to do great things. This should give all of us hope that God can also use us in amazing ways if we are yielded to him.

STRENGTHS AND ACCOMPLISHMENTS:
- He was one of the greatest leaders in the entire Old Testament.
- He was a man of great faith and courage in following God.
- He was an example of self-giving and humility.
- He was willing to accept wise counsel from God and others.

WEAKNESSES AND MISTAKES:
- He often acted impulsively without looking to God for advice.
- At times he became almost frozen with self-doubt.
- He displayed a lack of adequate personal boundaries.
- His failure to specifically follow God's command to bring forth water from a rock kept him out of the Promised Land.

LESSONS FROM HIS LIFE:
- The way to handle the ups and downs of life is to face them with faith in God and commitment to his plan.
- We don't have to be perfect to be greatly used by God; we can still be "in process."
- We need personal boundaries to avoid workaholism, depression, and burnout.

KEY VERSE:
"It was by faith that Moses left the land of Egypt, not fearing the king's anger. He kept right on going because he kept his eyes on the one who is invisible" (Hebrews 11:27).

Moses' story spans the books of Exodus, Leviticus, Numbers, and Deuteronomy. The name Moses, often associated with the law, is found throughout the rest of the Bible. Moses is also referred to at some length in Acts 7:20-40, 44 and Hebrews 11:23-29.

CHAPTER 5
Moses and Aaron Speak to Pharaoh
After this presentation to Israel's leaders, Moses and Aaron went and spoke to Pharaoh. They told him, "This is what the LORD, the God of Israel, says: Let my people go so they may hold a festival in my honor in the wilderness."

²"Is that so?" retorted Pharaoh. "And who is the LORD? Why should I listen to him and let Israel go? I don't know the LORD, and I will not let Israel go."

³But Aaron and Moses persisted. "The God of the Hebrews has met with us," they declared. "So let us take a three-day journey into the wilderness so we can offer sacrifices to the LORD our God. If we don't, he will kill us with a plague or with the sword."

⁴Pharaoh replied, "Moses and Aaron, why are you distracting the people from their tasks? Get back to work! ⁵Look, there are many of your people in the land, and you are stopping them from their work."

Making Bricks without Straw

⁶That same day Pharaoh sent this order to the Egyptian slave drivers and the Israelite foremen: ⁷"Do not supply any more straw for making bricks. Make the people get it themselves! ⁸But still require them to make the same number of bricks as before. Don't reduce the quota. They are lazy. That's why they are crying out, 'Let us go and offer sacrifices to our God.' ⁹Load them down with more work. Make them sweat! That will teach them to listen to lies!"

¹⁰So the slave drivers and foremen went out and told the people: "This is what Pharaoh says: I will not provide any more straw for you. ¹¹Go and get it yourselves. Find it wherever you can. But you must produce just as many bricks as before!" ¹²So the people scattered throughout the land of Egypt in search of stubble to use as straw.

¹³Meanwhile, the Egyptian slave drivers continued to push hard. "Meet your daily quota of bricks, just as you did when we provided you with straw!" they demanded. ¹⁴Then they whipped the Israelite foremen they had put in charge of the work crews.

"Why haven't you met your quotas either yesterday or today?" they demanded.

¹⁵So the Israelite foremen went to Pharaoh and pleaded with him. "Please don't treat your servants like this," they begged. ¹⁶"We are given no straw, but the slave drivers still demand, 'Make bricks!' We are being beaten, but it isn't our fault! Your own people are to blame!"

¹⁷But Pharaoh shouted, "You're just lazy! Lazy! That's why you're saying, 'Let us go and offer sacrifices to the LORD.' ¹⁸Now get back to work! No straw will be given to you, but you must still produce the full quota of bricks."

¹⁹The Israelite foremen could see that they were in serious trouble when they were told, "You must not reduce the number of bricks you make each day." ²⁰As they left Pharaoh's court, they confronted Moses and Aaron, who were waiting outside for them. ²¹The foremen said to them, "May the LORD judge and punish you for making us stink before Pharaoh and his officials. You have put a sword into their hands, an excuse to kill us!"

²²Then Moses went back to the LORD and protested, "Why have you brought all this trouble on your own people, Lord? Why did you send me? ²³Ever since I came to Pharaoh as your spokesman, he has been even more brutal to your people. And you have done nothing to rescue them!"

CHAPTER 6
Promises of Deliverance

Then the LORD told Moses, "Now you will see what I will do to Pharaoh. When he feels the force of my strong hand, he will let the people go. In fact, he will force them to leave his land!"

²And God said to Moses, "I am Yahweh— 'the LORD.'* ³I appeared to Abraham, to Isaac, and to Jacob as El-Shaddai—'God

6:2 *Yahweh* is a transliteration of the proper name *YHWH* that is sometimes rendered "Jehovah"; in this translation it is usually rendered "the LORD" (note the use of small capitals).

5:10-21 The Israelite foremen needed to understand how difficult the process toward their freedom would be. They were deeply discouraged by Pharaoh's additional demands because they had unrealistic hopes of an immediate and painless deliverance. They also became disillusioned about the leadership ability of Moses and Aaron. They needed wisdom to see their troubles with the long-range view in mind. These were only the first steps on the road to freedom. We need to be aware that the road to recovery is long and difficult. There are few, if any, immediate and painless cures. If we realize this, we will find the difficulties we face less discouraging.

5:22-23 Moses prayed to God with perplexed honesty. He faced a real problem. In following God's program for freeing Israel, the people encountered increased suffering. Moses, however, did not realize that God was preparing to force Pharaoh to let Israel go. God had not failed the test of trustworthiness. Gaining freedom is often a lengthy process. We need to recognize this as we seek recovery. If we do, we will be less likely to be discouraged by the obstacles we face along the way.

Almighty'*—but I did not reveal my name, Yahweh, to them. ⁴And I reaffirmed my covenant with them. Under its terms, I promised to give them the land of Canaan, where they were living as foreigners. ⁵You can be sure that I have heard the groans of the people of Israel, who are now slaves to the Egyptians. And I am well aware of my covenant with them.

⁶"Therefore, say to the people of Israel: 'I am the LORD. I will free you from your oppression and will rescue you from your slavery in Egypt. I will redeem you with a powerful arm and great acts of judgment. ⁷I will claim you as my own people, and I will be your God. Then you will know that I am the LORD your God who has freed you from your oppression in Egypt. ⁸I will bring you into the land I swore to give to Abraham, Isaac, and Jacob. I will give it to you as your very own possession. I am the LORD!'"

⁹So Moses told the people of Israel what the LORD had said, but they refused to listen anymore. They had become too discouraged by the brutality of their slavery.

¹⁰Then the LORD said to Moses, ¹¹"Go back to Pharaoh, the king of Egypt, and tell him to let the people of Israel leave his country."

¹²"But LORD!" Moses objected. "My own people won't listen to me anymore. How can I expect Pharaoh to listen? I'm such a clumsy speaker!*"

¹³But the LORD spoke to Moses and Aaron and gave them orders for the Israelites and for Pharaoh, the king of Egypt. The LORD commanded Moses and Aaron to lead the people of Israel out of Egypt.

The Ancestors of Moses and Aaron

¹⁴These are the ancestors of some of the clans of Israel:

The sons of Reuben, Israel's oldest son, were Hanoch, Pallu, Hezron, and Carmi.

Their descendants became the clans of Reuben.

¹⁵The sons of Simeon were Jemuel, Jamin, Ohad, Jakin, Zohar, and Shaul. (Shaul's mother was a Canaanite woman.) Their descendants became the clans of Simeon.

¹⁶These are the descendants of Levi, as listed in their family records: The sons of Levi were Gershon, Kohath, and Merari. (Levi lived to be 137 years old.)

¹⁷The descendants of Gershon included Libni and Shimei, each of whom became the ancestor of a clan.

¹⁸The descendants of Kohath included Amram, Izhar, Hebron, and Uzziel. (Kohath lived to be 133 years old.)

¹⁹The descendants of Merari included Mahli and Mushi.

These are the clans of the Levites, as listed in their family records.

²⁰Amram married his father's sister Jochebed, and she gave birth to his sons, Aaron and Moses. (Amram lived to be 137 years old.)

²¹The sons of Izhar were Korah, Nepheg, and Zicri.

²²The sons of Uzziel were Mishael, Elzaphan, and Sithri.

²³Aaron married Elisheba, the daughter of Amminadab and sister of Nahshon, and she gave birth to his sons, Nadab, Abihu, Eleazar, and Ithamar.

²⁴The sons of Korah were Assir, Elkanah, and Abiasaph. Their descendants became the clans of Korah.

²⁵Eleazar son of Aaron married one of the daughters of Putiel, and she gave birth to his son, Phinehas.

These are the ancestors of the Levite families, listed according to their clans.

²⁶The Aaron and Moses named in this list are the same ones to whom the LORD said,

6:3 *El-Shaddai,* which means "God Almighty," is the name for God used in Gen 17:1; 28:3; 35:11; 43:14; 48:3.
6:12 Hebrew *I have uncircumcised lips;* also in 6:30.

6:8-13 After suffering a number of setbacks, the Israelites were ready to give up. When we fail to realize how difficult the process toward freedom can be, it is all too easy to become discouraged and give up. At such times, patience and perseverance are absolutely essential. We also need to remember that difficulties and failures are often the back door to ultimate success.

6:14-27 To a great extent, Moses and Aaron were products of their family heritage, sketched briefly in the genealogy included here (6:14-25). Now they faced difficult opposition to their goal of freeing the Israelites. But out of their past came signs of hope, strengthening their courage to continue their quest for freedom. For example, God had promised Abraham and his descendants a land of their own, free from oppression. God's promises from the past gave Moses and Aaron the encouragement they needed to continue their fight for freedom. God's promises can do the same for us today.

"Lead the people of Israel out of the land of Egypt like an army." ²⁷It was Moses and Aaron who spoke to Pharaoh, the king of Egypt, about leading the people of Israel out of Egypt.

²⁸When the LORD spoke to Moses in the land of Egypt, ²⁹he said to him, "I am the LORD! Tell Pharaoh, the king of Egypt, everything I am telling you." ³⁰But Moses argued with the LORD, saying, "I can't do it! I'm such a clumsy speaker! Why should Pharaoh listen to me?"

CHAPTER 7
Aaron's Staff Becomes a Serpent
Then the LORD said to Moses, "Pay close attention to this. I will make you seem like God to Pharaoh, and your brother, Aaron, will be your prophet. ²Tell Aaron everything I command you, and Aaron must command Pharaoh to let the people of Israel leave his country. ³But I will make Pharaoh's heart stubborn so I can multiply my miraculous signs and wonders in the land of Egypt. ⁴Even then Pharaoh will refuse to listen to you. So I will bring down my fist on Egypt. Then I will rescue my forces—my people, the Israelites—from the land of Egypt with great acts of judgment. ⁵When I raise my powerful hand and bring out the Israelites, the Egyptians will know that I am the LORD."

⁶So Moses and Aaron did just as the LORD had commanded them. ⁷Moses was eighty years old, and Aaron was eighty-three when they made their demands to Pharaoh.

⁸Then the LORD said to Moses and Aaron, ⁹"Pharaoh will demand, 'Show me a miracle.' When he does this, say to Aaron, 'Take your staff and throw it down in front of Pharaoh, and it will become a serpent.*'"

¹⁰So Moses and Aaron went to Pharaoh and did what the LORD had commanded them. Aaron threw down his staff before Pharaoh and his officials, and it became a serpent! ¹¹Then Pharaoh called in his own wise men and sorcerers, and these Egyptian magicians did the same thing with their magic. ¹²They threw down their staffs, which also became serpents! But then Aaron's staff swallowed up their staffs. ¹³Pharaoh's heart, however, remained hard. He still refused to listen, just as the LORD had predicted.

A Plague of Blood
¹⁴Then the LORD said to Moses, "Pharaoh's heart is stubborn,* and he still refuses to let

7:9 Hebrew *tannin*, which elsewhere refers to a sea monster. Greek version translates it "dragon." 7:14 Hebrew *heavy*.

6:28-30 Once again we are reminded of God's insistence that Moses respond in faith, despite his fears and his perceived speech problem (6:30; see 4:10; 6:12). Throughout the process of the Exodus, God repeatedly challenged Moses' personal insecurities and his negative, self-defeating attitudes. Faith in a trustworthy God was the solution to this problem. We, too, need to trust God with our problems and insecurities; this is a key step in recovery.

7:1-5 Nowhere is the stubbornness of Pharaoh's heart sketched more vividly. Moses and Aaron were fully involved in the process of confronting this unyielding persecutor. At this point, their task of freeing the people must have seemed impossible. But God had assured them that their goal of freedom would be reached by his sovereign power. We may be battling with a powerful, unreasonable enemy, internally or externally. But when God desires something to happen, it will happen, no matter what the opposition.

7:7 Notice that Aaron is the older brother, but God called Moses to be the primary leader. This cut across the grain of cultural expectation. The firstborn was always considered the first in line for a position of power or influence. But God often chose unlikely people to accomplish his plans. Consider also Isaac, Jacob, Judah, Joseph, Gideon, and David. None of these was a firstborn son, but all were given a significant part to play in God's plan. God often does things that surprise us; he uses unlikely people. No matter what kinds of things we have done in the past, each of us has a special place in his plan.

7:8-13 When we decide to commit ourself to God, we can be assured of God's power within us, which is greater than any other. Here God shows his power to Pharaoh by turning Aaron's staff into a serpent. But in this case, as is often true in life, victory through God's power is not always immediate. Notice that Pharaoh's magicians also performed this same sign. But then the snake that had been Aaron's staff turned and devoured the others, showing that if we depend on God's power, we will find ultimate victory.

7:14–8:19 The first three plagues—blood (7:14-24), frogs (8:1-15), and gnats (8:16-19)—as intense as they were, did not turn Pharaoh from his cruel behavior. He still continued in his denial. At the height of the frog plague, he nearly relented, asking Moses and Aaron to pray to God on

the people go. [15]So go to Pharaoh in the morning as he goes down to the river. Stand on the bank of the Nile and meet him there. Be sure to take along the staff that turned into a snake. [16]Then announce to him, 'The LORD, the God of the Hebrews, has sent me to tell you, "Let my people go, so they can worship me in the wilderness." Until now, you have refused to listen to him. [17]So this is what the LORD says: "I will show you that I am the LORD." Look! I will strike the water of the Nile with this staff in my hand, and the river will turn to blood. [18]The fish in it will die, and the river will stink. The Egyptians will not be able to drink any water from the Nile.'"

[19]Then the LORD said to Moses: "Tell Aaron, 'Take your staff and raise your hand over the waters of Egypt—all its rivers, canals, ponds, and all the reservoirs. Turn all the water to blood. Everywhere in Egypt the water will turn to blood, even the water stored in wooden bowls and stone pots.'"

[20]So Moses and Aaron did just as the LORD commanded them. As Pharaoh and all of his officials watched, Aaron raised his staff and struck the water of the Nile. Suddenly, the whole river turned to blood! [21]The fish in the river died, and the water became so foul that the Egyptians couldn't drink it. There was blood everywhere throughout the land of Egypt. [22]But again the magicians of Egypt used their magic, and they, too, turned water into blood. So Pharaoh's heart remained hard. He refused to listen to Moses and Aaron, just as the LORD had predicted. [23]Pharaoh returned to his palace and put the whole thing out of his mind. [24]Then all the Egyptians dug along the riverbank to find drinking water, for they couldn't drink the water from the Nile.

[25]Seven days passed from the time the LORD struck the Nile.

CHAPTER 8
A Plague of Frogs

[1]*Then the LORD said to Moses, "Go back to Pharaoh and announce to him, 'This is what the LORD says: Let my people go, so they can worship me. [2]If you refuse to let them go, I will send a plague of frogs across your entire land. [3]The Nile River will swarm with frogs. They will come up out of the river and into your palace, even into your bedroom and onto your bed! They will enter the houses of your officials and your people. They will even jump into your ovens and your kneading bowls. [4]Frogs will jump on you, your people, and all your officials.'"

[5]*Then the LORD said to Moses, "Tell Aaron, 'Raise the staff in your hand over all the rivers, canals, and ponds of Egypt, and bring up frogs over all the land.'" [6]So Aaron raised his hand over the waters of Egypt, and frogs came up and covered the whole land! [7]But the magicians were able to do the same thing with their magic. They, too, caused frogs to come up on the land of Egypt.

[8]Then Pharaoh summoned Moses and Aaron and begged, "Plead with the LORD to take the frogs away from me and my people. I will let your people go, so they can offer sacrifices to the LORD."

[9]"You set the time!" Moses replied. "Tell me when you want me to pray for you, your officials, and your people. Then you and your houses will be rid of the frogs. They will remain only in the Nile River."

[10]"Do it tomorrow," Pharaoh said.

"All right," Moses replied, "it will be as you have said. Then you will know that there is no one like the LORD our God. [11]The frogs will leave you and your houses, your officials, and your people. They will remain only in the Nile River."

[12]So Moses and Aaron left Pharaoh's palace, and Moses cried out to the LORD about the frogs he had inflicted on Pharaoh. [13]And the LORD did just what Moses had predicted. The frogs in the houses, the courtyards, and the fields all died. [14]The Egyptians piled them into great heaps, and a terrible stench filled the land. [15]But when Pharaoh saw that relief had come, he became stubborn.* He refused to listen to Moses and Aaron, just as the LORD had predicted.

A Plague of Gnats

[16]So the LORD said to Moses, "Tell Aaron, 'Raise your staff and strike the ground. The

---

8:1 Verses 8:1-4 are numbered 7:26-29 in Hebrew text. 8:5 Verses 8:5-32 are numbered 8:1-28 in Hebrew text. 8:15 Hebrew *made his heart heavy;* also in 8:32.

---

his behalf (8:8-14). However, when things let up momentarily, he hardened his heart again (8:15). We must be careful to persevere to the end, not getting overconfident when things start to go well. We must realize our constant need for God even when things are going well, or we are doomed to failure in the long-term process toward freedom.

dust will turn into swarms of gnats throughout the land of Egypt.'" [17]So Moses and Aaron did just as the LORD had commanded them. When Aaron raised his hand and struck the ground with his staff, gnats infested the entire land, covering the Egyptians and their animals. All the dust in the land of Egypt turned into gnats. [18]Pharaoh's magicians tried to do the same thing with their secret arts, but this time they failed. And the gnats covered everyone, people and animals alike.

[19]"This is the finger of God!" the magicians exclaimed to Pharaoh. But Pharaoh's heart remained hard. He wouldn't listen to them, just as the LORD had predicted.

A Plague of Flies

[20]Then the LORD told Moses, "Get up early in the morning and stand in Pharaoh's way as he goes down to the river. Say to him, 'This is what the LORD says: Let my people go, so they can worship me. [21]If you refuse, then I will send swarms of flies on you, your officials, your people, and all the houses. The Egyptian homes will be filled with flies, and the ground will be covered with them. [22]But this time I will spare the region of Goshen, where my people live. No flies will be found there. Then you will know that I am the LORD and that I am present even in the heart of your land. [23]I will make a clear distinction between* my people and your people. This miraculous sign will happen tomorrow.'"

[24]And the LORD did just as he had said. A thick swarm of flies filled Pharaoh's palace and the houses of his officials. The whole land of Egypt was thrown into chaos by the flies.

[25]Pharaoh called for Moses and Aaron. "All right! Go ahead and offer sacrifices to your God," he said. "But do it here in this land."

[26]But Moses replied, "That wouldn't be right. The Egyptians detest the sacrifices that we offer to the LORD our God. Look, if we offer our sacrifices here where the Egyptians can see us, they will stone us. [27]We must take a three-day trip into the wilderness to offer sacrifices to the LORD our God, just as he has commanded us."

[28]"All right, go ahead," Pharaoh replied. "I will let you go into the wilderness to offer sacrifices to the LORD your God. But don't go too far away. Now hurry and pray for me."

[29]Moses answered, "As soon as I leave you, I will pray to the LORD, and tomorrow the swarms of flies will disappear from you and your officials and all your people. But I am warning you, Pharaoh, don't lie to us again and refuse to let the people go to sacrifice to the LORD."

[30]So Moses left Pharaoh's palace and pleaded with the LORD to remove all the flies. [31]And the LORD did as Moses asked and caused the swarms of flies to disappear from Pharaoh, his officials, and his people. Not a single fly remained. [32]But Pharaoh again became stubborn and refused to let the people go.

CHAPTER 9
A Plague against Livestock

"Go back to Pharaoh," the LORD commanded Moses. "Tell him, 'This is what the LORD, the God of the Hebrews, says: Let my people go, so they can worship me. [2]If you continue to hold them and refuse to let them go, [3]the hand of the LORD will strike all your livestock—your horses, donkeys, camels, cattle, sheep, and goats—with a deadly plague. [4]But the LORD will again make a distinction between the livestock of the Israelites and that of the Egyptians. Not a single one of Israel's animals will die! [5]The LORD has already set the time for the plague to begin. He has declared that he will strike the land tomorrow.'"

[6]And the LORD did just as he had said. The next morning all the livestock of the Egyptians died, but the Israelites didn't lose a single animal. [7]Pharaoh sent his officials to

8:23 As in Greek and Latin versions; Hebrew reads *I will set redemption between.*

8:20–9:12 The fourth, fifth, and sixth plagues—flies (8:20-32), death of Egyptian lifestock (9:1-7), and boils (9:8-12)—were similarly resisted by Pharaoh. However, during the detestable onslaught of flies, Pharaoh tried to bargain with Moses and God. He agreed to allow Israel to offer sacrifices to God, first in Egypt and then a short distance away in the wilderness. But Pharaoh made this concession on the grounds that Moses pray to God on his behalf to stop the plague (8:25-28). Moses did pray, but Pharaoh went back on his word, hardening his heart (8:29-32). Pharaoh failed on two counts. First, he tried to bargain with God to get what he wanted. God is more than willing to give us what is best for us, but we must accept his terms, not expect him to accept ours. Second, Pharaoh failed to keep his word with God. This could only lead to continued disaster.

investigate, and they discovered that the Israelites had not lost a single animal! But even so, Pharaoh's heart remained stubborn,* and he still refused to let the people go.

A Plague of Festering Boils

[8] Then the LORD said to Moses and Aaron, "Take handfuls of soot from a brick kiln, and have Moses toss it into the air while Pharaoh watches. [9] The ashes will spread like fine dust over the whole land of Egypt, causing festering boils to break out on people and animals throughout the land."

[10] So they took soot from a brick kiln and went and stood before Pharaoh. As Pharaoh watched, Moses threw the soot into the air, and boils broke out on people and animals alike. [11] Even the magicians were unable to stand before Moses, because the boils had broken out on them and all the Egyptians. [12] But the LORD hardened Pharaoh's heart, and just as the LORD had predicted to Moses, Pharaoh refused to listen.

A Plague of Hail

[13] Then the LORD said to Moses, "Get up early in the morning and stand before Pharaoh. Tell him, 'This is what the LORD, the God of the Hebrews, says: Let my people go, so they can worship me. [14] If you don't, I will send more plagues on you* and your officials and your people. Then you will know that there is no one like me in all the earth. [15] By now I could have lifted my hand and struck you and your people with a plague to wipe you off the face of the earth. [16] But I have spared you for a purpose—to show you my power* and to spread my fame throughout the earth. [17] But you still lord it over my people and refuse to let them go. [18] So tomorrow at this time I will send a hailstorm more devastating than any in all the history of Egypt. [19] Quick! Order your livestock and servants to come in from the fields to find shelter. Any person or animal left outside will die when the hail falls.'"

[20] Some of Pharaoh's officials were afraid because of what the LORD had said. They quickly brought their servants and livestock in from the fields. [21] But those who paid no attention to the word of the LORD left theirs out in the open.

[22] Then the LORD said to Moses, "Lift your hand toward the sky so hail may fall on the people, the livestock, and all the plants throughout the land of Egypt."

[23] So Moses lifted his staff toward the sky, and the LORD sent thunder and hail, and lightning flashed toward the earth. The LORD sent a tremendous hailstorm against all the land of Egypt. [24] Never in all the history of Egypt had there been a storm like that, with such devastating hail and continuous lightning. [25] It left all of Egypt in ruins. The hail struck down everything in the open field— people, animals, and plants alike. Even the trees were destroyed. [26] The only place without hail was the region of Goshen, where the people of Israel lived.

[27] Then Pharaoh quickly summoned Moses and Aaron. "This time I have sinned," he confessed. "The LORD is the righteous one, and my people and I are wrong. [28] Please beg the LORD to end this terrifying thunder and hail. We've had enough. I will let you go; you don't need to stay any longer."

[29] "All right," Moses replied. "As soon as I leave the city, I will lift my hands and pray to the LORD. Then the thunder and hail will stop, and you will know that the earth belongs to the LORD. [30] But I know that you and your officials still do not fear the LORD God."

[31] (All the flax and barley were ruined by the hail, because the barley had formed heads and the flax was budding. [32] But the wheat and the emmer wheat were spared, because they had not yet sprouted from the ground.)

[33] So Moses left Pharaoh's court and went out of the city. When he lifted his hands to the LORD, the thunder and hail stopped, and the downpour ceased. [34] But when Pharaoh saw that the rain, hail, and thunder had stopped, he and his officials sinned again,

9:7 Hebrew *heavy.* 9:14 Hebrew *on your heart.* 9:16 Greek version reads *to display my power in you;* compare Rom 9:17.

9:13-35 During the devastating plague of hail, Pharaoh went so far as to admit that "the LORD is the righteous one, and my people and I are wrong" (9:27). But after Moses prayed to God and the hail stopped, Pharaoh and the Egyptian officials again refused to do as they had promised. Pharaoh still was not willing to face the reality of God's sovereign power, even though he clearly had been convicted of his shortcomings. When we began the recovery process, we may have recognized that we were powerless in our circumstances. But as we saw improvement, some of us may have failed to take the second and third steps, giving our life over to God's helping power. If we refuse to depend wholeheartedly on God's power, we will surely continue to fail.

and Pharaoh again became stubborn.* ³⁵Because his heart was hard, Pharaoh refused to let the people leave, just as the LORD had predicted through Moses.

CHAPTER 10
A Plague of Locusts
Then the LORD said to Moses, "Return to Pharaoh and make your demands again. I have made him and his officials stubborn* so I can display my miraculous signs among them. ²I've also done it so you can tell your children and grandchildren about how I made a mockery of the Egyptians and about the signs I displayed among them—and so you will know that I am the LORD."

³So Moses and Aaron went to Pharaoh and said, "This is what the LORD, the God of the Hebrews, says: How long will you refuse to submit to me? Let my people go, so they can worship me. ⁴If you refuse, watch out! For tomorrow I will bring a swarm of locusts on your country. ⁵They will cover the land so that you won't be able to see the ground. They will devour what little is left of your crops after the hailstorm, including all the trees growing in the fields. ⁶They will overrun your palaces and the homes of your officials and all the houses in Egypt. Never in the history of Egypt have your ancestors seen a plague like this one!" And with that, Moses turned and left Pharaoh.

⁷Pharaoh's officials now came to Pharaoh and appealed to him. "How long will you let this man hold us hostage? Let the men go to worship the LORD their God! Don't you realize that Egypt lies in ruins?"

⁸So Moses and Aaron were brought back to Pharaoh. "All right," he told them, "go and worship the LORD your God. But who exactly will be going with you?"

⁹Moses replied, "We will all go—young and old, our sons and daughters, and our flocks and herds. We must all join together in celebrating a festival to the LORD."

¹⁰Pharaoh retorted, "The LORD will certainly need to be with you if I let you take your little ones! I can see through your evil plan. ¹¹Never! Only the men may go and worship the LORD, since that is what you requested." And Pharaoh threw them out of the palace.

¹²Then the LORD said to Moses, "Raise your hand over the land of Egypt to bring on the locusts. Let them cover the land and devour every plant that survived the hailstorm."

¹³So Moses raised his staff over Egypt, and the LORD caused an east wind to blow over the land all that day and through the night. When morning arrived, the east wind had brought the locusts. ¹⁴And the locusts swarmed over the whole land of Egypt, settling in dense swarms from one end of the country to the other. It was the worst locust plague in Egyptian history, and there has never been another one like it. ¹⁵For the locusts covered the whole country and darkened the land. They devoured every plant in the fields and all the fruit on the trees that had survived the hailstorm. Not a single leaf was left on the trees and plants throughout the land of Egypt.

¹⁶Pharaoh quickly summoned Moses and Aaron. "I have sinned against the LORD your God and against you," he confessed. ¹⁷"Forgive my sin, just this once, and plead with the LORD your God to take away this death from me."

¹⁸So Moses left Pharaoh's court and pleaded with the LORD. ¹⁹The LORD responded by shifting the wind, and the strong west wind blew the locusts into the Red Sea.* Not

9:34 Hebrew *made his heart heavy.* 10:1 Hebrew *have made his heart and his officials' hearts heavy.* 10:19 Hebrew *sea of reeds.*

10:2 Not only are the consequences of sin and dysfunctional qualities passed on from one generation to the next (see 20:5), so are positive patterns and a godly heritage (see 20:6). God's power over the Egyptians was to be celebrated by each successive generation of Israelites. The faith and spirit of God's people who experienced the Exodus would bolster the faith of their descendants, giving them the courage to conquer enemies in the future. God's powerful acts for his people can also give us hope as we face dependencies and problems that are too big for us. And remember, the victories we win with God's help will influence and strengthen our descendants far into the future.

10:1-20 During the plague of locusts, Pharaoh again attempted to bargain with God. He first consented to let only the men go out from Egypt to worship God (10:10-11), retaining the women and children as hostages. But the severity of the locust plague caused him to admit his sin and ask Moses to intercede before God (10:12-19). In the end, however, Pharaoh once again became stubborn (10:20), and he still refused to let them leave. His continued denial led him further and further away from obedience to God's will.

a single locust remained in all the land of Egypt. [20]But the LORD hardened Pharaoh's heart again, so he refused to let the people go.

A Plague of Darkness

[21]Then the LORD said to Moses, "Lift your hand toward heaven, and the land of Egypt will be covered with a darkness so thick you can feel it." [22]So Moses lifted his hand to the sky, and a deep darkness covered the entire land of Egypt for three days. [23]During all that time the people could not see each other, and no one moved. But there was light as usual where the people of Israel lived.

[24]Finally, Pharaoh called for Moses. "Go and worship the LORD," he said. "But leave your flocks and herds here. You may even take your little ones with you."

[25]"No," Moses said, "you must provide us with animals for sacrifices and burnt offerings to the LORD our God. [26]All our livestock must go with us, too; not a hoof can be left behind. We must choose our sacrifices for the LORD our God from among these animals. And we won't know how we are to worship the LORD until we get there."

[27]But the LORD hardened Pharaoh's heart once more, and he would not let them go. [28]"Get out of here!" Pharaoh shouted at Moses. "I'm warning you. Never come back to see me again! The day you see my face, you will die!"

[29]"Very well," Moses replied. "I will never see your face again."

CHAPTER 11
Death for Egypt's Firstborn

Then the LORD said to Moses, "I will strike Pharaoh and the land of Egypt with one more blow. After that, Pharaoh will let you leave this country. In fact, he will be so eager to get rid of you that he will force you all to leave. [2]Tell all the Israelite men and women to ask their Egyptian neighbors for articles of silver and gold." [3](Now the LORD had caused the Egyptians to look favorably on the people of Israel. And Moses was considered a very great man in the land of Egypt, respected by Pharaoh's officials and the Egyptian people alike.)

[4]Moses had announced to Pharaoh, "This is what the LORD says: At midnight tonight I will pass through the heart of Egypt. [5]All the firstborn sons will die in every family in Egypt, from the oldest son of Pharaoh, who sits on his throne, to the oldest son of his lowliest servant girl who grinds the flour. Even the firstborn of all the livestock will die. [6]Then a loud wail will rise throughout the land of Egypt, a wail like no one has heard before or will ever hear again. [7]But among the Israelites it will be so peaceful that not even a dog will bark. Then you will know that the LORD makes a distinction between the Egyptians and the Israelites. [8]All the officials of Egypt will run to me and fall to the ground before me. 'Please leave!' they will beg. 'Hurry! And take all your followers with you.' Only then will I go!" Then, burning with anger, Moses left Pharaoh.

[9]Now the LORD had told Moses earlier, "Pharaoh will not listen to you, but then I will do even more mighty miracles in the land of Egypt." [10]Moses and Aaron performed these miracles in Pharaoh's presence, but the LORD hardened Pharaoh's heart, and he wouldn't let the Israelites leave the country.

10:21-29 After three days of darkness, Pharaoh agreed to let all the Israelites leave Egypt to worship God, but he refused to let them take their livestock (10:24). While this was a further concession on Pharaoh's part, it still was far from wholehearted repentance. Moses' continued perseverance only incited Pharaoh to escalate the confrontation with dangerous threats (10:24-28). If we truly desire recovery, we must admit the reality of our problems and sins. If we cannot admit the problems we face, we can hardly ask God to help us with them.

11:1-3 People who are not directly involved in a dysfunctional or abusive relationship often evaluate things quite differently from those who are. While Pharaoh obviously hated and feared Moses and the Israelites, the majority of Egypt's leaders and populace did not share his feelings (11:2-3). A crucial step in accurately understanding the realities we face is to realize that not everyone has it in for us. Some will regard our progress toward recovery quite favorably; some will even cheer us on!

11:9-10 God gave Pharaoh numerous chances to soften his heart. The tough love God displayed in this progression of plagues eventually led the king to hit bottom emotionally (see 12:29-32). God often intervenes in our life in similar ways. When difficult times come, many of us become angry with God. It may be wise, however, to start listening. God may be giving us chances to find a new life. He will use the difficulties we face to show us our errors and lead us to correct our ways. Let's not, like Pharaoh, refuse God's intervention until it is too late. Let us learn God's hard lessons, realizing that he will help us through all the difficulties and pain.

CHAPTER 12
The First Passover

While the Israelites were still in the land of Egypt, the LORD gave the following instructions to Moses and Aaron: ²"From now on, this month will be the first month of the year for you. ³Announce to the whole community of Israel that on the tenth day of this month each family must choose a lamb or a young goat for a sacrifice, one animal for each household. ⁴If a family is too small to eat a whole animal, let them share with another family in the neighborhood. Divide the animal according to the size of each family and how much they can eat. ⁵The animal you select must be a one-year-old male, either a sheep or a goat, with no defects.

⁶"Take special care of this chosen animal until the evening of the fourteenth day of this first month. Then the whole assembly of the community of Israel must slaughter their lamb or young goat at twilight. ⁷They are to take some of the blood and smear it on the sides and top of the doorframes of the houses where they eat the animal. ⁸That same night they must roast the meat over a fire and eat it along with bitter salad greens and bread made without yeast. ⁹Do not eat any of the meat raw or boiled in water. The whole animal—including the head, legs, and internal organs—must be roasted over a fire. ¹⁰Do not leave any of it until the next morning. Burn whatever is not eaten before morning.

¹¹"These are your instructions for eating this meal: Be fully dressed,* wear your sandals, and carry your walking stick in hand. Eat the meal with urgency, for this is the LORD's Passover. ¹²On that night I will pass through the land of Egypt and strike down every firstborn son and firstborn male animal in the land of Egypt. I will execute judgment against all the gods of Egypt, for I am the LORD! ¹³But the blood on your doorposts will serve as a sign, marking the houses where you are staying. When I see the blood, I will pass over you. This plague of death will not touch you when I strike the land of Egypt.

¹⁴"This is a day to remember. Each year, from generation to generation, you must celebrate it as a special festival to the LORD. This is a law for all time. ¹⁵For seven days the bread you eat must be made without yeast. On the first day of the festival, remove every trace of yeast from your homes. Anyone who eats bread made with yeast during the seven days of the festival will be cut off from the community of Israel. ¹⁶On the first day of the festival and again on the seventh day, all the people must observe an official day for holy assembly. No work of any kind may be done on these days except in the preparation of food.

¹⁷"Celebrate this Festival of Unleavened Bread, for it will remind you that I brought your forces out of the land of Egypt on this very day. This festival will be a permanent law for you; celebrate this day from generation to generation. ¹⁸The bread you eat must be made without yeast from the evening of the fourteenth day of the first month until the evening of the twenty-first day of that month. ¹⁹During those seven days, there must be no trace of yeast in your homes. Anyone who eats anything made with yeast during this week will be cut off from the community of Israel. These regulations apply both to the foreigners living among you and to the native-born Israelites. ²⁰During those days you must not eat anything made with yeast. Wherever you live, eat only bread made without yeast."

²¹Then Moses called all the elders of Israel together and said to them, "Go, pick out a lamb or young goat for each of your families, and slaughter the Passover animal. ²²Drain the blood into a basin. Then take a bundle of hyssop branches and dip it into the blood. Brush the hyssop across the top and sides of the doorframes of your houses. And no one may go out through the door until morning. ²³For the LORD will pass through the land to strike down the Egyptians. But when he sees the blood on the top and sides of the doorframe, the LORD will pass over your home. He will not permit his death angel to enter your house and strike you down.

12:11 Hebrew *Bind up your loins.*

12:14-16 The Passover was to become an occasion of celebration for future generations of Israel. It would be a time to remember their deliverance from slavery. Part of building a new life involves replacing old unhealthy thoughts and actions with healthy new ones. This may include taking on new traditions that celebrate our recovery from past problems. These should emphasize the positive differences between our old dysfunctional existence and the healthy freedom we experience in our new life.

24"Remember, these instructions are a permanent law that you and your descendants must observe forever. 25When you enter the land the LORD has promised to give you, you will continue to observe this ceremony. 26Then your children will ask, 'What does this ceremony mean?' 27And you will reply, 'It is the Passover sacrifice to the LORD, for he passed over the houses of the Israelites in Egypt. And though he struck the Egyptians, he spared our families.' " When Moses had finished speaking, all the people bowed down to the ground and worshiped.

28So the people of Israel did just as the LORD had commanded through Moses and Aaron. 29And that night at midnight, the LORD struck down all the firstborn sons in the land of Egypt, from the firstborn son of Pharaoh, who sat on his throne, to the firstborn son of the prisoner in the dungeon. Even the firstborn of their livestock were killed. 30Pharaoh and all his officials and all the people of Egypt woke up during the night, and loud wailing was heard throughout the land of Egypt. There was not a single house where someone had not died.

Israel's Exodus from Egypt

31Pharaoh sent for Moses and Aaron during the night. "Get out!" he ordered. "Leave my people—and take the rest of the Israelites with you! Go and worship the LORD as you have requested. 32Take your flocks and herds, as you said, and be gone. Go, but bless me as you leave." 33All the Egyptians urged the people of Israel to get out of the land as quickly as possible, for they thought, "We will all die!"

34The Israelites took their bread dough before yeast was added. They wrapped their kneading boards in their cloaks and carried them on their shoulders. 35And the people of Israel did as Moses had instructed; they asked the Egyptians for clothing and articles of silver and gold. 36The LORD caused the Egyptians to look favorably on the Israelites, and they gave the Israelites whatever they asked for. So they stripped the Egyptians of their wealth!

37That night the people of Israel left Rameses and started for Succoth. There were about 600,000 men,* plus all the women and children. 38A rabble of non-Israelites went with them, along with great flocks and herds of livestock. 39For bread they baked flat cakes from the dough without yeast they had brought from Egypt. It was made without yeast because the people were driven out of Egypt in such a hurry that they had no time to prepare the bread or other food.

40The people of Israel had lived in Egypt* for 430 years. 41In fact, it was on the last day of the 430th year that all the LORD's forces left the land. 42On this night the LORD kept his promise to bring his people out of the land of Egypt. So this night belongs to him, and it must be commemorated every year by all the Israelites, from generation to generation.

Instructions for the Passover

43Then the LORD said to Moses and Aaron, "These are the instructions for the festival of Passover. No outsiders are allowed to eat the Passover meal. 44But any slave who has been purchased may eat it if he has been circumcised. 45Temporary residents and hired servants may not eat it. 46Each Passover lamb must be eaten in one house. Do not carry any of its meat outside, and do not break any of its bones. 47The whole community of Israel must celebrate this Passover festival.

48"If there are foreigners living among you who want to celebrate the LORD's Passover, let all their males be circumcised. Only then may they celebrate the Passover with you like any native-born Israelite. But no uncircumcised

12:37 Or *fighting men;* Hebrew reads *men on foot.* 12:40 Samaritan Pentateuch reads *in Canaan and Egypt;* Greek version reads *in Egypt and Canaan.*

12:24-27 Children are usually curious as to why their parents believe and do what they do. Children are quick to pick up on halfhearted or hypocritical actions. But they are also quick to learn when positive lessons and values are modeled and taught. The Israelites were to teach their children important lessons from the past, recalling God's great victories for their ancestors. This would then provide the groundwork for their faith in God, enabling them to step forward into life with a healthy confidence. We should remember that much of the present and future grows out of the past. Let us capitalize on the good things in the past to strengthen our prospects for the future.

12:28-51 After this final plague, the Israelites were not just allowed to leave; they were commanded to get out! In the pain and shock of his son's death, Pharaoh didn't attach any conditions to the Israelites' exodus. He only asked for Moses' blessing (12:32). God had worked out the timing and all the details necessary for the Exodus to take place. Similarly, the all-knowing and all-powerful God lays out the recovery process of those committed to his program.

male may ever eat the Passover meal. [49]This instruction applies to everyone, whether a native-born Israelite or a foreigner living among you."

[50]So all the people of Israel followed all the Lord's commands to Moses and Aaron. [51]On that very day the Lord brought the people of Israel out of the land of Egypt like an army.

CHAPTER 13
Dedication of the Firstborn
Then the Lord said to Moses, [2]"Dedicate to me every firstborn among the Israelites. The first offspring to be born, of both humans and animals, belongs to me."

[3]So Moses said to the people, "This is a day to remember forever—the day you left Egypt, the place of your slavery. Today the Lord has brought you out by the power of his mighty hand. (Remember, eat no food containing yeast.) [4]On this day in early spring, in the month of Abib,* you have been set free. [5]You must celebrate this event in this month each year after the Lord brings you into the land of the Canaanites, Hittites, Amorites, Hivites, and Jebusites. (He swore to your ancestors that he would give you this land—a land flowing with milk and honey.) [6]For seven days the bread you eat must be made without yeast. Then on the seventh day, celebrate a feast to the Lord. [7]Eat bread without yeast during those seven days. In fact, there must be no yeast bread or any yeast at all found within the borders of your land during this time.

[8]"On the seventh day you must explain to your children, 'I am celebrating what the Lord did for me when I left Egypt.' [9]This annual festival will be a visible sign to you, like a mark branded on your hand or your forehead. Let it remind you always to recite this teaching of the Lord: 'With a strong hand, the Lord rescued you from Egypt.'* [10]So observe the decree of this festival at the appointed time each year.

[11]"This is what you must do when the Lord fulfills the promise he swore to you and to your ancestors. When he gives you the land where the Canaanites now live, [12]you must present all firstborn sons and firstborn male animals to the Lord, for they belong to him. [13]A firstborn donkey may be bought back from the Lord by presenting a lamb or young goat in its place. But if you do not buy it back, you must break its neck. However, you must buy back every firstborn son.

[14]"And in the future, your children will ask you, 'What does all this mean?' Then you will tell them, 'With the power of his mighty hand, the Lord brought us out of Egypt, the place of our slavery. [15]Pharaoh stubbornly refused to let us go, so the Lord killed all the firstborn males throughout the land of Egypt, both people and animals. That is why I now sacrifice all the firstborn males to the Lord— except that the firstborn sons are always bought back.' [16]This ceremony will be like a mark branded on your hand or your forehead. It is a reminder that the power of the Lord's mighty hand brought us out of Egypt."

Israel's Wilderness Detour
[17]When Pharaoh finally let the people go, God did not lead them along the main road that runs through Philistine territory, even though that was the shortest route to the Promised Land. God said, "If the people are faced with a battle, they might change their

---

13:4 Hebrew *On this day in the month of Abib.* This first month of the ancient Hebrew lunar calendar usually occurs within the months of March and April. 13:9 Or *Let it remind you always to keep the instructions of the Lord on the tip of your tongue, because with a strong hand, the Lord rescued you from Egypt.*

13:1-2, 11-16 The consecration of the firstborn sons of Israel (see also 22:29-30) points to the important position of the firstborn in family dynamics. Since God had spared the lives of the firstborn sons of Israel during the Passover, in a very real sense they all belonged to him. As a result, the Israelites had to sacrifice a lamb to buy their firstborn sons back from God. All of our children should be viewed as being "on loan" from God. The public dedication of our children to God is a helpful tradition reminding us of this fact. When parents recognize this truth, they are well on the way toward raising children with healthy and accurate self-images.

13:17-18 Swinging southeast to the Red Sea was not the fastest route from Egypt to the Promised Land, but it was the route that God chose for the Israelites to follow. The shortest route between two points is not always the best. God's will often calls us to take the more scenic routes. Though longer and sometimes harder, these are often God's means of taking us through the next step in the recovery process. In the Israelites' case, they were given the opportunity to see God overcome a huge obstacle—the Red Sea. This gave them additional fuel for their faith, building their courage for the journey ahead. It also helped them avoid dangers in the land of the Philistines that they were not yet prepared to face.

minds and return to Egypt." [18]So God led them in a roundabout way through the wilderness toward the Red Sea.* Thus the Israelites left Egypt like an army ready for battle.*

[19]Moses took the bones of Joseph with him, for Joseph had made the sons of Israel swear to do this. He said, "God will certainly come to help you. When he does, you must take my bones with you from this place."

[20]The Israelites left Succoth and camped at Etham on the edge of the wilderness. [21]The LORD went ahead of them. He guided them during the day with a pillar of cloud, and he provided light at night with a pillar of fire. This allowed them to travel by day or by night. [22]And the LORD did not remove the pillar of cloud or pillar of fire from its place in front of the people.

CHAPTER 14

Then the LORD gave these instructions to Moses: [2]"Order the Israelites to turn back and camp by Pi-hahiroth between Migdol and the sea. Camp there along the shore, across from Baal-zephon. [3]Then Pharaoh will think, 'The Israelites are confused. They are trapped in the wilderness!' [4]And once again I will harden Pharaoh's heart, and he will chase after you.* I have planned this in order to display my glory through Pharaoh and his whole army. After this the Egyptians will know that I am the LORD!" So the Israelites camped there as they were told.

The Egyptians Pursue Israel

[5]When word reached the king of Egypt that the Israelites had fled, Pharaoh and his officials changed their minds. "What have we done, letting all those Israelite slaves get away?" they asked. [6]So Pharaoh harnessed his chariot and called up his troops. [7]He took with him 600 of Egypt's best chariots, along with the rest of the chariots of Egypt, each with its commander. [8]The LORD hardened the heart of Pharaoh, the king of Egypt, so he chased after the people of Israel, who had left with fists raised in defiance. [9]The Egyptians chased after them with all the forces in Pharaoh's army—all his horses and chariots, his charioteers, and his troops. The Egyptians caught up with the people of Israel as they were camped beside the shore near Pi-hahiroth, across from Baal-zephon.

[10]As Pharaoh approached, the people of Israel looked up and panicked when they saw the Egyptians overtaking them. They cried out to the LORD, [11]and they said to Moses, "Why did you bring us out here to die in the wilderness? Weren't there enough graves for us in Egypt? What have you done to us? Why did you make us leave Egypt? [12]Didn't we tell you this would happen while we were still in Egypt? We said, 'Leave us alone! Let us be slaves to the Egyptians. It's better to be a slave in Egypt than a corpse in the wilderness!'"

[13]But Moses told the people, "Don't be afraid. Just stand still and watch the LORD rescue you today. The Egyptians you see today will never be seen again. [14]The LORD himself will fight for you. Just stay calm."

Escape through the Red Sea

[15]Then the LORD said to Moses, "Why are you crying out to me? Tell the people to get moving! [16]Pick up your staff and raise your hand over the sea. Divide the water so the Israelites can walk through the middle of the sea on dry ground. [17]And I will harden the hearts of the Egyptians, and they will charge in after the Israelites. My great glory will be displayed through Pharaoh and his troops, his chariots, and his charioteers. [18]When my glory is

---

13:18a Hebrew *sea of reeds.* 13:18b Greek version reads *left Egypt in the fifth generation.* 14:4 Hebrew *after them.*

13:21-22 God guided his people out of slavery into a new life of freedom and responsibility by his visible presence in the pillar of cloud and pillar of fire. He led them to recover the promises he had given their ancestor, Abraham, centuries earlier. When we are committed to God, we, too, can count on his leading. He has sent his Holy Spirit to direct us (Galatians 5:18) and has promised to never fail us or forsake us (Hebrews 13:5).

14:1-9 The Israelites were between a rock and a hard place—the Red Sea on one side and the Egyptian army on the other. And though the Israelites had already seen God do great miracles in Egypt (7:1–12:51), it must have been hard for them to wait and see how God would save them from this ominous situation. Our situations may seem just as hopeless, but nothing is a hopeless dead end for God. He will always provide a door leading to the next step in his plan.

14:10-12 In all their fear the Israelites cried out to God for help. Their terrified complaints show that their faith in God was limited. But at least they took the right first steps—they admitted that they were powerless in the situation and then looked to God for help. They were honest about what they were feeling. As a result, their discouragement and fear were soon turned into amazement and rejoicing (14:21–15:21).

displayed through them, all Egypt will see my glory and know that I am the LORD!"

¹⁹Then the angel of God, who had been leading the people of Israel, moved to the rear of the camp. The pillar of cloud also moved from the front and stood behind them. ²⁰The cloud settled between the Egyptian and Israelite camps. As darkness fell, the cloud turned to fire, lighting up the night. But the Egyptians and Israelites did not approach each other all night.

²¹Then Moses raised his hand over the sea, and the LORD opened up a path through the water with a strong east wind. The wind blew all that night, turning the seabed into dry land. ²²So the people of Israel walked through the middle of the sea on dry ground, with walls of water on each side!

²³Then the Egyptians—all of Pharaoh's horses, chariots, and charioteers—chased them into the middle of the sea. ²⁴But just before dawn the LORD looked down on the Egyptian army from the pillar of fire and cloud, and he threw their forces into total confusion. ²⁵He twisted* their chariot wheels, making their chariots difficult to drive. "Let's get out of here—away from these Israelites!" the Egyptians shouted. "The LORD is fighting for them against Egypt!"

²⁶When all the Israelites had reached the other side, the LORD said to Moses, "Raise your hand over the sea again. Then the waters will rush back and cover the Egyptians and their chariots and charioteers." ²⁷So as the sun began to rise, Moses raised his hand over the sea, and the water rushed back into its usual place. The Egyptians tried to escape, but the LORD swept them into the sea. ²⁸Then the waters returned and covered all the chariots and charioteers—the entire army of Pharaoh. Of all the Egyptians who had chased the Israelites into the sea, not a single one survived.

²⁹But the people of Israel had walked through the middle of the sea on dry ground, as the water stood up like a wall on both sides. ³⁰That is how the LORD rescued Israel from the hand of the Egyptians that day. And the Israelites saw the bodies of the Egyptians washed up on the seashore. ³¹When the people of Isra-el saw the mighty power that the LORD had unleashed against the Egyptians, they were filled with awe before him. They put their faith in the LORD and in his servant Moses.

CHAPTER 15
A Song of Deliverance
Then Moses and the people of Israel sang this song to the LORD:

"I will sing to the LORD,
    for he has triumphed gloriously;
he has hurled both horse and rider
    into the sea.
²The LORD is my strength and my song;
    he has given me victory.
This is my God, and I will praise him—
    my father's God, and I will exalt him!
³The LORD is a warrior;
    Yahweh* is his name!
⁴Pharaoh's chariots and army
    he has hurled into the sea.
The finest of Pharaoh's officers
    are drowned in the Red Sea.*
⁵The deep waters gushed over them;
    they sank to the bottom like a stone.

⁶"Your right hand, O LORD,
    is glorious in power.
Your right hand, O LORD,
    smashes the enemy.
⁷In the greatness of your majesty,
    you overthrow those who rise against
      you.
You unleash your blazing fury;
    it consumes them like straw.
⁸At the blast of your breath,
    the waters piled up!
The surging waters stood straight like
    a wall;
    in the heart of the sea the deep waters
      became hard.

⁹"The enemy boasted, 'I will chase them
    and catch up with them.
I will plunder them
    and consume them.
I will flash my sword;
    my powerful hand will destroy them.'
¹⁰But you blew with your breath,
    and the sea covered them.

14:25 As in Greek version, Samaritan Pentateuch, and Syriac version; Hebrew reads *He removed.* 15:3 *Yahweh* is a transliteration of the proper name *YHWH* that is sometimes rendered "Jehovah"; in this translation it is usually rendered "the LORD" (note the use of small capitals). 15:4 Hebrew *sea of reeds;* also in 15:22.

15:1-21 Israel's escape through the Red Sea took a mighty miracle from God and an act of faith by the Israelites. Often the road to victory is not easy, but it is still worth it. There will be something to rejoice about in the end if we depend on God to help us through. When we have gained the victory, we need to stand up, sing, and rejoice, remembering God's miracles on our behalf.

They sank like lead
    in the mighty waters.

[11] "Who is like you among the gods,
    O LORD—
glorious in holiness,
    awesome in splendor,
    performing great wonders?
[12] You raised your right hand,
    and the earth swallowed our enemies.

[13] "With your unfailing love you lead
    the people you have redeemed.
In your might, you guide them
    to your sacred home.
[14] The peoples hear and tremble;
    anguish grips those who live in
      Philistia.
[15] The leaders of Edom are terrified;
    the nobles of Moab tremble.
All who live in Canaan melt away;
[16]   terror and dread fall upon them.
The power of your arm
    makes them lifeless as stone
until your people pass by, O LORD,
    until the people you purchased pass by.
[17] You will bring them in and plant them on
    your own mountain—
the place, O LORD, reserved for your
    own dwelling,
the sanctuary, O Lord, that your hands
    have established.
[18] The LORD will reign forever and ever!"

[19] When Pharaoh's horses, chariots, and charioteers rushed into the sea, the LORD brought the water crashing down on them. But the people of Israel had walked through the middle of the sea on dry ground!
[20] Then Miriam the prophet, Aaron's sister, took a tambourine and led all the women as they played their tambourines and danced. [21] And Miriam sang this song:

"Sing to the LORD,
    for he has triumphed gloriously;
he has hurled both horse and rider
    into the sea."

Bitter Water at Marah

[22] Then Moses led the people of Israel away from the Red Sea, and they moved out into the desert of Shur. They traveled in this desert for three days without finding any water. [23] When they came to the oasis of Marah, the water was too bitter to drink. So they called the place Marah (which means "bitter").

[24] Then the people complained and turned against Moses. "What are we going to drink?" they demanded. [25] So Moses cried out to the LORD for help, and the LORD showed him a piece of wood. Moses threw it into the water, and this made the water good to drink.

It was there at Marah that the LORD set before them the following decree as a standard to test their faithfulness to him. [26] He said, "If you will listen carefully to the voice of the LORD your God and do what is right in his sight, obeying his commands and keeping all his decrees, then I will not make you suffer any of the diseases I sent on the Egyptians; for I am the LORD who heals you."

[27] After leaving Marah, the Israelites traveled on to the oasis of Elim, where they found twelve springs and seventy palm trees. They camped there beside the water.

CHAPTER 16
Manna and Quail from Heaven

Then the whole community of Israel set out from Elim and journeyed into the wilderness of Sin,* between Elim and Mount Sinai. They arrived there on the fifteenth day of the second month, one month after leaving the land of Egypt.* [2] There, too, the whole

16:1a The geographical name *Sin* is related to *Sinai* and should not be confused with the English word *sin*.
16:1b The Exodus had occurred on the fifteenth day of the first month (see Num 33:3).

15:22-27 Those of us just beginning the recovery process often have short memories. We quickly forget the important victories that have brought us to our present state of freedom. We also may tend to fall back into reacting to crises as we did in the painful past. Despite God's recent victories on the Israelites' behalf, they still became desperate when their water ran out. And this happened only a few days after the miracle at the Red Sea! They were still unwilling or unable to exercise faith in God. Even so, God came through with an immediate, abundant provision for their need (see Ephesians 3:20).

16:1-36 Next to our need for water (15:22-27), our need for food is the most critical. Again, the Israelites failed to believe that God would meet their needs. They lacked faith in God's power and still didn't understand their privileges as God's people. But God faithfully provided for them anyway, and the people's faith was given further reason to grow. This example of God's gracious provision should encourage us to seek help during the wilderness periods of our own life.

community of Israel complained about Moses and Aaron.

³"If only the LORD had killed us back in Egypt," they moaned. "There we sat around pots filled with meat and ate all the bread we wanted. But now you have brought us into this wilderness to starve us all to death."

⁴Then the LORD said to Moses, "Look, I'm going to rain down food from heaven for you. Each day the people can go out and pick up as much food as they need for that day. I will test them in this to see whether or not they will follow my instructions. ⁵On the sixth day they will gather food, and when they prepare it, there will be twice as much as usual."

⁶So Moses and Aaron said to all the people of Israel, "By evening you will realize it was the LORD who brought you out of the land of Egypt. ⁷In the morning you will see the glory of the LORD, because he has heard your complaints, which are against him, not against us. What have we done that you should complain about us?" ⁸Then Moses added, "The LORD will give you meat to eat in the evening and bread to satisfy you in the morning, for he has heard all your complaints against him. What have we done? Yes, your complaints are against the LORD, not against us."

⁹Then Moses said to Aaron, "Announce this to the entire community of Israel: 'Present yourselves before the LORD, for he has heard your complaining.'" ¹⁰And as Aaron spoke to the whole community of Israel, they looked out toward the wilderness. There they could see the awesome glory of the LORD in the cloud.

¹¹Then the LORD said to Moses, ¹²"I have heard the Israelites' complaints. Now tell them, 'In the evening you will have meat to eat, and in the morning you will have all the bread you want. Then you will know that I am the LORD your God.'"

¹³That evening vast numbers of quail flew in and covered the camp. And the next morning the area around the camp was wet with dew. ¹⁴When the dew evaporated, a flaky substance as fine as frost blanketed the ground. ¹⁵The Israelites were puzzled when they saw it. "What is it?" they asked each other. They had no idea what it was.

And Moses told them, "It is the food the LORD has given you to eat. ¹⁶These are the LORD's instructions: Each household should gather as much as it needs. Pick up two quarts* for each person in your tent."

¹⁷So the people of Israel did as they were told. Some gathered a lot, some only a little. ¹⁸But when they measured it out,* everyone had just enough. Those who gathered a lot had nothing left over, and those who gathered only a little had enough. Each family had just what it needed.

¹⁹Then Moses told them, "Do not keep any of it until morning." ²⁰But some of them didn't listen and kept some of it until morning. But by then it was full of maggots and had a terrible smell. Moses was very angry with them.

²¹After this the people gathered the food morning by morning, each family according to its need. And as the sun became hot, the flakes they had not picked up melted and disappeared. ²²On the sixth day, they gathered twice as much as usual—four quarts* for each person instead of two. Then all the leaders of the community came and asked Moses for an explanation. ²³He told them, "This is what the LORD commanded: Tomorrow will be a day of complete rest, a holy Sabbath day set apart for the LORD. So bake or boil as much as you want today, and set aside what is left for tomorrow."

²⁴So they put some aside until morning, just as Moses had commanded. And in the morning the leftover food was wholesome and good, without maggots or odor. ²⁵Moses said, "Eat this food today, for today is a Sabbath day dedicated to the LORD. There will be no food on the ground today. ²⁶You may gather the food for six days, but the seventh day is the Sabbath. There will be no food on the ground that day."

²⁷Some of the people went out anyway on the seventh day, but they found no food. ²⁸The LORD asked Moses, "How long will these people refuse to obey my commands and instructions? ²⁹They must realize that the Sabbath is the LORD's gift to you. That is why he gives you a two-day supply on the sixth day, so there will be enough for two days. On the Sabbath day you must each stay in your place. Do not go out to pick up food on the seventh day." ³⁰So the people did not gather any food on the seventh day.

³¹The Israelites called the food manna.* It was white like coriander seed, and it tasted like honey wafers.

³²Then Moses said, "This is what the LORD

16:16 Hebrew *1 omer* [2.2 liters]; also in 16:32, 33. **16:18** Hebrew *measured it with an omer.* **16:22** Hebrew *2 omers* [4.4 liters]. **16:31** *Manna* means "What is it?" See 16:15.

has commanded: Fill a two-quart container with manna to preserve it for your descendants. Then later generations will be able to see the food I gave you in the wilderness when I set you free from Egypt."

[33]Moses said to Aaron, "Get a jar and fill it with two quarts of manna. Then put it in a sacred place before the LORD to preserve it for all future generations." [34]Aaron did just as the LORD had commanded Moses. He eventually placed it in the Ark of the Covenant—in front of the stone tablets inscribed with the terms of the covenant.* [35]So the people of Israel ate manna for forty years until they arrived at the land where they would settle. They ate manna until they came to the border of the land of Canaan.

[36]The container used to measure the manna was an omer, which was one-tenth of an ephah; it held about two quarts.*

CHAPTER 17
Water from the Rock
At the LORD's command, the whole community of Israel left the wilderness of Sin* and moved from place to place. Eventually they camped at Rephidim, but there was no water there for the people to drink. [2]So once more the people complained against Moses. "Give us water to drink!" they demanded.

"Quiet!" Moses replied. "Why are you complaining against me? And why are you testing the LORD?"

[3]But tormented by thirst, they continued to argue with Moses. "Why did you bring us out of Egypt? Are you trying to kill us, our children, and our livestock with thirst?"

[4]Then Moses cried out to the LORD, "What should I do with these people? They are ready to stone me!"

[5]The LORD said to Moses, "Walk out in front of the people. Take your staff, the one you used when you struck the water of the Nile, and call some of the elders of Israel to join you. [6]I will stand before you on the rock at Mount Sinai.* Strike the rock, and water will come gushing out. Then the people will be able to drink." So Moses struck the rock as he was told, and water gushed out as the elders looked on.

[7]Moses named the place Massah (which means "test") and Meribah (which means "arguing") because the people of Israel argued with Moses and tested the LORD by saying, "Is the LORD here with us or not?"

Israel Defeats the Amalekites
[8]While the people of Israel were still at Rephidim, the warriors of Amalek attacked them. [9]Moses commanded Joshua, "Choose some men to go out and fight the army of Amalek for us. Tomorrow, I will stand at the top of the hill, holding the staff of God in my hand."

[10]So Joshua did what Moses had commanded and fought the army of Amalek. Meanwhile, Moses, Aaron, and Hur climbed to the top of a nearby hill. [11]As long as Moses held up the staff in his hand, the Israelites had the advantage. But whenever he dropped his hand, the Amalekites gained the advantage. [12]Moses' arms soon became so tired he could no longer hold them up. So Aaron and Hur found a stone for him to sit on. Then they stood on each side of Moses, holding up his hands. So his hands held steady until sunset. [13]As a result, Joshua overwhelmed the army of Amalek in battle.

[14]After the victory, the LORD instructed Moses, "Write this down on a scroll as a permanent reminder, and read it aloud to Joshua: I will erase the memory of Amalek from under heaven." [15]Moses built an altar there and

---

16:34 Hebrew *He placed it in front of the Testimony;* see note on 25:16.   16:36 Hebrew *An omer is one-tenth of an ephah.*
17:1 The geographical name *Sin* is related to *Sinai* and should not be confused with the English word *sin.*
17:6 Hebrew *Horeb,* another name for Sinai.

17:1-7 As we begin the recovery process, we are often hindered repeatedly by the same old mistakes. We have certain weaknesses that haunt us time and again. The Israelites displayed this same tendency. They rebelled against Moses' leadership just because of a short-term lack of water (see 15:22-27). To make this place a monument to the people's lack of faith, Moses named it Massah (meaning "test") and Meribah (meaning "arguing"). By these names, the people would be reminded of their past mistakes, hopefully encouraging them to be wiser the next time. We need to be reminded of our past mistakes from time to time in order to avoid them in the future.
17:8-16 The people had just put God on trial, testing him and wondering whether he was with them (17:1-7). In response, God overwhelmed the Amalekite forces in battle. In so doing he employed an instructive visual aid. Moses stood upon a hill in full view of the people and the battlefield. When his hands were raised, the Israelite army prevailed. The raised hands did not speak of Moses' power but of God's empowering. Through such incidents, the Israelites learned that their freedom was dependent on their faith in God, not on their own strength.

named it Yahweh-Nissi (which means "the LORD is my banner"). [16]He said, "They have raised their fist against the LORD's throne, so now* the LORD will be at war with Amalek generation after generation."

CHAPTER 18
Jethro's Visit to Moses

Moses' father-in-law, Jethro, the priest of Midian, heard about everything God had done for Moses and his people, the Israelites. He heard especially about how the LORD had rescued them from Egypt.

[2]Earlier, Moses had sent his wife, Zipporah, and his two sons back to Jethro, who had taken them in. [3](Moses' first son was named Gershom,* for Moses had said when the boy was born, "I have been a foreigner in a foreign land." [4]His second son was named Eliezer,* for Moses had said, "The God of my ancestors was my helper; he rescued me from the sword of Pharaoh.") [5]Jethro, Moses' father-in-law, now came to visit Moses in the wilderness. He brought Moses' wife and two sons with him, and they arrived while Moses and the people were camped near the mountain of God. [6]Jethro had sent a message to Moses, saying, "I, Jethro, your father-in-law, am coming to see you with your wife and your two sons."

[7]So Moses went out to meet his father-in-law. He bowed low and kissed him. They asked about each other's welfare and then went into Moses' tent. [8]Moses told his father-in-law everything the LORD had done to Pharaoh and Egypt on behalf of Israel. He also told about all the hardships they had experienced along the way and how the LORD had rescued his people from all their troubles. [9]Jethro was delighted when he heard about all the good things the LORD had done for Israel as he rescued them from the hand of the Egyptians.

[10]"Praise the LORD," Jethro said, "for he has rescued you from the Egyptians and from Pharaoh. Yes, he has rescued Israel from the powerful hand of Egypt! [11]I know now that the LORD is greater than all other gods, because he rescued his people from the oppression of the proud Egyptians."

[12]Then Jethro, Moses' father-in-law, brought a burnt offering and sacrifices to God. Aaron and all the elders of Israel came out and joined him in a sacrificial meal in God's presence.

Jethro's Wise Advice

[13]The next day, Moses took his seat to hear the people's disputes against each other. They waited before him from morning till evening.

[14]When Moses' father-in-law saw all that Moses was doing for the people, he asked, "What are you really accomplishing here? Why are you trying to do all this alone while everyone stands around you from morning till evening?"

[15]Moses replied, "Because the people come to me to get a ruling from God. [16]When a dispute arises, they come to me, and I am the one who settles the case between the quarreling parties. I inform the people of God's decrees and give them his instructions."

[17]"This is not good!" Moses' father-in-law exclaimed. [18]"You're going to wear yourself out—and the people, too. This job is too heavy a burden for you to handle all by yourself. [19]Now listen to me, and let me give you a word of advice, and may God be with you. You should continue to be the people's representative before God, bringing their disputes to him. [20]Teach them God's decrees, and give them his instructions. Show them how to conduct their lives. [21]But select from all the people some capable, honest men who fear

---

17:16 Or *Hands have been lifted up to the LORD's throne, and now.* **18:3** *Gershom* sounds like a Hebrew term that means "a foreigner there." **18:4** *Eliezer* means "God is my helper."

18:1-12 Relationships between married children and their parents, especially in-laws, can often be difficult. It is crucial for married children to leave their parents (Genesis 2:24), physically and emotionally. This includes relating to our parents and in-laws on an adult level. It is also necessary to "honor" our parents (Exodus 20:12). The relationship between Moses and Jethro, characterized by honesty and mutual respect, is a good example for us to follow.

18:13-26 This episode reveals that Moses had a difficult time setting boundaries in his life. Jethro gave Moses some wise and creative advice, helping him to protect himself from the extensive demands of the people. But even this good advice did not solve this problem for Moses once and for all. His tendency to assume that God expected him to do everything (18:13-16) shows up later in a slightly different way (Numbers 11:10-17). There Moses appears near emotional burnout, just as Jethro had predicted (Exodus 18:17-18). We need to set appropriate boundaries in our own life, maximizing the use of the time and energy we have while also protecting ourself from burnout.

God and hate bribes. Appoint them as leaders over groups of one thousand, one hundred, fifty, and ten. ²²They should always be available to solve the people's common disputes, but have them bring the major cases to you. Let the leaders decide the smaller matters themselves. They will help you carry the load, making the task easier for you. ²³If you follow this advice, and if God commands you to do so, then you will be able to endure the pressures, and all these people will go home in peace."

²⁴Moses listened to his father-in-law's advice and followed his suggestions. ²⁵He chose capable men from all over Israel and appointed them as leaders over the people. He put them in charge of groups of one thousand, one hundred, fifty, and ten. ²⁶These men were always available to solve the people's common disputes. They brought the major cases to Moses, but they took care of the smaller matters themselves.

²⁷Soon after this, Moses said good-bye to his father-in-law, who returned to his own land.

CHAPTER 19
The LORD Reveals Himself at Sinai

Exactly two months after the Israelites left Egypt,* they arrived in the wilderness of Sinai. ²After breaking camp at Rephidim, they came to the wilderness of Sinai and set up camp there at the base of Mount Sinai.

³Then Moses climbed the mountain to appear before God. The LORD called to him from the mountain and said, "Give these instructions to the family of Jacob; announce it to the descendants of Israel: ⁴'You have seen what I did to the Egyptians. You know how I carried you on eagles' wings and brought you to myself. ⁵Now if you will obey me and keep my covenant, you will be my own special treasure from among all the peoples on earth; for all the earth belongs to me. ⁶And

you will be my kingdom of priests, my holy nation.' This is the message you must give to the people of Israel."

⁷So Moses returned from the mountain and called together the elders of the people and told them everything the LORD had commanded him. ⁸And all the people responded together, "We will do everything the LORD has commanded." So Moses brought the people's answer back to the LORD.

⁹Then the LORD said to Moses, "I will come to you in a thick cloud, Moses, so the people themselves can hear me when I speak with you. Then they will always trust you."

Moses told the LORD what the people had said. ¹⁰Then the LORD told Moses, "Go down and prepare the people for my arrival. Consecrate them today and tomorrow, and have them wash their clothing. ¹¹Be sure they are ready on the third day, for on that day the LORD will come down on Mount Sinai as all the people watch. ¹²Mark off a boundary all around the mountain. Warn the people, 'Be careful! Do not go up on the mountain or even touch its boundaries. Anyone who touches the mountain will certainly be put to death. ¹³No hand may touch the person or animal that crosses the boundary; instead, stone them or shoot them with arrows. They must be put to death.' However, when the ram's horn sounds a long blast, then the people may go up on the mountain.*"

¹⁴So Moses went down to the people. He consecrated them for worship, and they washed their clothes. ¹⁵He told them, "Get ready for the third day, and until then abstain from having sexual intercourse."

¹⁶On the morning of the third day, thunder roared and lightning flashed, and a dense cloud came down on the mountain. There was a long, loud blast from a ram's horn, and all the people trembled. ¹⁷Moses led them out from the camp to meet with God, and

19:1 Hebrew *In the third month after the Israelites left Egypt, on the very day*, i.e., two lunar months to the day after leaving Egypt. Compare Num 33:3. 19:13 Or *up to the mountain*.

19:2-6 Israel's new sense of identity and ability was to be founded upon its relationship with God. The Israelites had suffered under Egyptian bondage. Their sense of identity had been defined by that terrible experience. Now God had graciously delivered them and had brought them to himself. The people of Israel needed to see themselves as a kingdom of priests and a holy nation (19:6). They were no longer a nation of slaves. As we progress in recovery, we also need to see ourselves as people loved and blessed by God, not as slaves to our compulsions and dependencies.

19:7-8 When Moses returned from God's presence and asked for the people's response, they gave the right answer: "We will do everything the LORD has commanded" (19:8). But had they really counted the cost before giving their response (Luke 14:28)? It is difficult for people needing recovery to be completely honest with others, even with themselves. Their rapid-fire answer was probably motivated by a fearful desire to appease their terrifying God. It was not properly motivated by a wholehearted love for him.

they stood at the foot of the mountain. ¹⁸All of Mount Sinai was covered with smoke because the LORD had descended on it in the form of fire. The smoke billowed into the sky like smoke from a brick kiln, and the whole mountain shook violently. ¹⁹As the blast of the ram's horn grew louder and louder, Moses spoke, and God thundered his reply. ²⁰The LORD came down on the top of Mount Sinai and called Moses to the top of the mountain. So Moses climbed the mountain.

²¹Then the LORD told Moses, "Go back down and warn the people not to break through the boundaries to see the LORD, or they will die. ²²Even the priests who regularly come near to the LORD must purify themselves so that the LORD does not break out and destroy them."

²³"But LORD," Moses protested, "the people cannot come up to Mount Sinai. You already warned us. You told me, 'Mark off a boundary all around the mountain to set it apart as holy.'"

²⁴But the LORD said, "Go down and bring Aaron back up with you. In the meantime, do not let the priests or the people break through to approach the LORD, or he will break out and destroy them."

²⁵So Moses went down to the people and told them what the LORD had said.

CHAPTER 20
Ten Commandments for the Covenant Community

Then God gave the people all these instructions*:

²"I am the LORD your God, who rescued you from the land of Egypt, the place of your slavery.

³"You must not have any other god but me.

⁴"You must not make for yourself an idol of any kind or an image of anything in the heavens or on the earth or in the sea. ⁵You must not bow down to them or worship them, for I, the LORD your God, am a jealous God who will not tolerate your affection for any other gods. I lay the sins of the parents upon their children; the entire family is affected— even children in the third and fourth generations of those who reject me. ⁶But I lavish unfailing love for a thousand generations on those* who love me and obey my commands.

⁷"You must not misuse the name of the LORD your God. The LORD will not let you go unpunished if you misuse his name.

⁸"Remember to observe the Sabbath day by keeping it holy. ⁹You have six days each week for your ordinary work, ¹⁰but the seventh day is a Sabbath day of rest dedicated to the LORD your God. On that day no one in your household may do any work. This includes you, your sons and daughters, your male and female servants, your livestock, and any foreigners living among you. ¹¹For in six days the LORD made the heavens, the earth, the sea, and everything in them; but on the seventh day he rested. That is why the LORD blessed the Sabbath day and set it apart as holy.

¹²"Honor your father and mother. Then you will live a long, full life in the land the LORD your God is giving you.

¹³"You must not murder.

¹⁴"You must not commit adultery.

¹⁵"You must not steal.

20:1 Hebrew *all these words.*   20:6 Hebrew *for thousands of those.*

20:1-11 The first four of the Ten Commandments provided the Israelites with a few foundational principles to govern their relationship with God. They were not to worship any other gods (20:3), make idols of any kind (20:4-6), or misuse God's name (20:7). They were to remember to observe God's Sabbath day of rest (20:8-11). Each of these principles represents boundaries that God had set to define his relationship with his people. Jesus later summed up this vertical relationship as the greatest commandment: "You must love the Lord your God with all your heart, all your soul, and all your mind" (Matthew 22:37). Loving God includes living out a consistent faith and commitment to him.

20:12-17 The final six of the Ten Commandments deal with principles that define boundaries for healthy human relationships. Only the command to honor our parents (20:12; see also Ephesians 6:1-3) is stated positively. The other five are negative: Do not murder (20:13), commit adultery (20:14), steal (20:15), testify falsely against your neighbor (20:16), or covet anything belonging to your neighbor (20:17). Jesus summed up these human relational boundaries like this: "Love your neighbor as yourself" (Matthew 22:39). This great commandment assumes that we have cultivated a healthy self-respect and follow it up with loving actions that respect the boundaries of others.

¹⁶"You must not testify falsely against your neighbor.

¹⁷"You must not covet your neighbor's house. You must not covet your neighbor's wife, male or female servant, ox or donkey, or anything else that belongs to your neighbor."

¹⁸When the people heard the thunder and the loud blast of the ram's horn, and when they saw the flashes of lightning and the smoke billowing from the mountain, they stood at a distance, trembling with fear. ¹⁹And they said to Moses, "You speak to us, and we will listen. But don't let God speak directly to us, or we will die!"

²⁰"Don't be afraid," Moses answered them, "for God has come in this way to test you, and so that your fear of him will keep you from sinning!"

²¹As the people stood in the distance, Moses approached the dark cloud where God was.

Proper Use of Altars

²²And the LORD said to Moses, "Say this to the people of Israel: You saw for yourselves that I spoke to you from heaven. ²³Remember, you must not make any idols of silver or gold to rival me.

²⁴"Build for me an altar made of earth, and offer your sacrifices to me—your burnt offerings and peace offerings, your sheep and goats, and your cattle. Build my altar wherever I cause my name to be remembered, and I will come to you and bless you. ²⁵If you use stones to build my altar, use only natural, uncut stones. Do not shape the stones with a tool, for that would make the altar unfit for holy use. ²⁶And do not approach my altar by going up steps. If you do, someone might look up under your clothing and see your nakedness.

CHAPTER 21
Fair Treatment of Slaves

"These are the regulations you must present to Israel.

²"If you buy a Hebrew slave, he may serve for no more than six years. Set him free in the seventh year, and he will owe you nothing for his freedom. ³If he was single when he became your slave, he shall leave single. But if he was married before he became a slave, then his wife must be freed with him. ⁴"If his master gave him a wife while he was a slave and they had sons or daughters, then only the man will be free in the seventh year, but his wife and children will still belong to his master. ⁵But the slave may declare, 'I love

SELF PROTECTION

READ EXODUS 20:8-11

When we are in recovery we need to be especially careful to have all our faculties about us. If we allow ourself to get over-tired, we will be less able to cope with the demands of life. It will be harder for us to maintain sobriety, and we will be more susceptible to a relapse.

Rest is essential to the maintenance of any kind of balanced life. The Bible recognizes the importance of rest for people, for farmland, for animals, and for God himself. Weekly rest was even included as one of the Ten Commandments. God declared, "You have six days each week for your ordinary work, but the seventh day is a Sabbath day of rest dedicated to the LORD your God. On that day no one in your household may do any work. . . . For in six days the LORD made the heavens, the earth, the sea, and everything in them; but on the seventh day he rested. That is why the LORD blessed the Sabbath day and set it apart as holy" (Exodus 20:9-11). "The LORD then gave these instructions to Moses: 'Tell the people of Israel: "Be careful to keep my Sabbath day, for the Sabbath is a sign of the covenant between me and you from generation to generation. It is given so you may know that I am the LORD, who makes you holy"'" (Exodus 31:12-13).

God wants us to have the rest we need for a balanced life. As part of our recovery program we should include a weekly Sabbath or intermission. This should be a time to relax from our regular duties and allow our body to rest. It should also be a time of spiritual refreshment, a time to reflect on God's promises and remember that it is God who sustains us throughout the recovery process. *Turn to page 339, Ruth 2.*

my master, my wife, and my children. I don't want to go free.' ⁶If he does this, his master must present him before God.* Then his master must take him to the door or doorpost and publicly pierce his ear with an awl. After that, the slave will serve his master for life.

⁷"When a man sells his daughter as a slave, she will not be freed at the end of six years as the men are. ⁸If she does not satisfy her owner, he must allow her to be bought back again. But he is not allowed to sell her to foreigners, since he is the one who broke the contract with her. ⁹But if the slave's owner arranges for her to marry his son, he may no longer treat her as a slave but as a daughter.

¹⁰"If a man who has married a slave wife takes another wife for himself, he must not neglect the rights of the first wife to food, clothing, and sexual intimacy. ¹¹If he fails in any of these three obligations, she may leave as a free woman without making any payment.

Cases of Personal Injury

¹²"Anyone who assaults and kills another person must be put to death. ¹³But if it was simply an accident permitted by God, I will appoint a place of refuge where the slayer can run for safety. ¹⁴However, if someone deliberately kills another person, then the slayer must be dragged even from my altar and be put to death.

¹⁵"Anyone who strikes father or mother must be put to death.

¹⁶"Kidnappers must be put to death, whether they are caught in possession of their victims or have already sold them as slaves.

¹⁷"Anyone who dishonors* father or mother must be put to death.

¹⁸"Now suppose two men quarrel, and one hits the other with a stone or fist, and the injured person does not die but is confined to bed. ¹⁹If he is later able to walk outside again, even with a crutch, the assailant will not be punished but must compensate his victim for lost wages and provide for his full recovery.

²⁰"If a man beats his male or female slave with a club and the slave dies as a result, the owner must be punished. ²¹But if the slave recovers within a day or two, then the owner shall not be punished, since the slave is his property.

²²"Now suppose two men are fighting, and in the process they accidentally strike a pregnant woman so she gives birth prematurely.* If no further injury results, the man who struck the woman must pay the amount of compensation the woman's husband demands and the judges approve. ²³But if there is further injury, the punishment must match the injury: a life for a life, ²⁴an eye for an eye, a tooth for a tooth, a hand for a hand, a foot for a foot, ²⁵a burn for a burn, a wound for a wound, a bruise for a bruise.

²⁶"If a man hits his male or female slave in the eye and the eye is blinded, he must let the slave go free to compensate for the eye. ²⁷And if a man knocks out the tooth of his male or female slave, he must let the slave go free to compensate for the tooth.

²⁸"If an ox* gores a man or woman to death, the ox must be stoned, and its flesh may not be eaten. In such a case, however, the owner will not be held liable. ²⁹But suppose the ox had a reputation for goring, and the owner had been informed but failed to keep it under control. If the ox then kills someone, it must be stoned, and the owner must also be put to death. ³⁰However, the dead person's relatives may accept payment to compensate for the loss of life. The owner of the ox may redeem his life by paying whatever is demanded.

³¹"The same regulation applies if the ox gores a boy or a girl. ³²But if the ox gores a slave, either male or female, the animal's owner must pay the slave's owner thirty silver coins,* and the ox must be stoned.

³³"Suppose someone digs or uncovers a pit and fails to cover it, and then an ox or a donkey falls into it. ³⁴The owner of the pit must pay full compensation to the owner of the animal, but then he gets to keep the dead animal.

³⁵"If someone's ox injures a neighbor's ox

21:6 Or *before the judges.* 21:17 Greek version reads *Anyone who speaks disrespectfully of.* Compare Matt 15:4; Mark 7:10. 21:22 Or *so she has a miscarriage;* Hebrew reads *so her children come out.* 21:28 Or *bull,* or *cow;* also in 21:29-36. 21:32 Hebrew *30 shekels of silver,* about 12 ounces or 342 grams in weight.

21:12-27 These laws deal with the consequences of inappropriate, abusive behavior. Notice that compensation for wrong behavior is emphasized, making it clear that God holds us accountable for our actions. These laws reveal God's instructions for maintaining an orderly, healthy society when proper boundaries have been overstepped. They safeguard human relationships and personal identities while also recognizing the worth of life and property.
21:32 Thirty silver coins was likely the standard or average price for a slave in the ancient Near East. Yet as much as this may have been worth, it could not compare to the true value of a human

and the injured ox dies, then the two owners must sell the live ox and divide the price equally between them. They must also divide the dead animal. ³⁶But if the ox had a reputation for goring, yet its owner failed to keep it under control, he must pay full compensation—a live ox for the dead one—but he may keep the dead ox.

CHAPTER 22
Protection of Property

¹*"If someone steals an ox* or sheep and then kills or sells it, the thief must pay back five oxen for each ox stolen, and four sheep for each sheep stolen.

²*"If a thief is caught in the act of breaking into a house and is struck and killed in the process, the person who killed the thief is not guilty of murder. ³But if it happens in daylight, the one who killed the thief is guilty of murder.

"A thief who is caught must pay in full for everything he stole. If he cannot pay, he must be sold as a slave to pay for his theft. ⁴If someone steals an ox or a donkey or a sheep and it is found in the thief's possession, then the thief must pay double the value of the stolen animal.

⁵"If an animal is grazing in a field or vineyard and the owner lets it stray into someone else's field to graze, then the animal's owner must pay compensation from the best of his own grain or grapes.

⁶"If you are burning thornbushes and the fire gets out of control and spreads into another person's field, destroying the sheaves or the uncut grain or the whole crop, the one who started the fire must pay for the lost crop.

⁷"Suppose someone leaves money or goods with a neighbor for safekeeping, and they are stolen from the neighbor's house. If the thief is caught, the compensation is double the value of what was stolen. ⁸But if the thief is not caught, the neighbor must appear before God,* who will determine if he stole the property.

⁹"Suppose there is a dispute between two people who both claim to own a particular ox, donkey, sheep, article of clothing, or any lost property. Both parties must come before God, and the person whom God declares* guilty must pay double compensation to the other.

¹⁰"Now suppose someone leaves a donkey, ox, sheep, or any other animal with a neighbor for safekeeping, but it dies or is injured or is taken away, and no one sees what happened. ¹¹The neighbor must then take an oath in the presence of the LORD. If the LORD confirms that the neighbor did not steal the property, the owner must accept the verdict, and no payment will be required. ¹²But if the animal was indeed stolen, the guilty person must pay compensation to the owner. ¹³If it was torn to pieces by a wild animal, the remains of the carcass must be shown as evidence, and no compensation will be required.

¹⁴"If someone borrows an animal from a neighbor and it is injured or dies when the owner is absent, the person who borrowed it must pay full compensation. ¹⁵But if the owner was present, no compensation is required. And no compensation is required if the animal was rented, for this loss is covered by the rental fee.

Social Responsibility

¹⁶"If a man seduces a virgin who is not engaged to anyone and has sex with her, he

22:1a Verse 22:1 is numbered 21:37 in Hebrew text. 22:1b Or *bull, or cow;* also in 22:4, 9, 10. 22:2 Verses 22:2-31 are numbered 22:1-30 in Hebrew text. 22:8 Or *before the judges.* 22:9 Or *before the judges, and the person whom the judges declare.*

life created in God's image (Genesis 1:26-27). Oppressed people are often bound by a poor self-image. It would have been of interest to all slaves at that ancient time to learn that the Son of God would someday be betrayed for 30 pieces of silver (Matthew 26:15). He submitted to such humiliation so he could heal us from the life we lived in the past, breaking the bonds of our sins. He came to set us free, buying us back with his very life.

22:1-15 These regulations concerning restitution for property losses are related to the recovery issues of personal boundaries and accountability. We should be able to expect that our personal boundaries and property will be respected by others in society. We should also expect appropriate restitution when such boundaries are violated or our property destroyed. Accountability for actions that violate others is an important part of God's program for a healthy society.

22:16-28 There are certain behaviors that are brutally inhumane and therefore abominable to God and others. God has set clear boundaries in such cases and demands our accountability to them. The apostle Paul implied that such behavior, which is totally devoid of faith and commitment to God, not only brings self-destruction but also erodes the very fabric of society (Romans 1:18-32). Complete recovery demands that we refrain from irresponsible behavior and seek reconciliation with those we have wronged.

must pay the customary bride price and marry her. [17]But if her father refuses to let him marry her, the man must still pay him an amount equal to the bride price of a virgin.

[18]"You must not allow a sorceress to live.

[19]"Anyone who has sexual relations with an animal must certainly be put to death.

[20]"Anyone who sacrifices to any god other than the LORD must be destroyed.*

[21]"You must not mistreat or oppress foreigners in any way. Remember, you yourselves were once foreigners in the land of Egypt.

[22]"You must not exploit a widow or an orphan. [23]If you exploit them in any way and they cry out to me, then I will certainly hear their cry. [24]My anger will blaze against you, and I will kill you with the sword. Then your wives will be widows and your children fatherless.

[25]"If you lend money to any of my people who are in need, do not charge interest as a money lender would. [26]If you take your neighbor's cloak as security for a loan, you must return it before sunset. [27]This coat may be the only blanket your neighbor has. How can a person sleep without it? If you do not return it and your neighbor cries out to me for help, then I will hear, for I am merciful.

[28]"You must not dishonor God or curse any of your rulers.

[29]"You must not hold anything back when you give me offerings from your crops and your wine.

"You must give me your firstborn sons.

[30]"You must also give me the firstborn of your cattle, sheep, and goats. But leave the newborn animal with its mother for seven days; then give it to me on the eighth day.

[31]"You must be my holy people. Therefore, do not eat any animal that has been torn up and killed by wild animals. Throw it to the dogs.

CHAPTER 23
A Call for Justice

"You must not pass along false rumors. You must not cooperate with evil people by lying on the witness stand.

[2]"You must not follow the crowd in doing wrong. When you are called to testify in a dispute, do not be swayed by the crowd to twist justice. [3]And do not slant your testimony in favor of a person just because that person is poor.

[4]"If you come upon your enemy's ox or donkey that has strayed away, take it back to its owner. [5]If you see that the donkey of someone who hates you has collapsed under its load, do not walk by. Instead, stop and help.

[6]"In a lawsuit, you must not deny justice to the poor.

[7]"Be sure never to charge anyone falsely with evil. Never sentence an innocent or blameless person to death, for I never declare a guilty person to be innocent.

[8]"Take no bribes, for a bribe makes you ignore something that you clearly see. A bribe makes even a righteous person twist the truth.

[9]"You must not oppress foreigners. You know what it's like to be a foreigner, for you yourselves were once foreigners in the land of Egypt.

[10]"Plant and harvest your crops for six years, [11]but let the land be renewed and lie uncultivated during the seventh year. Then let the poor among you harvest whatever grows on its own. Leave the rest for wild animals to eat. The same applies to your vineyards and olive groves.

[12]"You have six days each week for your ordinary work, but on the seventh day you must stop working. This gives your ox and your donkey a chance to rest. It also allows your slaves and the foreigners living among you to be refreshed.

[13]"Pay close attention to all my instruc-

22:20 The Hebrew term used here refers to the complete consecration of things or people to the LORD, either by destroying them or by giving them as an offering.

23:1-8 This section is basically an expansion of 20:16, which prohibits false testimony. The truth will eventually be revealed (see 1 Timothy 5:24-25), so honesty is not only the right policy but also the smart one. Even if someone seems to be getting away with lies for a time, in the end that person will be held accountable and must still answer to God (Exodus 23:7).

23:10-19 God gave instructions concerning Sabbath regulations (see 20:8-11) and annual festivals for several reasons. First, these events were a time for worship, faith, and renewed commitment to God. Second, they were object lessons that pictured important spiritual truths for God's people. Third, they were times for rest; they protected God's people from overwork and imbalance. These events were designed to encourage the people's health—spiritually, emotionally, and physically. We also need regular times of worship, reflection, and rest.

tions. You must not call on the name of any other gods. Do not even speak their names.

Three Annual Festivals

[14]"Each year you must celebrate three festivals in my honor. [15]First, celebrate the Festival of Unleavened Bread. For seven days the bread you eat must be made without yeast, just as I commanded you. Celebrate this festival annually at the appointed time in early spring, in the month of Abib,* for that is the anniversary of your departure from Egypt. No one may appear before me without an offering.

[16]"Second, celebrate the Festival of Harvest,* when you bring me the first crops of your harvest.

"Finally, celebrate the Festival of the Final Harvest* at the end of the harvest season, when you have harvested all the crops from your fields. [17]At these three times each year, every man in Israel must appear before the Sovereign, the LORD.

[18]"You must not offer the blood of my sacrificial offerings together with any baked goods containing yeast. And do not leave the fat from the festival offerings until the next morning.

[19]"As you harvest your crops, bring the very best of the first harvest to the house of the LORD your God.

"You must not cook a young goat in its mother's milk.

A Promise of the LORD's Presence

[20]"See, I am sending an angel before you to protect you on your journey and lead you safely to the place I have prepared for you. [21]Pay close attention to him, and obey his instructions. Do not rebel against him, for he is my representative, and he will not forgive your rebellion. [22]But if you are careful to obey him, following all my instructions, then I will be an enemy to your enemies, and I will oppose those who oppose you. [23]For my angel will go before you and bring you into the land of the Amorites, Hittites, Perizzites, Canaanites, Hivites, and Jebusites, so you may live there. And I will destroy them completely.

23:15 Hebrew *appointed time in the month of Abib*. This first month of the ancient Hebrew lunar calendar usually occurs within the months of March and April.
23:16a Or *Festival of Weeks*. This was later called the Festival of Pentecost (see Acts 2:1). It is celebrated today as Shavuot (or Shabuoth). 23:16b Or *Festival of Ingathering*. This was later called the Festival of Shelters or Festival of Tabernacles (see Lev 23:33-36). It is celebrated today as Sukkot (or Succoth).

STEP 8

Making Restitution

BIBLE READING: Exodus 22:10-15

We made lists of all persons we had harmed and became willing to make amends to them all.

Dysfunctional family systems tend to affect people in a number of different ways. Some of us come to see ourselves as irresponsible and continually condemn ourselves. Others of us tend to admit that we are irresponsible but excuse ourselves because of all the things we have suffered. Still others of us may not even notice our irresponsible behaviors, but we have recurrent problems with other people because we fail to respect their property.

The Bible clearly states, "If someone borrows an animal from a neighbor and it is injured or dies when the owner is absent, the person who borrowed it must pay full compensation" (Exodus 22:14). David once wrote, "The wicked borrow and never repay, but the godly are generous givers" (Psalm 37:21).

The Bible tells us that it's important to take responsibility for the things we borrow. We may feel that we are being condemned as chronically evil if we have had a problem with irresponsibility. The word translated "the wicked" really means one who is morally wrong or a person who acts badly. God sees irresponsible behavior as bad action that can be corrected. He doesn't see us as hopelessly bad. Regardless of what we have been through, we are still held responsible to respect the property of others. We need to consider those we have harmed by being negligent or irresponsible with the use of their property. *Turn to page 139, Leviticus 4.*

tyndal.es/lrbstep8

²⁴You must not worship the gods of these nations or serve them in any way or imitate their evil practices. Instead, you must utterly destroy them and smash their sacred pillars.

²⁵ "You must serve only the LORD your God. If you do, I* will bless you with food and water, and I will protect you from illness. ²⁶There will be no miscarriages or infertility in your land, and I will give you long, full lives.

²⁷ "I will send my terror ahead of you and create panic among all the people whose lands you invade. I will make all your enemies turn and run. ²⁸I will send terror* ahead of you to drive out the Hivites, Canaanites, and Hittites. ²⁹But I will not drive them out in a single year, because the land would become desolate and the wild animals would multiply and threaten you. ³⁰I will drive them out a little at a time until your population has increased enough to take possession of the land. ³¹And I will fix your boundaries from the Red Sea to the Mediterranean Sea,* and from the eastern wilderness to the Euphrates River.* I will hand over to you the people now living in the land, and you will drive them out ahead of you.

³² "Make no treaties with them or their gods. ³³They must not live in your land, or they will cause you to sin against me. If you serve their gods, you will be caught in the trap of idolatry."

CHAPTER 24
Israel Accepts the LORD's Covenant

Then the LORD instructed Moses: "Come up here to me, and bring along Aaron, Nadab, Abihu, and seventy of Israel's elders. All of you must worship from a distance. ²Only Moses is allowed to come near to the LORD. The others must not come near, and none of the other people are allowed to climb up the mountain with him."

³Then Moses went down to the people and repeated all the instructions and regulations the LORD had given him. All the people answered with one voice, "We will do everything the LORD has commanded."

⁴Then Moses carefully wrote down all the LORD's instructions. Early the next morning Moses got up and built an altar at the foot of the mountain. He also set up twelve pillars, one for each of the twelve tribes of Israel. ⁵ Then he sent some of the young Israelite men to present burnt offerings and to sacrifice bulls as peace offerings to the LORD. ⁶Moses drained half the blood from these animals into basins. The other half he splattered against the altar.

⁷Then he took the Book of the Covenant and read it aloud to the people. Again they all responded, "We will do everything the LORD has commanded. We will obey."

⁸Then Moses took the blood from the basins and splattered it over the people, declaring, "Look, this blood confirms the covenant the LORD has made with you in giving you these instructions."

⁹ Then Moses, Aaron, Nadab, Abihu, and the seventy elders of Israel climbed up the mountain. ¹⁰There they saw the God of Israel. Under his feet there seemed to be a surface of brilliant blue lapis lazuli, as clear as

---

23:25 As in Greek and Latin versions; Hebrew reads *he.* 23:28 Often rendered *the hornet.* The meaning of the Hebrew is uncertain. 23:31a Hebrew *from the sea of reeds to the sea of the Philistines.* 23:31b Hebrew *from the wilderness to the river.*

23:32-33 The temptations of life within the Promised Land serve as a vivid illustration of how proper standards and boundaries can be tragically forgotten. The Israelites were warned about their tendency to make a good, clean start and then compromise their values and goals. They were warned not to make treaties with the people of the land. They were to push them right out, replacing them with communities of their own. In recovery it is easy to make a good start and then compromise, allowing certain "little" practices to go on unchecked. In the end, these things will spell disaster, eroding the new life we have started to build.

24:1-8 Although Israel's response to God's covenant was the same as before (see 19:8), they were now beginning to "count the cost" of their commitment to God. At this point they were called upon to make sacrifices to him. As they heard the cries of the animals being slaughtered and saw the sacrificial blood being splashed against the altar, surely they were reminded of how costly their redemption from Egypt had been. It was a clear reminder of God's gracious forgiveness, for God allowed these animals to die as payment for the people's infractions of the law. We should feel similar gratitude as we think of Jesus on the cross and realize that we are the ones who should have been there.

24:9-11 One of the best ways for us to see ourself as we actually are is to gain a clear view of God and his glory. The person who tends to glorify himself will quickly change his ways if he gets even a glimpse of God's awesome glory. On the other hand, the person who is self-deprecating needs

the sky itself. [11]And though these nobles of Israel gazed upon God, he did not destroy them. In fact, they ate a covenant meal, eating and drinking in his presence!

[12]Then the LORD said to Moses, "Come up to me on the mountain. Stay there, and I will give you the tablets of stone on which I have inscribed the instructions and commands so you can teach the people." [13]So Moses and his assistant Joshua set out, and Moses climbed up the mountain of God.

[14]Moses told the elders, "Stay here and wait for us until we come back. Aaron and Hur are here with you. If anyone has a dispute while I am gone, consult with them."

[15]Then Moses climbed up the mountain, and the cloud covered it. [16]And the glory of the LORD settled down on Mount Sinai, and the cloud covered it for six days. On the seventh day the LORD called to Moses from inside the cloud. [17]To the Israelites at the foot of the mountain, the glory of the LORD appeared at the summit like a consuming fire. [18]Then Moses disappeared into the cloud as he climbed higher up the mountain. He remained on the mountain forty days and forty nights.

CHAPTER 25
Offerings for the Tabernacle

The LORD said to Moses, [2]"Tell the people of Israel to bring me their sacred offerings. Accept the contributions from all whose hearts are moved to offer them. [3]Here is a list of sacred offerings you may accept from them:

gold, silver, and bronze;
[4] blue, purple, and scarlet thread;
fine linen and goat hair for cloth;
[5] tanned ram skins and fine goatskin leather;
acacia wood;

[6] olive oil for the lamps;
spices for the anointing oil and the fragrant incense;
[7] onyx stones, and other gemstones to be set in the ephod and the priest's chestpiece.

[8]"Have the people of Israel build me a holy sanctuary so I can live among them. [9]You must build this Tabernacle and its furnishings exactly according to the pattern I will show you.

Plans for the Ark of the Covenant

[10]"Have the people make an Ark of acacia wood—a sacred chest 45 inches long, 27 inches wide, and 27 inches high.* [11]Overlay it inside and outside with pure gold, and run a molding of gold all around it. [12]Cast four gold rings and attach them to its four feet, two rings on each side. [13]Make poles from acacia wood, and overlay them with gold. [14]Insert the poles into the rings at the sides of the Ark to carry it. [15]These carrying poles must stay inside the rings; never remove them. [16]When the Ark is finished, place inside it the stone tablets inscribed with the terms of the covenant,* which I will give to you.

[17]"Then make the Ark's cover—the place of atonement—from pure gold. It must be 45 inches long and 27 inches wide.* [18]Then make two cherubim from hammered gold, and place them on the two ends of the atonement cover. [19]Mold the cherubim on each end of the atonement cover, making it all of one piece of gold. [20]The cherubim will face each other and look down on the atonement cover. With their wings spread above it, they will protect it. [21]Place inside the Ark the stone tablets inscribed with the terms of the covenant, which I will give to you. Then put the atonement cover on top of the Ark.

25:10 Hebrew *2.5 cubits* [115 centimeters] *long, 1.5 cubits* [69 centimeters] *wide, and 1.5 cubits high.* **25:16** Hebrew *Place inside the Ark the Testimony;* similarly in 25:21. The Hebrew word for "testimony" refers to the terms of the LORD's covenant with Israel as written on stone tablets, and also to the covenant itself. **25:17** Hebrew *2.5 cubits* [115 centimeters] *long and 1.5 cubits* [69 centimeters] *wide.*

---

to understand that he is made in God's image (Genesis 1:26-27) and that he is destined to be in God's glorious presence forever (Revelation 21–22). One glimpse of God in his glory will heal both our pride and our self-deprecation, giving us a healthy and balanced self-assessment.

25:8-9 When Adam and Eve sinned in the garden, they created a terrible rift in the relationship between God and the human race. But God has spent the centuries since then reaching out to us, seeking to heal that relationship. God's declaration that he would dwell among the Israelites in a Tabernacle was a step in this process of reconciliation. God wanted to live among his people. The details of the pattern he laid out also show that God sets clear boundaries within which he relates to his people. Later, when Jesus Christ became a man, God's personal presence among the human race represented an even more personal relationship with us (John 1:14). God is in the business of reconciliation.

²²I will meet with you there and talk to you from above the atonement cover between the gold cherubim that hover over the Ark of the Covenant.* From there I will give you my commands for the people of Israel.

Plans for the Table

²³"Then make a table of acacia wood, 36 inches long, 18 inches wide, and 27 inches high.* ²⁴Overlay it with pure gold and run a gold molding around the edge. ²⁵Decorate it with a 3-inch border* all around, and run a gold molding along the border. ²⁶Make four gold rings for the table and attach them at the four corners next to the four legs. ²⁷Attach the rings near the border to hold the poles that are used to carry the table. ²⁸Make these poles from acacia wood, and overlay them with gold. ²⁹Make special containers of pure gold for the table—bowls, ladles, pitchers, and jars—to be used in pouring out liquid offerings. ³⁰Place the Bread of the Presence on the table to remain before me at all times.

Plans for the Lampstand

³¹"Make a lampstand of pure, hammered gold. Make the entire lampstand and its decorations of one piece—the base, center stem, lamp cups, buds, and petals. ³²Make it with six branches going out from the center stem, three on each side. ³³Each of the six branches will have three lamp cups shaped like almond blossoms, complete with buds and petals. ³⁴Craft the center stem of the lampstand with four lamp cups shaped like almond blossoms, complete with buds and petals. ³⁵There will also be an almond bud beneath each pair of branches where the six branches extend from the center stem. ³⁶The almond buds and branches must all be of one piece with the center stem, and they must be hammered from pure gold. ³⁷Then make the seven lamps for the lampstand, and set them so they reflect their light forward. ³⁸The lamp snuffers and trays must also be made of pure gold. ³⁹You will need seventy-five pounds* of pure gold for the lampstand and its accessories.

⁴⁰"Be sure that you make everything according to the pattern I have shown you here on the mountain.

CHAPTER 26

Plans for the Tabernacle

"Make the Tabernacle from ten curtains of finely woven linen. Decorate the curtains with blue, purple, and scarlet thread and with skillfully embroidered cherubim. ²These ten curtains must all be exactly the same size—42 feet long and 6 feet wide.* ³Join five of these curtains together to make one long curtain, then join the other five into a second long curtain. ⁴Put loops of blue yarn along the edge of the last curtain in each set. ⁵The fifty loops along the edge of one curtain are to match the fifty loops along the edge of the other curtain. ⁶Then make fifty gold clasps and fasten the long curtains together with the clasps. In this way, the Tabernacle will be made of one continuous piece.

⁷"Make eleven curtains of goat-hair cloth to serve as a tent covering for the Tabernacle. ⁸These eleven curtains must all be exactly the same size—45 feet long and 6 feet wide.* ⁹Join five of these curtains together to make one long curtain, and join the other six into a second long curtain. Allow 3 feet of material from the second set of curtains to hang over the front* of the sacred tent. ¹⁰Make fifty loops for one edge of each large curtain. ¹¹Then make fifty bronze clasps, and fasten the loops of the long curtains with the clasps. In this way, the tent covering will be made of one continuous piece. ¹²The remaining 3 feet* of this tent covering will be left to hang over the back of the Tabernacle. ¹³Allow 18 inches* of remaining material to hang down over each side, so the Tabernacle is completely covered. ¹⁴Complete the tent covering with a protective layer of tanned ram skins and a layer of fine goatskin leather.

¹⁵"For the framework of the Tabernacle, construct frames of acacia wood. ¹⁶Each frame must be 15 feet high and 27 inches wide,* ¹⁷with two pegs under each frame. Make all the frames identical. ¹⁸Make twenty of these frames to support the curtains on the south side of the Tabernacle. ¹⁹Also make forty silver bases—two bases under each frame, with the pegs fitting securely into the bases. ²⁰For the north side of the Tabernacle, make another twenty frames, ²¹with their forty silver bases, two bases under each frame. ²²Make six frames for the rear—the

25:22 Or Ark of the Testimony. 25:23 Hebrew 2 cubits [92 centimeters] long, 1 cubit [46 centimeters] wide, and 1.5 cubits [69 centimeters] high. 25:25 Hebrew a border of a handbreadth [8 centimeters]. 25:39 Hebrew 1 talent [34 kilograms]. 26:2 Hebrew 28 cubits [12.9 meters] long and 4 cubits [1.8 meters] wide. 26:8 Hebrew 30 cubits [13.8 meters] long and 4 cubits [1.8 meters] wide. 26:9 Hebrew Double over the sixth sheet at the front. 26:12 Hebrew The half sheet that is left over. 26:13 Hebrew 1 cubit [46 centimeters]. 26:16 Hebrew 10 cubits [4.6 meters] high and 1.5 cubits [69 centimeters] wide.

west side of the Tabernacle—²³along with two additional frames to reinforce the rear corners of the Tabernacle. ²⁴These corner frames will be matched at the bottom and firmly attached at the top with a single ring, forming a single corner unit. Make both of these corner units the same way. ²⁵So there will be eight frames at the rear of the Tabernacle, set in sixteen silver bases— two bases under each frame.

²⁶"Make crossbars of acacia wood to link the frames, five crossbars for the north side of the Tabernacle ²⁷and five for the south side. Also make five crossbars for the rear of the Tabernacle, which will face west. ²⁸The middle crossbar, attached halfway up the frames, will run all the way from one end of the Tabernacle to the other. ²⁹Overlay the frames with gold, and make gold rings to hold the crossbars. Overlay the crossbars with gold as well.

³⁰"Set up this Tabernacle according to the pattern you were shown on the mountain.

³¹"For the inside of the Tabernacle, make a special curtain of finely woven linen. Decorate it with blue, purple, and scarlet thread and with skillfully embroidered cherubim. ³²Hang this curtain on gold hooks attached to four posts of acacia wood. Overlay the posts with gold, and set them in four silver bases. ³³Hang the inner curtain from clasps, and put the Ark of the Covenant* in the room behind it. This curtain will separate the Holy Place from the Most Holy Place.

³⁴"Then put the Ark's cover—the place of atonement—on top of the Ark of the Covenant inside the Most Holy Place. ³⁵Place the table outside the inner curtain on the north side of the Tabernacle, and place the lampstand across the room on the south side.

³⁶"Make another curtain for the entrance to the sacred tent. Make it of finely woven linen and embroider it with exquisite designs, using blue, purple, and scarlet thread. ³⁷Craft five posts from acacia wood. Overlay them with gold, and hang the curtain from them with gold hooks. Cast five bronze bases for the posts.

CHAPTER 27
Plans for the Altar of Burnt Offering

"Using acacia wood, construct a square altar 7½ feet wide, 7½ feet long, and 4½ feet high.* ²Make horns for each of its four corners so that the horns and altar are all one piece. Overlay the altar with bronze. ³Make ash buckets, shovels, basins, meat forks, and firepans, all of bronze. ⁴Make a bronze grating for it, and attach four bronze rings at its four corners. ⁵Install the grating halfway down the side of the altar, under the ledge. ⁶For carrying the altar, make poles from acacia wood, and overlay them with bronze. ⁷Insert the poles through the rings on the two sides of the altar. ⁸The altar must be hollow, made from planks. Build it just as you were shown on the mountain.

Plans for the Courtyard

⁹"Then make the courtyard for the Tabernacle, enclosed with curtains made of finely woven linen. On the south side, make the curtains 150 feet long.* ¹⁰They will be held up by twenty posts set securely in twenty bronze bases. Hang the curtains with silver hooks and rings. ¹¹Make the curtains the same on the north side—150 feet of curtains held up by twenty posts set securely in bronze bases. Hang the curtains with silver hooks and rings. ¹²The curtains on the west end of the courtyard will be 75 feet long,* supported by ten posts set into ten bases. ¹³The east end of the courtyard, the front, will also be 75 feet long. ¹⁴The courtyard entrance will be on the east end, flanked by two curtains. The curtain on the right side will be 22½ feet long,* supported by three posts set into three bases. ¹⁵The curtain on the left side will also be 22½ feet long, supported by three posts set into three bases.

¹⁶"For the entrance to the courtyard, make a curtain that is 30 feet long.* Make it from finely woven linen, and decorate it with beautiful embroidery in blue, purple, and scarlet thread. Support it with four posts, each securely set in its own base. ¹⁷All the posts around the courtyard must have silver rings and hooks and bronze bases. ¹⁸So the entire courtyard will be 150 feet long and 75 feet wide, with curtain walls 7½ feet high,* made from finely woven linen. The bases for the posts will be made of bronze.

¹⁹"All the articles used in the rituals of the Tabernacle, including all the tent pegs used to support the Tabernacle and the courtyard curtains, must be made of bronze.

26:33 Or *Ark of the Testimony;* also in 26:34. 27:1 Hebrew *5 cubits* [2.3 meters] *wide, 5 cubits long, a square, and 3 cubits* [1.4 meters] *high.* 27:9 Hebrew *100 cubits* [46 meters]; also in 27:11. 27:12 Hebrew *50 cubits* [23 meters]; also in 27:13. 27:14 Hebrew *15 cubits* [6.9 meters]; also in 27:15. 27:16 Hebrew *20 cubits* [9.2 meters]. 27:18 Hebrew *100 cubits* [46 meters] *long and 50 by 50* [23 meters] *wide and 5 cubits* [2.3 meters] *high.*

Light for the Tabernacle

20 "Command the people of Israel to bring you pure oil of pressed olives for the light, to keep the lamps burning continually. 21The lampstand will stand in the Tabernacle, in front of the inner curtain that shields the Ark of the Covenant.* Aaron and his sons must keep the lamps burning in the LORD's presence all night. This is a permanent law for the people of Israel, and it must be observed from generation to generation.

CHAPTER 28
Clothing for the Priests

"Call for your brother, Aaron, and his sons, Nadab, Abihu, Eleazar, and Ithamar. Set them apart from the rest of the people of Israel so they may minister to me and be my priests. 2Make sacred garments for Aaron that are glorious and beautiful. 3Instruct all the skilled craftsmen whom I have filled with the spirit of wisdom. Have them make garments for Aaron that will distinguish him as a priest set apart for my service. 4These are the garments they are to make: a chestpiece, an ephod, a robe, a patterned tunic, a turban, and a sash. They are to make these sacred garments for your brother, Aaron, and his sons to wear when they serve me as priests. 5So give them fine linen cloth, gold thread, and blue, purple, and scarlet thread.

Design of the Ephod

6"The craftsmen must make the ephod of finely woven linen and skillfully embroider it with gold and with blue, purple, and scarlet thread. 7It will consist of two pieces, front and back, joined at the shoulders with two shoulder-pieces. 8The decorative sash will be made of the same materials: finely woven linen embroidered with gold and with blue, purple, and scarlet thread.

9"Take two onyx stones, and engrave on them the names of the tribes of Israel. 10Six names will be on each stone, arranged in the order of the births of the original sons of Israel. 11Engrave these names on the two stones in the same way a jeweler engraves a seal. Then mount the stones in settings of gold filigree. 12Fasten the two stones on the shoulder-pieces of the ephod as a reminder that Aaron represents the people of Israel. Aaron will carry these names on his shoulders as a constant reminder whenever he goes before the LORD. 13Make the settings of gold filigree, 14then braid two cords of pure gold and attach them to the filigree settings on the shoulders of the ephod.

Design of the Chestpiece

15"Then, with great skill and care, make a chestpiece to be worn for seeking a decision from God.* Make it to match the ephod, using finely woven linen embroidered with gold and with blue, purple, and scarlet thread. 16Make the chestpiece of a single piece of cloth folded to form a pouch nine inches* square. 17Mount four rows of gemstones* on it. The first row will contain a red carnelian, a pale-green peridot, and an emerald. 18The second row will contain a turquoise, a blue lapis lazuli, and a white moonstone. 19The third row will contain an orange jacinth, an agate, and a purple amethyst. 20The fourth row will contain a blue-green beryl, an onyx, and a green jasper. All these stones will be set in gold filigree. 21Each stone will represent one of the twelve sons of Israel, and the name of that tribe will be engraved on it like a seal.

22"To attach the chestpiece to the ephod, make braided cords of pure gold thread. 23Then make two gold rings and attach them to the top corners of the chestpiece. 24Tie the two gold cords to the two rings on the chestpiece. 25Tie the other ends of the cords to the gold settings on the shoulder-pieces of the ephod. 26Then make two more gold rings and attach them to the inside edges of the chestpiece next to the ephod. 27And make two more gold rings and attach them to the front of the ephod, below the shoulder-pieces, just above the knot where the decorative sash is fastened to the ephod. 28Then attach the bottom rings of the chestpiece to

27:21 Hebrew *in the Tent of Meeting, outside the inner curtain that is in front of the Testimony.* See note on 25:16. 28:15 Hebrew *a chestpiece for decision.* 28:16 Hebrew *1 span* [23 centimeters]. 28:17 The identification of some of these gemstones is uncertain.

27:20-21 God's command to keep the lamps burning throughout the hours of darkness indicates that God is a God of light (see 1 John 1:5). Under cover of darkness, it is difficult to judge reality and easier to hide the truth. God is not a God of darkness. He wants his people to be transparent, having integrity and faith. He wants them to be obedient to his program for living. That is what it means to live in the light of God's presence as Christ does (1 John 1:7).

the rings on the ephod with blue cords. This will hold the chestpiece securely to the ephod above the decorative sash.

29 "In this way, Aaron will carry the names of the tribes of Israel on the sacred chestpiece* over his heart when he goes into the Holy Place. This will be a continual reminder that he represents the people when he comes before the LORD. 30Insert the Urim and Thummim into the sacred chestpiece so they will be carried over Aaron's heart when he goes into the LORD's presence. In this way, Aaron will always carry over his heart the objects used to determine the LORD's will for his people whenever he goes in before the LORD.

Additional Clothing for the Priests

31 "Make the robe that is worn with the ephod from a single piece of blue cloth, 32with an opening for Aaron's head in the middle of it. Reinforce the opening with a woven collar* so it will not tear. 33Make pomegranates out of blue, purple, and scarlet yarn, and attach them to the hem of the robe, with gold bells between them. 34The gold bells and pomegranates are to alternate all around the hem. 35Aaron will wear this robe whenever he ministers before the LORD, and the bells will tinkle as he goes in and out of the LORD's presence in the Holy Place. If he wears it, he will not die.

36 "Next make a medallion of pure gold, and engrave it like a seal with these words: HOLY TO THE LORD. 37Attach the medallion with a blue cord to the front of Aaron's turban, where it must remain. 38Aaron must wear it on his forehead so he may take on himself any guilt of the people of Israel when they consecrate their sacred offerings. He must always wear it on his forehead so the LORD will accept the people.

39 "Weave Aaron's patterned tunic from fine linen cloth. Fashion the turban from this linen as well. Also make a sash, and decorate it with colorful embroidery.

40 "For Aaron's sons, make tunics, sashes, and special head coverings that are glorious and beautiful. 41Clothe your brother, Aaron, and his sons with these garments, and then anoint and ordain them. Consecrate them so they can serve as my priests. 42Also make linen undergarments for them, to be worn next to their bodies, reaching from their hips to their thighs. 43These must be worn whenever Aaron and his sons enter the Tabernacle* or approach the altar in the Holy Place to perform their priestly duties. Then they will not incur guilt and die. This is a permanent law for Aaron and all his descendants after him.

CHAPTER 29
Dedication of the Priests

"This is the ceremony you must follow when you consecrate Aaron and his sons to serve me as priests: Take a young bull and two rams with no defects. 2Then, using choice wheat flour and no yeast, make loaves of bread, thin cakes mixed with olive oil, and wafers spread with oil. 3Place them all in a single basket, and present them at the entrance of the Tabernacle, along with the young bull and the two rams.

4 "Present Aaron and his sons at the entrance of the Tabernacle,* and wash them with water. 5Dress Aaron in his priestly garments—the tunic, the robe worn with the ephod, the ephod itself, and the chestpiece. Then wrap the decorative sash of the ephod around him. 6Place the turban on his head, and fasten the sacred medallion to the turban. 7Then anoint him by pouring the anointing oil over his head. 8Next present his sons, and dress them in their tunics. 9Wrap the sashes around the waists of Aaron and his sons, and put their special head coverings on them. Then the right to the priesthood will be theirs by law forever. In this way, you will ordain Aaron and his sons.

10 "Bring the young bull to the entrance of the Tabernacle, where Aaron and his sons will lay their hands on its head. 11Then slaughter the bull in the LORD's presence at the entrance of the Tabernacle. 12Put some of its blood on the horns of the altar with your finger, and pour out the rest at the base of the altar. 13Take all the fat around the internal organs, the long lobe of the liver, and the two

28:29 Hebrew the chestpiece for decision; also in 28:30. See 28:15. 28:32 The meaning of the Hebrew is uncertain. 28:43 Hebrew Tent of Meeting. 29:4 Hebrew Tent of Meeting; also in 29:10, 11, 30, 32, 42, 44.

28:29-32 The priest's breastplate was inscribed with the names of Israel's tribes. This showed that the priest represented the nation and was spiritually responsible for the people. The Urim and Thummim were a means to determine the will of God in key decisions. Similarly, those in positions of responsibility must seriously and consistently seek God's will as they make decisions or be accountable for acting otherwise.

kidneys and the fat around them, and burn it all on the altar. [14]Then take the rest of the bull, including its hide, meat, and dung, and burn it outside the camp as a sin offering.

[15]"Next Aaron and his sons must lay their hands on the head of one of the rams. [16]Then slaughter the ram, and splatter its blood against all sides of the altar. [17]Cut the ram into pieces, and wash off the internal organs and the legs. Set them alongside the head and the other pieces of the body, [18]then burn the entire animal on the altar. This is a burnt offering to the LORD; it is a pleasing aroma, a special gift presented to the LORD.

[19]"Now take the other ram, and have Aaron and his sons lay their hands on its head. [20]Then slaughter it, and apply some of its blood to the right earlobes of Aaron and his sons. Also put it on the thumbs of their right hands and the big toes of their right feet. Splatter the rest of the blood against all sides of the altar. [21]Then take some of the blood from the altar and some of the anointing oil, and sprinkle it on Aaron and his sons and on their garments. In this way, they and their garments will be set apart as holy.

[22]"Since this is the ram for the ordination of Aaron and his sons, take the fat of the ram, including the fat of the broad tail, the fat around the internal organs, the long lobe of the liver, and the two kidneys and the fat around them, along with the right thigh. [23]Then take one round loaf of bread, one thin cake mixed with olive oil, and one wafer from the basket of bread without yeast that was placed in the LORD's presence. [24]Put all these in the hands of Aaron and his sons to be lifted up as a special offering to the LORD. [25]Afterward take the various breads from their hands, and burn them on the altar along with the burnt offering. It is a pleasing aroma to the LORD, a special gift for him. [26]Then take the breast of Aaron's ordination ram, and lift it up in the LORD's presence as a special offering to him. Then keep it as your own portion.

[27]"Set aside the portions of the ordination ram that belong to Aaron and his sons. This includes the breast and the thigh that were lifted up before the LORD as a special offering. [28]In the future, whenever the people of Israel lift up a peace offering, a portion of it must be set aside for Aaron and his descendants. This is their permanent right, and it is a sacred offering from the Israelites to the LORD.

[29]"Aaron's sacred garments must be preserved for his descendants who succeed him, and they will wear them when they are anointed and ordained. [30]The descendant who succeeds him as high priest will wear these clothes for seven days as he ministers in the Tabernacle and the Holy Place.

[31]"Take the ram used in the ordination ceremony, and boil its meat in a sacred place. [32]Then Aaron and his sons will eat this meat, along with the bread in the basket, at the Tabernacle entrance. [33]They alone may eat the meat and bread used for their purification* in the ordination ceremony. No one else may eat them, for these things are set apart and holy. [34]If any of the ordination meat or bread remains until the morning, it must be burned. It may not be eaten, for it is holy.

[35]"This is how you will ordain Aaron and his sons to their offices, just as I have commanded you. The ordination ceremony will go on for seven days. [36]Each day you must sacrifice a young bull as a sin offering to purify them, making them right with the LORD.* Afterward, cleanse the altar by purifying it*; make it holy by anointing it with oil. [37]Purify the altar, and consecrate it every day for seven days. After that, the altar will be absolutely holy, and whatever touches it will become holy.

[38]"These are the sacrifices you are to offer regularly on the altar. Each day, offer two lambs that are a year old, [39]one in the morning and the other in the evening. [40]With one of them, offer two quarts of choice flour mixed with one quart of pure oil of pressed olives; also, offer one quart of wine* as a liquid offering. [41]Offer the other lamb in the evening, along with the same offerings of flour and wine as in the morning. It will be a pleasing aroma, a special gift presented to the LORD.

[42]"These burnt offerings are to be made each day from generation to generation. Offer them in the LORD's presence at the Tabernacle entrance; there I will meet with you and speak with you. [43]I will meet the people of Israel there, in the place made holy by my glorious presence. [44]Yes, I will consecrate the Tabernacle and the altar, and I will consecrate Aaron and his sons to serve me as priests. [45]Then I will live among the people of Israel and be their God, [46]and they will know that I am the LORD their God. I am the one who brought them out of the land of Egypt so that I could live among them. I am the LORD their God.

29:33 Or *their atonement.* **29:36a** Or *to make atonement.* **29:36b** Or *by making atonement for it;* similarly in 29:37. **29:40** Hebrew *¹/₁₀ [of an ephah]* [2.2 liters] *of choice flour . . . ¼ of a hin* [1 liter] *of pure oil . . . ¼ of a hin of wine.*

CHAPTER 30
Plans for the Incense Altar

"Then make another altar of acacia wood for burning incense. ²Make it 18 inches square and 36 inches high,* with horns at the corners carved from the same piece of wood as the altar itself. ³Overlay the top, sides, and horns of the altar with pure gold, and run a gold molding around the entire altar. ⁴Make two gold rings, and attach them on opposite sides of the altar below the gold molding to hold the carrying poles. ⁵Make the poles of acacia wood and overlay them with gold. ⁶Place the incense altar just outside the inner curtain that shields the Ark of the Covenant,* in front of the Ark's cover—the place of atonement—that covers the tablets inscribed with the terms of the covenant.* I will meet with you there.

⁷"Every morning when Aaron maintains the lamps, he must burn fragrant incense on the altar. ⁸And each evening when he lights the lamps, he must again burn incense in the LORD's presence. This must be done from generation to generation. ⁹Do not offer any unholy incense on this altar, or any burnt offerings, grain offerings, or liquid offerings.

¹⁰"Once a year Aaron must purify* the altar by smearing its horns with blood from the offering made to purify the people from their sin. This will be a regular, annual event from generation to generation, for this is the LORD's most holy altar."

Money for the Tabernacle

¹¹Then the LORD said to Moses, ¹²"Whenever you take a census of the people of Israel, each man who is counted must pay a ransom for himself to the LORD. Then no plague will strike the people as you count them. ¹³Each person who is counted must give a small piece of silver as a sacred offering to the LORD. (This payment is half a shekel,* based on the sanctuary shekel, which equals twenty gerahs.) ¹⁴All who have reached their twentieth birthday must give this sacred offering to the LORD. ¹⁵When this offering is given to the LORD to purify your lives, making you right with him,* the rich must not give more than the specified amount, and the poor must not give less. ¹⁶Receive this ransom money from the Israelites, and use it for the care of the Tabernacle.* It will bring the Israelites to the LORD's attention, and it will purify your lives."

Plans for the Washbasin

¹⁷Then the LORD said to Moses, ¹⁸"Make a bronze washbasin with a bronze stand. Place it between the Tabernacle and the altar, and fill it with water. ¹⁹Aaron and his sons will wash their hands and feet there. ²⁰They must wash with water whenever they go into the Tabernacle to appear before the LORD and when they approach the altar to burn up their special gifts to the LORD—or they will die! ²¹They must always wash their hands and feet, or they will die. This is a permanent law for Aaron and his descendants, to be observed from generation to generation."

The Anointing Oil

²²Then the LORD said to Moses, ²³"Collect choice spices—12½ pounds of pure myrrh, 6¼ pounds of fragrant cinnamon, 6¼ pounds of fragrant calamus,* ²⁴and 12½ pounds of cassia*—as measured by the weight of the sanctuary shekel. Also get one gallon of olive oil.* ²⁵Like a skilled incense maker, blend these ingredients to make a holy anointing oil. ²⁶Use this sacred oil to anoint the Tabernacle, the Ark of the Covenant, ²⁷the table and all its utensils, the lampstand and all its accessories, the incense altar, ²⁸the altar of burnt offering and all its utensils, and the washbasin with its stand. ²⁹Consecrate them to make them absolutely holy. After this, whatever touches them will also become holy.

³⁰"Anoint Aaron and his sons also, consecrating them to serve me as priests. ³¹And say to the people of Israel, 'This holy anointing oil is reserved for me from generation to generation. ³²It must never be used to anoint anyone else, and you must never make any blend like it for yourselves. It is holy, and you must

---

30:2 Hebrew *1 cubit* [46 centimeters] *long and 1 cubit wide, a square, and 2 cubits* [92 centimeters] *high.* 30:6a Or *Ark of the Testimony;* also in 30:26. 30:6b Hebrew *that covers the Testimony;* see note on 25:16. 30:10 Or *make atonement for;* also in 30:10b. 30:13 Or *0.2 ounces* [6 grams]. 30:15 Or *to make atonement for your lives;* similarly in 30:16. 30:16 Hebrew *Tent of Meeting;* also in 30:18, 20, 26, 36. 30:23 Hebrew *500* [shekels] *[5.7 kilograms] of pure myrrh, 250* [shekels] *[2.9 kilograms] of fragrant cinnamon, 250* [shekels] *of fragrant calamus.* 30:24a Hebrew *500* [shekels] *[5.7 kilograms] of cassia.* 30:24b Hebrew *1 hin* [3.8 liters] *of olive oil.*

30:1-10 As graphic and compelling as the sacrificial system was, it still could provide only temporary atonement and forgiveness. These sacrifices and offerings effectively foreshadowed the final sacrifice of Christ (see John 1:29), but unlike Christ's sacrifice, they could not provide permanent forgiveness. Only through faith in Christ is such forgiveness possible.

treat it as holy. [33]Anyone who makes a blend like it or anoints someone other than a priest will be cut off from the community.'"

The Incense

[34]Then the LORD said to Moses, "Gather fragrant spices—resin droplets, mollusk shell, and galbanum—and mix these fragrant spices with pure frankincense, weighed out in equal amounts. [35]Using the usual techniques of the incense maker, blend the spices together and sprinkle them with salt to produce a pure and holy incense. [36]Grind some of the mixture into a very fine powder and put it in front of the Ark of the Covenant,* where I will meet with you in the Tabernacle. You must treat this incense as most holy. [37]Never use this formula to make this incense for yourselves. It is reserved for the LORD, and you must treat it as holy. [38]Anyone who makes incense like this for personal use will be cut off from the community."

CHAPTER 31
Craftsmen: Bezalel and Oholiab

Then the LORD said to Moses, [2]"Look, I have specifically chosen Bezalel son of Uri, grandson of Hur, of the tribe of Judah. [3]I have filled him with the Spirit of God, giving him great wisdom, ability, and expertise in all kinds of crafts. [4]He is a master craftsman, expert in working with gold, silver, and bronze. [5]He is skilled in engraving and mounting gemstones and in carving wood. He is a master at every craft!

[6]"And I have personally appointed Oholiab son of Ahisamach, of the tribe of Dan, to be his assistant. Moreover, I have given special skill to all the gifted craftsmen so they can make all the things I have commanded you to make:

[7] the Tabernacle;*
the Ark of the Covenant;*
the Ark's cover—the place of atonement;
all the furnishings of the Tabernacle;
[8] the table and its utensils;
the pure gold lampstand with all its
accessories;

the incense altar;
[9] the altar of burnt offering with all its
utensils;
the washbasin with its stand;
[10] the beautifully stitched garments—the
sacred garments for Aaron the priest,
and the garments for his sons to wear
as they minister as priests;
[11] the anointing oil;
the fragrant incense for the Holy Place.

The craftsmen must make everything as I have commanded you."

Instructions for the Sabbath

[12]The LORD then gave these instructions to Moses: [13]"Tell the people of Israel: 'Be careful to keep my Sabbath day, for the Sabbath is a sign of the covenant between me and you from generation to generation. It is given so you may know that I am the LORD, who makes you holy. [14]You must keep the Sabbath day, for it is a holy day for you. Anyone who desecrates it must be put to death; anyone who works on that day will be cut off from the community. [15]You have six days each week for your ordinary work, but the seventh day must be a Sabbath day of complete rest, a holy day dedicated to the LORD. Anyone who works on the Sabbath must be put to death. [16]The people of Israel must keep the Sabbath day by observing it from generation to generation. This is a covenant obligation for all time. [17]It is a permanent sign of my covenant with the people of Israel. For in six days the LORD made heaven and earth, but on the seventh day he stopped working and was refreshed.'"

[18]When the LORD finished speaking with Moses on Mount Sinai, he gave him the two stone tablets inscribed with the terms of the covenant,* written by the finger of God.

CHAPTER 32
The Gold Calf

When the people saw how long it was taking Moses to come back down the mountain, they gathered around Aaron. "Come on,"

30:36 Hebrew *in front of the Testimony;* see note on 25:16. **31:7a** Hebrew *the Tent of Meeting.* **31:7b** Hebrew *the Ark of the Testimony.* **31:18** Hebrew *the two tablets of the Testimony;* see note on 25:16.

31:12-17 Keeping the weekly Sabbath was to become a regular occurrence in the lives of the Israelites. This day was set apart for God as a day of special worship and for the people as a day of rest. In modern society the weekend is often considered a time to get away from our work. But we often fail to set aside a day for God as he intended. As we look forward to Sunday, let us look for ways to make it holy unto God as well as spiritually refreshing for us.
32:1-20 Israel shattered the second commandment by making the gold calf. God had clearly said, "You must not make for yourself an idol of any kind" (20:4-6). Weak-kneed Aaron tried to

they said, "make us some gods who can lead us. We don't know what happened to this fellow Moses, who brought us here from the land of Egypt."

²So Aaron said, "Take the gold rings from the ears of your wives and sons and daughters, and bring them to me."

³All the people took the gold rings from their ears and brought them to Aaron. ⁴Then Aaron took the gold, melted it down, and molded it into the shape of a calf. When the people saw it, they exclaimed, "O Israel, these are the gods who brought you out of the land of Egypt!"

⁵Aaron saw how excited the people were, so he built an altar in front of the calf. Then he announced, "Tomorrow will be a festival to the LORD!"

⁶The people got up early the next morning to sacrifice burnt offerings and peace offerings. After this, they celebrated with feasting and drinking, and they indulged in pagan revelry.

⁷The LORD told Moses, "Quick! Go down the mountain! Your people whom you brought from the land of Egypt have corrupted themselves. ⁸How quickly they have turned away from the way I commanded them to live! They have melted down gold and made a calf, and they have bowed down and sacrificed to it. They are saying, 'These are your gods, O Israel, who brought you out of the land of Egypt.'"

⁹Then the LORD said, "I have seen how stubborn and rebellious these people are. ¹⁰Now leave me alone so my fierce anger can blaze against them, and I will destroy them. Then I will make you, Moses, into a great nation."

¹¹But Moses tried to pacify the LORD his God. "O LORD!" he said. "Why are you so angry with your own people whom you brought

from the land of Egypt with such great power and such a strong hand? ¹²Why let the Egyptians say, 'Their God rescued them with the evil intention of slaughtering them in the mountains and wiping them from the face of the earth'? Turn away from your fierce anger. Change your mind about this terrible disaster you have threatened against your people! ¹³Remember your servants Abraham, Isaac, and Jacob.* You bound yourself with an oath to them, saying, 'I will make your descendants as numerous as the stars of heaven. And I will give them all of this land that I have promised to your descendants, and they will possess it forever.'"

¹⁴So the LORD changed his mind about the terrible disaster he had threatened to bring on his people.

¹⁵Then Moses turned and went down the mountain. He held in his hands the two stone tablets inscribed with the terms of the covenant.* They were inscribed on both sides, front and back. ¹⁶These tablets were God's work; the words on them were written by God himself.

¹⁷When Joshua heard the boisterous noise of the people shouting below them, he exclaimed to Moses, "It sounds like war in the camp!"

¹⁸But Moses replied, "No, it's not a shout of victory nor the wailing of defeat. I hear the sound of a celebration."

¹⁹When they came near the camp, Moses saw the calf and the dancing, and he burned with anger. He threw the stone tablets to the ground, smashing them at the foot of the mountain. ²⁰He took the calf they had made and burned it. Then he ground it into powder, threw it into the water, and forced the people to drink it.

²¹Finally, he turned to Aaron and demanded, "What did these people do to you to

---

32:13 Hebrew *Israel.* The names "Jacob" and "Israel" are often interchanged throughout the Old Testament, referring sometimes to the individual patriarch and sometimes to the nation. 32:15 Hebrew *the two tablets of the Testimony;* see note on 25:16.

---

put a good face on his blasphemy (32:22-24), but to no avail. The people's behavior represented a wholesale turning from their previously professed faith and commitment to God. This incident contains a warning to those who believe they have progressed so far in recovery that they are immune to failure (see 1 John 5:21). No matter how far we have come, we are never safe from the danger of a relapse.

32:21-29 Aaron reveals himself to be a "people pleaser." He caved in to the idolatrous desires of the Israelites rather than confront them with the reality of the sin in their lives. He also displayed a lack of honesty and an unwillingness to face the reality of his actions. To avoid his accountability to God and Moses he made a farfetched excuse for his behavior (32:22-24). The consequences of Aaron's failure were terrible, reaching far beyond his personal reprimand. Let us learn from Aaron's mistakes. We must defend and live out God's program, even when it is unpopular with the crowd. If we don't, the consequences for both us and the people around us could be terrible.

make you bring such terrible sin upon them?"

22 "Don't get so upset, my lord," Aaron replied. "You yourself know how evil these people are. 23 They said to me, 'Make us gods who will lead us. We don't know what happened to this fellow Moses, who brought us here from the land of Egypt.' 24 So I told them, 'Whoever has gold jewelry, take it off.' When they brought it to me, I simply threw it into the fire—and out came this calf!"

25 Moses saw that Aaron had let the people get completely out of control, much to the amusement of their enemies.* 26 So he stood at the entrance to the camp and shouted, "All of you who are on the LORD's side, come here and join me." And all the Levites gathered around him.

27 Moses told them, "This is what the LORD, the God of Israel, says: Each of you, take your swords and go back and forth from one end of the camp to the other. Kill everyone—even your brothers, friends, and neighbors." 28 The Levites obeyed Moses' command, and about 3,000 people died that day.

29 Then Moses told the Levites, "Today you have ordained yourselves* for the service of the LORD, for you obeyed him even though it meant killing your own sons and brothers. Today you have earned a blessing."

Moses Intercedes for Israel

30 The next day Moses said to the people, "You have committed a terrible sin, but I will go back up to the LORD on the mountain. Perhaps I will be able to obtain forgiveness* for your sin."

31 So Moses returned to the LORD and said, "Oh, what a terrible sin these people have committed. They have made gods of gold for themselves. 32 But now, if you will only forgive their sin—but if not, erase my name from the record you have written!"

33 But the LORD replied to Moses, "No, I will erase the name of everyone who has sinned against me. 34 Now go, lead the people to the place I told you about. Look! My angel will lead the way before you. And when I come to call the people to account, I will certainly hold them responsible for their sins."

35 Then the LORD sent a great plague upon the people because they had worshiped the calf Aaron had made.

CHAPTER 33

The LORD said to Moses, "Get going, you and the people you brought up from the land of Egypt. Go up to the land I swore to give to Abraham, Isaac, and Jacob. I told them, 'I will give this land to your descendants.' 2 And I will send an angel before you to drive out the Canaanites, Amorites, Hittites, Perizzites, Hivites, and Jebusites. 3 Go up to this land that flows with milk and honey. But I will not travel among you, for you are a stubborn and rebellious people. If I did, I would surely destroy you along the way."

4 When the people heard these stern words, they went into mourning and stopped wearing their jewelry and fine clothes. 5 For the LORD had told Moses to tell them, "You are a stubborn and rebellious people. If I were to travel with you for even a moment, I would destroy you. Remove your jewelry and fine clothes while I decide what to do with you." 6 So from the time they left Mount Sinai,* the Israelites wore no more jewelry or fine clothes.

7 It was Moses' practice to take the Tent of Meeting* and set it up some distance from

32:25 Or *out of control, and they mocked anyone who opposed them.* The meaning of the Hebrew is uncertain. 32:29 As in Greek and Latin versions; Hebrew reads *Today ordain yourselves.* 32:30 Or *to make atonement.* 33:6 Hebrew *Horeb,* another name for Sinai. 33:7 This "Tent of Meeting" is different from the Tabernacle described in chapters 26 and 36.

32:30-35 In the wake of the Israelites' horrible idolatry, Moses took on the role of a loving father toward them. In seeking atonement and forgiveness for the people's sins, Moses asked God to hold back the terrible consequences; he even suggested that he take the punishment upon himself. It is difficult for many parents and leaders to see that those under their charge must learn responsibility by facing the full consequences of their wrong choices. In this case, God required that these disobedient people suffer the ultimate consequence—death.

33:1-6 This display of emotion by God and the people's response is instructive. God reassured Israel that he would stand by his covenant commitments. He would give them the Promised Land and protect them through the time of its recovery. However, God became so angry with Israel because of their stubborn disobedience that he was forced to back away. While God was restraining his anger and deciding what to do with them, the people underwent a heart-wrenching self-examination, mourning their sins and repenting before God. Even when we have failed miserably, we can be assured that God's promises of reconciliation will stand. All we need to do is go to God openly with our sins, seeking his help to find a new way of life.

the camp. Everyone who wanted to make a request of the LORD would go to the Tent of Meeting outside the camp.

[8]Whenever Moses went out to the Tent of Meeting, all the people would get up and stand in the entrances of their own tents. They would all watch Moses until he disappeared inside. [9]As he went into the tent, the pillar of cloud would come down and hover at its entrance while the LORD spoke with Moses. [10]When the people saw the cloud standing at the entrance of the tent, they would stand and bow down in front of their own tents. [11]Inside the Tent of Meeting, the LORD would speak to Moses face to face, as one speaks to a friend. Afterward Moses would return to the camp, but the young man who assisted him, Joshua son of Nun, would remain behind in the Tent of Meeting.

Moses Sees the LORD's Glory

[12]One day Moses said to the LORD, "You have been telling me, 'Take these people up to the Promised Land.' But you haven't told me whom you will send with me. You have told me, 'I know you by name, and I look favorably on you.' [13]If it is true that you look favorably on me, let me know your ways so I may understand you more fully and continue to enjoy your favor. And remember that this nation is your very own people."

[14]The LORD replied, "I will personally go with you, Moses, and I will give you rest—everything will be fine for you."

[15]Then Moses said, "If you don't personally go with us, don't make us leave this place. [16]How will anyone know that you look favorably on me—on me and on your people—if you don't go with us? For your presence among us sets your people and me apart from all other people on the earth."

[17]The LORD replied to Moses, "I will indeed do what you have asked, for I look favorably on you, and I know you by name."

[18]Moses responded, "Then show me your glorious presence."

[19]The LORD replied, "I will make all my goodness pass before you, and I will call out my name, Yahweh,* before you. For I will show mercy to anyone I choose, and I will show compassion to anyone I choose. [20]But you may not look directly at my face, for no one may see me and live." [21]The LORD continued, "Look, stand near me on this rock. [22]As my glorious presence passes by, I will hide you in the crevice of the rock and cover you with my hand until I have passed by. [23]Then I will remove my hand and let you see me from behind. But my face will not be seen."

CHAPTER 34
A New Copy of the Covenant

Then the LORD told Moses, "Chisel out two stone tablets like the first ones. I will write on them the same words that were on the tablets you smashed. [2]Be ready in the morning to climb up Mount Sinai and present yourself to me on the top of the mountain. [3]No one else may come with you. In fact, no one is to appear anywhere on the mountain. Do not even let the flocks or herds graze near the mountain."

[4]So Moses chiseled out two tablets of stone like the first ones. Early in the morning he climbed Mount Sinai as the LORD had commanded him, and he carried the two stone tablets in his hands.

[5]Then the LORD came down in a cloud and

33:19 *Yahweh* is a transliteration of the proper name *YHWH* that is sometimes rendered "Jehovah"; in this translation it is usually rendered "the LORD" (note the use of small capitals).

33:12-23 When Moses asked to experience more of God's comforting presence and see his glory, he was not seeking to glorify himself. A clear vision of God is important for all of us to have. As we see him more clearly, we are better able to understand our own strengths and limitations. This scene shows Moses growing spiritually in a remarkable way. All of us should seek to know God better and to experience his presence in our life.

34:1-4 In spite of the horrible sin that the people of Israel had committed in making the gold calf (see 32:1-35), God was willing to give them another chance to commit themselves to him and obey his covenant. When Moses came down from Mount Sinai the first time, he smashed the tablets inscribed with the Ten Commandments (32:19). Now God displayed his amazing grace (34:6) by rewriting the tablets for his people. Our failures can never be so great that God will not forgive us.

34:5-7 When God announced the meaning of his name to Moses, he was explaining who he was. In ancient cultures the meaning of a person's name was understood to be a window into that person's character, not just a surface title. As we commit ourselves to God and let him change us, it is important that we get to know God's character. He is compassionate, gracious, patient, loving, trustworthy, forgiving, and just.

stood there with him; and he called out his own name, Yahweh.* [6]The LORD passed in front of Moses, calling out,

"Yahweh!* The LORD!
   The God of compassion and mercy!
I am slow to anger
   and filled with unfailing love and
      faithfulness.
[7]I lavish unfailing love to a thousand
      generations.*
   I forgive iniquity, rebellion, and sin.
But I do not excuse the guilty.
   I lay the sins of the parents upon their
      children and grandchildren;
the entire family is affected—
   even children in the third and fourth
      generations."

[8]Moses immediately threw himself to the ground and worshiped. [9]And he said, "O Lord, if it is true that I have found favor with you, then please travel with us. Yes, this is a stubborn and rebellious people, but please forgive our iniquity and our sins. Claim us as your own special possession."

[10]The LORD replied, "Listen, I am making a covenant with you in the presence of all your people. I will perform miracles that have never been performed anywhere in all the earth or in any nation. And all the people around you will see the power of the LORD—the awesome power I will display for you. [11]But listen carefully to everything I command you today. Then I will go ahead of you and drive out the Amorites, Canaanites, Hittites, Perizzites, Hivites, and Jebusites.

[12]"Be very careful never to make a treaty with the people who live in the land where you are going. If you do, you will follow their evil ways and be trapped. [13]Instead, you must break down their pagan altars, smash their sacred pillars, and cut down their Asherah poles. [14]You must worship no other gods, for the LORD, whose very name is Jealous, is a God who is jealous about his relationship with you.

[15]"You must not make a treaty of any kind with the people living in the land. They lust after their gods, offering sacrifices to them. They will invite you to join them in their sacrificial meals, and you will go with them. [16]Then you will accept their daughters, who

sacrifice to other gods, as wives for your sons. And they will seduce your sons to commit adultery against me by worshiping other gods. [17]You must not make any gods of molten metal for yourselves.

[18]"You must celebrate the Festival of Unleavened Bread. For seven days the bread you eat must be made without yeast, just as I commanded you. Celebrate this festival annually at the appointed time in early spring, in the month of Abib,* for that is the anniversary of your departure from Egypt.

[19]"The firstborn of every animal belongs to me, including the firstborn males* from your herds of cattle and your flocks of sheep and goats. [20]A firstborn donkey may be bought back from the LORD by presenting a lamb or young goat in its place. But if you do not buy it back, you must break its neck. However, you must buy back every firstborn son.

"No one may appear before me without an offering.

[21]"You have six days each week for your ordinary work, but on the seventh day you must stop working, even during the seasons of plowing and harvest.

[22]"You must celebrate the Festival of Harvest* with the first crop of the wheat harvest, and celebrate the Festival of the Final Harvest* at the end of the harvest season. [23]Three times each year every man in Israel must appear before the Sovereign, the LORD, the God of Israel. [24]I will drive out the other nations ahead of you and expand your territory, so no one will covet and conquer your land while you appear before the LORD your God three times each year.

[25]"You must not offer the blood of my sacrificial offerings together with any baked goods containing yeast. And none of the meat of the Passover sacrifice may be kept over until the next morning.

[26]"As you harvest your crops, bring the very best of the first harvest to the house of the LORD your God.

"You must not cook a young goat in its mother's milk."

[27]Then the LORD said to Moses, "Write down all these instructions, for they represent the terms of the covenant I am making with you and with Israel."

34:5 *Yahweh* is a transliteration of the proper name *YHWH* that is sometimes rendered "Jehovah"; in this translation it is usually rendered "the LORD" (note the use of small capitals). **34:6** See note on 34:5. **34:7** Hebrew *for thousands*. **34:18** Hebrew *appointed time in the month of Abib*. This first month of the ancient Hebrew lunar calendar usually occurs within the months of March and April. **34:19** As in Greek version; the meaning of the Hebrew word is uncertain. **34:22a** Hebrew *Festival of Weeks;* compare 23:16. This was later called the Festival of Pentecost. It is celebrated today as Shavuot (or Shabuoth). **34:22b** Or *Festival of Ingathering*. This was later called the Festival of Shelters or Festival of Tabernacles (see Lev 23:33-36). It is celebrated today as Sukkot (or Succoth).

[28]Moses remained there on the mountain with the LORD forty days and forty nights. In all that time he ate no bread and drank no water. And the LORD* wrote the terms of the covenant—the Ten Commandments*—on the stone tablets.

[29]When Moses came down Mount Sinai carrying the two stone tablets inscribed with the terms of the covenant,* he wasn't aware that his face had become radiant because he had spoken to the LORD. [30]So when Aaron and the people of Israel saw the radiance of Moses' face, they were afraid to come near him.

[31]But Moses called out to them and asked Aaron and all the leaders of the community to come over, and he talked with them. [32]Then all the people of Israel approached him, and Moses gave them all the instructions the LORD had given him on Mount Sinai. [33]When Moses finished speaking with them, he covered his face with a veil. [34]But whenever he went into the Tent of Meeting to speak with the LORD, he would remove the veil until he came out again. Then he would give the people whatever instructions the LORD had given him, [35]and the people of Israel would see the radiant glow of his face. So he would put the veil over his face until he returned to speak with the LORD.

CHAPTER 35
Instructions for the Sabbath

Then Moses called together the whole community of Israel and told them, "These are the instructions the LORD has commanded you to follow. [2]You have six days each week for your ordinary work, but the seventh day must be a Sabbath day of complete rest, a holy day dedicated to the LORD. Anyone who works on that day must be put to death. [3]You must not even light a fire in any of your homes on the Sabbath."

Offerings for the Tabernacle

[4]Then Moses said to the whole community of Israel, "This is what the LORD has commanded: [5]Take a sacred offering for the LORD. Let those with generous hearts present the following gifts to the LORD:

gold, silver, and bronze;
[6] blue, purple, and scarlet thread;
fine linen and goat hair for cloth;
[7] tanned ram skins and fine goatskin leather;
acacia wood;
[8] olive oil for the lamps;
spices for the anointing oil and the fragrant incense;
[9] onyx stones, and other gemstones to be set in the ephod and the priest's chestpiece.

[10]"Come, all of you who are gifted craftsmen. Construct everything that the LORD has commanded:

[11] the Tabernacle and its sacred tent, its covering, clasps, frames, crossbars, posts, and bases;
[12] the Ark and its carrying poles;
the Ark's cover—the place of atonement;
the inner curtain to shield the Ark;
[13] the table, its carrying poles, and all its utensils;
the Bread of the Presence;
[14] for light, the lampstand, its accessories, the lamp cups, and the olive oil for lighting;
[15] the incense altar and its carrying poles;
the anointing oil and fragrant incense;
the curtain for the entrance of the Tabernacle;
[16] the altar of burnt offering;
the bronze grating of the altar and its carrying poles and utensils;
the washbasin with its stand;
[17] the curtains for the walls of the courtyard;
the posts and their bases;
the curtain for the entrance to the courtyard;
[18] the tent pegs of the Tabernacle and courtyard and their ropes;

34:28a Hebrew *he.* 34:28b Hebrew *the ten words.* 34:29 Hebrew *the two tablets of the Testimony;* see note on 25:16.

34:29-35 Moses' experience in God's presence was transforming. God's holy presence was so radiant that it caused Moses' face to glow. But that was only one of the results of drawing so close to God. This experience gave Moses the faith he needed to continue leading the Israelites through the wilderness. Drawing close to God should also provide us with the strength we need to make it through our wilderness experiences.

35:4-9, 20-29 This freewill offering was given by the Israelites to show their commitment to God. Many of the other sacrifices and offerings in the laws of Moses were mandatory. They were required—almost like paying taxes. The freewill offering was completely voluntary and was to be used to finance and build the Tabernacle. All the people joyfully gave and in so doing, selflessly served God and each other.

¹⁹ the beautifully stitched garments for the priests to wear while ministering in the Holy Place—the sacred garments for Aaron the priest, and the garments for his sons to wear as they minister as priests."

²⁰So the whole community of Israel left Moses and returned to their tents. ²¹All whose hearts were stirred and whose spirits were moved came and brought their sacred offerings to the LORD. They brought all the materials needed for the Tabernacle,* for the performance of its rituals, and for the sacred garments. ²²Both men and women came, all whose hearts were willing. They brought to the LORD their offerings of gold—brooches, earrings, rings from their fingers, and necklaces. They presented gold objects of every kind as a special offering to the LORD. ²³All those who owned the following items willingly brought them: blue, purple, and scarlet thread; fine linen and goat hair for cloth; and tanned ram skins and fine goatskin leather. ²⁴And all who had silver and bronze objects gave them as a sacred offering to the LORD. And those who had acacia wood brought it for use in the project.

²⁵All the women who were skilled in sewing and spinning prepared blue, purple, and scarlet thread, and fine linen cloth. ²⁶All the women who were willing used their skills to spin the goat hair into yarn. ²⁷The leaders brought onyx stones and the special gemstones to be set in the ephod and the priest's chestpiece. ²⁸They also brought spices and olive oil for the light, the anointing oil, and the fragrant incense. ²⁹So the people of Israel—every man and woman who was eager to help in the work the LORD had given them through Moses—brought their gifts and gave them freely to the LORD.

³⁰Then Moses told the people of Israel, "The LORD has specifically chosen Bezalel son of Uri, grandson of Hur, of the tribe of Judah. ³¹The LORD has filled Bezalel with the Spirit of God, giving him great wisdom, ability, and expertise in all kinds of crafts. ³²He is a master craftsman, expert in working with gold, silver, and bronze. ³³He is skilled in engraving and mounting gemstones and in carving wood. He is a master at every craft. ³⁴And the LORD has given both him and Oholiab son of Ahisamach, of the tribe of Dan, the ability to teach their skills to others. ³⁵The LORD has given them special skills as engravers, designers, embroiderers in blue, purple, and scarlet thread on fine linen cloth, and weavers. They excel as craftsmen and as designers.

CHAPTER 36
"The LORD has gifted Bezalel, Oholiab, and the other skilled craftsmen with wisdom and ability to perform any task involved in building the sanctuary. Let them construct and furnish the Tabernacle, just as the LORD has commanded."

²So Moses summoned Bezalel and Oholiab and all the others who were specially gifted by the LORD and were eager to get to work. ³Moses gave them the materials donated by the people of Israel as sacred offerings for the completion of the sanctuary. But the people continued to bring additional gifts each morning. ⁴Finally the craftsmen who were working on the sanctuary left their work. ⁵They went to Moses and reported, "The people have given more than enough materials to complete the job the LORD has commanded us to do!"

⁶So Moses gave the command, and this message was sent throughout the camp: "Men and women, don't prepare any more gifts for the sanctuary. We have enough!" So the people stopped bringing their sacred offerings. ⁷Their contributions were more than enough to complete the whole project.

Building the Tabernacle
⁸The skilled craftsmen made ten curtains of finely woven linen for the Tabernacle. Then Bezalel* decorated the curtains with blue, purple, and scarlet thread and with skillfully embroidered cherubim. ⁹All ten curtains were exactly the same size—42 feet long and 6 feet wide.* ¹⁰Five of these curtains were joined together to make one long curtain, and the other five were joined to make a second long

35:21 Hebrew *Tent of Meeting.* 36:8 Hebrew *he;* also in 36:16, 20, 35. See 37:1. 36:9 Hebrew *28 cubits* [12.9 meters] *long and 4 cubits* [1.8 meters] *wide.*

35:30–36:3 People who are greatly gifted need to have a clear sense of their identity. Often such people can be described as either self-glorifying or self-deprecating. Neither is a healthy or accurate self-assessment, and neither is pleasing to God. There should be no sense of superiority or inferiority among God's people, since every member plays a unique and important role (1 Corinthians 12:12-27).

curtain. ¹¹He made fifty loops of blue yarn and put them along the edge of the last curtain in each set. ¹²The fifty loops along the edge of one curtain matched the fifty loops along the edge of the other curtain. ¹³Then he made fifty gold clasps and fastened the long curtains together with the clasps. In this way, the Tabernacle was made of one continuous piece.

¹⁴He made eleven curtains of goat-hair cloth to serve as a tent covering for the Tabernacle. ¹⁵These eleven curtains were all exactly the same size—45 feet long and 6 feet wide.* ¹⁶Bezalel joined five of these curtains together to make one long curtain, and the other six were joined to make a second long curtain. ¹⁷He made fifty loops for the edge of each large curtain. ¹⁸He also made fifty bronze clasps to fasten the long curtains together. In this way, the tent covering was made of one continuous piece. ¹⁹He completed the tent covering with a layer of tanned ram skins and a layer of fine goatskin leather.

²⁰For the framework of the Tabernacle, Bezalel constructed frames of acacia wood. ²¹Each frame was 15 feet high and 27 inches wide,* ²²with two pegs under each frame. All the frames were identical. ²³He made twenty of these frames to support the curtains on the south side of the Tabernacle. ²⁴He also made forty silver bases—two bases under each frame, with the pegs fitting securely into the bases. ²⁵For the north side of the Tabernacle, he made another twenty frames, ²⁶with their forty silver bases, two bases under each frame. ²⁷He made six frames for the rear—the west side of the Tabernacle—²⁸along with two additional frames to reinforce the rear corners of the Tabernacle. ²⁹These corner frames were matched at the bottom and firmly attached at the top with a single ring, forming a single corner unit. Both of these corner units were made the same way. ³⁰So there were eight frames at the rear of the Tabernacle, set in sixteen silver bases—two bases under each frame.

³¹Then he made crossbars of acacia wood to link the frames, five crossbars for the north side of the Tabernacle ³²and five for the south side. He also made five crossbars for the rear of the Tabernacle, which faced west. ³³He made the middle crossbar to attach halfway up the frames; it ran all the way from one end of the Tabernacle to the other. ³⁴He overlaid the frames with gold and made gold rings to hold the crossbars. Then he overlaid the crossbars with gold as well.

³⁵For the inside of the Tabernacle, Bezalel made a special curtain of finely woven linen. He decorated it with blue, purple, and scarlet thread and with skillfully embroidered cherubim. ³⁶For the curtain, he made four posts of acacia wood and four gold hooks. He overlaid the posts with gold and set them in four silver bases.

³⁷Then he made another curtain for the entrance to the sacred tent. He made it of finely woven linen and embroidered it with exquisite designs using blue, purple, and scarlet thread. ³⁸This curtain was hung on gold hooks attached to five posts. The posts with their decorated tops and hooks were overlaid with gold, and the five bases were cast from bronze.

CHAPTER 37
Building the Ark of the Covenant

Next Bezalel made the Ark of acacia wood—a sacred chest 45 inches long, 27 inches wide, and 27 inches high.* ²He overlaid it inside and outside with pure gold, and he ran a molding of gold all around it. ³He cast four gold rings and attached them to its four feet, two rings on each side. ⁴Then he made poles from acacia wood and overlaid them with gold. ⁵He inserted the poles into the rings at the sides of the Ark to carry it.

⁶Then he made the Ark's cover—the place of atonement—from pure gold. It was 45 inches long and 27 inches wide.* ⁷He made two cherubim from hammered gold and placed them on the two ends of the atonement cover. ⁸He molded the cherubim on each end of the atonement cover, making it all of one piece of gold. ⁹The cherubim

36:15 Hebrew *30 cubits* [13.8 meters] *long and 4 cubits* [1.8 meters] *wide.* 36:21 Hebrew *10 cubits* [4.6 meters] *high and 1.5 cubits* [69 centimeters] *wide.* 37:1 Hebrew *2.5 cubits* [115 centimeters] *long, 1.5 cubits* [69 centimeters] *wide, and 1.5 cubits high.* 37:6 Hebrew *2.5 cubits* [115 centimeters] *long and 1.5 cubits* [69 centimeters] *wide.*

37:1-9 High expectations are difficult for anyone to cope with, even for people with a great deal of ability. It is quite common for supremely gifted people to never approach their potential because they fear failure. The craftsman Bezalel did not allow the high expectations of others to hinder his work. Because God had filled him with his Spirit and given him unusual skills, he willingly used his gifts to glorify God, not only in building the Tabernacle but also in teaching others. Bezalel's life is a good example for us to live by today.

faced each other and looked down on the atonement cover. With their wings spread above it, they protected it.

Building the Table

[10]Then Bezalel* made the table of acacia wood, 36 inches long, 18 inches wide, and 27 inches high.* [11]He overlaid it with pure gold and ran a gold molding around the edge. [12]He decorated it with a 3-inch border* all around, and he ran a gold molding along the border. [13]Then he cast four gold rings for the table and attached them at the four corners next to the four legs. [14]The rings were attached near the border to hold the poles that were used to carry the table. [15]He made these poles from acacia wood and overlaid them with gold. [16]Then he made special containers of pure gold for the table—bowls, ladles, jars, and pitchers—to be used in pouring out liquid offerings.

Building the Lampstand

[17]Then Bezalel made the lampstand of pure, hammered gold. He made the entire lampstand and its decorations of one piece—the base, center stem, lamp cups, buds, and petals. [18]The lampstand had six branches going out from the center stem, three on each side. [19]Each of the six branches had three lamp cups shaped like almond blossoms, complete with buds and petals. [20]The center stem of the lampstand was crafted with four lamp cups shaped like almond blossoms, complete with buds and petals. [21]There was an almond bud beneath each pair of branches where the six branches extended from the center stem, all made of one piece. [22]The almond buds and branches were all of one piece with the center stem, and they were hammered from pure gold.

[23]He also made seven lamps for the lampstand, lamp snuffers, and trays, all of pure gold. [24]The entire lampstand, along with its accessories, was made from seventy-five pounds* of pure gold.

Building the Incense Altar

[25]Then Bezalel made the incense altar of acacia wood. It was 18 inches square and 36 inches high,* with horns at the corners carved from the same piece of wood as the altar itself. [26]He overlaid the top, sides, and horns of the altar with pure gold, and he ran a gold molding around the entire altar. [27]He made two gold rings and attached them on opposite sides of the altar below the gold molding to hold the carrying poles. [28]He made the poles of acacia wood and overlaid them with gold.

[29]Then he made the sacred anointing oil and the fragrant incense, using the techniques of a skilled incense maker.

CHAPTER 38

Building the Altar of Burnt Offering

Next Bezalel* used acacia wood to construct the square altar of burnt offering. It was 7½ feet wide, 7½ feet long, and 4½ feet high.* [2]He made horns for each of its four corners so that the horns and altar were all one piece. He overlaid the altar with bronze. [3]Then he made all the altar utensils of bronze—the ash buckets, shovels, basins, meat forks, and firepans. [4]Next he made a bronze grating and installed it halfway down the side of the altar, under the ledge. [5]He cast four rings and attached them to the corners of the bronze grating to hold the carrying poles. [6]He made the poles from acacia wood and overlaid them with bronze. [7]He inserted the poles through the rings on the sides of the altar. The altar was hollow and was made from planks.

Building the Washbasin

[8]Bezalel made the bronze washbasin and its bronze stand from bronze mirrors donated by the women who served at the entrance of the Tabernacle.*

Building the Courtyard

[9]Then Bezalel made the courtyard, which was enclosed with curtains made of finely woven linen. On the south side the curtains were 150 feet long.* [10]They were held up by twenty posts set securely in twenty bronze bases. He hung the curtains with silver hooks and rings. [11]He made a similar set of curtains for the north side—150 feet of curtains held up by twenty posts set securely in bronze bases. He hung the curtains with silver hooks and rings. [12]The curtains on the west end of the courtyard were 75 feet long,* hung with silver hooks and rings and supported by ten posts set into ten bases. [13]The east end, the front, was also 75 feet long.

37:10a Hebrew *he;* also in 37:17, 25. 37:10b Hebrew *2 cubits* [92 centimeters] *long, 1 cubit* [46 centimeters] *wide, and 1.5 cubits* [69 centimeters] *high.* 37:12 Hebrew *a border of a handbreadth* [8 centimeters]. 37:24 Hebrew *1 talent* [34 kilograms]. 37:25 Hebrew *1 cubit* [46 centimeters] *long and 1 cubit wide, a square, and 2 cubits* [92 centimeters] *high.* 38:1a Hebrew *he;* also in 38:8, 9. 38:1b Hebrew *5 cubits* [2.3 meters] *wide, 5 cubits long, a square, and 3 cubits* [1.4 meters] *high.* 38:8 Hebrew *Tent of Meeting;* also in 38:30. 38:9 Hebrew *100 cubits* [46 meters]; also in 38:11. 38:12 Hebrew *50 cubits* [23 meters]; also in 38:13.

¹⁴The courtyard entrance was on the east end, flanked by two curtains. The curtain on the right side was 22½ feet long* and was supported by three posts set into three bases. ¹⁵The curtain on the left side was also 22½ feet long and was supported by three posts set into three bases. ¹⁶All the curtains used in the courtyard were made of finely woven linen. ¹⁷Each post had a bronze base, and all the hooks and rings were silver. The tops of the posts of the courtyard were overlaid with silver, and the rings to hold up the curtains were made of silver.

¹⁸He made the curtain for the entrance to the courtyard of finely woven linen, and he decorated it with beautiful embroidery in blue, purple, and scarlet thread. It was 30 feet long, and its height was 7½ feet,* just like the curtains of the courtyard walls. ¹⁹It was supported by four posts, each set securely in its own bronze base. The tops of the posts were overlaid with silver, and the hooks and rings were also made of silver.

²⁰All the tent pegs used in the Tabernacle and courtyard were made of bronze.

Inventory of Materials

²¹This is an inventory of the materials used in building the Tabernacle of the Covenant.* The Levites compiled the figures, as Moses directed, and Ithamar son of Aaron the priest served as recorder. ²²Bezalel son of Uri, grandson of Hur, of the tribe of Judah, made everything just as the LORD had commanded Moses. ²³He was assisted by Oholiab son of Ahisamach, of the tribe of Dan, a craftsman expert at engraving, designing, and embroidering with blue, purple, and scarlet thread on fine linen cloth.

²⁴The people brought special offerings of gold totaling 2,193 pounds,* as measured by the weight of the sanctuary shekel. This gold was used throughout the Tabernacle.

²⁵The whole community of Israel gave 7,545 pounds* of silver, as measured by the weight of the sanctuary shekel. ²⁶This silver came from the tax collected from each man registered in the census. (The tax is one beka, which is half a shekel,* based on the sanctuary shekel.) The tax was collected from 603,550 men who had reached their twentieth birthday. ²⁷The hundred bases for the frames of the sanctuary walls and for the posts supporting the inner curtain required 7,500 pounds of silver, about 75 pounds for each base.* ²⁸The remaining 45 pounds* of silver was used to make the hooks and rings and to overlay the tops of the posts.

²⁹The people also brought as special offerings 5,310 pounds* of bronze, ³⁰which was used for casting the bases for the posts at the entrance to the Tabernacle, and for the bronze altar with its bronze grating and all the altar utensils. ³¹Bronze was also used to make the bases for the posts that supported the curtains around the courtyard, the bases for the curtain at the entrance of the courtyard, and all the tent pegs for the Tabernacle and the courtyard.

CHAPTER 39
Clothing for the Priests

The craftsmen made beautiful sacred garments of blue, purple, and scarlet cloth—clothing for Aaron to wear while ministering in the Holy Place, just as the LORD had commanded Moses.

38:14 Hebrew *15 cubits* [6.9 meters]; also in 38:15. **38:18** Hebrew *20 cubits* [9.2 meters] *long and 5 cubits* [2.3 meters] *high.* **38:21** Hebrew *the Tabernacle, the Tabernacle of the Testimony.* **38:24** Hebrew *29 talents and 730 shekels* [994 kilograms]. Each shekel weighed about 0.4 ounces. **38:25** Hebrew *100 talents and 1,775 shekels* [3,420 kilograms]. **38:26** Or *0.2 ounces* [6 grams]. **38:27** Hebrew *100 talents* [3,400 kilograms] *of silver, 1 talent* [34 kilograms] *for each base.* **38:28** Hebrew *1,775* [shekels] [20.2 kilograms]. **38:29** Hebrew *70 talents and 2,400 shekels* [2,407 kilograms].

38:21-31 The dollar value of the gold, silver, bronze, and other materials used to build the Tabernacle would be mind-boggling. But the value of the materials used does not reflect empty extravagance or showiness. It only illustrates how precious and invaluable the presence of God really is. We can see here that the people's faith had surpassed the point of hanging on to material things. They were beginning to learn to trust God as they shared the wealth that ensured their future security.
39:1-31 The priestly garments were ornate and detailed, in accordance with God's instructions to Moses. The intricate details point to the fact that a priest was to be holy—set apart for God (39:30). The death of Christ made it possible for all believers to become "royal priests" (1 Peter 2:9), for we are to be holy and pure, committed to God in everything we do. Like the priestly garments, our actions need to reflect externally what we are on the inside through Christ—holy and set apart.

Making the Ephod

[2]Bezalel* made the ephod of finely woven linen and embroidered it with gold and with blue, purple, and scarlet thread. [3]He made gold thread by hammering out thin sheets of gold and cutting it into fine strands. With great skill and care, he worked it into the fine linen with the blue, purple, and scarlet thread.

[4]The ephod consisted of two pieces, front and back, joined at the shoulders with two shoulder-pieces. [5]The decorative sash was made of the same materials: finely woven linen embroidered with gold and with blue, purple, and scarlet thread, just as the LORD had commanded Moses. [6]They mounted the two onyx stones in settings of gold filigree. The stones were engraved with the names of the tribes of Israel, just as a seal is engraved. [7]He fastened these stones on the shoulder-pieces of the ephod as a reminder that the priest represents the people of Israel. All this was done just as the LORD had commanded Moses.

Making the Chestpiece

[8]Bezalel made the chestpiece with great skill and care. He made it to match the ephod, using finely woven linen embroidered with gold and with blue, purple, and scarlet thread. [9]He made the chestpiece of a single piece of cloth folded to form a pouch nine inches* square. [10]They mounted four rows of gemstones* on it. The first row contained a red carnelian, a pale-green peridot, and an emerald. [11]The second row contained a turquoise, a blue lapis lazuli, and a white moonstone. [12]The third row contained an orange jacinth, an agate, and a purple amethyst. [13]The fourth row contained a blue-green beryl, an onyx, and a green jasper. All these stones were set in gold filigree. [14]Each stone represented one of the twelve sons of Israel, and the name of that tribe was engraved on it like a seal.

[15]To attach the chestpiece to the ephod, they made braided cords of pure gold thread. [16]They also made two settings of gold filigree and two gold rings and attached them to the top corners of the chestpiece. [17]They tied the two gold cords to the rings on the chestpiece. [18]They tied the other ends of the cords to the gold settings on the shoulder-pieces of the ephod. [19]Then they made two more gold rings and attached them to the inside edges of the chestpiece next to the ephod. [20]Then they made two more gold rings and attached them to the front of the ephod, below the shoulder-pieces, just above the knot where the decorative sash was fastened to the ephod. [21]They attached the bottom rings of the chestpiece to the rings on the ephod with blue cords. In this way, the chestpiece was held securely to the ephod above the decorative sash. All this was done just as the LORD had commanded Moses.

Additional Clothing for the Priests

[22]Bezalel made the robe that is worn with the ephod from a single piece of blue woven cloth, [23]with an opening for Aaron's head in the middle of it. The opening was reinforced with a woven collar* so it would not tear. [24]They made pomegranates of blue, purple, and scarlet yarn, and attached them to the hem of the robe. [25]They also made bells of pure gold and placed them between the pomegranates along the hem of the robe, [26]with bells and pomegranates alternating all around the hem. This robe was to be worn whenever the priest ministered before the LORD, just as the LORD had commanded Moses.

[27] They made tunics for Aaron and his sons from fine linen cloth. [28]The turban and the special head coverings were made of fine linen, and the undergarments were also made of finely woven linen. [29]The sashes were made of finely woven linen and embroidered with blue, purple, and scarlet thread, just as the LORD had commanded Moses.

[30]Finally, they made the sacred medallion—the badge of holiness—of pure gold. They engraved it like a seal with these words: HOLY TO THE LORD. [31]They attached the medallion with a blue cord to Aaron's turban, just as the LORD had commanded Moses.

Moses Inspects the Work

[32]And so at last the Tabernacle* was finished. The Israelites had done everything just as the LORD had commanded Moses. [33]And they brought the entire Tabernacle to Moses:

39:2 Hebrew *He;* also in 39:8, 22. 39:9 Hebrew *1 span* [23 centimeters]. 39:10 The identification of some of these gemstones is uncertain. 39:23 The meaning of the Hebrew is uncertain. 39:32 Hebrew *the Tabernacle, the Tent of Meeting;* also in 39:40.

39:33-43 The Tabernacle was completed, following all of God's instructions (39:32, 42-43). It had required a great deal of tedious work, but it had all been done God's way. This was not self-defeating perfectionism or a substandard "good-enough-for-God" mentality. Rather, it was the melding of faith, commitment to God, and perseverance. The successful building of the

the sacred tent with all its furnishings, clasps, frames, crossbars, posts, and bases; ³⁴ the tent coverings of tanned ram skins and fine goatskin leather; the inner curtain to shield the Ark; ³⁵ the Ark of the Covenant* and its carrying poles; the Ark's cover—the place of atonement; ³⁶ the table and all its utensils; the Bread of the Presence; ³⁷ the pure gold lampstand with its symmetrical lamp cups, all its accessories, and the olive oil for lighting; ³⁸ the gold altar; the anointing oil and fragrant incense; the curtain for the entrance of the sacred tent; ³⁹ the bronze altar; the bronze grating and its carrying poles and utensils; the washbasin with its stand; ⁴⁰ the curtains for the walls of the courtyard; the posts and their bases; the curtain for the entrance to the courtyard; the ropes and tent pegs; all the furnishings to be used in worship at the Tabernacle; ⁴¹ the beautifully stitched garments for the priests to wear while ministering in the Holy Place—the sacred garments for Aaron the priest, and the garments for his sons to wear as they minister as priests.

⁴² So the people of Israel followed all of the LORD's instructions to Moses. ⁴³ Then Moses inspected all their work. When he found it had been done just as the LORD had commanded him, he blessed them.

CHAPTER 40
The Tabernacle Completed
Then the LORD said to Moses, ²"Set up the Tabernacle* on the first day of the new year.*

³Place the Ark of the Covenant* inside, and install the inner curtain to enclose the Ark within the Most Holy Place. ⁴Then bring in the table, and arrange the utensils on it. And bring in the lampstand, and set up the lamps.

⁵"Place the gold incense altar in front of the Ark of the Covenant. Then hang the curtain at the entrance of the Tabernacle. ⁶Place the altar of burnt offering in front of the Tabernacle entrance. ⁷Set the washbasin between the Tabernacle* and the altar, and fill it with water. ⁸Then set up the courtyard around the outside of the tent, and hang the curtain for the courtyard entrance.

⁹"Take the anointing oil and anoint the Tabernacle and all its furnishings to consecrate them and make them holy. ¹⁰Anoint the altar of burnt offering and its utensils to consecrate them. Then the altar will become absolutely holy. ¹¹Next anoint the washbasin and its stand to consecrate them.

¹²"Present Aaron and his sons at the entrance of the Tabernacle, and wash them with water. ¹³Dress Aaron with the sacred garments and anoint him, consecrating him to serve me as a priest. ¹⁴Then present his sons and dress them in their tunics. ¹⁵Anoint them as you did their father, so they may also serve me as priests. With their anointing, Aaron's descendants are set apart for the priesthood forever, from generation to generation."

¹⁶Moses proceeded to do everything just as the LORD had commanded him. ¹⁷So the Tabernacle was set up on the first day of the first month of the second year. ¹⁸Moses erected the Tabernacle by setting down its bases, inserting the frames, attaching the crossbars, and setting up the posts. ¹⁹Then he spread the coverings over the Tabernacle framework and put on the protective layers, just as the LORD had commanded him.

²⁰He took the stone tablets inscribed with the terms of the covenant and placed them* inside the Ark. Then he attached the carrying poles to the Ark, and he set the Ark's cover—the place of atonement—on top of it. ²¹Then

39:35 Or *Ark of the Testimony.* **40:2a** Hebrew *the Tabernacle, the Tent of Meeting;* also in 40:6, 29. **40:2b** Hebrew *the first day of the first month.* This day of the ancient Hebrew lunar calendar occurred in March or April. **40:3** Or *Ark of the Testimony;* also in 40:5, 21. **40:7** Hebrew *Tent of Meeting;* also in 40:12, 22, 24, 26, 30, 32, 34, 35. **40:20** Hebrew *He placed the Testimony;* see note on 25:16.

Tabernacle was dependent on the Israelites' following God's program. A successful recovery is built upon the same principle.
40:1-33 Setting up the Tabernacle began a new life of worship for the Israelites. Undoubtedly, as with any large task, it had taken a great deal of patience and self-control to finish the job. This required that the Israelites delay their gratification, but it must also have made the victory celebration and worship all the more joyous. Sometimes recovery takes many years of delayed gratification, but in the end, the joyous freedom we experience is worth it.

he brought the Ark of the Covenant into the Tabernacle and hung the inner curtain to shield it from view, just as the LORD had commanded him.

²²Next Moses placed the table in the Tabernacle, along the north side of the Holy Place, just outside the inner curtain. ²³And he arranged the Bread of the Presence on the table before the LORD, just as the LORD had commanded him.

²⁴He set the lampstand in the Tabernacle across from the table on the south side of the Holy Place. ²⁵Then he lit the lamps in the LORD's presence, just as the LORD had commanded him. ²⁶He also placed the gold incense altar in the Tabernacle, in the Holy Place in front of the inner curtain. ²⁷On it he burned the fragrant incense, just as the LORD had commanded him.

²⁸He hung the curtain at the entrance of the Tabernacle, ²⁹and he placed the altar of burnt offering near the Tabernacle entrance. On it he offered a burnt offering and a grain offering, just as the LORD had commanded him.

³⁰Next Moses placed the washbasin between the Tabernacle and the altar. He filled it with water so the priests could wash themselves. ³¹Moses and Aaron and Aaron's sons used water from it to wash their hands and feet. ³²Whenever they approached the altar and entered the Tabernacle, they washed themselves, just as the LORD had commanded Moses.

³³Then he hung the curtains forming the courtyard around the Tabernacle and the altar. And he set up the curtain at the entrance of the courtyard. So at last Moses finished the work.

The LORD's Glory Fills the Tabernacle
³⁴Then the cloud covered the Tabernacle, and the glory of the LORD filled the Tabernacle. ³⁵Moses could no longer enter the Tabernacle because the cloud had settled down over it, and the glory of the LORD filled the Tabernacle.

³⁶Now whenever the cloud lifted from the Tabernacle, the people of Israel would set out on their journey, following it. ³⁷But if the cloud did not rise, they remained where they were until it lifted. ³⁸The cloud of the LORD hovered over the Tabernacle during the day, and at night fire glowed inside the cloud so the whole family of Israel could see it. This continued throughout all their journeys.

40:34-38 Israel could count on God's guiding presence in the Tabernacle all the way to the Promised Land. This new relationship with God provided the Israelites with the consistent challenge of self-examination and spiritual growth. Believers today follow Christ by faith, but those same challenges are present. God's guiding presence in our life should provide us with the strength and direction we need to progress in the recovery process.

REFLECTIONS ON **EXODUS**

insights FROM MOSES' LIFE

As we see in **Exodus 2:8-10**, God graciously allowed Moses to be raised by his real mother. Not only did that allow for his normal, healthy development, but it also gave Moses a true understanding of who he was—a Hebrew. Apparently the education he received in the Egyptian royal court never altered Moses' sense of identity with his people. As he grew to manhood, his desire to promote their freedom greatly influenced many of his actions and decisions.

In **Exodus 4:1-9** we see the series of miracles that God gave to Moses to show the Israelites in order to bolster their faith in Moses' message and mission. God does not normally use such wondrous signs to strengthen our faith, but he has performed one miracle that should give us all the encouragement we need. He raised Jesus Christ from the dead, showing that he is no slave to the destruction of sin and death (1 Corinthians 15:1-6). This miracle should give us all faith in God's promises and hope in the Good News he offers.

In **Exodus 4:13-17** we see how Moses tried desperately to escape God's call for his life. He didn't want to go back to Egypt as God's spokesman. He was apparently afraid to face the huge responsibility that this entailed. But God held Moses accountable to his divine plan. He laid out for Moses exactly how the mission in Egypt would be accomplished, despite Moses' presumed handicap. God has a special plan for each of us. If we let him, he will bring it to pass no matter what our weaknesses.

In **Exodus 4:29–5:3** Moses and Aaron approached the elders of Israel with God's message. This alone took a great deal of courage, but by doing so, they were able to encourage the elders to seek freedom from the Egyptians. In an even greater step of courage, they confronted Pharaoh, demanding that things be set straight. God's word to Moses and Aaron gave them the courage to act on behalf of others. Their courage also sparked courage in others, which, in turn, helped them take another step. Courage begets courage. Our own recovery, if properly shared, will inspire others to move forward as well. This in turn will strengthen us to move ahead even further.

In **Exodus 7:6-7** we are told that Moses was 80 years old and that Aaron was 83 when they confronted Pharaoh. The courage and faith demonstrated by Moses and Aaron despite the difficulties before them are doubly amazing when their age is considered. During this later season of life, many people try to avoid confrontations and other difficult challenges. But Moses and Aaron knowingly faced their trials head-on. The courage of Moses and Aaron in these situations provides an example for us to follow. We need to be willing to follow God's program no matter what—even if it means taking action when we would rather just sit back and enjoy the ride.

insights FROM PHARAOH'S LIFE

Egypt's pharaoh perfectly exemplified the persecutor-type personality. In **Exodus 5:3-9** we watch him as he bulldozed the legitimate boundaries of others to get his way. Then he failed to respond properly when he was honestly confronted about the way he was treating the Israelites. He became upset when Moses sought to set appropriate boundaries. Instead of examining himself, Pharaoh then accused the Israelites of being lazy and demanded even more of them. This kind of person is tough to deal with, but God proves here that people like this are no match for him.

In **Exodus 11:4-8** Moses warned Pharaoh of the final plague—the death of the firstborn. This plague would touch people from all levels of Egyptian society and their livestock as well. In ancient Egypt the role of the firstborn son was very important. The firstborn sons affected by this plague included Pharaoh's son, who was heir to the Egyptian throne. It was this plague that finally caused Pharaoh to hit bottom—at least temporarily. It took this severe loss to get the attention of his hard heart. Let us learn from Pharaoh's mistakes and face our problems while our losses are still recoverable. Continued denial can only lead to terrible suffering.

insights FROM ISRAEL'S EXODUS

In **Exodus 12:1-2** we learn how Israel began its escape from Egypt. Israel's exodus from Egypt marked a turning point for Israel. God's people were giving up their life of slavery and turning to a new life of responsibility and freedom. It is possible to build a new life that is so markedly different from the old one that we can declare a new phase or season of life. Such a "declaration of newness" can provide a new sense of identity and be a healthy boundary line, setting us apart from our past failures. At this point in their history the Israelites were declaring such a boundary line—a turning point. We may find it helpful to do the same thing, reinforcing the process of recovery in our life.

In **Exodus 12:3-13** we see that those who trusted God's promise and put the sacrificial blood over their doors were spared the loss of their firstborn sons. Similarly, we who have faith in the sacrifice of Jesus Christ, the ultimate Passover Lamb (John 1:36), are spared from eternal death (John 3:16). We also become brand-new people in Christ (2 Corinthians 5:17). God initiates and maintains the necessary spiritual and emotional recovery processes in our life if we are willing to trust him to do it.

In **Exodus 13:19** we see that Moses took Joseph's bones with him when the people journeyed to the Promised Land. Many years earlier Joseph had made his descendants promise that they would bring his body back to Canaan with them (Genesis 50:24-26). Joseph believed God's promise to Abraham that someday Canaan would belong to Abraham's descendants. Joseph was a godly example to his descendants; here we see that he was remembered 400 years after his death. Not everything in someone's family history is negative. The good things should be remembered and treasured, even as the bad ones must be faced and dealt with.

In **Exodus 14:13-31** a great miracle took place! God opened a dry path through the Red Sea so the people could cross. Notice that even with this amazing miracle, the Israelites had to respond in faith. They had to walk between the massive walls of water that could have become a tidal wave at any moment. This step of faith required commitment to God and surely resulted in the growth of the Israelites' faith. The miracles that God works in our life also require that we respond in faith, stepping out to receive all the blessings he desires for us.

insights DISCOVERED AT MOUNT SINAI

In **Exodus 19:12-23** we see that God set limits or boundaries beyond which the people of Israel, or even their livestock, were not to step. There was mortal danger for those who overstepped God's boundaries. The unauthorized approach into God's holy presence meant certain death. For us, the boundaries are not usually this clear. It is not so immediately obvious when one person violates the boundaries of another. But the consequences of violating these God-given boundaries can also be destructive. It is crucial for us to set personal boundaries as clearly and firmly as possible. We also need to respect the boundaries of others.

In **Exodus 20:18-20** we see how the people of Israel shook with fear before God's holy presence. Fear is an emotion that can be either healthy or unhealthy. When we fear danger or the consequences of inappropriate actions, it is a helpful guide. But when fear is constant or overwhelming and not connected to reality, it is unhealthy. The fear of God can be defined as thoughtful reverence for God; it is certainly a healthy emotion, based on the reality of God's holiness. Fear of God should result in a vibrant faith and motivate us to act according to God's program for our life.

insights FROM GOD'S LAWS

In **Exodus 21:2-11** God showed concern for people in bondage and granted them means of gaining their freedom. But as with any recovery situation involving a network of relationships, there were possible complications. Some people may have been affected adversely by the freeing of a slave and set out to stop the process. And when slaves were freed, they probably needed to learn some difficult lessons about living responsibly without a master to direct their thinking. In the recovery process, these same truths apply. Some of the people close to us may stand against our recovery because they benefit somehow from our bondage. Such obstacles must be overcome. We also need to learn to live responsibly and unselfishly as we begin our new life of freedom.

In **Exodus 21:5-6** God offered each slave the option of becoming a slave forever. This idea of being a slave for life by personal choice is also used in the New Testament to illustrate the commitment we should have to Jesus Christ (Philippians 1:1). Being a slave to a loving and gracious master is a wonderful thing. It has been said that we are all slaves to something— material things, alcohol, drugs, or any number of other things. But none of these masters is kind; they all sell us out to destruction. Only God truly loves his servants. He is the only master worthy of our voluntary, lifelong devotion and service.

According to **Exodus 21:28-36,** we are accountable not only for our own actions but for every-thing we own. Here, the Israelites were required to control their animals so the animals couldn't damage the property of others. Even if the owners were not directly involved in an incident, they were still held accountable for the actions of their livestock or members of their household. This kind of mature accountability serves as the basis for a just and responsible society.

In **Exodus 23:20-26** God promised the Israelites the protection of his angel and the instruc-tions necessary for living wisely as they journeyed toward the Promised Land. As we face recovery, God does the same for us. He is able to lead and protect us in ways we may never even know about. He has given us his Word, which contains instructions for living according to his program. If we do as he says and look to him for help, we will experience the fulfillment of his promises.

LEVITICUS

Rules . . . regulations . . . strange sacrifices—what could the God who requires such things be like? What relevance could these ancient laws possibly have for us? As we look closely at this lengthy list of rules and regulations, some comforting truths about our God and how he relates to us come through.

The book of Leviticus portrays a God who is awesome and holy; he is pure, clean, sinless, perfect. The numerous regulations given to the Israelites confirm this truth. The people needed to humbly obey God if they wanted to live in close fellowship with him. But despite his holiness, God reaches out to broken, sinful people. He provided a way—even though a difficult one—for the Israelites to recover from their past failures through a system of laws and sacrifices.

We all know that "a picture is worth a thousand words." Leviticus is filled with powerful images—pictures that show us both God's gracious character and the terrible consequences of sin. Could there be a more striking reminder of God's grace than the realization that God allowed a suffering, sacrificial animal to take our place? Could there be a more powerful way for us to visualize the consequences of sin than to watch the bloody death of that animal, suffering on our behalf?

The laws and sacrifices in Leviticus help us understand God's character: He is holy but gracious and forgiving. These sacrifices also foreshadow God's later provision of the perfect sacrifice— Jesus Christ. God calls us to obedience, but because he knows that we are far from perfect, he has provided the means for recovery and cleansing through the sacrificial death of Jesus Christ. Because of Jesus, we no longer need animal sacrifices to atone for our sins. Instead, it is through our believing in God's loving forgiveness and in Christ's power over sin and death that we are saved.

THE BOTTOM LINE

PURPOSE: To show that God desires to have personal fellowship with those who turn to him. Only through the channels of worship and personal obedience to God can we fully experience the cleansing and freedom he offers. AUTHOR: Moses. AUDIENCE: The people of Israel. DATE WRITTEN: Shortly after the events the book records, between 1445 and 1407 B.C. SETTING: Camped at Mount Sinai, the people of Israel are given God's special instructions. KEY VERSE: "I, the LORD, am the one who brought you up from the land of Egypt, that I might be your God. Therefore, you must be holy because I am holy" (11:45). KEY PLACE: Mount Sinai. KEY PEOPLE: Moses and Aaron.

RECOVERY THEMES

God's Holy Character: When we focus on God's gracious character, it is easy to forget that he is also terrifying, holy, and awesomely powerful. He is far above us in his majesty and power as well as in his actions and thoughts. As the book of Leviticus reminds us of God's holy power, we should be comforted by the fact that there is nothing he cannot do. But God's holiness never stops him from relating closely to his people. Though perfect and far greater than we are, he is still intimately concerned with each one of us and our progress along the road to recovery.

God's Loving Character: Even the sacrifices, which are so graphically detailed in this book, are an extension of God's love toward each of us. Over and over we encounter the sinfulness of human individuals. We are also repeatedly reminded of the holiness of God. Because of the great chasm between God's holiness and our sinfulness, something was needed to bridge the gap so that people could relate to God. In Old Testament times he graciously provided the sacrifices to bridge that gap, thus revealing his love for his people. This love was ultimately expressed when he sent his Son as a sacrifice to pay for our sins, making it possible for us to draw near to our holy God and receive eternal life.

The Power of Symbolism: For thousands of years God had been working to draw his chosen people back into a relationship with himself. A few followed the true God, but the majority were drawn to false gods. With the sacrifices, God's people had a graphic symbol not only of the costly consequences of their sins but also of God's love for them and his desire for them to draw near to him. We all need symbols to remind us of important truths from God's Word.

Our Need for Grace: When we see the power and majesty of God in Leviticus, we are confronted with our powerlessness to do anything about the problem of our sins. Just as the Israelites were powerless as slaves in Egypt, we are slaves to our human tendency toward sin and its destructive consequences. We need grace. We need help. So God, in his grace, set up a system of sacrifices that provided a means for the debts of sin to be paid. And God took his provision even one step further. He gave his only Son to die for us, a complete and eternal payment for all of our sins and failures.

CHAPTER 1
Procedures for the Burnt Offering

The LORD called to Moses from the Tabernacle* and said to him, ² "Give the following instructions to the people of Israel. When you present an animal as an offering to the LORD, you may take it from your herd of cattle or your flock of sheep and goats.

³ "If the animal you present as a burnt offering is from the herd, it must be a male with no defects. Bring it to the entrance of the Tabernacle so you* may be accepted by the LORD. ⁴Lay your hand on the animal's head, and the LORD will accept its death in your place to purify you, making you right with him.* ⁵ Then slaughter the young bull in the LORD's presence, and Aaron's sons, the priests, will present the animal's blood by splattering it against all sides of the altar that stands at the entrance to the Tabernacle. ⁶Then skin the animal and cut it into pieces. ⁷The sons of Aaron the priest will build a wood fire on the altar. ⁸They will arrange the pieces of the offering, including the head and fat, on the wood burning on the altar. ⁹But the internal organs and the legs must first be washed with water. Then the priest will burn the entire sacrifice on the altar as a burnt offering. It is a special gift, a pleasing aroma to the LORD.

1:1 Hebrew *Tent of Meeting;* also in 1:3, 5.   1:3 Or *it.*   1:4 Or *to make atonement for you.*

1:1 The very first words of this book, "The LORD called," reveal a God who seeks out and initiates relationships with people. Similar words are found in Genesis 3:9 (the same Hebrew word is used), where it says "the LORD God called" to Adam after he had disobeyed to offer him a way of recovery from his sin. Through God's instructions in Exodus and Leviticus, God provided Israel with more elaborate "object lessons" to remind them of how much he had done for them. God is still calling to us today, offering forgiveness, hope, and restored fellowship with him.
1:2-3 The offerings in Leviticus 1–3 are voluntary acts of worship, involving the free will of the individual. While God emphasizes the importance of committing our life to him and provides ways for us to do that, we must choose to act; he does not violate anyone's free will. By actively refusing or passively ignoring a relationship with God, we are choosing life without God's help and hope. The choice is ours!

¹⁰"If the animal you present as a burnt offering is from the flock, it may be either a sheep or a goat, but it must be a male with no defects. ¹¹Slaughter the animal on the north side of the altar in the LORD's presence, and Aaron's sons, the priests, will splatter its blood against all sides of the altar. ¹²Then cut the animal in pieces, and the priests will arrange the pieces of the offering, including the head and fat, on the wood burning on the altar. ¹³But the internal organs and the legs must first be washed with water. Then the priest will burn the entire sacrifice on the altar as a burnt offering. It is a special gift, a pleasing aroma to the LORD.

¹⁴"If you present a bird as a burnt offering to the LORD, choose either a turtledove or a young pigeon. ¹⁵The priest will take the bird to the altar, wring off its head, and burn it on the altar. But first he must drain its blood against the side of the altar. ¹⁶The priest must also remove the crop and the feathers* and throw them in the ashes on the east side of the altar. ¹⁷Then, grasping the bird by its wings, the priest will tear the bird open, but without tearing it apart. Then he will burn it as a burnt offering on the wood burning on the altar. It is a special gift, a pleasing aroma to the LORD.

CHAPTER 2
Procedures for the Grain Offering

"When you present grain as an offering to the LORD, the offering must consist of choice flour. You are to pour olive oil on it, sprinkle it with frankincense, ²and bring it to Aaron's sons, the priests. The priest will scoop out a handful of the flour moistened with oil, together with all the frankincense, and burn this representative portion on the altar. It is a special gift, a pleasing aroma to the LORD. ³The rest of the grain offering will then be given to Aaron and his sons. This offering will be considered a most holy part of the special gifts presented to the LORD.

⁴"If your offering is a grain offering baked in an oven, it must be made of choice flour, but without any yeast. It may be presented in the form of thin cakes mixed with olive oil or wafers spread with olive oil. ⁵If your grain offering is cooked on a griddle, it must be made of choice flour mixed with olive oil but without any yeast. ⁶Break it in pieces and pour olive oil on it; it is a grain offering. ⁷If your grain offering is prepared in a pan, it must be made of choice flour and olive oil.

⁸"No matter how a grain offering for the LORD has been prepared, bring it to the priest, who will present it at the altar. ⁹The priest will take a representative portion of the grain offering and burn it on the altar. It is a special gift, a pleasing aroma to the LORD. ¹⁰The rest of the grain offering will then be given to Aaron and his sons as their food. This offering will be considered a most holy part of the special gifts presented to the LORD.

¹¹"Do not use yeast in preparing any of the grain offerings you present to the LORD, because no yeast or honey may be burned as a special gift presented to the LORD. ¹²You may add yeast and honey to an offering of the first crops of your harvest, but these must never be offered on the altar as a pleasing aroma to the LORD. ¹³Season all your grain offerings with salt to remind you of God's eternal covenant. Never forget to add salt to your grain offerings.

¹⁴"If you present a grain offering to the LORD from the first portion of your harvest, bring fresh grain that is coarsely ground and roasted on a fire. ¹⁵Put olive oil on this grain offering, and sprinkle it with frankincense. ¹⁶The priest will take a representative portion of the grain moistened with oil, together with all the frankincense, and burn it as a special gift presented to the LORD.

1:16 Or *the crop and its contents.* The meaning of the Hebrew is uncertain.

2:1, 4, 14 The grain offering was to consist of *fine* flour or the *first* of the grain harvest. As an animal without defect was required for the other offerings, so the best of one's produce was to be offered here. God was reminding his people that he was worthy of more than just the leftovers; he deserved the best they could offer. God wanted their undivided devotion. In recovery, we cannot entrust ourself to God halfheartedly. We need to give ourself wholeheartedly over to him and his plan.
2:1-16 The grain offering (sometimes called the cereal or meal offering) is the only offering described here that does not involve a blood sacrifice. This offering was made up of the most common daily foods. It symbolized that the offerer had surrendered his whole life to God in recognition of all that God had provided. The recovery process often involves moving from an unhealthy overdependence on some substance or person to a healthy dependence on God. That commitment involves giving not only of ourself to God (the burnt offering) but also of the things of our everyday life (the grain offering).

CHAPTER 3
Procedures for the Peace Offering

"If you present an animal from the herd as a peace offering to the LORD, it may be a male or a female, but it must have no defects. ²Lay your hand on the animal's head, and slaughter it at the entrance of the Tabernacle.* Then Aaron's sons, the priests, will splatter its blood against all sides of the altar. ³The priest must present part of this peace offering as a special gift to the LORD. This includes all the fat around the internal organs, ⁴the two kidneys and the fat around them near the loins, and the long lobe of the liver. These must be removed with the kidneys, ⁵and Aaron's sons will burn them on top of the burnt offering on the wood burning on the altar. It is a special gift, a pleasing aroma to the LORD.

⁶"If you present an animal from the flock as a peace offering to the LORD, it may be a male or a female, but it must have no defects. ⁷If you present a sheep as your offering, bring it to the LORD, ⁸lay your hand on its head, and slaughter it in front of the Tabernacle. Aaron's sons will then splatter the sheep's blood against all sides of the altar. ⁹The priest must present the fat of this peace offering as a special gift to the LORD. This includes the fat of the broad tail cut off near the backbone, all the fat around the internal organs, ¹⁰the two kidneys and the fat around them near the loins, and the long lobe of the liver. These must be removed with the kidneys, ¹¹and the priest will burn them on the altar. It is a special gift of food presented to the LORD.

¹²"If you present a goat as your offering, bring it to the LORD, ¹³lay your hand on its head, and slaughter it in front of the Tabernacle. Aaron's sons will then splatter the goat's blood against all sides of the altar. ¹⁴The priest must present part of this offering as a special gift to the LORD. This includes all the fat around the internal organs, ¹⁵the two kidneys and the fat around them near the loins, and the long lobe of the liver. These must be removed with the kidneys, ¹⁶and the priest will burn them on the altar. It is a special gift of food, a pleasing aroma to the LORD. All the fat belongs to the LORD.

¹⁷"You must never eat any fat or blood. This is a permanent law for you, and it must be observed from generation to generation, wherever you live."

CHAPTER 4
Procedures for the Sin Offering

Then the LORD said to Moses, ²"Give the following instructions to the people of Israel. This is how you are to deal with those who sin unintentionally by doing anything that violates one of the LORD's commands.

³"If the high priest* sins, bringing guilt upon the entire community, he must give a sin offering for the sin he has committed. He

---

3:2 Hebrew *Tent of Meeting;* also in 3:8, 13.   4:3 Hebrew *the anointed priest;* also in 4:5, 16.

3:3-5 In ancient times the fat portions of the animal were considered the very best parts (Genesis 4:4; 45:18). As with the other offerings, God asked that the choice parts be reserved for him. This is a clear reminder that we need to bring our best to God, committing our life to him completely, no matter what the cost.

3:3-5 We are told that the peace offering would be "a special gift, a pleasing aroma to the LORD." God graciously established a way for the people to show their thanks and to give back some of the blessings he had bestowed upon them. Sometimes the way we live brings God a great deal of pain and causes separation from him. Our offerings of thanks to God are a special step toward reconciliation with him—they give him much joy. Reconciliation with God is an important step in recovery and leads toward a life filled with joy.

3:1-17 The peace offering (sometimes called the fellowship offering) was brought to God as an expression of thanks for his blessings, healing, or help in difficult times. The Hebrew word for peace *(shalom)* is a rich term that includes the ideas of physical health, emotional well-being, spiritual wholeness, and material prosperity. The person bringing the offering of thanksgiving was expressing faith and thanks that God had provided what was lacking in his life. It was an act of praise that God had restored him to completeness and harmony with both God and other people. How can we thank God for the peace he has brought into our life?

4:2 The meaning of the word for sin here is "to miss the mark." In the New Testament, the words of the apostle Paul tell us that "Everyone has sinned; we all fall short of God's glorious standard" (Romans 3:23). The Old and New Testament words for sin both emphasize the fact that it keeps us from experiencing the fullness of life that God wants us to enjoy. All of us have failed in some way, so God has provided a means for our healing and reconciliation. It is available to us through repentance and obedience to God's plan for healthy living.

4:3 The sin offering was not only for the average Israelite; it was for the priests as well. Even Israel's high priest was not exempt from sin and its consequences. The writer of Hebrews tells us

must present to the LORD a young bull with no defects. ⁴He must bring the bull to the LORD at the entrance of the Tabernacle,* lay his hand on the bull's head, and slaughter it before the LORD. ⁵The high priest will then take some of the bull's blood into the Tabernacle, ⁶dip his finger in the blood, and sprinkle it seven times before the LORD in front of the inner curtain of the sanctuary. ⁷The priest will then put some of the blood on the horns of the altar for fragrant incense that stands in the LORD's presence inside the Tabernacle. He will pour out the rest of the bull's blood at the base of the altar for burnt offerings at the entrance of the Tabernacle. ⁸Then the priest must remove all the fat of the bull to be offered as a sin offering. This includes all the fat around the internal organs, ⁹the two kidneys and the fat around them near the loins, and the long lobe of the liver. He must remove these along with the kidneys, ¹⁰just as he does with cattle offered as a peace offering, and burn them on the altar of burnt offerings. ¹¹But he must take whatever is left of the bull—its hide, meat, head, legs, internal organs, and dung—¹²and carry it away to a place outside the camp that is ceremonially clean, the place where the ashes are dumped. There, on the ash heap, he will burn it on a wood fire.

¹³"If the entire Israelite community sins by violating one of the LORD's commands, but the people don't realize it, they are still guilty. ¹⁴When they become aware of their sin, the people must bring a young bull as an offering for their sin and present it before the Tabernacle. ¹⁵The elders of the community must then lay their hands on the bull's head and slaughter it before the LORD. ¹⁶The high priest will then take some of the bull's blood into the Tabernacle, ¹⁷dip his finger in the blood, and sprinkle it seven times before the LORD in front of the inner curtain. ¹⁸He will then put some of the blood on the horns of the altar for fragrant incense that stands in the LORD's presence inside the Tabernacle. He will pour out the rest of the blood at the base of the altar for burnt offerings at the entrance of the Tabernacle. ¹⁹Then the priest must remove all the animal's fat and burn it on the altar, ²⁰just as he does with the bull offered as a sin offering for the high priest. Through this process, the priest will purify the people, making them right with the LORD,* and they will be forgiven. ²¹Then the priest must take what is left of the bull and carry it outside the camp and burn it there, just as is done with the sin offering for the high priest. This offering is for the sin of the entire congregation of Israel.

²²"If one of Israel's leaders sins by violating one of the commands of the LORD his God but doesn't realize it, he is still guilty. ²³When he becomes aware of his sin, he must bring as his offering a male goat with no defects. ²⁴He must lay his hand on the goat's head and slaughter it at the place where burnt offerings are slaughtered before the LORD. This is an offering for his sin. ²⁵Then the priest will dip his finger in the blood of the sin offering and put it on the horns of the altar for burnt offerings. He will pour out the rest of the blood at the base of the altar. ²⁶Then he must burn all the goat's fat on the altar, just as he does with the peace offering. Through this process, the priest will purify the leader from his sin, making him right with the LORD, and he will be forgiven.

²⁷"If any of the common people sin by violating one of the LORD's commands, but they don't realize it, they are still guilty. ²⁸When they become aware of their sin, they must bring as an offering for their sin a female goat with no defects. ²⁹They must lay a hand on the head of the sin offering and slaughter it at

4:4 Hebrew *Tent of Meeting;* also in 4:5, 7, 14, 16, 18.   4:20 Or *will make atonement for the people;* similarly in 4:26, 31, 35.

that we have a sinless high priest, Jesus, who is able to understand our weaknesses (Hebrews 4:14-16). So we are to boldly approach God in prayer, that we may receive mercy and find grace to help us in our times of need.

4:1–5:13 The sin offering brought atonement and provided forgiveness for an individual's sin against God. In contrast, the guilt offering (5:14–6:7) brought atonement for acts perpetrated against others. As we seek to recover from past sins and failures, it is clear that we must start by admitting our helplessness before God. We must begin by seeing that all sin is first of all committed against God, who created and loves those we have wronged. We need to echo David's prayer: "Against you, and you alone, have I sinned; I have done what is evil in your sight" (Psalm 51:4). The consequences of our sins, however, usually fall upon us or the people around us. Ultimately we must seek reconciliation with the people we have wronged and make any necessary restitution.

the place where burnt offerings are slaughtered. [30]Then the priest will dip his finger in the blood and put it on the horns of the altar for burnt offerings. He will pour out the rest of the blood at the base of the altar. [31]Then he must remove all the goat's fat, just as he does with the fat of the peace offering. He will burn the fat on the altar, and it will be a pleasing aroma to the LORD. Through this process, the priest will purify the people, making them right with the LORD, and they will be forgiven.

[32]"If the people bring a sheep as their sin offering, it must be a female with no defects. [33]They must lay a hand on the head of the sin offering and slaughter it at the place where burnt offerings are slaughtered. [34]Then the priest will dip his finger in the blood of the sin offering and put it on the horns of the altar for burnt offerings. He will pour out the rest of the blood at the base of the altar. [35]Then he must remove all the sheep's fat, just as he does with the fat of a sheep presented as a peace offering. He will burn the fat on the altar on top of the special gifts presented to the LORD. Through this process, the priest will purify the people from their sin, making them right with the LORD, and they will be forgiven.

CHAPTER 5
Sins Requiring a Sin Offering
"If you are called to testify about something you have seen or that you know about, it is sinful to refuse to testify, and you will be punished for your sin.

[2]"Or suppose you unknowingly touch something that is ceremonially unclean, such as the carcass of an unclean animal. When you realize what you have done, you must admit your defilement and your guilt. This is true whether it is a wild animal, a domestic animal, or an animal that scurries along the ground.

[3]"Or suppose you unknowingly touch something that makes a person unclean. When you realize what you have done, you must admit your guilt.

[4]"Or suppose you make a foolish vow of any kind, whether its purpose is for good or for bad. When you realize its foolishness, you must admit your guilt.

[5]"When you become aware of your guilt in any of these ways, you must confess your sin. [6]Then you must bring to the LORD as the penalty for your sin a female from the flock, either a sheep or a goat. This is a sin offering with which the priest will purify you from your sin, making you right with the LORD.*

[7]"But if you cannot afford to bring a sheep, you may bring to the LORD two turtledoves or two young pigeons as the penalty for your sin. One of the birds will be for a sin offering, and the other for a burnt offering. [8]You must bring them to the priest, who will present the first bird as the sin offering. He will wring its neck but without severing its head from the body. [9]Then he will sprinkle some of the blood of the sin offering against the sides of the altar, and the rest of the blood will be drained out at the base of the altar. This is an offering for sin. [10]The priest will then prepare the second bird as a burnt offering, following all the procedures that have been prescribed. Through this process the priest will purify you from your sin, making you right with the LORD, and you will be forgiven.

[11]"If you cannot afford to bring two turtledoves or two young pigeons, you may bring two quarts* of choice flour for your sin offering. Since it is an offering for sin, you must not moisten it with olive oil or put any frankincense on it. [12]Take the flour to the priest, who will scoop out a handful as a representative portion. He will burn it on the altar on top of the special gifts presented to the LORD. It is an offering for sin. [13]Through this process, the priest will purify those who are guilty of any of these sins, making them right with the LORD, and they will be forgiven. The rest of the flour will belong to the priest, just as with the grain offering."

Procedures for the Guilt Offering
[14]Then the LORD said to Moses, [15]"If one of you commits a sin by unintentionally defiling the LORD's sacred property, you must bring a guilt offering to the LORD. The offer-

---

5:6 Or *will make atonement for you for your sin;* similarly in 5:10, 13, 16, 18.   5:11 Hebrew *1/10 of an ephah* [2.2 liters].

5:14–6:7 The guilt offering was a special kind of sin offering. It was offered by a wrongdoer so he might receive forgiveness from God. That person must also make restitution for the pain or loss he had caused someone else. This offering held the wrongdoer accountable for his actions and paved the path toward his reconciliation with the wronged party. We, too, must consider the effects of our sins on others. Complete recovery demands that we seek reconciliation with God by asking for his forgiveness and making amends with the people we have wronged, wherever possible.

ing must be your own ram with no defects, or you may buy one of equal value with silver, as measured by the weight of the sanctuary shekel.* [16]You must make restitution for the sacred property you have harmed by paying for the loss, plus an additional 20 percent. When you give the payment to the priest, he will purify you with the ram sacrificed as a guilt offering, making you right with the LORD, and you will be forgiven.

[17]"Suppose you sin by violating one of the LORD's commands. Even if you are unaware of what you have done, you are guilty and will be punished for your sin. [18]For a guilt offering, you must bring to the priest your own ram with no defects, or you may buy one of equal value. Through this process the priest will purify you from your unintentional sin, making you right with the LORD, and you will be forgiven. [19]This is a guilt offering, for you have been guilty of an offense against the LORD."

CHAPTER 6
Sins Requiring a Guilt Offering
[1]*Then the LORD said to Moses, [2]"Suppose one of you sins against your associate and is unfaithful to the LORD. Suppose you cheat in a deal involving a security deposit, or you steal or commit fraud, [3]or you find lost property and lie about it, or you lie while swearing to tell the truth, or you commit any other such sin. [4]If you have sinned in any of these ways, you are guilty. You must give back whatever you stole, or the money you took by extortion, or the security deposit, or the lost property you found, [5]or anything obtained by swearing falsely. You must make restitution by paying the full price plus an additional 20 percent to the person you have harmed. On the same day you must present a guilt offering. [6]As a guilt offering to the LORD, you must bring to the priest your own ram with no defects, or you may buy one of equal value. [7]Through this process, the priest will purify you before the LORD, making you right with him,* and you will be forgiven for any of these sins you have committed."

Further Instructions for the Burnt Offering
[8]*Then the LORD said to Moses, [9]"Give Aaron and his sons the following instructions regarding the burnt offering. The burnt

5:15 Each shekel was about 0.4 ounces or 11 grams in weight. 6:1 Verses 6:1-7 are numbered 5:20-26 in Hebrew text. 6:7 Or *will make atonement for you before the LORD.* 6:8 Verses 6:8-30 are numbered 6:1-23 in Hebrew text.

STEP **8**

Unintentional Sins
BIBLE READING: Leviticus 4:1-28
We made lists of all persons we had harmed and became willing to make amends to them all.
As we have allowed our life to get out of control, we have probably hurt people without even realizing it. In fact, much of the pain we have caused has most likely been unintentional. Nevertheless, we still need to take responsibility for our actions by making amends.

When God gave the commandments, he included instructions for handling mistakes as well as intentional sins. He said, "Give the following instructions to the people of Israel. This is how you are to deal with those who sin unintentionally by doing anything that violates one of the LORD's commands. . . . If any of the common people sin by violating one of the LORD's commands, but they don't realize it, they are still guilty. When they become aware of their sin, they must bring as an offering for their sin a female goat with no defects" (Leviticus 4:2, 27-28). "But suppose you unintentionally fail to carry out all these commands that the LORD has given you. . . . If the mistake was made unintentionally, and the community was unaware of it, the whole community must present a young bull for a burnt offering . . . and they will be forgiven. For it was an unintentional sin, and they have corrected it with their offerings to the LORD" (Numbers 15:22-25).

We are responsible for the way our behavior has affected others. This is true even when we didn't realize we were hurting them. These unintentional sins need to be acknowledged and corrected as soon as we discover them. God forgives all our sins. In the recovery process, however, the unintentional sins need to be accounted for along with the more glaring ones. *Turn to page 153, Leviticus 16.*

offering must be left on top of the altar until the next morning, and the fire on the altar must be kept burning all night. [10]In the morning, after the priest on duty has put on his official linen clothing and linen undergarments, he must clean out the ashes of the burnt offering and put them beside the altar. [11]Then he must take off these garments, change back into his regular clothes, and carry the ashes outside the camp to a place that is ceremonially clean. [12]Meanwhile, the fire on the altar must be kept burning; it must never go out. Each morning the priest will add fresh wood to the fire and arrange the burnt offering on it. He will then burn the fat of the peace offerings on it. [13]Remember, the fire must be kept burning on the altar at all times. It must never go out.

Further Instructions for the Grain Offering

[14]"These are the instructions regarding the grain offering. Aaron's sons must present this offering to the LORD in front of the altar. [15]The priest on duty will take from the grain offering a handful of the choice flour moistened with olive oil, together with all the frankincense. He will burn this representative portion on the altar as a pleasing aroma to the LORD. [16]Aaron and his sons may eat the rest of the flour, but it must be baked without yeast and eaten in a sacred place within the courtyard of the Tabernacle.* [17]Remember, it must never be prepared with yeast. I have given it to the priests as their share of the special gifts presented to me. Like the sin offering and the guilt offering, it is most holy. [18]Any of Aaron's male descendants may eat from the special gifts presented to the LORD. This is their permanent right from generation to generation. Anyone or anything that touches these offerings will become holy."

Procedures for the Ordination Offering

[19]Then the LORD said to Moses, [20]"On the day Aaron and his sons are anointed, they must present to the LORD the standard grain offering of two quarts* of choice flour, half to be offered in the morning and half to be offered in the evening. [21]It must be carefully mixed with olive oil and cooked on a griddle. Then slice* this grain offering and present it as a pleasing aroma to the LORD. [22]In each generation, the high priest* who succeeds Aaron must prepare this same offering. It belongs to the LORD and must be burned up completely.

This is a permanent law. [23]All such grain offerings of a priest must be burned up entirely. None of it may be eaten."

Further Instructions for the Sin Offering

[24]Then the LORD said to Moses, [25]"Give Aaron and his sons the following instructions regarding the sin offering. The animal given as an offering for sin is a most holy offering, and it must be slaughtered in the LORD's presence at the place where the burnt offerings are slaughtered. [26]The priest who offers the sacrifice as a sin offering must eat his portion in a sacred place within the courtyard of the Tabernacle. [27]Anyone or anything that touches the sacrificial meat will become holy. If any of the sacrificial blood spatters on a person's clothing, the soiled garment must be washed in a sacred place. [28]If a clay pot is used to boil the sacrificial meat, it must then be broken. If a bronze pot is used, it must be scoured and thoroughly rinsed with water. [29]Any male from a priest's family may eat from this offering; it is most holy. [30]But the offering for sin may not be eaten if its blood was brought into the Tabernacle as an offering for purification* in the Holy Place. It must be completely burned with fire.

CHAPTER 7
Further Instructions for the Guilt Offering

"These are the instructions for the guilt offering. It is most holy. [2]The animal sacrificed as a guilt offering must be slaughtered at the place where the burnt offerings are slaughtered, and its blood must be splattered against all sides of the altar. [3]The priest will then offer all its fat on the altar, including the fat of the broad tail, the fat around the internal organs, [4]the two kidneys and the fat around them near the loins, and the long lobe of the liver. These are to be removed with the kidneys, [5]and the priests will burn them on the altar as a special gift presented to the LORD. This is the guilt offering. [6]Any male from a priest's family may eat the meat. It must be eaten in a sacred place, for it is most holy.

[7]"The same instructions apply to both the guilt offering and the sin offering. Both belong to the priest who uses them to purify someone, making that person right with the LORD.* [8]In the case of the burnt offering, the priest may keep the hide of the sacrificed animal. [9]Any grain offering that has been baked in an oven, prepared in a pan, or cooked on a

---

6:16 Hebrew *Tent of Meeting;* also in 6:26, 30. **6:20** Hebrew *1/10 of an ephah* [2.2 liters]. **6:21** The meaning of this Hebrew term is uncertain. **6:22** Hebrew *the anointed priest.* **6:30** Or *an offering to make atonement.* **7:7** Or *to make atonement.*

griddle belongs to the priest who presents it. [10]All other grain offerings, whether made of dry flour or flour moistened with olive oil, are to be shared equally among all the priests, the descendants of Aaron.

Further Instructions for the Peace Offering

[11]"These are the instructions regarding the different kinds of peace offerings that may be presented to the LORD. [12]If you present your peace offering as an expression of thanksgiving, the usual animal sacrifice must be accompanied by various kinds of bread made without yeast—thin cakes mixed with olive oil, wafers spread with oil, and cakes made of choice flour mixed with olive oil. [13]This peace offering of thanksgiving must also be accompanied by loaves of bread made with yeast. [14]One of each kind of bread must be presented as a gift to the LORD. It will then belong to the priest who splatters the blood of the peace offering against the altar. [15]The meat of the peace offering of thanksgiving must be eaten on the same day it is offered. None of it may be saved for the next morning.

[16]"If you bring an offering to fulfill a vow or as a voluntary offering, the meat must be eaten on the same day the sacrifice is offered, but whatever is left over may be eaten on the second day. [17]Any meat left over until the third day must be completely burned up. [18]If any of the meat from the peace offering is eaten on the third day, the person who presented it will not be accepted by the LORD. You will receive no credit for offering it. By then the meat will be contaminated; if you eat it, you will be punished for your sin.

[19]"Meat that touches anything ceremonially unclean may not be eaten; it must be completely burned up. The rest of the meat may be eaten, but only by people who are ceremonially clean. [20]If you are ceremonially unclean and you eat meat from a peace offering that was presented to the LORD, you will be cut off from the community. [21]If you touch anything that is unclean (whether it is human defilement or an unclean animal or any other unclean, detestable thing) and then eat meat from a peace offering presented to the LORD, you will be cut off from the community."

The Forbidden Blood and Fat

[22]Then the LORD said to Moses, [23]"Give the following instructions to the people of Israel. You must never eat fat, whether from cattle, sheep, or goats. [24]The fat of an animal found dead or torn to pieces by wild animals must never be eaten, though it may be used for any other purpose. [25]Anyone who eats fat from an animal presented as a special gift to the LORD will be cut off from the community. [26]No matter where you live, you must never consume the blood of any bird or animal. [27]Anyone who consumes blood will be cut off from the community."

A Portion for the Priests

[28]Then the LORD said to Moses, [29]"Give the following instructions to the people of Israel. When you present a peace offering to the LORD, bring part of it as a gift to the LORD. [30]Present it to the LORD with your own hands as a special gift to the LORD. Bring the fat of the animal, together with the breast, and lift up the breast as a special offering to the LORD. [31]Then the priest will burn the fat on the altar, but the breast will belong to Aaron and his descendants. [32]Give the right thigh of your peace offering to the priest as a gift. [33]The right thigh must always be given to the priest who offers the blood and the fat of the peace offering. [34]For I have reserved the breast of the special offering and the right thigh of the sacred offering for the priests. It is the permanent right of Aaron and his descendants to share in the peace offerings brought by the people of Israel. [35]This is their rightful share. The special gifts presented to the LORD have been reserved for Aaron and his descendants from the time they were set apart to serve the LORD as priests. [36]On the day they were anointed, the LORD commanded the Israelites to give these portions to the priests as their permanent share from generation to generation."

[37]These are the instructions for the burnt offering, the grain offering, the sin offering,

---

7:12-15 The most common type of peace offering was the offering of thanksgiving. It involved, in addition to the animal sacrifice, the presentation of various kinds of unleavened and leavened breads, part of which were sacrificed and part eaten in a communal meal. From this the Israelite believer learned the importance of a public expression of thanks to God. God wants us to praise him before others too. An excellent occasion for this is when he has given us a victory over sin. This public expression of gratitude to God will not only enhance our spiritual growth but be a first step toward helping others.

and the guilt offering, as well as the ordination offering and the peace offering. [38]The LORD gave these instructions to Moses on Mount Sinai when he commanded the Israelites to present their offerings to the LORD in the wilderness of Sinai.

CHAPTER 8
Ordination of the Priests
Then the LORD said to Moses, [2]"Bring Aaron and his sons, along with their sacred garments, the anointing oil, the bull for the sin offering, the two rams, and the basket of bread made without yeast, [3]and call the entire community of Israel together at the entrance of the Tabernacle.*"

[4]So Moses followed the LORD's instructions, and the whole community assembled at the Tabernacle entrance. [5]Moses announced to them, "This is what the LORD has commanded us to do!" [6]Then he presented Aaron and his sons and washed them with water. [7]He put the official tunic on Aaron and tied the sash around his waist. He dressed him in the robe, placed the ephod on him, and attached the ephod securely with its decorative sash. [8]Then Moses placed the chestpiece on Aaron and put the Urim and the Thummim inside it. [9]He placed the turban on Aaron's head and attached the gold medallion—the badge of holiness—to the front of the turban, just as the LORD had commanded him.

[10]Then Moses took the anointing oil and anointed the Tabernacle and everything in it, making them holy. [11]He sprinkled the oil on the altar seven times, anointing it and all its utensils, as well as the washbasin and its stand, making them holy. [12]Then he poured some of the anointing oil on Aaron's head, anointing him and making him holy for his work. [13]Next Moses presented Aaron's sons. He clothed them in their tunics, tied their sashes around them, and put their special head coverings on them, just as the LORD had commanded him.

[14]Then Moses presented the bull for the sin offering. Aaron and his sons laid their hands on the bull's head, [15]and Moses slaughtered it. Moses took some of the blood, and with his finger he put it on the four horns of the altar to purify it. He poured out the rest of the blood at the base of the altar. Through this process, he made the altar holy by purifying it.* [16]Then Moses took all the fat around the internal organs, the long lobe of the liver, and the two kidneys and the fat around them, and he burned it all on the altar. [17]He took the rest of the bull, including its hide, meat, and dung, and burned it on a fire outside the camp, just as the LORD had commanded him.

[18]Then Moses presented the ram for the burnt offering. Aaron and his sons laid their hands on the ram's head, [19]and Moses slaughtered it. Then Moses took the ram's blood and splattered it against all sides of the altar. [20]Then he cut the ram into pieces, and he burned the head, some of its pieces, and the fat on the altar. [21]After washing the internal organs and the legs with water, Moses burned the entire ram on the altar as a burnt offering. It was a pleasing aroma, a special gift presented to the LORD, just as the LORD had commanded him.

[22]Then Moses presented the other ram, which was the ram of ordination. Aaron and his sons laid their hands on the ram's head, [23]and Moses slaughtered it. Then Moses took some of its blood and applied it to the lobe of Aaron's right ear, the thumb of his right hand, and the big toe of his right foot. [24]Next Moses presented Aaron's sons and applied some of the blood to the lobes of their right ears, the thumbs of their right hands, and the big toes of their right feet. He then splattered the rest of the blood against all sides of the altar.

[25]Next Moses took the fat, including the fat of the broad tail, the fat around the internal organs, the long lobe of the liver, and the two kidneys and the fat around them, along with the right thigh. [26]On top of these he placed a thin cake of bread made without yeast, a cake of bread mixed with olive oil, and a wafer

---

8:3 Hebrew *Tent of Meeting;* also in 8:4, 31, 33, 35. 8:15 Or *by making atonement for it;* or *that offerings for purification might be made on it.*

8:1-4 Among the Israelites, the priest entered God's holy presence with the people's requests; he was the mediator between God and the people. God instituted the priesthood because he desired to have fellowship with his people. But the mediation of the priesthood was also a stern reminder that God is an awesome and holy God who cannot be approached lightly. Since we as believers are called "holy priests" (1 Peter 2:5), we may come boldly before God, offering him our life as a spiritual sacrifice. But as we approach him, we must be careful to remember that he is a holy God. God does not take sin lightly—neither should we.

spread with olive oil. All these were taken from the basket of bread made without yeast that was placed in the LORD's presence. [27]He put all these in the hands of Aaron and his sons, and he lifted these gifts as a special offering to the LORD. [28]Moses then took all the offerings back from them and burned them on the altar on top of the burnt offering. This was the ordination offering. It was a pleasing aroma, a special gift presented to the LORD. [29] Then Moses took the breast and lifted it up as a special offering to the LORD. This was Moses' portion of the ram of ordination, just as the LORD had commanded him.

[30]Next Moses took some of the anointing oil and some of the blood that was on the altar, and he sprinkled them on Aaron and his garments and on his sons and their garments. In this way, he made Aaron and his sons and their garments holy.

[31]Then Moses said to Aaron and his sons, "Boil the remaining meat of the offerings at the Tabernacle entrance, and eat it there, along with the bread that is in the basket of offerings for the ordination, just as I commanded when I said, 'Aaron and his sons will eat it.' [32]Any meat or bread that is left over must then be burned up. [33]You must not leave the Tabernacle entrance for seven days, for that is when the ordination ceremony will be completed. [34]Everything we have done today was commanded by the LORD in order to purify you, making you right with him.* [35]Now stay at the entrance of the Tabernacle day and night for seven

days, and do everything the LORD requires. If you fail to do this, you will die, for this is what the LORD has commanded." [36]So Aaron and his sons did everything the LORD had commanded through Moses.

CHAPTER 9
The Priests Begin Their Work

After the ordination ceremony, on the eighth day, Moses called together Aaron and his sons and the elders of Israel. [2]He said to Aaron, "Take a young bull for a sin offering and a ram for a burnt offering, both without defects, and present them to the LORD. [3]Then tell the Israelites, 'Take a male goat for a sin offering, and take a calf and a lamb, both a year old and without defects, for a burnt offering. [4]Also take a bull* and a ram for a peace offering and flour moistened with olive oil for a grain offering. Present all these offerings to the LORD because the LORD will appear to you today.'"

[5]So the people presented all these things at the entrance of the Tabernacle,* just as Moses had commanded. Then the whole community came forward and stood before the LORD. [6]And Moses said, "This is what the LORD has commanded you to do so that the glory of the LORD may appear to you."

[7] Then Moses said to Aaron, "Come to the altar and sacrifice your sin offering and your burnt offering to purify yourself and the people. Then present the offerings of the people to purify them, making them right with the LORD,* just as he has commanded."

8:34 Or to make atonement for you. 9:4 Or cow; also in 9:18, 19. 9:5 Hebrew Tent of Meeting; also in 9:23. 9:7 Or to make atonement for them.

8:30-36 Aaron and his sons were sprinkled with blood from the sacrifices. This symbolized their cleansing and reconciliation to God through the sacrificial death of the animal offering. The high price for their sin, the death of a living animal, would have been a poignant reminder of how important obedience was. The apostle Peter described believers as those who have been "cleansed by the blood of Jesus Christ" (1 Peter 1:2). Because of the high price paid for our sins— the sacrificial death of Christ on the cross—we ought to be living a life of obedience to his Word.

9:7 Because Aaron was the high priest, he offered sacrifices to make atonement for his sins and those of the people. But Jesus Christ, our High Priest, did more than offer sacrifices for us; he actually became our sin offering. He made all animal sacrifices obsolete by offering himself on the cross as the perfect sacrifice. And by sacrificially giving himself for others, he set a clear example for us to live by. His example should lead us to give ourself to others as a means to their healing and enrichment.

9:8-24 This account of Aaron's sacrifices reflects the actual order in which the various sacrifices were offered by an individual. The sin offering was first, showing the priority of confession and cleansing from sin before God. The following burnt or grain offering represented the worshiper's obedience in giving his or her life over to God. Then the peace offering was an expression of gratitude for a continuing walk with God. Similarly, our first step along the road to recovery from sin and failure must be the admission that we are hopeless on our own. The next step is the commitment of our life to God through Jesus Christ, our sacrifice. This is then followed by ongoing fellowship with God, accountability for sin, and spiritual growth.

⁸So Aaron went to the altar and slaughtered the calf as a sin offering for himself. ⁹His sons brought him the blood, and he dipped his finger in it and put it on the horns of the altar. He poured out the rest of the blood at the base of the altar. ¹⁰Then he burned on the altar the fat, the kidneys, and the long lobe of the liver from the sin offering, just as the LORD had commanded Moses. ¹¹The meat and the hide, however, he burned outside the camp.

¹²Next Aaron slaughtered the animal for the burnt offering. His sons brought him the blood, and he splattered it against all sides of the altar. ¹³Then they handed him each piece of the burnt offering, including the head, and he burned them on the altar. ¹⁴Then he washed the internal organs and the legs and burned them on the altar along with the rest of the burnt offering.

¹⁵Next Aaron presented the offerings of the people. He slaughtered the people's goat and presented it as an offering for their sin, just as he had first done with the offering for his own sin. ¹⁶Then he presented the burnt offering and sacrificed it in the prescribed way. ¹⁷He also presented the grain offering, burning a handful of the flour mixture on the altar, in addition to the regular burnt offering for the morning.

¹⁸Then Aaron slaughtered the bull and the ram for the people's peace offering. His sons brought him the blood, and he splattered it against all sides of the altar. ¹⁹Then he took the fat of the bull and the ram—the fat of the broad tail and from around the internal organs—along with the kidneys and the long lobes of the livers. ²⁰He placed these fat portions on top of the breasts of these animals and burned them on the altar. ²¹Aaron then lifted up the breasts and right thighs as a special offering to the LORD, just as Moses had commanded.

²²After that, Aaron raised his hands toward the people and blessed them. Then, after presenting the sin offering, the burnt offering, and the peace offering, he stepped down from the altar. ²³Then Moses and Aaron went into the Tabernacle, and when they came back out, they blessed the people again, and the glory of the LORD appeared to the whole community. ²⁴Fire blazed forth from the LORD's presence and consumed the burnt offering and the fat on the altar. When the people saw this, they shouted with joy and fell face down on the ground.

CHAPTER 10
The Sin of Nadab and Abihu

Aaron's sons Nadab and Abihu put coals of fire in their incense burners and sprinkled incense over them. In this way, they disobeyed the LORD by burning before him the wrong kind of fire, different than he had commanded. ²So fire blazed forth from the LORD's presence and burned them up, and they died there before the LORD.

³Then Moses said to Aaron, "This is what the LORD meant when he said,

'I will display my holiness
    through those who come near me.
I will display my glory
    before all the people.'"

And Aaron was silent.

⁴Then Moses called for Mishael and Elzaphan, Aaron's cousins, the sons of Aaron's uncle Uzziel. He said to them, "Come forward and carry away the bodies of your relatives from in front of the sanctuary to a place outside the camp." ⁵So they came forward and picked them up by their garments and carried them out of the camp, just as Moses had commanded.

⁶Then Moses said to Aaron and his sons Eleazar and Ithamar, "Do not show grief by leaving your hair uncombed* or by tearing your clothes. If you do, you will die, and the LORD's anger will strike the whole community of Israel. However, the rest of the Israelites, your relatives, may mourn because of the LORD's fiery destruction of Nadab and Abihu. ⁷But you must not leave the entrance of the Tabernacle* or you will die, for you have been anointed with the LORD's anointing oil." So they did as Moses commanded.

10:6 Or *by uncovering your heads.* 10:7 Hebrew *Tent of Meeting;* also in 10:9.

10:1-3 The sin and swift judgment of Aaron's two eldest sons indicate the greater responsibility of those who occupy positions of leadership and authority. Although the specifics of their sin are not explained in Scripture, it is likely that their wrong actions proceeded from wrong attitudes. Perhaps they believed that as leaders they were exempt from the moral law. While God's grace and long-suffering may often spare us from immediate judgment, we should be aware that we are accountable to him. When we become irresponsible and disobedient to God's plan, the consequences may be grave.

Instructions for Priestly Conduct

8Then the LORD said to Aaron, 9"You and your descendants must never drink wine or any other alcoholic drink before going into the Tabernacle. If you do, you will die. This is a permanent law for you, and it must be observed from generation to generation. 10You must distinguish between what is sacred and what is common, between what is ceremonially unclean and what is clean. 11And you must teach the Israelites all the decrees that the LORD has given them through Moses."

12Then Moses said to Aaron and his remaining sons, Eleazar and Ithamar, "Take what is left of the grain offering after a portion has been presented as a special gift to the LORD, and eat it beside the altar. Make sure it contains no yeast, for it is most holy. 13You must eat it in a sacred place, for it has been given to you and your descendants as your portion of the special gifts presented to the LORD. These are the commands I have been given. 14But the breast and thigh that were lifted up as a special offering may be eaten in any place that is ceremonially clean. These parts have been given to you and your descendants as your portion of the peace offerings presented by the people of Israel. 15You must lift up the thigh and breast as a special offering to the LORD, along with the fat of the special gifts. These parts will belong to you and your descendants as your permanent right, just as the LORD has commanded."

16Moses then asked them what had happened to the goat of the sin offering. When he discovered it had been burned up, he became very angry with Eleazar and Ithamar, Aaron's remaining sons. 17"Why didn't you eat the sin offering in the sacred area?" he demanded. "It is a holy offering! The LORD has given it to you to remove the guilt of the community and to purify the people, making them right with the LORD.* 18Since the animal's blood was not brought into the Holy Place, you should have eaten the meat in the sacred area as I ordered you."

19Then Aaron answered Moses, "Today my sons presented both their sin offering and their burnt offering to the LORD. And yet this tragedy has happened to me. If I had eaten the people's sin offering on such a tragic day as this, would the LORD have been pleased?" 20And when Moses heard this, he was satisfied.

CHAPTER 11
Ceremonially Clean and Unclean Animals

Then the LORD said to Moses and Aaron, 2"Give the following instructions to the people of Israel.

"Of all the land animals, these are the ones you may use for food. 3You may eat any animal that has completely split hooves and chews the cud. 4You may not, however, eat the following animals* that have split hooves or that chew the cud, but not both. The camel chews the cud but does not have split hooves, so it is ceremonially unclean for you. 5The hyrax* chews the cud but does not have split hooves, so it is unclean. 6The hare chews the cud but does not have split hooves, so it is unclean. 7The pig has evenly split hooves but does not chew the cud, so it is unclean. 8You may not eat the meat of these animals or even touch their carcasses. They are ceremonially unclean for you.

9"Of all the marine animals, these are ones you may use for food. You may eat anything from the water if it has both fins and scales, whether taken from salt water or from

10:17 Or *to make atonement for the people before the LORD.* 11:4 The identification of some of the animals, birds, and insects in this chapter is uncertain. 11:5 Or *coney,* or *rock badger.*

10:8-9 This passage about the use of wine or other intoxicating beverages illustrates the importance of self-control on the part of the priests. Because of the importance of their work and their example, God required certain boundaries and evidence of self-control. Alcohol would affect their ability to carry out the task God had called them to do. This illustrates our need for boundaries and self-control as we seek to carry an effective and positive testimony of God's love to others.
10:8-11 First, Aaron was told how to act (10:8-9); then he was told what to teach (10:10-11). This illustrates an important principle: Actions speak louder than words. God calls us to live in a way that will, by example, reinforce what we teach others. If we fail to live by what we teach, we may as well have never spoken.
11:1-47 The elaborate dietary laws in this section illustrate the fact that God's relationship with his people extends to even the practical areas of everyday living. While we are not bound by the specifics of these dietary standards, we know that God is just as interested in the details of our life. If our eating or drinking leads to excess, abuse, or poor health, God is interested. He also holds us accountable to deal with the problem. Personal holiness relates even to the mundane areas of our life.

streams. ¹⁰But you must never eat animals from the sea or from rivers that do not have both fins and scales. They are detestable to you. This applies both to little creatures that live in shallow water and to all creatures that live in deep water. ¹¹They will always be detestable to you. You must never eat their meat or even touch their dead bodies. ¹²Any marine animal that does not have both fins and scales is detestable to you.

¹³"These are the birds that are detestable to you. You must never eat them: the griffon vulture, the bearded vulture, the black vulture, ¹⁴the kite, falcons of all kinds, ¹⁵ravens of all kinds, ¹⁶the eagle owl, the short-eared owl, the seagull, hawks of all kinds, ¹⁷the little owl, the cormorant, the great owl, ¹⁸the barn owl, the desert owl, the Egyptian vulture, ¹⁹the stork, herons of all kinds, the hoopoe, and the bat.

²⁰"You must not eat winged insects that walk along the ground; they are detestable to you. ²¹You may, however, eat winged insects that walk along the ground and have jointed legs so they can jump. ²²The insects you are permitted to eat include all kinds of locusts, bald locusts, crickets, and grasshoppers. ²³All other winged insects that walk along the ground are detestable to you.

²⁴"The following creatures will make you ceremonially unclean. If any of you touch their carcasses, you will be defiled until evening. ²⁵If you pick up their carcasses, you must wash your clothes, and you will remain defiled until evening.

²⁶"Any animal that has split hooves that are not evenly divided or that does not chew the cud is unclean for you. If you touch the carcass of such an animal, you will be defiled. ²⁷Of the animals that walk on all fours, those that have paws are unclean. If you touch the carcass of such an animal, you will be defiled until evening. ²⁸If you pick up its carcass, you must wash your clothes, and you will remain defiled until evening. These animals are unclean for you.

²⁹"Of the small animals that scurry along the ground, these are unclean for you: the mole rat, the rat, large lizards of all kinds, ³⁰the gecko, the monitor lizard, the common lizard, the sand lizard, and the chameleon.

³¹All these small animals are unclean for you. If any of you touch the dead body of such an animal, you will be defiled until evening. ³²If such an animal dies and falls on something, that object will be unclean. This is true whether the object is made of wood, cloth, leather, or burlap. Whatever its use, you must dip it in water, and it will remain defiled until evening. After that, it will be ceremonially clean and may be used again.

³³"If such an animal falls into a clay pot, everything in the pot will be defiled, and the pot must be smashed. ³⁴If the water from such a container spills on any food, the food will be defiled. And any beverage in such a container will be defiled. ³⁵Any object on which the carcass of such an animal falls will be defiled. If it is an oven or hearth, it must be destroyed, for it is defiled, and you must treat it accordingly.

³⁶"However, if the carcass of such an animal falls into a spring or a cistern, the water will still be clean. But anyone who touches the carcass will be defiled. ³⁷If the carcass falls on seed grain to be planted in the field, the seed will still be considered clean. ³⁸But if the seed is wet when the carcass falls on it, the seed will be defiled.

³⁹"If an animal you are permitted to eat dies and you touch its carcass, you will be defiled until evening. ⁴⁰If you eat any of its meat or carry away its carcass, you must wash your clothes, and you will remain defiled until evening.

⁴¹"All small animals that scurry along the ground are detestable, and you must never eat them. ⁴²This includes all animals that slither along on their bellies, as well as those with four legs and those with many feet. All such animals that scurry along the ground are detestable, and you must never eat them. ⁴³Do not defile yourselves by touching them. You must not make yourselves ceremonially unclean because of them. ⁴⁴For I am the LORD your God. You must consecrate yourselves and be holy, because I am holy. So do not defile yourselves with any of these small animals that scurry along the ground. ⁴⁵For I, the LORD, am the one who brought you up from the land of Egypt, that I might be your

---

11:44 What does it mean to be holy? It doesn't mean just to have a pious attitude toward God. The Hebrew word literally means "to be set apart," both unto God and from sin. This chapter emphasizes the aspect of being set apart unto God. These dietary laws and other guidelines for daily living gave the Israelites a unique identity as God's people. God also calls us to a life of holiness, a life that clearly reflects God's standards.

God. Therefore, you must be holy because I am holy.

⁴⁶ "These are the instructions regarding land animals, birds, marine creatures, and animals that scurry along the ground. ⁴⁷ By these instructions you will know what is unclean and clean, and which animals may be eaten and which may not be eaten."

CHAPTER 12
Purification after Childbirth

The LORD said to Moses, ² "Give the following instructions to the people of Israel. If a woman becomes pregnant and gives birth to a son, she will be ceremonially unclean for seven days, just as she is unclean during her menstrual period. ³ On the eighth day the boy's foreskin must be circumcised. ⁴ After waiting thirty-three days, she will be purified from the bleeding of childbirth. During this time of purification, she must not touch anything that is set apart as holy. And she must not enter the sanctuary until her time of purification is over. ⁵ If a woman gives birth to a daughter, she will be ceremonially unclean for two weeks, just as she is unclean during her menstrual period. After waiting sixty-six days, she will be purified from the bleeding of childbirth.

⁶ "When the time of purification is completed for either a son or a daughter, the woman must bring a one-year-old lamb for a burnt offering and a young pigeon or turtledove for a purification offering. She must bring her offerings to the priest at the entrance of the Tabernacle.* ⁷ The priest will then present them to the LORD to purify her.* Then she will be ceremonially clean again after her bleeding at childbirth. These are the instructions for a woman after the birth of a son or a daughter.

⁸ "If a woman cannot afford to bring a lamb, she must bring two turtledoves or two young pigeons. One will be for the burnt offering and the other for the purification offering. The priest will sacrifice them to purify her, and she will be ceremonially clean."

CHAPTER 13
Serious Skin Diseases

The LORD said to Moses and Aaron, ² "If anyone has a swelling or a rash or discolored skin that might develop into a serious skin disease,* that person must be brought to Aaron the priest or to one of his sons.* ³ The priest will examine the affected area of the skin. If the hair in the affected area has turned white and the problem appears to be more than skin-deep, it is a serious skin disease, and the priest who examines it must pronounce the person ceremonially unclean.

⁴ "But if the affected area of the skin is only a white discoloration and does not appear to be more than skin-deep, and if the hair on the spot has not turned white, the priest will quarantine the person for seven days. ⁵ On the seventh day the priest will make another examination. If he finds the affected area has not changed and the problem has not spread on the skin, the priest will quarantine the person for seven more days. ⁶ On the seventh day the priest will make another examination. If he finds the affected area has faded and has not spread, the priest will pronounce the person ceremonially clean. It was only a rash. The person's clothing must be washed, and the person will be ceremonially clean. ⁷ But if the rash continues to spread after the person has been examined by the priest and has been pronounced clean, the infected person must return to be examined again. ⁸ If the priest finds that the rash has spread, he must pronounce the person ceremonially unclean, for it is indeed a skin disease.

⁹ "Anyone who develops a serious skin disease must go to the priest for an examination. ¹⁰ If the priest finds a white swelling on the skin, and some hair on the spot has turned white, and there is an open sore in the affected area, ¹¹ it is a chronic skin disease, and the priest must pronounce the person ceremonially unclean. In such cases the person need not be quarantined, for it is obvious that the skin is defiled by the disease. ¹² "Now suppose the disease has spread all

---

12:6 Hebrew *Tent of Meeting.* **12:7** Or *to make atonement for her;* also in 12:8. **13:2a** Traditionally rendered *leprosy.* The Hebrew word used throughout this passage is used to describe various skin diseases. **13:2b** Or *one of his descendants.*

13:1–15:33 These detailed health regulations excluded many Israelites from the larger society. They were banned from fellowship with others for being "ceremonially unclean." Lepers and prostitutes were automatically unclean, according to the law, and were thus ostracized. This fact should help us appreciate even more the compassionate heart of Jesus Christ. He healed lepers and the woman who had been hemorrhaging for 12 years; he talked with prostitutes and other outcasts. He cared most about the needy, the unclean. He considered it his work to show them the road to recovery and forgiveness.

over the person's skin, covering the body from head to foot. [13]When the priest examines the infected person and finds that the disease covers the entire body, he will pronounce the person ceremonially clean. Since the skin has turned completely white, the person is clean. [14]But if any open sores appear, the infected person will be pronounced ceremonially unclean. [15]The priest must make this pronouncement as soon as he sees an open sore, since open sores indicate the presence of a skin disease. [16]However, if the open sores heal and turn white like the rest of the skin, the person must return to the priest [17]for another examination. If the affected areas have indeed turned white, the priest will then pronounce the person ceremonially clean by declaring, 'You are clean!'

[18]"If anyone has a boil on the skin that has started to heal, [19]but a white swelling or a reddish white spot develops in its place, that person must go to the priest to be examined. [20]If the priest examines it and finds it to be more than skin-deep, and if the hair in the affected area has turned white, the priest must pronounce the person ceremonially unclean. The boil has become a serious skin disease. [21]But if the priest finds no white hair on the affected area and the problem appears to be no more than skin-deep and has faded, the priest must quarantine the person for seven days. [22]If during that time the affected area spreads on the skin, the priest must pronounce the person ceremonially unclean, because it is a serious disease. [23]But if the area grows no larger and does not spread, it is merely the scar from the boil, and the priest will pronounce the person ceremonially clean.

[24]"If anyone has suffered a burn on the skin and the burned area changes color, becoming either reddish white or shiny white, [25]the priest must examine it. If he finds that the hair in the affected area has turned white and the problem appears to be more than skin-deep, a skin disease has broken out in the burn. The priest must then pronounce the person ceremonially unclean, for it is clearly a serious skin disease. [26]But if the priest finds no white hair on the affected area and the problem appears to be no more than skin-deep and has faded, the priest must quarantine the infected person for seven days. [27]On the seventh day the priest must examine the person again. If the affected area has spread on the skin, the priest must pronounce that person ceremonially unclean, for it is clearly a serious skin disease.

[28]But if the affected area has not changed or spread on the skin and has faded, it is simply a swelling from the burn. The priest will then pronounce the person ceremonially clean, for it is only the scar from the burn.

[29]"If anyone, either a man or woman, has a sore on the head or chin, [30]the priest must examine it. If he finds it is more than skin-deep and has fine yellow hair on it, the priest must pronounce the person ceremonially unclean. It is a scabby sore of the head or chin. [31]If the priest examines the scabby sore and finds that it is only skin-deep but there is no black hair on it, he must quarantine the person for seven days. [32]On the seventh day the priest must examine the sore again. If he finds that the scabby sore has not spread, and there is no yellow hair on it, and it appears to be only skin-deep, [33]the person must shave off all hair except the hair on the affected area. Then the priest must quarantine the person for another seven days. [34]On the seventh day he will examine the sore again. If it has not spread and appears to be no more than skin-deep, the priest will pronounce the person ceremonially clean. The person's clothing must be washed, and the person will be ceremonially clean. [35]But if the scabby sore begins to spread after the person is pronounced clean, [36]the priest must do another examination. If he finds that the sore has spread, the priest does not need to look for yellow hair. The infected person is ceremonially unclean. [37]But if the color of the scabby sore does not change and black hair has grown on it, it has healed. The priest will then pronounce the person ceremonially clean.

[38]"If anyone, either a man or woman, has shiny white patches on the skin, [39]the priest must examine the affected area. If he finds that the shiny patches are only pale white, this is a harmless skin rash, and the person is ceremonially clean.

[40]"If a man loses his hair and his head becomes bald, he is still ceremonially clean. [41]And if he loses hair on his forehead, he simply has a bald forehead; he is still clean. [42]However, if a reddish white sore appears on the bald area on top of his head or on his forehead, this is a skin disease. [43]The priest must examine him, and if he finds swelling around the reddish white sore anywhere on the man's head and it looks like a skin disease, [44]the man is indeed infected with a skin disease and is unclean. The priest must pronounce him ceremonially unclean because of the sore on his head.

⁴⁵"Those who suffer from a serious skin disease must tear their clothing and leave their hair uncombed.* They must cover their mouth and call out, 'Unclean! Unclean!' ⁴⁶As long as the serious disease lasts, they will be ceremonially unclean. They must live in isolation in their place outside the camp.

Treatment of Contaminated Clothing

⁴⁷"Now suppose mildew* contaminates some woolen or linen clothing, ⁴⁸woolen or linen fabric, the hide of an animal, or anything made of leather. ⁴⁹If the contaminated area in the clothing, the animal hide, the fabric, or the leather article has turned greenish or reddish, it is contaminated with mildew and must be shown to the priest. ⁵⁰After examining the affected spot, the priest will put the article in quarantine for seven days. ⁵¹On the seventh day the priest must inspect it again. If the contaminated area has spread, the clothing or fabric or leather is clearly contaminated by a serious mildew and is ceremonially unclean. ⁵²The priest must burn the item—the clothing, the woolen or linen fabric, or piece of leather—for it has been contaminated by a serious mildew. It must be completely destroyed by fire.

⁵³"But if the priest examines it and finds that the contaminated area has not spread in the clothing, the fabric, or the leather, ⁵⁴the priest will order the object to be washed and then quarantined for seven more days. ⁵⁵Then the priest must examine the object again. If he finds that the contaminated area has not changed color after being washed, even if it did not spread, the object is defiled. It must be completely burned up, whether the contaminated spot* is on the inside or outside. ⁵⁶But if the priest examines it and finds that the contaminated area has faded after being washed, he must cut the spot from the clothing, the fabric, or the leather. ⁵⁷If the spot later reappears on the clothing, the fabric, or the leather article, the mildew is clearly spreading, and the contaminated object must be burned up. ⁵⁸But if the spot disappears from the clothing, the fabric, or the leather article after it has been washed, it must be washed again; then it will be ceremonially clean.

⁵⁹"These are the instructions for dealing with mildew that contaminates woolen or linen clothing or fabric or anything made of leather. This is how the priest will determine whether these items are ceremonially clean or unclean."

CHAPTER 14
Cleansing from Skin Diseases

And the LORD said to Moses, ²"The following instructions are for those seeking ceremonial purification from a skin disease.* Those who have been healed must be brought to the priest, ³who will examine them at a place outside the camp. If the priest finds that someone has been healed of a serious skin disease, ⁴he will perform a purification ceremony, using two live birds that are ceremonially clean, a stick of cedar,* some scarlet yarn, and a hyssop branch. ⁵The priest will order that one bird be slaughtered over a clay pot filled with fresh water. ⁶He will take the live bird, the cedar stick, the scarlet yarn, and the hyssop branch, and dip them into the blood of the bird that was slaughtered over the fresh water. ⁷The priest will then sprinkle the blood of the dead bird seven times on the person being purified of the skin disease. When the priest has purified the person, he will release the live bird in the open field to fly away.

⁸"The persons being purified must then wash their clothes, shave off all their hair, and bathe themselves in water. Then they will be ceremonially clean and may return to the camp. However, they must remain outside their tents for seven days. ⁹On the seventh day they must again shave all the hair from their heads, including the hair of the beard and eyebrows. They must also wash their clothes and bathe themselves in water. Then they will be ceremonially clean.

¹⁰"On the eighth day each person being purified must bring two male lambs and a one-year-old female lamb, all with no defects, along with a grain offering of six quarts* of choice flour moistened with olive oil, and a cup* of olive oil. ¹¹Then the officiating priest will present that person for purification, along with the offerings, before the LORD at the entrance of the Tabernacle.* ¹²The priest will take one of the male lambs and the olive oil and present them as a guilt offering, lifting them up as a special offering before the LORD. ¹³He will then slaughter the

13:45 Or *and uncover their heads.* 13:47 Traditionally rendered *leprosy.* The Hebrew term used throughout this passage is the same term used for the various skin diseases described in 13:1-46. 13:55 The meaning of the Hebrew is uncertain. 14:2 Traditionally rendered *leprosy;* see note on 13:2a. 14:4 Or *juniper;* also in 14:6, 49, 51. 14:10a Hebrew *³/₁₀ of an ephah* [6.6 liters]. 14:10b Hebrew *1 log* [0.3 liters]; also in 14:21. 14:11 Hebrew *Tent of Meeting;* also in 14:23.

male lamb in the sacred area where sin offerings and burnt offerings are slaughtered. As with the sin offering, the guilt offering belongs to the priest. It is a most holy offering. [14]The priest will then take some of the blood of the guilt offering and apply it to the lobe of the right ear, the thumb of the right hand, and the big toe of the right foot of the person being purified.

[15]"Then the priest will pour some of the olive oil into the palm of his own left hand. [16]He will dip his right finger into the oil in his palm and sprinkle some of it with his finger seven times before the LORD. [17]The priest will then apply some of the oil in his palm over the blood from the guilt offering that is on the lobe of the right ear, the thumb of the right hand, and the big toe of the right foot of the person being purified. [18]The priest will apply the oil remaining in his hand to the head of the person being purified. Through this process, the priest will purify* the person before the LORD.

[19]"Then the priest must present the sin offering to purify the person who was cured of the skin disease. After that, the priest will slaughter the burnt offering [20]and offer it on the altar along with the grain offering. Through this process, the priest will purify the person who was healed, and the person will be ceremonially clean.

[21]"But anyone who is too poor and cannot afford these offerings may bring one male lamb for a guilt offering, to be lifted up as a special offering for purification. The person must also bring two quarts* of choice flour moistened with olive oil for the grain offering and a cup of olive oil. [22]The offering must also include two turtledoves or two young pigeons, whichever the person can afford. One of the pair must be used for the sin offering and the other for a burnt offering. [23]On the eighth day of the purification ceremony, the person being purified must bring the offerings to the priest in the LORD's presence at the entrance of the Tabernacle. [24]The priest will take the lamb for the guilt offering, along with the olive oil, and lift them up as a special offering to the LORD. [25]Then the priest will slaughter the lamb for the guilt offering. He will take some of its blood and apply it to the lobe of the right ear, the thumb of the right hand, and the big toe of the right foot of the person being purified.

[26]"The priest will also pour some of the ol-

ive oil into the palm of his own left hand. [27]He will dip his right finger into the oil in his palm and sprinkle some of it seven times before the LORD. [28]The priest will then apply some of the oil in his palm over the blood from the guilt offering that is on the lobe of the right ear, the thumb of the right hand, and the big toe of the right foot of the person being purified. [29]The priest will apply the oil remaining in his hand to the head of the person being purified. Through this process, the priest will purify the person before the LORD.

[30]"Then the priest will offer the two turtledoves or the two young pigeons, whichever the person can afford. [31]One of them is for a sin offering and the other for a burnt offering, to be presented along with the grain offering. Through this process, the priest will purify the person before the LORD. [32]These are the instructions for purification for those who have recovered from a serious skin disease but who cannot afford to bring the offerings normally required for the ceremony of purification."

Treatment of Contaminated Houses

[33] Then the LORD said to Moses and Aaron, [34]"When you arrive in Canaan, the land I am giving you as your own possession, I may contaminate some of the houses in your land with mildew.* [35]The owner of such a house must then go to the priest and say, 'It appears that my house has some kind of mildew.' [36]Before the priest goes in to inspect the house, he must have the house emptied so nothing inside will be pronounced ceremonially unclean. [37]Then the priest will go in and examine the mildew on the walls. If he finds greenish or reddish streaks and the contamination appears to go deeper than the wall's surface, [38]the priest will step outside the door and put the house in quarantine for seven days. [39]On the seventh day the priest must return for another inspection. If he finds that the mildew on the walls of the house has spread, [40]the priest must order that the stones from those areas be removed. The contaminated material will then be taken outside the town to an area designated as ceremonially unclean. [41]Next the inside walls of the entire house must be scraped thoroughly and the scrapings dumped in the unclean place outside the town. [42]Other stones will be brought in to replace the ones that were removed, and the walls will be replastered.

14:18 Or *will make atonement for;* similarly in 14:19, 20, 21, 29, 31, 53.   14:21 Hebrew *1/10 of an ephah* [2.2 liters].
14:34 Traditionally rendered *leprosy;* see note on 13:47.

43"But if the mildew reappears after all the stones have been replaced and the house has been scraped and replastered, 44the priest must return and inspect the house again. If he finds that the mildew has spread, the walls are clearly contaminated with a serious mildew, and the house is defiled. 45It must be torn down, and all its stones, timbers, and plaster must be carried out of town to the place designated as ceremonially unclean. 46Those who enter the house during the period of quarantine will be ceremonially unclean until evening, 47and all who sleep or eat in the house must wash their clothing.

48"But if the priest returns for his inspection and finds that the mildew has not reappeared in the house after the fresh plastering, he will pronounce it clean because the mildew is clearly gone. 49To purify the house the priest must take two birds, a stick of cedar, some scarlet yarn, and a hyssop branch. 50He will slaughter one of the birds over a clay pot filled with fresh water. 51He will take the cedar stick, the hyssop branch, the scarlet yarn, and the live bird, and dip them into the blood of the slaughtered bird and into the fresh water. Then he will sprinkle the house seven times. 52When the priest has purified the house in exactly this way, 53he will release the live bird in the open fields outside the town. Through this process, the priest will purify the house, and it will be ceremonially clean.

54"These are the instructions for dealing with serious skin diseases,* including scabby sores; 55and mildew,* whether on clothing or in a house; 56and a swelling on the skin, a rash, or discolored skin. 57This procedure will determine whether a person or object is ceremonially clean or unclean.

"These are the instructions regarding skin diseases and mildew."

CHAPTER 15
Bodily Discharges

The LORD said to Moses and Aaron, 2"Give the following instructions to the people of Israel.

"Any man who has a bodily discharge is ceremonially unclean. 3This defilement is caused by his discharge, whether the discharge continues or stops. In either case the man is unclean. 4Any bed on which the man with the discharge lies and anything on which he sits will be ceremonially unclean.

5So if you touch the man's bed, you must wash your clothes and bathe yourself in water, and you will remain unclean until evening. 6If you sit where the man with the discharge has sat, you must wash your clothes and bathe yourself in water, and you will remain unclean until evening. 7If you touch the man with the discharge, you must wash your clothes and bathe yourself in water, and you will remain unclean until evening. 8If the man spits on you, you must wash your clothes and bathe yourself in water, and you will remain unclean until evening. 9Any saddle blanket on which the man rides will be ceremonially unclean. 10If you touch anything that was under the man, you will be unclean until evening. You must wash your clothes and bathe yourself in water, and you will remain unclean until evening. 11If the man touches you without first rinsing his hands, you must wash your clothes and bathe yourself in water, and you will remain unclean until evening. 12Any clay pot the man touches must be broken, and any wooden utensil he touches must be rinsed with water.

13"When the man with the discharge is healed, he must count off seven days for the period of purification. Then he must wash his clothes and bathe himself in fresh water, and he will be ceremonially clean. 14On the eighth day he must get two turtledoves or two young pigeons and come before the LORD at the entrance of the Tabernacle* and give his offerings to the priest. 15The priest will offer one bird for a sin offering and the other for a burnt offering. Through this process, the priest will purify* the man before the LORD for his discharge.

16"Whenever a man has an emission of semen, he must bathe his entire body in water, and he will remain ceremonially unclean until the next evening.* 17Any clothing or leather with semen on it must be washed in water, and it will remain unclean until evening. 18After a man and a woman have sexual intercourse, they must each bathe in water, and they will remain unclean until the next evening.

19"Whenever a woman has her menstrual period, she will be ceremonially unclean for seven days. Anyone who touches her during that time will be unclean until evening. 20Anything on which the woman lies or sits during the time of her period will be

14:54 Traditionally rendered *leprosy;* see note on 13:2a. 14:55 Traditionally rendered *leprosy;* see note on 13:47. 15:14 Hebrew *Tent of Meeting;* also in 15:29. 15:15 Or *will make atonement for;* also in 15:30. 15:16 Hebrew *until evening;* also in 15:18.

unclean. ²¹If any of you touch her bed, you must wash your clothes and bathe yourself in water, and you will remain unclean until evening. ²²If you touch any object she has sat on, you must wash your clothes and bathe yourself in water, and you will remain unclean until evening. ²³This includes her bed or any other object she has sat on; you will be unclean until evening if you touch it. ²⁴If a man has sexual intercourse with her and her blood touches him, her menstrual impurity will be transmitted to him. He will remain unclean for seven days, and any bed on which he lies will be unclean.

²⁵"If a woman has a flow of blood for many days that is unrelated to her menstrual period, or if the blood continues beyond the normal period, she is ceremonially unclean. As during her menstrual period, the woman will be unclean as long as the discharge continues. ²⁶Any bed she lies on and any object she sits on during that time will be unclean, just as during her normal menstrual period. ²⁷If any of you touch these things, you will be ceremonially unclean. You must wash your clothes and bathe yourself in water, and you will remain unclean until evening.

²⁸"When the woman's bleeding stops, she must count off seven days. Then she will be ceremonially clean. ²⁹On the eighth day she must bring two turtledoves or two young pigeons and present them to the priest at the entrance of the Tabernacle. ³⁰The priest will offer one for a sin offering and the other for a burnt offering. Through this process, the priest will purify her before the LORD for the ceremonial impurity caused by her bleeding.

³¹"This is how you will guard the people of Israel from ceremonial uncleanness. Otherwise they would die, for their impurity would defile my Tabernacle that stands among them. ³²These are the instructions for dealing with anyone who has a bodily discharge—a man who is unclean because of an emission of semen ³³or a woman during her menstrual period. It applies to any man or woman who has a bodily discharge, and to a man who has sexual intercourse with a woman who is ceremonially unclean."

CHAPTER 16
The Day of Atonement
The LORD spoke to Moses after the death of Aaron's two sons, who died after they entered the LORD's presence and burned the wrong kind of fire before him. ²The LORD said to Moses, "Warn your brother, Aaron, not to enter the Most Holy Place behind the inner curtain whenever he chooses; if he does, he will die. For the Ark's cover—the place of atonement—is there, and I myself am present in the cloud above the atonement cover.

³"When Aaron enters the sanctuary area, he must follow these instructions fully. He must bring a young bull for a sin offering and a ram for a burnt offering. ⁴He must put on his linen tunic and the linen undergarments worn next to his body. He must tie the linen sash around his waist and put the linen turban on his head. These are sacred garments, so he must bathe himself in water before he puts them on. ⁵Aaron must take from the community of Israel two male goats for a sin offering and a ram for a burnt offering.

⁶"Aaron will present his own bull as a sin offering to purify himself and his family, making them right with the LORD.* ⁷Then he must take the two male goats and present them to the LORD at the entrance of the Tabernacle.* ⁸He is to cast sacred lots to determine which goat will be reserved as an offering to the LORD and which will carry the sins of the people to the wilderness of Azazel. ⁹Aaron will then present as a sin offering the

16:6 Or *to make atonement for himself and his family;* similarly in 16:11, 17b, 24, 34. 16:7 Hebrew *Tent of Meeting;* also in 16:16, 17, 20, 23, 33.

16:1-22 The Day of Atonement is a thematic pivot point for the book of Leviticus. For the Israelites who participated in the ceremony with hearts of faith, this solemn day provided assurance that their past sins had been completely dealt with. Today, through the sacrificial work of Christ, we too can find assurance of forgiveness and a right standing before God. We can leave our past failures behind to build a new life governed by obedience to God's program.
16:15-19 The goat was slaughtered for the people's sin offering, and its blood was sprinkled on the lid of the Ark of the Covenant, sometimes called the "place of atonement" or "atonement cover." This yearly sacrifice atoned for the sins of the people, but it had to be offered again the following year. Hebrews 10:1-4 makes it clear that these sacrifices were not a permanent solution to the problem of sin; they were only a temporary measure. Jesus Christ has now provided a perfect and permanent sacrifice for our sins. Through faith, we can be assured of complete forgiveness—permanently!

goat chosen by lot for the LORD. ¹⁰The other goat, the scapegoat chosen by lot to be sent away, will be kept alive, standing before the LORD. When it is sent away to Azazel in the wilderness, the people will be purified and made right with the LORD.*

¹¹"Aaron will present his own bull as a sin offering to purify himself and his family, making them right with the LORD. After he has slaughtered the bull as a sin offering, ¹²he will fill an incense burner with burning coals from the altar that stands before the LORD. Then he will take two handfuls of fragrant powdered incense and will carry the burner and the incense behind the inner curtain. ¹³There in the LORD's presence he will put the incense on the burning coals so that a cloud of incense will rise over the Ark's cover—the place of atonement—that rests on the Ark of the Covenant.* If he follows these instructions, he will not die. ¹⁴Then he must take some of the blood of the bull, dip his finger in it, and sprinkle it on the east side of the atonement cover. He must sprinkle blood seven times with his finger in front of the atonement cover.

¹⁵"Then Aaron must slaughter the first goat as a sin offering for the people and carry its blood behind the inner curtain. There he will sprinkle the goat's blood over the atonement cover and in front of it, just as he did with the bull's blood. ¹⁶Through this process, he will purify* the Most Holy Place, and he will do the same for the entire Tabernacle, because of the defiling sin and rebellion of the Israelites. ¹⁷No one else is allowed inside the Tabernacle when Aaron enters it for the purification ceremony in the Most Holy Place. No one may enter until he comes out again after purifying himself, his family, and all the congregation of Israel, making them right with the LORD. ¹⁸"Then Aaron will come out to purify the altar that stands before the LORD. He will do this by taking some of the blood from the bull and the goat and putting it on each of the horns of the altar. ¹⁹Then he must sprinkle the blood with his finger seven times over the altar. In this way, he will cleanse it from Israel's defilement and make it holy.

²⁰"When Aaron has finished purifying the Most Holy Place and the Tabernacle and the altar, he must present the live goat. ²¹He will

16:10 Or *wilderness, it will make atonement for the people.*
16:13 Hebrew *that is above the Testimony.* The Hebrew word for "testimony" refers to the terms of the LORD's covenant with Israel as written on stone tablets, which were kept in the Ark, and also to the covenant itself.
16:16 Or *make atonement for;* similarly in 16:17a, 18, 20, 27, 33.

STEP 8

Scapegoats

BIBLE READING: Leviticus 16:20-22
We made lists of all persons we had harmed and became willing to make amends to them all.

It is natural to hope that the people we have hurt will think better of us once we have sought to make amends. We may fear that there are some who will never upgrade their opinions about us, no matter what we do. In reality they may not, especially if they have chosen to use us as scapegoats.

Before the coming of Jesus, the people of Israel were instructed to select a live goat that would carry away their sins. (Jesus became our scapegoat when he took our sins upon himself.) The priest was to place his hands on this goat and confess over it all the sins of the people. "He will lay both of his hands on the goat's head and confess over it all the wickedness, rebellion, and sins of the people of Israel. In this way, he will transfer the people's sins to the head of the goat. Then a man specially chosen for the task will drive the goat into the wilderness. As the goat goes into the wilderness, it will carry all the people's sins upon itself into a desolate land" (Leviticus 16:21-22).

Some of the people we have hurt will use us as their scapegoats. Since we have hurt them, they feel justified in sending us away with more than our share of the burden. They unconsciously place the blame for their pain on us so we can carry it away. As their scapegoats, we play the role of removing something they were unable to deal with in any other way. Because of this, they may never welcome us back. We should be prepared for this kind of response and realize that their behavior says more about them than it says about us. *Turn to page 829, Ecclesiastes 4.*

lay both of his hands on the goat's head and confess over it all the wickedness, rebellion, and sins of the people of Israel. In this way, he will transfer the people's sins to the head of the goat. Then a man specially chosen for the task will drive the goat into the wilderness. [22]As the goat goes into the wilderness, it will carry all the people's sins upon itself into a desolate land.

[23] "When Aaron goes back into the Tabernacle, he must take off the linen garments he was wearing when he entered the Most Holy Place, and he must leave the garments there. [24]Then he must bathe himself with water in a sacred place, put on his regular garments, and go out to sacrifice a burnt offering for himself and a burnt offering for the people. Through this process, he will purify himself and the people, making them right with the LORD. [25]He must then burn all the fat of the sin offering on the altar.

[26] "The man chosen to drive the scapegoat into the wilderness of Azazel must wash his clothes and bathe himself in water. Then he may return to the camp.

[27] "The bull and the goat presented as sin offerings, whose blood Aaron takes into the Most Holy Place for the purification ceremony, will be carried outside the camp. The animals' hides, internal organs, and dung are all to be burned. [28]The man who burns them must wash his clothes and bathe himself in water before returning to the camp.

[29] "On the tenth day of the appointed month in early autumn,* you must deny yourselves.* Neither native-born Israelites nor foreigners living among you may do any kind of work. This is a permanent law for you. [30]On that day offerings of purification will be made for you,* and you will be purified in the LORD's presence from all your sins. [31]It will be a Sabbath day of complete rest for you, and you must deny yourselves. This is a permanent law for you. [32]In future generations, the purification* ceremony will be performed by the priest who has been anointed and ordained to serve as high priest in place of his ancestor Aaron. He will put on the holy linen garments [33]and purify the Most Holy Place, the Tabernacle, the altar, the priests, and the entire congregation. [34]This is a permanent law for you, to purify the people of Israel from their sins, making them right with the LORD once each year."

Moses followed all these instructions exactly as the LORD had commanded him.

CHAPTER 17
Prohibitions against Eating Blood

Then the LORD said to Moses, [2]"Give the following instructions to Aaron and his sons and all the people of Israel. This is what the LORD has commanded.

[3] "If any native Israelite sacrifices a bull* or a lamb or a goat anywhere inside or outside the camp [4]instead of bringing it to the entrance of the Tabernacle* to present it as an offering to the LORD, that person will be as guilty as a murderer.* Such a person has shed blood and will be cut off from the community. [5] The purpose of this rule is to stop the Israelites from sacrificing animals in the open fields. It will ensure that they bring their sacrifices to the priest at the entrance of the Tabernacle, so he can present them to the LORD as peace offerings. [6]Then the priest will be able to splatter the blood against the LORD's altar at the entrance of the Tabernacle, and he will burn the fat as a pleasing aroma to the LORD. [7]The people must no longer be unfaithful to the LORD by offering sacrifices to the goat idols.* This is a permanent law for them, to be observed from generation to generation.

[8]"Give them this command as well. If any native Israelite or foreigner living among you offers a burnt offering or a sacrifice [9]but does not bring it to the entrance of the Tabernacle to offer it to the LORD, that person will be cut off from the community.

[10] "And if any native Israelite or foreigner

16:29a Hebrew *On the tenth day of the seventh month.* This day in the ancient Hebrew lunar calendar occurred in September or October. 16:29b Or *must fast;* also in 16:31. 16:30 Or *atonement will be made for you, to purify you.* 16:32 Or *atonement.* 17:3 Or *cow.* 17:4a Hebrew *Tent of Meeting;* also in 17:5, 6, 9. 17:4b Hebrew *will be guilty of blood.* 17:7 Or *goat demons.*

16:22 The innocent scapegoat was sent away, carrying with it the guilt of the entire Israelite nation. A dysfunctional family will often choose its own scapegoat from among its members. This person is loaded down with the guilt of the whole family and then ostracized. This frees the other members from their feelings of failure and gives them someone to blame. For those of us who have experienced this, it should encourage us to know that God has sent his Son to be a scapegoat for us. Although innocent, he has chosen to carry away the guilt of the entire human race. We need not shoulder our sin any longer; no human being should be expected to. We can hand it over to him.

living among you eats or drinks blood in any form, I will turn against that person and cut him off from the community of your people, [11] for the life of the body is in its blood. I have given you the blood on the altar to purify you, making you right with the LORD.* It is the blood, given in exchange for a life, that makes purification possible. [12] That is why I have said to the people of Israel, 'You must never eat or drink blood—neither you nor the foreigners living among you.'

[13] "And if any native Israelite or foreigner living among you goes hunting and kills an animal or bird that is approved for eating, he must drain its blood and cover it with earth. [14] The life of every creature is in its blood. That is why I have said to the people of Israel, 'You must never eat or drink blood, for the life of any creature is in its blood.' So whoever consumes blood will be cut off from the community.

[15] "And if any native-born Israelites or foreigners eat the meat of an animal that died naturally or was torn up by wild animals, they must wash their clothes and bathe themselves in water. They will remain ceremonially unclean until evening, but then they will be clean. [16] But if they do not wash their clothes and bathe themselves, they will be punished for their sin."

CHAPTER 18
Forbidden Sexual Practices

Then the LORD said to Moses, [2] "Give the following instructions to the people of Israel. I am the LORD your God. [3] So do not act like the people in Egypt, where you used to live, or like the people of Canaan, where I am taking you. You must not imitate their way of life. [4] You must obey all my regulations and be careful to obey my decrees, for I am the LORD your God. [5] If you obey my decrees and my regulations, you will find life through them. I am the LORD.

[6] "You must never have sexual relations with a close relative, for I am the LORD. [7] Do not violate your father by having sexual relations with your mother. She is your mother; you must not have sexual relations with her.

[8] "Do not have sexual relations with any of your father's wives, for this would violate your father.

[9] "Do not have sexual relations with your sister or half sister, whether she is your father's daughter or your mother's daughter, whether she was born into your household or someone else's.

[10] "Do not have sexual relations with your granddaughter, whether she is your son's daughter or your daughter's daughter, for this would violate yourself.

[11] "Do not have sexual relations with your stepsister, the daughter of any of your father's wives, for she is your sister.

[12] "Do not have sexual relations with your father's sister, for she is your father's close relative.

[13] "Do not have sexual relations with your mother's sister, for she is your mother's close relative.

[14] "Do not violate your uncle, your father's brother, by having sexual relations with his wife, for she is your aunt.

[15] "Do not have sexual relations with your daughter-in-law; she is your son's wife, so you must not have sexual relations with her.

[16] "Do not have sexual relations with your brother's wife, for this would violate your brother.

[17] "Do not have sexual relations with both a woman and her daughter. And do not take* her granddaughter, whether her son's daughter or her daughter's daughter, and have sexual relations with her. They are close relatives, and this would be a wicked act.

[18] "While your wife is living, do not marry

17:11 Or to make atonement for you. 18:17 Or do not marry.

18:4-5 God promises life to all those who live according to his program. The Hebrew expression for "you will find life" refers to finding contentment and enjoyment in life—living life to its fullest. While the personal moral standards in this section of Leviticus are quite restrictive, God's plan offers freedom beyond our wildest dreams. It is the paths of sin that are truly restrictive. When we obey God's standards, we are free to discover life as God intended it to be. His plan leads to peace and contentment through mature and satisfying relationships.

18:6-18 God instituted marriage as a foundational human relationship and forbade anything that might destroy it—incest included. Some societies in history have endorsed incestuous relationships, but they have suffered the tragic consequences. The people in such societies have suffered physical and mental abnormalities, which lead eventually to societal decline. God's purpose in setting boundaries for both personal and family life has always been to protect us from destruction. He desires to build families that promote healing and wholeness among their members.

her sister and have sexual relations with her, for they would be rivals.

19 "Do not have sexual relations with a woman during her period of menstrual impurity.

20 "Do not defile yourself by having sexual intercourse with your neighbor's wife.

21 "Do not permit any of your children to be offered as a sacrifice to Molech, for you must not bring shame on the name of your God. I am the LORD.

22 "Do not practice homosexuality, having sex with another man as with a woman. It is a detestable sin.

23 "A man must not defile himself by having sex with an animal. And a woman must not offer herself to a male animal to have intercourse with it. This is a perverse act.

24 "Do not defile yourselves in any of these ways, for the people I am driving out before you have defiled themselves in all these ways. 25 Because the entire land has become defiled, I am punishing the people who live there. I will cause the land to vomit them out. 26 You must obey all my decrees and regulations. You must not commit any of these detestable sins. This applies both to native-born Israelites and to the foreigners living among you.

27 "All these detestable activities are practiced by the people of the land where I am taking you, and this is how the land has become defiled. 28 So do not defile the land and give it a reason to vomit you out, as it will vomit out the people who live there now. 29 Whoever commits any of these detestable sins will be cut off from the community of Israel. 30 So obey my instructions, and do not defile yourselves by committing any of these detestable practices that were committed by

19:5 Or it.

the people who lived in the land before you. I am the LORD your God."

CHAPTER 19
Holiness in Personal Conduct

The LORD also said to Moses, 2 "Give the following instructions to the entire community of Israel. You must be holy because I, the LORD your God, am holy.

3 "Each of you must show great respect for your mother and father, and you must always observe my Sabbath days of rest. I am the LORD your God.

4 "Do not put your trust in idols or make metal images of gods for yourselves. I am the LORD your God.

5 "When you sacrifice a peace offering to the LORD, offer it properly so you* will be accepted by God. 6 The sacrifice must be eaten on the same day you offer it or on the next day. Whatever is left over until the third day must be completely burned up. 7 If any of the sacrifice is eaten on the third day, it will be contaminated, and I will not accept it. 8 Anyone who eats it on the third day will be punished for defiling what is holy to the LORD and will be cut off from the community.

9 "When you harvest the crops of your land, do not harvest the grain along the edges of your fields, and do not pick up what the harvesters drop. 10 It is the same with your grape crop—do not strip every last bunch of grapes from the vines, and do not pick up the grapes that fall to the ground. Leave them for the poor and the foreigners living among you. I am the LORD your God.

11 "Do not steal.

"Do not deceive or cheat one another.

12 "Do not bring shame on the name of

18:20 Fidelity in marriage is central to God's plan for society and family; it is one of the Ten Commandments (Exodus 20:14). Since the bond of marriage is a foundational building block of society, adultery is a blatant violation of a community's trust. Healthy relationships require self-control and the acceptance of self-imposed boundaries, but God didn't intend to deprive us of anything in marriage. God wants the marriage relationship to bring us joy and fulfillment.
19:1-4 God has commanded us to be holy; here, respect for our parents is mentioned as one aspect of holiness. Strained or dysfunctional family relationships can become one of the greatest barriers to the life of fulfillment and contentment God desires for us. Since God places a priority on respect within family relationships, we should do the same.
19:9-10 The laws given here (illustrated in the story of Ruth) show that God is concerned about poor people. There was a sense of community among the Israelites that went beyond the immediate family. The Israelites were commanded to give special considerations to the poor or underprivileged people among them. With so many needs among God's people today—physical, emotional, spiritual—we should be quick to respond. Only in an atmosphere of acceptance and love can the needs of others be discerned and truly met.
19:11-13, 35-37 God's program for successful living demands honesty in both word and deed. Dishonesty and misrepresentation lead to suspicion, mistrust, and hatred, ultimately destroying

your God by using it to swear falsely. I am the LORD.

¹³"Do not defraud or rob your neighbor.

"Do not make your hired workers wait until the next day to receive their pay.

¹⁴"Do not insult the deaf or cause the blind to stumble. You must fear your God; I am the LORD.

¹⁵"Do not twist justice in legal matters by favoring the poor or being partial to the rich and powerful. Always judge people fairly.

¹⁶"Do not spread slanderous gossip among your people.*

"Do not stand idly by when your neighbor's life is threatened. I am the LORD.

¹⁷"Do not nurse hatred in your heart for any of your relatives.* Confront people directly so you will not be held guilty for their sin.

¹⁸"Do not seek revenge or bear a grudge against a fellow Israelite, but love your neighbor as yourself. I am the LORD.

¹⁹"You must obey all my decrees.

"Do not mate two different kinds of animals. Do not plant your field with two different kinds of seed. Do not wear clothing woven from two different kinds of thread.

²⁰"If a man has sex with a slave girl whose freedom has never been purchased but who is committed to become another man's wife, he must pay full compensation to her master. But since she is not a free woman, neither the man nor the woman will be put to death. ²¹The man, however, must bring a ram as a guilt offering and present it to the LORD at the entrance of the Tabernacle.* ²²The priest will then purify him* before the LORD with the ram of the guilt offering, and the man's sin will be forgiven.

²³"When you enter the land and plant fruit trees, leave the fruit unharvested for the first three years and consider it forbidden.* Do not eat it. ²⁴In the fourth year the entire crop must be consecrated to the LORD as a celebration of praise. ²⁵Finally, in the fifth

year you may eat the fruit. If you follow this pattern, your harvest will increase. I am the LORD your God.

²⁶"Do not eat meat that has not been drained of its blood.

"Do not practice fortune-telling or witchcraft.

²⁷"Do not trim off the hair on your temples or trim your beards.

²⁸"Do not cut your bodies for the dead, and do not mark your skin with tattoos. I am the LORD.

²⁹"Do not defile your daughter by making her a prostitute, or the land will be filled with prostitution and wickedness.

³⁰"Keep my Sabbath days of rest, and show reverence toward my sanctuary. I am the LORD.

³¹"Do not defile yourselves by turning to mediums or to those who consult the spirits of the dead. I am the LORD your God.

³²"Stand up in the presence of the elderly, and show respect for the aged. Fear your God. I am the LORD.

³³"Do not take advantage of foreigners who live among you in your land. ³⁴Treat them like native-born Israelites, and love them as you love yourself. Remember that you were once foreigners living in the land of Egypt. I am the LORD your God.

³⁵"Do not use dishonest standards when measuring length, weight, or volume. ³⁶Your scales and weights must be accurate. Your containers for measuring dry materials or liquids must be accurate.* I am the LORD your God who brought you out of the land of Egypt.

³⁷"You must be careful to keep all of my decrees and regulations by putting them into practice. I am the LORD."

CHAPTER 20
Punishments for Disobedience

The LORD said to Moses, ²"Give the people of Israel these instructions, which apply both

---

19:16 Hebrew *Do not act as a merchant toward your own people.* 19:17 Hebrew *for your brother.* 19:21 Hebrew *Tent of Meeting.* 19:22 Or *make atonement for him.* 19:23 Hebrew *consider it uncircumcised.* 19:36 Hebrew *Use an honest ephah* [a dry measure] *and an honest hin* [a liquid measure].

---

our relationships. Human relationships can grow and thrive only if we are willing to tell the truth—the only real basis for trust between people. When there is honesty in our relationships, we can confidently look to others in times of need.

20:1-5 The earlier prohibition against worshiping Molech (18:21) is given again here in even stronger language. Most of the Israelites probably had nothing but contempt for this type of pagan worship, which included sacrificing children to this god. Yet Israel's history records that several centuries later, King Manasseh sacrificed his sons to this god, and no one even objected (2 Chronicles 33:6). Our life can be greatly tainted by the behavior of the people around us. Given enough time, their values may become ours. With God's help we need to stand by our commitment to the moral boundaries he has set up.

to native Israelites and to the foreigners living in Israel.

"If any of them offer their children as a sacrifice to Molech, they must be put to death. The people of the community must stone them to death. ³I myself will turn against them and cut them off from the community, because they have defiled my sanctuary and brought shame on my holy name by offering their children to Molech. ⁴And if the people of the community ignore those who offer their children to Molech and refuse to execute them, ⁵I myself will turn against them and their families and will cut them off from the community. This will happen to all who commit spiritual prostitution by worshiping Molech.

⁶"I will also turn against those who commit spiritual prostitution by putting their trust in mediums or in those who consult the spirits of the dead. I will cut them off from the community. ⁷So set yourselves apart to be holy, for I am the LORD your God. ⁸Keep all my decrees by putting them into practice, for I am the LORD who makes you holy.

⁹"Anyone who dishonors* father or mother must be put to death. Such a person is guilty of a capital offense.

¹⁰"If a man commits adultery with his neighbor's wife, both the man and the woman who have committed adultery must be put to death.

¹¹"If a man violates his father by having sex with one of his father's wives, both the man and the woman must be put to death, for they are guilty of a capital offense.

¹²"If a man has sex with his daughter-in-law, both must be put to death. They have committed a perverse act and are guilty of a capital offense.

¹³"If a man practices homosexuality, having sex with another man as with a woman, both men have committed a detestable act. They must both be put to death, for they are guilty of a capital offense.

¹⁴"If a man marries both a woman and her mother, he has committed a wicked act. The man and both women must be burned to death to wipe out such wickedness from among you.

¹⁵"If a man has sex with an animal, he must be put to death, and the animal must be killed.

¹⁶"If a woman presents herself to a male animal to have intercourse with it, she and the animal must both be put to death. You must kill both, for they are guilty of a capital offense.

¹⁷"If a man marries his sister, the daughter of either his father or his mother, and they have sexual relations, it is a shameful disgrace. They must be publicly cut off from the community. Since the man has violated his sister, he will be punished for his sin.

¹⁸"If a man has sexual relations with a woman during her menstrual period, both of them must be cut off from the community, for together they have exposed the source of her blood flow.

¹⁹"Do not have sexual relations with your aunt, whether your mother's sister or your father's sister. This would dishonor a close relative. Both parties are guilty and will be punished for their sin.

²⁰"If a man has sex with his uncle's wife, he has violated his uncle. Both the man and woman will be punished for their sin, and they will die childless.

²¹"If a man marries his brother's wife, it is an act of impurity. He has violated his brother, and the guilty couple will remain childless.

²²"You must keep all my decrees and regulations by putting them into practice; otherwise the land to which I am bringing you as your new home will vomit you out. ²³Do not live according to the customs of the people I am driving out before you. It is because they do these shameful things that I detest them. ²⁴But I have promised you, 'You will possess their land because I will give it to you as your possession—a land flowing with milk and honey.' I am the LORD your God, who has set you apart from all other people.

²⁵"You must therefore make a distinction between ceremonially clean and unclean animals, and between clean and unclean birds. You must not defile yourselves by eating any unclean animal or bird or creature that scurries along the ground. I have identified them as being unclean for you. ²⁶You must be holy because I, the LORD, am holy. I have set you apart from all other people to be my very own.

²⁷"Men and women among you who act as mediums or who consult the spirits of the dead must be put to death by stoning. They are guilty of a capital offense."

CHAPTER 21
Instructions for the Priests

The LORD said to Moses, "Give the following instructions to the priests, the descendants of Aaron.

20:9 Greek version reads *Anyone who speaks disrespectfully of*. Compare Matt 15:4; Mark 7:10.

"A priest must not make himself ceremonially unclean by touching the dead body of a relative. [2]The only exceptions are his closest relatives—his mother or father, son or daughter, brother, [3]or his virgin sister who depends on him because she has no husband. [4]But a priest must not defile himself and make himself unclean for someone who is related to him only by marriage.

[5]"The priests must not shave their heads or trim their beards or cut their bodies. [6]They must be set apart as holy to their God and must never bring shame on the name of God. They must be holy, for they are the ones who present the special gifts to the LORD, gifts of food for their God.

[7]"Priests may not marry a woman defiled by prostitution, and they may not marry a woman who is divorced from her husband, for the priests are set apart as holy to their God. [8]You must treat them as holy because they offer up food to your God. You must consider them holy because I, the LORD, am holy, and I make you holy.

[9]"If a priest's daughter defiles herself by becoming a prostitute, she also defiles her father's holiness, and she must be burned to death.

[10]"The high priest has the highest rank of all the priests. The anointing oil has been poured on his head, and he has been ordained to wear the priestly garments. He must never leave his hair uncombed* or tear his clothing. [11]He must not defile himself by going near a dead body. He may not make himself ceremonially unclean even for his father or mother. [12]He must not defile the sanctuary of his God by leaving it to attend to a dead person, for he has been made holy by the anointing oil of his God. I am the LORD.

[13]"The high priest may marry only a virgin. [14]He may not marry a widow, a woman who is divorced, or a woman who has defiled herself by prostitution. She must be a virgin from his own clan, [15]so that he will not dishonor his descendants among his clan, for I am the LORD who makes him holy."

[16]Then the LORD said to Moses, [17]"Give the following instructions to Aaron: In all future generations, none of your descendants who has any defect will qualify to offer food to his God. [18]No one who has a defect qualifies, whether he is blind, lame, disfigured, deformed, [19]or has a broken foot or arm, [20]or is hunchbacked or dwarfed, or has a defective eye, or skin sores or scabs, or damaged testicles. [21]No descendant of Aaron who has a defect may approach the altar to present special gifts to the LORD. Since he has a defect, he may not approach the altar to offer food to his God. [22]However, he may eat from the food offered to God, including the holy offerings and the most holy offerings. [23]Yet because of his physical defect, he may not enter the room behind the inner curtain or approach the altar, for this would defile my holy places. I am the LORD who makes them holy."

[24]So Moses gave these instructions to Aaron and his sons and to all the Israelites.

CHAPTER 22

The LORD said to Moses, [2]"Tell Aaron and his sons to be very careful with the sacred gifts that the Israelites set apart for me, so they do not bring shame on my holy name. I am the LORD. [3]Give them the following instructions.

"In all future generations, if any of your descendants is ceremonially unclean when he approaches the sacred offerings that the people of Israel consecrate to the LORD, he must be cut off from my presence. I am the LORD.

[4]"If any of Aaron's descendants has a skin disease* or any kind of discharge that makes him ceremonially unclean, he may not eat from the sacred offerings until he has been pronounced clean. He also becomes unclean by touching a corpse, or by having an emission of semen, [5]or by touching a small animal that is unclean, or by touching someone who is ceremonially unclean for any reason. [6]The man who is defiled in any of these ways will remain unclean until evening. He may not eat from the sacred offerings until he has bathed himself in water. [7]When the sun goes down, he will be ceremonially clean again and may eat from the sacred offerings, for this is his food. [8]He may not eat an animal that has died a natural death or has been

21:10 Or *never uncover his head.* 22:4 Traditionally rendered *leprosy;* see note on 13:2a.

21:7-8 The priest's personal life, including his marriage, was to be holy, reflecting his commitment to God. As believers, each of us is a part of Christ and our body is "the temple of the Holy Spirit" (1 Corinthians 6:15-20). Being holy includes setting healthy boundaries that will lead to purity in sexual relationships.

torn apart by wild animals, for this would defile him. I am the LORD.

⁹"The priests must follow my instructions carefully. Otherwise they will be punished for their sin and will die for violating my instructions. I am the LORD who makes them holy.

¹⁰"No one outside a priest's family may eat the sacred offerings. Even guests and hired workers in a priest's home are not allowed to eat them. ¹¹However, if the priest buys a slave for himself, the slave may eat from the sacred offerings. And if his slaves have children, they also may share his food. ¹²If a priest's daughter marries someone outside the priestly family, she may no longer eat the sacred offerings. ¹³But if she becomes a widow or is divorced and has no children to support her, and she returns to live in her father's home as in her youth, she may eat her father's food again. Otherwise, no one outside a priest's family may eat the sacred offerings.

¹⁴"Any such person who eats the sacred offerings without realizing it must pay the priest for the amount eaten, plus an additional 20 percent. ¹⁵The priests must not let the Israelites defile the sacred offerings brought to the LORD ¹⁶by allowing unauthorized people to eat them. This would bring guilt upon them and require them to pay compensation. I am the LORD who makes them holy."

Worthy and Unworthy Offerings

¹⁷And the LORD said to Moses, ¹⁸"Give Aaron and his sons and all the Israelites these instructions, which apply both to native Israelites and to the foreigners living among you.

"If you present a gift as a burnt offering to the LORD, whether it is to fulfill a vow or is a voluntary offering, ¹⁹you* will be accepted only if your offering is a male animal with no defects. It may be a bull, a ram, or a male goat. ²⁰Do not present an animal with defects, because the LORD will not accept it on your behalf.

²¹"If you present a peace offering to the LORD from the herd or the flock, whether it is to fulfill a vow or is a voluntary offering, you must offer a perfect animal. It may have no

defect of any kind. ²²You must not offer an animal that is blind, crippled, or injured, or that has a wart, a skin sore, or scabs. Such animals must never be offered on the altar as special gifts to the LORD. ²³If a bull* or lamb has a leg that is too long or too short, it may be offered as a voluntary offering, but it may not be offered to fulfill a vow. ²⁴If an animal has damaged testicles or is castrated, you may not offer it to the LORD. You must never do this in your own land, ²⁵and you must not accept such an animal from foreigners and then offer it as a sacrifice to your God. Such animals will not be accepted on your behalf, for they are mutilated or defective."

²⁶And the LORD said to Moses, ²⁷"When a calf or lamb or goat is born, it must be left with its mother for seven days. From the eighth day on, it will be acceptable as a special gift to the LORD. ²⁸But you must not slaughter a mother animal and her offspring on the same day, whether from the herd or the flock. ²⁹When you bring a thanksgiving offering to the LORD, sacrifice it properly so you will be accepted. ³⁰Eat the entire sacrificial animal on the day it is presented. Do not leave any of it until the next morning. I am the LORD.

³¹"You must faithfully keep all my commands by putting them into practice, for I am the LORD. ³²Do not bring shame on my holy name, for I will display my holiness among the people of Israel. I am the LORD who makes you holy. ³³It was I who rescued you from the land of Egypt, that I might be your God. I am the LORD."

CHAPTER 23
The Appointed Festivals

The LORD said to Moses, ²"Give the following instructions to the people of Israel. These are the LORD's appointed festivals, which you are to proclaim as official days for holy assembly.

³"You have six days each week for your ordinary work, but the seventh day is a Sabbath day of complete rest, an official day for holy assembly. It is the LORD's Sabbath day, and it must be observed wherever you live.

⁴"In addition to the Sabbath, these are the LORD's appointed festivals, the official days

22:19 Or *it.* 22:23 Or *cow.*

22:31-33 God calls us to remember his deliverance in the past so we can find strength to live for him in the present. He has graciously made it possible for us to be free from the power of our past sins. He has rescued us from Satan's kingdom and delivered us from our slavery to sin. He wants us to remember all he has done in the past so we can find courage to face the challenges ahead.

for holy assembly that are to be celebrated at their proper times each year.

Passover and the Festival of Unleavened Bread

5 "The LORD's Passover begins at sundown on the fourteenth day of the first month.* 6On the next day, the fifteenth day of the month, you must begin celebrating the Festival of Unleavened Bread. This festival to the LORD continues for seven days, and during that time the bread you eat must be made without yeast. 7On the first day of the festival, all the people must stop their ordinary work and observe an official day for holy assembly. 8For seven days you must present special gifts to the LORD. On the seventh day the people must again stop all their ordinary work to observe an official day for holy assembly."

Celebration of First Harvest

9Then the LORD said to Moses, 10"Give the following instructions to the people of Israel. When you enter the land I am giving you and you harvest its first crops, bring the priest a bundle of grain from the first cutting of your grain harvest. 11On the day after the Sabbath, the priest will lift it up before the LORD so it may be accepted on your behalf. 12On that same day you must sacrifice a one-year-old male lamb with no defects as a burnt offering to the LORD. 13With it you must present a grain offering consisting of four quarts* of choice flour moistened with olive oil. It will be a special gift, a pleasing aroma to the LORD. You must also offer one quart* of wine as a liquid offering. 14Do not eat any bread or roasted grain or fresh kernels on that day until you bring this offering to your God. This is a permanent law for you, and it must be observed from generation to generation wherever you live.

The Festival of Harvest

15 "From the day after the Sabbath—the day you bring the bundle of grain to be lifted up as a special offering—count off seven full weeks. 16Keep counting until the day after the seventh Sabbath, fifty days later. Then present an offering of new grain to the LORD. 17From wherever you live, bring two loaves of bread to be lifted up before the LORD as a special offering. Make these loaves from four quarts of choice flour, and bake them with yeast. They will be an offering to the LORD from the first of your crops. 18Along with the bread, present seven one-year-old male lambs with no defects, one young bull, and two rams as burnt offerings to the LORD. These burnt offerings, together with the grain offerings and liquid offerings, will be a special gift, a pleasing aroma to the LORD. 19Then you must offer one male goat as a sin offering and two one-year-old male lambs as a peace offering.

20 "The priest will lift up the two lambs as a special offering to the LORD, together with the loaves representing the first of your crops. These offerings, which are holy to the LORD, belong to the priests. 21That same day will be proclaimed an official day for holy assembly, a day on which you do no ordinary work. This is a permanent law for you, and it must be observed from generation to generation wherever you live.*

22 "When you harvest the crops of your land, do not harvest the grain along the edges of your fields, and do not pick up what the harvesters drop. Leave it for the poor and the foreigners living among you. I am the LORD your God."

The Festival of Trumpets

23The LORD said to Moses, 24"Give the following instructions to the people of Israel. On the first day of the appointed month in early autumn,* you are to observe a day of complete rest. It will be an official day for holy assembly, a day commemorated with loud blasts of a trumpet. 25You must do no ordinary work on that day. Instead, you are to present special gifts to the LORD."

23:5 This day in the ancient Hebrew lunar calendar occurred in late March, April, or early May. 23:13a Hebrew 2/10 of an ephah [4.4 liters]; also in 23:17. 23:13b Hebrew 1/4 of a hin [1 liter]. 23:21 This celebration, called the Festival of Harvest or the Festival of Weeks, was later called the Festival of Pentecost (see Acts 2:1). It is celebrated today as Shavuot (or Shabuoth). 23:24 Hebrew On the first day of the seventh month. This day in the ancient Hebrew lunar calendar occurred in September or October. This festival is celebrated today as Rosh Hashanah, the Jewish new year.

23:26-32 The yearly Day of Atonement festival was to be a day of complete and total rest as the Israelites made sacrifices and offerings to atone for their sins. Leviticus 1–7 contains specific instructions on how the Israelites were to worship God. In order for us to experience a true relationship with God, we must first acknowledge that Christ is our sacrificial lamb. John the Baptist introduced him as "the Lamb of God who takes away the sin of the world" (John 1:29). This initial step will enable us to worship God in spirit and in truth.

The Day of Atonement

²⁶Then the LORD said to Moses, ²⁷"Be careful to celebrate the Day of Atonement on the tenth day of that same month—nine days after the Festival of Trumpets.* You must observe it as an official day for holy assembly, a day to deny yourselves* and present special gifts to the LORD. ²⁸Do no work during that entire day because it is the Day of Atonement, when offerings of purification are made for you, making you right with* the LORD your God. ²⁹All who do not deny themselves that day will be cut off from God's people. ³⁰And I will destroy anyone among you who does any work on that day. ³¹You must not do any work at all! This is a permanent law for you, and it must be observed from generation to generation wherever you live. ³²This will be a Sabbath day of complete rest for you, and on that day you must deny yourselves. This day of rest will begin at sundown on the ninth day of the month and extend until sundown on the tenth day."

The Festival of Shelters

³³And the LORD said to Moses, ³⁴"Give the following instructions to the people of Israel. Begin celebrating the Festival of Shelters* on the fifteenth day of the appointed month— five days after the Day of Atonement.* This festival to the LORD will last for seven days. ³⁵On the first day of the festival you must proclaim an official day for holy assembly, when you do no ordinary work. ³⁶For seven days you must present special gifts to the LORD. The eighth day is another holy day on which you present your special gifts to the LORD. This will be a solemn occasion, and no ordinary work may be done that day.

³⁷("These are the LORD's appointed festivals. Celebrate them each year as official days for holy assembly by presenting special gifts to the LORD—burnt offerings, grain offerings, sacrifices, and liquid offerings—each on its proper day. ³⁸These festivals must be observed in addition to the LORD's regular Sabbath days, and the offerings are in addition to your personal gifts, the offerings you give to fulfill your vows, and the voluntary offerings you present to the LORD.)

³⁹"Remember that this seven-day festival to the LORD—the Festival of Shelters—begins on the fifteenth day of the appointed month,* after you have harvested all the produce of the land. The first day and the eighth day of the festival will be days of complete rest. ⁴⁰On the first day gather branches from magnificent trees*—palm fronds, boughs from leafy trees, and willows that grow by the streams. Then celebrate with joy before the LORD your God for seven days. ⁴¹You must observe this festival to the LORD for seven days every year. This is a permanent law for you, and it must be observed in the appointed month* from generation to generation. ⁴²For seven days you must live outside in little shelters. All native-born Israelites must live in shelters. ⁴³This will remind each new generation of Israelites that I made their ancestors live in shelters when I rescued them from the land of Egypt. I am the LORD your God."

⁴⁴So Moses gave the Israelites these instructions regarding the annual festivals of the LORD.

CHAPTER 24
Pure Oil and Holy Bread

The LORD said to Moses, ²"Command the people of Israel to bring you pure oil of pressed olives for the light, to keep the lamps burning continually. ³This is the lampstand that stands in the Tabernacle, in front of the inner curtain that shields the Ark of the Covenant.* Aaron must keep the lamps burning in the LORD's presence all

---

23:27a Hebrew *on the tenth day of the seventh month;* see 23:24 and the note there. This day in the ancient Hebrew lunar calendar occurred in September or October. It is celebrated today as Yom Kippur. 23:27b Or *to fast;* similarly in 23:29, 32. 23:28 Or *when atonement is made for you before.* 23:34a Or *Festival of Booths,* or *Festival of Tabernacles.* This was earlier called the Festival of the Final Harvest or Festival of Ingathering (see Exod 23:16b). It is celebrated today as Sukkot (or Succoth). 23:34b Hebrew *on the fifteenth day of the seventh month;* see 23:27a and the note there. 23:39 Hebrew *on the fifteenth day of the seventh month.* 23:40 Or *gather fruit from majestic trees.* 23:41 Hebrew *the seventh month.* 24:3 Hebrew *in the Tent of Meeting, outside the inner curtain of the Testimony;* see note on 16:13.

23:33-43 The Festival of Shelters, like Israel's other yearly feasts, was to remind the people of a crucial event in their history. Required for all native-born Israelites, the festival celebrated God's protective care of his people during their forty-year sojourn in the wilderness. It pictured God's tremendous grace in this "recovery period" after the Exodus from Egypt. This same God is faithful to us in our times of recovery from sin, and he extends his grace to us. We may not have a formal week of feasting to remember those times, but we should set aside one day each week to remember them and praise God for our spiritual growth.

night. This is a permanent law for you, and it must be observed from generation to generation. ⁴Aaron and the priests must tend the lamps on the pure gold lampstand continually in the LORD's presence.

⁵"You must bake twelve flat loaves of bread from choice flour, using four quarts* of flour for each loaf. ⁶Place the bread before the LORD on the pure gold table, and arrange the loaves in two stacks, with six loaves in each stack. ⁷Put some pure frankincense near each row to serve as a representative offering, a special gift presented to the LORD. ⁸Every Sabbath day this bread must be laid out before the LORD as a gift from the Israelites; it is an ongoing expression of the eternal covenant. ⁹The loaves of bread will belong to Aaron and his descendants, who must eat them in a sacred place, for they are most holy. It is the permanent right of the priests to claim this portion of the special gifts presented to the LORD."

An Example of Just Punishment

¹⁰One day a man who had an Israelite mother and an Egyptian father came out of his tent and got into a fight with one of the Israelite men. ¹¹During the fight, this son of an Israelite woman blasphemed the Name of the LORD* with a curse. So the man was brought to Moses for judgment. His mother was Shelomith, the daughter of Dibri of the tribe of Dan. ¹²They kept the man in custody until the LORD's will in the matter should become clear to them.

¹³Then the LORD said to Moses, ¹⁴"Take the blasphemer outside the camp, and tell all those who heard the curse to lay their hands on his head. Then let the entire community stone him to death. ¹⁵Say to the people of Israel: Those who curse their God will be punished for their sin. ¹⁶Anyone who blasphemes the Name of the LORD must be stoned to death by the whole community of Israel. Any native-born Israelite or foreigner among you who blasphemes the Name of the LORD must be put to death.

¹⁷"Anyone who takes another person's life must be put to death.

¹⁸"Anyone who kills another person's animal must pay for it in full—a live animal for the animal that was killed.

¹⁹"Anyone who injures another person must be dealt with according to the injury inflicted—²⁰a fracture for a fracture, an eye for an eye, a tooth for a tooth. Whatever anyone does to injure another person must be paid back in kind.

²¹"Whoever kills an animal must pay for it in full, but whoever kills another person must be put to death.

²²"This same standard applies both to native-born Israelites and to the foreigners living among you. I am the LORD your God."

²³After Moses gave all these instructions to the Israelites, they took the blasphemer outside the camp and stoned him to death. The Israelites did just as the LORD had commanded Moses.

CHAPTER 25
The Sabbath Year

While Moses was on Mount Sinai, the LORD said to him, ²"Give the following instructions to the people of Israel. When you have entered the land I am giving you, the land itself must observe a Sabbath rest before the LORD every seventh year. ³For six years you may plant your fields and prune your vineyards and harvest your crops, ⁴but during the seventh year the land must have a Sabbath year of complete rest. It is the LORD's Sabbath. Do not plant your fields or prune your vineyards during that year. ⁵And don't store away the crops that grow on their own or gather the grapes from your unpruned vines. The land must have a year of complete rest. ⁶But you may eat whatever the land produces on its own during its Sabbath. This applies to you, your male and female servants, your hired workers, and the temporary residents who live with you. ⁷Your livestock and the wild animals in your land will also be allowed to eat what the land produces.

24:5 Hebrew ²/₁₀ of an ephah [4.4 liters]. 24:11 Hebrew *the Name;* also in 24:16b.

25:1-7 The sabbatical year, like the weekly Sabbath day, was instituted by God as a special period of rest for the Israelites. Every seventh year was a time of rest for the land, animals, and people. Their rest from work was in itself an act of faith, proving that they believed God would provide for the coming year. It also gave them time to reflect on the fact that God was the true provider: Everything they owned ultimately came from his generous hand. When we realize this truth, we will be better able to commit ourself into God's hands. He is more than able to provide for our needs and help us as we continue in the recovery process.

The Year of Jubilee

8 "In addition, you must count off seven Sabbath years, seven sets of seven years, adding up to forty-nine years in all. 9Then on the Day of Atonement in the fiftieth year,* blow the ram's horn loud and long throughout the land. 10Set this year apart as holy, a time to proclaim freedom throughout the land for all who live there. It will be a jubilee year for you, when each of you may return to the land that belonged to your ancestors and return to your own clan. 11This fiftieth year will be a jubilee for you. During that year you must not plant your fields or store away any of the crops that grow on their own, and don't gather the grapes from your unpruned vines. 12It will be a jubilee year for you, and you must keep it holy. But you may eat whatever the land produces on its own. 13In the Year of Jubilee each of you may return to the land that belonged to your ancestors.

14 "When you make an agreement with your neighbor to buy or sell property, you must not take advantage of each other. 15When you buy land from your neighbor, the price you pay must be based on the number of years since the last jubilee. The seller must set the price by taking into account the number of years remaining until the next Year of Jubilee. 16The more years until the next jubilee, the higher the price; the fewer years, the lower the price. After all, the person selling the land is actually selling you a certain number of harvests. 17Show your fear of God by not taking advantage of each other. I am the LORD your God.

18 "If you want to live securely in the land, follow my decrees and obey my regulations. 19Then the land will yield large crops, and you will eat your fill and live securely in it. 20But you might ask, 'What will we eat during the seventh year, since we are not allowed to plant or harvest crops that year?' 21Be assured that I will send my blessing for you in the sixth year, so the land will produce a crop large enough for three years. 22When you plant your fields in the eighth year, you will still be eating from the large crop of the sixth year. In fact, you will still be eating from that large crop when the new crop is harvested in the ninth year.

Redemption of Property

23 "The land must never be sold on a permanent basis, for the land belongs to me. You are only foreigners and tenant farmers working for me. 24 "With every purchase of land you must grant the seller the right to buy it back. 25If one of your fellow Israelites falls into poverty and is forced to sell some family land, then a close relative should buy it back for him. 26If there is no close relative to buy the land, but the person who sold it gets enough money to buy it back, 27he then has the right to redeem it from the one who bought it. The price of the land will be discounted according to the number of years until the next Year of Jubilee. In this way the original owner can then return to the land. 28But if the original owner cannot afford to buy back the land, it will remain with the new owner until the next Year of Jubilee. In the jubilee year, the land must be returned to the original owners so they can return to their family land.

29 "Anyone who sells a house inside a walled town has the right to buy it back for a full year after its sale. During that year, the seller retains the right to buy it back. 30But if it is not bought back within a year, the sale of the house within the walled town cannot be reversed. It will become the permanent property of the buyer. It will not be returned to the original owner in the Year of Jubilee. 31But a house in a village—a settlement without fortified walls—will be treated like property in the countryside. Such a house may be bought back at any time, and it must be returned to the original owner in the Year of Jubilee.

32 "The Levites always have the right to buy back a house they have sold within the towns allotted to them. 33And any property that is sold by the Levites—all houses within the Le-

25:9 Hebrew *on the tenth day of the seventh month, on the Day of Atonement;* see 23:27a and the note there.

25:8-55 The Year of Jubilee took place every 50 years. At this time all the lands and possessions that had passed from one family to another during the previous 49 years were returned to the original owners. This reminded the Israelites that God was really the owner of all their possessions. They were only the managers. This would have curbed their tendency toward materialism. It would also provide families that had lost everything during the previous 50 years a chance for recovery. True contentment in life comes only when we see our material possessions as gifts from the hand of God. Jesus taught that we should give God first place in our life and live as he wants us to; then God will provide everything we need to live from day to day (Matthew 6:33).

vitical towns—must be returned in the Year of Jubilee. After all, the houses in the towns reserved for the Levites are the only property they own in all Israel. [34]The open pastureland around the Levitical towns may never be sold. It is their permanent possession.

Redemption of the Poor and Enslaved

[35]"If one of your fellow Israelites falls into poverty and cannot support himself, support him as you would a foreigner or a temporary resident and allow him to live with you. [36]Do not charge interest or make a profit at his expense. Instead, show your fear of God by letting him live with you as your relative. [37]Remember, do not charge interest on money you lend him or make a profit on food you sell him. [38]I am the LORD your God, who brought you out of the land of Egypt to give you the land of Canaan and to be your God.

[39]"If one of your fellow Israelites falls into poverty and is forced to sell himself to you, do not treat him as a slave. [40]Treat him instead as a hired worker or as a temporary resident who lives with you, and he will serve you only until the Year of Jubilee. [41]At that time he and his children will no longer be obligated to you, and they will return to their clans and go back to the land originally allotted to their ancestors. [42]The people of Israel are my servants, whom I brought out of the land of Egypt, so they must never be sold as slaves. [43]Show your fear of God by not treating them harshly.

[44]"However, you may purchase male and female slaves from among the nations around you. [45]You may also purchase the children of temporary residents who live among you, including those who have been born in your land. You may treat them as your property, [46]passing them on to your children as a permanent inheritance. You may treat them as slaves, but you must never treat your fellow Israelites this way.

[47]"Suppose a foreigner or temporary resident becomes rich while living among you. If any of your fellow Israelites fall into poverty and are forced to sell themselves to such a foreigner or to a member of his family, [48]they still retain the right to be bought back, even after they have been purchased. They may be bought back by a brother, [49]an uncle, or a cousin. In fact, anyone from the extended family may buy them back. They may also redeem themselves if they have prospered. [50]They will negotiate the price of their freedom with the person who bought them. The price will be based on the number of years from the time they were sold until the next Year of Jubilee—whatever it would cost to hire a worker for that period of time. [51]If many years still remain until the jubilee, they will repay the proper proportion of what they received when they sold themselves. [52]If only a few years remain until the Year of Jubilee, they will repay a small amount for their redemption. [53]The foreigner must treat them as workers hired on a yearly basis. You must not allow a foreigner to treat any of your fellow Israelites harshly. [54]If any Israelites have not been bought back by the time the Year of Jubilee arrives, they and their children must be set free at that time. [55]For the people of Israel belong to me. They are my servants, whom I brought out of the land of Egypt. I am the LORD your God.

CHAPTER 26
Blessings for Obedience

"Do not make idols or set up carved images, or sacred pillars, or sculptured stones in your land so you may worship them. I am the LORD your God. [2]You must keep my Sabbath days of rest and show reverence for my sanctuary. I am the LORD.

[3]"If you follow my decrees and are careful to obey my commands, [4]I will send you the seasonal rains. The land will then yield its crops, and the trees of the field will produce their fruit. [5]Your threshing season will overlap with the grape harvest, and your grape harvest will overlap with the season of planting grain. You will eat your fill and live securely in your own land.

[6]"I will give you peace in the land, and you will be able to sleep with no cause for fear. I will rid the land of wild animals and keep your enemies out of your land. [7]In fact, you will chase down your enemies and slaughter them with your swords. [8]Five of

---

25:35-38 God wanted the Israelites to be kind to those around them and supportive of those in need. Here, God demands generosity toward those stricken with poverty. The fellowship of God's people was always intended to be redemptive; those in need were to be cared for by those with plenty. This was true not only for physical needs but for emotional and spiritual needs as well. Recovery and rebuilding in our life will rarely happen if we have to do it all alone. It takes the support and encouragement of those in God's family who are closest to us.

you will chase a hundred, and a hundred of you will chase ten thousand! All your enemies will fall beneath your sword.

⁹"I will look favorably upon you, making you fertile and multiplying your people. And I will fulfill my covenant with you. ¹⁰You will have such a surplus of crops that you will need to clear out the old grain to make room for the new harvest! ¹¹I will live among you, and I will not despise you. ¹²I will walk among you; I will be your God, and you will be my people. ¹³I am the LORD your God, who brought you out of the land of Egypt so you would no longer be their slaves. I broke the yoke of slavery from your neck so you can walk with your heads held high.

Punishments for Disobedience

¹⁴"However, if you do not listen to me or obey all these commands, ¹⁵and if you break my covenant by rejecting my decrees, treating my regulations with contempt, and refusing to obey my commands, ¹⁶I will punish you. I will bring sudden terrors upon you—wasting diseases and burning fevers that will cause your eyes to fail and your life to ebb away. You will plant your crops in vain because your enemies will eat them. ¹⁷I will turn against you, and you will be defeated by your enemies. Those who hate you will rule over you, and you will run even when no one is chasing you!

¹⁸"And if, in spite of all this, you still disobey me, I will punish you seven times over for your sins. ¹⁹I will break your proud spirit by making the skies as unyielding as iron and the earth as hard as bronze. ²⁰All your work will be for nothing, for your land will yield no crops, and your trees will bear no fruit.

²¹"If even then you remain hostile toward me and refuse to obey me, I will inflict disaster on you seven times over for your sins. ²²I will send wild animals that will rob you of your children and destroy your livestock. Your numbers will dwindle, and your roads will be deserted.

²³"And if you fail to learn the lesson and continue your hostility toward me, ²⁴then I myself will be hostile toward you. I will personally strike you with calamity seven times over for your sins. ²⁵I will send armies against you to carry out the curse of the covenant you have broken. When you run to your towns for safety, I will send a plague to destroy you there, and you will be handed over to your enemies. ²⁶I will destroy your food supply, so that ten women will need only one oven to bake bread for their families. They will ration your food by weight, and though you have food to eat, you will not be satisfied.

²⁷"If in spite of all this you still refuse to listen and still remain hostile toward me, ²⁸then I will give full vent to my hostility. I myself will punish you seven times over for your sins. ²⁹Then you will eat the flesh of your own sons and daughters. ³⁰I will destroy your pagan shrines and knock down your places of worship. I will leave your lifeless corpses piled on top of your lifeless idols,* and I will despise you. ³¹I will make your cities desolate and destroy your places of pagan worship. I will take no pleasure in your offerings that should be a pleasing aroma to me. ³²Yes, I myself will devastate your land, and your enemies who come to occupy it will be appalled at what they see. ³³I will scatter you among the nations and bring out my sword against you. Your land will become desolate,

26:30 The Hebrew term (literally *round things*) probably alludes to dung.

26:11-13 God's promises of rewards for Israel's obedience are culminated in this powerful affirmation of his love for his people. Again, the Exodus is used as a reminder that God took them from bondage and humiliation and lifted them up to become a people of dignity. As we learn to obey him, God offers us the same hope of recovery. His deliverance can provide us with a new life of moral and spiritual dignity. God assures us of this by offering to bring Christ's personal presence into each Christian's life forever (Matthew 28:20).

26:14-39 Here God warns his people about what will happen to those who are disobedient to God's laws. After reading this, some might get the idea that God is harsh and unloving. It might seem that he delights in punishing those who refuse to do things his way. But this long list of warnings about the consequences of sin is really an extended love letter from God. God doesn't want us to suffer; he doesn't want to punish us. But God does understand the destructive consequences of sin. He knows that certain activities will cause suffering to us and to those around us. So he warns us away from them, giving us a plan to follow that will lead to healthy and joyful living. God's program, though viewed by some as restrictive, is actually the shortest path to a life of fulfillment.

and your cities will lie in ruins. ³⁴Then at last the land will enjoy its neglected Sabbath years as it lies desolate while you are in exile in the land of your enemies. Then the land will finally rest and enjoy the Sabbaths it missed. ³⁵As long as the land lies in ruins, it will enjoy the rest you never allowed it to take every seventh year while you lived in it.

³⁶"And for those of you who survive, I will demoralize you in the land of your enemies. You will live in such fear that the sound of a leaf driven by the wind will send you fleeing. You will run as though fleeing from a sword, and you will fall even when no one pursues you. ³⁷Though no one is chasing you, you will stumble over each other as though fleeing from a sword. You will have no power to stand up against your enemies. ³⁸You will die among the foreign nations and be devoured in the land of your enemies. ³⁹Those of you who survive will waste away in your enemies' lands because of their sins and the sins of their ancestors.

⁴⁰"But at last my people will confess their sins and the sins of their ancestors for betraying me and being hostile toward me. ⁴¹When I have turned their hostility back on them and brought them to the land of their enemies, then at last their stubborn hearts will be humbled, and they will pay for their sins. ⁴²Then I will remember my covenant with Jacob and my covenant with Isaac and my covenant with Abraham, and I will remember the land. ⁴³For the land must be abandoned to enjoy its years of Sabbath rest as it lies deserted. At last the people will pay for their sins, for they have continually rejected my regulations and despised my decrees.

⁴⁴"But despite all this, I will not utterly reject or despise them while they are in exile in the land of their enemies. I will not cancel my covenant with them by wiping them out, for I am the LORD their God. ⁴⁵For their sakes I will remember my ancient covenant with their ancestors, whom I brought out of the land of Egypt in the sight of all the nations, that I might be their God. I am the LORD."

⁴⁶These are the decrees, regulations, and instructions that the LORD gave through Moses on Mount Sinai as evidence of the relationship between himself and the Israelites.

CHAPTER 27
Redemption of Gifts Offered to the LORD

The LORD said to Moses, ²"Give the following instructions to the people of Israel. If anyone makes a special vow to dedicate someone to the LORD by paying the value of that person, ³here is the scale of values to be used. A man between the ages of twenty and sixty is valued at fifty shekels* of silver, as measured by the sanctuary shekel. ⁴A woman of that age is valued at thirty shekels* of silver. ⁵A boy between the ages of five and twenty is valued at twenty shekels of silver; a girl of that age is valued at ten shekels* of silver. ⁶A boy between the ages of one month and five years is valued at five shekels of silver; a girl of that age is valued at three shekels* of silver. ⁷A man older than sixty is valued at fifteen shekels of silver; a woman of that age is valued at ten shekels* of silver. ⁸If you desire to make such a vow but cannot afford to pay the required amount, take the person to the priest. He will determine the amount for you to pay based on what you can afford.

⁹"If your vow involves giving an animal that is acceptable as an offering to the LORD, any gift to the LORD will be considered holy. ¹⁰You may not exchange or substitute it for another animal—neither a good animal for a bad one nor a bad animal for a good one. But if you do exchange one animal for another, then both the original animal and its substitute will be considered holy. ¹¹If your vow involves an unclean animal—one that is not acceptable as an offering to the LORD—then you must bring the animal to the priest. ¹²He will assess its value, and his assessment will be final, whether high or low. ¹³If you want to buy back the animal, you must pay the value set by the priest, plus 20 percent.

¹⁴"If someone dedicates a house to the

27:3 Or *20 ounces* [570 grams]. 27:4 Or *12 ounces* [342 grams]. 27:5 Or *A boy . . . 8 ounces* [228 grams] *of silver; a girl . . . 4 ounces* [114 grams]. 27:6 Or *A boy . . . 2 ounces* [57 grams] *of silver; a girl . . . 1.2 ounces* [34 grams]. 27:7 Or *A man . . . 6 ounces* [171 grams] *of silver; a woman . . . 4 ounces* [114 grams].

26:40-42 Even after a harsh warning for those disobedient to his laws (26:14-39), God shows great love for his people in this promise of restoration. God delights in restoring those who repent. Christ came to earth, died, and was resurrected so that we could experience God's forgiveness. All we have to do is take the first step: "But if we confess our sins to him, he is faithful and just to forgive us our sins and to cleanse us from all wickedness" (1 John 1:9). Even if we have fallen away from him, God is still willing to help us begin the journey toward recovery.

LORD, the priest will come to assess its value. The priest's assessment will be final, whether high or low. [15] If the person who dedicated the house wants to buy it back, he must pay the value set by the priest, plus 20 percent. Then the house will again be his.

[16] "If someone dedicates to the LORD a piece of his family property, its value will be assessed according to the amount of seed required to plant it—fifty shekels of silver for a field planted with five bushels of barley seed.* [17] If the field is dedicated to the LORD in the Year of Jubilee, then the entire assessment will apply. [18] But if the field is dedicated after the Year of Jubilee, the priest will assess the land's value in proportion to the number of years left until the next Year of Jubilee. Its assessed value is reduced each year. [19] If the person who dedicated the field wants to buy it back, he must pay the value set by the priest, plus 20 percent. Then the field will again be legally his. [20] But if he does not want to buy it back, and it is sold to someone else, the field can no longer be bought back. [21] When the field is released in the Year of Jubilee, it will be holy, a field specially set apart* for the LORD. It will become the property of the priests.

[22] "If someone dedicates to the LORD a field he has purchased but which is not part of his family property, [23] the priest will assess its value based on the number of years left until the next Year of Jubilee. On that day he must give the assessed value of the land as a sacred donation to the LORD. [24] In the Year of Jubilee the field must be returned to the person from whom he purchased it, the one who inher-ited it as family property. [25] (All the payments must be measured by the weight of the sanc-tuary shekel,* which equals twenty gerahs.)

[26] "You may not dedicate a firstborn ani-mal to the LORD, for the firstborn of your cat-tle, sheep, and goats already belong to him. [27] However, you may buy back the firstborn of a ceremonially unclean animal by paying the priest's assessment of its worth, plus 20 percent. If you do not buy it back, the priest will sell it at its assessed value.

[28] "However, anything specially set apart for the LORD—whether a person, an animal, or family property—must never be sold or bought back. Anything devoted in this way has been set apart as holy, and it belongs to the LORD. [29] No person specially set apart for destruction may be bought back. Such a per-son must be put to death.

[30] "One-tenth of the produce of the land, whether grain from the fields or fruit from the trees, belongs to the LORD and must be set apart to him as holy. [31] If you want to buy back the LORD's tenth of the grain or fruit, you must pay its value, plus 20 percent. [32] Count off every tenth animal from your herds and flocks and set them apart for the LORD as holy. [33] You may not pick and choose between good and bad animals, and you may not substitute one for another. But if you do exchange one animal for another, then both the original animal and its substi-tute will be considered holy and cannot be bought back."

[34] These are the commands that the LORD gave through Moses on Mount Sinai for the Israelites.

27:16 Hebrew *50 shekels* [20 ounces or 570 grams] *of silver for a homer* [220 liters] *of barley seed.* 27:21 The Hebrew term used here refers to the complete consecration of things or people to the LORD, either by destroying them or by giving them as an offering; also in 27:28, 29. 27:25 Each shekel was about 0.4 ounces [11 grams] in weight.

REFLECTIONS ON LEVITICUS

insights FROM THE OFFERINGS

In **Leviticus 1:3-13** we see the first object lesson given to God's people—the burnt offering. By identifying himself with the offering, the person bringing the offering was committing his life to God in a fresh way. In Romans 12:1-2 Paul similarly spoke of presenting our body as a living sacrifice to God. This is an essential step in recovery and a step toward positive growth for anyone. Only when we place our life in God's hands will he be able to change us through his power.

Not every Israelite was financially able to bring a large animal sacrifice to God. In **Leviticus 1:10-14** we see that God allowed worshipers to bring smaller offerings (a sheep, goat, dove, or pigeon), as they were able. Joseph and Mary, the parents of Jesus, were evidently quite poor because they offered the smallest of the sacrifices (see Luke 2:24). We may feel we have very little to offer to God compared to other people, but he doesn't compare us with others. He asks that our worship and commitment to him simply reflect what he has given to us.

The sin offering, introduced in **Leviticus 4:1-2,** was not a voluntary act of worship but a required response to sin. God takes sin very seriously and holds us accountable for dealing with it through confession. Confession of sin is not just a voluntary activity; it is demanded by God and is a basic requirement for healthy, holy living.

The sin offering was not just for blatant, intentional sins. As we see in **Leviticus 4:2-3, 13, 22, 27,** it was also meant to deal with unintentional sins. God takes sin seriously—including the sins we aren't even aware of! God recognizes that even unintentional sins have grave consequences. We sometimes sin unintentionally against our children in the same ways that our parents sinned against us. Family sins can be passed on for generations. We need to carefully examine ourself before God on a regular basis and repent of every known sin in our life—with no excuses or denials. We can be thankful that God understands our human frailty and graciously provides ways for us to deal with it.

insights FROM THE PURIFICATION CEREMONY

The purification ceremony on the Day of Atonement, described first in **Leviticus 16,** is rich with meaning. The word *atonement* literally means "a making at one," as in *at-one-ment.* The underlying Hebrew term occurs in numerous other places and is often translated "to purify you . . . making you right" (see 1:4 and the textual note there). When the Israelites sinned, they became separated from God. But God graciously forgave them time after time, reconciling them to himself—making them "at one." God intends this for our life as well. He wants us to find forgiveness and purification for our sins and to be reconciled to him. God is in the business of restoring broken relationships. By means of forgiveness, he provides a way for the restoration of relationships broken by sin.

In **Leviticus 16:7-10, 15-22** we see two goats set apart for the purification ceremony. The first was associated with the people's sin and was sacrificed to God as a sin offering. The second goat, also associated with the sins of the people, was led into the wilderness and then released. This "scapegoat" took the sins of the people upon itself and carried them away. This illustrated the truth of Psalm 103:12, that God removes our sins "as far from us as the east is from the west."

God has done this through the ultimate scapegoat, Jesus Christ, who has taken all our sins upon himself. One of the most important steps in the process of recovery from sin and failure is learning to let it go. The fact that God himself has taken it away should help us as we do this.

insights FROM GOD'S LAWS

In **Leviticus 11:44-45** God forbade the Israelites to touch certain animals. God may have given this law for logical reasons, such as a concern for his people's health. It seems, however, that many of these laws were given for theological reasons so the Israelites might be different from the surrounding nations—"set apart" or "holy" unto God. While God may sometimes show us logical reasons for obeying him, this should not be our primary motivation for obedience. We are to obey him because he calls us to be different—"set apart" or "holy"—just as he is holy. And we can trust that his plan will lead us to discover the best life has to offer, whether what he asks seems logical to us or not.

Leviticus 18:1-5 sets the tone for the rest of the book. It affirms that God's relationship with his people was intended to affect the practical areas of their moral and spiritual lives. When we commit our life to God, we give God the opportunity to transform us. Spiritual growth can only come about, however, when we begin to live responsibly before God, handing over all our moral decisions to his wise direction.

In **Leviticus 18:4-5** we see the refrain "I am the Lord your God." This phrase appears more often in Leviticus than in any other book of the Bible. When God asked the Israelites to live holy lives, he knew that this would be difficult. God knew they would need a healthy fear of him to motivate them to obedience. So he continually reminded them of his identity as the Lord their God—the God who had revealed himself with terrifying power at Mount Sinai. Fear or respect for God is a good starting point if we want to live according to his plan. It should encourage us to know that this awesome God sent his Son to help us live according to that plan.

Incest (18:6-18), adultery (18:20), child sacrifice (18:21), homosexuality (18:22), and bestiality (18:23) were all practiced by godless societies in the ancient Near East. In **Leviticus 18:24-30** God tells us that these activities lead to the deterioration and destruction of society. It is only through a relationship with God that people are able to be morally pure and recover from the destructive effects of their sins. God's standards are given for our good.

In **Leviticus 19:1-2** God's call to holiness is repeated (see 11:44). God's holiness is the model and motivation for God's people to lead holy lives. God knows our weaknesses and our failures, yet he places before us the goal of his righteousness. It is only with Christ's help that we can reach this goal. Through his death we have cleansing from our failures and sins, and through his life (lived in us by the power of the Holy Spirit) we have the power to live a morally pure and holy life.

As we compare **Leviticus 19:18** and **19:33-34**, we see that the call to love one's neighbor was extended to include not only fellow Israelites but foreigners as well. This was a radical concept among the people of ancient times just as it is for us today. Jesus quoted this commandment as the second great commandment of the law (Matthew 22:39; Mark 12:31; Luke 10:27). It should be easier for us to have compassion on others if we remember that God had compassion on us and freed us from our slavery to sin.

NUMBERS

THE BIG PICTURE

This book has long been known as Numbers because it begins and ends with a census of Israel. However, the Hebrew name for the book, "In the Wilderness," better describes what the book is about. While in the wilderness, God's people experienced not only God's kindness and patience but also his holy discipline. They learned that their new freedom from Egyptian bondage included the responsibility to serve and obey God.

After their exodus from Egypt, the Israelites moved quickly through the wilderness to the edge of the Promised Land. But when they saw the strength of the people living there, they became afraid and refused to conquer it. As a result, they were sent back into the wilderness to wander for almost 40 years—just because they refused to act upon God's promises! Numbers ends with the Israelites again poised at the border of the Promised Land. Forty years of wilderness lessons had taught them that God's power was available to all who trusted and obeyed him.

The Israelites' experiences illustrate the importance of a practical faith in God. They show us the blessed fruits of obedience and the disastrous consequences of sin. We see how God's love is shown not only by his gracious forgiveness but also through his wise discipline and call to accountability.

It is usually in our wilderness experiences that we discover the true meaning of life, faith, and a personal relationship with God. God graciously offers us deliverance and cleansing, but our newfound freedom carries with it personal responsibility. We need to act on God's promises and follow the program he sets out for us. If we do, he will lead us through the wilderness; he will never allow us to wander forever.

THE BOTTOM LINE

PURPOSE: To demonstrate historically that God's great mercy and forgiveness toward his people are consistent with the firm, loving discipline he shows when they disobey. AUTHOR: Moses. AUDIENCE: The people of Israel. DATE WRITTEN: During and shortly after Israel's wilderness experience, between 1445 and 1406 B.C. SETTING: Beginning with a census at the Sinai encampment, Numbers follows the people of Israel during 38 years of wilderness wandering near Kadesh-barnea to the plains of Moab, just east of the Promised Land.
KEY VERSES: "Please, Lord, prove that your power is as great as you have claimed. For you said, 'The LORD is slow to anger and filled with unfailing love, forgiving every kind of sin and rebellion'" (14:17-18). KEY PLACES: Mount Sinai, Kadesh-barnea, Moab. KEY PEOPLE: Moses, Aaron, Caleb, Joshua.

RECOVERY THEMES

Experiencing the Wilderness: All of us wish that our recovery would involve a dramatic escape from slavery and immediate entrance into the Promised Land. We would love to leave out the wilderness experiences in between. But growth and recovery occur within the wilderness. It is in the wilderness that we come to terms with who we really are. We discover faith and the reality of God's faithfulness and patience. In the wilderness we discover that we cannot make it alone, that we need to turn our life over to God and depend on him. Numbers reveals the value of our own wilderness experiences as we progress in the recovery process.

The Importance of Faith: Faith is the opposite of self-sufficiency. The Israelites were confronted daily with the fact that if left to their own abilities, they would die in the wilderness. They were forced to live one day at a time, acting on their faith that God would provide what they needed each day. They needed a practical faith—one that looked to God for safety, food, and even health. When we enter the wilderness experiences of recovery, we need the same practical faith that allows us to live one day at a time.

Personal Accountability: The Israelites wandered in the wilderness for 40 years because they believed the report of the 10 faithless scouts instead of God's promises to deliver them from their enemies. Each wilderness step they took should have reminded them that they were responsible for their predicament. Most of them, however, chose to blame God and Moses instead. They refused to admit the truth—that they were wandering because of their own choices. We too are in our present circumstances because of choices we have made. We need to take personal responsibility for our life if we desire to progress along the road to recovery.

CHAPTER 1
Registration of Israel's Troops

A year after Israel's departure from Egypt, the LORD spoke to Moses in the Tabernacle* in the wilderness of Sinai. On the first day of the second month* of that year he said, ²"From the whole community of Israel, record the names of all the warriors by their clans and families. List all the men ³twenty years old or older who are able to go to war. You and Aaron must register the troops, ⁴and you will be assisted by one family leader from each tribe.

⁵"These are the tribes and the names of the leaders who will assist you:

Tribe	Leader
Reuben	Elizur son of Shedeur
⁶ Simeon	Shelumiel son of Zurishaddai
⁷ Judah	Nahshon son of Amminadab
⁸ Issachar	Nethanel son of Zuar
⁹ Zebulun	Eliab son of Helon

¹⁰ Ephraim son of Joseph . . . . Elishama son of Ammihud
Manasseh son of Joseph . . . . . . Gamaliel son of Pedahzur
¹¹ Benjamin . . . . Abidan son of Gideoni
¹² Dan . . . . Ahiezer son of Ammishaddai
¹³ Asher . . . . Pagiel son of Ocran
¹⁴ Gad . . . . Eliasaph son of Deuel
¹⁵ Naphtali . . . . Ahira son of Enan

¹⁶These are the chosen leaders of the community, the leaders of their ancestral tribes, the heads of the clans of Israel."

¹⁷So Moses and Aaron called together these chosen leaders, ¹⁸and they assembled the whole community of Israel on that very day.* All the people were registered according to their ancestry by their clans and families. The men of Israel who were twenty years old or older were listed one by one, ¹⁹just as the LORD had commanded Moses.

1:1a Hebrew *the Tent of Meeting.* 1:1b This day in the ancient Hebrew lunar calendar occurred in April or May.
1:18 Hebrew *on the first day of the second month;* see 1:1.

1:1 The expression "the LORD spoke," is similar to that found in the first verse of Leviticus and indicates God's personal interest in the lives of his people. He communicated clearly with his people, giving them instructions for healthy living. He was interested in the way they worshiped (Leviticus) as well as in the events of their daily lives (Numbers). He was interested in delivering and directing his people. This should remind us of his commitment to us today.
1:2-46 Taking a census of the Israelites prior to their journey to the Promised Land not only had organizational and military significance (1:3) but also served an important psychological purpose. As each individual identified his tribal and family background (1:18), it was a powerful reminder to the Israelites of their unity and common family heritage. This sense of unity would become essential as they faced the enemies and challenges ahead. Similarly, the assurance of support and unity within the family of Christ is critical for those who face wilderness periods in their life today (Philippians 2:1-3).

So Moses recorded their names in the wilderness of Sinai.

20-21This is the number of men twenty years old or older who were able to go to war, as their names were listed in the records of their clans and families*:

Tribe	Number
Reuben (Jacob's* oldest son)	46,500
22-23 Simeon	59,300
24-25 Gad	45,650
26-27 Judah	74,600
28-29 Issachar	54,400
30-31 Zebulun	57,400
32-33 Ephraim son of Joseph	40,500
34-35 Manasseh son of Joseph	32,200
36-37 Benjamin	35,400
38-39 Dan	62,700
40-41 Asher	41,500
42-43 Naphtali	53,400

44These were the men registered by Moses and Aaron and the twelve leaders of Israel, all listed according to their ancestral descent. 45They were registered by families—all the men of Israel who were twenty years old or older and able to go to war. 46The total number was 603,550.

47But this total did not include the Levites. 48For the LORD had said to Moses, 49"Do not include the tribe of Levi in the registration; do not count them with the rest of the Israelites. 50Put the Levites in charge of the Tabernacle of the Covenant,* along with all its furnishings and equipment. They must carry the Tabernacle and all its furnishings as you travel, and they must take care of it and camp around it. 51Whenever it is time for the Tabernacle to move, the Levites will take it down. And when it is time to stop, they will set it up again. But any unauthorized person who goes too near the Tabernacle must be put to death. 52Each tribe of Israel will camp in a designated area with its own family banner. 53But the Levites will camp around the Tabernacle of the Covenant to protect the community of Israel from the LORD's anger. The Levites are responsible to stand guard around the Tabernacle."

54So the Israelites did everything just as the LORD had commanded Moses.

CHAPTER 2
Organization for Israel's Camp

Then the LORD gave these instructions to Moses and Aaron: 2"When the Israelites set up camp, each tribe will be assigned its own area. The tribal divisions will camp beneath their family banners on all four sides of the Tabernacle,* but at some distance from it.

3-4"The divisions of Judah, Issachar, and Zebulun are to camp toward the sunrise on the east side of the Tabernacle, beneath their family banners. These are the names of the tribes, their leaders, and the numbers of their registered troops:

Tribe	Leader	Number
Judah	Nahshon son of Amminadab	74,600
5-6 Issachar	Nethanel son of Zuar	54,400
7-8 Zebulun	Eliab son of Helon	57,400

9So the total of all the troops on Judah's side of the camp is 186,400. These three tribes are to lead the way whenever the Israelites travel to a new campsite.

10-11"The divisions of Reuben, Simeon, and Gad are to camp on the south side of the Tabernacle, beneath their family banners. These are the names of the tribes, their leaders, and the numbers of their registered troops:

Tribe	Leader	Number
Reuben	Elizur son of Shedeur	46,500
12-13 Simeon	Shelumiel son of Zurishaddai	59,300
14-15 Gad	Eliasaph son of Deuel*	45,650

16So the total of all the troops on Reuben's side of the camp is 151,450. These three tribes will be second in line whenever the Israelites travel.

1:20-21a In the Hebrew text, this sentence (*This is the number of men twenty years old or older who were able to go to war, as their names were listed in the records of their clans and families*) is repeated in 1:22, 24, 26, 28, 30, 32, 34, 36, 38, 40, 42. 1:20-21b Hebrew *Israel's*. The names "Jacob" and "Israel" are often interchanged throughout the Old Testament, referring sometimes to the individual patriarch and sometimes to the nation. 1:50 Or *Tabernacle of the Testimony;* also in 1:53. 2:2 Hebrew *the Tent of Meeting;* also in 2:17. 2:14-15 As in many Hebrew manuscripts, Samaritan Pentateuch, and Latin Vulgate (see also 1:14); most Hebrew manuscripts read *son of Reuel*.

2:1-34 As they traveled and camped, the Israelites were to arrange themselves by tribe around the Tabernacle. God wanted the Israelites to keep him in constant focus, making him the center of all their thoughts and actions. Many of us try to face the challenges of life alone but find the battle overwhelming. It is only through the power of God, as we keep him constantly before us, that true victory and recovery can be realized.

17 "Then the Tabernacle, carried by the Levites, will set out from the middle of the camp. All the tribes are to travel in the same order that they camp, each in position under the appropriate family banner.

18-19 "The divisions of Ephraim, Manasseh, and Benjamin are to camp on the west side of the Tabernacle, beneath their family banners. These are the names of the tribes, their leaders, and the numbers of their registered troops:

Tribe	Leader	Number
Ephraim	Elishama son of Ammihud	40,500
20-21 Manasseh	Gamaliel son of Pedahzur	32,200
22-23 Benjamin	Abidan son of Gideoni	35,400

24 So the total of all the troops on Ephraim's side of the camp is 108,100. These three tribes will be third in line whenever the Israelites travel.

25-26 "The divisions of Dan, Asher, and Naphtali are to camp on the north side of the Tabernacle, beneath their family banners. These are the names of the tribes, their leaders, and the numbers of their registered troops:

Tribe	Leader	Number
Dan	Ahiezer son of Ammishaddai	62,700
27-28 Asher	Pagiel son of Ocran	41,500
29-30 Naphtali	Ahira son of Enan	53,400

31 So the total of all the troops on Dan's side of the camp is 157,600. These three tribes will be last, marching under their banners whenever the Israelites travel."

32 In summary, the troops of Israel listed by their families totaled 603,550. 33 But as the LORD had commanded, the Levites were not included in this registration. 34 So the people of Israel did everything as the LORD had commanded Moses. Each clan and family set up camp and marched under their banners exactly as the LORD had instructed them.

CHAPTER 3
Levites Appointed for Service

This is the family line of Aaron and Moses as it was recorded when the LORD spoke to Moses on Mount Sinai: 2 The names of Aaron's sons were Nadab (the oldest), Abihu, Eleazar, and Ithamar. 3 These sons of Aaron were anointed and ordained to minister as priests. 4 But Nadab and Abihu died in the LORD's presence in the wilderness of Sinai when they burned before the LORD the wrong kind of fire, different than he had commanded. Since they had no sons, this left only Eleazar and Ithamar to serve as priests with their father, Aaron.

5 Then the LORD said to Moses, 6 "Call forward the tribe of Levi, and present them to Aaron the priest to serve as his assistants. 7 They will serve Aaron and the whole community, performing their sacred duties in and around the Tabernacle.* 8 They will also maintain all the furnishings of the sacred tent,* serving in the Tabernacle on behalf of all the Israelites. 9 Assign the Levites to Aaron and his sons. They have been given from among all the people of Israel to serve as their assistants. 10 Appoint Aaron and his sons to carry out the duties of the priesthood. But any unauthorized person who goes too near the sanctuary must be put to death."

11 And the LORD said to Moses, 12 "Look, I have chosen the Levites from among the Israelites to serve as substitutes for all the firstborn sons of the people of Israel. The Levites belong to me, 13 for all the firstborn males are mine. On the day I struck down all the firstborn sons of the Egyptians, I set apart for myself all the firstborn in Israel, both of people and of animals. They are mine; I am the LORD."

Registration of the Levites

14 The LORD spoke again to Moses in the wilderness of Sinai. He said, 15 "Record the names of the members of the tribe of Levi by their families and clans. List every male who is one

---

3:7 Hebrew *around the Tent of Meeting, doing service at the Tabernacle.* 3:8 Hebrew *the Tent of Meeting;* also in 3:25.

3:1–4:49 This detailed organization of the Levites and priests illustrates the principle that God's calling is accompanied by responsibility and accountability. Out of Israel, God sovereignly chose one tribe (Levi), and out of that tribe he chose specific families to lead Israel in worship. With great privilege comes great responsibility. When God places us in a position of influence, we must not take it lightly. We need to recognize our responsibility to obey God and remember our accountability before him.

month old or older." ¹⁶So Moses listed them, just as the LORD had commanded.

¹⁷Levi had three sons, whose names were Gershon, Kohath, and Merari.
¹⁸The clans descended from Gershon were named after two of his descendants, Libni and Shimei.
¹⁹The clans descended from Kohath were named after four of his descendants, Amram, Izhar, Hebron, and Uzziel.
²⁰The clans descended from Merari were named after two of his descendants, Mahli and Mushi.

These were the Levite clans, listed according to their family groups.

²¹The descendants of Gershon were composed of the clans descended from Libni and Shimei. ²²There were 7,500 males one month old or older among these Gershonite clans. ²³They were assigned the area to the west of the Tabernacle for their camp. ²⁴The leader of the Gershonite clans was Eliasaph son of Lael. ²⁵These two clans were responsible to care for the Tabernacle, including the sacred tent with its layers of coverings, the curtain at its entrance, ²⁶the curtains of the courtyard that surrounded the Tabernacle and altar, the curtain at the courtyard entrance, the ropes, and all the equipment related to their use.

²⁷The descendants of Kohath were composed of the clans descended from Amram, Izhar, Hebron, and Uzziel. ²⁸There were 8,600* males one month old or older among these Kohathite clans. They were responsible for the care of the sanctuary, ²⁹and they were assigned the area south of the Tabernacle for their camp. ³⁰The leader of the Kohathite clans was Elizaphan son of Uzziel. ³¹These four clans were responsible for the care of the Ark, the table, the lampstand, the altars, the various articles used in the sanctuary, the inner curtain, and all the equipment related to their use. ³²Eleazar, son of Aaron the priest, was the chief administrator over all the Levites, with special responsibility for the oversight of the sanctuary.

³³The descendants of Merari were composed of the clans descended from Mahli and Mushi. ³⁴There were 6,200 males one month old or older among these Merarite clans. ³⁵They were assigned the area north of the Tabernacle for their camp. The leader of the Merarite clans was Zuriel son of Abihail.

³⁶These two clans were responsible for the care of the frames supporting the Tabernacle, the crossbars, the pillars, the bases, and all the equipment related to their use. ³⁷They were also responsible for the posts of the courtyard and all their bases, pegs, and ropes.

³⁸The area in front of the Tabernacle, in the east toward the sunrise,* was reserved for the tents of Moses and of Aaron and his sons, who had the final responsibility for the sanctuary on behalf of the people of Israel. Anyone other than a priest or Levite who went too near the sanctuary was to be put to death.

³⁹When Moses and Aaron counted the Levite clans at the LORD's command, the total number was 22,000 males one month old or older.

Redeeming the Firstborn Sons

⁴⁰Then the LORD said to Moses, "Now count all the firstborn sons in Israel who are one month old or older, and make a list of their names. ⁴¹The Levites must be reserved for me as substitutes for the firstborn sons of Israel; I am the LORD. And the Levites' livestock must be reserved for me as substitutes for the firstborn livestock of the whole nation of Israel."

⁴²So Moses counted the firstborn sons of the people of Israel, just as the LORD had commanded. ⁴³The number of firstborn sons who were one month old or older was 22,273.

⁴⁴Then the LORD said to Moses, ⁴⁵"Take the Levites as substitutes for the firstborn sons of the people of Israel. And take the livestock of the Levites as substitutes for the firstborn livestock of the people of Israel. The Levites belong to me; I am the LORD. ⁴⁶There are 273 more firstborn sons of Israel than there are Levites. To redeem these extra firstborn sons, ⁴⁷collect five pieces of silver* for each of them (each piece weighing the same as the sanctuary shekel, which equals twenty gerahs). ⁴⁸Give the silver to Aaron and his sons as the redemption price for the extra firstborn sons."

⁴⁹So Moses collected the silver for redeeming the firstborn sons of Israel who exceeded the number of Levites. ⁵⁰He collected 1,365 pieces of silver* on behalf of these firstborn sons of Israel (each piece weighing the same as the sanctuary shekel). ⁵¹And

3:28 Some Greek manuscripts read *8,300;* see total in 3:39. **3:38** Hebrew *toward the sunrise, in front of the Tent of Meeting.* **3:47** Hebrew *5 shekels* [2 ounces or 57 grams]. **3:50** Hebrew *1,365 [shekels] of silver.* [34 pounds or 15.5 kilograms].

Moses gave the silver for the redemption to Aaron and his sons, just as the LORD had commanded.

CHAPTER 4
Duties of the Kohathite Clan

Then the LORD said to Moses and Aaron, [2]"Record the names of the members of the clans and families of the Kohathite division of the tribe of Levi. [3]List all the men between the ages of thirty and fifty who are eligible to serve in the Tabernacle.*

[4]"The duties of the Kohathites at the Tabernacle will relate to the most sacred objects. [5]When the camp moves, Aaron and his sons must enter the Tabernacle first to take down the inner curtain and cover the Ark of the Covenant* with it. [6]Then they must cover the inner curtain with fine goatskin leather and spread over that a single piece of blue cloth. Finally, they must put the carrying poles of the Ark in place.

[7]"Next they must spread a blue cloth over the table where the Bread of the Presence is displayed, and on the cloth they will place the bowls, ladles, jars, pitchers, and the special bread. [8]They must spread a scarlet cloth over all of this, and finally a covering of fine goatskin leather on top of the scarlet cloth. Then they must insert the carrying poles into the table.

[9]"Next they must cover the lampstand with a blue cloth, along with its lamps, lamp snuffers, trays, and special jars of olive oil. [10]Then they must cover the lampstand and its accessories with fine goatskin leather and place the bundle on a carrying frame.

[11]"Next they must spread a blue cloth over the gold incense altar and cover this cloth with fine goatskin leather. Then they must attach the carrying poles to the altar. [12]They must take all the remaining furnishings of the sanctuary and wrap them in a blue cloth, cover them with fine goatskin leather, and place them on the carrying frame.

[13]"They must remove the ashes from the altar for sacrifices and cover the altar with a purple cloth. [14]All the altar utensils—the firepans, meat forks, shovels, basins, and all the containers—must be placed on the cloth, and a covering of fine goatskin leather must be spread over them. Finally, they must put the carrying poles in place. [15]The camp will be ready to move when Aaron and his sons have finished covering the sanctuary and all the sacred articles. The Kohathites will come and carry these things to the next destination. But they must not touch the sacred objects, or they will die. So these are the things from the Tabernacle that the Kohathites must carry.

[16]"Eleazar son of Aaron the priest will be responsible for the oil of the lampstand, the fragrant incense, the daily grain offering, and the anointing oil. In fact, Eleazar will be responsible for the entire Tabernacle and everything in it, including the sanctuary and its furnishings."

[17]Then the LORD said to Moses and Aaron, [18]"Do not let the Kohathite clans be destroyed from among the Levites! [19]This is what you must do so they will live and not die when they approach the most sacred objects. Aaron and his sons must always go in with them and assign a specific duty or load to each person. [20]The Kohathites must never enter the sanctuary to look at the sacred objects for even a moment, or they will die."

Duties of the Gershonite Clan

[21]And the LORD said to Moses, [22]"Record the names of the members of the clans and families of the Gershonite division of the tribe of Levi. [23]List all the men between the ages of thirty and fifty who are eligible to serve in the Tabernacle.

[24]"These Gershonite clans will be responsible for general service and carrying loads. [25]They must carry the curtains of the Tabernacle, the Tabernacle itself with its coverings, the outer covering of fine goatskin leather, and the curtain for the Tabernacle entrance. [26]They are also to carry the curtains for the courtyard walls that surround

4:3 Hebrew *the Tent of Meeting*; also in 4:4, 15, 23, 25, 28, 30, 31, 33, 35, 37, 39, 41, 43, 47.   4:5 Or *Ark of the Testimony*.

4:1-49 The efficient operation of the Israelite camp (especially the moving process) required detailed organization and cooperation. This chapter describes the responsibilities of the men of the Levite tribe. When each man cooperated and did his unique task, results were achieved. The ministry of the church today, especially in meeting some of the greatest human needs, requires a cooperative effort of people using their unique spiritual gifts to help others (1 Corinthians 12:7). Only then will we be able to reach those in need and provide the necessary environment for recovery and growth.

the Tabernacle and altar, the curtain across the courtyard entrance, the ropes, and all the equipment related to their use. The Gershonites are responsible for all these items. 27Aaron and his sons will direct the Gershonites regarding all their duties, whether it involves moving the equipment or doing other work. They must assign the Gershonites responsibility for the loads they are to carry. 28So these are the duties assigned to the Gershonite clans at the Tabernacle. They will be directly responsible to Ithamar son of Aaron the priest.

Duties of the Merarite Clan

29"Now record the names of the members of the clans and families of the Merarite division of the tribe of Levi. 30List all the men between the ages of thirty and fifty who are eligible to serve in the Tabernacle.

31"Their only duty at the Tabernacle will be to carry loads. They will carry the frames of the Tabernacle, the crossbars, the posts, and the bases; 32also the posts for the courtyard walls with their bases, pegs, and ropes; and all the accessories and everything else related to their use. Assign the various loads to each man by name. 33So these are the duties of the Merarite clans at the Tabernacle. They are directly responsible to Ithamar son of Aaron the priest."

Summary of the Registration

34So Moses, Aaron, and the other leaders of the community listed the members of the Kohathite division by their clans and families. 35The list included all the men between thirty and fifty years of age who were eligible for service in the Tabernacle, 36and the total number came to 2,750. 37So this was the total of all those from the Kohathite clans who were eligible to serve at the Tabernacle. Moses and Aaron listed them, just as the LORD had commanded through Moses.

38The Gershonite division was also listed by its clans and families. 39The list included all the men between thirty and fifty years of age who were eligible for service in the Tabernacle, 40and the total number came to 2,630. 41So this was the total of all those from the

Gershonite clans who were eligible to serve at the Tabernacle. Moses and Aaron listed them, just as the LORD had commanded.

42The Merarite division was also listed by its clans and families. 43The list included all the men between thirty and fifty years of age who were eligible for service in the Tabernacle, 44and the total number came to 3,200. 45So this was the total of all those from the Merarite clans who were eligible for service. Moses and Aaron listed them, just as the LORD had commanded through Moses.

46So Moses, Aaron, and the leaders of Israel listed all the Levites by their clans and families. 47All the men between thirty and fifty years of age who were eligible for service in the Tabernacle and for its transportation 48numbered 8,580. 49When their names were recorded, as the LORD had commanded through Moses, each man was assigned his task and told what to carry.

And so the registration was completed, just as the LORD had commanded Moses.

CHAPTER 5
Purity in Israel's Camp

The LORD gave these instructions to Moses: 2"Command the people of Israel to remove from the camp anyone who has a skin disease* or a discharge, or who has become ceremonially unclean by touching a dead person. 3This command applies to men and women alike. Remove them so they will not defile the camp in which I live among them." 4So the Israelites did as the LORD had commanded Moses and removed such people from the camp.

5Then the LORD said to Moses, 6"Give the following instructions to the people of Israel: If any of the people—men or women—betray the LORD by doing wrong to another person, they are guilty. 7They must confess their sin and make full restitution for what they have done, adding an additional 20 percent and returning it to the person who was wronged. 8But if the person who was wronged is dead, and there are no near relatives to whom restitution can be made, the payment belongs to the LORD and must be given to the priest. Those who are guilty

---

5:2 Traditionally rendered *leprosy*. The Hebrew word used here describes various skin diseases.

5:5-7 This command for dealing with sin emphasizes the same principles as do the sin and guilt offerings of Leviticus 4–5. God has provided clear steps for those who have violated others. These steps include admitting the wrong things we have done and providing restitution wherever possible. If we follow these simple steps, we will make significant progress toward recovery.

must also bring a ram as a sacrifice, and they will be purified and made right with the LORD.* [9]All the sacred offerings that the Israelites bring to a priest will belong to him. [10]Each priest may keep all the sacred donations that he receives."

Protecting Marital Faithfulness

[11]And the LORD said to Moses, [12]"Give the following instructions to the people of Israel.

"Suppose a man's wife goes astray, and she is unfaithful to her husband [13]and has sex with another man, but neither her husband nor anyone else knows about it. She has defiled herself, even though there was no witness and she was not caught in the act. [14]If her husband becomes jealous and is suspicious of his wife and needs to know whether or not she has defiled herself, [15]the husband must bring his wife to the priest. He must also bring an offering of two quarts* of barley flour to be presented on her behalf. Do not mix it with olive oil or frankincense, for it is a jealousy offering—an offering to prove whether or not she is guilty.

[16]"The priest will then present her to stand trial before the LORD. [17]He must take some holy water in a clay jar and pour into it dust he has taken from the Tabernacle floor. [18]When the priest has presented the woman before the LORD, he must unbind her hair and place in her hands the offering of proof—the jealousy offering to determine whether her husband's suspicions are justified. The priest will stand before her, holding the jar of bitter water that brings a curse to those who are guilty. [19]The priest will then put the woman under oath and say to her, 'If no other man has had sex with you, and you have not gone astray and defiled yourself while under your husband's authority, may you be immune from the effects of this bitter water that brings on the curse. [20]But if you have gone astray by being unfaithful to your husband, and have defiled yourself by having sex with another man—'

[21]"At this point the priest must put the woman under oath by saying, 'May the people know that the LORD's curse is upon you when he makes you infertile, causing your womb to shrivel* and your abdomen to swell. [22]Now may this water that brings the curse enter your body and cause your abdomen to swell and your womb to shrivel.*' And the woman will be required to say, 'Yes, let it be so.' [23]And the priest will write these curses on a piece of leather and wash them off into the bitter water. [24]He will make the woman drink the bitter water that brings on the curse. When the water enters her body, it will cause bitter suffering if she is guilty.

[25]"The priest will take the jealousy offering from the woman's hand, lift it up before the LORD, and carry it to the altar. [26]He will take a handful of the flour as a token portion and burn it on the altar, and he will require the woman to drink the water. [27]If she has defiled herself by being unfaithful to her husband, the water that brings on the curse will cause bitter suffering. Her abdomen will swell and her womb will shrink,* and her name will become a curse among her people. [28]But if she has not defiled herself and is pure, then she will be unharmed and will still be able to have children.

[29]"This is the ritual law for dealing with suspicion. If a woman goes astray and defiles herself while under her husband's authority, [30]or if a man becomes jealous and is suspicious that his wife has been unfaithful, the husband must present his wife before the LORD, and the priest will apply this entire ritual law to her. [31]The husband will be innocent of any guilt in this matter, but his wife will be held accountable for her sin."

CHAPTER 6
Nazirite Laws

Then the LORD said to Moses, [2]"Give the following instructions to the people of Israel.

"If any of the people, either men or women, take the special vow of a Nazirite,

5:8 Or *bring a ram for atonement, which will make atonement for them.*   5:15 Hebrew *1/10 of an ephah* [2.2 liters].
5:21 Hebrew *when he causes your thigh to waste away.*   5:22 Hebrew *and your thigh to waste away.*   5:27 Hebrew *and her thigh will waste away.*

5:11-15 The seriousness of adultery is underscored in this passage. Marriage was intended to be a picture of God's covenant relationship with his people. The ritual described in 5:16-31 was used to demonstrate guilt and was not simply a magic spell. God will forgive all sins, even adultery, as was shown by Christ's words to the adulterous woman (John 8:2-11). But his charge to her, "Go and sin no more," emphasizes that forgiveness carries with it a responsibility to live by God's standards. God's priorities for his people have always emphasized pure relationships, especially in marriage.

setting themselves apart to the LORD in a special way, [3] they must give up wine and other alcoholic drinks. They must not use vinegar made from wine or from other alcoholic drinks, they must not drink fresh grape juice, and they must not eat grapes or raisins. [4] As long as they are bound by their Nazirite vow, they are not allowed to eat or drink anything that comes from a grapevine—not even the grape seeds or skins.

[5] "They must never cut their hair throughout the time of their vow, for they are holy and set apart to the LORD. Until the time of their vow has been fulfilled, they must let their hair grow long. [6] And they must not go near a dead body during the entire period of their vow to the LORD. [7] Even if the dead person is their own father, mother, brother, or sister, they must not defile themselves, for the hair on their head is the symbol of their separation to God. [8] This requirement applies as long as they are set apart to the LORD.

[9] "If someone falls dead beside them, the hair they have dedicated will be defiled. They must wait for seven days and then shave their heads. Then they will be cleansed from their defilement. [10] On the eighth day they must bring two turtledoves or two young pigeons to the priest at the entrance of the Tabernacle.* [11] The priest will offer one of the birds for a sin offering and the other for a burnt offering. In this way, he will purify them* from the guilt they incurred through contact with the dead body. Then they must reaffirm their commitment and let their hair begin to grow again. [12] The days of their vow that were completed before their defilement no longer count. They must rededicate themselves to the LORD as a Nazirite for the full term of their vow, and each must bring a one-year-old male lamb for a guilt offering.

[13] "This is the ritual law for Nazirites. At the conclusion of their time of separation as Nazirites, they must each go to the entrance of the Tabernacle [14] and offer their sacrifices to the LORD: a one-year-old male lamb without defect for a burnt offering, a one-year-old female lamb without defect for a sin offering, a ram without defect for a peace offering, [15] a basket of bread made without yeast—cakes of choice flour mixed with olive oil and wafers spread with olive oil—along with their prescribed grain offerings and liquid offerings. [16] The priest will present these offerings before the LORD: first the sin offering and the burnt offering; [17] then the ram for a peace offering, along with the basket of bread made without yeast. The priest must also present the prescribed grain offering and liquid offering to the LORD.

[18] "Then the Nazirites will shave their heads at the entrance of the Tabernacle. They will take the hair that had been dedicated and place it on the fire beneath the peace-offering sacrifice. [19] After the Nazirite's head has been shaved, the priest will take for each of them the boiled shoulder of the ram, and he will take from the basket a cake and a wafer made without yeast. He will put them all into the Nazirite's hands. [20] Then the priest will lift them up as a special offering before the LORD. These are holy portions for the priest, along with the breast of the special offering and the thigh of the sacred offering that are lifted up before the LORD. After this ceremony the Nazirites may again drink wine.

[21] "This is the ritual law of the Nazirites, who vow to bring these offerings to the LORD. They may also bring additional offerings if they can afford it. And they must be careful to do whatever they vowed when they set themselves apart as Nazirites."

The Priestly Blessing

[22] Then the LORD said to Moses, [23] "Tell Aaron and his sons to bless the people of Israel with this special blessing:

6:10 Hebrew *the Tent of Meeting;* also in 6:13, 18.   6:11 Or *make atonement for them.*

6:3-4 The name *Nazirite* comes from a Hebrew word meaning "to separate." One aspect of this vow was separation from various activities and attitudes, symbolizing a person's willingness to set personal standards for himself during the time of the vow. This principle of personal accountability is always necessary for anyone who seeks to live a life pleasing to God. Self-discipline and self-examination both play key roles in our relationship with God as we continue the process of recovery.
6:5-8 An important aspect of the Nazirite vow was the separation *unto* God, dedicating one's life for his use. Romans 12:1 commands us to present our body as a living sacrifice to God. The Nazirite vow provided opportunities to do this on special occasions, but we are to give ourself to God regularly. Even in the most hopeless human situations, God gives hope. But that hope cannot come without our committing ourself to God through Jesus Christ.

24 'May the LORD bless you
and protect you.
25 May the LORD smile on you
and be gracious to you.
26 May the LORD show you his
favor
and give you his peace.'

27 Whenever Aaron and his sons bless the people of Israel in my name, I myself will bless them."

CHAPTER 7
Offerings of Dedication
On the day Moses set up the Tabernacle, he anointed it and set it apart as holy. He also anointed and set apart all its furnishings and the altar with its utensils. ²Then the leaders of Israel—the tribal leaders who had registered the troops—came and brought their offerings. ³Together they brought six large wagons and twelve oxen. There was a wagon for every two leaders and an ox for each leader. They presented these to the LORD in front of the Tabernacle.

⁴Then the LORD said to Moses, ⁵"Receive their gifts, and use these oxen and wagons for transporting the Tabernacle.* Distribute them among the Levites according to the work they have to do." ⁶So Moses took the wagons and oxen and presented them to the Levites. ⁷He gave two wagons and four oxen to the Gershonite division for their work, ⁸and he gave four wagons and eight oxen to the Merarite division for their work. All their work was done under the leadership of Ithamar son of Aaron the priest. ⁹But he gave none of the wagons or oxen to the Kohathite division, since they were required to carry the sacred objects of the Tabernacle on their shoulders.

¹⁰The leaders also presented dedication gifts for the altar at the time it was anointed. They each placed their gifts before the altar. ¹¹The LORD said to Moses, "Let one leader bring his gift each day for the dedication of the altar."

¹²On the first day Nahshon son of Amminadab, leader of the tribe of Judah, presented his offering.
¹³His offering consisted of a silver platter weighing 3¼ pounds and a silver basin weighing 1¾ pounds* (as measured by the weight of the sanctuary shekel). These were both filled with grain offerings of choice flour moistened with olive oil. ¹⁴He also brought a gold container weighing four ounces,* which was filled with incense. ¹⁵He brought a young bull, a ram, and a one-year-old male lamb for a burnt offering, ¹⁶and a male goat for a sin offering. ¹⁷For a peace offering he brought two bulls, five rams, five male goats, and five one-year-old male lambs. This was the offering brought by Nahshon son of Amminadab.

¹⁸On the second day Nethanel son of Zuar, leader of the tribe of Issachar, presented his offering.
¹⁹His offering consisted of a silver platter weighing 3¼ pounds and a silver basin weighing 1¾ pounds (as measured by the weight of the sanctuary shekel). These were both filled with grain offerings of choice flour moistened with olive oil. ²⁰He also brought a gold container weighing four ounces, which was filled with incense. ²¹He brought a young bull, a ram, and a one-year-old male lamb for a burnt

7:5 Hebrew *the Tent of Meeting;* also in 7:89. 7:13 Hebrew *silver platter weighing 130 [shekels]* [1.5 kilograms] *and a silver basin weighing 70 shekels* [800 grams]; also in 7:19, 25, 31, 37, 43, 49, 55, 61, 67, 73, 79, 85. 7:14 Hebrew *10 [shekels]* [114 grams]; also in 7:20, 26, 32, 38, 44, 50, 56, 62, 68, 74, 80, 86.

6:24-26 The simple words of this blessing reflect God's desire for all his people. He is the source of all blessings, grace, and peace in life; only through a relationship with God can we hope to experience the fullness of life described here. The blessing seems to build to its final word—*peace (shalom).* The Hebrew word for peace means much more than an absence of conflict. It implies a complete sense of well-being, health, and contentment. God offers this to anyone who is willing to follow him and especially to those whose lives have been bruised and broken.
7:1-88 The way we use our possessions is an important part of our accountability to God. This passage shows how God's ministry among his people often depends upon the personal gifts of individuals and families. An attitude of sacrifice and generosity is needed among us if we hope to meet the needs of others. Sometimes this sacrifice may involve giving physical gifts, as did each of the tribal leaders in this case. Sometimes it may involve giving of our time, as did the Levites. God asks that we bring a gift to him (7:11); the nature and amount of the gift are to be voluntary and from the heart.

offering, ²²and a male goat for a sin offering. ²³For a peace offering he brought two bulls, five rams, five male goats, and five one-year-old male lambs. This was the offering brought by Nethanel son of Zuar.

²⁴On the third day Eliab son of Helon, leader of the tribe of Zebulun, presented his offering.

²⁵His offering consisted of a silver platter weighing 3¼ pounds and a silver basin weighing 1¾ pounds (as measured by the weight of the sanctuary shekel). These were both filled with grain offerings of choice flour moistened with olive oil. ²⁶He also brought a gold container weighing four ounces, which was filled with incense. ²⁷He brought a young bull, a ram, and a one-year-old male lamb for a burnt offering, ²⁸and a male goat for a sin offering. ²⁹For a peace offering he brought two bulls, five rams, five male goats, and five one-year-old male lambs. This was the offering brought by Eliab son of Helon.

³⁰On the fourth day Elizur son of Shedeur, leader of the tribe of Reuben, presented his offering.

³¹His offering consisted of a silver platter weighing 3¼ pounds and a silver basin weighing 1¾ pounds (as measured by the weight of the sanctuary shekel). These were both filled with grain offerings of choice flour moistened with olive oil. ³²He also brought a gold container weighing four ounces, which was filled with incense. ³³He brought a young bull, a ram, and a one-year-old male lamb for a burnt offering, ³⁴and a male goat for a sin offering. ³⁵For a peace offering he brought two bulls, five rams, five male goats, and five one-year-old male lambs. This was the offering brought by Elizur son of Shedeur.

³⁶On the fifth day Shelumiel son of Zurishaddai, leader of the tribe of Simeon, presented his offering.

³⁷His offering consisted of a silver platter weighing 3¼ pounds and a silver basin weighing 1¾ pounds (as measured by the weight of the sanctuary shekel). These were both filled with grain offerings of choice flour moistened with olive oil. ³⁸He also brought a gold container weighing four ounces, which was filled

with incense. ³⁹He brought a young bull, a ram, and a one-year-old male lamb for a burnt offering, ⁴⁰and a male goat for a sin offering. ⁴¹For a peace offering he brought two bulls, five rams, five male goats, and five one-year-old male lambs. This was the offering brought by Shelumiel son of Zurishaddai.

⁴²On the sixth day Eliasaph son of Deuel, leader of the tribe of Gad, presented his offering.

⁴³His offering consisted of a silver platter weighing 3¼ pounds and a silver basin weighing 1¾ pounds (as measured by the weight of the sanctuary shekel). These were both filled with grain offerings of choice flour moistened with olive oil. ⁴⁴He also brought a gold container weighing four ounces, which was filled with incense. ⁴⁵He brought a young bull, a ram, and a one-year-old male lamb for a burnt offering, ⁴⁶and a male goat for a sin offering. ⁴⁷For a peace offering he brought two bulls, five rams, five male goats, and five one-year-old male lambs. This was the offering brought by Eliasaph son of Deuel.

⁴⁸On the seventh day Elishama son of Ammihud, leader of the tribe of Ephraim, presented his offering.

⁴⁹His offering consisted of a silver platter weighing 3¼ pounds and a silver basin weighing 1¾ pounds (as measured by the weight of the sanctuary shekel). These were both filled with grain offerings of choice flour moistened with olive oil. ⁵⁰He also brought a gold container weighing four ounces, which was filled with incense. ⁵¹He brought a young bull, a ram, and a one-year-old male lamb for a burnt offering, ⁵²and a male goat for a sin offering. ⁵³For a peace offering he brought two bulls, five rams, five male goats, and five one-year-old male lambs. This was the offering brought by Elishama son of Ammihud.

⁵⁴On the eighth day Gamaliel son of Pedahzur, leader of the tribe of Manasseh, presented his offering.

⁵⁵His offering consisted of a silver platter weighing 3¼ pounds and a silver basin weighing 1¾ pounds (as measured by the weight of the sanctuary shekel). These were both filled with grain offerings of choice flour moistened with olive oil. ⁵⁶He also brought a gold container

weighing four ounces, which was filled with incense. [57]He brought a young bull, a ram, and a one-year-old male lamb for a burnt offering, [58]and a male goat for a sin offering. [59]For a peace offering he brought two bulls, five rams, five male goats, and five one-year-old male lambs. This was the offering brought by Gamaliel son of Pedahzur.

[60]On the ninth day Abidan son of Gideoni, leader of the tribe of Benjamin, presented his offering.

[61]His offering consisted of a silver platter weighing 3¼ pounds and a silver basin weighing 1¾ pounds (as measured by the weight of the sanctuary shekel). These were both filled with grain offerings of choice flour moistened with olive oil. [62]He also brought a gold container weighing four ounces, which was filled with incense. [63]He brought a young bull, a ram, and a one-year-old male lamb for a burnt offering, [64]and a male goat for a sin offering. [65]For a peace offering he brought two bulls, five rams, five male goats, and five one-year-old male lambs. This was the offering brought by Abidan son of Gideoni.

[66]On the tenth day Ahiezer son of Ammishaddai, leader of the tribe of Dan, presented his offering.

[67]His offering consisted of a silver platter weighing 3¼ pounds and a silver basin weighing 1¾ pounds (as measured by the weight of the sanctuary shekel). These were both filled with grain offerings of choice flour moistened with olive oil. [68]He also brought a gold container weighing four ounces, which was filled with incense. [69]He brought a young bull, a ram, and a one-year-old male lamb for a burnt offering, [70]and a male goat for a sin offering. [71]For a peace offering he brought two bulls, five rams, five male goats, and five one-year-old male lambs. This was the offering brought by Ahiezer son of Ammishaddai.

[72]On the eleventh day Pagiel son of Ocran, leader of the tribe of Asher, presented his offering.

[73]His offering consisted of a silver platter weighing 3¼ pounds and a silver basin weighing 1¾ pounds (as measured by the weight of the sanctuary shekel). These were both filled with grain offerings of choice flour moistened with olive oil. [74]He also brought a gold container weighing four ounces, which was filled with incense. [75]He brought a young bull, a ram, and a one-year-old male lamb for a burnt offering, [76]and a male goat for a sin offering. [77]For a peace offering he brought two bulls, five rams, five male goats, and five one-year-old male lambs. This was the offering brought by Pagiel son of Ocran.

[78]On the twelfth day Ahira son of Enan, leader of the tribe of Naphtali, presented his offering. [79]His offering consisted of a silver platter weighing 3¼ pounds and a silver basin weighing 1¾ pounds (as measured by the weight of the sanctuary shekel). These were both filled with grain offerings of choice flour moistened with olive oil. [80]He also brought a gold container weighing four ounces, which was filled with incense. [81]He brought a young bull, a ram, and a one-year-old male lamb for a burnt offering, [82]and a male goat for a sin offering. [83]For a peace offering he brought two bulls, five rams, five male goats, and five one-year-old male lambs. This was the offering brought by Ahira son of Enan.

[84]So this was the dedication offering brought by the leaders of Israel at the time the altar was anointed: twelve silver platters, twelve silver basins, and twelve gold incense containers. [85]Each silver platter weighed 3¼ pounds, and each silver basin weighed 1¾ pounds. The total weight of the silver was 60 pounds* (as measured by the weight of the sanctuary shekel). [86]Each of the twelve gold containers that was filled with incense weighed four ounces (as measured by the weight of the sanctuary shekel). The total weight of the gold was three pounds.* [87]Twelve young bulls, twelve rams, and twelve one-year-old male lambs were donated for the burnt offerings, along with their prescribed grain offerings. Twelve male goats were brought for the sin offerings. [88]Twenty-four bulls, sixty rams, sixty male goats, and sixty one-year-old male lambs were donated for the peace offerings. This was the dedication offering for the altar after it was anointed.

[89]Whenever Moses went into the Tabernacle to speak with the LORD, he heard the voice speaking to him from between the

two cherubim above the Ark's cover—the place of atonement—that rests on the Ark of the Covenant.* The LORD spoke to him from there.

CHAPTER 8
Preparing the Lamps
The LORD said to Moses, ²"Give Aaron the following instructions: When you set up the seven lamps in the lampstand, place them so their light shines forward in front of the lampstand." ³So Aaron did this. He set up the seven lamps so they reflected their light forward, just as the LORD had commanded Moses. ⁴The entire lampstand, from its base to its decorative blossoms, was made of beaten gold. It was built according to the exact design the LORD had shown Moses.

The Levites Dedicated
⁵Then the LORD said to Moses, ⁶"Now set the Levites apart from the rest of the people of Israel and make them ceremonially clean. ⁷Do this by sprinkling them with the water of purification, and have them shave their entire body and wash their clothing. Then they will be ceremonially clean. ⁸Have them bring a young bull and a grain offering of choice flour moistened with olive oil, along with a second young bull for a sin offering. ⁹Then assemble the whole community of Israel, and present the Levites at the entrance of the Tabernacle.* ¹⁰When you present the Levites before the LORD, the people of Israel must lay their hands on them. ¹¹Raising his hands, Aaron must then present the Levites to the LORD as a special offering from the people of Israel, thus dedicating them to the LORD's service.
¹²"Next the Levites will lay their hands on the heads of the young bulls. Present one as a sin offering and the other as a burnt offering to the LORD, to purify the Levites and make

them right with the LORD.* ¹³Then have the Levites stand in front of Aaron and his sons, and raise your hands and present them as a special offering to the LORD. ¹⁴In this way, you will set the Levites apart from the rest of the people of Israel, and the Levites will belong to me. ¹⁵After this, they may go into the Tabernacle to do their work, because you have purified them and presented them as a special offering.
¹⁶"Of all the people of Israel, the Levites are reserved for me. I have claimed them for myself in place of all the firstborn sons of the Israelites; I have taken the Levites as their substitutes. ¹⁷For all the firstborn males among the people of Israel are mine, both of people and of animals. I set them apart for myself on the day I struck down all the firstborn sons of the Egyptians. ¹⁸Yes, I have claimed the Levites in place of all the firstborn sons of Israel. ¹⁹And of all the Israelites, I have assigned the Levites to Aaron and his sons. They will serve in the Tabernacle on behalf of the Israelites and make sacrifices to purify* the people so no plague will strike them when they approach the sanctuary."
²⁰So Moses, Aaron, and the whole community of Israel dedicated the Levites, carefully following all the LORD's instructions to Moses. ²¹The Levites purified themselves from sin and washed their clothes, and Aaron lifted them up and presented them to the LORD as a special offering. He then offered a sacrifice to purify them and make them right with the LORD.* ²²After that the Levites went into the Tabernacle to perform their duties, assisting Aaron and his sons. So they carried out all the commands that the LORD gave Moses concerning the Levites.
²³The LORD also instructed Moses, ²⁴"This is the rule the Levites must follow: They must begin serving in the Tabernacle at the

---

7:89 Or *Ark of the Testimony.* 8:9 Hebrew *the Tent of Meeting;* also in 8:15, 19, 22, 24, 26. 8:12 Or *to make atonement for the Levites.* 8:19 Or *make atonement for.* 8:21 Or *then made atonement for them to purify them.*

8:5-8, 12 This section focuses on the Levitical priests, noting several important aspects of their preparation for service. They were to be cleansed prior to service. The sin offering made on their behalf showed that even they, Israel's spiritual leaders, needed to be cleansed of sin. Only our great High Priest, Jesus Christ, serves in the priestly role without sin. Even though he is sinless, he can fully understand our weaknesses, so we need not fear approaching him in any time of need (Hebrews 4:14-16).
8:9-11, 13-16 The Levitical priests not only offered sacrifices and offerings to God, but they were to consider themselves "living sacrifices." Their lives were to be given completely over to God. The New Testament teaches that we are to consider ourselves as holy priests, each giving our life as a "living sacrifice" unto God (Romans 12:1-2; 1 Peter 2:5). A life founded on commitment to God contains the essential ingredients of a life filled with contentment and purpose.

age of twenty-five, [25] and they must retire at the age of fifty. [26] After retirement they may assist their fellow Levites by serving as guards at the Tabernacle, but they may not officiate in the service. This is how you must assign duties to the Levites."

CHAPTER 9
The Second Passover

A year after Israel's departure from Egypt, the LORD spoke to Moses in the wilderness of Sinai. In the first month* of that year he said, [2] "Tell the Israelites to celebrate the Passover at the prescribed time, [3] at twilight on the fourteenth day of the first month.* Be sure to follow all my decrees and regulations concerning this celebration."

[4] So Moses told the people to celebrate the Passover [5] in the wilderness of Sinai as twilight fell on the fourteenth day of the month. And they celebrated the festival there, just as the LORD had commanded Moses. [6] But some of the men had been ceremonially defiled by touching a dead body, so they could not celebrate the Passover that day. They came to Moses and Aaron that day [7] and said, "We have become ceremonially unclean by touching a dead body. But why should we be prevented from presenting the LORD's offering at the proper time with the rest of the Israelites?"

[8] Moses answered, "Wait here until I have received instructions for you from the LORD."

[9] This was the LORD's reply to Moses. [10] "Give the following instructions to the people of Israel: If any of the people now or in future generations are ceremonially unclean at Passover time because of touching a dead body, or if they are on a journey and cannot be present at the ceremony, they may still celebrate the LORD's Passover. [11] They must offer the Passover sacrifice one month later, at twilight on the fourteenth day of the second month.* They must eat the Passover lamb at that time with bitter salad greens and bread made without yeast. [12] They must not leave any of the lamb until the next morning, and they must not break any of its bones. They must follow all the normal regulations concerning the Passover.

[13] "But those who neglect to celebrate the Passover at the regular time, even though they are ceremonially clean and not away on a trip, will be cut off from the community of Israel. If they fail to present the LORD's offering at the proper time, they will suffer the consequences of their guilt. [14] And if foreigners living among you want to celebrate the Passover to the LORD, they must follow these same decrees and regulations. The same laws apply both to native-born Israelites and to the foreigners living among you."

The Fiery Cloud

[15] On the day the Tabernacle was set up, the cloud covered it.* But from evening until morning the cloud over the Tabernacle looked like a pillar of fire. [16] This was the regular pattern—at night the cloud that covered the Tabernacle had the appearance of fire. [17] Whenever the cloud lifted from over the sacred tent, the people of Israel would break camp and follow it. And wherever the cloud settled, the people of Israel would set up camp. [18] In this way, they traveled and camped at the LORD's command wherever he told them to go. Then they remained in their camp as long as the cloud stayed over the Tab-

9:1 The first month of the ancient Hebrew lunar calendar usually occurs within the months of March and April. 9:3 This day in the ancient Hebrew lunar calendar occurred in late March, April, or early May. 9:11 This day in the ancient Hebrew lunar calendar occurred in late April, May, or early June. 9:15 Hebrew *covered the Tabernacle, the Tent of the Testimony.*

9:1-14 The Passover was to be an annual feast for all the Israelites, a celebration of their deliverance from bondage in Egypt (Exodus 12:1-51). A problem arose, however, for those who were ceremonially unclean at the time of Passover. According to the strict standards of the law, they were not allowed to join in the celebration even though it was required of them. Moses brought this problem to God, who graciously instituted a second date of celebration for those who couldn't participate at the regular time. God wants each of us to participate in a relationship with him. We should not allow our failures and sins to keep us from coming to God. He has provided a means for us to come, no matter how "unclean" we may be. Our Passover lamb, Jesus Christ, was sacrificed on our behalf so we might enjoy an eternal relationship with God (1 Corinthians 5:7). Christ, through his death and resurrection, has taken away our sins (John 1:29), and it is through Christ that we bring glory to God by presenting our life to him (Romans 12:1).
9:15-23 As the cloud moved, so did the Israelites. They had to stay alert, watching each day for God's guidance. It was essential that the people trust God rather than make their own plans. This object lesson in obedience should be the description of our day-by-day walk with God—to trust in him completely and not in ourself (Proverbs 3:5-6).

ernacle. [19]If the cloud remained over the Tabernacle for a long time, the Israelites stayed and performed their duty to the LORD. [20]Sometimes the cloud would stay over the Tabernacle for only a few days, so the people would stay for only a few days, as the LORD commanded. Then at the LORD's command they would break camp and move on. [21]Sometimes the cloud stayed only overnight and lifted the next morning. But day or night, when the cloud lifted, the people broke camp and moved on. [22]Whether the cloud stayed above the Tabernacle for two days, a month, or a year, the people of Israel stayed in camp and did not move on. But as soon as it lifted, they broke camp and moved on. [23]So they camped or traveled at the LORD's command, and they did whatever the LORD told them through Moses.

CHAPTER 10
The Silver Trumpets

Now the LORD said to Moses, [2]"Make two trumpets of hammered silver for calling the community to assemble and for signaling the breaking of camp. [3]When both trumpets are blown, everyone must gather before you at the entrance of the Tabernacle.* [4]But if only one trumpet is blown, then only the leaders—the heads of the clans of Israel—must present themselves to you.

[5]"When you sound the signal to move on, the tribes camped on the east side of the Tabernacle must break camp and move forward. [6]When you sound the signal a second time, the tribes camped on the south will follow. You must sound short blasts as the signal for moving on. [7]But when you call the people to an assembly, blow the trumpets with a different signal. [8]Only the priests, Aaron's descendants, are allowed to blow the trumpets. This is a permanent law for you, to be observed from generation to generation.

[9]"When you arrive in your own land and go to war against your enemies who attack you, sound the alarm with the trumpets. Then the LORD your God will remember you and rescue you from your enemies. [10]Blow the trumpets in times of gladness, too, sounding them at your annual festivals and at the beginning of each month. And blow the trumpets over your burnt offerings and peace offerings. The trumpets will remind your God of his covenant with you. I am the LORD your God."

The Israelites Leave Sinai

[11]In the second year after Israel's departure from Egypt—on the twentieth day of the second month*—the cloud lifted from the Tabernacle of the Covenant.* [12]So the Israelites set out from the wilderness of Sinai and traveled on from place to place until the cloud stopped in the wilderness of Paran.

[13]When the people set out for the first time, following the instructions the LORD had given through Moses, [14]Judah's troops led the way. They marched behind their banner, and their leader was Nahshon son of Amminadab. [15]They were joined by the troops of the tribe of Issachar, led by Nethanel son of Zuar, [16]and the troops of the tribe of Zebulun, led by Eliab son of Helon.

[17]Then the Tabernacle was taken down, and the Gershonite and Merarite divisions of the Levites were next in the line of march, carrying the Tabernacle with them. [18]Reuben's troops went next, marching behind their banner. Their leader was Elizur son of Shedeur. [19]They were joined by the troops of the tribe of Simeon, led by Shelumiel son of Zurishaddai, [20]and the troops of the tribe of Gad, led by Eliasaph son of Deuel.

[21]Next came the Kohathite division of the Levites, carrying the sacred objects from the Tabernacle. Before they arrived at the next camp, the Tabernacle would already be set up at its new location. [22]Ephraim's troops went next, marching behind their banner. Their leader was Elishama son of Ammihud. [23]They were joined by the troops of the tribe of Manasseh, led by Gamaliel son of Pedahzur, [24]and the troops of the tribe of Benjamin, led by Abidan son of Gideoni.

10:3 Hebrew *Tent of Meeting.* 10:11a This day in the ancient Hebrew lunar calendar occurred in late April, May, or early June. 10:11b Or *Tabernacle of the Testimony.*

10:11-36 This section begins the account of the Israelites' journey through the wilderness on the way to the Promised Land. They were entering new territory on their way to building new lives, but the immediate results were not encouraging. As they set out for the Promised Land, they were not willing to trust God to lead and protect them. Their weak faith showed up in their impatience with God, which resulted in 38 years of wilderness wandering. Often, building a new life involves entering uncharted territory. It takes great patience to let God guide us each step of the way. Let us learn from the mistakes of the Israelites (1 Corinthians 10; Hebrews 3–4).

²⁵Dan's troops went last, marching behind their banner and serving as the rear guard for all the tribal camps. Their leader was Ahiezer son of Ammishaddai. ²⁶They were joined by the troops of the tribe of Asher, led by Pagiel son of Ocran, ²⁷and the troops of the tribe of Naphtali, led by Ahira son of Enan.

²⁸This was the order in which the Israelites marched, division by division.

²⁹One day Moses said to his brother-in-law, Hobab son of Reuel the Midianite, "We are on our way to the place the LORD promised us, for he said, 'I will give it to you.' Come with us and we will treat you well, for the LORD has promised wonderful blessings for Israel!"

³⁰But Hobab replied, "No, I will not go. I must return to my own land and family."

³¹"Please don't leave us," Moses pleaded. "You know the places in the wilderness where we should camp. Come, be our guide. ³²If you do, we'll share with you all the blessings the LORD gives us."

³³They marched for three days after leaving the mountain of the LORD, with the Ark of the LORD's Covenant moving ahead of them to show them where to stop and rest. ³⁴As they moved on each day, the cloud of the LORD hovered over them. ³⁵And whenever the Ark set out, Moses would shout, "Arise, O LORD, and let your enemies be scattered! Let them flee before you!" ³⁶And when the Ark was set down, he would say, "Return, O LORD, to the countless thousands of Israel!"

CHAPTER 11
The People Complain to Moses

Soon the people began to complain about their hardship, and the LORD heard everything they said. Then the LORD's anger blazed against them, and he sent a fire to rage among them, and he destroyed some of the people in the outskirts of the camp. ²Then the people screamed to Moses for help, and when he prayed to the LORD, the fire stopped. ³After that, the area was known as Taberah (which means "the place of burning"), because fire from the LORD had burned among them there.

⁴Then the foreign rabble who were traveling with the Israelites began to crave the good things of Egypt. And the people of Israel also began to complain. "Oh, for some meat!" they exclaimed. ⁵"We remember the fish we used to eat for free in Egypt. And we had all the cucumbers, melons, leeks, onions, and garlic we wanted. ⁶But now our appetites are gone. All we ever see is this manna!"

⁷The manna looked like small coriander seeds, and it was pale yellow like gum resin. ⁸The people would go out and gather it from the ground. They made flour by grinding it with hand mills or pounding it in mortars. Then they boiled it in a pot and made it into flat cakes. These cakes tasted like pastries baked with olive oil. ⁹The manna came down on the camp with the dew during the night.

¹⁰Moses heard all the families standing in the doorways of their tents whining, and the LORD became extremely angry. Moses was

10:35-36 Even though God's presence was with Israel, evidenced by the cloud and the Ark of the Covenant (10:33-34), Moses continually prayed for the well-being of his people. He was their intercessor and knew the importance of the ministry of prayer. Praying for others, especially for those who are in the process of recovery, is a resource often overlooked. But it may be our most effective means of laying hold of the awesome power of God.

11:1-3 Instead of trusting God to take care of them, the people started to complain. This first complaint against God is just one of many during their wilderness travels. God reacted quickly and harshly to their murmuring because it was seriously undermining the program of recovery God had given to them. Their complaining indicated their ingratitude, impatience, and lack of faith. The difficult process of going from Egyptian bondage to God's promised home in Canaan could only be accomplished if the people patiently trusted God to get them through. The same is true for us as we continue in the recovery process.

11:4-5 We are told here that a group of foreigners traveling with Israel began to complain. Notice that the complaints were then spread by the Israelites. This illustrates the importance of supportive company in the recovery process. One of Satan's strategies to undermine our faith may be the negative attitudes and comments of those around us. We need to avoid spending time with those who drag us down and seek out people who build us up and strengthen us.

11:10-15 When Moses complained angrily to God about his unpleasant circumstances, God didn't rebuke him; he evidently sympathized with his problem. God's response to Moses stands in stark contrast to the severe judgment he brought upon the Israelites for their complaints. God evidently saw that Moses' motives were pure and his faith, genuine; thus, he responded to Moses' honest cry for help. God is never afraid of the anger we may feel about situations we face. He expects honesty in our prayers.

AARON & MIRIAM

The pecking order in most families is established by order of birth—oldest to youngest. The family of Aaron, Miriam, and Moses started out this way, too. But with time it became clear that God had special plans for Moses. When Moses was born, his sister, Miriam, was given a special part in saving him from Pharaoh's decree demanding that all Hebrew baby boys die. Miriam continued to watch Moses from a distance as he grew up in Pharaoh's palace as the adopted son of Pharaoh's daughter. Still later, Miriam watched God raise up Moses to lead the Israelites out of their slavery in Egypt. Brother Aaron was also called to play a special role in the life of Moses. At one point Aaron was assigned to be his brother's spokesman. Later God called Aaron to be Israel's high priest.

Moses' older siblings became disturbed that God had chosen Moses and raised him to a level above themselves. At various times during Moses' life they criticized him openly. This displeased God greatly, for it undermined the leadership of the man he had chosen to lead his people. Aaron and Miriam had both been given important roles in the nation of Israel. Their jealousy toward Moses made them blind to the importance of their own gifts. God judged Miriam's criticism of Moses suddenly and harshly—with leprosy. People with this disease were doomed not only to a long and painful death but to banishment from society. It was only because of the intercessory prayer of brother Moses that Miriam was later healed by God (Numbers 12).

We must be careful not to confuse constructive criticism with sibling jealousy. Sibling jealousy left unaddressed can lead to the destruction of family and, in some cases, a much larger community. But when these problems are brought before God, he can restore even these relationships, just as he did for Aaron, Miriam, and Moses.

STRENGTHS AND ACCOMPLISHMENTS:
• Both were gifted to help the Israelites.
• Aaron was called by God to be Israel's first high priest.
• Miriam was an able leader and prophetess.

WEAKNESSES AND MISTAKES:
• Both were jealous of Moses' authority.
• Miriam openly criticized Moses' leadership.
• Both complained about Moses' marriage.
• Aaron allowed himself to be manipulated by the people.

LESSONS FROM THEIR LIVES:
• Order of birth doesn't necessarily define a person's responsibilities or level of success.
• God chooses his leaders according to his own criteria, not ours.
• The motives behind the criticism, not just the criticism itself, need to be dealt with.
• God gives us all special gifts, and he uses them to fulfill his plans.
• Jealousy of others can easily blind us to our own special gifts.

KEY VERSES:
"While they were at Hazeroth, Miriam and Aaron criticized Moses because he had married a Cushite woman. They said, 'Has the LORD spoken only through Moses? Hasn't he spoken through us, too?' But the LORD heard them" (Numbers 12:1-2).

The story of Aaron and Miriam is told throughout the book of Exodus. Aaron is also referred to in Leviticus, Numbers, Deuteronomy, and Hebrews 7:11. Miriam is mentioned in Numbers 12; 20; and Deuteronomy 24:9. Both are mentioned in 1 Chronicles 6:3 and Micah 6:4.

---

also very aggravated. [11]And Moses said to the LORD, "Why are you treating me, your servant, so harshly? Have mercy on me! What did I do to deserve the burden of all these people? [12]Did I give birth to them? Did I bring them into the world? Why did you tell me to carry them in my arms like a mother carries a nursing baby? How can I carry them to the land you swore to give their ancestors? [13]Where am I supposed to get meat for all these people? They keep whining to me, saying, 'Give us meat to eat!' [14]I can't carry all these people by myself! The load is far too heavy! [15]If this is how you intend to treat me, just go ahead and kill me. Do me a favor and spare me this misery!"

Moses Chooses Seventy Leaders
[16]Then the LORD said to Moses, "Gather before me seventy men who are recognized as elders and leaders of Israel. Bring them to the Tabernacle* to stand there with you. [17]I will come down and talk to you there. I will take some of the Spirit that is upon you,

11:16 Hebrew *the Tent of Meeting.*

and I will put the Spirit upon them also. They will bear the burden of the people along with you, so you will not have to carry it alone.

¹⁸"And say to the people, 'Purify yourselves, for tomorrow you will have meat to eat. You were whining, and the LORD heard you when you cried, "Oh, for some meat! We were better off in Egypt!" Now the LORD will give you meat, and you will have to eat it. ¹⁹And it won't be for just a day or two, or for five or ten or even twenty. ²⁰You will eat it for a whole month until you gag and are sick of it. For you have rejected the LORD, who is here among you, and you have whined to him, saying, "Why did we ever leave Egypt?"'"

²¹But Moses responded to the LORD, "There are 600,000 foot soldiers here with me, and yet you say, 'I will give them meat for a whole month!' ²²Even if we butchered all our flocks and herds, would that satisfy them? Even if we caught all the fish in the sea, would that be enough?"

²³Then the LORD said to Moses, "Has my arm lost its power? Now you will see whether or not my word comes true!"

²⁴So Moses went out and reported the LORD's words to the people. He gathered the seventy elders and stationed them around the Tabernacle.* ²⁵And the LORD came down in the cloud and spoke to Moses. Then he gave the seventy elders the same Spirit that was upon Moses. And when the Spirit rested upon them, they prophesied. But this never happened again.

²⁶Two men, Eldad and Medad, had stayed behind in the camp. They were listed among the elders, but they had not gone out to the Tabernacle. Yet the Spirit rested upon them as well, so they prophesied there in the camp. ²⁷A young man ran and reported to Moses, "Eldad and Medad are prophesying in the camp!"

²⁸Joshua son of Nun, who had been Moses' assistant since his youth, protested, "Moses, my master, make them stop!"

²⁹But Moses replied, "Are you jealous for my sake? I wish that all the LORD's people were prophets and that the LORD would put his Spirit upon them all!" ³⁰Then Moses returned to the camp with the elders of Israel.

The LORD Sends Quail

³¹Now the LORD sent a wind that brought quail from the sea and let them fall all around the camp. For miles in every direction there were quail flying about three feet above the ground.* ³²So the people went out and caught quail all that day and throughout the night and all the next day, too. No one gathered less than fifty bushels*! They spread the quail all around the camp to dry. ³³But while they were gorging themselves on the meat—while it was still in their mouths—the anger of the LORD blazed against the people, and he struck them with a severe plague. ³⁴So that place was called Kibroth-hattaavah (which means "graves of gluttony") because there they buried the people who had craved meat from Egypt. ³⁵From Kibroth-hattaavah the Israelites traveled to Hazeroth, where they stayed for some time.

CHAPTER 12
The Complaints of Miriam and Aaron

While they were at Hazeroth, Miriam and Aaron criticized Moses because he had married a Cushite woman. ²They said, "Has the LORD spoken only through Moses? Hasn't he spoken through us, too?" But the LORD heard them. ³(Now Moses was very humble—more humble than any other person on earth.)

⁴So immediately the LORD called to Moses, Aaron, and Miriam and said, "Go out to the Tabernacle,* all three of you!" So the three of them went to the Tabernacle. ⁵Then the LORD descended in the pillar of cloud and stood at the entrance of the Tabernacle.* "Aaron and Miriam!" he called, and they stepped forward. ⁶And the LORD said to them, "Now listen to what I say:

"If there were prophets among you,
 I, the LORD, would reveal myself in
 visions.

11:24 Hebrew *the tent;* also in 11:26. 11:31 Or *there were quail 3 feet* [2 cubits or 92 centimeters] *deep on the ground.* 11:32 Hebrew *10 homers* [2.2 kiloliters]. 12:4 Hebrew *the Tent of Meeting.* 12:5 Hebrew *the tent;* also in 12:10.

12:3-4 This parenthetical statement about Moses' humility is one of the most revealing evaluations of his character found in Scripture. He is described as being more humble than any other person on earth. This is essentially the same quality mentioned in the first beatitude: "God blesses those who . . . realize their need for him" (Matthew 5:3). Moses realized his need for God and knew he couldn't go it alone. His humility, evidenced in his great patience and perseverance, was a significant aspect of his leadership as he guided the Israelites through the wilderness. Our own humility is extremely important as we put our life into God's hands for recovery.

CALEB

Many of us seek the acceptance of others when we make decisions. We try not to admit it, but a careful examination of past decisions will probably show that we, like so many others, often side with the majority viewpoint. Unfortunately, in our world system, the majority viewpoint seldom gives God and his Word any consideration.

Caleb was an individual who saw things from God's perspective and stood against the majority opinion. Ten of the twelve scouts who had entered Canaan, a clear majority, believed that the Promised Land couldn't be conquered. They reported that the cities and towns were fortified and defended by terrible giants. They told the people that the task was hopeless, letting their fears and the majority opinion decide the course of action. But Caleb, along with Joshua, differed with the majority, embracing a godly, minority opinion. Caleb agreed that Canaan was well fortified and the task formidable. But he also believed that even the greatest enemies were no match for the mighty God of Israel. Caleb spoke out, calling the people to believe in God's promises. Caleb knew that with God's help, they could conquer all the obstacles and difficulties that the majority had reported.

Sadly, the people of Israel didn't listen to Caleb and Joshua and began to talk about stoning them. They followed the majority opinion and refused to take the land God had promised them. As a direct result, the entire nation of Israel was left to wander in the wilderness for nearly 40 years. Of all the adult Israelites who left Egypt, only Caleb and Joshua would enter the Promised Land.

It is so easy for us to focus on the obstacles in our own life—all those things that make change seem impossible. We can learn from Caleb, who believed God's word despite the obstacles before him. When the situation appeared hopeless, he knew that victory could come by turning his life and will over to the God who had promised him and his people victory. Caleb knew that self-worth could be found not in the approval of other people but only in the loving eyes of God. He had learned to live for God's approval, not the approval of others.

STRENGTHS AND ACCOMPLISHMENTS:
- He was one of the 12 hand-picked men sent into Canaan.
- He was able to express his faith in God even in the face of opposition.
- Despite overwhelming opposition he remained faithful to God and his promises.
- He remained faithful to Joshua and Moses throughout the wilderness wanderings.
- He based his self-worth on God's opinion, not on the opinions of others.

LESSONS FROM HIS LIFE:
- Right and wrong can never be based solely on the majority opinion.
- Boldness is appropriate in a God-centered life.
- An effective faith should be confirmed by both words and actions.
- Self-worth should not be based upon acceptance by the majority.

KEY VERSE:
"But my servant Caleb has a different attitude than the others have. He has remained loyal to me, so I will bring him into the land he explored. His descendants will possess their full share of that land" (Numbers 14:24).

Caleb's story is told in Numbers 13–14 and Joshua 14–15. He is also mentioned in Judges 1 and 1 Chronicles 4:15.

I would speak to them in dreams.
⁷But not with my servant Moses.
 Of all my house, he is the one
  I trust.
⁸I speak to him face to face,
 clearly, and not in riddles!
 He sees the LORD as he is.

So why were you not afraid
  to criticize my servant Moses?"

⁹The LORD was very angry with them, and he departed. ¹⁰As the cloud moved from above the Tabernacle, there stood Miriam, her skin as white as snow from leprosy.* When Aaron saw what had happened to

12:10 Or *with a skin disease.* The Hebrew word used here can describe various skin diseases.

her, [11]he cried out to Moses, "Oh, my master! Please don't punish us for this sin we have so foolishly committed. [12]Don't let her be like a stillborn baby, already decayed at birth."

[13]So Moses cried out to the LORD, "O God, I beg you, please heal her!"

[14]But the LORD said to Moses, "If her father had done nothing more than spit in her face, wouldn't she be defiled for seven days? So keep her outside the camp for seven days, and after that she may be accepted back."

[15]So Miriam was kept outside the camp for seven days, and the people waited until she was brought back before they traveled again. [16]Then they left Hazeroth and camped in the wilderness of Paran.

CHAPTER 13
Twelve Scouts Explore Canaan

The LORD now said to Moses, [2]"Send out men to explore the land of Canaan, the land I am giving to the Israelites. Send one leader from each of the twelve ancestral tribes." [3]So Moses did as the LORD commanded him. He sent out twelve men, all tribal leaders of Israel, from their camp in the wilderness of Paran. [4]These were the tribes and the names of their leaders:

Tribe	Leader
Reuben	Shammua son of Zaccur
[5] Simeon	Shaphat son of Hori
[6] Judah	Caleb son of Jephunneh
[7] Issachar	Igal son of Joseph
[8] Ephraim	Hoshea son of Nun
[9] Benjamin	Palti son of Raphu
[10] Zebulun	Gaddiel son of Sodi
[11] Manasseh son of Joseph	Gaddi son of Susi
[12] Dan	Ammiel son of Gemalli
[13] Asher	Sethur son of Michael
[14] Naphtali	Nahbi son of Vophsi
[15] Gad	Geuel son of Maki

[16]These are the names of the men Moses sent out to explore the land. (Moses called Hoshea son of Nun by the name Joshua.)

[17]Moses gave the men these instructions as he sent them out to explore the land: "Go north through the Negev into the hill country. [18]See what the land is like, and find out whether the people living there are strong or weak, few or many. [19]See what kind of land they live in. Is it good or bad? Do their towns have walls, or are they unprotected like open camps? [20]Is the soil fertile or poor? Are there many trees? Do your best to bring back samples of the crops you see." (It happened to be the season for harvesting the first ripe grapes.)

[21]So they went up and explored the land from the wilderness of Zin as far as Rehob, near Lebo-hamath. [22]Going north, they passed through the Negev and arrived at Hebron, where Ahiman, Sheshai, and Talmai—all descendants of Anak—lived. (The ancient town of Hebron was founded seven years before the Egyptian city of Zoan.) [23]When they came to the valley of Eshcol, they cut down a branch with a single cluster of grapes so large that it took two of them to carry it on a pole between them! They also brought back samples of the pomegranates and figs. [24]That place was called the valley of Eshcol (which means "cluster"), because of the cluster of grapes the Israelite men cut there.

The Scouting Report

[25]After exploring the land for forty days, the men returned [26]to Moses, Aaron, and the whole community of Israel at Kadesh in the wilderness of Paran. They reported to the whole community what they had seen and showed them the fruit they had taken from the land. [27]This was their report to Moses: "We entered the land you sent us to explore, and it is indeed a bountiful country—a land flowing with milk and honey. Here is the kind of fruit it produces. [28]But the people living there are powerful, and their towns are large and fortified. We even saw giants there, the descendants of Anak! [29]The Amalekites live in the Negev, and the Hittites, Jebusites, and Amorites live in the hill country. The Canaanites live along the coast of the Mediterranean Sea* and along the Jordan Valley."

[30]But Caleb tried to quiet the people as they stood before Moses. "Let's go at once to take the land," he said. "We can certainly conquer it!"

[31]But the other men who had explored the

13:29 Hebrew *the sea.*

13:30 The minority report of Caleb, and later that of Joshua (14:6-9), emphasized God's power to overcome even the greatest problems. Their faith enabled them to see problems not as obstacles but as opportunities for God to demonstrate his power. The basis for their faith was God's promise to rescue his people from their enemies (10:9). When we have an active faith in God, our view of life and its challenges will emphasize the positive rather than the negative.

land with him disagreed. "We can't go up against them! They are stronger than we are!" ³²So they spread this bad report about the land among the Israelites: "The land we traveled through and explored will devour anyone who goes to live there. All the people we saw were huge. ³³We even saw giants* there, the descendants of Anak. Next to them we felt like grasshoppers, and that's what they thought, too!"

CHAPTER 14
The People Rebel

Then the whole community began weeping aloud, and they cried all night. ²Their voices rose in a great chorus of protest against Moses and Aaron. "If only we had died in Egypt, or even here in the wilderness!" they complained. ³"Why is the LORD taking us to this country only to have us die in battle? Our wives and our little ones will be carried off as plunder! Wouldn't it be better for us to return to Egypt?" ⁴Then they plotted among themselves, "Let's choose a new leader and go back to Egypt!"

⁵Then Moses and Aaron fell face down on the ground before the whole community of Israel. ⁶Two of the men who had explored the land, Joshua son of Nun and Caleb son of Jephunneh, tore their clothing. ⁷They said to all the people of Israel, "The land we traveled through and explored is a wonderful land! ⁸And if the LORD is pleased with us, he will bring us safely into that land and give it to us. It is a rich land flowing with milk and honey. ⁹Do not rebel against the LORD, and don't be afraid of the people of the land. They are only helpless prey to us! They have no protection, but the LORD is with us! Don't be afraid of them!"

¹⁰But the whole community began to talk about stoning Joshua and Caleb. Then the glorious presence of the LORD appeared to all the Israelites at the Tabernacle.* ¹¹And the LORD said to Moses, "How long will these people treat me with contempt? Will they never believe me, even after all the miraculous signs I have done among them? ¹²I will

disown them and destroy them with a plague. Then I will make you into a nation greater and mightier than they are!"

Moses Intercedes for the People

¹³But Moses objected. "What will the Egyptians think when they hear about it?" he asked the LORD. "They know full well the power you displayed in rescuing your people from Egypt. ¹⁴Now if you destroy them, the Egyptians will send a report to the inhabitants of this land, who have already heard that you live among your people. They know, LORD, that you have appeared to your people face to face and that your pillar of cloud hovers over them. They know that you go before them in the pillar of cloud by day and the pillar of fire by night. ¹⁵Now if you slaughter all these people with a single blow, the nations that have heard of your fame will say, ¹⁶'The LORD was not able to bring them into the land he swore to give them, so he killed them in the wilderness.'

¹⁷"Please, Lord, prove that your power is as great as you have claimed. For you said,¹⁸'The LORD is slow to anger and filled with unfailing love, forgiving every kind of sin and rebellion. But he does not excuse the guilty. He lays the sins of the parents upon their children; the entire family is affected—even children in the third and fourth generations.' ¹⁹In keeping with your magnificent, unfailing love, please pardon the sins of this people, just as you have forgiven them ever since they left Egypt."

²⁰Then the LORD said, "I will pardon them as you have requested. ²¹But as surely as I live, and as surely as the earth is filled with the LORD's glory, ²²not one of these people will ever enter that land. They have all seen my glorious presence and the miraculous signs I performed both in Egypt and in the wilderness, but again and again they have tested me by refusing to listen to my voice. ²³They will never even see the land I swore to give their ancestors. None of those who have treated me with contempt will ever see

---

13:33 Hebrew *nephilim.* 14:10 Hebrew *the Tent of Meeting.*

13:33 The words of the ten men here reveal their perception of themselves: "Next to them we felt like grasshoppers, and that's what they thought, too!" The Israelites failed to see themselves as God saw them. They were his chosen people, backed by the promises of the Creator of the universe. God had promised to give them the land of Canaan. As we face life's greatest challenges, our self-perception needs to come from our faith in God not from the difficult problems we face. We need to realize that God loves us and has promised to help us overcome the adversity and sins in our life.

it. [24]But my servant Caleb has a different attitude than the others have. He has remained loyal to me, so I will bring him into the land he explored. His descendants will possess their full share of that land. [25]Now turn around, and don't go on toward the land where the Amalekites and Canaanites live. Tomorrow you must set out for the wilderness in the direction of the Red Sea.*"

The LORD Punishes the Israelites

[26]Then the LORD said to Moses and Aaron, [27]"How long must I put up with this wicked community and its complaints about me? Yes, I have heard the complaints the Israelites are making against me. [28]Now tell them this: 'As surely as I live, declares the LORD, I will do to you the very things I heard you say. [29]You will all drop dead in this wilderness! Because you complained against me, every one of you who is twenty years old or older and was included in the registration will die. [30]You will not enter and occupy the land I swore to give you. The only exceptions will be Caleb son of Jephunneh and Joshua son of Nun.

[31]"'You said your children would be carried off as plunder. Well, I will bring them safely into the land, and they will enjoy what you have despised. [32]But as for you, you will drop dead in this wilderness. [33]And your children will be like shepherds, wandering in the wilderness for forty years. In this way, they will pay for your faithlessness, until the last of you lies dead in the wilderness.

[34]"'Because your men explored the land for forty days, you must wander in the wilderness for forty years—a year for each day, suffering the consequences of your sins. Then you will discover what it is like to have me for an enemy.' [35]I, the LORD, have spoken! I will certainly do these things to every member of the community who has conspired against me. They will be destroyed here in this wilderness, and here they will die!"

[36]The ten men Moses had sent to explore the land—the ones who incited rebellion against the LORD with their bad report— [37]were struck dead with a plague before the LORD. [38]Of the twelve who had explored the land, only Joshua and Caleb remained alive.

[39]When Moses reported the LORD's words to all the Israelites, the people were filled with grief. [40]Then they got up early the next morning and went to the top of the range of hills. "Let's go," they said. "We realize that we have sinned, but now we are ready to enter the land the LORD has promised us."

[41]But Moses said, "Why are you now disobeying the LORD's orders to return to the wilderness? It won't work. [42]Do not go up into the land now. You will only be crushed by your enemies because the LORD is not with you. [43]When you face the Amalekites and Canaanites in battle, you will be slaughtered. The LORD will abandon you because you have abandoned the LORD."

[44]But the people defiantly pushed ahead toward the hill country, even though neither Moses nor the Ark of the LORD's Covenant left the camp. [45]Then the Amalekites and the Canaanites who lived in those hills came down and attacked them and chased them back as far as Hormah.

CHAPTER 15
Laws concerning Offerings

Then the LORD told Moses, [2]"Give the following instructions to the people of Israel.

"When you finally settle in the land I am giving you, [3]you will offer special gifts as a pleasing aroma to the LORD. These gifts may take the form of a burnt offering, a sacrifice to fulfill a vow, a voluntary offering, or an of-

14:25 Hebrew *sea of reeds.*

14:24 In contrast to the unbelief of the other Israelites, Caleb trusted God and obeyed him fully. The positive result of his faith was his entrance into the Promised Land, though he had to wait nearly 40 years. All the other adults except Joshua died as they wandered on their forty-year wilderness trek. If we seek recovery in our own strength, we will also wander in the wilderness and never experience the wholeness God desires for us. But if we step out, trusting God to lead and protect us, we will discover a new life. Notice that even Caleb and Joshua had to wander in the wilderness, but through perseverance and faith in God they finally arrived.

14:34-45 After Moses announced God's judgment, the Israelites showed superficial repentance. Then they tried to conquer parts of Canaan in their own strength, but their mission was unsuccessful. As we seek to overcome our dependencies and compulsions, we need to do it God's way, with God's timing and with God's help. The obstacles we face are too great to be tackled alone, but with God's help, nothing is impossible.

15:1-36 This restatement of many of the Levitical laws was intended to train the new generation concerning their accountability to God. They would be allowed to enter the Promised Land and

fering at any of your annual festivals, and they may be taken from your herds of cattle or your flocks of sheep and goats. ⁴When you present these offerings, you must also give the LORD a grain offering of two quarts* of choice flour mixed with one quart* of olive oil. ⁵For each lamb offered as a burnt offering or a special sacrifice, you must also present one quart of wine as a liquid offering.

⁶"If the sacrifice is a ram, give a grain offering of four quarts* of choice flour mixed with a third of a gallon* of olive oil, ⁷and give a third of a gallon of wine as a liquid offering. This will be a pleasing aroma to the LORD.

⁸"When you present a young bull as a burnt offering or as a sacrifice to fulfill a vow or as a peace offering to the LORD, ⁹you must also give a grain offering of six quarts* of choice flour mixed with two quarts* of olive oil, ¹⁰and give two quarts of wine as a liquid offering. This will be a special gift, a pleasing aroma to the LORD.

¹¹"Each sacrifice of a bull, ram, lamb, or young goat should be prepared in this way. ¹²Follow these instructions with each offering you present. ¹³All of you native-born Israelites must follow these instructions when you offer a special gift as a pleasing aroma to the LORD. ¹⁴And if any foreigners visit you or live among you and want to present a special gift as a pleasing aroma to the LORD, they must follow these same procedures. ¹⁵Native-born Israelites and foreigners are equal before the LORD and are subject to the same decrees. This is a permanent law for you, to be observed from generation to generation. ¹⁶The same instructions and regulations will apply both to you and to the foreigners living among you."

¹⁷Then the LORD said to Moses, ¹⁸"Give the following instructions to the people of Israel.

"When you arrive in the land where I am taking you, ¹⁹and you eat the crops that grow there, you must set some aside as a sacred offering to the LORD. ²⁰Present a cake from the first of the flour you grind, and set it aside as a sacred offering, as you do with the first grain from the threshing floor. ²¹Throughout the generations to come, you are to present a sacred offering to the LORD each year from the first of your ground flour.

²²"But suppose you unintentionally fail to carry out all these commands that the LORD has given you through Moses. ²³And suppose your descendants in the future fail to do everything the LORD has commanded through Moses. ²⁴If the mistake was made unintentionally, and the community was unaware of it, the whole community must present a young bull for a burnt offering as a pleasing aroma to the LORD. It must be offered along with its prescribed grain offering and liquid offering and with one male goat for a sin offering. ²⁵With it the priest will purify the whole community of Israel, making them right with the LORD,* and they will be forgiven. For it was an unintentional sin, and they have corrected it with their offerings to the LORD—the special gift and the sin offering. ²⁶The whole community of Israel will be forgiven, including the foreigners living among you, for all the people were involved in the sin.

²⁷"If one individual commits an unintentional sin, the guilty person must bring a one-year-old female goat for a sin offering. ²⁸The priest will sacrifice it to purify* the guilty person before the LORD, and that person will be forgiven. ²⁹These same instructions apply both to native-born Israelites and to the foreigners living among you.

³⁰"But those who brazenly violate the LORD's will, whether native-born Israelites or foreigners, have blasphemed the LORD, and they must be cut off from the community. ³¹Since they have treated the LORD's word with contempt and deliberately disobeyed his command, they must be completely cut off and suffer the punishment for their guilt."

Penalty for Breaking the Sabbath

³²One day while the people of Israel were in the wilderness, they discovered a man gathering wood on the Sabbath day. ³³The people who found him doing this took him before Moses, Aaron, and the rest of the community. ³⁴They held him in custody because they did not know what to do with him. ³⁵Then the

---

15:4a Hebrew *1/10 of an ephah* [2.2 liters]. 15:4b Hebrew *1/4 of a hin* [1 liter]; also in 15:5. 15:6a Hebrew *2/10 of an ephah* [4.4 liters]. 15:6b Hebrew *1/3 of a hin* [1.3 liters]; also in 15:7. 15:9a Hebrew *3/10 of an ephah* [6.6 liters]. 15:9b Hebrew *1/2 of a hin* [2 liters]; also in 15:10. 15:25 Or *will make atonement for the whole community of Israel.* 15:28 Or *to make atonement for.*

---

enjoy God's blessings. But they needed to realize that in their new life there, they would be accountable to God. Privilege always brings with it responsibility. God was affirming this principle with a new generation of Israelites.

LORD said to Moses, "The man must be put to death! The whole community must stone him outside the camp." [36]So the whole community took the man outside the camp and stoned him to death, just as the LORD had commanded Moses.

Tassels on Clothing
[37]Then the LORD said to Moses, [38]"Give the following instructions to the people of Israel: Throughout the generations to come you must make tassels for the hems of your clothing and attach them with a blue cord. [39]When you see the tassels, you will remember and obey all the commands of the LORD instead of following your own desires and defiling yourselves, as you are prone to do. [40]The tassels will help you remember that you must obey all my commands and be holy to your God. [41]I am the LORD your God who brought you out of the land of Egypt that I might be your God. I am the LORD your God!"

CHAPTER 16
Korah's Rebellion
One day Korah son of Izhar, a descendant of Kohath son of Levi, conspired with Dathan and Abiram, the sons of Eliab, and On son of Peleth, from the tribe of Reuben. [2]They incited a rebellion against Moses, along with 250 other leaders of the community, all prominent members of the assembly. [3]They united against Moses and Aaron and said, "You have gone too far! The whole community of Israel has been set apart by the LORD, and he is with all of us. What right do you have to act as though you are greater than the rest of the LORD's people?"

[4]When Moses heard what they were saying, he fell face down on the ground. [5]Then he said to Korah and his followers, "Tomorrow morning the LORD will show us who belongs to him* and who is holy. The LORD will allow only those whom he selects to enter his own presence. [6]Korah, you and all your followers must prepare your incense burners. [7]Light fires in them tomorrow, and burn incense before the LORD. Then we will see whom the LORD chooses as his holy one. You Levites are the ones who have gone too far!"

[8]Then Moses spoke again to Korah: "Now listen, you Levites! [9]Does it seem insignificant to you that the God of Israel has chosen you from among all the community of Israel to be near him so you can serve in the LORD's Tabernacle and stand before the people to minister to them? [10]Korah, he has already given this special ministry to you and your fellow Levites. Are you now demanding the priesthood as well? [11]The LORD is the one you and your followers are really revolting against! For who is Aaron that you are complaining about him?"

[12]Then Moses summoned Dathan and Abiram, the sons of Eliab, but they replied, "We refuse to come before you! [13]Isn't it enough that you brought us out of Egypt, a land flowing with milk and honey, to kill us here in this wilderness, and that you now treat us like your subjects? [14]What's more, you haven't brought us into another land flowing with milk and honey. You haven't given us a new homeland with fields and vineyards. Are you trying to fool these men?* We will not come."

[15]Then Moses became very angry and said to the LORD, "Do not accept their grain offerings! I have not taken so much as a donkey from them, and I have never hurt a single one of them." [16]And Moses said to Korah, "You and all your followers must come here tomorrow and present yourselves before the LORD. Aaron will also be here. [17]You and each

16:5 Greek version reads *God has visited and knows those who are his.* Compare 2 Tim 2:19. 16:14 Hebrew *Are you trying to put out the eyes of these men?*

15:37-41 The Israelites were required to wear tassels on the corners of their clothing. This reminded them constantly of their covenant relationship with God and the need to obey him. It was a visual reminder that their commitment to obey God was important in every realm of life. Although the New Testament does not command such a ritual for us today, the principle behind it is still helpful. As we commit our life to God, we need to realize that obedience to him is important in all areas of life.

16:1–17:13 The three stories in this section illustrate the priority of Aaron's priesthood in God's leadership of his people, the Israelites. God made it clear that Aaron was his chosen spiritual leader. Proper worship of God could come only through Aaron's high priesthood. The writer of Hebrews shows us that Jesus Christ is a high priest superior in every way to Aaron (Hebrews 4:1–10:39). As Aaron's budding rod demonstrated that he was chosen by God, so Christ's resurrection proved that he was to be the only mediator between God and people (1 Timothy 2:5). For us today, cleansing from sin and a proper approach to God can come only through a relationship with Christ (John 14:6). He alone makes it possible for us to be reconciled to God.

of your 250 followers must prepare an incense burner and put incense on it, so you can all present them before the LORD. Aaron will also bring his incense burner."

[18]So each of these men prepared an incense burner, lit the fire, and placed incense on it. Then they all stood at the entrance of the Tabernacle* with Moses and Aaron. [19]Meanwhile, Korah had stirred up the entire community against Moses and Aaron, and they all gathered at the Tabernacle entrance. Then the glorious presence of the LORD appeared to the whole community, [20]and the LORD said to Moses and Aaron, [21]"Get away from all these people so that I may instantly destroy them!"

[22]But Moses and Aaron fell face down on the ground. "O God," they pleaded, "you are the God who gives breath to all creatures. Must you be angry with all the people when only one man sins?"

[23]And the LORD said to Moses, [24]"Then tell all the people to get away from the tents of Korah, Dathan, and Abiram."

[25]So Moses got up and rushed over to the tents of Dathan and Abiram, followed by the elders of Israel. [26]"Quick!" he told the people. "Get away from the tents of these wicked men, and don't touch anything that belongs to them. If you do, you will be destroyed for their sins." [27]So all the people stood back from the tents of Korah, Dathan, and Abiram. Then Dathan and Abiram came out and stood at the entrances of their tents, together with their wives and children and little ones.

[28]And Moses said, "This is how you will know that the LORD has sent me to do all these things that I have done—for I have not done them on my own. [29]If these men die a natural death, or if nothing unusual happens, then the LORD has not sent me. [30]But if the LORD does something entirely new and the ground opens its mouth and swallows them and all their belongings, and they go down alive into the grave,* then you will know that these men have shown contempt for the LORD."

[31]He had hardly finished speaking the words when the ground suddenly split open beneath them. [32]The earth opened its mouth and swallowed the men, along with their households and all their followers who were standing with them, and everything they owned. [33]So they went down alive into the grave, along with all their belongings. The earth closed over them, and they all vanished from among the people of Israel. [34]All the people around them fled when they heard their screams. "The earth will swallow us, too!" they cried. [35]Then fire blazed forth from the LORD and burned up the 250 men who were offering incense.

[36]*And the LORD said to Moses, [37]"Tell Eleazar son of Aaron the priest to pull all the incense burners from the fire, for they are holy. Also tell him to scatter the burning coals. [38]Take the incense burners of these men who have sinned at the cost of their lives, and hammer the metal into a thin sheet to overlay the altar. Since these burners were used in the LORD's presence, they have become holy. Let them serve as a warning to the people of Israel."

[39]So Eleazar the priest collected the 250 bronze incense burners that had been used by the men who died in the fire, and the bronze was hammered into a thin sheet to overlay the altar. [40]This would warn the Israelites that no unauthorized person—no one who was not a descendant of Aaron—should ever enter the LORD's presence to burn incense. If anyone did, the same thing would happen to him as happened to Korah and his followers. So the LORD's instructions to Moses were carried out.

[41]But the very next morning the whole community of Israel began muttering again against Moses and Aaron, saying, "You have killed the LORD's people!" [42]As the community gathered to protest against Moses and Aaron, they turned toward the Tabernacle and saw that the cloud had covered it, and the glorious presence of the LORD appeared.

[43]Moses and Aaron came and stood in front of the Tabernacle, [44]and the LORD said to Moses, [45]"Get away from all these people so that I can instantly destroy them!" But Moses and Aaron fell face down on the ground.

[46]And Moses said to Aaron, "Quick, take an incense burner and place burning coals on it from the altar. Lay incense on it, and carry it out among the people to purify them and make them right with the LORD.* The LORD's anger is blazing against them—the plague has already begun."

[47]Aaron did as Moses told him and ran out among the people. The plague had already begun to strike down the people, but Aaron burned the incense and purified* the people.

16:18 Hebrew *the Tent of Meeting;* also in 16:19, 42, 43, 50. **16:30** Hebrew *into Sheol;* also in 16:33. **16:36** Verses 16:36-50 are numbered 17:1-15 in Hebrew text. **16:46** Or *to make atonement for them.* **16:47** Or *and made atonement for.*

[48] He stood between the dead and the living, and the plague stopped. [49] But 14,700 people died in that plague, in addition to those who had died in the affair involving Korah. [50] Then because the plague had stopped, Aaron returned to Moses at the entrance of the Tabernacle.

CHAPTER 17
The Budding of Aaron's Staff

[1]*Then the LORD said to Moses, [2] "Tell the people of Israel to bring you twelve wooden staffs, one from each leader of Israel's ancestral tribes, and inscribe each leader's name on his staff. [3] Inscribe Aaron's name on the staff of the tribe of Levi, for there must be one staff for the leader of each ancestral tribe. [4] Place these staffs in the Tabernacle in front of the Ark containing the tablets of the Covenant,* where I meet with you. [5] Buds will sprout on the staff belonging to the man I choose. Then I will finally put an end to the people's murmuring and complaining against you."

[6] So Moses gave the instructions to the people of Israel, and each of the twelve tribal leaders, including Aaron, brought Moses a staff. [7] Moses placed the staffs in the LORD's presence in the Tabernacle of the Covenant.* [8] When he went into the Tabernacle of the Covenant the next day, he found that Aaron's staff, representing the tribe of Levi, had sprouted, budded, blossomed, and produced ripe almonds!

[9] When Moses brought all the staffs out from the LORD's presence, he showed them to the people. Each man claimed his own staff. [10] And the LORD said to Moses: "Place Aaron's staff permanently before the Ark of the Covenant* to serve as a warning to rebels. This should put an end to their complaints against me and prevent any further deaths." [11] So Moses did as the LORD commanded him.

[12] Then the people of Israel said to Moses, "Look, we are doomed! We are dead! We are ruined! [13] Everyone who even comes close to the Tabernacle of the LORD dies. Are we all doomed to die?"

CHAPTER 18
Duties of Priests and Levites

Then the LORD said to Aaron: "You, your sons, and your relatives from the tribe of Levi will be held responsible for any offenses related to the sanctuary. But you and your sons alone will be held responsible for violations connected with the priesthood.

[2] "Bring your relatives of the tribe of Levi—your ancestral tribe—to assist you and your sons as you perform the sacred duties in front of the Tabernacle of the Covenant.* [3] But as the Levites go about all their assigned duties at the Tabernacle, they must be careful not to go near any of the sacred objects or the altar. If they do, both you and they will die. [4] The Levites must join you in fulfilling their responsibilities for the care and maintenance of the Tabernacle,* but no unauthorized person may assist you.

[5] "You yourselves must perform the sacred duties inside the sanctuary and at the altar. If you follow these instructions, the LORD's anger will never again blaze against the people of Israel. [6] I myself have chosen your fellow Levites from among the Israelites to be your special assistants. They are a gift to you, dedicated to the LORD for service in the Tabernacle. [7] But you and your sons, the priests, must personally handle all the priestly rituals associated with the altar and with everything behind the inner curtain. I am giving you the priesthood as your special privilege of service. Any unauthorized person who comes too near the sanctuary will be put to death."

Support for the Priests and Levites

[8] The LORD gave these further instructions to Aaron: "I myself have put you in charge of all the holy offerings that are brought to me by the people of Israel. I have given all these consecrated offerings to you and your sons as your permanent share. [9] You are allotted the portion of the most holy offerings that is not burned on the fire. This portion of all the most holy offerings—including the grain offerings, sin offerings, and guilt offerings—will be most holy, and it belongs to you and your sons. [10] You must eat it as a most holy offering. All the males may eat of it, and you must treat it as most holy.

[11] "All the sacred offerings and special offerings presented to me when the Israelites lift them up before the altar also belong to you. I have given them to you and to your sons and daughters as your permanent share. Any member of your family who is ceremonially clean may eat of these offerings.

17:1 Verses 17:1-13 are numbered 17:16-28 in Hebrew text. **17:4** Hebrew *in the Tent of Meeting before the Testimony*. The Hebrew word for "testimony" refers to the terms of the LORD's covenant with Israel as written on stone tablets, which were kept in the Ark, and also to the covenant itself. **17:7** Or *Tabernacle of the Testimony;* also in 17:8. **17:10** Hebrew *before the Testimony;* see note on 17:4. **18:2** Or *Tabernacle of the Testimony.* **18:4** Hebrew *the Tent of Meeting;* also in 18:6, 21, 22, 23, 31.

¹² "I also give you the harvest gifts brought by the people as offerings to the LORD—the best of the olive oil, new wine, and grain. ¹³All the first crops of their land that the people present to the LORD belong to you. Any member of your family who is ceremonially clean may eat this food.

¹⁴"Everything in Israel that is specially set apart for the LORD* also belongs to you.

¹⁵ "The firstborn of every mother, whether human or animal, that is offered to the LORD will be yours. But you must always redeem your firstborn sons and the firstborn of ceremonially unclean animals. ¹⁶Redeem them when they are one month old. The redemption price is five pieces of silver* (as measured by the weight of the sanctuary shekel, which equals twenty gerahs).

¹⁷ "However, you may not redeem the firstborn of cattle, sheep, or goats. They are holy and have been set apart for the LORD. Sprinkle their blood on the altar, and burn their fat as a special gift, a pleasing aroma to the LORD. ¹⁸The meat of these animals will be yours, just like the breast and right thigh that are presented by lifting them up as a special offering before the altar. ¹⁹Yes, I am giving you all these holy offerings that the people of Israel bring to the LORD. They are for you and your sons and daughters, to be eaten as your permanent share. This is an eternal and unbreakable covenant* between the LORD and you, and it also applies to your descendants."

²⁰And the LORD said to Aaron, "You priests will receive no allotment of land or share of property among the people of Israel. I am your share and your allotment. ²¹As for the tribe of Levi, your relatives, I will compensate them for their service in the Tabernacle. Instead of an allotment of land, I will give them the tithes from the entire land of Israel.

²² "From now on, no Israelites except priests or Levites may approach the Tabernacle. If they come too near, they will be judged guilty and will die. ²³Only the Levites may serve at the Tabernacle, and they will be held responsible for any offenses against it. This is a permanent law for you, to be observed from generation to generation. The Levites will receive no allotment of land among the Israelites, ²⁴because I have given them the Israelites' tithes, which have been presented as sacred offerings to the LORD. This will be the Levites' share. That is why I said they would receive no allotment of land among the Israelites."

²⁵The LORD also told Moses, ²⁶"Give these instructions to the Levites: When you receive from the people of Israel the tithes I have assigned as your allotment, give a tenth of the tithes you receive—a tithe of the tithe—to the LORD as a sacred offering. ²⁷The LORD will consider this offering to be your harvest offering, as though it were the first grain from your own threshing floor or wine from your own winepress. ²⁸You must present one-tenth of the tithe received from the Israelites as a sacred offering to the LORD. This is the LORD's sacred portion, and you must present it to Aaron the priest. ²⁹Be sure to give to the LORD the best portions of the gifts given to you.

³⁰"Also, give these instructions to the Levites: When you present the best part as your offering, it will be considered as though it came from your own threshing floor or winepress. ³¹You Levites and your families may eat this food anywhere you wish, for it is your compensation for serving in the Tabernacle. ³²You will not be considered guilty for accepting the LORD's tithes if you give the best portion to the priests. But be careful not to treat the holy gifts of the people of Israel as though they were common. If you do, you will die."

CHAPTER 19
The Water of Purification

The LORD said to Moses and Aaron, ²"Here is another legal requirement commanded by the LORD: Tell the people of Israel to bring you a red heifer, a perfect animal that has no defects and has never been yoked to a plow. ³Give it to Eleazar the priest, and it will be taken outside the camp and slaughtered in his presence. ⁴Eleazar will take some of its blood on his finger and sprinkle it seven times toward the front of the Tabernacle.* ⁵As Eleazar watches, the heifer must be burned—its hide, meat, blood, and dung. ⁶Eleazar the priest must then take a stick of cedar,* a hyssop branch, and some scarlet yarn and throw them into the fire where the heifer is burning.

⁷ "Then the priest must wash his clothes and bathe himself in water. Afterward he may return to the camp, though he will remain ceremonially unclean until evening. ⁸The man who burns the animal must also

---

18:14 The Hebrew term used here refers to the complete consecration of things or people to the LORD, either by destroying them or by giving them as an offering. **18:16** Hebrew *5 shekels* [2 ounces or 57 grams] *of silver.* **18:19** Hebrew *a covenant of salt.* **19:4** Hebrew *the Tent of Meeting.* **19:6** Or *juniper.*

wash his clothes and bathe himself in water, and he, too, will remain unclean until evening. ⁹Then someone who is ceremonially clean will gather up the ashes of the heifer and deposit them in a purified place outside the camp. They will be kept there for the community of Israel to use in the water for the purification ceremony. This ceremony is performed for the removal of sin. ¹⁰The man who gathers up the ashes of the heifer must also wash his clothes, and he will remain ceremonially unclean until evening. This is a permanent law for the people of Israel and any foreigners who live among them.

¹¹"All those who touch a dead human body will be ceremonially unclean for seven days. ¹²They must purify themselves on the third and seventh days with the water of purification; then they will be purified. But if they do not do this on the third and seventh days, they will continue to be unclean even after the seventh day. ¹³All those who touch a dead body and do not purify themselves in the proper way defile the LORD's Tabernacle, and they will be cut off from the community of Israel. Since the water of purification was not sprinkled on them, their defilement continues.

¹⁴"This is the ritual law that applies when someone dies inside a tent: All those who enter that tent and those who were inside when the death occurred will be ceremonially unclean for seven days. ¹⁵Any open container in the tent that was not covered with a lid is also defiled. ¹⁶And if someone in an open field touches the corpse of someone who was killed with a sword or who died a natural death, or if someone touches a human bone or a grave, that person will be defiled for seven days.

¹⁷"To remove the defilement, put some of the ashes from the burnt purification offering in a jar, and pour fresh water over them. ¹⁸Then someone who is ceremonially clean must take a hyssop branch and dip it into the water. That person must sprinkle the water on the tent, on all the furnishings in the tent, and on the people who were in the tent; also on the person who touched a human bone, or touched someone who was killed or who died naturally, or touched a grave. ¹⁹On the third and seventh days the person who is ceremonially clean must sprinkle the water on those who are defiled. Then on the seventh day the people being cleansed must wash their clothes and bathe themselves, and that evening they will be cleansed of their defilement.

²⁰"But those who become defiled and do not purify themselves will be cut off from the community, for they have defiled the sanctuary of the LORD. Since the water of purification has not been sprinkled on them, they remain defiled. ²¹This is a permanent law for the people. Those who sprinkle the water of purification must afterward wash their clothes, and anyone who then touches the water used for purification will remain defiled until evening. ²²Anything and anyone that a defiled person touches will be ceremonially unclean until evening."

CHAPTER 20
Moses Strikes the Rock
In the first month of the year,* the whole community of Israel arrived in the wilderness of Zin and camped at Kadesh. While they were there, Miriam died and was buried.

²There was no water for the people to drink at that place, so they rebelled against Moses and Aaron. ³The people blamed Moses and said, "If only we had died in the LORD's presence with our brothers! ⁴Why have you brought the congregation of the LORD's people into this wilderness to die, along with all our livestock? ⁵Why did you make us leave Egypt and bring us here to this terrible place? This land has no grain, no figs, no grapes, no pomegranates, and no water to drink!"

⁶Moses and Aaron turned away from the people and went to the entrance of the Tabernacle,* where they fell face down on the

---

20:1 The first month of the ancient Hebrew lunar calendar usually occurs within the months of March and April. The number of years since leaving Egypt is not specified. 20:6 Hebrew *the Tent of Meeting.*

20:2-13 After a water shortage, the Israelites started to complain again. The focus of this incident, however, was on the failure of Moses and Aaron. God severely judged Moses for not following God's instructions specifically and for using his own method to produce water. Aaron was judged because he evidently had a part in it. While the judgment seems severe, it illustrates the importance of obedience to God's Word, especially if we are in a leadership position. By disobeying God's specific instructions, Moses and Aaron exhibited attitudes of personal rebellion against God. Commitment to God's program cannot be a partway proposition. Despite Moses' great success in the past, this failure kept him out of the Promised Land.

ground. Then the glorious presence of the LORD appeared to them, [7]and the LORD said to Moses, [8]"You and Aaron must take the staff and assemble the entire community. As the people watch, speak to the rock over there, and it will pour out its water. You will provide enough water from the rock to satisfy the whole community and their livestock."

[9]So Moses did as he was told. He took the staff from the place where it was kept before the LORD. [10]Then he and Aaron summoned the people to come and gather at the rock. "Listen, you rebels!" he shouted. "Must we bring you water from this rock?" [11]Then Moses raised his hand and struck the rock twice with the staff, and water gushed out. So the entire community and their livestock drank their fill.

[12]But the LORD said to Moses and Aaron, "Because you did not trust me enough to demonstrate my holiness to the people of Israel, you will not lead them into the land I am giving them!" [13]This place was known as the waters of Meribah (which means "arguing") because there the people of Israel argued with the LORD, and there he demonstrated his holiness among them.

Edom Refuses Israel Passage

[14]While Moses was at Kadesh, he sent ambassadors to the king of Edom with this message:

"This is what your relatives, the people of Israel, say: You know all the hardships we have been through. [15]Our ancestors went down to Egypt, and we lived there a long time, and we and our ancestors were brutally mistreated by the Egyptians. [16]But when we cried out to the LORD, he heard us and sent an angel who brought us out of Egypt. Now we are camped at Kadesh, a town on the border of your land. [17]Please let us travel through your land. We will be careful not to go through your fields and vineyards. We won't even drink water from your wells. We will stay on the king's road and never leave it until we have passed through your territory."

[18]But the king of Edom said, "Stay out of my land, or I will meet you with an army!"

[19]The Israelites answered, "We will stay on the main road. If our livestock drink your water, we will pay for it. Just let us pass through your country. That's all we ask."

[20]But the king of Edom replied, "Stay out! You may not pass through our land." With that he mobilized his army and marched out against them with an imposing force. [21]Because Edom refused to allow Israel to pass through their country, Israel was forced to turn around.

The Death of Aaron

[22]The whole community of Israel left Kadesh and arrived at Mount Hor. [23]There, on the border of the land of Edom, the LORD said to Moses and Aaron, [24]"The time has come for Aaron to join his ancestors in death. He will not enter the land I am giving the people of Israel, because the two of you rebelled against my instructions concerning the water at Meribah. [25]Now take Aaron and his son Eleazar up Mount Hor. [26]There you will remove Aaron's priestly garments and put them on Eleazar, his son. Aaron will die there and join his ancestors."

[27]So Moses did as the LORD commanded. The three of them went up Mount Hor together as the whole community watched. [28]At the summit, Moses removed the priestly garments from Aaron and put them on Eleazar, Aaron's son. Then Aaron died there on top of the mountain, and Moses and Eleazar went back down. [29]When the people realized that Aaron had died, all Israel mourned for him thirty days.

CHAPTER 21
Victory over the Canaanites

The Canaanite king of Arad, who lived in the Negev, heard that the Israelites were

---

20:23-29 The death of Aaron, Israel's first high priest, was mourned by the people (20:29), but this wouldn't be the last of Israel's priestly funerals. The writer of Hebrews used this point to contrast the ministry of Jesus Christ with the ministry of human priests: "There were many priests under the old system, for death prevented them from remaining in office. But because Jesus lives forever, his priesthood lasts forever" (Hebrews 7:23-24). Our great High Priest will always be available to provide help for any problems we may have.

21:1-3 Victory! This first great success was the result of complete obedience to God's will. This victory, along with others that followed, began an important era in Israel's history. The Israelites were able to see the truth of Joshua and Caleb's advice—faith would bring victory over any enemy or obstacle. God delights in demonstrating his power in the lives of those who trust him to overcome life's obstacles. Our powerlessness over any problem can be covered by God's unlimited power to act on our behalf.

approaching on the road through Atharim. So he attacked the Israelites and took some of them as prisoners. ²Then the people of Israel made this vow to the LORD: "If you will hand these people over to us, we will completely destroy* all their towns." ³The LORD heard the Israelites' request and gave them victory over the Canaanites. The Israelites completely destroyed them and their towns, and the place has been called Hormah* ever since.

The Bronze Snake

⁴Then the people of Israel set out from Mount Hor, taking the road to the Red Sea* to go around the land of Edom. But the people grew impatient with the long journey, ⁵and they began to speak against God and Moses. "Why have you brought us out of Egypt to die here in the wilderness?" they complained. "There is nothing to eat here and nothing to drink. And we hate this horrible manna!"

⁶So the LORD sent poisonous snakes among the people, and many were bitten and died. ⁷Then the people came to Moses and cried out, "We have sinned by speaking against the LORD and against you. Pray that the LORD will take away the snakes." So Moses prayed for the people.

⁸Then the LORD told him, "Make a replica of a poisonous snake and attach it to a pole. All who are bitten will live if they simply look at it!" ⁹So Moses made a snake out of bronze and attached it to a pole. Then anyone who was bitten by a snake could look at the bronze snake and be healed!

Israel's Journey to Moab

¹⁰The Israelites traveled next to Oboth and camped there. ¹¹Then they went on to Iye-abarim, in the wilderness on the eastern border of Moab. ¹²From there they traveled to the valley of Zered Brook and set up camp. ¹³Then they moved out and camped on the far side of the Arnon River, in the wilderness adjacent to the territory of the Amorites. The Arnon is the boundary line between the Moabites and the Amorites. ¹⁴For this reason *The Book of the Wars of the LORD* speaks of "the town of Waheb in the area of Suphah, and the ravines of the Arnon River, ¹⁵and the ravines that extend as far as the settlement of Ar on the border of Moab."

¹⁶From there the Israelites traveled to Beer,* which is the well where the LORD said to Moses, "Assemble the people, and I will give them water." ¹⁷There the Israelites sang this song:

"Spring up, O well!
    Yes, sing its praises!
¹⁸Sing of this well,
    which princes dug,
which great leaders hollowed
        out
    with their scepters and staffs."

Then the Israelites left the wilderness and proceeded on through Mattanah, ¹⁹Nahaliel, and Bamoth. ²⁰After that they went to the valley in Moab where Pisgah Peak overlooks the wasteland.*

Victory over Sihon and Og

²¹The Israelites sent ambassadors to King Sihon of the Amorites with this message:

²²"Let us travel through your land. We will be careful not to go through your fields and vineyards. We won't even

---

21:2 The Hebrew term used here refers to the complete consecration of things or people to the LORD, either by destroying them or by giving them as an offering; also in 21:3. **21:3** *Hormah* means "destruction." **21:4** Hebrew *sea of reeds*. **21:16** *Beer* means "well." **21:20** Or *overlooks Jeshimon*.

21:4-9 In the New Testament book of John, Jesus used this incident as an illustration of what he did on our behalf: "And as Moses lifted up the bronze snake on a pole in the wilderness, so the Son of Man must be lifted up, so that everyone who believes in him will have eternal life" (John 3:14-15). Evident in both passages is God's saving grace, which provides salvation and healing for anyone who responds in faith. Healing did not come to everyone in Israel but only to those who by faith looked at the bronze snake on the pole. The apostle John makes it clear that personal forgiveness and victory over sin can come only to those who look to Christ on the cross. God provides the powerful means of recovery from sin and failure; we need to receive it in faith.

21:7 Notice here that Moses resumed his role as Israel's leader and mediator even after he was judged for his sin at Meribah. His failure undoubtedly brought him a great deal of personal pain and disappointment. He would lead several million Israelites to the Promised Land but would never enter it himself. In spite of this, Moses showed no bitter feelings toward God; neither did he neglect his responsibilities. His recovery from this personal failure and his continued faithful service are evidence of Moses' great faith and dependence upon God. Our mistakes don't disqualify us from future success; they provide opportunities for learning, growth, and dependence on God.

drink water from your wells. We will stay on the king's road until we have passed through your territory."

23But King Sihon refused to let them cross his territory. Instead, he mobilized his entire army and attacked Israel in the wilderness, engaging them in battle at Jahaz. 24But the Israelites slaughtered them with their swords and occupied their land from the Arnon River to the Jabbok River. They went only as far as the Ammonite border because the boundary of the Ammonites was fortified.*

25So Israel captured all the towns of the Amorites and settled in them, including the city of Heshbon and its surrounding villages. 26Heshbon had been the capital of King Sihon of the Amorites. He had defeated a former Moabite king and seized all his land as far as the Arnon River. 27Therefore, the ancient poets wrote this about him:

"Come to Heshbon and let it be rebuilt!
　　Let the city of Sihon be restored.
28 A fire flamed forth from Heshbon,
　　a blaze from the city of Sihon.
It burned the city of Ar in Moab;
　　it destroyed the rulers of the Arnon
　　heights.
29 What sorrow awaits you, O people
　　of Moab!
You are finished, O worshipers of
　　Chemosh!
Chemosh has left his sons as refugees,
　　his daughters as captives of Sihon, the
　　Amorite king.
30 We have utterly destroyed them,
　　from Heshbon to Dibon.
We have completely wiped them out
　　as far away as Nophah and Medeba.*"

31So the people of Israel occupied the territory of the Amorites. 32After Moses sent men to explore the Jazer area, they captured all the towns in the region and drove out the Amorites who lived there. 33Then they turned and marched up the road to Bashan, but King Og of Bashan and all his people attacked them at Edrei. 34The LORD said to Moses, "Do not be afraid of him, for I have handed him over to you, along with all his people and his land. Do the same to him as you did to King Sihon of the Amorites, who ruled in Heshbon." 35And Israel killed King Og, his sons, and all his subjects; not a single survivor remained. Then Israel occupied their land.

CHAPTER 22
Balak Sends for Balaam

Then the people of Israel traveled to the plains of Moab and camped east of the Jordan River, across from Jericho. 2Balak son of Zippor, the Moabite king, had seen everything the Israelites did to the Amorites. 3And when the people of Moab saw how many Israelites there were, they were terrified. 4The king of Moab said to the elders of Midian, "This mob will devour everything in sight, like an ox devours grass in the field!"

So Balak, king of Moab, 5sent messengers to call Balaam son of Beor, who was living in his native land of Pethor* near the Euphrates River.* His message said:

"Look, a vast horde of people has arrived from Egypt. They cover the face of the earth and are threatening me. 6Please come and curse these people for me because they are too powerful for me. Then perhaps I will be able to conquer them and drive them from the land. I know that blessings fall on any people you bless, and curses fall on people you curse."

7Balak's messengers, who were elders of Moab and Midian, set out with money to pay Balaam to place a curse upon Israel.* They went to Balaam and delivered Balak's message to him. 8"Stay here overnight," Balaam said. "In the morning I will tell you whatever the LORD directs me to say." So the officials from Moab stayed there with Balaam.

9 That night God came to Balaam and asked him, "Who are these men visiting you?"

10Balaam said to God, "Balak son of Zippor,

21:24 Or *because the terrain of the Ammonite frontier was rugged;* Hebrew reads *because the boundary of the Ammonites was strong.* 21:30 Or *until fire spread to Medeba.* The meaning of the Hebrew is uncertain. 22:5a Or *who was at Pethor in the land of the Amavites.* 22:5b Hebrew *the river.* 22:7 Hebrew *set out with the money of divination in their hand.*

22:1-20 Balaam was a Mesopotamian magician (Joshua 13:22) who was hired by Balak, king of Moab, to place a curse on Israel. King Balak wanted to prevent the Israelites from conquering Moab and the surrounding lands. Balaam, evidently a man of great spiritual stature, openly admitted that he had no power to go beyond the will of God. He could not place a curse on the people whom God desired to bless. This should help us realize that when it seems that everyone is against us, we can be sure that God can protect us and provide us with the wisdom to survive the toughest situations (James 1:2-5).

king of Moab, has sent me this message: [11]"Look, a vast horde of people has arrived from Egypt, and they cover the face of the earth. Come and curse these people for me. Then perhaps I will be able to stand up to them and drive them from the land.'"

[12]But God told Balaam, "Do not go with them. You are not to curse these people, for they have been blessed!"

[13]The next morning Balaam got up and told Balak's officials, "Go on home! The LORD will not let me go with you."

[14]So the Moabite officials returned to King Balak and reported, "Balaam refused to come with us." [15]Then Balak tried again. This time he sent a larger number of even more distinguished officials than those he had sent the first time. [16]They went to Balaam and delivered this message to him:

"This is what Balak son of Zippor says: Please don't let anything stop you from coming to help me. [17]I will pay you very well and do whatever you tell me. Just come and curse these people for me!"

[18]But Balaam responded to Balak's messengers, "Even if Balak were to give me his palace filled with silver and gold, I would be powerless to do anything against the will of the LORD my God. [19]But stay here one more night, and I will see if the LORD has anything else to say to me."

[20]That night God came to Balaam and told him, "Since these men have come for you, get up and go with them. But do only what I tell you to do."

Balaam and His Donkey

[21]So the next morning Balaam got up, saddled his donkey, and started off with the Moabite officials. [22]But God was angry that Balaam was going, so he sent the angel of the LORD to stand in the road to block his way. As Balaam and two servants were riding along, [23]Balaam's donkey saw the angel of the LORD standing in the road with a drawn sword in his hand. The donkey bolted off the road into a field, but Balaam beat it and turned it back onto the road. [24]Then the angel of the LORD stood at a place where the road narrowed between two vineyard walls. [25]When the donkey saw the angel of the LORD, it tried to squeeze by and crushed Balaam's foot against the wall. So Balaam beat the donkey again. [26]Then the angel of the LORD moved farther down the road and stood in a place too narrow for the donkey to get by at all. [27]This time when the donkey saw the angel, it lay down under Balaam. In a fit of rage Balaam beat the animal again with his staff.

[28]Then the LORD gave the donkey the ability to speak. "What have I done to you that deserves your beating me three times?" it asked Balaam.

[29]"You have made me look like a fool!" Balaam shouted. "If I had a sword with me, I would kill you!"

[30]"But I am the same donkey you have ridden all your life," the donkey answered. "Have I ever done anything like this before?"

"No," Balaam admitted.

[31]Then the LORD opened Balaam's eyes, and he saw the angel of the LORD standing in the roadway with a drawn sword in his hand. Balaam bowed his head and fell face down on the ground before him.

[32]"Why did you beat your donkey those three times?" the angel of the LORD demanded. "Look, I have come to block your way because you are stubbornly resisting me. [33]Three times the donkey saw me and shied away; otherwise, I would certainly have killed you by now and spared the donkey."

[34]Then Balaam confessed to the angel of the LORD, "I have sinned. I didn't realize you were standing in the road to block my way. I will return home if you are against my going."

[35]But the angel of the LORD told Balaam, "Go with these men, but say only what I tell you to say." So Balaam went on with Balak's officials. [36]When King Balak heard that Balaam was on the way, he went out to meet him at a Moabite town on the Arnon River at the farthest border of his land.

[37]"Didn't I send you an urgent invitation? Why didn't you come right away?" Balak asked Balaam. "Didn't you believe me when I said I would reward you richly?"

[38]Balaam replied, "Look, now I have come, but I have no power to say whatever I want. I

22:22-35 The humorous story of Balaam and his donkey illustrates Balaam's spiritual blindness with respect to the true God. As a specialist in divination, Balaam would often have relied upon signs from animals and nature to determine the future. In this situation, however, he had less spiritual perception than his donkey and was prevented from carrying out a diabolical plot against Israel. From Balaam we learn that even the greatest human wisdom often leads to spiritual blindness. True wisdom to face life's situations comes only from the sovereign, all-knowing God.

will speak only the message that God puts in my mouth." ³⁹Then Balaam accompanied Balak to Kiriath-huzoth, ⁴⁰where the king sacrificed cattle and sheep. He sent portions of the meat to Balaam and the officials who were with him. ⁴¹The next morning Balak took Balaam up to Bamoth-baal. From there he could see some of the people of Israel spread out below him.

CHAPTER 23
Balaam Blesses Israel

Then Balaam said to King Balak, "Build me seven altars here, and prepare seven young bulls and seven rams for me to sacrifice." ²Balak followed his instructions, and the two of them sacrificed a young bull and a ram on each altar.

³Then Balaam said to Balak, "Stand here by your burnt offerings, and I will go to see if the LORD will respond to me. Then I will tell you whatever he reveals to me." So Balaam went alone to the top of a bare hill, ⁴and God met him there. Balaam said to him, "I have prepared seven altars and have sacrificed a young bull and a ram on each altar."

⁵The LORD gave Balaam a message for King Balak. Then he said, "Go back to Balak and give him my message."

⁶So Balaam returned and found the king standing beside his burnt offerings with all the officials of Moab. ⁷This was the message Balaam delivered:

> "Balak summoned me to come from Aram;
>> the king of Moab brought me from the eastern hills.
> 'Come,' he said, 'curse Jacob for me!
>> Come and announce Israel's doom.'
> ⁸But how can I curse those
>> whom God has not cursed?
> How can I condemn those
>> whom the LORD has not condemned?
> ⁹I see them from the cliff tops;
>> I watch them from the hills.
> I see a people who live by themselves,
>> set apart from other nations.
> ¹⁰Who can count Jacob's descendants, as numerous as dust?
>> Who can count even a fourth of Israel's people?
> Let me die like the righteous;
>> let my life end like theirs."

¹¹Then King Balak demanded of Balaam, "What have you done to me? I brought you

STEP 3

Trusting God

BIBLE READING: Numbers 23:18-24

We made a decision to turn our wills and our lives over to the care of God.

It is not uncommon to link our perceptions about God to our childhood experiences with people who played powerful roles in our life. If we have been victimized in the past by people who were capricious, abusive, distant, uncaring, or incompetent, we may now anticipate these qualities in God.

Just because God is a power greater than we are and the people who victimized us represented a power greater than we were, we must not conclude that God will harm us if we entrust our life to him. Jesus tells us that he didn't entrust himself to men because he knew what was in their hearts. Nevertheless, he voluntarily turned his life over to the will of God the Father. "It is better to take refuge in the LORD than to trust in people" (Psalm 118:8).

We may have learned in the past that putting confidence in people brings only pain and disappointment. We can't let this keep us from ever trusting again. In working through Step Three we can make a healthy decision to turn our will and our life over to the only one who is worthy of being trusted. The Bible tells us, "God is not a man, so he does not lie. He is not human, so he does not change his mind" (Numbers 23:19). And God has said, "I will never fail you. I will never abandon you" (Hebrews 13:5).

We know that we can't make it all alone. But now we can stop being the victim. We can turn our life over to Someone who is really able to care for our needs. *Turn to page 255, Deuteronomy 30.*

tyndal.es/lrbstep3

to curse my enemies. Instead, you have blessed them!"

¹²But Balaam replied, "I will speak only the message that the LORD puts in my mouth."

Balaam's Second Message

¹³Then King Balak told him, "Come with me to another place. There you will see another part of the nation of Israel, but not all of them. Curse at least that many!" ¹⁴So Balak took Balaam to the plateau of Zophim on Pisgah Peak. He built seven altars there and offered a young bull and a ram on each altar.

¹⁵Then Balaam said to the king, "Stand here by your burnt offerings while I go over there to meet the LORD."

¹⁶And the LORD met Balaam and gave him a message. Then he said, "Go back to Balak and give him my message."

¹⁷So Balaam returned and found the king standing beside his burnt offerings with all the officials of Moab. "What did the LORD say?" Balak asked eagerly.

¹⁸This was the message Balaam delivered:

"Rise up, Balak, and listen!
Hear me, son of Zippor.
¹⁹God is not a man, so he does not lie.
He is not human, so he does not
change his mind.
Has he ever spoken and failed to act?
Has he ever promised and not carried it
through?
²⁰Listen, I received a command to bless;
God has blessed, and I cannot
reverse it!
²¹No misfortune is in his plan for Jacob;
no trouble is in store for Israel.
For the LORD their God is with them;
he has been proclaimed their king.
²²God brought them out of Egypt;
for them he is as strong as a wild ox.
²³No curse can touch Jacob;
no magic has any power against
Israel.

23:28 Or *overlooking Jeshimon.*

For now it will be said of Jacob,
'What wonders God has done for
Israel!'
²⁴These people rise up like a lioness,
like a majestic lion rousing itself.
They refuse to rest
until they have feasted on prey,
drinking the blood of the slaughtered!"

²⁵Then Balak said to Balaam, "Fine, but if you won't curse them, at least don't bless them!"

²⁶But Balaam replied to Balak, "Didn't I tell you that I can do only what the LORD tells me?"

Balaam's Third Message

²⁷Then King Balak said to Balaam, "Come, I will take you to one more place. Perhaps it will please God to let you curse them from there."

²⁸So Balak took Balaam to the top of Mount Peor, overlooking the wasteland.* ²⁹Balaam again told Balak, "Build me seven altars, and prepare seven young bulls and seven rams for me to sacrifice." ³⁰So Balak did as Balaam ordered and offered a young bull and a ram on each altar.

CHAPTER 24

By now Balaam realized that the LORD was determined to bless Israel, so he did not resort to divination as before. Instead, he turned and looked out toward the wilderness, ²where he saw the people of Israel camped, tribe by tribe. Then the Spirit of God came upon him, ³and this is the message he delivered:

"This is the message of Balaam son
of Beor,
the message of the man whose eyes see
clearly,
⁴the message of one who hears the words
of God,
who sees a vision from the Almighty,
who bows down with eyes wide open:

23:18-24 Through Balaam's second prophecy, God affirmed not only his sovereignty but also his truthful character: "God is not a man, so he does not lie. He is not human, so he does not change his mind." The future of Israel was secure because a sovereign God had chosen it for his glory and promised to bless it. The New Testament tells us that God chose us before the world was made and that he has blessed us with every spiritual blessing in Christ (Ephesians 1:3-14). Worldly wisdom, as illustrated by Balaam, cannot compare with the wisdom of God.

23:18-24 Israel's wilderness experience demonstrates not only the faithlessness of the Exodus generation but also the loving care of our sovereign God. Though the Israelites made numerous mistakes, God graciously led them to the Promised Land. Our life is also riddled with failures and sins, but God is still able and willing to lead us along the road to recovery.

⁵How beautiful are your tents, O Jacob;
  how lovely are your homes, O Israel!
⁶They spread before me like palm groves,*
  like gardens by the riverside.
They are like tall trees planted by the LORD,
  like cedars beside the waters.
⁷Water will flow from their buckets;
  their offspring have all they need.
Their king will be greater than Agag;
  their kingdom will be exalted.
⁸God brought them out of Egypt;
  for them he is as strong as a wild ox.
He devours all the nations that oppose
      him,
  breaking their bones in pieces,
  shooting them with arrows.
⁹Like a lion, Israel crouches and lies down;
  like a lioness, who dares to arouse her?
Blessed is everyone who blesses you,
      O Israel,
  and cursed is everyone who curses you."

¹⁰King Balak flew into a rage against Balaam. He angrily clapped his hands and shouted, "I called you to curse my enemies! Instead, you have blessed them three times. ¹¹Now get out of here! Go back home! I promised to reward you richly, but the LORD has kept you from your reward."

¹²Balaam told Balak, "Don't you remember what I told your messengers? I said, ¹³'Even if Balak were to give me his palace filled with silver and gold, I would be powerless to do anything against the will of the LORD.' I told you that I could say only what the LORD says! ¹⁴Now I am returning to my own people. But first let me tell you what the Israelites will do to your people in the future."

Balaam's Final Messages
¹⁵This is the message Balaam delivered:

"This is the message of Balaam son of Beor,
  the message of the man whose eyes see
      clearly,
¹⁶the message of one who hears the words
      of God,
  who has knowledge from the Most High,

who sees a vision from the Almighty,
  who bows down with eyes wide open:
¹⁷I see him, but not here and now.
  I perceive him, but far in the distant
      future.
A star will rise from Jacob;
  a scepter will emerge from Israel.
It will crush the heads of Moab's people,
  cracking the skulls* of the people of
      Sheth.
¹⁸Edom will be taken over,
  and Seir, its enemy, will be conquered,
  while Israel marches on in triumph.
¹⁹A ruler will rise in Jacob
  who will destroy the survivors of Ir."

²⁰Then Balaam looked over toward the people of Amalek and delivered this message:

"Amalek was the greatest of nations,
  but its destiny is destruction!"

²¹Then he looked over toward the Kenites and delivered this message:

"Your home is secure;
  your nest is set in the rocks.
²²But the Kenites will be destroyed
  when Assyria* takes you captive."

²³Balaam concluded his messages by saying:

"Alas, who can survive
  unless God has willed it?
²⁴Ships will come from the coasts of Cyprus*;
  they will oppress Assyria and afflict
      Eber,
  but they, too, will be utterly destroyed."

²⁵Then Balaam left and returned home, and Balak also went on his way.

CHAPTER 25
Moab Seduces Israel
While the Israelites were camped at Acacia Grove,* some of the men defiled themselves by having* sexual relations with local Moabite women. ²These women invited them to attend sacrifices to their gods, so the Israelites feasted with them and worshiped the gods of

24:6 Or *like a majestic valley.* 24:17 As in Samaritan Pentateuch; the meaning of the Hebrew word is uncertain. 24:22 Hebrew *Asshur;* also in 24:24. 24:24 Hebrew *Kittim.* 25:1a Hebrew *Shittim.* 25:1b As in Greek version; Hebrew reads *some of the men began having.*

25:1-18 Even after God's victory over the evil intentions of Balak, the Israelites were quickly seduced into Canaanite worship. Through this story we see how clever and diverse Satan's strategies are. When unsuccessful in his attack from the outside (22:1–24:25), he succeeded in bringing decay from within. Israelite participation in immoral Canaanite worship practices resulted in the judgment and death of 24,000 of God's people. This shows how important the personal morality of God's people is to him.

Moab. ³In this way, Israel joined in the worship of Baal of Peor, causing the LORD's anger to blaze against his people.

⁴The LORD issued the following command to Moses: "Seize all the ringleaders and execute them before the LORD in broad daylight, so his fierce anger will turn away from the people of Israel."

⁵So Moses ordered Israel's judges, "Each of you must put to death the men under your authority who have joined in worshiping Baal of Peor."

⁶Just then one of the Israelite men brought a Midianite woman into his tent, right before the eyes of Moses and all the people, as everyone was weeping at the entrance of the Tabernacle.* ⁷When Phinehas son of Eleazar and grandson of Aaron the priest saw this, he jumped up and left the assembly. He took a spear ⁸and rushed after the man into his tent. Phinehas thrust the spear all the way through the man's body and into the woman's stomach. So the plague against the Israelites was stopped, ⁹but not before 24,000 people had died.

¹⁰Then the LORD said to Moses, ¹¹"Phinehas son of Eleazar and grandson of Aaron the priest has turned my anger away from the Israelites by being as zealous among them as I was. So I stopped destroying all Israel as I had intended to do in my zealous anger. ¹²Now tell him that I am making my special covenant of peace with him. ¹³In this covenant, I give him and his descendants a permanent right to the priesthood, for in his zeal for me, his God, he purified the people of Israel, making them right with me.*"

¹⁴The Israelite man killed with the Midianite woman was named Zimri son of Salu, the leader of a family from the tribe of Simeon. ¹⁵The woman's name was Cozbi; she was the daughter of Zur, the leader of a Midianite clan.

¹⁶Then the LORD said to Moses, ¹⁷"Attack the Midianites and destroy them, ¹⁸because they assaulted you with deceit and tricked you into worshiping Baal of Peor, and because of Cozbi, the daughter of a Midianite leader, who was killed at the time of the plague because of what happened at Peor."

CHAPTER 26
The Second Registration of Israel's Troops

After the plague had ended,* the LORD said to Moses and to Eleazar son of Aaron the priest, ²"From the whole community of Israel, record the names of all the warriors by their families. List all the men twenty years old or older who are able to go to war."

³So there on the plains of Moab beside the Jordan River, across from Jericho, Moses and Eleazar the priest issued these instructions to the leaders of Israel: ⁴"List all the men of Israel twenty years old and older, just as the LORD commanded Moses."

This is the record of all the descendants of Israel who came out of Egypt.

The Tribe of Reuben

⁵These were the clans descended from the sons of Reuben, Jacob's* oldest son:

The Hanochite clan, named after their ancestor Hanoch.

The Palluite clan, named after their ancestor Pallu.

⁶ The Hezronite clan, named after their ancestor Hezron.

The Carmite clan, named after their ancestor Carmi.

⁷These were the clans of Reuben. Their registered troops numbered 43,730.

⁸Pallu was the ancestor of Eliab, ⁹and Eliab was the father of Nemuel, Dathan, and Abiram. This Dathan and Abiram are the same community leaders who conspired with Korah against Moses and Aaron, rebelling against the LORD. ¹⁰But the earth opened up its mouth and swallowed them with Korah, and fire devoured 250 of their followers. This served as a warning to the entire nation of Israel. ¹¹However, the sons of Korah did not die that day.

The Tribe of Simeon

¹²These were the clans descended from the sons of Simeon:

The Jemuelite clan, named after their ancestor Jemuel.*

The Jaminite clan, named after their ancestor Jamin.

25:6 Hebrew *the Tent of Meeting*. 25:13 Or *he made atonement for the people of Israel*. 26:1 The initial phrase in verse 26:1 is numbered 25:19 in Hebrew text. 26:5 Hebrew *Israel's;* see note on 1:20-21b. 26:12 As in Syriac version (see also Gen 46:10; Exod 6:15); Hebrew reads *Nemuelite . . . Nemuel*.

26:1-65 The census in chapter 1 was taken primarily for organizational purposes. This later census was intended to prepare Israel for the conquest of the Promised Land and the later division of property. The decrease in numbers from the census taken 40 years earlier was due primarily to the judgments suffered by Israel in the wilderness.

The Jakinite clan, named after their ancestor Jakin.
[13] The Zoharite clan, named after their ancestor Zohar.*
The Shaulite clan, named after their ancestor Shaul.

[14]These were the clans of Simeon. Their registered troops numbered 22,200.

The Tribe of Gad
[15]These were the clans descended from the sons of Gad:
The Zephonite clan, named after their ancestor Zephon.
The Haggite clan, named after their ancestor Haggi.
The Shunite clan, named after their ancestor Shuni.
[16] The Oznite clan, named after their ancestor Ozni.
The Erite clan, named after their ancestor Eri.
[17] The Arodite clan, named after their ancestor Arodi.*
The Arelite clan, named after their ancestor Areli.

[18]These were the clans of Gad. Their registered troops numbered 40,500.

The Tribe of Judah
[19]Judah had two sons, Er and Onan, who had died in the land of Canaan. [20]These were the clans descended from Judah's surviving sons:
The Shelanite clan, named after their ancestor Shelah.
The Perezite clan, named after their ancestor Perez.
The Zerahite clan, named after their ancestor Zerah.
[21]These were the subclans descended from the Perezites:
The Hezronites, named after their ancestor Hezron.
The Hamulites, named after their ancestor Hamul.

[22]These were the clans of Judah. Their registered troops numbered 76,500.

The Tribe of Issachar
[23]These were the clans descended from the sons of Issachar:

The Tolaite clan, named after their ancestor Tola.
The Puite clan, named after their ancestor Puah.*
[24] The Jashubite clan, named after their ancestor Jashub.
The Shimronite clan, named after their ancestor Shimron.

[25]These were the clans of Issachar. Their registered troops numbered 64,300.

The Tribe of Zebulun
[26]These were the clans descended from the sons of Zebulun:
The Seredite clan, named after their ancestor Sered.
The Elonite clan, named after their ancestor Elon.
The Jahleelite clan, named after their ancestor Jahleel.

[27]These were the clans of Zebulun. Their registered troops numbered 60,500.

The Tribe of Manasseh
[28]Two clans were descended from Joseph through Manasseh and Ephraim.
[29]These were the clans descended from Manasseh:
The Makirite clan, named after their ancestor Makir.
The Gileadite clan, named after their ancestor Gilead, Makir's son.
[30]These were the subclans descended from the Gileadites:
The Iezerites, named after their ancestor Iezer.
The Helekites, named after their ancestor Helek.
[31] The Asrielites, named after their ancestor Asriel.
The Shechemites, named after their ancestor Shechem.
[32] The Shemidaites, named after their ancestor Shemida.
The Hepherites, named after their ancestor Hepher.
[33] (One of Hepher's descendants, Zelophehad, had no sons, but his daughters' names were Mahlah, Noah, Hoglah, Milcah, and Tirzah.)
[34]These were the clans of Manasseh. Their registered troops numbered 52,700.

26:13 As in parallel texts at Gen 46:10 and Exod 6:15; Hebrew reads *Zerahite . . . Zerah.* 26:17 As in Samaritan Pentateuch and Greek and Syriac versions (see also Gen 46:16); Hebrew reads *Arod.* 26:23 As in Samaritan Pentateuch, Greek and Syriac versions, and Latin Vulgate (see also 1 Chr 7:1); Hebrew reads *The Punite clan, named after its ancestor Puvah.*

The Tribe of Ephraim

35 These were the clans descended from the sons of Ephraim:

The Shuthelahite clan, named after their ancestor Shuthelah.

The Bekerite clan, named after their ancestor Beker.

The Tahanite clan, named after their ancestor Tahan.

36 This was the subclan descended from the Shuthelahites:

The Eranites, named after their ancestor Eran.

37 These were the clans of Ephraim. Their registered troops numbered 32,500.

These clans of Manasseh and Ephraim were all descendants of Joseph.

The Tribe of Benjamin

38 These were the clans descended from the sons of Benjamin:

The Belaite clan, named after their ancestor Bela.

The Ashbelite clan, named after their ancestor Ashbel.

The Ahiramite clan, named after their ancestor Ahiram.

39 The Shuphamite clan, named after their ancestor Shupham.*

The Huphamite clan, named after their ancestor Hupham.

40 These were the subclans descended from the Belaites:

The Ardites, named after their ancestor Ard.*

The Naamites, named after their ancestor Naaman.

41 These were the clans of Benjamin. Their registered troops numbered 45,600.

The Tribe of Dan

42 These were the clans descended from the sons of Dan:

The Shuhamite clan, named after their ancestor Shuham.

43 These were the Shuhamite clans of Dan. Their registered troops numbered 64,400.

The Tribe of Asher

44 These were the clans descended from the sons of Asher:

The Imnite clan, named after their ancestor Imnah.

The Ishvite clan, named after their ancestor Ishvi.

The Beriite clan, named after their ancestor Beriah.

45 These were the subclans descended from the Beriites:

The Heberites, named after their ancestor Heber.

The Malkielites, named after their ancestor Malkiel.

46 Asher also had a daughter named Serah.

47 These were the clans of Asher. Their registered troops numbered 53,400.

The Tribe of Naphtali

48 These were the clans descended from the sons of Naphtali:

The Jahzeelite clan, named after their ancestor Jahzeel.

The Gunite clan, named after their ancestor Guni.

49 The Jezerite clan, named after their ancestor Jezer.

The Shillemite clan, named after their ancestor Shillem.

50 These were the clans of Naphtali. Their registered troops numbered 45,400.

Results of the Registration

51 In summary, the registered troops of all Israel numbered 601,730.

52 Then the LORD said to Moses, 53 "Divide the land among the tribes, and distribute the grants of land in proportion to the tribes' populations, as indicated by the number of names on the list. 54 Give the larger tribes more land and the smaller tribes less land, each group receiving a grant in proportion to the size of its population. 55 But you must assign the land by lot, and give land to each ancestral tribe according to the number of names on the list. 56 Each grant of land must be assigned by lot among the larger and smaller tribal groups."

The Tribe of Levi

57 This is the record of the Levites who were counted according to their clans:

The Gershonite clan, named after their ancestor Gershon.

The Kohathite clan, named after their ancestor Kohath.

26:39 As in some Hebrew manuscripts, Samaritan Pentateuch, Greek and Syriac versions, and Latin Vulgate; most Hebrew manuscripts read Shephupham. 26:40 As in Samaritan Pentateuch, some Greek manuscripts, and Latin Vulgate; Hebrew lacks named after their ancestor Ard.

The Merarite clan, named after their ancestor Merari.

[58]The Libnites, the Hebronites, the Mahlites, the Mushites, and the Korahites were all subclans of the Levites.

Now Kohath was the ancestor of Amram, [59]and Amram's wife was named Jochebed. She also was a descendant of Levi, born among the Levites in the land of Egypt. Amram and Jochebed became the parents of Aaron, Moses, and their sister, Miriam. [60]To Aaron were born Nadab, Abihu, Eleazar, and Ithamar. [61]But Nadab and Abihu died when they burned before the LORD the wrong kind of fire, different than he had commanded.

[62]The men from the Levite clans who were one month old or older numbered 23,000. But the Levites were not included in the registration of the rest of the people of Israel because they were not given an allotment of land when it was divided among the Israelites.

[63]So these are the results of the registration of the people of Israel as conducted by Moses and Eleazar the priest on the plains of Moab beside the Jordan River, across from Jericho. [64]Not one person on this list had been among those listed in the previous registration taken by Moses and Aaron in the wilderness of Sinai. [65]For the LORD had said of them, "They will all die in the wilderness." Not one of them survived except Caleb son of Jephunneh and Joshua son of Nun.

CHAPTER 27
The Daughters of Zelophehad

One day a petition was presented by the daughters of Zelophehad—Mahlah, Noah, Hoglah, Milcah, and Tirzah. Their father, Zelophehad, was a descendant of Hepher son of Gilead, son of Makir, son of Manasseh, son of Joseph. [2]These women stood before Moses, Eleazar the priest, the tribal leaders, and the entire community at the entrance of the Tabernacle.* [3]"Our father died in the wilderness," they said. "He was not among Ko-

rah's followers, who rebelled against the LORD; he died because of his own sin. But he had no sons. [4]Why should the name of our father disappear from his clan just because he had no sons? Give us property along with the rest of our relatives."

[5]So Moses brought their case before the LORD. [6]And the LORD replied to Moses, [7]"The claim of the daughters of Zelophehad is legitimate. You must give them a grant of land along with their father's relatives. Assign them the property that would have been given to their father.

[8]"And give the following instructions to the people of Israel: If a man dies and has no son, then give his inheritance to his daughters. [9]And if he has no daughter either, transfer his inheritance to his brothers. [10]If he has no brothers, give his inheritance to his father's brothers. [11]But if his father has no brothers, give his inheritance to the nearest relative in his clan. This is a legal requirement for the people of Israel, just as the LORD commanded Moses."

Joshua Chosen to Lead Israel

[12]One day the LORD said to Moses, "Climb one of the mountains east of the river,* and look out over the land I have given the people of Israel. [13]After you have seen it, you will die like your brother, Aaron, [14]for you both rebelled against my instructions in the wilderness of Zin. When the people of Israel rebelled, you failed to demonstrate my holiness to them at the waters." (These are the waters of Meribah at Kadesh* in the wilderness of Zin.)

[15]Then Moses said to the LORD, [16]"O LORD, you are the God who gives breath to all creatures. Please appoint a new man as leader for the community. [17]Give them someone who will guide them wherever they go and will lead them into battle, so the community of the LORD will not be like sheep without a shepherd."

[18]The LORD replied, "Take Joshua son of Nun, who has the Spirit in him, and lay your

27:2 Hebrew *the Tent of Meeting.* 27:12 Or *the mountains of Abarim.* 27:14 Hebrew *waters of Meribath-kadesh.*

27:12-23 The torch of Israel's leadership was passed from Moses to Joshua. Moses was able to view the land of Canaan (27:12-14) but was not allowed to enter it because of his earlier failure. Rather than being self-centered and overcome with disappointment, Moses' greatest concern was still for his people. The attitude reflected in his words reveal his godly character: "Please appoint a new man as leader for the community. Give them someone who will guide them wherever they go and will lead them into battle, so the community of the LORD will not be like sheep without a shepherd." Moses was content with God's plan for him. Like Moses, we must learn to be content with God's plan for us, even when it brings us temporary disappointments. God always desires what is best for us.

hands on him. [19]Present him to Eleazar the priest before the whole community, and publicly commission him to lead the people. [20]Transfer some of your authority to him so the whole community of Israel will obey him. [21]When direction from the LORD is needed, Joshua will stand before Eleazar the priest, who will use the Urim—one of the sacred lots cast before the LORD—to determine his will. This is how Joshua and the rest of the community of Israel will determine everything they should do."

[22]So Moses did as the LORD commanded. He presented Joshua to Eleazar the priest and the whole community. [23]Moses laid his hands on him and commissioned him to lead the people, just as the LORD had commanded through Moses.

CHAPTER 28
The Daily Offerings

The LORD said to Moses, [2]"Give these instructions to the people of Israel: The offerings you present as special gifts are a pleasing aroma to me; they are my food. See to it that they are brought at the appointed times and offered according to my instructions.

[3]"Say to the people: This is the special gift you must present to the LORD as your daily burnt offering. You must offer two one-year-old male lambs with no defects. [4]Sacrifice one lamb in the morning and the other in the evening. [5]With each lamb you must offer a grain offering of two quarts* of choice flour mixed with one quart* of pure oil of pressed olives. [6]This is the regular burnt offering instituted at Mount Sinai as a special gift, a pleasing aroma to the LORD. [7]Along with it you must present the proper liquid offering of one quart of alcoholic drink with each lamb, poured out in the Holy Place as an offering to the LORD. [8]Offer the second lamb in the evening with the same grain offering and

liquid offering. It, too, is a special gift, a pleasing aroma to the LORD.

The Sabbath Offerings

[9]"On the Sabbath day, sacrifice two one-year-old male lambs with no defects. They must be accompanied by a grain offering of four quarts* of choice flour moistened with olive oil, and a liquid offering. [10]This is the burnt offering to be presented each Sabbath day, in addition to the regular burnt offering and its accompanying liquid offering.

The Monthly Offerings

[11]"On the first day of each month, present an extra burnt offering to the LORD of two young bulls, one ram, and seven one-year-old male lambs, all with no defects. [12]These must be accompanied by grain offerings of choice flour moistened with olive oil—six quarts* with each bull, four quarts with the ram, [13]and two quarts* with each lamb. This burnt offering will be a special gift, a pleasing aroma to the LORD. [14]You must also present a liquid offering with each sacrifice: two quarts* of wine for each bull, a third of a gallon* for the ram, and one quart* for each lamb. Present this monthly burnt offering on the first day of each month throughout the year.

[15]"On the first day of each month, you must also offer one male goat for a sin offering to the LORD. This is in addition to the regular burnt offering and its accompanying liquid offering.

Offerings for the Passover

[16]"On the fourteenth day of the first month,* you must celebrate the LORD's Passover. [17]On the following day—the fifteenth day of the month—a joyous, seven-day festival will begin, but no bread made with yeast may be eaten. [18]The first day of the festival will be an

28:5a Hebrew ¹/₁₀ of an ephah [2.2 liters]; also in 28:13, 21, 29. **28:5b** Hebrew ¼ of a hin [1 liter]; also in 28:7.
28:9 Hebrew ²/₁₀ of an ephah [4.4 liters]; also in 28:12, 20, 28. **28:12** Hebrew ³/₁₀ of an ephah [6.6 liters]; also in 28:20, 28. **28:14a** Hebrew ½ of a hin [2 liters]. **28:14b** Hebrew ⅓ of a hin [1.3 liters]. **28:14c** Hebrew ¼ of a hin [1 liter].
28:16 This day in the ancient Hebrew lunar calendar occurred in late March, April, or early May.

28:1-2 Just as the offerings were to be brought regularly, so our fellowship with God should be regular and voluntary. It should be a continuous, moment-by-moment experience. God desires more than ritual worship; he invites us to have a personal, day-by-day relationship with him.
28:1-8 Only through continuous fellowship with God could God's people expect victory as they entered the Promised Land. This is probably the reason for repeating the instructions for the burnt offering here—a reaffirmation of its significance for the new generation. By bringing the offering, a person was committing his or her life to God in a fresh way. In a similar way, the apostle Paul called us to present our body as a living sacrifice to God (Romans 12:1). This is an essential step for our spiritual growth. Only when we place our life in God's hands will he be able to change us through his power.

official day for holy assembly, and no ordinary work may be done on that day. ¹⁹As a special gift you must present a burnt offering to the LORD—two young bulls, one ram, and seven one-year-old male lambs, all with no defects. ²⁰These will be accompanied by grain offerings of choice flour moistened with olive oil—six quarts with each bull, four quarts with the ram, ²¹and two quarts with each of the seven lambs. ²²You must also offer a male goat as a sin offering to purify yourselves and make yourselves right with the LORD.* ²³Present these offerings in addition to your regular morning burnt offering. ²⁴On each of the seven days of the festival, this is how you must prepare the food offering that is presented as a special gift, a pleasing aroma to the LORD. These will be offered in addition to the regular burnt offerings and liquid offerings. ²⁵The seventh day of the festival will be another official day for holy assembly, and no ordinary work may be done on that day.

Offerings for the Festival of Harvest

²⁶"At the Festival of Harvest,* when you present the first of your new grain to the LORD, you must call an official day for holy assembly, and you may do no ordinary work on that day. ²⁷Present a special burnt offering on that day as a pleasing aroma to the LORD. It will consist of two young bulls, one ram, and seven one-year-old male lambs. ²⁸These will be accompanied by grain offerings of choice flour moistened with olive oil—six quarts with each bull, four quarts with the ram, ²⁹and two quarts with each of the seven lambs. ³⁰Also, offer one male goat to purify yourselves and make yourselves right with the LORD. ³¹Prepare these special burnt offerings, along with their liquid offerings, in addition to the regular burnt offering and its accompanying grain offering. Be sure that all the animals you sacrifice have no defects.

CHAPTER 29
Offerings for the Festival of Trumpets

"Celebrate the Festival of Trumpets each year on the first day of the appointed month in early autumn.* You must call an official day for holy assembly, and you may do no ordinary work. ²On that day you must present a burnt offering as a pleasing aroma to the LORD. It will consist of one young bull, one ram, and seven one-year-old male lambs, all with no defects. ³These must be accompanied by grain offerings of choice flour moistened with olive oil—six quarts* with the bull, four quarts* with the ram, ⁴and two quarts* with each of the seven lambs. ⁵In addition, you must sacrifice a male goat as a sin offering to purify yourselves and make yourselves right with the LORD.* ⁶These special sacrifices are in addition to your regular monthly and daily burnt offerings, and they must be given with their prescribed grain offerings and liquid offerings. These offerings are given as a special gift to the LORD, a pleasing aroma to him.

Offerings for the Day of Atonement

⁷"Ten days later, on the tenth day of the same month,* you must call another holy assembly. On that day, the Day of Atonement, the people must go without food and must do no ordinary work. ⁸You must present a burnt offering as a pleasing aroma to the LORD. It will consist of one young bull, one ram, and seven one-year-old male lambs, all with no defects. ⁹These offerings must be accompanied by the prescribed grain offerings of choice flour moistened with olive oil—six quarts of choice flour with the bull, four quarts of choice flour with the ram, ¹⁰and two quarts of choice flour with each of the seven lambs. ¹¹You must also sacrifice one male goat for a sin offering. This is in addition to the sin offering of atonement and the regular daily burnt offering with its grain offering, and their accompanying liquid offerings.

Offerings for the Festival of Shelters

¹²"Five days later, on the fifteenth day of the same month,* you must call another holy assembly of all the people, and you may do no ordinary work on that day. It is the beginning of the Festival of Shelters,* a seven-day festival

---

28:22 Or *to make atonement for yourselves;* also in 28:30. 28:26 Hebrew *Festival of Weeks.* This was later called the Festival of Pentecost (see Acts 2:1). It is celebrated today as Shavuot (or Shabuoth). 29:1 Hebrew *the first day of the seventh month.* This day in the ancient Hebrew lunar calendar occurred in September or October. This festival is celebrated today as Rosh Hashanah, the Jewish new year. 29:3a Hebrew ³/10 *of an ephah* [6.6 liters]; also in 29:9, 14. 29:3b Hebrew ²/10 *of an ephah* [4.4 liters]; also in 29:9, 14. 29:4 Hebrew ¹/10 *of an ephah* [2.2 liters]; also in 29:10, 15. 29:5 Or *to make atonement for yourselves.* 29:7 Hebrew *On the tenth day of the seventh month;* see 29:1 and the note there. This day in the ancient Hebrew lunar calendar occurred in September or October. It is celebrated today as Yom Kippur. 29:12a Hebrew *On the fifteenth day of the seventh month;* see 29:1, 7 and the notes there. This day in the ancient Hebrew lunar calendar occurred in late September, October, or early November. 29:12b Or *Festival of Booths,* or *Festival of Tabernacles.* This was earlier called the Festival of the Final Harvest or Festival of Ingathering (see Exod 23:16b). It is celebrated today as Sukkot (or Succoth).

to the LORD. ¹³On the first day of the festival, you must present a burnt offering as a special gift, a pleasing aroma to the LORD. It will consist of thirteen young bulls, two rams, and fourteen one-year-old male lambs, all with no defects. ¹⁴Each of these offerings must be accompanied by a grain offering of choice flour moistened with olive oil—six quarts for each of the thirteen bulls, four quarts for each of the two rams, ¹⁵and two quarts for each of the fourteen lambs. ¹⁶You must also sacrifice a male goat as a sin offering, in addition to the regular burnt offering with its accompanying grain offering and liquid offering.

¹⁷"On the second day of this seven-day festival, sacrifice twelve young bulls, two rams, and fourteen one-year-old male lambs, all with no defects. ¹⁸Each of these offerings of bulls, rams, and lambs must be accompanied by its prescribed grain offering and liquid offering. ¹⁹You must also sacrifice a male goat as a sin offering, in addition to the regular burnt offering with its accompanying grain offering and liquid offering.

²⁰"On the third day of the festival, sacrifice eleven young bulls, two rams, and fourteen one-year-old male lambs, all with no defects. ²¹Each of these offerings of bulls, rams, and lambs must be accompanied by its prescribed grain offering and liquid offering. ²²You must also sacrifice a male goat as a sin offering, in addition to the regular burnt offering with its accompanying grain offering and liquid offering.

²³"On the fourth day of the festival, sacrifice ten young bulls, two rams, and fourteen one-year-old male lambs, all with no defects. ²⁴Each of these offerings of bulls, rams, and lambs must be accompanied by its prescribed grain offering and liquid offering. ²⁵You must also sacrifice a male goat as a sin offering, in addition to the regular burnt offering with its accompanying grain offering and liquid offering.

²⁶"On the fifth day of the festival, sacrifice nine young bulls, two rams, and fourteen one-year-old male lambs, all with no defects. ²⁷Each of these offerings of bulls, rams, and lambs must be accompanied by its prescribed grain offering and liquid offering. ²⁸You must also sacrifice a male goat as a sin offering, in addition to the regular burnt offering with its accompanying grain offering and liquid offering.

²⁹"On the sixth day of the festival, sacrifice eight young bulls, two rams, and fourteen one-year-old male lambs, all with no defects. ³⁰Each of these offerings of bulls, rams, and lambs must be accompanied by its prescribed grain offering and liquid offering. ³¹You must also sacrifice a male goat as a sin offering, in addition to the regular burnt offering with its accompanying grain offering and liquid offering.

³²"On the seventh day of the festival, sacrifice seven young bulls, two rams, and fourteen one-year-old male lambs, all with no defects. ³³Each of these offerings of bulls, rams, and lambs must be accompanied by its prescribed grain offering and liquid offering. ³⁴You must also sacrifice one male goat as a sin offering, in addition to the regular burnt offering with its accompanying grain offering and liquid offering.

³⁵"On the eighth day of the festival, proclaim another holy day. You must do no ordinary work on that day. ³⁶You must present a burnt offering as a special gift, a pleasing aroma to the LORD. It will consist of one young bull, one ram, and seven one-year-old male lambs, all with no defects. ³⁷Each of these offerings must be accompanied by its prescribed grain offering and liquid offering. ³⁸You must also sacrifice one male goat as a sin offering, in addition to the regular burnt offering with its accompanying grain offering and liquid offering.

³⁹"You must present these offerings to the LORD at your annual festivals. These are in addition to the sacrifices and offerings you present in connection with vows, or as voluntary offerings, burnt offerings, grain offerings, liquid offerings, or peace offerings."

⁴⁰*So Moses gave all of these instructions to the people of Israel as the LORD had commanded him.

CHAPTER 30
Laws concerning Vows

¹*Then Moses summoned the leaders of the tribes of Israel and told them, "This is what the LORD has commanded: ²A man who makes a vow to the LORD or makes a pledge under oath must never break it. He must do exactly what he said he would do.

³"If a young woman makes a vow to the LORD or a pledge under oath while she is still living at her father's home, ⁴and her father hears of the vow or pledge and does not object to it, then all her vows and pledges will stand. ⁵But if her father refuses to let her fulfill the vow or pledge on the day he hears of

---

29:40 Verse 29:40 is numbered 30:1 in Hebrew text. **30:1** Verses 30:1-16 are numbered 30:2-17 in Hebrew text.

it, then all her vows and pledges will become invalid. The LORD will forgive her because her father would not let her fulfill them.

⁶"Now suppose a young woman makes a vow or binds herself with an impulsive pledge and later marries. ⁷If her husband learns of her vow or pledge and does not object on the day he hears of it, her vows and pledges will stand. ⁸But if her husband refuses to accept her vow or impulsive pledge on the day he hears of it, he nullifies her commitments, and the LORD will forgive her. ⁹If, however, a woman is a widow or is divorced, she must fulfill all her vows and pledges.

¹⁰"But suppose a woman is married and living in her husband's home when she makes a vow or binds herself with a pledge. ¹¹If her husband hears of it and does not object to it, her vow or pledge will stand. ¹²But if her husband refuses to accept it on the day he hears of it, her vow or pledge will be nullified, and the LORD will forgive her. ¹³So her husband may either confirm or nullify any vows or pledges she makes to deny herself. ¹⁴But if he does not object on the day he hears of it, then he is agreeing to all her vows and pledges. ¹⁵If he waits more than a day and then tries to nullify a vow or pledge, he will be punished for her guilt."

¹⁶These are the regulations the LORD gave Moses concerning relationships between a man and his wife, and between a father and a young daughter who still lives at home.

CHAPTER 31
Conquest of the Midianites

Then the LORD said to Moses, ²"On behalf of the people of Israel, take revenge on the Midianites for leading them into idolatry. After that, you will die and join your ancestors."

³So Moses said to the people, "Choose some men, and arm them to fight the LORD's war of revenge against Midian. ⁴From each tribe of Israel, send 1,000 men into battle." ⁵So they chose 1,000 men from each tribe of Israel, a total of 12,000 men armed for battle. ⁶Then Moses sent them out, 1,000 men from each tribe, and Phinehas son of Eleazar the priest led them into battle. They carried along the holy objects of the sanctuary and the trumpets for sounding the charge. ⁷They attacked Midian as the LORD had commanded Moses, and they killed all the men. ⁸All five of the Midianite kings—Evi, Rekem, Zur, Hur, and Reba—died in the battle. They also killed Balaam son of Beor with the sword.

⁹Then the Israelite army captured the Midianite women and children and seized their cattle and flocks and all their wealth as plunder. ¹⁰They burned all the towns and villages where the Midianites had lived. ¹¹After they had gathered the plunder and captives, both people and animals, ¹²they brought them all to Moses and Eleazar the priest, and to the whole community of Israel, which was camped on the plains of Moab beside the Jordan River, across from Jericho. ¹³Moses, Eleazar the priest, and all the leaders of the community went to meet them outside the camp. ¹⁴But Moses was furious with all the generals and captains* who had returned from the battle.

¹⁵"Why have you let all the women live?" he demanded. ¹⁶"These are the very ones who followed Balaam's advice and caused the people of Israel to rebel against the LORD at Mount Peor. They are the ones who caused the plague to strike the LORD's people. ¹⁷So kill all the boys and all the women who have had intercourse with a man. ¹⁸Only the young girls who are virgins may live; you may keep them for yourselves. ¹⁹And all of you who have killed anyone or touched a dead body must stay outside the camp for seven days. You must purify yourselves and your captives on the third and seventh days. ²⁰Purify all your clothing, too, and everything made of leather, goat hair, or wood."

²¹Then Eleazar the priest said to the men who were in the battle, "The LORD has given Moses this legal requirement: ²²Anything made of gold, silver, bronze, iron, tin, or lead—²³that is, all metals that do not burn—must be passed through fire in order to be made ceremonially pure. These metal objects must then be further purified with the water of purification. But everything that burns must be purified by the water alone. ²⁴On the seventh day you must wash your clothes and be purified. Then you may return to the camp."

Division of the Plunder

²⁵And the LORD said to Moses, ²⁶"You and Eleazar the priest and the family leaders of each tribe are to make a list of all the plunder taken in the battle, including the people and animals. ²⁷Then divide the plunder into two parts, and give half to the men who fought the battle and half to the rest of the people. ²⁸From the army's portion, first give the LORD his share of the plunder—one of every 500 of

the prisoners and of the cattle, donkeys, sheep, and goats. ²⁹Give this share of the army's half to Eleazar the priest as an offering to the LORD. ³⁰From the half that belongs to the people of Israel, take one of every fifty of the prisoners and of the cattle, donkeys, sheep, goats, and other animals. Give this share to the Levites, who are in charge of maintaining the LORD's Tabernacle." ³¹So Moses and Eleazar the priest did as the LORD commanded Moses.

³²The plunder remaining from everything the fighting men had taken totaled 675,000 sheep and goats, ³³72,000 cattle, ³⁴61,000 donkeys, ³⁵and 32,000 virgin girls.

³⁶Half of the plunder was given to the fighting men. It totaled 337,500 sheep and goats, ³⁷of which 675 were the LORD's share; ³⁸36,000 cattle, of which 72 were the LORD's share; ³⁹30,500 donkeys, of which 61 were the LORD's share; ⁴⁰and 16,000 virgin girls, of whom 32 were the LORD's share. ⁴¹Moses gave all the LORD's share to Eleazar the priest, just as the LORD had directed him.

⁴²Half of the plunder belonged to the people of Israel, and Moses separated it from the half belonging to the fighting men. ⁴³It totaled 337,500 sheep and goats, ⁴⁴36,000 cattle, ⁴⁵30,500 donkeys, ⁴⁶and 16,000 virgin girls. ⁴⁷From the half-share given to the people, Moses took one of every fifty prisoners and animals and gave them to the Levites, who maintained the LORD's Tabernacle. All this was done as the LORD had commanded Moses.

⁴⁸Then all the generals and captains came to Moses ⁴⁹and said, "We, your servants, have accounted for all the men who went out to battle under our command; not one of us is missing! ⁵⁰So we are presenting the items of gold we captured as an offering to the LORD from our share of the plunder— armbands, bracelets, rings, earrings, and necklaces. This will purify our lives before the LORD and make us right with him.*"

⁵¹So Moses and Eleazar the priest received the gold from all the military commanders—all kinds of jewelry and crafted objects. ⁵²In all, the gold that the generals and captains presented as a gift to the LORD weighed about 420 pounds.* ⁵³All the fighting men had taken some of the plunder for themselves. ⁵⁴So Moses and Eleazar the priest accepted the gifts from the generals and captains and brought the gold to the Taber-nacle* as a reminder to the LORD that the people of Israel belong to him.

CHAPTER 32
The Tribes East of the Jordan

The tribes of Reuben and Gad owned vast numbers of livestock. So when they saw that the lands of Jazer and Gilead were ideally suited for their flocks and herds, ²they came to Moses, Eleazar the priest, and the other leaders of the community. They said, ³"Notice the towns of Ataroth, Dibon, Jazer, Nimrah, Heshbon, Elealeh, Sibmah,* Nebo, and Beon. ⁴The LORD has conquered this whole area for the community of Israel, and it is ideally suited for all our livestock. ⁵If we have found favor with you, please let us have this land as our property instead of giving us land across the Jordan River."

⁶"Do you intend to stay here while your brothers go across and do all the fighting?" Moses asked the men of Gad and Reuben. ⁷"Why do you want to discourage the rest of the people of Israel from going across to the land the LORD has given them? ⁸Your ancestors did the same thing when I sent them from Kadesh-barnea to explore the land. ⁹After they went up to the valley of Eshcol and explored the land, they discouraged the people of Israel from entering the land the LORD was giving them. ¹⁰Then the LORD was very angry with them, and he vowed, ¹¹'Of all those I rescued from Egypt, no one who is twenty years old or older will ever see the land I swore to give to Abraham, Isaac, and Jacob, for they have not obeyed me whole-heartedly. ¹²The only exceptions are Caleb son of Jephunneh the Kenizzite and Joshua son of Nun, for they have wholeheartedly followed the LORD.'

¹³"The LORD was angry with Israel and made them wander in the wilderness for forty years until the entire generation that sinned in the LORD's sight had died. ¹⁴But here you are, a brood of sinners, doing exactly the same thing! You are making the LORD even angrier with Israel. ¹⁵If you turn away from him like this and he abandons them again in the wilderness, you will be responsible for destroying this entire nation!"

¹⁶But they approached Moses and said, "We simply want to build pens for our livestock and fortified towns for our wives and children. ¹⁷Then we will arm ourselves and lead our fellow Israelites into battle until we

---

31:50 Or *will make atonement for our lives before the LORD.* **31:52** Hebrew *16,750 shekels* [191 kilograms]. **31:54** Hebrew *the Tent of Meeting.* **32:3** As in Samaritan Pentateuch and Greek version (see also 32:38); Hebrew reads *Sebam.*

have brought them safely to their land. Meanwhile, our families will stay in the fortified towns we build here, so they will be safe from any attacks by the local people. [18]We will not return to our homes until all the people of Israel have received their portions of land. [19]But we do not claim any of the land on the other side of the Jordan. We would rather live here on the east side and accept this as our grant of land."

[20]Then Moses said, "If you keep your word and arm yourselves for the LORD's battles, [21]and if your troops cross the Jordan and keep fighting until the LORD has driven out his enemies, [22]then you may return when the LORD has conquered the land. You will have fulfilled your duty to the LORD and to the rest of the people of Israel. And the land on the east side of the Jordan will be your property from the LORD. [23]But if you fail to keep your word, then you will have sinned against the LORD, and you may be sure that your sin will find you out. [24]Go ahead and build towns for your families and pens for your flocks, but do everything you have promised."

[25]Then the men of Gad and Reuben replied, "We, your servants, will follow your instructions exactly. [26]Our children, wives, flocks, and cattle will stay here in the towns of Gilead. [27]But all who are able to bear arms will cross over to fight for the LORD, just as you have said."

[28]So Moses gave orders to Eleazar the priest, Joshua son of Nun, and the leaders of the clans of Israel. [29]He said, "The men of Gad and Reuben who are armed for battle must cross the Jordan with you to fight for the LORD. If they do, give them the land of Gilead as their property when the land is conquered. [30]But if they refuse to arm themselves and cross over with you, then they must accept land with the rest of you in the land of Canaan."

[31]The tribes of Gad and Reuben said again, "We are your servants, and we will do as the LORD has commanded! [32]We will cross the Jordan into Canaan fully armed to fight for the LORD, but our property will be here on this side of the Jordan."

[33]So Moses assigned land to the tribes of Gad, Reuben, and half the tribe of Manasseh son of Joseph. He gave them the territory of King Sihon of the Amorites and the land of King Og of Bashan—the whole land with its cities and surrounding lands.

[34]The descendants of Gad built the towns of Dibon, Ataroth, Aroer, [35]Atroth-shophan, Jazer, Jogbehah, [36]Beth-nimrah, and Beth-haran. These were all fortified towns with pens for their flocks.

[37]The descendants of Reuben built the towns of Heshbon, Elealeh, Kiriathaim, [38]Nebo, Baal-meon, and Sibmah. They changed the names of some of the towns they conquered and rebuilt.

[39]Then the descendants of Makir of the tribe of Manasseh went to Gilead and conquered it, and they drove out the Amorites living there. [40]So Moses gave Gilead to the Makirites, descendants of Manasseh, and they settled there. [41]The people of Jair, another clan of the tribe of Manasseh, captured many of the towns in Gilead and changed the name of that region to the Towns of Jair.* [42]Meanwhile, a man named Nobah captured the town of Kenath and its surrounding villages, and he renamed that area Nobah after himself.

CHAPTER 33
Remembering Israel's Journey

This is the route the Israelites followed as they marched out of Egypt under the leadership of Moses and Aaron. [2]At the LORD's direction, Moses kept a written record of their progress. These are the stages of their march, identified by the different places where they stopped along the way.

[3]They set out from the city of Rameses in early spring—on the fifteenth day of the first month*—on the morning after the first Passover celebration. The people of Israel left defiantly, in full view of all the Egyptians. [4]Meanwhile, the Egyptians were burying all

32:41 Hebrew *Havvoth-jair.* 33:3 This day in the ancient Hebrew lunar calendar occurred in late March, April, or early May.

33:1-49 Moses sketched out Israel's wilderness itinerary to remind the new generation of how God had graciously protected them and their ancestors since their exodus from Egyptian bondage. It was important to reaffirm these truths in order for the Israelites to spiritually prepare for the many challenges ahead as they conquered the Promised Land. Reviewing God's past acts of faithfulness was often used by Israel's leaders to prepare the people for future challenges. Likewise, praising God for past victories and blessings (answered prayer, a helping hand, progress in recovery) is an excellent way for us to prepare for future challenges.

their firstborn sons, whom the LORD had killed the night before. The LORD had defeated the gods of Egypt that night with great acts of judgment!

⁵After leaving Rameses, the Israelites set up camp at Succoth.

⁶Then they left Succoth and camped at Etham on the edge of the wilderness.

⁷They left Etham and turned back toward Pi-hahiroth, opposite Baal-zephon, and camped near Migdol.

⁸They left Pi-hahiroth* and crossed the Red Sea* into the wilderness beyond. Then they traveled for three days into the Etham wilderness and camped at Marah.

⁹They left Marah and camped at Elim, where there were twelve springs of water and seventy palm trees.

¹⁰They left Elim and camped beside the Red Sea.*

¹¹They left the Red Sea and camped in the wilderness of Sin.*

¹²They left the wilderness of Sin and camped at Dophkah.

¹³They left Dophkah and camped at Alush.

¹⁴They left Alush and camped at Rephidim, where there was no water for the people to drink.

¹⁵They left Rephidim and camped in the wilderness of Sinai.

¹⁶They left the wilderness of Sinai and camped at Kibroth-hattaavah.

¹⁷They left Kibroth-hattaavah and camped at Hazeroth.

¹⁸They left Hazeroth and camped at Rithmah.

¹⁹They left Rithmah and camped at Rimmon-perez.

²⁰They left Rimmon-perez and camped at Libnah.

²¹They left Libnah and camped at Rissah.

²²They left Rissah and camped at Kehelathah.

²³They left Kehelathah and camped at Mount Shepher.

²⁴They left Mount Shepher and camped at Haradah.

²⁵They left Haradah and camped at Makheloth.

²⁶They left Makheloth and camped at Tahath.

²⁷They left Tahath and camped at Terah.

²⁸They left Terah and camped at Mithcah.

²⁹They left Mithcah and camped at Hashmonah.

³⁰They left Hashmonah and camped at Moseroth.

³¹They left Moseroth and camped at Bene-jaakan.

³²They left Bene-jaakan and camped at Hor-haggidgad.

³³They left Hor-haggidgad and camped at Jotbathah.

³⁴They left Jotbathah and camped at Abronah.

³⁵They left Abronah and camped at Ezion-geber.

³⁶They left Ezion-geber and camped at Kadesh in the wilderness of Zin.

³⁷They left Kadesh and camped at Mount Hor, at the border of Edom. ³⁸While they were at the foot of Mount Hor, Aaron the priest was directed by the LORD to go up the mountain, and there he died. This happened in midsummer, on the first day of the fifth month* of the fortieth year after Israel's departure from Egypt.

³⁹Aaron was 123 years old when he died there on Mount Hor.

⁴⁰At that time the Canaanite king of Arad, who lived in the Negev in the land of Canaan, heard that the people of Israel were approaching his land.

⁴¹Meanwhile, the Israelites left Mount Hor and camped at Zalmonah.

⁴² Then they left Zalmonah and camped at Punon.

⁴³ They left Punon and camped at Oboth.

⁴⁴They left Oboth and camped at Iye-abarim on the border of Moab.

⁴⁵They left Iye-abarim* and camped at Dibon-gad.

⁴⁶They left Dibon-gad and camped at Almon-diblathaim.

⁴⁷They left Almon-diblathaim and camped in the mountains east of the river,* near Mount Nebo.

⁴⁸They left the mountains east of the river and camped on the plains of Moab beside the Jordan River, across from Jericho.

⁴⁹Along the Jordan River they camped from Beth-jeshimoth as far as the meadows of Acacia* on the plains of Moab.

⁵⁰While they were camped near the Jordan River on the plains of Moab opposite Jericho,

---

33:8a As in many Hebrew manuscripts, Samaritan Pentateuch, and Latin Vulgate (see also 33:7; most Hebrew manuscripts read *left from in front of Hahiroth.* **33:8b** Hebrew *the sea.* **33:10** Hebrew *sea of reeds;* also in 33:11. **33:11** The geographical name *Sin* is related to *Sinai* and should not be confused with the English word *sin.* **33:38** This day in the ancient Hebrew lunar calendar occurred in July or August. **33:45** As in 33:44; Hebrew reads *Iyim,* another name for Iye-abarim. **33:47** Or *the mountains of Abarim;* also in 33:48. **33:49** Hebrew *as far as Abel-shittim.*

the LORD said to Moses, [51]"Give the following instructions to the people of Israel: When you cross the Jordan River into the land of Canaan, [52]you must drive out all the people living there. You must destroy all their carved and molten images and demolish all their pagan shrines. [53]Take possession of the land and settle in it, because I have given it to you to occupy. [54]You must distribute the land among the clans by sacred lot and in proportion to their size. A larger portion of land will be allotted to each of the larger clans, and a smaller portion will be allotted to each of the smaller clans. The decision of the sacred lot is final. In this way, the portions of land will be divided among your ancestral tribes. [55]But if you fail to drive out the people who live in the land, those who remain will be like splinters in your eyes and thorns in your sides. They will harass you in the land where you live. [56]And I will do to you what I had planned to do to them."

CHAPTER 34
Boundaries of the Land

Then the LORD said to Moses, [2]"Give these instructions to the Israelites: When you come into the land of Canaan, which I am giving you as your special possession, these will be the boundaries. [3]The southern portion of your country will extend from the wilderness of Zin, along the edge of Edom. The southern boundary will begin on the east at the Dead Sea.* [4]It will then run south past Scorpion Pass* in the direction of Zin. Its southernmost point will be Kadesh-barnea, from which it will go to Hazar-addar, and on to Azmon. [5]From Azmon the boundary will turn toward the Brook of Egypt and end at the Mediterranean Sea.*

[6]"Your western boundary will be the coastline of the Mediterranean Sea.

[7]"Your northern boundary will begin at the Mediterranean Sea and run east to Mount Hor, [8]then to Lebo-hamath, and on through Zedad [9]and Ziphron to Hazar-enan. This will be your northern boundary.

[10]"The eastern boundary will start at Hazar-enan and run south to Shepham, [11]then down to Riblah on the east side of Ain. From there the boundary will run down along the eastern edge of the Sea of Galilee,* [12]and then along the Jordan River to the Dead Sea. These are the boundaries of your land."

[13]Then Moses told the Israelites, "This territory is the homeland you are to divide among yourselves by sacred lot. The LORD has commanded that the land be divided among the nine and a half remaining tribes. [14]The families of the tribes of Reuben, Gad, and half the tribe of Manasseh have already received their grants of land [15]on the east side of the Jordan River, across from Jericho toward the sunrise."

Leaders to Divide the Land

[16]And the LORD said to Moses, [17]"Eleazar the priest and Joshua son of Nun are the men designated to divide the grants of land among the people. [18]Enlist one leader from each tribe to help them with the task. [19]These are the tribes and the names of the leaders:

Tribe	Leader
Judah	Caleb son of Jephunneh
[20] Simeon	Shemuel son of Ammihud
[21] Benjamin	Elidad son of Kislon
[22] Dan	Bukki son of Jogli
[23] Manasseh son of Joseph	Hanniel son of Ephod

34:3 Hebrew *Salt Sea;* also in 34:12. 34:4 Or *the ascent of Akrabbim.* 34:5 Hebrew *the sea;* also in 34:6, 7.
34:11 Hebrew *Sea of Kinnereth.*

33:55-56 Here God sternly warned his people to *completely* cleanse the Promised Land of ungodly nations. This will become a major theme in the book of Joshua. The Israelites failed to completely push out their Canaanite neighbors, and, as a result, became like them. New Testament writers also warned of the dangers of associating too closely with people who might draw us away from God and his program for living (1 Corinthians 10:1-33; Hebrews 3:1–4:16). We all are susceptible to being led astray by others. If we don't use wisdom in choosing our relationships, we may find ourself falling back into our old ways.
34:1-29 The boundaries given here were based on faith in God. The Israelites had to trust that God would help them conquer the Promised Land. This great chapter of anticipation recalls God's promise to Abraham: "And I will give the entire land of Canaan, where you now live as a foreigner, to you and to your descendants. It will be their possession forever, and I will be their God" (Genesis 17:8). Those who were obedient to God would see the fulfillment of this promise that had been made hundreds of years earlier. God fulfills his promises, even though it sometimes takes longer than we expect. We must learn to trust him, following his plan with patience and humility.

²⁴ Ephraim son of Joseph . . . . Kemuel
son of Shiphtan
²⁵ Zebulun . . . . Elizaphan son of Parnach
²⁶ Issachar . . . . Paltiel son of Azzan
²⁷ Asher . . . . Ahihud son of Shelomi
²⁸ Naphtali. . . . . . . Pedahel son of Ammihud

²⁹ These are the men the LORD has appointed to divide the grants of land in Canaan among the Israelites."

CHAPTER 35
Towns for the Levites
While Israel was camped beside the Jordan on the plains of Moab across from Jericho, the LORD said to Moses, ² "Command the people of Israel to give to the Levites from their property certain towns to live in, along with the surrounding pasturelands. ³ These towns will be for the Levites to live in, and the surrounding lands will provide pasture for their cattle, flocks, and other livestock. ⁴ The pastureland assigned to the Levites around these towns will extend 1,500 feet* from the town walls in every direction. ⁵ Measure off 3,000 feet* outside the town walls in every direction—east, south, west, north—with the town at the center. This area will serve as the larger pastureland for the towns.

⁶ "Six of the towns you give the Levites will be cities of refuge, where a person who has accidentally killed someone can flee for safety. In addition, give them forty-two other towns. ⁷ In all, forty-eight towns with the surrounding pastureland will be given to the Levites. ⁸ These towns will come from the property of the people of Israel. The larger tribes will give more towns to the Levites, while the smaller tribes will give fewer. Each tribe will give property in proportion to the size of its land."

Cities of Refuge
⁹ The LORD said to Moses, ¹⁰ "Give the following instructions to the people of Israel.

"When you cross the Jordan into the land of Canaan, ¹¹ designate cities of refuge to which people can flee if they have killed someone accidentally. ¹² These cities will be places of protection from a dead person's relatives who want to avenge the death. The slayer must not be put to death before being tried by the community. ¹³ Designate six cities of refuge for yourselves, ¹⁴ three on the east side of the Jordan River and three on the west in the land of Canaan. ¹⁵ These cities are for the protection of Israelites, foreigners living among you, and traveling merchants. Anyone who accidentally kills someone may flee there for safety.

¹⁶ "But if someone strikes and kills another person with a piece of iron, it is murder, and the murderer must be executed. ¹⁷ Or if someone with a stone in his hand strikes and kills another person, it is murder, and the murderer must be put to death. ¹⁸ Or if someone strikes and kills another person with a wooden object, it is murder, and the murderer must be put to death. ¹⁹ The victim's nearest relative is responsible for putting the murderer to death. When they meet, the avenger must put the murderer to death. ²⁰ So if someone hates another person and waits in ambush, then pushes him or throws something at him and he dies, it is murder. ²¹ Or if someone hates another person and hits him with a fist and he dies, it is murder. In such cases, the avenger must put the murderer to death when they meet.

²² "But suppose someone pushes another person without having shown previous hostility, or throws something that unintentionally hits another person, ²³ or accidentally drops a huge stone on someone, though they were not enemies, and the person dies. ²⁴ If this should happen, the community must follow these regulations in making a judgment between the slayer and the avenger, the victim's nearest relative: ²⁵ The community must protect the slayer from the avenger and must escort the slayer back to live in the city of refuge to which he fled. There he must remain until the death of the high priest, who was anointed with the sacred oil.

²⁶ "But if the slayer ever leaves the limits of the city of refuge, ²⁷ and the avenger finds him outside the city and kills him, it will not be considered murder. ²⁸ The slayer should

---

35:4 Hebrew *1,000 cubits* [460 meters]. **35:5** Hebrew *2,000 cubits* [920 meters].

35:9-34 God provided cities of refuge as places where a person who had caused an accidental death could get a fair hearing. According to the law, murderers were subject to the death penalty. Even those guilty of manslaughter could be avenged by a near relative of the victim. The cities of refuge provided safety for those who had accidently killed someone. This system demanded the strict moral accountability of every Israelite, but it also provided a way of escape for those who had sinned unintentionally. Although God is just, he is also gracious.

have stayed inside the city of refuge until the death of the high priest. But after the death of the high priest, the slayer may return to his own property. [29]These are legal requirements for you to observe from generation to generation, wherever you may live.

[30]"All murderers must be put to death, but only if evidence is presented by more than one witness. No one may be put to death on the testimony of only one witness. [31]Also, you must never accept a ransom payment for the life of someone judged guilty of murder and subject to execution; murderers must always be put to death. [32]And never accept a ransom payment from someone who has fled to a city of refuge, allowing a slayer to return to his property before the death of the high priest. [33]This will ensure that the land where you live will not be polluted, for murder pollutes the land. And no sacrifice except the execution of the murderer can purify the land from murder.* [34]You must not defile the land where you live, for I live there myself. I am the LORD, who lives among the people of Israel."

CHAPTER 36
Women Who Inherit Property

Then the heads of the clans of Gilead—descendants of Makir, son of Manasseh, son of Joseph—came to Moses and the family leaders of Israel with a petition. [2]They said, "Sir, the LORD instructed you to divide the land by sacred lot among the people of Israel. You were told by the LORD to give the grant of land owned by our brother Zelophehad to his daughters. [3]But if they marry men from

35:33 Or *can make atonement for murder.*

another tribe, their grants of land will go with them to the tribe into which they marry. In this way, the total area of our tribal land will be reduced. [4]Then when the Year of Jubilee comes, their portion of land will be added to that of the new tribe, causing it to be lost forever to our ancestral tribe."

[5]So Moses gave the Israelites this command from the LORD: "The claim of the men of the tribe of Joseph is legitimate. [6]This is what the LORD commands concerning the daughters of Zelophehad: Let them marry anyone they like, as long as it is within their own ancestral tribe. [7]None of the territorial land may pass from tribe to tribe, for all the land given to each tribe must remain within the tribe to which it was first allotted. [8]The daughters throughout the tribes of Israel who are in line to inherit property must marry within their tribe, so that all the Israelites will keep their ancestral property. [9]No grant of land may pass from one tribe to another; each tribe of Israel must keep its allotted portion of land."

[10]The daughters of Zelophehad did as the LORD commanded Moses. [11]Mahlah, Tirzah, Hoglah, Milcah, and Noah all married cousins on their father's side. [12]They married into the clans of Manasseh son of Joseph. Thus, their inheritance of land remained within their ancestral tribe.

[13]These are the commands and regulations that the LORD gave to the people of Israel through Moses while they were camped on the plains of Moab beside the Jordan River across from Jericho.

REFLECTIONS ON NUMBERS

insights FROM THE TABERNACLE

In **Numbers 1:1** we see that Moses met God in the Tabernacle. This tent provided a place for the people to worship and represented God's presence among the Israelites. God's permanent presence in our life today can be found through a personal relationship with Jesus Christ. The apostle John recorded the ultimate fulfillment of the Old Testament Tabernacle: "So the Word [Christ] became human and made his home ['tabernacled'] among us" (John 1:14). With Christ in our life, we have a tangible means of "meeting with God" each and every day. God's presence in us will provide us with the help we need as we progress in recovery.

insights FROM THE NAZIRITE VOW

In **Numbers 6:1-21** the Nazirite vow is explained. This was a special commitment or promise made to God by which people could prove their personal devotion to God and demonstrate their seriousness in following him. Vows, in general, were voluntary, including the Nazirite vow. God's endorsement of this voluntary practice emphasizes how much he delights in obedience that flows from the heart as opposed to strict compliance to a legalistic set of rules.

insights FROM THE WILDERNESS

When things got tough in the wilderness, the people wanted to go back to their life of bondage in Egypt. In **Numbers 11:4-6** the people seemed to think that slavery was better than what they had there in the wilderness. They had stopped seeing with the eyes of faith and had lost sight of their goal and of God's guiding presence. The recovery journey is much like Israel's experience in the wilderness. As things get tough, it is easy to look back at our old life with longing. We need to keep our eyes on God and his promises for us. If we do, he will eventually lead us to a new and better life.

We often fail to see our greatest blessings. God had supplied the people of Israel with miraculous provisions of food—manna from heaven. But in **Numbers 11:4-6** they revealed their discontent by complaining to God. They were blind to the fact that supplying millions of people with ample provisions in a desert was an awesome miracle. We may complain about our circumstances in life, especially as we seek recovery. We need to stop and examine all the wonderful blessings we have. Then we can continue in the recovery process with the positive attitude of faith and thanksgiving toward God, our great provider.

The scouting mission was undoubtedly planned to encourage Israel. They would see for themselves the richness of the land God had promised them. The scouts' report in **Numbers 13:25-29** began with a glorious description of the Promised Land. But the mood abruptly changed as the Israelites began to focus on the "giants" that stood between them and their new life there. They failed to recognize God's power to overcome obstacles, no matter how great. Because of their lack of faith, they had to wander in the wilderness nearly forty more years. In recovery we need to take our eyes off the obstacles and focus on God, whose power is sufficient for any "giants" we might face.

Numbers 33:50-53 beautifully illustrates the relationship between God's sovereignty and man's responsibility. God gave the Israelites specific instructions about what they were to do to conquer Canaan. Yet he also affirmed that he had already given them the land. God promises us victory over many adversaries, but his victory cannot be claimed without active participation on our part. We need to take responsibility for ourself as we travel the road to recovery, but we should also look to God for help and guidance every step of the way.

DEUTERONOMY

THE BIG PICTURE

A. LOOKING TOWARD THE PAST: LESSONS FROM HISTORY (1:1–4:43)
   1. Commencing a Life of Defeat (1:1-46)
   2. Continuing a Life of Defeat (2:1-37)
   3. Concluding a Life of Defeat (3:1–4:43)
B. LOOKING AT THE PRESENT: LESSONS FROM LAW (4:44–26:19)
   1. The Decalogue and Its Explanation (4:44–11:32)
   2. The Directions for Israel (12:1–26:19)
      a. Ceremonial laws (12:1–16:17)
      b. Civil laws (16:18–20:20)
      c. Cultural laws (21:1–26:19)
C. LOOKING TOWARD THE PROMISE: LESSONS FROM PROPHECY (27:1–34:12)
   1. Reward or Rejection (27:1–28:68)
   2. Removal or Repentance (29:1–30:20)
   3. Reminders and Remembrances (31:1–34:12)

What might we do after failing persistently for almost 40 years? How might we set out a new pattern for living? In this book, the Israelites were about to enter the Promised Land. But they had been there before—four decades earlier. They had failed to believe in God's promise to give them the land of Canaan. So God had allowed them to wander in the wilderness for almost 40 years.

The Israelites were rebuilding. They were trying to make sense of 40 "wasted" years. They were looking for ways to overcome the fear that had caused them to fail once before. They needed a controlling purpose, some practical steps, a few guidelines for action. In the book of Deuteronomy, Moses gave them the guidelines they needed.

Moses began by telling the people to learn from their history. He reminded them not only of their past failures but also of God's mighty acts on their behalf. He encouraged them to use their past experiences—both good and bad—to set their faith on fire. Next, Moses directed the people to think about their present circumstances. He reviewed God's laws, giving them detailed instructions on how to respond to the challenges of life. Finally, Moses called the people to look toward the future. What would be the results of obeying God? What would be the consequences of disobeying him?

Rebuilding a broken life is serious business. In Deuteronomy, God gives that subject his full attention. He gives us essential guidelines for God's plan of victory. He shows how we can gain direction from the past, guidance for the present, and hope for the future. Deuteronomy is a handbook for rebuilders.

THE BOTTOM LINE

PURPOSE: To assist God's people as they live in the present by reviewing what God has done in the past and considering what God has promised to do in the future. AUTHOR: Moses. AUDIENCE: The people of Israel. DATE WRITTEN: Just before Israel's entrance into the Promised Land, about 1406 or 1405 B.C. SETTING: The plains of Moab. KEY VERSE: "He brought us out of Egypt so he could give us this land he had sworn to give our ancestors" (6:23). KEY EVENTS: Three sermons by Moses. KEY PERSON: Moses.

RECOVERY THEMES

Learning from the Past: For 40 years the Israelites had lived out the consequences of their weak faith and disobedience. But instead of hiding their past mistakes, Moses brought them out into the open. The past holds many lessons for us. Recovery demands that we learn from past failures, but we must also remember God's mighty acts on our behalf. Remembering that God walks with us through the recovery process should provide hope for the future and strength for the present.

A Program for the Present: One of our fears in looking at the past is that we will continue to live out our past mistakes. Moses made it clear that we need to learn from the past in order to live successfully in the present. He also reviewed the laws that God had given the Israelites to help them relate to each other in healthy and responsible ways. In recovery, these clear guidelines, or steps, can help us learn how to live responsibly and healthily. God does not leave us clueless—he provides a program to guide us as we live one day at a time.

Hope for the Future: In many ways our future is based on what we have learned from the past and on how we live in the present. Our successes or failures may well depend upon whether or not we choose to follow God's program for recovery and wholeness in the present. But the future is also based on God's faithfulness to us. He is a God who loves us, forgives us, and redeems us from our slavery to sin. As we live each day in recovery, we can be assured that God's love and grace are a present reality, providing hope for the future.

Rebuilding: How exciting to be able to start over again! This should be our attitude whenever we fail—anticipating a new start! The air must have been filled with excitement as the Israelites listened to Moses and anticipated their entrance into the Promised Land. There is hope! We can begin again! And God's grace in that process is limitless. The Israelites had failed repeatedly and miserably for 40 years, but God had now brought them to the edge of the Promised Land! They had yet another chance to begin again.

CHAPTER 1
Introduction to Moses' First Address

These are the words that Moses spoke to all the people of Israel while they were in the wilderness east of the Jordan River. They were camped in the Jordan Valley* near Suph, between Paran on one side and Tophel, Laban, Hazeroth, and Di-zahab on the other.

²Normally it takes only eleven days to travel from Mount Sinai* to Kadesh-barnea, going by way of Mount Seir. ³But forty years after the Israelites left Egypt, on the first day of the eleventh month,* Moses addressed the people of Israel, telling them everything the LORD had commanded him to say. ⁴This took place after he had defeated King Sihon of the Amorites, who ruled in Heshbon, and at Edrei had defeated King Og of Bashan, who ruled in Ashtaroth.

⁵While the Israelites were in the land of Moab east of the Jordan River, Moses carefully explained the LORD's instructions as follows.

The Command to Leave Sinai

⁶"When we were at Mount Sinai, the LORD our God said to us, 'You have stayed at this mountain long enough. ⁷It is time to break camp and move on. Go to the hill country of the Amorites and to all the neighboring regions—the Jordan Valley, the hill country, the western foothills,* the Negev, and the coastal plain. Go to the land of the Canaanites and to Lebanon, and all the way to the great Euphrates River. ⁸Look, I am giving all this land to you! Go in and occupy it, for it is the land the LORD swore to give to your ancestors Abraham, Isaac, and Jacob, and to all their descendants.'"

1:1 Hebrew *the Arabah;* also in 1:7. 1:2 Hebrew *Horeb,* another name for Sinai; also in 1:6, 19. 1:3 Hebrew *In the fortieth year, on the first day of the eleventh month.* This day in the ancient Hebrew lunar calendar occurred in January or February. 1:7 Hebrew *the Shephelah.*

1:1-5 This is a book of new hope; it is all about making a fresh start. The Israelites' failures were behind them. Opportunities for rebuilding their lives, their communities, and their nation lay ahead. At last Israel stood on the threshold of the Promised Land. It had taken them forty years to accomplish an 11-day journey because of their willful disobedience and lack of faith. Moses took time to give them principles for rebuilding their lives in the Israelite community and in their relationship with God.

1:6 "You have stayed at this mountain long enough." In every life there are moments when it is essential to move on. Times come when action is necessary. When we stay too long at one place, we stagnate. In rebuilding a life, we must be careful to advance according to God's schedule—neither lagging behind nor running ahead.

Moses Appoints Leaders from Each Tribe

[9]Moses continued, "At that time I told you, 'You are too great a burden for me to carry all by myself. [10]The LORD your God has increased your population, making you as numerous as the stars! [11]And may the LORD, the God of your ancestors, multiply you a thousand times more and bless you as he promised! [12]But you are such a heavy load to carry! How can I deal with all your problems and bickering? [13]Choose some well-respected men from each tribe who are known for their wisdom and understanding, and I will appoint them as your leaders.'

[14]"Then you responded, 'Your plan is a good one.' [15]So I took the wise and respected men you had selected from your tribes and appointed them to serve as judges and officials over you. Some were responsible for a thousand people, some for a hundred, some for fifty, and some for ten.

[16]"At that time I instructed the judges, 'You must hear the cases of your fellow Israelites and the foreigners living among you. Be perfectly fair in your decisions [17]and impartial in your judgments. Hear the cases of those who are poor as well as those who are rich. Don't be afraid of anyone's anger, for the decision you make is God's decision. Bring me any cases that are too difficult for you, and I will handle them.'

[18]"At that time I gave you instructions about everything you were to do.

Scouts Explore the Land

[19]"Then, just as the LORD our God commanded us, we left Mount Sinai and traveled through the great and terrifying wilderness, as you yourselves remember, and headed toward the hill country of the Amorites. When we arrived at Kadesh-barnea, [20]I said to you, 'You have now reached the hill country of the Amorites that the LORD our God is giving us. [21]Look! He has placed the land in front of you. Go and occupy it as the LORD, the God of your ancestors, has promised you. Don't be afraid! Don't be discouraged!'

[22]"But you all came to me and said, 'First, let's send out scouts to explore the land for us. They will advise us on the best route to take and which towns we should enter.'

[23]"This seemed like a good idea to me, so I chose twelve scouts, one from each of your tribes. [24]They headed for the hill country and came to the valley of Eshcol and explored it. [25]They picked some of its fruit and brought it back to us. And they reported, 'The land the LORD our God has given us is indeed a good land.'

Israel's Rebellion against the LORD

[26]"But you rebelled against the command of the LORD your God and refused to go in. [27]You complained in your tents and said, 'The LORD must hate us. That's why he has brought us here from Egypt—to hand us over to the Amorites to be slaughtered. [28]Where can we go? Our brothers have demoralized us with their report. They tell us, "The people of the land are taller and more powerful than we are, and their towns are large, with walls rising high into the sky! We even saw giants there—the descendants of Anak!"'

[29]"But I said to you, 'Don't be shocked or afraid of them! [30]The LORD your God is going ahead of you. He will fight for you, just as you saw him do in Egypt. [31]And you saw how the LORD your God cared for you all along the way as you traveled through the wilderness, just as a father cares for his child. Now he has brought you to this place.'

[32]"But even after all he did, you refused to trust the LORD your God, [33]who goes before you looking for the best places to camp, guiding you with a pillar of fire by night and a pillar of cloud by day.

[34]"When the LORD heard your complaining, he became very angry. So he solemnly swore, [35]'Not one of you from this wicked generation will live to see the good land I swore to give your ancestors, [36]except Caleb son of Jephunneh. He will see this land because he has followed the LORD completely. I will give to him and his descendants some of the very land he explored during his scouting mission.'

[37]"And the LORD was also angry with me because of you. He said to me, 'Moses, not even you will enter the Promised Land! [38]Instead, your assistant, Joshua son of Nun, will lead the people into the land. Encourage him, for he will lead Israel as they take possession of it.

1:19-21 "Don't be afraid! Don't be discouraged!" The expression "Don't be afraid," along with its variations, is the most common command in Scripture. There are so many things to be afraid of. In challenging his people to a new course of action, God insisted that they cast away their fears. God was really asking his people to trust in him. If we can learn to turn our focus away from our circumstances toward God and his power, our helplessness and fears will soon melt away.

[39] I will give the land to your little ones—your innocent children. You were afraid they would be captured, but they will be the ones who occupy it. [40] As for you, turn around now and go on back through the wilderness toward the Red Sea.*'

[41] "Then you confessed, 'We have sinned against the LORD! We will go into the land and fight for it, as the LORD our God has commanded us.' So your men strapped on their weapons, thinking it would be easy to attack the hill country.

[42] "But the LORD told me to tell you, 'Do not attack, for I am not with you. If you go ahead on your own, you will be crushed by your enemies.'

[43] "This is what I told you, but you would not listen. Instead, you again rebelled against the LORD's command and arrogantly went into the hill country to fight. [44] But the Amorites who lived there came out against you like a swarm of bees. They chased and battered you all the way from Seir to Hormah. [45] Then you returned and wept before the LORD, but he refused to listen. [46] So you stayed there at Kadesh for a long time.

CHAPTER 2
Remembering Israel's Wanderings

"Then we turned around and headed back across the wilderness toward the Red Sea,* just as the LORD had instructed me, and we wandered around in the region of Mount Seir for a long time.

[2] "Then at last the LORD said to me, [3] 'You have been wandering around in this hill country long enough; turn to the north. [4] Give these orders to the people: "You will pass through the country belonging to your relatives the Edomites, the descendants of Esau, who live in Seir. The Edomites will feel threatened, so be careful. [5] Do not bother

them, for I have given them all the hill country around Mount Seir as their property, and I will not give you even one square foot of their land. [6] If you need food to eat or water to drink, pay them for it. [7] For the LORD your God has blessed you in everything you have done. He has watched your every step through this great wilderness. During these forty years, the LORD your God has been with you, and you have lacked nothing."'

[8] "So we bypassed the territory of our relatives, the descendants of Esau, who live in Seir. We avoided the road through the Arabah Valley that comes up from Elath and Ezion-geber.

"Then as we turned north along the desert route through Moab, [9] the LORD warned us, 'Do not bother the Moabites, the descendants of Lot, or start a war with them. I have given them Ar as their property, and I will not give you any of their land.'"

[10] (A race of giants called the Emites had once lived in the area of Ar. They were as strong and numerous and tall as the Anakites, another race of giants. [11] Both the Emites and the Anakites are also known as the Rephaites, though the Moabites call them Emites. [12] In earlier times the Horites had lived in Seir, but they were driven out and displaced by the descendants of Esau, just as Israel drove out the people of Canaan when the LORD gave Israel their land.)

[13] Moses continued, "Then the LORD said to us, 'Get moving. Cross the Zered Brook.' So we crossed the brook.

[14] "Thirty-eight years passed from the time we first left Kadesh-barnea until we finally crossed the Zered Brook! By then, all the men old enough to fight in battle had died in the wilderness, as the LORD had vowed would happen. [15] The LORD struck them down until

1:40 Hebrew *sea of reeds*. 2:1 Hebrew *sea of reeds*.

2:7 God was not rejecting his people when he consigned them to 40 years of wilderness wandering. He was lovingly guiding them in a way that would bring them some much-needed discipline. It is comforting to remember that even after we have failed, God continues to shower his loving care upon us. He may lead us through a time of difficult discipline, but he never leaves us during the hard times. He often allows the hard times for our own good. God protected the people of Israel in the wilderness even though they had rejected him. Even after our worst failures, when terrible consequences are bearing down on us, God is there.

2:14-15 Timing is often an essential element in God's plan. It is sometimes necessary for us to hit bottom before we can begin to rebuild our life. It was necessary for the Israelites to experience what seemed like total defeat in the wilderness before they could learn to trust God's plan and do things his way. We should be careful to learn from Israel's mistakes. Let us learn to give up our plans for life before we discover that the consequences are disastrous. We would be wise to accept God's program for healthy living.

they had all been eliminated from the community.

¹⁶ "When all the men of fighting age had died, ¹⁷ the LORD said to me, ¹⁸ 'Today you will cross the border of Moab at Ar ¹⁹ and enter the land of the Ammonites, the descendants of Lot. But do not bother them or start a war with them. I have given the land of Ammon to them as their property, and I will not give you any of their land.' "

²⁰ (That area was once considered the land of the Rephaites, who had lived there, though the Ammonites call them Zamzummites. ²¹ They were also as strong and numerous and tall as the Anakites. But the LORD destroyed them so the Ammonites could occupy their land. ²² He had done the same for the descendants of Esau who lived in Seir, for he destroyed the Horites so they could settle there in their place. The descendants of Esau live there to this day. ²³ A similar thing happened when the Caphtorites from Crete* invaded and destroyed the Avvites, who had lived in villages in the area of Gaza.)

²⁴ Moses continued, "Then the LORD said, 'Now get moving! Cross the Arnon Gorge. Look, I will hand over to you Sihon the Amorite, king of Heshbon, and I will give you his land. Attack him and begin to occupy the land. ²⁵ Beginning today I will make people throughout the earth terrified because of you. When they hear reports about you, they will tremble with dread and fear.' "

Victory over Sihon of Heshbon

²⁶ Moses continued, "From the wilderness of Kedemoth I sent ambassadors to King Sihon of Heshbon with this proposal of peace:

²⁷ 'Let us travel through your land. We will stay on the main road and won't turn off into the fields on either side. ²⁸ Sell us food to eat and water to drink, and we will pay for it. All we want is permission to pass through your land. ²⁹ The descendants of Esau who live in Seir allowed us to go through their country, and so did the Moabites, who live in Ar. Let us pass through until we cross the Jordan into the land the LORD our God is giving us.'

³⁰ "But King Sihon of Heshbon refused to allow us to pass through, because the LORD your God made Sihon stubborn and defiant so he could help you defeat him, as he has now done.

³¹ "Then the LORD said to me, 'Look, I have begun to hand King Sihon and his land over to you. Begin now to conquer and occupy his land.'

³² "Then King Sihon declared war on us and mobilized his forces at Jahaz. ³³ But the LORD our God handed him over to us, and we crushed him, his sons, and all his people. ³⁴ We conquered all his towns and completely destroyed* everyone—men, women, and children. Not a single person was spared. ³⁵ We took all the livestock as plunder for ourselves, along with anything of value from the towns we ransacked.

³⁶ "The LORD our God also helped us conquer Aroer on the edge of the Arnon Gorge, and the town in the gorge, and the whole area as far as Gilead. No town had walls too strong for us. ³⁷ However, we avoided the land of the Ammonites all along the Jabbok River and the towns in the hill country—all the places the LORD our God had commanded us to leave alone.

CHAPTER 3
Victory over Og of Bashan

"Next we turned and headed for the land of Bashan, where King Og and his entire army attacked us at Edrei. ²But the LORD told me, 'Do not be afraid of him, for I have given you victory over Og and his entire army, and I will give you all his land. Treat him just as you treated King Sihon of the Amorites, who ruled in Heshbon.'

³ "So the LORD our God handed King Og and all his people over to us, and we killed them all. Not a single person survived. ⁴ We conquered all sixty of his towns—the entire Argob region in his kingdom of Bashan. Not a single town escaped our conquest. ⁵ These towns were all fortified with high walls and barred gates. We also took many unwalled

2:23 Hebrew *from Caphtor*. 2:34 The Hebrew term used here refers to the complete consecration of things or people to the LORD, either by destroying them or by giving them as an offering.

3:1-2 The Israelites' resources were pitifully limited, but God gave them victory. It was not by their military strength but by God's power that they overcame the nation of Bashan. As we fit the pieces of our life back together, it is God's resources, not ours, that will bring success. Our powerlessness in life provides wonderful opportunities for God to demonstrate his power.

villages at the same time. [6]We completely destroyed* the kingdom of Bashan, just as we had destroyed King Sihon of Heshbon. We destroyed all the people in every town we conquered—men, women, and children alike. [7]But we kept all the livestock for ourselves and took plunder from all the towns.

[8]"So we took the land of the two Amorite kings east of the Jordan River—all the way from the Arnon Gorge to Mount Hermon. [9](Mount Hermon is called Sirion by the Sidonians, and the Amorites call it Senir.) [10]We had now conquered all the cities on the plateau and all Gilead and Bashan, as far as the towns of Salecah and Edrei, which were part of Og's kingdom in Bashan. [11](King Og of Bashan was the last survivor of the giant Rephaites. His bed was made of iron and was more than thirteen feet long and six feet wide.* It can still be seen in the Ammonite city of Rabbah.)

Land Division East of the Jordan

[12]"When we took possession of this land, I gave to the tribes of Reuben and Gad the territory beyond Aroer along the Arnon Gorge, plus half of the hill country of Gilead with its towns. [13]Then I gave the rest of Gilead and all of Bashan—Og's former kingdom—to the half-tribe of Manasseh. (This entire Argob region of Bashan used to be known as the land of the Rephaites. [14]Jair, a leader from the tribe of Manasseh, conquered the whole Argob region in Bashan, all the way to the border of the Geshurites and Maacathites. Jair renamed this region after himself, calling it the Towns of Jair,* as it is still known today.) [15]I gave Gilead to the clan of Makir. [16]But I also gave part of Gilead to the tribes of Reuben and Gad. The area I gave them extended from the middle of the Arnon Gorge in the south to the Jabbok River on the Ammonite frontier. [17]They also received the Jordan Valley, all the way from the Sea of Galilee down to the Dead Sea,* with the Jordan River serving as the western boundary. To the east were the slopes of Pisgah.

[18]"At that time I gave this command to the tribes that would live east of the Jordan: 'Although the LORD your God has given you this land as your property, all your fighting men must cross the Jordan ahead of your Israelite relatives, armed and ready to assist them. [19]Your wives, children, and numerous livestock, however, may stay behind in the towns I have given you. [20]When the LORD has given security to the rest of the Israelites, as he has to you, and when they occupy the land the LORD your God is giving them across the Jordan River, then you may all return here to the land I have given you.'

Moses Forbidden to Enter the Land

[21]"At that time I gave Joshua this charge: 'You have seen for yourself everything the LORD your God has done to these two kings. He will do the same to all the kingdoms on the west side of the Jordan. [22]Do not be afraid of the nations there, for the LORD your God will fight for you.'

[23]"At that time I pleaded with the LORD and said, [24]'O Sovereign LORD, you have only begun to show your greatness and the strength of your hand to me, your servant. Is there any god in heaven or on earth who can perform such great and mighty deeds as you do? [25]Please let me cross the Jordan to see the wonderful land on the other side, the beautiful hill country and the Lebanon mountains.'

[26]"But the LORD was angry with me because of you, and he would not listen to me. 'That's enough!' he declared. 'Speak of it no more. [27]But go up to Pisgah Peak, and look

---

3:6 The Hebrew term used here refers to the complete consecration of things or people to the LORD, either by destroying them or by giving them as an offering; also in 3:6b. **3:11** Hebrew *9 cubits* [4.1 meters] *long and 4 cubits* [1.8 meters] *wide.* **3:14** Hebrew *Havvoth-jair.* **3:17** Hebrew *from Kinnereth to the Sea of the Arabah, the Salt Sea.*

3:12-20 Three of the Israelite tribes, Reuben, Gad, and half of Manasseh, wanted land on the east side of the Jordan River, just outside the Promised Land. God allowed them to do this, but he also demanded that they follow through on their promises to fight in the conquest of Canaan. The other tribes had counted on their support, and their failure to help in the conquest might have created deep divisions within God's chosen nation. An important step in recovery is learning to take responsibility for our promises and decisions. This is important as we seek to reconcile, build, and maintain our relationships with others.

3:23-29 Even Moses was not exempt from God's requirements. As great as Moses was, God's commands still applied to him. We must never presume to be a "special case." We must not rationalize and excuse ourselves from God's program for healthy and holy living. Rather, we should seek out and then joyfully accept God's program for us. His plans are always in our best interest, even if they are not what we expect or want.

over the land in every direction. Take a good look, but you may not cross the Jordan River. [28]Instead, commission Joshua and encourage and strengthen him, for he will lead the people across the Jordan. He will give them all the land you now see before you as their possession.' [29]So we stayed in the valley near Beth-peor.

CHAPTER 4
Moses Urges Israel to Obey

"And now, Israel, listen carefully to these decrees and regulations that I am about to teach you. Obey them so that you may live, so you may enter and occupy the land that the LORD, the God of your ancestors, is giving you. [2]Do not add to or subtract from these commands I am giving you. Just obey the commands of the LORD your God that I am giving you.

[3]"You saw for yourself what the LORD did to you at Baal-peor. There the LORD your God destroyed everyone who had worshiped Baal, the god of Peor. [4]But all of you who were faithful to the LORD your God are still alive today—every one of you.

[5]"Look, I now teach you these decrees and regulations just as the LORD my God commanded me, so that you may obey them in the land you are about to enter and occupy. [6]Obey them completely, and you will display your wisdom and intelligence among the surrounding nations. When they hear all these decrees, they will exclaim, 'How wise and prudent are the people of this great nation!' [7]For what great nation has a god as near to them as the LORD our God is near to us whenever we call on him? [8]And what great nation has decrees and regulations as righteous and fair as this body of instructions that I am giving you today?

[9]"But watch out! Be careful never to forget what you yourself have seen. Do not let these memories escape from your mind as long as you live! And be sure to pass them on to your children and grandchildren. [10]Never forget the day when you stood before the LORD your God at Mount Sinai,* where he told me, 'Summon the people before me, and I will personally instruct them. Then they will learn to fear me as long as they live, and they will teach their children to fear me also.'

[11]"You came near and stood at the foot of the mountain, while flames from the mountain shot into the sky. The mountain was shrouded in black clouds and deep darkness. [12]And the LORD spoke to you from the heart of the fire. You heard the sound of his words but didn't see his form; there was only a voice. [13]He proclaimed his covenant—the Ten Commandments*—which he commanded you to keep, and which he wrote on two stone tablets. [14]It was at that time that the LORD commanded me to teach you his decrees and regulations so you would obey them in the land you are about to enter and occupy.

A Warning against Idolatry

[15]"But be very careful! You did not see the LORD's form on the day he spoke to you from the heart of the fire at Mount Sinai. [16]So do not corrupt yourselves by making an idol in any form—whether of a man or a woman, [17]an animal on the ground, a bird in the sky, [18]a small animal that scurries along the ground, or a fish in the deepest sea. [19]And when you look up into the sky and see the sun, moon, and stars—all the forces of heaven—don't be seduced into worshiping them. The LORD your God gave them to all the peoples of the earth. [20]Remember that the LORD rescued you from the iron-smelting furnace of Egypt in order to make you his very own people and his special possession, which is what you are today.

[21]"But the LORD was angry with me because of you. He vowed that I would not cross the Jordan River into the good land the LORD your God is giving you as your special

---

4:10 Hebrew *Horeb,* another name for Sinai; also in 4:15. 4:13 Hebrew *the ten words.*

4:2 God's directions are not to be tampered with. It is tempting to add to or take away from God's provisions. But if we are to have victory, we must accept God's way—as it is, not as we might wish it to be. These requirements were offered for Israel's guidance; they were a gracious provision of God's love. God, through his Word and loving presence in our life, also provides us with all we need to live with fulfillment and contentment.

4:15-19 God warned the Israelites time and again about the dangers of idolatry. Most of us aren't tempted to worship a carved figure or statue, but in our busy world, a multitude of other matters or things clamor for our attention and affection. It is sometimes difficult to remember that we owe our primary allegiance to God. He requires absolute faithfulness from his people; he will not be satisfied with second place in our life. If we desire victory over our dependencies or compulsions, we will need to put God in his rightful place—first.

possession. [22] You will cross the Jordan to occupy the land, but I will not. Instead, I will die here on the east side of the river. [23] So be careful not to break the covenant the LORD your God has made with you. Do not make idols of any shape or form, for the LORD your God has forbidden this. [24] The LORD your God is a devouring fire; he is a jealous God.

[25] "In the future, when you have children and grandchildren and have lived in the land a long time, do not corrupt yourselves by making idols of any kind. This is evil in the sight of the LORD your God and will arouse his anger.

[26] "Today I call on heaven and earth as witnesses against you. If you break my covenant, you will quickly disappear from the land you are crossing the Jordan to occupy. You will live there only a short time; then you will be utterly destroyed. [27] For the LORD will scatter you among the nations, where only a few of you will survive. [28] There, in a foreign land, you will worship idols made from wood and stone—gods that neither see nor hear nor eat nor smell. [29] But from there you will search again for the LORD your God. And if you search for him with all your heart and soul, you will find him.

[30] "In the distant future, when you are suffering all these things, you will finally return to the LORD your God and listen to what he tells you. [31] For the LORD your God is a merciful God; he will not abandon you or destroy you or forget the solemn covenant he made with your ancestors.

There Is Only One God

[32] "Now search all of history, from the time God created people on the earth until now, and search from one end of the heavens to the other. Has anything as great as this ever been seen or heard before? [33] Has any nation ever heard the voice of God* speaking from fire—as you did—and survived? [34] Has any other god dared to take a nation for himself out of another nation by means of trials, miraculous signs, wonders, war, a strong hand, a powerful arm, and terrifying acts? Yet that is what the LORD your God did for you in Egypt, right before your eyes.

[35] "He showed you these things so you would know that the LORD is God and there is no other. [36] He let you hear his voice from heaven so he could instruct you. He let you see his great fire here on earth so he could speak to you from it. [37] Because he loved your ancestors, he chose to bless their descendants, and he personally brought you out of Egypt with a great display of power. [38] He drove out nations far greater than you, so he could bring you in and give you their land as your special possession, as it is today.

[39] "So remember this and keep it firmly in mind: The LORD is God both in heaven and on earth, and there is no other. [40] If you obey all the decrees and commands I am giving you today, all will be well with you and your children. I am giving you these instructions so you will enjoy a long life in the land the LORD your God is giving you for all time."

Eastern Cities of Refuge

[41] Then Moses set apart three cities of refuge east of the Jordan River. [42] Anyone who killed another person unintentionally, without previous hostility, could flee there to live in safety. [43] These were the cities: Bezer on the wilderness plateau for the tribe of Reuben; Ramoth in Gilead for the tribe of Gad; Golan in Bashan for the tribe of Manasseh.

Introduction to Moses' Second Address

[44] This is the body of instruction that Moses presented to the Israelites. [45] These are the laws, decrees, and regulations that Moses gave to the people of Israel when they left Egypt, [46] and as they camped in the valley near Beth-peor east of the Jordan River. (This land was formerly occupied by the Amorites under King Sihon, who ruled from Heshbon. But Moses and the Israelites destroyed him and his people when they came up from Egypt. [47] Israel took possession of his land and that of King Og of Bashan—the two Amorite kings east of the Jordan. [48] So Israel conquered the entire area from Aroer at the edge of the Arnon Gorge all the way to Mount Sirion,* also called Mount Hermon. [49] And they conquered the eastern bank of the Jordan

4:33 Or *voice of a god.* 4:48 As in Syriac version (see also 3:9); Hebrew reads *Mount Sion.*

4:29-31 Here God reaffirms his compassion toward victims of painful circumstances and promises to come through for his people, even when they have failed him. He asks only that his people listen to him and follow his instructions for healthy, holy living. Our relationship with God is certain because it is based upon God's compassion for us, even when we don't deserve it. God is faithful; we can be sure he will come through for us.

River as far south as the Dead Sea,* below the slopes of Pisgah.)

CHAPTER 5
Ten Commandments for the Covenant Community

Moses called all the people of Israel together and said, "Listen carefully, Israel. Hear the decrees and regulations I am giving you today, so you may learn them and obey them!

²"The LORD our God made a covenant with us at Mount Sinai.* ³The LORD did not make this covenant with our ancestors, but with all of us who are alive today. ⁴At the mountain the LORD spoke to you face to face from the heart of the fire. ⁵I stood as an intermediary between you and the LORD, for you were afraid of the fire and did not want to approach the mountain. He spoke to me, and I passed his words on to you. This is what he said:

⁶"I am the LORD your God, who rescued you from the land of Egypt, the place of your slavery.

⁷"You must not have any other god but me.

⁸"You must not make for yourself an idol of any kind, or an image of anything in the heavens or on the earth or in the sea. ⁹You must not bow down to them or worship them, for I, the LORD your God, am a jealous God who will not tolerate your affection for any other gods. I lay the sins of the parents upon their children; the entire family is affected—even children in the third and fourth generations of those who reject me. ¹⁰But I lavish unfailing love for a thousand generations on those* who love me and obey my commands.

¹¹"You must not misuse the name of the LORD your God. The LORD will not let you go unpunished if you misuse his name.

¹²"Observe the Sabbath day by keeping it holy, as the LORD your God has commanded you. ¹³You have six days each week for your ordinary work, ¹⁴but the seventh day is a Sabbath day of rest dedicated to the LORD your God. On that day no one in your household may do any work. This includes you, your sons and daughters, your male and female servants, your oxen and donkeys and other livestock, and any foreigners living among you. All your male and female servants must rest as you do. ¹⁵Remember that you were once slaves in Egypt, but the LORD your God brought you out with his strong hand and powerful arm. That is why the LORD your God has commanded you to rest on the Sabbath day.

¹⁶"Honor your father and mother, as the LORD your God commanded you. Then you will live a long, full life in the land the LORD your God is giving you.

¹⁷"You must not murder.

¹⁸"You must not commit adultery.

¹⁹"You must not steal.

²⁰"You must not testify falsely against your neighbor.

²¹"You must not covet your neighbor's wife. You must not covet your neighbor's house or land, male or female servant, ox or donkey, or anything else that belongs to your neighbor.

²²"The LORD spoke these words to all of you assembled there at the foot of the mountain. He spoke with a loud voice from the heart of the fire, surrounded by clouds and

---

4:49 Hebrew *took the Arabah on the east side of the Jordan as far as the sea of the Arabah.* **5:2** Hebrew *Horeb,* another name for Sinai. **5:10** Hebrew *for thousands of those.*

5:6-21 God gave his people the Ten Commandments after reminding them that he had redeemed them from slavery in Egypt. These laws stated how God's redeemed people were expected to act; they contained a godly pattern of living for people of all ages. But they are not so much a collection of rules as a "job description"—a set of ideal goals. We are all gripped by the powerful effects of sin. God's laws describe the goals of the recovery process. We will be working on these our whole life. With self-discipline and God's gracious help, we will find that these commandments naturally become part of our life.

5:9-10 God is jealous of our affections, and when we fail to give him the proper place in our life, negative consequences always result. And we are not the only ones who will suffer; so will our children and grandchildren. God created us to live according to his program. By following it, we can have hope for our future and the future of our children and grandchildren. We need to start by putting God first in our life.

5:20 Honesty must be characteristic of everyone, especially those of us in recovery. Healthy living before God demands that we are honest *with* others and *about* others. Being honest in our relationships is a necessary requirement for reconciliation with the people we have wronged as well as with those who have wronged us.

deep darkness. This was all he said at that time, and he wrote his words on two stone tablets and gave them to me.

23 "But when you heard the voice from the heart of the darkness, while the mountain was blazing with fire, all your tribal leaders and elders came to me. 24They said, 'Look, the LORD our God has shown us his glory and greatness, and we have heard his voice from the heart of the fire. Today we have seen that God can speak to us humans, and yet we live! 25But now, why should we risk death again? If the LORD our God speaks to us again, we will certainly die and be consumed by this awesome fire. 26Can any living thing hear the voice of the living God from the heart of the fire as we did and yet survive? 27Go yourself and listen to what the LORD our God says. Then come and tell us everything he tells you, and we will listen and obey.'

28 "The LORD heard the request you made to me. And he said, 'I have heard what the people said to you, and they are right. 29Oh, that they would always have hearts like this, that they might fear me and obey all my commands! If they did, they and their descendants would prosper forever. 30Go and tell them, "Return to your tents." 31But you stand here with me so I can give you all my commands, decrees, and regulations. You must teach them to the people so they can obey them in the land I am giving them as their possession.'"

32 So Moses told the people, "You must be careful to obey all the commands of the LORD your God, following his instructions in every detail. 33Stay on the path that the LORD your God has commanded you to follow. Then you will live long and prosperous lives in the land you are about to enter and occupy.

CHAPTER 6
A Call for Wholehearted Commitment

"These are the commands, decrees, and regulations that the LORD your God com-

manded me to teach you. You must obey them in the land you are about to enter and occupy, 2and you and your children and grandchildren must fear the LORD your God as long as you live. If you obey all his decrees and commands, you will enjoy a long life. 3Listen closely, Israel, and be careful to obey. Then all will go well with you, and you will have many children in the land flowing with milk and honey, just as the LORD, the God of your ancestors, promised you.

4"Listen, O Israel! The LORD is our God, the LORD alone.* 5And you must love the LORD your God with all your heart, all your soul, and all your strength. 6And you must commit yourselves wholeheartedly to these commands that I am giving you today. 7Repeat them again and again to your children. Talk about them when you are at home and when you are on the road, when you are going to bed and when you are getting up. 8Tie them to your hands and wear them on your forehead as reminders. 9Write them on the doorposts of your house and on your gates.

10 "The LORD your God will soon bring you into the land he swore to give you when he made a vow to your ancestors Abraham, Isaac, and Jacob. It is a land with large, prosperous cities that you did not build. 11The houses will be richly stocked with goods you did not produce. You will draw water from cisterns you did not dig, and you will eat from vineyards and olive trees you did not plant. When you have eaten your fill in this land, 12be careful not to forget the LORD, who rescued you from slavery in the land of Egypt. 13You must fear the LORD your God and serve him. When you take an oath, you must use only his name.

14 "You must not worship any of the gods of neighboring nations, 15for the LORD your God, who lives among you, is a jealous God. His anger will flare up against you, and he will wipe you from the face of the earth. 16You must not test the LORD your God as you did

---

6:4 Or *The LORD our God is one LORD;* or *The LORD our God, the LORD is one;* or *The LORD is our God, the LORD is one.*

6:5 Here the Israelites were told to love God with all their heart, soul, and strength. Jesus called this the most important commandment in the Bible. If we love God, we will want to do everything he wants us to do. The nature of this love, however, is often misunderstood. In the Bible, love is not primarily an emotion. It is a decision that shows itself in appropriate actions. Thus, loving God entails the decision to follow God's program, looking to him constantly for help and forgiveness.

6:7 God's Word should be foremost in our thoughts when we get up in the morning or go to bed at night, when we are at home, at work, or on vacation. In other words, it should be a matter of constant and primary concern. We know that recovery is an all-day, everyday process. Following God's prescriptions for healthy living should help us as we progress in recovery, one day at a time.

when you complained at Massah. [17]You must diligently obey the commands of the LORD your God—all the laws and decrees he has given you. [18]Do what is right and good in the LORD's sight, so all will go well with you. Then you will enter and occupy the good land that the LORD swore to give your ancestors. [19]You will drive out all the enemies living in the land, just as the LORD said you would.

[20]"In the future your children will ask you, 'What is the meaning of these laws, decrees, and regulations that the LORD our God has commanded us to obey?'

[21]"Then you must tell them, 'We were Pharaoh's slaves in Egypt, but the LORD brought us out of Egypt with his strong hand. [22]The LORD did miraculous signs and wonders before our eyes, dealing terrifying blows against Egypt and Pharaoh and all his people. [23]He brought us out of Egypt so he could give us this land he had sworn to give our ancestors. [24]And the LORD our God commanded us to obey all these decrees and to fear him so he can continue to bless us and preserve our lives, as he has done to this day. [25]For we will be counted as righteous when we obey all the commands the LORD our God has given us.'

CHAPTER 7
The Privilege of Holiness

"When the LORD your God brings you into the land you are about to enter and occupy, he will clear away many nations ahead of you: the Hittites, Girgashites, Amorites, Canaanites, Perizzites, Hivites, and Jebusites. These seven nations are greater and more numerous than you. [2]When the LORD your God hands these nations over to you and

you conquer them, you must completely destroy* them. Make no treaties with them and show them no mercy. [3]You must not intermarry with them. Do not let your daughters and sons marry their sons and daughters, [4]for they will lead your children away from me to worship other gods. Then the anger of the LORD will burn against you, and he will quickly destroy you. [5]This is what you must do. You must break down their pagan altars and shatter their sacred pillars. Cut down their Asherah poles and burn their idols. [6]For you are a holy people, who belong to the LORD your God. Of all the people on earth, the LORD your God has chosen you to be his own special treasure.

[7]"The LORD did not set his heart on you and choose you because you were more numerous than other nations, for you were the smallest of all nations! [8]Rather, it was simply that the LORD loves you, and he was keeping the oath he had sworn to your ancestors. That is why the LORD rescued you with such a strong hand from your slavery and from the oppressive hand of Pharaoh, king of Egypt. [9]Understand, therefore, that the LORD your God is indeed God. He is the faithful God who keeps his covenant for a thousand generations and lavishes his unfailing love on those who love him and obey his commands. [10]But he does not hesitate to punish and destroy those who reject him. [11]Therefore, you must obey all these commands, decrees, and regulations I am giving you today.

[12]"If you listen to these regulations and faithfully obey them, the LORD your God will keep his covenant of unfailing love with you, as he promised with an oath to your

---

7:2 The Hebrew term used here refers to the complete consecration of things or people to the LORD, either by destroying them or by giving them as an offering; also in 7:26.

6:18 This is one of the biblical formulas for success: "Do what is right and good in the LORD's sight, so all will go well with you." It seems simple, but anyone who has tried it knows how hard it can be. God laid out a plan for successful and healthy living in the Israelite community. Most of these laws and principles apply to us as well. God has given us instructions for living a healthy, joy-filled life; he desires the best for us. This should encourage us as we seek to follow his program, as difficult as that may be. And we can know for certain that when God's instructions become too difficult for us, he is right there to help us.

7:6 The people whom God chooses have the responsibility to live a holy life. This has a negative aspect: It means that the believer is separated *away from* the defilement of the world. Probably of greater importance is the positive aspect: It means that we are separated *unto* God, chosen and set aside for his purposes. We are set apart for wholeness and balance, characteristics we all work toward in recovery.

7:7-8 Why did God choose to treat the Israelites in a special way? Was it because they deserved it? No! In fact, in some respects they deserved it less than others. He chose them as his own because he had promised his loving care to their ancestor Abraham and his descendants. He treated them kindly because he is a gracious God. God wants us all to be free from bondage, whether we are "good enough" or not. If there are any chains binding us, God's loving hands are ready to set us on the road toward freedom.

ancestors. [13]He will love you and bless you, and he will give you many children. He will give fertility to your land and your animals. When you arrive in the land he swore to give your ancestors, you will have large harvests of grain, new wine, and olive oil, and great herds of cattle, sheep, and goats. [14]You will be blessed above all the nations of the earth. None of your men or women will be childless, and all your livestock will bear young. [15]And the LORD will protect you from all sickness. He will not let you suffer from the terrible diseases you knew in Egypt, but he will inflict them on all your enemies!

[16]"You must destroy all the nations the LORD your God hands over to you. Show them no mercy, and do not worship their gods, or they will trap you. [17]Perhaps you will think to yourselves, 'How can we ever conquer these nations that are so much more powerful than we are?' [18]But don't be afraid of them! Just remember what the LORD your God did to Pharaoh and to all the land of Egypt. [19]Remember the great terrors the LORD your God sent against them. You saw it all with your own eyes! And remember the miraculous signs and wonders, and the strong hand and powerful arm with which he brought you out of Egypt. The LORD your God will use this same power against all the people you fear. [20]And then the LORD your God will send terror* to drive out the few survivors still hiding from you!

[21]"No, do not be afraid of those nations, for the LORD your God is among you, and he is a great and awesome God. [22]The LORD your God will drive those nations out ahead of you little by little. You will not clear them away all at once, otherwise the wild animals would multiply too quickly for you. [23]But the LORD your God will hand them over to you. He will throw them into complete confusion until they are destroyed. [24]He will put their kings in your power, and you will erase their names from the face of the earth. No one will be able to stand against you, and you will destroy them all.

[25]"You must burn their idols in fire, and you must not covet the silver or gold that covers them. You must not take it or it will become a trap to you, for it is detestable to the LORD your God. [26]Do not bring any detestable objects into your home, for then you will be destroyed, just like them. You must utterly detest such things, for they are set apart for destruction.

CHAPTER 8
A Call to Remember and Obey

"Be careful to obey all the commands I am giving you today. Then you will live and multiply, and you will enter and occupy the land the LORD swore to give your ancestors. [2]Remember how the LORD your God led you through the wilderness for these forty years, humbling you and testing you to prove your character, and to find out whether or not you would obey his commands. [3]Yes, he humbled you by letting you go hungry and then feeding you with manna, a food previously unknown to you and your ancestors. He did it to teach you that people do not live by bread alone; rather, we live by every word that comes from the mouth of the LORD. [4]For all these forty years your clothes didn't wear out, and your feet didn't blister or swell. [5]Think about it: Just as a parent disciplines a child, the LORD your God disciplines you for your own good.

[6]"So obey the commands of the LORD your God by walking in his ways and fearing him. [7]For the LORD your God is bringing you into a good land of flowing streams and pools of water, with fountains and springs that gush out in the valleys and hills. [8]It is a land of wheat and barley; of grapevines, fig trees, and pomegranates; of olive oil and honey. [9]It is a land where food is plentiful and nothing

---

7:20 Often rendered *the hornet.* The meaning of the Hebrew is uncertain.

7:22 Notice that the conquest was to take place a little at a time. God knew that throwing enemies out of the land had to be followed by immediate rebuilding. He would give his people new territory only when they were ready to move in and take advantage of the conquest. We need to recognize that recovery is a long-term process. We should not expect immediate success; instead, we should look for steady progress. God gives us victories as we are ready to take advantage of them and build on them. We must trust him to move us forward according to his timing.
8:2 God often uses the hard times in life to teach us important lessons. Here we see that he had a twofold purpose in Israel's 40 years of wandering. First, the trials were brought upon Israel to teach them humility. God wanted them to learn who they really were in relationship to him. Second, the trials were given to test the Israelites—so they could demonstrate what was really in their hearts. Sometimes God tests us in similar ways, pushing us to examine ourselves. We need to take advantage of the difficult times, using them as stepping-stones toward recovery.

is lacking. It is a land where iron is as common as stone, and copper is abundant in the hills. [10]When you have eaten your fill, be sure to praise the LORD your God for the good land he has given you.

[11]"But that is the time to be careful! Beware that in your plenty you do not forget the LORD your God and disobey his commands, regulations, and decrees that I am giving you today. [12]For when you have become full and prosperous and have built fine homes to live in, [13]and when your flocks and herds have become very large and your silver and gold have multiplied along with everything else, be careful! [14]Do not become proud at that time and forget the LORD your God, who rescued you from slavery in the land of Egypt. [15]Do not forget that he led you through the great and terrifying wilderness with its poisonous snakes and scorpions, where it was so hot and dry. He gave you water from the rock! [16]He fed you with manna in the wilderness, a food unknown to your ancestors. He did this to humble you and test you for your own good. [17]He did all this so you would never say to yourself, 'I have achieved this wealth with my own strength and energy.' [18]Remember the LORD your God. He is the one who gives you power to be successful, in order to fulfill the covenant he confirmed to your ancestors with an oath.

[19]"But I assure you of this: If you ever forget the LORD your God and follow other gods, worshiping and bowing down to them, you will certainly be destroyed. [20]Just as the LORD has destroyed other nations in your path, you also will be destroyed if you refuse to obey the LORD your God.

CHAPTER 9
Victory by God's Grace
"Listen, O Israel! Today you are about to cross the Jordan River to take over the land belonging to nations much greater and more powerful than you. They live in cities with

9:8 Hebrew *Horeb,* another name for Sinai.

walls that reach to the sky! [2]The people are strong and tall—descendants of the famous Anakite giants. You've heard the saying, 'Who can stand up to the Anakites?' [3]But recognize today that the LORD your God is the one who will cross over ahead of you like a devouring fire to destroy them. He will subdue them so that you will quickly conquer them and drive them out, just as the LORD has promised.

[4]"After the LORD your God has done this for you, don't say in your hearts, 'The LORD has given us this land because we are such good people!' No, it is because of the wickedness of the other nations that he is pushing them out of your way. [5]It is not because you are so good or have such integrity that you are about to occupy their land. The LORD your God will drive these nations out ahead of you only because of their wickedness, and to fulfill the oath he swore to your ancestors Abraham, Isaac, and Jacob. [6]You must recognize that the LORD your God is not giving you this good land because you are good, for you are not—you are a stubborn people.

Remembering the Gold Calf
[7]"Remember and never forget how angry you made the LORD your God out in the wilderness. From the day you left Egypt until now, you have been constantly rebelling against him. [8]Even at Mount Sinai* you made the LORD so angry he was ready to destroy you. [9]This happened when I was on the mountain receiving the tablets of stone inscribed with the words of the covenant that the LORD had made with you. I was there for forty days and forty nights, and all that time I ate no food and drank no water. [10]The LORD gave me the two tablets on which God had written with his own finger all the words he had spoken to you from the heart of the fire when you were assembled at the mountain.

[11]"At the end of the forty days and nights, the LORD handed me the two stone tablets

---

8:16-18 As we begin to experience some success in rebuilding our life, we should remember to give credit where credit is due. We must be careful to give God the glory. We must not selfishly claim what belongs to God alone, for this leads to proud self-sufficiency that invariably leads to a fall.

8:19-20 If we fail to obey God's instructions, we should expect his anger. These verses should challenge us to take careful inventory of our life. We need to determine those areas in us that need restructuring and renewal. God's wrath is not to be taken lightly. But if we are willing to change with his help, his grace is more than sufficient to help us overcome our problems.

9:3 This verse reminds us that if God is for us, who can be against us? God went ahead of his people to guide them and prepare the way for them. He destroyed Israel's national enemies. Is it too much to ask that God will vanquish the enemies in our life, too?

inscribed with the words of the covenant. [12]Then the LORD said to me, 'Get up! Go down immediately, for the people you brought out of Egypt have corrupted themselves. How quickly they have turned away from the way I commanded them to live! They have melted gold and made an idol for themselves!'

[13]"The LORD also said to me, 'I have seen how stubborn and rebellious these people are. [14]Leave me alone so I may destroy them and erase their name from under heaven. Then I will make a mighty nation of your descendants, a nation larger and more powerful than they are.'

[15]"So while the mountain was blazing with fire I turned and came down, holding in my hands the two stone tablets inscribed with the terms of the covenant. [16]There below me I could see that you had sinned against the LORD your God. You had melted gold and made a calf idol for yourselves. How quickly you had turned away from the path the LORD had commanded you to follow! [17]So I took the stone tablets and threw them to the ground, smashing them before your eyes.

[18]"Then, as before, I threw myself down before the LORD for forty days and nights. I ate no bread and drank no water because of the great sin you had committed by doing what the LORD hated, provoking him to anger. [19]I feared that the furious anger of the LORD, which turned him against you, would drive him to destroy you. But again he listened to me. [20]The LORD was so angry with Aaron that he wanted to destroy him, too. But I prayed for Aaron, and the LORD spared him. [21]I took your sin—the calf you had made—and I melted it down in the fire and ground it into fine dust. Then I threw the dust into the stream that flows down the mountain.

[22]"You also made the LORD angry at Taberah,* Massah,* and Kibroth-hattaavah.* [23]And at Kadesh-barnea the LORD sent you out with this command: 'Go up and take over the land I have given you.' But you rebelled against the command of the LORD your God and refused to put your trust in him or obey him. [24]Yes, you have been rebelling against the LORD as long as I have known you.

[25]"That is why I threw myself down before the LORD for forty days and nights—for the LORD said he would destroy you. [26]I prayed to the LORD and said, 'O Sovereign LORD, do not destroy them. They are your own people. They are your special possession, whom you redeemed from Egypt by your mighty power and your strong hand. [27]Please overlook the stubbornness and the awful sin of these people, and remember instead your servants Abraham, Isaac, and Jacob. [28]If you destroy these people, the Egyptians will say, "The Israelites died because the LORD wasn't able to bring them to the land he had promised to give them." Or they might say, "He destroyed them because he hated them; he deliberately took them into the wilderness to slaughter them." [29]But they are your people and your special possession, whom you brought out of Egypt by your great strength and powerful arm.'

CHAPTER 10
A New Copy of the Covenant

"At that time the LORD said to me, 'Chisel out two stone tablets like the first ones. Also make a wooden Ark—a sacred chest to store them in. Come up to me on the mountain, [2]and I will write on the tablets the same words that were on the ones you smashed. Then place the tablets in the Ark.'

[3]"So I made an Ark of acacia wood and cut two stone tablets like the first two. Then I went up the mountain with the tablets in my hand. [4]Once again the LORD wrote the Ten Commandments* on the tablets and gave them to me. They were the same words the LORD had spoken to you from the heart of the fire on the day you were assembled at the foot of the mountain. [5]Then I turned and came down the mountain and placed the

---

9:22a *Taberah* means "place of burning." See Num 11:1-3. 9:22b *Massah* means "place of testing." See Exod 17:1-7.
9:22c *Kibroth-hattaavah* means "graves of gluttony." See Num 11:31-34. 10:4 Hebrew *the ten words.*

9:18-29 Moses prayed to God, interceding for his people. In the process of recovery we will experience times of temporary failure. It is at these times that the intercession of God's people is vital to our continued success. We need to build relationships of support that will result in this kind of intercession for us before God.

10:1 The first stone tablets containing the law had been completely destroyed because of the people's failure. How encouraging to see that God instructed Moses to bring new ones so he could rewrite his instructions to the people. No matter how great our failures, God still seeks to reach out to us. God always gives humble people a chance to start again. But remember, this is a characteristic of God that should be appreciated not presumed upon.

tablets in the Ark of the Covenant, which I had made, just as the LORD commanded me. And the tablets are still there in the Ark."

6(The people of Israel set out from the wells of the people of Jaakan* and traveled to Moserah, where Aaron died and was buried. His son Eleazar ministered as high priest in his place. 7Then they journeyed to Gudgodah, and from there to Jotbathah, a land with many brooks and streams. 8At that time the LORD set apart the tribe of Levi to carry the Ark of the LORD's Covenant, and to stand before the LORD as his ministers, and to pronounce blessings in his name. These are their duties to this day. 9That is why the Levites have no share of property or possession of land among the other Israelite tribes. The LORD himself is their special possession, as the LORD your God told them.)

10"As for me, I stayed on the mountain in the LORD's presence for forty days and nights, as I had done the first time. And once again the LORD listened to my pleas and agreed not to destroy you. 11Then the LORD said to me, 'Get up and resume the journey, and lead the people to the land I swore to give to their ancestors, so they may take possession of it.'

A Call to Love and Obedience

12"And now, Israel, what does the LORD your God require of you? He requires only that you fear the LORD your God, and live in a way that pleases him, and love him and serve him with all your heart and soul. 13And you must always obey the LORD's commands and decrees that I am giving you today for your own good.

14"Look, the highest heavens and the earth and everything in it all belong to the LORD your God. 15Yet the LORD chose your ancestors as the objects of his love. And he chose you, their descendants, above all other nations, as is evident today. 16Therefore, change your hearts* and stop being stubborn.

17"For the LORD your God is the God of gods and Lord of lords. He is the great God, the mighty and awesome God, who shows no partiality and cannot be bribed. 18He ensures that orphans and widows receive justice. He shows love to the foreigners living among you and gives them food and clothing. 19So you, too, must show love to foreigners, for you yourselves were once foreigners in the land of Egypt. 20You must fear the LORD your God and worship him and cling to him. Your oaths must be in his name alone. 21He alone is your God, the only one who is worthy of your praise, the one who has done these mighty miracles that you have seen with your own eyes. 22When your ancestors went down into Egypt, there were only seventy of them. But now the LORD your God has made you as numerous as the stars in the sky!

CHAPTER 11

"You must love the LORD your God and always obey his requirements, decrees, regulations, and commands. 2Keep in mind that I am not talking now to your children, who have never experienced the discipline of the LORD your God or seen his greatness and his strong hand and powerful arm. 3They didn't see the miraculous signs and wonders he performed in Egypt against Pharaoh and all his land. 4They didn't see what the LORD did to the armies of Egypt and to their horses and chariots—how he drowned them in the Red Sea* as they were chasing you. He destroyed them, and they have not recovered to this very day!

5"Your children didn't see how the LORD cared for you in the wilderness until you

---

10:6 Or *set out from Beeroth of Bene-jaakan.*   10:16 Hebrew *circumcise the foreskin of your hearts.*   11:4 Hebrew *sea of reeds.*

10:12-13 God's pattern for godly living begins with a proper respect for him ("fear the LORD your God") and a healthy lifestyle ("live in a way that pleases him"). When we truly love God and are living his way, obedience to him is a natural response ("obey the LORD's commands and decrees"). Notice that God's laws are given to us for our own good. As a result of our obedience, we should have right attitudes and responses toward God ("love him and serve him"). Since God's pattern for living is in our best interest, we would be wise to follow it.

10:16 It is so easy to become hardened by circumstances; it's natural for us to respond to difficulties with stubbornness and rebellion. But here we are asked to keep our heart soft and our ears open to God. God desires to communicate with us; we need to be willing to listen and then follow through.

11:1 Obedience to God's instructions should be a direct result of our love for him. Love for God is the major motivating force in our obedience to the civil, ceremonial, and moral obligations he requests of us. Our love and obedience should be a natural response to the love he has shown to us.

arrived here. [6]They didn't see what he did to Dathan and Abiram (the sons of Eliab, a descendant of Reuben) when the earth opened its mouth in the Israelite camp and swallowed them, along with their households and tents and every living thing that belonged to them. [7]But you have seen the LORD perform all these mighty deeds with your own eyes!

The Blessings of Obedience

[8]"Therefore, be careful to obey every command I am giving you today, so you may have strength to go in and take over the land you are about to enter. [9]If you obey, you will enjoy a long life in the land the LORD swore to give to your ancestors and to you, their descendants—a land flowing with milk and honey! [10]For the land you are about to enter and take over is not like the land of Egypt from which you came, where you planted your seed and made irrigation ditches with your foot as in a vegetable garden. [11]Rather, the land you will soon take over is a land of hills and valleys with plenty of rain—[12]a land that the LORD your God cares for. He watches over it through each season of the year!

[13]"If you carefully obey the commands I am giving you today, and if you love the LORD your God and serve him with all your heart and soul, [14]then he will send the rains in their proper seasons—the early and late rains—so you can bring in your harvests of grain, new wine, and olive oil. [15]He will give you lush pastureland for your livestock, and you yourselves will have all you want to eat.

[16]"But be careful. Don't let your heart be deceived so that you turn away from the LORD and serve and worship other gods. [17]If you do, the LORD's anger will burn against you. He will shut up the sky and hold back the rain, and the ground will fail to produce its harvests. Then you will quickly die in that good land the LORD is giving you.

[18]"So commit yourselves wholeheartedly to these words of mine. Tie them to your hands and wear them on your forehead as reminders. [19]Teach them to your children. Talk about them when you are at home and when you are on the road, when you are going to bed and when you are getting up. [20]Write them on the doorposts of your house and on your gates, [21]so that as long as the sky remains above the earth, you and your children may flourish in the land the LORD swore to give your ancestors.

[22]"Be careful to obey all these commands I am giving you. Show love to the LORD your God by walking in his ways and holding tightly to him. [23]Then the LORD will drive out all the nations ahead of you, though they are much greater and stronger than you, and you will take over their land. [24]Wherever you set foot, that land will be yours. Your frontiers will stretch from the wilderness in the south to Lebanon in the north, and from the Euphrates River in the east to the Mediterranean Sea in the west.* [25]No one will be able to stand against you, for the LORD your God will cause the people to fear and dread you, as he promised, wherever you go in the whole land.

[26]"Look, today I am giving you the choice between a blessing and a curse! [27]You will be blessed if you obey the commands of the LORD your God that I am giving you today. [28]But you will be cursed if you reject the commands of the LORD your God and turn away from him and worship gods you have not known before.

[29]"When the LORD your God brings you into the land and helps you take possession of it, you must pronounce the blessing at Mount Gerizim and the curse at Mount Ebal. [30](These two mountains are west of the Jordan River in the land of the Canaanites who live in the Jordan Valley,* near the town of Gilgal, not far from the oaks of Moreh.) [31]For you are about to cross the Jordan River to take over the land the LORD your God is giving you. When you take that land and are living in it, [32]you must be careful to obey all the decrees and regulations I am giving you today.

CHAPTER 12
The LORD's Chosen Place for Worship

"These are the decrees and regulations you must be careful to obey when you live in the land that the LORD, the God of your ancestors, is giving you. You must obey them as long as you live.

[2]"When you drive out the nations that live there, you must destroy all the places where they worship their gods—high on the mountains, up on the hills, and under every green tree. [3]Break down their altars and smash their sacred pillars. Burn their Asherah poles and cut down their carved idols. Completely erase the names of their gods!

[4]"Do not worship the LORD your God in the way these pagan peoples worship their

11:24 Hebrew *to the western sea.* 11:30 Hebrew *the Arabah.*

gods. [5]Rather, you must seek the LORD your God at the place of worship he himself will choose from among all the tribes—the place where his name will be honored. [6]There you will bring your burnt offerings, your sacrifices, your tithes, your sacred offerings, your offerings to fulfill a vow, your voluntary offerings, and your offerings of the firstborn animals of your herds and flocks. [7]There you and your families will feast in the presence of the LORD your God, and you will rejoice in all you have accomplished because the LORD your God has blessed you.

[8]"Your pattern of worship will change. Today all of you are doing as you please, [9]because you have not yet arrived at the place of rest, the land the LORD your God is giving you as your special possession. [10]But you will soon cross the Jordan River and live in the land the LORD your God is giving you. When he gives you rest from all your enemies and you're living safely in the land, [11]you must bring everything I command you—your burnt offerings, your sacrifices, your tithes, your sacred offerings, and your offerings to fulfill a vow—to the designated place of worship, the place the LORD your God chooses for his name to be honored.

[12]"You must celebrate there in the presence of the LORD your God with your sons and daughters and all your servants. And remember to include the Levites who live in your towns, for they will receive no allotment of land among you. [13]Be careful not to sacrifice your burnt offerings just anywhere you like. [14]You may do so only at the place the LORD will choose within one of your tribal territories. There you must offer your burnt offerings and do everything I command you.

[15]"But you may butcher your animals and eat their meat in any town whenever you want. You may freely eat the animals with which the LORD your God blesses you. All of you, whether ceremonially clean or unclean, may eat that meat, just as you now eat gazelle and deer. [16]But you must not consume the blood. You must pour it out on the ground like water.

[17]"But you may not eat your offerings in your hometown—neither the tithe of your grain and new wine and olive oil, nor the firstborn of your flocks and herds, nor any offering to fulfill a vow, nor your voluntary offerings, nor your sacred offerings. [18]You must eat these in the presence of the LORD your God at the place he will choose. Eat them there with your children, your servants, and the Levites who live in your towns, celebrating in the presence of the LORD your God in all you do. [19]And be very careful never to neglect the Levites as long as you live in your land.

[20]"When the LORD your God expands your territory as he has promised, and you have the urge to eat meat, you may freely eat meat whenever you want. [21]It might happen that the designated place of worship—the place the LORD your God chooses for his name to be honored—is a long way from your home. If so, you may butcher any of the cattle, sheep, or goats the LORD has given you, and you may freely eat the meat in your hometown, as I have commanded you. [22]Anyone, whether ceremonially clean or unclean, may eat that meat, just as you do now with gazelle and deer. [23]But never consume the blood, for the blood is the life, and you must not consume the lifeblood with the meat. [24]Instead, pour out the blood on the ground like water. [25]Do not consume the blood, so that all may go well with you and your children after you, because you will be doing what pleases the LORD.

[26]"Take your sacred gifts and your offerings given to fulfill a vow to the place the LORD chooses. [27]You must offer the meat and blood of your burnt offerings on the altar of the LORD your God. The blood of your other sacrifices must be poured out on the altar of the LORD your God, but you may eat the meat. [28]Be careful to obey all my commands, so that all will go well with you and your children after you, because you will be doing what is good and pleasing to the LORD your God.

[29]"When the LORD your God goes ahead of you and destroys the nations and you drive them out and live in their land, [30]do not fall into the trap of following their customs and worshiping their gods. Do not inquire about their gods, saying, 'How do

---

12:4-5 A place of worship was essential to the well-being of God's people in the Old Testament. The Tabernacle and the Jerusalem Temple of later times provided that place. It is important for God's people in all times in history to have a place to worship God properly. The encouragement that can be found by meeting with other believers to worship God is helpful to any successful recovery program.

these nations worship their gods? I want to follow their example.' ³¹You must not worship the LORD your God the way the other nations worship their gods, for they perform for their gods every detestable act that the LORD hates. They even burn their sons and daughters as sacrifices to their gods.

³²*"So be careful to obey all the commands I give you. You must not add anything to them or subtract anything from them.

CHAPTER 13
A Warning against Idolatry

¹*"Suppose there are prophets among you or those who dream dreams about the future, and they promise you signs or miracles, ²and the predicted signs or miracles occur. If they then say, 'Come, let us worship other gods'—gods you have not known before— ³do not listen to them. The LORD your God is testing you to see if you truly love him with all your heart and soul. ⁴Serve only the LORD your God and fear him alone. Obey his commands, listen to his voice, and cling to him. ⁵The false prophets or visionaries who try to lead you astray must be put to death, for they encourage rebellion against the LORD your God, who redeemed you from slavery and brought you out of the land of Egypt. Since they try to lead you astray from the way the LORD your God commanded you to live, you must put them to death. In this way you will purge the evil from among you.

⁶"Suppose someone secretly entices you—even your brother, your son or daughter, your beloved wife, or your closest friend—and says, 'Let us go worship other gods'—gods that neither you nor your ancestors have known. ⁷They might suggest that you worship the gods of peoples who live nearby or who come from the ends of the earth. ⁸But do not give in or listen. Have no pity, and do not spare or protect them. ⁹You must put them to death! Strike the first blow yourself, and then all the people must join in. ¹⁰Stone the guilty ones to death because they have tried to draw you away from the LORD your God, who rescued you from the land of Egypt, the place of slavery. ¹¹Then all Israel will hear about it and be afraid, and no one will act so wickedly again.

¹²"When you begin living in the towns the LORD your God is giving you, you may hear ¹³that scoundrels among you are leading their fellow citizens astray by saying, 'Let us go worship other gods'—gods you have not known before. ¹⁴In such cases, you must examine the facts carefully. If you find that the report is true and such a detestable act has been committed among you, ¹⁵you must attack that town and completely destroy* all its inhabitants, as well as all the livestock. ¹⁶Then you must pile all the plunder in the middle of the open square and burn it. Burn the entire town as a burnt offering to the LORD your God. That town must remain a ruin forever; it may never be rebuilt. ¹⁷Keep none of the plunder that has been set apart for destruction. Then the LORD will turn from his fierce anger and be merciful to you. He will have compassion on you and make you a large nation, just as he swore to your ancestors.

¹⁸"The LORD your God will be merciful only if you listen to his voice and keep all his commands that I am giving you today, doing what pleases him.

CHAPTER 14
Ceremonially Clean and Unclean Animals

"Since you are the people of the LORD your God, never cut yourselves or shave the hair above your foreheads in mourning for the dead. ²You have been set apart as holy to the

---

12:32 Verse 12:32 is numbered 13:1 in Hebrew text. 13:1 Verses 13:1-18 are numbered 13:2-19 in Hebrew text. 13:15 The Hebrew term used here refers to the complete consecration of things or people to the LORD, either by destroying them or by giving them as an offering; similarly in 13:17.

12:32 When all else fails, follow the directions. So often we attempt to accomplish God's work our own way and in our own strength. It is quite possible to do the right thing in the wrong way or for the wrong reason. We are to follow God's directions, all of God's directions, and nothing but God's directions. Do it God's way. That is the divine prescription for physical, emotional, and spiritual recovery.

13:1-5 This warning about false prophets is as important today as it was in ancient times. We all know of individuals who have gained a wide following, but their teachings or lifestyles do not measure up to the truth of God's Word. As we seek recovery, we need to measure the teachings we choose to live by against God's truth. We must make certain that we are following God's standards and strategies for recovery and wholeness.

14:2 As children of God, we need to stand out; we need to be different. We should begin by realizing that nothing in our life is outside God's interest. Because God is holy, our life should be

LORD your God, and he has chosen you from all the nations of the earth to be his own special treasure.

³ "You must not eat any detestable animals that are ceremonially unclean. ⁴These are the animals* you may eat: the ox, the sheep, the goat, ⁵the deer, the gazelle, the roe deer, the wild goat, the addax, the antelope, and the mountain sheep.

⁶ "You may eat any animal that has completely split hooves and chews the cud, ⁷but if the animal doesn't have both, it may not be eaten. So you may not eat the camel, the hare, or the hyrax.* They chew the cud but do not have split hooves, so they are ceremonially unclean for you. ⁸And you may not eat the pig. It has split hooves but does not chew the cud, so it is ceremonially unclean for you. You may not eat the meat of these animals or even touch their carcasses.

⁹ "Of all the marine animals, you may eat whatever has both fins and scales. ¹⁰You may not, however, eat marine animals that do not have both fins and scales. They are ceremonially unclean for you.

¹¹ "You may eat any bird that is ceremonially clean. ¹²These are the birds you may not eat: the griffon vulture, the bearded vulture, the black vulture, ¹³the kite, the falcon, buzzards of all kinds, ¹⁴ravens of all kinds, ¹⁵the eagle owl, the short-eared owl, the seagull, hawks of all kinds, ¹⁶the little owl, the great owl, the barn owl, ¹⁷the desert owl, the Egyptian vulture, the cormorant, ¹⁸the stork, herons of all kinds, the hoopoe, and the bat.

¹⁹ "All winged insects that walk along the ground are ceremonially unclean for you and may not be eaten. ²⁰But you may eat any winged bird or insect that is ceremonially clean.

²¹ "You must not eat anything that has died a natural death. You may give it to a foreigner living in your town, or you may sell it to a stranger. But do not eat it yourselves, for you are set apart as holy to the LORD your God.

"You must not cook a young goat in its mother's milk.

The Giving of Tithes

²² "You must set aside a tithe of your crops— one-tenth of all the crops you harvest each year. ²³Bring this tithe to the designated place of worship—the place the LORD your God chooses for his name to be honored—and eat it there in his presence. This applies to your tithes of grain, new wine, olive oil, and the firstborn males of your flocks and herds. Doing this will teach you always to fear the LORD your God.

²⁴ "Now when the LORD your God blesses you with a good harvest, the place of worship he chooses for his name to be honored might be too far for you to bring the tithe. ²⁵If so, you may sell the tithe portion of your crops and herds, put the money in a pouch, and go to the place the LORD your God has chosen. ²⁶When you arrive, you may use the money to buy any kind of food you want— cattle, sheep, goats, wine, or other alcoholic drink. Then feast there in the presence of the LORD your God and celebrate with your household. ²⁷And do not neglect the Levites in your town, for they will receive no allotment of land among you.

²⁸ "At the end of every third year, bring the entire tithe of that year's harvest and store it in the nearest town. ²⁹Give it to the Levites, who will receive no allotment of land among you, as well as to the foreigners living among you, the orphans, and the widows in your towns, so they can eat and be satisfied. Then the LORD your God will bless you in all your work.

CHAPTER 15
Release for Debtors

"At the end of every seventh year you must cancel the debts of everyone who owes you money. ²This is how it must be done. Everyone must cancel the loans they have made to their fellow Israelites. They must not demand payment from their neighbors or relatives, for the LORD's time of release has arrived. ³This release from debt, however, applies only to your fellow Israelites—not to the foreigners living among you.

⁴ "There should be no poor among you, for the LORD your God will greatly bless you in the land he is giving you as a special possession. ⁵You will receive this blessing if you are careful to obey all the commands of the LORD your God that I am giving you today. ⁶The

---

14:4 The identification of some of the animals and birds listed in this chapter is uncertain. **14:7** Or *coney,* or *rock badger.*

---

characterized by holiness in all things. Those of us in recovery need to take a constant personal inventory, seeking to follow God's plan for achieving wholeness. This is an important part of following God's call to holy living.

LORD your God will bless you as he has promised. You will lend money to many nations but will never need to borrow. You will rule many nations, but they will not rule over you.

⁷"But if there are any poor Israelites in your towns when you arrive in the land the LORD your God is giving you, do not be hard-hearted or tightfisted toward them. ⁸Instead, be generous and lend them whatever they need. ⁹Do not be mean-spirited and refuse someone a loan because the year for canceling debts is close at hand. If you refuse to make the loan and the needy person cries out to the LORD, you will be considered guilty of sin. ¹⁰Give generously to the poor, not grudgingly, for the LORD your God will bless you in everything you do. ¹¹There will always be some in the land who are poor. That is why I am commanding you to share freely with the poor and with other Israelites in need.

Release for Hebrew Slaves
¹²"If a fellow Hebrew sells himself or herself to be your servant* and serves you for six years, in the seventh year you must set that servant free.

¹³"When you release a male servant, do not send him away empty-handed. ¹⁴Give him a generous farewell gift from your flock, your threshing floor, and your winepress. Share with him some of the bounty with which the LORD your God has blessed you. ¹⁵Remember that you were once slaves in the land of Egypt and the LORD your God redeemed you! That is why I am giving you this command.

¹⁶"But suppose your servant says, 'I will not leave you,' because he loves you and your family, and he has done well with you. ¹⁷In that case, take an awl and push it through his earlobe into the door. After that,

he will be your servant for life. And do the same for your female servants.

¹⁸"You must not consider it a hardship when you release your servants. Remember that for six years they have given you services worth double the wages of hired workers, and the LORD your God will bless you in all you do.

Sacrificing Firstborn Male Animals
¹⁹"You must set aside for the LORD your God all the firstborn males from your flocks and herds. Do not use the firstborn of your herds to work your fields, and do not shear the firstborn of your flocks. ²⁰Instead, you and your family must eat these animals in the presence of the LORD your God each year at the place he chooses. ²¹But if this firstborn animal has any defect, such as lameness or blindness, or if anything else is wrong with it, you must not sacrifice it to the LORD your God. ²²Instead, use it for food for your family in your hometown. Anyone, whether ceremonially clean or unclean, may eat it, just as anyone may eat a gazelle or deer. ²³But you must not consume the blood. You must pour it out on the ground like water.

CHAPTER 16
Passover and the Festival of Unleavened Bread
"In honor of the LORD your God, celebrate the Passover each year in the early spring, in the month of Abib,* for that was the month in which the LORD your God brought you out of Egypt by night. ²Your Passover sacrifice may be from either the flock or the herd, and it must be sacrificed to the LORD your God at the designated place of worship—the place he chooses for his name to be honored. ³Eat it with bread made without yeast. For seven

---

15:12 Or *If a Hebrew man or woman is sold to you.* 16:1 Hebrew *Observe the month of Abib, and keep the Passover unto the LORD your God.* Abib, the first month of the ancient Hebrew lunar calendar, usually occurs within the months of March and April.

15:16-18 At first glance, these verses seem to have little to do with us. But the servant who serves first out of necessity and then out of devotion is similar to us and the way we relate to God, our master. As believers, we often obey simply because it is required. But as we mature in our walk with God, our obedience grows out of our love for him. We soon come to realize that everything that God requires of us is for our own good. We need to be willing to be perpetual slaves to God and his recovery program, abandoning our old life of sin (Romans 6:15-23).

15:19 The Israelites were to give to God the first of anything they received. This is an important step for anyone seeking wholeness. It demands that we put God first in the area of our resources, which includes both time and money. This shows that we are aware that God is the source of our future provision and that we are willing to trust him for it. It is healthy to give up some of our wealth and any security it promises. Only when we trust God with our life can we begin to conquer the problems that are too big for us to face alone. This is where recovery starts.

16:1-8 When God delivered the Israelites from Egypt, he brought them out using signs and other wonders. The final plague resulted in the death of all Egypt's firstborn sons. But God "passed

days the bread you eat must be made without yeast, as when you escaped from Egypt in such a hurry. Eat this bread—the bread of suffering—so that as long as you live you will remember the day you departed from Egypt. [4]Let no yeast be found in any house throughout your land for those seven days. And when you sacrifice the Passover lamb on the evening of the first day, do not let any of the meat remain until the next morning.

[5]"You may not sacrifice the Passover in just any of the towns that the LORD your God is giving you. [6]You must offer it only at the designated place of worship—the place the LORD your God chooses for his name to be honored. Sacrifice it there in the evening as the sun goes down on the anniversary of your exodus from Egypt. [7]Roast the lamb and eat it in the place the LORD your God chooses. Then you may go back to your tents the next morning. [8]For the next six days you may not eat any bread made with yeast. On the seventh day proclaim another holy day in honor of the LORD your God, and no work may be done on that day.

The Festival of Harvest

[9]"Count off seven weeks from when you first begin to cut the grain at the time of harvest. [10]Then celebrate the Festival of Harvest* to honor the LORD your God. Bring him a voluntary offering in proportion to the blessings you have received from him. [11]This is a time to celebrate before the LORD your God at the designated place of worship he will choose for his name to be honored. Cele-brate with your sons and daughters, your male and female servants, the Levites from your towns, and the foreigners, orphans, and widows who live among you. [12]Remember that you were once slaves in Egypt, so be careful to obey all these decrees.

The Festival of Shelters

[13]"You must observe the Festival of Shelters* for seven days at the end of the harvest season, after the grain has been threshed and the grapes have been pressed. [14]This festival will be a happy time of celebrating with your sons and daughters, your male and female servants, and the Levites, foreigners, orphans, and widows from your towns. [15]For seven days you must celebrate this festival to honor the LORD your God at the place he chooses, for it is he who blesses you with bountiful harvests and gives you success in all your work. This festival will be a time of great joy for all.

[16]"Each year every man in Israel must celebrate these three festivals: the Festival of Unleavened Bread, the Festival of Harvest, and the Festival of Shelters. On each of these occasions, all men must appear before the LORD your God at the place he chooses, but they must not appear before the LORD without a gift for him. [17]All must give as they are able, according to the blessings given to them by the LORD your God.

Justice for the People

[18]"Appoint judges and officials for yourselves from each of your tribes in all the towns the

16:10 Hebrew *Festival of Weeks;* also in 16:16. This was later called the Festival of Pentecost (see Acts 2:1). It is celebrated today as Shavuot (or Shabuoth). 16:13 Or *Festival of Booths,* or *Festival of Tabernacles;* also in 16:16. This was earlier called the Festival of the Final Harvest or Festival of Ingathering (see Exod 23:16b). It is celebrated today as Sukkot (or Succoth).

over" the homes of the Israelites, sparing their firstborn sons. From then on God required that the Israelites give a sacrifice in place of all their firstborn sons. This was a constant reminder of how God had spared their children. This should also remind us that we have been "passed over" because of God's love for us. God gave the sacrifice of his firstborn Son, Jesus Christ, so we could be free of sin and its terrible consequences.

16:9-12 The Festival of Harvest (also called the Feast of Weeks or Pentecost) was a season of great joy among God's people. It came near the beginning of the harvest season and was a time of commemoration and rejoicing—a time to celebrate the gifts that God had given. It was also a time of fellowship, feasting, and sharing God's gifts with those in need. God ordained festivals so people would be brought together for mutual encouragement. As we seek to rebuild our life, we also need the fellowship of God's people to gain the strength that makes the rebuilding process possible. We need to join with others for mutual encouragement and celebration.

16:1-15 The times and seasons of Israel's religious life were spelled out in detail. As Israel became a more settled agricultural nation, the people's lives were even further defined by the year's weather patterns. They were given specific times to work and rest. They knew when to transact business and when to abstain. God had prescribed a regular and healthy pattern of rest and work for his people. We also need to take regular rest periods if we want our life to progress toward wholeness.

LORD your God is giving you. They must judge the people fairly. [19]You must never twist justice or show partiality. Never accept a bribe, for bribes blind the eyes of the wise and corrupt the decisions of the godly. [20]Let true justice prevail, so you may live and occupy the land that the LORD your God is giving you.

[21]"You must never set up a wooden Asherah pole beside the altar you build for the LORD your God. [22]And never set up sacred pillars for worship, for the LORD your God hates them.

CHAPTER 17

"Never sacrifice sick or defective cattle, sheep, or goats to the LORD your God, for he detests such gifts.

[2]"When you begin living in the towns the LORD your God is giving you, a man or woman among you might do evil in the sight of the LORD your God and violate the covenant. [3]For instance, they might serve other gods or worship the sun, the moon, or any of the stars—the forces of heaven— which I have strictly forbidden. [4]When you hear about it, investigate the matter thoroughly. If it is true that this detestable thing has been done in Israel, [5]then the man or woman who has committed such an evil act must be taken to the gates of the town and stoned to death. [6]But never put a person to death on the testimony of only one witness. There must always be two or three witnesses. [7]The witnesses must throw the first stones, and then all the people may join in. In this way, you will purge the evil from among you.

[8]"Suppose a case arises in a local court that is too hard for you to decide—for instance, whether someone is guilty of murder or only of manslaughter, or a difficult lawsuit, or a case involving different kinds of assault. Take such legal cases to the place the LORD your God will choose, [9]and present them to the Levitical priests or the judge on duty at that time. They will hear the case and declare the verdict. [10]You must carry out the verdict they announce and the sentence they prescribe at the place the LORD chooses. You must do exactly what they say. [11]After they have interpreted the law and declared their verdict, the sentence they impose must be fully executed; do not modify it in any way. [12]Anyone arrogant enough to reject the verdict of the judge or of the priest who represents the LORD your God must die. In this way you will purge the evil from Israel. [13]Then everyone else will hear about it and be afraid to act so arrogantly.

Guidelines for a King

[14]"You are about to enter the land the LORD your God is giving you. When you take it over and settle there, you may think, 'We should select a king to rule over us like the other nations around us.' [15]If this happens, be sure to select as king the man the LORD your God chooses. You must appoint a fellow Israelite; he may not be a foreigner.

[16]"The king must not build up a large stable of horses for himself or send his people to Egypt to buy horses, for the LORD has told you, 'You must never return to Egypt.' [17]The king must not take many wives for himself, because they will turn his heart away from the LORD. And he must not accumulate large amounts of wealth in silver and gold for himself.

[18]"When he sits on the throne as king, he must copy for himself this body of instruction on a scroll in the presence of the Levitical priests. [19]He must always keep that copy with him and read it daily as long as he lives. That way he will learn to fear the LORD his God by obeying all the terms of these instructions and decrees. [20]This regular reading will prevent him from becoming proud and acting as if he is above his fellow citizens. It will also prevent him from turning away from these commands in the smallest way. And it will ensure that he and his descendants will reign for many generations in Israel.

17:1 God should get the best we have. For the ancient Israelites, this was important with respect to their material sacrifices. How much more does the principle apply in terms of our offering our life to God as a living sacrifice (see Romans 12:1). We must do our best to preserve ourself for God's service. Recovery is an important part of this task.

17:8-13 Submission to authority is a concept that is largely lost in our culture, but it is consistent with biblical teaching. God is our supreme authority, but the Bible also makes it clear that we are to submit to the earthly authorities and governments God has placed over us (Romans 13:1-5; 1 Peter 2:13-14). Part of God's program for healthy living involves respecting and submitting to our authorities. "Anyone who rebels against authority is rebelling against what God has instituted" (Romans 13:2). When we do follow the laws set out for us by the government, we are bringing honor to God.

CHAPTER 18
Gifts for the Priests and Levites

"Remember that the Levitical priests—that is, the whole of the tribe of Levi—will receive no allotment of land among the other tribes in Israel. Instead, the priests and Levites will eat from the special gifts given to the LORD, for that is their share. ²They will have no land of their own among the Israelites. The LORD himself is their special possession, just as he promised them.

³"These are the parts the priests may claim as their share from the cattle, sheep, and goats that the people bring as offerings: the shoulder, the cheeks, and the stomach. ⁴You must also give to the priests the first share of the grain, the new wine, the olive oil, and the wool at shearing time. ⁵For the LORD your God chose the tribe of Levi out of all your tribes to minister in the LORD's name forever.

⁶"Suppose a Levite chooses to move from his town in Israel, wherever he is living, to the place the LORD chooses for worship. ⁷He may minister there in the name of the LORD his God, just like all his fellow Levites who are serving the LORD there. ⁸He may eat his share of the sacrifices and offerings, even if he also receives support from his family.

A Call to Holy Living

⁹"When you enter the land the LORD your God is giving you, be very careful not to imitate the detestable customs of the nations living there. ¹⁰For example, never sacrifice your son or daughter as a burnt offering.* And do not let your people practice fortune-telling, or use sorcery, or interpret omens, or engage in witchcraft, ¹¹or cast spells, or function as mediums or psychics, or call forth the spirits of the dead. ¹²Anyone who does these things is detestable to the LORD. It is because the other nations have done these detestable things that the LORD your God will drive them out ahead of you. ¹³But you must be blameless before the LORD your God. ¹⁴The nations you are about to displace consult sorcerers and fortune-tellers, but the LORD your God forbids you to do such things."

True and False Prophets

¹⁵Moses continued, "The LORD your God will raise up for you a prophet like me from among your fellow Israelites. You must listen to him. ¹⁶For this is what you yourselves requested of the LORD your God when you were assembled at Mount Sinai.* You said, 'Don't let us hear the voice of the LORD our God anymore or see this blazing fire, for we will die.'

¹⁷"Then the LORD said to me, 'What they have said is right. ¹⁸I will raise up a prophet like you from among their fellow Israelites. I will put my words in his mouth, and he will tell the people everything I command him. ¹⁹I will personally deal with anyone who will not listen to the messages the prophet proclaims on my behalf. ²⁰But any prophet who falsely claims to speak in my name or who speaks in the name of another god must die.'

²¹"But you may wonder, 'How will we know whether or not a prophecy is from the LORD?' ²²If the prophet speaks in the LORD's name but his prediction does not happen or come true, you will know that the LORD did not give that message. That prophet has spoken without my authority and need not be feared.

CHAPTER 19
Cities of Refuge

"When the LORD your God destroys the nations whose land he is giving you, you will take over their land and settle in their towns and homes. ²Then you must set apart three cities of refuge in the land the LORD your God is giving you. ³Survey the territory,* and divide the land the LORD your God is giving

---

18:10 Or *never make your son or daughter pass through the fire.* 18:16 Hebrew *Horeb,* another name for Sinai. 19:3 Or *Keep the roads in good repair.*

18:9-12 Beware of the occult. There is a resurgence of demonic activity in the world today. Many people think they can dabble in the occult without doing any harm, least of all to themselves. The Bible, however, condemns these activities in no uncertain terms. Mark this well: Meaningful spiritual or emotional growth is impossible for anyone who is taking part in occult activities.

19:1-7 In ancient Near Eastern societies, if a person killed someone, the deceased person's family had the right of vengeance, even if the killing was accidental. God's concern with justice in Israelite society led to his institution of cities of refuge. If a killing was accidental, the person guilty of manslaughter could run to one of these cities for safety from the avenging family. As we progress in recovery, we also need places where we can escape the pressing demands of life, places where we can find support as we begin the task of rebuilding. Recovery groups or church fellowship groups often serve as places of refuge for those in recovery.

you into three districts, with one of these cities in each district. Then anyone who has killed someone can flee to one of the cities of refuge for safety.

⁴"If someone kills another person unintentionally, without previous hostility, the slayer may flee to any of these cities to live in safety. ⁵For example, suppose someone goes into the forest with a neighbor to cut wood. And suppose one of them swings an ax to chop down a tree, and the ax head flies off the handle, killing the other person. In such cases, the slayer may flee to one of the cities of refuge to live in safety.

⁶"If the distance to the nearest city of refuge is too far, an enraged avenger might be able to chase down and kill the person who caused the death. Then the slayer would die unfairly, since he had never shown hostility toward the person who died. ⁷That is why I am commanding you to set aside three cities of refuge.

⁸"And if the LORD your God enlarges your territory, as he swore to your ancestors, and gives you all the land he promised them, ⁹you must designate three additional cities of refuge. (He will give you this land if you are careful to obey all the commands I have given you—if you always love the LORD your God and walk in his ways.) ¹⁰That way you will prevent the death of innocent people in the land the LORD your God is giving you as your special possession. You will not be held responsible for the death of innocent people.

¹¹"But suppose someone is hostile toward a neighbor and deliberately ambushes and murders him and then flees to one of the cities of refuge. ¹²In that case, the elders of the murderer's hometown must send agents to the city of refuge to bring him back and hand him over to the dead person's avenger to be put to death. ¹³Do not feel sorry for that murderer! Purge from Israel the guilt of murdering innocent people; then all will go well with you.

Concern for Justice

¹⁴"When you arrive in the land the LORD your God is giving you as your special possession, you must never steal anyone's land by moving the boundary markers your ancestors set up to mark their property.

¹⁵"You must not convict anyone of a crime on the testimony of only one witness. The facts of the case must be established by the testimony of two or three witnesses.

¹⁶"If a malicious witness comes forward and accuses someone of a crime, ¹⁷then both the accuser and accused must appear before the LORD by coming to the priests and judges in office at that time. ¹⁸The judges must investigate the case thoroughly. If the accuser has brought false charges against his fellow Israelite, ¹⁹you must impose on the accuser the sentence he intended for the other person. In this way, you will purge such evil from among you. ²⁰Then the rest of the people will hear about it and be afraid to do such an evil thing. ²¹You must show no pity for the guilty! Your rule should be life for life, eye for eye, tooth for tooth, hand for hand, foot for foot.

CHAPTER 20
Regulations concerning War

"When you go out to fight your enemies and you face horses and chariots and an army greater than your own, do not be afraid. The LORD your God, who brought you out of the land of Egypt, is with you! ²When you prepare for battle, the priest must come forward to speak to the troops. ³He will say to them, 'Listen to me, all you men of Israel! Do not be afraid as you go out to fight your enemies today! Do not lose heart or panic or tremble

---

19:14 It is important to God that we respect the property of others. This verse forbids the moving of landmarks, specifically addressing the issue of real estate rights. Physical landmarks are an important kind of personal boundary. As we relate to others, we need to be sure that we respect the legitimate boundaries they have set up, physical or emotional. As we take inventory of our wrongs, we should pay close attention to this boundary issue. In what ways have we trespassed in other people's lives?

19:21 Here is the law of retribution in its simplest form. Given this kind of context, the task of recovery would be virtually impossible. All the wrongs we have ever committed would have to be leveled against us for our guilt to be satisfied. How wonderful that God has provided his Son to take the punishment on our behalf. Recovery can take place only in the environment of grace created by the work of Jesus Christ.

20:1 "Do not be afraid." This great and encouraging imperative appears often in the Bible. It has occurred many times in this book without receiving any special notice, but here in the context of enemies it seems particularly significant. Even as we face impossible odds in recovery, we should not fear. God is able to bring about recovery for us against all odds.

before them. [4]For the LORD your God is going with you! He will fight for you against your enemies, and he will give you victory!'

[5]"Then the officers of the army must address the troops and say, 'Has anyone here just built a new house but not yet dedicated it? If so, you may go home! You might be killed in the battle, and someone else would dedicate your house. [6]Has anyone here just planted a vineyard but not yet eaten any of its fruit? If so, you may go home! You might die in battle, and someone else would eat the first fruit. [7]Has anyone here just become engaged to a woman but not yet married her? Well, you may go home and get married! You might die in the battle, and someone else would marry her.'

[8]"Then the officers will also say, 'Is anyone here afraid or worried? If you are, you may go home before you frighten anyone else.' [9]When the officers have finished speaking to their troops, they will appoint the unit commanders.

[10]"As you approach a town to attack it, you must first offer its people terms for peace. [11]If they accept your terms and open the gates to you, then all the people inside will serve you in forced labor. [12]But if they refuse to make peace and prepare to fight, you must attack the town. [13]When the LORD your God hands the town over to you, use your swords to kill every man in the town. [14]But you may keep for yourselves all the women, children, livestock, and other plunder. You may enjoy the plunder from your enemies that the LORD your God has given you.

[15]"But these instructions apply only to distant towns, not to the towns of the nations in the land you will enter. [16]In those towns that the LORD your God is giving you as a special possession, destroy every living thing. [17]You must completely destroy* the Hittites, Amorites, Canaanites, Perizzites, Hivites, and Jebusites, just as the LORD your God has commanded you. [18]This will prevent the people of the land from teaching you to imitate their detestable customs in the worship of their gods, which would cause you to sin deeply against the LORD your God.

[19]"When you are attacking a town and the war drags on, you must not cut down the trees with your axes. You may eat the fruit, but do not cut down the trees. Are the trees your enemies, that you should attack them?

[20]You may only cut down trees that you know are not valuable for food. Use them to make the equipment you need to attack the enemy town until it falls.

CHAPTER 21
Cleansing for Unsolved Murder

"When you are in the land the LORD your God is giving you, someone may be found murdered in a field, and you don't know who committed the murder. [2]In such a case, your elders and judges must measure the distance from the site of the crime to the nearby towns. [3]When the nearest town has been determined, that town's elders must select from the herd a heifer that has never been trained or yoked to a plow. [4]They must lead it down to a valley that has not been plowed or planted and that has a stream running through it. There in the valley they must break the heifer's neck. [5]Then the Levitical priests must step forward, for the LORD your God has chosen them to minister before him and to pronounce blessings in the LORD's name. They are to decide all legal and criminal cases.

[6]"The elders of the town must wash their hands over the heifer whose neck was broken. [7]Then they must say, 'Our hands did not shed this person's blood, nor did we see it happen. [8]O LORD, forgive your people Israel whom you have redeemed. Do not charge your people with the guilt of murdering an innocent person.' Then they will be absolved of the guilt of this person's blood. [9]By following these instructions, you will do what is right in the LORD's sight and will cleanse the guilt of murder from your community.

Marriage to a Captive Woman

[10]"Suppose you go out to war against your enemies and the LORD your God hands them over to you, and you take some of them as captives. [11]And suppose you see among the captives a beautiful woman, and you are attracted to her and want to marry her. [12]If this happens, you may take her to your home, where she must shave her head, cut her nails, [13]and change the clothes she was wearing when she was captured. She will stay in your home, but let her mourn for her father and mother for a full month. Then you may marry her, and you will be her husband and she will be your wife. [14]But if you marry her

20:17 The Hebrew term used here refers to the complete consecration of things or people to the LORD, either by destroying them or by giving them as an offering.

and she does not please you, you must let her go free. You may not sell her or treat her as a slave, for you have humiliated her.

Rights of the Firstborn

15 "Suppose a man has two wives, but he loves one and not the other, and both have given him sons. And suppose the firstborn son is the son of the wife he does not love. 16When the man divides his inheritance, he may not give the larger inheritance to his younger son, the son of the wife he loves, as if he were the firstborn son. 17He must recognize the rights of his oldest son, the son of the wife he does not love, by giving him a double portion. He is the first son of his father's virility, and the rights of the firstborn belong to him.

Dealing with a Rebellious Son

18 "Suppose a man has a stubborn and rebellious son who will not obey his father or mother, even though they discipline him. 19 In such a case, the father and mother must take the son to the elders as they hold court at the town gate. 20The parents must say to the elders, 'This son of ours is stubborn and rebellious and refuses to obey. He is a glutton and a drunkard.' 21Then all the men of his town must stone him to death. In this way, you will purge this evil from among you, and all Israel will hear about it and be afraid.

Various Regulations

22 "If someone has committed a crime worthy of death and is executed and hung on a tree,* 23the body must not remain hanging from the tree overnight. You must bury the body that same day, for anyone who is hung* is cursed in the sight of God. In this way, you will prevent the defilement of the land the LORD your God is giving you as your special possession.

CHAPTER 22

"If you see your neighbor's ox or sheep or goat wandering away, don't ignore your responsibility.* Take it back to its owner. 2If its owner does not live nearby or you don't know who the owner is, take it to your place and keep it until the owner comes looking for it. Then you must return it. 3Do the same if you find your neighbor's donkey, clothing, or anything else your neighbor loses. Don't ignore your responsibility.

4"If you see that your neighbor's donkey or ox has collapsed on the road, do not look the other way. Go and help your neighbor get it back on its feet!

5"A woman must not put on men's clothing, and a man must not wear women's clothing. Anyone who does this is detestable in the sight of the LORD your God.

6"If you happen to find a bird's nest in a tree or on the ground, and there are young ones or eggs in it with the mother sitting in the nest, do not take the mother with the young. 7You may take the young, but let the mother go, so that you may prosper and enjoy a long life.

8"When you build a new house, you must build a railing around the edge of its flat roof. That way you will not be considered guilty of murder if someone falls from the roof.

9"You must not plant any other crop between the rows of your vineyard. If you do, you are forbidden to use either the grapes from the vineyard or the other crop.

10"You must not plow with an ox and a donkey harnessed together.

11"You must not wear clothing made of wool and linen woven together.

12"You must put four tassels on the hem of the cloak with which you cover yourself—on the front, back, and sides.

21:22 Or *impaled on a pole;* similarly in 21:23. 21:23 Greek version reads *for everyone who is hung on a tree.* Compare Gal 3:13. 22:1 Hebrew *don't hide yourself;* similarly in 22:3.

21:18-21 Rebellious children are one of the most heartbreaking products of dysfunctional families. But sometimes, even when parents do the best they can, children still become rebellious and refuse to adhere to God's standards of conduct. In such cases, the Old Testament law offered this drastic measure. This law reveals how much God desires that we have healthy family relationships. He desires that proper authority structures be established early in each family so such radical measures are not necessary. If we have failed in the past, seeking reconciliation is an important step toward healing our family relationships.

22:5 One of the ugliest results of rebellion in our times is the confusion of sex roles. The Bible is unequivocal on this point: Don't reverse sex roles. Men, rejoice in your maleness. Women, celebrate your femaleness. Be the gender God intended you to be—in your appearance, in your clothing, and in your thinking. Outside of these parameters, meaningful recovery is impossible.

Regulations for Sexual Purity

¹³"Suppose a man marries a woman, but after sleeping with her, he turns against her ¹⁴and publicly accuses her of shameful conduct, saying, 'When I married this woman, I discovered she was not a virgin.' ¹⁵Then the woman's father and mother must bring the proof of her virginity to the elders as they hold court at the town gate. ¹⁶Her father must say to them, 'I gave my daughter to this man to be his wife, and now he has turned against her. ¹⁷He has accused her of shameful conduct, saying, "I discovered that your daughter was not a virgin." But here is the proof of my daughter's virginity.' Then they must spread her bed sheet before the elders. ¹⁸The elders must then take the man and punish him. ¹⁹They must also fine him 100 pieces of silver,* which he must pay to the woman's father because he publicly accused a virgin of Israel of shameful conduct. The woman will then remain the man's wife, and he may never divorce her.

²⁰"But suppose the man's accusations are true, and he can show that she was not a virgin. ²¹The woman must be taken to the door of her father's home, and there the men of the town must stone her to death, for she has committed a disgraceful crime in Israel by being promiscuous while living in her parents' home. In this way, you will purge this evil from among you.

²²"If a man is discovered committing adultery, both he and the woman must die. In this way, you will purge Israel of such evil.

²³"Suppose a man meets a young woman, a virgin who is engaged to be married, and he has sexual intercourse with her. If this happens within a town, ²⁴you must take both of them to the gates of that town and stone them to death. The woman is guilty because she did not scream for help. The man must die because he violated another man's wife. In this way, you will purge this evil from among you.

²⁵"But if the man meets the engaged woman out in the country, and he rapes her, then only the man must die. ²⁶Do nothing to the young woman; she has committed no crime worthy of death. She is as innocent as a murder victim. ²⁷Since the man raped her out in the country, it must be assumed that she screamed, but there was no one to rescue her.

²⁸"Suppose a man has intercourse with a young woman who is a virgin but is not engaged to be married. If they are discovered, ²⁹he must pay her father fifty pieces of silver.* Then he must marry the young woman because he violated her, and he may never divorce her as long as he lives.

³⁰★"A man must not marry his father's former wife, for this would violate his father.

CHAPTER 23

Regulations concerning Worship

¹★"If a man's testicles are crushed or his penis is cut off, he may not be admitted to the assembly of the LORD.

²"If a person is illegitimate by birth, neither he nor his descendants for ten generations may be admitted to the assembly of the LORD.

³"No Ammonite or Moabite or any of their descendants for ten generations may be admitted to the assembly of the LORD. ⁴These nations did not welcome you with food and water when you came out of Egypt. Instead, they hired Balaam son of Beor from Pethor in distant Aram-naharaim to curse you. ⁵But the LORD your God refused to listen to Balaam. He turned the intended curse into a blessing because the LORD your God loves you. ⁶As long as you live, you must never promote the welfare and prosperity of the Ammonites or Moabites.

⁷"Do not detest the Edomites or the Egyptians, because the Edomites are your relatives and you lived as foreigners among the Egyptians. ⁸The third generation of Edomites and Egyptians may enter the assembly of the LORD.

Miscellaneous Regulations

⁹"When you go to war against your enemies, be sure to stay away from anything that is impure.

22:19 Hebrew *100 [shekels] of silver,* about 2.5 pounds or 1.1 kilograms in weight. 22:29 Hebrew *50 [shekels] of silver,* about 1.25 pounds or 570 grams in weight. 22:30 Verse 22:30 is numbered 23:1 in Hebrew text. 23:1 Verses 23:1-25 are numbered 23:2-26 in Hebrew text.

22:13-30 The home is of vital concern to God. He cares about marital faithfulness and purity. He spells out all of these regulations to demonstrate that the marriage relationship is of great and holy importance. Those of us recovering from dysfunctional families need to understand God's pattern for marriage. Marital fidelity is the only means of establishing a healthy family where members are characterized by maturity and wholeness.

¹⁰ "Any man who becomes ceremonially defiled because of a nocturnal emission must leave the camp and stay away all day. ¹¹Toward evening he must bathe himself, and at sunset he may return to the camp.

¹² "You must have a designated area outside the camp where you can go to relieve yourself. ¹³Each of you must have a spade as part of your equipment. Whenever you relieve yourself, dig a hole with the spade and cover the excrement. ¹⁴The camp must be holy, for the LORD your God moves around in your camp to protect you and to defeat your enemies. He must not see any shameful thing among you, or he will turn away from you.

¹⁵ "If slaves should escape from their masters and take refuge with you, you must not hand them over to their masters. ¹⁶Let them live among you in any town they choose, and do not oppress them.

¹⁷ "No Israelite, whether man or woman, may become a temple prostitute. ¹⁸When you are bringing an offering to fulfill a vow, you must not bring to the house of the LORD your God any offering from the earnings of a prostitute, whether a man* or a woman, for both are detestable to the LORD your God.

¹⁹ "Do not charge interest on the loans you make to a fellow Israelite, whether you loan money, or food, or anything else. ²⁰You may charge interest to foreigners, but you may not charge interest to Israelites, so that the LORD your God may bless you in everything you do in the land you are about to enter and occupy.

²¹ "When you make a vow to the LORD your God, be prompt in fulfilling whatever you promised him. For the LORD your God demands that you promptly fulfill all your vows,

or you will be guilty of sin. ²²However, it is not a sin to refrain from making a vow. ²³But once you have voluntarily made a vow, be careful to fulfill your promise to the LORD your God.

²⁴ "When you enter your neighbor's vineyard, you may eat your fill of grapes, but you must not carry any away in a basket. ²⁵And when you enter your neighbor's field of grain, you may pluck the heads of grain with your hand, but you must not harvest it with a sickle.

CHAPTER 24

"Suppose a man marries a woman but she does not please him. Having discovered something wrong with her, he writes a document of divorce, hands it to her, and sends her away from his house. ²When she leaves his house, she is free to marry another man. ³But if the second husband also turns against her, writes a document of divorce, hands it to her, and sends her away, or if he dies, ⁴the first husband may not marry her again, for she has been defiled. That would be detestable to the LORD. You must not bring guilt upon the land the LORD your God is giving you as a special possession.

⁵ "A newly married man must not be drafted into the army or be given any other official responsibilities. He must be free to spend one year at home, bringing happiness to the wife he has married.

⁶ "It is wrong to take a set of millstones, or even just the upper millstone, as security for a loan, for the owner uses it to make a living.

⁷ "If anyone kidnaps a fellow Israelite and treats him as a slave or sells him, the kidnapper must die. In this way, you will purge the evil from among you.

23:18 Hebrew *a dog.*

23:17-18 Prostitution is singled out for special condemnation. Within the bounds of marriage is the only valid context for sex. In society today, sexual activity outside of marriage has become an accepted practice, and sexual purity is viewed as something to be embarrassed about. Healthy marriages must be founded on trust, which is based to a significant extent on sexual purity. God's program for healthy relationships demands that sexual activity be kept within marriage. If we have failed in this area, there is still hope for recovery, but the consequences of our failure will be far-reaching.

23:21-23 Being trustworthy is an absolute necessity for anyone in recovery. All enduring relationships are built on trust. When we make promises, we must keep them—even at great inconvenience to ourselves. Lying is a problem for many people. It breaks down relationships and eventually destroys them. We must realize that telling the truth is always best for us in the long run. The truth is one boundary we can never overstep without severe consequences.

24:1-4 Some might look at this regulation as proof that God supports divorce. On the contrary, God hates divorce (Malachi 2:16). Regulations like this were given to put controls on this unsatisfactory solution for disunity in marriage. Some of us may be recovering from a divorce. We can rest assured that God's grace is sufficient for our needs. We also need to reconcile any broken relationships that have resulted, asking and granting forgiveness where necessary.

8"In all cases involving serious skin diseases,* be careful to follow the instructions of the Levitical priests; obey all the commands I have given them. 9Remember what the LORD your God did to Miriam as you were coming from Egypt.

10"If you lend anything to your neighbor, do not enter his house to pick up the item he is giving as security. 11You must wait outside while he goes in and brings it out to you. 12If your neighbor is poor and gives you his cloak as security for a loan, do not keep the cloak overnight. 13Return the cloak to its owner by sunset so he can stay warm through the night and bless you, and the LORD your God will count you as righteous.

14"Never take advantage of poor and destitute laborers, whether they are fellow Israelites or foreigners living in your towns. 15You must pay them their wages each day before sunset because they are poor and are counting on it. If you don't, they might cry out to the LORD against you, and it would be counted against you as sin.

16"Parents must not be put to death for the sins of their children, nor children for the sins of their parents. Those deserving to die must be put to death for their own crimes.

17"True justice must be given to foreigners living among you and to orphans, and you must never accept a widow's garment as security for her debt. 18Always remember that you were slaves in Egypt and that the LORD your God redeemed you from your slavery. That is why I have given you this command.

19"When you are harvesting your crops and forget to bring in a bundle of grain from your field, don't go back to get it. Leave it for the foreigners, orphans, and widows. Then the LORD your God will bless you in all you do. 20When you beat the olives from your olive trees, don't go over the boughs twice. Leave the remaining olives for the foreigners, orphans, and widows. 21When you gather the grapes in your vineyard, don't glean the vines after they are picked. Leave the remaining grapes for the foreigners, orphans, and widows. 22Remember that you were slaves in the land of Egypt. That is why I am giving you this command.

CHAPTER 25

"Suppose two people take a dispute to court, and the judges declare that one is right and the other is wrong. 2If the person in the wrong is sentenced to be flogged, the judge must command him to lie down and be beaten in his presence with the number of lashes appropriate to the crime. 3But never give more than forty lashes; more than forty lashes would publicly humiliate your neighbor.

4"You must not muzzle an ox to keep it from eating as it treads out the grain.

5"If two brothers are living together on the same property and one of them dies without a son, his widow may not be married to anyone from outside the family. Instead, her husband's brother should marry her and have intercourse with her to fulfill the duties of a brother-in-law. 6The first son she bears to him will be considered the son of the dead brother, so that his name will not be forgotten in Israel.

7"But if the man refuses to marry his brother's widow, she must go to the town gate and say to the elders assembled there, 'My husband's brother refuses to preserve his brother's name in Israel—he refuses to fulfill the duties of a brother-in-law by marrying me.' 8The elders of the town will then summon him and talk with him. If he still refuses and says, 'I don't want to marry her,' 9the widow must walk over to him in the presence of the elders, pull his sandal from his foot, and spit in his face. Then she must declare, 'This is what happens to a man who refuses to provide his brother with children.' 10Ever afterward in Israel his family will be referred to as 'the family of the man whose sandal was pulled off'!

11"If two Israelite men get into a fight and the wife of one tries to rescue her husband by grabbing the testicles of the other man, 12you must cut off her hand. Show her no pity.

13"You must use accurate scales when you weigh out merchandise, 14and you must use full and honest measures. 15Yes, always use honest weights and measures, so that you may enjoy a long life in the land the LORD your God is giving you. 16All who cheat with dishonest weights and measures are detestable to the LORD your God.

17"Never forget what the Amalekites did to you as you came from Egypt. 18They attacked you when you were exhausted and weary, and they struck down those who were straggling behind. They had no fear of God. 19Therefore, when the LORD your God has given you rest from all your enemies in the land he is giving you as a special possession, you must destroy

24:8 Traditionally rendered *leprosy*. The Hebrew word used here can describe various skin diseases.

the Amalekites and erase their memory from under heaven. Never forget this!

CHAPTER 26
Harvest Offerings and Tithes

"When you enter the land the LORD your God is giving you as a special possession and you have conquered it and settled there, ²put some of the first produce from each crop you harvest into a basket and bring it to the designated place of worship—the place the LORD your God chooses for his name to be honored. ³Go to the priest in charge at that time and say to him, 'With this gift I acknowledge to the LORD your God that I have entered the land he swore to our ancestors he would give us.' ⁴The priest will then take the basket from your hand and set it before the altar of the LORD your God.

⁵"You must then say in the presence of the LORD your God, 'My ancestor Jacob was a wandering Aramean who went to live as a foreigner in Egypt. His family arrived few in number, but in Egypt they became a large and mighty nation. ⁶When the Egyptians oppressed and humiliated us by making us their slaves, ⁷we cried out to the LORD, the God of our ancestors. He heard our cries and saw our hardship, toil, and oppression. ⁸So the LORD brought us out of Egypt with a strong hand and powerful arm, with overwhelming terror, and with miraculous signs and wonders. ⁹He brought us to this place and gave us this land flowing with milk and honey! ¹⁰And now, O LORD, I have brought you the first portion of the harvest you have given me from the ground.' Then place the produce before the LORD your God, and bow to the ground in worship before him. ¹¹Afterward you may go and celebrate because of all the good things the LORD your God has given to you and your household. Remember to include the Levites and the foreigners living among you in the celebration.

¹²"Every third year you must offer a special tithe of your crops. In this year of the special tithe you must give your tithes to the Levites, foreigners, orphans, and widows, so that they will have enough to eat in your towns. ¹³Then you must declare in the presence of the LORD your God, 'I have taken the sacred gift from my house and have given it to the Levites, foreigners, orphans, and widows,

just as you commanded me. I have not violated or forgotten any of your commands. ¹⁴I have not eaten any of it while in mourning; I have not handled it while I was ceremonially unclean; and I have not offered any of it to the dead. I have obeyed the LORD my God and have done everything you commanded me. ¹⁵Now look down from your holy dwelling place in heaven and bless your people Israel and the land you swore to our ancestors to give us—a land flowing with milk and honey.'

A Call to Obey the LORD's Commands

¹⁶"Today the LORD your God has commanded you to obey all these decrees and regulations. So be careful to obey them wholeheartedly. ¹⁷You have declared today that the LORD is your God. And you have promised to walk in his ways, and to obey his decrees, commands, and regulations, and to do everything he tells you. ¹⁸The LORD has declared today that you are his people, his own special treasure, just as he promised, and that you must obey all his commands. ¹⁹And if you do, he will set you high above all the other nations he has made. Then you will receive praise, honor, and renown. You will be a nation that is holy to the LORD your God, just as he promised."

CHAPTER 27
The Altar on Mount Ebal

Then Moses and the leaders of Israel gave this charge to the people: "Obey all these commands that I am giving you today. ²When you cross the Jordan River and enter the land the LORD your God is giving you, set up some large stones and coat them with plaster. ³Write this whole body of instruction on them when you cross the river to enter the land the LORD your God is giving you—a land flowing with milk and honey, just as the LORD, the God of your ancestors, promised you. ⁴When you cross the Jordan, set up these stones at Mount Ebal and coat them with plaster, as I am commanding you today.

⁵"Then build an altar there to the LORD your God, using natural, uncut stones. You must not shape the stones with an iron tool. ⁶Build the altar of uncut stones, and use it to offer burnt offerings to the LORD your God. ⁷Also sacrifice peace offerings on it, and celebrate by feasting there before the LORD your

---

27:7 Joy is an important characteristic of a healthy and godly life. It is often looked upon as something nice to have but not absolutely necessary. This is not the Bible's perspective. God's

God. [8]You must clearly write all these instructions on the stones coated with plaster."

[9]Then Moses and the Levitical priests addressed all Israel as follows: "O Israel, be quiet and listen! Today you have become the people of the LORD your God. [10]So you must obey the LORD your God by keeping all these commands and decrees that I am giving you today."

Curses from Mount Ebal

[11]That same day Moses also gave this charge to the people: [12]"When you cross the Jordan River, the tribes of Simeon, Levi, Judah, Issachar, Joseph, and Benjamin must stand on Mount Gerizim to proclaim a blessing over the people. [13]And the tribes of Reuben, Gad, Asher, Zebulun, Dan, and Naphtali must stand on Mount Ebal to proclaim a curse.

[14]"Then the Levites will shout to all the people of Israel:

[15]'Cursed is anyone who carves or casts an idol and secretly sets it up. These idols, the work of craftsmen, are detestable to the LORD.'
 And all the people will reply, 'Amen.'

[16]'Cursed is anyone who dishonors father or mother.'
 And all the people will reply, 'Amen.'

[17]'Cursed is anyone who steals property from a neighbor by moving a boundary marker.'
 And all the people will reply, 'Amen.'

[18]'Cursed is anyone who leads a blind person astray on the road.'
 And all the people will reply, 'Amen.'

[19]'Cursed is anyone who denies justice to foreigners, orphans, or widows.'
 And all the people will reply, 'Amen.'

[20]'Cursed is anyone who has sexual intercourse with one of his father's wives, for he has violated his father.'
 And all the people will reply, 'Amen.'

[21]'Cursed is anyone who has sexual intercourse with an animal.'
 And all the people will reply, 'Amen.'

[22]'Cursed is anyone who has sexual intercourse with his sister, whether she is the daughter of his father or his mother.'
 And all the people will reply, 'Amen.'

[23]'Cursed is anyone who has sexual intercourse with his mother-in-law.'
 And all the people will reply, 'Amen.'

[24]'Cursed is anyone who attacks a neighbor in secret.'
 And all the people will reply, 'Amen.'

[25]'Cursed is anyone who accepts payment to kill an innocent person.'
 And all the people will reply, 'Amen.'

[26]'Cursed is anyone who does not affirm and obey the terms of these instructions.'
 And all the people will reply, 'Amen.'

CHAPTER 28
Blessings for Obedience

"If you fully obey the LORD your God and carefully keep all his commands that I am giving you today, the LORD your God will set you high above all the nations of the world. [2]You will experience all these blessings if you obey the LORD your God:

[3]Your towns and your fields
 will be blessed.
[4]Your children and your crops
 will be blessed.
 The offspring of your herds and flocks
 will be blessed.
[5]Your fruit baskets and breadboards
 will be blessed.
[6]Wherever you go and whatever you do,
 you will be blessed.

[7]"The LORD will conquer your enemies when they attack you. They will attack you from one direction, but they will scatter from you in seven!

Word calls us to live a joy-filled life (see also 12:12; 28:47-48). As we approach God in worship, it is possible to have joy even when experiencing the pain of recovery.

27:15-26 Sin never goes unpunished. God considers disobedience so grave that he even spells out its consequences. Those who disobey God's commandments will be cursed by God. Even negative passages like this remind us that God wants only our best. He wants us to obey because disobedience can only bring us suffering. This should encourage us to follow God's pattern for healthy living.

28:1-6 These verses reveal the one essential requirement for God's blessings—obedience. We are to obey God and respond to his commandments. There are considerable blessings for those who are obedient. Recovery demands that we seek to know God's will for us and then do it. Obedience to God's Word, the Bible, is a good place to start.

8"The LORD will guarantee a blessing on everything you do and will fill your storehouses with grain. The LORD your God will bless you in the land he is giving you.

9"If you obey the commands of the LORD your God and walk in his ways, the LORD will establish you as his holy people as he swore he would do. 10Then all the nations of the world will see that you are a people claimed by the LORD, and they will stand in awe of you.

11"The LORD will give you prosperity in the land he swore to your ancestors to give you, blessing you with many children, numerous livestock, and abundant crops. 12The LORD will send rain at the proper time from his rich treasury in the heavens and will bless all the work you do. You will lend to many nations, but you will never need to borrow from them. 13If you listen to these commands of the LORD your God that I am giving you today, and if you carefully obey them, the LORD will make you the head and not the tail, and you will always be on top and never at the bottom. 14You must not turn away from any of the commands I am giving you today, nor follow after other gods and worship them.

Curses for Disobedience

15"But if you refuse to listen to the LORD your God and do not obey all the commands and decrees I am giving you today, all these curses will come and overwhelm you:

16 Your towns and your fields
　　 will be cursed.
17 Your fruit baskets and breadboards
　　 will be cursed.
18 Your children and your crops
　　 will be cursed.
　　 The offspring of your herds and flocks
　　 will be cursed.
19 Wherever you go and whatever you do,
　　 you will be cursed.

20 "The LORD himself will send on you curses, confusion, and frustration in everything you do, until at last you are completely destroyed for doing evil and abandoning me. 21The LORD will afflict you with diseases until none of you are left in the land you are about to enter and occupy.

22The LORD will strike you with wasting diseases, fever, and inflammation, with scorching heat and drought, and with blight and mildew. These disasters will pursue you until you die. 23The skies above will be as unyielding as bronze, and the earth beneath will be as hard as iron. 24The LORD will change the rain that falls on your land into powder, and dust will pour down from the sky until you are destroyed.

25"The LORD will cause you to be defeated by your enemies. You will attack your enemies from one direction, but you will scatter from them in seven! You will be an object of horror to all the kingdoms of the earth. 26Your corpses will be food for all the scavenging birds and wild animals, and no one will be there to chase them away.

27"The LORD will afflict you with the boils of Egypt and with tumors, scurvy, and the itch, from which you cannot be cured. 28The LORD will strike you with madness, blindness, and panic. 29You will grope around in broad daylight like a blind person groping in the darkness, but you will not find your way. You will be oppressed and robbed continually, and no one will come to save you.

30"You will be engaged to a woman, but another man will sleep with her. You will build a house, but someone else will live in it. You will plant a vineyard, but you will never enjoy its fruit. 31Your ox will be butchered before your eyes, but you will not eat a single bite of the meat. Your donkey will be taken from you, never to be returned. Your sheep and goats will be given to your enemies, and no one will be there to help you. 32You will watch as your sons and daughters are taken away as slaves. Your heart will break for them, but you won't be able to help them. 33A foreign nation you have never heard about will eat the crops you worked so hard to grow. You will suffer under constant oppression and harsh treatment. 34You will go mad because of all the tragedy you see around you. 35The LORD will cover your knees and legs with incurable boils. In fact, you will be covered from head to foot.

36"The LORD will exile you and your king to a nation unknown to you and your ancestors. There in exile you will worship gods of

---

28:15-68 Just as obedience results in God's blessings, disobedience brings God's curse. We need to know what God's requirements are; then we must follow God's program in humble obedience. This passage outlines many of the negative consequences that come from disobeying God's plan. We would be wise to take this warning to heart.

wood and stone! [37]You will become an object of horror, ridicule, and mockery among all the nations to which the LORD sends you.

[38]"You will plant much but harvest little, for locusts will eat your crops. [39]You will plant vineyards and care for them, but you will not drink the wine or eat the grapes, for worms will destroy the vines. [40]You will grow olive trees throughout your land, but you will never use the olive oil, for the fruit will drop before it ripens. [41]You will have sons and daughters, but you will lose them, for they will be led away into captivity. [42]Swarms of insects will destroy your trees and crops.

[43]"The foreigners living among you will become stronger and stronger, while you become weaker and weaker. [44]They will lend money to you, but you will not lend to them. They will be the head, and you will be the tail!

[45]"If you refuse to listen to the LORD your God and to obey the commands and decrees he has given you, all these curses will pursue and overtake you until you are destroyed. [46]These horrors will serve as a sign and warning among you and your descendants forever. [47]If you do not serve the LORD your God with joy and enthusiasm for the abundant benefits you have received, [48]you will serve your enemies whom the LORD will send against you. You will be left hungry, thirsty, naked, and lacking in everything. The LORD will put an iron yoke on your neck, oppressing you harshly until he has destroyed you.

[49]"The LORD will bring a distant nation against you from the end of the earth, and it will swoop down on you like a vulture. It is a nation whose language you do not understand, [50]a fierce and heartless nation that shows no respect for the old and no pity for the young. [51]Its armies will devour your livestock and crops, and you will be destroyed. They will leave you no grain, new wine, olive oil, calves, or lambs, and you will starve to death. [52]They will attack your cities until all the fortified walls in your land—the walls you trusted to protect you—are knocked down. They will attack all the towns in the land the LORD your God has given you.

[53]"The siege and terrible distress of the enemy's attack will be so severe that you will eat the flesh of your own sons and daugh-ters, whom the LORD your God has given you. [54]The most tenderhearted man among you will have no compassion for his own brother, his beloved wife, and his surviving children. [55]He will refuse to share with them the flesh he is devouring—the flesh of one of his own children—because he has nothing else to eat during the siege and terrible distress that your enemy will inflict on all your towns. [56]The most tender and delicate woman among you—so delicate she would not so much as touch the ground with her foot—will be selfish toward the husband she loves and toward her own son or daughter. [57]She will hide from them the afterbirth and the new baby she has borne, so that she herself can secretly eat them. She will have nothing else to eat during the siege and terrible distress that your enemy will inflict on all your towns.

[58]"If you refuse to obey all the words of instruction that are written in this book, and if you do not fear the glorious and awesome name of the LORD your God, [59]then the LORD will overwhelm you and your children with indescribable plagues. These plagues will be intense and without relief, making you miserable and unbearably sick. [60]He will afflict you with all the diseases of Egypt that you feared so much, and you will have no relief. [61]The LORD will afflict you with every sickness and plague there is, even those not mentioned in this Book of Instruction, until you are destroyed. [62]Though you become as numerous as the stars in the sky, few of you will be left because you would not listen to the LORD your God.

[63]"Just as the LORD has found great pleasure in causing you to prosper and multiply, the LORD will find pleasure in destroying you. You will be torn from the land you are about to enter and occupy. [64]For the LORD will scatter you among all the nations from one end of the earth to the other. There you will worship foreign gods that neither you nor your ancestors have known, gods made of wood and stone! [65]There among those nations you will find no peace or place to rest. And the LORD will cause your heart to tremble, your eyesight to fail, and your soul to despair. [66]Your life will constantly hang in the balance. You will live night and day in fear,

---

28:66-67 These verses graphically depict a life devoid of satisfaction. This person dreads both night and day. When it is dark, he wishes for light. When it is light, he wishes for dark. This is one of the inevitable consequences of rejecting God's plan for healthy living. There is no lasting satisfaction outside of a real relationship with God and obedience to his will. Seeking God's will and following it without reservation are essential parts of the recovery process.

unsure if you will survive. [67] In the morning you will say, 'If only it were night!' And in the evening you will say, 'If only it were morning!' For you will be terrified by the awful horrors you see around you. [68] Then the LORD will send you back to Egypt in ships, to a destination I promised you would never see again. There you will offer to sell yourselves to your enemies as slaves, but no one will buy you."

CHAPTER 29

[1]*These are the terms of the covenant the LORD commanded Moses to make with the Israelites while they were in the land of Moab, in addition to the covenant he had made with them at Mount Sinai.*

Moses Reviews the Covenant

[2]*Moses summoned all the Israelites and said to them, "You have seen with your own eyes everything the LORD did in the land of Egypt to Pharaoh and to all his servants and to his whole country—[3] all the great tests of strength, the miraculous signs, and the amazing wonders. [4] But to this day the LORD has not given you minds that understand, nor eyes that see, nor ears that hear! [5] For forty years I led you through the wilderness, yet your clothes and sandals did not wear out. [6] You ate no bread and drank no wine or other alcoholic drink, but he provided for you so you would know that he is the LORD your God.

[7] "When we came here, King Sihon of Heshbon and King Og of Bashan came out to fight against us, but we defeated them. [8] We took their land and gave it to the tribes of Reuben and Gad and to the half-tribe of Manasseh as their grant of land.

[9] "Therefore, obey the terms of this covenant so that you will prosper in everything you do. [10] All of you—tribal leaders, elders, officers, all the men of Israel—are standing today in the presence of the LORD your God.

[11] Your little ones and your wives are with you, as well as the foreigners living among you who chop your wood and carry your water. [12] You are standing here today to enter into the covenant of the LORD your God. The LORD is making this covenant, including the curses. [13] By entering into the covenant today, he will establish you as his people and confirm that he is your God, just as he promised you and as he swore to your ancestors Abraham, Isaac, and Jacob.

[14] "But you are not the only ones with whom I am making this covenant with its curses. [15] I am making this covenant both with you who stand here today in the presence of the LORD our God, and also with the future generations who are not standing here today.

[16] "You remember how we lived in the land of Egypt and how we traveled through the lands of enemy nations as we left. [17] You have seen their detestable practices and their idols* made of wood, stone, silver, and gold. [18] I am making this covenant with you so that no one among you—no man, woman, clan, or tribe—will turn away from the LORD our God to worship these gods of other nations, and so that no root among you bears bitter and poisonous fruit.

[19] "Those who hear the warnings of this curse should not congratulate themselves, thinking, 'I am safe, even though I am following the desires of my own stubborn heart.' This would lead to utter ruin! [20] The LORD will never pardon such people. Instead his anger and jealousy will burn against them. All the curses written in this book will come down on them, and the LORD will erase their names from under heaven. [21] The LORD will separate them from all the tribes of Israel, to pour out on them all the curses of the covenant recorded in this Book of Instruction.

[22] "Then the generations to come, both your own descendants and the foreigners who come from distant lands, will see the devastation of the land and the diseases the

---

29:1a Verse 29:1 is numbered 28:69 in Hebrew text. 29:1b Hebrew *Horeb*, another name for Sinai. 29:2 Verses 29:2-29 are numbered 29:1-28 in Hebrew text. 29:17 The Hebrew term (literally *round things*) probably alludes to dung.

29:29 God does not hold us responsible for what we do not know, but he makes it clear that we are responsible for what we do know. This is not to say that God condones ignorance of his revealed Word; rather, we are required to be aware of its instructions. Only by seeking out God's will in Scripture and then following it with his gracious help will we be able to rebuild our life.
30:1 The Israelites were commanded to meditate upon God's will for them. They were to recognize that both blessings and curses came from his hand as a response to their obedience or disobedience. We, too, need to realize that everything in our life—good and bad—is part of God's plan for us. If we don't, we are only hiding from the truth. This world runs according to God's sovereign program. If we refuse to go along with it, we are only insisting on our destruction.

LORD inflicts on it. ²³They will exclaim, 'The whole land is devastated by sulfur and salt. It is a wasteland with nothing planted and nothing growing, not even a blade of grass. It is like the cities of Sodom and Gomorrah, Admah and Zeboiim, which the LORD destroyed in his intense anger.'

²⁴"And all the surrounding nations will ask, 'Why has the LORD done this to this land? Why was he so angry?'

²⁵"And the answer will be, 'This happened because the people of the land abandoned the covenant that the LORD, the God of their ancestors, made with them when he brought them out of the land of Egypt. ²⁶Instead, they turned away to serve and worship gods they had not known before, gods that were not from the LORD. ²⁷That is why the LORD's anger has burned against this land, bringing down on it every curse recorded in this book. ²⁸In great anger and fury the LORD uprooted his people from their land and banished them to another land, where they still live today!'

²⁹"The LORD our God has secrets known to no one. We are not accountable for them, but we and our children are accountable forever for all that he has revealed to us, so that we may obey all the terms of these instructions.

CHAPTER 30
A Call to Return to the LORD

"In the future, when you experience all these blessings and curses I have listed for you, and when you are living among the nations to which the LORD your God has exiled you, take to heart all these instructions. ²If at that time you and your children return to the LORD your God, and if you obey with all your heart and all your soul all the commands I have given you today, ³then the LORD your God will restore your fortunes. He will have mercy on you and gather you back from all the nations where he has scattered you. ⁴Even though you are banished to the ends of the earth,* the LORD your God will gather you from there and bring you back again. ⁵The LORD your God will return you to the land that belonged to your ancestors, and you will possess that land again. Then he will make you even more prosperous and numerous than your ancestors!

⁶"The LORD your God will change your heart* and the hearts of all your descendants, so that you will love him with all your heart and soul and so you may live! ⁷The

30:4 Hebrew *of the heavens.* 30:6 Hebrew *circumcise your heart.*

STEP 3

Free to Choose
BIBLE READING: Deuteronomy 30:15-20
We made a decision to turn our wills and our lives over to the care of God.
Everyone has a life-or-death decision to make. We have all been created with the supreme privilege of free will—the ability to choose. Even when we are in the bondage of our addictions, we still have choices confronting us. When we are in recovery, we face the nagging lure of falling back into our addictions. The freedom to choose brings with it the burden of the consequences of our choices. These choices affect our life and the lives of our children. Free will is our blessing and our responsibility!

God spoke through Moses, saying, "Now listen! Today I am giving you a choice between life and death, between prosperity and disaster. For I command you this day to love the LORD your God and to keep his commands, decrees, and regulations by walking in his ways. If you do this, you will live . . . and the LORD your God will bless you. . . . But if your heart turns away and you refuse to listen, . . . then I warn you now that you will certainly be destroyed. . . . Today I have given you the choice between life and death, between blessings and curses. Now I call on heaven and earth to witness the choice you make. Oh, that you would choose life, so that you and your descendants might live! You can make this choice by loving the LORD your God, obeying him, and committing yourself firmly to him. This is the key to your life" (Deuteronomy 30:15-20).

Although we may feel out of control with respect to our addictions, we can choose to set our heart in the direction of life. We can choose to love God and begin to follow his program. *Turn to page 721, Psalm 61.*

LORD your God will inflict all these curses on your enemies and on those who hate and persecute you. [8]Then you will again obey the LORD and keep all his commands that I am giving you today.

[9]"The LORD your God will then make you successful in everything you do. He will give you many children and numerous livestock, and he will cause your fields to produce abundant harvests, for the LORD will again delight in being good to you as he was to your ancestors. [10]The LORD your God will delight in you if you obey his voice and keep the commands and decrees written in this Book of Instruction, and if you turn to the LORD your God with all your heart and soul.

The Choice of Life or Death

[11]"This command I am giving you today is not too difficult for you, and it is not beyond your reach. [12]It is not kept in heaven, so distant that you must ask, 'Who will go up to heaven and bring it down so we can hear it and obey?' [13]It is not kept beyond the sea, so far away that you must ask, 'Who will cross the sea to bring it to us so we can hear it and obey?' [14]No, the message is very close at hand; it is on your lips and in your heart so that you can obey it.

[15]"Now listen! Today I am giving you a choice between life and death, between prosperity and disaster. [16]For I command you this day to love the LORD your God and to keep his commands, decrees, and regulations by walking in his ways. If you do this, you will live and multiply, and the LORD your God will bless you and the land you are about to enter and occupy.

[17]"But if your heart turns away and you refuse to listen, and if you are drawn away to serve and worship other gods, [18]then I warn you now that you will certainly be destroyed. You will not live a long, good life in the land you are crossing the Jordan to occupy.

[19]"Today I have given you the choice between life and death, between blessings and curses. Now I call on heaven and earth to witness the choice you make. Oh, that you would choose life, so that you and your descendants might live! [20]You can make this choice by loving the LORD your God, obeying him, and committing yourself firmly to him. This* is the key to your life. And if you love and obey the LORD, you will live long in the land the LORD swore to give your ancestors Abraham, Isaac, and Jacob."

CHAPTER 31
Joshua Becomes Israel's Leader

When Moses had finished giving these instructions* to all the people of Israel, [2]he said, "I am now 120 years old, and I am no longer able to lead you. The LORD has told me, 'You will not cross the Jordan River.' [3]But the LORD your God himself will cross over ahead of you. He will destroy the nations living there, and you will take possession of their land. Joshua will lead you across the river, just as the LORD promised.

[4]"The LORD will destroy the nations living in the land, just as he destroyed Sihon and Og, the kings of the Amorites. [5]The LORD will hand over to you the people who live there, and you must deal with them as I have commanded you. [6]So be strong and courageous! Do not be afraid and do not panic before them. For the LORD your God will personally go ahead of you. He will neither fail you nor abandon you."

[7]Then Moses called for Joshua, and as all Israel watched, he said to him, "Be strong and courageous! For you will lead these people into the land that the LORD swore to their ancestors he would give them. You are the one who will divide it among them as their grants of land. [8]Do not be afraid or discouraged, for the LORD will personally go ahead

30:20 Or *He.* 31:1 As in Dead Sea Scrolls and Greek version; Masoretic Text reads *Moses went and spoke.*

30:19 Again God urged his people to choose life. We are reminded here of the claim of Jesus Christ: "I am the way, the truth, and the life. No one can come to the Father except through me" (John 14:6). The way to life is choosing God and his gracious forgiveness through Jesus Christ. Our decision is important not only for us but for our children. Let's choose life and pass the gift of abundant life on to our children as well.

31:3 The Israelites were on the verge of entering the Promised Land. They needed a fresh reminder of God's strength and a promise of victory. Some may have been putting their confidence in Joshua. Others may have been depending on the strength of their armies. But no matter how strong we or our leaders might be, victory comes from God alone. Some enemies are too great for us. Our personal resources or support groups, though helpful, will never be adequate to gain complete victory over our dependencies. We must learn to trust God alone, for he is greater than any of the enemies we might face.

of you. He will be with you; he will neither fail you nor abandon you."

Public Reading of the Book of Instruction

[9]So Moses wrote this entire body of instruction in a book and gave it to the priests, who carried the Ark of the LORD's Covenant, and to the elders of Israel. [10]Then Moses gave them this command: "At the end of every seventh year, the Year of Release, during the Festival of Shelters, [11]you must read this Book of Instruction to all the people of Israel when they assemble before the LORD your God at the place he chooses. [12]Call them all together—men, women, children, and the foreigners living in your towns—so they may hear this Book of Instruction and learn to fear the LORD your God and carefully obey all the terms of these instructions. [13]Do this so that your children who have not known these instructions will hear them and will learn to fear the LORD your God. Do this as long as you live in the land you are crossing the Jordan to occupy."

Israel's Disobedience Predicted

[14]Then the LORD said to Moses, "The time has come for you to die. Call Joshua and present yourselves at the Tabernacle,* so that I may commission him there." So Moses and Joshua went and presented themselves at the Tabernacle. [15]And the LORD appeared to them in a pillar of cloud that stood at the entrance to the sacred tent.

[16]The LORD said to Moses, "You are about to die and join your ancestors. After you are gone, these people will begin to worship foreign gods, the gods of the land where they are going. They will abandon me and break my covenant that I have made with them. [17]Then my anger will blaze forth against them. I will abandon them, hiding my face from them, and they will be devoured. Terrible trouble will come down on them, and on that day they will say, 'These disasters have come down on us because God is no longer among us!' [18]At that time I will hide my face from them on account of all the evil they commit by worshiping other gods.

[19]"So write down the words of this song,

and teach it to the people of Israel. Help them learn it, so it may serve as a witness for me against them. [20]For I will bring them into the land I swore to give their ancestors—a land flowing with milk and honey. There they will become prosperous, eat all the food they want, and become fat. But they will begin to worship other gods; they will despise me and break my covenant. [21]And when great disasters come down on them, this song will stand as evidence against them, for it will never be forgotten by their descendants. I know the intentions of these people, even now before they have entered the land I swore to give them."

[22]So that very day Moses wrote down the words of the song and taught it to the Israelites.

[23]Then the LORD commissioned Joshua son of Nun with these words: "Be strong and courageous, for you must bring the people of Israel into the land I swore to give them. I will be with you."

[24]When Moses had finished writing this entire body of instruction in a book, [25]he gave this command to the Levites who carried the Ark of the LORD's Covenant: [26]"Take this Book of Instruction and place it beside the Ark of the Covenant of the LORD your God, so it may remain there as a witness against the people of Israel. [27]For I know how rebellious and stubborn you are. Even now, while I am still alive and am here with you, you have rebelled against the LORD. How much more rebellious will you be after my death!

[28]"Now summon all the elders and officials of your tribes, so that I can speak to them directly and call heaven and earth to witness against them. [29]I know that after my death you will become utterly corrupt and will turn from the way I have commanded you to follow. In the days to come, disaster will come down on you, for you will do what is evil in the LORD's sight, making him very angry with your actions."

The Song of Moses

[30]So Moses recited this entire song publicly to the assembly of Israel:

31:14 Hebrew *Tent of Meeting;* also in 31:14b.

31:23 This verse contains an important message for rebuilders. In spite of the difficulty of the task, we are told: "Be strong and courageous." The basis for this strength and courage is the marvelous promise "I will be with you." As we face the desperate challenges of recovery, we can find strength and courage in this message. Our God is a God who specializes in overcoming giant challenges (see 1 Samuel 17).

CHAPTER 32

1 "Listen, O heavens, and I will speak!
  Hear, O earth, the words that I say!
2 Let my teaching fall on you like rain;
  let my speech settle like dew.
Let my words fall like rain on tender grass,
  like gentle showers on young plants.
3 I will proclaim the name of the LORD;
  how glorious is our God!
4 He is the Rock; his deeds are perfect.
  Everything he does is just and fair.
He is a faithful God who does no wrong;
  how just and upright he is!

5 "But they have acted corruptly toward
    him;
  when they act so perversely,
are they really his children?*
  They are a deceitful and twisted
    generation.
6 Is this the way you repay the LORD,
  you foolish and senseless people?
Isn't he your Father who created you?
  Has he not made you and established
    you?
7 Remember the days of long ago;
  think about the generations past.
Ask your father, and he will inform you.
  Inquire of your elders, and they will
    tell you.
8 When the Most High assigned lands to
    the nations,
  when he divided up the human race,
he established the boundaries of the
    peoples
  according to the number in his
    heavenly court.*

9 "For the people of Israel belong to the
    LORD;
  Jacob is his special possession.
10 He found them in a desert land,
  in an empty, howling wasteland.
He surrounded them and watched over
    them;
  he guarded them as he would guard his
    own eyes.*

11 Like an eagle that rouses her chicks
  and hovers over her young,
so he spread his wings to take them up
  and carried them safely on his pinions.
12 The LORD alone guided them;
  they followed no foreign gods.
13 He let them ride over the highlands
  and feast on the crops of the fields.
He nourished them with honey from
    the rock
  and olive oil from the stony ground.
14 He fed them yogurt from the herd
  and milk from the flock,
  together with the fat of lambs.
He gave them choice rams from Bashan,
    and goats,
  together with the choicest wheat.
You drank the finest wine,
  made from the juice of grapes.

15 "But Israel* soon became fat and unruly;
  the people grew heavy, plump, and
    stuffed!
Then they abandoned the God who had
    made them;
  they made light of the Rock of their
    salvation.
16 They stirred up his jealousy by worshiping
    foreign gods;
  they provoked his fury with detestable
    deeds.
17 They offered sacrifices to demons, which
    are not God,
  to gods they had not known before,
to new gods only recently arrived,
  to gods their ancestors had never
    feared.
18 You neglected the Rock who had fathered
    you;
  you forgot the God who had given
    you birth.

19 "The LORD saw this and drew back,
  provoked to anger by his own sons and
    daughters.
20 He said, 'I will abandon them;
  then see what becomes of them.

32:5 The meaning of the Hebrew is uncertain. 32:8 As in Dead Sea Scrolls, which read *the number of the sons of God,* and Greek version, which reads *the number of the angels of God;* Masoretic Text reads *the number of the sons of Israel.* 32:10 Hebrew *as the pupil of his eye.* 32:15 Hebrew *Jeshurun,* a term of endearment for Israel.

32:3-4 An important part of spiritual growth is learning to worship God. An important part of worship is praise. Moses takes time to praise God for who he is—glorious, strong, perfect, just and fair, faithful, upright. We also need to take time to rejoice in who God is and praise him for his greatness. He is the Rock—our foundation for a stable life. His work in our life is perfect. We need to recognize God's ability to help us and then allow him to do his mighty work on our behalf.
32:11-13 As we go about the rebuilding process, we need to be assured of God's protection and guidance. These verses from Moses' song should offer just the certainty we need. God will protect us as we seek recovery and guide us toward a life filled with joy and freedom.

For they are a twisted generation,
  children without integrity.
21 They have roused my jealousy by
    worshiping things that are not God;
  they have provoked my anger with
    their useless idols.
  Now I will rouse their jealousy through
    people who are not even a people;
  I will provoke their anger through the
    foolish Gentiles.
22 For my anger blazes forth like fire
    and burns to the depths of the grave.*
  It devours the earth and all its crops
    and ignites the foundations of the
    mountains.
23 I will heap disasters upon them
    and shoot them down with my arrows.
24 I will weaken them with famine,
    burning fever, and deadly disease.
  I will send the fangs of wild beasts
    and poisonous snakes that glide in
    the dust.
25 Outside, the sword will bring death,
    and inside, terror will strike
  both young men and young women,
    both infants and the aged.
26 I would have annihilated them,
    wiping out even the memory of them.
27 But I feared the taunt of Israel's enemy,
    who might misunderstand and say,
  "Our own power has triumphed!
    The LORD had nothing to do with
    this!"'

28 "But Israel is a senseless nation;
    the people are foolish, without
    understanding.
29 Oh, that they were wise and could
    understand this!
  Oh, that they might know their fate!
30 How could one person chase a thousand
    of them,
    and two people put ten thousand to
    flight,
  unless their Rock had sold them,
    unless the LORD had given them up?
31 But the rock of our enemies is not like our
    Rock,
    as even they recognize.*
32 Their vine grows from the vine of Sodom,
    from the vineyards of Gomorrah.
  Their grapes are poison,
    and their clusters are bitter.

33 Their wine is the venom of serpents,
    the deadly poison of cobras.

34 "The LORD says, 'Am I not storing up
    these things,
    sealing them away in my treasury?
35 I will take revenge; I will pay them back.
    In due time their feet will slip.
  Their day of disaster will arrive,
    and their destiny will overtake them.'

36 "Indeed, the LORD will give justice to his
    people,
    and he will change his mind about*
    his servants,
  when he sees their strength is gone
    and no one is left, slave or free.
37 Then he will ask, 'Where are their gods,
    the rocks they fled to for refuge?
38 Where now are those gods,
    who ate the fat of their sacrifices
    and drank the wine of their offerings?
  Let those gods arise and help you!
    Let them provide you with shelter!
39 Look now; I myself am he!
    There is no other god but me!
  I am the one who kills and gives life;
    I am the one who wounds and heals;
    no one can be rescued from my
    powerful hand!
40 Now I raise my hand to heaven
    and declare, "As surely as I live,
41 when I sharpen my flashing sword
    and begin to carry out justice,
  I will take revenge on my enemies
    and repay those who reject me.
42 I will make my arrows drunk with blood,
    and my sword will devour flesh—
  the blood of the slaughtered and the
    captives,
    and the heads of the enemy leaders."'

43 "Rejoice with him, you heavens,
    and let all of God's angels worship
    him.*
  Rejoice with his people, you Gentiles,
    and let all the angels be strengthened in
    him.*
  For he will avenge the blood of his
    children*;
    he will take revenge against his
    enemies.
  He will repay those who hate him*
    and cleanse his people's land."

32:22 Hebrew *of Sheol.* 32:31 The meaning of the Hebrew is uncertain. Greek version reads *our enemies are fools.*
32:36 Or *will take revenge for.* 32:43a As in Dead Sea Scrolls and Greek version; Masoretic Text lacks the first two lines.
Compare Heb 1:6. 32:43b As in Greek version; Hebrew text lacks this sentence. Compare Romans 15:10. 32:43c As
in Dead Sea Scrolls and Greek version; Masoretic Text reads *his servants.* 32:43d As in Dead Sea Scrolls and Greek
version; Masoretic Text lacks this line.

[44]So Moses came with Joshua* son of Nun and recited all the words of this song to the people. [45]When Moses had finished reciting all these words to the people of Israel, [46]he added: "Take to heart all the words of warning I have given you today. Pass them on as a command to your children so they will obey every word of these instructions. [47]These instructions are not empty words—they are your life! By obeying them you will enjoy a long life in the land you will occupy when you cross the Jordan River."

Moses' Death Foretold

[48]That same day the LORD said to Moses, [49]"Go to Moab, to the mountains east of the river,* and climb Mount Nebo, which is across from Jericho. Look out across the land of Canaan, the land I am giving to the people of Israel as their own special possession. [50]Then you will die there on the mountain. You will join your ancestors, just as Aaron, your brother, died on Mount Hor and joined his ancestors. [51]For both of you betrayed me with the Israelites at the waters of Meribah at Kadesh* in the wilderness of Zin. You failed to demonstrate my holiness to the people of Israel there. [52]So you will see the land from a distance, but you may not enter the land I am giving to the people of Israel."

CHAPTER 33
Moses Blesses the People

This is the blessing that Moses, the man of God, gave to the people of Israel before his death:

[2] "The LORD came from Mount Sinai
and dawned upon us* from
    Mount Seir;
he shone forth from Mount Paran
and came from Meribah-kadesh
    with flaming fire at his right
    hand.*
[3] Indeed, he loves his people;*
all his holy ones are in his hands.
They follow in his steps
and accept his teaching.
[4] Moses gave us the LORD's instruction,
the special possession of the people of
    Israel.*

[5] The LORD became king in Israel*—
when the leaders of the people
    assembled,
when the tribes of Israel gathered as
    one."

[6]Moses said this about the tribe of Reuben:*

"Let the tribe of Reuben live and not die
    out,
though they are few in number."

[7]Moses said this about the tribe of Judah:

"O LORD, hear the cry of Judah
and bring them together as a people.
Give them strength to defend their
    cause;
help them against their enemies!"

[8]Moses said this about the tribe of Levi:

"O LORD, you have given your Thummim
    and Urim—the sacred lots—
to your faithful servants the Levites.*
You put them to the test at Massah
and struggled with them at the waters
    of Meribah.
[9] The Levites obeyed your word
and guarded your covenant.
They were more loyal to you
than to their own parents.
They ignored their relatives
and did not acknowledge their own
    children.
[10] They teach your regulations to Jacob;
they give your instructions to Israel.
They present incense before you
and offer whole burnt offerings on the
    altar.
[11] Bless the ministry of the Levites, O LORD,
and accept all the work of their hands.
Hit their enemies where it hurts the
    most;
strike down their foes so they never rise
    again."

[12]Moses said this about the tribe of Benjamin:

"The people of Benjamin are loved by the
    LORD
and live in safety beside him.
He surrounds them continuously
and preserves them from every
    harm."

32:44 Hebrew *Hoshea,* a variant name for Joshua. 32:49 Hebrew *the mountains of Abarim.* 32:51 Hebrew *waters of Meribath-kadesh.* 33:2a As in Greek and Syriac versions; Hebrew reads *upon them.* 33:2b Or *came from myriads of holy ones, from the south, from his mountain slopes.* The meaning of the Hebrew is uncertain. 33:3 As in Greek version; Hebrew reads *Indeed, lover of the peoples.* 33:4 Hebrew *of Jacob.* The names "Jacob" and "Israel" are often interchanged throughout the Old Testament, referring sometimes to the individual patriarch and sometimes to the nation. 33:5 Hebrew *in Jeshurun,* a term of endearment for Israel. 33:6 Hebrew lacks *Moses said this about the tribe of Reuben.* 33:8 As in Greek version; Hebrew lacks *the Levites.*

[13]Moses said this about the tribes of Joseph:

"May their land be blessed by the LORD
  with the precious gift of dew from the
    heavens
  and water from beneath the earth;
[14]with the rich fruit that grows in the sun,
  and the rich harvest produced each
    month;
[15]with the finest crops of the ancient
    mountains,
  and the abundance from the everlasting
    hills;
[16]with the best gifts of the earth and its
    bounty,
  and the favor of the one who appeared
    in the burning bush.
May these blessings rest on Joseph's head,
  crowning the brow of the prince among
    his brothers.
[17]Joseph has the majesty of a young bull;
  he has the horns of a wild ox.
He will gore distant nations,
  even to the ends of the earth.
This is my blessing for the multitudes
    of Ephraim
  and the thousands of Manasseh."

[18]Moses said this about the tribes of Zebulun
and Issachar*:

"May the people of Zebulun prosper in
    their travels.
  May the people of Issachar prosper at
    home in their tents.
[19]They summon the people to the mountain
  to offer proper sacrifices there.
They benefit from the riches of the sea
  and the hidden treasures in the sand."

[20]Moses said this about the tribe of Gad:

"Blessed is the one who enlarges Gad's
    territory!
  Gad is poised there like a lion
  to tear off an arm or a head.
[21]The people of Gad took the best land for
    themselves;
  a leader's share was assigned to them.
When the leaders of the people were
    assembled,
  they carried out the LORD's justice
  and obeyed his regulations for Israel."

[22]Moses said this about the tribe of Dan:

"Dan is a lion's cub,
  leaping out from Bashan."

[23]Moses said this about the tribe of Naphtali:

"O Naphtali, you are rich in favor
  and full of the LORD's blessings;
  may you possess the west and the
    south."

[24]Moses said this about the tribe of Asher:

"May Asher be blessed above other
    sons;
  may he be esteemed by his brothers;
  may he bathe his feet in olive oil.
[25]May the bolts of your gates be of iron and
    bronze;
  may you be secure all your days."

[26]"There is no one like the God of Israel.*
  He rides across the heavens to help
    you,
  across the skies in majestic splendor.
[27]The eternal God is your refuge,
  and his everlasting arms are under
    you.
He drives out the enemy before you;
  he cries out, 'Destroy them!'
[28]So Israel will live in safety,
  prosperous Jacob in security,
in a land of grain and new wine,
  while the heavens drop down dew.
[29]How blessed you are, O Israel!
  Who else is like you, a people saved by
    the LORD?
He is your protecting shield
  and your triumphant sword!
Your enemies will cringe before you,
  and you will stomp on their backs!"

CHAPTER 34
The Death of Moses
Then Moses went up to Mount Nebo from the
plains of Moab and climbed Pisgah Peak,
which is across from Jericho. And the LORD
showed him ²the whole land, from Gilead as
far as Dan; ²all the land of Naphtali; the land
of Ephraim and Manasseh; all the land of Judah, extending to the Mediterranean Sea*;
³the Negev; the Jordan Valley with Jericho—

33:18 Hebrew lacks *and Issachar.* **33:26** Hebrew *of Jeshurun,* a term of endearment for Israel. **34:2** Hebrew *the western sea.*

33:29 Here is another promise of God's saving help. He provides his people defense from their enemies and fights on their behalf. He assures them of ultimate victory. When our life is in disar- ray, it is comforting to know that God has genuine concern for our welfare. As we seek recovery, we can be sure that God is on our side.

the city of palms—as far as Zoar. ⁴Then the LORD said to Moses, "This is the land I promised on oath to Abraham, Isaac, and Jacob when I said, 'I will give it to your descendants.' I have now allowed you to see it with your own eyes, but you will not enter the land."

⁵So Moses, the servant of the LORD, died there in the land of Moab, just as the LORD had said. ⁶The LORD buried him* in a valley near Beth-peor in Moab, but to this day no one knows the exact place. ⁷Moses was 120 years old when he died, yet his eyesight was clear, and he was as strong as ever. ⁸The people of Israel mourned for Moses on the plains of Moab for thirty days, until the customary period of mourning was over.

⁹Now Joshua son of Nun was full of the spirit of wisdom, for Moses had laid his hands on him. So the people of Israel obeyed him, doing just as the LORD had commanded Moses.

¹⁰There has never been another prophet in Israel like Moses, whom the LORD knew face to face. ¹¹The LORD sent him to perform all the miraculous signs and wonders in the land of Egypt against Pharaoh, and all his servants, and his entire land. ¹²With mighty power, Moses performed terrifying acts in the sight of all Israel.

34:6 Hebrew *He buried him;* Samaritan Pentateuch and some Greek manuscripts read *They buried him.*

REFLECTIONS ON DEUTERONOMY

insights FROM THE PAST

After a generation of consistent failure, Moses found it necessary to go back to the basics. **Deuteronomy 1:1-5** tells us that as the Israelites were about to enter the Promised Land, they took time to read God's laws once again. The name *Deuteronomy* actually means "second law" or "repetition of the law." It was necessary for Moses to repeat God's instructions for the new generation of Israelites as they faced new living conditions and the accompanying temptations. God's instructions for living are good for every generation. We need to regularly review them as we face the temptations and difficulties of recovery.

In **Deuteronomy 1:32** Moses reminded the Israelites of their refusal to believe what God had told them. There is no better formula for failure. When we refuse to trust in God, no program for recovery will be successful for long. In this verse we are told why the Israelites were forced to wander in the wilderness for 40 years. They had refused to trust in God! God had the power to deliver them from their powerless condition, but the Israelites refused to take advantage of it. Believing God is essential for lasting success.

In **Deuteronomy 4:9** and other points in the following verses we see warning exclamations such as "Watch out!" No matter how secure we may feel in our righteousness, if we are unwary, we are in danger of falling. Here the Israelites were charged to remember what God had done for them. Remembering past victories and failures can help us guard against sin and failure in the present. The Israelites were instructed to pass their wisdom and experience on to the next generation. We also are to pass on to our children the wisdom learned from our experiences. This will give them a chance, if they choose to listen, to avoid some of the same mistakes we have made. God is concerned that godly attitudes and wisdom are passed on to each generation.

We see in **Deuteronomy 4:20** that God delivered Israel for a specific purpose. He forged Israel into a nation to be his chosen possession, and through this special nation God brought salvation to the whole world. Why has God delivered us? God's purpose for each of us is quite specific. We need to ask these questions: What does God want from us? Why did God save us? He may intend to use us to bring his saving grace into the lives of others who suffer from problems similar to ours.

In **Deuteronomy 4:34-40** we see a review of God's glorious work on Israel's behalf. Israel's many failures aren't even mentioned here. They are forgotten in the amazing story of how God led his people from slavery in Egypt to the Promised Land. God's plans for Israel succeeded in the long run, despite Israel's tendency to rebel against God and his program. Since we all fail on our recovery journey, Israel's history should be encouraging to us. God will continue to work with us, disciplining us when we need it, comforting us when we are discouraged. If we trust him, our own history will be a glorious account of our journey from slavery to freedom—all the failures and mistakes graciously forgotten.

The Israelites were about to end 40 difficult years of wilderness wandering. They were starting new lives and building a new nation. But when things start going well in life, it is easy to forget the help God has given us. In **Deuteronomy 6:10-13** Moses gave the Israelites a special warning. He told them to give God the respect and obedience he deserved. This was foundational for them in their efforts to continue rebuilding. As we begin to make progress in recovery, it is easy to forget that it is only by God's grace that we have come this far. We need to realize that without God's help, we will quickly regress. Continued respect for and obedience to God are necessary for our progress in recovery.

In **Deuteronomy 6:23** Moses reminded the people that God's purpose was to bring them from bondage into a new life of freedom. God brought them out so he could bring them into something much better. Most of us have suffered periods of bondage in our life. Maybe that is all we have known. We can be assured that when God leads us out of slavery, he has a much better life in store for us. As we are freed from our dependencies, he will give us new things to live for—good and healthy things. God is reminding us here that his people are delivered for a purpose and that recovery is part of that purpose.

insights FOR THE PRESENT

All relationships come with responsibilities. In **Deuteronomy 4:23-24** we are reminded that this is also true of our relationship with God. We cannot remake God as we would like him to be; we must relate to him as he is. As the only true God, he demands that we give him our full devotion. As with any relationship, we need to be faithful to God if we wish our relationship with him to remain strong. This book calls the Israelites to follow through on their responsibilities to God. The consequences of ignoring responsibilities in any relationship are great. Failing in our relationship with God results in even deeper problems.

In **Deuteronomy 5:1** Moses reminded the people of the importance of obedience. God's laws gave the Israelites clear guidance as to what God expected of them, presenting them with God's standard of excellence. These guidelines supplied a pattern for healthy living in virtually every area of life. But sadly, none of us is fully able to live up to God's standards (see Romans 3:23). Because of this, God has extended his grace to us, accepting us on the basis of Jesus Christ and his work. God's presence with us will provide us with the help we need. God's grace enables us to rebuild our life according to his standard.

In **Deuteronomy 5:5-6** Moses introduced the Ten Commandments by directing Israel's attention to the person of God, reminding the people that he was "the LORD" (*Yahweh* or *Jehovah*). This name is God's personal covenant name. It reminds us of his relationship with Abraham, Isaac, Jacob, and then with Moses and the nation of Israel. God is personal; he relates to us one-on-one. He states in Scripture, "I am the LORD your God." He is our God. Our personal relationship with God and our love for him should provide the motivation for our obedience to his laws.

In **Deuteronomy 6:6** it becomes clear that God's laws need more than our cursory attention. Thinking about God's program for healthy living just once or twice a week isn't enough. We are to think about God's laws constantly every day. In recovery we know the importance of living one day at a time. We need constant reminders if we are to overcome our dependencies and build a new life. God's plan for recovery must be reviewed constantly if we are to discover the freedom he promises.

In **Deuteronomy 7:9** we are reminded of God's steadfast faithfulness. He is a delivering and faithful God. He always keeps his promises. A major step in rebuilding our life is to take God at his word. His steadfast love is behind every response God makes toward us. Notice, however, that he also asks something of us. We must believe, love, and obey him.

insights FROM THE TEN COMMANDMENTS

In **Deuteronomy 5:7-8** we are commanded to put God first in our life. It is easy to let our priorities get out of balance. The important things are forgotten; the "urgent" things claim our attention, affection, and resources. If we are to build our life according to God's specifications, then God has to be our highest priority. Anything that comes before God in our life becomes a false god. We need to stay clear of anything that might come between us and God.

Deuteronomy 5:11 prohibits the use of God's name in any way that brings it dishonor. This is often understood to refer to using God's name in an exclamation of anger or disgust. Actually this commandment refers not primarily to speech but to life. As people who represent the name of God, we are responsible to act in ways that will bring him glory, not shame. Thus, when our actions and attitudes bring dishonor to God, this commandment is broken. We need to live with complete honesty in both word and deed, bringing honor rather than dishonor to God's name.

In **Deuteronomy 5:12-15** we are commanded to observe the Sabbath day of rest. God has placed a seven-day clock in our body. If we don't give it the rest it needs, the restructuring of our life will never be completely effective. Physical, emotional, and spiritual exhaustion will make it impossible for us to accomplish what our goals and plans call for. Although most of us do not celebrate the Old Testament Sabbath, our human makeup demands that we have at least one special day in seven—a day of rest.

In **Deuteronomy 5:16** we are commanded to honor our parents. This does not mean we should obey them blindly, never questioning their demands or actions. Some of us may have been abused by dysfunctional parents; obeying all their demands would only be destructive. Honoring our parents does, however, mean showing love toward them. This may mean that we must call them to account for their actions toward us when we are ready to take that step. It demands that we seek their best, bringing them honor. We should work to help them develop their honorable characteristics while not enabling their dishonorable ones.

In **Deuteronomy 5:18** we are commanded to remain faithful in marriage. Dysfunctional families are often the result of unfaithfulness on the part of one or both of the marriage partners. Many of the sexual difficulties and problems with venereal disease and AIDS could be avoided if this commandment were obeyed. A healthy marriage relationship requires 100 percent fidelity on the part of both partners. Rebuilding a shattered marriage can come about only through the trust that develops out of this kind of loving commitment.

In **Deuteronomy 5:19** we are commanded not to steal. Healthy interpersonal relationships require that people have respect for one another. Such respect includes the recognition and protection of the personal property belonging to others. Stealing of all kinds is completely forbidden by this commandment. Theft of property is primarily in view, but theft of ideas and theft of reputation are included as well. "Honesty is the best policy" because it is God's policy.

The commandment in **Deuteronomy 5:21** is different from the others because it forbids not only certain actions but certain attitudes as well. It insists that we carefully guard our thoughts. As we continue in recovery, we must learn to keep our thoughts in order. We need to live in the real world, not in a world of fantasy or self-deception.

insights FOR THE FUTURE

In **Deuteronomy 6:7** we are told specifically to share God's wisdom with our children. In recovery we often focus on the suffering that has been passed down to us from past generations. Here we are reminded that the blessings of God's Word should be passed on. Now is the time to break the cycle of suffering and pain! We can start by passing God's wisdom on to our children. This verse demands that we make God's Word an integral part of our life. We need to live it, not just speak it. We need to teach it, not just with our words but also with our lifestyle.

The Israelites were about to enter the Promised Land and probably feared the powerful enemies they would face. But in **Deuteronomy 7:21** God made it clear that he was sufficient for the task, no matter how great it might be. As we take hold of the opportunity of building a new life, we also face great obstacles to our progress. We need to trust in God's sufficiency to help us in our own conquests. He is capable of overcoming any obstacles we might face.

In **Deuteronomy 30:2-3** God offered this gracious message to his people who were living in defeat: Repent and be restored. Even though they had strayed from God's requirements, all they needed to do was to return to the Lord and obey him. Our wholehearted repentance brings God's wholehearted forgiveness. With God, it is never too late to make a new start in life.

In **Deuteronomy 30:15** God laid out a clear choice for his people. On the one hand were life and prosperity. On the other hand were death and disaster. Choosing God and his program leads to healthy living and an eternal life with God. Choosing against God leads to destruction and death. The choice we make here will lead to either recovery or destruction. The clear consequences should help us make the right choice. It's up to us!

JOSHUA

THE BIG PICTURE

A. SECURING THE FRUITS OF
   VICTORY (1:1–12:24)
   1. Inspiring the People
      (1:1–5:15)
   2. Implementing the Plan
      (6:1–11:23)
   3. Identifying the Progress
      (12:1-24)
B. SHARING THE FRUITS OF
   VICTORY (13:1–24:33)
   1. Ensuring Fair Compensation
      (13:1–19:51)
   2. Ensuring Full Cooperation
      (20:1–22:34)
   3. Ensuring Faithful
      Continuance (23:1–24:33)

God had miraculously used Moses to lead the people of Israel out of bondage in Egypt to the threshold of the Promised Land. But instead of conquering it, they had wandered in the wilderness for 40 years. The book of Joshua records how God brought the next generation of Israelites to the borders of Canaan under Joshua's leadership.

Joshua was ideal for the job of leading Israel. He was a gifted leader and had served as Moses' assistant for many years. The primary reason for his success, however, was not his leadership ability. It was his trust in God and his obedience to God's instructions. He constantly turned the attention of his people to the God who took care of them, who fought for them, who gave them the land. He recognized and declared that Israel's victories belonged to God alone.

The new generation of Israelites seemed to have recovered from their parents' lack of trust and tendency toward disobedience. Instead of resisting God's plan for conquest, they agreed to do everything that Joshua commanded. As a result, they witnessed miraculous victories won in the face of impossible odds. As the Israelites continued to believe and obey God, incredible things were done on their behalf. They soon discovered that God was worthy of their trust.

It is hard for some of us to believe that God has a plan for our recovery or that he is able to bring it about. But such doubts are not grounded in the truth. God does care about us, and he is able to lead us to amazing victories over our most powerful enemies. Remembering this truth should help us to step out in faith and follow God's program for victorious living.

THE BOTTOM LINE

PURPOSE: To reveal the importance of trusting and obeying God in the difficult process of achieving both physical and spiritual goals. AUTHOR: The book's author is anonymous, though tradition attributes much of it to Joshua. AUDIENCE: The people of Israel. DATE WRITTEN: Probably sometime between 1375 and 1300 B.C., soon after the events recorded. SETTING: Initially in the wilderness east of the Jordan River, but primarily in the Promised Land. KEY VERSES: "Be strong and courageous, for you are the one who will lead these people. . . . Be strong and very courageous. Be careful to obey all the instructions Moses gave you. Do not deviate from them, turning either to the right or to the left. Then you will be successful in everything you do" (1:6-7). KEY PLACES: Jordan River, Gilgal, Jericho, Ai, Shiloh, Shechem. KEY PEOPLE: Joshua, Rahab, Caleb.

RECOVERY THEMES

Recovery Is Ongoing: How wonderful it would be to be completely recovered—to have arrived! That's one of our fantasies, and certainly one that the Israelites must have had. The first generation had not made it into the Promised Land. But this group had followed God's plan and conquered the land. What could possibly go wrong now? They may have said, "We're in the Promised Land at last—finally we can relax!" But the exact opposite was true. Their work had just begun! The same is true for us. When we think we have arrived, we have probably just begun the journey to recovery. We need to recognize that recovery is a lifelong process.

The Conflict with Evil: God commanded his people to completely conquer the land of Canaan and its people. His concern was to purify the land from evil people and practices. The Israelites were the people of God's promise. They were to judge evil and be a blessing to all nations. But to accomplish this, they had to be on guard against the evil around them. The ever-present fact of evil is one reason why recovery can never be complete. We cannot eliminate evil from our lives; many have tried. But if we escape the evil forces on the outside of us, we are confronted with the evil that lies within us. We must be ever watchful of the old patterns in our life that could destroy our chances for recovery.

Obedience Is Ongoing: God had given the Israelites instructions for every area of their lives. Joshua was obedient; the people sometimes wavered and were inconsistent. This brought trouble. But what was true in Joshua's day is still true for us. The more we trust and believe God, the more we will want to obey him. The more we obey him, the greater our joy, regardless of our circumstances. Obedience to God is not something to be resisted; it is the only pathway to a life filled with joy.

The Importance of Communication: Communication is extremely important in relationships characterized by stability and peace. The eastern tribes had built a large monument in Canaan before crossing the Jordan River. This act was misunderstood by the western tribes, who perceived it as an act of rebellion against God. War between the tribes seemed inevitable, but fighting was averted by a simple conversation between the groups involved. After understanding was established, the reason for battle no longer existed. We often misinterpret the actions and words of others, which results in confusion and conflict. Open and honest communication is a prerequisite for overcoming confusion and establishing peace.

CHAPTER 1
The LORD's Charge to Joshua

After the death of Moses the LORD's servant, the LORD spoke to Joshua son of Nun, Moses' assistant. He said, ²"Moses my servant is dead. Therefore, the time has come for you to lead these people, the Israelites, across the Jordan River into the land I am giving them. ³I promise you what I promised Moses: 'Wherever you set foot, you will be on land I have given you—⁴from the Negev wilderness in the south to the Lebanon mountains in the north, from the Euphrates River in the east to the Mediterranean Sea* in the west, including all the land of the Hittites.' ⁵No one will be able to stand against you as long as you live. For I will be with you as I was with Moses. I will not fail you or abandon you.

⁶"Be strong and courageous, for you are the one who will lead these people to possess all the land I swore to their ancestors I would

1:4 Hebrew *the Great Sea.*

1:1-9 Joshua may have been devastated by the death of Moses, his close friend, mentor, and father figure. But he was immediately thrust into a leadership role for which he undoubtedly felt unworthy and unprepared. How could Joshua ever fill the shoes of the man who had talked to God face to face (Exodus 33:11)? Joshua dared not show fear before the people, or they would have lost confidence in his ability to lead them to victory. He needed to demonstrate a bold obedience to God's commands in order to ensure success. Joshua was able to do this because he was willing to turn his life and will over to God.

1:10-15 In his new role as commander in chief of Israel's armies, Joshua commanded his subordinates to prepare their people for the new and difficult venture that lay before them. He then reminded the Reubenites, Gadites, and the half-tribe of Manasseh of their promise to Moses to fight side by side with their fellow Israelites until all the land had been conquered (see Numbers 32:1-32). Quite understandably, Joshua was concerned to know whether they would stand with or defect from the main body of the people. If they defected, war might have broken out or, at the very least, discouragement might have set in among the people of Israel. We need to continue to guard ourselves, evaluating, watching for seeds of discouragement.

READ JOSHUA 1:1-9

GOD grant me the serenity to accept the things I cannot change the courage to change the things I can and the wisdom to know the difference AMEN

There probably have been times when we all had high hopes for a promising life—before those hopes were dashed. But then, through the crazy and chaotic circumstances of growing up, we learned to settle for a life that was far less than what we had once hoped for.

God led the nation of Israel out of bondage in Egypt, through the wilderness, and to the edge of the Promised Land. But as the Israelites stood on the border looking into the fruitful and prosperous land of Canaan, they lacked the faith and courage to go in because of the scouts' reports of the powerful "giants" living there. Joshua was one of the few who had the faith to enter, but because of the others, he was held back. Forty years later the chance came again. Just before he entered the land, the Lord told him, "This is my command—be strong and courageous! Do not be afraid or discouraged. For the LORD your God is with you wherever you go" (Joshua 1:9).

We may have concluded that a good and healthy life is reserved for people who are better or stronger than we are, but there is a Promised Land for each one of us. Jeremiah 29:11 says: "'For I know the plans I have for you,' says the LORD. 'They are plans for good and not for disaster, to give you a future and a hope.'" We need to be courageous. We need to believe that there can be good things in life for us. We, too, can be encouraged that regardless of our own past failures and those of our family, we can start again. We can find our way out of the chaos of the wilderness into the Promised Land of productive and healthy living. *Turn to page 309, Judges 5.*

give them. [7]Be strong and very courageous. Be careful to obey all the instructions Moses gave you. Do not deviate from them, turning either to the right or to the left. Then you will be successful in everything you do. [8]Study this Book of Instruction continually. Meditate on it day and night so you will be sure to obey everything written in it. Only then will you prosper and succeed in all you do. [9]This is my command—be strong and courageous! Do not be afraid or discouraged. For the LORD your God is with you wherever you go."

Joshua's Charge to the Israelites

[10]Joshua then commanded the officers of Israel, [11]"Go through the camp and tell the people to get their provisions ready. In three days you will cross the Jordan River and take possession of the land the LORD your God is giving you."

[12]Then Joshua called together the tribes of Reuben, Gad, and the half-tribe of Manasseh. He told them, [13]"Remember what Moses, the servant of the LORD, commanded you: 'The LORD your God is giving you a place of rest. He has given you this land.' [14]Your wives, children, and livestock may remain here in the land Moses assigned to you on the east side of the Jordan River. But your strong warriors, fully armed, must lead the other tribes across the Jordan to help them conquer their territory. Stay with them [15]until the LORD gives them rest, as he has given you rest, and until they, too, possess the land the LORD your God is giving them. Only then may you return and settle here on the east side of the Jordan River in the land that Moses, the servant of the LORD, assigned to you."

[16]They answered Joshua, "We will do whatever you command us, and we will go wherever you send us. [17]We will obey you just

as we obeyed Moses. And may the LORD your God be with you as he was with Moses. [18]Anyone who rebels against your orders and does not obey your words and everything you command will be put to death. So be strong and courageous!"

CHAPTER 2
Rahab Protects the Spies

Then Joshua secretly sent out two spies from the Israelite camp at Acacia Grove.* He instructed them, "Scout out the land on the other side of the Jordan River, especially around Jericho." So the two men set out and came to the house of a prostitute named Rahab and stayed there that night.

[2]But someone told the king of Jericho, "Some Israelites have come here tonight to spy out the land." [3]So the king of Jericho sent orders to Rahab: "Bring out the men who have come into your house, for they have come here to spy out the whole land."

[4]Rahab had hidden the two men, but she replied, "Yes, the men were here earlier, but I didn't know where they were from. [5]They left the town at dusk, as the gates were about to close. I don't know where they went. If you hurry, you can probably catch up with them." [6](Actually, she had taken them up to the roof and hidden them beneath bundles of flax she had laid out.) [7]So the king's men went looking for the spies along the road leading to the shallow crossings of the Jordan River. And as soon as the king's men had left, the gate of Jericho was shut.

[8]Before the spies went to sleep that night, Rahab went up on the roof to talk with them. [9]"I know the LORD has given you this land," she told them. "We are all afraid of you. Everyone in the land is living in terror. [10]For we have heard how the LORD made a dry path for you through the Red Sea* when you left Egypt. And we know what you did to Sihon and Og, the two Amorite kings east of the Jordan River, whose people you completely destroyed.* [11]No wonder our hearts have melted in fear! No one has the courage to fight after hearing such things. For the LORD your God is the supreme God of the heavens above and the earth below.

[12]"Now swear to me by the LORD that you will be kind to me and my family since I have helped you. Give me some guarantee that [13]when Jericho is conquered, you will let me live, along with my father and mother, my brothers and sisters, and all their families."

[14]"We offer our own lives as a guarantee for your safety," the men agreed. "If you don't betray us, we will keep our promise and be kind to you when the LORD gives us the land."

[15]Then, since Rahab's house was built into the town wall, she let them down by a rope through the window. [16]"Escape to the hill country," she told them. "Hide there for three days from the men searching for you. Then, when they have returned, you can go on your way."

[17]Before they left, the men told her, "We will be bound by the oath we have taken only if you follow these instructions. [18]When we come into the land, you must leave this scarlet rope hanging from the window through which you let us down. And all your family members—your father, mother, brothers, and all your relatives—must be here inside the house. [19]If they go out into the street and are killed, it will not be our fault. But if anyone lays a hand on people inside this house, we will accept the responsibility for their death. [20]If you betray us, however, we are not bound by this oath in any way."

2:1 Hebrew *Shittim*. 2:10a Hebrew *sea of reeds*. 2:10b The Hebrew term used here refers to the complete consecration of things or people to the LORD, either by destroying them or by giving them as an offering.

2:1-7 Joshua wisely determined to first discover the strength of his enemies, the people of the city of Jericho, before setting out to encounter them in battle (see Luke 14:31-32). Rahab, a prostitute and a citizen of Jericho, also made a wise decision when she took a stand for the God of Israel by assisting and protecting the spies sent by Joshua. Rahab displayed courage when she turned away from the security and praise of the world she knew and risked following the true God, of whom she knew little. It always takes courage to make changes in our life, especially when those changes take us into the unknown.

2:15-21 Rahab completed her chosen task of helping the spies by providing them with a rope, a window hidden from sight, and a plan (hide three days in the hills) for their safe return to their people. The spies, in turn, established the ground rules of responsibility for Rahab and her family. They outlined the specific requirements for the safety of Rahab's family and the consequences of betrayal. Rahab is an excellent example of how God can use each of us, no matter what terrible things we may have done in the past.

²¹"I accept your terms," she replied. And she sent them on their way, leaving the scarlet rope hanging from the window.

²²The spies went up into the hill country and stayed there three days. The men who were chasing them searched everywhere along the road, but they finally returned without success.

²³Then the two spies came down from the hill country, crossed the Jordan River, and reported to Joshua all that had happened to them. ²⁴"The LORD has given us the whole land," they said, "for all the people in the land are terrified of us."

CHAPTER 3
The Israelites Cross the Jordan

Early the next morning Joshua and all the Israelites left Acacia Grove* and arrived at the banks of the Jordan River, where they camped before crossing. ²Three days later the Israelite officers went through the camp, ³giving these instructions to the people: "When you see the Levitical priests carrying the Ark of the Covenant of the LORD your God, move out from your positions and follow them. ⁴Since you have never traveled this way before, they will guide you. Stay about a half mile* behind them, keeping a clear distance between you and the Ark. Make sure you don't come any closer."

⁵Then Joshua told the people, "Purify yourselves, for tomorrow the LORD will do great wonders among you."

⁶In the morning Joshua said to the priests, "Lift up the Ark of the Covenant and lead the people across the river." And so they started out and went ahead of the people.

⁷The LORD told Joshua, "Today I will begin to make you a great leader in the eyes of all the Israelites. They will know that I am with you, just as I was with Moses. ⁸Give this command to the priests who carry the Ark of the Covenant: 'When you reach the banks of the Jordan River, take a few steps into the river and stop there.'"

⁹So Joshua told the Israelites, "Come and listen to what the LORD your God says. ¹⁰Today you will know that the living God is among you. He will surely drive out the Canaanites, Hittites, Hivites, Perizzites, Girgashites, Amorites, and Jebusites ahead of you. ¹¹Look, the Ark of the Covenant, which belongs to the Lord of the whole earth, will lead you across the Jordan River! ¹²Now choose twelve men from the tribes of Israel, one from each tribe. ¹³The priests will carry the Ark of the LORD, the Lord of all the earth. As soon as their feet touch the water, the flow of water will be cut off upstream, and the river will stand up like a wall."

¹⁴So the people left their camp to cross the Jordan, and the priests who were carrying the Ark of the Covenant went ahead of them. ¹⁵It was the harvest season, and the Jordan was overflowing its banks. But as soon as the feet of the priests who were carrying the Ark touched the water at the river's edge, ¹⁶the water above that point began backing up a great distance away at a town called Adam, which is near Zarethan. And the water below that point flowed on to the Dead Sea* until the riverbed was dry. Then all the people crossed over near the town of Jericho.

¹⁷Meanwhile, the priests who were carrying the Ark of the LORD's Covenant stood on dry ground in the middle of the riverbed as the people passed by. They waited there until the whole nation of Israel had crossed the Jordan on dry ground.

3:1 Hebrew *Shittim.* 3:4 Hebrew *about 2,000 cubits* [920 meters]. 3:16 Hebrew *the sea of the Arabah, the Salt Sea.*

3:1-6 These were anxious times for Joshua and the Israelites. They set out to the Promised Land but then had to delay their entrance for three full days while their leaders gave them instructions. Those instructions, moreover, dealt with the physical and the spiritual realms. The people were commanded (1) to remain approximately a half mile behind the Ark of the Covenant when the priests carried it (i.e., they were not to run ahead of God but were to receive their direction from God) and (2) to purify themselves (i.e., they were to dedicate themselves to God, remaining close to him to see what great things he would do). No doubt it was as difficult then as it is now to follow God's plan rather than to rebel and go our own way.

3:7-14 God would drive out the enemies of Israel if the Israelites were obedient to him. Furthermore, so the people could see the power of God at work, the priests, acting by faith, had to carry the Ark of the Covenant and stand with their feet in the Jordan River. Would God leave Joshua looking foolish, or would God act in the way he had promised? Joshua did not doubt God but had the priests stand in the river. The Jordan River was at flood stage and extremely dangerous, if not impossible, to cross without God's help. Often God places us where we must either stand for him or show that we don't really trust him. If we trust in God, we can be sure that he will never disappoint us.

CHAPTER 4
Memorials to the Jordan Crossing

When all the people had crossed the Jordan, the LORD said to Joshua, ²"Now choose twelve men, one from each tribe. ³Tell them, 'Take twelve stones from the very place where the priests are standing in the middle of the Jordan. Carry them out and pile them up at the place where you will camp tonight.'"

⁴So Joshua called together the twelve men he had chosen—one from each of the tribes of Israel. ⁵He told them, "Go into the middle of the Jordan, in front of the Ark of the LORD your God. Each of you must pick up one stone and carry it out on your shoulder—twelve stones in all, one for each of the twelve tribes of Israel. ⁶We will use these stones to build a memorial. In the future your children will ask you, 'What do these stones mean?' ⁷Then you can tell them, 'They remind us that the Jordan River stopped flowing when the Ark of the LORD's Covenant went across.' These stones will stand as a memorial among the people of Israel forever."

⁸So the men did as Joshua had commanded them. They took twelve stones from the middle of the Jordan River, one for each tribe, just as the LORD had told Joshua. They carried them to the place where they camped for the night and constructed the memorial there.

⁹Joshua also set up another pile of twelve stones in the middle of the Jordan, at the place where the priests who carried the Ark of the Covenant were standing. And they are there to this day.

¹⁰The priests who were carrying the Ark stood in the middle of the river until all of the LORD's commands that Moses had given to Joshua were carried out. Meanwhile, the people hurried across the riverbed. ¹¹And when everyone was safely on the other side, the priests crossed over with the Ark of the LORD as the people watched.

¹²The armed warriors from the tribes of Reuben, Gad, and the half-tribe of Manasseh led the Israelites across the Jordan, just as Moses had directed. ¹³These armed men—about 40,000 strong—were ready for battle, and the LORD was with them as they crossed over to the plains of Jericho.

¹⁴That day the LORD made Joshua a great leader in the eyes of all the Israelites, and for the rest of his life they revered him as much as they had revered Moses.

¹⁵The LORD had said to Joshua, ¹⁶"Command the priests carrying the Ark of the Covenant* to come up out of the riverbed." ¹⁷So Joshua gave the command. ¹⁸As soon as the priests carrying the Ark of the LORD's Covenant came up out of the riverbed and their feet were on high ground, the water of the Jordan returned and overflowed its banks as before.

¹⁹The people crossed the Jordan on the tenth day of the first month.* Then they camped at Gilgal, just east of Jericho. ²⁰It

---

4:16 Hebrew *Ark of the Testimony.* 4:19 This day in the ancient Hebrew lunar calendar occurred in late March, April, or early May.

4:1-7 The priests faithfully remained standing in the riverbed until the more than 2 million people had crossed into the Promised Land. Joshua, at the command of God, then sent 12 men back to the place where the priests were standing. Those men were to collect one stone per tribe to set up a memorial that would remind them, their children, and their children's children of what God had done on their behalf as they moved into the Promised Land. The stones would serve as a visible reminder of God's great power should the people ever become discouraged when they faced powerful enemies in the future. If we take time to review our life, we also will find small reminders, monuments, of God's presence with us.

4:8-14 Joshua took a direct interest in remembering the glory of God and in honoring the faith of the priests by personally erecting a permanent memorial in the middle of the river. When the crossing was completed, God raised Joshua to a new status in the eyes of the people—he was honored in the same way his predecessor Moses had been. Sometimes it helps to record the events where God provided a way when everything appeared hopeless. These written accounts can then become our monuments to God's faithfulness and can be reviewed and celebrated in times of doubt.

5:1-9 The Amorite kings were terrified of the power of the God of Israel, but they did not turn to him for help. The people of Israel, however, took steps to ensure that their relationship with God was as it should be. Because God commanded it, they circumcised all the males among them. As a result, God took away their shame when they submitted to the painful act of circumcision. Fortunately, we do not have to go through a physical cutting to be rid of our shame. But we do have to go through the painful process of acknowledging our failures and allowing God to remove the shame from us. This process can sometimes be so painful that we are tempted to deny our shame rather than allow God to remove it.

JOSHUA

We all have experienced the frustration of knowing the truth but having no one believe us. Few of us, however, have had to live with the consequences of this for almost 40 years.

Joshua was one of the 12 Israelites chosen to scout out the land of Canaan. Tremendous responsibility came along with this job. Their report on what they saw would help over a million people make a decision about entering the Promised Land. When the twelve scouts gave their reports, ten said it would be impossible to conquer the land. Their understanding of God was limited by their weak faith; it was distorted. On the other hand, Joshua and Caleb agreed that the task would be difficult, but they urged the people to trust God to help them. They saw God as loving, powerful, and able to lead them safely into the Promised Land.

The people rebelled against God and sided with the majority report. In doing so, they ran from the responsibility of turning their wills and their lives over to God and following him. The result of their irresponsibility was tragic: A whole generation—with the exception of Joshua and Caleb—died in the desert.

Three important principles are illustrated in Joshua's life. First, what we think about God has a powerful effect upon what we do. Second, ever since Adam's fall, human beings have had to endure pain whether they accept responsibility or decline it. Third, our decisions to accept or run away from responsibility determine the types of pain we experience and the effect they will have on us. Joshua experienced significant pain despite putting God first in his life. But that pain did not bring his destruction. God used it to develop him into one of the most effective leaders in all of history.

Many of us think that we can escape pain by avoiding responsibility and its demands. What we fail to realize is that in running away from responsibility, we often experience a much deeper pain than we would have if we had only accepted it in the first place.

STRENGTHS AND ACCOMPLISHMENTS:
- Joshua was a wise and gifted military strategist.
- When faced with life's challenges, he sought God's direction.
- He was not afraid to go against popular opinion.
- He led the Israelites into the Promised Land.
- He believed God's promises despite opposition.

LESSONS FROM HIS LIFE:
- Despite opposition, it is always best to follow God.
- Those we choose as mentors have a profound effect on us.
- Solid preparation and encouragement are keys to training a leader.

KEY VERSE:
"But if you refuse to serve the LORD, then choose today whom you will serve. Would you prefer the gods your ancestors served beyond the Euphrates? Or will it be the gods of the Amorites in whose land you now live? But as for me and my family, we will serve the LORD" (24:15).

Joshua's story is told in Exodus 17; 24; 32–33; Numbers 11; 13–14, 26–27, 32–34; Deuteronomy 1; 3; 31; 34; and the book of Joshua. He is also mentioned in Judges 1–2; 1 Kings 16:34; 1 Chronicles 7:27; and Hebrews 4:8.

---

was there at Gilgal that Joshua piled up the twelve stones taken from the Jordan River.

²¹Then Joshua said to the Israelites, "In the future your children will ask, 'What do these stones mean?' ²²Then you can tell them, 'This is where the Israelites crossed the Jordan on dry ground.' ²³For the LORD your God dried up the river right before your eyes, and he kept it dry until you were all across, just as he did at the Red Sea* when he dried it up until we had all

crossed over. ²⁴He did this so all the nations of the earth might know that the LORD's hand is powerful, and so you might fear the LORD your God forever."

CHAPTER 5
When all the Amorite kings west of the Jordan and all the Canaanite kings who lived along the Mediterranean coast* heard how the LORD had dried up the Jordan River so

4:23 Hebrew *sea of reeds.* 5:1 Hebrew *along the sea.*

the people of Israel could cross, they lost heart and were paralyzed with fear because of them.

Israel Reestablishes Covenant Ceremonies

²At that time the LORD told Joshua, "Make flint knives and circumcise this second generation of Israelites.*" ³So Joshua made flint knives and circumcised the entire male population of Israel at Gibeath-haaraloth.*

⁴Joshua had to circumcise them because all the men who were old enough to fight in battle when they left Egypt had died in the wilderness. ⁵Those who left Egypt had all been circumcised, but none of those born after the Exodus, during the years in the wilderness, had been circumcised. ⁶The Israelites had traveled in the wilderness for forty years until all the men who were old enough to fight in battle when they left Egypt had died. For they had disobeyed the LORD, and the LORD vowed he would not let them enter the land he had sworn to give us—a land flowing with milk and honey. ⁷So Joshua circumcised their sons—those who had grown up to take their fathers' places—for they had not been circumcised on the way to the Promised Land. ⁸After all the males had been circumcised, they rested in the camp until they were healed.

⁹Then the LORD said to Joshua, "Today I have rolled away the shame of your slavery in Egypt." So that place has been called Gilgal* to this day.

¹⁰While the Israelites were camped at Gilgal on the plains of Jericho, they celebrated Passover on the evening of the fourteenth day of the first month.* ¹¹The very next day they began to eat unleavened bread and roasted grain harvested from the land. ¹²No manna appeared on the day they first ate from the crops of the land, and it was never seen again. So from that time on the Israelites ate from the crops of Canaan.

The LORD's Commander Confronts Joshua

¹³When Joshua was near the town of Jericho, he looked up and saw a man standing in front of him with sword in hand. Joshua went up to him and demanded, "Are you friend or foe?"

¹⁴"Neither one," he replied. "I am the commander of the LORD's army."

At this, Joshua fell with his face to the ground in reverence. "I am at your command," Joshua said. "What do you want your servant to do?"

¹⁵The commander of the LORD's army replied, "Take off your sandals, for the place where you are standing is holy." And Joshua did as he was told.

CHAPTER 6
The Fall of Jericho

Now the gates of Jericho were tightly shut because the people were afraid of the Israelites. No one was allowed to go out or in. ²But the LORD said to Joshua, "I have given you Jericho, its king, and all its strong warriors. ³You and your fighting men should march around the town once a day for six days. ⁴Seven priests will walk ahead of the Ark, each carrying a ram's horn. On the seventh day you are to march around the town seven times, with the priests blowing the horns. ⁵When you hear the priests give one long blast on the rams' horns, have all the people shout as loud as they can. Then the walls of the town will collapse, and the people can charge straight into the town."

⁶So Joshua called together the priests and said, "Take up the Ark of the LORD's Cov-

---

5:2 Or *circumcise the Israelites a second time.* 5:3 *Gibeath-haaraloth* means "hill of foreskins." 5:9 *Gilgal* sounds like the Hebrew word *galal,* meaning "to roll." 5:10 This day in the ancient Hebrew lunar calendar occurred in late March, April, or early May.

5:13-15 Note two important considerations regarding the identity of the commander of the Lord's army: (1) He accepted worship when Joshua bowed down to him, and (2) the place where he stood was considered holy ground (compare Exodus 3:1-6). This commander, therefore, was more than a man and more than an angel; this Captain was none other than God himself. When Joshua recognized who the stranger was, he quickly deferred all claims of leadership to him. If each of us could acknowledge our powerlessness without God and relinquish control to God as Joshua did, we would avoid many of the self-inflicted wounds that hurt us. Fortunately, it is never too late to acknowledge God's lordship over us and allow him to lead us in life's battles.

6:1-14 Israel was ready to attack, but God told them to wait. God required his people to do something that on the surface seemed very foolish. They were commanded to march around the city day after day. The Israelites obeyed God and persisted in their faith, not fully understanding how God would destroy the walls of Jericho. When there are seemingly unbreakable barriers along the road to recovery, God can make those barriers crumble down, allowing us to be victorious. But we need to do things his way, even if we don't always understand why.

RAHAB & FAMILY

It is amazing that a pagan prostitute would demonstrate even rudimentary trust in God. Because she believed, Joshua found an unlikely ally waiting within the city walls of Jericho. As the trumpets blared and the people thunderously marched, Rahab gathered her parents, brothers, and sisters about her in anticipation of rescue. A single scarlet cord tied to her window alerted the conquerors to spare the people within. Thanks to her surprising faith, her family was plucked from the ruins.

Given her line of work, Rahab surely wasn't accustomed to setting boundaries upon her behavior. She probably wasn't even aware of her personal sin. Her faith, like her job, was likely born of necessity. She was, above all, practical, and it made sense to believe in this powerful Hebrew God. She watched as fear paralyzed her people, and she recognized her own powerlessness in the situation. Jericho's fall was inevitable. The God who parted seas could surely topple walls. Her ability to see reality also prompted her to faith.

Aiding Joshua's men was a risky business, yet Rahab acted with courage and daring. She proved herself faithful by concealing the spies and giving them vital information. Her strategy of deceiving the king might be questioned, although nowhere in Scripture is she criticized for her methods. Instead, she is extolled as an example of righteousness and faith.

Following the rescue, God gave Rahab what she probably never dreamed possible in Jericho: the opportunity to break with the past and build a new life. Rahab and her relatives found a home among the Israelites, but there was more. She married Salmon and was blessed with a son, Boaz. Boaz would become the great-grandfather of King David, from whose line Jesus descended. Rahab's transformation proves once again that God is in the business of turning lives around. Rahab shines as a stellar example of a second chance, a forgiven past, and a recovered life. Though our recovery story may not be as dramatic, God is able to pick up broken pieces and facilitate fresh beginnings.

STRENGTHS AND ACCOMPLISHMENTS:
- Rahab's faith in God was made visible by her actions.
- Rahab had a deep love and concern for her family.
- She recognized the hopeless reality of her situation and was willing to turn from her old life of sin to a new life of faith.
- She sought help from the right source: God and his people.

WEAKNESSES AND MISTAKES:
- Rahab's initial trust in God seems to have been motivated by pragmatism and fear rather than loving gratitude.

LESSONS FROM HER LIFE:
- God is alive and available to facilitate fresh starts when we are willing to cooperate with his plans.
- Nothing is impossible with God.
- A proper view of God should convince us of his power and worth.

KEY VERSE:
"It was by faith that Rahab the prostitute was not destroyed with the people in her city who refused to obey God" (Hebrews 11:31).

Rahab's story is told in Joshua 2:1-21; 6:17-25. She is also mentioned in Matthew 1:5; Hebrews 11:31; and James 2:25.

---

enant, and assign seven priests to walk in front of it, each carrying a ram's horn." [7]Then he gave orders to the people: "March around the town, and the armed men will lead the way in front of the Ark of the LORD."

[8]After Joshua spoke to the people, the seven priests with the rams' horns started marching in the presence of the LORD, blowing the horns as they marched. And the Ark of the LORD's Covenant followed behind them. [9]Some of the armed men marched in front of the priests with the horns and some behind the Ark, with the priests continually blowing the horns. [10]"Do not shout; do not even talk," Joshua commanded. "Not a single word from any of you until I tell you to shout. Then shout!" [11]So the Ark of the LORD was carried around the town once that day, and then everyone returned to spend the night in the camp.

¹²Joshua got up early the next morning, and the priests again carried the Ark of the LORD. ¹³The seven priests with the rams' horns marched in front of the Ark of the LORD, blowing their horns. Again the armed men marched both in front of the priests with the horns and behind the Ark of the LORD. All this time the priests were blowing their horns. ¹⁴On the second day they again marched around the town once and returned to the camp. They followed this pattern for six days.

¹⁵On the seventh day the Israelites got up at dawn and marched around the town as they had done before. But this time they went around the town seven times. ¹⁶The seventh time around, as the priests sounded the long blast on their horns, Joshua commanded the people, "Shout! For the LORD has given you the town! ¹⁷Jericho and everything in it must be completely destroyed* as an offering to the LORD. Only Rahab the prostitute and the others in her house will be spared, for she protected our spies.

¹⁸"Do not take any of the things set apart for destruction, or you yourselves will be completely destroyed, and you will bring trouble on the camp of Israel. ¹⁹Everything made from silver, gold, bronze, or iron is sacred to the LORD and must be brought into his treasury."

²⁰When the people heard the sound of the rams' horns, they shouted as loud as they could. Suddenly, the walls of Jericho collapsed, and the Israelites charged straight into the town and captured it. ²¹They completely destroyed everything in it with their swords—men and women, young and old, cattle, sheep, goats, and donkeys.

²²Meanwhile, Joshua said to the two spies, "Keep your promise. Go to the prostitute's house and bring her out, along with all her family."

²³The men who had been spies went in and brought out Rahab, her father, mother, brothers, and all the other relatives who were with her. They moved her whole family to a safe place near the camp of Israel.

²⁴Then the Israelites burned the town and everything in it. Only the things made from silver, gold, bronze, or iron were kept for the treasury of the LORD's house. ²⁵So Joshua spared Rahab the prostitute and her relatives who were with her in the house, because she had hidden the spies Joshua sent to Jericho. And she lives among the Israelites to this day.

²⁶At that time Joshua invoked this curse:

"May the curse of the LORD fall on anyone
    who tries to rebuild the town of Jericho.
At the cost of his firstborn son,
    he will lay its foundation.
At the cost of his youngest son,
    he will set up its gates."

²⁷So the LORD was with Joshua, and his reputation spread throughout the land.

CHAPTER 7
Ai Defeats the Israelites
But Israel violated the instructions about the things set apart for the LORD.* A man named Achan had stolen some of these dedicated things, so the LORD was very angry with the Israelites. Achan was the son of Carmi, a descendant of Zimri* son of Zerah, of the tribe of Judah.

²Joshua sent some of his men from Jericho

6:17 The Hebrew term used here refers to the complete consecration of things or people to the LORD, either by destroying them or by giving them as an offering; similarly in 6:18, 21. 7:1a The Hebrew term used here refers to the complete consecration of things or people to the LORD, either by destroying them or by giving them as an offering; similarly in 7:11, 12, 13, 15. 7:1b As in parallel text at 1 Chr 2:6; Hebrew reads Zabdi. Also in 7:17, 18.

6:15-21 Once more Israel experienced delayed gratification. On the seventh day just before initiating the attack, the people of Israel were required to march seven times around the city. They were also prohibited from enjoying the spoils of victory, which were to be dedicated to God—they were not to steal from God. Finally Israel was given the go-ahead. In obedience to God, they pressed the attack and secured the victory, destroying their enemies completely. Learning to delay gratification is a major step toward maturity, both in our faith and in our recovery. God calls us to trust him and wait on him, especially when our every urge is to move ahead without delay.

7:1-9 The Israelites grew overconfident from their victory at Jericho and attacked the small city of Ai without first consulting God. Their small force was soundly defeated because God was angry at Israel because of Achan's disobedience. Israel as a whole became utterly demoralized. Even Joshua was afraid and confused by what had happened. We must be careful not to take back control of our life once we see what God can do when he is in control. On our own, we may allow some seemingly insignificant area of our life to lead us away from God's plan with disastrous results. We are to submit our whole life to his control.

to spy out the town of Ai, east of Bethel, near Beth-aven. ³When they returned, they told Joshua, "There's no need for all of us to go up there; it won't take more than two or three thousand men to attack Ai. Since there are so few of them, don't make all our people struggle to go up there."

⁴So approximately 3,000 warriors were sent, but they were soundly defeated. The men of Ai ⁵chased the Israelites from the town gate as far as the quarries,* and they killed about thirty-six who were retreating down the slope. The Israelites were paralyzed with fear at this turn of events, and their courage melted away.

⁶Joshua and the elders of Israel tore their clothing in dismay, threw dust on their heads, and bowed face down to the ground before the Ark of the LORD until evening. ⁷Then Joshua cried out, "Oh, Sovereign LORD, why did you bring us across the Jordan River if you are going to let the Amorites kill us? If only we had been content to stay on the other side! ⁸Lord, what can I say now that Israel has fled from its enemies? ⁹For when the Canaanites and all the other people living in the land hear about it, they will surround us and wipe our name off the face of the earth. And then what will happen to the honor of your great name?"

¹⁰But the LORD said to Joshua, "Get up! Why are you lying on your face like this? ¹¹Israel has sinned and broken my covenant! They have stolen some of the things that I commanded must be set apart for me. And they have not only stolen them but have lied about it and hidden the things among their own belongings. ¹²That is why the Israelites are running from their enemies in defeat. For now Israel itself has been set apart for destruction. I will not remain with you any longer unless you destroy the things among you that were set apart for destruction.

¹³"Get up! Command the people to purify themselves in preparation for tomorrow. For this is what the LORD, the God of Israel, says: Hidden among you, O Israel, are things set apart for the LORD. You will never defeat your enemies until you remove these things from among you.

¹⁴"In the morning you must present yourselves by tribes, and the LORD will point out the tribe to which the guilty man belongs. That tribe must come forward with its clans, and the LORD will point out the guilty clan. That clan will then come forward, and the LORD will point out the guilty family. Finally, each member of the guilty family must come forward one by one. ¹⁵The one who has stolen what was set apart for destruction will himself be burned with fire, along with everything he has, for he has broken the covenant of the LORD and has done a horrible thing in Israel."

Achan's Sin

¹⁶Early the next morning Joshua brought the tribes of Israel before the LORD, and the tribe of Judah was singled out. ¹⁷Then the clans of Judah came forward, and the clan of Zerah was singled out. Then the families of Zerah came forward, and the family of Zimri was singled out. ¹⁸Every member of Zimri's family was brought forward person by person, and Achan was singled out.

¹⁹Then Joshua said to Achan, "My son, give glory to the LORD, the God of Israel, by telling the truth. Make your confession and tell me what you have done. Don't hide it from me."

²⁰Achan replied, "It is true! I have sinned against the LORD, the God of Israel. ²¹Among the plunder I saw a beautiful robe from Babylon,* 200 silver coins,* and a bar of gold weighing more than a pound.* I wanted them so much that I took them. They are hidden in the ground beneath my tent, with the silver buried deeper than the rest."

7:5 Or *as far as Shebarim.* **7:21a** Hebrew *Shinar.* **7:21b** Hebrew *200 shekels of silver,* about 5 pounds or 2.3 kilograms in weight. **7:21c** Hebrew *50 shekels,* about 20 ounces or 570 grams in weight.

7:20-26 Once Achan was identified as the guilty party, he confessed his sin, but his confession came too late. Had he confessed earlier, he might have prevented the Israelite defeat and the death of his family members. After having Achan and his family stoned to death, Joshua erected another monument of stones (see 4:9, 20). This monument, however, was not to commemorate God's great power of deliverance but to be a reminder that the sin of one person can negatively impact the well-being of many people. Perhaps each of us should write down when and where we rebelled against God and how that impacted our life and the lives of those around us. If we are to learn from our mistakes, we must remember not only the result but also the steps that led to our turning away from God.

²²So Joshua sent some men to make a search. They ran to the tent and found the stolen goods hidden there, just as Achan had said, with the silver buried beneath the rest. ²³They took the things from the tent and brought them to Joshua and all the Israelites. Then they laid them on the ground in the presence of the LORD.

²⁴Then Joshua and all the Israelites took Achan, the silver, the robe, the bar of gold, his sons, daughters, cattle, donkeys, sheep, goats, tent, and everything he had, and they brought them to the valley of Achor. ²⁵Then Joshua said to Achan, "Why have you brought trouble on us? The LORD will now bring trouble on you." And all the Israelites stoned Achan and his family and burned their bodies. ²⁶They piled a great heap of stones over Achan, which remains to this day. That is why the place has been called the Valley of Trouble* ever since. So the LORD was no longer angry.

CHAPTER 8
The Israelites Defeat Ai

Then the LORD said to Joshua, "Do not be afraid or discouraged. Take all your fighting men and attack Ai, for I have given you the king of Ai, his people, his town, and his land. ²You will destroy them as you destroyed Jericho and its king. But this time you may keep the plunder and the livestock for yourselves. Set an ambush behind the town."

³So Joshua and all the fighting men set out to attack Ai. Joshua chose 30,000 of his best warriors and sent them out at night ⁴with these orders: "Hide in ambush close behind the town and be ready for action. ⁵When our main army attacks, the men of Ai will come out to fight as they did before, and we will run away from them. ⁶We will let them chase us until we have drawn them away from the town. For they will say, 'The Israelites are running away from us as they did before.' Then, while we are running from them, ⁷you will jump up from your ambush and take possession of the town, for the LORD your God will give it to you. ⁸Set the town on fire, as the LORD has commanded. You have your orders."

⁹So they left and went to the place of ambush between Bethel and the west side of Ai. But Joshua remained among the people in the camp that night. ¹⁰Early the next morning Joshua roused his men and started toward Ai, accompanied by the elders of Israel. ¹¹All the fighting men who were with Joshua marched in front of the town and camped on the north side of Ai, with a valley between them and the town. ¹²That night Joshua sent about 5,000 men to lie in ambush between Bethel and Ai, on the west side of the town. ¹³So they stationed the main army north of the town and the ambush west of the town. Joshua himself spent that night in the valley.

¹⁴When the king of Ai saw the Israelites across the valley, he and all his army hurried out early in the morning and attacked the Israelites at a place overlooking the Jordan Valley.* But he didn't realize there was an ambush behind the town. ¹⁵Joshua and the Israelite army fled toward the wilderness as though they were badly beaten. ¹⁶Then all the men in the town were called out to chase after them. In this way, they were lured away from the town. ¹⁷There was not a man left in Ai or Bethel* who did not chase after the Israelites, and the town was left wide open.

¹⁸Then the LORD said to Joshua, "Point the spear in your hand toward Ai, for I will hand the town over to you." Joshua did as he was commanded. ¹⁹As soon as Joshua gave this signal, all the men in ambush jumped up from their position and poured into the town. They quickly captured it and set it on fire.

²⁰When the men of Ai looked behind them,

7:26 Hebrew *valley of Achor.* 8:14 Hebrew *the Arabah.* 8:17 Some manuscripts lack *or Bethel.*

8:1-9 Once again God gave Joshua detailed plans to follow. With this guidance, Joshua used his God-given reasoning to assess the situation and develop a detailed strategy to defeat his enemies. For such a plan to succeed, the soldiers had to exercise discipline and self-control, attacking only when the enemy was most vulnerable. Thus, by using God's methods, Joshua and his people demonstrated that they had learned from their defeat and had grown spiritually. God's plans often require discipline and self-control, which can only be attained through work and struggle. The ability to say no to our human urges places us in reach of God's divine plan.
8:10-23 The Israelites executed God's plan exactly as he had given it to them. Joshua relied on God in the midst of the battle, and God gave the Israelites victory. When our desires and impulses lead us away from God, it may help to remember that Joshua's faith in God did not result in a life free from battles. The battles were to be fought and won through continued reliance on God. Like Joshua, we need to persevere with God's strength and resist the tendency to run from our own personal battles.

smoke from the town was filling the sky, and they had nowhere to go. For the Israelites who had fled in the direction of the wilderness now turned on their pursuers. ²¹When Joshua and all the other Israelites saw that the ambush had succeeded and that smoke was rising from the town, they turned and attacked the men of Ai. ²²Meanwhile, the Israelites who were inside the town came out and attacked the enemy from the rear. So the men of Ai were caught in the middle, with Israelite fighters on both sides. Israel attacked them, and not a single person survived or escaped. ²³Only the king of Ai was taken alive and brought to Joshua.

²⁴When the Israelite army finished chasing and killing all the men of Ai in the open fields, they went back and finished off everyone inside. ²⁵So the entire population of Ai, including men and women, was wiped out that day—12,000 in all. ²⁶For Joshua kept holding out his spear until everyone who had lived in Ai was completely destroyed.* ²⁷Only the livestock and the treasures of the town were not destroyed, for the Israelites kept these as plunder for themselves, as the LORD had commanded Joshua. ²⁸So Joshua burned the town of Ai,* and it became a permanent mound of ruins, desolate to this very day.

²⁹Joshua impaled the king of Ai on a sharpened pole and left him there until evening. At sunset the Israelites took down the body, as Joshua commanded, and threw it in front of the town gate. They piled a great heap of stones over him that can still be seen today.

The LORD's Covenant Renewed

³⁰Then Joshua built an altar to the LORD, the God of Israel, on Mount Ebal. ³¹He followed the commands that Moses the LORD's servant had written in the Book of Instruction: "Make me an altar from stones that are uncut and have not been shaped with iron tools."* Then on the altar they presented burnt offerings and peace offerings to the LORD. ³²And as the

Israelites watched, Joshua copied onto the stones of the altar* the instructions Moses had given them.

³³Then all the Israelites—foreigners and native-born alike—along with the elders, officers, and judges, were divided into two groups. One group stood in front of Mount Gerizim, the other in front of Mount Ebal. Each group faced the other, and between them stood the Levitical priests carrying the Ark of the LORD's Covenant. This was all done according to the commands that Moses, the servant of the LORD, had previously given for blessing the people of Israel.

³⁴Joshua then read to them all the blessings and curses Moses had written in the Book of Instruction. ³⁵Every word of every command that Moses had ever given was read to the entire assembly of Israel, including the women and children and the foreigners who lived among them.

CHAPTER 9
The Gibeonites Deceive Israel

Now all the kings west of the Jordan River heard about what had happened. These were the kings of the Hittites, Amorites, Canaanites, Perizzites, Hivites, and Jebusites, who lived in the hill country, in the western foothills,* and along the coast of the Mediterranean Sea* as far north as the Lebanon mountains. ²These kings combined their armies to fight as one against Joshua and the Israelites.

³But when the people of Gibeon heard what Joshua had done to Jericho and Ai, ⁴they resorted to deception to save themselves. They sent ambassadors to Joshua, loading their donkeys with weathered saddlebags and old, patched wineskins. ⁵They put on worn-out, patched sandals and ragged clothes. And the bread they took with them was dry and moldy. ⁶When they arrived at the camp of Israel at Gilgal, they told Joshua and the men of Israel, "We have

---

8:26 The Hebrew term used here refers to the complete consecration of things or people to the LORD, either by destroying them or by giving them as an offering. 8:28 Ai means "ruin." 8:31 Exod 20:25; Deut 27:5-6. 8:32 Hebrew *onto the stones.* 9:1a Hebrew *the Shephelah.* 9:1b Hebrew *the Great Sea.*

9:1-15 Frightened by Israel's success over Jericho and Ai, the kings of the southern coastal regions formed a coalition to attack Israel. The Gibeonites, however, took a different tactic. Recognizing their helplessness before Israel, they wisely but deceptively sought peace. By establishing a peace treaty, they avoided becoming Israel's next victims. The Israelites, however, failed to investigate the Gibeonite situation thoroughly and did not seek God's guidance. They entered into a covenant that was a violation of God's command (see Exodus 23:31-33). We must always examine the agreements we make and the relationships we form. We must ask ourselves whether God would approve of them at this particular time. A seemingly right relationship at the wrong time could produce ungodly results.

come from a distant land to ask you to make a peace treaty with us."

⁷The Israelites replied to these Hivites, "How do we know you don't live nearby? For if you do, we cannot make a treaty with you."

⁸They replied, "We are your servants."

"But who are you?" Joshua demanded. "Where do you come from?"

⁹They answered, "Your servants have come from a very distant country. We have heard of the might of the LORD your God and of all he did in Egypt. ¹⁰We have also heard what he did to the two Amorite kings east of the Jordan River—King Sihon of Heshbon and King Og of Bashan (who lived in Ashtaroth). ¹¹So our elders and all our people instructed us, 'Take supplies for a long journey. Go meet with the people of Israel and tell them, "We are your servants; please make a treaty with us."'

¹²"This bread was hot from the ovens when we left our homes. But now, as you can see, it is dry and moldy. ¹³These wineskins were new when we filled them, but now they are old and split open. And our clothing and sandals are worn out from our very long journey."

¹⁴So the Israelites examined their food, but they did not consult the LORD. ¹⁵Then Joshua made a peace treaty with them and guaranteed their safety, and the leaders of the community ratified their agreement with a binding oath.

¹⁶Three days after making the treaty, they learned that these people actually lived nearby! ¹⁷The Israelites set out at once to investigate and reached their towns in three days. The names of these towns were Gibeon, Kephirah, Beeroth, and Kiriath-jearim. ¹⁸But the Israelites did not attack the towns, for the Israelite leaders had made a vow to them in the name of the LORD, the God of Israel.

The people of Israel grumbled against their leaders because of the treaty. ¹⁹But the leaders replied, "Since we have sworn an oath in the presence of the LORD, the God of Israel, we cannot touch them. ²⁰This is what we must do. We must let them live, for divine anger would come upon us if we broke our oath. ²¹Let them live." So they made them woodcutters and water carriers for the entire community, as the Israelite leaders directed.

²²Joshua called together the Gibeonites and said, "Why did you lie to us? Why did you say that you live in a distant land when you live right here among us? ²³May you be cursed! From now on you will always be servants who cut wood and carry water for the house of my God."

²⁴They replied, "We did it because we—your servants—were clearly told that the LORD your God commanded his servant Moses to give you this entire land and to destroy all the people living in it. So we feared greatly for our lives because of you. That is why we have done this. ²⁵Now we are at your mercy—do to us whatever you think is right."

²⁶So Joshua did not allow the people of Israel to kill them. ²⁷But that day he made the Gibeonites the woodcutters and water carriers for the community of Israel and for the altar of the LORD—wherever the LORD would choose to build it. And that is what they do to this day.

CHAPTER 10
Israel Defeats the Southern Armies
Adoni-zedek, king of Jerusalem, heard that Joshua had captured and completely destroyed* Ai and killed its king, just as he had destroyed the town of Jericho and killed its king. He also learned that the Gibeonites had made peace with Israel and were now their allies. ²He and his people became very afraid when they heard all this because Gibeon was

---

10:1 The Hebrew term used here refers to the complete consecration of things or people to the LORD, either by destroying them or by giving them as an offering; also in 10:28, 35, 37, 39, 40.

9:16-27 The leaders of Israel accepted their mistake and honored God by adhering to the conditions of the treaty. Likewise, the Gibeonites, who had confessed their deception, willingly accepted the consequences of their actions and gave up their freedom in exchange for their lives, becoming servants of Israel. We are all aware that the effects of some decisions last a lifetime. We, too, have given up freedom in order to save our life. We need to remember that the decision to live in God's will results in *true* freedom, whereas "freedom" apart from God often leads to addictive behaviors.

10:1-11 The troubles associated with the undesirable treaty with Gibeon were compounded—Israel now had to fight on behalf of the Gibeonites. Israel accepted its obligation, and God promised Israel victory over all five kings. Although Joshua achieved success, his real victory came from God. God killed more of the enemy with hailstones than the entire Israelite army did with their weapons. If we examine our accomplishments, we will find that while we were working so hard, God was preparing a way that allowed us to do more than we could have ever done alone.

a large town—as large as the royal cities and larger than Ai. And the Gibeonite men were strong warriors.

³So King Adoni-zedek of Jerusalem sent messengers to several other kings: Hoham of Hebron, Piram of Jarmuth, Japhia of Lachish, and Debir of Eglon. ⁴"Come and help me destroy Gibeon," he urged them, "for they have made peace with Joshua and the people of Israel." ⁵So these five Amorite kings combined their armies for a united attack. They moved all their troops into place and attacked Gibeon.

⁶The men of Gibeon quickly sent messengers to Joshua at his camp in Gilgal. "Don't abandon your servants now!" they pleaded. "Come at once! Save us! Help us! For all the Amorite kings who live in the hill country have joined forces to attack us."

⁷So Joshua and his entire army, including his best warriors, left Gilgal and set out for Gibeon. ⁸"Do not be afraid of them," the LORD said to Joshua, "for I have given you victory over them. Not a single one of them will be able to stand up to you."

⁹Joshua traveled all night from Gilgal and took the Amorite armies by surprise. ¹⁰The LORD threw them into a panic, and the Israelites slaughtered great numbers of them at Gibeon. Then the Israelites chased the enemy along the road to Beth-horon, killing them all along the way to Azekah and Makkedah. ¹¹As the Amorites retreated down the road from Beth-horon, the LORD destroyed them with a terrible hailstorm from heaven that continued until they reached Azekah. The hail killed more of the enemy than the Israelites killed with the sword.

¹²On the day the LORD gave the Israelites victory over the Amorites, Joshua prayed to the LORD in front of all the people of Israel. He said,

"Let the sun stand still over Gibeon,
 and the moon over the valley of Aijalon."

¹³So the sun stood still and the moon stayed in place until the nation of Israel had defeated its enemies.

Is this event not recorded in *The Book of Jashar**? The sun stayed in the middle of the sky, and it did not set as on a normal day.* ¹⁴There has never been a day like this one before or since, when the LORD answered such a prayer. Surely the LORD fought for Israel that day!

¹⁵Then Joshua and the Israelite army returned to their camp at Gilgal.

Joshua Kills the Five Southern Kings

¹⁶During the battle the five kings escaped and hid in a cave at Makkedah. ¹⁷When Joshua heard that they had been found, ¹⁸he issued this command: "Cover the opening of the cave with large rocks, and place guards at the entrance to keep the kings inside. ¹⁹The rest of you continue chasing the enemy and cut them down from the rear. Don't give them a chance to get back to their towns, for the LORD your God has given you victory over them."

²⁰So Joshua and the Israelite army continued the slaughter and completely crushed the enemy. They totally wiped out the five armies except for a tiny remnant that managed to reach their fortified towns. ²¹Then the Israelites returned safely to Joshua in the camp at Makkedah. After that, no one dared to speak even a word against Israel.

²²Then Joshua said, "Remove the rocks covering the opening of the cave, and bring the five kings to me." ²³So they brought the five kings out of the cave—the kings of Jerusalem, Hebron, Jarmuth, Lachish, and Eglon. ²⁴When they brought them out, Joshua told the commanders of his army, "Come and put your feet on the kings' necks." And they did as they were told.

²⁵"Don't ever be afraid or discouraged," Joshua told his men. "Be strong and courageous, for the LORD is going to do this to all

10:13a Or *The Book of the Upright.* 10:13b Or *did not set for about a whole day.*

It is foolish to believe that all we have and are comes from our own effort and ability. Acknowledging God's hand in our past accomplishments allows us to hold onto God's hand more firmly in the face of future challenges.

10:12-15 Joshua's faith was rewarded by God's action. Joshua prayed that God would supernaturally provide additional daylight hours to press the battle on to complete victory over the Amorite nation. God responded to Joshua's prayer by causing the sun and the moon to keep their respective positions in the sky until God himself claimed victory for Israel. For centuries, unbelievers have tried to explain away this miraculous example of God's divine intervention into the lives of his people. Our human nature drives us to find an explanation outside of God's power. We tend to explain away the times when God miraculously intervenes in our life. God does not call us to be ignorant, but we must be careful that we do not allow intellect to rob us of faith.

of your enemies." ²⁶Then Joshua killed each of the five kings and impaled them on five sharpened poles, where they hung until evening.

²⁷As the sun was going down, Joshua gave instructions for the bodies of the kings to be taken down from the poles and thrown into the cave where they had been hiding. Then they covered the opening of the cave with a pile of large rocks, which remains to this very day.

Israel Destroys the Southern Towns

²⁸That same day Joshua captured and destroyed the town of Makkedah. He killed everyone in it, including the king, leaving no survivors. He destroyed them all, and he killed the king of Makkedah as he had killed the king of Jericho. ²⁹Then Joshua and the Israelites went to Libnah and attacked it. ³⁰There, too, the LORD gave them the town and its king. He killed everyone in it, leaving no survivors. Then Joshua killed the king of Libnah as he had killed the king of Jericho.

³¹From Libnah, Joshua and the Israelites went to Lachish and attacked it. ³²Here again, the LORD gave them Lachish. Joshua took it on the second day and killed everyone in it, just as he had done at Libnah. ³³During the attack on Lachish, King Horam of Gezer arrived with his army to help defend the town. But Joshua's men killed him and his army, leaving no survivors.

³⁴Then Joshua and the Israelite army went on to Eglon and attacked it. ³⁵They captured it that day and killed everyone in it. He completely destroyed everyone, just as he had done at Lachish. ³⁶From Eglon, Joshua and the Israelite army went up to Hebron and attacked it. ³⁷They captured the town and killed everyone in it, including its king, leaving no survivors. They did the same thing to all of its surrounding villages. And just as he had done at Eglon, he completely destroyed the entire population.

³⁸Then Joshua and the Israelites turned back and attacked Debir. ³⁹He captured the town, its king, and all of its surrounding villages. He completely destroyed everyone in it, leaving no survivors. He did to Debir and its king just what he had done to Hebron and to Libnah and its king.

⁴⁰So Joshua conquered the whole region—the kings and people of the hill country, the Negev, the western foothills,* and the mountain slopes. He completely destroyed everyone in the land, leaving no survivors, just as the LORD, the God of Israel, had commanded. ⁴¹Joshua slaughtered them from Kadesh-barnea to Gaza and from the region around the town of Goshen up to Gibeon. ⁴²Joshua conquered all these kings and their land in a single campaign, for the LORD, the God of Israel, was fighting for his people.

⁴³Then Joshua and the Israelite army returned to their camp at Gilgal.

CHAPTER 11
Israel Defeats the Northern Armies

When King Jabin of Hazor heard what had happened, he sent messages to the following kings: King Jobab of Madon; the king of Shimron; the king of Acshaph; ²all the kings of the northern hill country; the kings in the Jordan Valley south of Galilee*; the kings in the Galilean foothills*; the kings of Naphoth-dor on the west; ³the kings of Canaan, both east and west; the kings of the Amorites, the Hittites, the Perizzites, the Jebusites in the hill country, and the Hivites in the towns on the slopes of Mount Hermon in the land of Mizpah.

⁴All these kings came out to fight. Their combined armies formed a vast horde. And with all their horses and chariots, they covered the landscape like the sand on the seashore. ⁵The kings joined forces and established their camp around the water near Merom to fight against Israel.

⁶Then the LORD said to Joshua, "Do not be afraid of them. By this time tomorrow I will hand all of them over to Israel as dead men. Then you must cripple their horses and burn their chariots."

10:40 Hebrew *the Shephelah.* 11:2a Hebrew *in the Arabah south of Kinnereth.* 11:2b Hebrew *the Shephelah;* also in 11:16.

11:1-9 Once again the situation looked hopelessly bleak for Joshua and Israel. Yet one more time God reminded Joshua that he should act boldly because he, God, would accomplish the seemingly impossible. So Joshua and his troops obeyed God and courageously attacked when the enemy least expected it. God, as he had promised, gave Israel the victory. When the situations we face seem hopeless, we can look back to the example of Joshua and his people. God prevailed even when the prospects for victory were bleak. God has not changed. His power to take what we have and do great things with it continues and far exceeds whatever we could do or even imagine.

[7]So Joshua and all his fighting men traveled to the water near Merom and attacked suddenly. [8]And the LORD gave them victory over their enemies. The Israelites chased them as far as Greater Sidon and Misrephoth-maim, and eastward into the valley of Mizpah, until not one enemy warrior was left alive. [9]Then Joshua crippled the horses and burned all the chariots, as the LORD had instructed.

[10]Joshua then turned back and captured Hazor and killed its king. (Hazor had at one time been the capital of all these kingdoms.) [11]The Israelites completely destroyed* every living thing in the city, leaving no survivors. Not a single person was spared. And then Joshua burned the city.

[12]Joshua slaughtered all the other kings and their people, completely destroying them, just as Moses, the servant of the LORD, had commanded. [13]But the Israelites did not burn any of the towns built on mounds except Hazor, which Joshua burned. [14]And the Israelites took all the plunder and livestock of the ravaged towns for themselves. But they killed all the people, leaving no survivors. [15]As the LORD had commanded his servant Moses, so Moses commanded Joshua. And Joshua did as he was told, carefully obeying all the commands that the LORD had given to Moses.

[16]So Joshua conquered the entire region—the hill country, the entire Negev, the whole area around the town of Goshen, the western foothills, the Jordan Valley,* the mountains of Israel, and the Galilean foothills. [17]The Israelite territory now extended all the way from Mount Halak, which leads up to Seir in the south, as far north as Baal-gad at the foot of Mount Hermon in the valley of Lebanon. Joshua killed all the kings of those territories, [18]waging war for a long time to accomplish this. [19]No one in this region made peace with the Israelites except the Hivites of Gibeon. All the others were defeated. [20]For the LORD hardened their hearts and caused them to fight the Israelites. So they were completely destroyed without mercy, as the LORD had commanded Moses.

[21]During this period Joshua destroyed all the descendants of Anak, who lived in the hill country of Hebron, Debir, Anab, and the entire hill country of Judah and Israel. He killed them all and completely destroyed their towns. [22]None of the descendants of Anak were left in all the land of Israel, though some still remained in Gaza, Gath, and Ashdod.

[23]So Joshua took control of the entire land, just as the LORD had instructed Moses. He gave it to the people of Israel as their special possession, dividing the land among the tribes. So the land finally had rest from war.

CHAPTER 12
Kings Defeated East of the Jordan

These are the kings east of the Jordan River who had been killed by the Israelites and whose land was taken. Their territory extended from the Arnon Gorge to Mount Hermon and included all the land east of the Jordan Valley.*

[2]King Sihon of the Amorites, who lived in Heshbon, was defeated. His kingdom included Aroer, on the edge of the Arnon Gorge, and extended from the middle of the Arnon Gorge to the Jabbok River, which serves as a border for the Ammonites. This territory included the southern half of the territory of Gilead. [3]Sihon also controlled the Jordan Valley and regions to the east—from as far north as the Sea of Galilee to as far south as the Dead Sea,* including the road to Beth-jeshimoth and southward to the slopes of Pisgah.

[4]King Og of Bashan, the last of the Rephaites, lived at Ashtaroth and Edrei. [5]He ruled a

---

11:11 The Hebrew term used here refers to the complete consecration of things or people to the LORD, either by destroying them or by giving them as an offering; also in 11:12, 20, 21. **11:16** Hebrew *the Shephelah, the Arabah.* **12:1** Hebrew *the Arabah;* also in 12:3, 8. **12:3** Hebrew *from the Sea of Kinnereth to the Sea of the Arabah, which is the Salt Sea.*

11:16-22 Entering new territories in the Promised Land was not easy. There were battles over a prolonged period of time that pitted the people of Israel against enemies who were entrenched in the land. Some of these enemies were the descendants of Anak, the giants who had frightened the scouts Moses sent into the land (see Numbers 13:25–14:25). By God's power, however, Israel conquered its worst fears. Whatever we fear the most today is easily handled by God's power. It is truly incredible that it takes so long for us to realize what is so obvious: God has the power to turn defeat into victory, producing maximum results from minimal faith and obedience.

12:1-24 Recounting God's great works in the past was a constant practice of the Israelites. In this instance, they recalled not only the victories of their present leader, Joshua, but also those of their previous leader, Moses. These recollections of victories served both as reminders of the great works God had done and as springboards for trusting God to act on Israel's behalf in future times of difficulty. We can become living reminders of the great things that can be realized through God's strength.

territory stretching from Mount Hermon to Salecah in the north and to all of Bashan in the east, and westward to the borders of the kingdoms of Geshur and Maacah. This territory included the northern half of Gilead, as far as the boundary of King Sihon of Heshbon.

⁶Moses, the servant of the LORD, and the Israelites had destroyed the people of King Sihon and King Og. And Moses gave their land as a possession to the tribes of Reuben, Gad, and the half-tribe of Manasseh.

Kings Defeated West of the Jordan

⁷The following is a list of the kings that Joshua and the Israelite armies defeated on the west side of the Jordan, from Baal-gad in the valley of Lebanon to Mount Halak, which leads up to Seir. (Joshua gave this land to the tribes of Israel as their possession, ⁸including the hill country, the western foothills,* the Jordan Valley, the mountain slopes, the Judean wilderness, and the Negev. The people who lived in this region were the Hittites, the Amorites, the Canaanites, the Perizzites, the Hivites, and the Jebusites.) These are the kings Israel defeated:

⁹ The king of Jericho
  The king of Ai, near Bethel
¹⁰ The king of Jerusalem
  The king of Hebron
¹¹ The king of Jarmuth
  The king of Lachish
¹² The king of Eglon
  The king of Gezer
¹³ The king of Debir
  The king of Geder
¹⁴ The king of Hormah
  The king of Arad
¹⁵ The king of Libnah
  The king of Adullam
¹⁶ The king of Makkedah
  The king of Bethel
¹⁷ The king of Tappuah
  The king of Hepher
¹⁸ The king of Aphek
  The king of Lasharon
¹⁹ The king of Madon

  The king of Hazor
²⁰ The king of Shimron-meron
  The king of Acshaph
²¹ The king of Taanach
  The king of Megiddo
²² The king of Kedesh
  The king of Jokneam in Carmel
²³ The king of Dor in the town of
    Naphoth-dor*
  The king of Goyim in Gilgal*
²⁴ The king of Tirzah.

In all, thirty-one kings were defeated.

CHAPTER 13
The Land Yet to Be Conquered

When Joshua was an old man, the LORD said to him, "You are growing old, and much land remains to be conquered. ²This is the territory that remains: all the regions of the Philistines and the Geshurites, ³and the larger territory of the Canaanites, extending from the stream of Shihor on the border of Egypt, northward to the boundary of Ekron. It includes the territory of the five Philistine rulers of Gaza, Ashdod, Ashkelon, Gath, and Ekron. The land of the Avvites ⁴in the south also remains to be conquered. In the north, the following area has not yet been conquered: all the land of the Canaanites, including Mearah (which belongs to the Sidonians), stretching northward to Aphek on the border of the Amorites; ⁵the land of the Gebalites and all of the Lebanon mountain area to the east, from Baal-gad below Mount Hermon to Lebo-hamath; ⁶and all the hill country from Lebanon to Misrephoth-maim, including all the land of the Sidonians.

"I myself will drive these people out of the land ahead of the Israelites. So be sure to give this land to Israel as a special possession, just as I have commanded you. ⁷Include all this territory as Israel's possession when you divide this land among the nine tribes and the half-tribe of Manasseh."

The Land Divided East of the Jordan

⁸Half the tribe of Manasseh and the tribes of Reuben and Gad had already received their

---

12:8 Hebrew *the Shephelah*. **12:23a** Hebrew *Naphath-dor*, a variant spelling of Naphoth-dor. **12:23b** Greek version reads *Goyim in Galilee*.

13:8-13 As we move from south to north on the east side of the Jordan River, the territories inherited by the tribes of Reuben, Gad, and the half-tribe of Manasseh are listed. However, Israel failed to trust God sufficiently to drive out the people of Geshur and Maacah. Even though we are tempted to blame God when things don't turn out, we should look first at where our faith has failed rather than at where we think God has failed.

grants of land on the east side of the Jordan, for Moses, the servant of the LORD, had previously assigned this land to them.

[9]Their territory extended from Aroer on the edge of the Arnon Gorge (including the town in the middle of the gorge) to the plain beyond Medeba, as far as Dibon. [10]It also included all the towns of King Sihon of the Amorites, who had reigned in Heshbon, and extended as far as the borders of Ammon. [11]It included Gilead, the territory of the kingdoms of Geshur and Maacah, all of Mount Hermon, all of Bashan as far as Salecah, [12]and all the territory of King Og of Bashan, who had reigned in Ashtaroth and Edrei. King Og was the last of the Rephaites, for Moses had attacked them and driven them out. [13]But the Israelites failed to drive out the people of Geshur and Maacah, so they continue to live among the Israelites to this day.

An Allotment for the Tribe of Levi

[14]Moses did not assign any allotment of land to the tribe of Levi. Instead, as the LORD had promised them, their allotment came from the offerings burned on the altar to the LORD, the God of Israel.

The Land Given to the Tribe of Reuben

[15]Moses had assigned the following area to the clans of the tribe of Reuben.

[16]Their territory extended from Aroer on the edge of the Arnon Gorge (including the town in the middle of the gorge) to the plain beyond Medeba. [17]It included Heshbon and the other towns on the plain—Dibon, Bamoth- baal, Beth-baal-meon, [18]Jahaz, Kedemoth, Mephaath, [19]Kiriathaim, Sibmah, Zereth-shahar on the hill above the valley, [20]Beth-peor, the slopes of Pisgah, and Beth-jeshimoth.

[21]The land of Reuben also included all the towns of the plain and the entire kingdom of Sihon. Sihon was the Amorite king who had reigned in Heshbon and was killed by Moses along with the leaders of Midian—Evi, Rekem, Zur, Hur, and Reba—princes living in the region who were allied with Sihon. [22]The Israelites had also killed Balaam son of Beor, who used magic to tell the future. [23]The Jordan River marked the western boundary for the tribe of Reuben. The towns and their surrounding villages in this area were given as a homeland to the clans of the tribe of Reuben.

The Land Given to the Tribe of Gad

[24]Moses had assigned the following area to the clans of the tribe of Gad.

[25]Their territory included Jazer, all the towns of Gilead, and half of the land of Ammon, as far as the town of Aroer just west of* Rabbah. [26]It extended from Heshbon to Ramath-mizpeh and Betonim, and from Mahanaim to the territory of Lo-debar.* [27]In the valley were Beth-haram, Beth-nimrah, Succoth, Zaphon, and the rest of the kingdom of King Sihon of Heshbon. The western boundary ran along the Jordan River, extended as far north as the tip of the Sea of Galilee,* and then turned eastward. [28]The towns and their surrounding villages in this area were given as a homeland to the clans of the tribe of Gad.

The Land Given to the Half-Tribe of Manasseh

[29]Moses had assigned the following area to the clans of the half-tribe of Manasseh.

[30]Their territory extended from Mahanaim, including all of Bashan, all the former kingdom of King Og, and the sixty towns of Jair in Bashan. [31]It also included half of Gilead and King Og's royal cities of Ashtaroth and Edrei. All this was given to the clans of the descendants of Makir, who was Manasseh's son.

13:25 Hebrew *in front of.* 13:26 Hebrew *Li-debir,* apparently a variant spelling of Lo-debar (compare 2 Sam 9:4; 17:27; Amos 6:13). 13:27 Hebrew *Sea of Kinnereth.*

13:15-32 So no one could mistakenly believe that God did not give the tribes east of the Jordan an inheritance equal to that of tribes living in the Promised Land, a detailed listing of the territories granted to the tribes of Reuben, Gad, and the half-tribe of Manasseh is offered here. Even though these tribes were physically separated from their fellow Israelites west of the Jordan, they were not to be separated spiritually. In discouraging times when we see only problems, it can be helpful to make a detailed list of what God has provided for each of us. As we become aware of our many gifts from God, it becomes more and more difficult to be disheartened over temporary inconveniences. The God who provided the blessings of yesterday is there for us today.

³²These are the allotments Moses had made while he was on the plains of Moab, across the Jordan River, east of Jericho. ³³But Moses gave no allotment of land to the tribe of Levi, for the LORD, the God of Israel, had promised that he himself would be their allotment.

CHAPTER 14
The Land Divided West of the Jordan

The remaining tribes of Israel received land in Canaan as allotted by Eleazar the priest, Joshua son of Nun, and the tribal leaders. ²These nine and a half tribes received their grants of land by means of sacred lots, in accordance with the LORD's command through Moses. ³Moses had already given a grant of land to the two and a half tribes on the east side of the Jordan River, but he had given the Levites no such allotment. ⁴The descendants of Joseph had become two separate tribes—Manasseh and Ephraim. And the Levites were given no land at all, only towns to live in with surrounding pasturelands for their livestock and all their possessions. ⁵So the land was distributed in strict accordance with the LORD's commands to Moses.

Caleb Requests His Land

⁶A delegation from the tribe of Judah, led by Caleb son of Jephunneh the Kenizzite, came to Joshua at Gilgal. Caleb said to Joshua, "Remember what the LORD said to Moses, the man of God, about you and me when we were at Kadesh-barnea. ⁷I was forty years old when Moses, the servant of the LORD, sent me from Kadesh-barnea to explore the land of Canaan. I returned and gave an honest report, ⁸but my brothers who went with me frightened the people from entering the Promised Land. For my part, I wholeheartedly followed the LORD

my God. ⁹So that day Moses solemnly promised me, 'The land of Canaan on which you were just walking will be your grant of land and that of your descendants forever, because you wholeheartedly followed the LORD my God.'

¹⁰"Now, as you can see, the LORD has kept me alive and well as he promised for all these forty-five years since Moses made this promise—even while Israel wandered in the wilderness. Today I am eighty-five years old. ¹¹I am as strong now as I was when Moses sent me on that journey, and I can still travel and fight as well as I could then. ¹²So give me the hill country that the LORD promised me. You will remember that as scouts we found the descendants of Anak living there in great, walled towns. But if the LORD is with me, I will drive them out of the land, just as the LORD said."

¹³So Joshua blessed Caleb son of Jephunneh and gave Hebron to him as his portion of land. ¹⁴Hebron still belongs to the descendants of Caleb son of Jephunneh the Kenizzite because he wholeheartedly followed the LORD, the God of Israel. ¹⁵(Previously Hebron had been called Kiriath-arba. It had been named after Arba, a great hero of the descendants of Anak.)

And the land had rest from war.

CHAPTER 15
The Land Given to the Tribe of Judah

The allotment for the clans of the tribe of Judah reached southward to the border of Edom, as far south as the wilderness of Zin.

²The southern boundary began at the south bay of the Dead Sea,* ³ran south of Scorpion Pass* into the wilderness of Zin, and then went south of Kadesh-barnea to

15:2 Hebrew *the Salt Sea;* also in 15:5. 15:3 Hebrew *Akrabbim.*

14:1-5 The leaders of Israel did not forget God's command given by Moses; they were obedient to it, which resulted in the total and proper apportionment of the Promised Land. As it was for the Levites who settled on the east side of the Jordan, so it was for those Levites who served God in the Promised Land. The Levites received no specific territory for an inheritance—God himself was their inheritance. God, however, did not leave them homeless to roam the countryside, but he gave them cities in which to live and pasturelands to manage. What a great reminder to us. When we focus on what we have or don't have, we often forget that our greatest inheritance is God himself.

14:6-15 Advanced age did not deter Caleb from seeking the inheritance promised to him by God as a reward for his faith when he and Joshua had served under Moses as scouts in the Promised Land (see Numbers 14:24). Age alone does not make a person feel or act old. In fact, Caleb willingly sought to enter into battle against some of the more powerful armies that inhabited the land. Because he trusted God fully, Caleb succeeded in securing his promised inheritance. We need to realize that in our own life, if God wants to grant us victory over any problem we encounter, that victory is already secured.

Hezron. Then it went up to Addar, where it turned toward Karka. [4]From there it passed to Azmon until it finally reached the Brook of Egypt, which it followed to the Mediterranean Sea.* This was their* southern boundary.

[5]The eastern boundary extended along the Dead Sea to the mouth of the Jordan River.

The northern boundary began at the bay where the Jordan River empties into the Dead Sea, [6]went up from there to Beth-hoglah, then proceeded north of Beth-arabah to the Stone of Bohan. (Bohan was Reuben's son.) [7]From that point it went through the valley of Achor to Debir, turning north toward Gilgal, which is across from the slopes of Adummim on the south side of the valley. From there the boundary extended to the springs at En-shemesh and on to En-rogel. [8]The boundary then passed through the valley of Ben-Hinnom, along the southern slopes of the Jebusites, where the city of Jerusalem is located. Then it went west to the top of the mountain above the valley of Hinnom, and on up to the northern end of the valley of Rephaim. [9]From there the boundary extended from the top of the mountain to the spring at the waters of Nephtoah,* and from there to the towns on Mount Ephron. Then it turned toward Baalah (that is, Kiriath-jearim). [10]The boundary circled west of Baalah to Mount Seir, passed along to the town of Kesalon on the northern slope of Mount Jearim, and went down to Beth-shemesh and on to Timnah. [11]The boundary then proceeded to the slope of the hill north of Ekron, where it turned toward Shikkeron and Mount Baalah. It passed Jabneel and ended at the Mediterranean Sea.

[12]The western boundary was the shoreline of the Mediterranean Sea.*

These are the boundaries for the clans of the tribe of Judah.

The Land Given to Caleb

[13]The LORD commanded Joshua to assign some of Judah's territory to Caleb son of Jephunneh. So Caleb was given the town of Kiriath-arba (that is, Hebron), which had been named after Anak's ancestor. [14]Caleb drove out the three groups of Anakites—the descendants of Sheshai, Ahiman, and Talmai, the sons of Anak.

[15]From there he went to fight against the people living in the town of Debir (formerly called Kiriath-sepher). [16]Caleb said, "I will give my daughter Acsah in marriage to the one who attacks and captures Kiriath-sepher." [17]Othniel, the son of Caleb's brother Kenaz, was the one who conquered it, so Acsah became Othniel's wife.

[18]When Acsah married Othniel, she urged him* to ask her father for a field. As she got down off her donkey, Caleb asked her, "What's the matter?"

[19]She said, "Give me another gift. You have already given me land in the Negev; now please give me springs of water, too." So Caleb gave her the upper and lower springs.

The Towns Allotted to Judah

[20]This was the homeland allocated to the clans of the tribe of Judah.

15:4a Hebrew *the sea;* also in 15:11. 15:4b Hebrew *your.* 15:9 Or *the spring at Me-nephtoah.* 15:12 Hebrew *the Great Sea;* also in 15:47. 15:18 Some Greek manuscripts read *he urged her.*

15:16-19 Caleb desired that not just any man marry his daughter Achsah; he wanted a son-in-law who by faith would trust God for victory over the city of Debir. Othniel took up Caleb's challenge and defeated Debir. For his efforts, Othniel received Acsah as his wife. The challenge here for our life and the lives of our children is to place faith in God as a number-one priority. So many problem relationships could be avoided if we would only seek out those strong in faith rather than those with prestige, power, or money.

15:20-63 Of all the tribes who received an inheritance, the greatest amount of information concerning any tribe's inheritance was recorded for Judah. The importance of the tribe of Judah may account for this. Judah was chosen to be the son of Jacob from whom future kings of Israel would arise and through whose lineage the Messiah would be born (see Genesis 49:10). Merely being part of such an important tribe, however, did not guarantee faith or success. Despite God's promise of victory to those who obey him fully (see Deuteronomy 28:1-7), some of the tribe of Judah apparently lacked sufficient faith in God to drive out the inhabitants of Jerusalem. Today, what areas of our life have been taken over by habits, mistakes, and addictions? If we put our full faith in God, he will give us victory.

²¹The towns of Judah situated along the borders of Edom in the extreme south were Kabzeel, Eder, Jagur, ²²Kinah, Dimonah, Adadah, ²³Kedesh, Hazor, Ithnan, ²⁴Ziph, Telem, Bealoth, ²⁵Hazor-hadattah, Kerioth-hezron (that is, Hazor), ²⁶Amam, Shema, Moladah, ²⁷Hazar-gaddah, Heshmon, Beth-pelet, ²⁸Hazar-shual, Beersheba, Biziothiah, ²⁹Baalah, Iim, Ezem, ³⁰Eltolad, Kesil, Hormah, ³¹Ziklag, Madmannah, Sansannah, ³²Lebaoth, Shilhim, Ain, and Rimmon—twenty-nine towns with their surrounding villages.

³³The following towns situated in the western foothills* were also given to Judah: Eshtaol, Zorah, Ashnah, ³⁴Zanoah, En-gannim, Tappuah, Enam, ³⁵Jarmuth, Adullam, Socoh, Azekah, ³⁶Shaaraim, Adithaim, Gederah, and Gederothaim—fourteen towns with their surrounding villages.

³⁷Also included were Zenan, Hadashah, Migdal-gad, ³⁸Dilean, Mizpeh, Joktheel, ³⁹Lachish, Bozkath, Eglon, ⁴⁰Cabbon, Lahmam, Kitlish, ⁴¹Gederoth, Beth-dagon, Naamah, and Makkedah—sixteen towns with their surrounding villages.

⁴²Besides these, there were Libnah, Ether, Ashan, ⁴³Iphtah, Ashnah, Nezib, ⁴⁴Keilah, Aczib, and Mareshah—nine towns with their surrounding villages.

⁴⁵The territory of the tribe of Judah also included Ekron and its surrounding settlements and villages. ⁴⁶From Ekron the boundary extended west and included the towns near Ashdod with their surrounding villages. ⁴⁷It also included Ashdod with its surrounding settlements and villages and Gaza with its settlements and villages, as far as the Brook of Egypt and along the coast of the Mediterranean Sea.

⁴⁸Judah also received the following towns in the hill country: Shamir, Jattir, Socoh, ⁴⁹Dannah, Kiriath-sannah (that is, Debir), ⁵⁰Anab, Eshtemoh, Anim,

⁵¹Goshen, Holon, and Giloh—eleven towns with their surrounding villages.

⁵²Also included were the towns of Arab, Dumah, Eshan, ⁵³Janim, Beth-tappuah, Aphekah, ⁵⁴Humtah, Kiriath-arba (that is, Hebron), and Zior—nine towns with their surrounding villages.

⁵⁵Besides these, there were Maon, Carmel, Ziph, Juttah, ⁵⁶Jezreel, Jokdeam, Zanoah, ⁵⁷Kain, Gibeah, and Timnah—ten towns with their surrounding villages.

⁵⁸In addition, there were Halhul, Beth-zur, Gedor, ⁵⁹Maarath, Beth-anoth, and Eltekon—six towns with their surrounding villages.

⁶⁰There were also Kiriath-baal (that is, Kiriath-jearim) and Rabbah—two towns with their surrounding villages.

⁶¹In the wilderness there were the towns of Beth-arabah, Middin, Secacah, ⁶²Nibshan, the City of Salt, and En-gedi—six towns with their surrounding villages.

⁶³But the tribe of Judah could not drive out the Jebusites, who lived in the city of Jerusalem, so the Jebusites live there among the people of Judah to this day.

CHAPTER 16
The Land Given to Ephraim and West Manasseh

The allotment for the descendants of Joseph extended from the Jordan River near Jericho, east of the springs of Jericho, through the wilderness and into the hill country of Bethel. ²From Bethel (that is, Luz)* it ran over to Ataroth in the territory of the Arkites. ³Then it descended westward to the territory of the Japhletites as far as Lower Beth-horon, then to Gezer and over to the Mediterranean Sea.*

⁴This was the homeland allocated to the families of Joseph's sons, Manasseh and Ephraim.

15:33 Hebrew *the Shephelah.* 16:2 As in Greek version (also see 18:13); Hebrew reads *From Bethel to Luz.* 16:3 Hebrew *the sea;* also in 16:6, 8.

16:1-10 A godly person's descendants often reap numerous benefits from that person's life. Because God had used Joseph to deliver his father, Jacob, and his family from a famine that almost certainly would have destroyed them, Jacob honored Joseph by "adopting" Joseph's two sons (Ephraim and Manasseh) and making them equal in status to Jacob's own sons (Genesis 48:1-5). Thus, of the 12 sons of Jacob, Joseph's lineage was granted the privilege of being considered two tribes for the purpose of receiving an inheritance. Our faith and the life we develop around our faith will have ramifications for our family in generations to come. There is no greater inheritance to pass on than to have lived a life of faith in prayerful submission to God.

The Land Given to Ephraim

⁵The following territory was given to the clans of the tribe of Ephraim.

The boundary of their homeland began at Ataroth-addar in the east. From there it ran to Upper Beth-horon, ⁶then on to the Mediterranean Sea. From Micmethath on the north, the boundary curved eastward past Taanath-shiloh to the east of Janoah. ⁷From Janoah it turned southward to Ataroth and Naarah, touched Jericho, and ended at the Jordan River. ⁸From Tappuah the boundary extended westward, following the Kanah Ravine to the Mediterranean Sea. This is the homeland allocated to the clans of the tribe of Ephraim.

⁹In addition, some towns with their surrounding villages in the territory allocated to the half-tribe of Manasseh were set aside for the tribe of Ephraim. ¹⁰They did not drive the Canaanites out of Gezer, however, so the people of Gezer live as slaves among the people of Ephraim to this day.

CHAPTER 17
The Land Given to West Manasseh

The next allotment of land was given to the half-tribe of Manasseh, the descendants of Joseph's older son. Makir, the firstborn son of Manasseh, was the father of Gilead. Because his descendants were experienced soldiers, the regions of Gilead and Bashan on the east side of the Jordan had already been given to them. ²So the allotment on the west side of the Jordan was for the remaining families within the clans of the tribe of Manasseh: Abiezer, Helek, Asriel, Shechem, Hepher, and Shemida. These clans represent the male descendants of Manasseh son of Joseph.

³However, Zelophehad, a descendant of Hepher son of Gilead, son of Makir, son of Manasseh, had no sons. He had only daughters, whose names were Mahlah, Noah, Hoglah, Milcah, and Tirzah. ⁴These women

came to Eleazar the priest, Joshua son of Nun, and the Israelite leaders and said, "The LORD commanded Moses to give us a grant of land along with the men of our tribe."

So Joshua gave them a grant of land along with their uncles, as the LORD had commanded. ⁵As a result, Manasseh's total allocation came to ten parcels of land, in addition to the land of Gilead and Bashan across the Jordan River, ⁶because the female descendants of Manasseh received a grant of land along with the male descendants. (The land of Gilead was given to the rest of the male descendants of Manasseh.)

⁷The boundary of the tribe of Manasseh extended from the border of Asher to Micmethath, near Shechem. Then the boundary went south from Micmethath to the settlement near the spring of Tappuah. ⁸The land surrounding Tappuah belonged to Manasseh, but the town of Tappuah itself, on the border of Manasseh's territory, belonged to the tribe of Ephraim. ⁹From the spring of Tappuah, the boundary of Manasseh followed the Kanah Ravine to the Mediterranean Sea.* Several towns south of the ravine were inside Manasseh's territory, but they actually belonged to the tribe of Ephraim. ¹⁰In general, however, the land south of the ravine belonged to Ephraim, and the land north of the ravine belonged to Manasseh. Manasseh's boundary ran along the northern side of the ravine and ended at the Mediterranean Sea. North of Manasseh was the territory of Asher, and to the east was the territory of Issachar.

¹¹The following towns within the territory of Issachar and Asher, however, were given to Manasseh: Beth-shan,* Ibleam, Dor (that is, Naphoth-dor),* Endor, Taanach, and Megiddo, each with their surrounding settlements.

¹²But the descendants of Manasseh were unable to occupy these towns because the

---

17:9 Hebrew *the sea;* also in 17:10. **17:11a** Hebrew *Beth-shean,* a variant spelling of Beth-shan; also in 17:16.
17:11b The meaning of the Hebrew here is uncertain.

17:1-6 The daughters of Zelophehad demonstrated true faith in God, believing that he would fulfill his promise of an inheritance to them. They based their confidence on an earlier ruling by Moses (which ultimately had come from God) that gave them their father's inheritance because he had no sons to receive it (Numbers 27:1-7). So the faith of Zelophehad's daughters was rewarded with land. God is the rewarder of faith. The reward may not always come in the form of land or possessions, but it will come in forms that far exceed the temporal values of material goods.

Canaanites were determined to stay in that region. ¹³Later, however, when the Israelites became strong enough, they forced the Canaanites to work as slaves. But they did not drive them out of the land.

¹⁴The descendants of Joseph came to Joshua and asked, "Why have you given us only one portion of land as our homeland when the LORD has blessed us with so many people?"

¹⁵Joshua replied, "If there are so many of you, and if the hill country of Ephraim is not large enough for you, clear out land for yourselves in the forest where the Perizzites and Rephaites live."

¹⁶The descendants of Joseph responded, "It's true that the hill country is not large enough for us. But all the Canaanites in the lowlands have iron chariots, both those in Beth-shan and its surrounding settlements and those in the valley of Jezreel. They are too strong for us."

¹⁷Then Joshua said to the tribes of Ephraim and Manasseh, the descendants of Joseph, "Since you are so large and strong, you will be given more than one portion. ¹⁸The forests of the hill country will be yours as well. Clear as much of the land as you wish, and take possession of its farthest corners. And you will drive out the Canaanites from the valleys, too, even though they are strong and have iron chariots."

18:1 Hebrew *Tent of Meeting.*

CHAPTER 18
The Allotments of the Remaining Land

Now that the land was under Israelite control, the entire community of Israel gathered at Shiloh and set up the Tabernacle.* ²But there remained seven tribes who had not yet been allotted their grants of land.

³Then Joshua asked them, "How long are you going to wait before taking possession of the remaining land the LORD, the God of your ancestors, has given to you? ⁴Select three men from each tribe, and I will send them out to explore the land and map it out. They will then return to me with a written report of their proposed divisions of their new homeland. ⁵Let them divide the land into seven sections, excluding Judah's territory in the south and Joseph's territory in the north. ⁶And when you record the seven divisions of the land and bring them to me, I will cast sacred lots in the presence of the LORD our God to assign land to each tribe.

⁷"The Levites, however, will not receive any allotment of land. Their role as priests of the LORD is their allotment. And the tribes of Gad, Reuben, and the half-tribe of Manasseh won't receive any more land, for they have already received their grant of land, which Moses, the servant of the LORD, gave them on the east side of the Jordan River."

⁸As the men started on their way to map

17:14-18 Even though they did not trust God enough to drive out all of their enemies and secure all the land of their inheritance (see 16:10; 17:12-13), the tribes of Ephraim and Manasseh complained that they did not have enough land in which to live. They also complained that the enemies in the land of their inheritance were too strong for them to defeat. Joshua generously granted them their request for additional land but at the same time challenged them to fulfill their responsibility to drive out the Canaanites. The erosion of God's best always occurs when our wills interfere with his. We come to believe we know so much and then recklessly destroy what God has provided. We must seek God, his will, and his power. If we do not, we may spend a lifetime compensating for mistakes made outside of his will.

18:1-10 Despite a general rest from war, the various tribes of Israel had not yet claimed their inheritance. Joshua chided them for their failure to recover that which God had apportioned to them. He then gave practical guidance as to how the remaining tribes should divide up the land. The tribes who earlier had not aggressively claimed their inheritance finally took action and followed Joshua's advice. Sometimes we need to be spurred to action by others. Maybe we don't have the courage to act—or perhaps we don't realize that we need to. But we should listen to the advice of wise, godly leaders, recognizing that they can see our situation more objectively than we can.

18:5-8 Rolling dice, or casting lots, to determine God's will was one means God used to communicate with his Old Testament people (see Leviticus 16:8-10; Numbers 26:55-56; Jonah 1:7). Lots normally were either stones or sticks with identification marks that were placed into the fold of a garment or into a vessel and shaken until one fell out. The one that came out indicated God's will. It is sad to see some today continuing to make decisions as if they were rolling dice to discover God's will. We don't need to roll dice; we have God's Word to form the foundation of every decision we make.

out the land, Joshua commanded them, "Go and explore the land and write a description of it. Then return to me, and I will assign the land to the tribes by casting sacred lots here in the presence of the LORD at Shiloh." ⁹The men did as they were told and mapped the entire territory into seven sections, listing the towns in each section. They made a written record and then returned to Joshua in the camp at Shiloh. ¹⁰And there at Shiloh, Joshua cast sacred lots in the presence of the LORD to determine which tribe should have each section.

The Land Given to Benjamin

¹¹The first allotment of land went to the clans of the tribe of Benjamin. It lay between the territory assigned to the tribes of Judah and Joseph.

¹²The northern boundary of Benjamin's land began at the Jordan River, went north of the slope of Jericho, then west through the hill country and the wilderness of Beth-aven. ¹³From there the boundary went south to Luz (that is, Bethel) and proceeded down to Ataroth-addar on the hill that lies south of Lower Beth-horon.

¹⁴The boundary then made a turn and swung south along the western edge of the hill facing Beth-horon, ending at the village of Kiriath-baal (that is, Kiriath-jearim), a town belonging to the tribe of Judah. This was the western boundary.

¹⁵The southern boundary began at the outskirts of Kiriath-jearim. From that western point it ran* to the spring at the waters of Nephtoah,* ¹⁶and down to the base of the mountain beside the valley of Ben-Hinnom, at the northern end of the valley of Rephaim. From there it went down the valley of Hinnom, crossing south of the slope where the Jebusites lived, and continued down to En-rogel. ¹⁷From En-rogel the boundary proceeded in a northerly direction and came to En-shemesh and on to Geliloth (which is across from the slopes of Adummim). Then it went down to the Stone of Bohan. (Bohan was Reuben's son.) ¹⁸From there it passed along the north side of the slope overlooking the Jordan Valley.* The border then went down into the valley, ¹⁹ran past the north slope of Beth-hoglah, and ended at the north bay of the Dead Sea,* which is the southern end of the Jordan River. This was the southern boundary.

²⁰The eastern boundary was the Jordan River.

These were the boundaries of the homeland allocated to the clans of the tribe of Benjamin.

The Towns Given to Benjamin

²¹These were the towns given to the clans of the tribe of Benjamin.

Jericho, Beth-hoglah, Emek-keziz, ²²Beth-arabah, Zemaraim, Bethel, ²³Avvim, Parah, Ophrah, ²⁴Kephar-ammoni, Ophni, and Geba—twelve towns with their surrounding villages. ²⁵Also Gibeon, Ramah, Beeroth, ²⁶Mizpah, Kephirah, Mozah, ²⁷Rekem, Irpeel, Taralah, ²⁸Zela, Haeleph, the Jebusite town (that is, Jerusalem), Gibeah, and Kiriath-jearim*—fourteen towns with their surrounding villages. This was the homeland allocated to the clans of the tribe of Benjamin.

CHAPTER 19
The Land Given to Simeon

The second allotment of land went to the clans of the tribe of Simeon. Their homeland was surrounded by Judah's territory.

²Simeon's homeland included Beersheba, Sheba, Moladah, ³Hazar-shual, Balah, Ezem, ⁴Eltolad, Bethul, Hormah, ⁵Ziklag, Beth-marcaboth, Hazar-susah, ⁶Beth-lebaoth, and Sharuhen—thirteen

---

18:15a Or *From there it went to Mozah.* The meaning of the Hebrew is uncertain. **18:15b** Or *the spring at Me-nephtoah.* **18:18** Hebrew *overlooking the Arabah,* or *overlooking Beth-arabah.* **18:19** Hebrew *Salt Sea.* **18:28** As in Greek version; Hebrew reads *Kiriath.*

19:1-16 The inheritance of the tribe of Simeon was carved out from the southern sector of the land of Judah, which previously had received more land than it required (see 15:1-62). Although several cities were transferred from Judah to Simeon, none of those cities were taken away from Caleb and his family. By contrast, Zebulun's inheritance was in the northern region of the Promised Land, a region that one day would be the site of the hometown of the Messiah (i.e., Nazareth; see Matthew 2:23). There must have been tremendous temptation for each tribe to compare its inheritance with the others rather than to see their allotment as ordained by God. True faith frees us to accept God's provision as perfectly planned for us, whether it seems great or small.

towns with their surrounding villages. ⁷It also included Ain, Rimmon, Ether, and Ashan—four towns with their villages, ⁸including all the surrounding villages as far south as Baalath-beer (also known as Ramah of the Negev).

This was the homeland allocated to the clans of the tribe of Simeon. ⁹Their allocation of land came from part of what had been given to Judah because Judah's territory was too large for them. So the tribe of Simeon received an allocation within the territory of Judah.

The Land Given to Zebulun

¹⁰The third allotment of land went to the clans of the tribe of Zebulun.

The boundary of Zebulun's homeland started at Sarid. ¹¹From there it went west, going past Maralah, touching Dabbesheth, and proceeding to the brook east of Jokneam. ¹²In the other direction, the boundary went east from Sarid to the border of Kisloth-tabor, and from there to Daberath and up to Japhia. ¹³Then it continued east to Gath-hepher, Eth-kazin, and Rimmon and turned toward Neah. ¹⁴The northern boundary of Zebulun passed Hannathon and ended at the valley of Iphtah-el. ¹⁵The towns in these areas included Kattath, Nahalal, Shimron, Idalah, and Bethlehem—twelve towns with their surrounding villages.

¹⁶The homeland allocated to the clans of the tribe of Zebulun included these towns and their surrounding villages.

The Land Given to Issachar

¹⁷The fourth allotment of land went to the clans of the tribe of Issachar.

¹⁸Its boundaries included the following towns: Jezreel, Kesulloth, Shunem, ¹⁹Hapharaim, Shion, Anaharath, ²⁰Rabbith, Kishion, Ebez, ²¹Remeth, En-gannim, En-haddah, and Beth-pazzez. ²²The boundary also touched Tabor, Shahazumah, and Beth-shemesh, ending at the Jordan River—sixteen towns with their surrounding villages.

²³The homeland allocated to the clans of the tribe of Issachar included these towns and their surrounding villages.

The Land Given to Asher

²⁴The fifth allotment of land went to the clans of the tribe of Asher.

²⁵Its boundaries included these towns: Helkath, Hali, Beten, Acshaph, ²⁶Allammelech, Amad, and Mishal. The boundary on the west touched Carmel and Shihor-libnath, ²⁷then it turned east toward Beth-dagon, and ran as far as Zebulun in the valley of Iphtah-el, going north to Beth-emek and Neiel. It then continued north to Cabul, ²⁸Abdon,* Rehob, Hammon, Kanah, and as far as Greater Sidon. ²⁹Then the boundary turned toward Ramah and the fortress of Tyre, where it turned toward Hosah and came to the Mediterranean Sea.* The territory also included Mehebel, Aczib, ³⁰Ummah, Aphek, and Rehob—twenty-two towns with their surrounding villages.

³¹The homeland allocated to the clans of the tribe of Asher included these towns and their surrounding villages.

The Land Given to Naphtali

³²The sixth allotment of land went to the clans of the tribe of Naphtali.

³³Its boundary ran from Heleph, from the oak at Zaanannim, and extended across to Adami-nekeb, Jabneel, and as far as Lakkum, ending at the Jordan River. ³⁴The western boundary ran past Aznoth-tabor, then to Hukkok, and touched the border of Zebulun in the south, the border of Asher on the west, and the Jordan River* on the east. ³⁵The fortified towns

19:28 As in some Hebrew manuscripts (see also 21:30); most Hebrew manuscripts read *Ebron*. **19:29** Hebrew *the sea*. **19:34** Hebrew *and Judah at the Jordan River*.

19:24-39 Neither Asher nor Naphtali was successful in driving out its enemies (see Judges 1:31-33). Failing to remove all the nations dwelling in the Promised Land proved costly for the Israelites. Instead of converting those whom they failed to destroy to God, the people of Israel were drawn away from God to serve the idols of those heathen nations. Those nations, in turn, would become like thorns in Israel's side (see Deuteronomy 31:16-20; Judges 2:1-3, 11-14). It is essential that we drive out our family's enemies so future generations won't have to battle them. Whether our enemies take the form of alcoholism, drug use, sexual abuse, or other problems, we must resolve them rather than hand the legacy down to our children and grandchildren.

included in this territory were Ziddim, Zer, Hammath, Rakkath, Kinnereth, ³⁶Adamah, Ramah, Hazor, ³⁷Kedesh, Edrei, En-hazor, ³⁸Yiron, Migdal-el, Horem, Beth-anath, and Beth-shemesh— nineteen towns with their surrounding villages.

³⁹The homeland allocated to the clans of the tribe of Naphtali included these towns and their surrounding villages.

The Land Given to Dan

⁴⁰The seventh allotment of land went to the clans of the tribe of Dan.

⁴¹The land allocated as their homeland included the following towns: Zorah, Eshtaol, Ir-shemesh, ⁴²Shaalabbin, Aijalon, Ithlah, ⁴³Elon, Timnah, Ekron, ⁴⁴Eltekeh, Gibbethon, Baalath, ⁴⁵Jehud, Bene-berak, Gath-rimmon, ⁴⁶Me-jarkon, Rakkon, and the territory across from Joppa.

⁴⁷But the tribe of Dan had trouble taking possession of their land,* so they attacked the town of Laish.* They captured it, slaughtered its people, and settled there. They renamed the town Dan after their ancestor.

⁴⁸The homeland allocated to the clans of the tribe of Dan included these towns and their surrounding villages.

The Land Given to Joshua

⁴⁹After all the land was divided among the tribes, the Israelites gave a piece of land to Joshua as his allocation. ⁵⁰For the LORD had said he could have any town he wanted. He chose Timnath-serah in the hill country of Ephraim. He rebuilt the town and lived there.

⁵¹These are the territories that Eleazar the priest, Joshua son of Nun, and the tribal leaders allocated as grants of land to the tribes of Israel by casting sacred lots in the presence of the LORD at the entrance of the Tabernacle* at Shiloh. So the division of the land was completed.

CHAPTER 20
The Cities of Refuge

The LORD said to Joshua, ²"Now tell the Israelites to designate the cities of refuge, as I instructed Moses. ³Anyone who kills another person accidentally and unintentionally can run to one of these cities; they will be places of refuge from relatives seeking revenge for the person who was killed.

⁴"Upon reaching one of these cities, the one who caused the death will appear before the elders at the city gate and present his case. They must allow him to enter the city and give him a place to live among them. ⁵If the relatives of the victim come to avenge the killing, the leaders must not release the slayer to them, for he killed the other person unintentionally and without previous hostility. ⁶But the slayer must stay in that city and be tried by the local assembly, which will render a judgment. And he must continue to live in that city until the death of the high priest who was in office at the time of the accident. After that, he is free to return to his own home in the town from which he fled."

⁷The following cities were designated as cities of refuge: Kedesh of Galilee, in the hill country of Naphtali; Shechem, in the hill country of Ephraim; and Kiriath-arba (that is, Hebron), in the hill country of Judah. ⁸On the east side of the Jordan River, across from Jericho, the following cities were designated: Bezer, in the wilderness plain of the tribe of Reuben; Ramoth in Gilead, in the territory of the tribe of Gad; and Golan in Bashan, in the land of the tribe of Manasseh. ⁹These cities were set apart for all the Israelites as well as the foreigners living among them. Anyone who accidentally killed another person

19:47a Or *had trouble holding on to their land.* **19:47b** Hebrew *Leshem,* a variant spelling of Laish. **19:51** Hebrew *Tent of Meeting.*

20:1-6 The six cities of refuge show God's design to protect the innocent. Anyone who accidentally killed another (without hatred or intention) could escape to a city of refuge where his case would be tried by the leaders of that city. If proven innocent, the individual was required to remain as a protected person within the city until the current high priest of Israel died. At the death of the high priest, the protected person was free to leave without fear of retribution. If found guilty of intentional murder, however, he was put to death (see Numbers 35:16-21, 29-34). Many of us go through life with no place of refuge. We carry our burdens from problem to problem, repeating our sins of the past. Churches and recovery groups can be refuges where we can come together and share our pain so we no longer have to be victimized by it. God is a God of grace; anyone seeking him will find refuge.

could take refuge in one of these cities. In this way, they could escape being killed in revenge prior to standing trial before the local assembly.

CHAPTER 21
The Towns Given to the Levites

Then the leaders of the tribe of Levi came to consult with Eleazar the priest, Joshua son of Nun, and the leaders of the other tribes of Israel. [2]They came to them at Shiloh in the land of Canaan and said, "The LORD commanded Moses to give us towns to live in and pasturelands for our livestock." [3]So by the command of the LORD the people of Israel gave the Levites the following towns and pasturelands out of their own grants of land.

[4]The descendants of Aaron, who were members of the Kohathite clan within the tribe of Levi, were allotted thirteen towns that were originally assigned to the tribes of Judah, Simeon, and Benjamin. [5]The other families of the Kohathite clan were allotted ten towns from the tribes of Ephraim, Dan, and the half-tribe of Manasseh.

[6]The clan of Gershon was allotted thirteen towns from the tribes of Issachar, Asher, Naphtali, and the half-tribe of Manasseh in Bashan.

[7]The clan of Merari was allotted twelve towns from the tribes of Reuben, Gad, and Zebulun.

[8]So the Israelites obeyed the LORD's command to Moses and assigned these towns and pasturelands to the Levites by casting sacred lots.

[9]The Israelites gave the following towns from the tribes of Judah and Simeon [10]to the descendants of Aaron, who were members of the Kohathite clan within the tribe of Levi, since the sacred lot fell to them first: [11]Kiriatharba (that is, Hebron), in the hill country of Judah, along with its surrounding pasturelands. (Arba was an ancestor of Anak.) [12]But the open fields beyond the town and the surrounding villages were given to Caleb son of Jephunneh as his possession.

[13]The following towns with their pasturelands were given to the descendants of Aaron the priest: Hebron (a city of refuge for those who accidentally killed someone), Libnah,

[14]Jattir, Eshtemoa, [15]Holon, Debir, [16]Ain, Juttah, and Beth-shemesh—nine towns from these two tribes.

[17]From the tribe of Benjamin the priests were given the following towns with their pasturelands: Gibeon, Geba, [18]Anathoth, and Almon—four towns. [19]So in all, thirteen towns with their pasturelands were given to the priests, the descendants of Aaron.

[20]The rest of the Kohathite clan from the tribe of Levi was allotted the following towns and pasturelands from the tribe of Ephraim: [21]Shechem in the hill country of Ephraim (a city of refuge for those who accidentally killed someone), Gezer, [22]Kibzaim, and Beth-horon—four towns.

[23]The following towns and pasturelands were allotted to the priests from the tribe of Dan: Eltekeh, Gibbethon, [24]Aijalon, and Gath-rimmon—four towns.

[25]The half-tribe of Manasseh allotted the following towns with their pasturelands to the priests: Taanach and Gath-rimmon—two towns. [26]So in all, ten towns with their pasturelands were given to the rest of the Kohathite clan.

[27]The descendants of Gershon, another clan within the tribe of Levi, received the following towns with their pasturelands from the half-tribe of Manasseh: Golan in Bashan (a city of refuge for those who accidentally killed someone) and Be-eshterah—two towns.

[28]From the tribe of Issachar they received the following towns with their pasturelands: Kishion, Daberath, [29]Jarmuth, and En-gannim—four towns.

[30]From the tribe of Asher they received the following towns with their pasturelands: Mishal, Abdon, [31]Helkath, and Rehob—four towns.

[32]From the tribe of Naphtali they received the following towns with their pasturelands: Kedesh in Galilee (a city of refuge for those who accidentally killed someone), Hammoth-dor, and Kartan—three towns. [33]So in all, thirteen towns with their pasturelands were allotted to the clan of Gershon.

[34]The rest of the Levites—the Merari clan— were given the following towns with their pasturelands from the tribe of Zebulun: Jok-

21:1-8 The Levites patiently waited for the other tribes to receive their inheritance before reminding Eleazar and Joshua of God's command that the tribes of Israel were to give to the Levites cities in which to live as an inheritance (see Numbers 35:1-8). Israel, in obedience to God's command, fulfilled its responsibility to God and to the tribe of Levi. Acting responsibly toward others brings honor not only to them and to ourselves but to God.

neam, Kartah, [35]Dimnah, and Nahalal—four towns.

[36]From the tribe of Reuben they received the following towns with their pasturelands: Bezer, Jahaz,* [37]Kedemoth, and Mephaath—four towns.

[38]From the tribe of Gad they received the following towns with their pasturelands: Ramoth in Gilead (a city of refuge for those who accidentally killed someone), Mahanaim, [39]Heshbon, and Jazer—four towns. [40]So in all, twelve towns were allotted to the clan of Merari.

[41]The total number of towns and pasturelands within Israelite territory given to the Levites came to forty-eight. [42]Every one of these towns had pasturelands surrounding it.

[43]So the LORD gave to Israel all the land he had sworn to give their ancestors, and they took possession of it and settled there. [44]And the LORD gave them rest on every side, just as he had solemnly promised their ancestors. None of their enemies could stand against them, for the LORD helped them conquer all their enemies. [45]Not a single one of all the good promises the LORD had given to the family of Israel was left unfulfilled; everything he had spoken came true.

CHAPTER 22
The Eastern Tribes Return Home
Then Joshua called together the tribes of Reuben, Gad, and the half-tribe of Manasseh. [2]He told them, "You have done as Moses, the servant of the LORD, commanded you, and you have obeyed every order I have given you. [3]During all this time you have not deserted the other tribes. You have been careful to obey the commands of the LORD your God right up to the present day. [4]And now

the LORD your God has given the other tribes rest, as he promised them. So go back home to the land that Moses, the servant of the LORD, gave you as your possession on the east side of the Jordan River. [5]But be very careful to obey all the commands and the instructions that Moses gave to you. Love the LORD your God, walk in all his ways, obey his commands, hold firmly to him, and serve him with all your heart and all your soul." [6]So Joshua blessed them and sent them away, and they went home.

[7]Moses had given the land of Bashan, east of the Jordan River, to the half-tribe of Manasseh. (The other half of the tribe was given land west of the Jordan.) As Joshua sent them away and blessed them, [8]he said to them, "Go back to your homes with the great wealth you have taken from your enemies—the vast herds of livestock, the silver, gold, bronze, and iron, and the large supply of clothing. Share the plunder with your relatives."

[9]So the men of Reuben, Gad, and the half-tribe of Manasseh left the rest of Israel at Shiloh in the land of Canaan. They started the journey back to their own land of Gilead, the territory that belonged to them according to the LORD's command through Moses.

The Eastern Tribes Build an Altar
[10]But while they were still in Canaan, and when they came to a place called Geliloth* near the Jordan River, the men of Reuben, Gad, and the half-tribe of Manasseh stopped to build a large and imposing altar.

[11]The rest of Israel heard that the people of Reuben, Gad, and the half-tribe of Manasseh had built an altar at Geliloth at

21:36 Hebrew *Jahzah*, a variant spelling of Jahaz. 22:10 Or *to the circle of stones;* similarly in 22:11.

21:43-45 God accomplished for the people of Israel all that he said he would do. The Israelites, for their part, had taken the land for their possession, so God gave them rest from their enemies. Furthermore, whenever the people served God faithfully and were obedient to his commands, he conquered even the most powerful of their enemies. Israel's problems arose only when they had sinned against God or had failed to act courageously in faith. Today, each of us faces the same challenge to remain faithful. The Israelites are profound examples of the need for us to continue to turn our life over to God.

22:10-20 Outraged that the tribes east of the Jordan had seemingly so quickly turned away from the God of their fathers and set up another altar of worship, the tribes living in the Promised Land prepared to go to war against their kinsmen. Before war broke out, however, wisdom prevailed, and a delegation was sent by the tribes living in the land to challenge the Transjordan tribes to return to God. The delegation boldly confronted their brothers, reminding them of the consequences of past rebellions against God (see Numbers 25:1-9; Joshua 7:1-26) and offering to let these tribes live with them in the Promised Land. Though it is often difficult and painful, we must confront others at times so that all of us can maintain faith. This is why recovery is never an individual process; others must be involved to both encourage and confront.

the edge of the land of Canaan, on the west side of the Jordan River. [12]So the whole community of Israel gathered at Shiloh and prepared to go to war against them. [13]First, however, they sent a delegation led by Phinehas son of Eleazar, the priest, to talk with the tribes of Reuben, Gad, and the half-tribe of Manasseh. [14]In this delegation were ten leaders of Israel, one from each of the ten tribes, and each the head of his family within the clans of Israel.

[15]When they arrived in the land of Gilead, they said to the tribes of Reuben, Gad, and the half-tribe of Manasseh, [16]"The whole community of the LORD demands to know why you are betraying the God of Israel. How could you turn away from the LORD and build an altar for yourselves in rebellion against him? [17]Was our sin at Peor not enough? To this day we are not fully cleansed of it, even after the plague that struck the entire community of the LORD. [18]And yet today you are turning away from following the LORD. If you rebel against the LORD today, he will be angry with all of us tomorrow.

[19]"If you need the altar because the land you possess is defiled, then join us in the LORD's land, where the Tabernacle of the LORD is situated, and share our land with us. But do not rebel against the LORD or against us by building an altar other than the one true altar of the LORD our God. [20]Didn't divine anger fall on the entire community of Israel when Achan, a member of the clan of Zerah, sinned by stealing the things set apart for the LORD*? He was not the only one who died because of his sin."

[21]Then the people of Reuben, Gad, and the half-tribe of Manasseh answered the heads of the clans of Israel: [22]"The LORD, the Mighty One, is God! The LORD, the Mighty One, is God! He knows the truth, and may Israel know it, too! We have not built the altar in treacherous rebellion against the LORD. If we have done so, do not spare our lives this day. [23]If we have built an altar for ourselves to turn away from the LORD or to offer burnt offerings or grain offerings or peace offerings, may the LORD himself punish us.

[24]"The truth is, we have built this altar because we fear that in the future your descendants will say to ours, 'What right do you have to worship the LORD, the God of Israel? [25]The LORD has placed the Jordan River as a barrier between our people and you people of Reuben and Gad. You have no claim to the LORD.' So your descendants may prevent our descendants from worshiping the LORD.

[26]"So we decided to build the altar, not for burnt offerings or sacrifices, [27]but as a memorial. It will remind our descendants and your descendants that we, too, have the right to worship the LORD at his sanctuary with our burnt offerings, sacrifices, and peace offerings. Then your descendants will not be able to say to ours, 'You have no claim to the LORD.'

[28]"If they say this, our descendants can reply, 'Look at this copy of the LORD's altar that our ancestors made. It is not for burnt offerings or sacrifices; it is a reminder of the relationship both of us have with the LORD.' [29]Far be it from us to rebel against the LORD or turn away from him by building our own altar for burnt offerings, grain offerings, or sacrifices. Only the altar of the LORD our God that stands in front of the Tabernacle may be used for that purpose."

[30]When Phinehas the priest and the leaders of the community—the heads of the clans of Israel—heard this from the tribes of

---

22:20 The Hebrew term used here refers to the complete consecration of things or people to the LORD, either by destroying them or by giving them as an offering.

22:21-29 The Reubenites, the Gadites, and the half-tribe of Manasseh responded in amazement. They explained their actions in order to reestablish their immediate relationship with the rest of Israel. Their actions had been taken to ensure that future generations would know that the tribes east of the Jordan also worshiped the one true God of Israel. In this case, confrontation was effective. Even though it does not always bring the desired response, it is an important step in the recovery process.

22:30-34 The leaders of the delegation of Israel listened carefully to the words of their brothers. As a result, the western leaders changed their attitude of anger toward the tribes of Reuben, Gad, and the half-tribe of Manasseh to one of reconciliation and joy. The leaders then praised God for the faithfulness of their eastern brothers and declared peace, thus averting the potential civil war. The east-bank altar thereafter was referred to as "Witness" because it was a reminder to all of Israel that the Lord is God. The objective of confrontation always needs to be a loving reconciliation, even though that may not always be the outcome.

Reuben, Gad, and the half-tribe of Manasseh, they were satisfied. [31]Phinehas son of Eleazar, the priest, replied to them, "Today we know the LORD is among us because you have not committed this treachery against the LORD as we thought. Instead, you have rescued Israel from being destroyed by the hand of the LORD."

[32]Then Phinehas son of Eleazar, the priest, and the other leaders left the tribes of Reuben and Gad in Gilead and returned to the land of Canaan to tell the Israelites what had happened. [33]And all the Israelites were satisfied and praised God and spoke no more of war against Reuben and Gad.

[34]The people of Reuben and Gad named the altar "Witness,"* for they said, "It is a witness between us and them that the LORD is our God, too."

CHAPTER 23
Joshua's Final Words to Israel

The years passed, and the LORD had given the people of Israel rest from all their enemies. Joshua, who was now very old, [2]called together all the elders, leaders, judges, and officers of Israel. He said to them, "I am now a very old man. [3]You have seen everything the LORD your God has done for you during my lifetime. The LORD your God has fought for you against your enemies. [4]I have allotted to you as your homeland all the land of the nations yet unconquered, as well as the land of those we have already conquered—from the Jordan River to the Mediterranean Sea* in the west. [5]This land will be yours, for the LORD your God will himself drive out all the people living there now. You will take possession of their land, just as the LORD your God promised you.

[6]"So be very careful to follow everything Moses wrote in the Book of Instruction. Do not deviate from it, turning either to the right or to the left. [7]Make sure you do not associate with the other people still remaining in the land. Do not even mention the names of their gods, much less swear by them or serve them or worship them. [8]Rather, cling tightly to the LORD your God as you have done until now.

[9]"For the LORD has driven out great and powerful nations for you, and no one has yet been able to defeat you. [10]Each one of you will put to flight a thousand of the enemy, for the LORD your God fights for you, just as he has promised. [11]So be very careful to love the LORD your God.

[12]"But if you turn away from him and cling to the customs of the survivors of these nations remaining among you, and if you intermarry with them, [13]then know for certain that the LORD your God will no longer drive them out of your land. Instead, they will be a snare and a trap to you, a whip for your backs and thorny brambles in your eyes, and you will vanish from this good land the LORD your God has given you.

[14]"Soon I will die, going the way of everything on earth. Deep in your hearts you know that every promise of the LORD your God has come true. Not a single one has failed! [15]But as surely as the LORD your God has given you the good things he promised, he will also bring disaster on you if you disobey him. He will completely destroy you from this good land he has given you. [16]If you break the covenant of the LORD your God by worshiping and serving other gods, his anger will burn against you, and you will quickly vanish from the good land he has given you."

22:34 Some manuscripts lack this word. 23:4 Hebrew *the Great Sea.*

23:1-7 Joshua reminded the Israelites that the God of Israel was the one who had given them all their victories, that all of the Promised Land had been apportioned as God had said it would be, and that God would continue to defeat Israel's enemies so his people would live at peace in the land. The people, therefore, were not to forsake God or ever turn to the false gods of the nations living within the land. The Israelites' walk with God was an ongoing process, just like our own progression in recovery.

23:14-16 Joshua spoke the truth: God had not failed Israel in the past. All that God said he would do, he did, and all of Israel knew that to be a fact. Joshua then issued a warning to the people. Just as God had blessed them because of their acts of obedience, as he had promised, so too would he judge them harshly if they broke their covenant with him and worshiped other gods. In fact, if they were disobedient to God, he would not even hesitate to drive them from the Promised Land, the land he had fought to give them. In a loving relationship, others will hold us accountable for our actions, not because they want to "get" us but because they want what is best for us.

CHAPTER 24
The LORD's Covenant Renewed

Then Joshua summoned all the tribes of Israel to Shechem, including their elders, leaders, judges, and officers. So they came and presented themselves to God.

²Joshua said to the people, "This is what the LORD, the God of Israel, says: Long ago your ancestors, including Terah, the father of Abraham and Nahor, lived beyond the Euphrates River,* and they worshiped other gods. ³But I took your ancestor Abraham from the land beyond the Euphrates and led him into the land of Canaan. I gave him many descendants through his son Isaac. ⁴To Isaac I gave Jacob and Esau. To Esau I gave the mountains of Seir, while Jacob and his children went down into Egypt.

⁵"Then I sent Moses and Aaron, and I brought terrible plagues on Egypt; and afterward I brought you out as a free people. ⁶But when your ancestors arrived at the Red Sea,* the Egyptians chased after you with chariots and charioteers. ⁷When your ancestors cried out to the LORD, I put darkness between you and the Egyptians. I brought the sea crashing down on the Egyptians, drowning them. With your very own eyes you saw what I did. Then you lived in the wilderness for many years.

⁸"Finally, I brought you into the land of the Amorites on the east side of the Jordan. They fought against you, but I destroyed them before you. I gave you victory over them, and you took possession of their land. ⁹Then Balak son of Zippor, king of Moab, started a war against Israel. He summoned Balaam son of Beor to curse you, ¹⁰but I would not listen to him. Instead, I made Balaam bless you, and so I rescued you from Balak.

¹¹"When you crossed the Jordan River and came to Jericho, the men of Jericho fought against you, as did the Amorites, the Perizzites, the Canaanites, the Hittites, the Girgashites, the Hivites, and the Jebusites. But I gave you victory over them. ¹²And I sent terror* ahead of you to drive out the two kings of the Amorites. It was not your swords or bows that brought you victory. ¹³I gave you land you had not worked on, and I gave you towns you did not build—the towns where you are now living. I gave you vineyards and olive groves for food, though you did not plant them.

¹⁴"So fear the LORD and serve him wholeheartedly. Put away forever the idols your ancestors worshiped when they lived beyond the Euphrates River and in Egypt. Serve the LORD alone. ¹⁵But if you refuse to serve the LORD, then choose today whom you will serve. Would you prefer the gods your ancestors served beyond the Euphrates? Or will it be the gods of the Amorites in whose land you now live? But as for me and my family, we will serve the LORD."

¹⁶The people replied, "We would never abandon the LORD and serve other gods. ¹⁷For the LORD our God is the one who rescued us and our ancestors from slavery in the land of Egypt. He performed mighty miracles before our very eyes. As we traveled through the wilderness among our enemies, he preserved us. ¹⁸It was the LORD who drove out the Amorites and the other nations living here in the land. So we, too, will serve the LORD, for he alone is our God."

¹⁹Then Joshua warned the people, "You are not able to serve the LORD, for he is a holy and jealous God. He will not forgive your rebellion and your sins. ²⁰If you abandon the LORD and serve other gods, he will turn against you and destroy you, even though he has been so good to you."

24:2 Hebrew *the river;* also in 24:3, 14, 15. 24:6 Hebrew *sea of reeds.* 24:12 Often rendered *the hornet.* The meaning of the Hebrew is uncertain.

24:1-13 Speaking on behalf of God, Joshua declared that everything of lasting value that had been done for Israel had been accomplished by God alone. What greater evidence of these truths do we need than this account of God's strength and the results that come from acting faithfully to achieve his will? Joshua's story is not unique. Each of us is a living testimony either to what God can do when we are faithful or to the tragedy that occurs when we are not.

24:14-18 Joshua concluded by challenging the people to serve the true God and to reject the gods their ancestors had so foolishly served in the wilderness and in Egypt. He then mockingly suggested that if the people were so unwise as to not worship the God of Israel as the only true God, then they should choose to serve either the gods of the Euphrates region or the gods of those heathen nations living in the Promised Land. Joshua and his family, however, would serve the God of Israel. The people responded positively to Joshua's challenge and declared their undying commitment to the one true God. Each day we make a decision whom we will serve, either God or this world. What a wonderful experience to be able to firmly assert that you will serve only the Lord!

²¹But the people answered Joshua, "No, we will serve the LORD!"

²²"You are a witness to your own decision," Joshua said. "You have chosen to serve the LORD."

"Yes," they replied, "we are witnesses to what we have said."

²³"All right then," Joshua said, "destroy the idols among you, and turn your hearts to the LORD, the God of Israel."

²⁴The people said to Joshua, "We will serve the LORD our God. We will obey him alone."

²⁵So Joshua made a covenant with the people that day at Shechem, committing them to follow the decrees and regulations of the LORD. ²⁶Joshua recorded these things in the Book of God's Instructions. As a reminder of their agreement, he took a huge stone and rolled it beneath the terebinth tree beside the Tabernacle of the LORD.

²⁷Joshua said to all the people, "This stone has heard everything the LORD said to us. It will be a witness to testify against you if you go back on your word to God."

²⁸Then Joshua sent all the people away to their own homelands.

Leaders Buried in the Promised Land

²⁹After this, Joshua son of Nun, the servant of the LORD, died at the age of 110. ³⁰They buried him in the land he had been allocated, at Timnath-serah in the hill country of Ephraim, north of Mount Gaash.

³¹The people of Israel served the LORD throughout the lifetime of Joshua and of the elders who outlived him—those who had personally experienced all that the LORD had done for Israel.

³²The bones of Joseph, which the Israelites had brought along with them when they left Egypt, were buried at Shechem, in the parcel of ground Jacob had bought from the sons of Hamor for 100 pieces of silver.* This land was located in the territory allotted to the descendants of Joseph.

³³Eleazar son of Aaron also died. He was buried in the hill country of Ephraim, in the town of Gibeah, which had been given to his son Phinehas.

24:32 Hebrew *100 kesitahs;* the value or weight of the kesitah is no longer known.

24:29-33 The great men of Israel had died—Moses, prior to Israel's entry into the Promised Land, and now, after the completion of the initial phase of Israel's conquest, Joshua and Eleazar the priest. How would the Israelites react to the death of Joshua, who left them without an apparent successor? They responded by serving God. They also demonstrated their commitment to God by burying Joseph's bones in the Promised Land as a testimony to his faith and to God's faithfulness to his people (see Genesis 50:25; Exodus 13:19; Hebrews 11:22). We might ask ourselves this question: Would someone burying our bones do so as a testimony to our faith—or to our faithlessness? If it is faithlessness, we can change that testimony by turning to God today. If it is faith, we must persevere.

REFLECTIONS ON JOSHUA

insights FROM RAHAB'S LIFE
In **Joshua 2:8-14** Rahab willingly admitted her hopeless condition before the God of Israel. She and all the people of Jericho saw no way of escape from the certain doom that was coming from the hands of those who served God. Yet, instead of attempting to pursue a hopeless cause as did the others around her, Rahab sought mercy from the only source of help available. Moreover, she was able to secure an effective relationship with the spies on the basis of mutual trust.

In **Joshua 6:22-25** we see that Joshua remembered the promise his spies had made to Rahab the prostitute. He commanded his men to fulfill that promise and to provide safe passage for her and those with her. Following the total destruction of Jericho, Rahab and her relatives began a new life with Israel because they had served God by protecting the spies. God's provision for Rahab should be significant to each of us. God honored her faith and obedience. Since Rahab was a prostitute, he obviously wasn't honoring her perfection. Rahab is a bold reminder that we can just come to God as we are and don't need to try to fix ourselves before we come.

insights FROM ISRAEL'S CEREMONIES OF REMEMBRANCE
Joshua 5:15-24 tells us that Israel's leaders set up a monument to God at Gilgal with the stones from the Jordan River. Joshua explained that this would serve as a reminder of the miracle God had done—the drying up of the flooded Jordan River. This miracle was reminiscent of the way God had delivered Israel 40 years earlier when he let the Israelites cross the Red Sea on dry ground (see Exodus 14). We must remember that God is all-powerful and cares for us. Knowing that God has rescued us in the past can help us trust in his ability to save us today.

In **Joshua 5:10-12** we find the Israelites celebrating the Passover—a remembrance of God's deliverance of his people from Egypt 40 years earlier. This undoubtedly bolstered the Israelites' faith as they faced the many battles ahead. We are told that God's miraculous provision of manna was stopped at this time. Now that the Israelites owned a productive land, they no longer needed food from heaven. This was a reminder that God would provide his people with what they needed in various ways, depending on the circumstances, and that they would have to trust him to do so in the future. God works with us in different ways at varying stages of the recovery process. Too often we resent God for not continuing to treat us as newborns in the faith. When life isn't easy, it is not a sign of God's abandonment. It is a sign that he is ready for us to grow in wisdom and faith. God often calls us to struggle in order to grow.

After the great victory recorded in **Joshua 8:24-35**, the people built a monument to God and erected an altar to him at Mount Ebal. At that time, Joshua had the words of the law, the blessings and curses (i.e., boundaries), read to the people to remind them of how God expected them to act in the Promised Land. In setting boundaries for our own behavior, we tend to either make them too rigid or not develop healthy boundaries at all. Today, just as in Joshua's day, healthy boundaries are formed as we adhere to the teaching of God's Word.

In **Joshua 11:1-9**, Joshua declared that the tribes east of the Jordan had faithfully fulfilled their responsibilities. They had delayed the gratification of enjoying their own reward so their brothers could receive what God had promised to them. Joshua then reminded them that they were always to love and obey God. Although there was much sorrow at leaving their kinsmen who lived west of the Jordan, there undoubtedly was also much joy for the Reubenites, Gadites, and the half-tribe of Manasseh since they were finally going home to their families. As they crossed the Jordan, the eastern tribes set up a monument to remind themselves and their western cousins of the kinship between the eastern and western tribes and of their loyalty to God.

Joshua understood the holiness of God, but he also was aware of the sinful tendencies of the Israelites. So in **Joshua 24:19-28**, he compelled the people to proclaim once again that they would follow God and that their words would be an eternal witness to their decision. To cement that commitment, Joshua, who had been a rock of faith before God throughout his life, recognized the importance of leaving one more permanent stone memorial as a reminder to the greatness and faithfulness of God. A record of our decision to follow God can be helpful to us in times of temptation. It can remind us that we were serious about that decision and that we are accountable for our actions.

insights FROM JOSHUA'S LIFE
In **Joshua 7:10-12**, God displayed his anger with Israel, chastising Joshua for the sin that still existed among the people. The Israelites needed to realize that victory was impossible for those who disobeyed God. We also must realize that our sins don't affect us alone. Our family, friends, co-workers, and any number of others are all affected by our choices and lifestyle. God wants us to confess our mistakes to each other rather than hide in shame. Only then will we be able to overcome the sins in our life.

In **Joshua 10:16-27**, after learning of the capture of the five kings, Joshua wisely commanded his troops not to "rest on their laurels" or refuse to strive for continued victories but to complete the mission God had given them. Later, while encouraging the Israelites for future battles, Joshua concluded his message by slaying the five kings and hanging them on five trees until evening, so that all would see the victory that God had given. As we publicly acknowledge God's work in our life, others can be reminded of God's presence in their lives and of the victories God has promised them.

In **Joshua 10:29-42** we are reminded that Joshua led the people from city to city and from victory to victory. With each day came new success as enemy after enemy was defeated. Each battle was fought in accordance with the commands of God. We see that no enemy will ever prove too strong for God to defeat. If God could handle these great armies, we can certainly trust him to handle our personal problems. We can allow him to work by daily submitting to his plan. Often we do not experience victory over our struggles because after some initial progress, we forget about trusting God and go into battle alone, under our own power. We must never be satisfied with one victory when God has a lifetime of victories planned for us.

Despite Joshua's advanced age, **Joshua 13:1** tells us that God placed additional challenges before him. Retirement from doing God's will is not an option. We are called to follow God's will throughout our life, until God's time for us to finish the race toward victory finally arrives (2 Timothy 4:6-8).

In **Joshua 19:49-50**, Joshua was permitted to select a city for his inheritance. He could have chosen any city in the Promised Land, but he chose to live within the territory of Ephraim, the tribe from which he had come (see Numbers 13:8, 16). Joshua remembered his roots and honored his extended family with his decision. We lose our way when we forget where we've come from. Although our roots are not perfect, we can celebrate what is good about them and honor God in doing so.

In **Joshua 23:8-13**, Joshua continued to challenge the Israelites to maintain a strong faith in God, remembering that God had accomplished a great work in defeating the powerful nations of the land on Israel's behalf. God gives all the courage and strength we need to succeed against all odds. In return, we are to love him with full commitment, knowing that if we turn away from the true God to other so-called gods, God will no longer fight on our side. Each of us will be tempted at times to turn our life over to a false god that promises to immediately gratify our urges. But in the Bible we discover that such "promises" are false. If we want success, we must follow the one true God.

JUDGES

THE BIG PICTURE

A. PROLOGUE: A PATTERN OF UNFINISHED RECOVERY (1:1–3:6)
1. Not Fully Dealing with the Issues (1:1–2:5)
2. Making the Same Mistake Over and Over (2:6–3:6)

B. CASE HISTORIES: THE UPS AND DOWNS OF INCOMPLETE RECOVERY (3:7–16:31)
1. Rescued by Othniel, Ehud, and Shamgar (3:7-31)
2. Rescued by Deborah and Barak (4:1–5:31)
3. Rescued by Gideon (6:1–8:35)
4. Rescued from Abimelech, the "In-house" Abuser (9:1-57)
5. Rescued by Tola, Jair, Jephthah, Ibzan, Elon, and Abdon (10:1–12:15)
6. Rescued by Samson (13:1–16:31)

C. EPILOGUE: CLASSIC EXAMPLES OF GOING YOUR OWN WAY IN DENIAL (17:1–21:25)
1. "Doing Your Own Thing" Religiously (17:1–18:31)
2. "Doing Your Own Thing" Morally (19:1–21:25)

The conquest of the Promised Land under Joshua had been a miraculous success. It wasn't long, however, before the people forgot what had made it all possible—faith in God and obedience to his commands. They became trapped in a four-step spiritual cycle: (1) They fell into sin, (2) they were enslaved by an oppressor, (3) they cried out to God for help, and (4) God sent a leader (or judge) to deliver them. At the end of each painful round, there was a temporary period of faithfulness and stability. But soon, most of the people slipped back into the same vicious cycle of relapse.

The book of Judges shows what happens to a society when its citizens do whatever they choose (17:6). The people of Israel refused to learn from their past mistakes. They blinded themselves to the needs of others and to the commands of God. As a result, they became trapped by their individual delusions and brought suffering on themselves and the people around them. They refused to follow the path to freedom by obeying God's program for righteous and healthy living. Doing things our way still leads to enslavement and suffering; following God's program is the only path to freedom.

Let us learn from Israel's mistakes. We would be wise to note that Israel's failures often came after great victories. Success is sometimes the first step toward a fall. We must humbly take inventory of our activities and relationships, keeping our eyes on God and obeying his will for us. But when we do fail, we can be sure that God will listen to our cries for help. He wants to deliver us once again.

THE BOTTOM LINE

PURPOSE: To show how tragic an incomplete recovery program can be and how dysfunctional patterns tend to continue from one generation to the next. And to show how God is ready to lift us up when we look to him for help. AUTHOR: Tradition attributes it to Samuel, though it could have been one of his contemporaries. AUDIENCE: The people of Israel. DATE WRITTEN: Probably between 1050 and 1000 B.C. SETTING: Various parts of the Promised Land of Israel. KEY VERSE: "In those days Israel had no king; all the people did whatever seemed right in their own eyes" (17:6). KEY PLACES: Israel, Aram, Moab, Midian, Ammon, Philistia. KEY PEOPLE AND RELATIONSHIPS: Othniel, Ehud, Deborah and Barak, Gideon, Abimelech, Jephthah, Samson and Delilah.

RECOVERY THEMES

The Danger of Pride: It is so easy to think we have "arrived." The Israelites had arrived in the Promised Land, their physical destination. What did they have to worry about now? After all, they were God's chosen people. They still had to learn, however, that "pride ends in humiliation" (Proverbs 29:23). In the book of Judges, the Israelites discovered repeatedly that overconfidence leads to relapse. What was true back then is still true today. Recovery is an ongoing process that requires vigilant self-examination. To be sustained in recovery demands that we depend on God one day at a time.

The Cycle of Failure: Why do intelligent people fall repeatedly to the same tragic mistakes? One unhealthy marriage ends in divorce only to be followed by another bad marriage and divorce. The process of recovery from an addiction only ends in a relapse. Again and again, God delivered the Israelites from their troubles. For short periods of time, the people gratefully guarded their faith and were consistent in worship. But then their overconfidence set them up for additional failure. The frequency with which such cyclical failures occur almost makes one think such patterns are inevitable. They are not inevitable; they are the result of failing to realize that recovery is a lifelong process and that we continually need help.

Suffering the Consequences: God did not protect his people from the painful consequences of their actions. He allowed them to suffer the consequences so they could learn some valuable lessons. Facing the consequences of our actions can be a healthy part of the recovery process. Every time the Israelites hit bottom and admitted their helplessness, God moved in and delivered them. If they had continually depended on God and admitted their helplessness, they would have been able to break the cycle permanently. We never outgrow the early steps of recovery. We are powerless to handle the chaos in our life, and we need to continually turn our whole life over to God.

God Uses Flawed People: A number of the heroes in Judges were most notable for their flaws. Barak refused to fight for God without the help of the prophetess, Deborah. Gideon needed numerous affirmations before he would step out in faith for God. Samson's flaws are legendary, but God still used him to fight the enemies of Israel. We do not need to be perfect in order to call upon God and receive help. We do not need to be perfect to be used by God for his glory. We simply need to see and admit our need for him. We cannot earn God's blessing; we simply receive his gifts of grace.

CHAPTER 1
Judah and Simeon Conquer the Land

After the death of Joshua, the Israelites asked the LORD, "Which tribe should go first to attack the Canaanites?"

²The LORD answered, "Judah, for I have given them victory over the land."

³The men of Judah said to their relatives from the tribe of Simeon, "Join with us to fight against the Canaanites living in the territory allotted to us. Then we will help you conquer your territory." So the men of Simeon went with Judah.

⁴When the men of Judah attacked, the LORD gave them victory over the Canaanites and Perizzites, and they killed 10,000 enemy warriors at the town of Bezek. ⁵While at Bezek they encountered King Adoni-bezek and fought against him, and the Canaanites and Perizzites were defeated. ⁶Adoni-bezek escaped, but the Israelites soon captured him and cut off his thumbs and big toes.

⁷Adoni-bezek said, "I once had seventy kings with their thumbs and big toes cut off, eating scraps from under my table. Now God has paid me back for what I did to them." They took him to Jerusalem, and he died there.

⁸The men of Judah attacked Jerusalem and captured it, killing all its people and setting the city on fire. ⁹Then they went down to fight the Canaanites living in the hill country, the Negev, and the western foothills.* ¹⁰Judah marched against the Canaanites in Hebron (formerly called Kiriath-arba), defeating the forces of Sheshai, Ahiman, and Talmai.

¹¹From there they went to fight against the people living in the town of Debir (formerly

1:9 Hebrew *the Shephelah.*

1:1ff The book of Judges gives us an idea of the courage it takes to enter new territory in life. Even though much of the Promised Land (see Genesis 15:18-21) had already been taken under Joshua's leadership, it was still necessary to address the present reality of the enemies still living there. Only when the conquest was completed could the people of Israel focus on building new lives in their new land. In the same way, it is important that we conquer and control our dependencies before we try to build a new life.

called Kiriath-sepher). [12]Caleb said, "I will give my daughter Acsah in marriage to the one who attacks and captures Kiriath-sepher." [13]Othniel, the son of Caleb's younger brother, Kenaz, was the one who conquered it, so Acsah became Othniel's wife.

[14]When Acsah married Othniel, she urged him* to ask her father for a field. As she got down off her donkey, Caleb asked her, "What's the matter?"

[15]She said, "Let me have another gift. You have already given me land in the Negev; now please give me springs of water, too." So Caleb gave her the upper and lower springs.

[16]When the tribe of Judah left Jericho— the city of palms—the Kenites, who were descendants of Moses' father-in-law, traveled with them into the wilderness of Judah. They settled among the people there, near the town of Arad in the Negev.

[17]Then Judah joined with Simeon to fight against the Canaanites living in Zephath, and they completely destroyed* the town. So the town was named Hormah.* [18]In addition, Judah captured the towns of Gaza, Ashkelon, and Ekron, along with their surrounding territories.

Israel Fails to Conquer the Land

[19]The LORD was with the people of Judah, and they took possession of the hill country. But they failed to drive out the people living in the plains, who had iron chariots. [20]The town of Hebron was given to Caleb as Moses had promised. And Caleb drove out the people living there, who were descendants of the three sons of Anak.

[21]The tribe of Benjamin, however, failed to drive out the Jebusites, who were living in Jerusalem. So to this day the Jebusites live in Jerusalem among the people of Benjamin.

[22]The descendants of Joseph attacked the town of Bethel, and the LORD was with them. [23]They sent men to scout out Bethel (formerly known as Luz). [24]They confronted a man coming out of the town and said to him, "Show us a way into the town, and we will have mercy on you." [25]So he showed them a way in, and they killed everyone in the town except that man and his family. [26]Later the man moved to the land of the Hittites, where he built a town. He named it Luz, which is its name to this day.

[27]The tribe of Manasseh failed to drive out the people living in Beth-shan,* Taanach, Dor, Ibleam, Megiddo, and all their surrounding settlements, because the Canaanites were determined to stay in that region. [28]When the Israelites grew stronger, they forced the Canaanites to work as slaves, but they never did drive them completely out of the land.

[29]The tribe of Ephraim failed to drive out the Canaanites living in Gezer, so the Canaanites continued to live there among them.

[30]The tribe of Zebulun failed to drive out the residents of Kitron and Nahalol, so the Canaanites continued to live among them. But the Canaanites were forced to work as slaves for the people of Zebulun.

[31]The tribe of Asher failed to drive out the residents of Acco, Sidon, Ahlab, Aczib, Helbah, Aphik, and Rehob. [32]Instead, the people of Asher moved in among the Canaanites, who controlled the land, for they failed to drive them out.

[33]Likewise, the tribe of Naphtali failed to drive out the residents of Beth-shemesh and Beth-anath. Instead, they moved in among the Canaanites, who controlled the land. Nevertheless, the people of Beth-shemesh and Beth-anath were forced to work as slaves for the people of Naphtali.

[34]As for the tribe of Dan, the Amorites forced them back into the hill country and would not let them come down into the plains. [35]The Amorites were determined to stay in Mount Heres, Aijalon, and Shaalbim, but when the descendants of Joseph became stronger, they forced the Amorites to work as slaves. [36]The boundary of the Amorites ran from Scorpion Pass* to Sela and continued upward from there.

1:14 Greek version and Latin Vulgate read *he urged her.* 1:17a The Hebrew term used here refers to the complete consecration of things or people to the LORD, either by destroying them or by giving them as an offering. 1:17b *Hormah* means "destruction." 1:27 Hebrew *Beth-shean,* a variant spelling of Beth-shan. 1:36 Hebrew *Akrabbim.*

1:19-36 The last half of this chapter shows how incomplete Israel's conquest of the Promised Land really was. God had promised to be with them and guide them in this difficult process. As they displayed courage and faith in God, God indeed brought them numerous victories. But lack of perseverance and faltering courage stopped God's people short of their goal. We must also persevere and place our faith in God if we desire to recover fully.

CHAPTER 2
The LORD's Messenger Comes to Bokim
The angel of the LORD went up from Gilgal to Bokim and said to the Israelites, "I brought you out of Egypt into this land that I swore to give your ancestors, and I said I would never break my covenant with you. [2]For your part, you were not to make any covenants with the people living in this land; instead, you were to destroy their altars. But you disobeyed my command. Why did you do this? [3]So now I declare that I will no longer drive out the people living in your land. They will be thorns in your sides,* and their gods will be a constant temptation to you."

[4]When the angel of the LORD finished speaking to all the Israelites, the people wept loudly. [5]So they called the place Bokim (which means "weeping"), and they offered sacrifices there to the LORD.

The Death of Joshua
[6]After Joshua sent the people away, each of the tribes left to take possession of the land allotted to them. [7]And the Israelites served the LORD throughout the lifetime of Joshua and the leaders who outlived him—those who had seen all the great things the LORD had done for Israel.

[8]Joshua son of Nun, the servant of the LORD, died at the age of 110. [9]They buried him in the land he had been allocated, at Timnath-serah* in the hill country of Ephraim, north of Mount Gaash.

Israel Disobeys the LORD
[10]After that generation died, another generation grew up who did not acknowledge the LORD or remember the mighty things he had done for Israel.

[11]The Israelites did evil in the LORD's sight and served the images of Baal. [12]They abandoned the LORD, the God of their ancestors, who had brought them out of Egypt. They went after other gods, worshiping the gods of the people around them. And they angered the LORD. [13]They abandoned the LORD to serve Baal and the images of Ashtoreth. [14]This made the LORD burn with anger against Israel, so he handed them over to raiders who stole their possessions. He turned them over to their enemies all around, and they were no longer able to resist them. [15]Every time Israel went out to battle, the LORD fought against them, causing them to be defeated, just as he had warned. And the people were in great distress.

The LORD Rescues His People
[16]Then the LORD raised up judges to rescue the Israelites from their attackers. [17]Yet Israel did not listen to the judges but prostituted themselves by worshiping other gods. How quickly they turned away from the path of their ancestors, who had walked in obedience to the LORD's commands.

[18]Whenever the LORD raised up a judge over Israel, he was with that judge and rescued the people from their enemies throughout the judge's lifetime. For the LORD took pity on his people, who were burdened by oppression and suffering. [19]But when the judge died, the people returned to their corrupt ways, behaving worse than those who had lived before them. They went after other gods, serving and worshiping them. And they refused to give up their evil practices and stubborn ways.

[20]So the LORD burned with anger against Israel. He said, "Because these people have violated my covenant, which I made with their ancestors, and have ignored my commands,

---

2:3 Hebrew *They will be in your sides;* compare Num 33:55.   2:9 As in parallel text at Josh 24:30; Hebrew reads *Timnath-heres,* a variant spelling of Timnath-serah.

2:1-5 The angel of the Lord stated in no uncertain terms that the foundational reason for Israel's half-completed conquest of the Promised Land was their halfhearted commitment to God. They had allowed the altars of the various Canaanite peoples to remain, and those moral temptations repeatedly became points of failure for God's people. To the Israelites' credit, they repented, attempting to set things right with God. No matter what we have done, we can turn to God. God will forgive us, but we must ask for that forgiveness.

2:11-19 This cycle of short-term recovery is echoed throughout Judges. Because of prolonged denial of their sin, the people repeatedly fell into spiritual and physical slavery to their enemies. In their misery, they finally admitted their helplessness by praying to God. Then and only then did God provide the judges to free them from oppression. Tragically, it was only a matter of time before Israel repeated the same mistakes. We cannot stand alone against our dependencies. We must rely upon God, who will support us and sustain us in our recovery efforts with his gracious power. God is waiting for our cries if we fall, and he will respond with the help we need.

2:20–3:6 God used the wicked nations in the land to test the Israelites' obedience. God did not use these tests spitefully, in order to catch the Israelites and punish them. He only wanted to show

[21]I will no longer drive out the nations that Joshua left unconquered when he died. [22]I did this to test Israel—to see whether or not they would follow the ways of the LORD as their ancestors did." [23]That is why the LORD left those nations in place. He did not quickly drive them out or allow Joshua to conquer them all.

CHAPTER 3
The Nations Left in Canaan

These are the nations that the LORD left in the land to test those Israelites who had not experienced the wars of Canaan. [2]He did this to teach warfare to generations of Israelites who had no experience in battle. [3]These are the nations: the Philistines (those living under the five Philistine rulers), all the Canaanites, the Sidonians, and the Hivites living in the mountains of Lebanon from Mount Baal-hermon to Lebo-hamath. [4]These people were left to test the Israelites—to see whether they would obey the commands the LORD had given to their ancestors through Moses.

[5]So the people of Israel lived among the Canaanites, Hittites, Amorites, Perizzites, Hivites, and Jebusites, [6]and they intermarried with them. Israelite sons married their daughters, and Israelite daughters were given in marriage to their sons. And the Israelites served their gods.

Othniel Becomes Israel's Judge

[7]The Israelites did evil in the LORD's sight. They forgot about the LORD their God, and they served the images of Baal and the Asherah poles. [8]Then the LORD burned with anger against Israel, and he turned them over to King Cushan-rishathaim of Aram-naharaim.* And the Israelites served Cushan-rishathaim for eight years.

[9]But when the people of Israel cried out to the LORD for help, the LORD raised up a rescuer to save them. His name was Othniel, the son of Caleb's younger brother, Kenaz. [10]The Spirit of the LORD came upon him, and he became Israel's judge. He went to war against King Cushan-rishathaim of Aram, and the LORD gave Othniel victory over him. [11]So there was peace in the land for forty years. Then Othniel son of Kenaz died.

Ehud Becomes Israel's Judge

[12]Once again the Israelites did evil in the LORD's sight, and the LORD gave King Eglon of Moab control over Israel because of their evil. [13]Eglon enlisted the Ammonites and Amalekites as allies, and then he went out and defeated Israel, taking possession of Jericho, the city of palms. [14]And the Israelites served Eglon of Moab for eighteen years.

[15]But when the people of Israel cried out to the LORD for help, the LORD again raised up a rescuer to save them. His name was Ehud son of Gera, a left-handed man of the tribe of Benjamin. The Israelites sent Ehud to deliver their tribute money to King Eglon of Moab. [16]So Ehud made a double-edged dagger that was about a foot* long, and he strapped it to his right thigh, keeping it hidden under his clothing. [17]He brought the tribute money to Eglon, who was very fat.

[18]After delivering the payment, Ehud started home with those who had helped carry the tribute. [19]But when Ehud reached the stone idols near Gilgal, he turned back. He came to Eglon and said, "I have a secret message for you."

So the king commanded his servants, "Be quiet!" and he sent them all out of the room.

[20]Ehud walked over to Eglon, who was sitting alone in a cool upstairs room. And Ehud said, "I have a message from God for you!" As King Eglon rose from his seat, [21]Ehud reached with his left hand, pulled out the dagger

---

3:8 *Aram-naharaim* means "Aram of the two rivers," thought to have been located between the Euphrates and Balih Rivers in northwestern Mesopotamia. 3:16 Hebrew *gomed*, the length of which is uncertain.

---

them the painful consequences of living apart from his will. If we are experiencing pain and turmoil now, God may be testing us. Are we following his will? Are our addictions getting the better of us and keeping us from doing what we know is right? If so, we can turn to God and ask him to rescue us.
3:7-10 Notice that Othniel's rescue of Israel from Syrian oppression was governed by the power of the Holy Spirit, or "the Spirit of the LORD." As believers, we have the Holy Spirit living in us (1 Corinthians 6:19) and directing us (Galatians 5:18). He is always there to give us guidance, encouragement, and power as we face our problems.
3:11-30 It was Ehud's distinctiveness as a left-handed warrior that made possible his assassination of Eglon, the Moabite king. If he had been right-handed, his weapon would have been found. People often view their unique characteristics as liabilities rather than assets. God has made us the way we are for a purpose. We should not complain about our differences; we should use our unique abilities to help others and to serve God. God isn't running an assembly line; he custom-builds all of his people. (See 1 Corinthians 12 for a discussion of the differences among God's people.)

strapped to his right thigh, and plunged it into the king's belly. ²²The dagger went so deep that the handle disappeared beneath the king's fat. So Ehud did not pull out the dagger, and the king's bowels emptied.* ²³Then Ehud closed and locked the doors of the room and escaped down the latrine.*

²⁴After Ehud was gone, the king's servants returned and found the doors to the upstairs room locked. They thought he might be using the latrine in the room, ²⁵so they waited. But when the king didn't come out after a long delay, they became concerned and got a key. And when they opened the doors, they found their master dead on the floor.

²⁶While the servants were waiting, Ehud escaped, passing the stone idols on his way to Seirah. ²⁷When he arrived in the hill country of Ephraim, Ehud sounded a call to arms. Then he led a band of Israelites down from the hills.

²⁸"Follow me," he said, "for the LORD has given you victory over Moab your enemy." So they followed him. And the Israelites took control of the shallow crossings of the Jordan River across from Moab, preventing anyone from crossing.

²⁹They attacked the Moabites and killed about 10,000 of their strongest and most able-bodied warriors. Not one of them escaped. ³⁰So Moab was conquered by Israel that day, and there was peace in the land for eighty years.

Shamgar Becomes Israel's Judge

³¹After Ehud, Shamgar son of Anath rescued Israel. He once killed 600 Philistines with an ox goad.

CHAPTER 4
Deborah Becomes Israel's Judge

After Ehud's death, the Israelites again did evil in the LORD's sight. ²So the LORD turned them over to King Jabin of Hazor, a Canaanite king. The commander of his army was Sisera, who lived in Harosheth-haggoyim. ³Sisera, who had 900 iron chariots, ruthlessly oppressed the Israelites for twenty years. Then the people of Israel cried out to the LORD for help.

⁴Deborah, the wife of Lappidoth, was a prophet who was judging Israel at that time. ⁵She would sit under the Palm of Deborah, between Ramah and Bethel in the hill country of Ephraim, and the Israelites would go to her for judgment. ⁶One day she sent for Barak son of Abinoam, who lived in Kedesh in the land of Naphtali. She said to him, "This is what the LORD, the God of Israel, commands you: Call out 10,000 warriors from the tribes of Naphtali and Zebulun at Mount Tabor. ⁷And I will call out Sisera, commander of Jabin's army, along with his chariots and warriors, to the Kishon River. There I will give you victory over him."

⁸Barak told her, "I will go, but only if you go with me."

⁹"Very well," she replied, "I will go with you. But you will receive no honor in this venture, for the LORD's victory over Sisera will be at the hands of a woman." So Deborah went with Barak to Kedesh. ¹⁰At Kedesh, Barak called together the tribes of Zebulun and Naphtali, and 10,000 warriors went up with him. Deborah also went with him.

¹¹Now Heber the Kenite, a descendant of Moses' brother-in-law* Hobab, had moved away from the other members of his tribe and pitched his tent by the oak of Zaanannim near Kedesh.

¹²When Sisera was told that Barak son of Abinoam had gone up to Mount Tabor, ¹³he called for all 900 of his iron chariots and all of his warriors, and they marched from Harosheth-haggoyim to the Kishon River.

¹⁴Then Deborah said to Barak, "Get ready! This is the day the LORD will give you victory over Sisera, for the LORD is marching ahead of you." So Barak led his 10,000 warriors down the slopes of Mount Tabor into battle. ¹⁵When Barak attacked, the LORD threw Sisera and all his chariots and warriors into a panic. Sisera leaped down from his chariot and escaped on foot. ¹⁶Then Barak chased the chariots and the enemy army all the way to Harosheth-haggoyim, killing all of Sisera's warriors. Not a single one was left alive.

¹⁷Meanwhile, Sisera ran to the tent of Jael,

3:22 Or *and it came out behind.* 3:23 Or *and went out through the porch;* the meaning of the Hebrew is uncertain. 4:11 Or *father-in-law.*

4:4-9 Until this time, Deborah had served as a prophetess of God in Israel. Here she was called to take part in a military campaign to overthrow the Canaanite oppressors. Though this was new ground for her, she didn't hesitate for a minute. She trusted that God would care for and direct her. Barak, however, put more trust in Deborah than in God. Because of Barak's lack of faith, God had to accomplish his task through another. We have the potential to assist others who are recovering from situations that have plagued us in the past. But if we don't demonstrate the courage to lead, God may decide not to use us.

DEBORAH & BARAK

In a lawless, enemy-occupied country, one woman became a "mother for Israel" (5:7). Chosen by God, Deborah gained national prominence as a prophetess and judge during one of her country's blackest hours. Considering Israel's male-dominated culture, it was remarkable that a woman would be selected for such a task, but Deborah was a remarkable woman. She never hesitated to assume leadership, nor was she reluctant to later risk her life in a military campaign. She was full of faith, courage, and confidence in God's power and promises. She turned her life over to God, making herself available to him and trusting him for the outcome.

Under God's direction, Deborah called Barak of Kedesh to assemble 10,000 men at Mount Tabor to draw the enemy into battle. Barak was reluctant. This reluctance may have been prompted by insecurity, self-doubt, lack of faith, fear, concern over the reliability of Deborah's message, or even simple pragmatism in the face of terrible odds. Nonetheless, Barak did step out in faith, leading his outmanned and outclassed troops against a formidable foe. But the battle was the Lord's. The Kenite woman Jael wrapped up the loose ends of the victory by killing Sisera in his sleep.

Barak's reticence had the expected repercussions. He was not only denied the honor of dispatching his enemy but he saw the privilege go to a female foreigner. Still, no mention of Barak's lapse is made in the epic song in chapter 5. It is also Barak, despite his timidity, who is found among the heroes of faith in Hebrews 11. It was his final obedience, not his initial hesitance, that God found significant. The same is true for us. God always commends our commitments while forgetting our failures. He did this with Barak and continues to do so for all those who trust him.

STRENGTHS AND ACCOMPLISHMENTS:
- As a female, Deborah held a rare position of leadership in a male-dominated culture.
- Deborah's confidence in God gave her courage in difficult situations.
- Despite initial reluctance, Barak demonstrated obedience to God.
- Together, Deborah and Barak led the Israelites to overthrow their Canaanite oppressors.

WEAKNESSES AND MISTAKES:
- Barak hesitated before obeying God.

LESSONS FROM THEIR LIVES:
- Deborah's prominence demonstrates the value of women in God's sight.
- Lack of faith and obedience leads to oppression.
- God forgets the failures as he commends obedience and trust.
- A society's well-being depends on its faithfulness to God.

KEY VERSES:
"There were few people left in the villages of Israel—until Deborah arose as a mother for Israel. . . . Arise, Barak! Lead your captives away, son of Abinoam!" (Judges 5:7, 12).

The story of Deborah and Barak is told in Judges 4–5. Barak is also mentioned in Hebrews 11:32.

---

the wife of Heber the Kenite, because Heber's family was on friendly terms with King Jabin of Hazor. ¹⁸Jael went out to meet Sisera and said to him, "Come into my tent, sir. Come in. Don't be afraid." So he went into her tent, and she covered him with a blanket.

¹⁹"Please give me some water," he said. "I'm thirsty." So she gave him some milk from a leather bag and covered him again.

²⁰"Stand at the door of the tent," he told her. "If anybody comes and asks you if there is anyone here, say no."

²¹But when Sisera fell asleep from exhaustion, Jael quietly crept up to him with a ham-

mer and tent peg in her hand. Then she drove the tent peg through his temple and into the ground, and so he died.

²²When Barak came looking for Sisera, Jael went out to meet him. She said, "Come, and I will show you the man you are looking for." So he followed her into the tent and found Sisera lying there dead, with the tent peg through his temple.

²³So on that day Israel saw God defeat Jabin, the Canaanite king. ²⁴And from that time on Israel became stronger and stronger against King Jabin until they finally destroyed him.

CHAPTER 5
The Song of Deborah

On that day Deborah and Barak son of Abinoam sang this song:

2 "Israel's leaders took charge,
and the people gladly followed.
Praise the LORD!

3 "Listen, you kings!
Pay attention, you mighty rulers!
For I will sing to the LORD.
I will make music to the LORD, the God
of Israel.

4 "LORD, when you set out from Seir
and marched across the fields of Edom,
the earth trembled,
and the cloudy skies poured down rain.

5 The mountains quaked in the presence of
the LORD,
the God of Mount Sinai—
in the presence of the LORD,
the God of Israel.

6 "In the days of Shamgar son of Anath,
and in the days of Jael,
people avoided the main roads,
and travelers stayed on winding
pathways.

7 There were few people left in the villages
of Israel*—
until Deborah arose as a mother for
Israel.

8 When Israel chose new gods,
war erupted at the city gates.
Yet not a shield or spear could be seen
among forty thousand warriors in
Israel!

9 My heart is with the commanders of Israel,
with those who volunteered for war.
Praise the LORD!

10 "Consider this, you who ride on fine
donkeys,
you who sit on fancy saddle blankets,
and you who walk along the road.

11 Listen to the village musicians*
gathered at the watering holes.
They recount the righteous victories
of the LORD
and the victories of his villagers in Israel.
Then the people of the LORD
marched down to the city gates.

12 "Wake up, Deborah, wake up!
Wake up, wake up, and sing a song!
Arise, Barak!
Lead your captives away, son of
Abinoam!

13 "Down from Tabor marched the few
against the nobles.
The people of the LORD marched down
against mighty warriors.

14 They came down from Ephraim—
a land that once belonged to the
Amalekites;
they followed you, Benjamin, with
your troops.
From Makir the commanders marched
down;
from Zebulun came those who carry a
commander's staff.

15 The princes of Issachar were with Deborah
and Barak.
They followed Barak, rushing into the
valley.
But in the tribe of Reuben
there was great indecision.*

16 Why did you sit at home among the
sheepfolds—
to hear the shepherds whistle for their
flocks?
Yes, in the tribe of Reuben
there was great indecision.

17 Gilead remained east of the Jordan.
And why did Dan stay home?
Asher sat unmoved at the seashore,

5:7 The meaning of the Hebrew is uncertain. 5:11 The meaning of the Hebrew is uncertain. 5:15 As in some Hebrew manuscripts and Syriac version, which read *searchings of heart*; Masoretic Text reads *resolve of heart*.

5:7, 12, 15 In this song of victory, the role of Deborah is emphasized. Women in ancient Israel rarely rose to positions of leadership. But Deborah's courage and faith in God made her an ideal prophetess. Then she was called to lead the forces of Israel against the oppressive Canaanites. What tremendous faith it must have taken for Deborah to assume this unlikely position! Victory can come even when God puts us in positions we are uncomfortable with. We must trust God's promises to us. "Is anything too hard for the LORD?" (Genesis 18:14).

5:24-27 The other heroine of this beautiful song is Jael. Notice that Barak, who had faltered in regard to God's call, is barely mentioned. It took amazing courage for Jael to do away with Sisera. Even though her husband Heber was an ally of the Canaanites (4:17), Jael displayed her faith in the God of Israel by siding with the Israelites, executing the commander of the oppressing army. This act of courage delivered many from bondage, giving them an opportunity to build a new life. If we expect any changes to take place in our life, we must take action against our oppressors.

GOD grant me the serenity
to accept the things I cannot change
the courage to change the things I can
and the wisdom to know the difference
AMEN

There are times when chaos reigns in our life because others are not willing or able to fulfill their God-given roles. When this happens, we often suffer from lack of leadership and protection. We may feel frustrated and angry.

The time of the judges was full of confusion for Israel. Instead of obeying God's law, "the people did whatever seemed right in their own eyes" (17:6). They were oppressed by tyrants, one of whom was King Jabin of Hazor. The commander of the Canaanite army ruled by Jabin was Sisera, who "ruthlessly oppressed the Israelites for twenty years" (4:3). At this time God chose Deborah to be a judge. Her job was to decide the disputes of the people.

One day Deborah summoned a man named Barak and told him that God would use him to defeat the army of Sisera. "Barak told her, 'I will go, but only if you go with me'" (4:8). So Deborah agreed to go along, but she said, "But you will receive no honor in this venture, for the LORD's victory over Sisera will be at the hands of a woman" (4:9). Barak lacked the faith to take on the responsibilities God had chosen him for. In the end, Sisera did die at the hands of a woman. In the victory song, Deborah was honored. They sang, "There were few people left in the villages of Israel—until Deborah arose as a mother for Israel" (5:7).

When others don't fulfill their rightful duties and roles, we have the option of finding a way to cope, with God's help. Deborah compensated for Barak's lack of faith. We don't have to endure the ongoing effects of other people's limitations. And we don't have to accept the painful circumstances that their weaknesses create. *Turn to page 313, Judges 7.*

---

remaining in his harbors.
¹⁸ But Zebulun risked his life,
   as did Naphtali, on the heights of the
      battlefield.

¹⁹ "The kings of Canaan came and fought,
   at Taanach near Megiddo's springs,
   but they carried off no silver treasures.
²⁰ The stars fought from heaven.
   The stars in their orbits fought against
      Sisera.
²¹ The Kishon River swept them away—
   that ancient torrent, the Kishon.
   March on with courage, my soul!
²² Then the horses' hooves hammered the
      ground,
   the galloping, galloping of Sisera's
      mighty steeds.
²³ 'Let the people of Meroz be cursed,' said
   the angel of the LORD.

'Let them be utterly cursed,
   because they did not come to help the
      LORD—
   to help the LORD against the mighty
      warriors.'

²⁴ "Most blessed among women is Jael,
   the wife of Heber the Kenite.
   May she be blessed above all women
      who live in tents.
²⁵ Sisera asked for water,
   and she gave him milk.
   In a bowl fit for nobles,
   she brought him yogurt.
²⁶ Then with her left hand she reached for
      a tent peg,
   and with her right hand for the
      workman's hammer.
   She struck Sisera with the hammer,
   crushing his head.

309

With a shattering blow, she pierced his
  temples.
27 He sank, he fell,
  he lay still at her feet.
And where he sank,
  there he died.

28 "From the window Sisera's mother
  looked out.
Through the window she watched for
  his return, saying,
'Why is his chariot so long in coming?
Why don't we hear the sound of chariot
  wheels?'

29 "Her wise women answer,
  and she repeats these words to herself:
30 'They must be dividing the captured
    plunder—
  with a woman or two for every man.
There will be colorful robes for Sisera,
  and colorful, embroidered robes for me.
Yes, the plunder will include
  colorful robes embroidered on both
    sides.'

31 "LORD, may all your enemies die like Sisera!
  But may those who love you rise like
    the sun in all its power!"

Then there was peace in the land for forty
years.

CHAPTER 6
Gideon Becomes Israel's Judge

The Israelites did evil in the LORD's sight. So
the LORD handed them over to the Midianites
for seven years. 2 The Midianites were so cruel
that the Israelites made hiding places for
themselves in the mountains, caves, and
strongholds. 3 Whenever the Israelites planted
their crops, marauders from Midian, Amalek,
and the people of the east would attack Israel,
4 camping in the land and destroying crops as
far away as Gaza. They left the Israelites with
nothing to eat, taking all the sheep, goats,
cattle, and donkeys. 5 These enemy hordes,
coming with their livestock and tents, were as
thick as locusts; they arrived on droves of
camels too numerous to count. And they
stayed until the land was stripped bare. 6 So Israel was reduced to starvation by the Midianites. Then the Israelites cried out to the LORD
for help.

7 When they cried out to the LORD because
of Midian, 8 the LORD sent a prophet to the Israelites. He said, "This is what the LORD, the
God of Israel, says: I brought you up out of
slavery in Egypt. 9 I rescued you from the
Egyptians and from all who oppressed you. I
drove out your enemies and gave you their
land. 10 I told you, 'I am the LORD your God.
You must not worship the gods of the Amorites, in whose land you now live.' But you
have not listened to me."

11 Then the angel of the LORD came and sat
beneath the great tree at Ophrah, which belonged to Joash of the clan of Abiezer. Gideon
son of Joash was threshing wheat at the bottom of a winepress to hide the grain from the
Midianites. 12 The angel of the LORD appeared
to him and said, "Mighty hero, the LORD is
with you!"

13 "Sir," Gideon replied, "if the LORD is with
us, why has all this happened to us? And where
are all the miracles our ancestors told us about?
Didn't they say, 'The LORD brought us up out of
Egypt'? But now the LORD has abandoned us
and handed us over to the Midianites."

14 Then the LORD turned to him and said,
"Go with the strength you have, and rescue
Israel from the Midianites. I am sending
you!"

15 "But Lord," Gideon replied, "how can I
rescue Israel? My clan is the weakest in the
whole tribe of Manasseh, and I am the least
in my entire family!"

16 The LORD said to him, "I will be with

6:11-15 Gideon responded to the angel's message with little faith or hope. He was so used to the
oppression of the Midianites that he had little confidence that things could ever be any different.
Not only did Gideon view himself as weak and insignificant, he also viewed God with distrust, as
being unfaithful to his covenant people. This is a typical response of a person trying to cope with
terrible circumstances. We become so worn down by continuous pain that we lose hope of ever
breaking free. We are deeply aware of our helplessness. But this is the starting point for recovery.
Gideon had admitted that he was helpless; now he only needed to discover that God was able to
deliver him.

6:22-40 Gideon's responses to God alternated between faith and fear. It took courage to build the
altars to God and to tear down the altar to Baal. He also blew the trumpet of assembly for those
who would fight for God. Yet his fears limited him to destroying the place of idol worship in the
middle of the night and questioning God's leadership (as seen in the fleece incident). Similarly many
of us use any excuse we can think of to not face what we fear. Fear is healthy; it can warn us of
dangers and prompt us to be careful. But it should not stop us from doing what we know is right.

GIDEON

In times of trouble, we often search for the thunder and lightning of God's voice and direction. Mistakenly, we think that God will provide us with the solutions we seek in some spectacular way. The truth of the matter is that the answers often lie within us.

Gideon struggled in his commitment to God. Day in and day out he sought food and shelter for his family in a land constantly raided by hostile invaders. Gideon was under extreme pressure to remain resourceful in the face of his enemies. His deliverance came in an unexpected way.

God called Gideon to deliver the Israelites from the rule of their oppressors. Like many of us, Gideon felt inadequate in the face of a great task. He obeyed, but his doubts kept him dragging his feet. He waited time and again for confirmations of what God had already told him to do.

Many of us feel weak and think we are a failure. We question God's interest in our life or our situation. Just as Gideon already had the talents and resourcefulness that God needed, often we already have within us what God needs to overcome our obstacles. Even when our faith wavers, God empowers us as we act.

STRENGTHS AND ACCOMPLISHMENTS:
- Gideon acted on his growing convictions, even when his faith wavered.
- He was responsible, even when times were difficult.
- He led 300 men to defeat 135,000 Midianites.

WEAKNESSES AND MISTAKES:
- Gideon was afraid to trust God because of his personal limitations.
- He failed to influence his family to follow after God's ways.
- He made a symbol from Midianite gold that was used for ungodly worship.

LESSONS FROM HIS LIFE:
- God gives us more responsibility as we are faithful.
- God uses each of us despite our personal limitations.
- Even in the wake of great victory, we are still capable of making mistakes.

KEY VERSE:
"The LORD said to him, 'I will be with you. And you will destroy the Midianites as if you were fighting against one man'" (Judges 6:16).

Gideon's story is told in Judges 6–8. Gideon is also mentioned in Hebrews 11:32.

---

you. And you will destroy the Midianites as if you were fighting against one man."

[17]Gideon replied, "If you are truly going to help me, show me a sign to prove that it is really the LORD speaking to me. [18]Don't go away until I come back and bring my offering to you."

He answered, "I will stay here until you return."

[19]Gideon hurried home. He cooked a young goat, and with a basket* of flour he baked some bread without yeast. Then, carrying the meat in a basket and the broth in a pot, he brought them out and presented them to the angel, who was under the great tree.

[20]The angel of God said to him, "Place the meat and the unleavened bread on this rock, and pour the broth over it." And Gideon did as he was told. [21]Then the angel of the LORD touched the meat and bread with the tip of the staff in his hand, and fire flamed up from the rock and consumed all he had brought. And the angel of the LORD disappeared.

[22]When Gideon realized that it was the angel of the LORD, he cried out, "Oh, Sovereign LORD, I'm doomed! I have seen the angel of the LORD face to face!"

[23]"It is all right," the LORD replied. "Do not be afraid. You will not die." [24]And Gideon built an altar to the LORD there and named it Yahweh-Shalom (which means "the LORD is peace"). The altar remains in Ophrah in the land of the clan of Abiezer to this day.

[25]That night the LORD said to Gideon, "Take the second bull from your father's herd, the one that is seven years old. Pull down your father's altar to Baal, and cut down the Asherah pole standing beside it. [26]Then build an altar to the LORD your God here on this hilltop sanctuary, laying the stones carefully. Sacrifice the bull as a burnt

6:19 Hebrew *an ephah* [20 quarts or 22 liters].

offering on the altar, using as fuel the wood of the Asherah pole you cut down."

27So Gideon took ten of his servants and did as the LORD had commanded. But he did it at night because he was afraid of the other members of his father's household and the people of the town.

28Early the next morning, as the people of the town began to stir, someone discovered that the altar of Baal had been broken down and that the Asherah pole beside it had been cut down. In their place a new altar had been built, and on it were the remains of the bull that had been sacrificed. 29The people said to each other, "Who did this?" And after asking around and making a careful search, they learned that it was Gideon, the son of Joash.

30"Bring out your son," the men of the town demanded of Joash. "He must die for destroying the altar of Baal and for cutting down the Asherah pole."

31But Joash shouted to the mob that confronted him, "Why are you defending Baal? Will you argue his case? Whoever pleads his case will be put to death by morning! If Baal truly is a god, let him defend himself and destroy the one who broke down his altar!" 32From then on Gideon was called Jerub-baal, which means "Let Baal defend himself," because he broke down Baal's altar.

Gideon Asks for a Sign

33Soon afterward the armies of Midian, Amalek, and the people of the east formed an alliance against Israel and crossed the Jordan, camping in the valley of Jezreel. 34Then the Spirit of the LORD clothed Gideon with power. He blew a ram's horn as a call to arms, and the men of the clan of Abiezer came to him. 35He also sent messengers throughout Manasseh, Asher, Zebulun, and Naphtali, summoning their warriors, and all of them responded.

36Then Gideon said to God, "If you are truly going to use me to rescue Israel as you promised, 37prove it to me in this way. I will put a wool fleece on the threshing floor tonight. If the fleece is wet with dew in the

morning but the ground is dry, then I will know that you are going to help me rescue Israel as you promised." 38And that is just what happened. When Gideon got up early the next morning, he squeezed the fleece and wrung out a whole bowlful of water.

39Then Gideon said to God, "Please don't be angry with me, but let me make one more request. Let me use the fleece for one more test. This time let the fleece remain dry while the ground around it is wet with dew." 40So that night God did as Gideon asked. The fleece was dry in the morning, but the ground was covered with dew.

CHAPTER 7
Gideon Defeats the Midianites

So Jerub-baal (that is, Gideon) and his army got up early and went as far as the spring of Harod. The armies of Midian were camped north of them in the valley near the hill of Moreh. 2The LORD said to Gideon, "You have too many warriors with you. If I let all of you fight the Midianites, the Israelites will boast to me that they saved themselves by their own strength. 3Therefore, tell the people, 'Whoever is timid or afraid may leave this mountain* and go home.'" So 22,000 of them went home, leaving only 10,000 who were willing to fight.

4But the LORD told Gideon, "There are still too many! Bring them down to the spring, and I will test them to determine who will go with you and who will not." 5When Gideon took his warriors down to the water, the LORD told him, "Divide the men into two groups. In one group put all those who cup water in their hands and lap it up with their tongues like dogs. In the other group put all those who kneel down and drink with their mouths in the stream." 6Only 300 of the men drank from their hands. All the others got down on their knees and drank with their mouths in the stream.

7The LORD told Gideon, "With these 300 men I will rescue you and give you victory over the Midianites. Send all the others home." 8So Gideon collected the provisions and rams' horns of the other warriors and

---

7:3 Hebrew *may leave Mount Gilead.* The identity of Mount Gilead is uncertain in this context. It is perhaps used here as another name for Mount Gilboa.

7:4-7 In further streamlining the fighting force from 10,000 to 300, God demonstrated to Gideon that he was looking for men who most consistently faced the reality of their present circumstances, keeping watch for the enemy while drinking. Facing the present reality is crucial to success in the recovery process. If we are constantly in touch with reality, we will not fall victim to sneak attacks—we will expect struggles with temptation. We can only combat our problems when we remain alert.

GOD grant me the serenity to accept the things I cannot change the courage to change the things I can and the wisdom to know the difference AMEN

We may begin to believe that we are destined to bondage, poverty, and failure. When we persist in this view of our life, we give up the possibility of change. We settle for just trying to survive. We live in fear and shame, filling up with resentment as our life remains in the pit. We need to overcome these kinds of negative assumptions about ourself.

Our first impression of Gideon is of a discouraged young man with little self-respect. His family was the poorest in a small tribe, and he was the least in his family. We first see him as he was threshing wheat in a winepress, hiding the little grain he had from his Midianite oppressors. An angel appeared and called to him, "Mighty hero, the LORD is with you!" (Judges 6:12). Gideon didn't look or feel like a mighty hero, but God could see his potential. By the end of the story, Gideon had become the deliverer of his people (Judges 6—8). His first step toward success was to see himself as God saw him—a mighty warrior. Then he was able to hope in the possibility of freedom.

We, too, must begin by finding the courage to see ourselves in a new light and to summon up hope for a better life. Then as God gives us the strength, we can set about pursuing freedom from the bondage that surrounds us and our family. ***Turn to page 363, 1 Samuel 15.***

For those of us who have lived in bondage to addictive/compulsive behaviors, loss of self-respect is a familiar feeling. It is easy to begin to see ourselves as chronically weak, small, even hopeless.

---

sent them home. But he kept the 300 men with him.

The Midianite camp was in the valley just below Gideon. ⁹That night the LORD said, "Get up! Go down into the Midianite camp, for I have given you victory over them! ¹⁰But if you are afraid to attack, go down to the camp with your servant Purah. ¹¹Listen to what the Midianites are saying, and you will be greatly encouraged. Then you will be eager to attack."

So Gideon took Purah and went down to the edge of the enemy camp. ¹²The armies of Midian, Amalek, and the people of the east had settled in the valley like a swarm of locusts. Their camels were like grains of sand on the seashore—too many to count! ¹³Gideon crept up just as a man was telling his companion about a dream. The man said, "I had this dream, and in my dream a loaf of barley bread came tumbling down into the Midianite camp. It hit a tent, turned it over, and knocked it flat!"

¹⁴His companion answered, "Your dream can mean only one thing—God has given Gideon son of Joash, the Israelite, victory over Midian and all its allies!"

¹⁵When Gideon heard the dream and its interpretation, he bowed in worship before the LORD.* Then he returned to the Israelite camp and shouted, "Get up! For the LORD has given you victory over the Midianite hordes!" ¹⁶He divided the 300 men into three groups and gave each man a ram's horn and a clay jar with a torch in it.

¹⁷Then he said to them, "Keep your eyes on me. When I come to the edge of the camp, do just as I do. ¹⁸As soon as I and those with me blow the rams' horns, blow your horns, too, all around the entire camp, and shout, 'For the LORD and for Gideon!'"

¹⁹It was just after midnight,* after the changing of the guard, when Gideon and the 100 men with him reached the edge of the Midianite camp. Suddenly, they blew the

---

7:15 As in Greek version; Hebrew reads *he bowed.* 7:19 Hebrew *at the beginning of the second watch.*

rams' horns and broke their clay jars. ²⁰Then all three groups blew their horns and broke their jars. They held the blazing torches in their left hands and the horns in their right hands, and they all shouted, "A sword for the LORD and for Gideon!"

²¹Each man stood at his position around the camp and watched as all the Midianites rushed around in a panic, shouting as they ran to escape. ²²When the 300 Israelites blew their rams' horns, the LORD caused the warriors in the camp to fight against each other with their swords. Those who were not killed fled to places as far away as Beth-shittah near Zererah and to the border of Abel-meholah near Tabbath.

²³Then Gideon sent for the warriors of Naphtali, Asher, and Manasseh, who joined in chasing the army of Midian. ²⁴Gideon also sent messengers throughout the hill country of Ephraim, saying, "Come down to attack the Midianites. Cut them off at the shallow crossings of the Jordan River at Beth-barah."

So all the men of Ephraim did as they were told. ²⁵They captured Oreb and Zeeb, the two Midianite commanders, killing Oreb at the rock of Oreb, and Zeeb at the winepress of Zeeb. And they continued to chase the Midianites. Afterward the Israelites brought the heads of Oreb and Zeeb to Gideon, who was by the Jordan River.

CHAPTER 8
Gideon Kills Zebah and Zalmunna

Then the people of Ephraim asked Gideon, "Why have you treated us this way? Why didn't you send for us when you first went out to fight the Midianites?" And they argued heatedly with Gideon.

²But Gideon replied, "What have I accomplished compared to you? Aren't even the leftover grapes of Ephraim's harvest better than the entire crop of my little clan of Abiezer? ³God gave you victory over Oreb and

Zeeb, the commanders of the Midianite army. What have I accomplished compared to that?" When the men of Ephraim heard Gideon's answer, their anger subsided.

⁴Gideon then crossed the Jordan River with his 300 men, and though exhausted, they continued to chase the enemy. ⁵When they reached Succoth, Gideon asked the leaders of the town, "Please give my warriors some food. They are very tired. I am chasing Zebah and Zalmunna, the kings of Midian."

⁶But the officials of Succoth replied, "Catch Zebah and Zalmunna first, and then we will feed your army."

⁷So Gideon said, "After the LORD gives me victory over Zebah and Zalmunna, I will return and tear your flesh with the thorns and briers from the wilderness."

⁸From there Gideon went up to Peniel* and again asked for food, but he got the same answer. ⁹So he said to the people of Peniel, "After I return in victory, I will tear down this tower."

¹⁰By this time Zebah and Zalmunna were in Karkor with about 15,000 warriors—all that remained of the allied armies of the east, for 120,000 had already been killed. ¹¹Gideon circled around by the caravan route east of Nobah and Jogbehah, taking the Midianite army by surprise. ¹²Zebah and Zalmunna, the two Midianite kings, fled, but Gideon chased them down and captured all their warriors.

¹³After this, Gideon returned from the battle by way of Heres Pass. ¹⁴There he captured a young man from Succoth and demanded that he write down the names of all the seventy-seven officials and elders in the town. ¹⁵Gideon then returned to Succoth and said to the leaders, "Here are Zebah and Zalmunna. When we were here before, you taunted me, saying, 'Catch Zebah and Zalmunna first, and then we will feed your exhausted army.'" ¹⁶Then Gideon took the elders of the town and taught them a lesson,

8:8 Hebrew *Penuel*, a variant spelling of Peniel; also in 8:9, 17.

7:24–8:3 Gideon's patient handling of the temperamental Ephraimite leaders reflects a great deal of progress in overcoming his feelings of personal inadequacy (6:15). In contrast to the anger of Ephraim's leaders, Gideon displayed great self-control and wisdom as a leader. He was willing to go to great lengths to set things straight. Self-control and wisdom are important elements of the recovery process.

8:4-21 This pursuit and execution of the Midianite kings are a striking example of perseverance on Gideon's part. In clear contrast to the tribes of Israel who had failed to finish the job of driving out the Canaanites, Gideon continued until the Midianite forces were completely defeated. He reversed the previous oppressive situation completely, opening the doorway to a new life of freedom for Israel. We should follow Gideon's example, doing all we can to escape oppression from our dependencies. God will help us to accomplish this; then he will help us go on to build a new life.

punishing them with thorns and briers from the wilderness. [17]He also tore down the tower of Peniel and killed all the men in the town.

[18]Then Gideon asked Zebah and Zalmunna, "The men you killed at Tabor—what were they like?"

"Like you," they replied. "They all had the look of a king's son."

[19]"They were my brothers, the sons of my own mother!" Gideon exclaimed. "As surely as the LORD lives, I wouldn't kill you if you hadn't killed them."

[20]Turning to Jether, his oldest son, he said, "Kill them!" But Jether did not draw his sword, for he was only a boy and was afraid.

[21]Then Zebah and Zalmunna said to Gideon, "Be a man! Kill us yourself!" So Gideon killed them both and took the royal ornaments from the necks of their camels.

Gideon's Sacred Ephod

[22]Then the Israelites said to Gideon, "Be our ruler! You and your son and your grandson will be our rulers, for you have rescued us from Midian."

[23]But Gideon replied, "I will not rule over you, nor will my son. The LORD will rule over you! [24]However, I do have one request—that each of you give me an earring from the plunder you collected from your fallen enemies." (The enemies, being Ishmaelites, all wore gold earrings.)

[25]"Gladly!" they replied. They spread out a cloak, and each one threw in a gold earring he had gathered from the plunder. [26]The weight of the gold earrings was forty-three pounds,* not including the royal ornaments and pendants, the purple clothing worn by the kings of Midian, or the chains around the necks of their camels.

[27]Gideon made a sacred ephod from the gold and put it in Ophrah, his hometown. But soon all the Israelites prostituted themselves by worshiping it, and it became a trap for Gideon and his family.

[28]That is the story of how the people of Israel defeated Midian, which never recovered. Throughout the rest of Gideon's lifetime—about forty years—there was peace in the land.

[29]Then Gideon* son of Joash returned home. [30]He had seventy sons born to him, for he had many wives. [31]He also had a concubine in Shechem, who gave birth to a son, whom he named Abimelech. [32]Gideon died when he was very old, and he was buried in the grave of his father, Joash, at Ophrah in the land of the clan of Abiezer.

[33]As soon as Gideon died, the Israelites prostituted themselves by worshiping the images of Baal, making Baal-berith their god. [34]They forgot the LORD their God, who had rescued them from all their enemies surrounding them. [35]Nor did they show any loyalty to the family of Jerub-baal (that is, Gideon), despite all the good he had done for Israel.

CHAPTER 9
Abimelech Rules over Shechem

One day Gideon's* son Abimelech went to Shechem to visit his uncles—his mother's brothers. He said to them and to the rest of his mother's family, [2]"Ask the leading citizens of Shechem whether they want to be ruled by all seventy of Gideon's sons or by one man. And remember that I am your own flesh and blood!"

8:26 Hebrew *1,700 [shekels]* [19.4 kilograms]. 8:29 Hebrew *Jerub-baal;* see 6:32. 9:1 Hebrew *Jerub-baal's* (see 6:32); also in 9:2, 24.

8:22-35 Once again the Israelites turned from the true God and worshiped idols. The ephod Gideon made to commemorate the defeat of the Midianites was soon worshiped by the people. And later, after Gideon's death, the Israelites went back to worshiping Baal and Baal-berith. The people still did not recognize the cycle of disobedience and oppression. We must not be like the Israelites but should learn from our past experiences. When tempted to return to old addictions, we need to remember the consequences of those behaviors and persevere in recovery.

9:1-57 Abimelech, Gideon's son by a concubine (8:31), proved to be the opposite of his father. Gideon rightly refused kingship over Israel; Abimelech not only demanded it, but he also attempted to kill anyone who stood in his way. Abimelech died as violently as he lived. None of the faith, patience, and honesty that characterized Gideon is seen in Abimelech, perhaps indicating serious deficiencies in his childhood years. Even someone who demonstrates strong leadership ability outside the home environment needs to take care to positively influence his or her children as well. If children do not spend time with godly parental examples, they may grow up with no positive role models to follow. If we don't teach our children to walk in God's ways, they may grow up to flout them, like Abimelech. But neither should we blame our childhood environment for the mistakes we have made. Even if we have grown up in a dysfunctional family, we still have hope for recovery through Jesus Christ.

[3]So Abimelech's uncles gave his message to all the citizens of Shechem on his behalf. And after listening to this proposal, the people of Shechem decided in favor of Abimelech because he was their relative. [4]They gave him seventy silver coins from the temple of Baal-berith, which he used to hire some reckless troublemakers who agreed to follow him. [5]He went to his father's home at Ophrah, and there, on one stone, they killed all seventy of his half brothers, the sons of Gideon.* But the youngest brother, Jotham, escaped and hid.

[6]Then all the leading citizens of Shechem and Beth-millo called a meeting under the oak beside the pillar* at Shechem and made Abimelech their king.

Jotham's Parable

[7]When Jotham heard about this, he climbed to the top of Mount Gerizim and shouted,

"Listen to me, citizens of Shechem!
　　Listen to me if you want God to listen
　　　to you!
[8] Once upon a time the trees decided to
　　　choose a king.
　　First they said to the olive tree,
　　　'Be our king!'
[9] But the olive tree refused, saying,
　　'Should I quit producing the olive oil
　　　that blesses both God and people,
　　　just to wave back and forth over the
　　　　trees?'
[10] "Then they said to the fig tree,
　　　'You be our king!'
[11] But the fig tree also refused, saying,
　　'Should I quit producing my sweet fruit
　　　just to wave back and forth over the
　　　　trees?'
[12] "Then they said to the grapevine,
　　　'You be our king!'
[13] But the grapevine also refused, saying,
　　'Should I quit producing the wine
　　　that cheers both God and people,
　　　just to wave back and forth over the
　　　　trees?'
[14] "Then all the trees finally turned to the
　　　thornbush and said,
　　　'Come, you be our king!'
[15] And the thornbush replied to the trees,
　　'If you truly want to make me your king,
　　　come and take shelter in my shade.
　　If not, let fire come out from me
　　　and devour the cedars of Lebanon.'"

[16]Jotham continued, "Now make sure you have acted honorably and in good faith by making Abimelech your king, and that you have done right by Gideon and all of his descendants. Have you treated him with the honor he deserves for all he accomplished? [17]For he fought for you and risked his life when he rescued you from the Midianites. [18]But today you have revolted against my father and his descendants, killing his seventy sons on one stone. And you have chosen his slave woman's son, Abimelech, to be your king just because he is your relative.

[19]"If you have acted honorably and in good faith toward Gideon and his descendants today, then may you find joy in Abimelech, and may he find joy in you. [20]But if you have not acted in good faith, then may fire come out from Abimelech and devour the leading citizens of Shechem and Beth-millo; and may fire come out from the citizens of Shechem and Beth-millo and devour Abimelech!"

[21]Then Jotham escaped and lived in Beer because he was afraid of his brother Abimelech.

Shechem Rebels against Abimelech

[22]After Abimelech had ruled over Israel for three years, [23]God sent a spirit that stirred up trouble between Abimelech and the leading citizens of Shechem, and they revolted. [24]God was punishing Abimelech for murdering Gideon's seventy sons, and the citizens of Shechem for supporting him in this treachery of murdering his brothers. [25]The citizens of Shechem set an ambush for Abimelech on the hilltops and robbed everyone who passed that way. But someone warned Abimelech about their plot.

[26]One day Gaal son of Ebed moved to Shechem with his brothers and gained the confidence of the leading citizens of Shechem. [27]During the annual harvest festival at Shechem, held in the temple of the local god, the wine flowed freely, and everyone began cursing Abimelech. [28]"Who is Abimelech?" Gaal shouted. "He's not a true son of Shechem,* so why should we be his servants? He's merely the son of Gideon, and this Zebul is merely his deputy. Serve the true sons of Hamor, the founder of Shechem. Why should we serve Abimelech? [29]If I were in charge here, I would get rid of Abimelech. I would say* to him, 'Get some soldiers, and come out and fight!'"

9:5 Hebrew *Jerub-baal* (see 6:32); also in 9:16, 19, 28, 57.　9:6 The meaning of the Hebrew is uncertain.　9:28 Hebrew *Who is Shechem?*　9:29 As in Greek version; Hebrew reads *And he said.*

[30]But when Zebul, the leader of the city, heard what Gaal was saying, he was furious. [31]He sent messengers to Abimelech in Arumah,* telling him, "Gaal son of Ebed and his brothers have come to live in Shechem, and now they are inciting the city to rebel against you. [32]Come by night with an army and hide out in the fields. [33]In the morning, as soon as it is daylight, attack the city. When Gaal and those who are with him come out against you, you can do with them as you wish."

[34]So Abimelech and all his men went by night and split into four groups, stationing themselves around Shechem. [35]Gaal was standing at the city gates when Abimelech and his army came out of hiding. [36]When Gaal saw them, he said to Zebul, "Look, there are people coming down from the hilltops!"

Zebul replied, "It's just the shadows on the hills that look like men."

[37]But again Gaal said, "No, people are coming down from the hills.* And another group is coming down the road past the Diviners' Oak.*"

[38]Then Zebul turned on him and asked, "Now where is that big mouth of yours? Wasn't it you that said, 'Who is Abimelech, and why should we be his servants?' The men you mocked are right outside the city! Go out and fight them!"

[39]So Gaal led the leading citizens of Shechem into battle against Abimelech. [40]But Abimelech chased him, and many of Shechem's men were wounded and fell along the road as they retreated to the city gate. [41]Abimelech returned to Arumah, and Zebul drove Gaal and his brothers out of Shechem.

[42]The next day the people of Shechem went out into the fields to battle. When Abimelech heard about it, [43]he divided his men into three groups and set an ambush in the fields. When Abimelech saw the people coming out of the city, he and his men jumped up from their hiding places and attacked them. [44]Abimelech and his group stormed the city gate to keep the men of Shechem from getting back in, while Abimelech's other two groups cut them down in the fields. [45]The battle went on all day before Abimelech finally captured the city. He killed the people, leveled the city, and scattered salt all over the ground.

[46]When the leading citizens who lived in the tower of Shechem heard what had happened, they ran and hid in the temple of Baal-berith.* [47]Someone reported to Abimelech that the citizens had gathered in the temple, [48]so he led his forces to Mount Zalmon. He took an ax and chopped some branches from a tree, then put them on his shoulder. "Quick, do as I have done!" he told his men. [49]So each of them cut down some branches, following Abimelech's example. They piled the branches against the walls of the temple and set them on fire. So all the people who had lived in the tower of Shechem died— about 1,000 men and women.

[50]Then Abimelech attacked the town of Thebez and captured it. [51]But there was a strong tower inside the town, and all the men and women—the entire population— fled to it. They barricaded themselves in and climbed up to the roof of the tower. [52]Abimelech followed them to attack the tower. But as he prepared to set fire to the entrance, [53]a woman on the roof dropped a millstone that landed on Abimelech's head and crushed his skull.

[54]He quickly said to his young armor bearer, "Draw your sword and kill me! Don't let it be said that a woman killed Abimelech!" So the young man ran him through with his sword, and he died. [55]When Abimelech's men saw that he was dead, they disbanded and returned to their homes.

[56]In this way, God punished Abimelech for the evil he had done against his father by murdering his seventy brothers. [57]God also punished the men of Shechem for all their evil. So the curse of Jotham son of Gideon was fulfilled.

CHAPTER 10
Tola Becomes Israel's Judge
After Abimelech died, Tola son of Puah, son of Dodo, was the next person to rescue Israel. He was from the tribe of Issachar but lived in the

9:31 Or *in secret;* Hebrew reads *in Tormah;* compare 9:41. 9:37a Or *the center of the land.* 9:37b Hebrew *Elon-meonenim.* 9:46 Hebrew *El-berith,* another name for Baal-berith; compare 9:4.

10:1-18 After suffering under Abimelech's leadership (Judges 9), Israel experienced 45 stable years under the leadership of Tola and Jair. But Israel's spiritual recovery was still by no means complete. In fact, after Jair died, the Israelites' denial of their sins was so strong that it took them 18 years to admit their helplessness and look to God for help. If we are honest with ourself, we will not have to suffer 18 years before realizing the consequences of our dependencies. It should be obvious when we start straying from God's will. If we keep our eyes open, we will be able to take immediate steps to get back on the right path.

town of Shamir in the hill country of Ephraim. ²He judged Israel for twenty-three years. When he died, he was buried in Shamir.

Jair Becomes Israel's Judge

³After Tola died, Jair from Gilead judged Israel for twenty-two years. ⁴His thirty sons rode around on thirty donkeys, and they owned thirty towns in the land of Gilead, which are still called the Towns of Jair.* ⁵When Jair died, he was buried in Kamon.

The Ammonites Oppress Israel

⁶Again the Israelites did evil in the LORD's sight. They served the images of Baal and Ashtoreth, and the gods of Aram, Sidon, Moab, Ammon, and Philistia. They abandoned the LORD and no longer served him at all. ⁷So the LORD burned with anger against Israel, and he turned them over to the Philistines and the Ammonites, ⁸who began to oppress them that year. For eighteen years they oppressed all the Israelites east of the Jordan River in the land of the Amorites (that is, in Gilead). ⁹The Ammonites also crossed to the west side of the Jordan and attacked Judah, Benjamin, and Ephraim.

The Israelites were in great distress. ¹⁰Finally, they cried out to the LORD for help, saying, "We have sinned against you because we have abandoned you as our God and have served the images of Baal."

¹¹The LORD replied, "Did I not rescue you from the Egyptians, the Amorites, the Ammonites, the Philistines, ¹²the Sidonians, the Amalekites, and the Maonites? When they oppressed you, you cried out to me for help, and I rescued you. ¹³Yet you have abandoned me and served other gods. So I will not rescue you anymore. ¹⁴Go and cry out to the gods you have chosen! Let them rescue you in your hour of distress!"

¹⁵But the Israelites pleaded with the LORD and said, "We have sinned. Punish us as you see fit, only rescue us today from our enemies." ¹⁶Then the Israelites put aside their foreign gods and served the LORD. And he was grieved by their misery.

¹⁷At that time the armies of Ammon had

10:4 Hebrew *Havvoth-jair.*

gathered for war and were camped in Gilead, and the people of Israel assembled and camped at Mizpah. ¹⁸The leaders of Gilead said to each other, "Whoever attacks the Ammonites first will become ruler over all the people of Gilead."

CHAPTER 11
Jephthah Becomes Israel's Judge

Now Jephthah of Gilead was a great warrior. He was the son of Gilead, but his mother was a prostitute. ²Gilead's wife also had several sons, and when these half brothers grew up, they chased Jephthah off the land. "You will not get any of our father's inheritance," they said, "for you are the son of a prostitute." ³So Jephthah fled from his brothers and lived in the land of Tob. Soon he had a band of worthless rebels following him.

⁴At about this time, the Ammonites began their war against Israel. ⁵When the Ammonites attacked, the elders of Gilead sent for Jephthah in the land of Tob. ⁶The elders said, "Come and be our commander! Help us fight the Ammonites!"

⁷But Jephthah said to them, "Aren't you the ones who hated me and drove me from my father's house? Why do you come to me now when you're in trouble?"

⁸"Because we need you," the elders replied. "If you lead us in battle against the Ammonites, we will make you ruler over all the people of Gilead."

⁹Jephthah said to the elders, "Let me get this straight. If I come with you and if the LORD gives me victory over the Ammonites, will you really make me ruler over all the people?"

¹⁰"The LORD is our witness," the elders replied. "We promise to do whatever you say."

¹¹So Jephthah went with the elders of Gilead, and the people made him their ruler and commander of the army. At Mizpah, in the presence of the LORD, Jephthah repeated what he had said to the elders.

¹²Then Jephthah sent messengers to the king of Ammon, asking, "Why have you come out to fight against my land?"

¹³The king of Ammon answered Jeph-

11:12-28 Jephthah displayed great self-control by patiently confronting the Ammonite king about his attacks upon Israel. Considering the hunger for power that propels most oppressive people, it was unlikely that Jephthah would be able to persuade the Ammonites to stop their unprovoked attacks. Still, he argued his case well, even though it was totally disregarded. We are called to try to make peace and speak the truth. It is not our responsibility, however, if others do not listen to us. We can only try to get them to see the truth.

thah's messengers, "When the Israelites came out of Egypt, they stole my land from the Arnon River to the Jabbok River and all the way to the Jordan. Now then, give back the land peaceably."

[14]Jephthah sent this message back to the Ammonite king:

[15]"This is what Jephthah says: Israel did not steal any land from Moab or Ammon. [16]When the people of Israel arrived at Kadesh on their journey from Egypt after crossing the Red Sea,* [17]they sent messengers to the king of Edom asking for permission to pass through his land. But their request was denied. Then they asked the king of Moab for similar permission, but he wouldn't let them pass through either. So the people of Israel stayed in Kadesh.

[18]"Finally, they went around Edom and Moab through the wilderness. They traveled along Moab's eastern border and camped on the other side of the Arnon River. But they never once crossed the Arnon River into Moab, for the Arnon was the border of Moab.

[19]"Then Israel sent messengers to King Sihon of the Amorites, who ruled from Heshbon, asking for permission to cross through his land to get to their destination. [20]But King Sihon didn't trust Israel to pass through his land. Instead, he mobilized his army at Jahaz and attacked them. [21]But the LORD, the God of Israel, gave his people victory over King Sihon. So Israel took control of all the land of the Amorites, who lived in that region, [22]from the Arnon River to the Jabbok River, and from the eastern wilderness to the Jordan.

[23]"So you see, it was the LORD, the God of Israel, who took away the land from the Amorites and gave it to Israel. Why, then, should we give it back to you? [24]You keep whatever your god Chemosh gives you, and we will keep whatever the LORD our God gives us. [25]Are you any better than Balak son of Zippor, king of Moab? Did he try to make a case against Israel for disputed land? Did he go to war against them?

[26]"Israel has been living here for 300 years, inhabiting Heshbon and its surrounding settlements, all the way to Aroer and its settlements, and in all the towns along the Arnon River. Why have you made no effort to recover it before now? [27]Therefore, I have not sinned against you. Rather, you have wronged me by attacking me. Let the LORD, who is judge, decide today which of us is right—Israel or Ammon."

[28]But the king of Ammon paid no attention to Jephthah's message.

Jephthah's Vow

[29]At that time the Spirit of the LORD came upon Jephthah, and he went throughout the land of Gilead and Manasseh, including Mizpah in Gilead, and from there he led an army against the Ammonites. [30]And Jephthah made a vow to the LORD. He said, "If you give me victory over the Ammonites, [31]I will give to the LORD whatever comes out of my house to meet me when I return in triumph. I will sacrifice it as a burnt offering."

[32]So Jephthah led his army against the Ammonites, and the LORD gave him victory. [33]He crushed the Ammonites, devastating about twenty towns from Aroer to an area near Minnith and as far away as Abel-keramim. In this way Israel defeated the Ammonites.

[34]When Jephthah returned home to Mizpah, his daughter came out to meet him, playing on a tambourine and dancing for joy. She was his one and only child; he had no other sons or daughters. [35]When he saw her, he tore his clothes in anguish. "Oh, my daughter!" he cried out. "You have completely destroyed me! You've brought disaster on me! For I have made a vow to the LORD, and I cannot take it back."

[36]And she said, "Father, if you have made a vow to the LORD, you must do to me what you have vowed, for the LORD has given you a great victory over your enemies, the Ammonites. [37]But first let me do this one thing: Let me go up and roam in the hills and weep

11:16 Hebrew *sea of reeds.*

11:29-40 Jephthah's recovery and leadership were guided by the Holy Spirit, but he still made a foolish mistake. His vow, which was an attempt to "cut a deal" with God to ensure military victory, is a classic example of what it means to "stifle the Holy Spirit" (1 Thessalonians 5:19). Jephthah lived to regret the vow made in the heat of the crisis. Often we do the same thing. We beg for God to fulfill some shortsighted goal, and in obtaining it, we miss God's best.

with my friends for two months, because I will die a virgin."

³⁸"You may go," Jephthah said. And he sent her away for two months. She and her friends went into the hills and wept because she would never have children. ³⁹When she returned home, her father kept the vow he had made, and she died a virgin.

So it has become a custom in Israel ⁴⁰for young Israelite women to go away for four days each year to lament the fate of Jephthah's daughter.

CHAPTER 12
Ephraim Fights with Jephthah
Then the people of Ephraim mobilized an army and crossed over the Jordan River to Zaphon. They sent this message to Jephthah: "Why didn't you call for us to help you fight against the Ammonites? We are going to burn down your house with you in it!"

²Jephthah replied, "I summoned you at the beginning of the dispute, but you refused to come! You failed to help us in our struggle against Ammon. ³So when I realized you weren't coming, I risked my life and went to battle without you, and the LORD gave me victory over the Ammonites. So why have you now come to fight me?"

⁴The people of Ephraim responded, "You men of Gilead are nothing more than fugitives from Ephraim and Manasseh." So Jephthah gathered all the men of Gilead and attacked the men of Ephraim and defeated them.

⁵Jephthah captured the shallow crossings of the Jordan River, and whenever a fugitive from Ephraim tried to go back across, the men of Gilead would challenge him. "Are you a member of the tribe of Ephraim?" they would ask. If the man said, "No, I'm not," ⁶they would tell him to say "Shibboleth." If

he was from Ephraim, he would say "Sibboleth," because people from Ephraim cannot pronounce the word correctly. Then they would take him and kill him at the shallow crossings of the Jordan. In all, 42,000 Ephraimites were killed at that time.

⁷Jephthah judged Israel for six years. When he died, he was buried in one of the towns of Gilead.

Ibzan Becomes Israel's Judge
⁸After Jephthah died, Ibzan from Bethlehem judged Israel. ⁹He had thirty sons and thirty daughters. He sent his daughters to marry men outside his clan, and he brought in thirty young women from outside his clan to marry his sons. Ibzan judged Israel for seven years. ¹⁰When he died, he was buried at Bethlehem.

Elon Becomes Israel's Judge
¹¹After Ibzan died, Elon from the tribe of Zebulun judged Israel for ten years. ¹²When he died, he was buried at Aijalon in Zebulun.

Abdon Becomes Israel's Judge
¹³After Elon died, Abdon son of Hillel, from Pirathon, judged Israel. ¹⁴He had forty sons and thirty grandsons, who rode on seventy donkeys. He judged Israel for eight years. ¹⁵When he died, he was buried at Pirathon in Ephraim, in the hill country of the Amalekites.

CHAPTER 13
The Birth of Samson
Again the Israelites did evil in the LORD's sight, so the LORD handed them over to the Philistines, who oppressed them for forty years.

²In those days a man named Manoah from the tribe of Dan lived in the town of Zorah.

12:1-7 This tragic incident is in many ways a replay of Gideon's confrontation with the angry Ephraimites in Judges 8:1-3. The outcome, however, is very different because of the way Jephthah mishandled the situation. Instead of the humble self-control and patience shown by Gideon, Jephthah responded in angry pride. As a result, war erupted between Gilead and Ephraim, and the two tribes were unable to enjoy a relationship like the one forged with Ephraim by Gideon.

12:8-15 The brief mention of the leadership of Ibzan, Elon, and Abdon might be taken to mean that they were less significant judges. However, each of them actually ruled longer than Jephthah: Ibzan, seven years; Elon, ten years; and Abdon, eight years. Apparently, events during their terms of leadership were not as tumultuous. The point here is that people should not base their self-worth or sense of accomplishment on whether or not they "make the headlines."

13:1-14 The instructions given by the angel to Manoah and his wife are similar to those given to Zechariah and Elizabeth, parents of John the Baptist (Luke 1:5-15). Both sets of parents were commanded to raise their children for special tasks for God. In fact, even these parents' actions before their sons were born were very significant. All parents should be aware of how closely related their own actions and outlooks are to the sense of identity each of their children will have as an adult.

SAMSON & DELILAH

The New Testament describes Samson as a man of faith. It mentions neither his failures nor his great strength. Though he possessed great physical strength, he was a moral weakling—following his own selfish desires and ignoring God. Samson spent most of his life pursuing his own goals, but in the end he finally admitted his need and cried out to God for help.

It seems that after the first three episodes of betrayal, Samson would have known not to trust Delilah. But like many of us, Samson thought that giving in to manipulation was an expression of love. He chose to please Delilah and get what he wanted from her rather than obey God and deliver his people. Delilah chose to use her relationship with Samson for her own gain. It was clearly a dysfunctional relationship. Most of us have experienced the pain of being used, and we have undoubtedly used others. We have also known the agony of being betrayed.

It will do no good to look at Samson and think about what he did not accomplish. We are often victimized in our own life by thoughts of what might have been. Samson shows us that as long as we have life, we have hope. It is never too late to turn our life over to God and allow him to redeem us and restore what has been lost. In spite of his failures, Samson is listed as a champion of faith in Hebrews 11. In spite of our failures, we, too, can be champions of faith as God continues to work out recovery in our life.

STRENGTHS AND ACCOMPLISHMENTS:
* Samson was called by God even before his birth.
* He is listed in the Hall of Faith (Hebrews 11).
* Samson believed God.
* He began to free his people from the Philistines.

WEAKNESSES AND MISTAKES:
* Samson abused the gift of strength God had given him.
* He was motivated by revenge rather than by righteousness.
* He allowed lust to cloud his thinking.
* Delilah valued riches over relationships.
* She betrayed Samson and lied to him.

LESSONS FROM THEIR LIVES:
* There is great danger in trusting our God-given abilities rather than trusting God himself.
* There is a price to be paid for sin.
* We must be careful to do what is right, not just what we want to do.
* God uses us in spite of our failures.

KEY VERSE:
"Then Samson prayed to the LORD, 'Sovereign LORD, remember me again. O God, please strengthen me just one more time. With one blow let me pay back the Philistines for the loss of my two eyes'" (Judges 16:28).

The story of Samson is found in Judges 13—16, and his relationship with Delilah is described in Judges 16. Samson is also mentioned in Hebrews 11:32.

His wife was unable to become pregnant, and they had no children. ³The angel of the LORD appeared to Manoah's wife and said, "Even though you have been unable to have children, you will soon become pregnant and give birth to a son. ⁴So be careful; you must not drink wine or any other alcoholic drink nor eat any forbidden food.* ⁵You will become pregnant and give birth to a son, and his hair must never be cut. For he will be dedicated to God as a Nazirite from birth. He will begin to rescue Israel from the Philistines."

⁶The woman ran and told her husband, "A man of God appeared to me! He looked like one of God's angels, terrifying to see. I didn't ask where he was from, and he didn't tell me his name. ⁷But he told me, 'You will become pregnant and give birth to a son. You must not drink wine or any other alcoholic drink nor eat any forbidden food. For your son will be dedicated to God as a Nazirite from the moment of his birth until the day of his death.'"

⁸Then Manoah prayed to the LORD, saying, "Lord, please let the man of God come back to us again and give us more instructions about this son who is to be born."

⁹God answered Manoah's prayer, and the angel of God appeared once again to his wife as she was sitting in the field. But her husband, Manoah, was not with her. ¹⁰So she quickly ran and told her husband, "The man who appeared to me the other day is here again!"

13:4 Hebrew *any unclean thing;* also in 13:7, 14.

¹¹Manoah ran back with his wife and asked, "Are you the man who spoke to my wife the other day?"

"Yes," he replied, "I am."

¹²So Manoah asked him, "When your words come true, what kind of rules should govern the boy's life and work?"

¹³The angel of the LORD replied, "Be sure your wife follows the instructions I gave her. ¹⁴She must not eat grapes or raisins, drink wine or any other alcoholic drink, or eat any forbidden food."

¹⁵Then Manoah said to the angel of the LORD, "Please stay here until we can prepare a young goat for you to eat."

¹⁶"I will stay," the angel of the LORD replied, "but I will not eat anything. However, you may prepare a burnt offering as a sacrifice to the LORD." (Manoah didn't realize it was the angel of the LORD.)

¹⁷Then Manoah asked the angel of the LORD, "What is your name? For when all this comes true, we want to honor you."

¹⁸"Why do you ask my name?" the angel of the LORD replied. "It is too wonderful for you to understand."

¹⁹Then Manoah took a young goat and a grain offering and offered it on a rock as a sacrifice to the LORD. And as Manoah and his wife watched, the LORD did an amazing thing. ²⁰As the flames from the altar shot up toward the sky, the angel of the LORD ascended in the fire. When Manoah and his wife saw this, they fell with their faces to the ground.

²¹The angel did not appear again to Manoah and his wife. Manoah finally realized it was the angel of the LORD, ²²and he said to his wife, "We will certainly die, for we have seen God!"

²³But his wife said, "If the LORD were going to kill us, he wouldn't have accepted our burnt offering and grain offering. He wouldn't have appeared to us and told us this wonderful thing and done these miracles."

²⁴When her son was born, she named him Samson. And the LORD blessed him as he grew up. ²⁵And the Spirit of the LORD began to stir him while he lived in Mahaneh-dan, which is located between the towns of Zorah and Eshtaol.

CHAPTER 14
Samson's Riddle

One day when Samson was in Timnah, one of the Philistine women caught his eye. ²When he returned home, he told his father and mother, "A young Philistine woman in Timnah caught my eye. I want to marry her. Get her for me."

³His father and mother objected. "Isn't there even one woman in our tribe or among all the Israelites you could marry?" they asked. "Why must you go to the pagan Philistines to find a wife?"

But Samson told his father, "Get her for me! She looks good to me." ⁴His father and mother didn't realize the LORD was at work in this, creating an opportunity to work against the Philistines, who ruled over Israel at that time.

⁵As Samson and his parents were going down to Timnah, a young lion suddenly attacked Samson near the vineyards of Timnah. ⁶At that moment the Spirit of the LORD came powerfully upon him, and he ripped the lion's jaws apart with his bare hands. He did it as easily as if it were a young goat. But he didn't tell his father or mother about it. ⁷When Samson arrived in Timnah, he talked with the woman and was very pleased with her.

⁸Later, when he returned to Timnah for the wedding, he turned off the path to look at the carcass of the lion. And he found that a swarm of bees had made some honey in the carcass. ⁹He scooped some of the honey into his hands and ate it along the way. He also gave some to his father and mother, and they ate it. But he didn't tell them he had taken the honey from the carcass of the lion.

¹⁰As his father was making final arrangements for the marriage, Samson threw a

---

13:24–14:4 Samson is living proof that someone can grow up in a godly home under the blessing of the Lord and still have major issues to face. Even the working of the Spirit of God in Samson's life did not protect him from his biggest blind spot: foreign women. Fortunately, God used even Samson's weaknesses to bring glory to himself. Unfortunately, Samson did not understand his unhealthy attraction to be a point of weakness. Samson's problem with foreign women is symbolic of many who struggle today. God will provide us with an abundant life if we are willing to give up or avoid our "forbidden fruit." This fruit differs for each person. We should ask God to help us see what things or activities are stumbling blocks for us. Only when God has helped us uncover and remove the stumbling blocks from our life can we continue in the recovery process.

14:10-20 During the wedding feast, Samson foolishly bet that his guests could not solve his riddle. After being manipulated by his new wife and losing the wager, Samson slaughtered other

party at Timnah, as was the custom for elite young men. [11]When the bride's parents* saw him, they selected thirty young men from the town to be his companions.

[12]Samson said to them, "Let me tell you a riddle. If you solve my riddle during these seven days of the celebration, I will give you thirty fine linen robes and thirty sets of festive clothing. [13]But if you can't solve it, then you must give me thirty fine linen robes and thirty sets of festive clothing."

"All right," they agreed, "let's hear your riddle."

[14]So he said:

"Out of the one who eats came something
    to eat;
  out of the strong came something
    sweet."

Three days later they were still trying to figure it out. [15]On the fourth* day they said to Samson's wife, "Entice your husband to explain the riddle for us, or we will burn down your father's house with you in it. Did you invite us to this party just to make us poor?"

[16]So Samson's wife came to him in tears and said, "You don't love me; you hate me! You have given my people a riddle, but you haven't told me the answer."

"I haven't even given the answer to my father or mother," he replied. "Why should I tell you?" [17]So she cried whenever she was with him and kept it up for the rest of the celebration. At last, on the seventh day he told her the answer because she was tormenting him with her nagging. Then she explained the riddle to the young men.

[18]So before sunset of the seventh day, the men of the town came to Samson with their answer:

"What is sweeter than honey?
  What is stronger than a lion?"

Samson replied, "If you hadn't plowed with my heifer, you wouldn't have solved my riddle!"

[19]Then the Spirit of the LORD came powerfully upon him. He went down to the town of Ashkelon, killed thirty men, took their belongings, and gave their clothing to the men who had solved his riddle. But Samson was furious about what had happened, and he went back home to live with his father and mother. [20]So his wife was given in marriage to the man who had been Samson's best man at the wedding.

CHAPTER 15
Samson's Vengeance on the Philistines

Later on, during the wheat harvest, Samson took a young goat as a present to his wife. He said, "I'm going into my wife's room to sleep with her," but her father wouldn't let him in.

[2]"I truly thought you must hate her," her father explained, "so I gave her in marriage to your best man. But look, her younger sister is even more beautiful than she is. Marry her instead."

[3]Samson said, "This time I cannot be blamed for everything I am going to do to you Philistines." [4]Then he went out and caught 300 foxes. He tied their tails together in pairs, and he fastened a torch to each pair of tails. [5]Then he lit the torches and let the foxes run through the grain fields of the Philistines. He burned all their grain to the ground, including the sheaves and the uncut grain. He also destroyed their vineyards and olive groves.

[6]"Who did this?" the Philistines demanded.

"Samson," was the reply, "because his father-in-law from Timnah gave Samson's wife to be married to his best man." So the Philistines went and got the woman and her father and burned them to death.

14:11 Hebrew *they.* 14:15 As in Greek version; Hebrew reads *seventh.*

Philistines to get the garments he needed for payment. His actions clearly showed his volatile and dangerous personality. Samson possessed the maturity of a young boy stuffed inside an incredibly strong and gifted adult exterior. Often we aspire to be like people with great physical beauty, only to find that they are shallow of character. We must never forget how much God values who we are on the inside. God looks at people's heart, not their appearance (1 Samuel 16:7).
14:19–15:8 The motive of angry revenge dominated Samson's personality and actions more and more. Because of what the Philistines had done to him, he destroyed much of their wheat and other crops. Then he turned his rage on the Philistines themselves, killing many of them. There are many "rage-aholics" who, like Samson, desperately need recovery. Otherwise, they will destroy themselves, as Samson later did, and hurt the people they love. God calls us to take our hurts and give them to him while forgiving those who hurt us. Revenge never adequately repays the victimizer. In fact, it only causes the one who was hurt to be victimized again.

7"Because you did this," Samson vowed, "I won't rest until I take my revenge on you!" 8So he attacked the Philistines with great fury and killed many of them. Then he went to live in a cave in the rock of Etam.

9The Philistines retaliated by setting up camp in Judah and spreading out near the town of Lehi. 10The men of Judah asked the Philistines, "Why are you attacking us?"

The Philistines replied, "We've come to capture Samson. We've come to pay him back for what he did to us."

11So 3,000 men of Judah went down to get Samson at the cave in the rock of Etam. They said to Samson, "Don't you realize the Philistines rule over us? What are you doing to us?"

But Samson replied, "I only did to them what they did to me."

12But the men of Judah told him, "We have come to tie you up and hand you over to the Philistines."

"All right," Samson said. "But promise that you won't kill me yourselves."

13"We will only tie you up and hand you over to the Philistines," they replied. "We won't kill you." So they tied him up with two new ropes and brought him up from the rock.

14As Samson arrived at Lehi, the Philistines came shouting in triumph. But the Spirit of the LORD came powerfully upon Samson, and he snapped the ropes on his arms as if they were burnt strands of flax, and they fell from his wrists. 15Then he found the jawbone of a recently killed donkey. He picked it up and killed 1,000 Philistines with it. 16Then Samson said,

"With the jawbone of a donkey,
    I've piled them in heaps!
With the jawbone of a donkey,
    I've killed a thousand men!"

17When he finished his boasting, he threw away the jawbone; and the place was named Jawbone Hill.*

18Samson was now very thirsty, and he cried out to the LORD, "You have accomplished this great victory by the strength of your servant. Must I now die of thirst and fall into the hands of these pagans?" 19So God caused water to gush out of a hollow in the ground at Lehi, and Samson was revived as he drank. Then he named that place "The Spring of the One Who Cried Out,"* and it is still in Lehi to this day.

20Samson judged Israel for twenty years during the period when the Philistines dominated the land.

CHAPTER 16
Samson Carries Away Gaza's Gates

One day Samson went to the Philistine town of Gaza and spent the night with a prostitute. 2Word soon spread* that Samson was there, so the men of Gaza gathered together and waited all night at the town gates. They kept quiet during the night, saying to themselves, "When the light of morning comes, we will kill him."

3But Samson stayed in bed only until midnight. Then he got up, took hold of the doors of the town gate, including the two posts, and lifted them up, bar and all. He put them on his shoulders and carried them all the way to the top of the hill across from Hebron.

Samson and Delilah

4Some time later Samson fell in love with a woman named Delilah, who lived in the valley of Sorek. 5The rulers of the Philistines went to her and said, "Entice Samson to tell you what makes him so strong and how he can be overpowered and tied up securely.

15:17 Hebrew *Ramath-lehi.* 15:19 Hebrew *En-hakkore.* 16:2 As in Greek and Syriac versions and Latin Vulgate; Hebrew lacks *Word soon spread.*

15:18-20 Samson was left emotionally and physically drained after his victory over the Philistines. He now complained to God, perhaps exaggerating his situation ("Must I now die of thirst?"). After a major victory in our life, we may feel emotionally or physically spent. But we must not stop and become discouraged. This will only lead to failure. We should rely on God's power to strengthen us and meet our needs. Then we can be ready to face the next battle in the recovery process.

16:4-17 The love affair between Samson and Delilah is one of the saddest examples of a dysfunctional relationship in history. We are told that Samson did love Delilah (v. 4), but Delilah clearly valued money above their relationship. It should have been obvious to Samson that Delilah was working with the Philistines to destroy him. But to get the physical pleasures he craved, Samson led Delilah on, staying in a situation he should have run from. He blindly believed he was virtually indestructible. This left him open to utter humiliation and suffering. If we hope to succeed in recovery, we need to recognize our weaknesses and avoid situations where we are vulnerable.

Then each of us will give you 1,100 pieces* of silver."

6So Delilah said to Samson, "Please tell me what makes you so strong and what it would take to tie you up securely."

7Samson replied, "If I were tied up with seven new bowstrings that have not yet been dried, I would become as weak as anyone else."

8So the Philistine rulers brought Delilah seven new bowstrings, and she tied Samson up with them. 9She had hidden some men in one of the inner rooms of her house, and she cried out, "Samson! The Philistines have come to capture you!" But Samson snapped the bowstrings as a piece of string snaps when it is burned by a fire. So the secret of his strength was not discovered.

10Afterward Delilah said to him, "You've been making fun of me and telling me lies! Now please tell me how you can be tied up securely."

11Samson replied, "If I were tied up with brand-new ropes that had never been used, I would become as weak as anyone else."

12So Delilah took new ropes and tied him up with them. The men were hiding in the inner room as before, and again Delilah cried out, "Samson! The Philistines have come to capture you!" But again Samson snapped the ropes from his arms as if they were thread.

13Then Delilah said, "You've been making fun of me and telling me lies! Now tell me how you can be tied up securely."

Samson replied, "If you were to weave the seven braids of my hair into the fabric on your loom and tighten it with the loom shuttle, I would become as weak as anyone else."

So while he slept, Delilah wove the seven braids of his hair into the fabric. 14Then she tightened it with the loom shuttle.* Again she cried out, "Samson! The Philistines have come to capture you!" But Samson woke up, pulled back the loom shuttle, and yanked his hair away from the loom and the fabric.

15Then Delilah pouted, "How can you tell me, 'I love you,' when you don't share your secrets with me? You've made fun of me three times now, and you still haven't told me what makes you so strong!" 16She tormented him with her nagging day after day until he was sick to death of it.

16:5 Hebrew *1,100 [shekels]*, about 28 pounds or 12.5 kilograms in weight. 16:13-14 As in Greek version and Latin Vulgate; Hebrew lacks *I would become as weak as anyone else. / So while he slept, Delilah wove the seven braids of his hair into the fabric.* 14Then she tightened it with the loom shuttle.

STEP 1

Dangerous Self-Deception
BIBLE READING: Judges 16:1-31
We admitted that we were powerless over our problems—that our lives had become unmanageable.
When we refuse to admit our powerlessness we are only deceiving ourselves. The lies we tell ourselves and others are familiar: "I can stop any time I want to." "I'm in control; this *one* won't hurt anything." And all the while, we are inching closer to disaster.

Samson was one of Israel's judges. As a child, he had been dedicated to God, and God had gifted him with supernatural strength. But Samson had a lifelong weakness—the way he related to women. Samson was especially blinded to the dangers he faced in his relationship with Delilah. His enemies were paying her to discover the secret of his strength. Three times she begged Samson to tell her his secret. Each time she set him up and tried to hand him over to the enemy. Three times Samson lied to her and was able to escape. But each time he got closer to telling her the truth. Finally, Samson revealed his secret, was taken captive, and died a slave in enemy hands.

Samson's real problem can be found in the lies he told himself. By not admitting his powerlessness, he remained blind to the obvious danger that his pride and desire for beautiful foreign women were leading him into. This caused him to gradually inch his way toward an untimely death.

We need to be careful not to fall into a similar trap. As we learn to acknowledge our powerlessness over our addictive/compulsive tendencies daily, we will become more aware of behaviors that will likely lead us to destruction. *Turn to page 471, 2 Kings 5.*

¹⁷Finally, Samson shared his secret with her. "My hair has never been cut," he confessed, "for I was dedicated to God as a Nazirite from birth. If my head were shaved, my strength would leave me, and I would become as weak as anyone else."

¹⁸Delilah realized he had finally told her the truth, so she sent for the Philistine rulers. "Come back one more time," she said, "for he has finally told me his secret." So the Philistine rulers returned with the money in their hands. ¹⁹Delilah lulled Samson to sleep with his head in her lap, and then she called in a man to shave off the seven locks of his hair. In this way she began to bring him down,* and his strength left him.

²⁰Then she cried out, "Samson! The Philistines have come to capture you!"

When he woke up, he thought, "I will do as before and shake myself free." But he didn't realize the LORD had left him.

²¹So the Philistines captured him and gouged out his eyes. They took him to Gaza, where he was bound with bronze chains and forced to grind grain in the prison.

²²But before long, his hair began to grow back.

Samson's Final Victory

²³The Philistine rulers held a great festival, offering sacrifices and praising their god, Dagon. They said, "Our god has given us victory over our enemy Samson!"

²⁴When the people saw him, they praised their god, saying, "Our god has delivered our enemy to us! The one who killed so many of us is now in our power!"

²⁵Half drunk by now, the people demanded, "Bring out Samson so he can amuse

us!" So he was brought from the prison to amuse them, and they had him stand between the pillars supporting the roof.

²⁶Samson said to the young servant who was leading him by the hand, "Place my hands against the pillars that hold up the temple. I want to rest against them." ²⁷Now the temple was completely filled with people. All the Philistine rulers were there, and there were about 3,000 men and women on the roof who were watching as Samson amused them.

²⁸Then Samson prayed to the LORD, "Sovereign LORD, remember me again. O God, please strengthen me just one more time. With one blow let me pay back the Philistines for the loss of my two eyes." ²⁹Then Samson put his hands on the two center pillars that held up the temple. Pushing against them with both hands, ³⁰he prayed, "Let me die with the Philistines." And the temple crashed down on the Philistine rulers and all the people. So he killed more people when he died than he had during his entire lifetime.

³¹Later his brothers and other relatives went down to get his body. They took him back home and buried him between Zorah and Eshtaol, where his father, Manoah, was buried. Samson had judged Israel for twenty years.

CHAPTER 17
Micah's Idols

There was a man named Micah, who lived in the hill country of Ephraim. ²One day he said to his mother, "I heard you place a curse on the person who stole 1,100 pieces* of silver from you. Well, I have the money. I was the one who took it."

"The LORD bless you for admitting it," his

16:19 Or *she began to torment him.* Greek version reads *He began to grow weak.* 17:2 Hebrew *1,100 [shekels],* about 28 pounds or 12.5 kilograms in weight.

16:22-31 It took the loss of his physical sight for Samson to gain personal and spiritual insight. But that was not the end of the story. In his prayer to God, Samson finally admitted his helplessness and committed himself into God's hands. Notice that Samson accomplished more in his God-appointed death than in his entire self-centered life. And despite Samson's serious flaws, he was remembered as a man of faith (see Hebrews 11:32). We can only imagine how Samson would have altered history had he been committed to God throughout his life. We need to examine our life for missed opportunities and then determine not to miss them when they arise again.

17:1-6 We can summarize all of the events of Judges 17–21 in 17:6: "In those days Israel had no king; all the people did whatever seemed right in their own eyes." This statement also applies to the do-it-yourself idolatry of Micah. Without a king or any well-defined enforcement of God's laws, there were almost no limits or boundaries placed upon the people. In Micah's case, true worship was mocked by the making of idols (see Exodus 20:4) and the creation of a private priesthood. When we ignore God's commands for our life, we also mock God. Showing God proper respect entails following God's will for our life. If we do this, we can avoid self-destructive actions like those of the Israelites in the following chapters.

mother replied. ³He returned the money to her, and she said, "I now dedicate these silver coins to the LORD. In honor of my son, I will have an image carved and an idol cast."

⁴So when he returned the money to his mother, she took 200 silver coins and gave them to a silversmith, who made them into an image and an idol. And these were placed in Micah's house. ⁵Micah set up a shrine for the idol, and he made a sacred ephod and some household idols. Then he installed one of his sons as his personal priest.

⁶In those days Israel had no king; all the people did whatever seemed right in their own eyes.

⁷One day a young Levite, who had been living in Bethlehem in Judah, arrived in that area. ⁸He had left Bethlehem in search of another place to live, and as he traveled, he came to the hill country of Ephraim. He happened to stop at Micah's house as he was traveling through. ⁹"Where are you from?" Micah asked him.

He replied, "I am a Levite from Bethlehem in Judah, and I am looking for a place to live."

¹⁰"Stay here with me," Micah said, "and you can be a father and priest to me. I will give you ten pieces of silver* a year, plus a change of clothes and your food." ¹¹The Levite agreed to this, and the young man became like one of Micah's sons.

¹²So Micah installed the Levite as his personal priest, and he lived in Micah's house. ¹³"I know the LORD will bless me now," Micah said, "because I have a Levite serving as my priest."

CHAPTER 18
Idolatry in the Tribe of Dan

Now in those days Israel had no king. And the tribe of Dan was trying to find a place where they could settle, for they had not yet moved into the land assigned to them when the land was divided among the tribes of Israel. ²So the men of Dan chose from their clans five capable warriors from the towns of Zorah and Eshtaol to scout out a land for them to settle in.

When these warriors arrived in the hill country of Ephraim, they came to Micah's house and spent the night there. ³While at Micah's house, they recognized the young Levite's accent, so they went over and asked him, "Who brought you here, and what are you doing in this place? Why are you here?" ⁴He told them about his agreement with Micah and that he had been hired as Micah's personal priest.

⁵Then they said, "Ask God whether or not our journey will be successful."

⁶"Go in peace," the priest replied. "For the LORD is watching over your journey."

⁷So the five men went on to the town of Laish, where they noticed the people living carefree lives, like the Sidonians; they were peaceful and secure.* The people were also wealthy because their land was very fertile. And they lived a great distance from Sidon and had no allies nearby.

⁸When the men returned to Zorah and Eshtaol, their relatives asked them, "What did you find?"

⁹The men replied, "Come on, let's attack

17:10 Hebrew *10 [shekels] of silver,* about 4 ounces or 114 grams in weight. **18:7** The meaning of the Hebrew is uncertain.

17:7-13 The depth of the self-deception, or religious denial, in Israel during this time is clearly seen here. Not only was Micah not rebuked by the priest from Bethlehem for his open idolatry, but the priest actually accepted Micah's job offer! This arrangement stood counter to God's clearly revealed will on the matter of worship in Israel. But Micah believed it would bring him great blessing anyway. He was either ignorant of God's laws or chose to ignore them. God has shown us in the Bible all that we need to know about healthy living. We are responsible to know what God desires of us and then to follow through on it.

18:2-6 The Danites were initially surprised, then intrigued, by Micah's arrangement of hiring a personal priest. Their first questions seem to indicate that they knew this arrangement was not right. But they liked the idea of having a personal hot line to God, especially after being told that their present mission would be successful. Sadly, it appears that Micah's priest spoke only for himself, not for God. The spiritual denial only increased on both sides. When confronted by something that is wrong or inappropriate, we must not compromise, even if there are apparent benefits.

18:7-20 When the city of Laish appeared to be a promising solution to their problem (having no land of their own), the Danites concluded that Micah's priest had spoken for God. Thus, when they came to Micah's house again, they stole his idols and hired his priest. Obviously, this priest felt no sense of accountability to God. After making the wrong decision to become Micah's priest, the young man had no problem becoming the priest to a whole tribe. We all know that the direction of our first step often affects the direction of the following steps. In order to remain free from our dependencies, we should make sure that each step is in the direction of recovery.

them! We have seen the land, and it is very good. What are you waiting for? Don't hesitate to go and take possession of it. ¹⁰When you get there, you will find the people living carefree lives. God has given us a spacious and fertile land, lacking in nothing!"

¹¹So 600 men from the tribe of Dan, armed with weapons of war, set out from Zorah and Eshtaol. ¹²They camped at a place west of Kiriath-jearim in Judah, which is called Mahaneh-dan* to this day. ¹³Then they went on from there into the hill country of Ephraim and came to the house of Micah.

¹⁴The five men who had scouted out the land around Laish explained to the others, "These buildings contain a sacred ephod, as well as some household idols, a carved image, and a cast idol. What do you think you should do?" ¹⁵Then the five men turned off the road and went over to Micah's house, where the young Levite lived, and greeted him kindly. ¹⁶As the 600 armed warriors from the tribe of Dan stood at the entrance of the gate, ¹⁷the five scouts entered the shrine and removed the carved image, the sacred ephod, the household idols, and the cast idol. Meanwhile, the priest was standing at the gate with the 600 armed warriors.

¹⁸When the priest saw the men carrying all the sacred objects out of Micah's shrine, he said, "What are you doing?"

¹⁹"Be quiet and come with us," they said. "Be a father and priest to all of us. Isn't it better to be a priest for an entire tribe and clan of Israel than for the household of just one man?"

²⁰The young priest was quite happy to go with them, so he took along the sacred ephod, the household idols, and the carved image. ²¹They turned and started on their way again, placing their children, livestock, and possessions in front of them.

²²When the people from the tribe of Dan were quite a distance from Micah's house, the people who lived near Micah came chasing after them. ²³They were shouting as they caught up with them. The men of Dan turned

around and said to Micah, "What's the matter? Why have you called these men together and chased after us like this?"

²⁴"What do you mean, 'What's the matter?'" Micah replied. "You've taken away all the gods I have made, and my priest, and I have nothing left!"

²⁵The men of Dan said, "Watch what you say! There are some short-tempered men around here who might get angry and kill you and your family." ²⁶So the men of Dan continued on their way. When Micah saw that there were too many of them for him to attack, he turned around and went home.

²⁷Then, with Micah's idols and his priest, the men of Dan came to the town of Laish, whose people were peaceful and secure. They attacked with swords and burned the town to the ground. ²⁸There was no one to rescue the people, for they lived a great distance from Sidon and had no allies nearby. This happened in the valley near Beth-rehob.

Then the people of the tribe of Dan rebuilt the town and lived there. ²⁹They renamed the town Dan after their ancestor, Israel's son, but it had originally been called Laish.

³⁰Then they set up the carved image, and they appointed Jonathan son of Gershom, son of Moses,* as their priest. This family continued as priests for the tribe of Dan until the Exile. ³¹So Micah's carved image was worshiped by the tribe of Dan as long as the Tabernacle of God remained at Shiloh.

CHAPTER 19
The Levite and His Concubine

Now in those days Israel had no king. There was a man from the tribe of Levi living in a remote area of the hill country of Ephraim. One day he brought home a woman from Bethlehem in Judah to be his concubine. ²But she became angry with him* and returned to her father's home in Bethlehem.

After about four months, ³her husband set out for Bethlehem to speak personally to her and persuade her to come back. He took with him a servant and a pair of donkeys. When he

---

18:12 *Mahaneh-dan* means "the camp of Dan." 18:30 As in an ancient Hebrew tradition, some Greek manuscripts, and Latin Vulgate; Masoretic Text reads *son of Manasseh.* 19:2 Or *she was unfaithful to him.*

18:22-31 This episode is a classic example of an angry confrontation between people who desperately need to change. Micah, the original idolater, asserted that he had been wronged because his idols and personal priest had been taken. The aggressive Danites responded with threats and intimidation. As a result, the Danites set up an elaborate long-term worship system as a rival to true worship in Israel. Micah's original "small mistake" had now spread and ensnared an entire tribe of Israel. We should be aware that small mistakes in our own life often have repercussions in the lives of others around us.

arrived at* her father's house, her father saw him and welcomed him. [4]Her father urged him to stay awhile, so he stayed three days, eating, drinking, and sleeping there.

[5]On the fourth day the man was up early, ready to leave, but the woman's father said to his son-in-law, "Have something to eat before you go." [6]So the two men sat down together and had something to eat and drink. Then the woman's father said, "Please stay another night and enjoy yourself." [7]The man got up to leave, but his father-in-law kept urging him to stay, so he finally gave in and stayed the night.

[8]On the morning of the fifth day he was up early again, ready to leave, and again the woman's father said, "Have something to eat; then you can leave later this afternoon." So they had another day of feasting. [9]Later, as the man and his concubine and servant were preparing to leave, his father-in-law said, "Look, it's almost evening. Stay the night and enjoy yourself. Tomorrow you can get up early and be on your way."

[10]But this time the man was determined to leave. So he took his two saddled donkeys and his concubine and headed in the direction of Jebus (that is, Jerusalem). [11]It was late in the day when they neared Jebus, and the man's servant said to him, "Let's stop at this Jebusite town and spend the night there." [12]"No," his master said, "we can't stay in this foreign town where there are no Israelites. Instead, we will go on to Gibeah. [13]Come on, let's try to get as far as Gibeah or Ramah, and we'll spend the night in one of those towns." [14]So they went on. The sun was setting as they came to Gibeah, a town in the land of Benjamin, [15]so they stopped there to spend the night. They rested in the town square, but no one took them in for the night.

[16]That evening an old man came home from his work in the fields. He was from the hill country of Ephraim, but he was living in Gibeah, where the people were from the tribe of Benjamin. [17]When he saw the travelers sitting in the town square, he asked them where they were from and where they were going.

[18]"We have been in Bethlehem in Judah," the man replied. "We are on our way to a remote area in the hill country of Ephraim, which is my home. I traveled to Bethlehem, and now I'm returning home.* But no one has taken us in for the night, [19]even though we have everything we need. We have straw and feed for our donkeys and plenty of bread and wine for ourselves."

[20]"You are welcome to stay with me," the old man said. "I will give you anything you might need. But whatever you do, don't spend the night in the square." [21]So he took them home with him and fed the donkeys. After they washed their feet, they ate and drank together.

[22]While they were enjoying themselves, a crowd of troublemakers from the town surrounded the house. They began beating at the door and shouting to the old man, "Bring out the man who is staying with you so we can have sex with him."

[23]The old man stepped outside to talk to them. "No, my brothers, don't do such an evil thing. For this man is a guest in my house, and such a thing would be shameful. [24]Here, take my virgin daughter and this man's concubine. I will bring them out to you, and you can abuse them and do whatever you like. But don't do such a shameful thing to this man."

[25]But they wouldn't listen to him. So the Levite took hold of his concubine and pushed her out the door. The men of the town abused her all night, taking turns raping her until morning. Finally, at dawn they let her go. [26]At daybreak the woman returned to the house where her husband was staying. She collapsed at the door of the house and lay there until it was light.

[27]When her husband opened the door to leave, there lay his concubine with her

---

19:3 As in Greek version; Hebrew reads *When she brought him to.* 19:18 As in Greek version (see also 19:29); Hebrew reads *now I'm going to the Tabernacle of the LORD.*

19:11-29 This tragic episode represents the moral low point of the book of Judges. Notice the similarities between the Levite's experience with the Benjamites and Lot's experience with the men of Sodom in Genesis 19. This incident is even worse because the uncaring Levite actually gave up his concubine to save his own skin. Have we sacrificed the health and stability of our family so we could engage in a selfish lifestyle? If so, we should accept responsibility for the consequences. The Levite blamed the Benjamites and did not recognize his responsibility in the tragedy. If drugs, alcohol, or some other problem is harming our loved ones, we need to accept our part in the process. When we recognize that we are accountable, we can begin to get the help we need.

hands on the threshold. [28]He said, "Get up! Let's go!" But there was no answer.* So he put her body on his donkey and took her home.

[29]When he got home, he took a knife and cut his concubine's body into twelve pieces. Then he sent one piece to each tribe throughout all the territory of Israel.

[30]Everyone who saw it said, "Such a horrible crime has not been committed in all the time since Israel left Egypt. Think about it! What are we going to do? Who's going to speak up?"

CHAPTER 20
Israel's War with Benjamin

Then all the Israelites were united as one man, from Dan in the north to Beersheba in the south, including those from across the Jordan in the land of Gilead. The entire community assembled in the presence of the LORD at Mizpah. [2]The leaders of all the people and all the tribes of Israel—400,000 warriors armed with swords—took their positions in the assembly of the people of God. [3](Word soon reached the land of Benjamin that the other tribes had gone up to Mizpah.) The Israelites then asked how this terrible crime had happened.

[4]The Levite, the husband of the woman who had been murdered, said, "My concubine and I came to spend the night in Gibeah, a town that belongs to the people of Benjamin. [5]That night some of the leading citizens of Gibeah surrounded the house, planning to kill me, and they raped my concubine until she was dead. [6]So I cut her body into twelve pieces and sent the pieces throughout the territory assigned to Israel, for these men have committed a terrible and shameful crime. [7]Now then, all of you—the entire community of Israel—must decide here and now what should be done about this!"

[8]And all the people rose to their feet in unison and declared, "None of us will return home! No, not even one of us! [9]Instead, this is what we will do to Gibeah; we will draw lots to decide who will attack it. [10]One-tenth of the men* from each tribe will be chosen to supply the warriors with food, and the rest of us will take revenge on Gibeah* of Benjamin for this shameful thing they have done in Israel." [11]So all the Israelites were completely united, and they gathered together to attack the town.

[12]The Israelites sent messengers to the tribe of Benjamin, saying, "What a terrible thing has been done among you! [13]Give up those evil men, those troublemakers from Gibeah, so we can execute them and purge Israel of this evil."

But the people of Benjamin would not listen. [14]Instead, they came from their towns and gathered at Gibeah to fight the Israelites. [15]In all, 26,000 of their warriors armed with swords arrived in Gibeah to join the 700 elite troops who lived there. [16]Among Benjamin's elite troops, 700 were left-handed, and each of them could sling a rock and hit a target within a hairsbreadth without missing. [17]Israel had 400,000 experienced soldiers armed with swords, not counting Benjamin's warriors.

[18]Before the battle the Israelites went to Bethel and asked God, "Which tribe should go first to attack the people of Benjamin?"

The LORD answered, "Judah is to go first."

[19]So the Israelites left early the next morning and camped near Gibeah. [20]Then they advanced toward Gibeah to attack the men of Benjamin. [21]But Benjamin's warriors, who were defending the town, came out and killed 22,000 Israelites on the battlefield that day.

[22]But the Israelites encouraged each other and took their positions again at the same place they had fought the previous day. [23]For they had gone up to Bethel and wept in the presence of the LORD until evening. They had asked the LORD, "Should we fight against our relatives from Benjamin again?"

And the LORD had said, "Go out and fight against them."

[24]So the next day they went out again to fight against the men of Benjamin, [25]but the men of Benjamin killed another 18,000 Isra-

---

19:28 Greek version adds *for she was dead.* **20:10a** Hebrew *10 men from every hundred, 100 men from every thousand, and 1,000 men from every 10,000.* **20:10b** Hebrew *Geba*, in this case a variant spelling of Gibeah; also in 20:33.

20:8-25 We are often highly resistant to the fact that we are in need of recovery. The tribe of Benjamin foolishly denied the sins of Gibeah and self-righteously set out to defend its honor. They were unwilling to admit that there was sin in their midst. This story is a powerful illustration of denial and its consequences. We often hide our problems, denying the need for help until it is too late. We would be wise to humbly admit our sin and seek to make things right. If the Benjamites had been willing to discipline Gibeah, the rest of the tribe could have remained strong. But they let their pride keep them from confession and were, as a result, almost destroyed.

elites, all of whom were experienced with the sword.

²⁶Then all the Israelites went up to Bethel and wept in the presence of the LORD and fasted until evening. They also brought burnt offerings and peace offerings to the LORD. ²⁷The Israelites went up seeking direction from the LORD. (In those days the Ark of the Covenant of God was in Bethel, ²⁸and Phinehas son of Eleazar and grandson of Aaron was the priest.) The Israelites asked the LORD, "Should we fight against our relatives from Benjamin again, or should we stop?"

The LORD said, "Go! Tomorrow I will hand them over to you."

²⁹So the Israelites set an ambush all around Gibeah. ³⁰They went out on the third day and took their positions at the same place as before. ³¹When the men of Benjamin came out to attack, they were drawn away from the town. And as they had done before, they began to kill the Israelites. About thirty Israelites died in the open fields and along the roads, one leading to Bethel and the other leading back to Gibeah.

³²Then the warriors of Benjamin shouted, "We're defeating them as we did before!" But the Israelites had planned in advance to run away so that the men of Benjamin would chase them along the roads and be drawn away from the town.

³³When the main group of Israelite warriors reached Baal-tamar, they turned and took up their positions. Meanwhile, the Israelites hiding in ambush to the west* of Gibeah jumped up to fight. ³⁴There were 10,000 elite Israelite troops who advanced against Gibeah. The fighting was so heavy that Benjamin didn't realize the impending disaster. ³⁵So the LORD helped Israel defeat Benjamin, and that day the Israelites killed 25,100 of Benjamin's warriors, all of whom were experienced swordsmen. ³⁶Then the men of Benjamin saw that they were beaten.

The Israelites had retreated from Benjamin's warriors in order to give those hiding in ambush more room to maneuver against Gibeah. ³⁷Then those who were hiding rushed in from all sides and killed everyone in the town. ³⁸They had arranged to send up a large cloud of smoke from the town as a signal. ³⁹When the Israelites saw the smoke, they turned and attacked Benjamin's warriors.

By that time Benjamin's warriors had killed about thirty Israelites, and they shouted, "We're defeating them as we did in the first battle!" ⁴⁰But when the warriors of Benjamin looked behind them and saw the smoke rising into the sky from every part of the town, ⁴¹the men of Israel turned and attacked. At this point the men of Benjamin became terrified, because they realized disaster was close at hand. ⁴²So they turned around and fled before the Israelites toward the wilderness. But they couldn't escape the battle, and the people who came out of the nearby towns were also killed.* ⁴³The Israelites surrounded the men of Benjamin and chased them relentlessly, finally overtaking them east of Gibeah.* ⁴⁴That day 18,000 of Benjamin's strongest warriors died in battle. ⁴⁵The survivors fled into the wilderness toward the rock of Rimmon, but Israel killed 5,000 of them along the road. They continued the chase until they had killed another 2,000 near Gidom.

⁴⁶So that day the tribe of Benjamin lost 25,000 strong warriors armed with swords, ⁴⁷leaving only 600 men who escaped to the rock of Rimmon, where they lived for four months. ⁴⁸And the Israelites returned and slaughtered every living thing in all the towns—the people, the livestock, and everything they found. They also burned down all the towns they came to.

20:33 As in Greek and Syriac versions and Latin Vulgate; Hebrew reads *hiding in the open space.* 20:42 Or *battle, for the people from the nearby towns also came out and killed them.* 20:43 The meaning of the Hebrew is uncertain.

20:26-41 The rest of the Israelites were willing to seriously examine themselves and commit themselves to God and his guidance. These steps of corporate recovery led to a painful yet decisive victory. God used the Benjamites' resistant pride to lead them into an ambush in which they lost almost all their troops (see 20:14-15). When we are confronted by others about our dependencies or wrong behaviors, we should acknowledge the problem and face reality before our denial of the situation destroys us.

21:1-12 In the heat of anger or strong emotions, many people needing recovery or moving through the recovery process make rash or unrealistic vows. Here the Israelites were forced to keep their vows because they were made publicly and before God. They had not learned from Jephthah's tragic mistake of making a thoughtless vow (11:30-31, 34-39). This reveals a great lack of wisdom and self-control. Promises are made to be kept. We should not make promises that we will regret or refuse to carry out later.

CHAPTER 21
Israel Provides Wives for Benjamin

The Israelites had vowed at Mizpah, "We will never give our daughters in marriage to a man from the tribe of Benjamin." ²Now the people went to Bethel and sat in the presence of God until evening, weeping loudly and bitterly. ³"O LORD, God of Israel," they cried out, "why has this happened in Israel? Now one of our tribes is missing from Israel!"

⁴Early the next morning the people built an altar and presented their burnt offerings and peace offerings on it. ⁵Then they said, "Who among the tribes of Israel did not join us at Mizpah when we held our assembly in the presence of the LORD?" At that time they had taken a solemn oath in the LORD's presence, vowing that anyone who refused to come would be put to death.

⁶The Israelites felt sorry for their brother Benjamin and said, "Today one of the tribes of Israel has been cut off. ⁷How can we find wives for the few who remain, since we have sworn by the LORD not to give them our daughters in marriage?"

⁸So they asked, "Who among the tribes of Israel did not join us at Mizpah when we assembled in the presence of the LORD?" And they discovered that no one from Jabesh-gilead had attended the assembly. ⁹For after they counted all the people, no one from Jabesh-gilead was present.

¹⁰So the assembly sent 12,000 of their best warriors to Jabesh-gilead with orders to kill everyone there, including women and children. ¹¹"This is what you are to do," they said. "Completely destroy* all the males and every woman who is not a virgin." ¹²Among the residents of Jabesh-gilead they found 400 young virgins who had never slept with a man, and they brought them to the camp at Shiloh in the land of Canaan.

¹³The Israelite assembly sent a peace delegation to the remaining people of Benjamin who were living at the rock of Rimmon. ¹⁴Then the men of Benjamin returned to their homes, and the 400 women of Jabesh-gilead who had been spared were given to them as wives. But there were not enough women for all of them.

¹⁵The people felt sorry for Benjamin because the LORD had made this gap among the tribes of Israel. ¹⁶So the elders of the assembly asked, "How can we find wives for the few who remain, since the women of the tribe of Benjamin are dead? ¹⁷There must be heirs for the survivors so that an entire tribe of Israel is not wiped out. ¹⁸But we cannot give them our own daughters in marriage because we have sworn with a solemn oath that anyone who does this will fall under God's curse."

¹⁹Then they thought of the annual festival of the LORD held in Shiloh, south of Lebonah and north of Bethel, along the east side of the road that goes from Bethel to Shechem. ²⁰They told the men of Benjamin who still needed wives, "Go and hide in the vineyards. ²¹When you see the young women of Shiloh come out for their dances, rush out from the vineyards, and each of you can take one of them home to the land of Benjamin to be your wife! ²²And when their fathers and brothers come to us in protest, we will tell them, 'Please be sympathetic. Let them have your daughters, for we didn't find wives for all of them when we destroyed Jabesh-gilead. And you are not guilty of breaking the vow since you did not actually give your daughters to them in marriage.'"

²³So the men of Benjamin did as they were told. Each man caught one of the women as she danced in the celebration and carried her off to be his wife. They returned to their own land, and they rebuilt their towns and lived in them.

²⁴Then the people of Israel departed by tribes and families, and they returned to their own homes.

²⁵In those days Israel had no king; all the people did whatever seemed right in their own eyes.

21:11 The Hebrew term used here refers to the complete consecration of things or people to the LORD, either by destroying them or by giving them as an offering.

21:10-24 Frequently those needing recovery are willing to do whatever it takes to survive without necessarily facing their root problems. There was no hint of repentance or commitment to God on the part of the Benjamites here, just the desire to survive. In feeling sorry for the remnant of Benjamin, the rest of Israel used very questionable ways of "making it up to them." While it is very commendable to help others, it should not be done wrongly or strictly out of guilt.

REFLECTIONS ON JUDGES

insights FROM GIDEON'S LIFE

There are frequently background issues, such as the way people view themselves or their family's status, involved in recovery. Gideon's response to God in **Judges 6:15-16** and his fear and hesitation later were likely related to feelings of inadequacy. God offered his power (because of Gideon's commitment to him) as the means of dealing decisively with such issues. A troubled past or a low family status may seem like a good excuse for doing nothing and hiding in comfortable (though detrimental) situations. But God says that he will be with us to help us carry out whatever tasks we have been assigned. All we need to do is trust in him.

In **Judges 7:1-7**, Gideon's forces were already outnumbered by the enemy, but God limited their numbers even more. In the end, only 300 men would go to fight the Midianites. From a human standpoint, this put Israel at an impossible disadvantage. But God had limited their numbers for a reason: He wanted to show Israel that his power was sufficient no matter what the odds. Undoubtedly, Gideon became nervous as his army began to dwindle before his very eyes. But instead of walking out on God, he proceeded with an even stronger commitment to God's plan. It is amazing how much can be accomplished with fewer resources and a stronger commitment to God's will. When we turn our life over to God each day, he can do more with us than with thousands of uncommitted soldiers.

The miraculous victory recorded in **Judges 7:8-23** illustrates some of the resources available to us in recovery. Certainly the person seeking recovery needs to know that it is possible to overcome great odds with God's power. Perhaps equally important is the realization that the oppressor or abuser in many situations will prove to be self-destructive. The abusive cycle, which may have seemed impossible to break, may actually be surprisingly fragile as we face it with God's help.

insights FROM JEPHTHAH'S LIFE

We often suffer ridicule because of our family background or other factors that are completely beyond our control. As we see in **Judges 11:1-11**, Jephthah apparently possessed considerable courage and natural leadership ability. But he was sensitive to having been rejected and sought to secure his position in Gilead even before the battle with the Ammonites. While Jephthah seemed confident in his ability as God's instrument to bring about freedom, he apparently still needed to forgive the people of Gilead and gain a more balanced self-understanding. Like Jephthah, we may have been taunted by others because of our family background or other problems beyond our control. We, too, need to forgive those people, put those events behind us, and then move on to the tasks to which God has called us.

insights FROM SAMSON'S LIFE

In **Judges 13:15-23**, the interaction between Samson's parents and the angel demonstrates their balanced sense of self-esteem. They had been called for the high purpose of raising a child uniquely gifted to serve God. They also had been allowed to live even though they had looked upon God. Their giving of sacrifices indicated their proper sense of faith, humility, and thankfulness before God. Likewise, we may be called to do special things for God or his people. We should remember that we are serving God and that he is allowing us to do these things. Knowing this should temper any exaggerated sense of self-worth we may be tempted to feel.

As we see in **Judges 14:5-9**, even early in life, Samson was insensitive to the vows that defined his relationship with God. Samson's Nazirite vow forbade his contact with anything dead (see Numbers 6), but Samson killed a lion and then revisited the carcass. It was indeed the Spirit of the Lord that strengthened him, but Samson was very capable of abusing his God-given ability. There is very little evidence of commitment to God at this point in Samson's life. Having been raised as a "special child," he was self-centered. This sinful self-obsession was the ruin of Samson as it is the ruin of too many people today.

As evidenced in **Judges 15:1-17**, Samson was the most contradictory of Israel's judges. Called to be a Nazirite, he violently killed and destroyed, flouting his previous "separation" before God (see Numbers 6). He would justify extreme actions, which in reality were based almost totally on angry vengeance. He also led a largely solitary, lonely existence for periods of time. Samson was far from ideal. Yet God still used him to begin the conquest of the neighboring Philistines, a task that would be finished much later by King David.

Unless we face and deal with our recovery issues, they will continue to reemerge throughout our life. Samson's weakness in regard to foreign women reasserted itself in **Judges 16:1-3**. Samson was known as a judge in Israel, a position of great respect and responsibility. Yet he exposed himself to both shame and danger—not to mention sin—by going to the prostitute in Gaza. Again, his strength and courage rescued him. But as we see later, Samson mistakenly believed that he could handle his weakness on his own. None of us can fight our dependencies alone. We may get by for a while, even racking up some impressive victories, but eventually we will fall prey to temptation. We need to lean upon God and other people for the support we need.

It is sad when a person in need of recovery finally hits bottom. For years Samson had steered around the potential disasters caused by his extreme behavior and anger. But in **Judges 16:18-21** Delilah used her knowledge about Samson to destroy him. Before facing the flaws in his life and then building a proper sense of identity and a new life, Samson was forced to admit his helplessness as a tortured Philistine slave. He had deserted God by his actions, and God's strength had left him. We don't need to hit bottom—we can face and defeat our problems before anything catastrophic happens by simply admitting our weaknesses before God and asking him for his help.

insights FROM THE TRIBE OF DAN
In **Judges 18:1-2** the tribe of Dan was looking for the easy way out. This kind of behavior is typical of people in need of recovery. The Danites had long been unable to evict the Amorites from the land allotted to them under Joshua (Judges 1:34). So they gave up persevering toward that God-given goal. Instead, they sent scouts in search of an easier area to conquer that offered significant advantages to the Danites. There is no indication that the tribe ever considered the reasons for their previous defeat or that they had sought to learn from it. They looked for an easier solution that led them even further away from God, who could have given them victory.

RUTH

THE BIG PICTURE

A. THE BOTTOM DROPS OUT IN LIFE (1:1-5)

B. THE BEGINNING OF THE LONG ROAD TO RECOVERY (1:6-22)

C. THE SEEN PROCESS AND THE UNSEEN PROVISION IN RECOVERY (2:1-23)

D. THE FASHION OF REALITY IN AN OLD-FASHIONED LOVE STORY (3:1-18)

E. THE JOY OF FULFILLED RELATIONSHIPS (4:1-17)

F. THE LONG-TERM CONSEQUENCES OF SHORT-TERM CHOICES (4:18-22)

In the time of the judges, Naomi and her family moved to neighboring Moab to escape a severe famine in Israel. Naomi's husband died there, and her sons married Moabite women. In time, both of her sons also died, leaving Naomi destitute and alone, far from her relatives in Israel. One daughter-in-law, Orpah, returned to her own family; the other one, Ruth, stayed with Naomi to comfort her in her grief.

Grief is hard work; it is painful. People who are grieving need others to grieve with them and comfort them. Ruth's faithfulness to her mother-in-law during this time is indeed striking. She gave up the security of her family in Moab to move and face a future of probable loneliness and poverty in a foreign land. But Ruth's faithfulness yielded the fruits of God's blessing, and Naomi experienced God's comfort and love through her.

Together Ruth and Naomi trusted God to help them, and God came through in his own time. The circumstances through which their desperate needs were met reveal God's unseen hand at work. God led Naomi and Ruth back to Israel, where Ruth met Boaz, her future husband. Not only did Ruth find security and love, but the sadness of Naomi's heart was replaced with joy.

We have all experienced some kind of loss. There are times when we might feel as if the future is hopeless, even after we have given it over to God. As we grieve, we may feel abandoned and bitter toward God and the people around us. But we can rest in the fact that God is still with us—even when our emotions scream the opposite message—and that he is working on our behalf behind the scenes.

THE BOTTOM LINE

PURPOSE: To show that people who turn their life over to God can make an extraordinary impact on others and find peace and serenity in their own life. AUTHOR: Tradition names Samuel as the author, but it could have been a writer during the reign of David or Solomon. AUDIENCE: The people of Israel. DATE WRITTEN: Sometime between 1020 and 930 B.C. SETTING: During the period of the judges. KEY VERSE: "But Ruth replied, 'Don't ask me to leave you and turn back. Wherever you go, I will go; wherever you live, I will live. Your people will be my people, and your God will be my God'" (1:16). KEY PLACES: Bethlehem, Moab. KEY PEOPLE AND RELATIONSHIPS: Naomi and Ruth, Ruth and Boaz, Naomi and Obed.

RECOVERY THEMES

Facing Our Losses: In the grief process we face the agonizing reality of our losses. This takes time and a great deal of emotional energy. Because it is so hard, our tendency is to try to shut out the pain. We want to ignore what has happened, keep a stiff upper lip, and smile at all costs. Avoiding the difficult process of grief does not produce growth and healing. Naomi felt embittered and abandoned by God. She faced her loss honestly and allowed herself to grieve. This was an important step toward her healing.

Comfort in Grief: The bottom fell out of Ruth's and Naomi's life. The easy way out for Ruth would have been to leave Naomi in her poverty and go back to the security of her own family. But Ruth trusted the God of Israel and chose to stay with Naomi. Naomi and Ruth received great comfort from each other. Those who are grieving need people who will mourn with them and help them bear their grief. During painful times, God often uses other people to bring us comfort.

God's Plan: This story reveals an important link in God's plan for the redemption of our broken world. God used the faithfulness and integrity of Ruth, Naomi, and Boaz to first bring about their own healing and then to bring a child they named Obed into the world. This baby would become the grandfather of King David and the ancestor of Jesus the Messiah, through whom we all can find forgiveness and healing from the destructive forces of sin. The faithfulness of these three individuals has made possible the spiritual healing of the human race.

Difficult Times: It is easy to think that if circumstances were just a little better, recovery would be easier. But the test of any recovery process is how well it works when times are bad. The book of Ruth tells us about a family that suffered extreme losses. First Naomi's husband died, then both of her sons. One daughter-in-law returned home to her family, but the other one stayed in this seemingly hopeless situation. Ruth refused to let difficult times determine the outcome of her future.

CHAPTER 1
Elimelech Moves His Family to Moab

In the days when the judges ruled in Israel, a severe famine came upon the land. So a man from Bethlehem in Judah left his home and went to live in the country of Moab, taking his wife and two sons with him. ²The man's name was Elimelech, and his wife was Naomi. Their two sons were Mahlon and Kilion. They were Ephrathites from Bethlehem in the land of Judah. And when they reached Moab, they settled there.

³Then Elimelech died, and Naomi was left with her two sons. ⁴The two sons married Moabite women. One married a woman named Orpah, and the other a woman named Ruth. But about ten years later, ⁵both Mahlon and Kilion died. This left Naomi alone, without her two sons or her husband.

Naomi and Ruth Return

⁶Then Naomi heard in Moab that the LORD had blessed his people in Judah by giving them good crops again. So Naomi and her daughters-in-law got ready to leave Moab to return to her homeland. ⁷With her two daughters-in-law she set out from the place where she had been living, and they took the road that would lead them back to Judah.

⁸But on the way, Naomi said to her two daughters-in-law, "Go back to your mothers' homes. And may the LORD reward you for your kindness to your husbands and to me. ⁹May the LORD bless you with the security of another marriage." Then she kissed them good-bye, and they all broke down and wept.

¹⁰"No," they said. "We want to go with you to your people."

¹¹But Naomi replied, "Why should you go

1:1-5 Elimelech and his family decided to move from Bethlehem to Moab to escape difficult circumstances. They fled political instability, economic problems, and famine. But there is a strange silence regarding their trust in God; nothing is said of their seeking God's guidance. The decision to move to Moab had disastrous immediate and long-term consequences. Similar consequences often result when we attempt to escape difficult or painful circumstances without God's direction. In recovery it is important for us to face our painful circumstances and, with God's help, overcome them.

1:16-18 Ruth's desire to remain close to Naomi was actually a step of faith. Naomi had no financial security, no family members nearby for support or protection. By staying with Naomi, Ruth was cutting herself off from her own family, land, and culture. She was essentially committing her life into God's hands. After making her commitment to Naomi, Ruth stood by her, doing all she could to provide food and help for her mother-in-law. The process of recovery is not an easy road. We must realize this before we commit to it; otherwise we will be tempted to give up when things get tough. But, as with Ruth, sticking to our commitments will always yield great rewards in the long run.

RUTH, NAOMI, & BOAZ

What could be more emotionally devastating than to experience widowhood, the death of two children, and poverty all at one time? Any one of these shocking losses would be enough to overwhelm most of us. Together, however, these losses would likely cause any of us to break beneath the mountain of grief.

Naomi and her daughter-in-law Ruth dug out from under their mountain of despair hand in hand. Faced with a hopeless situation, Ruth chose to stay with Naomi even though Naomi had little to offer her. She also committed herself to Naomi's God. God saw Ruth through that difficult period of uncertainty to the point of healing and readiness for marriage to Boaz.

As Naomi traveled through the grief process to recovery, she experienced anger, depression, and a sense that God had dealt her bitter blows and then abandoned her. She felt hopeless and initially could not understand Ruth's faith. But after Ruth's God-given success gleaning in Boaz's field, Naomi's outlook changed dramatically. She was able to see that God was at work helping them rebuild their lives. The marriage of Ruth and Boaz brought joyful fulfillment to Naomi; once again Naomi had not only a son but later a grandson!

Boaz was wonderfully gentle and wise. Although strong and successful, he was sensitive and concerned about the needs of those around him. He was immediately interested in Ruth and Naomi's situation, while still carefully maintaining Ruth's dignity. Perhaps a widower himself and likely some years older than Ruth, Boaz also displayed admirable self-control and respect for Ruth. He chose the path of delayed gratification in their relationship rather than a sexual compromise.

God led Naomi and Ruth to a new life filled with promise for the future. The son of Ruth and Boaz would become the grandfather of King David and the ancestor of Jesus the Messiah. They could never have known that their simple acts of faith would lead to the salvation and blessing of millions! God may have significant plans for us and our descendants, too. All we need to do is trust God and obey his will for us.

STRENGTHS AND ACCOMPLISHMENTS:
* Naomi and Ruth's relationship was centered on God.
* Ruth and Naomi were committed to each other.
* Ruth's actions were characterized by faith, loyalty, and boldness.
* Boaz was sensitive, generous, and full of integrity.

LESSONS FROM THEIR LIVES:
* Trust is the necessary foundation for a healthy relationship.
* Grieving is the process that helps us recover from losses.
* Those who are grieving need people to stand by them.
* God is intimately involved in our grief.

KEY VERSE:
"Don't ask me to leave you and turn back. Wherever you go, I will go; wherever you live, I will live. Your people will be my people, and your God will be my God" (1:16).

The story of Ruth, Naomi, and Boaz is told in the book of Ruth. Boaz and Ruth are mentioned in Matthew 1:5, and Boaz is referred to in 1 Chronicles 2:11-12 and Luke 3:23-38.

---

on with me? Can I still give birth to other sons who could grow up to be your husbands? ¹²No, my daughters, return to your parents' homes, for I am too old to marry again. And even if it were possible, and I were to get married tonight and bear sons, then what? ¹³Would you wait for them to grow up and refuse to marry someone else? No, of course not, my daughters! Things are far more bitter for

me than for you, because the LORD himself has raised his fist against me."

¹⁴And again they wept together, and Orpah kissed her mother-in-law good-bye. But Ruth clung tightly to Naomi. ¹⁵"Look," Naomi said to her, "your sister-in-law has gone back to her people and to her gods. You should do the same."

¹⁶But Ruth replied, "Don't ask me to leave

you and turn back. Wherever you go, I will go; wherever you live, I will live. Your people will be my people, and your God will be my God. [17]Wherever you die, I will die, and there I will be buried. May the LORD punish me severely if I allow anything but death to separate us!" [18]When Naomi saw that Ruth was determined to go with her, she said nothing more.

[19]So the two of them continued on their journey. When they came to Bethlehem, the entire town was excited by their arrival. "Is it really Naomi?" the women asked.

[20]"Don't call me Naomi," she responded. "Instead, call me Mara,* for the Almighty has made life very bitter for me. [21]I went away full, but the LORD has brought me home empty. Why call me Naomi when the LORD has caused me to suffer* and the Almighty has sent such tragedy upon me?"

[22]So Naomi returned from Moab, accompanied by her daughter-in-law Ruth, the young Moabite woman. They arrived in Bethlehem in late spring, at the beginning of the barley harvest.

CHAPTER 2
Ruth Works in Boaz's Field
Now there was a wealthy and influential man in Bethlehem named Boaz, who was a relative of Naomi's husband, Elimelech.

[2]One day Ruth the Moabite said to Naomi, "Let me go out into the harvest fields to pick up the stalks of grain left behind by anyone who is kind enough to let me do it."

Naomi replied, "All right, my daughter, go ahead." [3]So Ruth went out to gather grain behind the harvesters. And as it happened, she found herself working in a field that belonged to Boaz, the relative of her father-in-law, Elimelech.

[4]While she was there, Boaz arrived from Bethlehem and greeted the harvesters. "The LORD be with you!" he said.

"The LORD bless you!" the harvesters replied.

[5]Then Boaz asked his foreman, "Who is that young woman over there? Who does she belong to?"

[6]And the foreman replied, "She is the young woman from Moab who came back with Naomi. [7]She asked me this morning if she could gather grain behind the harvesters. She has been hard at work ever since, except for a few minutes' rest in the shelter."

[8]Boaz went over and said to Ruth, "Listen, my daughter. Stay right here with us when you gather grain; don't go to any other fields. Stay right behind the young women working in my field. [9]See which part of the field they are harvesting, and then follow them. I have warned the young men not to treat you roughly. And when you are thirsty, help yourself to the water they have drawn from the well."

[10]Ruth fell at his feet and thanked him warmly. "What have I done to deserve such kindness?" she asked. "I am only a foreigner."

[11]"Yes, I know," Boaz replied. "But I also know about everything you have done for your mother-in-law since the death of your husband. I have heard how you left your father and mother and your own land to live here among complete strangers. [12]May the LORD, the God of Israel, under whose wings you have come to take refuge, reward you fully for what you have done."

[13]"I hope I continue to please you, sir," she replied. "You have comforted me by speaking so kindly to me, even though I am not one of your workers."

1:20 Naomi means "pleasant"; Mara means "bitter." 1:21 Or has testified against me.

2:1-3, 18-23 We must never forget that God is in charge of the recovery process. Ruth was guided by God into Boaz's field, though at the time she was unaware of it. Later Naomi recognized God's guidance. Throughout this story God was hard at work behind the scenes, whether the people involved recognized it or not. God often works the same way with us. He leads us to meet people and make decisions that make all the difference for us. It is only later that we see that God was leading us all the way. Knowing that God works in this way should encourage us as we face the challenges and unknowns in our life.

2:4-17 This passage beautifully illustrates one of the Bible's most encouraging and reassuring promises: "God . . . will supply all your needs" (Philippians 4:19). Naomi and Ruth needed food, so Ruth went in search of it. As she stepped out in faith, persevering in her commitment to Naomi, God provided what she needed—a place to gather grain in an atmosphere of safety and respect. God led her to the field of Boaz, a man of outstanding character—honest and willing to help others without demanding anything in return. When we experience such fortunate "coincidences" and helpful new relationships in life, we need to thank God for his provision.

¹⁴At mealtime Boaz called to her, "Come over here, and help yourself to some food. You can dip your bread in the sour wine." So she sat with his harvesters, and Boaz gave her some roasted grain to eat. She ate all she wanted and still had some left over.

¹⁵When Ruth went back to work again, Boaz ordered his young men, "Let her gather grain right among the sheaves without stopping her. ¹⁶And pull out some heads of barley from the bundles and drop them on purpose for her. Let her pick them up, and don't give her a hard time!"

¹⁷So Ruth gathered barley there all day, and when she beat out the grain that evening, it filled an entire basket.* ¹⁸She carried it back into town and showed it to her mother-in-law. Ruth also gave her the roasted grain that was left over from her meal.

¹⁹"Where did you gather all this grain today?" Naomi asked. "Where did you work? May the LORD bless the one who helped you!"

So Ruth told her mother-in-law about the man in whose field she had worked. She said, "The man I worked with today is named Boaz."

²⁰"May the LORD bless him!" Naomi told her daughter-in-law. "He is showing his kindness to us as well as to your dead husband.* That man is one of our closest relatives, one of our family redeemers."

²¹Then Ruth* said, "What's more, Boaz even told me to come back and stay with his harvesters until the entire harvest is completed."

²²"Good!" Naomi exclaimed. "Do as he said, my daughter. Stay with his young women right through the whole harvest. You might be harassed in other fields, but you'll be safe with him."

²³So Ruth worked alongside the women in Boaz's fields and gathered grain with them until the end of the barley harvest. Then she continued working with them through the wheat harvest in early summer. And all the while she lived with her mother-in-law.

CHAPTER 3
Ruth at the Threshing Floor

One day Naomi said to Ruth, "My daughter, it's time that I found a permanent home for you, so that you will be provided for. ²Boaz is a close relative of ours, and he's been very kind by letting you gather grain with his young women. Tonight he will be winnowing

2:17 Hebrew *it was about an ephah* [20 quarts or 22 liters]. 2:20 Hebrew *to the living and to the dead.* 2:21 Hebrew *Ruth the Moabite.*

LOVE

READ RUTH 2:4-18

"Please love me!" Isn't this the whispered cry of our heart? We may not want to admit it for fear of rejection, but we all are hungry for love. Some of us are starving for affection because of previous losses. We gather whatever crumbs we can find to fill that hunger deep inside.

Ruth was a young woman who had known loss and hunger. Her husband died, leaving her without any means of emotional or physical sustenance. She followed her mother-in-law, Naomi, to a foreign land and gathered leftover grain from the harvested fields just to have enough to stay alive. Boaz, the man who owned the fields, was a relative who could marry Ruth, if he so chose, and fulfill her needs for love and protection. Naomi told her to go to the threshing floor where Boaz was sleeping and curl up at his feet. Culturally, this displayed a request to be taken care of. Boaz was quite happy to find Ruth there and later married her, providing the love and provision she had lost and longed for.

As we turn our life over to God, we need to venture toward developing healthy love relationships with people and with God. It's scary to say, "Please love me," but it's worth the risk. If we don't satisfy our hunger for love in a legitimate way, we will be driven back toward our addictive/compulsive behaviors. We can be sure that when we "curl up" at the feet of Jesus, he will be glad to find us there. He will provide for us, protect us, and love us. *Turn to page 359, 1 Samuel 13.*

barley at the threshing floor. [3]Now do as I tell you—take a bath and put on perfume and dress in your nicest clothes. Then go to the threshing floor, but don't let Boaz see you until he has finished eating and drinking. [4]Be sure to notice where he lies down; then go and uncover his feet and lie down there. He will tell you what to do."

[5]"I will do everything you say," Ruth replied. [6]So she went down to the threshing floor that night and followed the instructions of her mother-in-law.

[7]After Boaz had finished eating and drinking and was in good spirits, he lay down at the far end of the pile of grain and went to sleep. Then Ruth came quietly, uncovered his feet, and lay down. [8]Around midnight Boaz suddenly woke up and turned over. He was surprised to find a woman lying at his feet! [9]"Who are you?" he asked.

"I am your servant Ruth," she replied. "Spread the corner of your covering over me, for you are my family redeemer."

[10]"The LORD bless you, my daughter!" Boaz exclaimed. "You are showing even more family loyalty now than you did before, for you have not gone after a younger man, whether rich or poor. [11]Now don't worry about a thing, my daughter. I will do what is necessary, for everyone in town knows you are a virtuous woman. [12]But while it's true that I am one of your family redeemers, there is another man who is more closely related

to you than I am. [13]Stay here tonight, and in the morning I will talk to him. If he is willing to redeem you, very well. Let him marry you. But if he is not willing, then as surely as the LORD lives, I will redeem you myself! Now lie down here until morning."

[14]So Ruth lay at Boaz's feet until the morning, but she got up before it was light enough for people to recognize each other. For Boaz had said, "No one must know that a woman was here at the threshing floor." [15]Then Boaz said to her, "Bring your cloak and spread it out." He measured six scoops* of barley into the cloak and placed it on her back. Then he* returned to the town.

[16]When Ruth went back to her mother-in-law, Naomi asked, "What happened, my daughter?"

Ruth told Naomi everything Boaz had done for her, [17]and she added, "He gave me these six scoops of barley and said, 'Don't go back to your mother-in-law empty-handed.'"

[18]Then Naomi said to her, "Just be patient, my daughter, until we hear what happens. The man won't rest until he has settled things today."

CHAPTER 4
Boaz Marries Ruth

Boaz went to the town gate and took a seat there. Just then the family redeemer he had mentioned came by, so Boaz called out to him, "Come over here and sit down, friend. I

3:15a Hebrew *six measures,* an unknown quantity. 3:15b Most Hebrew manuscripts read *he;* many Hebrew manuscripts, Syriac version, and Latin Vulgate read *she.*

3:6-14 This is one of the great biblical examples of how the truth, clear personal boundaries, and self-respect can protect people in a tempting situation. Both Ruth and Boaz, though in a delicate and compromising situation, chose to do what was right. They avoided the sexual gratification that many couples would have embraced; they refused to yield to the "chemistry" of the moment. They considered the long-term consequences of sexual activity outside the bounds of marriage. Notice how Boaz showed an unselfish concern for Ruth's safety (3:13) and her reputation (3:14).

3:15-18 Earlier Boaz had provided abundantly for the short-term needs of Ruth and Naomi, but now that the harvest was over he gave them additional provisions. Naomi recognized in Boaz's generous gifts his willingness to be responsible for Ruth (and Naomi) according to the stipulations of God's law (Deuteronomy 25:5-10). God provided for Naomi and Ruth through his wise laws and through a man who was willing to obey them. God has given his Word to us for guidance. We need to follow through on his program if we hope to help others in recovery or to continue in recovery ourself.

4:1-10 As we watch Boaz negotiate, it is clear that he was a wise and shrewd man. He did not lie or manipulate the circumstances, though he clearly sought a specific outcome. Boaz wisely anticipated the greedy response of Naomi's closer kinsman. This other man wanted the inheritance of Ruth's dead husband but had no desire to care for Ruth or to father her children and care for them. When faced with the facts, he saw that the economic advantages of taking Ruth's case were limited, possibly even detrimental. He did not want to be held accountable to God's law and the economic loss it might entail. We must be careful not only to seek the advantages in our relationships but also to accept the responsibilities. Like Boaz, we need to seek what is best for the people close to us.

want to talk to you." So they sat down together. ²Then Boaz called ten leaders from the town and asked them to sit as witnesses. ³And Boaz said to the family redeemer, "You know Naomi, who came back from Moab. She is selling the land that belonged to our relative Elimelech. ⁴I thought I should speak to you about it so that you can redeem it if you wish. If you want the land, then buy it here in the presence of these witnesses. But if you don't want it, let me know right away, because I am next in line to redeem it after you."

The man replied, "All right, I'll redeem it."

⁵Then Boaz told him, "Of course, your purchase of the land from Naomi also requires that you marry Ruth, the Moabite widow. That way she can have children who will carry on her husband's name and keep the land in the family."

⁶"Then I can't redeem it," the family redeemer replied, "because this might endanger my own estate. You redeem the land; I cannot do it."

⁷Now in those days it was the custom in Israel for anyone transferring a right of purchase to remove his sandal and hand it to the other party. This publicly validated the transaction. ⁸So the other family redeemer drew off his sandal as he said to Boaz, "You buy the land."

⁹Then Boaz said to the elders and to the crowd standing around, "You are witnesses that today I have bought from Naomi all the property of Elimelech, Kilion, and Mahlon. ¹⁰And with the land I have acquired Ruth, the Moabite widow of Mahlon, to be my wife. This way she can have a son to carry on the family name of her dead husband and to inherit the family property here in his hometown. You are all witnesses today."

¹¹Then the elders and all the people standing in the gate replied, "We are witnesses! May the LORD make this woman who is coming into your home like Rachel and Leah, from whom all the nation of Israel descended! May you prosper in Ephrathah and be famous in Bethlehem. ¹²And may the LORD give you descendants by this young woman who will be like those of our ancestor Perez, the son of Tamar and Judah."

The Descendants of Boaz

¹³So Boaz took Ruth into his home, and she became his wife. When he slept with her, the LORD enabled her to become pregnant, and she gave birth to a son. ¹⁴Then the women of the town said to Naomi, "Praise the LORD, who has now provided a redeemer for your family! May this child be famous in Israel. ¹⁵May he restore your youth and care for you in your old age. For he is the son of your daughter-in-law who loves you and has been better to you than seven sons!"

¹⁶Naomi took the baby and cuddled him to her breast. And she cared for him as if he were her own. ¹⁷The neighbor women said, "Now at last Naomi has a son again!" And they named him Obed. He became the father of Jesse and the grandfather of David.

¹⁸This is the genealogical record of their ancestor Perez:

Perez was the father of Hezron.
¹⁹ Hezron was the father of Ram.
Ram was the father of Amminadab.
²⁰ Amminadab was the father of Nahshon.
Nahshon was the father of Salmon.*
²¹ Salmon was the father of Boaz.
Boaz was the father of Obed.
²² Obed was the father of Jesse.
Jesse was the father of David.

4:20 As in some Greek manuscripts (see also 4:21); Hebrew reads *Salma.*

4:18-22 Hidden in this family tree is powerful evidence that God uses fallible people to bring about his good will. Perez was the first of David's ancestors mentioned; he was the illegitimate son of Judah and his daughter-in-law, Tamar (Genesis 38:1-30). Boaz was the son of Salmon, whose wife was Rahab, a prostitute in Jericho (Joshua 2:1-24; Matthew 1:5). Ruth was a foreigner from Moab, not even one of God's chosen people. God used these people, far from ideal according to human standards, to produce Israel's greatest king, David, and the world's only Savior, Jesus Christ. Knowing this truth should give us hope. No matter what we've done or how we've lived in the past, God can use us significantly if we are willing to put ourself in his hands.

REFLECTIONS ON RUTH

insights FROM THE STORY OF RUTH

Ruth 1:6-22 shows us the painful beginnings of the recovery process. In choosing to leave Moab, Naomi was admitting her powerlessness. She displayed brutal honesty as she advised her daughters-in-law to return to their family of origin. Naomi knew that she would be unable to support them in the years ahead. But she also knew that in sending them away, she was dismissing her last vestige of support and security. As bleak as the situation was, Naomi was willing to summon the courage to build a new life. Too often our desire for short-term security prevents us from stepping out in faith. We cling to the people and things that help us feel secure. This, however, only keeps us from turning everything over to God. As a result, we often miss God's best for us.

In **Ruth 3:1-7** Naomi's plan to find a husband for her daughter-in-law may seem a little strange to us. However, it was based on a scriptural provision for the protection of widows (Deuteronomy 25:5-10). God had assigned the responsibility of caring for a widow to the dead husband's brothers or near relatives. Since Boaz was a near relative to Ruth's dead husband, he was bound by the law to do something to help her. Ruth trusted Naomi's advice and took another courageous step of faith and obedience, following God's program for rebuilding her life. God often provides direction for us in his Word, but that doesn't mean our life will automatically work out. We need to takes steps of faith and obedience, following his plan for recovery.

As we see in **Ruth 4:11-17**, Ruth's and Naomi's recovery from loneliness and destitution ends happily. Naomi, who had lost her family (1:4-5), had a family once again. Ruth, who had lost her husband and all hope of a prosperous future (1:8-9), was given a husband, a son, and hope for the future. It is interesting to note that Ruth's sacrificial lifestyle brought recovery not only to herself and Naomi but to all of us. Boaz and Ruth had a son named Obed, and he became the ancestor of Jesus Christ, who has provided the means for all of us to recover from the destructive effects of sin.

1 SAMUEL

THE BIG PICTURE

A. FINISHING WITH THE OLD—
   SAMUEL, THE LAST JUDGE
   (1:1–12:25)
   1. God's Man Is Brought on the
      Scene (1:1–3:21)
   2. The Problems Continue—
      War with the Philistines
      (4:1–7:17)
   3. A King Is Requested, Chosen,
      and Anointed (8:1–11:15)
   4. Samuel's Retirement
      (12:1-25)
B. STARTING WITH THE NEW—
   SAUL, THE FIRST KING
   (13:1–31:13)
   1. The Sudden Failure of Saul as
      Leader (13:1–15:35)
   2. A New Leader
      Appears—David
      (16:1–17:58)
   3. Saul's Obsession with David
      (18:1–30:31)
   4. The Death of Saul (31:1-13)

The book of 1 Samuel begins with the birth of the prophet Samuel and ends with the death of King Saul. It contains a catalog of lives for us to learn from—some exemplary, others not. Samuel was born in the time of the judges, when "people did whatever seemed right in their own eyes" (Judges 17:6). The people were far from God. Eli was high priest, but the flaws in his leadership can be seen in the dysfunctions of his own family. Since Israel lacked strong spiritual leadership, God chose Samuel and prepared him to lead the Israelites back to God.

Near the end of Samuel's ministry, the people demanded a king; they wanted to be like the surrounding nations. God was not pleased with Israel's demand, but he chose Saul to lead them anyway. Saul, though a man of great potential, was self-centered and disobedient; he never achieved what God had intended for him.

While Saul was still king, Samuel anointed David to be the next king. David became a national hero by killing Goliath, and he won numerous other great battles with God's help. But when Saul realized that David was in line for the throne, he was consumed by bitterness and tried to kill him. Finally, faced with defeat in battle, Saul took his own life.

This book portrays some who moved toward God and toward wholeness and others who moved away from God and toward disaster. Jealousy, bitterness, and disobedience destroyed the life of King Saul. But forgiveness, trust, and obedience brought David great success. This book clearly shows that the only way to wholeness is by trusting and obeying God and following his program.

THE BOTTOM LINE

PURPOSE: To track Israel's transition from the period of the judges to the era of kingly rule. AUTHOR: Unknown, but probably most of it was written by Samuel. Nathan and Gad were also contributors. AUDIENCE: The people of Israel. DATE WRITTEN: The book was probably started during Samuel's lifetime and finished around 930 B.C. SETTING: In Israel, between 1120 and 971 B.C. KEY VERSE: "What is more pleasing to the LORD: your burnt offerings and sacrifices or your obedience to his voice? Listen! Obedience is better than sacrifice" (15:22). KEY PLACES: Shiloh, Gilgal, Ramah, Bethlehem, Gath, Adullam, Hebron, the wilderness of Judah, Ziklag, Endor, Beth-shan. KEY PEOPLE AND RELATIONSHIPS: Samuel and Eli, Samuel and Saul, and Samuel and David.

RECOVERY THEMES

Dependence on God: Of the three men prominent in the books of Samuel (Samuel, Saul, and David), only two (Samuel and David) truly depended on God. The third, Saul, started out well, but his faith in God never matured. When God chose Saul as the first king, Saul clearly had the potential for greatness. But instead of obeying God and trusting him for success, Saul acted out of self-sufficiency and ended up a tragic failure. When we experience success in life or when someone threatens our success, we need to keep our eyes on God. He is the giver of all success and the only one who can help us continue in it.

Strength in Weakness: No matter how weak we may be, God is able to work through us to do mighty things. When young David killed the giant Goliath in God's name, David's weakness became a funnel for God's power. Jonathan and his bodyguard virtually destroyed a vast Philistine army with God's help—a task impossible from a human perspective! There is only one way to begin the process of recovery: We must admit our powerlessness. Then God can step into our life and supply us with all the power we need to follow his will in recovery.

Necessity of Obedience: Again we are confronted with the importance of obedience for those who want to recover. To God, "obedience is better than sacrifice" (15:22). In Saul's case, his lack of obedience led to his downfall. David, on the other hand, was a man after God's own heart. He trusted and obeyed God. Even when he could have killed Saul, he refused because Saul was God's anointed king. And even though David failed and sinned, he repented and turned back to God. Be encouraged. No one can live a flawless life, but we do need to trust God and do our best to obey him.

Consequences of Disobedience: When Eli, Samuel, Saul, and David disobeyed God, they all faced tragic consequences. Their sin affected not only themselves but also their children. Saul's disobedience destroyed not only himself but the majority of his family. Saul had various opportunities to get his life back on track, but his self-centered heart blocked him from looking to God for help and healing. Saul's lack of faith and obedience resulted in a bitter life and tragic death.

CHAPTER 1
Elkanah and His Family

There was a man named Elkanah who lived in Ramah in the region of Zuph* in the hill country of Ephraim. He was the son of Jeroham, son of Elihu, son of Tohu, son of Zuph, of Ephraim. ²Elkanah had two wives, Hannah and Peninnah. Peninnah had children, but Hannah did not.

³Each year Elkanah would travel to Shiloh to worship and sacrifice to the LORD of Heaven's Armies at the Tabernacle. The priests of the LORD at that time were the two sons of Eli—Hophni and Phinehas. ⁴On the days Elkanah presented his sacrifice, he would give portions of the meat to Peninnah and each of her children. ⁵And though he loved Hannah, he would give her only one choice portion* because the LORD had given her no children. ⁶So Peninnah would taunt Hannah and make fun of her because the LORD had kept her from having children. ⁷Year after year it was the same—Peninnah would taunt Hannah as they went to the Tabernacle.* Each time, Hannah would be reduced to tears and would not even eat.

⁸"Why are you crying, Hannah?" Elkanah would ask. "Why aren't you eating? Why be

1:1 As in Greek version; Hebrew reads *in Ramathaim-zophim*; compare 1:19. 1:5 Or *And because he loved Hannah, he would give her a choice portion.* The meaning of the Hebrew is uncertain. 1:7 Hebrew *the house of the LORD;* also in 1:24.

1:9-11 In these verses Hannah breathed a beautiful prayer through her tears. She admitted her helplessness and acknowledged her need of a Power greater than herself. In faith she not only committed her infertility to God, but she also vowed to surrender to God's service the son he might give her (1:11). All of us must realize that without God's intervention we are helpless to overcome any of the problems or dependencies we might have. Learning to give up control and wholly depend upon God is a step we all need to take.

1:12-18 Hannah's prayer was misunderstood by Eli the priest, who assumed she was drunk. In reality she was taking a vital step toward recovery by admitting her helplessness and committing her infertility to God. Sadly, attempts toward recovery are often misinterpreted, and the insensitive responses we experience can be disheartening. To her credit, Hannah persevered despite the criticism she received. Eli soon recognized Hannah's integrity and encouraged her in her prayer (1:17). No matter what discouragement we may face in recovery, we must persevere. God will support us, even if the people around us do not.

HANNAH

Living in a dysfunctional family does not automatically mean that an individual will turn away from God. Neither does turning to God guarantee that the problems of a destructive family situation will go away. Reaching out to God, however, does ensure that we will have a far better chance of coping despite the devastating circumstances.

Hannah lived in a difficult family situation. As was typical in the Israelite culture during the times of the judges, Elkanah, her husband, had a second wife named Peninnah. Such a relationship, although it may have met certain needs, almost inevitably would lead to problems.

Elkanah foolishly played favorites—he loved Hannah more than Peninnah. He was apparently unaware of the negative impact his partiality had on the relationship between his wives. Peninnah became jealous of Hannah and got back at her by flaunting the fact that she had children while Hannah did not. Bearing children in ancient Israel gave the mother both personal fulfillment and social status.

Hannah reacted with bitter anguish. No amount of comforting by her husband could relieve her pain—she wanted a child. In desperation, on a yearly pilgrimage to the Tabernacle, Hannah silently poured out her grief to God. She pleaded for a son and vowed to dedicate the child to God for his entire life. After admitting her helplessness and her need for utter dependence on God, Hannah returned home with a renewed spiritual confidence that God would grant her request. When God did give her a son, she named him Samuel, offered a prayer of praise to God, and fulfilled her vow by dedicating Samuel to God's service. God, in turn, blessed Hannah with additional children. Our only hope is to turn our life over to God, regardless of the circumstances, and then allow him to work recovery and healing within us.

STRENGTHS AND ACCOMPLISHMENTS:
- Hannah turned her life and her will over to God in her time of need.
- Hannah prayed from the heart.
- Hannah carried out her vow, even though it was costly.

WEAKNESSES AND MISTAKES:
- Hannah allowed the circumstances of her life to dictate her feelings and her sense of worth.

LESSONS FROM HER LIFE:
- We should turn our life over to God before our situation becomes unbearable.
- God ultimately is the only one who can fulfill our needs.
- Keeping our vows to God sustains a close relationship with him, allowing him to shower us with his blessings.

KEY VERSE:
"Hannah was in deep anguish, crying bitterly as she prayed to the LORD" (1 Samuel 1:10).

Hannah's story is told in 1 Samuel 1:1–2:21.

---

downhearted just because you have no children? You have me—isn't that better than having ten sons?"

Hannah's Prayer for a Son

⁹Once after a sacrificial meal at Shiloh, Hannah got up and went to pray. Eli the priest was sitting at his customary place beside the entrance of the Tabernacle.* ¹⁰Hannah was in deep anguish, crying bitterly as she prayed to the LORD. ¹¹And she made this vow: "O LORD of Heaven's Armies, if you will look upon my sorrow and answer my prayer and give me a son, then I will give him back to you. He will be yours for his entire lifetime, and as a sign that he has been dedicated to the LORD, his hair will never be cut.*"

¹²As she was praying to the LORD, Eli watched her. ¹³Seeing her lips moving but hearing no sound, he thought she had been drinking. ¹⁴"Must you come here drunk?" he demanded. "Throw away your wine!"

¹⁵"Oh no, sir!" she replied. "I haven't been drinking wine or anything stronger. But I am very discouraged, and I was pouring out my heart to the LORD. ¹⁶Don't think I am a wicked woman! For I have been praying out of great anguish and sorrow."

¹⁷"In that case," Eli said, "go in peace!

1:9 Hebrew *the Temple of the LORD.* 1:11 Some manuscripts add *He will drink neither wine nor intoxicants.*

May the God of Israel grant the request you have asked of him."

18"Oh, thank you, sir!" she exclaimed. Then she went back and began to eat again, and she was no longer sad.

Samuel's Birth and Dedication

19The entire family got up early the next morning and went to worship the LORD once more. Then they returned home to Ramah. When Elkanah slept with Hannah, the LORD remembered her plea, 20and in due time she gave birth to a son. She named him Samuel,* for she said, "I asked the LORD for him."

21The next year Elkanah and his family went on their annual trip to offer a sacrifice to the LORD and to keep his vow. 22But Hannah did not go. She told her husband, "Wait until the boy is weaned. Then I will take him to the Tabernacle and leave him there with the LORD permanently.*"

23"Whatever you think is best," Elkanah agreed. "Stay here for now, and may the LORD help you keep your promise.*" So she stayed home and nursed the boy until he was weaned.

24When the child was weaned, Hannah took him to the Tabernacle in Shiloh. They brought along a three-year-old bull* for the sacrifice and a basket* of flour and some wine. 25After sacrificing the bull, they brought the boy to Eli. 26"Sir, do you remember me?" Hannah asked. "I am the very woman who stood here several years ago praying to the LORD. 27I asked the LORD to give me this boy, and he has granted my request. 28Now I am giving him to the LORD, and he will belong to the LORD his whole life." And they* worshiped the LORD there.

CHAPTER 2
Hannah's Prayer of Praise

Then Hannah prayed:

"My heart rejoices in the LORD!
    The LORD has made me strong.*
Now I have an answer for my enemies;
    I rejoice because you rescued me.
2No one is holy like the LORD!
    There is no one besides you;
    there is no Rock like our God.

3"Stop acting so proud and haughty!
    Don't speak with such arrogance!
For the LORD is a God who knows what
        you have done;
    he will judge your actions.
4The bow of the mighty is now broken,
    and those who stumbled are now
        strong.
5Those who were well fed are now starving,
    and those who were starving are
        now full.
The childless woman now has seven
        children,
    and the woman with many children
        wastes away.
6The LORD gives both death and life;
    he brings some down to the grave* but
        raises others up.
7The LORD makes some poor and others
        rich;
    he brings some down and lifts
        others up.
8He lifts the poor from the dust
    and the needy from the garbage dump.
He sets them among princes,
    placing them in seats of honor.
For all the earth is the LORD's,
    and he has set the world in order.

1:20 *Samuel* sounds like the Hebrew term for "asked of God" or "heard by God." 1:22 Some manuscripts add *I will offer him as a Nazirite for all time.* 1:23 As in Dead Sea Scrolls and Greek version; Masoretic Text reads *may the LORD keep his promise.* 1:24a As in Dead Sea Scrolls, Greek and Syriac versions; Masoretic Text reads *three bulls.* 1:24b Hebrew *and an ephah* [20 quarts or 22 liters]. 1:28 Hebrew *he.* 2:1 Hebrew *has exalted my horn.* 2:6 Hebrew *to Sheol.*

2:1-3 Note Hannah's prayer of rejoicing: "My heart rejoices in the LORD! The LORD has made me strong!" (2:1). She praised the one responsible for her deliverance—God himself. He had delivered her from the trauma of infertility and gave her a son. After Hannah gave Samuel into God's service, he blessed her with other children (2:21). This certainly would have lightened the burden of seeing her firstborn son only once a year (2:19). Obedience was surely difficult, even painful, but it was for the good of Hannah and Samuel, and ultimately for the good of all Israel. Obedience to God, as painful as it might be at times, will ultimately bring us joy. It will also bring blessings to the people close to us.

2:12-17 Eli's sons sinned greatly by treating God's offerings with contempt. They failed to realize that the sacrifices were God's provision for the people's recovery from sin. They stole meat from the sacrifices for their own personal use rather than for their healing and purification. God has provided for our recovery by giving the ultimate sacrifice on our behalf. If we treat Christ with contempt by refusing to follow his recovery program, we are as guilty as Eli's sons (Hebrews 10:26-29). Let us show proper respect for the compassion, love, and power that God has shown to us through Christ! Let us wholeheartedly embrace his provision for our healing.

SAMUEL

As soon as Samuel was weaned from Hannah, who had cried out to God for a child, she gave him back to God. Samuel learned the various duties of the priesthood from Eli, Israel's high priest. During his lifetime, Samuel served as a priest, a prophet, and Israel's last judge. He was a godly man who transformed the office of judge from that of a crisis military leader to a stable position of leadership just short of kingship.

But Samuel was human and had his blind spots. When the people asked to have a king like other countries, Samuel took this request as rejection of his own leadership. What Samuel didn't hear was the people's complaint that his sons, whom he had appointed as judges in his place, "accepted bribes and perverted justice" (8:3). The people hadn't rejected Samuel; they had rejected God's leadership and the leadership of Samuel's corrupt sons.

Perhaps Samuel was deaf to the people's complaints about his sons because he was blind to their corrupt ways. We often develop blind spots from dysfunctional situations within our family. If Samuel had heard the people's complaints and corrected the problem, things might have been different. When we feel rejection, it should be a signal to evaluate carefully what is being said. In spite of his family issues, however, Samuel was a great man of faith and one of the greatest leaders in Israel's history.

STRENGTHS AND ACCOMPLISHMENTS:
* Samuel was sensitive to God's voice.
* He was the last and greatest judge in Israel.
* He commanded great respect from the people of Israel.

WEAKNESSES AND MISTAKES:
* He failed to lead his sons to a close relationship with God.

LESSONS FROM HIS LIFE:
* The feeling of rejection can blind us to God's truth.
* Who we are with God is more important than what we accomplish in life.

KEY VERSES:
"As Samuel grew up, the LORD was with him, and everything Samuel said proved to be reliable. And all Israel, from Dan in the north to Beersheba in the south, knew that Samuel was confirmed as a prophet of the LORD" (1 Samuel 3:19-20).

Samuel's story is found in 1 Samuel 1:1—25:1; 28. He is mentioned in Psalm 99:6; Jeremiah 15:1; Acts 3:24; 13:20; Hebrews 11:32.

---

⁹ "He will protect his faithful ones,
   but the wicked will disappear in
      darkness.
No one will succeed by strength alone.
¹⁰   Those who fight against the LORD will be
      shattered.
He thunders against them from heaven;
   the LORD judges throughout the earth.
He gives power to his king;
   he increases the strength* of his
      anointed one."

¹¹Then Elkanah returned home to Ramah without Samuel. And the boy served the LORD by assisting Eli the priest.

Eli's Wicked Sons

¹²Now the sons of Eli were scoundrels who had no respect for the LORD ¹³or for their duties as priests. Whenever anyone offered a sacrifice, Eli's sons would send over a servant with a three-pronged fork. While the meat of the sacrificed animal was still boiling, ¹⁴the servant would stick the fork into the pot and demand that whatever it brought up be given to Eli's sons. All the Israelites who came to worship at Shiloh were treated this way. ¹⁵Sometimes the servant would come even before the animal's fat had been burned on the altar. He would demand raw meat before it had been boiled so that it could be used for roasting.

¹⁶The man offering the sacrifice might reply, "Take as much as you want, but the fat must be burned first." Then the servant would demand, "No, give it to me now, or I'll take it by force." ¹⁷So the sin of these young men was very serious in the LORD's sight, for they treated the LORD's offerings with contempt.

¹⁸But Samuel, though he was only a boy, served the LORD. He wore a linen garment like that of a priest.* ¹⁹Each year his mother made a small coat for him and brought it to him when she came with her husband for the sacrifice. ²⁰Before they returned home,

2:10 Hebrew *he exalts the horn.* 2:18 Hebrew *He wore a linen ephod.*

Eli would bless Elkanah and his wife and say, "May the LORD give you other children to take the place of this one she gave to the LORD.*" [21]And the LORD blessed Hannah, and she conceived and gave birth to three sons and two daughters. Meanwhile, Samuel grew up in the presence of the LORD.

[22]Now Eli was very old, but he was aware of what his sons were doing to the people of Israel. He knew, for instance, that his sons were seducing the young women who assisted at the entrance of the Tabernacle.* [23]Eli said to them, "I have been hearing reports from all the people about the wicked things you are doing. Why do you keep sinning? [24]You must stop, my sons! The reports I hear among the LORD's people are not good. [25]If someone sins against another person, God* can mediate for the guilty party. But if someone sins against the LORD, who can intercede?" But Eli's sons wouldn't listen to their father, for the LORD was already planning to put them to death.

[26]Meanwhile, the boy Samuel grew taller and grew in favor with the LORD and with the people.

A Warning for Eli's Family

[27]One day a man of God came to Eli and gave him this message from the LORD: "I revealed myself* to your ancestors when they were Pharaoh's slaves in Egypt. [28]I chose your ancestor Aaron* from among all the tribes of Israel to be my priest, to offer sacrifices on my altar, to burn incense, and to wear the priestly vest* as he served me. And I assigned the sacrificial offerings to you priests. [29]So why do you scorn my sacrifices and offerings? Why do you give your sons more honor than you give me—for you and they have become fat from the best offerings of my people Israel!

[30]"Therefore, the LORD, the God of Israel, says: I promised that your branch of the tribe of Levi* would always be my priests. But I will honor those who honor me, and I will despise those who think lightly of me. [31]The time is coming when I will put an end to your family, so it will no longer serve as my

priests. All the members of your family will die before their time. None will reach old age. [32]You will watch with envy as I pour out prosperity on the people of Israel. But no members of your family will ever live out their days. [33]The few not cut off from serving at my altar will survive, but only so their eyes can go blind and their hearts break, and their children will die a violent death.* [34]And to prove that what I have said will come true, I will cause your two sons, Hophni and Phinehas, to die on the same day!

[35]"Then I will raise up a faithful priest who will serve me and do what I desire. I will establish his family, and they will be priests to my anointed kings forever. [36]Then all of your surviving family will bow before him, begging for money and food. 'Please,' they will say, 'give us jobs among the priests so we will have enough to eat.' "

CHAPTER 3
The LORD Speaks to Samuel

Meanwhile, the boy Samuel served the LORD by assisting Eli. Now in those days messages from the LORD were very rare, and visions were quite uncommon.

[2]One night Eli, who was almost blind by now, had gone to bed. [3]The lamp of God had not yet gone out, and Samuel was sleeping in the Tabernacle* near the Ark of God. [4]Suddenly the LORD called out, "Samuel!"

"Yes?" Samuel replied. "What is it?" [5]He got up and ran to Eli. "Here I am. Did you call me?"

"I didn't call you," Eli replied. "Go back to bed." So he did.

[6]Then the LORD called out again, "Samuel!"

Again Samuel got up and went to Eli. "Here I am. Did you call me?"

"I didn't call you, my son," Eli said. "Go back to bed."

[7]Samuel did not yet know the LORD because he had never had a message from the LORD before. [8]So the LORD called a third time, and once more Samuel got up and went to Eli. "Here I am. Did you call me?"

2:20 As in Dead Sea Scrolls and Greek version; Masoretic Text reads *this one he requested of the LORD.* 2:22 Hebrew *Tent of Meeting.* Some manuscripts lack this entire sentence. 2:25 Or *the judges.* 2:27 As in Greek and Syriac versions; Hebrew reads *Did I reveal myself.* 2:28a Hebrew *your father.* 2:28b Hebrew *an ephod.* 2:30 Hebrew *that your house and your father's house.* 2:33 As in Dead Sea Scrolls and Greek version, which read *die by the sword;* Masoretic Text reads *die like mortals.* 3:3 Hebrew *the Temple of the LORD.*

3:1-10 Learning to listen to God's voice is an important part of the recovery process (Isaiah 30:21; Hebrews 5:11). God spoke directly to young Samuel, and he speaks to us clearly and relevantly through the Holy Spirit and his Word (James 1:22). We need to listen to God's voice as we study to understand the truths in the Bible. There we will find the wisdom and direction we need to progress in recovery.

Then Eli realized it was the LORD who was calling the boy. [9]So he said to Samuel, "Go and lie down again, and if someone calls again, say, 'Speak, LORD, your servant is listening.'" So Samuel went back to bed.

[10]And the LORD came and called as before, "Samuel! Samuel!"

And Samuel replied, "Speak, your servant is listening."

[11]Then the LORD said to Samuel, "I am about to do a shocking thing in Israel. [12]I am going to carry out all my threats against Eli and his family, from beginning to end. [13]I have warned him that judgment is coming upon his family forever, because his sons are blaspheming God* and he hasn't disciplined them. [14]So I have vowed that the sins of Eli and his sons will never be forgiven by sacrifices or offerings."

Samuel Speaks for the LORD

[15]Samuel stayed in bed until morning, then got up and opened the doors of the Tabernacle* as usual. He was afraid to tell Eli what the LORD had said to him. [16]But Eli called out to him, "Samuel, my son."

"Here I am," Samuel replied.

[17]"What did the LORD say to you? Tell me everything. And may God strike you and even kill you if you hide anything from me!" [18]So Samuel told Eli everything; he didn't hold anything back. "It is the LORD's will," Eli replied. "Let him do what he thinks best."

[19]As Samuel grew up, the LORD was with him, and everything Samuel said proved to be reliable. [20]And all Israel, from Dan in the north to Beersheba in the south, knew that Samuel was confirmed as a prophet of the LORD. [21]The LORD continued to appear at Shiloh and gave messages to Samuel there at the Tabernacle. [4:1]And Samuel's words went out to all the people of Israel.

CHAPTER 4
The Philistines Capture the Ark

At that time Israel was at war with the Philistines. The Israelite army was camped near Ebenezer, and the Philistines were at Aphek.

[2]The Philistines attacked and defeated the army of Israel, killing 4,000 men. [3]After the battle was over, the troops retreated to their camp, and the elders of Israel asked, "Why did the LORD allow us to be defeated by the Philistines?" Then they said, "Let's bring the Ark of the Covenant of the LORD from Shiloh. If we carry it into battle with us, it* will save us from our enemies."

[4]So they sent men to Shiloh to bring the Ark of the Covenant of the LORD of Heaven's Armies, who is enthroned between the cherubim. Hophni and Phinehas, the sons of Eli, were also there with the Ark of the Covenant of God. [5]When all the Israelites saw the Ark of the Covenant of the LORD coming into the camp, their shout of joy was so loud it made the ground shake!

[6]"What's going on?" the Philistines asked. "What's all the shouting about in the Hebrew camp?" When they were told it was because the Ark of the LORD had arrived, [7]they panicked. "The gods have* come into their camp!" they cried. "This is a disaster! We have never had to face anything like this before! [8]Help! Who can save us from these mighty gods of Israel? They are the same gods who destroyed the Egyptians with plagues when Israel was in the wilderness. [9]Fight as never before, Philistines! If you don't, we will become the Hebrews' slaves just as they have been ours! Stand up like men and fight!"

[10]So the Philistines fought desperately, and Israel was defeated again. The slaughter was great; 30,000 Israelite soldiers died that day. The survivors turned and fled to their tents. [11]The Ark of God was captured, and Hophni and Phinehas, the two sons of Eli, were killed.

The Death of Eli

[12]A man from the tribe of Benjamin ran from the battlefield and arrived at Shiloh later that same day. He had torn his clothes and put dust on his head to show his grief. [13]Eli was waiting beside the road to hear the news of the battle, for his heart trembled for the safety

---

3:13 As in Greek version; Hebrew reads *his sons have made themselves contemptible.* **3:15** Hebrew *the house of the LORD.* **4:3** Or *he.* **4:7** Or *A god has.*

3:16-18 Samuel's honesty is obvious as he comes clean, telling Eli everything. He even told Eli the devastating truth about the priest's own family and the suffering they would endure. He confronted Eli with his failure, stating clearly the truth God had given him. Such forthrightness must be part of any recovery program. As we discover the truth about ourself and others through God's Word, we will need to speak that truth to others, confronting them in love for their encouragement and spiritual growth. This will never be easy, but it is an important part of any loving relationship.

of the Ark of God. When the messenger arrived and told what had happened, an outcry resounded throughout the town.

[14]"What is all the noise about?" Eli asked.

The messenger rushed over to Eli, [15]who was ninety-eight years old and blind. [16]He said to Eli, "I have just come from the battlefield—I was there this very day."

"What happened, my son?" Eli demanded.

[17]"Israel has been defeated by the Philistines," the messenger replied. "The people have been slaughtered, and your two sons, Hophni and Phinehas, were also killed. And the Ark of God has been captured."

[18]When the messenger mentioned what had happened to the Ark of God, Eli fell backward from his seat beside the gate. He broke his neck and died, for he was old and overweight. He had been Israel's judge for forty years.

[19]Eli's daughter-in-law, the wife of Phinehas, was pregnant and near her time of delivery. When she heard that the Ark of God had been captured and that her father-in-law and husband were dead, she went into labor and gave birth. [20]She died in childbirth, but before she passed away the midwives tried to encourage her. "Don't be afraid," they said. "You have a baby boy!" But she did not answer or pay attention to them.

[21]She named the child Ichabod (which means "Where is the glory?"), for she said, "Israel's glory is gone." She named him this because the Ark of God had been captured

and because her father-in-law and husband were dead. [22]Then she said, "The glory has departed from Israel, for the Ark of God has been captured."

CHAPTER 5
The Ark in Philistia

After the Philistines captured the Ark of God, they took it from the battleground at Ebenezer to the town of Ashdod. [2]They carried the Ark of God into the temple of Dagon and placed it beside an idol of Dagon. [3]But when the citizens of Ashdod went to see it the next morning, Dagon had fallen with his face to the ground in front of the Ark of the LORD! So they took Dagon and put him in his place again. [4]But the next morning the same thing happened—Dagon had fallen face down before the Ark of the LORD again. This time his head and hands had broken off and were lying in the doorway. Only the trunk of his body was left intact. [5]That is why to this day neither the priests of Dagon nor anyone who enters the temple of Dagon in Ashdod will step on its threshold.

[6]Then the LORD's heavy hand struck the people of Ashdod and the nearby villages with a plague of tumors.* [7]When the people realized what was happening, they cried out, "We can't keep the Ark of the God of Israel here any longer! He is against us! We will all be destroyed along with Dagon, our god." [8]So they called together the rulers of the

---

5:6 Greek version and Latin Vulgate read *tumors; and rats appeared in their land, and death and destruction were throughout the city.*

4:16-22 Eli and his family, and indeed the entire nation of Israel, suffered the terrible consequences of disobedience. Eli and his sons died; the Ark of the Covenant, the symbol of God's glorious presence with Israel, was captured by foreigners. This may remind us of how the refusal to abandon our selfish, addictive lifestyle brings suffering upon our family and the people close to us. This is illustrated in Eli's family by Eli's daughter-in-law. With her final words she named her baby Ichabod, meaning "where is the glory?" (4:21-22), for the glory of God had departed from Israel. Before she died she acknowledged her hopelessness, but it was much too late for her and her family. The process of life recovery is not easy; it involves surrender, loss, pain, and difficulty. Yet the death of this young woman and the shattering of Eli's family should warn us about what is at stake if we do not persevere in our quest for recovery.

5:1-4 The ignoble fate of the Philistine idol Dagon illustrates that Israel's God is greater than all other gods (Jeremiah 32:27; 33:2; 1 John 4:4). Anything that controls us has become a "god" in our life, whether it is drugs, drink, sex, power, or money. We should be encouraged knowing that God is stronger than any of the false idols we might serve. If we seek God and follow his recovery program, he will set us free from our addictions so that we may serve him, the only God worthy of our affection.

5:6-12 Physical suffering (5:6, 9, 12) was a direct consequence of the disrespect the Philistines showed toward the true God (5:1-12). The parallels to today are unmistakable. By setting up addictions as gods in our life, we show disrespect to the true God. We also violate God's laws by living selfishly and hurting the people close to us. Many—though not all—who violate God's standards experience physical repercussions. Often it is precisely this suffering that prompts us to seek help. So it was with the Philistines.

Philistine towns and asked, "What should we do with the Ark of the God of Israel?"

The rulers discussed it and replied, "Move it to the town of Gath." So they moved the Ark of the God of Israel to Gath. [9]But when the Ark arrived at Gath, the LORD's heavy hand fell on its men, young and old; he struck them with a plague of tumors, and there was a great panic.

[10]So they sent the Ark of God to the town of Ekron, but when the people of Ekron saw it coming they cried out, "They are bringing the Ark of the God of Israel here to kill us, too!" [11]The people summoned the Philistine rulers again and begged them, "Please send the Ark of the God of Israel back to its own country, or it* will kill us all." For the deadly plague from God had already begun, and great fear was sweeping across the town. [12]Those who didn't die were afflicted with tumors; and the cry from the town rose to heaven.

CHAPTER 6
The Philistines Return the Ark

The Ark of the LORD remained in Philistine territory seven months in all. [2]Then the Philistines called in their priests and diviners and asked them, "What should we do about the Ark of the LORD? Tell us how to return it to its own country."

[3]"Send the Ark of the God of Israel back with a gift," they were told. "Send a guilt offering so the plague will stop. Then, if you are healed, you will know it was his hand that caused the plague."

[4]"What sort of guilt offering should we send?" they asked.

And they were told, "Since the plague has struck both you and your five rulers, make five gold tumors and five gold rats, just like those that have ravaged your land. [5]Make these things to show honor to the God of Israel. Perhaps then he will stop afflicting you, your gods, and your land. [6]Don't be stubborn and rebellious as Pharaoh and the Egyptians were. By the time God was finished with them, they were eager to let Israel go.

[7]"Now build a new cart, and find two cows that have just given birth to calves. Make sure the cows have never been yoked to a cart. Hitch the cows to the cart, but shut their calves away from them in a pen. [8]Put the Ark of the LORD on the cart, and beside it place a chest containing the gold rats and gold tumors you are sending as a guilt offering. Then let the cows go wherever they want. [9]If they cross the border of our land and go to Beth-shemesh, we will know it was the LORD who brought this great disaster upon us. If they don't, we will know it was not his hand that caused the plague. It came simply by chance."

[10]So these instructions were carried out. Two cows were hitched to the cart, and their newborn calves were shut up in a pen. [11]Then the Ark of the LORD and the chest containing the gold rats and gold tumors were placed on the cart. [12]And sure enough, without veering off in other directions, the cows went straight along the road toward Beth-shemesh, lowing as they went. The Philistine rulers followed them as far as the border of Beth-shemesh.

[13]The people of Beth-shemesh were harvesting wheat in the valley, and when they saw the Ark, they were overjoyed! [14]The cart came into the field of a man named Joshua and stopped beside a large rock. So the people broke up the wood of the cart for a fire and killed the cows and sacrificed them to the LORD as a burnt offering. [15]Several men of the tribe of Levi lifted the Ark of the LORD and the chest containing the gold rats and gold tumors from the cart and placed them on the large rock. Many sacrifices and burnt offerings were offered to the LORD that day by the people of Beth-shemesh. [16]The five Philistine rulers watched all this and then returned to Ekron that same day.

[17]The five gold tumors sent by the Philistines as a guilt offering to the LORD were gifts from the rulers of Ashdod, Gaza, Ashkelon, Gath, and Ekron. [18]The five gold rats represented the five Philistine towns and their surrounding villages, which were controlled by the five rulers. The large rock* at Beth-shemesh, where they set the Ark of the LORD, still stands in the field of Joshua as a witness to what happened there.

5:11 Or *he.* 6:18 As in some Hebrew manuscripts and Greek version; most Hebrew manuscripts read *great meadow* or *Abel-haggedolah.*

6:6 As the Philistine leaders looked for a way to get rid of the Ark, their priests reminded them of the high cost of Pharaoh's resistance to God years earlier in Egypt. This object lesson is for us as well. The refusal to move toward recovery is costly. Stubbornness and willfulness often carry the hefty price tags of wrecked lives, broken relationships, and unreconciled pasts.

The Ark Moved to Kiriath-Jearim

¹⁹But the LORD killed seventy men* from Beth-shemesh because they looked into the Ark of the LORD. And the people mourned greatly because of what the LORD had done. ²⁰"Who is able to stand in the presence of the LORD, this holy God?" they cried out. "Where can we send the Ark from here?"

²¹So they sent messengers to the people at Kiriath-jearim and told them, "The Philistines have returned the Ark of the LORD. Come here and get it!"

CHAPTER 7

So the men of Kiriath-jearim came to get the Ark of the LORD. They took it to the hillside home of Abinadab and ordained Eleazar, his son, to be in charge of it. ²The Ark remained in Kiriath-jearim for a long time—twenty years in all. During that time all Israel mourned because it seemed the LORD had abandoned them.

Samuel Leads Israel to Victory

³Then Samuel said to all the people of Israel, "If you want to return to the LORD with all your hearts, get rid of your foreign gods and your images of Ashtoreth. Turn your hearts to the LORD and obey him alone; then he will rescue you from the Philistines." ⁴So the Israelites got rid of their images of Baal and Ashtoreth and worshiped only the LORD.

⁵Then Samuel told them, "Gather all of Israel to Mizpah, and I will pray to the LORD for you." ⁶So they gathered at Mizpah and, in a great ceremony, drew water from a well and poured it out before the LORD. They also went without food all day and confessed that they had sinned against the LORD. (It was at Mizpah that Samuel became Israel's judge.)

⁷When the Philistine rulers heard that Israel had gathered at Mizpah, they mobilized their army and advanced. The Israelites were badly frightened when they learned that the Philistines were approaching. ⁸"Don't stop pleading with the LORD our God to save us from the Philistines!" they begged Samuel. ⁹So Samuel took a young lamb and offered it to the LORD as a whole burnt offering. He pleaded with the LORD to help Israel, and the LORD answered him.

¹⁰Just as Samuel was sacrificing the burnt offering, the Philistines arrived to attack Israel. But the LORD spoke with a mighty voice of thunder from heaven that day, and the Philistines were thrown into such confusion

---

6:19 As in a few Hebrew manuscripts; most Hebrew manuscripts read *70 men, 50,000 men.* Perhaps the text should be understood to read *the LORD killed 70 men and 50 oxen.*

6:19 This seems a harsh judgment, but it carries with it a reminder of the high cost of disobedience. Here the Israelites were held accountable to the instructions God had given them regarding the treatment of the Ark. Either they were ignorant of these instructions or they chose to ignore them. In the Bible God has given us instructions for healthy living. When we fail to follow God's program, out of either ignorance or choice, the consequences will be devastating. Neglecting God's instructions proved fatal for this group of Israelites. The same consequence may await us if we fail to listen to God and heed his Word.

7:7-11 The people of Israel were helpless as they faced the attacking Philistines. They didn't know what to do, so they turned to Samuel for help. Samuel did the only thing possible: He asked God for help. God answered by giving Israel an overwhelming victory over the Philistines. This is how our own recovery begins. We realize that we are helpless against our enemies of addiction and dependency, so we turn to God for help. We can be sure that God will come through for us if we admit our helplessness and commit our life to him.

7:12 The fact that Samuel set up a stone and named it Ebenezer, which means "the stone of help," should remind us of two principles: First, God's help in the past is a promise of help in the future. God offers much more than a onetime antidote or a quick fix. He offers a continual remedy and is our source of strength as we rebuild our life. Second, the fact that God's help is available daily should help us see that we need to look to him every day. The secret to recovery is to recognize that it happens one day at a time. If we depend on God daily, we will find the strength and grace to endure and achieve the victory.

8:3-5 Like the sons of Eli, Samuel's sons also failed to set boundaries on their behavior. They were greedy for money, taking bribes and perverting justice (8:3), actions for which they were held accountable. Their disobedience surely embarrassed their father, but it also prompted a national outcry for governmental change (8:5). Because of failure in the leadership, the people rejected God's rule through the judges and demanded what all the surrounding nations had—a king. One wonders what might have happened if Samuel's sons had been able to delay their gratification and had acted more responsibly. Clearly God will not allow sin to continue unpunished, especially among those he has put in leadership positions.

SAUL

Saul's story is a tragic one. He was a man with great potential for leadership, but he failed miserably. He allowed his fearfulness, disobedience, and self-sufficiency to come between him and God's plan for his life.

At the beginning of his career, Saul was a shy and reluctant leader. He was found hiding in the baggage when Samuel called the people together to publicly anoint him as king. Saul's humble, restrained style worked well in the early days of his rule, but he came to a point in his life where he had to decide to either follow or fight against God's authority. Unfortunately, Saul made the wrong choice.

During his reign, Saul had his greatest successes when he obeyed God. His greatest failures resulted from acting on his own. Even his weaknesses, though, could have been used by God if Saul had recognized them and left them in God's hands.

Like Saul, we are faced with the choice of turning our life and will over to God or continuing to fight his plan for us. As with Saul, our answer to that choice sets the course of our life.

STRENGTHS AND ACCOMPLISHMENTS:
- Saul's family and troops were always loyal to him.
- When he obeyed God, his leadership and courage were great.
- He had a striking, charismatic appearance.

WEAKNESSES AND MISTAKES:
- He was driven by fear that led to disobedience.
- He was a people pleaser.
- He disobeyed God in crucial situations.

LESSONS FROM HIS LIFE:
- God desires heartfelt obedience, not ritualistic, routine actions.
- Though costly, obedience to God is always best.

KEY VERSE:
"Rebellion is as sinful as witchcraft, and stubbornness is as bad as worshiping idols. So because you have rejected the command of the LORD, he has rejected you as king" (1 Samuel 15:23).

Saul's story is told in 1 Samuel 9–31. He is also mentioned in Acts 13:21.

---

that the Israelites defeated them. ¹¹The men of Israel chased them from Mizpah to a place below Beth-car, slaughtering them all along the way.

¹²Samuel then took a large stone and placed it between the towns of Mizpah and Jeshanah.* He named it Ebenezer (which means "the stone of help"), for he said, "Up to this point the LORD has helped us!"

¹³So the Philistines were subdued and didn't invade Israel again for some time. And throughout Samuel's lifetime, the LORD's powerful hand was raised against the Philistines. ¹⁴The Israelite villages near Ekron and Gath that the Philistines had captured were restored to Israel, along with the rest of the territory that the Philistines had taken. And there was peace between Israel and the Amorites in those days.

¹⁵Samuel continued as Israel's judge for the rest of his life. ¹⁶Each year he traveled around, setting up his court first at Bethel, then at Gilgal, and then at Mizpah. He judged the people of Israel at each of these places. ¹⁷Then he would return to his home at Ramah, and he

would hear cases there, too. And Samuel built an altar to the LORD at Ramah.

CHAPTER 8
Israel Requests a King

As Samuel grew old, he appointed his sons to be judges over Israel. ²Joel and Abijah, his oldest sons, held court in Beersheba. ³But they were not like their father, for they were greedy for money. They accepted bribes and perverted justice.

⁴Finally, all the elders of Israel met at Ramah to discuss the matter with Samuel. ⁵"Look," they told him, "you are now old, and your sons are not like you. Give us a king to judge us like all the other nations have."

⁶Samuel was displeased with their request and went to the LORD for guidance. ⁷"Do everything they say to you," the LORD replied, "for they are rejecting me, not you. They don't want me to be their king any longer. ⁸Ever since I brought them from Egypt they have continually abandoned me and followed other gods. And now they are

7:12 As in Greek and Syriac versions; Hebrew reads *Shen*.

353

giving you the same treatment. ⁹Do as they ask, but solemnly warn them about the way a king will reign over them."

Samuel Warns against a Kingdom

¹⁰So Samuel passed on the LORD's warning to the people who were asking him for a king. ¹¹"This is how a king will reign over you," Samuel said. "The king will draft your sons and assign them to his chariots and his charioteers, making them run before his chariots. ¹²Some will be generals and captains in his army,* some will be forced to plow in his fields and harvest his crops, and some will make his weapons and chariot equipment. ¹³The king will take your daughters from you and force them to cook and bake and make perfumes for him. ¹⁴He will take away the best of your fields and vineyards and olive groves and give them to his own officials. ¹⁵He will take a tenth of your grain and your grape harvest and distribute it among his officers and attendants. ¹⁶He will take your male and female slaves and demand the finest of your cattle* and donkeys for his own use. ¹⁷He will demand a tenth of your flocks, and you will be his slaves. ¹⁸When that day comes, you will beg for relief from this king you are demanding, but then the LORD will not help you."

¹⁹But the people refused to listen to Samuel's warning. "Even so, we still want a king," they said. ²⁰"We want to be like the nations around us. Our king will judge us and lead us into battle."

²¹So Samuel repeated to the LORD what the people had said, ²²and the LORD replied, "Do as they say, and give them a king." Then Samuel agreed and sent the people home.

CHAPTER 9
Saul Meets Samuel

There was a wealthy, influential man named Kish from the tribe of Benjamin. He was the son of Abiel, son of Zeror, son of Becorath, son of Aphiah, of the tribe of Benjamin. ²His son Saul was the most handsome man in Israel—head and shoulders taller than anyone else in the land.

³One day Kish's donkeys strayed away, and he told Saul, "Take a servant with you, and go look for the donkeys." ⁴So Saul took one of the servants and traveled through the hill country of Ephraim, the land of Shalishah, the Shaalim area, and the entire land of Benjamin, but they couldn't find the donkeys anywhere.

⁵Finally, they entered the region of Zuph, and Saul said to his servant, "Let's go home. By now my father will be more worried about us than about the donkeys!"

⁶But the servant said, "I've just thought of something! There is a man of God who lives here in this town. He is held in high honor by all the people because everything he says comes true. Let's go find him. Perhaps he can tell us which way to go."

⁷"But we don't have anything to offer him," Saul replied. "Even our food is gone, and we don't have a thing to give him."

⁸"Well," the servant said, "I have one small silver piece.* We can at least offer it to the man of God and see what happens!" ⁹(In those days if people wanted a message from God, they would say, "Let's go and ask the seer," for prophets used to be called seers.)

¹⁰"All right," Saul agreed, "let's try it!" So they started into the town where the man of God lived.

8:12 Hebrew *commanders of thousands and commanders of fifties.* 8:16 As in Greek version; Hebrew reads *young men.*
9:8 Hebrew ¼ *shekel of silver,* about 0.1 ounces or 3 grams in weight.

8:18-20 The Israelites refused to listen to Samuel's God-given advice, and they were soon saddled with a less-than-satisfactory ruler—Saul. Wanting to be like the other nations, they clamored for a king and found out the hard way that what they wanted wasn't necessarily what they needed. God's dealings with his people suggest two lessons: (1) The road to recovery is often lengthened when a deliberate choice is made to go against wise counsel (Psalm 106:13-15); (2) the constant pressure to be like everyone else makes it difficult to gain freedom and experience recovery. God may even allow us to have our own way in a situation so he can show us the ultimate folly of it.

9:2 Saul was certainly a man of impressive physical attributes, but in his case, his "gifts" were detrimental rather than helpful. People gifted with beauty, intelligence, great size or strength often fall into the trap of self-sufficiency. They begin to think they can go it alone. This attitude only stands in the way of achieving God's success. Pride and notions of personal potential may prevent us from ever becoming humble enough to admit that we have needs. Saul looked good on paper, but he allowed his "strengths" to stand in the way of his only means of success—God's help. We must be careful to avoid this pitfall if we hope to succeed in recovery.

[11]As they were climbing the hill to the town, they met some young women coming out to draw water. So Saul and his servant asked, "Is the seer here today?"

[12]"Yes," they replied. "Stay right on this road. He is at the town gates. He has just arrived to take part in a public sacrifice up at the place of worship. [13]Hurry and catch him before he goes up there to eat. The guests won't begin eating until he arrives to bless the food."

[14]So they entered the town, and as they passed through the gates, Samuel was coming out toward them to go up to the place of worship.

[15]Now the LORD had told Samuel the previous day, [16]"About this time tomorrow I will send you a man from the land of Benjamin. Anoint him to be the leader of my people, Israel. He will rescue them from the Philistines, for I have looked down on my people in mercy and have heard their cry."

[17]When Samuel saw Saul, the LORD said, "That's the man I told you about! He will rule my people."

[18]Just then Saul approached Samuel at the gateway and asked, "Can you please tell me where the seer's house is?"

[19]"I am the seer!" Samuel replied. "Go up to the place of worship ahead of me. We will eat there together, and in the morning I'll tell you what you want to know and send you on your way. [20]And don't worry about those donkeys that were lost three days ago, for they have been found. And I am here to tell you that you and your family are the focus of all Israel's hopes."

[21]Saul replied, "But I'm only from the tribe of Benjamin, the smallest tribe in Israel, and my family is the least important of all the families of that tribe! Why are you talking like this to me?"

[22]Then Samuel brought Saul and his servant into the hall and placed them at the head of the table, honoring them above the thirty special guests. [23]Samuel then instructed the cook to bring Saul the finest cut of meat, the piece that had been set aside for the guest of honor. [24]So the cook brought in the meat and placed it before Saul. "Go ahead and eat it," Samuel said. "I was saving it for you even before I invited these others!" So Saul ate with Samuel that day.

[25]When they came down from the place of worship and returned to town, Samuel took Saul up to the roof of the house and prepared a bed for him there.* [26]At daybreak the next morning, Samuel called to Saul, "Get up! It's time you were on your way." So Saul got ready, and he and Samuel left the house together. [27]When they reached the edge of town, Samuel told Saul to send his servant on ahead. After the servant was gone, Samuel said, "Stay here, for I have received a special message for you from God."

CHAPTER 10
Samuel Anoints Saul as King

Then Samuel took a flask of olive oil and poured it over Saul's head. He kissed Saul and said, "I am doing this because the LORD has appointed you to be the ruler over Israel, his special possession.* [2]When you leave me today, you will see two men beside Rachel's tomb at Zelzah, on the border of Benjamin. They will tell you that the donkeys have been found and that your father has stopped worrying about them and is now worried about you. He is asking, 'Have you seen my son?'

[3]"When you get to the oak of Tabor, you will see three men coming toward you who are on their way to worship God at Bethel. One will be bringing three young goats, another will have three loaves of bread, and the

---

9:25 As in Greek version; Hebrew reads *and talked with him there.* 10:1 Greek version reads *over Israel. And you will rule over the LORD's people and save them from their enemies around them. This will be the sign to you that the LORD has appointed you to be leader over his special possession.*

9:14-17 Notice that Samuel approached at the very moment Saul entered the town. This should remind us of how perfect God's timing is in the events of our own life! He often leads us to meet people or experience events that hasten the recovery process. If we see this to be true as we look back on our life, we should thank God for his direction (Psalms 37:23-24; 138:8; Proverbs 3:5-6; Isaiah 48:17).

10:1 As Samuel anointed Saul king over Israel, he was also burying his personal dreams. Samuel was the last of the judges; his sons would never share his honor. But despite his disappointment, Samuel found the courage to follow God's will instead of his own. He was willing to lay aside his plans and even to assist in the process of helping Saul become king. Assisting others on the road to a new life sometimes means that we must give up some personal dreams of our own. But if we are following God's will, helping others will turn out to be the surest way to discover a new life for ourself.

third will be carrying a wineskin full of wine. [4]They will greet you and offer you two of the loaves, which you are to accept.

[5]"When you arrive at Gibeah of God,* where the garrison of the Philistines is located, you will meet a band of prophets coming down from the place of worship. They will be playing a harp, a tambourine, a flute, and a lyre, and they will be prophesying. [6]At that time the Spirit of the LORD will come powerfully upon you, and you will prophesy with them. You will be changed into a different person. [7]After these signs take place, do what must be done, for God is with you. [8]Then go down to Gilgal ahead of me. I will join you there to sacrifice burnt offerings and peace offerings. You must wait for seven days until I arrive and give you further instructions."

Samuel's Signs Are Fulfilled

[9]As Saul turned and started to leave, God gave him a new heart, and all Samuel's signs were fulfilled that day. [10]When Saul and his servant arrived at Gibeah, they saw a group of prophets coming toward them. Then the Spirit of God came powerfully upon Saul, and he, too, began to prophesy. [11]When those who knew Saul heard about it, they exclaimed, "What? Is even Saul a prophet? How did the son of Kish become a prophet?"

[12]And one of those standing there said, "Can anyone become a prophet, no matter who his father is?"* So that is the origin of the saying "Is even Saul a prophet?"

[13]When Saul had finished prophesying, he went up to the place of worship. [14]"Where have you been?" Saul's uncle asked him and his servant.

"We were looking for the donkeys," Saul replied, "but we couldn't find them. So we went to Samuel to ask him where they were."

[15]"Oh? And what did he say?" his uncle asked.

[16]"He told us that the donkeys had already been found," Saul replied. But Saul didn't tell his uncle what Samuel said about the kingdom.

Saul Is Acclaimed King

[17]Later Samuel called all the people of Israel to meet before the LORD at Mizpah. [18]And he said, "This is what the LORD, the God of Israel, has declared: I brought you from Egypt and rescued you from the Egyptians and from all of the nations that were oppressing you. [19]But though I have rescued you from your misery and distress, you have rejected your God today and have said, 'No, we want a king instead!' Now, therefore, present yourselves before the LORD by tribes and clans."

[20]So Samuel brought all the tribes of Israel before the LORD, and the tribe of Benjamin was chosen by lot. [21]Then he brought each family of the tribe of Benjamin before the LORD, and the family of the Matrites was chosen. And finally Saul son of Kish was chosen from among them. But when they looked for him, he had disappeared! [22]So they asked the LORD, "Where is he?"

And the LORD replied, "He is hiding among the baggage." [23]So they found him and brought him out, and he stood head and shoulders above anyone else.

[24]Then Samuel said to all the people, "This is the man the LORD has chosen as your king. No one in all Israel is like him!"

And all the people shouted, "Long live the king!"

[25]Then Samuel told the people what the rights and duties of a king were. He wrote them down on a scroll and placed it before the LORD. Then Samuel sent the people home again.

[26]When Saul returned to his home at Gibeah, a group of men whose hearts God had touched went with him. [27]But there were some scoundrels who complained, "How can this man save us?" And they scorned him and refused to bring him gifts. But Saul ignored them.

[Nahash, king of the Ammonites, had been grievously oppressing the people of Gad and Reuben who lived east of the Jordan River. He gouged out the right eye of each of the Israelites living there, and he didn't allow anyone to come and rescue them. In fact, of all the

10:5 Hebrew *Gibeath-haelohim.* 10:12 Hebrew *said, "Who is their father?"*

10:26 The phrase "whose hearts God had touched" points to a critical phase in the recovery process. God touched Saul's life, and then he touched several individuals to support Saul in his new role. These words recall a verse in the New Testament: "Jesus came over and touched them. 'Get up,' he said. 'Don't be afraid'" (Matthew 17:7). The touch of God's healing hand enables us to deal with the past, persist in the present, and find direction for the future. Starting anew means that we must first come to God for the salvation he offers in Jesus Christ (John 3:16); then we must depend on him for sustenance and strength (John 15:4-7).

Israelites east of the Jordan, there wasn't a single one whose right eye Nahash had not gouged out. But there were 7,000 men who had escaped from the Ammonites, and they had settled in Jabesh-gilead.]*

CHAPTER 11
Saul Defeats the Ammonites
About a month later,* King Nahash of Ammon led his army against the Israelite town of Jabesh-gilead. But all the citizens of Jabesh asked for peace. "Make a treaty with us, and we will be your servants," they pleaded.

²"All right," Nahash said, "but only on one condition. I will gouge out the right eye of every one of you as a disgrace to all Israel!"

³"Give us seven days to send messengers throughout Israel!" replied the elders of Jabesh. "If no one comes to save us, we will agree to your terms."

⁴When the messengers came to Gibeah of Saul and told the people about their plight, everyone broke into tears. ⁵Saul had been plowing a field with his oxen, and when he returned to town, he asked, "What's the matter? Why is everyone crying?" So they told him about the message from Jabesh.

⁶Then the Spirit of God came powerfully upon Saul, and he became very angry. ⁷He took two oxen and cut them into pieces and sent the messengers to carry them throughout Israel with this message: "This is what will happen to the oxen of anyone who refuses to follow Saul and Samuel into battle!" And the LORD made the people afraid of Saul's anger, and all of them came out together as one. ⁸When Saul mobilized them at Bezek, he found that there were 300,000 men from Israel and 30,000* men from Judah.

⁹So Saul sent the messengers back to Jabesh-gilead to say, "We will rescue you by noontime tomorrow!" There was great joy throughout the town when that message arrived!

¹⁰The men of Jabesh then told their enemies, "Tomorrow we will come out to you, and you can do to us whatever you wish."

¹¹But before dawn the next morning, Saul arrived, having divided his army into three detachments. He launched a surprise attack against the Ammonites and slaughtered them the whole morning. The remnant of their army was so badly scattered that no two of them were left together.

¹²Then the people exclaimed to Samuel, "Now where are those men who said, 'Why should Saul rule over us?' Bring them here, and we will kill them!"

¹³But Saul replied, "No one will be executed today, for today the LORD has rescued Israel!"

¹⁴Then Samuel said to the people, "Come, let us all go to Gilgal to renew the kingdom." ¹⁵So they all went to Gilgal, and in a solemn ceremony before the LORD they made Saul king. Then they offered peace offerings to the LORD, and Saul and all the Israelites were filled with joy.

CHAPTER 12
Samuel's Farewell Address
Then Samuel addressed all Israel: "I have done as you asked and given you a king. ²Your king is now your leader. I stand here before you—an old, gray-haired man—and my sons serve you. I have served as your leader from the time I was a boy to this very day. ³Now testify against me in the presence of the LORD and before his anointed one. Whose ox or donkey have I stolen? Have I ever cheated any of you? Have I ever oppressed you? Have I ever taken a bribe and perverted justice? Tell me and I will make right whatever I have done wrong."

⁴"No," they replied, "you have never cheated or oppressed us, and you have never taken even a single bribe."

⁵"The LORD and his anointed one are my witnesses today," Samuel declared, "that my hands are clean."

"Yes, he is a witness," they replied.

⁶"It was the LORD who appointed Moses and Aaron," Samuel continued. "He brought your ancestors out of the land of Egypt.

10:27 This paragraph, which is not included in the Masoretic Text, is found in Dead Sea Scroll 4QSamᵃ. 11:1 As in Dead Sea Scroll 4QSamᵃ and Greek version; Masoretic Text lacks *About a month later.* 11:8 Dead Sea Scrolls and Greek version read *70,000.*

11:13-15 Saul proclaimed, "Today the LORD has rescued Israel!" (11:13). Following their victory over the Ammonites, Saul, Samuel, and the people confirmed Saul's kingship at Gilgal (11:14-15). Likewise, it is often a good idea for us to go public with our commitments so we feel responsible for them and be held accountable by others. Platform speeches aren't usually necessary. Generally, confiding in a few trusted friends will do, as long as they will follow through and confront us when we slip up.

7Now stand here quietly before the LORD as I remind you of all the great things the LORD has done for you and your ancestors.

8"When the Israelites were* in Egypt and cried out to the LORD, he sent Moses and Aaron to rescue them from Egypt and to bring them into this land. 9But the people soon forgot about the LORD their God, so he handed them over to Sisera, the commander of Hazor's army, and also to the Philistines and to the king of Moab, who fought against them.

10"Then they cried to the LORD again and confessed, 'We have sinned by turning away from the LORD and worshiping the images of Baal and Ashtoreth. But we will worship you and you alone if you will rescue us from our enemies.' 11Then the LORD sent Gideon,* Bedan,* Jephthah, and Samuel* to save you, and you lived in safety.

12"But when you were afraid of Nahash, the king of Ammon, you came to me and said that you wanted a king to reign over you, even though the LORD your God was already your king. 13All right, here is the king you have chosen. You asked for him, and the LORD has granted your request.

14"Now if you fear and worship the LORD and listen to his voice, and if you do not rebel against the LORD's commands, then both you and your king will show that you recognize the LORD as your God. 15But if you rebel against the LORD's commands and refuse to listen to him, then his hand will be as heavy upon you as it was upon your ancestors.

16"Now stand here and see the great thing the LORD is about to do. 17You know that it does not rain at this time of the year during the wheat harvest. I will ask the LORD to send thunder and rain today. Then you will realize how wicked you have been in asking the LORD for a king!"

18So Samuel called to the LORD, and the LORD sent thunder and rain that day. And all the people were terrified of the LORD and of Samuel. 19"Pray to the LORD your God for us, or we will die!" they all said to Samuel. "For now we have added to our sins by asking for a king."

20"Don't be afraid," Samuel reassured them. "You have certainly done wrong, but make sure now that you worship the LORD with all your heart, and don't turn your back on him. 21Don't go back to worshiping worthless idols that cannot help or rescue you—they are totally useless! 22The LORD will not abandon his people, because that would dishonor his great name. For it has pleased the LORD to make you his very own people.

23"As for me, I will certainly not sin against the LORD by ending my prayers for you. And I will continue to teach you what is good and right. 24But be sure to fear the LORD and faithfully serve him. Think of all the wonderful

---

12:8 Hebrew *When Jacob was.* The names "Jacob" and "Israel" are often interchanged throughout the Old Testament, referring sometimes to the individual patriarch and sometimes to the nation. **12:11a** Hebrew *Jerub-baal,* another name for Gideon; see Judg 6:32. **12:11b** Greek and Syriac versions read *Barak.* **12:11c** Greek and Syriac versions read *Samson.*

12:14-15 Life is filled with choices, and the Bible is filled with clear direction on how to make decisions in line with God's program. A wise decision maker always shows proper respect for God, worshiping and serving him and obeying his commands (12:14). A poor decision maker will fail to keep God's desires and requirements in focus (12:15). Following God's program will reap positive long-term consequences, even though it may look difficult in the short run. Disobedience to God's revealed instructions will invariably lead us into bondage and the need for recovery.

12:20 Samuel exhorted the Israelites to not be afraid and to hang in there. He was calling the people to persevere in recovering from past failure. He didn't downplay their past sin; in fact, he reminded them of it. But he also called them to escape the mire of guilt and past failure. He emphasized the positive, saying, "Make sure now that you worship the LORD with all your heart, and don't turn your back on him." It is important to recognize past sins in our life, but it is even more important to look ahead to a positive future. As the process continues, it is vital to remember that a new life is not built overnight.

13:8-14 When we take our eyes off God and look at the circumstances around us, we often want to act with impatience or indiscretion. Confronted by the seemingly insurmountable threat of the Philistine army and afraid that more of his men would desert him, Saul acted irresponsibly by offering a burnt sacrifice himself rather than waiting until a priest arrived. He failed to trust in God's timing and thus disobeyed one of God's commands. The consequences for taking things into his own hands were great: His descendants would be denied the right to rule in Israel. Being patient when things seem to be running behind schedule is sometimes the most difficult part of recovery. We need to be true to God's program, even when it seems to be going too slowly. God's way is always the best way.

things he has done for you. ²⁵But if you continue to sin, you and your king will be swept away."

CHAPTER 13
Continued War with Philistia
Saul was thirty* years old when he became king, and he reigned for forty-two years.*

²Saul selected 3,000 special troops from the army of Israel and sent the rest of the men home. He took 2,000 of the chosen men with him to Micmash and the hill country of Bethel. The other 1,000 went with Saul's son Jonathan to Gibeah in the land of Benjamin.

³Soon after this, Jonathan attacked and defeated the garrison of Philistines at Geba. The news spread quickly among the Philistines. So Saul blew the ram's horn throughout the land, saying, "Hebrews, hear this! Rise up in revolt!" ⁴All Israel heard the news that Saul had destroyed the Philistine garrison at Geba and that the Philistines now hated the Israelites more than ever. So the entire Israelite army was summoned to join Saul at Gilgal.

⁵The Philistines mustered a mighty army of 3,000* chariots, 6,000 charioteers, and as many warriors as the grains of sand on the seashore! They camped at Micmash east of Beth-aven. ⁶The men of Israel saw what a tight spot they were in; and because they were hard pressed by the enemy, they tried to hide in caves, thickets, rocks, holes, and cisterns. ⁷Some of them crossed the Jordan River and escaped into the land of Gad and Gilead.

Saul's Disobedience and Samuel's Rebuke
Meanwhile, Saul stayed at Gilgal, and his men were trembling with fear. ⁸Saul waited there seven days for Samuel, as Samuel had instructed him earlier, but Samuel still didn't come. Saul realized that his troops were rapidly slipping away. ⁹So he demanded, "Bring me the burnt offering and the peace offerings!" And Saul sacrificed the burnt offering himself.

¹⁰Just as Saul was finishing with the burnt offering, Samuel arrived. Saul went out to meet and welcome him, ¹¹but Samuel said, "What is this you have done?"

Saul replied, "I saw my men scattering from me, and you didn't arrive when you said you would, and the Philistines are at Micmash ready for battle. ¹²So I said, 'The

13:1a As in a few Greek manuscripts; the number is missing in the Hebrew. 13:1b Hebrew *reigned . . . and two;* the number is incomplete in the Hebrew. Compare Acts 13:21. 13:5 As in Greek and Syriac versions; Hebrew reads *30,000.*

PEER PRESSURE

READ 1 SAMUEL 13:1-14
We are all susceptible to the negative influences of others. We get pushed into rushed decisions by peer pressure and often find ourselves in trouble as a result. This weakness should alert us to a defect in our own life and our need for help.

Saul had this defect but refused God's help. Samuel had told the Israelites at Saul's coronation that if they all obeyed God's commands all would be well (1 Samuel 12:14). But Saul allowed his men to pressure him into disobedience. Israel was at war. In the midst of battle it was customary to have a priest offer sacrifices; Samuel had promised Saul that he would come at an appointed time to do this. Saul waited for a while but began to feel pressured because his troops were leaving him. He knew that it was against God's law for him to offer sacrifices, but he decided he could wait no longer and did it himself.

Just as Saul finished his sacrifice, Samuel arrived. "'How foolish!' Samuel exclaimed. 'You have not kept the command the LORD your God gave you. Had you kept it, the LORD would have established your kingdom over Israel forever. But now your kingdom must end, for the LORD has sought out a man after his own heart. The LORD has already appointed him to be the leader of his people, because you have not kept the LORD's command'" (1 Samuel 13:13-14). Saul would suffer the consequences of his disobedience.

If Saul had delayed his action just one more hour, he would have kept his kingdom. Our tendency to be unduly influenced by others needs to be replaced with strength from God and faith in his plan. *Turn to page 361, 1 Samuel 14.*

Philistines are ready to march against us at Gilgal, and I haven't even asked for the LORD's help!' So I felt compelled to offer the burnt offering myself before you came."

[13]"How foolish!" Samuel exclaimed. "You have not kept the command the LORD your God gave you. Had you kept it, the LORD would have established your kingdom over Israel forever. [14]But now your kingdom must end, for the LORD has sought out a man after his own heart. The LORD has already appointed him to be the leader of his people, because you have not kept the LORD's command."

Israel's Military Disadvantage

[15]Samuel then left Gilgal and went on his way, but the rest of the troops went with Saul to meet the army. They went up from Gilgal to Gibeah in the land of Benjamin.* When Saul counted the men who were still with him, he found only 600 were left! [16]Saul and Jonathan and the troops with them were staying at Geba in the land of Benjamin. The Philistines set up their camp at Micmash. [17]Three raiding parties soon left the camp of the Philistines. One went north toward Ophrah in the land of Shual, [18]another went west to Beth-horon, and the third moved toward the border above the valley of Zeboim near the wilderness.

[19]There were no blacksmiths in the land of Israel in those days. The Philistines wouldn't allow them for fear they would make swords and spears for the Hebrews. [20]So whenever the Israelites needed to sharpen their plowshares, picks, axes, or sickles,* they had to take them to a Philistine blacksmith. [21]The charges were as follows: a quarter of an ounce* of silver for sharpening a plowshare or a pick, and an eighth of an ounce* for sharpening an ax or making the point of an ox goad. [22]So on the day of the battle none of the people of Israel had a sword or spear, except for Saul and Jonathan.

[23]The pass at Micmash had meanwhile been secured by a contingent of the Philistine army.

CHAPTER 14
Jonathan's Daring Plan

One day Jonathan said to his armor bearer, "Come on, let's go over to where the Philistines have their outpost." But Jonathan did not tell his father what he was doing.

[2]Meanwhile, Saul and his 600 men were camped on the outskirts of Gibeah, around the pomegranate tree* at Migron. [3]Among Saul's men was Ahijah the priest, who was wearing the ephod, the priestly vest. Ahijah was the son of Ichabod's brother Ahitub, son of Phinehas, son of Eli, the priest of the LORD who had served at Shiloh.

No one realized that Jonathan had left the Israelite camp. [4]To reach the Philistine outpost, Jonathan had to go down between two rocky cliffs that were called Bozez and Seneh. [5]The cliff on the north was in front of Micmash, and the one on the south was in front of Geba. [6]"Let's go across to the outpost of those pagans," Jonathan said to his armor bearer. "Perhaps the LORD will help us, for nothing can hinder the LORD. He can win a battle whether he has many warriors or only a few!"

[7]"Do what you think is best," the armor bearer replied. "I'm with you completely, whatever you decide."

[8]"All right then," Jonathan told him. "We

13:15 As in Greek version; Hebrew reads *Samuel then left Gilgal and went to Gibeah in the land of Benjamin.* 13:20 As in Greek version; Hebrew reads *or plowshares.* 13:21a Hebrew *1 pim* [8 grams]. 13:21b Hebrew *1/3 [of a shekel]* [4 grams]. 14:2 Or *around the rock of Rimmon;* compare Judg 20:45, 47; 21:13.

14:6-14 God gives people who trust him victory in impossible situations. Jonathan's confidence in God prompted him to step out in faith and tackle incredible odds. His faith and courage were rewarded with an amazing victory (14:13). Sadly, many of us never trust God enough to discover what he can do and the joy this brings. Notice that Jonathan did not take his step of faith alone; he was accompanied by a bodyguard. Similarly, recovery is not something we can accomplish by ourself. We need support—friends who, like Jonathan's companion, will exclaim, "I'm with you completely" (14:7). Significant relationships are not to be shunned "until we get better"; often God uses people to help us get there.

14:19-20 Saul's indecision as he heard the battle in the Philistine camp caused a great deal of confusion among his troops. He was waiting for a clear message from God about what to do. Eventually he found that he had no alternative but to attack, building on Jonathan's victory (14:13-15). Saul's course of action should have been obvious. His rather insincere hesitation shows us that there is a time to pray and a time to act. We must avoid trying to be "spiritual" when it is time to take action. We don't need to pray about obvious things. We already know what people, places, and activities to avoid. Some things are obvious and must be pursued without delay.

will cross over and let them see us. ⁹If they say to us, 'Stay where you are or we'll kill you,' then we will stop and not go up to them. ¹⁰But if they say, 'Come on up and fight,' then we will go up. That will be the LORD's sign that he will help us defeat them."

¹¹When the Philistines saw them coming, they shouted, "Look! The Hebrews are crawling out of their holes!" ¹²Then the men from the outpost shouted to Jonathan, "Come on up here, and we'll teach you a lesson!"

"Come on, climb right behind me," Jonathan said to his armor bearer, "for the LORD will help us defeat them!"

¹³So they climbed up using both hands and feet, and the Philistines fell before Jonathan, and his armor bearer killed those who came behind them. ¹⁴They killed some twenty men in all, and their bodies were scattered over about half an acre.*

¹⁵Suddenly, panic broke out in the Philistine army, both in the camp and in the field, including even the outposts and raiding parties. And just then an earthquake struck, and everyone was terrified.

Israel Defeats the Philistines

¹⁶Saul's lookouts in Gibeah of Benjamin saw a strange sight—the vast army of Philistines began to melt away in every direction.* ¹⁷"Call the roll and find out who's missing," Saul ordered. And when they checked, they found that Jonathan and his armor bearer were gone.

¹⁸Then Saul shouted to Ahijah, "Bring the ephod here!" For at that time Ahijah was wearing the ephod in front of the Israelites.* ¹⁹But while Saul was talking to the priest, the confusion in the Philistine camp grew louder and louder. So Saul said to the priest, "Never mind; let's get going!"*

²⁰Then Saul and all his men rushed out to the battle and found the Philistines killing each other. There was terrible confusion everywhere. ²¹Even the Hebrews who had previously gone over to the Philistine army revolted and joined in with Saul, Jonathan, and the rest of the Israelites. ²²Likewise, the men of Israel who were hiding in the hill country of Ephraim joined the chase when they saw the Philistines running away. ²³So the LORD saved Israel that day, and the battle continued to rage even beyond Beth-aven.

14:14 Hebrew *half a yoke;* a "yoke" was the amount of land plowed by a pair of yoked oxen in one day. 14:16 As in Greek version; Hebrew reads *they went and there.* 14:18 As in some Greek manuscripts; Hebrew reads *"Bring the Ark of God."* For at that time the Ark of God was with the Israelites. 14:19 Hebrew *Withdraw your hand.*

SELF-PROTECTION

READ 1 SAMUEL 14:1-12, 20-29
We once used our addictions to find comfort and help us cope with life's daily battles. In recovery, we may have become so focused on the battle at hand that we have neglected our basic physical needs. We may have forgotten our need to enjoy some of the sweet things of life. Failure to take care of ourself can leave us weak and vulnerable.

During a difficult battle, King Saul had declared, "'Let a curse fall on anyone who eats before evening—before I have full revenge on my enemies.' . . . But Jonathan had not heard his father's command, and he dipped the end of his stick into a piece of honeycomb and ate the honey. After he had eaten it, he felt refreshed. But one of the men saw him and said, 'Your father made the army take a strict oath that anyone who eats food today will be cursed. That is why everyone is weary and faint.' 'My father has made trouble for us all!' Jonathan exclaimed. 'A command like that only hurts us. See how refreshed I am now'" (1 Samuel 14:24-29).

When we are in recovery, we already feel deprived. We need to make sure that we are being good to ourself in healthy ways, eating good food and tasting some of the sweet things that life naturally provides. Recovery isn't a time for unnecessary deprivation. If we become too hungry physically or emotionally, we'll find that we are weary and less able to fight the battles we face each day. ***Turn to page 403, 2 Samuel 13.***

Saul's Foolish Oath

24Now the men of Israel were pressed to exhaustion that day, because Saul had placed them under an oath, saying, "Let a curse fall on anyone who eats before evening—before I have full revenge on my enemies." So no one ate anything all day, 25even though they had all found honeycomb on the ground in the forest. 26They didn't dare touch the honey because they all feared the oath they had taken.

27But Jonathan had not heard his father's command, and he dipped the end of his stick into a piece of honeycomb and ate the honey. After he had eaten it, he felt refreshed.* 28But one of the men saw him and said, "Your father made the army take a strict oath that anyone who eats food today will be cursed. That is why everyone is weary and faint."

29"My father has made trouble for us all!" Jonathan exclaimed. "A command like that only hurts us. See how refreshed I am now that I have eaten this little bit of honey. 30If the men had been allowed to eat freely from the food they found among our enemies, think how many more Philistines we could have killed!"

31They chased and killed the Philistines all day from Micmash to Aijalon, growing more and more faint. 32That evening they rushed for the battle plunder and butchered the sheep, goats, cattle, and calves, but they ate them without draining the blood. 33Someone reported to Saul, "Look, the men are sinning against the LORD by eating meat that still has blood in it."

"That is very wrong," Saul said. "Find a large stone and roll it over here. 34Then go out among the troops and tell them, 'Bring the cattle, sheep, and goats here to me. Kill them here, and drain the blood before you eat them. Do not sin against the LORD by eating meat with the blood still in it.'"

So that night all the troops brought their animals and slaughtered them there. 35Then Saul built an altar to the LORD; it was the first of the altars he built to the LORD.

36Then Saul said, "Let's chase the Philistines all night and plunder them until sunrise. Let's destroy every last one of them."

His men replied, "We'll do whatever you think is best."

But the priest said, "Let's ask God first."

37So Saul asked God, "Should we go after the Philistines? Will you help us defeat them?" But God made no reply that day.

38Then Saul said to the leaders, "Something's wrong! I want all my army commanders to come here. We must find out what sin was committed today. 39I vow by the name of the LORD who rescued Israel that the sinner will surely die, even if it is my own son Jonathan!" But no one would tell him what the trouble was.

40Then Saul said, "Jonathan and I will stand over here, and all of you stand over there."

And the people responded to Saul, "Whatever you think is best."

41Then Saul prayed, "O LORD, God of Israel, please show us who is guilty and who is innocent.*" Then they cast sacred lots, and Jonathan and Saul were chosen as the guilty ones, and the people were declared innocent.

42Then Saul said, "Now cast lots again and choose between me and Jonathan." And Jonathan was shown to be the guilty one.

43"Tell me what you have done," Saul demanded of Jonathan.

"I tasted a little honey," Jonathan admitted. "It was only a little bit on the end of my stick. Does that deserve death?"

44"Yes, Jonathan," Saul said, "you must die! May God strike me and even kill me if you do not die for this."

45But the people broke in and said to Saul, "Jonathan has won this great victory for Israel. Should he die? Far from it! As surely as the LORD lives, not one hair on his head will be touched, for God helped him do a great deed today." So the people rescued Jonathan, and he was not put to death.

46Then Saul called back the army from chasing the Philistines, and the Philistines returned home.

Saul's Military Successes

47Now when Saul had secured his grasp on Israel's throne, he fought against his enemies in every direction—against Moab, Ammon, Edom, the kings of Zobah, and the Philistines. And wherever he turned, he was victorious.* 48He performed great deeds and conquered the Amalekites, saving Israel from all those who had plundered them.

49Saul's sons included Jonathan, Ishbosheth,* and Malkishua. He also had two daughters: Merab, who was older, and Michal. 50Saul's wife was Ahinoam, the daughter of Ahimaaz. The commander of Saul's army was

14:27 Or *his eyes brightened;* similarly in 14:29. **14:41** Greek version adds *If the fault is with me or my son Jonathan, respond with Urim; but if the men of Israel are at fault, respond with Thummim.* **14:47** As in Greek version; Hebrew reads *he acted wickedly.* **14:49** Hebrew *Ishvi,* a variant name for Ishbosheth; also known as Esh-baal.

GOD grant me the serenity to accept the things I cannot change the courage to change the things I can and the wisdom to know the difference

A M E N

We need serenity to be able to accept the consequences of our actions. We may tend to feel wrongly accused and deny our wrongdoings or try to justify them. Unless we are willing to take responsibility for past failures, there is no hope for recovery.

Saul was the first king of Israel. At his coronation the people were told, "Now if you fear and worship the LORD and listen to his voice, and if you do not rebel against the LORD's commands, then both you and your king will show that you recognize the LORD as your God" (1 Samuel 12:14). But Saul and the people disobeyed God. "Then the LORD said to Samuel, 'I am sorry that I ever made Saul king, for he has not been loyal to me and has refused to obey my command'" (15:10-11). When Samuel confronted Saul, he denied doing any wrong and put up his defenses. So Samuel replied, "Rebellion is as sinful as witchcraft, and stubbornness as bad as worshiping idols. So because you have rejected the command of the LORD, he has rejected you as king" (15:23). Saul then led his entire family and country into years of civil war as he fought to remain king. He finally died at his own hand, surrounded by enemy troops. His three sons died with him.

There is no escaping the consequences of our actions. God can give us the serenity about our past failures if we are willing to take responsibility for them and ask for God's forgiveness. When we face this with courage, we may well spare ourself and our loved ones many years of additional pain. *Turn to page 367, 1 Samuel 17.*

Abner, the son of Saul's uncle Ner. ⁵¹Saul's father, Kish, and Abner's father, Ner, were both sons of Abiel.

⁵²The Israelites fought constantly with the Philistines throughout Saul's lifetime. So whenever Saul observed a young man who was brave and strong, he drafted him into his army.

CHAPTER 15
Saul Defeats the Amalekites

One day Samuel said to Saul, "It was the LORD who told me to anoint you as king of his people, Israel. Now listen to this message from the LORD! ²This is what the LORD of Heaven's Armies has declared: I have decided to settle accounts with the nation of Amalek for opposing Israel when they came from Egypt. ³Now go and completely destroy* the entire Amalekite nation—men, women, children, babies, cattle, sheep, goats, camels, and donkeys."

⁴So Saul mobilized his army at Telaim. There were 200,000 soldiers from Israel and 10,000 men from Judah. ⁵Then Saul and his army went to a town of the Amalekites and lay in wait in the valley. ⁶Saul sent this warning to the Kenites: "Move away from where the Amalekites live, or you will die with them. For you showed kindness to all the people of Israel when they came up from Egypt." So the Kenites packed up and left.

⁷Then Saul slaughtered the Amalekites from Havilah all the way to Shur, east of Egypt. ⁸He captured Agag, the Amalekite king, but completely destroyed everyone else. ⁹Saul and his men spared Agag's life and kept the best of the sheep and goats, the cattle, the fat calves, and the lambs—everything, in fact,

15:3 The Hebrew term used here refers to the complete consecration of things or people to the LORD, either by destroying them or by giving them as an offering; also in 15:8, 9, 15, 18, 20, 21.

that appealed to them. They destroyed only what was worthless or of poor quality.

The LORD Rejects Saul

[10]Then the LORD said to Samuel, [11]"I am sorry that I ever made Saul king, for he has not been loyal to me and has refused to obey my command." Samuel was so deeply moved when he heard this that he cried out to the LORD all night.

[12]Early the next morning Samuel went to find Saul. Someone told him, "Saul went to the town of Carmel to set up a monument to himself; then he went on to Gilgal."

[13]When Samuel finally found him, Saul greeted him cheerfully. "May the LORD bless you," he said. "I have carried out the LORD's command!"

[14]"Then what is all the bleating of sheep and goats and the lowing of cattle I hear?" Samuel demanded.

[15]"It's true that the army spared the best of the sheep, goats, and cattle," Saul admitted. "But they are going to sacrifice them to the LORD your God. We have destroyed everything else."

[16]Then Samuel said to Saul, "Stop! Listen to what the LORD told me last night!"

"What did he tell you?" Saul asked.

[17]And Samuel told him, "Although you may think little of yourself, are you not the leader of the tribes of Israel? The LORD has anointed you king of Israel. [18]And the LORD sent you on a mission and told you, 'Go and completely destroy the sinners, the Amalekites, until they are all dead.' [19]Why haven't you obeyed the LORD? Why did you rush for the plunder and do what was evil in the LORD's sight?"

[20]"But I did obey the LORD," Saul insisted. "I carried out the mission he gave me. I brought back King Agag, but I destroyed everyone else. [21]Then my troops brought in the best of the sheep, goats, cattle, and plunder to sacrifice to the LORD your God in Gilgal."

[22]But Samuel replied,

"What is more pleasing to the LORD:
  your burnt offerings and sacrifices
  or your obedience to his voice?
Listen! Obedience is better than sacrifice,
  and submission is better than offering
  the fat of rams.
[23]Rebellion is as sinful as witchcraft,
  and stubbornness as bad as worshiping idols.
So because you have rejected the
  command of the LORD,
  he has rejected you as king."

Saul Pleads for Forgiveness

[24]Then Saul admitted to Samuel, "Yes, I have sinned. I have disobeyed your instructions and the LORD's command, for I was afraid of the people and did what they demanded. [25]But now, please forgive my sin and come back with me so that I may worship the LORD."

[26]But Samuel replied, "I will not go back with you! Since you have rejected the LORD's command, he has rejected you as king of Israel."

[27]As Samuel turned to go, Saul tried to hold him back and tore the hem of his robe. [28]And Samuel said to him, "The LORD has torn the kingdom of Israel from you today and has given it to someone else—one who is better than you. [29]And he who is the Glory of Israel will not lie, nor will he change his mind, for he is not human that he should change his mind!"

[30]Then Saul pleaded again, "I know I have sinned. But please, at least honor me before the elders of my people and before Israel by coming back with me so that I may worship the LORD your God." [31]So Samuel finally

---

15:16-21 Samuel confronted Saul in his denial, but it didn't help. Instead of admitting his failure to obey God's instructions, Saul continued in denial, rationalizing his disobedience. Denial and rationalization are two of the biggest enemies to recovery. God places a premium on honesty. Saul sought to excuse himself by his intention to bring sacrifices to God. God does not want our pious prayers and religious activities unless they are accompanied by a humble and obedient heart. Hiding the sins in our life with pious words and deeds is no substitute for confessing our sins and allowing God to cleanse us.

15:22-30 Samuel's words pierced Saul's callous heart like surgical steel (15:22-23). As we seek recovery, nothing can take the place of obedience to God. Everything hinges on an obedient heart; this was where Saul had failed so miserably. He tried to cover his sins with religious activities, promising to offer sacrifices to God. But God was more interested in Saul's confession and obedience than in his sacrifice. Saul's obvious regret spurred him to grasp vainly at Samuel's robe (15:27). But reality proved painful; God's rejection of Saul after so many second chances was real. At this point, complete recovery for Saul had become virtually impossible (15:28-29).

agreed and went back with him, and Saul worshiped the LORD.

Samuel Executes King Agag

³²Then Samuel said, "Bring King Agag to me." Agag arrived full of hope, for he thought, "Surely the worst is over, and I have been spared!"* ³³But Samuel said, "As your sword has killed the sons of many mothers, now your mother will be childless." And Samuel cut Agag to pieces before the LORD at Gilgal.

³⁴Then Samuel went home to Ramah, and Saul returned to his house at Gibeah of Saul. ³⁵Samuel never went to meet with Saul again, but he mourned constantly for him. And the LORD was sorry he had ever made Saul king of Israel.

CHAPTER 16
Samuel Anoints David as King

Now the LORD said to Samuel, "You have mourned long enough for Saul. I have rejected him as king of Israel, so fill your flask with olive oil and go to Bethlehem. Find a man named Jesse who lives there, for I have selected one of his sons to be my king."

²But Samuel asked, "How can I do that? If Saul hears about it, he will kill me."

"Take a heifer with you," the LORD replied, "and say that you have come to make a sacrifice to the LORD. ³Invite Jesse to the sacrifice, and I will show you which of his sons to anoint for me."

⁴So Samuel did as the LORD instructed. When he arrived at Bethlehem, the elders of the town came trembling to meet him. "What's wrong?" they asked. "Do you come in peace?"

⁵"Yes," Samuel replied. "I have come to sacrifice to the LORD. Purify yourselves and come with me to the sacrifice." Then Samuel per-

formed the purification rite for Jesse and his sons and invited them to the sacrifice, too.

⁶When they arrived, Samuel took one look at Eliab and thought, "Surely this is the LORD's anointed!"

⁷But the LORD said to Samuel, "Don't judge by his appearance or height, for I have rejected him. The LORD doesn't see things the way you see them. People judge by outward appearance, but the LORD looks at the heart."

⁸Then Jesse told his son Abinadab to step forward and walk in front of Samuel. But Samuel said, "This is not the one the LORD has chosen." ⁹Next Jesse summoned Shimea,* but Samuel said, "Neither is this the one the LORD has chosen." ¹⁰In the same way all seven of Jesse's sons were presented to Samuel. But Samuel said to Jesse, "The LORD has not chosen any of these." ¹¹Then Samuel asked, "Are these all the sons you have?"

"There is still the youngest," Jesse replied. "But he's out in the fields watching the sheep and goats."

"Send for him at once," Samuel said. "We will not sit down to eat until he arrives."

¹²So Jesse sent for him. He was dark and handsome, with beautiful eyes.

And the LORD said, "This is the one; anoint him."

¹³So as David stood there among his brothers, Samuel took the flask of olive oil he had brought and anointed David with the oil. And the Spirit of the LORD came powerfully upon David from that day on. Then Samuel returned to Ramah.

David Serves in Saul's Court

¹⁴Now the Spirit of the LORD had left Saul, and the LORD sent a tormenting spirit* that filled him with depression and fear.

¹⁵Some of Saul's servants said to him, "A

15:32 Dead Sea Scrolls and Greek version read *Agag arrived hesitantly, for he thought, "Surely this is the bitterness of death."* 16:9 Hebrew *Shammah,* a variant spelling of Shimea; compare 1 Chr 2:13; 20:7. 16:14 Or *an evil spirit;* also in 16:15, 16, 23.

16:1 Samuel was paralyzed by despair over Saul's failure, but God intervened and pointed Samuel toward a new venture. Saul had failed as king, but God had another man in mind for the job. It has been said that when the past is quarreling with the present there can be no future. We all need to quit living in the past after we have learned its lessons. There is a time for all of us to proceed to new assignments and goals. Recovery involves letting go of what was in the past so we can take hold of what is in the present and begin building a new life for the future.

16:6-13 God's choice of the man who would succeed Saul undoubtedly surprised Samuel. God tells us how he judges the value of individuals. It is not the physical gifts of strength or beauty that make people great. God judges people by their "heart." It is not what we see that is important; it is who a person is inside. Most of us are not models of physical perfection, so it comes as a relief that God does not judge us this way. Saul had failed, despite his external attractiveness. God is concerned with our humility and obedience—requirements for anyone who hopes to succeed in recovery.

tormenting spirit from God is troubling you. [16]Let us find a good musician to play the harp whenever the tormenting spirit troubles you. He will play soothing music, and you will soon be well again."

[17]"All right," Saul said. "Find me someone who plays well, and bring him here."

[18]One of the servants said to Saul, "One of Jesse's sons from Bethlehem is a talented harp player. Not only that—he is a brave warrior, a man of war, and has good judgment. He is also a fine-looking young man, and the LORD is with him."

[19]So Saul sent messengers to Jesse to say, "Send me your son David, the shepherd." [20]Jesse responded by sending David to Saul, along with a young goat, a donkey loaded with bread, and a wineskin full of wine.

[21]So David went to Saul and began serving him. Saul loved David very much, and David became his armor bearer. [22]Then Saul sent word to Jesse asking, "Please let David remain in my service, for I am very pleased with him."

[23]And whenever the tormenting spirit from God troubled Saul, David would play the harp. Then Saul would feel better, and the tormenting spirit would go away.

CHAPTER 17
Goliath Challenges the Israelites
The Philistines now mustered their army for battle and camped between Socoh in Judah and Azekah at Ephes-dammim. [2]Saul countered by gathering his Israelite troops near the valley of Elah. [3]So the Philistines and Israelites faced each other on opposite hills, with the valley between them.

[4]Then Goliath, a Philistine champion from Gath, came out of the Philistine ranks to face the forces of Israel. He was over nine feet* tall! [5]He wore a bronze helmet, and his bronze coat of mail weighed 125 pounds.* [6]He also wore bronze leg armor, and he carried a bronze javelin on his shoulder. [7]The shaft of his spear was as heavy and thick as a weaver's beam, tipped with an iron spear-

head that weighed 15 pounds.* His armor bearer walked ahead of him carrying a shield.

[8]Goliath stood and shouted a taunt across to the Israelites. "Why are you all coming out to fight?" he called. "I am the Philistine champion, but you are only the servants of Saul. Choose one man to come down here and fight me! [9]If he kills me, then we will be your slaves. But if I kill him, you will be our slaves! [10]I defy the armies of Israel today! Send me a man who will fight me!" [11]When Saul and the Israelites heard this, they were terrified and deeply shaken.

Jesse Sends David to Saul's Camp
[12]Now David was the son of a man named Jesse, an Ephrathite from Bethlehem in the land of Judah. Jesse was an old man at that time, and he had eight sons. [13]Jesse's three oldest sons—Eliab, Abinadab, and Shimea*— had already joined Saul's army to fight the Philistines. [14]David was the youngest son. David's three oldest brothers stayed with Saul's army, [15]but David went back and forth so he could help his father with the sheep in Bethlehem.

[16]For forty days, every morning and evening, the Philistine champion strutted in front of the Israelite army.

[17]One day Jesse said to David, "Take this basket* of roasted grain and these ten loaves of bread, and carry them quickly to your brothers. [18]And give these ten cuts of cheese to their captain. See how your brothers are getting along, and bring back a report on how they are doing.*" [19]David's brothers were with Saul and the Israelite army at the valley of Elah, fighting against the Philistines.

[20]So David left the sheep with another shepherd and set out early the next morning with the gifts, as Jesse had directed him. He arrived at the camp just as the Israelite army was leaving for the battlefield with shouts and battle cries. [21]Soon the Israelite and Philistine forces stood facing each other, army against army. [22]David left his things

---

17:4 Hebrew *6 cubits and 1 span* [which totals about 9.75 feet or 3 meters]; Dead Sea Scrolls and Greek version read *4 cubits and 1 span* [which totals about 6.75 feet or 2 meters]. 17:5 Hebrew *5,000 shekels* [57 kilograms]. 17:7 Hebrew *600 shekels* [6.8 kilograms]. 17:13 Hebrew *Shammah*, a variant spelling of Shimea; compare 1 Chr 2:13; 20:7. 17:17 Hebrew *ephah* [20 quarts or 22 liters]. 17:18 Hebrew *and take their pledge.*

17:32-37 David was confident that God would deliver him from Goliath's wrath, no matter how improbable it may have seemed. David was a young shepherd boy, armed with sticks and stones. Goliath was a giant of a man, armed with a great sword and spear. In human terms, David didn't have a chance; but with God, he couldn't lose. God is able to provide the victory to all who are willing to trust him. We all face giants in our life, problems that are too big to face alone. But even when the odds are stacked against us, we can't lose if God is on our side.

READ 1 SAMUEL 17:20-47

GOD grant me the serenity
to accept the things I cannot change
the courage to change the things I can
and the wisdom to know the difference
AMEN

There will be times in our life when right and wrong stand in stark contrast. Even when we know what is right and how things should be changed, the power may seem to be on the wrong side.

We may feel powerless even though we know we are standing for what is right. But even when this is true, we still shouldn't give up. Sometimes situations where we feel powerless can prompt action that changes everything for the better.

David watched as "Goliath, the Philistine champion from Gath, came out from the Philistine ranks. Then David heard him shout his usual taunt to the army of Israel. As soon as the Israelite army saw him, they began to run away in fright. 'Have you seen the giant?' the men asked. 'He comes out each day to defy Israel'" (1 Samuel 17:23-25). David convinced the king to let him fight the giant his own way. He shouted to Goliath, "You come to me with sword, spear, and javelin, but I come to you in the name of the LORD of Heaven's Armies—the God of the armies of Israel, whom you have defied. Today the LORD will conquer you" (17:45-46).

The Israelite soldiers saw themselves as helpless victims. Their powerlessness paralyzed them, so they just stood there and took the abuse. David took courageous action to recover their dignity. There are times when we need courage and God's help to fight against the tendency to remain a victim. We need to stand up for our human dignity and respond in new ways if we are to claim the victory. *Turn to page 375, 1 Samuel 24.*

---

with the keeper of supplies and hurried out to the ranks to greet his brothers. 23As he was talking with them, Goliath, the Philistine champion from Gath, came out from the Philistine ranks. Then David heard him shout his usual taunt to the army of Israel.

24As soon as the Israelite army saw him, they began to run away in fright. 25"Have you seen the giant?" the men asked. "He comes out each day to defy Israel. The king has offered a huge reward to anyone who kills him. He will give that man one of his daughters for a wife, and the man's entire family will be exempted from paying taxes!"

26David asked the soldiers standing nearby, "What will a man get for killing this Philistine and ending his defiance of Israel? Who is this pagan Philistine anyway, that he is allowed to defy the armies of the living God?"

27And these men gave David the same re-

ply. They said, "Yes, that is the reward for killing him."

28But when David's oldest brother, Eliab, heard David talking to the men, he was angry. "What are you doing around here anyway?" he demanded. "What about those few sheep you're supposed to be taking care of? I know about your pride and deceit. You just want to see the battle!"

29"What have I done now?" David replied. "I was only asking a question!" 30He walked over to some others and asked them the same thing and received the same answer. 31Then David's question was reported to King Saul, and the king sent for him.

David Kills Goliath

32"Don't worry about this Philistine," David told Saul. "I'll go fight him!"

33"Don't be ridiculous!" Saul replied.

"There's no way you can fight this Philistine and possibly win! You're only a boy, and he's been a man of war since his youth."

[34] But David persisted. "I have been taking care of my father's sheep and goats," he said. "When a lion or a bear comes to steal a lamb from the flock, [35] I go after it with a club and rescue the lamb from its mouth. If the animal turns on me, I catch it by the jaw and club it to death. [36] I have done this to both lions and bears, and I'll do it to this pagan Philistine, too, for he has defied the armies of the living God! [37] The LORD who rescued me from the claws of the lion and the bear will rescue me from this Philistine!"

Saul finally consented. "All right, go ahead," he said. "And may the LORD be with you!"

[38] Then Saul gave David his own armor—a bronze helmet and a coat of mail. [39] David put it on, strapped the sword over it, and took a step or two to see what it was like, for he had never worn such things before.

"I can't go in these," he protested to Saul. "I'm not used to them." So David took them off again. [40] He picked up five smooth stones from a stream and put them into his shepherd's bag. Then, armed only with his shepherd's staff and sling, he started across the valley to fight the Philistine.

[41] Goliath walked out toward David with his shield bearer ahead of him, [42] sneering in contempt at this ruddy-faced boy. [43] "Am I a dog," he roared at David, "that you come at me with a stick?" And he cursed David by the names of his gods. [44] "Come over here, and I'll give your flesh to the birds and wild animals!" Goliath yelled.

[45] David replied to the Philistine, "You come to me with sword, spear, and javelin, but I come to you in the name of the LORD of Heaven's Armies—the God of the armies of Israel, whom you have defied. [46] Today the LORD will conquer you, and I will kill you and cut off your head. And then I will give the dead bodies of your men to the birds and wild animals, and the whole world will know that there is a God in Israel! [47] And everyone assembled here will know that the LORD rescues his people, but not with sword and spear. This is the LORD's battle, and he will give you to us!"

[48] As Goliath moved closer to attack, David quickly ran out to meet him. [49] Reaching into his shepherd's bag and taking out a stone, he hurled it with his sling and hit the Philistine in the forehead. The stone sank in, and Goliath stumbled and fell face down on the ground.

[50] So David triumphed over the Philistine with only a sling and a stone, for he had no sword. [51] Then David ran over and pulled Goliath's sword from its sheath. David used it to kill him and cut off his head.

Israel Routs the Philistines
When the Philistines saw that their champion was dead, they turned and ran. [52] Then the men of Israel and Judah gave a great shout of triumph and rushed after the Philistines, chasing them as far as Gath* and the gates of Ekron. The bodies of the dead and wounded Philistines were strewn all along the road from Shaaraim, as far as Gath and Ekron. [53] Then the Israelite army returned and plundered the deserted Philistine camp. [54] (David took the Philistine's head to Jerusalem, but he stored the man's armor in his own tent.)

[55] As Saul watched David go out to fight the Philistine, he asked Abner, the commander of his army, "Abner, whose son is this young man?"

"I really don't know," Abner declared.

[56] "Well, find out who he is!" the king told him.

[57] As soon as David returned from killing Goliath, Abner brought him to Saul with the Philistine's head still in his hand. [58] "Tell me about your father, young man," Saul said.

And David replied, "His name is Jesse, and we live in Bethlehem."

CHAPTER 18
Saul Becomes Jealous of David
After David had finished talking with Saul, he met Jonathan, the king's son. There was an immediate bond between them, for Jonathan loved David. [2] From that day on Saul kept

17:52 As in some Greek manuscripts; Hebrew reads *a valley.*

17:45-47 As David squared off against Goliath, he knew that in human terms, he didn't have a chance. His courage came from his recognition that the battle belonged to God. Like David, we are helpless in the battles we face without God's intervention. But with God, the victory is certain. **18:1-4** God graciously provided David with a close friend in the person of Jonathan. This friendship later helped David survive Saul's various attempts on his life. God created us to be close to people and to need their companionship and help. The importance of a significant friend to whom one can be accountable during recovery cannot be overestimated. Recovery is not possible without accountability.

DAVID & JONATHAN

It is amazing that David and Jonathan formed one of the greatest friendships in history! There were vast differences between the two. The oldest son of King Saul, Jonathan was heir apparent to the throne of Israel. He was an experienced soldier, distinguished for his courage in battle. He was probably 15 years older than David.

David, on the other hand, was the youngest son of Jesse and was a shepherd in the town of Bethlehem. When Jonathan first met him, David was probably a teenager and looked the part of the junior shepherd boy. Although he demonstrated the bold heart of a warrior when he defeated Goliath, he was primarily known as a talented musician in King Saul's court.

There seem to be two basic ingredients that shaped this unlikely relationship: (1) They shared a common faith and commitment to God, and (2) they loved each other unconditionally.

Their friendship was put to the test, however. David was anointed by Samuel, the prophet, to succeed Saul as king. As a result, Saul tried repeatedly to kill David. This placed Jonathan at odds with his father. He risked himself to protect and encourage David, the one who would take his place as Israel's future king. No wonder David grieved so deeply at Jonathan's untimely death! It is a gift to have a friend who loves unconditionally. Building these relationships in our life is invaluable in recovery for ourself and for others.

STRENGTHS AND ACCOMPLISHMENTS:
- David and Jonathan were men of faith and courage.
- They loved each other unconditionally.
- They demonstrated great perseverance in their friendship.
- Jonathan was one of David's greatest encouragers.

LESSONS FROM THEIR LIVES:
- Mutual commitment to God and unconditional love for each other are vital ingredients in relationships.
- Difficulties can test and strengthen relationships.
- Encouragement vitalizes any relationship.

KEY VERSE:
"Jonathan went to find David and encouraged him to stay strong in his faith in God" (1 Samuel 23:16).

The story of David and Jonathan is told in 1 Samuel 18–31. It is remembered by David in 2 Samuel 1 and 9.

David with him and wouldn't let him return home. [3]And Jonathan made a solemn pact with David, because he loved him as he loved himself. [4]Jonathan sealed the pact by taking off his robe and giving it to David, together with his tunic, sword, bow, and belt.

[5]Whatever Saul asked David to do, David did it successfully. So Saul made him a commander over the men of war, an appointment that was welcomed by the people and Saul's officers alike.

[6]When the victorious Israelite army was returning home after David had killed the Philistine, women from all the towns of Israel came out to meet King Saul. They sang and danced for joy with tambourines and cymbals.* [7]This was their song:

"Saul has killed his thousands,
    and David his ten thousands!"

[8]This made Saul very angry. "What's this?" he said. "They credit David with ten thousands and me with only thousands. Next they'll be making him their king!" [9]So from that time on Saul kept a jealous eye on David.

[10]The very next day a tormenting spirit* from God overwhelmed Saul, and he began to rave in his house like a madman. David was playing the harp, as he did each day. But Saul had a spear in his hand, [11]and he suddenly hurled it at David, intending to pin him to the wall. But David escaped him twice.

[12]Saul was then afraid of David, for the LORD was with David and had turned away from Saul. [13]Finally, Saul sent him away and appointed him commander over 1,000 men, and David faithfully led his troops into battle.

18:6 The type of instrument represented by the word *cymbals* is uncertain. 18:10 Or *an evil spirit*.

¹⁴David continued to succeed in everything he did, for the LORD was with him. ¹⁵When Saul recognized this, he became even more afraid of him. ¹⁶But all Israel and Judah loved David because he was so successful at leading his troops into battle.

David Marries Saul's Daughter

¹⁷One day Saul said to David, "I am ready to give you my older daughter, Merab, as your wife. But first you must prove yourself to be a real warrior by fighting the LORD's battles." For Saul thought, "I'll send him out against the Philistines and let them kill him rather than doing it myself."

¹⁸"Who am I, and what is my family in Israel that I should be the king's son-in-law?" David exclaimed. "My father's family is nothing!" ¹⁹So* when the time came for Saul to give his daughter Merab in marriage to David, he gave her instead to Adriel, a man from Meholah.

²⁰In the meantime, Saul's daughter Michal had fallen in love with David, and Saul was delighted when he heard about it. ²¹"Here's another chance to see him killed by the Philistines!" Saul said to himself. But to David he said, "Today you have a second chance to become my son-in-law!"

²²Then Saul told his men to say to David, "The king really likes you, and so do we. Why don't you accept the king's offer and become his son-in-law?"

²³When Saul's men said these things to David, he replied, "How can a poor man from a humble family afford the bride price for the daughter of a king?"

²⁴When Saul's men reported this back to the king, ²⁵he told them, "Tell David that all I want for the bride price is 100 Philistine foreskins! Vengeance on my enemies is all I really want." But what Saul had in mind was that David would be killed in the fight.

²⁶David was delighted to accept the offer. Before the time limit expired, ²⁷he and his men went out and killed 200 Philistines. Then David fulfilled the king's requirement by presenting all their foreskins to him. So Saul gave his daughter Michal to David to be his wife.

²⁸When Saul realized that the LORD was with David and how much his daughter Michal loved him, ²⁹Saul became even more afraid of him, and he remained David's enemy for the rest of his life.

³⁰Every time the commanders of the Philistines attacked, David was more successful against them than all the rest of Saul's officers. So David's name became very famous.

CHAPTER 19
Saul Tries to Kill David

Saul now urged his servants and his son Jonathan to assassinate David. But Jonathan, because of his strong affection for David, ²told him what his father was planning. "Tomorrow morning," he warned him, "you must find a hiding place out in the fields. ³I'll ask my father to go out there with me, and I'll talk to him about you. Then I'll tell you everything I can find out."

⁴The next morning Jonathan spoke with his father about David, saying many good things about him. "The king must not sin against his servant David," Jonathan said. "He's never done anything to harm you. He has always helped you in any way he could. ⁵Have you forgotten about the time he risked his life to kill the Philistine giant and how the LORD brought a great victory to all Israel as a result? You were certainly happy about it then. Why should you murder an innocent man like David? There is no reason for it at all!"

⁶So Saul listened to Jonathan and vowed, "As surely as the LORD lives, David will not be killed."

⁷Afterward Jonathan called David and told him what had happened. Then he brought David to Saul, and David served in the court as before.

⁸War broke out again after that, and David led his troops against the Philistines. He attacked them with such fury that they all ran away.

⁹But one day when Saul was sitting at home, with spear in hand, the tormenting spirit* from the LORD suddenly came upon him again. As David played his harp, ¹⁰Saul hurled his spear at David. But David dodged

18:19 Or *But.* **19:9** Or *evil spirit.*

19:1-2 Since David was a threat to Saul's dynasty, Jonathan could conceivably have felt threatened by David. Yet Jonathan displayed no such smallness or insecurity. Instead he helped his friend, not only warning David of Saul's intentions but also assisting in his escape. True friends are never swayed by self-interest; they are willing to help, even if they must make personal sacrifices to do so. A good friend will be there to help in a crisis.

out of the way, and leaving the spear stuck in the wall, he fled and escaped into the night.

Michal Saves David's Life

¹¹Then Saul sent troops to watch David's house. They were told to kill David when he came out the next morning. But Michal, David's wife, warned him, "If you don't escape tonight, you will be dead by morning." ¹²So she helped him climb out through a window, and he fled and escaped. ¹³Then she took an idol* and put it in his bed, covered it with blankets, and put a cushion of goat's hair at its head.

¹⁴When the troops came to arrest David, she told them he was sick and couldn't get out of bed.

¹⁵But Saul sent the troops back to get David. He ordered, "Bring him to me in his bed so I can kill him!" ¹⁶But when they came to carry David out, they discovered that it was only an idol in the bed with a cushion of goat's hair at its head.

¹⁷"Why have you betrayed me like this and let my enemy escape?" Saul demanded of Michal.

"I had to," Michal replied. "He threatened to kill me if I didn't help him."

¹⁸So David escaped and went to Ramah to see Samuel, and he told him all that Saul had done to him. Then Samuel took David with him to live at Naioth. ¹⁹When the report reached Saul that David was at Naioth in Ramah, ²⁰he sent troops to capture him. But when they arrived and saw Samuel leading a group of prophets who were prophesying, the Spirit of God came upon Saul's men, and they also began to prophesy. ²¹When Saul heard what had happened, he sent other troops, but they, too, prophesied! The same thing happened a third time. ²²Finally, Saul himself went to Ramah and arrived at the great well in Secu. "Where are Samuel and David?" he demanded.

"They are at Naioth in Ramah," someone told him.

19:13 Hebrew *teraphim;* also in 19:16.

²³But on the way to Naioth in Ramah the Spirit of God came even upon Saul, and he, too, began to prophesy all the way to Naioth! ²⁴He tore off his clothes and lay naked on the ground all day and all night, prophesying in the presence of Samuel. The people who were watching exclaimed, "What? Is even Saul a prophet?"

CHAPTER 20
Jonathan Helps David

David now fled from Naioth in Ramah and found Jonathan. "What have I done?" he exclaimed. "What is my crime? How have I offended your father that he is so determined to kill me?"

²"That's not true!" Jonathan protested. "You're not going to die. He always tells me everything he's going to do, even the little things. I know my father wouldn't hide something like this from me. It just isn't so!"

³Then David took an oath before Jonathan and said, "Your father knows perfectly well about our friendship, so he has said to himself, 'I won't tell Jonathan—why should I hurt him?' But I swear to you that I am only a step away from death! I swear it by the LORD and by your own soul!"

⁴"Tell me what I can do to help you," Jonathan exclaimed.

⁵David replied, "Tomorrow we celebrate the new moon festival. I've always eaten with the king on this occasion, but tomorrow I'll hide in the field and stay there until the evening of the third day. ⁶If your father asks where I am, tell him I asked permission to go home to Bethlehem for an annual family sacrifice. ⁷If he says, 'Fine!' you will know all is well. But if he is angry and loses his temper, you will know he is determined to kill me. ⁸Show me this loyalty as my sworn friend—for we made a solemn pact before the LORD—or kill me yourself if I have sinned against your father. But please don't betray me to him!"

⁹"Never!" Jonathan exclaimed. "You know

19:18 In dire straits, David fled to his mentor, Samuel. Where we go when we are in trouble often reveals the kind of person we are. Samuel was one of the great spiritual leaders in Israel's history. David's decision to go to Samuel for help reveals his wisdom and desire to rely on God. In the recovery process it is important that we find people who will help us stay on track and lead us to depend on God for help.

20:4 David was exceedingly blessed to have a friend like Jonathan. After hearing of David's difficulties, he responded, "Tell me what I can do to help you!" Reliable and resourceful, Jonathan was ready to be supportive in helping David through this crisis. His willing response should challenge all of us who have loved ones in the process of recovery. We should be available to help others as they seek victory over their dependencies.

that if I had the slightest notion my father was planning to kill you, I would tell you at once."

¹⁰Then David asked, "How will I know whether or not your father is angry?"

¹¹"Come out to the field with me," Jonathan replied. And they went out there together. ¹²Then Jonathan told David, "I promise by the LORD, the God of Israel, that by this time tomorrow, or the next day at the latest, I will talk to my father and let you know at once how he feels about you. If he speaks favorably about you, I will let you know. ¹³But if he is angry and wants you killed, may the LORD strike me and even kill me if I don't warn you so you can escape and live. May the LORD be with you as he used to be with my father. ¹⁴And may you treat me with the faithful love of the LORD as long as I live. But if I die, ¹⁵treat my family with this faithful love, even when the LORD destroys all your enemies from the face of the earth."

¹⁶So Jonathan made a solemn pact with David,* saying, "May the LORD destroy all your enemies!" ¹⁷And Jonathan made David reaffirm his vow of friendship again, for Jonathan loved David as he loved himself.

¹⁸Then Jonathan said, "Tomorrow we celebrate the new moon festival. You will be missed when your place at the table is empty. ¹⁹The day after tomorrow, toward evening, go to the place where you hid before, and wait there by the stone pile.* ²⁰I will come out and shoot three arrows to the side of the stone pile as though I were shooting at a target. ²¹Then I will send a boy to bring the arrows back. If you hear me tell him, 'They're on this side,' then you will know, as surely as the LORD lives, that all is well, and there is no trouble. ²²But if I tell him, 'Go farther—the arrows are still ahead of you,' then it will mean that you must leave immediately, for the LORD is sending you away. ²³And may the LORD make us keep our promises to each other, for he has witnessed them."

²⁴So David hid himself in the field, and when the new moon festival began, the king sat down to eat. ²⁵He sat at his usual place against the wall, with Jonathan sitting opposite him* and Abner beside him. But David's place was empty. ²⁶Saul didn't say anything about it that day, for he said to himself, "Something must have made David ceremonially unclean." ²⁷But when David's place

was empty again the next day, Saul asked Jonathan, "Why hasn't the son of Jesse been here for the meal either yesterday or today?"

²⁸Jonathan replied, "David earnestly asked me if he could go to Bethlehem. ²⁹He said, 'Please let me go, for we are having a family sacrifice. My brother demanded that I be there. So please let me get away to see my brothers.' That's why he isn't here at the king's table."

³⁰Saul boiled with rage at Jonathan. "You stupid son of a whore!"* he swore at him. "Do you think I don't know that you want him to be king in your place, shaming yourself and your mother? ³¹As long as that son of Jesse is alive, you'll never be king. Now go and get him so I can kill him!"

³²"But why should he be put to death?" Jonathan asked his father. "What has he done?" ³³Then Saul hurled his spear at Jonathan, intending to kill him. So at last Jonathan realized that his father was really determined to kill David.

³⁴Jonathan left the table in fierce anger and refused to eat on that second day of the festival, for he was crushed by his father's shameful behavior toward David.

³⁵The next morning, as agreed, Jonathan went out into the field and took a young boy with him to gather his arrows. ³⁶"Start running," he told the boy, "so you can find the arrows as I shoot them." So the boy ran, and Jonathan shot an arrow beyond him. ³⁷When the boy had almost reached the arrow, Jonathan shouted, "The arrow is still ahead of you. ³⁸Hurry, hurry, don't wait." So the boy quickly gathered up the arrows and ran back to his master. ³⁹He, of course, suspected nothing; only Jonathan and David understood the signal. ⁴⁰Then Jonathan gave his bow and arrows to the boy and told him to take them back to town.

⁴¹As soon as the boy was gone, David came out from where he had been hiding near the stone pile.* Then David bowed three times to Jonathan with his face to the ground. Both of them were in tears as they embraced each other and said good-bye, especially David.

⁴²At last Jonathan said to David, "Go in peace, for we have sworn loyalty to each other in the LORD's name. The LORD is the witness of a bond between us and our children forever." Then David left, and Jonathan returned to the town.*

20:16 Hebrew *with the house of David.* 20:19 Hebrew *the stone Ezel.* The meaning of the Hebrew is uncertain. 20:25 As in Greek version; Hebrew reads *with Jonathan standing.* 20:30 Hebrew *You son of a perverse and rebellious woman.* 20:41 As in Greek version; Hebrew reads *near the south edge.* 20:42 This sentence is numbered 21:1 in Hebrew text.

CHAPTER 21
David Runs from Saul

[1]*David went to the town of Nob to see Ahimelech the priest. Ahimelech trembled when he saw him. "Why are you alone?" he asked. "Why is no one with you?"

[2]"The king has sent me on a private matter," David said. "He told me not to tell anyone why I am here. I have told my men where to meet me later. [3]Now, what is there to eat? Give me five loaves of bread or anything else you have."

[4]"We don't have any regular bread," the priest replied. "But there is the holy bread, which you can have if your young men have not slept with any women recently."

[5]"Don't worry," David replied. "I never allow my men to be with women when we are on a campaign. And since they stay clean even on ordinary trips, how much more on this one!"

[6]Since there was no other food available, the priest gave him the holy bread—the Bread of the Presence that was placed before the LORD in the Tabernacle. It had just been replaced that day with fresh bread.

[7]Now Doeg the Edomite, Saul's chief herdsman, was there that day, having been detained before the LORD.*

[8]David asked Ahimelech, "Do you have a spear or sword? The king's business was so urgent that I didn't even have time to grab a weapon!"

[9]"I only have the sword of Goliath the Philistine, whom you killed in the valley of Elah," the priest replied. "It is wrapped in a cloth behind the ephod. Take that if you want it, for there is nothing else here."

"There is nothing like it!" David replied. "Give it to me!"

[10]So David escaped from Saul and went to King Achish of Gath. [11]But the officers of Achish were unhappy about his being there. "Isn't this David, the king of the land?" they asked. "Isn't he the one the people honor with dances, singing,

'Saul has killed his thousands,
  and David his ten thousands'?"

[12]David heard these comments and was very afraid of what King Achish of Gath might do to him. [13]So he pretended to be insane, scratching on doors and drooling down his beard.

[14]Finally, King Achish said to his men, "Must you bring me a madman? [15]We already have enough of them around here! Why should I let someone like this be my guest?"

CHAPTER 22
David at the Cave of Adullam

So David left Gath and escaped to the cave of Adullam. Soon his brothers and all his other relatives joined him there. [2]Then others began coming—men who were in trouble or in debt or who were just discontented—until David was the captain of about 400 men.

[3]Later David went to Mizpeh in Moab, where he asked the king, "Please allow my father and mother to live here with you until I know what God is going to do for me." [4]So David's parents stayed in Moab with the king during the entire time David was living in his stronghold.

[5]One day the prophet Gad told David, "Leave the stronghold and return to the land of Judah." So David went to the forest of Hereth.

[6]The news of his arrival in Judah soon reached Saul. At the time, the king was sitting beneath the tamarisk tree on the hill at Gibeah, holding his spear and surrounded by his officers.

[7]"Listen here, you men of Benjamin!" Saul shouted to his officers when he heard the news. "Has that son of Jesse promised every one of you fields and vineyards? Has he promised to make you all generals and

21:1 Verses 21:1-15 are numbered 21:2-16 in Hebrew text. 21:7 The meaning of the Hebrew is uncertain.

21:1-2 The book of Proverbs tells us: "There are six things the LORD hates—no, seven things he detests: haughty eyes, a lying tongue, hands that kill the innocent, a heart that plots evil, feet that race to do wrong, a false witness who pours out lies, a person who sows discord in a family" (Proverbs 6:16-19). In his encounter with Ahimelech, David revealed that he was capable of making wrong choices. He lied, and his single lie led to others (1 Samuel 21:9-15). In the end this seemingly small falsehood, even though told for a good cause, proved costly—85 innocent priests lost their lives (22:18-20). God values honesty. Even minor indiscretions can have devastating effects on the lives of others, especially the people close to us (Ephesians 4:25).

22:1 David's family joined him in the cave of Adullam. Recovery is a family project, involving our loved ones and a network of supportive friends and fellow strugglers. Companionship should not be shunned in a crisis. God never wants us to go it alone.

captains in his army?* [8]Is that why you have conspired against me? For not one of you told me when my own son made a solemn pact with the son of Jesse. You're not even sorry for me. Think of it! My own son—encouraging him to kill me, as he is trying to do this very day!"

[9]Then Doeg the Edomite, who was standing there with Saul's men, spoke up. "When I was at Nob," he said, "I saw the son of Jesse talking to the priest, Ahimelech son of Ahitub. [10]Ahimelech consulted the LORD for him. Then he gave him food and the sword of Goliath the Philistine."

The Slaughter of the Priests

[11]King Saul immediately sent for Ahimelech and all his family, who served as priests at Nob. [12]When they arrived, Saul shouted at him, "Listen to me, you son of Ahitub!"

"What is it, my king?" Ahimelech asked.

[13]"Why have you and the son of Jesse conspired against me?" Saul demanded. "Why did you give him food and a sword? Why have you consulted God for him? Why have you encouraged him to kill me, as he is trying to do this very day?"

[14]"But sir," Ahimelech replied, "is anyone among all your servants as faithful as David, your son-in-law? Why, he is the captain of your bodyguard and a highly honored member of your household! [15]This was certainly not the first time I had consulted God for him! May the king not accuse me and my family in this matter, for I knew nothing at all of any plot against you."

[16]"You will surely die, Ahimelech, along with your entire family!" the king shouted.

[17]And he ordered his bodyguards, "Kill these priests of the LORD, for they are allies and conspirators with David! They knew he was running away from me, but they didn't tell me!" But Saul's men refused to kill the LORD's priests.

[18]Then the king said to Doeg, "You do it." So Doeg the Edomite turned on them and killed them that day, eighty-five priests in all, still wearing their priestly garments. [19]Then he went to Nob, the town of the priests, and killed the priests' families—men and women, children and babies—and all the cattle, donkeys, sheep, and goats.

[20]Only Abiathar, one of the sons of Ahimelech, escaped and fled to David. [21]When he told David that Saul had killed the priests of the LORD, [22]David exclaimed, "I knew it! When I saw Doeg the Edomite there that day, I knew he was sure to tell Saul. Now I have caused the death of all your father's family. [23]Stay here with me, and don't be afraid. I will protect you with my own life, for the same person wants to kill us both."

CHAPTER 23
David Protects the Town of Keilah

One day news came to David that the Philistines were at Keilah stealing grain from the threshing floors. [2]David asked the LORD, "Should I go and attack them?"

"Yes, go and save Keilah," the LORD told him.

[3]But David's men said, "We're afraid even here in Judah. We certainly don't want to go to Keilah to fight the whole Philistine army!"

[4]So David asked the LORD again, and again the LORD replied, "Go down to Keilah, for I will help you conquer the Philistines."

22:7 Hebrew *commanders of thousands and commanders of hundreds?*

22:16-18 The priests in this passage are the innocent victims of Saul's mental illness, David's lie (21:2), and Doeg's desire to be accepted. David's apparently inconsequential lie became the catalyst for the sins of others. It gave Saul the opportunity to act in an unbalanced way. It gave Doeg the chance to try to get some attention. Sometimes the small lies we tell can be compounded by the failures of others to bring great suffering to innocent people. In such times, telling the truth will often stop the sins of others rather than perpetuating or compounding them. Honesty is always the best policy.

23:14-15 The wonderful little phrase "but God didn't let Saul find [David]" must not be overlooked. Saul pursued David, but God protected, provided for, and preserved David's life. During the difficult years of running from Saul, David must have often felt alone and abandoned by God. But here we are told that God was working to protect David throughout that time. Even when things look bad for us, God is with us, protecting us in ways we do not even know. He is indeed worthy of our confidence and trust.

23:16-18 Once Jonathan located David, he encouraged him to find his strength in God. Jonathan was aware of the fearsome difficulties David faced, but he also knew that God was equal to the task of overcoming them. We often face problems too big for us to handle alone, but God is bigger than the worst of them. At times we may wonder how we can help our struggling friends. We can always do what Jonathan did for David. We can remind them that God is with them and that he is greater than any problem they might face.

GOD grant me the serenity to accept the things I cannot change the courage to change the things I can and the wisdom to know the difference

AMEN

When we are working to make changes in our life and relationships, we may not always be certain of what to do. When we face confusing situations, we need to rely on God's wisdom to help us make our decisions.

King Saul's jealousy and abuse made young David's life miserable. Saul knew that God had chosen David to be king instead of him. Although David was a loyal subject, Saul tried to kill him. Once, when David was hiding in a cave, King Saul came in without knowing David was there. "'Now's your opportunity!' David's men whispered to him. 'Today the LORD is telling you, "I will certainly put your enemy into your power, to do with as you wish."' So David crept forward and cut off a piece of the hem of Saul's robe. But then David's conscience began bothering him because he had cut Saul's robe. 'The LORD knows I shouldn't have done that to my lord the king,' he said to his men. 'The LORD forbid that I should do this to my lord the king and attack the LORD's anointed one, for the LORD himself has chosen him.' So David restrained his men and did not let them kill Saul" (1 Samuel 24:4-7).

David knew what God expected of him in this situation, and he chose to obey God. In trying to obey God, it is important to know what his will is in a given situation. When we aren't sure what to do, we can see if the Bible gives us any guidance on a similar situation. Then we will have a clear view of what it means to be truly obedient to God. *Turn to page 377, 1 Samuel 25.*

---

[5]So David and his men went to Keilah. They slaughtered the Philistines and took all their livestock and rescued the people of Keilah. [6]Now when Abiathar son of Ahimelech fled to David at Keilah, he brought the ephod with him.

[7]Saul soon learned that David was at Keilah. "Good!" he exclaimed. "We've got him now! God has handed him over to me, for he has trapped himself in a walled town!" [8]So Saul mobilized his entire army to march to Keilah and besiege David and his men.

[9]But David learned of Saul's plan and told Abiathar the priest to bring the ephod and ask the LORD what he should do. [10]Then David prayed, "O LORD, God of Israel, I have heard that Saul is planning to come and destroy Keilah because I am here. [11]Will the leaders of Keilah betray me to him?* And will

23:11 Some manuscripts lack the first sentence of 23:11.

Saul actually come as I have heard? O LORD, God of Israel, please tell me."

And the LORD said, "He will come."

[12]Again David asked, "Will the leaders of Keilah betray me and my men to Saul?"

And the LORD replied, "Yes, they will betray you."

David Hides in the Wilderness

[13]So David and his men—about 600 of them now—left Keilah and began roaming the countryside. Word soon reached Saul that David had escaped, so he didn't go to Keilah after all. [14]David now stayed in the strongholds of the wilderness and in the hill country of Ziph. Saul hunted him day after day, but God didn't let Saul find him.

[15]One day near Horesh, David received the news that Saul was on the way to Ziph to

search for him and kill him. [16]Jonathan went to find David and encouraged him to stay strong in his faith in God. [17]"Don't be afraid," Jonathan reassured him. "My father will never find you! You are going to be the king of Israel, and I will be next to you, as my father, Saul, is well aware." [18]So the two of them renewed their solemn pact before the LORD. Then Jonathan returned home, while David stayed at Horesh.

[19]But now the men of Ziph went to Saul in Gibeah and betrayed David to him. "We know where David is hiding," they said. "He is in the strongholds of Horesh on the hill of Hakilah, which is in the southern part of Jeshimon. [20]Come down whenever you're ready, O king, and we will catch him and hand him over to you!"

[21]"The LORD bless you," Saul said. "At last someone is concerned about me! [22]Go and check again to be sure of where he is staying and who has seen him there, for I know that he is very crafty. [23]Discover his hiding places, and come back when you are sure. Then I'll go with you. And if he is in the area at all, I'll track him down, even if I have to search every hiding place in Judah!" [24]So the men of Ziph returned home ahead of Saul.

Meanwhile, David and his men had moved into the wilderness of Maon in the Arabah Valley south of Jeshimon. [25]When David heard that Saul and his men were searching for him, he went even farther into the wilderness to the great rock, and he remained there in the wilderness of Maon. But Saul kept after him in the wilderness.

[26]Saul and David were now on opposite sides of a mountain. Just as Saul and his men began to close in on David and his men, [27]an urgent message reached Saul that the Philistines were raiding Israel again. [28]So Saul quit chasing David and returned to fight the Philistines. Ever since that time, the place where David was camped has been called the Rock of Escape.* [29]*David then went to live in the strongholds of En-gedi.

CHAPTER 24
David Spares Saul's Life

[1]*After Saul returned from fighting the Philistines, he was told that David had gone into the wilderness of En-gedi. [2]So Saul chose 3,000 elite troops from all Israel and went to search for David and his men near the rocks of the wild goats.

[3]At the place where the road passes some sheepfolds, Saul went into a cave to relieve himself. But as it happened, David and his men were hiding farther back in that very cave!

[4]"Now's your opportunity!" David's men whispered to him. "Today the LORD is telling you, 'I will certainly put your enemy into your power, to do with as you wish.'" So David crept forward and cut off a piece of the hem of Saul's robe.

[5]But then David's conscience began bothering him because he had cut Saul's robe. [6]He said to his men, "The LORD forbid that I should do this to my lord the king. I shouldn't attack the LORD's anointed one, for the LORD himself has chosen him." [7]So David restrained his men and did not let them kill Saul.

After Saul had left the cave and gone on his way, [8]David came out and shouted after him, "My lord the king!" And when Saul looked around, David bowed low before him.

[9]Then he shouted to Saul, "Why do you listen to the people who say I am trying to harm you? [10]This very day you can see with your own eyes it isn't true. For the LORD placed you at my mercy back there in the cave. Some of my men told me to kill you, but I spared you. For I said, 'I will never harm the king—he is the LORD's anointed one.' [11]Look, my father, at what I have in my hand. It is a piece of the hem of your robe! I cut it off, but I didn't kill you. This proves that I am not trying to harm you and that I have not sinned against you, even though you have been hunting for me to kill me. [12]"May the LORD judge between us. Per-

23:28 Hebrew *Sela-hammahlekoth.* 23:29 Verse 23:29 is numbered 24:1 in Hebrew text. 24:1 Verses 24:1-22 are numbered 24:2-23 in Hebrew text.

24:4-6 David refused to follow the counsel of his men and kill Saul. Even the act of cutting off a piece of Saul's robe troubled the younger man's conscience. Despite all that had happened, David still respected the king and his position as God's anointed one. Despite the temptation to hurt Saul and Saul's obvious vulnerability, David wisely restrained himself. David's intelligent response suggests two principles vital to the recovery process: (1) We need to assess the advice we get from the people around us, even from our close friends; (2) we must be tuned in to what God desires for a particular situation, not just what might be the easy way out.

READ 1 SAMUEL 25:18-39

GOD grant me the serenity
to accept the things I cannot change
the courage to change the things I can
and the wisdom to know the difference
AMEN

When other people put us at risk or cause us pain, we may feel as if there's nothing we can do. We may be used to the role of victim. But there are ways to maintain our dignity and sanity even in the most oppressive circumstances.

Abigail is a good example of someone who didn't give in to helplessness but had the wisdom to know what she could and couldn't change. Her husband, Nabal (meaning "fool"), was "crude and mean in all his dealings" (1 Samuel 25:3). Before David became king, Nabal insulted his troops to the point that David and his men were on their way to kill him and anyone who got in their way. Through some fast thinking and even faster talking, Abigail protected her family. She convinced David not to take vengeance into his own hands. A few weeks later Nabal died of natural (or perhaps supernatural) causes, and Abigail became David's wife.

We cannot always change other people. It takes wisdom and courage to accept this truth. But even when we can't change them, we can still change the situation to protect ourself from the effects of their behavior. Acceptance of another's addiction or personality does not mean that we have to accept being the victim of that person's wrongs. We can give up our crusade to change the other person without giving up our right to be treated with dignity. ***Turn to page 407, 2 Samuel 15.***

haps the LORD will punish you for what you are trying to do to me, but I will never harm you. ¹³As that old proverb says, 'From evil people come evil deeds.' So you can be sure I will never harm you. ¹⁴Who is the king of Israel trying to catch anyway? Should he spend his time chasing one who is as worthless as a dead dog or a single flea? ¹⁵May the LORD therefore judge which of us is right and punish the guilty one. He is my advocate, and he will rescue me from your power!"

¹⁶When David had finished speaking, Saul called back, "Is that really you, my son David?" Then he began to cry. ¹⁷And he said to David, "You are a better man than I am, for you have repaid me good for evil. ¹⁸Yes, you have been amazingly kind to me today, for when the LORD put me in a place where you could have killed me, you didn't do it. ¹⁹Who else would let his enemy get away when he had him in his power? May the LORD reward you well for the kindness you have shown me today. ²⁰And now I realize that you are

surely going to be king, and that the kingdom of Israel will flourish under your rule. ²¹Now swear to me by the LORD that when that happens you will not kill my family and destroy my line of descendants!"

²²So David promised this to Saul with an oath. Then Saul went home, but David and his men went back to their stronghold.

CHAPTER 25
The Death of Samuel
Now Samuel died, and all Israel gathered for his funeral. They buried him at his house in Ramah.

Nabal Angers David
Then David moved down to the wilderness of Maon.* ²There was a wealthy man from Maon who owned property near the town of Carmel. He had 3,000 sheep and 1,000 goats, and it was sheep-shearing time. ³This man's name was Nabal, and his wife, Abigail, was a sensible and beautiful woman. But Nabal, a

25:1 As in Greek version (see also 25:2); Hebrew reads *Paran*.

descendant of Caleb, was crude and mean in all his dealings.

[4] When David heard that Nabal was shearing his sheep, [5] he sent ten of his young men to Carmel with this message for Nabal: [6] "Peace and prosperity to you, your family, and everything you own! [7] I am told that it is sheep-shearing time. While your shepherds stayed among us near Carmel, we never harmed them, and nothing was ever stolen from them. [8] Ask your own men, and they will tell you this is true. So would you be kind to us, since we have come at a time of celebration? Please share any provisions you might have on hand with us and with your friend David." [9] David's young men gave this message to Nabal in David's name, and they waited for a reply.

[10] "Who is this fellow David?" Nabal sneered to the young men. "Who does this son of Jesse think he is? There are lots of servants these days who run away from their masters. [11] Should I take my bread and my water and my meat that I've slaughtered for my shearers and give it to a band of outlaws who come from who knows where?"

[12] So David's young men returned and told him what Nabal had said. [13] "Get your swords!" was David's reply as he strapped on his own. Then 400 men started off with David, and 200 remained behind to guard their equipment.

[14] Meanwhile, one of Nabal's servants went to Abigail and told her, "David sent messengers from the wilderness to greet our master, but he screamed insults at them. [15] These men have been very good to us, and we never suffered any harm from them. Nothing was stolen from us the whole time they were with us. [16] In fact, day and night they were like a wall of protection to us and the sheep. [17] You need to know this and figure out what to do, for there is going to be trouble for our master and his whole family. He's so ill-tempered that no one can even talk to him!"

[18] Abigail wasted no time. She quickly gathered 200 loaves of bread, two wineskins full of wine, five sheep that had been slaughtered, nearly a bushel* of roasted grain, 100 clusters of raisins, and 200 fig cakes. She packed them on donkeys [19] and said to her servants, "Go on ahead. I will follow you shortly." But she didn't tell her husband Nabal what she was doing.

[20] As she was riding her donkey into a mountain ravine, she saw David and his men coming toward her. [21] David had just been saying, "A lot of good it did to help this fellow. We protected his flocks in the wilderness, and nothing he owned was lost or stolen. But he has repaid me evil for good. [22] May God strike me and kill me* if even one man of his household is still alive tomorrow morning!"

Abigail Intercedes for Nabal

[23] When Abigail saw David, she quickly got off her donkey and bowed low before him. [24] She fell at his feet and said, "I accept all blame in this matter, my lord. Please listen to what I have to say. [25] I know Nabal is a wicked and ill-tempered man; please don't pay any attention to him. He is a fool, just as his name suggests.* But I never even saw the young men you sent.

[26] "Now, my lord, as surely as the LORD lives and you yourself live, since the LORD has kept you from murdering and taking vengeance into your own hands, let all your enemies and those who try to harm you be as cursed as Nabal is. [27] And here is a present that I, your servant, have brought to you and your young men. [28] Please forgive me if I have offended you in any way. The LORD will surely reward you with a lasting dynasty, for you are fighting the LORD's battles. And you have not done wrong throughout your entire life.

[29] "Even when you are chased by those who seek to kill you, your life is safe in the care of the LORD your God, secure in his treasure pouch! But the lives of your enemies will disappear like stones shot from a sling! [30] When the LORD has done all he promised and has made you leader of Israel, [31] don't let this be a blemish on your record. Then your conscience won't have to bear the staggering burden of needless bloodshed and vengeance. And when the LORD has done these great things for you, please remember me, your servant!"

[32] David replied to Abigail, "Praise the LORD, the God of Israel, who has sent you to meet me today! [33] Thank God for your good sense! Bless you for keeping me from murder and from carrying out vengeance with my own hands. [34] For I swear by the LORD, the God of Israel, who has kept me from hurting you, that if you had not hurried out to meet me, not one of Nabal's men would still be alive tomorrow morning." [35] Then David accepted her present and told her, "Return home in peace. I have heard what you said. We will not kill your husband."

25:18 Hebrew 5 seahs [36.5 liters]. 25:22 As in Greek version; Hebrew reads May God strike and kill the enemies of David. 25:25 The name Nabal means "fool."

³⁶When Abigail arrived home, she found that Nabal was throwing a big party and was celebrating like a king. He was very drunk, so she didn't tell him anything about her meeting with David until dawn the next day. ³⁷In the morning when Nabal was sober, his wife told him what had happened. As a result he had a stroke,* and he lay paralyzed on his bed like a stone. ³⁸About ten days later, the LORD struck him, and he died.

David Marries Abigail

³⁹When David heard that Nabal was dead, he said, "Praise the LORD, who has avenged the insult I received from Nabal and has kept me from doing it myself. Nabal has received the punishment for his sin." Then David sent messengers to Abigail to ask her to become his wife.

⁴⁰When the messengers arrived at Carmel, they told Abigail, "David has sent us to take you back to marry him."

⁴¹She bowed low to the ground and responded, "I, your servant, would be happy to marry David. I would even be willing to become a slave, washing the feet of his servants!" ⁴²Quickly getting ready, she took along five of her servant girls as attendants, mounted her donkey, and went with David's messengers. And so she became his wife. ⁴³David also married Ahinoam from Jezreel, making both of them his wives. ⁴⁴Saul, meanwhile, had given his daughter Michal, David's wife, to a man from Gallim named Palti son of Laish.

CHAPTER 26
David Spares Saul Again

Now some men from Ziph came to Saul at Gibeah to tell him, "David is hiding on the hill of Hakilah, which overlooks Jeshimon."

25:37 Hebrew *his heart failed him.*

²So Saul took 3,000 of Israel's elite troops and went to hunt him down in the wilderness of Ziph. ³Saul camped along the road beside the hill of Hakilah, near Jeshimon, where David was hiding. When David learned that Saul had come after him into the wilderness, ⁴he sent out spies to verify the report of Saul's arrival.

⁵David slipped over to Saul's camp one night to look around. Saul and Abner son of Ner, the commander of his army, were sleeping inside a ring formed by the slumbering warriors. ⁶"Who will volunteer to go in there with me?" David asked Ahimelech the Hittite and Abishai son of Zeruiah, Joab's brother.

"I'll go with you," Abishai replied. ⁷So David and Abishai went right into Saul's camp and found him asleep, with his spear stuck in the ground beside his head. Abner and the soldiers were lying asleep around him.

⁸"God has surely handed your enemy over to you this time!" Abishai whispered to David. "Let me pin him to the ground with one thrust of the spear; I won't need to strike twice!"

⁹"No!" David said. "Don't kill him. For who can remain innocent after attacking the LORD's anointed one? ¹⁰Surely the LORD will strike Saul down someday, or he will die of old age or in battle. ¹¹The LORD forbid that I should kill the one he has anointed! But take his spear and that jug of water beside his head, and then let's get out of here!"

¹²So David took the spear and jug of water that were near Saul's head. Then he and Abishai got away without anyone seeing them or even waking up, because the LORD had put Saul's men into a deep sleep.

¹³David climbed the hill opposite the camp until he was at a safe distance. ¹⁴Then

---

25:36-38 *Nabal* means "fool"; here Nabal demonstrated how appropriate his name was. His self-centeredness kept him from fulfilling an act of common courtesy that was expected in ancient Israel. David and his band had protected Nabal and his herds from foreign marauders, so they expected that he would give them supplies. But Nabal lived to satisfy his own appetites, with little regard for others. His selfish bravado nearly resulted in the deaths of many innocent employees. Only the intervention of his wife, Abigail, prevented a disaster. Most of us have a little of Nabal in us; we are somewhat foolish at times. Our dependencies drive us to make decisions that are destructive to us and to those around us. An important part of recovery is taking inventory of the foolishness in our life. Nabal's end should encourage us to do so.

26:8-11 The advice of even loyal friends can sometimes get us into trouble. Abishai recommended the murder of Saul, but David was unwilling to accept the consequences of assassinating God's chosen king (26:9-11). He wisely placed boundaries on the behavior of his men and left Saul alone. David knew that Saul's judgment belonged in God's hands, and he wisely left it there. As we seek reconciliation with people, we may need to give up our tendency to judge others and allow God to be the judge. This is an important step in the process of forgiveness and reconciliation.

he shouted down to the soldiers and to Abner son of Ner, "Wake up, Abner!"

"Who is it?" Abner demanded.

¹⁵"Well, Abner, you're a great man, aren't you?" David taunted. "Where in all Israel is there anyone as mighty? So why haven't you guarded your master the king when someone came to kill him? ¹⁶This isn't good at all! I swear by the LORD that you and your men deserve to die, because you failed to protect your master, the LORD's anointed! Look around! Where are the king's spear and the jug of water that were beside his head?"

¹⁷Saul recognized David's voice and called out, "Is that you, my son David?"

And David replied, "Yes, my lord the king. ¹⁸Why are you chasing me? What have I done? What is my crime? ¹⁹But now let my lord the king listen to his servant. If the LORD has stirred you up against me, then let him accept my offering. But if this is simply a human scheme, then may those involved be cursed by the LORD. For they have driven me from my home, so I can no longer live among the LORD's people, and they have said, 'Go, worship pagan gods.' ²⁰Must I die on foreign soil, far from the presence of the LORD? Why has the king of Israel come out to search for a single flea? Why does he hunt me down like a partridge on the mountains?"

²¹Then Saul confessed, "I have sinned. Come back home, my son, and I will no longer try to harm you, for you valued my life today. I have been a fool and very, very wrong."

²²"Here is your spear, O king," David replied. "Let one of your young men come over and get it. ²³The LORD gives his own reward for doing good and for being loyal, and I refused to kill you even when the LORD placed you in my power, for you are the LORD's anointed one. ²⁴Now may the LORD value my life, even as I have valued yours today. May he rescue me from all my troubles."

²⁵And Saul said to David, "Blessings on you, my son David. You will do many heroic deeds, and you will surely succeed." Then David went away, and Saul returned home.

CHAPTER 27
David among the Philistines

But David kept thinking to himself, "Someday Saul is going to get me. The best thing I can do is escape to the Philistines. Then Saul will stop hunting for me in Israelite territory, and I will finally be safe."

²So David took his 600 men and went over and joined Achish son of Maoch, the king of Gath. ³David and his men and their families settled there with Achish at Gath. David brought his two wives along with him—Ahinoam from Jezreel and Abigail, Nabal's widow from Carmel. ⁴Word soon reached Saul that David had fled to Gath, so he stopped hunting for him.

⁵One day David said to Achish, "If it is all right with you, we would rather live in one of the country towns instead of here in the royal city."

⁶So Achish gave him the town of Ziklag (which still belongs to the kings of Judah to this day), ⁷and they lived there among the Philistines for a year and four months.

⁸David and his men spent their time raiding the Geshurites, the Girzites, and the Amalekites—people who had lived near Shur, toward the land of Egypt, since ancient times. ⁹David did not leave one person alive in the villages he attacked. He took the sheep, goats, cattle, donkeys, camels, and clothing before returning home to see King Achish.

¹⁰"Where did you make your raid today?" Achish would ask.

And David would reply, "Against the south of Judah, the Jerahmeelites, and the Kenites."

¹¹No one was left alive to come to Gath and tell where he had really been. This happened again and again while he was living among the Philistines. ¹²Achish believed

---

26:17-21 Too little, too late. We hear from Saul's lips words that should have been uttered much earlier: (1) "I have sinned"; (2) "I have been a fool"; (3) "I have been . . . very, very wrong." Such honest admissions reflect the concerns of a personal inventory—the basis for repentance, forgiveness, and reconciliation. These are essential parts of the recovery process.

27:1 David's fearful thoughts were not consistent with God's promises. He knew that God had a special plan for his life, which included kingship over Israel. After years of running for his life, however, David seems to have become discouraged. Motivated by fear, he moved to the land of the Philistines where he encountered some compromising situations (28:1-2; 29:1-7). David needed to persevere in his trust. God had protected him up until that point and was perfectly capable of continuing that protection. Recovery is never a short-term process, but after years of struggling it is sometimes tempting to step away from God's program. If we desire God's help and success, we must persevere.

David and thought to himself, "By now the people of Israel must hate him bitterly. Now he will have to stay here and serve me forever!"

CHAPTER 28
Saul Consults a Medium

About that time the Philistines mustered their armies for another war with Israel. King Achish told David, "You and your men will be expected to join me in battle."

²"Very well!" David agreed. "Now you will see for yourself what we can do."

Then Achish told David, "I will make you my personal bodyguard for life."

³Meanwhile, Samuel had died, and all Israel had mourned for him. He was buried in Ramah, his hometown. And Saul had banned from the land of Israel all mediums and those who consult the spirits of the dead.

⁴The Philistines set up their camp at Shunem, and Saul gathered all the army of Israel and camped at Gilboa. ⁵When Saul saw the vast Philistine army, he became frantic with fear. ⁶He asked the LORD what he should do, but the LORD refused to answer him, either by dreams or by sacred lots* or by the prophets. ⁷Saul then said to his advisers, "Find a woman who is a medium, so I can go and ask her what to do."

His advisers replied, "There is a medium at Endor."

⁸So Saul disguised himself by wearing ordinary clothing instead of his royal robes. Then he went to the woman's home at night, accompanied by two of his men.

"I have to talk to a man who has died," he said. "Will you call up his spirit for me?"

⁹"Are you trying to get me killed?" the woman demanded. "You know that Saul has outlawed all the mediums and all who consult the spirits of the dead. Why are you setting a trap for me?"

¹⁰But Saul took an oath in the name of the LORD and promised, "As surely as the LORD

lives, nothing bad will happen to you for doing this."

¹¹Finally, the woman said, "Well, whose spirit do you want me to call up?"

"Call up Samuel," Saul replied.

¹²When the woman saw Samuel, she screamed, "You've deceived me! You are Saul!"

¹³"Don't be afraid!" the king told her. "What do you see?"

"I see a god* coming up out of the earth," she said.

¹⁴"What does he look like?" Saul asked.

"He is an old man wrapped in a robe," she replied. Saul realized it was Samuel, and he fell to the ground before him.

¹⁵"Why have you disturbed me by calling me back?" Samuel asked Saul.

"Because I am in deep trouble," Saul replied. "The Philistines are at war with me, and God has left me and won't reply by prophets or dreams. So I have called for you to tell me what to do."

¹⁶But Samuel replied, "Why ask me, since the LORD has left you and has become your enemy? ¹⁷The LORD has done just as he said he would. He has torn the kingdom from you and given it to your rival, David. ¹⁸The LORD has done this to you today because you refused to carry out his fierce anger against the Amalekites. ¹⁹What's more, the LORD will hand you and the army of Israel over to the Philistines tomorrow, and you and your sons will be here with me. The LORD will bring down the entire army of Israel in defeat."

²⁰Saul fell full length on the ground, paralyzed with fright because of Samuel's words. He was also faint with hunger, for he had eaten nothing all day and all night.

²¹When the woman saw how distraught he was, she said, "Sir, I obeyed your command at the risk of my life. ²²Now do what I say, and let me give you a little something to eat so you can regain your strength for the trip back."

28:6 Hebrew *by Urim*. **28:13** Or *gods*.

28:1-2 Compromising our convictions often leaves us with hard choices. David had left Israel to hide among the Philistines and was now reaping the consequences. He was asked to join the Philistines in a battle against his own people. David had to deal with a difficult decision that God probably never intended him to face. When we make decisions apart from God and his Word, we may end up in unfortunate situations. We need to keep God at the center of our decisions and carefully consider the likely consequences of our actions before we make a decision.

28:7-8 Saul's final act of rebellion involved witchcraft, which the Bible unequivocally condemns. In his desperation, Saul sought the guidance of spirits of the dead. Instead of finding help there, however, they only confirmed his destruction. The world of the occult will never yield true recovery and must be avoided at all cost.

²³But Saul refused to eat anything. Then his advisers joined the woman in urging him to eat, so he finally yielded and got up from the ground and sat on the couch.

²⁴The woman had been fattening a calf, so she hurried out and killed it. She took some flour, kneaded it into dough and baked unleavened bread. ²⁵She brought the meal to Saul and his advisers, and they ate it. Then they went out into the night.

CHAPTER 29
The Philistines Reject David

The entire Philistine army now mobilized at Aphek, and the Israelites camped at the spring in Jezreel. ²As the Philistine rulers were leading out their troops in groups of hundreds and thousands, David and his men marched at the rear with King Achish. ³But the Philistine commanders demanded, "What are these Hebrews doing here?"

And Achish told them, "This is David, the servant of King Saul of Israel. He's been with me for years, and I've never found a single fault in him from the day he arrived until today."

⁴But the Philistine commanders were angry. "Send him back to the town you've given him!" they demanded. "He can't go into the battle with us. What if he turns against us in battle and becomes our adversary? Is there any better way for him to reconcile himself with his master than by handing our heads over to him? ⁵Isn't this the same David about whom the women of Israel sing in their dances,

'Saul has killed his thousands,
   and David his ten thousands'?"

⁶So Achish finally summoned David and said to him, "I swear by the LORD that you have been a trustworthy ally. I think you should go with me into battle, for I've never found a single flaw in you from the day you arrived until today. But the other Philistine rulers won't hear of it. ⁷Please don't upset them, but go back quietly."

⁸"What have I done to deserve this treatment?" David demanded. "What have you ever found in your servant, that I can't go and fight the enemies of my lord the king?"

⁹But Achish insisted, "As far as I'm concerned, you're as perfect as an angel of God. But the Philistine commanders are afraid to have you with them in the battle. ¹⁰Now get up early in the morning, and leave with your men as soon as it gets light."

¹¹So David and his men headed back into the land of the Philistines, while the Philistine army went on to Jezreel.

CHAPTER 30
David Destroys the Amalekites

Three days later, when David and his men arrived home at their town of Ziklag, they found that the Amalekites had made a raid into the Negev and Ziklag; they had crushed Ziklag and burned it to the ground. ²They had carried off the women and children and everyone else but without killing anyone.

³When David and his men saw the ruins and realized what had happened to their families, ⁴they wept until they could weep no more. ⁵David's two wives, Ahinoam from Jezreel and Abigail, the widow of Nabal from Carmel, were among those captured. ⁶David was now in great danger because all his men were very bitter about losing their sons and daughters, and they began to talk of stoning him. But David found strength in the LORD his God.

⁷Then he said to Abiathar the priest, "Bring me the ephod!" So Abiathar brought it. ⁸Then David asked the LORD, "Should I chase after this band of raiders? Will I catch them?"

And the LORD told him, "Yes, go after them. You will surely recover everything that was taken from you!"

⁹So David and his 600 men set out, and they came to the brook Besor. ¹⁰But 200 of

---

29:1-10 David's move to Philistia was a compromising one. His safety there depended on his relationship with King Achish, who asked David to fight against the Israelites. Here Achish released David from his service. God delivered David from the consequences of his earlier decision. God's love is great! He often provides us with a way to escape difficult circumstances, even ones of our own making (see 1 Corinthians 10:13). But remember this: When God provides the way for us to escape a compromising situation, it is still our responsibility to take it.

30:1-6 During David's and his men's time away from Ziklag, marauders had come and stolen their belongings and kidnapped their families. In this crisis David shows us where to go for direction and hope: "David found strength in the LORD his God" (30:6). David knew where to go in a crisis. Entrusting our life to God, no matter how dire our circumstances, is an important step in recovery.

the men were too exhausted to cross the brook, so David continued the pursuit with 400 men.

[11]Along the way they found an Egyptian man in a field and brought him to David. They gave him some bread to eat and water to drink. [12]They also gave him part of a fig cake and two clusters of raisins, for he hadn't had anything to eat or drink for three days and nights. Before long his strength returned.

[13]"To whom do you belong, and where do you come from?" David asked him.

"I am an Egyptian—the slave of an Amalekite," he replied. "My master abandoned me three days ago because I was sick. [14]We were on our way back from raiding the Kerethites in the Negev, the territory of Judah, and the land of Caleb, and we had just burned Ziklag."

[15]"Will you lead me to this band of raiders?" David asked.

The young man replied, "If you take an oath in God's name that you will not kill me or give me back to my master, then I will guide you to them."

[16]So he led David to them, and they found the Amalekites spread out across the fields, eating and drinking and dancing with joy because of the vast amount of plunder they had taken from the Philistines and the land of Judah. [17]David and his men rushed in among them and slaughtered them throughout that night and the entire next day until evening. None of the Amalekites escaped except 400 young men who fled on camels. [18]David got back everything the Amalekites had taken, and he rescued his two wives. [19]Nothing was missing: small or great, son or daughter, nor anything else that had been taken. David brought everything back. [20]He also recovered all the flocks and herds, and his men drove them ahead of the other livestock. "This plunder belongs to David!" they said.

[21]Then David returned to the brook Besor and met up with the 200 men who had been left behind because they were too exhausted to go with him. They went out to meet David and his men, and David greeted them joy-

30:29 Greek version reads *Carmel*.

fully. [22]But some evil troublemakers among David's men said, "They didn't go with us, so they can't have any of the plunder we recovered. Give them their wives and children, and tell them to be gone."

[23]But David said, "No, my brothers! Don't be selfish with what the LORD has given us. He has kept us safe and helped us defeat the band of raiders that attacked us. [24]Who will listen when you talk like this? We share and share alike—those who go to battle and those who guard the equipment." [25]From then on David made this a decree and regulation for Israel, and it is still followed today.

[26]When he arrived at Ziklag, David sent part of the plunder to the elders of Judah, who were his friends. "Here is a present for you, taken from the LORD's enemies," he said.

[27]The gifts were sent to the people of the following towns David had visited: Bethel, Ramoth-negev, Jattir, [28]Aroer, Siphmoth, Eshtemoa, [29]Racal,* the towns of the Jerahmeelites, the towns of the Kenites, [30]Hormah, Borashan, Athach, [31]Hebron, and all the other places David and his men had visited.

CHAPTER 31
The Death of Saul

Now the Philistines attacked Israel, and the men of Israel fled before them. Many were slaughtered on the slopes of Mount Gilboa. [2]The Philistines closed in on Saul and his sons, and they killed three of his sons—Jonathan, Abinadab, and Malkishua. [3]The fighting grew very fierce around Saul, and the Philistine archers caught up with him and wounded him severely.

[4]Saul groaned to his armor bearer, "Take your sword and kill me before these pagan Philistines come to run me through and taunt and torture me."

But his armor bearer was afraid and would not do it. So Saul took his own sword and fell on it. [5]When his armor bearer realized that Saul was dead, he fell on his own sword and died beside the king. [6]So Saul, his three sons, and his armor bearer, and his troops all died together that same day.

[7]When the Israelites on the other side of

31:3-4 Suicide was the tragic end of a man who never learned to repent. Recovery would have been possible for Saul if he had admitted his helplessness, committed his life to God, and allowed God to change him. He never allowed anyone to assist him in matters of accountability and spiritual growth. He never learned to depend upon God. He never felt the courage or a real desire to change. As a result, his life stands as a monument to squandered potential. Saul's tragic end should give us ample reason to embrace God's program for recovery.

the Jezreel Valley and beyond the Jordan saw that the Israelite army had fled and that Saul and his sons were dead, they abandoned their towns and fled. So the Philistines moved in and occupied their towns.

⁸The next day, when the Philistines went out to strip the dead, they found the bodies of Saul and his three sons on Mount Gilboa. ⁹So they cut off Saul's head and stripped off his armor. Then they proclaimed the good news of Saul's death in their pagan temple and to the people throughout the land of Philistia. ¹⁰They placed his armor in the temple of the Ashtoreths, and they fastened his body to the wall of the city of Beth-shan.

¹¹But when the people of Jabesh-gilead heard what the Philistines had done to Saul, ¹²all their mighty warriors traveled through the night to Beth-shan and took the bodies of Saul and his sons down from the wall. They brought them to Jabesh, where they burned the bodies. ¹³Then they took their bones and buried them beneath the tamarisk tree at Jabesh, and they fasted for seven days.

REFLECTIONS ON 1 SAMUEL

insights FROM HANNAH'S LIFE

In ancient times, much of a woman's self-worth was built upon her ability to bear children. As is clear from **1 Samuel 1:1-8**, Hannah's childless state brought her a great deal of pain. To make matters worse, Elkanah's second wife, Peninnah, ridiculed Hannah for her infertility. Certainly Hannah had tried everything humanly possible to become pregnant. She was at the end of her rope, helpless to change her situation. She was unable to see that a fulfilling life could be found without children. Her husband, Elkanah, tried to intervene, reminding Hannah of his unconditional love for her (1:8), but Hannah was unable to accept his comfort. Hannah had come to the point of acknowledging her helplessness, the first step toward her recovery.

Samuel's birth, mentioned in **1 Samuel 1:19-20**, shows us that God is a listening God. He solved Hannah's crisis by giving her a son. She named him Samuel, meaning "asked of God." This would have been a constant reminder that God had heard Hannah's cries and answered. We can be confident that when we ask God for anything in line with his will (1 John 5:14), he hears us, too. No problem is ever too big for him to solve (Jeremiah 32:27).

In **1 Samuel 1:24-28** the time came for Hannah to fulfill her vow to God. Letting go of her little son must certainly have been painful. But Hannah recognized her accountability to God and unselfishly fulfilled her promise by releasing her much-loved son into his service. Her choice reflected her gratitude and her confidence in God, who had given Samuel to her in the first place. When we make commitments to God and others, we need to follow through on them. If we do, no matter how hard it may be, God will help us and bless our efforts. After Hannah gave up Samuel to God's service, God blessed her with additional children.

Hannah continued her prayer of praise in **1 Samuel 2:4-10**, thanking God for blessing her. She said, "Those who stumbled are now strong" (2:4). God provided not only the deliverance but also the strength for recovery. He gave Hannah the strength to persevere in the process, to seek freedom, to adopt new attitudes, to fulfill responsibilities, to set things straight, to build a new life. Such honest praise of God's power will naturally burst forth as we admit our helplessness and commit our life to God. As we surrender ourself, the Holy Spirit is freed to do his good work in us.

In **1 Samuel 2:20-21** we see that Hannah was blessed with additional children. God is in the business of blessing his people beyond their requests and expectations (Ephesians 3:20).

insights FROM ELI'S LIFE

In **1 Samuel 2:23-34** Eli exercised "tough love" as he confronted his sons about their blatant sin. He surely hoped they would make significant changes in their lives. Unfortunately, they didn't listen to their father. The young men refused to set boundaries on their behavior, and they displayed no desire to change. Their choice to go their own way brought dire conse-quences—ultimately, physical death (2:25, 34; 4:11). Eli, too, made a choice: He opted to ignore his sons' continued disobedience. Thus the high priest failed in his responsibility to God and was eventually judged for it. Eli was told that his descendants would bring him tears of grief and would die in the prime of life. What a bitter harvest we reap when we refuse to turn from tempta-tion and embrace God's power for change.

insights FROM SAMUEL'S LIFE

Samuel's exhortation to the Israelites in **1 Samuel 7:3-4** gives us a clear picture of what is involved in the recovery process. He tells them (1) to get rid of their foreign gods and idols, (2) to deter-mine to obey God, and (3) to worship him only. Those of us in recovery are called to do the same. First we must get rid of all the idols in our life—anything that drives or controls us. This involves a deep self-examination, an honest assessment of motives and priorities, and a realization of our own helplessness and disobedience. Then we must commit ourself to God, recognizing our accountability before him and before the people close to us. This will necessitate reconciling the past and setting it straight. We must come clean, letting God wash away our filth and lies. Samuel promised the Israelites that their obedience would result in their deliverance from the Philistines. We, too, can rest assured that God will facilitate a fresh start in our life as we respond properly to his principles and priorities.

In **1 Samuel 12:8-11** Samuel reviewed Israel's history and described the cycle of sin, crisis, and deliverance that was evident in the book of Judges. The Israelites sinned, and the consequences led them to enslavement. Helpless to shake their oppressors, the people cried out to God, admit-ting their sins of disobedience. By recognizing their helplessness, the Israelites were freed to turn to the only one who could help them, God himself. Then God provided a delivering judge to lead the people out of bondage. The crisis stage described by Samuel is similar to our experience of "hitting bottom." When we do that, we recognize our helplessness and with God's help begin the process of recovery.

In **1 Samuel 12:23-25**, Samuel identified failure to pray for the people as a sin against God. This shows the depth of his sense of accountability to God and his feelings of responsibility for the people. His spiritual maturity manifested itself in his desire to help others; he said, "I will continue to teach you what is good and right" (12:23). Indeed, Samuel outlined the people's program for recovery that they might gain freedom: (1) "fear the LORD," (2) "faithfully serve him," and (3) "think of all the wonderful things he has done for you" (12:24). Samuel concluded by warning the people of the dire consequences of refusing to obey God (12:25). We would all do well to heed Samuel's words.

insights FROM SAUL'S LIFE

Saul said in **1 Samuel 14:24-25**, "before I have full revenge on my enemies." This comment gives us a clue that Saul was on a downhill slide spiritually. Earlier he had declared, "Today the LORD has rescued Israel!" (11:13). But here he has changed his tune; no longer did he see God as the vital entity in the victory. The battle had become Saul's; the enemies were no longer God's enemies but Saul's. Thus the victory would belong to Saul and not to God. When we begin to take credit for our progress in recovery, we have already begun to regress toward failure. We must always remember that the enemies we face are too big for us unless we seek victory through God's help.

In **1 Samuel 15:10-15** God was grieved because Saul had followed his own inclinations rather than God's clear instructions. God's principles for healthy living call us to obey his instructions, to make a clean break with the past, and to refuse to compromise. Saul exhibited none of these prin-ciples. He chose to spare King Agag and the finest animals instead of destroying everything as God had commanded (15:8-9). He even built a monument to himself rather than pay tribute to God for the miraculous victory (15:12). When confronted by Samuel, Saul tried to justify his actions (15:15), but making excuses has never paved the way to a new life. We must accept responsibility for our actions if we desire to grow. Until we stop making excuses for our behavior, there is no hope for recovery.

In **1 Samuel 15:32-33** we see that Saul was not willing to obey God completely; he spared King Agag against God's express orders. The execution of Agag by Samuel reminds us that a successful recovery demands a distinct break with the past and complete obedience to God's program. The past must be put to death if we hope to progress in recovery.

insights FROM DAVID'S LIFE

Notice in **1 Samuel 17:32-37** that David's courage was, in part, based on God's help in David's previous battles with lions and bears. David had learned to trust God in his smaller battles, giving him the faith he needed to confront Goliath. It is easy to overlook our smaller victories and forget about the help God gave us during such times. We would be wise to take account of our victories, no matter how small, and allow them to build our courage and faith for the battles still ahead.

In **1 Samuel 23:1-9** David repeatedly looked to God for direction in his life. He had grown accustomed to trusting God for direction during times of crisis. When God commanded David to lead his men against the Philistines at Keilah, David's men were afraid to act on that command. So David went to God a second time, and God affirmed his first command but also added a reassuring message: "I will help you conquer the Philistines" (23:4). Like David and his men, we may respond with fear to God's direction in our life. But we can be sure that when God tells us to do something, he will stand by us each step of the way and help us gain the victory.

In **1 Samuel 23:24-28**, it appeared that Saul would finally capture David. But God intervened and Saul was forced to return home to defend against Philistine raids. After experiencing this, it is no surprise that David wrote these words: "The LORD himself watches over you! The LORD stands beside you as your protective shade. The sun will not harm you by day, nor the moon at night. The LORD keeps you from all harm and watches over your life. The LORD keeps watch over you as you come and go, both now and forever" (Psalm 121:5-8). God is in the business of protecting his own.

Though at times David appears a model of self-restraint, we see in **1 Samuel 25:12-13** that he was capable of giving in to impatience. In reacting to Nabal's poor manners, David failed to consult with God before taking action. He made a hasty decision while he was angry and upset. Such impulsiveness frequently results in mistakes with long-term consequences. Thankfully, God sent Abigail to prevent David from acting unwisely (25:32). When we are angry and tempted to act impulsively, we need to calm down and listen to what God has to say to us.

2 SAMUEL

THE BIG PICTURE

A. DAVID'S TRIUMPHS
   (1:1–10:19)
   1. Reigning in Hebron over
      Judah (1:1–4:12)
   2. Reigning in Jerusalem over
      All Israel (5:1–10:19)
B. DAVID'S TROUBLES
   (11:1–12:31)
   1. David's Sexual Sin (11:1-27)
   2. Nathan's Intervention by
      Confrontation (12:1-31)
C. THE CONSEQUENCES OF
   DAVID'S SINS (13:1–20:26)
   1. The Dysfunction in David's
      Family (13:1–18:33)
   2. The Problems in David's
      Kingdom (19:1–20:26)
D. CONCLUSION (21:1–24:25)
   1. Famine and War (21:1-22)
   2. David's Song (22:1-51)
   3. David's Tribute (23:1-39)
   4. David's Final Failure and
      Recovery (24:1-25)

The book of 2 Samuel tells the story of King David, one of the most notable people in the Bible. In the opening verses, David received word that both Jonathan and Saul had been killed in battle. The Israelite army had fled in defeat, and thousands of soldiers were dead or wounded on the battlefield. Samuel the prophet, David's mentor, was no longer around to give him comfort or advice. David had lost most of the people he had depended on. Yet in the wake of such losses, life for David was really just beginning.

In spite of his grief, David managed the kingdom's affairs brilliantly after Saul's death. He demonstrated patience and kindness toward the northern tribes during the reign of Ish-bosheth. He wisely established the capital in Jerusalem, a neutral city. He brought the Ark of the Covenant back to Jerusalem. His victories over the Philistines led to further consolidation of the kingdom.

Unfortunately, David did not do as well at managing the affairs of his heart. In the midst of his political success, he made some terrible mistakes. He fell into adultery and committed murder, which later led to incest and rebellion within his own family. This all culminated in the near destruction of his family and the kingdom he had so skillfully built.

But God did not allow David's mistakes to destroy the nation. He sent the prophet Nathan to initiate a recovery program for David; Nathan's intervention brought the king to repentance. David was humble and willing to accept God's word of correction. He was willing to learn from his mistakes and for the rest of his life continued to look to God for strength and help.

THE BOTTOM LINE

PURPOSE: To record the history of King David, who, despite his personal failings, was a man who sought after God. AUTHOR: Unknown, though the book includes writings from the prophets Nathan and Gad. AUDIENCE: The people of Israel. DATE WRITTEN: Sometime after David's death, around 930 B.C. SETTING: The land of Palestine. KEY VERSES: "Then King David . . . prayed, 'Who am I, O Sovereign LORD, and what is my family, that you have brought me this far? And now, Sovereign LORD, in addition to everything else, you speak of giving your servant a lasting dynasty! . . . What more can I say to you?'" (7:18-20). KEY PLACES: Hebron, Jerusalem, Bahurim, Mahanaim. KEY PEOPLE AND RELATIONSHIPS: David with Joab, Abner, Michal, Bathsheba, Nathan, Amnon, Absalom, and Mephibosheth.

RECOVERY THEMES

Recovery Follows Failure: There is life after failure; David's biography proves that fact. His list of sins included murder and adultery, not to mention neglect of his family. If anyone should have been written off in God's plan, it was David. But David's important place in history proves that God uses fallible people to work his will. God's grace is adequate for even the greatest failures.

Justice with Mercy: David was a just king, and his justice was always tempered by mercy. He demonstrated this when he refused to strike back at Saul, even while being chased by him. He revealed it when he punished the murderers of Abner and Ish-bosheth, even though these men had been his enemies. He never rejoiced in wrongdoing—even when it brought him personal advantage. And when David himself sinned, he accepted God's judgment as right and just. David's attitudes and actions were grounded in his relationship with our just and merciful God. God had been fair with him, so David was fair with his people. God had been merciful toward him, so David freely dispensed mercy to others.

Accepting Reality: When Nathan confronted him about his sin, David accepted the truth. When reminded of the consequences of his sin, he repented with sorrow. Recovery is based on willingness to accept reality. When our life is out of control, we need to acknowledge God's sovereignty and our great need for him. The secret to David's recovery was his dependence on God and his ability to accept the truth about his sin.

The Seriousness of Sin: David did not get away with his sin; it brought serious consequences. The baby born to David and Bathsheba died soon after his birth. Within David's own family, incest was followed by murder. His favorite son, Absalom, rebelled and was killed by David's own men. David had experienced the joy of God's blessing. But he also knew the depths of sorrow that resulted from the bad choices he made.

CHAPTER 1
David Learns of Saul's Death

After the death of Saul, David returned from his victory over the Amalekites and spent two days in Ziklag. ²On the third day a man arrived from Saul's army camp. He had torn his clothes and put dirt on his head to show that he was in mourning. He fell to the ground before David in deep respect.

³"Where have you come from?" David asked.

"I escaped from the Israelite camp," the man replied.

⁴"What happened?" David demanded. "Tell me how the battle went."

The man replied, "Our entire army fled from the battle. Many of the men are dead, and Saul and his son Jonathan are also dead."

⁵"How do you know Saul and Jonathan are dead?" David demanded of the young man.

⁶The man answered, "I happened to be on Mount Gilboa, and there was Saul leaning on his spear with the enemy chariots and charioteers closing in on him. ⁷When he turned and saw me, he cried out for me to come to him. 'How can I help?' I asked him.

⁸"He responded, 'Who are you?'

"'I am an Amalekite,' I told him.

⁹"Then he begged me, 'Come over here and put me out of my misery, for I am in terrible pain and want to die.'

¹⁰"So I killed him," the Amalekite told David, "for I knew he couldn't live. Then I took his crown and his armband, and I have brought them here to you, my lord."

¹¹David and his men tore their clothes in sorrow when they heard the news. ¹²They mourned and wept and fasted all day for Saul and his son Jonathan, and for the LORD's army and the nation of Israel, because they had died by the sword that day.

¹³Then David said to the young man who had brought the news, "Where are you from?"

And he replied, "I am a foreigner, an Amalekite, who lives in your land."

¹⁴"Why were you not afraid to kill the LORD's anointed one?" David asked.

¹⁵Then David said to one of his men, "Kill

1:8-10 The record of Saul's suicide in 1 Samuel 31:4 raises questions about the truth of the Amalekite's claims. More than likely, the man was lying in hopes of receiving a reward from David. He did receive his reward—death. Deceit is often a harbinger of disaster; honesty is always the best policy.

1:11-27 The honest outpouring of grief by David and his men over the deaths of Saul, Jonathan, and the other men of Israel was no sign of weakness. Instead, it indicated the love, respect, and sorrow they felt for their fallen countrymen. Sincere expressions of emotion are invaluable in the healing process. We don't need to be afraid of displaying our emotions.

him!" So the man thrust his sword into the Amalekite and killed him. [16]"You have condemned yourself," David said, "for you yourself confessed that you killed the LORD's anointed one."

David's Song for Saul and Jonathan

[17]Then David composed a funeral song for Saul and Jonathan, [18]and he commanded that it be taught to the people of Judah. It is known as the Song of the Bow, and it is recorded in *The Book of Jashar.**

[19]Your pride and joy, O Israel, lies dead on the hills!
  Oh, how the mighty heroes have fallen!
[20]Don't announce the news in Gath,
  don't proclaim it in the streets of Ashkelon,
or the daughters of the Philistines will rejoice
  and the pagans will laugh in triumph.
[21]O mountains of Gilboa,
  let there be no dew or rain upon you,
  nor fruitful fields producing offerings of grain.*
For there the shield of the mighty heroes was defiled;
  the shield of Saul will no longer be anointed with oil.
[22]The bow of Jonathan was powerful,
  and the sword of Saul did its mighty work.
They shed the blood of their enemies
  and pierced the bodies of mighty heroes.
[23]How beloved and gracious were Saul and Jonathan!
  They were together in life and in death.
They were swifter than eagles,
  stronger than lions.
[24]O women of Israel, weep for Saul,
  for he dressed you in luxurious scarlet clothing,
  in garments decorated with gold.
[25]Oh, how the mighty heroes have fallen in battle!
  Jonathan lies dead on the hills.

[26]How I weep for you, my brother Jonathan!
  Oh, how much I loved you!
And your love for me was deep,
  deeper than the love of women!
[27]Oh, how the mighty heroes have fallen!
  Stripped of their weapons, they lie dead.

CHAPTER 2
David Anointed King of Judah

After this, David asked the LORD, "Should I move back to one of the towns of Judah?"

"Yes," the LORD replied.

Then David asked, "Which town should I go to?"

"To Hebron," the LORD answered.

[2]David's two wives were Ahinoam from Jezreel and Abigail, the widow of Nabal from Carmel. So David and his wives [3]and his men and their families all moved to Judah, and they settled in the villages near Hebron. [4]Then the men of Judah came to David and anointed him king over the people of Judah.

When David heard that the men of Jabesh-gilead had buried Saul, [5]he sent them this message: "May the LORD bless you for being so loyal to your master Saul and giving him a decent burial. [6]May the LORD be loyal to you in return and reward you with his unfailing love! And I, too, will reward you for what you have done. [7]Now that Saul is dead, I ask you to be my strong and loyal subjects like the people of Judah, who have anointed me as their new king."

Ishbosheth Proclaimed King of Israel

[8]But Abner son of Ner, the commander of Saul's army, had already gone to Mahanaim with Saul's son Ishbosheth.* [9]There he proclaimed Ishbosheth king over Gilead, Jezreel, Ephraim, Benjamin, the land of the Ashurites, and all the rest of Israel.

[10]Ishbosheth, Saul's son, was forty years old when he became king, and he ruled from Mahanaim for two years. Meanwhile, the people of Judah remained loyal to David. [11]David made Hebron his capital, and he ruled as king of Judah for seven and a half years.

1:18 Or *The Book of the Upright.* **1:21** The meaning of the Hebrew is uncertain. **2:8** *Ishbosheth* is another name for Esh-baal.

2:1-11 We often make our greatest mistakes in situations where we are eager to act. After years as a fugitive, David must have burned with excitement at the thought of finally assuming Israel's throne. Yet he accepted a continued delay of his gratification and waited to take charge of the northern Israelite tribes at a later time. He listened to God's instructions and became king of only one tribe—Judah. We would be wise to learn from David's patience and trust in God.

War between Israel and Judah

[12]One day Abner led Ishbosheth's troops from Mahanaim to Gibeon. [13]About the same time, Joab son of Zeruiah led David's troops out and met them at the pool of Gibeon. The two groups sat down there, facing each other from opposite sides of the pool.

[14]Then Abner suggested to Joab, "Let's have a few of our warriors fight hand to hand here in front of us."

"All right," Joab agreed. [15]So twelve men were chosen to fight from each side—twelve men of Benjamin representing Ishbosheth son of Saul, and twelve representing David. [16]Each one grabbed his opponent by the hair and thrust his sword into the other's side so that all of them died. So this place at Gibeon has been known ever since as the Field of Swords.*

[17]A fierce battle followed that day, and Abner and the men of Israel were defeated by the forces of David.

The Death of Asahel

[18]Joab, Abishai, and Asahel—the three sons of Zeruiah—were among David's forces that day. Asahel could run like a gazelle, [19]and he began chasing Abner. He pursued him relentlessly, not stopping for anything. [20]When Abner looked back and saw him coming, he called out, "Is that you, Asahel?"

"Yes, it is," he replied.

[21]"Go fight someone else!" Abner warned. "Take on one of the younger men, and strip him of his weapons." But Asahel kept right on chasing Abner.

[22]Again Abner shouted to him, "Get away from here! I don't want to kill you. How could I ever face your brother Joab again?"

[23]But Asahel refused to turn back, so Abner thrust the butt end of his spear through Asahel's stomach, and the spear came out through his back. He stumbled to the ground and died there. And everyone who came by that spot stopped and stood still when they saw Asahel lying there.

[24]When Joab and Abishai found out what had happened, they set out after Abner. The sun was just going down as they arrived at the hill of Ammah near Giah, along the road to the wilderness of Gibeon. [25]Abner's troops from the tribe of Benjamin regrouped there at the top of the hill to take a stand.

[26]Abner shouted down to Joab, "Must we always be killing each other? Don't you realize that bitterness is the only result? When will you call off your men from chasing their Israelite brothers?"

[27]Then Joab said, "God only knows what would have happened if you hadn't spoken, for we would have chased you all night if necessary." [28]So Joab blew the ram's horn, and his men stopped chasing the troops of Israel.

[29]All that night Abner and his men retreated through the Jordan Valley.* They crossed the Jordan River, traveling all through the morning,* and didn't stop until they arrived at Mahanaim.

[30]Meanwhile, Joab and his men also returned home. When Joab counted his casualties, he discovered that only 19 men were missing in addition to Asahel. [31]But 360 of Abner's men had been killed, all from the tribe of Benjamin. [32]Joab and his men took Asahel's body to Bethlehem and buried him there in his father's tomb. Then they traveled all night and reached Hebron at daybreak.

CHAPTER 3

That was the beginning of a long war between those who were loyal to Saul and those loyal to David. As time passed David became stronger and stronger, while Saul's dynasty became weaker and weaker.

David's Sons Born in Hebron

[2]These are the sons who were born to David in Hebron:

The oldest was Amnon, whose mother was Ahinoam from Jezreel.
[3] The second was Daniel,* whose mother was Abigail, the widow of Nabal from Carmel.
The third was Absalom, whose mother was Maacah, the daughter of Talmai, king of Geshur.

2:16 Hebrew *Helkath-hazzurim.* 2:29a Hebrew *the Arabah.* 2:29b Or *continued on through the Bithron.* The meaning of the Hebrew is uncertain. 3:3 As in parallel text at 1 Chr 3:1 (see also Greek version, which reads *Daluia,* and possible support by Dead Sea Scrolls); Hebrew reads *Kileab.*

2:30-31 What a tragic picture! Hundreds died in a needless conflict between related tribes. This tragedy was the fruit of a divided nation and unwise leadership on the part of Joab. Often our families suffer in the same way. If conflicts are not dealt with properly and family leaders make decisions driven by passion, suffering and pain are sure to result. This should be a warning for us to seek restoration early before the consequences bring destruction that cannot be repaired.

⁴ The fourth was Adonijah, whose mother was Haggith.

The fifth was Shephatiah, whose mother was Abital.

⁵ The sixth was Ithream, whose mother was Eglah, David's wife.

These sons were all born to David in Hebron.

Abner Joins Forces with David

⁶As the war between the house of Saul and the house of David went on, Abner became a powerful leader among those loyal to Saul. ⁷One day Ishbosheth,* Saul's son, accused Abner of sleeping with one of his father's concubines, a woman named Rizpah, daughter of Aiah.

⁸Abner was furious. "Am I some Judean dog to be kicked around like this?" he shouted. "After all I have done for your father, Saul, and his family and friends by not handing you over to David, is this my reward—that you find fault with me about this woman? ⁹May God strike me and even kill me if I don't do everything I can to help David get what the LORD has promised him! ¹⁰I'm going to take Saul's kingdom and give it to David. I will establish the throne of David over Israel as well as Judah, all the way from Dan in the north to Beersheba in the south." ¹¹Ishbosheth didn't dare say another word because he was afraid of what Abner might do.

¹²Then Abner sent messengers to David, saying, "Doesn't the entire land belong to you? Make a solemn pact with me, and I will help turn over all of Israel to you."

¹³"All right," David replied, "but I will not negotiate with you unless you bring back my wife Michal, Saul's daughter, when you come."

¹⁴David then sent this message to Ishbosheth, Saul's son: "Give me back my wife Michal, for I bought her with the lives* of 100 Philistines."

¹⁵So Ishbosheth took Michal away from her husband, Palti* son of Laish. ¹⁶Palti followed along behind her as far as Bahurim, weeping as he went. Then Abner told him, "Go back home!" So Palti returned.

¹⁷Meanwhile, Abner had consulted with the elders of Israel. "For some time now," he told them, "you have wanted to make David your king. ¹⁸Now is the time! For the LORD has said, 'I have chosen David to save my people Israel from the hands of the Philistines and from all their other enemies.'" ¹⁹Abner also spoke with the men of Benjamin. Then he went to Hebron to tell David that all the people of Israel and Benjamin had agreed to support him.

²⁰When Abner and twenty of his men came to Hebron, David entertained them with a great feast. ²¹Then Abner said to David, "Let me go and call an assembly of all Israel to support my lord the king. They will make a covenant with you to make you their king, and you will rule over everything your heart desires." So David sent Abner safely on his way.

Joab Murders Abner

²²But just after David had sent Abner away in safety, Joab and some of David's troops returned from a raid, bringing much plunder with them. ²³When Joab arrived, he was told that Abner had just been there visiting the king and had been sent away in safety.

²⁴Joab rushed to the king and demanded, "What have you done? What do you mean by letting Abner get away? ²⁵You know perfectly well that he came to spy on you and find out everything you're doing!"

²⁶Joab then left David and sent messengers to catch up with Abner, asking him to return. They found him at the well of Sirah and brought him back, though David knew nothing about it. ²⁷When Abner arrived back at

3:7 *Ishbosheth* is another name for Esh-baal. **3:14** Hebrew *the foreskins*. **3:15** As in 1 Sam 25:44; Hebrew reads *Paltiel,* a variant spelling of Palti.

3:17-18 Abner displayed the courage to take an unpopular stand and make an important change in his life. He advised the elders of the northern tribes to take the necessary steps to make David their king. Good intentions are worthless until they are translated into actions, and Abner understood this. One of the major steps of recovery involves not only wanting change but taking active steps to pursue it. Abner's exhortation, "Now is the time!" (3:18), is a clarion call to all who want to progress toward a balanced life.

3:27 Joab chose to harbor deep bitterness toward Abner and sought revenge rather than look for a new start in life. It would have been better if Joab had let go of painful past events; instead, he chose to avenge his brother's death. His rash act of vengeance against Abner brought a curse upon his family and embarrassment and grief to his king. True recovery requires that we seek release from the past, no matter how painful it may be. This can only be done as we learn to forgive the people who have wronged us. Forgiveness, though difficult, is the only sure path toward freedom from a painful past.

Hebron, Joab took him aside at the gateway as if to speak with him privately. But then he stabbed Abner in the stomach and killed him in revenge for killing his brother Asahel.

[28]When David heard about it, he declared, "I vow by the LORD that I and my kingdom are forever innocent of this crime against Abner son of Ner. [29]Joab and his family are the guilty ones. May the family of Joab be cursed in every generation with a man who has open sores or leprosy* or who walks on crutches* or dies by the sword or begs for food!"

[30]So Joab and his brother Abishai killed Abner because Abner had killed their brother Asahel at the battle of Gibeon.

David Mourns Abner's Death

[31]Then David said to Joab and all those who were with him, "Tear your clothes and put on burlap. Mourn for Abner." And King David himself walked behind the procession to the grave. [32]They buried Abner in Hebron, and the king and all the people wept at his graveside. [33]Then the king sang this funeral song for Abner:

"Should Abner have died as fools die?
[34] Your hands were not bound;
    your feet were not chained.
No, you were murdered—
    the victim of a wicked plot."

All the people wept again for Abner. [35]David had refused to eat anything on the day of the funeral, and now everyone begged him to eat. But David had made a vow, saying, "May God strike me and even kill me if I eat anything before sundown."

[36]This pleased the people very much. In fact, everything the king did pleased them! [37]So everyone in Judah and all Israel understood that David was not responsible for Abner's murder.

[38]Then King David said to his officials, "Don't you realize that a great commander has fallen today in Israel? [39]And even though I am the anointed king, these two sons of Zeruiah—Joab and Abishai—are too strong

for me to control. So may the LORD repay these evil men for their evil deeds."

CHAPTER 4
The Murder of Ishbosheth

When Ishbosheth,* Saul's son, heard about Abner's death at Hebron, he lost all courage, and all Israel became paralyzed with fear. [2]Now there were two brothers, Baanah and Recab, who were captains of Ishbosheth's raiding parties. They were sons of Rimmon, a member of the tribe of Benjamin who lived in Beeroth. The town of Beeroth is now part of Benjamin's territory [3]because the original people of Beeroth fled to Gittaim, where they still live as foreigners.

[4](Saul's son Jonathan had a son named Mephibosheth,* who was crippled as a child. He was five years old when the report came from Jezreel that Saul and Jonathan had been killed in battle. When the child's nurse heard the news, she picked him up and fled. But as she hurried away, she dropped him, and he became crippled.)

[5]One day Recab and Baanah, the sons of Rimmon from Beeroth, went to Ishbosheth's house around noon as he was taking his midday rest. [6]The doorkeeper, who had been sifting wheat, became drowsy and fell asleep. So Recab and Baanah slipped past her.* [7]They went into the house and found Ishbosheth sleeping on his bed. They struck and killed him and cut off his head. Then, taking his head with them, they fled across the Jordan Valley* through the night. [8]When they arrived at Hebron, they presented Ishbosheth's head to David. "Look!" they exclaimed to the king. "Here is the head of Ishbosheth, the son of your enemy Saul who tried to kill you. Today the LORD has given my lord the king revenge on Saul and his entire family!"

[9]But David said to Recab and Baanah, "The LORD, who saves me from all my enemies, is my witness. [10]Someone once told me, 'Saul is dead,' thinking he was bringing me good news. But I seized him and killed him at Ziklag. That's the reward I gave him for his

---

3:29a Or *or a contagious skin disease.* The Hebrew word used here can describe various skin diseases. **3:29b** Or *who is effeminate;* Hebrew reads *who handles a spindle.* **4:1** *Ishbosheth* is another name for Esh-baal. **4:4** *Mephibosheth* is another name for Merib-baal. **4:6** As in Greek version; Hebrew reads *So they went into the house pretending to fetch wheat, but they stabbed him in the stomach. Then Recab and Baanah escaped.* **4:7** Hebrew *the Arabah.*

4:9 David acknowledged God as the source of his deliverance. This is crucial in the process of recovery. If we cannot give God the credit for our victories, it is obvious that we never really gave our life over to him in the first place. We need to give credit where credit is due. Praising God for our victories is a good way to show how much we depend on him and appreciate his help.

news! [11]How much more should I reward evil men who have killed an innocent man in his own house and on his own bed? Shouldn't I hold you responsible for his blood and rid the earth of you?"

[12]So David ordered his young men to kill them, and they did. They cut off their hands and feet and hung their bodies beside the pool in Hebron. Then they took Ishbosheth's head and buried it in Abner's tomb in Hebron.

CHAPTER 5
David Becomes King of All Israel

Then all the tribes of Israel went to David at Hebron and told him, "We are your own flesh and blood. [2]In the past,* when Saul was our king, you were the one who really led the forces of Israel. And the LORD told you, 'You will be the shepherd of my people Israel. You will be Israel's leader.'"

[3]So there at Hebron, King David made a covenant before the LORD with all the elders of Israel. And they anointed him king of Israel.

[4]David was thirty years old when he began to reign, and he reigned forty years in all. [5]He had reigned over Judah from Hebron for seven years and six months, and from Jerusalem he reigned over all Israel and Judah for thirty-three years.

David Captures Jerusalem

[6]David then led his men to Jerusalem to fight against the Jebusites, the original inhabitants of the land who were living there. The Jebusites taunted David, saying, "You'll never get in here! Even the blind and lame could keep you out!" For the Jebusites thought they were safe. [7]But David captured the fortress of Zion, which is now called the City of David.

[8]On the day of the attack, David said to his troops, "I hate those 'lame' and 'blind' Jebusites.* Whoever attacks them should strike by going into the city through the water tunnel.*" That is the origin of the saying, "The blind and the lame may not enter the house."*

[9]So David made the fortress his home, and he called it the City of David. He extended the city, starting at the supporting terraces* and working inward. [10]And David became more and more powerful, because the LORD God of Heaven's Armies was with him.

[11]Then King Hiram of Tyre sent messengers to David, along with cedar timber and carpenters and stonemasons, and they built David a palace. [12]And David realized that the LORD had confirmed him as king over Israel and had blessed his kingdom for the sake of his people Israel.

[13]After moving from Hebron to Jerusalem, David married more concubines and wives, and they had more sons and daughters. [14]These are the names of David's sons who were born in Jerusalem: Shammua, Shobab, Nathan, Solomon, [15]Ibhar, Elishua, Nepheg, Japhia, [16]Elishama, Eliada, and Eliphelet.

David Conquers the Philistines

[17]When the Philistines heard that David had been anointed king of Israel, they mobilized all their forces to capture him. But David was told they were coming, so he went into the stronghold. [18]The Philistines arrived and spread out across the valley of Rephaim. [19]So David asked the LORD, "Should I go out to fight the Philistines? Will you hand them over to me?"

The LORD replied to David, "Yes, go ahead. I will certainly hand them over to you."

[20]So David went to Baal-perazim and defeated the Philistines there. "The LORD did

---

5:2 Or *For some time.* 5:8a Or *Those 'lame' and 'blind' Jebusites hate me.* 5:8b Or *with scaling hooks.* The meaning of the Hebrew is uncertain. 5:8c The meaning of this saying is uncertain. 5:9 Hebrew *the millo.* The meaning of the Hebrew is uncertain.

5:6-8 The arrogant Jebusites thought their city was invincible: "You'll never get in here! Even the blind and lame could keep you out!" As we progress in recovery, it is easy to assume that we are immune to a dramatic reversal. Then we are shocked when it happens, as were the Jebusites. "But David captured the fortress of Zion." We would be wise to be humble and keep alert so we will not fall.

5:13 At the height of David's political progress, he began to build his harem. This was customary for kings in the ancient Near East, but his decision to be like other kings carried a price tag with it. In later years, conflict between David's many children almost destroyed both king and kingdom. Since polygamy was customary in Old Testament times, no moral judgment is cast here. But the consequences of family strife are attested to numerous times in Scripture. Sometimes God's plan will lead us away from the norms of the society around us. If so, we can either seek God's ideal or suffer the consequences.

it!" David exclaimed. "He burst through my enemies like a raging flood!" So he named that place Baal-perazim (which means "the Lord who bursts through"). ²¹The Philistines had abandoned their idols there, so David and his men confiscated them.

²²But after a while the Philistines returned and again spread out across the valley of Rephaim. ²³And again David asked the LORD what to do. "Do not attack them straight on," the LORD replied. "Instead, circle around behind and attack them near the poplar* trees. ²⁴When you hear a sound like marching feet in the tops of the poplar trees, be on the alert! That will be the signal that the LORD is moving ahead of you to strike down the Philistine army." ²⁵So David did what the LORD commanded, and he struck down the Philistines all the way from Gibeon* to Gezer.

CHAPTER 6
Moving the Ark to Jerusalem

Then David again gathered all the elite troops in Israel, 30,000 in all. ²He led them to Baalah of Judah* to bring back the Ark of God, which bears the name of the LORD of Heaven's Armies,* who is enthroned between the cherubim. ³They placed the Ark of God on a new cart and brought it from Abinadab's house, which was on a hill. Uzzah and Ahio, Abinadab's sons, were guiding the cart ⁴that carried the Ark of God.* Ahio walked in front of the Ark. ⁵David and all the people of Israel were celebrating before the LORD, singing songs* and playing all kinds of musical instruments—lyres, harps, tambourines, castanets, and cymbals.

⁶But when they arrived at the threshing floor of Nacon, the oxen stumbled, and Uzzah reached out his hand and steadied the Ark of God. ⁷Then the LORD's anger was aroused against Uzzah, and God struck him dead because of this.* So Uzzah died right there beside the Ark of God.

⁸David was angry because the LORD's anger had burst out against Uzzah. He named that place Perez-uzzah (which means "to burst out against Uzzah"), as it is still called today.

⁹David was now afraid of the LORD, and he asked, "How can I ever bring the Ark of the LORD back into my care?" ¹⁰So David decided not to move the Ark of the LORD into the City of David. Instead, he took it to the house of Obed-edom of Gath. ¹¹The Ark of the LORD remained there in Obed-edom's house for three months, and the LORD blessed Obed-edom and his entire household.

¹²Then King David was told, "The LORD has blessed Obed-edom's household and everything he has because of the Ark of God." So David went there and brought the Ark of God from the house of Obed-edom to the City of David with a great celebration. ¹³After the men who were carrying the Ark of the LORD had gone six steps, David sacrificed a bull and a fattened calf. ¹⁴And David danced before the LORD with all his might, wearing a priestly garment.* ¹⁵So David and all the people of Israel brought up the Ark of the LORD with shouts of joy and the blowing of rams' horns.

Michal's Contempt for David

¹⁶But as the Ark of the LORD entered the City of David, Michal, the daughter of Saul,

---

5:23 Or *aspen,* or *balsam;* also in 5:24. The exact identification of this tree is uncertain. 5:25 As in Greek version (see also 1 Chr 14:16); Hebrew reads *Geba.* 6:2a Hebrew *Baale of Judah,* another name for Kiriath-jearim; compare 1 Chr 13:6. 6:2b Or *the Ark of God where the Name is proclaimed—the name of the LORD of Heaven's Armies.* 6:4 As in Dead Sea Scrolls and some Greek manuscripts; Masoretic Text reads ⁴*and they brought it from Abinadab's house, which was on a hill, with the Ark of God.* 6:5 As in Dead Sea Scrolls and Greek version (see also 1 Chr 13:8); Masoretic Text reads *before the LORD with all manner of cypress wood.* 6:7 As in Dead Sea Scrolls; Masoretic Text reads *because of his irreverence.* 6:14 Hebrew *a linen ephod.*

6:1-8 David desired to bring the Ark of the Covenant, the symbol of God's presence, to Jerusalem. But he failed to follow God's specific instructions for transporting it (Exodus 25:10-15; Numbers 4:5-15). He probably hadn't ever read God's laws concerning the Ark, but God's Word was available to him. There are serious consequences for failing to honor God by not following his instructions. We are responsible for knowing what God desires of us; such knowledge will enable us to act according to his will. The Bible is our primary source for discovering God's plan for healthy living.
6:16-23 Michal's anger was probably driven by far more than her embarrassment at David's conduct. Over the years, Michal had been a pawn on the chessboard of David's life. After Michal had been married to David for a short time, her father, King Saul, gave her to another man to spite David. In later kingdom negotiations David won her back, but then she found herself just one wife among many. Her life is a tragic example of how people can be used by others. Michal's anger at the injustice she had suffered affected her ability to enjoy the present. The same thing can happen to us; we need to uncover the pain in our life and allow God to free us from the past.

DAVID, MICHAL, & BATHSHEBA

David failed in many of his relationships. He tended to avoid conflict and therefore did not deal with some important issues in his life. David's first wife, Michal, was the daughter of King Saul. Their marriage was right out of a fairy tale. The king's beautiful daughter married the onetime shepherd boy turned great war hero, who was also the most talented musician of his day. Their early relationship appeared to be fine, but over time difficulties developed. Michal was separated from David for several years when Saul gave her to another man to spite David. Later David won her back but brought her into a house filled with his other wives. Their relationship was never truly reestablished after Michal's return; they apparently kept the pain of their separation to themselves and from each other.

Michal exploded at David for dancing before the Ark as he celebrated its return to Jerusalem (6:16). It seems that her bitterness and frustration over the years of separation and neglect had built to the boiling point. Unfortunately, there is no indication that they ever tried to heal their damaged marriage relationship. Instead, they seem to have settled into destructive silence.

David complicated his life further by his infatuation and adultery with Bathsheba (11:1-27). This sin led to a tangled web of deceit involving Uriah's murder and a rushed marriage to the pregnant Bathsheba. This string of self-induced tragedies left a cloud of shame that hung over David throughout the rest of his life. David's own children would repeat his mistakes, bringing further suffering to the royal family and the nation as a whole.

With all his mistakes, why was David considered more righteous than Saul, his predecessor? His heart was open before God, and he was willing to accept God's correction in his life. After each failure, he was willing to admit the truth, accept the consequences, and receive God's forgiveness. Even in the midst of his failures, pain, and grief, he remained a man whose primary desire was to know God. Like David, all of us have made mistakes. We can learn much from him about recovering from the bad choices we have made.

STRENGTHS AND ACCOMPLISHMENTS:
- In the beginning, David and Michal had a strong marriage.
- David kept an open relationship with God.
- David was always willing to admit his failures and accept God's correction.

WEAKNESSES AND MISTAKES:
- David and Michal did not communicate effectively.
- David avoided family conflict and the resolution of problems.
- David allowed immediate gratification to lead him into sin with Bathsheba.
- By hiding his sin of adultery, David was driven deeper into sin.

LESSONS FROM THEIR LIVES:
- A good marriage can be destroyed by unresolved issues.
- Communication must be a high priority in any relationship.
- One mistake usually leads to others.
- No matter how great our sin, God is willing to forgive us if we repent.

KEY VERSES:
"As the deer pants for streams of water, so I long for you, O God. I thirst for God, the living God" (Psalm 42:1-2).

David and Michal's story is told in 1 Samuel 18–19; 25; 2 Samuel 3; 6; 1 Chronicles 15:29. David and Bathsheba's story is told in 2 Samuel 11—1 Kings 1.

---

looked down from her window. When she saw King David leaping and dancing before the LORD, she was filled with contempt for him.

¹⁷They brought the Ark of the LORD and set it in its place inside the special tent David had prepared for it. And David sacrificed burnt offerings and peace offerings to the LORD. ¹⁸When he had finished his sacrifices, David blessed the people in the name of the LORD of Heaven's Armies. ¹⁹Then he gave to every Israelite man and woman in the crowd a loaf of bread, a cake of dates,* and a cake of raisins. Then all the people returned to their homes.

²⁰When David returned home to bless his own family, Michal, the daughter of Saul,

6:19 Or *a portion of meat.* The meaning of the Hebrew is uncertain.

came out to meet him. She said in disgust, "How distinguished the king of Israel looked today, shamelessly exposing himself to the servant girls like any vulgar person might do!"

[21]David retorted to Michal, "I was dancing before the LORD, who chose me above your father and all his family! He appointed me as the leader of Israel, the people of the LORD, so I celebrate before the LORD. [22]Yes, and I am willing to look even more foolish than this, even to be humiliated in my own eyes! But those servant girls you mentioned will indeed think I am distinguished!" [23]So Michal, the daughter of Saul, remained childless throughout her entire life.

CHAPTER 7
The LORD's Covenant Promise to David

When King David was settled in his palace and the LORD had given him rest from all the surrounding enemies, [2]the king summoned Nathan the prophet. "Look," David said, "I am living in a beautiful cedar palace,* but the Ark of God is out there in a tent!"

[3]Nathan replied to the king, "Go ahead and do whatever you have in mind, for the LORD is with you."

[4]But that same night the LORD said to Nathan,

[5]"Go and tell my servant David, 'This is what the LORD has declared: Are you the one to build a house for me to live in? [6]I have never lived in a house, from the day I brought the Israelites out of Egypt until this very day. I have always moved from one place to another with a tent and a Tabernacle as my dwelling. [7]Yet no matter where I have gone with the Israelites, I have never once complained to Israel's tribal leaders, the shepherds of my people Israel. I have never asked them, "Why haven't you built me a beautiful cedar house?"'

[8]"Now go and say to my servant David,

'This is what the LORD of Heaven's Armies has declared: I took you from tending sheep in the pasture and selected you to be the leader of my people Israel. [9]I have been with you wherever you have gone, and I have destroyed all your enemies before your eyes. Now I will make your name as famous as anyone who has ever lived on the earth! [10]And I will provide a homeland for my people Israel, planting them in a secure place where they will never be disturbed. Evil nations won't oppress them as they've done in the past, [11]starting from the time I appointed judges to rule my people Israel. And I will give you rest from all your enemies.

"'Furthermore, the LORD declares that he will make a house for you—a dynasty of kings! [12]For when you die and are buried with your ancestors, I will raise up one of your descendants, your own offspring, and I will make his kingdom strong. [13]He is the one who will build a house—a temple—for my name. And I will secure his royal throne forever. [14]I will be his father, and he will be my son. If he sins, I will correct and discipline him with the rod, like any father would do. [15]But my favor will not be taken from him as I took it from Saul, whom I removed from your sight. [16]Your house and your kingdom will continue before me* for all time, and your throne will be secure forever.'"

[17]So Nathan went back to David and told him everything the LORD had said in this vision.

David's Prayer of Thanks

[18]Then King David went in and sat before the LORD and prayed,

"Who am I, O Sovereign LORD, and what is my family, that you have brought me this far? [19]And now, Sovereign LORD, in

---

7:2 Hebrew *a house of cedar*. **7:16** As in Greek version and some Hebrew manuscripts; Masoretic Text reads *before you*.

7:9-16 God may have refused David's request to build the temple, but as we see here, God had an even better plan (Proverbs 3:4-6). God's plan involved establishing the Davidic covenant, which included the promise of an eternal kingdom with a descendant upon its throne forever. David was called upon to delay his desire to build a temple and to exercise patience and faith. There may be times when we have to wait patiently for our dream of recovery to become reality. But God has a special plan for each of us, and when it unfolds, we can be sure it will be better than what we had hoped for.

7:18-29 A vital step in any successful recovery program involves recognizing God's authority in our life and allowing him to direct our plans. In this beautiful prayer, David called God "LORD" no

addition to everything else, you speak of giving your servant a lasting dynasty! Do you deal with everyone this way, O Sovereign LORD?*

20"What more can I say to you? You know what your servant is really like, Sovereign LORD. 21Because of your promise and according to your will, you have done all these great things and have made them known to your servant.

22"How great you are, O Sovereign LORD! There is no one like you. We have never even heard of another God like you! 23What other nation on earth is like your people Israel? What other nation, O God, have you redeemed from slavery to be your own people? You made a great name for yourself when you redeemed your people from Egypt. You performed awesome miracles and drove out the nations and gods that stood in their way.* 24You made Israel your very own people forever, and you, O LORD, became their God.

25"And now, O LORD God, I am your servant; do as you have promised concerning me and my family. Confirm it as a promise that will last forever. 26And may your name be honored forever so that everyone will say, 'The LORD of Heaven's Armies is God over Israel!' And may the house of your servant David continue before you forever.

27"O LORD of Heaven's Armies, God of Israel, I have been bold enough to pray this prayer to you because you have revealed all this to your servant, saying, 'I will build a house for you—a dynasty of kings!' 28For you are God, O Sovereign LORD. Your words are truth, and you have promised these good things to your servant. 29And now, may it please you to bless the house of your servant, so that it may continue forever before you. For you

have spoken, and when you grant a blessing to your servant, O Sovereign LORD, it is an eternal blessing!"

CHAPTER 8
David's Military Victories

After this, David defeated and subdued the Philistines by conquering Gath, their largest town.* 2David also conquered the land of Moab. He made the people lie down on the ground in a row, and he measured them off in groups with a length of rope. He measured off two groups to be executed for every one group to be spared. The Moabites who were spared became David's subjects and paid him tribute money.

3David also destroyed the forces of Hadadezer son of Rehob, king of Zobah, when Hadadezer marched out to strengthen his control along the Euphrates River. 4David captured 1,000 chariots, 7,000 charioteers,* and 20,000 foot soldiers. He crippled all the chariot horses except enough for 100 chariots.

5When Arameans from Damascus arrived to help King Hadadezer, David killed 22,000 of them. 6Then he placed several army garrisons in Damascus, the Aramean capital, and the Arameans became David's subjects and paid him tribute money. So the LORD made David victorious wherever he went.

7David brought the gold shields of Hadadezer's officers to Jerusalem, 8along with a large amount of bronze from Hadadezer's towns of Tebah* and Berothai.

9When King Toi of Hamath heard that David had destroyed the entire army of Hadadezer, 10he sent his son Joram to congratulate King David for his successful campaign. Hadadezer and Toi had been enemies and were often at war. Joram presented David with many gifts of silver, gold, and bronze.

11King David dedicated all these gifts to the LORD, as he did with the silver and gold from the other nations he had defeated—12from

---

7:19 Or *This is your instruction for all humanity, O Sovereign LORD.* 7:23 As in Greek version (see also 1 Chr 17:21); Hebrew reads *You made a name for yourself and awesome miracles for your land in the sight of your people, whom you redeemed from Egypt, the nations and their gods.* 8:1 Hebrew *by conquering Metheg-ammah,* a name that means "the bridle," possibly referring to the size of the town or the tribute money taken from it. Compare 1 Chr 18:1. 8:4 As in Dead Sea Scrolls and Greek version (see also 1 Chr 18:4); Masoretic Text reads *captured 1,700 charioteers.* 8:8 As in some Greek manuscripts (see also 1 Chr 18:8); Hebrew reads *Betah.*

---

fewer than 11 times. David realized that God was his master and that following God's will was of utmost importance. By submitting to God's will and looking to him for help, we will discover the power we need to overcome our difficulties.

7:27-29 David took the time to review God's promises to him. God's Word is filled with promises for us, and God delights as we plead those promises before him in prayer. This can be especially helpful in the midst of a crisis. Not that God needs reminding, but our memories can usually stand some refreshing.

Edom,* Moab, Ammon, Philistia, and Amalek—and from Hadadezer son of Rehob, king of Zobah.

¹³So David became even more famous when he returned from destroying 18,000 Edomites* in the Valley of Salt. ¹⁴He placed army garrisons throughout Edom, and all the Edomites became David's subjects. In fact, the LORD made David victorious wherever he went.

¹⁵So David reigned over all Israel and did what was just and right for all his people. ¹⁶Joab son of Zeruiah was commander of the army. Jehoshaphat son of Ahilud was the royal historian. ¹⁷Zadok son of Ahitub and Ahimelech son of Abiathar were the priests. Seraiah was the court secretary. ¹⁸Benaiah son of Jehoiada was captain of the king's bodyguard.* And David's sons served as priestly leaders.*

CHAPTER 9
David's Kindness to Mephibosheth

One day David asked, "Is anyone in Saul's family still alive—anyone to whom I can show kindness for Jonathan's sake?" ²He summoned a man named Ziba, who had been one of Saul's servants. "Are you Ziba?" the king asked.

"Yes sir, I am," Ziba replied.

³The king then asked him, "Is anyone still alive from Saul's family? If so, I want to show God's kindness to them."

Ziba replied, "Yes, one of Jonathan's sons is still alive. He is crippled in both feet."

⁴"Where is he?" the king asked.

"In Lo-debar," Ziba told him, "at the home of Makir son of Ammiel."

⁵So David sent for him and brought him from Makir's home. ⁶His name was Mephibosheth*; he was Jonathan's son and Saul's grandson. When he came to David, he bowed low to the ground in deep respect. David said, "Greetings, Mephibosheth."

Mephibosheth replied, "I am your servant."

⁷"Don't be afraid!" David said. "I intend to show kindness to you because of my promise to your father, Jonathan. I will give you all the property that once belonged to your grandfather Saul, and you will eat here with me at the king's table!"

⁸Mephibosheth bowed respectfully and exclaimed, "Who is your servant, that you should show such kindness to a dead dog like me?"

⁹Then the king summoned Saul's servant Ziba and said, "I have given your master's grandson everything that belonged to Saul and his family. ¹⁰You and your sons and servants are to farm the land for him to produce food for your master's household.* But Mephibosheth, your master's grandson, will eat here at my table." (Ziba had fifteen sons and twenty servants.)

¹¹Ziba replied, "Yes, my lord the king; I am your servant, and I will do all that you have commanded." And from that time on, Mephibosheth ate regularly at David's table,* like one of the king's own sons.

¹²Mephibosheth had a young son named

8:12 As in a few Hebrew manuscripts and Greek and Syriac versions (see also 8:14; 1 Chr 18:11); most Hebrew manuscripts read *Aram.* 8:13 As in a few Hebrew manuscripts and Greek and Syriac versions (see also 8:14; 1 Chr 18:12); most Hebrew manuscripts read *Arameans.* 8:18a Hebrew *of the Kerethites and Pelethites.* 8:18b Hebrew *David's sons were priests;* compare parallel text at 1 Chr 18:17. 9:6 *Mephibosheth* is another name for Merib-baal. 9:10 As in Greek version; Hebrew reads *your master's grandson.* 9:11 As in Greek version; Hebrew reads *my table.*

9:1-7 David had promised to treat Saul's family well for the sake of his friend Jonathan. Though many years had passed since the promise had been given, David was true to it. He honored the memory of Jonathan by offering Mephibosheth a place in his household. David stood by his word and did what he could to set right a painful conflict from his past. Being responsible for our promises and dealing with past conflicts are important aspects of the recovery process.

10:1-5 Hanun was needlessly suspicious of the motives of David's men. As a result, he treated them shamefully and brought a great deal of needless bloodshed upon his people. Hanun's suspicions led him to distrust others and negated David's attempts to forge a productive relationship. Allowing our fears to shape our conclusions can often lead to unnecessary conflict and a disruption of possible positive relationships. Much time, effort, and energy are wasted when we respond with suspicion and fear to the friendly overtures of other people.

10:11-12 Joab gave wise counsel to Abishai before going to battle. First he devised a simple strategy of attack. Then he recognized God's role in the process. As we struggle with our adversaries, these principles can prove helpful. First we need a plan or program to follow; God's Word is filled with valuable insights for healthy living. We also need to recognize that no matter how good our plans, we still need God's help to succeed. God wants us to have victory: "May the LORD's will be done."

Mica. From then on, all the members of Ziba's household were Mephibosheth's servants. ¹³And Mephibosheth, who was crippled in both feet, lived in Jerusalem and ate regularly at the king's table.

CHAPTER 10
David Defeats the Ammonites
Some time after this, King Nahash* of the Ammonites died, and his son Hanun became king. ²David said, "I am going to show loyalty to Hanun just as his father, Nahash, was always loyal to me." So David sent ambassadors to express sympathy to Hanun about his father's death.

But when David's ambassadors arrived in the land of Ammon, ³the Ammonite commanders said to Hanun, their master, "Do you really think these men are coming here to honor your father? No! David has sent them to spy out the city so they can come in and conquer it!" ⁴So Hanun seized David's ambassadors and shaved off half of each man's beard, cut off their robes at the buttocks, and sent them back to David in shame.

⁵When David heard what had happened, he sent messengers to tell the men, "Stay at Jericho until your beards grow out, and then come back." For they felt deep shame because of their appearance.

⁶When the people of Ammon realized how seriously they had angered David, they sent and hired 20,000 Aramean foot soldiers from the lands of Beth-rehob and Zobah, 1,000 from the king of Maacah, and 12,000 from the land of Tob. ⁷When David heard about this, he sent Joab and all his warriors to fight them. ⁸The Ammonite troops came out and drew up their battle lines at the entrance of the city gate, while the Arameans from Zobah and Rehob and the men from Tob and Maacah positioned themselves to fight in the open fields.

⁹When Joab saw that he would have to fight on both the front and the rear, he chose some of Israel's elite troops and placed them under his personal command to fight the Arameans in the fields. ¹⁰He left the rest of the army under the command of his brother Abishai, who was to attack the Ammonites. ¹¹"If the Arameans are too strong for me, then come over and help me," Joab told his brother. "And if the Ammonites are too strong for you, I will come and help you. ¹²Be courageous! Let us fight bravely for our people

10:1 As in parallel text at 1 Chr 19:1; Hebrew reads *the king.*

STEP 9

Keeping Promises
BIBLE READING: 2 Samuel 9:1-9
We made direct amends to such people wherever possible, except when to do so would injure them or others.
How many people are still living in the shadow of our unkept promises? Is it too late to go back now and try to make it up to them?

King David had made a promise to his friend Jonathan. "One day David asked, 'Is anyone in Saul's family still alive—anyone to whom I can show kindness for Jonathan's sake?'" (2 Samuel 9:1).

Jonathan's only living son, Mephibosheth, had lived a long time with the pain of David's unkept promise. It had shaped his lifestyle, his emotional condition, and the way he thought about himself. His grandfather, King Saul, had mistreated David before David became king. Perhaps Mephibosheth was afraid that David would mistreat him because of his grandfather. Perhaps he had begun to take the guilt of his grandfather's sins upon himself. Generations of fear and guilt had been laid upon Mephibosheth— until David remembered and fulfilled his promise.

There are probably people we know who have been affected by promises we have failed to keep. It is important that we try to fulfill whatever promises we have made. When we can't, the least we can do is ask what our neglect meant to those we disappointed and apologize for not keeping our promise. *Turn to page 1051, Ezekiel 33.*

and the cities of our God. May the LORD's will be done."

¹³When Joab and his troops attacked, the Arameans began to run away. ¹⁴And when the Ammonites saw the Arameans running, they ran from Abishai and retreated into the city. After the battle was over, Joab returned to Jerusalem.

¹⁵The Arameans now realized that they were no match for Israel. So when they regrouped, ¹⁶they were joined by additional Aramean troops summoned by Hadadezer from the other side of the Euphrates River.* These troops arrived at Helam under the command of Shobach, the commander of Hadadezer's forces.

¹⁷When David heard what was happening, he mobilized all Israel, crossed the Jordan River, and led the army to Helam. The Arameans positioned themselves in battle formation and fought against David. ¹⁸But again the Arameans fled from the Israelites. This time David's forces killed 700 charioteers and 40,000 foot soldiers,* including Shobach, the commander of their army. ¹⁹When all the kings allied with Hadadezer saw that they had been defeated by Israel, they surrendered to Israel and became their subjects. After that, the Arameans were afraid to help the Ammonites.

CHAPTER 11
David and Bathsheba

In the spring of the year,* when kings normally go out to war, David sent Joab and the Israelite army to fight the Ammonites. They destroyed the Ammonite army and laid siege to the city of Rabbah. However, David stayed behind in Jerusalem.

²Late one afternoon, after his midday rest, David got out of bed and was walking on the roof of the palace. As he looked out over the city, he noticed a woman of unusual beauty taking a bath. ³He sent someone to find out who she was, and he was told, "She is Bathsheba, the daughter of Eliam and the wife of Uriah the Hittite." ⁴Then David sent messengers to get her; and when she came to the palace, he slept with her. She had just completed the purification rites after having her menstrual period. Then she returned home. ⁵Later, when Bathsheba discovered that she was pregnant, she sent David a message, saying, "I'm pregnant."

⁶Then David sent word to Joab: "Send me Uriah the Hittite." So Joab sent him to David. ⁷When Uriah arrived, David asked him how Joab and the army were getting along and how the war was progressing. ⁸Then he told Uriah, "Go on home and relax.*" David even sent a gift to Uriah after he had left the palace. ⁹But Uriah didn't go home. He slept that night at the palace entrance with the king's palace guard.

¹⁰When David heard that Uriah had not gone home, he summoned him and asked, "What's the matter? Why didn't you go home last night after being away for so long?"

¹¹Uriah replied, "The Ark and the armies of Israel and Judah are living in tents,* and Joab and my master's men are camping in the open fields. How could I go home to wine and dine and sleep with my wife? I swear that I would never do such a thing."

¹²"Well, stay here today," David told him, "and tomorrow you may return to the army." So Uriah stayed in Jerusalem that day and the next. ¹³Then David invited him to dinner and got him drunk. But even then he couldn't get Uriah to go home to his wife. Again he slept at the palace entrance with the king's palace guard.

10:16 Hebrew *the river.* 10:18 As in some Greek manuscripts (see also 1 Chr 19:18); Hebrew reads *charioteers.*
11:1 Hebrew *At the turn of the year.* The first day of the year in the ancient Hebrew lunar calendar occurred in March or April. 11:8 Hebrew *and wash your feet,* an expression that may also have a connotation of ritualistic washing.
11:11 Or *at Succoth.*

11:1-5 David chose to stay home and rest instead of leading his men into battle. That was his first mistake. One sleepless night, the king saw Bathsheba bathing on a nearby rooftop. David didn't have to watch her; he chose to do so. This was his second mistake. After indulging his visual lust, David gratified his sexual desire and committed adultery. This was his third mistake. Idle times frequently get us into trouble. Staying busy with healthy activities can do much to keep us from temptation and sin. We also need to diligently select what we allow ourselves to watch or think about. Failure in our thought life will usually lead to a fall.

11:14-17 Since Uriah refused to sleep with his wife, which would have covered for Bathsheba's adulterous pregnancy, David engineered Uriah's death. One hidden sin almost always leads to another. Only when we confess our sins and bring them out into the open can we be free of the destructive cycle. In recovery we must admit our wrongs to God, ourself, and another person. This is an important step in breaking free from our past failures.

David Arranges for Uriah's Death

[14]So the next morning David wrote a letter to Joab and gave it to Uriah to deliver. [15]The letter instructed Joab, "Station Uriah on the front lines where the battle is fiercest. Then pull back so that he will be killed." [16]So Joab assigned Uriah to a spot close to the city wall where he knew the enemy's strongest men were fighting. [17]And when the enemy soldiers came out of the city to fight, Uriah the Hittite was killed along with several other Israelite soldiers.

[18]Then Joab sent a battle report to David. [19]He told his messenger, "Report all the news of the battle to the king. [20]But he might get angry and ask, 'Why did the troops go so close to the city? Didn't they know there would be shooting from the walls? [21]Wasn't Abimelech son of Gideon* killed at Thebez by a woman who threw a millstone down on him from the wall? Why would you get so close to the wall?' Then tell him, 'Uriah the Hittite was killed, too.'"

[22]So the messenger went to Jerusalem and gave a complete report to David. [23]"The enemy came out against us in the open fields," he said. "And as we chased them back to the city gate, [24]the archers on the wall shot arrows at us. Some of the king's men were killed, including Uriah the Hittite."

[25]"Well, tell Joab not to be discouraged," David said. "The sword devours this one today and that one tomorrow! Fight harder next time, and conquer the city!"

[26]When Uriah's wife heard that her husband was dead, she mourned for him. [27]When the period of mourning was over, David sent for her and brought her to the palace, and she became one of his wives. Then she gave birth to a son. But the LORD was displeased with what David had done.

CHAPTER 12

Nathan Rebukes David

So the LORD sent Nathan the prophet to tell David this story: "There were two men in a certain town. One was rich, and one was poor. [2]The rich man owned a great many sheep and cattle. [3]The poor man owned nothing but one little lamb he had bought. He raised that little lamb, and it grew up with his children. It ate from the man's own plate and drank from his cup. He cuddled it in his arms like a baby daughter. [4]One day a guest arrived at the home of the rich man. But instead of killing an animal from his own flock or herd, he took the poor man's lamb and killed it and prepared it for his guest."

[5]David was furious. "As surely as the LORD lives," he vowed, "any man who would do such a thing deserves to die! [6]He must repay four lambs to the poor man for the one he stole and for having no pity."

[7]Then Nathan said to David, "You are that man! The LORD, the God of Israel, says: I anointed you king of Israel and saved you from the power of Saul. [8]I gave you your master's house and his wives and the kingdoms of Israel and Judah. And if that had not been enough, I would have given you much, much more. [9]Why, then, have you despised the word of the LORD and done this horrible deed? For you have murdered Uriah the Hittite with the sword of the Ammonites and stolen his wife. [10]From this time on, your family will live by the sword because you have despised me by taking Uriah's wife to be your own.

[11]"This is what the LORD says: Because of what you have done, I will cause your own household to rebel against you. I will give your wives to another man before your very eyes, and he will go to bed with them in public view. [12]You did it secretly, but I will make this happen to you openly in the sight of all Israel."

David Confesses His Guilt

[13]Then David confessed to Nathan, "I have sinned against the LORD."

Nathan replied, "Yes, but the LORD has forgiven you, and you won't die for this sin. [14]Nevertheless, because you have shown utter contempt for the word of the LORD* by doing this, your child will die."

[15]After Nathan returned to his home, the

11:21 Hebrew *son of Jerub-besheth*. Jerub-besheth is a variation on the name Jerub-baal, which is another name for Gideon; see Judg 6:32. 12:14 As in Dead Sea Scrolls; Masoretic Text reads *the enemies of the LORD.*

12:1-7 God chose his prophet Nathan to intervene after David's failure. Notice how Nathan used a story to broach the subject with David. After David had become emotionally involved, Nathan turned to direct confrontation: "You are that man!" Nathan hoped that this piercing declaration would help David realize the serious nature of his sin and cause him to repent. Nathan's wise intervention serves as a model for us. He confronted David with the terrible reality of his acts, but he did it in such a way that David would listen. As we take part in the recovery process, we may be called to participate in the recovery of others; wise intervention is a part of this task.

LORD sent a deadly illness to the child of David and Uriah's wife. [16]David begged God to spare the child. He went without food and lay all night on the bare ground. [17]The elders of his household pleaded with him to get up and eat with them, but he refused.

[18]Then on the seventh day the child died. David's advisers were afraid to tell him. "He wouldn't listen to reason while the child was ill," they said. "What drastic thing will he do when we tell him the child is dead?"

[19]When David saw them whispering, he realized what had happened. "Is the child dead?" he asked.

"Yes," they replied, "he is dead."

[20]Then David got up from the ground, washed himself, put on lotions,* and changed his clothes. He went to the Tabernacle and worshiped the LORD. After that, he returned to the palace and was served food and ate.

[21]His advisers were amazed. "We don't understand you," they told him. "While the child was still living, you wept and refused to eat. But now that the child is dead, you have stopped your mourning and are eating again."

[22]David replied, "I fasted and wept while the child was alive, for I said, 'Perhaps the LORD will be gracious to me and let the child live.' [23]But why should I fast when he is dead? Can I bring him back again? I will go to him one day, but he cannot return to me."

[24]Then David comforted Bathsheba, his wife, and slept with her. She became pregnant and gave birth to a son, and David* named him Solomon. The LORD loved the child [25]and sent word through Nathan the prophet that they should name him Jedidiah (which means "beloved of the LORD"), as the LORD had commanded.*

David Captures Rabbah

[26]Meanwhile, Joab was fighting against Rabbah, the capital of Ammon, and he captured the royal fortifications.* [27]Joab sent messengers to tell David, "I have fought against Rabbah and captured its water supply.* [28]Now bring the rest of the army and capture the city. Otherwise, I will capture it and get credit for the victory."

[29]So David gathered the rest of the army and went to Rabbah, and he fought against it and captured it. [30]David removed the crown from the king's head,* and it was placed on his own head. The crown was made of gold and set with gems, and it weighed seventy-five pounds.* David took a vast amount of plunder from the city. [31]He also made slaves of the people of Rabbah and forced them to labor with* saws, iron picks, and iron axes, and to work in the brick kilns.* That is how he dealt with the people of all the Ammonite towns. Then David and all the army returned to Jerusalem.

CHAPTER 13
The Rape of Tamar

Now David's son Absalom had a beautiful sister named Tamar. And Amnon, her half brother, fell desperately in love with her. [2]Amnon became so obsessed with Tamar that he became ill. She was a virgin, and Amnon thought he could never have her.

[3]But Amnon had a very crafty friend—his cousin Jonadab. He was the son of David's brother Shimea.* [4]One day Jonadab said to Amnon, "What's the trouble? Why should the son of a king look so dejected morning after morning?"

So Amnon told him, "I am in love with Tamar, my brother Absalom's sister."

12:20 Hebrew *anointed himself.* **12:24** Hebrew *he;* an alternate Hebrew reading and some Hebrew manuscripts read *she.* **12:25** As in Greek version; Hebrew reads *because of the LORD.* **12:26** Or *the royal city.* **12:27** Or *captured the city of water.* **12:30a** Or *from the head of Milcom* (as in Greek version). Milcom, also called Molech, was the god of the Ammonites. **12:30b** Hebrew *1 talent* [34 kilograms]. **12:31a** Hebrew *He also brought out the people [of Rabbah] and put them under.* **12:31b** Hebrew *and he made them pass through the brick kilns.* **13:3** Hebrew *Shimeah* (also in 13:32), a variant spelling of Shimea; compare 1 Chr 2:13.

12:29-31 After the death of Bathsheba's child, David returned to his proper role by leading the attack on Rabbah. He should have been attacking this city at the time he sinned with Bathsheba (11:1). To David's credit, even though he had made some poor choices, he made a dramatic comeback. He went back to doing the things he should have been doing all along. After a relapse, we would be wise to follow David's example.

13:14-16 Amnon's selfish lust brought terrible consequences. Tamar's future was destroyed, and her hopes for a good marriage were dashed. Amnon had to live with his guilt, and he soon would be murdered for his actions (13:29). Amnon also discovered the bitter taste of sexual activity driven by selfish desire. His self-centered "love" turned to hate within minutes. These contradictory feelings are often experienced by people in the throes of an addiction. Alternately we embrace and despise the activity or substance that controls us.

⁵"Well," Jonadab said, "I'll tell you what to do. Go back to bed and pretend you are ill. When your father comes to see you, ask him to let Tamar come and prepare some food for you. Tell him you'll feel better if she prepares it as you watch and feeds you with her own hands."

⁶So Amnon lay down and pretended to be sick. And when the king came to see him, Amnon asked him, "Please let my sister Tamar come and cook my favorite dish* as I watch. Then I can eat it from her own hands." ⁷So David agreed and sent Tamar to Amnon's house to prepare some food for him.

⁸When Tamar arrived at Amnon's house, she went to the place where he was lying down so he could watch her mix some dough. Then she baked his favorite dish for him. ⁹But when she set the serving tray before him, he refused to eat. "Everyone get out of here," Amnon told his servants. So they all left.

¹⁰Then he said to Tamar, "Now bring the food into my bedroom and feed it to me here." So Tamar took his favorite dish to him. ¹¹But as she was feeding him, he grabbed her and demanded, "Come to bed with me, my darling sister."

¹²"No, my brother!" she cried. "Don't be foolish! Don't do this to me! Such wicked things aren't done in Israel. ¹³Where could I go in my shame? And you would be called one of the greatest fools in Israel. Please, just speak to the king about it, and he will let you marry me."

¹⁴But Amnon wouldn't listen to her, and since he was stronger than she was, he raped her. ¹⁵Then suddenly Amnon's love turned to hate, and he hated her even more than he had loved her. "Get out of here!" he snarled at her.

¹⁶"No, no!" Tamar cried. "Sending me away now is worse than what you've already done to me."

But Amnon wouldn't listen to her. ¹⁷He shouted for his servant and demanded, "Throw this woman out, and lock the door behind her!"

¹⁸So the servant put her out and locked the door behind her. She was wearing a long, beautiful robe,* as was the custom in those days for the king's virgin daughters. ¹⁹But now Tamar tore her robe and put ashes on her head. And then, with her face in her hands, she went away crying.

13:6 Or a couple of cakes; also in 13:8, 10. 13:18 Or a robe with sleeves, or an ornamented robe. The meaning of the Hebrew is uncertain.

HONESTY

READ 2 SAMUEL 13:1-24
When past injustices have caused us pain, we often seek to bury them in the deep recesses of our mind. Being dishonest with ourself this way, however, almost always allows pain from the past to translate into mistakes and suffering in the future. We often become powerless against the strength of our inner turmoil. We lose control of the very feelings we have tried to hide.

Absalom became powerless against his hatred and rage. They ultimately controlled his life to the point that he fought to overthrow his own father's rule. He was outraged when his half brother raped his sister, Tamar. When King David did nothing to avenge his daughter, Absalom vowed revenge in his heart. He waited until the time was right and murdered the guilty brother. This sequence of abuse, family secrecy, denial, unprocessed feelings, and revenge destroyed Absalom's relationship with his father. Absalom never forgave David, and he died in a military rebellion against David (2 Samuel 13:1–18:33).

We may use our addictive/compulsive behaviors to distract us from the unresolved pain within us. There may be so many strong emotions that we don't know how to process appropriately, so we simply try to stuff them down inside. Eventually these feelings are expressed in some way. We need to be honest about our past hurts, express our feelings, confront the guilty, and work through forgiveness. If we try to ignore these hurts, we will be controlled by our explosive hidden emotions. ***Turn to page 455, 1 Kings 19.***

²⁰Her brother Absalom saw her and asked, "Is it true that Amnon has been with you? Well, my sister, keep quiet for now, since he's your brother. Don't you worry about it." So Tamar lived as a desolate woman in her brother Absalom's house.

²¹When King David heard what had happened, he was very angry.* ²²And though Absalom never spoke to Amnon about this, he hated Amnon deeply because of what he had done to his sister.

Absalom's Revenge on Amnon

²³Two years later, when Absalom's sheep were being sheared at Baal-hazor near Ephraim, Absalom invited all the king's sons to come to a feast. ²⁴He went to the king and said, "My sheep-shearers are now at work. Would the king and his servants please come to celebrate the occasion with me?"

²⁵The king replied, "No, my son. If we all came, we would be too much of a burden on you." Absalom pressed him, but the king would not come, though he gave Absalom his blessing.

²⁶"Well, then," Absalom said, "if you can't come, how about sending my brother Amnon with us?"

"Why Amnon?" the king asked. ²⁷But Absalom kept on pressing the king until he finally agreed to let all his sons attend, including Amnon. So Absalom prepared a feast fit for a king.*

²⁸Absalom told his men, "Wait until Amnon gets drunk; then at my signal, kill him! Don't be afraid. I'm the one who has given the command. Take courage and do it!" ²⁹So at Absalom's signal they murdered Amnon. Then the other sons of the king jumped on their mules and fled.

³⁰As they were on the way back to Jerusalem, this report reached David: "Absalom has killed all the king's sons; not one is left alive!" ³¹The king got up, tore his robe, and threw himself on the ground. His advisers also tore their clothes in horror and sorrow.

³²But just then Jonadab, the son of David's brother Shimea, arrived and said, "No, don't believe that all the king's sons have been killed! It was only Amnon! Absalom has been plotting this ever since Amnon raped his sister Tamar. ³³No, my lord the king, your sons aren't all dead! It was only Amnon." ³⁴Meanwhile Absalom escaped.

Then the watchman on the Jerusalem wall saw a great crowd coming down the hill on the road from the west. He ran to tell the king, "I see a crowd of people coming from the Horonaim road along the side of the hill."*

³⁵"Look!" Jonadab told the king. "There they are now! The king's sons are coming, just as I said."

³⁶They soon arrived, weeping and sobbing, and the king and all his servants wept bitterly with them. ³⁷And David mourned many days for his son Amnon.

Absalom fled to his grandfather, Talmai son of Ammihud, the king of Geshur. ³⁸He stayed there in Geshur for three years. ³⁹And King David,* now reconciled to Amnon's death, longed to be reunited with his son Absalom.*

CHAPTER 14
Joab Arranges for Absalom's Return
Joab realized how much the king longed to see Absalom. ²So he sent for a woman from Tekoa who had a reputation for great wisdom. He said to her, "Pretend you are in mourning; wear mourning clothes and don't put on lotions.* Act like a woman who has

---

13:21 Dead Sea Scrolls and Greek version add *But he did not punish his son Amnon, because he loved him, for he was his firstborn.* 13:27 As in Greek and Latin versions (compare also Dead Sea Scrolls); the Hebrew text lacks this sentence. 13:34 As in Greek version; Hebrew lacks this sentence. 13:39a Dead Sea Scrolls and Greek version read *And the spirit of the king.* 13:39b Or *no longer felt a need to go out after Absalom.* 14:2 Hebrew *don't anoint yourself with oil.*

13:21-24 David was enraged when he first heard of Amnon's sin, but he never did anything about it. Perhaps he felt uncomfortable confronting Amnon, since he had also failed in this area. David's failure to intervene allowed the matter to fester, and eventually it exploded when Absalom murdered Amnon to avenge his sister's rape (13:29). When someone close to us acts irresponsibly, it is easy to allow our initial rage or concern to subside. Selective denial is often easier for us than confrontation. This was how David handled Amnon's sin, but the consequences to his family were devastating.

14:1-20 Joab, with the help of a woman from Tekoa, intervened in the conflict between David and Absalom. When we are living in denial and ignoring festering problems in our life, God often uses other people to confront us with the real issues. This wise woman gently opened David's eyes to the situation and suggested that he restore his relationship with Absalom. David humbly listened and took steps to bring Absalom home from exile. When God provides wise counsel, we should humbly listen and then act accordingly.

AMNON & TAMAR

People can be destroyed emotionally by rape, incest, or any kind of sexual abuse. Breaking God's laws about sexual behavior always causes devastation in people's lives. One tragic example of this is the scandal concerning Amnon and Tamar.

Amnon was David's oldest son, and Tamar was Amnon's half sister. Amnon's sin took root in his imagination. He chose to nurture his fantasy until he shared it with a cousin, who suggested a way to make this fantasy a reality. Then Amnon chose to satisfy his desire, and he raped Tamar. He blinded himself to the consequences that were sure to follow.

Tamar felt violated, abandoned, and shameful. Amnon's fleeting pleasure very likely cost Tamar the honorable future expected for a king's daughter. When Absalom, Tamar's full brother, was informed about what happened, he was filled with rage. Absalom plotted and killed Amnon. Jonadab, the cousin, lost his integrity; Tamar lost her purity; Amnon lost his life; and David lost his son. These are just some of the consequences of Amnon's sin.

David headed a dysfunctional family. He failed to confront Amnon about his sin, perhaps because David had failed by committing a sexual sin with Bathsheba. Many of us know the painful consequences of being part of a family like this. Tamar's family responded to her crisis with silence, deception, rage, and denial. Amnon's sin had terrible consequences, and David's failure to deal directly with that sin only compounded the devastation.

STRENGTHS AND ACCOMPLISHMENTS:
- Though victimized, Tamar displayed strength of character.

WEAKNESSES AND MISTAKES:
- Amnon mistook lust for love, allowing temptation to overwhelm him.
- Amnon acted on some very unwise counsel.
- Amnon failed to take responsibility for his actions.
- King David was unwilling to confront the problem.

LESSONS FROM THEIR LIVES:
- All of our moral choices have long-term, eternal consequences.
- We must carefully consider from whom to seek advice.
- If we don't deal with sin immediately, its consequences will be compounded.
- The mistakes of parents are often repeated by their children.

KEY VERSE:
"'No, my brother!' she cried. 'Don't be foolish! Don't do this to me! Such wicked things aren't done in Israel'" (2 Samuel 13:12).

The story of Amnon and Tamar is told in 2 Samuel 13. Amnon is also mentioned in 2 Samuel 3:2. Both are mentioned in David's family tree in 1 Chronicles 3.

---

been mourning for the dead for a long time. ³Then go to the king and tell him the story I am about to tell you." Then Joab told her what to say.

⁴When the woman from Tekoa approached* the king, she bowed with her face to the ground in deep respect and cried out, "O king! Help me!"

⁵"What's the trouble?" the king asked.

"Alas, I am a widow!" she replied. "My husband is dead. ⁶My two sons had a fight out in the field. And since no one was there to stop it, one of them was killed. ⁷Now the rest of the family is demanding, 'Let us have your son. We will execute him for murdering his brother. He doesn't deserve to inherit his family's property.' They want to extinguish the only coal I have left, and my husband's name and family will disappear from the face of the earth."

⁸"Leave it to me," the king told her. "Go home, and I'll see to it that no one touches him."

⁹"Oh, thank you, my lord the king," the woman from Tekoa replied. "If you are criticized for helping me, let the blame fall on me and on my father's house, and let the king and his throne be innocent."

¹⁰"If anyone objects," the king said, "bring him to me. I can assure you he will never harm you again!"

¹¹Then she said, "Please swear to me by the LORD your God that you won't let anyone take vengeance against my son. I want no more bloodshed."

"As surely as the LORD lives," he replied, "not a hair on your son's head will be disturbed!"

¹²"Please allow me to ask one more thing of my lord the king," she said.

14:4 As in many Hebrew manuscripts and Greek and Syriac versions; Masoretic Text reads *spoke to*.

"Go ahead and speak," he responded.

[13]She replied, "Why don't you do as much for the people of God as you have promised to do for me? You have convicted yourself in making this decision, because you have refused to bring home your own banished son. [14]All of us must die eventually. Our lives are like water spilled out on the ground, which cannot be gathered up again. But God does not just sweep life away; instead, he devises ways to bring us back when we have been separated from him.

[15]"I have come to plead with my lord the king because people have threatened me. I said to myself, 'Perhaps the king will listen to me [16]and rescue us from those who would cut us off from the inheritance* God has given us. [17]Yes, my lord the king will give us peace of mind again.' I know that you are like an angel of God in discerning good from evil. May the LORD your God be with you."

[18]"I must know one thing," the king replied, "and tell me the truth."

"Yes, my lord the king," she responded.

[19]"Did Joab put you up to this?"

And the woman replied, "My lord the king, how can I deny it? Nobody can hide anything from you. Yes, Joab sent me and told me what to say. [20]He did it to place the matter before you in a different light. But you are as wise as an angel of God, and you understand everything that happens among us!"

[21]So the king sent for Joab and told him, "All right, go and bring back the young man Absalom."

[22]Joab bowed with his face to the ground in deep respect and said, "At last I know that I have gained your approval, my lord the king, for you have granted me this request!"

[23]Then Joab went to Geshur and brought Absalom back to Jerusalem. [24]But the king gave this order: "Absalom may go to his own house, but he must never come into my presence." So Absalom did not see the king.

Absalom Reconciled to David

[25]Now Absalom was praised as the most handsome man in all Israel. He was flawless from head to foot. [26]He cut his hair only once a year, and then only because it was so heavy. When he weighed it out, it came to five pounds!* [27]He had three sons and one daughter. His daughter's name was Tamar, and she was very beautiful.

[28]Absalom lived in Jerusalem for two years, but he never got to see the king. [29]Then Absalom sent for Joab to ask him to intercede for him, but Joab refused to come. Absalom sent for him a second time, but again Joab refused to come. [30]So Absalom said to his servants, "Go and set fire to Joab's barley field, the field next to mine." So they set his field on fire, as Absalom had commanded.

[31]Then Joab came to Absalom at his house and demanded, "Why did your servants set my field on fire?"

[32]And Absalom replied, "Because I wanted you to ask the king why he brought me back from Geshur if he didn't intend to see me. I might as well have stayed there. Let me see the king; if he finds me guilty of anything, then let him kill me."

[33]So Joab told the king what Absalom had said. Then at last David summoned Absalom, who came and bowed low before the king, and the king kissed him.

CHAPTER 15
Absalom's Rebellion

After this, Absalom bought a chariot and horses, and he hired fifty bodyguards to run ahead of him. [2]He got up early every morning and went out to the gate of the city.

14:16 Or *the property;* or *the people.* 14:26 Hebrew *200 shekels* [2.3 kilograms] *by the royal standard.*

14:28-33 Absalom had been in limbo for five years. He was exiled for three years in Geshur. Then he spent two years in Jerusalem without speaking to his father. Finally Absalom resorted to theatrics to force contact with his father. But his reunion with David was far too stilted and formal for genuine reconciliation. No tears were shed; no brokenness was evidenced; no effort was made to set things straight. The relationship between father and son was never restored. It seems that David gave Absalom only partial forgiveness. This led to bondage and bitterness between them and was probably worse than David's giving no forgiveness at all. True forgiveness and reconciliation are an essential part of the recovery process.

15:7-10 For Absalom, it had been eleven years since the rape of Tamar, nine years since his murder of Amnon, six years since his return to Jerusalem, and four years since his awkward reunion with David. He had given up hope of ever being truly reconciled with his father. Using religion as a cover, Absalom led an open rebellion against David. In recovery we are called to seek reconciliation with the people we have wronged. We must be careful not to delay; if we wait too long, we may suffer as David did.

READ 2 SAMUEL 15:1-26

GOD grant me the serenity
to accept the things I cannot change
the courage to change the things I can
and the wisdom to know the difference
AMEN

Sometimes in recovery we're on top of the world; we feel as though our problems are licked for good. At such times, it is tempting to relax and stop living one day at a time. But then life surprises us with an unexpected problem.

King David had reached a pinnacle of success. He had killed giants, won battles, captured the hearts of his people, and overcome enemies on every side. While he was in this comfortable position, he was surprised by a rebellion led by his own son: "A messenger soon arrived in Jerusalem to tell David, 'All Israel has joined Absalom in a conspiracy against you!' 'Then we must flee at once, or it will be too late!' David urged his men. 'Hurry! If we get out of the city before Absalom arrives, both we and the city of Jerusalem will be spared from disaster.' . . . 'If the LORD sees fit,' David said, 'he will bring me back to see the Ark and the Tabernacle again. But if he is through with me, then let him do what seems best to him'" (2 Samuel 15:13-14, 25-26).

King David wisely accepted the reality at hand and responded to the situation as it was, not as he wished it to be. It seems that David was a little out of the habit of relying on God day by day, but he quickly placed his life back in God's hands. God did protect him and returned him to the throne in Jerusalem. When life hits us with unexpected threats, we, too, should be reminded that our life needs to be in God's hands. *Turn to page 537, 1 Chronicles 28.*

When people brought a case to the king for judgment, Absalom would ask where in Israel they were from, and they would tell him their tribe. ³Then Absalom would say, "You've really got a strong case here! It's too bad the king doesn't have anyone to hear it. ⁴I wish I were the judge. Then everyone could bring their cases to me for judgment, and I would give them justice!"

⁵When people tried to bow before him, Absalom wouldn't let them. Instead, he took them by the hand and kissed them. ⁶Absalom did this with everyone who came to the king for judgment, and so he stole the hearts of all the people of Israel.

⁷After four years,* Absalom said to the king, "Let me go to Hebron to offer a sacrifice to the LORD and fulfill a vow I made to him. ⁸For while your servant was at Geshur in Aram, I promised to sacrifice to the LORD in Hebron* if he would bring me back to Jerusalem."

⁹"All right," the king told him. "Go and fulfill your vow."

So Absalom went to Hebron. ¹⁰But while he was there, he sent secret messengers to all the tribes of Israel to stir up a rebellion against the king. "As soon as you hear the ram's horn," his message read, "you are to say, 'Absalom has been crowned king in Hebron.'" ¹¹He took 200 men from Jerusalem with him as guests, but they knew nothing of his intentions. ¹²While Absalom was offering the sacrifices, he sent for Ahithophel, one of David's counselors who lived in Giloh. Soon many others also joined Absalom, and the conspiracy gained momentum.

David Escapes from Jerusalem

¹³A messenger soon arrived in Jerusalem to tell David, "All Israel has joined Absalom in a conspiracy against you!"

¹⁴"Then we must flee at once, or it will be

15:7 As in Greek and Syriac versions; Hebrew reads *forty years.* 15:8 As in some Greek manuscripts; Hebrew lacks *in Hebron.*

407

too late!" David urged his men. "Hurry! If we get out of the city before Absalom arrives, both we and the city of Jerusalem will be spared from disaster."

¹⁵"We are with you," his advisers replied. "Do what you think is best."

¹⁶So the king and all his household set out at once. He left no one behind except ten of his concubines to look after the palace. ¹⁷The king and all his people set out on foot, pausing at the last house ¹⁸to let all the king's men move past to lead the way. There were 600 men from Gath who had come with David, along with the king's bodyguard.*

¹⁹Then the king turned and said to Ittai, a leader of the men from Gath, "Why are you coming with us? Go on back to King Absalom, for you are a guest in Israel, a foreigner in exile. ²⁰You arrived only recently, and should I force you today to wander with us? I don't even know where we will go. Go on back and take your kinsmen with you, and may the LORD show you his unfailing love and faithfulness.*"

²¹But Ittai said to the king, "I vow by the LORD and by your own life that I will go wherever my lord the king goes, no matter what happens—whether it means life or death."

²²David replied, "All right, come with us." So Ittai and all his men and their families went along.

²³Everyone cried loudly as the king and his followers passed by. They crossed the Kidron Valley and then went out toward the wilderness.

²⁴Zadok and all the Levites also came along, carrying the Ark of the Covenant of God. They set down the Ark of God, and Abiathar offered sacrifices* until everyone had passed out of the city.

²⁵Then the king instructed Zadok to take the Ark of God back into the city. "If the LORD sees fit," David said, "he will bring me back to see the Ark and the Tabernacle* again. ²⁶But if he is through with me, then let him do what seems best to him."

²⁷The king also told Zadok the priest, "Look,* here is my plan. You and Abiathar* should return quietly to the city with your son Ahimaaz and Abiathar's son Jonathan. ²⁸I will stop at the shallows of the Jordan River* and wait there for a report from you." ²⁹So Zadok and Abiathar took the Ark of God back to the city and stayed there.

³⁰David walked up the road to the Mount of Olives, weeping as he went. His head was covered and his feet were bare as a sign of mourning. And the people who were with him covered their heads and wept as they climbed the hill. ³¹When someone told David that his adviser Ahithophel was now backing Absalom, David prayed, "O LORD, let Ahithophel give Absalom foolish advice!"

³²When David reached the summit of the Mount of Olives where people worshiped God, Hushai the Arkite was waiting there for him. Hushai had torn his clothing and put dirt on his head as a sign of mourning. ³³But David told him, "If you go with me, you will only be a burden. ³⁴Return to Jerusalem and tell Absalom, 'I will now be your adviser, O king, just as I was your father's adviser in the past.' Then you can frustrate and counter Ahithophel's advice. ³⁵Zadok and Abiathar, the priests, will be there. Tell them about the plans being made in the king's palace, ³⁶and they will send their sons Ahimaaz and Jonathan to tell me what is going on."

³⁷So David's friend Hushai returned to Jerusalem, getting there just as Absalom arrived.

CHAPTER 16
David and Ziba
When David had gone a little beyond the summit of the Mount of Olives, Ziba, the servant of Mephibosheth,* was waiting there for him. He had two donkeys loaded with 200 loaves of bread, 100 clusters of raisins, 100 bunches of summer fruit, and a wineskin full of wine.

²"What are these for?" the king asked Ziba.

15:18 Hebrew *the Kerethites and Pelethites.* 15:20 As in Greek version; Hebrew reads *and may unfailing love and faithfulness go with you.* 15:24 Or *Abiathar went up.* 15:25 Hebrew *and his dwelling place.* 15:27a As in Greek version; Hebrew reads *Are you a seer?* or *Do you see?* 15:27b Hebrew lacks *and Abiathar;* compare 15:29. 15:28 Hebrew *at the crossing points of the wilderness.* 16:1 *Mephibosheth* is another name for Merib-baal.

15:19-22 As we face difficult trials in life, faithful friends can be our greatest assets. Ittai had led a foreign contingent of David's army for many years. As a foreigner, he could have returned to Jerusalem and declared his allegiance to Absalom. But despite a probable tragic outcome, he stood by David. We need to seek out and cultivate true friends who will come alongside us and support us in recovery, even when things are tough. Sometimes the crucible of affliction helps us to see who our real friends are. It may also strengthen relationships that were not close previously, as in the case of David and Ittai.

ABSALOM

Without true forgiveness, bitterness will inevitably tear our relationships apart. No relationship or family will hold together for long if the people are unable to grant forgiveness evidenced in both word and deed. Incomplete forgiveness can sometimes secure a semblance of peace within a family, but when that forgiveness is not seen in the way we live, true reconciliation will never result. Absalom, the third son of King David, suffered much and also caused much suffering because true forgiveness was not part of his life.

Early in his life, Absalom discovered that his sister, Tamar, had been raped by his half brother Amnon. Absalom harbored hatred toward Amnon for two years until he finally killed him. Soon thereafter, Absalom fled to the protection of his grandfather Talmai, king of Geshur, to avoid the wrath of his father, David. After three years, David relented and permitted Absalom to return to Jerusalem, but it wasn't until two years after Absalom's return that David finally spoke with Absalom. Apparently little was said between them, and David continued to ignore his son.

Although David and Absalom seemed happy to see each other at their reunion, the scars of isolation ran deep. Absalom was never able to regain the love he once had for his father or the relationship he longed for. In fact, Absalom spent the rest of his life scheming against his father; his life ended while he led a rebellion against King David. Absalom's life is an example of the wasted years and the broken hearts that can result when we fail to deal directly and decisively with major issues within our family.

WEAKNESSES AND MISTAKES:
- Absalom never once turned to God for guidance.
- Absalom took the law into his own hands.
- Absalom harbored hatred against those who crossed him.

LESSONS FROM HIS LIFE:
- Incomplete forgiveness destroys relationships.
- Words of forgiveness must be proven by actions.
- Delaying forgiveness may render reconciliation almost impossible.
- The sins of parents are often repeated by their children and grandchildren.

KEY VERSE:
"And though Absalom never spoke to Amnon about this, he hated Amnon deeply because of what he had done to his sister" (2 Samuel 13:22).

Absalom's story is told in 2 Samuel 13–19. He is also mentioned in 2 Samuel 3:3 and 1 Chronicles 3:2.

Ziba replied, "The donkeys are for the king's people to ride on, and the bread and summer fruit are for the young men to eat. The wine is for those who become exhausted in the wilderness."

[3] "And where is Mephibosheth, Saul's grandson?" the king asked him.

"He stayed in Jerusalem," Ziba replied. "He said, 'Today I will get back the kingdom of my grandfather Saul.'"

[4] "In that case," the king told Ziba, "I give you everything Mephibosheth owns."

"I bow before you," Ziba replied. "May I always be pleasing to you, my lord the king."

Shimei Curses David

[5] As King David came to Bahurim, a man came out of the village cursing them. It was Shimei son of Gera, from the same clan as Saul's family. [6] He threw stones at the king and the king's officers and all the mighty warriors who surrounded him. [7] "Get out of here, you murderer, you scoundrel!" he shouted at David. [8] "The LORD is paying you back for all the bloodshed in Saul's clan. You stole his throne, and now the LORD has given it to your son Absalom. At last you will taste some of your own medicine, for you are a murderer!"

[9] "Why should this dead dog curse my lord the king?" Abishai son of Zeruiah demanded. "Let me go over and cut off his head!"

[10] "No!" the king said. "Who asked your opinion, you sons of Zeruiah! If the LORD has told him to curse me, who are you to stop him?"

[11] Then David said to Abishai and to all

his servants, "My own son is trying to kill me. Doesn't this relative of Saul* have even more reason to do so? Leave him alone and let him curse, for the LORD has told him to do it. ¹²And perhaps the LORD will see that I am being wronged* and will bless me because of these curses today." ¹³So David and his men continued down the road, and Shimei kept pace with them on a nearby hillside, cursing and throwing stones and dirt at David.

¹⁴The king and all who were with him grew weary along the way, so they rested when they reached the Jordan River.*

Ahithophel Advises Absalom

¹⁵Meanwhile, Absalom and all the army of Israel arrived at Jerusalem, accompanied by Ahithophel. ¹⁶When David's friend Hushai the Arkite arrived, he went immediately to see Absalom. "Long live the king!" he exclaimed. "Long live the king!"

¹⁷"Is this the way you treat your friend David?" Absalom asked him. "Why aren't you with him?"

¹⁸"I'm here because I belong to the man who is chosen by the LORD and by all the men of Israel," Hushai replied. ¹⁹"And anyway, why shouldn't I serve you? Just as I was your father's adviser, now I will be your adviser!"

²⁰Then Absalom turned to Ahithophel and asked him, "What should I do next?"

²¹Ahithophel told him, "Go and sleep with your father's concubines, for he has left them here to look after the palace. Then all Israel will know that you have insulted your father beyond hope of reconciliation, and they will throw their support to you." ²²So they set up a tent on the palace roof where everyone could see it, and Absalom went in and had sex with his father's concubines.

²³Absalom followed Ahithophel's advice, just as David had done. For every word Ahithophel spoke seemed as wise as though it had come directly from the mouth of God.

CHAPTER 17

Now Ahithophel urged Absalom, "Let me choose 12,000 men to start out after David tonight. ²I will catch up with him while he is weary and discouraged. He and his troops will panic, and everyone will run away. Then I will kill only the king, ³and I will bring all the people back to you as a bride returns to her husband. After all, it is only one man's life that you seek.* Then you will be at peace with all the people." ⁴This plan seemed good to Absalom and to all the elders of Israel.

Hushai Counters Ahithophel's Advice

⁵But then Absalom said, "Bring in Hushai the Arkite. Let's see what he thinks about this." ⁶When Hushai arrived, Absalom told him what Ahithophel had said. Then he asked, "What is your opinion? Should we follow Ahithophel's advice? If not, what do you suggest?"

⁷"Well," Hushai replied to Absalom, "this time Ahithophel has made a mistake. ⁸You know your father and his men; they are mighty warriors. Right now they are as enraged as a mother bear who has been robbed of her cubs. And remember that your father is an experienced man of war. He won't be spending the night among the troops. ⁹He has probably already hidden in some pit or cave. And when he comes out and attacks and a few of your men fall, there will be panic among your troops, and the word will spread that Absalom's men are being slaughtered. ¹⁰Then even the bravest soldiers, though they have the heart of a lion, will be paralyzed with fear. For all Israel knows what a mighty warrior your father is and how courageous his men are.

¹¹"I recommend that you mobilize the entire army of Israel, bringing them from as far away as Dan in the north and Beersheba in the south. That way you will have an army as numerous as the sand on the seashore. And I advise that you personally lead the troops. ¹²When we find David, we'll fall on him like dew that falls on the ground. Then neither he nor any of his men will be left alive. ¹³And

---

16:11 Hebrew *this Benjaminite.* 16:12 As in Greek and Syriac versions; Hebrew reads *see my iniquity.* 16:14 As in Greek version (see also 17:16); Hebrew reads *when they reached their destination.* 17:3 As in Greek version; Hebrew reads *like the return of all is the man whom you seek.*

16:5-12 What did David get for 30 years of successful, sacrificial leadership? Stones and curses. Notice that David refused to seek revenge against Shimei. He was well aware of his own failures and was willing to accept Shimei's criticism. He was beyond the point of denial. David put himself in God's hands, trusting that God would do what was right—whether it meant judgment or deliverance. As we experience failure in our life, we need to follow David's example. We must put ourself in God's hands; he will always do what is best for us.

if David were to escape into some town, you will have all Israel there at your command. Then we can take ropes and drag the walls of the town into the nearest valley until every stone is torn down."

[14]Then Absalom and all the men of Israel said, "Hushai's advice is better than Ahithophel's." For the LORD had determined to defeat the counsel of Ahithophel, which really was the better plan, so that he could bring disaster on Absalom!

Hushai Warns David to Escape

[15]Hushai told Zadok and Abiathar, the priests, what Ahithophel had said to Absalom and the elders of Israel and what he himself had advised instead. [16]"Quick!" he told them. "Find David and urge him not to stay at the shallows of the Jordan River* tonight. He must go across at once into the wilderness beyond. Otherwise he will die and his entire army with him."

[17]Jonathan and Ahimaaz had been staying at En-rogel so as not to be seen entering and leaving the city. Arrangements had been made for a servant girl to bring them the message they were to take to King David. [18]But a boy spotted them at En-rogel, and he told Absalom about it. So they quickly escaped to Bahurim, where a man hid them down inside a well in his courtyard. [19]The man's wife put a cloth over the top of the well and scattered grain on it to dry in the sun; so no one suspected they were there.

[20]When Absalom's men arrived, they asked her, "Have you seen Ahimaaz and Jonathan?"

The woman replied, "They were here, but they crossed over the brook." Absalom's men looked for them without success and returned to Jerusalem.

[21]Then the two men crawled out of the well and hurried on to King David. "Quick!" they told him, "cross the Jordan tonight!" And they told him how Ahithophel had advised that he be captured and killed. [22]So David and all the people with him went across

the Jordan River during the night, and they were all on the other bank before dawn.

[23]When Ahithophel realized that his advice had not been followed, he saddled his donkey, went to his hometown, set his affairs in order, and hanged himself. He died there and was buried in the family tomb.

[24]David soon arrived at Mahanaim. By now, Absalom had mobilized the entire army of Israel and was leading his troops across the Jordan River. [25]Absalom had appointed Amasa as commander of his army, replacing Joab, who had been commander under David. (Amasa was Joab's cousin. His father was Jether,* an Ishmaelite.* His mother, Abigail daughter of Nahash, was the sister of Joab's mother, Zeruiah.) [26]Absalom and the Israelite army set up camp in the land of Gilead.

[27]When David arrived at Mahanaim, he was warmly greeted by Shobi son of Nahash, who came from Rabbah of the Ammonites, and by Makir son of Ammiel from Lo-debar, and by Barzillai of Gilead from Rogelim. [28]They brought sleeping mats, cooking pots, serving bowls, wheat and barley, flour and roasted grain, beans, lentils, [29]honey, butter, sheep, goats, and cheese for David and those who were with him. For they said, "You must all be very hungry and tired and thirsty after your long march through the wilderness."

CHAPTER 18
Absalom's Defeat and Death

David now mustered the men who were with him and appointed generals and captains* to lead them. [2]He sent the troops out in three groups, placing one group under Joab, one under Joab's brother Abishai son of Zeruiah, and one under Ittai, the man from Gath. The king told his troops, "I am going out with you."

[3]But his men objected strongly. "You must not go," they urged. "If we have to turn and run—and even if half of us die—it will make no difference to Absalom's troops; they will be looking only for you. You are worth 10,000 of us,* and it is better that you

---

17:16 Hebrew *at the crossing points of the wilderness.* **17:25a** Hebrew *Ithra,* a variant spelling of Jether. **17:25b** As in some Greek manuscripts (see also 1 Chr 2:17); Hebrew reads *an Israelite.* **18:1** Hebrew *appointed commanders of thousands and commanders of hundreds.* **18:3** As in two Hebrew manuscripts and some Greek and Latin manuscripts; most Hebrew manuscripts read *Now there are 10,000 like us.*

17:14 No matter how strong our enemies are, they can never thwart God's plan. God used Hushai to lead Absalom toward disaster. God was working behind the scenes to protect David and give him a chance to recover his losses. As we continue in recovery, God will accomplish his purposes for us. We can trust that he will work behind the scenes on our behalf, supporting us in the recovery process in ways we'll never know.

stay here in the town and send help if we need it."

4"If you think that's the best plan, I'll do it," the king answered. So he stood alongside the gate of the town as all the troops marched out in groups of hundreds and of thousands.

5And the king gave this command to Joab, Abishai, and Ittai: "For my sake, deal gently with young Absalom." And all the troops heard the king give this order to his commanders.

6So the battle began in the forest of Ephraim, 7and the Israelite troops were beaten back by David's men. There was a great slaughter that day, and 20,000 men laid down their lives. 8The battle raged all across the countryside, and more men died because of the forest than were killed by the sword.

9During the battle, Absalom happened to come upon some of David's men. He tried to escape on his mule, but as he rode beneath the thick branches of a great tree, his hair* got caught in the tree. His mule kept going and left him dangling in the air. 10One of David's men saw what had happened and told Joab, "I saw Absalom dangling from a great tree."

11"What?" Joab demanded. "You saw him there and didn't kill him? I would have rewarded you with ten pieces of silver* and a hero's belt!"

12"I would not kill the king's son for even a thousand pieces of silver,*" the man replied to Joab. "We all heard the king say to you and Abishai and Ittai, 'For my sake, please spare young Absalom.' 13And if I had betrayed the king by killing his son—and the king would certainly find out who did it—you yourself would be the first to abandon me."

14"Enough of this nonsense," Joab said. Then he took three daggers and plunged them into Absalom's heart as he dangled, still alive, in the great tree. 15Ten of Joab's young armor bearers then surrounded Absalom and killed him.

16Then Joab blew the ram's horn, and his men returned from chasing the army of Israel. 17They threw Absalom's body into a deep pit in the forest and piled a great heap of stones over it. And all Israel fled to their homes.

18During his lifetime, Absalom had built a monument to himself in the King's Valley, for he said, "I have no son to carry on my name." He named the monument after himself, and it is known as Absalom's Monument to this day.

David Mourns Absalom's Death

19Then Zadok's son Ahimaaz said, "Let me run to the king with the good news that the LORD has rescued him from his enemies."

20"No," Joab told him, "it wouldn't be good news to the king that his son is dead. You can be my messenger another time, but not today."

21Then Joab said to a man from Ethiopia,* "Go tell the king what you have seen." The man bowed and ran off.

22But Ahimaaz continued to plead with Joab, "Whatever happens, please let me go, too."

"Why should you go, my son?" Joab replied. "There will be no reward for your news."

23"Yes, but let me go anyway," he begged.

Joab finally said, "All right, go ahead." So Ahimaaz took the less demanding route by way of the plain and ran to Mahanaim ahead of the Ethiopian.

24While David was sitting between the inner and outer gates of the town, the watchman climbed to the roof of the gateway by the wall. As he looked, he saw a lone man running toward them. 25He shouted the news down to David, and the king replied, "If he is alone, he has news."

As the messenger came closer, 26the watchman saw another man running toward them. He shouted down, "Here comes another one!"

The king replied, "He also will have news."

27"The first man runs like Ahimaaz son of Zadok," the watchman said.

18:9 Hebrew *his head*. 18:11 Hebrew *10 [shekels] of silver*, about 4 ounces or 114 grams in weight. 18:12 Hebrew *1,000 [shekels] of silver*, about 25 pounds or 11.4 kilograms in weight. 18:21 Hebrew *from Cush;* similarly in 18:23, 31, 32.

18:15 Absalom died a tragic death—a rebel and the victim of a broken relationship with his father. He was the product of an unreconciled past. If we are driven by painful emotions or events from our past, we may also find ourself fighting unnecessary battles and end up in an early grave. As with Absalom, we may not be completely to blame for our broken relationships. Yet we still are responsible to deal with the issues and seek reconciliation. If we don't, we will probably destroy ourself and bring all the people close to us down as well.

"He is a good man and comes with good news," the king replied.

[28]Then Ahimaaz cried out to the king, "Everything is all right!" He bowed before the king with his face to the ground and said, "Praise to the LORD your God, who has handed over the rebels who dared to stand against my lord the king."

[29]"What about young Absalom?" the king demanded. "Is he all right?"

Ahimaaz replied, "When Joab told me to come, there was a lot of commotion. But I didn't know what was happening."

[30]"Wait here," the king told him. So Ahimaaz stepped aside.

[31]Then the man from Ethiopia arrived and said, "I have good news for my lord the king. Today the LORD has rescued you from all those who rebelled against you."

[32]"What about young Absalom?" the king demanded. "Is he all right?"

And the Ethiopian replied, "May all of your enemies, my lord the king, both now and in the future, share the fate of that young man!"

[33]*The king was overcome with emotion. He went up to the room over the gateway and burst into tears. And as he went, he cried, "O my son Absalom! My son, my son Absalom! If only I had died instead of you! O Absalom, my son, my son."

CHAPTER 19
Joab Rebukes the King

[1]*Word soon reached Joab that the king was weeping and mourning for Absalom. [2]As all the people heard of the king's deep grief for his son, the joy of that day's victory was turned into deep sadness. [3]They crept back into the town that day as though they were ashamed and had deserted in battle. [4]The king covered his face with his hands and kept on crying, "O my son Absalom! O Absalom, my son, my son!"

[5]Then Joab went to the king's room and said to him, "We saved your life today and the lives of your sons, your daughters, and your wives and concubines. Yet you act like this, making us feel ashamed of ourselves. [6]You seem to love those who hate you and hate those who love you. You have made it clear today that your commanders and troops mean nothing to you. It seems that if Absalom had lived and all of us had died, you would be pleased. [7]Now go out there and congratulate your troops, for I swear by the LORD that if you don't go out, not a single one of them will remain here tonight. Then you will be worse off than ever before."

[8]So the king went out and took his seat at the town gate, and as the news spread throughout the town that he was there, everyone went to him.

Meanwhile, the Israelites who had supported Absalom fled to their homes. [9]And throughout all the tribes of Israel there was much discussion and argument going on. The people were saying, "The king rescued us from our enemies and saved us from the Philistines, but Absalom chased him out of the country. [10]Now Absalom, whom we anointed to rule over us, is dead. Why not ask David to come back and be our king again?"

[11]Then King David sent Zadok and Abiathar, the priests, to say to the elders of Judah, "Why are you the last ones to welcome back the king into his palace? For I have heard that all Israel is ready. [12]You are my relatives, my own tribe, my own flesh and blood! So why are you the last ones to welcome back the king?" [13]And David told them to tell Amasa, "Since you are my own flesh and blood, like Joab, may God strike me and even kill me if I do not appoint you as commander of my army in his place."

[14]Then Amasa* convinced all the men of Judah, and they responded unanimously.

18:33 Verse 18:33 is numbered 19:1 in Hebrew text. **19:1** Verses 19:1-43 are numbered 19:2-44 in Hebrew text. **19:14** Or *David;* Hebrew reads *he.*

18:32-33 David could have avoided this great sorrow had he been willing to forgive, to set things straight, and to restore his relationship with Absalom. David had failed to seek reconciliation, and now it was too late. He could never have Absalom back; he could never make things right with him. Once again, as earlier with Amnon, we see that the consequences of sin live long after the act itself. We also see the importance of reconciliation if we want to enjoy a peaceful future.

19:5-7 Joab was courageous to confront David about his improper behavior. David had failed to thank his men for standing loyal to him throughout the civil war. They deserved his grateful congratulations. Instead, David was mourning the loss of his son, who had also been his enemy. Joab's intervention probably saved David's still-shaky kingdom. The criticism of a friend is sometimes the right medicine to prompt us to proper action (Proverbs 27:6).

They sent word to the king, "Return to us, and bring back all who are with you."

David's Return to Jerusalem

[15]So the king started back to Jerusalem. And when he arrived at the Jordan River, the people of Judah came to Gilgal to meet him and escort him across the river. [16]Shimei son of Gera, the man from Bahurim in Benjamin, hurried across with the men of Judah to welcome King David. [17]A thousand other men from the tribe of Benjamin were with him, including Ziba, the chief servant of the house of Saul, and Ziba's fifteen sons and twenty servants. They rushed down to the Jordan to meet the king. [18]They crossed the shallows of the Jordan to bring the king's household across the river, helping him in every way they could.

David's Mercy to Shimei

As the king was about to cross the river, Shimei fell down before him. [19]"My lord the king, please forgive me," he pleaded. "Forget the terrible thing your servant did when you left Jerusalem. May the king put it out of his mind. [20]I know how much I sinned. That is why I have come here today, the very first person in all Israel* to greet my lord the king."

[21]Then Abishai son of Zeruiah said, "Shimei should die, for he cursed the LORD's anointed king!"

[22]"Who asked your opinion, you sons of Zeruiah!" David exclaimed. "Why have you become my adversary* today? This is not a day for execution, for today I am once again the king of Israel!" [23]Then, turning to Shimei, David vowed, "Your life will be spared."

David's Kindness to Mephibosheth

[24]Now Mephibosheth,* Saul's grandson, came down from Jerusalem to meet the king. He had not cared for his feet, trimmed his beard, or washed his clothes since the day the king left Jerusalem. [25]"Why didn't you come with me, Mephibosheth?" the king asked him.

[26]Mephibosheth replied, "My lord the king, my servant Ziba deceived me. I told him, 'Saddle my donkey* so I can go with the king.' For as you know I am crippled. [27]Ziba has slandered me by saying that I refused to come. But I know that my lord the king is like an angel of God, so do what you think is best. [28]All my relatives and I could expect only death from you, my lord, but instead you have honored me by allowing me to eat at your own table! What more can I ask?"

[29]"You've said enough," David replied. "I've decided that you and Ziba will divide your land equally between you."

[30]"Give him all of it," Mephibosheth said. "I am content just to have you safely back again, my lord the king!"

David's Kindness to Barzillai

[31]Barzillai of Gilead had come down from Rogelim to escort the king across the Jordan. [32]He was very old—eighty years of age—and very wealthy. He was the one who had provided food for the king during his stay in Mahanaim. [33]"Come across with me and live in Jerusalem," the king said to Barzillai. "I will take care of you there."

[34]"No," he replied, "I am far too old to go with the king to Jerusalem. [35]I am eighty years old today, and I can no longer enjoy anything. Food and wine are no longer tasty, and I cannot hear the singers as they sing. I would only be a burden to my lord the king. [36]Just to go across the Jordan River with the king is all the honor I need! [37]Then let me return again to die in my own town, where my father and mother are buried. But here is your servant, my son Kimham. Let him go with my lord the king and receive whatever you want to give him."

[38]"Good," the king agreed. "Kimham will go with me, and I will help him in any way you would like. And I will do for you anything you want." [39]So all the people crossed the Jordan with the king. After David had blessed Barzillai and kissed him, Barzillai returned to his own home.

[40]The king then crossed over to Gilgal, taking Kimham with him. All the troops of Judah and half the troops of Israel escorted the king on his way.

19:20 Hebrew *in the house of Joseph.* 19:22 Or *my prosecutor.* 19:24 *Mephibosheth* is another name for Merib-baal. 19:26 As in Greek, Syriac, and Latin versions; Hebrew reads *I will saddle a donkey for myself.*

19:18-20 Shimei, trying to reconcile his relationship with King David, asked that David forgive and forget the stones and insults he had hurled during Absalom's rebellion. Shimei wanted to be set free from the burden of his past mistakes so he could build a solid future. God offers us this kind of forgiveness when we come to his Son, Jesus. Through him our sins are forgiven and forgotten; we are given the opportunity to start over again with a clean slate.

An Argument over the King

⁴¹But all the men of Israel complained to the king, "The men of Judah stole the king and didn't give us the honor of helping take you, your household, and all your men across the Jordan."

⁴²The men of Judah replied, "The king is one of our own kinsmen. Why should this make you angry? We haven't eaten any of the king's food or received any special favors!"

⁴³"But there are ten tribes in Israel," the others replied. "So we have ten times as much right to the king as you do. What right do you have to treat us with such contempt? Weren't we the first to speak of bringing him back to be our king again?" The argument continued back and forth, and the men of Judah spoke even more harshly than the men of Israel.

CHAPTER 20
The Revolt of Sheba

There happened to be a troublemaker there named Sheba son of Bicri, a man from the tribe of Benjamin. Sheba blew a ram's horn and began to chant:

"Down with the dynasty of David!
    We have no interest in the son of Jesse.
Come on, you men of Israel,
    back to your homes!"

²So all the men of Israel deserted David and followed Sheba son of Bicri. But the men of Judah stayed with their king and escorted him from the Jordan River to Jerusalem.

³When David came to his palace in Jerusalem, he took the ten concubines he had left to look after the palace and placed them in seclusion. Their needs were provided for, but he no longer slept with them. So each of them lived like a widow until she died.

⁴Then the king told Amasa, "Mobilize the army of Judah within three days, and report back at that time." ⁵So Amasa went out to notify Judah, but it took him longer than the time he had been given.

⁶Then David said to Abishai, "Sheba son of Bicri is going to hurt us more than Absalom did. Quick, take my troops and chase after him before he gets into a fortified town where we can't reach him."

⁷So Abishai and Joab,* together with the king's bodyguard* and all the mighty warriors, set out from Jerusalem to go after

Sheba. ⁸As they arrived at the great stone in Gibeon, Amasa met them. Joab was wearing his military tunic with a dagger strapped to his belt. As he stepped forward to greet Amasa, he slipped the dagger from its sheath.*

⁹"How are you, my cousin?" Joab said and took him by the beard with his right hand as though to kiss him. ¹⁰Amasa didn't notice the dagger in his left hand, and Joab stabbed him in the stomach with it so that his insides gushed out onto the ground. Joab did not need to strike again, and Amasa soon died. Joab and his brother Abishai left him lying there and continued after Sheba.

¹¹One of Joab's young men shouted to Amasa's troops, "If you are for Joab and David, come and follow Joab." ¹²But Amasa lay in his blood in the middle of the road, and Joab's man saw that everyone was stopping to stare at him. So he pulled him off the road into a field and threw a cloak over him. ¹³With Amasa's body out of the way, everyone went on with Joab to capture Sheba son of Bicri.

¹⁴Meanwhile, Sheba traveled through all the tribes of Israel and eventually came to the town of Abel-beth-maacah. All the members of his own clan, the Bicrites,* assembled for battle and followed him into the town. ¹⁵When Joab's forces arrived, they attacked Abel-beth-maacah. They built a siege ramp against the town's fortifications and began battering down the wall. ¹⁶But a wise woman in the town called out to Joab, "Listen to me, Joab. Come over here so I can talk to you." ¹⁷As he approached, the woman asked, "Are you Joab?"

"I am," he replied.

So she said, "Listen carefully to your servant."

"I'm listening," he said.

¹⁸Then she continued, "There used to be a saying, 'If you want to settle an argument, ask advice at the town of Abel.' ¹⁹I am one who is peace loving and faithful in Israel. But you are destroying an important town in Israel.* Why do you want to devour what belongs to the LORD?"

²⁰And Joab replied, "Believe me, I don't want to devour or destroy your town! ²¹That's not my purpose. All I want is a man named Sheba son of Bicri from the hill country of Ephraim, who has revolted against King David. If you hand over this one man to me, I will leave the town in peace."

"All right," the woman replied, "we will

20:7a Hebrew *So Joab's men.* 20:7b Hebrew *the Kerethites and Pelethites;* also in 20:23. 20:8 Hebrew *As he stepped forward, it fell out.* 20:14 As in Greek and Latin versions; Hebrew reads *All the B erites.* 20:19 Hebrew *a town that is a mother in Israel.*

throw his head over the wall to you." ²²Then the woman went to all the people with her wise advice, and they cut off Sheba's head and threw it out to Joab. So he blew the ram's horn and called his troops back from the attack. They all returned to their homes, and Joab returned to the king at Jerusalem.

²³Now Joab was the commander of the army of Israel. Benaiah son of Jehoiada was captain of the king's bodyguard. ²⁴Adoniram* was in charge of forced labor. Jehoshaphat son of Ahilud was the royal historian. ²⁵Sheva was the court secretary. Zadok and Abiathar were the priests. ²⁶And Ira, a descendant of Jair, was David's personal priest.

CHAPTER 21
David Avenges the Gibeonites

There was a famine during David's reign that lasted for three years, so David asked the LORD about it. And the LORD said, "The famine has come because Saul and his family are guilty of murdering the Gibeonites."

²So the king summoned the Gibeonites. They were not part of Israel but were all that was left of the nation of the Amorites. The people of Israel had sworn not to kill them, but Saul, in his zeal for Israel and Judah, had tried to wipe them out. ³David asked them, "What can I do for you? How can I make amends so that you will bless the LORD's people again?"

⁴"Well, money can't settle this matter between us and the family of Saul," the Gibeonites replied. "Neither can we demand the life of anyone in Israel."

"What can I do then?" David asked. "Just tell me and I will do it for you."

⁵Then they replied, "It was Saul who planned to destroy us, to keep us from having any place at all in the territory of Israel. ⁶So let seven of Saul's sons be handed over to us, and we will execute them before the LORD at Gibeon, on the mountain of the LORD.*"

"All right," the king said, "I will do it."

⁷The king spared Jonathan's son Mephibosheth,* who was Saul's grandson, because of the oath David and Jonathan had sworn before the LORD. ⁸But he gave them Saul's two sons Armoni and Mephibosheth, whose mother was Rizpah daughter of Aiah. He also gave them the five sons of Saul's daughter Merab,* the wife of Adriel son of Barzillai from Meholah. ⁹The men of Gibeon executed them on the mountain before the LORD. So all seven of them died together at the beginning of the barley harvest.

¹⁰Then Rizpah daughter of Aiah, the mother of two of the men, spread burlap on a rock and stayed there the entire harvest season. She prevented the scavenger birds from tearing at their bodies during the day and stopped wild animals from eating them at night. ¹¹When David learned what Rizpah, Saul's concubine, had done, ¹²he went to the people of Jabesh-gilead and retrieved the bones of Saul and his son Jonathan. (When the Philistines had killed Saul and Jonathan on Mount Gilboa, the people of Jabesh-gilead stole their bodies from the public square of Beth-shan, where the Philistines had hung them.) ¹³So David obtained the bones of Saul and Jonathan, as well as the bones of the men the Gibeonites had executed.

¹⁴Then the king ordered that they bury the bones in the tomb of Kish, Saul's father, at the town of Zela in the land of Benjamin. After that, God ended the famine in the land.

Battles against Philistine Giants

¹⁵Once again the Philistines were at war with Israel. And when David and his men were in the thick of battle, David became weak and exhausted. ¹⁶Ishbi-benob was a descendant of the giants*; his bronze spearhead weighed more than seven pounds,* and he was armed with a new sword. He had cornered David and was about to kill him. ¹⁷But Abishai son of

20:24 As in Greek version (see also 1 Kgs 4:6; 5:14); Hebrew reads *Adoram.* 21:6 As in Greek version (see also 21:9); Hebrew reads *at Gibeah of Saul, the chosen of the LORD.* 21:7 *Mephibosheth* is another name for Merib-baal. 21:8 As in a few Hebrew and Greek manuscripts and Syriac version (see also 1 Sam 18:19); most Hebrew manuscripts read *Michal.* 21:16a Or *a descendant of the Rapha;* also in 21:18, 20, 22. 21:16b Hebrew *300 [shekels]* [3.4 kilograms].

21:1-14 The land of Israel suffered a drought because King Saul had broken a treaty with the Gibeonites. The consequences of Saul's mistake lingered long after he had perpetrated it. Sometimes we allow things to remain hidden in our life that serve as barriers to God's blessings. We need to take steps to remove these barriers. When the Israelites did this, God answered prayers on behalf of the land and its people.

21:16-17 Accepting our limitations is a critical mark of maturity. David acknowledged his diminishing physical strength and agreed to stay away from battle. Sometimes our pride will not allow

Zeruiah came to David's rescue and killed the Philistine. Then David's men declared, "You are not going out to battle with us again! Why risk snuffing out the light of Israel?"

18After this, there was another battle against the Philistines at Gob. As they fought, Sibbecai from Hushah killed Saph, another descendant of the giants.

19During another battle at Gob, Elhanan son of Jair* from Bethlehem killed the brother of Goliath of Gath.* The handle of his spear was as thick as a weaver's beam!

20In another battle with the Philistines at Gath, they encountered a huge man* with six fingers on each hand and six toes on each foot, twenty-four in all, who was also a descendant of the giants. 21But when he defied and taunted Israel, he was killed by Jonathan, the son of David's brother Shimea.*

22These four Philistines were descendants of the giants of Gath, but David and his warriors killed them.

CHAPTER 22
David's Song of Praise

David sang this song to the LORD on the day the LORD rescued him from all his enemies and from Saul. 2He sang:

"The LORD is my rock, my fortress, and
    my savior;
3 my God is my rock, in whom I find
    protection.
He is my shield, the power that saves me,
    and my place of safety.
He is my refuge, my savior,
    the one who saves me from violence.
4I called on the LORD, who is worthy
    of praise,
and he saved me from my enemies.

5"The waves of death overwhelmed me;
    floods of destruction swept over me.
6The grave* wrapped its ropes around me;
    death laid a trap in my path.
7But in my distress I cried out to the LORD;
    yes, I cried to my God for help.
He heard me from his sanctuary;
    my cry reached his ears.

8"Then the earth quaked and trembled.
    The foundations of the heavens shook;
    they quaked because of his anger.
9Smoke poured from his nostrils;
    fierce flames leaped from his mouth.
    Glowing coals blazed forth from him.
10He opened the heavens and came down;
    dark storm clouds were beneath
      his feet.
11Mounted on a mighty angelic being,*
    he flew,
    soaring* on the wings of the wind.
12He shrouded himself in darkness,
    veiling his approach with dense
      rain clouds.
13A great brightness shone around him,
    and burning coals* blazed forth.
14The LORD thundered from heaven;
    the voice of the Most High resounded.
15He shot arrows and scattered his enemies;
    his lightning flashed, and they were
      confused.
16Then at the command of the LORD,
    at the blast of his breath,
the bottom of the sea could be seen,
    and the foundations of the earth were
      laid bare.

17"He reached down from heaven and
    rescued me;
he drew me out of deep waters.

21:19a As in parallel text at 1 Chr 20:5; Hebrew reads *son of Jaare-oregim.* 21:19b As in parallel text at 1 Chr 20:5; Hebrew reads *killed Goliath of Gath.* 21:20 As in parallel text at 1 Chr 20:6; Hebrew reads *a Midianite.* 21:21 As in parallel text at 1 Chr 20:7; Hebrew reads *Shimei,* a variant spelling of Shimea. 22:6 Hebrew *Sheol.* 22:11a Hebrew *a cherub.* 22:11b As in some Hebrew manuscripts (see also Ps 18:10); other Hebrew manuscripts read *appearing.* 22:13 Or *and lightning bolts.*

---

us to admit our limitations, and we try to do things we are not capable of doing. We might think we are strong enough to persevere on our own in recovery, even in unsafe contexts. Such an attitude will only lead to a fall. We would be wise to follow David's example and admit there are certain things we cannot and should not try to do.

22:1 David had lived a fruitful life, full of service to God. He had certainly had his problems and made his share of mistakes, but he had trusted God through them all. Here, near the end of his life, David still had a song for God, full of unabashed, authentic praise. No matter what we've been through in our life, we need to regularly remember the victories God has given us and praise him for his healing love in guiding us through the recovery process.

22:17-18 Through it all, David was able to recognize God's hand in his life. He knew that God had reached down, taken hold of him, and drawn him out of deep waters. Even at the end of his life he recognized his helplessness and God's sovereignty. Although this is one of the first requirements in recovery, it is something we should never forget.

18 He rescued me from my powerful enemies,
from those who hated me and were too strong for me.
19 They attacked me at a moment when I was in distress,
but the LORD supported me.
20 He led me to a place of safety;
he rescued me because he delights in me.
21 The LORD rewarded me for doing right;
he restored me because of my innocence.
22 For I have kept the ways of the LORD;
I have not turned from my God to follow evil.
23 I have followed all his regulations;
I have never abandoned his decrees.
24 I am blameless before God;
I have kept myself from sin.
25 The LORD rewarded me for doing right.
He has seen my innocence.
26 "To the faithful you show yourself faithful;
to those with integrity you show integrity.
27 To the pure you show yourself pure,
but to the crooked you show yourself shrewd.
28 You rescue the humble,
but your eyes watch the proud and humiliate them.
29 O LORD, you are my lamp.
The LORD lights up my darkness.
30 In your strength I can crush an army;
with my God I can scale any wall.
31 "God's way is perfect.
All the LORD's promises prove true.
He is a shield for all who look to him for protection.
32 For who is God except the LORD?
Who but our God is a solid rock?
33 God is my strong fortress,
and he makes my way perfect.
34 He makes me as surefooted as a deer,
enabling me to stand on mountain heights.

35 He trains my hands for battle;
he strengthens my arm to draw a bronze bow.
36 You have given me your shield of victory;
your help* has made me great.
37 You have made a wide path for my feet
to keep them from slipping.
38 "I chased my enemies and destroyed them;
I did not stop until they were conquered.
39 I consumed them;
I struck them down so they did not get up;
they fell beneath my feet.
40 You have armed me with strength for the battle;
you have subdued my enemies under my feet.
41 You placed my foot on their necks.
I have destroyed all who hated me.
42 They looked for help, but no one came to their rescue.
They even cried to the LORD, but he refused to answer.
43 I ground them as fine as the dust of the earth;
I trampled them* in the gutter like dirt.
44 "You gave me victory over my accusers.
You preserved me as the ruler over nations;
people I don't even know now serve me.
45 Foreign nations cringe before me;
as soon as they hear of me, they submit.
46 They all lose their courage
and come trembling* from their strongholds.
47 "The LORD lives! Praise to my Rock!
May God, the Rock of my salvation, be exalted!
48 He is the God who pays back those who harm me;
he brings down the nations under me
49 and delivers me from my enemies.

22:36 As in Dead Sea Scrolls; Masoretic Text reads *your answering.* 22:43 As in Dead Sea Scrolls (see also Ps 18:42); Masoretic Text reads *I crushed and trampled them.* 22:46 As in parallel text at Ps 18:45; Hebrew reads *come girding themselves.*

23:5 Through all of David's ups and downs God had stood by him. God had promised David that he would father a dynasty that would rule forever. There must have been times when David wondered if that would ever happen. He had seen his kingdom crumbling and his sons tearing each other apart, but he knew that God could sustain his promises. David's faith remained strong, even toward the end of his life. Today God promises hope and forgiveness for us. We can be sure, no matter how bad things may seem at times, that he is faithful to his promises.

You hold me safe beyond the reach of my
  enemies;
  you save me from violent opponents.
⁵⁰ For this, O LORD, I will praise you among
  the nations;
  I will sing praises to your name.
⁵¹ You give great victories to your king;
  you show unfailing love to your
    anointed,
  to David and all his descendants
    forever."

CHAPTER 23
David's Last Words

These are the last words of David:

"David, the son of Jesse, speaks—
  David, the man who was raised up so
    high,
  David, the man anointed by the God
    of Jacob,
  David, the sweet psalmist of Israel.*

² "The Spirit of the LORD speaks through
  me;
  his words are upon my tongue.
³ The God of Israel spoke.
  The Rock of Israel said to me:
  'The one who rules righteously,
    who rules in the fear of God,
⁴ is like the light of morning at sunrise,
  like a morning without clouds,
  like the gleaming of the sun
    on new grass after rain.'

⁵ "Is it not my family God has chosen?
  Yes, he has made an everlasting
    covenant with me.
  His agreement is arranged and guaranteed
    in every detail.
  He will ensure my safety and success.
⁶ But the godless are like thorns to be
    thrown away,
  for they tear the hand that touches
    them.
⁷ One must use iron tools to chop them
    down;
  they will be totally consumed by fire."

David's Mightiest Warriors

⁸ These are the names of David's mightiest
warriors. The first was Jashobeam the Hacmonite,* who was leader of the Three*—the
three mightiest warriors among David's men.

23:1 Or *the favorite subject of the songs of Israel;* or *the
favorite of the Strong One of Israel.* 23:8a As in parallel
text at 1 Chr 11:11; Hebrew reads *Josheb-basshebeth the
Tahkemonite.* 23:8b As in Greek and Latin versions (see
also 1 Chr 11:11); the meaning of the Hebrew is
uncertain.

STEP 11

A New Hiding Place

BIBLE READING: 2 Samuel 22:1-33

**We sought through prayer and medita-
tion to improve our conscious contact
with God, praying only for knowledge of
his will for us and the power to carry that
out.**

In the past we used our addiction as a
hiding place when life became overwhelming. Now that we are in recovery, life
can at times feel even more overwhelming.
We'll need a new place of refuge to escape
the storms and find protection.

King David experienced many battles.
He said of God: "The LORD is my rock, my
fortress, and my savior; my God is my rock,
in whom I find protection. He is my shield,
the power that saves me, and my place of
safety. . . . I called on the LORD, who is
worthy of praise, and he saved me from my
enemies. The waves of death overwhelmed
me; floods of destruction swept over me.
The grave wrapped its ropes around me;
death laid a trap in my path. But in my
distress I cried out to the LORD; yes, I cried
to my God for help. He heard me from his
sanctuary; my cry reached his ears. . . . He
is a shield for all who look to him for
protection. For who is God except the
LORD? Who but our God is a solid rock?
God is my strong fortress, and he makes my
way perfect" (2 Samuel 22:2-7, 31-33).

There will always be times when we feel
the need for a safe place, the need to run
and hide. God can be that hiding place.
When we were in distress, surrounded by
"waves of death" in our old life of sin, we
called to God for help. He heard our cries
and brought us to a place of safety. He's
always there, ready to shield and protect
us whenever we call on him. *Turn to page
697, Psalm 27.*

tyndal.es/lrbstep11

He once used his spear to kill 800 enemy warriors in a single battle.*

⁹Next in rank among the Three was Eleazar son of Dodai, a descendant of Ahoah. Once Eleazar and David stood together against the Philistines when the entire Israelite army had fled. ¹⁰He killed Philistines until his hand was too tired to lift his sword, and the LORD gave him a great victory that day. The rest of the army did not return until it was time to collect the plunder!

¹¹Next in rank was Shammah son of Agee from Harar. One time the Philistines gathered at Lehi and attacked the Israelites in a field full of lentils. The Israelite army fled, ¹²but Shammah* held his ground in the middle of the field and beat back the Philistines. So the LORD brought about a great victory.

¹³Once during the harvest, when David was at the cave of Adullam, the Philistine army was camped in the valley of Rephaim. The Three (who were among the Thirty—an elite group among David's fighting men) went down to meet him there. ¹⁴David was staying in the stronghold at the time, and a Philistine detachment had occupied the town of Bethlehem.

¹⁵David remarked longingly to his men, "Oh, how I would love some of that good water from the well by the gate in Bethlehem." ¹⁶So the Three broke through the Philistine lines, drew some water from the well by the gate in Bethlehem, and brought it back to David. But he refused to drink it. Instead, he poured it out as an offering to the LORD. ¹⁷"The LORD forbid that I should drink this!" he exclaimed. "This water is as precious as the blood of these men* who risked their lives to bring it to me." So David did not drink it. These are examples of the exploits of the Three.

David's Thirty Mighty Men

¹⁸Abishai son of Zeruiah, the brother of Joab, was the leader of the Thirty.* He once used his spear to kill 300 enemy warriors in a single battle. It was by such feats that he became as famous as the Three. ¹⁹Abishai was the most famous of the Thirty* and was their commander, though he was not one of the Three.

²⁰There was also Benaiah son of Jehoiada, a valiant warrior* from Kabzeel. He did many heroic deeds, which included killing two champions* of Moab. Another time, on a snowy day, he chased a lion down into a pit and killed it. ²¹Once, armed only with a club, he killed an imposing Egyptian warrior who was armed with a spear. Benaiah wrenched the spear from the Egyptian's hand and killed him with it. ²²Deeds like these made Benaiah as famous as the Three mightiest warriors. ²³He was more honored than the other members of the Thirty, though he was not one of the Three. And David made him captain of his bodyguard.

²⁴Other members of the Thirty included:

Asahel, Joab's brother;
Elhanan son of Dodo from Bethlehem;
25 Shammah from Harod;
Elika from Harod;
26 Helez from Pelon*;
Ira son of Ikkesh from Tekoa;
27 Abiezer from Anathoth;
Sibbecai* from Hushah;
28 Zalmon from Ahoah;
Maharai from Netophah;
29 Heled* son of Baanah from Netophah;
Ithai* son of Ribai from Gibeah (in the land of Benjamin);
30 Benaiah from Pirathon;
Hurai* from Nahale-gaash*;
31 Abi-albon from Arabah;
Azmaveth from Bahurim;
32 Eliahba from Shaalbon;
the sons of Jashen;
Jonathan ³³son of Shagee* from Harar;
Ahiam son of Sharar from Harar;
34 Eliphelet son of Ahasbai from Maacah;
Eliam son of Ahithophel from Giloh;
35 Hezro from Carmel;
Paarai from Arba;
36 Igal son of Nathan from Zobah;
Bani from Gad;

23:8c As in some Greek manuscripts (see also 1 Chr 11:11); the meaning of the Hebrew is uncertain, though it might be rendered *the Three. It was Adino the Eznite who killed 800 men at one time.* 23:12 Hebrew *he.* 23:17 Hebrew *Shall I drink the blood of these men?* 23:18 As in a few Hebrew manuscripts and Syriac version; most Hebrew manuscripts read *the Three.* 23:19 As in Syriac version; Hebrew reads *the Three.* 23:20a Or *son of Jehoiada, son of Ish-hai.* 23:20b Hebrew *two of Ariel.* 23:26 As in parallel text at 1 Chr 11:27 (see also 1 Chr 27:10); Hebrew reads *from Palti.* 23:27 As in some Greek manuscripts (see also 1 Chr 11:29); Hebrew reads *Mebunnai.* 23:29a As in some Hebrew manuscripts (see also 1 Chr 11:30); most Hebrew manuscripts read *Heleb.* 23:29b As in parallel text at 1 Chr 11:31; Hebrew reads *Ittai.* 23:30a As in some Greek manuscripts (see also 1 Chr 11:32); Hebrew reads *Hiddai.* 23:30b Or *from the ravines of Gaash.* 23:33 As in parallel text at 1 Chr 11:34; Hebrew reads *Jonathan, Shammah;* some Greek manuscripts read *Jonathan son of Shammah.*

37 Zelek from Ammon;
  Naharai from Beeroth, the armor bearer
    of Joab son of Zeruiah;
38 Ira from Jattir;
  Gareb from Jattir;
39 Uriah the Hittite.

There were thirty-seven in all.

CHAPTER 24
David Takes a Census

Once again the anger of the LORD burned against Israel, and he caused David to harm them by taking a census. "Go and count the people of Israel and Judah," the LORD told him.

2 So the king said to Joab and the commanders* of the army, "Take a census of all the tribes of Israel—from Dan in the north to Beersheba in the south—so I may know how many people there are."

3 But Joab replied to the king, "May the LORD your God let you live to see a hundred times as many people as there are now! But why, my lord the king, do you want to do this?"

4 But the king insisted that they take the census, so Joab and the commanders of the army went out to count the people of Israel. 5 First they crossed the Jordan and camped at Aroer, south of the town in the valley, in the direction of Gad. Then they went on to Jazer, 6 then to Gilead in the land of Tahtim-hodshi* and to Dan-jaan and around to Sidon. 7 Then they came to the fortress of Tyre, and all the towns of the Hivites and Canaanites. Finally, they went south to Judah* as far as Beersheba.

8 Having gone through the entire land for nine months and twenty days, they returned to Jerusalem. 9 Joab reported the number of people to the king. There were 800,000 capable warriors in Israel who could handle a sword, and 500,000 in Judah.

Judgment for David's Sin

10 But after he had taken the census, David's conscience began to bother him. And he said to the LORD, "I have sinned greatly by taking this census. Please forgive my guilt, LORD, for doing this foolish thing."

11 The next morning the word of the LORD came to the prophet Gad, who was David's seer. This was the message: 12 "Go and say to David, 'This is what the LORD says: I will give you three choices. Choose one of these punishments, and I will inflict it on you.'"

13 So Gad came to David and asked him, "Will you choose three* years of famine throughout your land, three months of fleeing from your enemies, or three days of severe plague throughout your land? Think this over and decide what answer I should give the LORD who sent me."

14 "I'm in a desperate situation!" David replied to Gad. "But let us fall into the hands of the LORD, for his mercy is great. Do not let me fall into human hands."

15 So the LORD sent a plague upon Israel that morning, and it lasted for three days.* A total of 70,000 people died throughout the nation, from Dan in the north to Beersheba in the south. 16 But as the angel was preparing to destroy Jerusalem, the LORD relented and said to the death angel, "Stop! That is enough!" At that moment the angel of the LORD was by the threshing floor of Araunah the Jebusite.

17 When David saw the angel, he said to the LORD, "I am the one who has sinned and done wrong! But these people are as innocent as sheep—what have they done? Let your anger fall against me and my family."

David Builds an Altar

18 That day Gad came to David and said to him, "Go up and build an altar to the LORD on the threshing floor of Araunah the Jebusite."

24:2 As in Greek version (see also 24:4 and 1 Chr 21:2); Hebrew reads *Joab the commander.* 24:6 Greek version reads *to Gilead and to Kadesh in the land of the Hittites.* 24:7 Or *they went to the Negev of Judah.* 24:13 As in Greek version (see also 1 Chr 21:12); Hebrew reads *seven.* 24:15 Hebrew *for the designated time.*

24:10 David sinned again. But notice how sensitive his conscience was; he quickly admitted his failure. David was clearly less than perfect, even now. Yet he was greatly used and deeply loved by God. This reality should encourage all of us. No one is perfect! God never requires perfection; he looks for a humble willingness to accept correction. God's grace is extended to everyone who comes to him without pretense.

24:15-25 Once again, David's sin brought tremendous suffering upon innocent people. Yet David responded properly and brought restitution. The book ends with David at his altar, his fellowship with God restored. We should be aware that the consequences of our sins and disobedience will touch the people around us. This is especially true if we are leaders— whether parents, teachers, or pastors.

[19]So David went up to do what the LORD had commanded him. [20]When Araunah saw the king and his men coming toward him, he came and bowed before the king with his face to the ground. [21]"Why have you come, my lord the king?" Araunah asked.

David replied, "I have come to buy your threshing floor and to build an altar to the LORD there, so that he will stop the plague."

[22]"Take it, my lord the king, and use it as you wish," Araunah said to David. "Here are oxen for the burnt offering, and you can use the threshing boards and ox yokes for wood to build a fire on the altar. [23]I will give it all to you, Your Majesty, and may the LORD your God accept your sacrifice."

[24]But the king replied to Araunah, "No, I insist on buying it, for I will not present burnt offerings to the LORD my God that have cost me nothing." So David paid him fifty pieces of silver* for the threshing floor and the oxen.

[25]David built an altar there to the LORD and sacrificed burnt offerings and peace offerings. And the LORD answered his prayer for the land, and the plague on Israel was stopped.

24:24 Hebrew *50 shekels of silver*, about 20 ounces or 570 grams in weight.

REFLECTIONS ON 2 SAMUEL

insights FROM DAVID'S LIFE

David was anointed king of Israel years before his ascension to the throne. David's crowning in **2 Samuel 5:3-5** is a reminder that God is faithful to his promises. Notice that God's promises to David were not fulfilled right away. He had to wait for many difficult years. Much of that time he was a fugitive without a home or a country. During that time, God supplied David with the help he needed to survive. The recovery process is never easy; it usually takes a lifetime. But God supplies his strength and protection as we continue in recovery.

In his initial attempt at retrieving the Ark, David had failed miserably. So in **2 Samuel 6:12-15**, David turned to the Scriptures to see what God said on the matter. Then he set everything straight, meticulously following God's instructions for moving the Ark. As he and the Israelites moved the Ark in the proper way, they discovered that the formerly terrifying task became an activity full of joy. When we do things God's way, we will discover that even trying situations can become occasions for joy.

David's admission in **2 Samuel 12:9-13**, "I have sinned against the LORD," was the right response to his wrongdoing. It was an acknowledgment of David's accountability before God. Spurred on by Nathan's appeal, he had started the process leading to recovery, which involves confrontation, conviction, confession, and cleansing (Psalm 51). Notice, however, that despite David's humble confession, he would still have to face terrible consequences (12:10-12). Confession only starts the process toward a new life; we still must face the consequences of our past actions. But we can be sure that as we rely on God and build for a productive future, he will help us overcome difficulties arising from the past.

insights FROM AMNON'S RAPE OF TAMAR

The consequences of our mistakes often remain long after they have been forgiven. David had pursued Bathsheba with no thought to the consequences. In **2 Samuel 13:1-2** Amnon pursued an incestuous relationship with his half sister, Tamar. This was an indirect consequence of David's earlier moral failure. Amnon became obsessed with his quest to seduce Tamar, and he satisfied his lust, much as his father had done before him. We must remember that our children learn by watching what we do. Our actions for good or bad may have consequences for future generations.

God has given us many good things to enjoy, but all of them need to be enjoyed in the proper contexts. There is only one right context for sexual intimacy, and that is marriage. God's Word gives us guidelines for having a healthy sexual relationship. God calls us to lives of discipline, delayed gratification, and self-control. Lasting sexual satisfaction can be found only in the context of a committed marriage. In **2 Samuel 13:13** Tamar showed that she was aware of this truth as she tried to escape her attacker by appealing to his reason. Amnon, however, was too obsessed to stop and listen to her.

As we see from **2 Samuel 13:20**, Tamar was left a desolate woman and probably never married. Her situation should remind us of the price paid by people close to those who manifest addictive behavior. Sometimes we try to deny the pain we may have caused others. But recovery demands that we take inventory of the wrongs we have committed and seek to restore our relationships and bring healing to the lives of those we have wronged.

Two years passed after Tamar's rape, but David did nothing about Amnon's sin. David's failure to confront his son and restore family unity planted the seeds of vengeance and murder. As we see in **2 Samuel 13:37-39**, David also allowed three more years to go by without communicating with Absalom, who had avenged his sister's rape by killing Amnon and then fleeing. The result was a broken relationship that grew into a kingdom torn by rebellion. Forgiveness and the restoration of relationships are two primary concerns in recovery. David's disregard for these principles brought painful consequences upon his family and his kingdom.

1 KINGS

THE BIG PICTURE

A. THE UNITED KINGDOM: PRIDE PRECEDES THE FALL (1:1–11:43)
  1. Fulfillment: Going from Good to Great (1:1–2:46)
  2. Greed: Serving Self before God (3:1–8:66)
  3. Denial: Running Away from Reality (9:1–11:43)
B. THE DIVIDED KINGDOM: A NATION SELF-DESTRUCTS (12:1–22:53)
  1. Rebellion: A Failure to "Let Go" (12:1–14:31)
  2. Indecision: An Attitude of Apathy (15:1–16:34)
  3. Recovery: God's Intervention (17:1–19:21)
  4. Refusal: God's Warning Ignored (20:1–22:53)

The book of 1 Kings was originally part of a larger book that also included 2 Kings. It recorded Israel's history from the last days of King David to the demise of the northern and southern kingdoms. As 1 Kings begins, Israel was still one nation under Solomon's rule, and the people were following God. Solomon led the nation to a position of world prominence, and his wisdom became legendary. Kings and queens from foreign lands traveled great distances just to meet him.

But like so many of us, the success of Solomon and the nation led the Israelites to self-sufficiency and pride. They turned their backs on the God who had blessed them so richly. This led to strife and a divided kingdom that was ruled by a series of dysfunctional, corrupt kings. The people wandered from God and began to worship idols, ignoring the laws that God had given them.

Yet throughout this period of prideful rebellion, God continued to reach out to his people. Godly kings like Asa and prophets like Elijah called the people to turn their lives over to God, and some responded. Elijah's confrontation with Ahab and Jezebel was a dramatic example of how God called disobedient kings to account for their actions. Elijah, though a flawed human being, won many great victories for God through faith.

This book is filled with examples of people who trusted God and received his help. It is also filled with accounts of people who disobeyed God and suffered the consequences of their rebellion. But even when the people disobeyed, God never gave up on them. He did everything he could to draw them back into a healthy, vibrant relationship with himself.

THE BOTTOM LINE

PURPOSE: To record the history of Solomon and the early kings of the divided kingdom and to illustrate the blessings of obeying God and the negative consequences of disobeying him. AUTHOR: Unknown; possibly Jeremiah, Ezra, or Ezekiel. AUDIENCE: The people of Israel in Babylonian exile. DATE WRITTEN: Sometime between 560 and 538 B.C. SETTING: The united kingdom of Israel under Solomon; then the kingdoms of Israel and Judah. KEY VERSES: "As for you, if you will follow me with integrity and godliness, as David your father did, obeying all my commands, decrees, and regulations, then I will establish the throne of your dynasty over Israel forever" (9:4-5). KEY PEOPLE: David, Solomon, Rehoboam, Jeroboam, Elijah, Ahab, Jezebel.

RECOVERY THEMES

The Dangers of Success: Solomon achieved everything he could ever have desired—wealth, success, prestige, and power. His life illustrates that success often leads to failure, especially when we claim sole responsibility for our achievements. In recovery, when we think we have it made, we are probably on the way to a fall. In his success, Solomon became proud and stubborn before God. He refused to hear the warnings God gave him and later suffered the consequences (see 11:9-11).

Dysfunction across Generations: David's weakness with women became a weakness in Solomon. Solomon set no boundaries on his sexual behavior. As dysfunctions cross over into the next generation, they are often intensified and become even more destructive. In David's case, his sin with Bathsheba led to painful consequences within his family. In Solomon's case, his lust for women resulted in his marrying many foreign wives who led him into idolatry. This ultimately led his people away from God, affecting the whole nation of Israel.

Our Vulnerability to Relapse: We are often the most vulnerable to relapse when life is going well. Solomon's experience illustrates this truth. He was warned by God on several occasions, but because everything in his life was going so well, he didn't listen. He began to think he was beyond needing to take regular inventory of his life. Perhaps he believed he could do fine without God's help. One thing is guaranteed: "Pride goes before destruction, and haughtiness before a fall" (Proverbs 16:18).

The Importance of Accountability: Recovery is impossible without God's help. Each of us needs to be accountable to someone who will be honest with us. Such a person will confront us and help us see where potential problems are lurking. When Solomon stopped listening to God, no one could get his attention. The same was true of the kings who followed him—they were accountable to no one. They were too proud to listen to God's word to them through the prophets. The result was sin and failure in their lives, which led to sin among their people. We would be wise to humble ourself and be open to wise counsel.

CHAPTER 1
David in His Old Age

King David was now very old, and no matter how many blankets covered him, he could not keep warm. [2]So his advisers told him, "Let us find a young virgin to wait on you and look after you, my lord. She will lie in your arms and keep you warm."

[3]So they searched throughout the land of Israel for a beautiful girl, and they found Abishag from Shunem and brought her to the king. [4]The girl was very beautiful, and she looked after the king and took care of him. But the king had no sexual relations with her.

Adonijah Claims the Throne

[5]About that time David's son Adonijah, whose mother was Haggith, began boasting, "I will make myself king." So he provided himself with chariots and charioteers and recruited fifty men to run in front of him.

[6]Now his father, King David, had never disciplined him at any time, even by asking, "Why are you doing that?" Adonijah had been born next after Absalom, and he was very handsome.

[7]Adonijah took Joab son of Zeruiah and Abiathar the priest into his confidence, and they agreed to help him become king. [8]But Zadok the priest, Benaiah son of Jehoiada, Nathan the prophet, Shimei, Rei, and David's personal bodyguard refused to support Adonijah.

[9]Adonijah went to the Stone of Zoheleth* near the spring of En-rogel, where he sacrificed sheep, cattle, and fattened calves. He invited all his brothers—the other sons of King David—and all the royal officials of Judah. [10]But he did not invite Nathan the prophet or Benaiah or the king's bodyguard or his brother Solomon.

[11]Then Nathan went to Bathsheba, Solo-

1:9 Or *to the Serpent's Stone;* Greek version supports reading *Zoheleth* as a proper name.

1:5-6 This conflict between Adonijah and Solomon was one result of King David's earlier mistakes. We are told here that David had never disciplined his son Adonijah. David's failure as a father led to several conflicts among his sons. Solomon was the son of David and Bathsheba, whose relationship began with adultery, deceit, and murder. Despite the painful start of their relationship, Bathsheba became David's favorite wife, and he appointed their son Solomon to be king. It is interesting that God used David's many failures to work his divine will for Israel. Solomon became the wisest and most powerful of all of Israel's kings. We have all made mistakes. As we seek recovery, we can trust God to take our life—good aspects and bad—and make something good out of it.

mon's mother, and asked her, "Haven't you heard that Haggith's son, Adonijah, has made himself king, and our lord David doesn't even know about it? [12]If you want to save your own life and the life of your son Solomon, follow my advice. [13]Go at once to King David and say to him, 'My lord the king, didn't you make a vow and say to me, "Your son Solomon will surely be the next king and will sit on my throne"? Why then has Adonijah become king?' [14]And while you are still talking with him, I will come and confirm everything you have said."

[15]So Bathsheba went into the king's bedroom. (He was very old now, and Abishag was taking care of him.) [16]Bathsheba bowed down before the king.

"What can I do for you?" he asked her.

[17]She replied, "My lord, you made a vow before the LORD your God when you said to me, 'Your son Solomon will surely be the next king and will sit on my throne.' [18]But instead, Adonijah has made himself king, and my lord the king does not even know about it. [19]He has sacrificed many cattle, fattened calves, and sheep, and he has invited all the king's sons to attend the celebration. He also invited Abiathar the priest and Joab, the commander of the army. But he did not invite your servant Solomon. [20]And now, my lord the king, all Israel is waiting for you to announce who will become king after you. [21]If you do not act, my son Solomon and I will be treated as criminals as soon as my lord the king has died."

[22]While she was still speaking with the king, Nathan the prophet arrived. [23]The king's officials told him, "Nathan the prophet is here to see you."

Nathan went in and bowed before the king with his face to the ground. [24]Nathan asked, "My lord the king, have you decided that Adonijah will be the next king and that he will sit on your throne? [25]Today he has sacrificed many cattle, fattened calves, and sheep, and he has invited all the king's sons to attend the celebration. He also invited the commanders of the army and Abiathar the priest. They are feasting and drinking with him and shouting, 'Long live King Adonijah!' [26]But he did not invite me or Zadok the priest or Benaiah or your servant

Solomon. [27]Has my lord the king really done this without letting any of his officials know who should be the next king?"

David Makes Solomon King

[28]King David responded, "Call Bathsheba!" So she came back in and stood before the king. [29]And the king repeated his vow: "As surely as the LORD lives, who has rescued me from every danger, [30]your son Solomon will be the next king and will sit on my throne this very day, just as I vowed to you before the LORD, the God of Israel."

[31]Then Bathsheba bowed down with her face to the ground before the king and exclaimed, "May my lord King David live forever!"

[32]Then King David ordered, "Call Zadok the priest, Nathan the prophet, and Benaiah son of Jehoiada." When they came into the king's presence, [33]the king said to them, "Take Solomon and my officials down to Gihon Spring. Solomon is to ride on my own mule. [34]There Zadok the priest and Nathan the prophet are to anoint him king over Israel. Blow the ram's horn and shout, 'Long live King Solomon!' [35]Then escort him back here, and he will sit on my throne. He will succeed me as king, for I have appointed him to be ruler over Israel and Judah."

[36]"Amen!" Benaiah son of Jehoiada replied. "May the LORD, the God of my lord the king, decree that it happen. [37]And may the LORD be with Solomon as he has been with you, my lord the king, and may he make Solomon's reign even greater than yours!"

[38]So Zadok the priest, Nathan the prophet, Benaiah son of Jehoiada, and the king's bodyguard* took Solomon down to Gihon Spring, with Solomon riding on King David's own mule. [39]There Zadok the priest took the flask of olive oil from the sacred tent and anointed Solomon with the oil. Then they sounded the ram's horn and all the people shouted, "Long live King Solomon!" [40]And all the people followed Solomon into Jerusalem, playing flutes and shouting for joy. The celebration was so joyous and noisy that the earth shook with the sound.

[41]Adonijah and his guests heard the celebrating and shouting just as they were

1:38 Hebrew *the Kerethites and Pelethites;* also in 1:44.

1:28-40 Nathan the prophet and Zadok the priest anointed Solomon king under the orders of King David. David realized that he was going to die soon and took care of his responsibility to secure the throne for Solomon. Unwisely, many of us put off the task of providing for the future of our family. Planning for the inevitability of death is not being morbid; it is part of being responsible.

finishing their banquet. When Joab heard the sound of the ram's horn, he asked, "What's going on? Why is the city in such an uproar?"

⁴²And while he was still speaking, Jonathan son of Abiathar the priest arrived. "Come in," Adonijah said to him, "for you are a good man. You must have good news."

⁴³"Not at all!" Jonathan replied. "Our lord King David has just declared Solomon king! ⁴⁴The king sent him down to Gihon Spring with Zadok the priest, Nathan the prophet, and Benaiah son of Jehoiada, protected by the king's bodyguard. They had him ride on the king's own mule, ⁴⁵and Zadok and Nathan have anointed him at Gihon Spring as the new king. They have just returned, and the whole city is celebrating and rejoicing. That's what all the noise is about. ⁴⁶What's more, Solomon is now sitting on the royal throne as king. ⁴⁷And all the royal officials have gone to King David and congratulated him, saying, 'May your God make Solomon's fame even greater than your own, and may Solomon's reign be even greater than yours!' Then the king bowed his head in worship as he lay in his bed, ⁴⁸and he said, 'Praise the LORD, the God of Israel, who today has chosen a successor to sit on my throne while I am still alive to see it.'"

⁴⁹Then all of Adonijah's guests jumped up in panic from the banquet table and quickly scattered. ⁵⁰Adonijah was afraid of Solomon, so he rushed to the sacred tent and grabbed on to the horns of the altar. ⁵¹Word soon reached Solomon that Adonijah had seized the horns of the altar in fear, and that he was pleading, "Let King Solomon swear today that he will not kill me!"

⁵²Solomon replied, "If he proves himself to be loyal, not a hair on his head will be touched. But if he makes trouble, he will die." ⁵³So King Solomon summoned Adonijah, and they brought him down from the altar. He came and bowed respectfully before King Solomon, who dismissed him, saying, "Go on home."

CHAPTER 2
David's Final Instructions to Solomon

As the time of King David's death approached, he gave this charge to his son Solomon:

²"I am going where everyone on earth must someday go. Take courage and be a man. ³Observe the requirements of the LORD your God, and follow all his ways. Keep the decrees, commands, regulations, and laws written in the Law of Moses so that you will be successful in all you do and wherever you go. ⁴If you do this, then the LORD will keep the promise he made to me. He told me, 'If your descendants live as they should and follow me faithfully with all their heart and soul, one of them will always sit on the throne of Israel.'

⁵"And there is something else. You know what Joab son of Zeruiah did to me when he murdered my two army commanders, Abner son of Ner and Amasa son of Jether. He pretended that it was an act of war, but it was done in a time of peace,* staining his belt and sandals with innocent blood.* ⁶Do with

2:5a Or *He murdered them during a time of peace as revenge for deaths they had caused in time of war.* 2:5b As in some Greek and Old Latin manuscripts; Hebrew reads *with the blood of war.*

1:41-53 Adonijah, as David's oldest living son, expected to take Israel's throne and, for a few hours, apparently held the kingship. When Solomon finally gained control, it was expected that he would kill his rival. But Solomon showed great mercy and forgiveness to Adonijah. He gave Adonijah a chance to prove whether or not he was worthy of forgiveness. When we are attacked at a personal level, it is natural to seek revenge. Granting forgiveness demands great strength of character. We need to turn our revenge over to God; failing to forgive will only slow the recovery process.

2:1-12 David instructed his son Solomon how to rule and whom to trust. David advised his son to keep his eyes on God. Solomon learned who his allies and enemies were. As parents, we need to sit down and talk with our children, just as David did with Solomon. This will increase our children's respect for us and help equip them to face the challenges ahead.

2:13-25 Adonijah again plotted to take the throne by asking that Solomon allow him to marry David's nurse, Abishag. In ancient times, sleeping with one of the king's wives was tantamount to making a claim to the throne. Bathsheba was apparently unaware of Adonijah's plot and took his request to Solomon. But Solomon understood the true nature of Adonijah's request and ordered his execution, fulfilling his earlier promise (1:52). Solomon showed strength by living up to his previous promise. Likewise, we need to live up to any promises we make. This will help us maintain the boundaries we have set and protect our interests and the interests of the people we are responsible for.

SOLOMON

Our society and the "American dream" are built on a strong work ethic: The harder we work, the greater our chances for success. But if unchecked, the positive work ethic can deteriorate into workaholism— devoting all our time to the job, perhaps even becoming "addicted" to work. We sacrifice healthy family relationships, friendships, and our spiritual life just to achieve more and advance in our profession.

Following the death of King David, Solomon became king of Israel. Solomon faced several revolts early in his reign, but he soon consolidated his power base and took firm control over his kingdom. Then God promised to give Solomon anything he desired; Solomon chose wisdom so he could rule his people wisely. God was pleased with Solomon's selfless choice, so he gave this young king honor, wealth, and a long life in addition to the wisdom he requested.

Solomon became a workaholic. He started by building the Temple. Then he built his palace and fortified his country against intruders. All of these projects were done on an enormous scale, even by today's standards. In order to accomplish these tasks, Solomon sacrificed important relationships with his people, his family, and his God. He taxed his people heavily and required them to work hard on his building projects. He failed to teach his son Rehoboam how to use wisdom to rule the people. He also stopped listening to God and disobeyed him by marrying numerous pagan women and by worshiping their gods.

In our busyness with work and achievements, it is easy to forget the source of our strengths and successes. We must remember that God is the top priority in our life, followed by our family. Whenever anything else is placed above these, we sacrifice everything and are headed for trouble.

STRENGTHS AND ACCOMPLISHMENTS:
- Solomon was the wisest man who ever lived.
- He passed his wisdom on by writing numerous proverbs and psalms.
- He built God's Temple in Jerusalem.
- He completed many difficult long-term projects.

WEAKNESSES AND MISTAKES:
- Solomon compromised his relationship with God by marrying foreign women.
- He worshiped the gods of his foreign wives.
- He placed loyalty to his work above loyalty to God.
- He drained the people of their resources in order to achieve his goals.

LESSONS FROM HIS LIFE:
- If we reject God's plan, we will fail no matter how much practical wisdom we have.
- Obedience to God is the beginning of personal success.
- We must do what we can to encourage our children to establish a relationship with God.

KEY VERSE:
"'Wasn't this exactly what led King Solomon of Israel into sin?' I demanded. 'There was no king from any nation who could compare to him, and God loved him and made him king over all Israel. But even he was led into sin by his foreign wives'" (Nehemiah 13:26).

Solomon's story is told in 2 Samuel 12:24; 1 Kings 1—11; 1 Chronicles 28—2 Chronicles 10. He is also mentioned in Nehemiah 13:26; Matthew 6:29; 12:42.

---

him what you think best, but don't let him grow old and go to his grave in peace.*

⁷"Be kind to the sons of Barzillai of Gilead. Make them permanent guests at your table, for they took care of me when I fled from your brother Absalom.

⁸"And remember Shimei son of Gera, the man from Bahurim in Benjamin. He cursed me with a terrible curse as I was fleeing to Mahanaim. When he came down to meet me at the Jordan River, I swore by the LORD that I would not kill him. ⁹But that oath does not make him innocent. You are a wise man, and

you will know how to arrange a bloody death for him.*"

¹⁰Then David died and was buried with his ancestors in the City of David. ¹¹David had reigned over Israel for forty years, seven of them in Hebron and thirty-three in Jerusalem. ¹²Solomon became king and sat on the throne of David his father, and his kingdom was firmly established.

Solomon Establishes His Rule

¹³One day Adonijah, whose mother was Haggith, came to see Bathsheba, Solomon's

2:6 Hebrew *don't let his white head go down to Sheol in peace.* **2:9** Hebrew *how to bring his white head down to Sheol in blood.*

mother. "Have you come with peaceful intentions?" she asked him.

"Yes," he said, "I come in peace. [14]In fact, I have a favor to ask of you."

"What is it?" she asked.

[15]He replied, "As you know, the kingdom was rightfully mine; all Israel wanted me to be the next king. But the tables were turned, and the kingdom went to my brother instead; for that is the way the LORD wanted it. [16]So now I have just one favor to ask of you. Please don't turn me down."

"What is it?" she asked.

[17]He replied, "Speak to King Solomon on my behalf, for I know he will do anything you request. Ask him to let me marry Abishag, the girl from Shunem."

[18]"All right," Bathsheba replied. "I will speak to the king for you."

[19]So Bathsheba went to King Solomon to speak on Adonijah's behalf. The king rose from his throne to meet her, and he bowed down before her. When he sat down on his throne again, the king ordered that a throne be brought for his mother, and she sat at his right hand.

[20]"I have one small request to make of you," she said. "I hope you won't turn me down."

"What is it, my mother?" he asked. "You know I won't refuse you."

[21]"Then let your brother Adonijah marry Abishag, the girl from Shunem," she replied.

[22]"How can you possibly ask me to give Abishag to Adonijah?" King Solomon demanded. "You might as well ask me to give him the kingdom! You know that he is my older brother, and that he has Abiathar the priest and Joab son of Zeruiah on his side."

[23]Then King Solomon made a vow before the LORD: "May God strike me and even kill me if Adonijah has not sealed his fate with this request. [24]The LORD has confirmed me and placed me on the throne of my father, David; he has established my dynasty as he promised. So as surely as the LORD lives, Adonijah will die this very day!" [25]So King Solomon ordered Benaiah son of Jehoiada to execute him, and Adonijah was put to death.

[26]Then the king said to Abiathar the priest,

"Go back to your home in Anathoth. You deserve to die, but I will not kill you now, because you carried the Ark of the Sovereign LORD for David my father and you shared all his hardships." [27]So Solomon deposed Abiathar from his position as priest of the LORD, thereby fulfilling the prophecy the LORD had given at Shiloh concerning the descendants of Eli.

[28]Joab had not joined Absalom's earlier rebellion, but he had joined Adonijah's rebellion. So when Joab heard about Adonijah's death, he ran to the sacred tent of the LORD and grabbed on to the horns of the altar. [29]When this was reported to King Solomon, he sent Benaiah son of Jehoiada to execute him.

[30]Benaiah went to the sacred tent of the LORD and said to Joab, "The king orders you to come out!"

But Joab answered, "No, I will die here."

So Benaiah returned to the king and told him what Joab had said.

[31]"Do as he said," the king replied. "Kill him there beside the altar and bury him. This will remove the guilt of Joab's senseless murders from me and from my father's family. [32]The LORD will repay him* for the murders of two men who were more righteous and better than he. For my father knew nothing about the deaths of Abner son of Ner, commander of the army of Israel, and of Amasa son of Jether, commander of the army of Judah. [33]May their blood be on Joab and his descendants forever, and may the LORD grant peace forever to David, his descendants, his dynasty, and his throne."

[34]So Benaiah son of Jehoiada returned to the sacred tent and killed Joab, and he was buried at his home in the wilderness. [35]Then the king appointed Benaiah to command the army in place of Joab, and he installed Zadok the priest to take the place of Abiathar.

[36]The king then sent for Shimei and told him, "Build a house here in Jerusalem and live there. But don't step outside the city to go anywhere else. [37]On the day you so much as cross the Kidron Valley, you will surely die; and your blood will be on your own head."

[38]Shimei replied, "Your sentence is fair; I

2:32 Hebrew *will return his blood on his own head.*

2:26-46 Solomon showed respect for his father's wisdom by having Joab and Shimei killed. Two things were accomplished by these deaths: (1) David's name was cleared of the wicked acts committed by these men; (2) Solomon cleared his kingdom of the enemies within. We all have enemies in our life—addictions, unforgiveness, guilt. These need to be completely removed if we want to recover and prosper.

will do whatever my lord the king commands." So Shimei lived in Jerusalem for a long time.

[39]But three years later two of Shimei's slaves ran away to King Achish son of Maacah of Gath. When Shimei learned where they were, [40]he saddled his donkey and went to Gath to search for them. When he found them, he brought them back to Jerusalem.

[41]Solomon heard that Shimei had left Jerusalem and had gone to Gath and returned. [42]So the king sent for Shimei and demanded, "Didn't I make you swear by the LORD and warn you not to go anywhere else or you would surely die? And you replied, 'The sentence is fair; I will do as you say.' [43]Then why haven't you kept your oath to the LORD and obeyed my command?"

[44]The king also said to Shimei, "You certainly remember all the wicked things you did to my father, David. May the LORD now bring that evil on your own head. [45]But may I, King Solomon, receive the LORD's blessings, and may one of David's descendants always sit on this throne in the presence of the LORD." [46]Then, at the king's command, Benaiah son of Jehoiada took Shimei outside and killed him.

So the kingdom was now firmly in Solomon's grip.

CHAPTER 3
Solomon Asks for Wisdom

Solomon made an alliance with Pharaoh, the king of Egypt, and married one of his daughters. He brought her to live in the City of David until he could finish building his palace and the Temple of the LORD and the wall around the city. [2]At that time the people of Israel sacrificed their offerings at local places of worship, for a temple honoring the name of the LORD had not yet been built.

[3]Solomon loved the LORD and followed all the decrees of his father, David, except that Solomon, too, offered sacrifices and burned incense at the local places of worship. [4]The most important of these places of worship was at Gibeon, so the king went there and sacrificed 1,000 burnt offerings. [5]That night the LORD appeared to Solomon in a dream, and God said, "What do you want? Ask, and I will give it to you!"

[6]Solomon replied, "You showed great and faithful love to your servant my father, David, because he was honest and true and faithful to you. And you have continued to show this great and faithful love to him today by giving him a son to sit on his throne.

[7]"Now, O LORD my God, you have made me king instead of my father, David, but I am like a little child who doesn't know his way around. [8]And here I am in the midst of your own chosen people, a nation so great and numerous they cannot be counted! [9]Give me an understanding heart so that I can govern your people well and know the difference between right and wrong. For who by himself is able to govern this great people of yours?"

[10]The Lord was pleased that Solomon had asked for wisdom. [11]So God replied, "Because you have asked for wisdom in governing my people with justice and have not asked for a long life or wealth or the death of your enemies—[12]I will give you what you asked for! I will give you a wise and understanding heart such as no one else has had or ever will have! [13]And I will also give you what you did not ask for—riches and fame! No other king in all the world will be compared to you for the rest of your life! [14]And if you follow me and obey my decrees and my commands as your father, David, did, I will give you a long life."

[15]Then Solomon woke up and realized it had been a dream. He returned to Jerusalem and stood before the Ark of the Lord's Covenant, where he sacrificed burnt offerings and peace offerings. Then he invited all his officials to a great banquet.

Solomon Judges Wisely

[16]Some time later two prostitutes came to the king to have an argument settled. [17]"Please, my lord," one of them began, "this woman and I live in the same house. I gave birth to a

---

3:3-15 God approached Solomon in a dream and told him he could have anything he wanted. Solomon asked for wisdom and discernment so he could rule his people well. God was pleased with Solomon and granted him his wish, adding to it wealth and honor. Solomon put his concern for his people before the fulfillment of his own desires. His selfless attitude brought him blessings beyond belief. Often the road to personal blessing is a life lived selflessly for others.

3:16-28 Solomon was put in a difficult situation. Two women claimed to be the mother of the same child. Obviously one of the women was lying, but which one? This was a major test for Solomon's wisdom. Solomon handled the situation wisely, and the child was returned to his real mother. Solomon had been given the special gift of wisdom to maintain peace in his kingdom. We all have gifts to offer others and need to use these gifts to the best of our ability.

baby while she was with me in the house. [18]Three days later this woman also had a baby. We were alone; there were only two of us in the house.

[19]"But her baby died during the night when she rolled over on it. [20]Then she got up in the night and took my son from beside me while I was asleep. She laid her dead child in my arms and took mine to sleep beside her. [21]And in the morning when I tried to nurse my son, he was dead! But when I looked more closely in the morning light, I saw that it wasn't my son at all."

[22]Then the other woman interrupted, "It certainly was your son, and the living child is mine."

"No," the first woman said, "the living child is mine, and the dead one is yours." And so they argued back and forth before the king.

[23]Then the king said, "Let's get the facts straight. Both of you claim the living child is yours, and each says that the dead one belongs to the other. [24]All right, bring me a sword." So a sword was brought to the king.

[25]Then he said, "Cut the living child in two, and give half to one woman and half to the other!"

[26]Then the woman who was the real mother of the living child, and who loved him very much, cried out, "Oh no, my lord! Give her the child—please do not kill him!"

But the other woman said, "All right, he will be neither yours nor mine; divide him between us!"

[27]Then the king said, "Do not kill the child, but give him to the woman who wants him to live, for she is his mother!"

[28]When all Israel heard the king's decision, the people were in awe of the king, for they saw the wisdom God had given him for rendering justice.

CHAPTER 4
Solomon's Officials and Governors

King Solomon now ruled over all Israel, [2]and these were his high officials:

Azariah son of Zadok was the priest.
[3] Elihoreph and Ahijah, the sons of Shisha, were court secretaries.
Jehoshaphat son of Ahilud was the royal historian.
[4] Benaiah son of Jehoiada was commander of the army.

Zadok and Abiathar were priests.
[5]Azariah son of Nathan was in charge of the district governors.
Zabud son of Nathan, a priest, was a trusted adviser to the king.
[6] Ahishar was manager of the palace property.
Adoniram son of Abda was in charge of forced labor.

[7]Solomon also had twelve district governors who were over all Israel. They were responsible for providing food for the king's household. Each of them arranged provisions for one month of the year. [8]These are the names of the twelve governors:

Ben-hur, in the hill country of Ephraim.
[9] Ben-deker, in Makaz, Shaalbim, Beth-shemesh, and Elon-bethhanan.
[10] Ben-hesed, in Arubboth, including Socoh and all the land of Hepher.
[11] Ben-abinadab, in all of Naphoth-dor.* (He was married to Taphath, one of Solomon's daughters.)
[12] Baana son of Ahilud, in Taanach and Megiddo, all of Beth-shan* near Zarethan below Jezreel, and all the territory from Beth-shan to Abel-meholah and over to Jokmeam.
[13] Ben-geber, in Ramoth-gilead, including the Towns of Jair (named for Jair of the tribe of Manasseh*) in Gilead, and in the Argob region of Bashan, including sixty large fortified towns with bronze bars on their gates.
[14] Ahinadab son of Iddo, in Mahanaim.
[15] Ahimaaz, in Naphtali. (He was married to Basemath, another of Solomon's daughters.)
[16] Baana son of Hushai, in Asher and in Aloth.
[17] Jehoshaphat son of Paruah, in Issachar.
[18] Shimei son of Ela, in Benjamin.
[19] Geber son of Uri, in the land of Gilead,* including the territories of King Sihon of the Amorites and King Og of Bashan.
There was also one governor over the land of Judah.*

Solomon's Prosperity and Wisdom

[20]The people of Judah and Israel were as numerous as the sand on the seashore. They were very contented, with plenty to eat and

4:11 Hebrew *Naphath-dor,* a variant spelling of Naphoth-dor. 4:12 Hebrew *Beth-shean,* a variant spelling of Beth-shan; also in 4:12b. 4:13 Hebrew *Jair son of Manasseh;* compare 1 Chr 2:22. 4:19a Greek version reads *of Gad;* compare 4:13. 4:19b As in some Greek manuscripts; Hebrew lacks *of Judah.* The meaning of the Hebrew is uncertain.

drink. ²¹*Solomon ruled over all the kingdoms from the Euphrates River* in the north to the land of the Philistines and the border of Egypt in the south. The conquered peoples of those lands sent tribute money to Solomon and continued to serve him throughout his lifetime.

²²The daily food requirements for Solomon's palace were 150 bushels of choice flour and 300 bushels of meal*; ²³also 10 oxen from the fattening pens, 20 pasture-fed cattle, 100 sheep or goats, as well as deer, gazelles, roe deer, and choice poultry.*

²⁴Solomon's dominion extended over all the kingdoms west of the Euphrates River, from Tiphsah to Gaza. And there was peace on all his borders. ²⁵During the lifetime of Solomon, all of Judah and Israel lived in peace and safety. And from Dan in the north to Beersheba in the south, each family had its own home and garden.*

²⁶Solomon had 4,000* stalls for his chariot horses, and he had 12,000 horses.*

²⁷The district governors faithfully provided food for King Solomon and his court; each made sure nothing was lacking during the month assigned to him. ²⁸They also brought the necessary barley and straw for the royal horses in the stables.

²⁹God gave Solomon very great wisdom and understanding, and knowledge as vast as the sands of the seashore. ³⁰In fact, his wisdom exceeded that of all the wise men of the East and the wise men of Egypt. ³¹He was wiser than anyone else, including Ethan the Ezrahite and the sons of Mahol—Heman, Calcol, and Darda. His fame spread throughout all the surrounding nations. ³²He composed some 3,000 proverbs and wrote 1,005 songs. ³³He could speak with authority about all kinds of plants, from the great cedar of Lebanon to the tiny hyssop that grows from cracks in a wall. He could also speak about animals, birds, small creatures, and fish. ³⁴And kings from every nation sent their ambassadors to listen to the wisdom of Solomon.

CHAPTER 5
Preparations for Building the Temple

¹*King Hiram of Tyre had always been a loyal friend of David. When Hiram learned that David's son Solomon was the new king of Israel, he sent ambassadors to congratulate him.

²Then Solomon sent this message back to Hiram:

³"You know that my father, David, was not able to build a Temple to honor the name of the LORD his God because of the many wars waged against him by surrounding nations. He could not build until the LORD gave him victory over all his enemies. ⁴But now the LORD my God has given me peace on every side; I have no enemies, and all is well. ⁵So I am planning to build a Temple to honor the name of the LORD my God, just as he had instructed my father, David. For the LORD told him, 'Your son, whom I will place on your throne, will build the Temple to honor my name.'

⁶"Therefore, please command that cedars from Lebanon be cut for me. Let my men work alongside yours, and I will pay your men whatever wages you ask. As you know, there is no one among us who can cut timber like you Sidonians!"

⁷When Hiram received Solomon's message, he was very pleased and said, "Praise

---

4:21a Verses 4:21-34 are numbered 5:1-14 in Hebrew text. 4:21b Hebrew *the river;* also in 4:24. 4:22 Hebrew *30 cors* [6.6 kiloliters] *of choice flour and 60 cors* [13.2 kiloliters] *of meal.* 4:23 Or *and fattened geese.* 4:25 Hebrew *each family lived under its own grapevine and under its own fig tree.* 4:26a As in some Greek manuscripts (see also 2 Chr 9:25); Hebrew reads *40,000.* 4:26b Or *12,000 charioteers.* 5:1 Verses 5:1-18 are numbered 5:15-32 in Hebrew text.

4:29-34 Teaching others what we know is one of the greatest gifts we can offer others. Solomon had been given wisdom by God (3:11-12). Instead of being "puffed up" at this point in his life, he chose to share his wealth of knowledge with others. People came from other countries to listen and learn from the wisdom God had given Solomon. All of us in recovery have been "gifted" with a special kind of knowledge. We know the guilt of failure, along with tidbits of wisdom for recovery. We can share our experiences and victories with others, helping them make the journey with us.
5:1-12 The benefits of a strong relationship can reach even beyond death. King David had established a sound relationship with Hiram of Tyre. Solomon continued that relationship and enjoyed its numerous benefits. Solomon's great building projects could never have been achieved alone. Hiram provided some of the expertise and many of the materials needed. God may have chosen people to encourage us and provide us with resources we need for recovery. We need to allow God to use these people in our life.

the LORD today for giving David a wise son to be king of the great nation of Israel." [8]Then he sent this reply to Solomon:

"I have received your message, and I will supply all the cedar and cypress timber you need. [9]My servants will bring the logs from the Lebanon mountains to the Mediterranean Sea* and make them into rafts and float them along the coast to whatever place you choose. Then we will break the rafts apart so you can carry the logs away. You can pay me by supplying me with food for my household."

[10]So Hiram supplied as much cedar and cypress timber as Solomon desired. [11]In return, Solomon sent him an annual payment of 100,000 bushels* of wheat for his household and 110,000 gallons* of pure olive oil. [12]So the LORD gave wisdom to Solomon, just as he had promised. And Hiram and Solomon made a formal alliance of peace.

[13]Then King Solomon conscripted a labor force of 30,000 men from all Israel. [14]He sent them to Lebanon in shifts, 10,000 every month, so that each man would be one month in Lebanon and two months at home. Adoniram was in charge of this labor force. [15]Solomon also had 70,000 common laborers, 80,000 quarry workers in the hill country, [16]and 3,600* foremen to supervise the work. [17]At the king's command, they quarried large blocks of high-quality stone and shaped them to make the foundation of the Temple. [18]Men from the city of Gebal helped Solomon's and Hiram's builders prepare the timber and stone for the Temple.

CHAPTER 6
Solomon Builds the Temple

It was in midspring, in the month of Ziv,* during the fourth year of Solomon's reign, that he began to construct the Temple of the LORD. This was 480 years after the people of Israel were rescued from their slavery in the land of Egypt.

[2]The Temple that King Solomon built for the LORD was 90 feet long, 30 feet wide, and 45 feet high.* [3]The entry room at the front of the Temple was 30 feet* wide, running across the entire width of the Temple. It projected outward 15 feet* from the front of the Temple. [4]Solomon also made narrow recessed windows throughout the Temple.

[5]He built a complex of rooms against the outer walls of the Temple, all the way around the sides and rear of the building. [6]The complex was three stories high, the bottom floor being 7½ feet wide, the second floor 9 feet wide, and the top floor 10½ feet wide.* The rooms were connected to the walls of the Temple by beams resting on ledges built out from the wall. So the beams were not inserted into the walls themselves.

[7]The stones used in the construction of the Temple were finished at the quarry, so there was no sound of hammer, ax, or any other iron tool at the building site.

[8]The entrance to the bottom floor* was on the south side of the Temple. There were winding stairs going up to the second floor, and another flight of stairs between the second and third floors. [9]After completing the Temple structure, Solomon put in a ceiling made of cedar beams and planks. [10]As already

---

5:9 Hebrew *the sea.* 5:11a Hebrew *20,000 cors* [4,400 kiloliters]. 5:11b As in Greek version, which reads *20,000 baths* [420 kiloliters] (see also 2 Chr 2:10); Hebrew reads *20 cors,* about 1,000 gallons or 4.4 kiloliters in volume. 5:16 As in some Greek manuscripts (see also 2 Chr 2:2, 18); Hebrew reads *3,300.* 6:1 Hebrew *It was in the month of Ziv, which is the second month.* This month of the ancient Hebrew lunar calendar usually occurs within the months of April and May. 6:2 Hebrew *60 cubits* [27.6 meters] *long, 20 cubits* [9.2 meters] *wide, and 30 cubits* [13.8 meters] *high.* 6:3a Hebrew *20 cubits* [9.2 meters]; also in 6:16, 20. 6:3b Hebrew *10 cubits* [4.6 meters]. 6:6 Hebrew *the bottom floor being 5 cubits* [2.3 meters] *wide, the second floor 6 cubits* [2.8 meters] *wide, and the top floor 7 cubits* [3.2 meters] *wide.* 6:8 As in Greek version; Hebrew reads *middle floor.*

5:13-14 It is necessary to set priorities in life. Solomon recognized this when he set up laborers' shifts of one month at work and two months at home (5:14). This schedule showed that Solomon placed great importance on the family. Whenever we set up schedules at work, home, and church, we need to examine the impact those schedules have on our family. Too often we strive for material things and lose what is much more precious—wonderful memories and warm family relationships.

6:1-10 Respect for God is of primary importance in a relationship with him. Solomon showed respect for God in the great amount of detail that was taken to design the Temple. No construction sounds were heard at the site of the Temple in order to show God respect (6:7). Solomon and the people worked painstakingly to accomplish this task. How willing are we to show God the respect he deserves? We need to make God our first priority rather than put him on a long list of obligations.

stated, he built a complex of rooms along the sides of the building, attached to the Temple walls by cedar timbers. Each story of the complex was 7½ feet* high.

[11]Then the LORD gave this message to Solomon: [12]"Concerning this Temple you are building, if you keep all my decrees and regulations and obey all my commands, I will fulfill through you the promise I made to your father, David. [13]I will live among the Israelites and will never abandon my people Israel."

The Temple's Interior

[14]So Solomon finished building the Temple. [15]The entire inside, from floor to ceiling, was paneled with wood. He paneled the walls and ceilings with cedar, and he used planks of cypress for the floors. [16]He partitioned off an inner sanctuary—the Most Holy Place—at the far end of the Temple. It was 30 feet deep and was paneled with cedar from floor to ceiling. [17]The main room of the Temple, outside the Most Holy Place, was 60 feet* long. [18]Cedar paneling completely covered the stone walls throughout the Temple, and the paneling was decorated with carvings of gourds and open flowers.

[19]He prepared the inner sanctuary at the far end of the Temple, where the Ark of the LORD's Covenant would be placed. [20]This inner sanctuary was 30 feet long, 30 feet wide, and 30 feet high. He overlaid the inside with solid gold. He also overlaid the altar made of cedar.* [21]Then Solomon overlaid the rest of the Temple's interior with solid gold, and he made gold chains to protect the entrance* to the Most Holy Place. [22]So he finished overlaying the entire Temple with gold, including the altar that belonged to the Most Holy Place.

[23]He made two cherubim of wild olive* wood, each 15 feet* tall, and placed them in the inner sanctuary. [24]The wingspan of each of the cherubim was 15 feet, each wing being 7½ feet* long. [25]The two cherubim were identical in shape and size; [26]each was 15 feet tall. [27]He placed them side by side in the inner sanctuary of the Temple. Their outspread wings reached from wall to wall, while their inner wings touched at the center of the room. [28]He overlaid the two cherubim with gold.

[29]He decorated all the walls of the inner sanctuary and the main room with carvings of cherubim, palm trees, and open flowers. [30]He overlaid the floor in both rooms with gold.

[31]For the entrance to the inner sanctuary, he made double doors of wild olive wood with five-sided doorposts.* [32]These double doors were decorated with carvings of cherubim, palm trees, and open flowers. The doors, including the decorations of cherubim and palm trees, were overlaid with gold.

[33]Then he made four-sided doorposts of wild olive wood for the entrance to the Temple. [34]There were two folding doors of cypress wood, and each door was hinged to fold back upon itself. [35]These doors were decorated with carvings of cherubim, palm trees, and open flowers—all overlaid evenly with gold.

[36]The walls of the inner courtyard were built so that there was one layer of cedar beams between every three layers of finished stone.

[37]The foundation of the LORD's Temple was laid in midspring, in the month of Ziv,* during the fourth year of Solomon's reign. [38]The entire building was completed in every detail by midautumn, in the month of Bul,* during the eleventh year of his reign. So it took seven years to build the Temple.

CHAPTER 7
Solomon Builds His Palace

Solomon also built a palace for himself, and it took him thirteen years to complete the construction.

[2]One of Solomon's buildings was called the Palace of the Forest of Lebanon. It was

---

6:10 Hebrew *5 cubits* [2.3 meters].   6:17 Hebrew *40 cubits* [18.4 meters].   6:20 Or *overlaid the altar with cedar.* The meaning of the Hebrew is uncertain.   6:21 Or *to draw curtains across.* The meaning of the Hebrew is uncertain. 6:23a Or *pine;* Hebrew reads *oil tree;* also in 6:31, 33.   6:23b Hebrew *10 cubits* [4.6 meters]; also in 6:24, 25. 6:24 Hebrew *5 cubits* [2.3 meters].   6:31 The meaning of the Hebrew is uncertain.   6:37 Hebrew *was laid in the month of Ziv.* This month of the ancient Hebrew lunar calendar usually occurs within the months of April and May. 6:38 Hebrew *by the month of Bul, which is the eighth month.* This month of the ancient Hebrew lunar calendar usually occurs within the months of October and November.

6:11-13 God promised Solomon that he would be present with Israel as long as the people chose to obey his laws. Often we forget that obedience is the key to our inheritance of God's promises. We complain that God has failed us, but we do so from a position of disobedience. God, unlike man, is always faithful to his promises, including those promises that give us hope for recovery. We need to be faithful to God if we desire his promises to bear fruit in our life.

150 feet long, 75 feet wide, and 45 feet high.* There were four rows of cedar pillars, and great cedar beams rested on the pillars. ³The hall had a cedar roof. Above the beams on the pillars were forty-five side rooms,* arranged in three tiers of fifteen each. ⁴On each end of the long hall were three rows of windows facing each other. ⁵All the doorways and oorposts* had rectangular frames and were arranged in sets of three, facing each other.

⁶Solomon also built the Hall of Pillars, which was 75 feet long and 45 feet wide.* There was a porch in front, along with a canopy supported by pillars.

⁷Solomon also built the throne room, known as the Hall of Justice, where he sat to hear legal matters. It was paneled with cedar from floor to ceiling.* ⁸Solomon's living quarters surrounded a courtyard behind this hall, and they were constructed the same way. He also built similar living quarters for Pharaoh's daughter, whom he had married.

⁹From foundation to eaves, all these buildings were built from huge blocks of high-quality stone, cut with saws and trimmed to exact measure on all sides. ¹⁰Some of the huge foundation stones were 15 feet long, and some were 12 feet* long. ¹¹The blocks of high-quality stone used in the walls were also cut to measure, and cedar beams were also used. ¹²The walls of the great courtyard were built so that there was one layer of cedar beams between every three layers of finished stone, just like the walls of the inner courtyard of the LORD's Temple with its entry room.

Furnishings for the Temple

¹³King Solomon then asked for a man named Huram* to come from Tyre. ¹⁴He was half Israelite, since his mother was a widow from the tribe of Naphtali, and his father had been a craftsman in bronze from Tyre. Huram was extremely skillful and talented in any work in bronze, and he came to do all the metal work for King Solomon.

¹⁵Huram cast two bronze pillars, each 27 feet tall and 18 feet in circumference.*

¹⁶For the tops of the pillars he cast bronze capitals, each 7½ feet* tall. ¹⁷Each capital was decorated with seven sets of latticework and interwoven chains. ¹⁸He also encircled the latticework with two rows of pomegranates to decorate the capitals over the pillars. ¹⁹The capitals on the columns inside the entry room were shaped like water lilies, and they were six feet* tall. ²⁰The capitals on the two pillars had 200 pomegranates in two rows around them, beside the rounded surface next to the latticework. ²¹Huram set the pillars at the entrance of the Temple, one toward the south and one toward the north. He named the one on the south Jakin, and the one on the north Boaz.* ²²The capitals on the pillars were shaped like water lilies. And so the work on the pillars was finished.

²³Then Huram cast a great round basin, 15 feet across from rim to rim, called the Sea. It was 7½ feet deep and about 45 feet in circumference.* ²⁴It was encircled just below its rim by two rows of decorative gourds. There were about six gourds per foot* all the way around, and they were cast as part of the basin.

²⁵The Sea was placed on a base of twelve bronze oxen,* all facing outward. Three faced north, three faced west, three faced south, and three faced east, and the Sea rested on them. ²⁶The walls of the Sea were about three inches* thick, and its rim flared out like a cup and resembled a water lily blossom. It could hold about 11,000 gallons* of water.

²⁷Huram also made ten bronze water carts, each 6 feet long, 6 feet wide, and 4½ feet tall.* ²⁸They were constructed with side panels braced with crossbars. ²⁹Both the panels and the crossbars were decorated with carved lions, oxen, and cherubim. Above and below the lions and oxen were wreath decorations. ³⁰Each of these carts had four bronze wheels and bronze axles. There were supporting posts for the bronze basins at the corners of the carts; these supports were decorated on each side with carvings of wreaths. ³¹The top of each cart had a rounded frame for the basin. It projected 1½ feet* above the cart's top

7:2 Hebrew 100 cubits [46 meters] long, 50 cubits [23 meters] wide, and 30 cubits [13.8 meters] high. 7:3 Or 45 rafters, or 45 beams, or 45 pillars. The architectural details in 7:2-6 can be interpreted in many different ways. 7:5 Greek version reads windows. 7:6 Hebrew 50 cubits [23 meters] long and 30 cubits [13.8 meters] wide. 7:7 As in Syriac version and Latin Vulgate; Hebrew reads from floor to floor. 7:10 Hebrew 10 cubits [4.6 meters] . . . 8 cubits [3.7 meters]. 7:13 Hebrew Hiram (also in 7:40, 45); compare 2 Chr 2:13. This is not the same person mentioned in 5:1. 7:15 Hebrew 18 cubits [8.3 meters] tall and 12 cubits [5.5 meters] in circumference. 7:16 Hebrew 5 cubits [2.3 meters]. 7:19 Hebrew 4 cubits [1.8 meters]; also in 7:38. 7:21 Jakin probably means "he establishes"; Boaz probably means "in him is strength." 7:23 Hebrew 10 cubits [4.6 meters] across. . . . 5 cubits [2.3 meters] deep and 30 cubits [13.8 meters] in circumference. 7:24 Or 20 gourds per meter; Hebrew reads 10 per cubit. 7:25 Hebrew 12 oxen; compare 2 Kgs 16:17, which specifies bronze oxen. 7:26a Hebrew a handbreadth [8 centimeters]. 7:26b Hebrew 2,000 baths [42 kiloliters]. 7:27 Hebrew 4 cubits [1.8 meters] long, 4 cubits wide, and 3 cubits [1.4 meters] high. 7:31a Hebrew a cubit [46 centimeters].

like a round pedestal, and its opening was 2¼ feet* across; it was decorated on the outside with carvings of wreaths. The panels of the carts were square, not round. ³²Under the panels were four wheels that were connected to axles that had been cast as one unit with the cart. The wheels were 2¼ feet in diameter ³³and were similar to chariot wheels. The axles, spokes, rims, and hubs were all cast from molten bronze.

³⁴There were handles at each of the four corners of the carts, and these, too, were cast as one unit with the cart. ³⁵Around the top of each cart was a rim nine inches wide.* The corner supports and side panels were cast as one unit with the cart. ³⁶Carvings of cherubim, lions, and palm trees decorated the panels and corner supports wherever there was room, and there were wreaths all around. ³⁷All ten water carts were the same size and were made alike, for each was cast from the same mold.

³⁸Huram also made ten smaller bronze basins, one for each cart. Each basin was six feet across and could hold 220 gallons* of water. ³⁹He set five water carts on the south side of the Temple and five on the north side. The great bronze basin called the Sea was placed near the southeast corner of the Temple. ⁴⁰He also made the necessary washbasins, shovels, and bowls.

So at last Huram completed everything King Solomon had assigned him to make for the Temple of the LORD:

⁴¹ the two pillars;
the two bowl-shaped capitals on top of the pillars;
the two networks of interwoven chains that decorated the capitals;
⁴² the 400 pomegranates that hung from the chains on the capitals (two rows of pomegranates for each of the chain networks that decorated the capitals on top of the pillars);
⁴³ the ten water carts holding the ten basins;
⁴⁴ the Sea and the twelve oxen under it;
⁴⁵ the ash buckets, the shovels, and the bowls.

Huram made all these things of burnished bronze for the Temple of the LORD, just as King Solomon had directed. ⁴⁶The king had them cast in clay molds in the Jordan Valley between Succoth and Zarethan. ⁴⁷Solomon did not weigh all these things because there were so many; the weight of the bronze could not be measured.

⁴⁸Solomon also made all the furnishings of the Temple of the LORD:

the gold altar;
the gold table for the Bread of the Presence;
⁴⁹ the lampstands of solid gold, five on the south and five on the north, in front of the Most Holy Place;
the flower decorations, lamps, and tongs—all of gold;
⁵⁰ the small bowls, lamp snuffers, bowls, ladles, and incense burners—all of solid gold;
the doors for the entrances to the Most Holy Place and the main room of the Temple, with their fronts overlaid with gold.

⁵¹So King Solomon finished all his work on the Temple of the LORD. Then he brought all the gifts his father, David, had dedicated—the silver, the gold, and the various articles—and he stored them in the treasuries of the LORD's Temple.

CHAPTER 8
The Ark Brought to the Temple
Solomon then summoned to Jerusalem the elders of Israel and all the heads of the tribes—the leaders of the ancestral families of the Israelites. They were to bring the Ark of the LORD's Covenant to the Temple from its location in the City of David, also known as Zion. ²So all the men of Israel assembled before King Solomon at the annual Festival of Shelters, which is held in early autumn in the month of Ethanim.*

³When all the elders of Israel arrived, the priests picked up the Ark. ⁴The priests and Levites brought up the Ark of the LORD along with the special tent* and all the sacred items that had been in it. ⁵There, before the Ark, King Solomon and the entire community of Israel sacrificed so many sheep, goats, and cattle that no one could keep count!

⁶Then the priests carried the Ark of the LORD's Covenant into the inner sanctuary of the Temple—the Most Holy Place—and placed it beneath the wings of the cherubim.

7:31b Hebrew *1½ cubits* [69 centimeters]; also in 7:32. **7:35** Hebrew *half a cubit wide* [23 centimeters]. **7:38** Hebrew *40 baths* [840 liters]. **8:2** Hebrew *at the festival in the month Ethanim, which is the seventh month.* The Festival of Shelters began on the fifteenth day of the seventh month of the ancient Hebrew lunar calendar. This day occurred in late September, October, or early November. **8:4** Hebrew *the Tent of Meeting;* i.e., the tent mentioned in 2 Sam 6:17 and 1 Chr 16:1.

[7]The cherubim spread their wings over the Ark, forming a canopy over the Ark and its carrying poles. [8]These poles were so long that their ends could be seen from the Holy Place, which is in front of the Most Holy Place, but not from the outside. They are still there to this day. [9]Nothing was in the Ark except the two stone tablets that Moses had placed in it at Mount Sinai,* where the LORD made a covenant with the people of Israel when they left the land of Egypt.

[10]When the priests came out of the Holy Place, a thick cloud filled the Temple of the LORD. [11]The priests could not continue their service because of the cloud, for the glorious presence of the LORD filled the Temple of the LORD.

Solomon Praises the LORD

[12]Then Solomon prayed, "O LORD, you have said that you would live in a thick cloud of darkness. [13]Now I have built a glorious Temple for you, a place where you can live forever!*"

[14]Then the king turned around to the entire community of Israel standing before him and gave this blessing: [15]"Praise the LORD, the God of Israel, who has kept the promise he made to my father, David. For he told my father, [16]'From the day I brought my people Israel out of Egypt, I have never chosen a city among any of the tribes of Israel as the place where a Temple should be built to honor my name. But I have chosen David to be king over my people Israel.'"

[17]Then Solomon said, "My father, David, wanted to build this Temple to honor the name of the LORD, the God of Israel. [18]But the LORD told him, 'You wanted to build the Temple to honor my name. Your intention is good, [19]but you are not the one to do it. One of your own sons will build the Temple to honor me.'

[20]"And now the LORD has fulfilled the promise he made, for I have become king in my father's place, and now I sit on the throne of Israel, just as the LORD promised. I have built this Temple to honor the name of the LORD, the God of Israel. [21]And I have prepared a place there for the Ark, which contains the covenant that the LORD made with our ancestors when he brought them out of Egypt."

Solomon's Prayer of Dedication

[22]Then Solomon stood before the altar of the LORD in front of the entire community of Israel. He lifted his hands toward heaven, [23]and he prayed,

"O LORD, God of Israel, there is no God like you in all of heaven above or on the earth below. You keep your covenant and show unfailing love to all who walk before you in wholehearted devotion. [24]You have kept your promise to your servant David, my father. You made that promise with your own mouth, and with your own hands you have fulfilled it today.

[25]"And now, O LORD, God of Israel, carry out the additional promise you made to your servant David, my father. For you said to him, 'If your descendants guard their behavior and faithfully follow me as you have done, one of them will always sit on the throne of Israel.' [26]Now, O God of Israel, fulfill this promise to your servant David, my father.

[27]"But will God really live on earth? Why, even the highest heavens cannot contain you. How much less this Temple I have built! [28]Nevertheless, listen to my prayer and my plea, O LORD my God. Hear the cry and the prayer that your servant is making to you today. [29]May you watch over this Temple night and day, this place where you have said, 'My name will be there.' May you always hear the prayers I make toward this place. [30]May you hear the humble and earnest requests from me and your people Israel when we pray toward this place. Yes, hear us from heaven where you live, and when you hear, forgive.

[31]"If someone wrongs another person and is required to take an oath of innocence in front of your altar in this Temple, [32]then hear from heaven and judge between your servants—the accuser and the accused. Punish the guilty as they deserve. Acquit the innocent because of their innocence.

[33]"If your people Israel are defeated by their enemies because they have sinned against you, and if they turn to you and acknowledge your name and pray to you here in this Temple, [34]then hear from heaven and forgive the sin of your people Israel and return them to this land you gave their ancestors.

[35]"If the skies are shut up and there is no rain because your people have sinned against you, and if they pray toward this

8:9 Hebrew *at Horeb,* another name for Sinai. 8:13 Some Greek texts add the line *Is this not written in the Book of Jashar?*

Temple and acknowledge your name and turn from their sins because you have punished them, [36]then hear from heaven and forgive the sins of your servants, your people Israel. Teach them to follow the right path, and send rain on your land that you have given to your people as their special possession.

[37]"If there is a famine in the land or a plague or crop disease or attacks of locusts or caterpillars, or if your people's enemies are in the land besieging their towns—whatever disaster or disease there is—[38]and if your people Israel pray about their troubles, raising their hands toward this Temple, [39]then hear from heaven where you live, and forgive. Give your people what their actions deserve, for you alone know each human heart. [40]Then they will fear you as long as they live in the land you gave to our ancestors.

[41]"In the future, foreigners who do not belong to your people Israel will hear of you. They will come from distant lands because of your name, [42]for they will hear of your great name and your strong hand and your powerful arm. And when they pray toward this Temple, [43]then hear from heaven where you live, and grant what they ask of you. In this way, all the people of the earth will come to know and fear you, just as your own people Israel do. They, too, will know that this Temple I have built honors your name.

[44]"If your people go out where you send them to fight their enemies, and if they pray to the LORD by turning toward this city you have chosen and toward this Temple I have built to honor your name, [45]then hear their prayers from heaven and uphold their cause.

[46]"If they sin against you—and who has never sinned?—you might become angry with them and let their enemies conquer them and take them captive to their land far away or near. [47]But in that land of exile, they might turn to you in repentance and pray, 'We have sinned, done evil, and acted wickedly.' [48]If they turn to you with their whole heart and soul in the land of their enemies and pray toward the land you gave to their ancestors—toward this city you have chosen, and toward this Temple I have built to honor your name—[49]then hear their prayers and their petition from heaven where you live, and uphold their cause. [50]Forgive your people who have sinned against you. Forgive all the offenses they have committed against you. Make their captors merciful to them, [51]for they are your people—your special possession—whom you brought out of the iron-smelting furnace of Egypt.

[52]"May your eyes be open to my requests and to the requests of your people Israel. May you hear and answer them whenever they cry out to you. [53]For when you brought our ancestors out of Egypt, O Sovereign LORD, you told your servant Moses that you had set Israel apart from all the nations of the earth to be your own special possession."

The Dedication of the Temple
[54]When Solomon finished making these prayers and petitions to the LORD, he stood up in front of the altar of the LORD, where he had been kneeling with his hands raised toward heaven. [55]He stood and in a loud voice blessed the entire congregation of Israel:

[56]"Praise the LORD who has given rest to his people Israel, just as he promised. Not one word has failed of all the wonderful promises he gave through his servant Moses. [57]May the LORD our God be with us as he was with our ancestors; may he never leave us or abandon us. [58]May he give us the desire to do his will in everything and to obey all the commands, decrees, and regulations that he

---

8:46-53 Intercessory prayer is an important part of any relationship with God. Solomon showed that he understood this when he prayed for himself and the people. He asked God to have mercy on them before they had even made any mistakes (8:46-50). Intercessory prayer is important for us, too. When we feel that we can't resist temptation any longer, we can find strength from the prayers of others. We should ask at least one person to pray for us as we go through recovery. That person can also hold us accountable for our actions.

8:56-60 Solomon's prayer provides us with a good example to follow. It can be divided into six steps: (1) He began by praising God (8:56); (2) he requested God's presence (8:57); (3) he asked for help to do God's will (8:58); (4) he pledged to obey God in all things (8:58); (5) he asked God to remember his prayer and fulfill his daily needs (8:59); and (6) he prayed that all people would come to know God (8:60). These are all important aspects of a recovery program that reflects the truth of God's Word.

gave our ancestors. [59]And may these words that I have prayed in the presence of the LORD be before him constantly, day and night, so that the LORD our God may give justice to me and to his people Israel, according to each day's needs. [60]Then people all over the earth will know that the LORD alone is God and there is no other. [61]And may you be completely faithful to the LORD our God. May you always obey his decrees and commands, just as you are doing today."

[62]Then the king and all Israel with him offered sacrifices to the LORD. [63]Solomon offered to the LORD a peace offering of 22,000 cattle and 120,000 sheep and goats. And so the king and all the people of Israel dedicated the Temple of the LORD.

[64]That same day the king consecrated the central area of the courtyard in front of the LORD's Temple. He offered burnt offerings, grain offerings, and the fat of peace offerings there, because the bronze altar in the LORD's presence was too small to hold all the burnt offerings, grain offerings, and the fat of the peace offerings.

[65]Then Solomon and all Israel celebrated the Festival of Shelters* in the presence of the LORD our God. A large congregation had gathered from as far away as Lebo-hamath in the north and the Brook of Egypt in the south. The celebration went on for fourteen days in all—seven days for the dedication of the altar and seven days for the Festival of Shelters.* [66]After the festival was over,* Solomon sent the people home. They blessed the king and went to their homes joyful and glad because the LORD had been good to his servant David and to his people Israel.

CHAPTER 9
The LORD's Response to Solomon

So Solomon finished building the Temple of the LORD, as well as the royal palace. He completed everything he had planned to do.

[2]Then the LORD appeared to Solomon a second time, as he had done before at Gibeon. [3]The LORD said to him,

"I have heard your prayer and your petition. I have set this Temple apart to be holy—this place you have built where my name will be honored forever. I will always watch over it, for it is dear to my heart.

[4]"As for you, if you will follow me with integrity and godliness, as David your father did, obeying all my commands, decrees, and regulations, [5]then I will establish the throne of your dynasty over Israel forever. For I made this promise to your father, David: 'One of your descendants will always sit on the throne of Israel.'

[6]"But if you or your descendants abandon me and disobey the commands and decrees I have given you, and if you serve and worship other gods, [7]then I will uproot Israel from this land that I have given them. I will reject this Temple that I have made holy to honor my name. I will make Israel an object of mockery and ridicule among the nations. [8]And though this Temple is impressive now, all who pass by will be appalled and will gasp in horror. They will ask, 'Why did the LORD do such terrible things to this land and to this Temple?' [9]And the answer will be, 'Because his people abandoned the LORD their God, who brought their ancestors out of Egypt, and they worshiped other gods instead and bowed down to them. That is why the LORD has brought all these disasters on them.'"

Solomon's Agreement with Hiram

[10]It took Solomon twenty years to build the LORD's Temple and his own royal palace. At

8:65a Hebrew *the festival;* see note on 8:2. 8:65b Hebrew *seven days and seven days, fourteen days;* compare parallel text at 2 Chr 7:8-10. 8:66 Hebrew *On the eighth day,* probably referring to the day following the seven-day Festival of Shelters; compare parallel text at 2 Chr 7:9-10.

9:1-9 God promised to extend to Solomon and his descendants the promises he had given to David. But with the promises came added responsibilities. God would not bless his people unless they chose to serve him and live according to his plan. If Israel worshiped other gods, they would lose their position of blessing (9:6). We are often given warning signs before we sin. The Bible, friends, and our conscience all warn us of inappropriate behavior. Unfortunately, like Solomon and Israel, we often ignore the warnings and then must suffer the consequences.

9:10-28 Upon completing the Temple and the palace (9:10), Solomon did not take time out for God and family. He also failed to give his labor force a chance to rest. Instead, he went on a building spree. Solomon built the fortresses of Hazor, Megiddo, and Gezer and extended the fortified walls of Jerusalem to protect the Temple and palace (9:15). Solomon exhibited many of the

the end of that time, [11]he gave twenty towns in the land of Galilee to King Hiram of Tyre. (Hiram had previously provided all the cedar and cypress timber and gold that Solomon had requested.) [12]But when Hiram came from Tyre to see the towns Solomon had given him, he was not at all pleased with them. [13]"What kind of towns are these, my brother?" he asked. So Hiram called that area Cabul (which means "worthless"), as it is still known today. [14]Nevertheless, Hiram paid* Solomon 9,000 pounds* of gold.

Solomon's Many Achievements

[15]This is the account of the forced labor that King Solomon conscripted to build the LORD's Temple, the royal palace, the supporting terraces,* the wall of Jerusalem, and the cities of Hazor, Megiddo, and Gezer. [16](Pharaoh, the king of Egypt, had attacked and captured Gezer, killing the Canaanite population and burning it down. He gave the city to his daughter as a wedding gift when she married Solomon. [17]So Solomon rebuilt the city of Gezer.) He also built up the towns of Lower Beth-horon, [18]Baalath, and Tamar* in the wilderness within his land. [19]He built towns as supply centers and constructed towns where his chariots and horses* could be stationed. He built everything he desired in Jerusalem and Lebanon and throughout his entire realm.

[20]There were still some people living in the land who were not Israelites, including Amorites, Hittites, Perizzites, Hivites, and Jebusites. [21]These were descendants of the nations whom the people of Israel had not completely destroyed.* So Solomon conscripted them as slaves, and they serve as forced laborers to this day. [22]But Solomon did not conscript any of the Israelites for forced labor. Instead, he assigned them to serve as fighting men, government officials, officers and captains in his army, commanders of his chariots, and charioteers. [23]Solomon appointed 550 of them to supervise the people working on his various projects.

[24]Solomon moved his wife, Pharaoh's daughter, from the City of David to the new palace he had built for her. Then he constructed the supporting terraces.

[25]Three times each year Solomon presented burnt offerings and peace offerings on the altar he had built for the LORD. He also burned incense to the LORD. And so he finished the work of building the Temple.

[26]King Solomon also built a fleet of ships at Ezion-geber, a port near Elath* in the land of Edom, along the shore of the Red Sea.* [27]Hiram sent experienced crews of sailors to sail the ships with Solomon's men. [28]They sailed to Ophir and brought back to Solomon some sixteen tons* of gold.

CHAPTER 10
Visit of the Queen of Sheba

When the queen of Sheba heard of Solomon's fame, which brought honor to the name of the LORD,* she came to test him with hard questions. [2]She arrived in Jerusalem with a large group of attendants and a great caravan of camels loaded with spices, large quantities of gold, and precious jewels. When she met with Solomon, she talked with him about everything she had on her mind. [3]Solomon had answers for all her questions; nothing was too hard for the king to explain to her. [4]When the queen of Sheba realized how very wise Solomon was, and when she saw the palace he had built, [5]she was overwhelmed. She was also amazed at the food on his tables, the organization of

9:14a Or *For Hiram had paid.* 9:14b Hebrew *120 talents* [4,000 kilograms]. 9:15 Hebrew *the millo;* also in 9:24. The meaning of the Hebrew is uncertain. 9:18 An alternate reading in the Masoretic Text reads *Tadmor.* 9:19 Or *and charioteers.* 9:21 The Hebrew term used here refers to the complete consecration of things or people to the LORD, either by destroying them or by giving them as an offering. 9:26a As in Greek version (see also 2 Kgs 14:22; 16:6); Hebrew reads *Eloth,* a variant spelling of Elath. 9:26b Hebrew *sea of reeds.* 9:28 Hebrew *420 talents* [14 metric tons]. 10:1 Or *which was due to the name of the LORD.* The meaning of the Hebrew is uncertain.

characteristics of a workaholic. He sacrificed his relationships with God, his family, and his people to fulfill his compulsion to build. His son Rehoboam suffered many of the consequences resulting from Solomon's driving personality. The people rebelled against Rehoboam because he promised to maintain the heavy burdens of labor and taxes initiated by Solomon (12:1-11).
10:1-13 When the queen of Sheba visited Solomon, she wanted to confirm all the rumors she had heard concerning his wealth and wisdom. She tested him with "hard questions" and toured the palace. After verifying the reports of Solomon's greatness for herself, she became an admirer of Solomon and his God. Testing others is sometimes necessary, especially if reports of their achievements seem incredible or unbelievable. We should test their claims to see if (1) the reports are accurate and if (2) they are from God. Often when something seems too good to be true, it is.

his officials and their splendid clothing, the cup-bearers, and the burnt offerings Solomon made at the Temple of the LORD.

⁶She exclaimed to the king, "Everything I heard in my country about your achievements* and wisdom is true! ⁷I didn't believe what was said until I arrived here and saw it with my own eyes. In fact, I had not heard the half of it! Your wisdom and prosperity are far beyond what I was told. ⁸How happy your people* must be! What a privilege for your officials to stand here day after day, listening to your wisdom! ⁹Praise the LORD your God, who delights in you and has placed you on the throne of Israel. Because of the LORD's eternal love for Israel, he has made you king so you can rule with justice and righteousness."

¹⁰Then she gave the king a gift of 9,000 pounds* of gold, great quantities of spices, and precious jewels. Never again were so many spices brought in as those the queen of Sheba gave to King Solomon.

¹¹(In addition, Hiram's ships brought gold from Ophir, and they also brought rich cargoes of red sandalwood* and precious jewels. ¹²The king used the sandalwood to make railings for the Temple of the LORD and the royal palace, and to construct lyres and harps for the musicians. Never before or since has there been such a supply of sandalwood.)

¹³King Solomon gave the queen of Sheba whatever she asked for, besides all the customary gifts he had so generously given. Then she and all her attendants returned to their own land.

Solomon's Wealth and Splendor

¹⁴Each year Solomon received about 25 tons* of gold. ¹⁵This did not include the additional revenue he received from merchants and traders, all the kings of Arabia, and the governors of the land.

¹⁶King Solomon made 200 large shields of hammered gold, each weighing more than fifteen pounds.* ¹⁷He also made 300 smaller

shields of hammered gold, each weighing nearly four pounds.* The king placed these shields in the Palace of the Forest of Lebanon.

¹⁸Then the king made a huge throne, decorated with ivory and overlaid with fine gold. ¹⁹The throne had six steps and a rounded back. There were armrests on both sides of the seat, and the figure of a lion stood on each side of the throne. ²⁰There were also twelve other lions, one standing on each end of the six steps. No other throne in all the world could be compared with it!

²¹All of King Solomon's drinking cups were solid gold, as were all the utensils in the Palace of the Forest of Lebanon. They were not made of silver, for silver was considered worthless in Solomon's day!

²²The king had a fleet of trading ships of Tarshish that sailed with Hiram's fleet. Once every three years the ships returned, loaded with gold, silver, ivory, apes, and peacocks.*

²³So King Solomon became richer and wiser than any other king on earth. ²⁴People from every nation came to consult him and to hear the wisdom God had given him. ²⁵Year after year everyone who visited brought him gifts of silver and gold, clothing, weapons, spices, horses, and mules.

²⁶Solomon built up a huge force of chariots and horses.* He had 1,400 chariots and 12,000 horses. He stationed some of them in the chariot cities and some near him in Jerusalem. ²⁷The king made silver as plentiful in Jerusalem as stone. And valuable cedar timber was as common as the sycamore-fig trees that grow in the foothills of Judah.* ²⁸Solomon's horses were imported from Egypt* and from Cilicia*; the king's traders acquired them from Cilicia at the standard price. ²⁹At that time chariots from Egypt could be purchased for 600 pieces of silver,* and horses for 150 pieces of silver.* They were then exported to the kings of the Hittites and the kings of Aram.

10:6 Hebrew *your words.* 10:8 Greek and Syriac versions and Latin Vulgate read *your wives.* 10:10 Hebrew *120 talents* [4,000 kilograms]. 10:11 Hebrew *almug wood;* also in 10:12. 10:14 Hebrew *666 talents* [23 metric tons]. 10:16 Hebrew *600 [shekels] of gold* [6.8 kilograms]. 10:17 Hebrew *3 minas* [1.8 kilograms]. 10:22 Or *and baboons.* 10:26 Or *charioteers;* also in 10:26b. 10:27 Hebrew *the Shephelah.* 10:28a Possibly *Muzur,* a district near Cilicia; also in 10:29. 10:28b Hebrew *Kue,* probably another name for Cilicia. 10:29a Hebrew *600 [shekels] of silver,* about 15 pounds or 6.8 kilograms in weight. 10:29b Hebrew *150 [shekels],* about 3.8 pounds or 1.7 kilograms in weight.

10:23 In the Old Testament a person's wealth often resulted from a good relationship with God. Throughout the earlier part of Solomon's life, this was the case. As Solomon grew older, however, his wealth led him to trust in himself rather than in God. We also have this tendency to allow our material wealth and pride to lead us away from God. We must remember that everything we have, even life itself, is a gift from God. As we succeed in recovery, we must remember to give God the credit he deserves. If we begin to think we did it alone, we are headed for trouble.

CHAPTER 11
Solomon's Many Wives
Now King Solomon loved many foreign women. Besides Pharaoh's daughter, he married women from Moab, Ammon, Edom, Sidon, and from among the Hittites. [2]The LORD had clearly instructed the people of Israel, "You must not marry them, because they will turn your hearts to their gods." Yet Solomon insisted on loving them anyway. [3]He had 700 wives of royal birth and 300 concubines. And in fact, they did turn his heart away from the LORD.

[4]In Solomon's old age, they turned his heart to worship other gods instead of being completely faithful to the LORD his God, as his father, David, had been. [5]Solomon worshiped Ashtoreth, the goddess of the Sidonians, and Molech,* the detestable god of the Ammonites. [6]In this way, Solomon did what was evil in the LORD's sight; he refused to follow the LORD completely, as his father, David, had done.

[7]On the Mount of Olives, east of Jerusalem,* he even built a pagan shrine for Chemosh, the detestable god of Moab, and another for Molech, the detestable god of the Ammonites. [8]Solomon built such shrines for all his foreign wives to use for burning incense and sacrificing to their gods.

[9]The LORD was very angry with Solomon, for his heart had turned away from the LORD, the God of Israel, who had appeared to him twice. [10]He had warned Solomon specifically about worshiping other gods, but Solomon did not listen to the LORD's command. [11]So now the LORD said to him, "Since you have not kept my covenant and have disobeyed my decrees, I will surely tear the kingdom away from you and give it to one of your servants. [12]But for the sake of your father, David, I will not do this while you are still alive. I will take the kingdom away from your son. [13]And even so, I will not take away the entire kingdom; I will let him be king of one tribe, for the sake of my servant David and for the sake of Jerusalem, my chosen city."

Solomon's Adversaries
[14]Then the LORD raised up Hadad the Edomite, a member of Edom's royal family, to be Solomon's adversary. [15]Years before, David had defeated Edom. Joab, his army commander, had stayed to bury some of the Israelite soldiers who had died in battle. While there, they killed every male in Edom. [16]Joab and the army of Israel had stayed there for six months, killing them.

[17]But Hadad and a few of his father's royal officials escaped and headed for Egypt. (Hadad was just a boy at the time.) [18]They set out from Midian and went to Paran, where others joined them. Then they traveled to Egypt and went to Pharaoh, who gave them a home, food, and some land. [19]Pharaoh grew very fond of Hadad, and he gave him his wife's sister in marriage—the sister of Queen Tahpenes. [20]She bore him a son named Genubath. Tahpenes raised him* in Pharaoh's palace among Pharaoh's own sons.

[21]When the news reached Hadad in Egypt that David and his commander Joab were both dead, he said to Pharaoh, "Let me return to my own country."

[22]"Why?" Pharaoh asked him. "What do you lack here that makes you want to go home?"

"Nothing," he replied. "But even so, please let me return home."

[23]God also raised up Rezon son of Eliada as Solomon's adversary. Rezon had fled from his master, King Hadadezer of Zobah, [24]and

11:5 Hebrew *Milcom*, a variant spelling of Molech; also in 11:33. 11:7 Hebrew *On the mountain east of Jerusalem*. 11:20 As in Greek version; Hebrew reads *weaned him*.

11:1-13 Solomon broke God's commands concerning interaction with foreign peoples (Exodus 23:32-33) by marrying women from Moab, Edom, and other nations (11:1). God had prohibited marriage with the people of Canaan because he knew that they would lead the Israelites to worship other gods. Not only did Solomon begin to worship other gods, but he even built altars to them (11:7-8). God became angry and punished Solomon for his disobedience (11:9-13). It is tempting to do things our own way without seeing what God says. When we do this, we shouldn't be surprised when problems arise. God is calling attention to our mistakes, hoping we will turn back to him and his offer to rescue us.

11:14-25 For years God had allowed Solomon to rule in peace. God had put down the threat of hostile neighbors so a man who was not a warrior could build his Temple (1 Chronicles 28:2-3). But as Solomon turned his back on God, he was confronted with foreign enemies, such as Hadad (11:14) and Rezon (11:23). The problems we now face are often consequences of choices we have already made. Before blaming others for our situation, we should examine our past. We may find that we are the one responsible.

had become the leader of a gang of rebels. After David conquered Hadadezer, Rezon and his men fled to Damascus, where he became king. 25Rezon was Israel's bitter adversary for the rest of Solomon's reign, and he made trouble, just as Hadad did. Rezon hated Israel intensely and continued to reign in Aram.

Jeroboam Rebels against Solomon

26Another rebel leader was Jeroboam son of Nebat, one of Solomon's own officials. He came from the town of Zeredah in Ephraim, and his mother was Zeruah, a widow.

27This is the story behind his rebellion. Solomon was rebuilding the supporting terraces* and repairing the walls of the city of his father, David. 28Jeroboam was a very capable young man, and when Solomon saw how industrious he was, he put him in charge of the labor force from the tribes of Ephraim and Manasseh, the descendants of Joseph.

29One day as Jeroboam was leaving Jerusalem, the prophet Ahijah from Shiloh met him along the way. Ahijah was wearing a new cloak. The two of them were alone in a field, 30and Ahijah took hold of the new cloak he was wearing and tore it into twelve pieces. 31Then he said to Jeroboam, "Take ten of these pieces, for this is what the LORD, the God of Israel, says: 'I am about to tear the kingdom from the hand of Solomon, and I will give ten of the tribes to you! 32But I will leave him one tribe for the sake of my servant David and for the sake of Jerusalem, which I have chosen out of all the tribes of Israel. 33For Solomon has* abandoned me and worshiped Ashtoreth, the goddess of the Sidonians; Chemosh, the god of Moab; and Molech, the god of the Ammonites. He has not followed my ways and done what is pleasing in my sight. He has not obeyed my

decrees and regulations as David his father did.

34" 'But I will not take the entire kingdom from Solomon at this time. For the sake of my servant David, the one whom I chose and who obeyed my commands and decrees, I will keep Solomon as leader for the rest of his life. 35But I will take the kingdom away from his son and give ten of the tribes to you. 36His son will have one tribe so that the descendants of David my servant will continue to reign, shining like a lamp in Jerusalem, the city I have chosen to be the place for my name. 37And I will place you on the throne of Israel, and you will rule over all that your heart desires. 38If you listen to what I tell you and follow my ways and do whatever I consider to be right, and if you obey my decrees and commands, as my servant David did, then I will always be with you. I will establish an enduring dynasty for you as I did for David, and I will give Israel to you. 39Because of Solomon's sin I will punish the descendants of David—though not forever.'"

40Solomon tried to kill Jeroboam, but he fled to King Shishak of Egypt and stayed there until Solomon died.

Summary of Solomon's Reign

41The rest of the events in Solomon's reign, including all his deeds and his wisdom, are recorded in *The Book of the Acts of Solomon.* 42Solomon ruled in Jerusalem over all Israel for forty years. 43When he died, he was buried in the City of David, named for his father. Then his son Rehoboam became the next king.

CHAPTER 12
The Northern Tribes Revolt

Rehoboam went to Shechem, where all Israel had gathered to make him king. 2When Jero-

---

11:27 Hebrew *the millo.* The meaning of the Hebrew is uncertain. 11:33 As in Greek, Syriac, and Latin Vulgate; Hebrew reads *For they have.*

11:26-40 The greatest consequence of Solomon's sins was realized after his death—Israel divided. God raised up Jeroboam as the first king of the northern kingdom of Israel. Solomon attempted to kill Jeroboam to try to prevent God's will from coming about (11:40). Solomon's decisions were obviously being driven by an inaccurate self-perception. He had begun to believe that his actions could rewrite the will of God. No matter how rich, popular, or important we might become, we will never be able to change what God has said will happen. How often do we fall prey to the sin of thinking we can outmaneuver God?

11:41–12:1 Solomon's life ended, and his son Rehoboam inherited the throne. Before David died, he had given his son Solomon advice on how to run the kingdom (see 2:1-12). But Solomon failed to do this with his son. Rehoboam was left to rule without the counsel of his father. Fathers must never underestimate the value of helping their children as the children take on new responsibilities. Fathers have valuable contributions to make, contributions that can save their children the pain of learning the lessons on their own.

boam son of Nebat heard of this, he returned from Egypt,* for he had fled to Egypt to escape from King Solomon. ³The leaders of Israel summoned him, and Jeroboam and the whole assembly of Israel went to speak with Rehoboam. ⁴"Your father was a hard master," they said. "Lighten the harsh labor demands and heavy taxes that your father imposed on us. Then we will be your loyal subjects."

⁵Rehoboam replied, "Give me three days to think this over. Then come back for my answer." So the people went away.

⁶Then King Rehoboam discussed the matter with the older men who had counseled his father, Solomon. "What is your advice?" he asked. "How should I answer these people?"

⁷The older counselors replied, "If you are willing to be a servant to these people today and give them a favorable answer, they will always be your loyal subjects."

⁸But Rehoboam rejected the advice of the older men and instead asked the opinion of the young men who had grown up with him and were now his advisers. ⁹"What is your advice?" he asked them. "How should I answer these people who want me to lighten the burdens imposed by my father?"

¹⁰The young men replied, "This is what you should tell those complainers who want a lighter burden: 'My little finger is thicker than my father's waist! ¹¹Yes, my father laid heavy burdens on you, but I'm going to make them even heavier! My father beat you with whips, but I will beat you with scorpions!'"

¹²Three days later Jeroboam and all the people returned to hear Rehoboam's decision, just as the king had ordered. ¹³But Rehoboam spoke harshly to the people, for he rejected the advice of the older counselors ¹⁴and followed the counsel of his younger advisers. He told the people, "My father laid heavy burdens on you, but I'm going to make them even heavier! My father beat you with whips, but I will beat you with scorpions!"

¹⁵So the king paid no attention to the people. This turn of events was the will of the LORD, for it fulfilled the LORD's message to Jeroboam son of Nebat through the prophet Ahijah from Shiloh.

¹⁶When all Israel realized that the king had refused to listen to them, they responded,

"Down with the dynasty of David!
    We have no interest in the son of Jesse.
Back to your homes, O Israel!
    Look out for your own house,
        O David!"

So the people of Israel returned home. ¹⁷But Rehoboam continued to rule over the Israelites who lived in the towns of Judah.

¹⁸King Rehoboam sent Adoniram,* who was in charge of forced labor, to restore order, but the people of Israel stoned him to death. When this news reached King Rehoboam, he quickly jumped into his chariot and fled to Jerusalem. ¹⁹And to this day the northern tribes of Israel have refused to be ruled by a descendant of David.

²⁰When the people of Israel learned of Jeroboam's return from Egypt, they called an assembly and made him king over all Israel. So only the tribe of Judah remained loyal to the family of David.

Shemaiah's Prophecy

²¹When Rehoboam arrived at Jerusalem, he mobilized the men of Judah and the tribe of Benjamin—180,000 select troops—to fight against the men of Israel and to restore the kingdom to himself.

²²But God said to Shemaiah, the man of God, ²³"Say to Rehoboam son of Solomon, king of Judah, and to all the people of Judah and Benjamin, and to the rest of the people,

12:2 As in Greek version and Latin Vulgate (see also 2 Chr 10:2); Hebrew reads *he lived in Egypt.* 12:18 As in some Greek manuscripts and Syriac version (see also 4:6; 5:14); Hebrew reads *Adoram.*

12:6-14 Rehoboam was wise to ask for counsel (12:6). He made a mistake, however, in rejecting the advice of his father's wise counselors. Counsel should always be measured against the principles set forth in Scripture. Had Rehoboam done this, he would have seen that the advice of his peers (12:9-11) was unwise. We need to carefully weigh the counsel we receive, asking God for the wisdom to know what is right.

12:15-33 Both kings who followed Solomon, Jeroboam and Rehoboam, made foolish, self-serving decisions. Rehoboam followed his selfish inclinations, which led to the division of the kingdom (12:15-17). Jeroboam was so afraid of losing his kingdom (even though God appointed him king) that he broke God's laws. He made idols for the people to worship so they wouldn't have to go to Jerusalem to worship. The selfish attitudes of these men led the entire nation toward sin. We must realize that our decisions always touch the lives of others. We should measure our decisions by God's truth and by how they will affect others.

²⁴"This is what the LORD says: Do not fight against your relatives, the Israelites. Go back home, for what has happened is my doing!'" So they obeyed the message of the LORD and went home, as the LORD had commanded.

Jeroboam Makes Gold Calves

²⁵Jeroboam then built up the city of Shechem in the hill country of Ephraim, and it became his capital. Later he went and built up the town of Peniel.*

²⁶Jeroboam thought to himself, "Unless I am careful, the kingdom will return to the dynasty of David. ²⁷When these people go to Jerusalem to offer sacrifices at the Temple of the LORD, they will again give their allegiance to King Rehoboam of Judah. They will kill me and make him their king instead."

²⁸So on the advice of his counselors, the king made two gold calves. He said to the people,* "It is too much trouble for you to worship in Jerusalem. Look, Israel, these are the gods who brought you out of Egypt!"

²⁹He placed these calf idols in Bethel and in Dan—at either end of his kingdom. ³⁰But this became a great sin, for the people worshiped the idols, traveling as far north as Dan to worship the one there.

³¹Jeroboam also erected buildings at the pagan shrines and ordained priests from the common people—those who were not from the priestly tribe of Levi. ³²And Jeroboam instituted a religious festival in Bethel, held on the fifteenth day of the eighth month,* in imitation of the annual Festival of Shelters in Judah. There at Bethel he himself offered sacrifices to the calves he had made, and he appointed priests for the pagan shrines he had made. ³³So on the fifteenth day of the eighth month, a day that he himself had designated, Jeroboam offered sacrifices on the altar at Bethel. He instituted a religious festival for Israel, and he went up to the altar to burn incense.

CHAPTER 13
A Prophet Denounces Jeroboam

At the LORD's command, a man of God from Judah went to Bethel, arriving there just as Jeroboam was approaching the altar to burn incense. ²Then at the LORD's command, he shouted, "O altar, altar! This is what the LORD says: A child named Josiah will be born into the dynasty of David. On you he will sacrifice the priests from the pagan shrines who come here to burn incense, and human bones will be burned on you." ³That same day the man of God gave a sign to prove his message. He said, "The LORD has promised to give this sign: This altar will split apart, and its ashes will be poured out on the ground."

⁴When King Jeroboam heard the man of God speaking against the altar at Bethel, he pointed at him and shouted, "Seize that man!" But instantly the king's hand became paralyzed in that position, and he couldn't pull it back. ⁵At the same time a wide crack appeared in the altar, and the ashes poured out, just as the man of God had predicted in his message from the LORD.

⁶The king cried out to the man of God, "Please ask the LORD your God to restore my hand again!" So the man of God prayed to the LORD, and the king's hand was restored and he could move it again.

⁷Then the king said to the man of God, "Come to the palace with me and have something to eat, and I will give you a gift."

⁸But the man of God said to the king, "Even if you gave me half of everything you own, I would not go with you. I would not eat or drink anything in this place. ⁹For the LORD gave me this command: 'You must not eat or drink anything while you are there, and do not return to Judah by the same way you came.'" ¹⁰So he left Bethel and went home another way.

¹¹As it happened, there was an old prophet living in Bethel, and his sons* came home and told him what the man of God had done in Bethel that day. They also told their father what the man had said to the king. ¹²The old prophet asked them, "Which way did he go?" So they showed their father* which road the man of God had taken. ¹³"Quick, saddle the donkey," the old man said. So they saddled the donkey for him, and he mounted it.

¹⁴Then he rode after the man of God and found him sitting under a great tree. The old prophet asked him, "Are you the man of God who came from Judah?"

"Yes, I am," he replied.

¹⁵Then he said to the man of God, "Come home with me and eat some food."

¹⁶"No, I cannot," he replied. "I am not allowed to eat or drink anything here in this place. ¹⁷For the LORD gave me this command: 'You must not eat or drink anything while you are there, and do not return to Judah by the same way you came.'"

12:25 Hebrew Penuel, a variant spelling of Peniel. 12:28 Hebrew to them. 12:32 This day of the ancient Hebrew lunar calendar occurred in late October or early November, exactly one month after the annual Festival of Shelters in Judah (see Lev 23:34). 13:11 As in Greek version; Hebrew reads son. 13:12 As in Greek version; Hebrew reads They had seen.

¹⁸But the old prophet answered, "I am a prophet, too, just as you are. And an angel gave me this command from the LORD: 'Bring him home with you so he can have something to eat and drink.' " But the old man was lying to him. ¹⁹So they went back together, and the man of God ate and drank at the prophet's home.

²⁰Then while they were sitting at the table, a command from the LORD came to the old prophet. ²¹He cried out to the man of God from Judah, "This is what the LORD says: You have defied the word of the LORD and have disobeyed the command the LORD your God gave you. ²²You came back to this place and ate and drank where he told you not to eat or drink. Because of this, your body will not be buried in the grave of your ancestors."

²³After the man of God had finished eating and drinking, the old prophet saddled his own donkey for him, ²⁴and the man of God started off again. But as he was traveling along, a lion came out and killed him. His body lay there on the road, with the donkey and the lion standing beside it. ²⁵People who passed by saw the body lying in the road and the lion standing beside it, and they went and reported it in Bethel, where the old prophet lived.

²⁶When the prophet heard the report, he said, "It is the man of God who disobeyed the LORD's command. The LORD has fulfilled his word by causing the lion to attack and kill him."

²⁷Then the prophet said to his sons, "Saddle a donkey for me." So they saddled a donkey, ²⁸and he went out and found the body lying in the road. The donkey and lion were still standing there beside it, for the lion had not eaten the body nor attacked the donkey. ²⁹So the prophet laid the body of the man of God on the donkey and took it back to the town to mourn over him and bury him. ³⁰He laid the body in his own grave, crying out in grief, "Oh, my brother!"

³¹Afterward the prophet said to his sons, "When I die, bury me in the grave where the man of God is buried. Lay my bones beside his bones. ³²For the message the LORD told him to proclaim against the altar in Bethel and against the pagan shrines in the towns of Samaria will certainly come true."

³³But even after this, Jeroboam did not turn from his evil ways. He continued to choose priests from the common people. He appointed anyone who wanted to become a priest for the pagan shrines. ³⁴This became a great sin and resulted in the utter destruction of Jeroboam's dynasty from the face of the earth.

CHAPTER 14
Ahijah's Prophecy against Jeroboam

At that time Jeroboam's son Abijah became very sick. ²So Jeroboam told his wife, "Disguise yourself so that no one will recognize you as my wife. Then go to the prophet Ahijah at Shiloh—the man who told me I would become king. ³Take him a gift of ten loaves of bread, some cakes, and a jar of honey, and ask him what will happen to the boy."

⁴So Jeroboam's wife went to Ahijah's home at Shiloh. He was an old man now and could no longer see. ⁵But the LORD had told Ahijah, "Jeroboam's wife will come here, pretending to be someone else. She will ask you about her son, for he is very sick. Give her the answer I give you."

⁶So when Ahijah heard her footsteps at the door, he called out, "Come in, wife of Jeroboam! Why are you pretending to be someone else?" Then he told her, "I have bad news for you. ⁷Give your husband,

13:33-34 Persistence in doing good is admirable. Persistence in doing wrong displays arrogance and is sure to result in great harm. Jeroboam's apostasy demonstrates just how harmful persistence can be when a person does wrong. After he was warned of God's coming wrath (13:1-32), Jeroboam violated God's commands about the priesthood (Numbers 3:10) by choosing unqualified people as priests. Without accountable relationships, all of us tend to start down the wrong track. We would be wise to find trustworthy friends who will hold us accountable to the truth in God's Word.
14:1-11 Here we see a good example of the dangers of codependency. Jeroboam had made deceit a regular practice during his reign over Israel. As his son was lying on his deathbed, Jeroboam asked his codependent wife to deceive the prophet Abijah by disguising herself. The result of their sin was the destruction of their family. We often cause our spouse to participate in our dependency by consciously or unconsciously asking for his or her help in some way. Jeroboam's wife should have confronted Jeroboam about his sinful ways. Instead, she enabled his sin, and the results were destructive. A spouse's confrontation, though difficult, can often initiate a person's recovery and deliver a family from great suffering.

Jeroboam, this message from the LORD, the God of Israel: 'I promoted you from the ranks of the common people and made you ruler over my people Israel. [8]I ripped the kingdom away from the family of David and gave it to you. But you have not been like my servant David, who obeyed my commands and followed me with all his heart and always did whatever I wanted. [9]You have done more evil than all who lived before you. You have made other gods for yourself and have made me furious with your gold calves. And since you have turned your back on me, [10]I will bring disaster on your dynasty and will destroy every one of your male descendants, slave and free alike, anywhere in Israel. I will burn up your royal dynasty as one burns up trash until it is all gone. [11]The members of Jeroboam's family who die in the city will be eaten by dogs, and those who die in the field will be eaten by vultures. I, the LORD, have spoken.'"

[12]Then Ahijah said to Jeroboam's wife, "Go on home, and when you enter the city, the child will die. [13]All Israel will mourn for him and bury him. He is the only member of your family who will have a proper burial, for this child is the only good thing that the LORD, the God of Israel, sees in the entire family of Jeroboam.

[14]"In addition, the LORD will raise up a king over Israel who will destroy the family of Jeroboam. This will happen today, even now! [15]Then the LORD will shake Israel like a reed whipped about in a stream. He will uproot the people of Israel from this good land that he gave their ancestors and will scatter them beyond the Euphrates River,* for they have angered the LORD with the Asherah poles they have set up for worship. [16]He will abandon Israel because Jeroboam sinned and made Israel sin along with him."

[17]So Jeroboam's wife returned to Tirzah, and the child died just as she walked through the door of her home. [18]And all Israel buried him and mourned for him, as the LORD had promised through the prophet Ahijah.

[19]The rest of the events in Jeroboam's reign, including all his wars and how he ruled, are recorded in *The Book of the History of the Kings of Israel.* [20]Jeroboam reigned in Israel twenty-two years. When Jeroboam died, his son Nadab became the next king.

Rehoboam Rules in Judah

[21]Meanwhile, Rehoboam son of Solomon was king in Judah. He was forty-one years old when he became king, and he reigned seventeen years in Jerusalem, the city the LORD had chosen from among all the tribes of Israel as the place to honor his name. Rehoboam's mother was Naamah, an Ammonite woman.

[22]During Rehoboam's reign, the people of Judah did what was evil in the LORD's sight, provoking his anger with their sin, for it was even worse than that of their ancestors. [23]For they also built for themselves pagan shrines and set up sacred pillars and Asherah poles on every high hill and under every green tree. [24]There were even male and female shrine prostitutes throughout the land. The people imitated the detestable practices of the pagan nations the LORD had driven from the land ahead of the Israelites.

[25]In the fifth year of King Rehoboam's reign, King Shishak of Egypt came up and attacked Jerusalem. [26]He ransacked the treasuries of the LORD's Temple and the royal palace; he stole everything, including all the gold shields Solomon had made. [27]King Rehoboam later replaced them with bronze shields as substitutes, and he entrusted them to the care of the commanders of the guard who protected the entrance to the royal palace. [28]Whenever the king went to the Temple of the LORD, the guards would also take the shields and then return them to the guardroom.

[29]The rest of the events in Rehoboam's reign and everything he did are recorded in *The Book of the History of the Kings of Judah.* [30]There was constant war between Rehoboam and Jeroboam. [31]When Rehoboam died, he was buried among his ancestors in the City of David. His mother was Naamah, an Ammonite woman. Then his son Abijam* became the next king.

14:15 Hebrew *the river.* 14:31 Also known as *Abijah.*

14:22–15:3 Children learn from their parents. Rehoboam learned from Solomon that idol worship was all right. So when Rehoboam became king, idol worship flourished. When Rehoboam's son Abijam became king, he followed in the footsteps of his father, committing "the same sins as his father before him" (15:3). We may not realize how deeply our addictions affect others, but here we can see that Solomon's worship of idols led his son and grandson to disobey God also. What are our children learning from our behaviors and attitudes?

CHAPTER 15
Abijam Rules in Judah

Abijam* began to rule over Judah in the eighteenth year of Jeroboam's reign in Israel. [2]He reigned in Jerusalem three years. His mother was Maacah, the granddaughter of Absalom.*

[3]He committed the same sins as his father before him, and he was not faithful to the LORD his God, as his ancestor David had been. [4]But for David's sake, the LORD his God allowed his descendants to continue ruling, shining like a lamp, and he gave Abijam a son to rule after him in Jerusalem. [5]For David had done what was pleasing in the LORD's sight and had obeyed the LORD's commands throughout his life, except in the affair concerning Uriah the Hittite.

[6]There was war between Abijam and Jeroboam* throughout Abijam's reign. [7]The rest of the events in Abijam's reign and everything he did are recorded in *The Book of the History of the Kings of Judah.* There was constant war between Abijam and Jeroboam. [8]When Abijam died, he was buried in the City of David. Then his son Asa became the next king.

Asa Rules in Judah

[9]Asa began to rule over Judah in the twentieth year of Jeroboam's reign in Israel. [10]He reigned in Jerusalem forty-one years. His grandmother* was Maacah, the granddaughter of Absalom.

[11]Asa did what was pleasing in the LORD's sight, as his ancestor David had done. [12]He banished the male and female shrine prostitutes from the land and got rid of all the idols* his ancestors had made. [13]He even deposed his grandmother Maacah from her position as queen mother because she had made an obscene Asherah pole. He cut down her obscene pole and burned it in the Kidron Valley. [14]Although the pagan shrines were not removed, Asa's heart remained completely faithful to the LORD throughout his life. [15]He brought into the Temple of the LORD the silver and gold and the various items that he and his father had dedicated.

[16]There was constant war between King Asa of Judah and King Baasha of Israel. [17]King Baasha of Israel invaded Judah and fortified Ramah in order to prevent anyone from entering or leaving King Asa's territory in Judah.

[18]Asa responded by removing all the silver and gold that was left in the treasuries of the Temple of the LORD and the royal palace. He sent it with some of his officials to Benhadad son of Tabrimmon, son of Hezion, the king of Aram, who was ruling in Damascus, along with this message:

[19]"Let there be a treaty* between you and me like the one between your father and my father. See, I am sending you a gift of silver and gold. Break your treaty with King Baasha of Israel so that he will leave me alone."

[20]Ben-hadad agreed to King Asa's request and sent the commanders of his army to attack the towns of Israel. They conquered the towns of Ijon, Dan, Abel-beth-maacah, and all Kinnereth, and all the land of Naphtali. [21]As soon as Baasha of Israel heard what was happening, he abandoned his project of fortifying Ramah and withdrew to Tirzah. [22]Then King Asa sent an order throughout Judah, requiring that everyone, without exception, help to carry away the building stones and timbers that Baasha had been using to fortify Ramah. Asa used these materials to fortify the town of Geba in Benjamin and the town of Mizpah.

[23]The rest of the events in Asa's reign—the extent of his power, everything he did, and the names of the cities he built—are recorded in *The Book of the History of the Kings of Judah.* In his old age his feet became diseased. [24]When Asa died, he was buried with his ancestors in the City of David.

Then Jehoshaphat, Asa's son, became the next king.

15:1 Also known as *Abijah.* 15:2 Hebrew *Abishalom* (also in 15:10), a variant spelling of Absalom; compare 2 Chr 11:20. 15:6 As in a few Hebrew and Greek manuscripts; most Hebrew manuscripts read *between Rehoboam and Jeroboam.* 15:10 Or *The queen mother;* Hebrew reads *His mother* (also in 15:13); compare 15:2. 15:12 The Hebrew term (literally *round things*) probably alludes to dung. 15:19 As in Greek version; Hebrew reads *There is a treaty.*

15:9-13 Courage is needed to confront generations of corruption and dysfunctional behavior in any family. Asa showed courage when he confronted the sins of his forefathers by deciding to serve God. Asa's changes included destroying idols and deposing his grandmother from her position as queen mother. In the early years of his reign, Asa leaves us with a wonderful example of how to go about the rebuilding process.

Nadab Rules in Israel

²⁵Nadab son of Jeroboam began to rule over Israel in the second year of King Asa's reign in Judah. He reigned in Israel two years. ²⁶But he did what was evil in the LORD's sight and followed the example of his father, continuing the sins that Jeroboam had led Israel to commit.

²⁷Then Baasha son of Ahijah, from the tribe of Issachar, plotted against Nadab and assassinated him while he and the Israelite army were laying siege to the Philistine town of Gibbethon. ²⁸Baasha killed Nadab in the third year of King Asa's reign in Judah, and he became the next king of Israel.

²⁹He immediately slaughtered all the descendants of King Jeroboam, so that not one of the royal family was left, just as the LORD had promised concerning Jeroboam by the prophet Ahijah from Shiloh. ³⁰This was done because Jeroboam had provoked the anger of the LORD, the God of Israel, by the sins he had committed and the sins he had led Israel to commit.

³¹The rest of the events in Nadab's reign and everything he did are recorded in *The Book of the History of the Kings of Israel.*

Baasha Rules in Israel

³²There was constant war between King Asa of Judah and King Baasha of Israel. ³³Baasha son of Ahijah began to rule over all Israel in the third year of King Asa's reign in Judah. Baasha reigned in Tirzah twenty-four years. ³⁴But he did what was evil in the LORD's sight and followed the example of Jeroboam, continuing the sins that Jeroboam had led Israel to commit.

CHAPTER 16

This message from the LORD was delivered to King Baasha by the prophet Jehu son of Hanani: ²"I lifted you out of the dust to make you ruler of my people Israel, but you have followed the evil example of Jeroboam. You have provoked my anger by causing my people Israel to sin. ³So now I will destroy you and your family, just as I destroyed the descendants of Jeroboam son of Nebat. ⁴The members of Baasha's family who die in the city will be eaten by dogs, and those who die in the field will be eaten by vultures."

⁵The rest of the events in Baasha's reign and the extent of his power are recorded in *The Book of the History of the Kings of Israel.* ⁶When Baasha died, he was buried in Tirzah. Then his son Elah became the next king.

⁷The message from the LORD against Baasha and his family came through the prophet Jehu son of Hanani. It was delivered because Baasha had done what was evil in the LORD's sight (just as the family of Jeroboam had done), and also because Baasha had destroyed the family of Jeroboam. The LORD's anger was provoked by Baasha's sins.

Elah Rules in Israel

⁸Elah son of Baasha began to rule over Israel in the twenty-sixth year of King Asa's reign in Judah. He reigned in the city of Tirzah for two years.

⁹Then Zimri, who commanded half of the royal chariots, made plans to kill him. One day in Tirzah, Elah was getting drunk at the home of Arza, the supervisor of the palace. ¹⁰Zimri walked in and struck him down and killed him. This happened in the twenty-

---

15:25-31 Nadab continued to lead Israel into sin as his father, Jeroboam, had done before him. Leadership must be taken seriously because leaders are ultimately responsible for their followers. As a result of the irresponsible leadership of Jeroboam, God destroyed him and his descendants (15:28-30). Leadership and responsibility go hand in hand; so do recovery and responsibility. If we desire to succeed in recovery, we need to take responsibility for our actions. Then we need to make the appropriate changes in our life.

15:32-34 Baasha is a good example of a person in denial. Baasha ruled in Israel at the same time Asa reigned in Judah (15:32-33). Baasha surely was aware of Asa's reforms and the resultant blessings. He had also seen the sin of his forefathers and the trouble it had caused. But apparently he was blind to the facts, for he repeated the sins of his fathers (15:34). We need to search our life for areas where denial may be keeping us from making an accurate inventory. Otherwise we will never be able to deal with our problems.

16:8-10 Alcohol and drug abuse is often driven by the desire to escape the realities we don't want to face. Every year people die, families are torn apart, careers are ruined, and lives are shattered by unhealthy dependencies. God used Elah to demonstrate the dangers of alcoholism. Probably too intoxicated to defend himself, Elah was killed easily by Zimri (16:10). Alcohol affects our judgment and our reflexes. How many lives could be saved if we would all learn from Elah's mistake?

AHAB & JEZEBEL

Oddly enough, bad role models can be as valuable to us as good ones. Their behavior provides clear guidance on how *not* to act. The consequences they suffer also provide a warning for any who might imitate them. We can often observe the actions of dysfunctional people and plot a healthy course by doing exactly the opposite.

Ahab and Jezebel were bad role models. Ahab was an exceedingly evil and oppressive king, and his wife, Jezebel, taught him things about evil that he would never have dreamed of alone. It is not as if Ahab and Jezebel had no opportunities to understand and pursue recovery. Again and again, the prophet Elijah confronted them about their wicked dealings; again and again they rebutted his efforts to start them on the road to recovery.

Finally, Elijah's confrontation made a difference in Ahab's life. After Jezebel's outrageous scheme allowed Ahab to possess the vineyard of Naboth, Elijah predicted Ahab's violent death. At that point, Ahab greatly humbled himself and went about in deep mourning. He seemed to have hit bottom and began to move toward recovery. There is, however, no record of further progress before Ahab's death in battle.

Jezebel, on the other hand, never made even the slightest move toward God and his ways. Whenever she was defeated by Elijah, she merely redoubled her efforts to maintain her idolatry and get her own way. No wonder her name has become a byword for evil among God's people.

Like most people involved in evil, Ahab and Jezebel surrounded themselves with people of like mind. They avoided and punished people who held them accountable. When we are involved in destructive behavior, we also prefer the comforting darkness of sin and sinful friends. Recovery requires that we break with the past and our destructive relationships. We should listen to the people who love us and who love God enough to hold us accountable for our actions.

WEAKNESSES AND MISTAKES:
- Ahab was the most evil king of Israel.
- Ahab married Jezebel, a pagan woman.
- Ahab allowed Jezebel to practice and promote idol worship in Israel.
- Ahab got depressed when he couldn't get what he wanted.
- Jezebel attempted to stamp out the worship of the true God.

LESSONS FROM THEIR LIVES:
- Human ability, wealth, power, and tenacity will lead us down a dead-end street if we ignore God's plan for us.
- Commitment to false gods will bring us little help; we must be committed to the true God through faith in Jesus Christ.

KEY VERSE:
"No one else so completely sold himself to what was evil in the LORD's sight as Ahab did under the influence of his wife Jezebel" (1 Kings 21:25).

Ahab and Jezebel's story is told in 1 Kings 16—22. Jezebel's story concludes in 2 Kings 9. Ahab is also mentioned in 2 Chronicles 18; 21—22; Micah 6:16.

---

seventh year of King Asa's reign in Judah. Then Zimri became the next king.

¹¹Zimri immediately killed the entire royal family of Baasha, leaving him not even a single male child. He even destroyed distant relatives and friends. ¹²So Zimri destroyed the dynasty of Baasha as the LORD had promised through the prophet Jehu. ¹³This happened because of all the sins Baasha and his son Elah had committed, and because of the sins they led Israel to commit. They provoked the anger of the LORD, the God of Israel, with their worthless idols.

¹⁴The rest of the events in Elah's reign and everything he did are recorded in *The Book of the History of the Kings of Israel.*

Zimri Rules in Israel

¹⁵Zimri began to rule over Israel in the twenty-seventh year of King Asa's reign in Judah, but his reign in Tirzah lasted only seven days. The army of Israel was then

attacking the Philistine town of Gibbethon. [16]When they heard that Zimri had committed treason and had assassinated the king, that very day they chose Omri, commander of the army, as the new king of Israel. [17]So Omri led the entire army of Israel up from Gibbethon to attack Tirzah, Israel's capital. [18]When Zimri saw that the city had been taken, he went into the citadel of the palace and burned it down over himself and died in the flames. [19]For he, too, had done what was evil in the LORD's sight. He followed the example of Jeroboam in all the sins he had committed and led Israel to commit.

[20]The rest of the events in Zimri's reign and his conspiracy are recorded in *The Book of the History of the Kings of Israel*.

Omri Rules in Israel

[21]But now the people of Israel were split into two factions. Half the people tried to make Tibni son of Ginath their king, while the other half supported Omri. [22]But Omri's supporters defeated the supporters of Tibni. So Tibni was killed, and Omri became the next king.

[23]Omri began to rule over Israel in the thirty-first year of King Asa's reign in Judah. He reigned twelve years in all, six of them in Tirzah. [24]Then Omri bought the hill now known as Samaria from its owner, Shemer, for 150 pounds of silver.* He built a city on it and called the city Samaria in honor of Shemer.

[25]But Omri did what was evil in the LORD's sight, even more than any of the kings before him. [26]He followed the example of Jeroboam son of Nebat in all the sins he had committed and led Israel to commit. The people provoked the anger of the LORD, the God of Israel, with their worthless idols.

[27]The rest of the events in Omri's reign, the extent of his power, and everything he did are recorded in *The Book of the History of the Kings of Israel*. [28]When Omri died, he was buried in Samaria. Then his son Ahab became the next king.

Ahab Rules in Israel

[29]Ahab son of Omri began to rule over Israel in the thirty-eighth year of King Asa's reign in Judah. He reigned in Samaria twenty-two years. [30]But Ahab son of Omri did what was evil in the LORD's sight, even more than any of the kings before him. [31]And as though it were not enough to follow the sinful example of Jeroboam, he married Jezebel, the daughter of King Ethbaal of the Sidonians, and he began to bow down in worship of Baal. [32]First Ahab built a temple and an altar for Baal in Samaria. [33]Then he set up an Asherah pole. He did more to provoke the anger of the LORD, the God of Israel, than any of the other kings of Israel before him.

[34]It was during his reign that Hiel, a man from Bethel, rebuilt Jericho. When he laid its foundations, it cost him the life of his oldest son, Abiram. And when he completed it and set up its gates, it cost him the life of his youngest son, Segub.* This all happened according to the message from the LORD concerning Jericho spoken by Joshua son of Nun.

CHAPTER 17
Elijah Fed by Ravens

Now Elijah, who was from Tishbe in Gilead, told King Ahab, "As surely as the LORD, the God of Israel, lives—the God I serve—there will be no dew or rain during the next few years until I give the word!"

[2]Then the LORD said to Elijah, [3]"Go to the east and hide by Kerith Brook, near where it enters the Jordan River. [4]Drink from the brook and eat what the ravens bring you, for I have commanded them to bring you food."

[5]So Elijah did as the LORD told him and camped beside Kerith Brook, east of the Jordan. [6]The ravens brought him bread and

---

16:24 Hebrew *for 2 talents* [68 kilograms] *of silver.* 16:34 An ancient Hebrew scribal tradition reads *He killed his oldest son when he laid its foundations, and he killed his youngest son when he set up its gates.*

16:15-20 Zimri had the shortest reign (seven days) of all the kings of Israel. Omri led the army of Israel against Zimri at Tirzah; seeing that his end was near, Zimri committed suicide. Like those before him, Zimri was an evil king. But even at the end, he had time to call upon God to save him. But rather than submit to almighty God or face the judgment of his people, Zimri took his own life. When it looks like there is no way out of our problems, we need not take such a drastic measure. We should always start by turning to God for help.

16:29-31 A descending spiral well illustrates how we tend to fall progressively deeper into trouble unless we take steps to turn things around. God uses the story of the kings of Israel to illuminate this principle to us. Ahab continued the downward spiral; he was more wicked than any other king before him. Ahab and his forefathers serve as a reminder that problems left unresolved will continue and even worsen until confronted and resolved.

meat each morning and evening, and he drank from the brook. [7]But after a while the brook dried up, for there was no rainfall anywhere in the land.

The Widow at Zarephath

[8]Then the LORD said to Elijah, [9]"Go and live in the village of Zarephath, near the city of Sidon. I have instructed a widow there to feed you."

[10]So he went to Zarephath. As he arrived at the gates of the village, he saw a widow gathering sticks, and he asked her, "Would you please bring me a little water in a cup?" [11]As she was going to get it, he called to her, "Bring me a bite of bread, too."

[12]But she said, "I swear by the LORD your God that I don't have a single piece of bread in the house. And I have only a handful of flour left in the jar and a little cooking oil in the bottom of the jug. I was just gathering a few sticks to cook this last meal, and then my son and I will die."

[13]But Elijah said to her, "Don't be afraid! Go ahead and do just what you've said, but make a little bread for me first. Then use what's left to prepare a meal for yourself and your son. [14]For this is what the LORD, the God of Israel, says: There will always be flour and olive oil left in your containers until the time when the LORD sends rain and the crops grow again!"

[15]So she did as Elijah said, and she and Elijah and her family continued to eat for many days. [16]There was always enough flour and olive oil left in the containers, just as the LORD had promised through Elijah.

[17]Some time later the woman's son became sick. He grew worse and worse, and finally he died. [18]Then she said to Elijah, "O man of God, what have you done to me? Have you come here to point out my sins and kill my son?"

[19]But Elijah replied, "Give me your son." And he took the child's body from her arms, carried him up the stairs to the room where he was staying, and laid the body on his bed. [20]Then Elijah cried out to the LORD, "O LORD my God, why have you brought tragedy to this widow who has opened her home to me, causing her son to die?"

[21]And he stretched himself out over the child three times and cried out to the LORD, "O LORD my God, please let this child's life return to him." [22]The LORD heard Elijah's prayer, and the life of the child returned, and he revived! [23]Then Elijah brought him down from the upper room and gave him to his mother. "Look!" he said. "Your son is alive!"

[24]Then the woman told Elijah, "Now I know for sure that you are a man of God, and that the LORD truly speaks through you."

CHAPTER 18
The Contest on Mount Carmel

Later on, in the third year of the drought, the LORD said to Elijah, "Go and present yourself to King Ahab. Tell him that I will soon send rain!" [2]So Elijah went to appear before Ahab.

Meanwhile, the famine had become very severe in Samaria. [3]So Ahab summoned Obadiah, who was in charge of the palace. (Obadiah was a devoted follower of the LORD. [4]Once when Jezebel had tried to kill all the LORD's prophets, Obadiah had hidden 100 of them in two caves. He put fifty prophets in each cave and supplied them with food and water.) [5]Ahab said to Obadiah, "We must check every spring and valley in the land to see if we can find enough grass to save at least some of my horses and mules." [6]So they divided the land between them. Ahab went one way by himself, and Obadiah went another way by himself.

[7]As Obadiah was walking along, he suddenly saw Elijah coming toward him. Obadiah recognized him at once and bowed low to the ground before him. "Is it really you, my lord Elijah?" he asked.

[8]"Yes, it is," Elijah replied. "Now go and tell your master, 'Elijah is here.'"

[9]"Oh, sir," Obadiah protested, "what harm

17:8-16 The widow of Zarephath demonstrated the delivering power of faith. She and her son faced starvation, but still she shared the last of her food with Elijah. She believed that God would come through, so she gave up her last resource for survival. The result was her deliverance. God provided for her need. When we are powerless—at the end of our rope—all we need to do is call out to God. He will take care of us and deliver us from our dependencies if we are willing to trust him.

17:17-24 When the widow lost her son, her first impulse was to blame it on her own sin. God showed her that this was not the case by bringing her son back to life. Personal tragedy is not always the result of something we have done. We must be careful not to blame ourselves without just cause. And we should never blame God. Instead, we should see what we can learn from the situation.

have I done to you that you are sending me to my death at the hands of Ahab? [10]For I swear by the LORD your God that the king has searched every nation and kingdom on earth from end to end to find you. And each time he was told, 'Elijah isn't here,' King Ahab forced the king of that nation to swear to the truth of his claim. [11]And now you say, 'Go and tell your master, "Elijah is here."' [12]But as soon as I leave you, the Spirit of the LORD will carry you away to who knows where. When Ahab comes and cannot find you, he will kill me. Yet I have been a true servant of the LORD all my life. [13]Has no one told you, my lord, about the time when Jezebel was trying to kill the LORD's prophets? I hid 100 of them in two caves and supplied them with food and water. [14]And now you say, 'Go and tell your master, "Elijah is here."' Sir, if I do that, Ahab will certainly kill me."

[15]But Elijah said, "I swear by the LORD Almighty, in whose presence I stand, that I will present myself to Ahab this very day."

[16]So Obadiah went to tell Ahab that Elijah had come, and Ahab went out to meet Elijah. [17]When Ahab saw him, he exclaimed, "So, is it really you, you troublemaker of Israel?"

[18]"I have made no trouble for Israel," Elijah replied. "You and your family are the troublemakers, for you have refused to obey the commands of the LORD and have worshiped the images of Baal instead. [19]Now summon all Israel to join me at Mount Carmel, along with the 450 prophets of Baal and the 400 prophets of Asherah who are supported by Jezebel.*"

[20]So Ahab summoned all the people of Israel and the prophets to Mount Carmel. [21]Then Elijah stood in front of them and said, "How much longer will you waver, hobbling between two opinions? If the LORD is God, follow him! But if Baal is God, then follow him!" But the people were completely silent.

[22]Then Elijah said to them, "I am the only prophet of the LORD who is left, but Baal has 450 prophets. [23]Now bring two bulls. The prophets of Baal may choose whichever one

they wish and cut it into pieces and lay it on the wood of their altar, but without setting fire to it. I will prepare the other bull and lay it on the wood on the altar, but not set fire to it. [24]Then call on the name of your god, and I will call on the name of the LORD. The god who answers by setting fire to the wood is the true God!" And all the people agreed.

[25]Then Elijah said to the prophets of Baal, "You go first, for there are many of you. Choose one of the bulls, and prepare it and call on the name of your god. But do not set fire to the wood."

[26]So they prepared one of the bulls and placed it on the altar. Then they called on the name of Baal from morning until noontime, shouting, "O Baal, answer us!" But there was no reply of any kind. Then they danced, hobbling around the altar they had made.

[27]About noontime Elijah began mocking them. "You'll have to shout louder," he scoffed, "for surely he is a god! Perhaps he is daydreaming, or is relieving himself.* Or maybe he is away on a trip, or is asleep and needs to be wakened!"

[28]So they shouted louder, and following their normal custom, they cut themselves with knives and swords until the blood gushed out. [29]They raved all afternoon until the time of the evening sacrifice, but still there was no sound, no reply, no response.

[30]Then Elijah called to the people, "Come over here!" They all crowded around him as he repaired the altar of the LORD that had been torn down. [31]He took twelve stones, one to represent each of the tribes of Israel,* [32]and he used the stones to rebuild the altar in the name of the LORD. Then he dug a trench around the altar large enough to hold about three gallons.* [33]He piled wood on the altar, cut the bull into pieces, and laid the pieces on the wood.*

Then he said, "Fill four large jars with water, and pour the water over the offering and the wood."

[34]After they had done this, he said, "Do the same thing again!" And when they were finished, he said, "Now do it a third time!"

18:19 Hebrew *who eat at Jezebel's table.* **18:27** Or *is busy somewhere else,* or *is engaged in business.* **18:31** Hebrew *each of the tribes of the sons of Jacob to whom the LORD had said, "Your name will be Israel."* **18:32** Hebrew *2 seahs [14.6 liters] of seed.* **18:33** Verse 18:34 in the Hebrew text begins here.

18:22-39 "The odds are against us" is a common phrase in our society. Few enjoy being the underdog, the one that the odds are against. The underdog here was Elijah, who was greatly outnumbered by the prophets of Baal. Elijah trusted God to be with him in what has become one of the greatest spiritual victories of all time. When God is on our side, we are always a majority. No dependency or problem will ever be able to stop our progress. "If God is for us, who can ever be against us?" (Romans 8:31).

So they did as he said, ³⁵and the water ran around the altar and even filled the trench.

³⁶At the usual time for offering the evening sacrifice, Elijah the prophet walked up to the altar and prayed, "O LORD, God of Abraham, Isaac, and Jacob,* prove today that you are God in Israel and that I am your servant. Prove that I have done all this at your command. ³⁷O LORD, answer me! Answer me so these people will know that you, O LORD, are God and that you have brought them back to yourself."

³⁸Immediately the fire of the LORD flashed down from heaven and burned up the young bull, the wood, the stones, and the dust. It even licked up all the water in the trench! ³⁹And when all the people saw it, they fell face down on the ground and cried out, "The LORD—he is God! Yes, the LORD is God!"

⁴⁰Then Elijah commanded, "Seize all the prophets of Baal. Don't let a single one escape!" So the people seized them all, and Elijah took them down to the Kishon Valley and killed them there.

Elijah Prays for Rain

⁴¹Then Elijah said to Ahab, "Go get something to eat and drink, for I hear a mighty rainstorm coming!"

⁴²So Ahab went to eat and drink. But Elijah climbed to the top of Mount Carmel and bowed low to the ground and prayed with his face between his knees.

⁴³Then he said to his servant, "Go and look out toward the sea."

The servant went and looked, then returned to Elijah and said, "I didn't see anything."

Seven times Elijah told him to go and look. ⁴⁴Finally the seventh time, his servant told him, "I saw a little cloud about the size of a man's hand rising from the sea."

Then Elijah shouted, "Hurry to Ahab and tell him, 'Climb into your chariot and go back home. If you don't hurry, the rain will stop you!'"

⁴⁵And soon the sky was black with clouds. A heavy wind brought a terrific rainstorm, and Ahab left quickly for Jezreel. ⁴⁶Then the LORD gave special strength to Elijah. He tucked his cloak into his belt* and ran ahead of Ahab's chariot all the way to the entrance of Jezreel.

18:36 Hebrew *and Israel.* The names "Jacob" and "Israel" are often interchanged throughout the Old Testament, referring sometimes to the individual patriarch and sometimes to the nation. **18:46** Hebrew *He bound up his loins.*

PERFECTIONISM

READ 1 KINGS 19:1-21
People who are perfectionists tend to see the world in black and white. We often feel like we're superhuman, able to take on anything—until we discover a flaw. Then we come crashing down and consider ourself completely worthless. This "all or nothing" way of thinking can be very dangerous to the recovery process.

The prophet Elijah is one of the great heroes of the Bible. If anyone had reason to feel superhuman, it was he. His prayers brought a lengthy drought upon Israel— and later brought fire down from heaven, humiliating Queen Jezebel and her priests of Baal. But even Elijah could have a bad day. Let's consider his reaction after being threatened by Jezebel. "'I have had enough, LORD,' he said. 'Take my life. . . . I have zealously served the LORD God Almighty. But the people of Israel have broken their covenant with you, torn down your altars, and killed every one of your prophets. I am the only one left, and now they are trying to kill me, too'" (1 Kings 19:4, 10). Then God told him that there were "7,000 others in Israel who have never bowed down to Baal or kissed him!" (19:18).

Like Elijah, if we're perfectionists, we may think that we are above everyone else. We work very hard to please God and other people, but we can grow dangerously discouraged if things don't seem to work. This tendency is something for us to watch for while working on Step Four. If we don't allow ourself to be less than perfect, we may find that we are at great risk when life reminds us that we are only human after all. ***Turn to page 655, Job 19.***

CHAPTER 19
Elijah Flees to Sinai

When Ahab got home, he told Jezebel everything Elijah had done, including the way he had killed all the prophets of Baal. ²So Jezebel sent this message to Elijah: "May the gods strike me and even kill me if by this time tomorrow I have not killed you just as you killed them."

³Elijah was afraid and fled for his life. He went to Beersheba, a town in Judah, and he left his servant there. ⁴Then he went on alone into the wilderness, traveling all day. He sat down under a solitary broom tree and prayed that he might die. "I have had enough, LORD," he said. "Take my life, for I am no better than my ancestors who have already died."

⁵Then he lay down and slept under the broom tree. But as he was sleeping, an angel touched him and told him, "Get up and eat!" ⁶He looked around and there beside his head was some bread baked on hot stones and a jar of water! So he ate and drank and lay down again.

⁷Then the angel of the LORD came again and touched him and said, "Get up and eat some more, or the journey ahead will be too much for you."

⁸So he got up and ate and drank, and the food gave him enough strength to travel forty days and forty nights to Mount Sinai,* the mountain of God. ⁹There he came to a cave, where he spent the night.

The LORD Speaks to Elijah

But the LORD said to him, "What are you doing here, Elijah?"

¹⁰Elijah replied, "I have zealously served the LORD God Almighty. But the people of Israel have broken their covenant with you, torn down your altars, and killed every one of your prophets. I am the only one left, and now they are trying to kill me, too."

¹¹"Go out and stand before me on the mountain," the LORD told him. And as Elijah stood there, the LORD passed by, and a mighty windstorm hit the mountain. It was such a terrible blast that the rocks were torn loose, but the LORD was not in the wind. After the wind there was an earthquake, but the LORD was not in the earthquake. ¹²And after the earthquake there was a fire, but the LORD was not in the fire. And after the fire there was the sound of a gentle whisper. ¹³When Elijah heard it, he wrapped his face in his cloak and went out and stood at the entrance of the cave.

And a voice said, "What are you doing here, Elijah?"

¹⁴He replied again, "I have zealously served the LORD God Almighty. But the people of Israel have broken their covenant with you, torn down your altars, and killed every one of your prophets. I am the only one left, and now they are trying to kill me, too."

¹⁵Then the LORD told him, "Go back the same way you came, and travel to the wilderness of Damascus. When you arrive there, anoint Hazael to be king of Aram. ¹⁶Then anoint Jehu grandson of Nimshi* to be king of Israel, and anoint Elisha son of Shaphat from the town of Abel-meholah to replace you as my prophet. ¹⁷Anyone who escapes from Hazael will be killed by Jehu, and those who escape Jehu will be killed by Elisha! ¹⁸Yet I will preserve 7,000 others in Israel who have never bowed down to Baal or kissed him!"

The Call of Elisha

¹⁹So Elijah went and found Elisha son of Shaphat plowing a field. There were twelve teams of oxen in the field, and Elisha was plowing with the twelfth team. Elijah went over to him and threw his cloak across his shoulders and then walked away. ²⁰Elisha left the oxen standing there, ran after Elijah, and said to him, "First let me go and kiss my

19:8 Hebrew *to Horeb,* another name for Sinai. 19:16 Hebrew *descendant of Nimshi;* compare 2 Kgs 9:2, 14.

19:1-4 After our greatest victories, we are often the most vulnerable to a fall. Elijah had just won an amazing victory with God's help, but suddenly he became so discouraged that he wanted to die. He had already forgotten the power God had displayed on Mount Carmel. We often do the same thing. As we depend on God's power, we progress in the recovery process. But suddenly opposition comes our way or we are overcome by temptation. We begin to wish we could die. Let us learn from Elijah. We would be wise to consider our victories as warning signs, times when we should renew our dependence on God. This will help us experience one success after another.
19:5-18 Self-doubt is common to all of us. Elijah doubted himself when he was on the run from Jezebel. God dealt with Elijah in a loving, patient manner by reassuring him that he was not alone. Reassurance and rest are a solid prescription for someone afflicted with self-doubt. We need to build a community of support to help us through the difficult times of recovery. Without the help of others, it will be impossible for us to succeed.

father and mother good-bye, and then I will go with you!"

Elijah replied, "Go on back, but think about what I have done to you."

²¹So Elisha returned to his oxen and slaughtered them. He used the wood from the plow to build a fire to roast their flesh. He passed around the meat to the townspeople, and they all ate. Then he went with Elijah as his assistant.

CHAPTER 20
Ben-Hadad Attacks Samaria

About that time King Ben-hadad of Aram mobilized his army, supported by the chariots and horses of thirty-two allied kings. They went to besiege Samaria, the capital of Israel, and launched attacks against it. ²Ben-hadad sent messengers into the city to relay this message to King Ahab of Israel: "This is what Ben-hadad says: ³'Your silver and gold are mine, and so are your wives and the best of your children!'"

⁴"All right, my lord the king," Israel's king replied. "All that I have is yours!"

⁵Soon Ben-hadad's messengers returned again and said, "This is what Ben-hadad says: 'I have already demanded that you give me your silver, gold, wives, and children. ⁶But about this time tomorrow I will send my officials to search your palace and the homes of your officials. They will take away everything you consider valuable!'"

⁷Then Ahab summoned all the elders of the land and said to them, "Look how this man is stirring up trouble! I already agreed with his demand that I give him my wives and children and silver and gold."

⁸"Don't give in to any more demands," all the elders and the people advised.

⁹So Ahab told the messengers from Ben-hadad, "Say this to my lord the king: 'I will give you everything you asked for the first time, but I cannot accept this last demand of yours.'" So the messengers returned to Ben-hadad with that response.

¹⁰Then Ben-hadad sent this message to Ahab: "May the gods strike me and even kill me if there remains enough dust from Sa-

maria to provide even a handful for each of my soldiers."

¹¹The king of Israel sent back this answer: "A warrior putting on his sword for battle should not boast like a warrior who has already won."

¹²Ahab's reply reached Ben-hadad and the other kings as they were drinking in their tents.* "Prepare to attack!" Ben-hadad commanded his officers. So they prepared to attack the city.

Ahab's Victory over Ben-Hadad

¹³Then a certain prophet came to see King Ahab of Israel and told him, "This is what the LORD says: Do you see all these enemy forces? Today I will hand them all over to you. Then you will know that I am the LORD."

¹⁴Ahab asked, "How will he do it?"

And the prophet replied, "This is what the LORD says: The troops of the provincial commanders will do it."

"Should we attack first?" Ahab asked.

"Yes," the prophet answered.

¹⁵So Ahab mustered the troops of the 232 provincial commanders. Then he called out the rest of the army of Israel, some 7,000 men. ¹⁶About noontime, as Ben-hadad and the thirty-two allied kings were still in their tents drinking themselves into a stupor, ¹⁷the troops of the provincial commanders marched out of the city as the first contingent.

As they approached, Ben-hadad's scouts reported to him, "Some troops are coming from Samaria."

¹⁸"Take them alive," Ben-hadad commanded, "whether they have come for peace or for war."

¹⁹But Ahab's provincial commanders and the entire army had now come out to fight. ²⁰Each Israelite soldier killed his Aramean opponent, and suddenly the entire Aramean army panicked and fled. The Israelites chased them, but King Ben-hadad and a few of his charioteers escaped on horses. ²¹However, the king of Israel destroyed the other horses and chariots and slaughtered the Arameans.

20:12 Or *in Succoth;* also in 20:16.

20:10-21 A common result of drug and alcohol abuse is impaired reasoning. This was demonstrated by Ben-hadad, who was drinking when Ahab's refusal to surrender arrived. He and the other kings of his coalition were drunk. Ben-hadad was soundly surprised by Ahab's attack in the middle of the day. While Ben-hadad survived, his men did not. Substance abuse does not mix with a victorious life.

²²Afterward the prophet said to King Ahab, "Get ready for another attack. Begin making plans now, for the king of Aram will come back next spring.*"

Ben-Hadad's Second Attack

²³After their defeat, Ben-hadad's officers said to him, "The Israelite gods are gods of the hills; that is why they won. But we can beat them easily on the plains. ²⁴Only this time replace the kings with field commanders! ²⁵Recruit another army like the one you lost. Give us the same number of horses, chariots, and men, and we will fight against them on the plains. There's no doubt that we will beat them." So King Ben-hadad did as they suggested.

²⁶The following spring he called up the Aramean army and marched out against Israel, this time at Aphek. ²⁷Israel then mustered its army, set up supply lines, and marched out for battle. But the Israelite army looked like two little flocks of goats in comparison to the vast Aramean forces that filled the countryside!

²⁸Then the man of God went to the king of Israel and said, "This is what the LORD says: The Arameans have said, 'The LORD is a god of the hills and not of the plains.' So I will defeat this vast army for you. Then you will know that I am the LORD."

²⁹The two armies camped opposite each other for seven days, and on the seventh day the battle began. The Israelites killed 100,000 Aramean foot soldiers in one day. ³⁰The rest fled into the town of Aphek, but the wall fell on them and killed another 27,000. Ben-hadad fled into the town and hid in a secret room.

³¹Ben-hadad's officers said to him, "Sir, we have heard that the kings of Israel are merciful. So let's humble ourselves by wearing burlap around our waists and putting ropes on our heads, and surrender to the king of Israel. Then perhaps he will let you live."

³²So they put on burlap and ropes, and they went to the king of Israel and begged, "Your servant Ben-hadad says, 'Please let me live!'"

The king of Israel responded, "Is he still alive? He is my brother!"

³³The men took this as a good sign and quickly picked up on his words. "Yes," they said, "your brother Ben-hadad!"

"Go and get him," the king of Israel told them. And when Ben-hadad arrived, Ahab invited him up into his chariot.

³⁴Ben-hadad told him, "I will give back the towns my father took from your father, and you may establish places of trade in Damascus, as my father did in Samaria."

Then Ahab said, "I will release you under these conditions." So they made a new treaty, and Ben-hadad was set free.

A Prophet Condemns Ahab

³⁵Meanwhile, the LORD instructed one of the group of prophets to say to another man, "Hit me!" But the man refused to hit the prophet. ³⁶Then the prophet told him, "Because you have not obeyed the voice of the LORD, a lion will kill you as soon as you leave me." And when he had gone, a lion did attack and kill him.

³⁷Then the prophet turned to another man and said, "Hit me!" So he struck the prophet and wounded him.

³⁸The prophet placed a bandage over his eyes to disguise himself and then waited beside the road for the king. ³⁹As the king passed by, the prophet called out to him, "Sir, I was in the thick of battle, and suddenly a man brought me a prisoner. He said, 'Guard this man; if for any reason he gets away, you will either die or pay a fine of seventy-five pounds* of silver!' ⁴⁰But while I was busy doing something else, the prisoner disappeared!"

"Well, it's your own fault," the king replied. "You have brought the judgment on yourself."

⁴¹Then the prophet quickly pulled the bandage from his eyes, and the king of Israel recognized him as one of the prophets. ⁴²The prophet said to him, "This is what the LORD

20:22 Hebrew *at the turn of the year;* similarly in 20:26. The first day of the year in the ancient Hebrew lunar calendar occurred in March or April. **20:39** Hebrew *1 talent* [34 kilograms].

20:35-43 When we reject God's will in favor of our own, we are headed for trouble. Ahab was commanded to execute Ben-hadad, but he allowed him to live. He saw Ben-hadad as a possible ally against Assyria. The result of Ahab's disobedience was eventually his death. We must learn to obey God's Word in every detail. Only then can we live a healthy life. If God calls us to remove certain things from our life, we must act immediately. Allowing them to remain will lead to our eventual destruction.

says: Because you have spared the man I said must be destroyed,* now you must die in his place, and your people will die instead of his people." ⁴³So the king of Israel went home to Samaria angry and sullen.

CHAPTER 21
Naboth's Vineyard

Now there was a man named Naboth, from Jezreel, who owned a vineyard in Jezreel beside the palace of King Ahab of Samaria. ²One day Ahab said to Naboth, "Since your vineyard is so convenient to my palace, I would like to buy it to use as a vegetable garden. I will give you a better vineyard in exchange, or if you prefer, I will pay you for it."

³But Naboth replied, "The LORD forbid that I should give you the inheritance that was passed down by my ancestors."

⁴So Ahab went home angry and sullen because of Naboth's answer. The king went to bed with his face to the wall and refused to eat!

⁵"What's the matter?" his wife Jezebel asked him. "What's made you so upset that you're not eating?"

⁶"I asked Naboth to sell me his vineyard or trade it, but he refused!" Ahab told her.

⁷"Are you the king of Israel or not?" Jezebel demanded. "Get up and eat something, and don't worry about it. I'll get you Naboth's vineyard!"

⁸So she wrote letters in Ahab's name, sealed them with his seal, and sent them to the elders and other leaders of the town where Naboth lived. ⁹In her letters she commanded: "Call the citizens together for a time of fasting, and give Naboth a place of honor. ¹⁰And then seat two scoundrels across from him who will accuse him of cursing God and the king. Then take him out and stone him to death."

¹¹So the elders and other town leaders followed the instructions Jezebel had written in the letters. ¹²They called for a fast and put Naboth at a prominent place before the people. ¹³Then the two scoundrels came and sat down across from him. And they accused Naboth before all the people, saying, "He cursed God and the king." So he was dragged outside the town and stoned to death. ¹⁴The town leaders then sent word to Jezebel, "Naboth has been stoned to death."

¹⁵When Jezebel heard the news, she said to Ahab, "You know the vineyard Naboth wouldn't sell you? Well, you can have it now! He's dead!" ¹⁶So Ahab immediately went down to the vineyard of Naboth to claim it.

¹⁷But the LORD said to Elijah,* ¹⁸"Go down to meet King Ahab of Israel, who rules in Samaria. He will be at Naboth's vineyard in Jezreel, claiming it for himself. ¹⁹Give him this message: 'This is what the LORD says: Wasn't it enough that you killed Naboth? Must you rob him, too? Because you have done this, dogs will lick your blood at the very place where they licked the blood of Naboth!'"

²⁰"So, my enemy, you have found me!" Ahab exclaimed to Elijah.

"Yes," Elijah answered, "I have come because you have sold yourself to what is evil in the LORD's sight. ²¹So now the LORD says,* 'I will bring disaster on you and consume you. I will destroy every one of your male descendants, slave and free alike, anywhere in Israel! ²²I am going to destroy your family as I did the family of Jeroboam son of Nebat and the family of Baasha son of Ahijah, for you have made me very angry and have led Israel into sin.'

²³"And regarding Jezebel, the LORD says, 'Dogs will eat Jezebel's body at the plot of land in Jezreel.*'

20:42 The Hebrew term used here refers to the complete consecration of things or people to the LORD, either by destroying them or by giving them as an offering. 21:17 Hebrew *Elijah the Tishbite;* also in 21:28. 21:21 As in Greek version; Hebrew lacks *So now the LORD says.* 21:23 As in several Hebrew manuscripts, Syriac, and Latin Vulgate (see also 2 Kgs 9:26, 36); most Hebrew manuscripts read *at the city wall.*

21:1-6 Ahab tried to use his power as king to force Naboth to sell him his vineyard, but Naboth refused. Even though Ahab was the king of Israel, he could not force Naboth to sell the land. He had to abide by God's laws. Ahab had been worshiping idols, but he still recognized God as an authority in his life. If we are in a position of power, we must remember that we will have to answer to God for our actions. Are we following his commands?

21:7-14 Jezebel's need to "have it all" drove her to plot the death of an innocent man. An obsession, such as greed, can severely taint our sense of right and wrong as evidenced by the murder of Naboth. Many of us are enslaved to a compulsive behavior that leads to a multitude of other sins. We must begin the journey toward recovery by recognizing that this behavior is a real problem. Then we can give our compulsions and dependencies over to God and seek to follow his program for healthy living.

²⁴"The members of Ahab's family who die in the city will be eaten by dogs, and those who die in the field will be eaten by vultures."

²⁵(No one else so completely sold himself to what was evil in the LORD's sight as Ahab did under the influence of his wife Jezebel. ²⁶His worst outrage was worshiping idols* just as the Amorites had done—the people whom the LORD had driven out from the land ahead of the Israelites.)

²⁷But when Ahab heard this message, he tore his clothing, dressed in burlap, and fasted. He even slept in burlap and went about in deep mourning.

²⁸Then another message from the LORD came to Elijah: ²⁹"Do you see how Ahab has humbled himself before me? Because he has done this, I will not do what I promised during his lifetime. It will happen to his sons; I will destroy his dynasty."

CHAPTER 22
Jehoshaphat and Ahab

For three years there was no war between Aram and Israel. ²Then during the third year, King Jehoshaphat of Judah went to visit King Ahab of Israel. ³During the visit, the king of Israel said to his officials, "Do you realize that the town of Ramoth-gilead belongs to us? And yet we've done nothing to recapture it from the king of Aram!"

⁴Then he turned to Jehoshaphat and asked, "Will you join me in battle to recover Ramoth-gilead?"

Jehoshaphat replied to the king of Israel, "Why, of course! You and I are as one. My troops are your troops, and my horses are your horses." ⁵Then Jehoshaphat added, "But first let's find out what the LORD says."

⁶So the king of Israel summoned the prophets, about 400 of them, and asked them, "Should I go to war against Ramoth-gilead, or should I hold back?"

They all replied, "Yes, go right ahead! The Lord will give the king victory."

⁷But Jehoshaphat asked, "Is there not also a prophet of the LORD here? We should ask him the same question."

⁸The king of Israel replied to Jehoshaphat, "There is one more man who could consult the LORD for us, but I hate him. He never prophesies anything but trouble for me! His name is Micaiah son of Imlah."

Jehoshaphat replied, "That's not the way a king should talk! Let's hear what he has to say."

⁹So the king of Israel called one of his officials and said, "Quick! Bring Micaiah son of Imlah."

Micaiah Prophesies against Ahab

¹⁰King Ahab of Israel and King Jehoshaphat of Judah, dressed in their royal robes, were sitting on thrones at the threshing floor near the gate of Samaria. All of Ahab's prophets were prophesying there in front of them. ¹¹One of them, Zedekiah son of Kenaanah, made some iron horns and proclaimed, "This is what the LORD says: With these horns you will gore the Arameans to death!"

¹²All the other prophets agreed. "Yes," they said, "go up to Ramoth-gilead and be victorious, for the LORD will give the king victory!"

¹³Meanwhile, the messenger who went to get Micaiah said to him, "Look, all the prophets are promising victory for the king. Be sure that you agree with them and promise success."

¹⁴But Micaiah replied, "As surely as the LORD lives, I will say only what the LORD tells me to say."

¹⁵When Micaiah arrived before the king, Ahab asked him, "Micaiah, should we go to war against Ramoth-gilead, or should we hold back?"

Micaiah replied sarcastically, "Yes, go up and be victorious, for the LORD will give the king victory!"

¹⁶But the king replied sharply, "How many times must I demand that you speak only the truth to me when you speak for the LORD?"

¹⁷Then Micaiah told him, "In a vision I saw all Israel scattered on the mountains, like sheep without a shepherd. And the LORD said, 'Their master has been killed.* Send them home in peace.'"

¹⁸"Didn't I tell you?" the king of Israel exclaimed to Jehoshaphat. "He never prophesies anything but trouble for me."

¹⁹Then Micaiah continued, "Listen to what the LORD says! I saw the LORD sitting on his throne with all the armies of heaven around him, on his right and on his left. ²⁰And the LORD said, 'Who can entice Ahab to go into battle against Ramoth-gilead so he can be killed?'

"There were many suggestions, ²¹and finally a spirit approached the LORD and said, 'I can do it!'

²²"'How will you do this?' the LORD asked.

21:26 The Hebrew term (literally *round things*) probably alludes to dung.   22:17 Hebrew *These people have no master.*

"And the spirit replied, 'I will go out and inspire all of Ahab's prophets to speak lies.'

" 'You will succeed,' said the LORD. 'Go ahead and do it.'

²³"So you see, the LORD has put a lying spirit in the mouths of all your prophets. For the LORD has pronounced your doom."

²⁴Then Zedekiah son of Kenaanah walked up to Micaiah and slapped him across the face. "Since when did the Spirit of the LORD leave me to speak to you?" he demanded.

²⁵And Micaiah replied, "You will find out soon enough when you are trying to hide in some secret room!"

²⁶"Arrest him!" the king of Israel ordered. "Take him back to Amon, the governor of the city, and to my son Joash. ²⁷Give them this order from the king: 'Put this man in prison, and feed him nothing but bread and water until I return safely from the battle!' "

²⁸But Micaiah replied, "If you return safely, it will mean that the LORD has not spoken through me!" Then he added to those standing around, "Everyone mark my words!"

The Death of Ahab

²⁹So King Ahab of Israel and King Jehoshaphat of Judah led their armies against Ramoth-gilead. ³⁰The king of Israel said to Jehoshaphat, "As we go into battle, I will disguise myself so no one will recognize me, but you wear your royal robes." So the king of Israel disguised himself, and they went into battle.

³¹Meanwhile, the king of Aram had issued these orders to his thirty-two chariot commanders: "Attack only the king of Israel. Don't bother with anyone else!" ³²So when the Aramean chariot commanders saw Jehoshaphat in his royal robes, they went after him. "There is the king of Israel!" they shouted. But when Jehoshaphat called out, ³³the chariot commanders realized he was not the king of Israel, and they stopped chasing him.

³⁴An Aramean soldier, however, randomly shot an arrow at the Israelite troops and hit the king of Israel between the joints of his ar-

mor. "Turn the horses* and get me out of here!" Ahab groaned to the driver of his chariot. "I'm badly wounded!"

³⁵The battle raged all that day, and the king remained propped up in his chariot facing the Arameans. The blood from his wound ran down to the floor of his chariot, and as evening arrived he died. ³⁶Just as the sun was setting, the cry ran through his troops: "We're done for! Run for your lives!"

³⁷So the king died, and his body was taken to Samaria and buried there. ³⁸Then his chariot was washed beside the pool of Samaria, and dogs came and licked his blood at the place where the prostitutes bathed,* just as the LORD had promised.

³⁹The rest of the events in Ahab's reign and everything he did, including the story of the ivory palace and the towns he built, are recorded in *The Book of the History of the Kings of Israel*. ⁴⁰So Ahab died, and his son Ahaziah became the next king.

Jehoshaphat Rules in Judah

⁴¹Jehoshaphat son of Asa began to rule over Judah in the fourth year of King Ahab's reign in Israel. ⁴²Jehoshaphat was thirty-five years old when he became king, and he reigned in Jerusalem twenty-five years. His mother was Azubah, the daughter of Shilhi.

⁴³Jehoshaphat was a good king, following the example of his father, Asa. He did what was pleasing in the LORD's sight. *During his reign, however, he failed to remove all the pagan shrines, and the people still offered sacrifices and burned incense there. ⁴⁴Jehoshaphat also made peace with the king of Israel.

⁴⁵The rest of the events in Jehoshaphat's reign, the extent of his power, and the wars he waged are recorded in *The Book of the History of the Kings of Judah*. ⁴⁶He banished from the land the rest of the male and female shrine prostitutes, who still continued their practices from the days of his father, Asa.

⁴⁷(There was no king in Edom at that time, only a deputy.)

22:34 Hebrew *Turn your hand.* 22:38 Or *his blood, and the prostitutes bathed [in it];* or *his blood, and they washed his armor.* 22:43 Verses 22:43b-53 are numbered 22:44-54 in Hebrew text.

22:30-40 Whatever God says will happen, will happen. Ahab disguised himself in battle so he wouldn't be killed, but he was shot by a stray arrow. Notice that the prophecy in 21:19 came true, three years after it was given. Justice is served by God in his timing, not ours. People may seem to get away with sin and denial for a while, but eventually their deeds will catch up with them.

22:41-43 Jehoshaphat was a good king who built on the positive steps of his father, Asa. Successful parenting involves modeling godly standards of conduct for our children. As our children watch us take steps toward recovery, they will learn about God's power of deliverance and the blessings that result from trust and obedience.

⁴⁸Jehoshaphat also built a fleet of trading ships* to sail to Ophir for gold. But the ships never set sail, for they met with disaster in their home port of Ezion-geber. ⁴⁹At one time Ahaziah son of Ahab had proposed to Jehoshaphat, "Let my men sail with your men in the ships." But Jehoshaphat refused the request.

⁵⁰When Jehoshaphat died, he was buried with his ancestors in the City of David. Then his son Jehoram became the next king.

22:48 Hebrew *fleet of ships of Tarshish.*

Ahaziah Rules in Israel

⁵¹Ahaziah son of Ahab began to rule over Israel in the seventeenth year of King Jehoshaphat's reign in Judah. He reigned in Samaria two years. ⁵²But he did what was evil in the LORD's sight, following the example of his father and mother and the example of Jeroboam son of Nebat, who had led Israel to sin. ⁵³He served Baal and worshiped him, provoking the anger of the LORD, the God of Israel, just as his father had done.

2 KINGS

THE BIG PICTURE

A. ISRAEL'S EXILE TO ASSYRIA: FROM DENIAL TO UTTER DEFEAT (1:1–17:41)
   1. Confrontation by Elijah and Elisha (1:1–13:25)
   2. Israel's Sin and Denial Leads to Defeat (14:1–17:41)
B. JUDAH'S EXILE TO BABYLON: REPEATED TRAGEDY FOR GOD'S PEOPLE (18:1–25:30)
   1. Fathers and Sons: Choices for Recovery or Oppression (18:1–23:30)
   2. The Last Stages of Denial and Defeat (23:31–25:30)

The book of 2 Kings was originally part of a larger book that also included 1 Kings. It recorded Israel's history from the end of David's reign to the demise of both its kingdoms. The book of 2 Kings opens with Israel already divided into northern and southern kingdoms. It records a succession of kings, many of them ungodly, and the inevitable movement of both kingdoms toward destruction and exile. First the northern kingdom fell to Assyria. Then the southern kingdom fell to Babylon.

The progression of events in 2 Kings could easily be likened to the gathering darkness at nightfall. The people suffered from a progressive darkening of a spiritual nature—denial and unbelief that led to spiritual darkness. Along the way, there were prophets like Elijah, Elisha, and Isaiah—and kings like Hezekiah and Josiah—who did their best to brighten the horizon by restoring God's way among the people. But eventually the influence of many godless kings brought destruction.

The writer of Kings wanted to make sure that the exiled Israelites learned from the mistakes of their parents. By narrating the events of their past, he showed how disobedience brought destruction and was the cause of their tragic plight. The people had disobeyed God, despite God's repeated attempts to get their attention through his prophets and a few godly kings.

The consequences for Israel's chronic sin were tragic and seemingly irreparable: The Temple was destroyed; David's royal line no longer ruled in Jerusalem; and the people were exiled from their homeland. Despite the gloomy ending of this book, however, the story of God's people will continue with rebuilding and restoration. There is always hope for the future.

THE BOTTOM LINE

PURPOSE: To record the final years of the northern and southern kingdoms and to demonstrate that prolonged denial and disobedience to God's program are destructive. AUTHOR: Unknown; possibly Jeremiah or another writer from the period of Babylonian exile (sixth century B.C.). AUDIENCE: The people of Israel in Babylonian exile. DATE WRITTEN: Sometime between 560 and 538 B.C. SETTING: The divided kingdoms of Israel and Judah, with concluding scenes in Babylonian exile. KEY VERSE: "But the Israelites would not listen. They were as stubborn as their ancestors who had refused to believe in the LORD their God" (17:14). KEY PEOPLE AND RELATIONSHIPS: Elijah with Elisha, Hezekiah, Sennacherib, Isaiah, Manasseh, Josiah, and Nebuchadnezzar.

RECOVERY THEMES

The Power of Denial: Nothing is as frustrating as dealing with people in denial. No matter how well we may argue a point—no matter how good the evidence—it is impossible to penetrate their defenses. Of the thirty-nine kings that Israel and Judah had between them after the death of Solomon, only eight of them responded to the truth of God. The others, in spite of all the evidence presented by the prophets, continued in denial and refused to admit the sin in their life. As a result, the good kings spent most of their time undoing the evil of their predecessors.

A Model of Intervention: As we see how patient God was with Israel, it is important that we don't mistake his patience for indifference. God did confront these evil kings through his prophets, through miracles, and through his Word (see 22:8-13). God was active, confronting the sins of Israel and Judah, seeking to lovingly intervene with the truth. Looking back at the events in this book, it seems difficult to understand why the kings and the people were so rebellious. That is our warning. We also need to see that God is still constantly and lovingly seeking to confront his people with the truth. That is our hope.

Hitting Bottom: Sometimes interventions don't work. That was the case with both Israel and Judah. Their denial continued to the bitter end, and even when the northern kingdom was conquered and its people exiled, the people of the southern kingdom failed to change their sinful ways. Hitting bottom is not only painful; it can also be dangerous. It has a profound effect on people's lives. If we want to avoid the pain and destruction of hitting bottom, we would be wise to heed the interventions of God and the people close to us.

God's Care for Us: The fact that God cares for his people is proven time and again in Israel's history and is especially emphasized in the book of Kings. Numerous times God sought to stop Israel's slide toward destruction. He confronted wicked kings and punished their continued sin. But they failed to respond with repentance to God's "tough love." God also gives us many chances to heed his message of hope and recovery. Sometimes we might be tempted to mistake his patience for indifference, but we can be sure that God is never indifferent toward his people. His love may sometimes be expressed in patience, but eventually it will be shown in judgment.

CHAPTER 1
Elijah Confronts King Ahaziah

After King Ahab's death, the land of Moab rebelled against Israel.

²One day Israel's new king, Ahaziah, fell through the latticework of an upper room at his palace in Samaria and was seriously injured. So he sent messengers to the temple of Baal-zebub, the god of Ekron, to ask whether he would recover.

³But the angel of the LORD told Elijah, who was from Tishbe, "Go and confront the messengers of the king of Samaria and ask them, 'Is there no God in Israel? Why are you going to Baal-zebub, the god of Ekron, to ask whether the king will recover? ⁴Now, therefore, this is what the LORD says: You will never

1:8 Or *He was wearing clothing made of hair.*

leave the bed you are lying on; you will surely die.'" So Elijah went to deliver the message.

⁵When the messengers returned to the king, he asked them, "Why have you returned so soon?"

⁶They replied, "A man came up to us and told us to go back to the king and give him this message. 'This is what the LORD says: Is there no God in Israel? Why are you sending men to Baal-zebub, the god of Ekron, to ask whether you will recover? Therefore, because you have done this, you will never leave the bed you are lying on; you will surely die.'"

⁷"What sort of man was he?" the king demanded. "What did he look like?"

⁸They replied, "He was a hairy man,* and he wore a leather belt around his waist."

1:2-5 Ahaziah sought guidance for recovery from the wrong spiritual source, and God made his error clear in no uncertain terms. Not everything passed off as spiritual guidance is "the real thing." God is not pleased with those who know better but still attempt recovery through "alternative resources" such as the New Age movement today. God is the only valid source of help for recovery.

1:5-17 Ahaziah sought to silence Elijah and persisted in trying to capture the prophet even after God had destroyed his first two military detachments. Ahaziah's denial was amazingly powerful, and as it deepened, Ahaziah failed to see the innocent lives he was throwing away. We, like Ahaziah, often fail to notice the toll that our denial takes on the people around us. Admitting our dependencies will not only help us recover but will also stop us from hurting the people close to us.

ELIJAH & ELISHA

Most of us know people whom we admire greatly. If we are fortunate, one or more of these people may be close enough to serve as a mentor for us in some way. Elisha had a relationship of this kind with Elijah. Elisha was the student; Elijah was the teacher. Both had a heart for God, though their ministries were very different.

Elijah's ministry was primarily confrontational—he had to reprove and prophesy against King Ahab. He prophesied a three-year drought; he destroyed the priests of Baal who were employed by Ahab; and he prophesied Ahab's death after Ahab killed Naboth for his vineyard. Elijah also served people: God miraculously provided food for a widow and later raised her son from the dead through Elijah.

Elisha witnessed many of the events in Elijah's life and learned much about God's power. Elisha learned that God would soon be taking Elijah to heaven, so he determined to stay with Elijah as long as possible. Because Elisha was present when Elijah was taken to heaven in a whirlwind, he became Elijah's rightful successor, no doubt believing he would follow in Elijah's ministry. But God had something else in mind.

Elisha's ministry was primarily one of comforting, not confrontation. He purified poisoned water, provided drinking water for King Jehoram, provided oil for a widow, cured a poisonous stew, multiplied food to feed 100 people, cured a leper, prophesied the birth of a son to a Shunammite woman, and later raised that son from the dead.

Elisha did not get angry at God for directing his ministry to the common people, even though Elijah had dealt primarily with rulers. He accepted his mission and followed God in all he did. We can learn from Elisha and accept God's calling without envying the greatness or importance our mentors may have achieved. All work is important to God, and we need to do everything we can to bring honor to him.

STRENGTHS AND ACCOMPLISHMENTS:
- Both men were bold in serving God in the face of formidable enemies.
- Elisha determined to secure God's blessing on his life and ministry.

WEAKNESSES AND MISTAKES:
- Elijah allowed victory to leave him isolated and vulnerable to despair.
- Elijah became fearful rather than turn to God when threatened by powerful enemies.

LESSONS FROM THEIR LIVES:
- We are to serve God with total commitment, without fear of the consequences.
- God is able to defeat all our enemies.
- We are most vulnerable to failure after our greatest victories.

KEY VERSE:
"And Elisha replied, 'Please let me inherit a double share of your spirit and become your successor'" (2 Kings 2:9).

Elijah's and Elisha's stories are told in 1 Kings 17–19; 21; 2 Kings 1–10; 13; 2 Chronicles 21. Elijah is mentioned in Malachi 4:5; Matthew 11:14; 17:1-5; 27:47-49; Mark 6:15; 8:28; 9:2-13; 15:35-36; Luke 1:17; 4:25-26; 9:8, 19, 28-31; John 1:21, 24-25; Romans 11:2-3; James 5:17. Elisha is mentioned in Luke 4:27.

"Elijah from Tishbe!" the king exclaimed.

⁹Then he sent an army captain with fifty soldiers to arrest him. They found him sitting on top of a hill. The captain said to him, "Man of God, the king has commanded you to come down with us."

¹⁰But Elijah replied to the captain, "If I am a man of God, let fire come down from heaven and destroy you and your fifty men!" Then fire fell from heaven and killed them all.

¹¹So the king sent another captain with fifty men. The captain said to him, "Man of God, the king demands that you come down at once."

¹²Elijah replied, "If I am a man of God, let fire come down from heaven and destroy you and your fifty men!" And again the fire of God fell from heaven and killed them all.

¹³Once more the king sent a third captain with fifty men. But this time the captain went up the hill and fell to his knees before Elijah. He pleaded with him, "O man of God, please spare my life and the lives of these, your fifty servants. ¹⁴See how the fire from heaven came down and destroyed the first two groups. But now please spare my life!"

¹⁵Then the angel of the LORD said to

Elijah, "Go down with him, and don't be afraid of him." So Elijah got up and went with him to the king.

¹⁶And Elijah said to the king, "This is what the LORD says: Why did you send messengers to Baal-zebub, the god of Ekron, to ask whether you will recover? Is there no God in Israel to answer your question? Therefore, because you have done this, you will never leave the bed you are lying on; you will surely die."

¹⁷So Ahaziah died, just as the LORD had promised through Elijah. Since Ahaziah did not have a son to succeed him, his brother Joram* became the next king. This took place in the second year of the reign of Jehoram son of Jehoshaphat, king of Judah.

¹⁸The rest of the events in Ahaziah's reign and everything he did are recorded in *The Book of the History of the Kings of Israel.*

CHAPTER 2
Elijah Taken into Heaven

When the LORD was about to take Elijah up to heaven in a whirlwind, Elijah and Elisha were traveling from Gilgal. ²And Elijah said to Elisha, "Stay here, for the LORD has told me to go to Bethel."

But Elisha replied, "As surely as the LORD lives and you yourself live, I will never leave you!" So they went down together to Bethel.

³The group of prophets from Bethel came to Elisha and asked him, "Did you know that the LORD is going to take your master away from you today?"

"Of course I know," Elisha answered. "But be quiet about it."

⁴Then Elijah said to Elisha, "Stay here, for the LORD has told me to go to Jericho."

But Elisha replied again, "As surely as the LORD lives and you yourself live, I will never leave you." So they went on together to Jericho.

⁵Then the group of prophets from Jericho came to Elisha and asked him, "Did you know that the LORD is going to take your master away from you today?"

"Of course I know," Elisha answered. "But be quiet about it."

⁶Then Elijah said to Elisha, "Stay here, for the LORD has told me to go to the Jordan River."

But again Elisha replied, "As surely as the LORD lives and you yourself live, I will never leave you." So they went on together.

⁷Fifty men from the group of prophets also went and watched from a distance as Elijah and Elisha stopped beside the Jordan River. ⁸Then Elijah folded his cloak together and struck the water with it. The river divided, and the two of them went across on dry ground!

⁹When they came to the other side, Elijah said to Elisha, "Tell me what I can do for you before I am taken away."

And Elisha replied, "Please let me inherit a double share of your spirit and become your successor."

¹⁰"You have asked a difficult thing," Elijah replied. "If you see me when I am taken from you, then you will get your request. But if not, then you won't."

¹¹As they were walking along and talking, suddenly a chariot of fire appeared, drawn by horses of fire. It drove between the two men, separating them, and Elijah was carried by a whirlwind into heaven. ¹²Elisha saw it and cried out, "My father! My father! I see the chariots and charioteers of Israel!" And as they disappeared from sight, Elisha tore his clothes in distress.

¹³Elisha picked up Elijah's cloak, which had fallen when he was taken up. Then Elisha returned to the bank of the Jordan River. ¹⁴He struck the water with Elijah's cloak and cried out, "Where is the LORD, the

---

1:17 Hebrew *Jehoram,* a variant spelling of Joram.

2:1-7 Elijah was Elisha's mentor; it must have been difficult for Elisha to accept the fact that Elijah was about to be taken away from him. But instead of denying or refusing to deal with Elijah's imminent departure, Elisha made the most of his last moments with his mentor, staying with him until Elijah was carried away into heaven. If we can admit that we may lose someone, we will be better able to cope with the loss when the time comes. Our ability to deal with future difficulties will be affected by our willingness to face the realities at hand.

2:8-14 It is difficult to get beyond the physical loss of a loved one, especially when it's someone we have greatly admired. The trauma of such a loss, however, can be minimized through our faith in God. We can know that our loved ones are in God's hands if they have trusted their life to God through Jesus Christ. We, too, are in God's hands as we follow his program for recovery. When we lose someone close, God has not abandoned us—rather, he is there ready to comfort us with his love and compassion. Recognizing this positive reality can help us go on with our life until God grants us a heavenly promotion of our own.

God of Elijah?" Then the river divided, and Elisha went across.

¹⁵When the group of prophets from Jericho saw from a distance what happened, they exclaimed, "Elijah's spirit rests upon Elisha!" And they went to meet him and bowed to the ground before him. ¹⁶"Sir," they said, "just say the word and fifty of our strongest men will search the wilderness for your master. Perhaps the Spirit of the LORD has left him on some mountain or in some valley."

"No," Elisha said, "don't send them." ¹⁷But they kept urging him until they shamed him into agreeing, and he finally said, "All right, send them." So fifty men searched for three days but did not find Elijah. ¹⁸Elisha was still at Jericho when they returned. "Didn't I tell you not to go?" he asked.

Elisha's First Miracles

¹⁹One day the leaders of the town of Jericho visited Elisha. "We have a problem, my lord," they told him. "This town is located in pleasant surroundings, as you can see. But the water is bad, and the land is unproductive."

²⁰Elisha said, "Bring me a new bowl with salt in it." So they brought it to him. ²¹Then he went out to the spring that supplied the town with water and threw the salt into it. And he said, "This is what the LORD says: I have purified this water. It will no longer cause death or infertility.*" ²²And the water has remained pure ever since, just as Elisha said.

²³Elisha left Jericho and went up to Bethel. As he was walking along the road, a group of boys from the town began mocking and making fun of him. "Go away, baldy!" they chanted. "Go away, baldy!" ²⁴Elisha turned around and looked at them, and he cursed them in the name of the LORD. Then two bears came out of the woods and mauled forty-two of them. ²⁵From there Elisha went to Mount Carmel and finally returned to Samaria.

CHAPTER 3
War between Israel and Moab

Ahab's son Joram* began to rule over Israel in the eighteenth year of King Jehoshaphat's reign in Judah. He reigned in Samaria twelve years. ²He did what was evil in the LORD's sight, but not to the same extent as his father and mother. He at least tore down the sacred pillar of Baal that his father had set up. ³Nevertheless, he continued in the sins that Jeroboam son of Nebat had committed and led the people of Israel to commit.

⁴King Mesha of Moab was a sheep breeder. He used to pay the king of Israel an annual tribute of 100,000 lambs and the wool of 100,000 rams. ⁵But after Ahab's death, the king of Moab rebelled against the king of Israel. ⁶So King Joram promptly mustered the army of Israel and marched from Samaria. ⁷On the way, he sent this message to King Jehoshaphat of Judah: "The king of Moab has rebelled against me. Will you join me in battle against him?"

And Jehoshaphat replied, "Why, of course! You and I are as one. My troops are your troops, and my horses are your horses." ⁸Then Jehoshaphat asked, "What route will we take?"

"We will attack from the wilderness of Edom," Joram replied.

⁹The king of Edom and his troops joined

2:21 Or *or make the land unproductive;* Hebrew reads *or barrenness.* 3:1 Hebrew *Jehoram,* a variant spelling of Joram; also in 3:6.

2:13-15 We all recognize the warping impact that a dysfunctional hero can have on us. But we should also realize that a godly mentor can make a significant positive impact. Here, for example, Elisha took over where Elijah left off. Elisha was recognized as Elijah's successor. He lived with the same faith and commitment as his mentor. We, too, need to seek out godly examples who will help us put God first in our life.

3:1-3 Taking a first step toward recovery is not enough by itself. It was truly a positive move when Joram tore down the sacred pillar of Baal, but it did not constitute full spiritual recovery in any sense. Whatever motivated Joram to destroy the pillar was not heartfelt enough to bring about a complete break from idolatry. He had not come to the point of admitting his helplessness and turning to the true God in faith.

3:5-14 Even a flirtation with recovery will often result in further intervention by God. Here King Joram's foray into the wilderness of Edom brought him and his thirsty troops near the point of helplessness. In their predicament, they consulted Elisha the prophet for insight. He challenged Joram's idolatry and urged the desperate king to be aware of the godly influence of King Jehoshaphat of Judah. We should not ignore the godly people God has placed in our life. They may be there to encourage us to take additional steps toward recovery.

them, and all three armies traveled along a roundabout route through the wilderness for seven days. But there was no water for the men or their animals.

¹⁰"What should we do?" the king of Israel cried out. "The LORD has brought the three of us here to let the king of Moab defeat us."

¹¹But King Jehoshaphat of Judah asked, "Is there no prophet of the LORD with us? If there is, we can ask the LORD what to do through him."

One of King Joram's officers replied, "Elisha son of Shaphat is here. He used to be Elijah's personal assistant.*"

¹²Jehoshaphat said, "Yes, the LORD speaks through him." So the king of Israel, King Jehoshaphat of Judah, and the king of Edom went to consult with Elisha.

¹³"Why are you coming to me?"* Elisha asked the king of Israel. "Go to the pagan prophets of your father and mother!"

But King Joram of Israel said, "No! For it was the LORD who called us three kings here— only to be defeated by the king of Moab!"

¹⁴Elisha replied, "As surely as the LORD Almighty lives, whom I serve, I wouldn't even bother with you except for my respect for King Jehoshaphat of Judah. ¹⁵Now bring me someone who can play the harp."

While the harp was being played, the power* of the LORD came upon Elisha, ¹⁶and he said, "This is what the LORD says: This dry valley will be filled with pools of water! ¹⁷You will see neither wind nor rain, says the LORD, but this valley will be filled with water. You will have plenty for yourselves and your cattle and other animals. ¹⁸But this is only a simple thing for the LORD, for he will make you victorious over the army of Moab! ¹⁹You will conquer the best of their towns, even the fortified ones. You will cut down all their good trees, stop up all their springs, and ruin all their good land with stones."

²⁰The next day at about the time when the morning sacrifice was offered, water sud-denly appeared! It was flowing from the direction of Edom, and soon there was water everywhere.

²¹Meanwhile, when the people of Moab heard about the three armies marching against them, they mobilized every man who was old enough to strap on a sword, and they stationed themselves along their border. ²²But when they got up the next morning, the sun was shining across the water, making it appear red to the Moabites—like blood. ²³"It's blood!" the Moabites exclaimed. "The three armies must have attacked and killed each other! Let's go, men of Moab, and collect the plunder!"

²⁴But when the Moabites arrived at the Israelite camp, the army of Israel rushed out and attacked them until they turned and ran. The army of Israel chased them into the land of Moab, destroying everything as they went.* ²⁵They destroyed the towns, covered their good land with stones, stopped up all the springs, and cut down all the good trees. Finally, only Kir-hareseth and its stone walls were left, but men with slings surrounded and attacked it.

²⁶When the king of Moab saw that he was losing the battle, he led 700 of his swordsmen in a desperate attempt to break through the enemy lines near the king of Edom, but they failed. ²⁷Then the king of Moab took his oldest son, who would have been the next king, and sacrificed him as a burnt offering on the wall. So there was great anger against Israel,* and the Israelites withdrew and returned to their own land.

CHAPTER 4
Elisha Helps a Poor Widow
One day the widow of a member of the group of prophets came to Elisha and cried out, "My husband who served you is dead, and you know how he feared the LORD. But now a creditor has come, threatening to take my two sons as slaves."

3:11 Hebrew *He used to pour water on the hands of Elijah.* 3:13 Hebrew *What is there in common between you and me?* 3:15 Hebrew *the hand.* 3:24 The meaning of the Hebrew is uncertain. 3:27 Or *So Israel's anger was great.* The meaning of the Hebrew is uncertain.

3:16-20 God had a battle plan devised for Joram: The king had only to admit he needed help; God was there to ensure the victory. God always has a plan to rescue us; he provides the resources and guidance we need. We just need to admit that we are helpless and turn to him for help.
4:1-7 People willing to pursue recovery can count on the fact that when they are "at the end of their rope," God is holding on to them. He is the God of limitless resources, who can provide incredibly when we are in need. As was true with the widow and her sons, God sometimes waits to act until the last minute in order to stretch our faith. Then, when he comes through, our faith in his power is strengthened for the battles ahead.

²"What can I do to help you?" Elisha asked. "Tell me, what do you have in the house?"

"Nothing at all, except a flask of olive oil," she replied.

³And Elisha said, "Borrow as many empty jars as you can from your friends and neighbors. ⁴Then go into your house with your sons and shut the door behind you. Pour olive oil from your flask into the jars, setting each one aside when it is filled."

⁵So she did as she was told. Her sons kept bringing jars to her, and she filled one after another. ⁶Soon every container was full to the brim!

"Bring me another jar," she said to one of her sons.

"There aren't any more!" he told her. And then the olive oil stopped flowing.

⁷When she told the man of God what had happened, he said to her, "Now sell the olive oil and pay your debts, and you and your sons can live on what is left over."

Elisha and the Woman from Shunem

⁸One day Elisha went to the town of Shunem. A wealthy woman lived there, and she urged him to come to her home for a meal. After that, whenever he passed that way, he would stop there for something to eat.

⁹She said to her husband, "I am sure this man who stops in from time to time is a holy man of God. ¹⁰Let's build a small room for him on the roof and furnish it with a bed, a table, a chair, and a lamp. Then he will have a place to stay whenever he comes by."

¹¹One day Elisha returned to Shunem, and he went up to this upper room to rest. ¹²He said to his servant Gehazi, "Tell the woman from Shunem I want to speak to her." When she appeared, ¹³Elisha said to Gehazi, "Tell her, 'We appreciate the kind concern you have shown us. What can we do for you? Can we put in a good word for you to the king or to the commander of the army?'"

"No," she replied, "my family takes good care of me."

¹⁴Later Elisha asked Gehazi, "What can we do for her?"

Gehazi replied, "She doesn't have a son, and her husband is an old man."

¹⁵"Call her back again," Elisha told him. When the woman returned, Elisha said to her as she stood in the doorway, ¹⁶"Next year at this time you will be holding a son in your arms!"

"No, my lord!" she cried. "O man of God, don't deceive me and get my hopes up like that."

¹⁷But sure enough, the woman soon became pregnant. And at that time the following year she had a son, just as Elisha had said.

¹⁸One day when her child was older, he went out to help his father, who was working with the harvesters. ¹⁹Suddenly he cried out, "My head hurts! My head hurts!"

His father said to one of the servants, "Carry him home to his mother."

²⁰So the servant took him home, and his mother held him on her lap. But around noontime he died. ²¹She carried him up and laid him on the bed of the man of God, then shut the door and left him there. ²²She sent a message to her husband: "Send one of the servants and a donkey so that I can hurry to the man of God and come right back."

²³"Why go today?" he asked. "It is neither a new moon festival nor a Sabbath."

But she said, "It will be all right."

²⁴So she saddled the donkey and said to the servant, "Hurry! Don't slow down unless I tell you to."

²⁵As she approached the man of God at Mount Carmel, Elisha saw her in the distance. He said to Gehazi, "Look, the woman from Shunem is coming. ²⁶Run out to meet her and ask her, 'Is everything all right with you, your husband, and your child?'"

"Yes," the woman told Gehazi, "everything is fine."

²⁷But when she came to the man of God at the mountain, she fell to the ground before him and caught hold of his feet. Gehazi began to push her away, but the man of God said, "Leave her alone. She is deeply troubled, but the LORD has not told me what it is."

²⁸Then she said, "Did I ask you for a son,

4:8-37 Elisha did two amazing miracles in these verses: (1) He promised that a woman unable to bear children would have a child; (2) after the child died, he brought him back to life. The God who performed these miracles is also able to provide all the power we need for recovery. Notice that God often uses people like Elisha to bring about new or renewed life. We should be aware of this, accepting God's gifts through the people chosen to help us along the way. We must remember, too, that God may also use us to touch the lives of others in need.

my lord? And didn't I say, 'Don't deceive me and get my hopes up'?"

²⁹Then Elisha said to Gehazi, "Get ready to travel*; take my staff and go! Don't talk to anyone along the way. Go quickly and lay the staff on the child's face."

³⁰But the boy's mother said, "As surely as the LORD lives and you yourself live, I won't go home unless you go with me." So Elisha returned with her.

³¹Gehazi hurried on ahead and laid the staff on the child's face, but nothing happened. There was no sign of life. He returned to meet Elisha and told him, "The child is still dead."

³²When Elisha arrived, the child was indeed dead, lying there on the prophet's bed. ³³He went in alone and shut the door behind him and prayed to the LORD. ³⁴Then he lay down on the child's body, placing his mouth on the child's mouth, his eyes on the child's eyes, and his hands on the child's hands. And as he stretched out on him, the child's body began to grow warm again! ³⁵Elisha got up, walked back and forth across the room once, and then stretched himself out again on the child. This time the boy sneezed seven times and opened his eyes!

³⁶Then Elisha summoned Gehazi. "Call the child's mother!" he said. And when she came in, Elisha said, "Here, take your son!" ³⁷She fell at his feet and bowed before him, overwhelmed with gratitude. Then she took her son in her arms and carried him downstairs.

Miracles during a Famine

³⁸Elisha now returned to Gilgal, and there was a famine in the land. One day as the group of prophets was seated before him, he said to his servant, "Put a large pot on the fire, and make some stew for the rest of the group."

³⁹One of the young men went out into the field to gather herbs and came back with a pocketful of wild gourds. He shredded them and put them into the pot without realizing they were poisonous. ⁴⁰Some of the stew was served to the men. But after they had eaten a

bite or two they cried out, "Man of God, there's poison in this stew!" So they would not eat it.

⁴¹Elisha said, "Bring me some flour." Then he threw it into the pot and said, "Now it's all right; go ahead and eat." And then it did not harm them.

⁴²One day a man from Baal-shalishah brought the man of God a sack of fresh grain and twenty loaves of barley bread made from the first grain of his harvest. Elisha said, "Give it to the people so they can eat."

⁴³"What?" his servant exclaimed. "Feed a hundred people with only this?"

But Elisha repeated, "Give it to the people so they can eat, for this is what the LORD says: Everyone will eat, and there will even be some left over!" ⁴⁴And when they gave it to the people, there was plenty for all and some left over, just as the LORD had promised.

CHAPTER 5
The Healing of Naaman

The king of Aram had great admiration for Naaman, the commander of his army, because through him the LORD had given Aram great victories. But though Naaman was a mighty warrior, he suffered from leprosy.*

²At this time Aramean raiders had invaded the land of Israel, and among their captives was a young girl who had been given to Naaman's wife as a maid. ³One day the girl said to her mistress, "I wish my master would go to see the prophet in Samaria. He would heal him of his leprosy."

⁴So Naaman told the king what the young girl from Israel had said. ⁵"Go and visit the prophet," the king of Aram told him. "I will send a letter of introduction for you to take to the king of Israel." So Naaman started out, carrying as gifts 750 pounds of silver, 150 pounds of gold,* and ten sets of clothing. ⁶The letter to the king of Israel said: "With this letter I present my servant Naaman. I want you to heal him of his leprosy."

⁷When the king of Israel read the letter, he tore his clothes in dismay and said, "This

---

4:29 Hebrew *Bind up your loins.* 5:1 Or *from a contagious skin disease.* The Hebrew word used here and throughout this passage can describe various skin diseases. 5:5 Hebrew *10 talents* [340 kilograms] *of silver, 6,000* [shekels] [68 kilograms] *of gold.*

5:1-8 People who are hurting deeply enough will try almost anything to find relief. For Naaman, the commander of the Aramean army, looking for help from a prophet in Israel was a desperate long shot. Naaman was willing to sacrifice prestige and wealth to find healing for his terrible disease. Naaman was healed of his leprosy, but not because he was willing to offer a reward. The real issue was not how much it cost; it was more important that he went to the only one who could really help him—the one true God.

man sends me a leper to heal! Am I God, that I can give life and take it away? I can see that he's just trying to pick a fight with me."

⁸But when Elisha, the man of God, heard that the king of Israel had torn his clothes in dismay, he sent this message to him: "Why are you so upset? Send Naaman to me, and he will learn that there is a true prophet here in Israel."

⁹So Naaman went with his horses and chariots and waited at the door of Elisha's house. ¹⁰But Elisha sent a messenger out to him with this message: "Go and wash yourself seven times in the Jordan River. Then your skin will be restored, and you will be healed of your leprosy."

¹¹But Naaman became angry and stalked away. "I thought he would certainly come out to meet me!" he said. "I expected him to wave his hand over the leprosy and call on the name of the LORD his God and heal me! ¹²Aren't the rivers of Damascus, the Abana and the Pharpar, better than any of the rivers of Israel? Why shouldn't I wash in them and be healed?" So Naaman turned and went away in a rage.

¹³But his officers tried to reason with him and said, "Sir,* if the prophet had told you to do something very difficult, wouldn't you have done it? So you should certainly obey him when he says simply, 'Go and wash and be cured!' " ¹⁴So Naaman went down to the Jordan River and dipped himself seven times, as the man of God had instructed him. And his skin became as healthy as the skin of a young child, and he was healed!

¹⁵Then Naaman and his entire party went back to find the man of God. They stood before him, and Naaman said, "Now I know that there is no God in all the world except in Israel. So please accept a gift from your servant."

¹⁶But Elisha replied, "As surely as the LORD lives, whom I serve, I will not accept any gifts." And though Naaman urged him to take the gift, Elisha refused.

¹⁷Then Naaman said, "All right, but please allow me to load two of my mules with earth from this place, and I will take it back home with me. From now on I will never again offer burnt offerings or sacrifices to any other god except the LORD. ¹⁸However, may the LORD pardon me in this one thing: When my master the king goes into the temple of the god Rimmon to worship there and leans on my arm, may the LORD pardon me when I bow, too."

5:13 Hebrew *My father.*

STEP 1

A Humble Beginning

BIBLE READING: 2 Kings 5:1-15

We admitted that we were powerless over our problems—that our lives had become unmanageable.

It can be very humiliating to admit that we are powerless, especially if we are used to being in control. We may be powerful in some areas of our life, but out of control in terms of our addictive/compulsive behaviors. If we refuse to admit our powerlessness, we may lose everything. That one unmanageable part of our life may infect and destroy everything else.

The experiences of Aramean army commander Naaman illustrate how this is true. He was a powerful military and political figure, a man of wealth, position, and power. He also had leprosy, which promised to bring about the loss of everything he held dear. Lepers were made outcasts from their families and from society. Ultimately, they faced a slow, painful, and disgraceful death.

Naaman heard about a prophet in Israel who could heal him. He found the prophet, and the prophet told him that in order to be healed he needed to dip himself seven times in the Jordan River. Naaman went away outraged, having expected that his power would buy him an instant and easy cure. In the end, however, he acknowledged his powerlessness, followed the instructions, and recovered completely.

Our "diseases" are as life threatening as the leprosy of Naaman's day. They slowly separate us from our family and lead toward the destruction of everything important to us. There is no instant or easy cure. The only answer is to admit our powerlessness, humble ourself, and submit to the process that will eventually bring recovery. *Turn to page 643, Job 6.*

¹⁹"Go in peace," Elisha said. So Naaman started home again.

The Greed of Gehazi

²⁰But Gehazi, the servant of Elisha, the man of God, said to himself, "My master should not have let this Aramean get away without accepting any of his gifts. As surely as the LORD lives, I will chase after him and get something from him." ²¹So Gehazi set off after Naaman.

When Naaman saw Gehazi running after him, he climbed down from his chariot and went to meet him. "Is everything all right?" Naaman asked.

²²"Yes," Gehazi said, "but my master has sent me to tell you that two young prophets from the hill country of Ephraim have just arrived. He would like 75 pounds* of silver and two sets of clothing to give to them."

²³"By all means, take twice as much* silver," Naaman insisted. He gave him two sets of clothing, tied up the money in two bags, and sent two of his servants to carry the gifts for Gehazi. ²⁴But when they arrived at the citadel,* Gehazi took the gifts from the servants and sent the men back. Then he went and hid the gifts inside the house.

²⁵When he went in to his master, Elisha asked him, "Where have you been, Gehazi?"

"I haven't been anywhere," he replied.

²⁶But Elisha asked him, "Don't you realize that I was there in spirit when Naaman stepped down from his chariot to meet you? Is this the time to receive money and clothing, olive groves and vineyards, sheep and cattle, and male and female servants? ²⁷Because you have done this, you and your descendants will suffer from Naaman's leprosy forever." When Gehazi left the room, he was covered with leprosy; his skin was white as snow.

CHAPTER 6
The Floating Ax Head

One day the group of prophets came to Elisha and told him, "As you can see, this place where we meet with you is too small. ²Let's go down to the Jordan River, where there are plenty of logs. There we can build a new place for us to meet."

"All right," he told them, "go ahead."

³"Please come with us," someone suggested.

"I will," he said. ⁴So he went with them.

When they arrived at the Jordan, they began cutting down trees. ⁵But as one of them was cutting a tree, his ax head fell into the river. "Oh, sir!" he cried. "It was a borrowed ax!"

⁶"Where did it fall?" the man of God asked. When he showed him the place, Elisha cut a stick and threw it into the water at that spot. Then the ax head floated to the surface. ⁷"Grab it," Elisha said. And the man reached out and grabbed it.

Elisha Traps the Arameans

⁸When the king of Aram was at war with Israel, he would confer with his officers and say, "We will mobilize our forces at such and such a place."

⁹But immediately Elisha, the man of God, would warn the king of Israel, "Do not go near that place, for the Arameans are planning to mobilize their troops there." ¹⁰So the king of Israel would send word to the place indicated by the man of God. Time and again Elisha warned the king, so that he would be on the alert there.

¹¹The king of Aram became very upset over this. He called his officers together and demanded, "Which of you is the traitor? Who has been informing the king of Israel of my plans?"

¹²"It's not us, my lord the king," one of the

5:22 Hebrew *1 talent* [34 kilograms]. **5:23** Hebrew *take 2 talents* [150 pounds or 68 kilograms]. **5:24** Hebrew *the Ophel.*

5:20-27 The shameful example of Gehazi and the resulting consequences he faced should serve as a warning to us. Those of us in recovery need to be aware that there are people who would try to take advantage of us as we experience the joy of recovery. Those working in the recovery field need to be careful not to take advantage of people as they experience the excitement of recovery. God is never pleased with this kind of exploitation.

6:1-7 By helping the prophet retrieve the borrowed ax head, God revealed his concern for the day-to-day needs of his people. He also showed how concerned he was for the maintenance of relationships. In ancient times, an ax head was extremely valuable; losing such an item would have resulted in conflict between the borrower and the lender. So Elisha's miracle helped the young prophets not only with their building project but also with the maintenance of their relationships. Maintaining healthy relationships is essential to the recovery process. God will support us in those relationships if we are willing to ask him for help.

officers replied. "Elisha, the prophet in Israel, tells the king of Israel even the words you speak in the privacy of your bedroom!"

[13]"Go and find out where he is," the king commanded, "so I can send troops to seize him."

And the report came back: "Elisha is at Dothan." [14]So one night the king of Aram sent a great army with many chariots and horses to surround the city.

[15]When the servant of the man of God got up early the next morning and went outside, there were troops, horses, and chariots everywhere. "Oh, sir, what will we do now?" the young man cried to Elisha.

[16]"Don't be afraid!" Elisha told him. "For there are more on our side than on theirs!" [17]Then Elisha prayed, "O LORD, open his eyes and let him see!" The LORD opened the young man's eyes, and when he looked up, he saw that the hillside around Elisha was filled with horses and chariots of fire.

[18]As the Aramean army advanced toward him, Elisha prayed, "O LORD, please make them blind." So the LORD struck them with blindness as Elisha had asked.

[19]Then Elisha went out and told them, "You have come the wrong way! This isn't the right city! Follow me, and I will take you to the man you are looking for." And he led them to the city of Samaria.

[20]As soon as they had entered Samaria, Elisha prayed, "O LORD, now open their eyes and let them see." So the LORD opened their eyes, and they discovered that they were in the middle of Samaria.

[21]When the king of Israel saw them, he shouted to Elisha, "My father, should I kill them? Should I kill them?"

[22]"Of course not!" Elisha replied. "Do we kill prisoners of war? Give them food and drink and send them home again to their master."

[23]So the king made a great feast for them and then sent them home to their master. Af-

ter that, the Aramean raiders stayed away from the land of Israel.

Ben-Hadad Besieges Samaria

[24]Some time later, however, King Ben-hadad of Aram mustered his entire army and besieged Samaria. [25]As a result, there was a great famine in the city. The siege lasted so long that a donkey's head sold for eighty pieces of silver, and a cup of dove's dung sold for five pieces* of silver.

[26]One day as the king of Israel was walking along the wall of the city, a woman called to him, "Please help me, my lord the king!"

[27]He answered, "If the LORD doesn't help you, what can I do? I have neither food from the threshing floor nor wine from the press to give you." [28]But then the king asked, "What is the matter?"

She replied, "This woman said to me: 'Come on, let's eat your son today, then we will eat my son tomorrow.' [29]So we cooked my son and ate him. Then the next day I said to her, 'Kill your son so we can eat him,' but she has hidden her son."

[30]When the king heard this, he tore his clothes in despair. And as the king walked along the wall, the people could see that he was wearing burlap under his robe next to his skin. [31]"May God strike me and even kill me if I don't separate Elisha's head from his shoulders this very day," the king vowed.

[32]Elisha was sitting in his house with the elders of Israel when the king sent a messenger to summon him. But before the messenger arrived, Elisha said to the elders, "A murderer has sent a man to cut off my head. When he arrives, shut the door and keep him out. We will soon hear his master's steps following him."

[33]While Elisha was still saying this, the messenger arrived. And the king* said, "All this misery is from the LORD! Why should I wait for the LORD any longer?"

6:25 Hebrew *sold for 80 [shekels]* [2 pounds or 0.9 kilograms] *of silver, and ¼ of a cab* [0.3 liters] *of dove's dung sold for 5 [shekels]* [2 ounces or 57 grams]. *Dove's dung may be a variety of wild vegetable.* 6:33 Hebrew *he.*

6:14-20 Elisha's servant was terrified by the awesome Aramean army because he couldn't see the help available to him. He was totally unaware of the great army of heavenly soldiers on his side. As we face the difficult task of recovery, we may be tempted to give up; our enemies may seem too powerful to overcome. But as we begin to see through the eyes of faith, we will discover the awesome power available to us. God's power is far greater than that of any enemy we might face. If we admit our powerlessness and trust God for help, we will find his power more than sufficient for our needs.

CHAPTER 7

Elisha replied, "Listen to this message from the LORD! This is what the LORD says: By this time tomorrow in the markets of Samaria, six quarts of choice flour will cost only one piece of silver,* and twelve quarts of barley grain will cost only one piece of silver.*"

[2]The officer assisting the king said to the man of God, "That couldn't happen even if the LORD opened the windows of heaven!"

But Elisha replied, "You will see it happen with your own eyes, but you won't be able to eat any of it!"

Lepers Visit the Enemy Camp

[3]Now there were four men with leprosy* sitting at the entrance of the city gates. "Why should we sit here waiting to die?" they asked each other. [4]"We will starve if we stay here, but with the famine in the city, we will starve if we go back there. So we might as well go out and surrender to the Aramean army. If they let us live, so much the better. But if they kill us, we would have died anyway."

[5]So at twilight they set out for the camp of the Arameans. But when they came to the edge of the camp, no one was there! [6]For the Lord had caused the Aramean army to hear the clatter of speeding chariots and the galloping of horses and the sounds of a great army approaching. "The king of Israel has hired the Hittites and Egyptians* to attack us!" they cried to one another. [7]So they panicked and ran into the night, abandoning their tents, horses, donkeys, and everything else, as they fled for their lives.

[8]When the lepers arrived at the edge of the camp, they went into one tent after another, eating and drinking wine; and they carried off silver and gold and clothing and hid it. [9]Finally, they said to each other, "This is not right. This is a day of good news, and we aren't sharing it with anyone! If we wait until morning, some calamity will certainly fall upon us. Come on, let's go back and tell the people at the palace."

[10]So they went back to the city and told the gatekeepers what had happened. "We went out to the Aramean camp," they said, "and no one was there! The horses and donkeys were tethered and the tents were all in order, but there wasn't a single person around!" [11]Then the gatekeepers shouted the news to the people in the palace.

Israel Plunders the Camp

[12]The king got out of bed in the middle of the night and told his officers, "I know what has happened. The Arameans know we are starving, so they have left their camp and have hidden in the fields. They are expecting us to leave the city, and then they will take us alive and capture the city."

[13]One of his officers replied, "We had better send out scouts to check into this. Let them take five of the remaining horses. If something happens to them, it will be no worse than if they stay here and die with the rest of us."

[14]So two chariots with horses were prepared, and the king sent scouts to see what had happened to the Aramean army. [15]They went all the way to the Jordan River, following a trail of clothing and equipment that the Arameans had thrown away in their mad rush to escape. The scouts returned and told the king about it. [16]Then the people of Samaria rushed out and plundered the Aramean camp. So it was true that six quarts of choice flour were sold that day for one piece of silver, and twelve quarts of barley grain were sold for one piece of silver, just as the LORD had promised. [17]The king appointed his officer to control the traffic at the gate, but he was knocked down and trampled to death as the people rushed out.

So everything happened exactly as the man of God had predicted when the king came to his house. [18]The man of God had said to the king, "By this time tomorrow in the markets of Samaria, six quarts of choice flour will cost one piece of silver, and twelve quarts of barley grain will cost one piece of silver."

[19]The king's officer had replied, "That

7:1a Hebrew *1 seah* [7.3 liters] *of choice flour will cost 1 shekel* [0.4 ounces or 11 grams]; also in 7:16, 18. 7:1b Hebrew *2 seahs* [14.6 liters] *of barley grain will cost 1 shekel* [0.4 ounces or 11 grams]; also in 7:16, 18. 7:3 Or *with a contagious skin disease.* The Hebrew word used here and throughout this passage can describe various skin diseases. 7:6 Possibly *and the people of Muzur,* a district near Cilicia.

7:1-20 Many who stand on the brink of recovery never progress, because as much as they desire victory, they believe it to be impossible. The officer of Israel tragically missed his opportunity for victory and freedom because of his unbelief. The obstacles to recovery are never too great for God. But if we fail to believe this, we may be destroyed by the obstacles that God could easily have removed. By looking to God for help and placing our life in his hands, we can enjoy victorious blessings beyond our wildest dreams!

couldn't happen even if the LORD opened the windows of heaven!" And the man of God had said, "You will see it happen with your own eyes, but you won't be able to eat any of it!" [20]And so it was, for the people trampled him to death at the gate!

CHAPTER 8
The Woman from Shunem Returns Home

Elisha had told the woman whose son he had brought back to life, "Take your family and move to some other place, for the LORD has called for a famine on Israel that will last for seven years." [2]So the woman did as the man of God instructed. She took her family and settled in the land of the Philistines for seven years.

[3]After the famine ended she returned from the land of the Philistines, and she went to see the king about getting back her house and land. [4]As she came in, the king was talking with Gehazi, the servant of the man of God. The king had just said, "Tell me some stories about the great things Elisha has done." [5]And Gehazi was telling the king about the time Elisha had brought a boy back to life. At that very moment, the mother of the boy walked in to make her appeal to the king about her house and land.

"Look, my lord the king!" Gehazi exclaimed. "Here is the woman now, and this is her son—the very one Elisha brought back to life!"

[6]"Is this true?" the king asked her. And she told him the story. So he directed one of his officials to see that everything she had lost was restored to her, including the value of any crops that had been harvested during her absence.

Hazael Murders Ben-Hadad

[7]Elisha went to Damascus, the capital of Aram, where King Ben-hadad lay sick. When someone told the king that the man of God

had come, [8]the king said to Hazael, "Take a gift to the man of God. Then tell him to ask the LORD, 'Will I recover from this illness?'"

[9]So Hazael loaded down forty camels with the finest products of Damascus as a gift for Elisha. He went to him and said, "Your servant Ben-hadad, the king of Aram, has sent me to ask, 'Will I recover from this illness?'"

[10]And Elisha replied, "Go and tell him, 'You will surely recover.' But actually the LORD has shown me that he will surely die!" [11]Elisha stared at Hazael* with a fixed gaze until Hazael became uneasy.* Then the man of God started weeping.

[12]"What's the matter, my lord?" Hazael asked him.

Elisha replied, "I know the terrible things you will do to the people of Israel. You will burn their fortified cities, kill their young men with the sword, dash their little children to the ground, and rip open their pregnant women!"

[13]Hazael responded, "How could a nobody like me* ever accomplish such great things?"

Elisha answered, "The LORD has shown me that you are going to be the king of Aram."

[14]When Hazael left Elisha and went back, the king asked him, "What did Elisha tell you?"

And Hazael replied, "He told me that you will surely recover."

[15]But the next day Hazael took a blanket, soaked it in water, and held it over the king's face until he died. Then Hazael became the next king of Aram.

Jehoram Rules in Judah

[16]Jehoram son of King Jehoshaphat of Judah began to rule over Judah in the fifth year of the reign of Joram son of Ahab, king of Israel. [17]Jehoram was thirty-two years old when he became king, and he reigned in Jerusalem eight years. [18]But Jehoram followed the example of the kings of Israel and was as

8:11a Hebrew *He stared at him.* 8:11b The meaning of the Hebrew is uncertain. 8:13 Hebrew *a dog.*

8:7-15 Recovery in the fullest sense cannot proceed when people refuse to handle things honestly. Elisha knew that King Ben-hadad could have come to physical "recovery" if he had been allowed to do so. But Hazael would not let this happen because of his own desire to dominate and control. Likewise, many people working toward recovery are hindered, even cruelly prevented, from reaching their goal by those around them who prefer to dominate them. We need to surround ourself with people who will honestly support and encourage us in the recovery process.
8:16-22 During King Jehoram's relatively brief rule over Judah, we see the actions and fruits of dysfunctional leadership. In spite of God's great patience with Jehoram (8:19), he continued to follow in the evil ways of his father-in-law, Ahab. When Jehoram found himself in dire straits, his army abandoned him. He was left alone to cope with his loss of Moab. If we resist God and oppress others, we can expect to be deserted by the people closest to us. We would be wise to learn from the sad consequences that resulted from Jehoram's wicked behavior.

wicked as King Ahab, for he had married one of Ahab's daughters. So Jehoram did what was evil in the LORD's sight. [19]But the LORD did not want to destroy Judah, for he had promised his servant David that his descendants would continue to rule, shining like a lamp forever.

[20]During Jehoram's reign, the Edomites revolted against Judah and crowned their own king. [21]So Jehoram* went with all his chariots to attack the town of Zair.* The Edomites surrounded him and his chariot commanders, but he went out at night and attacked them* under cover of darkness. But Jehoram's army deserted him and fled to their homes. [22]So Edom has been independent from Judah to this day. The town of Libnah also revolted about that same time.

[23]The rest of the events in Jehoram's reign and everything he did are recorded in *The Book of the History of the Kings of Judah.* [24]When Jehoram died, he was buried with his ancestors in the City of David. Then his son Ahaziah became the next king.

Ahaziah Rules in Judah

[25]Ahaziah son of Jehoram began to rule over Judah in the twelfth year of the reign of Joram son of Ahab, king of Israel.

[26]Ahaziah was twenty-two years old when he became king, and he reigned in Jerusalem one year. His mother was Athaliah, a granddaughter of King Omri of Israel. [27]Ahaziah followed the evil example of King Ahab's family. He did what was evil in the LORD's sight, just as Ahab's family had done, for he was related by marriage to the family of Ahab.

[28]Ahaziah joined Joram son of Ahab in his war against King Hazael of Aram at Ramoth-gilead. When the Arameans wounded King Joram in the battle, [29]he returned to Jezreel

to recover from the wounds he had received at Ramoth.* Because Joram was wounded, King Ahaziah of Judah went to Jezreel to visit him.

CHAPTER 9
Jehu Anointed King of Israel

Meanwhile, Elisha the prophet had summoned a member of the group of prophets. "Get ready to travel,"* he told him, "and take this flask of olive oil with you. Go to Ramoth-gilead, [2]and find Jehu son of Jehoshaphat, son of Nimshi. Call him into a private room away from his friends, [3]and pour the oil over his head. Say to him, 'This is what the LORD says: I anoint you to be the king over Israel.' Then open the door and run for your life!"

[4]So the young prophet did as he was told and went to Ramoth-gilead. [5]When he arrived there, he found Jehu sitting around with the other army officers. "I have a message for you, Commander," he said.

"For which one of us?" Jehu asked.

"For you, Commander," he replied.

[6]So Jehu left the others and went into the house. Then the young prophet poured the oil over Jehu's head and said, "This is what the LORD, the God of Israel, says: I anoint you king over the LORD's people, Israel. [7]You are to destroy the family of Ahab, your master. In this way, I will avenge the murder of my prophets and all the LORD's servants who were killed by Jezebel. [8]The entire family of Ahab must be wiped out. I will destroy every one of his male descendants, slave and free alike, anywhere in Israel. [9]I will destroy the family of Ahab as I destroyed the families of Jeroboam son of Nebat and of Baasha son of Ahijah. [10]Dogs will eat Ahab's wife Jezebel at the plot of land in Jezreel, and no one will

---

8:21a Hebrew *Joram,* a variant spelling of Jehoram; also in 8:23, 24. **8:21b** Greek version reads *Seir.* **8:21c** Or *he went out and escaped.* The meaning of the Hebrew is uncertain. **8:29** Hebrew *Ramah,* a variant spelling of Ramoth. **9:1** Hebrew *Bind up your loins.*

9:1-26 Joram was king of Israel, but he failed to command heartfelt loyalty from his troops. Instead, he manipulated them through fear. Jehu, however, had friends who risked their lives to be loyal servants of their friend who would also soon be their king. When Joram's riders met Jehu, they allied with him, seeing an escape from their evil, oppressive master. If we are to expect loyalty from those around us, we need to be honest and fair with them. Loyalty is based on respect and admiration, not fear.

9:1–10:36 This extended account of the fulfillment of Elijah's earlier prophecy about the eventual destruction of evil King Ahab's family (see 1 Kings 21:21-24) should encourage those who have suffered under oppressive or abusive situations. When we have been victimized, we may wonder why God has allowed our oppressors to go unpunished. Here we see that eventually God does punish sin. No one will ever get away with it forever. God delays his judgment to give people more time to repent (see 2 Peter 3:9), but his patience does run out. After giving plenty of opportunities to repent, God always acts decisively to justly punish perpetrators like Ahab's family.

bury her." Then the young prophet opened the door and ran.

[11]Jehu went back to his fellow officers, and one of them asked him, "What did that madman want? Is everything all right?"

"You know how a man like that babbles on," Jehu replied.

[12]"You're hiding something," they said. "Tell us."

So Jehu told them, "He said to me, 'This is what the LORD says: I have anointed you to be king over Israel.'"

[13]Then they quickly spread out their cloaks on the bare steps and blew the ram's horn, shouting, "Jehu is king!"

Jehu Kills Joram and Ahaziah

[14]So Jehu son of Jehoshaphat, son of Nimshi, led a conspiracy against King Joram. (Now Joram had been with the army at Ramoth-gilead, defending Israel against the forces of King Hazael of Aram. [15]But King Joram* was wounded in the fighting and returned to Jezreel to recover from his wounds.) So Jehu told the men with him, "If you want me to be king, don't let anyone leave town and go to Jezreel to report what we have done."

[16]Then Jehu got into a chariot and rode to Jezreel to find King Joram, who was lying there wounded. King Ahaziah of Judah was there, too, for he had gone to visit him. [17]The watchman on the tower of Jezreel saw Jehu and his company approaching, so he shouted to Joram, "I see a company of troops coming!"

"Send out a rider to ask if they are coming in peace," King Joram ordered.

[18]So a horseman went out to meet Jehu and said, "The king wants to know if you are coming in peace."

Jehu replied, "What do you know about peace? Fall in behind me!"

The watchman called out to the king, "The messenger has met them, but he's not returning."

[19]So the king sent out a second horseman. He rode up to them and said, "The king wants to know if you come in peace."

Again Jehu answered, "What do you know about peace? Fall in behind me!"

[20]The watchman exclaimed, "The messenger has met them, but he isn't returning either! It must be Jehu son of Nimshi, for he's driving like a madman."

[21]"Quick! Get my chariot ready!" King Joram commanded.

Then King Joram of Israel and King Ahaziah of Judah rode out in their chariots to meet Jehu. They met him at the plot of land that had belonged to Naboth of Jezreel. [22]King Joram demanded, "Do you come in peace, Jehu?"

Jehu replied, "How can there be peace as long as the idolatry and witchcraft of your mother, Jezebel, are all around us?"

[23]Then King Joram turned the horses around* and fled, shouting to King Ahaziah, "Treason, Ahaziah!" [24]But Jehu drew his bow and shot Joram between the shoulders. The arrow pierced his heart, and he sank down dead in his chariot.

[25]Jehu said to Bidkar, his officer, "Throw him into the plot of land that belonged to Naboth of Jezreel. Do you remember when you and I were riding along behind his father, Ahab? The LORD pronounced this message against him: [26]'I solemnly swear that I will repay him here on this plot of land, says the LORD, for the murder of Naboth and his sons that I saw yesterday.' So throw him out on Naboth's property, just as the LORD said."

[27]When King Ahaziah of Judah saw what was happening, he fled along the road to Beth-haggan. Jehu rode after him, shouting, "Shoot him, too!" So they shot Ahaziah* in his chariot at the Ascent of Gur, near Ibleam. He was able to go on as far as Megiddo, but he died there. [28]His servants took him by chariot to Jerusalem, where they buried him with his ancestors in the City of David. [29]Ahaziah had become king over Judah in the eleventh year of the reign of Joram son of Ahab.

The Death of Jezebel

[30]When Jezebel, the queen mother, heard that Jehu had come to Jezreel, she painted her eyelids and fixed her hair and sat at a window. [31]When Jehu entered the gate of the palace, she shouted at him, "Have you come in peace, you murderer? You're just like Zimri, who murdered his master!"*

[32]Jehu looked up and saw her at the window and shouted, "Who is on my side?" And two or three eunuchs looked out at him. [33]"Throw her down!" Jehu yelled. So they threw her out the window, and her blood spattered against the wall and on the horses. And Jehu trampled her body under his horses' hooves.

[34]Then Jehu went into the palace and ate

9:15 Hebrew *Jehoram,* a variant spelling of Joram; also in 9:17, 21, 22, 23, 24. **9:23** Hebrew *turned his hands.* **9:27** As in Greek and Syriac versions; Hebrew lacks *So they shot Ahaziah.* **9:31** See 1 Kgs 16:9-10, where Zimri killed his master, King Elah.

and drank. Afterward he said, "Someone go and bury this cursed woman, for she is the daughter of a king." 35But when they went out to bury her, they found only her skull, her feet, and her hands.

36When they returned and told Jehu, he stated, "This fulfills the message from the LORD, which he spoke through his servant Elijah from Tishbe: 'At the plot of land in Jezreel, dogs will eat Jezebel's body. 37Her remains will be scattered like dung on the plot of land in Jezreel, so that no one will be able to recognize her.'"

CHAPTER 10
Jehu Kills Ahab's Family

Ahab had seventy sons living in the city of Samaria. So Jehu wrote letters and sent them to Samaria, to the elders and officials of the city,* and to the guardians of King Ahab's sons. He said, 2"The king's sons are with you, and you have at your disposal chariots, horses, a fortified city, and weapons. As soon as you receive this letter, 3select the best qualified of your master's sons to be your king, and prepare to fight for Ahab's dynasty."

4But they were paralyzed with fear and said, "We've seen that two kings couldn't stand against this man! What can we do?"

5So the palace and city administrators, together with the elders and the guardians of the king's sons, sent this message to Jehu: "We are your servants and will do anything you tell us. We will not make anyone king; do whatever you think is best."

6Jehu responded with a second letter: "If you are on my side and are going to obey me, bring the heads of your master's sons to me at Jezreel by this time tomorrow." Now the seventy sons of the king were being cared for by the leaders of Samaria, where they had been raised since childhood. 7When the letter arrived, the leaders killed all seventy of the king's sons. They placed their heads in baskets and presented them to Jehu at Jezreel.

8A messenger went to Jehu and said, "They have brought the heads of the king's sons."

So Jehu ordered, "Pile them in two heaps at the entrance of the city gate, and leave them there until morning."

9In the morning he went out and spoke to the crowd that had gathered around them. "You are not to blame," he told them. "I am the one who conspired against my master and killed him. But who killed all these? 10You can be sure that the message of the LORD that was spoken concerning Ahab's family will not fail. The LORD declared through his servant Elijah that this would happen." 11Then Jehu killed all who were left of Ahab's relatives living in Jezreel and all his important officials, his personal friends, and his priests. So Ahab was left without a single survivor.

12Then Jehu set out for Samaria. Along the way, while he was at Beth-eked of the Shepherds, 13he met some relatives of King Ahaziah of Judah. "Who are you?" he asked them.

And they replied, "We are relatives of King Ahaziah. We are going to visit the sons of King Ahab and the sons of the queen mother."

14"Take them alive!" Jehu shouted to his men. And they captured all forty-two of them and killed them at the well of Beth-eked. None of them escaped.

15When Jehu left there, he met Jehonadab son of Recab, who was coming to meet him. After they had greeted each other, Jehu said to him, "Are you as loyal to me as I am to you?"

"Yes, I am," Jehonadab replied.

"If you are," Jehu said, "then give me your hand." So Jehonadab put out his hand, and Jehu helped him into the chariot. 16Then Jehu said, "Now come with me, and see how devoted I am to the LORD." So Jehonadab rode along with him.

17When Jehu arrived in Samaria, he killed everyone who was left there from Ahab's

10:1 As in some Greek manuscripts and Latin Vulgate (see also 10:6); Hebrew reads *of Jezreel*.

10:1-12 This gory account appears to have been motivated by commitment to God's will, as earlier expressed by the prophecy of Elijah about the destruction of Ahab's family (10:10; see 1 Kings 21:21-24). Although later events show that Jehu was probably not serious about spiritual recovery, he at least seems to have acted responsibly and with accountability toward God and his people (10:9-10). However, he went too far in his killing spree (see Hosea 1:4-5). In our zeal to recover, we may go beyond what is necessary, being swept up in the emotion of the situation. Compulsive behavior can be devastating, even if we think we are doing it for the right reasons.

family, just as the LORD had promised through Elijah.

Jehu Kills the Priests of Baal

[18]Then Jehu called a meeting of all the people of the city and said to them, "Ahab's worship of Baal was nothing compared to the way I will worship him! [19]Therefore, summon all the prophets and worshipers of Baal, and call together all his priests. See to it that every one of them comes, for I am going to offer a great sacrifice to Baal. Anyone who fails to come will be put to death." But Jehu's cunning plan was to destroy all the worshipers of Baal.

[20]Then Jehu ordered, "Prepare a solemn assembly to worship Baal!" So they did. [21]He sent messengers throughout all Israel summoning those who worshiped Baal. They all came—not a single one remained behind—and they filled the temple of Baal from one end to the other. [22]And Jehu instructed the keeper of the wardrobe, "Be sure that every worshiper of Baal wears one of these robes." So robes were given to them.

[23]Then Jehu went into the temple of Baal with Jehonadab son of Recab. Jehu said to the worshipers of Baal, "Make sure no one who worships the LORD is here—only those who worship Baal." [24]So they were all inside the temple to offer sacrifices and burnt offerings. Now Jehu had stationed eighty of his men outside the building and had warned them, "If you let anyone escape, you will pay for it with your own life."

[25]As soon as Jehu had finished sacrificing the burnt offering, he commanded his guards and officers, "Go in and kill all of them. Don't let a single one escape!" So they killed them all with their swords, and the guards and officers dragged their bodies outside.* Then Jehu's men went into the innermost fortress* of the temple of Baal. [26]They dragged out the sacred pillar* used in the worship of Baal and burned it. [27]They smashed the sacred pillar and wrecked the temple of Baal, converting it into a public toilet, as it remains to this day.

[28]In this way, Jehu destroyed every trace of Baal worship from Israel. [29]He did not, however, destroy the gold calves at Bethel and Dan, with which Jeroboam son of Nebat had caused Israel to sin.

[30]Nonetheless the LORD said to Jehu, "You have done well in following my instructions to destroy the family of Ahab. Therefore, your descendants will be kings of Israel down to the fourth generation." [31]But Jehu did not obey the Law of the LORD, the God of Israel, with all his heart. He refused to turn from the sins that Jeroboam had led Israel to commit.

The Death of Jehu

[32]At about that time the LORD began to cut down the size of Israel's territory. King Hazael conquered several sections of the country [33]east of the Jordan River, including all of Gilead, Gad, Reuben, and Manasseh. He conquered the area from the town of Aroer by the Arnon Gorge to as far north as Gilead and Bashan.

[34]The rest of the events in Jehu's reign—everything he did and all his achievements—are recorded in *The Book of the History of the Kings of Israel.*

[35]When Jehu died, he was buried in Samaria. Then his son Jehoahaz became the next king. [36]In all, Jehu reigned over Israel from Samaria for twenty-eight years.

10:25a Or *and they left their bodies lying there;* or *and they threw them out into the outermost court.* 10:25b Hebrew *city.*
10:26 As in Greek and Syriac versions and Latin Vulgate; Hebrew reads *sacred pillars.*

10:18-29 Even in this crowning victory over Ahab's legacy of Baal worship, two troubling defects in Jehu's personality and actions are seen: (1) Jehu was not honest about why he wanted the Baal worshipers to gather (10:18-25); he manipulated them with a lie. (2) He got rid of the Baal worship in the northern kingdom but not all the false worship (10:26-29). The process of recovery can proceed only with honesty and wholehearted commitment to God. We will never recover if we tell only part of the truth or if we change only part of our life.
10:30-33 It is entirely possible to please God in some parts of our life and displease him greatly in others. Jehu honored God by destroying Ahab's family, and he was blessed for it. But his divided spiritual allegiance prevented the full recovery of the northern kingdom (10:31). Because there was no clean break from the sinful worship patterns established long before by King Jeroboam, God allowed Israel to move closer to hitting bottom (10:31-33). We, too, need to turn our entire life over to God's control. The areas we refuse to commit to God could very well be the roots of our addictions or compulsions.

CHAPTER 11
Queen Athaliah Rules in Judah

When Athaliah, the mother of King Ahaziah of Judah, learned that her son was dead, she began to destroy the rest of the royal family. [2]But Ahaziah's sister Jehosheba, the daughter of King Jehoram,* took Ahaziah's infant son, Joash, and stole him away from among the rest of the king's children, who were about to be killed. She put Joash and his nurse in a bedroom, and they hid him from Athaliah, so the child was not murdered. [3]Joash remained hidden in the Temple of the LORD for six years while Athaliah ruled over the land.

Revolt against Athaliah

[4]In the seventh year of Athaliah's reign, Jehoiada the priest summoned the commanders, the Carite mercenaries, and the palace guards to come to the Temple of the LORD. He made a solemn pact with them and made them swear an oath of loyalty there in the LORD's Temple; then he showed them the king's son.

[5]Jehoiada told them, "This is what you must do. A third of you who are on duty on the Sabbath are to guard the royal palace itself. [6]Another third of you are to stand guard at the Sur Gate. And the final third must stand guard behind the palace guard. These three groups will all guard the palace. [7]The other two units who are off duty on the Sabbath must stand guard for the king at the LORD's Temple. [8]Form a bodyguard around the king and keep your weapons in hand. Kill anyone who tries to break through. Stay with the king wherever he goes."

[9]So the commanders did everything as Jehoiada the priest ordered. The commanders took charge of the men reporting for duty that Sabbath, as well as those who were going off duty. They brought them all to Jehoiada the priest, [10]and he supplied them with the spears and small shields that had once belonged to King David and were stored in the Temple of the LORD. [11]The palace guards stationed themselves around the king, with their weapons ready. They formed a line from the south side of the Temple around to the north side and all around the altar.

[12]Then Jehoiada brought out Joash, the king's son, placed the crown on his head, and presented him with a copy of God's laws.* They anointed him and proclaimed him king, and everyone clapped their hands and shouted, "Long live the king!"

The Death of Athaliah

[13]When Athaliah heard the noise made by the palace guards and the people, she hurried to the LORD's Temple to see what was happening. [14]When she arrived, she saw the newly crowned king standing in his place of authority by the pillar, as was the custom at times of coronation. The commanders and trumpeters were surrounding him, and people from all over the land were rejoicing and blowing trumpets. When Athaliah saw all this, she tore her clothes in despair and shouted, "Treason! Treason!"

[15]Then Jehoiada the priest ordered the commanders who were in charge of the troops, "Take her to the soldiers in front of the Temple,* and kill anyone who tries to rescue her." For the priest had said, "She must not be killed in the Temple of the LORD." [16]So they seized her and led her out to the gate

11:2 Hebrew *Joram,* a variant spelling of Jehoram. 11:12 Or *a copy of the covenant.* 11:15 Or *Bring her out from between the ranks;* or *Take her out of the Temple precincts.* The meaning of the Hebrew is uncertain.

11:1-3 Recovery is a difficult, even terrifying, alternative for many who must live near ruthless oppressors or abusive personalities. Such highly dysfunctional personalities will attempt to do anything to get their way and to solidify their rule by intimidation. Jehosheba must have feared Athaliah's wrath when she stole young Josiah away, thus thwarting the new queen's murderous plans. In spite of this, however, she acted on faith, trusting God to take care of her. The flaw in Athaliah's "reign of terror" was her failure to believe God's promises to David and his line (see 2 Samuel 7:12-16). Young Joash's survival was not only God's will but also a manifestation of God's ongoing care of his chosen people. We, like Jehosheba, must trust in God's care for us and take the steps necessary for recovery.

11:4-21 Jehoiada's faith was the catalyst for Judah's move toward recovery. The process of anointing Joash and proclaiming him the rightful ruler was undergirded by Jehoiada's courage. Jehoiada desired to restore Judah to a right relationship with God. Under his direction, the people and king agreed to worship God, follow God's commands, and destroy the altars to false gods. Through the agreement they set up, all the people were responsible for the nation's recovery, and everyone was held accountable. Courage to change our situation and personal accountability to others are necessary parts of any successful recovery program.

where horses enter the palace grounds, and she was killed there.

Jehoiada's Religious Reforms

[17] Then Jehoiada made a covenant between the LORD and the king and the people that they would be the LORD's people. He also made a covenant between the king and the people. [18] And all the people of the land went over to the temple of Baal and tore it down. They demolished the altars and smashed the idols to pieces, and they killed Mattan the priest of Baal in front of the altars.

Jehoiada the priest stationed guards at the Temple of the LORD. [19] Then the commanders, the Carite mercenaries, the palace guards, and all the people of the land escorted the king from the Temple of the LORD. They went through the gate of the guards and into the palace, and the king took his seat on the royal throne. [20] So all the people of the land rejoiced, and the city was peaceful because Athaliah had been killed at the king's palace.

[21]*Joash* was seven years old when he became king.

CHAPTER 12
Joash Repairs the Temple

[1]*Joash* began to rule over Judah in the seventh year of King Jehu's reign in Israel. He reigned in Jerusalem forty years. His mother was Zibiah from Beersheba. [2] All his life Joash did what was pleasing in the LORD's sight because Jehoiada the priest instructed him. [3] Yet even so, he did not destroy the pagan shrines, and the people still offered sacrifices and burned incense there.

[4] One day King Joash said to the priests, "Collect all the money brought as a sacred offering to the LORD's Temple, whether it is a regular assessment, a payment of vows, or a voluntary gift. [5] Let the priests take some of that money to pay for whatever repairs are needed at the Temple."

[6] But by the twenty-third year of Joash's reign, the priests still had not repaired the Temple. [7] So King Joash called for Jehoiada and the other priests and asked them, "Why haven't you repaired the Temple? Don't use any more money for your own needs. From now on, it must all be spent on Temple repairs." [8] So the priests agreed not to accept any more money from the people, and they also agreed to let others take responsibility for repairing the Temple.

[9] Then Jehoiada the priest bored a hole in the lid of a large chest and set it on the right-hand side of the altar at the entrance of the Temple of the LORD. The priests guarding the entrance put all of the people's contributions into the chest. [10] Whenever the chest became full, the court secretary and the high priest counted the money that had been brought to the LORD's Temple and put it into bags. [11] Then they gave the money to the construction supervisors, who used it to pay the people working on the LORD's Temple—the carpenters, the builders, [12] the masons, and the stonecutters. They also used the money to buy the timber and the finished stone needed for repairing the LORD's Temple, and they paid any other expenses related to the Temple's restoration.

[13] The money brought to the Temple was not used for making silver bowls, lamp snuffers, basins, trumpets, or other articles of gold or silver for the Temple of the LORD. [14] It was paid to the workmen, who used it for the Temple repairs. [15] No accounting of this money was required from the construction supervisors, because they were honest and trustworthy men. [16] However, the money that was contributed for guilt offerings and sin offerings was not brought into the LORD's Temple. It was given to the priests for their own use.

The End of Joash's Reign

[17] About this time King Hazael of Aram went to war against Gath and captured it. Then he

---

11:21a Verse 11:21 is numbered 12:1 in Hebrew text. **11:21b** Hebrew *Jehoash,* a variant spelling of Joash. **12:1a** Verses 12:1-21 are numbered 12:2-22 in Hebrew text. **12:1b** Hebrew *Jehoash,* a variant spelling of Joash; also in 12:2, 4, 6, 7, 18.

12:4-16 The difficult task of repairing the Temple was an important part of Judah's spiritual recovery. Yet raising the money to rebuild proved difficult. The priests and people were not willing to make the sacrifices necessary to get the job done. So Joash made the priests accountable for the money the people contributed. With this system of accountability the people of Judah were able to accomplish the renovation process. This should remind us that accountability and concrete planning are necessary for a successful rebuilding program. Without them, we would probably take the path of least resistance and make little progress toward recovery.

turned to attack Jerusalem. [18]King Joash collected all the sacred objects that Jehoshaphat, Jehoram, and Ahaziah, the previous kings of Judah, had dedicated, along with what he himself had dedicated. He sent them all to Hazael, along with all the gold in the treasuries of the LORD's Temple and the royal palace. So Hazael called off his attack on Jerusalem.

[19]The rest of the events in Joash's reign and everything he did are recorded in *The Book of the History of the Kings of Judah.*

[20]Joash's officers plotted against him and assassinated him at Beth-millo on the road to Silla. [21]The assassins were Jozacar* son of Shimeath and Jehozabad son of Shomer—both trusted advisers. Joash was buried with his ancestors in the City of David. Then his son Amaziah became the next king.

CHAPTER 13
Jehoahaz Rules in Israel

Jehoahaz son of Jehu began to rule over Israel in the twenty-third year of King Joash's reign in Judah. He reigned in Samaria seventeen years. [2]But he did what was evil in the LORD's sight. He followed the example of Jeroboam son of Nebat, continuing the sins that Jeroboam had led Israel to commit. [3]So the LORD was very angry with Israel, and he allowed King Hazael of Aram and his son Ben-hadad to defeat them repeatedly.

[4]Then Jehoahaz prayed for the LORD's help, and the LORD heard his prayer, for he could see how severely the king of Aram was oppressing Israel. [5]So the LORD provided someone to rescue the Israelites from the tyranny of the Arameans. Then Israel lived in safety again as they had in former days.

[6]But they continued to sin, following the evil example of Jeroboam. They also allowed the Asherah pole in Samaria to remain standing. [7]Finally, Jehoahaz's army was reduced to 50 charioteers, 10 chariots, and 10,000 foot soldiers. The king of Aram had killed the others, trampling them like dust under his feet.

[8]The rest of the events in Jehoahaz's reign—everything he did and the extent of his power—are recorded in *The Book of the History of the Kings of Israel.* [9]When Jehoahaz died, he was buried in Samaria. Then his son Jehoash* became the next king.

Jehoash Rules in Israel

[10]Jehoash son of Jehoahaz began to rule over Israel in the thirty-seventh year of King Joash's reign in Judah. He reigned in Samaria sixteen years. [11]But he did what was evil in the LORD's sight. He refused to turn from the sins that Jeroboam son of Nebat had led Israel to commit.

[12]The rest of the events in Jehoash's reign and everything he did, including the extent of his power and his war with King Amaziah of Judah, are recorded in *The Book of the History of the Kings of Israel.* [13]When Jehoash

12:21 As in Greek and Syriac versions; Hebrew reads *Jozabad.* 13:9 Hebrew *Joash,* a variant spelling of Jehoash; also in 13:10, 12, 13, 14, 25.

12:17-18 Joash had made great strides toward leading Israel into spiritual recovery. But here we see that his faith wavered easily when he was put in a difficult situation. Under threat of Aramean attack, he gave away the Temple treasury to pay off King Hazael of Aram. He failed to turn to God, who was capable of delivering his people from the Arameans, and sought his own human solution. The consequences were great national losses and a perpetuation of faithless living (see 2 Chronicles 24:17-18). Even after great success, we are still susceptible to giving in to fear and denial. We need to trust God to defeat the "enemies" in our life. Trying to fight them on our own will only invest them with greater power.

13:1-7 The experience of King Jehoahaz of Israel is a solemn case study of what happens when you "play around" with recovery. Jehoahaz apparently was humbled by his consistent defeats by the Arameans. He admitted he was powerless and turned to God, the all-important first step of recovery. But after God graciously granted relief and freedom, Jehoahaz fell back into his old dysfunctional patterns again. The consequences of his actions then led to the near collapse of his rule. When we hit bottom, it is relatively easy to give things over to God—we have nothing worth holding on to. True recovery is only possible when we leave our life in God's hands—even when things are going well.

13:10-19 King Jehoash of Israel was another individual who started the recovery process but didn't go far enough. Though he was a king who "did what was evil in the LORD's sight," Jehoash was greatly touched emotionally when the prophet Elisha was about to die. He expressed his great respect and grief for Elisha. But when Elisha gave Jehoash instructions that would lead him to victory over Aram, Jehoash followed them halfheartedly, thus limiting his progress. Anything less than complete commitment to the recovery process will result in incomplete recovery.

died, he was buried in Samaria with the kings of Israel. Then his son Jeroboam II became the next king.

Elisha's Final Prophecy

[14]When Elisha was in his last illness, King Jehoash of Israel visited him and wept over him. "My father! My father! I see the chariots and charioteers of Israel!" he cried.

[15]Elisha told him, "Get a bow and some arrows." And the king did as he was told. [16]Elisha told him, "Put your hand on the bow," and Elisha laid his own hands on the king's hands.

[17]Then he commanded, "Open that eastern window," and he opened it. Then he said, "Shoot!" So he shot an arrow. Elisha proclaimed, "This is the LORD's arrow, an arrow of victory over Aram, for you will completely conquer the Arameans at Aphek."

[18]Then he said, "Now pick up the other arrows and strike them against the ground." So the king picked them up and struck the ground three times. [19]But the man of God was angry with him. "You should have struck the ground five or six times!" he exclaimed. "Then you would have beaten Aram until it was entirely destroyed. Now you will be victorious only three times."

[20]Then Elisha died and was buried.

Groups of Moabite raiders used to invade the land each spring. [21]Once when some Israelites were burying a man, they spied a band of these raiders. So they hastily threw the corpse into the tomb of Elisha and fled. But as soon as the body touched Elisha's bones, the dead man revived and jumped to his feet!

[22]King Hazael of Aram had oppressed Israel during the entire reign of King Jehoahaz. [23]But the LORD was gracious and merciful to the people of Israel, and they were not totally destroyed. He pitied them because of his covenant with Abraham, Isaac, and Jacob. And to this day he still has not completely destroyed them or banished them from his presence.

[24]King Hazael of Aram died, and his son Ben-hadad became the next king. [25]Then Jehoash son of Jehoahaz recaptured from Ben-hadad son of Hazael the towns that had been taken from Jehoash's father, Jehoahaz. Jehoash defeated Ben-hadad on three occasions, and he recovered the Israelite towns.

CHAPTER 14
Amaziah Rules in Judah

Amaziah son of Joash began to rule over Judah in the second year of the reign of King Jehoash* of Israel. [2]Amaziah was twenty-five years old when he became king, and he reigned in Jerusalem twenty-nine years. His mother was Jehoaddin from Jerusalem. [3]Amaziah did what was pleasing in the LORD's sight, but not like his ancestor David. Instead, he followed the example of his father, Joash. [4]Amaziah did not destroy the pagan shrines, and the people still offered sacrifices and burned incense there.

[5]When Amaziah was well established as king, he executed the officials who had assassinated his father. [6]However, he did not kill the children of the assassins, for he obeyed the command of the LORD as written by Moses in the Book of the Law: "Parents must not be put to death for the sins of their children, nor children for the sins of their parents. Those deserving to die must be put to death for their own crimes."*

[7]Amaziah also killed 10,000 Edomites in the Valley of Salt. He also conquered Sela and changed its name to Joktheel, as it is called to this day.

[8]One day Amaziah sent messengers with this challenge to Israel's king Jehoash, the son of Jehoahaz and grandson of Jehu: "Come and meet me in battle!"*

[9]But King Jehoash of Israel replied to King Amaziah of Judah with this story: "Out in the Lebanon mountains, a thistle sent a message to a mighty cedar tree: 'Give your

14:1 Hebrew *Joash,* a variant spelling of Jehoash; also in 14:13, 23, 27. 14:6 Deut 24:16. 14:8 Hebrew *Come, let us look one another in the face.*

14:1-7 Amaziah of Judah demonstrated how a parent's behavior often has a significant impact on his children's behavior. Amaziah "followed the example of his father, Joash." Joash's strengths and weaknesses were evidenced in the behavior of his son Amaziah. Notable was their blind spot in regard to the shrines of false worship (12:3; 14:4). Perhaps it is best to say that Amaziah's commitment to God was mostly defined by Joash's commitment. We need to remember that our children are watching us and may well follow suit. Learning to trust God and obey his program for godly and healthy living is more than just a personal victory. It is an opportunity to leave a godly legacy for our children and grandchildren.

daughter in marriage to my son.' But just then a wild animal of Lebanon came by and stepped on the thistle, crushing it!

[10]"You have indeed defeated Edom, and you are proud of it. But be content with your victory and stay at home! Why stir up trouble that will only bring disaster on you and the people of Judah?"

[11]But Amaziah refused to listen, so King Jehoash of Israel mobilized his army against King Amaziah of Judah. The two armies drew up their battle lines at Beth-shemesh in Judah. [12]Judah was routed by the army of Israel, and its army scattered and fled for home. [13]King Jehoash of Israel captured Judah's king, Amaziah son of Joash and grandson of Ahaziah, at Beth-shemesh. Then he marched to Jerusalem, where he demolished 600 feet* of Jerusalem's wall, from the Ephraim Gate to the Corner Gate. [14]He carried off all the gold and silver and all the articles from the Temple of the LORD. He also seized the treasures from the royal palace, along with hostages, and then returned to Samaria.

[15]The rest of the events in Jehoash's reign and everything he did, including the extent of his power and his war with King Amaziah of Judah, are recorded in *The Book of the History of the Kings of Israel*. [16]When Jehoash died, he was buried in Samaria with the kings of Israel. And his son Jeroboam II became the next king.

[17]King Amaziah of Judah lived for fifteen years after the death of King Jehoash of Israel. [18]The rest of the events in Amaziah's reign are recorded in *The Book of the History of the Kings of Judah*.

[19]There was a conspiracy against Amaziah's life in Jerusalem, and he fled to Lachish. But his enemies sent assassins after him, and they killed him there. [20]They brought his body back to Jerusalem on a horse, and he was buried with his ancestors in the City of David.

[21]All the people of Judah had crowned Amaziah's sixteen-year-old son, Uzziah,* as king in place of his father, Amaziah. [22]After his father's death, Uzziah rebuilt the town of Elath and restored it to Judah.

Jeroboam II Rules in Israel

[23]Jeroboam II, the son of Jehoash, began to rule over Israel in the fifteenth year of King Amaziah's reign in Judah. He reigned in Samaria forty-one years. [24]He did what was evil in the LORD's sight. He refused to turn from the sins that Jeroboam son of Nebat had led Israel to commit. [25]Jeroboam II recovered the territories of Israel between Lebo-hamath and the Dead Sea,* just as the LORD, the God of Israel, had promised through Jonah son of Amittai, the prophet from Gath-hepher.

[26]For the LORD saw the bitter suffering of everyone in Israel, and that there was no one in Israel, slave or free, to help them. [27]And because the LORD had not said he would blot out the name of Israel completely, he used Jeroboam II, the son of Jehoash, to save them.

[28]The rest of the events in the reign of Jeroboam II and everything he did—including the extent of his power, his wars, and how he recovered for Israel both Damascus and Hamath, which had belonged to Judah*—are recorded in *The Book of the History of the Kings of Israel*. [29]When Jeroboam II died, he was buried in Samaria* with the kings of Israel. Then his son Zechariah became the next king.

CHAPTER 15
Uzziah Rules in Judah

Uzziah* son of Amaziah began to rule over Judah in the twenty-seventh year of the reign of King Jeroboam II of Israel. [2]He was sixteen years old when he became king, and he reigned in Jerusalem fifty-two years. His mother was Jecoliah from Jerusalem.

[3]He did what was pleasing in the LORD's sight, just as his father, Amaziah, had done. [4]But he did not destroy the pagan shrines, and the people still offered sacrifices and

---

14:13 Hebrew *400 cubits* [180 meters]. **14:21** Hebrew *Azariah,* a variant spelling of Uzziah. **14:25** Hebrew *the sea of the Arabah.* **14:28** Or *to Yaudi.* The meaning of the Hebrew is uncertain. **14:29** As in some Greek manuscripts; Hebrew lacks *he was buried in Samaria.* **15:1** Hebrew *Azariah,* a variant spelling of Uzziah; also in 15:6, 7, 8, 17, 23, 27.

14:23-27 God, in his sovereignty, can use oppressive or abusive personalities as part of his wider plan. God allowed the evil reign of King Jeroboam II to last 41 years only because God had a special purpose for him (14:23-26). Even though Jeroboam II had no discernible faith or commitment to God, God used him as his instrument to maintain the independence of the northern kingdom for the time being. This perspective may help those in recovery understand why God does not always immediately punish an oppressive personality; God may have something special for this person to do.

burned incense there. ⁵The LORD struck the king with leprosy,* which lasted until the day he died. He lived in isolation in a separate house. The king's son Jotham was put in charge of the royal palace, and he governed the people of the land.

⁶The rest of the events in Uzziah's reign and everything he did are recorded in *The Book of the History of the Kings of Judah.* ⁷When Uzziah died, he was buried with his ancestors in the City of David. And his son Jotham became the next king.

Zechariah Rules in Israel

⁸Zechariah son of Jeroboam II began to rule over Israel in the thirty-eighth year of King Uzziah's reign in Judah. He reigned in Samaria six months. ⁹Zechariah did what was evil in the LORD's sight, as his ancestors had done. He refused to turn from the sins that Jeroboam son of Nebat had led Israel to commit. ¹⁰Then Shallum son of Jabesh conspired against Zechariah, assassinated him in public,* and became the next king.

¹¹The rest of the events in Zechariah's reign are recorded in *The Book of the History of the Kings of Israel.* ¹²So the LORD's message to Jehu came true: "Your descendants will be kings of Israel down to the fourth generation."

Shallum Rules in Israel

¹³Shallum son of Jabesh began to rule over Israel in the thirty-ninth year of King Uzziah's reign in Judah. Shallum reigned in Samaria only one month. ¹⁴Then Menahem son of Gadi went to Samaria from Tirzah and assassinated him, and he became the next king.

¹⁵The rest of the events in Shallum's reign, including his conspiracy, are recorded in *The Book of the History of the Kings of Israel.*

Menahem Rules in Israel

¹⁶At that time Menahem destroyed the town of Tappuah* and all the surrounding countryside as far as Tirzah, because its citizens refused to surrender the town. He killed the entire population and ripped open the pregnant women.

¹⁷Menahem son of Gadi began to rule over Israel in the thirty-ninth year of King Uzziah's reign in Judah. He reigned in Samaria ten years. ¹⁸But Menahem did what was evil in the LORD's sight. During his entire reign, he refused to turn from the sins that Jeroboam son of Nebat had led Israel to commit.

¹⁹Then King Tiglath-pileser* of Assyria invaded the land. But Menahem paid him thirty-seven tons* of silver to gain his support in tightening his grip on royal power. ²⁰Menahem extorted the money from the rich of Israel, demanding that each of them pay fifty pieces* of silver to the king of Assyria. So the king of Assyria turned from attacking Israel and did not stay in the land.

²¹The rest of the events in Menahem's reign and everything he did are recorded in *The Book of the History of the Kings of Israel.* ²²When Menahem died, his son Pekahiah became the next king.

Pekahiah Rules in Israel

²³Pekahiah son of Menahem began to rule over Israel in the fiftieth year of King Uzziah's reign in Judah. He reigned in Samaria two years. ²⁴But Pekahiah did what was evil in the LORD's sight. He refused to turn from the sins that Jeroboam son of Nebat had led Israel to commit.

²⁵Then Pekah son of Remaliah, the commander of Pekahiah's army, conspired against him. With fifty men from Gilead,

---

15:5 Or *with a contagious skin disease.* The Hebrew word used here and throughout this passage can describe various skin diseases. **15:10** Or *at Ibleam.* **15:16** As in some Greek manuscripts; Hebrew reads *Tiphsah.* **15:19a** Hebrew *Pul,* another name for Tiglath-pileser. **15:19b** Hebrew *1,000 talents* [34 metric tons]. **15:20** Hebrew *50 shekels* [20 ounces or 570 grams].

15:8-12 Jeroboam II's long, evil reign could not guarantee stability or power of the northern kingdom when his equally evil son, Zechariah, became king. God allowed Zechariah to rule only six months before he was assassinated (15:10). God had kept the word of judgment he had made against Jehu generations before (15:12; see 10:30); this was the end of his primarily evil line of descendants. Jehu's failure had led to the failure of his descendants. Unless we seek recovery now, the results may be disastrous for our children and grandchildren.

15:13-14, 23-25 The reigns of kings Shallum and Pekahiah of the northern kingdom show us what often happens to oppressive personalities who refuse to face their need for recovery. Both were assassinated after very brief reigns. Shallum had been an assassin himself, so he died the same way he had risen to power (15:10). Pekahiah was killed by someone very close to him (15:25). If we tend to be oppressive in our relationships, we need to be careful—these people may tire of our abuse and either destroy us or abandon us to our misery.

Pekah assassinated the king, along with Argob and Arieh, in the citadel of the palace at Samaria. And Pekah reigned in his place.

²⁶The rest of the events in Pekahiah's reign and everything he did are recorded in *The Book of the History of the Kings of Israel.*

Pekah Rules in Israel

²⁷Pekah son of Remaliah began to rule over Israel in the fifty-second year of King Uzziah's reign in Judah. He reigned in Samaria twenty years. ²⁸But Pekah did what was evil in the LORD's sight. He refused to turn from the sins that Jeroboam son of Nebat had led Israel to commit.

²⁹During Pekah's reign, King Tiglath-pileser of Assyria attacked Israel again, and he captured the towns of Ijon, Abel-beth-maacah, Janoah, Kedesh, and Hazor. He also conquered the regions of Gilead, Galilee, and all of Naphtali, and he took the people to Assyria as captives. ³⁰Then Hoshea son of Elah conspired against Pekah and assassinated him. He began to rule over Israel in the twentieth year of Jotham son of Uzziah.

³¹The rest of the events in Pekah's reign and everything he did are recorded in *The Book of the History of the Kings of Israel.*

Jotham Rules in Judah

³²Jotham son of Uzziah began to rule over Judah in the second year of King Pekah's reign in Israel. ³³He was twenty-five years old when he became king, and he reigned in Jerusalem sixteen years. His mother was Jerusha, the daughter of Zadok.

16:3 Or *even making his son pass through the fire.*

³⁴Jotham did what was pleasing in the LORD's sight. He did everything his father, Uzziah, had done. ³⁵But he did not destroy the pagan shrines, and the people still offered sacrifices and burned incense there. He rebuilt the upper gate of the Temple of the LORD.

³⁶The rest of the events in Jotham's reign and everything he did are recorded in *The Book of the History of the Kings of Judah.* ³⁷In those days the LORD began to send King Rezin of Aram and King Pekah of Israel to attack Judah. ³⁸When Jotham died, he was buried with his ancestors in the City of David. And his son Ahaz became the next king.

CHAPTER 16
Ahaz Rules in Judah

Ahaz son of Jotham began to rule over Judah in the seventeenth year of King Pekah's reign in Israel. ²Ahaz was twenty years old when he became king, and he reigned in Jerusalem sixteen years. He did not do what was pleasing in the sight of the LORD his God, as his ancestor David had done. ³Instead, he followed the example of the kings of Israel, even sacrificing his own son in the fire.* In this way, he followed the detestable practices of the pagan nations the LORD had driven from the land ahead of the Israelites. ⁴He offered sacrifices and burned incense at the pagan shrines and on the hills and under every green tree.

⁵Then King Rezin of Aram and King Pekah of Israel came up to attack Jerusalem. They besieged Ahaz but could not conquer him.

15:32-38 The reign of King Jotham of Judah—first as governor under his father Uzziah (15:5) and then in his own right (15:32-33)—was a "mixed bag." He exemplified faith and commitment to God up to a point, as had his predecessors. He gave attention to God's Temple. But he did not destroy the pagan shrines and false worship in Judah (15:34-35), so God "turned up the heat." God allowed Aram and Israel to attack (15:37) in order to shatter Jotham's denial. God sometimes brings trials into our life to alert us to our denial.

16:1-4 It was only a matter of time before the halfhearted attempts at recovery by Judah's kings would cause great damage. Ahaz's reign wasn't even a mixed bag. He completely denied his need for God and disobeyed God's laws, even sacrificing his own son to pagan gods (16:3). The partial recovery of many generations had a cumulative impact on the later generations. Children can quickly see through the hypocrisy of a halfhearted recovery. This may cause them to reject everything we stand for—especially the good things. What kind of example are we setting for our children?

16:5-9 King Ahaz paid tribute to the king of Assyria, placing his trust in the human resources at his disposal. In seeking human solutions to the conflict, however, he failed to trust God to help him. The peace that Ahaz established in Judah was dependent on the payment of money. When Ahaz's son Hezekiah refused to pay tribute money to Assyria, Assyria attacked (see 18:7, 13), but God protected Hezekiah and his kingdom. Had Ahaz turned to God for help, the peace he sought would have been unconditional—built upon the unchanging power and presence of God. We also need to ask God for help as we continue in recovery. Looking for human help may be disappointing. Some people may help us only for what they get in return.

HEZEKIAH

Hezekiah inherited a kingdom that his father had led into social, economic, and spiritual decline. Upon his ascension to the throne, Hezekiah courageously implemented sweeping reforms. He reopened the Temple, which his father had nailed shut, and he abolished idolatry throughout the land. He followed God's instructions to the letter, with two exceptions.

First, Hezekiah took credit for the blessings that God had given to him and to the nation of Israel. Hezekiah proudly displayed the wealth of his kingdom to the Babylonians, who would eventually conquer the kingdom of Judah. It was not really Hezekiah's wealth; it belonged to God.

Second, he failed in his task as a father. He spent little time teaching Manasseh, his son and heir, godly ways. When Manasseh became king, he reversed all his father's righteous reforms. The idol worship instituted during Manasseh's reign initiated one of the great spiritual declines in Israel's history. The prophet Jeremiah pinned Judah's ultimate demise on Manasseh, giving him the reputation as the most evil of all Judah's kings (Jeremiah 15:4).

Hezekiah's failures are easy to repeat. We can look at our possessions, status, and progress in recovery and think that we have achieved it all, forgetting that God was the one who gave them to us. We can get caught up in work, activities, even the things we do for God, and forget that our primary task is to prepare the next generation to follow in the path of righteousness. What we have learned from the past and are learning in the present must be communicated to the leaders of the future. Jesus illustrated the importance of this by spending quality time with his disciples—his hope for the future. We need to follow Jesus' example, not Hezekiah's.

STRENGTHS AND ACCOMPLISHMENTS:
- Hezekiah instituted sweeping spiritual and political reforms.
- He had a powerful prayer life.
- He maintained a consistent personal relationship with God.

WEAKNESSES AND MISTAKES:
- Hezekiah failed to train his son and protect the reforms he had instituted.
- He showed Judah's wealth to Babylonian messengers and took credit for it.

LESSONS FROM HIS LIFE:
- We must teach our family what we learn in recovery if we want to protect them from our past failures.
- When we turn our life over to God, amazing results will occur.

KEY VERSES:
"And Hezekiah prayed this prayer before the LORD: . . . 'It is true, LORD, that the kings of Assyria . . . have thrown the gods of these nations into the fire and burned them. . . . They were not gods at all—only idols of wood and stone shaped by human hands. Now, O LORD our God, rescue us . . . ; then all the kingdoms of the earth will know that you alone, O LORD, are God'" (2 Kings 19:15, 17-19).

Hezekiah's story is told in 2 Kings 16–20; 2 Chronicles 28–32; Isaiah 36–39. He is mentioned in 1 Chronicles 3:10-14; 4:40-41; Proverbs 25:1; Isaiah 1:1; Jeremiah 15:4; 26:18-19; Hosea 1:1; Micah 1:1; Zephaniah 1:1; Matthew 1:9-10.

6At that time the king of Edom* recovered the town of Elath for Edom.* He drove out the people of Judah and sent Edomites* to live there, as they do to this day.

7King Ahaz sent messengers to King Tiglath-pileser of Assyria with this message: "I am your servant and your vassal.* Come up and rescue me from the attacking armies of Aram and Israel." 8Then Ahaz took the silver and gold from the Temple of the LORD and the palace treasury and sent it as a payment to the Assyrian king. 9So the king of Assyria attacked the Aramean capital of Damascus and led its population away as captives, resettling them in Kir. He also killed King Rezin.

10King Ahaz then went to Damascus to meet with King Tiglath-pileser of Assyria. While he was there, he took special note of the altar. Then he sent a model of the altar to Uriah the priest, along with its design in full detail. 11Uriah followed the king's instructions and built an altar just like it, and it was ready before the king returned from Damascus. 12When the king returned, he

16:6a As in Latin Vulgate; Hebrew reads *Rezin king of Aram.* 16:6b As in Latin Vulgate; Hebrew reads *Aram.* 16:6c As in Greek version, Latin Vulgate, and an alternate reading of the Masoretic Text; the other alternate reads *Arameans.* 16:7 Hebrew *your son.*

inspected the altar and made offerings on it. [13]He presented a burnt offering and a grain offering, he poured out a liquid offering, and he sprinkled the blood of peace offerings on the altar.

[14]Then King Ahaz removed the old bronze altar from its place in front of the LORD's Temple, between the entrance and the new altar, and placed it on the north side of the new altar. [15]He told Uriah the priest, "Use the new altar* for the morning sacrifices of burnt offering, the evening grain offering, the king's burnt offering and grain offering, and the burnt offerings of all the people, as well as their grain offerings and liquid offerings. Sprinkle the blood from all the burnt offerings and sacrifices on the new altar. The bronze altar will be for my personal use only." [16]Uriah the priest did just as King Ahaz commanded him.

[17]Then the king removed the side panels and basins from the portable water carts. He also removed the great bronze basin called the Sea from the backs of the bronze oxen and placed it on the stone pavement. [18]In deference to the king of Assyria, he also removed the canopy that had been constructed inside the palace for use on the Sabbath day,* as well as the king's outer entrance to the Temple of the LORD.

[19]The rest of the events in Ahaz's reign and everything he did are recorded in *The Book of the History of the Kings of Judah.* [20]When Ahaz died, he was buried with his ancestors in the City of David. Then his son Hezekiah became the next king.

CHAPTER 17
Hoshea Rules in Israel

Hoshea son of Elah began to rule over Israel in the twelfth year of King Ahaz's reign in Judah. He reigned in Samaria nine years. [2]He did what was evil in the LORD's sight, but not to the same extent as the kings of Israel who ruled before him.

[3]King Shalmaneser of Assyria attacked King Hoshea, so Hoshea was forced to pay heavy tribute to Assyria. [4]But Hoshea stopped paying the annual tribute and conspired against the king of Assyria by asking King So of Egypt* to help him shake free of Assyria's power. When the king of Assyria discovered this treachery, he seized Hoshea and put him in prison.

Samaria Falls to Assyria

[5]Then the king of Assyria invaded the entire land, and for three years he besieged the city of Samaria. [6]Finally, in the ninth year of King Hoshea's reign, Samaria fell, and the people of Israel were exiled to Assyria. They were settled in colonies in Halah, along the banks of the Habor River in Gozan, and in the cities of the Medes.

[7]This disaster came upon the people of Israel because they worshiped other gods. They sinned against the LORD their God, who had brought them safely out of Egypt and had rescued them from the power of Pharaoh, the king of Egypt. [8]They had followed the practices of the pagan nations the LORD had driven from the land ahead of them, as well as the practices the kings of Israel had introduced. [9]The people of Israel had also secretly done many things that were not pleasing to the LORD their God. They built pagan shrines for themselves in all their towns, from the smallest outpost to the largest walled city. [10]They set up sacred pillars and Asherah poles at the top of every hill and under every green tree. [11]They offered sacrifices on all the hilltops, just like the nations the LORD had driven from the land ahead of them. So the people of Israel had done many evil things, arousing the LORD's anger. [12]Yes, they worshiped idols,* despite the LORD's specific and repeated warnings.

[13]Again and again the LORD had sent his prophets and seers to warn both Israel and Judah: "Turn from all your evil ways. Obey my commands and decrees—the entire law that I commanded your ancestors to obey,

---

16:15 Hebrew *the great altar.* 16:18 The meaning of the Hebrew is uncertain. 17:4 Or *by asking the king of Egypt at Sais.* 17:12 The Hebrew term (literally *round things*) probably alludes to dung.

17:1-23 This chapter records the progressive degeneration of the northern kingdom of Israel leading to its destruction and exile. The reign of Hoshea was the straw that broke the camel's back. He led Israel through its final climactic period of sinful denial, which ended in Assyrian exile (17:1-7). Notice that the nation of Judah is criticized for making the same mistakes, following the same evil path toward judgment and exile (17:18-19). The southern kingdom of Judah should have seen the consequences of Israel's disobedience and then pursued recovery. Have we ever criticized others for their addictions and noted the consequences of their actions? If we have, we should be careful to head in the opposite direction. We must avoid Judah's terrible mistake.

and that I gave you through my servants the prophets."

¹⁴But the Israelites would not listen. They were as stubborn as their ancestors who had refused to believe in the LORD their God. ¹⁵They rejected his decrees and the covenant he had made with their ancestors, and they despised all his warnings. They worshiped worthless idols, so they became worthless themselves. They followed the example of the nations around them, disobeying the LORD's command not to imitate them.

¹⁶They rejected all the commands of the LORD their God and made two calves from metal. They set up an Asherah pole and worshiped Baal and all the forces of heaven. ¹⁷They even sacrificed their own sons and daughters in the fire.* They consulted fortune-tellers and practiced sorcery and sold themselves to evil, arousing the LORD's anger.

¹⁸Because the LORD was very angry with Israel, he swept them away from his presence. Only the tribe of Judah remained in the land. ¹⁹But even the people of Judah refused to obey the commands of the LORD their God, for they followed the evil practices that Israel had introduced. ²⁰The LORD rejected all the descendants of Israel. He punished them by handing them over to their attackers until he had banished Israel from his presence.

²¹For when the LORD* tore Israel away from the kingdom of David, they chose Jeroboam son of Nebat as their king. But Jeroboam drew Israel away from following the LORD and made them commit a great sin. ²²And the people of Israel persisted in all the evil ways of Jeroboam. They did not turn from these sins ²³until the LORD finally swept them away from his presence, just as all his prophets had warned. So Israel was exiled from their land to Assyria, where they remain to this day.

Foreigners Settle in Israel

²⁴The king of Assyria transported groups of people from Babylon, Cuthah, Avva, Hamath, and Sepharvaim and resettled them in the towns of Samaria, replacing the people of Israel. They took possession of Samaria and lived in its towns. ²⁵But since these foreign settlers did not worship the LORD when they first arrived, the LORD sent lions among them, which killed some of them.

²⁶So a message was sent to the king of Assyria: "The people you have sent to live in the towns of Samaria do not know the religious customs of the God of the land. He has sent lions among them to destroy them because they have not worshiped him correctly."

²⁷The king of Assyria then commanded, "Send one of the exiled priests back to Samaria. Let him live there and teach the new residents the religious customs of the God of the land." ²⁸So one of the priests who had been exiled from Samaria returned to Bethel and taught the new residents how to worship the LORD.

²⁹But these various groups of foreigners also continued to worship their own gods. In town after town where they lived, they placed their idols at the pagan shrines that the people of Samaria had built. ³⁰Those from Babylon worshiped idols of their god Succoth-benoth. Those from Cuthah worshiped their god Nergal. And those from Hamath worshiped Ashima. ³¹The Avvites worshiped their gods Nibhaz and Tartak. And the people from Sepharvaim even burned their own children as sacrifices to their gods Adrammelech and Anammelech.

³²These new residents worshiped the LORD, but they also appointed from among themselves all sorts of people as priests to offer sacrifices at their places of worship. ³³And though they worshiped the LORD, they continued to follow their own gods according to the religious customs of the nations from which they came. ³⁴And this is still going on today. They continue to follow their former practices instead of truly worshiping the LORD and obeying the decrees, regulations, instructions, and commands he gave the descendants of Jacob, whose name he changed to Israel.

³⁵For the LORD had made a covenant with the descendants of Jacob and commanded them: "Do not worship any other gods or bow before them or serve them or offer sacrifices to them. ³⁶But worship only the LORD, who brought you out of Egypt with great strength and a powerful arm. Bow down to him alone, and offer sacrifices only to him. ³⁷Be careful at all times to obey the decrees, regulations, instructions, and commands that he wrote for you. You must not worship other gods. ³⁸Do not forget the covenant I made with you, and do not worship other gods. ³⁹You must worship only the LORD your God. He is the one who will rescue you from all your enemies."

⁴⁰But the people would not listen and continued to follow their former practices. ⁴¹So

---

17:17 Or *They even made their sons and daughters pass through the fire.* **17:21** Hebrew *he;* compare 1 Kgs 11:31-32.

while these new residents worshiped the LORD, they also worshiped their idols. And to this day their descendants do the same.

CHAPTER 18
Hezekiah Rules in Judah

Hezekiah son of Ahaz began to rule over Judah in the third year of King Hoshea's reign in Israel. ²He was twenty-five years old when he became king, and he reigned in Jerusalem twenty-nine years. His mother was Abijah,* the daughter of Zechariah. ³He did what was pleasing in the LORD's sight, just as his ancestor David had done. ⁴He removed the pagan shrines, smashed the sacred pillars, and cut down the Asherah poles. He broke up the bronze serpent that Moses had made, because the people of Israel had been offering sacrifices to it. The bronze serpent was called Nehushtan.*

⁵Hezekiah trusted in the LORD, the God of Israel. There was no one like him among all the kings of Judah, either before or after his time. ⁶He remained faithful to the LORD in everything, and he carefully obeyed all the commands the LORD had given Moses. ⁷So the LORD was with him, and Hezekiah was successful in everything he did. He revolted against the king of Assyria and refused to pay him tribute. ⁸He also conquered the Philistines as far distant as Gaza and its territory, from their smallest outpost to their largest walled city.

⁹During the fourth year of Hezekiah's reign, which was the seventh year of King Hoshea's reign in Israel, King Shalmaneser of Assyria attacked the city of Samaria and began a siege against it. ¹⁰Three years later, during the sixth year of King Hezekiah's reign and the ninth year of King Hoshea's reign in Israel, Samaria fell. ¹¹At that time the king of Assyria exiled the Israelites to Assyria and placed them in colonies in Halah, along the banks of the Habor River in Gozan, and in the cities of the Medes. ¹²For they refused to listen to the LORD their God and obey him. Instead, they violated his covenant—all the laws that Moses the LORD's servant had commanded them to obey.

Assyria Invades Judah

¹³In the fourteenth year of King Hezekiah's reign,* King Sennacherib of Assyria came to attack the fortified towns of Judah and conquered them. ¹⁴King Hezekiah sent this message to the king of Assyria at Lachish: "I have done wrong. I will pay whatever tribute money you demand if you will only withdraw." The king of Assyria then demanded a settlement of more than eleven tons of silver and one ton of gold.* ¹⁵To gather this amount, King Hezekiah used all the silver stored in the Temple of the LORD and in the palace treasury. ¹⁶Hezekiah even stripped the gold from the doors of the LORD's Temple and from the doorposts he had overlaid with gold, and he gave it all to the Assyrian king.

¹⁷Nevertheless, the king of Assyria sent his commander in chief, his field commander, and his chief of staff* from Lachish with a huge army to confront King Hezekiah in Jerusalem. The Assyrians took up a position beside the aqueduct that feeds water into the upper pool, near the road leading to the field where cloth is washed.* ¹⁸They summoned King Hezekiah, but the king sent these officials to meet with them: Eliakim son of Hilkiah, the palace administrator; Shebna the court secretary; and Joah son of Asaph, the royal historian.

18:2 As in parallel text at 2 Chr 29:1; Hebrew reads *Abi,* a variant spelling of Abijah. **18:4** *Nehushtan* sounds like the Hebrew terms that mean "snake," "bronze," and "unclean thing." **18:13** The fourteenth year of Hezekiah's reign was 701 B.C. **18:14** Hebrew *300 talents* [10 metric tons] *of silver and 30 talents* [1 metric ton] *of gold.* **18:17a** Or *the rabshakeh;* also in 18:19, 26, 27, 28, 37. **18:17b** Or *bleached.*

18:1-8 King Hezekiah made a radical break from the evil ways of his father, Ahaz. Hezekiah's stated faith and commitment to the Lord gave him the courage to stand against Judah's sinful past and take significant steps to rebuild his kingdom God's way (18:5). His honesty in assessing the spiritual state of his kingdom and his willingness to break from its sinful ways made him one of Judah's greatest kings (18:6-7). Because he was faithful to the Lord in everything, the Lord caused him to be successful. If we want to succeed in recovery, we also must honestly admit our failures and do all we can to rebuild our life God's way.

18:9-16 Although Hezekiah was one of Judah's best kings, he responded exactly as his father had at the threat of the Assyrian invasion. Hezekiah trusted God with the smaller things, but at the threat of invasion, he looked elsewhere for help. Rather than trusting the God who gave him his kingdom, Hezekiah trusted the very enemy who was attacking him. Our addictions have the same effect on us. We choose to trust in the things that are ruining our life rather than in the God who created us and desires recovery for us. Putting our life into God's hands is the only way to experience true deliverance.

Sennacherib Threatens Jerusalem

[19] Then the Assyrian king's chief of staff told them to give this message to Hezekiah:

"This is what the great king of Assyria says: What are you trusting in that makes you so confident? [20] Do you think that mere words can substitute for military skill and strength? Who are you counting on, that you have rebelled against me? [21] On Egypt? If you lean on Egypt, it will be like a reed that splinters beneath your weight and pierces your hand. Pharaoh, the king of Egypt, is completely unreliable!

[22] "But perhaps you will say to me, 'We are trusting in the LORD our God!' But isn't he the one who was insulted by Hezekiah? Didn't Hezekiah tear down his shrines and altars and make everyone in Judah and Jerusalem worship only at the altar here in Jerusalem?

[23] "I'll tell you what! Strike a bargain with my master, the king of Assyria. I will give you 2,000 horses if you can find that many men to ride on them! [24] With your tiny army, how can you think of challenging even the weakest contingent of my master's troops, even with the help of Egypt's chariots and charioteers? [25] What's more, do you think we have invaded your land without the LORD's direction? The LORD himself told us, 'Attack this land and destroy it!'"

[26] Then Eliakim son of Hilkiah, Shebna, and Joah said to the Assyrian chief of staff, "Please speak to us in Aramaic, for we understand it well. Don't speak in Hebrew,* for the people on the wall will hear."

[27] But Sennacherib's chief of staff replied, "Do you think my master sent this message only to you and your master? He wants all the people to hear it, for when we put this city under siege, they will suffer along with you. They will be so hungry and thirsty that they will eat their own dung and drink their own urine."

[28] Then the chief of staff stood and shouted in Hebrew to the people on the wall, "Listen to this message from the great king of Assyria! [29] This is what the king says: Don't let Hezekiah deceive you. He will never be able to rescue you from my power. [30] Don't let him fool you into trusting in the LORD by saying, 'The LORD will surely rescue us. This city will never fall into the hands of the Assyrian king!'

[31] "Don't listen to Hezekiah! These are the terms the king of Assyria is offering: Make peace with me—open the gates and come out. Then each of you can continue eating from your own grapevine and fig tree and drinking from your own well. [32] Then I will arrange to take you to another land like this one—a land of grain and new wine, bread and vineyards, olive groves and honey. Choose life instead of death!

"Don't listen to Hezekiah when he tries to mislead you by saying, 'The LORD will rescue us!' [33] Have the gods of any other nations ever saved their people from the king of Assyria? [34] What happened to the gods of Hamath and Arpad? And what about the gods of Sepharvaim, Hena, and Ivvah? Did any god rescue Samaria from my power? [35] What god of any nation has ever been able to save its people from my power? So what makes you think that the LORD can rescue Jerusalem from me?"

[36] But the people were silent and did not utter a word because Hezekiah had commanded them, "Do not answer him."

[37] Then Eliakim son of Hilkiah, the palace administrator; Shebna the court secretary; and Joah son of Asaph, the royal historian, went back to Hezekiah. They tore their clothes in despair, and they went in to see the king and told him what the Assyrian chief of staff had said.

CHAPTER 19

Hezekiah Seeks the LORD's Help

When King Hezekiah heard their report, he tore his clothes and put on burlap and went into the Temple of the LORD. [2] And he sent Eliakim the palace administrator, Shebna the court secretary, and the leading priests, all dressed in burlap, to the prophet Isaiah son

---

18:26 Hebrew *in the dialect of Judah;* also in 18:28.

19:2-34 As Hezekiah faced this impossible situation, he humbly turned to God for help. God answered Hezekiah's desperate plea and delivered his people from a formidable enemy. In this case, God didn't roar in with blaring trumpets or a terrifying earthquake. The enemy army was quietly lured from its siege of Jerusalem. We may wish for an instant, miraculous deliverance from our problems, but it doesn't usually happen that way. God most often uses quiet resources—the steady support of a friend, the encouragement of a support group, the quiet leading of the Holy Spirit—to strengthen us in recovery.

of Amoz. ³They told him, "This is what King Hezekiah says: Today is a day of trouble, insults, and disgrace. It is like when a child is ready to be born, but the mother has no strength to deliver the baby. ⁴But perhaps the LORD your God has heard the Assyrian chief of staff,* sent by the king to defy the living God, and will punish him for his words. Oh, pray for those of us who are left!"

⁵After King Hezekiah's officials delivered the king's message to Isaiah, ⁶the prophet replied, "Say to your master, 'This is what the LORD says: Do not be disturbed by this blasphemous speech against me from the Assyrian king's messengers. ⁷Listen! I myself will move against him,* and the king will receive a message that he is needed at home. So he will return to his land, where I will have him killed with a sword.'"

⁸Meanwhile, the Assyrian chief of staff left Jerusalem and went to consult the king of Assyria, who had left Lachish and was attacking Libnah.

⁹Soon afterward King Sennacherib received word that King Tirhakah of Ethiopia* was leading an army to fight against him. Before leaving to meet the attack, he sent messengers back to Hezekiah in Jerusalem with this message:

¹⁰"This message is for King Hezekiah of Judah. Don't let your God, in whom you trust, deceive you with promises that Jerusalem will not be captured by the king of Assyria. ¹¹You know perfectly well what the kings of Assyria have done wherever they have gone. They have completely destroyed everyone who stood in their way! Why should you be any different? ¹²Have the gods of other nations rescued them—such nations as Gozan, Haran, Rezeph, and the people of Eden who were in Tel-assar? My predecessors destroyed them all! ¹³What happened to the king of Hamath and the king of Arpad? What happened to the kings of Sepharvaim, Hena, and Ivvah?"

¹⁴After Hezekiah received the letter from the messengers and read it, he went up to the LORD's Temple and spread it out before the LORD. ¹⁵And Hezekiah prayed this prayer before the LORD: "O LORD, God of Israel, you are enthroned between the mighty cherubim! You alone are God of all the kingdoms of the earth. You alone created the heavens and the earth. ¹⁶Bend down, O LORD, and listen!

Open your eyes, O LORD, and see! Listen to Sennacherib's words of defiance against the living God.

¹⁷"It is true, LORD, that the kings of Assyria have destroyed all these nations. ¹⁸And they have thrown the gods of these nations into the fire and burned them. But of course the Assyrians could destroy them! They were not gods at all—only idols of wood and stone shaped by human hands. ¹⁹Now, O LORD our God, rescue us from his power; then all the kingdoms of the earth will know that you alone, O LORD, are God."

Isaiah Predicts Judah's Deliverance

²⁰Then Isaiah son of Amoz sent this message to Hezekiah: "This is what the LORD, the God of Israel, says: I have heard your prayer about King Sennacherib of Assyria. ²¹And the LORD has spoken this word against him:

"The virgin daughter of Zion
    despises you and laughs at you.
The daughter of Jerusalem
    shakes her head in derision as you flee.

²² "Whom have you been defying and
        ridiculing?
    Against whom did you raise your voice?
    At whom did you look with such haughty
        eyes?
    It was the Holy One of Israel!
²³ By your messengers you have defied the
        Lord.
    You have said, 'With my many chariots
I have conquered the highest
        mountains—
    yes, the remotest peaks of Lebanon.
I have cut down its tallest cedars
    and its finest cypress trees.
I have reached its farthest corners
    and explored its deepest forests.
²⁴ I have dug wells in many foreign lands
    and refreshed myself with their water.
With the sole of my foot
    I stopped up all the rivers of Egypt!'

²⁵ "But have you not heard?
    I decided this long ago.
Long ago I planned it,
    and now I am making it happen.
I planned for you to crush fortified cities
    into heaps of rubble.
²⁶ That is why their people have so little
        power
    and are so frightened and confused.
They are as weak as grass,

19:4 Or *the rabshakeh;* also in 19:8. 19:7 Hebrew *I will put a spirit in him.* 19:9 Hebrew *of Cush.*

as easily trampled as tender green
shoots.
They are like grass sprouting on a
housetop,
scorched before it can grow lush
and tall.

²⁷ "But I know you well—
where you stay
and when you come and go.
I know the way you have raged against
me.
²⁸ And because of your raging against me
and your arrogance, which I have heard
for myself,
I will put my hook in your nose
and my bit in your mouth.
I will make you return
by the same road on which you came."

²⁹ Then Isaiah said to Hezekiah, "Here is the
proof that what I say is true:

"This year you will eat only what grows
up by itself,
and next year you will eat what springs
up from that.
But in the third year you will plant crops
and harvest them;
you will tend vineyards and eat their
fruit.
³⁰ And you who are left in Judah,
who have escaped the ravages of the
siege,
will put roots down in your own soil
and will grow up and flourish.
³¹ For a remnant of my people will spread
out from Jerusalem,
a group of survivors from Mount Zion.
The passionate commitment of the LORD
of Heaven's Armies*
will make this happen!

³²"And this is what the LORD says about the
king of Assyria:

"His armies will not enter Jerusalem.
They will not even shoot an arrow at it.
They will not march outside its gates with
their shields
nor build banks of earth against its
walls.
³³ The king will return to his own country
by the same road on which he came.
He will not enter this city,
says the LORD.
³⁴ For my own honor and for the sake of my
servant David,
I will defend this city and protect it."

³⁵That night the angel of the LORD went
out to the Assyrian camp and killed 185,000
Assyrian soldiers. When the surviving
Assyrians* woke up the next morning, they
found corpses everywhere. ³⁶Then King
Sennacherib of Assyria broke camp and returned to his own land. He went home to his
capital of Nineveh and stayed there.

³⁷One day while he was worshiping in the
temple of his god Nisroch, his sons*
Adrammelech and Sharezer killed him with
their swords. They then escaped to the land
of Ararat, and another son, Esarhaddon, became the next king of Assyria.

CHAPTER 20
Hezekiah's Sickness and Recovery
About that time Hezekiah became deathly
ill, and the prophet Isaiah son of Amoz went
to visit him. He gave the king this message:
"This is what the LORD says: Set your affairs
in order, for you are going to die. You will
not recover from this illness."

²When Hezekiah heard this, he turned his
face to the wall and prayed to the LORD, ³"Remember, O LORD, how I have always been
faithful to you and have served you single-
mindedly, always doing what pleases you."
Then he broke down and wept bitterly.

19:31 As in Greek and Syriac versions, Latin Vulgate, and an alternate reading of the Masoretic Text (see also Isa
37:32); the other alternate reads *the LORD.* 19:35 Hebrew *When they.* 19:37 As in Greek version and an alternate
reading of the Masoretic Text (see also Isa 37:38); the other alternate reading lacks *his sons.*

19:35-37 All of the Assyrian general's boasting about his army's strength could not keep it from
being destroyed by God. Those needing recovery are often terrified in the face of brutal human
power, especially if they have been previously abused. Some of us feel powerless against the
persistent enemies that lie within. But such oppressors or problems, no matter how great, stand
no chance at all against God's power; he will ultimately overcome them.
20:1-11 Hezekiah pleaded with God to spare his life, reminding God of his previous consistent
faith and commitment to God. So Hezekiah was granted another 15 years of life. God also
performed a great miracle as proof of his promise of life to Hezekiah, who seems to have been
greatly troubled by doubt and possibly even depression at this point. Although God may not
make the sun go backward for us, we should never doubt that he will rescue us if we honestly cry
out to him.

[4]But before Isaiah had left the middle court-yard,* this message came to him from the LORD: [5]"Go back to Hezekiah, the leader of my people. Tell him, 'This is what the LORD, the God of your ancestor David, says: I have heard your prayer and seen your tears. I will heal you, and three days from now you will get out of bed and go to the Temple of the LORD. [6]I will add fifteen years to your life, and I will rescue you and this city from the king of Assyria. I will defend this city for my own honor and for the sake of my servant David.'"

[7]Then Isaiah said, "Make an ointment from figs." So Hezekiah's servants spread the oint-ment over the boil, and Hezekiah recovered!

[8]Meanwhile, Hezekiah had said to Isaiah, "What sign will the LORD give to prove that he will heal me and that I will go to the Tem-ple of the LORD three days from now?"

[9]Isaiah replied, "This is the sign from the LORD to prove that he will do as he promised. Would you like the shadow on the sundial to go forward ten steps or backward ten steps?*"

[10]"The shadow always moves forward," Hezekiah replied, "so that would be easy. Make it go ten steps backward instead." [11]So Isaiah the prophet asked the LORD to do this, and he caused the shadow to move ten steps backward on the sundial* of Ahaz!

Envoys from Babylon

[12]Soon after this, Merodach-baladan* son of Baladan, king of Babylon, sent Hezekiah his best wishes and a gift, for he had heard that Hezekiah had been very sick. [13]Hezekiah re-ceived the Babylonian envoys and showed them everything in his treasure-houses—the silver, the gold, the spices, and the aromatic oils. He also took them to see his armory and showed them everything in his royal treasur-ies! There was nothing in his palace or king-dom that Hezekiah did not show them.

[14]Then Isaiah the prophet went to King Hezekiah and asked him, "What did those men want? Where were they from?"

Hezekiah replied, "They came from the distant land of Babylon."

[15]"What did they see in your palace?" Isa-iah asked.

"They saw everything," Hezekiah replied. "I showed them everything I own—all my royal treasuries."

[16]Then Isaiah said to Hezekiah, "Listen to this message from the LORD: [17]The time is coming when everything in your palace—all the treasures stored up by your ancestors un-til now—will be carried off to Babylon. Noth-ing will be left, says the LORD. [18]Some of your very own sons will be taken away into exile. They will become eunuchs who will serve in the palace of Babylon's king."

[19]Then Hezekiah said to Isaiah, "This mes-sage you have given me from the LORD is good." For the king was thinking, "At least there will be peace and security during my lifetime."

[20]The rest of the events in Hezekiah's reign, including the extent of his power and how he built a pool and dug a tunnel* to bring water into the city, are recorded in *The Book of the History of the Kings of Judah.* [21]Hezekiah died, and his son Manasseh be-came the next king.

CHAPTER 21
Manasseh Rules in Judah

Manasseh was twelve years old when he became king, and he reigned in Jerusalem

20:4 As in Greek version and an alternate reading in the Masoretic Text; the other alternate reads *the middle of the city.* 20:9 Or *The shadow on the sundial has gone forward ten steps; do you want it to go backward ten steps?* 20:11 Hebrew *the steps.* 20:12 As in some Hebrew manuscripts and Greek and Syriac versions (see also Isa 39:1); Masoretic Text reads *Berodach-baladan.* 20:20 Hebrew *watercourse.*

20:12-21 Hezekiah made a major mistake that seriously set back his recovery. When the delega-tion from the rising nation of Babylon came to Jerusalem, Hezekiah put on the most impressive show possible. Not only that, he took the credit for all his wealth instead of giving the glory to God (20:15). The unconsidered consequences of his prideful actions came to painful fruition in the Babylonian exile (23:36—25:30). When we become prideful about our accomplishments, we show that we have forgotten the true source of our success—God. We must remain humble if we want God to help us. He can't work in a life that isn't surrendered to him.
21:1-17 Manasseh reversed all the positive steps Hezekiah instituted for Judah's national recovery. Because of Manasseh's totally evil, oppressive reign, God declared that Judah would inevitably be exiled. Judah would follow the northern kingdom of Israel into exile just as they had followed them into sin. By the end of Manasseh's fifty-five-year reign, the possibility of meaningful recovery in Judah seemed very dim. (Even in the midst of such evil, God displayed his love for his people yet again. When Manasseh hit bottom, he cried out to God for renewal, and God granted him victory [see 2 Chronicles 33:12-17]. No matter what the circumstances, there is always hope for recovery.) Those who submit to our leadership may suffer consequences for our mistakes. This truth should cause us to think twice before abandoning the recovery process.

fifty-five years. His mother was Hephzibah. [2]He did what was evil in the LORD's sight, following the detestable practices of the pagan nations that the LORD had driven from the land ahead of the Israelites. [3]He rebuilt the pagan shrines his father, Hezekiah, had destroyed. He constructed altars for Baal and set up an Asherah pole, just as King Ahab of Israel had done. He also bowed before all the powers of the heavens and worshiped them.

[4]He built pagan altars in the Temple of the LORD, the place where the LORD had said, "My name will remain in Jerusalem forever." [5]He built these altars for all the powers of the heavens in both courtyards of the LORD's Temple. [6]Manasseh also sacrificed his own son in the fire.* He practiced sorcery and divination, and he consulted with mediums and psychics. He did much that was evil in the LORD's sight, arousing his anger.

[7]Manasseh even made a carved image of Asherah and set it up in the Temple, the very place where the LORD had told David and his son Solomon: "My name will be honored forever in this Temple and in Jerusalem—the city I have chosen from among all the tribes of Israel. [8]If the Israelites will be careful to obey my commands—all the laws my servant Moses gave them—I will not send them into exile from this land that I gave their ancestors." [9]But the people refused to listen, and Manasseh led them to do even more evil than the pagan nations that the LORD had destroyed when the people of Israel entered the land.

[10]Then the LORD said through his servants the prophets: [11]"King Manasseh of Judah has done many detestable things. He is even more wicked than the Amorites, who lived in this land before Israel. He has caused the people of Judah to sin with his idols.* [12]So this is what the LORD, the God of Israel, says: I will bring such disaster on Jerusalem and Judah that the ears of those who hear about it will tingle with horror. [13]I will judge Jerusalem by the same standard I used for Samaria and the same measure* I used for the family of Ahab. I will wipe away the people of Jerusalem as one wipes a dish and turns it upside down. [14]Then I will reject even the remnant of my own people who are left, and I will hand them over as plunder for their enemies. [15]For they have done great evil in my sight and have angered me ever since their ancestors came out of Egypt."

[16]Manasseh also murdered many innocent people until Jerusalem was filled from one end to the other with innocent blood. This was in addition to the sin that he caused the people of Judah to commit, leading them to do evil in the LORD's sight.

[17]The rest of the events in Manasseh's reign and everything he did, including the sins he committed, are recorded in *The Book of the History of the Kings of Judah*. [18]When Manasseh died, he was buried in the palace garden, the garden of Uzza. Then his son Amon became the next king.

Amon Rules in Judah

[19]Amon was twenty-two years old when he became king, and he reigned in Jerusalem two years. His mother was Meshullemeth, the daughter of Haruz from Jotbah. [20]He did what was evil in the LORD's sight, just as his father, Manasseh, had done. [21]He followed the example of his father, worshiping the same idols his father had worshiped. [22]He abandoned the LORD, the God of his ancestors, and he refused to follow the LORD's ways.

[23]Then Amon's own officials conspired against him and assassinated him in his palace. [24]But the people of the land killed all those who had conspired against King Amon, and they made his son Josiah the next king.

[25]The rest of the events in Amon's reign and what he did are recorded in *The Book of the History of the Kings of Judah*. [26]He was buried in his tomb in the garden of Uzza. Then his son Josiah became the next king.

21:6 Or *also made his son pass through the fire.* 21:11 The Hebrew term (literally *round things*) probably alludes to dung; also in 21:21. 21:13 Hebrew *the same plumb line I used for Samaria and the same plumb bob.*

21:19-26 King Amon of Judah was a carbon copy of his father, Manasseh, with one exception: Manasseh, toward the end of his life, repented of his evil ways; Amon, "unlike his father, . . . did not humble himself before the LORD. Instead, Amon sinned even more" (2 Chronicles 33:23). God had allowed Manasseh's abusive oppression to continue for many years, but he did not do the same for Amon; God destroyed Amon after only two years. Lovingly, God would promote yet one more cycle of recovery in Judah and offer relief from Judah's self-destructive unbelief and false worship. Josiah, Amon's young son, became the initiator and primary instrument for a major cycle of recovery among God's people (22:1–23:30).

CHAPTER 22
Josiah Rules in Judah

Josiah was eight years old when he became king, and he reigned in Jerusalem thirty-one years. His mother was Jedidah, the daughter of Adaiah from Bozkath. [2]He did what was pleasing in the LORD's sight and followed the example of his ancestor David. He did not turn away from doing what was right.

[3]In the eighteenth year of his reign, King Josiah sent Shaphan son of Azaliah and grandson of Meshullam, the court secretary, to the Temple of the LORD. He told him, [4]"Go to Hilkiah the high priest and have him count the money the gatekeepers have collected from the people at the LORD's Temple. [5]Entrust this money to the men assigned to supervise the restoration of the LORD's Temple. Then they can use it to pay workers to repair the Temple. [6]They will need to hire carpenters, builders, and masons. Also have them buy the timber and the finished stone needed to repair the Temple. [7]But don't require the construction supervisors to keep account of the money they receive, for they are honest and trustworthy men."

Hilkiah Discovers God's Law

[8]Hilkiah the high priest said to Shaphan the court secretary, "I have found the Book of the Law in the LORD's Temple!" Then Hilkiah gave the scroll to Shaphan, and he read it.

[9]Shaphan went to the king and reported, "Your officials have turned over the money collected at the Temple of the LORD to the workers and supervisors at the Temple." [10]Shaphan also told the king, "Hilkiah the priest has given me a scroll." So Shaphan read it to the king.

[11]When the king heard what was written in the Book of the Law, he tore his clothes in despair. [12]Then he gave these orders to Hilkiah the priest, Ahikam son of Shaphan, Acbor son of Micaiah, Shaphan the court secretary, and Asaiah the king's personal adviser: [13]"Go to the Temple and speak to the LORD for me and for the people and for all Judah. Inquire about the words written in this scroll that has been found. For the LORD's great anger is burning against us because our ancestors have not obeyed the words in this scroll. We have not been doing everything it says we must do."

[14]So Hilkiah the priest, Ahikam, Acbor, Shaphan, and Asaiah went to the New Quarter* of Jerusalem to consult with the prophet Huldah. She was the wife of Shallum son of Tikvah, son of Harhas, the keeper of the Temple wardrobe.

[15]She said to them, "The LORD, the God of Israel, has spoken! Go back and tell the man who sent you, [16]'This is what the LORD says: I am going to bring disaster on this city* and its people. All the words written in the scroll that the king of Judah has read will come true. [17]For my people have abandoned me and offered sacrifices to pagan gods, and I am very angry with them for everything they have done. My anger will burn against this place, and it will not be quenched.'

[18]"But go to the king of Judah who sent you to seek the LORD and tell him: 'This is what the LORD, the God of Israel, says concerning the message you have just heard: [19]You were sorry and humbled yourself before the LORD when you heard what I said against this city and its people—that this land would be cursed and become desolate. You tore your clothing in despair and wept before me in repentance. And I have indeed heard you, says the LORD. [20]So I will not send the promised disaster until after you have

22:14 Or *the Second Quarter,* a newer section of Jerusalem. Hebrew reads *the Mishneh.* 22:16 Hebrew *this place;* also in 22:19, 20.

22:1-7 Almost two hundred years before Josiah, King Joash of Judah had undertaken repairs of the Temple in a strikingly similar way (12:4-14). Josiah instituted Judah's last major recovery before its final demise. Recovery often has its ups and downs, but the ultimate effect needs to be positive. In Judah, however, the effect was negative. Overall, the great reforms and good intentions of the few good kings were negated by the activities of the bad ones. In recovery, we must persevere. We cannot have an occasional victory and then backslide for extended periods. An uncommitted approach to recovery will ultimately lead to destruction.

22:8-20 In spite of Josiah's heartfelt reforms in Judah, there would still be serious long-term consequences for the nation's sin. But Judah's destruction would be postponed significantly because of Josiah's humble faith and obedience. While it may seem unfair to hold the people of Judah responsible for what they didn't know about God's laws, which had been lost, that's the way it often is in recovery. We may never have read the Bible and acquired the wisdom it contains, but we are still accountable to its truth. God's plan is clearly stated in his Word; all we have to do is read it. God's standards are absolute; there is no excuse for not following his ways.

died and been buried in peace. You will not see the disaster I am going to bring on this city.'"

So they took her message back to the king.

CHAPTER 23
Josiah's Religious Reforms

Then the king summoned all the elders of Judah and Jerusalem. [2]And the king went up to the Temple of the LORD with all the people of Judah and Jerusalem, along with the priests and the prophets—all the people from the least to the greatest. There the king read to them the entire Book of the Covenant that had been found in the LORD's Temple. [3]The king took his place of authority beside the pillar and renewed the covenant in the LORD's presence. He pledged to obey the LORD by keeping all his commands, laws, and decrees with all his heart and soul. In this way, he confirmed all the terms of the covenant that were written in the scroll, and all the people pledged themselves to the covenant.

[4]Then the king instructed Hilkiah the high priest and the priests of the second rank and the Temple gatekeepers to remove from the LORD's Temple all the articles that were used to worship Baal, Asherah, and all the powers of the heavens. The king had all these things burned outside Jerusalem on the terraces of the Kidron Valley, and he carried the ashes away to Bethel. [5]He did away with the idolatrous priests, who had been appointed by the previous kings of Judah, for they had offered sacrifices at the pagan shrines throughout Judah and even in the vicinity of Jerusalem. They had also offered sacrifices to Baal, and to the sun, the moon, the constellations, and to all the powers of the heavens. [6]The king removed the Asherah pole from the LORD's Temple and took it outside Jerusalem to the Kidron Valley, where he burned it. Then he ground the ashes of the pole to dust and threw the dust over the graves of the people. [7]He also tore down the living quarters of the male and female shrine prostitutes that were inside the Temple of the LORD, where the women wove coverings for the Asherah pole.

[8]Josiah brought to Jerusalem all the priests who were living in other towns of Judah. He also defiled the pagan shrines, where they had offered sacrifices—all the way from Geba to Beersheba. He destroyed the shrines at the entrance to the gate of Joshua, the governor of Jerusalem. This gate was located to the left of the city gate as one enters the city. [9]The priests who had served at the pagan shrines were not allowed to serve at* the LORD's altar in Jerusalem, but they were allowed to eat unleavened bread with the other priests.

[10]Then the king defiled the altar of Topheth in the valley of Ben-Hinnom, so no one could ever again use it to sacrifice a son or daughter in the fire* as an offering to Molech. [11]He removed from the entrance of the LORD's Temple the horse statues that the former kings of Judah had dedicated to the sun. They were near the quarters of Nathan-melech the eunuch, an officer of the court.* The king also burned the chariots dedicated to the sun.

[12]Josiah tore down the altars that the kings of Judah had built on the palace roof above the upper room of Ahaz. The king destroyed the altars that Manasseh had built in the two courtyards of the LORD's Temple. He smashed them to bits* and scattered the pieces in the Kidron Valley. [13]The king also desecrated the pagan shrines east of Jerusalem, to the south of the Mount of Corruption, where King Solomon of Israel had built shrines for Ashtoreth, the detestable goddess of the Sidonians; and for Chemosh, the detestable god of the Moabites; and for Molech,* the vile god of the Ammonites. [14]He smashed the sacred pillars and cut down the Asherah poles. Then he desecrated these places by scattering human bones over them.

[15]The king also tore down the altar at Bethel—the pagan shrine that Jeroboam son of Nebat had made when he caused Israel to sin. He burned down the shrine and ground it to dust, and he burned the Asherah pole.

23:9 Hebrew *did not come up to.* 23:10 Or *to make a son or daughter pass through the fire.* 23:11 The meaning of the Hebrew is uncertain. 23:12 Or *He quickly removed them.* 23:13 Hebrew *Milcom,* a variant spelling of Molech.

23:1-20 The revival under Josiah was no halfhearted recovery. It was unlike the moderate but incomplete process of recovery achieved by many of Judah's earlier kings; Josiah concluded that there could be no middle ground. As a strong statement of proper boundaries and limits, Josiah destroyed all aspects of the long-standing idol worship. He also went to great lengths to reinstitute proper worship of the true God, indicating his faith and commitment. Limits and boundaries are necessary if we want to recover. We have to know where the boundary lines are and stay within them.

¹⁶Then Josiah turned around and noticed several tombs in the side of the hill. He ordered that the bones be brought out, and he burned them on the altar at Bethel to desecrate it. (This happened just as the LORD had promised through the man of God when Jeroboam stood beside the altar at the festival.)

Then Josiah turned and looked up at the tomb of the man of God* who had predicted these things. ¹⁷"What is that monument over there?" Josiah asked.

And the people of the town told him, "It is the tomb of the man of God who came from Judah and predicted the very things that you have just done to the altar at Bethel!"

¹⁸Josiah replied, "Leave it alone. Don't disturb his bones." So they did not burn his bones or those of the old prophet from Samaria.

¹⁹Then Josiah demolished all the buildings at the pagan shrines in the towns of Samaria, just as he had done at Bethel. They had been built by the various kings of Israel and had made the LORD* very angry. ²⁰He executed the priests of the pagan shrines on their own altars, and he burned human bones on the altars to desecrate them. Finally, he returned to Jerusalem.

Josiah Celebrates Passover

²¹King Josiah then issued this order to all the people: "You must celebrate the Passover to the LORD your God, as required in this Book of the Covenant." ²²There had not been a Passover celebration like that since the time when the judges ruled in Israel, nor throughout all the years of the kings of Israel and Judah. ²³But in the eighteenth year of King Josiah's reign, this Passover was celebrated to the LORD in Jerusalem.

²⁴Josiah also got rid of the mediums and psychics, the household gods, the idols,* and every other kind of detestable practice, both in Jerusalem and throughout the land of Ju-

dah. He did this in obedience to the laws written in the scroll that Hilkiah the priest had found in the LORD's Temple. ²⁵Never before had there been a king like Josiah, who turned to the LORD with all his heart and soul and strength, obeying all the laws of Moses. And there has never been a king like him since.

²⁶Even so, the LORD was very angry with Judah because of all the wicked things Manasseh had done to provoke him. ²⁷For the LORD said, "I will also banish Judah from my presence just as I have banished Israel. And I will reject my chosen city of Jerusalem and the Temple where my name was to be honored."

²⁸The rest of the events in Josiah's reign and all his deeds are recorded in *The Book of the History of the Kings of Judah.*

²⁹While Josiah was king, Pharaoh Neco, king of Egypt, went to the Euphrates River to help the king of Assyria. King Josiah and his army marched out to fight him,* but King Neco* killed him when they met at Megiddo. ³⁰Josiah's officers took his body back in a chariot from Megiddo to Jerusalem and buried him in his own tomb. Then the people of the land anointed Josiah's son Jehoahaz and made him the next king.

Jehoahaz Rules in Judah

³¹Jehoahaz was twenty-three years old when he became king, and he reigned in Jerusalem three months. His mother was Hamutal, the daughter of Jeremiah from Libnah. ³²He did what was evil in the LORD's sight, just as his ancestors had done.

³³Pharaoh Neco put Jehoahaz in prison at Riblah in the land of Hamath to prevent him from ruling* in Jerusalem. He also demanded that Judah pay 7,500 pounds of silver and 75 pounds of gold* as tribute.

Jehoiakim Rules in Judah

³⁴Pharaoh Neco then installed Eliakim, another of Josiah's sons, to reign in place of his

23:16 As in Greek version; Hebrew lacks *when Jeroboam stood beside the altar at the festival. Then Josiah turned and looked up at the tomb of the man of God.* 23:19 As in Greek and Syriac versions and Latin Vulgate; Hebrew lacks *the LORD.* 23:24 The Hebrew term (literally *round things*) probably alludes to dung. 23:29a Or *Josiah went out to meet him.* 23:29b Hebrew *he.* 23:33a The meaning of the Hebrew is uncertain. 23:33b Hebrew *100 talents* [3,400 kilograms] *of silver and 1 talent* [34 kilograms] *of gold.*

23:31-35 The evil character of King Jehoahaz, Josiah's son, may well imply a flaw in Josiah's life. The fact that Jehoahaz was evil (23:32), unlike his righteous father, may indicate that Josiah was not attentive or available to his children. Perhaps he was too busy initiating his reforms in Judah to pass on his faith and commitment to God to his children. While children may be able to see the godly things parents do, they may follow evil ways if they are not loved and nurtured. We need to balance family time with the time we take for recovery. If we don't, all our gains may be lost in the next generation. Our steps of self-improvement can easily become detrimental to our family's ultimate chances for recovery.

father, and he changed Eliakim's name to Jehoiakim. Jehoahaz was taken to Egypt as a prisoner, where he died.

[35] In order to get the silver and gold demanded as tribute by Pharaoh Neco, Jehoiakim collected a tax from the people of Judah, requiring them to pay in proportion to their wealth.

[36] Jehoiakim was twenty-five years old when he became king, and he reigned in Jerusalem eleven years. His mother was Zebidah, the daughter of Pedaiah from Rumah. [37] He did what was evil in the LORD's sight, just as his ancestors had done.

CHAPTER 24

During Jehoiakim's reign, King Nebuchadnezzar of Babylon invaded the land of Judah. Jehoiakim surrendered and paid him tribute for three years but then rebelled. [2] Then the LORD sent bands of Babylonian,* Aramean, Moabite, and Ammonite raiders against Judah to destroy it, just as the LORD had promised through his prophets. [3] These disasters happened to Judah because of the LORD's command. He had decided to banish Judah from his presence because of the many sins of Manasseh, [4] who had filled Jerusalem with innocent blood. The LORD would not forgive this.

[5] The rest of the events in Jehoiakim's reign and all his deeds are recorded in *The Book of the History of the Kings of Judah.* [6] When Jehoiakim died, his son Jehoiachin became the next king.

[7] The king of Egypt did not venture out of his country after that, for the king of Babylon captured the entire area formerly claimed by Egypt—from the Brook of Egypt to the Euphrates River.

Jehoiachin Rules in Judah

[8] Jehoiachin was eighteen years old when he became king, and he reigned in Jerusalem

three months. His mother was Nehushta, the daughter of Elnathan from Jerusalem. [9] Jehoiachin did what was evil in the LORD's sight, just as his father had done.

[10] During Jehoiachin's reign, the officers of King Nebuchadnezzar of Babylon came up against Jerusalem and besieged it. [11] Nebuchadnezzar himself arrived at the city during the siege. [12] Then King Jehoiachin, along with the queen mother, his advisers, his commanders, and his officials, surrendered to the Babylonians.

In the eighth year of Nebuchadnezzar's reign, he took Jehoiachin prisoner. [13] As the LORD had said beforehand, Nebuchadnezzar carried away all the treasures from the LORD's Temple and the royal palace. He stripped away* all the gold objects that King Solomon of Israel had placed in the Temple. [14] King Nebuchadnezzar took all of Jerusalem captive, including all the commanders and the best of the soldiers, craftsmen, and artisans—10,000 in all. Only the poorest people were left in the land.

[15] Nebuchadnezzar led King Jehoiachin away as a captive to Babylon, along with the queen mother, his wives and officials, and all Jerusalem's elite. [16] He also exiled 7,000 of the best troops and 1,000 craftsmen and artisans, all of whom were strong and fit for war. [17] Then the king of Babylon installed Mattaniah, Jehoiachin's* uncle, as the next king, and he changed Mattaniah's name to Zedekiah.

Zedekiah Rules in Judah

[18] Zedekiah was twenty-one years old when he became king, and he reigned in Jerusalem eleven years. His mother was Hamutal, the daughter of Jeremiah from Libnah. [19] But Zedekiah did what was evil in the LORD's sight, just as Jehoiakim had done. [20] These things happened because of the LORD's anger

24:2 Or *Chaldean.* 24:13 Or *He cut apart.* 24:17 Hebrew *his.*

23:36—24:4 The reign of King Jehoiakim of Judah was basically an eleven-year military and political nightmare. Rather than admit his hopeless situation and turn to God, Jehoiakim tried to maneuver his way out of each successive crisis. As disaster after disaster befell Jehoiakim, his denial only deepened. He continued to trust in his own power and sank deeper into despair. There is no need to continue in our nightmare. If we stop our denial and accept the hopelessness of our situation, we can turn to God for help. He will help us break out of our downward spiral.

24:18—25:7 It is sad to watch a person in the advanced stages of denial. It is sadder still to observe a large group of people who deny the painful reality of their situation—they were captives. Even under the Babylonian puppet king Zedekiah, Judah attempted yet another rebellion against Babylon instead of turning to God. The continued denial of Zedekiah's true situation led to his cruel treatment by the Babylonians when he was finally exiled (25:7). Our continued denial will almost always lead us further into dark consequences. The sooner we admit our true predicament, the sooner we can recover.

against the people of Jerusalem and Judah, until he finally banished them from his presence and sent them into exile.

The Fall of Jerusalem

Zedekiah rebelled against the king of Babylon.

CHAPTER 25

So on January 15,* during the ninth year of Zedekiah's reign, King Nebuchadnezzar of Babylon led his entire army against Jerusalem. They surrounded the city and built siege ramps against its walls. ²Jerusalem was kept under siege until the eleventh year of King Zedekiah's reign.

³By July 18 in the eleventh year of Zedekiah's reign,* the famine in the city had become very severe, and the last of the food was entirely gone. ⁴Then a section of the city wall was broken down. Since the city was surrounded by the Babylonians,* the soldiers waited for nightfall and escaped* through the gate between the two walls behind the king's garden. Then they headed toward the Jordan Valley.*

⁵But the Babylonian* troops chased the king and overtook him on the plains of Jericho, for his men had all deserted him and scattered. ⁶They captured the king and took him to the king of Babylon at Riblah, where they pronounced judgment upon Zedekiah. ⁷They made Zedekiah watch as they slaughtered his sons. Then they gouged out Zedekiah's eyes, bound him in bronze chains, and led him away to Babylon.

The Temple Destroyed

⁸On August 14 of that year,* which was the nineteenth year of King Nebuchadnezzar's reign, Nebuzaradan, the captain of the guard and an official of the Babylonian king, arrived in Jerusalem. ⁹He burned down the Temple of the LORD, the royal palace, and all the houses of Jerusalem. He destroyed all the important buildings* in the city. ¹⁰Then he supervised the entire Babylonian army as they tore down the walls of Jerusalem on every side. ¹¹Then Nebuzaradan, the captain of the guard, took as exiles the rest of the people who remained in the city, the defectors who had declared their allegiance to the king of Babylon, and the rest of the population. ¹²But the captain of the guard allowed some of the poorest people to stay behind to care for the vineyards and fields.

¹³The Babylonians broke up the bronze pillars in front of the LORD's Temple, the bronze water carts, and the great bronze basin called the Sea, and they carried all the bronze away to Babylon. ¹⁴They also took all the ash buckets, shovels, lamp snuffers, ladles, and all the other bronze articles used for making sacrifices at the Temple. ¹⁵The captain of the guard also took the incense burners and basins, and all the other articles made of pure gold or silver.

¹⁶The weight of the bronze from the two pillars, the Sea, and the water carts was too great to be measured. These things had been made for the LORD's Temple in the days of Solomon. ¹⁷Each of the pillars was 27 feet* tall. The bronze capital on top of each pillar was 7½ feet* high and was decorated with a network of bronze pomegranates all the way around.

¹⁸Nebuzaradan, the captain of the guard, took with him as prisoners Seraiah the high priest, Zephaniah the priest of the second rank, and the three chief gatekeepers. ¹⁹And from among the people still hiding in the city, he took an officer who had been in charge of the Judean army; five of the king's personal advisers; the army commander's

---

25:1 Hebrew *on the tenth day of the tenth month,* of the ancient Hebrew lunar calendar. A number of events in 2 Kings can be cross-checked with dates in surviving Babylonian records and related accurately to our modern calendar. This day was January 15, 588 B.C. 25:3 Hebrew *By the ninth day of the [fourth] month* [in the eleventh year of Zedekiah's reign] (compare Jer 39:2; 52:6 and the notes there). This day was July 18, 586 B.C.; also see note on 25:1. 25:4a Or *the Chaldeans;* also in 25:13, 25, 26. 25:4b As in Greek version (see also Jer 39:4; 52:7); Hebrew lacks *escaped.* 25:4c Hebrew *the Arabah.* 25:5 Or *Chaldean;* also in 25:10, 24. 25:8 Hebrew *On the seventh day of the fifth month,* of the ancient Hebrew lunar calendar. This day was August 14, 586 B.C.; also see note on 25:1. 25:9 Or *destroyed the houses of all the important people.* 25:17a Hebrew *18 cubits* [8.3 meters]. 25:17b As in parallel texts at 1 Kgs 7:16, 2 Chr 3:15, and Jer 52:22, all of which read *5 cubits* [2.3 meters]; Hebrew reads *3 cubits,* which is 4.5 feet or 1.4 meters.

25:8-26 Judah had now hit bottom in the most literal sense. King Nebuchadnezzar ordered Jerusalem, the once-proud capital of Judah, to be destroyed. He plundered the city and Temple, carrying all its valuables off to Babylon. Realistically, corporate recovery for Judah was now impossible. What was needed was a full-scale resurrection for God's people. If we have hit bottom, we may need to discover the new life offered by Jesus Christ. "Anyone who belongs to Christ has become a new person. The old life is gone; a new life has begun!" (2 Corinthians 5:17). For Christ to take away our sins and give us a new start, all we need to do is repent and ask him into our life.

chief secretary, who was in charge of recruitment; and sixty other citizens. [20]Nebuzaradan, the captain of the guard, took them all to the king of Babylon at Riblah. [21]And there at Riblah, in the land of Hamath, the king of Babylon had them all put to death. So the people of Judah were sent into exile from their land.

Gedaliah Governs in Judah

[22]Then King Nebuchadnezzar appointed Gedaliah son of Ahikam and grandson of Shaphan as governor over the people he had left in Judah. [23]When all the army commanders and their men learned that the king of Babylon had appointed Gedaliah as governor, they went to see him at Mizpah. These included Ishmael son of Nethaniah, Johanan son of Kareah, Seraiah son of Tanhumeth the Netophathite, Jezaniah* son of the Maacathite, and all their men.

[24]Gedaliah vowed to them that the Babylonian officials meant them no harm. "Don't be afraid of them. Live in the land and serve the king of Babylon, and all will go well for you," he promised.

[25]But in midautumn of that year,* Ishmael son of Nethaniah and grandson of Elishama, who was a member of the royal family, went to Mizpah with ten men and killed Gedaliah. He also killed all the Judeans and Babylonians who were with him at Mizpah.

[26]Then all the people of Judah, from the least to the greatest, as well as the army commanders, fled in panic to Egypt, for they were afraid of what the Babylonians would do to them.

Hope for Israel's Royal Line

[27]In the thirty-seventh year of the exile of King Jehoiachin of Judah, Evil-merodach ascended to the Babylonian throne. He was kind to* Jehoiachin and released him* from prison on April 2 of that year.* [28]He spoke kindly to Jehoiachin and gave him a higher place than all the other exiled kings in Babylon. [29]He supplied Jehoiachin with new clothes to replace his prison garb and allowed him to dine in the king's presence for the rest of his life. [30]So the king gave him a regular food allowance as long as he lived.

25:23 As in parallel text at Jer 40:8; Hebrew reads *Jaazaniah,* a variant spelling of Jezaniah. 25:25 Hebrew *in the seventh month,* of the ancient Hebrew lunar calendar. This month occurred within the months of October and November 586 B.C.; also see note on 25:1. 25:27a Hebrew *He raised the head of.* 25:27b As in some Hebrew manuscripts and Greek and Syriac versions (see also Jer 52:31); Masoretic Text lacks *released him.* 25:27c Hebrew *on the twenty-seventh day of the twelfth month,* of the ancient Hebrew lunar calendar. This day was April 2, 561 B.C.; also see note on 25:1.

25:27-30 The kindness Evil-merodach showed to captive King Jehoiachin brings a glimmer of hope to the tragic conclusion of 2 Kings. With the Babylonian exile came the destruction of Jerusalem and an end to the rule of the Davidic kings. The exiled people lost all hope that God was still with them. They probably thought that God's promises to them through Abraham and David were no longer valid. When they heard that Jehoiachin, one of David's descendants, was being treated well in exile, however, hope must have been stirred in their heavy hearts. Perhaps God's promises were still valid! The continued story of rebuilding after the Exile shows us that this was true. God still planned for his people's restoration. Through this broken nation the King of kings, Jesus the Messiah, would be born. No matter how terrible the situation is that we face, there is hope for the future. Our sins have been paid for by the work of God's Son; God is still in the business of restoration.

REFLECTIONS ON 2 KINGS

insights FROM THE MINISTRY OF ELISHA
Strong-willed people, especially leaders who are used to getting their way, have a hard time humbling themselves to enter recovery. What Elisha asked Naaman to do in **2 Kings 5:9-15** was simple, but it was very undignified. Elisha certainly didn't do things the way Naaman thought they should be done. Fortunately, Naaman was not so angry and resistant that he was unwilling to listen to the advice of his officers. By following Elisha's instructions, Naaman was healed and found physical "recovery" and apparently entered the initial phase of spiritual recovery by recognizing the power of the only true God.

The power and patience of God in relation to recovery are both evident in **2 Kings 13:20-23**. God's reviving power, found even in the dead body of Elisha (13:21), can empower a comeback in life even when a person thinks "it's all over." The patience of God is tied to his covenant made with Abraham and his successors (13:22-23). Except for God's great covenant loyalty, the northern kingdom would have been destroyed long before its fall to Assyria in 722 B.C. God offers us a covenant through Jesus Christ, through whom we are forgiven and empowered to become God's children. God will care for anyone who believes in his Son's name. We should accept that promise and let him guide us as we work toward recovery.

insights FROM THE LIVES OF JUDAH'S KINGS
The forty-year reign of King Joash of Judah was a time of substantial personal and national recovery. Yet, as much of a model of faith as Joash was, we see in **2 Kings 12:1-3** that he never completely destroyed the places of idol worship—the shrines on the hills. Since recovery is a lifelong process, we must not stop when we start to feel good. Our goal should be *complete* recovery, not just recovery in a few areas. We need to ask God to give us the strength and patience to gain back our entire life. Stopping too early will only lead to regression and failure.

The tragic incident related in **2 Kings 14:8-14** illustrates the dangers of overconfidence. After defeating the Edomites, King Amaziah of Judah picked a fight with Israel—a fight that ended in disaster. It is easy to become overconfident in our own abilities after winning a major victory—we feel invincible! But we must proceed with caution because we may be letting our emotions blind us to reality. Recovery is a long and difficult process, and we are setting ourself up for failure if we think the rest of the road will be effortless. We need to continually recognize our need for God's helping hand.

We see in **2 Kings 15:1-7** that King Uzziah of Judah followed in the footsteps of his father, Amaziah (14:1-20), and his grandfather, Joash of Judah (12:1-21). Like them, he displayed a basic faith and commitment to God (15:3). But, also like them, he tolerated false worship at the pagan hilltop shrines (15:4). As a result, even though his reign lasted 52 years, for Uzziah it was mostly sad and solitary because God judged his halfhearted recovery by giving him leprosy (15:5). Partial commitment to recovery will never bring complete results; only full devotion to the process will give lasting healing.

In **2 Kings 18:17–19:1** King Hezekiah of Judah bought off Assyrian invaders, but it was only a matter of time before the enemy would come back for more. The Assyrian representative knew that Hezekiah had failed to trust God in the earlier crisis. So he used that very issue in his attempt to intimidate the Judeans into surrendering. It was a terrible situation to face, but at least it led Hezekiah to a point of helplessness and surrender to God. He had no choice but to turn to God for help and pursue recovery. Even if our situation looks hopeless, it is never too late to turn to God for help. God may have led us to this very place just so we would turn to him for deliverance.

1 CHRONICLES

THE BIG PICTURE

A. ANTICIPATING DAVID'S REIGN
(1:1–9:44)
B. THE REIGN OF DAVID
(10:1–29:30)
1. The Passing of Saul (10:1-14)
2. The Accession of David
(11:1–12:40)
3. David and the Ark of the
Covenant (13:1–17:27)
4. The Account of David's Wars
(18:1–20:8)
5. The Census Taken by David
(21:1-30)
6. The Arrangements for the
Temple (22:1–29:30)

The book of 1 Chronicles was originally part of a larger book that also included 2 Chronicles. It recorded Israel's history, starting with a genealogy of Adam's descendants and ending with Israel in Babylonian captivity. This condensed history of Israel was written to give the Israelites hope as they sought to rebuild their nation after the Exile.

The primary focus of 1 Chronicles is the reign of King David, who is presented as an ideal for the people to follow. The writer quickly glosses over David's faults and focuses on the positive aspects of his reign. We see David here as God saw him—a man after God's own heart.

The first nine chapters of 1 Chronicles record the ancestry of Israel from the dawn of history to the time of Israel's return from Babylon. The list emphasizes the royal line of David, which had remained unbroken even through the terrible years of exile. This would have encouraged the Jews as they sought to rebuild their broken nation. While in exile, many had begun to think that God had abandoned them. The survival of David's descendants would have given them hope for the future.

The last half of 1 Chronicles records the events of David's reign, emphasizing his role in leading the people to worship God. Although David was not allowed to build God's Temple, God promised to build a royal "house" for him, pledging that David's descendants would reign forever. This promise was the basis for Israel's hope upon their return from exile. They could see that David's descendants were still among them. It was clear that despite Israel's past disobedience, God had not abandoned them. God was in the process of rebuilding his chosen people.

THE BOTTOM LINE

PURPOSE: To record the history of David's reign and to encourage and admonish the people of Israel as they sought to rebuild after the Babylonian exile. AUTHOR: Unknown; ancient tradition suggests that Ezra was the author. AUDIENCE: The people of Israel after their return from exile in Babylon. DATE WRITTEN: Approximately 430 B.C. SETTING: The period of David's reign over Israel, the eleventh century B.C. KEY VERSE: "And David realized that the LORD had confirmed him as king over Israel and had greatly blessed his kingdom for the sake of his people Israel" (14:2). KEY PEOPLE: David, Solomon.

RECOVERY THEMES

The Power of Grace: David's life story is filled with examples of God's grace. David was not a stranger to sin. In the books of 1 and 2 Samuel we saw him commit adultery and murder. In this book David proved to be impulsive, even when his intentions were good. He failed to listen to God's plan for bringing the Ark to Jerusalem, which led to the death of Uzzah. The main theme of this book, however, is not David's failures but his ability to learn from those failures. David had a heart that accepted God's correction and understood his loving forgiveness. It was David's openness to God's grace that set him apart from the other kings of Israel. David knew the joy of forgiveness.

The Importance of Worship: David knew how to worship. The spiritual part of him was an open book before God. A life that ignores or neglects the spiritual is a life that is barren of purpose and weak in resolve. All recovery must include the spiritual aspect, or it will be anemic and unsuccessful. David shows us that spiritual issues and worship are central to our life. He also makes it very clear that worship is not only private; it also involves our meeting together with others.

Recovery beyond Our Personal Recovery: David would never enjoy much of what he set up during his lifetime. He invested his time and possessions in things that would minister to others for centuries into the future. He collected materials for the Temple and organized the priests and Levites for their work there. He was able to see beyond himself to the needs of others. As we journey toward recovery, we need to look beyond ourself and see that when we experience healing and growth, we affect not only our own life but also the lives of those who follow us.

Learning to Accept No for an Answer: David had great plans for Israel. He was a dreamer; he could envision great things ahead. But God had his own plans for David. While David assumed that he would build a temple for Israel, God said no. So often, when God says no to us, we withdraw, argue, or feel rejected. Growth and recovery involve learning not only to say no but also to accept the no that might come from God or from others. When God denied David's desire to build the Temple, he promised in turn that he would build an eternal dynasty from David's lineage.

CHAPTER 1
From Adam to Noah's Sons
The descendants of Adam were Seth, Enosh, [2]Kenan, Mahalalel, Jared, [3]Enoch, Methuselah, Lamech, [4]and Noah.
The sons of Noah were* Shem, Ham, and Japheth.

Descendants of Japheth
[5]The descendants of Japheth were Gomer, Magog, Madai, Javan, Tubal, Meshech, and Tiras.
[6]The descendants of Gomer were Ashkenaz, Riphath,* and Togarmah.

[7]The descendants of Javan were Elishah, Tarshish, Kittim, and Rodanim.

Descendants of Ham
[8]The descendants of Ham were Cush, Mizraim,* Put, and Canaan.
[9]The descendants of Cush were Seba, Havilah, Sabtah, Raamah, and Sabteca. The descendants of Raamah were Sheba and Dedan. [10]Cush was also the ancestor of Nimrod, who was the first heroic warrior on earth.
[11]Mizraim was the ancestor of the Ludites, Anamites, Lehabites, Naphtuhites,

---

1:4 As in Greek version (see also Gen 5:3-32); Hebrew lacks *The sons of Noah were.* 1:6 As in some Hebrew manuscripts and Greek version (see also Gen 10:3); most Hebrew manuscripts read *Diphath.* 1:8 Or *Egypt;* also in 1:11.

1:1 As the father of the human race, Adam is the "head of our family," so to speak. The account of his life in Eden's perfect environment is given in Genesis 2–3. We often are prone to blame our environment or family background for the mistakes we make. Adam was no different. Although he couldn't very well use his family background as an excuse for his sin, he did try to pin the blame on Eve—and even on God for creating Eve (Genesis 3:12). Blaming our environment or circumstances for the sins we commit will never lead to recovery. Each of us must accept responsibility for our past mistakes and take steps to correct them.
1:1 Adam, Seth, Enosh . . . Notice that neither Cain nor Abel follows Adam in the genealogy of Israel. Genesis 4 records how Cain committed the first murder by killing his brother, Abel. One of the consequences of Adam's and Eve's first sin was their dysfunctional family. It is encouraging, however, that despite Cain's and Abel's failure to leave descendants in Israel's ancestry, God provided Adam's broken family with a new start. He gave them another son named Seth.

¹²Pathrusites, Casluhites, and the Caphtorites, from whom the Philistines came.*
¹³Canaan's oldest son was Sidon, the ancestor of the Sidonians. Canaan was also the ancestor of the Hittites,* ¹⁴Jebusites, Amorites, Girgashites, ¹⁵Hivites, Arkites, Sinites, ¹⁶Arvadites, Zemarites, and Hamathites.

Descendants of Shem

¹⁷The descendants of Shem were Elam, Asshur, Arphaxad, Lud, and Aram.
The descendants of Aram were* Uz, Hul, Gether, and Mash.*
¹⁸Arphaxad was the father of Shelah.
Shelah was the father of Eber.
¹⁹Eber had two sons. The first was named Peleg (which means "division"), for during his lifetime the people of the world were divided into different language groups. His brother's name was Joktan.
²⁰Joktan was the ancestor of Almodad, Sheleph, Hazarmaveth, Jerah, ²¹Hadoram, Uzal, Diklah, ²²Obal,* Abimael, Sheba, ²³Ophir, Havilah, and Jobab. All these were descendants of Joktan.
²⁴So this is the family line descended from Shem: Arphaxad, Shelah,* ²⁵Eber, Peleg, Reu, ²⁶Serug, Nahor, Terah, ²⁷and Abram, later known as Abraham.

Descendants of Abraham

²⁸The sons of Abraham were Isaac and Ishmael. ²⁹These are their genealogical records:
The sons of Ishmael were Nebaioth (the oldest), Kedar, Adbeel, Mibsam, ³⁰Mishma, Dumah, Massa, Hadad, Tema, ³¹Jetur, Naphish, and Kedemah. These were the sons of Ishmael.

³²The sons of Keturah, Abraham's concubine, were Zimran, Jokshan, Medan, Midian, Ishbak, and Shuah.
The sons of Jokshan were Sheba and Dedan.
³³The sons of Midian were Ephah, Epher, Hanoch, Abida, and Eldaah.

All these were descendants of Abraham through his concubine Keturah.

Descendants of Isaac

³⁴Abraham was the father of Isaac. The sons of Isaac were Esau and Israel.*

Descendants of Esau

³⁵The sons of Esau were Eliphaz, Reuel, Jeush, Jalam, and Korah.
³⁶The descendants of Eliphaz were Teman, Omar, Zepho,* Gatam, Kenaz, and Amalek, who was born to Timna.*
³⁷The descendants of Reuel were Nahath, Zerah, Shammah, and Mizzah.

Original Peoples of Edom

³⁸The descendants of Seir were Lotan, Shobal, Zibeon, Anah, Dishon, Ezer, and Dishan.
³⁹The descendants of Lotan were Hori and Hemam.* Lotan's sister was named Timna.
⁴⁰The descendants of Shobal were Alvan,* Manahath, Ebal, Shepho,* and Onam.
The descendants of Zibeon were Aiah and Anah.
⁴¹The son of Anah was Dishon.
The descendants of Dishon were Hemdan,* Eshban, Ithran, and Keran.
⁴²The descendants of Ezer were Bilhan, Zaavan, and Akan.*
The descendants of Dishan* were Uz and Aran.

Rulers of Edom

⁴³These are the kings who ruled in the land of Edom before any king ruled over the Israelites*:

Bela son of Beor, who ruled from his city of Dinhabah.
⁴⁴When Bela died, Jobab son of Zerah from Bozrah became king in his place.
⁴⁵When Jobab died, Husham from the land of the Temanites became king in his place.
⁴⁶When Husham died, Hadad son of Bedad became king in his place and ruled from the city of Avith. He was the one who destroyed the Midianite army in the land of Moab.

1:12 Hebrew *Casluhites, from whom the Philistines came, Caphtorites.* See Jer 47:4; Amos 9:7. **1:13** Hebrew *ancestor of Heth.* **1:17a** As in one Hebrew manuscript and some Greek manuscripts (see also Gen 10:23); most Hebrew manuscripts lack *The descendants of Aram were.* **1:17b** As in parallel text at Gen 10:23; Hebrew reads *and Meshech.* **1:22** As in some Hebrew manuscripts and Syriac version (see also Gen 10:28); most Hebrew manuscripts read *Ebal.* **1:24** Some Greek manuscripts read *Arphaxad, Cainan, Shelah.* See notes on Gen 10:24; 11:12-13. **1:34** *Israel* is the name that God gave to Jacob. **1:36a** As in many Hebrew manuscripts and a few Greek manuscripts (see also Gen 36:11); most Hebrew manuscripts read *Zephi.* **1:36b** As in some Greek manuscripts (see also Gen 36:12); Hebrew reads *Kenaz, Timna, and Amalek.* **1:39** As in parallel text at Gen 36:22; Hebrew reads *and Homam.* **1:40a** As in many Hebrew manuscripts and a few Greek manuscripts (see also Gen 36:23); most Hebrew manuscripts read *Alian.* **1:40b** As in some Hebrew manuscripts (see also Gen 36:23); most Hebrew manuscripts read *Shephi.* **1:41** As in many Hebrew manuscripts and some Greek manuscripts (see also Gen 36:26); most Hebrew manuscripts read *Hamran.* **1:42a** As in many Hebrew and Greek manuscripts (see also Gen 36:27); most Hebrew manuscripts read *Jaakan.* **1:42b** Hebrew *Dishon;* compare 1:38 and parallel text at Gen 36:28. **1:43** Or *before an Israelite king ruled over them.*

⁴⁷When Hadad died, Samlah from the city of Masrekah became king in his place. ⁴⁸When Samlah died, Shaul from the city of Rehoboth-on-the-River became king in his place. ⁴⁹When Shaul died, Baal-hanan son of Acbor became king in his place. ⁵⁰When Baal-hanan died, Hadad became king in his place and ruled from the city of Pau.* His wife was Mehetabel, the daughter of Matred and granddaughter of Me-zahab. ⁵¹Then Hadad died.

The clan leaders of Edom were Timna, Alvah,* Jetheth, ⁵²Oholibamah, Elah, Pinon, ⁵³Kenaz, Teman, Mibzar, ⁵⁴Magdiel, and Iram. These are the clan leaders of Edom.

CHAPTER 2
Descendants of Israel
The sons of Israel* were Reuben, Simeon, Levi, Judah, Issachar, Zebulun, ²Dan, Joseph, Benjamin, Naphtali, Gad, and Asher.

Descendants of Judah
³Judah had three sons from Bathshua, a Canaanite woman. Their names were Er, Onan, and Shelah. But the LORD saw that the oldest son, Er, was a wicked man, so he killed him. ⁴Later Judah had twin sons from Tamar, his widowed daughter-in-law. Their names were Perez and Zerah. So Judah had five sons in all.

⁵The sons of Perez were Hezron and Hamul.
⁶The sons of Zerah were Zimri, Ethan, Heman, Calcol, and Darda*—five in all.
⁷The son of Carmi (a descendant of Zimri) was Achan,* who brought disaster on Israel by taking plunder that had been set apart for the LORD.*
⁸The son of Ethan was Azariah.

From Judah's Grandson Hezron to David
⁹The sons of Hezron were Jerahmeel, Ram, and Caleb.*
¹⁰ Ram was the father of Amminadab. Amminadab was the father of Nahshon, a leader of Judah.
¹¹ Nahshon was the father of Salmon.* Salmon was the father of Boaz.
¹² Boaz was the father of Obed. Obed was the father of Jesse.
¹³Jesse's first son was Eliab, his second was Abinadab, his third was Shimea, ¹⁴his fourth was Nethanel, his fifth was Raddai, ¹⁵his sixth was Ozem, and his seventh was David.

¹⁶Their sisters were named Zeruiah and Abigail. Zeruiah had three sons named Abishai, Joab, and Asahel. ¹⁷Abigail married a man named Jether, an Ishmaelite, and they had a son named Amasa.

Other Descendants of Hezron
¹⁸Hezron's son Caleb had sons from his wife Azubah and from Jerioth.* Her sons were named Jesher, Shobab, and Ardon. ¹⁹After Azubah died, Caleb married Ephrathah,* and they had a son named Hur. ²⁰Hur was the father of Uri. Uri was the father of Bezalel.
²¹When Hezron was sixty years old, he married Gilead's sister, the daughter of Makir. They had a son named Segub. ²²Segub was the father of Jair, who ruled twenty-three towns in the land of Gilead. ²³(But Geshur and Aram captured the Towns of Jair* and also took Kenath and its sixty surrounding villages.) All these were descendants of Makir, the father of Gilead.
²⁴Soon after Hezron died in the town of

1:50 As in many Hebrew manuscripts, some Greek manuscripts, Syriac version, and Latin Vulgate (see also Gen 36:39); most Hebrew manuscripts read *Pai.* **1:51** As in an alternate reading of the Masoretic Text (see also Gen 36:40); the other alternate reads *Aliah.* **2:1** *Israel* is the name that God gave to Jacob. **2:6** As in many Hebrew manuscripts, some Greek manuscripts, and Syriac version (see also 1 Kgs 4:31); Hebrew reads *Dara.* **2:7a** Hebrew *Achar;* compare Josh 7:1. *Achar* means "disaster." **2:7b** The Hebrew term used here refers to the complete consecration of things or people to the LORD, either by destroying them or by giving them as an offering. **2:9** Hebrew *Kelubai,* a variant spelling of Caleb; compare 2:18. **2:11** As in Greek version (see also Ruth 4:20); Hebrew reads *Salma.* **2:18** Or *Caleb had a daughter named Jerioth from his wife, Azubah.* The meaning of the Hebrew is uncertain. **2:19** Hebrew *Ephrath,* a variant spelling of Ephrathah; compare 2:50 and 4:4. **2:23** Or *captured Havvoth-jair.*

2:3-15 For most of us, these verses contain a boring list of people in David's ancestry, the family line of the promised Messiah. Among these, however, are hidden stories of God's grace. The Messiah's line comes through an illegitimate union between Judah and Tamar (2:4; see Genesis 38). The line passes through Salmon (2:11), who fathered Boaz through Rahab, a former Canaanite prostitute from Jericho (Joshua 2:1; Matthew 1:5). And Boaz (1 Chronicles 2:11-12) bore Obed through Ruth, a Moabite woman (Ruth 1–4). God used numerous people, some less than ideal or even unsavory, to bring the Messiah into the world. God can also use us significantly, no matter how terrible our past experiences or circumstances may be.

Caleb-ephrathah, his wife Abijah gave birth to a son named Ashhur (the father of* Tekoa).

Descendants of Hezron's Son Jerahmeel

25 The sons of Jerahmeel, the oldest son of Hezron, were Ram (the firstborn), Bunah, Oren, Ozem, and Ahijah. 26 Jerahmeel had a second wife named Atarah. She was the mother of Onam.

27 The sons of Ram, the oldest son of Jerahmeel, were Maaz, Jamin, and Eker. 28 The sons of Onam were Shammai and Jada.

The sons of Shammai were Nadab and Abishur. 29 The sons of Abishur and his wife Abihail were Ahban and Molid. 30 The sons of Nadab were Seled and Appaim. Seled died without children, 31 but Appaim had a son named Ishi. The son of Ishi was Sheshan. Sheshan had a descendant named Ahlai.

32 The sons of Jada, Shammai's brother, were Jether and Jonathan. Jether died without children, 33 but Jonathan had two sons named Peleth and Zaza.

These were all descendants of Jerahmeel. 34 Sheshan had no sons, though he did have daughters. He also had an Egyptian servant named Jarha. 35 Sheshan gave one of his daughters to be the wife of Jarha, and they had a son named Attai.

36 Attai was the father of Nathan. Nathan was the father of Zabad. 37 Zabad was the father of Ephlal. Ephlal was the father of Obed. 38 Obed was the father of Jehu. Jehu was the father of Azariah. 39 Azariah was the father of Helez. Helez was the father of Eleasah. 40 Eleasah was the father of Sismai. Sismai was the father of Shallum. 41 Shallum was the father of Jekamiah. Jekamiah was the father of Elishama.

Descendants of Hezron's Son Caleb

42 The descendants of Caleb, the brother of Jerahmeel, included Mesha (the firstborn), who became the father of Ziph. Caleb's descendants also included the sons of Mareshah, the father of Hebron.* 43 The sons of Hebron were Korah, Tappuah, Rekem, and Shema. 44 Shema was the father of Raham. Raham was the father of Jorkeam. Rekem was the father of Shammai. 45 The son of Shammai was Maon. Maon was the father of Beth-zur. 46 Caleb's concubine Ephah gave birth to Haran, Moza, and Gazez. Haran was the father of Gazez. 47 The sons of Jahdai were Regem, Jotham, Geshan, Pelet, Ephah, and Shaaph. 48 Another of Caleb's concubines, Maacah, gave birth to Sheber and Tirhanah. 49 She also gave birth to Shaaph (the father of Madmannah) and Sheva (the father of Macbenah and Gibea). Caleb also had a daughter named Acsah. 50 These were all descendants of Caleb.

Descendants of Caleb's Son Hur

The sons of Hur, the oldest son of Caleb's wife Ephrathah, were Shobal (the founder of Kiriath-jearim), 51 Salma (the founder of Bethlehem), and Hareph (the founder of Beth-gader). 52 The descendants of Shobal (the founder of Kiriath-jearim) were Haroeh, half the Manahathites, 53 and the families of Kiriath-jearim—the Ithrites, Puthites, Shumathites, and Mishraites, from whom came the people of Zorah and Eshtaol. 54 The descendants of Salma were the people of Bethlehem, the Netophathites, Atroth-beth-joab, the other half of the Manahathites, the Zorites, 55 and the families of scribes living at Jabez—the Tirathites, Shimeathites, and Sucathites. All these were Kenites who descended from Hammath, the father of the family of Recab.*

2:24 Or *the founder of;* also in 2:42, 45, 49. 2:42 Or *who founded Hebron.* The meaning of the Hebrew is uncertain. 2:55 Or *the founder of Beth-recab.*

2:42-55 God rewards faith. This entire section is devoted to the family of Caleb, one of the 12 spies Moses sent into Canaan. Caleb, along with Joshua, brought back a positive report based entirely upon his faith in God's provision. Caleb refused to be discouraged by difficult obstacles, believing that God could overcome anything he might face. We need not be stopped by the difficult circumstances we face in the recovery process. Like Caleb, we should remember that God is able to overcome anything we might face. God is the source of true victory.

CHAPTER 3
Descendants of David

These are the sons of David who were born in Hebron:

The oldest was Amnon, whose mother was Ahinoam from Jezreel.

The second was Daniel, whose mother was Abigail from Carmel.

2 The third was Absalom, whose mother was Maacah, the daughter of Talmai, king of Geshur.

The fourth was Adonijah, whose mother was Haggith.

3 The fifth was Shephatiah, whose mother was Abital.

The sixth was Ithream, whose mother was Eglah, David's wife.

4These six sons were born to David in Hebron, where he reigned seven and a half years.

Then David reigned another thirty-three years in Jerusalem. 5The sons born to David in Jerusalem included Shammua,* Shobab, Nathan, and Solomon. Their mother was Bathsheba,* the daughter of Ammiel. 6David also had nine other sons: Ibhar, Elishua,* Elpelet,* 7Nogah, Nepheg, Japhia, 8Elishama, Eliada, and Eliphelet.

9These were the sons of David, not including his sons born to his concubines. Their sister was named Tamar.

Descendants of Solomon

10The descendants of Solomon were Rehoboam, Abijah, Asa, Jehoshaphat, 11Jehoram,* Ahaziah, Joash, 12Amaziah, Uzziah,* Jotham, 13Ahaz, Hezekiah, Manasseh, 14Amon, and Josiah.

15The sons of Josiah were Johanan (the oldest), Jehoiakim (the second), Zedekiah (the third), and Jehoahaz* (the fourth).

16The successors of Jehoiakim were his son Jehoiachin and his brother Zedekiah.*

Descendants of Jehoiachin

17The sons of Jehoiachin,* who was taken prisoner by the Babylonians, were Shealtiel, 18Malkiram, Pedaiah, Shenazzar, Jekamiah, Hoshama, and Nedabiah.

19The sons of Pedaiah were Zerubbabel and Shimei.

The sons of Zerubbabel were Meshullam and Hananiah. (Their sister was Shelomith.) 20His five other sons were Hashubah, Ohel, Berekiah, Hasadiah, and Jushab-hesed.

21The sons of Hananiah were Pelatiah and Jeshaiah. Jeshaiah's son was Rephaiah. Rephaiah's son was Arnan. Arnan's son was Obadiah. Obadiah's son was Shecaniah.

22The descendants of Shecaniah were Shemaiah and his sons, Hattush, Igal, Bariah, Neariah, and Shaphat—six in all.

23The sons of Neariah were Elioenai, Hizkiah, and Azrikam—three in all.

24The sons of Elioenai were Hodaviah, Eliashib, Pelaiah, Akkub, Johanan, Delaiah, and Anani—seven in all.

CHAPTER 4
Other Descendants of Judah

The descendants of Judah were Perez, Hezron, Carmi, Hur, and Shobal.

2Shobal's son Reaiah was the father of Jahath. Jahath was the father of Ahumai and Lahad. These were the families of the Zorathites.

3The descendants of* Etam were Jezreel, Ishma, Idbash, their sister Hazzelelponi, 4Penuel (the father of* Gedor), and Ezer (the father of Hushah). These were the descendants of Hur (the firstborn of Ephrathah), the ancestor of Bethlehem.

5Ashhur (the father of Tekoa) had two wives, named Helah and Naarah. 6Naarah gave birth to Ahuzzam, Hepher, Temeni, and Haahashtari. 7Helah gave birth to Zereth, Izhar,* Ethnan, 8and Koz, who

3:5a As in Syriac version (see also 14:4; 2 Sam 5:14); Hebrew reads *Shimea.* 3:5b Hebrew *Bathshua,* a variant spelling of Bathsheba. 3:6a As in some Hebrew and Greek manuscripts (see also 14:5-7 and 2 Sam 5:15); most Hebrew manuscripts read *Elishama.* 3:6b Hebrew *Eliphelet;* compare parallel text at 14:5-7. 3:11 Hebrew *Joram,* a variant spelling of Jehoram. 3:12 Hebrew *Azariah,* a variant spelling of Uzziah. 3:15 Hebrew *Shallum,* another name for Jehoahaz. 3:16 Hebrew *The sons of Jehoiakim were his son Jeconiah* [a variant spelling of Jehoiachin] *and his son Zedekiah.* 3:17 Hebrew *Jeconiah,* a variant spelling of Jehoiachin. 4:3 As in Greek version; Hebrew reads *father of.* The meaning of the Hebrew is uncertain. 4:4 Or *the founder of;* also in 4:5, 12, 14, 17, 18, and perhaps other instances where the text reads *the father of.* 4:7 As in an alternate reading in the Masoretic Text (see also Latin Vulgate); the other alternate and the Greek version read *Zohar.*

3:1-24 This chapter is entirely devoted to the family of David. As such, it is the most important of the genealogies—the line of the promised Messiah. Many of these names are cited in the New Testament genealogies of Jesus in the books of Matthew and Luke. Just as the entire Old Testament looks forward to the Messiah, Jesus, we also must look to him if we hope to experience meaningful recovery.

became the ancestor of Anub, Zobebah, and all the families of Aharhel son of Harum.

⁹There was a man named Jabez who was more honorable than any of his brothers. His mother named him Jabez* because his birth had been so painful. ¹⁰He was the one who prayed to the God of Israel, "Oh, that you would bless me and expand my territory! Please be with me in all that I do, and keep me from all trouble and pain!" And God granted him his request.

¹¹Kelub (the brother of Shuhah) was the father of Mehir. Mehir was the father of Eshton. ¹²Eshton was the father of Beth-rapha, Paseah, and Tehinnah. Tehinnah was the father of Ir-nahash. These were the descendants of Recah.

¹³The sons of Kenaz were Othniel and Seraiah. Othniel's sons were Hathath and Meonothai.* ¹⁴Meonothai was the father of Ophrah. Seraiah was the father of Joab, the founder of the Valley of Craftsmen,* so called because they were craftsmen.

¹⁵The sons of Caleb son of Jephunneh were Iru, Elah, and Naam. The son of Elah was Kenaz.

¹⁶The sons of Jehallelel were Ziph, Ziphah, Tiria, and Asarel.

¹⁷The sons of Ezrah were Jether, Mered, Epher, and Jalon. One of Mered's wives became* the mother of Miriam, Shammai, and Ishbah (the father of Eshtemoa). ¹⁸He married a woman from Judah, who became the mother of Jered (the father of Gedor), Heber (the father of Soco), and Jekuthiel (the father of Zanoah). Mered also married Bithia, a daughter of Pharaoh, and she bore him children.

¹⁹Hodiah's wife was the sister of Naham. One of her sons was the father of Keilah the Garmite, and another was the father of Eshtemoa the Maacathite.

²⁰The sons of Shimon were Amnon, Rinnah, Ben-hanan, and Tilon.

The descendants of Ishi were Zoheth and Ben-zoheth.

Descendants of Judah's Son Shelah

²¹Shelah was one of Judah's sons. The descendants of Shelah were Er (the father of Lecah); Laadah (the father of Mareshah); the families of linen workers at Beth-ashbea; ²²Jokim; the men of Cozeba; and Joash and Saraph, who ruled over Moab and Jashubi-lehem. These names all come from ancient records. ²³They were the pottery makers who lived in Netaim and Gederah. They lived there and worked for the king.

Descendants of Simeon

²⁴The sons of Simeon were Jemuel,* Jamin, Jarib, Zohar,* and Shaul.

²⁵The descendants of Shaul were Shallum, Mibsam, and Mishma.

²⁶The descendants of Mishma were Hammuel, Zaccur, and Shimei.

²⁷Shimei had sixteen sons and six daughters, but none of his brothers had large families. So Simeon's tribe never grew as large as the tribe of Judah.

²⁸They lived in Beersheba, Moladah, Hazar-shual, ²⁹Bilhah, Ezem, Tolad, ³⁰Bethuel, Hormah, Ziklag, ³¹Beth-marcaboth, Hazar-susim, Beth-biri, and Shaaraim. These towns were under their control until the time of King David. ³²Their descendants also lived in Etam, Ain, Rimmon, Token, and Ashan—five towns ³³and their surrounding villages as far away as Baalath.* This was their territory, and these names are listed in their genealogical records.

³⁴Other descendants of Simeon included Meshobab, Jamlech, Joshah son of Amaziah, ³⁵Joel, Jehu son of Joshibiah, son of Seraiah, son of Asiel, ³⁶Elioenai, Jaakobah, Jeshohaiah, Asaiah, Adiel, Jesimiel, Benaiah, ³⁷and Ziza son of

---

4:9 *Jabez* sounds like a Hebrew word meaning "distress" or "pain." **4:13** As in some Greek manuscripts and Latin Vulgate; Hebrew lacks *and Meonothai.* **4:14** Or *Joab, the father of Ge-harashim.* **4:17** Or *Jether's wife became;* Hebrew reads *She became.* **4:24a** As in Syriac version (see also Gen 46:10; Exod 6:15); Hebrew reads *Nemuel.* **4:24b** As in parallel texts at Gen 46:10 and Exod 6:15; Hebrew reads *Zerah.* **4:33** As in some Greek manuscripts (see also Josh 19:8); Hebrew reads *Baal.*

4:9-10 Jabez is another example of faith. In the midst of his difficulties and in spite of his name (meaning "distress" or "pain"), Jabez looked to God for the solution to his problems. He prayed that God would keep him from fulfilling the meaning of his name. This is a worthwhile prayer. People in recovery must be careful not to cause pain to others; instead they should try to be a blessing to them.

Shiphi, son of Allon, son of Jedaiah, son of Shimri, son of Shemaiah.

38These were the names of some of the leaders of Simeon's wealthy clans. Their families grew, 39and they traveled to the region of Gerar,* in the east part of the valley, seeking pastureland for their flocks. 40They found lush pastures there, and the land was spacious, quiet and peaceful.

Some of Ham's descendants had been living in that region. 41But during the reign of King Hezekiah of Judah, these leaders of Simeon invaded the region and completely destroyed* the homes of the descendants of Ham and of the Meunites. No trace of them remains today. They killed everyone who lived there and took the land for themselves, because they wanted its good pastureland for their flocks. 42Five hundred of these invaders from the tribe of Simeon went to Mount Seir, led by Pelatiah, Neariah, Rephaiah, and Uzziel—all sons of Ishi. 43They destroyed the few Amalekites who had survived, and they have lived there ever since.

CHAPTER 5
Descendants of Reuben
The oldest son of Israel* was Reuben. But since he dishonored his father by sleeping with one of his father's concubines, his birthright was given to the sons of his brother Joseph. For this reason, Reuben is not listed in the genealogical records as the firstborn son. 2The descendants of Judah became the most powerful tribe and provided a ruler for the nation,* but the birthright belonged to Joseph.

3The sons of Reuben, the oldest son of Israel, were Hanoch, Pallu, Hezron, and Carmi.
4The descendants of Joel were Shemaiah, Gog, Shimei, 5Micah, Reaiah, Baal, 6and Beerah. Beerah was the leader of the Reubenites when they were taken into captivity by King Tiglath-pileser* of Assyria.

7Beerah's* relatives are listed in their genealogical records by their clans: Jeiel (the leader), Zechariah, 8and Bela son of Azaz, son of Shema, son of Joel.
The Reubenites lived in the area that stretches from Aroer to Nebo and Baal-meon. 9And since they had so many livestock in the land of Gilead, they spread east toward the edge of the desert that stretches to the Euphrates River.
10During the reign of Saul, the Reubenites defeated the Hagrites in battle. Then they moved into the Hagrite settlements all along the eastern edge of Gilead.

Descendants of Gad
11Next to the Reubenites, the descendants of Gad lived in the land of Bashan as far east as Salecah. 12Joel was the leader in the land of Bashan, and Shapham was second-in-command, followed by Janai and Shaphat.
13Their relatives, the leaders of seven other clans, were Michael, Meshullam, Sheba, Jorai, Jacan, Zia, and Eber. 14These were all descendants of Abihail son of Huri, son of Jaroah, son of Gilead, son of Michael, son of Jeshishai, son of Jahdo, son of Buz. 15Ahi son of Abdiel, son of Guni, was the leader of their clans.

16The Gadites lived in the land of Gilead, in Bashan and its villages, and throughout all the pasturelands of Sharon. 17All of these were listed in the genealogical records during the days of King Jotham of Judah and King Jeroboam of Israel.

The Tribes East of the Jordan
18There were 44,760 capable warriors in the armies of Reuben, Gad, and the half-tribe of Manasseh. They were all skilled in combat and armed with shields, swords, and bows. 19They waged war against the Hagrites, the Jeturites, the Naphishites, and the Nodabites. 20They cried out to God during the battle, and he answered their prayer because they trusted

---

4:39 As in Greek version; Hebrew reads *Gedor.* 4:41 The Hebrew term used here refers to the complete consecration of things or people to the LORD, either by destroying them or by giving them as an offering. 5:1 *Israel* is the name that God gave to Jacob. 5:2 Or *and from Judah came a prince.* 5:6 Hebrew *Tilgath-pilneser,* a variant spelling of Tiglath-pileser; also in 5:26. 5:7 Hebrew *His.*

5:1 After plowing through all these names, people usually wonder, *Why are these lists in the Bible?* Each of these names represents an individual and, in some cases, a family. It is obvious from this that God values individuals and uses them to work his plan. Most of these people never made a significant impact on history. Some of them were far from ideal. We don't have to look far to realize that God cares for us—no matter who we are or what we've done. This should be a comforting message for us as we seek to rebuild our life.

in him. So the Hagrites and all their allies were defeated. ²¹The plunder taken from the Hagrites included 50,000 camels, 250,000 sheep and goats, 2,000 donkeys, and 100,000 captives. ²²Many of the Hagrites were killed in the battle because God was fighting against them. The people of Reuben, Gad, and Manasseh lived in their land until they were taken into exile.

²³The half-tribe of Manasseh was very large and spread through the land from Bashan to Baal-hermon, Senir, and Mount Hermon. ²⁴These were the leaders of their clans: Epher,* Ishi, Eliel, Azriel, Jeremiah, Hodaviah, and Jahdiel. These men had a great reputation as mighty warriors and leaders of their clans.

²⁵But these tribes were unfaithful to the God of their ancestors. They worshiped the gods of the nations that God had destroyed. ²⁶So the God of Israel caused King Pul of Assyria (also known as Tiglath-pileser) to invade the land and take away the people of Reuben, Gad, and the half-tribe of Manasseh as captives. The Assyrians exiled them to Halah, Habor, Hara, and the Gozan River, where they remain to this day.

CHAPTER 6
The Priestly Line

¹*The sons of Levi were Gershon, Kohath, and Merari.
²The descendants of Kohath included Amram, Izhar, Hebron, and Uzziel.
³The children of Amram were Aaron, Moses, and Miriam.
The sons of Aaron were Nadab, Abihu, Eleazar, and Ithamar.
⁴ Eleazar was the father of Phinehas. Phinehas was the father of Abishua.
⁵ Abishua was the father of Bukki. Bukki was the father of Uzzi.
⁶ Uzzi was the father of Zerahiah. Zerahiah was the father of Meraioth.
⁷ Meraioth was the father of Amariah. Amariah was the father of Ahitub.

⁸ Ahitub was the father of Zadok. Zadok was the father of Ahimaaz.
⁹ Ahimaaz was the father of Azariah. Azariah was the father of Johanan.
¹⁰ Johanan was the father of Azariah, the high priest at the Temple* built by Solomon in Jerusalem.
¹¹ Azariah was the father of Amariah. Amariah was the father of Ahitub.
¹² Ahitub was the father of Zadok. Zadok was the father of Shallum.
¹³ Shallum was the father of Hilkiah. Hilkiah was the father of Azariah.
¹⁴ Azariah was the father of Seraiah. Seraiah was the father of Jehozadak,
¹⁵who went into exile when the LORD sent the people of Judah and Jerusalem into captivity under Nebuchadnezzar.

The Levite Clans

¹⁶*The sons of Levi were Gershon,* Kohath, and Merari.
¹⁷The descendants of Gershon included Libni and Shimei.
¹⁸The descendants of Kohath included Amram, Izhar, Hebron, and Uzziel.
¹⁹The descendants of Merari included Mahli and Mushi.

The following were the Levite clans, listed according to their ancestral descent:

²⁰The descendants of Gershon included Libni, Jahath, Zimmah, ²¹Joah, Iddo, Zerah, and Jeatherai.
²²The descendants of Kohath included Amminadab, Korah, Assir, ²³Elkanah, Abiasaph,* Assir, ²⁴Tahath, Uriel, Uzziah, and Shaul.
²⁵The descendants of Elkanah included Amasai, Ahimoth, ²⁶Elkanah, Zophai, Nahath, ²⁷Eliab, Jeroham, Elkanah, and Samuel.*
²⁸The sons of Samuel were Joel* (the older) and Abijah (the second).

5:24 As in Greek version and Latin Vulgate; Hebrew reads *and Epher.* 6:1 Verses 6:1-15 are numbered 5:27-41 in Hebrew text. 6:10 Hebrew *the house.* 6:16a Verses 6:16-81 are numbered 6:1-66 in Hebrew text. 6:16b Hebrew *Gershom,* a variant spelling of Gershon (see 6:1); also in 6:17, 20, 43, 62, 71. 6:23 Hebrew *Ebiasaph,* a variant spelling of Abiasaph (also in 6:37); compare parallel text at Exod 6:24. 6:27 As in some Greek manuscripts (see also 6:33-34); Hebrew lacks *and Samuel.* 6:28 As in some Greek manuscripts and the Syriac version (see also 6:33 and 1 Sam 8:2); Hebrew lacks *Joel.*

6:1-30 This chapter contains the priestly genealogy. It is vital to have access to God. In the Old Testament the priests represented the people before God. Whenever any breach in fellowship occurred, the priests served as mediators to effect reconciliation between God and the people. In the New Testament Jesus Christ is our mediator before God. This truth is where all recovery begins. Christ makes it possible for us to deal with our sins and draw close to God. But recovery does not end there. We also need to be accountable to others who will support us in the recovery process. Without them, our growth will slow down and eventually stagnate.

29 The descendants of Merari included Mahli, Libni, Shimei, Uzzah, 30Shimea, Haggiah, and Asaiah.

The Temple Musicians

31David assigned the following men to lead the music at the house of the LORD after the Ark was placed there. 32They ministered with music at the Tabernacle* until Solomon built the Temple of the LORD in Jerusalem. They carried out their work, following all the regulations handed down to them. 33These are the men who served, along with their sons:

Heman the musician was from the clan of Kohath. His genealogy was traced back through Joel, Samuel, 34Elkanah, Jeroham, Eliel, Toah, 35Zuph, Elkanah, Mahath, Amasai, 36Elkanah, Joel, Azariah, Zephaniah, 37Tahath, Assir, Abiasaph, Korah, 38Izhar, Kohath, Levi, and Israel.*

39Heman's first assistant was Asaph from the clan of Gershon.* Asaph's genealogy was traced back through Berekiah, Shimea, 40Michael, Baaseiah, Malkijah, 41Ethni, Zerah, Adaiah, 42Ethan, Zimmah, Shimei, 43Jahath, Gershon, and Levi.

44Heman's second assistant was Ethan from the clan of Merari. Ethan's genealogy was traced back through Kishi, Abdi, Malluch, 45Hashabiah, Amaziah, Hilkiah, 46Amzi, Bani, Shemer, 47Mahli, Mushi, Merari, and Levi.

48Their fellow Levites were appointed to various other tasks in the Tabernacle, the house of God.

Aaron's Descendants

49Only Aaron and his descendants served as priests. They presented the offerings on the altar of burnt offering and the altar of incense, and they performed all the other duties related to the Most Holy Place. They made atonement for Israel by doing every-thing that Moses, the servant of God, had commanded them.

50The descendants of Aaron were Eleazar, Phinehas, Abishua, 51Bukki, Uzzi, Zerahiah, 52Meraioth, Amariah, Ahitub, 53Zadok, and Ahimaaz.

Territory for the Levites

54This is a record of the towns and territory assigned by means of sacred lots to the descendants of Aaron, who were from the clan of Kohath. 55This territory included Hebron and its surrounding pasturelands in Judah, 56but the fields and outlying areas belonging to the city were given to Caleb son of Jephunneh. 57So the descendants of Aaron were given the following towns, each with its pasturelands: Hebron (a city of refuge),* Libnah, Jattir, Eshtemoa, 58Holon,* Debir, 59Ain,* Juttah,* and Beth-shemesh. 60And from the territory of Benjamin they were given Gibeon,* Geba, Alemeth, and Anathoth, each with its pasturelands. So thirteen towns were given to the descendants of Aaron. 61The remaining descendants of Kohath received ten towns from the territory of the half-tribe of Manasseh by means of sacred lots.

62The descendants of Gershon received by sacred lots thirteen towns from the territories of Issachar, Asher, Naphtali, and from the Bashan area of Manasseh, east of the Jordan.

63The descendants of Merari received by sacred lots twelve towns from the territories of Reuben, Gad, and Zebulun.

64So the people of Israel assigned all these towns and pasturelands to the Levites. 65The towns in the territories of Judah, Simeon, and Benjamin, mentioned above, were assigned to them by means of sacred lots.

66The descendants of Kohath were given the following towns from the territory of Ephraim, each with its pasturelands: 67Shechem (a city of refuge in the hill country

6:32 Hebrew *the Tabernacle, the Tent of Meeting.* 6:38 *Israel* is the name that God gave to Jacob. 6:39 Hebrew lacks *from the clan of Gershon;* see 6:43. 6:57 As in parallel text at Josh 21:13; Hebrew reads *were given the cities of refuge: Hebron, and the following towns, each with its pasturelands.* 6:58 As in parallel text at Josh 21:15; Masoretic Text reads *Hilez;* other manuscripts read *Hilen.* 6:59a As in parallel text at Josh 21:16; Hebrew reads *Ashan.* 6:59b As in Syriac version (see also Josh 21:16); Hebrew lacks *Juttah.* 6:60 As in parallel text at Josh 21:17; Hebrew lacks *Gibeon.*

6:31-48 These verses contain a genealogy of the family that led the people in worship. Music and singing were vital parts of serving God in the Temple, calling the people to joyfully express their thanks to God. Our worship of God needs to contain joy. Joy is an aspect of worship that is often ignored during the recovery process. Worship must never become an arduous task— it should be a happy response to a good and loving God. Worship does not need to be an elaborate ceremony. It can begin with simple thanks for God's grace, power, and rich blessings in our life.

of Ephraim),* Gezer, [68]Jokmeam, Beth-horon, [69]Aijalon, and Gath-rimmon. [70]The remaining descendants of Kohath were assigned the towns of Aner and Bileam from the territory of the half-tribe of Manasseh, each with its pasturelands.

[71]The descendants of Gershon received the towns of Golan (in Bashan) and Ashtaroth from the territory of the half-tribe of Manasseh, each with its pasturelands. [72]From the territory of Issachar, they were given Kedesh, Daberath, [73]Ramoth, and Anem, each with its pasturelands. [74]From the territory of Asher, they received Mashal, Abdon, [75]Hukok, and Rehob, each with its pasturelands. [76]From the territory of Naphtali, they were given Kedesh in Galilee, Hammon, and Kiriathaim, each with its pasturelands.

[77]The remaining descendants of Merari received the towns of Jokneam, Kartah,* Rimmon,* and Tabor from the territory of Zebulun, each with its pasturelands. [78]From the territory of Reuben, east of the Jordan River opposite Jericho, they received Bezer (a desert town), Jahaz,* [79]Kedemoth, and Mephaath, each with its pasturelands. [80]And from the territory of Gad, they received Ramoth in Gilead, Mahanaim, [81]Heshbon, and Jazer, each with its pasturelands.

CHAPTER 7
Descendants of Issachar

The four sons of Issachar were Tola, Puah, Jashub, and Shimron.

[2]The sons of Tola were Uzzi, Rephaiah, Jeriel, Jahmai, Ibsam, and Shemuel. Each of them was the leader of an ancestral clan. At the time of King David, the total number of mighty warriors listed in the records of these clans was 22,600.

[3]The son of Uzzi was Izrahiah. The sons of Izrahiah were Michael, Obadiah, Joel, and Isshiah. These five became the leaders of clans. [4]All of them had many wives and many sons, so the total number of men available for military service among their descendants was 36,000.

[5]The total number of mighty warriors from all the clans of the tribe of Issachar was 87,000. All of them were listed in their genealogical records.

Descendants of Benjamin

[6]Three of Benjamin's sons were Bela, Beker, and Jediael.

[7]The five sons of Bela were Ezbon, Uzzi, Uzziel, Jerimoth, and Iri. Each of them was the leader of an ancestral clan. The total number of mighty warriors from these clans was 22,034, as listed in their genealogical records.

[8]The sons of Beker were Zemirah, Joash, Eliezer, Elioenai, Omri, Jeremoth, Abijah, Anathoth, and Alemeth. [9]Each of them was the leader of an ancestral clan. The total number of mighty warriors and leaders from these clans was 20,200, as listed in their genealogical records.

[10]The son of Jediael was Bilhan. The sons of Bilhan were Jeush, Benjamin, Ehud, Kenaanah, Zethan, Tarshish, and Ahishahar. [11]Each of them was the leader of an ancestral clan. From these clans the total number of mighty warriors ready for war was 17,200.

[12]The sons of Ir were Shuppim and Huppim. Hushim was the son of Aher.

Descendants of Naphtali

[13]The sons of Naphtali were Jahzeel,* Guni, Jezer, and Shillem.* They were all descendants of Jacob's concubine Bilhah.

Descendants of Manasseh

[14]The descendants of Manasseh through his Aramean concubine included Asriel. She also bore Makir, the father of Gilead. [15]Makir found wives for* Huppim and Shuppim. Makir had a sister named Maacah. One of his descendants was Zelophehad, who had only daughters.

[16]Makir's wife, Maacah, gave birth to a son whom she named Peresh. His brother's name was Sheresh. The sons of Peresh were Ulam and Rakem. [17]The son of Ulam was Bedan. All these were considered Gileadites, descendants of Makir son of Manasseh.

[18]Makir's sister Hammoleketh gave birth to Ishhod, Abiezer, and Mahlah.

[19]The sons of Shemida were Ahian, Shechem, Likhi, and Aniam.

6:66-67 As in parallel text at Josh 21:21. Hebrew text reads *were given the cities of refuge: Shechem in the hill country of Ephraim, and the following towns, each with its pasturelands.* 6:77a As in Greek version (see also Josh 21:34); Hebrew lacks *Jokneam, Kartah.* 6:77b As in Greek version (see also Josh 19:13); Hebrew reads *Rimmono.* 6:78 Hebrew *Jahzah*, a variant spelling of Jahaz. 7:13a As in parallel text at Gen 46:24; Hebrew reads *Jahziel*, a variant spelling of Jahzeel. 7:13b As in some Hebrew and Greek manuscripts (see also Gen 46:24; Num 26:49); most Hebrew manuscripts read *Shallum.* 7:15 Or *Makir took a wife from.* The meaning of the Hebrew is uncertain.

Descendants of Ephraim

20The descendants of Ephraim were Shuthelah, Bered, Tahath, Eleadah, Tahath, 21Zabad, Shuthelah, Ezer, and Elead. These two were killed trying to steal livestock from the local farmers near Gath. 22Their father, Ephraim, mourned for them a long time, and his relatives came to comfort him. 23Afterward Ephraim slept with his wife, and she became pregnant and gave birth to a son. Ephraim named him Beriah* because of the tragedy his family had suffered. 24He had a daughter named Sheerah. She built the towns of Lower and Upper Beth-horon and Uzzen-sheerah.

25The descendants of Ephraim included Rephah, Resheph, Telah, Tahan, 26Ladan, Ammihud, Elishama, 27Nun, and Joshua.

28The descendants of Ephraim lived in the territory that included Bethel and its surrounding towns to the south, Naaran to the east, Gezer and its villages to the west, and Shechem and its surrounding villages to the north as far as Ayyah and its towns. 29Along the border of Manasseh were the towns of Beth-shan,* Taanach, Megiddo, Dor, and their surrounding villages. The descendants of Joseph son of Israel* lived in these towns.

Descendants of Asher

30The sons of Asher were Imnah, Ishvah, Ishvi, and Beriah. They had a sister named Serah.

31The sons of Beriah were Heber and Malkiel (the father of Birzaith).

32The sons of Heber were Japhlet, Shomer, and Hotham. They had a sister named Shua.

33The sons of Japhlet were Pasach, Bimhal, and Ashvath.

34The sons of Shomer were Ahi,* Rohgah, Hubbah, and Aram.

35The sons of his brother Helem* were Zophah, Imna, Shelesh, and Amal.

36The sons of Zophah were Suah, Harnepher, Shual, Beri, Imrah, 37Bezer, Hod, Shamma, Shilshah, Ithran,* and Beera.

38The sons of Jether were Jephunneh, Pispah, and Ara.

39The sons of Ulla were Arah, Hanniel, and Rizia.

40Each of these descendants of Asher was the head of an ancestral clan. They were all select men—mighty warriors and outstanding leaders. The total number of men available for military service was 26,000, as listed in their genealogical records.

CHAPTER 8
Descendants of Benjamin

Benjamin's first son was Bela, the second was Ashbel, the third was Aharah, 2the fourth was Nohah, and the fifth was Rapha.

3The sons of Bela were Addar, Gera, Abihud,* 4Abishua, Naaman, Ahoah, 5Gera, Shephuphan, and Huram.

6The sons of Ehud, leaders of the clans living at Geba, were exiled to Manahath. 7Ehud's sons were Naaman, Ahijah, and Gera. Gera, who led them into exile, was the father of Uzza and Ahihud.*

8After Shaharaim divorced his wives Hushim and Baara, he had children in the land of Moab. 9His wife Hodesh gave birth to Jobab, Zibia, Mesha, Malcam, 10Jeuz, Sakia, and Mirmah. These sons all became the leaders of clans.

11Shaharaim's wife Hushim had already given birth to Abitub and Elpaal. 12The sons of Elpaal were Eber, Misham, Shemed (who built the towns of Ono and Lod and their nearby villages), 13Beriah, and Shema. They were the leaders of the clans living in Aijalon, and they drove out the inhabitants of Gath.

14Ahio, Shashak, Jeremoth, 15Zebadiah, Arad, Eder, 16Michael, Ishpah, and Joha were the sons of Beriah.

17Zebadiah, Meshullam, Hizki, Heber, 18Ishmerai, Izliah, and Jobab were the sons of Elpaal.

7:23 *Beriah* sounds like a Hebrew term meaning "tragedy" or "misfortune." 7:29a Hebrew *Beth-shean,* a variant spelling of Beth-shan. 7:29b *Israel* is the name that God gave to Jacob. 7:34 Or *The sons of Shomer, his brother, were.* 7:35 Possibly another name for *Hotham;* compare 7:32. 7:37 Possibly another name for *Jether;* compare 7:38. 8:3 Possibly *Gera the father of Ehud;* compare 8:6. 8:7 Or *Gera, that is Heglam, was the father of Uzza and Ahihud.*

8:1-33 When the people demanded a king, God gave them Saul. This is his personal genealogy. Even though he was well received by the people, it soon became obvious that he was attempting to build Israel with only human resources. Any project, either on a personal or a national level, must have divine resources if anything lasting is to result. This is a lesson that we all need to apply to our life as we continue in recovery.

[19]Jakim, Zicri, Zabdi, [20]Elienai, Zillethai, Eliel, [21]Adaiah, Beraiah, and Shimrath were the sons of Shimei.
[22]Ishpan, Eber, Eliel, [23]Abdon, Zicri, Hanan, [24]Hananiah, Elam, Anthothijah, [25]Iphdeiah, and Penuel were the sons of Shashak.
[26]Shamsherai, Shehariah, Athaliah, [27]Jaareshiah, Elijah, and Zicri were the sons of Jeroham.
[28]These were the leaders of the ancestral clans; they were listed in their genealogical records, and they all lived in Jerusalem.

The Family of Saul

[29]Jeiel* (the father of* Gibeon) lived in the town of Gibeon. His wife's name was Maacah, [30]and his oldest son was named Abdon. Jeiel's other sons were Zur, Kish, Baal, Ner,* Nadab, [31]Gedor, Ahio, Zechariah,* [32]and Mikloth, who was the father of Shimeam.* All these families lived near each other in Jerusalem.
[33] Ner was the father of Kish.
Kish was the father of Saul.
Saul was the father of Jonathan, Malkishua, Abinadab, and Esh-baal.
[34] Jonathan was the father of Merib-baal.
Merib-baal was the father of Micah.
[35] Micah was the father of Pithon, Melech, Tahrea,* and Ahaz.
[36] Ahaz was the father of Jadah.*
Jadah was the father of Alemeth, Azmaveth, and Zimri.
Zimri was the father of Moza.
[37] Moza was the father of Binea.
Binea was the father of Rephaiah.*

Rephaiah was the father of Eleasah.
Eleasah was the father of Azel.
[38]Azel had six sons: Azrikam, Bokeru, Ishmael, Sheariah, Obadiah, and Hanan. These were the sons of Azel.
[39]Azel's brother Eshek had three sons: the first was Ulam, the second was Jeush, and the third was Eliphelet. [40]Ulam's sons were all mighty warriors and expert archers. They had many sons and grandsons—150 in all.

All these were descendants of Benjamin.

CHAPTER 9

So all Israel was listed in the genealogical records in *The Book of the Kings of Israel*.

The Returning Exiles

The people of Judah were exiled to Babylon because they were unfaithful to the LORD. [2]The first of the exiles to return to their property in their former towns were priests, Levites, Temple servants, and other Israelites. [3]Some of the people from the tribes of Judah, Benjamin, Ephraim, and Manasseh came and settled in Jerusalem.

[4]One family that returned was that of Uthai son of Ammihud, son of Omri, son of Imri, son of Bani, a descendant of Perez son of Judah.
[5]Others returned from the Shilonite clan, including Asaiah (the oldest) and his sons.
[6]From the Zerahite clan, Jeuel returned with his relatives.
In all, 690 families from the tribe of Judah returned.

8:29a As in some Greek manuscripts (see also 9:35); Hebrew lacks *Jeiel*. **8:29b** Or *the founder of*. **8:30** As in some Greek manuscripts (see also 9:36); Hebrew lacks *Ner*. **8:31** As in parallel text at 9:37; Hebrew reads *Zeker*, a variant spelling of Zechariah. **8:32** As in parallel text at 9:38; Hebrew reads *Shimeah*, a variant spelling of Shimeam. **8:35** As in parallel text at 9:41; Hebrew reads *Tarea*, a variant spelling of Tahrea. **8:36** As in parallel text at 9:42; Hebrew reads *Jehoaddah*, a variant spelling of Jadah. **8:37** As in parallel text at 9:43; Hebrew reads *Raphah*, a variant spelling of Rephaiah.

9:1 We are reminded of the primary reason for Judah's punishment in exile: The people had turned from God and worshiped idols. The idols in our life can often lead us into similar exile. As an addiction or compulsion takes over our life, our values get distorted. We forget about God, our family, and the other important things in life. As a result, we may lose everything. But just as Judah was restored through the Babylonian exile, we can also find restoration through the exiles we may experience. Even if our life is filled with memories of past sins and failures, God has the power to give us a new start. All we need to do is ask him.
9:1-44 This chapter contains a record of the Jews who returned to Judah after the Babylonian exile (see 2 Kings 25:21). The books of Chronicles were written to encourage these people as they returned and rebuilt their nation after their seventy-year exile. The Temple had been destroyed, and the Davidic line of kings had been discontinued. It must have been a great encouragement for them to see that they were still God's people. God had made promises to their ancestors, and though the people had gone through hard times, God's promises were still valid for them. In Scripture, God gives numerous promises to his people. God's promises are for all of us in Christ to embrace, no matter what we have done or suffered in the past. We, too, are the people of God.

[7]From the tribe of Benjamin came Sallu son of Meshullam, son of Hodaviah, son of Hassenuah; [8]Ibneiah son of Jeroham; Elah son of Uzzi, son of Micri; and Meshullam son of Shephatiah, son of Reuel, son of Ibnijah.

[9]These men were all leaders of clans, and they were listed in their genealogical records. In all, 956 families from the tribe of Benjamin returned.

The Returning Priests

[10]Among the priests who returned were Jedaiah, Jehoiarib, Jakin, [11]Azariah son of Hilkiah, son of Meshullam, son of Zadok, son of Meraioth, son of Ahitub. Azariah was the chief officer of the house of God. [12]Other returning priests were Adaiah son of Jeroham, son of Pashhur, son of Malkijah, and Maasai son of Adiel, son of Jahzerah, son of Meshullam, son of Meshillemith, son of Immer.

[13]In all, 1,760 priests returned. They were heads of clans and very able men. They were responsible for ministering at the house of God.

The Returning Levites

[14]The Levites who returned were Shemaiah son of Hasshub, son of Azrikam, son of Hashabiah, a descendant of Merari; [15]Bakbakkar; Heresh; Galal; Mattaniah son of Mica, son of Zicri, son of Asaph; [16]Obadiah son of Shemaiah, son of Galal, son of Jeduthun; and Berekiah son of Asa, son of Elkanah, who lived in the area of Netophah.

[17]The gatekeepers who returned were Shallum, Akkub, Talmon, Ahiman, and their relatives. Shallum was the chief gatekeeper. [18]Prior to this time, they were responsible for the King's Gate on the east side. These men served as gatekeepers for the camps of the Levites. [19]Shallum was the son of Kore, a descendant of Abiasaph,* from the clan of Korah. He and his relatives, the Korahites, were responsible for guarding the entrance to the sanctuary, just as their ancestors had guarded the Tabernacle in the camp of the LORD.

[20]Phinehas son of Eleazar had been in charge of the gatekeepers in earlier times, and the LORD had been with him. [21]And later Zechariah son of Meshelemiah was responsible for guarding the entrance to the Tabernacle.*

[22]In all, there were 212 gatekeepers in those days, and they were listed according to the genealogies in their villages. David and Samuel the seer had appointed their ancestors because they were reliable men. [23]These gatekeepers and their descendants, by their divisions, were responsible for guarding the entrance to the house of the LORD when that house was a tent. [24]The gatekeepers were stationed on all four sides—east, west, north, and south. [25]Their relatives in the villages came regularly to share their duties for seven-day periods.

[26]The four chief gatekeepers, all Levites, were trusted officials, for they were responsible for the rooms and treasuries at the house of God. [27]They would spend the night around the house of God, since it was their duty to guard it and to open the gates every morning.

[28]Some of the gatekeepers were assigned to care for the various articles used in worship. They checked them in and out to avoid any loss. [29]Others were responsible for the furnishings, the items in the sanctuary, and the supplies, such as choice flour, wine, olive oil, frankincense, and spices. [30]But it was the priests who blended the spices. [31]Mattithiah, a Levite and the oldest son of Shallum the Korahite, was entrusted with baking the bread used in the offerings. [32]And some members of the clan of Kohath were in charge of preparing the bread to be set on the table each Sabbath day.

[33]The musicians, all prominent Levites, lived at the Temple. They were exempt from other responsibilities since they were on duty at all hours. [34]All these men lived in Jerusalem. They were the heads of Levite families and were listed as prominent leaders in their genealogical records.

King Saul's Family Tree

[35]Jeiel (the father of* Gibeon) lived in the town of Gibeon. His wife's name was Maacah, [36]and his oldest son was named Abdon. Jeiel's other sons were Zur, Kish, Baal, Ner, Nadab, [37]Gedor, Ahio, Zechariah, and Mikloth. [38]Mikloth was the father of Shimeam. All these families lived near each other in Jerusalem.

[39] Ner was the father of Kish.
Kish was the father of Saul.

9:19 Hebrew *Ebiasaph,* a variant spelling of Abiasaph; compare Exod 6:24. **9:21** Hebrew *Tent of Meeting.* **9:35** Or *the founder of.*

Saul was the father of Jonathan,
Malkishua, Abinadab, and Esh-baal.
⁴⁰ Jonathan was the father of Merib-baal.
Merib-baal was the father of Micah.
⁴¹ The sons of Micah were Pithon, Melech,
Tahrea, and Ahaz.*
⁴² Ahaz was the father of Jadah.*
Jadah was the father of Alemeth,
Azmaveth, and Zimri.
Zimri was the father of Moza.
⁴³ Moza was the father of Binea.
Binea's son was Rephaiah.
Rephaiah's son was Eleasah.
Eleasah's son was Azel.
⁴⁴Azel had six sons, whose names were
Azrikam, Bokeru, Ishmael, Sheariah,
Obadiah, and Hanan. These were the
sons of Azel.

CHAPTER 10
The Death of King Saul

Now the Philistines attacked Israel, and the
men of Israel fled before them. Many were
slaughtered on the slopes of Mount Gilboa.
²The Philistines closed in on Saul and his
sons, and they killed three of his sons—Jonathan, Abinadab, and Malkishua. ³The fighting grew very fierce around Saul, and the
Philistine archers caught up with him and
wounded him.

⁴Saul groaned to his armor bearer, "Take
your sword and kill me before these pagan
Philistines come to taunt and torture me."
But his armor bearer was afraid and would

not do it. So Saul took his own sword and
fell on it. ⁵When his armor bearer realized
that Saul was dead, he fell on his own sword
and died. ⁶So Saul and his three sons died
there together, bringing his dynasty to an
end.

⁷When all the Israelites in the Jezreel Valley
saw that their army had fled and that Saul
and his sons were dead, they abandoned
their towns and fled. So the Philistines
moved in and occupied their towns.

⁸The next day, when the Philistines went
out to strip the dead, they found the bodies
of Saul and his sons on Mount Gilboa. ⁹So
they stripped off Saul's armor and cut off his
head. Then they proclaimed the good news
of Saul's death before their idols and to the
people throughout the land of Philistia.
¹⁰They placed his armor in the temple of
their gods, and they fastened his head to the
temple of Dagon.

¹¹But when everyone in Jabesh-gilead
heard about everything the Philistines had
done to Saul, ¹²all their mighty warriors
brought the bodies of Saul and his sons back
to Jabesh. Then they buried their bones beneath the great tree at Jabesh, and they
fasted for seven days.

¹³So Saul died because he was unfaithful to
the LORD. He failed to obey the LORD's command, and he even consulted a medium ¹⁴instead of asking the LORD for guidance. So the
LORD killed him and turned the kingdom
over to David son of Jesse.

9:41 As in Syriac version and Latin Vulgate (see also 8:35); Hebrew lacks *and Ahaz.* 9:42 As in some Hebrew
manuscripts and Greek version (see also 8:36); Hebrew reads *Jarah.*

10:1-10 Here is a horrifying account of personal defeat. Like many people in the process of recovery, Saul had started out well. At first he was humble and willing to follow the leadership of the
prophet Samuel. But he began to take matters into his own hands. Once he started on the downward spiral, he added rebellion to rebellion. The final outcome was the defeat described here.
We need to be careful! We are capable of starting down this same path toward complete disaster.
We must never forget to ask God to join us in the journey toward recovery—each and every
day.
10:11-12 In spite of Saul's failure and downfall, the men of Jabesh-gilead remembered the kindness that Saul had shown toward them (see 1 Samuel 11). They were loyal to his memory and, at
great personal risk, rescued the bodies of Saul and his three sons. Even when a person is down
and out, we should remember that he or she needs loyalty and encouragement as much or more
than ever. We need to remember the people who have stuck by us through recovery and remain
loyal to them, even through the worst of times.
10:13-14 As we face problems, we must be careful of where we go for help. God is the only true
source of help. In many cases looking elsewhere will prove fatal. This was true in Saul's case.
Notice that Saul's sin, which cost him the throne, was not simply disobedience and rebellion.
Saul's primary mistake was his failure to seek God for help. Instead, he went to an evil source that
was forbidden by God (see 1 Samuel 28). God is waiting to help us. All we need to do is recognize our helplessness and call out to him. Looking to the occult and other sources for help will
always spell disaster.

CHAPTER 11

David Becomes King of All Israel

Then all Israel gathered before David at Hebron and told him, "We are your own flesh and blood. ²In the past,* even when Saul was king, you were the one who really led the forces of Israel. And the LORD your God told you, 'You will be the shepherd of my people Israel. You will be the leader of my people Israel.'"

³So there at Hebron, David made a covenant before the LORD with all the elders of Israel. And they anointed him king of Israel, just as the LORD had promised through Samuel.

David Captures Jerusalem

⁴Then David and all Israel went to Jerusalem (or Jebus, as it used to be called), where the Jebusites, the original inhabitants of the land, were living. ⁵The people of Jebus taunted David, saying, "You'll never get in here!" But David captured the fortress of Zion, which is now called the City of David.

⁶David had said to his troops, "Whoever is first to attack the Jebusites will become the commander of my armies!" And Joab, the son of David's sister Zeruiah, was first to attack, so he became the commander of David's armies.

⁷David made the fortress his home, and that is why it is called the City of David. ⁸He extended the city from the supporting terraces* to the surrounding area, while Joab rebuilt the rest of Jerusalem. ⁹And David became more and more powerful, because the LORD of Heaven's Armies was with him.

David's Mightiest Warriors

¹⁰These are the leaders of David's mighty warriors. Together with all Israel, they decided to make David their king, just as the LORD had promised concerning Israel.

¹¹Here is the record of David's mightiest warriors: The first was Jashobeam the Hacmonite, who was leader of the Three—the mightiest warriors among David's men.* He once used his spear to kill 300 enemy warriors in a single battle.

¹²Next in rank among the Three was Eleazar son of Dodai,* a descendant of Ahoah. ¹³He was with David when the Philistines gathered for battle at Pas-dammim and attacked the Israelites in a field full of barley. The Israelite army fled, ¹⁴but Eleazar and David* held their ground in the middle of the field and beat back the Philistines. So the LORD saved them by giving them a great victory.

¹⁵Once when David was at the rock near the cave of Adullam, the Philistine army was camped in the valley of Rephaim. The Three (who were among the Thirty—an elite group among David's fighting men) went down to meet him there. ¹⁶David was staying in the stronghold at the time, and a Philistine detachment had occupied the town of Bethlehem.

¹⁷David remarked longingly to his men, "Oh, how I would love some of that good water from the well by the gate in Bethlehem." ¹⁸So the Three broke through the Philistine lines, drew some water from the well by the gate in Bethlehem, and brought it back to David. But David refused to drink it. Instead, he poured it out as an offering to

---

11:2 Or *For some time.* 11:8 Hebrew *the millo.* The meaning of the Hebrew is uncertain. 11:11 As in some Greek manuscripts (see also 2 Sam 23:8); Hebrew reads *leader of the Thirty,* or *leader of the captains.* 11:12 As in parallel text at 2 Sam 23:9 (see also 1 Chr 27:4); Hebrew reads *Dodo,* a variant spelling of Dodai. 11:14 Hebrew *they.*

11:1-3 With every God-given opportunity comes a God-given responsibility. This is clear in the career of David, the man after God's own heart. The people of Israel pledged themselves as his subjects. In this relationship, the people had a perfect right to look to David for military leadership and personal protection. This is not an unhealthy state of dependency but a proper definition of roles. When God gives us opportunities to help others, we need to realize that with the position of leadership comes a responsibility to "shepherd" God's people.

11:4-7 These verses recount David's capture of the city of Jerusalem, which would soon become the spiritual center of worship for Israel. This place remained the focal point for Israel's worship for centuries and is important in the thinking of Jews to this day. For all individuals facing recovery, a spiritual center for corporate worship is extremely important. God has provided us with the worshiping community—the church—for proper healing. Through the church or other appropriate support groups, God encourages us, giving us the strength we need to persevere in the process of recovery.

11:9 All of us desire success of one kind or another. Here the Bible attributes David's amazing success to his strong relationship with God. True success is only possible when God is empowering the individual. If we achieve personal greatness but are spiritually bankrupt, our efforts will have been in vain. True success in life can only be achieved when we put God first. Everything else in life is secondary.

the LORD. [19]"God forbid that I should drink this!" he exclaimed. "This water is as precious as the blood of these men* who risked their lives to bring it to me." So David did not drink it. These are examples of the exploits of the Three.

David's Thirty Mighty Men

[20]Abishai, the brother of Joab, was the leader of the Thirty.* He once used his spear to kill 300 enemy warriors in a single battle. It was by such feats that he became as famous as the Three. [21]Abishai was the most famous of the Thirty and was their commander, though he was not one of the Three.

[22]There was also Benaiah son of Jehoiada, a valiant warrior from Kabzeel. He did many heroic deeds, which included killing two champions* of Moab. Another time, on a snowy day, he chased a lion down into a pit and killed it. [23]Once, armed only with a club, he killed an Egyptian warrior who was 7½ feet* tall and who was armed with a spear as thick as a weaver's beam. Benaiah wrenched the spear from the Egyptian's hand and killed him with it. [24]Deeds like these made Benaiah as famous as the three mightiest warriors. [25]He was more honored than the other members of the Thirty, though he was not one of the Three. And David made him captain of his bodyguard.

[26]David's mighty warriors also included:

Asahel, Joab's brother;
Elhanan son of Dodo from Bethlehem;
[27] Shammah from Harod;*
Helez from Pelon;
[28] Ira son of Ikkesh from Tekoa;
Abiezer from Anathoth;
[29] Sibbecai from Hushah;
Zalmon* from Ahoah;
[30] Maharai from Netophah;
Heled son of Baanah from Netophah;
[31] Ithai son of Ribai from Gibeah (in the land of Benjamin);
Benaiah from Pirathon;
[32] Hurai from near Nahale-gaash*;
Abi-albon* from Arabah;
[33] Azmaveth from Bahurim*;
Eliahba from Shaalbon;
[34] the sons of Jashen* from Gizon;
Jonathan son of Shagee from Harar;
[35] Ahiam son of Sharar* from Harar;
Eliphal son of Ur;
[36] Hepher from Mekerah;
Ahijah from Pelon;
[37] Hezro from Carmel;
Paarai* son of Ezbai;
[38] Joel, the brother of Nathan;
Mibhar son of Hagri;
[39] Zelek from Ammon;
Naharai from Beeroth, the armor bearer of Joab son of Zeruiah;
[40] Ira from Jattir;
Gareb from Jattir;
[41] Uriah the Hittite;
Zabad son of Ahlai;
[42] Adina son of Shiza, the Reubenite leader who had thirty men with him;
[43] Hanan son of Maacah;
Joshaphat from Mithnah;
[44] Uzzia from Ashtaroth;
Shama and Jeiel, the sons of Hotham, from Aroer;
[45] Jediael son of Shimri;
Joha, his brother, from Tiz;
[46] Eliel from Mahavah;
Jeribai and Joshaviah, the sons of Elnaam;
Ithmah from Moab;
[47] Eliel and Obed;
Jaasiel from Zobah.*

CHAPTER 12
Warriors Join David's Army

The following men joined David at Ziklag while he was hiding from Saul son of Kish. They were among the warriors who fought beside David in battle. [2]All of them were expert archers, and they could shoot arrows or sling stones with their left hand as well as their right. They were all relatives of Saul

---

11:19 Hebrew *Shall I drink the lifeblood of these men?* 11:20 As in Syriac version; Hebrew reads *the Three;* also in 11:21. 11:22 Or *two sons of Ariel.* 11:23 Hebrew *5 cubits* [2.3 meters]. 11:27 As in parallel text at 2 Sam 23:25; Hebrew reads *Shammoth from Haror.* 11:29 As in parallel text at 2 Sam 23:28; Hebrew reads *Ilai.* 11:32a Or *from the ravines of Gaash.* 11:32b As in parallel text at 2 Sam 23:31; Hebrew reads *Abiel.* 11:33 As in parallel text at 2 Sam 23:31; Hebrew reads *Baharum.* 11:34 As in parallel text at 2 Sam 23:32; Hebrew reads *sons of Hashem.* 11:35 As in parallel text at 2 Sam 23:33; Hebrew reads *son of Sacar.* 11:37 As in parallel text at 2 Sam 23:35; Hebrew reads *Naarai.* 11:47 Or *the Mezobaite.*

12:1-7 All these warriors were well prepared for conflict. Proper preparation is a necessary step for winning any battle. Any of us in the process of rebuilding our life will encounter conflict. The example of David's warriors should encourage us to be prepared. We would be wise to draw close to God. When we are armed with God's armor, we will be prepared to fight life's battles (see Ephesians 6:10-18).

from the tribe of Benjamin. ³Their leader was Ahiezer son of Shemaah from Gibeah; his brother Joash was second-in-command. These were the other warriors:

Jeziel and Pelet, sons of Azmaveth;
Beracah;
Jehu from Anathoth;
⁴ Ishmaiah from Gibeon, a famous warrior and leader among the Thirty;
*Jeremiah, Jahaziel, Johanan, and Jozabad from Gederah;
⁵ Eluzai, Jerimoth, Bealiah, Shemariah, and Shephatiah from Haruph;
⁶ Elkanah, Isshiah, Azarel, Joezer, and Jashobeam, who were Korahites;
⁷ Joelah and Zebadiah, sons of Jeroham from Gedor.

⁸Some brave and experienced warriors from the tribe of Gad also defected to David while he was at the stronghold in the wilderness. They were expert with both shield and spear, as fierce as lions and as swift as deer on the mountains.

⁹ Ezer was their leader.
Obadiah was second.
Eliab was third.
¹⁰ Mishmannah was fourth.
Jeremiah was fifth.
¹¹ Attai was sixth.
Eliel was seventh.
¹² Johanan was eighth.
Elzabad was ninth.
¹³ Jeremiah was tenth.
Macbannai was eleventh.

¹⁴These warriors from Gad were army commanders. The weakest among them could take on a hundred regular troops, and the strongest could take on a thousand! ¹⁵These were the men who crossed the Jordan River during its seasonal flooding at the beginning of the year and drove out all the people living in the lowlands on both the east and west banks.

¹⁶Others from Benjamin and Judah came to David at the stronghold. ¹⁷David went out to meet them and said, "If you have come in peace to help me, we are friends. But if you have come to betray me to my enemies when I am innocent, then may the God of our ancestors see it and punish you."

¹⁸Then the Spirit came upon Amasai, the leader of the Thirty, and he said,

"We are yours, David!
    We are on your side, son of Jesse.
Peace and prosperity be with you,
    and success to all who help you,
    for your God is the one who helps you."

So David let them join him, and he made them officers over his troops.

¹⁹Some men from Manasseh defected from the Israelite army and joined David when he set out with the Philistines to fight against Saul. But as it turned out, the Philistine rulers refused to let David and his men go with them. After much discussion, they sent them back, for they said, "It will cost us our heads if David switches loyalties to Saul and turns against us."

²⁰Here is a list of the men from Manasseh who defected to David as he was returning to Ziklag: Adnah, Jozabad, Jediael, Michael, Jozabad, Elihu, and Zillethai. Each commanded 1,000 troops from the tribe of Manasseh. ²¹They helped David chase down bands of raiders, for they were all brave and able warriors who became commanders in his army. ²²Day after day more men joined David until he had a great army, like the army of God.

²³These are the numbers of armed warriors who joined David at Hebron. They were all eager to see David become king instead of Saul, just as the LORD had promised.

12:4 Verses 12:4b-40 are numbered 12:5-41 in Hebrew text.

12:16-18 This group of warriors came to David, wanting to submit to his leadership. During the period of anarchy experienced in Israel after Saul's death, many desperately sought direction for their lives. David gave this band of warriors the direction they needed. We all desire our life to be meaningful. These volunteers were not only anxious to serve, but they were also empowered by the Holy Spirit. We often forget that spiritual empowerment is vital if we desire to accomplish anything significant in life, including recovery. "It is not by force nor by strength, but by my Spirit, says the LORD of Heaven's Armies" (Zechariah 4:6). If we hope to move forward in recovery, we must do it with God's power.

12:18 Under spiritual direction, Amasai proclaimed peace to David. How can there be peace in the midst of conflict? The Hebrew word for peace *(shalom)* conveys the idea of completeness, including physical safety and spiritual well-being. It is a peace based on the fact of God's presence, not on the surrounding circumstances. As such, this peace can be enjoyed even during warfare. No matter what personal conflicts we face, we can find peace and comfort in acknowledging daily that God is in complete control of our life.

²⁴From the tribe of Judah, there were 6,800 warriors armed with shields and spears. ²⁵From the tribe of Simeon, there were 7,100 brave warriors. ²⁶From the tribe of Levi, there were 4,600 warriors. ²⁷This included Jehoiada, leader of the family of Aaron, who had 3,700 under his command. ²⁸This also included Zadok, a brave young warrior, with 22 members of his family who were all officers. ²⁹From the tribe of Benjamin, Saul's relatives, there were 3,000 warriors. Most of the men from Benjamin had remained loyal to Saul until this time. ³⁰From the tribe of Ephraim, there were 20,800 brave warriors, each highly respected in his own clan. ³¹From the half-tribe of Manasseh west of the Jordan, 18,000 men were designated by name to help David become king. ³²From the tribe of Issachar, there were 200 leaders of the tribe with their relatives. All these men understood the signs of the times and knew the best course for Israel to take. ³³From the tribe of Zebulun, there were 50,000 skilled warriors. They were fully armed and prepared for battle and completely loyal to David. ³⁴From the tribe of Naphtali, there were 1,000 officers and 37,000 warriors armed with shields and spears. ³⁵From the tribe of Dan, there were 28,600 warriors, all prepared for battle. ³⁶From the tribe of Asher, there were 40,000 trained warriors, all prepared for battle. ³⁷From the east side of the Jordan River—where the tribes of Reuben and Gad and the half-tribe of Manasseh lived—there were 120,000 troops armed with every kind of weapon.

³⁸All these men came in battle array to Hebron with the single purpose of making David the king over all Israel. In fact, everyone in Israel agreed that David should be their king. ³⁹They feasted and drank with David for three days, for preparations had been made by their relatives for their arrival. ⁴⁰And people from as far away as Issachar, Zebulun, and Naphtali brought food on donkeys, camels, mules, and oxen. Vast supplies of flour, fig cakes, clusters of raisins, wine, olive oil, cattle, sheep, and goats were brought to the celebration. There was great joy throughout the land of Israel.

CHAPTER 13
David Attempts to Move the Ark

David consulted with all his officials, including the generals and captains of his army.* ²Then he addressed the entire assembly of Israel as follows: "If you approve and if it is the will of the LORD our God, let us send messages to all the Israelites throughout the land, including the priests and Levites in their towns and pasturelands. Let us invite them to come and join us. ³It is time to bring back the Ark of our God, for we neglected it during the reign of Saul."

⁴The whole assembly agreed to this, for the people could see it was the right thing to do. ⁵So David summoned all Israel, from the Shihor Brook of Egypt in the south all the way to the town of Lebo-hamath in the north, to join in bringing the Ark of God from Kiriath-jearim. ⁶Then David and all Israel went to Baalah of Judah (also called Kiriath-jearim) to bring back the Ark of God, which bears the name* of the LORD who is enthroned between the cherubim. ⁷They placed the Ark of God on a new cart and brought it from Abinadab's house. Uzzah and Ahio were guiding the cart. ⁸David and all Israel were celebrating before God with all their might, singing songs and playing all kinds of musical instruments—lyres, harps, tambourines, cymbals, and trumpets.

⁹But when they arrived at the threshing

13:1 Hebrew *the commanders of thousands and of hundreds.* 13:6 Or *the Ark of God, where the Name is proclaimed—the name.*

13:1-10 Here we see David doing a good thing but in the wrong way. God had prescribed the exact method of moving the Ark of the Covenant (Exodus 25:10-15; Numbers 4:5-15). David used the expedient way—and the results were catastrophic! God's clear guidelines were ignored. As we progress in recovery, we can fall into the same trap. We must be extremely careful of the means selected in the recovery process. Recovery is clearly within God's will, but we need to go about it with God's plan in mind. If we don't, we will have to suffer the consequences.

13:9-11 We must take great care as we deal with the obstacles we face along the path to recovery. We are prone to do the first thing that comes to us—almost a knee-jerk reaction. But some things are absolutely forbidden by God. Uzzah discovered this basic principle too late. In dealing with barriers to recovery, we must be careful to do things God's way; otherwise, the results could be disastrous.

floor of Nacon,* the oxen stumbled, and Uzzah reached out his hand to steady the Ark. ¹⁰Then the LORD's anger was aroused against Uzzah, and he struck him dead because he had laid his hand on the Ark. So Uzzah died there in the presence of God.

¹¹David was angry because the LORD's anger had burst out against Uzzah. He named that place Perez-uzzah (which means "to burst out against Uzzah"), as it is still called today.

¹²David was now afraid of God, and he asked, "How can I ever bring the Ark of God back into my care?" ¹³So David did not move the Ark into the City of David. Instead, he took it to the house of Obed-edom of Gath. ¹⁴The Ark of God remained there in Obed-edom's house for three months, and the LORD blessed the household of Obed-edom and everything he owned.

CHAPTER 14
David's Palace and Family
Then King Hiram of Tyre sent messengers to David, along with cedar timber, and stonemasons and carpenters to build him a palace. ²And David realized that the LORD had confirmed him as king over Israel and had greatly blessed his kingdom for the sake of his people Israel.

³Then David married more wives in Jerusalem, and they had more sons and daughters. ⁴These are the names of David's sons who were born in Jerusalem: Shammua, Shobab, Nathan, Solomon, ⁵Ibhar, Elishua, Elpelet,

⁶Nogah, Nepheg, Japhia, ⁷Elishama, Eliada,* and Eliphelet.

David Conquers the Philistines
⁸When the Philistines heard that David had been anointed king over all Israel, they mobilized all their forces to capture him. But David was told they were coming, so he marched out to meet them. ⁹The Philistines arrived and made a raid in the valley of Rephaim. ¹⁰So David asked God, "Should I go out to fight the Philistines? Will you hand them over to me?"

The LORD replied, "Yes, go ahead. I will hand them over to you."

¹¹So David and his troops went up to Baal-perazim and defeated the Philistines there. "God did it!" David exclaimed. "He used me to burst through my enemies like a raging flood!" So they named that place Baal-perazim (which means "the Lord who bursts through"). ¹²The Philistines had abandoned their gods there, so David gave orders to burn them.

¹³But after a while the Philistines returned and raided the valley again. ¹⁴And once again David asked God what to do. "Do not attack them straight on," God replied. "Instead, circle around behind and attack them near the poplar* trees. ¹⁵When you hear a sound like marching feet in the tops of the poplar trees, go out and attack! That will be the signal that God is moving ahead of you to strike down the Philistine army." ¹⁶So David did what

13:9 As in parallel text at 2 Sam 6:6; Hebrew reads *Kidon.* 14:7 Hebrew *Beeliada,* a variant spelling of Eliada; compare 3:8 and parallel text at 2 Sam 5:16. 14:14 Or *aspen,* or *balsam;* also in 14:15. The exact identification of this tree is uncertain.

13:13-14 We often experience setbacks when we attempt to accomplish something good. Such was the case here. David wanted to take the Ark to Jerusalem, but the death of Uzzah brought his project to a standstill. The good thing went undone because God's requirements were not observed. We often experience similar setbacks in recovery because we try to achieve things our own way. We forget to seek God's will in the recovery process. God is concerned not only that we reach the goal but that we go about it in the right way.

14:1-2 God gave great success to David. Everything he did had a positive outcome. Here we see one reason why God blessed him so much: God wanted to give joy to his people. By helping David, God was helping the whole nation of Israel. When God gives us success in recovery, he is probably doing it first of all because he loves us. But our success could also be the source of comfort and help to many others who suffer in similar ways. As Step Twelve advises, we need to reach out to help others as we become able. We may discover that God gave us victory so we could become a source of help and joy to others.

14:8 Enemies seem to gather against us as soon as we gain victory in any area of our life. When David became king, Israel's old enemies, the Philistines, began to attack. When we experience success, we become the target of the Devil's power, of our own fleshly desires, and even of the people close to us. Some of our loved ones may even feel threatened by the changes taking place in our life. For this reason we must never forget our vulnerability. Each day we should look to God for protection against relapse.

14:16-17 David did as God commanded, and God granted him success. Simple obedience was the key to David's victory. It is important here that we do not misunderstand and look at God as a

God commanded, and they struck down the Philistine army all the way from Gibeon to Gezer.

[17]So David's fame spread everywhere, and the LORD caused all the nations to fear David.

CHAPTER 15
Preparing to Move the Ark
David now built several buildings for himself in the City of David. He also prepared a place for the Ark of God and set up a special tent for it. [2]Then he commanded, "No one except the Levites may carry the Ark of God. The LORD has chosen them to carry the Ark of the LORD and to serve him forever."

[3]Then David summoned all Israel to Jerusalem to bring the Ark of the LORD to the place he had prepared for it. [4]This is the number of the descendants of Aaron (the priests) and the Levites who were called together:

[5]From the clan of Kohath, 120, with Uriel as their leader.

[6]From the clan of Merari, 220, with Asaiah as their leader.

[7]From the clan of Gershon,* 130, with Joel as their leader.

[8]From the descendants of Elizaphan, 200, with Shemaiah as their leader.

[9]From the descendants of Hebron, 80, with Eliel as their leader.

[10]From the descendants of Uzziel, 112, with Amminadab as their leader.

[11]Then David summoned the priests, Zadok and Abiathar, and these Levite leaders: Uriel, Asaiah, Joel, Shemaiah, Eliel, and Amminadab. [12]He said to them, "You are the leaders of the Levite families. You must purify yourselves and all your fellow Levites, so you can bring the Ark of the LORD, the God of Israel, to the place I have prepared for it. [13]Because you

Levites did not carry the Ark the first time, the anger of the LORD our God burst out against us. We failed to ask God how to move it properly." [14]So the priests and the Levites purified themselves in order to bring the Ark of the LORD, the God of Israel, to Jerusalem. [15]Then the Levites carried the Ark of God on their shoulders with its carrying poles, just as the LORD had instructed Moses.

[16]David also ordered the Levite leaders to appoint a choir of Levites who were singers and musicians to sing joyful songs to the accompaniment of harps, lyres, and cymbals. [17]So the Levites appointed Heman son of Joel along with his fellow Levites: Asaph son of Berekiah, and Ethan son of Kushaiah from the clan of Merari. [18]The following men were chosen as their assistants: Zechariah, Jaaziel,* Shemiramoth, Jehiel, Unni, Eliab, Benaiah, Maaseiah, Mattithiah, Eliphelehu, Mikneiah, and the gatekeepers—Obed-edom and Jeiel.

[19]The musicians Heman, Asaph, and Ethan were chosen to sound the bronze cymbals. [20]Zechariah, Aziel, Shemiramoth, Jehiel, Unni, Eliab, Maaseiah, and Benaiah were chosen to play the harps.* [21]Mattithiah, Eliphelehu, Mikneiah, Obed-edom, Jeiel, and Azaziah were chosen to play the lyres.* [22]Kenaniah, the head Levite, was chosen as the choir leader because of his skill.

[23]Berekiah and Elkanah were chosen to guard* the Ark. [24]Shebaniah, Joshaphat, Nethanel, Amasai, Zechariah, Benaiah, and Eliezer—all of whom were priests—were chosen to blow the trumpets as they marched in front of the Ark of God. Obed-edom and Jehiah were chosen to guard the Ark.

Moving the Ark to Jerusalem
[25]Then David and the elders of Israel and the generals of the army* went to the house of Obed-edom to bring the Ark of the LORD's

---

15:7 Hebrew *Gershom,* a variant spelling of Gershon. **15:18** As in several Hebrew manuscripts and Greek version (see also parallel lists in 15:20; 16:5); Masoretic Text reads *Zechariah ben Jaaziel.* **15:20** Hebrew adds *according to Alamoth,* which is probably a musical term. The meaning of the Hebrew is uncertain. **15:21** Hebrew adds *according to the Sheminith,* which is probably a musical term. The meaning of the Hebrew is uncertain. **15:23** Hebrew *chosen as gatekeepers for;* also in 15:24. **15:25** Hebrew *the commanders of thousands.*

"push-button" deity who will act or react based on a set formula. Some teach that if we have enough faith or if we follow certain instructions, we will experience an immediate cure. This is not always true. Sometimes our obedience will bring new and difficult circumstances. When hard times fall repeatedly upon us, we need not fear that God has rejected us. Sometimes he uses such situations to work his will in us. We can be sure that God will always stand with us, even if he doesn't always give us an immediate cure.

15:25 What happens when victory is finally achieved? What are the emotions? What are the reactions? This verse says that these people did their work "with a great celebration." The joy of accomplishing God's will is one of the sweetest joys of all. Celebration is an essential element in the life of a believer. Even as we go through the difficult and often painful process of recovery, we can and should celebrate God's love and faithfulness to us.

Covenant up to Jerusalem with a great celebration. ²⁶And because God was clearly helping the Levites as they carried the Ark of the LORD's Covenant, they sacrificed seven bulls and seven rams.

²⁷David was dressed in a robe of fine linen, as were all the Levites who carried the Ark, and also the singers, and Kenaniah the choir leader. David was also wearing a priestly garment.* ²⁸So all Israel brought up the Ark of the LORD's Covenant with shouts of joy, the blowing of rams' horns and trumpets, the crashing of cymbals, and loud playing on harps and lyres.

²⁹But as the Ark of the LORD's Covenant entered the City of David, Michal, the daughter of Saul, looked down from her window. When she saw King David skipping about and laughing with joy, she was filled with contempt for him.

CHAPTER 16

They brought the Ark of God and placed it inside the special tent David had prepared for it. And they presented burnt offerings and peace offerings to God. ²When he had finished his sacrifices, David blessed the people in the name of the LORD. ³Then he gave to every man and woman in all Israel a loaf of bread, a cake of dates,* and a cake of raisins.

⁴David appointed the following Levites to lead the people in worship before the Ark of the LORD—to invoke his blessings, to give thanks, and to praise the LORD, the God of Israel. ⁵Asaph, the leader of this group, sounded the cymbals. Second to him was Zechariah, followed by Jeiel, Shemiramoth, Jehiel, Mattithiah, Eliab, Benaiah, Obed-edom, and Jeiel. They played the harps and lyres. ⁶The priests, Benaiah and Jahaziel, played the trumpets regularly before the Ark of God's Covenant.

David's Song of Praise

⁷On that day David gave to Asaph and his fellow Levites this song of thanksgiving to the LORD:

⁸ Give thanks to the LORD and proclaim his greatness.
   Let the whole world know what he has done.
⁹ Sing to him; yes, sing his praises.
   Tell everyone about his wonderful deeds.
¹⁰ Exult in his holy name;
   rejoice, you who worship the LORD.
¹¹ Search for the LORD and for his strength;
   continually seek him.
¹² Remember the wonders he has performed,
   his miracles, and the rulings he has given,
¹³ you children of his servant Israel,
   you descendants of Jacob, his chosen ones.

¹⁴ He is the LORD our God.
   His justice is seen throughout the land.

15:27 Hebrew *a linen ephod.* 16:3 Or *a portion of meat.* The meaning of the Hebrew is uncertain.

15:27-29 In modern America there seems to be the ingrained notion that people, especially men, should hide their true emotions. Many Christians support this idea, believing they should be stoic and not show their emotions. Contrary to this popular view, God's Word insists that we be honest about our feelings. David displayed an intense emotional outburst, "skipping about and laughing with joy." We should be willing to display our feelings. Tears of sorrow or joy should never be totally absent from our life experiences.

15:29 Even though God has given us emotions and encourages us to express them honestly, there will always be those who disapprove when feelings are demonstrated. When David's wife Michal saw him in the emotional celebration of his victory, she "was filled with contempt." It is true that some expressions of emotion are inappropriate. But when we discover appropriate avenues of expression, we should not hesitate to express our feelings.

16:1-3 When God's will is accomplished, celebration should be an automatic response. We should celebrate each victory we have, no matter how small it may be. When David finally brought the Ark to Jerusalem, he threw a great celebration and blessed the people in the name of the Lord. The whole city enjoyed a happy time of worship, and David brought out refreshments for everyone. Appropriate celebrations along the way will affirm our progress and encourage us to move forward once again.

16:8-13 In times of victory or defeat, recovery or relapse, God remains the same. Our response to him in all circumstances should include thanksgiving and praise. There is never an inappropriate time to seek God; indeed, verse 11 enjoins us to continually seek his strength. This imperative must be observed by each of us in recovery.

16:14-22 Sometimes we are tempted to think that God has somehow lost control of things. We are not the only ones who have felt this way. At times during Israel's history God seemed far

15 Remember his covenant forever—
    the commitment he made to a
    thousand generations.
16 This is the covenant he made with
    Abraham
    and the oath he swore to Isaac.
17 He confirmed it to Jacob as a decree,
    and to the people of Israel as a
    never-ending covenant:
18 "I will give you the land of Canaan
    as your special possession."

19 He said this when you were few in
    number,
    a tiny group of strangers in Canaan.
20 They wandered from nation to nation,
    from one kingdom to another.
21 Yet he did not let anyone oppress them.
    He warned kings on their behalf:
22 "Do not touch my chosen people,
    and do not hurt my prophets."

23 Let the whole earth sing to the LORD!
    Each day proclaim the good news that
    he saves.
24 Publish his glorious deeds among the
    nations.
    Tell everyone about the amazing things
    he does.
25 Great is the LORD! He is most worthy of
    praise!
    He is to be feared above all gods.
26 The gods of other nations are mere
    idols,
    but the LORD made the heavens!
27 Honor and majesty surround him;
    strength and joy fill his dwelling.

28 O nations of the world, recognize the
    LORD,
    recognize that the LORD is glorious and
    strong.
29 Give to the LORD the glory he deserves!
    Bring your offering and come into his
    presence.
    Worship the LORD in all his holy splendor.
30 Let all the earth tremble before him.
    The world stands firm and cannot be
    shaken.

31 Let the heavens be glad, and the earth
    rejoice!

Tell all the nations, "The LORD
    reigns!"
32 Let the sea and everything in it shout his
    praise!
    Let the fields and their crops burst out
    with joy!
33 Let the trees of the forest sing for joy
    before the LORD,
    for he is coming to judge the earth.

34 Give thanks to the LORD, for he is good!
    His faithful love endures forever.
35 Cry out, "Save us, O God of our
    salvation!
    Gather and rescue us from among
    the nations,
    so we can thank your holy name
    and rejoice and praise you."

36 Praise the LORD, the God of Israel,
    who lives from everlasting to
    everlasting!

And all the people shouted "Amen!" and
praised the LORD.

Worship at Jerusalem and Gibeon

37 David arranged for Asaph and his fellow Levites to serve regularly before the Ark of the LORD's Covenant, doing whatever needed to be done each day. 38 This group included Obed-edom (son of Jeduthun), Hosah, and sixty-eight other Levites as gatekeepers.

39 Meanwhile, David stationed Zadok the priest and his fellow priests at the Tabernacle of the LORD at the place of worship in Gibeon, where they continued to minister before the LORD. 40 They sacrificed the regular burnt offerings to the LORD each morning and evening on the altar set aside for that purpose, obeying everything written in the Law of the LORD, as he had commanded Israel. 41 David also appointed Heman, Jeduthun, and the others chosen by name to give thanks to the LORD, for "his faithful love endures forever." 42 They used their trumpets, cymbals, and other instruments to accompany their songs of praise to God.* And the sons of Jeduthun were appointed as gatekeepers.

43 Then all the people returned to their

16:42 Or *to accompany the sacred music;* or *to accompany singing to God.*

away; God's plan for his people must have seemed obscure and distant. But as time passed it became clear that God had been with Israel the whole time—even as they wandered in the wilderness. God used the difficult times to work out his plan. Sometimes crises and emergencies occur that seem beyond God's sovereign control. We can be sure that even in such times God is there and in control! We must learn to rest in our knowledge of God's goodness and love.

homes, and David turned and went home to bless his own family.

CHAPTER 17
The LORD's Covenant Promise to David

When David was settled in his palace, he summoned Nathan the prophet. "Look," David said, "I am living in a beautiful cedar palace,* but the Ark of the LORD's Covenant is out there under a tent!"

[2]Nathan replied to David, "Do whatever you have in mind, for God is with you."

[3]But that same night God said to Nathan,

[4]"Go and tell my servant David, 'This is what the LORD has declared: You are not the one to build a house for me to live in. [5]I have never lived in a house, from the day I brought the Israelites out of Egypt until this very day. My home has always been a tent, moving from one place to another in a Tabernacle. [6]Yet no matter where I have gone with the Israelites, I have never once complained to Israel's leaders, the shepherds of my people. I have never asked them, "Why haven't you built me a beautiful cedar house?"'

[7]"Now go and say to my servant David, 'This is what the LORD of Heaven's Armies has declared: I took you from tending sheep in the pasture and selected you to be the leader of my people Israel. [8]I have been with you wherever you have gone, and I have destroyed all your enemies before your eyes. Now I will make your name as famous as anyone who has ever lived on the earth! [9]And I will provide a homeland for my people Israel, planting them in a secure place where they will never be disturbed. Evil nations won't oppress them as they've done in the past, [10]starting from the time I appointed judges to rule my people Israel. And I will defeat all your enemies.

"'Furthermore, I declare that the LORD will build a house for you—a dynasty of kings! [11]For when you die and join your ancestors, I will raise up one of your descendants, one of your sons, and I will make his kingdom strong. [12]He is the one who will build a house—a temple—for me. And I will secure his throne forever. [13]I will be his father, and he will be my son. I will never take my favor from him as I took it from the one who ruled before you. [14]I will confirm him as king over my house and my kingdom for all time, and his throne will be secure forever.'"

[15]So Nathan went back to David and told him everything the LORD had said in this vision.

David's Prayer of Thanks

[16]Then King David went in and sat before the LORD and prayed,

"Who am I, O LORD God, and what is my family, that you have brought me this far? [17]And now, O God, in addition to everything else, you speak of giving your servant a lasting dynasty! You speak as though I were someone very great,* O LORD God!

[18]"What more can I say to you about the way you have honored me? You know what your servant is really like. [19]For the sake of your servant, O LORD,

17:1 Hebrew *a house of cedar.* 17:17 The meaning of the Hebrew is uncertain.

17:1-2 Have you ever had a great idea? In these verses, David had a wonderful idea: He wanted to build God a temple to house the Ark. David's idea to build a temple was a good one, but, like all good ideas, it had to pass a test. It needed to conform to God's will and timing. Even our best ideas or plans will fail if we act counter to God's program for us. We must learn to seek God's will and submit to his plan if we desire to succeed in recovery.

17:3-4 It is easy to become enamored with our own plans. We must remember, however, that God has veto power over even our best ideas. Nathan, who had approved the idea of a temple earlier, discovered that the timing was wrong. We tend to believe that if we desire a good thing, God's timing for it is now! Sometimes in recovery, progress may not come as quickly or smoothly as we would like it to. But we must learn that the only successful recovery program is one submitted to God's control and timing.

17:9-13 As always, God had a better idea. David wanted to build God a house—that was a good idea. But God assigned that job to Solomon, David's son. More important, God promised to build a "house" for David—a dynasty that would reign forever. From that dynasty came David's greater son, Jesus Christ, who provides salvation to all who are willing to receive it! This promise to David has become a promise to all who need to recover from the powerful effects of sin.

and according to your will, you have done all these great things and have made them known.

20"O LORD, there is no one like you. We have never even heard of another God like you! 21What other nation on earth is like your people Israel? What other nation, O God, have you redeemed from slavery to be your own people? You made a great name for yourself when you redeemed your people from Egypt. You performed awesome miracles and drove out the nations that stood in their way. 22You chose Israel to be your very own people forever, and you, O LORD, became their God.

23"And now, O LORD, I am your servant; do as you have promised concerning me and my family. May it be a promise that will last forever. 24And may your name be established and honored forever so that everyone will say, 'The LORD of Heaven's Armies, the God of Israel, is Israel's God!' And may the house of your servant David continue before you forever.

25"O my God, I have been bold enough to pray to you because you have revealed to your servant that you will build a house for him—a dynasty of kings! 26For you are God, O LORD. And you have promised these good things to your servant. 27And now, it has pleased you to bless the house of your servant, so that it will continue forever before you. For when you grant a blessing, O LORD, it is an eternal blessing!"

CHAPTER 18
David's Military Victories

After this, David defeated and subdued the Philistines by conquering Gath and its surrounding towns. 2David also conquered the land of Moab, and the Moabites who were spared became David's subjects and paid him tribute money.

3David also destroyed the forces of Hadadezer, king of Zobah, as far as Hamath,* when Hadadezer marched out to strengthen his control along the Euphrates River. 4David captured 1,000 chariots, 7,000 charioteers, and 20,000 foot soldiers. He crippled all the chariot horses except enough for 100 chariots.

5When Arameans from Damascus arrived to help King Hadadezer, David killed 22,000 of them. 6Then he placed several army garrisons* in Damascus, the Aramean capital, and the Arameans became David's subjects and paid him tribute money. So the LORD made David victorious wherever he went.

7David brought the gold shields of Hadadezer's officers to Jerusalem, 8along with a large amount of bronze from Hadadezer's towns of Tebah* and Cun. Later Solomon melted the bronze and molded it into the great bronze basin called the Sea, the pillars, and the various bronze articles used at the Temple.

9When King Toi* of Hamath heard that David had destroyed the entire army of King Hadadezer of Zobah, 10he sent his son Joram* to congratulate King David for his successful campaign. Hadadezer and Toi had been enemies and were often at war. Joram presented David with many gifts of gold, silver, and bronze.

11King David dedicated all these gifts to the LORD, along with the silver and gold he had taken from the other nations—from Edom, Moab, Ammon, Philistia, and Amalek.

12Abishai son of Zeruiah destroyed 18,000 Edomites in the Valley of Salt. 13He placed army garrisons in Edom, and all the Edomites became David's subjects. In fact, the LORD made David victorious wherever he went.

14So David reigned over all Israel and did what was just and right for all his people. 15Joab son of Zeruiah was commander of the army. Jehoshaphat son of Ahilud was the royal historian. 16Zadok son of Ahitub and

18:3 The meaning of the Hebrew is uncertain. 18:6 As in Greek version and Latin Vulgate (see also 2 Sam 8:6); Hebrew lacks *several army garrisons*. 18:8 Hebrew reads *Tibhath,* a variant spelling of Tebah; compare parallel text at 2 Sam 8:8. 18:9 As in parallel text at 2 Sam 8:9; Hebrew reads *Tou;* also in 18:10. 18:10 As in parallel text at 2 Sam 8:10; Hebrew reads *Hadoram,* a variant spelling of Joram.

18:4 Why did David cripple the horses? God had commanded that Israel's kings never build up large stables of horses (Deuteronomy 17:16). God wanted Israel to depend on him for protection, not on great armies of chariots and horses. This is an important principle for us to keep in mind. Only God can truly protect us and give us the power to overcome our dependencies and compulsions. We must be sure that as we rely on human systems to support our recovery, we don't forget to seek God and lean on him. Our personal resources are never sufficient for success; we must learn to depend on God's power.

Ahimelech* son of Abiathar were the priests. Seraiah* was the court secretary. [17]Benaiah son of Jehoiada was captain of the king's bodyguard.* And David's sons served as the king's chief assistants.

CHAPTER 19
David Defeats the Ammonites
Some time after this, King Nahash of the Ammonites died, and his son Hanun* became king. [2]David said, "I am going to show loyalty to Hanun because his father, Nahash, was always loyal to me." So David sent messengers to express sympathy to Hanun about his father's death.

But when David's ambassadors arrived in the land of Ammon, [3]the Ammonite commanders said to Hanun, "Do you really think these men are coming here to honor your father? No! David has sent them to spy out the land so they can come in and conquer it!" [4]So Hanun seized David's ambassadors and shaved them, cut off their robes at the buttocks, and sent them back to David in shame.

[5]When David heard what had happened to the men, he sent messengers to tell them, "Stay at Jericho until your beards grow out, and then come back." For they felt deep shame because of their appearance.

[6]When the people of Ammon realized how seriously they had angered David, Hanun and the Ammonites sent 75,000 pounds* of silver to hire chariots and charioteers from Aram-naharaim, Aram-maacah, and Zobah. [7]They also hired 32,000 chariots and secured the support of the king of Maacah and his army. These forces camped at Medeba, where they were joined by the Ammonite troops that Hanun had recruited from his own towns. [8]When David heard about this, he sent Joab and all his warriors to fight them. [9]The Ammonite troops came out and drew up their battle lines at the entrance of the city, while the other kings positioned themselves to fight in the open fields.

[10]When Joab saw that he would have to fight on both the front and the rear, he chose some of Israel's elite troops and placed them under his personal command to fight the Arameans in the fields. [11]He left the rest of the army under the command of his brother Abishai, who was to attack the Ammonites. [12]"If the Arameans are too strong for me, then come over and help me," Joab told his brother. "And if the Ammonites are too strong for you, I will help you. [13]Be courageous! Let us fight bravely for our people and the cities of our God. May the LORD's will be done."

[14]When Joab and his troops attacked, the Arameans began to run away. [15]And when the Ammonites saw the Arameans running, they also ran from Abishai and retreated into the city. Then Joab returned to Jerusalem.

[16]The Arameans now realized that they were no match for Israel, so they sent messengers and summoned additional Aramean troops from the other side of the Euphrates River.* These troops were under the command of Shobach,* the commander of Hadadezer's forces.

[17]When David heard what was happening, he mobilized all Israel, crossed the Jordan

18:16a As in some Hebrew manuscripts, Syriac version, and Latin Vulgate (see also 2 Sam 8:17); most Hebrew manuscripts read *Abimelech.* 18:16b As in parallel text at 2 Sam 8:17; Hebrew reads *Shavsha.* 18:17 Hebrew *of the Kerethites and Pelethites.* 19:1 As in parallel text at 2 Sam 10:1; Hebrew lacks *Hanun.* 19:6 Hebrew *1,000 talents* [34,000 kilograms]. 19:16a Hebrew *the river.* 19:16b As in parallel text at 2 Sam 10:16; Hebrew reads *Shophach;* also in 19:18.

19:1-4 The distrust of Hanun's men caused them to misread David's friendly overtures. So instead of building a strong relationship with Israel, they created a destructive one. We often make the same mistake, especially if we have been disappointed by the people we love. If we are lied to, we learn to distrust others. This may cause us to cut off even the healthy relationships offered to us. We must learn how to discern between the people we can trust and those we can't. Honest relationships are extremely important; we cannot afford to alienate the people who will support us in the recovery process.

19:5 In this very delicate situation, David showed deep sensitivity to the embarrassment of his ambassadors. He gave them time to recover their dignity before returning home. Surely there is a lesson here for all of us. Like David, we need to exhibit sensitivity to others as they deal with embarrassing issues. This is part of learning to support others in recovery.

19:13 Joab's words are worth remembering. He called his men to act, but he also recognized that ultimately God was in control. In recovery we need to keep the same tension before us. We are responsible to act. We must strike out boldly to seek recovery. Yet we are ultimately powerless and in desperate need of God's help. We need to continually leave things in God's hands and seek his will. As we face the trials of recovery, we can rest assured of God's power to help, but we also need to take responsibility for our situations and act accordingly.

River, and positioned his troops in battle formation. Then David engaged the Arameans in battle, and they fought against him. [18]But again the Arameans fled from the Israelites. This time David's forces killed 7,000 charioteers and 40,000 foot soldiers, including Shobach, the commander of their army. [19]When Hadadezer's allies saw that they had been defeated by Israel, they surrendered to David and became his subjects. After that, the Arameans were no longer willing to help the Ammonites.

CHAPTER 20
David Captures Rabbah
In the spring of the year,* when kings normally go out to war, Joab led the Israelite army in successful attacks against the land of the Ammonites. In the process he laid siege to the city of Rabbah, attacking and destroying it. However, David stayed behind in Jerusalem.

[2]Then David went to Rabbah and removed the crown from the king's head,* and it was placed on his own head. The crown was made of gold and set with gems, and he found that it weighed seventy-five pounds.* David took a vast amount of plunder from the city. [3]He also made slaves of the people of Rabbah and forced them to labor with saws, iron picks, and iron axes.* That is how David dealt with the people of all the Ammonite towns. Then David and all the army returned to Jerusalem.

Battles against Philistine Giants
[4]After this, war broke out with the Philistines at Gezer. As they fought, Sibbecai from Hushah killed Saph,* a descendant of the giants,* and so the Philistines were subdued.

[5]During another battle with the Philistines, Elhanan son of Jair killed Lahmi, the brother of Goliath of Gath. The handle of Lahmi's spear was as thick as a weaver's beam!

[6]In another battle with the Philistines at Gath, they encountered a huge man with six fingers on each hand and six toes on each foot, twenty-four in all, who was also a descendant of the giants. [7]But when he defied and taunted Israel, he was killed by Jonathan, the son of David's brother Shimea.

[8]These Philistines were descendants of the giants of Gath, but David and his warriors killed them.

CHAPTER 21
David Takes a Census
Satan rose up against Israel and caused David to take a census of the people of Israel. [2]So David said to Joab and the commanders of the army, "Take a census of all the people of Israel—from Beersheba in the south to Dan in the north—and bring me a report so I may know how many there are."

[3]But Joab replied, "May the LORD increase the number of his people a hundred times over! But why, my lord the king, do you want to do this? Are they not all your servants? Why must you cause Israel to sin?"

[4]But the king insisted that they take the census, so Joab traveled throughout all Israel to count the people. Then he returned to Jerusalem [5]and reported the number of people to David. There were 1,100,000 warriors in all Israel who could handle a sword, and 470,000 in Judah. [6]But Joab did not include the tribes of Levi and Benjamin in the census because he was so distressed at what the king had made him do.

20:1 Hebrew *At the turn of the year.* The first day of the year in the ancient Hebrew lunar calendar occurred in March or April. 20:2a Or *from the head of Milcom* (as in Greek version and Latin Vulgate). Milcom, also called Molech, was the god of the Ammonites. 20:2b Hebrew *1 talent* [34 kilograms]. 20:3 As in parallel text at 2 Sam 12:31; Hebrew reads *and cut them with saws, iron picks, and saws.* 20:4a As in parallel text at 2 Sam 21:18; Hebrew reads *Sippai.* 20:4b Hebrew *descendant of the Rephaites;* also in 20:6, 8.

20:1-8 David understood who his enemies were, and he acted accordingly. With God's help he overcame each one in turn. We often make the mistake of allowing enemies into our life. We welcome people and activities dangerous to our health and well-being and treat them as our friends. We need to learn from David. In spiritual battle, we need to identify our enemies and act accordingly.

21:1 As we read of David's life, we would probably identify David's greatest sins as adultery, betrayal, and murder. But God's evaluation of David's greatest sin seems somewhat different. Although God punished David for his acts of adultery and murder, the punishment David suffered for his census was far greater and more widespread. What was wrong with counting the people? David did so to assess their human strength. He put his trust in Israel's numbers and the army it could muster. He had forgotten that with God's help, they needed no army at all to achieve victory. We often make the same mistake. We seek to do things in our own strength, rather than depend on God's. Seeking recovery through human strength alone will only end in disaster.

Judgment for David's Sin

[7]God was very displeased with the census, and he punished Israel for it. [8]Then David said to God, "I have sinned greatly by taking this census. Please forgive my guilt for doing this foolish thing."

[9]Then the LORD spoke to Gad, David's seer. This was the message: [10]"Go and say to David, 'This is what the LORD says: I will give you three choices. Choose one of these punishments, and I will inflict it on you.'"

[11]So Gad came to David and said, "These are the choices the LORD has given you. [12]You may choose three years of famine, three months of destruction by the sword of your enemies, or three days of severe plague as the angel of the LORD brings devastation throughout the land of Israel. Decide what answer I should give the LORD who sent me."

[13]"I'm in a desperate situation!" David replied to Gad. "But let me fall into the hands of the LORD, for his mercy is very great. Do not let me fall into human hands."

[14]So the LORD sent a plague upon Israel, and 70,000 people died as a result. [15]And God sent an angel to destroy Jerusalem. But just as the angel was preparing to destroy it, the LORD relented and said to the death angel, "Stop! That is enough!" At that moment the angel of the LORD was standing by the threshing floor of Araunah* the Jebusite.

[16]David looked up and saw the angel of the LORD standing between heaven and earth with his sword drawn, reaching out over Jerusalem. So David and the leaders of Israel put on burlap to show their deep distress and fell face down on the ground. [17]And David said to God, "I am the one who called for the census! I am the one who has sinned and done wrong! But these people are as innocent as sheep—what have they done? O LORD my God, let your anger fall against me and my family, but do not destroy your people."

David Builds an Altar

[18]Then the angel of the LORD told Gad to instruct David to go up and build an altar to the LORD on the threshing floor of Araunah the Jebusite. [19]So David went up to do what the LORD had commanded him through Gad. [20]Araunah, who was busy threshing wheat at the time, turned and saw the angel there. His four sons, who were with him, ran away and hid. [21]When Araunah saw David approaching, he left his threshing floor and bowed before David with his face to the ground.

[22]David said to Araunah, "Let me buy this threshing floor from you at its full price. Then I will build an altar to the LORD there, so that he will stop the plague."

[23]"Take it, my lord the king, and use it as you wish," Araunah said to David. "I will give the oxen for the burnt offerings, and the threshing boards for wood to build a fire on the altar, and the wheat for the grain offering. I will give it all to you."

[24]But King David replied to Araunah, "No, I insist on buying it for the full price. I will not take what is yours and give it to the LORD. I will not present burnt offerings that have cost me nothing!" [25]So David gave Araunah 600 pieces of gold* in payment for the threshing floor.

[26]David built an altar there to the LORD and sacrificed burnt offerings and peace offerings. And when David prayed, the LORD answered him by sending fire from heaven to burn up the offering on the altar. [27]Then the LORD spoke to the angel, who put the sword back into its sheath.

[28]When David saw that the LORD had answered his prayer, he offered sacrifices there at Araunah's threshing floor. [29]At that time the Tabernacle of the LORD and the altar of burnt offering that Moses had made in the wilderness were located at the place of worship in Gibeon. [30]But David was not able to

---

21:15 As in parallel text at 2 Sam 24:16; Hebrew reads *Ornan*, another name for Araunah; also in 21:18-28.
21:25 Hebrew *600 shekels of gold*, about 15 pounds or 6.8 kilograms in weight.

21:9-13 Have you ever been trapped by a dilemma? All the options open to you seem to be bad. David faced a dilemma where all three choices would bring terrible consequences. God offered him (1) three years of famine, (2) three months of destruction by Israel's enemies, or (3) three days of a deadly plague. David chose the plague, and even though 70,000 men died, he had made the best choice. May God deliver us from situations where all of the options have severe consequences!

21:17 It is a terrible thing, but very often our personal sins have consequences in the lives of other people. David was aware that the people of his kingdom would suffer for his personal sin. It is heartrending to read David's admission of guilt as he accepted full responsibility for his sin. Then he prayed diligently for the rescue of his people. When people close to us suffer because of our sins, we should pray that God would give them special grace to overcome the consequences of our failures.

go there to inquire of God, because he was terrified by the drawn sword of the angel of the LORD.

CHAPTER 22

Then David said, "This will be the location for the Temple of the LORD God and the place of the altar for Israel's burnt offerings!"

Preparations for the Temple

²So David gave orders to call together the foreigners living in Israel, and he assigned them the task of preparing finished stone for building the Temple of God. ³David provided large amounts of iron for the nails that would be needed for the doors in the gates and for the clamps, and he gave more bronze than could be weighed. ⁴He also provided innumerable cedar logs, for the men of Tyre and Sidon had brought vast amounts of cedar to David.

⁵David said, "My son Solomon is still young and inexperienced. And since the Temple to be built for the LORD must be a magnificent structure, famous and glorious throughout the world, I will begin making preparations for it now." So David collected vast amounts of building materials before his death.

⁶Then David sent for his son Solomon and instructed him to build a Temple for the LORD, the God of Israel. ⁷"My son, I wanted to build a Temple to honor the name of the LORD my God," David told him. ⁸"But the LORD said to me, 'You have killed many men in the battles you have fought. And since you have shed so much blood in my sight, you will not be the one to build a Temple to honor my name. ⁹But you will have a son who will be a man of peace. I will give him peace with his enemies in all the surrounding lands. His name will be Solomon,* and I will give peace and quiet to Israel during his reign. ¹⁰He is the one who will build a Temple to honor my name. He will be my son, and I will be his father. And I will secure the throne of his kingdom over Israel forever.'

¹¹"Now, my son, may the LORD be with you and give you success as you follow his directions in building the Temple of the LORD your God. ¹²And may the LORD give you wisdom and understanding, that you may obey the Law of the LORD your God as you rule over Israel. ¹³For you will be successful if you carefully obey the decrees and regulations that the LORD gave to Israel through Moses. Be strong and courageous; do not be afraid or lose heart!

¹⁴"I have worked hard to provide materials for building the Temple of the LORD—nearly 4,000 tons of gold, 40,000 tons of silver,* and so much iron and bronze that it cannot be weighed. I have also gathered timber and stone for the walls, though you may need to add more. ¹⁵You have a large number of skilled stonemasons and carpenters and craftsmen of every kind. ¹⁶You have expert goldsmiths and silversmiths and workers of bronze and iron. Now begin the work, and may the LORD be with you!"

¹⁷Then David ordered all the leaders of Israel to assist Solomon in this project. ¹⁸"The LORD your God is with you," he declared. "He has given you peace with the surrounding nations. He has handed them over to me, and they are now subject to the LORD and his people. ¹⁹Now seek the LORD your God with all your heart and soul. Build the sanctuary of the LORD God so that you can bring the Ark of the LORD's Covenant and the holy vessels of God into the Temple built to honor the LORD's name."

CHAPTER 23
Duties of the Levites

When David was an old man, he appointed his son Solomon to be king over Israel. ²David summoned all the leaders of Israel, together with the priests and Levites. ³All the Levites who were thirty years old or older were counted, and the total came to 38,000. ⁴Then David said, "From all the Levites,

---

22:9 *Solomon* sounds like and is probably derived from the Hebrew word for "peace." **22:14** Hebrew *100,000 talents* [3,400 metric tons] *of gold, 1,000,000 talents* [34,000 metric tons] *of silver.*

22:1-5 Although David would never build the Temple, he collected numerous materials for the project. A whole chapter is dedicated to David's preparations for building the Temple. What does this have to do with recovery? Any rebuilding project needs careful planning and the necessary materials and resources to get the job done. We need to assess our needs and seek the help and resources that will support us in the recovery process.

22:6-19 We are told of some of the spiritual preparations necessary for building the Temple. Material preparations are essential for any building or rebuilding project, but the spiritual preparations are even more important. Just as David helped Solomon define the goals and procedures for building the Temple, so must we define these same elements for our recovery program.

24,000 will supervise the work at the Temple of the LORD. Another 6,000 will serve as officials and judges. [5]Another 4,000 will work as gatekeepers, and 4,000 will praise the LORD with the musical instruments I have made." [6]Then David divided the Levites into divisions named after the clans descended from the three sons of Levi—Gershon, Kohath, and Merari.

The Gershonites

[7]The Gershonite family units were defined by their lines of descent from Libni* and Shimei, the sons of Gershon. [8]Three of the descendants of Libni were Jehiel (the family leader), Zetham, and Joel. [9]These were the leaders of the family of Libni.

Three of the descendants of Shimei were Shelomoth, Haziel, and Haran. [10]Four other descendants of Shimei were Jahath, Ziza,* Jeush, and Beriah. [11]Jahath was the family leader, and Ziza was next. Jeush and Beriah were counted as a single family because neither had many sons.

The Kohathites

[12]Four of the descendants of Kohath were Amram, Izhar, Hebron, and Uzziel. [13]The sons of Amram were Aaron and Moses. Aaron and his descendants were set apart to dedicate the most holy things, to offer sacrifices in the LORD's presence, to serve the LORD, and to pronounce blessings in his name forever.

[14]As for Moses, the man of God, his sons were included with the tribe of Levi. [15]The sons of Moses were Gershom and Eliezer. [16]The descendants of Gershom included Shebuel, the family leader. [17]Eliezer had only one son, Rehabiah, the family leader. Rehabiah had numerous descendants.

[18]The descendants of Izhar included Shelomith, the family leader.

[19]The descendants of Hebron included Jeriah (the family leader), Amariah (the second), Jahaziel (the third), and Jekameam (the fourth). [20]The descendants of Uzziel included Micah (the family leader) and Isshiah (the second).

The Merarites

[21]The descendants of Merari included Mahli and Mushi.

The sons of Mahli were Eleazar and Kish. [22]Eleazar died with no sons, only daughters. His daughters married their cousins, the sons of Kish. [23]Three of the descendants of Mushi were Mahli, Eder, and Jerimoth.

[24]These were the descendants of Levi by clans, the leaders of their family groups, registered carefully by name. Each had to be twenty years old or older to qualify for service in the house of the LORD. [25]For David said, "The LORD, the God of Israel, has given us peace, and he will always live in Jerusalem. [26]Now the Levites will no longer need to carry the Tabernacle and its furnishings from place to place." [27]In accordance with David's

23:7 Hebrew *Ladan* (also in 23:8, 9), a variant spelling of Libni; compare 6:17. 23:10 As in Greek version and Latin Vulgate (see also 23:11); Hebrew reads *Zina*.

23:1-2 At a certain point in his life, David stepped down from his position of responsibility. Since many of us derive our sense of self-worth from our activities, this is often a difficult thing to do. But none of us can take responsibility for everything. There are some matters that we are not capable of handling. We may need to relinquish some of our burdens to others. This is an important issue in recovery. We need to determine our limits and then stand by them. Being "responsible" to the point of imbalance can be just as destructive as being irresponsible.

23:3-23 The Levites were called to serve in God's Temple, and here the program for their service is outlined. In order for the Levites to work effectively, a detailed system had to be set up. Duties had to be defined and assigned. In recovery we also need to define our relationships and responsibilities in ways that are workable and fair. When expectations are clear, our relationships will run more smoothly. Understanding our role in our family or organizations is essential to make sense of our life.

23:24-31 This is a new job description for Levites. Some of the traditional Levitical tasks were no longer necessary. They no longer needed to transport the Tabernacle. To deal with changes in the times, the role of the Levites was adjusted. Such changes were still under God's control. The role we play in our relationships also changes with time. We may have been dysfunctional in our marriage and family; now that we are in recovery we will experience some changes. We need to be willing to assess our former role in relationships and make the changes needed to function effectively where God places us.

final instructions, all the Levites twenty years old or older were registered for service. [28]The work of the Levites was to assist the priests, the descendants of Aaron, as they served at the house of the LORD. They also took care of the courtyards and side rooms, helped perform the ceremonies of purification, and served in many other ways in the house of God. [29]They were in charge of the sacred bread that was set out on the table, the choice flour for the grain offerings, the wafers made without yeast, the cakes cooked in olive oil, and the other mixed breads. They were also responsible to check all the weights and measures. [30]And each morning and evening they stood before the LORD to sing songs of thanks and praise to him. [31]They assisted with the burnt offerings that were presented to the LORD on Sabbath days, at new moon celebrations, and at all the appointed festivals. The required number of Levites served in the LORD's presence at all times, following all the procedures they had been given.

[32]And so, under the supervision of the priests, the Levites watched over the Tabernacle and the Temple* and faithfully carried out their duties of service at the house of the LORD.

CHAPTER 24
Duties of the Priests

This is how Aaron's descendants, the priests, were divided into groups for service. The sons of Aaron were Nadab, Abihu, Eleazar, and Ithamar. [2]But Nadab and Abihu died before their father, and they had no sons. So only Eleazar and Ithamar were left to carry on as priests.

[3]With the help of Zadok, who was a descendant of Eleazar, and of Ahimelech, who was a descendant of Ithamar, David divided Aaron's descendants into groups according to their various duties. [4]Eleazar's descendants were divided into sixteen groups and Ithamar's into eight, for there were more family leaders among the descendants of Eleazar. [5]All tasks were assigned to the various groups by means of sacred lots so that no preference would be shown, for there were many qualified officials serving God in the sanctuary from among the descendants of both Eleazar and Ithamar. [6]Shemaiah son of Nethanel, a Levite, acted as secretary and wrote down the names and assignments in the presence of the king, the officials, Zadok

the priest, Ahimelech son of Abiathar, and the family leaders of the priests and Levites. The descendants of Eleazar and Ithamar took turns casting lots.

[7] The first lot fell to Jehoiarib.
The second lot fell to Jedaiah.
[8] The third lot fell to Harim.
The fourth lot fell to Seorim.
[9] The fifth lot fell to Malkijah.
The sixth lot fell to Mijamin.
[10] The seventh lot fell to Hakkoz.
The eighth lot fell to Abijah.
[11] The ninth lot fell to Jeshua.
The tenth lot fell to Shecaniah.
[12] The eleventh lot fell to Eliashib.
The twelfth lot fell to Jakim.
[13] The thirteenth lot fell to Huppah.
The fourteenth lot fell to Jeshebeab.
[14] The fifteenth lot fell to Bilgah.
The sixteenth lot fell to Immer.
[15] The seventeenth lot fell to Hezir.
The eighteenth lot fell to Happizzez.
[16] The nineteenth lot fell to Pethahiah.
The twentieth lot fell to Jehezkel.
[17] The twenty-first lot fell to Jakin.
The twenty-second lot fell to Gamul.
[18] The twenty-third lot fell to Delaiah.
The twenty-fourth lot fell to Maaziah.

[19]Each group carried out its appointed duties in the house of the LORD according to the procedures established by their ancestor Aaron in obedience to the commands of the LORD, the God of Israel.

Family Leaders among the Levites

[20]These were the other family leaders descended from Levi:

From the descendants of Amram, the leader was Shebuel.*
From the descendants of Shebuel, the leader was Jehdeiah.
[21] From the descendants of Rehabiah, the leader was Isshiah.
[22] From the descendants of Izhar, the leader was Shelomith.*
From the descendants of Shelomith, the leader was Jahath.
[23] From the descendants of Hebron, Jeriah was the leader,* Amariah was second, Jahaziel was third, and Jekameam was fourth.
[24] From the descendants of Uzziel, the leader was Micah.

23:32 Hebrew *the Tent of Meeting and the sanctuary.* 24:20 Hebrew *Shubael* (also in 24:20b), a variant spelling of Shebuel; compare 23:16 and 26:24. 24:22 Hebrew *Shelomoth* (also in 24:22b), a variant spelling of Shelomith; compare 23:18. 24:23 Hebrew *From the descendants of Jeriah;* compare 23:19.

From the descendants of Micah, the leader was Shamir, 25along with Isshiah, the brother of Micah.

From the descendants of Isshiah, the leader was Zechariah.

26 From the descendants of Merari, the leaders were Mahli and Mushi.

From the descendants of Jaaziah, the leader was Beno.

27 From the descendants of Merari through Jaaziah, the leaders were Beno, Shoham, Zaccur, and Ibri.

28 From the descendants of Mahli, the leader was Eleazar, though he had no sons.

29 From the descendants of Kish, the leader was Jerahmeel.

30 From the descendants of Mushi, the leaders were Mahli, Eder, and Jerimoth.

These were the descendants of Levi in their various families. 31Like the descendants of Aaron, they were assigned to their duties by means of sacred lots, without regard to age or rank. Lots were drawn in the presence of King David, Zadok, Ahimelech, and the family leaders of the priests and the Levites.

CHAPTER 25
Duties of the Musicians
David and the army commanders then appointed men from the families of Asaph, Heman, and Jeduthun to proclaim God's messages to the accompaniment of lyres, harps, and cymbals. Here is a list of their names and their work:

2From the sons of Asaph, there were Zaccur, Joseph, Nethaniah, and Asarelah. They worked under the direction of their father, Asaph, who proclaimed God's messages by the king's orders.

3From the sons of Jeduthun, there were Gedaliah, Zeri, Jeshaiah, Shimei,* Hashabiah, and Mattithiah, six in all. They worked under the direction of their father, Jeduthun, who proclaimed God's messages to the accompaniment of the lyre, offering thanks and praise to the LORD.

4From the sons of Heman, there were Bukkiah, Mattaniah, Uzziel, Shubael,*

Jerimoth, Hananiah, Hanani, Eliathah, Giddalti, Romamti-ezer, Joshbekashah, Mallothi, Hothir, and Mahazioth. 5All these were the sons of Heman, the king's seer, for God had honored him with fourteen sons and three daughters.

6All these men were under the direction of their fathers as they made music at the house of the LORD. Their responsibilities included the playing of cymbals, harps, and lyres at the house of God. Asaph, Jeduthun, and Heman reported directly to the king. 7They and their families were all trained in making music before the LORD, and each of them— 288 in all—was an accomplished musician. 8The musicians were appointed to their term of service by means of sacred lots, without regard to whether they were young or old, teacher or student.

9 The first lot fell to Joseph of the Asaph clan and twelve of his sons and relatives.*

The second lot fell to Gedaliah and twelve of his sons and relatives.

10 The third lot fell to Zaccur and twelve of his sons and relatives.

11 The fourth lot fell to Zeri* and twelve of his sons and relatives.

12 The fifth lot fell to Nethaniah and twelve of his sons and relatives.

13 The sixth lot fell to Bukkiah and twelve of his sons and relatives.

14 The seventh lot fell to Asarelah* and twelve of his sons and relatives.

15 The eighth lot fell to Jeshaiah and twelve of his sons and relatives.

16 The ninth lot fell to Mattaniah and twelve of his sons and relatives.

17 The tenth lot fell to Shimei and twelve of his sons and relatives.

18 The eleventh lot fell to Uzziel* and twelve of his sons and relatives.

19 The twelfth lot fell to Hashabiah and twelve of his sons and relatives.

20 The thirteenth lot fell to Shubael and twelve of his sons and relatives.

21 The fourteenth lot fell to Mattithiah and twelve of his sons and relatives.

22 The fifteenth lot fell to Jerimoth* and twelve of his sons and relatives.

23 The sixteenth lot fell to Hananiah and twelve of his sons and relatives.

25:3 As in one Hebrew manuscript and some Greek manuscripts (see also 25:17); most Hebrew manuscripts lack *Shimei.* 25:4 Hebrew *Shebuel,* a variant spelling of Shubael; compare 25:20. 25:9 As in Greek version; Hebrew lacks *and twelve of his sons and relatives.* 25:11 Hebrew *Izri,* a variant spelling of Zeri; compare 25:3. 25:14 Hebrew *Jesarelah,* a variant spelling of Asarelah; compare 25:2. 25:18 Hebrew *Azarel,* a variant spelling of Uzziel; compare 25:4. 25:22 Hebrew *Jeremoth,* a variant spelling of Jerimoth; compare 25:4.

²⁴ The seventeenth lot fell to Joshbekashah*
and twelve of his sons and relatives.

²⁵ The eighteenth lot fell to Hanani and
twelve of his sons and relatives.

²⁶ The nineteenth lot fell to Mallothi and
twelve of his sons and relatives.

²⁷ The twentieth lot fell to Eliathah and
twelve of his sons and relatives.

²⁸ The twenty-first lot fell to Hothir and
twelve of his sons and relatives.

²⁹ The twenty-second lot fell to Giddalti and
twelve of his sons and relatives.

³⁰ The twenty-third lot fell to Mahazioth
and twelve of his sons and relatives.

³¹ The twenty-fourth lot fell to
Romamti-ezer and twelve of his sons
and relatives.

CHAPTER 26
Duties of the Gatekeepers

These are the divisions of the gatekeepers:

From the Korahites, there was Meshelemiah
son of Kore, of the family of Abiasaph.*
²The sons of Meshelemiah were Zechariah
(the oldest), Jediael (the second),
Zebadiah (the third), Jathniel (the
fourth), ³Elam (the fifth), Jehohanan (the
sixth), and Eliehoenai (the seventh).

⁴The sons of Obed-edom, also gatekeepers,
were Shemaiah (the oldest), Jehozabad
(the second), Joah (the third), Sacar (the
fourth), Nethanel (the fifth), ⁵Ammiel
(the sixth), Issachar (the seventh), and
Peullethai (the eighth). God had richly
blessed Obed-edom.

⁶Obed-edom's son Shemaiah had sons
with great ability who earned positions of
great authority in the clan. ⁷Their names
were Othni, Rephael, Obed, and Elzabad.
Their relatives, Elihu and Semakiah, were
also very capable men.

⁸All of these descendants of
Obed-edom, including their sons and
grandsons—sixty-two of them in
all—were very capable men, well
qualified for their work.

⁹Meshelemiah's eighteen sons and relatives
were also very capable men.

¹⁰Hosah, of the Merari clan, appointed
Shimri as the leader among his sons,
though he was not the oldest. ¹¹His other
sons included Hilkiah (the second),
Tebaliah (the third), and Zechariah (the
fourth). Hosah's sons and relatives, who
served as gatekeepers, numbered thirteen
in all.

¹²These divisions of the gatekeepers were
named for their family leaders, and like the
other Levites, they served at the house of the
LORD. ¹³They were assigned by families for
guard duty at the various gates, without regard to age or training, for it was all decided
by means of sacred lots.

¹⁴The responsibility for the east gate went
to Meshelemiah* and his group. The north
gate was assigned to his son Zechariah, a
man of unusual wisdom. ¹⁵The south gate
went to Obed-edom, and his sons were put
in charge of the storehouse. ¹⁶Shuppim and
Hosah were assigned the west gate and the
gateway leading up to the Temple.* Guard
duties were divided evenly. ¹⁷Six Levites were
assigned each day to the east gate, four to the
north gate, four to the south gate, and two
pairs at the storehouse. ¹⁸Six were assigned
each day to the west gate, four to the gateway leading up to the Temple, and two to the
courtyard.*

¹⁹These were the divisions of the gatekeepers from the clans of Korah and Merari.

Treasurers and Other Officials

²⁰Other Levites, led by Ahijah, were in charge
of the treasuries of the house of God and the
treasuries of the gifts dedicated to the LORD.
²¹From the family of Libni* in the clan of
Gershon, Jehiel* was the leader. ²²The sons of
Jehiel, Zetham and his brother Joel, were in
charge of the treasuries of the house of the
LORD.

²³These are the leaders that descended
from Amram, Izhar, Hebron, and Uzziel:

25:24 Hebrew *Joshbekasha*, a variant spelling of Joshbekashah; compare 25:4. 26:1 As in Greek version (see also
Exod 6:24); Hebrew reads *Asaph*. 26:14 Hebrew *Shelemiah*, a variant spelling of Meshelemiah; compare 26:2.
26:16 Or *the gate of Shalleketh on the upper road* (also in 26:18). The meaning of the Hebrew is uncertain. 26:18 Or
the colonnade. The meaning of the Hebrew is uncertain. 26:21a Hebrew *Ladan*, a variant spelling of Libni; compare
6:17. 26:21b Hebrew *Jehieli* (also in 26:22), a variant spelling of Jehiel; compare 23:8.

26:1-32 God wants all kinds of people to serve him. Not everyone is a musician or a worship
leader. Not everyone is gifted with a golden tongue. This chapter reminds us that all of God's
people are important to him. Duties that we might consider mundane—those of the greeters,
ushers, financial officers, and others—are of great importance. God values our service even if few
people ever become aware of it.

[24]From the clan of Amram, Shebuel was a descendant of Gershom son of Moses. He was the chief officer of the treasuries. [25]His relatives through Eliezer were Rehabiah, Jeshaiah, Joram, Zicri, and Shelomoth.

[26]Shelomoth and his relatives were in charge of the treasuries containing the gifts that King David, the family leaders, and the generals and captains* and other officers of the army had dedicated to the LORD. [27]These men dedicated some of the plunder they had gained in battle to maintain the house of the LORD. [28]Shelomoth* and his relatives also cared for the gifts dedicated to the LORD by Samuel the seer, Saul son of Kish, Abner son of Ner, and Joab son of Zeruiah. All the other dedicated gifts were in their care, too.

[29]From the clan of Izhar came Kenaniah. He and his sons were given administrative responsibilities* over Israel as officials and judges.

[30]From the clan of Hebron came Hashabiah. He and his relatives—1,700 capable men—were put in charge of the Israelite lands west of the Jordan River. They were responsible for all matters related to the things of the LORD and the service of the king in that area.

[31]Also from the clan of Hebron came Jeriah,* who was the leader of the Hebronites according to the genealogical records. (In the fortieth year of David's reign, a search was made in the records, and capable men from the clan of Hebron were found at Jazer in the land of Gilead.) [32]There were 2,700 capable men among the relatives of Jeriah. King David sent them to the east side of the Jordan River and put them in charge of the tribes of Reuben and Gad and the half-tribe of Manasseh. They were responsible for all matters related to God and to the king.

CHAPTER 27
Military Commanders and Divisions

This is the list of Israelite generals and captains,* and their officers, who served the king by supervising the army divisions that were on duty each month of the year. Each division served for one month and had 24,000 troops.

[2]Jashobeam son of Zabdiel was commander of the first division of 24,000 troops, which was on duty during the first month. [3]He was a descendant of Perez and was in charge of all the army officers for the first month.

[4]Dodai, a descendant of Ahoah, was commander of the second division of 24,000 troops, which was on duty during the second month. Mikloth was his chief officer.

[5]Benaiah son of Jehoiada the priest was commander of the third division of 24,000 troops, which was on duty during the third month. [6]This was the Benaiah who commanded David's elite military group known as the Thirty. His son Ammizabad was his chief officer.

[7]Asahel, the brother of Joab, was commander of the fourth division of 24,000 troops, which was on duty during the fourth month. Asahel was succeeded by his son Zebadiah.

[8]Shammah* the Izrahite was commander of the fifth division of 24,000 troops, which was on duty during the fifth month.

[9]Ira son of Ikkesh from Tekoa was commander of the sixth division of 24,000 troops, which was on duty during the sixth month.

[10]Helez, a descendant of Ephraim from Pelon, was commander of the seventh division of 24,000 troops, which was on duty during the seventh month.

[11]Sibbecai, a descendant of Zerah from Hushah, was commander of the eighth division of 24,000 troops, which was on duty during the eighth month.

26:26 Hebrew *the commanders of thousands and of hundreds.* 26:28 Hebrew *Shelomith,* a variant spelling of Shelomoth. 26:29 Or *were given outside work;* or *were given work away from the Temple area.* 26:31 Hebrew *Jerijah,* a variant spelling of Jeriah; compare 23:19. 27:1 Hebrew *commanders of thousands and of hundreds.* 27:8 Hebrew *Shamhuth,* a variant spelling of Shammah; compare 11:27 and 2 Sam 23:25.

27:1-34 If we want to succeed in the rebuilding process, we need to submit to some kind of authority structure. As believers we need to place ourselves under the authority of a local church body. We need to be accountable to others. This chapter establishes the proper lines of authority for the people of Israel. This should remind us of the importance of accountability in the rebuilding process.

Full recovery doesn't stop when our broken parts are repaired. It includes building a new life that is free, full, and rich. Fear of failure, humiliation, or disappointment can keep us from seeking life in all its fullness. It takes courage to dream of the life we truly desire.

King David dreamed of building a magnificent temple, the likes of which the world had never seen. In commissioning his son Solomon to do the work David said, "Every part of this plan . . . was given to me in writing from the hand of the LORD. . . . Be strong and courageous, and do the work. Don't be afraid or discouraged, for the LORD God, my God, is with you. He will not fail you or forsake you" (1 Chronicles 28:19-20). The apostle Paul said, "We are carefully joined together in him, becoming a holy temple for the Lord" (Ephesians 2:21).

Just as David dreamed of building a magnificent temple, we can dare to dream of building a magnificent new life. God has the blueprints already drawn up. It's natural to fear that if we allow ourself to hope, we will only be disappointed again or that we might start and fail, suffering public humiliation. But we need only to "be strong and courageous, and do the work." We need not be afraid or discouraged by the size of the task, for "God, who began the good work within you, will continue his work until it is finally finished" (Philippians 1:6). *Turn to page 557, 2 Chronicles 15.*

---

¹²Abiezer from Anathoth in the territory of Benjamin was commander of the ninth division of 24,000 troops, which was on duty during the ninth month. ¹³Maharai, a descendant of Zerah from Netophah, was commander of the tenth division of 24,000 troops, which was on duty during the tenth month. ¹⁴Benaiah from Pirathon in Ephraim was commander of the eleventh division of 24,000 troops, which was on duty during the eleventh month. ¹⁵Heled,* a descendant of Othniel from Netophah, was commander of the twelfth division of 24,000 troops, which was on duty during the twelfth month.

Leaders of the Tribes
¹⁶The following were the tribes of Israel and their leaders:

Tribe	Leader
Reuben	Eliezer son of Zicri
Simeon	Shephatiah son of Maacah
¹⁷Levi	Hashabiah son of Kemuel
Aaron (the priests)	Zadok
¹⁸Judah	Elihu (a brother of David)
Issachar	Omri son of Michael
¹⁹Zebulun	Ishmaiah son of Obadiah
Naphtali	Jeremoth son of Azriel
²⁰Ephraim	Hoshea son of Azaziah
Manasseh (west)	Joel son of Pedaiah
²¹Manasseh in Gilead (east)	Iddo son of Zechariah
Benjamin	Jaasiel son of Abner
²²Dan	Azarel son of Jeroham

These were the leaders of the tribes of Israel. ²³When David took his census, he did not count those who were younger than twenty years of age, because the LORD had promised to make the Israelites as numerous as the stars in heaven. ²⁴Joab son of Zeruiah began the census but never finished it because* the anger of God fell on Israel. The total number was never recorded in King David's official records.

27:15 Hebrew *Heldai,* a variant spelling of Heled; compare 11:30 and 2 Sam 23:29. 27:24 Or *never finished it, and yet.*

Officials of David's Kingdom

25Azmaveth son of Adiel was in charge of the palace treasuries.

Jonathan son of Uzziah was in charge of the regional treasuries throughout the towns, villages, and fortresses of Israel.

26Ezri son of Kelub was in charge of the field workers who farmed the king's lands.

27Shimei from Ramah was in charge of the king's vineyards.

Zabdi from Shepham was responsible for the grapes and the supplies of wine.

28Baal-hanan from Geder was in charge of the king's olive groves and sycamore-fig trees in the foothills of Judah.*

Joash was responsible for the supplies of olive oil.

29Shitrai from Sharon was in charge of the cattle on the Sharon Plain.

Shaphat son of Adlai was responsible for the cattle in the valleys.

30Obil the Ishmaelite was in charge of the camels.

Jehdeiah from Meronoth was in charge of the donkeys.

31Jaziz the Hagrite was in charge of the king's flocks of sheep and goats.

All these officials were overseers of King David's property.

32Jonathan, David's uncle, was a wise counselor to the king, a man of great insight, and a scribe. Jehiel the Hacmonite was responsible for teaching the king's sons. 33Ahithophel was the royal adviser. Hushai the Arkite was the king's friend. 34Ahithophel was succeeded by Jehoiada son of Benaiah and by Abiathar. Joab was commander of the king's army.

CHAPTER 28

David's Instructions to Solomon

David summoned all the officials of Israel to Jerusalem—the leaders of the tribes, the commanders of the army divisions, the other generals and captains,* the overseers of the royal property and livestock, the palace officials, the mighty men, and all the other brave warriors in the kingdom. 2David rose to his feet and said: "My brothers and my people! It was my desire to build a temple where the Ark of the LORD's Covenant, God's footstool, could rest permanently. I made the necessary preparations for building it, 3but God said to me, 'You must not build a temple to honor my name, for you are a warrior and have shed much blood.'

4"Yet the LORD, the God of Israel, has chosen me from among all my father's family to be king over Israel forever. For he has chosen the tribe of Judah to rule, and from among the families of Judah he chose my father's family. And from among my father's sons the LORD was pleased to make me king over all Israel. 5And from among my sons—for the LORD has given me many—he chose Solomon to succeed me on the throne of Israel and to rule over the LORD's kingdom. 6He said to me, 'Your son Solomon will build my Temple and its courtyards, for I have chosen him as my son, and I will be his father. 7And if he continues to obey my commands and regulations as he does now, I will make his kingdom last forever.'

8"So now, with God as our witness, and in the sight of all Israel—the LORD's assembly—I give you this charge. Be careful to obey all the commands of the LORD your God, so that you may continue to possess this good land and leave it to your children as a permanent inheritance.

9"And Solomon, my son, learn to know the God of your ancestors intimately. Worship and serve him with your whole heart and a willing mind. For the LORD sees every heart and knows every plan and thought. If you seek him, you will find him. But if you forsake him, he will reject you forever. 10So take this seriously. The LORD has chosen you to build a Temple as his sanctuary. Be strong, and do the work."

11Then David gave Solomon the plans for the Temple and its surroundings, including the entry room, the storerooms, the upstairs rooms, the inner rooms, and the inner sanctuary—which was the place of atonement. 12David also gave Solomon all the plans he had in mind* for the courtyards of the LORD's Temple, the outside rooms, the treasuries, and the rooms for the gifts dedicated to the

27:28 Hebrew *the Shephelah.* 28:1 Hebrew *the commanders of thousands and commanders of hundreds.* 28:12 Or *the plans of the spirit that was with him.*

28:8-10 David took the time to pass God's wisdom on to Solomon. He began by acknowledging God's promise of a dynasty that would rule Israel forever. But David recognized that in order to receive the blessings of this great promise, Solomon and his descendants were responsible to obey God's commands. Likewise, obedience to God's will is the only pathway to blessing for us and for our descendants.

LORD. [13]The king also gave Solomon the instructions concerning the work of the various divisions of priests and Levites in the Temple of the LORD. And he gave specifications for the items in the Temple that were to be used for worship.

[14]David gave instructions regarding how much gold and silver should be used to make the items needed for service. [15]He told Solomon the amount of gold needed for the gold lampstands and lamps, and the amount of silver for the silver lampstands and lamps, depending on how each would be used. [16]He designated the amount of gold for the table on which the Bread of the Presence would be placed and the amount of silver for other tables.

[17]David also designated the amount of gold for the solid gold meat hooks used to handle the sacrificial meat and for the basins, pitchers, and dishes, as well as the amount of silver for every dish. [18]He designated the amount of refined gold for the altar of incense. Finally, he gave him a plan for the LORD's "chariot"—the gold cherubim* whose wings were stretched out over the Ark of the LORD's Covenant. [19]"Every part of this plan," David told Solomon, "was given to me in writing from the hand of the LORD.*"

[20]Then David continued, "Be strong and courageous, and do the work. Don't be afraid or discouraged, for the LORD God, my God, is with you. He will not fail you or forsake you. He will see to it that all the work related to the Temple of the LORD is finished correctly. [21]The various divisions of priests and Levites will serve in the Temple of God. Others with skills of every kind will volunteer, and the officials and the entire nation are at your command."

CHAPTER 29
Gifts for Building the Temple

Then King David turned to the entire assembly and said, "My son Solomon, whom God has clearly chosen as the next king of Israel, is still young and inexperienced. The work ahead of him is enormous, for the Temple he will build is not for mere mortals—it is for the LORD God himself! [2]Using every resource at my command, I have gathered as much as I could for building the Temple of my God. Now there is enough gold, silver, bronze, iron, and wood, as well as great quantities of onyx, other precious stones, costly jewels, and all kinds of fine stone and marble.

[3]"And now, because of my devotion to the Temple of my God, I am giving all of my own private treasures of gold and silver to help in the construction. This is in addition to the building materials I have already collected for his holy Temple. [4]I am donating more than 112 tons of gold* from Ophir and 262 tons of refined silver* to be used for overlaying the walls of the buildings [5]and for the other gold and silver work to be done by the craftsmen. Now then, who will follow my example and give offerings to the LORD today?"

[6]Then the family leaders, the leaders of the tribes of Israel, the generals and captains of the army,* and the king's administrative officers all gave willingly. [7]For the construction of the Temple of God, they gave about 188 tons of gold,* 10,000 gold coins,* 375 tons of silver,* 675 tons of bronze,* and 3,750 tons of iron.* [8]They also contributed numerous precious stones, which were deposited in the treasury of the house of the LORD under the care of Jehiel, a descendant of Gershon. [9]The people rejoiced over the offerings, for they had given freely and

---

28:18 Hebrew *for the gold cherub chariot.* **28:19** Or *was written under the direction of the LORD.* **29:4a** Hebrew *3,000 talents* [102 metric tons] *of gold.* **29:4b** Hebrew *7,000 talents* [238 metric tons] *of silver.* **29:6** Hebrew *the commanders of thousands and commanders of hundreds.* **29:7a** Hebrew *5,000 talents* [170 metric tons] *of gold.* **29:7b** Hebrew *10,000 darics* [a Persian coin] *of gold,* about 185 pounds or 84 kilograms in weight. **29:7c** Hebrew *10,000 talents* [340 metric tons] *of silver.* **29:7d** Hebrew *18,000 talents* [612 metric tons] *of bronze.* **29:7e** Hebrew *100,000 talents* [3,400 metric tons] *of iron.*

28:19 God gave David a plan for building the Temple in Jerusalem. David passed it on to Solomon, who would complete the project. God also has a plan for each of us, and his blueprint includes our recovery. Each of us is a "temple" of the Holy Spirit (1 Corinthians 6:19); God actually dwells inside all his people. We are responsible to rebuild our life in a way worthy of the one who dwells within us. Let us seek God's plan for healthy living and do everything we can to rebuild according to that plan.

29:3 Setting proper priorities is necessary in recovery. We need to put God first in our life. We also need to help others. David gave out of his own wealth and energy. His personal treasures would help support the work of God in Israel. His giving would also contribute to the blessings received by people worshiping at the Temple for generations to come.

wholeheartedly to the LORD, and King David was filled with joy.

David's Prayer of Praise

[10]Then David praised the LORD in the presence of the whole assembly:

"O LORD, the God of our ancestor Israel,* may you be praised forever and ever! [11]Yours, O LORD, is the greatness, the power, the glory, the victory, and the majesty. Everything in the heavens and on earth is yours, O LORD, and this is your kingdom. We adore you as the one who is over all things. [12]Wealth and honor come from you alone, for you rule over everything. Power and might are in your hand, and at your discretion people are made great and given strength.

[13]"O our God, we thank you and praise your glorious name! [14]But who am I, and who are my people, that we could give anything to you? Everything we have has come from you, and we give you only what you first gave us! [15]We are here for only a moment, visitors and strangers in the land as our ancestors were before us. Our days on earth are like a passing shadow, gone so soon without a trace.

[16]"O LORD our God, even this material we have gathered to build a Temple to honor your holy name comes from you! It all belongs to you! [17]I know, my God, that you examine our hearts and rejoice when you find integrity there. You know I have done all this with good motives, and I have watched your people offer their gifts willingly and joyously.

[18]"O LORD, the God of our ancestors Abraham, Isaac, and Israel, make your people always want to obey you. See to it that their love for you never changes. [19]Give my son Solomon the wholehearted desire to obey all your commands, laws, and decrees, and to do everything necessary to build this Temple, for which I have made these preparations."

[20]Then David said to the whole assembly, "Give praise to the LORD your God!" And the entire assembly praised the LORD, the God of their ancestors, and they bowed low and knelt before the LORD and the king.

Solomon Named as King

[21]The next day they brought 1,000 bulls, 1,000 rams, and 1,000 male lambs as burnt offerings to the LORD. They also brought liquid offerings and many other sacrifices on behalf of all Israel. [22]They feasted and drank in the LORD's presence with great joy that day.

And again they crowned David's son Solomon as their new king. They anointed him before the LORD as their leader, and they anointed Zadok as priest. [23]So Solomon took the throne of the LORD in place of his father, David, and he succeeded in everything, and all Israel obeyed him. [24]All the officials, the warriors, and the sons of King David pledged their loyalty to King Solomon. [25]And the LORD exalted Solomon in the sight of all Israel, and he gave Solomon greater royal splendor than any king in Israel before him.

Summary of David's Reign

[26]So David son of Jesse reigned over all Israel. [27]He reigned over Israel for forty years, seven of them in Hebron and thirty-three in Jerusalem. [28]He died at a ripe old age, having enjoyed long life, wealth, and honor. Then his son Solomon ruled in his place.

[29]All the events of King David's reign, from beginning to end, are written in *The Record of Samuel the Seer, The Record of Nathan the Prophet,* and *The Record of Gad the Seer.* [30]These accounts include the mighty deeds of his reign and everything that happened to him and to Israel and to all the surrounding kingdoms.

29:10 *Israel* is the name that God gave to Jacob.

29:11-12 David's prayer of praise is filled with truths important for recovery. It recognizes that God is the source of all true success. It ascribes all greatness, power, glory, victory, and majesty to him. It recognizes that God is the source of all riches and honor; God is sovereign over everything. These are essential truths. We must daily affirm the truth that God is our source of strength. We are helpless on our own, but God is more than able to help us overcome the problems that assail us.

2 CHRONICLES

THE BIG PICTURE

A. THE REIGN OF SOLOMON
(1:1–9:31)
B. THE DOWNWARD SLIDE OF
THE KINGS (10:1–36:4)
1. Rehoboam (10:1–13:22)
2. Asa (14:1–16:14)
3. Jehoshaphat
(17:1–20:37)
4. Jehoram and Athaliah
(21:1–22:12)
5. Joash (23:1–24:27)
6. Amaziah (25:1-28)
7. Uzziah (26:1-23)
8. Jotham (27:1-9)
9. Ahaz (28:1-27)
10. Hezekiah (29:1–32:33)
11. Manasseh (33:1-25)
12. Josiah (34:1–35:27)
13. Sons of Josiah
(36:1-14)
  a. Jehoahaz (36:1-4)
  b. Jehoiakim (36:5-8)
  c. Grandson, Jehoiachin
    (36:9-10)
  d. Zedekiah (36:11-14)
C. JUDAH EXILED TO BABYLON
(36:5-21)
D. THE DECREE OF HOPE
(36:22-23)

The book of 2 Chronicles was originally part of a larger book that also included 1 Chronicles. It recorded Israel's history starting with a genealogy of Adam's descendants and ending with Israel in Babylonian captivity. This condensed history was written to give Israel hope as they sought to rebuild their nation after the Babylonian exile.

Second Chronicles begins on a high note, recording Solomon's great success in building God's Temple in Jerusalem. But after his good start, Solomon made some mistakes that were intensified by his son and successor, Rehoboam, which led to Israel's division into two kingdoms. Successive kings of David's royal descendants in the southern kingdom exhibited varying degrees of success or failure. Some attempted to break from the dysfunctional patterns and lead the people to examine their lives and turn back to God. Through these kings, God brought revival and renewal to Judah. But the kings who set their hearts against God led the people back into sinful ways. As a result, the kingdom of Judah was conquered, and the people were taken captive by Babylonian armies.

Second Chronicles follows David's royal line on a slow but steady decline toward destruction and exile. But when things look their blackest, the final verses leave us with a message of hope. King Cyrus of Persia, stirred by the Spirit of God, issued a decree allowing the Jerusalem Temple to be rebuilt. This would have shown the Jews seeking to rebuild Israel that God had been working behind the scenes on their behalf. Despite their past failures and lack of faith, God was graciously working to bring about their recovery.

THE BOTTOM LINE

PURPOSE: To record the history of Judah's kings, both those who obeyed God and those who sinned against him. Their examples would encourage and admonish the people to rebuild their nation according to God's program. AUTHOR: Unknown; Jewish tradition attributes it to Ezra. AUDIENCE: The people of Israel after their return from exile in Babylon. DATE WRITTEN: Approximately 430 B.C. SETTING: The kingdom of Judah between Solomon's reign (979 B.C.) and the decree of Cyrus (539 B.C.). KEY VERSE: "Then if my people who are called by my name will humble themselves and pray and seek my face and turn from their wicked ways, I will hear from heaven and will forgive their sins and restore their land" (7:14). KEY EVENTS: The spiritual revivals that occurred under Asa, Jehoshaphat, Joash, Hezekiah, and Josiah.

RECOVERY THEMES

The Necessity of Faithfulness: When a king came along who was faithful to God, the people followed his lead and experienced recovery and restoration. But the victories of one day did not mean that the people would automatically win the trials of the next. They had to persevere in their faithfulness through each new day. When the path of faithfulness was forsaken, the people returned to their false gods and false worship. Their disobedience stood in sharp contrast to their faithfulness in earlier days. When the principles they learned were not continually incorporated into their daily lives, they experienced only shallow recovery, which quickly eroded as temptations presented themselves.

God Is the Focus of True Recovery: This book was written to encourage the Jews after their return from Babylonian exile. In their humiliating captivity, the people had hit bottom. As they returned to rebuild their Temple, land, and nation, God wanted them to learn that any successful rebuilding program centered around the true worship of God. A recovery program that does not begin and end with God's power becomes empty and weak. We need to learn the lesson that the Israelites struggled to grasp throughout their history: Genuine recovery begins, survives, and continues through complete dependence upon God.

The Ups and Downs of Recovery: We might think that God is pleased with us only when we make steady progress in recovery. If we slip backward, even a little, it is easy to feel that everything is lost. But for all of us, recovery has its ups and downs. In this book we see the Israelites following a recovery pattern that will eventually lead to destruction. They take three steps backward and then only one step forward. But if we can make more steps forward than we do backward, we are on the right track. The recovery process will continue as long as we depend on God for strength and guidance.

With God There Is Always Hope: Even when things seem bleakest, God is at work. When we are overwhelmed by circumstances and feel that God has forsaken us, it might help to remember that we are feeling what the people of Judah must have felt in Babylon—that all is lost! We might be encouraged as we look at the surprising reversal of their circumstances. In the midst of their despair, King Cyrus of Persia sent out a proclamation that allowed God's people to return to Jerusalem to rebuild their Temple. When our life is turned over to God, we can be confident that even in our darkest hours, God is at work. There is hope!

CHAPTER 1
Solomon Asks for Wisdom

Solomon son of David took firm control of his kingdom, for the LORD his God was with him and made him very powerful.

²Solomon called together all the leaders of Israel—the generals and captains of the army,* the judges, and all the political and clan leaders. ³Then he led the entire assembly to the place of worship in Gibeon, for God's Tabernacle* was located there. (This was the Tabernacle that Moses, the LORD's servant, had made in the wilderness.)

⁴David had already moved the Ark of God from Kiriath-jearim to the tent he had prepared for it in Jerusalem. ⁵But the bronze altar made by Bezalel son of Uri and grandson of Hur was there* at Gibeon in front of the Tabernacle of the LORD. So Solomon and the people gathered in front of it to consult the LORD.* ⁶There in front of the Tabernacle, Solomon went up to the bronze altar in the LORD's presence and sacrificed 1,000 burnt offerings on it.

⁷That night God appeared to Solomon and said, "What do you want? Ask, and I will give it to you!"

⁸Solomon replied to God, "You showed great and faithful love to David, my father, and now you have made me king in his place. ⁹O LORD God, please continue to keep your promise to David my father, for you

1:2 Hebrew *the commanders of thousands and of hundreds.* 1:3 Hebrew *Tent of Meeting;* also in 1:6, 13. 1:5a As in Greek version and Latin Vulgate, and some Hebrew manuscripts. Masoretic Text reads *he placed.* 1:5b Hebrew *to consult him.*

1:1 We all want to succeed, whether at escaping destructive patterns or at establishing positive habits. At the outset of this book, God gave Solomon unprecedented success in everything he did. But notice that Solomon's success depended on God's presence with him. Our success in recovery is impossible without God's helping presence in our life. We must recognize this if we hope to make progress.

1:7 What might we request if God gave us this offer? Solomon asked for wisdom, passing over wealth or power. Solomon made a request that would serve the best interests of his people. God was pleased with Solomon's selfless attitude and rewarded him with more power and wealth than Solomon could ever have wished for. In recovery we also need to delay gratification in our

have made me king over a people as numerous as the dust of the earth! [10]Give me the wisdom and knowledge to lead them properly,* for who could possibly govern this great people of yours?"

[11]God said to Solomon, "Because your greatest desire is to help your people, and you did not ask for wealth, riches, fame, or even the death of your enemies or a long life, but rather you asked for wisdom and knowledge to properly govern my people—[12]I will certainly give you the wisdom and knowledge you requested. But I will also give you wealth, riches, and fame such as no other king has had before you or will ever have in the future!"

[13]Then Solomon returned to Jerusalem from the Tabernacle at the place of worship in Gibeon, and he reigned over Israel.

[14]Solomon built up a huge force of chariots and horses.* He had 1,400 chariots and 12,000 horses. He stationed some of them in the chariot cities and some near him in Jerusalem. [15]The king made silver and gold as plentiful in Jerusalem as stone. And valuable cedar timber was as common as the sycamore-fig trees that grow in the foothills of Judah.* [16]Solomon's horses were imported from Egypt* and from Cilicia*; the king's traders acquired them from Cilicia at the standard price. [17]At that time chariots from Egypt could be purchased for 600 pieces of silver,* and horses for 150 pieces of silver.* They were then exported to the kings of the Hittites and the kings of Aram.

CHAPTER 2
Preparations for Building the Temple

[1]*Solomon decided to build a Temple to honor the name of the LORD, and also a royal palace for himself. [2]*He enlisted a force of 70,000 laborers, 80,000 men to quarry stone in the hill country, and 3,600 foremen.

[3]Solomon also sent this message to King Hiram* at Tyre:

"Send me cedar logs as you did for my father, David, when he was building his palace. [4]I am about to build a Temple to honor the name of the LORD my God. It will be a place set apart to burn fragrant incense before him, to display the special sacrificial bread, and to sacrifice burnt offerings each m7orning and evening, on the Sabbaths, at new moon celebrations, and at the other appointed festivals of the LORD our God. He has commanded Israel to do these things forever.

[5]"This must be a magnificent Temple because our God is greater than all other gods. [6]But who can really build him a worthy home? Not even the highest heavens can contain him! So who am I to consider building a Temple for him, except as a place to burn sacrifices to him?

[7]"So send me a master craftsman who can work with gold, silver, bronze, and iron, as well as with purple, scarlet, and blue cloth. He must be a skilled engraver who can work with the craftsmen of

1:10 Hebrew *to go out and come in before this people.* 1:14 Or *charioteers;* also in 1:14b. 1:15 Hebrew *the Shephelah.* 1:16a Possibly *Muzur,* a district near Cilicia; also in 1:17. 1:16b Hebrew *Kue,* probably another name for Cilicia. 1:17a Hebrew *600 [shekels] of silver,* about 15 pounds or 6.8 kilograms in weight. 1:17b Hebrew *150 [shekels],* about 3.8 pounds or 1.7 kilograms in weight. 2:1 Verse 2:1 is numbered 1:18 in Hebrew text. 2:2 Verses 2:2-18 are numbered 2:1-17 in Hebrew text. 2:3 Hebrew *Huram,* a variant spelling of Hiram; also in 2:11.

decisions. We need to realize that short-term pleasure often yields trouble in the long run. A wise decision demands consideration of the long-term consequences and whether or not we are in agreement with God's will. Keeping God's will in focus as we make decisions always yields the greatest rewards.

2:1 Solomon was anxious to fulfill the plans God had for him. He began by building the Temple— a huge, seemingly impossible, task. God has certain tasks ordained for each of us; the task of recovery may be the place we should start. Some of these tasks will be difficult; some may even seem impossible! But with God's help, we will be able to accomplish them.

2:5 Solomon's achievements for God were great. Here we are told why: "This must be a magnificent Temple because our God is greater than all other gods." The deeper our relationship with God, the more we will realize how much he deserves our obedience and service. The realization of God's great power and love should give us courage as we face the difficult task of recovery. As we seek to rebuild, we will discover that God's power is sufficient for the task.

2:6 This verse reminds us of how great God really is. He is far greater than we can even imagine or understand. Solomon's Temple was one of the great triumphs of the ancient world, but even it was not good enough for God. God's greatness may discourage some of us. Why would such a great God bother with us? We need to learn that though God is great, he is also loving and gracious. He reaches out to sinful, weak people like us to bring us restoration. As great as God is, he certainly does not lack the power we need to reach the goal of recovery.

Judah and Jerusalem who were selected by my father, David.

[8]"Also send me cedar, cypress, and red sandalwood* logs from Lebanon, for I know that your men are without equal at cutting timber in Lebanon. I will send my men to help them. [9]An immense amount of timber will be needed, for the Temple I am going to build will be very large and magnificent. [10]In payment for your woodcutters, I will send 100,000 bushels of crushed wheat, 100,000 bushels of barley,* 110,000 gallons of wine, and 110,000 gallons of olive oil.*"

[11]King Hiram sent this letter of reply to Solomon:

"It is because the LORD loves his people that he has made you their king! [12]Praise the LORD, the God of Israel, who made the heavens and the earth! He has given King David a wise son, gifted with skill and understanding, who will build a Temple for the LORD and a royal palace for himself.

[13]"I am sending you a master craftsman named Huram-abi, who is extremely talented. [14]His mother is from the tribe of Dan in Israel, and his father is from Tyre. He is skillful at making things from gold, silver, bronze, and iron, and he also works with stone and wood. He can work with purple, blue, and scarlet cloth and fine linen. He is also an engraver and can follow any design given to him. He will work with your craftsmen and those appointed by my lord David, your father.

[15]"Send along the wheat, barley, olive oil, and wine that my lord has mentioned. [16]We will cut whatever timber you need from the Lebanon mountains and will float the logs in rafts down the coast of the Mediterranean Sea* to Joppa. From there you can transport the logs up to Jerusalem."

[17]Solomon took a census of all foreigners in the land of Israel, like the census his father had taken, and he counted 153,600. [18]He assigned 70,000 of them as common laborers, 80,000 as quarry workers in the hill country, and 3,600 as foremen.

CHAPTER 3
Solomon Builds the Temple

So Solomon began to build the Temple of the LORD in Jerusalem on Mount Moriah, where the LORD had appeared to David, his father. The Temple was built on the threshing floor of Araunah* the Jebusite, the site that David had selected. [2]The construction began in midspring,* during the fourth year of Solomon's reign.

[3]These are the dimensions Solomon used for the foundation of the Temple of God (using the old standard of measurement).* It was 90 feet long and 30 feet wide.* [4]The entry room at the front of the Temple was 30 feet* wide, running across the entire width of the Temple, and 30 feet* high. He overlaid the inside with pure gold.

[5]He paneled the main room of the Temple with cypress wood, overlaid it with fine gold, and decorated it with carvings of palm trees and chains. [6]He decorated the walls of the Temple with beautiful jewels and with gold from the land of Parvaim. [7]He overlaid the beams, thresholds, walls, and doors throughout the Temple with gold, and he carved figures of cherubim on the walls.

[8]He made the Most Holy Place 30 feet wide, corresponding to the width of the Temple, and 30 feet deep. He overlaid its interior with 23 tons* of fine gold. [9]The gold nails that were used weighed 20 ounces* each. He also overlaid the walls of the upper rooms with gold.

[10]He made two figures shaped like cherubim, overlaid them with gold, and placed them in the Most Holy Place. [11]The total wingspan of the two cherubim standing side by side was 30 feet. One wing of the first fig-

---

2:8 Or *juniper*; Hebrew reads *algum*, perhaps a variant spelling of *almug*; compare 9:10-11 and parallel text at 1 Kgs 10:11-12. 2:10a Hebrew *20,000 cors* [4,400 kiloliters] *of crushed wheat, 20,000 cors of barley.* 2:10b Hebrew *20,000 baths* [420 kiloliters] *of wine, and 20,000 baths of olive oil.* 2:16 Hebrew *the sea.* 3:1 Hebrew reads *Ornan,* a variant spelling of Araunah; compare 2 Sam 24:16. 3:2 Hebrew *on the second [day] of the second month.* This day of the ancient Hebrew lunar calendar occurred in April or May. 3:3a The "old standard of measurement" was a cubit equal to 18 inches [46 centimeters]. The new standard was a cubit of approximately 21 inches [53 centimeters]. 3:3b Hebrew *60 cubits* [27.6 meters] *long and 20 cubits* [9.2 meters] *wide.* 3:4a Hebrew *20 cubits* [9.2 meters]; also in 3:8, 11, 13. 3:4b As in some Greek and Syriac manuscripts, which read *20 cubits* [9.2 meters]; Hebrew reads *120 [cubits],* which is 180 feet or 55 meters. 3:8 Hebrew *600 talents* [20.4 metric tons]. 3:9 Hebrew *50 shekels* [570 grams].

3:3-17 This begins a description of the Temple's specifications. We are overwhelmed by the immense wealth required to build it. Large projects always require great resources. This is especially true in personal recovery projects. God is the only one with sufficient resources for the huge task of personal recovery. We need to learn to depend on his power.

ure was 7½ feet* long, and it touched the Temple wall. The other wing, also 7½ feet long, touched one of the wings of the second figure. ¹²In the same way, the second figure had one wing 7½ feet long that touched the opposite wall. The other wing, also 7½ feet long, touched the wing of the first figure. ¹³So the wingspan of the two cherubim side by side was 30 feet. They stood on their feet and faced out toward the main room of the Temple.

¹⁴Across the entrance of the Most Holy Place he hung a curtain made of fine linen, decorated with blue, purple, and scarlet thread and embroidered with figures of cherubim.

¹⁵For the front of the Temple, he made two pillars that were 27 feet* tall, each topped by a capital extending upward another 7½ feet. ¹⁶He made a network of interwoven chains* and used them to decorate the tops of the pillars. He also made 100 decorative pomegranates and attached them to the chains. ¹⁷Then he set up the two pillars at the entrance of the Temple, one to the south of the entrance and the other to the north. He named the one on the south Jakin, and the one on the north Boaz.*

CHAPTER 4
Furnishings for the Temple

Solomon* also made a bronze altar 30 feet long, 30 feet wide, and 15 feet high.* ²Then he cast a great round basin, 15 feet across from rim to rim, called the Sea. It was 7½ feet deep and about 45 feet in circumference.* ³It was encircled just below its rim by two rows of figures that resembled oxen. There were about six oxen per foot* all the way around, and they were cast as part of the basin.

⁴The Sea was placed on a base of twelve bronze oxen, all facing outward. Three faced north, three faced west, three faced south, and three faced east, and the Sea rested on them. ⁵The walls of the Sea were about three inches* thick, and its rim flared out like a cup and resembled a water lily blossom. It could hold about 16,500 gallons* of water.

⁶He also made ten smaller basins for washing the utensils for the burnt offerings. He set five on the south side and five on the north. But the priests washed themselves in the Sea.

⁷He then cast ten gold lampstands according to the specifications that had been given, and he put them in the Temple. Five were placed against the south wall, and five were placed against the north wall.

⁸He also built ten tables and placed them in the Temple, five along the south wall and five along the north wall. Then he molded 100 gold basins.

⁹He then built a courtyard for the priests, and also the large outer courtyard. He made doors for the courtyard entrances and overlaid them with bronze. ¹⁰The great bronze basin called the Sea was placed near the southeast corner of the Temple.

¹¹Huram-abi also made the necessary washbasins, shovels, and bowls.

So at last Huram-abi completed everything King Solomon had assigned him to make for the Temple of God:

¹² the two pillars;
   the two bowl-shaped capitals on top of the pillars;
   the two networks of interwoven chains that decorated the capitals;
¹³ the 400 pomegranates that hung from the chains on the capitals (two rows of pomegranates for each of the chain

---

3:11 Hebrew *5 cubits* [2.3 meters]; also in 3:11b, 12, 15. 3:15 As in Syriac version (see also 1 Kgs 7:15; 2 Kgs 25:17; Jer 52:21), which reads *18 cubits* [8.3 meters]; Hebrew reads *35 cubits*, which is 52.5 feet or 16.5 meters. 3:16 Hebrew *He made chains in the inner sanctuary.* The meaning of the Hebrew is uncertain. 3:17 *Jakin* probably means "he establishes"; *Boaz* probably means "in him is strength." 4:1a Or *Huram-abi;* Hebrew reads *He.* 4:1b Hebrew *20 cubits* [9.2 meters] *long, 20 cubits wide, and 10 cubits* [4.6 meters] *high.* 4:2 Hebrew *10 cubits* [4.6 meters] *across . . . 5 cubits* [2.3 meters] *deep and 30 cubits* [13.8 meters] *in circumference.* 4:3 Or *20 oxen per meter;* Hebrew reads *10 per cubit.* 4:5a Hebrew *a handbreadth* [8 centimeters]. 4:5b Hebrew *3,000 baths* [63 kiloliters].

4:1 Immediately upon entering the Temple area, worshipers encountered a great bronze altar. This object would remind them that each individual was in great need of forgiveness. Here many animal sacrifices were offered in payment for the people's sins. Before any approach to God was possible, forgiveness had to be achieved through sacrifice. God has made it possible for us to approach him through the death and resurrection of his Son. Even as we approach God for forgiveness, we also need to seek restoration with the people we have wronged. Only by seeking forgiveness will we ever break free from the bondage of our past failures.

4:2 The bronze basin is the item of furniture corresponding to the Tabernacle's washbasin (Exodus 30:17-21). Before approaching God in the Temple or making sacrifices at the altar, the priests were required to wash their hands and feet so they would be ceremonially clean. We, too, need to be cleansed of our impurities before we can approach God. How wonderful to remember that our sins can daily be forgiven through Christ!

networks that decorated the capitals on top of the pillars);

14 the water carts holding the basins;

15 the Sea and the twelve oxen under it;

16 the ash buckets, the shovels, the meat hooks, and all the related articles.

Huram-abi made all these things of burnished bronze for the Temple of the LORD, just as King Solomon had directed. 17The king had them cast in clay molds in the Jordan Valley between Succoth and Zarethan.* 18Solomon used such great quantities of bronze that its weight could not be determined.

19Solomon also made all the furnishings for the Temple of God:

the gold altar;

the tables for the Bread of the Presence;

20 the lampstands and their lamps of solid gold, to burn in front of the Most Holy Place as prescribed;

21 the flower decorations, lamps, and tongs—all of the purest gold;

22 the lamp snuffers, bowls, ladles, and incense burners—all of solid gold;

the doors for the entrances to the Most Holy Place and the main room of the Temple, overlaid with gold.

CHAPTER 5

So Solomon finished all his work on the Temple of the LORD. Then he brought all the gifts his father, David, had dedicated— the silver, the gold, and the various articles—and he stored them in the treasuries of the Temple of God.

The Ark Brought to the Temple

2Solomon then summoned to Jerusalem the elders of Israel and all the heads of tribes— the leaders of the ancestral families of Israel.

They were to bring the Ark of the LORD's Covenant to the Temple from its location in the City of David, also known as Zion. 3So all the men of Israel assembled before the king at the annual Festival of Shelters, which is held in early autumn.*

4When all the elders of Israel arrived, the Levites picked up the Ark. 5The priests and Levites brought up the Ark along with the special tent* and all the sacred items that had been in it. 6There, before the Ark, King Solomon and the entire community of Israel sacrificed so many sheep, goats, and cattle that no one could keep count!

7Then the priests carried the Ark of the LORD's Covenant into the inner sanctuary of the Temple—the Most Holy Place—and placed it beneath the wings of the cherubim. 8The cherubim spread their wings over the Ark, forming a canopy over the Ark and its carrying poles. 9These poles were so long that their ends could be seen from the Holy Place,* which is in front of the Most Holy Place, but not from the outside. They are still there to this day. 10Nothing was in the Ark except the two stone tablets that Moses had placed in it at Mount Sinai,* where the LORD made a covenant with the people of Israel when they left Egypt.

11Then the priests left the Holy Place. All the priests who were present had purified themselves, whether or not they were on duty that day. 12And the Levites who were musicians—Asaph, Heman, Jeduthun, and all their sons and brothers—were dressed in fine linen robes and stood at the east side of the altar playing cymbals, lyres, and harps. They were joined by 120 priests who were playing trumpets. 13The trumpeters and singers performed together in unison to praise and give thanks to the LORD. Accompanied

---

4:17 As in parallel text at 1 Kgs 7:46; Hebrew reads *Zeredah*. 5:3 Hebrew *at the festival that is in the seventh month*. The Festival of Shelters began on the fifteenth day of the seventh month of the ancient Hebrew lunar calendar. This day occurred in late September, October, or early November. 5:5 Hebrew *the Tent of Meeting*; i.e., the tent mentioned in 2 Sam 6:17 and 1 Chr 16:1. 5:9 As in some Hebrew manuscripts and Greek version (see also 1 Kgs 8:8); Masoretic Text reads *from the Ark*. 5:10 Hebrew *Horeb*, another name for Sinai.

4:20 Light was needed in the Temple's dark interior. Even as the Holy Place would have been dark were it not for the lampstand, so would our life be in total darkness without the presence of the "Light of the World"—Jesus Christ (see John 8:12).

5:13 The trumpets sounded with joy! The singers happily sang out their praises to God. What a beautiful celebration! We must remember to respond with thanksgiving and praise to God for the victories in our life. It is dangerous to emphasize our problems so much that we forget to express joy for God's cures!

5:13-14 As the people praised God, his glorious presence appeared and filled the Temple. For us to have any hope for recovery, God must be present in our life. No matter what we set out to do, God's help is necessary for success. No wonder God's people responded with such a joyful celebration. They were assured that God was with them! This fact alone gave them confidence in a future filled with joy and success.

by trumpets, cymbals, and other instruments, they raised their voices and praised the LORD with these words:

> "He is good!
> His faithful love endures forever!"

At that moment a thick cloud filled the Temple of the LORD. ¹⁴The priests could not continue their service because of the cloud, for the glorious presence of the LORD filled the Temple of God.

CHAPTER 6
Solomon Praises the LORD
Then Solomon prayed, "O LORD, you have said that you would live in a thick cloud of darkness. ²Now I have built a glorious Temple for you, a place where you can live forever!"

³Then the king turned around to the entire community of Israel standing before him and gave this blessing: ⁴"Praise the LORD, the God of Israel, who has kept the promise he made to my father, David. For he told my father, ⁵'From the day I brought my people out of the land of Egypt, I have never chosen a city among any of the tribes of Israel as the place where a Temple should be built to honor my name. Nor have I chosen a king to lead my people Israel. ⁶But now I have chosen Jerusalem as the place for my name to be honored, and I have chosen David to be king over my people Israel.'"

⁷Then Solomon said, "My father, David, wanted to build this Temple to honor the name of the LORD, the God of Israel. ⁸But the LORD told him, 'You wanted to build the Temple to honor my name. Your intention is good, ⁹but you are not the one to do it. One of your own sons will build the Temple to honor me.'

¹⁰"And now the LORD has fulfilled the promise he made, for I have become king in my father's place, and now I sit on the throne of Israel, just as the LORD promised. I have built this Temple to honor the name of the LORD, the God of Israel. ¹¹There I have placed the Ark, which contains the covenant that the LORD made with the people of Israel."

Solomon's Prayer of Dedication
¹²Then Solomon stood before the altar of the LORD in front of the entire community of Israel, and he lifted his hands in prayer. ¹³Now Solomon had made a bronze platform 7½ feet long, 7½ feet wide, and 4½ feet high* and had placed it at the center of the Temple's outer courtyard. He stood on the platform, and then he knelt in front of the entire community of Israel and lifted his hands toward heaven. ¹⁴He prayed,

"O LORD, God of Israel, there is no God like you in all of heaven and earth. You keep your covenant and show unfailing love to all who walk before you in wholehearted devotion. ¹⁵You have kept your promise to your servant David, my father. You made that promise with your own mouth, and with your own hands you have fulfilled it today.

¹⁶"And now, O LORD, God of Israel, carry out the additional promise you made to your servant David, my father. For you said to him, 'If your descendants guard their behavior and faithfully follow my Law as you have done, one of them will always sit on the throne of Israel.' ¹⁷Now, O LORD, God of Israel, fulfill this promise to your servant David.

¹⁸"But will God really live on earth among people? Why, even the highest heavens cannot contain you. How much less this Temple I have built! ¹⁹Nevertheless, listen to my prayer and my plea, O LORD my God. Hear the cry and the prayer that your servant is making to you. ²⁰May you watch over this Temple day and night, this place where you have said you would put your name. May you always hear the prayers I make toward this place. ²¹May you hear the humble and earnest requests from me and your people Israel when we pray toward this place. Yes, hear us from heaven where you live, and when you hear, forgive.

6:13 Hebrew *5 cubits* [2.3 meters] *long, 5 cubits wide, and 3 cubits* [1.4 meters] *high.*

6:14 We often become impressed by trendy strategies that claim they can solve all our problems. New techniques or programs promise to accomplish great changes in our life. Usually these programs are filled with human wisdom that urges us to fix our problems by our own strength. This verse reminds us that there is no substitute for God. He alone is able to empower us for recovery. God's promises are realized only when we submit to God's will. Although God gives us the power to recover, he also asks that we put our life into his hands.

²²"If someone wrongs another person and is required to take an oath of innocence in front of your altar at this Temple, ²³then hear from heaven and judge between your servants—the accuser and the accused. Pay back the guilty as they deserve. Acquit the innocent because of their innocence.

²⁴"If your people Israel are defeated by their enemies because they have sinned against you, and if they turn back and acknowledge your name and pray to you here in this Temple, ²⁵then hear from heaven and forgive the sin of your people Israel and return them to this land you gave to them and to their ancestors.

²⁶"If the skies are shut up and there is no rain because your people have sinned against you, and if they pray toward this Temple and acknowledge your name and turn from their sins because you have punished them, ²⁷then hear from heaven and forgive the sins of your servants, your people Israel. Teach them to follow the right path, and send rain on your land that you have given to your people as their special possession.

²⁸"If there is a famine in the land or a plague or crop disease or attacks of locusts or caterpillars, or if your people's enemies are in the land besieging their towns—whatever disaster or disease there is—²⁹and if your people Israel pray about their troubles or sorrow, raising their hands toward this Temple, ³⁰then hear from heaven where you live, and forgive. Give your people what their actions deserve, for you alone know each human heart. ³¹Then they will fear you and walk in your ways as long as they live in the land you gave to our ancestors.

³²"In the future, foreigners who do not belong to your people Israel will hear of you. They will come from distant lands when they hear of your great name and your strong hand and your powerful arm. And when they pray toward this Temple, ³³then hear from heaven where you live, and grant what they ask of you. In this way, all the people of the earth will come

to know and fear you, just as your own people Israel do. They, too, will know that this Temple I have built honors your name.

³⁴"If your people go out where you send them to fight their enemies, and if they pray to you by turning toward this city you have chosen and toward this Temple I have built to honor your name, ³⁵then hear their prayers from heaven and uphold their cause.

³⁶"If they sin against you—and who has never sinned?—you might become angry with them and let their enemies conquer them and take them captive to a foreign land far away or near. ³⁷But in that land of exile, they might turn to you in repentance and pray, 'We have sinned, done evil, and acted wickedly.' ³⁸If they turn to you with their whole heart and soul in the land of their captivity and pray toward the land you gave to their ancestors—toward this city you have chosen, and toward this Temple I have built to honor your name—³⁹then hear their prayers and their petitions from heaven where you live, and uphold their cause. Forgive your people who have sinned against you.

⁴⁰"O my God, may your eyes be open and your ears attentive to all the prayers made to you in this place.

⁴¹"And now arise, O LORD God, and enter
> your resting place,
> along with the Ark, the symbol of
> your power.
> May your priests, O LORD God, be
> clothed with salvation;
> may your loyal servants rejoice in
> your goodness.
⁴²O LORD God, do not reject the king you
> have anointed.
> Remember your unfailing love for
> your servant David."

CHAPTER 7
The Dedication of the Temple

When Solomon finished praying, fire flashed down from heaven and burned up the burnt offerings and sacrifices, and the glorious

---

6:36-40 Prayer is one of our greatest privileges! Solomon pleaded with God, asking him to listen to his people's cries for help and forgiveness. Today we need not plead with God to listen. Jesus Christ, the Son of God, now mediates our conversations with God. We can approach God at any time through Jesus, whose sacrificial death made reconciliation with God possible. Solomon had to plead that his prayers would be heard, but we are absolutely assured of a hearing!

7:1-3 God sent fire down from heaven to consume the offerings and sacrifices and to show that the new Temple was acceptable to him. The people's response was powerful: They fell on their

presence of the LORD filled the Temple. ²The priests could not enter the Temple of the LORD because the glorious presence of the LORD filled it. ³When all the people of Israel saw the fire coming down and the glorious presence of the LORD filling the Temple, they fell face down on the ground and worshiped and praised the LORD, saying,

"He is good!
His faithful love endures forever!"

⁴Then the king and all the people offered sacrifices to the LORD. ⁵King Solomon offered a sacrifice of 22,000 cattle and 120,000 sheep and goats. And so the king and all the people dedicated the Temple of God. ⁶The priests took their assigned positions, and so did the Levites who were singing, "His faithful love endures forever!" They accompanied the singing with music from the instruments King David had made for praising the LORD. Across from the Levites, the priests blew the trumpets, while all Israel stood.

⁷Solomon then consecrated the central area of the courtyard in front of the LORD's Temple. He offered burnt offerings and the fat of peace offerings there, because the bronze altar he had built could not hold all the burnt offerings, grain offerings, and sacrificial fat.

⁸For the next seven days Solomon and all Israel celebrated the Festival of Shelters.* A large congregation had gathered from as far away as Lebo-hamath in the north and the Brook of Egypt in the south. ⁹On the eighth day they had a closing ceremony, for they had celebrated the dedication of the altar for seven days and the Festival of Shelters for seven days. ¹⁰Then at the end of the celebration,* Solomon sent the people home. They were all joyful and glad because the LORD had been so good to David and to Solomon and to his people Israel.

The LORD's Response to Solomon

¹¹So Solomon finished the Temple of the LORD, as well as the royal palace. He completed everything he had planned to do in the construction of the Temple and the palace. ¹²Then one night the LORD appeared to Solomon and said,

"I have heard your prayer and have chosen this Temple as the place for making sacrifices. ¹³At times I might shut up the heavens so that no rain falls, or command grasshoppers to devour your crops, or send plagues among you. ¹⁴Then if my people who are called by my name will humble themselves and pray and seek my face and turn from their wicked ways, I will hear from heaven and will forgive their sins and restore their land. ¹⁵My eyes will be open and my ears attentive to every prayer made in this place. ¹⁶For I have chosen this Temple and set it apart to be holy—a place where my name will be honored forever. I will always watch over it, for it is dear to my heart.

¹⁷"As for you, if you faithfully follow me as David your father did, obeying all my commands, decrees, and regulations, ¹⁸then I will establish the throne of your dynasty. For I made this covenant with your father, David, when I said, 'One of your descendants will always rule over Israel.'

¹⁹"But if you or your descendants abandon me and disobey the decrees and commands I have given you, and if you serve and worship other gods, ²⁰then I will uproot the people from this land that I have given them. I will reject this Temple that I have made holy to honor my name. I will make it an object of mockery and ridicule among the nations. ²¹And though this Temple is impressive now, all who pass by will be appalled. They will ask, 'Why did the LORD do such terrible things to this land and to this Temple?'

²²"And the answer will be, 'Because his people abandoned the LORD, the God of their ancestors, who brought them out of Egypt, and they worshiped other gods

---

7:8 Hebrew *the festival* (also in 7:9); see note on 5:3. **7:10** Hebrew *Then on the twenty-third day of the seventh month.* This day of the ancient Hebrew lunar calendar occurred in October or early November.

---

faces in worship and praise to God. Their response was the right one after completing such a monumental task as building the Temple: They affirmed God's goodness as they thanked him for his love and faithfulness. As we experience great victory in our life, we also need to affirm God's goodness.

7:14 This verse contains one of God's greatest promises to Israel. Although this promise was given specifically to Old Testament Israel, we know that through Jesus Christ, God does listen to our prayers, and he does forgive our sins as we confess them. It is part of God's nature to be forgiving. This fact should give us great comfort as we seek to deal with our past failures.

instead and bowed down to them. That is why he has brought all these disasters on them.'"

CHAPTER 8
Solomon's Many Achievements

It took Solomon twenty years to build the LORD's Temple and his own royal palace. At the end of that time, ²Solomon turned his attention to rebuilding the towns that King Hiram* had given him, and he settled Israelites in them.

³Solomon also fought against the town of Hamath-zobah and conquered it. ⁴He rebuilt Tadmor in the wilderness and built towns in the region of Hamath as supply centers. ⁵He fortified the towns of Upper Beth-horon and Lower Beth-horon, rebuilding their walls and installing barred gates. ⁶He also rebuilt Baalath and other supply centers and constructed towns where his chariots and horses* could be stationed. He built everything he desired in Jerusalem and Lebanon and throughout his entire realm.

⁷There were still some people living in the land who were not Israelites, including the Hittites, Amorites, Perizzites, Hivites, and Jebusites. ⁸These were descendants of the nations whom the people of Israel had not destroyed. So Solomon conscripted them for his labor force, and they serve as forced laborers to this day. ⁹But Solomon did not conscript any of the Israelites for his labor force. Instead, he assigned them to serve as fighting men, officers in his army, commanders of his chariots, and charioteers. ¹⁰King Solomon appointed 250 of them to supervise the people.

¹¹Solomon moved his wife, Pharaoh's daughter, from the City of David to the new palace he had built for her. He said, "My wife must not live in King David's palace, for the Ark of the LORD has been there, and it is holy ground."

¹²Then Solomon presented burnt offerings to the LORD on the altar he had built for him in front of the entry room of the Temple. ¹³He offered the sacrifices for the Sabbaths, the new moon festivals, and the three annual festivals—the Passover celebration, the Festival of Harvest,* and the Festival of Shelters—as Moses had commanded.

¹⁴In assigning the priests to their duties, Solomon followed the regulations of his father, David. He also assigned the Levites to lead the people in praise and to assist the priests in their daily duties. And he assigned the gatekeepers to their gates by their divisions, following the commands of David, the man of God. ¹⁵Solomon did not deviate in any way from David's commands concerning the priests and Levites and the treasuries.

¹⁶So Solomon made sure that all the work related to building the Temple of the LORD was carried out, from the day its foundation was laid to the day of its completion.

¹⁷Later Solomon went to Ezion-geber and Elath,* ports along the shore of the Red Sea* in the land of Edom. ¹⁸Hiram sent him ships commanded by his own officers and manned by experienced crews of sailors. These ships sailed to Ophir with Solomon's men and brought back to Solomon almost seventeen tons* of gold.

CHAPTER 9
Visit of the Queen of Sheba

When the queen of Sheba heard of Solomon's fame, she came to Jerusalem to test him with hard questions. She arrived with a large group

---

8:2 Hebrew *Huram,* a variant spelling of Hiram; also in 8:18. 8:6 Or *and charioteers.* 8:13 Or *Festival of Weeks.* 8:17a As in Greek version (see also 2 Kgs 14:22; 16:6); Hebrew reads *Eloth,* a variant spelling of Elath. 8:17b As in parallel text at 1 Kgs 9:26; Hebrew reads *the sea.* 8:18 Hebrew *450 talents* [15.3 metric tons].

8:3 Even for Solomon, whose name means "peaceful," some conflict was necessary. As we work toward recovery, we must admit that conflict is a part of life. Admitting this truth is an important step for all of us in recovery. If we believe that the world should be a bed of roses, we are living in denial. A successful recovery program recognizes that we are in a constant state of warfare against the forces that stand against us. If we fail to recognize this and don't prepare for the battle, our chances for recovery are minimal.

8:11 In Solomon's day it was common for a head of state to confirm a treaty with a foreign king by marrying one of his daughters. Solomon accepted this worldly practice and married numerous foreign wives to validate his treaties with the surrounding nations. This practice eventually led Solomon into idolatry. We may be tempted to seek recovery through the latest recovery fad. If any recovery practice or belief system denies God's Word or leads us away from God, we need to avoid it at any cost.

8:16 It is a glorious feeling to complete a worthwhile project. Many Bible scholars feel that Solomon's greatest accomplishment was the building of the Temple. He did it for God's purposes and in God's way. This is the only kind of building project that honors God.

of attendants and a great caravan of camels loaded with spices, large quantities of gold, and precious jewels. When she met with Solomon, she talked with him about everything she had on her mind. ²Solomon had answers for all her questions; nothing was too hard for him to explain to her. ³When the queen of Sheba realized how wise Solomon was, and when she saw the palace he had built, ⁴she was overwhelmed. She was also amazed at the food on his tables, the organization of his officials and their splendid clothing, the cup-bearers and their robes, and the burnt offerings* Solomon made at the Temple of the LORD.

⁵She exclaimed to the king, "Everything I heard in my country about your achievements* and wisdom is true! ⁶I didn't believe what was said until I arrived here and saw it with my own eyes. In fact, I had not heard the half of your great wisdom! It is far beyond what I was told. ⁷How happy your people must be! What a privilege for your officials to stand here day after day, listening to your wisdom! ⁸Praise the LORD your God, who delights in you and has placed you on the throne as king to rule for him. Because God loves Israel and desires this kingdom to last forever, he has made you king over them so you can rule with justice and righteousness."

⁹Then she gave the king a gift of 9,000 pounds* of gold, great quantities of spices, and precious jewels. Never before had there been spices as fine as those the queen of Sheba gave to King Solomon.

¹⁰(In addition, the crews of Hiram and Solomon brought gold from Ophir, and they also brought red sandalwood* and precious jewels. ¹¹The king used the sandalwood to make steps* for the Temple of the LORD and the royal palace, and to construct lyres and harps for the musicians. Never before had such beautiful things been seen in Judah.)

¹²King Solomon gave the queen of Sheba whatever she asked for—gifts of greater value than the gifts she had given him. Then she and all her attendants returned to their own land.

Solomon's Wealth and Splendor

¹³Each year Solomon received about 25 tons* of gold. ¹⁴This did not include the additional revenue he received from merchants and traders. All the kings of Arabia and the governors of the provinces also brought gold and silver to Solomon.

¹⁵King Solomon made 200 large shields of hammered gold, each weighing more than 15 pounds.* ¹⁶He also made 300 smaller shields of hammered gold, each weighing more than 7½ pounds.* The king placed these shields in the Palace of the Forest of Lebanon.

¹⁷Then the king made a huge throne, decorated with ivory and overlaid with pure gold. ¹⁸The throne had six steps, with a footstool of gold. There were armrests on both sides of the seat, and the figure of a lion stood on each side of the throne. ¹⁹There were also twelve other lions, one standing on each end of the six steps. No other throne in all the world could be compared with it!

²⁰All of King Solomon's drinking cups were solid gold, as were all the utensils in the Palace of the Forest of Lebanon. They were not made of silver, for silver was considered worthless in Solomon's day!

²¹The king had a fleet of trading ships of Tarshish manned by the sailors sent by Hiram.* Once every three years the ships returned, loaded with gold, silver, ivory, apes, and peacocks.*

²²So King Solomon became richer and wiser than any other king on earth. ²³Kings from every nation came to consult him and to hear the wisdom God had given him. ²⁴Year after year everyone who visited brought him gifts of silver and gold, clothing, weapons, spices, horses, and mules.

²⁵Solomon had 4,000 stalls for his horses and chariots, and he had 12,000 horses.* He stationed some of them in the chariot cities, and some near him in Jerusalem. ²⁶He ruled over all the kings from the Euphrates River* in the north to the land of the Philistines

---

9:4 As in Greek and Syriac versions (see also 1 Kgs 10:5); Hebrew reads *and the ascent.* 9:5 Hebrew *your words.* 9:9 Hebrew *120 talents* [4,000 kilograms]. 9:10 Hebrew *algum wood* (also in 9:11); perhaps a variant spelling of *almug.* Compare parallel text at 1 Kgs 10:11-12. 9:11 Or *gateways.* The meaning of the Hebrew is uncertain. 9:13 Hebrew *666 talents* [23 metric tons]. 9:15 Hebrew *600 [shekels] of hammered gold* [6.8 kilograms]. 9:16 Hebrew *300 [shekels] of gold* [3.4 kilograms]. 9:21a Hebrew *Huram,* a variant spelling of Hiram. 9:21b Or *and baboons.* 9:25 Or *12,000 charioteers.* 9:26 Hebrew *the river.*

9:25 When we seek security from any strategy or resource outside of God himself, we are in grave danger. David refused to trust in horses and the military advantages they offered (1 Chronicles 18:4; see Deuteronomy 17:16). Unfortunately, Solomon did not follow his father's example. We will never succeed in recovery until we learn that God alone is capable of leading us to victory. No other resource is capable of supporting us as we experience the trials of rebuilding our life.

and the border of Egypt in the south. [27]The king made silver as plentiful in Jerusalem as stone. And valuable cedar timber was as common as the sycamore-fig trees that grow in the foothills of Judah.* [28]Solomon's horses were imported from Egypt* and many other countries.

Summary of Solomon's Reign

[29]The rest of the events of Solomon's reign, from beginning to end, are recorded in *The Record of Nathan the Prophet,* and *The Prophecy of Ahijah from Shiloh,* and also in *The Visions of Iddo the Seer,* concerning Jeroboam son of Nebat. [30]Solomon ruled in Jerusalem over all Israel for forty years. [31]When he died, he was buried in the City of David, named for his father. Then his son Rehoboam became the next king.

CHAPTER 10

The Northern Tribes Revolt

Rehoboam went to Shechem, where all Israel had gathered to make him king. [2]When Jeroboam son of Nebat heard of this, he returned from Egypt, for he had fled to Egypt to escape from King Solomon. [3]The leaders of Israel summoned him, and Jeroboam and all Israel went to speak with Rehoboam. [4]"Your father was a hard master," they said. "Lighten the harsh labor demands and heavy taxes that your father imposed on us. Then we will be your loyal subjects."

[5]Rehoboam replied, "Come back in three days for my answer." So the people went away.

[6]Then King Rehoboam discussed the matter with the older men who had counseled his father, Solomon. "What is your advice?" he asked. "How should I answer these people?"

[7]The older counselors replied, "If you are good to these people and do your best to please them and give them a favorable answer, they will always be your loyal subjects."

[8]But Rehoboam rejected the advice of the older men and instead asked the opinion of the young men who had grown up with him and were now his advisers. [9]"What is your advice?" he asked them. "How should I answer these people who want me to lighten the burdens imposed by my father?"

[10]The young men replied, "This is what you should tell those complainers who want a lighter burden: 'My little finger is thicker than my father's waist! [11]Yes, my father laid heavy burdens on you, but I'm going to make them even heavier! My father beat you with whips, but I will beat you with scorpions!'"

[12]Three days later Jeroboam and all the people returned to hear Rehoboam's decision, just as the king had ordered. [13]But Rehoboam spoke harshly to them, for he rejected the advice of the older counselors [14]and followed the counsel of his younger advisers. He told the people, "My father laid* heavy burdens on you, but I'm going to make them even heavier! My father beat you with whips, but I will beat you with scorpions!"

[15]So the king paid no attention to the people. This turn of events was the will of God, for it fulfilled the LORD's message to Jeroboam son of Nebat through the prophet Ahijah from Shiloh.

[16]When all Israel realized* that the king had refused to listen to them, they responded,

"Down with the dynasty of David!
 We have no interest in the son of Jesse.
Back to your homes, O Israel!
 Look out for your own house,
  O David!"

So all the people of Israel returned home. [17]But Rehoboam continued to rule over the Israelites who lived in the towns of Judah.

9:27 Hebrew *the Shephelah.* 9:28 Possibly *Muzur,* a district near Cilicia. 10:14 As in Greek version and many Hebrew manuscripts (see also 1 Kgs 12:14); Masoretic Text reads *I will lay.* 10:16 As in Syriac version, Latin Vulgate, and many Hebrew manuscripts (see also 1 Kgs 12:16); Masoretic Text lacks *realized.*

10:1-14 Rehoboam followed some foolish advice in responding to what seemed a reasonable request. Advice is cheap. We will always have people trying to tell us how to live. Sometimes that advice will be godly; other times it will be foolish. Before heeding the advice of any individual, we should look at the fruits of that person's own life. Where have that person's decisions led him or her? Also check whether or not the advice is in line with God's revealed will. If it contradicts God's Word, it must be rejected.

10:15-16 Responding to Rehoboam's foolish decision, the people rebelled and split the kingdom of Israel in two. Two wrongs never make a right. The consequences that followed the rebellion and division were far more harmful to Israel than were the foolish actions of Rehoboam. Their actions eventually led the northern tribes away from God and toward destruction. We are often tempted to take rash measures when we are mistreated by others or when they fail to take our claims seriously. Before doing anything, we must prayerfully and carefully consider the long-term consequences.

[18]King Rehoboam sent Adoniram,* who was in charge of forced labor, to restore order, but the people of Israel stoned him to death. When this news reached King Rehoboam, he quickly jumped into his chariot and fled to Jerusalem. [19]And to this day the northern tribes of Israel have refused to be ruled by a descendant of David.

CHAPTER 11
Shemaiah's Prophecy
When Rehoboam arrived at Jerusalem, he mobilized the men of Judah and Benjamin—180,000 select troops—to fight against Israel and to restore the kingdom to himself.

[2]But the LORD said to Shemaiah, the man of God, [3]"Say to Rehoboam son of Solomon, king of Judah, and to all the Israelites in Judah and Benjamin: [4]"This is what the LORD says: Do not fight against your relatives. Go back home, for what has happened is my doing!'" So they obeyed the message of the LORD and did not fight against Jeroboam.

Rehoboam Fortifies Judah
[5]Rehoboam remained in Jerusalem and fortified various towns for the defense of Judah. [6]He built up Bethlehem, Etam, Tekoa, [7]Bethzur, Soco, Adullam, [8]Gath, Mareshah, Ziph, [9]Adoraim, Lachish, Azekah, [10]Zorah, Aijalon, and Hebron. These became the fortified towns of Judah and Benjamin. [11]Rehoboam strengthened their defenses and stationed commanders in them, and he stored supplies of food, olive oil, and wine. [12]He also put shields and spears in these towns as a further safety measure. So only Judah and Benjamin remained under his control.

[13]But all the priests and Levites living among the northern tribes of Israel sided with Rehoboam. [14]The Levites even abandoned their pasturelands and property and moved to Judah and Jerusalem, because Jeroboam and his sons would not allow them to serve the LORD as priests. [15]Jeroboam appointed his own priests to serve at the pagan shrines, where they worshiped the goat and calf idols he had made. [16]From all the tribes of Israel, those who sincerely wanted to worship the LORD, the God of Israel, followed the Levites to Jerusalem, where they could offer sacrifices to the LORD, the God of their ancestors. [17]This strengthened the kingdom of Judah, and for three years they supported Rehoboam son of Solomon, for during those years they faithfully followed in the footsteps of David and Solomon.

Rehoboam's Family
[18]Rehoboam married his cousin Mahalath, the daughter of David's son Jerimoth and of Abihail, the daughter of Eliab son of Jesse. [19]Mahalath had three sons—Jeush, Shemariah, and Zaham.

[20]Later Rehoboam married another cousin, Maacah, the granddaughter of Absalom.

10:18 Hebrew *Hadoram,* a variant spelling of Adoniram; compare 1 Kgs 4:6; 5:14; 12:18.

10:18-19 When Rehoboam sent Adoniram, who was in charge of the labor force, to restore order among the rebels, he was headed for trouble. The northern tribes had rebelled mainly because of the forced labor demanded by Solomon. This automatically caused the rebels to explode. When we seek reconciliation with the people we have wronged, we should do so wisely. We should look for common ground and build on it. We should not foolishly emphasize differences that will impair the recovery process.

11:1-12 Rehoboam was tempted to take matters into his own hands. He was preparing to attack Jeroboam and the northern kingdom when God's messenger came to warn him against the invasion. To Rehoboam's credit, he listened to God and abandoned his plans. Our plans and programs likewise need to be subject to God's leading. We need to be ready to change course based on the directions God gives us. If we try to do things our own way, the outcome could often be disastrous.

11:15 Most of us try to justify our actions, and it is tempting to use religion to do this. Jeroboam ordained false priests to provide religious respectability for his kingdom. We often do the same thing when we face difficulties in our life. We attempt to justify our actions by finding something in the Bible to support us or by naming some religious authority who agrees with our position. Doing this, however, usually only compounds our problems by defending our sins. In recovery, we must take inventory of our failures and seek, with God's help, to make restitution and take steps to avoid repeating our mistakes.

11:20-23 The families of most of Israel's kings show us what a family should not be like. Rehoboam was no exception. His multiple marriages led to favoritism and, apparently, rivalry among his sons. To maintain peace in his family, Rehoboam had to give his sons positions of responsibility in separate cities. Evidently the conflict in his family was somewhat explosive. Rehoboam's solution was certainly a wise one, though it was only a "Band-Aid solution." The real problem was rooted in his family relationships. Families that are forced to deal with multiple marriages, whether due to polygamy or divorce, always suffer.

Maacah gave birth to Abijah, Attai, Ziza, and Shelomith. 21Rehoboam loved Maacah more than any of his other wives and concubines. In all, he had eighteen wives and sixty concubines, and they gave birth to twenty-eight sons and sixty daughters.

22Rehoboam appointed Maacah's son Abijah as leader among the princes, making it clear that he would be the next king. 23Rehoboam also wisely gave responsibilities to his other sons and stationed some of them in the fortified towns throughout the land of Judah and Benjamin. He provided them with generous provisions, and he found many wives for them.

CHAPTER 12
Egypt Invades Judah
But when Rehoboam was firmly established and strong, he abandoned the Law of the LORD, and all Israel followed him in this sin. 2Because they were unfaithful to the LORD, King Shishak of Egypt came up and attacked Jerusalem in the fifth year of King Rehoboam's reign. 3He came with 1,200 chariots, 60,000 horses,* and a countless army of foot soldiers, including Libyans, Sukkites, and Ethiopians.* 4Shishak conquered Judah's fortified towns and then advanced to attack Jerusalem.

5The prophet Shemaiah then met with Rehoboam and Judah's leaders, who had all fled to Jerusalem because of Shishak. Shemaiah told them, "This is what the LORD says: You have abandoned me, so I am abandoning you to Shishak."

6Then the leaders of Israel and the king humbled themselves and said, "The LORD is right in doing this to us!"

7When the LORD saw their change of heart, he gave this message to Shemaiah: "Since the people have humbled themselves, I will not completely destroy them and will soon give them some relief. I will not use Shishak to pour out my anger on Jerusalem. 8But they will become his subjects, so they will know the difference between serving me and serving earthly rulers."

9So King Shishak of Egypt came up and attacked Jerusalem. He ransacked the treasuries of the LORD's Temple and the royal palace; he stole everything, including all the gold shields Solomon had made. 10King Rehoboam later replaced them with bronze shields as substitutes, and he entrusted them to the care of the commanders of the guard who protected the entrance to the royal palace. 11Whenever the king went to the Temple of the LORD, the guards would also take the shields and then return them to the guardroom. 12Because Rehoboam humbled himself, the LORD's anger was turned away, and he did not destroy him completely. There were still some good things in the land of Judah.

Summary of Rehoboam's Reign
13King Rehoboam firmly established himself in Jerusalem and continued to rule. He was forty-one years old when he became king, and he reigned seventeen years in Jerusalem, the city the LORD had chosen from among all the tribes of Israel as the place to honor his name. Rehoboam's mother was Naamah, a woman from Ammon. 14But he was an evil king, for he did not seek the LORD with all his heart.

12:3a Or *charioteers,* or *horsemen.* 12:3b Hebrew *and Cushites.*

12:1-4 When things begin to go well in our life, we need to sound the alarm! With success comes the danger of self-sufficiency. When Rehoboam became established and began to feel secure, he forsook his obligation to lead the people closer to God. As a result, the whole nation fell into sin and was defeated by the Egyptians. In recovery, the same thing tends to happen. When things are going well, we begin to relax. We need to stay alert, realizing that good times often make us more vulnerable to a fall.

12:5 Turning from God has its consequences. Rehoboam had failed to lead his people in godly ways. As a result, they were abandoned by God. The prophet Shemaiah gave God's message in no uncertain terms: "You have abandoned me, so I am abandoning you." God loves us and wants us to live a life that honors him. We cannot sin with impunity. Sin always brings destructive consequences. The most terrible consequence of all might be abandonment by God, without whom recovery is impossible. If we have failed and sought forgiveness, however, God will help us deal with our past failures.

12:13-15 How might our epitaph read? What have we done in our life that is worth remembering? How will people remember our relationship with God when we die? Rehoboam's epitaph reads: "He was an evil king, for he did not seek the LORD with all his heart." Sadly, we spend too little time really seeking God. That is one reason recovery is so difficult for us. When we die, our wealth and achievements will soon be forgotten. Our relationship with God and the things we do for him are the only things that will last. We would be wise to put our energy into things of eternal value.

[15]The rest of the events of Rehoboam's reign, from beginning to end, are recorded in *The Record of Shemaiah the Prophet* and *The Record of Iddo the Seer*, which are part of the genealogical record. Rehoboam and Jeroboam were continually at war with each other. [16]When Rehoboam died, he was buried in the City of David. Then his son Abijah became the next king.

CHAPTER 13
Abijah's War with Jeroboam

Abijah began to rule over Judah in the eighteenth year of Jeroboam's reign in Israel. [2]He reigned in Jerusalem three years. His mother was Maacah,* the daughter of Uriel from Gibeah.

Then war broke out between Abijah and Jeroboam. [3]Judah, led by King Abijah, fielded 400,000 select warriors, while Jeroboam mustered 800,000 select troops from Israel.

[4]When the army of Judah arrived in the hill country of Ephraim, Abijah stood on Mount Zemaraim and shouted to Jeroboam and all Israel: "Listen to me! [5]Don't you realize that the LORD, the God of Israel, made a lasting covenant* with David, giving him and his descendants the throne of Israel forever? [6]Yet Jeroboam son of Nebat, a mere servant of David's son Solomon, rebelled against his master. [7]Then a whole gang of scoundrels joined him, defying Solomon's son Rehoboam when he was young and inexperienced and could not stand up to them.

[8]"Do you really think you can stand against the kingdom of the LORD that is led by the descendants of David? You may have a vast army, and you have those gold calves that Jeroboam made as your gods. [9]But you have chased away the priests of the LORD (the descendants of Aaron) and the Levites, and you have appointed your own priests, just like the pagan nations. You let anyone become a priest these days! Whoever comes to be dedicated with a young bull and seven rams can become a priest of these so-called gods of yours!

[10]"But as for us, the LORD is our God, and we have not abandoned him. Only the descendants of Aaron serve the LORD as priests, and the Levites alone may help them in their work. [11]They present burnt offerings and fragrant incense to the LORD every morning and evening. They place the Bread of the Presence on the holy table, and they light the gold lampstand every evening. We are following the instructions of the LORD our God, but you have abandoned him. [12]So you see, God is with us. He is our leader. His priests blow their trumpets and lead us into battle against you. O people of Israel, do not fight against the LORD, the God of your ancestors, for you will not succeed!"

[13]Meanwhile, Jeroboam had secretly sent part of his army around behind the men of Judah to ambush them. [14]When Judah realized that they were being attacked from the front and the rear, they cried out to the LORD for help. Then the priests blew the trumpets, [15]and the men of Judah began to shout. At the sound of their battle cry, God defeated Jeroboam and all Israel and routed them before Abijah and the army of Judah.

[16]The Israelite army fled from Judah, and God handed them over to Judah in defeat. [17]Abijah and his army inflicted heavy losses on them; 500,000 of Israel's select troops were killed that day. [18]So Judah defeated Israel on that occasion because they trusted in the LORD, the God of their ancestors. [19]Abijah and his army pursued Jeroboam's troops and captured some of his towns, including

13:2 As in most Greek manuscripts and Syriac version (see also 2 Chr 11:20-21; 1 Kgs 15:2); Hebrew reads *Micaiah,* a variant spelling of Maacah. 13:5 Hebrew *a covenant of salt.*

13:1-9 Abijah was about to go into a battle in which his army was vastly outnumbered. But instead of giving in to fear, he stood firm because of his faith in God's promises. In the process of recovery we will battle many difficult situations. If we try to face them alone, we will fail. We need to stand on the many promises God has given us in Scripture and trust him to deliver us. We must learn to live by faith when it is impossible to live by sight.

13:10-14 When the going gets tough, it is a good idea to have God on our side. Abijah said, "The LORD is our God, and we have not abandoned him." If we draw close to God, he will draw close to us. As we encounter difficulties or negative patterns in our life, we will certainly need his help to win the battles we face.

13:18-20 There is great danger in rebelling against God. Sometimes it may seem that God is not paying attention—people seem to get away with murder. But what we sow, we will eventually reap. Jeroboam seemed to be successful, but eventually his sins caught up with him. He was soundly defeated by a small army from Judah, which was set firmly in God's hands. Sin has inevitable consequences. We must root it out of our life before it leads us to destruction.

Bethel, Jeshanah, and Ephron, along with their surrounding villages.

²⁰So Jeroboam of Israel never regained his power during Abijah's lifetime, and finally the LORD struck him down and he died. ²¹Meanwhile, Abijah of Judah grew more and more powerful. He married fourteen wives and had twenty-two sons and sixteen daughters.

²²The rest of the events of Abijah's reign, including his words and deeds, are recorded in *The Commentary of Iddo the Prophet.*

CHAPTER 14
Early Years of Asa's Reign

¹*When Abijah died, he was buried in the City of David. Then his son Asa became the next king. There was peace in the land for ten years. ²*Asa did what was pleasing and good in the sight of the LORD his God. ³He removed the foreign altars and the pagan shrines. He smashed the sacred pillars and cut down the Asherah poles. ⁴He commanded the people of Judah to seek the LORD, the God of their ancestors, and to obey his law and his commands. ⁵Asa also removed the pagan shrines, as well as the incense altars from every one of Judah's towns. So Asa's kingdom enjoyed a period of peace. ⁶During those peaceful years, he was able to build up the fortified towns throughout Judah. No one tried to make war against him at this time, for the LORD was giving him rest from his enemies.

⁷Asa told the people of Judah, "Let us build towns and fortify them with walls, towers, gates, and bars. The land is still ours because we sought the LORD our God, and he has given us peace on every side." So they went ahead with these projects and brought them to completion.

⁸King Asa had an army of 300,000 warriors from the tribe of Judah, armed with large shields and spears. He also had an army of 280,000 warriors from the tribe of Benjamin, armed with small shields and bows. Both armies were composed of well-trained fighting men.

⁹Once an Ethiopian* named Zerah attacked Judah with an army of 1,000,000 men* and 300 chariots. They advanced to the town of Mareshah, ¹⁰so Asa deployed his armies for battle in the valley north of Mareshah.* ¹¹Then Asa cried out to the LORD his God, "O LORD, no one but you can help the powerless against the mighty! Help us, O LORD our God, for we trust in you alone. It is in your name that we have come against this vast horde. O LORD, you are our God; do not let mere men prevail against you!"

¹²So the LORD defeated the Ethiopians* in the presence of Asa and the army of Judah, and the enemy fled. ¹³Asa and his army pursued them as far as Gerar, and so many Ethiopians fell that they were unable to rally. They were destroyed by the LORD and his army, and the army of Judah carried off a vast amount of plunder.

¹⁴While they were at Gerar, they attacked all the towns in that area, and terror from the LORD came upon the people there. As a result, a vast amount of plunder was taken from these towns, too. ¹⁵They also attacked the camps of herdsmen and captured many sheep, goats, and camels before finally returning to Jerusalem.

CHAPTER 15
Asa's Religious Reforms

Then the Spirit of God came upon Azariah son of Oded, ²and he went out to meet King

---

14:1 Verse 14:1 is numbered 13:23 in the Hebrew text.   14:2 Verses 14:2-15 are numbered 14:1-14 in Hebrew text.
14:9a Hebrew *a Cushite.*   14:9b Or *an army of thousands and thousands;* Hebrew reads *an army of a thousand thousands.*
14:10 As in Greek version; Hebrew reads *valley of Zephathah near Mareshah.*   14:12 Hebrew *Cushites;* also in 14:13.

14:1-2 The world's measure of success is not the same as God's measure. Every action, attitude, decision, and feeling needs to be measured by the criterion suggested by Asa's life. "Asa did what was pleasing and good in the sight of the LORD his God." Obedience to the revealed will of God is an essential step in the rebuilding process. If we are unwilling to obey God's program, there is little hope for recovery.

14:9-15 Asa was about to be overwhelmed by a mighty enemy army, but he cried out to God, admitting his powerlessness. This was his first step toward victory. Asa was willing to trust that God would deliver him. God comes through when we admit our weakness and look to him for help, but we need to take that all-important first step.

15:4 God is a forgiving God. No matter how deep the stain of sin upon the people of Israel, God forgave them when they chose to repent. We may have failed so often that we believe we are beyond the point of God's forgiveness and care. It is never too late to turn to God! When we cry out for help, he will respond with restoration and forgiveness. Then he will give us the courage we need to deal with the problems before us.

GOD grant me the serenity
to accept the things I cannot change
the courage to change the things I can
and the wisdom to know the difference
AMEN

There comes a point in recovery when we need to face ourself. We need to acknowledge the wrongs we have committed and the harm we have caused. It takes courage to make the preparations necessary to allow God to change our life and our relationships in ways that support the recovery process.

King Asa lived at a time when the people of Israel had given themselves over to the worship of idols. They had turned away from God and the way of life they knew to be right. A messenger of God told the king: "'The LORD will stay with you as long as you stay with him! Whenever you seek him, you will find him. But if you abandon him, he will abandon you.' . . . When Asa heard this message . . . he took courage and removed all the idols in the land. . . . And he repaired the altar of the LORD" (2 Chronicles 15:2, 8). Asa even removed his grandmother from her position of power because she had been influential in Israel's idolatry.

Allowing God to work on all our character defects takes courage because the changes he makes in us will affect every part of our lives. The time will come when we need to crush and burn the "idols" we have served, to go against the crowd, to make a commitment to God, and even to separate ourself from those who don't contribute to our recovery. When we do these things, we will find that God will be there for us, encouraging us as we set things straight. *Turn to page 577, 2 Chronicles 32.*

Asa as he was returning from the battle. "Listen to me, Asa!" he shouted. "Listen, all you people of Judah and Benjamin! The LORD will stay with you as long as you stay with him! Whenever you seek him, you will find him. But if you abandon him, he will abandon you. ³For a long time Israel was without the true God, without a priest to teach them, and without the Law to instruct them. ⁴But whenever they were in trouble and turned to the LORD, the God of Israel, and sought him out, they found him.

⁵"During those dark times, it was not safe to travel. Problems troubled the people of every land. ⁶Nation fought against nation, and city against city, for God was troubling them with every kind of problem. ⁷But as for you, be strong and courageous, for your work will be rewarded."

⁸When Asa heard this message from Azariah the prophet,* he took courage and removed all the detestable idols from the land of Judah and Benjamin and in the towns he had captured in the hill country of Ephraim. And he repaired the altar of the LORD, which stood in front of the entry room of the LORD's Temple.

⁹Then Asa called together all the people of Judah and Benjamin, along with the people of Ephraim, Manasseh, and Simeon who had settled among them. For many from Israel had moved to Judah during Asa's reign when they saw that the LORD his God was with him. ¹⁰The people gathered at Jerusalem in late spring,* during the fifteenth year of Asa's reign.

¹¹On that day they sacrificed to the LORD 700 cattle and 7,000 sheep and goats from the plunder they had taken in the battle. ¹²Then they entered into a covenant to seek the LORD,

15:8 As in Syriac version and Latin Vulgate (see also 15:1); Hebrew reads *from Oded the prophet.* 15:10 Hebrew *in the third month.* This month of the ancient Hebrew lunar calendar usually occurs within the months of May and June.

the God of their ancestors, with all their heart and soul. ¹³They agreed that anyone who refused to seek the LORD, the God of Israel, would be put to death—whether young or old, man or woman. ¹⁴They shouted out their oath of loyalty to the LORD with trumpets blaring and rams' horns sounding. ¹⁵All in Judah were happy about this covenant, for they had entered into it with all their heart. They earnestly sought after God, and they found him. And the LORD gave them rest from their enemies on every side.

¹⁶King Asa even deposed his grandmother* Maacah from her position as queen mother because she had made an obscene Asherah pole. He cut down her obscene pole, broke it up, and burned it in the Kidron Valley. ¹⁷Although the pagan shrines were not removed from Israel, Asa's heart remained completely faithful throughout his life. ¹⁸He brought into the Temple of God the silver and gold and the various items that he and his father had dedicated.

¹⁹So there was no more war until the thirty-fifth year of Asa's reign.

CHAPTER 16
Final Years of Asa's Reign
In the thirty-sixth year of Asa's reign, King Baasha of Israel invaded Judah and fortified Ramah in order to prevent anyone from entering or leaving King Asa's territory in Judah. ²Asa responded by removing the silver and gold from the treasuries of the Temple of the LORD and the royal palace. He sent it to King Ben-hadad of Aram, who was ruling in Damascus, along with this message:

³"Let there be a treaty* between you and me like the one between your father and my father. See, I am sending you silver and gold. Break your treaty with King Baasha of Israel so that he will leave me alone."

⁴Ben-hadad agreed to King Asa's request and sent the commanders of his army to attack the towns of Israel. They conquered the towns of Ijon, Dan, Abel-beth-maacah,* and all the store cities in Naphtali. ⁵As soon as Baasha of Israel heard what was happening, he abandoned his project of fortifying Ramah and stopped all work on it. ⁶Then King Asa called out all the men of Judah to carry away the building stones and timbers that Baasha had been using to fortify Ramah. Asa used these materials to fortify the towns of Geba and Mizpah.

⁷At that time Hanani the seer came to King Asa and told him, "Because you have put your trust in the king of Aram instead of in the LORD your God, you missed your chance to destroy the army of the king of Aram. ⁸Don't you remember what happened to the Ethiopians* and Libyans and their vast army, with all of their chariots and charioteers?* At that time you relied on the LORD, and he handed them over to you. ⁹The eyes of the LORD search the whole earth in order to strengthen those whose hearts are fully committed to him. What a fool you have been! From now on you will be at war."

¹⁰Asa became so angry with Hanani for saying this that he threw him into prison and put him in stocks. At that time Asa also began to oppress some of his people.

Summary of Asa's Reign
¹¹The rest of the events of Asa's reign, from beginning to end, are recorded in *The Book of the Kings of Judah and Israel.* ¹²In the thirty-ninth year of his reign, Asa developed a serious foot disease. Yet even with the severity of his disease, he did not seek the LORD's help but turned only to his physicians. ¹³So he died in the forty-first year of his reign. ¹⁴He was buried in the tomb he had carved out for himself in the City of David. He was laid on a bed perfumed with sweet

15:16 Hebrew *his mother.* 16:3 As in Greek version; Hebrew reads *There is a treaty.* 16:4 As in parallel text at 1 Kgs 15:20; Hebrew reads *Abel-maim,* another name for Abel-beth-maacah. 16:8a Hebrew *Cushites.* 16:8b Or *and horsemen?*

16:7-9 Hanani rebuked Asa for depending on the king of Aram instead of trusting in God. No matter what the odds, God could have delivered Judah without the help of Syria's army. We must learn that God is the only one able to deliver us from our dependencies. Though there is an overwhelming array of individuals and programs to help us deal with our problems, none of these programs or people is sufficient without God's help. We need to put our trust in him.

16:10 When someone honestly points out problems or failures in our life, we have a choice to make. Either we humbly try to discover the truth behind the charges, or we become angry and take revenge. When Hanani rebuked Asa for hiring the Arameans, the king immediately made the wrong response—he punished Hanani. He should have listened to God's corrective message. As we take inventory of our life, we need to humbly acknowledge our failures. If we don't, our efforts in recovery will ultimately fail.

spices and fragrant ointments, and the people built a huge funeral fire in his honor.

CHAPTER 17
Jehoshaphat Rules in Judah
Then Jehoshaphat, Asa's son, became the next king. He strengthened Judah to stand against any attack from Israel. ²He stationed troops in all the fortified towns of Judah, and he assigned additional garrisons to the land of Judah and to the towns of Ephraim that his father, Asa, had captured.

³The LORD was with Jehoshaphat because he followed the example of his father's early years* and did not worship the images of Baal. ⁴He sought his father's God and obeyed his commands instead of following the evil practices of the kingdom of Israel. ⁵So the LORD established Jehoshaphat's control over the kingdom of Judah. All the people of Judah brought gifts to Jehoshaphat, so he became very wealthy and highly esteemed. ⁶He was deeply committed to* the ways of the LORD. He removed the pagan shrines and Asherah poles from Judah.

⁷In the third year of his reign Jehoshaphat sent his officials to teach in all the towns of Judah. These officials included Ben-hail, Obadiah, Zechariah, Nethanel, and Micaiah. ⁸He sent Levites along with them, including Shemaiah, Nethaniah, Zebadiah, Asahel, Shemiramoth, Jehonathan, Adonijah, Tobijah, and Tob-adonijah. He also sent out the priests Elishama and Jehoram. ⁹They took copies of the Book of the Law of the LORD and traveled around through all the towns of Judah, teaching the people.

¹⁰Then the fear of the LORD fell over all the surrounding kingdoms so that none of them wanted to declare war on Jehoshaphat.

¹¹Some of the Philistines brought him gifts and silver as tribute, and the Arabs brought 7,700 rams and 7,700 male goats.

¹²So Jehoshaphat became more and more powerful and built fortresses and storage cities throughout Judah. ¹³He stored numerous supplies in Judah's towns and stationed an army of seasoned troops at Jerusalem. ¹⁴His army was enrolled according to ancestral clans.

From Judah there were 300,000 troops organized in units of 1,000, under the command of Adnah. ¹⁵Next in command was Jehohanan, who commanded 280,000 troops. ¹⁶Next was Amasiah son of Zicri, who volunteered for the LORD's service, with 200,000 troops under his command.

¹⁷From Benjamin there were 200,000 troops equipped with bows and shields. They were under the command of Eliada, a veteran soldier. ¹⁸Next in command was Jehozabad, who commanded 180,000 armed men.

¹⁹These were the troops stationed in Jerusalem to serve the king, besides those Jehoshaphat stationed in the fortified towns throughout Judah.

CHAPTER 18
Jehoshaphat and Ahab
Jehoshaphat enjoyed great riches and high esteem, and he made an alliance with Ahab of Israel by having his son marry Ahab's daughter. ²A few years later he went to Samaria to visit Ahab, who prepared a great banquet for him and his officials. They butchered great numbers of sheep, goats, and cattle for the feast. Then Ahab enticed

---

17:3 Some Hebrew manuscripts read *the example of his father, David.* **17:6** Hebrew *His heart was courageous in.*

17:3-4 The role models we follow make a tremendous difference in how we respond to the challenges we face. It is refreshing to discover that Jehoshaphat chose a positive role model to give direction to his life. Based on the work of his worthy exemplar, Jehoshaphat instituted excellent reforms in Judah. We must be careful not to follow those whose path leads away from the heart of God. We need to look up to people who will lead us to make positive steps in recovery.

17:5-6 We can learn a lot about people by the way they find fulfillment in life. Jehoshaphat "was deeply committed to the ways of the LORD." That commitment was evidenced as he led his kingdom on the path of recovery from idolatry and sin. We can only imagine the joy he experienced as he broke down the idols and pagan shrines in his land! Like Jehoshaphat, we need to begin by being committed to God's ways. We can be sure that this commitment will lead to success in following God's program for recovery.

17:7-9 Notice that Jehoshaphat used the Word of God as the foundation for his reforms. As we attempt to effect changes in our life, we also need God's Word to direct the changes we make. Scripture furnishes the only adequate foundation for change in our life. We must study it so we can learn God's will for us and make use of the power God offers us in recovery.

Jehoshaphat to join forces with him to recover Ramoth-gilead.

³"Will you go with me to Ramoth-gilead?" King Ahab of Israel asked King Jehoshaphat of Judah.

Jehoshaphat replied, "Why, of course! You and I are as one, and my troops are your troops. We will certainly join you in battle." ⁴Then Jehoshaphat added, "But first let's find out what the LORD says."

⁵So the king of Israel summoned the prophets, 400 of them, and asked them, "Should we go to war against Ramoth-gilead, or should I hold back?"

They all replied, "Yes, go right ahead! God will give the king victory."

⁶But Jehoshaphat asked, "Is there not also a prophet of the LORD here? We should ask him the same question."

⁷The king of Israel replied to Jehoshaphat, "There is one more man who could consult the LORD for us, but I hate him. He never prophesies anything but trouble for me! His name is Micaiah son of Imlah."

Jehoshaphat replied, "That's not the way a king should talk! Let's hear what he has to say."

⁸So the king of Israel called one of his officials and said, "Quick! Bring Micaiah son of Imlah."

Micaiah Prophesies against Ahab

⁹King Ahab of Israel and King Jehoshaphat of Judah, dressed in their royal robes, were sitting on thrones at the threshing floor near the gate of Samaria. All of Ahab's prophets were prophesying there in front of them. ¹⁰One of them, Zedekiah son of Kenaanah, made some iron horns and proclaimed, "This is what the LORD says: With these horns you will gore the Arameans to death!"

¹¹All the other prophets agreed. "Yes," they said, "go up to Ramoth-gilead and be victorious, for the LORD will give the king victory!"

¹²Meanwhile, the messenger who went to get Micaiah said to him, "Look, all the prophets are promising victory for the king. Be sure that you agree with them and promise success."

¹³But Micaiah replied, "As surely as the LORD lives, I will say only what my God says."

¹⁴When Micaiah arrived before the king, Ahab asked him, "Micaiah, should we go to war against Ramoth-gilead, or should I hold back?"

Micaiah replied sarcastically, "Yes, go up and be victorious, for you will have victory over them!"

¹⁵But the king replied sharply, "How many times must I demand that you speak only the truth to me when you speak for the LORD?"

¹⁶Then Micaiah told him, "In a vision I saw all Israel scattered on the mountains, like sheep without a shepherd. And the LORD said, 'Their master has been killed.* Send them home in peace.'"

¹⁷"Didn't I tell you?" the king of Israel exclaimed to Jehoshaphat. "He never prophesies anything but trouble for me."

¹⁸Then Micaiah continued, "Listen to what the LORD says! I saw the LORD sitting on his throne with all the armies of heaven around him, on his right and on his left. ¹⁹And the LORD said, 'Who can entice King Ahab of Israel to go into battle against Ramoth-gilead so he can be killed?'

"There were many suggestions, ²⁰and finally a spirit approached the LORD and said, 'I can do it!'

"'How will you do this?' the LORD asked.

²¹"And the spirit replied, 'I will go out and inspire all of Ahab's prophets to speak lies.'

"'You will succeed,' said the LORD. 'Go ahead and do it.'

²²"So you see, the LORD has put a lying

18:16 Hebrew *These people have no master.*

18:3-5 Generally when a project is undertaken, companions and allies must be chosen. But there is grave danger in choosing the wrong allies. Jehoshaphat's alliance with Ahab almost caused his undoing (18:28-32). Jehoshaphat not only allied himself with Ahab, but he declared himself in complete agreement with this godless king: "You and I are as one." Companions in recovery are necessary; we cannot accomplish it alone. But choosing the wrong companions can be as destructive as having no companions at all.
18:3-7 Ahab called upon a false prophet; as a result, he got false information. Jehoshaphat wanted to discover what God had to say, so he looked for a true prophet. False prophets told the people whatever they wanted to hear. True prophets spoke God's word whether the people liked it or not. As we seek God's will in Scripture, we must be careful not to reject messages we don't like. Sometimes the path toward victory is difficult and we have to do things we don't want to do. In the long run, however, God's way is the only sure way to recovery. Looking for quick and easy solutions to our problems will never yield permanent results.

spirit in the mouths of your prophets. For the LORD has pronounced your doom."

²³Then Zedekiah son of Kenaanah walked up to Micaiah and slapped him across the face. "Since when did the Spirit of the LORD leave me to speak to you?" he demanded.

²⁴And Micaiah replied, "You will find out soon enough when you are trying to hide in some secret room!"

²⁵"Arrest him!" the king of Israel ordered. "Take him back to Amon, the governor of the city, and to my son Joash. ²⁶Give them this order from the king: 'Put this man in prison, and feed him nothing but bread and water until I return safely from the battle!'"

²⁷But Micaiah replied, "If you return safely, it will mean that the LORD has not spoken through me!" Then he added to those standing around, "Everyone mark my words!"

The Death of Ahab

²⁸So King Ahab of Israel and King Jehoshaphat of Judah led their armies against Ramoth-gilead. ²⁹The king of Israel said to Jehoshaphat, "As we go into battle, I will disguise myself so no one will recognize me, but you wear your royal robes." So the king of Israel disguised himself, and they went into battle.

³⁰Meanwhile, the king of Aram had issued these orders to his chariot commanders: "Attack only the king of Israel! Don't bother with anyone else." ³¹So when the Aramean chariot commanders saw Jehoshaphat in his royal robes, they went after him. "There is the king of Israel!" they shouted. But Jehoshaphat called out, and the LORD saved him. God helped him by turning the attackers away from him. ³²As soon as the chariot commanders realized he was not the king of Israel, they stopped chasing him.

³³An Aramean soldier, however, randomly shot an arrow at the Israelite troops and hit the king of Israel between the joints of his armor. "Turn the horses* and get me out of here!" Ahab groaned to the driver of the chariot. "I'm badly wounded!"

³⁴The battle raged all that day, and the king of Israel propped himself up in his chariot facing the Arameans. In the evening, just as the sun was setting, he died.

CHAPTER 19
Jehoshaphat Appoints Judges

When King Jehoshaphat of Judah arrived safely home in Jerusalem, ²Jehu son of Hanani the seer went out to meet him. "Why should you help the wicked and love those who hate the LORD?" he asked the king. "Because of what you have done, the LORD is very angry with you. ³Even so, there is some good in you, for you have removed the Asherah poles throughout the land, and you have committed yourself to seeking God."

⁴Jehoshaphat lived in Jerusalem, but he went out among the people, traveling from Beersheba to the hill country of Ephraim, encouraging the people to return to the LORD, the God of their ancestors. ⁵He appointed judges throughout the nation in all the fortified towns, ⁶and he said to them, "Always think carefully before pronouncing judgment. Remember that you do not judge to please people but to please the LORD. He will be with you when you render the verdict in each case. ⁷Fear the LORD and judge with integrity, for the LORD our God does not tolerate perverted justice, partiality, or the taking of bribes."

⁸In Jerusalem, Jehoshaphat appointed

18:33 Hebrew *Turn your hand.*

18:31-34 After hearing God's warning to abandon his plans, Ahab took precautions so he would not be killed in battle. He disguised himself as a common soldier so he wouldn't be a target of the enemy. In spite of crafty preparations, Ahab was killed by a "chance" arrow. He believed that he could escape God's will, but in trying to do so, he sealed his own doom. When God directs us through his Word or through wise counsel, we should listen. Following God's will for us, no matter how hard that may be, is the only way to recovery.

19:1-2 When we make wrong alliances and trust in fallible sources of human strength and ability, we will suffer the consequences. The prophet Jehu met Jehoshaphat to proclaim a message of judgment. Because of Jehoshaphat's cooperation with Ahab, he would have to bear the consequences. We should take this as a warning. Our alliances need to be with people who will encourage us in God's program for recovery. Seeking help from anyone else will lead to negative consequences and suffering.

19:5-7 These verses give us excellent instructions for correcting wrong situations in our life. Judah's judicial system was corrupt, but rather than despairing, Jehoshaphat did something about it. He challenged the judges to pay attention to God's way. He reminded them that the fear of God and his justice was the only proper motivation for action. God's ways should also direct our decisions in recovery. We must seek his wisdom in the Scriptures.

some of the Levites and priests and clan leaders in Israel to serve as judges* for cases involving the LORD's regulations and for civil disputes. 9These were his instructions to them: "You must always act in the fear of the LORD, with faithfulness and an undivided heart. 10Whenever a case comes to you from fellow citizens in an outlying town, whether a murder case or some other violation of God's laws, commands, decrees, or regulations, you must warn them not to sin against the LORD, so that he will not be angry with you and them. Do this and you will not be guilty.

11"Amariah the high priest will have final say in all cases involving the LORD. Zebadiah son of Ishmael, a leader from the tribe of Judah, will have final say in all civil cases. The Levites will assist you in making sure that justice is served. Take courage as you fulfill your duties, and may the LORD be with those who do what is right."

CHAPTER 20
War with Surrounding Nations

After this, the armies of the Moabites, Ammonites, and some of the Meunites* declared war on Jehoshaphat. 2Messengers came and told Jehoshaphat, "A vast army from Edom* is marching against you from beyond the Dead Sea.* They are already at Hazazon-tamar." (This was another name for En-gedi.)

3Jehoshaphat was terrified by this news and begged the LORD for guidance. He also ordered everyone in Judah to begin fasting. 4So people from all the towns of Judah came to Jerusalem to seek the LORD's help.

5Jehoshaphat stood before the community of Judah and Jerusalem in front of the new courtyard at the Temple of the LORD. 6He prayed, "O LORD, God of our ancestors, you alone are the God who is in heaven. You are ruler of all the kingdoms of the earth. You are powerful and mighty; no one can stand against you! 7O our God, did you not drive out those who lived in this land when your people Israel arrived? And did you not give this land forever to the descendants of your friend Abraham? 8Your people settled here and built this Temple to honor your name. 9They said, 'Whenever we are faced with any calamity such as war,* plague, or famine, we can come to stand in your presence before this Temple where your name is honored. We can cry out to you to save us, and you will hear us and rescue us.'

10"And now see what the armies of Ammon, Moab, and Mount Seir are doing. You would not let our ancestors invade those nations when Israel left Egypt, so they went around them and did not destroy them. 11Now see how they reward us! For they have come to throw us out of your land, which you gave us as an inheritance. 12O our God, won't you stop them? We are powerless against this mighty army that is about to attack us. We do not know what to do, but we are looking to you for help."

13As all the men of Judah stood before the LORD with their little ones, wives, and children, 14the Spirit of the LORD came upon one of the men standing there. His name was Jahaziel son of Zechariah, son of Benaiah, son of Jeiel, son of Mattaniah, a Levite who was a descendant of Asaph.

15He said, "Listen, all you people of Judah and Jerusalem! Listen, King Jehoshaphat! This is what the LORD says: Do not be afraid! Don't

19:8 As in Greek version; the meaning of the Hebrew is uncertain. 20:1 As in some Greek manuscripts (see also 26:7); Hebrew repeats *Ammonites.* 20:2a As in one Hebrew manuscript; most Hebrew manuscripts and ancient versions read *Aram.* 20:2b Hebrew *the sea.* 20:9 Or *sword of judgment;* or *sword, judgment.*

19:11 Jehoshaphat appointed people to make final decisions for justice in the land. He wanted to make sure that the people would be treated justly and that the truth would never be hidden. As we inventory our life, we must judge our past performances by God's standards of justice. We must also look honestly at our failures, avoiding our tendency for denial. If we, like Jehoshaphat, are committed to the truth, we will build the foundation for a successful recovery.

20:6-9 God is in charge of our world! He is master over everything! Trust in his sovereignty is the basis for victory in recovery. As we learn to believe in God's control, even when things aren't going our way, our life can be serene in the midst of conflict. We can know that God desires what is best for us. Seeking his will and consistently obeying his direction for our life will always lead to a successful recovery.

20:15 If God is on our side, even the greatest difficulties will not stand in the way of victory. Just as God's messenger Jahaziel spoke to the people of Israel, urging them to trust in God's power to deliver them, God speaks to us in the Bible. He calls upon us to trust in him. The most common command in all of Scripture is "Do not be afraid!" God often pronounces this command when the surrounding circumstances are terrible. God shows us repeatedly that no matter how terrible the circumstances, he is able to give us victory. All we need to do is trust him.

be discouraged by this mighty army, for the battle is not yours, but God's. ¹⁶Tomorrow, march out against them. You will find them coming up through the ascent of Ziz at the end of the valley that opens into the wilderness of Jeruel. ¹⁷But you will not even need to fight. Take your positions; then stand still and watch the LORD's victory. He is with you, O people of Judah and Jerusalem. Do not be afraid or discouraged. Go out against them tomorrow, for the LORD is with you!"

¹⁸Then King Jehoshaphat bowed low with his face to the ground. And all the people of Judah and Jerusalem did the same, worshiping the LORD. ¹⁹Then the Levites from the clans of Kohath and Korah stood to praise the LORD, the God of Israel, with a very loud shout.

²⁰Early the next morning the army of Judah went out into the wilderness of Tekoa. On the way Jehoshaphat stopped and said, "Listen to me, all you people of Judah and Jerusalem! Believe in the LORD your God, and you will be able to stand firm. Believe in his prophets, and you will succeed."

²¹After consulting the people, the king appointed singers to walk ahead of the army, singing to the LORD and praising him for his holy splendor. This is what they sang:

"Give thanks to the LORD;
  his faithful love endures forever!"

²²At the very moment they began to sing and give praise, the LORD caused the armies of Ammon, Moab, and Mount Seir to start fighting among themselves. ²³The armies of Moab and Ammon turned against their allies from Mount Seir and killed every one of them. After they had destroyed the army of Seir, they began attacking each other. ²⁴So when the army of Judah arrived at the lookout point in the wilderness, all they saw were dead bodies lying on the ground as far as they could see. Not a single one of the enemy had escaped.

²⁵King Jehoshaphat and his men went out to gather the plunder. They found vast amounts of equipment, clothing,* and other valuables—more than they could carry. There was so much plunder that it took them three days just to collect it all! ²⁶On the fourth day they gathered in the Valley of Blessing,* which got its name that day because the people praised and thanked the LORD there. It is still called the Valley of Blessing today.

²⁷Then all the men returned to Jerusalem, with Jehoshaphat leading them, overjoyed that the LORD had given them victory over their enemies. ²⁸They marched into Jerusalem to the music of harps, lyres, and trumpets, and they proceeded to the Temple of the LORD.

²⁹When all the surrounding kingdoms heard that the LORD himself had fought against the enemies of Israel, the fear of God came over them. ³⁰So Jehoshaphat's kingdom was at peace, for his God had given him rest on every side.

Summary of Jehoshaphat's Reign

³¹So Jehoshaphat ruled over the land of Judah. He was thirty-five years old when he became king, and he reigned in Jerusalem twenty-five years. His mother was Azubah, the daughter of Shilhi.

³²Jehoshaphat was a good king, following the ways of his father, Asa. He did what was pleasing in the LORD's sight. ³³During his reign, however, he failed to remove all the pagan shrines, and the people never fully committed themselves to follow the God of their ancestors.

³⁴The rest of the events of Jehoshaphat's reign, from beginning to end, are recorded in *The Record of Jehu Son of Hanani,* which is included in *The Book of the Kings of Israel.*

³⁵Some time later King Jehoshaphat of Judah made an alliance with King Ahaziah of Israel, who was very wicked.* ³⁶Together they built a fleet of trading ships* at the port of Ezion-geber. ³⁷Then Eliezer son of Dodavahu from Mareshah prophesied against Jehoshaphat. He said, "Because you have allied yourself with King Ahaziah, the LORD will destroy your work." So the ships met with disaster and never put out to sea.*

20:25 As in some Hebrew manuscripts and Latin Vulgate; most Hebrew manuscripts read *corpses.* 20:26 Hebrew *valley of Beracah.* 20:35 Or *who made him do what was wicked.* 20:36 Hebrew *fleet of ships that could go to Tarshish.* 20:37 Hebrew *never set sail for Tarshish.*

20:17 It is hard for some of us to give up control. We want to do things our way, and we want the credit for success! God told the people of Judah to stand still and watch as he gave them a great victory. In recovery we must learn to give our battles to God. Whether we like it or not, we cannot win them alone. With God's help, however, no enemy is too large or too terrible. If we are willing to put our life into God's hands, God will give us victory.

CHAPTER 21
Jehoram Rules in Judah

When Jehoshaphat died, he was buried with his ancestors in the City of David. Then his son Jehoram became the next king.

²Jehoram's brothers—the other sons of Jehoshaphat—were Azariah, Jehiel, Zechariah, Azariahu, Michael, and Shephatiah; all these were the sons of Jehoshaphat king of Judah.* ³Their father had given each of them valuable gifts of silver, gold, and costly items, and also some of Judah's fortified towns. However, he designated Jehoram as the next king because he was the oldest. ⁴But when Jehoram had become solidly established as king, he killed all his brothers and some of the other leaders of Judah.

⁵Jehoram was thirty-two years old when he became king, and he reigned in Jerusalem eight years. ⁶But Jehoram followed the example of the kings of Israel and was as wicked as King Ahab, for he had married one of Ahab's daughters. So Jehoram did what was evil in the LORD's sight. ⁷But the LORD did not want to destroy David's dynasty, for he had made a covenant with David and promised that his descendants would continue to rule, shining like a lamp forever.

⁸During Jehoram's reign, the Edomites revolted against Judah and crowned their own king. ⁹So Jehoram went out with his full army and all his chariots. The Edomites surrounded him and his chariot commanders, but he went out at night and attacked them* under cover of darkness. ¹⁰Even so, Edom has been independent from Judah to this day. The town of Libnah also revolted about that same time. All this happened because Jehoram had abandoned the LORD, the God of his ancestors. ¹¹He had built pagan shrines in the hill country of Judah and had led the people of Jerusalem and Judah to give themselves to pagan gods and to go astray.

¹²Then Elijah the prophet wrote Jehoram this letter:

"This is what the LORD, the God of your ancestor David, says: You have not followed the good example of your father, Jehoshaphat, or your grandfather King Asa of Judah. ¹³Instead, you have been as evil as the kings of Israel. You have led the people of Jerusalem and Judah to worship idols, just as King Ahab did in Israel. And you have even killed your own brothers, men who were better than you. ¹⁴So now the LORD is about to strike you, your people, your children, your wives, and all that is yours with a heavy blow. ¹⁵You yourself will suffer with a severe intestinal disease that will get worse each day until your bowels come out."

¹⁶Then the LORD stirred up the Philistines and the Arabs, who lived near the Ethiopians,* to attack Jehoram. ¹⁷They marched against Judah, broke down its defenses, and carried away everything of value in the royal palace, including the king's sons and his wives. Only his youngest son, Ahaziah,* was spared.

¹⁸After all this, the LORD struck Jehoram with an incurable intestinal disease. ¹⁹The disease grew worse and worse, and at the end of two years it caused his bowels to come out, and he died in agony. His people did not build a great funeral fire to honor him as they had done for his ancestors.

²⁰Jehoram was thirty-two years old when he became king, and he reigned in Jerusalem eight years. No one was sorry when he died. They buried him in the City of David, but not in the royal cemetery.

21:2 Masoretic Text reads *of Israel;* also in 21:4. The author of Chronicles sees Judah as representative of the true Israel. (Some Hebrew manuscripts, Greek and Syriac versions, and Latin Vulgate read *of Judah.*) 21:9 Or *he went out and escaped.* The meaning of the Hebrew is uncertain. 21:16 Hebrew *the Cushites.* 21:17 Hebrew *Jehoahaz,* a variant spelling of Ahaziah; compare 22:1.

21:6-7 What an amazing contrast between father and son! Here we are told about the faithlessness of Jehoram. He patterned his reign after the kings of the northern kingdom, and he even married one of wicked King Ahab's daughters. The consequences of turning from God are exhibited in Jehoram's failures. We should be encouraged, however, to see that Jehoram's actions could never negate God's promises. No matter how badly we have failed, God will restore us if we turn back to him.

21:18-20 Jehoram's life of rebellion against God and his failure to fulfill his royal responsibilities led to a tragic end. He was disowned and undesired by his own people—they didn't even give him an honorable burial. We can only wonder what would have happened had Jehoram renewed his relationship with God and reconciled himself with his people. Rejecting God's program leads to failure and shame. God's way is the only way to achieve true recovery.

CHAPTER 22
Ahaziah Rules in Judah
Then the people of Jerusalem made Ahaziah, Jehoram's youngest son, their next king, since the marauding bands who came with the Arabs* had killed all the older sons. So Ahaziah son of Jehoram reigned as king of Judah.

²Ahaziah was twenty-two* years old when he became king, and he reigned in Jerusalem one year. His mother was Athaliah, a granddaughter of King Omri. ³Ahaziah also followed the evil example of King Ahab's family, for his mother encouraged him in doing wrong. ⁴He did what was evil in the LORD's sight, just as Ahab's family had done. They even became his advisers after the death of his father, and they led him to ruin.

⁵Following their evil advice, Ahaziah joined Joram,* the son of King Ahab of Israel, in his war against King Hazael of Aram at Ramoth-gilead. When the Arameans* wounded Joram in the battle, ⁶he returned to Jezreel to recover from the wounds he had received at Ramoth.* Because Joram was wounded, King Ahaziah* of Judah went to Jezreel to visit him.

⁷But God had decided that this visit would be Ahaziah's downfall. While he was there, Ahaziah went out with Joram to meet Jehu grandson of Nimshi,* whom the LORD had appointed to destroy the dynasty of Ahab. ⁸While Jehu was executing judgment against the family of Ahab, he happened to meet some of Judah's officials and Ahaziah's relatives* who were traveling with Ahaziah. So Jehu killed them all. ⁹Then Jehu's men searched for Ahaziah, and they found him hiding in the city of Samaria. They brought him to Jehu, who killed him. Ahaziah was given a decent burial because the people said, "He was the grandson of Jehoshaphat—a man who sought the LORD with all his heart." But none of the surviving members of Ahaziah's family was capable of ruling the kingdom.

Queen Athaliah Rules in Judah
¹⁰When Athaliah, the mother of King Ahaziah of Judah, learned that her son was dead, she began to destroy the rest of Judah's royal family. ¹¹But Ahaziah's sister Jehosheba,* the daughter of King Jehoram, took Ahaziah's infant son, Joash, and stole him away from among the rest of the king's children, who were about to be killed. She put Joash and his nurse in a bedroom. In this way, Jehosheba, wife of Jehoiada the priest and sister of Ahaziah, hid the child so that Athaliah could not murder him. ¹²Joash remained hidden in the Temple of God for six years while Athaliah ruled over the land.

CHAPTER 23
Revolt against Athaliah
In the seventh year of Athaliah's reign, Jehoiada the priest decided to act. He

---

22:1 Or *marauding bands of Arabs.* 22:2 As in some Greek manuscripts and Syriac version (see also 2 Kgs 8:26); Hebrew reads *forty-two.* 22:5a Hebrew *Jehoram,* a variant spelling of Joram; also in 22:6, 7. 22:5b As in two Hebrew manuscripts and Latin Vulgate (see also 2 Kgs 8:28); Masoretic Text reads *the archers.* 22:6a Hebrew *Ramah,* a variant spelling of Ramoth. 22:6b As in some Hebrew manuscripts, Greek and Syriac versions, and Latin Vulgate (see also 2 Kgs 8:29); most Hebrew manuscripts read *Azariah.* 22:7 Hebrew *descendant of Nimshi;* compare 2 Kgs 9:2, 14. 22:8 As in Greek version (see also 2 Kgs 10:13); Hebrew reads *and sons of the brothers of Ahaziah.* 22:11 As in parallel text at 2 Kgs 11:2; Hebrew lacks *Ahaziah's sister* and reads *Jehoshabeath* [a variant spelling of Jehosheba].

22:2-4 It is a terrible thing to follow a bad example and listen to foolish advice. Ahaziah had a poisoned heritage and surroundings. His grandparents were Ahab and Jezebel. His mother was godless Athaliah, who served as his chief adviser. Sadly, Ahaziah never turned to God to receive the gift of forgiveness and reconciliation. We may have a heritage similar to Ahaziah's. If so, it is reassuring to know that through Christ, we can overcome the legacy of even the worst environment or family background.

22:5 Outside of God's direct assistance, it is difficult to overcome family pressures. Just as Jehoshaphat of Judah had joined forces with Ahab of Israel, Ahaziah of Judah teamed up with his uncle Joram of Israel against the Syrians. This was a difficult situation. We do owe special allegiance to our family, but not if they try to lead us away from God and his will for our life.

22:10-12 Again and again we are reminded of the truth that God is sovereign. Everything was against Jehosheba and young Joash. They escaped the bloodbath of Jehu and then avoided Athaliah's slaughter of Ahaziah's family. As we face difficult circumstances, we can find encouragement in the fact that God is ultimately in control. If we entrust our life to him, he will lead us through even the darkest situations.

23:1-11 Some people claim that when we trust God to deliver us, we need not make any further preparations. This is not what we see in Scripture. Even when we entrust our life to God, he still expects us to take action. To accomplish God's will, Jehoiada made painstaking plans. He did everything necessary to restore the royal dynasty of David to Judah's throne. Sometimes doing right requires careful planning and even using force. We need to trust that God will lead us to act in godly ways to fulfill his will in our life.

summoned his courage and made a pact with five army commanders: Azariah son of Jeroham, Ishmael son of Jehohanan, Azariah son of Obed, Maaseiah son of Adaiah, and Elishaphat son of Zicri. ²These men traveled secretly throughout Judah and summoned the Levites and clan leaders in all the towns to come to Jerusalem. ³They all gathered at the Temple of God, where they made a solemn pact with Joash, the young king.

Jehoiada said to them, "Here is the king's son! The time has come for him to reign! The LORD has promised that a descendant of David will be our king. ⁴This is what you must do. When you priests and Levites come on duty on the Sabbath, a third of you will serve as gatekeepers. ⁵Another third will go over to the royal palace, and the final third will be at the Foundation Gate. Everyone else should stay in the courtyards of the LORD's Temple. ⁶Remember, only the priests and Levites on duty may enter the Temple of the LORD, for they are set apart as holy. The rest of the people must obey the LORD's instructions and stay outside. ⁷You Levites, form a bodyguard around the king and keep your weapons in hand. Kill anyone who tries to enter the Temple. Stay with the king wherever he goes."

⁸So the Levites and all the people of Judah did everything as Jehoiada the priest ordered. The commanders took charge of the men reporting for duty that Sabbath, as well as those who were going off duty. Jehoiada the priest did not let anyone go home after their shift ended. ⁹Then Jehoiada supplied the commanders with the spears and the large and small shields that had once belonged to King David and were stored in the Temple of God. ¹⁰He stationed all the people around the king, with their weapons ready. They formed a line from the south side of the Temple around to the north side and all around the altar.

¹¹Then Jehoiada and his sons brought out Joash, the king's son, placed the crown on his head, and presented him with a copy of God's laws.* They anointed him and pro-claimed him king, and everyone shouted, "Long live the king!"

The Death of Athaliah

¹²When Athaliah heard the noise of the people running and the shouts of praise to the king, she hurried to the LORD's Temple to see what was happening. ¹³When she arrived, she saw the newly crowned king standing in his place of authority by the pillar at the Temple entrance. The commanders and trumpeters were surrounding him, and people from all over the land were rejoicing and blowing trumpets. Singers with musical instruments were leading the people in a great celebration. When Athaliah saw all this, she tore her clothes in despair and shouted, "Treason! Treason!"

¹⁴Then Jehoiada the priest ordered the commanders who were in charge of the troops, "Take her to the soldiers in front of the Temple,* and kill anyone who tries to rescue her." For the priest had said, "She must not be killed in the Temple of the LORD." ¹⁵So they seized her and led her out to the entrance of the Horse Gate on the palace grounds, and they killed her there.

Jehoiada's Religious Reforms

¹⁶Then Jehoiada made a covenant between himself and the king and the people that they would be the LORD's people. ¹⁷And all the people went over to the temple of Baal and tore it down. They demolished the altars and smashed the idols, and they killed Mattan the priest of Baal in front of the altars.

¹⁸Jehoiada now put the priests and Levites in charge of the Temple of the LORD, following all the directions given by David. He also commanded them to present burnt offerings to the LORD, as prescribed by the Law of Moses, and to sing and rejoice as David had instructed. ¹⁹He also stationed gatekeepers at the gates of the LORD's Temple to keep out those who for any reason were ceremonially unclean.

²⁰Then the commanders, nobles, rulers,

23:11 Or *a copy of the covenant.* 23:14 Or *Bring her out from between the ranks;* or *Take her out of the Temple precincts.* The meaning of the Hebrew is uncertain.

23:15-17 After the overthrow of the usurper Athaliah, Jehoiada led the people of Judah to renew their relationship with God. After times of relapse and rebellion, we need to revive our commitment to God. He is always willing to offer us a fresh start—no matter how constant or how deep our failures have been.

23:20-21 The results of conflict are not always negative. After the overthrow of Athaliah, the people rejoiced and there was peace in Jerusalem. We should use conflicts to pinpoint the problems in our life and take steps to root them out. Hiding from conflict or denying its existence will never lead to personal growth or to victory over our dependency.

and all the people of the land escorted the king from the Temple of the LORD. They went through the upper gate and into the palace, and they seated the king on the royal throne. [21]So all the people of the land rejoiced, and the city was peaceful because Athaliah had been killed.

CHAPTER 24
Joash Repairs the Temple

Joash was seven years old when he became king, and he reigned in Jerusalem forty years. His mother was Zibiah from Beersheba. [2]Joash did what was pleasing in the LORD's sight throughout the lifetime of Jehoiada the priest. [3]Jehoiada chose two wives for Joash, and he had sons and daughters.

[4]At one point Joash decided to repair and restore the Temple of the LORD. [5]He summoned the priests and Levites and gave them these instructions: "Go to all the towns of Judah and collect the required annual offerings, so that we can repair the Temple of your God. Do not delay!" But the Levites did not act immediately.

[6]So the king called for Jehoiada the high priest and asked him, "Why haven't you demanded that the Levites go out and collect the Temple taxes from the towns of Judah and from Jerusalem? Moses, the servant of the LORD, levied this tax on the community of Israel in order to maintain the Tabernacle of the Covenant.*"

[7]Over the years the followers of wicked Athaliah had broken into the Temple of God, and they had used all the dedicated things from the Temple of the LORD to worship the images of Baal.

[8]So now the king ordered a chest to be made and set outside the gate leading to the Temple of the LORD. [9]Then a proclamation was sent throughout Judah and Jerusalem, telling the people to bring to the LORD the tax that Moses, the servant of God, had required of the Israelites in the wilderness. [10]This pleased all the leaders and the people, and they gladly brought their money and filled the chest with it.

[11]Whenever the chest became full, the Levites would carry it to the king's officials. Then the court secretary and an officer of the high priest would come and empty the chest and take it back to the Temple again. This went on day after day, and a large amount of money was collected. [12]The king and Jehoiada gave the money to the construction supervisors, who hired masons and carpenters to restore the Temple of the LORD. They also hired metalworkers, who made articles of iron and bronze for the LORD's Temple.

[13]The men in charge of the renovation worked hard and made steady progress. They restored the Temple of God according to its original design and strengthened it. [14]When all the repairs were finished, they brought the remaining money to the king and Jehoiada. It was used to make various articles for the Temple of the LORD—articles for worship services and for burnt offerings, including ladles and other articles made of gold and silver. And the burnt offerings were sacrificed continually in the Temple of the LORD during the lifetime of Jehoiada the priest.

[15]Jehoiada lived to a very old age, finally dying at 130. [16]He was buried among the kings in the City of David, because he had done so much good in Israel for God and his Temple.

Jehoiada's Reforms Reversed

[17]But after Jehoiada's death, the leaders of Judah came and bowed before King Joash

24:6 Hebrew *Tent of the Testimony.*

24:1-2 When we are ill equipped or unprepared for any role in life, it is important that we find a godly mentor to give us direction. The boy-king Joash was greatly blessed to have Jehoiada to guide him in his early decisions. The old priest kept Joash going in the right direction, leading him in the ways of God. In recovery, all of us need the help of a godly mentor who knows what we are going through. We must avoid the tendency to "go it alone" and allow God to use others to help us in recovery.

24:4-5 Not only must we be committed to doing God's will, but we must also be committed to doing things when God wants them done. Procrastinating when God has shown us what he requires is a form of disobedience. Plans to do God's will "tomorrow" should never be mistaken for obedience. If we know what God wants us to do, we need to get on with it!

24:17-22 After Jehoiada died, Joash turned away from God. Jehoiada's son Zechariah rebuked Joash for his failure to obey God's laws. Joash was unwilling to face the truth about his behavior and even killed Zechariah to hide from it. When we are confronted with our sins, it is tempting to deny their existence. As we take inventory, we need to do so honestly. When confronted with our sins, we need to admit them and then take steps to eliminate them from our life.

and persuaded him to listen to their advice. [18]They decided to abandon the Temple of the LORD, the God of their ancestors, and they worshiped Asherah poles and idols instead! Because of this sin, divine anger fell on Judah and Jerusalem. [19]Yet the LORD sent prophets to bring them back to him. The prophets warned them, but still the people would not listen.

[20]Then the Spirit of God came upon Zechariah son of Jehoiada the priest. He stood before the people and said, "This is what God says: Why do you disobey the LORD's commands and keep yourselves from prospering? You have abandoned the LORD, and now he has abandoned you!"

[21]Then the leaders plotted to kill Zechariah, and King Joash ordered that they stone him to death in the courtyard of the LORD's Temple. [22]That was how King Joash repaid Jehoiada for his loyalty—by killing his son. Zechariah's last words as he died were, "May the LORD see what they are doing and avenge my death!"

The End of Joash's Reign

[23]In the spring of the year* the Aramean army marched against Joash. They invaded Judah and Jerusalem and killed all the leaders of the nation. Then they sent all the plunder back to their king in Damascus. [24]Although the Arameans attacked with only a small army, the LORD helped them conquer the much larger army of Judah. The people of Judah had abandoned the LORD, the God of their ancestors, so judgment was carried out against Joash.

[25]The Arameans withdrew, leaving Joash severely wounded. But his own officials plotted to kill him for murdering the son* of Jehoiada the priest. They assassinated him as he lay in bed. Then he was buried in the City of David, but not in the royal cemetery. [26]The assassins were Jozacar,* the son of an Ammonite woman named Shimeath, and Jehozabad, the son of a Moabite woman named Shomer.*

[27]The account of the sons of Joash, the prophecies about him, and the record of his restoration of the Temple of God are written in *The Commentary on the Book of the Kings*. His son Amaziah became the next king.

CHAPTER 25
Amaziah Rules in Judah

Amaziah was twenty-five years old when he became king, and he reigned in Jerusalem twenty-nine years. His mother was Jehoaddin* from Jerusalem. [2]Amaziah did what was pleasing in the LORD's sight, but not wholeheartedly.

[3]When Amaziah was well established as king, he executed the officials who had assassinated his father. [4]However, he did not kill the children of the assassins, for he obeyed the command of the LORD as written by Moses in the Book of the Law: "Parents must not be put to death for the sins of their children, nor children for the sins of their parents. Those deserving to die must be put to death for their own crimes."*

[5]Then Amaziah organized the army, assigning generals and captains* for all Judah and Benjamin. He took a census and found

---

24:23 Hebrew *At the turn of the year*. The first day of the year in the ancient Hebrew lunar calendar occurred in March or April. **24:25** As in Greek version and Latin Vulgate; Hebrew reads *sons*. **24:26a** As in parallel text at 2 Kgs 12:21; Hebrew reads *Zabad*. **24:26b** As in parallel text at 2 Kgs 12:21; Hebrew reads *Shimrith*, a variant spelling of Shomer. **25:1** As in parallel text at 2 Kgs 14:2; Hebrew reads *Jehoaddan*, a variant spelling of Jehoaddin. **25:4** Deut 24:16. **25:5** Hebrew *commanders of thousands and commanders of hundreds*.

25:1-2 When it came to God's evaluation, Amaziah's grade was good—but not great. He did the right things, but he failed to do them with the right attitude. As we follow God's program for healthy living, we need to do it wholeheartedly. We need to seek God sincerely. If we are just going through the motions with hopes of receiving God's blessings, our progress in recovery will be slow and temporary at best.

25:4 Here we are reminded that we all must take responsibility for our own sins. Many of us in recovery may realize that much of what we suffer is a result of our parents' mistakes. It is easy to use this as an excuse for our failures, but this is a big mistake. We need to take responsibility for our own failures. This is part of taking a personal inventory. We must take the responsibility for the sin in our life and take steps to remove it. We alone are responsible before God for our actions.

25:5-8 As Amaziah faced a powerful enemy, he thought it was a good idea to hire mercenaries from the northern kingdom. But God told Amaziah to send all the foreign troops home and to trust him for the outcome. As we face the difficult process of recovery, we may be tempted to try every human resource available to support us. We must be careful to limit the resources we use to the ones that recognize our need for God's help.

that he had an army of 300,000 select troops, twenty years old and older, all trained in the use of spear and shield. [6]He also paid about 7,500 pounds* of silver to hire 100,000 experienced fighting men from Israel.

[7]But a man of God came to him and said, "Your Majesty, do not hire troops from Israel, for the LORD is not with Israel. He will not help those people of Ephraim! [8]If you let them go with your troops into battle, you will be defeated by the enemy no matter how well you fight. God will overthrow you, for he has the power to help you or to trip you up."

[9]Amaziah asked the man of God, "But what about all that silver I paid to hire the army of Israel?"

The man of God replied, "The LORD is able to give you much more than this!" [10]So Amaziah discharged the hired troops and sent them back to Ephraim. This made them very angry with Judah, and they returned home in a great rage.

[11]Then Amaziah summoned his courage and led his army to the Valley of Salt, where they killed 10,000 Edomite troops from Seir. [12]They captured another 10,000 and took them to the top of a cliff and threw them off, dashing them to pieces on the rocks below.

[13]Meanwhile, the hired troops that Amaziah had sent home raided several of the towns of Judah between Samaria and Beth-horon. They killed 3,000 people and carried off great quantities of plunder.

[14]When King Amaziah returned from slaughtering the Edomites, he brought with him idols taken from the people of Seir. He set them up as his own gods, bowed down in front of them, and offered sacrifices to them! [15]This made the LORD very angry, and he sent a prophet to ask, "Why do you turn to gods who could not even save their own people from you?"

[16]But the king interrupted him and said, "Since when have I made you the king's counselor? Be quiet now before I have you killed!"

So the prophet stopped with this warning: "I know that God has determined to destroy you because you have done this and have refused to accept my counsel."

[17]After consulting with his advisers, King Amaziah of Judah sent this challenge to Israel's king Jehoash,* the son of Jehoahaz and grandson of Jehu: "Come and meet me in battle!"*

[18]But King Jehoash of Israel replied to King Amaziah of Judah with this story: "Out in the Lebanon mountains, a thistle sent a message to a mighty cedar tree: 'Give your daughter in marriage to my son.' But just then a wild animal of Lebanon came by and stepped on the thistle, crushing it!

[19]"You are saying, 'I have defeated Edom,' and you are very proud of it. But my advice is to stay at home. Why stir up trouble that will only bring disaster on you and the people of Judah?"

[20]But Amaziah refused to listen, for God was determined to destroy him for turning to the gods of Edom. [21]So King Jehoash of Israel mobilized his army against King Amaziah of Judah. The two armies drew up their battle lines at Beth-shemesh in Judah. [22]Judah was routed by the army of Israel, and its army scattered and fled for home. [23]King Jehoash of Israel captured Judah's king, Amaziah son of Joash and grandson of Ahaziah, at Beth-shemesh. Then he brought him to Jerusalem, where he demolished 600 feet* of Jerusalem's wall, from the Ephraim Gate to the Corner Gate. [24]He carried off all the gold and silver and all the articles from the Temple of God that had been in the care of Obed-edom. He also seized the treasures of the royal palace, along with hostages, and then returned to Samaria.

[25]King Amaziah of Judah lived for fifteen years after the death of King Jehoash of Israel. [26]The rest of the events in Amaziah's reign, from beginning to end, are recorded in *The Book of the Kings of Judah and Israel.*

[27]After Amaziah turned away from the LORD, there was a conspiracy against his life in Jerusalem, and he fled to Lachish. But his enemies sent assassins after him, and they killed him there. [28]They brought his body back on a horse, and he was buried with his ancestors in the City of David.*

CHAPTER 26
Uzziah Rules in Judah

All the people of Judah had crowned Amaziah's sixteen-year-old son, Uzziah, as king in place of his father. [2]After his father's death, Uzziah rebuilt the town of Elath* and restored it to Judah.

[3]Uzziah was sixteen years old when he

25:6 Hebrew *100 talents* [3,400 kilograms]. 25:17a Hebrew *Joash*, a variant spelling of Jehoash; also in 25:18, 21, 23, 25. 25:17b Hebrew *Come, let us look one another in the face.* 25:23 Hebrew *400 cubits* [180 meters]. 25:28 As in some Hebrew manuscripts and other ancient versions (see also 2 Kgs 14:20); most Hebrew manuscripts read *the city of Judah.* 26:2 As in Greek version (see also 2 Kgs 14:22; 16:6); Hebrew reads *Eloth*, a variant spelling of Elath.

became king, and he reigned in Jerusalem fifty-two years. His mother was Jecoliah from Jerusalem. ⁴He did what was pleasing in the LORD's sight, just as his father, Amaziah, had done. ⁵Uzziah sought God during the days of Zechariah, who taught him to fear God.* And as long as the king sought guidance from the LORD, God gave him success.

⁶Uzziah declared war on the Philistines and broke down the walls of Gath, Jabneh, and Ashdod. Then he built new towns in the Ashdod area and in other parts of Philistia. ⁷God helped him in his wars against the Philistines, his battles with the Arabs of Gur,* and his wars with the Meunites. ⁸The Meunites* paid annual tribute to him, and his fame spread even to Egypt, for he had become very powerful.

⁹Uzziah built fortified towers in Jerusalem at the Corner Gate, at the Valley Gate, and at the angle in the wall. ¹⁰He also constructed forts in the wilderness and dug many water cisterns, because he kept great herds of livestock in the foothills of Judah* and on the plains. He was also a man who loved the soil. He had many workers who cared for his farms and vineyards, both on the hillsides and in the fertile valleys.

¹¹Uzziah had an army of well-trained warriors, ready to march into battle, unit by unit. This army had been mustered and organized by Jeiel, the secretary of the army, and his assistant, Maaseiah. They were under the direction of Hananiah, one of the king's officials. ¹²These regiments of mighty warriors were commanded by 2,600 clan leaders. ¹³The army consisted of 307,500 men, all elite troops. They were prepared to assist the king against any enemy. ¹⁴Uzziah provided the entire army with shields, spears, helmets, coats of mail, bows, and sling stones. ¹⁵And he built structures on the walls of Jerusalem, designed by experts to protect those who shot arrows and hurled large stones* from the towers and the corners of the wall. His fame spread far and wide, for the LORD gave him marvelous help, and he became very powerful.

Uzziah's Sin and Punishment

¹⁶But when he had become powerful, he also became proud, which led to his downfall. He sinned against the LORD his God by entering the sanctuary of the LORD's Temple and personally burning incense on the incense altar. ¹⁷Azariah the high priest went in after him with eighty other priests of the LORD, all brave men. ¹⁸They confronted King Uzziah and said, "It is not for you, Uzziah, to burn incense to the LORD. That is the work of the priests alone, the descendants of Aaron who are set apart for this work. Get out of the sanctuary, for you have sinned. The LORD God will not honor you for this!"

¹⁹Uzziah, who was holding an incense burner, became furious. But as he was standing there raging at the priests before the incense altar in the LORD's Temple, leprosy* suddenly broke out on his forehead. ²⁰When Azariah the high priest and all the other priests saw the leprosy, they rushed him out. And the king himself was eager to get out because the LORD had struck him. ²¹So King Uzziah had leprosy until the day he died. He lived in isolation in a separate house, for he was excluded from the Temple of the LORD. His son Jotham was put in charge of the royal palace, and he governed the people of the land.

²²The rest of the events of Uzziah's reign, from beginning to end, are recorded by the prophet Isaiah son of Amoz. ²³When Uzziah died, he was buried with his ancestors; his grave was in a nearby burial field belonging to the kings, for the people said, "He had leprosy." And his son Jotham became the next king.

26:5 As in Syriac and Greek versions; Hebrew reads *who instructed him in divine visions.* 26:7 As in Greek version; Hebrew reads *Gur-baal.* 26:8 As in Greek version; Hebrew reads *Ammonites.* Compare 26:7. 26:10 Hebrew *the Shephelah.* 26:15 Or *to shoot arrows and hurl large stones.* 26:19 Or *a contagious skin disease.* The Hebrew word used here and throughout this passage can describe various skin diseases.

26:14-16 When everything is going great, we are tempted to feel that we don't need God. Surely this was Uzziah's primary problem. As he became successful, he forgot that he needed God's help. We need to learn from Uzziah's mistake. When things begin to go well for us in recovery, it is easy to think we can go it alone. But as soon as we start to think this way, we are headed for a fall.

26:16-20 Uzziah had begun his reign so well; he had the potential of being one of the greatest kings in Judah's history. God blessed him in practically everything he did. But then he became proud and entered the Temple sanctuary, something only the priests were allowed to do. Uzziah discovered an important truth—we cannot sin without suffering the consequences.

CHAPTER 27
Jotham Rules in Judah

Jotham was twenty-five years old when he became king, and he reigned in Jerusalem sixteen years. His mother was Jerusha, the daughter of Zadok.

²Jotham did what was pleasing in the LORD's sight. He did everything his father, Uzziah, had done, except that Jotham did not sin by entering the Temple of the LORD. But the people continued in their corrupt ways.

³Jotham rebuilt the upper gate of the Temple of the LORD. He also did extensive rebuilding on the wall at the hill of Ophel. ⁴He built towns in the hill country of Judah and constructed fortresses and towers in the wooded areas. ⁵Jotham went to war against the Ammonites and conquered them. Over the next three years he received from them an annual tribute of 7,500 pounds* of silver, 50,000 bushels of wheat, and 50,000 bushels of barley.*

⁶King Jotham became powerful because he was careful to live in obedience to the LORD his God.

⁷The rest of the events of Jotham's reign, including all his wars and other activities, are recorded in *The Book of the Kings of Israel and Judah*. ⁸He was twenty-five years old when he became king, and he reigned in Jerusalem sixteen years. ⁹When Jotham died, he was buried in the City of David. And his son Ahaz became the next king.

CHAPTER 28
Ahaz Rules in Judah

Ahaz was twenty years old when he became king, and he reigned in Jerusalem sixteen years. He did not do what was pleasing in the sight of the LORD, as his ancestor David had done. ²Instead, he followed the example of the kings of Israel. He cast metal images for the worship of Baal. ³He offered sacrifices in the valley of Ben-Hinnom, even sacrificing his own sons in the fire.* In this way, he followed the detestable practices of the pagan nations the LORD had driven from the land ahead of the Israelites. ⁴He offered sacrifices and burned incense at the pagan shrines and on the hills and under every green tree.

⁵Because of all this, the LORD his God allowed the king of Aram to defeat Ahaz and to exile large numbers of his people to Damascus. The armies of the king of Israel also defeated Ahaz and inflicted many casualties on his army. ⁶In a single day Pekah son of Remaliah, Israel's king, killed 120,000 of Judah's troops, all of them experienced warriors, because they had abandoned the LORD, the God of their ancestors. ⁷Then Zicri, a warrior from Ephraim, killed Maaseiah, the king's son; Azrikam, the king's palace commander; and Elkanah, the king's second-in-command. ⁸The armies of Israel captured 200,000 women and children from Judah and seized tremendous amounts of plunder, which they took back to Samaria.

⁹But a prophet of the LORD named Oded was there in Samaria when the army of Israel returned home. He went out to meet them and said, "The LORD, the God of your ancestors, was angry with Judah and let you defeat them. But you have gone too far, killing them without mercy, and all heaven is disturbed. ¹⁰And now you are planning to make slaves of these people from Judah and Jerusalem. What about your own sins against the LORD your God? ¹¹Listen to me and return these prisoners you have taken, for they are your own relatives. Watch out, because now

---

27:5a Hebrew *100 talents* [3,400 kilograms]. **27:5b** Hebrew *10,000 cors* [2,200 kiloliters] *of wheat, and 10,000 cors of barley.* **28:3** Or *even making his sons pass through the fire.*

27:6 What makes a person great? This verse shows us that Jotham's success was a direct result of his obedience to God. When we are faithful to God's ways, God will lead us to a victorious and productive life. We must remember, however, that God's view of greatness might not correspond with ours.

28:1-2 The northern kingdom of Israel had been vanquished by the Assyrians. Many of its people had been taken into captivity and would never return. How foolish for Ahaz, king of the southern kingdom of Judah, to follow the wicked example of the kings of the northern kingdom! He could see where their behavior had led them (see 2 Kings 15:29; 16:1; 17:5). We need to be careful about whom we choose to emulate.

28:3-4 Ahaz hadn't learned that the pagan customs of the surrounding nations were not appropriate or helpful. In fact, these activities eventually led to his own destruction (28:22-23). It is tempting to try recovery programs that prescribe activities or beliefs that contradict God's Word, especially if they seem to be working for people we know. We must measure any program against the truth of God's Word and remember that true recovery can only be achieved through God's power.

the LORD's fierce anger has been turned against you!"

[12]Then some of the leaders of Israel*—Azariah son of Jehohanan, Berekiah son of Meshillemoth, Jehizkiah son of Shallum, and Amasa son of Hadlai—agreed with this and confronted the men returning from battle. [13]"You must not bring the prisoners here!" they declared. "We cannot afford to add to our sins and guilt. Our guilt is already great, and the LORD's fierce anger is already turned against Israel."

[14]So the warriors released the prisoners and handed over the plunder in the sight of the leaders and all the people. [15]Then the four men just mentioned by name came forward and distributed clothes from the plunder to the prisoners who were naked. They provided clothing and sandals to wear, gave them enough food and drink, and dressed their wounds with olive oil. They put those who were weak on donkeys and took all the prisoners back to their own people in Jericho, the city of palms. Then they returned to Samaria.

Ahaz Closes the Temple

[16]At that time King Ahaz of Judah asked the king of Assyria for help. [17]The armies of Edom had again invaded Judah and taken captives. [18]And the Philistines had raided towns located in the foothills of Judah* and in the Negev of Judah. They had already captured and occupied Beth-shemesh, Aijalon, Gederoth, Soco with its villages, Timnah with its villages, and Gimzo with its villages. [19]The LORD was humbling Judah because of King Ahaz of Judah,* for he had encouraged his people to sin and had been utterly unfaithful to the LORD.

[20]So when King Tiglath-pileser* of Assyria arrived, he attacked Ahaz instead of helping him. [21]Ahaz took valuable items from the LORD's Temple, the royal palace, and from the homes of his officials and gave them to the king of Assyria as tribute. But this did not help him.

[22]Even during this time of trouble, King Ahaz continued to reject the LORD. [23]He offered sacrifices to the gods of Damascus who had defeated him, for he said, "Since these gods helped the kings of Aram, they will help me, too, if I sacrifice to them." But instead, they led to his ruin and the ruin of all Judah.

[24]The king took the various articles from the Temple of God and broke them into pieces. He shut the doors of the LORD's Temple so that no one could worship there, and he set up altars to pagan gods in every corner of Jerusalem. [25]He made pagan shrines in all the towns of Judah for offering sacrifices to other gods. In this way, he aroused the anger of the LORD, the God of his ancestors.

[26]The rest of the events of Ahaz's reign and everything he did, from beginning to end, are recorded in *The Book of the Kings of Judah and Israel*. [27]When Ahaz died, he was buried in Jerusalem but not in the royal cemetery of the kings of Judah. Then his son Hezekiah became the next king.

CHAPTER 29
Hezekiah Rules in Judah

Hezekiah was twenty-five years old when he became the king of Judah, and he reigned in Jerusalem twenty-nine years. His mother was Abijah, the daughter of Zechariah. [2]He did what was pleasing in the LORD's sight, just as his ancestor David had done.

Hezekiah Reopens the Temple

[3]In the very first month of the first year of his reign, Hezekiah reopened the doors of the Temple of the LORD and repaired them. [4]He summoned the priests and Levites to meet

---

28:12 Hebrew *Ephraim*, referring to the northern kingdom of Israel. 28:18 Hebrew *the Shephelah*. 28:19 Masoretic Text reads *of Israel;* also in 28:23, 27. The author of Chronicles sees Judah as representative of the true Israel. (Some Hebrew manuscripts and Greek version read *of Judah.*) 28:20 Hebrew *Tilgath-pilneser,* a variant spelling of Tiglath-pileser.

29:1-2 Hezekiah received a high commendation indeed: He followed the example of his ancestor David. For the kings of Judah, King David was the measure of success. As we seek to rebuild our life, we need to find worthy role models. David is an ideal role model, for though he made many mistakes, he was always willing to humbly admit his failures and seek reconciliation with God and other people.

29:3-5 Hezekiah began his reign the right way—with steps toward recovery. His father had led Judah into sin and idolatry. The Temple had been closed, and its worship discontinued. Hezekiah recognized his father's failures and set out to make changes. He opened the Temple's doors and enjoined the priests to purify themselves and reinstitute the proper worship activities. When our life is filled with problems, denial is not the way to make things better. We need to act like Hezekiah did; he assessed the problems and deficiencies of his kingdom and then did what he could to change them.

him at the courtyard east of the Temple. ⁵He said to them, "Listen to me, you Levites! Purify yourselves, and purify the Temple of the LORD, the God of your ancestors. Remove all the defiled things from the sanctuary. ⁶Our ancestors were unfaithful and did what was evil in the sight of the LORD our God. They abandoned the LORD and his dwelling place; they turned their backs on him. ⁷They also shut the doors to the Temple's entry room, and they snuffed out the lamps. They stopped burning incense and presenting burnt offerings at the sanctuary of the God of Israel.

⁸"That is why the LORD's anger has fallen upon Judah and Jerusalem. He has made them an object of dread, horror, and ridicule, as you can see with your own eyes. ⁹Because of this, our fathers have been killed in battle, and our sons and daughters and wives have been captured. ¹⁰But now I will make a covenant with the LORD, the God of Israel, so that his fierce anger will turn away from us. ¹¹My sons, do not neglect your duties any longer! The LORD has chosen you to stand in his presence, to minister to him, and to lead the people in worship and present offerings to him."

¹²Then these Levites got right to work:

From the clan of Kohath: Mahath son of Amasai and Joel son of Azariah.
From the clan of Merari: Kish son of Abdi and Azariah son of Jehallelel.
From the clan of Gershon: Joah son of Zimmah and Eden son of Joah.
¹³ From the family of Elizaphan: Shimri and Jeiel.
From the family of Asaph: Zechariah and Mattaniah.
¹⁴ From the family of Heman: Jehiel and Shimei.
From the family of Jeduthun: Shemaiah and Uzziel.

¹⁵These men called together their fellow Levites, and they all purified themselves. Then they began to cleanse the Temple of the LORD, just as the king had commanded. They were careful to follow all the LORD's instructions in their work. ¹⁶The priests went into the sanctuary of the Temple of the LORD to cleanse it, and they took out to the Temple courtyard all the defiled things they found. From there the Levites carted it all out to the Kidron Valley.

¹⁷They began the work in early spring, on the first day of the new year,* and in eight days they had reached the entry room of the LORD's Temple. Then they purified the Temple of the LORD itself, which took another eight days. So the entire task was completed in sixteen days.

The Temple Rededication

¹⁸Then the Levites went to King Hezekiah and gave him this report: "We have cleansed the entire Temple of the LORD, the altar of burnt offering with all its utensils, and the table of the Bread of the Presence with all its utensils. ¹⁹We have also recovered all the items discarded by King Ahaz when he was unfaithful and closed the Temple. They are now in front of the altar of the LORD, purified and ready for use."

²⁰Early the next morning King Hezekiah gathered the city officials and went to the Temple of the LORD. ²¹They brought seven bulls, seven rams, and seven male lambs as a burnt offering, together with seven male goats as a sin offering for the kingdom, for the Temple, and for Judah. The king commanded the priests, who were descendants of Aaron, to sacrifice the animals on the altar of the LORD.

²²So they killed the bulls, and the priests took the blood and sprinkled it on the altar. Next they killed the rams and sprinkled their blood on the altar. And finally, they did the same with the male lambs. ²³The male goats for the sin offering were then brought before the king and the assembly of people, who laid their hands on them. ²⁴The priests then killed the goats as a sin offering and sprinkled their blood on the altar to make atonement for the sins of all Israel. The king had specifically commanded that this burnt offering and sin offering should be made for all Israel.

²⁵King Hezekiah then stationed the Levites at the Temple of the LORD with cymbals, lyres, and harps. He obeyed all the commands that the LORD had given to King David through Gad, the king's seer, and the prophet Nathan. ²⁶The Levites then took their positions around the Temple with the instruments of David, and the priests took their positions with the trumpets.

²⁷Then Hezekiah ordered that the burnt offering be placed on the altar. As the burnt offering was presented, songs of praise to the

29:17 Hebrew *on the first day of the first month.* This day in the ancient Hebrew lunar calendar occurred in March or early April, 715 B.C.

LORD were begun, accompanied by the trumpets and other instruments of David, the former king of Israel. [28]The entire assembly worshiped the LORD as the singers sang and the trumpets blew, until all the burnt offerings were finished. [29]Then the king and everyone with him bowed down in worship. [30]King Hezekiah and the officials ordered the Levites to praise the LORD with the psalms written by David and by Asaph the seer. So they offered joyous praise and bowed down in worship.

[31]Then Hezekiah declared, "Now that you have consecrated yourselves to the LORD, bring your sacrifices and thanksgiving offerings to the Temple of the LORD." So the people brought their sacrifices and thanksgiving offerings, and all whose hearts were willing brought burnt offerings, too. [32]The people brought to the LORD 70 bulls, 100 rams, and 200 male lambs for burnt offerings. [33]They also brought 600 cattle and 3,000 sheep and goats as sacred offerings.

[34]But there were too few priests to prepare all the burnt offerings. So their relatives the Levites helped them until the work was finished and more priests had been purified, for the Levites had been more conscientious about purifying themselves than the priests had been. [35]There was an abundance of burnt offerings, along with the usual liquid offerings, and a great deal of fat from the many peace offerings.

So the Temple of the LORD was restored to service. [36]And Hezekiah and all the people rejoiced because of what God had done for the people, for everything had been accomplished so quickly.

CHAPTER 30
Preparations for Passover

King Hezekiah now sent word to all Israel and Judah, and he wrote letters of invitation to the people of Ephraim and Manasseh. He asked everyone to come to the Temple of the LORD at Jerusalem to celebrate the Passover of the LORD, the God of Israel. [2]The king, his officials, and all the community of Jerusalem decided to celebrate Passover a month later than usual.* [3]They were unable to celebrate it at the prescribed time because not enough priests could be purified by then, and the people had not yet assembled at Jerusalem.

[4]This plan for keeping the Passover seemed right to the king and all the people. [5]So they sent a proclamation throughout all Israel, from Beersheba in the south to Dan in the north, inviting everyone to come to Jerusalem to celebrate the Passover of the LORD, the God of Israel. The people had not been celebrating it in great numbers as required in the Law.

[6]At the king's command, runners were sent throughout Israel and Judah. They carried letters that said:

"O people of Israel, return to the LORD, the God of Abraham, Isaac, and Israel,* so that he will return to the few of us who have survived the conquest of the Assyrian kings. [7]Do not be like your ancestors and relatives who abandoned the LORD, the God of their ancestors, and became an object of derision, as you yourselves can see. [8]Do not be stubborn, as they were, but submit yourselves to the LORD. Come to his Temple, which he has set apart as holy forever. Worship the LORD your God so that his fierce anger will turn away from you.

[9]"For if you return to the LORD, your relatives and your children will be treated mercifully by their captors, and they will be able to return to this land. For the LORD your God is gracious and merciful. If you return to him, he will not continue to turn his face from you."

Celebration of Passover

[10]The runners went from town to town throughout Ephraim and Manasseh and as far as the territory of Zebulun. But most of the people just laughed at the runners and made fun of them. [11]However, some people from Asher, Manasseh, and Zebulun humbled themselves and went to Jerusalem. [12]At the same time, God's hand was on the

---

30:2 Hebrew *in the second month*. Passover was normally observed in the first month (of the ancient Hebrew lunar calendar). 30:6 *Israel* is the name that God gave to Jacob.

30:6-8 Hezekiah called his people to break from the dysfunctional patterns set by their ancestors. Hezekiah had already broken from the patterns set by his father. He was the ideal person to call his people to do the same because he knew exactly where they were coming from. Some people feel absolutely imprisoned by the failures and wrong patterns set by their family. But there is hope for all who trust God. We don't need to be bound by others' failures. We can recover if we are willing to place our life in God's hands.

people in the land of Judah, giving them all one heart to obey the orders of the king and his officials, who were following the word of the LORD. [13]So a huge crowd assembled at Jerusalem in midspring* to celebrate the Festival of Unleavened Bread. [14]They set to work and removed the pagan altars from Jerusalem. They took away all the incense altars and threw them into the Kidron Valley.

[15]On the fourteenth day of the second month, one month later than usual,* the people slaughtered the Passover lamb. This shamed the priests and Levites, so they purified themselves and brought burnt offerings to the Temple of the LORD. [16]Then they took their places at the Temple as prescribed in the Law of Moses, the man of God. The Levites brought the sacrificial blood to the priests, who then sprinkled it on the altar.

[17]Since many of the people had not purified themselves, the Levites had to slaughter their Passover lamb for them, to set them apart for the LORD. [18]Most of those who came from Ephraim, Manasseh, Issachar, and Zebulun had not purified themselves. But King Hezekiah prayed for them, and they were allowed to eat the Passover meal anyway, even though this was contrary to the requirements of the Law. For Hezekiah said, "May the LORD, who is good, pardon those [19]who decide to follow the LORD, the God of their ancestors, even though they are not properly cleansed for the ceremony." [20]And the LORD listened to Hezekiah's prayer and healed the people.

[21]So the people of Israel who were present in Jerusalem joyously celebrated the Festival of Unleavened Bread for seven days. Each day the Levites and priests sang to the LORD,

accompanied by loud instruments.* [22]Hezekiah encouraged all the Levites regarding the skill they displayed as they served the LORD. The celebration continued for seven days. Peace offerings were sacrificed, and the people gave thanks to the LORD, the God of their ancestors.

[23]The entire assembly then decided to continue the festival another seven days, so they celebrated joyfully for another week. [24]King Hezekiah gave the people 1,000 bulls and 7,000 sheep and goats for offerings, and the officials donated 1,000 bulls and 10,000 sheep and goats. Meanwhile, many more priests purified themselves.

[25]The entire assembly of Judah rejoiced, including the priests, the Levites, all who came from the land of Israel, the foreigners who came to the festival, and all those who lived in Judah. [26]There was great joy in the city, for Jerusalem had not seen a celebration like this one since the days of Solomon, King David's son. [27]Then the priests and Levites stood and blessed the people, and God heard their prayer from his holy dwelling in heaven.

CHAPTER 31
Hezekiah's Religious Reforms
When the festival ended, the Israelites who attended went to all the towns of Judah, Benjamin, Ephraim, and Manasseh, and they smashed all the sacred pillars, cut down the Asherah poles, and removed the pagan shrines and altars. After this, the Israelites returned to their own towns and homes.

[2]Hezekiah then organized the priests and Levites into divisions to offer the burnt offerings and peace offerings, and to worship and

---

30:13 Hebrew *in the second month.* The second month of the ancient Hebrew lunar calendar usually occurs within the months of April and May. 30:15 Hebrew *On the fourteenth day of the second month.* Passover normally began on the fourteenth day of the first month (see Lev 23:5). 30:21 Or *sang to the LORD with all their strength.*

30:17-19 God is awesome and holy; he is sinless and perfect. We can approach him only because he graciously allows us to do so. In Old Testament times, one had to follow prescribed procedures in seeking God. Hezekiah prayed on behalf of those whose preparations were not as complete as they should have been. Now we can all approach God directly because of what Christ has done on our behalf.

31:2 Hezekiah illustrates another important element of recovery. He ensured constant praise to God by setting up structures and personnel to lead the people in worship. Here is an element that is often lacking in our recovery programs. We must never forget to thank God for his help as we seek to overcome the problems in our life. Praising the one who makes recovery possible is essential to a healthy recovery.

31:4-8 Sometimes doing good is a thankless task. Hezekiah made certain that encouragement was given to the people who took part in Judah's recovery process. When the people gave sacrificially to God, Hezekiah thanked them for their generosity. How necessary it is for anyone in recovery to be part of a comforting and strengthening fellowship. We need to give and receive the encouragement necessary for a successful recovery.

give thanks and praise to the LORD at the gates of the Temple. ³The king also made a personal contribution of animals for the daily morning and evening burnt offerings, the weekly Sabbath festivals, the monthly new moon festivals, and the annual festivals as prescribed in the Law of the LORD. ⁴In addition, he required the people in Jerusalem to bring a portion of their goods to the priests and Levites, so they could devote themselves fully to the Law of the LORD.

⁵When the people of Israel heard these requirements, they responded generously by bringing the first share of their grain, new wine, olive oil, honey, and all the produce of their fields. They brought a large quantity—a tithe of all they produced. ⁶The people who had moved to Judah from Israel, and the people of Judah themselves, brought in the tithes of their cattle, sheep, and goats and a tithe of the things that had been dedicated to the LORD their God, and they piled them up in great heaps. ⁷They began piling them up in late spring, and the heaps continued to grow until early autumn.* ⁸When Hezekiah and his officials came and saw these huge piles, they thanked the LORD and his people Israel!

⁹"Where did all this come from?" Hezekiah asked the priests and Levites.

¹⁰And Azariah the high priest, from the family of Zadok, replied, "Since the people began bringing their gifts to the LORD's Temple, we have had enough to eat and plenty to spare. The LORD has blessed his people, and all this is left over."

¹¹Hezekiah ordered that storerooms be prepared in the Temple of the LORD. When this was done, ¹²the people faithfully brought all the gifts, tithes, and other items dedicated for use in the Temple. Conaniah the Levite was put in charge, assisted by his brother Shimei. ¹³The supervisors under them were Jehiel, Azaziah, Nahath, Asahel, Jerimoth, Jozabad, Eliel, Ismakiah, Mahath, and Benaiah. These appointments were made by King Hezekiah and Azariah, the chief official in the Temple of God.

¹⁴Kore son of Imnah the Levite, who was the gatekeeper at the East Gate, was put in charge of distributing the voluntary offerings given to God, the gifts, and the things that had been dedicated to the LORD. ¹⁵His faithful assistants were Eden, Miniamin, Jeshua, Shemaiah, Amariah, and Shecaniah. They distributed the gifts among the families of priests in their towns by their divisions, dividing the gifts fairly among old and young alike. ¹⁶They distributed the gifts to all males three years old or older, regardless of their place in the genealogical records. The distribution went to all who would come to the LORD's Temple to perform their daily duties according to their divisions. ¹⁷They distributed gifts to the priests who were listed by their families in the genealogical records, and to the Levites twenty years old or older who were listed according to their jobs and their divisions. ¹⁸Food allotments were also given to the families of all those listed in the genealogical records, including their little babies, wives, sons, and daughters. For they had all been faithful in purifying themselves.

¹⁹As for the priests, the descendants of Aaron, who were living in the open villages around the towns, men were appointed by name to distribute portions to every male among the priests and to all the Levites listed in the genealogical records.

²⁰In this way, King Hezekiah handled the distribution throughout all Judah, doing what was pleasing and good in the sight of the LORD his God. ²¹In all that he did in the service of the Temple of God and in his efforts to follow God's laws and commands, Hezekiah sought his God wholeheartedly. As a result, he was very successful.

CHAPTER 32
Assyria Invades Judah

After Hezekiah had faithfully carried out this work, King Sennacherib of Assyria invaded Judah. He laid siege to the fortified towns, giving orders for his army to break through their walls. ²When Hezekiah realized that

---

31:7 Hebrew *in the third month . . . until the seventh month.* The third month of the ancient Hebrew lunar calendar usually occurs within the months of May and June; the seventh month usually occurs within September and October.

32:3-6 Trust in God—and work hard to do his will. Hezekiah gives us an excellent example of how we should act in recovery—with both faith and hard work. He knew that only God could deliver Judah from the Assyrian invasion, but that didn't stop him from doing what he could to protect Jerusalem. One of the engineering marvels of the ancient world is Hezekiah's tunnel, which brought water into the city from a spring outside the city walls. This ensured a steady water supply during a siege. There is no question that Hezekiah trusted God for victory, but he made certain that he did all he could to prepare for the invasion.

READ 2 CHRONICLES 32:1-19

GOD grant me the serenity to accept the things I cannot change the courage to change the things I can and the wisdom to know the difference A M E N

Boundaries are the limits we set for our protection. Recovery involves repairing or building healthy boundaries that have become weak, defective, or torn down through abuse.

In Bible times each city was fortified by boundary walls that served as protection from outside enemies. If these walls were weak or broken, there was grave danger of invasion and destruction. At one point in Israel's history an enemy was threatening to attack Jerusalem. King Hezekiah "strengthened his defenses by repairing all the broken sections of the wall, erecting towers, and constructing a second wall outside the first. [He] . . . . encouraged them by saying: 'Be strong and courageous! . . . We have the LORD our God to help us and to fight our battles for us!' Hezekiah's words greatly encouraged the people" (2 Chronicles 32:5-8).

For some of us, our boundaries have grown weak as we have let people walk all over us or as we have let down our guard against our own destructive behaviors.

Part of the recovery process involves repairing our boundaries. We can also construct a second wall of defense by developing a strong support network around us. We will still need to be brave and remember that no matter what enemies we face in the form of destructive behaviors, there is someone on our side who is far greater. This should bring us great encouragement. *Turn to page 759, Psalm 111.*

Sennacherib also intended to attack Jerusalem, ³he consulted with his officials and military advisers, and they decided to stop the flow of the springs outside the city. ⁴They organized a huge work crew to stop the flow of the springs, cutting off the brook that ran through the fields. For they said, "Why should the kings of Assyria come here and find plenty of water?"

⁵Then Hezekiah worked hard at repairing all the broken sections of the wall, erecting towers, and constructing a second wall outside the first. He also reinforced the supporting terraces* in the City of David and manufactured large numbers of weapons and shields. ⁶He appointed military officers over the people and assembled them before him in the square at the city gate. Then Hezekiah encouraged them by saying: ⁷"Be strong and courageous! Don't be afraid or discouraged because of the king of Assyria or

his mighty army, for there is a power far greater on our side! ⁸He may have a great army, but they are merely men. We have the LORD our God to help us and to fight our battles for us!" Hezekiah's words greatly encouraged the people.

Sennacherib Threatens Jerusalem
⁹While King Sennacherib of Assyria was still besieging the town of Lachish, he sent his officers to Jerusalem with this message for Hezekiah and all the people in the city:

¹⁰"This is what King Sennacherib of Assyria says: What are you trusting in that makes you think you can survive my siege of Jerusalem? ¹¹Hezekiah has said, 'The LORD our God will rescue us from the king of Assyria.' Surely Hezekiah is misleading you, sentencing you to death by famine and thirst! ¹²Don't you realize

32:5 Hebrew *the millo.* The meaning of the Hebrew is uncertain.

577

that Hezekiah is the very person who destroyed all the LORD's shrines and altars? He commanded Judah and Jerusalem to worship only at the altar at the Temple and to offer sacrifices on it alone.

¹³"Surely you must realize what I and the other kings of Assyria before me have done to all the people of the earth! Were any of the gods of those nations able to rescue their people from my power? ¹⁴Which of their gods was able to rescue its people from the destructive power of my predecessors? What makes you think your God can rescue you from me? ¹⁵Don't let Hezekiah deceive you! Don't let him fool you like this! I say it again—no god of any nation or kingdom has ever yet been able to rescue his people from me or my ancestors. How much less will your God rescue you from my power!"

¹⁶And Sennacherib's officers further mocked the LORD God and his servant Hezekiah, heaping insult upon insult. ¹⁷The king also sent letters scorning the LORD, the God of Israel. He wrote, "Just as the gods of all the other nations failed to rescue their people from my power, so the God of Hezekiah will also fail." ¹⁸The Assyrian officials who brought the letters shouted this in Hebrew* to the people gathered on the walls of the city, trying to terrify them so it would be easier to capture the city. ¹⁹These officers talked about the God of Jerusalem as though he were one of the pagan gods, made by human hands.

²⁰Then King Hezekiah and the prophet Isaiah son of Amoz cried out in prayer to God in heaven. ²¹And the LORD sent an angel who destroyed the Assyrian army with all its commanders and officers. So Sennacherib was forced to return home in disgrace to his own land. And when he entered the temple of his god, some of his own sons killed him there with a sword.

²²That is how the LORD rescued Hezekiah and the people of Jerusalem from King Sennacherib of Assyria and from all the oth-

ers who threatened them. So there was peace throughout the land. ²³From then on King Hezekiah became highly respected among all the surrounding nations, and many gifts for the LORD arrived at Jerusalem, with valuable presents for King Hezekiah, too.

Hezekiah's Sickness and Recovery

²⁴About that time Hezekiah became deathly ill. He prayed to the LORD, who healed him and gave him a miraculous sign. ²⁵But Hezekiah did not respond appropriately to the kindness shown him, and he became proud. So the LORD's anger came against him and against Judah and Jerusalem. ²⁶Then Hezekiah humbled himself and repented of his pride, as did the people of Jerusalem. So the LORD's anger did not fall on them during Hezekiah's lifetime.

²⁷Hezekiah was very wealthy and highly honored. He built special treasury buildings for his silver, gold, precious stones, and spices, and for his shields and other valuable items. ²⁸He also constructed many storehouses for his grain, new wine, and olive oil; and he made many stalls for his cattle and pens for his flocks of sheep and goats. ²⁹He built many towns and acquired vast flocks and herds, for God had given him great wealth. ³⁰He blocked up the upper spring of Gihon and brought the water down through a tunnel to the west side of the City of David. And so he succeeded in everything he did.

³¹However, when ambassadors arrived from Babylon to ask about the remarkable events that had taken place in the land, God withdrew from Hezekiah in order to test him and to see what was really in his heart.

Summary of Hezekiah's Reign

³²The rest of the events in Hezekiah's reign and his acts of devotion are recorded in *The Vision of the Prophet Isaiah Son of Amoz*, which is included in *The Book of the Kings of Judah and Israel*. ³³When Hezekiah died, he was buried in the upper area of the royal cemetery, and all Judah and Jerusalem honored him at his death. And his son Manasseh became the next king.

32:18 Hebrew *in the dialect of Judah.*

32:20-22 Perhaps the most overlooked resource in the recovery process is prayer. God does hear and answer the call of his people. He does not always send an immediate and miraculous rescue as he did for Hezekiah, but he always answers. God's intervention in this instance is clear. By any human estimation, Sennacherib should have won this battle, but with God fighting on Judah's side, the Assyrian king returned home in disgrace. God is just as able to help us in our "impossible" battles.

CHAPTER 33
Manasseh Rules in Judah

Manasseh was twelve years old when he became king, and he reigned in Jerusalem fifty-five years. [2]He did what was evil in the LORD's sight, following the detestable practices of the pagan nations that the LORD had driven from the land ahead of the Israelites. [3]He rebuilt the pagan shrines his father, Hezekiah, had broken down. He constructed altars for the images of Baal and set up Asherah poles. He also bowed before all the powers of the heavens and worshiped them.

[4]He built pagan altars in the Temple of the LORD, the place where the LORD had said, "My name will remain in Jerusalem forever." [5]He built these altars for all the powers of the heavens in both courtyards of the LORD's Temple. [6]Manasseh also sacrificed his own sons in the fire* in the valley of Ben-Hinnom. He practiced sorcery, divination, and witchcraft, and he consulted with mediums and psychics. He did much that was evil in the LORD's sight, arousing his anger.

[7]Manasseh even took a carved idol he had made and set it up in God's Temple, the very place where God had told David and his son Solomon: "My name will be honored forever in this Temple and in Jerusalem—the city I have chosen from among all the tribes of Israel. [8]If the Israelites will be careful to obey my commands—all the laws, decrees, and regulations given through Moses—I will not send them into exile from this land that I set aside for your ancestors." [9]But Manasseh led the people of Judah and Jerusalem to do even more evil than the pagan nations that the LORD had destroyed when the people of Israel entered the land.

[10]The LORD spoke to Manasseh and his people, but they ignored all his warnings. [11]So the LORD sent the commanders of the Assyrian armies, and they took Manasseh prisoner. They put a ring through his nose, bound him in bronze chains, and led him away to Babylon. [12]But while in deep distress, Manasseh sought the LORD his God and sincerely humbled himself before the God of his ancestors. [13]And when he prayed, the LORD listened to him and was moved by his request. So the LORD brought Manasseh back to Jerusalem and to his kingdom. Then Manasseh finally realized that the LORD alone is God!

[14]After this Manasseh rebuilt the outer wall of the City of David, from west of the Gihon Spring in the Kidron Valley to the Fish Gate, and continuing around the hill of Ophel. He built the wall very high. And he stationed his military officers in all of the fortified towns of Judah. [15]Manasseh also removed the foreign gods and the idol from the LORD's Temple. He tore down all the altars he had built on the hill where the Temple stood and all the altars that were in Jerusalem, and he dumped them outside the city. [16]Then he restored the altar of the LORD and sacrificed peace offerings and thanksgiving offerings on it. He also encouraged the people of Judah to worship the LORD, the God of Israel. [17]However, the people still sacrificed at the pagan shrines, though only to the LORD their God.

[18]The rest of the events of Manasseh's reign, his prayer to God, and the words the seers spoke to him in the name of the LORD, the God of Israel, are recorded in *The Book of the Kings of Israel.* [19]Manasseh's prayer, the account of the way God answered him, and an account of all his sins and unfaithfulness are recorded in *The Record of the Seers.** It includes a list of the locations where he built pagan shrines and set up Asherah poles and idols before he humbled himself and repented. [20]When Manasseh died, he was buried in his palace. Then his son Amon became the next king.

Amon Rules in Judah

[21]Amon was twenty-two years old when he became king, and he reigned in Jerusalem two years. [22]He did what was evil in the LORD's sight, just as his father, Manasseh, had done. He worshiped and sacrificed to all

---

33:6 Or *also made his sons pass through the fire.*   33:19 Or *The Record of Hozai.*

33:1-2 There is biting irony in these verses. Manasseh followed the patterns of the pagan nations—the very ones over whom God had demonstrated his superiority. Manasseh insisted on a program that had already proved inadequate. In the recovery process, there are some things that will never work. We need to make sure that the program we follow reflects God's truth as revealed in the Bible.

33:12-13 God placed Manasseh into such dire straits that there was nothing else he could do but seek God. Even though Manasseh had been one of Judah's most evil kings, he was forgiven and restored when he recognized his powerless state and cried out humbly to God for help. God will do no less for each of us today. Sin and failure will ultimately lead us into difficult circumstances. When this happens, we need to run into God's open and forgiving arms.

the idols his father had made. ²³But unlike his father, he did not humble himself before the LORD. Instead, Amon sinned even more.

²⁴Then Amon's own officials conspired against him and assassinated him in his palace. ²⁵But the people of the land killed all those who had conspired against King Amon, and they made his son Josiah the next king.

CHAPTER 34
Josiah Rules in Judah

Josiah was eight years old when he became king, and he reigned in Jerusalem thirty-one years. ²He did what was pleasing in the LORD's sight and followed the example of his ancestor David. He did not turn away from doing what was right.

³During the eighth year of his reign, while he was still young, Josiah began to seek the God of his ancestor David. Then in the twelfth year he began to purify Judah and Jerusalem, destroying all the pagan shrines, the Asherah poles, and the carved idols and cast images. ⁴He ordered that the altars of Baal be demolished and that the incense altars which stood above them be broken down. He also made sure that the Asherah poles, the carved idols, and the cast images were smashed and scattered over the graves of those who had sacrificed to them. ⁵He burned the bones of the pagan priests on their own altars, and so he purified Judah and Jerusalem.

⁶He did the same thing in the towns of Manasseh, Ephraim, and Simeon, even as far as Naphtali, and in the regions* all around them. ⁷He destroyed the pagan altars and the Asherah poles, and he crushed the idols into dust. He cut down all the incense altars throughout the land of Israel. Finally, he returned to Jerusalem.

⁸In the eighteenth year of his reign, after he had purified the land and the Temple,

Josiah appointed Shaphan son of Azaliah, Maaseiah the governor of Jerusalem, and Joah son of Joahaz, the royal historian, to repair the Temple of the LORD his God. ⁹They gave Hilkiah the high priest the money that had been collected by the Levites who served as gatekeepers at the Temple of God. The gifts were brought by people from Manasseh, Ephraim, and from all the remnant of Israel, as well as from all Judah, Benjamin, and the people of Jerusalem.

¹⁰He entrusted the money to the men assigned to supervise the restoration of the LORD's Temple. Then they paid the workers who did the repairs and renovation of the Temple. ¹¹They hired carpenters and builders, who purchased finished stone for the walls and timber for the rafters and beams. They restored what earlier kings of Judah had allowed to fall into ruin.

¹²The workers served faithfully under the leadership of Jahath and Obadiah, Levites of the Merarite clan, and Zechariah and Meshullam, Levites of the Kohathite clan. Other Levites, all of whom were skilled musicians, ¹³were put in charge of the laborers of the various trades. Still others assisted as secretaries, officials, and gatekeepers.

Hilkiah Discovers God's Law

¹⁴While they were bringing out the money collected at the LORD's Temple, Hilkiah the priest found the Book of the Law of the LORD that was written by Moses. ¹⁵Hilkiah said to Shaphan the court secretary, "I have found the Book of the Law in the LORD's Temple!" Then Hilkiah gave the scroll to Shaphan.

¹⁶Shaphan took the scroll to the king and reported, "Your officials are doing everything they were assigned to do. ¹⁷The money that was collected at the Temple of the LORD has been turned over to the supervisors and

---

34:6 As in Syriac version. Hebrew reads *in their temples,* or *in their ruins.* The meaning of the Hebrew is uncertain.

34:14-19 Even the Scriptures had been lost during the years of spiritual decline. After more than 70 years of not having God's Word, the people had forgotten how God wanted them to live. They had no idea what they were doing wrong or how to please God. Without the Bible, it is impossible to effect proper changes in our life. We need definite standards of right and wrong. Without God's Word, it is all too easy for such things to become matters of individual opinion. Today whole systems of faith are based on opinions—what people want to hear rather than what God says. To succeed in recovery, our program must be based on God's standards set out for us in the Bible.

34:21 As soon as Josiah heard what God expected of his people, he took inventory of the situation in Judah. He was open and willing to admit how poorly he and the people measured up against God's standards. Josiah's humility and honesty here are truly exemplary. He did not try to hide his sins or the sins of his nation. He had no layers of denial to overcome. He openly admitted his failures and sought to change things immediately. As we take inventory in our life, we need to display the same kind of honest humility.

JOSIAH

Normally the sinful patterns of the parents are duplicated in succeeding generations. Even those who do not want to be like their parents usually turn out to be amazingly similar in their behavior and personality. But it is possible for us to break out of this ongoing spiral of sinful habits by depending on God to help us make wise personal choices and face reality in our life.

Josiah was a young king who chose to stand against a virtual tidal wave of disobedience fostered by his grandfather, Manasseh, and his father, Amon. Breaking from this downward spiral was particularly difficult since Josiah had little knowledge to guide his actions. The Scriptures containing God's laws had been lost for years. But when Hilkiah, the high priest, discovered the Scriptures in the Temple, young Josiah immediately initiated a recovery program for himself and his people.

It is fair to say that Josiah grew up in a dysfunctional and destructive situation. Idolatry and other forms of sinful behavior were an established norm. Josiah had to begin by discovering what God's ideals for living were. Then he was able to establish his own recovery and intervene in the sinful affairs of his nation. In time he was able to break the cycle of sin that had ensnared Israel. He had faith, commitment to God, and the courage to pursue both personal and national recovery.

In making his difficult choices, Josiah sought to "cut loose" from the sins of the past and build a new life for himself and the people of Judah. Breaking from long-standing evil practices enabled Judah to proceed with positive reforms and a closer relationship with God. That included one of the most joyful Passover celebrations that Israel had ever known. Josiah was not a perfect man, but he was a true champion of recovery. His stand for God's way made a significant impact on the lives of his people.

STRENGTHS AND ACCOMPLISHMENTS:
- Josiah undertook the long, painful process of personal and national recovery.
- He did away with idolatry and led the people to renew their commitment to God.
- His heart was open to God's will, and he was obedient to God's commands.

WEAKNESSES AND MISTAKES:
- Josiah fought an unnecessary battle against King Neco of Egypt, which resulted in his untimely death.

LESSONS FROM HIS LIFE:
- We are never too young to pursue recovery and help others around us.
- One person of faith and courage can have a profound influence in a dysfunctional context.

KEY VERSE:
"Never before had there been a king like Josiah, who turned to the LORD with all his heart and soul and strength" (2 Kings 23:25).

Josiah's story is told in 2 Kings 21:24–23:30 and 2 Chronicles 33:25–35:26. He is also mentioned in Jeremiah 1:1; 3:6; 22:11-18; Zephaniah 1:1; Zechariah 12:11; Matthew 1:10-11.

---

workmen." [18]Shaphan also told the king, "Hilkiah the priest has given me a scroll." So Shaphan read it to the king.

[19]When the king heard what was written in the Law, he tore his clothes in despair. [20]Then he gave these orders to Hilkiah, Ahikam son of Shaphan, Acbor son of Micaiah,* Shaphan the court secretary, and Asaiah the king's personal adviser: [21]"Go to the Temple and speak to the LORD for me and for all the remnant of Israel and Judah. Inquire about the words written in the scroll that has been found. For the LORD's great anger has been poured out on us because our ancestors have not obeyed the word of the LORD. We have not been doing everything this scroll says we must do."

[22]So Hilkiah and the other men went to the New Quarter* of Jerusalem to consult with the prophet Huldah. She was the wife of Shallum son of Tikvah, son of Harhas,* the keeper of the Temple wardrobe.

[23]She said to them, "The LORD, the God of

34:20 As in parallel text at 2 Kgs 22:12; Hebrew reads *Abdon son of Micah.* **34:22a** Or *the Second Quarter,* a newer section of Jerusalem. Hebrew reads *the Mishneh.* **34:22b** As in parallel text at 2 Kgs 22:14; Hebrew reads *son of Tokhath, son of Hasrah.*

Israel, has spoken! Go back and tell the man who sent you, ²⁴"This is what the LORD says: I am going to bring disaster on this city* and its people. All the curses written in the scroll that was read to the king of Judah will come true. ²⁵For my people have abandoned me and offered sacrifices to pagan gods, and I am very angry with them for everything they have done. My anger will be poured out on this place, and it will not be quenched.'

²⁶"But go to the king of Judah who sent you to seek the LORD and tell him: 'This is what the LORD, the God of Israel, says concerning the message you have just heard: ²⁷You were sorry and humbled yourself before God when you heard his words against this city and its people. You humbled yourself and tore your clothing in despair and wept before me in repentance. And I have indeed heard you, says the LORD. ²⁸So I will not send the promised disaster until after your have died and been buried in peace. You yourself will not see the disaster I am going to bring on this city and its people.'"

So they took her message back to the king.

Josiah's Religious Reforms
²⁹Then the king summoned all the elders of Judah and Jerusalem. ³⁰And the king went up to the Temple of the LORD with all the people of Judah and Jerusalem, along with the priests and the Levites—all the people from the greatest to the least. There the king read to them the entire Book of the Covenant that had been found in the LORD's Temple. ³¹The king took his place of authority beside the pillar and renewed the covenant in the LORD's presence. He pledged to obey the LORD by keeping all his commands, laws, and decrees with all his heart and soul. He promised to obey all the terms of the covenant that were written in the scroll. ³²And he required everyone in Jerusalem and the people of Benjamin to make a similar pledge. The people of Jerusalem did so, renewing their covenant with God, the God of their ancestors.

³³So Josiah removed all detestable idols from the entire land of Israel and required

everyone to worship the LORD their God. And throughout the rest of his lifetime, they did not turn away from the LORD, the God of their ancestors.

CHAPTER 35
Josiah Celebrates Passover
Then Josiah announced that the Passover of the LORD would be celebrated in Jerusalem, and so the Passover lamb was slaughtered on the fourteenth day of the first month.* ²Josiah also assigned the priests to their duties and encouraged them in their work at the Temple of the LORD. ³He issued this order to the Levites, who were to teach all Israel and who had been set apart to serve the LORD: "Put the holy Ark in the Temple that was built by Solomon son of David, the king of Israel. You no longer need to carry it back and forth on your shoulders. Now spend your time serving the LORD your God and his people Israel. ⁴Report for duty according to the family divisions of your ancestors, following the directions of King David of Israel and the directions of his son Solomon.

⁵"Then stand in the sanctuary at the place appointed for your family division and help the families assigned to you as they bring their offerings to the Temple. ⁶Slaughter the Passover lambs, purify yourselves, and prepare to help those who come. Follow all the directions that the LORD gave through Moses."

⁷Then Josiah provided 30,000 lambs and young goats for the people's Passover offerings, along with 3,000 cattle, all from the king's own flocks and herds. ⁸The king's officials also made willing contributions to the people, priests, and Levites. Hilkiah, Zechariah, and Jehiel, the administrators of God's Temple, gave the priests 2,600 lambs and young goats and 300 cattle as Passover offerings. ⁹The Levite leaders—Conaniah and his brothers Shemaiah and Nethanel, as well as Hashabiah, Jeiel, and Jozabad—gave 5,000 lambs and young goats and 500 cattle to the Levites for their Passover offerings.

¹⁰When everything was ready for the Passover celebration, the priests and the Levites

---

34:24 Hebrew *this place;* also in 34:27, 28. 35:1 This day in the ancient Hebrew lunar calendar was April 5, 622 B.C.

35:1-2 Josiah encouraged the priests in their Temple activities. Encouragement is extremely important for anyone in a recovery situation. The priests were unaccustomed to leading the people in worship. They needed encouragement to face new and difficult tasks. We are unaccustomed to living without the support of our dependency. As we face life directly, without our normal means of escape, we need the encouragement and support of others. Recovery must never be undertaken alone.

took their places, organized by their divisions, as the king had commanded. ¹¹The Levites then slaughtered the Passover lambs and presented the blood to the priests, who sprinkled the blood on the altar while the Levites prepared the animals. ¹²They divided the burnt offerings among the people by their family groups, so they could offer them to the LORD as prescribed in the Book of Moses. They did the same with the cattle. ¹³Then they roasted the Passover lambs as prescribed; and they boiled the holy offerings in pots, kettles, and pans, and brought them out quickly so the people could eat them.

¹⁴Afterward the Levites prepared Passover offerings for themselves and for the priests— the descendants of Aaron—because the priests had been busy from morning till night offering the burnt offerings and the fat portions. The Levites took responsibility for all these preparations.

¹⁵The musicians, descendants of Asaph, were in their assigned places, following the commands that had been given by David, Asaph, Heman, and Jeduthun, the king's seer. The gatekeepers guarded the gates and did not need to leave their posts of duty, for their Passover offerings were prepared for them by their fellow Levites.

¹⁶The entire ceremony for the LORD's Passover was completed that day. All the burnt offerings were sacrificed on the altar of the LORD, as King Josiah had commanded. ¹⁷All the Israelites present in Jerusalem celebrated Passover and the Festival of Unleavened Bread for seven days. ¹⁸Never since the time of the prophet Samuel had there been such a Passover. None of the kings of Israel had ever kept a Passover as Josiah did, involving all the priests and Levites, all the people of Jerusalem, and people from all over Judah and Israel. ¹⁹This Passover was celebrated in the eighteenth year of Josiah's reign.

Josiah Dies in Battle

²⁰After Josiah had finished restoring the Temple, King Neco of Egypt led his army up from Egypt to do battle at Carchemish on the Euphrates River, and Josiah and his army marched out to fight him.* ²¹But King Neco sent messengers to Josiah with this message:

"What do you want with me, king of Judah? I have no quarrel with you today! I am on my way to fight another nation, and God has told me to hurry! Do not interfere with God, who is with me, or he will destroy you."

²²But Josiah refused to listen to Neco, to whom God had indeed spoken, and he would not turn back. Instead, he disguised himself and led his army into battle on the plain of Megiddo. ²³But the enemy archers hit King Josiah with their arrows and wounded him. He cried out to his men, "Take me from the battle, for I am badly wounded!"

²⁴So they lifted Josiah out of his chariot and placed him in another chariot. Then they brought him back to Jerusalem, where he died. He was buried there in the royal cemetery. And all Judah and Jerusalem mourned for him. ²⁵The prophet Jeremiah composed funeral songs for Josiah, and to this day choirs still sing these sad songs about his death. These songs of sorrow have become a tradition and are recorded in *The Book of Laments.*

²⁶The rest of the events of Josiah's reign and his acts of devotion (carried out according to what was written in the Law of the LORD), ²⁷from beginning to end—all are recorded in *The Book of the Kings of Israel and Judah.*

CHAPTER 36
Jehoahaz Rules in Judah

Then the people of the land took Josiah's son Jehoahaz and made him the next king in Jerusalem.

²Jehoahaz* was twenty-three years old when he became king, and he reigned in Jerusalem three months.

³Then he was deposed by the king of Egypt, who demanded that Judah pay 7,500 pounds of silver and 75 pounds of gold* as tribute.

Jehoiakim Rules in Judah

⁴The king of Egypt then installed Eliakim, the brother of Jehoahaz, as the next king of Judah and Jerusalem, and he changed Eliakim's name to Jehoiakim. Then Neco took Jehoahaz to Egypt as a prisoner.

⁵Jehoiakim was twenty-five years old when he became king, and he reigned in Jerusalem eleven years. He did what was evil in the sight of the LORD his God.

⁶Then King Nebuchadnezzar of Babylon came to Jerusalem and captured it, and he bound Jehoiakim in bronze chains and led him away to Babylon. ⁷Nebuchadnezzar also

35:20 Or *Josiah went out to meet him.* 36:2 Hebrew *Joahaz,* a variant spelling of Jehoahaz; also in 36:4. 36:3 Hebrew *100 talents* [3,400 kilograms] *of silver and 1 talent* [34 kilograms] *of gold.*

took some of the treasures from the Temple of the LORD, and he placed them in his palace* in Babylon.

⁸The rest of the events in Jehoiakim's reign, including all the evil things he did and everything found against him, are recorded in *The Book of the Kings of Israel and Judah*. Then his son Jehoiachin became the next king.

Jehoiachin Rules in Judah

⁹Jehoiachin was eighteen* years old when he became king, and he reigned in Jerusalem three months and ten days. Jehoiachin did what was evil in the LORD's sight.

¹⁰In the spring of the year* King Nebuchadnezzar took Jehoiachin to Babylon. Many treasures from the Temple of the LORD were also taken to Babylon at that time. And Nebuchadnezzar installed Jehoiachin's uncle,* Zedekiah, as the next king in Judah and Jerusalem.

Zedekiah Rules in Judah

¹¹Zedekiah was twenty-one years old when he became king, and he reigned in Jerusalem eleven years. ¹²But Zedekiah did what was evil in the sight of the LORD his God, and he refused to humble himself when the prophet Jeremiah spoke to him directly from the LORD. ¹³He also rebelled against King Nebuchadnezzar, even though he had taken an oath of loyalty in God's name. Zedekiah was a hard and stubborn man, refusing to turn to the LORD, the God of Israel.

¹⁴Likewise, all the leaders of the priests and the people became more and more unfaithful. They followed all the pagan practices of the surrounding nations, desecrating the Temple of the LORD that had been consecrated in Jerusalem.

¹⁵The LORD, the God of their ancestors, repeatedly sent his prophets to warn them, for he had compassion on his people and his Temple. ¹⁶But the people mocked these messengers of God and despised their words. They scoffed at the prophets until the LORD's anger could no longer be restrained and nothing could be done.

The Fall of Jerusalem

¹⁷So the LORD brought the king of Babylon against them. The Babylonians* killed Judah's young men, even chasing after them into the Temple. They had no pity on the people, killing both young men and young women, the old and the infirm. God handed all of them over to Nebuchadnezzar. ¹⁸The king took home to Babylon all the articles, large and small, used in the Temple of God, and the treasures from both the LORD's Temple and from the palace of the king and his officials. ¹⁹Then his army burned the Temple of God, tore down the walls of Jerusalem, burned all the palaces, and completely destroyed everything of value.* ²⁰The few who survived were taken as exiles to Babylon, and they became servants to the king and his sons until the kingdom of Persia came to power.

²¹So the message of the LORD spoken through Jeremiah was fulfilled. The land finally enjoyed its Sabbath rest, lying desolate until the seventy years were fulfilled, just as the prophet had said.

Cyrus Allows the Exiles to Return

²²In the first year of King Cyrus of Persia,* the LORD fulfilled the prophecy he had given through Jeremiah.* He stirred the heart of Cyrus to put this proclamation in writing and to send it throughout his kingdom:

36:7 Or *temple.* **36:9** As in one Hebrew manuscript, some Greek manuscripts, and Syriac version (see also 2 Kgs 24:8); most Hebrew manuscripts read *eight.* **36:10a** Hebrew *At the turn of the year.* The first day of this year in the ancient Hebrew lunar calendar was April 13, 597 B.C. **36:10b** As in parallel text at 2 Kgs 24:17; Hebrew reads *brother,* or *relative.* **36:17** Or *Chaldeans.* **36:19** Or *destroyed all the valuable articles from the Temple.* **36:22a** The first year of Cyrus's reign over Babylon was 538 B.C. **36:22b** See Jer 25:11-12; 29:10.

36:14-20 We can never ignore God's will without suffering the consequences. Under Zedekiah the people ignored God's laws and even persecuted the prophets who were sent to remind them of their failure. Is it any wonder that the Temple was destroyed and the people of Judah were exiled to Babylon? As we discover God's will in the Bible, we need to act on it. His plan will direct us toward recovery and healing. Ignoring his way will surely lead to destruction.

36:22-23 These chronicles of woe and doom end with a note of amazing hope. Jerusalem had been destroyed; the Temple had been torn down; the nation had been defeated; the population had been exiled. Yet the chronicler leaves a burning challenge before God's people. From their exile in Babylon, they were given an opportunity to rebuild, renew, recover, and restore. The books of Chronicles were written for people who had returned to rebuild their Temple and nation. This final passage would show them that despite their ancestors' failures, God is faithful to his promises. He would help them recover from centuries of failure. God holds out the same opportunity for us. With his help, we, too, can pursue and succeed in recovery.

²³"This is what King Cyrus of Persia says:
"The LORD, the God of heaven, has given me all the kingdoms of the earth. He has appointed me to build him a Temple at Jerusalem, which is in Judah. Any of you who are his people may go there for this task. And may the LORD your God be with you!"

REFLECTIONS ON 2 CHRONICLES

insights FROM GOD'S PRIESTS AND PROPHETS

The priests of the northern kingdom found themselves in a difficult position when King Jeroboam ascended to Israel's throne. In **2 Chronicles 11:13-17** King Rehoboam ousted the true priests and replaced them with priests who would support his program. The true priests surely wanted to stay in the land of their childhood, but it was obvious that the northern kingdom had turned from God. They moved to the southern kingdom where true worship was, for the time being, still being maintained. We often face similar decisions. We may have to choose between a good job and a healthy or comfortable environment for our family. We would be wise to do as the priests did. They maintained their relationship with God at the cost of personal stability and comfort. Our relationship with God should shape all the decisions we make.

In **2 Chronicles 15:1-8** God sent a prophet to warn King Asa of Judah that sin would bring suffering to his kingdom but that trust and obedience would bring blessing. Asa responded to God's warning with appropriate action. He destroyed the idols in his kingdom and rebuilt the altar of God. We also receive warnings from God. He speaks to us through the Bible, through people, and through our conscience. We need to listen for his direction and then act appropriately. Regular times of meditation on God's Word and prayer should help us be more sensitive to God's leading.

It is often costly to be absolutely faithful to God, but it is worth it. In **2 Chronicles 18:13-27** the prophet Micaiah knew that he would get into trouble if he told King Ahab that he should abandon his plans to attack Ramoth-gilead. At first, Micaiah seemingly supported Ahab's plans, but in the end, he took a stand and told the truth. When God speaks to us in his Word or by some other means, we need to do things his way. We must stand for the truth no matter what the people around us are thinking and doing. God's way is always the best way.

insights FROM THE VICTORIES OF JUDAH'S KINGS

Taking God at his word is not always easy, especially when God's promises seem impossible. In the face of Jeroboam's massive armies, King Abijah of Judah had good reason to doubt God's promises. Practically speaking, the army of Judah didn't have a chance. But as we see in **2 Chronicles 13:5-9**, King Abijah still trusted God's promises for the kingly line of David. The positive results of Abijah's trust should encourage us. When God makes a promise, we should have no doubt that he will keep it.

King Hezekiah of Judah had his armies; he had made elaborate preparations for defense. But in **2 Chronicles 32:7-8** we see that he didn't trust any of these to bring him victory. It is clear that

Hezekiah looked only to God for success. We are prone to depend on our own resources in a crisis. This, however, is never the way to experience success in recovery. We are powerless over our dependency; only God has the power we need for victory.

When things are in ruin and disarray, it is necessary to rebuild, repair, and clean up. As we see in **2 Chronicles 34:3-11**, such was the situation in Jerusalem at the beginning of King Josiah's reign. During the godless years of King Manasseh, worship of God at the Temple had been discontinued. The Temple itself had fallen into disrepair. Josiah committed the nation's resources to the restoration of the Temple. We, too, need to set aside significant resources for the difficult task of recovery. It will demand a great deal of commitment and sacrifice, but no matter what we give up, the gains will be well worth the cost.

Hearing God's Word is important, but we must act on what we hear. If we refuse to act, the hearing is all in vain. In **2 Chronicles 34:31-32** King Josiah pledged himself to obey God's revealed will after hearing the Scriptures. Not only did he do so as an individual, but he also called his people to do likewise. In recovery, we must hear the Word of God and then act on it. Without action, change is impossible; recovery demands that we act—now!

insights FROM THE FAILURES OF JUDAH'S KINGS
In **2 Chronicles 16:12-14** King Asa's feet became seriously diseased; he sought only a human solution to his problem. Despite the measures he took, Asa's condition worsened and he died. Asa failed to look to God for help. In times of trouble, God is often the last resource we turn to. We are willing to try every new human solution that comes along to fix our problems. Such solutions will never give us true victory. God alone can do that. We should go to him first.

It is always more important for parents to be godly examples for their children than it is for them to give extravagant gifts. In **2 Chronicles 21:1-6** we see that King Jehoshaphat of Judah gave his children great wealth, but apparently he did little to teach or guide them. Our roles as parents include much more than supplying our children's material needs. Children need comfort, direction, and the gift of godly values.

It is a terrible thing for an individual to do evil. It is far more terrible for such a person to lead others into evil. We see in **2 Chronicles 33:9** that King Manasseh of Judah was guilty on both counts. He was even worse than the pagan kings who lived nearby. We must be careful to never lead others into evil. If we have already done so, making restitution demands that we make every effort to lead them out again.

In the final assessment in **2 Chronicles 36:4-8**, King Jehoiakim's reign is condemned as evil. By the world's standards, he might have been considered successful. He reigned 11 years through a very difficult time, and he weathered the change of empires when Babylon defeated Assyria and began its period of world domination. But worldly success is never the final measure. If we fail to live according to God's program, our disobedience will doom us to ultimate failure. In the end, Jehoiakim was exiled to Babylon.

insights FROM THE PERSPECTIVE OF GENESIS
In the book of Genesis, we first learn of the feud between Jacob and Esau. Jacob's descendants became the Israelites, and Esau's descendants became the Edomites. Here in **2 Chronicles 21:8-10** the family feud was still going on hundreds of years later. This should be a lesson to us: The conflicts that we fail to resolve may be passed on to our descendants. For their sake, we must confront and resolve our broken relationships here and now.

EZRA

THE BIG PICTURE

A. REBUILDING THE PLACE
(1:1–6:22)
1. The First Exiles Return
(1:1–2:70)
2. The Attempt to Rebuild the
Temple (3:1-13)
3. The Discouragement of the
People (4:1-24)
4. The Joy of the People at the
Rebuilt Temple (5:1–6:22)
B. REBUILDING THE PEOPLE
(7:1–10:44)
1. The Second Group of Exiles
Returns with Ezra (7:1–8:36)
2. The Sins of the People
(9:1-15)
3. The People Confess Their
Sins (10:1-44)

The book of Ezra picks up Israel's history where 2 Chronicles leaves off, nearly 50 years after Jerusalem was destroyed by Babylon. During those 50 years, King Nebuchadnezzar of Babylon died. After his glorious reign, the empire slowly declined until it was conquered by Persia. It was King Cyrus of Persia who wrote the proclamation allowing the exiled Jews to return to Jerusalem to rebuild the Temple (see 2 Chronicles 36:22-23; Ezra 1:1-3).

The book of Ezra records two great journeys toward recovery from the Babylonian exile. The first journey (1:1–6:22) took place immediately after the proclamation of Cyrus and was led by Zerubbabel, one of King David's descendants. Under his direction the Temple was rebuilt over a twenty-year period. The priest Jeshua and the prophets Haggai and Zechariah encouraged the people in this task. The second journey (7:1–10:44) was led by Ezra almost 60 years after the Temple's completion.

Ezra was one of the great men of the Old Testament. He was a scribe, a teacher, and a priest. Tradition assigns most of Chronicles, Ezra, Nehemiah, and Psalm 119 to his hand. Ezra shows us what it means to turn one's life over to God. His desire to know God better motivated him to study God's Word, to believe it, and to obey it. First we need to learn what God's will is; then we need to take action, following the program he lays out for us. But Ezra didn't stop with seeking spiritual growth in his own life. He returned to Jerusalem and led the returned Jews in rebuilding their lives as well. Ezra provides a model of how we are to carry the message of hope to those still living in bondage.

THE BOTTOM LINE

PURPOSE: To record how the people rebuilt their lives and nation after their exile in Babylon. AUTHOR: Not stated; probably Ezra. AUDIENCE: The people of Israel after their return from exile in Babylon. DATE WRITTEN: Around the year 446 B.C. SETTING: Ezra picks up where 2 Chronicles left off, covering the period from the decree of Cyrus (538 B.C.) through Ezra's return and reformation (457 B.C.). KEY VERSE: "Get up, for it is your duty to tell us how to proceed in setting things straight. We are behind you, so be strong and take action" (10:4). KEY PEOPLE: Zerubbabel, Haggai, Zechariah, Ezra.

RECOVERY THEMES

God's Provision for Recovery: God shows his mercy to every one of us. In his love, he desires our restoration and recovery, not only from our sins but from the consequences of those sins. When we are in captivity to our sins, whether they are addictions or compulsive behaviors, we are never far from God's love and mercy. God is waiting to help us. All we need to do is admit our hopeless situation and come to him for strength and forgiveness. When we know we are helpless, we are closest to his powerful arm. In the book of Ezra we see various examples of how God empowered his people to do what they could never have done without him. All they had to do was give themselves over to his plan.

Resistance to Recovery: There will always be those who do not want to see us recover from "captivity." People who were associated with our old lifestyle may fight against the recovery process, just as those within Jerusalem fought against rebuilding the Temple. But the most dangerous form of opposition is often found within ourself. Even though we truly do want to be healed, there is always a part of us that rebels against the good. This does not make us evil, but we need to be aware of this part of our inner selves. We don't have to obey this inclination. When we turn our will over to God, we become people who "are no longer slaves to sin," but "slaves to righteous living" (Romans 6:6, 18).

Starting Over: In the face of opposition, the people of God were not only hindered in their work, but they ultimately had to stop the rebuilding process. The same thing often happens to us. Discouragement sets in. We begin to feel like everything we've done was to no avail. In the book of Ezra the work stopped for ten years. To be blocked from the recovery process for ten years could be devastating, giving us a feeling of hopelessness. But we can be encouraged; starting over is always part of God's plan for us. He is patient and long-suffering, and he comes to the aid of those who seek him. As we look at the history of the Jewish people, we see it is a history of new beginnings. God is also the God of new beginnings!

The Importance of Action: It is one thing to talk about recovery and rebuilding; it is quite another to actually do it! God is interested in our *actions.* The main characters in this book are all people of action. They didn't sit around and discuss rebuilding the Temple; they organized themselves and started working. The task must have appeared overwhelming at first. But by taking things one day at a time, one step at a time, even overwhelming tasks became possible. The first step is always the most difficult, with the next step almost as hard. Sometimes each step is difficult, but we must focus on today's task and take action, trusting that God will empower us along each step of the away.

CHAPTER 1
Cyrus Allows the Exiles to Return

In the first year of King Cyrus of Persia,* the LORD fulfilled the prophecy he had given through Jeremiah.* He stirred the heart of Cyrus to put this proclamation in writing and to send it throughout his kingdom:

²"This is what King Cyrus of Persia says: "The LORD, the God of heaven, has given me all the kingdoms of the earth. He has appointed me to build him a Temple at Jerusalem, which is in Judah. ³Any of you who are his people may go to Jerusalem in Judah to rebuild this Temple of the LORD, the God of Israel, who lives in Jerusalem. And may your God be with you! ⁴Wherever this Jewish remnant is found, let their neighbors contribute toward their expenses by giving them

1:1a The first year of Cyrus's reign over Babylon was 538 B.C. 1:1b See Jer 25:11-12; 29:10.

1:1 All of us need something we can count on. The Jews in exile counted on Jeremiah's prophecy—that their captivity would last only 70 years (70 years passed between the destruction of the Temple by the Babylonians [2 Kings 25:9; 2 Chronicles 36:19] and the completion of the new Temple [6:10-15]). Today, God has promises for us, too. If we accept Jesus as our Savior, the Holy Spirit will comfort us and help us. We will become a "new person"—leaving our old ways behind (2 Corinthians 5:17). Although our problems may seem overwhelming today, God has provided a way of deliverance through Christ's death and resurrection.
1:3 When we are in recovery, we need to respond to the opportunities that arise. The Jews had been living in Babylonian exile for many years. King Cyrus gave them an open invitation to return to Jerusalem to rebuild their nation—and their lives. Well over 40,000 brave people made the journey home; others remained behind in exile. God, through the work of Christ, has given each of us an open invitation to leave our personal exile of sinfulness. God is greater than Cyrus, and he is inviting us to rebuild. Will we respond to the opportunity?

silver and gold, supplies for the journey, and livestock, as well as a voluntary offering for the Temple of God in Jerusalem."

[5] Then God stirred the hearts of the priests and Levites and the leaders of the tribes of Judah and Benjamin to go to Jerusalem to rebuild the Temple of the LORD. [6] And all their neighbors assisted by giving them articles of silver and gold, supplies for the journey, and livestock. They gave them many valuable gifts in addition to all the voluntary offerings.

[7] King Cyrus himself brought out the articles that King Nebuchadnezzar had taken from the LORD's Temple in Jerusalem and had placed in the temple of his own gods. [8] Cyrus directed Mithredath, the treasurer of Persia, to count these items and present them to Sheshbazzar, the leader of the exiles returning to Judah.* [9] This is a list of the items that were returned:

gold basins	30
silver basins	1,000
silver incense burners*	29
[10] gold bowls	30
silver bowls	410
other items	1,000

[11] In all, there were 5,400 articles of gold and silver. Sheshbazzar brought all of these along when the exiles went from Babylon to Jerusalem.

CHAPTER 2
Exiles Who Returned with Zerubbabel
Here is the list of the Jewish exiles of the provinces who returned from their captivity. King Nebuchadnezzar had deported them to Babylon, but now they returned to Jerusalem and the other towns in Judah where they originally lived. [2] Their leaders were Zerubbabel, Jeshua, Nehemiah, Seraiah, Reelaiah, Mordecai, Bilshan, Mispar, Bigvai, Rehum, and Baanah.

This is the number of the men of Israel who returned from exile:

[3] The family of Parosh	2,172
[4] The family of Shephatiah	372
[5] The family of Arah	775
[6] The family of Pahath-moab (descendants of Jeshua and Joab)	2,812
[7] The family of Elam	1,254
[8] The family of Zattu	945
[9] The family of Zaccai	760
[10] The family of Bani	642
[11] The family of Bebai	623
[12] The family of Azgad	1,222
[13] The family of Adonikam	666
[14] The family of Bigvai	2,056
[15] The family of Adin	454
[16] The family of Ater (descendants of Hezekiah)	98
[17] The family of Bezai	323
[18] The family of Jorah	112
[19] The family of Hashum	223
[20] The family of Gibbar	95
[21] The people of Bethlehem	123
[22] The people of Netophah	56
[23] The people of Anathoth	128
[24] The people of Beth-azmaveth*	42
[25] The people of Kiriath-jearim,* Kephirah, and Beeroth	743
[26] The people of Ramah and Geba	621
[27] The people of Micmash	122
[28] The people of Bethel and Ai	223
[29] The citizens of Nebo	52
[30] The citizens of Magbish	156
[31] The citizens of West Elam*	1,254
[32] The citizens of Harim	320
[33] The citizens of Lod, Hadid, and Ono	725
[34] The citizens of Jericho	345
[35] The citizens of Senaah	3,630

[36] These are the priests who returned from exile:

The family of Jedaiah (through the line of Jeshua)	973
[37] The family of Immer	1,052
[38] The family of Pashhur	1,247
[39] The family of Harim	1,017

[40] These are the Levites who returned from exile:

1:8 Hebrew *Sheshbazzar, the prince of Judah.* 1:9 The meaning of this Hebrew word is uncertain. 2:24 As in parallel text at Neh 7:28; Hebrew reads *Azmaveth.* 2:25 As in some Hebrew manuscripts and Greek version (see also Neh 7:29); Hebrew reads *Kiriath-arim.* 2:31 Or *of the other Elam.*

1:4-6 It is important to have people to encourage and enable us in the recovery process. The Jews who were returning to their homeland were given gifts of money and supplies by their neighbors—most likely non-Jews as well as the Jews who had elected to remain in Babylon. Had those making the return trip not been given assistance, they might not have had the motivation or strength to see the mission through.

[41]
[42]

[43]The descendants of the following Temple servants returned from exile:
Ziha, Hasupha, Tabbaoth,
[44] Keros, Siaha, Padon,
[45] Lebanah, Hagabah, Akkub,
[46] Hagab, Shalmai,* Hanan,
[47] Giddel, Gahar, Reaiah,
[48] Rezin, Nekoda, Gazzam,
[49] Uzza, Paseah, Besai,
[50] Asnah, Meunim, Nephusim,
[51] Bakbuk, Hakupha, Harhur,
[52] Bazluth, Mehida, Harsha,
[53] Barkos, Sisera, Temah,
[54] Neziah, and Hatipha.

[55]The descendants of these servants of King Solomon returned from exile:
Sotai, Hassophereth, Peruda,
[56] Jaalah, Darkon, Giddel,
[57] Shephatiah, Hattil, Pokereth-hazzebaim, and Ami.

[58]In all, the Temple servants and the descendants of Solomon's servants numbered 392.

[59]Another group returned at this time from the towns of Tel-melah, Tel-harsha, Kerub, Addan, and Immer. However, they could not prove that they or their families were descendants of Israel. [60]This group included the families of Delaiah, Tobiah, and Nekoda—a total of 652 people.

[61]Three families of priests—Hobaiah, Hakkoz, and Barzillai—also returned. (This Barzillai had married a woman who was a descendant of Barzillai of Gilead, and he had taken her family name.) [62]They searched for their names in the genealogical records, but they were not found, so they were disqualified from serving as priests. [63]The governor told them not to eat the priests' share of food from the sacrifices until a priest could consult the LORD about the matter by using the Urim and Thummim—the sacred lots.

[64]So a total of 42,360 people returned to Judah, [65]in addition to 7,337 servants and 200 singers, both men and women. [66]They took with them 736 horses, 245 mules, [67]435 camels, and 6,720 donkeys.

[68]When they arrived at the Temple of the LORD in Jerusalem, some of the family leaders made voluntary offerings toward the rebuilding of God's Temple on its original site, [69]and each leader gave as much as he could. The total of their gifts came to 61,000 gold coins,* 6,250 pounds* of silver, and 100 robes for the priests.

[70]So the priests, the Levites, the singers, the gatekeepers, the Temple servants, and some of the common people settled in villages near Jerusalem. The rest of the people returned to their own towns throughout Israel.

CHAPTER 3
The Altar Is Rebuilt

In early autumn,* when the Israelites had settled in their towns, all the people assembled in Jerusalem with a unified purpose. [2]Then Jeshua son of Jehozadak* joined his fellow priests and Zerubbabel son of Shealtiel with his family in rebuilding the altar of the God of Israel. They wanted to sacrifice burnt offerings on it, as instructed in the Law of Moses, the man of God. [3]Even though the people were afraid of the local residents, they rebuilt the altar at its old site. Then they began to sacrifice burnt offerings on the altar to the LORD each morning and evening.

[4]They celebrated the Festival of Shelters as prescribed in the Law, sacrificing the number of burnt offerings specified for each day of the festival. [5]They also offered the regular burnt offerings and the offerings required for the new moon celebrations and the annual festivals as prescribed by the LORD. The people also gave voluntary offerings to the LORD.

2:46 As in an alternate reading of the Masoretic Text (see also Neh 7:48); the other alternate reads *Shamlai*. **2:69a** Hebrew *61,000 darics of gold*, about 1,100 pounds or 500 kilograms in weight. **2:69b** Hebrew *5,000 minas* [3,000 kilograms]. **3:1** Hebrew *In the seventh month*. The year is not specified, so it may have been during Cyrus's first year (538 B.C.) or second year (537 B.C.). The seventh month of the ancient Hebrew lunar calendar occurred within the months of September/October 538 B.C. and October/November 537 B.C. **3:2** Hebrew *Jozadak*, a variant spelling of Jehozadak; also in 3:8.

3:1-2 The Temple had been destroyed many years earlier, so there was no altar for burning sacrifices. The people's means of reconciliation with God had been discontinued; their spiritual lives had been cut off. So before the people could proceed with the rebuilding, they needed to straighten out their relationship with God. These verses show how the Israelites reestablished the sacrifices as a means of reconciliation. Such reconciliation is necessary for all of us in recovery. This has been made eternally possible for us through the sacrifice of Jesus Christ.

[6]Fifteen days before the Festival of Shelters began,* the priests had begun to sacrifice burnt offerings to the LORD. This was even before they had started to lay the foundation of the LORD's Temple.

The People Begin to Rebuild the Temple

[7]Then the people hired masons and carpenters and bought cedar logs from the people of Tyre and Sidon, paying them with food, wine, and olive oil. The logs were brought down from the Lebanon mountains and floated along the coast of the Mediterranean Sea* to Joppa, for King Cyrus had given permission for this.

[8]The construction of the Temple of God began in midspring,* during the second year after they arrived in Jerusalem. The work force was made up of everyone who had returned from exile, including Zerubbabel son of Shealtiel, Jeshua son of Jehozadak and his fellow priests, and all the Levites. The Levites who were twenty years old or older were put in charge of rebuilding the LORD's Temple. [9]The workers at the Temple of God were supervised by Jeshua with his sons and relatives, and Kadmiel and his sons, all descendants of Hodaviah.* They were helped in this task by the Levites of the family of Henadad.

[10]When the builders completed the foundation of the LORD's Temple, the priests put on their robes and took their places to blow their trumpets. And the Levites, descendants of Asaph, clashed their cymbals to praise the LORD, just as King David had prescribed. [11]With praise and thanks, they sang this song to the LORD:

"He is so good!
His faithful love for Israel endures forever!"

Then all the people gave a great shout, praising the LORD because the foundation of the LORD's Temple had been laid.

[12]But many of the older priests, Levites, and other leaders who had seen the first Temple wept aloud when they saw the new Temple's foundation. The others, however, were shouting for joy. [13]The joyful shouting and weeping mingled together in a loud noise that could be heard far in the distance.

CHAPTER 4
Enemies Oppose the Rebuilding

The enemies of Judah and Benjamin heard that the exiles were rebuilding a Temple to the LORD, the God of Israel. [2]So they approached Zerubbabel and the other leaders and said, "Let us build with you, for we worship your God just as you do. We have sacrificed to him ever since King Esarhaddon of Assyria brought us here."

[3]But Zerubbabel, Jeshua, and the other leaders of Israel replied, "You may have no part in this work. We alone will build the Temple for the LORD, the God of Israel, just as King Cyrus of Persia commanded us."

3:6 Hebrew *On the first day of the seventh month.* This day in the ancient Hebrew lunar calendar occurred in September or October. The Festival of Shelters began on the fifteenth day of the seventh month. 3:7 Hebrew *the sea.* 3:8 Hebrew *in the second month.* This month in the ancient Hebrew lunar calendar occurred within the months of April and May 536 B.C. 3:9 Hebrew *sons of Judah* (i.e., *bene Yehudah*). *Bene* might also be read here as the proper name Binnui; *Yehudah* is probably another name for Hodaviah. Compare 2:40; Neh 7:43; 1 Esdras 5:58.

3:10-11 Having already built an altar for the sacrifices, the people began rebuilding the Temple itself. Notice that they praised God and celebrated after having laid only the Temple's foundation. Big jobs always seem easier and less intimidating when we break them up into smaller steps. When we face overwhelming or long-term projects such as recovery, we should take pleasure in completing one step at a time. Realizing that we have completed one phase will encourage us to keep going.

3:12 Some of the old people remembered the first Temple and wept when they saw the foundation of the new Temple. This Temple obviously would never match the glory of Solomon's Temple built during Israel's golden age; their expectations were too high. Though Israel would never regain its previous status in the world, God promised that the new Jerusalem would be the center of God's eternal Kingdom (see Revelation 21). If our expectations are too high or unrealistic, they may cause us to relapse. We need to focus on how far we have come, not on how far we have to go. We may never be able to regain our previous position in life, but that should not discourage us and make us want to give up the recovery process. A life lived in recovery is always better than one lived in sin, no matter how much less spectacular it may be.

4:1-3 When God's work begins in a great way, enemies almost invariably rise up against it. There will be adversaries against our work as we establish positive patterns in our life. It is interesting that the enemies of the Temple's rebuilding came in the guise of helpers. We must reject any assistance in the recovery process that is not God approved and God centered.

[4]Then the local residents tried to discourage and frighten the people of Judah to keep them from their work. [5]They bribed agents to work against them and to frustrate their plans. This went on during the entire reign of King Cyrus of Persia and lasted until King Darius of Persia took the throne.*

Later Opposition under Xerxes and Artaxerxes

[6]Years later when Xerxes* began his reign, the enemies of Judah wrote a letter of accusation against the people of Judah and Jerusalem.

[7]Even later, during the reign of King Artaxerxes of Persia,* the enemies of Judah, led by Bishlam, Mithredath, and Tabeel, sent a letter to Artaxerxes in the Aramaic language, and it was translated for the king.

[8]*Rehum the governor and Shimshai the court secretary wrote the letter, telling King Artaxerxes about the situation in Jerusalem. [9]They greeted the king for all their colleagues—the judges and local leaders, the people of Tarpel, the Persians, the Babylonians, and the people of Erech and Susa (that is, Elam). [10]They also sent greetings from the rest of the people whom the great and noble Ashurbanipal* had deported and relocated in Samaria and throughout the neighboring lands of the province west of the Euphrates River.* [11]This is a copy of their letter:

"To King Artaxerxes, from your loyal subjects in the province west of the Euphrates River.

[12]"The king should know that the Jews who came here to Jerusalem from Babylon are rebuilding this rebellious and evil city. They have already laid the foundation and will soon finish its walls. [13]And the king should know that if this city is rebuilt and its walls are completed, it will be much to your disadvantage, for the Jews will then refuse to pay their tribute, customs, and tolls to you. [14]"Since we are your loyal subjects* and

do not want to see the king dishonored in this way, we have sent the king this information. [15]We suggest that a search be made in your ancestors' records, where you will discover what a rebellious city this has been in the past. In fact, it was destroyed because of its long and troublesome history of revolt against the kings and countries who controlled it. [16]We declare to the king that if this city is rebuilt and its walls are completed, the province west of the Euphrates River will be lost to you."

[17]Then King Artaxerxes sent this reply:

"To Rehum the governor, Shimshai the court secretary, and their colleagues living in Samaria and throughout the province west of the Euphrates River. Greetings.

[18]"The letter you sent has been translated and read to me. [19]I ordered a search of the records and have found that Jerusalem has indeed been a hotbed of insurrection against many kings. In fact, rebellion and revolt are normal there! [20]Powerful kings have ruled over Jerusalem and the entire province west of the Euphrates River, receiving tribute, customs, and tolls. [21]Therefore, issue orders to have these men stop their work. That city must not be rebuilt except at my express command. [22]Be diligent, and don't neglect this matter, for we must not permit the situation to harm the king's interests."

[23]When this letter from King Artaxerxes was read to Rehum, Shimshai, and their colleagues, they hurried to Jerusalem. Then, with a show of strength, they forced the Jews to stop building.

The Rebuilding Resumes

[24]So the work on the Temple of God in Jerusalem had stopped, and it remained at a

---

4:5 Darius reigned 521–486 B.C. **4:6** Hebrew *Ahasuerus,* another name for Xerxes. He reigned 486–465 B.C. **4:7** Artaxerxes reigned 465–424 B.C. **4:8** The original text of 4:8–6:18 is in Aramaic. **4:10a** Aramaic *Osnappar,* another name for Ashurbanipal. **4:10b** Aramaic *the province beyond the river;* also in 4:11, 16, 17, 20. **4:14** Aramaic *Since we eat the salt of the palace.*

4:17-23 Often obstacles are placed in the way of rebuilding. In this case it was a work-restraining order from Artaxerxes. Today, we must accept the reality that many will not be supportive of our recovery efforts. We must never allow such people to stand in the way of our recovery.

4:24 Whether it was a legitimate reason or the workers were taking an easy way out, the rebuilding work on God's Temple ceased. How often in our own life have outward difficulties stopped our positive progress? We need to guard against interruptions. It is often hard to get back on track once we have stopped or slowed down.

standstill until the second year of the reign of King Darius of Persia.*

CHAPTER 5

At that time the prophets Haggai and Zechariah son of Iddo prophesied to the Jews in Judah and Jerusalem. They prophesied in the name of the God of Israel who was over them. [2]Zerubbabel son of Shealtiel and Jeshua son of Jehozadak* responded by starting again to rebuild the Temple of God in Jerusalem. And the prophets of God were with them and helped them.

[3]But Tattenai, governor of the province west of the Euphrates River,* and Shethar-bozenai and their colleagues soon arrived in Jerusalem and asked, "Who gave you permission to rebuild this Temple and restore this structure?" [4]They also asked for* the names of all the men working on the Temple. [5]But because their God was watching over them, the leaders of the Jews were not prevented from building until a report was sent to Darius and he returned his decision.

Tattenai's Letter to King Darius

[6]This is a copy of the letter that Tattenai the governor, Shethar-bozenai, and the other officials of the province west of the Euphrates River sent to King Darius:

[7]"To King Darius. Greetings.

[8]"The king should know that we went to the construction site of the Temple of the great God in the province of Judah. It is being rebuilt with specially prepared stones, and timber is being laid in its walls. The work is going forward with great energy and success.

[9]"We asked the leaders, 'Who gave you permission to rebuild this Temple and restore this structure?' [10]And we demanded their names so that we could tell you who the leaders were.

[11]"This was their answer: 'We are the servants of the God of heaven and earth, and we are rebuilding the Temple that was built here many years ago by a great king of Israel. [12]But because our ancestors angered the God of heaven, he abandoned them to King Nebuchadnezzar of Babylon,* who destroyed this Temple and exiled the people to Babylonia. [13]However, King Cyrus of Babylon,* during the first year of his reign, issued a decree that the Temple of God should be rebuilt. [14]King Cyrus returned the gold and silver cups that Nebuchadnezzar had taken from the Temple of God in Jerusalem and had placed in the temple of Babylon. These cups were taken from that temple and presented to a man named Sheshbazzar, whom King Cyrus appointed as governor of Judah. [15]The king instructed him to return the cups to their place in Jerusalem and to rebuild the Temple of God there on its original site. [16]So this Sheshbazzar came and laid the foundations of the Temple of God in Jerusalem. The people have been working on it ever since, though it is not yet completed.'

[17]"Therefore, if it pleases the king, we request that a search be made in the royal archives of Babylon to discover whether King Cyrus ever issued a decree to rebuild God's Temple in Jerusalem. And then let the king send us his decision in this matter."

CHAPTER 6
Darius Approves the Rebuilding

So King Darius issued orders that a search be made in the Babylonian archives, which were stored in the treasury. [2]But it was at the fortress at Ecbatana in the province of Media that a scroll was found. This is what it said:

4:24 The second year of Darius's reign was 520 B.C. The narrative started in 4:1-5 is resumed at verse 24. **5:2** Aramaic *Jozadak*, a variant spelling of Jehozadak. **5:3** Aramaic *the province beyond the river*; also in 5:6. **5:4** As in one Hebrew manuscript and Greek and Syriac versions; Masoretic Text reads *Then we told them.* **5:12** Aramaic *Nebuchadnezzar the Chaldean.* **5:13** King Cyrus of Persia is here identified as the king of Babylon because Persia had conquered the Babylonian Empire.

5:1 In this verse God gave the people fresh encouragement to build. He sent the prophets Haggai and Zechariah to encourage the people to finish their project. These prophets told the people what God wanted them to do. In this case it was not the proper time to have a Bible study or a prayer meeting. It was time for them to roll up their sleeves and get to work! There will be times when study and prayer are appropriate, but there will also be times that require immediate action. If God says go, we must go!
5:3-5 Again the work went smoothly; the people had begun to work with enthusiasm and joy. But again, enemies tried to halt the rebuilding. This time, the Jews did not stop their rebuilding task. God was their heavenly foreman, lovingly supervising their work. God cares about us and the outcome of our recovery. If he cared for the rebuilding of the Temple back then, surely he cares for the rebuilding of our life—his living temple—today (see 1 Corinthians 3:16-17).

"Memorandum:

3"In the first year of King Cyrus's reign, a decree was sent out concerning the Temple of God at Jerusalem.

"Let the Temple be rebuilt on the site where Jews used to offer their sacrifices, using the original foundations. Its height will be ninety feet, and its width will be ninety feet.* 4Every three layers of specially prepared stones will be topped by a layer of timber. All expenses will be paid by the royal treasury. 5Furthermore, the gold and silver cups, which were taken to Babylon by Nebuchadnezzar from the Temple of God in Jerusalem, must be returned to Jerusalem and put back where they belong. Let them be taken back to the Temple of God."

6So King Darius sent this message:

"Now therefore, Tattenai, governor of the province west of the Euphrates River,* and Shethar-bozenai, and your colleagues and other officials west of the Euphrates River—stay away from there! 7Do not disturb the construction of the Temple of God. Let it be rebuilt on its original site, and do not hinder the governor of Judah and the elders of the Jews in their work.

8"Moreover, I hereby decree that you are to help these elders of the Jews as they rebuild this Temple of God. You must pay the full construction costs, without delay, from my taxes collected in the province west of the Euphrates River so that the work will not be interrupted.

9"Give the priests in Jerusalem whatever is needed in the way of young bulls, rams, and male lambs for the burnt offerings presented to the God of heaven. And without fail, provide them with as much wheat, salt, wine, and olive oil as they need each day. 10Then they will be able to offer acceptable sacrifices to the God of heaven and pray for the welfare of the king and his sons.

11"Those who violate this decree in any way will have a beam pulled from their house. Then they will be lifted up and impaled on it, and their house will be reduced to a pile of rubble.* 12May the God who has chosen the city of Jerusalem as the place to honor his name destroy any king or nation that violates this command and destroys this Temple.

"I, Darius, have issued this decree. Let it be obeyed with all diligence."

The Temple's Dedication

13Tattenai, governor of the province west of the Euphrates River, and Shethar-bozenai and their colleagues complied at once with the command of King Darius. 14So the Jewish elders continued their work, and they were greatly encouraged by the preaching of the prophets Haggai and Zechariah son of Iddo. The Temple was finally finished, as had been commanded by the God of Israel and decreed by Cyrus, Darius, and Artaxerxes, the kings of Persia. 15The Temple was completed on March 12,* during the sixth year of King Darius's reign.

16The Temple of God was then dedicated with great joy by the people of Israel, the priests, the Levites, and the rest of the people who had returned from exile. 17During the dedication ceremony for the Temple of God, 100 young bulls, 200 rams, and 400 male lambs were sacrificed. And 12 male goats were presented as a sin offering for the twelve tribes of Israel. 18Then the priests and Levites were divided into their various divi-

---

6:3 Aramaic *Its height will be 60 cubits* [27.6 meters], *and its width will be 60 cubits.* It is commonly held that this verse should be emended to read: "Its height will be 30 cubits [45 feet or 13.8 meters], its length will be 60 cubits [90 feet or 27.6 meters], and its width will be 20 cubits [30 feet or 9.2 meters]"; compare 1 Kgs 6:2. The emendation regarding the width is supported by the Syriac version. **6:6** Aramaic *the province beyond the river;* also in 6:6b, 8, 13. **6:11** Aramaic *a dunghill.* **6:15** Aramaic *on the third day of the month Adar,* of the ancient Hebrew lunar calendar. A number of events in Ezra can be cross-checked with dates in surviving Persian records and related accurately to our modern calendar. This day was March 12, 515 B.C.

6:14-15 Sometimes (almost always) the recovery process takes more time than we had originally planned. It took more than 20 years, but the Temple was finally finished. The long process had been sometimes frustrating, sometimes disillusioning, always difficult. But it was done, and every minute of work had been worth it! Restoration of our life is not easy either, but the end result will make the difficult process worth it.

6:15-19 After the long, drawn-out process of rebuilding the Temple was finally over, what was the people's response to success? First, they acknowledged God in the entire project. Second, they formally recognized the completion in a dedication ceremony. Third, they celebrated this victory with great joy. We, too, need to celebrate our victories in recovery. What is worth celebrating more than a life brought back into a right relationship with God and other people?

sions to serve at the Temple of God in Jerusalem, as prescribed in the Book of Moses.

Celebration of Passover

[19]On April 21* the returned exiles celebrated Passover. [20]The priests and Levites had purified themselves and were ceremonially clean. So they slaughtered the Passover lamb for all the returned exiles, for their fellow priests, and for themselves. [21]The Passover meal was eaten by the people of Israel who had returned from exile and by the others in the land who had turned from their immoral customs to worship the LORD, the God of Israel. [22]Then they celebrated the Festival of Unleavened Bread for seven days. There was great joy throughout the land because the LORD had caused the king of Assyria* to be favorable to them, so that he helped them to rebuild the Temple of God, the God of Israel.

CHAPTER 7
Ezra Arrives in Jerusalem

Many years later, during the reign of King Artaxerxes of Persia,* there was a man named Ezra. He was the son* of Seraiah, son of Azariah, son of Hilkiah, [2]son of Shallum, son of Zadok, son of Ahitub, [3]son of Amariah, son of Azariah, son* of Meraioth, [4]son of Zerahiah, son of Uzzi, son of Bukki, [5]son of Abishua, son of Phinehas, son of Eleazar, son of Aaron the high priest.* [6]This Ezra was a scribe who was well versed in the Law of Moses, which the LORD, the God of Israel, had given to the people of Israel. He

came up to Jerusalem from Babylon, and the king gave him everything he asked for, because the gracious hand of the LORD his God was on him. [7]Some of the people of Israel, as well as some of the priests, Levites, singers, gatekeepers, and Temple servants, traveled up to Jerusalem with him in the seventh year of King Artaxerxes' reign.

[8]Ezra arrived in Jerusalem in August* of that year. [9]He had arranged to leave Babylon on April 8, the first day of the new year,* and he arrived at Jerusalem on August 4,* for the gracious hand of his God was on him. [10]This was because Ezra had determined to study and obey the Law of the LORD and to teach those decrees and regulations to the people of Israel.

Artaxerxes' Letter to Ezra

[11]King Artaxerxes had given a copy of the following letter to Ezra, the priest and scribe who studied and taught the commands and decrees of the LORD to Israel:

[12]*"From Artaxerxes, the king of kings, to Ezra the priest, the teacher of the law of the God of heaven. Greetings.

[13]"I decree that any of the people of Israel in my kingdom, including the priests and Levites, may volunteer to return to Jerusalem with you. [14]I and my council of seven hereby instruct you to conduct an inquiry into the situation in Judah and Jerusalem, based on your God's law, which is in your hand. [15]We

---

6:19 Hebrew *On the fourteenth day of the first month,* of the ancient Hebrew lunar calendar. This day was April 21, 515 B.C.; also see note on 6:15. **6:22** King Darius of Persia is here identified as the king of Assyria because Persia had conquered the Babylonian Empire, which included the earlier Assyrian Empire. **7:1a** Artaxerxes reigned 465–424 B.C. **7:1b** Or *descendant;* see 1 Chr 6:14. **7:3** Or *descendant;* see 1 Chr 6:6-10. **7:5** Or *the first priest.* **7:8** Hebrew *in the fifth month.* This month in the ancient Hebrew lunar calendar occurred within the months of August and September 458 B.C. **7:9a** Hebrew *on the first day of the first month,* of the ancient Hebrew lunar calendar. This day was April 8, 458 B.C.; also see note on 6:15. **7:9b** Hebrew *on the first day of the fifth month,* of the ancient Hebrew lunar calendar. This day was August 4, 458 B.C.; also see note on 6:15. **7:12** The original text of 7:12-26 is in Aramaic.

6:20 Before they could lead the people in worshiping God, it was necessary for the priests and Levites to purify themselves. They had to be ceremonially clean. Now purification is available to all through Jesus Christ. When we trust in Jesus, he purifies us and allows us to commune with him.
7:7 Surprisingly, when the initial invitation to rebuild was made by Cyrus (1:1-3), many of the people failed to respond. They chose to remain in a depressing, though comfortable, lifestyle instead of making the long, hard journey back to Jerusalem to rebuild the Temple and nation. We often choose what is comfortable over what we know is best for us. Recovery is a long, hard journey, but it is far better than the option of continued slavery. Happily, when given a second chance to return to their homeland 80 years later, much of the Jewish population that had remained in Babylon decided to go with Ezra. Eighty years is a long time to wait for a second chance at recovery; we need to take God's offer the first time around.
7:10 What a noble aspiration is recorded here! This careful student of the Scriptures had prepared his heart to seek what God was saying through his Word. Then he was obedient to its requirements. Ezra also wanted to teach the people the truths he had discovered and share God's laws with the people of Israel. It is natural for us to share something that we believe to be worthwhile. We should want to share our testimony of recovery to lead others to overcome their dependency.

also commission you to take with you silver and gold, which we are freely presenting as an offering to the God of Israel who lives in Jerusalem.

¹⁶"Furthermore, you are to take any silver and gold that you may obtain from the province of Babylon, as well as the voluntary offerings of the people and the priests that are presented for the Temple of their God in Jerusalem. ¹⁷These donations are to be used specifically for the purchase of bulls, rams, male lambs, and the appropriate grain offerings and liquid offerings, all of which will be offered on the altar of the Temple of your God in Jerusalem. ¹⁸Any silver and gold that is left over may be used in whatever way you and your colleagues feel is the will of your God.

¹⁹"But as for the cups we are entrusting to you for the service of the Temple of your God, deliver them all to the God of Jerusalem. ²⁰If you need anything else for your God's Temple or for any similar needs, you may take it from the royal treasury.

²¹"I, Artaxerxes the king, hereby send this decree to all the treasurers in the province west of the Euphrates River*: 'You are to give Ezra, the priest and teacher of the law of the God of heaven, whatever he requests of you. ²²You are to give him up to 7,500 pounds* of silver, 500 bushels* of wheat, 550 gallons of wine, 550 gallons of olive oil,* and an unlimited supply of salt. ²³Be careful to provide whatever the God of heaven demands for his Temple, for why should we risk bringing God's anger against the realm of the king and his sons? ²⁴I also decree that no priest, Levite, singer, gatekeeper, Temple servant, or other worker in this Temple of God will be required to pay tribute, customs, or tolls of any kind.'

²⁵"And you, Ezra, are to use the wisdom your God has given you to appoint magistrates and judges who know your God's laws to govern all the people in the province west of the Euphrates River. Teach the law to anyone who does not know it. ²⁶Anyone who refuses to obey the law of your God and the law of the king will be punished immediately, either by death, banishment, confiscation of goods, or imprisonment."

Ezra Praises the LORD

²⁷Praise the LORD, the God of our ancestors, who made the king want to beautify the Temple of the LORD in Jerusalem! ²⁸And praise him for demonstrating such unfailing love to me by honoring me before the king, his council, and all his mighty nobles! I felt encouraged because the gracious hand of the LORD my God was on me. And I gathered some of the leaders of Israel to return with me to Jerusalem.

CHAPTER 8
Exiles Who Returned with Ezra

Here is a list of the family leaders and the genealogies of those who came with me from Babylon during the reign of King Artaxerxes:

² From the family of Phinehas: Gershom.
From the family of Ithamar: Daniel.
From the family of David: Hattush, ³a descendant of Shecaniah.
From the family of Parosh: Zechariah and 150 other men were registered.
⁴ From the family of Pahath-moab: Eliehoenai son of Zerahiah and 200 other men.
⁵ From the family of Zattu*: Shecaniah son of Jahaziel and 300 other men.
⁶ From the family of Adin: Ebed son of Jonathan and 50 other men.
⁷ From the family of Elam: Jeshaiah son of Athaliah and 70 other men.
⁸ From the family of Shephatiah: Zebadiah son of Michael and 80 other men.
⁹ From the family of Joab: Obadiah son of Jehiel and 218 other men.
¹⁰ From the family of Bani*: Shelomith son of Josiphiah and 160 other men.

7:21 Aramaic *the province beyond the river;* also in 7:25. **7:22a** Aramaic *100 talents* [3,400 kilograms]. **7:22b** Aramaic *100 cors* [22 kiloliters]. **7:22c** Aramaic *100 baths* [2.1 kiloliters] *of wine, 100 baths of olive oil.* **8:5** As in some Greek manuscripts (see also 1 Esdras 8:32); Hebrew lacks *Zattu.* **8:10** As in some Greek manuscripts (see also 1 Esdras 8:36); Hebrew lacks *Bani.*

7:27-28 Many obstacles stood in the way of Ezra's dream of leading the people to learn and obey God's Word. Not the least of these was a governmental one, but God worked in the heart of Artaxerxes to provide permission and resources for Ezra's mission. These two verses record Ezra's prayer of thanks to God. The progress we make is due only to God's love for us. We should praise him for the good work he is accomplishing in our life.

11 From the family of Bebai: Zechariah son of Bebai and 28 other men. 12 From the family of Azgad: Johanan son of Hakkatan and 110 other men. 13 From the family of Adonikam, who came later*: Eliphelet, Jeuel, Shemaiah, and 60 other men. 14 From the family of Bigvai: Uthai, Zaccur,* and 70 other men.

Ezra's Journey to Jerusalem

15 I assembled the exiles at the Ahava Canal, and we camped there for three days while I went over the lists of the people and the priests who had arrived. I found that not one Levite had volunteered to come along. 16 So I sent for Eliezer, Ariel, Shemaiah, Elnathan, Jarib, Elnathan, Nathan, Zechariah, and Meshullam, who were leaders of the people. I also sent for Joiarib and Elnathan, who were men of discernment. 17 I sent them to Iddo, the leader of the Levites at Casiphia, to ask him and his relatives and the Temple servants to send us ministers for the Temple of God at Jerusalem.

18 Since the gracious hand of our God was on us, they sent us a man named Sherebiah, along with eighteen of his sons and brothers. He was a very astute man and a descendant of Mahli, who was a descendant of Levi son of Israel.* 19 They also sent Hashabiah, together with Jeshaiah from the descendants of Merari, and twenty of his sons and brothers, 20 and 220 Temple servants. The Temple servants were assistants to the Levites—a group of Temple workers first instituted by King David and his officials. They were all listed by name.

21 And there by the Ahava Canal, I gave orders for all of us to fast and humble ourselves before our God. We prayed that he would give us a safe journey and protect us, our children, and our goods as we traveled. 22 For I was ashamed to ask the king for soldiers and horsemen* to accompany us and protect us from enemies along the way. After all, we had told the king, "Our God's hand of protection is on all who worship him, but his fierce anger rages against those who abandon him." 23 So we fasted and earnestly prayed that our God would take care of us, and he heard our prayer.

24 I appointed twelve leaders of the priests—Sherebiah, Hashabiah, and ten other priests—25 to be in charge of transporting the silver, the gold, the gold bowls, and the other items that the king, his council, his officials, and all the people of Israel had presented for the Temple of God. 26 I weighed the treasure as I gave it to them and found the totals to be as follows:

24 tons* of silver,
7,500 pounds* of silver articles,
7,500 pounds of gold,
27 20 gold bowls, equal in value to 1,000 gold coins,*
2 fine articles of polished bronze, as precious as gold.

28 And I said to these priests, "You and these treasures have been set apart as holy to the LORD. This silver and gold is a voluntary offering to the LORD, the God of our ancestors. 29 Guard these treasures well until you present them to the leading priests, the Levites, and the leaders of Israel, who will weigh them at the storerooms of the LORD's Temple in Jerusalem." 30 So the priests and the Levites accepted the task of transporting these treasures of silver and gold to the Temple of our God in Jerusalem.

8:13 Or who were the last of his family. 8:14 As in Greek and Syriac versions and an alternative reading of the Masoretic Text; the other alternate reads Zabbud. 8:18 Israel is the name that God gave to Jacob. 8:22 Or charioteers. 8:26a Hebrew 650 talents [22 metric tons]. 8:26b Hebrew 100 talents [3,400 kilograms]; also in 8:26c. 8:27 Hebrew 1,000 darics, about 19 pounds or 8.6 kilograms in weight.

8:15-20 Recovery generally requires careful preparation and the wise advice of godly people. Ezra knew that his primary task was a spiritual one. These verses detail some of the preparations he made. Here he arranged for a team of experts (the priests and Levites) to assist him. We will never be able to recover on our own. We need God's help, and we also need others who will encourage and advise us on how to proceed.
8:24-30 Ezra's group had to transport a great deal of money to Jerusalem, and Ezra made provisions for its safekeeping. He set up guidelines of accountability; the priests took up the responsibility. In recovery, we must set up measures of accountability for ourselves. We need to establish goals and then find someone to hold us accountable to them.
8:31-33 Finally Ezra arrived in Jerusalem. He had overcome many obstacles—evidently they had faced considerable danger on the road. It is interesting that the first thing he did upon arrival was to rest for three days. If we are exhausted or emotionally burned out when we begin a project, the task will seem much tougher than it really is. We need to get proper rest, develop patience, and gain godly perspectives.

³¹We broke camp at the Ahava Canal on April 19* and started off to Jerusalem. And the gracious hand of our God protected us and saved us from enemies and bandits along the way. ³²So we arrived safely in Jerusalem, where we rested for three days.

³³On the fourth day after our arrival, the silver, gold, and other valuables were weighed at the Temple of our God and entrusted to Meremoth son of Uriah the priest and to Eleazar son of Phinehas, along with Jozabad son of Jeshua and Noadiah son of Binnui—both of whom were Levites. ³⁴Everything was accounted for by number and weight, and the total weight was officially recorded.

³⁵Then the exiles who had come out of captivity sacrificed burnt offerings to the God of Israel. They presented twelve bulls for all the people of Israel, as well as ninety-six rams and seventy-seven male lambs. They also offered twelve male goats as a sin offering. All this was given as a burnt offering to the LORD. ³⁶The king's decrees were delivered to his highest officers and the governors of the province west of the Euphrates River,* who then cooperated by supporting the people and the Temple of God.

CHAPTER 9
Ezra's Prayer concerning Intermarriage

When these things had been done, the Jewish leaders came to me and said, "Many of the people of Israel, and even some of the priests and Levites, have not kept themselves separate from the other peoples living in the land. They have taken up the detestable practices of the Canaanites, Hittites, Perizzites, Jebusites, Ammonites, Moabites, Egyptians, and Amorites. ²For the men of Israel have married women from these people and have taken them as wives for their sons. So the holy race has become polluted by these mixed marriages. Worse yet, the leaders and officials have led the way in this outrage."

³When I heard this, I tore my cloak and my shirt, pulled hair from my head and beard, and sat down utterly shocked. ⁴Then all who trembled at the words of the God of Israel came and sat with me because of this outrage committed by the returned exiles. And I sat there utterly appalled until the time of the evening sacrifice.

⁵At the time of the sacrifice, I stood up from where I had sat in mourning with my clothes torn. I fell to my knees and lifted my hands to the LORD my God. ⁶I prayed,

"O my God, I am utterly ashamed; I blush to lift up my face to you. For our sins are piled higher than our heads, and our guilt has reached to the heavens. ⁷From the days of our ancestors until now, we have been steeped in sin. That is why we and our kings and our priests have been at the mercy of the pagan kings of the land. We have been killed, captured, robbed, and disgraced, just as we are today.

⁸"But now we have been given a brief moment of grace, for the LORD our God has allowed a few of us to survive as a remnant. He has given us security in this holy place. Our God has brightened our eyes and granted us some relief from our slavery. ⁹For we were slaves, but in his unfailing love our God did not abandon us in our slavery. Instead, he caused the kings of Persia to treat us favorably. He revived us so we could rebuild the

---

8:31 Hebrew *on the twelfth day of the first month,* of the ancient Hebrew lunar calendar. This day was April 19, 458 B.C.; also see note on 6:15. 8:36 Hebrew *the province beyond the river.*

9:1-2 God called Abraham's descendants, the Hebrews, to be his special people. He set them apart to bring his Son into the world through them. He intended them to be holy—unique among all the other peoples on earth. Ezra discovered that God's special people were compromising their uniqueness and calling through intermarriage with the neighboring pagans. God has called us to be his people, too, through a relationship with Jesus Christ. We should not blend in with the unbelievers around us; we must remain clearly identifiable as God's special people.
9:3 Upon realizing the people's sin, Ezra responded with deep mourning. He was heartbroken that the people had forgotten their special calling and the obligations it entailed. As people of God, we must remember that we also have certain responsibilities before God. The temptation to procrastinate in dealing with tough issues in our life is strong. But God wants us to tackle these issues head-on, remembering that he is there to give us strength and encouragement.
9:6-15 Ezra's prayer of confession followed his mourning. He freely admitted the sins of the people and pleaded with God for their restoration. He realized that until they removed this major obstacle to their spiritual success by confessing their sin, they would never achieve the victory that God intended for them. Often we hold on to some areas of our life that prevent us from experiencing everything that God has in store for us. What areas do we need to confess and turn over to God's control? We should act immediately so we can get on with the recovery process.

Temple of our God and repair its ruins. He has given us a protective wall in Judah and Jerusalem.

10"And now, O our God, what can we say after all of this? For once again we have abandoned your commands! 11Your servants the prophets warned us when they said, 'The land you are entering to possess is totally defiled by the detestable practices of the people living there. From one end to the other, the land is filled with corruption. 12Don't let your daughters marry their sons! Don't take their daughters as wives for your sons. Don't ever promote the peace and prosperity of those nations. If you follow these instructions, you will be strong and will enjoy the good things the land produces, and you will leave this prosperity to your children forever.'

13"Now we are being punished because of our wickedness and our great guilt. But we have actually been punished far less than we deserve, for you, our God, have allowed some of us to survive as a remnant. 14But even so, we are again breaking your commands and intermarrying with people who do these detestable things. Won't your anger be enough to destroy us, so that even this little remnant no longer survives? 15O LORD, God of Israel, you are just. We come before you in our guilt as nothing but an escaped remnant, though in such a condition none of us can stand in your presence."

CHAPTER 10
The People Confess Their Sin

While Ezra prayed and made this confession, weeping and lying face down on the ground in front of the Temple of God, a very large crowd of people from Israel—men, women, and children—gathered and wept bitterly with him. 2Then Shecaniah son of Jehiel, a descendant of Elam, said to Ezra, "We have been unfaithful to our God, for we have married these pagan women of the land. But in spite of this there is hope for Israel. 3Let us now make a covenant with our God to divorce our pagan wives and to send them away with their children. We will follow the advice given by you and by the others who respect the commands of our God. Let it be done according to the Law of God. 4Get up, for it is your duty to tell us how to proceed in setting things straight. We are behind you, so be strong and take action."

5So Ezra stood up and demanded that the leaders of the priests and the Levites and all the people of Israel swear that they would do as Shecaniah had said. And they all swore a solemn oath. 6Then Ezra left the front of the Temple of God and went to the room of Jehohanan son of Eliashib. He spent the night* there without eating or drinking anything. He was still in mourning because of the unfaithfulness of the returned exiles.

7Then a proclamation was made throughout Judah and Jerusalem that all the exiles should come to Jerusalem. 8Those who failed to come within three days would, if the leaders and elders so decided, forfeit all their property and be expelled from the assembly of the exiles.

9Within three days, all the people of Judah and Benjamin had gathered in Jerusalem. This took place on December 19,* and all the people were sitting in the square before the Temple of God. They were trembling both because of the seriousness of the matter and because it was raining. 10Then Ezra the priest stood and said to them: "You have committed a terrible sin. By marrying pagan women, you have increased Israel's guilt. 11So now confess your sin to the LORD, the God of your

---

10:6 As in parallel text at 1 Esdras 9:2; Hebrew reads *He went.* 10:9 Hebrew *on the twentieth day of the ninth month,* of the ancient Hebrew lunar calendar. This day was December 19, 458 B.C.; also see note on 6:15.

10:2 It was all very well and good for Ezra to confess the sins of the people, but until the people themselves confessed their sin, the victory could not take place. If we do nothing about the areas in our life that are out of control, we will never move forward. We must submit these parts to God and then take action against them.
10:3 The people did not stop at mere confession; they vowed to reform. It is never enough to just acknowledge that we have unacceptable patterns in our life. Just like these people did, we must follow our confession with action. This is the purpose of recovery—to take active steps to eliminate sinful and destructive behaviors from our life.
10:10-12 Heartily, the people responded, "We must do as you say!" They recognized their special privileges and responsibilities as God's people. When they admitted that they needed to obey God, they found victory! Ezra was successful in his recovery mission to the nation! We, too, can know such victory if we follow God's will for our life and trust him to see us through.

ancestors, and do what he demands. Separate yourselves from the people of the land and from these pagan women."

¹²Then the whole assembly raised their voices and answered, "Yes, you are right; we must do as you say!" ¹³Then they added, "This isn't something that can be done in a day or two, for many of us are involved in this extremely sinful affair. And this is the rainy season, so we cannot stay out here much longer. ¹⁴Let our leaders act on behalf of us all. Let everyone who has a pagan wife come at a scheduled time, accompanied by the leaders and judges of his city, so that the fierce anger of our God concerning this affair may be turned away from us."

¹⁵Only Jonathan son of Asahel and Jahzeiah son of Tikvah opposed this course of action, and they were supported by Meshullam and Shabbethai the Levite.

¹⁶So this was the plan they followed. Ezra selected leaders to represent their families, designating each of the representatives by name. On December 29,* the leaders sat down to investigate the matter. ¹⁷By March 27, the first day of the new year,* they had finished dealing with all the men who had married pagan wives.

Those Guilty of Intermarriage
¹⁸These are the priests who had married pagan wives:

From the family of Jeshua son of Jehozadak* and his brothers: Maaseiah, Eliezer, Jarib, and Gedaliah. ¹⁹They vowed to divorce their wives, and they each acknowledged their guilt by offering a ram as a guilt offering.

²⁰From the family of Immer: Hanani and Zebadiah.

²¹From the family of Harim: Maaseiah, Elijah, Shemaiah, Jehiel, and Uzziah.

²²From the family of Pashhur: Elioenai, Maaseiah, Ishmael, Nethanel, Jozabad, and Elasah.

²³These are the Levites who were guilty: Jozabad, Shimei, Kelaiah (also called Kelita), Pethahiah, Judah, and Eliezer.

²⁴This is the singer who was guilty: Eliashib.

These are the gatekeepers who were guilty: Shallum, Telem, and Uri.

²⁵These are the other people of Israel who were guilty:

From the family of Parosh: Ramiah, Izziah, Malkijah, Mijamin, Eleazar, Hashabiah,* and Benaiah.

²⁶From the family of Elam: Mattaniah, Zechariah, Jehiel, Abdi, Jeremoth, and Elijah.

²⁷From the family of Zattu: Elioenai, Eliashib, Mattaniah, Jeremoth, Zabad, and Aziza.

²⁸From the family of Bebai: Jehohanan, Hananiah, Zabbai, and Athlai.

²⁹From the family of Bani: Meshullam, Malluch, Adaiah, Jashub, Sheal, and Jeremoth.

³⁰From the family of Pahath-moab: Adna, Kelal, Benaiah, Maaseiah, Mattaniah, Bezalel, Binnui, and Manasseh.

³¹From the family of Harim: Eliezer, Ishijah, Malkijah, Shemaiah, Shimeon, ³²Benjamin, Malluch, and Shemariah.

³³From the family of Hashum: Mattenai, Mattattah, Zabad, Eliphelet, Jeremai, Manasseh, and Shimei.

³⁴From the family of Bani: Maadai, Amram, Uel, ³⁵Benaiah, Bedeiah, Keluhi, ³⁶Vaniah, Meremoth, Eliashib, ³⁷Mattaniah, Mattenai, and Jaasu.

³⁸From the family of Binnui*: Shimei, ³⁹Shelemiah, Nathan, Adaiah, ⁴⁰Macnadebai, Shashai, Sharai, ⁴¹Azarel, Shelemiah, Shemariah, ⁴²Shallum, Amariah, and Joseph.

⁴³From the family of Nebo: Jeiel, Mattithiah, Zabad, Zebina, Jaddai, Joel, and Benaiah.

⁴⁴Each of these men had a pagan wife, and some even had children by these wives.*

10:16 Hebrew *On the first day of the tenth month,* of the ancient Hebrew lunar calendar. This day was December 29, 458 B.C.; also see note on 6:15.   10:17 Hebrew *By the first day of the first month,* of the ancient Hebrew lunar calendar. This day was March 27, 457 B.C.; also see note on 6:15.   10:18 Hebrew *Jozadak,* a variant spelling of Jehozadak. 10:25 As in parallel text at 1 Esdras 9:26; Hebrew reads *Malkijah.*   10:37-38 As in Greek version; Hebrew reads *Jaasu,* ³⁸*Bani, Binnui.*   10:44 Or *and they sent them away with their children.* The meaning of the Hebrew is uncertain.

NEHEMIAH

THE BIG PICTURE

A. REBUILDING THE WALL
(1:1–7:73)
1. Nehemiah's Call (1:1–2:8)
2. Nehemiah's Preparations
(2:9–3:32)
3. Nehemiah's Problems
(4:1–6:14)
    a. Derision—answered by
prayer (4:1-6)
    b. Discouragement—
answered by
communication (4:7-23)
    c. Greed—answered by
confrontation (5:1-19)
    d. Personal attacks—
answered by dependence
on God (6:1-14)
4. Nehemiah's Perseverance
(6:15–7:73)
B. REBUILDING THE WORKERS
(8:1–12:47)
1. Ezra Leads in Revival (8:1-18)
2. The Role of Confession
(9:1-38)
3. The Response of the People
(10:1–10:39)
4. Nehemiah Establishes
Policies (11:1–12:47)
C. REBUILDING THE WORSHIP
(13:1-31)

A secure environment is helpful for any rebuilding project. When we lack physical safety and emotional stability, it is difficult to concentrate on the job at hand. The people of Jerusalem had no physical security. Their city wall had been piles of rubble for over a hundred years. The Temple had been rebuilt many years before, but the wall around Jerusalem was still in disrepair and the gates had been burned. Walls are important boundaries. They protect and shelter inhabitants who live inside and repel destructive intruders from outside. In the ancient Near East, a city without walls was vulnerable to raids and all kinds of harassment—it was unthinkable! It was in this unstable situation that Ezra encouraged the Jews to rebuild their nation and their lives.

At this time, Nehemiah worked as the cup-bearer for King Artaxerxes of Persia. When Nehemiah heard about the situation that Ezra faced in Jerusalem, he literally sat down and wept.

Nehemiah decided to approach King Artaxerxes about the problem, and he was given permission to lead a third group of Jews back to Jerusalem. He took responsibility for encouraging the people to rebuild the wall of Jerusalem. Nehemiah's organizational skills and leadership abilities overcame both internal and external resistance to the rebuilding project. In the end, by trusting God and pulling together, the people completed the task of rebuilding the wall.

When the work was completed, Nehemiah joined with Ezra to encourage the people to rebuild their lives, their culture, and proper worship of God. Together, with God's help, they led the people in the recovery of their spiritual heritage.

THE BOTTOM LINE

PURPOSE: To describe the rebuilding of the wall of Jerusalem and the continued spiritual rebuilding of the people. AUTHOR: Nehemiah; Ezra probably served as an editor. AUDIENCE: The people of Israel after their return from exile in Babylon. DATE WRITTEN: The dates of Nehemiah's first administration were 445–432 B.C., during which time this book was probably written. SETTING: The city of Jerusalem. KEY VERSES: "They confessed their own sins and the sins of their ancestors. They remained standing in place for three hours while the Book of the Law of the LORD their God was read aloud to them. Then for three more hours they confessed their sins and worshiped the LORD their God" (9:2-3). KEY PEOPLE: Ezra, Nehemiah.

RECOVERY THEMES

The Importance of Boundaries: Nehemiah's rebuilding of the wall of Jerusalem illustrates the importance of personal boundaries in our life. When we don't have boundaries, other people may feel as if they can control us, and they usually can. Our identity becomes confused with the identities of others till we lose touch with who we really are. The Jews living in Jerusalem after the return from Babylon lacked physical boundaries of protection. They were at the mercy of the people living nearby. The task of rebuilding Jerusalem's boundaries met with opposition, for with a wall, the people of Jerusalem would be able to defend themselves against their enemies. Rebuilding the wall was a difficult task for Nehemiah, as it is for us, but we must have protective boundaries.

The Importance of Confrontation: Often, directly confronting a person in the wrong is the best way to remedy a bad situation. Several times Nehemiah's enemies tried to undermine his work through lies and deceit. Each time, Nehemiah was direct in confronting the lies, going right to the source of the problem. He did not allow himself to get discouraged or overwhelmed by the difficulties. Instead, each time something came up as a potential roadblock to God's work, Nehemiah faced the issue squarely and honestly. Then he stayed with the problem until it was resolved.

The Danger of Discouragement: As a wise leader, Nehemiah knew that the discouragement of the people was one of his biggest enemies, just as it is for us. When we get discouraged, we are open to defeat, giving the enemy victory for a period of time. Nehemiah shows us that we need to be on guard against discouragement, making certain that we are building into our life protection and healthy relationships, and that we have a heart that seeks after God.

The Power of Confession and Worship: We have a vivid picture in this book of the power of confession and the role of worship in our recovery. Not many days after the end of the Festival of Shelters (chapter 8), the people returned for another celebration (chapters 9–10). This one was to celebrate the recovery of not only the Temple but also the city of Jerusalem. They started their celebration by listening to the Word of God and confessing not only their own sins but the sins of their ancestors. This kind of confession brings healing and prepares us for true worship, genuine recovery, and joyous celebration.

CHAPTER 1

These are the memoirs of Nehemiah son of Hacaliah.

Nehemiah's Concern for Jerusalem

In late autumn, in the month of Kislev, in the twentieth year of King Artaxerxes' reign,* I was at the fortress of Susa. ²Hanani, one of my brothers, came to visit me with some other men who had just arrived from Judah. I asked them about the Jews who had returned there from captivity and about how things were going in Jerusalem.

³They said to me, "Things are not going well for those who returned to the province of Judah. They are in great trouble and disgrace. The wall of Jerusalem has been torn down, and the gates have been destroyed by fire."

⁴When I heard this, I sat down and wept. In fact, for days I mourned, fasted, and prayed to the God of heaven. ⁵Then I said,

"O LORD, God of heaven, the great and awesome God who keeps his covenant of unfailing love with those who love him

---

1:1 Hebrew *In the month of Kislev of the twentieth year.* A number of dates in the book of Nehemiah can be cross-checked with dates in surviving Persian records and related accurately to our modern calendar. This month of the ancient Hebrew lunar calendar occurred within the months of November and December 446 B.C. The *twentieth year* probably refers to the reign of King Artaxerxes I; compare 2:1; 5:14.

1:4-11 For believers, prayer is often an untapped resource or the last resort after every other possibility has been exhausted. It is refreshing to notice that for Nehemiah, prayer was his immediate response. He knew that if the situation was to be corrected, God would be the one to accomplish it! This is a powerful reminder for us: We should fall on our knees so we don't fall on our face.

1:11 Recovery can never be a solitary procedure. Other people must be involved. Cooperation has to be sought. Sometimes even permission has to be obtained. In this case, Nehemiah recognized the need for the king's favor; before asking the king, he asked God to secure the necessary response from him. Like Nehemiah, we should determine whose help we need and then prayerfully ask for their assistance.

NEHEMIAH

Recovery is the process of rebuilding a life, often from a point near complete destruction. Nehemiah, the great rebuilder of Jerusalem, leaves us an excellent biblical example of how to pursue and enhance the recovery process.

Nehemiah did not let the long-delayed recovery of Jerusalem discourage him. He realized that it was never too late for God's people to begin the process. Nehemiah's actions were direct and forceful, always based on the realities at hand. His faith, wisdom, and courage kept him focused on his goal, despite considerable opposition. Leaders like Sanballat and Tobiah, who had dominated the land of Judah for some time, used various means to discourage the progress of Nehemiah and the Jews. Painful differences among the Jews themselves also had to be confronted along the way. But all of the obstacles were overcome as the people worked to build a new, more secure life.

The wall of Jerusalem was completed in a miraculous 52 days! Soon after this first victory, Nehemiah directed the people toward a second phase of recovery. He called upon the great teacher Ezra to lead the people in a study of the Scriptures. Confronted by God's Word, they tearfully repented of their sins and the sins of their ancestors. Ezra, Nehemiah, and the other leaders encouraged the people to be filled with joy because God was with them.

Even now, however, the Israelites had not learned all the painful lessons of recovery. After Nehemiah went back to Babylon, the people returned once again to their sinful ways. When Nehemiah returned to Jerusalem, he had to put the Jews back on the path toward recovery. This example of short-term recovery and relapse ends the story of Nehemiah on a very realistic note. There will be times when we all fall back into familiar, though destructive, patterns. We should be encouraged to realize that no matter how often we fail, God is still waiting to lead us back to his way of life.

STRENGTHS AND ACCOMPLISHMENTS:
- Nehemiah was a man of prayer and unshakable commitment to God.
- He was an effective administrator and an even greater visionary.
- He was secure in himself and had the ability to withstand criticism.
- He had the faith and perseverance to help the people complete the rebuilding process for Jerusalem and the nation.

LESSONS FROM HIS LIFE:
- Prayerful intervention, a realistic vision, and commitment to God are helpful aids to recovery.
- Confronting and overcoming obstacles to recovery can actually provide momentum for the process.
- The completion of one phase of recovery should motivate us to pursue the next step in the process.
- A relapse should be viewed as a step toward renewed recovery.

KEY VERSES:
"O LORD, God of heaven, . . . listen to my prayer! Look down and see me praying night and day for your people Israel" (Nehemiah 1:5-6).

Nehemiah's story is told in the book of Nehemiah. He is also mentioned in Ezra 2:2.

---

and obey his commands, ⁶listen to my prayer! Look down and see me praying night and day for your people Israel. I confess that we have sinned against you. Yes, even my own family and I have sinned! ⁷We have sinned terribly by not obeying the commands, decrees, and regulations that you gave us through your servant Moses.

⁸"Please remember what you told your servant Moses: 'If you are unfaithful to me, I will scatter you among the nations. ⁹But if you return to me and obey my commands and live by them, then even if you are exiled to the ends of the earth,* I will bring you back to the place I have chosen for my name to be honored.'

¹⁰"The people you rescued by your great power and strong hand are your servants. ¹¹O Lord, please hear my prayer! Listen to the prayers of those of us who delight in honoring you. Please grant me success today by making the

1:9 Hebrew *of the heavens.*

king favorable to me.* Put it into his heart to be kind to me."

In those days I was the king's cup-bearer.

CHAPTER 2
Nehemiah Goes to Jerusalem

Early the following spring, in the month of Nisan,* during the twentieth year of King Artaxerxes' reign, I was serving the king his wine. I had never before appeared sad in his presence. [2]So the king asked me, "Why are you looking so sad? You don't look sick to me. You must be deeply troubled."

Then I was terrified, [3]but I replied, "Long live the king! How can I not be sad? For the city where my ancestors are buried is in ruins, and the gates have been destroyed by fire."

[4]The king asked, "Well, how can I help you?"

With a prayer to the God of heaven, [5]I replied, "If it please the king, and if you are pleased with me, your servant, send me to Judah to rebuild the city where my ancestors are buried."

[6]The king, with the queen sitting beside him, asked, "How long will you be gone? When will you return?" After I told him how long I would be gone, the king agreed to my request.

[7]I also said to the king, "If it please the king, let me have letters addressed to the governors of the province west of the Euphrates River,* instructing them to let me travel safely through their territories on my way to Judah. [8]And please give me a letter addressed to Asaph, the manager of the king's forest, instructing him to give me timber. I will need it to make beams for the gates of the Temple fortress, for the city walls, and for a house for myself." And the king granted these requests, because the gracious hand of God was on me.

[9]When I came to the governors of the province west of the Euphrates River, I delivered the king's letters to them. The king, I should add, had sent along army officers and horsemen* to protect me. [10]But when Sanballat the Horonite and Tobiah the Ammonite official heard of my arrival, they were very displeased that someone had come to help the people of Israel.

Nehemiah Inspects Jerusalem's Wall

[11]So I arrived in Jerusalem. Three days later, [12]I slipped out during the night, taking only a few others with me. I had not told anyone about the plans God had put in my heart for Jerusalem. We took no pack animals with us except the donkey I was riding. [13]After dark I went out through the Valley Gate, past the Jackal's Well,* and over to the Dung Gate to inspect the broken walls and burned gates. [14]Then I went to the Fountain Gate and to the King's Pool, but my donkey couldn't get through the rubble. [15]So, though it was still dark, I went up the Kidron Valley* instead, inspecting the wall before I turned back and entered again at the Valley Gate.

[16]The city officials did not know I had been out there or what I was doing, for I had not yet said anything to anyone about my plans. I had not yet spoken to the Jewish leaders—the priests, the nobles, the officials, or anyone else in the administration. [17]But now I said to them, "You know very well what trouble we are in. Jerusalem lies in ruins, and its gates have been destroyed by fire. Let us rebuild the wall of Jerusalem and end this disgrace!" [18]Then I told them about how the gracious hand of God had been on me, and about my conversation with the king.

They replied at once, "Yes, let's rebuild the wall!" So they began the good work.

[19]But when Sanballat, Tobiah, and Geshem the Arab heard of our plan, they scoffed contemptuously. "What are you doing? Are you rebelling against the king?" they asked.

1:11 Hebrew *today in the sight of this man.* 2:1 Hebrew *In the month of Nisan.* This month of the ancient Hebrew lunar calendar occurred within the months of April and May 445 B.C. 2:7 Hebrew *the province beyond the river;* also in 2:9. 2:9 Or *charioteers.* 2:13 Or *Serpent's Well.* 2:15 Hebrew *the valley.*

2:4-8 In answer to Nehemiah's prayer to God, the king's immediate response was one of encouragement and assistance. One wonders how Artaxerxes would have responded had Nehemiah not first approached God on this matter. Prayer changes things. Prayer changes people. Prayer is a supernatural power at our disposal that enables us to accomplish God's supernatural will. If we try to do things on our own, the odds are against us; we will probably fail. If we try something with God's help, we will definitely succeed.

2:11-16 Taking inventory is one of the first tasks in any rebuilding project. As soon as Nehemiah arrived in Jerusalem, he made a nighttime inspection of the city's broken walls. Each of us in recovery needs to take an honest look at all the circumstances, problems, and resources before us. This is essential for selecting the proper strategy for correcting the problems we face.

[20]I replied, "The God of heaven will help us succeed. We, his servants, will start rebuilding this wall. But you have no share, legal right, or historic claim in Jerusalem."

CHAPTER 3
Rebuilding the Wall of Jerusalem

Then Eliashib the high priest and the other priests started to rebuild at the Sheep Gate. They dedicated it and set up its doors, building the wall as far as the Tower of the Hundred, which they dedicated, and the Tower of Hananel. [2]People from the town of Jericho worked next to them, and beyond them was Zaccur son of Imri.

[3]The Fish Gate was built by the sons of Hassenaah. They laid the beams, set up its doors, and installed its bolts and bars. [4]Meremoth son of Uriah and grandson of Hakkoz repaired the next section of wall. Beside him were Meshullam son of Berekiah and grandson of Meshezabel, and then Zadok son of Baana. [5]Next were the people from Tekoa, though their leaders refused to work with the construction supervisors.

[6]The Old City Gate* was repaired by Joiada son of Paseah and Meshullam son of Besodeiah. They laid the beams, set up its doors, and installed its bolts and bars. [7]Next to them were Melatiah from Gibeon, Jadon from Meronoth, people from Gibeon, and people from Mizpah, the headquarters of the governor of the province west of the Euphrates River.* [8]Next was Uzziel son of Harhaiah, a goldsmith by trade, who also worked on the wall. Beyond him was Hananiah, a manufacturer of perfumes. They left out a section of Jerusalem as they built the Broad Wall.*

[9]Rephaiah son of Hur, the leader of half the district of Jerusalem, was next to them on the wall. [10]Next Jedaiah son of Harumaph repaired the wall across from his own house, and next to him was Hattush son of Hashabneiah. [11]Then came Malkijah son of Harim and Hasshub son of Pahath-moab, who repaired another section of the wall and the Tower of the Ovens. [12]Shallum son of

Hallohesh and his daughters repaired the next section. He was the leader of the other half of the district of Jerusalem.

[13]The Valley Gate was repaired by the people from Zanoah, led by Hanun. They set up its doors and installed its bolts and bars. They also repaired the 1,500 feet* of wall to the Dung Gate.

[14]The Dung Gate was repaired by Malkijah son of Recab, the leader of the Beth-hakkerem district. He rebuilt it, set up its doors, and installed its bolts and bars.

[15]The Fountain Gate was repaired by Shallum* son of Col-hozeh, the leader of the Mizpah district. He rebuilt it, roofed it, set up its doors, and installed its bolts and bars. Then he repaired the wall of the pool of Siloam* near the king's garden, and he rebuilt the wall as far as the stairs that descend from the City of David. [16]Next to him was Nehemiah son of Azbuk, the leader of half the district of Beth-zur. He rebuilt the wall from a place across from the tombs of David's family as far as the water reservoir and the House of the Warriors.

[17]Next to him, repairs were made by a group of Levites working under the supervision of Rehum son of Bani. Then came Hashabiah, the leader of half the district of Keilah, who supervised the building of the wall on behalf of his own district. [18]Next down the line were his countrymen led by Binnui* son of Henadad, the leader of the other half of the district of Keilah.

[19]Next to them, Ezer son of Jeshua, the leader of Mizpah, repaired another section of wall across from the ascent to the armory near the angle in the wall. [20]Next to him was Baruch son of Zabbai, who zealously repaired an additional section from the angle to the door of the house of Eliashib the high priest. [21]Meremoth son of Uriah and grandson of Hakkoz rebuilt another section of the wall extending from the door of Eliashib's house to the end of the house.

[22]The next repairs were made by the priests from the surrounding region. [23]After them,

---

3:6 Or *The Mishneh Gate,* or *The Jeshanah Gate.* **3:7** Hebrew *the province beyond the river.* **3:8** Or *They fortified Jerusalem up to the Broad Wall.* **3:13** Hebrew *1,000 cubits* [460 meters]. **3:15a** As in Syriac version; Hebrew reads *Shallun.* **3:15b** Hebrew *pool of Shelah,* another name for the pool of Siloam. **3:18** As in a few Hebrew manuscripts, some Greek manuscripts, and Syriac version (see also 3:24; 10:9); most Hebrew manuscripts read *Bavvai.*

3:1-32 Rebuilding the entire wall of Jerusalem was an enormous task. But Nehemiah had a plan to make it easier: He divided the work and assigned it to different groups of people. This way the people felt responsible for their section, and no one got burned out working on the entire task. There is a lesson here for us. As we face the challenge of recovery, we may become discouraged by the immensity of the task. But if we break up the process into smaller steps—a day or a week or a month at a time—the task will look less intimidating.

Benjamin and Hasshub repaired the section across from their house, and Azariah son of Maaseiah and grandson of Ananiah repaired the section across from his house. 24Next was Binnui son of Henadad, who rebuilt another section of the wall from Azariah's house to the angle and the corner. 25Palal son of Uzai carried on the work from a point opposite the angle and the tower that projects up from the king's upper house beside the court of the guard. Next to him were Pedaiah son of Parosh, 26with the Temple servants living on the hill of Ophel, who repaired the wall as far as a point across from the Water Gate to the east and the projecting tower. 27Then came the people of Tekoa, who repaired another section across from the great projecting tower and over to the wall of Ophel.

28Above the Horse Gate, the priests repaired the wall. Each one repaired the section immediately across from his own house. 29Next Zadok son of Immer also rebuilt the wall across from his own house, and beyond him was Shemaiah son of Shecaniah, the gatekeeper of the East Gate. 30Next Hananiah son of Shelemiah and Hanun, the sixth son of Zalaph, repaired another section, while Meshullam son of Berekiah rebuilt the wall across from where he lived. 31Malkijah, one of the goldsmiths, repaired the wall as far as the housing for the Temple servants and merchants, across from the Inspection Gate. Then he continued as far as the upper room at the corner. 32The other goldsmiths and merchants repaired the wall from that corner to the Sheep Gate.

CHAPTER 4
Enemies Oppose the Rebuilding

1*Sanballat was very angry when he learned that we were rebuilding the wall. He flew into a rage and mocked the Jews, 2saying in front of his friends and the Samarian army officers, "What does this bunch of poor, feeble Jews think they're doing? Do they think they can build the wall in a single day by just offering a few sacrifices?* Do they actually think they can make something of stones from a rubbish heap—and charred ones at that?"

3Tobiah the Ammonite, who was standing beside him, remarked, "That stone wall would collapse if even a fox walked along the top of it!"

4Then I prayed, "Hear us, our God, for we are being mocked. May their scoffing fall back on their own heads, and may they themselves become captives in a foreign land! 5Do not ignore their guilt. Do not blot out their sins, for they have provoked you to anger here in front of* the builders."

6At last the wall was completed to half its height around the entire city, for the people had worked with enthusiasm.

7*But when Sanballat and Tobiah and the Arabs, Ammonites, and Ashdodites heard that the work was going ahead and that the gaps in the wall of Jerusalem were being repaired, they were furious. 8They all made plans to come and fight against Jerusalem and throw us into confusion. 9But we prayed to our God and guarded the city day and night to protect ourselves.

10Then the people of Judah began to complain, "The workers are getting tired, and there is so much rubble to be moved. We will never be able to build the wall by ourselves."

11Meanwhile, our enemies were saying, "Before they know what's happening, we will swoop down on them and kill them and end their work."

12The Jews who lived near the enemy came and told us again and again, "They will come from all directions and attack us!"* 13So I placed armed guards behind the lowest parts of the wall in the exposed areas. I stationed the people to stand guard by families, armed with swords, spears, and bows.

4:1 Verses 4:1-6 are numbered 3:33-38 in Hebrew text. 4:2 The meaning of the Hebrew is uncertain. 4:5 Or *for they have thrown insults in the face of.* 4:7 Verses 4:7-23 are numbered 4:1-17 in Hebrew text. 4:12 The meaning of the Hebrew is uncertain.

4:1-4 When we start the recovery process, we will face many kinds of opposition. Nehemiah was no exception. One kind of opposition he faced was ridicule. The sarcasm expressed by Sanballat and Tobiah must have stung. But Nehemiah did not focus on the ridicule; he continued to look to God. We, too, should look to God when we are taunted. The ridicule of others may be motivated by their desire to continue dominating us or by their jealousy over our victories in recovery.

4:10 Rubble can be very disheartening in itself. With every remodeling project, trash accumulates. This is true not only for physical rebuilding but for emotional and spiritual recovery as well. The garbage was getting in the way of the workmen, and they were discouraged by it. We may experience the same discouragement as some of the unresolved emotional garbage from the past still remains. We must recognize the garbage, resolve the problem, and then remove the rubble so we can continue on the path to recovery.

[14]Then as I looked over the situation, I called together the nobles and the rest of the people and said to them, "Don't be afraid of the enemy! Remember the Lord, who is great and glorious, and fight for your brothers, your sons, your daughters, your wives, and your homes!"

[15]When our enemies heard that we knew of their plans and that God had frustrated them, we all returned to our work on the wall. [16]But from then on, only half my men worked while the other half stood guard with spears, shields, bows, and coats of mail. The leaders stationed themselves behind the people of Judah [17]who were building the wall. The laborers carried on their work with one hand supporting their load and one hand holding a weapon. [18]All the builders had a sword belted to their side. The trumpeter stayed with me to sound the alarm.

[19]Then I explained to the nobles and officials and all the people, "The work is very spread out, and we are widely separated from each other along the wall. [20]When you hear the blast of the trumpet, rush to wherever it is sounding. Then our God will fight for us!"

[21]We worked early and late, from sunrise to sunset. And half the men were always on guard. [22]I also told everyone living outside the walls to stay in Jerusalem. That way they and their servants could help with guard duty at night and work during the day. [23]During this time, none of us—not I, nor my relatives, nor my servants, nor the guards who were with me—ever took off our clothes. We carried our weapons with us at all times, even when we went for water.*

CHAPTER 5
Nehemiah Defends the Oppressed
About this time some of the men and their wives raised a cry of protest against their fellow Jews. [2]They were saying, "We have such large families. We need more food to survive."

[3]Others said, "We have mortgaged our fields, vineyards, and homes to get food during the famine."

[4]And others said, "We have had to borrow money on our fields and vineyards to pay our taxes. [5]We belong to the same family as those who are wealthy, and our children are just like theirs. Yet we must sell our children into slavery just to get enough money to live. We have already sold some of our daughters, and we are helpless to do anything about it, for our fields and vineyards are already mortgaged to others."

[6]When I heard their complaints, I was very angry. [7]After thinking it over, I spoke out against these nobles and officials. I told them, "You are hurting your own relatives by charging interest when they borrow money!" Then I called a public meeting to deal with the problem.

[8]At the meeting I said to them, "We are doing all we can to redeem our Jewish relatives who have had to sell themselves to pagan foreigners, but you are selling them back into slavery again. How often must we redeem them?" And they had nothing to say in their defense.

[9]Then I pressed further, "What you are doing is not right! Should you not walk in the fear of our God in order to avoid being mocked by enemy nations? [10]I myself, as well as my brothers and my workers, have been lending the people money and grain, but now let us stop this business of charging interest. [11]You must restore their fields, vineyards, olive groves, and homes to them this very day. And repay the interest you charged when you lent them money, grain, new wine, and olive oil."

[12]They replied, "We will give back everything and demand nothing more from the people. We will do as you say." Then I called the priests and made the nobles and officials swear to do what they had promised.

[13]I shook out the folds of my robe and said, "If you fail to keep your promise, may God shake you like this from your homes and from your property!"

The whole assembly responded, "Amen," and they praised the LORD. And the people did as they had promised.

4:23 Or *Each carried his weapon in his right hand.* Hebrew reads *Each his weapon the water.* The meaning of the Hebrew is uncertain.

5:1-5 The previous attack had come from the outside; now a new attack came from within. The rebuilding was costing too much! We experience the same emotions as the Jews felt. In overcoming our dependency, we have to give up some of the things that have brought us security. When times get bad, we may wish we had our addiction back to comfort us, even though we know it was harmful. But in order to rebuild the walls of our life, some pain and sacrifice are necessary. The cost of recovery is worth what we will receive in return—freedom.

¹⁴For the entire twelve years that I was governor of Judah—from the twentieth year to the thirty-second year of the reign of King Artaxerxes*—neither I nor my officials drew on our official food allowance. ¹⁵The former governors, in contrast, had laid heavy burdens on the people, demanding a daily ration of food and wine, besides forty pieces* of silver. Even their assistants took advantage of the people. But because I feared God, I did not act that way.

¹⁶I also devoted myself to working on the wall and refused to acquire any land. And I required all my servants to spend time working on the wall. ¹⁷I asked for nothing, even though I regularly fed 150 Jewish officials at my table, besides all the visitors from other lands! ¹⁸The provisions I paid for each day included one ox, six choice sheep or goats, and a large number of poultry. And every ten days we needed a large supply of all kinds of wine. Yet I refused to claim the governor's food allowance because the people already carried a heavy burden.

¹⁹Remember, O my God, all that I have done for these people, and bless me for it.

CHAPTER 6
Continued Opposition to Rebuilding

Sanballat, Tobiah, Geshem the Arab, and the rest of our enemies found out that I had finished rebuilding the wall and that no gaps remained—though we had not yet set up the doors in the gates. ²So Sanballat and Geshem sent a message asking me to meet them at one of the villages* in the plain of Ono.

But I realized they were plotting to harm me, ³so I replied by sending this message to them: "I am engaged in a great work, so I can't come. Why should I stop working to come and meet with you?"

⁴Four times they sent the same message, and each time I gave the same reply. ⁵The fifth time, Sanballat's servant came with an open letter in his hand, ⁶and this is what it said:

"There is a rumor among the surrounding nations, and Geshem* tells me it is true, that you and the Jews are planning to rebel and that is why you are building the wall. According to his reports, you plan to be their king. ⁷He also reports that you have appointed prophets in Jerusalem to proclaim about you, 'Look! There is a king in Judah!'

"You can be very sure that this report will get back to the king, so I suggest that you come and talk it over with me."

⁸I replied, "There is no truth in any part of your story. You are making up the whole thing."

⁹They were just trying to intimidate us, imagining that they could discourage us and stop the work. So I continued the work with even greater determination.*

¹⁰Later I went to visit Shemaiah son of Delaiah and grandson of Mehetabel, who was confined to his home. He said, "Let us meet together inside the Temple of God and bolt the doors shut. Your enemies are coming to kill you tonight."

¹¹But I replied, "Should someone in my position run from danger? Should someone in my position enter the Temple to save his life? No, I won't do it!" ¹²I realized that God had not spoken to him, but that he had uttered this prophecy against me because Tobiah and Sanballat had hired him. ¹³They were hoping to intimidate me and make me sin. Then they would be able to accuse and discredit me.

¹⁴Remember, O my God, all the evil things that Tobiah and Sanballat have

5:14 That is, 445–433 B.C. 5:15 Hebrew *40 shekels* [1 pound or 456 grams]. 6:2 As in Greek version; Hebrew reads *at Kephirim.* 6:6 Hebrew *Gashmu,* a variant spelling of Geshem. 6:9 As in Greek version; Hebrew reads *But now to strengthen my hands.*

5:14-19 Leadership by example is the most difficult, yet the most effective, way to lead. Nehemiah gave up many of his rightful privileges in order to be a godly example. Nehemiah did not insist on his own rights. Rather, he was willing to sacrifice them for the good of the people as a part of his response to God.

6:1-2 As the work neared completion, the enemies resorted to trickery—under the guise of negotiation. As we seek to work out a godly program, God's enemies may not be excited about us completing it. We should not allow others to distract us from the goal of recovery; they may be diverting us from the path to recovery because they do not want us to succeed.

6:3 Nehemiah had set his mind to the task; he had a singleness of purpose. When his enemies tried to lure him away from his labor, he answered with the ringing statement, "I am engaged in a great work, so I can't come." He allowed nothing to deter him from his purpose. Each of us needs to ask God for such singleness of purpose because we, too, are "engaged in a great work."

done. And remember Noadiah the prophet and all the prophets like her who have tried to intimidate me.

The Builders Complete the Wall

[15]So on October 2* the wall was finished—just fifty-two days after we had begun. [16]When our enemies and the surrounding nations heard about it, they were frightened and humiliated. They realized this work had been done with the help of our God.

[17]During those fifty-two days, many letters went back and forth between Tobiah and the nobles of Judah. [18]For many in Judah had sworn allegiance to him because his father-in-law was Shecaniah son of Arah, and his son Jehohanan was married to the daughter of Meshullam son of Berekiah. [19]They kept telling me about Tobiah's good deeds, and then they told him everything I said. And Tobiah kept sending threatening letters to intimidate me.

CHAPTER 7

After the wall was finished and I had set up the doors in the gates, the gatekeepers, singers, and Levites were appointed. [2]I gave the responsibility of governing Jerusalem to my brother Hanani, along with Hananiah, the commander of the fortress, for he was a faithful man who feared God more than most. [3]I said to them, "Do not leave the gates open during the hottest part of the day.* And even while the gatekeepers are on duty, have them shut and bar the doors. Appoint the residents of Jerusalem to act as guards, everyone on a regular watch. Some will serve at sentry posts and some in front of their own homes."

Nehemiah Registers the People

[4]At that time the city was large and spacious, but the population was small, and none of the houses had been rebuilt. [5]So my God gave me the idea to call together all the nobles and leaders of the city, along with the ordinary citizens, for registration. I had found the genealogical record of those who had first returned to Judah. This is what was written there:

[6]Here is the list of the Jewish exiles of the provinces who returned from their captivity. King Nebuchadnezzar had deported them to Babylon, but now they returned to Jerusalem and the other towns in Judah where they originally lived. [7]Their leaders were Zerubbabel, Jeshua, Nehemiah, Seraiah,* Reelaiah,* Nahamani, Mordecai, Bilshan, Mispar,* Bigvai, Rehum,* and Baanah.

This is the number of the men of Israel who returned from exile:

[8] The family of Parosh	2,172
[9] The family of Shephatiah	372
[10] The family of Arah	652
[11] The family of Pahath-moab (descendants of Jeshua and Joab)	2,818
[12] The family of Elam	1,254
[13] The family of Zattu	845
[14] The family of Zaccai	760
[15] The family of Bani*	648
[16] The family of Bebai	628
[17] The family of Azgad	2,322
[18] The family of Adonikam	667
[19] The family of Bigvai	2,067
[20] The family of Adin	655
[21] The family of Ater (descendants of Hezekiah)	98

6:15 Hebrew *on the twenty-fifth day of the month Elul,* of the ancient Hebrew lunar calendar. This day was October 2, 445 B.C.; also see note on 1:1. 7:3 Or *Keep the gates of Jerusalem closed until the sun is hot.* 7:7a As in parallel text at Ezra 2:2; Hebrew reads *Azariah.* 7:7b As in parallel text at Ezra 2:2; Hebrew reads *Raamiah.* 7:7c As in parallel text at Ezra 2:2; Hebrew reads *Mispereth.* 7:7d As in parallel text at Ezra 2:2; Hebrew reads *Nehum.* 7:15 As in parallel text at Ezra 2:10; Hebrew reads *Binnui.*

6:15-16 After overcoming all kinds of evil opposition, the building of the wall was completed in a record 52 days. A job that had not been done for almost a hundred years was finished within two months because God had helped the workers. If we have delayed in starting the recovery process and now think it is too late, we should remember Nehemiah. He took a long-neglected task and completed it in a short period of time. It is never too late to begin recovery if we go about it with God's help.
7:1-4 After the great project was completed, Nehemiah did not quit working. He carefully organized the people for further defense of the city. Those living in Jerusalem were to act as guards, keeping watch over the sections of the wall nearest their homes. Nehemiah wanted God's people to be safe and have a safe environment for their individual building projects. Our recovery calls for ongoing attention to the details of the process. Though we may have made the step of breaking with our addiction, we must be on guard for lapses in our resolve or attacks from those who don't want us to succeed.

²² The family of Hashum. 328
²³ The family of Bezai 324
²⁴ The family of Jorah*. 112
²⁵ The family of Gibbar*. 95
²⁶ The people of Bethlehem and
    Netophah 188
²⁷ The people of Anathoth 128
²⁸ The people of Beth-azmaveth 42
²⁹ The people of Kiriath-jearim, Kephirah,
    and Beeroth 743
³⁰ The people of Ramah and Geba 621
³¹ The people of Micmash 122
³² The people of Bethel and Ai. 123
³³ The people of West Nebo* 52
³⁴ The citizens of West Elam* 1,254
³⁵ The citizens of Harim 320
³⁶ The citizens of Jericho. 345
³⁷ The citizens of Lod, Hadid, and Ono . . 721
³⁸ The citizens of Senaah. 3,930

³⁹ These are the priests who returned from exile:

The family of Jedaiah
    (through the line of Jeshua) 973
⁴⁰ The family of Immer 1,052
⁴¹ The family of Pashhur. 1,247
⁴² The family of Harim. 1,017

⁴³ These are the Levites who returned from exile:

The families of Jeshua and Kadmiel
    (descendants of Hodaviah*) 74
⁴⁴ The singers of the family of Asaph . . . 148
⁴⁵ The gatekeepers of the families of Shallum,
    Ater, Talmon, Akkub, Hatita,
    and Shobai. 138

⁴⁶ The descendants of the following Temple servants returned from exile:
Ziha, Hasupha, Tabbaoth,
⁴⁷ Keros, Siaha,* Padon,
⁴⁸ Lebanah, Hagabah, Shalmai,
⁴⁹ Hanan, Giddel, Gahar,
⁵⁰ Reaiah, Rezin, Nekoda,

⁵¹ Gazzam, Uzza, Paseah,
⁵² Besai, Meunim, Nephusim,*
⁵³ Bakbuk, Hakupha, Harhur,
⁵⁴ Bazluth,* Mehida, Harsha,
⁵⁵ Barkos, Sisera, Temah,
⁵⁶ Neziah, and Hatipha.

⁵⁷ The descendants of these servants of King Solomon returned from exile:
Sotai, Hassophereth, Peruda,*
⁵⁸ Jaalah,* Darkon, Giddel,
⁵⁹ Shephatiah, Hattil, Pokereth-hazzebaim, and Ami.*

⁶⁰ In all, the Temple servants and the descendants of Solomon's servants numbered 392.

⁶¹ Another group returned at this time from the towns of Tel-melah, Tel-harsha, Kerub, Addan,* and Immer. However, they could not prove that they or their families were descendants of Israel. ⁶² This group included the families of Delaiah, Tobiah, and Nekoda—a total of 642 people.

⁶³ Three families of priests—Hobaiah, Hakkoz, and Barzillai—also returned. (This Barzillai had married a woman who was a descendant of Barzillai of Gilead, and he had taken her family name.) ⁶⁴ They searched for their names in the genealogical records, but they were not found, so they were disqualified from serving as priests. ⁶⁵ The governor told them not to eat the priests' share of food from the sacrifices until a priest could consult the LORD about the matter by using the Urim and Thummim—the sacred lots.

⁶⁶ So a total of 42,360 people returned to Judah, ⁶⁷ in addition to 7,337 servants and 245 singers, both men and women. ⁶⁸ They took with them 736 horses, 245 mules,* ⁶⁹ 435 camels, and 6,720 donkeys.

7:24 As in parallel text at Ezra 2:18; Hebrew reads *Hariph.* **7:25** As in parallel text at Ezra 2:20; Hebrew reads *Gibeon.* **7:33** Or *of the other Nebo.* **7:34** Or *of the other Elam.* **7:43** As in parallel text at Ezra 2:40; Hebrew reads *Hodevah.* **7:47** As in parallel text at Ezra 2:44; Hebrew reads *Sia.* **7:52** As in parallel text at Ezra 2:50; Hebrew reads *Nephushesim.* **7:54** As in parallel text at Ezra 2:52; Hebrew reads *Bazlith.* **7:57** As in parallel text at Ezra 2:55; Hebrew reads *Sotai, Sophereth, Perida.* **7:58** As in parallel text at Ezra 2:56; Hebrew reads *Jaala.* **7:59** As in parallel text at Ezra 2:57; Hebrew reads *Amon.* **7:61** As in parallel text at Ezra 2:59; Hebrew reads *Addon.* **7:68** As in some Hebrew manuscripts (see also Ezra 2:66); most Hebrew manuscripts lack this verse. Verses 7:69-73 are numbered 7:68-72 in Hebrew text.

8:7-8 Not only did Ezra publicly read the Scriptures; he also chose a team that was responsible for the public teaching of the Word. This group of men assisted the people in understanding what the Bible meant and how to apply it to their lives. Success in recovery always involves the study of Scripture and its application to our life. The Bible tells us that we "have no excuse for not knowing God" (Romans 1:19-20)—even not having the Scriptures is no excuse. Without Scripture, however, it would be difficult to discern God's purpose in our life. Those of us who do have God's Word are responsible to live according to God's will and to help others understand what God expects of them.

⁷⁰Some of the family leaders gave gifts for the work. The governor gave to the treasury 1,000 gold coins,* 50 gold basins, and 530 robes for the priests. ⁷¹The other leaders gave to the treasury a total of 20,000 gold coins* and some 2,750 pounds* of silver for the work. ⁷²The rest of the people gave 20,000 gold coins, about 2,500 pounds* of silver, and 67 robes for the priests.

⁷³So the priests, the Levites, the gatekeepers, the singers, the Temple servants, and some of the common people settled near Jerusalem. The rest of the people returned to their own towns throughout Israel.

CHAPTER 8
Ezra Reads the Law
In October,* when the Israelites had settled in their towns, ⁸:¹all the people assembled with a unified purpose at the square just inside the Water Gate. They asked Ezra the scribe to bring out the Book of the Law of Moses, which the LORD had given for Israel to obey.

²So on October 8* Ezra the priest brought the Book of the Law before the assembly, which included the men and women and all the children old enough to understand. ³He faced the square just inside the Water Gate from early morning until noon and read aloud to everyone who could understand. All the people listened closely to the Book of the Law.

⁴Ezra the scribe stood on a high wooden platform that had been made for the occasion. To his right stood Mattithiah, Shema, Anaiah, Uriah, Hilkiah, and Maaseiah. To his left stood Pedaiah, Mishael, Malkijah, Hashum, Hashbaddanah, Zechariah, and Meshullam. ⁵Ezra stood on the platform in full view of all the people. When they saw him open the book, they all rose to their feet.

⁶Then Ezra praised the LORD, the great God, and all the people chanted, "Amen! Amen!" as they lifted their hands. Then they bowed down and worshiped the LORD with their faces to the ground.

7:70 Hebrew *1,000 darics of gold,* about 19 pounds or 8.6 kilograms in weight. 7:71a Hebrew *20,000 darics of gold,* about 375 pounds or 170 kilograms in weight; also in 7:72. 7:71b Hebrew *2,200 minas* [1,300 kilograms]. 7:72 Hebrew *2,000 minas* [1,200 kilograms]. 7:73 Hebrew *in the seventh month.* This month of the ancient Hebrew lunar calendar occurred within the months of October and November 445 B.C. 8:2 Hebrew *on the first day of the seventh month,* of the ancient Hebrew lunar calendar. This day was October 8, 445 B.C.; also see note on 1:1.

STEP 4

Facing the Sadness
BIBLE READING: Nehemiah 8:7-10
We made a searching and fearless moral inventory of ourselves.
Most of us falter at the prospect of making an honest personal inventory. Rationalizations and excuses for avoiding this step abound. The bottom line is that we know there is an enormous amount of sadness awaiting us, and we fear the pain that facing the sadness will bring.

The Jewish exiles who returned to Jerusalem after captivity in Babylon had lost touch with God. During the Exile, they hadn't been taught his laws, so naturally, they hadn't practiced them either. After rebuilding the city wall and the Temple, the priests gathered the people together to read the Book of the Law. The people were overwhelmed with grief and began weeping, because their lives in no way measured up.

The priests said to the people, "Don't mourn or weep on such a day as this! For today is a sacred day before the LORD your God. . . . Go and celebrate with a feast of rich foods and sweet drinks, and share gifts of food with people who have nothing prepared. . . . Don't be dejected and sad, for the joy of the LORD is your strength!" (Nehemiah 8:9-10). The next day marked the beginning of the Festival of Shelters, a required Jewish feast celebrating the Israelites' escape from bondage in Egypt and God's care for them while they wandered in the wilderness.

When we set out to face the pain and sadness of making a moral inventory, we will need the "joy of the LORD" to give us strength. This joy comes from recognizing, even celebrating, God's ability to bring us out of bondage and care for us as we pass through the sadness toward a new way of life. *Turn to page 613, Nehemiah 9.*

[7]The Levites—Jeshua, Bani, Sherebiah, Jamin, Akkub, Shabbethai, Hodiah, Maaseiah, Kelita, Azariah, Jozabad, Hanan, and Pelaiah—then instructed the people in the Law while everyone remained in their places. [8]They read from the Book of the Law of God and clearly explained the meaning of what was being read, helping the people understand each passage.

[9]Then Nehemiah the governor, Ezra the priest and scribe, and the Levites who were interpreting for the people said to them, "Don't mourn or weep on such a day as this! For today is a sacred day before the LORD your God." For the people had all been weeping as they listened to the words of the Law.

[10]And Nehemiah* continued, "Go and celebrate with a feast of rich foods and sweet drinks, and share gifts of food with people who have nothing prepared. This is a sacred day before our Lord. Don't be dejected and sad, for the joy of the LORD is your strength!"

[11]And the Levites, too, quieted the people, telling them, "Hush! Don't weep! For this is a sacred day." [12]So the people went away to eat and drink at a festive meal, to share gifts of food, and to celebrate with great joy because they had heard God's words and understood them.

The Festival of Shelters

[13]On October 9* the family leaders of all the people, together with the priests and Levites, met with Ezra the scribe to go over the Law in greater detail. [14]As they studied the Law, they discovered that the LORD had commanded through Moses that the Israelites should live in shelters during the festival to be held that month.* [15]He had said that a proclamation should be made throughout their towns and in Jerusalem, telling the people to go to the hills to get branches from olive, wild olive,* myrtle, palm, and other leafy trees. They were to use these branches to make shelters in which they would live during the festival, as prescribed in the Law.

[16]So the people went out and cut branches and used them to build shelters on the roofs of their houses, in their courtyards, in the courtyards of God's Temple, or in the squares just inside the Water Gate and the Ephraim Gate. [17]So everyone who had returned from captivity lived in these shelters during the festival, and they were all filled with great joy! The Israelites had not celebrated like this since the days of Joshua* son of Nun.

[18]Ezra read from the Book of the Law of God on each of the seven days of the festival. Then on the eighth day they held a solemn assembly, as was required by law.

CHAPTER 9
The People Confess Their Sins

On October 31* the people assembled again, and this time they fasted and dressed in burlap and sprinkled dust on their heads. [2]Those of Israelite descent separated themselves from all foreigners as they confessed their own sins and the sins of their ancestors. [3]They remained standing in place for three hours* while the Book of the Law of the LORD their God was read aloud to them. Then for three more hours they confessed their sins and worshiped the LORD their God. [4]The Levites—Jeshua, Bani, Kadmiel, Shebaniah, Bunni, Sherebiah, Bani, and Kenani—stood on the stairway of the Levites and cried out to the LORD their God with loud voices.

[5]Then the leaders of the Levites—Jeshua, Kadmiel, Bani, Hashabneiah, Sherebiah, Hodiah, Shebaniah, and Pethahiah—called out to the people: "Stand up and praise the LORD your God, for he lives from everlasting to everlasting!" Then they prayed:

8:10 Hebrew *he.* **8:13** Hebrew *On the second day,* of the seventh month of the ancient Hebrew lunar calendar. This day was October 9, 445 B.C.; also see notes on 1:1 and 8:2. **8:14** Hebrew *in the seventh month.* This month of the ancient Hebrew lunar calendar usually occurs within the months of September and October. See Lev 23:39-43. **8:15** Or *pine;* Hebrew reads *oil tree.* **8:17** Hebrew *Jeshua,* a variant spelling of Joshua. **9:1** Hebrew *On the twenty-fourth day of that same month,* the seventh month of the ancient Hebrew lunar calendar. This day was October 31, 445 B.C.; also see notes on 1:1 and 8:2. **9:3** Hebrew *for a quarter of a day.*

8:12 The people expressed great joy at understanding God's words. They went out rejoicing. They weren't excited about just *hearing* God's words; they were excited because they *understood* God's words. They were overwhelmed by God's power and his great love for them. The same message is true for us today: God is all powerful, and he loves us. God sent his Son to die for our sins so we can live with him forever. Understanding this message should bring us great joy.

9:1-3 Joy was not the people's only response to the Scriptures. Their fresh understanding of the Bible brought about their repentance. They confessed their sins and expressed deep sorrow for disobeying God. They also confessed the sins of their ancestors—a necessary step for us as well if we are to break the dysfunctional patterns of our family's past. When we repent, we recognize and admit our disobedience. Only then can we turn our life and addiction over to God.

"May your glorious name be praised! May it be exalted above all blessing and praise!

6"You alone are the LORD. You made the skies and the heavens and all the stars. You made the earth and the seas and everything in them. You preserve them all, and the angels of heaven worship you.

7"You are the LORD God, who chose Abram and brought him from Ur of the Chaldeans and renamed him Abraham. 8When he had proved himself faithful, you made a covenant with him to give him and his descendants the land of the Canaanites, Hittites, Amorites, Perizzites, Jebusites, and Girgashites. And you have done what you promised, for you are always true to your word.

9"You saw the misery of our ancestors in Egypt, and you heard their cries from beside the Red Sea.* 10You displayed miraculous signs and wonders against Pharaoh, his officials, and all his people, for you knew how arrogantly they were treating our ancestors. You have a glorious reputation that has never been forgotten. 11You divided the sea for your people so they could walk through on dry land! And then you hurled their enemies into the depths of the sea. They sank like stones beneath the mighty waters. 12You led our ancestors by a pillar of cloud during the day and a pillar of fire at night so that they could find their way.

13"You came down at Mount Sinai and spoke to them from heaven. You gave them regulations and instructions that were just, and decrees and commands that were good. 14You instructed them concerning your holy Sabbath. And you commanded them, through Moses your servant, to obey all your commands, decrees, and instructions.

15"You gave them bread from heaven when they were hungry and water from the rock when they were thirsty. You commanded them to go and take possession of the land you had sworn to give them.

16"But our ancestors were proud and stubborn, and they paid no attention to your commands. 17They refused to obey and did not remember the miracles you had done for them. Instead, they became stubborn and appointed a leader to take them back to their slavery in Egypt.* But you are a God of forgiveness, gracious

9:9 Hebrew *sea of reeds.* 9:17 As in Greek version; Hebrew reads *in their rebellion.*

STEP 4

Confession

BIBLE READING: Nehemiah 9:1-3

We made a searching and fearless moral inventory of ourselves.

As we make our moral inventory, we will probably find ourself listing our destructive habits, our defects of character, the wrongs we have done, the consequences of wrong choices that we now live with, and the hurts we have caused others. It's like sifting through all the garbage in our past. This is painful, but it is a necessary part of throwing away those rotten habits and behaviors that, if not dealt with, will almost certainly spoil the rest of our life.

The returned Jewish exiles "confessed their own sins." This phrase speaks volumes. The idea of confession involves not only owning up to one's sins but being truly sorry for them as well. Sins are offenses against God, including any transgressions against his will. The natural follow-up to true confession, after owning up to our sins and bemoaning them before God, is to turn from them. The Israelites' confession can serve as a model for us to follow as we take our moral inventory. We can list the occasions of our offenses, our destructive habits, and the consequences we have brought into our life and the lives of others. Then, after accounting for all the garbage, we can "take out the trash."

In their confession, the Israelites owned, bemoaned, and then discarded their sins. After this they were better able to make a new start. We can "own" the garbage in our own life by taking personal responsibility for our choices and actions. We can "bemoan" it by allowing ourself to grieve. We can "discard" it by leaving it behind and turning toward the future. *Turn to page 615, Nehemiah 9.*

and merciful, slow to become angry, and rich in unfailing love. You did not abandon them, [18]even when they made an idol shaped like a calf and said, 'This is your god who brought you out of Egypt!' They committed terrible blasphemies.

[19]"But in your great mercy you did not abandon them to die in the wilderness. The pillar of cloud still led them forward by day, and the pillar of fire showed them the way through the night. [20]You sent your good Spirit to instruct them, and you did not stop giving them manna from heaven or water for their thirst. [21]For forty years you sustained them in the wilderness, and they lacked nothing. Their clothes did not wear out, and their feet did not swell!

[22]"Then you helped our ancestors conquer kingdoms and nations, and you placed your people in every corner of the land.* They took over the land of King Sihon of Heshbon and the land of King Og of Bashan. [23]You made their descendants as numerous as the stars in the sky and brought them into the land you had promised to their ancestors.

[24]"They went in and took possession of the land. You subdued whole nations before them. Even the Canaanites, who inhabited the land, were powerless! Your people could deal with these nations and their kings as they pleased. [25]Our ancestors captured fortified cities and fertile land. They took over houses full of good things, with cisterns already dug and vineyards and olive groves and fruit trees in abundance. So they ate until they were full and grew fat and enjoyed themselves in all your blessings.

[26]"But despite all this, they were disobedient and rebelled against you. They turned their backs on your Law, they killed your prophets who warned them to return to you, and they committed terrible blasphemies. [27]So you handed them over to their enemies, who made them suffer. But in their time of trouble they cried to you, and you heard them from heaven. In your great mercy, you sent them liberators who rescued them from their enemies.

[28]"But as soon as they were at peace, your people again committed evil in your sight, and once more you let their enemies conquer them. Yet whenever your people turned and cried to you again for help, you listened once more from heaven. In your wonderful mercy, you rescued them many times!

[29]"You warned them to return to your Law, but they became proud and obstinate and disobeyed your commands. They did not follow your regulations, by which people will find life if only they obey. They stubbornly turned their backs on you and refused to listen. [30]In your love, you were patient with them for many years. You sent your Spirit, who warned them through the prophets. But still they wouldn't listen! So once again you allowed the peoples of the land to conquer them. [31]But in your great mercy, you did not destroy them completely or abandon them forever. What a gracious and merciful God you are!

[32]"And now, our God, the great and mighty and awesome God, who keeps his covenant of unfailing love, do not let all the hardships we have suffered seem insignificant to you. Great trouble has come upon us and upon our kings and leaders and priests and prophets and ancestors—all of your people—from the days when the kings of Assyria first triumphed over us until now. [33]Every time you punished us you were being just. We have sinned greatly, and you gave us only what we deserved. [34]Our kings, leaders, priests, and ancestors did not obey your Law or listen to the warnings in your commands and laws. [35]Even while they had their own kingdom, they did not serve you, though you showered your goodness on them. You gave them a large, fertile land, but they refused to turn from their wickedness.

[36]"So now today we are slaves in the land of plenty that you gave our ancestors for their enjoyment! We are slaves here in this good land. [37]The lush produce of this

9:22 The meaning of the Hebrew is uncertain.

9:38 Every believer needs to be part of a specific structure of accountability. To establish such accountability, the religious leaders in Israel formally wrote out this pact; the leaders pledged themselves to be accountable to God and to each other. We must not try to live a godly life by ourself. We need others to uplift us, encourage us, and pray for us.

land piles up in the hands of the kings whom you have set over us because of our sins. They have power over us and our livestock. We serve them at their pleasure, and we are in great misery."

The People Agree to Obey
38*The people responded, "In view of all this,* we are making a solemn promise and putting it in writing. On this sealed document are the names of our leaders and Levites and priests."

CHAPTER 10
1*The document was ratified and sealed with the following names:

The governor:
Nehemiah son of Hacaliah, and also Zedekiah.
2The following priests:
Seraiah, Azariah, Jeremiah, 3Pashhur, Amariah, Malkijah, 4Hattush, Shebaniah, Malluch, 5Harim, Meremoth, Obadiah, 6Daniel, Ginnethon, Baruch, 7Meshullam, Abijah, Mijamin, 8Maaziah, Bilgai, and Shemaiah. These were the priests.
9The following Levites:
Jeshua son of Azaniah, Binnui from the family of Henadad, Kadmiel, 10and their fellow Levites: Shebaniah, Hodiah, Kelita, Pelaiah, Hanan, 11Mica, Rehob, Hashabiah, 12Zaccur, Sherebiah, Shebaniah, 13Hodiah, Bani, and Beninu.
14The following leaders:
Parosh, Pahath-moab, Elam, Zattu, Bani, 15Bunni, Azgad, Bebai, 16Adonijah, Bigvai, Adin, 17Ater, Hezekiah, Azzur, 18Hodiah, Hashum, Bezai, 19Hariph, Anathoth, Nebai, 20Magpiash, Meshullam, Hezir, 21Meshezabel, Zadok, Jaddua, 22Pelatiah, Hanan, Anaiah, 23Hoshea, Hananiah, Hasshub, 24Hallohesh, Pilha, Shobek, 25Rehum, Hashabnah, Maaseiah, 26Ahiah, Hanan, Anan, 27Malluch, Harim, and Baanah.

The Vow of the People
28Then the rest of the people—the priests, Levites, gatekeepers, singers, Temple servants, and all who had separated themselves from the pagan people of the land in order to obey the Law of God, together with their wives, sons, daughters, and all who were old enough to understand—29joined their leaders and

9:38a Verse 9:38 is numbered 10:1 in Hebrew text.
9:38b Or In spite of all this.   10:1 Verses 10:1-39 are numbered 10:2-40 in Hebrew text.

STEP 4

Family Influence
BIBLE READING: Nehemiah 9:34-38
We made a searching and fearless moral inventory of ourselves.
Our family of origin has had an influence on who we are today. Some of us want to pretend that our family was, or is, nearly perfect. Others of us may tend to avoid responsibility for our actions by blaming our family. Whatever the case, when we think about our own life, we also need to deal with our family and the effects its members have had on who we are today.

We are told that the returned Jewish exiles "confessed their own sins and the sins of their ancestors" (Nehemiah 9:2). They blamed their ancestors for their captivity and the difficult situation they were facing. They said, "[Our ancestors] refused to turn from their wickedness. So now today we are slaves in the land of plenty that you gave our ancestors for their enjoyment! . . . We serve [conquering kings] at their pleasure, and we are in great misery" (Nehemiah 9:35-37).

It's all right to admit the truth about what brought us into bondage. This might very well involve the wrongs committed by our parents and other family members. It's perfectly all right to express our anger and regret over what has been done to us. We have a right to hold others accountable and grieve over the negative effects their actions have had on our life. That is all part of the real picture. It's not all right, however, to use this as an excuse for our wrong choices or for staying in bondage. Our relatives may be partly responsible for bringing us to this point, but we are responsible for moving on to a better place for ourself and our family.
Turn to page 1207, Matthew 7.

bound themselves with an oath. They swore a curse on themselves if they failed to obey the Law of God as issued by his servant Moses. They solemnly promised to carefully follow all the commands, regulations, and decrees of the LORD our Lord:

30"We promise not to let our daughters marry the pagan people of the land, and not to let our sons marry their daughters. 31"We also promise that if the people of the land should bring any merchandise or grain to be sold on the Sabbath or on any other holy day, we will refuse to buy it. Every seventh year we will let our land rest, and we will cancel all debts owed to us. 32"In addition, we promise to obey the command to pay the annual Temple tax of one-eighth of an ounce of silver* for the care of the Temple of our God. 33This will provide for the Bread of the Presence; for the regular grain offerings and burnt offerings; for the offerings on the Sabbaths, the new moon celebrations, and the annual festivals; for the holy offerings; and for the sin offerings to make atonement for Israel. It will provide for everything necessary for the work of the Temple of our God. 34"We have cast sacred lots to determine when—at regular times each year—the families of the priests, Levites, and the common people should bring wood to God's Temple to be burned on the altar of the LORD our God, as is written in the Law. 35"We promise to bring the first part of every harvest to the LORD's Temple year after year—whether it be a crop from the soil or from our fruit trees. 36We agree to give God our oldest sons and the firstborn of all our herds and flocks, as prescribed in the Law. We will present them to the priests who minister in the Temple of our God. 37We will store the produce in the storerooms of the Temple of our God. We will bring the best of our flour and other grain offerings, the best of our fruit, and the best of our new wine and olive oil. And we promise to bring to the Levites a tenth of everything our land produces, for it is the Levites who collect the tithes in all our rural towns.

38"A priest—a descendant of Aaron—will be with the Levites as they receive these tithes. And a tenth of all that is collected as tithes will be delivered by the Levites to the Temple of our God and placed in the storerooms. 39The people and the Levites must bring these offerings of grain, new wine, and olive oil to the storerooms and place them in the sacred containers near the ministering priests, the gatekeepers, and the singers.

"We promise together not to neglect the Temple of our God."

CHAPTER 11
The People Occupy Jerusalem

The leaders of the people were living in Jerusalem, the holy city. A tenth of the people from the other towns of Judah and Benjamin were chosen by sacred lots to live there, too, while the rest stayed where they were. 2And the people commended everyone who volunteered to resettle in Jerusalem.

3Here is a list of the names of the provincial officials who came to live in Jerusalem. (Most of the people, priests, Levites, Temple servants, and descendants of Solomon's servants continued to live in their own homes in the various towns of Judah, 4but some of the people from Judah and Benjamin resettled in Jerusalem.)

From the tribe of Judah:
Athaiah son of Uzziah, son of Zechariah, son of Amariah, son of Shephatiah, son of Mahalalel, of the family of Perez. 5Also Maaseiah son of Baruch, son of Col-hozeh, son of Hazaiah, son of Adaiah, son of Joiarib, son of Zechariah, of the family of Shelah.* 6There were 468 descendants of Perez who lived in Jerusalem—all outstanding men.

7From the tribe of Benjamin:
Sallu son of Meshullam, son of Joed, son of Pedaiah, son of Kolaiah, son of Maaseiah, son of Ithiel, son of Jeshaiah. 8After him were Gabbai and Sallai and a

10:32 Hebrew *tax of 1/3 of a shekel* [4 grams]. 11:5 Hebrew *son of the Shilonite.*

10:39 Here the people agreed to not neglect the Temple, God's dwelling place among them. Today we have a temple to care for, too—our body. "Don't you realize that your body is the temple of the Holy Spirit, who lives in you and was given to you by God? You do not belong to yourself" (1 Corinthians 6:19). We should take care of our body and treat it with respect because God's Holy Spirit dwells within it. To mistreat our body with an addiction is to mistreat God's own dwelling place.

total of 928 relatives. ⁹Their chief officer was Joel son of Zicri, who was assisted by Judah son of Hassenuah, second-in-command over the city.
¹⁰From the priests:
Jedaiah son of Joiarib; Jakin; ¹¹and Seraiah son of Hilkiah, son of Meshullam, son of Zadok, son of Meraioth, son of Ahitub, the supervisor of the Temple of God.
¹²Also 822 of their associates, who worked at the Temple. Also Adaiah son of Jeroham, son of Pelaliah, son of Amzi, son of Zechariah, son of Pashhur, son of Malkijah, ¹³along with 242 of his associates, who were heads of their families. Also Amashsai son of Azarel, son of Ahzai, son of Meshillemoth, son of Immer, ¹⁴and 128 of his* outstanding associates. Their chief officer was Zabdiel son of Haggedolim.
¹⁵From the Levites:
Shemaiah son of Hasshub, son of Azrikam, son of Hashabiah, son of Bunni.
¹⁶Also Shabbethai and Jozabad, who were in charge of the work outside the Temple of God. ¹⁷Also Mattaniah son of Mica, son of Zabdi, a descendant of Asaph, who led in thanksgiving and prayer. Also Bakbukiah, who was Mattaniah's assistant, and Abda son of Shammua, son of Galal, son of Jeduthun. ¹⁸In all, there were 284 Levites in the holy city.
¹⁹From the gatekeepers:
Akkub, Talmon, and 172 of their associates, who guarded the gates.

²⁰The other priests, Levites, and the rest of the Israelites lived wherever their family inheritance was located in any of the towns of Judah. ²¹The Temple servants, however, whose leaders were Ziha and Gishpa, all lived on the hill of Ophel.
²²The chief officer of the Levites in Jerusalem was Uzzi son of Bani, son of Hashabiah, son of Mattaniah, son of Mica, a descendant of Asaph, whose family served as singers at God's Temple. ²³Their daily responsibilities were carried out according to the terms of a royal command.
²⁴Pethahiah son of Meshezabel, a descendant of Zerah son of Judah, was the royal adviser in all matters of public administration.
²⁵As for the surrounding villages with their open fields, some of the people of Judah lived in Kiriath-arba with its settlements, Dibon with its settlements, and Jekabzeel with its villages. ²⁶They also lived in Jeshua, Moladah, Beth-pelet, ²⁷Hazar-shual, Beersheba with its settlements, ²⁸Ziklag, and Meconah with its settlements. ²⁹They also lived in En-rimmon, Zorah, Jarmuth, ³⁰Zanoah, and Adullam with their surrounding villages. They also lived in Lachish with its nearby fields and Azekah with its surrounding villages. So the people of Judah were living all the way from Beersheba in the south to the valley of Hinnom.
³¹Some of the people of Benjamin lived at Geba, Micmash, Aija, and Bethel with its settlements. ³²They also lived in Anathoth, Nob, Ananiah, ³³Hazor, Ramah, Gittaim, ³⁴Hadid, Zeboim, Neballat, ³⁵Lod, Ono, and the Valley of Craftsmen.* ³⁶Some of the Levites who lived in Judah were sent to live with the tribe of Benjamin.

CHAPTER 12
A History of the Priests and Levites
Here is the list of the priests and Levites who returned with Zerubbabel son of Shealtiel and Jeshua the high priest:

Seraiah, Jeremiah, Ezra,
² Amariah, Malluch, Hattush,
³ Shecaniah, Harim,* Meremoth,
⁴ Iddo, Ginnethon,* Abijah,
⁵ Miniamin, Moadiah,* Bilgah,
⁶ Shemaiah, Joiarib, Jedaiah,
⁷ Sallu, Amok, Hilkiah, and Jedaiah.
These were the leaders of the priests and their associates in the days of Jeshua.

⁸The Levites who returned with them were Jeshua, Binnui, Kadmiel, Sherebiah, Judah, and Mattaniah, who with his associates was in charge of the songs of thanksgiving. ⁹Their associates, Bakbukiah and Unni, stood opposite them during the service.

¹⁰ Jeshua the high priest was the father of Joiakim.
Joiakim was the father of Eliashib.
Eliashib was the father of Joiada.
¹¹ Joiada was the father of Johanan.*
Johanan was the father of Jaddua.

¹²Now when Joiakim was high priest, the family leaders of the priests were as follows:

Meraiah was leader of the family of Seraiah.
Hananiah was leader of the family of Jeremiah.

11:14 As in Greek version; Hebrew reads *their.* 11:35 Or *and Ge-harashim.* 12:3 Hebrew *Rehum;* compare 7:42; 12:15; Ezra 2:39. 12:4 As in some Hebrew manuscripts and Latin Vulgate (see also 12:16); most Hebrew manuscripts read *Ginnethoi.* 12:5 Hebrew *Mijamin, Maadiah;* compare 12:17. 12:11 Hebrew *Jonathan;* compare 12:22.

[13] Meshullam was leader of the family of Ezra.
Jehohanan was leader of the family of Amariah.
[14] Jonathan was leader of the family of Malluch.*
Joseph was leader of the family of Shecaniah.*
[15] Adna was leader of the family of Harim.
Helkai was leader of the family of Meremoth.*
[16] Zechariah was leader of the family of Iddo.
Meshullam was leader of the family of Ginnethon.
[17] Zicri was leader of the family of Abijah.
There was also a* leader of the family of Miniamin.
Piltai was leader of the family of Moadiah.
[18] Shammua was leader of the family of Bilgah.
Jehonathan was leader of the family of Shemaiah.
[19] Mattenai was leader of the family of Joiarib.
Uzzi was leader of the family of Jedaiah.
[20] Kallai was leader of the family of Sallu.*
Eber was leader of the family of Amok.
[21] Hashabiah was leader of the family of Hilkiah.
Nethanel was leader of the family of Jedaiah.

[22] A record of the Levite families was kept during the years when Eliashib, Joiada, Johanan, and Jaddua served as high priest. Another record of the priests was kept during the reign of Darius the Persian.* [23] A record of the heads of the Levite families was kept in *The Book of History* down to the days of Johanan, the grandson* of Eliashib.

[24] These were the family leaders of the Levites: Hashabiah, Sherebiah, Jeshua, Binnui,* Kadmiel, and other associates, who stood opposite them during the ceremonies of praise and thanksgiving, one section responding to the other, as commanded by David, the man of God. [25] This included Mattaniah, Bakbukiah, and Obadiah.

Meshullam, Talmon, and Akkub were the gatekeepers in charge of the storerooms at the gates. [26] These all served in the days of Joiakim son of Jeshua, son of Jehozadak,* and in the days of Nehemiah the governor and of Ezra the priest and scribe.

Dedication of Jerusalem's Wall

[27] For the dedication of the new wall of Jerusalem, the Levites throughout the land were asked to come to Jerusalem to assist in the ceremonies. They were to take part in the joyous occasion with their songs of thanksgiving and with the music of cymbals, harps, and lyres. [28] The singers were brought together from the region around Jerusalem and from the villages of the Netophathites. [29] They also came from Beth-gilgal and the rural areas near Geba and Azmaveth, for the singers had built their own settlements around Jerusalem. [30] The priests and Levites first purified themselves; then they purified the people, the gates, and the wall.

[31] I led the leaders of Judah to the top of the wall and organized two large choirs to give thanks. One of the choirs proceeded southward* along the top of the wall to the Dung Gate. [32] Hoshaiah and half the leaders of Judah followed them, [33] along with Azariah, Ezra, Meshullam, [34] Judah, Benjamin, Shemaiah, and Jeremiah. [35] Then came some priests who played trumpets, including Zechariah son of Jonathan, son of Shemaiah, son of Mattaniah, son of Micaiah, son of Zaccur, a descendant of Asaph. [36] And Zechariah's colleagues were Shemaiah, Azarel, Milalai, Gilalai, Maai, Nethanel, Judah, and Hanani. They used the musical instruments prescribed by David, the man of God. Ezra the scribe led this procession. [37] At the Fountain Gate they went straight up the steps on

---

12:14a As in Greek version (see also 10:4; 12:2); Hebrew reads *Malluchi*.   12:14b As in many Hebrew manuscripts, some Greek manuscripts, and Syriac version (see also 12:3); most Hebrew manuscripts read *Shebaniah*.   12:15 As in some Greek manuscripts (see also 12:3); Hebrew reads *Meraioth*.   12:17 Hebrew lacks the name of this family leader.
12:20 Hebrew *Sallai*; compare 12:7.   12:22 *Darius the Persian* is probably Darius II, who reigned 423–404 B.C., or possibly Darius III, who reigned 336–331 B.C.   12:23 Hebrew *descendant*; compare 12:10-11.   12:24 Hebrew *son of* (i.e., *ben*), which should probably be read here as the proper name Binnui; compare Ezra 3:9 and the note there.
12:26 Hebrew *Jozadak*, a variant spelling of Jehozadak.   12:31 Hebrew *to the right*.

12:27 As God's people, we have the privilege and the reason to celebrate. All the worship leaders were called upon to come to Jerusalem to dedicate the new wall. This was to be the most joyful occasion in Israel in over half a century! We should take time to joyfully dedicate in our life both the building of healthy boundaries and the tearing down of walls that prevent us from being authentic.

the ascent of the city wall toward the City of David. They passed the house of David and then proceeded to the Water Gate on the east.

[38]The second choir giving thanks went northward* around the other way to meet them. I followed them, together with the other half of the people, along the top of the wall past the Tower of the Ovens to the Broad Wall, [39]then past the Ephraim Gate to the Old City Gate,* past the Fish Gate and the Tower of Hananel, and on to the Tower of the Hundred. Then we continued on to the Sheep Gate and stopped at the Guard Gate.

[40]The two choirs that were giving thanks then proceeded to the Temple of God, where they took their places. So did I, together with the group of leaders who were with me. [41]We went together with the trumpet-playing priests—Eliakim, Maaseiah, Miniamin, Micaiah, Elioenai, Zechariah, and Hananiah—[42]and the singers—Maaseiah, Shemaiah, Eleazar, Uzzi, Jehohanan, Malkijah, Elam, and Ezer. They played and sang loudly under the direction of Jezrahiah the choir director.

[43]Many sacrifices were offered on that joyous day, for God had given the people cause for great joy. The women and children also participated in the celebration, and the joy of the people of Jerusalem could be heard far away.

Provisions for Temple Worship
[44]On that day men were appointed to be in charge of the storerooms for the offerings, the first part of the harvest, and the tithes. They were responsible to collect from the fields outside the towns the portions required by the Law for the priests and Levites. For all the people of Judah took joy in the priests and Levites and their work. [45]They

performed the service of their God and the service of purification, as commanded by David and his son Solomon, and so did the singers and the gatekeepers. [46]The custom of having choir directors to lead the choirs in hymns of praise and thanksgiving to God began long ago in the days of David and Asaph. [47]So now, in the days of Zerubbabel and of Nehemiah, all Israel brought a daily supply of food for the singers, the gatekeepers, and the Levites. The Levites, in turn, gave a portion of what they received to the priests, the descendants of Aaron.

CHAPTER 13
Nehemiah's Various Reforms
On that same day, as the Book of Moses was being read to the people, the passage was found that said no Ammonite or Moabite should ever be permitted to enter the assembly of God.* [2]For they had not provided the Israelites with food and water in the wilderness. Instead, they hired Balaam to curse them, though our God turned the curse into a blessing. [3]When this passage of the Law was read, all those of foreign descent were immediately excluded from the assembly.

[4]Before this had happened, Eliashib the priest, who had been appointed as supervisor of the storerooms of the Temple of our God and who was also a relative of Tobiah, [5]had converted a large storage room and placed it at Tobiah's disposal. The room had previously been used for storing the grain offerings, the frankincense, various articles for the Temple, and the tithes of grain, new wine, and olive oil (which were prescribed for the Levites, the singers, and the gatekeepers), as well as the offerings for the priests.

[6]I was not in Jerusalem at that time, for I had returned to King Artaxerxes of Babylon in

12:38 Hebrew *to the left.* 12:39 Or *the Mishneh Gate,* or *the Jeshanah Gate.* 13:1 See Deut 23:3-6.

13:1-3, 23-30 For the people of Israel to accomplish God's purpose of being the nation to bring the Messiah into the world, it was necessary for them to remain pure. They were not to mix with the godless population around them, and those with mixed ancestry were not allowed in the Temple. But some of the Israelites had intermarried. Nehemiah had to purge the nation of foreigners so Israel would not be contaminated by false religions. The recovery process is either strengthened or weakened by our relationships. As we mature, we may need to sacrifice some of our "friends" for the sake of our long-term goal.

13:4-9 Close relationships with God's enemies are never acceptable. In this hideous case, one of the Temple administrators provided a room within the Temple for Tobiah, one of Nehemiah's chief opponents (see 2:10; 4:7-8; 6:1-2). From this strategic location in the very heart of Jerusalem, Tobiah could have undermined God's authority and his place in the Israelites' lives. Each of us must evaluate the health of our relationships and act accordingly, to either terminate or nurture them. If we allow people into our life who do not recognize God as Lord of their life, we are allowing ourself to be influenced for evil. Much of the work we have done in recovery could be negated by even one such relationship.

the thirty-second year of his reign,* though I later asked his permission to return. [7]When I arrived back in Jerusalem, I learned about Eliashib's evil deed in providing Tobiah with a room in the courtyards of the Temple of God. [8]I became very upset and threw all of Tobiah's belongings out of the room. [9]Then I demanded that the rooms be purified, and I brought back the articles for God's Temple, the grain offerings, and the frankincense.

[10]I also discovered that the Levites had not been given their prescribed portions of food, so they and the singers who were to conduct the worship services had all returned to work their fields. [11]I immediately confronted the leaders and demanded, "Why has the Temple of God been neglected?" Then I called all the Levites back again and restored them to their proper duties. [12]And once more all the people of Judah began bringing their tithes of grain, new wine, and olive oil to the Temple storerooms.

[13]I assigned supervisors for the storerooms: Shelemiah the priest, Zadok the scribe, and Pedaiah, one of the Levites. And I appointed Hanan son of Zaccur and grandson of Mattaniah as their assistant. These men had an excellent reputation, and it was their job to make honest distributions to their fellow Levites.

[14]Remember this good deed, O my God, and do not forget all that I have faithfully done for the Temple of my God and its services.

[15]In those days I saw men of Judah treading out their winepresses on the Sabbath. They were also bringing in grain, loading it on donkeys, and bringing their wine, grapes, figs, and all sorts of produce to Jerusalem to sell on the Sabbath. So I rebuked them for selling their produce on that day. [16]Some men from Tyre, who lived in Jerusalem, were bringing in fish and all kinds of merchandise. They were selling it on the Sabbath to the people of Judah—and in Jerusalem at that!

[17]So I confronted the nobles of Judah. "Why are you profaning the Sabbath in this evil way?" I asked. [18]"Wasn't it just this sort of thing that your ancestors did that caused our God to bring all this trouble upon us and our city? Now you are bringing even more wrath upon Israel by permitting the Sabbath to be desecrated in this way!"

[19]Then I commanded that the gates of Jerusalem should be shut as darkness fell every Friday evening,* not to be opened until the Sabbath ended. I sent some of my own servants to guard the gates so that no merchandise could be brought in on the Sabbath day. [20]The merchants and tradesmen with a variety of wares camped outside Jerusalem once or twice. [21]But I spoke sharply to them and said, "What are you doing out here, camping around the wall? If you do this again, I will arrest you!" And that was the last time they came on the Sabbath. [22]Then I commanded the Levites to purify themselves and to guard the gates in order to preserve the holiness of the Sabbath.

Remember this good deed also, O my God! Have compassion on me according to your great and unfailing love.

[23]About the same time I realized that some of the men of Judah had married women from Ashdod, Ammon, and Moab. [24]Furthermore, half their children spoke the language of Ashdod or of some other people and could not speak the language of Judah at all. [25]So I confronted them and called down curses on them. I beat some of them and pulled out their hair. I made them swear in the name of God that they would not let their children intermarry with the pagan people of the land.

[26]"Wasn't this exactly what led King Solomon of Israel into sin?" I demanded. "There was no king from any nation who could compare to him, and God loved him and made him king over all Israel. But even he was led into sin by his foreign wives. [27]How could you even think of committing this sinful deed and acting unfaithfully toward God by marrying foreign women?"

[28]One of the sons of Joiada son of Eliashib the high priest had married a daughter of Sanballat the Horonite, so I banished him from my presence.

13:6 King Artaxerxes of Persia is here identified as the king of Babylon because Persia had conquered the Babylonian Empire. The thirty-second year of Artaxerxes was 433 B.C. 13:19 Hebrew *on the day before the Sabbath.*

13:14, 22, 31 Nehemiah was a great rebuilder. He reconstructed the wall of Jerusalem. He helped the people rebuild their broken lives. There is no question that God gave credit for these deeds to this good and faithful servant. God will honor our attempts to rebuild, too. We will also experience God's compassion in our life.

²⁹Remember them, O my God, for they have defiled the priesthood and the solemn vows of the priests and Levites.

³⁰So I purged out everything foreign and assigned tasks to the priests and Levites, making certain that each knew his work. ³¹I also made sure that the supply of wood for the altar and the first portions of the harvest were brought at the proper times.

Remember this in my favor, O my God.

REFLECTIONS ON **NEHEMIAH**

insights FROM THE MINISTRY OF NEHEMIAH

Great affliction and reproach! Ruins and wreckage! In **Nehemiah 1:1-4** we see a situation that demanded rebuilding and recovery. When Nehemiah heard of the circumstances in Jerusalem, he was immediately touched. He wanted to do something about it. As we take inventory of our own life, we must take careful note of what areas need specific work. Rebuilding cannot take place until we know where to begin.

In **Nehemiah 2:17-18** Nehemiah performed a ministry of encouragement. He was completely honest about the people's problems; he didn't deny or underestimate their needs. Then he reminded them of God's powerful hand and challenged them to get on with the work. We all need a Nehemiah in our life—someone who will honestly tell us what needs fixing and who will then stick close to help us complete the task. How do we handle ridicule and disdain? In **Nehemiah 4:4-9** Nehemiah offers us a magnificent example. In such times, it is essential that we seek God and keep on guard. Nehemiah countered ridicule with prayer. Not only did he pray, but he also set a twenty-four-hour watch, guarding against an attack day and night. While it is important to pray to God for help with our life, we must also be on the lookout for physical attacks from our enemies. Prayer must be balanced with action. One person can't do everything. In **Nehemiah 4:14-18** Nehemiah recognized this and divided the tasks of defense and construction. This illustrates the truth that exterior attacks don't disappear just because we are busy focusing on our spiritual interior. We need to be prepared for attacks from external enemies who will try to take advantage of our busyness. This is especially true in recovery.

insights FROM THE MINISTRY OF EZRA

In **Nehemiah 8:1-5** Ezra took on the essential task of spiritual rebuilding in the lives of the citizens. Now that the wall of Jerusalem had been rebuilt and its streets were safe, Ezra was able to give attention to the reading of the law. It is imperative to remember that the Bible contains the directions and resources for rebuilding broken lives. While we may obtain physical recovery, it is also necessary to recover spiritually (through salvation by belief in Jesus Christ) to remain free from our addiction. God is the foundation on which we must build our new life.

insights FROM THE PEOPLE'S EXPERIENCE OF WORSHIP

In **Nehemiah 8:9-10** we find an example of God's people openly expressing their emotions. Elsewhere in the Bible we see that Job expressed his emotions to his friends; King David poured out his heart in his many psalms, pleading with God to rescue him; and Jesus showed emotions, crying on occasion (see John 11). God expects us to be open and honest in our expressions of emotion. Too often, out of fear of appearing weak, we refuse to express our emotions, only to have them grow in intensity and haunt us for years. Venting our emotions is the best way to overcome the grief or despair we experience.

In **Nehemiah 9:4-38** we read pure, unmitigated words of praise to God. As the Levites sang this beautiful hymn, they gloried in the person of God—who he was and what he had done. There is something therapeutic in recognizing God for who he is. We can gain much by reading the words of this hymn of praise and by making the words our own.

ESTHER

THE BIG PICTURE

A. ESTHER BECOMES QUEEN
   (1:1–2:23)
   1. Dethronement of Vashti
      (1:1-22)
   2. Enthronement of Esther
      (2:1-23)
B. A THREAT AGAINST GOD'S
   PEOPLE (3:1–7:10)
   1. The Rise of the Enemy of
      God's People (3:1-15)
   2. The Commitment of a
      Leader of God's People
      (4:1–5:14)
   3. The Fall of the Enemy of
      God's People (6:1–7:10)
C. MORDECAI SECURES THEIR
   RECOVERY (8:1–10:3)
   1. The Plan of a Rescue
      Operation (8:1-17)
   2. The Process of a Rescue
      Operation (9:1-32)
   3. The Product of a Rescue
      Operation (10:1-3)

The book of Esther tells a story about God's loving care for his people during the Babylonian exile. Although nearly 50,000 Jews had returned to Jerusalem with Zerubbabel to rebuild the Temple, the majority had remained in Babylonia, which by this time was ruled by Persia. Esther was raised among the Jewish community in exile. The Persian king Xerxes deposed his queen for disobedience and later held a contest to find a new queen. Esther was chosen.

Soon after Esther became queen, the king appointed Haman, an Agagite, to the position of second in command. All people in the empire were expected to bow down to show him respect. Mordecai, Esther's older cousin, refused to bow down; this so enraged Haman that he had the king enact an irrevocable edict sentencing all Jews to death. Neither the king nor Haman knew that Esther was among the people doomed by the edict. Through Mordecai's prodding, Esther secured the king's favor to deliver her people and brought about Haman's demise.

In the Hebrew Bible, God's name never actually appears in this story. Yet throughout the book we see God's quiet yet effective activity behind the scenes. We see him work through different individuals who are willing to trust him. He brought Esther to a position of influence at just the right time and gave her the courage to act. Esther could have remained selfishly silent. Instead, she risked her life and became an instrument of great deliverance. Even though God's presence is not always obvious in our life, we can be sure that he is behind the scenes, working to protect us and lead us to recovery.

THE BOTTOM LINE

PURPOSE: To demonstrate God's loving care for his people and his sovereignty over history and to record the origins of the Jewish holiday of Purim. AUTHOR: Unknown; it may have been written by Mordecai or Ezra. AUDIENCE: The people of Israel after the Babylonian exile. DATE WRITTEN: Approximately 470 B.C.; Esther became queen in 479. SETTING: In Susa, the capital of Medo-Persia. KEY VERSE: "If you keep quiet at a time like this, deliverance and relief for the Jews will arise from some other place, but you and your relatives will die. Who knows if perhaps you were made queen for just such a time as this?" (4:14). KEY PEOPLE AND RELATIONSHIPS: Esther with Mordecai, Haman, King Xerxes, Queen Vashti.

RECOVERY THEMES

Hope for the Helpless: When we recognize that we are powerless over our problems, we are in a place of great opportunity if we turn things over to God. This was exactly the experience of Esther, Mordecai, and the Jews during their exile under Persian rule. They were in captivity. Their lives were out of their own control and under the control of Persian rulers. It was in this situation of helplessness that God worked through Esther and Mordecai to bring amazing deliverance to God's people. When we put ourself in God's hands, our success will be defined by God's power, not our weakness.

God's Faithfulness: When we turn our life and our will over to God, we can take courage. We can expect him to display his power in carrying out his will in our life. As we unite our will with his, we benefit from his faithfulness. He does this in spite of our doubts and even in spite of our desires. One of the great lessons we can learn from Esther is how God acts on our behalf even when we are unaware of what he is doing. He is a God who can be trusted to underwrite the recovery process, for even when we are faithless, he always remains faithful!

The Emptiness of Hatred: Haman was driven by racial prejudice and hatred. In the blindness of his own hatred, Haman determined his own punishment and died the death he had planned for the one he hated— Mordecai. Racial hatred is always sinful. It is sinful because it denies the intrinsic value of God's creation. When we hate in this way, we end up with an awful emptiness that works toward our destruction through bitterness and isolation.

Dealing with Pressures: It takes great wisdom and patience to survive in a world that does not acknowledge God or is little concerned with the recovery process. Mordecai shows us how to resist the pressures around us: He learned all he could about the Persian system and law but never compromised his own integrity. He continued to respect what was true and good. He was obedient to the God of all truth and was able to show wisdom in the face of everyday pressures.

CHAPTER 1
The King's Banquet

These events happened in the days of King Xerxes,* who reigned over 127 provinces stretching from India to Ethiopia.* ²At that time Xerxes ruled his empire from his royal throne at the fortress of Susa. ³In the third year of his reign, he gave a banquet for all his nobles and officials. He invited all the military officers of Persia and Media as well as the princes and nobles of the provinces. ⁴The celebration lasted 180 days—a tremendous display of the opulent wealth of his empire and the pomp and splendor of his majesty.

⁵When it was all over, the king gave a banquet for all the people, from the greatest to the least, who were in the fortress of Susa. It lasted for seven days and was held in the courtyard of the palace garden. ⁶The courtyard was beautifully decorated with white cotton curtains and blue hangings, which were fastened with white linen cords and purple ribbons to silver rings embedded in marble pillars. Gold and silver couches stood on a mosaic pavement of porphyry, marble, mother-of-pearl, and other costly stones.

⁷Drinks were served in gold goblets of many designs, and there was an abundance of royal wine, reflecting the king's generosity. ⁸By edict of the king, no limits were placed on the drinking, for the king had instructed all his palace officials to serve each man as much as he wanted.

⁹At the same time, Queen Vashti gave a banquet for the women in the royal palace of King Xerxes.

1:1a Hebrew *Ahasuerus*, another name for Xerxes; also throughout the book of Esther. Xerxes reigned 486–465 B.C.
1:1b Hebrew *to Cush.*

1:1-8 Having only recently established his kingdom, King Xerxes attempted to curry the favor of his leaders (perhaps to assure their allegiance for an upcoming war) by holding a six-month celebration at Susa, the royal winter residence. Following the celebration, the king threw a banquet for all the palace personnel—"from the greatest to the least." Although it was customary for the king to control how much wine each person drank, Xerxes let all the party-goers determine this for themselves. He set no limits on the wine consumption, nor did he force anyone to drink a minimum amount. Xerxes must have been showing respect for those people whose cultures prohibited the consumption or abuse of alcohol. Those of us trying to overcome alcohol abuse would do well to have friends that show the same respect for us.

ESTHER & MORDECAI

Many of us find ourselves in situations where cruel, unfortunate experiences seem to be the norm. We feel powerless to act—to either defend ourself or help anyone else. We may wonder how we got there or why. Esther must have felt this way at times. She lived in a community of exiled Jews in Babylonia, far from her homeland of Israel. She was a Jewish foreigner; her people were dominated by pagan Persian rulers. Esther was also an orphan; she was adopted by her older cousin Mordecai, a prominent figure in the exiled Jewish community.

When Esther was probably no more than in her late teens, King Xerxes, ruler of the Persian Empire, deposed his queen and held a mandatory, empire-wide beauty contest to find a replacement. Esther, forced to compete in the contest by the king's decree, was selected to join the king's harem and be his queen. But Mordecai instructed her not to tell anyone of her Jewish descent.

Even as queen to Xerxes, Esther was hardly in a wonderful situation. She was one among many wives and concubines. She would not see her husband for months at a time. Xerxes was hardly an ideal husband. He was known to depose or kill the people close to him at a mere whim. Being close to Xerxes was anything but a comfortable position. Esther, as one of God's chosen people, must have often wondered why she had become queen.

A man named Haman rose to the position of prime minister, and Esther's cousin Mordecai enraged Haman by not bowing down to him. To get revenge, Haman sought the destruction of all the Jews in the Persian Empire. When Mordecai learned of Haman's plan to kill the Jews, he went to Esther for help. Esther risked her life by approaching Xerxes without an appointment to plead with him to have mercy on her people. Before doing so, however, she called for a three-day fast by all the Jews in the city. This shows that she trusted God, even though she did not mention him by name. She must have spend those three days in prayer for God's protection as she went unbidden before the king. Her prayers were answered. Within a few days, Esther had succeeded in delivering her people from death. God was in control.

Esther may not have initially known why she was chosen to be queen, but God made his reason known soon enough: She was there to save her people from destruction. God used Esther and Mordecai to work his will in a difficult situation. We may not know why we are in certain circumstances, but God has a purpose and a plan for each of us. God may use us, as powerless as we may feel, to work his will in the lives of many.

STRENGTHS AND ACCOMPLISHMENTS:
- Both of them showed great courage and careful planning.
- Esther was open to wise advice from Mordecai.
- Esther's beauty and character endeared her to King Xerxes.
- Esther placed the lives of her people above her own.
- Mordecai refused to bow down to Haman, disregarding the possible consequences.

LESSONS FROM THEIR LIVES:
- Following God often means that we have to sacrifice our own security.
- We can trust that God will protect his people.
- God may put us in certain circumstances in order to benefit or even rescue others.
- God uses powerless people to work his powerful and perfect will.

KEY VERSE: "If you keep quiet at a time like this, deliverance and relief for the Jews will arise from some other place, but you and your relatives will die. Who knows if perhaps you were made queen for just such a time as this?" (Esther 4:14).

Esther and Mordecai's story is told in the book of Esther.

Queen Vashti Deposed

[10]On the seventh day of the feast, when King Xerxes was in high spirits because of the wine, he told the seven eunuchs who attended him—Mehuman, Biztha, Harbona, Bigtha, Abagtha, Zethar, and Carcas—[11]to bring Queen Vashti to him with the royal crown on her head. He wanted the nobles and all the other men to gaze on her beauty, for she was a very beautiful woman. [12]But when they conveyed the king's order to Queen Vashti, she refused to come. This made the king furious, and he burned with anger.

[13]He immediately consulted with his wise advisers, who knew all the Persian laws and customs, for he always asked their advice. [14]The names of these men were Carshena, Shethar, Admatha, Tarshish, Meres, Marsena, and Memucan—seven nobles of Persia and Media. They met with the king regularly and held the highest positions in the empire.

[15]"What must be done to Queen Vashti?" the king demanded. "What penalty does the law provide for a queen who refuses to obey the king's orders, properly sent through his eunuchs?"

[16]Memucan answered the king and his nobles, "Queen Vashti has wronged not only the king but also every noble and citizen throughout your empire. [17]Women everywhere will begin to despise their husbands when they learn that Queen Vashti has refused to appear before the king. [18]Before this day is out, the wives of all the king's nobles throughout Persia and Media will hear what the queen did and will start treating their husbands the same way. There will be no end to their contempt and anger.

[19]"So if it please the king, we suggest that you issue a written decree, a law of the Persians and Medes that cannot be revoked. It should order that Queen Vashti be forever banished from the presence of King Xerxes, and that the king should choose another queen more worthy than she. [20]When this decree is published throughout the king's vast empire, husbands everywhere, whatever their rank, will receive proper respect from their wives!"

[21]The king and his nobles thought this made good sense, so he followed Memucan's counsel. [22]He sent letters to all parts of the empire, to each province in its own script and language, proclaiming that every man should be the ruler of his own home and should say whatever he pleases.*

CHAPTER 2
Esther Becomes Queen

But after Xerxes' anger had subsided, he began thinking about Vashti and what she had done and the decree he had made. [2]So his personal attendants suggested, "Let us search the empire to find beautiful young virgins for the king. [3]Let the king appoint agents in each province to bring these beautiful young women into the royal harem at the fortress of Susa. Hegai, the king's eunuch in charge of the harem, will see that they are all given beauty treatments. [4]After that, the young woman who most pleases the king will be made queen instead of Vashti." This advice was very appealing to the king, so he put the plan into effect.

[5]At that time there was a Jewish man in the fortress of Susa whose name was Mordecai son of Jair. He was from the tribe of Benjamin and was a descendant of Kish and Shimei. [6]His family* had been among those who, with King Jehoiachin* of Judah, had been exiled from Jerusalem to Babylon by King Nebuchadnezzar. [7]This man had a very beautiful and lovely young cousin, Hadassah, who was also called Esther. When her father and mother died, Mordecai adopted her into his family and raised her as his own daughter.

[8]As a result of the king's decree, Esther, along with many other young women, was brought to the king's harem at the fortress of Susa and placed in Hegai's care. [9]Hegai was very impressed with Esther and treated her kindly. He quickly ordered a special menu for her and provided her with beauty treatments. He also assigned her seven maids specially chosen from the king's palace, and he moved her and her maids into the best place in the harem.

[10]Esther had not told anyone of her na-

1:22 Or *and should speak in the language of his own people.* 2:6a Hebrew *He.* 2:6b Hebrew *Jeconiah,* a variant spelling of Jehoiachin.

1:13-22 The king's advisers evaluated the situation regarding Vashti's disobedience and, realizing the far-reaching effects that such an act could have, suggested that quick and final action be taken at once. Anxious to please his allies, the king had made an unwise request of Vashti, which she had refused, and now he had to live with the consequences. We need to carefully evaluate the requests we make of others, realizing that we may be compromising their rights or desires.

tionality and family background, because Mordecai had directed her not to do so. [11]Every day Mordecai would take a walk near the courtyard of the harem to find out about Esther and what was happening to her.

[12]Before each young woman was taken to the king's bed, she was given the prescribed twelve months of beauty treatments—six months with oil of myrrh, followed by six months with special perfumes and ointments. [13]When it was time for her to go to the king's palace, she was given her choice of whatever clothing or jewelry she wanted to take from the harem. [14]That evening she was taken to the king's private rooms, and the next morning she was brought to the second harem,* where the king's wives lived. There she would be under the care of Shaashgaz, the king's eunuch in charge of the concubines. She would never go to the king again unless he had especially enjoyed her and requested her by name.

[15]Esther was the daughter of Abihail, who was Mordecai's uncle. (Mordecai had adopted his younger cousin Esther.) When it was Esther's turn to go to the king, she accepted the advice of Hegai, the eunuch in charge of the harem. She asked for nothing except what he suggested, and she was admired by everyone who saw her.

[16]Esther was taken to King Xerxes at the royal palace in early winter* of the seventh year of his reign. [17]And the king loved Esther more than any of the other young women. He was so delighted with her that he set the royal crown on her head and declared her queen instead of Vashti. [18]To celebrate the occasion, he gave a great banquet in Esther's honor for all his nobles and officials, declaring a public holiday for the provinces and giving generous gifts to everyone.

[19]Even after all the young women had been transferred to the second harem* and Mordecai had become a palace official,* [20]Esther continued to keep her family background and nationality a secret. She was still following Mordecai's directions, just as she did when she lived in his home.

Mordecai's Loyalty to the King

[21]One day as Mordecai was on duty at the king's gate, two of the king's eunuchs, Bigthana* and Teresh—who were guards at the door of the king's private quarters—became angry at King Xerxes and plotted to assassinate him. [22]But Mordecai heard about the plot and gave the information to Queen Esther. She then told the king about it and gave Mordecai credit for the report. [23]When an investigation was made and Mordecai's story was found to be true, the two men were impaled on a sharpened pole. This was all recorded in *The Book of the History of King Xerxes' Reign.*

CHAPTER 3
Haman's Plot against the Jews

Some time later King Xerxes promoted Haman son of Hammedatha the Agagite over all the other nobles, making him the most powerful official in the empire. [2]All the king's officials would bow down before Haman to show him respect whenever he passed by, for so the king had commanded. But Mordecai refused to bow down or show him respect.

[3]Then the palace officials at the king's gate asked Mordecai, "Why are you disobeying the king's command?" [4]They spoke to him

---

2:14 Or *to another part of the harem.* 2:16 Hebrew *in the tenth month, the month of Tebeth.* A number of dates in the book of Esther can be cross-checked with dates in surviving Persian records and related accurately to our modern calendar. This month of the ancient Hebrew lunar calendar occurred within the months of December 479 B.C. and January 478 B.C. 2:19a The meaning of the Hebrew is uncertain. 2:19b Hebrew *and Mordecai was sitting in the gate of the king.* 2:21 Hebrew *Bigthan;* compare 6:2.

2:21-23 When Mordecai learned of the guards' plan to kill Xerxes, he reported their plot to Queen Esther. Even though he had done something worthy of great honor, Mordecai received no recognition at the time (see 6:1-3). Sometimes the good decisions we make in recovery are rewarded only by our own sense of integrity. Knowing that we made a right decision before God should be enough for us to continue on the right path.

3:1-7 When Haman heard that Mordecai refused to bow before him, he became furious. Haman wanted revenge for Mordecai's insubordination, so he sought the destruction of all the Jews. His desire to destroy the whole nation may have been due to his family's (the Agagites) feud with Mordecai's tribe (the Benjamites; see 1 Samuel 15 for the story of King Saul and King Agag). This illustrates how a legacy of hatred can affect a person's judgment. Haman took drastic measures to settle a conflict that had begun over 500 years earlier. Do we have unsettled disagreements with others? If so, we need to forgive them so we can get on with our life and avoid having our children fight our battles long after we are gone.

day after day, but still he refused to comply with the order. So they spoke to Haman about this to see if he would tolerate Mordecai's conduct, since Mordecai had told them he was a Jew.

⁵When Haman saw that Mordecai would not bow down or show him respect, he was filled with rage. ⁶He had learned of Mordecai's nationality, so he decided it was not enough to lay hands on Mordecai alone. Instead, he looked for a way to destroy all the Jews throughout the entire empire of Xerxes.

⁷So in the month of April,* during the twelfth year of King Xerxes' reign, lots were cast in Haman's presence (the lots were called *purim*) to determine the best day and month to take action. And the day selected was March 7, nearly a year later.*

⁸Then Haman approached King Xerxes and said, "There is a certain race of people scattered through all the provinces of your empire who keep themselves separate from everyone else. Their laws are different from those of any other people, and they refuse to obey the laws of the king. So it is not in the king's interest to let them live. ⁹If it please the king, issue a decree that they be destroyed, and I will give 10,000 large sacks* of silver to the government administrators to be deposited in the royal treasury."

¹⁰The king agreed, confirming his decision by removing his signet ring from his finger and giving it to Haman son of Hammedatha the Agagite, the enemy of the Jews. ¹¹The king said, "The money and the people are both yours to do with as you see fit."

¹²So on April 17* the king's secretaries were summoned, and a decree was written exactly as Haman dictated. It was sent to the king's highest officers, the governors of the respective provinces, and the nobles of each province in their own scripts and languages. The decree was written in the name of King Xerxes and sealed with the king's signet ring. ¹³Dispatches were sent by swift messengers into all the provinces of the empire, giving the order that all Jews—young and old, including women and children—must be killed, slaughtered, and annihilated on a single day. This was scheduled to happen on March 7 of the next year.* The property of the Jews would be given to those who killed them.

¹⁴A copy of this decree was to be issued as law in every province and proclaimed to all peoples, so that they would be ready to do their duty on the appointed day. ¹⁵At the king's command, the decree went out by swift messengers, and it was also proclaimed in the fortress of Susa. Then the king and Haman sat down to drink, but the city of Susa fell into confusion.

CHAPTER 4
Mordecai Requests Esther's Help

When Mordecai learned about all that had been done, he tore his clothes, put on burlap and ashes, and went out into the city, crying with a loud and bitter wail. ²He went as far as the gate of the palace, for no one was allowed to enter the palace gate while wearing clothes of mourning. ³And as news of the king's decree reached all the provinces, there was great mourning among the Jews. They fasted, wept, and wailed, and many people lay in burlap and ashes.

3:7a Hebrew *in the first month, the month of Nisan.* This month of the ancient Hebrew lunar calendar occurred within the months of April and May 474 B.C.; also see note on 2:16. 3:7b As in 3:13, which reads *the thirteenth day of the twelfth month, the month of Adar;* Hebrew reads *in the twelfth month,* of the ancient Hebrew lunar calendar. The date selected was March 7, 473 B.C.; also see note on 2:16. 3:9 Hebrew *10,000 talents,* about 375 tons or 340 metric tons in weight. 3:12 Hebrew *On the thirteenth day of the first month,* of the ancient Hebrew lunar calendar. This day was April 17, 474 B.C.; also see note on 2:16. 3:13 Hebrew *on the thirteenth day of the twelfth month, the month of Adar,* of the ancient Hebrew lunar calendar. The date selected was March 7, 473 B.C.; also see note on 2:16.

3:8-15 Without mentioning them by name, Haman convinced the king to allow him to destroy the Jews because they followed different customs and disobeyed the king's laws. Irresponsibly, without investigating such a serious matter, the king gave Haman complete authority to implement his plan. We should always check out the requests of others, especially when the requests have major implications.

4:1-8 Mordecai and the Jews throughout the empire sensed the hopelessness of their situation and put on mourning clothes. When Esther learned that Mordecai was wailing at the palace gate, she dispatched a servant to determine the reasons for Mordecai's anguish. In a straightforward manner, Mordecai disclosed the gravity of the situation. Realizing our hopelessness is a significant step in the recovery process. Had Mordecai denied the truth of Haman's edict, he and the Jews would have faced certain death.

[4] When Queen Esther's maids and eunuchs came and told her about Mordecai, she was deeply distressed. She sent clothing to him to replace the burlap, but he refused it. [5] Then Esther sent for Hathach, one of the king's eunuchs who had been appointed as her attendant. She ordered him to go to Mordecai and find out what was troubling him and why he was in mourning. [6] So Hathach went out to Mordecai in the square in front of the palace gate.

[7] Mordecai told him the whole story, including the exact amount of money Haman had promised to pay into the royal treasury for the destruction of the Jews. [8] Mordecai gave Hathach a copy of the decree issued in Susa that called for the death of all Jews. He asked Hathach to show it to Esther and explain the situation to her. He also asked Hathach to direct her to go to the king to beg for mercy and plead for her people. [9] So Hathach returned to Esther with Mordecai's message.

[10] Then Esther told Hathach to go back and relay this message to Mordecai: [11] "All the king's officials and even the people in the provinces know that anyone who appears before the king in his inner court without being invited is doomed to die unless the king holds out his gold scepter. And the king has not called for me to come to him for thirty days." [12] So Hathach* gave Esther's message to Mordecai.

[13] Mordecai sent this reply to Esther: "Don't think for a moment that because you're in the palace you will escape when all other Jews are killed. [14] If you keep quiet at a time like this, deliverance and relief for the Jews will arise from some other place, but you and your relatives will die. Who knows if

4:12 As in Greek version; Hebrew reads *they*.

perhaps you were made queen for just such a time as this?"

[15] Then Esther sent this reply to Mordecai: [16] "Go and gather together all the Jews of Susa and fast for me. Do not eat or drink for three days, night or day. My maids and I will do the same. And then, though it is against the law, I will go in to see the king. If I must die, I must die." [17] So Mordecai went away and did everything as Esther had ordered him.

CHAPTER 5
Esther's Request to the King

On the third day of the fast, Esther put on her royal robes and entered the inner court of the palace, just across from the king's hall. The king was sitting on his royal throne, facing the entrance. [2] When he saw Queen Esther standing there in the inner court, he welcomed her and held out the gold scepter to her. So Esther approached and touched the end of the scepter.

[3] Then the king asked her, "What do you want, Queen Esther? What is your request? I will give it to you, even if it is half the kingdom!"

[4] And Esther replied, "If it please the king, let the king and Haman come today to a banquet I have prepared for the king."

[5] The king turned to his attendants and said, "Tell Haman to come quickly to a banquet, as Esther has requested." So the king and Haman went to Esther's banquet.

[6] And while they were drinking wine, the king said to Esther, "Now tell me what you really want. What is your request? I will give it to you, even if it is half the kingdom!"

[7] Esther replied, "This is my request and deepest wish. [8] If I have found favor with the king, and if it pleases the king to grant my

4:9-17 At first Esther wanted to deny the facts about Haman's edict. She focused on her fear that she might be killed for approaching the king uninvited. In doing so, she failed to see the long-term consequences that could result if she refused to act. Esther finally consented to help her people by approaching the volatile Xerxes, even though she didn't know if he would accept her or have her killed. "I will go in to see the king. If I must die, I must die" (4:16) reveals Esther's faith in God and her selflessness. We need to trust God to deliver us from our dependencies. We must also look to others for their support and prayers. Like Esther, we need people praying for us if we hope to succeed.

5:1-8 Esther courageously faced the danger of approaching the king without first being summoned. Her fears proved unfounded, however, for the king expressed his willingness to fulfill whatever requests she might make. Esther asked the king and Haman to two banquets before making her request, knowing that the king would be more receptive to her petition after two great feasts. We need to ask God to help us select the right people to help us in the recovery process and look for ways to show our appreciation to them, but we must not compromise our own position to gain their favor.

request and do what I ask, please come with Haman tomorrow to the banquet I will prepare for you. Then I will explain what this is all about."

Haman's Plan to Kill Mordecai

⁹Haman was a happy man as he left the banquet! But when he saw Mordecai sitting at the palace gate, not standing up or trembling nervously before him, Haman became furious. ¹⁰However, he restrained himself and went on home.

Then Haman gathered together his friends and Zeresh, his wife, ¹¹and boasted to them about his great wealth and his many children. He bragged about the honors the king had given him and how he had been promoted over all the other nobles and officials. ¹²Then Haman added, "And that's not all! Queen Esther invited only me and the king himself to the banquet she prepared for us. And she has invited me to dine with her and the king again tomorrow!" ¹³Then he added, "But this is all worth nothing as long as I see Mordecai the Jew just sitting there at the palace gate."

¹⁴So Haman's wife, Zeresh, and all his friends suggested, "Set up a sharpened pole that stands seventy-five feet* tall, and in the morning ask the king to impale Mordecai on it. When this is done, you can go on your merry way to the banquet with the king." This pleased Haman, and he ordered the pole set up.

CHAPTER 6
The King Honors Mordecai

That night the king had trouble sleeping, so he ordered an attendant to bring the book of

5:14 Hebrew *50 cubits* [23 meters].

the history of his reign so it could be read to him. ²In those records he discovered an account of how Mordecai had exposed the plot of Bigthana and Teresh, two of the eunuchs who guarded the door to the king's private quarters. They had plotted to assassinate King Xerxes.

³"What reward or recognition did we ever give Mordecai for this?" the king asked.

His attendants replied, "Nothing has been done for him."

⁴"Who is that in the outer court?" the king inquired. As it happened, Haman had just arrived in the outer court of the palace to ask the king to impale Mordecai on the pole he had prepared.

⁵So the attendants replied to the king, "Haman is out in the court."

"Bring him in," the king ordered. ⁶So Haman came in, and the king said, "What should I do to honor a man who truly pleases me?"

Haman thought to himself, "Whom would the king wish to honor more than me?" ⁷So he replied, "If the king wishes to honor someone, ⁸he should bring out one of the king's own royal robes, as well as a horse that the king himself has ridden—one with a royal emblem on its head. ⁹Let the robes and the horse be handed over to one of the king's most noble officials. And let him see that the man whom the king wishes to honor is dressed in the king's robes and led through the city square on the king's horse. Have the official shout as they go, 'This is what the king does for someone he wishes to honor!'"

¹⁰"Excellent!" the king said to Haman. "Quick! Take the robes and my horse, and do just as you have said for Mordecai the Jew,

5:9-14 Totally oblivious to Queen Esther's plans to thwart his evil schemes, Haman was overjoyed at being so highly honored by her. Yet even under such auspicious circumstances, Haman could not fully enjoy himself because he wanted still more. More than anything else, he wanted Mordecai to bow down to him; in fact, Haman became obsessed with it. We shouldn't allow what we don't have to overshadow what we do have. The desire to have everything might cost us the riches we already have.

6:1-6 Even though some time had gone by, the king felt a responsibility to acknowledge his gratitude to Mordecai for saving his life. Expressing gratitude is important in the recovery process. It shows others that we appreciate their help and that we are not fooling ourselves by thinking our progress was accomplished on our own. We should continually express our thanks to those who have helped us in recovery: God, family, friends, and employers.

6:6-12 Thinking the king was going to honor him, Haman recommended a public display. Haman must have been livid when he was ordered to honor Mordecai according to the plan he himself had outlined. Perhaps Haman's hatred of Mordecai was sparked because Haman had a difficult time honoring others. Showing respect to others would have been a blow to his ego. We should make sure our sense of self-worth does not depend on what others think of us. Once we realize that true self-worth is based on God's acceptance, we can stop competing with others and enjoy them for who they are.

who sits at the gate of the palace. Leave out nothing you have suggested!"

[11]So Haman took the robes and put them on Mordecai, placed him on the king's own horse, and led him through the city square, shouting, "This is what the king does for someone he wishes to honor!" [12]Afterward Mordecai returned to the palace gate, but Haman hurried home dejected and completely humiliated.

[13]When Haman told his wife, Zeresh, and all his friends what had happened, his wise advisers and his wife said, "Since Mordecai—this man who has humiliated you—is of Jewish birth, you will never succeed in your plans against him. It will be fatal to continue opposing him."

[14]While they were still talking, the king's eunuchs arrived and quickly took Haman to the banquet Esther had prepared.

CHAPTER 7
The King Executes Haman

So the king and Haman went to Queen Esther's banquet. [2]On this second occasion, while they were drinking wine, the king again said to Esther, "Tell me what you want, Queen Esther. What is your request? I will give it to you, even if it is half the kingdom!"

[3]Queen Esther replied, "If I have found favor with the king, and if it pleases the king to grant my request, I ask that my life and the lives of my people will be spared. [4]For my people and I have been sold to those who would kill, slaughter, and annihilate us. If we had merely been sold as slaves, I could remain quiet, for that would be too trivial a matter to warrant disturbing the king."

[5]"Who would do such a thing?" King Xerxes demanded. "Who would be so presumptuous as to touch you?"

7:9 Hebrew *50 cubits* [23 meters].

[6]Esther replied, "This wicked Haman is our adversary and our enemy." Haman grew pale with fright before the king and queen. [7]Then the king jumped to his feet in a rage and went out into the palace garden.

Haman, however, stayed behind to plead for his life with Queen Esther, for he knew that the king intended to kill him. [8]In despair he fell on the couch where Queen Esther was reclining, just as the king was returning from the palace garden.

The king exclaimed, "Will he even assault the queen right here in the palace, before my very eyes?" And as soon as the king spoke, his attendants covered Haman's face, signaling his doom.

[9]Then Harbona, one of the king's eunuchs, said, "Haman has set up a sharpened pole that stands seventy-five feet* tall in his own courtyard. He intended to use it to impale Mordecai, the man who saved the king from assassination."

"Then impale Haman on it!" the king ordered. [10]So they impaled Haman on the pole he had set up for Mordecai, and the king's anger subsided.

CHAPTER 8
A Decree to Help the Jews

On that same day King Xerxes gave the property of Haman, the enemy of the Jews, to Queen Esther. Then Mordecai was brought before the king, for Esther had told the king how they were related. [2]The king took off his signet ring—which he had taken back from Haman—and gave it to Mordecai. And Esther appointed Mordecai to be in charge of Haman's property.

[3]Then Esther went again before the king, falling down at his feet and begging him with tears to stop the evil plot devised by

---

7:1-6 Esther presented her petition to the king, seeking his help in saving her and her people from death. After explaining this life-threatening situation, she wisely waited to see how the king would respond. Noting his rage, she boldly proceeded to denounce Haman as the enemy of her people. Wisely evaluating situations before jumping in further is often necessary. Waiting for the proper timing is much easier than trying to repair damage done by being impetuous.

7:7-10 Haman did not seek forgiveness or make amends for his heinous acts. In his terror, Haman lost his self-control and committed the impropriety of falling upon Queen Esther's couch, which the king perceived as an attempted assault on the queen. Had Haman asked for forgiveness and explained the matter to the king, he might have been spared. Xerxes condemned Haman to death. There is always a chance for forgiveness and recovery. God will always forgive us, no matter what we have done. But the responsibility to ask for forgiveness is ours.

8:1-6 Esther received Haman's property, and Mordecai became prime minister; but still the Jewish people were in danger because of the edict. Once again Esther approached Xerxes, this time asking for a reversal of Haman's decree. Like Esther, we shouldn't stop with our own recovery. If others still suffer from their addiction, we should help them escape the disastrous effects of sin.

Haman the Agagite against the Jews. ⁴Again the king held out the gold scepter to Esther. So she rose and stood before him.

⁵Esther said, "If it please the king, and if I have found favor with him, and if he thinks it is right, and if I am pleasing to him, let there be a decree that reverses the orders of Haman son of Hammedatha the Agagite, who ordered that Jews throughout all the king's provinces should be destroyed. ⁶For how can I endure to see my people and my family slaughtered and destroyed?"

⁷Then King Xerxes said to Queen Esther and Mordecai the Jew, "I have given Esther the property of Haman, and he has been impaled on a pole because he tried to destroy the Jews. ⁸Now go ahead and send a message to the Jews in the king's name, telling them whatever you want, and seal it with the king's signet ring. But remember that whatever has already been written in the king's name and sealed with his signet ring can never be revoked."

⁹So on June 25* the king's secretaries were summoned, and a decree was written exactly as Mordecai dictated. It was sent to the Jews and to the highest officers, the governors, and the nobles of all the 127 provinces stretching from India to Ethiopia.* The decree was written in the scripts and languages of all the peoples of the empire, including that of the Jews. ¹⁰The decree was written in the name of King Xerxes and sealed with the king's signet ring. Mordecai sent the dispatches by swift messengers, who rode fast horses especially bred for the king's service.

¹¹The king's decree gave the Jews in every city authority to unite to defend their lives. They were allowed to kill, slaughter, and annihilate anyone of any nationality or province who might attack them or their children and wives, and to take the property of their enemies. ¹²The day chosen for this event throughout all the provinces of King Xerxes was March 7 of the next year.*

¹³A copy of this decree was to be issued as law in every province and proclaimed to all peoples, so that the Jews would be ready to take revenge on their enemies on the appointed day. ¹⁴So urged on by the king's command, the messengers rode out swiftly on fast horses bred for the king's service. The same decree was also proclaimed in the fortress of Susa.

¹⁵Then Mordecai left the king's presence, wearing the royal robe of blue and white, the great crown of gold, and an outer cloak of fine linen and purple. And the people of Susa celebrated the new decree. ¹⁶The Jews were filled with joy and gladness and were honored everywhere. ¹⁷In every province and city, wherever the king's decree arrived, the Jews rejoiced and had a great celebration and declared a public festival and holiday. And many of the people of the land became Jews themselves, for they feared what the Jews might do to them.

CHAPTER 9
The Victory of the Jews

So on March 7* the two decrees of the king were put into effect. On that day, the enemies of the Jews had hoped to overpower them, but quite the opposite happened. It was the Jews who overpowered their enemies. ²The Jews gathered in their cities throughout all the king's provinces to attack anyone who tried to harm them. But no one could make a stand against them, for everyone was afraid of them. ³And all the nobles of the provinces, the highest officers, the governors, and the royal officials helped the Jews for fear of Mordecai. ⁴For Mordecai had been promoted in the king's palace, and his fame spread throughout all the provinces as he became more and more powerful.

⁵So the Jews went ahead on the appointed

8:9a Hebrew *on the twenty-third day of the third month, the month of Sivan,* of the ancient Hebrew lunar calendar. This day was June 25, 474 B.C.; also see note on 2:16. 8:9b Hebrew *to Cush.* 8:12 Hebrew *the thirteenth day of the twelfth month, the month of Adar,* of the ancient Hebrew lunar calendar. The date selected was March 7, 473 B.C.; also see note on 2:16. 9:1 Hebrew *on the thirteenth day of the twelfth month, the month of Adar,* of the ancient Hebrew lunar calendar. This day was March 7, 473 B.C.; also see note on 2:16.

8:7-14 As before (see 3:10), King Xerxes abdicated his management responsibility. This time he put Esther and Mordecai in charge, allowing them to do as they pleased. We should make sure that those to whom we entrust responsibility are dependable. If we ask friends to hold us accountable or help us, we must be able to rely on their commitment to us and to God. If our friends are not trustworthy, we may be doing ourself more harm than good by asking them for their help.

9:5-15 The Jews were finally able to defend themselves from their enemies. Notice that the Jews exhibited self-control by not plundering their enemies' goods even though they had the right to do so (see 8:11). This was a wise move; the Jews could not be accused of rationalizing their slaughter as

day and struck down their enemies with the sword. They killed and annihilated their enemies and did as they pleased with those who hated them. [6]In the fortress of Susa itself, the Jews killed 500 men. [7]They also killed Parshandatha, Dalphon, Aspatha, [8]Poratha, Adalia, Aridatha, [9]Parmashta, Arisai, Aridai, and Vaizatha—[10]the ten sons of Haman son of Hammedatha, the enemy of the Jews. But they did not take any plunder.

[11]That very day, when the king was informed of the number of people killed in the fortress of Susa, [12]he called for Queen Esther. He said, "The Jews have killed 500 men in the fortress of Susa alone, as well as Haman's ten sons. If they have done that here, what has happened in the rest of the provinces? But now, what more do you want? It will be granted to you; tell me and I will do it."

[13]Esther responded, "If it please the king, give the Jews in Susa permission to do again tomorrow as they have done today, and let the bodies of Haman's ten sons be impaled on a pole."

[14]So the king agreed, and the decree was announced in Susa. And they impaled the bodies of Haman's ten sons. [15]Then the Jews at Susa gathered together on March 8* and killed 300 more men, and again they took no plunder.

[16]Meanwhile, the other Jews throughout the king's provinces had gathered together to defend their lives. They gained relief from all their enemies, killing 75,000 of those who hated them. But they did not take any plunder. [17]This was done throughout the provinces on March 7, and on March 8 they rested,* celebrating their victory with a day of feasting and gladness. [18](The Jews at Susa killed their enemies on March 7 and again on March 8, then rested on March 9,* making that their day of feasting and gladness.) [19]So to this day, rural Jews living in remote villages celebrate an annual festival and holiday on the appointed day in late winter,* when they rejoice and send gifts of food to each other.

The Festival of Purim

[20]Mordecai recorded these events and sent letters to the Jews near and far, throughout all the provinces of King Xerxes, [21]calling on them to celebrate an annual festival on these two days.* [22]He told them to celebrate these days with feasting and gladness and by giving gifts of food to each other and presents to the poor. This would commemorate a time when the Jews gained relief from their enemies, when their sorrow was turned into gladness and their mourning into joy.

[23]So the Jews accepted Mordecai's proposal and adopted this annual custom. [24]Haman son of Hammedatha the Agagite, the enemy of the Jews, had plotted to crush and destroy them on the date determined by casting lots (the lots were called *purim*). [25]But when Esther came before the king, he issued a decree causing Haman's evil plot to backfire, and Haman and his sons were impaled on a sharpened pole. [26]That is why this celebration is called Purim, because it is the ancient word for casting lots.

So because of Mordecai's letter and because of what they had experienced, [27]the Jews throughout the realm agreed to inaugurate this tradition and to pass it on to their descendants and to all who became Jews. They declared they would never fail to celebrate these two prescribed days at the appointed time each year. [28]These days would

---

9:15 Hebrew *the fourteenth day of the month of Adar,* of the Hebrew lunar calendar. This day was March 8, 473 B.C.; also see note on 2:16. 9:17 Hebrew *on the thirteenth day of the month of Adar, and on the fourteenth day they rested.* These days were March 7 and 8, 473 B.C.; also see note on 2:16. 9:18 Hebrew *killed their enemies on the thirteenth day and the fourteenth day, and then rested on the fifteenth day,* of the Hebrew month of Adar. 9:19 Hebrew *on the fourteenth day of the month of Adar.* This day of the Hebrew lunar calendar occurs in February or March. 9:21 Hebrew *on the fourteenth and fifteenth days of Adar,* of the ancient Hebrew lunar calendar.

---

a cover for becoming rich. We need not always embrace every advantage that the law allows. Sometimes it's wise to sacrifice some of our rights to make a statement about our motives.
9:16-19 Upon completing their task, the Jews throughout the empire spontaneously and joyfully celebrated their survival. There is nothing wrong with celebrating a great victory, whether it is emotional, spiritual, or physical. If we have been delivered from an addiction or have overcome an emotional problem, we need to rejoice and celebrate! Proper celebration is not only fun, but it brings glory to God and helps us recharge our batteries for the battles that still lie ahead.
9:20-28 Mordecai formalized what originally had been a spur-of-the-moment celebration into an annual event. He named this deliverance of the Jews as an official holiday—Purim. This would remind the Jews annually of their deliverance from near destruction. It is often helpful for us to establish special days to commemorate the important victories in our life. Such days would serve as reminders of how we were delivered from near self-destruction.

be remembered and kept from generation to generation and celebrated by every family throughout the provinces and cities of the empire. This Festival of Purim would never cease to be celebrated among the Jews, nor would the memory of what happened ever die out among their descendants.

[29]Then Queen Esther, the daughter of Abihail, along with Mordecai the Jew, wrote another letter putting the queen's full authority behind Mordecai's letter to establish the Festival of Purim. [30]Letters wishing peace and security were sent to the Jews throughout the 127 provinces of the empire of Xerxes. [31]These letters established the Festival of Purim—an annual celebration of these days at the appointed time, decreed by both Mordecai the Jew and Queen Esther. (The people decided to observe this festival, just as they had decided for themselves and their descendants to establish the times of fasting and mourning.) [32]So the command of Esther confirmed the practices of Purim, and it was all written down in the records.

CHAPTER 10
The Greatness of Xerxes and Mordecai

King Xerxes imposed a tribute throughout his empire, even to the distant coastlands. [2]His great achievements and the full account of the greatness of Mordecai, whom the king had promoted, are recorded in *The Book of the History of the Kings of Media and Persia.* [3]Mordecai the Jew became the prime minister, with authority next to that of King Xerxes himself. He was very great among the Jews, who held him in high esteem, because he continued to work for the good of his people and to speak up for the welfare of all their descendants.

10:1-3 Mordecai became known as a great prime minister, no doubt because for his fairness and godliness. Although the book ends with the Jews enjoying much success, it never once mentions God. Yet despite this seeming oversight, God's handiwork—his timing, his deliverance, and his encouragement—can be seen throughout the book. God truly works behind the scenes to ensure the full recovery and ultimate success of his people.

JOB

THE BIG PICTURE

A. THE PAIN BEGINS (1:1–2:13)
1. The World of a Faithful Man (1:1-5)
2. The World of a Faithless Angel (1:6-7)
3. God's Choice for Faithfulness (1:8-12)
4. The Trial Begins (1:13–2:10)
5. The Only Friendly Visit (2:11-13)

B. A MAN FORSAKEN (3:1–37:24)
1. Round One: Undependable Friends (3:1–14:22)
2. Round Two: Unnerving Theologies (15:1–21:34)
3. Round Three: Misguided Cures (22:1–26:14)
4. A Painful Remembrance (27:1–31:40)
5. A Self-Appointed Spokesman (32:1–37:24)

C. A VOICE OUT OF THE STORM (38:1–41:34)

D. SPIRITUAL RECOVERY: EYES THAT SEE GOD (42:1-6)

E. PHYSICAL RECOVERY: A NEW BEGINNING (42:7-17)

The book of Job addresses head-on the problem of the suffering of the innocent. At its opening, Job was a prosperous man, greatly blessed by God. But God allowed one disaster after another to fall on Job. We are told that Job's suffering was the result of a spiritual conflict, not because of any failure on Job's part. But Job, his wife, and his friends were never made aware of this. They were left to struggle with the pain and ask the age-old question *why.*

Job was confused by the devastating losses he had experienced. Even after taking a rigorous inventory of his life, he could find nothing to warrant the punishment he was receiving. Amidst his confusion, however, he displayed an amazing faith in God, despite short lapses of anger and despair. Job's wife reacted to his suffering as we often do in such situations—she pointed an angry finger at God. The four visiting friends approached Job's suffering with the orthodox theology of their day, which considered all suffering to be the direct result of sin. They could think of no other reason for Job's suffering except his denial of some hidden sin.

The book's prologue makes it clear that Job was innocent. The solutions offered by his friends were clearly wrong. Why did God allow Job to suffer? Job was never given a lucid answer. He did learn, however, to stand humbly and trustingly before his Creator. God alone knows and understands all things. Life brings hurts, and there are no guarantees that we will escape them. But through suffering we can learn to live by faith rather than by our own strength. We can learn that even when suffering leads us to doubt, God is still with us.

THE BOTTOM LINE

PURPOSE: To provide an intimate look into the struggles of a man dealing with the problem of human suffering. AUTHOR: The author is unknown, though either Job or Elihu may have written the initial record. AUDIENCE: The people of Israel. DATE WRITTEN: The date of the book's written completion is unknown. The events probably belong to the patriarchal period (2000–1800 B.C.). SETTING: The land of Uz, probably located in either northeastern Palestine or northwestern Arabia. KEY VERSES: "But as for me, I know that my Redeemer lives, and he will stand upon the earth at last. And after my body has decayed, yet in my body I will see God!" (19:25-26). KEY PEOPLE AND RELATIONSHIPS: Job; his wife; and his four friends Eliphaz, Bildad, Zophar, and Elihu.

RECOVERY THEMES

Dealing with Unfairness: We live in a world filled with injustice and unfairness. The Bible recognizes this hard fact. Joseph suffered unfairly at the hands of his brothers and Potiphar's wife. David suffered unjustly for many years at the hands of King Saul. And here, through no fault of his own, Job lost his possessions, his family, and his health. Job wondered why God was allowing him to suffer, but he never got a clear answer. He did, however, through his struggles come to know God in a new and deeper way. Even though we face unfairness in our world, we can still use those opportunities to learn more about trusting God.

Honesty with Our Emotions: In the book of Job we discover that it is all right to cry, to doubt, to fear, to question, to need, and to wrestle with the very essence of our existence. As our heart cries out against injustice and pain, the book of Job reassures us of the importance of being honest with God. When we are angry, we should tell him. When we are afraid, we should reach out to him. God understands our strong feelings. He is never put off or threatened by our anger. In fact, God longs for us to be open and honest with him. He wants to participate even in the darkest parts of our life. Only then will we be able to come to him with all our heart. Only then will he be able to bring us the healing and hope he longs to give.

God's Goodness: God is all-knowing and all-powerful. His will for each of us is perfect. But he doesn't always act in ways we can understand. Very often he seems to do things that contradict his justice in the world. As Job suffered, his friends believed his pain was the result of something he had done. Job knew this was not the case. Yet he could not help wondering why he had to suffer so much pain. It would have been easy for Job to wholeheartedly reject God for the apparent injustice he was suffering. But Job still knew that God was good, and, despite lapses of anger and despair, Job trusted that in the end God would deal with him fairly.

The Importance of Trust: When our life is going smoothly, trust is easy. The tests of trust always come when our life stops making sense. Job's attitude is a very real example of how trust needs to work in our life. Everything Job enjoyed had been stripped away for no reason that he could discover or understand. In spite of this, Job never gave up on God. He never placed hope in his experience, his wisdom, his friends, or his wealth. His trust was in God, even though he couldn't understand everything he was going through. God alone is sufficient to help us deal with the ambiguities in life. We can trust in him.

CHAPTER 1
Prologue

There once was a man named Job who lived in the land of Uz. He was blameless—a man of complete integrity. He feared God and stayed away from evil. ²He had seven sons and three daughters. ³He owned 7,000 sheep, 3,000 camels, 500 teams of oxen, and 500 female donkeys. He also had many servants. He was, in fact, the richest person in that entire area.

⁴Job's sons would take turns preparing feasts in their homes, and they would also invite their three sisters to celebrate with them. ⁵When these celebrations ended— sometimes after several days—Job would purify his children. He would get up early in the morning and offer a burnt offering for each of them. For Job said to himself, "Perhaps my children have sinned and have cursed God in their hearts." This was Job's regular practice.

Job's First Test

⁶One day the members of the heavenly court* came to present themselves before the LORD, and the Accuser, Satan,* came with them. ⁷"Where have you come from?" the LORD asked Satan.

Satan answered the LORD, "I have been patrolling the earth, watching everything that's going on."

⁸Then the LORD asked Satan, "Have you noticed my servant Job? He is the finest man in all the earth. He is blameless—a man of complete integrity. He fears God and stays away from evil."

⁹Satan replied to the LORD, "Yes, but Job has good reason to fear God. ¹⁰You have always put a wall of protection around him

1:6a Hebrew *the sons of God.* **1:6b** Hebrew *and the satan;* similarly throughout this chapter.

1:1-5 Job's lifestyle and heart are revealed to us during this brief introduction. We are told (1:1) and then shown (1:4-5) that Job loved God and desired to lead his children to do the same. This fact will help us understand the rest of the narrative properly. Job's innocence is firmly established at the beginning of the book so we won't question it as he is judged by his friends.

JOB, HIS FAMILY & FRIENDS

Responding to tragedy is never easy. Maybe it's the terrible sense of loss we feel. Perhaps it's the desire to know *why* that leaves us feeling alienated and alone. Was it something we did? Was it someone else's fault? Why did God allow it to happen? These questions often go unanswered. For many of us, as we make our moral inventory and dig up the layers of denial in our life, we realize that our suffering has resulted from our own addictive behaviors. But in Job's case this wasn't true. He was a godly man with healthy family relationships. He was willing to honestly examine his life but could find no particular failures or deficiencies. When Job lost everything—wealth and family—in one day, the question *why* was especially appropriate.

Yet even after his great losses, Job continued to glorify God. Very soon after losing everything he owned, he also lost his good health. Why was all this happening, especially to such a good person? That was the question in the minds of Job, his wife, and the friends who visited Job in his misery. Such a question is often asked but ultimately unanswerable from our limited human standpoint. We must work through this question as we seek to navigate our way through the tragedies we face in our life.

We, the readers, know that Job's sufferings resulted from discussions between God and Satan (1:6-12; 2:1-7). But Job and the others had no idea what was happening in the unseen spiritual realm; they could only guess or theorize. Job's friends believed that he was living in denial, hiding sins and failures that were the cause of his suffering. Job, knowing his heart was pure, could not go along with the explanations of his friends. But still, he had no real answer for the nagging question, *why*. As time passed, Job grew increasingly upset and confused, until even he began to question God's sense of justice.

Job eventually lost his debate with God. While God never explained fully to Job why the disasters had befallen him, he did bring Job to the point of self-examination. This expanded Job's understanding of God and gave him the proper perspective to continue life. Neither Job nor any other person who has suffered a serious loss can ever fully understand why such a catastrophe happens. But if we are willing to trust the God of recovery and put our life in his powerful hands, balanced restoration can take place as it did in Job's life.

STRENGTHS AND ACCOMPLISHMENTS:
- Job was rightly known for his godliness.
- Job proved himself to be a good father and husband.
- Job is also justly famous for his patience and perseverance.
- Job's friends had good intentions as they visited him.

WEAKNESSES AND MISTAKES:
- Job's friends made their judgments based on outward appearances, without truly understanding the situation.
- Job's wife let her losses come between her and God.
- Job displayed some pride that needed to be dealt with.

LESSONS FROM THEIR LIVES:
- Disasters touch the lives of even the most moral or godly people.
- When we sustain a major loss, we should not deny our anger; instead, we should work through it.
- In times of loss we must not let pride stand in the way of an honest personal inventory.

KEY VERSE:
"You know about Job, a man of great endurance. You can see how the Lord was kind to him at the end, for the Lord is full of tenderness and mercy" (James 5:11).

The story of Job, his family, and friends is told in the book of Job. He is also referred to in Ezekiel 14:14, 20 and James 5:11.

---

and his home and his property. You have made him prosper in everything he does. Look how rich he is! ¹¹But reach out and take away everything he has, and he will surely curse you to your face!"

¹²"All right, you may test him," the LORD said to Satan. "Do whatever you want with everything he possesses, but don't harm him physically." So Satan left the LORD's presence.

¹³One day when Job's sons and daughters were feasting at the oldest brother's house, ¹⁴a messenger arrived at Job's home with this news: "Your oxen were plowing, with the donkeys feeding beside them, ¹⁵when the Sabeans raided us. They stole all the animals and killed all the farmhands. I am the only one who escaped to tell you."

¹⁶While he was still speaking, another messenger arrived with this news: "The fire of God has fallen from heaven and burned up your sheep and all the shepherds. I am the only one who escaped to tell you."

¹⁷While he was still speaking, a third messenger arrived with this news: "Three bands of Chaldean raiders have stolen your camels and killed your servants. I am the only one who escaped to tell you."

¹⁸While he was still speaking, another messenger arrived with this news: "Your sons and daughters were feasting in their oldest brother's home. ¹⁹Suddenly, a powerful wind swept in from the wilderness and hit the house on all sides. The house collapsed, and all your children are dead. I am the only one who escaped to tell you."

²⁰Job stood up and tore his robe in grief. Then he shaved his head and fell to the ground to worship. ²¹He said,

"I came naked from my mother's womb,
  and I will be naked when I leave.
The LORD gave me what I had,
  and the LORD has taken it away.
Praise the name of the LORD!"

²²In all of this, Job did not sin by blaming God.

CHAPTER 2
Job's Second Test

One day the members of the heavenly court* came again to present themselves before the LORD, and the Accuser, Satan,* came with them. ²"Where have you come from?" the LORD asked Satan.

Satan answered the LORD, "I have been patrolling the earth, watching everything that's going on."

³Then the LORD asked Satan, "Have you noticed my servant Job? He is the finest man in all the earth. He is blameless—a man of complete integrity. He fears God and stays away from evil. And he has maintained his integrity, even though you urged me to harm him without cause."

⁴Satan replied to the LORD, "Skin for skin! A man will give up everything he has to save his life. ⁵But reach out and take away his health, and he will surely curse you to your face!"

⁶"All right, do with him as you please," the LORD said to Satan. "But spare his life." ⁷So Satan left the LORD's presence, and he struck Job with terrible boils from head to foot.

⁸Job scraped his skin with a piece of broken pottery as he sat among the ashes. ⁹His wife said to him, "Are you still trying to maintain your integrity? Curse God and die."

¹⁰But Job replied, "You talk like a foolish woman. Should we accept only good things from the hand of God and never anything bad?" So in all this, Job said nothing wrong.

Job's Three Friends Share His Anguish

¹¹When three of Job's friends heard of the tragedy he had suffered, they got together

2:1a Hebrew *the sons of God.* 2:1b Hebrew *and the satan;* similarly throughout this chapter.

1:13-19 In what seems to be only a few hours' time, everything Job had held significant was stripped away. The pain must have seemed intolerable; the grief, beyond solace. Even though Job mourned his loss, however, his identity was not wrapped up in his possessions. Do we ever get caught in that trap, building our sense of self-worth on what we own—our home, cars, job, or wealth? If those were taken away, how would we feel? Self-esteem must be based on the fact that God loves us so much that he sent his Son, Jesus, to die for us while we were still sinners (Romans 5:8). God's love can never be taken away from us.

2:1-3 It is important to realize that Satan has no authority apart from God's consent. He is only permitted to test God's beloved ones; he is not permitted to devour them. When we undergo trials, we should realize that God won't let us be destroyed; if we trust God, he will help us face our trials. He wants us to grow in our faith and glorify his name, no matter what difficulties we may be called upon to endure.

2:9-10 It is one thing to lose our physical comforts; it is quite another to lose the support of a spouse. In times of great loss, we desperately need the support of our loved ones. We need our spouse's vote of confidence when no one else is there. The only mention of Job's wife comes at the start of his affliction. She was bitter and unable to share in his pain. As a spouse experiences tough times in recovery, we need to be careful not to taunt or ridicule or minimize. He or she needs our support, not our anger or frustration.

and traveled from their homes to comfort and console him. Their names were Eliphaz the Temanite, Bildad the Shuhite, and Zophar the Naamathite. ¹²When they saw Job from a distance, they scarcely recognized him. Wailing loudly, they tore their robes and threw dust into the air over their heads to show their grief. ¹³Then they sat on the ground with him for seven days and nights. No one said a word to Job, for they saw that his suffering was too great for words.

CHAPTER 3
Job's First Speech

At last Job spoke, and he cursed the day of his birth. ²He said:

³ "Let the day of my birth be erased,
   and the night I was conceived.
⁴ Let that day be turned to darkness.
   Let it be lost even to God on high,
   and let no light shine on it.
⁵ Let the darkness and utter gloom claim
      that day for its own.
   Let a black cloud overshadow it,
   and let the darkness terrify it.
⁶ Let that night be blotted off the calendar,
      never again to be counted among the
         days of the year,
      never again to appear among the
         months.
⁷ Let that night be childless.
   Let it have no joy.
⁸ Let those who are experts at cursing—
      whose cursing could rouse Leviathan*—
   curse that day.
⁹ Let its morning stars remain dark.
   Let it hope for light, but in vain;
   may it never see the morning light.

¹⁰ Curse that day for failing to shut my
      mother's womb,
   for letting me be born to see all this
      trouble.
¹¹ "Why wasn't I born dead?
   Why didn't I die as I came from the
      womb?
¹² Why was I laid on my mother's lap?
   Why did she nurse me at her breasts?
¹³ Had I died at birth, I would now be at
      peace.
   I would be asleep and at rest.
¹⁴ I would rest with the world's kings and
      prime ministers,
   whose great buildings now lie in ruins.
¹⁵ I would rest with princes, rich in gold,
   whose palaces were filled with silver.
¹⁶ Why wasn't I buried like a stillborn child,
   like a baby who never lives to see the
      light?
¹⁷ For in death the wicked cause no trouble,
   and the weary are at rest.
¹⁸ Even captives are at ease in death,
   with no guards to curse them.
¹⁹ Rich and poor are both there,
   and the slave is free from his master.

²⁰ "Oh, why give light to those in misery,
   and life to those who are bitter?
²¹ They long for death, and it won't come.
   They search for death more eagerly
      than for hidden treasure.
²² They're filled with joy when they finally
      die,
   and rejoice when they find the grave.
²³ Why is life given to those with no future,
   those God has surrounded with
      difficulties?
²⁴ I cannot eat for sighing;
   my groans pour out like water.

3:8 The identification of Leviathan is disputed, ranging from an earthly creature to a mythical sea monster in ancient literature.

3:1-19 Even though Job had known amazing success and happiness, he couldn't remember what it had been like. A common element of suffering is a loss of perspective. No matter how hard we try to maintain our point of view, it is difficult to separate yesterday's celebrations from today's devastation. But even so, it is comforting to remember that God, who loves us more than we can even imagine, will always be there for us when we need him.

3:20-23 Like most sufferers, Job asked *why*. Unfortunately, the answer to that question is often reserved for eternity. We must learn to trust God and stay faithful to him even if we never receive an explanation for our suffering. Sometimes we will never know why things happen as they do. We can be sure, though, that God is with us in the pain. We can begin the healing process by entrusting our life to God and to his will for us.

3:24-26 Although Job had lived an exemplary life, he faced great suffering. Job thought that he wouldn't have to face this kind of suffering because he had avoided certain behaviors. He had no idea, however, of the supernatural events that had precipitated his misery. Like Job, we may be surprised to find that we are suffering, especially after we have been faithfully following a recovery program. But God has a reason for allowing all the events in our life. We need to persevere in our trust and realize that God's will for us will ultimately bring us great joy.

25 What I always feared has happened
     to me.
     What I dreaded has come true.
26 I have no peace, no quietness.
     I have no rest; only trouble comes."

CHAPTER 4
Eliphaz's First Response to Job
Then Eliphaz the Temanite replied to Job:

2 "Will you be patient and let me say
     a word?
     For who could keep from speaking
     out?

3 "In the past you have encouraged many
     people;
     you have strengthened those who were
     weak.
4 Your words have supported those who
     were falling;
     you encouraged those with shaky
     knees.
5 But now when trouble strikes, you lose
     heart.
     You are terrified when it touches you.
6 Doesn't your reverence for God give you
     confidence?
     Doesn't your life of integrity give you
     hope?

7 "Stop and think! Do the innocent die?
     When have the upright been
     destroyed?
8 My experience shows that those who
     plant trouble
     and cultivate evil will harvest the same.
9 A breath from God destroys them.
     They vanish in a blast of his anger.

10 The lion roars and the wildcat snarls,
     but the teeth of strong lions will be
     broken.
11 The fierce lion will starve for lack
     of prey,
     and the cubs of the lioness will be
     scattered.

12 "This truth was given to me in secret,
     as though whispered in my ear.
13 It came to me in a disturbing vision at
     night,
     when people are in a deep sleep.
14 Fear gripped me,
     and my bones trembled.
15 A spirit* swept past my face,
     and my hair stood on end.*
16 The spirit stopped, but I couldn't see its
     shape.
     There was a form before my eyes.
     In the silence I heard a voice say,
17 'Can a mortal be innocent before God?
     Can anyone be pure before the
     Creator?'

18 "If God does not trust his own angels
     and has charged his messengers with
     foolishness,
19 how much less will he trust people made
     of clay!
     They are made of dust, crushed as easily
     as a moth.
20 They are alive in the morning but dead
     by evening,
     gone forever without a trace.
21 Their tent-cords are pulled and the tent
     collapses,
     and they die in ignorance.

4:15a Or *wind;* also in 4:16. **4:15b** Or *its wind sent shivers up my spine.*

4:1-6 One thing suffering people don't need is harsh words of judgment, especially from their friends. Most of us are aware of the wrong things we have done and want to make things right. We don't need to be told that our behavior is disappointing to God. Our Father knows better than anyone the pain we experience. He is not a distant observer of our life but an intimate companion. When we try to comfort suffering friends or family members, we should let them go through the grief process. Then we can encourage them with the message of God's forgiveness—the only real hope for recovery.

4:7-11 We know that a man reaps what he sows—at least in theory. We cannot, however, offer these verses as a universal reason for suffering. First, God deals with us by grace, not as we "deserve." Second, suffering is not always a tool of judgment. It can be used to strengthen our faith. Just as gold must be melted to get the impurities out, so we must go through trials to purify our faith.

4:7-21 There are few things more frustrating than a friend who claims to know what is happening to us, why it is happening, and how we should respond. Job wasn't outside God's favor. He wasn't disobedient and unwilling to follow God. Job was a sufferer, and he needed his friends to trust what they knew about him. Job needed people to share his pain and help him grieve. We don't have to come up with all the answers to effectively comfort our friends. We just have to lovingly support them as they face difficult times.

CHAPTER 5
Eliphaz's Response Continues
¹ "Cry for help, but will anyone answer you?
   Which of the angels* will help you?
² Surely resentment destroys the fool,
   and jealousy kills the simple.
³ I have seen that fools may be successful
   for the moment,
   but then comes sudden disaster.
⁴ Their children are abandoned far from
   help;
   they are crushed in court with no one
   to defend them.
⁵ The hungry devour their harvest,
   even when it is guarded by brambles.*
   The thirsty pant after their wealth.*
⁶ But evil does not spring from the soil,
   and trouble does not sprout from the
   earth.
⁷ People are born for trouble
   as readily as sparks fly up from a fire.

⁸ "If I were you, I would go to God
   and present my case to him.
⁹ He does great things too marvelous to
   understand.
   He performs countless miracles.
¹⁰ He gives rain for the earth
   and water for the fields.
¹¹ He gives prosperity to the poor
   and protects those who suffer.
¹² He frustrates the plans of schemers
   so the work of their hands will not
   succeed.
¹³ He traps the wise in their own cleverness
   so their cunning schemes are thwarted.
¹⁴ They find it is dark in the daytime,
   and they grope at noon as if it were
   night.
¹⁵ He rescues the poor from the cutting
   words of the strong,
   and rescues them from the clutches of
   the powerful.
¹⁶ And so at last the poor have hope,
   and the snapping jaws of the wicked
   are shut.

¹⁷ "But consider the joy of those corrected
   by God!
   Do not despise the discipline of the
   Almighty when you sin.
¹⁸ For though he wounds, he also bandages.
   He strikes, but his hands also heal.
¹⁹ From six disasters he will rescue you;
   even in the seventh, he will keep you
   from evil.
²⁰ He will save you from death in time of
   famine,
   from the power of the sword in time
   of war.
²¹ You will be safe from slander
   and have no fear when destruction
   comes.
²² You will laugh at destruction and famine;
   wild animals will not terrify you.
²³ You will be at peace with the stones of the
   field,
   and its wild animals will be at peace
   with you.
²⁴ You will know that your home is safe.
   When you survey your possessions,
   nothing will be missing.
²⁵ You will have many children;
   your descendants will be as plentiful
   as grass!
²⁶ You will go to the grave at a ripe old age,
   like a sheaf of grain harvested at the
   proper time!

²⁷ "We have studied life and found all this to
   be true.
   Listen to my counsel, and apply it to
   yourself."

5:1 Hebrew *the holy ones.* 5:5a The meaning of the Hebrew for this phrase is uncertain. 5:5b As in Greek and Syriac versions; Hebrew reads *A snare snatches their wealth.*

5:8-16 As we seek to comfort others we must avoid saying, "If I were you, . . ." No matter what we have experienced in the past, we can never really understand what other people are going through. We have no idea how we would respond if placed in their exact situation. We would be wise to respond to another's suffering like this: "Tell me how you're feeling" or "Show me how to stand with you in your grief."

5:17 Eliphaz assumed that Job was rejecting God's discipline. Though Job was not being disciplined by God here, Eliphaz was correct in saying that we should welcome God's correction. God wants only the best for us, and he will discipline us in order to get us back in line with his will. But we shouldn't assume that every experience of suffering in our life is correction from God.

5:27 The greatest personal resource we possess as believers is the indwelling of the Holy Spirit. In addition to being our intimate connection with God (Romans 8:26-27), he is our counselor, our teacher, our guide, our strength (see John 14:16-17, 26; 16:13; James 4:5-6). Eliphaz made the mistake of trying to play the role of the Holy Spirit in Job's life. If we ever find ourself doing the same thing to comfort our friends, we should opt instead to sit quietly with them, as Job's friends did at first. They came across as more sympathetic when their mouths were shut.

CHAPTER 6
Job's Second Speech: A Response to Eliphaz
Then Job spoke again:

2 "If my misery could be weighed
  and my troubles be put on the scales,
3 they would outweigh all the sands of the
    sea.
  That is why I spoke impulsively.
4 For the Almighty has struck me down
    with his arrows.
  Their poison infects my spirit.
  God's terrors are lined up against me.
5 Don't I have a right to complain?
  Don't wild donkeys bray when they
    find no grass,
  and oxen bellow when they have no
    food?
6 Don't people complain about unsalted
    food?
  Does anyone want the tasteless white of
    an egg?*
7 My appetite disappears when I look at it;
  I gag at the thought of eating it!

8 "Oh, that I might have my request,
  that God would grant my desire.
9 I wish he would crush me.
  I wish he would reach out his hand and
    kill me.
10 At least I can take comfort in this:
  Despite the pain,
  I have not denied the words of the Holy
    One.

11 But I don't have the strength
    to endure.
  I have nothing to live for.
12 Do I have the strength of a stone?
  Is my body made of bronze?
13 No, I am utterly helpless,
  without any chance of success.

14 "One should be kind to a fainting
    friend,
  but you accuse me without any fear of
    the Almighty.*
15 My brothers, you have proved as
    unreliable as a seasonal brook
  that overflows its banks in the spring
16   when it is swollen with ice and melting
    snow.
17 But when the hot weather arrives, the
    water disappears.
  The brook vanishes in the heat.
18 The caravans turn aside to be refreshed,
  but there is nothing to drink, so they
    die.
19 The caravans from Tema search for this
    water;
  the travelers from Sheba hope to
    find it.
20 They count on it but are disappointed.
  When they arrive, their hopes are
    dashed.
21 You, too, have given no help.
  You have seen my calamity, and you are
    afraid.

6:6 Or the tasteless juice of the mallow plant? 6:14 Or friend, / or he might lose his fear of the Almighty.

6:14-21 Friends are very important. When we are hurting, we depend on them to listen, to weep, to support, to just be with us. If ever Job needed a friend, it was now. Yet Job found Eliphaz's friendship as undependable as a brook. Job was deeply disappointed in Eliphaz's failure to support him in his pain. Eliphaz was long on advice but short on compassion—an excellent example of how *not* to treat those we are trying to comfort. When our friends try to comfort us, we should tell them how they can help us. If we are called upon to comfort others, we need to be sensitive to their needs.

6:30 Job stated that if he had sinned, he would have admitted it. He wanted to know just what he had done to deserve punishment. Job kept a good moral inventory of his acts and couldn't find anything wrong. We need to keep accurate records of our actions, too. If there is sin in our life, we need to confess it. If we have wronged someone, we need to make restitution. Denying the facts will not help us in the recovery process.

7:1-5 Whether we suffer from physical pain, the loss of a spouse, a disappointing career, divorce, loneliness, depression, an estranged loved one, alcoholism, or any kind of addiction, nights are difficult. At least in the daylight hours, our work or other activities can help take our mind off our situation. When night falls and we are alone, the reality of our pain stares us in the face with no distractions. It is then that we can talk to God about our pain. He will listen and comfort us. We are never alone—we can always talk to God through prayer.

7:11-21 Here, Job turned to petition God. Even though he was in anguish, he recognized that God was the only one who could take away the pain. Whether or not the pain we feel is a result of our own sins, God is there to comfort us. His timing may not be what we would consider ideal, but God's perspective and timing are always best. We can trust God to rescue us—but in his time, not ours.

²² But why? Have I ever asked you for a gift?
Have I begged for anything of yours for
myself?
²³ Have I asked you to rescue me from my
enemies,
or to save me from ruthless people?
²⁴ Teach me, and I will keep quiet.
Show me what I have done wrong.
²⁵ Honest words can be painful,
but what do your criticisms amount to?
²⁶ Do you think your words are convincing
when you disregard my cry of
desperation?
²⁷ You would even send an orphan into
slavery*
or sell a friend.
²⁸ Look at me!
Would I lie to your face?
²⁹ Stop assuming my guilt,
for I have done no wrong.
³⁰ Do you think I am lying?
Don't I know the difference between
right and wrong?

CHAPTER 7

¹ "Is not all human life a struggle?
Our lives are like that of a hired hand,
² like a worker who longs for the shade,
like a servant waiting to be paid.
³ I, too, have been assigned months of
futility,
long and weary nights of misery.
⁴ Lying in bed, I think, 'When will it be
morning?'
But the night drags on, and I toss till
dawn.
⁵ My body is covered with maggots and
scabs.
My skin breaks open, oozing with pus.

Job Cries Out to God

⁶ "My days fly faster than a weaver's
shuttle.
They end without hope.
⁷ O God, remember that my life is but a
breath,
and I will never again feel happiness.
⁸ You see me now, but not for long.
You will look for me, but I will be gone.
⁹ Just as a cloud dissipates and vanishes,
those who die* will not come back.
¹⁰ They are gone forever from their home—
never to be seen again.

¹¹ "I cannot keep from speaking.
I must express my anguish.

6:27 Hebrew *even gamble over an orphan.* 7:9 Hebrew
who go down to Sheol.

STEP 1

Hope amidst Suffering

BIBLE READING: Job 6:2-13

**We admitted that we were powerless
over our problems—that our lives had
become unmanageable.**

There are times when we are so confused
and overwhelmed by the pain in our life
that we wish we could die. No matter what
we do, we are powerless to change things
for the better. The weight of the pain and
sadness seems too heavy to bear. We can't
see why our heart doesn't just break and
allow death to free us.

Job felt that way. He'd lost everything,
even though he had always done what was
right. His ten children were dead. He had
lost his business, his riches, and his health.
And all this happened in a matter of days!
He was left with a sharp-tongued wife and
three friends who blamed him for his own
misfortune. Job cried out, "If my misery
could be weighed and my troubles be put
on the scales, they would outweigh all the
sands of the sea. . . . Oh, that I might have
my request, that God would grant my
desire. I wish he would crush me. I wish he
would reach out his hand and kill me. . . . I
don't have the strength to endure. I have
nothing to live for. Do I have the strength
of a stone? Is my body made of bronze?
No, I am utterly helpless, without any
chance of success" (Job 6:2-3, 8-9, 11-13).

Job didn't know that the end of his life
would be even better than the beginning.
God eventually restored everything Job had
lost, and then some. "Then he died, an old
man who had lived a long, full life" (Job
42:17). Even when we're pressed to the
point of death, there is still hope that our
life will change. Our recovery could be so
complete that the final lines written about
us might read: "At last he or she died, after
living a long, full life." We must remember:
Life can be good again! *Turn to page 1267,
Mark 10.*

My bitter soul must complain.
¹² Am I a sea monster or a dragon
    that you must place me under guard?
¹³ I think, 'My bed will comfort me,
    and sleep will ease my misery,'
¹⁴ but then you shatter me with dreams
    and terrify me with visions.
¹⁵ I would rather be strangled—
    rather die than suffer like this.
¹⁶ I hate my life and don't want to go on
    living.
  Oh, leave me alone for my few
    remaining days.

¹⁷ "What are people, that you should make
    so much of us,
  that you should think of us so often?
¹⁸ For you examine us every morning
    and test us every moment.
¹⁹ Why won't you leave me alone,
    at least long enough for me to swallow!
²⁰ If I have sinned, what have I done to you,
    O watcher of all humanity?
  Why make me your target?
    Am I a burden to you?*
²¹ Why not just forgive my sin
    and take away my guilt?
  For soon I will lie down in the dust and die.
    When you look for me, I will be gone."

CHAPTER 8
Bildad's First Response to Job
Then Bildad the Shuhite replied to Job:

² "How long will you go on like this?
    You sound like a blustering wind.
³ Does God twist justice?
    Does the Almighty twist what is right?
⁴ Your children must have sinned against
    him,
  so their punishment was well deserved.
⁵ But if you pray to God
    and seek the favor of the Almighty,
⁶ and if you are pure and live with integrity,
  he will surely rise up and restore your
    happy home.

⁷ And though you started with little,
    you will end with much.

⁸ "Just ask the previous generation.
  Pay attention to the experience of our
    ancestors.
⁹ For we were born but yesterday and know
    nothing.
  Our days on earth are as fleeting as a
    shadow.
¹⁰ But those who came before us will teach
    you.
  They will teach you the wisdom of old.

¹¹ "Can papyrus reeds grow tall without a
    marsh?
  Can marsh grass flourish without water?
¹² While they are still flowering, not ready to
    be cut,
  they begin to wither more quickly than
    grass.
¹³ The same happens to all who forget God.
  The hopes of the godless evaporate.
¹⁴ Their confidence hangs by a thread.
  They are leaning on a spider's web.
¹⁵ They cling to their home for security, but
    it won't last.
  They try to hold it tight, but it will not
    endure.
¹⁶ The godless seem like a lush plant
    growing in the sunshine,
  its branches spreading across the garden.
¹⁷ Its roots grow down through a pile of
    stones;
  it takes hold on a bed of rocks.
¹⁸ But when it is uprooted,
    it's as though it never existed!
¹⁹ That's the end of its life,
    and others spring up from the earth to
    replace it.

²⁰ "But look, God will not reject a person of
    integrity,
  nor will he lend a hand to the wicked.
²¹ He will once again fill your mouth with
    laughter

7:20 As in Greek version; Hebrew reads *target, so that I am a burden to myself?*

8:1-7 "You're getting what you deserve." This is perhaps the most unkind remark we might ever make to one who is suffering. In some cases it might be true. Foolish choices do often lead to painful consequences. But if we always got what we deserved, all of us would soon be destroyed. Sometimes our suffering is not a consequence of sin at all. Bildad showed his ignorance of God's ways when he tried to connect Job's loss to some hidden sin. We need to be careful not to judge a person who is suffering a setback, for we may not know the whole story. Only God truly knows and understands a person and his or her circumstances.

8:8-22 Bildad was correct in some of his theology, but he erred in the application of his knowledge. God saw Job as blameless and upright (see 1:8; 2:3), not as unfaithful or disobedient. Job's suffering was not the result of a wayward life. It is not our job to guess the purpose of another person's pain. It is our job to offer comfort and support.

and your lips with shouts of joy.
²²Those who hate you will be clothed with
shame,
and the home of the wicked will be
destroyed."

CHAPTER 9
Job's Third Speech: A Response to Bildad
Then Job spoke again:

²"Yes, I know all this is true in principle.
But how can a person be declared
innocent in God's sight?
³If someone wanted to take God to court,*
would it be possible to answer him even
once in a thousand times?
⁴For God is so wise and so mighty.
Who has ever challenged him
successfully?

⁵"Without warning, he moves the
mountains,
overturning them in his anger.
⁶He shakes the earth from its place,
and its foundations tremble.
⁷If he commands it, the sun won't rise
and the stars won't shine.
⁸He alone has spread out the heavens
and marches on the waves of the sea.
⁹He made all the stars—the Bear and
Orion,
the Pleiades and the constellations of
the southern sky.
¹⁰He does great things too marvelous to
understand.
He performs countless miracles.

¹¹"Yet when he comes near, I cannot see
him.
When he moves by, I do not see
him go.
¹²If he snatches someone in death, who can
stop him?
Who dares to ask, 'What are you
doing?'
¹³And God does not restrain his anger.
Even the monsters of the sea* are
crushed beneath his feet.

¹⁴"So who am I, that I should try to answer
God
or even reason with him?
¹⁵Even if I were right, I would have no
defense.
I could only plead for mercy.
¹⁶And even if I summoned him and he
responded,
I'm not sure he would listen to me.
¹⁷For he attacks me with a storm
and repeatedly wounds me without
cause.
¹⁸He will not let me catch my breath,
but fills me instead with bitter sorrows.
¹⁹If it's a question of strength, he's the
strong one.
If it's a matter of justice, who dares to
summon him* to court?
²⁰Though I am innocent, my own mouth
would pronounce me guilty.
Though I am blameless, it* would prove
me wicked.

²¹"I am innocent,
but it makes no difference to me—
I despise my life.
²²Innocent or wicked, it is all the same
to God.
That's why I say, 'He destroys both the
blameless and the wicked.'
²³When a plague* sweeps through,
he laughs at the death of the innocent.
²⁴The whole earth is in the hands of the
wicked,
and God blinds the eyes of the judges.
If he's not the one who does it, who is?

²⁵"My life passes more swiftly than a
runner.
It flees away without a glimpse of
happiness.
²⁶It disappears like a swift papyrus boat,
like an eagle swooping down on its
prey.
²⁷If I decided to forget my complaints,
to put away my sad face and be
cheerful,
²⁸I would still dread all the pain,

9:3 Or *If God wanted to take someone to court.* 9:13 Hebrew *the helpers of Rahab,* the name of a mythical sea monster that represents chaos in ancient literature. 9:19 As in Greek version; Hebrew reads *me.* 9:20 Or *he.* 9:23 Or *disaster.*

9:1-20 Job knew more than he understood. He knew about God's sovereignty and justice and that no man is blameless when seen in the light of God's perfection. What he didn't understand is that God is merciful and that it is only by grace that we do not receive our deserved fates, which would be far worse than Job's sufferings. When we feel that God isn't being fair, we should remember that if he were, we would never be able to enter his presence. When God is "unfair," it is always on the side of mercy.

for I know you will not find me
  innocent, O God.
²⁹ Whatever happens, I will be found guilty.
  So what's the use of trying?
³⁰ Even if I were to wash myself with soap
  and clean my hands with lye,
³¹ you would plunge me into a muddy
    ditch,
  and my own filthy clothing would
    hate me.

³² "God is not a mortal like me,
  so I cannot argue with him or take him
    to trial.
³³ If only there were a mediator between us,
  someone who could bring us together.
³⁴ The mediator could make God stop
    beating me,
  and I would no longer live in terror of
    his punishment.
³⁵ Then I could speak to him without fear,
  but I cannot do that in my own
    strength.

CHAPTER 10
Job Frames His Plea to God
¹ "I am disgusted with my life.
  Let me complain freely.
  My bitter soul must complain.
² I will say to God, 'Don't simply
    condemn me—
  tell me the charge you are bringing
    against me.
³ What do you gain by oppressing me?
  Why do you reject me, the work of your
    own hands,
  while smiling on the schemes of the
    wicked?
⁴ Are your eyes like those of a human?
  Do you see things only as people see
    them?

⁵ Is your lifetime only as long as ours?
  Is your life so short
⁶ that you must quickly probe for my guilt
  and search for my sin?
⁷ Although you know I am not guilty,
  no one can rescue me from your
    hands.

⁸ "'You formed me with your hands; you
    made me,
  yet now you completely destroy me.
⁹ Remember that you made me
    from dust—
  will you turn me back to dust
    so soon?
¹⁰ You guided my conception
  and formed me in the womb.*
¹¹ You clothed me with skin and flesh,
  and you knit my bones and sinews
    together.
¹² You gave me life and showed me your
    unfailing love.
  My life was preserved by your care.

¹³ "'Yet your real motive—
  your true intent—
¹⁴ was to watch me, and if I sinned,
  you would not forgive my guilt.
¹⁵ If I am guilty, too bad for me;
  and even if I'm innocent, I can't hold
    my head high,
  because I am filled with shame and
    misery.
¹⁶ And if I hold my head high, you hunt me
    like a lion
  and display your awesome power
    against me.
¹⁷ Again and again you witness against me.
  You pour out your growing anger
    on me
  and bring fresh armies against me.

10:10 Hebrew *You poured me out like milk / and curdled me like cheese.*

9:32-35 Job lamented the absence of a mediator to stand between himself and God. We need
not make that same plea; God has sent a mediator—Jesus Christ. We can take our cases directly to
God because Jesus' death gave us access to God's presence. When we feel as if we cannot stand
any more pain, we can go to Jesus with our requests for peace. He will listen to us and answer our
prayers, although he might not do it the way we think he should or according to our timetable.
God is perfect. Perfect peace and recovery come in his time and by his methods.
10:1-17 Job took a respite from measuring his pain and began to direct his thoughts toward God.
This subtle change would become a catalyst for his growth, though he was not yet able to sense
any relief. So often we talk *about* God or *about* our feelings. A critical step in healing is to address
our helpless cries *to* God. He does not despise our grief; he welcomes its expressions.
10:1-22 There are those who teach that depression is a negative emotion. They say that if we
have sufficient faith, we need not be depressed. Job gives us an honest account of one man's
overwhelming grief. When we feel depressed, it is healthy to explore and express the emotions
locked up inside us—especially the so-called negative ones. By expressing them, we are often
released from their devastating effects.

18 "'Why, then, did you deliver me from my
  mother's womb?
  Why didn't you let me die at birth?
19 It would be as though I had never existed,
  going directly from the womb to the
  grave.
20 I have only a few days left, so leave me
  alone,
  that I may have a moment of comfort
21 before I leave—never to return—
  for the land of darkness and utter
  gloom.
22 It is a land as dark as midnight,
  a land of gloom and confusion,
  where even the light is dark as
  midnight.'"

CHAPTER 11
Zophar's First Response to Job
Then Zophar the Naamathite replied to Job:

2 "Shouldn't someone answer this torrent
  of words?
  Is a person proved innocent just by a
  lot of talking?
3 Should I remain silent while you
  babble on?
  When you mock God, shouldn't
  someone make you ashamed?
4 You claim, 'My beliefs are pure,'
  and 'I am clean in the sight of God.'
5 If only God would speak;
  if only he would tell you what he
  thinks!
6 If only he would tell you the secrets of
  wisdom,
  for true wisdom is not a simple
  matter.
  Listen! God is doubtless punishing you
  far less than you deserve!

7 "Can you solve the mysteries of God?
  Can you discover everything about the
  Almighty?
8 Such knowledge is higher than the
  heavens—
  and who are you?
  It is deeper than the underworld*—
  what do you know?
9 It is broader than the earth
  and wider than the sea.
10 If God comes and puts a person in
  prison
  or calls the court to order, who can stop
  him?
11 For he knows those who are false,
  and he takes note of all their sins.
12 An empty-headed person won't become
  wise
  any more than a wild donkey can bear a
  human child.*

13 "If only you would prepare your heart
  and lift up your hands to him
  in prayer!
14 Get rid of your sins,
  and leave all iniquity behind you.
15 Then your face will brighten with
  innocence.
  You will be strong and free of fear.
16 You will forget your misery;
  it will be like water flowing away.
17 Your life will be brighter than the
  noonday.
  Even darkness will be as bright as
  morning.
18 Having hope will give you courage.
  You will be protected and will rest in
  safety.
19 You will lie down unafraid,
  and many will look to you for help.

11:8 Hebrew *than Sheol.* 11:12 Or *than a wild male donkey can bear a tame colt.*

10:18-22 Before leaving this world, Jesus assured the disciples that they and we have a place with him in eternity (see John 14:1-4). He gave them a picture of hope that they could hold on to in their impending grief. When we suffer, sometimes hope seems far away. Job couldn't imagine a future of light when he felt so enveloped in darkness. But we can—we have Jesus' promise.
11:7-12 Zophar knew something about God, but his knowledge was limited. God is indeed sovereign, and no one can oppose him and hope to win. But Job wasn't opposing God; he was trying to make sense of his suffering. Just as God allowed Job to meditate on his suffering, he will allow us time to understand why some things happen to us. We may never find a clear answer, but our faith in God will grow if we learn from our trials and trust God in them, rather than complain at each new trial.
11:13-20 As we devote our heart to God in prayer and confess our sins, we will experience a deepening fellowship with him. But this fellowship with God never eliminates all our suffering. Pain is part of life, whether we are close to God or rebellious against him. Zophar's theology could not allow the possibility that Job could suffer and still be righteous. We need to trust in God simply because of who he is revealed to be. Our faith should never be measured solely by our own experiences.

20 But the wicked will be blinded.
   They will have no escape.
   Their only hope is death."

CHAPTER 12
Job's Fourth Speech: A Response to Zophar
Then Job spoke again:

2 "You people really know everything,
     don't you?
   And when you die, wisdom will die
     with you!
3 Well, I know a few things myself—
   and you're no better than I am.
   Who doesn't know these things you've
     been saying?
4 Yet my friends laugh at me,
   for I call on God and expect an answer.
   I am a just and blameless man,
     yet they laugh at me.
5 People who are at ease mock those in
     trouble.
   They give a push to people who are
     stumbling.
6 But robbers are left in peace,
   and those who provoke God live in
     safety—
   though God keeps them in his
     power.*

7 "Just ask the animals, and they will teach
     you.
   Ask the birds of the sky, and they will
     tell you.
8 Speak to the earth, and it will instruct
     you.
   Let the fish in the sea speak to you.
9 For they all know
   that my disaster* has come from the
     hand of the LORD.
10 For the life of every living thing is in his
     hand,
   and the breath of every human being.

11 The ear tests the words it hears
     just as the mouth distinguishes between
       foods.
12 Wisdom belongs to the aged,
   and understanding to the old.

13 "But true wisdom and power are found
     in God;
   counsel and understanding are his.
14 What he destroys cannot be rebuilt.
   When he puts someone in prison,
     there is no escape.
15 If he holds back the rain, the earth
     becomes a desert.
   If he releases the waters, they flood the
     earth.
16 Yes, strength and wisdom are his;
   deceivers and deceived are both in his
     power.
17 He leads counselors away, stripped of
     good judgment;
   wise judges become fools.
18 He removes the royal robe of kings.
   They are led away with ropes around
     their waist.
19 He leads priests away, stripped
     of status;
   he overthrows those with long years
     in power.
20 He silences the trusted adviser
   and removes the insight of the
     elders.
21 He pours disgrace upon princes
   and disarms the strong.

22 "He uncovers mysteries hidden in
     darkness;
   he brings light to the deepest
     gloom.
23 He builds up nations, and he destroys
     them.
   He expands nations, and he abandons
     them.

12:6 Or *safety—those who try to manipulate God*. The meaning of the Hebrew is uncertain. 12:9 Hebrew *that this*.

12:1-6 Job becomes wiser and wiser because of his pain. He understood well the dilemma faced by Zophar and his companions: "People who are at ease mock those in trouble." Theirs was a very comfortable theology: If we are good, God blesses with wealth and comfort. If we are bad, God punishes with poverty and suffering. But as we see here, their assumptions were far from the truth. Job knew that he was innocent of wrongdoing, yet he suffered greatly. His sufferings gave him the perspective he needed for a better understanding of God and the way he works in our world. Unlike his friends, Job knew that suffering was not always a punishment for sin. Like Job, we should use our difficult times to lead us to a deeper understanding of God.
12:7-25 Job explored the sovereign nature of God. He recognized that God is powerful; man is not. Herein lies one of the most difficult lessons for all of us to learn—God is in ultimate control. Humility does not come easily to us. In our culture, we greatly value power and authority. But we are often powerless over our circumstances and unable to change our life—only God can do that. Realizing this truth carries us through the first two steps of recovery: recognizing that our life is unmanageable, and acknowledging that only God is able to change it.

²⁴ He strips kings of understanding
    and leaves them wandering in a
      pathless wasteland.
²⁵ They grope in the darkness without a
    light.
    He makes them stagger like drunkards.

CHAPTER 13
Job Wants to Argue His Case with God
¹ "Look, I have seen all this with my own
    eyes
    and heard it with my own ears, and
      now I understand.
² I know as much as you do.
    You are no better than I am.
³ As for me, I would speak directly to the
    Almighty.
    I want to argue my case with God
      himself.
⁴ As for you, you smear me with lies.
    As physicians, you are worthless
      quacks.
⁵ If only you could be silent!
    That's the wisest thing you could do.
⁶ Listen to my charge;
    pay attention to my arguments.

⁷ "Are you defending God with lies?
    Do you make your dishonest arguments
      for his sake?
⁸ Will you slant your testimony in his
    favor?
    Will you argue God's case for him?
⁹ What will happen when he finds out what
    you are doing?
    Can you fool him as easily as you fool
      people?
¹⁰ No, you will be in trouble with him
    if you secretly slant your testimony in
      his favor.
¹¹ Doesn't his majesty terrify you?
    Doesn't your fear of him overwhelm
      you?
¹² Your platitudes are as valuable as ashes.
    Your defense is as fragile as a
      clay pot.

¹³ "Be silent now and leave me alone.
    Let me speak, and I will face the
      consequences.
¹⁴ Why should I put myself in mortal
    danger*
    and take my life in my own hands?
¹⁵ God might kill me, but I have no other
    hope.*
    I am going to argue my case with him.
¹⁶ But this is what will save me—I am not
    godless.
    If I were, I could not stand before
      him.

¹⁷ "Listen closely to what I am about
    to say.
    Hear me out.
¹⁸ I have prepared my case;
    I will be proved innocent.
¹⁹ Who can argue with me over this?
    And if you prove me wrong, I will
      remain silent and die.

Job Asks How He Has Sinned
²⁰ "O God, grant me these two things,
    and then I will be able to face you.
²¹ Remove your heavy hand from me,
    and don't terrify me with your
      awesome presence.
²² Now summon me, and I will answer!
    Or let me speak to you, and you reply.
²³ Tell me, what have I done wrong?
    Show me my rebellion and my sin.
²⁴ Why do you turn away from me?
    Why do you treat me as your enemy?
²⁵ Would you terrify a leaf blown by the
    wind?
    Would you chase dry straw?

²⁶ "You write bitter accusations against me
    and bring up all the sins of my youth.
²⁷ You put my feet in stocks.
    You examine all my paths.
    You trace all my footprints.
²⁸ I waste away like rotting wood,
    like a moth-eaten coat.

13:14 Hebrew *Why should I take my flesh in my teeth.* **13:15** An alternate reading in the Masoretic Text reads *God might kill me, but I hope in him.*

13:1-13 Job was clearly angry with his accusers. He saw them as obstacles to his own conversation with God. Like Job's friends, we often find it easy to speak for God when we feel insecure with the circumstances we face. We need to recognize that we never have the whole story on any one situation. God rarely appoints us as intercessors or spokespersons for him. We must be careful that we do not impede someone else's recovery by presuming to speak for God.
13:24 Job asked God to show him what he had done wrong. Job had completed a personal moral inventory and had come up with no reasons for his punishment. We often have areas of denial in our own life and hesitate to be truly honest about our failures. We need to find the courage to admit any weaknesses we have so we can eliminate all the barriers to the recovery process.

CHAPTER 14

1 "How frail is humanity!
How short is life, how full of trouble!
2 We blossom like a flower and then wither.
Like a passing shadow, we quickly disappear.
3 Must you keep an eye on such a frail creature
and demand an accounting from me?
4 Who can bring purity out of an impure person?
No one!
5 You have decided the length of our lives.
You know how many months we will live,
and we are not given a minute longer.
6 So leave us alone and let us rest!
We are like hired hands, so let us finish our work in peace.

7 "Even a tree has more hope!
If it is cut down, it will sprout again
and grow new branches.
8 Though its roots have grown old in the earth
and its stump decays,
9 at the scent of water it will bud
and sprout again like a new seedling.

10 "But when people die, their strength is gone.
They breathe their last, and then where are they?
11 As water evaporates from a lake
and a river disappears in drought,

12 people are laid to rest and do not rise again.
Until the heavens are no more, they will not wake up
nor be roused from their sleep.

13 "I wish you would hide me in the grave*
and forget me there until your anger has passed.
But mark your calendar to think of me again!
14 Can the dead live again?
If so, this would give me hope through all my years of struggle,
and I would eagerly await the release of death.
15 You would call and I would answer,
and you would yearn for me, your handiwork.
16 For then you would guard my steps,
instead of watching for my sins.
17 My sins would be sealed in a pouch,
and you would cover my guilt.

18 "But instead, as mountains fall and crumble
and as rocks fall from a cliff,
19 as water wears away the stones
and floods wash away the soil,
so you destroy people's hope.
20 You always overpower them, and they pass from the scene.
You disfigure them in death and send them away.

14:13 Hebrew *in Sheol.*

14:1-12 We are very fortunate to live after the time of Jesus Christ. We have seen grace demonstrated firsthand, and we have experienced the power of the risen Christ in our life. Job understood much, but he couldn't quite grasp the idea of eternal life. Our days in the flesh are both numbered and final, and this disturbed Job. Our hope in a future life with Christ should make our troubles here on earth more bearable. We can know with certainty that our sufferings here are not permanent.

14:13-19 We all face times when we simply want to hide from distress and defeat; Job was no exception. He pleaded with God for the chance to hide until renewal came. We need to realize that God wasn't punishing Job or taking pleasure in his anguish. He was allowing Job to pass through a fiery trial. God knows the end result of our suffering and despair—faith that is purer than gold (see 1 Peter 1:6-8). We must look past the difficult times and hope for the positive effects God desires to work in us. This should encourage us as we face difficult times.

15:1-16 Eliphaz didn't like Job's attitude. He mistook Job's words of grief for words of pride—foolish words. Be careful not to minimize the importance of expressed grief. Grieving is necessary in order to move from despair to hope and to get on with life. We would do well to steer clear of the judgmental attitudes exhibited by Job's friends.

15:17-35 Eliphaz thought he had *the* explanation for Job's misery: Suffering was reserved for the ungodly; therefore, Job was a wicked man, charging at God with a shield of his own making. Why would Eliphaz speak so to Job? What made him think Job was wicked? We may be tempted to adopt Eliphaz's theory as long as things are going well for us. But when things get tough and there is no clear cause for our suffering, his theory will no longer comfort us. Hopefully we are not as callous about the pain of others as Eliphaz was. If we are, we will probably bring more harm than help to our friends.

²¹ They never know if their children grow
up in honor
or sink to insignificance.
²² They suffer painfully;
their life is full of trouble."

CHAPTER 15
Eliphaz's Second Response to Job
Then Eliphaz the Temanite replied:

² "A wise man wouldn't answer with such
empty talk!
You are nothing but a windbag.
³ The wise don't engage in empty chatter.
What good are such words?
⁴ Have you no fear of God,
no reverence for him?
⁵ Your sins are telling your mouth what
to say.
Your words are based on clever
deception.
⁶ Your own mouth condemns you,
not I.
Your own lips testify against you.

⁷ "Were you the first person ever born?
Were you born before the hills were
made?
⁸ Were you listening at God's secret
council?
Do you have a monopoly on wisdom?
⁹ What do you know that we don't?
What do you understand that we
do not?
¹⁰ On our side are aged, gray-haired men
much older than your father!

¹¹ "Is God's comfort too little for you?
Is his gentle word not enough?
¹² What has taken away your reason?
What has weakened your vision,*
¹³ that you turn against God
and say all these evil things?
¹⁴ Can any mortal be pure?
Can anyone born of a woman be just?
¹⁵ Look, God does not even trust the
angels.*
Even the heavens are not absolutely
pure in his sight.
¹⁶ How much less pure is a corrupt and
sinful person
with a thirst for wickedness!

¹⁷ "If you will listen, I will show you.
I will answer you from my own
experience.
¹⁸ And it is confirmed by the reports
of wise men

15:12 Or *Why do your eyes flash with anger;* Hebrew reads
Why do your eyes blink. 15:15 Hebrew *the holy ones.*

STEP 2

Persistent Seeking
BIBLE READING: Job 14:1-6
**We came to believe that a Power greater
than ourselves could restore us to sanity.**
One thing that may make it hard to believe
in God is that life often seems unfair to us.
We didn't ask to be born into a dysfunctional family! We didn't have any say over
the abuses and injustices we have suffered!
We didn't choose our predisposition toward
addiction. And yet we are held accountable
for things we can't control on our own.
This makes it hard to initially turn to God as
the Power to restore our sanity. He seems
unreasonable in his demands.

Job understood these feelings. In the
midst of his suffering he said, "How frail is
humanity! How short is life, how full of
trouble! We blossom like a flower and then
wither. Like a passing shadow, we quickly
disappear. Must you keep an eye on such a
frail creature and demand an accounting
from me? Who can bring purity out of an
impure person?" (Job 14:1-4). These are
good questions—ones that most of us have
asked in one form or another. Job persisted
in his questioning because deep inside he
believed God to be good and fair, even
though life wasn't. He was honest with his
emotions and questions, but he never
stopped seeking God.

There is a good answer to the question
Job posed, one that will satisfy both our
heart and our mind. It will be found,
however, only by those who are willing to
work through the pain and unfairness of life
and still seek God. Those who seek him will
find him. In God's loving arms, they will
also find the answers they seek. ***Turn to page
1081, Daniel 4.***

tyndal.es/lrbstep2

who have heard the same thing from
their fathers—
¹⁹ from those to whom the land was given
long before any foreigners arrived.

²⁰ "The wicked writhe in pain throughout
their lives.
Years of trouble are stored up for the
ruthless.
²¹ The sound of terror rings in their ears,
and even on good days they fear the
attack of the destroyer.
²² They dare not go out into the darkness
for fear they will be murdered.
²³ They wander around, saying, 'Where can I
find bread?'*
They know their day of destruction is
near.
²⁴ That dark day terrifies them.
They live in distress and anguish,
like a king preparing for battle.
²⁵ For they shake their fists at God,
defying the Almighty.
²⁶ Holding their strong shields,
they defiantly charge against him.

²⁷ "These wicked people are heavy and
prosperous;
their waists bulge with fat.
²⁸ But their cities will be ruined.
They will live in abandoned houses
that are ready to tumble down.
²⁹ Their riches will not last,
and their wealth will not endure.
Their possessions will no longer spread
across the horizon.

³⁰ "They will not escape the darkness.
The burning sun will wither their
shoots,
and the breath of God will destroy
them.
³¹ Let them no longer fool themselves by
trusting in empty riches,
for emptiness will be their only reward.
³² They will be cut down in the prime
of life;
their branches will never again be
green.
³³ They will be like a vine whose grapes are
harvested too early,

like an olive tree that loses its blossoms
before the fruit can form.
³⁴ For the godless are barren.
Their homes, enriched through bribery,
will burn.
³⁵ They conceive trouble and give birth to
evil.
Their womb produces deceit."

CHAPTER 16
Job's Fifth Speech: A Response to Eliphaz
Then Job spoke again:

² "I have heard all this before.
What miserable comforters you are!
³ Won't you ever stop blowing hot air?
What makes you keep on talking?
⁴ I could say the same things if you were in
my place.
I could spout off criticism and shake my
head at you.
⁵ But if it were me, I would encourage you.
I would try to take away your grief.
⁶ Instead, I suffer if I defend myself,
and I suffer no less if I refuse to speak.

⁷ "O God, you have ground me down
and devastated my family.
⁸ As if to prove I have sinned, you've
reduced me to skin and bones.
My gaunt flesh testifies against me.
⁹ God hates me and angrily tears me apart.
He snaps his teeth at me
and pierces me with his eyes.
¹⁰ People jeer and laugh at me.
They slap my cheek in contempt.
A mob gathers against me.
¹¹ God has handed me over to sinners.
He has tossed me into the hands of the
wicked.

¹² "I was living quietly until he
shattered me.
He took me by the neck and broke me
in pieces.
Then he set me up as his target,
¹³ and now his archers surround me.
His arrows pierce me without mercy.
The ground is wet with my blood.*
¹⁴ Again and again he smashes against me,
charging at me like a warrior.

15:23 Greek version reads *He is appointed to be food for a vulture.* 16:13 Hebrew *my gall.*

16:1-5 Most of us have known "miserable comforters": those who give advice, those who offer
solutions, those who lecture us concerning our failures and mistakes. They generally mean well,
but they know little about comfort. Paul tells us that the comfort we offer should grow out of the
wealth of comfort we have received from God (2 Corinthians 1:3-7). We should note the ways we
have been comforted by God; this will help us comfort the people we love.

¹⁵ I wear burlap to show my grief.
   My pride lies in the dust.
¹⁶ My eyes are red with weeping;
   dark shadows circle my eyes.
¹⁷ Yet I have done no wrong,
   and my prayer is pure.

¹⁸ "O earth, do not conceal my blood.
   Let it cry out on my behalf.
¹⁹ Even now my witness is in heaven.
   My advocate is there on high.
²⁰ My friends scorn me,
   but I pour out my tears to God.
²¹ I need someone to mediate between God
      and me,
   as a person mediates between friends.
²² For soon I must go down that road
   from which I will never return.

CHAPTER 17
Job Continues to Defend His Innocence
¹ "My spirit is crushed,
   and my life is nearly snuffed out.
   The grave is ready to receive me.
² I am surrounded by mockers.
   I watch how bitterly they taunt me.

³ "You must defend my innocence,
      O God,
   since no one else will stand up
      for me.
⁴ You have closed their minds to
      understanding,
   but do not let them triumph.
⁵ They betray their friends for their own
      advantage,
   so let their children faint with
      hunger.

⁶ "God has made a mockery of me among
      the people;
   they spit in my face.

17:13 Hebrew *to Sheol;* also in 17:16.

⁷ My eyes are swollen with weeping,
   and I am but a shadow of my former
      self.
⁸ The virtuous are horrified when they
      see me.
   The innocent rise up against the
      ungodly.
⁹ The righteous keep moving forward,
   and those with clean hands become
      stronger and stronger.

¹⁰ "As for all of you, come back with a better
      argument,
   though I still won't find a wise man
      among you.
¹¹ My days are over.
   My hopes have disappeared.
   My heart's desires are broken.
¹² These men say that night is day;
   they claim that the darkness is light.
¹³ What if I go to the grave*
   and make my bed in darkness?
¹⁴ What if I call the grave my father,
   and the maggot my mother or my
      sister?
¹⁵ Where then is my hope?
   Can anyone find it?
¹⁶ No, my hope will go down with me to the
      grave.
   We will rest together in the dust!"

CHAPTER 18
Bildad's Second Response to Job
Then Bildad the Shuhite replied:

² "How long before you stop talking?
   Speak sense if you want us to answer!
³ Do you think we are mere animals?
   Do you think we are stupid?
⁴ You may tear out your hair in anger,
   but will that destroy the earth?
   Will it make the rocks tremble?

16:18–17:2 How frightening death can be to those who are unaware of God's glorious hope! Job knew God. He even knew that God was his advocate and friend. But the glory of eternity hadn't yet been revealed to God's people. Though we have God's Word, we, too, fear giving up our mortal body. This world is the home we know; eternity is the home that awaits us.

17:3-12 Friends are often most supportive at the beginning of our tough times. Later they attempt to instruct or judge us. Sometimes they just disappear altogether. Job confronted the meaningless words of his accusers. Unlike his friends, Job offered no explanations for his pain. All he knew was that his heart was heavy, and his friends offered heartless words. If our friends provide us with no comfort, we should either ask them to leave or give them some direction as to how they can help.

18:1-21 We can see Job's frustration as he longed for just a little comfort from his friends. Bildad wanted to know why Job offered speeches and why he regarded the words of his friends as stupid. The answer is fairly simple: Job's friends didn't know what they were talking about. We should never burden our suffering friends with unnecessary guilt. God is the only one in the position to judge. We should support, not judge, our friends in need.

5 "Surely the light of the wicked will be
    snuffed out.
  The sparks of their fire will not glow.
6 The light in their tent will grow dark.
  The lamp hanging above them will be
    quenched.
7 The confident stride of the wicked will be
    shortened.
  Their own schemes will be their
    downfall.
8 The wicked walk into a net.
  They fall into a pit.
9 A trap grabs them by the heel.
  A snare holds them tight.
10 A noose lies hidden on the ground.
  A rope is stretched across their path.

11 "Terrors surround the wicked
  and trouble them at every step.
12 Hunger depletes their strength,
  and calamity waits for them to stumble.
13 Disease eats their skin;
  death devours their limbs.
14 They are torn from the security of their
    homes
  and are brought down to the king of
    terrors.
15 The homes of the wicked will burn down;
  burning sulfur rains on their houses.
16 Their roots will dry up,
  and their branches will wither.
17 All memory of their existence will fade
    from the earth;
  no one will remember their names.
18 They will be thrust from light into
    darkness,
  driven from the world.
19 They will have neither children nor
    grandchildren,
  nor any survivor in the place where
    they lived.
20 People in the west are appalled at their
    fate;

people in the east are horrified.
21 They will say, 'This was the home of a
    wicked person,
  the place of one who rejected God.'"

CHAPTER 19
Job's Sixth Speech: A Response to Bildad
Then Job spoke again:

2 "How long will you torture me?
  How long will you try to crush me with
    your words?
3 You have already insulted me ten times.
  You should be ashamed of treating me
    so badly.
4 Even if I have sinned,
  that is my concern, not yours.
5 You think you're better than I am,
  using my humiliation as evidence of
    my sin.
6 But it is God who has wronged me,
  capturing me in his net.*

7 "I cry out, 'Help!' but no one answers me.
  I protest, but there is no justice.
8 God has blocked my way so I cannot
    move.
  He has plunged my path into darkness.
9 He has stripped me of my honor
  and removed the crown from my
    head.
10 He has demolished me on every side, and
    I am finished.
  He has uprooted my hope like a fallen
    tree.
11 His fury burns against me;
  he counts me as an enemy.
12 His troops advance.
  They build up roads to attack me.
  They camp all around my tent.

13 "My relatives stay far away,
  and my friends have turned
    against me.

19:6 Or *for I am like a city under siege.*

19:23-27 Job's spiritual growth should encourage us as we struggle with our own pain. As we grieve over losses in this world, we learn to see the reality of eternity. Once Job saw death as unrelenting darkness and gloom (see 10:20-22); now he testifies to a living Redeemer. The Hebrew word translated "Redeemer" here can also mean "vindicator." By saying "I know that my Redeemer lives," Job was saying, in effect, "I trust that God will someday clear my name of these supposed sins my friends think I'm guilty of." Job had faith that God would clear his name and that he would eventually see God face to face. We, too, have a living Redeemer—Jesus Christ. Though we are not as blameless as Job was, Jesus has redeemed us through his life, death, and resurrection. If we believe in him, he will rescue us from eternal darkness.
19:28-29 If we live by judgment and condemnation, Job reminds us that we are in danger of punishment. It is critical that we recognize grace. It is by grace that we are saved, and it is by grace that we live in this world. We need to remember that we will be judged by the measure with which we judge others (Matthew 7:1-5; James 2:12-13).

¹⁴ My family is gone,
  and my close friends have
    forgotten me.
¹⁵ My servants and maids consider me
    a stranger.
  I am like a foreigner to them.
¹⁶ When I call my servant, he doesn't come;
  I have to plead with him!
¹⁷ My breath is repulsive to my wife.
  I am rejected by my own family.
¹⁸ Even young children despise me.
  When I stand to speak, they turn their
    backs on me.
¹⁹ My close friends detest me.
  Those I loved have turned against me.
²⁰ I have been reduced to skin and bones
  and have escaped death by the skin of
    my teeth.

²¹ "Have mercy on me, my friends, have
    mercy,
  for the hand of God has struck me.
²² Must you also persecute me, like God
    does?
  Haven't you chewed me up enough?

²³ "Oh, that my words could be recorded.
  Oh, that they could be inscribed on a
    monument,
²⁴ carved with an iron chisel and filled with
    lead,
  engraved forever in the rock.

²⁵ "But as for me, I know that my Redeemer
    lives,
  and he will stand upon the earth at last.
²⁶ And after my body has decayed,
  yet in my body I will see God!*
²⁷ I will see him for myself.
  Yes, I will see him with my own eyes.
  I am overwhelmed at the thought!

²⁸ "How dare you go on persecuting me,
  saying, 'It's his own fault'?
²⁹ You should fear punishment yourselves,
  for your attitude deserves punishment.
  Then you will know that there is indeed
    a judgment."

CHAPTER 20
Zophar's Second Response to Job
Then Zophar the Naamathite replied:

² "I must reply
  because I am greatly disturbed.
³ I've had to endure your insults,
  but now my spirit prompts me to reply.

19:26 Or *without my body I will see God!* The meaning of
the Hebrew is uncertain.

FAITH

READ JOB 19:8-27
When we experience pain and loss because
of something that is beyond our control,
we may feel like God is our enemy. The
anger and confusion we may feel don't
need to destroy our faith. We may never
grasp why God allows such trials, but at
such times we need to wholly trust in God,
who is sovereign and will not allow us to
suffer more than we can bear.

Job felt this way, too. He said, "God has
blocked my way so I cannot move. He has
plunged my path into darkness. He has
stripped me of my honor and removed the
crown from my head. He has demolished
me on every side, and I am finished. He has
uprooted my hope like a fallen tree. His
fury burns against me; he counts me as an
enemy. His troops advance. They build up
roads to attack me. They camp all around
my tent. . . . My close friends detest me.
Those I loved have turned against me. I
have been reduced to skin and bones and
have escaped death by the skin of my
teeth. . . . Oh, that my words could be
recorded. Oh, that they could be inscribed
on a monument, carved with an iron chisel
and filled with lead, engraved forever in
the rock" (Job 19:8-24).

Despite Job's confusion and pain, he was
able to conclude his complaint with a
statement of his faith in God: "But as for
me, I know that my Redeemer lives, and he
will stand upon the earth at last. And after
my body has decayed, yet in my body I will
see God! I will see him for myself. Yes, I will
see him with my own eyes. I am
overwhelmed at the thought!" (Job
19:25-27). God is on our side, even if we
can't see it right now. *Turn to page 685,
Psalm 8.*

4 "Don't you realize that from the
   beginning of time,
      ever since people were first placed on
      the earth,
5 the triumph of the wicked has been short
   lived
      and the joy of the godless has been
      only temporary?
6 Though the pride of the godless reaches to
   the heavens
      and their heads touch the clouds,
7 yet they will vanish forever,
      thrown away like their own dung.
   Those who knew them will ask,
      'Where are they?'
8 They will fade like a dream and not be
   found.
      They will vanish like a vision in the
      night.
9 Those who once saw them will see them
   no more.
      Their families will never see them
      again.
10 Their children will beg from the poor,
      for they must give back their stolen
      riches.
11 Though they are young,
      their bones will lie in the dust.

12 "They enjoyed the sweet taste of
   wickedness,
      letting it melt under their tongue.
13 They savored it,
      holding it long in their mouths.
14 But suddenly the food in their bellies
   turns sour,
      a poisonous venom in their stomach.
15 They will vomit the wealth they swallowed.
      God won't let them keep it down.
16 They will suck the poison of cobras.
      The viper will kill them.
17 They will never again enjoy streams of
   olive oil
      or rivers of milk and honey.
18 They will give back everything they
   worked for.

20:25 Hebrew *with gall.*

Their wealth will bring them no joy.
19 For they oppressed the poor and left them
   destitute.
      They foreclosed on their homes.
20 They were always greedy and never
   satisfied.
      Nothing remains of all the things they
      dreamed about.
21 Nothing is left after they finish gorging
   themselves.
      Therefore, their prosperity will not
      endure.

22 "In the midst of plenty, they will run into
   trouble
      and be overcome by misery.
23 May God give them a bellyful of trouble.
      May God rain down his anger upon
      them.
24 When they try to escape an iron weapon,
      a bronze-tipped arrow will pierce them.
25 The arrow is pulled from their back,
      and the arrowhead glistens with
      blood.*
   The terrors of death are upon them.
26   Their treasures will be thrown into
      deepest darkness.
   A wildfire will devour their goods,
      consuming all they have left.
27 The heavens will reveal their guilt,
      and the earth will testify against them.
28 A flood will sweep away their house.
      God's anger will descend on them in
      torrents.
29 This is the reward that God gives the
   wicked.
      It is the inheritance decreed by God."

CHAPTER 21
Job's Seventh Speech: A Response to Zophar
Then Job spoke again:

2 "Listen closely to what I am saying.
      That's one consolation you can
      give me.

20:4-29 Imagine asking Zophar to paint a portrait of God. What images would we see? Zophar would probably paint an angry God dealing heavy blows against the ungodly. Where is the God who is patient and kind, compassionate and slow to anger? Where is the God whose love is unfailing? If we have any doubts as to God's compassion, we need only look to Christ. He gave his own life so that we could be forgiven and have fellowship with him. "Since [God] did not spare even his own Son but gave him up for us all, won't he also give us everything else?" (Romans 8:32).

21:1-21 Job refuted his friend's arguments by saying that the wicked succeed, have large families, great wealth, and long lives. He said that "the light of the wicked never seems to be extinguished." If there are exceptions to the assumptions of Job's friends, there are exceptions to

³ Bear with me, and let me speak.
  After I have spoken, you may resume
    mocking me.

⁴ "My complaint is with God, not with
    people.
  I have good reason to be so impatient.
⁵ Look at me and be stunned.
  Put your hand over your mouth in
    shock.
⁶ When I think about what I am saying,
    I shudder.
  My body trembles.

⁷ "Why do the wicked prosper,
  growing old and powerful?
⁸ They live to see their children grow up
    and settle down,
  and they enjoy their grandchildren.
⁹ Their homes are safe from every fear,
  and God does not punish them.
¹⁰ Their bulls never fail to breed.
  Their cows bear calves and never
    miscarry.
¹¹ They let their children frisk about like
    lambs.
  Their little ones skip and dance.
¹² They sing with tambourine and harp.
  They celebrate to the sound of the flute.
¹³ They spend their days in prosperity,
  then go down to the grave* in peace.
¹⁴ And yet they say to God, 'Go away.
  We want no part of you and your ways.
¹⁵ Who is the Almighty, and why should we
    obey him?
  What good will it do us to pray?'
¹⁶ (They think their prosperity is of their
    own doing,
  but I will have nothing to do with that
    kind of thinking.)

¹⁷ "Yet the light of the wicked never seems
    to be extinguished.
  Do they ever have trouble?
  Does God distribute sorrows to them in
    anger?
¹⁸ Are they driven before the wind like
    straw?

Are they carried away by the storm like
    chaff?
  Not at all!

¹⁹ "'Well,' you say, 'at least God will punish
    their children!'
  But I say he should punish the ones
    who sin,
  so that they understand his judgment.
²⁰ Let them see their destruction with their
    own eyes.
  Let them drink deeply of the anger of
    the Almighty.
²¹ For they will not care what happens to
    their family
  after they are dead.

²² "But who can teach a lesson to God,
  since he judges even the most
    powerful?
²³ One person dies in prosperity,
  completely comfortable and secure,
²⁴ the picture of good health,
  vigorous and fit.
²⁵ Another person dies in bitter poverty,
  never having tasted the good life.
²⁶ But both are buried in the same dust,
  both eaten by the same maggots.

²⁷ "Look, I know what you're thinking.
  I know the schemes you plot
    against me.
²⁸ You will tell me of rich and wicked
    people
  whose houses have vanished because
    of their sins.
²⁹ But ask those who have been around,
  and they will tell you the truth.
³⁰ Evil people are spared in times of calamity
  and are allowed to escape disaster.
³¹ No one criticizes them openly
  or pays them back for what they have
    done.
³² When they are carried to the grave,
  an honor guard keeps watch at their
    tomb.
³³ A great funeral procession goes to the
    cemetery.

21:13 Hebrew *to Sheol.*

---

the rule that the godly will not suffer. Of course we know that those who seem to get away with evil acts without punishment here on earth will be judged in heaven. We should take comfort in the fact that though we may endure hardships here on earth, in heaven we will be comforted (see Luke 16:19-31).

21:22-26 Job examined the futility of this world's treasures firsthand. His discovery was simple: Those who have known great prosperity meet the same end as those who have known poverty. All will die; all bodies will return to the dust. The treasures we store up in this world will meet the same fate. Earthly conditions don't matter all that much from an eternal perspective. We should store our treasures in heaven, not on earth (see Matthew 6:19-21).

Many pay their respects as the body is
laid to rest,
and the earth gives sweet repose.

34 "How can your empty clichés
comfort me?
All your explanations are lies!"

CHAPTER 22
Eliphaz's Third Response to Job
Then Eliphaz the Temanite replied:

2 "Can a person do anything to help God?
Can even a wise person be helpful to
him?
3 Is it any advantage to the Almighty if you
are righteous?
Would it be any gain to him if you were
perfect?
4 Is it because you're so pious that he
accuses you
and brings judgment against you?
5 No, it's because of your wickedness!
There's no limit to your sins.

6 "For example, you must have lent money
to your friend
and demanded clothing as security.
Yes, you stripped him to the bone.
7 You must have refused water for the
thirsty
and food for the hungry.
8 You probably think the land belongs to
the powerful
and only the privileged have a right
to it!
9 You must have sent widows away
empty-handed
and crushed the hopes of orphans.
10 That is why you are surrounded by traps
and tremble from sudden fears.
11 That is why you cannot see in the
darkness,
and waves of water cover you.

12 "God is so great—higher than the
heavens,

higher than the farthest stars.
13 But you reply, 'That's why God can't see
what I am doing!
How can he judge through the thick
darkness?
14 For thick clouds swirl about him, and he
cannot see us.
He is way up there, walking on the
vault of heaven.'

15 "Will you continue on the old paths
where evil people have walked?
16 They were snatched away in the prime of
life,
the foundations of their lives washed
away.
17 For they said to God, 'Leave us alone!
What can the Almighty do to us?'
18 Yet he was the one who filled their homes
with good things,
so I will have nothing to do with that
kind of thinking.

19 "The righteous will be happy to see the
wicked destroyed,
and the innocent will laugh in
contempt.
20 They will say, 'See how our enemies have
been destroyed.
The last of them have been consumed
in the fire.'

21 "Submit to God, and you will have
peace;
then things will go well for you.
22 Listen to his instructions,
and store them in your heart.
23 If you return to the Almighty, you will be
restored—
so clean up your life.
24 If you give up your lust for money
and throw your precious gold into the
river,
25 the Almighty himself will be your
treasure.
He will be your precious silver!

22:1-10 Eliphaz listed sins he was sure Job had committed at one time or another. It is easy for us to project our own sins on other people, claiming others to be guilty of the mistakes we have made. Eliphaz may have been guilty of these sins and perhaps was making himself feel better by condemning Job for them. We must be careful how we react to the problems or sins of others. Are we being honest with them? Are we using defense mechanisms to soothe our own guilt? If so, we need to stop denying our faults, confess our sins, and start down the road to recovery.
22:21-25 While Eliphaz's advice didn't apply to Job, it is clearly applicable to many of us. The pain we suffer as a consequence of our dependencies should tell us that our way of coping with life is not working. We may have tried living without God, but then we discovered that it led to disaster. All we need to do is give our life over to God, and he will help us in the process of recovery. We can find all we were searching for in God. He is our comfort, our hope, and our "treasure."

26 "Then you will take delight in the
 Almighty
  and look up to God.
27 You will pray to him, and he will hear
 you,
  and you will fulfill your vows to him.
28 You will succeed in whatever you choose
 to do,
  and light will shine on the road ahead
   of you.
29 If people are in trouble and you say, 'Help
 them,'
  God will save them.
30 Even sinners will be rescued;
  they will be rescued because your hands
   are pure."

CHAPTER 23
Job's Eighth Speech: A Response to Eliphaz
Then Job spoke again:

2 "My complaint today is still a bitter one,
  and I try hard not to groan aloud.
3 If only I knew where to find God,
  I would go to his court.
4 I would lay out my case
  and present my arguments.
5 Then I would listen to his reply
  and understand what he says to me.
6 Would he use his great power to argue
 with me?
  No, he would give me a fair hearing.
7 Honest people can reason with him,
  so I would be forever acquitted by my
   judge.
8 I go east, but he is not there.
  I go west, but I cannot find him.
9 I do not see him in the north, for he is
 hidden.
  I look to the south, but he is concealed.

10 "But he knows where I am going.
  And when he tests me, I will come out
   as pure as gold.
11 For I have stayed on God's paths;
  I have followed his ways and not
   turned aside.

12 I have not departed from his commands,
  but have treasured his words more than
   daily food.
13 But once he has made his decision, who
 can change his mind?
  Whatever he wants to do, he does.
14 So he will do to me whatever he has
 planned.
  He controls my destiny.
15 No wonder I am so terrified in his
 presence.
  When I think of it, terror grips me.
16 God has made me sick at heart;
  the Almighty has terrified me.
17 Darkness is all around me;
  thick, impenetrable darkness is
   everywhere.

CHAPTER 24
Job Asks Why the Wicked Are Not Punished
1 "Why doesn't the Almighty bring the
 wicked to judgment?
  Why must the godly wait for him in
   vain?
2 Evil people steal land by moving the
 boundary markers.
  They steal livestock and put them in
   their own pastures.
3 They take the orphan's donkey
  and demand the widow's ox as security
   for a loan.
4 The poor are pushed off the path;
  the needy must hide together for safety.
5 Like wild donkeys in the wilderness,
  the poor must spend all their time
   looking for food,
  searching even in the desert for food for
   their children.
6 They harvest a field they do not own,
  and they glean in the vineyards of the
   wicked.
7 All night they lie naked in the cold,
  without clothing or covering.
8 They are soaked by mountain showers,
  and they huddle against the rocks for
   want of a home.

23:1-17 Throughout his trials, Job was always honest about what he was thinking and feeling.
Strong emotions are a natural part of our responses to this life. In and of themselves they should
not be labeled either "good" or "bad." We should give our friends, our family, and our God the
gift of honest expression. We should let them know how we feel and what we think. This will
make us feel better, too. As we vent our emotions in positive ways, we will be set free from the
tensions that build up inside us.
24:1-25 Why aren't the faithful rewarded or even protected? Why don't exploiters meet a speedy
punishment? Where is God when we cry for help? As we face momentous losses, we are often
compelled to rediscover the foundations of our faith. Job probed the whole realms of God's
justice, judgment, and timing and came to a humble conclusion: God's ways are just. We are
often confused by his timing, but his ways are ultimately just.

9 "The wicked snatch a widow's child from
  her breast,
    taking the baby as security for a loan.
10 The poor must go about naked, without
  any clothing.
    They harvest food for others while they
    themselves are starving.
11 They press out olive oil without being
  allowed to taste it,
    and they tread in the winepress as they
    suffer from thirst.
12 The groans of the dying rise from the city,
  and the wounded cry for help,
    yet God ignores their moaning.

13 "Wicked people rebel against the light.
  They refuse to acknowledge its ways
  or stay in its paths.
14 The murderer rises in the early dawn
  to kill the poor and needy;
    at night he is a thief.
15 The adulterer waits for the twilight,
  saying, 'No one will see me then.'
    He hides his face so no one will know
    him.
16 Thieves break into houses at night
  and sleep in the daytime.
    They are not acquainted with the light.
17 The black night is their morning.
  They ally themselves with the terrors of
  the darkness.

18 "But they disappear like foam down a
  river.
    Everything they own is cursed,
    and they are afraid to enter their own
    vineyards.
19 The grave* consumes sinners
  just as drought and heat consume
  snow.
20 Their own mothers will forget them.
  Maggots will find them sweet to eat.

24:19 Hebrew *Sheol*.

No one will remember them.
  Wicked people are broken like a tree in
  the storm.
21 They cheat the woman who has no son to
  help her.
    They refuse to help the needy widow.

22 "God, in his power, drags away the rich.
  They may rise high, but they have no
  assurance of life.
23 They may be allowed to live in security,
  but God is always watching them.
24 And though they are great now,
  in a moment they will be gone like all
  others,
    cut off like heads of grain.
25 Can anyone claim otherwise?
  Who can prove me wrong?"

CHAPTER 25
Bildad's Third Response to Job
Then Bildad the Shuhite replied:

2 "God is powerful and dreadful.
  He enforces peace in the heavens.
3 Who is able to count his heavenly army?
  Doesn't his light shine on all the earth?
4 How can a mortal be innocent before
  God?
    Can anyone born of a woman be pure?
5 God is more glorious than the moon;
  he shines brighter than the stars.
6 In comparison, people are maggots;
  we mortals are mere worms."

CHAPTER 26
Job's Ninth Speech: A Response to Bildad
Then Job spoke again:

2 "How you have helped the powerless!
  How you have saved the weak!
3 How you have enlightened my stupidity!
  What wise advice you have offered!

24:22-25 Our need for security affects our decisions, attitudes, and actions every day. Each of us has a working definition of security, and we fear anything that threatens it. Job's entire foundation in this world had been shaken, and yet he learned an important lesson about security. Real security doesn't lie in what this world has to offer; it lies in the consistency, the justice, the faithfulness, and the overwhelming power and love of God.

25:1-6 Bildad described a god who thought little of man, but that is not our God. We are made "wonderfully complex" (see Psalm 139:14), crowned with glory and honor (see Psalm 8:5), and fashioned in the image of a God who gives good gifts to his children. No matter how difficult our life may be, we can count on God's love, commitment, patience, and compassion. We have great worth in God's eyes.

26:1-14 It is difficult for us to admit our powerlessness. We spend years building the illusion that we are in control, only to face events that make it clear that we have no control at all. This is the first step in any recovery from a dependency or compulsion. Job was powerless over his situation. We, too, are powerless over our dependency and the circumstances that fuel it. But when we call on God for help, we will find he is merciful and willing to help us.

⁴Where have you gotten all these wise
  sayings?
  Whose spirit speaks through you?

⁵"The dead tremble—
  those who live beneath the waters.
⁶The underworld* is naked in God's
  presence.
  The place of destruction* is uncovered.
⁷God stretches the northern sky over
  empty space
  and hangs the earth on nothing.
⁸He wraps the rain in his thick clouds,
  and the clouds don't burst with the
  weight.
⁹He covers the face of the moon,*
  shrouding it with his clouds.
¹⁰He created the horizon when he separated
  the waters;
  he set the boundary between day and
  night.
¹¹The foundations of heaven tremble;
  they shudder at his rebuke.
¹²By his power the sea grew calm.
  By his skill he crushed the great sea
  monster.*
¹³His Spirit made the heavens beautiful,
  and his power pierced the gliding
  serpent.
¹⁴These are just the beginning of all that he
  does,
  merely a whisper of his power.
  Who, then, can comprehend the
  thunder of his power?"

CHAPTER 27
Job's Final Speech
Job continued speaking:

²"I vow by the living God, who has taken
  away my rights,
  by the Almighty who has embittered
  my soul—
³As long as I live,
  while I have breath from God,
⁴my lips will speak no evil,
  and my tongue will speak no lies.
⁵I will never concede that you are right;
  I will defend my integrity until I die.

⁶I will maintain my innocence without
  wavering.
  My conscience is clear for as long
  as I live.

⁷"May my enemy be punished like the
  wicked,
  my adversary like those who do evil.
⁸For what hope do the godless have when
  God cuts them off
  and takes away their life?
⁹Will God listen to their cry
  when trouble comes upon them?
¹⁰Can they take delight in the Almighty?
  Can they call to God at any time?
¹¹I will teach you about God's power.
  I will not conceal anything concerning
  the Almighty.
¹²But you have seen all this,
  yet you say all these useless things to me.

¹³"This is what the wicked will receive from
  God;
  this is their inheritance from the
  Almighty.
¹⁴They may have many children,
  but the children will die in war or
  starve to death.
¹⁵Those who survive will die of a plague,
  and not even their widows will mourn
  them.

¹⁶"Evil people may have piles of money
  and may store away mounds of
  clothing.
¹⁷But the righteous will wear that clothing,
  and the innocent will divide that money.
¹⁸The wicked build houses as fragile as a
  spider's web,*
  as flimsy as a shelter made of branches.
¹⁹The wicked go to bed rich
  but wake to find that all their wealth
  is gone.
²⁰Terror overwhelms them like a flood,
  and they are blown away in the storms
  of the night.
²¹The east wind carries them away, and they
  are gone.
  It sweeps them away.

26:6a Hebrew *Sheol.* **26:6b** Hebrew *Abaddon.* **26:9** Or *covers his throne.* **26:12** Hebrew *Rahab*, the name of a mythical sea monster that represents chaos in ancient literature. **27:18** As in Greek and Syriac versions (see also 8:14); Hebrew reads *a moth.*

27:1-4 Job vowed that he would not speak against God—yet he had suffered despite his innocence! Most of us readily denounce God as unjust, even when we are clearly suffering the consequences of our actions. This is denial in its greatest form—insisting that we have done nothing wrong and blaming our fair and merciful God. To recover successfully, we need to take inventory of our life and see where we have deviated from God's will. Then we need to submit to God's control and ask him to work with us to overcome our dependency.

²² It whirls down on them without
  mercy.
  They struggle to flee from its power.
²³ But everyone jeers at them
  and mocks them.

CHAPTER 28
Job Speaks of Wisdom and Understanding

¹ "People know where to mine silver
  and how to refine gold.
² They know where to dig iron from the
  earth
  and how to smelt copper from rock.
³ They know how to shine light in the
  darkness
  and explore the farthest regions of the
  earth
  as they search in the dark for ore.
⁴ They sink a mine shaft into the earth
  far from where anyone lives.
  They descend on ropes, swinging back
  and forth.
⁵ Food is grown on the earth above,
  but down below, the earth is melted as
  by fire.
⁶ Here the rocks contain precious lapis
  lazuli,
  and the dust contains gold.
⁷ These are treasures no bird of prey
  can see,
  no falcon's eye observe.
⁸ No wild animal has walked upon these
  treasures;
  no lion has ever set his paw there.
⁹ People know how to tear apart flinty
  rocks
  and overturn the roots of mountains.
¹⁰ They cut tunnels in the rocks
  and uncover precious stones.
¹¹ They dam up the trickling streams
  and bring to light the hidden treasures.

¹² "But do people know where to find
  wisdom?
  Where can they find understanding?
¹³ No one knows where to find it,*
  for it is not found among the living.
¹⁴ 'It is not here,' says the ocean.

'Nor is it here,' says the sea.
¹⁵ It cannot be bought with gold.
  It cannot be purchased with silver.
¹⁶ It's worth more than all the gold
  of Ophir,
  greater than precious onyx or lapis
  lazuli.
¹⁷ Wisdom is more valuable than gold and
  crystal.
  It cannot be purchased with jewels
  mounted in fine gold.
¹⁸ Coral and jasper are worthless in trying to
  get it.
  The price of wisdom is far above
  rubies.
¹⁹ Precious peridot from Ethiopia* cannot be
  exchanged for it.
  It's worth more than the purest gold.

²⁰ "But do people know where to find
  wisdom?
  Where can they find understanding?
²¹ It is hidden from the eyes of all
  humanity.
  Even the sharp-eyed birds in the sky
  cannot discover it.
²² Destruction* and Death say,
  'We've heard only rumors of where
  wisdom can be found.'

²³ "God alone understands the way to
  wisdom;
  he knows where it can be found,
²⁴ for he looks throughout the whole
  earth
  and sees everything under the
  heavens.
²⁵ He decided how hard the winds should
  blow
  and how much rain should fall.
²⁶ He made the laws for the rain
  and laid out a path for the lightning.
²⁷ Then he saw wisdom and evaluated it.
  He set it in place and examined it
  thoroughly.
²⁸ And this is what he says to all
  humanity:
  'The fear of the Lord is true wisdom;
  to forsake evil is real understanding.'"

28:13 As in Greek version; Hebrew reads *knows its value.* 28:19 Hebrew *from Cush.* 28:22 Hebrew *Abaddon.*

28:28 "The fear of the Lord is true wisdom; to forsake evil is real understanding." This is God's message to man—that wisdom is found only in God and his ways. But how do we know what God wants of us? God has given us his truth in the Bible. We are responsible to study it and discover what he expects of us. We should ask God to show us his truth and then take the time to listen as God reveals his truth to us. He will give us the strength and encouragement we need to follow his program for recovery (see James 1:5).

CHAPTER 29
Job Speaks of His Former Blessings
Job continued speaking:

2 "I long for the years gone by
  when God took care of me,
3 when he lit up the way before me
  and I walked safely through the
    darkness.
4 When I was in my prime,
  God's friendship was felt in my home.
5 The Almighty was still with me,
  and my children were around me.
6 My steps were awash in cream,
  and the rocks gushed olive oil for me.

7 "Those were the days when I went to the
    city gate
  and took my place among the honored
    leaders.
8 The young stepped aside when they
    saw me,
  and even the aged rose in respect at my
    coming.
9 The princes stood in silence
  and put their hands over their mouths.
10 The highest officials of the city stood
    quietly,
  holding their tongues in respect.

11 "All who heard me praised me.
  All who saw me spoke well of me.
12 For I assisted the poor in their need
  and the orphans who required help.
13 I helped those without hope, and they
    blessed me.
  And I caused the widows' hearts to sing
    for joy.
14 Everything I did was honest.
  Righteousness covered me like a robe,
  and I wore justice like a turban.
15 I served as eyes for the blind
  and feet for the lame.

16 I was a father to the poor
  and assisted strangers who needed help.
17 I broke the jaws of godless oppressors
  and plucked their victims from their
    teeth.

18 "I thought, 'Surely I will die surrounded
    by my family
  after a long, good life.*
19 For I am like a tree whose roots reach the
    water,
  whose branches are refreshed with
    the dew.
20 New honors are constantly bestowed
    on me,
  and my strength is continually
    renewed.'

21 "Everyone listened to my advice.
  They were silent as they waited for me
    to speak.
22 And after I spoke, they had nothing to
    add,
  for my counsel satisfied them.
23 They longed for me to speak as people
    long for rain.
  They drank my words like a refreshing
    spring rain.
24 When they were discouraged, I smiled at
    them.
  My look of approval was precious
    to them.
25 Like a chief, I told them what to do.
  I lived like a king among his troops
  and comforted those who mourned.

CHAPTER 30
Job Speaks of His Anguish
1 "But now I am mocked by people younger
    than I,
  by young men whose fathers are
  not worthy to run with my
    sheepdogs.

29:18 Hebrew *after I have counted my days like sand.*

29:1-3 Job found comfort in remembering the days when God had taken care of him. Those were days when Job felt secure. As hard as it is for us to believe, God continues to take care of us when we suffer. Even when the suffering is brought on by our own actions, he is there, waiting for us to call on him for deliverance.

29:4-17 Here we can almost see Job's countenance change as he recalled the joy of days gone by. A smile, a tear, a glow of contentment all passed on his face at his remembrance of a godly life. Where once Job cursed his birth (see 3:1-26), he now remembered the good times. By reflecting on better times in our life, we can begin to feel hope again. We were happy once. If we trust God, we can be sure that we will be happy again.

29:18-19 Our life now may be very different from what we had hoped it would be. We certainly didn't plan on becoming addicted to anything. But even though we have failed to fulfill our youthful dreams, we don't have to give up hope. Once we admit we have problems, things can still be fixed. But first we have to give our life over to God—only he can overcome the dependency that controls us. It is never too late to get our life back on track.

2 A lot of good they are to me—
those worn-out wretches!

3 They are gaunt from poverty and hunger.
They claw the dry ground in desolate
wastelands.

4 They pluck wild greens from among the
bushes
and eat from the roots of broom trees.

5 They are driven from human society,
and people shout at them as if they
were thieves.

6 So now they live in frightening ravines,
in caves and among the rocks.

7 They sound like animals howling among
the bushes,
huddled together beneath the nettles.

8 They are nameless fools,
outcasts from society.

9 "And now they mock me with vulgar
songs!
They taunt me!

10 They despise me and won't come near me,
except to spit in my face.

11 For God has cut my bowstring.
He has humbled me,
so they have thrown off all restraint.

12 These outcasts oppose me to my face.
They send me sprawling
and lay traps in my path.

13 They block my road
and do everything they can to
destroy me.
They know I have no one to help me.

14 They come at me from all directions.
They jump on me when I am down.

15 I live in terror now.
My honor has blown away in the wind,
and my prosperity has vanished like a
cloud.

16 "And now my life seeps away.
Depression haunts my days.

17 At night my bones are filled with pain,
which gnaws at me relentlessly.

18 With a strong hand, God grabs my shirt.*

He grips me by the collar of my coat.

19 He has thrown me into the mud.
I'm nothing more than dust and ashes.

20 "I cry to you, O God, but you don't
answer.
I stand before you, but you don't even
look.

21 You have become cruel toward me.
You use your power to persecute me.

22 You throw me into the whirlwind
and destroy me in the storm.

23 And I know you are sending me to my
death—
the destination of all who live.

24 "Surely no one would turn against the
needy
when they cry for help in their trouble.

25 Did I not weep for those in trouble?
Was I not deeply grieved for the needy?

26 So I looked for good, but evil came
instead.
I waited for the light, but darkness fell.

27 My heart is troubled and restless.
Days of suffering torment me.

28 I walk in gloom, without sunlight.
I stand in the public square and cry for
help.

29 Instead, I am considered a brother to
jackals
and a companion to owls.

30 My skin has turned dark,
and my bones burn with fever.

31 My harp plays sad music,
and my flute accompanies those who
weep.

CHAPTER 31
Job's Final Protest of Innocence

1 "I made a covenant with my eyes
not to look with lust at a young
woman.

2 For what has God above chosen for us?
What is our inheritance from the
Almighty on high?

30:18 As in Greek version; Hebrew reads *hand, my garment is disfigured.*

30:16-31 When we are depressed, we tend to speak as Job spoke here. As we turn to God, displaying our raw emotions, God does hear. We have only to read Jeremiah, Lamentations, Psalms, and the words of Jesus as he approached his death to realize the emotional agony that accompanies suffering. God hears our complaints and cherishes our openness. It is only as we openly communicate with God that we can truly ask for his forgiveness and maintain an honest relationship with him.

30:20 As his suffering continued, Job began to feel certain that God wasn't listening. Job hadn't considered the possibility that God wasn't responding simply because Job wasn't giving him the chance to answer. We, like Job, may talk about God or even talk to God, but we don't usually stop long enough to let him talk to us. God speaks to us through his Word, the Bible, and through the Holy Spirit during our times of prayer and meditation. We need to be still and wait for God to speak to our heart.

³ Isn't it calamity for the wicked
  and misfortune for those who do evil?
⁴ Doesn't he see everything I do
  and every step I take?

⁵ "Have I lied to anyone
  or deceived anyone?
⁶ Let God weigh me on the scales of justice,
  for he knows my integrity.
⁷ If I have strayed from his pathway,
  or if my heart has lusted for what my
    eyes have seen,
  or if I am guilty of any other sin,
⁸ then let someone else eat the crops I have
    planted.
  Let all that I have planted be uprooted.

⁹ "If my heart has been seduced by a
    woman,
  or if I have lusted for my neighbor's
    wife,
¹⁰ then let my wife serve* another man;
  let other men sleep with her.
¹¹ For lust is a shameful sin,
  a crime that should be punished.
¹² It is a fire that burns all the way to hell.*
  It would wipe out everything I own.

¹³ "If I have been unfair to my male or
    female servants
  when they brought their complaints
    to me,
¹⁴ how could I face God?
  What could I say when he
    questioned me?
¹⁵ For God created both me and my servants.
  He created us both in the womb.

¹⁶ "Have I refused to help the poor,
  or crushed the hopes of widows?
¹⁷ Have I been stingy with my food
  and refused to share it with orphans?
¹⁸ No, from childhood I have cared for
    orphans like a father,
  and all my life I have cared for widows.
¹⁹ Whenever I saw the homeless without
    clothes
  and the needy with nothing to wear,
²⁰ did they not praise me

31:10 Hebrew *grind for.* 31:12 Hebrew *to Abaddon.*

for providing wool clothing to keep
  them warm?
²¹ "If I raised my hand against an orphan,
  knowing the judges would take my
    side,
²² then let my shoulder be wrenched out of
    place!
  Let my arm be torn from its socket!
²³ That would be better than facing God's
    judgment.
  For if the majesty of God opposes me,
    what hope is there?

²⁴ "Have I put my trust in money
  or felt secure because of my gold?
²⁵ Have I gloated about my wealth
  and all that I own?

²⁶ "Have I looked at the sun shining in the
    skies,
  or the moon walking down its silver
    pathway,
²⁷ and been secretly enticed in my heart
  to throw kisses at them in worship?
²⁸ If so, I should be punished by the judges,
  for it would mean I had denied the God
    of heaven.

²⁹ "Have I ever rejoiced when disaster struck
    my enemies,
  or become excited when harm came
    their way?
³⁰ No, I have never sinned by cursing
    anyone
  or by asking for revenge.

³¹ "My servants have never said,
  'He let others go hungry.'
³² I have never turned away a stranger
  but have opened my doors to everyone.

³³ "Have I tried to hide my sins like other
    people do,
  concealing my guilt in my heart?
³⁴ Have I feared the crowd
  or the contempt of the masses,
  so that I kept quiet and stayed indoors?

³⁵ "If only someone would listen to me!
  Look, I will sign my name to my
    defense.

31:35-36 Job wanted God to show him his failure. He was tired and wished desperately for some kind of resolution to his suffering. Job had already taken a critical inventory and found no clear reason for his suffering. He wanted God to explain what was going on. He was open to any explanation, even the possibility of his own guilt. In recovery we need Job's attitude as we make our personal inventory. Realizing our need for change, we need to honestly examine our life and pray that God will reveal any wrongs we have committed.

Let the Almighty answer me.
Let my accuser write out the charges
against me.
[36] I would face the accusation proudly.
I would wear it like a crown.
[37] For I would tell him exactly what I have
done.
I would come before him like a prince.

[38] "If my land accuses me
and all its furrows cry out together,
[39] or if I have stolen its crops
or murdered its owners,
[40] then let thistles grow on that land instead
of wheat,
and weeds instead of barley."

Job's words are ended.

CHAPTER 32
Elihu Responds to Job's Friends
Job's three friends refused to reply further to
him because he kept insisting on his
innocence.
[2] Then Elihu son of Barakel the Buzite, of
the clan of Ram, became angry. He was angry
because Job refused to admit that he had
sinned and that God was right in punishing
him. [3] He was also angry with Job's three
friends, for they made God* appear to be
wrong by their inability to answer Job's arguments. [4] Elihu had waited for the others to
speak to Job because they were older than he.
[5] But when he saw that they had no further
reply, he spoke out angrily. [6] Elihu son of
Barakel the Buzite said,

"I am young and you are old,
so I held back from telling you what I
think.
[7] I thought, 'Those who are older should
speak,
for wisdom comes with age.'
[8] But there is a spirit* within people,

the breath of the Almighty within
them,
that makes them intelligent.
[9] Sometimes the elders are not wise.
Sometimes the aged do not understand
justice.
[10] So listen to me,
and let me tell you what I think.

[11] "I have waited all this time,
listening very carefully to your
arguments,
listening to you grope for words.
[12] I have listened,
but not one of you has refuted Job
or answered his arguments.
[13] And don't tell me, 'He is too wise for us.
Only God can convince him.'
[14] If Job had been arguing with me,
I would not answer with your kind of
logic!
[15] You sit there baffled,
with nothing more to say.
[16] Should I continue to wait, now that you
are silent?
Must I also remain silent?
[17] No, I will say my piece.
I will speak my mind.
[18] For I am full of pent-up words,
and the spirit within me urges me on.
[19] I am like a cask of wine without a vent,
like a new wineskin ready to burst!
[20] I must speak to find relief,
so let me give my answers.
[21] I won't play favorites
or try to flatter anyone.
[22] For if I tried flattery,
my Creator would soon destroy me.

CHAPTER 33
Elihu Presents His Case against Job
[1] "Listen to my words, Job;
pay attention to what I have to say.

32:3 As in ancient Hebrew scribal tradition; the Masoretic Text reads Job. 32:8 Or Spirit; also in 32:18.

32:6-20 There will always be people like Elihu, who think they have all the answers. They will give us reasons for our actions and condemn our lifestyle, thinking that wisdom has been given to them alone. But we need to be careful about listening to these people. We need to consider: (1) Do they have our best interests at heart? (2) Do their words build us up or tear us down? (3) Is what they are saying from God? If any of these questions can be answered no, then they are not the people to help us in the recovery process. Elihu meant well, but his words, like those of Job's other three friends, did little to help Job cope with his suffering.
33:1-5 Elihu set himself up as someone with an upright heart who spoke sincerely, and yet he accused Job of being prideful for making the same claim (see 33:8-11). The sins we accuse others of are often the very sins we commit. This defense mechanism is called projection—we project our areas of weakness or sin onto others. As we identify a particular fault in someone else, we need to ask ourself, "Am I guilty of this, too?" If we hope to progress in recovery, we need to be honest and pinpoint the areas of denial in our own life.

[2] Now that I have begun to speak,
let me continue.
[3] I speak with all sincerity;
I speak the truth.
[4] For the Spirit of God has made me,
and the breath of the Almighty gives
me life.
[5] Answer me, if you can;
make your case and take your stand.
[6] Look, you and I both belong to God.
I, too, was formed from clay.
[7] So you don't need to be afraid of me.
I won't come down hard on you.

[8] "You have spoken in my hearing,
and I have heard your very words.
[9] You said, 'I am pure; I am without sin;
I am innocent; I have no guilt.
[10] God is picking a quarrel with me,
and he considers me his enemy.
[11] He puts my feet in the stocks
and watches my every move.'

[12] "But you are wrong, and I will show
you why.
For God is greater than any human
being.
[13] So why are you bringing a charge against
him?
Why say he does not respond to
people's complaints?
[14] For God speaks again and again,
though people do not recognize it.
[15] He speaks in dreams, in visions of the
night,
when deep sleep falls on people
as they lie in their beds.
[16] He whispers in their ears
and terrifies them with warnings.
[17] He makes them turn from doing wrong;
he keeps them from pride.
[18] He protects them from the grave,
from crossing over the river of death.

[19] "Or God disciplines people with pain on
their sickbeds,
with ceaseless aching in their bones.
[20] They lose their appetite
for even the most delicious food.
[21] Their flesh wastes away,

and their bones stick out.
[22] They are at death's door;
the angels of death wait for them.

[23] "But if an angel from heaven appears—
a special messenger to intercede for a
person
and declare that he is upright—
[24] he will be gracious and say,
'Rescue him from the grave,
for I have found a ransom for his life.'
[25] Then his body will become as healthy
as a child's,
firm and youthful again.
[26] When he prays to God,
he will be accepted.
And God will receive him with joy
and restore him to good standing.
[27] He will declare to his friends,
'I sinned and twisted the truth,
but it was not worth it.*
[28] God rescued me from the grave,
and now my life is filled with light.'

[29] "Yes, God does these things
again and again for people.
[30] He rescues them from the grave
so they may enjoy the light of life.
[31] Mark this well, Job. Listen to me,
for I have more to say.
[32] But if you have anything to say, go ahead.
Speak, for I am anxious to see you
justified.
[33] But if not, then listen to me.
Keep silent and I will teach you
wisdom!"

CHAPTER 34
Elihu Accuses Job of Arrogance
Then Elihu said:

[2] "Listen to me, you wise men.
Pay attention, you who have
knowledge.
[3] Job said, 'The ear tests the words it hears
just as the mouth distinguishes between
foods.'
[4] So let us discern for ourselves what
is right;
let us learn together what is good.

33:27 Greek version reads *but he* [God] *did not punish me as my sin deserved.*

34:1-15 Elihu, like Job's other friends, believed that external circumstances are a measuring stick for the quality of a person's faith. If Job was suffering, then he was getting what he deserved. But Elihu's assumptions were clearly wrong. Job's grief was not the consequence of a sinful past; it was a testimony to God's faith in his servant Job. As we face the temptation to revert to our dependency, we should remember that the pain we suffer testifies to our faith and our desire to stay free from addiction. When we are tempted, God "will not allow the temptation to be more than [we] can stand" (1 Corinthians 10:13).

⁵ For Job also said, 'I am innocent,
but God has taken away my rights.
⁶ I am innocent, but they call me a liar.
My suffering is incurable, though I have
not sinned.'

⁷ "Tell me, has there ever been a man like
Job,
with his thirst for irreverent talk?
⁸ He chooses evil people as companions.
He spends his time with wicked men.
⁹ He has even said, 'Why waste time
trying to please God?'

¹⁰ "Listen to me, you who have
understanding.
Everyone knows that God doesn't sin!
The Almighty can do no wrong.
¹¹ He repays people according to their deeds.
He treats people as they deserve.
¹² Truly, God will not do wrong.
The Almighty will not twist justice.
¹³ Did someone else put the world in his
care?
Who set the whole world in place?
¹⁴ If God were to take back his spirit
and withdraw his breath,
¹⁵ all life would cease,
and humanity would turn again to
dust.

¹⁶ "Now listen to me if you are wise.
Pay attention to what I say.
¹⁷ Could God govern if he hated justice?
Are you going to condemn the
almighty judge?
¹⁸ For he says to kings, 'You are wicked,'
and to nobles, 'You are unjust.'
¹⁹ He doesn't care how great a person
may be,
and he pays no more attention to the
rich than to the poor.
He made them all.
²⁰ In a moment they die.
In the middle of the night they pass
away;
the mighty are removed without
human hand.

²¹ "For God watches how people live;
he sees everything they do.
²² No darkness is thick enough

to hide the wicked from his eyes.
²³ We don't set the time
when we will come before God in
judgment.
²⁴ He brings the mighty to ruin without
asking anyone,
and he sets up others in their place.
²⁵ He knows what they do,
and in the night he overturns and
destroys them.
²⁶ He strikes them down because they are
wicked,
doing it openly for all to see.
²⁷ For they turned away from following him.
They have no respect for any of his
ways.
²⁸ They cause the poor to cry out, catching
God's attention.
He hears the cries of the needy.
²⁹ But if he chooses to remain quiet,
who can criticize him?
When he hides his face, no one can find
him,
whether an individual or a nation.
³⁰ He prevents the godless from ruling
so they cannot be a snare to the people.

³¹ "Why don't people say to God, 'I have
sinned,
but I will sin no more'?
³² Or 'I don't know what evil I have
done—tell me.
If I have done wrong, I will stop at
once'?

³³ "Must God tailor his justice to your
demands?
But you have rejected him!
The choice is yours, not mine.
Go ahead, share your wisdom with us.
³⁴ After all, bright people will tell me,
and wise people will hear me say,
³⁵ 'Job speaks out of ignorance;
his words lack insight.'
³⁶ Job, you deserve the maximum penalty
for the wicked way you have talked.
³⁷ For you have added rebellion to your sin;
you show no respect,
and you speak many angry words
against God."

34:16-33 Elihu displayed his misunderstanding of God in a variety of ways. According to Elihu,
God watches our actions, takes note of our deeds, and punishes us without need of further examination. This is not the God of the Bible. God looks at the heart, is endlessly patient, and is slow to
anger and quick to forgive. No one would be able to stand before Elihu's god and find mercy. But
anyone who honestly submits to the true God through his Son, Jesus, will find mercy (see Psalm
130).

CHAPTER 35
Elihu Reminds Job of God's Justice
Then Elihu said:

2 "Do you think it is right for you to claim,
  'I am righteous before God'?
3 For you also ask, 'What's in it for me?
  What's the use of living a righteous
    life?'

4 "I will answer you
  and all your friends, too.
5 Look up into the sky,
  and see the clouds high above you.
6 If you sin, how does that affect God?
  Even if you sin again and again,
  what effect will it have on him?
7 If you are good, is this some great gift to
    him?
  What could you possibly give him?
8 No, your sins affect only people like
    yourself,
  and your good deeds also affect only
    humans.

9 "People cry out when they are oppressed.
  They groan beneath the power of the
    mighty.
10 Yet they don't ask, 'Where is God my
    Creator,
  the one who gives songs in the
    night?
11 Where is the one who makes us smarter
    than the animals
  and wiser than the birds of the sky?'
12 And when they cry out, God does not
    answer
  because of their pride.
13 But it is wrong to say God doesn't listen,
  to say the Almighty isn't concerned.
14 You say you can't see him,
  but he will bring justice if you will only
    wait.*
15 You say he does not respond to sinners
    with anger
  and is not greatly concerned about
    wickedness.*

16 But you are talking nonsense, Job.
  You have spoken like a fool."

CHAPTER 36
Elihu continued speaking:

2 "Let me go on, and I will show you the
    truth.
  For I have not finished defending God!
3 I will present profound arguments
  for the righteousness of my Creator.
4 I am telling you nothing but the truth,
  for I am a man of great knowledge.

5 "God is mighty, but he does not despise
    anyone!
  He is mighty in both power and
    understanding.
6 He does not let the wicked live
  but gives justice to the afflicted.
7 He never takes his eyes off the innocent,
  but he sets them on thrones with
    kings
  and exalts them forever.
8 If they are bound in chains
  and caught up in a web of trouble,
9 he shows them the reason.
  He shows them their sins of pride.
10 He gets their attention
  and commands that they turn from
    evil.

11 "If they listen and obey God,
  they will be blessed with prosperity
    throughout their lives.
  All their years will be pleasant.
12 But if they refuse to listen to him,
  they will cross over the river of death,
  dying from lack of understanding.
13 For the godless are full of resentment.
  Even when he punishes them,
  they refuse to cry out to him for help.
14 They die when they are young,
  after wasting their lives in immoral
    living.
15 But by means of their suffering, he rescues
  those who suffer.

35:13-14 These verses can also be translated as follows: 13*Indeed, God doesn't listen to their empty plea; / the Almighty is not concerned. /* 14*How much less will he listen when you say you don't see him, / and that your case is before him and you're waiting for justice.* 35:15 As in Greek and Latin versions; the meaning of this Hebrew word is uncertain.

36:5-12 The logic of man is very different from the logic of God. In our mind, justice is simple. When we are good, we should be rewarded. When we sin, we should be punished. When our enemies sin, they should be judged. Elihu spoke well of the majesty and glory of God (see 36:22-26), but he seemed to know little about God's true nature. God is willing to forgive each of us, no matter what we have done or who we are. If we feel we have failed too deeply to be forgiven, we should search the New Testament for people whom God has forgiven—adulterers, homosexuals, alcoholics, thieves (1 Corinthians 6:9-11). No one is ever beyond the reach of God's forgiveness.

For he gets their attention through
adversity.

16 "God is leading you away from danger,
Job,
to a place free from distress.
He is setting your table with the best
food.
17 But you are obsessed with whether the
godless will be judged.
Don't worry, judgment and justice will
be upheld.
18 But watch out, or you may be seduced by
wealth.*
Don't let yourself be bribed into sin.
19 Could all your wealth*
or all your mighty efforts
keep you from distress?
20 Do not long for the cover of night,
for that is when people will be
destroyed.*
21 Be on guard! Turn back from evil,
for God sent this suffering
to keep you from a life of evil.

Elihu Reminds Job of God's Power

22 "Look, God is all-powerful.
Who is a teacher like him?
23 No one can tell him what to do,
or say to him, 'You have done wrong.'
24 Instead, glorify his mighty works,
singing songs of praise.
25 Everyone has seen these things,
though only from a distance.

26 "Look, God is greater than we can
understand.
His years cannot be counted.
27 He draws up the water vapor
and then distills it into rain.
28 The rain pours down from the clouds,
and everyone benefits.
29 Who can understand the spreading of the
clouds
and the thunder that rolls forth from
heaven?
30 See how he spreads the lightning around
him
and how it lights up the depths
of the sea.

31 By these mighty acts he nourishes* the
people,
giving them food in abundance.
32 He fills his hands with lightning bolts
and hurls each at its target.
33 The thunder announces his presence;
the storm announces his indignant
anger.*

CHAPTER 37

1 "My heart pounds as I think of this.
It trembles within me.
2 Listen carefully to the thunder of God's
voice
as it rolls from his mouth.
3 It rolls across the heavens,
and his lightning flashes in every
direction.
4 Then comes the roaring of the thunder—
the tremendous voice of his majesty.
He does not restrain it when he speaks.
5 God's voice is glorious in the thunder.
We can't even imagine the greatness of
his power.

6 "He directs the snow to fall on the earth
and tells the rain to pour down.
7 Then everyone stops working
so they can watch his power.
8 The wild animals take cover
and stay inside their dens.
9 The stormy wind comes from its chamber,
and the driving winds bring the cold.
10 God's breath sends the ice,
freezing wide expanses of water.
11 He loads the clouds with moisture,
and they flash with his lightning.
12 The clouds churn about at his direction.
They do whatever he commands
throughout the earth.
13 He makes these things happen either to
punish people
or to show his unfailing love.

14 "Pay attention to this, Job.
Stop and consider the wonderful
miracles of God!
15 Do you know how God controls the
storm
and causes the lightning to flash from
his clouds?

36:18 Or *But don't let your anger lead you to mockery.* 36:19 Or *Could all your cries for help.* 36:16-20 The meaning of
the Hebrew in this passage is uncertain. 36:31 Or *he governs.* 36:33 Or *even the cattle know when a storm is coming.*
The meaning of the Hebrew is uncertain.

37:1-24 God would soon deliver a speech similar to Elihu's, but the words will carry a much
different connotation (see 38–41). God is the Creator, the Almighty One, but he is not beyond
our reach. He has made himself available to each of us, even when we fall desperately short of his
glorious ideal.

16 Do you understand how he moves the clouds
with wonderful perfection and skill?
17 When you are sweltering in your clothes
and the south wind dies down and everything is still,
18 he makes the skies reflect the heat like a bronze mirror.
Can you do that?

19 "So teach the rest of us what to say to God.
We are too ignorant to make our own arguments.
20 Should God be notified that I want to speak?
Can people even speak when they are confused?*
21 We cannot look at the sun,
for it shines brightly in the sky
when the wind clears away the clouds.
22 So also, golden splendor comes from the mountain of God.*
He is clothed in dazzling splendor.
23 We cannot imagine the power of the Almighty;
but even though he is just and righteous,
he does not destroy us.
24 No wonder people everywhere fear him.
All who are wise show him reverence.*"

CHAPTER 38
The LORD Challenges Job

Then the LORD answered Job from the whirlwind:

2 "Who is this that questions my wisdom with such ignorant words?
3 Brace yourself like a man,
because I have some questions for you,
and you must answer them.

4 "Where were you when I laid the foundations of the earth?
Tell me, if you know so much.
5 Who determined its dimensions
and stretched out the surveying line?
6 What supports its foundations,
and who laid its cornerstone
7 as the morning stars sang together

and all the angels* shouted for joy?

8 "Who kept the sea inside its boundaries
as it burst from the womb,
9 and as I clothed it with clouds
and wrapped it in thick darkness?
10 For I locked it behind barred gates,
limiting its shores.
11 I said, 'This far and no farther will you come.
Here your proud waves must stop!'

12 "Have you ever commanded the morning to appear
and caused the dawn to rise in the east?
13 Have you made daylight spread to the ends of the earth,
to bring an end to the night's wickedness?
14 As the light approaches,
the earth takes shape like clay pressed beneath a seal;
it is robed in brilliant colors.*
15 The light disturbs the wicked
and stops the arm that is raised in violence.

16 "Have you explored the springs from which the seas come?
Have you explored their depths?
17 Do you know where the gates of death are located?
Have you seen the gates of utter gloom?
18 Do you realize the extent of the earth?
Tell me about it if you know!

19 "Where does light come from,
and where does darkness go?
20 Can you take each to its home?
Do you know how to get there?
21 But of course you know all this!
For you were born before it was all created,
and you are so very experienced!

22 "Have you visited the storehouses of the snow
or seen the storehouses of hail?
23 (I have reserved them as weapons for the time of trouble,
for the day of battle and war.)

37:20 Or *speak without being swallowed up?* 37:22 Or *from the north; or from the abode.* 37:24 As in Greek version; Hebrew reads *He is not impressed by the wise.* 38:7 Hebrew *the sons of God.* 38:14 Or *its features stand out like folds in a robe.*

38:2–39:30 God used a series of questions to illustrate how little Job knew about creation and God's ways. If Job knew nothing of these mysteries, how could he know anything about God's character? All Job could do was worship and trust God. We, too, wonder why we suffer. We wonder why bad things happen to us and those we love. But like Job, we are finite and cannot understand the ways of our infinite God. All we can do is praise him and await his deliverance.

²⁴ Where is the path to the source of light?
Where is the home of the east wind?

²⁵ "Who created a channel for the torrents
of rain?
Who laid out the path for the
lightning?
²⁶ Who makes the rain fall on barren land,
in a desert where no one lives?
²⁷ Who sends rain to satisfy the parched
ground
and make the tender grass spring up?

²⁸ "Does the rain have a father?
Who gives birth to the dew?
²⁹ Who is the mother of the ice?
Who gives birth to the frost from the
heavens?
³⁰ For the water turns to ice as hard as rock,
and the surface of the water freezes.

³¹ "Can you direct the movement of the
stars—
binding the cluster of the Pleiades
or loosening the cords of Orion?
³² Can you direct the constellations through
the seasons
or guide the Bear with her cubs across
the heavens?
³³ Do you know the laws of the universe?
Can you use them to regulate the earth?

³⁴ "Can you shout to the clouds
and make it rain?
³⁵ Can you make lightning appear
and cause it to strike as you direct?
³⁶ Who gives intuition to the heart
and instinct to the mind?
³⁷ Who is wise enough to count all the
clouds?
Who can tilt the water jars of heaven
³⁸ when the parched ground is dry
and the soil has hardened into clods?

³⁹ "Can you stalk prey for a lioness
and satisfy the young lions' appetites
⁴⁰ as they lie in their dens
or crouch in the thicket?
⁴¹ Who provides food for the ravens
when their young cry out to God
and wander about in hunger?

CHAPTER 39
The LORD's Challenge Continues

¹ "Do you know when the wild goats give
birth?
Have you watched as deer are born in
the wild?
² Do you know how many months they
carry their young?

Are you aware of the time of their
delivery?
³ They crouch down to give birth to their
young
and deliver their offspring.
⁴ Their young grow up in the open fields,
then leave home and never return.

⁵ "Who gives the wild donkey its freedom?
Who untied its ropes?
⁶ I have placed it in the wilderness;
its home is the wasteland.
⁷ It hates the noise of the city
and has no driver to shout at it.
⁸ The mountains are its pastureland,
where it searches for every blade of grass.

⁹ "Will the wild ox consent to being tamed?
Will it spend the night in your stall?
¹⁰ Can you hitch a wild ox to a plow?
Will it plow a field for you?
¹¹ Given its strength, can you trust it?
Can you leave and trust the ox to do
your work?
¹² Can you rely on it to bring home your grain
and deliver it to your threshing floor?

¹³ "The ostrich flaps her wings grandly,
but they are no match for the feathers
of the stork.
¹⁴ She lays her eggs on top of the earth,
letting them be warmed in the dust.
¹⁵ She doesn't worry that a foot might crush
them
or a wild animal might destroy them.
¹⁶ She is harsh toward her young,
as if they were not her own.
She doesn't care if they die.
¹⁷ For God has deprived her of wisdom.
He has given her no understanding.
¹⁸ But whenever she jumps up to run,
she passes the swiftest horse with its
rider.

¹⁹ "Have you given the horse its strength
or clothed its neck with a flowing mane?
²⁰ Did you give it the ability to leap like a
locust?
Its majestic snorting is terrifying!
²¹ It paws the earth and rejoices in its
strength
when it charges out to battle.
²² It laughs at fear and is unafraid.
It does not run from the sword.
²³ The arrows rattle against it,
and the spear and javelin flash.
²⁴ It paws the ground fiercely
and rushes forward into battle when
the ram's horn blows.

²⁵ It snorts at the sound of the horn.
  It senses the battle in the distance.
  It quivers at the captain's commands
    and the noise of battle.

²⁶ "Is it your wisdom that makes the hawk
    soar
  and spread its wings toward the south?
²⁷ Is it at your command that the eagle rises
    to the heights to make its nest?
²⁸ It lives on the cliffs,
    making its home on a distant, rocky
      crag.
²⁹ From there it hunts its prey,
    keeping watch with piercing eyes.
³⁰ Its young gulp down blood.
    Where there's a carcass, there you'll
      find it."

CHAPTER 40
Then the LORD said to Job,

² "Do you still want to argue with the
    Almighty?
  You are God's critic, but do you have
    the answers?"

Job Responds to the LORD
³ Then Job replied to the LORD,

⁴ "I am nothing—how could I ever find the
    answers?
  I will cover my mouth with my hand.
⁵ I have said too much already.
  I have nothing more to say."

The LORD Challenges Job Again
⁶ Then the LORD answered Job from the
whirlwind:

⁷ "Brace yourself like a man,
  because I have some questions for you,
  and you must answer them.

⁸ "Will you discredit my justice
  and condemn me just to prove you are
    right?

⁹ Are you as strong as God?
  Can you thunder with a voice like his?
¹⁰ All right, put on your glory and splendor,
  your honor and majesty.
¹¹ Give vent to your anger.
  Let it overflow against the proud.
¹² Humiliate the proud with a glance;
  walk on the wicked where they stand.
¹³ Bury them in the dust.
  Imprison them in the world of the
    dead.
¹⁴ Then even I would praise you,
  for your own strength would save you.

¹⁵ "Take a look at Behemoth,*
  which I made, just as I made you.
  It eats grass like an ox.
¹⁶ See its powerful loins
  and the muscles of its belly.
¹⁷ Its tail is as strong as a cedar.
  The sinews of its thighs are knit tightly
    together.
¹⁸ Its bones are tubes of bronze.
  Its limbs are bars of iron.
¹⁹ It is a prime example of God's handiwork,
  and only its Creator can threaten it.
²⁰ The mountains offer it their best food,
  where all the wild animals play.
²¹ It lies under the lotus plants,*
  hidden by the reeds in the marsh.
²² The lotus plants give it shade
  among the willows beside the stream.
²³ It is not disturbed by the raging river,
  not concerned when the swelling
    Jordan rushes around it.
²⁴ No one can catch it off guard
  or put a ring in its nose and lead it
    away.

CHAPTER 41
The LORD's Challenge Continues
¹ *"Can you catch Leviathan* with a hook
  or put a noose around its jaw?
² Can you tie it with a rope through the
    nose

40:15 The identification of Behemoth is disputed, ranging from an earthly creature to a mythical sea monster in ancient literature. **40:21** Or *bramble bushes;* also in 40:22. **41:1a** Verses 41:1-8 are numbered 40:25-32 in Hebrew text. **41:1b** The identification of Leviathan is disputed, ranging from an earthly creature to a mythical sea monster in ancient literature.

40:1–41:34 God used the majesty and power of his creation to remind Job that God is the only one who can save. If Job could not even overpower created beings such as the crocodile, how could Job save himself from the God who created the crocodile? Everything under heaven belongs to God, including Job. God never did give Job an explanation for his suffering; God only let Job know that he was ultimately in control. We may be suffering unfairly because of an abusive family member or because of codependency with an addict. We may never know why we have to go through the pain, but we need to realize that God is in control of our life. Our faith in him will be rewarded—if not in this life, then in the next.

or pierce its jaw with a spike?
³Will it beg you for mercy
 or implore you for pity?
⁴Will it agree to work for you,
 to be your slave for life?
⁵Can you make it a pet like a bird,
 or give it to your little girls to play with?
⁶Will merchants try to buy it
 to sell it in their shops?
⁷Will its hide be hurt by spears
 or its head by a harpoon?
⁸If you lay a hand on it,
 you will certainly remember the battle
  that follows.
 You won't try that again!
⁹*No, it is useless to try to capture it.
 The hunter who attempts it will be
  knocked down.
¹⁰And since no one dares to disturb it,
 who then can stand up to me?
¹¹Who has given me anything that I need
  to pay back?
 Everything under heaven is mine.

¹²"I want to emphasize Leviathan's limbs
 and its enormous strength and graceful
  form.
¹³Who can strip off its hide,
 and who can penetrate its double layer
  of armor?*
¹⁴Who could pry open its jaws?
 For its teeth are terrible!
¹⁵The scales on its back are like* rows of
  shields
 tightly sealed together.
¹⁶They are so close together
 that no air can get between them.
¹⁷Each scale sticks tight to the next.
 They interlock and cannot be
  penetrated.

¹⁸"When it sneezes, it flashes light!
 Its eyes are like the red of dawn.
¹⁹Lightning leaps from its mouth;
 flames of fire flash out.
²⁰Smoke streams from its nostrils
 like steam from a pot heated over
  burning rushes.
²¹Its breath would kindle coals,
 for flames shoot from its mouth.

²²"The tremendous strength in Leviathan's
  neck
 strikes terror wherever it goes.
²³Its flesh is hard and firm
 and cannot be penetrated.
²⁴Its heart is hard as rock,
 hard as a millstone.
²⁵When it rises, the mighty are afraid,
 gripped by terror.
²⁶No sword can stop it,
 no spear, dart, or javelin.
²⁷Iron is nothing but straw to that creature,
 and bronze is like rotten wood.
²⁸Arrows cannot make it flee.
 Stones shot from a sling are like bits of
  grass.
²⁹Clubs are like a blade of grass,
 and it laughs at the swish of javelins.
³⁰Its belly is covered with scales as sharp as
  glass.
 It plows up the ground as it drags
  through the mud.

³¹"Leviathan makes the water boil with its
  commotion.
 It stirs the depths like a pot of ointment.
³²The water glistens in its wake,
 making the sea look white.
³³Nothing on earth is its equal,
 no other creature so fearless.
³⁴Of all the creatures, it is the proudest.
 It is the king of beasts."

CHAPTER 42
Job Responds to the LORD
Then Job replied to the LORD:

²"I know that you can do anything,
 and no one can stop you.
³You asked, 'Who is this that questions my
  wisdom with such ignorance?'
 It is I—and I was talking about things I
  knew nothing about,
 things far too wonderful for me.
⁴You said, 'Listen and I will speak!
 I have some questions for you,
 and you must answer them.'
⁵I had only heard about you before,

41:9 Verses 41:9-34 are numbered 41:1-26 in Hebrew text. 41:13 As in Greek version; Hebrew reads *its bridle?*
41:15 As in some Greek manuscripts and Latin Vulgate; Hebrew reads *Its pride is in its.*

42:1-6 Job ventured to answer God, and his reply was filled with gratitude. Where Job had once only heard about God, here he actually saw him—the loving, merciful, all-powerful, majestic Creator. This man, who was known as "blameless" and "a man of complete integrity" before his suffering, was now even greater because of that suffering. God is good: He gives us good gifts, he works good from all things, and his intentions for us are always good (Romans 8:28). Suffering is a privilege when through it we grow closer to God (Philippians 1:29; 3:10).

but now I have seen you with my own
   eyes.
⁶I take back everything I said,
   and I sit in dust and ashes to show my
   repentance."

Conclusion: The LORD Blesses Job

⁷After the LORD had finished speaking to
Job, he said to Eliphaz the Temanite: "I am
angry with you and your two friends, for
you have not spoken accurately about me,
as my servant Job has. ⁸So take seven bulls
and seven rams and go to my servant Job
and offer a burnt offering for yourselves. My
servant Job will pray for you, and I will accept his prayer on your behalf. I will not
treat you as you deserve, for you have not
spoken accurately about me, as my servant
Job has." ⁹So Eliphaz the Temanite, Bildad
the Shuhite, and Zophar the Naamathite
did as the LORD commanded them, and the
LORD accepted Job's prayer.

¹⁰When Job prayed for his friends, the
LORD restored his fortunes. In fact, the LORD
gave him twice as much as before! ¹¹Then all
his brothers, sisters, and former friends came
and feasted with him in his home. And they
consoled him and comforted him because of
all the trials the LORD had brought against
him. And each of them brought him a gift of
money* and a gold ring.

¹²So the LORD blessed Job in the second
half of his life even more than in the beginning. For now he had 14,000 sheep, 6,000
camels, 1,000 teams of oxen, and 1,000 female donkeys. ¹³He also gave Job seven more
sons and three more daughters. ¹⁴He named
his first daughter Jemimah, the second
Keziah, and the third Keren-happuch. ¹⁵In all
the land no women were as lovely as the
daughters of Job. And their father put them
into his will along with their brothers.

¹⁶Job lived 140 years after that, living to
see four generations of his children and
grandchildren. ¹⁷Then he died, an old man
who had lived a long, full life.

42:11 Hebrew *a kesitah;* the value or weight of the kesitah is no longer known.

42:7-9 How thankful Job's friends must have been that God was not going to deal with them
according to their rules but by grace. They spoke without wisdom or accuracy. They spoke from
their fear. They used another man's weakness to bolster their own self-esteem. But Job prayed for
them, and God forgave them. God is still waiting to forgive us and restore our fellowship with
him when we make mistakes. We shouldn't let our past actions and attitudes keep us from knowing the true God.

42:10-17 The fact that God restored and even doubled Job's wealth is incidental. Even if Job had
continued in his pain, God would still have been—and still be—in control of the universe. Job
probably wouldn't have complained because he recognized that he would be rewarded when he
died and went to be with God. We have the same promise. Whether our pain has been caused by
our dependency or by the dysfunctional people around us, God is controlling our life and will
reward us in eternity if we submit to his plan. God's future blessings for us will be greater than
anything we could ever imagine!

REFLECTIONS ON JOB

insights INTO SATAN'S ACTIVITY

In **Job 1:8-13** we find that God knew the heart of his servant Job and of Satan, the accuser. The stage was set as God volunteered Job to be the one who would prove Satan wrong. How could God have used Job this way? It seems somewhat cruel. Perhaps the answer lies in the way we understand suffering. We usually see suffering as an almost crippling tragedy. But for God, suffering is a pathway to maturity (see Romans 5:3-4; James 1:2-4). God used Job's suffering to bring him even greater blessings and strength in the end. We can be sure that God is working his good in our life, even in the midst of our pain.

In **Job 2:4-6** Satan made a keen observation about the character of man. We may grieve when confronted by the loss of possessions, power, friends, or even family; but when confronted by physical illness, we curse God. Sadly, Satan had a good point. It is difficult to maintain the proper perspective when we are physically afflicted. As we suffer the physical effects of addiction, we may feel that God hates us or that he is punishing us. We should be aware, however, that he may be using our pain to lead us away from our destructive life-style and into recovery.

insights ABOUT JOB'S RELATIONSHIP WITH GOD

We may never know how we'll respond to tragedy until we face it. From Job's response in **Job 1:20-22**, we learn why God labeled him a good man who "fears God and will have nothing to do with evil." Job chose to worship God, even in his grief. He chose to make an offering of faith at a time when he needed God the most. When we suffer a loss, praising God for his sovereignty and generosity in allowing us to have the possessions or loved ones for a period of time is often the last thing we feel like doing—but it is the proper response to God.

Job received some comfort from the fact that he hadn't disobeyed God. Even while he was in intense pain, we find in **Job 6:8-13** that he was concerned about his relationship with God. The opposite is often true with us: We suffer and no longer care about God or his laws. Discouragement touches our spiritual life rather quickly, and the more pain we feel, the quicker we give up on God. But we see from Job's example that when we suffer, we should focus our thoughts on God, our only hope for salvation.

In **Job 13:14-19** Job argued his case with God. He had confidence in his righteousness and decided to do something about his circumstances. God is never offended by our strong feelings. He welcomes the honest expression of our emotions as we seek to draw closer to him. We, too, must decide to do something about our circumstances. We can sit and wallow in our misery, or we can take a chance and try to change things. We would be wise to begin as Job did—with a heart-to-heart talk with God.

Job recognized in **Job 14:4** that no person can make himself pure. This statement reflects the very heart of God's message of grace. Who can make something pure out of something inherently impure? Only our gracious God, and he has done so through the death and resurrection of Jesus. Through him we are holy, just as God himself is holy.

insights ABOUT GIVING AND RECEIVING COMFORT

In **Job 2:11-13** the three friends saw Job's pain from a distance and were overwhelmed. Then they gave him the best gift they had to offer—they wept and shared silently in his grief. When others are suffering, we often feel that we have to say something comforting, sympathetic, or advisory. But what they may really need is for us to just be with them and experience their pain.

Eliphaz acted like God's prophet sent to straighten out Job's life. He claimed in **Job 5:1-7** to know more about Job than even Job knew! Not all of Eliphaz's words were false, but he spoke about things he didn't fully understand. It is always easier to analyze than to empathize, because to feel empathy means to put ourself in the position of the sufferer. This can be quite frightening—especially if our friends are suffering from something that could also happen to us.

Eliphaz's testimony about God in **Job 5:18-26** was not incorrect, but it was insensitive. Job was not doubting God's sovereignty or faithfulness; he was simply mourning his loss. He had, after all, suddenly lost his children, as well as his wealth and health. Like Job, we need to grieve for a period of time. Grief is not an abnormal emotion; it is necessary if we are to move on with our life.

Job's frustration reached a breaking point in **Job 19:1-7**. His friends had repeatedly accused him of sin but had yet to prove any of it. Job knew in his heart that he was not being punished for some hidden, willful sin. He just wanted some comfort and understanding. Sufferers long to be understood. They need comfort, not judgment. We need to keep this in mind as we seek to help our friends who are grieving losses in their lives.

insights ABOUT GRIEF AND SUFFERING

Suffering has a way of stripping us of the protective shield we create to hide behind. As we openly display our pain, we can no longer pretend that things are all right. Job was grieving deeply in **Job 6:1-7**. He felt wounded by God and had no reason to pretend that his pain was not significant. When we can no longer hide our pain, we can talk about it. We can get our emotions out in the open where we can deal with them.

In **Job 11:1-6** Zophar made it clear that he didn't like Job's expressions of grief. To Zophar, Job's words were sacrilegious and unfaithful. God, however, understands our grief. When people are hurting, God does not turn away from their words or tears. Intimacy, brokenness, and honesty are part of the purpose for our pain. When we are powerless over our circumstances, we need to give our life over to God's sovereign care. He will lead us out of the painful situations we are facing.

PSALMS

THE BIG PICTURE

A. PSALMS OF PREPARATION AND PROMISE (1–41)

B. PSALMS OF PETITION AND PRESERVATION (42–72)

C. PSALMS OF PROBLEMS AND POWER (73–89)

D. PSALMS OF PERIL AND PROTECTION (90–106)

E. PSALMS OF PERFECTION AND PRAISE (107–150)

It is impossible to adequately summarize the richness contained in the book of Psalms. It was Israel's hymnal, containing hymns of praise to God for personal and national salvation, and contains the laments of God's people in difficult situations. It was Israel's prayer book. The psalmists looked to God in moments of private despair and times of national suffering. Amidst their difficulties, they found release by lifting their heartfelt laments and praises to God.

The psalms are for us, too. They are brimming with honest emotion. Through them we can pour out our anguish and adoration, our suffering and confessions, our hopes and fears. Through some we may openly question God's actions or his apparent lack of action. Through others we might express our pain, heartache, and discouragement. Through still others we may praise God as he frees us from oppression and sin. Each psalm is an expression of the heart. None of them is a neat little package of answers tied up with a pretty bow. They are living documents, a collection of spiritual diaries from people who honestly sought God's gracious help.

We will find that the psalms may be read at many different levels, depending on the problems we face. They may function as deterrents to keep us out of trouble, as guides to help us through our problems, as reminders of the one who actually delivers us, or as beacons of hope to encourage us in perplexing or painful situations. Through the psalms we share in the hopes and failures of the entire human race. Yet as we read them, we are also ushered into the very presence of our loving and merciful God.

THE BOTTOM LINE

PURPOSE: To demonstrate that God is holy and loving and intimately involved in every aspect of our human experience. AUTHORS: David wrote seventy-three psalms; Asaph wrote twelve; the sons of Korah wrote nine; Solomon wrote two; Heman (with the sons of Korah), Ethan, and Moses each wrote one; fifty-one psalms are anonymous. AUDIENCE: The people of Israel. DATE WRITTEN: The psalms were written between 1440 and 586 B.C. SETTING: Though the psalms are not generally concerned with recording history, many of them were inspired by historical events. KEY VERSE: "Let everything that breathes sing praises to the LORD! Praise the LORD!" (150:6). KEY PLACE: The Temple in Jerusalem. KEY PEOPLE: David, Asaph, Solomon, Heman, the sons of Korah, Ethan, and Moses.

RECOVERY THEMES

Truth Brings Healing: Above everything else, the psalmists were honest about their experiences and feelings. Again and again they testified to God's faithfulness in hearing and responding to their words of honest confession or praise. It is so easy to try and hedge on the truth, even when we pray to God. This, however, is always a dead end. Only the truth can bring us into the kind of relationship with God that will result in true healing. When we face the truth about our sins and failures and recognize that we are powerless over them, God will meet us where we are and guide us in the path of recovery and healing.

Legitimate Doubts and Complaints: Most of us act as if doubt is an unforgivable sin. We do everything we can to hide it from God. But God knows all about our doubts. The psalmists were honest about their doubts and brought them straight to God. They were also honest in their complaints. There is a place for complaining before God—it helps us to bring our raw feelings and doubts out into the open. But just as the psalmists did, we will find that our complaining is followed by an affirmation of faith. If we hide our doubts about God, we will be sure to drift away from him. But if we honestly express them to him, even complaining about his apparent failures in our life, we will discover that our faith is renewed. As happened with the psalmists, our complaints will be followed by words of praise.

God's Power of Deliverance: We can count on the fact that God is all-powerful, and he always chooses to act at the best possible time. God is sovereign over every situation. The psalmists testify repeatedly that God is able to overcome the despair and pain in life and that he is always in control. This kind of faith didn't come easily to them. They struggled with this truth, often questioning God's presence in their lives, just as we do. But in the end, their questions were always replaced by praises that affirmed the fact of God's powerful presence.

The Necessity of Forgiveness: Many of the psalms are intense prayers asking God for forgiveness. What the psalmists discovered was that they could be open and honest before God about their failures, emotions, and weaknesses, because God had promised to forgive them. As we experience God's forgiveness, we move away from our dependencies and feelings of alienation and guilt and into an intimate and loving relationship with God. God's antidote to our past failures—no matter how terrible our sins—is always forgiveness!

BOOK ONE (Psalms 1–41)

PSALM 1

¹ Oh, the joys of those who do not
    follow the advice of the wicked,
    or stand around with sinners,
    or join in with mockers.
² But they delight in the law of the LORD,
    meditating on it day and night.
³ They are like trees planted along the
        riverbank,
    bearing fruit each season.
Their leaves never wither,
    and they prosper in all they do.

⁴ But not the wicked!
They are like worthless chaff, scattered
    by the wind.

⁵ They will be condemned at the time
        of judgment.
Sinners will have no place among the
        godly.
⁶ For the LORD watches over the path
        of the godly,
    but the path of the wicked leads to
        destruction.

PSALM 2

¹ Why are the nations so angry?
    Why do they waste their time with
        futile plans?
² The kings of the earth prepare for battle;
    the rulers plot together
against the LORD
    and against his anointed one.

1:1-6 Turning our will over to God means turning away from the kind of people who draw us into temptation. There is no better source for wisdom and direction than the Word of God. When we fail to study and apply God's Word, we tend to drift through life. We are tossed around by every new fad or philosophy that comes our way. Recognizing our sins and being willing to change our sinful habits is the only way to avoid God's judgment. God wants to help us live a godly life. But if we refuse to work on removing the character defects that slow the recovery process, we will certainly suffer the consequences.
2:1-6 If God is in charge of the world, why do we continually try to do things our own way? Fighting God's program is useless and foolish. Many turn from God because they think it involves

3 "Let us break their chains," they cry,
    "and free ourselves from slavery
        to God."

4 But the one who rules in heaven laughs.
    The Lord scoffs at them.
5 Then in anger he rebukes them,
    terrifying them with his fierce fury.
6 For the Lord declares, "I have placed my
        chosen king on the throne
    in Jerusalem,* on my holy
        mountain."

7 The king proclaims the LORD's decree:
    "The LORD said to me, 'You are my
        son.*
    Today I have become your
        Father.*
8 Only ask, and I will give you the
        nations as your inheritance,
    the whole earth as your possession.
9 You will break* them with an
        iron rod
    and smash them like clay pots.'"

10 Now then, you kings, act wisely!
    Be warned, you rulers of the earth!
11 Serve the LORD with reverent fear,
    and rejoice with trembling.
12 Submit to God's royal son,* or he will
        become angry,
    and you will be destroyed in the midst
        of all your activities—
    for his anger flares up in an instant.
    But what joy for all who take refuge
        in him!

PSALM 3
*A psalm of David, regarding the time David fled from
his son Absalom.*

1 O LORD, I have so many enemies;
    so many are against me.

2 So many are saying,
    "God will never rescue him!"   *Interlude**

3 But you, O LORD, are a shield around me;
    you are my glory, the one who holds
        my head high.
4 I cried out to the LORD,
    and he answered me from his holy
        mountain.   *Interlude*

5 I lay down and slept,
    yet I woke up in safety,
    for the LORD was watching over me.
6 I am not afraid of ten thousand enemies
    who surround me on every side.

7 Arise, O LORD!
    Rescue me, my God!
    Slap all my enemies in the face!
    Shatter the teeth of the wicked!
8 Victory comes from you, O LORD.
    May you bless your people.   *Interlude*

PSALM 4
*For the choir director: A psalm of David, to be
accompanied by stringed instruments.*

1 Answer me when I call to you,
    O God who declares me innocent.
    Free me from my troubles.
    Have mercy on me and hear my prayer.

2 How long will you people ruin my
        reputation?
    How long will you make groundless
        accusations?
    How long will you continue your lies?
                                    Interlude
3 You can be sure of this:
    The LORD set apart the godly for
        himself.
    The LORD will answer when I call to
        him.

2:6 Hebrew *on Zion.* 2:7a Or *Son;* also in 2:12. 2:7b Or *Today I reveal you as my son.* 2:9 Greek version reads *rule.*
Compare Rev 2:27. 2:12 The meaning of the Hebrew is uncertain. 3:2 Hebrew *Selah.* The meaning of this word is
uncertain, though it is probably a musical or literary term. It is rendered *Interlude* throughout the Psalms.

becoming his slave. But if we reject God's rule in our life, we will invariably become a slave to
someone or something else. The foolish man who rejects God's rule soon falls into a prison of sin
and destruction. The only way we can be in tune with God's plan and receive his help is to accept
his loving rule in our life.
3:1-4 Even David, a righteous man, recognized problems in his life that had become unmanageable. When we fail, even our friends sometimes begin to think we are beyond God's help. David,
however, knew otherwise. He looked to God for help and encouragement. Calling out to God to
increase our knowledge of him is one of the most important steps in the recovery process.
3:5-8 God comforted David so much that he could sleep in the face of his troubles. What is more,
David's worries and anxieties vanished when he focused his thoughts fully on God; he could view
life as though all of his problems had been eliminated. By placing his problems in God's hands,
David had made the most important step toward solving them. True deliverance and happiness
come when we acknowledge God as our helper and the source of our strength.

4 Don't sin by letting anger control you.
   Think about it overnight and remain
      silent.   *Interlude*
5 Offer sacrifices in the right spirit,
   and trust the LORD.

6 Many people say, "Who will show us
      better times?"
   Let your face smile on us, LORD.
7 You have given me greater joy
      than those who have abundant harvests
      of grain and new wine.
8 In peace I will lie down and sleep,
   for you alone, O LORD, will keep me
      safe.

PSALM 5

*For the choir director: A psalm of David, to be
accompanied by the flute.*

1 O LORD, hear me as I pray;
   pay attention to my groaning.
2 Listen to my cry for help, my King and
   my God,
   for I pray to no one but you.
3 Listen to my voice in the morning,
   LORD.
   Each morning I bring my requests to
   you and wait expectantly.

4 O God, you take no pleasure in
   wickedness;
   you cannot tolerate the sins of the
   wicked.
5 Therefore, the proud may not stand in
   your presence,

5:9 Greek version reads *with lies.* Compare Rom 3:13.

   for you hate all who do evil.
6 You will destroy those who tell lies.
   The LORD detests murderers and
      deceivers.

7 Because of your unfailing love, I can enter
      your house;
   I will worship at your Temple with
      deepest awe.
8 Lead me in the right path, O LORD,
   or my enemies will conquer me.
   Make your way plain for me to follow.

9 My enemies cannot speak a truthful
      word.
   Their deepest desire is to destroy
      others.
   Their talk is foul, like the stench from an
      open grave.
   Their tongues are filled with flattery.*
10 O God, declare them guilty.
   Let them be caught in their own
      traps.
   Drive them away because of their many
      sins,
   for they have rebelled against you.

11 But let all who take refuge in you
      rejoice;
   let them sing joyful praises forever.
   Spread your protection over them,
      that all who love your name may be
      filled with joy.
12 For you bless the godly, O LORD;
   you surround them with your shield
      of love.

4:4-5 Turning our will over to God is not a onetime experience; it is a moment-by-moment decision to keep our mind fixed on doing God's will. Today we don't sacrifice animals on an altar to
please God, but we can offer God our life as a living sacrifice. In order to do this, we must seek
out and then follow God's plan for holy and healthy living.
4:6-8 Many people around us cannot see God at work in our life; they see only our past failures.
But as we seek God and with his help make changes, our success in recovery will allow others to
see God's power. True joy comes from God—a joy that is greater than all the gladness the world
can produce. Nothing will bring us more peaceful nights of sleep than the knowledge that God is
with us and helping us to progress in recovery.
5:1-7 We have probably tried just about everything to escape our slavery to destructive habits.
David understood how foolish it was to look for help from anything or anyone else but God. One
by one, he brought his needs daily to God. David understood that God would not accept the
prayers of one who was trusting in himself and continuing in his sin. When we trust God for help
in our moment-by-moment walk of obedience, his wall of protection surrounds us wherever we
go and whatever we do.
5:8-12 David requested God's guidance because he knew that God's plan for him was the only
way to avoid the destructive traps he faced. Our old friends, like David's enemies, will tell us the
big lie—that one more sin won't hurt us. Their words sound good, but their lives prove that they
are slaves to sin and that they are headed for destruction. In the midst of these snares of the
world, we can always find protection by trusting in God.

PSALM 6

For the choir director: A psalm of David, to be accompanied by an eight-stringed instrument. *

¹ O LORD, don't rebuke me in your anger
   or discipline me in your rage.
² Have compassion on me, LORD, for I am
      weak.
   Heal me, LORD, for my bones are in
      agony.
³ I am sick at heart.
   How long, O LORD, until you
      restore me?

⁴ Return, O LORD, and rescue me.
   Save me because of your unfailing love.
⁵ For the dead do not remember you.
   Who can praise you from the grave?*

⁶ I am worn out from sobbing.
   All night I flood my bed with weeping,
      drenching it with my tears.
⁷ My vision is blurred by grief;
   my eyes are worn out because of all my
      enemies.

⁸ Go away, all you who do evil,
   for the LORD has heard my weeping.
⁹ The LORD has heard my plea;
   the LORD will answer my prayer.
¹⁰ May all my enemies be disgraced and
      terrified.
   May they suddenly turn back in shame.

PSALM 7

A psalm of David, which he sang to the LORD concerning Cush of the tribe of Benjamin.*

¹ I come to you for protection, O LORD my
      God.
   Save me from my persecutors—rescue
      me!
² If you don't, they will maul me like a lion,
   tearing me to pieces with no one to
      rescue me.

³ O LORD my God, if I have done wrong
   or am guilty of injustice,
⁴ if I have betrayed a friend
   or plundered my enemy without cause,
⁵ then let my enemies capture me.
   Let them trample me into the ground
   and drag my honor in the dust.

                                    Interlude

⁶ Arise, O LORD, in anger!
   Stand up against the fury of my
      enemies!
   Wake up, my God, and bring justice!
⁷ Gather the nations before you.
   Rule over them from on high.
⁸   The LORD judges the nations.
   Declare me righteous, O LORD,
      for I am innocent, O Most High!
⁹ End the evil of those who are wicked,
   and defend the righteous.
   For you look deep within the mind and
      heart,
   O righteous God.

¹⁰ God is my shield,
   saving those whose hearts are true and
      right.
¹¹ God is an honest judge.
   He is angry with the wicked every day.
¹² If a person does not repent,
   God* will sharpen his sword;
   he will bend and string his bow.
¹³ He will prepare his deadly weapons
   and shoot his flaming arrows.

¹⁴ The wicked conceive evil;
   they are pregnant with trouble
   and give birth to lies.
¹⁵ They dig a deep pit to trap others,
   then fall into it themselves.
¹⁶ The trouble they make for others backfires
      on them.

6:TITLE Hebrew *with stringed instruments; according to the sheminith.* 6:5 Hebrew *from Sheol?* 7:TITLE Hebrew *A shiggaion,* probably indicating a musical setting for the psalm. 7:12 Hebrew *he.*

6:1-5 Although we might want instant relief from the anguish of temptation, it doesn't usually come immediately. But when we realize that we are powerless over our dependency or compulsion, we have taken the first step toward recovery. Once we have acknowledged that God has the power to help us, we have taken the second step. Knowing about these important steps, however, is never enough to help us avoid destruction. We need to act on them, too.

6:6-10 Even though we may be suffering greatly, we can have confidence that God answers our prayers. God will always hear our petitions and rescue us. We should be as bold as David is here, claiming victory at the end of his prayer. Prayer should not be a last-ditch tactic; it should be the basis for our battles for recovery.

7:11-16 God is patient, but there is a limit to how long he will tolerate those who continue to rebel against him. When we choose to live in ways that run counter to God's program, we will quickly discover that our problems only grow worse. The plans we make to achieve personal success at the expense of others will destroy us in the end. We will only fall prey to our own schemes (see 9:15).

The violence they plan falls on their own heads.

¹⁷ I will thank the LORD because he is just;
I will sing praise to the name of the LORD Most High.

PSALM 8

*For the choir director: A psalm of David, to be accompanied by a stringed instrument.**

¹ O LORD, our Lord, your majestic name fills the earth!
Your glory is higher than the heavens.
² You have taught children and infants to tell of your strength,*
silencing your enemies and all who oppose you.

³ When I look at the night sky and see the work of your fingers—
the moon and the stars you set in place—
⁴ what are mere mortals that you should think about them,
human beings that you should care for them?*
⁵ Yet you made them only a little lower than God*
and crowned them* with glory and honor.

⁶ You gave them charge of everything you made,
putting all things under their authority—
⁷ the flocks and the herds and all the wild animals,
⁸ the birds in the sky, the fish in the sea, and everything that swims the ocean currents.

⁹ O LORD, our Lord, your majestic name fills the earth!

PSALM 9

For the choir director: A psalm of David, to be sung to the tune "Death of the Son."

¹ I will praise you, LORD, with all my heart;
I will tell of all the marvelous things you have done.
² I will be filled with joy because of you.
I will sing praises to your name, O Most High.

³ My enemies retreated;
they staggered and died when you appeared.
⁴ For you have judged in my favor;
from your throne you have judged with fairness.
⁵ You have rebuked the nations and destroyed the wicked;

8:TITLE Hebrew *according to the gittith.* **8:2** Greek version reads *to give you praise.* Compare Matt 21:16. **8:4** Hebrew *what is man that you should think of him, / the son of man that you should care for him?* **8:5a** Or *Yet you made them only a little lower than the angels;* Hebrew reads *Yet you made him* [i.e., man] *a little lower than Elohim.* **8:5b** Hebrew *him* [i.e., man]; similarly in 8:6.

8:3-9 Many of our problems are rooted in our low self-esteem. Perhaps we were never listened to as children. Or maybe we were abused by people who had authority over us. Whatever the roots of our problems, we are now probably overly sensitive to the attacks of others. We see here that God has made us to be fantastic beings with great honor and authority. We should never sell ourselves short. Self-esteem should be based on what God thinks of us—not on what others say about us.

9:1-6 As we experience God's help and begin to change our life for the better, we have the responsibility to carry the message of deliverance to others so their lives can be changed, too. As we allow God to help us overcome the defects in our character, others will see what God has done for us and may also receive the gift of hope. Our painful struggles with our addictions and compulsions and our victories through God's help can be a source of encouragement and guidance to others whose lives are headed toward destruction.

9:15-20 The people who set traps for others will ultimately be trapped themselves. God ensures that such people do not succeed in the long run. Those who realize they need God's help and turn to him will receive it; those who try to control their problems alone will ultimately fail. If we think we are in control of our own destiny or the destinies of others, we have a terrible surprise in store. One day God will step in and demonstrate who is truly in control. Since God is ultimately in control, the only wise plan to follow is God's plan.

10:1-11 God sometimes seems far away when temptation is strong. In truth, he is never far from us. Temptation sometimes becomes strongest when our godless friends seem to be able to do things without getting trapped the way we do. We tend to follow along and end up in trouble. We need to realize that even though our friends seem to do well and be in control at the moment, they are headed for serious trouble; they just don't realize it yet. We need to make sure that the apparent successes of others don't lead us away from God's program for healthy living.

you have erased their names forever.
⁶ The enemy is finished, in endless ruins;
  the cities you uprooted are now
    forgotten.

⁷ But the LORD reigns forever,
  executing judgment from his throne.
⁸ He will judge the world with justice
  and rule the nations with fairness.
⁹ The LORD is a shelter for the oppressed,
  a refuge in times of trouble.
¹⁰ Those who know your name trust in you,
  for you, O LORD, do not abandon those
    who search for you.

¹¹ Sing praises to the LORD who reigns in
    Jerusalem.*
  Tell the world about his unforgettable
    deeds.
¹² For he who avenges murder cares for the
    helpless.
  He does not ignore the cries of those
    who suffer.

¹³ LORD, have mercy on me.
  See how my enemies torment me.
  Snatch me back from the jaws of death.
¹⁴ Save me so I can praise you publicly at
    Jerusalem's gates,
  so I can rejoice that you have rescued
    me.

¹⁵ The nations have fallen into the pit they
    dug for others.
  Their own feet have been caught in the
    trap they set.
¹⁶ The LORD is known for his justice.
  The wicked are trapped by their own
    deeds.   *Quiet Interlude*

¹⁷ The wicked will go down to the grave.*
  This is the fate of all the nations who
    ignore God.
¹⁸ But the needy will not be ignored forever;
  the hopes of the poor will not always be
    crushed.

¹⁹ Arise, O LORD!
  Do not let mere mortals defy you!
  Judge the nations!
²⁰ Make them tremble in fear, O LORD.
  Let the nations know they are merely
    human.   *Interlude*

PSALM 10
¹ O LORD, why do you stand so far away?
  Why do you hide when I am in
    trouble?

9:11 Hebrew *Zion;* also in 9:14. **9:16** Hebrew *Higgaion
Selah.* The meaning of this phrase is uncertain.
9:17 Hebrew *to Sheol.*

SELF-PERCEPTION

READ PSALM 8:1-9

We develop our sense of self-perception by
noticing how the important people in our
life see us. If we grew up in a dysfunctional
family, their skewed view of us probably
warped our ability to see ourself as we truly
are in God's eyes. Understanding how God
sees us and the value he has placed on us
can help us overcome the negative
self-perception that many of us have
developed.

  King David was amazed as he thought
about how much God valued him. He said,
"What are mere mortals that you should
think about them, human beings that you
should care for them? Yet you made them
only a little lower than God and crowned
them with glory and honor. You gave them
charge of everything you made, putting all
things under their authority" (Psalm 8:4-6).
"How precious are your thoughts about
me, O God! They cannot be numbered! I
can't even count them; they outnumber
the grains of sand! And when I wake up,
you are still with me!" (Psalm 139:17-18).
God demonstrated how precious we are
in his sight by sending Jesus to give his life
for us.

  God wants us to realize how precious we
are to him and to see ourself in the light of
his love. Consider this: If God considered
us worthy of giving up the most precious
thing he had (his only Son), what does that
say about how valuable we are to him?
Turn to page 701, Psalm 32.

Turn to page 701, Psalm 32.

2 The wicked arrogantly hunt down the
poor.
Let them be caught in the evil they
plan for others.
3 For they brag about their evil desires;
they praise the greedy and curse the
LORD.

4 The wicked are too proud to seek God.
They seem to think that God
is dead.
5 Yet they succeed in everything they do.
They do not see your punishment
awaiting them.
They sneer at all their enemies.
6 They think, "Nothing bad will ever
happen to us!
We will be free of trouble forever!"

7 Their mouths are full of cursing, lies, and
threats.*
Trouble and evil are on the tips of their
tongues.
8 They lurk in ambush in the villages,
waiting to murder innocent people.
They are always searching for helpless
victims.
9 Like lions crouched in hiding,
they wait to pounce on the helpless.
Like hunters they capture the helpless
and drag them away in nets.
10 Their helpless victims are crushed;
they fall beneath the strength of the
wicked.
11 The wicked think, "God isn't
watching us!
He has closed his eyes and won't even
see what we do!"

12 Arise, O LORD!
Punish the wicked, O God!
Do not ignore the helpless!
13 Why do the wicked get away with
despising God?
They think, "God will never call us to
account."

10:7 Greek version reads *cursing and bitterness.* Compare Rom 3:14.

14 But you see the trouble and grief they
cause.
You take note of it and punish them.
The helpless put their trust in you.
You defend the orphans.

15 Break the arms of these wicked, evil
people!
Go after them until the last one is
destroyed.
16 The LORD is king forever and ever!
The godless nations will vanish from
the land.
17 LORD, you know the hopes of the helpless.
Surely you will hear their cries and
comfort them.
18 You will bring justice to the orphans and
the oppressed,
so mere people can no longer terrify
them.

PSALM 11
For the choir director: A psalm of David.

1 I trust in the LORD for protection.
So why do you say to me,
"Fly like a bird to the mountains for
safety!
2 The wicked are stringing their bows
and fitting their arrows on the
bowstrings.
They shoot from the shadows
at those whose hearts are right.
3 The foundations of law and order have
collapsed.
What can the righteous do?"

4 But the LORD is in his holy Temple;
the LORD still rules from heaven.
He watches everyone closely,
examining every person on earth.
5 The LORD examines both the righteous
and the wicked.
He hates those who love violence.
6 He will rain down blazing coals and
burning sulfur on the wicked,

10:13-18 Even when it appears that God is blind to the evil deeds of others, we can be sure that one day he will respond with judgment. Those who drag others into sin will be judged harshly by God (see Luke 17:1-3). At times God works quietly behind the scenes, helping those who admit their helplessness to overcome the enemies and problems they face. When we humble ourself and put our trust in God, we can have hope that one day God will give us a full recovery.
11:1-3 Security from temptation can only be found in God; running elsewhere for help—to merely human sources and programs—will never do any long-term good. If we turn only to human resources for help, the people and situations that endanger us will cause us to fall when we are most vulnerable. They will destroy us when the human resources we depend on are unavailable. God is always with us. If we put our trust in him, we will never be without the means to overcome temptation.

punishing them with scorching winds.
[7] For the righteous LORD loves justice.
The virtuous will see his face.

PSALM 12
*For the choir director: A psalm of David, to be
accompanied by an eight-stringed instrument.* *

[1] Help, O LORD, for the godly are fast
disappearing!
The faithful have vanished from the
earth!
[2] Neighbors lie to each other,
speaking with flattering lips and
deceitful hearts.
[3] May the LORD cut off their flattering lips
and silence their boastful tongues.
[4] They say, "We will lie to our hearts'
content.
Our lips are our own—who can stop us?"

[5] The LORD replies, "I have seen violence
done to the helpless,
and I have heard the groans of the poor.
Now I will rise up to rescue them,
as they have longed for me to do."
[6] The LORD's promises are pure,
like silver refined in a furnace,
purified seven times over.
[7] Therefore, LORD, we know you will protect
the oppressed,
preserving them forever from this lying
generation,
[8] even though the wicked strut about,
and evil is praised throughout the land.

PSALM 13
For the choir director: A psalm of David.

[1] O LORD, how long will you forget me?
Forever?

How long will you look the other way?
[2] How long must I struggle with anguish in
my soul,
with sorrow in my heart every day?
How long will my enemy have the
upper hand?

[3] Turn and answer me, O LORD my God!
Restore the sparkle to my eyes, or I will
die.
[4] Don't let my enemies gloat, saying, "We
have defeated him!"
Don't let them rejoice at my downfall.

[5] But I trust in your unfailing love.
I will rejoice because you have rescued
me.
[6] I will sing to the LORD
because he is good to me.

PSALM 14
For the choir director: A psalm of David.

[1] Only fools say in their hearts,
"There is no God."
They are corrupt, and their actions are
evil;
not one of them does good!

[2] The LORD looks down from heaven
on the entire human race;
he looks to see if anyone is truly wise,
if anyone seeks God.
[3] But no, all have turned away;
all have become corrupt.*
No one does good,
not a single one!

[4] Will those who do evil never learn?
They eat up my people like bread
and wouldn't think of praying to
the LORD.

12:TITLE Hebrew *according to the sheminith.* **14:3** Greek version reads *have become useless.* Compare Rom 3:12.

12:5-8 We need not worry about the harm that liars may bring us. God has promised to protect us from those who try to destroy us. People make a grave mistake if they don't understand that God is not like us—his words are pure. He never deceives, nor does he ever fail to keep his promises. God has offered to protect us from the wicked if we but ask. If we really want to avoid tempting situations, God offers us his protection.

13:1-6 The recovery process is often long, with seemingly interminable stretches of spiritual barrenness. At times we may be convinced that God has forgotten us completely. We may feel overwhelmed by our problems and baffled that God has done nothing to help. David began this psalm with similar feelings. Then he demonstrated a helpful way of dealing with the temptation to give in to discouragement. We can turn our focus away from our problems and on to God. When we turn our thoughts to God, we will see that he is already at work in us to complete the recovery process and to fill us with joy.

14:1-3 Our refusal to believe in God is the first step toward failure in recovery. Unless we can accept that there is a God who is concerned about us, there is no hope for us. The psalmist gave us a good term to describe the people who refuse to believe in God—*fools.* The world is filled with evil-minded fools, but we don't have to be like them. We prove we are not such people by deciding to turn our will over to God.

⁵Terror will grip them,
　for God is with those who obey him.
⁶The wicked frustrate the plans of the
　　oppressed,
　but the LORD will protect his people.

⁷Who will come from Mount Zion to
　　rescue Israel?
　When the LORD restores his people,
　Jacob will shout with joy, and Israel will
　　rejoice.

PSALM 15
A psalm of David.

¹Who may worship in your sanctuary,
　LORD?
　Who may enter your presence on your
　　holy hill?
²Those who lead blameless lives and do
　　what is right,
　speaking the truth from sincere hearts.
³Those who refuse to gossip
　or harm their neighbors
　or speak evil of their friends.
⁴Those who despise flagrant sinners,
　and honor the faithful followers of the
　　LORD,
　and keep their promises even when it
　　hurts.
⁵Those who lend money without charging
　　interest,
　and who cannot be bribed to lie about
　　the innocent.
　Such people will stand firm forever.

PSALM 16
A psalm* of David.

¹Keep me safe, O God,
　for I have come to you for refuge.

²I said to the LORD, "You are my Master!
　Every good thing I have comes from
　　you."
³The godly people in the land
　are my true heroes!
　I take pleasure in them!
⁴Troubles multiply for those who chase
　　after other gods.
　I will not take part in their sacrifices
　　of blood
　or even speak the names of their gods.

⁵LORD, you alone are my inheritance, my
　　cup of blessing.
　You guard all that is mine.
⁶The land you have given me is a pleasant
　　land.
　What a wonderful inheritance!

⁷I will bless the LORD who guides me;
　even at night my heart instructs me.
⁸I know the LORD is always with me.
　I will not be shaken, for he is right
　　beside me.

⁹No wonder my heart is glad, and I rejoice.*
　My body rests in safety.
¹⁰For you will not leave my soul among the
　　dead*
　or allow your holy one* to rot in the
　　grave.
¹¹You will show me the way of life,
　granting me the joy of your presence
　and the pleasures of living with you
　　forever.*

PSALM 17
A prayer of David.

¹O LORD, hear my plea for justice.
　Listen to my cry for help.

16:TITLE Hebrew *miktam.* This may be a literary or musical term. **16:9** Greek version reads *and my tongue shouts his praises.* Compare Acts 2:26. **16:10a** Hebrew *in Sheol.* **16:10b** Or *your Holy One.* **16:11** Greek version reads *You have shown me the way of life, / and you will fill me with the joy of your presence.* Compare Acts 2:28.

15:1-3 If we want to experience recovery, we must be committed to honesty, integrity, and right living. We must quit lying to ourself and to others, and we must stop doing things that hurt other people. These are all essential elements of any effective personal inventory if we hope to bring reconciliation to our relationships.
16:1-6 Strength and security come from God alone; he is the only one who can restore us to right living. We can often draw strength from those who are trying to do God's will. As we recover, we can offer that strength to others. If we look to God as the source of our strength and joy, he will never disappoint us. People and other sources of pleasure will let us down, but God will not.
16:7-11 As we seek through prayer and meditation to improve our relationship with God, we will find in his Word not only peace of mind and heart but also good counsel that will keep us from falling into sin. Knowing that God is with us and that he will never abandon us should be a constant source of joy and peace. An important principle of recovery is realizing that God is with us—here and now—and that he promises to be with us through all eternity.
17:1-5 Taking a careful personal inventory of our life is absolutely necessary for complete recovery. If we refuse to examine our life, we will encounter numerous obstacles that will stand in the way of

Pay attention to my prayer,
for it comes from honest lips.
[2] Declare me innocent,
for you see those who do right.

[3] You have tested my thoughts and
examined my heart in the night.
You have scrutinized me and found
nothing wrong.
I am determined not to sin in what
I say.
[4] I have followed your commands,
which keep me from following cruel
and evil people.
[5] My steps have stayed on your path;
I have not wavered from following
you.

[6] I am praying to you because I know you
will answer, O God.
Bend down and listen as I pray.
[7] Show me your unfailing love in
wonderful ways.
By your mighty power you rescue
those who seek refuge from their
enemies.
[8] Guard me as you would guard your own
eyes.*
Hide me in the shadow of your wings.
[9] Protect me from wicked people who
attack me,
from murderous enemies who surround
me.
[10] They are without pity.
Listen to their boasting!
[11] They track me down and surround me,
watching for the chance to throw me
to the ground.
[12] They are like hungry lions, eager to tear
me apart—
like young lions hiding in ambush.

[13] Arise, O LORD!
Stand against them, and bring them to
their knees!
Rescue me from the wicked with your
sword!

17:8 Hebrew *as the pupil of your eye.* 18:5 Hebrew *Sheol.*

[14] By the power of your hand,
O LORD,
destroy those who look to this world for
their reward.
But satisfy the hunger of your treasured
ones.
May their children have plenty,
leaving an inheritance for their
descendants.
[15] Because I am righteous, I will see you.
When I awake, I will see you face to
face and be satisfied.

PSALM 18

*For the choir director: A psalm of David, the servant
of the LORD. He sang this song to the LORD on the
day the LORD rescued him from all his enemies and
from Saul. He sang:*

[1] I love you, LORD;
you are my strength.
[2] The LORD is my rock, my fortress, and my
savior;
my God is my rock, in whom I find
protection.
He is my shield, the power that saves me,
and my place of safety.
[3] I called on the LORD, who is worthy of
praise,
and he saved me from my enemies.

[4] The ropes of death entangled me;
floods of destruction swept over me.
[5] The grave* wrapped its ropes around me;
death laid a trap in my path.
[6] But in my distress I cried out to the LORD;
yes, I prayed to my God for help.
He heard me from his sanctuary;
my cry to him reached his ears.

[7] Then the earth quaked and trembled.
The foundations of the mountains
shook;
they quaked because of his anger.
[8] Smoke poured from his nostrils;
fierce flames leaped from his mouth.
Glowing coals blazed forth from him.

---

our recovery program. As we learn to live as we should, we can have confidence that God will
respond to our cries for help. We must follow through on our commitment by avoiding
involvement with the people who draw us toward the evil things that have overwhelmed us in the
past.
18:6-15 The psalmist used very graphic language here to show how serious God is about helping
those who turn to him for help. The psalmist knew that he would be delivered—not because he
was strong or deserving of God's help but because God loved him and was powerful enough to
arouse all the forces of nature to help him. If God is on our side, no enemy is too great. We can
always experience victory by depending on God's delivering hand.

⁹ He opened the heavens and came down;
dark storm clouds were beneath his
feet.
¹⁰ Mounted on a mighty angelic being,* he
flew,
soaring on the wings of the wind.
¹¹ He shrouded himself in darkness,
veiling his approach with dark rain
clouds.
¹² Thick clouds shielded the brightness
around him
and rained down hail and burning
coals.*
¹³ The LORD thundered from heaven;
the voice of the Most High resounded
amid the hail and burning coals.
¹⁴ He shot his arrows and scattered his
enemies;
great bolts of lightning flashed, and
they were confused.
¹⁵ Then at your command, O LORD,
at the blast of your breath,
the bottom of the sea could be seen,
and the foundations of the earth were
laid bare.

¹⁶ He reached down from heaven and
rescued me;
he drew me out of deep waters.
¹⁷ He rescued me from my powerful enemies,
from those who hated me and were too
strong for me.
¹⁸ They attacked me at a moment when I
was in distress,
but the LORD supported me.
¹⁹ He led me to a place of safety;
he rescued me because he delights
in me.
²⁰ The LORD rewarded me for doing right;
he restored me because of my
innocence.
²¹ For I have kept the ways of the LORD;
I have not turned from my God to
follow evil.
²² I have followed all his regulations;

I have never abandoned his decrees.
²³ I am blameless before God;
I have kept myself from sin.
²⁴ The LORD rewarded me for doing right.
He has seen my innocence.

²⁵ To the faithful you show yourself faithful;
to those with integrity you show
integrity.
²⁶ To the pure you show yourself pure,
but to the crooked you show yourself
shrewd.
²⁷ You rescue the humble,
but you humiliate the proud.
²⁸ You light a lamp for me.
The LORD, my God, lights up my
darkness.
²⁹ In your strength I can crush an army;
with my God I can scale any wall.

³⁰ God's way is perfect.
All the LORD's promises prove true.
He is a shield for all who look to him
for protection.
³¹ For who is God except the LORD?
Who but our God is a solid rock?
³² God arms me with strength,
and he makes my way perfect.
³³ He makes me as surefooted as a deer,
enabling me to stand on mountain
heights.
³⁴ He trains my hands for battle;
he strengthens my arm to draw a
bronze bow.
³⁵ You have given me your shield of victory.
Your right hand supports me;
your help* has made me great.
³⁶ You have made a wide path for my feet
to keep them from slipping.

³⁷ I chased my enemies and caught them;
I did not stop until they were
conquered.
³⁸ I struck them down so they could not
get up;
they fell beneath my feet.

18:10 Hebrew *a cherub.* 18:12 Or *and lightning bolts;* also in 18:13. 18:35 Hebrew *your humility;* compare 2 Sam 22:36.

18:16-19 When the psalmist realized his helplessness and turned his life over to God, God came to his aid. Many of us have known this truth as a theological principle, but now we are beginning to experience it in our own life. We also are given a clear warning in these verses. Our enemies or temptations always attack us when we are most vulnerable. A careful moral inventory helps us see what our weaknesses are and when temptation will most likely attack. Then we need to evaluate the situations we encounter and decide which ones should be avoided.

18:37-42 We cannot fight the battles between us and our dependency alone. Although at times we may feel that our efforts are overcoming the things that cripple and destroy us, we soon realize that it is God who gives us the strength to fight these battles. Once we bring God into our battles, we begin to experience victory in the places where we were defeated in the past. God alone can guarantee a permanent victory.

³⁹ You have armed me with strength for the
    battle;
    you have subdued my enemies under
      my feet.
⁴⁰ You placed my foot on their necks.
    I have destroyed all who hated me.
⁴¹ They called for help, but no one came to
    their rescue.
    They even cried to the LORD, but he
      refused to answer.
⁴² I ground them as fine as dust in the
    wind.
    I swept them into the gutter like dirt.
⁴³ You gave me victory over my accusers.
    You appointed me ruler over nations;
    people I don't even know now serve
      me.
⁴⁴ As soon as they hear of me, they submit;
    foreign nations cringe before me.
⁴⁵ They all lose their courage
    and come trembling from their
      strongholds.

⁴⁶ The LORD lives! Praise to my Rock!
    May the God of my salvation be
      exalted!
⁴⁷ He is the God who pays back those who
    harm me;
    he subdues the nations under me
⁴⁸   and rescues me from my enemies.
    You hold me safe beyond the reach of my
      enemies;
    you save me from violent opponents.
⁴⁹ For this, O LORD, I will praise you among
    the nations;
    I will sing praises to your name.
⁵⁰ You give great victories to your king;
    you show unfailing love to your
      anointed,
    to David and all his descendants
      forever.

19:3 Or *There is no speech or language where their voice is not heard.*

PSALM 19
For the choir director: A psalm of David.

¹ The heavens proclaim the glory of God.
    The skies display his craftsmanship.
² Day after day they continue to speak;
    night after night they make him
      known.
³ They speak without a sound or word;
    their voice is never heard.*
⁴ Yet their message has gone throughout
    the earth,
    and their words to all the world.

God has made a home in the heavens for
    the sun.
⁵ It bursts forth like a radiant bridegroom
    after his wedding.
    It rejoices like a great athlete eager to
      run the race.
⁶ The sun rises at one end of the heavens
    and follows its course to the other end.
    Nothing can hide from its heat.

⁷ The instructions of the LORD are perfect,
    reviving the soul.
    The decrees of the LORD are trustworthy,
    making wise the simple.
⁸ The commandments of the LORD
    are right,
    bringing joy to the heart.
    The commands of the LORD are clear,
    giving insight for living.
⁹ Reverence for the LORD is pure,
    lasting forever.
    The laws of the LORD are true;
    each one is fair.
¹⁰ They are more desirable than gold,
    even the finest gold.
    They are sweeter than honey,
    even honey dripping from
      the comb.

18:43-50 The successes that God gives us can be a strong encouragement to others. In recovery we are called upon to share our victories with others. As we do, we will also be carrying the message of his saving power and love to those who are listening. This may be all it takes to give them the courage to go on. They will see God's transforming power in our life and begin to hope that God can do the same for them. Because of who God is and what he does for us, we should constantly give him thanks and praise for the way he helps us.

19:1-6 No one can rightly say that he or she has never heard about God (see Romans 1:20). His power can be seen throughout our physical world. Even the sun, though silent in the skies, declares every day what God has done. All humans benefit from the sun, and, whether they like it or not, they cannot hide from the message it declares to all the world. God is not a figment of our imagination. He is with us right now, and he desires to help us through the recovery process.

19:7-11 Adhering to God's laws will produce wholeness in our life. Applying God's truth revives our inner being and gives insight—even to the least of us—into how we should live. His Word is not a burden that robs us of the good things of life (see Matthew 11:29-30). Instead, it transforms us and replaces our discouragement with joy.

¹¹ They are a warning to your servant,
    a great reward for those who obey
      them.
¹² How can I know all the sins lurking in
      my heart?
    Cleanse me from these hidden faults.
¹³ Keep your servant from deliberate sins!
    Don't let them control me.
  Then I will be free of guilt
    and innocent of great sin.

¹⁴ May the words of my mouth
    and the meditation of my heart
  be pleasing to you,
    O Lord, my rock and my redeemer.

PSALM 20
For the choir director: A psalm of David.

¹ In times of trouble, may the Lord answer
    your cry.
  May the name of the God of Jacob keep
    you safe from all harm.
² May he send you help from his
    sanctuary
  and strengthen you from Jerusalem.*
³ May he remember all your gifts
    and look favorably on your burnt
    offerings.   *Interlude*

⁴ May he grant your heart's desires
    and make all your plans succeed.
⁵ May we shout for joy when we hear of
    your victory
  and raise a victory banner in the name
    of our God.
  May the Lord answer all your prayers.

⁶ Now I know that the Lord rescues his
    anointed king.
  He will answer him from his holy
    heaven
  and rescue him by his great power.

20:2 Hebrew *Zion.*

⁷ Some nations boast of their chariots and
    horses,
  but we boast in the name of the Lord
    our God.
⁸ Those nations will fall down and collapse,
  but we will rise up and stand firm.

⁹ Give victory to our king, O Lord!
  Answer our cry for help.

PSALM 21
For the choir director: A psalm of David.

¹ How the king rejoices in your strength,
    O Lord!
  He shouts with joy because you give
    him victory.
² For you have given him his heart's desire;
  you have withheld nothing he
    requested.   *Interlude*

³ You welcomed him back with success and
    prosperity.
  You placed a crown of finest gold
    on his head.
⁴ He asked you to preserve his life,
    and you granted his request.
  The days of his life stretch on forever.
⁵ Your victory brings him great honor,
    and you have clothed him with
    splendor and majesty.
⁶ You have endowed him with eternal
    blessings
  and given him the joy of your presence.
⁷ For the king trusts in the Lord.
  The unfailing love of the Most High
    will keep him from stumbling.

⁸ You will capture all your enemies.
  Your strong right hand will seize all
    who hate you.
⁹ You will throw them in a flaming furnace
    when you appear.

20:1-3 The psalmist counted on God's presence at all times to protect him, especially when his problems were most intense. The Bible is full of stories of people who were helped by God in times of trouble: Abraham, Joseph, Moses, Joshua, David, Peter, Paul. If God helped all these people when they needed him, he can also protect all of us. Knowing we need his help, we must remain steadfast in our decision to turn our will and our life over to his care.

20:4-9 God is more than able to give us our greatest desires—even recovery from the consequences of our past mistakes (see Ephesians 3:20). Unlike those who trust in their own power to overcome their problems, we can place our trust in God. As a result, we have hope in the future because God will help us when we call out to him.

21:1-6 As we thoroughly evaluate our life, we realize that our strength comes from God as we seek him through prayer and meditation. He wants to give each of us a life that has eternal value and meaning. As we experience this, we will begin to understand that true joy is an outgrowth of being in God's presence. This should motivate us to spend time with God through prayer and meditation. We need to draw close to him, not just for what he can do for us but for who he is.

The LORD will consume them in his anger;
    fire will devour them.
¹⁰ You will wipe their children from the face
    of the earth;
    they will never have descendants.
¹¹ Although they plot against you,
    their evil schemes will never succeed.
¹² For they will turn and run
    when they see your arrows aimed at
    them.
¹³ Rise up, O LORD, in all your power.
    With music and singing we celebrate
    your mighty acts.

PSALM 22

For the choir director: A psalm of David, to be sung to the tune "Doe of the Dawn."

¹ My God, my God, why have you
    abandoned me?
    Why are you so far away when I groan
    for help?
² Every day I call to you, my God, but you
    do not answer.
    Every night I lift my voice, but I find
    no relief.

³ Yet you are holy,
    enthroned on the praises of Israel.
⁴ Our ancestors trusted in you,
    and you rescued them.
⁵ They cried out to you and were saved.
    They trusted in you and were never
    disgraced.

⁶ But I am a worm and not a man.
    I am scorned and despised by all!
⁷ Everyone who sees me mocks me.
    They sneer and shake their heads,
    saying,
⁸ "Is this the one who relies on the LORD?

Then let the LORD save him!
If the LORD loves him so much,
    let the LORD rescue him!"

⁹ Yet you brought me safely from my
    mother's womb
    and led me to trust you at my mother's
    breast.
¹⁰ I was thrust into your arms at my birth.
    You have been my God from the
    moment I was born.

¹¹ Do not stay so far from me,
    for trouble is near,
    and no one else can help me.
¹² My enemies surround me like a herd of
    bulls;
    fierce bulls of Bashan have hemmed
    me in!
¹³ Like lions they open their jaws against me,
    roaring and tearing into their prey.
¹⁴ My life is poured out like water,
    and all my bones are out of joint.
My heart is like wax,
    melting within me.
¹⁵ My strength has dried up like sunbaked
    clay.
    My tongue sticks to the roof of my
    mouth.
    You have laid me in the dust and left
    me for dead.
¹⁶ My enemies surround me like a pack of
    dogs;
    an evil gang closes in on me.
    They have pierced* my hands and feet.
¹⁷ I can count all my bones.
    My enemies stare at me and gloat.
¹⁸ They divide my garments among
    themselves
    and throw dice* for my clothing.

22:16 As in some Hebrew manuscripts and Greek and Syriac versions; most Hebrew manuscripts read *They are like a lion at.* **22:18** Hebrew *cast lots.*

22:1-5 We all have experienced feelings of abandonment. The words in the first verse were repeated by Jesus Christ as he hung on the cross, indicating that even he experienced isolation from God the Father (see Matthew 27:46; Mark 15:34). When we feel cut off from God, we may be tempted to question his existence or doubt that he is able to rescue us. At such times, we must rely on facts not feelings. We must remember who God is and what he has done for us in the past.

22:6-11 When things aren't going well, we may experience low self-esteem, feeling like a "worm." But God cares for us and will help us. Others may mock us, doubting that God can really save us. We should ignore these people because we know God is there to rescue us. He has helped before, ever since our birth, and he will surely continue to help us through the low points in our life.

22:12-21 For many of us, these verses describe the results of our addiction. People may torment us, making fun of our problems. The physical pain described here reminds us of the effects of drugs or alcohol, or the symptoms of withdrawal. When we seek recovery, we have the help of a God who understands our pain. Jesus Christ experienced similar conditions during his earthly life; he also had to face death. He was surrounded, crucified, gawked at, and stripped of his dignity. Jesus knows how we feel, and he is with us through each step in the recovery process.

¹⁹ O LORD, do not stay far away!
    You are my strength; come quickly to
      my aid!
²⁰ Save me from the sword;
    spare my precious life from these dogs.
²¹ Snatch me from the lion's jaws
    and from the horns of these wild oxen.

²² I will proclaim your name to my brothers
    and sisters.*
    I will praise you among your assembled
      people.
²³ Praise the LORD, all you who fear him!
    Honor him, all you descendants of
      Jacob!
    Show him reverence, all you
      descendants of Israel!
²⁴ For he has not ignored or belittled the
      suffering of the needy.
    He has not turned his back on them,
    but has listened to their cries for help.

²⁵ I will praise you in the great assembly.
    I will fulfill my vows in the presence of
      those who worship you.
²⁶ The poor will eat and be satisfied.
    All who seek the LORD will praise him.
    Their hearts will rejoice with everlasting
      joy.
²⁷ The whole earth will acknowledge the
      LORD and return to him.
    All the families of the nations will bow
      down before him.
²⁸ For royal power belongs to the LORD.
    He rules all the nations.

²⁹ Let the rich of the earth feast and
      worship.
    Bow before him, all who are mortal,
    all whose lives will end as dust.
³⁰ Our children will also serve him.
    Future generations will hear about the
      wonders of the Lord.
³¹ His righteous acts will be told to those not
    yet born.

22:22 Hebrew *my brothers.* 23:4 Or *the dark valley of death.*

They will hear about everything he has
    done.

PSALM 23
A psalm of David.

¹ The LORD is my shepherd;
    I have all that I need.
² He lets me rest in green meadows;
    he leads me beside peaceful streams.
³   He renews my strength.
 He guides me along right paths,
    bringing honor to his name.
⁴ Even when I walk
    through the darkest valley,*
 I will not be afraid,
    for you are close beside me.
 Your rod and your staff
    protect and comfort me.
⁵ You prepare a feast for me
    in the presence of my enemies.
 You honor me by anointing my head with
    oil.
 My cup overflows with blessings.
⁶ Surely your goodness and unfailing love
    will pursue me
 all the days of my life,
 and I will live in the house of the LORD
    forever.

PSALM 24
A psalm of David.

¹ The earth is the LORD's, and everything
    in it.
 The world and all its people belong
    to him.
² For he laid the earth's foundation on the
    seas
 and built it on the ocean depths.

³ Who may climb the mountain of the
    LORD?
 Who may stand in his holy place?
⁴ Only those whose hands and hearts are
    pure,

23:1-6 God is our shepherd, and he knows what we need even better than we do. God wants us to have what is best for us. As long as we make him our shepherd, he will lead us to places of safety. He knows how to direct us away from places where we may be tempted to stumble. Even when we fall, he can deliver us from our failure, pain, and suffering. God will help us avoid the places where we have stumbled in the past and guide us as we journey toward recovery.
24:1-2 Some of us may feel that there is no power great enough to deliver us from the terrible circumstances we have fallen into. In these verses, however, we see a God who has enough power to create and control the entire universe. We know from his Word that God desires to support us in the process of recovery from sin and its terrible consequences. God is more than able to help us overcome our dependency and lead us to freedom. We must bring our failures to him and ask him to help us deal with our defects of character.

who do not worship idols
and never tell lies.
5 They will receive the LORD's blessing
and have a right relationship with God
their savior.
6 Such people may seek you
and worship in your presence, O God
of Jacob.*   Interlude

7 Open up, ancient gates!
Open up, ancient doors,
and let the King of glory enter.
8 Who is the King of glory?
The LORD, strong and mighty;
the LORD, invincible in battle.
9 Open up, ancient gates!
Open up, ancient doors,
and let the King of glory enter.
10 Who is the King of glory?
The LORD of Heaven's Armies—
he is the King of glory.   Interlude

PSALM 25*
A psalm of David.

1 O LORD, I give my life to you.
2   I trust in you, my God!
Do not let me be disgraced,
or let my enemies rejoice in my defeat.
3 No one who trusts in you will ever be
disgraced,
but disgrace comes to those who try to
deceive others.

4 Show me the right path, O LORD;
point out the road for me to follow.
5 Lead me by your truth and teach me,
for you are the God who saves me.
All day long I put my hope in you.
6 Remember, O LORD, your compassion and
unfailing love,
which you have shown from long
ages past.
7 Do not remember the rebellious sins of
my youth.
Remember me in the light of your
unfailing love,
for you are merciful, O LORD.

8 The LORD is good and does what
is right;
he shows the proper path to those who
go astray.
9 He leads the humble in doing right,
teaching them his way.
10 The LORD leads with unfailing love and
faithfulness
all who keep his covenant and obey his
demands.

11 For the honor of your name,
O LORD,
forgive my many, many sins.
12 Who are those who fear the LORD?
He will show them the path they
should choose.
13 They will live in prosperity,
and their children will inherit
the land.
14 The LORD is a friend to those who fear
him.
He teaches them his covenant.
15 My eyes are always on the LORD,
for he rescues me from the traps of my
enemies.

16 Turn to me and have mercy,
for I am alone and in deep
distress.
17 My problems go from bad to
worse.
Oh, save me from them all!
18 Feel my pain and see my trouble.
Forgive all my sins.
19 See how many enemies I have
and how viciously they hate me!
20 Protect me! Rescue my life from
them!
Do not let me be disgraced, for in
you I take refuge.
21 May integrity and honesty
protect me,
for I put my hope in you.

22 O God, ransom Israel
from all its troubles.

24:6 As in two Hebrew manuscripts and Greek and Syriac versions; most Hebrew manuscripts read *O Jacob*.
25 This psalm is a Hebrew acrostic poem; each verse begins with a successive letter of the Hebrew alphabet.

25:1-7 When we place our faith in God, we can trust him to care for us and help us overcome the things in our life that would destroy us. We need to ask him to show us how to live according to his truth. Because of his great love and compassion, he will forgive our past sins when we ask him to. And while forgiveness for our sins is important, it is also important for us to forgive others who have harmed us. As we forgive others, we can release our anger and focus on our own recovery.
25:8-10 We need to let God change us, yet we cannot expect him to work his transformation in our life if we are still proud and unwilling to admit that we are helpless apart from him. The first step in recovery is humbly admitting that we are powerless over our dependency. Only after we do this can we experience God's healing work in our life.

PSALM 26
A psalm of David.

¹ Declare me innocent, O LORD,
  for I have acted with integrity;
  I have trusted in the LORD without
    wavering.
² Put me on trial, LORD, and cross-examine
    me.
  Test my motives and my heart.
³ For I am always aware of your unfailing
    love,
  and I have lived according to your
    truth.
⁴ I do not spend time with liars
  or go along with hypocrites.
⁵ I hate the gatherings of those who
    do evil,
  and I refuse to join in with the wicked.
⁶ I wash my hands to declare my
    innocence.
  I come to your altar, O LORD,
⁷ singing a song of thanksgiving
  and telling of all your wonders.
⁸ I love your sanctuary, LORD,
  the place where your glorious presence
    dwells.

⁹ Don't let me suffer the fate of sinners.
  Don't condemn me along with
    murderers.
¹⁰ Their hands are dirty with evil schemes,
  and they constantly take bribes.
¹¹ But I am not like that; I live with
    integrity.
  So redeem me and show me mercy.
¹² Now I stand on solid ground,
  and I will publicly praise the LORD.

PSALM 27
A psalm of David.

¹ The LORD is my light and my salvation—
  so why should I be afraid?
The LORD is my fortress, protecting me
    from danger,
  so why should I tremble?
² When evil people come to devour me,
  when my enemies and foes attack me,
  they will stumble and fall.
³ Though a mighty army surrounds me,
  my heart will not be afraid.
Even if I am attacked,
  I will remain confident.

⁴ The one thing I ask of the LORD—
  the thing I seek most—
is to live in the house of the LORD all the
    days of my life,
  delighting in the LORD's perfections
  and meditating in his Temple.
⁵ For he will conceal me there when
    troubles come;
  he will hide me in his sanctuary.
He will place me out of reach on a high
    rock.
⁶ Then I will hold my head high
  above my enemies who surround me.
At his sanctuary I will offer sacrifices with
    shouts of joy,
  singing and praising the LORD with
    music.

⁷ Hear me as I pray, O LORD.
  Be merciful and answer me!
⁸ My heart has heard you say, "Come and
    talk with me."

26:1-7 Even if we stumble, we must keep trying to live an honest and open life, doing all we can to discover and fulfill God's will for us. We don't have to fear God's judgment, since he loves us— even with all our faults. As we seek God's will for us, we also need to avoid the people who will lead us back into our destructive lifestyle. Nothing good can come from trying to associate with those who formerly dragged us down. We also need to avoid the situations and activities that could tempt us and lead to an eventual fall.

27:11-14 Because temptations press in around us, we need to learn how God wants us to act in the midst of such pressures. He wants to become the stabilizing factor in our life. Apart from him we have no power against the things that once put us in bondage. We must determine, one day at a time, to follow God, patiently and confidently waiting for him to protect and lead us.

28:1-5 The decision to turn our life over to God for his care is an important step in recovery. We won't find the answers to life's problems anywhere else. The best way to avoid the judgment that will fall on those who lead others astray is to stay away from them. If we don't avoid the people and situations of our past failures, we will almost always get trapped by the same old mistakes and dependencies.

28:6-9 God expects us to do our part in recovery, but we know that only he can empower us to stand against the pressures that seem to drive us back into our old ways. Knowing that God is our strength and will give us victory over our bad habits should fill our heart with great joy and encouragement. Even when we feel we are powerless and can't go on, God is waiting for us to run into his open and powerful arms.

And my heart responds, "LORD, I am
coming."
⁹ Do not turn your back on me.
Do not reject your servant in anger.
You have always been my helper.
Don't leave me now; don't abandon me,
O God of my salvation!
¹⁰ Even if my father and mother abandon me,
the LORD will hold me close.

¹¹ Teach me how to live, O LORD.
Lead me along the right path,
for my enemies are waiting for me.
¹² Do not let me fall into their hands.
For they accuse me of things I've never
done;
with every breath they threaten me
with violence.
¹³ Yet I am confident I will see the LORD's
goodness
while I am here in the land of the
living.

¹⁴ Wait patiently for the LORD.
Be brave and courageous.
Yes, wait patiently for the LORD.

PSALM 28
A psalm of David.

¹ I pray to you, O LORD, my rock.
Do not turn a deaf ear to me.
For if you are silent,
I might as well give up and die.
² Listen to my prayer for mercy
as I cry out to you for help,
as I lift my hands toward your holy
sanctuary.

³ Do not drag me away with the wicked—
with those who do evil—
those who speak friendly words to their
neighbors
while planning evil in their hearts.
⁴ Give them the punishment they so richly
deserve!
Measure it out in proportion to their
wickedness.
Pay them back for all their evil deeds!
Give them a taste of what they have
done to others.
⁵ They care nothing for what the LORD has
done
or for what his hands have made.
So he will tear them down,
and they will never be rebuilt!

⁶ Praise the LORD!
For he has heard my cry
for mercy.

Thirst for God
BIBLE READING: Psalm 27:1-6
**We sought through prayer and medita-
tion to improve our conscious contacts
with God, praying only for knowledge of
his will for us and the power to carry that
out.**
Most of us initially turn to God for the help
he can give us, namely, his power to free us
from the power of our dependency. We may
be surprised to find that, as time passes, we
turn to God out of a desire to be near him.
As we discover how wonderful he is and
how much he loves us, we draw near to him
because of the joy we experience in his
presence.

King David gave us a glimpse into his
relationship with God, saying, "The one
thing I ask of the LORD—the thing I seek
most—is to live in the house of the LORD all
the days of my life, delighting in the LORD's
perfections and meditating in his Temple.
For he will conceal me there when troubles
come; he will hide me in his sanctuary. He
will place me out of reach on a high rock.
Then I will hold my head high above my
enemies who surround me. At his sanctuary
I will offer sacrifices with shouts of joy, singing and praising the LORD with music"
(Psalm 27:4-6).

David found great joy by improving his
conscious contact with God. God is always
there, but we are not always aware of his
presence. Our relationship with God usually
begins with his meeting our desperate
needs. But when we begin to focus on
getting to know God as an end in itself, we
will discover that he will give us what we
have always desired—the joy of being close
to our loving Creator. Then we will see
that he can be trusted with every area of
our life. *Turn to page 723, Psalm 65.*

[7] The LORD is my strength and shield.
  I trust him with all my heart.
He helps me, and my heart is filled
    with joy.
  I burst out in songs of thanksgiving.

[8] The LORD gives his people strength.
  He is a safe fortress for his anointed
    king.
[9] Save your people!
  Bless Israel, your special possession.*
Lead them like a shepherd,
  and carry them in your arms
    forever.

PSALM 29
A psalm of David.

[1] Honor the LORD, you heavenly beings*;
  honor the LORD for his glory and
    strength.
[2] Honor the LORD for the glory of his name.
  Worship the LORD in the splendor of his
    holiness.
[3] The voice of the LORD echoes above
    the sea.
  The God of glory thunders.
  The LORD thunders over the mighty
    sea.
[4] The voice of the LORD is powerful;
  the voice of the LORD is majestic.
[5] The voice of the LORD splits the mighty
    cedars;
  the LORD shatters the cedars of
    Lebanon.
[6] He makes Lebanon's mountains skip like a
    calf;
  he makes Mount Hermon* leap like a
    young wild ox.
[7] The voice of the LORD strikes
  with bolts of lightning.

[8] The voice of the LORD makes the barren
    wilderness quake;
  the LORD shakes the wilderness of
    Kadesh.
[9] The voice of the LORD twists mighty oaks*
  and strips the forests bare.
In his Temple everyone shouts, "Glory!"

[10] The LORD rules over the floodwaters.
  The LORD reigns as king forever.
[11] The LORD gives his people strength.
  The LORD blesses them with peace.

PSALM 30
*A psalm of David. A song for the dedication of the
Temple.*

[1] I will exalt you, LORD, for you rescued me.
  You refused to let my enemies triumph
    over me.
[2] O LORD my God, I cried to you for help,
  and you restored my health.
[3] You brought me up from the grave,*
    O LORD.
  You kept me from falling into the pit
    of death.

[4] Sing to the LORD, all you godly ones!
  Praise his holy name.
[5] For his anger lasts only a moment,
  but his favor lasts a lifetime!
Weeping may last through the night,
  but joy comes with the morning.

[6] When I was prosperous, I said,
  "Nothing can stop me now!"
[7] Your favor, O LORD, made me as secure as
    a mountain.
  Then you turned away from me, and I
    was shattered.

[8] I cried out to you, O LORD.
  I begged the Lord for mercy, saying,

28:9 Hebrew *Bless your inheritance.* 29:1 Hebrew *you sons of God.* 29:6 Hebrew *Sirion,* another name for Mount
Hermon. 29:9 Or *causes the deer to writhe in labor.* 30:3 Hebrew *from Sheol.*

29:1-9 In this psalm we are reminded of God's great power over the natural world. Yet even
though his majesty is greater than any words can describe, he knows and loves each one of us.
Knowing how powerless we are over the problems we face should make us realize that we need
to turn our life over to him, the one who is all-powerful. He is the only one able and willing to
help us.

30:1-5 What joy and gratitude we feel when God picks us up and does not allow our problems to
defeat or destroy us! One of the hard lessons to learn during recovery is how to delay gratification. We may go through some long, dark nights struggling with temptation before we experience the joy of victory. But the Lord will not let our enemy triumph over us. When we do finally
overcome, the joy of success will only be that much sweeter.

30:6-9 Sometimes we may be in the most danger when everything in our life is going well. We
tend to become overconfident; we think nothing can happen to us. But pride and arrogance
usually come before a fall. Sometimes God allows us to go our own way and suffer the consequences so we will learn that we can't make it alone. We will succeed in recovery only when we
learn to rely completely on God and follow his recovery program.

9 "What will you gain if I die,
 if I sink into the grave?
Can my dust praise you?
 Can it tell of your faithfulness?
10 Hear me, LORD, and have mercy on me.
 Help me, O LORD."

11 You have turned my mourning into
 joyful dancing.
 You have taken away my clothes of
 mourning and clothed me with joy,
12 that I might sing praises to you and not
 be silent.
 O LORD my God, I will give you thanks
 forever!

PSALM 31
For the choir director: A psalm of David.

1 O LORD, I have come to you for
 protection;
 don't let me be disgraced.
 Save me, for you do what is right.
2 Turn your ear to listen to me;
 rescue me quickly.
 Be my rock of protection,
 a fortress where I will be safe.
3 You are my rock and my fortress.
 For the honor of your name, lead me
 out of this danger.
4 Pull me from the trap my enemies set
 for me,
 for I find protection in you alone.
5 I entrust my spirit into your hand.
 Rescue me, LORD, for you are a faithful
 God.

6 I hate those who worship worthless idols.
 I trust in the LORD.
7 I will be glad and rejoice in your unfailing
 love,
 for you have seen my troubles,
 and you care about the anguish of my
 soul.
8 You have not handed me over to my
 enemies
 but have set me in a safe place.

31:17 Hebrew *in Sheol.*

9 Have mercy on me, LORD, for I am in
 distress.
 Tears blur my eyes.
 My body and soul are withering
 away.
10 I am dying from grief;
 my years are shortened by sadness.
 Sin has drained my strength;
 I am wasting away from within.
11 I am scorned by all my enemies
 and despised by my neighbors—
 even my friends are afraid to come
 near me.
 When they see me on the street,
 they run the other way.
12 I am ignored as if I were dead,
 as if I were a broken pot.
13 I have heard the many rumors about me,
 and I am surrounded by terror.
 My enemies conspire against me,
 plotting to take my life.

14 But I am trusting you, O LORD,
 saying, "You are my God!"
15 My future is in your hands.
 Rescue me from those who hunt me
 down relentlessly.
16 Let your favor shine on your servant.
 In your unfailing love, rescue me.
17 Don't let me be disgraced, O LORD,
 for I call out to you for help.
 Let the wicked be disgraced;
 let them lie silent in the grave.*
18 Silence their lying lips—
 those proud and arrogant lips that
 accuse the godly.

19 How great is the goodness
 you have stored up for those who
 fear you.
 You lavish it on those who come to you
 for protection,
 blessing them before the watching
 world.
20 You hide them in the shelter of your
 presence,

31:9-13 These verses reflect the heavy toll that sin takes on our life. When we fall into its bondage, everything begins to fall apart. Friends and neighbors avoid us, afraid to come near us. The psalmist understood how we might feel when caught in the trap of sin and continual failure. But he also knew that God is merciful and ready to help us when we call out to him. God is willing to forgive and empower us if we will only look to him for help.
31:19-22 Old friends can drag us down with their "accusing tongues," sometimes without meaning to do so. God can protect us from harm if we allow him to take control of our life. In our distress we may wrongly assume that we are alone; yet God is always there, answering our cries for help. No situation is too tough for God to handle. If we rely on him, he will guide us away from our old life of sin and toward recovery, hiding us "in the shelter of [his] presence."

safe from those who conspire against
them.
You shelter them in your presence,
far from accusing tongues.

²¹ Praise the LORD,
for he has shown me the wonders of his
unfailing love.
He kept me safe when my city was
under attack.
²² In panic I cried out,
"I am cut off from the LORD!"
But you heard my cry for mercy
and answered my call for help.

²³ Love the LORD, all you godly ones!
For the LORD protects those who are
loyal to him,
but he harshly punishes the arrogant.
²⁴ So be strong and courageous,
all you who put your hope in
the LORD!

PSALM 32
A psalm* of David.

¹ Oh, what joy for those
whose disobedience is forgiven,
whose sin is put out of sight!
² Yes, what joy for those
whose record the LORD has cleared of
guilt,*
whose lives are lived in complete
honesty!
³ When I refused to confess my sin,
my body wasted away,
and I groaned all day long.
⁴ Day and night your hand of discipline
was heavy on me.

My strength evaporated like water in
the summer heat.   *Interlude*
⁵ Finally, I confessed all my sins to you
and stopped trying to hide my guilt.
I said to myself, "I will confess my
rebellion to the LORD."
And you forgave me! All my guilt is
gone.   *Interlude*
⁶ Therefore, let all the godly pray to you
while there is still time,
that they may not drown in the
floodwaters of judgment.
⁷ For you are my hiding place;
you protect me from trouble.
You surround me with songs of victory.
Interlude
⁸ The LORD says, "I will guide you along the
best pathway for your life.
I will advise you and watch over you.
⁹ Do not be like a senseless horse or mule
that needs a bit and bridle to keep it
under control."
¹⁰ Many sorrows come to the wicked,
but unfailing love surrounds those who
trust the LORD.
¹¹ So rejoice in the LORD and be glad, all you
who obey him!
Shout for joy, all you whose hearts are
pure!

PSALM 33
¹ Let the godly sing for joy to the LORD;
it is fitting for the pure to praise him.
² Praise the LORD with melodies on the lyre;
make music for him on the ten-stringed
harp.

32:TITLE Hebrew *maskil*. This may be a literary or musical term. **32:2** Greek version reads *of sin*. Compare Rom 4:7.

32:1-4 When we get serious about our past sins, admitting each of them and seeking to make amends, we will probably find that most people are willing to forgive us. Making amends for our past failures and reconciling our relationships is an important part of the recovery process. We see in this psalm that being reconciled to God begins as we admit our sins to him. He will forgive us; we can count on it! When we try to hide our sins from God, our life becomes dysfunctional and miserable. Our inner beings become tied up in knots, and we once again begin to lose control. Why fight it? Confessing our sins to God is the first step toward having a joyful heart.
32:5-9 Like David, we need to confess our sins before God and admit them to the people we have wronged. By doing so, we set a good example for others who are also having a hard time admitting their sins to God. We also set our heart free of the destructive grip of guilt and can reestablish the healthy relationships we all need for a full recovery. God wants to give us a full and productive life, but we must respond willingly to his commands.
33:1-11 Such a powerful God is worthy of our trust and praise. The God who spoke the universe into existence is able to re-create us, and he is filled with tender love for us. He can heal us of the defects that have brought such destruction to us and the people we love. All he asks is that we turn our life over to him so he can work these changes in us.

³ Sing a new song of praise to him;
   play skillfully on the harp, and sing
      with joy.
⁴ For the word of the LORD holds true,
   and we can trust everything he does.
⁵ He loves whatever is just and good;
   the unfailing love of the LORD fills
      the earth.

⁶ The LORD merely spoke,
   and the heavens were created.
He breathed the word,
   and all the stars were born.
⁷ He assigned the sea its boundaries
   and locked the oceans in vast reservoirs.
⁸ Let the whole world fear the LORD,
   and let everyone stand in awe of him.
⁹ For when he spoke, the world began!
   It appeared at his command.

¹⁰ The LORD frustrates the plans of the
      nations
   and thwarts all their schemes.
¹¹ But the LORD's plans stand firm forever;
   his intentions can never be shaken.

¹² What joy for the nation whose God is the
      LORD,
   whose people he has chosen as his
      inheritance.

¹³ The LORD looks down from heaven
   and sees the whole human race.
¹⁴ From his throne he observes
   all who live on the earth.
¹⁵ He made their hearts,
   so he understands everything they do.
¹⁶ The best-equipped army cannot save a
      king,
   nor is great strength enough to save
      a warrior.
¹⁷ Don't count on your warhorse to give
      you victory—
   for all its strength, it cannot save you.

¹⁸ But the LORD watches over those who
      fear him,
   those who rely on his unfailing love.
¹⁹ He rescues them from death
   and keeps them alive in times
      of famine.

²⁰ We put our hope in the LORD.
   He is our help and our shield.
²¹ In him our hearts rejoice,
   for we trust in his holy name.
²² Let your unfailing love surround
      us, LORD,
   for our hope is in you alone.

HONESTY

READ PSALM 32:1-11

Living a lie is miserable. We may know from personal experience the heavy burden of trying to hide a secret life. If we are avoiding God and withdrawing from people because we fear being found out, we are living in needless agony.

Moses understood the price one must pay for trying to live a lie. He prayed, "We wither beneath your anger; we are overwhelmed by your fury. You spread out our sins before you—our secret sins—and you see them all. We live our lives beneath your wrath, ending our years with a groan" (Psalm 90:7-9). David showed us the other side. "Oh, what joy for those whose disobedience is forgiven, whose sin is put out of sight! Yes, what joy for those whose record the LORD has cleared of guilt, whose lives are lived in complete honesty! When I refused to confess my sin, my body wasted away, and I groaned all day long. Day and night your hand of discipline was heavy on me. My strength evaporated like water in the summer heat. Finally, I confessed all my sins to you and stopped trying to hide my guilt. I said to myself, 'I will confess my rebellion to the LORD.' And you forgave me! All my guilt is gone. Therefore, let all the godly pray to you while there is still time, that they may not drown in the floodwaters of judgment" (Psalm 32:1-6).

Why should we live with the weight of dishonesty when relief is available to us? God already knows our secret sins anyway. Why continue to suffer needless agony when we can be set free? *Turn to page 709, Psalm 42.*

PSALM 34*

A psalm of David, regarding the time he pretended to be insane in front of Abimelech, who sent him away.

¹ I will praise the LORD at all times.
  I will constantly speak his praises.
² I will boast only in the LORD;
  let all who are helpless take heart.
³ Come, let us tell of the LORD's greatness;
  let us exalt his name together.

⁴ I prayed to the LORD, and he
    answered me.
  He freed me from all my fears.
⁵ Those who look to him for help will be
    radiant with joy;
  no shadow of shame will darken their
    faces.
⁶ In my desperation I prayed, and the LORD
    listened;
  he saved me from all my troubles.
⁷ For the angel of the LORD is a guard;
  he surrounds and defends all who fear
    him.

⁸ Taste and see that the LORD is good.
  Oh, the joys of those who take refuge in
    him!
⁹ Fear the LORD, you his godly people,
  for those who fear him will have all
    they need.
¹⁰ Even strong young lions sometimes go
    hungry,
  but those who trust in the LORD will
    lack no good thing.

¹¹ Come, my children, and listen to me,
  and I will teach you to fear the LORD.
¹² Does anyone want to live a life
  that is long and prosperous?
¹³ Then keep your tongue from speaking evil
  and your lips from telling lies!
¹⁴ Turn away from evil and do good.
  Search for peace, and work to
    maintain it.

¹⁵ The eyes of the LORD watch over those
    who do right;
  his ears are open to their cries for help.

¹⁶ But the LORD turns his face against those
    who do evil;
  he will erase their memory from the
    earth.
¹⁷ The LORD hears his people when they call
    to him for help.
  He rescues them from all their troubles.
¹⁸ The LORD is close to the brokenhearted;
  he rescues those whose spirits are
    crushed.

¹⁹ The righteous person faces many troubles,
  but the LORD comes to the rescue each
    time.
²⁰ For the LORD protects the bones of the
    righteous;
  not one of them is broken!

²¹ Calamity will surely destroy the wicked,
  and those who hate the righteous will
    be punished.
²² But the LORD will redeem those who serve
    him.
  No one who takes refuge in him will be
    condemned.

PSALM 35

A psalm of David.

¹ O LORD, oppose those who oppose me.
  Fight those who fight against me.
² Put on your armor, and take up your
    shield.
  Prepare for battle, and come to my aid.
³ Lift up your spear and javelin
  against those who pursue me.
  Let me hear you say,
    "I will give you victory!"
⁴ Bring shame and disgrace on those trying
    to kill me;
  turn them back and humiliate those
    who want to harm me.
⁵ Blow them away like chaff in the wind—
  a wind sent by the angel of the LORD.
⁶ Make their path dark and slippery,
  with the angel of the LORD pursuing
    them.

34 This psalm is a Hebrew acrostic poem; each verse begins with a successive letter of the Hebrew alphabet.

34:1-7 When we experience deliverance through God's power, it should be natural for us to praise him and share the good news with others. If we care about other people who suffer as we did, we would be selfish not to tell how God has delivered us. Boasting about our God and the help he has given us is one kind of boasting that is good. This kind of godly boasting will not only encourage others in the recovery process, but it will also strengthen our faith in God.
34:8-14 If we have gone through life trusting in our own judgment, we may find it hard to commit ourself to God and his plan for us. But when we trust the Lord and honor him, he has promised to supply all our needs. He has the power and the wisdom we need to have victory in our struggles over sin and temptation.

[7] I did them no wrong, but they laid a trap
for me.
I did them no wrong, but they dug a pit
to catch me.
[8] So let sudden ruin come upon them!
Let them be caught in the trap they set
for me!
Let them be destroyed in the pit they
dug for me.

[9] Then I will rejoice in the LORD.
I will be glad because he rescues me.
[10] With every bone in my body I will praise
him:
"LORD, who can compare with you?
Who else rescues the helpless from the
strong?
Who else protects the helpless and poor
from those who rob them?"

[11] Malicious witnesses testify against me.
They accuse me of crimes I know
nothing about.
[12] They repay me evil for good.
I am sick with despair.
[13] Yet when they were ill, I grieved for them.
I denied myself by fasting for them,
but my prayers returned unanswered.
[14] I was sad, as though they were my friends
or family,
as if I were grieving for my own mother.
[15] But they are glad now that I am in
trouble;
they gleefully join together against me.
I am attacked by people I don't even know;
they slander me constantly.
[16] They mock me and call me names;
they snarl at me.

[17] How long, O Lord, will you look on and
do nothing?
Rescue me from their fierce attacks.
Protect my life from these lions!
[18] Then I will thank you in front of the great
assembly.
I will praise you before all the people.

[19] Don't let my treacherous enemies rejoice
over my defeat.
Don't let those who hate me without
cause gloat over my sorrow.
[20] They don't talk of peace;
they plot against innocent people who
mind their own business.
[21] They shout, "Aha! Aha!
With our own eyes we saw him do it!"

[22] O LORD, you know all about this.
Do not stay silent.
Do not abandon me now, O Lord.
[23] Wake up! Rise to my defense!
Take up my case, my God and my Lord.
[24] Declare me not guilty, O LORD my God,
for you give justice.
Don't let my enemies laugh about me
in my troubles.
[25] Don't let them say, "Look, we got what we
wanted!
Now we will eat him alive!"

[26] May those who rejoice at my troubles
be humiliated and disgraced.
May those who triumph over me
be covered with shame and dishonor.
[27] But give great joy to those who came to
my defense.
Let them continually say, "Great is the
LORD,
who delights in blessing his servant
with peace!"
[28] Then I will proclaim your justice,
and I will praise you all day long.

PSALM 36

*For the choir director: A psalm of David, the servant
of the LORD.*

[1] Sin whispers to the wicked, deep within
their hearts.*
They have no fear of God at all.
[2] In their blind conceit,
they cannot see how wicked they
really are.
[3] Everything they say is crooked and deceitful.

36:1 As in some Hebrew manuscripts and Syriac version, which read *in his heart.* Masoretic Text reads *in my heart.*

35:17-28 In this psalm David expressed feelings of desperation; he felt that God had forgotten him. At times we feel the same. But when relief comes, we should, like David, encourage others who are having the same desperate feelings by telling them of God's goodness. The whole world seems to conspire against us when we are fighting to stay free from our dependency and compulsions. We need to keep crying out to God for his wisdom and power to help us continue to do what is right. When those who have stood with us see our progress, they will rejoice with us as we tell them about the goodness of the Lord.
36:1-4 Sins and repeated failures have taken a toll on our life. Sometimes we aren't fully aware of how deceitful we have been or how much damage our sin has done to us and to others. That is why it is important to examine our life carefully as we take moral inventory so that God can begin to help us change the things that need to be changed.

They refuse to act wisely or do good.
4 They lie awake at night, hatching sinful
plots.
Their actions are never good.
They make no attempt to turn from
evil.

5 Your unfailing love, O LORD, is as vast as
the heavens;
your faithfulness reaches beyond the
clouds.
6 Your righteousness is like the mighty
mountains,
your justice like the ocean depths.
You care for people and animals alike,
O LORD.
7 How precious is your unfailing love,
O God!
All humanity finds shelter
in the shadow of your wings.
8 You feed them from the abundance of
your own house,
letting them drink from your river of
delights.
9 For you are the fountain of life,
the light by which we see.

10 Pour out your unfailing love on those
who love you;
give justice to those with honest hearts.
11 Don't let the proud trample me
or the wicked push me around.
12 Look! Those who do evil have fallen!
They are thrown down, never to rise
again.

PSALM 37*
A psalm of David.

1 Don't worry about the wicked
or envy those who do wrong.
2 For like grass, they soon fade away.
Like spring flowers, they soon wither.

3 Trust in the LORD and do good.
Then you will live safely in the land
and prosper.
4 Take delight in the LORD,
and he will give you your heart's
desires.

5 Commit everything you do to the LORD.
Trust him, and he will help you.
6 He will make your innocence radiate like
the dawn,
and the justice of your cause will shine
like the noonday sun.

7 Be still in the presence of the LORD,
and wait patiently for him to act.
Don't worry about evil people who
prosper
or fret about their wicked schemes.

8 Stop being angry!
Turn from your rage!
Do not lose your temper—
it only leads to harm.
9 For the wicked will be destroyed,
but those who trust in the LORD will
possess the land.

10 Soon the wicked will disappear.
Though you look for them, they will be
gone.
11 The lowly will possess the land
and will live in peace and prosperity.

12 The wicked plot against the godly;
they snarl at them in defiance.
13 But the Lord just laughs,
for he sees their day of judgment
coming.

14 The wicked draw their swords
and string their bows
to kill the poor and the oppressed,
to slaughter those who do right.
15 But their swords will stab their own
hearts,
and their bows will be broken.

16 It is better to be godly and have little
than to be evil and rich.
17 For the strength of the wicked will be
shattered,
but the LORD takes care of the godly.
18 Day by day the LORD takes care of the
innocent,
and they will receive an inheritance
that lasts forever.
19 They will not be disgraced in hard times;

37 This psalm is a Hebrew acrostic poem; each stanza begins with a successive letter of the Hebrew alphabet.

37:1-7 Do not worry about or envy those who seem to get away with doing wrong things. Their moments of glory will soon be over, and like grass, they will soon "fade away." We need to do things that have lasting value—faithfully serving God and helping the people around us. God's formula for our success is that we develop a relationship with him and determine to serve him in everything we do. Then, in God's perfect timing, we will experience the true joy God promises and freedom from the guilt heaped upon us by others.

even in famine they will have more
than enough.
20 But the wicked will die.
The LORD's enemies are like flowers
in a field—
they will disappear like smoke.
21 The wicked borrow and never repay,
but the godly are generous givers.
22 Those the LORD blesses will possess the
land,
but those he curses will die.
23 The LORD directs the steps of the godly.
He delights in every detail of their
lives.
24 Though they stumble, they will never fall,
for the LORD holds them by the hand.
25 Once I was young, and now I am old.
Yet I have never seen the godly
abandoned
or their children begging for bread.
26 The godly always give generous loans to
others,
and their children are a blessing.
27 Turn from evil and do good,
and you will live in the land forever.
28 For the LORD loves justice,
and he will never abandon the godly.

He will keep them safe forever,
but the children of the wicked will die.
29 The godly will possess the land
and will live there forever.
30 The godly offer good counsel;
they teach right from wrong.
31 They have made God's law their own,
so they will never slip from his path.
32 The wicked wait in ambush for the
godly,
looking for an excuse to kill them.
33 But the LORD will not let the wicked
succeed
or let the godly be condemned when
they are put on trial.

34 Put your hope in the LORD.
Travel steadily along his path.
He will honor you by giving you
the land.
You will see the wicked destroyed.
35 I have seen wicked and ruthless people
flourishing like a tree in its native soil.
36 But when I looked again, they were gone!
Though I searched for them, I could
not find them!
37 Look at those who are honest and good,
for a wonderful future awaits those who
love peace.
38 But the rebellious will be destroyed;
they have no future.
39 The LORD rescues the godly;
he is their fortress in times of trouble.
40 The LORD helps them,
rescuing them from the wicked.
He saves them,
and they find shelter in him.

PSALM 38
A psalm of David, asking God to remember him.

1 O LORD, don't rebuke me in your anger
or discipline me in your rage!
2 Your arrows have struck deep,
and your blows are crushing me.
3 Because of your anger, my whole body is
sick;
my health is broken because of my sins.
4 My guilt overwhelms me—
it is a burden too heavy to bear.
5 My wounds fester and stink
because of my foolish sins.
6 I am bent over and racked with pain.
All day long I walk around filled with
grief.
7 A raging fever burns within me,
and my health is broken.
8 I am exhausted and completely
crushed.
My groans come from an anguished
heart.

37:27-31 God's plan for godly living is the only means to a healthy life. If we really desire to
follow God, we must "turn from evil" and saturate our mind with the truth of his Word. God's
truth should be the foundation for our life. It helps us to know right from wrong and to make
wise decisions. Living according to God's program will lead to healthy relationships and freedom
from the dependencies that bind us.
38:1-8 God's judgment against our sinful habits may seem very harsh, but even his toughest
discipline is intended for our ultimate good. Sin has consequences; God allows us to experience
the painful results of our sins in order to encourage us to turn to him. Our suffering will only
worsen unless we turn from our sins and commit our life to God. Only he can help us overcome
our sinful habits and reestablish our relationships. We would be wise to learn from our suffering
rather than be destroyed by it.

⁹ You know what I long for, Lord;
      you hear my every sigh.
¹⁰ My heart beats wildly, my strength fails,
      and I am going blind.
¹¹ My loved ones and friends stay away,
      fearing my disease.
   Even my own family stands at a
      distance.
¹² Meanwhile, my enemies lay traps
      to kill me.
   Those who wish me harm make plans
      to ruin me.
   All day long they plan their treachery.

¹³ But I am deaf to all their threats.
   I am silent before them as one who
      cannot speak.
¹⁴ I choose to hear nothing,
      and I make no reply.
¹⁵ For I am waiting for you, O LORD.
   You must answer for me, O Lord my
      God.
¹⁶ I prayed, "Don't let my enemies gloat
      over me
   or rejoice at my downfall."

¹⁷ I am on the verge of collapse,
      facing constant pain.
¹⁸ But I confess my sins;
   I am deeply sorry for what I have
      done.
¹⁹ I have many aggressive enemies;
      they hate me without reason.
²⁰ They repay me evil for good
      and oppose me for pursuing good.
²¹ Do not abandon me, O LORD.
   Do not stand at a distance, my God.
²² Come quickly to help me,
   O Lord my savior.

PSALM 39
For Jeduthun, the choir director: A psalm of David.

¹ I said to myself, "I will watch what I do
      and not sin in what I say.
   I will hold my tongue
      when the ungodly are around me."
² But as I stood there in silence—
      not even speaking of good things—
   the turmoil within me grew worse.
³ The more I thought about it,
      the hotter I got,
   igniting a fire of words:
⁴ "LORD, remind me how brief my time on
      earth will be.
   Remind me that my days are
      numbered—
   how fleeting my life is.
⁵ You have made my life no longer than the
      width of my hand.
   My entire lifetime is just a moment to
      you;
   at best, each of us is but a breath."
                                    Interlude

⁶ We are merely moving shadows,
      and all our busy rushing ends in
         nothing.
   We heap up wealth,
      not knowing who will spend it.
⁷ And so, Lord, where do I put my hope?
      My only hope is in you.
⁸ Rescue me from my rebellion.
   Do not let fools mock me.
⁹ I am silent before you; I won't say a word,
      for my punishment is from you.
¹⁰ But please stop striking me!
   I am exhausted by the blows from
      your hand.
¹¹ When you discipline us for our sins,

38:11-22 As we fall deeper into our addictions, our loved ones and friends may turn away from us, which can make the people who approve of our dependency and problems even more powerful in our life. We may find that being with these people draws us deeper and deeper into a destructive trap. If we hope to recover, we need to avoid the people who want us to remain trapped by our sinful habits. If everyone else has abandoned us, we may find this hard to do. We should begin by looking to God for help and seek godly companions. Staying close to God demands that we confess our sins and do what is right. This should then lead to healthy relationships in our life.

39:1-7 At times we may become frustrated and explode in anger just as David did in this psalm. We should not be afraid to do this. If we feel afraid, alone, and abandoned, we should voice our feelings of anger and confusion. As we do this, we are admitting our helplessness. This is the first step in turning to God, through whom we can gain a true perspective on life. God is never threatened by our strong emotions. It is our apathy and pride that disturb him the most.

39:8-13 As we suffer God's punishment in our life, there is no point in trying to escape it. The only wise thing to do is beg for mercy. When God reproves us for our sins, we soon learn that everything we hold dear—our family and friends, even our life—is ultimately under his divine control. Rather than trying to rationalize our sins, we need to confess them. God is ready and willing to forgive anyone who comes to him with a humble heart. In confessing our sins and failures to God, we are taking an important step in the process of recovery.

you consume like a moth what is
    precious to us.
Each of us is but a breath.   *Interlude*

[12] Hear my prayer, O Lord!
    Listen to my cries for help!
    Don't ignore my tears.
For I am your guest—
    a traveler passing through,
    as my ancestors were before me.
[13] Leave me alone so I can smile again
    before I am gone and exist no more.

PSALM 40
For the choir director: A psalm of David.

[1] I waited patiently for the Lord to
    help me,
    and he turned to me and heard my cry.
[2] He lifted me out of the pit of despair,
    out of the mud and the mire.
He set my feet on solid ground
    and steadied me as I walked along.
[3] He has given me a new song to sing,
    a hymn of praise to our God.
Many will see what he has done and be
    amazed.
    They will put their trust in the Lord.

[4] Oh, the joys of those who trust the Lord,
    who have no confidence in the proud
    or in those who worship idols.
[5] O Lord my God, you have performed
    many wonders for us.
Your plans for us are too numerous
    to list.
You have no equal.
If I tried to recite all your wonderful deeds,
    I would never come to the end of them.

[6] You take no delight in sacrifices or
    offerings.
Now that you have made me listen, I
    finally understand*—
you don't require burnt offerings or sin
    offerings.

[7] Then I said, "Look, I have come.
    As is written about me in the Scriptures:
[8] I take joy in doing your will, my God,
    for your instructions are written on my
    heart."

[9] I have told all your people about your
    justice.
I have not been afraid to speak out,
    as you, O Lord, well know.
[10] I have not kept the good news of your
    justice hidden in my heart;
I have talked about your faithfulness
    and saving power.
I have told everyone in the great assembly
    of your unfailing love and faithfulness.

[11] Lord, don't hold back your tender mercies
    from me.
Let your unfailing love and faithfulness
    always protect me.
[12] For troubles surround me—
    too many to count!
My sins pile up so high
    I can't see my way out.
They outnumber the hairs on my head.
    I have lost all courage.

[13] Please, Lord, rescue me!
    Come quickly, Lord, and help me.
[14] May those who try to destroy me
    be humiliated and put to shame.
May those who take delight in my
    trouble
    be turned back in disgrace.
[15] Let them be horrified by their shame,
    for they said, "Aha! We've got him
    now!"

[16] But may all who search for you
    be filled with joy and gladness in you.
May those who love your salvation
    repeatedly shout, "The Lord is
    great!"
[17] As for me, since I am poor and needy,
    let the Lord keep me in his thoughts.

40:6 Greek text reads *You have given me a body.* Compare Heb 10:5.

40:1-5 God's timing is always worth waiting for. If we look to him for help, he will rescue us from destruction and despair and from the things that hold us down. He will also bring stability to our life so we can move forward again with confidence and joy. If we are to experience God's best for our life (which far exceeds anything we can imagine), we need to rely on him alone and avoid any entanglements with those who could lead us away from God and his plan for us.

40:11-17 Recovery is rarely a once-and-for-all thing. The psalmist apparently experienced deliverance from depression (40:1), but then a few verses later he expressed frustration at his numerous troubles (40:12). Every time he felt entrapped, he called out to God for help. This is an important lesson for us to learn as we struggle on the road to full recovery. God will respond as many times as we call out to him. We, however, should never use this as an excuse to return to our sin time and time again. We need to do what we can to avoid the people and situations that we know will lead us into trouble.

You are my helper and my savior.
O my God, do not delay.

PSALM 41
For the choir director: A psalm of David.

[1] Oh, the joys of those who are kind to the poor!
The LORD rescues them when they are in trouble.
[2] The LORD protects them
and keeps them alive.
He gives them prosperity in the land
and rescues them from their enemies.
[3] The LORD nurses them when they are sick
and restores them to health.

[4] "O LORD," I prayed, "have mercy on me.
Heal me, for I have sinned against you."
[5] But my enemies say nothing but evil about me.
"How soon will he die and be forgotten?" they ask.
[6] They visit me as if they were my friends,
but all the while they gather gossip,
and when they leave, they spread it everywhere.
[7] All who hate me whisper about me,
imagining the worst.
[8] "He has some fatal disease," they say.
"He will never get out of that bed!"
[9] Even my best friend, the one I trusted completely,
the one who shared my food, has turned against me.

[10] LORD, have mercy on me.
Make me well again, so I can pay them back!
[11] I know you are pleased with me,
for you have not let my enemies triumph over me.
[12] You have preserved my life because I am innocent;
you have brought me into your presence forever.

[13] Praise the LORD, the God of Israel,
who lives from everlasting to everlasting.
Amen and amen!

BOOK TWO (Psalms 42–72)

PSALM 42
For the choir director: A psalm* of the descendants of Korah.

[1] As the deer longs for streams of water,
so I long for you, O God.
[2] I thirst for God, the living God.
When can I go and stand before him?
[3] Day and night I have only tears for food,
while my enemies continually taunt me, saying,
"Where is this God of yours?"

[4] My heart is breaking
as I remember how it used to be:

42:TITLE Hebrew *maskil*. This may be a literary or musical term.

41:1-3 As we work through the process of recovery, it is easy to become blind to the needs of others as we focus on our own needs and feelings. Recovery demands that we reach out to help others in need. Because of the things we have suffered, we are uniquely gifted to help other people seeking freedom from their dependency. As we reach out to others, we will experience God's help when we are emotionally down or physically sick, or when we face seemingly hopeless situations.

41:4-9 Many people wish us well as we seek to recover. Others, however, seem to hover over us, constantly trying to predict our next failure. We will feel pressure from such people when our relationship with God is weak. At such vulnerable moments, our enemies may seem hard at work trying to ruin our life through deception, lies, and discouraging words. We must keep focused on God; he will never let us down.

42:1-3 We probably developed many destructive appetites during our days of rebellion against God. The solution to this problem is to make God the only object of our desires. The psalmist paints a beautiful picture of the person who longs to be close to God. The language he uses could easily describe the craving we feel for our addiction. We need to realize that only God can satisfy our deepest needs and that our addiction will never bring us real satisfaction. It may temporarily numb the pain, but in the end it will destroy us. If we turn to God, he will help us to change our desires. We can learn to make him the object of our heart's deepest longings.

43:1-5 As we work through the recovery process, those who are ungodly may treat us unfairly. During such times we must look to God, our only dependable source of strength and encouragement. As we turn our life over to him and seek his wisdom and strength, we will find the help we need. We must learn, as the psalmist did, to find strength by reading God's Word and allowing him to restore our joy. As our relationship with God grows stronger, we will discover the means for reconciling our broken relationships.

I walked among the crowds of worshipers,
  leading a great procession to the house
    of God,
singing for joy and giving thanks
  amid the sound of a great celebration!

⁵ Why am I discouraged?
  Why is my heart so sad?
I will put my hope in God!
  I will praise him again—
    my Savior and ⁶my God!

Now I am deeply discouraged,
  but I will remember you—
even from distant Mount Hermon, the
    source of the Jordan,
  from the land of Mount Mizar.
⁷ I hear the tumult of the raging seas
  as your waves and surging tides sweep
    over me.
⁸ But each day the LORD pours his unfailing
    love upon me,
  and through each night I sing his songs,
    praying to God who gives me life.

⁹ "O God my rock," I cry,
  "Why have you forgotten me?
Why must I wander around in grief,
  oppressed by my enemies?"
¹⁰ Their taunts break my bones.
  They scoff, "Where is this God of
    yours?"

¹¹ Why am I discouraged?
  Why is my heart so sad?
I will put my hope in God!
  I will praise him again—
    my Savior and my God!

PSALM 43
¹ Declare me innocent, O God!
  Defend me against these ungodly
    people.
  Rescue me from these unjust liars.
² For you are God, my only safe haven.
  Why have you tossed me aside?
Why must I wander around in grief,
  oppressed by my enemies?
³ Send out your light and your truth;
  let them guide me.
Let them lead me to your holy
    mountain,
  to the place where you live.
⁴ There I will go to the altar of God,
  to God—the source of all my joy.
I will praise you with my harp,
  O God, my God!

⁵ Why am I discouraged?
  Why is my heart so sad?

HOPE

READ PSALM 42:1-11

During bad times we may get lost in our memories of the "good old days." We may struggle with conflicting emotions, teetering between the extremes of depression and hope.

The psalmist reflected these emotions when he said to himself, "My heart is breaking as I remember how it used to be: I walked among the crowds of worshipers, leading a great procession to the house of God, singing for joy and giving thanks amid the sound of a great celebration! Why am I discouraged? Why is my heart so sad? I will put my hope in God! . . . I will remember you. . . . I hear the tumult of the raging seas as your waves and surging tides sweep over me. But each day the LORD pours his unfailing love upon me, and through each night I sing his songs, praying to God who gives me life. . . . Why am I discouraged? Why is my heart so sad? I will put my hope in God! I will praise him again—my Savior and my God!" (Psalm 42:4-8, 11).

Look how the psalmist improved his conscious contact with God. He talked to himself, commanding his emotions to "hope in God!" He repeated "I will praise him again," even though he didn't feel like it at the time. In the dark times he sang songs, thought about God's steadfast love, and prayed. We can do these things, too.
Turn to page 751, Psalm 103.

709

I will put my hope in God!
  I will praise him again—
  my Savior and my God!

PSALM 44

For the choir director: A psalm* of the descendants of Korah.

¹ O God, we have heard it with our own
      ears—
  our ancestors have told us
of all you did in their day,
  in days long ago:
² You drove out the pagan nations by your
      power
  and gave all the land to our ancestors.
You crushed their enemies
  and set our ancestors free.
³ They did not conquer the land with their
      swords;
  it was not their own strong arm that
      gave them victory.
It was your right hand and strong arm
  and the blinding light from your face
      that helped them,
  for you loved them.

⁴ You are my King and my God.
  You command victories for Israel.*
⁵ Only by your power can we push back our
      enemies;
  only in your name can we trample our
      foes.
⁶ I do not trust in my bow;
  I do not count on my sword to save me.
⁷ You are the one who gives us victory over
      our enemies;
  you disgrace those who hate us.
⁸ O God, we give glory to you all day long
  and constantly praise your name.

Interlude

⁹ But now you have tossed us aside in
      dishonor.
  You no longer lead our armies to battle.
¹⁰ You make us retreat from our enemies
  and allow those who hate us to plunder
      our land.
¹¹ You have butchered us like sheep
  and scattered us among the nations.

¹² You sold your precious people for a
      pittance,
  making nothing on the sale.
¹³ You let our neighbors mock us.
  We are an object of scorn and derision
      to those around us.
¹⁴ You have made us the butt of their jokes;
  they shake their heads at us in scorn.
¹⁵ We can't escape the constant humiliation;
  shame is written across our faces.
¹⁶ All we hear are the taunts of our mockers.
  All we see are our vengeful enemies.

¹⁷ All this has happened though we have not
      forgotten you.
  We have not violated your covenant.
¹⁸ Our hearts have not deserted you.
  We have not strayed from your path.
¹⁹ Yet you have crushed us in the jackal's
      desert home.
  You have covered us with darkness and
      death.
²⁰ If we had forgotten the name of our God
  or spread our hands in prayer to
      foreign gods,
²¹ God would surely have known it,
  for he knows the secrets of every heart.
²² But for your sake we are killed every day;
  we are being slaughtered like sheep.

²³ Wake up, O Lord! Why do you sleep?
  Get up! Do not reject us forever.
²⁴ Why do you look the other way?
  Why do you ignore our suffering and
      oppression?
²⁵ We collapse in the dust,
  lying face down in the dirt.
²⁶ Rise up! Help us!
  Ransom us because of your unfailing
      love.

PSALM 45

For the choir director: A love song to be sung to the tune "Lilies." A psalm* of the descendants of Korah.

¹ Beautiful words stir my heart.
  I will recite a lovely poem about the
      king,
  for my tongue is like the pen of a
      skillful poet.

44:TITLE Hebrew *maskil.* This may be a literary or musical term. **44:4** Hebrew *for Jacob.* The names "Jacob" and "Israel" are often interchanged throughout the Old Testament, referring sometimes to the individual patriarch and sometimes to the nation. **45:TITLE** Hebrew *maskil.* This may be a literary or musical term.

44:1-7 There are always valuable lessons to be learned from our spiritual predecessors. Those who have progressed farther in the struggle of life and recovery can share how God brought them help and deliverance. The victories God has given others should encourage us, but we must put into practice the principles they share. If we don't act on what we learn, we will never experience the victories they have told us about.

² You are the most handsome of all.
  Gracious words stream from your lips.
  God himself has blessed you forever.
³ Put on your sword, O mighty warrior!
  You are so glorious, so majestic!
⁴ In your majesty, ride out to victory,
  defending truth, humility, and
  justice.
  Go forth to perform awe-inspiring
  deeds!
⁵ Your arrows are sharp, piercing your
  enemies' hearts.
  The nations fall beneath your feet.

⁶ Your throne, O God,* endures forever and
  ever.
  You rule with a scepter of justice.
⁷ You love justice and hate evil.
  Therefore God, your God, has anointed
  you,
  pouring out the oil of joy on you more
  than on anyone else.
⁸ Myrrh, aloes, and cassia perfume your
  robes.
  In ivory palaces the music of strings
  entertains you.
⁹ Kings' daughters are among your noble
  women.
  At your right side stands the queen,
  wearing jewelry of finest gold from
  Ophir!

¹⁰ Listen to me, O royal daughter; take to
  heart what I say.
  Forget your people and your family far
  away.
¹¹ For your royal husband delights in your
  beauty;
  honor him, for he is your lord.
¹² The princess of Tyre* will shower you with
  gifts.
  The wealthy will beg your favor.
¹³ The bride, a princess, looks glorious
  in her golden gown.
¹⁴ In her beautiful robes, she is led to the
  king,
  accompanied by her bridesmaids.

¹⁵ What a joyful and enthusiastic procession
  as they enter the king's palace!
¹⁶ Your sons will become kings like their
  father.
  You will make them rulers over many
  lands.
¹⁷ I will bring honor to your name in every
  generation.
  Therefore, the nations will praise you
  forever and ever.

PSALM 46

*For the choir director: A song of the descendants of
Korah, to be sung by soprano voices.* *

¹ God is our refuge and strength,
  always ready to help in times of trouble.
² So we will not fear when earthquakes
  come
  and the mountains crumble into the
  sea.
³ Let the oceans roar and foam.
  Let the mountains tremble as the
  waters surge!   *Interlude*

⁴ A river brings joy to the city of our God,
  the sacred home of the Most High.
⁵ God dwells in that city; it cannot be
  destroyed.
  From the very break of day, God will
  protect it.
⁶ The nations are in chaos,
  and their kingdoms crumble!
  God's voice thunders,
  and the earth melts!
⁷ The LORD of Heaven's Armies is here
  among us;
  the God of Israel* is our fortress.
                        Interlude

⁸ Come, see the glorious works of the LORD:
  See how he brings destruction upon the
  world.
⁹ He causes wars to end throughout the
  earth.
  He breaks the bow and snaps the spear;
  he burns the shields with fire.

45:6 Or *Your divine throne.* 45:12 Hebrew *The daughter of Tyre.* 46:TITLE Hebrew *according to alamoth.* 46:7 Hebrew *of
Jacob;* also in 46:11. See note on 44:4.

46:1-6 God is more than able to protect us no matter how strong the pull of temptation might
be. If we try to resist temptation in our own strength, we have good reason to fear. But if God is
with us, we have no reason to be afraid. God's river of mercy and strength flows just for us when
we are weak and thirsty. No power can draw us out of the circle of his protection once we take
refuge in him.
46:7-11 God, the commander of the heavenly armies, is here among us. If we put our life in his
hands, we can rest, confident that he will protect us. He knows our weaknesses and can
strengthen us in the needed areas, helping us to overcome the attacks we face each day. Our
enemies may be strong, but God is far more powerful than anything that might assail us.

¹⁰ "Be still, and know that I am God!
  I will be honored by every nation.
  I will be honored throughout the
    world."

¹¹ The LORD of Heaven's Armies is here
    among us;
  the God of Israel is our fortress.

Interlude

PSALM 47
*For the choir director: A psalm of the descendants of
Korah.*

¹ Come, everyone! Clap your hands!
  Shout to God with joyful praise!
² For the LORD Most High is awesome.
  He is the great King of all the earth.
³ He subdues the nations before us,
  putting our enemies beneath our feet.
⁴ He chose the Promised Land as our
    inheritance,
  the proud possession of Jacob's
    descendants, whom he loves.

Interlude

⁵ God has ascended with a mighty shout.
  The LORD has ascended with trumpets
    blaring.
⁶ Sing praises to God, sing praises;
  sing praises to our King, sing
    praises!
⁷ For God is the King over all the earth.
  Praise him with a psalm.*
⁸ God reigns above the nations,
  sitting on his holy throne.
⁹ The rulers of the world have gathered
    together
  with the people of the God of Abraham.
  For all the kings of the earth belong to
    God.
  He is highly honored everywhere.

PSALM 48
A song. A psalm of the descendants of Korah.

¹ How great is the LORD,
  how deserving of praise,
  in the city of our God,

which sits on his holy mountain!
² It is high and magnificent;
  the whole earth rejoices to see it!
  Mount Zion, the holy mountain,*
    is the city of the great King!
³ God himself is in Jerusalem's towers,
  revealing himself as its defender.

⁴ The kings of the earth joined forces
  and advanced against the city.
⁵ But when they saw it, they were stunned;
  they were terrified and ran away.
⁶ They were gripped with terror
  and writhed in pain like a woman in
    labor.
⁷ You destroyed them like the mighty ships
    of Tarshish
  shattered by a powerful east wind.

⁸ We had heard of the city's glory,
  but now we have seen it ourselves—
  the city of the LORD of Heaven's
    Armies.
  It is the city of our God;
  he will make it safe forever.   *Interlude*

⁹ O God, we meditate on your unfailing
    love
  as we worship in your Temple.
¹⁰ As your name deserves, O God,
  you will be praised to the ends of the
    earth.
  Your strong right hand is filled with
    victory.
¹¹ Let the people on Mount Zion rejoice.
  Let all the towns of Judah be glad
  because of your justice.

¹² Go, inspect the city of Jerusalem.*
  Walk around and count the many
    towers.
¹³ Take note of the fortified walls,
  and tour all the citadels,
  that you may describe them
  to future generations.
¹⁴ For that is what God is like.
  He is our God forever and ever,
  and he will guide us until we die.

47:7 Hebrew *maskil*. This may be a literary or musical term. 48:2 Or *Mount Zion, in the far north;* Hebrew reads *Mount
Zion, the heights of Zaphon.* 48:12 Hebrew *Zion.*

47:1-9 Victories, great and small, should be shared with others who are struggling. The psalmist
made it a goal to encourage others, reminding them how good and powerful God is and inviting
them to join him in praising our awesome God.
48:9-14 We must worship God and meditate on how he has brought us victory over the problems that once held us in bondage and defeat. An important part of the recovery process involves
seeking God through prayer and meditation, actions that help us to develop confidence in God.
We are told to meditate on God's unfailing love for us. He will be our guide and strength as we
face the struggles of recovery.

PSALM 49

For the choir director: A psalm of the descendants of Korah.

[1] Listen to this, all you people!
    Pay attention, everyone in the world!
[2] High and low,
    rich and poor—listen!
[3] For my words are wise,
    and my thoughts are filled with insight.
[4] I listen carefully to many proverbs
    and solve riddles with inspiration from
        a harp.

[5] Why should I fear when trouble comes,
    when enemies surround me?
[6] They trust in their wealth
    and boast of great riches.
[7] Yet they cannot redeem themselves from
        death*
    by paying a ransom to God.
[8] Redemption does not come so easily,
    for no one can ever pay enough
[9] to live forever
    and never see the grave.

[10] Those who are wise must finally die,
    just like the foolish and senseless,
    leaving all their wealth behind.
[11] The grave* is their eternal home,
    where they will stay forever.
They may name their estates after
        themselves,
[12]   but their fame will not last.
    They will die, just like animals.
[13] This is the fate of fools,
    though they are remembered as
        being wise.*   *Interlude*

[14] Like sheep, they are led to the grave,*
    where death will be their shepherd.
In the morning the godly will rule over
        them.
    Their bodies will rot in the grave,
    far from their grand estates.

[15] But as for me, God will redeem my life.
    He will snatch me from the power of
        the grave.   *Interlude*
[16] So don't be dismayed when the wicked
        grow rich
    and their homes become ever more
        splendid.
[17] For when they die, they take nothing with
        them.
    Their wealth will not follow them into
        the grave.
[18] In this life they consider themselves
        fortunate
    and are applauded for their success.
[19] But they will die like all before them
    and never again see the light of day.
[20] People who boast of their wealth don't
        understand;
    they will die, just like animals.

PSALM 50

A psalm of Asaph.

[1] The LORD, the Mighty One, is God,
    and he has spoken;
he has summoned all humanity
    from where the sun rises to where
        it sets.
[2] From Mount Zion, the perfection of
        beauty,
    God shines in glorious radiance.
[3] Our God approaches,
    and he is not silent.
Fire devours everything in his way,
    and a great storm rages around
        him.
[4] He calls on the heavens above and earth
        below
    to witness the judgment of his
        people.
[5] "Bring my faithful people to me—
    those who made a covenant with me by
        giving sacrifices."

49:7 Some Hebrew manuscripts read *no one can redeem the life of another.* **49:11** As in Greek and Syriac versions; Hebrew reads *Their inward [thought].* **49:13** The meaning of the Hebrew is uncertain. **49:14** Hebrew *Sheol;* also in 49:14b, 15.

49:5-13 We need to respect our addictions and compulsions, remembering how they once caused us to lose control. But we do not need to fear them, because God won't allow our destruction as long as we trust in him and follow his program for godly living. The only way we can repay God for his deliverance is to show gratitude and share the good news with others. Although some may seem to prosper and escape the consequences of their wrongdoings in this life, they will leave all their wealth behind and face judgment in the next (see 37:12-17). This should be a warning to us not to spend too much time envying others (37:1).

50:1-6 These verses portray God's judgment of the wicked with powerful images of thunder and fire. Judgment is coming to those who refuse to recognize God's authority. God is good, but he must deal with those who have harmed others or he would not be a just God after all. Because he is just, we need to take careful inventory of our life, doing our best to right all the wrongs we have committed.

⁶Then let the heavens proclaim his justice,
    for God himself will be the judge.

Interlude

⁷"O my people, listen as I speak.
    Here are my charges against you,
        O Israel:
    I am God, your God!
⁸I have no complaint about your sacrifices
    or the burnt offerings you constantly
        offer.
⁹But I do not need the bulls from your
        barns
    or the goats from your pens.
¹⁰For all the animals of the forest are mine,
    and I own the cattle on a thousand
        hills.
¹¹I know every bird on the mountains,
    and all the animals of the field are mine.
¹²If I were hungry, I would not tell you,
    for all the world is mine and everything
        in it.
¹³Do I eat the meat of bulls?
    Do I drink the blood of goats?
¹⁴Make thankfulness your sacrifice to God,
    and keep the vows you made to the
        Most High.
¹⁵Then call on me when you are in trouble,
    and I will rescue you,
    and you will give me glory."

¹⁶But God says to the wicked:
    "Why bother reciting my decrees
    and pretending to obey my covenant?
¹⁷For you refuse my discipline
    and treat my words like trash.
¹⁸When you see thieves, you approve of
        them,

    and you spend your time with
        adulterers.
¹⁹Your mouth is filled with wickedness,
    and your tongue is full of lies.
²⁰You sit around and slander your brother—
    your own mother's son.
²¹While you did all this, I remained silent,
    and you thought I didn't care.
    But now I will rebuke you,
        listing all my charges against you.
²²Repent, all of you who forget me,
    or I will tear you apart,
    and no one will help you.
²³But giving thanks is a sacrifice that truly
        honors me.
    If you keep to my path,
    I will reveal to you the salvation of God."

PSALM 51

*For the choir director: A psalm of David, regarding
the time Nathan the prophet came to him after David
had committed adultery with Bathsheba.*

¹Have mercy on me, O God,
    because of your unfailing love.
Because of your great compassion,
    blot out the stain of my sins.
²Wash me clean from my guilt.
    Purify me from my sin.
³For I recognize my rebellion;
    it haunts me day and night.
⁴Against you, and you alone, have I
        sinned;
    I have done what is evil in your sight.
You will be proved right in what
        you say,
    and your judgment against me
        is just.*

51:4 Greek version reads *and you will win your case in court.* Compare Rom 3:4.

50:16-23 People who deceive, slander, lie, and encourage others to follow immoral lifestyles cannot ignore God's Word for long. God sees what goes on, and, just because he is silent does not mean he doesn't care. One day he will present his case against them, and judgment will follow. The way to avoid such an end is to worship God with thanksgiving and follow him in what he says in his Word.

51:5-9 If we fail to admit and confess our sins, they will continue to burden us with destructive guilt and rob us of joy. We need to learn to confess and forsake our sins immediately. Then we need to seek God's wisdom as to how we can make amends for the wrongs we have done to others. We won't be able to progress in the recovery process or reach out to others until we seek forgiveness for our past failures. Some people may not readily forgive us, but we can be sure God will.

51:10-13 David had already seen what happened when God removed his Spirit from King Saul—it was the beginning of his bitter downfall (1 Samuel 15–19). David wrote this psalm of repentance after he committed adultery with Bathsheba and then arranged for her husband's death (2 Samuel 11–12). On the surface, David's sins were far worse than Saul's. Why did God forgive David and offer him restoration? David was humble and broken about his sin. He admitted it and asked for God's help and forgiveness. Saul was never willing to admit his sins; he continued in denial. If we try to hide or deny our sins, we are in grave danger of judgment. But if we are sensitive to our sins and humbly seek God's forgiveness, there is hope for us, no matter how great our past sins. God will remove any taint of guilt and restore our joy.

⁵ For I was born a sinner—
   yes, from the moment my mother
      conceived me.
⁶ But you desire honesty from the womb,*
   teaching me wisdom even there.

⁷ Purify me from my sins,* and I will be clean;
   wash me, and I will be whiter than
      snow.
⁸ Oh, give me back my joy again;
   you have broken me—
      now let me rejoice.
⁹ Don't keep looking at my sins.
   Remove the stain of my guilt.
¹⁰ Create in me a clean heart, O God.
   Renew a loyal spirit within me.
¹¹ Do not banish me from your presence,
   and don't take your Holy Spirit*
      from me.

¹² Restore to me the joy of your
      salvation,
   and make me willing to obey you.
¹³ Then I will teach your ways to rebels,
   and they will return to you.
¹⁴ Forgive me for shedding blood, O God
      who saves;
   then I will joyfully sing of your
      forgiveness.
¹⁵ Unseal my lips, O Lord,
   that my mouth may praise you.

¹⁶ You do not desire a sacrifice, or I would
      offer one.
   You do not want a burnt offering.
¹⁷ The sacrifice you desire is a broken spirit.
   You will not reject a broken and
      repentant heart, O God.
¹⁸ Look with favor on Zion and help her;
   rebuild the walls of Jerusalem.
¹⁹ Then you will be pleased with sacrifices
      offered in the right spirit—
   with burnt offerings and whole burnt
      offerings.
   Then bulls will again be sacrificed on
      your altar.

PSALM 52

For the choir director: A psalm of David, regarding
the time Doeg the Edomite said to Saul, "David has
gone to see Ahimelech."*

¹ Why do you boast about your crimes,
      great warrior?
   Don't you realize God's justice
      continues forever?

51:6 Or *from the heart;* Hebrew reads *in the inward parts.*
51:7 Hebrew *Purify me with the hyssop branch.* 51:11 Or
your spirit of holiness. 52:TITLE Hebrew *maskil.* This may
be a literary or musical term.

STEP 6

Healing the Brokenness

BIBLE READING: Psalm 51:16-19

**We were entirely ready to have God
remove all these defects of character.**
If we have sincerely practiced the previous
steps, we have probably found enough pain
inside ourself to break our heart. Facing the
fact that brokenness is part of the human
condition can be crushing. But if we have
arrived at this point, it is probably a sign
that we are ready for God to change us.

As a young man, King David wasn't ready
for God to change his character because he
didn't recognize that it had defects. He
prayed, "Don't let me suffer the fate of
sinners. . . . I am not like that; I live with
integrity. So redeem me and show me
mercy" (Psalm 26:9-11). He approached
God on the basis of his own merit.

It wasn't until later in his life when he was
confronted with his sins of adultery and
murder that he was able to say, "For I was
born a sinner—yes, from the moment my
mother conceived me" (Psalm 51:5). He
also said, "You do not desire a sacrifice, or I
would offer one. . . . The sacrifice you desire
is a broken spirit. You will not reject a
broken and repentant heart, O God" (Psalm
51:16-17).

Jesus taught that "God blesses those who
mourn, for they will be comforted"
(Matthew 5:4). God isn't looking for
evidence of how good we are or how hard
we try. He only wants us to mourn over our
sins and admit our brokenness. Then he will
not ignore our needs but will forgive us,
comfort us, and cleanse us. *Turn to page 913,
Isaiah 55.*

[2] All day long you plot destruction.
  Your tongue cuts like a sharp razor;
  you're an expert at telling lies.
[3] You love evil more than good
  and lies more than truth. *Interlude*

[4] You love to destroy others with your
    words,
  you liar!
[5] But God will strike you down once and
    for all.
  He will pull you from your home
  and uproot you from the land
    of the living. *Interlude*

[6] The righteous will see it and be amazed.
  They will laugh and say,
[7] "Look what happens to mighty warriors
  who do not trust in God.
  They trust their wealth instead
  and grow more and more bold in their
    wickedness."

[8] But I am like an olive tree, thriving in the
    house of God.
  I will always trust in God's unfailing
    love.
[9] I will praise you forever, O God,
  for what you have done.
  I will trust in your good name
  in the presence of your faithful people.

PSALM 53
For the choir director: A meditation; a psalm of
David.*

[1] Only fools say in their hearts,
  "There is no God."
  They are corrupt, and their actions are
    evil;
  not one of them does good!

[2] God looks down from heaven
  on the entire human race;
  he looks to see if anyone is truly wise,
  if anyone seeks God.
[3] But no, all have turned away;
  all have become corrupt.*
  No one does good,
  not a single one!

[4] Will those who do evil never learn?
  They eat up my people like bread
  and wouldn't think of praying to God.
[5] Terror will grip them,
  terror like they have never known
    before.
  God will scatter the bones of your
    enemies.
  You will put them to shame, for God
  has rejected them.

[6] Who will come from Mount Zion to
    rescue Israel?
  When God restores his people,
  Jacob will shout with joy, and Israel
  will rejoice.

PSALM 54
For the choir director: A psalm of David, regarding
the time the Ziphites came and said to Saul, "We
know where David is hiding." To be accompanied by
stringed instruments.*

[1] Come with great power, O God, and
    rescue me!
  Defend me with your might.
[2] Listen to my prayer, O God.
  Pay attention to my plea.
[3] For strangers are attacking me;
  violent people are trying to kill me.
  They care nothing for God. *Interlude*

53:TITLE Hebrew *According to mahalath; a maskil.* These may be literary or musical terms. 53:3 Greek version reads
have become useless. Compare Rom 3:12. 54:TITLE Hebrew *maskil.* This may be a literary or musical term.

52:5-9 In the past we may have valued people for the enjoyment and excitement we experienced
while we were with them. We lived for the pleasure and fun of the present moment. With time,
however, it became clear that such a lifestyle always led to painful long-term consequences. We
see in this psalm that God is able and willing to snatch us out of the dangerous situations we may
have gotten ourselves into. A consistent prayer life can help us keep the right perspective about
the world and give us patience and hope as we look to the future.
53:1-6 Believing in God is essential in the recovery journey. Ignoring God's plan for healthy living
brings only trouble and suffering. We have become prisoners of our own desires, powerless to
escape without God's help. Seeing the damage that rebellion has done should cause us to spend
time in prayer. Our own powerlessness should serve as a constant reminder of our need for God's
powerful presence in our life.
54:1-7 We will almost certainly face opposition from people who don't understand what recovery
is all about or who feel threatened by it. The words of this psalm should be our prayer for deliverance at such times. God is our rescuer and helper, who will cause our enemies to fall into their
own traps. Our response to God's deliverance from those who are against us should be worship
and thanks.

⁴But God is my helper.
  The Lord keeps me alive!
⁵May the evil plans of my enemies be
    turned against them.
  Do as you promised and put an end
    to them.

⁶I will sacrifice a voluntary offering to you;
  I will praise your name, O Lord,
    for it is good.
⁷For you have rescued me from my
    troubles
  and helped me to triumph over my
    enemies.

PSALM 55

For the choir director: A psalm* of David, to be
accompanied by stringed instruments.

¹Listen to my prayer, O God.
  Do not ignore my cry for help!
²Please listen and answer me,
  for I am overwhelmed by my troubles.
³My enemies shout at me,
  making loud and wicked threats.
  They bring trouble on me
  and angrily hunt me down.

⁴My heart pounds in my chest.
  The terror of death assaults me.
⁵Fear and trembling overwhelm me,
  and I can't stop shaking.
⁶Oh, that I had wings like a dove;
  then I would fly away and rest!
⁷I would fly far away
  to the quiet of the wilderness.
                                    Interlude

⁸How quickly I would escape—
  far from this wild storm of hatred.

⁹Confuse them, Lord, and frustrate their
    plans,
  for I see violence and conflict in the
    city.
¹⁰Its walls are patrolled day and night
    against invaders,
  but the real danger is wickedness within
    the city.

¹¹Everything is falling apart;
  threats and cheating are rampant in the
    streets.

¹²It is not an enemy who taunts me—
  I could bear that.
  It is not my foes who so arrogantly insult
    me—
  I could have hidden from them.
¹³Instead, it is you—my equal,
  my companion and close friend.
¹⁴What good fellowship we once enjoyed
  as we walked together to the house of
    God.

¹⁵Let death stalk my enemies;
  let the grave* swallow them alive,
  for evil makes its home within them.

¹⁶But I will call on God,
  and the Lord will rescue me.
¹⁷Morning, noon, and night
  I cry out in my distress,
  and the Lord hears my voice.
¹⁸He ransoms me and keeps me safe
  from the battle waged against me,
  though many still oppose me.
¹⁹God, who has ruled forever,
  will hear me and humble them.
                                    Interlude
  For my enemies refuse to change their
    ways;
  they do not fear God.

²⁰As for my companion, he betrayed his
    friends;
  he broke his promises.
²¹His words are as smooth as butter,
  but in his heart is war.
  His words are as soothing as lotion,
  but underneath are daggers!

²²Give your burdens to the Lord,
  and he will take care of you.
  He will not permit the godly to slip
    and fall.
²³But you, O God, will send the
    wicked

55:TITLE Hebrew *maskil.* This may be a literary or musical term. **55:15** Hebrew *let Sheol.*

55:16-19 During recovery our relationship with God is extremely important. At times he may be
the only friend we have. David was confident that God would rescue and deliver him from his
problems. He also depended on God to keep him safe from others who opposed him. With God
as our friend and helper, there is hope for recovery no matter what circumstances we have to
face.
55:20-22 David's anguish caused him to think about the pain he had suffered at the betrayal of
an old friend. Old friends may say all the right words, but deep down they probably want us to
continue practicing destructive habits with them. The solution for David, and for us, is to give our
burdens to God. He is able to strengthen us, encourage us, and keep us from falling.

down to the pit of destruction.
Murderers and liars will die young,
    but I am trusting you to save me.

PSALM 56

For the choir director: A psalm of David, regarding
the time the Philistines seized him in Gath. To be
sung to the tune "Dove on Distant Oaks."*

¹O God, have mercy on me,
    for people are hounding me.
    My foes attack me all day long.
²I am constantly hounded by those who
    slander me,
    and many are boldly attacking me.
³But when I am afraid,
    I will put my trust in you.
⁴I praise God for what he has promised.
    I trust in God, so why should I be
    afraid?
    What can mere mortals do to me?
⁵They are always twisting what I say;
    they spend their days plotting to
    harm me.
⁶They come together to spy on me—
    watching my every step, eager to kill me.
⁷Don't let them get away with their
    wickedness;
    in your anger, O God, bring them down.

⁸You keep track of all my sorrows.*
    You have collected all my tears in your
    bottle.
    You have recorded each one in your
    book.
⁹My enemies will retreat when I call to you
    for help.
    This I know: God is on my side!
¹⁰I praise God for what he has promised;
    yes, I praise the LORD for what he has
    promised.
¹¹I trust in God, so why should I be afraid?
    What can mere mortals do to me?
¹²I will fulfill my vows to you, O God,
    and will offer a sacrifice of thanks for
    your help.

¹³For you have rescued me from death;
    you have kept my feet from slipping.
So now I can walk in your presence,
    O God,
    in your life-giving light.

PSALM 57

For the choir director: A psalm of David, regarding
the time he fled from Saul and went into the cave. To
be sung to the tune "Do Not Destroy!"*

¹Have mercy on me, O God, have
    mercy!
    I look to you for protection.
I will hide beneath the shadow of your
    wings
    until the danger passes by.
²I cry out to God Most High,*
    to God who will fulfill his purpose
    for me.
³He will send help from heaven to rescue
    me,
    disgracing those who hound me. *Interlude*
My God will send forth his unfailing love
    and faithfulness.

⁴I am surrounded by fierce lions
    who greedily devour human prey—
whose teeth pierce like spears and
    arrows,
    and whose tongues cut like swords.

⁵Be exalted, O God, above the highest
    heavens!
    May your glory shine over all the
    earth.

⁶My enemies have set a trap for me.
    I am weary from distress.
They have dug a deep pit in my path,
    but they themselves have fallen into it.
    Interlude
⁷My heart is confident in you, O God;
    my heart is confident.
    No wonder I can sing your
    praises!

56:TITLE Hebrew *miktam*. This may be a literary or musical term. **56:8** Or *my wanderings.* **57:TITLE** Hebrew *miktam*.
This may be a literary or musical term. **57:2** Hebrew *Elohim-Elyon*.

56:8-13 As we keep our thoughts focused on God and trust him, we will find, as the psalmist did,
that God is on our side. Even when our struggles are most difficult, God knows all our pain, and
he will do his part. We, however, must fulfill our responsibilities of being obedient to God's
revealed will. His program is always best for us in the long run.
57:1-3 When we understand the mercy and unfailing love of God, we find comfort in turning to
him in times of trouble, knowing that he will surround us with his protection until the storm is
past. God is faithful and will always be there for us. Understanding and acting upon this truth are
essential for progressing in recovery.
57:7-11 Here the psalmist demonstrates an important principle for recovery: After experiencing
God's help, we should be thankful and share what God has done for us with others. In fact, this

8 Wake up, my heart!
   Wake up, O lyre and harp!
   I will wake the dawn with my song.
9 I will thank you, Lord, among all the
   people.
   I will sing your praises among the
   nations.
10 For your unfailing love is as high as the
   heavens.
   Your faithfulness reaches to the clouds.
11 Be exalted, O God, above the highest
   heavens.
   May your glory shine over all the earth.

PSALM 58
For the choir director: A psalm of David, to be sung
to the tune "Do Not Destroy!"*

1 Justice—do you rulers* know the meaning
   of the word?
   Do you judge the people fairly?
2 No! You plot injustice in your hearts.
   You spread violence throughout the
   land.
3 These wicked people are born sinners;
   even from birth they have lied and
   gone their own way.
4 They spit venom like deadly snakes;
   they are like cobras that refuse to listen,
5 ignoring the tunes of the snake charmers,
   no matter how skillfully they play.
6 Break off their fangs, O God!
   Smash the jaws of these lions, O LORD!
7 May they disappear like water into thirsty
   ground.
   Make their weapons useless in their
   hands.*
8 May they be like snails that dissolve into
   slime,
   like a stillborn child who will never see
   the sun.
9 God will sweep them away, both young
   and old,
   faster than a pot heats over burning
   thorns.

10 The godly will rejoice when they see
   injustice avenged.
   They will wash their feet in the blood of
   the wicked.
11 Then at last everyone will say,
   "There truly is a reward for those who
   live for God;
   surely there is a God who judges justly
   here on earth."

PSALM 59
For the choir director: A psalm of David, regarding
the time Saul sent soldiers to watch David's house in
order to kill him. To be sung to the tune "Do Not
Destroy!"*

1 Rescue me from my enemies, O God.
   Protect me from those who have come
   to destroy me.
2 Rescue me from these criminals;
   save me from these murderers.
3 They have set an ambush for me.
   Fierce enemies are out there waiting,
   LORD,
   though I have not sinned or offended
   them.
4 I have done nothing wrong,
   yet they prepare to attack me.
   Wake up! See what is happening and
   help me!
5 O LORD God of Heaven's Armies, the God
   of Israel,
   wake up and punish those hostile
   nations.
   Show no mercy to wicked traitors.
                                        Interlude

6 They come out at night,
   snarling like vicious dogs
   as they prowl the streets.
7 Listen to the filth that comes from their
   mouths;
   their words cut like swords.
   "After all, who can hear us?" they sneer.
8 But LORD, you laugh at them.
   You scoff at all the hostile nations.

58:TITLE Hebrew *miktam*. This may be a literary or musical term. 58:1 Or *you gods*. 58:7 Or *Let them be trodden down
and wither like grass*. The meaning of the Hebrew is uncertain. 59:TITLE Hebrew *miktam*. This may be a literary or
musical term.

---

should be the natural response of our grateful hearts. This will not only encourage others in the
recovery process but also help in our own journey toward recovery.
58:1-5 The world is unfair and unjust. We shouldn't expect everything to go our way; nor should
we allow our anger at apparent injustices to cause us to compromise. Regardless of how others
act, God still expects us to make amends for the mistakes we have made. He is the only one in the
position to ultimately judge whether things are fair or unfair.
59:1-4 Our enemies may not be people—they may be alcohol or some other addictive substance,
abuse, pornography, or a dysfunctional family. Whatever our enemies are, we should realize that they
are capable of destroying us. The wisest thing we can do is to call out to God for help. He is the only
one really capable of helping and protecting us; he is our "place of safety . . . in distress" (59:16).

⁹ You are my strength; I wait for you to
    rescue me,
      for you, O God, are my fortress.
¹⁰ In his unfailing love, my God will stand
    with me.
    He will let me look down in triumph on
    all my enemies.
¹¹ Don't kill them, for my people soon forget
    such lessons;
    stagger them with your power, and
    bring them to their knees,
    O Lord our shield.
¹² Because of the sinful things they say,
    because of the evil that is on
    their lips,
    let them be captured by their pride,
    their curses, and their lies.
¹³ Destroy them in your anger!
    Wipe them out completely!
    Then the whole world will know
    that God reigns in Israel.*   *Interlude*
¹⁴ My enemies come out at night,
    snarling like vicious dogs
    as they prowl the streets.
¹⁵ They scavenge for food
    but go to sleep unsatisfied.*
¹⁶ But as for me, I will sing about your
    power.
    Each morning I will sing with joy about
    your unfailing love.
    For you have been my refuge,
    a place of safety when I am in
    distress.
¹⁷ O my Strength, to you I sing praises,
    for you, O God, are my refuge,
    the God who shows me unfailing
    love.

PSALM 60

For the choir director: A psalm of David useful for
teaching, regarding the time David fought
Aram-naharaim and Aram-zobah, and Joab returned
and killed 12,000 Edomites in the Valley of Salt. To
be sung to the tune "Lily of the Testimony."*

¹ You have rejected us, O God, and broken
    our defenses.
    You have been angry with us; now
    restore us to your favor.
² You have shaken our land and split it
    open.
    Seal the cracks, for the land trembles.
³ You have been very hard on us,
    making us drink wine that sent us
    reeling.
⁴ But you have raised a banner for those
    who fear you—
    a rallying point in the face of attack.
                     Interlude
⁵ Now rescue your beloved people.
    Answer and save us by your power.
⁶ God has promised this by his
    holiness*:
    "I will divide up Shechem with joy.
    I will measure out the valley
    of Succoth.
⁷ Gilead is mine,
    and Manasseh, too.
    Ephraim, my helmet, will produce my
    warriors,
    and Judah, my scepter, will produce
    my kings.
⁸ But Moab, my washbasin, will become
    my servant,
    and I will wipe my feet on Edom
    and shout in triumph over Philistia."

59:13 Hebrew *in Jacob*. See note on 44:4. **59:15** Or *and growl if they don't get enough.* **60:TITLE** Hebrew *miktam*. This
may be a literary or musical term. **60:6** Or *in his sanctuary.*

60:1-4 When God shows his anger because of our sins, we feel both rejected and overwhelmed.
It is at such times that we need to repent and renew our fellowship with him. The consequences
of our sins and mistakes often hurt others as well, and we ought to be sensitive to that fact and
do our best to make amends. Discipline is never easy to take, but in the midst of it, God provides
us with the direction we need to regain his favor and protection. He has revealed his program for
spiritual recovery in his Word.

61:1-8 Wherever we are, whatever circumstances we face, we can turn to God for help. He will
hear our prayer and protect us with his divine presence. He is our safety and our refuge. We can
confidently ask him for help because he has proven himself to be a deliverer of those who love
him who are under enemy attack. He is our loving protector, who blesses us and gives our life
meaning as we fulfill our vows to live for him daily.

62:1-8 When we face problems that we cannot overcome alone, the wisest thing to do is wait
quietly for God to defend us. We will never totally escape our problems and temptations, but God
is with us at all times. He is more than capable of overcoming our most powerful adversaries—all
we have to do is ask him. We can rely on him not only for deliverance in times of trouble but also
for strength when things are going well and our guard is down. As we realize these truths, we
should encourage others to place their confidence in God. As we reach out to help others, we are
strengthened by sharing with them the good news of God's salvation.

⁹ Who will bring me into the fortified city?
Who will bring me victory over Edom?
¹⁰ Have you rejected us, O God?
Will you no longer march with our armies?
¹¹ Oh, please help us against our enemies,
for all human help is useless.
¹² With God's help we will do mighty things,
for he will trample down our foes.

PSALM 61

For the choir director: A psalm of David, to be accompanied by stringed instruments.

¹ O God, listen to my cry!
Hear my prayer!
² From the ends of the earth,
I cry to you for help
when my heart is overwhelmed.
Lead me to the towering rock of safety,
³ for you are my safe refuge,
a fortress where my enemies cannot
reach me.
⁴ Let me live forever in your sanctuary,
safe beneath the shelter of your wings!
Interlude

⁵ For you have heard my vows, O God.
You have given me an inheritance
reserved for those who fear your
name.
⁶ Add many years to the life of the king!
May his years span the generations!
⁷ May he reign under God's protection
forever.
May your unfailing love and
faithfulness watch over him.
⁸ Then I will sing praises to your name
forever
as I fulfill my vows each day.

PSALM 62

For Jeduthun, the choir director: A psalm of David.

¹ I wait quietly before God,
for my victory comes from him.
² He alone is my rock and my salvation,
my fortress where I will never be
shaken.

³ So many enemies against one man—
all of them trying to kill me.
To them I'm just a broken-down wall
or a tottering fence.
⁴ They plan to topple me from my high
position.
They delight in telling lies about me.
They praise me to my face
but curse me in their hearts. *Interlude*

STEP 3

Giving Up Control

BIBLE READING: Psalm 61:1-8

We made a decision to turn our wills and our lives over to the care of God.

The thought of turning our will and our life over can be attractive. When we give in to our dependencies and compulsions, aren't we giving control over to another power? Aren't we in some way giving up personal responsibility for our life? When we are overwhelmed and want to escape, our addiction can make us feel strong, safe, attractive, powerful, happy. So, in a sense, we are very comfortable with the thought of giving up control of our will and our life.

We can take steps to change our focus and turn our life over to God instead of reverting to the hiding places of the past. The apostle Paul touched on this contrast when he said, "Don't be drunk with wine, because that will ruin your life. Instead, be filled with the Holy Spirit" (Ephesians 5:18).

When we are overwhelmed and in need of some kind of escape, we have a new place to turn. King David declared, "The LORD is a shelter for the oppressed, a refuge in times of trouble. Those who know your name trust in you, for you, O LORD, do not abandon those who search for you" (Psalm 9:9-10).

David also wrote, "From the ends of the earth, I cry to you for help when my heart is overwhelmed. Lead me to the towering rock of safety, for you are my safe refuge, a fortress where my enemies cannot reach me" (Psalm 61:2-3). *Turn to page 909, Isaiah 54.*

5 Let all that I am wait quietly before God,
 for my hope is in him.
6 He alone is my rock and my salvation,
 my fortress where I will not be shaken.
7 My victory and honor come from God
 alone.
 He is my refuge, a rock where no enemy
 can reach me.
8 O my people, trust in him at all times.
 Pour out your heart to him,
 for God is our refuge. *Interlude*

9 Common people are as worthless as a puff
 of wind,
 and the powerful are not what they
 appear to be.
 If you weigh them on the scales,
 together they are lighter than a breath
 of air.
10 Don't make your living by extortion
 or put your hope in stealing.
 And if your wealth increases,
 don't make it the center of your life.

11 God has spoken plainly,
 and I have heard it many times:
 Power, O God, belongs to you;
12 unfailing love, O Lord, is yours.
 Surely you repay all people
 according to what they have done.

PSALM 63
*A psalm of David, regarding a time when David was
in the wilderness of Judah.*

1 O God, you are my God;
 I earnestly search for you.
 My soul thirsts for you;
 my whole body longs for you
 in this parched and weary land
 where there is no water.
2 I have seen you in your sanctuary
 and gazed upon your power and glory.
3 Your unfailing love is better than life
 itself;
 how I praise you!

4 I will praise you as long as I live,
 lifting up my hands to you in prayer.
5 You satisfy me more than the richest feast.
 I will praise you with songs of joy.

6 I lie awake thinking of you,
 meditating on you through the night.
7 Because you are my helper,
 I sing for joy in the shadow of your
 wings.
8 I cling to you;
 your strong right hand holds me
 securely.

9 But those plotting to destroy me will
 come to ruin.
 They will go down into the depths of
 the earth.
10 They will die by the sword
 and become the food of jackals.
11 But the king will rejoice in God.
 All who swear to tell the truth will
 praise him,
 while liars will be silenced.

PSALM 64
For the choir director: A psalm of David.

1 O God, listen to my complaint.
 Protect my life from my enemies'
 threats.
2 Hide me from the plots of this evil mob,
 from this gang of wrongdoers.
3 They sharpen their tongues like swords
 and aim their bitter words like arrows.
4 They shoot from ambush at the innocent,
 attacking suddenly and fearlessly.
5 They encourage each other to do evil
 and plan how to set their traps in secret.
 "Who will ever notice?" they ask.
6 As they plot their crimes, they say,
 "We have devised the perfect plan!"
 Yes, the human heart and mind are
 cunning.

7 But God himself will shoot them with his
 arrows,

63:1-5 The more difficult our life is and the more severe the temptations we face, the more important God becomes to us. When we are at our weakest, God's power takes on added significance for us. We begin to discover how precious his compassionate care toward us really is. He is worthy of all our praise, for only he can satisfy our deepest longings.

64:7-10 God knows exactly where our enemies are, and thus he is able to help us thwart their attacks. Our part in the recovery process is to turn our life and will over to God for his care. He can't help us without our cooperation. As we allow God to work on our behalf, others will be amazed at what he has done for us. As we share the good news of God's marvelous deeds, our victories will be cause for the hope and celebration of others, too.

65:5-13 God is more than able to respond to our need for deliverance because he is the one God who made the majestic mountains of this world. If he can take care of the earth and water it, bringing forth bountiful harvests, we can be sure he can take care of us.

suddenly striking them down.
⁸ Their own tongues will ruin them,
　and all who see them will shake their
　　heads in scorn.
⁹ Then everyone will be afraid;
　they will proclaim the mighty acts of
　　God
　and realize all the amazing things he
　　does.
¹⁰ The godly will rejoice in the LORD
　and find shelter in him.
And those who do what is right
　will praise him.

PSALM 65
For the choir director: A song. A psalm of David.

¹ What mighty praise, O God,
　belongs to you in Zion.
We will fulfill our vows to you,
²　for you answer our prayers.
　All of us must come to you.
³ Though we are overwhelmed by our sins,
　you forgive them all.
⁴ What joy for those you choose to bring
　　near,
　those who live in your holy courts.
What festivities await us
　inside your holy Temple.

⁵ You faithfully answer our prayers with
　　awesome deeds,
　O God our savior.
You are the hope of everyone on earth,
　even those who sail on distant seas.
⁶ You formed the mountains by your power
　and armed yourself with mighty
　　strength.
⁷ You quieted the raging oceans
　with their pounding waves
　and silenced the shouting of the
　　nations.
⁸ Those who live at the ends of the earth
　stand in awe of your wonders.
From where the sun rises to where it sets,
　you inspire shouts of joy.

⁹ You take care of the earth and water it,
　making it rich and fertile.
The river of God has plenty of water;
　it provides a bountiful harvest of grain,
　for you have ordered it so.
¹⁰ You drench the plowed ground with rain,
　melting the clods and leveling the
　　ridges.
You soften the earth with showers
　and bless its abundant crops.
¹¹ You crown the year with a bountiful
　harvest;

STEP 11

Joy in God's Presence
BIBLE READING: Psalm 65:1-4
**We sought through prayer and medita-
tion to improve our conscious contacts
with God, praying only for knowledge of
his will for us and the power to carry that
out.**
Most of us need to desire something before
we will wholeheartedly seek after it. Until
we realize how much God loves us and
cares about the details of our life, we probably won't have the desire to pray to him.
Until we sincerely believe that he has
completely forgiven us, we will be ashamed
to face him. If we hold to our misconceptions about God, this step will be a formidable chore rather than a joy.

　The life of King David should give us
hope. After he had come face to face with
his own sinfulness, he was able to sing,
"What mighty praise, O God, belongs to
you in Zion. We will fulfill our vows to you,
for you answer our prayers. All of us must
come to you. Though we are overwhelmed
by our sins, you forgive them all. What joy
for those you choose to bring near, those
who live in your holy courts. What festivities
await us inside your holy Temple" (Psalm
65:1-4). God wants us to be like those who
lived and served in his Temple, walking
freely into his presence. He wants us to
know that we are welcome and valued
before him. (See also Matthew 10:29-31.)

　God is always present with us and can be
a source of joy and happiness for us now.
We can look forward to spending time with
him and living in his presence every day.
Turn to page 753, Psalm 105.

even the hard pathways overflow with
abundance.
¹²The grasslands of the wilderness become a
lush pasture,
and the hillsides blossom with joy.
¹³The meadows are clothed with flocks of
sheep,
and the valleys are carpeted with grain.
They all shout and sing for joy!

PSALM 66

For the choir director: A song. A psalm.

¹Shout joyful praises to God, all the earth!
²   Sing about the glory of his name!
Tell the world how glorious he is.
³Say to God, "How awesome are your deeds!
Your enemies cringe before your
mighty power.
⁴Everything on earth will worship you;
they will sing your praises,
shouting your name in glorious songs."
Interlude

⁵Come and see what our God has done,
what awesome miracles he performs for
people!
⁶He made a dry path through the Red Sea,*
and his people went across on foot.
There we rejoiced in him.
⁷For by his great power he rules forever.
He watches every movement of the
nations;
let no rebel rise in defiance.   *Interlude*

⁸Let the whole world bless our God
and loudly sing his praises.
⁹Our lives are in his hands,
and he keeps our feet from stumbling.
¹⁰You have tested us, O God;
you have purified us like silver.
¹¹You captured us in your net
and laid the burden of slavery on our
backs.
¹²Then you put a leader over us.*
We went through fire and flood,
but you brought us to a place of great
abundance.

¹³Now I come to your Temple with burnt
offerings
to fulfill the vows I made to you—
¹⁴yes, the sacred vows that I made
when I was in deep trouble.
¹⁵That is why I am sacrificing burnt
offerings to you—
the best of my rams as a pleasing
aroma,
and a sacrifice of bulls and male goats.
Interlude

¹⁶Come and listen, all you who fear God,
and I will tell you what he did for me.
¹⁷For I cried out to him for help,
praising him as I spoke.
¹⁸If I had not confessed the sin in my heart,
the Lord would not have listened.
¹⁹But God did listen!
He paid attention to my prayer.
²⁰Praise God, who did not ignore my prayer
or withdraw his unfailing love
from me.

PSALM 67

*For the choir director: A song. A psalm, to be
accompanied by stringed instruments.*

¹May God be merciful and bless us.
May his face smile with favor
on us.   *Interlude*

²May your ways be known throughout the
earth,
your saving power among people
everywhere.
³May the nations praise you, O God.
Yes, may all the nations praise you.
⁴Let the whole world sing for joy,
because you govern the nations with
justice
and guide the people of the whole
world.   *Interlude*

⁵May the nations praise you, O God.
Yes, may all the nations praise you.
⁶Then the earth will yield its harvests,
and God, our God, will richly bless us.

66:6 Hebrew *the sea.* 66:12 Or *You made people ride over our heads.*

66:1-7 When God demonstrates his power and his care for us, we need to share what he has
done with others. We are not alone in our troubles. Some of our struggling friends face the same
problems we do. Seeing us praise God for his deliverance can become a source of hope and inspiration for them as they seek victory over their dependencies.
67:1-7 We are called to share with others the good news of God's powerful deliverance and his
plan of salvation for all. This should not be thought of as a chore to avoid. It should be a natural
expression of our joy at being delivered from forces too powerful for us to handle alone. Without
God's help, we could never resist the tempting call of our addictions. But with his help we can live
with freedom and joy. Let us celebrate and spread the news of God's powerful deliverance!

⁷Yes, God will bless us,
   and people all over the world will
      fear him.

PSALM 68
For the choir director: A song. A psalm of David.

¹Rise up, O God, and scatter your enemies.
   Let those who hate God run for their
      lives.
²Blow them away like smoke.
   Melt them like wax in a fire.
   Let the wicked perish in the presence
      of God.
³But let the godly rejoice.
   Let them be glad in God's presence.
   Let them be filled with joy.
⁴Sing praises to God and to his name!
   Sing loud praises to him who rides the
      clouds.*
   His name is the LORD—
      rejoice in his presence!

⁵Father to the fatherless, defender of
      widows—
   this is God, whose dwelling is holy.
⁶God places the lonely in families;
   he sets the prisoners free and gives
      them joy.
   But he makes the rebellious live in a
      sun-scorched land.

⁷O God, when you led your people out
      from Egypt,
   when you marched through the dry
      wasteland,   *Interlude*
⁸the earth trembled, and the heavens
      poured down rain
   before you, the God of Sinai,
   before God, the God of Israel.
⁹You sent abundant rain, O God,
   to refresh the weary land.
¹⁰There your people finally settled,
   and with a bountiful harvest,
      O God,
   you provided for your needy people.

¹¹The Lord gives the word,
   and a great army* brings the good
      news.
¹²Enemy kings and their armies flee,
   while the women of Israel divide the
      plunder.

¹³Even those who lived among the
      sheepfolds found treasures—
   doves with wings of silver
   and feathers of gold.
¹⁴The Almighty scattered the enemy kings
   like a blowing snowstorm on Mount
      Zalmon.

¹⁵The mountains of Bashan are majestic,
   with many peaks stretching high into
      the sky.
¹⁶Why do you look with envy, O rugged
      mountains,
   at Mount Zion, where God has chosen
      to live,
   where the LORD himself will live
      forever?

¹⁷Surrounded by unnumbered thousands of
      chariots,
   the Lord came from Mount Sinai into
      his sanctuary.
¹⁸When you ascended to the heights,
   you led a crowd of captives.
   You received gifts from the people,
   even from those who rebelled against
      you.
   Now the LORD God will live among us
      there.

¹⁹Praise the Lord; praise God our savior!
   For each day he carries us in his arms.
                                 Interlude
²⁰Our God is a God who saves!
   The Sovereign LORD rescues us from
      death.

²¹But God will smash the heads of his
      enemies,
   crushing the skulls of those who love
      their guilty ways.
²²The Lord says, "I will bring my enemies
      down from Bashan;
   I will bring them up from the depths of
      the sea.
²³You, my people, will wash* your feet in
      their blood,
   and even your dogs will get their share!"

²⁴Your procession has come into view,
      O God—
   the procession of my God and King as
      he goes into the sanctuary.

68:4 Or *rides through the deserts.* **68:11** Or *a host of women.* **68:23** As in Greek and Syriac versions; Hebrew reads
shatter.

68:1-6 There is no security for those who act like rebels in opposition to God. When life has
beaten us down, God wants us to know we can find a loving family among his people. He himself
is like a father to us, a loving deliverer who sets us free from the traps in which we are caught.

²⁵ Singers are in front, musicians behind;
 between them are young women
 playing tambourines.
²⁶ Praise God, all you people of Israel;
 praise the Lord, the source of Israel's
 life.
²⁷ Look, the little tribe of Benjamin leads
 the way.
 Then comes a great throng of rulers
 from Judah
 and all the rulers of Zebulun and
 Naphtali.

²⁸ Summon your might, O God.*
 Display your power, O God, as you have
 in the past.
²⁹ The kings of the earth are bringing
 tribute
 to your Temple in Jerusalem.
³⁰ Rebuke these enemy nations—
 these wild animals lurking in the reeds,
 this herd of bulls among the weaker
 calves.
 Make them bring bars of silver in humble
 tribute.
 Scatter the nations that delight in war.
³¹ Let Egypt come with gifts of precious
 metals*;
 let Ethiopia* bring tribute to God.
³² Sing to God, you kingdoms of the earth.
 Sing praises to the Lord.   *Interlude*
³³ Sing to the one who rides across the
 ancient heavens,
 his mighty voice thundering from the
 sky.
³⁴ Tell everyone about God's power.
 His majesty shines down on Israel;
 his strength is mighty in the heavens.
³⁵ God is awesome in his sanctuary.

The God of Israel gives power and
 strength to his people.

Praise be to God!

PSALM 69

For the choir director: A psalm of David, to be sung to the tune "Lilies."

¹ Save me, O God,
 for the floodwaters are up to my neck.
² Deeper and deeper I sink into the mire;
 I can't find a foothold.
 I am in deep water,
 and the floods overwhelm me.
³ I am exhausted from crying for help;
 my throat is parched.
 My eyes are swollen with weeping,
 waiting for my God to help me.
⁴ Those who hate me without cause
 outnumber the hairs on my head.
 Many enemies try to destroy me with lies,
 demanding that I give back what I
 didn't steal.

⁵ O God, you know how foolish I am;
 my sins cannot be hidden from you.
⁶ Don't let those who trust in you be
 ashamed because of me,
 O Sovereign Lord of Heaven's Armies.
 Don't let me cause them to be humiliated,
 O God of Israel.
⁷ For I endure insults for your sake;
 humiliation is written all over my face.
⁸ Even my own brothers pretend they don't
 know me;
 they treat me like a stranger.

⁹ Passion for your house has consumed me,
 and the insults of those who insult you
 have fallen on me.

68:28 As in some Hebrew manuscripts and Greek and Syriac versions; most Hebrew manuscripts read *Your God has commanded your strength.* 68:31a Or *of rich cloth.* 68:31b Hebrew *Cush.*

68:24-31 When God helps us gain control over our inner enemies, praise should naturally flow from our lips. The best gifts we can bring to God are our life and our praise. As we thank God for delivering us from our dependencies and problems, others will be encouraged to admit their need for God and call out to him for help.

69:1-4, 13 As he wrote this psalm, David felt as if his problems were drowning him. It seemed that everyone was attacking him and no one was around to take his side. We often feel the same desperation as we work through the process of recovery. In times like these, we should do what David did—cry out to God for help, submit to his will, and entrust our life to his care.

69:5-8 David knew how important it was to recognize his sins and to admit them to God. This is an essential step toward recovery in our own life. We must accept responsibility for what we have done in the past. Then, like David, we should turn to God for forgiveness and restoration.

69:9-12 David's visible repentance and desire to change his life brought him intense ridicule. He became a laughingstock among those who opposed God. Even the town drunks ridiculed him. As we confess our failures and turn our life over to God, we may experience similar scorn. We may deserve some of the ridicule we receive; it may take people awhile to believe that the changes in our life are real. During such trials we should remember that God is more concerned about rebuilding our character than he is about restoring our reputation.

¹⁰When I weep and fast,
 they scoff at me.
¹¹When I dress in burlap to show
  sorrow,
 they make fun of me.
¹²I am the favorite topic of town gossip,
 and all the drunks sing about me.

¹³But I keep praying to you, LORD,
 hoping this time you will show me
  favor.
 In your unfailing love, O God,
 answer my prayer with your sure
  salvation.
¹⁴Rescue me from the mud;
 don't let me sink any deeper!
 Save me from those who hate me,
 and pull me from these deep waters.
¹⁵Don't let the floods overwhelm me,
 or the deep waters swallow me,
 or the pit of death devour me.

¹⁶Answer my prayers, O LORD,
 for your unfailing love is wonderful.
 Take care of me,
 for your mercy is so plentiful.
¹⁷Don't hide from your servant;
 answer me quickly, for I am in deep
  trouble!
¹⁸Come and redeem me;
 free me from my enemies.

¹⁹You know of my shame, scorn, and
  disgrace.
 You see all that my enemies are doing.
²⁰Their insults have broken my heart,
 and I am in despair.
 If only one person would show some pity;
 if only one would turn and comfort me.
²¹But instead, they give me poison* for food;
 they offer me sour wine for my thirst.

²²Let the bountiful table set before them
  become a snare
 and their prosperity become a trap.*
²³Let their eyes go blind so they cannot see,
 and make their bodies shake
  continually.*
²⁴Pour out your fury on them;
 consume them with your burning
  anger.

²⁵Let their homes become desolate
 and their tents be deserted.
²⁶To the one you have punished, they add
  insult to injury;
 they add to the pain of those you have
  hurt.
²⁷Pile their sins up high,
 and don't let them go free.
²⁸Erase their names from the Book of Life;
 don't let them be counted among the
  righteous.

²⁹I am suffering and in pain.
 Rescue me, O God, by your saving
  power.
³⁰Then I will praise God's name with
  singing,
 and I will honor him with
  thanksgiving.
³¹For this will please the LORD more than
  sacrificing cattle,
 more than presenting a bull with its
  horns and hooves.
³²The humble will see their God at work
  and be glad.
 Let all who seek God's help be
  encouraged.
³³For the LORD hears the cries of the needy;
 he does not despise his imprisoned
  people.

³⁴Praise him, O heaven and earth,
 the seas and all that move in them.
³⁵For God will save Jerusalem*
 and rebuild the towns of Judah.
 His people will live there
 and settle in their own land.
³⁶The descendants of those who obey him
  will inherit the land,
 and those who love him will live there
  in safety.

PSALM 70
For the choir director: A psalm of David, asking God to remember him.

¹Please, God, rescue me!
 Come quickly, LORD, and help me.
²May those who try to kill me
 be humiliated and put to shame.

69:21 Or *gall.* 69:22 Greek version reads *Let their bountiful table set before them become a snare, / a trap that makes them think all is well. / Let their blessings cause them to stumble, / and let them get what they deserve.* Compare Rom 11:9. 69:23 Greek version reads *and let their backs be bent forever.* Compare Rom 11:10. 69:35 Hebrew *Zion.*

70:1-5 This prayer by David is short and to the point. He cried out to God for help in the face of an emergency. It is possible to pray at any time, and it is especially appropriate when faced with a sudden temptation or dilemma. For many of us, prayer is the last solution we think of in times of trouble. We try any number of human solutions before looking to God for help. We would be wise to always pray about everything (see Philippians 4:6).

May those who take delight in my trouble
  be turned back in disgrace.
[3] Let them be horrified by their shame,
  for they said, "Aha! We've got him now!"
[4] But may all who search for you
  be filled with joy and gladness in you.
May those who love your salvation
  repeatedly shout, "God is great!"
[5] But as for me, I am poor and needy;
  please hurry to my aid, O God.
You are my helper and my savior;
  O LORD, do not delay.

PSALM 71

[1] O LORD, I have come to you for
    protection;
  don't let me be disgraced.
[2] Save me and rescue me,
  for you do what is right.
Turn your ear to listen to me,
  and set me free.
[3] Be my rock of safety
  where I can always hide.
Give the order to save me,
  for you are my rock and my fortress.
[4] My God, rescue me from the power of the
    wicked,
  from the clutches of cruel oppressors.
[5] O Lord, you alone are my hope.
  I've trusted you, O LORD, from
    childhood.
[6] Yes, you have been with me from birth;
  from my mother's womb you have
    cared for me.
No wonder I am always praising you!

[7] My life is an example to many,
  because you have been my strength and
    protection.
[8] That is why I can never stop praising you;
  I declare your glory all day long.
[9] And now, in my old age, don't set me
    aside.
  Don't abandon me when my strength is
    failing.
[10] For my enemies are whispering against me.
  They are plotting together to kill me.

71:15 Or *though I cannot count it.*

[11] They say, "God has abandoned him.
  Let's go and get him,
  for no one will help him now."

[12] O God, don't stay away.
  My God, please hurry to help me.
[13] Bring disgrace and destruction on my
    accusers.
  Humiliate and shame those who want
    to harm me.
[14] But I will keep on hoping for your help;
  I will praise you more and more.
[15] I will tell everyone about your
    righteousness.
  All day long I will proclaim your saving
    power,
  though I am not skilled with words.*
[16] I will praise your mighty deeds,
    O Sovereign LORD.
  I will tell everyone that you alone are
    just.

[17] O God, you have taught me from my
    earliest childhood,
  and I constantly tell others about the
    wonderful things you do.
[18] Now that I am old and gray,
  do not abandon me, O God.
Let me proclaim your power to this new
    generation,
  your mighty miracles to all who come
    after me.

[19] Your righteousness, O God, reaches to the
    highest heavens.
  You have done such wonderful things.
  Who can compare with you, O God?
[20] You have allowed me to suffer much
    hardship,
  but you will restore me to life again
  and lift me up from the depths of the
    earth.
[21] You will restore me to even greater honor
  and comfort me once again.

[22] Then I will praise you with music on the
    harp,

71:1-8 The psalmist often described God as his refuge or protecting rock—a place of safety in times of difficulty and trial. The psalmist gave heartfelt praise for God's protection from birth. His life was an example to many. One way we can show the reality of God's power to others is to praise and thank him for his deliverance. Let us learn from David's praise and pass the same lesson on to the people around us.
71:9-12 We all face difficult times, especially as we undergo the recovery process. As we struggle with our dependency, our strength often drains to its lowest possible level. When we are powerless, we should seek God's watchful care. He has the power we need to overcome even the most devastating problems.

because you are faithful to your
promises, O my God.
I will sing praises to you with a lyre,
O Holy One of Israel.
²³ I will shout for joy and sing your
praises,
for you have ransomed me.
²⁴ I will tell about your righteous deeds
all day long,
for everyone who tried to hurt me
has been shamed and humiliated.

PSALM 72
A psalm of Solomon.

¹ Give your love of justice to the king,
O God,
and righteousness to the king's son.
² Help him judge your people in the right
way;
let the poor always be treated fairly.
³ May the mountains yield prosperity for
all,
and may the hills be fruitful.
⁴ Help him to defend the poor,
to rescue the children of the needy,
and to crush their oppressors.
⁵ May they fear you* as long as the sun
shines,
as long as the moon remains in the sky.
Yes, forever!

⁶ May the king's rule be refreshing like
spring rain on freshly cut grass,
like the showers that water the earth.
⁷ May all the godly flourish during his
reign.
May there be abundant prosperity until
the moon is no more.
⁸ May he reign from sea to sea,
and from the Euphrates River* to the
ends of the earth.
⁹ Desert nomads will bow before him;
his enemies will fall before him in the
dust.
¹⁰ The western kings of Tarshish and other
distant lands
will bring him tribute.
The eastern kings of Sheba and Seba
will bring him gifts.

¹¹ All kings will bow before him,
and all nations will serve him.
¹² He will rescue the poor when they cry to
him;
he will help the oppressed, who have
no one to defend them.
¹³ He feels pity for the weak and the needy,
and he will rescue them.
¹⁴ He will redeem them from oppression and
violence,
for their lives are precious to him.

¹⁵ Long live the king!
May the gold of Sheba be given
to him.
May the people always pray for him
and bless him all day long.
¹⁶ May there be abundant grain throughout
the land,
flourishing even on the hilltops.
May the fruit trees flourish like the trees
of Lebanon,
and may the people thrive like grass in
a field.
¹⁷ May the king's name endure forever;
may it continue as long as the sun
shines.
May all nations be blessed through him
and bring him praise.

¹⁸ Praise the LORD God, the God of Israel,
who alone does such wonderful things.
¹⁹ Praise his glorious name forever!
Let the whole earth be filled with his
glory.
Amen and amen!

²⁰ (This ends the prayers of David son of
Jesse.)

BOOK THREE (Psalms 73–89)

PSALM 73
A psalm of Asaph.

¹ Truly God is good to Israel,
to those whose hearts are pure.
² But as for me, I almost lost my footing.
My feet were slipping, and I was almost
gone.
³ For I envied the proud

72:5 Greek version reads *May they endure.* 72:8 Hebrew *the river.*

72:12-14 God acts on behalf of those who have no power to free themselves from their problems. He helps those who are oppressed and have no one to defend them. He has great love and
compassion for those who are weak and needy. As we face our addiction, we know what it means
to be powerless. Alone, we are helpless to overcome the temptations of our dependency. But with
God's help, there is always hope for us. His power can help us overcome any problems we face,
and he wants to see us through the hard times to a new life of freedom and joy.

when I saw them prosper despite their
wickedness.
⁴They seem to live such painless lives;
their bodies are so healthy and strong.
⁵They don't have troubles like other people;
they're not plagued with problems like
everyone else.
⁶They wear pride like a jeweled necklace
and clothe themselves with cruelty.
⁷These fat cats have everything
their hearts could ever wish for!
⁸They scoff and speak only evil;
in their pride they seek to crush others.
⁹They boast against the very heavens,
and their words strut throughout the
earth.
¹⁰And so the people are dismayed and
confused,
drinking in all their words.
¹¹"What does God know?" they ask.
"Does the Most High even know what's
happening?"
¹²Look at these wicked people—
enjoying a life of ease while their riches
multiply.

¹³Did I keep my heart pure for nothing?
Did I keep myself innocent for no
reason?
¹⁴I get nothing but trouble all day long;
every morning brings me pain.

¹⁵If I had really spoken this way to others,
I would have been a traitor to your
people.
¹⁶So I tried to understand why the wicked
prosper.
But what a difficult task it is!
¹⁷Then I went into your sanctuary, O God,
and I finally understood the destiny of
the wicked.
¹⁸Truly, you put them on a slippery path
and send them sliding over the cliff to
destruction.

¹⁹In an instant they are destroyed,
completely swept away by terrors.
²⁰When you arise, O Lord,
you will laugh at their silly ideas
as a person laughs at dreams in the
morning.
²¹Then I realized that my heart was
bitter,
and I was all torn up inside.
²²I was so foolish and ignorant—
I must have seemed like a senseless
animal to you.
²³Yet I still belong to you;
you hold my right hand.
²⁴You guide me with your counsel,
leading me to a glorious destiny.
²⁵Whom have I in heaven but you?
I desire you more than anything on
earth.
²⁶My health may fail, and my spirit may
grow weak,
but God remains the strength of my
heart;
he is mine forever.

²⁷Those who desert him will perish,
for you destroy those who abandon
you.
²⁸But as for me, how good it is to be near
God!
I have made the Sovereign LORD my
shelter,
and I will tell everyone about the
wonderful things you do.

PSALM 74
A psalm* of Asaph.

¹O God, why have you rejected us
so long?
Why is your anger so intense against
the sheep of your own pasture?

74:TITLE Hebrew *maskil.* This may be a literary or musical term.

73:13-20 The psalmist had begun to wonder whether following God's program was worth it. It
seemed to him that evil people were happy and prosperous. It didn't seem to make sense. But then
the psalmist came to his senses as he thought about the destiny of the wicked. God's justice will ultimately be served. We all know that our addiction seemed to work for a while, but with time, it
became destructive. God's plan is the only recovery program leading to wholeness and eternal life
with him. We would be wise to follow his plan no matter how difficult it may seem to us at present.
73:21-24 The psalmist had begun to think that God was unjust and had a hard time believing
that God was loving and good. In these verses, however, he realized how foolish he had been.
God was waiting to restore his relationship with the doubting psalmist. We need God's help if we
want to succeed in recovery. But if we cannot believe that God is good, we will hardly be able to
entrust him with our life. Like the psalmist, we need to realize that God does love us and that his
plan for us is for the best. If we trust in God and seek to follow his will for us, he will keep on
guiding us with his good counsel.

2 Remember that we are the people you
chose long ago,
the tribe you redeemed as your own
special possession!
And remember Jerusalem,* your home
here on earth.
3 Walk through the awful ruins of the city;
see how the enemy has destroyed your
sanctuary.

4 There your enemies shouted their
victorious battle cries;
there they set up their battle standards.
5 They swung their axes
like woodcutters in a forest.
6 With axes and picks,
they smashed the carved paneling.
7 They burned your sanctuary to the
ground.
They defiled the place that bears your
name.
8 Then they thought, "Let's destroy
everything!"
So they burned down all the places
where God was worshiped.

9 We no longer see your miraculous signs.
All the prophets are gone,
and no one can tell us when it will end.
10 How long, O God, will you allow our
enemies to insult you?
Will you let them dishonor your name
forever?
11 Why do you hold back your strong right
hand?
Unleash your powerful fist and destroy
them.

12 You, O God, are my king from ages past,
bringing salvation to the earth.
13 You split the sea by your strength
and smashed the heads of the sea
monsters.
14 You crushed the heads of Leviathan*
and let the desert animals eat him.

15 You caused the springs and streams to
gush forth,
and you dried up rivers that never run
dry.
16 Both day and night belong to you;
you made the starlight* and the sun.
17 You set the boundaries of the earth,
and you made both summer and winter.

18 See how these enemies insult you, LORD.
A foolish nation has dishonored your
name.
19 Don't let these wild beasts destroy your
turtledoves.
Don't forget your suffering people
forever.

20 Remember your covenant promises,
for the land is full of darkness and
violence!
21 Don't let the downtrodden be humiliated
again.
Instead, let the poor and needy praise
your name.

22 Arise, O God, and defend your cause.
Remember how these fools insult you
all day long.
23 Don't overlook what your enemies have
said
or their growing uproar.

PSALM 75

*For the choir director: A psalm of Asaph. A song to be
sung to the tune "Do Not Destroy!"*

1 We thank you, O God!
We give thanks because you are near.
People everywhere tell of your
wonderful deeds.

2 God says, "At the time I have planned,
I will bring justice against the wicked.
3 When the earth quakes and its people live
in turmoil,

74:2 Hebrew *Mount Zion.* 74:14 The identification of Leviathan is disputed, ranging from an earthly creature to a
mythical sea monster in ancient literature. 74:16 Or *moon;* Hebrew reads *light.*

74:12-23 God has proven himself over and over as a God who is able to deliver us. He has shown
his power by his control over our enemies, over ferocious animals, and over nature itself. We
therefore can call on him and be confident that he is able to overcome all the problems we face.
He will be faithful to his Word, watching over us even as we walk through the darkest valleys in
this life.
75:1-5 Once we turn our life and will over to God, we begin to see evidence of his care for us.
But pride is a powerful enemy. It keeps us from turning to God or others to get help and perpetu-
ates our tendency for denial. God shows the wrath of his judgment against the proud and boastful, who consider themselves self-sufficient. We were never created to stand alone and make our
own way in life. God created us to fit into his plan for the created universe. God's program for
righteous and healthy living has been given for our benefit and joy.

I am the one who keeps its foundations
firm.   *Interlude*

⁴ "I warned the proud, 'Stop your boasting!'
I told the wicked, 'Don't raise your fists!
⁵ Don't raise your fists in defiance at the
heavens
or speak with such arrogance.'"
⁶ For no one on earth—from east or west,
or even from the wilderness—
should raise a defiant fist.*
⁷ It is God alone who judges;
he decides who will rise and who will
fall.
⁸ For the LORD holds a cup in his hand
that is full of foaming wine mixed with
spices.
He pours out the wine in judgment,
and all the wicked must drink it,
draining it to the dregs.

⁹ But as for me, I will always proclaim what
God has done;
I will sing praises to the God of Jacob.
¹⁰ For God says, "I will break the strength of
the wicked,
but I will increase the power of the
godly."

PSALM 76

*For the choir director: A psalm of Asaph. A song to be
accompanied by stringed instruments.*

¹ God is honored in Judah;
his name is great in Israel.
² Jerusalem* is where he lives;
Mount Zion is his home.
³ There he has broken the fiery arrows of
the enemy,
the shields and swords and weapons
of war.   *Interlude*

⁴ You are glorious and more majestic
than the everlasting mountains.*
⁵ Our boldest enemies have been
plundered.
They lie before us in the sleep
of death.
No warrior could lift a hand against us.
⁶ At the blast of your breath, O God of
Jacob,
their horses and chariots lay still.

⁷ No wonder you are greatly feared!
Who can stand before you when your
anger explodes?
⁸ From heaven you sentenced your
enemies;
the earth trembled and stood silent
before you.
⁹ You stand up to judge those who do evil,
O God,
and to rescue the oppressed of the
earth.   *Interlude*
¹⁰ Human defiance only enhances your
glory,
for you use it as a weapon.*

¹¹ Make vows to the LORD your God, and
keep them.
Let everyone bring tribute to the
Awesome One.
¹² For he breaks the pride of princes,
and the kings of the earth fear him.

PSALM 77

For Jeduthun, the choir director: A psalm of Asaph.

¹ I cry out to God; yes, I shout.
Oh, that God would listen to me!
² When I was in deep trouble,
I searched for the Lord.

75:6 Hebrew *should lift.* 76:2 Hebrew *Salem,* another name for Jerusalem. 76:4 As in Greek version; Hebrew reads
than mountains filled with beasts of prey. 76:10 The meaning of the Hebrew is uncertain.

75:6-10 Our desire to be greater than others is another great enemy of our soul. The psalmist
understood that it was God who elevates one person and demotes another. We must leave issues
of promotion in God's hands. His promise to punish the wicked is given first to cause them to
turn away from their evil ways and also to assure those who suffer at the hands of wicked people
that God hasn't forgotten them.
76:11-12 As we think about the people we have harmed and make plans for reconciliation, we
need to follow through on our plans. We often make promises to act but then fail to do so. If we
expect to reconcile our relationships, we need to follow through on our promises. The same principle holds true with God. If we make a promise to him, refusing to follow through will only lead
to further pain and separation from him. God expects us to fulfill our vows. All relationships are
based on trust. Unless we learn to be trustworthy, our relationships will be shaky, and our efforts
in recovery are doomed to failure.
77:1-4 As he wrote these verses, the psalmist became so distressed that he couldn't even pray!
The same thing often happens to us. When we are discouraged, we need to be more persistent in
our prayers. God is the only one who can really help us. When our life is out of control, God is
able to help us slow down and put the pieces back together again.

All night long I prayed, with hands lifted
toward heaven,
but my soul was not comforted.
³ I think of God, and I moan,
overwhelmed with longing for
his help. *Interlude*

⁴ You don't let me sleep.
I am too distressed even to pray!
⁵ I think of the good old days,
long since ended,
⁶ when my nights were filled with joyful
songs.
I search my soul and ponder the
difference now.
⁷ Has the Lord rejected me forever?
Will he never again be kind to me?
⁸ Is his unfailing love gone forever?
Have his promises permanently failed?
⁹ Has God forgotten to be gracious?
Has he slammed the door on his
compassion? *Interlude*

¹⁰ And I said, "This is my fate;
the Most High has turned his hand
against me."
¹¹ But then I recall all you have done,
O LORD;
I remember your wonderful deeds of
long ago.
¹² They are constantly in my thoughts.
I cannot stop thinking about your
mighty works.

¹³ O God, your ways are holy.
Is there any god as mighty as you?
¹⁴ You are the God of great wonders!
You demonstrate your awesome power
among the nations.
¹⁵ By your strong arm, you redeemed your
people,
the descendants of Jacob and Joseph. *Interlude*

¹⁶ When the Red Sea* saw you, O God,
its waters looked and trembled!
The sea quaked to its very depths.
¹⁷ The clouds poured down rain;
the thunder rumbled in the sky.
Your arrows of lightning flashed.
¹⁸ Your thunder roared from the whirlwind;
the lightning lit up the world!

The earth trembled and shook.
¹⁹ Your road led through the sea,
your pathway through the mighty
waters—
a pathway no one knew was there!
²⁰ You led your people along that road like a
flock of sheep,
with Moses and Aaron as their
shepherds.

PSALM 78
A psalm* of Asaph.

¹ O my people, listen to my instructions.
Open your ears to what I am saying,
²   for I will speak to you in a parable.
I will teach you hidden lessons from our
past—
³   stories we have heard and known,
stories our ancestors handed down
to us.
⁴ We will not hide these truths from our
children;
we will tell the next generation
about the glorious deeds of the LORD,
about his power and his mighty
wonders.
⁵ For he issued his laws to Jacob;
he gave his instructions to Israel.
He commanded our ancestors
to teach them to their children,
⁶ so the next generation might know
them—
even the children not yet born—
and they in turn will teach their own
children.
⁷ So each generation should set its hope
anew on God,
not forgetting his glorious miracles
and obeying his commands.
⁸ Then they will not be like their
ancestors—
stubborn, rebellious, and unfaithful,
refusing to give their hearts to God.

⁹ The warriors of Ephraim, though armed
with bows,
turned their backs and fled on the day
of battle.
¹⁰ They did not keep God's covenant
and refused to live by his instructions.

77:16 Hebrew *the waters.* 78:TITLE Hebrew *maskil.* This may be a literary or musical term.

78:9-12 God's people, although well equipped to defeat their enemies in the Promised Land, failed to carry out God's commands. When they should have boldly pressed forward, they ran from the conflict like cowards. This failure was undoubtedly prompted by the fact that they forgot God's past acts of power on behalf of his people. When we fail to believe in God's power, because of either unbelief or pride, we are bound to fail.

¹¹ They forgot what he had done—
    the great wonders he had shown them,
¹² the miracles he did for their ancestors
    on the plain of Zoan in the land of
    Egypt.
¹³ For he divided the sea and led them
    through,
    making the water stand up like walls!
¹⁴ In the daytime he led them by a cloud,
    and all night by a pillar of fire.
¹⁵ He split open the rocks in the wilderness
    to give them water, as from a gushing
    spring.
¹⁶ He made streams pour from the rock,
    making the waters flow down like a
    river!

¹⁷ Yet they kept on sinning against him,
    rebelling against the Most High in the
    desert.
¹⁸ They stubbornly tested God in their
    hearts,
    demanding the foods they craved.
¹⁹ They even spoke against God himself,
    saying,
    "God can't give us food in the
    wilderness.
²⁰ Yes, he can strike a rock so water gushes
    out,
    but he can't give his people bread and
    meat."
²¹ When the LORD heard them, he was
    furious.
    The fire of his wrath burned against
    Jacob.
    Yes, his anger rose against Israel,
²² for they did not believe God
    or trust him to care for them.
²³ But he commanded the skies to open;
    he opened the doors of heaven.
²⁴ He rained down manna for them to eat;
    he gave them bread from heaven.
²⁵ They ate the food of angels!
    God gave them all they could hold.
²⁶ He released the east wind in the heavens

and guided the south wind by his
    mighty power.
²⁷ He rained down meat as thick as dust—
    birds as plentiful as the sand on the
    seashore!
²⁸ He caused the birds to fall within their
    camp
    and all around their tents.
²⁹ The people ate their fill.
    He gave them what they craved.
³⁰ But before they satisfied their craving,
    while the meat was yet in their mouths,
³¹ the anger of God rose against them,
    and he killed their strongest men.
    He struck down the finest of Israel's
    young men.

³² But in spite of this, the people kept
    sinning.
    Despite his wonders, they refused to
    trust him.
³³ So he ended their lives in failure,
    their years in terror.
³⁴ When God began killing them,
    they finally sought him.
    They repented and took God seriously.
³⁵ Then they remembered that God was
    their rock,
    that God Most High* was their
    redeemer.
³⁶ But all they gave him was lip service;
    they lied to him with their tongues.
³⁷ Their hearts were not loyal to him.
    They did not keep his covenant.
³⁸ Yet he was merciful and forgave their sins
    and did not destroy them all.
    Many times he held back his anger
    and did not unleash his fury!
³⁹ For he remembered that they were merely
    mortal,
    gone like a breath of wind that never
    returns.

⁴⁰ Oh, how often they rebelled against him
    in the wilderness

78:35 Hebrew *El-Elyon*.

78:17-33 God's anger against his rebellious people increased because they continually complained and refused to trust him to deliver them from their wilderness experience. We should pray that this won't happen to us. In spite of our unbelief, God is still merciful to us, giving us benefits we don't deserve (see Exodus 16:4-5; Numbers 11:31). The people had all they could ever want, but because they still rebelled against him, God sent a plague that terrified them and cut down many of them in the prime of their lives (see Numbers 11:32-33). Rebellion will cause our life to end in failure, too.

78:34-39 God knows that we are human, with all the imperfections and frailties of mortal beings. He is compassionate toward us, forgiving our sins and often turning away his judgment as he did to his people in the wilderness. His goodness should encourage us and make us more willing to commit our life to him.

and grieved his heart in that dry
  wasteland.
⁴¹ Again and again they tested God's
  patience
  and provoked the Holy One of Israel.
⁴² They did not remember his power
  and how he rescued them from their
    enemies.
⁴³ They did not remember his miraculous
    signs in Egypt,
  his wonders on the plain of Zoan.
⁴⁴ For he turned their rivers into blood,
  so no one could drink from the streams.
⁴⁵ He sent vast swarms of flies to consume
    them
  and hordes of frogs to ruin them.
⁴⁶ He gave their crops to caterpillars;
  their harvest was consumed by locusts.
⁴⁷ He destroyed their grapevines with hail
  and shattered their sycamore-figs with
    sleet.
⁴⁸ He abandoned their cattle to the hail,
  their livestock to bolts of lightning.
⁴⁹ He loosed on them his fierce anger—
  all his fury, rage, and hostility.
  He dispatched against them
  a band of destroying angels.
⁵⁰ He turned his anger against them;
  he did not spare the Egyptians' lives
  but ravaged them with the plague.
⁵¹ He killed the oldest son in each Egyptian
    family,
  the flower of youth throughout the
    land of Egypt.*
⁵² But he led his own people like a flock of
    sheep,
  guiding them safely through the
    wilderness.
⁵³ He kept them safe so they were not afraid;
  but the sea covered their enemies.
⁵⁴ He brought them to the border of his
    holy land,
  to this land of hills he had won for
    them.
⁵⁵ He drove out the nations before them;
  he gave them their inheritance by lot.
  He settled the tribes of Israel into their
    homes.
⁵⁶ But they kept testing and rebelling against
  God Most High.

78:51 Hebrew *in the tents of Ham.*

They did not obey his laws.
⁵⁷ They turned back and were as faithless as
    their parents.
  They were as undependable as a
    crooked bow.
⁵⁸ They angered God by building shrines to
    other gods;
  they made him jealous with their idols.
⁵⁹ When God heard them, he was very angry,
  and he completely rejected Israel.
⁶⁰ Then he abandoned his dwelling at
    Shiloh,
  the Tabernacle where he had lived
    among the people.
⁶¹ He allowed the Ark of his might to be
    captured;
  he surrendered his glory into enemy
    hands.
⁶² He gave his people over to be butchered
    by the sword,
  because he was so angry with his own
    people—his special possession.
⁶³ Their young men were killed by fire;
  their young women died before singing
    their wedding songs.
⁶⁴ Their priests were slaughtered,
  and their widows could not mourn
    their deaths.

⁶⁵ Then the Lord rose up as though waking
    from sleep,
  like a warrior aroused from a drunken
    stupor.
⁶⁶ He routed his enemies
  and sent them to eternal shame.
⁶⁷ But he rejected Joseph's descendants;
  he did not choose the tribe of Ephraim.
⁶⁸ He chose instead the tribe of Judah,
  and Mount Zion, which he loved.
⁶⁹ There he built his sanctuary as high as the
    heavens,
  as solid and enduring as the earth.
⁷⁰ He chose his servant David,
  calling him from the sheep pens.
⁷¹ He took David from tending the ewes and
    lambs
  and made him the shepherd of Jacob's
    descendants—
  God's own people, Israel.
⁷² He cared for them with a true heart
  and led them with skillful hands.

78:59-64 Sin has devastating consequences. God loves us, but our persistent disobedience sometimes causes him to turn away from us and allow our enemies to defeat us. If we are wise, we will
understand what has happened, admit our sins and failures, and commit our life again to God's
care and control.

PSALM 79
A psalm of Asaph.

¹O God, pagan nations have conquered
    your land,
    your special possession.
They have defiled your holy Temple
    and made Jerusalem a heap of ruins.
²They have left the bodies of your servants
    as food for the birds of heaven.
The flesh of your godly ones
    has become food for the wild animals.
³Blood has flowed like water all around
    Jerusalem;
    no one is left to bury the dead.
⁴We are mocked by our neighbors,
    an object of scorn and derision to those
    around us.

⁵O LORD, how long will you be angry with
    us? Forever?
    How long will your jealousy burn like
    fire?
⁶Pour out your wrath on the nations that
    refuse to acknowledge you—
    on kingdoms that do not call upon
    your name.
⁷For they have devoured your people
    Israel,*
    making the land a desolate wilderness.
⁸Do not hold us guilty for the sins of our
    ancestors!
    Let your compassion quickly meet our
    needs,
    for we are on the brink of despair.

⁹Help us, O God of our salvation!
    Help us for the glory of your name.
Save us and forgive our sins
    for the honor of your name.
¹⁰Why should pagan nations be allowed to
    scoff,
    asking, "Where is their God?"
Show us your vengeance against the
    nations,
    for they have spilled the blood of your
    servants.
¹¹Listen to the moaning of the prisoners.

Demonstrate your great power by
    saving those condemned to die.
¹²O Lord, pay back our neighbors seven
    times
    for the scorn they have hurled at you.
¹³Then we your people, the sheep of your
    pasture,
    will thank you forever and ever,
    praising your greatness from generation
    to generation.

PSALM 80
*For the choir director: A psalm of Asaph, to be sung to
the tune "Lilies of the Covenant."*

¹Please listen, O Shepherd of Israel,
    you who lead Joseph's descendants like
    a flock.
O God, enthroned above the cherubim,
    display your radiant glory
²   to Ephraim, Benjamin, and Manasseh.
Show us your mighty power.
    Come to rescue us!

³Turn us again to yourself, O God.
    Make your face shine down upon us.
    Only then will we be saved.
⁴O LORD God of Heaven's Armies,
    how long will you be angry with our
    prayers?
⁵You have fed us with sorrow
    and made us drink tears by the
    bucketful.
⁶You have made us the scorn* of
    neighboring nations.
    Our enemies treat us as a joke.

⁷Turn us again to yourself, O God of
    Heaven's Armies.
    Make your face shine down upon us.
    Only then will we be saved.
⁸You brought us from Egypt like a
    grapevine;
    you drove away the pagan nations and
    transplanted us into your land.
⁹You cleared the ground for us,
    and we took root and filled the land.
¹⁰Our shade covered the mountains;

79:7 Hebrew *devoured Jacob.* See note on 44:4. 80:6 As in Syriac version; Hebrew reads *the strife.*

79:5-13 As we face hard times, we need to be open to the possibility that God may be allowing
our difficulties so we will turn from sin. If that is true, we need to plead for God's mercy and
forgiveness so we can be restored to wholeness. God delivers us from the controlling influences of
our life not merely to give us freedom but also to bring him honor and to have others recognize
his greatness. It is our responsibility to spread the good news of God's deliverance.
80:9-13 God does marvelous works for us. He frees us from bondage, removes barriers from our
life, and firmly establishes us, doing all he can to help us grow and prosper spiritually. When we
begin to act as if we don't need God, he may cut us back down to size and allow our

our branches covered the mighty
cedars.
¹¹ We spread our branches west to the
Mediterranean Sea;
our shoots spread east to the Euphrates
River.*
¹² But now, why have you broken down our
walls
so that all who pass by may steal our
fruit?
¹³ The wild boar from the forest devours it,
and the wild animals feed on it.

¹⁴ Come back, we beg you, O God of
Heaven's Armies.
Look down from heaven and see our
plight.
Take care of this grapevine
¹⁵ that you yourself have planted,
this son you have raised for yourself.
¹⁶ For we are chopped up and burned by our
enemies.
May they perish at the sight of your
frown.
¹⁷ Strengthen the man you love,
the son of your choice.
¹⁸ Then we will never abandon you again.
Revive us so we can call on your name
once more.

¹⁹ Turn us again to yourself, O LORD God of
Heaven's Armies.
Make your face shine down upon us.
Only then will we be saved.

PSALM 81

*For the choir director: A psalm of Asaph, to be
accompanied by a stringed instrument.**

¹ Sing praises to God, our strength.
Sing to the God of Jacob.
² Sing! Beat the tambourine.
Play the sweet lyre and the harp.

³ Blow the ram's horn at new moon,
and again at full moon to call a festival!
⁴ For this is required by the decrees
of Israel;
it is a regulation of the God of Jacob.
⁵ He made it a law for Israel*
when he attacked Egypt to set us free.

I heard an unknown voice say,
⁶ "Now I will take the load from your
shoulders;
I will free your hands from their heavy
tasks.
⁷ You cried to me in trouble, and I saved
you;
I answered out of the thundercloud
and tested your faith when there
was no water at Meribah.   *Interlude*

⁸ "Listen to me, O my people, while I give
you stern warnings.
O Israel, if you would only listen to me!
⁹ You must never have a foreign god;
you must not bow down before a false
god.
¹⁰ For it was I, the LORD your God,
who rescued you from the land of
Egypt.
Open your mouth wide, and I will fill it
with good things.

¹¹ "But no, my people wouldn't listen.
Israel did not want me around.
¹² So I let them follow their own stubborn
desires,
living according to their own ideas.
¹³ Oh, that my people would listen to me!
Oh, that Israel would follow me,
walking in my paths!
¹⁴ How quickly I would then subdue their
enemies!
How soon my hands would be upon
their foes!

80:11 Hebrew *west to the sea, . . . east to the river.* 81:TITLE Hebrew *according to the gittith.* 81:5 Hebrew *for Joseph.*

---

enemies—internal or external—to take advantage of us. Recovery is a lifelong process. Our
relationship with God should also last a lifetime. We need to realize that without God's help, we are
in danger of falling, even when we seem to be doing well. Our progress in recovery and our
relationship with God need our constant attention.
80:14-19 When we are beaten down, we must plead for God's mercy and his restorative work in
our life. Even though we feel overwhelmed by our suffering, we should remember that God can
end all that caused us so much pain. As he strengthens and restores us to wholeness, he wants us
to share the good news about deliverance with others. As we share the message of God's deliverance, others will begin to hope in God's power, and we will be strengthened as well by the hope
we bring to others.
81:6-10 With great power, God takes the burdens away from his people and delivers them when
they cry out to him. God warns us over and over not to allow any person or thing to take his
place in our life. Trusting any resource or power other than God is foolishness. He is far more
powerful than any other possible means of deliverance. Only he can satisfy our deepest needs; all
we need to do is look to him for help.

[15] Those who hate the LORD would cringe
before him;
they would be doomed forever.
[16] But I would feed you with the finest
wheat.
I would satisfy you with wild honey
from the rock."

PSALM 82
A psalm of Asaph.

[1] God presides over heaven's court;
he pronounces judgment on the
heavenly beings:
[2] "How long will you hand down unjust
decisions
by favoring the wicked?   *Interlude*

[3] "Give justice to the poor and the orphan;
uphold the rights of the oppressed and
the destitute.
[4] Rescue the poor and helpless;
deliver them from the grasp of evil
people.
[5] But these oppressors know nothing;
they are so ignorant!
They wander about in darkness,
while the whole world is shaken to the
core.
[6] I say, 'You are gods;
you are all children of the Most High.
[7] But you will die like mere mortals
and fall like every other ruler.'"

[8] Rise up, O God, and judge the earth,
for all the nations belong to you.

PSALM 83
A song. A psalm of Asaph.

[1] O God, do not be silent!
Do not be deaf.
Do not be quiet, O God.
[2] Don't you hear the uproar of your
enemies?

Don't you see that your arrogant
enemies are rising up?
[3] They devise crafty schemes against your
people;
they conspire against your precious
ones.
[4] "Come," they say, "let us wipe out Israel
as a nation.
We will destroy the very memory of its
existence."
[5] Yes, this was their unanimous decision.
They signed a treaty as allies against
you—
[6] these Edomites and Ishmaelites;
Moabites and Hagrites;
[7] Gebalites, Ammonites, and Amalekites;
and people from Philistia and Tyre.
[8] Assyria has joined them, too,
and is allied with the descendants
of Lot.   *Interlude*

[9] Do to them as you did to the Midianites
and as you did to Sisera and Jabin at the
Kishon River.
[10] They were destroyed at Endor,
and their decaying corpses fertilized the
soil.
[11] Let their mighty nobles die as Oreb and
Zeeb did.
Let all their princes die like Zebah and
Zalmunna,
[12] for they said, "Let us seize for our own use
these pasturelands of God!"
[13] O my God, scatter them like tumbleweed,
like chaff before the wind!
[14] As a fire burns a forest
and as a flame sets mountains ablaze,
[15] chase them with your fierce storm;
terrify them with your tempest.
[16] Utterly disgrace them
until they submit to your name,
O LORD.
[17] Let them be ashamed and terrified forever.
Let them die in disgrace.

82:1-4 God executes judgment among his people and holds accountable particularly those who
deal unfairly with the helpless and the destitute. Many will have to answer for things they have
done that caused others to stumble and become addicted to a harmful, controlling influence. If
we have led others astray, part of making amends may be to help them face their problems and
to share the good news of God's deliverance with them.
83:1-8 Encountering problems in our life should motivate us to call out to God for help. All the
forces of evil seem to conspire against us as we face temptation. God doesn't want us to fail; he is
there to help us. But we need to become aware of the things that weaken and defeat us. By
avoiding them, we will find temptation easier to deal with. God's program for healthy living is
designed for this very thing—to lead us away from temptation.
83:13-18 Nothing can stand against God. He created everything that exists, and he alone is
sovereign over all the world. When we are trying to live for him, our enemies are his enemies, and
we can count on him to deal with them on our behalf.

¹⁸ Then they will learn that you alone are
      called the Lord,
   that you alone are the Most High,
   supreme over all the earth.

PSALM 84

*For the choir director: A psalm of the descendants of
Korah, to be accompanied by a stringed instrument.* *

¹ How lovely is your dwelling place,
   O Lord of Heaven's Armies.
² I long, yes, I faint with longing
   to enter the courts of the Lord.
   With my whole being, body and soul,
   I will shout joyfully to the living God.
³ Even the sparrow finds a home,
   and the swallow builds her nest and
      raises her young
   at a place near your altar,
   O Lord of Heaven's Armies, my King
      and my God!
⁴ What joy for those who can live in your
      house,
   always singing your praises.   *Interlude*

⁵ What joy for those whose strength comes
      from the Lord,
   who have set their minds on a
      pilgrimage to Jerusalem.
⁶ When they walk through the Valley of
      Weeping,*
   it will become a place of refreshing
      springs.
   The autumn rains will clothe it with
      blessings.
⁷ They will continue to grow stronger,
   and each of them will appear before
      God in Jerusalem.*

⁸ O Lord God of Heaven's Armies, hear my
      prayer.
   Listen, O God of Jacob.   *Interlude*

⁹ O God, look with favor upon the king,
      our shield!
   Show favor to the one you have
      anointed.

¹⁰ A single day in your courts
   is better than a thousand anywhere
      else!
   I would rather be a gatekeeper in the
      house of my God
   than live the good life in the homes of
      the wicked.
¹¹ For the Lord God is our sun and our
      shield.
   He gives us grace and glory.
   The Lord will withhold no good thing
      from those who do what is right.
¹² O Lord of Heaven's Armies,
   what joy for those who trust in you.

PSALM 85

*For the choir director: A psalm of the descendants of
Korah.*

¹ Lord, you poured out blessings on your
      land!
   You restored the fortunes of Israel.*
² You forgave the guilt of your people—
   yes, you covered all their sins.
                                  Interlude
³ You held back your fury.
   You kept back your blazing anger.

⁴ Now restore us again, O God of our
      salvation.
   Put aside your anger against us once
      more.
⁵ Will you be angry with us always?
   Will you prolong your wrath to all
      generations?
⁶ Won't you revive us again,
   so your people can rejoice in you?

84:title Hebrew *according to the gittith.* 84:6 Or *Valley of Poplars;* Hebrew reads *valley of Baca.* 84:7 Hebrew *Zion.*
85:1 Hebrew *of Jacob.* See note on 44:4.

84:1-4 Beauty is found wherever the all-powerful God resides. Although God rules with great
power, he also cares for the seemingly insignificant things of the world—even sparrows and swallows. True blessing and joy come to us when we choose to live in his presence. As we entrust our
life to God and do our best to follow his will for us, we will discover the blessings of living in the
presence of our righteous and loving God.
84:8-12 A single day in the presence of God is far better than a thousand lifetimes apart from
him. The security, peace, and love that God offers are greater than anything we could receive
from people. When we find that the initial pleasures of our addiction have faded and the promises
of our dependency haven't come true, we can turn to God, and he will fill our soul with true
happiness.
85:1-3 It is hard enough to deal with the sins that have us entrapped; how much worse we make
it by having to live with a bad conscience. Great relief comes when God helps us regain control
and we realize that he has forgiven our sins. All we need to do is confess our sins to God and
accept the forgiveness he offers.

[7] Show us your unfailing love, O LORD,
  and grant us your salvation.

[8] I listen carefully to what God the LORD is
    saying,
  for he speaks peace to his faithful
    people.
  But let them not return to their foolish
    ways.
[9] Surely his salvation is near to those who
    fear him,
  so our land will be filled with his glory.

[10] Unfailing love and truth have met
    together.
  Righteousness and peace have kissed!
[11] Truth springs up from the earth,
  and righteousness smiles down from
    heaven.
[12] Yes, the LORD pours down his blessings.
  Our land will yield its bountiful harvest.
[13] Righteousness goes as a herald before him,
  preparing the way for his steps.

PSALM 86
A prayer of David.

[1] Bend down, O LORD, and hear my prayer;
  answer me, for I need your help.
[2] Protect me, for I am devoted to you.
  Save me, for I serve you and trust you.
  You are my God.
[3] Be merciful to me, O Lord,
  for I am calling on you constantly.
[4] Give me happiness, O Lord,
  for I give myself to you.
[5] O Lord, you are so good, so ready to
    forgive,
  so full of unfailing love for all who ask
    for your help.
[6] Listen closely to my prayer, O LORD;
  hear my urgent cry.
[7] I will call to you whenever I'm in trouble,
  and you will answer me.

[8] No pagan god is like you, O Lord.
  None can do what you do!
[9] All the nations you made
  will come and bow before you, Lord;
  they will praise your holy name.
[10] For you are great and perform wonderful
    deeds.
  You alone are God.

[11] Teach me your ways, O LORD,
  that I may live according to your truth!
  Grant me purity of heart,
  so that I may honor you.
[12] With all my heart I will praise you, O Lord
    my God.
  I will give glory to your name forever,
[13] for your love for me is very great.
  You have rescued me from the depths
    of death.*

[14] O God, insolent people rise up against me;
  a violent gang is trying to kill me.
  You mean nothing to them.
[15] But you, O Lord,
  are a God of compassion and mercy,
  slow to get angry
  and filled with unfailing love and
    faithfulness.
[16] Look down and have mercy on me.
  Give your strength to your servant;
  save me, the son of your servant.
[17] Send me a sign of your favor.
  Then those who hate me will be put to
    shame,
  for you, O LORD, help and comfort me.

PSALM 87
A song. A psalm of the descendants of Korah.

[1] On the holy mountain
  stands the city founded by the LORD.
[2] He loves the city of Jerusalem
  more than any other city
    in Israel.*

86:13 Hebrew *of Sheol.* 87:2 Hebrew *He loves the gates of Zion more than all the dwellings of Jacob.* See note on 44:4.

86:1-5 Even though we may be trying to serve and trust God, we still may be bound by addictions and problems from which we need deliverance. Sometimes the answers don't come quickly, and though we pray constantly, nothing seems to happen. We may become impatient and begin to wonder if God will ever act. God will ultimately respond with forgiveness and compassion to all who call upon him. Sometimes, though, we may have to wait awhile before we experience changes in our life.
86:11-17 We only know God's will as we seek to know him through prayer and the study of his Word. The more we know about God, the more we know what he expects of us. As we get to know God better, we will discover that he gives us not only direction but also the strength and encouragement we need to walk the pathway he has chosen for us.
87:1-7 Because of God's kindness, we all can be citizens of Jerusalem, the city for which God had special love and concern. In the Old Testament, Jerusalem was known as God's dwelling place on earth and the seat of his rule. Since the coming of Jesus Christ, God comes to dwell in our heart.

³O city of God,
what glorious things are said of you!
Interlude

⁴I will count Egypt* and Babylon among
those who know me—
also Philistia and Tyre, and even distant
Ethiopia.*
They have all become citizens of
Jerusalem!
⁵Regarding Jerusalem* it will be said,
"Everyone enjoys the rights of
citizenship there."
And the Most High will personally bless
this city.
⁶When the LORD registers the nations, he
will say,
"They have all become citizens of
Jerusalem." *Interlude*

⁷The people will play flutes* and sing,
"The source of my life springs from
Jerusalem!"

PSALM 88

For the choir director: A psalm of the descendants of Korah. A song to be sung to the tune "The Suffering of Affliction." A psalm* of Heman the Ezrahite.

¹O LORD, God of my salvation,
I cry out to you by day.
I come to you at night.
²Now hear my prayer;
listen to my cry.
³For my life is full of troubles,
and death* draws near.
⁴I am as good as dead,
like a strong man with no strength
left.
⁵They have left me among the dead,
and I lie like a corpse in a grave.
I am forgotten,
cut off from your care.

⁶You have thrown me into the lowest pit,
into the darkest depths.
⁷Your anger weighs me down;
with wave after wave you have
engulfed me. *Interlude*

⁸You have driven my friends away
by making me repulsive to them.
I am in a trap with no way of escape.
⁹ My eyes are blinded by my tears.
Each day I beg for your help, O LORD;
I lift my hands to you for mercy.
¹⁰Are your wonderful deeds of any use to
the dead?
Do the dead rise up and praise you?
Interlude

¹¹Can those in the grave declare your
unfailing love?
Can they proclaim your faithfulness in
the place of destruction?*
¹²Can the darkness speak of your wonderful
deeds?
Can anyone in the land of forgetfulness
talk about your righteousness?
¹³O LORD, I cry out to you.
I will keep on pleading day by day.
¹⁴O LORD, why do you reject me?
Why do you turn your face from me?

¹⁵I have been sick and close to death since
my youth.
I stand helpless and desperate before
your terrors.
¹⁶Your fierce anger has overwhelmed me.
Your terrors have paralyzed me.
¹⁷They swirl around me like floodwaters all
day long.
They have engulfed me completely.
¹⁸You have taken away my companions and
loved ones.
Darkness is my closest friend.

87:4a Hebrew *Rahab*, the name of a mythical sea monster that represents chaos in ancient literature. The name is used here as a poetic name for Egypt. **87:4b** Hebrew *Cush*. **87:5** Hebrew *Zion*. **87:7** Or *will dance*. **88:TITLE** Hebrew *maskil*. This may be a literary or musical term. **88:3** Hebrew *Sheol*. **88:11** Hebrew *in Abaddon?*

He loves us and longs to direct our decisions and actions through his Holy Spirit. It is a privilege to be called God's beloved and to be considered citizens of his Kingdom. It means he cares for us and wants us to enjoy living in his presence.

88:1-5 All of us who have struggled with an addiction know what it means to feel hopeless and overwhelmed by troubles. It is comforting to know that God listens to our cries. We are privileged to have the Bible, which tells us about God and his power to help us when we call out to him. No situation is hopeless for those who call out to God. When we feel helpless and abandoned, we need to look to God and hope in his deliverance.

88:6-12 In these verses, the psalmist felt that God's anger was heavily upon him. It is important to remember that God allows us to stumble and fall, giving us opportunities to learn personally about the consequences of sin. But we should also remember that God does not cause us to fall. Natural consequences should be expected when we sin. If we are suffering because of our sins and failures, we should use the opportunity to learn from the past and turn to God.

PSALM 89

A psalm* of Ethan the Ezrahite.

¹ I will sing of the LORD's unfailing love forever!
    Young and old will hear of your faithfulness.
² Your unfailing love will last forever.
    Your faithfulness is as enduring as the heavens.

³ The LORD said, "I have made a covenant with David, my chosen servant.
    I have sworn this oath to him:
⁴ 'I will establish your descendants as kings forever;
    they will sit on your throne from now until eternity.'"   *Interlude*
⁵ All heaven will praise your great wonders, LORD;
    myriads of angels will praise you for your faithfulness.
⁶ For who in all of heaven can compare with the LORD?
    What mightiest angel is anything like the LORD?
⁷ The highest angelic powers stand in awe of God.
    He is far more awesome than all who surround his throne.
⁸ O LORD God of Heaven's Armies!
    Where is there anyone as mighty as you, O LORD?
    You are entirely faithful.

⁹ You rule the oceans.
    You subdue their storm-tossed waves.
¹⁰ You crushed the great sea monster.*
    You scattered your enemies with your mighty arm.
¹¹ The heavens are yours, and the earth is yours;
    everything in the world is yours—you created it all.
¹² You created north and south.
    Mount Tabor and Mount Hermon praise your name.
¹³ Powerful is your arm!
    Strong is your hand!
    Your right hand is lifted high in glorious strength.

¹⁴ Righteousness and justice are the foundation of your throne.
    Unfailing love and truth walk before you as attendants.
¹⁵ Happy are those who hear the joyful call to worship,
    for they will walk in the light of your presence, LORD.
¹⁶ They rejoice all day long in your wonderful reputation.
    They exult in your righteousness.
¹⁷ You are their glorious strength.
    It pleases you to make us strong.
¹⁸ Yes, our protection comes from the LORD,
    and he, the Holy One of Israel, has given us our king.

¹⁹ Long ago you spoke in a vision to your faithful people.
    You said, "I have raised up a warrior.
    I have selected him from the common people to be king.
²⁰ I have found my servant David.
    I have anointed him with my holy oil.
²¹ I will steady him with my hand;
    with my powerful arm I will make him strong.
²² His enemies will not defeat him,
    nor will the wicked overpower him.
²³ I will beat down his adversaries before him
    and destroy those who hate him.
²⁴ My faithfulness and unfailing love will be with him,
    and by my authority he will grow in power.
²⁵ I will extend his rule over the sea,
    his dominion over the rivers.
²⁶ And he will call out to me, 'You are my Father,
    my God, and the Rock of my salvation.'
²⁷ I will make him my firstborn son,
    the mightiest king on earth.
²⁸ I will love him and be kind to him forever;
    my covenant with him will never end.
²⁹ I will preserve an heir for him;
    his throne will be as endless as the days of heaven.

89:title Hebrew *maskil*. This may be a literary or musical term. **89:10** Hebrew *Rahab*, the name of a mythical sea monster that represents chaos in ancient literature.

89:11-18 God created and sustains everything that exists. He is extremely powerful, and he displays righteousness, truth, justice, and unfailing love. When we are powerless, it only makes sense to turn to God. He has the power we need to overcome our dependencies. As we remain close to him and do his will, we will experience deliverance and discover true freedom.

³⁰ But if his descendants forsake my
  instructions
  and fail to obey my regulations,
³¹ if they do not obey my decrees
  and fail to keep my commands,
³² then I will punish their sin with the rod,
  and their disobedience with beating.
³³ But I will never stop loving him
  nor fail to keep my promise to him.
³⁴ No, I will not break my covenant;
  I will not take back a single word I said.
³⁵ I have sworn an oath to David,
  and in my holiness I cannot lie:
³⁶ His dynasty will go on forever;
  his kingdom will endure as the sun.
³⁷ It will be as eternal as the moon,
  my faithful witness in the sky!"

Interlude

³⁸ But now you have rejected him and cast
  him off.
  You are angry with your anointed king.
³⁹ You have renounced your covenant with
  him;
  you have thrown his crown in the dust.
⁴⁰ You have broken down the walls
  protecting him
  and ruined every fort defending him.
⁴¹ Everyone who comes along has robbed
  him,
  and he has become a joke to his
  neighbors.
⁴² You have strengthened his enemies
  and made them all rejoice.
⁴³ You have made his sword useless
  and refused to help him in battle.
⁴⁴ You have ended his splendor
  and overturned his throne.
⁴⁵ You have made him old before his time
  and publicly disgraced him. *Interlude*

⁴⁶ O LORD, how long will this go on?
  Will you hide yourself forever?
  How long will your anger burn like fire?
⁴⁷ Remember how short my life is,
  how empty and futile this human
  existence!
⁴⁸ No one can live forever; all will die.

89:48 Hebrew *of Sheol.*

No one can escape the power of the
  grave.* *Interlude*

⁴⁹ Lord, where is your unfailing love?
  You promised it to David with a faithful
  pledge.
⁵⁰ Consider, Lord, how your servants are
  disgraced!
  I carry in my heart the insults of so
  many people.
⁵¹ Your enemies have mocked me, O LORD;
  they mock your anointed king
  wherever he goes.

⁵² Praise the LORD forever!
  Amen and amen!

BOOK FOUR (Psalms 90–106)

PSALM 90
A prayer of Moses, the man of God.

¹ Lord, through all the generations
  you have been our home!
² Before the mountains were born,
  before you gave birth to the earth and
  the world,
  from beginning to end, you are God.

³ You turn people back to dust, saying,
  "Return to dust, you mortals!"
⁴ For you, a thousand years are as a passing
  day,
  as brief as a few night hours.
⁵ You sweep people away like dreams that
  disappear.
  They are like grass that springs up in
  the morning.
⁶ In the morning it blooms and flourishes,
  but by evening it is dry and withered.
⁷ We wither beneath your anger;
  we are overwhelmed by your fury.
⁸ You spread out our sins before you—
  our secret sins—and you see them all.
⁹ We live our lives beneath your wrath,
  ending our years with a groan.

¹⁰ Seventy years are given to us!
  Some even live to eighty.

89:38-45 Although God at times may seem to abandon his people and act toward them in anger,
he is just doing what he promised to do. He said he would bless us if we obey and punish us if we
disobey. We sometimes find it hard to understand why God lets some people be seemingly in
perfect control of their life, while we are hopelessly out of control. Deep down, we know the
answer: Unless God is in control of a person's life, nothing of ultimate good will ever come of it.
90:10-12 Remembering that life is short and often filled with sorrow, we should ask God how he
wants us to spend our days and concentrate on making our life count for something. We have
wasted enough time creating our own problems. We should focus now on growing in wisdom
and making positive changes in our life so we can accomplish things for God.

But even the best years are filled with pain
and trouble;
soon they disappear, and we fly away.
[11] Who can comprehend the power of your
anger?
Your wrath is as awesome as the fear
you deserve.
[12] Teach us to realize the brevity of life,
so that we may grow in wisdom.

[13] O LORD, come back to us!
How long will you delay?
Take pity on your servants!
[14] Satisfy us each morning with your
unfailing love,
so we may sing for joy to the end
of our lives.
[15] Give us gladness in proportion to our
former misery!
Replace the evil years with good.
[16] Let us, your servants, see you work again;
let our children see your glory.
[17] And may the Lord our God show us his
approval
and make our efforts successful.
Yes, make our efforts successful!

PSALM 91
[1] Those who live in the shelter of the Most
High
will find rest in the shadow of the
Almighty.
[2] This I declare about the LORD:
He alone is my refuge, my place of safety;
he is my God, and I trust him.
[3] For he will rescue you from every trap
and protect you from deadly disease.
[4] He will cover you with his feathers.
He will shelter you with his wings.
His faithful promises are your armor
and protection.

[5] Do not be afraid of the terrors of the
night,
nor the arrow that flies in the day.
[6] Do not dread the disease that stalks in
darkness,
nor the disaster that strikes at midday.
[7] Though a thousand fall at your side,
though ten thousand are dying around
you,
these evils will not touch you.
[8] Just open your eyes,
and see how the wicked are punished.

[9] If you make the LORD your refuge,
if you make the Most High your shelter,
[10] no evil will conquer you;
no plague will come near your home.
[11] For he will order his angels
to protect you wherever you go.
[12] They will hold you up with their hands
so you won't even hurt your foot on a
stone.
[13] You will trample upon lions and cobras;
you will crush fierce lions and serpents
under your feet!

[14] The LORD says, "I will rescue those who
love me.
I will protect those who trust in my
name.
[15] When they call on me, I will answer;
I will be with them in trouble.
I will rescue and honor them.
[16] I will reward them with a long life
and give them my salvation."

PSALM 92
A psalm. A song to be sung on the Sabbath Day.

[1] It is good to give thanks to the LORD,
to sing praises to the Most High.

90:13-17 Our restoration to wholeness and health depends on our cooperation with God. Only
he can give us the power to be what we ought to be. But God won't force changes on us; we
must want to change. We must begin through prayer and Bible study. We can ask God to make
us willing to change and to give us the strength to follow through with action.
91:1-4 When we discover that we are powerless to fight our addiction alone, we become weak
like little children. We feel helpless to protect ourself, caught in a whirlwind of our own making.
We turn to God our rescuer because there is nowhere else to go. How comforting to know that
when we cry out, God will rescue us and protect us as a mother bird protects her young. Our
powerful defender will never fail us if we turn to him for shelter and safety.
91:10-16 We will escape danger because God protects us as his chosen ones. Sometimes his
protection comes through angels, who are given the responsibility of caring for us and keeping us
safe. Sometimes God may use other, more natural, means. As we cry out to him for help, he will be
with us in our troubles and rescue us. Ultimately, he will bring us into his eternal presence forever.
92:1-4 It is a necessary part of recovery to praise God for all he has done for us, to proclaim his
unfailing love and his faithfulness to us. He brings us abiding joy. As we experience his faithfulness
in our life, praise and thanks should be our natural responses. Our praise will serve as a declaration
to others of God's power to deliver us from the bondage of addiction.

² It is good to proclaim your unfailing love
in the morning,
your faithfulness in the evening,
³ accompanied by a ten-stringed
instrument, a harp,
and the melody of a lyre.

⁴ You thrill me, LORD, with all you have
done for me!
I sing for joy because of what you have
done.
⁵ O LORD, what great works you do!
And how deep are your thoughts.
⁶ Only a simpleton would not know,
and only a fool would not understand
this:
⁷ Though the wicked sprout like weeds
and evildoers flourish,
they will be destroyed forever.

⁸ But you, O LORD, will be exalted forever.
⁹ Your enemies, LORD, will surely perish;
all evildoers will be scattered.
¹⁰ But you have made me as strong as
a wild ox.
You have anointed me with the finest
oil.
¹¹ My eyes have seen the downfall of my
enemies;
my ears have heard the defeat of my
wicked opponents.
¹² But the godly will flourish like palm trees
and grow strong like the cedars of
Lebanon.
¹³ For they are transplanted to the LORD's
own house.
They flourish in the courts of our God.
¹⁴ Even in old age they will still produce fruit;
they will remain vital and green.
¹⁵ They will declare, "The LORD is just!
He is my rock!
There is no evil in him!"

PSALM 93

¹ The LORD is king! He is robed in majesty.
Indeed, the LORD is robed in majesty
and armed with strength.
The world stands firm
and cannot be shaken.

94:7 Hebrew *of Jacob*. See note on 44:4.

² Your throne, O LORD, has stood from time
immemorial.
You yourself are from the everlasting
past.
³ The floods have risen up, O LORD.
The floods have roared like thunder;
the floods have lifted their pounding
waves.
⁴ But mightier than the violent raging of
the seas,
mightier than the breakers on the
shore—
the LORD above is mightier than these!
⁵ Your royal laws cannot be changed.
Your reign, O LORD, is holy forever and
ever.

PSALM 94

¹ O LORD, the God of vengeance,
O God of vengeance, let your glorious
justice shine forth!
² Arise, O Judge of the earth.
Give the proud what they deserve.
³ How long, O LORD?
How long will the wicked be allowed to
gloat?
⁴ How long will they speak with
arrogance?
How long will these evil people boast?
⁵ They crush your people, LORD,
hurting those you claim as your own.
⁶ They kill widows and foreigners
and murder orphans.
⁷ "The LORD isn't looking," they say,
"and besides, the God of Israel* doesn't
care."

⁸ Think again, you fools!
When will you finally catch on?
⁹ Is he deaf—the one who made your ears?
Is he blind—the one who formed your
eyes?
¹⁰ He punishes the nations—won't he also
punish you?
He knows everything—doesn't he also
know what you are doing?
¹¹ The LORD knows people's thoughts;
he knows they are worthless!

93:1-5 The Lord is more powerful than the mighty oceans. Surely such a God is able to help us
exercise control over our universe—our life. He always keeps his promises. Since he has said he
will help us if we turn to him, we can count on it.
94:8-10 The voice of the tempter says, "No one will know or care if we have just one more
moment of pleasure." Here we are reminded that God is neither deaf nor blind. Neither are the
people who know us well. "Just one more" always translates into a disastrous downfall. Remembering that God knows what we are doing and that he cares about us should encourage us to
stand against the temptations we face.

¹²Joyful are those you discipline, LORD,
  those you teach with your instructions.
¹³You give them relief from troubled times
  until a pit is dug to capture the wicked.
¹⁴The LORD will not reject his people;
  he will not abandon his special
  possession.
¹⁵Judgment will again be founded on
  justice,
  and those with virtuous hearts will
  pursue it.

¹⁶Who will protect me from the wicked?
  Who will stand up for me against
  evildoers?
¹⁷Unless the LORD had helped me,
  I would soon have settled in the silence
  of the grave.
¹⁸I cried out, "I am slipping!"
  but your unfailing love, O LORD,
  supported me.
¹⁹When doubts filled my mind,
  your comfort gave me renewed hope
  and cheer.

²⁰Can unjust leaders claim that God is on
  their side—
  leaders whose decrees permit injustice?
²¹They gang up against the righteous
  and condemn the innocent to death.
²²But the LORD is my fortress;
  my God is the mighty rock where
  I hide.
²³God will turn the sins of evil people back
  on them.
  He will destroy them for their sins.
  The LORD our God will destroy them.

PSALM 95
¹Come, let us sing to the LORD!
  Let us shout joyfully to the Rock of our
  salvation.
²Let us come to him with thanksgiving.
  Let us sing psalms of praise to him.

³For the LORD is a great God,
  a great King above all gods.
⁴He holds in his hands the depths of the
  earth
  and the mightiest mountains.
⁵The sea belongs to him, for he made it.
  His hands formed the dry land, too.

⁶Come, let us worship and bow down.
  Let us kneel before the LORD our maker,
⁷ for he is our God.
We are the people he watches over,
  the flock under his care.

If only you would listen to his voice
  today!
⁸The LORD says, "Don't harden your hearts
  as Israel did at Meribah,
  as they did at Massah in the wilderness.
⁹For there your ancestors tested and tried
  my patience,
  even though they saw everything I did.
¹⁰For forty years I was angry with them, and
  I said,
  'They are a people whose hearts turn away
  from me.
  They refuse to do what I tell them.'
¹¹So in my anger I took an oath:
  'They will never enter my place of
  rest.'"

PSALM 96
¹Sing a new song to the LORD!
  Let the whole earth sing to the LORD!
²Sing to the LORD; praise his name.
  Each day proclaim the good news that
  he saves.
³Publish his glorious deeds among the
  nations.
  Tell everyone about the amazing things
  he does.
⁴Great is the LORD! He is most worthy of
  praise!
  He is to be feared above all gods.

94:16-23 In the final analysis, we can count on no one but God to stand up for us against our enemies. He is our fortress and mighty rock. When we stumble into temptation, he is there to keep us from falling. Because he is our defender, he does not allow sin to destroy us beyond hope. Knowing that God is so intimately involved in our life should encourage us to live for him.
95:1-7 We all know how frightening it is to lose control of our life. For this very reason, we may hesitate to entrust ourself to God. Can he be trusted? God wants us to remember that when we surrender our life to him, he regards us with the same concern that a kind shepherd feels for his sheep. If a watchful shepherd is around, the sheep have little to fear.
96:1-9 The way we live demonstrates what we believe about God. If we stay in our prison of sin, we show that we are either unaware of God's power to save us or indifferent about him and the help he offers. If we seek his help to escape the bondage of sin and share the joyful news of recovery with others, we show our gratitude to God and reveal the beauty of a changed life. The world is filled with "remedies" for our problems. Many of them are helpful, but none can offer us the power we need for real change. Only God is mighty enough to offer that kind of help.

⁵The gods of other nations are mere idols,
 but the LORD made the heavens!
⁶Honor and majesty surround him;
 strength and beauty fill his sanctuary.

⁷O nations of the world, recognize the
 LORD;
 recognize that the LORD is glorious and
 strong.
⁸Give to the LORD the glory he deserves!
 Bring your offering and come into his
 courts.
⁹Worship the LORD in all his holy
 splendor.
 Let all the earth tremble before him.
¹⁰Tell all the nations, "The LORD reigns!"
 The world stands firm and cannot be
 shaken.
 He will judge all peoples fairly.

¹¹Let the heavens be glad, and the earth
 rejoice!
 Let the sea and everything in it shout
 his praise!
¹²Let the fields and their crops burst out
 with joy!
 Let the trees of the forest sing for joy
¹³before the LORD, for he is coming!
 He is coming to judge the earth.
 He will judge the world with justice,
 and the nations with his truth.

PSALM 97

¹The LORD is king!
 Let the earth rejoice!
 Let the farthest coastlands be glad.
²Dark clouds surround him.
 Righteousness and justice are the
 foundation of his throne.
³Fire spreads ahead of him
 and burns up all his foes.
⁴His lightning flashes out across the
 world.
 The earth sees and trembles.
⁵The mountains melt like wax before the
 LORD,
 before the Lord of all the earth.

97:8 Hebrew *Zion.*

⁶The heavens proclaim his righteousness;
 every nation sees his glory.
⁷Those who worship idols are disgraced—
 all who brag about their worthless gods—
 for every god must bow to him.
⁸Jerusalem* has heard and rejoiced,
 and all the towns of Judah are glad
 because of your justice, O LORD!
⁹For you, O LORD, are supreme over all the
 earth;
 you are exalted far above all gods.

¹⁰You who love the LORD, hate evil!
 He protects the lives of his godly people
 and rescues them from the power of the
 wicked.
¹¹Light shines on the godly,
 and joy on those whose hearts are right.
¹²May all who are godly rejoice in the LORD
 and praise his holy name!

PSALM 98
A psalm.

¹Sing a new song to the LORD,
 for he has done wonderful deeds.
 His right hand has won a mighty
 victory;
 his holy arm has shown his saving
 power!
²The LORD has announced his victory
 and has revealed his righteousness to
 every nation!
³He has remembered his promise to love
 and be faithful to Israel.
 The ends of the earth have seen the
 victory of our God.

⁴Shout to the LORD, all the earth;
 break out in praise and sing for joy!
⁵Sing your praise to the LORD with the
 harp,
 with the harp and melodious song,
⁶with trumpets and the sound of the ram's
 horn.
 Make a joyful symphony before the
 LORD, the King!

97:10-12 God desires to help us, and he wants us to hate our sin as he does. He helps those who hate evil and want to please him. God has placed a very close link between happiness and holiness. If we want real joy, we need to commit our life to the Lord and his program for joyful and holy living.

98:1-3 God revealed his power to the whole world by rescuing the people of Israel. Today he shows his power by delivering us from our addiction and hopeless problems. We can win impossible battles, just as the Israelites did, because God is powerful and active in our life. Having found victory, we can share with others our stories of God's deliverance. This will give them the hope and wisdom they need to experience God's help in their own lives.

⁷ Let the sea and everything in it shout his
    praise!
  Let the earth and all living things
    join in.
⁸ Let the rivers clap their hands in glee!
  Let the hills sing out their songs of joy
⁹ before the LORD,
  for he is coming to judge the earth.
  He will judge the world with justice,
    and the nations with fairness.

PSALM 99

¹ The LORD is king!
    Let the nations tremble!
  He sits on his throne between the
    cherubim.
    Let the whole earth quake!
² The LORD sits in majesty in Jerusalem,*
    exalted above all the nations.
³ Let them praise your great and awesome
    name.
    Your name is holy!
⁴ Mighty King, lover of justice,
    you have established fairness.
  You have acted with justice
    and righteousness throughout
    Israel.*
⁵ Exalt the LORD our God!
    Bow low before his feet, for he is holy!

⁶ Moses and Aaron were among his priests;
    Samuel also called on his name.
  They cried to the LORD for help,
    and he answered them.
⁷ He spoke to Israel from the pillar of cloud,
    and they followed the laws and decrees
    he gave them.
⁸ O LORD our God, you answered them.
    You were a forgiving God to them,
    but you punished them when they
    went wrong.

⁹ Exalt the LORD our God,
    and worship at his holy mountain in
    Jerusalem,
  for the LORD our God is holy!

PSALM 100
A psalm of thanksgiving.

¹ Shout with joy to the LORD, all the earth!
²   Worship the LORD with gladness.
    Come before him, singing with joy.
³ Acknowledge that the LORD is God!
    He made us, and we are his.*
    We are his people, the sheep of his
    pasture.
⁴ Enter his gates with thanksgiving;
    go into his courts with praise.
    Give thanks to him and praise his name.
⁵ For the LORD is good.
    His unfailing love continues forever,
    and his faithfulness continues to each
    generation.

PSALM 101
A psalm of David.

¹ I will sing of your love and justice, LORD.
    I will praise you with songs.
² I will be careful to live a blameless life—
    when will you come to help me?
  I will lead a life of integrity
    in my own home.
³ I will refuse to look at
    anything vile and vulgar.
  I hate all who deal crookedly;
    I will have nothing to do with them.
⁴ I will reject perverse ideas
    and stay away from every evil.
⁵ I will not tolerate people who slander
    their neighbors.
  I will not endure conceit and
    pride.

99:2 Hebrew *Zion.* 99:4 Hebrew *Jacob.* See note on 44:4. 100:3 As in an alternate reading in the Masoretic Text;
the other alternate and some ancient versions read *and not we ourselves.*

99:1-9 Even though God is a God of love, he is also holy and righteous. His love causes him to
show mercy toward us, but his holiness means that we can't please him if we continue in sin. We
must not presume upon God's loving and forgiving nature, for he also loves justice. Continuing in
sin will result in terrible consequences. Our experiences of God's delivering power should motivate us to live for him with all our strength.

100:1-5 We always have reasons to rejoice: We live in God's presence, under his continual care,
and we experience his love each day. Each time we come into his presence, our heart should be
filled with gratitude and praise. God never stops showering us with his love; he always keeps his
promise to help us when we call on him.

101:1-5 Staying free from the sin that used to entrap us depends on our staying close to God and
staying away from every evil. It is vital that we not waste our time following a recovery program
that tries to undermine our faith in God. We must learn to be discerning about the activities we
become involved in. Like the psalmist, we must not tolerate anyone in our life who does not value
the things of God and who may slander us because of our faith in Christ.

⁶I will search for faithful people
   to be my companions.
Only those who are above reproach
   will be allowed to serve me.
⁷I will not allow deceivers to serve in my
   house,
   and liars will not stay in my presence.
⁸My daily task will be to ferret out the
   wicked
   and free the city of the LORD from their
   grip.

PSALM 102

A prayer of one overwhelmed with trouble, pouring
out problems before the LORD.

¹LORD, hear my prayer!
   Listen to my plea!
²Don't turn away from me
   in my time of distress.
Bend down to listen,
   and answer me quickly when I call to
   you.
³For my days disappear like smoke,
   and my bones burn like red-hot coals.
⁴My heart is sick, withered like grass,
   and I have lost my appetite.
⁵Because of my groaning,
   I am reduced to skin and bones.
⁶I am like an owl in the desert,
   like a little owl in a far-off wilderness.
⁷I lie awake,
   lonely as a solitary bird on the roof.
⁸My enemies taunt me day after day.
   They mock and curse me.
⁹I eat ashes for food.
   My tears run down into my drink
¹⁰because of your anger and wrath.
   For you have picked me up and thrown
   me out.
¹¹My life passes as swiftly as the evening
   shadows.
   I am withering away like grass.

¹²But you, O LORD, will sit on your throne
   forever.

102:13 Hebrew *Zion;* also in 102:16.

Your fame will endure to every
   generation.
¹³You will arise and have mercy on
   Jerusalem*—
   and now is the time to pity her,
   now is the time you promised to help.
¹⁴For your people love every stone in her
   walls
   and cherish even the dust in her streets.
¹⁵Then the nations will tremble before the
   LORD.
   The kings of the earth will tremble
   before his glory.
¹⁶For the LORD will rebuild Jerusalem.
   He will appear in his glory.
¹⁷He will listen to the prayers of the
   destitute.
   He will not reject their pleas.

¹⁸Let this be recorded for future generations,
   so that a people not yet born will praise
   the LORD.
¹⁹Tell them the LORD looked down
   from his heavenly sanctuary.
   He looked down to earth from heaven
²⁰   to hear the groans of the prisoners,
   to release those condemned to die.
²¹And so the LORD's fame will be celebrated
   in Zion,
   his praises in Jerusalem,
²²when multitudes gather together
   and kingdoms come to worship the LORD.

²³He broke my strength in midlife,
   cutting short my days.
²⁴But I cried to him, "O my God, who lives
   forever,
   don't take my life while I am so young!
²⁵Long ago you laid the foundation of the
   earth
   and made the heavens with your hands.
²⁶They will perish, but you remain forever;
   they will wear out like old clothing.
You will change them like a garment
   and discard them.

102:1-7 When we are heartsick and beaten down by the events of life, we can run to God with our urgent requests. At times we may lose our appetite and feel pain like red-hot coals in our bones. Our energy—our very life—withers like grass under the scorching sun. When there is no other solution, God is still able to deliver us. We need to admit our powerlessness in the situation and trust God to help us through the pain.
102:17-22 God responds to people who are downtrodden and in distress. Sometimes we may feel that God is too busy or too distant, but he is always intimately concerned about us and will not reject our requests. He wants us to have a joyful and meaningful relationship with him—that's what he created us for! When we admit our helplessness and turn to God, he will come through for us in one way or another. Then our only natural response to him will be one of joyful praise; we should also want to tell others about what God has done for us.

27 But you are always the same;
    you will live forever.
28 The children of your people
    will live in security.
   Their children's children
    will thrive in your presence."

PSALM 103
A psalm of David.

1 Let all that I am praise the LORD;
    with my whole heart, I will praise his
    holy name.
2 Let all that I am praise the LORD;
    may I never forget the good things he
    does for me.
3 He forgives all my sins
    and heals all my diseases.
4 He redeems me from death
    and crowns me with love and tender
    mercies.
5 He fills my life with good things.
    My youth is renewed like the eagle's!

6 The LORD gives righteousness
    and justice to all who are treated
    unfairly.

7 He revealed his character to Moses
    and his deeds to the people of Israel.
8 The LORD is compassionate and merciful,
    slow to get angry and filled with
    unfailing love.
9 He will not constantly accuse us,
    nor remain angry forever.
10 He does not punish us for all our sins;
    he does not deal harshly with us, as we
    deserve.
11 For his unfailing love toward those who
    fear him
    is as great as the height of the heavens
    above the earth.
12 He has removed our sins as far from us
    as the east is from the west.
13 The LORD is like a father to his children,
    tender and compassionate to those who
    fear him.

14 For he knows how weak we are;
    he remembers we are only dust.
15 Our days on earth are like grass;
    like wildflowers, we bloom and die.
16 The wind blows, and we are gone—
    as though we had never been here.
17 But the love of the LORD remains forever
    with those who fear him.
   His salvation extends to the children's
    children
18 of those who are faithful to his
    covenant,
   of those who obey his commandments!

19 The LORD has made the heavens his
    throne;
    from there he rules over everything.

20 Praise the LORD, you angels,
    you mighty ones who carry out his
    plans,
    listening for each of his commands.
21 Yes, praise the LORD, you armies of angels
    who serve him and do his will!
22 Praise the LORD, everything he has created,
    everything in all his kingdom.

    Let all that I am praise the LORD.

PSALM 104
1 Let all that I am praise the LORD.

   O LORD my God, how great you are!
    You are robed with honor and majesty.
2   You are dressed in a robe of light.
   You stretch out the starry curtain of the
    heavens;
3   you lay out the rafters of your home in
    the rain clouds.
   You make the clouds your chariot;
    you ride upon the wings of the wind.
4 The winds are your messengers;
    flames of fire are your servants.*

5 You placed the world on its foundation
    so it would never be moved.
6 You clothed the earth with floods of water,
    water that covered even the mountains.

104:4 Greek version reads *He sends his angels like the winds, / his servants like flames of fire.* Compare Heb 1:7.

103:13-18 As a loving father cares for his children, God has compassion on all who call on him. He is sensitive to our needs and treats us lovingly because he understands our weaknesses and the transitory nature of our life. God's love never ceases for those who fear him. By obediently serving him now, we can be assured that his love will touch not only our own life but also the lives of our children and grandchildren.

104:1-26 God created us as well as this world and all its creatures. He created the world to function according to his plan. God also created us to function best—to live joyful and healthy lives—when we do things his way. When we follow our own path, we will suffer painful consequences. If we seek to live according to God's program revealed in the Bible, we will discover the way to live in peace and harmony with God, other people, and the world we live in.

⁷At your command, the water fled;
   at the sound of your thunder, it hurried
      away.
⁸Mountains rose and valleys sank
   to the levels you decreed.
⁹Then you set a firm boundary for the seas,
   so they would never again cover the
      earth.

¹⁰You make springs pour water into the
      ravines,
   so streams gush down from the
      mountains.
¹¹They provide water for all the animals,
   and the wild donkeys quench their
      thirst.
¹²The birds nest beside the streams
   and sing among the branches of the
      trees.
¹³You send rain on the mountains from
      your heavenly home,
   and you fill the earth with the fruit of
      your labor.
¹⁴You cause grass to grow for the livestock
   and plants for people to use.
   You allow them to produce food from the
      earth—
¹⁵   wine to make them glad,
   olive oil to soothe their skin,
   and bread to give them strength.
¹⁶The trees of the LORD are well cared for—
   the cedars of Lebanon that he planted.
¹⁷There the birds make their nests,
   and the storks make their homes in the
      cypresses.
¹⁸High in the mountains live the wild goats,
   and the rocks form a refuge for the
      hyraxes.*

¹⁹You made the moon to mark the
      seasons,
   and the sun knows when to set.
²⁰You send the darkness, and it becomes
      night,
   when all the forest animals prowl
      about.
²¹Then the young lions roar for their prey,
   stalking the food provided by God.
²²At dawn they slink back
   into their dens to rest.
²³Then people go off to their work,
   where they labor until evening.

²⁴O LORD, what a variety of things you have
      made!
   In wisdom you have made them all.
   The earth is full of your creatures.

104:18 Or *coneys,* or *rock badgers.*

FORGIVENESS

READ PSALM 103:1-22

We may have a hard time believing in God's forgiveness. We may think, *After all I've done, I don't think anyone can completely forgive me.* Maybe we feel that we have done such horrible things or hurt people so badly that there's no way our sins could ever be blotted out entirely. Even if we could be forgiven, who could ever *forget* the things we have done?

When we think of people we know—the people we have hurt—perhaps these fears are well founded. But when it comes to forgiveness from God, we need to remember that his ways are higher than our ways. The psalmist wrote, "[God] does not punish us for all our sins; he does not deal harshly with us, as we deserve. For his unfailing love toward those who fear him is as great as the height of the heavens above the earth. He has removed our sins as far from us as the east is from the west" (Psalm 103:10-12). God has said, "Come now, let's settle this. . . . Though your sins are like scarlet, I will make them as white as snow. Though they are red like crimson, I will make them as white as wool" (Isaiah 1:18). "I—yes, I alone—will blot out your sins for my own sake and will never think of them again" (Isaiah 43:25).

Part of the recovery process is accepting complete forgiveness from God. When we come to God through the atoning blood of Jesus Christ, his forgiveness is complete. We may keep track of our failures, adding every one to the long list we have written out against ourself. But God doesn't keep lists of our past sins; in his eyes we are clean. *Turn to page 803, Proverbs 15.*

²⁵ Here is the ocean, vast and wide,
teeming with life of every kind,
both large and small.
²⁶ See the ships sailing along,
and Leviathan,* which you made to
play in the sea.

²⁷ They all depend on you
to give them food as they need it.
²⁸ When you supply it, they gather it.
You open your hand to feed them,
and they are richly satisfied.
²⁹ But if you turn away from them, they
panic.
When you take away their breath,
they die and turn again to dust.
³⁰ When you give them your breath,* life is
created,
and you renew the face of the earth.

³¹ May the glory of the LORD continue
forever!
The LORD takes pleasure in all he has
made!
³² The earth trembles at his glance;
the mountains smoke at his touch.

³³ I will sing to the LORD as long as I live.
I will praise my God to my last breath!
³⁴ May all my thoughts be pleasing to him,
for I rejoice in the LORD.
³⁵ Let all sinners vanish from the face of the
earth;
let the wicked disappear forever.

Let all that I am praise the LORD.

Praise the LORD!

PSALM 105

¹ Give thanks to the LORD and proclaim his
greatness.
Let the whole world know what he has
done.
² Sing to him; yes, sing his praises.

Tell everyone about his wonderful
deeds.
³ Exult in his holy name;
rejoice, you who worship the LORD.
⁴ Search for the LORD and for his strength;
continually seek him.
⁵ Remember the wonders he has
performed,
his miracles, and the rulings he has
given,
⁶ you children of his servant Abraham,
you descendants of Jacob, his chosen
ones.

⁷ He is the LORD our God.
His justice is seen throughout the land.
⁸ He always stands by his covenant—
the commitment he made to a
thousand generations.
⁹ This is the covenant he made with
Abraham
and the oath he swore to Isaac.
¹⁰ He confirmed it to Jacob as a decree,
and to the people of Israel as a
never-ending covenant:
¹¹ "I will give you the land of Canaan
as your special possession."

¹² He said this when they were few in
number,
a tiny group of strangers in Canaan.
¹³ They wandered from nation to nation,
from one kingdom to another.
¹⁴ Yet he did not let anyone oppress them.
He warned kings on their behalf:
¹⁵ "Do not touch my chosen people,
and do not hurt my prophets."

¹⁶ He called for a famine on the land
of Canaan,
cutting off its food supply.
¹⁷ Then he sent someone to Egypt ahead
of them—
Joseph, who was sold as a slave.

104:26 The identification of Leviathan is disputed, ranging from an earthly creature to a mythical sea monster in ancient literature. **104:30** Or *When you send your Spirit.*

104:27-35 God controls the destinies of all beings; every living being depends on him for food and life. We need to realize that if we withdraw ourself from God's presence, from his control and care, we are without hope, just as the natural world would be without hope if God should withdraw himself from it.

105:5-15 God always keeps his word. He fulfills all his promises. God promised Abraham and Jacob that their descendants would inherit the land of Canaan. Generations after Jacob's death, the Israelites entered Canaan. Sometimes God's promises take time to be fulfilled. In recovery we often grow impatient with our slow progress. At times we may think the entire process is hopeless and be tempted to give up. We need to realize that recovery takes time, but this does not mean God is not working on our behalf. We should also remember that the benefits of our efforts in recovery will touch not only our own life but also the lives of our descendants. Let us embrace God's recovery promises for the long haul.

¹⁸They bruised his feet with fetters
   and placed his neck in an iron collar.
¹⁹Until the time came to fulfill his dreams,*
   the LORD tested Joseph's character.
²⁰Then Pharaoh sent for him and set him
      free;
   the ruler of the nation opened his
      prison door.
²¹Joseph was put in charge of all the king's
      household;
   he became ruler over all the king's
      possessions.
²²He could instruct* the king's aides as he
      pleased
   and teach the king's advisers.

²³Then Israel arrived in Egypt;
   Jacob lived as a foreigner in the land
      of Ham.
²⁴And the LORD multiplied the people of
      Israel
   until they became too mighty for their
      enemies.
²⁵Then he turned the Egyptians against the
      Israelites,
   and they plotted against the LORD's
      servants.
²⁶But the LORD sent his servant Moses,
   along with Aaron, whom he had chosen.
²⁷They performed miraculous signs among
      the Egyptians,
   and wonders in the land of Ham.
²⁸The LORD blanketed Egypt in darkness,
   for they had defied* his commands to
      let his people go.
²⁹He turned their water into blood,
   poisoning all the fish.
³⁰Then frogs overran the land
   and even invaded the king's bedrooms.
³¹When the LORD spoke, flies descended on
      the Egyptians,
   and gnats swarmed across Egypt.
³²He sent them hail instead of rain,
   and lightning flashed over the land.
³³He ruined their grapevines and fig trees
   and shattered all the trees.
³⁴He spoke, and hordes of locusts came—
   young locusts beyond number.
³⁵They ate up everything green in the land,
   destroying all the crops in their fields.
³⁶Then he killed the oldest son in each
      Egyptian home,
   the pride and joy of each family.
³⁷The LORD brought his people out of Egypt,
   loaded with silver and gold;

105:19 Hebrew *his word.* **105:22** As in Greek and Syriac versions; Hebrew reads *bind* or *imprison.* **105:28** As in Greek and Syriac versions; Hebrew reads *had not defied.*

STEP 11

Finding God
BIBLE READING: Psalm 105:1-9
We sought through prayer and meditation to improve our conscious contacts with God, praying only for knowledge of his will for us and the power to carry that out.

As we work through the Twelve Steps, we spend a lot of time looking back. We often think about the wrong things we have done in the past. As we proceed in the recovery process, we will need strength to move along the path God wants us to follow. Part of this strength will come as we visualize God's constant presence with us.

The psalmist wrote, "Give thanks to the LORD and proclaim his greatness. Let the whole world know what he has done. . . . Remember the wonders he has performed, his miracles and the rulings he has given. . . . He is the LORD our God. His justice is seen throughout the land. He always stands by his covenant—the commitment he made to a thousand generations" (Psalm 105:1, 5-8).

From now on when we look back, we should concentrate on seeing the "wonders he has performed" and remember "his miracles and the rulings he has given." We can look around to find his goodness "throughout the land" and look forward to the fulfillment of his promises. In prayer, we should thank God for what he has done, seek him for the strength we need today, and ask him to fulfill his promises for tomorrow. In meditation, we need to remember our victories, ponder God's presence with us today, and consider his faithfulness and the hope he gives us for tomorrow. *Turn to page 765, Psalm 119.*

and not one among the tribes of Israel
even stumbled.
[38] Egypt was glad when they were gone,
for they feared them greatly.
[39] The LORD spread a cloud above them as a
covering
and gave them a great fire to light the
darkness.
[40] They asked for meat, and he sent them
quail;
he satisfied their hunger with
manna—bread from heaven.
[41] He split open a rock, and water gushed
out
to form a river through the dry
wasteland.
[42] For he remembered his sacred promise
to his servant Abraham.
[43] So he brought his people out of Egypt
with joy,
his chosen ones with rejoicing.
[44] He gave his people the lands of pagan
nations,
and they harvested crops that others
had planted.
[45] All this happened so they would follow
his decrees
and obey his instructions.

Praise the LORD!

PSALM 106
[1] Praise the LORD!

Give thanks to the LORD, for he is good!
His faithful love endures forever.
[2] Who can list the glorious miracles of the
LORD?
Who can ever praise him enough?

[3] There is joy for those who deal justly with
others
and always do what is right.
[4] Remember me, LORD, when you show
favor to your people;
come near and rescue me.
[5] Let me share in the prosperity of your
chosen ones.
Let me rejoice in the joy of your people;
let me praise you with those who are
your heritage.
[6] Like our ancestors, we have sinned.
We have done wrong! We have acted
wickedly!
[7] Our ancestors in Egypt
were not impressed by the LORD's
miraculous deeds.
They soon forgot his many acts of
kindness to them.
Instead, they rebelled against him
at the Red Sea.*
[8] Even so, he saved them—
to defend the honor of his name
and to demonstrate his mighty power.
[9] He commanded the Red Sea* to dry up.
He led Israel across the sea as if it were
a desert.
[10] So he rescued them from their enemies
and redeemed them from their foes.
[11] Then the water returned and covered their
enemies;
not one of them survived.
[12] Then his people believed his promises.
Then they sang his praise.
[13] Yet how quickly they forgot what he had
done!
They wouldn't wait for his counsel!

106:7 Hebrew *at the sea, the sea of reeds.* 106:9 Hebrew *sea of reeds;* also in 106:22.

105:39-45 God is able to care for his people. He responds to our prayers—even our complaints—
and meets all our needs that no one else could possibly fill. His ultimate purpose is to make us
faithful and obedient to his laws. As he helps us be faithful and obedient to his plan, he will fill us
with joy. These verses are of special comfort to us in recovery. As we admit our faults to God, we
can know that he is listening. As we seek to live according to his will, he will fill us with joy and
fulfillment. As we entrust our life to God, we can be sure we are in good hands.
106:6-12 The psalmist reflected on the failures of the present generation in Israel and the
mistakes of past generations. In recovery we must do the same. Our failures are often closely tied
to the mistakes of our parents and grandparents. We need to look back and forgive those who
have hurt us. Then we should honestly assess our own mistakes, taking responsibility for them
and seeking forgiveness from those we have hurt. Just as God revealed his goodness by rescuing
the Israelites from their enemies, he will forgive us and support us in the recovery process.
106:13-15 We all get discouraged when we fail. Like the people of Israel, we sometimes have very
short memories. We learn a lesson one day, only to forget it the next. After failing repeatedly, we
need to remember that God has pulled us through in the past, and he is able and willing to do it
again. God is always willing to help us if we are sincerely sorry and truly desire to change. We
must be careful, however, not to test God's patience to the breaking point. If we sin willfully, we
will suffer the consequences.

¹⁴ In the wilderness their desires ran wild,
   testing God's patience in that dry
   wasteland.
¹⁵ So he gave them what they asked for,
   but he sent a plague along with it.
¹⁶ The people in the camp were jealous
   of Moses
   and envious of Aaron, the LORD's holy
   priest.
¹⁷ Because of this, the earth opened up;
   it swallowed Dathan
   and buried Abiram and the other rebels.
¹⁸ Fire fell upon their followers;
   a flame consumed the wicked.

¹⁹ The people made a calf at Mount Sinai*;
   they bowed before an image made of
   gold.
²⁰ They traded their glorious God
   for a statue of a grass-eating bull.
²¹ They forgot God, their savior,
   who had done such great things in
   Egypt—
²² such wonderful things in the land of Ham,
   such awesome deeds at the Red Sea.
²³ So he declared he would destroy them.
   But Moses, his chosen one, stepped
   between the LORD and the people.
   He begged him to turn from his anger
   and not destroy them.

²⁴ The people refused to enter the pleasant
   land,
   for they wouldn't believe his promise to
   care for them.
²⁵ Instead, they grumbled in their tents
   and refused to obey the LORD.
²⁶ Therefore, he solemnly swore
   that he would kill them in the
   wilderness,
²⁷ that he would scatter their descendants*
   among the nations,
   exiling them to distant lands.

²⁸ Then our ancestors joined in the worship
   of Baal at Peor;
   they even ate sacrifices offered to the
   dead!
²⁹ They angered the LORD with all these
   things,
   so a plague broke out among them.

³⁰ But Phinehas had the courage to
   intervene,
   and the plague was stopped.
³¹ So he has been regarded as a righteous
   man
   ever since that time.

³² At Meribah, too, they angered the LORD,
   causing Moses serious trouble.
³³ They made Moses angry,*
   and he spoke foolishly.

³⁴ Israel failed to destroy the nations
   in the land,
   as the LORD had commanded them.
³⁵ Instead, they mingled among the pagans
   and adopted their evil customs.
³⁶ They worshiped their idols,
   which led to their downfall.
³⁷ They even sacrificed their sons
   and their daughters to the demons.
³⁸ They shed innocent blood,
   the blood of their sons and daughters.
   By sacrificing them to the idols of
   Canaan,
   they polluted the land with murder.
³⁹ They defiled themselves by their evil deeds,
   and their love of idols was adultery in
   the LORD's sight.

⁴⁰ That is why the LORD's anger burned
   against his people,
   and he abhorred his own special
   possession.
⁴¹ He handed them over to pagan nations,
   and they were ruled by those who
   hated them.
⁴² Their enemies crushed them
   and brought them under their cruel
   power.
⁴³ Again and again he rescued them,
   but they chose to rebel against him,
   and they were finally destroyed by their
   sin.
⁴⁴ Even so, he pitied them in their distress
   and listened to their cries.
⁴⁵ He remembered his covenant with them
   and relented because of his unfailing
   love.
⁴⁶ He even caused their captors
   to treat them with kindness.

106:19 Hebrew *at Horeb*, another name for Sinai. 106:27 As in Syriac version; Hebrew reads *he would cause their descendants to fall*. 106:33 Hebrew *They embittered his spirit*.

106:40-46 God hates sin. When we continue in our sinful ways, we shouldn't expect him to be pleased with us. God's judgment sometimes follows swiftly and may come from unexpected sources. Our sins will eventually destroy us. Yet God never abandons us forever. His goal is still to free us from the bondage of our sins.

⁴⁷ Save us, O LORD our God!
Gather us back from among the nations,
so we can thank your holy name
and rejoice and praise you.

⁴⁸ Praise the LORD, the God of Israel,
who lives from everlasting to
everlasting!
Let all the people say, "Amen!"

Praise the LORD!

BOOK FIVE (Psalms 107–150)

PSALM 107
¹ Give thanks to the LORD, for he is good!
His faithful love endures forever.
² Has the LORD redeemed you? Then speak
out!
Tell others he has redeemed you from
your enemies.
³ For he has gathered the exiles from many
lands,
from east and west,
from north and south.*

⁴ Some wandered in the wilderness,
lost and homeless.
⁵ Hungry and thirsty,
they nearly died.
⁶ "LORD, help!" they cried in their trouble,
and he rescued them from their
distress.
⁷ He led them straight to safety,
to a city where they could live.
⁸ Let them praise the LORD for his great love
and for the wonderful things he has
done for them.
⁹ For he satisfies the thirsty
and fills the hungry with good things.

¹⁰ Some sat in darkness and deepest gloom,
imprisoned in iron chains of misery.
¹¹ They rebelled against the words of God,
scorning the counsel of the Most High.
¹² That is why he broke them with hard
labor;

107:3 Hebrew *and sea.*

they fell, and no one was there to help
them.
¹³ "LORD, help!" they cried in their trouble,
and he saved them from their distress.
¹⁴ He led them from the darkness and
deepest gloom;
he snapped their chains.
¹⁵ Let them praise the LORD for his
great love
and for the wonderful things he has
done for them.
¹⁶ For he broke down their prison gates of
bronze;
he cut apart their bars of iron.

¹⁷ Some were fools; they rebelled
and suffered for their sins.
¹⁸ They couldn't stand the thought of food,
and they were knocking on death's
door.
¹⁹ "LORD, help!" they cried in their trouble,
and he saved them from their distress.
²⁰ He sent out his word and healed them,
snatching them from the door of death.
²¹ Let them praise the LORD for his great love
and for the wonderful things he has
done for them.
²² Let them offer sacrifices of thanksgiving
and sing joyfully about his glorious
acts.

²³ Some went off to sea in ships,
plying the trade routes of the world.
²⁴ They, too, observed the LORD's power in
action,
his impressive works on the deepest
seas.
²⁵ He spoke, and the winds rose,
stirring up the waves.
²⁶ Their ships were tossed to the heavens
and plunged again to the depths;
the sailors cringed in terror.
²⁷ They reeled and staggered like drunkards
and were at their wits' end.
²⁸ "LORD, help!" they cried in their trouble,
and he saved them from their distress.

107:10-20 When we reject God and his plan, we live in spiritual darkness; we are like prisoners in chains. God punishes evil acts with heavy penalties, including God's divine punishment and the natural consequences of disobedience. The psalmist's announcement of punishment, however, should not leave us in despair; his comments end on a hopeful note. If we come to our senses and ask God for his deliverance, he will help us escape from bondage and heal us.
107:23-32 Sometimes we may feel that we are in a small ship plowing through stormy seas and about to go under. Bad memories and a sense of failure make our world seem dark and hopeless. The longer the storm rages, the more we fear and lose all hope of rescue. But when we cry out to God in our trouble, he will turn our storm-tossed life into a calm and peaceful sea and restore our joy. We must turn to him for help, follow his plan for healthy living, and patiently await his deliverance.

²⁹ He calmed the storm to a whisper
  and stilled the waves.
³⁰ What a blessing was that stillness
  as he brought them safely into harbor!
³¹ Let them praise the LORD for his great love
  and for the wonderful things he has
  done for them.
³² Let them exalt him publicly before the
  congregation
  and before the leaders of the nation.

³³ He changes rivers into deserts,
  and springs of water into dry, thirsty
  land.
³⁴ He turns the fruitful land into salty
  wastelands,
  because of the wickedness of those who
  live there.
³⁵ But he also turns deserts into pools of
  water,
  the dry land into springs of water.
³⁶ He brings the hungry to settle there
  and to build their cities.
³⁷ They sow their fields, plant their
  vineyards,
  and harvest their bumper crops.
³⁸ How he blesses them!
  They raise large families there,
  and their herds of livestock increase.

³⁹ When they decrease in number and
  become impoverished
  through oppression, trouble, and
  sorrow,
⁴⁰ the LORD pours contempt on their princes,
  causing them to wander in trackless
  wastelands.
⁴¹ But he rescues the poor from trouble
  and increases their families like flocks
  of sheep.
⁴² The godly will see these things and be
  glad,
  while the wicked are struck silent.
⁴³ Those who are wise will take all this to
  heart;
  they will see in our history the faithful
  love of the LORD.

108:7 Or *in his sanctuary.*

PSALM 108
A song. A psalm of David.

¹ My heart is confident in you, O God;
  no wonder I can sing your praises with
  all my heart!
² Wake up, lyre and harp!
  I will wake the dawn with my song.
³ I will thank you, LORD, among all the
  people.
  I will sing your praises among the
  nations.
⁴ For your unfailing love is higher than the
  heavens.
  Your faithfulness reaches to the
  clouds.
⁵ Be exalted, O God, above the highest
  heavens.
  May your glory shine over all the
  earth.

⁶ Now rescue your beloved people.
  Answer and save us by your power.
⁷ God has promised this by his holiness*:
  "I will divide up Shechem with joy.
  I will measure out the valley of Succoth.
⁸ Gilead is mine,
  and Manasseh, too.
  Ephraim, my helmet, will produce my
  warriors,
  and Judah, my scepter, will produce
  my kings.
⁹ But Moab, my washbasin, will become
  my servant,
  and I will wipe my feet on Edom
  and shout in triumph over Philistia."

¹⁰ Who will bring me into the fortified city?
  Who will bring me victory over Edom?
¹¹ Have you rejected us, O God?
  Will you no longer march with our
  armies?
¹² Oh, please help us against our enemies,
  for all human help is useless.
¹³ With God's help we will do mighty
  things,
  for he will trample down our foes.

108:1-5 Morning is a wonderful time to praise God. Now that we are in recovery, our nights may
seem long, but each addiction-free day should fill our heart with joy. We should let our joy spill
out as a message of hope to others in need. Our testimony of God's faithfulness may lead others
to the joy we are beginning to experience in the process of recovery.
108:6-13 There is no resource for true recovery other than the strength offered by our gracious
God. It is futile to rely on anyone else for our victory, since God alone can give us the power to
overcome our dependencies and compulsions. Ultimately he is the one who conquers our
enemies and helps us do "mighty things." We must admit our powerlessness and turn our life
over to his care and direction.

PSALM 109
For the choir director: A psalm of David.

1 O God, whom I praise,
  don't stand silent and aloof
2 while the wicked slander me
  and tell lies about me.
3 They surround me with hateful words
  and fight against me for no reason.
4 I love them, but they try to destroy me
  with accusations
  even as I am praying for them!
5 They repay evil for good,
  and hatred for my love.

6 They say,* "Get an evil person to turn
  against him.
  Send an accuser to bring him to trial.
7 When his case comes up for judgment,
  let him be pronounced guilty.
  Count his prayers as sins.
8 Let his years be few;
  let someone else take his position.
9 May his children become fatherless,
  and his wife a widow.
10 May his children wander as beggars
  and be driven from* their ruined
  homes.
11 May creditors seize his entire estate,
  and strangers take all he has earned.
12 Let no one be kind to him;
  let no one pity his fatherless children.
13 May all his offspring die.
  May his family name be blotted out
  in the next generation.
14 May the LORD never forget the sins of his
  fathers;
  may his mother's sins never be erased
  from the record.
15 May the LORD always remember
  these sins,
  and may his name disappear from
  human memory.
16 For he refused all kindness to others;
  he persecuted the poor and needy,
  and he hounded the brokenhearted
  to death.

17 He loved to curse others;
  now you curse him.
  He never blessed others;
  now don't you bless him.
18 Cursing is as natural to him as his
  clothing,
  or the water he drinks,
  or the rich food he eats.
19 Now may his curses return and cling to
  him like clothing;
  may they be tied around him like
  a belt."

20 May those curses become the LORD's
  punishment
  for my accusers who speak evil of me.
21 But deal well with me, O Sovereign LORD,
  for the sake of your own reputation!
  Rescue me
  because you are so faithful and good.
22 For I am poor and needy,
  and my heart is full of pain.
23 I am fading like a shadow at dusk;
  I am brushed off like a locust.
24 My knees are weak from fasting,
  and I am skin and bones.
25 I am a joke to people everywhere;
  when they see me, they shake their
  heads in scorn.

26 Help me, O LORD my God!
  Save me because of your unfailing
  love.
27 Let them see that this is your doing,
  that you yourself have done it, LORD.
28 Then let them curse me if they like,
  but you will bless me!
  When they attack me, they will be
  disgraced!
  But I, your servant, will go right on
  rejoicing!
29 May my accusers be clothed with disgrace;
  may their humiliation cover them
  like a cloak.
30 But I will give repeated thanks to the
  LORD,
  praising him to everyone.

109:6 Hebrew lacks *They say.* **109:10** As in Greek version; Hebrew reads *and seek.*

109:1-5 We all know what it feels like to be condemned by others—sometimes unjustly. Sometimes we are attacked by painful memories of the abuse we may have suffered. It is then we need to turn to God for relief. He will fill our heart with his love and help us to forgive those who speak hateful words against us. We can rest in him and do our best to love those who hurt us.
109:21-31 It takes great humility to entrust our life to God. One of the most difficult parts of recovery, as God's children, is to admit how helpless we are to overcome our powerful dependency alone. We have all discovered what happens when we try to do things our own way: We become enslaved to our own desires and appetites. Dependence on God and his program is the only road to true freedom. We need to remember, however, that although God calls us to be childlike in spirit, he does not want us to be childish in behavior.

GOD grant me the serenity
to accept the things I cannot change
the courage to change the things I can
and the wisdom to know the difference

AMEN

When we lack wisdom, the storms of life can be devastating. When we find our life is in pieces, we may realize that we have acted unwisely and want to change, but where do we start?

"Fear of the LORD," the psalmist wrote, "is the foundation of true wisdom. All who obey his commandments will grow in wisdom" (Psalm 111:10). God has given us clear instructions for our life in his Word. When we fear God and are willing to accept his instructions as the basis for all of our decisions, we have a good starting point.

Jesus said, "Anyone who listens to my teaching and follows it is wise, like a person who builds a house on solid rock. Though the rain comes in torrents and the floodwaters rise and the winds beat against that house, it won't collapse, because it is built on bedrock" (Matthew 7:24-25). Listening to what the Bible says is the next step toward walking in wisdom. Filling our mind with God's instructions will help lead us to follow them. This will also help us turn away from the things forbidden by God. The book of Job tells us, "The fear of the Lord is true wisdom; to forsake evil is real understanding" (Job 28:28).

Turning our life over to God is a wise move! Like most aspects of recovery, walking in wisdom is a process that we grow into. These three elements are the groundwork: reverence for God, listening to his instructions, and following them. *Turn to page 775, Psalm 139.*

---

³¹ For he stands beside the needy,
   ready to save them from those who
   condemn them.

PSALM 110
A psalm of David.

¹ The LORD said to my Lord,*
   "Sit in the place of honor at my right
   hand
until I humble your enemies,
   making them a footstool under your
   feet."

² The LORD will extend your powerful
   kingdom from Jerusalem*;
   you will rule over your enemies.
³ When you go to war,
   your people will serve you willingly.
You are arrayed in holy garments,
   and your strength will be renewed each
   day like the morning dew.

⁴ The LORD has taken an oath and will not
   break his vow:
   "You are a priest forever in the order
   of Melchizedek."

⁵ The Lord stands at your right hand to
   protect you.
He will strike down many kings when
   his anger erupts.
⁶ He will punish the nations
   and fill their lands with corpses;
he will shatter heads over the whole
   earth.
⁷ But he himself will be refreshed from
   brooks along the way.
He will be victorious.

PSALM 111*
¹ Praise the LORD!

I will thank the LORD with all my heart
   as I meet with his godly people.

110:1 Or *my lord.* **110:2** Hebrew *Zion.* **111** This psalm is a Hebrew acrostic poem; after the introductory note of praise, each line begins with a successive letter of the Hebrew alphabet.

² How amazing are the deeds of
the LORD!
All who delight in him should ponder
them.
³ Everything he does reveals his glory and
majesty.
His righteousness never fails.
⁴ He causes us to remember his wonderful
works.
How gracious and merciful is our LORD!
⁵ He gives food to those who fear him;
he always remembers his covenant.
⁶ He has shown his great power to his
people
by giving them the lands of other
nations.
⁷ All he does is just and good,
and all his commandments are
trustworthy.
⁸ They are forever true,
to be obeyed faithfully and with
integrity.
⁹ He has paid a full ransom for his people.
He has guaranteed his covenant with
them forever.
What a holy, awe-inspiring name
he has!
¹⁰ Fear of the LORD is the foundation of true
wisdom.
All who obey his commandments will
grow in wisdom.

Praise him forever!

PSALM 112*
¹ Praise the LORD!

How joyful are those who fear the LORD
and delight in obeying his commands.
² Their children will be successful
everywhere;

an entire generation of godly people
will be blessed.
³ They themselves will be wealthy,
and their good deeds will last
forever.
⁴ Light shines in the darkness for the
godly.
They are generous, compassionate, and
righteous.
⁵ Good comes to those who lend money
generously
and conduct their business fairly.
⁶ Such people will not be overcome by evil.
Those who are righteous will be long
remembered.
⁷ They do not fear bad news;
they confidently trust the LORD to care
for them.
⁸ They are confident and fearless
and can face their foes triumphantly.
⁹ They share freely and give generously to
those in need.
Their good deeds will be remembered
forever.
They will have influence and honor.
¹⁰ The wicked will see this and be infuriated.
They will grind their teeth in anger;
they will slink away, their hopes
thwarted.

PSALM 113
¹ Praise the LORD!

Yes, give praise, O servants of the LORD.
Praise the name of the LORD!
² Blessed be the name of the LORD
now and forever.
³ Everywhere—from east to west—
praise the name of the LORD.
⁴ For the LORD is high above the nations;
his glory is higher than the heavens.

112 This psalm is a Hebrew acrostic poem; after the introductory note of praise, each line begins with a successive letter of the Hebrew alphabet.

111:9-10 God ransomed his people, the Israelites, first by making a covenant with them and then by delivering them time after time from their enemies. God has ransomed us, too, from the penalty of our sins by paying a very dear price—his own Son! God made this ultimate sacrifice so we, unworthy though we are, can be restored to godly and joyful lives. This should encourage us as we seek recovery. God wants it to happen even more than we do! That's why we can safely entrust our life into his hands. God has proven how strongly he desires our recovery by giving his own Son to suffer on our behalf.

112:5-10 Our best chance of success in overcoming our habits, our bad thought patterns, and the hurts in our life is to keep our eyes on God. Making good changes in our life won't make everyone happy. Some of our old enemies—and our old friends who used to lead us astray—will wonder why we no longer relate to them as we did. Some of them may even criticize us or think we are snobbish. As a result, we may find the process of recovery lonely at first. In times like these, we must look to God, who is always with us. With his help we will find new relationships that will strengthen us and learn how to reconcile our old relationships so they will support us in the recovery process.

⁵ Who can be compared with the LORD our
    God,
    who is enthroned on high?
⁶ He stoops to look down
    on heaven and on earth.
⁷ He lifts the poor from the dust
    and the needy from the garbage dump.
⁸ He sets them among princes,
    even the princes of his own people!
⁹ He gives the childless woman a family,
    making her a happy mother.

Praise the LORD!

PSALM 114

¹ When the Israelites escaped from Egypt—
    when the family of Jacob left that
        foreign land—
² the land of Judah became God's sanctuary,
    and Israel became his kingdom.

³ The Red Sea* saw them coming and
        hurried out of their way!
    The water of the Jordan River turned
        away.
⁴ The mountains skipped like rams,
    the hills like lambs!
⁵ What's wrong, Red Sea, that made you
        hurry out of their way?
    What happened, Jordan River, that you
        turned away?
⁶ Why, mountains, did you skip like rams?
    Why, hills, like lambs?

⁷ Tremble, O earth, at the presence of the
        Lord,
    at the presence of the God of Jacob.
⁸ He turned the rock into a pool
        of water;
    yes, a spring of water flowed from
        solid rock.

114:3 Hebrew *the sea;* also in 114:5.

PSALM 115

¹ Not to us, O LORD, not to us,
    but to your name goes all the glory
    for your unfailing love and faithfulness.
² Why let the nations say,
    "Where is their God?"
³ Our God is in the heavens,
    and he does as he wishes.
⁴ Their idols are merely things of silver and
        gold,
    shaped by human hands.
⁵ They have mouths but cannot speak,
    and eyes but cannot see.
⁶ They have ears but cannot hear,
    and noses but cannot smell.
⁷ They have hands but cannot feel,
    and feet but cannot walk,
    and throats but cannot make a sound.
⁸ And those who make idols are just like
        them,
    as are all who trust in them.

⁹ O Israel, trust the LORD!
    He is your helper and your shield.
¹⁰ O priests, descendants of Aaron, trust the
        LORD!
    He is your helper and your shield.
¹¹ All you who fear the LORD, trust the LORD!
    He is your helper and your shield.

¹² The LORD remembers us and will bless us.
    He will bless the people of Israel
    and bless the priests, the descendants of
        Aaron.
¹³ He will bless those who fear the LORD,
    both great and lowly.

¹⁴ May the LORD richly bless
    both you and your children.
¹⁵ May you be blessed by the LORD,
    who made heaven and earth.

113:5-9 Only God can restore us to sanity and right living, and he alone can lift us up. We may not sit "among princes," but we can return to society with dignity when we allow God to help us regain control of our life.

114:1-6 There is no end to the miracles God can perform on behalf of those who seek refuge in him. To bring courage to his readers, the psalmist listed some of God's amazing acts of deliverance in Israel's history. As we face difficulties, we can recall events of God's deliverance—in biblical history or in our own life. This will give us the hope we need to persevere in recovery; it will help us entrust our life into God's hands without reservation. God is truly awesome, worthy of our respect, obedience, and praise.

115:1-8 God is the only real resource for recovery. We have probably tried a number of recovery plans, but if God is not a central part of our program, we won't experience a lasting recovery. Some of us look for help in every new fad that comes along. If we don't ask God for help, all the recovery resources are useless—they are only man-made plans, as powerless as idols. Recovery is never easy. If we hear of a plan that is easy or quick, someone is probably just after our money. God alone knows what we need and has the power to lift us out of our painful circumstances and give us a life of meaning and joy. His program is our only way to a healthy life.

¹⁶ The heavens belong to the LORD,
    but he has given the earth to all
    humanity.
¹⁷ The dead cannot sing praises to the LORD,
    for they have gone into the silence of
    the grave.
¹⁸ But we can praise the LORD
    both now and forever!

    Praise the LORD!

PSALM 116

¹ I love the LORD because he hears my voice
    and my prayer for mercy.
² Because he bends down to listen,
    I will pray as long as I have breath!
³ Death wrapped its ropes around me;
    the terrors of the grave* overtook me.
    I saw only trouble and sorrow.
⁴ Then I called on the name of the LORD:
    "Please, LORD, save me!"
⁵ How kind the LORD is! How good he is!
    So merciful, this God of ours!
⁶ The LORD protects those of childlike faith;
    I was facing death, and he saved me.
⁷ Let my soul be at rest again,
    for the LORD has been good to me.
⁸ He has saved me from death,
    my eyes from tears,
    my feet from stumbling.
⁹ And so I walk in the LORD's presence
    as I live here on earth!
¹⁰ I believed in you, so I said,
    "I am deeply troubled, LORD."
¹¹ In my anxiety I cried out to you,
    "These people are all liars!"
¹² What can I offer the LORD
    for all he has done for me?
¹³ I will lift up the cup of salvation
    and praise the LORD's name for
    saving me.
¹⁴ I will keep my promises to the LORD
    in the presence of all his people.

¹⁵ The LORD cares deeply
    when his loved ones die.

116:3 Hebrew *of Sheol.*

¹⁶ O LORD, I am your servant;
    yes, I am your servant, born into your
    household;
    you have freed me from my chains.
¹⁷ I will offer you a sacrifice of thanksgiving
    and call on the name of the LORD.
¹⁸ I will fulfill my vows to the LORD
    in the presence of all his people—
¹⁹ in the house of the LORD
    in the heart of Jerusalem.

    Praise the LORD!

PSALM 117

¹ Praise the LORD, all you nations.
    Praise him, all you people of the earth.
² For his unfailing love for us is powerful;
    the LORD's faithfulness endures
    forever.

    Praise the LORD!

PSALM 118

¹ Give thanks to the LORD, for he is good!
    His faithful love endures forever.

² Let all Israel repeat:
    "His faithful love endures forever."
³ Let Aaron's descendants, the priests,
    repeat:
    "His faithful love endures forever."
⁴ Let all who fear the LORD repeat:
    "His faithful love endures forever."

⁵ In my distress I prayed to the LORD,
    and the LORD answered me and set me
    free.
⁶ The LORD is for me, so I will have
    no fear.
    What can mere people do to me?
⁷ Yes, the LORD is for me; he will help me.
    I will look in triumph at those who
    hate me.
⁸ It is better to take refuge in the LORD
    than to trust in people.
⁹ It is better to take refuge in the LORD
    than to trust in princes.

116:1-9 How wonderful that God hears and answers the prayers of those who turn to him in distress! When we were in the grip of our dependency or addiction, we may have been blind to the fact that we were in danger of losing our reputation, our friends, or even our life. But then we called out to the Lord, and he saved us. The natural response to this realization should be praise to God.

116:10-19 We will never be able to repay God for what he has done for us. But we can at least show our gratitude by fulfilling the promises we made to him when we called out to him for help. God thinks of us as his precious children, so we should thank him by keeping our promises to him. This may include making sure everyone knows it is God who deserves the credit for our deliverance.

¹⁰Though hostile nations surrounded me,
   I destroyed them all with the authority
      of the LORD.
¹¹Yes, they surrounded and attacked me,
   but I destroyed them all with the
      authority of the LORD.
¹²They swarmed around me like bees;
   they blazed against me like a crackling
      fire.
   But I destroyed them all with the
      authority of the LORD.
¹³My enemies did their best to kill me,
   but the LORD rescued me.
¹⁴The LORD is my strength and my song;
   he has given me victory.
¹⁵Songs of joy and victory are sung in the
      camp of the godly.
   The strong right arm of the LORD has
      done glorious things!
¹⁶The strong right arm of the LORD is raised
      in triumph.
   The strong right arm of the LORD has
      done glorious things!
¹⁷I will not die; instead, I will live
   to tell what the LORD has done.
¹⁸The LORD has punished me severely,
   but he did not let me die.

¹⁹Open for me the gates where the
      righteous enter,
   and I will go in and thank the LORD.
²⁰These gates lead to the presence of the
      LORD,
   and the godly enter there.
²¹I thank you for answering my prayer
   and giving me victory!

²²The stone that the builders rejected
   has now become the cornerstone.
²³This is the LORD's doing,
   and it is wonderful to see.
²⁴This is the day the LORD has made.
   We will rejoice and be glad in it.
²⁵Please, LORD, please save us.
   Please, LORD, please give us success.

²⁶Bless the one who comes in the name of
      the LORD.
   We bless you from the house of the
      LORD.
²⁷The LORD is God, shining upon us.
   Take the sacrifice and bind it with cords
      on the altar.
²⁸You are my God, and I will praise you!
   You are my God, and I will exalt you!

²⁹Give thanks to the LORD, for he
      is good!
   His faithful love endures forever.

PSALM 119*

Aleph
¹Joyful are people of integrity,
   who follow the instructions of the
      LORD.
²Joyful are those who obey his laws
   and search for him with all their hearts.
³They do not compromise with evil,
   and they walk only in his paths.
⁴You have charged us
   to keep your commandments
      carefully.
⁵Oh, that my actions would consistently
   reflect your decrees!
⁶Then I will not be ashamed
   when I compare my life with your
      commands.
⁷As I learn your righteous regulations,
   I will thank you by living as I should!
⁸I will obey your decrees.
   Please don't give up on me!

Beth
⁹How can a young person stay pure?
   By obeying your word.
¹⁰I have tried hard to find you—
   don't let me wander from your
      commands.
¹¹I have hidden your word in my heart,
   that I might not sin against you.

119 This psalm is a Hebrew acrostic poem; there are twenty-two stanzas, one for each successive letter of the Hebrew alphabet. Each of the eight verses within each stanza begins with the Hebrew letter named in its heading.

118:22-25 God's ways are not the same as our ways. What people may cast aside as unfit for use, God uses to do awe-inspiring work. This can be true for us, too. We may feel that our life is beyond repair or that God would never use us for anything significant. God often uses the most unlikely people to work his greatest miracles, proving to the world that he is at work. As willing vessels of God's power, we can be transformed to impact others far beyond our wildest dreams. To do this, we must entrust our life to God.

119:9-16 Obedience to God's Word produces wholeness; it seems only logical that we should do all we can to follow it. This is a significant part of seeking God's will for us. In the Bible, God has left clear guidelines for how he expects us to live. He has also promised that he will help us to carry out his will if we only ask him. Studying and applying God's Word should become a joyful experience that will implant God's truth firmly in our mind and heart.

¹²I praise you, O LORD;
   teach me your decrees.
¹³I have recited aloud
   all the regulations you have given us.
¹⁴I have rejoiced in your laws
   as much as in riches.
¹⁵I will study your commandments
   and reflect on your ways.
¹⁶I will delight in your decrees
   and not forget your word.

Gimel

¹⁷Be good to your servant,
   that I may live and obey your word.
¹⁸Open my eyes to see
   the wonderful truths in your
      instructions.
¹⁹I am only a foreigner in the land.
   Don't hide your commands from me!
²⁰I am always overwhelmed
   with a desire for your regulations.
²¹You rebuke the arrogant;
   those who wander from your
      commands are cursed.
²²Don't let them scorn and insult me,
   for I have obeyed your laws.
²³Even princes sit and speak against me,
   but I will meditate on your decrees.
²⁴Your laws please me;
   they give me wise advice.

Daleth

²⁵I lie in the dust;
   revive me by your word.
²⁶I told you my plans, and you
      answered.
   Now teach me your decrees.
²⁷Help me understand the meaning of your
      commandments,
   and I will meditate on your wonderful
      deeds.
²⁸I weep with sorrow;
   encourage me by your word.
²⁹Keep me from lying to myself;
   give me the privilege of knowing your
      instructions.

³⁰I have chosen to be faithful;
   I have determined to live by your
      regulations.
³¹I cling to your laws.
   LORD, don't let me be put to shame!
³²I will pursue your commands,
   for you expand my understanding.

He

³³Teach me your decrees, O LORD;
   I will keep them to the end.
³⁴Give me understanding and I will obey
      your instructions;
   I will put them into practice with all
      my heart.
³⁵Make me walk along the path of your
      commands,
   for that is where my happiness is found.
³⁶Give me an eagerness for your laws
   rather than a love for money!
³⁷Turn my eyes from worthless things,
   and give me life through your word.*
³⁸Reassure me of your promise,
   made to those who fear you.
³⁹Help me abandon my shameful ways;
   for your regulations are good.
⁴⁰I long to obey your commandments!
   Renew my life with your goodness.

Waw

⁴¹LORD, give me your unfailing love,
   the salvation that you promised me.
⁴²Then I can answer those who taunt me,
   for I trust in your word.
⁴³Do not snatch your word of truth
      from me,
   for your regulations are my only hope.
⁴⁴I will keep on obeying your instructions
   forever and ever.
⁴⁵I will walk in freedom,
   for I have devoted myself to your
      commandments.
⁴⁶I will speak to kings about your laws,
   and I will not be ashamed.
⁴⁷How I delight in your commands!
   How I love them!

119:37 Some manuscripts read *in your ways.*

119:17-24 With God's guidance, we can learn truths from his Word that will lead us safely through the uncharted territories of life. Because God rebukes those who do not follow his teaching, we need to seek his forgiveness for those times we have strayed from his commands. We must not let our problems inhibit our study of God's Word. Without God's wisdom and guidance, we lack the insight we need to experience a successful recovery.

119:57-64 In recovery we are called to seek out God's will for our life. The Bible should be the first place we look. Yet we must not merely listen to his Word and study his principles. We also need to take appropriate action once God's will is known (see James 1:22-25). If we learn God's will but fail to act on it, we are no better off than we were before. Recovery demands that we act—now!

48 I honor and love your commands.
  I meditate on your decrees.

Zayin

49 Remember your promise to me;
  it is my only hope.
50 Your promise revives me;
  it comforts me in all my troubles.
51 The proud hold me in utter contempt,
  but I do not turn away from your
    instructions.
52 I meditate on your age-old regulations;
  O LORD, they comfort me.
53 I become furious with the wicked,
  because they reject your instructions.
54 Your decrees have been the theme of my
    songs
  wherever I have lived.
55 I reflect at night on who you are, O LORD;
  therefore, I obey your instructions.
56 This is how I spend my life:
  obeying your commandments.

Heth

57 LORD, you are mine!
  I promise to obey your words!
58 With all my heart I want your blessings.
  Be merciful as you promised.
59 I pondered the direction of my life,
  and I turned to follow your laws.
60 I will hurry, without delay,
  to obey your commands.
61 Evil people try to drag me into sin,
  but I am firmly anchored to your
    instructions.
62 I rise at midnight to thank you
  for your just regulations.
63 I am a friend to anyone who fears you—
  anyone who obeys your
    commandments.
64 O LORD, your unfailing love fills the earth;
  teach me your decrees.

Teth

65 You have done many good things for me,
    LORD,
  just as you promised.
66 I believe in your commands;
  now teach me good judgment and
    knowledge.
67 I used to wander off until you
    disciplined me;
  but now I closely follow your word.
68 You are good and do only good;
  teach me your decrees.
69 Arrogant people smear me with lies,
  but in truth I obey your
    commandments with all
    my heart.

STEP 11

Powerful Secrets

BIBLE READING: Psalm 119:1-11

We sought through prayer and meditation to improve our conscious contacts with God, praying only for knowledge of his will for us and the power to carry that out.

The secrets we hide have enormous power in our life. How many of our addictive/compulsive behaviors have been hidden or covered up? When we took the step and admitted the exact nature of our addiction to another person, we were probably amazed at the way the addiction lost its power as it was exposed. The power of hidden behaviors and secrets can work for us as well as against us.

The psalmist wrote this prayer to God: "I have hidden your word in my heart, that I might not sin against you" (Psalm 119:11). If we "hide" God's Word in our heart by memorizing and meditating on it, we will find new power to keep our mind and heart clean.

The power of secrets will also work to our advantage in our prayer life. Jesus taught us that "when you pray, go away by yourself, shut the door behind you, and pray to your Father in private. Then your Father, who sees everything, will reward you" (Matthew 6:6). When we begin to spend time shut away with God in prayer and meditation, we'll find that power working for us. *Turn to page 891, Isaiah 40.*

[70] Their hearts are dull and stupid,
  but I delight in your instructions.
[71] My suffering was good for me,
  for it taught me to pay attention to
    your decrees.
[72] Your instructions are more valuable to me
  than millions in gold and silver.

Yodh

[73] You made me; you created me.
  Now give me the sense to follow your
    commands.
[74] May all who fear you find in me a cause
    for joy,
  for I have put my hope in your word.
[75] I know, O LORD, that your regulations are
    fair;
  you disciplined me because I needed it.
[76] Now let your unfailing love comfort me,
  just as you promised me, your servant.
[77] Surround me with your tender mercies so
    I may live,
  for your instructions are my delight.
[78] Bring disgrace upon the arrogant people
    who lied about me;
  meanwhile, I will concentrate on your
    commandments.
[79] Let me be united with all who fear you,
  with those who know your laws.
[80] May I be blameless in keeping your
    decrees;
  then I will never be ashamed.

Kaph

[81] I am worn out waiting for your rescue,
  but I have put my hope in your word.
[82] My eyes are straining to see your promises
    come true.
  When will you comfort me?
[83] I am shriveled like a wineskin in the
    smoke,
  but I have not forgotten to obey your
    decrees.
[84] How long must I wait?
  When will you punish those who
    persecute me?
[85] These arrogant people who hate your
    instructions
  have dug deep pits to trap me.

[86] All your commands are trustworthy.
  Protect me from those who hunt me
    down without cause.
[87] They almost finished me off,
  but I refused to abandon your
    commandments.
[88] In your unfailing love, spare my life;
  then I can continue to obey your laws.

Lamedh

[89] Your eternal word, O LORD,
  stands firm in heaven.
[90] Your faithfulness extends to every
    generation,
  as enduring as the earth you created.
[91] Your regulations remain true to this day,
  for everything serves your plans.
[92] If your instructions hadn't sustained me
    with joy,
  I would have died in my misery.
[93] I will never forget your commandments,
  for by them you give me life.
[94] I am yours; rescue me!
  For I have worked hard at obeying your
    commandments.
[95] Though the wicked hide along the way to
    kill me,
  I will quietly keep my mind on your
    laws.
[96] Even perfection has its limits,
  but your commands have no limit.

Mem

[97] Oh, how I love your instructions!
  I think about them all day long.
[98] Your commands make me wiser than my
    enemies,
  for they are my constant guide.
[99] Yes, I have more insight than my
    teachers,
  for I am always thinking of your laws.
[100] I am even wiser than my elders,
  for I have kept your commandments.
[101] I have refused to walk on any evil path,
  so that I may remain obedient to your
    word.
[102] I haven't turned away from your
    regulations,
  for you have taught me well.

119:71-72 We should be thankful when God disciplines us for our sins. Painful as it may be, discipline drives us back to his truth, which is far more valuable than all the riches of this world. God wants us only what is best for us. We would be wise to learn from God's discipline rather than fight it. It is given for our betterment, not our destruction.

119:73-77 As we obey God's revealed commands, people will begin to see the changes in our life and praise God. All of God's work—even his discipline—is done because of his goodness and faithfulness. God wants us to live joyfully. We need to seek God's will and do our best, with his help, to follow it. As God transforms us, we will become a living testimony of God's power to transform broken lives.

¹⁰³How sweet your words taste to me;
   they are sweeter than honey.
¹⁰⁴Your commandments give me
      understanding;
   no wonder I hate every false way
      of life.

Nun

¹⁰⁵Your word is a lamp to guide my feet
   and a light for my path.
¹⁰⁶I've promised it once, and I'll promise it
      again:
   I will obey your righteous regulations.
¹⁰⁷I have suffered much, O LORD;
   restore my life again as you promised.
¹⁰⁸LORD, accept my offering of praise,
   and teach me your regulations.
¹⁰⁹My life constantly hangs in the balance,
   but I will not stop obeying your
      instructions.
¹¹⁰The wicked have set their traps for me,
   but I will not turn from your
      commandments.
¹¹¹Your laws are my treasure;
   they are my heart's delight.
¹¹²I am determined to keep your decrees
   to the very end.

Samekh

¹¹³I hate those with divided loyalties,
   but I love your instructions.
¹¹⁴You are my refuge and my shield;
   your word is my source of hope.
¹¹⁵Get out of my life, you evil-minded
      people,
   for I intend to obey the commands
      of my God.
¹¹⁶LORD, sustain me as you promised, that
      I may live!
   Do not let my hope be crushed.
¹¹⁷Sustain me, and I will be rescued;
   then I will meditate continually on
      your decrees.
¹¹⁸But you have rejected all who stray from
      your decrees.
   They are only fooling themselves.
¹¹⁹You skim off the wicked of the earth like
      scum;
   no wonder I love to obey your laws!
¹²⁰I tremble in fear of you;
   I stand in awe of your regulations.

Ayin

¹²¹Don't leave me to the mercy of my
      enemies,
   for I have done what is just and right.
¹²²Please guarantee a blessing for me.
   Don't let the arrogant oppress me!
¹²³My eyes strain to see your rescue,
   to see the truth of your promise
      fulfilled.
¹²⁴I am your servant; deal with me in
      unfailing love,
   and teach me your decrees.
¹²⁵Give discernment to me, your servant;
   then I will understand your laws.
¹²⁶LORD, it is time for you to act,
   for these evil people have violated your
      instructions.
¹²⁷Truly, I love your commands
   more than gold, even the finest gold.
¹²⁸Each of your commandments is right.
   That is why I hate every false way.

Pe

¹²⁹Your laws are wonderful.
   No wonder I obey them!
¹³⁰The teaching of your word gives light,
   so even the simple can understand.
¹³¹I pant with expectation,
   longing for your commands.
¹³²Come and show me your mercy,
   as you do for all who love your name.
¹³³Guide my steps by your word,
   so I will not be overcome by evil.
¹³⁴Ransom me from the oppression of evil
      people;
   then I can obey your commandments.
¹³⁵Look upon me with love;
   teach me your decrees.
¹³⁶Rivers of tears gush from my eyes
   because people disobey your
      instructions.

Tsadhe

¹³⁷O LORD, you are righteous,
   and your regulations are fair.
¹³⁸Your laws are perfect
   and completely trustworthy.
¹³⁹I am overwhelmed with indignation,
   for my enemies have disregarded
      your words.

119:124-128 Until we turn to God for help, we will never be rescued or have sure guidance for our life. Following God's plan for recovery will not be easy, but we can count on his help. Like the psalmist, we should ask God to teach us his principles. When we are under pressure, we may be tempted to abandon God's principles. Before returning to our old, destructive behaviors, we should turn to God, asking him to help us do what is right. God wants us to recover. He is willing to provide not only the plan but also the encouragement we need to follow it.

[140]Your promises have been thoroughly
tested;
that is why I love them so much.
[141]I am insignificant and despised,
but I don't forget your commandments.
[142]Your justice is eternal,
and your instructions are perfectly true.
[143]As pressure and stress bear down on me,
I find joy in your commands.
[144]Your laws are always right;
help me to understand them so I may
live.

Qoph

[145]I pray with all my heart; answer me, LORD!
I will obey your decrees.
[146]I cry out to you; rescue me,
that I may obey your laws.
[147]I rise early, before the sun is up;
I cry out for help and put my hope in
your words.
[148]I stay awake through the night,
thinking about your promise.
[149]In your faithful love, O LORD, hear my cry;
let me be revived by following your
regulations.
[150]Lawless people are coming to attack me;
they live far from your instructions.
[151]But you are near, O LORD,
and all your commands are true.
[152]I have known from my earliest days
that your laws will last forever.

Resh

[153]Look upon my suffering and rescue me,
for I have not forgotten your
instructions.
[154]Argue my case; take my side!
Protect my life as you promised.
[155]The wicked are far from rescue,
for they do not bother with your
decrees.
[156]LORD, how great is your mercy;
let me be revived by following your
regulations.
[157]Many persecute and trouble me,
yet I have not swerved from your laws.
[158]Seeing these traitors makes me sick at
heart,
because they care nothing for your
word.
[159]See how I love your commandments,
LORD.

Give back my life because of your
unfailing love.
[160]The very essence of your words is truth;
all your just regulations will stand
forever.

Shin

[161]Powerful people harass me without cause,
but my heart trembles only at your
word.
[162]I rejoice in your word
like one who discovers a great treasure.
[163]I hate and abhor all falsehood,
but I love your instructions.
[164]I will praise you seven times a day
because all your regulations are just.
[165]Those who love your instructions have
great peace
and do not stumble.
[166]I long for your rescue, LORD,
so I have obeyed your commands.
[167]I have obeyed your laws,
for I love them very much.
[168]Yes, I obey your commandments and laws
because you know everything I do.

Taw

[169]O LORD, listen to my cry;
give me the discerning mind you
promised.
[170]Listen to my prayer;
rescue me as you promised.
[171]Let praise flow from my lips,
for you have taught me your decrees.
[172]Let my tongue sing about your word,
for all your commands are right.
[173]Give me a helping hand,
for I have chosen to follow your
commandments.
[174]O LORD, I have longed for your rescue,
and your instructions are my delight.
[175]Let me live so I can praise you,
and may your regulations help me.
[176]I have wandered away like a lost sheep;
come and find me,
for I have not forgotten your
commands.

PSALM 120

A song for pilgrims ascending to Jerusalem.

[1]I took my troubles to the LORD;
I cried out to him, and he answered my
prayer.

119:153-160 As we entrust our life to God, he restores us to wholeness. We can be sure that he
will stand with us and protect us from those who persecute us. We can count on him to encourage us when the recovery process becomes difficult or painful. As we seek out God's will in his
Word, we will discover the joyful truth: He is willing and able to restore us to wholeness!

² Rescue me, O LORD, from liars
    and from all deceitful people.
³ O deceptive tongue, what will God do to
        you?
    How will he increase your punishment?
⁴ You will be pierced with sharp arrows
    and burned with glowing coals.

⁵ How I suffer in far-off Meshech.
    It pains me to live in distant Kedar.
⁶ I am tired of living
    among people who hate peace.
⁷ I search for peace;
    but when I speak of peace, they want
        war!

PSALM 121
A song for pilgrims ascending to Jerusalem.

¹ I look up to the mountains—
    does my help come from there?
² My help comes from the LORD,
    who made heaven and earth!

³ He will not let you stumble;
    the one who watches over you will not
        slumber.
⁴ Indeed, he who watches over Israel
    never slumbers or sleeps.

⁵ The LORD himself watches over you!
    The LORD stands beside you as your
        protective shade.
⁶ The sun will not harm you by day,
    nor the moon at night.

⁷ The LORD keeps you from all harm
    and watches over your life.
⁸ The LORD keeps watch over you as you
        come and go,
    both now and forever.

PSALM 122
*A song for pilgrims ascending to Jerusalem. A psalm
of David.*

¹ I was glad when they said to me,
    "Let us go to the house of the LORD."
² And now here we are,
    standing inside your gates, O Jerusalem.
³ Jerusalem is a well-built city;
    its seamless walls cannot be breached.

⁴ All the tribes of Israel—the LORD's
        people—
    make their pilgrimage here.
    They come to give thanks to the name of
        the LORD,
    as the law requires of Israel.
⁵ Here stand the thrones where judgment
        is given,
    the thrones of the dynasty
        of David.

⁶ Pray for peace in Jerusalem.
    May all who love this city prosper.
⁷ O Jerusalem, may there be peace within
        your walls
    and prosperity in your palaces.
⁸ For the sake of my family and friends,
        I will say,
    "May you have peace."
⁹ For the sake of the house of the LORD our
        God,
    I will seek what is best for you,
        O Jerusalem.

PSALM 123
A song for pilgrims ascending to Jerusalem.

¹ I lift my eyes to you,
    O God, enthroned in heaven.
² We keep looking to the LORD our God for
        his mercy,
    just as servants keep their eyes on their
        master,
    as a slave girl watches her mistress for
        the slightest signal.
³ Have mercy on us, LORD, have mercy,
    for we have had our fill of contempt.
⁴ We have had more than our fill of the
        scoffing of the proud
    and the contempt of the arrogant.

PSALM 124
*A song for pilgrims ascending to Jerusalem. A psalm
of David.*

¹ What if the LORD had not been on our
        side?
    Let all Israel repeat:
² What if the LORD had not been on
        our side
    when people attacked us?

121:1-8 God alone is able to give us victory over our dependency. He watches over us day and
night, placing us under his umbrella of protection. He guards us against the dangers that threaten
to destroy our life and keeps us from evil.
124:1-8 Without God, there is no hope of deliverance and freedom. If he is not helping us fight
our battles, we will be overwhelmed by our powerful addiction. We should respond to God's
gracious deliverance by praising him for what he has done for us. This is the first step toward
sharing the good news of God's love and power with others.

³They would have swallowed us alive
   in their burning anger.
⁴The waters would have engulfed us;
   a torrent would have overwhelmed us.
⁵Yes, the raging waters of their fury
   would have overwhelmed our very
   lives.

⁶Praise the LORD,
   who did not let their teeth tear us apart!
⁷We escaped like a bird from a hunter's
   trap.
   The trap is broken, and we are free!
⁸Our help is from the LORD,
   who made heaven and earth.

PSALM 125
A song for pilgrims ascending to Jerusalem.

¹Those who trust in the LORD are as secure
   as Mount Zion;
   they will not be defeated but will
   endure forever.
²Just as the mountains surround Jerusalem,
   so the LORD surrounds his people, both
   now and forever.
³The wicked will not rule the land of the
   godly,
   for then the godly might be tempted to
   do wrong.
⁴O LORD, do good to those who are
   good,
   whose hearts are in tune with you.
⁵But banish those who turn to crooked
   ways, O LORD.
   Take them away with those who do
   evil.

May Israel have peace!

PSALM 126
A song for pilgrims ascending to Jerusalem.

¹When the LORD brought back his exiles
   to Jerusalem,*
   it was like a dream!

126:1 Hebrew *Zion.*

²We were filled with laughter,
   and we sang for joy.
And the other nations said,
   "What amazing things the LORD has
   done for them."
³Yes, the LORD has done amazing things
   for us!
   What joy!

⁴Restore our fortunes, LORD,
   as streams renew the desert.
⁵Those who plant in tears
   will harvest with shouts of joy.
⁶They weep as they go to plant their seed,
   but they sing as they return with the
   harvest.

PSALM 127
*A song for pilgrims ascending to Jerusalem. A psalm
of Solomon.*

¹Unless the LORD builds a house,
   the work of the builders is wasted.
Unless the LORD protects a city,
   guarding it with sentries will do no
   good.
²It is useless for you to work so hard
   from early morning until late at night,
anxiously working for food to eat;
   for God gives rest to his loved ones.

³Children are a gift from the LORD;
   they are a reward from him.
⁴Children born to a young man
   are like arrows in a warrior's hands.
⁵How joyful is the man whose quiver is full
   of them!
   He will not be put to shame when he
   confronts his accusers at the city
   gates.

PSALM 128
A song for pilgrims ascending to Jerusalem.

¹How joyful are those who fear the LORD—
   all who follow his ways!

126:1-6 This psalm was written in response to the return of the Jewish exiles from captivity. God enabled his people to recover from their many sins by leading them through a period of painful exile. During this exile, they confessed their sins and returned to God. Then God allowed them to return to their homeland. This can be our story too. As we experience God's restoration, our tears will turn to joy and we can sing our own songs of praise. Change never comes overnight, but God promises to complete the transformation in our life when the time is right.
127:1 As we seek to rebuild our life, we must make sure God is involved in the building process. Without him, we have no hope for success. The forces that tear at our life are too strong for us to handle alone. Yet God is able to protect us as the rebuilding goes on, and he will direct us each step of the way. Recovery programs that fail to keep God at the center of our life will only lead to disappointment and deeper suffering. Unless God is supporting us in the recovery process, all our efforts are useless.

[2] You will enjoy the fruit of your labor.
How joyful and prosperous you
will be!
[3] Your wife will be like a fruitful grapevine,
flourishing within your home.
Your children will be like vigorous young
olive trees
as they sit around your table.
[4] That is the LORD's blessing
for those who fear him.

[5] May the LORD continually bless you from
Zion.
May you see Jerusalem prosper as long
as you live.
[6] May you live to enjoy your grandchildren.
May Israel have peace!

PSALM 129
A song for pilgrims ascending to Jerusalem.

[1] From my earliest youth my enemies have
persecuted me.
Let all Israel repeat this:
[2] From my earliest youth my enemies have
persecuted me,
but they have never defeated me.
[3] My back is covered with cuts,
as if a farmer had plowed long furrows.
[4] But the LORD is good;
he has cut me free from the ropes
of the ungodly.

[5] May all who hate Jerusalem*
be turned back in shameful defeat.
[6] May they be as useless as grass on a
rooftop,
turning yellow when only half grown,
[7] ignored by the harvester,
despised by the binder.
[8] And may those who pass by
refuse to give them this blessing:
"The LORD bless you;
we bless you in the LORD's name."

PSALM 130
A song for pilgrims ascending to Jerusalem.

[1] From the depths of despair, O LORD,
I call for your help.
[2] Hear my cry, O Lord.
Pay attention to my prayer.

[3] LORD, if you kept a record of our sins,
who, O Lord, could ever survive?
[4] But you offer forgiveness,
that we might learn to fear you.

[5] I am counting on the LORD;
yes, I am counting on him.
I have put my hope in his word.
[6] I long for the Lord
more than sentries long for the dawn,
yes, more than sentries long for the
dawn.

[7] O Israel, hope in the LORD;
for with the LORD there is unfailing
love.
His redemption overflows.
[8] He himself will redeem Israel
from every kind of sin.

PSALM 131
*A song for pilgrims ascending to Jerusalem. A psalm
of David.*

[1] LORD, my heart is not proud;
my eyes are not haughty.
I don't concern myself with matters too
great
or too awesome for me to grasp.
[2] Instead, I have calmed and quieted myself,
like a weaned child who no longer cries
for its mother's milk.
Yes, like a weaned child is my soul
within me.

[3] O Israel, put your hope in the LORD—
now and always.

PSALM 132
A song for pilgrims ascending to Jerusalem.

[1] LORD, remember David
and all that he suffered.
[2] He made a solemn promise to the LORD.
He vowed to the Mighty One of Israel,*
[3] "I will not go home;
I will not let myself rest.
[4] I will not let my eyes sleep
nor close my eyelids in slumber
[5] until I find a place to build a house
for the LORD,
a sanctuary for the Mighty One of
Israel."

129:5 Hebrew *Zion.* **132:2** Hebrew *of Jacob;* also in 132:5. See note on 44:4.

130:1-8 When we cry out to God, we want quick answers. We should be thankful that God does
not respond on the basis of our worthiness. If he did, we would receive nothing but judgment.
God forgives us of every kind of sin so we might worship him with a thankful heart. He desires our
recovery from the sinful forces that beset us; he will deliver us when we call out to him.

⁶We heard that the Ark was in Ephrathah;
  then we found it in the distant
    countryside of Jaar.
⁷Let us go to the sanctuary of the LORD;
  let us worship at the footstool of his
    throne.
⁸Arise, O LORD, and enter your resting place,
  along with the Ark, the symbol of your
    power.
⁹May your priests be clothed in godliness;
  may your loyal servants sing for joy.
¹⁰For the sake of your servant David,
  do not reject the king you have
    anointed.
¹¹The LORD swore an oath to David
  with a promise he will never take
    back:
  "I will place one of your descendants
    on your throne.
¹²If your descendants obey the terms of my
    covenant
  and the laws that I teach them,
  then your royal line
    will continue forever and ever."

¹³For the LORD has chosen Jerusalem*;
  he has desired it for his home.
¹⁴"This is my resting place forever," he said.
  "I will live here, for this is the home
    I desired.
¹⁵I will bless this city and make it prosperous;
  I will satisfy its poor with food.
¹⁶I will clothe its priests with godliness;
  its faithful servants will sing for joy.
¹⁷Here I will increase the power of David;
  my anointed one will be a light for my
    people.
¹⁸I will clothe his enemies with shame,
  but he will be a glorious king."

PSALM 133
A song for pilgrims ascending to Jerusalem. A psalm of David.

¹How wonderful and pleasant it is
  when brothers live together in
    harmony!

132:13 Hebrew *Zion.* 134:3 Hebrew *Zion.*

²For harmony is as precious as the
    anointing oil
  that was poured over Aaron's head,
  that ran down his beard
  and onto the border of his robe.
³Harmony is as refreshing as the dew from
    Mount Hermon
  that falls on the mountains of Zion.
  And there the LORD has pronounced his
    blessing,
  even life everlasting.

PSALM 134
A song for pilgrims ascending to Jerusalem.

¹Oh, praise the LORD, all you servants
    of the LORD,
  you who serve at night in the house of
    the LORD.
²Lift your hands toward the sanctuary,
  and praise the LORD.

³May the LORD, who made heaven and
    earth,
  bless you from Jerusalem.*

PSALM 135
¹Praise the LORD!

Praise the name of the LORD!
  Praise him, you who serve the LORD,
²you who serve in the house of the LORD,
  in the courts of the house of
    our God.

³Praise the LORD, for the LORD is good;
  celebrate his lovely name with music.
⁴For the LORD has chosen Jacob for
    himself,
  Israel for his own special treasure.

⁵I know the greatness of the LORD—
  that our Lord is greater than any other
    god.
⁶The LORD does whatever pleases him
  throughout all heaven and earth,
  and on the seas and in their depths.
⁷He causes the clouds to rise over the
    whole earth.

133:1-3 Reconciling our human relationships is an important part of the recovery process. We need the people in our life to give us encouragement to overcome our pain and to stand with us against the temptations we face. There is nothing quite like human fellowship and friendship, and God wants to bless us through other people. The kind of friends most helpful to us in recovery are those who are trying to live godly lives.
135:1-13 Knowing that God has chosen us as his own should give us the confidence to call on him when we are in trouble. All through the Old Testament we see evidence of God working to save his people. Because God is all-powerful and "does whatever pleases him" throughout the earth, he can help us when we call on him. In his greatness, no problem is too great for him to solve.

He sends the lightning with the rain
and releases the wind from his
storehouses.

8 He destroyed the firstborn in each
Egyptian home,
both people and animals.
9 He performed miraculous signs and
wonders in Egypt
against Pharaoh and all his people.
10 He struck down great nations
and slaughtered mighty kings—
11 Sihon king of the Amorites,
Og king of Bashan,
and all the kings of Canaan.
12 He gave their land as an inheritance,
a special possession to his people
Israel.

13 Your name, O LORD, endures forever;
your fame, O LORD, is known to every
generation.
14 For the LORD will give justice to his people
and have compassion on his
servants.

15 The idols of the nations are merely things
of silver and gold,
shaped by human hands.
16 They have mouths but cannot speak,
and eyes but cannot see.
17 They have ears but cannot hear,
and mouths but cannot breathe.
18 And those who make idols are just like
them,
as are all who trust in them.

19 O Israel, praise the LORD!
O priests—descendants of
Aaron—praise the LORD!
20 O Levites, praise the LORD!
All you who fear the LORD, praise the
LORD!
21 The LORD be praised from Zion,
for he lives here in Jerusalem.

Praise the LORD!

PSALM 136

1 Give thanks to the LORD, for he
is good!
His faithful love endures forever.

136:13 Hebrew *sea of reeds;* also in 136:15.

2 Give thanks to the God of gods.
His faithful love endures forever.
3 Give thanks to the Lord of lords.
His faithful love endures forever.
4 Give thanks to him who alone does
mighty miracles.
His faithful love endures forever.
5 Give thanks to him who made the
heavens so skillfully.
His faithful love endures forever.
6 Give thanks to him who placed the earth
among the waters.
His faithful love endures forever.
7 Give thanks to him who made the
heavenly lights—
His faithful love endures forever.
8 the sun to rule the day,
His faithful love endures forever.
9 and the moon and stars to rule the night.
His faithful love endures forever.

10 Give thanks to him who killed the
firstborn of Egypt.
His faithful love endures forever.
11 He brought Israel out of Egypt.
His faithful love endures forever.
12 He acted with a strong hand and powerful
arm.
His faithful love endures forever.
13 Give thanks to him who parted the Red
Sea.*
His faithful love endures forever.
14 He led Israel safely through,
His faithful love endures forever.
15 but he hurled Pharaoh and his army into
the Red Sea.
His faithful love endures forever.
16 Give thanks to him who led his people
through the wilderness.
His faithful love endures forever.
17 Give thanks to him who struck down
mighty kings.
His faithful love endures forever.
18 He killed powerful kings—
His faithful love endures forever.
19 Sihon king of the Amorites,
His faithful love endures forever.
20 and Og king of Bashan.
His faithful love endures forever.

136:16-26 Struggling with a powerful addiction might be compared to walking through a wilderness. But if we entrust our life to him, God is able to lead us to victory, just as he led the Israelites through the wilderness. God never abandons us when we are humbled by our enemies—whether internal or external. Instead, he frees us from their clutches because his faithful love for us "endures forever."

²¹ God gave the land of these kings as an
inheritance—
His faithful love endures forever.
²² a special possession to his servant Israel.
His faithful love endures forever.

²³ He remembered us in our weakness.
His faithful love endures forever.
²⁴ He saved us from our enemies.
His faithful love endures forever.
²⁵ He gives food to every living thing.
His faithful love endures forever.
²⁶ Give thanks to the God of heaven.
His faithful love endures forever.

PSALM 137

¹ Beside the rivers of Babylon, we sat and
wept
as we thought of Jerusalem.*
² We put away our harps,
hanging them on the branches of
poplar trees.
³ For our captors demanded a song
from us.
Our tormentors insisted on a joyful
hymn:
"Sing us one of those songs of Jerusalem!"
⁴ But how can we sing the songs of the LORD
while in a pagan land?

⁵ If I forget you, O Jerusalem,
let my right hand forget how to play
the harp.
⁶ May my tongue stick to the roof of my
mouth
if I fail to remember you,
if I don't make Jerusalem my greatest
joy.

⁷ O LORD, remember what the Edomites did
on the day the armies of Babylon
captured Jerusalem.

137:1 Hebrew *Zion;* also in 137:3.

"Destroy it!" they yelled.
"Level it to the ground!"
⁸ O Babylon, you will be destroyed.
Happy is the one who pays you back
for what you have done to us.
⁹ Happy is the one who takes your
babies
and smashes them against the rocks!

PSALM 138
A psalm of David.

¹ I give you thanks, O LORD, with all my
heart;
I will sing your praises before the gods.
² I bow before your holy Temple as I
worship.
I praise your name for your unfailing
love and faithfulness;
for your promises are backed
by all the honor of your name.
³ As soon as I pray, you answer me;
you encourage me by giving me
strength.

⁴ Every king in all the earth will thank you,
LORD,
for all of them will hear your words.
⁵ Yes, they will sing about the LORD's ways,
for the glory of the LORD is very great.
⁶ Though the LORD is great, he cares for the
humble,
but he keeps his distance from the
proud.

⁷ Though I am surrounded by troubles,
you will protect me from the anger of
my enemies.
You reach out your hand,
and the power of your right hand
saves me.
⁸ The LORD will work out his plans for my
life—

138:6-8 God responds favorably to humility, but he keeps his distance from the proud, who think
they have no need of him. When we remain humble and seek his face, he will renew our strength
and give us power over our enemies. How wonderful to know that the Lord is working out his
plans for our life, and he will never fail us.

139:6-12 God is everywhere. We can never escape from his presence. Such knowledge should
keep us from falling into sin and encourage us to follow him, knowing he is there to help us. He is
not limited by space, nor is he limited by time. He is with us day and night to strengthen and
support us.

139:13-18 The power of our dependency is often rooted in low self-esteem. These verses reveal
an exciting fact: Each of us is an amazing creature—"wonderfully complex "! More than that,
God is constantly thinking about us! We are so precious to him that he has recorded every day of
our life in a book. We may have been taught, in one way or another, that we were no good. We
began to believe this message, and now we have fallen into various destructive methods to deal
with the pain. When we see ourself as God sees us, much of the pain that drives our dependency
will fall away.

READ PSALM 139:1-16

GOD grant me the serenity
to accept the things I cannot change
the courage to change the things I can
and the wisdom to know the difference

A M E N

Many of us have spent our life trying to be someone we are not. Our addictive/compulsive behaviors may be only a desperate attempt to escape from ourself. Maybe we have difficulty accepting our personality, our appearance, our handicap, or even our talents.

Perhaps we spend our energy and time trying to be what other people want us to be because we feel that who we are is not enough. We may do all we can to separate from our inner being because we are so deeply ashamed of who we are. Self-hatred is a defect of character that needs to be removed. It breeds the sin of covetousness—that is, longing to be in someone else's situation or have what they have. The psalmist wrote, "Thank you for making me so wonderfully complex! Your workmanship is marvelous—how well I know it" (Psalm 139:14). Saying we are God's "workmanship" means that we are unique and beautiful masterpieces—works of divine poetry. Beauty and value are designed into the very fiber of our being by virtue of our Creator.

One important step in the recovery process is to allow God to re-move our self-hatred, helping us to value ourself for who we are. We have been miraculously created, and we are treasured by God. This has been true since the time we were in our mother's womb, long be-fore we could *do* anything to earn it! As we begin to see how unique and special we are—embraced and accepted by God himself—our strides toward recovery should grow faster and longer. *Turn to page 787, Proverbs 2.*

for your faithful love, O LORD, endures
forever.
Don't abandon me, for you made me.

PSALM 139
For the choir director: A psalm of David.

¹O LORD, you have examined my heart
and know everything about me.
²You know when I sit down or stand up.
You know my thoughts even when I'm
far away.
³You see me when I travel
and when I rest at home.
You know everything I do.
⁴You know what I am going to say
even before I say it, LORD.
⁵You go before me and follow me.
You place your hand of blessing
on my head.
⁶Such knowledge is too wonderful for me,
too great for me to understand!

139:8 Hebrew *to Sheol.*

⁷I can never escape from your Spirit!
I can never get away from your
presence!
⁸If I go up to heaven, you are there;
if I go down to the grave,* you are
there.
⁹If I ride the wings of the morning,
if I dwell by the farthest oceans,
¹⁰even there your hand will guide me,
and your strength will support me.
¹¹I could ask the darkness to hide me
and the light around me to become
night—
¹² but even in darkness I cannot hide
from you.
To you the night shines as bright as day.
Darkness and light are the same to you.

¹³You made all the delicate, inner parts of
my body
and knit me together in my mother's
womb.

¹⁴ Thank you for making me so wonderfully
  complex!
  Your workmanship is marvelous—how
  well I know it.
¹⁵ You watched me as I was being formed in
  utter seclusion,
  as I was woven together in the dark of
  the womb.
¹⁶ You saw me before I was born.
  Every day of my life was recorded in
  your book.
  Every moment was laid out
  before a single day had passed.

¹⁷ How precious are your thoughts about
  me,* O God.
  They cannot be numbered!
¹⁸ I can't even count them;
  they outnumber the grains of sand!
  And when I wake up,
  you are still with me!

¹⁹ O God, if only you would destroy the
  wicked!
  Get out of my life, you murderers!
²⁰ They blaspheme you;
  your enemies misuse your name.
²¹ O LORD, shouldn't I hate those who hate
  you?
  Shouldn't I despise those who oppose
  you?
²² Yes, I hate them with total hatred,
  for your enemies are my enemies.

²³ Search me, O God, and know my heart;
  test me and know my anxious
  thoughts.
²⁴ Point out anything in me that offends
  you,
  and lead me along the path of
  everlasting life.

PSALM 140
For the choir director: A psalm of David.

¹ O LORD, rescue me from evil people.
  Protect me from those who are violent,
² those who plot evil in their hearts

139:17 Or *How precious to me are your thoughts.*

and stir up trouble all day long.
³ Their tongues sting like a snake;
  the venom of a viper drips from
  their lips.   *Interlude*

⁴ O LORD, keep me out of the hands of the
  wicked.
  Protect me from those who are violent,
  for they are plotting against me.
⁵ The proud have set a trap to catch me;
  they have stretched out a net;
  they have placed traps all along
  the way.   *Interlude*

⁶ I said to the LORD, "You are my God!"
  Listen, O LORD, to my cries for mercy!
⁷ O Sovereign LORD, the strong one who
  rescued me,
  you protected me on the day of battle.
⁸ LORD, do not let evil people have their
  way.
  Do not let their evil schemes succeed,
  or they will become proud.   *Interlude*

⁹ Let my enemies be destroyed
  by the very evil they have planned
  for me.
¹⁰ Let burning coals fall down on their
  heads.
  Let them be thrown into the fire
  or into watery pits from which they
  can't escape.
¹¹ Don't let liars prosper here in our land.
  Cause great disasters to fall on the
  violent.

¹² But I know the LORD will help those they
  persecute;
  he will give justice to the poor.
¹³ Surely righteous people are praising your
  name;
  the godly will live in your presence.

PSALM 141
A psalm of David.

¹ O LORD, I am calling to you. Please hurry!
  Listen when I cry to you for help!

140:1-5 We need God's protection against those who might cause our destruction. Some people like to stir up trouble and may trap us and entice us to return to the poisonous dependency that led to our downfall in the first place. More than ever, we need God to keep us from being caught in their hidden snares. We are never out of the danger zone and may never totally escape the siren call of our addiction. We must commit ourself to staying close to God, the only one who can keep us safe.
141:1-10 When the flaming desire for our addiction is upon us, we need God's help to put out the fire. God can take away our desire for destructive and evil things. When temptation is so strong that we can't stand up against it, God will help us find a way to escape (see 1 Corinthians 10:13). We should not hesitate to call a Christian friend for prayer and support when we feel

[2] Accept my prayer as incense offered to
you,
and my upraised hands as an evening
offering.

[3] Take control of what I say, O LORD,
and guard my lips.
[4] Don't let me drift toward evil
or take part in acts of wickedness.
Don't let me share in the delicacies
of those who do wrong.

[5] Let the godly strike me!
It will be a kindness!
If they correct me, it is soothing medicine.
Don't let me refuse it.

But I pray constantly
against the wicked and their deeds.
[6] When their leaders are thrown down from
a cliff,
the wicked will listen to my words and
find them true.
[7] Like rocks brought up by a plow,
the bones of the wicked will lie
scattered without burial.*
[8] I look to you for help, O Sovereign LORD.
You are my refuge; don't let them
kill me.
[9] Keep me from the traps they have set
for me,
from the snares of those who
do wrong.
[10] Let the wicked fall into their own nets,
but let me escape.

PSALM 142
A psalm of David, regarding his experience in the
cave. A prayer.*

[1] I cry out to the LORD;
I plead for the LORD's mercy.
[2] I pour out my complaints before him
and tell him all my troubles.
[3] When I am overwhelmed,
you alone know the way I should turn.

Wherever I go,
my enemies have set traps for me.
[4] I look for someone to come and help me,
but no one gives me a passing
thought!
No one will help me;
no one cares a bit what happens to me.
[5] Then I pray to you, O LORD.
I say, "You are my place of refuge.
You are all I really want in life.
[6] Hear my cry,
for I am very low.
Rescue me from my persecutors,
for they are too strong for me.
[7] Bring me out of prison
so I can thank you.
The godly will crowd around me,
for you are good to me."

PSALM 143
A psalm of David.

[1] Hear my prayer, O LORD;
listen to my plea!
Answer me because you are faithful and
righteous.
[2] Don't put your servant on trial,
for no one is innocent before you.
[3] My enemy has chased me.
He has knocked me to the ground
and forces me to live in darkness like
those in the grave.
[4] I am losing all hope;
I am paralyzed with fear.
[5] I remember the days of old.
I ponder all your great works
and think about what you have done.
[6] I lift my hands to you in prayer.
I thirst for you as parched land thirsts
for rain.   *Interlude*

[7] Come quickly, LORD, and answer me,
for my depression deepens.
Don't turn away from me,
or I will die.

141:7 Hebrew *our bones will be scattered at the mouth of Sheol.* **142:TITLE** Hebrew *maskil.* This may be a literary or
musical term.

weak. During times of stress, we need to allow God to be our defender, to keep us safe from the
snares of evil people.
142:1-7 Suffering should drive us to God, not to despair. We should freely express our feelings to
God about the trials we experience. Many former friends don't really care what happens to us,
but God cares about us. Surrendering our life to him is the thing to do when our dependencies
begin to get the better of us. God is our place of refuge. Only he can help us escape from the
bondage of our sins and surround us with godly people who can encourage and strengthen us.
143:5-12 Our addiction often makes it hard to think of anything but the present. We may have
lost all hope, and our depression is deepening. It is very important in recovery that we recall times
in the past when God helped us overcome our addiction. As we spend time in prayer, his gracious
Spirit will lead us forward and show us how to live.

[8] Let me hear of your unfailing love each
    morning,
    for I am trusting you.
Show me where to walk,
    for I give myself to you.
[9] Rescue me from my enemies, LORD;
    I run to you to hide me.
[10] Teach me to do your will,
    for you are my God.
May your gracious Spirit lead me forward
    on a firm footing.
[11] For the glory of your name, O LORD,
    preserve my life.
    Because of your faithfulness, bring me
    out of this distress.
[12] In your unfailing love, silence all my
    enemies
    and destroy all my foes,
    for I am your servant.

PSALM 144
A psalm of David.

[1] Praise the LORD, who is my rock.
    He trains my hands for war
    and gives my fingers skill for battle.
[2] He is my loving ally and my fortress,
    my tower of safety, my rescuer.
He is my shield, and I take refuge
    in him.
    He makes the nations* submit to me.

[3] O LORD, what are human beings that you
    should notice them,
    mere mortals that you should think
    about them?
[4] For they are like a breath of air;
    their days are like a passing shadow.

[5] Open the heavens, LORD, and come
    down.
    Touch the mountains so they billow
    smoke.
[6] Hurl your lightning bolts and scatter your
    enemies!
    Shoot your arrows and confuse them!
[7] Reach down from heaven and rescue me;
    rescue me from deep waters,

from the power of my enemies.
[8] Their mouths are full of lies;
    they swear to tell the truth, but they
    lie instead.

[9] I will sing a new song to you, O God!
    I will sing your praises with a
    ten-stringed harp.
[10] For you grant victory to kings!
    You rescued your servant David from
    the fatal sword.
[11] Save me!
    Rescue me from the power of my
    enemies.
Their mouths are full of lies;
    they swear to tell the truth, but they
    lie instead.

[12] May our sons flourish in their youth
    like well-nurtured plants.
May our daughters be like graceful pillars,
    carved to beautify a palace.
[13] May our barns be filled
    with crops of every kind.
May the flocks in our fields multiply by
    the thousands,
    even tens of thousands,
[14]   and may our oxen be loaded down
    with produce.
May there be no enemy breaking through
    our walls,
    no going into captivity,
    no cries of alarm in our town squares.
[15] Yes, joyful are those who live like this!
    Joyful indeed are those whose God
    is the LORD.

PSALM 145*
A psalm of praise of David.

[1] I will exalt you, my God and King,
    and praise your name forever and ever.
[2] I will praise you every day;
    yes, I will praise you forever.
[3] Great is the LORD! He is most worthy
    of praise!
    No one can measure his greatness.

144:2 Some manuscripts read *my people.* 145 This psalm is a Hebrew acrostic poem; each verse (including 13b)
begins with a successive letter of the Hebrew alphabet.

144:3-8 One mystery we will never understand in this life is why God would ever concern himself
with us. The greater mystery is how he could ever love us when we are overwhelmed by destructive addictions or compulsions. Why is God so good to us? Why does he continually rescue us? It
is God's nature to do this—he is a loving, gracious, and merciful God. He wants the best for his
creation. We need to act on God's promises to us and rejoice in his unlimited kindness.
145:1-7 Praise is an effective weapon against the temptations of our dependency. Keeping our
mind focused on God and praising him are helpful weapons against our addiction. Our praise of
God's work in our life can bring joy and encouragement to others.

⁴Let each generation tell its children of
your mighty acts;
let them proclaim your power.
⁵I will meditate on your majestic, glorious
splendor
and your wonderful miracles.
⁶Your awe-inspiring deeds will be on every
tongue;
I will proclaim your greatness.
⁷Everyone will share the story of your
wonderful goodness;
they will sing with joy about your
righteousness.

⁸The LORD is merciful and compassionate,
slow to get angry and filled with
unfailing love.
⁹The LORD is good to everyone.
He showers compassion on all his
creation.
¹⁰All of your works will thank you, LORD,
and your faithful followers will praise
you.
¹¹They will speak of the glory of your
kingdom;
they will give examples of your
power.
¹²They will tell about your mighty deeds
and about the majesty and glory of
your reign.
¹³For your kingdom is an everlasting
kingdom.
You rule throughout all generations.

The LORD always keeps his promises;
he is gracious in all he does.*
¹⁴The LORD helps the fallen
and lifts those bent beneath their
loads.
¹⁵The eyes of all look to you in hope;
you give them their food as they
need it.
¹⁶When you open your hand,
you satisfy the hunger and thirst of
every living thing.

¹⁷The LORD is righteous in everything he
does;
he is filled with kindness.
¹⁸The LORD is close to all who call on him,
yes, to all who call on him in truth.
¹⁹He grants the desires of those who fear
him;
he hears their cries for help and rescues
them.
²⁰The LORD protects all those who love him,
but he destroys the wicked.

²¹I will praise the LORD,
and may everyone on earth bless his
holy name
forever and ever.

PSALM 146

¹Praise the LORD!

Let all that I am praise the LORD.
² I will praise the LORD as long as
I live.
I will sing praises to my God with my
dying breath.

³Don't put your confidence in powerful
people;
there is no help for you there.
⁴When they breathe their last, they return
to the earth,
and all their plans die with them.
⁵But joyful are those who have the God of
Israel* as their helper,
whose hope is in the LORD their God.
⁶He made heaven and earth,
the sea, and everything in them.
He keeps every promise forever.
⁷He gives justice to the oppressed
and food to the hungry.
The LORD frees the prisoners.
⁸ The LORD opens the eyes of the blind.
The LORD lifts up those who are weighed
down.
The LORD loves the godly.
⁹The LORD protects the foreigners
among us.

145:13 As in Dead Sea Scrolls and Greek and Syriac versions; the Masoretic Text lacks the final two lines of this verse.
146:5 Hebrew *of Jacob.* See note on 44:4.

145:8-13 God showers us with his gifts and often withholds the judgment we deserve. Although
he hates our sin, he does not react with anger. Instead, he shows us great compassion. Someday
all creation will recognize what God has done and will praise him. We are part of the host that will
be examples of his great power, especially his work of deliverance in our own life.
146:5-9 God made all things and cares about all his creation, even the most lowly. He gives
justice to the oppressed, feeds the hungry, and frees the prisoners. He alone can restore us to
sanity when sin has caused us to lose control of our life. We may think no one else cares about us,
but we can be assured that God does. He even watches over those who have no one else to care
for them.

He cares for the orphans and widows,
but he frustrates the plans of the
wicked.
[10] The LORD will reign forever.
He will be your God, O Jerusalem,*
throughout the generations.

Praise the LORD!

PSALM 147

[1] Praise the LORD!

How good to sing praises to our God!
How delightful and how fitting!
[2] The LORD is rebuilding Jerusalem
and bringing the exiles back
to Israel.
[3] He heals the brokenhearted
and bandages their wounds.
[4] He counts the stars
and calls them all by name.
[5] How great is our Lord! His power is
absolute!
His understanding is beyond
comprehension!
[6] The LORD supports the humble,
but he brings the wicked down into
the dust.
[7] Sing out your thanks to the LORD;
sing praises to our God with a harp.
[8] He covers the heavens with clouds,
provides rain for the earth,
and makes the grass grow in mountain
pastures.
[9] He gives food to the wild animals
and feeds the young ravens when they
cry.
[10] He takes no pleasure in the strength of a
horse
or in human might.
[11] No, the LORD's delight is in those who fear
him,
those who put their hope in his
unfailing love.

146:10 Hebrew *Zion.* 147:17 Hebrew *like bread crumbs.*

[12] Glorify the LORD, O Jerusalem!
Praise your God, O Zion!
[13] For he has strengthened the bars of your
gates
and blessed your children within your
walls.
[14] He sends peace across your nation
and satisfies your hunger with the
finest wheat.
[15] He sends his orders to the world—
how swiftly his word flies!
[16] He sends the snow like white wool;
he scatters frost upon the ground like
ashes.
[17] He hurls the hail like stones.*
Who can stand against his freezing
cold?
[18] Then, at his command, it all melts.
He sends his winds, and the ice thaws.
[19] He has revealed his words to Jacob,
his decrees and regulations to Israel.
[20] He has not done this for any other
nation;
they do not know his regulations.

Praise the LORD!

PSALM 148

[1] Praise the LORD!

Praise the LORD from the heavens!
Praise him from the skies!
[2] Praise him, all his angels!
Praise him, all the armies of heaven!
[3] Praise him, sun and moon!
Praise him, all you twinkling stars!
[4] Praise him, skies above!
Praise him, vapors high above the
clouds!
[5] Let every created thing give praise to the
LORD,
for he issued his command, and they
came into being.
[6] He set them in place forever and ever.
His decree will never be revoked.

147:2-11 God can restore us to wholeness again. We need to turn to him instead of withering away in our remorse. There is always hope when we honor God in our life because there is nothing greater than God's power. He is able to heal us and provide for all our needs and is never overwhelmed by the dependency that we call our enemy.
147:12-20 God is our defender and peacemaker, the one who meets all of our needs. Since he is the creator and sustainer of all nature, we should have no doubt about his ability to care for us once we commit our life to him. He is worthy of our trust.
148:1-14 God deserves our praise for all the good we receive day by day. Not the least of these benefits is the help he gives us in restoring our life to health and sanity. There was a time when we felt out of control; now God is making us strong. That should give us ample reason to join the rest of the universe in a chorus of ceaseless praise.

7 Praise the LORD from the earth,
you creatures of the ocean depths,
8 fire and hail, snow and clouds,*
wind and weather that obey him,
9 mountains and all hills,
fruit trees and all cedars,
10 wild animals and all livestock,
small scurrying animals and birds,
11 kings of the earth and all people,
rulers and judges of the earth,
12 young men and young women,
old men and children.

13 Let them all praise the name of the LORD.
For his name is very great;
his glory towers over the earth and
heaven!
14 He has made his people strong,
honoring his faithful ones—
the people of Israel who are close
to him.

Praise the LORD!

PSALM 149
1 Praise the LORD!

Sing to the LORD a new song.
Sing his praises in the assembly of the
faithful.

2 O Israel, rejoice in your Maker.
O people of Jerusalem,* exult in your
King.
3 Praise his name with dancing,
accompanied by tambourine and harp.
4 For the LORD delights in his people;

148:8 Or *mist,* or *smoke.* **149:2** Hebrew *Zion.*

he crowns the humble with victory.
5 Let the faithful rejoice that he honors
them.
Let them sing for joy as they lie
on their beds.

6 Let the praises of God be in their mouths,
and a sharp sword in their hands—
7 to execute vengeance on the nations
and punishment on the peoples,
8 to bind their kings with shackles
and their leaders with iron chains,
9 to execute the judgment written against
them.
This is the glorious privilege of his
faithful ones.

Praise the LORD!

PSALM 150
1 Praise the LORD!

Praise God in his sanctuary;
praise him in his mighty heaven!
2 Praise him for his mighty works;
praise his unequaled greatness!
3 Praise him with a blast of the ram's horn;
praise him with the lyre and harp!
4 Praise him with the tambourine and
dancing;
praise him with strings and flutes!
5 Praise him with a clash of cymbals;
praise him with loud clanging cymbals.
6 Let everything that breathes sing praises
to the LORD!

Praise the LORD!

149:1-9 It should not be hard to commit our life to God. He is the one who gives us salvation and helps the humble and needy—people just like us. Knowing that he cares for us should cause us to rejoice and sing his praises. God always wants the best for us. All we need to do is turn our life over to him.

150:1-6 One of the best ways to praise God is with our life, including submitting to his will for us and sharing the Good News with others. All of us are recipients of God's loving forgiveness and restoration. Every living creature—each of us—has ample reason to praise our wonderful and gracious God. "Let everything that breathes sing praises to the LORD! Praise the LORD!"

REFLECTIONS ON PSALMS

insights INTO GOD'S PROTECTION

In **Psalm 4:1-3** David rejoiced about God's powerful protection. In times of distress our merciful God is the perfect haven of rest. He is listening, and he hears our cries for help. God wants us to put our trust in him. We insult him when we trust in our own resources or anything else to deliver us from our problems. When we turn our will and life over to God, we become his own chosen ones, whom he promises to hear when we call out to him.

In **Psalm 7:3-11** David looked to God to defend him against the slanderous judgments of his enemies. Those who attack us or try to undermine the recovery process through lies are not just our enemies; they are God's enemies, too. We can count on him to deal with our common enemies if we are doing what we can to avoid temptation. We ought to hate the things God hates. We don't need to try to defend our choices when we are choosing the right paths; God has promised to be our defense.

In **Psalm 18:30-36** David praised God for his ability to protect those who looked to him for help. God will protect us if we are willing to admit our weaknesses and depend on him. He will empower us to do what is right in difficult situations and give us the ability to walk without stumbling, even when the path is slippery. God also equips his people for spiritual warfare, enabling us to use the shield of salvation and other powerful weapons. If we will only ask him to help us, God will protect us from temptations that could lead to our defeat.

In **Psalm 27:1-6** David praised God for the protection and hope he provided. We have nothing to fear in this life if we put our complete trust in God as our guide, deliverer, and protector. With God on our side, there is no need for us to be drawn away by the evil people who formerly led us astray. If we maintain our close contact with God, we can be assured that when problems come, he will watch over us, make our way secure, and draw us even closer to himself.

In **Psalm 31:1-5** David's words exhibit his dependence on God in times of danger and stress. God is our strong refuge, our rock of safety—the one we can turn to when we feel overwhelmed by temptations and dangers. Because we know he will always do what is right, we can with confidence turn our will and our life over to his care.

In **Psalm 56:1-7** David trusted God to take care of him during a time of great danger. When we are terrified by tempting or dangerous circumstances, we need to turn our life and our will over to God. We need to trust him and his promises. He is able to strengthen us so we won't fall again. Sometimes the enemy we face is obvious. At other times the attacks are very subtle, so we need to be careful.

insights INTO GOD'S DELIVERANCE

David probably wrote **Psalm 9:7-14** soon after a great victory over the Philistines. David praised God for delivering him from powerful enemies. God is merciful; he is always ready to help those who are oppressed by their enemies. In God's perfect timing, those who are oppressed will find comfort and encouragement if they put their trust in him. Because God never forsakes those who trust him, we should praise him and tell others that he has rescued us. As we remember his faithfulness to us in our times of distress, we will be able to take this message of encouragement to others.

After lamenting the oppressive acts of wicked people, David, in **Psalm 14:4-7**, expressed his confidence that God could deliver him from their clutches. Many of our problems may have been caused by someone else. Someone may have taken advantage of us without considering our feelings. We can find comfort in two facts. First, God will judge the people who have hurt us; we don't have to hold on to our anger and hatred. Second, God is with us; he is there to see us through the recovery process from beginning to end. In his perfect timing God will rescue us.

David wrote **Psalm 18:1-5** soon after God delivered him from his enemies. God is more than able to deliver us from our problems. He is our source of strength, our rock, and the one on whom we must rely as we seek freedom from our bondage. The psalmist learned that his decision to cry out to God for help was a wise choice. We, too, can experience God's deliverance. We should start by admitting our helplessness, the first step in recovery. Then we can look to God to give us the help we need to overcome our dependency.

In **Psalm 31:14-18** the psalmist shared his confidence that God alone could deliver him from his troubles. He also realized that without God's help he would suffer humiliation. God is the only one able to solve our problems. He is willing to help us overcome the people and situations that once dragged us down. We need to make sure he is at the center of our life as we continue in recovery.

In **Psalm 42:4-11** the psalmist honestly shared his feelings of depression. He felt God had forsaken him. Then he declared his faith in God and again put his hope in God. He struggled with his emotions—between despair and faith—and he was always honest about his feelings. In the process of recovery, we may experience times of deep depression. But God wants us to remember that even as floods of trouble pour over us, we should keep trusting him. We should feel free to express our feelings to God. As we spill out our complaints to him, he will pour over us waves of his steadfast love.

In **Psalm 57:4-6** David witnessed God's faithful help and love in times of trouble. Our dependencies and compulsions are never easy to handle. In fact, without God's help, they are impossible to handle. But God is far more powerful than all our internal and external enemies combined. He rules over heaven and earth and is able and willing to thwart the plans of our enemies.

David wrote **Psalm 60:6-12** during a time of war and affirmed that his help came from God alone. We can turn to God for deliverance because he has promised to help us. God reminds us that we still belong to him, no matter how great our failures in the past. He still offers a good life for any who are willing to do their best to follow his divine program. He can still give us victory if we allow him to help us fight our battles against temptation.

In **Psalm 76:1-12** we learn that God is able to overcome even the most powerful opposition we might face. He can use evil deeds to bring about his own plans for good. God's power is far greater than we can imagine. He is able to overcome even our greatest problems. All we need to do is turn our dependency over to him and entrust our life to his care. When he fights for us, none of our enemies—past, present, or future—can stand against us.

In **Psalm 104:19-24** the psalmist praised God for his amazing control over the created world. God uses the sun to regulate the days and nights and the moon to mark the seasons. Such power and control over the physical world should encourage us that when we commit our life to God, we have committed ourself to someone who has the power to help us.

In **Psalm 109:16-20** David spoke to God about the undeserved attacks he was forced to endure. All of us have suffered injustice; we all know the feelings that accompany innocent suffering. When we are hurt without just cause, we may be tempted to lash out in revenge. This will never resolve our pain or hurts. We need to let go of our anger; it will only lead to more suffering. We can trust God to work his justice according to his timetable. God will ultimately return the same kind of evil done to the innocent to those who are guilty. God is the best judge; judgment against the sins of others is best left up to him.

insights INTO GOD'S FORGIVENESS

In **Psalm 103:8-12** David praised God for his great love and kindness. We should be encouraged by the knowledge that God loves us enough to not only forgive our sins but also put them behind him forever—"as far . . . as the east is from the west." We have all failed; our mistakes have hurt other people and damaged or destroyed our relationships. Sometimes others have a hard time forgiving us, even when we seek to make amends. God, on the other hand, is waiting to forgive us. All we have to do is confess our sins and turn our life over to him. Knowing that God has forgiven us should give us the courage to continue seeking reconciliation with the people we have wronged.

insights INTO THE VALUE OF CONFESSION

In **Psalm 15:1-5** David reflected on how God's way of doing things leads to stability and peace. If we want to progress in recovery, we must never compromise with sin, whether it's our own or someone else's. No matter how painful it might be, we must confess the sin in our life or, in some cases, confront others with theirs. Many times our sins have caused a great deal of pain and loss to the people close to us. We need to become more sensitive to the wrongs we have committed and be specific in our personal inventory. This will help us escape the cycle of sin we are caught in and protect the people we love from further hurt.

In **Psalm 18:25-29** David recognized God's desire to bestow mercy on those who are merciful toward others and repentant of their sins. When we are ready to admit our wrongs to God and to others and when we show mercy to others, God is merciful toward us. We do great harm to ourselves and to others when we are too proud to admit our failures. But God is always ready to help us when we acknowledge who he is.

In **Psalm 19:12-14** David asked God to reveal any hidden sins in his life—to break through any denial he might have. He was taking a moral inventory and asked God to help him do this with absolute honesty. Because we tend to be blind to our sinful disposition, we need God to clarify our thinking—to reveal any sin that is working its deception within us and to keep us from deliberately doing wrong. When our thought life is right with God, our actions will be right also.

In **Psalm 38:9-16** the psalmist recognized how hideous he had become because of his sins. He turned to the only one who was listening—indeed, the only one who could help—God. The longer we remain in sin, the more disabled we become. Our heart pounds in fear, our energy ebbs away, and our ability to see ourselves as we really are becomes distorted. Even our closest friends and family members steer clear of us for fear we might drag them down. We must recognize how helpless we are in the face of our problems and turn to God for help. He is always ready to give us a helping hand.

David wrote **Psalm 51:16-19** after being convicted of adultery with Bathsheba. He realized that no number of sacrifices would cover his sins if he wasn't sorry for what he had done. He knew that God would grant him forgiveness if he honestly confessed his sins. We don't earn forgiveness from God. He is happy to give it to us if we only admit our failures and seek to make changes in our life. God is concerned more with our heartfelt attitudes than outward acts of repentance that do not reflect our true feelings. God is never fooled by these insincere acts of repentance. He wants us to take responsibility for our sins and seek forgiveness and restoration. There is always hope for us if we are willing to repent, as David did, and seek God's forgiveness. God is looking for people with humble hearts, not perfect records.

insights INTO THE VALUE OF PRAISE

In **Psalm 30:10-12** David concluded his request for deliverance with words of praise to God. Staying close to God through prayer and meditation is an important part of recovery. God wants us to succeed in recovery—he wants it even more than we do. He wants us to have a meaningful life filled with purpose and joy. When God helps us, we should not hesitate to praise him; like David, we should "sing praises to [God] and not be silent." Praising God out loud is an excellent way to tell others about God's work in our life. Sharing our experiences of deliverance will encourage others to persevere in recovery as well as strengthen our own resolves.

After experiencing God's deliverance, David spoke in **Psalm 40:9-10** about how he shared this good news with others. The news about our deliverance needs to be shared with others who are struggling. God is righteous, faithful, and able to deliver others from their bondage, just as he delivered us. As we share our victories with others, we will discover that not only will they be encouraged, but we will be strengthened as well.

Through **Psalm 111:1-8** the psalmist illustrated what it means to fulfill Step Twelve in recovery. God's work in our life has a twofold purpose: to accomplish our deliverance from bondage and to demonstrate God's power to others who need his help. Sharing the good news of God's deliverance will help others and will also strengthen us, giving us the encouragement we need to avoid relapses.

In **Psalm 112:1-4** the psalmist sang out in exuberant praise to God. When we decide to turn our life over to God and commit ourself to do his will, we will experience the joy this passage speaks of. Our children and grandchildren, too, will reap the benefits of a godly heritage. When times get tough and we are unsure of what to do, God will reveal his path to us. For our part, we need to tell others about what God has given us. This will not only bring hope to other hurting people; it will also strengthen our own program for recovery.

PROVERBS

THE BIG PICTURE

Common sense—the idea sounds so folksy and simple. Oddly enough, however, we seem to have less and less of it. Perhaps it's because we are too busy or distant to learn from our parents and grandparents. Just as common sense is rare, godly wisdom is also a quality hard to find. The book of Proverbs can be a helpful resource to fill the void left by the lack of wisdom and common sense in society today. By reading and heeding the wise words of Proverbs, we can avoid many common destructive mistakes that come so naturally from our ignorance, denial, and pride.

Although he made numerous costly mistakes, Solomon was the wisest person who ever lived. Because Solomon valued wisdom so highly, he collected many wise proverbs and compiled them into a guidebook of insight and counsel. Solomon was by no means the only wise man of his day. Agur and Lemuel, also known for their wisdom, are credited with the book's final chapters.

Solomon was particularly aware of the need for young people to develop proper priorities, boundaries, and behavior patterns. But young people were not Solomon's only concern. His collection of wisdom is invaluable to people of all ages and occupations. King Hezekiah later found the collection so important that he assigned his men to edit an installment of Solomon's proverbs (see 25:1), speaking to issues such as honesty, limits, and healthy relationships.

As dysfunctional thinking and relationships become more prevalent in society, the godly wisdom offered by Proverbs is desperately needed. Its precious nuggets of life-changing counsel are there for us to discover and use. All of us, no matter how great our failures or hurts, can proceed far down the path of healing by following the God-given wisdom of Proverbs.

THE BOTTOM LINE

PURPOSE: To offer God-given wisdom for protection against dysfunctional behaviors and ungodly practices. AUTHOR: Solomon collected or wrote most of the book; Agur and Lemuel were responsible for the final chapters. AUDIENCE: The people of Israel. DATE WRITTEN: Much of the book was compiled during Solomon's reign (970–930 B.C.); it probably took its final form during Hezekiah's reign (715–686 B.C.). SETTING: This is a book of wise sayings related to the priorities and problems of everyday life. KEY VERSE: "Fear of the LORD is the foundation of true knowledge, but fools despise wisdom and discipline" (1:7). KEY PEOPLE AND RELATIONSHIPS: Parents and children, husbands and wives, leaders and citizens, people and God, with warnings against unhealthy and sinful relationships.

RECOVERY THEMES

The Importance of Common Sense: Any good recovery program is filled with common sense and wisdom. If our addictive behavior has roots in our early life, we may have missed the opportunity of learning both common sense and wisdom. In recovery we seek to learn what we have missed; the book of Proverbs is a primary source. In contrast to a person with common sense is the fool, who is portrayed as a stubborn, willful person who either hates or ignores God. Our own path of recovery should be paved with the common sense found in Proverbs.

The Power of Priorities: We all have priorities, whether we're aware of them or not. So it's never a question of having priorities but rather of straightening them out. A big part of the recovery process involves sorting out our priorities, turning them over to God, and getting them to line up with his will. As our priorities become reflections of God's will, we will progress in recovery and avoid destructive relapses. The book of Proverbs contains wisdom and practical advice that reflect God's desires for us. If we follow this advice, we will discover a significant part of God's will for our life.

The Role of Boundaries: A big part of setting personal boundaries in our life is knowing how and when to say no. Solomon recorded for us a large number of situations where saying no is the wisest option—family situations, sexual situations, monetary situations, business situations, and social situations. As we take these proverbs and make them a part of us, we will develop clearer boundaries and have a better sense of when we should say no.

Building Healthy Relationships: The recovery process will only be as successful as the health of our relationships. We may have the best of intentions, but if we are surrounded with unhealthy relationships, we are headed nowhere. The book of Proverbs gives us sound advice for building healthy relationships with friends, family, and coworkers. We are called to be consistent and tactful and to use self-discipline. If we hope to build the kind of relationships that will help us love and follow God, high moral standards are essential, for us and for those close to us.

CHAPTER 1
The Purpose of Proverbs

These are the proverbs of Solomon, David's son, king of Israel.

² Their purpose is to teach people wisdom and discipline,
   to help them understand the insights of the wise.
³ Their purpose is to teach people to live disciplined and successful lives,
   to help them do what is right, just, and fair.
⁴ These proverbs will give insight to the simple,
   knowledge and discernment to the young.

⁵ Let the wise listen to these proverbs and become even wiser.
   Let those with understanding receive guidance
⁶ by exploring the meaning in these proverbs and parables,
   the words of the wise and their riddles.

⁷ Fear of the LORD is the foundation of true knowledge,
   but fools despise wisdom and discipline.

A Father's Exhortation: Acquire Wisdom

⁸ My child,* listen when your father corrects you.
   Don't neglect your mother's instruction.

1:8 Hebrew *My son;* also in 1:10, 15.

1:2-9 The purpose for writing down these proverbs was to teach people foundational principles in wisdom, discipline, and good conduct and in doing what is right, just, and fair. The first step to attaining this kind of wisdom is the hardest: trusting and showing reverence ("fear") for God. This means admitting that we need help and then allowing God to guide and care for us (see 3:5; 9:10; 14:26-27; 15:16, 33; 19:23).

1:20-23 Wisdom is personified here, calling out to all who would choose to follow her. There is no real secret to obtaining wisdom; all we have to do is ask for it. "If you need wisdom, ask our generous God, and he will give it to you. He will not rebuke you for asking" (James 1:5). Unlike experience, which we never get until *after* we need it, God's wisdom is available to us as soon as we are willing to listen to him and obey his plan for our life.

GOD grant me the serenity
to accept the things I cannot change
the courage to change the things I can
and the wisdom to know the difference

AMEN

In recovery we come to realize that we are influenced by the people close to us. We welcome the support of those who are farther along the road to recovery. We may rely heavily on the encouragement of our sponsor or others who are supportive of our new way of life.

We will also come to see the negative influence of associating with people who are still living the kind of life from which we are trying to escape. Part of our self-inventory may include considering those with whom we choose to spend our time and how these decisions contribute to our progress in recovery. In Proverbs we are told that "wisdom will enter your heart, and knowledge will fill you with joy. Wise choices will watch over you. Understanding will keep you safe. Wisdom will save you from evil people, from those whose words are twisted. These men turn from the right way to walk down dark and evil paths. They take pleasure in doing wrong, and they enjoy the twisted ways of evil" (Proverbs 2:10-14). We are encouraged to "follow the steps of good men instead, and stay on the paths of the righteous. For only the godly will live in the land, and those who have integrity will remain in it. But the wicked will be removed from the land, and the treacherous will be uprooted" (Proverbs 2:20-22).

Are we exercising wisdom by following the steps of those who are living the kind of life we truly desire? If we do this, we will find our life filled with joy. We will also be spared the loss and destruction that await those who continue down darkened pathways and do not enter into recovery. *Turn to page 789, Proverbs 3.*

---

9 What you learn from them will crown you
     with grace
   and be a chain of honor around your
     neck.

10 My child, if sinners entice you,
     turn your back on them!
11 They may say, "Come and join us.
     Let's hide and kill someone!
     Just for fun, let's ambush the innocent!
12 Let's swallow them alive, like the grave*;
     let's swallow them whole, like those
       who go down to the pit of death.
13 Think of the great things we'll get!
     We'll fill our houses with all the stuff
       we take.
14 Come, throw in your lot with us;
     we'll all share the loot."

15 My child, don't go along with them!
     Stay far away from their paths.

1:12 Hebrew *like Sheol.*

16 They rush to commit evil deeds.
     They hurry to commit murder.
17 If a bird sees a trap being set,
     it knows to stay away.
18 But these people set an ambush for
       themselves;
     they are trying to get themselves killed.
19 Such is the fate of all who are greedy for
       money;
     it robs them of life.

Wisdom Shouts in the Streets
20 Wisdom shouts in the streets.
     She cries out in the public square.
21 She calls to the crowds along the main
       street,
     to those gathered in front of the city
       gate:
22 "How long, you simpletons,
     will you insist on being simpleminded?

How long will you mockers relish your
mocking?
How long will you fools hate
knowledge?
²³ Come and listen to my counsel.
I'll share my heart with you
and make you wise.

²⁴ "I called you so often, but you wouldn't
come.
I reached out to you, but you paid no
attention.
²⁵ You ignored my advice
and rejected the correction I offered.
²⁶ So I will laugh when you are in
trouble!
I will mock you when disaster overtakes
you—
²⁷ when calamity overtakes you like a storm,
when disaster engulfs you like a
cyclone,
and anguish and distress overwhelm you.

²⁸ "When they cry for help, I will not
answer.
Though they anxiously search for me,
they will not find me.
²⁹ For they hated knowledge
and chose not to fear the LORD.
³⁰ They rejected my advice
and paid no attention when I corrected
them.
³¹ Therefore, they must eat the bitter fruit of
living their own way,
choking on their own schemes.
³² For simpletons turn away from me—to
death.
Fools are destroyed by their own
complacency.
³³ But all who listen to me will live in peace,
untroubled by fear
of harm."

2:1 Hebrew *My son.*

CHAPTER 2
The Benefits of Wisdom
¹ My child,* listen to what I say,
and treasure my commands.
² Tune your ears to wisdom,
and concentrate on understanding.
³ Cry out for insight,
and ask for understanding.
⁴ Search for them as you would for
silver;
seek them like hidden treasures.
⁵ Then you will understand what it means
to fear the LORD,
and you will gain knowledge of God.
⁶ For the LORD grants wisdom!
From his mouth come knowledge and
understanding.
⁷ He grants a treasure of common sense to
the honest.
He is a shield to those who walk with
integrity.
⁸ He guards the paths of the just
and protects those who are faithful
to him.

⁹ Then you will understand what is right,
just, and fair,
and you will find the right way to go.
¹⁰ For wisdom will enter your heart,
and knowledge will fill you with joy.
¹¹ Wise choices will watch over you.
Understanding will keep you safe.

¹² Wisdom will save you from evil people,
from those whose words are twisted.
¹³ These men turn from the right way
to walk down dark paths.
¹⁴ They take pleasure in doing wrong,
and they enjoy the twisted ways
of evil.
¹⁵ Their actions are crooked,
and their ways are wrong.

2:1-9 Wisdom is like a hidden treasure that is found only by those who search for it. God will
grant us wisdom and good sense. He will also protect us and instruct us on how to make good
decisions. We may not have made great decisions in the past, and now we may be suffering the
consequences of those decisions. But when we put our trust in God, he will guide us in the decisions we should make in order to experience a full recovery.
2:20-22 While we may try to do good, our dependencies are utterly evil. We know what our
addictions have cost us: our jobs, friends, families, health, sanity. Now we want to change our life
patterns to escape our enslavement. God tells us here that if we get on the right track, we can still
enjoy life to the fullest. We may be tempted at times to stray from the path of recovery, but here
we are reminded that our addictions will eventually lead to destruction. Recovery is the only real
option we have.
3:5-6 What a promise! God will guide us on the right pathway of life if we put our trust in him
rather than try to do it on our own. Putting God first means turning our life and will over to him.
Surrendering to his leadership is humbling, but it is the only way for us to lead a good life.

GOD grant me the serenity
to accept the things I cannot change
the courage to change the things I can
and the wisdom to know the difference

AMEN

Unfortunately, the things we turned to could not satisfy our deepest needs or desires. Our needs are legitimate. What must be changed is the tendency to go the wrong way to try to meet those needs. The Bible says, "My child, don't lose sight of common sense and discernment. Hang on to them, for they will refresh your soul. They are like jewels on a necklace. They keep you safe on your way, and your feet will not stumble" (Proverbs 3:21-23).

None of us set out to become addicted to something. We were seeking something else—escape from pain, perhaps, or something to make up for our losses and brokenness—or maybe we had a subconscious desire for self-destruction.

Godly wisdom leads to great benefits in life. As we seek wisdom, we will find the other things we desire. "Joyful is the person who finds wisdom, the one who gains understanding. For wisdom is more profitable than silver, and her wages are better than gold. Wisdom is more precious than rubies; nothing you desire can compare with her. She offers you long life in her right hand, and riches and honor in her left. She will guide you down delightful paths; all her ways are satisfying" (Proverbs 3:13-17). As we change our focus and begin to seek after wisdom, we will find our life more fulfilled and secure. Godly wisdom will also help us avoid the destructive paths we have previously taken as we tried to fulfill our unmet needs and desires. *Turn to page 791, Proverbs 4.*

---

16 Wisdom will save you from the immoral woman,
　　from the seductive words of the promiscuous woman.
17 She has abandoned her husband
　　and ignores the covenant she made before God.
18 Entering her house leads to death;
　　it is the road to the grave.*
19 The man who visits her is doomed.
　　He will never reach the paths of life.
20 Follow the steps of good men instead,
　　and stay on the paths of the righteous.
21 For only the godly will live in the land,
　　and those with integrity will remain in it.
22 But the wicked will be removed from the land,
　　and the treacherous will be uprooted.

CHAPTER 3
Trusting in the LORD
1 My child,* never forget the things I have taught you.
　　Store my commands in your heart.
2 If you do this, you will live many years,
　　and your life will be satisfying.
3 Never let loyalty and kindness leave you!
　　Tie them around your neck as a reminder.
　　Write them deep within your heart.
4 Then you will find favor with both God and people,
　　and you will earn a good reputation.
5 Trust in the LORD with all your heart;
　　do not depend on your own understanding.
6 Seek his will in all you do,
　　and he will show you which path to take.

2:18 Hebrew *to the spirits of the dead.*　3:1 Hebrew *My son;* also in 3:11, 21.

7 Don't be impressed with your own wisdom.
  Instead, fear the LORD and turn away
  from evil.
8 Then you will have healing for your body
  and strength for your bones.

9 Honor the LORD with your wealth
  and with the best part of everything
  you produce.
10 Then he will fill your barns with grain,
  and your vats will overflow with good
  wine.

11 My child, don't reject the LORD's
  discipline,
  and don't be upset when he corrects you.
12 For the LORD corrects those he loves,
  just as a father corrects a child in whom
  he delights.*

13 Joyful is the person who finds wisdom,
  the one who gains understanding.
14 For wisdom is more profitable than silver,
  and her wages are better than gold.
15 Wisdom is more precious than rubies;
  nothing you desire can compare with her.
16 She offers you long life in her right hand,
  and riches and honor in her left.
17 She will guide you down delightful paths;
  all her ways are satisfying.
18 Wisdom is a tree of life to those who
  embrace her;
  happy are those who hold her tightly.

19 By wisdom the LORD founded the earth;
  by understanding he created the
  heavens.
20 By his knowledge the deep fountains of
  the earth burst forth,
  and the dew settles beneath the night
  sky.

21 My child, don't lose sight of common
  sense and discernment.
  Hang on to them,

22 for they will refresh your soul.
  They are like jewels on a necklace.
23 They keep you safe on your way,
  and your feet will not stumble.
24 You can go to bed without fear;
  you will lie down and sleep soundly.
25 You need not be afraid of sudden disaster
  or the destruction that comes upon the
  wicked,
26 for the LORD is your security.
  He will keep your foot from being
  caught in a trap.

27 Do not withhold good from those who
  deserve it
  when it's in your power to help them.
28 If you can help your neighbor now, don't
  say,
  "Come back tomorrow, and then I'll
  help you."

29 Don't plot harm against your neighbor,
  for those who live nearby trust you.
30 Don't pick a fight without reason,
  when no one has done you harm.
31 Don't envy violent people
  or copy their ways.
32 Such wicked people are detestable to the
  LORD,
  but he offers his friendship to the godly.
33 The LORD curses the house of the wicked,
  but he blesses the home of the upright.
34 The LORD mocks the mockers
  but is gracious to the humble.*
35 The wise inherit honor,
  but fools are put to shame!

CHAPTER 4
A Father's Wise Advice
1 My children,* listen when your father
  corrects you.

3:12 Greek version reads *loves, / and he punishes those he accepts as his children.* Compare Heb 12:6. 3:34 Greek version reads *The LORD opposes the proud / but gives grace to the humble.* Compare Jas 4:6; 1 Pet 5:5. 4:1 Hebrew *My sons.*

3:11-12 When God disciplines us, he is not doing so because he hates us or likes to see us suffer. He is correcting us because he loves us and doesn't want us to go any farther into our sin. Those of us who have had abusive parents may not be able to easily grasp the concept of a loving, nurturing God, because the parental figures we have known were anything but loving. To help us see the true nature of God, we need to look to the Gospels and examine the love Jesus had for others. When we understand that Jesus and God are one and the same, we can more readily understand that God loves us and has our best interests in mind as he disciplines us.
4:11-19 We are all influenced by our environment. We become like our friends. That is why we are warned here to stay away from those who do evil deeds. It is easy to become desensitized to sin. If we spend too much time with people who have few moral boundaries, we will begin to think and act as they do. Slipping back into our dependency will be a very natural thing. However, by spending time with godly people, we will find the encouragement we need to continue in recovery and enjoy the life God intended for us.

GOD grant me the serenity to accept the things I cannot change the courage to change the things I can and the wisdom to know the difference AMEN

Many of us grew up in a dysfunctional family. Our parents scarcely seemed to care about us at all, let alone provide wise guidance for us. This deprivation can leave us wondering how we can fill the void in our life.

Some people grew up in a family where they received wise advice and where wisdom was modeled and taught by their parents. But if we haven't, we may feel like the rest of the human race has passed us by. Some of us feel anger, resentment, and shame because we had little guidance and never learned how to make wise choices. We may ask ourselves, Shouldn't someone have shown me the way? Ideally, all of us should have had wise and godly instruction. The book of Proverbs records a father's godly instruction to his son: "For I, too, was once my father's son, tenderly loved as my mother's only child. My father taught me, 'Take my words to heart. Get wisdom; develop good judgment. Don't forget my words or turn away from them. Don't turn your back on wisdom, for she will protect you. Love her, and she will guard you'" (Proverbs 4:3-6).

For those of us who were neglected and given little or no guidance by our parents, it's not too late. We have a Father in heaven who is eager to give us the wisdom we need. James advised: "If you need wisdom, ask our generous God, and he will give it to you" (James 1:5). Our heavenly Father loves us tenderly, as a parent should. He is always there for us, waiting to give us the wisdom we need whenever we ask for it. *Turn to page 1137, Jonah 4.*

Pay attention and learn good judgment,
²for I am giving you good guidance.
Don't turn away from my instructions.
³For I, too, was once my father's son,
tenderly loved as my mother's only child.

⁴My father taught me,
"Take my words to heart.
Follow my commands, and you will live.
⁵Get wisdom; develop good judgment.
Don't forget my words or turn away from them.
⁶Don't turn your back on wisdom, for she will protect you.
Love her, and she will guard you.
⁷Getting wisdom is the wisest thing you can do!

And whatever else you do, develop good judgment.
⁸If you prize wisdom, she will make you great.
Embrace her, and she will honor you.
⁹She will place a lovely wreath on your head;
she will present you with a beautiful crown."

¹⁰My child,* listen to me and do as I say,
and you will have a long, good life.
¹¹I will teach you wisdom's ways
and lead you in straight paths.
¹²When you walk, you won't be held back;
when you run, you won't stumble.
¹³Take hold of my instructions; don't let them go.
Guard them, for they are the key to life.

4:10 Hebrew *My son;* also in 4:20.

¹⁴ Don't do as the wicked do,
and don't follow the path of evildoers.
¹⁵ Don't even think about it; don't go that
way.
Turn away and keep moving.
¹⁶ For evil people can't sleep until they've
done their evil deed for the day.
They can't rest until they've caused
someone to stumble.
¹⁷ They eat the food of wickedness
and drink the wine of violence!

¹⁸ The way of the righteous is like the first
gleam of dawn,
which shines ever brighter until the full
light of day.
¹⁹ But the way of the wicked is like total
darkness.
They have no idea what they are
stumbling over.

²⁰ My child, pay attention to what I say.
Listen carefully to my words.
²¹ Don't lose sight of them.
Let them penetrate deep into your heart,
²² for they bring life to those who find them,
and healing to their whole body.

²³ Guard your heart above all else,
for it determines the course of your life.

²⁴ Avoid all perverse talk;
stay away from corrupt speech.

²⁵ Look straight ahead,
and fix your eyes on what lies before
you.
²⁶ Mark out a straight path for your feet;
stay on the safe path.
²⁷ Don't get sidetracked;
keep your feet from following evil.

CHAPTER 5
Avoid Immoral Women

¹ My son, pay attention to my wisdom;
listen carefully to my wise counsel.

² Then you will show discernment,
and your lips will express what you've
learned.
³ For the lips of an immoral woman are as
sweet as honey,
and her mouth is smoother than oil.
⁴ But in the end she is as bitter as poison,
as dangerous as a double-edged sword.
⁵ Her feet go down to death;
her steps lead straight to the grave.*
⁶ For she cares nothing about the path to
life.
She staggers down a crooked trail and
doesn't realize it.

⁷ So now, my sons, listen to me.
Never stray from what I am about to
say:
⁸ Stay away from her!
Don't go near the door of her house!
⁹ If you do, you will lose your honor
and will lose to merciless people all you
have achieved.
¹⁰ Strangers will consume your wealth,
and someone else will enjoy the fruit of
your labor.
¹¹ In the end you will groan in anguish
when disease consumes your body.
¹² You will say, "How I hated discipline!
If only I had not ignored all the
warnings!
¹³ Oh, why didn't I listen to my teachers?
Why didn't I pay attention to my
instructors?
¹⁴ I have come to the brink of utter ruin,
and now I must face public disgrace."

¹⁵ Drink water from your own well—
share your love only with your wife.*
¹⁶ Why spill the water of your springs in the
streets,
having sex with just anyone?*
¹⁷ You should reserve it for yourselves.
Never share it with strangers.

5:5 Hebrew *to Sheol.* 5:15 Hebrew *Drink water from your own cistern, / flowing water from your own well.* 5:16 Hebrew
Why spill your springs in the streets, / your streams in the city squares?

4:23-27 The warning to guard our heart is also a warning to not give in to the temptation of
sinful pleasures of any kind. Indulging in sin is pleasurable at first, but in the end its promise is
empty and bitter. Sin may satisfy short-term desires, but its consequences are long term. Returning to our addiction may make us feel better for the moment, but it will damage (maybe even
undo) our progress in the recovery process.
5:1-23 Sexual temptation is often very hard to resist, even if we are aware of the dangers and
consequences of promiscuous sex. Sex outside of marriage is against God's law, whether we are
married or not. Throughout the book of Proverbs there are warnings against promiscuity (see
2:16-19; 6:25-35; 7:6-27; 22:14; 23:27-28). Unfaithfulness can destroy family life and physical
health, and it may result in pregnancy. If sex is among our addictions, we must *run* from any situations where we might be tempted to sin. We should also seek help from a support group or a
counselor.

¹⁸ Let your wife be a fountain of blessing for
you.
Rejoice in the wife of your youth.
¹⁹ She is a loving deer, a graceful doe.
Let her breasts satisfy you always.
May you always be captivated by her
love.
²⁰ Why be captivated, my son, by an
immoral woman,
or fondle the breasts of a promiscuous
woman?
²¹ For the LORD sees clearly what a man
does,
examining every path he takes.
²² An evil man is held captive by his own
sins;
they are ropes that catch and hold
him.
²³ He will die for lack of self-control;
he will be lost because of his great
foolishness.

CHAPTER 6
Lessons for Daily Life
¹ My child,* if you have put up security for
a friend's debt
or agreed to guarantee the debt of a
stranger—
² if you have trapped yourself by your
agreement
and are caught by what you said—
³ follow my advice and save yourself,
for you have placed yourself at your
friend's mercy.
Now swallow your pride;
go and beg to have your name erased.
⁴ Don't put it off; do it now!
Don't rest until you do.
⁵ Save yourself like a gazelle escaping
from a hunter,
like a bird fleeing from a net.

⁶ Take a lesson from the ants, you
lazybones.
Learn from their ways and become
wise!

6:1 Hebrew *My son.*

⁷ Though they have no prince
or governor or ruler to make them
work,
⁸ they labor hard all summer,
gathering food for the winter.
⁹ But you, lazybones, how long will you
sleep?
When will you wake up?
¹⁰ A little extra sleep, a little more slumber,
a little folding of the hands to rest—
¹¹ then poverty will pounce on you like a
bandit;
scarcity will attack you like an armed
robber.

¹² What are worthless and wicked people
like?
They are constant liars,
¹³ signaling their deceit with a wink of the
eye,
a nudge of the foot, or the wiggle of
fingers.
¹⁴ Their perverted hearts plot evil,
and they constantly stir up trouble.
¹⁵ But they will be destroyed suddenly,
broken in an instant beyond all hope of
healing.

¹⁶ There are six things the LORD hates—
no, seven things he detests:
¹⁷ haughty eyes,
a lying tongue,
hands that kill the innocent,
¹⁸ a heart that plots evil,
feet that race to do wrong,
¹⁹ a false witness who pours out lies,
a person who sows discord in a family.

²⁰ My son, obey your father's commands,
and don't neglect your mother's
instruction.
²¹ Keep their words always in your heart.
Tie them around your neck.
²² When you walk, their counsel will lead
you.
When you sleep, they will protect you.
When you wake up, they will advise
you.

6:16-19 The seven things God hates are things that stand against recovery. They violate our
well-being. Haughtiness is being too proud to begin recovery by admitting we need God's help
(Step One). Lying is failing to take inventory of our life and admit our wrongs (Steps Four and
Five). Plotting evil is going in the opposite direction of those who repent of their sins and ask God
to cleanse their heart (Steps Six and Seven). Murder is the opposite of asking forgiveness and
making amends (Steps Eight and Nine). Racing to do wrong is the opposite of being eager to do
right by seeking to know God and do his will (Step Eleven). Bearing false witness and sowing
discord among brothers are contrary to carrying the true message of peace to those who are hurting (Step Twelve).

²³ For their command is a lamp
and their instruction a light;
their corrective discipline
is the way to life.
²⁴ It will keep you from the immoral woman,
from the smooth tongue of a
promiscuous woman.
²⁵ Don't lust for her beauty.
Don't let her coy glances seduce you.
²⁶ For a prostitute will bring you to poverty,*
but sleeping with another man's wife
will cost you your life.
²⁷ Can a man scoop a flame into his lap
and not have his clothes catch on fire?
²⁸ Can he walk on hot coals
and not blister his feet?
²⁹ So it is with the man who sleeps with
another man's wife.
He who embraces her will not go
unpunished.

³⁰ Excuses might be found for a thief
who steals because he is starving.
³¹ But if he is caught, he must pay back
seven times what he stole,
even if he has to sell everything in his
house.
³² But the man who commits adultery is an
utter fool,
for he destroys himself.
³³ He will be wounded and disgraced.
His shame will never be erased.
³⁴ For the woman's jealous husband will be
furious,
and he will show no mercy when he
takes revenge.
³⁵ He will accept no compensation,
nor be satisfied with a payoff of any
size.

CHAPTER 7
Another Warning about Immoral Women

¹ Follow my advice, my son;
always treasure my commands.
² Obey my commands and live!
Guard my instructions as you guard
your own eyes.*
³ Tie them on your fingers as a reminder.
Write them deep within your heart.

⁴ Love wisdom like a sister;
make insight a beloved member of your
family.
⁵ Let them protect you from an affair with
an immoral woman,

from listening to the flattery of a
promiscuous woman.
⁶ While I was at the window of my house,
looking through the curtain,
⁷ I saw some naive young men,
and one in particular who lacked
common sense.
⁸ He was crossing the street near the house
of an immoral woman,
strolling down the path by her house.
⁹ It was at twilight, in the evening,
as deep darkness fell.
¹⁰ The woman approached him,
seductively dressed and sly of heart.
¹¹ She was the brash, rebellious type,
never content to stay at home.
¹² She is often in the streets and markets,
soliciting at every corner.
¹³ She threw her arms around him and
kissed him,
and with a brazen look she said,
¹⁴ "I've just made my peace offerings
and fulfilled my vows.
¹⁵ You're the one I was looking for!
I came out to find you, and here you
are!
¹⁶ My bed is spread with beautiful blankets,
with colored sheets of Egyptian linen.
¹⁷ I've perfumed my bed
with myrrh, aloes, and cinnamon.
¹⁸ Come, let's drink our fill of love until
morning.
Let's enjoy each other's caresses,
¹⁹ for my husband is not home.
He's away on a long trip.
²⁰ He has taken a wallet full of money with
him
and won't return until later this
month.*"
²¹ So she seduced him with her pretty
speech
and enticed him with her flattery.
²² He followed her at once,
like an ox going to the slaughter.
He was like a stag caught in a trap,*
²³   awaiting the arrow that would pierce its
heart.
He was like a bird flying into a snare,
little knowing it would cost him his life.

²⁴ So listen to me, my sons,
and pay attention to my words.
²⁵ Don't let your hearts stray away toward
her.
Don't wander down her wayward path.

6:26 Hebrew *to a loaf of bread.* 7:2 Hebrew *as the pupil of your eye.* 7:20 Hebrew *until the moon is full.* 7:22 As in Greek and Syriac versions; Hebrew reads *slaughter, as shackles are for the discipline of a fool.*

²⁶ For she has been the ruin of many;
   many men have been her victims.
²⁷ Her house is the road to the grave.*
   Her bedroom is the den of death.

CHAPTER 8
Wisdom Calls for a Hearing
¹ Listen as Wisdom calls out!
   Hear as understanding raises her voice!
² On the hilltop along the road,
   she takes her stand at the crossroads.
³ By the gates at the entrance to the town,
   on the road leading in, she cries aloud,
⁴ "I call to you, to all of you!
   I raise my voice to all people.
⁵ You simple people, use good judgment.
   You foolish people, show some
   understanding.
⁶ Listen to me! For I have important things
   to tell you.
   Everything I say is right,
⁷ for I speak the truth
   and detest every kind of deception.
⁸ My advice is wholesome.
   There is nothing devious or crooked
   in it.
⁹ My words are plain to anyone with
   understanding,
   clear to those with knowledge.
¹⁰ Choose my instruction rather than silver,
   and knowledge rather than pure gold.
¹¹ For wisdom is far more valuable than
   rubies.
   Nothing you desire can compare
   with it.
¹² "I, Wisdom, live together with good
   judgment.
   I know where to discover knowledge
   and discernment.
¹³ All who fear the LORD will hate evil.
   Therefore, I hate pride and arrogance,
   corruption and perverse speech.
¹⁴ Common sense and success belong to me.
   Insight and strength are mine.
¹⁵ Because of me, kings reign,
   and rulers make just decrees.
¹⁶ Rulers lead with my help,
   and nobles make righteous judgments.*

¹⁷ "I love all who love me.
   Those who search will surely find me.
¹⁸ I have riches and honor,
   as well as enduring wealth and justice.
¹⁹ My gifts are better than gold, even the
   purest gold,
   my wages better than sterling silver!
²⁰ I walk in righteousness,
   in paths of justice.
²¹ Those who love me inherit wealth.
   I will fill their treasuries.

²² "The LORD formed me from the beginning,
   before he created anything else.
²³ I was appointed in ages past,
   at the very first, before the earth began.
²⁴ I was born before the oceans were created,
   before the springs bubbled forth their
   waters.
²⁵ Before the mountains were formed,
   before the hills, I was born—
²⁶ before he had made the earth and fields
   and the first handfuls of soil.
²⁷ I was there when he established the
   heavens,
   when he drew the horizon on the oceans.
²⁸ I was there when he set the clouds above,
   when he established springs deep in the
   earth.
²⁹ I was there when he set the limits
   of the seas,
   so they would not spread beyond their
   boundaries.
   And when he marked off the earth's
   foundations,
³⁰   I was the architect at his side.
   I was his constant delight,
   rejoicing always in his presence.
³¹ And how happy I was with the world he
   created;
   how I rejoiced with the human family!

³² "And so, my children,* listen to me,
   for all who follow my ways are joyful.
³³ Listen to my instruction and be wise.
   Don't ignore it.
³⁴ Joyful are those who listen to me,
   watching for me daily at my gates,
   waiting for me outside my home!

7:27 Hebrew *to Sheol*. 8:16 Some Hebrew manuscripts and Greek version read *and nobles are judges over the earth*.
8:32 Hebrew *my sons*.

8:22-36 Solomon portrayed wisdom as a personal being who existed with God before the earth
was created and who was the "architect" for Creation. This may be an allusion to Jesus the
Messiah, who, according to the book of John, was the Word that not only "already existed . . . in
the beginning with God," but "was God," and "created everything" (John 1:1-3). Colossians 1:16
says that "Through [Christ] God created everything in the heavenly realms and on earth." Those
who in faith listen to Christ and follow his wisdom will find eternal life and favor with God (see
John 5:24). Following Christ's instructions for our life is our only means of recovery.

³⁵ For whoever finds me finds life
  and receives favor from the LORD.
³⁶ But those who miss me injure themselves.
  All who hate me love death."

CHAPTER 9

¹ Wisdom has built her house;
  she has carved its seven columns.
² She has prepared a great banquet,
  mixed the wines, and set the table.
³ She has sent her servants to invite
  everyone to come.
  She calls out from the heights
  overlooking the city.
⁴ "Come in with me," she urges the simple.
  To those who lack good judgment,
  she says,
⁵ "Come, eat my food,
  and drink the wine I have mixed.
⁶ Leave your simple ways behind, and begin
  to live;
  learn to use good judgment."

⁷ Anyone who rebukes a mocker will get an
  insult in return.
  Anyone who corrects the wicked will
  get hurt.
⁸ So don't bother correcting mockers;
  they will only hate you.
  But correct the wise,
  and they will love you.
⁹ Instruct the wise,
  and they will be even wiser.
  Teach the righteous,
  and they will learn even more.

¹⁰ Fear of the LORD is the foundation of
  wisdom.
  Knowledge of the Holy One results in
  good judgment.
¹¹ Wisdom will multiply your days
  and add years to your life.
¹² If you become wise, you will be the one to
  benefit.
  If you scorn wisdom, you will be the
  one to suffer.

9:18 Hebrew *in Sheol.* 10:1 Hebrew *son;* also in 10:1b.

Folly Calls for a Hearing

¹³ The woman named Folly is brash.
  She is ignorant and doesn't know it.
¹⁴ She sits in her doorway
  on the heights overlooking the city.
¹⁵ She calls out to men going by
  who are minding their own business.
¹⁶ "Come in with me," she urges the simple.
  To those who lack good judgment, she
  says,
¹⁷ "Stolen water is refreshing;
  food eaten in secret tastes the best!"
¹⁸ But little do they know that the dead are
  there.
  Her guests are in the depths of the
  grave.*

CHAPTER 10
The Proverbs of Solomon
The proverbs of Solomon:

A wise child* brings joy to a father;
  a foolish child brings grief to a mother.

² Tainted wealth has no lasting value,
  but right living can save your life.

³ The LORD will not let the godly go hungry,
  but he refuses to satisfy the craving of
  the wicked.

⁴ Lazy people are soon poor;
  hard workers get rich.

⁵ A wise youth harvests in the summer,
  but one who sleeps during harvest is a
  disgrace.

⁶ The godly are showered with blessings;
  the words of the wicked conceal violent
  intentions.

⁷ We have happy memories of the godly,
  but the name of a wicked person rots
  away.

⁸ The wise are glad to be instructed,
  but babbling fools fall flat on their
  faces.

9:7-8 When someone tries to help us and correct us, we have two choices. We can either listen and learn as the wise person does, or we can get angry and rebel as the mocker does. To mock and hate those who are concerned for us is to deny that we have a problem. If we are wise, we will be honest enough to admit that we have a problem and we need help. This attitude enables recovery. Mockers will reject good advice and be overtaken by their sins.
10:6 In this and many of the proverbs Solomon contrasts good and evil people by the way they live and the consequences they suffer. This basic principle is repeated often: Moral living is good for us. One key to doing what is right is having an accurate self-concept. As we begin to see ourself as God sees us, we see that we are loved and valued, and we will want to apply the principles of wisdom to our life.

⁹ People with integrity walk safely,
but those who follow crooked paths
will be exposed.

¹⁰ People who wink at wrong cause trouble,
but a bold reproof promotes peace.*

¹¹ The words of the godly are a life-giving
fountain;
the words of the wicked conceal violent
intentions.

¹² Hatred stirs up quarrels,
but love makes up for all offenses.

¹³ Wise words come from the lips of people
with understanding,
but those lacking sense will be beaten
with a rod.

¹⁴ Wise people treasure knowledge,
but the babbling of a fool invites
disaster.

¹⁵ The wealth of the rich is their fortress;
the poverty of the poor is their
destruction.

¹⁶ The earnings of the godly enhance their
lives,
but evil people squander their money
on sin.

¹⁷ People who accept discipline are on the
pathway to life,
but those who ignore correction will go
astray.

¹⁸ Hiding hatred makes you a liar;
slandering others makes you a fool.

¹⁹ Too much talk leads to sin.
Be sensible and keep your mouth shut.

²⁰ The words of the godly are like sterling
silver;
the heart of a fool is worthless.

²¹ The words of the godly encourage many,
but fools are destroyed by their lack of
common sense.

²² The blessing of the LORD makes a person
rich,
and he adds no sorrow with it.

²³ Doing wrong is fun for a fool,
but living wisely brings pleasure to the
sensible.

²⁴ The fears of the wicked will be fulfilled;
the hopes of the godly will be granted.

²⁵ When the storms of life come, the wicked
are whirled away,
but the godly have a lasting foundation.

²⁶ Lazy people irritate their employers,
like vinegar to the teeth or smoke
in the eyes.

²⁷ Fear of the LORD lengthens one's life,
but the years of the wicked are cut
short.

²⁸ The hopes of the godly result in
happiness,
but the expectations of the wicked
come to nothing.

²⁹ The way of the LORD is a stronghold to
those with integrity,
but it destroys the wicked.

³⁰ The godly will never be disturbed,
but the wicked will be removed from
the land.

³¹ The mouth of the godly person gives wise
advice,
but the tongue that deceives will be
cut off.

³² The lips of the godly speak helpful words,
but the mouth of the wicked speaks
perverse words.

CHAPTER 11
¹ The LORD detests the use of dishonest
scales,
but he delights in accurate weights.

10:10 As in Greek version; Hebrew reads *but babbling fools fall flat on their faces.*

10:25 A building's foundation keeps it from falling in a storm or strong wind. Without a solid, lasting foundation, tall buildings wouldn't last very long. We encounter all sorts of "storms" along the road to recovery. Whether or not we can stand fast through the many storms we encounter depends on the strength of our "foundation" of faith. Our foundation—that is, our trust in God—will support and steady us so we can get through even the toughest cyclones. When we encounter difficulties, it is a real challenge to weather the storms and learn what God is teaching us through them. For people of faith, such trials are opportunities for personal growth (see James 1:2-4).

11:1-3 These verses underscore the importance of being honest. In recovery, we need to be honest—with ourself and with others. We need to honestly admit that we can't control our addiction (Step One). We need to be honest as we compile our moral inventory (Steps Four and Ten), and we need to honestly admit to God and others exactly what we have done wrong (Step Five).

[2] Pride leads to disgrace,
but with humility comes wisdom.

[3] Honesty guides good people;
dishonesty destroys treacherous people.

[4] Riches won't help on the day of judgment,
but right living can save you from death.

[5] The godly are directed by honesty;
the wicked fall beneath their load of sin.

[6] The godliness of good people rescues
them;
the ambition of treacherous people
traps them.

[7] When the wicked die, their hopes die with
them,
for they rely on their own feeble strength.

[8] The godly are rescued from trouble,
and it falls on the wicked instead.

[9] With their words, the godless destroy their
friends,
but knowledge will rescue the
righteous.

[10] The whole city celebrates when the godly
succeed;
they shout for joy when the wicked die.

[11] Upright citizens are good for a city and
make it prosper,
but the talk of the wicked tears it apart.

[12] It is foolish to belittle one's neighbor;
a sensible person keeps quiet.

[13] A gossip goes around telling secrets,
but those who are trustworthy can keep
a confidence.

[14] Without wise leadership, a nation falls;
there is safety in having many advisers.

[15] There's danger in putting up security for a
stranger's debt;
it's safer not to guarantee another
person's debt.

[16] A gracious woman gains respect,
but ruthless men gain only wealth.

[17] Your kindness will reward you,
but your cruelty will destroy you.

[18] Evil people get rich for the moment,
but the reward of the godly will last.

[19] Godly people find life;
evil people find death.

[20] The LORD detests people with crooked
hearts,
but he delights in those with integrity.

[21] Evil people will surely be punished,
but the children of the godly will go
free.

[22] A beautiful woman who lacks discretion
is like a gold ring in a pig's snout.

[23] The godly can look forward to a reward,
while the wicked can expect only
judgment.

[24] Give freely and become more wealthy;
be stingy and lose everything.

[25] The generous will prosper;
those who refresh others will
themselves be refreshed.

[26] People curse those who hoard their grain,
but they bless the one who sells in time
of need.

[27] If you search for good, you will find favor;
but if you search for evil, it will find
you!

[28] Trust in your money and down you go!
But the godly flourish like leaves in
spring.

[29] Those who bring trouble on their families
inherit the wind.
The fool will be a servant to the wise.

[30] The seeds of good deeds become a tree of
life;
a wise person wins friends.*

[31] If the righteous are rewarded here on
earth,
what will happen to wicked sinners?*

11:30 Or *and those who win souls are wise.* 11:31 Greek version reads *If the righteous are barely saved, / what will
happen to godless sinners?* Compare 1 Pet 4:18.

11:24-25 Some of us may wonder how we can be expected to give anything away. We may have
lost everything, or perhaps we just feel too empty and tired to reach out. It might be refreshing to
realize that we have a special gift to give others in recovery—encouragement. When we share our
victories, and even our failures, others will be strengthened for their battles ahead. That is what
Step Twelve is all about. As we share our message with others who are in recovery, they will gain
the insight and encouragement they need for their own success. We, in turn, will be encouraged
to stay away from our dependency because of what our recovery has come to mean to others.

CHAPTER 12

¹ To learn, you must love discipline;
it is stupid to hate correction.

² The LORD approves of those who are good,
but he condemns those who plan
wickedness.

³ Wickedness never brings stability,
but the godly have deep roots.

⁴ A worthy wife is a crown for her husband,
but a disgraceful woman is like cancer
in his bones.

⁵ The plans of the godly are just;
the advice of the wicked is treacherous.

⁶ The words of the wicked are like a
murderous ambush,
but the words of the godly save lives.

⁷ The wicked die and disappear,
but the family of the godly stands firm.

⁸ A sensible person wins admiration,
but a warped mind is despised.

⁹ Better to be an ordinary person with a
servant
than to be self-important but have no
food.

¹⁰ The godly care for their animals,
but the wicked are always cruel.

¹¹ A hard worker has plenty of food,
but a person who chases fantasies has
no sense.

¹² Thieves are jealous of each other's loot,
but the godly are well rooted and bear
their own fruit.

¹³ The wicked are trapped by their own
words,
but the godly escape such trouble.

¹⁴ Wise words bring many benefits,
and hard work brings rewards.

¹⁵ Fools think their own way is right,
but the wise listen to others.

¹⁶ A fool is quick-tempered,
but a wise person stays calm when
insulted.

¹⁷ An honest witness tells the truth;
a false witness tells lies.

¹⁸ Some people make cutting remarks,
but the words of the wise bring healing.

¹⁹ Truthful words stand the test of time,
but lies are soon exposed.

²⁰ Deceit fills hearts that are plotting evil;
joy fills hearts that are planning peace!

²¹ No harm comes to the godly,
but the wicked have their fill of trouble.

²² The LORD detests lying lips,
but he delights in those who tell the
truth.

²³ The wise don't make a show of their
knowledge,
but fools broadcast their foolishness.

²⁴ Work hard and become a leader;
be lazy and become a slave.

²⁵ Worry weighs a person down;
an encouraging word cheers a person up.

²⁶ The godly give good advice to their
friends;*
the wicked lead them astray.

²⁷ Lazy people don't even cook the game
they catch,
but the diligent make use of everything
they find.

²⁸ The way of the godly leads to life;
that path does not lead to death.

CHAPTER 13

¹ A wise child accepts a parent's discipline;*
a mocker refuses to listen to correction.

² Wise words will win you a good meal,
but treacherous people have an appetite
for violence.

12:26 Or *The godly are cautious in friendship*; or *The godly are freed from evil*. The meaning of the Hebrew is uncertain.
13:1 Hebrew *A wise son accepts his father's discipline*.

12:15 Changing patterns of behavior that led us into bondage or recovering from emotional trauma requires the help of people we trust and respect (see 12:26; 15:22; 19:20). We cannot live successfully alone. Wise people listen to good advice from others; fools do not. Growing toward spiritual and emotional maturity is a process that requires the help of trustworthy people who can guide us with care and hold us accountable as we try to make changes.
12:16 It is foolish to lose our temper when we are insulted. We demonstrate maturity by using self-control and staying calm. By doing so, we can lovingly offer needed correction to the offender, provide a chance to build intimacy in the relationship, and keep our heart free of resentment.

3 Those who control their tongue will have
    a long life;
  opening your mouth can ruin
    everything.

4 Lazy people want much but get little,
  but those who work hard will prosper.

5 The godly hate lies;
  the wicked cause shame and disgrace.

6 Godliness guards the path of the
    blameless,
  but the evil are misled by sin.

7 Some who are poor pretend to be rich;
  others who are rich pretend to be poor.

8 The rich can pay a ransom for their lives,
  but the poor won't even get threatened.

9 The life of the godly is full of light and joy,
  but the light of the wicked will be
    snuffed out.

10 Pride leads to conflict;
  those who take advice are wise.

11 Wealth from get-rich-quick schemes
    quickly disappears;
  wealth from hard work grows over time.

12 Hope deferred makes the heart sick,
  but a dream fulfilled is a tree of life.

13 People who despise advice are asking for
    trouble;
  those who respect a command will
    succeed.

14 The instruction of the wise is like a
    life-giving fountain;
  those who accept it avoid the snares of
    death.

15 A person with good sense is respected;
  a treacherous person is headed for
    destruction.*

16 Wise people think before they act;
  fools don't—and even brag about their
    foolishness.

17 An unreliable messenger stumbles into
    trouble,
  but a reliable messenger brings healing.

18 If you ignore criticism, you will end in
    poverty and disgrace;
  if you accept correction, you will be
    honored.

19 It is pleasant to see dreams come true,
  but fools refuse to turn from evil to
    attain them.

20 Walk with the wise and become wise;
  associate with fools and get in trouble.

21 Trouble chases sinners,
  while blessings reward the righteous.

22 Good people leave an inheritance to their
    grandchildren,
  but the sinner's wealth passes to the
    godly.

23 A poor person's farm may produce much
    food,
  but injustice sweeps it all away.

24 Those who spare the rod of discipline hate
    their children.
  Those who love their children care
    enough to discipline them.

25 The godly eat to their hearts' content,
  but the belly of the wicked goes hungry.

CHAPTER 14

1 A wise woman builds her home,
  but a foolish woman tears it down with
    her own hands.

2 Those who follow the right path fear the
  Lord;

13:15 As in Greek version; Hebrew reads *the way of the treacherous is lasting.*

13:6 It should not surprise us that evil deeds destroy people, and sin results in painful consequences. Drug or alcohol abuse will destroy the body; lying will ruin a person's reputation;
gambling will put one in the poorhouse. To avoid the inevitable results of sinful behavior, we need
to commit our life to the Lord, who is able to give us victory over our addictions and compulsions. Following God's way leads to happiness and gives positive direction to our life.
13:9 Leaving a destructive past to join a recovery program based on God's principles is like walking out of the darkness and into the light. Those who enter the light see their need for help and
the reality of a loving God who wants to help them. They can no longer hide their deeds in the
darkness of denial and deceit. They must honestly deal with the issues the light has exposed.
13:20 Since we become like the company we keep, it is important to have wise, godly friends we
respect. Being involved in a support group is so important to personal growth and recovery.
When we are struggling in a certain area, it's helpful to know that we are not alone and that
others share our pain. It also helps to see fellow strugglers model the qualities that will help us
overcome our obstacles—honesty, perseverance, and accountability.

those who take the wrong path despise him.

[3] A fool's proud talk becomes a rod that beats him,
but the words of the wise keep them safe.

[4] Without oxen a stable stays clean,
but you need a strong ox for a large harvest.

[5] An honest witness does not lie;
a false witness breathes lies.

[6] A mocker seeks wisdom and never finds it,
but knowledge comes easily to those with understanding.

[7] Stay away from fools,
for you won't find knowledge on their lips.

[8] The prudent understand where they are going,
but fools deceive themselves.

[9] Fools make fun of guilt,
but the godly acknowledge it and seek reconciliation.

[10] Each heart knows its own bitterness,
and no one else can fully share its joy.

[11] The house of the wicked will be destroyed,
but the tent of the godly will flourish.

[12] There is a path before each person that seems right,
but it ends in death.

[13] Laughter can conceal a heavy heart,
but when the laughter ends, the grief remains.

[14] Backsliders get what they deserve;
good people receive their reward.

[15] Only simpletons believe everything they're told!
The prudent carefully consider their steps.

[16] The wise are cautious* and avoid danger;
fools plunge ahead with reckless confidence.

[17] Short-tempered people do foolish things,
and schemers are hated.

[18] Simpletons are clothed with foolishness,*
but the prudent are crowned with knowledge.

[19] Evil people will bow before good people;
the wicked will bow at the gates of the godly.

[20] The poor are despised even by their neighbors,
while the rich have many "friends."

[21] It is a sin to belittle one's neighbor;
blessed are those who help the poor.

[22] If you plan to do evil, you will be lost;
if you plan to do good, you will receive unfailing love and faithfulness.

[23] Work brings profit,
but mere talk leads to poverty!

[24] Wealth is a crown for the wise;
the effort of fools yields only foolishness.

[25] A truthful witness saves lives,
but a false witness is a traitor.

[26] Those who fear the LORD are secure;
he will be a refuge for their children.

[27] Fear of the LORD is a life-giving fountain;
it offers escape from the snares of death.

[28] A growing population is a king's glory;
a prince without subjects has nothing.

[29] People with understanding control their anger;
a hot temper shows great foolishness.

[30] A peaceful heart leads to a healthy body;
jealousy is like cancer in the bones.

14:16 Hebrew *The wise fear.* 14:18 Or *inherit foolishness.*

14:15 Trusting God to direct us through the advice of others is an important step in recovery. Solomon, however, gave a wise note of caution here: Don't trust others blindly. A healthy trust in others is developed gradually and carefully. This can only happen as we determine when it is safe for us to be vulnerable and if the guidance we are receiving is godly. If any advice is contrary to the truth revealed in the Bible, it should be disregarded, no matter who gave it.
14:26-27 "Fear of the LORD" is integral in any twelve-step program. Steps Two, Three, Six, Seven, and Eleven all have to do directly with trusting God and drawing closer to him. God will give us strength and power that we never could have experienced if we had refused to follow his plan for us. He is our security, our strength, and our source of life. If we haven't given our life to Jesus yet, we must do it now. Any hope of recovery depends on a relationship with him.

³¹ Those who oppress the poor insult their
Maker,
but helping the poor honors him.

³² The wicked are crushed by disaster,
but the godly have a refuge when they
die.

³³ Wisdom is enshrined in an understanding
heart;
wisdom is not* found among fools.

³⁴ Godliness makes a nation great,
but sin is a disgrace to any people.

³⁵ A king rejoices in wise servants
but is angry with those who disgrace
him.

CHAPTER 15

¹ A gentle answer deflects anger,
but harsh words make tempers flare.

² The tongue of the wise makes knowledge
appealing,
but the mouth of a fool belches out
foolishness.

³ The LORD is watching everywhere,
keeping his eye on both the evil and
the good.

⁴ Gentle words are a tree of life;
a deceitful tongue crushes the spirit.

⁵ Only a fool despises a parent's* discipline;
whoever learns from correction
is wise.

⁶ There is treasure in the house of the godly,
but the earnings of the wicked bring
trouble.

⁷ The lips of the wise give good advice;
the heart of a fool has none to give.

⁸ The LORD detests the sacrifice of the
wicked,
but he delights in the prayers of the
upright.

⁹ The LORD detests the way of the wicked,
but he loves those who pursue godliness.

¹⁰ Whoever abandons the right path will be
severely disciplined;
whoever hates correction will die.

¹¹ Even Death and Destruction* hold no
secrets from the LORD.
How much more does he know the
human heart!

¹² Mockers hate to be corrected,
so they stay away from the wise.

¹³ A glad heart makes a happy face;
a broken heart crushes the spirit.

¹⁴ A wise person is hungry for knowledge,
while the fool feeds on trash.

¹⁵ For the despondent, every day brings
trouble;
for the happy heart, life is a continual
feast.

¹⁶ Better to have little, with fear for the LORD,
than to have great treasure and inner
turmoil.

¹⁷ A bowl of vegetables with someone you
love
is better than steak with someone you
hate.

14:33 As in Greek and Syriac versions; Hebrew lacks *not*. 15:5 Hebrew *father's*. 15:11 Hebrew *Sheol and Abaddon*.

15:14 We must be careful what we feed our mind. If we are "hungry for knowledge," we will not only live according to God's plan, but we will also love and study his Word, which is "more valuable . . . than millions in gold and silver" (Psalm 119:72). When our thoughts dwell on unhealthy things—things that draw us away from God—we are feeding on "trash." Filling our mind with evil thoughts, words, or images will only hinder us in the recovery process. Instead, we are commanded to "fix [our] thoughts on what is true, and honorable, and right, and pure, and lovely, and admirable. Think about things that are excellent and worthy of praise" (Philippians 4:8).
15:31-32 If we really want to learn and grow, we must be willing to be held accountable by receiving constructive criticism from others (see 13:18; 15:5; 25:12). For many of us it is hard to receive reproof because even when it is shared in love, it hurts. Our tendency may be to ignore correction to avoid the hurt or to collapse emotionally because we are devastated by a word of constructive criticism. We would be wise to ask for feedback from people we respect so we can learn from our mistakes and grow in understanding and maturity.
16:2 We are incredibly good at rationalizing our actions and motives so that others don't know why we are doing things. This is dangerous because soon we may begin to believe what we are telling others. For those of us who have a drinking problem, for instance, it is easy to deny it. We claim that we really don't need to drink or that we only drink to be social. We may even have "proved" to everyone that we don't have a problem—everyone, that is, except God. He knows all our actions, our motives, and our excuses. He is the only one who can make full recovery possible.

18 A hot-tempered person starts fights;
   a cool-tempered person stops them.

19 A lazy person's way is blocked with briers,
   but the path of the upright is an open
   highway.

20 Sensible children bring joy to their father;
   foolish children despise their mother.

21 Foolishness brings joy to those with no
   sense;
   a sensible person stays on the right
   path.

22 Plans go wrong for lack of advice;
   many advisers bring success.

23 Everyone enjoys a fitting reply;
   it is wonderful to say the right thing at
   the right time!

24 The path of life leads upward for the wise;
   they leave the grave* behind.

25 The LORD tears down the house of the
   proud,
   but he protects the property of widows.

26 The LORD detests evil plans,
   but he delights in pure words.

27 Greed brings grief to the whole family,
   but those who hate bribes will live.

28 The heart of the godly thinks carefully
   before speaking;
   the mouth of the wicked overflows with
   evil words.

29 The LORD is far from the wicked,
   but he hears the prayers of the
   righteous.

30 A cheerful look brings joy to the heart;
   good news makes for good health.

31 If you listen to constructive criticism,
   you will be at home among the wise.

32 If you reject discipline, you only harm
   yourself;
   but if you listen to correction, you grow
   in understanding.

33 Fear of the LORD teaches wisdom;
   humility precedes honor.

CHAPTER 16
1 We can make our own plans,
   but the LORD gives the right answer.

2 People may be pure in their own eyes,
   but the LORD examines their motives.

15:24 Hebrew *Sheol*.

SELF-PROTECTION

READ PROVERBS 15:16-33
In recovery we learn new ways of seeing things, new ways of responding, and new guidelines for making decisions. Our old patterns of thinking and living didn't work very well. Now that we are establishing new patterns, we will need wise counselors. They will listen as we share our struggles with them, and they will supply the support and wisdom we need.

King Solomon gave this advice: "Plans go wrong for lack of advice; many advisers bring success" (Proverbs 15:22). "There is safety in having many advisers" (Proverbs 11:14). King David looked to God's Word for counsel saying, "Your laws please me; they give me wise advice" (Psalm 119:24). Isaiah prophesied about Jesus the Messiah, saying, "For a child is born to us, a son is given to us. The government will rest on his shoulders. And he will be called: Wonderful Counselor, Mighty God, Everlasting Father, Prince of Peace" (Isaiah 9:6). God is our ultimate source of wise counsel.

When we surround ourself with dependable and wise counselors, we are developing a safety net. Good counsel can come from the Bible and from godly people. When we admit our wrongs to other people, they can become a source of counsel for us. They may be professionals who understand addiction and recovery. They may be people who know us and measure their advice by godly principles. Or perhaps they are people who have experienced what we are now going through. Find someone! But above all, trust in God as your ultimate source of wise counsel. *Turn to page 827, Ecclesiastes 3.*

³ Commit your actions to the LORD,
and your plans will succeed.

⁴ The LORD has made everything for his
own purposes,
even the wicked for a day of disaster.

⁵ The LORD detests the proud;
they will surely be punished.

⁶ Unfailing love and faithfulness make
atonement for sin.
By fearing the LORD, people avoid evil.

⁷ When people's lives please the LORD,
even their enemies are at peace with
them.

⁸ Better to have little, with godliness,
than to be rich and dishonest.

⁹ We can make our plans,
but the LORD determines our steps.

¹⁰ The king speaks with divine wisdom;
he must never judge unfairly.

¹¹ The LORD demands accurate scales and
balances;
he sets the standards for fairness.

¹² A king detests wrongdoing,
for his rule is built on justice.

¹³ The king is pleased with words from
righteous lips;
he loves those who speak honestly.

¹⁴ The anger of the king is a deadly threat;
the wise will try to appease it.

¹⁵ When the king smiles, there is life;
his favor refreshes like a spring rain.

¹⁶ How much better to get wisdom than
gold,
and good judgment than silver!

¹⁷ The path of the virtuous leads away from
evil;
whoever follows that path is safe.

16:33 Hebrew *We may cast lots.*

¹⁸ Pride goes before destruction,
and haughtiness before a fall.

¹⁹ Better to live humbly with the poor
than to share plunder with the proud.

²⁰ Those who listen to instruction will
prosper;
those who trust the LORD will be joyful.

²¹ The wise are known for their
understanding,
and pleasant words are persuasive.

²² Discretion is a life-giving fountain to
those who possess it,
but discipline is wasted on fools.

²³ From a wise mind comes wise speech;
the words of the wise are persuasive.

²⁴ Kind words are like honey—
sweet to the soul and healthy for the
body.

²⁵ There is a path before each person that
seems right,
but it ends in death.

²⁶ It is good for workers to have an appetite;
an empty stomach drives them on.

²⁷ Scoundrels create trouble;
their words are a destructive blaze.

²⁸ A troublemaker plants seeds of strife;
gossip separates the best of friends.

²⁹ Violent people mislead their companions,
leading them down a harmful path.

³⁰ With narrowed eyes, people plot evil;
with a smirk, they plan their mischief.

³¹ Gray hair is a crown of glory;
it is gained by living a godly life.

³² Better to be patient than powerful;
better to have self-control than to
conquer a city.

³³ We may throw the dice,*
but the LORD determines how they fall.

16:9 It is important that we entrust the future to God, but we also need to make plans—for our steps in recovery, for our retirement savings, for our life. Responsible trust in God means taking action to secure what we need in life, while letting God's Word and his Spirit guide us in our preparations. Saying "God will provide" and then sitting passively, waiting for God to take care of us, is often an excuse for laziness. We need to get moving and let God direct our steps in the process.

16:33 There is no such thing as luck. Everything that happens to us, even the seemingly random roll of the dice, is under the watchful eye and guiding hand of our sovereign God. It is a challenge to our faith to trust that God is truly in control and that he cares about all the details of our life. But it is encouraging to remember that "God causes everything to work together for the good of those who love God and are called according to his purpose for them" (Romans 8:28).

CHAPTER 17

¹ Better a dry crust eaten in peace
    than a house filled with feasting—and
      conflict.

² A wise servant will rule over the master's
    disgraceful son
    and will share the inheritance of the
      master's children.

³ Fire tests the purity of silver and gold,
    but the LORD tests the heart.

⁴ Wrongdoers eagerly listen to gossip;
    liars pay close attention to slander.

⁵ Those who mock the poor insult their
    Maker;
    those who rejoice at the misfortune of
      others will be punished.

⁶ Grandchildren are the crowning glory of
    the aged;
    parents* are the pride of their children.

⁷ Eloquent words are not fitting for a fool;
    even less are lies fitting for a ruler.

⁸ A bribe is like a lucky charm;
    whoever gives one will prosper!

⁹ Love prospers when a fault is forgiven,
    but dwelling on it separates close friends.

¹⁰ A single rebuke does more for a person of
    understanding
    than a hundred lashes on the back
      of a fool.

¹¹ Evil people are eager for rebellion,
    but they will be severely punished.

¹² It is safer to meet a bear robbed of her cubs
    than to confront a fool caught in
      foolishness.

¹³ If you repay good with evil,
    evil will never leave your house.

¹⁴ Starting a quarrel is like opening a
    floodgate,
    so stop before a dispute breaks out.

¹⁵ Acquitting the guilty and condemning the
    innocent—
    both are detestable to the LORD.

¹⁶ It is senseless to pay to educate
    a fool,
    since he has no heart for learning.

¹⁷ A friend is always loyal,
    and a brother is born to help in time
      of need.

¹⁸ It's poor judgment to guarantee another
    person's debt
    or put up security for a friend.

¹⁹ Anyone who loves to quarrel loves sin;
    anyone who trusts in high walls invites
      disaster.

²⁰ The crooked heart will not prosper;
    the lying tongue tumbles into
      trouble.

²¹ It is painful to be the parent of a fool;
    there is no joy for the father of
      a rebel.

²² A cheerful heart is good medicine,
    but a broken spirit saps a person's
      strength.

²³ The wicked take secret bribes
    to pervert the course of justice.

²⁴ Sensible people keep their eyes glued on
    wisdom,
    but a fool's eyes wander to the ends of
      the earth.

²⁵ Foolish children* bring grief to their
    father
    and bitterness to the one who gave
      them birth.

²⁶ It is wrong to punish the godly for being
    good
    or to flog leaders for being honest.

²⁷ A truly wise person uses few words;
    a person with understanding is
      even-tempered.

17:6 Hebrew *fathers.* 17:25 Hebrew *A foolish son.*

17:9 The last thing we need to hear in recovery is how badly we have messed up our life. We are well aware of our mistakes and are ashamed of things we have done. But by confessing our sins and repenting, we receive God's forgiveness and cleansing. He has forgotten our sins and has removed them "as far from us as the east is from the west" (Psalm 103:12). If God has forgiven and forgotten our past mistakes, we have no need to be reminded of them. If friends bring up the past, we need to ignore them and not feel guilty for what we have done. The guilt we feel may drag us back into our old lifestyle.

17:17 A true friend will stick beside us during the hard times. Without a relationship with that kind of friend, recovery and growth can't take place. We all need to be able to express our needs and concerns to someone who will care, pray, and encourage us in our efforts to change.

28 Even fools are thought wise when they
keep silent;
with their mouths shut, they seem
intelligent.

CHAPTER 18

1 Unfriendly people care only about
themselves;
they lash out at common sense.

2 Fools have no interest in understanding;
they only want to air their own
opinions.

3 Doing wrong leads to disgrace,
and scandalous behavior brings
contempt.

4 Wise words are like deep waters;
wisdom flows from the wise like a
bubbling brook.

5 It is not right to acquit the guilty
or deny justice to the innocent.

6 Fools' words get them into constant
quarrels;
they are asking for a beating.

7 The mouths of fools are their ruin;
they trap themselves with their lips.

8 Rumors are dainty morsels
that sink deep into one's heart.

9 A lazy person is as bad as
someone who destroys things.

10 The name of the LORD is a strong fortress;
the godly run to him and are safe.

11 The rich think of their wealth as a strong
defense;
they imagine it to be a high wall of
safety.

12 Haughtiness goes before destruction;
humility precedes honor.

13 Spouting off before listening to the facts
is both shameful and foolish.

18:18 Hebrew *Casting lots.*

14 The human spirit can endure a sick body,
but who can bear a crushed spirit?

15 Intelligent people are always ready to
learn.
Their ears are open for knowledge.

16 Giving a gift can open doors;
it gives access to important people!

17 The first to speak in court sounds right—
until the cross-examination begins.

18 Flipping a coin* can end arguments;
it settles disputes between powerful
opponents.

19 An offended friend is harder to win back
than a fortified city.
Arguments separate friends like a gate
locked with bars.

20 Wise words satisfy like a good meal;
the right words bring satisfaction.

21 The tongue can bring death or life;
those who love to talk will reap the
consequences.

22 The man who finds a wife finds a treasure,
and he receives favor from the LORD.

23 The poor plead for mercy;
the rich answer with insults.

24 There are "friends" who destroy each
other,
but a real friend sticks closer than a
brother.

CHAPTER 19

1 Better to be poor and honest
than to be dishonest and a fool.

2 Enthusiasm without knowledge is no
good;
haste makes mistakes.

3 People ruin their lives by their own
foolishness
and then are angry at the LORD.

18:1 The self-indulgent person lacks the ability to delay gratification. If we are self-indulgent, we
end up satisfying our whims but never meeting our real needs. Rather than demanding our own
way, it is healthier to take the time to reflect on what is truly important to us and to appropriately
seek to have those needs met.
18:12 When we are filled with pride, we cannot see our weaknesses. We build walls of denial that
are almost impregnable. If we cannot admit our faults, they will never be corrected, and we will
suffer the consequences. On the other hand, humility opens the door for correction. When we
honestly evaluate our life, we can see our weaknesses and take steps to improve and correct
them. This may be painful now, but it will be much more bearable than the pain of a life
destroyed by a dependency and a compulsion.

4 Wealth makes many "friends";
poverty drives them all away.

5 A false witness will not go unpunished,
nor will a liar escape.

6 Many seek favors from a ruler;
everyone is the friend of a person who
gives gifts!

7 The relatives of the poor despise them;
how much more will their friends avoid
them!
Though the poor plead with them,
their friends are gone.

8 To acquire wisdom is to love yourself;
people who cherish understanding will
prosper.

9 A false witness will not go unpunished,
and a liar will be destroyed.

10 It isn't right for a fool to live in luxury
or for a slave to rule over princes!

11 Sensible people control their temper;
they earn respect by overlooking
wrongs.

12 The king's anger is like a lion's roar,
but his favor is like dew on the grass.

13 A foolish child* is a calamity to a father;
a quarrelsome wife is as annoying as
constant dripping.

14 Fathers can give their sons an inheritance
of houses and wealth,
but only the LORD can give an
understanding wife.

15 Lazy people sleep soundly,
but idleness leaves them hungry.

16 Keep the commandments and keep your
life;
despising them leads to death.

17 If you help the poor, you are lending to
the LORD—
and he will repay you!

18 Discipline your children while there is
hope.
Otherwise you will ruin their lives.

19:13 Hebrew *son;* also in 19:27.

19 Hot-tempered people must pay the
penalty.
If you rescue them once, you will have
to do it again.

20 Get all the advice and instruction you
can,
so you will be wise the rest of your life.

21 You can make many plans,
but the LORD's purpose will prevail.

22 Loyalty makes a person attractive.
It is better to be poor than dishonest.

23 Fear of the LORD leads to life,
bringing security and protection from
harm.

24 Lazy people take food in their hand
but don't even lift it to their mouth.

25 If you punish a mocker, the simpleminded
will learn a lesson;
if you correct the wise, they will be all
the wiser.

26 Children who mistreat their father or
chase away their mother
are an embarrassment and a public
disgrace.

27 If you stop listening to instruction, my
child,
you will turn your back on knowledge.

28 A corrupt witness makes a mockery of
justice;
the mouth of the wicked gulps down
evil.

29 Punishment is made for mockers,
and the backs of fools are made to be
beaten.

CHAPTER 20
1 Wine produces mockers; alcohol leads
to brawls.
Those led astray by drink cannot
be wise.

2 The king's fury is like a lion's roar;
to rouse his anger is to risk
your life.

19:19 If we rescue impatient friends from their problems once, we will probably rescue them again and again. They will become used to being rescued and will live irresponsibly without suffering the consequences of their behavior. We may even become codependent, addicted to the pattern of avoiding our own needs and gaining a sense of importance by helping others in their need. This harms us and the people who need our help. Though it is painful to do, we must let others feel the effects of their addiction. The pain of those experiences may bring them to admit their problems and seek recovery.

³ Avoiding a fight is a mark of honor;
   only fools insist on quarreling.

⁴ Those too lazy to plow in the right season
   will have no food at the harvest.

⁵ Though good advice lies deep within the
   heart,
   a person with understanding will draw
   it out.

⁶ Many will say they are loyal friends,
   but who can find one who is truly
   reliable?

⁷ The godly walk with integrity;
   blessed are their children who follow
   them.

⁸ When a king sits in judgment, he weighs
   all the evidence,
   distinguishing the bad from the good.

⁹ Who can say, "I have cleansed my heart;
   I am pure and free from sin"?

¹⁰ False weights and unequal measures*—
   the LORD detests double standards of
   every kind.

¹¹ Even children are known by the way
   they act,
   whether their conduct is pure, and
   whether it is right.

¹² Ears to hear and eyes to see—
   both are gifts from the LORD.

¹³ If you love sleep, you will end in poverty.
   Keep your eyes open, and there will be
   plenty to eat!

¹⁴ The buyer haggles over the price, saying,
   "It's worthless,"
   then brags about getting a bargain!

¹⁵ Wise words are more valuable
   than much gold and many rubies.

¹⁶ Get security from someone who
   guarantees a stranger's debt.
   Get a deposit if he does it for
   foreigners.*

¹⁷ Stolen bread tastes sweet,
   but it turns to gravel in the mouth.

¹⁸ Plans succeed through good counsel;
   don't go to war without wise advice.

¹⁹ A gossip goes around telling secrets,
   so don't hang around with chatterers.

²⁰ If you insult your father or mother,
   your light will be snuffed out in total
   darkness.

²¹ An inheritance obtained too early in life
   is not a blessing in the end.

²² Don't say, "I will get even for this wrong."
   Wait for the LORD to handle the matter.

²³ The LORD detests double standards;
   he is not pleased by dishonest scales.

²⁴ The LORD directs our steps,
   so why try to understand everything
   along the way?

²⁵ Don't trap yourself by making a rash
   promise to God
   and only later counting the cost.

²⁶ A wise king scatters the wicked like wheat,
   then runs his threshing wheel over
   them.

²⁷ The LORD's light penetrates the human
   spirit,*
   exposing every hidden motive.

20:10 Hebrew *A stone and a stone, an ephah and an ephah.* 20:16 An alternate reading in the Masoretic Text is *for a promiscuous woman.* 20:27 Or *The human spirit is the LORD's light.*

20:9 None of us is without sin, but we can receive God's forgiveness through confession and repentance. An important step in recovery involves taking a moral inventory of our life, which is a big job! Many of our sins were committed unconsciously and will require real soul-searching to uncover. Since we have such a strong tendency to sin, we will need to take several inventories. We can be sure, however, that each time we confess our sins to God, he will be faithful in forgiving us.

20:22 Seeking revenge against people who have hurt us will never satisfy our anger; it will only add fuel to the fire. The cycle of retribution often lasts a long time, sometimes for years after both parties have forgotten the origin of the conflict. To overcome our anger, we need to start the process of forgiveness right away. We may need to confront our offender in love and seek to resolve the conflict through mutual understanding. If reconciliation is not possible, it is best to give the matter to God and his ultimate justice. Either way, we need to put the sin behind us and move on with our life.

20:27 God intends for our conscience to be like a searchlight that illuminates our life, helping us take our moral inventory. When exposing sin, the godly conscience doesn't condemn and blame,

28 Unfailing love and faithfulness protect the
king;
his throne is made secure through love.

29 The glory of the young is their strength;
the gray hair of experience is the
splendor of the old.

30 Physical punishment cleanses away evil;*
such discipline purifies the heart.

CHAPTER 21

1 The king's heart is like a stream of water
directed by the LORD;
he guides it wherever he pleases.

2 People may be right in their own eyes,
but the LORD examines their heart.

3 The LORD is more pleased when we do
what is right and just
than when we offer him sacrifices.

4 Haughty eyes, a proud heart,
and evil actions are all sin.

5 Good planning and hard work lead to
prosperity,
but hasty shortcuts lead to poverty.

6 Wealth created by a lying tongue
is a vanishing mist and a deadly trap.*

7 The violence of the wicked sweeps them
away,
because they refuse to do what is just.

8 The guilty walk a crooked path;
the innocent travel a straight road.

9 It's better to live alone in the corner of an
attic
than with a quarrelsome wife in a
lovely home.

10 Evil people desire evil;
their neighbors get no mercy from them.

11 If you punish a mocker, the simpleminded
become wise;
if you instruct the wise, they will be all
the wiser.

12 The Righteous One* knows what is going
on in the homes of the wicked;
he will bring disaster on them.

13 Those who shut their ears to the cries
of the poor
will be ignored in their own time of
need.

14 A secret gift calms anger;
a bribe under the table pacifies fury.

15 Justice is a joy to the godly,
but it terrifies evildoers.

16 The person who strays from common
sense
will end up in the company of the dead.

17 Those who love pleasure become poor;
those who love wine and luxury will
never be rich.

18 The wicked are punished in place of the
godly,
and traitors in place of the honest.

19 It's better to live alone in the desert
than with a quarrelsome, complaining
wife.

20 The wise have wealth and luxury,
but fools spend whatever they get.

21 Whoever pursues righteousness and
unfailing love
will find life, righteousness, and honor.

22 The wise conquer the city of the strong
and level the fortress in which they
trust.

23 Watch your tongue and keep your mouth
shut,
and you will stay out of trouble.

24 Mockers are proud and haughty;
they act with boundless arrogance.

25 Despite their desires, the lazy will come
to ruin,
for their hands refuse to work.

20:30 The meaning of the Hebrew is uncertain. 21:6 As in Greek version; Hebrew reads *mist for those who seek death.*
21:12 Or *The righteous man.*

but it doesn't overlook sin either. Instead it realizes that sin is not good for us and it causes pain to
others. When we feel that something is not right about our actions, our conscience is probably
speaking to us, shining its light on our sins. Once we know that sins are there, we can confess
them, repent, and be forgiven.
21:5 Recovery is spelled P-A-T-I-E-N-C-E! We often feel as if we are plodding along, just one short
step at a time. Sometimes we even have to repeat steps we have already completed. To experience real change in our life will almost always be a slow process. It takes time to put the principles
of recovery into practice. A "quick fix" recovery program will not have lasting results because it
will never give us the time we need to make the steps an integral part of our life.

26 Some people are always greedy for more,
 but the godly love to give!

27 The sacrifice of an evil person is
 detestable,
 especially when it is offered with wrong
 motives.

28 A false witness will be cut off,
 but a credible witness will be allowed
 to speak.

29 The wicked bluff their way through,
 but the virtuous think before they act.

30 No human wisdom or understanding
 or plan
 can stand against the LORD.

31 The horse is prepared for the day of battle,
 but the victory belongs to the LORD.

CHAPTER 22
1 Choose a good reputation over great
 riches;
 being held in high esteem is better than
 silver or gold.

2 The rich and poor have this in common:
 The LORD made them both.

3 A prudent person foresees danger and
 takes precautions.
 The simpleton goes blindly on and
 suffers the consequences.

4 True humility and fear of the LORD
 lead to riches, honor, and long life.

5 Corrupt people walk a thorny, treacherous
 road;
 whoever values life will avoid it.

6 Direct your children onto the right path,
 and when they are older, they will not
 leave it.

7 Just as the rich rule the poor,
 so the borrower is servant to the lender.

8 Those who plant injustice will harvest
 disaster,
 and their reign of terror will come to an
 end.*

9 Blessed are those who are generous,
 because they feed the poor.

10 Throw out the mocker, and fighting goes,
 too.
 Quarrels and insults will disappear.

11 Whoever loves a pure heart and gracious
 speech
 will have the king as a friend.

12 The LORD preserves those with knowledge,
 but he ruins the plans of the
 treacherous.

13 The lazy person claims, "There's a lion out
 there!
 If I go outside, I might be killed!"

14 The mouth of an immoral woman is a
 dangerous trap;
 those who make the LORD angry will
 fall into it.

15 A youngster's heart is filled with
 foolishness,
 but physical discipline will drive it far
 away.

16 A person who gets ahead by oppressing
 the poor
 or by showering gifts on the rich will
 end in poverty.

Sayings of the Wise
17 Listen to the words of the wise;
 apply your heart to my instruction.
18 For it is good to keep these sayings
 in your heart
 and always ready on your lips.
19 I am teaching you today—yes, you—
 so you will trust in the LORD.
20 I have written thirty sayings* for you,
 filled with advice and knowledge.

22:8 The Greek version includes an additional proverb: *God blesses a man who gives cheerfully, / but his worthless deeds will come to an end.* Compare 2 Cor 9:7. 22:20 Or *excellent sayings;* the meaning of the Hebrew is uncertain.

22:6 The most important part of being parents is teaching our children to follow a godly lifestyle.
If children learn to respect authority and obey God while they are young, they will stay on that
path when they are older. We may have grown up in a dysfunctional family where godly values
were shunned or laughed at, and now we can see how that led to our codependent lifestyle.
But our children deserve better; they need all the advantages of a moral and loving family
environment.
22:17-19 Here Solomon repeated one of his favorite themes in Proverbs: Trust in the Lord. He
alone is the source of perfect love and truth. It is only by surrendering to him that we can experience true love and discover how our life should be lived.

²¹ In this way, you may know the truth
   and take an accurate report to those
      who sent you.

²² Don't rob the poor just because you can,
   or exploit the needy in court.
²³ For the LORD is their defender.
   He will ruin anyone who ruins them.

²⁴ Don't befriend angry people
   or associate with hot-tempered people,
²⁵ or you will learn to be like them
   and endanger your soul.

²⁶ Don't agree to guarantee another person's
      debt
   or put up security for someone else.
²⁷ If you can't pay it,
   even your bed will be snatched from
      under you.

²⁸ Don't cheat your neighbor by moving the
      ancient boundary markers
   set up by previous generations.

²⁹ Do you see any truly competent workers?
   They will serve kings
   rather than working for ordinary people.

CHAPTER 23
¹ While dining with a ruler,
   pay attention to what is put
      before you.
² If you are a big eater,
   put a knife to your throat;
³ don't desire all the delicacies,
   for he might be trying to trick you.

⁴ Don't wear yourself out trying to get rich.
   Be wise enough to know when to quit.
⁵ In the blink of an eye wealth disappears,
   for it will sprout wings
   and fly away like an eagle.

⁶ Don't eat with people who are stingy;
   don't desire their delicacies.

⁷ They are always thinking about how
      much it costs.*
   "Eat and drink," they say, but they
      don't mean it.
⁸ You will throw up what little you've eaten,
   and your compliments will be wasted.

⁹ Don't waste your breath on fools,
   for they will despise the wisest advice.

¹⁰ Don't cheat your neighbor by moving the
      ancient boundary markers;
   don't take the land of defenseless
      orphans.
¹¹ For their Redeemer* is strong;
   he himself will bring their charges
      against you.

¹² Commit yourself to instruction;
   listen carefully to words of knowledge.

¹³ Don't fail to discipline your children.
   The rod of punishment won't kill them.
¹⁴ Physical discipline
   may well save them from death.*

¹⁵ My child,* if your heart is wise,
   my own heart will rejoice!
¹⁶ Everything in me will celebrate
   when you speak what is right.

¹⁷ Don't envy sinners,
   but always continue to fear the LORD.
¹⁸ You will be rewarded for this;
   your hope will not be disappointed.

¹⁹ My child, listen and be wise:
   Keep your heart on the right course.
²⁰ Do not carouse with drunkards
   or feast with gluttons,
²¹ for they are on their way to poverty,
   and too much sleep clothes them
      in rags.

²² Listen to your father, who gave you life,
   and don't despise your mother when
      she is old.

23:7 The meaning of the Hebrew is uncertain. 23:11 Or *redeemer.* 23:14 Hebrew *from Sheol.* 23:15 Hebrew *My son;*
also in 23:19.

23:4-5 Perhaps the most common and unrecognized addiction in our culture today is greed or
materialism. Many people weary themselves trying to get more and more money so they can buy
more goods and do more things. The pleasure that money buys is only temporary; it doesn't
satisfy the longings of our heart. The wise learn the secret of delayed gratification and resist the
greedy impulses that bring quick and fleeting pleasure. Instead they seek to have their needs met
through a healthy relationship with God and with others.
23:10-11 Unfortunately, those of us who were not adequately cared for as children often get
taken advantage of as adults. Because we have been abandoned, neglected, or violated by people
who were supposed to love and care for us, we have trouble discerning when it's safe to trust
others. We often allow others to abuse our rights so we will be liked. We need help learning to set
boundaries to protect us from people who might take advantage of our vulnerability. We need to
look for godly people who will help us draw healthy boundaries in our life.

²³ Get the truth and never sell it;
also get wisdom, discipline, and good
judgment.
²⁴ The father of godly children has cause
for joy.
What a pleasure to have children who
are wise.*
²⁵ So give your father and mother joy!
May she who gave you birth be happy.

²⁶ O my son, give me your heart.
May your eyes take delight in following
my ways.
²⁷ A prostitute is a dangerous trap;
a promiscuous woman is as dangerous
as falling into a narrow well.
²⁸ She hides and waits like a robber,
eager to make more men unfaithful.

²⁹ Who has anguish? Who has sorrow?
Who is always fighting? Who is always
complaining?
Who has unnecessary bruises? Who has
bloodshot eyes?
³⁰ It is the one who spends long hours in the
taverns,
trying out new drinks.
³¹ Don't gaze at the wine, seeing how red
it is,
how it sparkles in the cup, how
smoothly it goes down.
³² For in the end it bites like a poisonous
snake;
it stings like a viper.
³³ You will see hallucinations,
and you will say crazy things.
³⁴ You will stagger like a sailor tossed at sea,
clinging to a swaying mast.
³⁵ And you will say, "They hit me, but I
didn't feel it.
I didn't even know it when they beat
me up.
When will I wake up
so I can look for another drink?"

CHAPTER 24

¹ Don't envy evil people
or desire their company.
² For their hearts plot violence,
and their words always stir up trouble.

³ A house is built by wisdom
and becomes strong through good sense.
⁴ Through knowledge its rooms are filled
with all sorts of precious riches and
valuables.

⁵ The wise are mightier than the strong,*
and those with knowledge grow
stronger and stronger.
⁶ So don't go to war without wise guidance;
victory depends on having many
advisers.

⁷ Wisdom is too lofty for fools.
Among leaders at the city gate, they
have nothing to say.

⁸ A person who plans evil
will get a reputation as a troublemaker.
⁹ The schemes of a fool are sinful;
everyone detests a mocker.

¹⁰ If you fail under pressure,
your strength is too small.

¹¹ Rescue those who are unjustly sentenced
to die;
save them as they stagger to their
death.
¹² Don't excuse yourself by saying, "Look,
we didn't know."
For God understands all hearts, and he
sees you.
He who guards your soul knows you knew.
He will repay all people as their actions
deserve.

¹³ My child,* eat honey, for it is good,
and the honeycomb is sweet to the
taste.

23:24 Hebrew *to have a wise son.* **24:5** As in Greek version; Hebrew reads *A wise man is strength.* **24:13** Hebrew *My son;* also in 24:21.

23:26-35 Three thousand years haven't changed the fact that alcohol and sex are still two of the most alluring and destructive addictions. They promise pleasure and escape from our troubles, but in the end they result in shame and embarrassment. The only real escape from our troubles, including alcohol abuse and sexual sin, is Jesus Christ. When we turn our life over to him and turn from our sins, addictions, and dependencies, we are freed to pursue a godly lifestyle. The temptations will still be there, but now we have God working with us to help us resist them. He will help us persevere in our recovery program.
24:8 This verse is not saying that planning and doing evil are the same thing. But evil actions are born of wrong motives. It is wise to take a moral inventory, not just of our actions but also of our motives. Confessing a sinful *action* is like pulling a weed but leaving the roots; it will reappear in time. Confessing a sinful *motive* is like pulling a weed out by its roots; the source of the trouble is gone.

¹⁴ In the same way, wisdom is sweet to your
soul.
If you find it, you will have a bright
future,
and your hopes will not be cut short.

¹⁵ Don't wait in ambush at the home of the
godly,
and don't raid the house where the
godly live.
¹⁶ The godly may trip seven times, but they
will get up again.
But one disaster is enough to overthrow
the wicked.

¹⁷ Don't rejoice when your enemies fall;
don't be happy when they stumble.
¹⁸ For the LORD will be displeased with you
and will turn his anger away from them.

¹⁹ Don't fret because of evildoers;
don't envy the wicked.
²⁰ For evil people have no future;
the light of the wicked will be snuffed
out.

²¹ My child, fear the LORD and the king.
Don't associate with rebels,
²² for disaster will hit them suddenly.
Who knows what punishment will come
from the LORD and the king?

More Sayings of the Wise
²³ Here are some further sayings of the wise:

It is wrong to show favoritism when
passing judgment.
²⁴ A judge who says to the wicked, "You are
innocent,"
will be cursed by many people and
denounced by the nations.
²⁵ But it will go well for those who convict
the guilty;
rich blessings will be showered on them.

²⁶ An honest answer
is like a kiss of friendship.

²⁷ Do your planning and prepare your fields
before building your house.

²⁸ Don't testify against your neighbors
without cause;

don't lie about them.
²⁹ And don't say, "Now I can pay them back
for what they've done to me!
I'll get even with them!"

³⁰ I walked by the field of a lazy person,
the vineyard of one with no common
sense.
³¹ I saw that it was overgrown with nettles.
It was covered with weeds,
and its walls were broken down.
³² Then, as I looked and thought about it,
I learned this lesson:
³³ A little extra sleep, a little more slumber,
a little folding of the hands to rest—
³⁴ then poverty will pounce on you like a
bandit;
scarcity will attack you like an armed
robber.

CHAPTER 25
More Proverbs of Solomon
These are more proverbs of Solomon, col-
lected by the advisers of King Hezekiah of
Judah.

² It is God's privilege to conceal things
and the king's privilege to discover
them.

³ No one can comprehend the height of
heaven, the depth of the earth,
or all that goes on in the king's mind!

⁴ Remove the impurities from silver,
and the sterling will be ready for the
silversmith.
⁵ Remove the wicked from the king's court,
and his reign will be made secure by
justice.

⁶ Don't demand an audience with the king
or push for a place among the great.
⁷ It's better to wait for an invitation to the
head table
than to be sent away in public disgrace.

Just because you've seen something,
⁸ don't be in a hurry to go to court.
For what will you do in the end
if your neighbor deals you a shameful
defeat?

24:15-16 Recovery is a process of being restored again and again. Though we may be tripped up
by sin or fall down many times, those who belong to God will have the strength and help to get
up again and move forward. God is forgiving and patient with us in our failings, and he is quick
to help us back on our feet.
24:30-34 Just as financial poverty comes to those who are lazy, emotional impoverishment comes
to those who neglect to work on themselves. As we work on our life, weeding out destructive
patterns and sowing the principles of recovery, we will reap a harvest of growth and recovery.
Those of us who are lazy, however, will find our soul overgrown with weeds.

⁹ When arguing with your neighbor,
don't betray another person's secret.
¹⁰ Others may accuse you of gossip,
and you will never regain your good
reputation.

¹¹ Timely advice is lovely,
like golden apples in a silver basket.
¹² To one who listens, valid criticism
is like a gold earring or other gold
jewelry.

¹³ Trustworthy messengers refresh like snow
in summer.
They revive the spirit of their employer.

¹⁴ A person who promises a gift but doesn't
give it
is like clouds and wind that bring no
rain.

¹⁵ Patience can persuade a prince,
and soft speech can break bones.

¹⁶ Do you like honey?
Don't eat too much, or it will make you
sick!

¹⁷ Don't visit your neighbors too often,
or you will wear out your welcome.

¹⁸ Telling lies about others
is as harmful as hitting them with an ax,
wounding them with a sword,
or shooting them with a sharp arrow.

¹⁹ Putting confidence in an unreliable
person in times of trouble
is like chewing with a broken tooth or
walking on a lame foot.

²⁰ Singing cheerful songs to a person with a
heavy heart
is like taking someone's coat in cold
weather
or pouring vinegar in a wound.*

²¹ If your enemies are hungry, give them
food to eat.
If they are thirsty, give them water to
drink.

²² You will heap burning coals of shame on
their heads,
and the LORD will reward you.

²³ As surely as a north wind brings rain,
so a gossiping tongue causes anger!

²⁴ It's better to live alone in the corner of an
attic
than with a quarrelsome wife in a
lovely home.

²⁵ Good news from far away
is like cold water to the thirsty.

²⁶ If the godly give in to the wicked,
it's like polluting a fountain or
muddying a spring.

²⁷ It's not good to eat too much honey,
and it's not good to seek honors for
yourself.

²⁸ A person without self-control
is like a city with broken-down walls.

CHAPTER 26
¹ Honor is no more associated with fools
than snow with summer or rain with
harvest.

² Like a fluttering sparrow or a darting
swallow,
an undeserved curse will not land on its
intended victim.

³ Guide a horse with a whip, a donkey with
a bridle,
and a fool with a rod to his back!

⁴ Don't answer the foolish arguments of
fools,
or you will become as foolish as they are.

⁵ Be sure to answer the foolish arguments of
fools,
or they will become wise in their own
estimation.

⁶ Trusting a fool to convey a message
is like cutting off one's feet or drinking
poison!

25:20 As in Greek version; Hebrew reads *pouring vinegar on soda.*

25:17 We have all known "cling-ons," people who cling to anyone who seems to care for them. Generally, they have been deprived of understanding, love, and respect. The "clingee" ends up feeling suffocated and pulls away, which confirms the cling-on's original insecurity. New and loving relationships in themselves don't make up for our past negative relationships. Recovery from childhood deprivations is a process that must also include working through past issues. Otherwise, our new relationships will follow the same destructive patterns as those in the past.
25:20 People who are troubled need empathy, not just halfhearted attempts to cheer them up. By showing that we understand and sincerely care about their feelings, we comfort them and give them the strength to make needed changes in their life.

⁷ A proverb in the mouth of a fool
    is as useless as a paralyzed leg.

⁸ Honoring a fool
    is as foolish as tying a stone to a
    slingshot.

⁹ A proverb in the mouth of a fool
    is like a thorny branch brandished
    by a drunk.

¹⁰ An employer who hires a fool or a
    bystander
    is like an archer who shoots at
    random.

¹¹ As a dog returns to its vomit,
    so a fool repeats his foolishness.

¹² There is more hope for fools
    than for people who think they are
    wise.

¹³ The lazy person claims, "There's a lion on
    the road!
    Yes, I'm sure there's a lion out there!"

¹⁴ As a door swings back and forth on its
    hinges,
    so the lazy person turns over in bed.

¹⁵ Lazy people take food in their hand
    but don't even lift it to their mouth.

¹⁶ Lazy people consider themselves smarter
    than seven wise counselors.

¹⁷ Interfering in someone else's argument
    is as foolish as yanking a dog's ears.

¹⁸ Just as damaging
    as a madman shooting a deadly weapon
¹⁹ is someone who lies to a friend
    and then says, "I was only joking."

²⁰ Fire goes out without wood,
    and quarrels disappear when gossip
    stops.

²¹ A quarrelsome person starts fights
    as easily as hot embers light charcoal or
    fire lights wood.

²² Rumors are dainty morsels
    that sink deep into one's heart.

²³ Smooth* words may hide a wicked
    heart,
    just as a pretty glaze covers a
    clay pot.

²⁴ People may cover their hatred with
    pleasant words,
    but they're deceiving you.
²⁵ They pretend to be kind, but don't believe
    them.
    Their hearts are full of many evils.*
²⁶ While their hatred may be concealed by
    trickery,
    their wrongdoing will be exposed in
    public.

²⁷ If you set a trap for others,
    you will get caught in it yourself.
    If you roll a boulder down on others,
    it will crush you instead.

²⁸ A lying tongue hates its victims,
    and flattering words cause ruin.

CHAPTER 27

¹ Don't brag about tomorrow,
    since you don't know what the day will
    bring.

² Let someone else praise you, not your
    own mouth—
    a stranger, not your own lips.

³ A stone is heavy and sand is weighty,
    but the resentment caused by a fool is
    even heavier.

⁴ Anger is cruel, and wrath is like a flood,
    but jealousy is even more dangerous.

⁵ An open rebuke
    is better than hidden love!

⁶ Wounds from a sincere friend
    are better than many kisses from an
    enemy.

⁷ A person who is full refuses honey,
    but even bitter food tastes sweet to the
    hungry.

⁸ A person who strays from home
    is like a bird that strays from
    its nest.

⁹ The heartfelt counsel of a friend
    is as sweet as perfume and incense.

26:23 As in Greek version; Hebrew reads *Burning.*   26:25 Hebrew *seven evils.*

26:11 We almost invariably repeat the patterns of the past; our old problems revisit us again and again. It is easy to slip back into our addiction; that is why we need to be diligent in the recovery process. When we relax in our recovery program, we are setting ourself up for a relapse into our old lifestyle. Only through perseverance will we be able to overcome our dependency.

¹⁰ Never abandon a friend—
   either yours or your father's.
When disaster strikes, you won't have to
   ask your brother for assistance.
   It's better to go to a neighbor than to a
   brother who lives far away.

¹¹ Be wise, my child,* and make my heart
   glad.
   Then I will be able to answer my critics.

¹² A prudent person foresees danger and
   takes precautions.
   The simpleton goes blindly on and
   suffers the consequences.

¹³ Get security from someone who
   guarantees a stranger's debt.
   Get a deposit if he does it for
   foreigners.*

¹⁴ A loud and cheerful greeting early in the
   morning
   will be taken as a curse!

¹⁵ A quarrelsome wife is as annoying
   as constant dripping on a rainy day.

¹⁶ Stopping her complaints is like trying to
   stop the wind
   or trying to hold something with
   greased hands.

¹⁷ As iron sharpens iron,
   so a friend sharpens a friend.

¹⁸ As workers who tend a fig tree are allowed
   to eat the fruit,
   so workers who protect their employer's
   interests will be rewarded.

¹⁹ As a face is reflected in water,
   so the heart reflects the real person.

²⁰ Just as Death and Destruction* are never
   satisfied,
   so human desire is never satisfied.

²¹ Fire tests the purity of silver and gold,
   but a person is tested by being
   praised.*

²² You cannot separate fools from their
   foolishness,
   even though you grind them like grain
   with mortar and pestle.

²³ Know the state of your flocks,
   and put your heart into caring for your
   herds,

²⁴ for riches don't last forever,
   and the crown might not be passed to
   the next generation.

²⁵ After the hay is harvested and the new
   crop appears
   and the mountain grasses are
   gathered in,

²⁶ your sheep will provide wool for clothing,
   and your goats will provide the price of
   a field.

²⁷ And you will have enough goats' milk for
   yourself,
   your family, and your servant girls.

CHAPTER 28

¹ The wicked run away when no one is
   chasing them,
   but the godly are as bold as lions.

² When there is moral rot within
   a nation, its government topples
   easily.
   But wise and knowledgeable leaders
   bring stability.

³ A poor person who oppresses the poor
   is like a pounding rain that destroys the
   crops.

⁴ To reject the law is to praise the wicked;
   to obey the law is to fight them.

27:11 Hebrew *my son.* 27:13 As in Greek and Latin versions (see also 20:16); Hebrew reads *for a promiscuous woman.*
27:20 Hebrew *Sheol and Abaddon.* 27:21 Or *by flattery.*

27:10 Friends are an important resource in recovery. We need people to whom we can be accountable and to whom we can turn in times of need—friends who are honest with us and have our best interests at heart. Just as we want our friends to stick by us in times of crisis, we should also support them when they need help. If we are there for others, we will have our own support network in place whenever we need help.
27:20 The desire referred to here is lust or greed—for things like sexual gratification, materialism, power, or prestige. Although satisfying these desires can be pleasurable, it is not fulfilling in the long run because these are false substitutes for deeper needs such as love, intimacy, and security. As time passes we will need more and more of our "drugs" of choice to make us feel good, and we will gradually become enslaved to our impulses.
27:21 One way to evaluate our self-perception is to note our responses when others praise us. If we discount compliments, this probably means that we suffer from a poor self-image. If we gloat in the praise we receive, we probably have an inflated self-image. The healthy response to praise is to receive it graciously and balance it with a humble awareness of our weaknesses.

⁵ Evil people don't understand justice,
  but those who follow the LORD
    understand completely.

⁶ Better to be poor and honest
  than to be dishonest and rich.

⁷ Young people who obey the law are wise;
  those with wild friends bring shame to
    their parents.*

⁸ Income from charging high interest rates
  will end up in the pocket of someone
    who is kind to the poor.

⁹ God detests the prayers
  of a person who ignores the law.

¹⁰ Those who lead good people along an evil
      path
    will fall into their own trap,
  but the honest will inherit good things.

¹¹ Rich people may think they are wise,
  but a poor person with discernment can
    see right through them.

¹² When the godly succeed, everyone is glad.
  When the wicked take charge, people
    go into hiding.

¹³ People who conceal their sins will not
      prosper,
  but if they confess and turn from them,
    they will receive mercy.

¹⁴ Blessed are those who fear to do wrong,*
  but the stubborn are headed for serious
    trouble.

¹⁵ A wicked ruler is as dangerous to
      the poor
    as a roaring lion or an attacking bear.

¹⁶ A ruler with no understanding will
      oppress his people,
  but one who hates corruption will have
    a long life.

¹⁷ A murderer's tormented conscience will
    drive him into the grave.
  Don't protect him!

¹⁸ The blameless will be rescued from harm,
  but the crooked will be suddenly
    destroyed.

¹⁹ A hard worker has plenty of food,
  but a person who chases fantasies ends
    up in poverty.

²⁰ The trustworthy person will get a rich
      reward,
  but a person who wants quick riches
    will get into trouble.

²¹ Showing partiality is never good,
  yet some will do wrong for a mere piece
    of bread.

²² Greedy people try to get rich quick
  but don't realize they're headed for
    poverty.

²³ In the end, people appreciate honest
      criticism
  far more than flattery.

²⁴ Anyone who steals from his father and
      mother
  and says, "What's wrong with that?"
  is no better than a murderer.

²⁵ Greed causes fighting;
  trusting the LORD leads to prosperity.

²⁶ Those who trust their own insight are
      foolish,
  but anyone who walks in wisdom is
    safe.

²⁷ Whoever gives to the poor will lack
      nothing,
  but those who close their eyes to
    poverty will be cursed.

²⁸ When the wicked take charge, people go
      into hiding.
  When the wicked meet disaster, the
    godly flourish.

CHAPTER 29
¹ Whoever stubbornly refuses to accept
    criticism
  will suddenly be destroyed beyond
    recovery.

² When the godly are in authority, the
    people rejoice.
  But when the wicked are in power, they
    groan.

28:7 Hebrew *their father.* **28:14** Or *those who fear the LORD;* Hebrew reads *those who fear.*

28:13 This verse contains wisdom essential to recovery and change. We must proceed with recovery by honestly assessing our mistakes, confessing our wrongs to God and to one another, resolving to avoid such mistakes in the future, and asking God to change our heart. It is humbling to admit and confess our sins, and it is alarming to commit to change; but that's the only way we can recover from our dependency and get another chance at life.

³ The man who loves wisdom brings joy to
his father,
but if he hangs around with prostitutes,
his wealth is wasted.

⁴ A just king gives stability to his nation,
but one who demands bribes destroys it.

⁵ To flatter friends
is to lay a trap for their feet.

⁶ Evil people are trapped by sin,
but the righteous escape, shouting for
joy.

⁷ The godly care about the rights of the poor;
the wicked don't care at all.

⁸ Mockers can get a whole town agitated,
but the wise will calm anger.

⁹ If a wise person takes a fool to court,
there will be ranting and ridicule but no
satisfaction.

¹⁰ The bloodthirsty hate blameless people,
but the upright seek to help them.*

¹¹ Fools vent their anger,
but the wise quietly hold it back.

¹² If a ruler pays attention to liars,
all his advisers will be wicked.

¹³ The poor and the oppressor have this in
common—
the LORD gives sight to the eyes of both.

¹⁴ If a king judges the poor fairly,
his throne will last forever.

¹⁵ To discipline a child produces wisdom,
but a mother is disgraced by an
undisciplined child.

¹⁶ When the wicked are in authority, sin
flourishes,
but the godly will live to see their
downfall.

¹⁷ Discipline your children, and they will
give you peace of mind
and will make your heart glad.

¹⁸ When people do not accept divine
guidance, they run wild.
But whoever obeys the law is joyful.

¹⁹ Words alone will not discipline a servant;
the words may be understood, but they
are not heeded.

²⁰ There is more hope for a fool
than for someone who speaks without
thinking.

²¹ A servant pampered from childhood
will become a rebel.

²² An angry person starts fights;
a hot-tempered person commits all
kinds of sin.

²³ Pride ends in humiliation,
while humility brings honor.

²⁴ If you assist a thief, you only hurt
yourself.
You are sworn to tell the truth, but you
dare not testify.

²⁵ Fearing people is a dangerous trap,
but trusting the LORD means safety.

²⁶ Many seek the ruler's favor,
but justice comes from the LORD.

²⁷ The righteous despise the unjust;
the wicked despise the godly.

CHAPTER 30
The Sayings of Agur
The sayings of Agur son of Jakeh contain this
message.*

I am weary, O God;
I am weary and worn out,
O God.*

29:10 Or *The bloodthirsty hate blameless people, / and they seek to kill the upright;* Hebrew reads *The bloodthirsty hate blameless people; / as for the upright, they seek their life.* **30:1a** Or *son of Jakeh from Massa;* or *son of Jakeh, an oracle.* **30:1b** The Hebrew can also be translated *The man declares this to Ithiel, / to Ithiel and to Ucal.*

29:15, 17 Children cannot grow up to be responsible adults if they are never disciplined, corrected, and held accountable for their actions. Children who are not held accountable fail to learn how to protect themselves from the negative influences of sin. Children who are punished inconsistently, in anger, or in the absence of a loving relationship will become rebellious toward authority and will resist accountability (see 22:15; 23:13-14). We must be consistent and fair in disciplining our children if they are to reap the benefits.
29:23 Pride always sets us up for humiliation. Pride tells us, "I'm strong; I don't need anyone's help." It blinds us to our weaknesses and prevents us from seeking the people and the help we need. Humility says, "I need improvement; could you help me?" Those of us who maintain a humble perspective, realizing that we are weak and vulnerable, will look for the help and support we need for a successful recovery. Humility will protect us from the devastation of a relapse.

2 I am too stupid to be human,
and I lack common sense.
3 I have not mastered human wisdom,
nor do I know the Holy One.

4 Who but God goes up to heaven and
comes back down?
Who holds the wind in his fists?
Who wraps up the oceans in his cloak?
Who has created the whole wide
world?
What is his name—and his son's name?
Tell me if you know!

5 Every word of God proves true.
He is a shield to all who come to him
for protection.
6 Do not add to his words,
or he may rebuke you and expose you
as a liar.

7 O God, I beg two favors from you;
let me have them before I die.
8 First, help me never to tell a lie.
Second, give me neither poverty nor
riches!
Give me just enough to satisfy my
needs.
9 For if I grow rich, I may deny you and say,
"Who is the LORD?"
And if I am too poor, I may steal and
thus insult God's holy name.

10 Never slander a worker to the employer,
or the person will curse you, and you
will pay for it.

11 Some people curse their father
and do not thank their mother.
12 They are pure in their own eyes,
but they are filthy and unwashed.
13 They look proudly around,
casting disdainful glances.
14 They have teeth like swords
and fangs like knives.

They devour the poor from the earth
and the needy from among humanity.

15 The leech has two suckers
that cry out, "More, more!"*

There are three things that are never
satisfied—
no, four that never say, "Enough!":
16 the grave,*
the barren womb,
the thirsty desert,
the blazing fire.

17 The eye that mocks a father
and despises a mother's instructions
will be plucked out by ravens of the valley
and eaten by vultures.

18 There are three things that amaze me—
no, four things that I don't understand:
19 how an eagle glides through the sky,
how a snake slithers on a rock,
how a ship navigates the ocean,
how a man loves a woman.

20 An adulterous woman consumes a man,
then wipes her mouth and says,
"What's wrong with that?"

21 There are three things that make the earth
tremble—
no, four it cannot endure:
22 a slave who becomes a king,
an overbearing fool who prospers,
23 a bitter woman who finally gets a
husband,
a servant girl who supplants her mistress.

24 There are four things on earth that are
small but unusually wise:
25 Ants—they aren't strong,
but they store up food all summer.
26 Hyraxes*—they aren't powerful,
but they make their homes among the
rocks.

30:15 Hebrew *two daughters who cry out, "Give, give!"* **30:16** Hebrew *Sheol.* **30:26** Or *Coneys,* or *Rock badgers.*

30:5 The words of God, including these principles in Proverbs, are true and offer protection to those who live by them. Living by God's truth demands that we honestly admit our need for God's wisdom and that we seek to live by it. This will not be easy, and it may not be popular. But walking in God's light will place us under God's protection and care, a necessity for any successful recovery. **30:11-12** It is easier to blame others for our problems than it is to admit them. Many of our problems do have roots in the failures of others. Our parents may have failed to love and discipline us as they should have. But these problems have been compounded by bad decisions that we have made. Our sufferings are usually caused by a combination of factors, including the sins of others and our own sins. We cannot change the failures of others. We cannot blame our mother or father for our wrong choices. Blame does nothing to speed up our recovery process. We can, however, change our own attitudes and actions that have perpetuated the suffering. Maturity comes as we take responsibility for our problems by forgiving those who have wronged us and by seeking forgiveness for our own sins.

²⁷ Locusts—they have no king,
    but they march in formation.
²⁸ Lizards—they are easy to catch,
    but they are found even in kings'
        palaces.

²⁹ There are three things that walk with
        stately stride—
    no, four that strut about:
³⁰ the lion, king of animals, who won't turn
        aside for anything,
³¹   the strutting rooster,
    the male goat,
    a king as he leads his army.

³² If you have been a fool by being proud or
        plotting evil,
    cover your mouth in shame.

³³ As the beating of cream yields butter
    and striking the nose causes bleeding,
    so stirring up anger causes quarrels.

CHAPTER 31
The Sayings of King Lemuel
The sayings of King Lemuel contain this
message,* which his mother taught him.

² O my son, O son of my womb,
    O son of my vows,
³ do not waste your strength on women,
    on those who ruin kings.

⁴ It is not for kings, O Lemuel, to guzzle
        wine.
    Rulers should not crave alcohol.
⁵ For if they drink, they may forget
        the law
    and not give justice to the oppressed.
⁶ Alcohol is for the dying,
    and wine for those in bitter distress.
⁷ Let them drink to forget their poverty
    and remember their troubles no more.

⁸ Speak up for those who cannot speak for
        themselves;
    ensure justice for those being crushed.
⁹ Yes, speak up for the poor and helpless,
    and see that they get justice.

A Wife of Noble Character
¹⁰* Who can find a virtuous and capable
        wife?
    She is more precious than rubies.
¹¹ Her husband can trust her,
    and she will greatly enrich his life.
¹² She brings him good, not harm,
    all the days of her life.

¹³ She finds wool and flax
    and busily spins it.
¹⁴ She is like a merchant's ship,
    bringing her food from afar.
¹⁵ She gets up before dawn to prepare
        breakfast for her household
    and plan the day's work for her servant
        girls.

¹⁶ She goes to inspect a field and buys it;
    with her earnings she plants a
        vineyard.
¹⁷ She is energetic and strong,
    a hard worker.
¹⁸ She makes sure her dealings are
        profitable;
    her lamp burns late into the night.

¹⁹ Her hands are busy spinning thread,
    her fingers twisting fiber.
²⁰ She extends a helping hand to the poor
    and opens her arms to the needy.
²¹ She has no fear of winter for her
        household,
    for everyone has warm* clothes.

²² She makes her own bedspreads.
    She dresses in fine linen and purple
        gowns.
²³ Her husband is well known at the city
        gates,
    where he sits with the other civic
        leaders.
²⁴ She makes belted linen garments
    and sashes to sell to the merchants.

²⁵ She is clothed with strength and
        dignity,
    and she laughs without fear of the
        future.

31:1 Or of Lemuel, king of Massa; or of King Lemuel, an oracle. 31:10 Verses 10-31 comprise a Hebrew acrostic poem; each verse begins with a successive letter of the Hebrew alphabet. 31:21 As in Greek and Latin versions; Hebrew reads scarlet.

31:10-31 Some women compare themselves to the wife described in this chapter and feel inadequate. Actually, the woman of Proverbs 31 is a description of the *ideal* wife. No wife has ever or will ever completely measure up to all these standards. A wife should not fall into the perfectionist's trap of striving to measure up to these ideal standards. This will inevitably lead to frustration and despair. Instead, a woman should accept herself for who she is and commit to allowing God to transform her more and more into his likeness. As she grows to be more like him, she will naturally exhibit many of the characteristics of this ideal wife.

²⁶ When she speaks, her words are wise,
    and she gives instructions with
        kindness.
²⁷ She carefully watches everything in her
        household
    and suffers nothing from laziness.
²⁸ Her children stand and bless her.
    Her husband praises her:

²⁹ "There are many virtuous and
        capable women in the world,
    but you surpass them all!"

³⁰ Charm is deceptive, and beauty does not last;
    but a woman who fears the LORD will be
        greatly praised.
³¹ Reward her for all she has done.
    Let her deeds publicly declare her praise.

REFLECTIONS ON PROVERBS

insights INTO OUR RELATIONSHIPS WITH GOD AND OTHERS

As we see in **Proverbs 1:29-33**, many people choose to live as they please. They give in to their sinful impulses without thinking about God's will for them. It is foolish to fall to temptations just to feel good momentarily or escape emotional pain for a while. That path will only lead to addiction and fear. It will also lead us away from God, the only one who can really satisfy our deepest needs. The path to secure freedom and peace is narrow and requires listening to God's wisdom and exercising self-control. Recovery is a process, not a "quick fix."

According to **Proverbs 10:4-5**, there is little hope for people who are not willing to work hard. Recovery from damaged emotions or addictive patterns is hard work. It requires persevering through each step in the process. But in recovery we will discover that effort alone is not sufficient. We need the faith to reach out and seize the opportunities that God brings our way. God shows his grace and goodness to us by providing chances for us to exercise our faith. He will also provide us with his spiritual support, wisdom, and encouragement as we seek to obey his will for our life.

Proverbs 12:25 reminds us of the value of encouragement. When people feel troubled or burdened, few things can help them more than a few words of encouragement. We don't necessarily need to give them a pep talk or an it's-gonna-be-all-right speech. Just letting them know that we are there for them and that we love them and are praying for them may be all they need. Real comfort comes from feeling understood, not from hollow words and cliches.

In **Proverbs 13:17** we are reminded of the importance of reliable communication. It is an essential ingredient in any successful recovery program. We need to be honest with ourself, God, and those who are helping us. If we hold anything back, others will not be able to help us completely. If we keep any areas of our addiction hidden, it will ruin the progress we have already made. Just as a war can't be won with inaccurate intelligence reports, giving inaccurate information in recovery will keep us from conquering our dependency.

We see in **Proverbs 14:2** that sin brings dishonor to God. This is one of the most important motivations we have for seeking recovery from our dependency. If we are truly seeking after God, we will want to obey and honor him. Like children who want to please their parents, we should want to recover so we can please God, our heavenly Father.

insights FOR EVERYDAY LIFE AND RECOVERY

The words in **Proverbs 10:24** speak of a self-fulfilling prophecy: What we expect to happen will happen. How we look at life often affects what actually happens in our life. If we assume that our chances for recovery are hopeless, we have already doomed our recovery program to failure. But if we approach recovery with a positive outlook, trusting in God to see us through, we will progress in the recovery process.

Proverbs 13:11 emphasizes the importance of hard work. Just as hard work can produce material riches, it can also produce spiritual riches. Yet few are willing to persevere through pain and difficulty until the job is done. It is easier to roll the dice and go for the "quick fix." There are no shortcuts to recovery or maturity. The roads to these goals are long, with many small steps that need to be taken over and over again.

As we see in **Proverbs 13:16**, it is wise to process our thoughts and feelings before we act (see also 14:8). Acting on impulses can get us into trouble. Those struggling with addictions to things like drugs, food, sex, work, gambling, or shopping know this well. These kinds of addictions start when we give in to impulses that make us feel good for the moment. The only problem is that the moment doesn't last because the impulsive behaviors don't meet our real needs. It is important to evaluate our real needs and find constructive ways to meet those needs so we can get past our addictive behaviors and find peace.

One thing in life is sure: We will face constant change. As we live in our changing world, it is important that we learn to accept the things that we cannot change. **Proverbs 14:30** reminds us of how important it is for us to find emotional serenity in this life. This is impossible if we fail to accept the things that we cannot change or control. We cannot change the past, but we must make peace with it by seeking to be forgiven and then to forgive others. True, it is easier to remain a victim of the past and seethe with jealousy or bitterness over those who were given advantages that we weren't given. Yet as we are freed from our past, we can put more energy into making positive changes for the future.

The eyes and ears that Solomon was talking about in **Proverbs 20:12** are called perception and understanding. Accurately sensing what is going on within us and around us is the beginning of recovery from an addictive or unhealthy lifestyle in which pain and feelings were avoided or repressed. Only by allowing the painful realities of our life to touch us will we be able to admit we need help and begin the healing process of recovery.

We would be wise to listen to the warning in **Proverbs 20:25**. Impulsive promises to change don't work because they are not made wholeheartedly. They come from people who know what they should do but don't really want to change. Counting the cost involves seriously examining what the promise requires of us and then being willing to fulfill the promise. If we don't want to change but realize that we probably need to, it is helpful to ask God to make us willing to change. It is only when we totally want to follow through with our promises that we will be able to.

We often look with envy at people who indulge in sinful pleasures. **Proverbs 23:17-18** warns us to avoid the temptation to do this. Such people do whatever they choose without regard for how their actions affect others (see 24:1, 19-20). They seem to have easy and pleasurable lives. Those who live righteously, however, seem to have it harder—at least initially. But as they move along the pathway to godly living, they have more fulfilling and meaningful lives. There is also an eternal perspective to be considered: Those who follow God will receive blessings in heaven, but those who live for themselves will face eternal separation from God.

ECCLESIASTES

THE BIG PICTURE

A. PROLOGUE: THE FUTILITY OF LIFE (1:1-2)

B. PROOF OF THE FUTILITY OF LIFE IN A FALLEN WORLD (1:3–6:12)

C. COPING WITH LIFE IN A FALLEN WORLD (7:1–12:8)

D. EPILOGUE: LIFE IN A FALLEN WORLD BEGINS AND ENDS WITH GOD (12:9-14)

Sometimes the events of life just don't fit together into coherent, meaningful patterns. How can we make sense of a past filled with sexual abuse? Why did God allow us to grow up in a home with an alcoholic? How does being the victim of physical abuse play a part in God's plan? All of these questions are multiplied when we see how our painful experiences have led us to make bad decisions. We see that we have perpetuated the destruction by attempting to compensate for being sinned against in our developmental years.

The Teacher in Ecclesiastes was searching for the key that would unlock the door to life's meaning. The first part of Ecclesiastes gives us the Teacher's conclusion: "Under the sun," that is, on this side of eternity, some things just don't make sense. After recognizing this basic truth, he advised that we enjoy life the best we can considering the circumstances. We are called to recognize that life is God's good gift to us. The Teacher's final conclusion, which admonishes us to reverence God and obey his commands, puts life into perspective. It creates the necessary boundaries to hold us back from selfish hedonism, while still allowing us to enjoy the good things in life.

Since life is God's good gift to be enjoyed, not a puzzle to be solved, Ecclesiastes helps us cope with our humanity. There will be some things in life that we will never understand. Rather than attempt to understand the inscrutable events in our life, the Teacher counsels us to enjoy the parts of life that do make sense and to entrust the rest to God's care.

THE BOTTOM LINE

PURPOSE: To show us that life is God's good gift to be enjoyed responsibly, not a puzzle that must be solved. AUTHOR: Attributed to Solomon, although the Hebrew text doesn't clearly name him as the author. AUDIENCE: The people of Israel. DATE WRITTEN: Possibly written toward the end of Solomon's life, around 935 B.C. SETTING: The writer evaluated what he had done in his life and pondered the relative value of his activities and accomplishments. KEY VERSE: "Here now is my final conclusion: Fear God and obey his commands, for this is everyone's duty" (12:13). SPECIAL FEATURES: The book uses a variety of literary forms: poems and couplets, proverbs, parables, and pointed questions.

RECOVERY THEMES

The Paralysis of Analysis: The Teacher's search for meaning was almost like a scientific experiment. He seemed desperate to explain life's ambiguities; he tried every human solution available before finally turning it all over to God. We need to beware of the paralysis that can set in when we get caught up in analyzing our situation and seeking human solutions to our problems. It's too easy to get lost on the way and never reach the right conclusion: Our life and will must be turned over to God. Only then will we be able to make true progress in recovery.

Some Things Will Never Make Sense: The Teacher's diligent search for understanding and meaning was ultimately futile, for we will never understand some things in life. We all recognize that we suffer because of our bad decisions, but it is also true that some failures were influenced by a past that we couldn't control. Our sufferings, both past and present, just don't seem to be fair in an ultimate sense. We need to stop trying to make sense of it all. Some things will remain a puzzle and will make sense only in eternity. We must take responsible steps toward recovery and seek God's help now. We can only trust that God will love and care for us through the difficult and seemingly meaningless problems we are forced to deal with in this life.

Only God Can Fill Our Emptiness: Ecclesiastes provides us with an accurate picture of the emptiness of our search for answers and meaning apart from God. All around us, people still pursue the same empty goals, looking at wealth, pleasure, and success for the answers to life's emptiness. We may have postponed or been sidetracked in the recovery process by the same futile searching. Solomon's experience shows us that until we turn our life over to God, our search will lead only to emptiness. God is the only one who can fill our restless, searching heart.

Life Is to Be Enjoyed Responsibly: The Teacher assessed life very honestly. He was not down on life—only on the futility of seeking happiness and fulfillment apart from God. The Teacher affirmed the value of knowledge, relationships, work, and even pleasure as long as they were put in proper perspective. We are to seek balance in our life, knowing that meaning can be found only through our relationship with God. Recovery is enhanced when we see that life is a gift from God. When he is at the center of all we do—including recovery—we will find joy during our short time here on earth.

CHAPTER 1
These are the words of the Teacher,* King David's son, who ruled in Jerusalem.

Everything Is Meaningless

²"Everything is meaningless," says the Teacher, "completely meaningless!"

³What do people get for all their hard work under the sun? ⁴Generations come and generations go, but the earth never changes. ⁵The sun rises and the sun sets, then hurries around to rise again. ⁶The wind blows south, and then turns north. Around and around it goes, blowing in circles. ⁷Rivers run into the sea, but the sea is never full. Then the water returns again to the rivers and flows out again to the sea. ⁸Everything is wearisome beyond description. No matter how much we see, we are never satisfied. No matter how much we hear, we are not content.

⁹History merely repeats itself. It has all been done before. Nothing under the sun is truly new. ¹⁰Sometimes people say, "Here is something new!" But actually it is old; nothing is ever truly new. ¹¹We don't remember what happened in the past, and in future generations, no one will remember what we are doing now.

1:1 Hebrew *Qoheleth;* this term is rendered "the Teacher" throughout this book.

1:2 Life and its various activities are not meaningless in an absolute sense. They are only meaningless or futile when we make them the ultimate goal of our existence. For example, work is not wholly worthless (2:17-24); elsewhere in Ecclesiastes we are encouraged to enjoy our work (3:9-11, 22). But work is meaningless if we use it to give our life its ultimate meaning. Only God can give true meaning to all our activities "under the sun."

1:3-11 The Teacher began his search for meaning in life by looking at nature. In the ancient world, people looked to nature to reveal life's mysteries, since it was the arena in which the gods supposedly expressed themselves. He concluded from nature that life is wearying and tiresome, filled with seemingly endless repetition. Even when we make God the center of our life, we cannot escape its natural grind. Yet as we seek to follow God's will, our godly perspective lets us see beyond the bounds of our natural world. This will help us cope with life's difficulties.

The Teacher Speaks: The Futility of Wisdom

[12]I, the Teacher, was king of Israel, and I lived in Jerusalem. [13]I devoted myself to search for understanding and to explore by wisdom everything being done under heaven. I soon discovered that God has dealt a tragic existence to the human race. [14]I observed everything going on under the sun, and really, it is all meaningless—like chasing the wind.

[15]What is wrong cannot be made right.
What is missing cannot be recovered.

[16]I said to myself, "Look, I am wiser than any of the kings who ruled in Jerusalem before me. I have greater wisdom and knowledge than any of them." [17]So I set out to learn everything from wisdom to madness and folly. But I learned firsthand that pursuing all this is like chasing the wind.

[18]The greater my wisdom, the greater my grief.
To increase knowledge only increases sorrow.

CHAPTER 2
The Futility of Pleasure

I said to myself, "Come on, let's try pleasure. Let's look for the 'good things' in life." But I found that this, too, was meaningless. [2]So I said, "Laughter is silly. What good does it do to seek pleasure?" [3]After much thought, I decided to cheer myself with wine. And while still seeking wisdom, I clutched at foolishness. In this way, I tried to experience the only happiness most people find during their brief life in this world.

[4]I also tried to find meaning by building huge homes for myself and by planting beau-

2:12 The meaning of the Hebrew is uncertain.

tiful vineyards. [5]I made gardens and parks, filling them with all kinds of fruit trees. [6]I built reservoirs to collect the water to irrigate my many flourishing groves. [7]I bought slaves, both men and women, and others were born into my household. I also owned large herds and flocks, more than any of the kings who had lived in Jerusalem before me. [8]I collected great sums of silver and gold, the treasure of many kings and provinces. I hired wonderful singers, both men and women, and had many beautiful concubines. I had everything a man could desire!

[9]So I became greater than all who had lived in Jerusalem before me, and my wisdom never failed me. [10]Anything I wanted, I would take. I denied myself no pleasure. I even found great pleasure in hard work, a reward for all my labors. [11]But as I looked at everything I had worked so hard to accomplish, it was all so meaningless—like chasing the wind. There was nothing really worthwhile anywhere.

The Wise and the Foolish

[12]So I decided to compare wisdom with foolishness and madness (for who can do this better than I, the king?*). [13]I thought, "Wisdom is better than foolishness, just as light is better than darkness. [14]For the wise can see where they are going, but fools walk in the dark." Yet I saw that the wise and the foolish share the same fate. [15]Both will die. So I said to myself, "Since I will end up the same as the fool, what's the value of all my wisdom? This is all so meaningless!" [16]For the wise and the foolish both die. The wise will not be remembered any longer than

1:12-15 The Teacher continued his search for meaning through wisdom. Instead of finding meaning, however, he discovered the limits of his wisdom. Wisdom brings grief, and knowledge increases sorrow (1:18) because we are that much more in touch with the realities of our fallen world. As we face recovery, we are not surprised by this. We have experienced many of life's harsh realities. True wisdom ultimately leads us back to God. Only by trusting God and obeying him will we find any meaningful direction and joy in this life.

2:1-3 The Teacher tried the pleasure escapes of laughter and alcohol. Had drugs been available in his day as they are now, he may also have tried them. But these things ultimately couldn't satisfy his search for meaning. Seeking to escape our pain through pleasure leads to substance abuse and addiction. Only God can give us the strength and purpose for a meaningful life. We need to trust him and patiently follow his program for healthy living.

2:4-11 The Teacher next tried to find meaning by building a personal empire. After experiencing incredible success, however, he concluded that it did not give ultimate meaning to his life; all the pieces of life's puzzle didn't fit together. Many of us have made success the basis for meaning in our life. We are driven to higher and higher goals only to find emptiness in each new success. Many of us even put off recovery, fearing that it might interfere with our career. We need to realize that true success can only be found in seeking God's help in recovery. He alone is able to give meaning to our broken life.

the fool. In the days to come, both will be forgotten.

[17]So I came to hate life because everything done here under the sun is so troubling. Everything is meaningless—like chasing the wind.

The Futility of Work

[18]I came to hate all my hard work here on earth, for I must leave to others everything I have earned. [19]And who can tell whether my successors will be wise or foolish? Yet they will control everything I have gained by my skill and hard work under the sun. How meaningless! [20]So I gave up in despair, questioning the value of all my hard work in this world.

[21]Some people work wisely with knowledge and skill, then must leave the fruit of their efforts to someone who hasn't worked for it. This, too, is meaningless, a great tragedy. [22]So what do people get in this life for all their hard work and anxiety? [23]Their days of labor are filled with pain and grief; even at night their minds cannot rest. It is all meaningless.

[24]So I decided there is nothing better than to enjoy food and drink and to find satisfaction in work. Then I realized that these pleasures are from the hand of God. [25]For who can eat or enjoy anything apart from him?* [26]God gives wisdom, knowledge, and joy to those who please him. But if a sinner becomes wealthy, God takes the wealth away and gives it to those who please him. This, too, is meaningless—like chasing the wind.

2:25 As in Greek and Syriac versions; Hebrew reads *apart from me?*

CHAPTER 3
A Time for Everything

[1]For everything there is a season,
a time for every activity under heaven.
[2]A time to be born and a time to die.
A time to plant and a time to harvest.
[3]A time to kill and a time to heal.
A time to tear down and a time to build up.
[4]A time to cry and a time to laugh.
A time to grieve and a time to dance.
[5]A time to scatter stones and a time to gather stones.
A time to embrace and a time to turn away.
[6]A time to search and a time to quit searching.
A time to keep and a time to throw away.
[7]A time to tear and a time to mend.
A time to be quiet and a time to speak.
[8]A time to love and a time to hate.
A time for war and a time for peace.

[9]What do people really get for all their hard work? [10]I have seen the burden God has placed on us all. [11]Yet God has made everything beautiful for its own time. He has planted eternity in the human heart, but even so, people cannot see the whole scope of God's work from beginning to end. [12]So I concluded there is nothing better than to be happy and enjoy ourselves as long as we can. [13]And people should eat and drink and enjoy the fruits of their labor, for these are gifts from God.

[14]And I know that whatever God does is

2:24-26 The alternative to neurotic commitment to work is the enjoyment of life as God's good gift. This includes enjoying our work, while not allowing it to become the key to meaning in our life. This is the first of the Teacher's admonitions to take life less seriously and enjoy it more. Life is too short to waste on the treadmill of ever increasing professional accomplishments. In the larger scheme of things, our accomplishments will not last. We need to take the time to enjoy the gifts that God gives us.

3:1-8 Analyzing each of these "times" would most likely miss the Teacher's point. These are figures of speech that present two opposite extremes and include the entire spectrum between them. For instance, there is a time to be born and a time to die (3:2), but the emphasis is on the lifetime in between. There is a time for everything because God has set the times. All of life is part of a well-orchestrated symphony for which God has written the music. An essential part of recovery is seeking out God's plan for us and then following it.

3:12-15 Here the Teacher gives us a practical alternative to the desperate search for ultimate meaning in life. We are to responsibly enjoy life as God's good gift to us. The Teacher wanted people to enjoy life more and to spend less time and energy trying to make sense of it all. Verse 14 sets parameters around our enjoyment of life. Everything we do must be done with the recognition that God is in charge. Our actions should demonstrate our respect for him. This will prevent our enjoyment of life from becoming selfish hedonism.

final. Nothing can be added to it or taken from it. God's purpose is that people should fear him. [15]What is happening now has happened before, and what will happen in the future has happened before, because God makes the same things happen over and over again.

The Injustices of Life

[16]I also noticed that under the sun there is evil in the courtroom. Yes, even the courts of law are corrupt! [17]I said to myself, "In due season God will judge everyone, both good and bad, for all their deeds."

[18]I also thought about the human condition—how God proves to people that they are like animals. [19]For people and animals share the same fate—both breathe* and both must die. So people have no real advantage over the animals. How meaningless! [20]Both go to the same place—they came from dust and they return to dust. [21]For who can prove that the human spirit goes up and the spirit of animals goes down into the earth? [22]So I saw that there is nothing better for people than to be happy in their work. That is our lot in life. And no one can bring us back to see what happens after we die.

CHAPTER 4

Again, I observed all the oppression that takes place under the sun. I saw the tears of the oppressed, with no one to comfort them. The oppressors have great power, and their victims are helpless. [2]So I concluded that the dead are better off than the living. [3]But most fortunate of all are those who are not yet born. For they have not seen all the evil that is done under the sun.

[4]Then I observed that most people are motivated to success because they envy their neighbors. But this, too, is meaningless—like chasing the wind.

[5]"Fools fold their idle hands,
    leading them to ruin."

[6]And yet,

"Better to have one handful with
    quietness
than two handfuls with hard work
    and chasing the wind."

The Advantages of Companionship

[7]I observed yet another example of something meaningless under the sun. [8]This is the case of a man who is all alone, without a child or a brother, yet who works hard to

3:19 Or both have the same spirit.

DENIAL

READ ECCLESIASTES 3:16–4:1
Some of us avoid or cope with our own pain by trying to fix the world. We try to right every wrong, heal every wound, point out every injustice. We spend our time demanding that the world system reform. We may also dedicate ourselves to rescuing and reforming those we love. Our zealousness to set the world right can be a means of denying that we are powerless to do so.

Solomon said, "I also noticed that under the sun there is evil in the courtroom. Yes, even the courts of law are corrupt! I said to myself, 'In due season God will judge everyone, both good and bad, for all their deeds.' . . . I observed all the oppression that takes place under the sun. I saw the tears of the oppressed, with no one to comfort them. The oppressors have great power, and their victims are helpless" (Ecclesiastes 3:16-17; 4:1). Solomon saw that the world was not as it should be. He also recognized that it was ultimately God's job to judge the injustices in our world.

When we set out to save the world, we err by taking on a role that belongs to God. What we gain by taking on such a massive task is the guarantee that we will always be busy. Then we will never have the time or energy to face our own issues. The Bible makes it clear that the world will never be right until Jesus Christ returns to make it so. We need to accept the fact that we are powerless to do his job. This does not mean that we should turn a blind eye to the world's problems. When we focus on our own recovery, fixing ourself instead of everyone else, we will be more effective in helping others. ***Turn to page 945, Jeremiah 9.***

gain as much wealth as he can. But then he asks himself, "Who am I working for? Why am I giving up so much pleasure now?" It is all so meaningless and depressing.

⁹Two people are better off than one, for they can help each other succeed. ¹⁰If one person falls, the other can reach out and help. But someone who falls alone is in real trouble. ¹¹Likewise, two people lying close together can keep each other warm. But how can one be warm alone? ¹²A person standing alone can be attacked and defeated, but two can stand back-to-back and conquer. Three are even better, for a triple-braided cord is not easily broken.

The Futility of Political Power

¹³It is better to be a poor but wise youth than an old and foolish king who refuses all advice. ¹⁴Such a youth could rise from poverty and succeed. He might even become king, though he has been in prison. ¹⁵But then everyone rushes to the side of yet another youth* who replaces him. ¹⁶Endless crowds stand around him,* but then another generation grows up and rejects him, too. So it is all meaningless—like chasing the wind.

CHAPTER 5
Approaching God with Care

¹*As you enter the house of God, keep your ears open and your mouth shut. It is evil to make mindless offerings to God. ²*Don't make rash promises, and don't be hasty in bringing matters before God. After all, God is in heaven, and you are here on earth. So let your words be few.

³Too much activity gives you restless dreams; too many words make you a fool.

⁴When you make a promise to God, don't delay in following through, for God takes no pleasure in fools. Keep all the promises you make to him. ⁵It is better to say nothing than to make a promise and not keep it. ⁶Don't let your mouth make you sin. And don't defend yourself by telling the Temple messenger that the promise you made was a mistake. That would make God angry, and he might wipe out everything you have achieved.

⁷Talk is cheap, like daydreams and other useless activities. Fear God instead.

The Futility of Wealth

⁸Don't be surprised if you see a poor person being oppressed by the powerful and if justice is being miscarried throughout the land. For every official is under orders from higher up, and matters of justice get lost in red tape and bureaucracy. ⁹Even the king milks the land for his own profit!*

¹⁰Those who love money will never have enough. How meaningless to think that wealth brings true happiness! ¹¹The more you have, the more people come to help you

---

4:15 Hebrew *the second youth*. 4:16 Hebrew *There is no end to all the people, to all those who are before them.* 5:1 Verse 5:1 is numbered 4:17 in Hebrew text. 5:2 Verses 5:2-20 are numbered 5:1-19 in Hebrew text. 5:9 The meaning of the Hebrew in verses 8 and 9 is uncertain.

4:9-12 Supportive friends and healthy relationships are absolutely necessary for successful recovery. When we fall down, we need help to get up again. If we stand alone, we are especially vulnerable to inner enemies. We must learn to trust others, to reach out to others, and to admit our need for others. This will give us added strength, wisdom, and protection against our dependencies and compulsions.

4:13-16 Climbing the ladder of success will never unlock the door to life's meaning. Success is always temporary. Someone else will inherit our work, and ultimately it will be forgotten. We must avoid the trap of living for success. Our relationships with God and with other people are of far greater importance. Reconciling and building our relationships will lead to true success and joy.

5:10-17 The Teacher here addressed living to accumulate wealth. As is true of all addictions, enough is never enough. This is one reason wealth is not the key to happiness and meaning in life. Here we are given additional reasons to avoid searching for wealth: (1) The more money we have, the more we spend, saving nothing (5:11); (2) the greater our financial empire, the more we will worry about it (5:12); (3) we can't take any of it with us when we die (5:13-17). God never intended for us to live for our possessions. We need to make our relationships with God and others our primary concerns.

5:18-20 Here we see an alternative to materialism: Celebrate the beauty of God's gift of life and its simple pleasures. Being healthy and content with what we have are gifts from God. The Teacher makes his point by stating that people who are not satisfied with their lives are worse off than stillborn babies (6:3-6). Though the Teacher probably exaggerated to make his point, his message is clear. The celebration and enjoyment of life are extremely important. The process of recovery is often very painful. We need to take the time to enjoy life's simple pleasures to gain strength for the battles we face.

spend it. So what good is wealth—except perhaps to watch it slip through your fingers!

¹²People who work hard sleep well, whether they eat little or much. But the rich seldom get a good night's sleep.

¹³There is another serious problem I have seen under the sun. Hoarding riches harms the saver. ¹⁴Money is put into risky investments that turn sour, and everything is lost. In the end, there is nothing left to pass on to one's children. ¹⁵We all come to the end of our lives as naked and empty-handed as on the day we were born. We can't take our riches with us.

¹⁶And this, too, is a very serious problem. People leave this world no better off than when they came. All their hard work is for nothing—like working for the wind. ¹⁷Throughout their lives, they live under a cloud—frustrated, discouraged, and angry.

¹⁸Even so, I have noticed one thing, at least, that is good. It is good for people to eat, drink, and enjoy their work under the sun during the short life God has given them, and to accept their lot in life. ¹⁹And it is a good thing to receive wealth from God and the good health to enjoy it. To enjoy your work and accept your lot in life—this is indeed a gift from God. ²⁰God keeps such people so busy enjoying life that they take no time to brood over the past.

CHAPTER 6

There is another serious tragedy I have seen under the sun, and it weighs heavily on humanity. ²God gives some people great wealth and honor and everything they could ever want, but then he doesn't give them the chance to enjoy these things. They die, and someone else, even a stranger, ends up enjoying their wealth! This is meaningless—a sickening tragedy.

³A man might have a hundred children and live to be very old. But if he finds no satisfaction in life and doesn't even get a decent burial, it would have been better for him to be born dead. ⁴His birth would have been meaningless, and he would have ended in darkness. He wouldn't even have had a name, ⁵and he would never have seen the sun or known of its existence. Yet he would have had more peace than in growing up to be an unhappy man. ⁶He might live a thousand years twice over but still not find contentment. And since he must die like everyone else—well, what's the use?

⁷All people spend their lives scratching for

STEP 8

Overcoming Loneliness

BIBLE READING: Ecclesiastes 4:9-12

We made lists of all persons we had harmed and became willing to make amends to them all.

Loneliness and isolation go along with the guilt and shame we feel about who we are or what we have done. We may feel so cut off from others that we feel lonely even when we are around other people. Guilt, fear of being hurt, and self-hatred can make us unable to believe in the love others have for us. We can feel all alone in the struggle even when there are people beside us who want to help. Being willing to accept their love is part of the preparation for making amends.

Wise King Solomon observed: "Two people are better off than one, for they can help each other succeed. If one person falls, the other can reach out and help. But someone who falls alone is in real trouble. Likewise, two people lying close together can keep each other warm. But how can one be warm alone? A person standing alone can be attacked and defeated, but two can stand back-to-back and conquer. Three are even better, for a triple-braided cord is not easily broken" (Ecclesiastes 4:9-12).

Loneliness can break us and defeat us in the recovery process. When we prepare to make amends, we also need to prepare our heart to accept whatever love, support, or friendship is offered in return. These supportive relationships, along with God's supporting hand, will strengthen our life considerably. With our friends and God joining with us to form a "triple-braided cord," we will not be easily broken or turned from the path to recovery. *Turn to page 1225, Matthew 18.*

food, but they never seem to have enough. [8]So are wise people really better off than fools? Do poor people gain anything by being wise and knowing how to act in front of others?

[9]Enjoy what you have rather than desiring what you don't have. Just dreaming about nice things is meaningless—like chasing the wind.

The Future—Determined and Unknown

[10]Everything has already been decided. It was known long ago what each person would be. So there's no use arguing with God about your destiny.

[11]The more words you speak, the less they mean. So what good are they?

[12]In the few days of our meaningless lives, who knows how our days can best be spent? Our lives are like a shadow. Who can tell what will happen on this earth after we are gone?

CHAPTER 7
Wisdom for Life
[1]A good reputation is more valuable than
  costly perfume.
  And the day you die is better than the
  day you are born.
[2]Better to spend your time at funerals than
  at parties.
  After all, everyone dies—
  so the living should take this
  to heart.
[3]Sorrow is better than laughter,
  for sadness has a refining influence
  on us.
[4]A wise person thinks a lot about death,
  while a fool thinks only about having a
  good time.

[5]Better to be criticized by a wise person
  than to be praised by a fool.
[6]A fool's laughter is quickly gone,
  like thorns crackling in a fire.
  This also is meaningless.

[7]Extortion turns wise people into fools,
  and bribes corrupt the heart.

[8]Finishing is better than starting.
  Patience is better than pride.

[9]Control your temper,
  for anger labels you a fool.

[10]Don't long for "the good old days."
  This is not wise.

[11]Wisdom is even better when you have
    money.
  Both are a benefit as you go through
    life.
[12]Wisdom and money can get you almost
    anything,
  but only wisdom can save your life.

[13]Accept the way God does things,
  for who can straighten what he has
    made crooked?
[14]Enjoy prosperity while you can,
  but when hard times strike, realize that
    both come from God.
  Remember that nothing is certain in
    this life.

The Limits of Human Wisdom
[15]I have seen everything in this meaningless life, including the death of good young people and the long life of wicked people. [16]So don't be too good or too wise! Why destroy yourself? [17]On the other hand, don't be too wicked either. Don't be a fool! Why die before your time? [18]Pay attention to these

6:12 Sometimes our situation seems hopeless. No matter what we do, everything seems painful and ultimately meaningless. "Who knows how our days can best be spent?" We certainly don't, but God does. If we faithfully follow his program for healthy living, we can have hope for the future. We need to recognize our hopeless state and place our life in God's hands. We often allow our lack of understanding or lack of material resources to discourage us. We should realize that if we trust and obey God, our lack of understanding or wealth need not get in the way of a rich and joyful life.

7:1 The writing style of Ecclesiastes shifts radically here, as does the Teacher's emphasis. The message is presented by using proverbs—short pithy statements of wisdom. We are given wisdom for coping with everyday life in a fallen world. The Teacher's search for the meaning of life has essentially ended.

7:13-14 God is in control of our world. He created it and the laws that govern it. So following his plan makes sense. Doing things his way will lead to harmony with God, other people, and the world we live in. We will never understand everything about our world or why things happen; some things in life will never make sense. But God is in control. By trusting him and obeying his plan for healthy living we can live a productive and joyful life. Living at odds with God's plan will only lead to increased suffering and eventual destruction.

instructions, for anyone who fears God will avoid both extremes.*

[19]One wise person is stronger than ten leading citizens of a town!

[20]Not a single person on earth is always good and never sins.

[21]Don't eavesdrop on others—you may hear your servant curse you. [22]For you know how often you yourself have cursed others.

[23]I have always tried my best to let wisdom guide my thoughts and actions. I said to myself, "I am determined to be wise." But it didn't work. [24]Wisdom is always distant and difficult to find. [25]I searched everywhere, determined to find wisdom and to understand the reason for things. I was determined to prove to myself that wickedness is stupid and that foolishness is madness.

[26]I discovered that a seductive woman* is a trap more bitter than death. Her passion is a snare, and her soft hands are chains. Those who are pleasing to God will escape her, but sinners will be caught in her snare.

[27]"This is my conclusion," says the Teacher. "I discovered this after looking at the matter from every possible angle. [28]Though I have searched repeatedly, I have not found what I was looking for. Only one out of a thousand men is virtuous, but not one woman! [29]But I did find this: God created people to be virtuous, but they have each turned to follow their own downward path."

CHAPTER 8

[1]How wonderful to be wise,
    to analyze and interpret things.
Wisdom lights up a person's face,
    softening its harshness.

Obedience to the King

[2]Obey the king since you vowed to God that you would. [3]Don't try to avoid doing your duty, and don't stand with those who plot evil, for the king can do whatever he wants. [4]His command is backed by great power. No one can resist or question it. [5]Those who obey him will not be punished. Those who are wise will find a time and a way to do what is right, [6]for there is a time and a way for everything, even when a person is in trouble.

[7]Indeed, how can people avoid what they don't know is going to happen? [8]None of us can hold back our spirit from departing. None of us has the power to prevent the day of our death. There is no escaping that obligation, that dark battle. And in the face of death, wickedness will certainly not rescue the wicked.

The Wicked and the Righteous

[9]I have thought deeply about all that goes on here under the sun, where people have the power to hurt each other. [10]I have seen wicked people buried with honor. Yet they were the very ones who frequented the Temple and are now praised* in the same city where they committed their crimes! This, too, is meaningless. [11]When a crime is not punished quickly, people feel it is safe to do wrong. [12]But even though a person sins a hundred times and still lives a long time, I know that those who fear God will be better off. [13]The wicked will not prosper, for they do not fear God. Their days will never grow long like the evening shadows.

[14]And this is not all that is meaningless in our world. In this life, good people are often treated as though they were wicked, and wicked people are often treated as though they were good. This is so meaningless!

[15]So I recommend having fun, because there is nothing better for people in this world than to eat, drink, and enjoy life. That way they will experience some happiness

---

7:18 Or *will follow them both.* 7:26 Hebrew *a woman.* 8:10 As in some Hebrew manuscripts and Greek version; many Hebrew manuscripts read *and are forgotten.*

7:21-22 We are to listen selectively, being careful about what we take to heart. Many of us grew up in a dysfunctional family and had to submit to constant negative criticism. Many of the messages we received just weren't true. We may need to stop listening to people who have been instrumental in destroying our self-esteem. This is not to say that we should filter out *constructive* criticism. We must learn to tell the difference between legitimate and false criticism, which is necessary for making our personal moral inventory.

8:14 The Teacher noticed something that just didn't make sense. Some good people suffer, and some wicked people prosper. Here we are advised not to trouble our mind with problems we cannot solve. We never have the whole picture. Only God knows the reasons behind everything. This should help us trust in God's plan for our life. Knowing that we can trust God to lead us through life's ambiguities, we should enjoy the simple pleasures. Some things will never make sense, but we should enjoy what we can understand rather than despairing about the things we cannot (8:15-17).

along with all the hard work God gives them under the sun.

[16]In my search for wisdom and in my observation of people's burdens here on earth, I discovered that there is ceaseless activity, day and night. [17]I realized that no one can discover everything God is doing under the sun. Not even the wisest people discover everything, no matter what they claim.

CHAPTER 9
Death Comes to All

This, too, I carefully explored: Even though the actions of godly and wise people are in God's hands, no one knows whether God will show them favor. [2]The same destiny ultimately awaits everyone, whether righteous or wicked, good or bad,* ceremonially clean or unclean, religious or irreligious. Good people receive the same treatment as sinners, and people who make promises to God are treated like people who don't.

[3]It seems so wrong that everyone under the sun suffers the same fate. Already twisted by evil, people choose their own mad course, for they have no hope. There is nothing ahead but death anyway. [4]There is hope only for the living. As they say, "It's better to be a live dog than a dead lion!"

[5]The living at least know they will die, but the dead know nothing. They have no further reward, nor are they remembered. [6]Whatever they did in their lifetime—loving, hating, envying—is all long gone. They no longer play a part in anything here on earth. [7]So go ahead. Eat your food with joy, and drink your wine with a happy heart, for God approves of this! [8]Wear fine clothes, with a splash of cologne!

[9]Live happily with the woman you love through all the meaningless days of life that God has given you under the sun. The wife God gives you is your reward for all your earthly toil. [10]Whatever you do, do well. For when you go to the grave,* there will be no work or planning or knowledge or wisdom.

[11]I have observed something else under the sun. The fastest runner doesn't always win the race, and the strongest warrior doesn't always win the battle. The wise sometimes go hungry, and the skillful are not necessarily wealthy. And those who are educated don't always lead successful lives. It is all decided by chance, by being in the right place at the right time.

[12]People can never predict when hard times might come. Like fish in a net or birds in a trap, people are caught by sudden tragedy.

Thoughts on Wisdom and Folly

[13]Here is another bit of wisdom that has impressed me as I have watched the way our world works. [14]There was a small town with only a few people, and a great king came with his army and besieged it. [15]A poor, wise man knew how to save the town, and so it was rescued. But afterward no one thought to thank him. [16]So even though wisdom is better than strength, those who are wise will be despised if they are poor. What they say will not be appreciated for long.

[17]Better to hear the quiet words of a wise
    person
than the shouts of a foolish king.
[18]Better to have wisdom than weapons
    of war,
but one sinner can destroy much that
    is good.

CHAPTER 10
[1]As dead flies cause even a bottle of
    perfume to stink,
so a little foolishness spoils great
    wisdom and honor.

[2]A wise person chooses the right road;
    a fool takes the wrong one.

[3]You can identify fools
    just by the way they walk down the
    street!

9:2 As in Greek and Syriac versions and Latin Vulgate; Hebrew lacks *or bad.* 9:10 Hebrew *to Sheol.*

9:7-10 Because life is short, we should enjoy it fully, and whatever we do, do well. The Teacher recognized that life "under the sun" was not the end of the story, but he never minimized the importance of our days here. God wants us to enjoy the friends and family he has given us. We may sometimes feel that our life is insignificant in the larger scheme of things, but we need to realize that our everyday life does make a difference. God will use us to touch the lives of others if we follow his program. This is one of the greatest lessons of recovery.
9:13-18 Even though wisdom in itself cannot give meaning to our life, it is clearly preferred over foolishness. This reinforces the view that wisdom is not meaningless in an absolute sense. Wisdom helps us avoid destructive pitfalls in life, though it is limited for the purpose of putting the pieces of the puzzle of life together.

[4] If your boss is angry at you, don't quit!
A quiet spirit can overcome even great
mistakes.

The Ironies of Life

[5] There is another evil I have seen under the
sun. Kings and rulers make a grave mistake
[6] when they give great authority to foolish
people and low positions to people of proven
worth. [7] I have even seen servants riding
horseback like princes—and princes walking
like servants!

[8] When you dig a well,
you might fall in.
When you demolish an old wall,
you could be bitten by a snake.
[9] When you work in a quarry,
stones might fall and crush you.
When you chop wood,
there is danger with each stroke
of your ax.

[10] Using a dull ax requires great strength,
so sharpen the blade.
That's the value of wisdom;
it helps you succeed.

[11] If a snake bites before you charm it,
what's the use of being a snake charmer?

[12] Wise words bring approval,
but fools are destroyed by their own
words.

[13] Fools base their thoughts on foolish
assumptions,
so their conclusions will be wicked
madness;
[14] they chatter on and on.

No one really knows what is going
to happen;
no one can predict the future.

[15] Fools are so exhausted by a little work
that they can't even find their way
home.

[16] What sorrow for the land ruled by a
servant,*
the land whose leaders feast in the
morning.

[17] Happy is the land whose king is a noble
leader
and whose leaders feast at the proper
time
to gain strength for their work, not
to get drunk.

[18] Laziness leads to a sagging roof;
idleness leads to a leaky house.

[19] A party gives laughter,
wine gives happiness,
and money gives everything!

[20] Never make light of the king, even in
your thoughts.
And don't make fun of the powerful,
even in your own bedroom.
For a little bird might deliver your
message
and tell them what you said.

CHAPTER 11

The Uncertainties of Life

[1] Send your grain across the seas,
and in time, profits will flow back
to you.*
[2] But divide your investments among many
places,*
for you do not know what risks might
lie ahead.

[3] When clouds are heavy, the rains come
down.
Whether a tree falls north or south, it
stays where it falls.

[4] Farmers who wait for perfect weather
never plant.
If they watch every cloud, they never
harvest.

[5] Just as you cannot understand the path of
the wind or the mystery of a tiny baby growing in its mother's womb,* so you cannot
understand the activity of God, who does all
things. [6] Plant your seed in the morning and keep
busy all afternoon, for you don't know if
profit will come from one activity or another—or maybe both.

10:16 Or *a child.* **11:1** Or *Give generously, / for your gifts will return to you later.* Hebrew reads *Throw your bread on the waters, / for after many days you will find it again.* **11:2** Hebrew *among seven or even eight.* **11:5** Some manuscripts read *Just as you cannot understand how breath comes to a tiny baby in its mother's womb.*

11:5-6 For the last time in this book, the Teacher reminds us of the limits of our understanding. In light of this, he counsels diligence: even though we do not know the outcome of our labor, we must keep busy. We will never understand all the events in our life. We may never really under-stand our dependency or compulsion. But God has given us instructions to follow. We need to be diligent as we obey our faithful and loving God.

Advice for Young and Old

[7]Light is sweet; how pleasant to see a new day dawning.

[8]When people live to be very old, let them rejoice in every day of life. But let them also remember there will be many dark days. Everything still to come is meaningless.

[9]Young people,* it's wonderful to be young! Enjoy every minute of it. Do everything you want to do; take it all in. But remember that you must give an account to God for everything you do. [10]So refuse to worry, and keep your body healthy. But remember that youth, with a whole life before you, is meaningless.

CHAPTER 12

Don't let the excitement of youth cause you to forget your Creator. Honor him in your youth before you grow old and say, "Life is not pleasant anymore." [2]Remember him before the light of the sun, moon, and stars is dim to your old eyes, and rain clouds continually darken your sky. [3]Remember him before your legs—the guards of your house—start to tremble; and before your shoulders—the strong men—stoop. Remember him before your teeth—your few remaining servants— stop grinding; and before your eyes—the women looking through the windows—see dimly.

[4]Remember him before the door to life's opportunities is closed and the sound of work fades. Now you rise at the first chirping of the birds, but then all their sounds will grow faint.

[5]Remember him before you become fearful of falling and worry about danger in the streets; before your hair turns white like an almond tree in bloom, and you drag along without energy like a dying grasshopper, and the caperberry no longer inspires sexual desire. Remember him before you near the grave, your everlasting home, when the mourners will weep at your funeral.

[6]Yes, remember your Creator now while you are young, before the silver cord of life snaps and the golden bowl is broken. Don't wait until the water jar is smashed at the spring and the pulley is broken at the well. [7]For then the dust will return to the earth, and the spirit will return to God who gave it.

Concluding Thoughts about the Teacher

[8]"Everything is meaningless," says the Teacher, "completely meaningless."

[9]Keep this in mind: The Teacher was considered wise, and he taught the people everything he knew. He listened carefully to many proverbs, studying and classifying them. [10]The Teacher sought to find just the right words to express truths clearly.*

[11]The words of the wise are like cattle prods—painful but helpful. Their collected sayings are like a nail-studded stick with which a shepherd* drives the sheep.

[12]But, my child,* let me give you some further advice: Be careful, for writing books is endless, and much study wears you out.

[13]That's the whole story. Here now is my final conclusion: Fear God and obey his commands, for this is everyone's duty. [14]God will judge us for everything we do, including every secret thing, whether good or bad.

11:9 Hebrew *Young man.* 12:10 Or *sought to write what was upright and true.* 12:11 Or *one shepherd.* 12:12 Hebrew *my son.*

12:1 Our relationship with God is foundational for coping with life in a fallen world. We need to do more than just acknowledge a higher power. We need to make him the center of our life. Everything we do and say should be inspired by his presence in us. We are to remember God in our youth, because it gets harder to change as we get older. This is a call to immediate action— the younger, the better! The older we are, the more urgent it is for us to act. We need to seek out God's will and then do our best to follow it. This may begin with the decision to get into a recovery program.

12:2-7 These verses describe the physical effects in the process of aging. Eyesight is lost (12:2-3); the muscles and bones deteriorate (12:3); hearing fades (12:4); fear sets in, and vitality is lost (12:5); our life becomes more and more fragile (12:6); and our bodies return to dust (12:7). Our addiction often causes these characteristics long before they would naturally happen. God desires that we experience the richest life possible. Yet we can be sure that he will be with us as we face physical deterioration, just as he walked with us in the days of our youth.

12:13-14 These final verses remind us of the importance of our relationship with God as we live in this fallen world. Life is filled with ambiguity; there are many things that we will never understand. But God knows the big picture; he knows the future. If we follow his program—obeying his commandments with his help—we will discover joy amidst the ambiguity. As we seek to follow his will, we will discover the only path toward true recovery.

REFLECTIONS ON ECCLESIASTES

insights ABOUT WORK AND SUCCESS

In **Ecclesiastes 2:1-11** the Teacher shows how living for personal success or pleasure will ultimately cause us to come up empty. Notice how the first person pronouns—*I, me, my*—dominate
this section. The Teacher was committed to the gratification of self-interest as a means of making
sense of life. The ultimate failure of this approach to discovering meaning is an important lesson
for us. We need to realize that living for self is ultimately self-destructive. Until we learn this, we
will find it unnatural to reach out to help others, an essential step in recovery.

In **Ecclesiastes 2:17-23** the Teacher addresses the workaholic. Work is valuable, even necessary,
to our well-being (Genesis 2:15; Ecclesiastes 2:24), yet a compulsive commitment to work will
lead to destruction. The Teacher gives us a number of reasons why looking to work for ultimate
meaning is a fruitless endeavor: (1) We don't know who will succeed us in our work (2:17-20);
(2) the one who inherits our work will not have the same passion for it as we did (2:21); and
(3) workaholism carries a higher emotional and physical cost than its benefits (2:22-23).

Ecclesiastes 4:7-8 makes it clear that if we allow work to control our life, we will end up alone.
This compulsion will cut us off from the significant relationships necessary to enjoy life. In later
years, even if we are successful, we will probably have no one to enjoy it with. It is very important
that we reconcile and strengthen the relationships God has given us. This is important for our
recovery and ultimate enjoyment of life.

insights INTO OUR IDENTITY AS HUMAN BEINGS

We are told in **Ecclesiastes 3:11** that eternity has been planted in our heart. This refers to our
innate human desire for ultimate meaning in life. Yet in this life, our perspective and understanding are limited. We can't always understand why we suffer. It is like looking at the underside of an
Oriental rug. All we see are knots and loose ends; we can only faintly make out the rug's pattern.
This is a key issue in recovery. We must not allow the things we can't understand to drag us
down. God tells us in the Bible how to live with joy and meaning.

insights ABOUT GOD

Ecclesiastes 5:1-3 assumes an important truth: God is approachable. He has established ways for
us to draw near to him. In the Old Testament, people approached God by worshiping him in the
Temple. Now that Jesus Christ has come, we can approach God directly wherever we are. He
desires to help us as we struggle with recovery. We are warned about how we should come before
God. We must never make rash promises or take him for granted. We are to approach him with
humble reverence and a grateful heart.

insights FOR REAL LIFE

We are reminded in **Ecclesiastes 5:4-7** of how important our commitments are. When we make a
commitment to God or another person, we need to take it very seriously. This reflects an important principle in recovery—being accountable for the promises we make. If we fail to keep our

commitment to recovery, we will cause the people close to us even deeper pain. We also will be headed for destruction. It might help us to realize that God takes the commitment we make very seriously.

In **Ecclesiastes 7:15-17** the Teacher does not suggest that we compromise our commitment to righteousness. We all know how destructive sin can be. This was probably the Teacher's way of suggesting that we avoid extremes in all areas of our life. But it also serves as a literal warning against being so heavenly minded that we are no earthly good. We can become so caught up in following the letter of the law that we fail to fulfill the spirit of the law. There are dangers in being too "religious."

SONG OF SONGS

THE BIG PICTURE

A. COURTSHIP (1:1–3:5)
B. MARRIAGE CEREMONY AND CONSUMMATION (3:6–5:1)
C. CONFLICT AND SEPARATION (5:2–6:13)
D. RESOLUTION AND STRENGTHENING OF LOVE (7:1–8:14)

No other book in the Bible describes the sexual relationship in such detail and with such affirmation as Song of Songs. Ironically, in our society the Bible is often thought to deny the importance of the sexual relationship. God is clearly not embarrassed by the topic. In fact, he is the one who created it in the first place! Thus it stands to reason that he is also the best qualified to tell us how to experience sex with the greatest fulfillment.

Song of Songs is characterized by the use of rich, figurative language that helps the lovers express the inexpressible about each other. The words are full of passion and emotion, and the figures of speech are designed to paint visual pictures so we can share in the emotional experience of the lovers.

The song develops a history of the relationship between Solomon and the young woman. It is not a continuous history, but a series of seemingly isolated snapshots. The couple meets and their love matures through courtship. Then the reader is taken to the wedding ceremony and the wedding night. At an unspecified later time, the couple encounters conflict, and in the course of its resolution, they passionately renew their commitment to each other.

The words of each lover clearly focus on the physical aspects of married love. Even the way Solomon and his bride praise each other focuses almost exclusively on their physical attributes. They have come to see each other as thoroughly beautiful. Marriage in general illustrates the love relationship between Christ and the church (see Ephesians 5:25-33), and Solomon's song has often been used as an illustration of God's love for his people. The primary focus of the Song of Songs, however, is the celebration of sexual love in the context of marriage.

THE BOTTOM LINE

PURPOSE: To tell of the love between a bridegroom (King Solomon) and his bride, affirming the sanctity of marriage and the richness of physical love. AUTHOR: Solomon. AUDIENCE: The people of Israel. DATE WRITTEN: Probably during the early part of Solomon's reign. SETTING: Jerusalem and the surrounding countryside. KEY VERSE: "I am my lover's, and my lover is mine. He browses among the lilies" (6:3). KEY PEOPLE AND RELATIONSHIPS: Solomon, his bride, and the young women of Jerusalem.

RECOVERY THEMES

The Beauty of God's Creation: Our past experiences may have limited our ability to see the many beautiful things that God has created for us to enjoy. When we have been sexually abused or molested, our legitimate boundaries have been destroyed. The sexual experience becomes an experience of pain and fear. Song of Songs helps us to see again what has been taken away from us—a physical love that is shameless and beautiful, even in God's eyes. We can pray that God will heal our memories and emotions so that we can see the beauty in what he has created.

The Joy of Committed Love: Our culture's understanding of love is largely distorted and twisted. It is a form of love that is driven by selfish desires, and it usually causes the people involved to be exploited or abused in some way. In Song of Songs we see the beauty of a committed love, a love that is protected by God-given boundaries. Sexual intercourse was designed by God as a holy means of celebrating love, producing children, and experiencing pleasure within the boundaries of marriage. As we seek to recover God's design in our life, we need to recover God's design for our sexuality.

The Realities of Love: Solomon did not just paint an idealized picture of marital bliss. If he had, he would have played into our own fantasies of ideal relationships and left us disappointed with the realities we all face. There will always be problems in any love relationship. As time passes, feelings of loneliness, indifference, and even isolation may be experienced. They are natural parts of most long-term love relationships. In his love song, Solomon revealed the difficult realities we all may face in the marriage relationship.

Conflict Should Lead to Recommitment: Just as Solomon revealed the challenging realities of love, he also showed us how to deal with those realities. As conflict entered Solomon's love relationship, the solution was ultimately found: perseverance, honesty, and communication. The same is true for us. Any long-term relationship will include conflict. If we learn to face our conflicts and communicate about them, we will find that doing so leads to reconciliation, recommitment, and refreshed romance. We must not let walls grow between us and the people we love. We need to face and deal with the problems before they become too large to manage.

CHAPTER 1

This is Solomon's song of songs, more wonderful than any other.

Young Woman*
2 Kiss me and kiss me again,
for your love is sweeter than wine.
3 How fragrant your cologne;
your name is like its spreading fragrance.
No wonder all the young women love you!
4 Take me with you; come, let's run!
The king has brought me into his bedroom.

Young Women of Jerusalem
How happy we are for you, O king.
We praise your love even more than wine.

Young Woman
How right they are to adore you.

5 I am dark but beautiful,
O women of Jerusalem—
dark as the tents of Kedar,
dark as the curtains of Solomon's tents.
6 Don't stare at me because I am dark—
the sun has darkened my skin.
My brothers were angry with me;
they forced me to care for their vineyards,
so I couldn't care for myself—my own vineyard.
7 Tell me, my love, where are you leading your flock today?
Where will you rest your sheep at noon?

1:1 The headings identifying the speakers are not in the original text, though the Hebrew usually gives clues by means of the gender of the person speaking.

1:6 Apparently the bride came from a somewhat dysfunctional family. Her domineering brothers forced her to work in the family's vineyards, something that was apparently not normally done. She was forced to neglect herself. Many of us have had similar experiences. We may have been abused by family members, and we now try to cover our painful scars and memories by any number of destructive behaviors. As we seek approval, we become enslaved to others and neglect our own well-beings to fill the emptiness inside. No matter how ugly we feel, God cares about us and loves us. We need to learn to trust him and obey his loving plan for our life.

For why should I wander like a prostitute*
among your friends and their flocks?

Young Man
8 If you don't know, O most beautiful
woman,
follow the trail of my flock,
and graze your young goats by the
shepherds' tents.
9 You are as exciting, my darling,
as a mare among Pharaoh's stallions.
10 How lovely are your cheeks;
your earrings set them afire!
How lovely is your neck,
enhanced by a string of jewels.
11 We will make for you earrings of gold
and beads of silver.

Young Woman
12 The king is lying on his couch,
enchanted by the fragrance of my
perfume.
13 My lover is like a sachet of myrrh
lying between my breasts.
14 He is like a bouquet of sweet henna
blossoms
from the vineyards of En-gedi.

Young Man
15 How beautiful you are, my darling,
how beautiful!
Your eyes are like doves.

Young Woman
16 You are so handsome, my love,
pleasing beyond words!
The soft grass is our bed;
17 fragrant cedar branches are the beams
of our house,
and pleasant smelling firs are the
rafters.

CHAPTER 2
Young Woman
1 I am the spring crocus blooming on the
Sharon Plain,*
the lily of the valley.

Young Man
2 Like a lily among thistles
is my darling among young women.

Young Woman
3 Like the finest apple tree in the orchard
is my lover among other young men.
I sit in his delightful shade
and taste his delicious fruit.
4 He escorts me to the banquet hall;
it's obvious how much he loves me.
5 Strengthen me with raisin cakes,
refresh me with apples,
for I am weak with love.
6 His left arm is under my head,
and his right arm embraces me.

7 Promise me, O women of Jerusalem,
by the gazelles and wild deer,
not to awaken love until the time is
right.*

8 Ah, I hear my lover coming!
He is leaping over the mountains,
bounding over the hills.
9 My lover is like a swift gazelle
or a young stag.
Look, there he is behind the wall,
looking through the window,
peering into the room.

10 My lover said to me,
"Rise up, my darling!
Come away with me, my fair one!
11 Look, the winter is past,
and the rains are over and gone.
12 The flowers are springing up,

1:7 Hebrew *like a veiled woman.* 2:1 Traditionally rendered *I am the rose of Sharon.* Sharon Plain is a region in the coastal plain of Palestine. 2:7 Or *not to awaken love until it is ready.*

1:9-17 This is the first of many sections of mutual praise and admiration between the bride and groom. Their passionate descriptions of each other undoubtedly remind us of when we met and fell in love with our spouse. There was no hint of criticism or sarcasm, two common elements in any deteriorating relationship. Notice especially the creative ways they compliment each other. Our relationships are extremely important to the recovery process. We might learn a few lessons here that will help us to reconcile and maintain the relationships God has given us.
2:7 Although she delighted in simply being with her groom, the bride desired sexual restraint until the proper time—until marriage. This restraint was difficult for her; she implored her friends to help her control her desire until the wedding night. The assumption of the book is that sex should occur only within the parameters of marriage. In recovery, we all need boundaries to give our life direction. In the Bible God has provided us with healthy boundaries. Marriage is a boundary that defines the proper context for sexual activity. We would be wise to develop friendships that will support the marriage relationship and any other boundaries important to the recovery process.

the season of singing birds* has
come,
and the cooing of turtledoves fills the
air.
¹³ The fig trees are forming young fruit,
and the fragrant grapevines are
blossoming.
Rise up, my darling!
Come away with me, my fair one!"

Young Man
¹⁴ My dove is hiding behind the rocks,
behind an outcrop on the cliff.
Let me see your face;
let me hear your voice.
For your voice is pleasant,
and your face is lovely.

Young Women of Jerusalem
¹⁵ Catch all the foxes,
those little foxes,
before they ruin the vineyard of love,
for the grapevines are blossoming!

Young Woman
¹⁶ My lover is mine, and I am his.
He browses among the lilies.
¹⁷ Before the dawn breezes blow
and the night shadows flee,
return to me, my love, like a gazelle
or a young stag on the rugged
mountains.*

CHAPTER 3
Young Woman
¹ One night as I lay in bed, I yearned for
my lover.
I yearned for him, but he did not
come.
² So I said to myself, "I will get up and
roam the city,
searching in all its streets and squares.
I will search for the one I love."
So I searched everywhere but did not
find him.

³ The watchmen stopped me as they made
their rounds,
and I asked, "Have you seen the one
I love?"
⁴ Then scarcely had I left them
when I found my love!
I caught and held him tightly,
then I brought him to my mother's
house,
into my mother's bed, where I had
been conceived.

⁵ Promise me, O women of Jerusalem,
by the gazelles and wild deer,
not to awaken love until the time is
right.*

Young Women of Jerusalem
⁶ Who is this sweeping in from the
wilderness
like a cloud of smoke?
Who is it, fragrant with myrrh and
frankincense
and every kind of spice?
⁷ Look, it is Solomon's carriage,
surrounded by sixty heroic men,
the best of Israel's soldiers.
⁸ They are all skilled swordsmen,
experienced warriors.
Each wears a sword on his thigh,
ready to defend the king against an
attack in the night.
⁹ King Solomon's carriage is built
of wood imported from Lebanon.
¹⁰ Its posts are silver,
its canopy gold;
its cushions are purple.
It was decorated with love
by the young women of Jerusalem.

Young Woman
¹¹ Come out to see King Solomon,
young women of Jerusalem.*
He wears the crown his mother gave him
on his wedding day,
his most joyous day.

2:12 Or *the season of pruning vines.* 2:17 Or *on the hills of Bether.* 3:5 Or *not to awaken love until it is ready.*
3:11 Hebrew *of Zion.*

3:6-11 As was customary in ancient Israel, the groom came to the bride's home in an elaborate
procession. After the ceremony and wedding feast, the newly married couple went to the groom's
home to consummate the marriage. They did not live with his parents, as was typical of other
cultures of the ancient Near East. Genesis 2:24 insists that both bride and groom leave their
respective families and form a new household, setting proper boundaries with both sets of
parents. If our parents have had negative effects on us, our progress in recovery may demand that
we set stronger boundaries between us and them. This may be instrumental in freeing us from
some of our destructive patterns.

CHAPTER 4

Young Man

¹ You are beautiful, my darling,
   beautiful beyond words.
Your eyes are like doves
   behind your veil.
Your hair falls in waves,
   like a flock of goats winding down the
      slopes of Gilead.
² Your teeth are as white as sheep,
   recently shorn and freshly washed.
Your smile is flawless,
   each tooth matched with its twin.*
³ Your lips are like scarlet ribbon;
   your mouth is inviting.
Your cheeks are like rosy pomegranates
   behind your veil.
⁴ Your neck is as beautiful as the tower
      of David,
   jeweled with the shields of a thousand
      heroes.
⁵ Your breasts are like two fawns,
   twin fawns of a gazelle grazing among
      the lilies.
⁶ Before the dawn breezes blow
   and the night shadows flee,
I will hurry to the mountain of myrrh
   and to the hill of frankincense.
⁷ You are altogether beautiful, my darling,
   beautiful in every way.

⁸ Come with me from Lebanon, my bride,
   come with me from Lebanon.
Come down* from Mount Amana,
   from the peaks of Senir and Hermon,
where the lions have their dens
   and leopards live among the hills.
⁹ You have captured my heart,
   my treasure,* my bride.

You hold it hostage with one glance
      of your eyes,
   with a single jewel of your necklace.
¹⁰ Your love delights me,
   my treasure, my bride.
Your love is better than wine,
   your perfume more fragrant than
      spices.
¹¹ Your lips are as sweet as nectar, my bride.
   Honey and milk are under your
      tongue.
Your clothes are scented
   like the cedars of Lebanon.

¹² You are my private garden, my treasure,
      my bride,
   a secluded spring, a hidden fountain.
¹³ Your thighs shelter a paradise of
      pomegranates
   with rare spices—
henna with nard,
¹⁴   nard and saffron,
   fragrant calamus and cinnamon,
with all the trees of frankincense,
   myrrh, and aloes,
   and every other lovely spice.
¹⁵ You are a garden fountain,
   a well of fresh water
   streaming down from Lebanon's
      mountains.

Young Woman

¹⁶ Awake, north wind!
   Rise up, south wind!
Blow on my garden
   and spread its fragrance all
      around.
Come into your garden, my love;
   taste its finest fruits.

4:2 Hebrew *Not one is missing; each has a twin.* **4:8** Or *Look down.* **4:9** Hebrew *my sister;* also in 4:10, 12.

4:1-7 Solomon described his bride from a lover's perspective. Although she may not have been considered attractive by the general public or even by herself (see 1:6), he saw her as beautiful. Solomon's figures of speech sometimes confuse us, but in the ancient culture these were glowing compliments. For instance, when he said her hair was "like a flock of goats winding down the slopes of Gilead" (4:1), he meant that her hair was long and flowing, and it glistened like goats frolicking in the evening sun. No matter how broken and sinful we are, God sees past our flaws to our possibilities. Jesus Christ paid for all our sins and mistakes through his death and resurrection. Because of this, God can look on us as lovingly as this lover looks on his bride.

4:12-15 The bride's virginity is compared to a garden, a spring, and a fountain, all of which have been inaccessible to Solomon until now. The couple's sexual enjoyment is compared to choice fruits that have come out of her garden. Many of us may suffer from the pain of a "garden" or "spring" that has been violated by others. We may feel that our sexuality has been spoiled beyond recovery. As the One who created our sexuality, however, God is capable of restoring it. Notice that each of the symbols used here—the garden, the spring, and the fountain—are symbols of recurring freshness. Even after times of destruction, they soon return to their original condition. With God's help, our sexuality can also be restored to its original beauty.

CHAPTER 5

Young Man
¹ I have entered my garden, my treasure,*
    my bride!
I gather myrrh with my spices
and eat honeycomb with my honey.
I drink wine with my milk.

Young Women of Jerusalem
Oh, lover and beloved, eat and drink!
Yes, drink deeply of your love!

Young Woman
² I slept, but my heart was awake,
    when I heard my lover knocking and
        calling:
"Open to me, my treasure, my darling,
    my dove, my perfect one.
My head is drenched with dew,
    my hair with the dampness of the
        night."

³ But I responded,
"I have taken off my robe.
    Should I get dressed again?
I have washed my feet.
    Should I get them soiled?"

⁴ My lover tried to unlatch the door,
    and my heart thrilled within me.
⁵ I jumped up to open the door for my love,
    and my hands dripped with perfume.
My fingers dripped with lovely myrrh
    as I pulled back the bolt.

5:1 Hebrew *my sister;* also in 5:2.

⁶ I opened to my lover,
    but he was gone!
    My heart sank.
I searched for him
    but could not find him anywhere.
I called to him,
    but there was no reply.
⁷ The night watchmen found me
    as they made their rounds.
They beat and bruised me
    and stripped off my veil,
    those watchmen on the walls.

⁸ Make this promise, O women of
        Jerusalem—
If you find my lover,
    tell him I am weak with love.

Young Women of Jerusalem
⁹ Why is your lover better than all others,
    O woman of rare beauty?
What makes your lover so special
    that we must promise this?

Young Woman
¹⁰ My lover is dark and dazzling,
    better than ten thousand others!
¹¹ His head is finest gold,
    his wavy hair is black as a raven.
¹² His eyes sparkle like doves
    beside springs of water;
they are set like jewels
    washed in milk.

5:1 Solomon delighted in his sexual relationship with his bride. He realized that people were created for sexual enjoyment—and celebrated that truth. We are often given the impression that God considers the sexual relationship a necessary evil. This is far from the truth. God gave sex as a gift to be enjoyed within marriage. Regaining a healthy view of sex is one of the most difficult problems in recovery, especially if we have been sexually abused. It is not difficult to see how sex can begin to seem very ugly when practiced outside the proper bounds. If we have suffered sexual abuse, we need to look to God for healing and strength. He will help us redefine the boundaries we need for healthy relationships.

5:2-8 It is not clear how much time had elapsed since the couple's wedding night, but enough time had passed for the realities of married life to set in. Indifference and emotional distance were likely at the root of the conflict here. The bride had gone to bed when her husband arrived and wanted to be with her (5:2-3). She failed to expend the necessary effort to respond to his initiative, so he felt rejected and left, leaving her downcast. We need to be aware of the dangers of indifference in marriage. It happens slowly and is often hard to detect until it is already quite far along. A strong marriage relationship is extremely helpful in the recovery process. We need to strengthen our relationships, especially the marriage relationship, by seeking reconciliation and forgiveness wherever necessary.

5:9-16 The young women of Jerusalem forced the young bride to remember all she loved about her husband. She began with his physical attributes and concluded by calling him her lover and her friend (5:16). Even though these descriptions emphasize the physical relationship, the couple had apparently also cultivated a solid friendship. Sexual relationships are often selfishly motivated and often don't last unless built upon the foundation of a deeper selfless friendship. We must evaluate our relationships carefully and avoid those that are motivated by our selfish desire for pleasure. God designed our sexuality to bring us joy within the context of marriage.

[13] His cheeks are like gardens of spices
    giving off fragrance.
His lips are like lilies,
    perfumed with myrrh.
[14] His arms are like rounded bars of gold,
    set with beryl.
His body is like bright ivory,
    glowing with lapis lazuli.
[15] His legs are like marble pillars
    set in sockets of finest gold.
His posture is stately,
    like the noble cedars of Lebanon.
[16] His mouth is sweetness itself;
    he is desirable in every way.
Such, O women of Jerusalem,
    is my lover, my friend.

CHAPTER 6
Young Women of Jerusalem
[1] Where has your lover gone,
    O woman of rare beauty?
Which way did he turn
    so we can help you find him?

Young Woman
[2] My lover has gone down to his garden,
    to his spice beds,
to browse in the gardens
    and gather the lilies.
[3] I am my lover's, and my lover is mine.
    He browses among the lilies.

Young Man
[4] You are beautiful, my darling,
    like the lovely city of Tirzah.
Yes, as beautiful as Jerusalem,
    as majestic as an army with billowing
    banners.
[5] Turn your eyes away,
    for they overpower me.
Your hair falls in waves,
    like a flock of goats winding down the
    slopes of Gilead.
[6] Your teeth are as white as sheep
    that are freshly washed.
Your smile is flawless,
    each tooth matched with its twin.*

[7] Your cheeks are like rosy pomegranates
    behind your veil.
[8] Even among sixty queens
    and eighty concubines
    and countless young women,
[9] I would still choose my dove, my perfect
    one—
    the favorite of her mother,
    dearly loved by the one who bore her.
The young women see her and praise her;
    even queens and royal concubines sing
    her praises:
[10] "Who is this, arising like the dawn,
    as fair as the moon,
as bright as the sun,
    as majestic as an army with billowing
    banners?"

Young Woman
[11] I went down to the grove of walnut trees
    and out to the valley to see the new
    spring growth,
to see whether the grapevines had
    budded
    or the pomegranates were in bloom.
[12] Before I realized it,
    my strong desires had taken me to the
    chariot of a noble man.*

Young Women of Jerusalem
[13] *Return, return to us, O maid of Shulam.
    Come back, come back, that we may
    see you again.

Young Man
Why do you stare at this young woman of
    Shulam,
    as she moves so gracefully between two
    lines of dancers?*

CHAPTER 7
[1] *How beautiful are your sandaled feet,
    O queenly maiden.
Your rounded thighs are like jewels,
    the work of a skilled craftsman.
[2] Your navel is perfectly formed
    like a goblet filled with mixed wine.

6:6 Hebrew *Not one is missing; each has a twin.* **6:12** Or *to the royal chariots of my people,* or *to the chariots of Amminadab. The meaning of the Hebrew is uncertain.* **6:13a** Verse 6:13 is numbered 7:1 in Hebrew text. **6:13b** Or *as you would at the movements of two armies?* or *as you would at the dance of Mahanaim? The meaning of the Hebrew is uncertain.* **7:1** Verses 7:1-13 are numbered 7:2-14 in Hebrew text.

7:1-9 Solomon's praise of his bride continues. As the couple matured in their love, the passion did not diminish. This is not to say that relationships should go on at a fevered pitch constantly, but it indicates that passionate love can last as a marriage matures. All relationships go through periods of ebb and flow. It is important for the recovery process that we maintain our relationships. We need to do all we can to assess the wrongs we have done against others and to achieve reconciliation and stability.

Between your thighs lies a mound
of wheat
bordered with lilies.
³ Your breasts are like two fawns,
twin fawns of a gazelle.
⁴ Your neck is as beautiful as an ivory
tower.
Your eyes are like the sparkling pools in
Heshbon
by the gate of Bath-rabbim.
Your nose is as fine as the tower of
Lebanon
overlooking Damascus.
⁵ Your head is as majestic as Mount Carmel,
and the sheen of your hair radiates
royalty.
The king is held captive by its tresses.
⁶ Oh, how beautiful you are!
How pleasing, my love, how full of
delights!
⁷ You are slender like a palm tree,
and your breasts are like its clusters of
fruit.
⁸ I said, "I will climb the palm tree
and take hold of its fruit."
May your breasts be like grape clusters,
and the fragrance of your breath like
apples.
⁹ May your kisses be as exciting as the best
wine—

Young Woman
Yes, wine that goes down smoothly for my
lover,
flowing gently over lips and teeth.*
¹⁰ I am my lover's,
and he claims me as his own.
¹¹ Come, my love, let us go out to
the fields
and spend the night among the
wildflowers.*

¹² Let us get up early and go to the vineyards
to see if the grapevines have budded,
if the blossoms have opened,
and if the pomegranates have bloomed.
There I will give you my love.
¹³ There the mandrakes give off their
fragrance,
and the finest fruits are at our door,
new delights as well as old,
which I have saved for you, my lover.

CHAPTER 8
Young Woman
¹ Oh, I wish you were my brother,
who nursed at my mother's breasts.
Then I could kiss you no matter who was
watching,
and no one would criticize me.
² I would bring you to my childhood home,
and there you would teach me.*
I would give you spiced wine to drink,
my sweet pomegranate wine.
³ Your left arm would be under my head,
and your right arm would embrace me.

⁴ Promise me, O women of Jerusalem,
not to awaken love until the time is
right.*

Young Women of Jerusalem
⁵ Who is this sweeping in from the desert,
leaning on her lover?

Young Woman
I aroused you under the apple tree,
where your mother gave you birth,
where in great pain she delivered you.
⁶ Place me like a seal over your heart,
like a seal on your arm.
For love is as strong as death,
its jealousy* as enduring as
the grave.*

7:9 As in Greek and Syriac versions and Latin Vulgate; Hebrew reads *over lips of sleepers.*   7:11 Or *in the villages.*
8:2 Or *there she will teach me.*   8:4 Or *not to awaken love until it is ready.*   8:6a Or *its passion.*   8:6b Hebrew as *Sheol.*

7:10-13 Here the young woman took the initiative, inviting her husband to come with her out to
the fields and vineyards, where they would celebrate their love. The romantic setting among the
wildflowers (7:11) would certainly have made for many tender moments. How often do we go
out of our way to create romance in our marriage? Solomon and his bride should inspire us to do
what we can to put some sparkle back into our marriage relationship.
8:6-7 This eloquent statement describing committed love shows the renewed fervor of a love
that endures and resolves conflict. The seal, or signet ring, symbolized Solomon's commitment to
his bride. The jealousy mentioned in 8:6 is a positive emotion; it speaks of the accountability
shared between Solomon and his bride. Their commitment was so strong that there would be
serious consequences for anyone who threatened it. Given his vast wealth, Solomon knew from
experience about the value of love over riches. True love can never be bought; it must be cultivated. Relationships characterized by commitment, love, and accountability are needed if we
hope to succeed in recovery.

Love flashes like fire,
  the brightest kind of flame.
[7] Many waters cannot quench love,
  nor can rivers drown it.
If a man tried to buy love
  with all his wealth,
  his offer would be utterly scorned.

The Young Woman's Brothers
[8] We have a little sister
  too young to have breasts.
What will we do for our sister
  if someone asks to marry her?
[9] If she is a virgin, like a wall,
  we will protect her with a silver
    tower.
But if she is promiscuous, like a swinging
    door,
  we will block her door with a cedar bar.

Young Woman
[10] I was a virgin, like a wall;
  now my breasts are like towers.

When my lover looks at me,
  he is delighted with what he sees.

[11] Solomon has a vineyard at Baal-hamon,
  which he leases out to tenant farmers.
Each of them pays a thousand pieces of
    silver
  for harvesting its fruit.
[12] But my vineyard is mine to give,
  and Solomon need not pay a thousand
    pieces of silver.
But I will give two hundred pieces
  to those who care for its vines.

Young Man
[13] O my darling, lingering in the gardens,
  your companions are fortunate to hear
    your voice.
Let me hear it, too!

Young Woman
[14] Come away, my love! Be like a gazelle
  or a young stag on the mountains of
    spices.

8:8-12 These verses assume that sexual expression is to be limited to the marriage relationship. The young woman's brothers desired to protect their sister and keep her chaste prior to her marriage. Sexual activity outside the marriage commitment is always destructive. It may bring pleasure for a while, but it will never lead to stability and fulfillment. We need to build relationships characterized by trust and honesty and keep sexual activity in the marriage context. This will help immensely as we seek recovery from the various problems we face.

ISAIAH

THE BIG PICTURE

A. MESSAGE OF CONFRON-
TATION TO JUDAH (1:1–39:8)
1. Judah Is Confronted about Its
Sin (1:1–12:6)
2. God Judges Judah's
Oppressors (13:1–23:18)
3. A Promise of God's Final
Victory (24:1–27:13)
4. Judah's Choice of Recovery
or Disaster (28:1–31:9)
5. Salvation Is Coming, but the
Path Is Hard (32:1–35:10)
6. Historical Interlude:
Hezekiah's Tests (36:1–39:8)
B. MESSAGE OF HOPE TO
BABYLONIAN EXILES
(40:1–66:24)
1. A Promise of God's
Deliverance (40:1–48:22)
2. Deliverance through a
Suffering Servant
(49:1–55:13)
3. Israel's Eventual Exaltation
(56:1–66:24)

Though it is never easy to face the truth, truth brings healing. God spoke through Isaiah to address the denial of the people of Judah. Over the centuries they had become addicted to the false promises of idolatry. They had developed self-destructive patterns of behavior that included oppressing the poor, accepting bribes, and lying to get what they wanted. Although repeatedly confronted by Isaiah, they refused to admit their sins. Instead, they blamed God for their sufferings and wondered why he refused to bless them.

The first part of Isaiah (1:1–39:8) is dominated by a message of judgment. The empire of Assyria had recently destroyed the northern kingdom of Israel and now threatened to destroy Judah. God told the people of Judah that deliverance would come, but only if they repented of their sins and turned to him for help. The people of Judah trusted in God only superficially and sought to save themselves through clever political alliances, first with Assyria and then with Egypt. Their human attempts to escape the suffering of exile could never bring permanent deliverance. God did allow Judah to survive the attacks of Egypt and Assyria, but a few generations later, Judah was crushed by the rising power of Babylon.

The second part of Isaiah (40:1–66:24) is dominated by a message of hope. In spite of Judah's unworthiness, God promised that he would lead his people out of Babylonian captivity. He also foretold the miracle of salvation through the Suffering Servant and his ultimate cosmic victory culminating in a new heaven and a new earth. Through the words of Isaiah we discover that God's ultimate purpose for his people is always their blessing and recovery.

THE BOTTOM LINE

PURPOSE: To confront the people of Judah with their sin and denial and to inspire them to rebuild their lives based on God's promises. AUTHOR: The prophet Isaiah. AUDIENCE: Isaiah 1–39 was spoken to the people of Judah before their exile; Isaiah 40–66 recorded a message of hope to future generations of exiled Jews. DATE WRITTEN: The book includes oracles given throughout Isaiah's ministry (740–680 B.C.). SETTING: The land of Judah before its destruction by Babylon. KEY VERSE: "But he was pierced for our rebellion, crushed for our sins. He was beaten so we could be whole. He was whipped so we could be healed" (53:5). KEY PLACES: Judah, Egypt, Assyria, Babylonia, and Persia. KEY PEOPLE AND RELATIONSHIPS: Isaiah with Kings Ahaz and Hezekiah of Judah and with King Cyrus of Persia.

RECOVERY THEMES

The Truth Brings Healing: Because the truth hurts, we often try to protect ourself from it. When Isaiah told the people of Judah the truth about their sins, they acted as we often do—they chose to hide in their denial. They refused to admit that they had sinned. In doing so, they also refused to experience the healing power of truth. Our recovery program will be effective only if we open ourself to the truth regardless of how painful that might be.

Denial Leads to Blaming: Instead of admitting their sins and responding to that truth, the people of Judah blamed God for the terrible consequences of their sins. If we continue in denial, we will also become expert blamers. If we desire to progress in recovery, however, we need to take responsibility for our actions. The painful circumstances that we suffer are often direct consequences of our own failures.

Recovery through Confrontation: God had a program for Judah's recovery: He confronted them with the truth of their sins. Isaiah's words of confrontation, however, were punctuated by the message of God's love and hope. The model of confrontation found in the book of Isaiah can help us as we intervene in the lives of the people we love who are trapped by their addictions. Our words of confrontation need to be balanced by words and actions that demonstrate our genuine love and forgiveness. Angry confrontation causes greater conflict and further destruction.

The Importance of Action: God is not an enabler. As we see in the book of Isaiah, God takes our actions very seriously. He does for us what we are unable to do for ourself, but then he leaves the rest to us. Isaiah told the people that despite their impending doom, God would deliver them from Babylonian captivity. God provided the way, but the people had to take the steps to leave. When our prayers for recovery are not answered, it may be time for us to act. Often, it is only after acting in faith that we are able to see what God has already accomplished for us.

CHAPTER 1

These are the visions that Isaiah son of Amoz saw concerning Judah and Jerusalem. He saw these visions during the years when Uzziah, Jotham, Ahaz, and Hezekiah were kings of Judah.*

A Message for Rebellious Judah

² Listen, O heavens! Pay attention, earth!
    This is what the LORD says:
"The children I raised and cared for
    have rebelled against me.
³ Even an ox knows its owner,
    and a donkey recognizes its master's
        care—
    but Israel doesn't know its master.
    My people don't recognize my care for
        them."
⁴ Oh, what a sinful nation they are—

1:1 These kings reigned from 792 to 686 B.C.

loaded down with a burden of guilt.
They are evil people,
    corrupt children who have rejected the
        LORD.
They have despised the Holy One of Israel
    and turned their backs on him.

⁵ Why do you continue to invite
        punishment?
    Must you rebel forever?
Your head is injured,
    and your heart is sick.
⁶ You are battered from head to foot—
    covered with bruises, welts, and
        infected wounds—
    without any soothing ointments or
        bandages.
⁷ Your country lies in ruins,
    and your towns are burned.

1:5-6 Because the people of Judah were in denial and refused to admit their sins, they continued to suffer. When we continue to deny our sins and refuse to admit our need of God's cleansing and forgiveness, we often suffer in ways we wouldn't have to. We often reap destructive consequences when we try to manage our own life. God wants us to know that in his presence we can safely start to deal with truth and come out of denial. We must trust him to bring us healing and forgiveness. **1:9-20** Although the people of Judah were very "religious," they were accused of being as evil as the people of Sodom and Gomorrah. They gave sacrifices to pay for their sins, but they felt no remorse. They needed to take moral inventories, acknowledge the depth of their sins, and turn to God for cleansing and renewal. Religious activity is no substitute for a genuine life with God. It is only when we honestly confess our sins and ask God to help us that he will make us "as white as snow."

ISAIAH

God called Isaiah to be a prophet in "the year King Uzziah died" (Isaiah 6:1), and his ministry extended over forty years (740–700 B.C.). He prophesied during the reigns of four kings of Judah: Uzziah, Jotham, Ahaz, and Hezekiah. Isaiah's name means "the Lord will save," a meaning especially appropriate since throughout his book he speaks of God's gracious promises of comfort and deliverance.

Isaiah was married and had a family. His sons were given symbolic names: *Shear-jashub* means "a remnant will return"; *Maher-shalal-hash-baz* means "swift to plunder and quick to spoil." These names carried messages from God to the people of Judah. Isaiah recognized that his sons ultimately belonged to God. This indicates that his family life was not only consistent with his vocation but also intimately interwoven with it.

All that we know about the prophet indicates that he was one of the greatest men of his time. His book is an undisputed masterpiece that reveals an author of considerable intelligence and education. Tradition holds that Isaiah belonged to a family of some rank. This would explain his easy access to the king. Because of this man's greatness, it may be difficult for us to relate to him. Isaiah was a man of God and a statesman. He had the soul of an artist, and he was steadfast in his obedience to God.

Although Isaiah had many gifts, his success was primarily a fruit of his humility and faithfulness to God's will for his life. When God called him, Isaiah had an overwhelming sense of his own sinfulness. He started where we need to start: He admitted his sins and turned to God for cleansing and deliverance. When God revealed his will for Isaiah, the prophet pursued God's plan with determination. He spoke and lived out God's will for him despite opposition. As a result, God used him to confront his people with their sins and to comfort them as they faced a painful future. Through his words and life, Isaiah has blazed a trail for us to follow for our spiritual growth and recovery.

STRENGTHS AND ACCOMPLISHMENTS:
- Isaiah was a gifted speaker and author, and is considered the greatest of the Old Testament prophets.
- He followed God's will for his life with determination.
- He recognized his personal need for healing and received God's help.
- He was sensitive yet strong in his convictions.
- He was faithful to God's call despite great opposition and discouragement.

LESSONS FROM HIS LIFE:
- Our healing begins when we admit our sins and turn to God.
- We can decide to follow God's will and remain faithful to that decision.
- God has gifted each of us, and he will help and lead us as we place our trust in him.

KEY VERSE:
"Then I heard the LORD asking, 'Whom should I send as a messenger to this people? Who will go for us?' I said, 'Here I am. Send me'" (Isaiah 6:8).

The story of Isaiah is told in the book of Isaiah. He is also mentioned in 2 Kings 18–20. His name is also found in the New Testament, where he is recognized for having foretold the coming of the Messiah.

Foreigners plunder your fields before
　　your eyes
　　and destroy everything they see.
⁸ Beautiful Jerusalem* stands abandoned
　　like a watchman's shelter in a vineyard,
　　like a lean-to in a cucumber field after the
　　　　harvest,
　　like a helpless city under siege.
⁹ If the LORD of Heaven's Armies
　　had not spared a few of us,*

we would have been wiped out like
　　Sodom,
　　destroyed like Gomorrah.
¹⁰ Listen to the LORD, you leaders
　　of "Sodom."
　　Listen to the law of our God, people
　　of "Gomorrah."
¹¹ "What makes you think I want all your
　　sacrifices?"
　　says the LORD.

1:8 Hebrew *The daughter of Zion.* **1:9** Greek version reads *a few of our children.* Compare Rom 9:29.

"I am sick of your burnt offerings of rams
and the fat of fattened cattle.
I get no pleasure from the blood
of bulls and lambs and goats.
¹²When you come to worship me,
who asked you to parade through my
courts with all your ceremony?
¹³Stop bringing me your meaningless gifts;
the incense of your offerings disgusts
me!
As for your celebrations of the new moon
and the Sabbath
and your special days for fasting—
they are all sinful and false.
I want no more of your pious
meetings.
¹⁴I hate your new moon celebrations and
your annual festivals.
They are a burden to me. I cannot
stand them!
¹⁵When you lift up your hands in prayer,
I will not look.
Though you offer many prayers, I will
not listen,
for your hands are covered with the
blood of innocent victims.
¹⁶Wash yourselves and be clean!
Get your sins out of my sight.
Give up your evil ways.
¹⁷Learn to do good.
Seek justice.
Help the oppressed.
Defend the cause of orphans.
Fight for the rights of widows.

¹⁸"Come now, let's settle this,"
says the LORD.
"Though your sins are like scarlet,
I will make them as white as snow.
Though they are red like crimson,
I will make them as white as wool.
¹⁹If you will only obey me,
you will have plenty to eat.
²⁰But if you turn away and refuse to listen,
you will be devoured by the sword of
your enemies.
I, the LORD, have spoken!"

Unfaithful Jerusalem

²¹See how Jerusalem, once so faithful,
has become a prostitute.
Once the home of justice and
righteousness,
she is now filled with murderers.
²²Once like pure silver,

you have become like worthless slag.
Once so pure,
you are now like watered-down wine.
²³Your leaders are rebels,
the companions of thieves.
All of them love bribes
and demand payoffs,
but they refuse to defend the cause of
orphans
or fight for the rights of widows.

²⁴Therefore, the Lord, the LORD of Heaven's
Armies,
the Mighty One of Israel, says,
"I will take revenge on my enemies
and pay back my foes!
²⁵I will raise my fist against you.
I will melt you down and skim off your
slag.
I will remove all your impurities.
²⁶Then I will give you good judges again
and wise counselors like you used to
have.
Then Jerusalem will again be called the
Home of Justice
and the Faithful City."

²⁷Zion will be restored by justice;
those who repent will be revived by
righteousness.
²⁸But rebels and sinners will be completely
destroyed,
and those who desert the LORD will be
consumed.

²⁹You will be ashamed of your idol
worship
in groves of sacred oaks.
You will blush because you worshiped
in gardens dedicated to idols.
³⁰You will be like a great tree with withered
leaves,
like a garden without water.
³¹The strongest among you will disappear
like straw;
their evil deeds will be the spark that
sets it on fire.
They and their evil works will burn up
together,
and no one will be able to put out the
fire.

CHAPTER 2
The LORD's Future Reign

This is a vision that Isaiah son of Amoz saw
concerning Judah and Jerusalem:

2:1-5 At the end of history, the entire human race will finally acknowledge that God is supreme.
Judah was called to live in light of that future reality. We, too, are called to walk in the light and

2 In the last days, the mountain of the
LORD's house
will be the highest of all—
the most important place on earth.
It will be raised above the other hills,
and people from all over the world will
stream there to worship.
3 People from many nations will come and
say,
"Come, let us go up to the mountain of
the LORD,
to the house of Jacob's God.
There he will teach us his ways,
and we will walk in his paths."
For the LORD's teaching will go out from
Zion;
his word will go out from Jerusalem.
4 The LORD will mediate between nations
and will settle international disputes.
They will hammer their swords into
plowshares
and their spears into pruning hooks.
Nation will no longer fight against nation,
nor train for war anymore.

A Warning of Judgment

5 Come, descendants of Jacob,
let us walk in the light of the LORD!
6 For the LORD has rejected his people,
the descendants of Jacob,
because they have filled their land with
practices from the East
and with sorcerers, as the Philistines do.
They have made alliances with pagans.
7 Israel is full of silver and gold;
there is no end to its treasures.
Their land is full of warhorses;
there is no end to its chariots.
8 Their land is full of idols;
the people worship things they have
made
with their own hands.
9 So now they will be humbled,
and all will be brought low—
do not forgive them.
10 Crawl into caves in the rocks.

2:16 Hebrew *every ship of Tarshish.*

Hide in the dust
from the terror of the LORD
and the glory of his majesty.
11 Human pride will be brought down,
and human arrogance will be humbled.
Only the LORD will be exalted
on that day of judgment.

12 For the LORD of Heaven's Armies
has a day of reckoning.
He will punish the proud and mighty
and bring down everything that is
exalted.
13 He will cut down the tall cedars of
Lebanon
and all the mighty oaks of Bashan.
14 He will level all the high mountains
and all the lofty hills.
15 He will break down every high tower
and every fortified wall.
16 He will destroy all the great trading ships*
and every magnificent vessel.
17 Human pride will be humbled,
and human arrogance will be brought
down.
Only the LORD will be exalted
on that day of judgment.

18 Idols will completely disappear.
19 When the LORD rises to shake the earth,
his enemies will crawl into holes in the
ground.
They will hide in caves in the rocks
from the terror of the LORD
and the glory of his majesty.
20 On that day of judgment they will
abandon the gold and silver idols
they made for themselves to worship.
They will leave their gods to the rodents
and bats,
21 while they crawl away into caverns
and hide among the jagged rocks in the
cliffs.
They will try to escape the terror of the
LORD
and the glory of his majesty
as he rises to shake the earth.

give up our addictions, compulsions, and other sinful attractions that draw our attention away from
God. We need to obey God's Word and live according to his will for us. As we do, we will be able to
restore our present life and also share in God's eternal Kingdom.
2:6-22 Isaiah declared that when God sets up his Kingdom, the people who have put their trust
in anything other than God will be humbled and hide to try to escape the terror of the Lord. By
putting our trust in God, not in any human program or plan, we will have no reason to be
ashamed or afraid when he fully reveals his awesome power. Any human program or item that we
may trust in will one day be destroyed. It is foolish to depend on things like subliminal tapes, crystals, or any other technique that excludes God and his power.

22 Don't put your trust in mere humans.
    They are as frail as breath.
    What good are they?

CHAPTER 3
Judgment against Judah

1 The Lord, the LORD of Heaven's Armies,
    will take away from Jerusalem and
    Judah
everything they depend on:
    every bit of bread
    and every drop of water,
2 all their heroes and soldiers,
    judges and prophets,
    fortune-tellers and elders,
3 army officers and high officials,
    advisers, skilled sorcerers, and
    astrologers.

4 I will make boys their leaders,
    and toddlers their rulers.
5 People will oppress each other—
    man against man,
    neighbor against neighbor.
Young people will insult their elders,
    and vulgar people will sneer at the
    honorable.

6 In those days a man will say to his
    brother,
"Since you have a coat, you be our
    leader!
Take charge of this heap of ruins!"
7 But he will reply,
    "No! I can't help.
I don't have any extra food or clothes.
    Don't put me in charge!"

8 For Jerusalem will stumble,
    and Judah will fall,
because they speak out against the LORD
    and refuse to obey him.
    They provoke him to his face.

9 The very look on their faces gives them
    away.
They display their sin like the people of
    Sodom
and don't even try to hide it.
They are doomed!
    They have brought destruction upon
    themselves.

10 Tell the godly that all will be well for
    them.
They will enjoy the rich reward they
    have earned!
11 But the wicked are doomed,
    for they will get exactly what they
    deserve.

12 Childish leaders oppress my people,
    and women rule over them.
O my people, your leaders mislead you;
    they send you down the wrong road.

13 The LORD takes his place in court
    and presents his case against his people.*
14 The LORD comes forward to pronounce
    judgment
    on the elders and rulers of his people:
"You have ruined Israel, my vineyard.
    Your houses are filled with things stolen
    from the poor.
15 How dare you crush my people,
    grinding the faces of the poor into the
    dust?"
    demands the Lord, the LORD of
    Heaven's Armies.

A Warning to Jerusalem

16 The LORD says, "Beautiful Zion* is
    haughty:
craning her elegant neck,
    flirting with her eyes,
walking with dainty steps,
    tinkling her ankle bracelets.

3:13 As in Greek and Syriac versions; Hebrew reads *against the peoples.* 3:16 Or *The women of Zion* (with
corresponding changes to plural forms through verse 24); Hebrew reads *The daughters of Zion;* also in 3:17.

3:1-8 God was going to crush Judah and Jerusalem because the people had refused to obey him.
They had refused to listen to God's warnings, so something drastic was needed to shake them out
of their denial. We often ignore the warnings God sends us and continue our dependency or
addiction. God may need to send a catastrophe to get us back on the right track. Continuing on
our present path will only lead to our destruction. We must heed his warnings before it is too late.
God wants us to have a joyful and meaningful life.
3:9-26 The sins of Sodom and Gomorrah were hideous, so God had utterly destroyed those cities
(see Genesis 19). Being compared to wicked Sodom should have made the Israelites realize how
evil they had become, but they weren't even ashamed of the comparison. They weren't denying
their sins; they delighted in them. Have we reached the point where we are proud of our addiction and flaunt our sinful behavior? If so, we may be trying to make ourself believe that our
dependent lifestyle really is fulfilling. But we shouldn't fool ourselves. God is willing to help us
recover and return to him if we ask him.

[17] So the Lord will send scabs on her head;
the LORD will make beautiful Zion
bald."

[18] On that day of judgment
the Lord will strip away everything that
makes her beautiful:
ornaments, headbands, crescent
necklaces,
[19] earrings, bracelets, and veils;
[20] scarves, ankle bracelets, sashes,
perfumes, and charms;
[21] rings, jewels,
[22] party clothes, gowns, capes, and
purses;
[23] mirrors, fine linen garments,
head ornaments, and shawls.

[24] Instead of smelling of sweet perfume, she
will stink.
She will wear a rope for a sash,
and her elegant hair will fall out.
She will wear rough burlap instead of rich
robes.
Shame will replace her beauty.*
[25] The men of the city will be killed with
the sword,
and her warriors will die in battle.
[26] The gates of Zion will weep and mourn.
The city will be like a ravaged woman,
huddled on the ground.

CHAPTER 4
In that day so few men will be left that seven
women will fight for each man, saying, "Let
us all marry you! We will provide our own
food and clothing. Only let us take your
name so we won't be mocked as old maids."

A Promise of Restoration
[2] But in that day, the branch* of the LORD
will be beautiful and glorious;
the fruit of the land will be the pride and
glory
of all who survive in Israel.
[3] All who remain in Zion
will be a holy people—

those who survive the destruction of
Jerusalem
and are recorded among the living.
[4] The Lord will wash the filth from
beautiful Zion*
and cleanse Jerusalem of its bloodstains
with the hot breath of fiery judgment.
[5] Then the LORD will provide shade for
Mount Zion
and all who assemble there.
He will provide a canopy of cloud during
the day
and smoke and flaming fire at night,
covering the glorious land.
[6] It will be a shelter from daytime heat
and a hiding place from storms and
rain.

CHAPTER 5
A Song about the LORD's Vineyard
[1] Now I will sing for the one I love
a song about his vineyard:
My beloved had a vineyard
on a rich and fertile hill.
[2] He plowed the land, cleared its stones,
and planted it with the best vines.
In the middle he built a watchtower
and carved a winepress in the nearby
rocks.
Then he waited for a harvest of sweet
grapes,
but the grapes that grew were bitter.

[3] Now, you people of Jerusalem and Judah,
you judge between me and my
vineyard.
[4] What more could I have done for my
vineyard
that I have not already done?
When I expected sweet grapes,
why did my vineyard give me bitter
grapes?

[5] Now let me tell you
what I will do to my vineyard:
I will tear down its hedges
and let it be destroyed.

3:24 As in Dead Sea Scrolls; Masoretic Text reads *robes / because instead of beauty.*   **4:2** Or *the Branch.*   **4:4** Or *from the women of Zion;* Hebrew reads *from the daughters of Zion.*

4:2-4 God wants his people to be characterized by self-respect, honor, and righteousness. Developing those qualities, however, sometimes includes a scorching purification process. Facing up to and dealing with the reality of our inadequacies, dysfunctions, addictions, and compulsive behaviors are neither easy nor painless, but the end God has prepared for us is worth the price.
5:1-7 God provides us with all we need for a fruitful, functional life, but when we reject him and abandon his way, our life becomes unmanageable, unfruitful, and dysfunctional. If we desire a normal, healthy life, we can ask God for his aid and turn our life over to him. With God's help, our life will someday bear "sweet grapes," fruit that is pleasing to God.

I will break down its walls
and let the animals trample it.
⁶I will make it a wild place
where the vines are not pruned and the
ground is not hoed,
a place overgrown with briers and
thorns.
I will command the clouds
to drop no rain on it.

⁷The nation of Israel is the vineyard of the
LORD of Heaven's Armies.
The people of Judah are his pleasant
garden.
He expected a crop of justice,
but instead he found oppression.
He expected to find righteousness,
but instead he heard cries of violence.

Judah's Guilt and Judgment

⁸What sorrow for you who buy up house
after house and field after field,
until everyone is evicted and you live
alone in the land.
⁹But I have heard the LORD of Heaven's
Armies
swear a solemn oath:
"Many houses will stand deserted;
even beautiful mansions will be
empty.
¹⁰Ten acres* of vineyard will not produce
even six gallons* of wine.
Ten baskets of seed will yield only one
basket* of grain."

¹¹What sorrow for those who get up early in
the morning
looking for a drink of alcohol
and spend long evenings drinking
wine
to make themselves flaming drunk.
¹²They furnish wine and lovely music at
their grand parties—
lyre and harp, tambourine and flute—
but they never think about the LORD
or notice what he is doing.

¹³So my people will go into exile far away
because they do not know me.
Those who are great and honored will
starve,
and the common people will die of
thirst.
¹⁴The grave* is licking its lips in
anticipation,
opening its mouth wide.
The great and the lowly
and all the drunken mob will be
swallowed up.
¹⁵Humanity will be destroyed, and people
brought down;
even the arrogant will lower their eyes
in humiliation.
¹⁶But the LORD of Heaven's Armies will be
exalted by his justice.
The holiness of God will be displayed
by his righteousness.
¹⁷In that day lambs will find good
pastures,
and fattened sheep and young goats*
will feed among the ruins.

¹⁸What sorrow for those who drag their sins
behind them
with ropes made of lies,
who drag wickedness behind them like
a cart!
¹⁹They even mock God and say,
"Hurry up and do something!
We want to see what you can do.
Let the Holy One of Israel carry out his
plan,
for we want to know what it is."

²⁰What sorrow for those who say
that evil is good and good is evil,
that dark is light and light is dark,
that bitter is sweet and sweet is bitter.
²¹What sorrow for those who are wise in
their own eyes
and think themselves so clever.
²²What sorrow for those who are heroes at
drinking wine
and boast about all the alcohol they
can hold.
²³They take bribes to let the wicked
go free,
and they punish the innocent.

5:10a Hebrew *A ten yoke,* that is, the area of land plowed by ten teams of oxen in one day. 5:10b Hebrew *a bath*
[21 liters]. 5:10c Hebrew *A homer* [5 bushels or 220 liters] *of seed will yield only an ephah* [20 quarts or 22 liters].
5:14 Hebrew *Sheol.* 5:17 As in Greek version; Hebrew reads *and strangers.*

5:20-23 When we reject God, our perception of right and wrong becomes distorted. We call our
compulsion good, and we become abusive to others. We don't view reality correctly because we
have abandoned the one who made reality. To see things in the proper light again, we need to
read the Bible—God's Word to us—and talk to God through prayer. As we improve our conscious
contacts with God, we will discover his will for us and receive clearer understandings of his
truth.

²⁴Therefore, just as fire licks up stubble
   and dry grass shrivels in the flame,
so their roots will rot
   and their flowers wither.
For they have rejected the law of
   the LORD of Heaven's Armies;
   they have despised the word of the
      Holy One of Israel.
²⁵That is why the LORD's anger burns
      against his people,
   and why he has raised his fist to crush
      them.
The mountains tremble,
   and the corpses of his people litter the
      streets like garbage.
But even then the LORD's anger is not
      satisfied.
   His fist is still poised to strike!

²⁶He will send a signal to distant nations
      far away
   and whistle to those at the ends of the
      earth.
They will come racing toward Jerusalem.
²⁷They will not get tired or stumble.
   They will not stop for rest or sleep.
Not a belt will be loose,
   not a sandal strap broken.
²⁸Their arrows will be sharp
   and their bows ready for battle.
Sparks will fly from their horses' hooves,
   and the wheels of their chariots will
      spin like a whirlwind.
²⁹They will roar like lions,
   like the strongest of lions.
Growling, they will pounce on their
      victims and carry them off,
   and no one will be there to rescue them.
³⁰They will roar over their victims on that
      day of destruction

6:1 King Uzziah died in 740 B.C.

like the roaring of the sea.
If someone looks across the land,
   only darkness and distress will be seen;
   even the light will be darkened by
      clouds.

CHAPTER 6
Isaiah's Cleansing and Call

It was in the year King Uzziah died* that I saw the Lord. He was sitting on a lofty throne, and the train of his robe filled the Temple. ²Attending him were mighty seraphim, each having six wings. With two wings they covered their faces, with two they covered their feet, and with two they flew. ³They were calling out to each other,

   "Holy, holy, holy is the LORD of Heaven's
      Armies!
   The whole earth is filled with his glory!"

⁴Their voices shook the Temple to its foundations, and the entire building was filled with smoke.

⁵Then I said, "It's all over! I am doomed, for I am a sinful man. I have filthy lips, and I live among a people with filthy lips. Yet I have seen the King, the LORD of Heaven's Armies."

⁶Then one of the seraphim flew to me with a burning coal he had taken from the altar with a pair of tongs. ⁷He touched my lips with it and said, "See, this coal has touched your lips. Now your guilt is removed, and your sins are forgiven."

⁸Then I heard the Lord asking, "Whom should I send as a messenger to this people? Who will go for us?"

I said, "Here I am. Send me."

⁹And he said, "Yes, go, and say to this people,

5:24-30 Just as God promised that enemy nations would invade Israel as judgment for its sins, he will also use the destruction sin brings to our life when we refuse to acknowledge our sins and try to run our life without God. Eventually, God's words proved true—Israel was invaded by Assyria, and the Israelites were taken into exile (2 Kings 17:21-23). We, too, may have to face some disaster before we finally admit that our life is unmanageable without God; but once we do, healing can begin.

6:1-8 Isaiah's recognition of his own uncleanness did not disqualify him from a relationship with God and a life of service to him. In contrast, it set the stage for his cleansing and commission into service. When we hide our sins and failures, we negate the possibility of real recovery. When we admit them, God can cleanse, restore, and use us.

6:8 God is not looking for people who are perfect or who pretend to be perfect. He is looking for people who can say with Isaiah, "Here I am. Send me." If we are willing to turn our past failures over to God, he will not allow them to stand in the way of his plans for us and our future.

6:9-13 Being fruitful does not necessarily mean we have to be a great success in human terms. We need not feel compelled to achieve or look good to others; Isaiah certainly did not. His goal was to fulfill God's will. Our aim, like Isaiah's, should be to be faithful to God's calling, not to measure up to the world's standards.

'Listen carefully, but do not understand.
    Watch closely, but learn nothing.'
[10] Harden the hearts of these people.
    Plug their ears and shut their eyes.
That way, they will not see with their
    eyes,
    nor hear with their ears,
nor understand with their hearts
    and turn to me for healing."*

[11] Then I said, "Lord, how long will this go
on?"
    And he replied,

"Until their towns are empty,
    their houses are deserted,
    and the whole country is a wasteland;
[12] until the LORD has sent everyone away,
    and the entire land of Israel lies
    deserted.
[13] If even a tenth—a remnant—survive,
    it will be invaded again and burned.
But as a terebinth or oak tree leaves a
    stump when it is cut down,
    so Israel's stump will be a holy
    seed."

CHAPTER 7
A Message for Ahaz

When Ahaz, son of Jotham and grandson
of Uzziah, was king of Judah, King Rezin of
Syria* and Pekah son of Remaliah, the king of
Israel, set out to attack Jerusalem. However,
they were unable to carry out their plan.

[2] The news had come to the royal court of
Judah: "Syria is allied with Israel* against
us!" So the hearts of the king and his people
trembled with fear, like trees shaking in a
storm.

[3] Then the LORD said to Isaiah, "Take your
son Shear-jashub* and go out to meet King
Ahaz. You will find him at the end of the aqueduct that feeds water into the upper pool,
near the road leading to the field where cloth
is washed.* [4] Tell him to stop worrying. Tell
him he doesn't need to fear the fierce anger

of those two burned-out embers, King Rezin
of Syria and Pekah son of Remaliah. [5] Yes, the
kings of Syria and Israel are plotting against
him, saying, [6] 'We will attack Judah and capture it for ourselves. Then we will install the
son of Tabeel as Judah's king.' [7] But this is
what the Sovereign LORD says:

"This invasion will never happen;
    it will never take place;
[8] for Syria is no stronger than its capital,
    Damascus,
    and Damascus is no stronger than its
    king, Rezin.
As for Israel, within sixty-five years
    it will be crushed and completely
    destroyed.
[9] Israel is no stronger than its capital,
    Samaria,
    and Samaria is no stronger than its
    king, Pekah son of Remaliah.
Unless your faith is firm,
    I cannot make you stand firm."

The Sign of Immanuel

[10] Later, the LORD sent this message to King
Ahaz: [11] "Ask the LORD your God for a sign of
confirmation, Ahaz. Make it as difficult as
you want—as high as heaven or as deep as
the place of the dead.*"

[12] But the king refused. "No," he said, "I
will not test the LORD like that."

[13] Then Isaiah said, "Listen well, you royal
family of David! Isn't it enough to exhaust
human patience? Must you exhaust the patience of my God as well? [14] All right then,
the Lord himself will give you the sign.
Look! The virgin* will conceive a child! She
will give birth to a son and will call him Immanuel (which means 'God is with us'). [15] By
the time this child is old enough to choose
what is right and reject what is wrong, he
will be eating yogurt* and honey. [16] For before the child is that old, the lands of the
two kings you fear so much will both be
deserted.

6:9-10 Greek version reads *And he said, "Go and say to this people, / 'When you hear what I say, you will not understand. / When you see what I do, you will not comprehend.' / For the hearts of these people are hardened, / and their ears cannot hear, / and they have closed their eyes— / so their eyes cannot see, / and their ears cannot hear, / and their hearts cannot understand, / and they cannot turn to me and let me heal them."* Compare Matt 13:14-15; Mark 4:12; Luke 8:10; Acts 26:26-27.
7:1 Hebrew *Aram;* also in 7:2, 4, 5, 8. **7:2** Hebrew *Ephraim,* referring to the northern kingdom of Israel; also in 7:5, 8, 9, 17. **7:3a** *Shear-jashub* means "A remnant will return." **7:3b** Or *bleached.* **7:11** Hebrew *as deep as Sheol.* **7:14** Or *young woman.* **7:15** Or *curds;* also in 7:22.

7:10-12 Ahaz continued in denial and did so with a religious cover-up. Instead of admitting that
he didn't believe God or want to obey him, Ahaz claimed that he didn't want to test God. God is
never bothered by our requests; he welcomes them and is waiting to help us. God is a personal
God who cares deeply for each of us. He sent his Son to die so that we could be close to him. Fear
of bothering God is never a good excuse for not requesting his help.

[17]"Then the LORD will bring things on you, your nation, and your family unlike anything since Israel broke away from Judah. He will bring the king of Assyria upon you!"

[18]In that day the LORD will whistle for the army of southern Egypt and for the army of Assyria. They will swarm around you like flies and bees. [19]They will come in vast hordes and settle in the fertile areas and also in the desolate valleys, caves, and thorny places. [20]In that day the Lord will hire a "razor" from beyond the Euphrates River*—the king of Assyria—and use it to shave off everything: your land, your crops, and your people.*

[21]In that day a farmer will be fortunate to have a cow and two sheep or goats left. [22]Nevertheless, there will be enough milk for everyone because so few people will be left in the land. They will eat their fill of yogurt and honey. [23]In that day the lush vineyards, now worth 1,000 pieces of silver,* will become patches of briers and thorns. [24]The entire land will become a vast expanse of briers and thorns, a hunting ground overrun by wildlife. [25]No one will go to the fertile hillsides where the gardens once grew, for briers and thorns will cover them. Cattle, sheep, and goats will graze there.

CHAPTER 8
The Coming Assyrian Invasion
Then the LORD said to me, "Make a large signboard and clearly write this name on it: Maher-shalal-hash-baz.*" [2]I asked Uriah the priest and Zechariah son of Jeberekiah, both known as honest men, to witness my doing this.

[3]Then I slept with my wife, and she became pregnant and gave birth to a son. And the LORD said, "Call him Maher-shalal-hash-baz. [4]For before this child is old enough to say 'Papa' or 'Mama,' the king of Assyria will carry away both the abundance of Damascus and the riches of Samaria."

[5]Then the LORD spoke to me again and said, [6]"My care for the people of Judah is like the gently flowing waters of Shiloah, but they have rejected it. They are rejoicing over what will happen to* King Rezin and King Pekah.* [7]Therefore, the Lord will overwhelm them with a mighty flood from the Euphrates River*—the king of Assyria and all his glory. This flood will overflow all its channels [8]and sweep into Judah until it is chin deep. It will spread its wings, submerging your land from one end to the other, O Immanuel.

[9]"Huddle together, you nations, and
> be terrified.
Listen, all you distant lands.
Prepare for battle, but you will be crushed!
> Yes, prepare for battle, but you will be
> crushed!
[10]Call your councils of war, but they
> will be worthless.
Develop your strategies, but they will
> not succeed.
For God is with us!*"

A Call to Trust the LORD
[11]The LORD has given me a strong warning not to think like everyone else does. He said,

[12]"Don't call everything a conspiracy, like
> they do,

7:20a Hebrew *the river.* 7:20b Hebrew *shave off the head, the hair of the legs, and the beard.* 7:23 Hebrew *1,000 [shekels] of silver,* about 25 pounds or 11.4 kilograms in weight. 8:1 *Maher-shalal-hash-baz* means "Swift to plunder and quick to carry away." 8:6a Or *They are rejoicing because of.* 8:6b Hebrew *and the son of Remaliah.* 8:7 Hebrew *the river.* 8:10 Hebrew *Immanuel!*

7:17-25 Confronted with the challenge of invasion from the coalition of Israel and Aram, Ahaz rejected Isaiah's call to trust God and tried to solve the problem his own way: He called on Assyria for protection (2 Kings 16:7-8). Assyria, however, later turned on Judah and greatly damaged God's nation and people (2 Chronicles 32:1). We have experienced this with our addiction. The things we originally used to help us cope with our problems—alcohol, drugs, sex, lies—have now taken over our life and are destroying us. It is not too late to call on the resource we should have turned to in the first place—God.

8:6-8 Asking Assyria for protection seemed like a good solution to Judah's leaders, but the long-term consequences would be disastrous. The Assyrian armies eventually attacked Judah and destroyed the land. This could have been avoided had the leaders heeded God's warning. If our recovery program is based on anything other than God and his principles, we may wind up in greater peril later. Unlike Judah, we should seek a recovery plan that includes God.

8:11-15 Isaiah was being pressured to go along with a human plan; God had nothing to do with it. To reject the king's plan, however, amounted to treason, and the king's advisers probably stressed this to Isaiah to get him to agree. We, too, will face pressure to follow ungodly plans, often leading us back into our addiction. When our "friends" try to coerce us to follow their ways, we shouldn't fear their rejection if we don't go along with them. God says that if we fear him, we need not fear anything else—not friends, coworkers, or family.

and don't live in dread of what
frightens them.
[13] Make the LORD of Heaven's Armies holy in
your life.
He is the one you should fear.
He is the one who should make you
tremble.
[14]   He will keep you safe.
But to Israel and Judah
he will be a stone that makes people
stumble,
a rock that makes them fall.
And for the people of Jerusalem
he will be a trap and a snare.
[15] Many will stumble and fall,
never to rise again.
They will be snared and captured."

[16] Preserve the teaching of God;
entrust his instructions to those who
follow me.
[17] I will wait for the LORD,
who has turned away from the
descendants of Jacob.
I will put my hope in him.

[18] I and the children the LORD has given me
serve as signs and warnings to Israel from the
LORD of Heaven's Armies who dwells in his
Temple on Mount Zion.

[19] Someone may say to you, "Let's ask the
mediums and those who consult the spirits
of the dead. With their whisperings and mut-
terings, they will tell us what to do." But
shouldn't people ask God for guidance?
Should the living seek guidance from the
dead?

[20] Look to God's instructions and teachings! People who contradict his word are
completely in the dark. [21] They will go from
one place to another, weary and hungry. And
because they are hungry, they will rage and
curse their king and their God. They will
look up to heaven [22] and down at the earth,
but wherever they look, there will be trouble

and anguish and dark despair. They will be
thrown out into the darkness.

CHAPTER 9
Hope in the Messiah

[1] *Nevertheless, that time of darkness and despair will not go on forever. The land of
Zebulun and Naphtali will be humbled, but
there will be a time in the future when Galilee of the Gentiles, which lies along the road
that runs between the Jordan and the sea,
will be filled with glory.

[2] *The people who walk in darkness
will see a great light.
For those who live in a land of deep
darkness,*
a light will shine.
[3] You will enlarge the nation of Israel,
and its people will rejoice.
They will rejoice before you
as people rejoice at the harvest
and like warriors dividing the plunder.
[4] For you will break the yoke of their
slavery
and lift the heavy burden from their
shoulders.
You will break the oppressor's rod,
just as you did when you destroyed the
army of Midian.
[5] The boots of the warrior
and the uniforms bloodstained by war
will all be burned.
They will be fuel for the fire.

[6] For a child is born to us,
a son is given to us.
The government will rest on his
shoulders.
And he will be called:
Wonderful Counselor,* Mighty God,
Everlasting Father, Prince of Peace.
[7] His government and its peace
will never end.

9:1 Verse 9:1 is numbered 8:23 in Hebrew text. 9:2a Verses 9:2-21 are numbered 9:1-20 in Hebrew text. 9:2b Greek
version reads *a land where death casts its shadow.* Compare Matt 4:16. 9:6 Or *Wonderful, Counselor.*

9:6 God's promise to send a Counselor and Prince of Peace was fulfilled with the birth of Jesus
Christ. Christ is the one to whom we can turn for deep healing and recovery. He is the Wonderful
Counselor, who can help us sort through the inner mess of our life and guide us into truth and
reality. He is the Mighty God, who can supply us with the power to stay on the path of recovery.
He is the Everlasting Father, who can love us more deeply than any earthly father can. He is the
Prince of Peace, who can fill us with peace and make us whole.
9:7 God brings justice and peace to the world and to troubled people. Although injustice seems
to prevail here on earth and we may suffer from abuses that are not our fault, we can be assured
that justice will be served—if not in this lifetime, then in the next. We can have God's peace if we
trust in him and give him all our worries, cares, hopes, and ambitions. To have peace in recovery,
we need to ask God to help us through it.

He will rule with fairness and justice from
the throne of his ancestor David
for all eternity.
The passionate commitment of the LORD
of Heaven's Armies
will make this happen!

The LORD's Anger against Israel

[8] The Lord has spoken out against Jacob;
his judgment has fallen upon Israel.
[9] And the people of Israel* and Samaria,
who spoke with such pride and
arrogance,
will soon know it.
[10] They said, "We will replace the broken
bricks of our ruins with finished
stone,
and replant the felled sycamore-fig trees
with cedars."

[11] But the LORD will bring Rezin's enemies
against Israel
and stir up all their foes.
[12] The Syrians* from the east and the
Philistines from the west
will bare their fangs and devour Israel.
But even then the LORD's anger will not be
satisfied.
His fist is still poised to strike.

[13] For after all this punishment, the people
will still not repent.
They will not seek the LORD of Heaven's
Armies.
[14] Therefore, in a single day the LORD will
destroy both the head and the tail,
the noble palm branch and the lowly
reed.
[15] The leaders of Israel are the head,
and the lying prophets are the tail.
[16] For the leaders of the people have misled
them.
They have led them down the path of
destruction.
[17] That is why the Lord takes no pleasure in
the young men
and shows no mercy even to the
widows and orphans.
For they are all wicked hypocrites,
and they all speak foolishness.

But even then the LORD's anger will not be
satisfied.
His fist is still poised to strike.

[18] This wickedness is like a brushfire.
It burns not only briers and thorns
but also sets the forests ablaze.
Its burning sends up clouds
of smoke.
[19] The land will be blackened
by the fury of the LORD of Heaven's
Armies.
The people will be fuel for the fire,
and no one will spare even his own
brother.
[20] They will attack their neighbor on the
right
but will still be hungry.
They will devour their neighbor on the
left
but will not be satisfied.
In the end they will even eat their own
children.*
[21] Manasseh will feed on Ephraim,
Ephraim will feed on Manasseh,
and both will devour Judah.
But even then the LORD's anger will not be
satisfied.
His fist is still poised to strike.

CHAPTER 10

[1] What sorrow awaits the unjust
judges
and those who issue unfair laws.
[2] They deprive the poor of justice
and deny the rights of the needy
among my people.
They prey on widows
and take advantage of orphans.
[3] What will you do when I punish you,
when I send disaster upon you from a
distant land?
To whom will you turn for help?
Where will your treasures be safe?
[4] You will stumble along as prisoners
or lie among the dead.
But even then the LORD's anger will not be
satisfied.
His fist is still poised to strike.

9:9 Hebrew *of Ephraim,* referring to the northern kingdom of Israel. 9:12 Hebrew *Arameans.* 9:20 Or *eat their own arms.*

10:1-19 The abused person can find comfort in the theological truth in these verses: (1) God can sovereignly use evil people to work good within his plan (10:5-11; here Assyria is God's instrument in disciplining Judah), and (2) God will punish evildoers (10:12-19; Assyria). It is a comfort to know that God will hold our abusers accountable (so we can release our hatred) and that he can even use their evil actions for our ultimate good.

Judgment against Assyria

⁵ "What sorrow awaits Assyria, the rod of
    my anger.
  I use it as a club to express my anger.
⁶ I am sending Assyria against a godless
    nation,
  against a people with whom I am angry.
  Assyria will plunder them,
    trampling them like dirt beneath its feet.
⁷ But the king of Assyria will not
    understand that he is my tool;
  his mind does not work that way.
  His plan is simply to destroy,
    to cut down nation after nation.
⁸ He will say,
  'Each of my princes will soon be a king.
⁹ We destroyed Calno just as we did
    Carchemish.
  Hamath fell before us as Arpad did.
  And we destroyed Samaria just as we
    did Damascus.
¹⁰ Yes, we have finished off many a kingdom
    whose gods were greater than those in
    Jerusalem and Samaria.
¹¹ So we will defeat Jerusalem and her gods,
    just as we destroyed Samaria with hers.'"

¹²After the Lord has used the king of Assyria to accomplish his purposes on Mount Zion and in Jerusalem, he will turn against the king of Assyria and punish him—for he is proud and arrogant. ¹³He boasts,

"By my own powerful arm I have done
    this.
  With my own shrewd wisdom I
    planned it.
  I have broken down the defenses of nations
    and carried off their treasures.
  I have knocked down their kings like a
    bull.
¹⁴ I have robbed their nests of riches
    and gathered up kingdoms as a farmer
    gathers eggs.
  No one can even flap a wing against me
    or utter a peep of protest."

¹⁵ But can the ax boast greater power than
    the person who uses it?
  Is the saw greater than the person who
    saws?

Can a rod strike unless a hand moves it?
  Can a wooden cane walk by itself?
¹⁶ Therefore, the Lord, the Lᴏʀᴅ of Heaven's
    Armies,
  will send a plague among Assyria's
    proud troops,
  and a flaming fire will consume its
    glory.
¹⁷ The Lᴏʀᴅ, the Light of Israel, will be a fire;
    the Holy One will be a flame.
  He will devour the thorns and briers with
    fire,
  burning up the enemy in a single night.
¹⁸ The Lᴏʀᴅ will consume Assyria's glory
    like a fire consumes a forest in a fruitful
    land;
  it will waste away like sick people in a
    plague.
¹⁹ Of all that glorious forest, only a few trees
    will survive—
  so few that a child could count them!

Hope for the Lᴏʀᴅ's People

²⁰ In that day the remnant left in Israel,
    the survivors in the house of Jacob,
  will no longer depend on allies
    who seek to destroy them.
  But they will faithfully trust the Lᴏʀᴅ,
    the Holy One of Israel.
²¹ A remnant will return;*
    yes, the remnant of Jacob will return to
    the Mighty God.
²² But though the people of Israel are as
    numerous
    as the sand of the seashore,
  only a remnant of them will return.
  The Lᴏʀᴅ has rightly decided to destroy
    his people.
²³ Yes, the Lord, the Lᴏʀᴅ of Heaven's Armies,
    has already decided to destroy the
    entire land.*

²⁴So this is what the Lord, the Lᴏʀᴅ of Heaven's Armies, says: "O my people in Zion, do not be afraid of the Assyrians when they oppress you with rod and club as the Egyptians did long ago. ²⁵In a little while my anger against you will end, and then my anger will rise up to destroy them." ²⁶The Lᴏʀᴅ of Heaven's Armies will lash them with his

---

10:21 Hebrew *Shear-jashub;* see 7:3; 8:18. **10:22-23** Greek version reads *only a remnant of them will be saved. / For he will carry out his sentence quickly and with finality and righteousness; / for God will carry out his sentence upon all the world with finality.* Compare Rom 9:27-28.

10:20 The people of Judah looked to Assyria for help in their military crisis, and Assyria would later oppress Judah. In a similar way, we look to addictive substances and behaviors and to unhealthy relationships to deliver us, and then we are victimized by our inadequate saviors. We must learn, as did the people of Judah, that only God is worthy of our trust.

whip, as he did when Gideon triumphed over the Midianites at the rock of Oreb, or when the LORD's staff was raised to drown the Egyptian army in the sea.

²⁷ In that day the LORD will end the bondage of his people.
He will break the yoke of slavery
and lift it from their shoulders.*

²⁸ Look, the Assyrians are now at Aiath.
They are passing through Migron
and are storing their equipment at Micmash.
²⁹ They are crossing the pass
and are camping at Geba.
Fear strikes the town of Ramah.
All the people of Gibeah, the
hometown of Saul,
are running for their lives.
³⁰ Scream in terror,
you people of Gallim!
Shout out a warning to Laishah.
Oh, poor Anathoth!
³¹ There go the people of Madmenah, all fleeing.
The citizens of Gebim are trying to hide.
³² The enemy stops at Nob for the rest of that day.
He shakes his fist at beautiful Mount Zion, the mountain of Jerusalem.

³³ But look! The Lord, the LORD of Heaven's Armies,
will chop down the mighty tree of Assyria with great power!
He will cut down the proud.
That lofty tree will be brought down.
³⁴ He will cut down the forest trees with an ax.
Lebanon will fall to the Mighty One.*

CHAPTER 11
A Branch from David's Line
¹ Out of the stump of David's family* will grow a shoot—

yes, a new Branch bearing fruit from the old root.
² And the Spirit of the LORD will rest on him—
the Spirit of wisdom and understanding,
the Spirit of counsel and might,
the Spirit of knowledge and the fear of the LORD.
³ He will delight in obeying the LORD.
He will not judge by appearance
nor make a decision based on hearsay.
⁴ He will give justice to the poor
and make fair decisions for the exploited.
The earth will shake at the force of his word,
and one breath from his mouth will destroy the wicked.
⁵ He will wear righteousness like a belt
and truth like an undergarment.

⁶ In that day the wolf and the lamb will live together;
the leopard will lie down with the baby goat.
The calf and the yearling will be safe with the lion,
and a little child will lead them all.
⁷ The cow will graze near the bear.
The cub and the calf will lie down together.
The lion will eat hay like a cow.
⁸ The baby will play safely near the hole of a cobra.
Yes, a little child will put its hand in a nest of deadly snakes without harm.
⁹ Nothing will hurt or destroy in all my holy mountain,
for as the waters fill the sea,
so the earth will be filled with people who know the LORD.

¹⁰ In that day the heir to David's throne*
will be a banner of salvation to all the world.
The nations will rally to him,
and the land where he lives will be a glorious place.*

10:27 As in Greek version; Hebrew reads *The yoke will be broken, / for you have grown so fat.* 10:34 Or *with an ax / as even the mighty trees of Lebanon fall.* 11:1 Hebrew *the stump of the line of Jesse.* Jesse was King David's father. 11:10a Hebrew *the root of Jesse.* 11:10b Greek version reads *In that day the heir to David's throne* [literally *the root of Jesse*] *will come, / and he will rule over the Gentiles. / They will place their hopes on him.* Compare Rom 15:12.

11:1-10 We may feel deep insecurities and hurt over the abuse, misunderstandings, and injustices we have suffered at the hands of others. Our hope is in God, who will come again and rule the world in justice and truth. He will straighten out all the inequities of the past. When God's Kingdom is established, we will not have anything to fear: "Nothing will hurt or destroy in all [God's] holy mountain" (11:9).

11 In that day the Lord will reach out his
hand a second time
to bring back the remnant of his
people—
those who remain in Assyria and northern
Egypt;
in southern Egypt, Ethiopia,* and
Elam;
in Babylonia,* Hamath, and all the
distant coastlands.
12 He will raise a flag among the nations
and assemble the exiles of Israel.
He will gather the scattered people of
Judah
from the ends of the earth.

13 Then at last the jealousy between Israel*
and Judah will end.
They will not be rivals anymore.
14 They will join forces to swoop down on
Philistia to the west.
Together they will attack and plunder
the nations to the east.
They will occupy the lands of Edom and
Moab,
and Ammon will obey them.
15 The LORD will make a dry path through
the gulf of the Red Sea.*
He will wave his hand over the
Euphrates River,*
sending a mighty wind to divide it into
seven streams
so it can easily be crossed on foot.
16 He will make a highway for the remnant
of his people,
the remnant coming from Assyria,
just as he did for Israel long ago
when they returned from Egypt.

CHAPTER 12
Songs of Praise for Salvation

1 In that day you will sing:
"I will praise you, O LORD!
You were angry with me, but not any
more.
Now you comfort me.
2 See, God has come to save me.
I will trust in him and not be afraid.
The LORD GOD is my strength and my
song;
he has given me victory."

3 With joy you will drink deeply
from the fountain of salvation!
4 In that wonderful day you will sing:
"Thank the LORD! Praise his name!
Tell the nations what he has done.
Let them know how mighty he is!
5 Sing to the LORD, for he has done
wonderful things.
Make known his praise around the
world.
6 Let all the people of Jerusalem* shout his
praise with joy!
For great is the Holy One of Israel who
lives among you."

CHAPTER 13
A Message about Babylon

Isaiah son of Amoz received this message
concerning the destruction of Babylon:

2 "Raise a signal flag on a bare hilltop.
Call up an army against Babylon.
Wave your hand to encourage them
as they march into the palaces of the
high and mighty.
3 I, the LORD, have dedicated these soldiers
for this task.

11:11a Hebrew *in Pathros, Cush*. 11:11b Hebrew *in Shinar*. 11:13 Hebrew *Ephraim*, referring to the northern kingdom of Israel. 11:15a Hebrew *will destroy the tongue of the sea of Egypt*. 11:15b Hebrew *the river*. 12:6 Hebrew *Zion*.

11:11-16 God's power to restore dysfunctional families is great. The family of Israel had fallen. Many had been scattered among the nations in the Dispersion. The nations of Israel and Judah were locked in destructive patterns of jealousy. Out of this mess, God promised to bring restoration and unity. He can do the same for us. If our family is broken because of abuse, addiction, jealousy, etc., God can unify and heal it. First we must begin the recovery process with open communication and complete trust in God.

12:1-6 Once we turn our life over to God, we can rejoice in his salvation. God was angry with us, but now he comforts, heals, and strengthens us. We will want to share with others our joy and the story of how God has saved us, making "known his praise around the world." This is Step Twelve, carrying the message to others who are in need of recovery.

13:1–14:2 Babylon would come under God's judgment. God's anger at the sin of unrepentant people is clearly displayed. God is not, however, like an angry, abusive parent whose anger and punishment do not accurately correspond to a child's behavior. God shows judgment toward unrepentant unbelievers, but to those who believe in him, he shows mercy (14:1).

13:1–23:18 These chapters deal with God's judgment on the unbelieving nations. Two lessons stand out for those of us on the path of recovery. First, evildoers will receive God's judgment. If

Yes, I have called mighty warriors to
express my anger,
and they will rejoice when I am
exalted."

[4] Hear the noise on the mountains!
Listen, as the vast armies march!
It is the noise and shouting of many
nations.
The LORD of Heaven's Armies has called
this army together.
[5] They come from distant countries,
from beyond the farthest horizons.
They are the LORD's weapons to carry out
his anger.
With them he will destroy the whole
land.

[6] Scream in terror, for the day of the LORD
has arrived—
the time for the Almighty to destroy.
[7] Every arm is paralyzed with fear.
Every heart melts,
[8]   and people are terrified.
Pangs of anguish grip them,
like those of a woman in labor.
They look helplessly at one another,
their faces aflame with fear.

[9] For see, the day of the LORD is coming—
the terrible day of his fury and fierce
anger.
The land will be made desolate,
and all the sinners destroyed with it.
[10] The heavens will be black above them;
the stars will give no light.
The sun will be dark when it rises,
and the moon will provide no light.

[11] "I, the LORD, will punish the world for
its evil
and the wicked for their sin.
I will crush the arrogance of the proud
and humble the pride of the mighty.
[12] I will make people scarcer than gold—
more rare than the fine gold of Ophir.
[13] For I will shake the heavens.
The earth will move from its place
when the LORD of Heaven's Armies
displays his wrath
in the day of his fierce anger."

[14] Everyone in Babylon will run about like a
hunted gazelle,
like sheep without a shepherd.
They will try to find their own people
and flee to their own land.
[15] Anyone who is captured will be cut down—
run through with a sword.
[16] Their little children will be dashed to
death before their eyes.
Their homes will be sacked, and their
wives will be raped.

[17] "Look, I will stir up the Medes against
Babylon.
They cannot be tempted by silver
or bribed with gold.
[18] The attacking armies will shoot down the
young men with arrows.
They will have no mercy on helpless
babies
and will show no compassion for
children."

[19] Babylon, the most glorious of kingdoms,
the flower of Chaldean pride,
will be devastated like Sodom and
Gomorrah
when God destroyed them.
[20] Babylon will never be inhabited again.
It will remain empty for generation
after generation.
Nomads will refuse to camp there,
and shepherds will not bed down their
sheep.
[21] Desert animals will move into the ruined
city,
and the houses will be haunted by
howling creatures.
Owls will live among the ruins,
and wild goats will go there to dance.
[22] Hyenas will howl in its fortresses,
and jackals will make dens in its
luxurious palaces.
Babylon's days are numbered;
its time of destruction will soon arrive.

CHAPTER 14
A Taunt for Babylon's King
But the LORD will have mercy on the descendants of Jacob. He will choose Israel as his
special people once again. He will bring
them back to settle once again in their own
land. And people from many different nations will come and join them there and

we have been seriously hurt by certain people, we can release them into God's hands. We need not
hold on to our pain and seek revenge because we know that God will deal with them. Second,
those who reject God and think they can manage alone will find they are headed for destruction.
We need to surrender our life to God so we can be saved from our dependency now and be with
God in eternity.

unite with the people of Israel.* [2]The nations of the world will help the people of Israel to return, and those who come to live in the LORD's land will serve them. Those who captured Israel will themselves be captured, and Israel will rule over its enemies.

[3]In that wonderful day when the LORD gives his people rest from sorrow and fear, from slavery and chains, [4]you will taunt the king of Babylon. You will say,

"The mighty man has been destroyed.
    Yes, your insolence* is ended.
[5]For the LORD has crushed your wicked power
    and broken your evil rule.
[6]You struck the people with endless blows of rage
    and held the nations in your angry grip
    with unrelenting tyranny.
[7]But finally the earth is at rest and quiet.
    Now it can sing again!
[8]Even the trees of the forest—
    the cypress trees and the cedars of Lebanon—
    sing out this joyous song:
'Since you have been cut down,
    no one will come now to cut us down!'

[9]"In the place of the dead* there is excitement
    over your arrival.
The spirits of world leaders and mighty kings long dead
    stand up to see you.
[10]With one voice they all cry out,
    'Now you are as weak as we are!
[11]Your might and power were buried with you.*
    The sound of the harp in your palace has ceased.
Now maggots are your sheet,
    and worms your blanket.'

[12]"How you are fallen from heaven,
    O shining star, son of the morning!
You have been thrown down to the earth,
    you who destroyed the nations of the world.

[13]For you said to yourself,
    'I will ascend to heaven and set my throne above God's stars.
I will preside on the mountain of the gods far away in the north.*
[14]I will climb to the highest heavens and be like the Most High.'
[15]Instead, you will be brought down to the place of the dead,
    down to its lowest depths.
[16]Everyone there will stare at you and ask,
    'Can this be the one who shook the earth
    and made the kingdoms of the world tremble?
[17]Is this the one who destroyed the world and made it into a wasteland?
Is this the king who demolished the world's greatest cities
    and had no mercy on his prisoners?'

[18]"The kings of the nations lie in stately glory,
    each in his own tomb,
[19]but you will be thrown out of your grave like a worthless branch.
Like a corpse trampled underfoot,
    you will be dumped into a mass grave with those killed in battle.
You will descend to the pit.
[20]   You will not be given a proper burial,
for you have destroyed your nation
    and slaughtered your people.
The descendants of such an evil person will never again receive honor.
[21]Kill this man's children!
    Let them die because of their father's sins!
They must not rise and conquer the earth, filling the world with their cities."

[22]This is what the LORD of Heaven's Armies says:
"I, myself, have risen against Babylon!
I will destroy its children and its children's children,"
    says the LORD.
[23]"I will make Babylon a desolate place of owls,
    filled with swamps and marshes.

14:1 Hebrew *the house of Jacob.* The names "Jacob" and "Israel" are often interchanged throughout the Old Testament, referring sometimes to the individual patriarch and sometimes to the nation. 14:4 As in Dead Sea Scrolls; the meaning of the Masoretic Text is uncertain. 14:9 Hebrew *Sheol;* also in 14:15. 14:11 Hebrew *were brought down to Sheol.* 14:13 Or *on the heights of Zaphon.*

14:12-20 Pride was the root of the problem with Babylon and its king. We, too, must beware of this deadly sin. Healthy self-esteem is proper, but the sin of pride makes us think we are better than others, even God. Sometimes our pride is an unhealthy attempt to cover up deep insecurities that can be dealt with only by God's love and grace.

I will sweep the land with the broom
of destruction.
I, the LORD of Heaven's Armies, have
spoken!"

A Message about Assyria

²⁴The LORD of Heaven's Armies has sworn
this oath:

"It will all happen as I have planned.
It will be as I have decided.
²⁵I will break the Assyrians when they are in
Israel;
I will trample them on my mountains.
My people will no longer be their slaves
nor bow down under their heavy loads.
²⁶I have a plan for the whole earth,
a hand of judgment upon all the
nations.
²⁷The LORD of Heaven's Armies has spoken—
who can change his plans?
When his hand is raised,
who can stop him?"

A Message about Philistia

²⁸This message came to me the year King
Ahaz died:*

²⁹Do not rejoice, you Philistines,
that the rod that struck you is broken—
that the king who attacked you is dead.
For from that snake a more poisonous
snake will be born,
a fiery serpent to destroy you!
³⁰I will feed the poor in my pasture;
the needy will lie down in peace.
But as for you, I will wipe you out with
famine
and destroy the few who remain.
³¹Wail at the gates! Weep in the cities!
Melt with fear, you Philistines!
A powerful army comes like smoke from
the north.
Each soldier rushes forward eager to
fight.

³²What should we tell the Philistine mes-
sengers? Tell them,

"The LORD has built Jerusalem*;
its walls will give refuge to his
oppressed people."

CHAPTER 15
A Message about Moab

This message came to me concerning Moab:

In one night the town of Ar will be
leveled,
and the city of Kir will be destroyed.
²Your people will go to their temple in
Dibon to mourn.
They will go to their sacred shrines to
weep.
They will wail for the fate of Nebo and
Medeba,
shaving their heads in sorrow and
cutting off their beards.
³They will wear burlap as they wander the
streets.
From every home and public square
will come the sound of wailing.
⁴The people of Heshbon and Elealeh will
cry out;
their voices will be heard as far away
as Jahaz!
The bravest warriors of Moab will cry out
in utter terror.
They will be helpless with fear.

⁵My heart weeps for Moab.
Its people flee to Zoar and
Eglath-shelishiyah.
Weeping, they climb the road to
Luhith.
Their cries of distress can be heard all
along the road to Horonaim.
⁶Even the waters of Nimrim are dried up!
The grassy banks are scorched.
The tender plants are gone;
nothing green remains.
⁷The people grab their possessions
and carry them across the Ravine
of Willows.
⁸A cry of distress echoes through the land
of Moab

14:28 King Ahaz died in 715 B.C. 14:32 Hebrew *Zion.*

14:26-27 We would be foolish to ignore God and his moral laws and still hope that life will go
well. The Assyrians thought just that, but they were denying reality. God is sovereign over the
whole earth and will uphold his moral laws and purposes whether we believe them or not. Since
this is the reality of the matter, we need to follow God and his laws. Even if we have ignored God
all our life, it is not too late to turn to him and start obeying him now.
15:2-4 The Moabites lamented their suffering, but they never recognized their sins or asked God to
forgive them. We face a similar danger in recovery. Unless we admit our sins and dependency to God
and others, we may never get beyond feeling sorry for ourself. Bemoaning the suffering brought on by
our dependency is helpful only if it leads to action that results in changes in our behavior.

from one end to the other—
from Eglaim to Beer-elim.
⁹ The stream near Dibon* runs red with
blood,
but I am still not finished with Dibon!
Lions will hunt down the survivors—
both those who try to escape
and those who remain behind.

CHAPTER 16

¹ Send lambs from Sela as tribute
to the ruler of the land.
Send them through the desert
to the mountain of beautiful Zion.
² The women of Moab are left like homeless
birds
at the shallow crossings of the Arnon
River.
³ "Help us," they cry.
"Defend us against our enemies.
Protect us from their relentless attack.
Do not betray us now that we have
escaped.
⁴ Let our refugees stay among you.
Hide them from our enemies until the
terror is past."

When oppression and destruction have
ended
and enemy raiders have disappeared,
⁵ then God will establish one of David's
descendants as king.
He will rule with mercy and truth.
He will always do what is just
and be eager to do what is right.

⁶ We have heard about proud Moab—
about its pride and arrogance and rage.
But all that boasting has disappeared.
⁷ The entire land of Moab weeps.
Yes, everyone in Moab mourns
for the cakes of raisins from Kir-hareseth.
They are all gone now.
⁸ The farms of Heshbon are abandoned;
the vineyards at Sibmah are deserted.

The rulers of the nations have broken
down Moab—
that beautiful grapevine.
Its tendrils spread north as far as the town
of Jazer
and trailed eastward into the wilderness.
Its shoots reached so far west
that they crossed over the Dead Sea.*

⁹ So now I weep for Jazer and the vineyards
of Sibmah;
my tears will flow for Heshbon and
Elealeh.
There are no more shouts of joy
over your summer fruits and harvest.
¹⁰ Gone now is the gladness,
gone the joy of harvest.
There will be no more singing in the vineyards,
no more happy shouts,
no treading of grapes in the winepresses.
I have ended all their harvest joys.
¹¹ My heart's cry for Moab is like a lament
on a harp.
I am filled with anguish for Kir-hareseth.*
¹² The people of Moab will worship at their
pagan shrines,
but it will do them no good.
They will cry to the gods in their temples,
but no one will be able to save them.

¹³ The LORD has already said these things
about Moab in the past. ¹⁴ But now the LORD
says, "Within three years, counting each
day,* the glory of Moab will be ended. From
its great population, only a feeble few will be
left alive."

CHAPTER 17
A Message about Damascus and Israel
This message came to me concerning Damascus:

"Look, the city of Damascus will
disappear!
It will become a heap of ruins.
² The towns of Aroer will be deserted.
Flocks will graze in the streets and lie
down undisturbed,

15:9 As in Dead Sea Scrolls, some Greek manuscripts, and Latin Vulgate; Masoretic Text reads *Dimon*; also in 15:9b.
16:8 Hebrew *the sea.* 16:11 Hebrew *Kir-heres,* a variant spelling of Kir-hareseth. 16:14 Hebrew *Within three years, as
a servant bound by contract would count them.*

16:3-5 This exhortation to Judah could well be applied to our communities and their dealings with
hurting people. Have we opened our doors to those with addictions—abused, dysfunctional, and
hurting people—so they can find refuge, counsel, and help in an environment of love and grace?
16:12 Judgment would come to humble the people of Moab and force them to deal with their
sins truthfully. Instead of turning to God, they would turn to idols that had no power to help. The
people of Moab are like those of us who need recovery but refuse it. Instead of turning to God,
we may turn to workaholism, perfectionism, or substance abuse. These "solutions," however, will
only add to our problems. God is always there to help us if we only turn to him.

with no one to chase them away.

³ The fortified towns of Israel* will also be
destroyed,
and the royal power of Damascus will
end.
All that remains of Syria*
will share the fate of Israel's departed
glory,"
declares the LORD of Heaven's Armies.

⁴ "In that day Israel's* glory will grow dim;
its robust body will waste away.
⁵ The whole land will look like a grainfield
after the harvesters have gathered the
grain.
It will be desolate,
like the fields in the valley of Rephaim
after the harvest.
⁶ Only a few of its people will be left,
like stray olives left on a tree after the
harvest.
Only two or three remain in the highest
branches,
four or five scattered here and there on
the limbs,"
declares the LORD, the God of Israel.

⁷ Then at last the people will look to their
Creator
and turn their eyes to the Holy One
of Israel.
⁸ They will no longer look to their idols for
help
or worship what their own hands have
made.
They will never again bow down to their
Asherah poles
or worship at the pagan shrines they
have built.
⁹ Their largest cities will be like a deserted
forest,
like the land the Hivites and Amorites
abandoned*
when the Israelites came here so long ago.
It will be utterly desolate.
¹⁰ Why? Because you have turned from the
God who can save you.
You have forgotten the Rock who can
hide you.
So you may plant the finest grapevines

and import the most expensive
seedlings.
¹¹ They may sprout on the day you set
them out;
yes, they may blossom on the very
morning you plant them,
but you will never pick any grapes from
them.
Your only harvest will be a load of grief
and unrelieved pain.

¹² Listen! The armies of many nations
roar like the roaring of the sea.
Hear the thunder of the mighty forces
as they rush forward like thundering
waves.
¹³ But though they thunder like breakers on
a beach,
God will silence them, and they will
run away.
They will flee like chaff scattered by the
wind,
like a tumbleweed whirling before
a storm.
¹⁴ In the evening Israel waits in terror,
but by dawn its enemies are dead.
This is the just reward of those who
plunder us,
a fitting end for those who destroy us.

CHAPTER 18
A Message about Ethiopia
¹ Listen, Ethiopia*—land of fluttering
sails*
that lies at the headwaters of the Nile,
² that sends ambassadors
in swift boats down the river.

Go, swift messengers!
Take a message to a tall, smooth-skinned
people,
who are feared far and wide
for their conquests and destruction,
and whose land is divided by rivers.

³ All you people of the world,
everyone who lives on the earth—
when I raise my battle flag on the
mountain, look!
When I blow the ram's horn, listen!
⁴ For the LORD has told me this:

17:3a Hebrew *of Ephraim,* referring to the northern kingdom of Israel. 17:3b Hebrew *Aram.* 17:4 Hebrew *Jacob's.* See
note on 14:1. 17:9 As in Greek version; Hebrew reads *like places of the wood and the highest bough.* 18:1a Hebrew
Cush. 18:1b Or *land of many locusts;* Hebrew reads *land of whirring wings.*

17:3-7 It would take almost complete destruction before the people of Israel would respect God
and follow him. Hopefully we won't wait until our life is devastated before turning to God for
help. The sooner we admit that our life is unmanageable, the sooner we can ask God to rescue us.

"I will watch quietly from my dwelling
   place—
   as quietly as the heat rises on a summer
      day,
   or as the morning dew forms during the
      harvest."
⁵ Even before you begin your attack,
   while your plans are ripening like grapes,
the LORD will cut off your new growth
   with pruning shears.
He will snip off and discard your
   spreading branches.
⁶ Your mighty army will be left dead in the
      fields
   for the mountain vultures and wild
      animals.
The vultures will tear at the corpses all
   summer.
   The wild animals will gnaw at the
      bones all winter.

⁷ At that time the LORD of Heaven's Armies
   will receive gifts
   from this land divided by rivers,
from this tall, smooth-skinned people,
   who are feared far and wide for their
      conquests and destruction.
They will bring the gifts to Jerusalem,*
   where the LORD of Heaven's Armies
      dwells.

CHAPTER 19
A Message about Egypt
This message came to me concerning Egypt:

   Look! The LORD is advancing against Egypt,
      riding on a swift cloud.
   The idols of Egypt tremble.
      The hearts of the Egyptians melt with
         fear.

² "I will make Egyptian fight against
      Egyptian—
   brother against brother,
neighbor against neighbor,
   city against city,
   province against province.
³ The Egyptians will lose heart,
   and I will confuse their plans.

They will plead with their idols for
   wisdom
   and call on spirits, mediums, and
      those who consult the spirits of the
         dead.
⁴ I will hand Egypt over
   to a hard, cruel master.
A fierce king will rule them,"
   says the Lord, the LORD of Heaven's
      Armies.

⁵ The waters of the Nile will fail to rise and
      flood the fields.
   The riverbed will be parched and dry.
⁶ The canals of the Nile will dry up,
   and the streams of Egypt will stink
      with rotting reeds and rushes.
⁷ All the greenery along the riverbank
   and all the crops along the river
   will dry up and blow away.
⁸ The fishermen will lament for lack of work.
   Those who cast hooks into the Nile will
      groan,
   and those who use nets will lose heart.
⁹ There will be no flax for the harvesters,
   no thread for the weavers.
¹⁰ They will be in despair,
   and all the workers will be sick at heart.

¹¹ What fools are the officials of Zoan!
   Their best counsel to the king of Egypt
      is stupid and wrong.
Will they still boast to Pharaoh of their
      wisdom?
   Will they dare brag about all their wise
      ancestors?
¹² Where are your wise counselors, Pharaoh?
   Let them tell you what God plans,
   what the LORD of Heaven's Armies is
      going to do to Egypt.
¹³ The officials of Zoan are fools,
   and the officials of Memphis* are
      deluded.
   The leaders of the people
      have led Egypt astray.
¹⁴ The LORD has sent a spirit of foolishness
      on them,
   so all their suggestions are wrong.

18:7 Hebrew *to Mount Zion.* 19:13 Hebrew *Noph.*

18:7 The enemy nation of Ethiopia would one day come to Jerusalem to worship God. This
reminds us that God can do the unexpected and seemingly impossible. What things in our life
look impossible? Is it recovering from an addiction, restoring a relationship, putting past abuses
behind us? Whatever the situation, God can bring healing. "Is anything too hard for the LORD?"
(Genesis 18:14).
19:11-14 The wisdom of the Egyptians turned out to be foolish. The wise men counted on their
own logic and were deceived. True wisdom comes from God alone. Our plans will succeed only if
we ask God for assistance and rely on him to show us the proper way to live.

They cause Egypt to stagger
like a drunk in his vomit.
¹⁵There is nothing Egypt can do.
All are helpless—
the head and the tail,
the noble palm branch and the lowly reed.

¹⁶In that day the Egyptians will be as weak as women. They will cower in fear beneath the upraised fist of the LORD of Heaven's Armies. ¹⁷Just to speak the name of Israel will terrorize them, for the LORD of Heaven's Armies has laid out his plans against them.

¹⁸In that day five of Egypt's cities will follow the LORD of Heaven's Armies. They will even begin to speak Hebrew, the language of Canaan. One of these cities will be Heliopolis, the City of the Sun.*

¹⁹In that day there will be an altar to the LORD in the heart of Egypt, and there will be a monument to the LORD at its border. ²⁰It will be a sign and a witness that the LORD of Heaven's Armies is worshiped in the land of Egypt. When the people cry to the LORD for help against those who oppress them, he will send them a savior who will rescue them. ²¹The LORD will make himself known to the Egyptians. Yes, they will know the LORD and will give their sacrifices and offerings to him. They will make a vow to the LORD and will keep it. ²²The LORD will strike Egypt, and then he will bring healing. For the Egyptians will turn to the LORD, and he will listen to their pleas and heal them.

²³In that day Egypt and Assyria will be connected by a highway. The Egyptians and Assyrians will move freely between their lands, and they will both worship God. ²⁴In that day Israel will be the third, along with Egypt and Assyria, a blessing in the midst of the earth. ²⁵For the LORD of Heaven's Armies will say, "Blessed be Egypt, my people. Blessed be Assyria, the land I have made. Blessed be Israel, my special possession!"

CHAPTER 20
A Message about Egypt and Ethiopia

In the year when King Sargon of Assyria sent his commander in chief to capture the Philistine city of Ashdod,* ²the LORD told Isaiah son of Amoz, "Take off the burlap you have been wearing, and remove your sandals." Isaiah did as he was told and walked around naked and barefoot.

³Then the LORD said, "My servant Isaiah has been walking around naked and barefoot for the last three years. This is a sign—a symbol of the terrible troubles I will bring upon Egypt and Ethiopia.* ⁴For the king of Assyria will take away the Egyptians and Ethiopians* as prisoners. He will make them walk naked and barefoot, both young and old, their buttocks bared, to the shame of Egypt. ⁵Then the Philistines will be thrown into panic, for they counted on the power of Ethiopia and boasted of their allies in Egypt! ⁶They will say, 'If this can happen to Egypt, what chance do we have? We were counting on Egypt to protect us from the king of Assyria.'"

CHAPTER 21
A Message about Babylon

This message came to me concerning Babylon—the desert by the sea*:

Disaster is roaring down on you from
the desert,
like a whirlwind sweeping in from the
Negev.
²I see a terrifying vision:
I see the betrayer betraying,
the destroyer destroying.
Go ahead, you Elamites and Medes,
attack and lay siege.
I will make an end
to all the groaning Babylon caused.
³My stomach aches and burns with pain.
Sharp pangs of anguish are upon me,
like those of a woman in labor.
I grow faint when I hear what God is
planning;
I am too afraid to look.
⁴My mind reels and my heart races.
I longed for evening to come,
but now I am terrified of the dark.

⁵Look! They are preparing a great feast.
They are spreading rugs for people
to sit on.

19:18 Or *will be the City of Destruction.* 20:1 Ashdod was captured by Assyria in 711 B.C. 20:3 Hebrew *Cush;* also in 20:5. 20:4 Hebrew *Cushites.* 21:1 Hebrew *concerning the desert by the sea.*

21:5 The Babylonians continued in denial. Their destruction would be imminent, but they would not face up to reality. They would be feasting when they should have been preparing for battle. As a result, they would fall to the Medes and Persians without a fight (see Daniel 5). Like the Babylonians, we won't know when disaster might strike. We could be reveling in our addiction when *bam!* a catastrophe hits us. If we turn our life and addiction over to God, we may yet be able to avoid some of the destructive consequences that would otherwise come.

Everyone is eating and drinking.
But quick! Grab your shields and prepare
for battle.
You are being attacked!

[6] Meanwhile, the Lord said to me,
"Put a watchman on the city wall.
Let him shout out what he sees.
[7] He should look for chariots
drawn by pairs of horses,
and for riders on donkeys and camels.
Let the watchman be fully alert."

[8] Then the watchman* called out,
"Day after day I have stood on the
watchtower, my lord.
Night after night I have remained
at my post.
[9] Now at last—look!
Here comes a man in a chariot
with a pair of horses!"
Then the watchman said,
"Babylon is fallen, fallen!
All the idols of Babylon
lie broken on the ground!"
[10] O my people, threshed and winnowed,
I have told you everything the LORD of
Heaven's Armies has said,
everything the God of Israel has told me.

A Message about Edom

[11] This message came to me concerning
Edom*:

Someone from Edom* keeps calling to me,
"Watchman, how much longer until
morning?
When will the night be over?"
[12] The watchman replies,
"Morning is coming, but night will soon
return.
If you wish to ask again, then come
back and ask."

A Message about Arabia

[13] This message came to me concerning Arabia:

O caravans from Dedan,
hide in the deserts of Arabia.

[14] O people of Tema,
bring water to these thirsty people,
food to these weary refugees.
[15] They have fled from the sword,
from the drawn sword,
from the bent bow
and the terrors of battle.

[16] The Lord said to me, "Within a year,
counting each day,* all the glory of Kedar
will come to an end. [17] Only a few of its courageous archers will survive. I, the LORD, the
God of Israel, have spoken!"

CHAPTER 22
A Message about Jerusalem
This message came to me concerning Jerusalem—the Valley of Vision*:

What is happening?
Why is everyone running to the
rooftops?
[2] The whole city is in a terrible uproar.
What do I see in this reveling city?
Bodies are lying everywhere,
killed not in battle but by famine and
disease.
[3] All your leaders have fled.
They surrendered without resistance.
The people tried to slip away,
but they were captured, too.
[4] That's why I said, "Leave me alone to
weep;
do not try to comfort me.
Let me cry for my people
as I watch them being destroyed."

[5] Oh, what a day of crushing defeat!
What a day of confusion and terror
brought by the Lord, the LORD of Heaven's
Armies,
upon the Valley of Vision!
The walls of Jerusalem have been broken,
and cries of death echo from the
mountainsides.
[6] Elamites are the archers,
with their chariots and charioteers.
The men of Kir hold up the shields.

21:8 As in Dead Sea Scrolls and Syriac version; Masoretic Text reads *a lion.* 21:11a Hebrew *Dumah,* which means
"silence" or "stillness." It is a wordplay on the word *Edom.* 21:11b Hebrew *Seir,* another name for Edom.
21:16 Hebrew *Within a year, as a servant bound by contract would count it.* Some ancient manuscripts read *Within three
years,* as in 16:14. 22:1 Hebrew *concerning the Valley of Vision.*

22:1-11 The people of Judah were threatened with destruction. They responded by taking inventory of their situation and weaponry, but they overlooked one thing—God. They still believed
they could withstand the enemy on their own. We do the same thing. While our dependency is
about to ruin us, we try to handle it on our own. We neglect to turn to the only resource that can
truly help—God. The first steps to recovery include admitting that we are powerless over our
problems and recognizing that we can succeed only with God.

⁷Chariots fill your beautiful valleys,
  and charioteers storm your gates.
⁸Judah's defenses have been stripped away.
  You run to the armory* for your weapons.
⁹You inspect the breaks in the walls of
    Jerusalem.*
  You store up water in the lower pool.
¹⁰You survey the houses and tear some down
  for stone to strengthen the walls.
¹¹Between the city walls, you build a
    reservoir
  for water from the old pool.
But you never ask for help from the One
    who did all this.
  You never considered the One who
    planned this long ago.

¹²At that time the Lord, the LORD of
    Heaven's Armies,
  called you to weep and mourn.
He told you to shave your heads in sorrow
    for your sins
  and to wear clothes of burlap to show
    your remorse.
¹³But instead, you dance and play;
  you slaughter cattle and kill sheep.
  You feast on meat and drink wine.
You say, "Let's feast and drink,
  for tomorrow we die!"

¹⁴The LORD of Heaven's Armies has revealed
this to me: "Till the day you die, you will
never be forgiven for this sin." That is the
judgment of the Lord, the LORD of Heaven's
Armies.

A Message for Shebna

¹⁵This is what the Lord, the LORD of Heaven's
Armies, said to me: "Confront Shebna, the
palace administrator, and give him this
message:

¹⁶"Who do you think you are,
  and what are you doing here,
  building a beautiful tomb for yourself—

a monument high up in the rock?
¹⁷For the LORD is about to hurl you away,
    mighty man.
  He is going to grab you,
¹⁸crumple you into a ball,
  and toss you away into a distant, barren
    land.
There you will die,
  and your glorious chariots will be
    broken and useless.
  You are a disgrace to your master!

¹⁹"Yes, I will drive you out of office," says
the LORD. "I will pull you down from your
high position. ²⁰And then I will call my servant Eliakim son of Hilkiah to replace you. ²¹I
will dress him in your royal robes and will
give him your title and your authority. And
he will be a father to the people of Jerusalem
and Judah. ²²I will give him the key to the
house of David—the highest position in the
royal court. When he opens doors, no one
will be able to close them; when he closes
doors, no one will be able to open them. ²³He
will bring honor to his family name, for I will
drive him firmly in place like a nail in the
wall. ²⁴They will give him great responsibility, and he will bring honor to even the lowliest members of his family.*"

²⁵But the LORD of Heaven's Armies also says:
"The time will come when I will pull out the
nail that seemed so firm. It will come out and
fall to the ground. Everything it supports will
fall with it. I, the LORD, have spoken!"

CHAPTER 23
A Message about Tyre
This message came to me concerning Tyre:

Wail, you trading ships of Tarshish,
  for the harbor and houses of Tyre are
    gone!
The rumors you heard in Cyprus*
  are all true.

22:8 Hebrew *to the House of the Forest;* see 1 Kgs 7:2-5. 22:9 Hebrew *the city of David.* 22:24 Hebrew *They will hang on
him all the glory of his father's house: its offspring and offshoots, all its lesser vessels, from the bowls to all the jars.*
23:1 Hebrew *Kittim;* also in 23:12.

22:12-14 Ignoring our problems doesn't make them go away. The opposite happens—they get
worse because we have put off dealing with them. If we have turned to alcohol, drugs, food, or
some other addiction, we have actually increased our problems. Instead of giving up hope (as
Judah did), we should turn to God and seek his help. If we trust the promises he has given us in
the Bible, there is no reason to give up—God is faithful!
23:1-12 God pronounced judgment on the prosperous merchant city of Tyre because of its pride.
Pride is not wrong when it is positive self-esteem ("I was proud of my son's winning home run"),
but it is disastrous when it is arrogance like Tyre's, which said, in effect, "I don't need God. I can
make my life prosper by my own efforts." We need to constantly take personal inventory and
make sure we have not replaced our dependence on God with unrealistic and arrogant confidence in ourself.

² Mourn in silence, you people of the coast
    and you merchants of Sidon.
Your traders crossed the sea,*
³   sailing over deep waters.
They brought you grain from Egypt*
    and harvests from along the Nile.
You were the marketplace of the world.

⁴ But now you are put to shame, city of
    Sidon,
    for Tyre, the fortress of the sea, says,*
"Now I am childless;
    I have no sons or daughters."
⁵ When Egypt hears the news about Tyre,
    there will be great sorrow.
⁶ Send word now to Tarshish!
Wail, you people who live in distant
    lands!
⁷ Is this silent ruin all that is left of your
    once joyous city?
    What a long history was yours!
    Think of all the colonists you sent to
    distant places.

⁸ Who has brought this disaster on Tyre,
    that great creator of kingdoms?
Her traders were all princes,
    her merchants were nobles.
⁹ The LORD of Heaven's Armies has done it
    to destroy your pride
    and bring low all earth's nobility.
¹⁰ Come, people of Tarshish,
    sweep over the land like the flooding
    Nile,
    for Tyre is defenseless.*
¹¹ The LORD held out his hand over the sea
    and shook the kingdoms of the earth.
He has spoken out against Phoenicia,*
    ordering that her fortresses be
    destroyed.
¹² He says, "Never again will you rejoice,
    O daughter of Sidon, for you have been
    crushed.
Even if you flee to Cyprus,
    you will find no rest."

¹³ Look at the land of Babylonia*—
    the people of that land are gone!

The Assyrians have handed Babylon over
    to the wild animals of the desert.
They have built siege ramps against its
    walls,
    torn down its palaces,
    and turned it to a heap of rubble.
¹⁴ Wail, you ships of Tarshish,
    for your harbor is destroyed!

¹⁵ For seventy years, the length of a king's
life, Tyre will be forgotten. But then the city
will come back to life as in the song about
the prostitute:

¹⁶ Take a harp and walk the streets,
    you forgotten harlot.
Make sweet melody and sing your songs
    so you will be remembered again.

¹⁷ Yes, after seventy years the LORD will revive Tyre. But she will be no different than
she was before. She will again be a prostitute
to all kingdoms around the world. ¹⁸ But in
the end her profits will be given to the LORD.
Her wealth will not be hoarded but will provide good food and fine clothing for the
LORD's priests.

CHAPTER 24
Destruction of the Earth
¹ Look! The LORD is about to destroy the
    earth
    and make it a vast wasteland.
He devastates the surface of the earth
    and scatters the people.
² Priests and laypeople,
    servants and masters,
    maids and mistresses,
    buyers and sellers,
    lenders and borrowers,
    bankers and debtors—none will be
    spared.
³ The earth will be completely emptied and
    looted.
    The LORD has spoken!

⁴ The earth mourns and dries up,
    and the land wastes away and wither.

23:2 As in Dead Sea Scrolls and Greek version; Masoretic Text reads *Those who have gone over the sea have filled you.*
23:3 Hebrew *from Shihor,* a branch of the Nile River. 23:4 Or *for the god of the sea says;* Hebrew reads *for the sea, the*
fortress of the sea, says. 23:10 The meaning of the Hebrew in this verse is uncertain. 23:11 Hebrew *Canaan.*
23:13 Or *Chaldea.*

23:13-18 After 70 years Tyre would rebuild and return to her old ways of seducing the nations to
materialism and idolatry. Without genuine recovery, we, too, go back to our old destructive
patterns. Our recovery aim needs to be more than just freedom from drugs or alcohol. We need a
whole new life, with God as the foundation. Jesus said that when we follow him we are like a
person who builds a house on rock. Even though the storms of life constantly assail us, we will
stand firm (see Matthew 7:24-27).
24:4-7 Our sins do not affect only us; they affect our family, our friends, our nation, and even our
planet. It is sobering to realize that what we do has such a great impact on the world. Our whole

Even the greatest people on earth waste
away.
⁵ The earth suffers for the sins of its people,
for they have twisted God's
instructions,
violated his laws,
and broken his everlasting covenant.
⁶ Therefore, a curse consumes the earth.
Its people must pay the price for their
sin.
They are destroyed by fire,
and only a few are left alive.
⁷ The grapevines waste away,
and there is no new wine.
All the merrymakers sigh and mourn.
⁸ The cheerful sound of tambourines is
stilled;
the happy cries of celebration are heard
no more.
The melodious chords of the harp are
silent.
⁹ Gone are the joys of wine and song;
alcoholic drink turns bitter in the
mouth.
¹⁰ The city writhes in chaos;
every home is locked to keep out
intruders.
¹¹ Mobs gather in the streets, crying out for
wine.
Joy has turned to gloom.
Gladness has been banished from the
land.
¹² The city is left in ruins,
its gates battered down.
¹³ Throughout the earth the story is the
same—
only a remnant is left,
like the stray olives left on the tree
or the few grapes left on the vine after
harvest.

¹⁴ But all who are left shout and sing for joy.
Those in the west praise the LORD's
majesty.
¹⁵ In eastern lands, give glory to the LORD.
In the lands beyond the sea, praise the
name of the LORD, the God of Israel.

¹⁶ We hear songs of praise from the ends
of the earth,
songs that give glory to the Righteous
One!

But my heart is heavy with grief.
Weep for me, for I wither away.
Deceit still prevails,
and treachery is everywhere.
¹⁷ Terror and traps and snares will be your
lot,
you people of the earth.
¹⁸ Those who flee in terror will fall into
a trap,
and those who escape the trap will be
caught in a snare.

Destruction falls like rain from the
heavens;
the foundations of the earth shake.
¹⁹ The earth has broken up.
It has utterly collapsed;
it is violently shaken.
²⁰ The earth staggers like a drunk.
It trembles like a tent in a storm.
It falls and will not rise again,
for the guilt of its rebellion is very
heavy.

²¹ In that day the LORD will punish the gods
in the heavens
and the proud rulers of the nations
on earth.
²² They will be rounded up and put in
prison.
They will be shut up in prison
and will finally be punished.
²³ Then the glory of the moon will
wane,
and the brightness of the sun
will fade,
for the LORD of Heaven's Armies will rule
on Mount Zion.
He will rule in great glory in
Jerusalem,
in the sight of all the leaders of his
people.

country is suffering the effects of alcoholism, drug addiction, infidelity, etc., and these problems
seem to be getting worse. Recovery is important to us and to our loved ones, but there is even
more at stake than we often realize. If each of us would successfully complete the recovery
program, dependency and addiction would decline, and society would benefit and begin a
recovery process of its own.
24:17-20 The people were in denial about their circumstances; Isaiah said that they would get
what they deserved—traps and snares, destruction and collapse. We, too, "get what's coming to
us" when we ignore the warning signs and continue in our dependencies and compulsions. To
deny the results of our dependency is to invite disaster into our life. When we are honest with
ourself, we can see that what we are doing is wrong and take steps to recover.

CHAPTER 25
Praise for Judgment and Salvation

¹ O LORD, I will honor and praise your
name,
for you are my God.
You do such wonderful things!
You planned them long ago,
and now you have accomplished them.
² You turn mighty cities into heaps of ruins.
Cities with strong walls are turned to
rubble.
Beautiful palaces in distant lands
disappear
and will never be rebuilt.
³ Therefore, strong nations will declare your
glory;
ruthless nations will fear you.

⁴ But you are a tower of refuge to the poor,
O LORD,
a tower of refuge to the needy in
distress.
You are a refuge from the storm
and a shelter from the heat.
For the oppressive acts of ruthless people
are like a storm beating against a wall,
⁵   or like the relentless heat of the desert.
But you silence the roar of foreign
nations.
As the shade of a cloud cools relentless
heat,
so the boastful songs of ruthless people
are stilled.

⁶ In Jerusalem,* the LORD of Heaven's
Armies
will spread a wonderful feast
for all the people of the world.
It will be a delicious banquet
with clear, well-aged wine and choice
meat.
⁷ There he will remove the cloud of gloom,
the shadow of death that hangs over
the earth.
⁸ He will swallow up death forever!
The Sovereign LORD will wipe away all
tears.

He will remove forever all insults and
mockery
against his land and people.
The LORD has spoken!

⁹ In that day the people will proclaim,
"This is our God!
We trusted in him, and he saved us!
This is the LORD, in whom we trusted.
Let us rejoice in the salvation he
brings!"
¹⁰ For the LORD's hand of blessing will rest
on Jerusalem.
But Moab will be crushed.
It will be like straw trampled down and
left to rot.
¹¹ God will push down Moab's people
as a swimmer pushes down water with
his hands.
He will end their pride
and all their evil works.
¹² The high walls of Moab will be
demolished.
They will be brought down to the
ground,
down into the dust.

CHAPTER 26
A Song of Praise to the LORD

In that day, everyone in the land of Judah
will sing this song:

Our city is strong!
We are surrounded by the walls of
God's salvation.
² Open the gates to all who are righteous;
allow the faithful to enter.
³ You will keep in perfect peace
all who trust in you,
all whose thoughts are fixed on you!
⁴ Trust in the LORD always,
for the LORD GOD is the eternal Rock.
⁵ He humbles the proud
and brings down the arrogant city.
He brings it down to the dust.
⁶ The poor and oppressed trample it
underfoot,
and the needy walk all over it.

25:6 Hebrew *On this mountain;* also in 25:10.

25:1-5 God will comfort those who trust in him and punish those who ignore him. He is a shelter
from the storms of life to those of us who have established a relationship with God. No matter
what we have done to mess up our life before, we can rely on God to strengthen us and keep us
from our dependency. If we haven't yet asked God to take control of our unmanageable life, there
is still time. No one is too far gone to receive God's mercy.
26:3 When our mind is absorbed with memories of abuse, failure, or shame, we are full of anxiety
and turmoil, whether we were victims or the main perpetrators of wrong. But when we learn to
work through the past and fix our thoughts on the Lord, we can receive his perfect peace.

⁷ But for those who are righteous,
    the way is not steep and rough.
You are a God who does what is right,
    and you smooth out the path ahead of
        them.
⁸ LORD, we show our trust in you by
        obeying your laws;
    our heart's desire is to glorify your
        name.
⁹ In the night I search for you;
    in the morning* I earnestly seek you.
For only when you come to judge the
        earth
    will people learn what is right.
¹⁰ Your kindness to the wicked
    does not make them do good.
Although others do right, the wicked keep
        doing wrong
    and take no notice of the LORD's
        majesty.
¹¹ O LORD, they pay no attention to your
        upraised fist.
Show them your eagerness to defend
        your people.
Then they will be ashamed.
    Let your fire consume your enemies.

¹² LORD, you will grant us peace;
    all we have accomplished is really from
        you.
¹³ O LORD our God, others have ruled us,
    but you alone are the one we worship.
¹⁴ Those we served before are dead and
        gone.
    Their departed spirits will never return!
You attacked them and destroyed them,
    and they are long forgotten.
¹⁵ O LORD, you have made our nation great;
    yes, you have made us great.
You have extended our borders,
    and we give you the glory!

¹⁶ LORD, in distress we searched for you.
    We prayed beneath the burden of your
        discipline.
¹⁷ Just as a pregnant woman
    writhes and cries out in pain as she
        gives birth,
    so were we in your presence, LORD.
¹⁸ We, too, writhe in agony,
    but nothing comes of our suffering.
We have not given salvation to the earth,
    nor brought life into the world.
¹⁹ But those who die in the LORD will live;
    their bodies will rise again!
Those who sleep in the earth
    will rise up and sing for joy!
For your life-giving light will fall like dew
    on your people in the place of the dead!

Restoration for Israel

²⁰ Go home, my people,
    and lock your doors!
Hide yourselves for a little while
    until the LORD's anger has passed.
²¹ Look! The LORD is coming from heaven
    to punish the people of the earth for
        their sins.
The earth will no longer hide those who
        have been killed.
    They will be brought out for all to see.

CHAPTER 27

In that day the LORD will take his terrible,
swift sword and punish Leviathan,* the
swiftly moving serpent, the coiling, writhing
serpent. He will kill the dragon of the sea.

² "In that day,
    sing about the fruitful vineyard.
³ I, the LORD, will watch over it,
    watering it carefully.

26:9 Hebrew *within me.* 27:1 The identification of Leviathan is disputed, ranging from an earthly creature to a mythical sea monster in ancient literature.

26:12-15 These verses summarize the recovery process. The Israelites, enslaved by foreign powers, admitted their sins and turned to God for salvation. They were willing to put aside their old ways, and God came to their rescue. The people praised God for what he had done to deliver them. Recovery for us will follow the same pattern. Our enslavement comes from alcohol, drugs, sex, pride—anything that takes us out of God's control. We need to admit our false dependencies, whatever they may be, and turn to God for help.

27:1 Leviathan was a mythical sea monster that was opposed to God. Its mention here is symbolic: God will destroy his enemies, especially Satan, God's chief rival. This is encouraging to those struggling with drugs, alcohol, sexual sins, eating disorders, or other dependencies that seem like oppressive monsters. God can vanquish these creatures that live in the depths of our life if we call to him for help.

27:2-3 God said he would take care of his people, just as a farmer takes care of his vineyard. God would provide the nourishment and keep enemies away. That truth is the same for us today as it was for the Israelites. God will protect us if we surrender to his power. Once we admit our sins to him, he will help us resist the lure of our dependency.

Day and night I will watch so no one can
  harm it.
4 My anger will be gone.
If I find briers and thorns growing,
  I will attack them;
I will burn them up—
5 unless they turn to me for help.
Let them make peace with me;
  yes, let them make peace with me."
6 The time is coming when Jacob's
  descendants will take root.
Israel will bud and blossom
  and fill the whole earth with fruit!

7 Has the LORD struck Israel
  as he struck her enemies?
Has he punished her
  as he punished them?
8 No, but he exiled Israel to call her to
  account.
She was exiled from her land
  as though blown away in a storm from
  the east.
9 The LORD did this to purge Israel's*
  wickedness,
  to take away all her sin.
As a result, all the pagan altars will be
  crushed to dust.
No Asherah pole or pagan shrine will be
  left standing.
10 The fortified towns will be silent and
  empty,
  the houses abandoned, the streets
  overgrown with weeds.
Calves will graze there,
  chewing on twigs and branches.
11 The people are like the dead branches of a
  tree,
  broken off and used for kindling
  beneath the cooking pots.
Israel is a foolish and stupid nation,
  for its people have turned away from
  God.
Therefore, the one who made them
  will show them no pity or mercy.

12 Yet the time will come when the LORD
will gather them together like handpicked
grain. One by one he will gather them—from

the Euphrates River* in the east to the Brook
of Egypt in the west. 13 In that day the great
trumpet will sound. Many who were dying
in exile in Assyria and Egypt will return to Jerusalem to worship the LORD on his holy
mountain.

CHAPTER 28
A Message about Samaria
1 What sorrow awaits the proud city of
  Samaria—
  the glorious crown of the drunks of
  Israel.*
It sits at the head of a fertile valley,
  but its glorious beauty will fade like a
  flower.
It is the pride of a people
  brought down by wine.
2 For the Lord will send a mighty army
  against it.
Like a mighty hailstorm and a torrential
  rain,
they will burst upon it like a surging flood
  and smash it to the ground.
3 The proud city of Samaria—
  the glorious crown of the drunks of
  Israel*—
  will be trampled beneath its enemies'
  feet.
4 It sits at the head of a fertile valley,
  but its glorious beauty will fade like a
  flower.
Whoever sees it will snatch it up,
  as an early fig is quickly picked and
  eaten.

5 Then at last the LORD of Heaven's Armies
  will himself be Israel's glorious crown.
He will be the pride and joy
  of the remnant of his people.
6 He will give a longing for justice
  to their judges.
He will give great courage
  to their warriors who stand at the gates.

7 Now, however, Israel is led by drunks
  who reel with wine and stagger with
  alcohol.

27:9 Hebrew *Jacob's*. See note on 14:1. 27:12 Hebrew *the river*. 28:1 Hebrew *What sorrow awaits the crowning glory of the drunks of Ephraim,* referring to Samaria, capital of the northern kingdom of Israel. 28:3 Hebrew *The crowning glory of the drunks of Ephraim;* see note on 28:1.

28:1-6 The pleasures of our addiction are like a crown of flowers whose beauty quickly fades. The highs we experience quickly fade and leave us wanting. In contrast, God is an unfading crown of glory to those who obey his commands. He is able to fill our life completely, and the joy he gives us will last throughout eternity.
28:7-13 Judah's leaders refused to listen to Isaiah's message because it seemed they were being treated like babies (28:9-10); by doing so, they rejected God's saving rest. We, too, can get so

The priests and prophets stagger with
    alcohol
and lose themselves in wine.
They reel when they see visions
    and stagger as they render decisions.
[8] Their tables are covered with vomit;
    filth is everywhere.
[9] "Who does the LORD think we are?" they
    ask.
    "Why does he speak to us like this?
Are we little children,
    just recently weaned?
[10] He tells us everything over and over—
one line at a time,
    one line at a time,
a little here,
    and a little there!"

[11] So now God will have to speak to his people
    through foreign oppressors who speak a
    strange language!
[12] God has told his people,
    "Here is a place of rest;
    let the weary rest here.
This is a place of quiet rest."
    But they would not listen.
[13] So the LORD will spell out his message for
    them again,
one line at a time,
    one line at a time,
a little here,
    and a little there,
so that they will stumble and fall.
    They will be injured, trapped, and
    captured.

[14] Therefore, listen to this message from the
    LORD,
    you scoffing rulers in Jerusalem.
[15] You boast, "We have struck a bargain to
    cheat death
and have made a deal to dodge the
    grave.*
The coming destruction can never
    touch us,

for we have built a strong refuge made
    of lies and deception."

[16] Therefore, this is what the Sovereign LORD
    says:
"Look! I am placing a foundation stone
    in Jerusalem,*
    a firm and tested stone.
It is a precious cornerstone that is safe to
    build on.
    Whoever believes need never be shaken.*
[17] I will test you with the measuring line of
    justice
    and the plumb line of righteousness.
Since your refuge is made of lies,
    a hailstorm will knock it down.
Since it is made of deception,
    a flood will sweep it away.
[18] I will cancel the bargain you made to
    cheat death,
    and I will overturn your deal to dodge
    the grave.
When the terrible enemy sweeps through,
    you will be trampled into the ground.
[19] Again and again that flood will come,
    morning after morning,
day and night,
    until you are carried away."

This message will bring terror to your
    people.
[20] The bed you have made is too short
    to lie on.
    The blankets are too narrow to cover you.
[21] The LORD will come as he did against the
    Philistines at Mount Perazim
    and against the Amorites at Gibeon.
He will come to do a strange thing;
    he will come to do an unusual deed:
[22] For the Lord, the LORD of Heaven's
    Armies,
    has plainly said that he is determined to
    crush the whole land.
So scoff no more,
    or your punishment will be even greater.

28:15 Hebrew *Sheol*; also in 28:18.   **28:16a** Hebrew *in Zion*.   **28:16b** Greek version reads *Look! I am placing a stone in the foundation of Jerusalem* [literally *Zion*], / *a precious cornerstone for its foundation, chosen for great honor.* / *Anyone who trusts in him will never be disgraced.* Compare Rom 9:33; 1 Pet 2:6.

---

caught up in our addiction and dysfunctional behavior that we belittle God's way of recovery, considering it too simple and old-fashioned. However, the truth is that God has graciously provided the only means for any recovery. When we reject his message and his methods, we harm only ourself. **28:14-22** The rulers of Jerusalem were in total denial. They thought they were in full control and could stand against the Assyrians. But they were about to fall to the overwhelming scourge of God's judgment through Assyria. Likewise, we err when we are confronted by God's corrections and yet we declare that there is no trouble we cannot handle. We cannot overpower God, and it is foolish to try. When King David sinned and faced judgment (see 2 Samuel 24), he said, "Let us fall into the hands of the LORD, for his mercy is great. Do not let me fall into human hands" (2 Samuel 24:14). God will show us mercy if we truly repent and turn from our destructive ways.

²³ Listen to me;
   listen, and pay close attention.
²⁴ Does a farmer always plow and never sow?
   Is he forever cultivating the soil and
      never planting?
²⁵ Does he not finally plant his seeds—
   black cumin, cumin, wheat, barley, and
      emmer wheat—
   each in its proper way,
   and each in its proper place?
²⁶ The farmer knows just what to do,
   for God has given him understanding.
²⁷ A heavy sledge is never used to thresh
      black cumin;
   rather, it is beaten with a light stick.
   A threshing wheel is never rolled on
      cumin;
   instead, it is beaten lightly with a flail.
²⁸ Grain for bread is easily crushed,
   so he doesn't keep on pounding it.
   He threshes it under the wheels of a cart,
   but he doesn't pulverize it.
²⁹ The LORD of Heaven's Armies is a
      wonderful teacher,
   and he gives the farmer great wisdom.

CHAPTER 29
A Message about Jerusalem
¹ "What sorrow awaits Ariel,* the City of
      David.
   Year after year you celebrate your feasts.
² Yet I will bring disaster upon you,
   and there will be much weeping and
      sorrow.
   For Jerusalem will become what her name
      Ariel means—
   an altar covered with blood.
³ I will be your enemy,
   surrounding Jerusalem and attacking its
      walls.
   I will build siege towers
   and destroy it.
⁴ Then deep from the earth you will speak;
   from low in the dust your words will
      come.
   Your voice will whisper from the ground
   like a ghost conjured up from the grave.

⁵ "But suddenly, your ruthless enemies will
      be crushed
   like the finest of dust.

Your many attackers will be driven away
   like chaff before the wind.
   Suddenly, in an instant,
⁶   I, the LORD of Heaven's Armies, will act
      for you
   with thunder and earthquake and great
      noise,
   with whirlwind and storm and
      consuming fire.
⁷ All the nations fighting against Jerusalem*
   will vanish like a dream!
   Those who are attacking her walls
   will vanish like a vision in the night.
⁸ A hungry person dreams of eating
   but wakes up still hungry.
   A thirsty person dreams of drinking
   but is still faint from thirst when
      morning comes.
   So it will be with your enemies,
   with those who attack Mount Zion."

⁹ Are you amazed and incredulous?
   Don't you believe it?
   Then go ahead and be blind.
   You are stupid, but not from wine!
   You stagger, but not from liquor!
¹⁰ For the LORD has poured out on you a
      spirit of deep sleep.
   He has closed the eyes of your prophets
   and visionaries.

¹¹All the future events in this vision are
like a sealed book to them. When you give it
to those who can read, they will say, "We
can't read it because it is sealed." ¹²When you
give it to those who cannot read, they will
say, "We don't know how to read."

¹³ And so the Lord says,
   "These people say they are mine.
   They honor me with their lips,
   but their hearts are far from me.
   And their worship of me
   is nothing but man-made rules learned
      by rote.*
¹⁴ Because of this, I will once again astound
      these hypocrites
   with amazing wonders.
   The wisdom of the wise will pass away,
   and the intelligence of the intelligent
   will disappear."

29:1 Ariel sounds like a Hebrew term that means "hearth" or "altar." 29:7 Hebrew Ariel. 29:13 Greek version reads
Their worship is a farce, / for they teach man-made ideas as commands from God. Compare Mark 7:7.

29:5-8 God is able to rescue us from certain death. He miraculously saved Jerusalem from its
enemies when all hope had been lost. He will miraculously save us from our dependency when
we ask him to. If God can save an entire nation from destruction and save the whole world from
sin through his Son, he certainly can rescue us from our addiction.

¹⁵ What sorrow awaits those who try to hide
their plans from the LORD,
who do their evil deeds in the dark!
"The LORD can't see us," they say.
"He doesn't know what's going on!"
¹⁶ How foolish can you be?
He is the Potter, and he is certainly
greater than you, the clay!
Should the created thing say of the one
who made it,
"He didn't make me"?
Does a jar ever say,
"The potter who made me is stupid"?

¹⁷ Soon—and it will not be very long—
the forests of Lebanon will become a
fertile field,
and the fertile field will yield bountiful
crops.
¹⁸ In that day the deaf will hear words read
from a book,
and the blind will see through the
gloom and darkness.
¹⁹ The humble will be filled with fresh joy
from the LORD.
The poor will rejoice in the Holy One
of Israel.
²⁰ The scoffer will be gone,
the arrogant will disappear,
and those who plot evil will be killed.
²¹ Those who convict the innocent
by their false testimony will disappear.
A similar fate awaits those who use
trickery to pervert justice
and who tell lies to destroy the innocent.

²²That is why the LORD, who redeemed Abraham, says to the people of Israel,*

"My people will no longer be ashamed
or turn pale with fear.

29:22 Hebrew *of Jacob*. See note on 14:1.

²³ For when they see their many children
and all the blessings I have given them,
they will recognize the holiness of the
Holy One of Jacob.
They will stand in awe of the God of
Israel.
²⁴ Then the wayward will gain
understanding,
and complainers will accept instruction.

CHAPTER 30
Judah's Worthless Treaty with Egypt
¹ "What sorrow awaits my rebellious
children,"
says the LORD.
"You make plans that are contrary to
mine.
You make alliances not directed by my
Spirit,
thus piling up your sins.
² For without consulting me,
you have gone down to Egypt for help.
You have put your trust in Pharaoh's
protection.
You have tried to hide in his shade.
³ But by trusting Pharaoh, you will be
humiliated,
and by depending on him, you will be
disgraced.
⁴ For though his power extends to Zoan
and his officials have arrived in Hanes,
⁵ all who trust in him will be ashamed.
He will not help you.
Instead, he will disgrace you."

⁶This message came to me concerning the
animals in the Negev:

The caravan moves slowly
across the terrible desert to Egypt—
donkeys weighed down with riches

29:15-16 We can hide nothing from God; he knows all that we have done, are doing, and will
do. When we try to hide things from God, we often succeed only in hiding them from ourself. We
must take an inventory of our life and admit our weaknesses to God, to ourself, and to others so
we can get help to overcome our problem. We tell God not to inform him (he knows already),
but to hand our life over to him. Once we do this, we will have the help of the almighty God.
30:1-5 In its quest for national recovery, Judah sought help from Egypt, not from God. God
warned Judah's leaders that their plan would only bring defeat because Egypt couldn't save them.
God alone had the power to deliver them. Our recovery program should include God. When we
put our trust in people or new fad programs, we will fail. To attempt anything apart from God will
only lead to failure and increased suffering.
30:6-11 When we sin, we usually try to avoid what God has to say. Deep inside we know what
God thinks and how it hurts him to see our behavior. But if we admit that to ourself, we become
convicted, feeling guilty about our actions and recognizing that we need to change. Instead of
wanting to hear God's truth, we want to hear people say that we are doing all right, that we have
no problems. To continue in denial will eventually lead to ruin; there will come a point when it is
too late to admit the truth of God's Word. It is important to accept the truth from God because a
little pain now is better than much pain later.

and camels loaded with treasure—
all to pay for Egypt's protection.
They travel through the wilderness,
a place of lionesses and lions,
a place where vipers and poisonous
snakes live.
All this, and Egypt will give you nothing
in return.
⁷ Egypt's promises are worthless!
Therefore, I call her Rahab—
the Harmless Dragon.*

A Warning for Rebellious Judah

⁸ Now go and write down these words.
Write them in a book.
They will stand until the end of time
as a witness
⁹ that these people are stubborn rebels
who refuse to pay attention to the
LORD's instructions.
¹⁰ They tell the seers,
"Stop seeing visions!"
They tell the prophets,
"Don't tell us what is right.
Tell us nice things.
Tell us lies.
¹¹ Forget all this gloom.
Get off your narrow path.
Stop telling us about your
'Holy One of Israel.'"

¹²This is the reply of the Holy One of Israel:

"Because you despise what I tell you
and trust instead in oppression and lies,
¹³ calamity will come upon you suddenly—
like a bulging wall that bursts and falls.
In an instant it will collapse
and come crashing down.
¹⁴ You will be smashed like a piece of pottery—
shattered so completely that
there won't be a piece big enough
to carry coals from a fireplace
or a little water from the well."

¹⁵ This is what the Sovereign LORD,
the Holy One of Israel, says:
"Only in returning to me
and resting in me will you be saved.
In quietness and confidence is your
strength.
But you would have none of it.
¹⁶ You said, 'No, we will get our help from
Egypt.
They will give us swift horses for riding
into battle.'
But the only swiftness you are going to see

is the swiftness of your enemies chasing
you!
¹⁷ One of them will chase a thousand of you.
Five of them will make all of you flee.
You will be left like a lonely flagpole
on a hill
or a tattered banner on a distant
mountaintop."

Blessings for the LORD's People

¹⁸ So the LORD must wait for you to come to
him
so he can show you his love and
compassion.
For the LORD is a faithful God.
Blessed are those who wait for his help.

¹⁹ O people of Zion, who live in Jerusalem,
you will weep no more.
He will be gracious if you ask for help.
He will surely respond to the sound of
your cries.
²⁰ Though the Lord gave you adversity for
food
and suffering for drink,
he will still be with you to teach you.
You will see your teacher with your own
eyes.
²¹ Your own ears will hear him.
Right behind you a voice will say,
"This is the way you should go,"
whether to the right or to the left.
²² Then you will destroy all your silver idols
and your precious gold images.
You will throw them out like filthy rags,
saying to them, "Good riddance!"

²³Then the LORD will bless you with rain at
planting time. There will be wonderful harvests and plenty of pastureland for your livestock. ²⁴The oxen and donkeys that till the
ground will eat good grain, its chaff blown
away by the wind. ²⁵In that day, when your
enemies are slaughtered and the towers fall,
there will be streams of water flowing down
every mountain and hill. ²⁶The moon will be
as bright as the sun, and the sun will be
seven times brighter—like the light of seven
days in one! So it will be when the LORD begins to heal his people and cure the wounds
he gave them.

²⁷ Look! The LORD is coming from far away,
burning with anger,
surrounded by thick, rising smoke.
His lips are filled with fury;
his words consume like fire.

30:7 Hebrew *Rahab who sits still.* Rahab is the name of a mythical sea monster that represents chaos in ancient
literature. The name is used here as a poetic name for Egypt.

28 His hot breath pours out like a flood
    up to the neck of his enemies.
He will sift out the proud nations for
    destruction.
He will bridle them and lead them
    away to ruin.

29 But the people of God will sing a song
    of joy,
    like the songs at the holy festivals.
You will be filled with joy,
    as when a flutist leads a group
      of pilgrims
to Jerusalem, the mountain of the LORD—
    to the Rock of Israel.
30 And the LORD will make his majestic
    voice heard.
He will display the strength of his
    mighty arm.
It will descend with devouring flames,
    with cloudbursts, thunderstorms, and
    huge hailstones.
31 At the LORD's command, the Assyrians
    will be shattered.
He will strike them down with his
    royal scepter.
32 And as the LORD strikes them with his
    rod of punishment,*
his people will celebrate with
    tambourines and harps.
Lifting his mighty arm, he will fight
    the Assyrians.
33 Topheth—the place of burning—
    has long been ready for the Assyrian
    king;
    the pyre is piled high with wood.
The breath of the LORD, like fire from
    a volcano,
    will set it ablaze.

CHAPTER 31
The Futility of Relying on Egypt
1 What sorrow awaits those who look to
    Egypt for help,
    trusting their horses, chariots, and
      charioteers
  and depending on the strength of
    human armies

instead of looking to the LORD,
    the Holy One of Israel.
2 In his wisdom, the LORD will send great
    disaster;
he will not change his mind.
He will rise against the wicked
    and against their helpers.
3 For these Egyptians are mere humans, not
    God!
    Their horses are puny flesh, not mighty
      spirits!
When the LORD raises his fist against them,
    those who help will stumble,
and those being helped will fall.
    They will all fall down and die together.

4 But this is what the LORD has told me:

"When a strong young lion
    stands growling over a sheep it has
      killed,
it is not frightened by the shouts and noise
    of a whole crowd of shepherds.
In the same way, the LORD of Heaven's
    Armies
    will come down and fight on Mount Zion.
5 The LORD of Heaven's Armies will hover
    over Jerusalem
    and protect it like a bird protecting its
      nest.
He will defend and save the city;
    he will pass over it and rescue it."

6 Though you are such wicked rebels, my
people, come and return to the LORD. 7 I know
the glorious day will come when each of you
will throw away the gold idols and silver images your sinful hands have made.

8 "The Assyrians will be destroyed,
    but not by the swords of men.
The sword of God will strike them,
    and they will panic and flee.
The strong young Assyrians
    will be taken away as captives.
9 Even the strongest will quake with terror,
    and princes will flee when they see your
      battle flags,"
says the LORD, whose fire burns in Zion,
    whose flame blazes from Jerusalem.

30:32 As in some Hebrew manuscripts and Syriac version; Masoretic Text reads *with the founded rod.*

31:1-5 Judah turned to Egypt instead of God for help, and destruction followed. Egypt can symbolize for us all those things we turn to for relief from our pain: work, sex, alcohol, drugs, food, unhealthy relationships. They look good, like the mighty chariots and horses of Egypt, but their help is just as illusory. Only God can bring us true deliverance.

31:6-9 We might think that with such rebellion and stubbornness in Judah, God would have become fed up with them and written them off. Incredibly, God continued to invite the Israelites to return to him and find his blessings. What an encouragement this is for us, especially if we have begun to wonder if God still cares about us after our repeated failures. God wants all of us to turn to him and find salvation.

CHAPTER 32
Israel's Ultimate Deliverance

¹ Look, a righteous king is coming!
And honest princes will rule under him.
² Each one will be like a shelter from the
wind
and a refuge from the storm,
like streams of water in the desert
and the shadow of a great rock in a
parched land.

³ Then everyone who has eyes will be able
to see the truth,
and everyone who has ears will be able
to hear it.
⁴ Even the hotheads will be full of sense
and understanding.
Those who stammer will speak out
plainly.
⁵ In that day ungodly fools will not be
heroes.
Scoundrels will not be respected.
⁶ For fools speak foolishness
and make evil plans.
They practice ungodliness
and spread false teachings about the
LORD.
They deprive the hungry of food
and give no water to the thirsty.
⁷ The smooth tricks of scoundrels are evil.
They plot crooked schemes.
They lie to convict the poor,
even when the cause of the poor is just.
⁸ But generous people plan to do what is
generous,
and they stand firm in their generosity.

⁹ Listen, you women who lie around in
ease.
Listen to me, you who are so smug.
¹⁰ In a short time—just a little more than a
year—
you careless ones will suddenly begin
to care.
For your fruit crops will fail,
and the harvest will never take place.
¹¹ Tremble, you women of ease;
throw off your complacency.
Strip off your pretty clothes,
and put on burlap to show your grief.
¹² Beat your breasts in sorrow for your
bountiful farms
and your fruitful grapevines.
¹³ For your land will be overgrown with
thorns and briers.
Your joyful homes and happy towns
will be gone.
¹⁴ The palace and the city will be deserted,
and busy towns will be empty.
Wild donkeys will frolic and flocks will
graze
in the empty forts* and watchtowers
¹⁵ until at last the Spirit is poured out
on us from heaven.
Then the wilderness will become a fertile
field,
and the fertile field will yield bountiful
crops.

¹⁶ Justice will rule in the wilderness
and righteousness in the fertile field.
¹⁷ And this righteousness will bring peace.
Yes, it will bring quietness and
confidence forever.
¹⁸ My people will live in safety, quietly at
home.
They will be at rest.
¹⁹ Even if the forest should be destroyed
and the city torn down,
²⁰ the LORD will greatly bless his people.
Wherever they plant seed, bountiful
crops will spring up.
Their cattle and donkeys will graze
freely.

CHAPTER 33
A Message about Assyria

¹ What sorrow awaits you Assyrians, who
have destroyed others*

32:14 Hebrew *the Ophel.* 33:1 Hebrew *What sorrow awaits you, O destroyer.* The Hebrew text does not specifically
name Assyria as the object of the prophecy in this chapter.

32:1-2 This King who was to come is Jesus—we don't have to wait for him. The future blessings
described in these verses are ours now. The Jews were asked to trust in help that was yet to come.
We can trust in help that has already come; it is ours for the asking. To claim God's aid, we need
to (1) confess Jesus as our Savior, realizing that he died and rose again; (2) ask for forgiveness for
our sins and addictions; and (3) give God control of our life so he can release us from our dependency.
33:1 Assyria's foreign policy was based on a double standard—lies told *to* Assyria were punished
while lies told *by* Assyria were overlooked. This hypocrisy will be judged by God. God hates lies as
much today as he did then. He will hold us responsible for our lies. Our relationships will be
destroyed by them. If we want a good reputation, we must be honest with everyone and fulfill
our promises.

but have never been destroyed
yourselves.
You betray others,
but you have never been betrayed.
When you are done destroying,
you will be destroyed.
When you are done betraying,
you will be betrayed.
² But LORD, be merciful to us,
for we have waited for you.
Be our strong arm each day
and our salvation in times of trouble.
³ The enemy runs at the sound of your
voice.
When you stand up, the nations flee!
⁴ Just as caterpillars and locusts strip the
fields and vines,
so the fallen army of Assyria will be
stripped!

⁵ Though the LORD is very great and lives in
heaven,
he will make Jerusalem* his home of
justice and righteousness.
⁶ In that day he will be your sure
foundation,
providing a rich store of salvation,
wisdom, and knowledge.
The fear of the LORD will be your
treasure.

⁷ But now your brave warriors weep in
public.
Your ambassadors of peace cry in bitter
disappointment.
⁸ Your roads are deserted;
no one travels them anymore.
The Assyrians have broken their peace
treaty
and care nothing for the promises they
made before witnesses.*
They have no respect for anyone.
⁹ The land of Israel wilts in mourning.
Lebanon withers with shame.
The plain of Sharon is now a wilderness.
Bashan and Carmel have been
plundered.

¹⁰ But the LORD says: "Now I will stand up.
Now I will show my power and might.
¹¹ You Assyrians produce nothing but dry
grass and stubble.
Your own breath will turn to fire and
consume you.
¹² Your people will be burned up completely,
like thornbushes cut down and tossed
in a fire.

¹³ Listen to what I have done, you nations
far away!
And you that are near, acknowledge my
might!"

¹⁴ The sinners in Jerusalem shake with fear.
Terror seizes the godless.
"Who can live with this devouring fire?"
they cry.
"Who can survive this all-consuming
fire?"
¹⁵ Those who are honest and fair,
who refuse to profit by fraud,
who stay far away from bribes,
who refuse to listen to those who plot
murder,
who shut their eyes to all enticement to
do wrong—
¹⁶ these are the ones who will dwell on high.
The rocks of the mountains will be their
fortress.
Food will be supplied to them,
and they will have water in abundance.

¹⁷ Your eyes will see the king in all his
splendor,
and you will see a land that stretches
into the distance.
¹⁸ You will think back to this time of terror,
asking,
"Where are the Assyrian officers
who counted our towers?
Where are the bookkeepers
who recorded the plunder taken from
our fallen city?"
¹⁹ You will no longer see these fierce, violent
people
with their strange, unknown language.

²⁰ Instead, you will see Zion as a place of
holy festivals.
You will see Jerusalem, a city quiet and
secure.
It will be like a tent whose ropes are taut
and whose stakes are firmly fixed.
²¹ The LORD will be our Mighty One.
He will be like a wide river of protection
that no enemy can cross,
that no enemy ship can sail upon.
²² For the LORD is our judge,
our lawgiver, and our king.
He will care for us and save us.
²³ The enemies' sails hang loose
on broken masts with useless tackle.
Their treasure will be divided by the
people of God.
Even the lame will take their share!

33:5 Hebrew *Zion;* also in 33:14.   33:8 As in Dead Sea Scrolls; Masoretic Text reads *care nothing for the cities.*

24 The people of Israel will no longer say,
  "We are sick and helpless,"
  for the LORD will forgive their sins.

CHAPTER 34
A Message for the Nations
1 Come here and listen, O nations of the
    earth.
  Let the world and everything in it hear
    my words.
2 For the LORD is enraged against the
    nations.
  His fury is against all their armies.
  He will completely destroy* them,
    dooming them to slaughter.
3 Their dead will be left unburied,
    and the stench of rotting bodies will fill
    the land.
  The mountains will flow with their
    blood.
4 The heavens above will melt away
    and disappear like a rolled-up scroll.
  The stars will fall from the sky
    like withered leaves from a grapevine,
    or shriveled figs from a fig tree.

5 And when my sword has finished its work
    in the heavens,
  it will fall upon Edom,
    the nation I have marked for
    destruction.
6 The sword of the LORD is drenched with
    blood
    and covered with fat—
  with the blood of lambs and goats,
    with the fat of rams prepared for
    sacrifice.
  Yes, the LORD will offer a sacrifice in the
    city of Bozrah.
  He will make a mighty slaughter in
    Edom.
7 Even men as strong as wild oxen will
    die—
  the young men alongside the veterans.

The land will be soaked with blood
  and the soil enriched with fat.

8 For it is the day of the LORD's revenge,
    the year when Edom will be paid back
    for all it did to Israel.*
9 The streams of Edom will be filled with
    burning pitch,
  and the ground will be covered with
    fire.
10 This judgment on Edom will never end;
    the smoke of its burning will rise
    forever.
  The land will lie deserted from generation
    to generation.
  No one will live there anymore.
11 It will be haunted by the desert owl and
    the screech owl,
    the great owl and the raven.*
  For God will measure that land carefully;
    he will measure it for chaos and
    destruction.
12 It will be called the Land of Nothing,
    and all its nobles will soon be gone.*
13 Thorns will overrun its palaces;
    nettles and thistles will grow in its forts.
  The ruins will become a haunt for jackals
    and a home for owls.
14 Desert animals will mingle there with
    hyenas,
    their howls filling the night.
  Wild goats will bleat at one another
    among the ruins,
    and night creatures* will come there to
    rest.
15 There the owl will make her nest and lay
    her eggs.
  She will hatch her young and cover
    them with her wings.
  And the buzzards will come,
    each one with its mate.

16 Search the book of the LORD,
    and see what he will do.

34:2 The Hebrew term used here refers to the complete consecration of things or people to the LORD, either by
destroying them or by giving them as an offering; similarly in 34:5. 34:8 Hebrew *to Zion*. 34:11 The identification
of some of these birds is uncertain. 34:12 The meaning of the Hebrew is uncertain. 34:14 Hebrew *Lilith*, possibly a
reference to a mythical demon of the night.

33:24 God will forgive the sins of the sick and helpless people who turn to him. That is wonderful
news for us. We have all committed sins, some of which have led to our addiction, as an escape
from the guilt we feel. We don't need the drugs, alcohol, work, or anything else to feel better
about ourself. God will heal us, forgiving our sins and blessing us. Once God has forgiven us, we
no longer need to feel guilt. Our sins are gone—God will never remember them again.
34:1-17 God's judgment of Edom reminds us that rejecting God and his program brings disaster.
It may mean physical destruction (such as the deterioration of our health), emotional destruction,
and/or eternal destruction after we die. Accepting God and his plan for our life will ensure that we
finish life on the right path, and we will enjoy God's presence throughout eternity.

Not one of these birds and animals will be
missing,
and none will lack a mate,
for the LORD has promised this.
His Spirit will make it all come true.
[17] He has surveyed and divided the land
and deeded it over to those creatures.
They will possess it forever,
from generation to generation.

CHAPTER 35
Hope for Restoration
[1] Even the wilderness and desert will be
glad in those days.
The wasteland will rejoice and blossom
with spring crocuses.
[2] Yes, there will be an abundance of flowers
and singing and joy!
The deserts will become as green as the
mountains of Lebanon,
as lovely as Mount Carmel or the plain
of Sharon.
There the LORD will display his glory,
the splendor of our God.
[3] With this news, strengthen those who
have tired hands,
and encourage those who have weak
knees.
[4] Say to those with fearful hearts,
"Be strong, and do not fear,
for your God is coming to destroy your
enemies.
He is coming to save you."

[5] And when he comes, he will open the
eyes of the blind
and unplug the ears of the deaf.
[6] The lame will leap like a deer,
and those who cannot speak will sing
for joy!

Springs will gush forth in the wilderness,
and streams will water the wasteland.
[7] The parched ground will become a pool,
and springs of water will satisfy the
thirsty land.
Marsh grass and reeds and rushes will
flourish
where desert jackals once lived.

[8] And a great road will go through that
once deserted land.
It will be named the Highway of
Holiness.
Evil-minded people will never travel on it.
It will be only for those who walk in
God's ways;
fools will never walk there.
[9] Lions will not lurk along its course,
nor any other ferocious beasts.
There will be no other dangers.
Only the redeemed will walk on it.
[10] Those who have been ransomed by the
LORD will return.
They will enter Jerusalem* singing,
crowned with everlasting joy.
Sorrow and mourning will disappear,
and they will be filled with joy and
gladness.

CHAPTER 36
Assyria Invades Judah
In the fourteenth year of King Hezekiah's
reign,* King Sennacherib of Assyria came to
attack the fortified towns of Judah and conquered them. [2] Then the king of Assyria sent
his chief of staff* from Lachish with a huge
army to confront King Hezekiah in Jerusalem. The Assyrians took up a position beside
the aqueduct that feeds water into the upper

35:10 Hebrew *Zion.* 36:1 The fourteenth year of Hezekiah's reign was 701 B.C. 36:2a Or *the rabshakeh;* also in 36:4,
11, 12, 22.

35:3-7 God proclaims a message of hope to all who are discouraged, frightened, or injured. God
will save us and strengthen our weaknesses; that is his promise. Part of this has already been
fulfilled (see Jesus' healing ministry throughout the Gospels), and we can ask God for his healing
and salvation. The other part of this will be fulfilled at the end of history when Christ returns.
Following God means that we can ask him to help us recover in this lifetime and share eternal
glory with him in the next.
35:8-10 This Highway of Holiness was God's recovery program for his people. He provided a way
for them to return from exile. God also provides those who follow him with a passage through
the desert of pain and suffering and into his presence. The road is without danger because God is
traveling with us. We are not alone as we fight against our addictions and compulsions—God is
with us, giving us strength to resist the temptations.
36:1-12 The Assyrians conquered Jerusalem and mocked Judah for thinking they could find deliverance through trusting in God. In a similar way, people may mock us for thinking our hope for
recovery comes from God. "That's a religious cop-out," they say. "Face reality." The reality is that
God loves us, cares about us, and wants the best for us. The reality is that God is the only one
who can effect recovery at all. To trust in anything else is to deny reality.

pool, near the road leading to the field where cloth is washed.*

³These are the officials who went out to meet with them: Eliakim son of Hilkiah, the palace administrator; Shebna the court secretary; and Joah son of Asaph, the royal historian.

Sennacherib Threatens Jerusalem

⁴Then the Assyrian king's chief of staff told them to give this message to Hezekiah:

"This is what the great king of Assyria says: What are you trusting in that makes you so confident? ⁵Do you think* that mere words can substitute for military skill and strength? Who are you counting on, that you have rebelled against me? ⁶On Egypt? If you lean on Egypt, it will be like a reed that splinters beneath your weight and pierces your hand. Pharaoh, the king of Egypt, is completely unreliable!

⁷"But perhaps you will say to me, 'We are trusting in the LORD our God!' But isn't he the one who was insulted by Hezekiah? Didn't Hezekiah tear down his shrines and altars and make everyone in Judah and Jerusalem worship only at the altar here in Jerusalem?

⁸"I'll tell you what! Strike a bargain with my master, the king of Assyria. I will give you 2,000 horses if you can find that many men to ride on them! ⁹With your tiny army, how can you think of challenging even the weakest contingent of my master's troops, even with the help of Egypt's chariots and charioteers? ¹⁰What's more, do you think we have invaded your land without the LORD's direction? The LORD himself told us, 'Attack this land and destroy it!'"

¹¹Then Eliakim, Shebna, and Joah said to the Assyrian chief of staff, "Please speak to us in Aramaic, for we understand it well. Don't speak in Hebrew,* for the people on the wall will hear."

¹²But Sennacherib's chief of staff replied,

"Do you think my master sent this message only to you and your master? He wants all the people to hear it, for when we put this city under siege, they will suffer along with you. They will be so hungry and thirsty that they will eat their own dung and drink their own urine."

¹³Then the chief of staff stood and shouted in Hebrew to the people on the wall, "Listen to this message from the great king of Assyria! ¹⁴This is what the king says: Don't let Hezekiah deceive you. He will never be able to rescue you. ¹⁵Don't let him fool you into trusting in the LORD by saying, 'The LORD will surely rescue us. This city will never fall into the hands of the Assyrian king!'

¹⁶"Don't listen to Hezekiah! These are the terms the king of Assyria is offering: Make peace with me—open the gates and come out. Then each of you can continue eating from your own grapevine and fig tree and drinking from your own well. ¹⁷Then I will arrange to take you to another land like this one—a land of grain and new wine, bread and vineyards.

¹⁸"Don't let Hezekiah mislead you by saying, 'The LORD will rescue us!' Have the gods of any other nations ever saved their people from the king of Assyria? ¹⁹What happened to the gods of Hamath and Arpad? And what about the gods of Sepharvaim? Did any god rescue Samaria from my power? ²⁰What god of any nation has ever been able to save its people from my power? So what makes you think that the LORD can rescue Jerusalem from me?"

²¹But the people were silent and did not utter a word because Hezekiah had commanded them, "Do not answer him."

²²Then Eliakim son of Hilkiah, the palace administrator; Shebna the court secretary; and Joah son of Asaph, the royal historian, went back to Hezekiah. They tore their clothes in despair, and they went in to see the king and told him what the Assyrian chief of staff had said.

36:2b Or *bleached.* 36:5 As in Dead Sea Scrolls (see also 2 Kgs 18:20); Masoretic Text reads *Do I think.* 36:11 Hebrew *in the dialect of Judah;* also in 36:13.

36:13-22 The king of Assyria appealed to the people of Jerusalem to trust him instead of God to care for them. That's tantamount to asking the three little pigs to trust the big, bad wolf and open the door to let him in. We are enticed to trust the things to which we are addicted, instead of turning to God for help, in spite of the fact that they are our enemies bent on our destruction. It is imperative that we stop believing the lies our addiction tells us and begin trusting God.

CHAPTER 37
Hezekiah Seeks the LORD's Help

When King Hezekiah heard their report, he tore his clothes and put on burlap and went into the Temple of the LORD. ²And he sent Eliakim the palace administrator, Shebna the court secretary, and the leading priests, all dressed in burlap, to the prophet Isaiah son of Amoz. ³They told him, "This is what King Hezekiah says: Today is a day of trouble, insults, and disgrace. It is like when a child is ready to be born, but the mother has no strength to deliver the baby. ⁴But perhaps the LORD your God has heard the Assyrian chief of staff,* sent by the king to defy the living God, and will punish him for his words. Oh, pray for those of us who are left!"

⁵After King Hezekiah's officials delivered the king's message to Isaiah, ⁶the prophet replied, "Say to your master, 'This is what the LORD says: Do not be disturbed by this blasphemous speech against me from the Assyrian king's messengers. ⁷Listen! I myself will move against him,* and the king will receive a message that he is needed at home. So he will return to his land, where I will have him killed with a sword.'"

⁸Meanwhile, the Assyrian chief of staff left Jerusalem and went to consult the king of Assyria, who had left Lachish and was attacking Libnah.

⁹Soon afterward King Sennacherib received word that King Tirhakah of Ethiopia* was leading an army to fight against him. Before leaving to meet the attack, he sent messengers back to Hezekiah in Jerusalem with this message:

¹⁰"This message is for King Hezekiah of Judah. Don't let your God, in whom you trust, deceive you with promises that Jerusalem will not be captured by the king of Assyria. ¹¹You know perfectly well what the kings of Assyria have done wherever they have gone. They have completely destroyed everyone who stood in their way! Why should you be any different? ¹²Have the gods of other nations rescued them—such nations as Gozan, Haran, Rezeph, and the people of Eden who were in Tel-assar? My predecessors destroyed them all! ¹³What happened to the king of Hamath and the king of Arpad? What happened to the kings of Sepharvaim, Hena, and Ivvah?"

¹⁴After Hezekiah received the letter from the messengers and read it, he went up to the LORD's Temple and spread it out before the LORD. ¹⁵And Hezekiah prayed this prayer before the LORD: ¹⁶"O LORD of Heaven's Armies, God of Israel, you are enthroned between the mighty cherubim! You alone are God of all the kingdoms of the earth. You alone created the heavens and the earth. ¹⁷Bend down, O LORD, and listen! Open your eyes, O LORD, and see! Listen to Sennacherib's words of defiance against the living God.

¹⁸"It is true, LORD, that the kings of Assyria have destroyed all these nations. ¹⁹And they have thrown the gods of these nations into the fire and burned them. But of course the Assyrians could destroy them! They were not gods at all—only idols of wood and stone shaped by human hands. ²⁰Now, O LORD our God, rescue us from his power; then all the kingdoms of the earth will know that you alone, O LORD, are God.*"

Isaiah Predicts Judah's Deliverance

²¹Then Isaiah son of Amoz sent this message to Hezekiah: "This is what the LORD, the God of Israel, says: Because you prayed about King Sennacherib of Assyria, ²²the LORD has spoken this word against him:

37:4 Or *the rabshakeh;* also in 37:8.   **37:7** Hebrew *I will put a spirit in him.*   **37:9** Hebrew *of Cush.*   **37:20** As in Dead Sea Scrolls (see also 2 Kgs 19:19); Masoretic Text reads *you alone are the LORD.*

37:1-4 Hezekiah shows us the right thing to do when we face overwhelming trouble. He humbled himself before God, prayed about the problem, and sought help from a godly person. Too often we deny the seriousness of our problems and refuse to turn to God or others for help. But recovery is not possible without asking God for help and without the encouragement and guidance of godly friends.

37:8-20 The king of Assyria tried to dissuade Hezekiah from trusting God by lumping the God of Israel together with the false gods of the people he had already conquered. Hezekiah recognized that those gods were man-made and easy to destroy but that Israel's God was real and able to rescue his people. Our addiction is powerful and may have resisted our human attempts to overcome it. Recovery programs that ignore God's power function as false gods in our life and fail us. But God is different. He is all-powerful; he created the world and can do anything he desires. No addiction can stand against God's powerful, transforming work in our life.

"The virgin daughter of Zion
    despises you and laughs at you.
The daughter of Jerusalem
    shakes her head in derision as you flee.

23 "Whom have you been defying and
        ridiculing?
    Against whom did you raise your voice?
    At whom did you look with such haughty
        eyes?
    It was the Holy One of Israel!
24 By your messengers you have defied the
        Lord.
    You have said, 'With my many chariots
    I have conquered the highest
        mountains—
        yes, the remotest peaks of Lebanon.
    I have cut down its tallest cedars
        and its finest cypress trees.
    I have reached its farthest heights
        and explored its deepest forests.
25 I have dug wells in many foreign lands*
        and refreshed myself with their water.
    With the sole of my foot,
        I stopped up all the rivers of Egypt!'

26 "But have you not heard?
    I decided this long ago.
    Long ago I planned it,
        and now I am making it happen.
    I planned for you to crush fortified cities
        into heaps of rubble.
27 That is why their people have so little
        power
        and are so frightened and confused.
    They are as weak as grass,
        as easily trampled as tender green
        shoots.
    They are like grass sprouting on a
        housetop,
        scorched* before it can grow lush and
        tall.

28 "But I know you well—
        where you stay
    and when you come and go.
    I know the way you have raged against
        me.
29 And because of your raging against me
        and your arrogance, which I have heard
        for myself,

I will put my hook in your nose
    and my bit in your mouth.
I will make you return
    by the same road on which you came."

30 Then Isaiah said to Hezekiah, "Here is the proof that what I say is true:

"This year you will eat only what grows
        up by itself,
    and next year you will eat what springs
        up from that.
But in the third year you will plant crops
        and harvest them;
    you will tend vineyards and eat their
        fruit.
31 And you who are left in Judah,
    who have escaped the ravages of the
        siege,
    will put roots down in your own soil
        and grow up and flourish.
32 For a remnant of my people will spread
        out from Jerusalem,
    a group of survivors from Mount Zion.
    The passionate commitment of the LORD
        of Heaven's Armies
    will make this happen!

33 "And this is what the LORD says about the king of Assyria:

"'His armies will not enter Jerusalem.
    They will not even shoot an arrow at it.
They will not march outside its gates with
        their shields
    nor build banks of earth against its
        walls.
34 The king will return to his own country
        by the same road on which he came.
He will not enter this city,'
    says the LORD.
35 'For my own honor and for the sake of my
        servant David,
    I will defend this city and protect it.'"

36 That night the angel of the LORD went out to the Assyrian camp and killed 185,000 Assyrian soldiers. When the surviving Assyrians* woke up the next morning, they found corpses everywhere. 37 Then King Sennacherib of Assyria broke camp and returned

37:25 As in Dead Sea Scrolls (see also 2 Kgs 19:24); Masoretic Text lacks *in many foreign lands*. 37:27 As in Dead Sea Scrolls and some Greek manuscripts (see also 2 Kgs 19:26); most Hebrew manuscripts read *like a terraced field*. 37:36 Hebrew *When they*.

37:33-38 What an impossible situation! Jerusalem was surrounded and besieged by the army of the largest empire on earth. All the Assyrians had to do was starve out Jerusalem, and success would be theirs. But God had other plans; he is not bound by what seems possible to man. He can deliver those who trust in him from the most hopeless situations.

to his own land. He went home to his capital of Nineveh and stayed there.

³⁸One day while he was worshiping in the temple of his god Nisroch, his sons Adrammelech and Sharezer killed him with their swords. They then escaped to the land of Ararat, and another son, Esarhaddon, became the next king of Assyria.

CHAPTER 38
Hezekiah's Sickness and Recovery

About that time Hezekiah became deathly ill, and the prophet Isaiah son of Amoz went to visit him. He gave the king this message: "This is what the LORD says: 'Set your affairs in order, for you are going to die. You will not recover from this illness.'"

²When Hezekiah heard this, he turned his face to the wall and prayed to the LORD, ³"Remember, O LORD, how I have always been faithful to you and have served you single-mindedly, always doing what pleases you." Then he broke down and wept bitterly.

⁴Then this message came to Isaiah from the LORD: ⁵"Go back to Hezekiah and tell him, 'This is what the LORD, the God of your ancestor David, says: I have heard your prayer and seen your tears. I will add fifteen years to your life, ⁶and I will rescue you and this city from the king of Assyria. Yes, I will defend this city.

⁷"'And this is the sign from the LORD to prove that he will do as he promised: ⁸I will cause the sun's shadow to move ten steps backward on the sundial* of Ahaz!'" So the shadow on the sundial moved backward ten steps.

Hezekiah's Poem of Praise

⁹When King Hezekiah was well again, he wrote this poem:

¹⁰I said, "In the prime of my life,
    must I now enter the place of the
      dead?*
  Am I to be robbed of the rest of my
    years?"

¹¹I said, "Never again will I see the LORD
    GOD
  while still in the land of the living.
  Never again will I see my friends
    or be with those who live in this world.
¹²My life has been blown away
  like a shepherd's tent in a storm.
  It has been cut short,
    as when a weaver cuts cloth from a
      loom.
  Suddenly, my life was over.
¹³I waited patiently all night,
  but I was torn apart as though by lions.
  Suddenly, my life was over.
¹⁴Delirious, I chattered like a swallow or a
    crane,
  and then I moaned like a mourning
    dove.
  My eyes grew tired of looking to heaven
    for help.
  I am in trouble, Lord. Help me!"

¹⁵But what could I say?
  For he himself sent this sickness.
  Now I will walk humbly throughout my
    years
  because of this anguish I have felt.
¹⁶Lord, your discipline is good,
  for it leads to life and health.
  You restore my health
  and allow me to live!
¹⁷Yes, this anguish was good for me,
  for you have rescued me from death
  and forgiven all my sins.
¹⁸For the dead* cannot praise you;
  they cannot raise their voices in praise.
  Those who go down to the grave
    can no longer hope in your
      faithfulness.
¹⁹Only the living can praise you as I do
    today.
  Each generation tells of your
    faithfulness to the next.
²⁰Think of it—the LORD is ready to heal me!
  I will sing his praises with instruments
every day of my life
  in the Temple of the LORD.

38:8 Hebrew *the steps.* 38:10 Hebrew *enter the gates of Sheol?* 38:18 Hebrew *Sheol.*

38:1-8 Hezekiah's situation seemed totally hopeless. God had even told him that his life was over. We are reminded that no situation, however hopeless it seems, is beyond God's ability to help. Hezekiah cried out to God in prayer, and God spared his life. We are never without hope because our God is a God of power and mercy. When we admit our hopelessness and ask him to save us, he will.

38:10-22 Hezekiah saw that his illness was actually good for him because it enabled him to find God's healing and deliverance. Often our suffering results in some good because it breaks our selfishness and helps us realize that we need God. We should take a moral inventory and see if we are living for God or for ourself. If God is not Lord of our life, now is a great time to put him there.

[21]Isaiah had said to Hezekiah's servants, "Make an ointment from figs and spread it over the boil, and Hezekiah will recover."

[22]And Hezekiah had asked, "What sign will prove that I will go to the Temple of the LORD?"

CHAPTER 39
Envoys from Babylon

Soon after this, Merodach-baladan son of Baladan, king of Babylon, sent Hezekiah his best wishes and a gift. He had heard that Hezekiah had been very sick and that he had recovered. [2]Hezekiah was delighted with the Babylonian envoys and showed them everything in his treasure-houses—the silver, the gold, the spices, and the aromatic oils. He also took them to see his armory and showed them everything in his royal treasuries! There was nothing in his palace or kingdom that Hezekiah did not show them.

[3]Then Isaiah the prophet went to King Hezekiah and asked him, "What did those men want? Where were they from?"

Hezekiah replied, "They came from the distant land of Babylon."

[4]"What did they see in your palace?" asked Isaiah.

"They saw everything," Hezekiah replied. "I showed them everything I own—all my royal treasuries."

[5]Then Isaiah said to Hezekiah, "Listen to this message from the LORD of Heaven's Armies: [6]'The time is coming when everything in your palace—all the treasures stored up by your ancestors until now—will be carried off to Babylon. Nothing will be left,' says the LORD. [7]Some of your very own sons will be taken away into exile. They will become eunuchs who will serve in the palace of Babylon's king.'"

[8]Then Hezekiah said to Isaiah, "This message you have given me from the LORD is good." For the king was thinking, "At least there will be peace and security during my lifetime."

CHAPTER 40
Comfort for God's People

[1]"Comfort, comfort my people,"
    says your God.
[2]"Speak tenderly to Jerusalem.
Tell her that her sad days are gone
    and her sins are pardoned.
Yes, the LORD has punished her twice over
    for all her sins."

[3]Listen! It's the voice of someone shouting,
"Clear the way through the wilderness
    for the LORD!
Make a straight highway through the
        wasteland
    for our God!
[4]Fill in the valleys,
    and level the mountains and hills.
Straighten the curves,
    and smooth out the rough places.
[5]Then the glory of the LORD will be
        revealed,
    and all people will see it together.
The LORD has spoken!"*

[6]A voice said, "Shout!"
    I asked, "What should I shout?"

"Shout that people are like the grass.
    Their beauty fades as quickly
    as the flowers in a field.

40:3-5 Greek version reads *He is a voice shouting in the wilderness, / "Prepare the way for the LORD's coming! / Clear a road for our God! / Fill in the valleys, / and level the mountains and hills. / And then the glory of the LORD will be revealed, / and all people will see the salvation sent from God. / The LORD has spoken!"* Compare Matt 3:3; Mark 1:3; Luke 3:4-6.

39:1-7 Hezekiah foolishly received the Babylonians and showed them the extent of his treasury; he failed to perceive that they would be the next conquerors of Judah. We often fail to discern the things that are our true enemies, and we get into unhealthy relationships and activities that end up destroying us. To avoid this pitfall, we need to ask ourself one question: Would God approve of these relationships, activities, habits, or environments?

40:1-5 After the judgments of chapters 1–39, God's message to his people is one of comfort and blessing. God never gives up on us, no matter how bad the things we have done. The punishments will end, and God will restore us to a loving relationship with himself. To join him in a relationship means to clear out the obstacles in our life: sin, pride, addiction, hypocrisy, greed. When those obstacles are dealt with, we are free to become the people God wants us to be.

40:9-17 When we doubt God's power, we need to remember that he is the Creator and will "rule with a powerful arm." He has perfect wisdom and is greater than any person or nation. When we doubt that God can really help us overcome our dependency, we need to remember that he is bigger and more powerful than anything on earth. And this God is also compassionate and loving. He will carry us (his lambs) in his arms and "gently lead" us down the road to recovery because he loves us.

⁷The grass withers and the flowers fade
  beneath the breath of the Lord.
  And so it is with people.
⁸The grass withers and the flowers fade,
  but the word of our God stands
    forever."

⁹O Zion, messenger of good news,
  shout from the mountaintops!
  Shout it louder, O Jerusalem.*
  Shout, and do not be afraid.
  Tell the towns of Judah,
    "Your God is coming!"
¹⁰Yes, the Sovereign Lord is coming in
    power.
  He will rule with a powerful arm.
  See, he brings his reward with him as
    he comes.
¹¹He will feed his flock like a shepherd.
  He will carry the lambs in his arms,
holding them close to his heart.
  He will gently lead the mother sheep
    with their young.

The Lord Has No Equal
¹²Who else has held the oceans in his hand?
  Who has measured off the heavens
    with his fingers?
  Who else knows the weight of the earth
    or has weighed the mountains and hills
      on a scale?
¹³Who is able to advise the Spirit of the
    Lord?*
  Who knows enough to give him advice
    or teach him?
¹⁴Has the Lord ever needed anyone's
    advice?
  Does he need instruction about what
    is good?
  Did someone teach him what is right
    or show him the path of justice?

¹⁵No, for all the nations of the world
  are but a drop in the bucket.
  They are nothing more
    than dust on the scales.
  He picks up the whole earth
    as though it were a grain of sand.
¹⁶All the wood in Lebanon's forests
  and all Lebanon's animals would not
    be enough
  to make a burnt offering worthy of our
    God.
¹⁷The nations of the world are worth
    nothing to him.

40:9 Or *O messenger of good news, shout to Zion from the
mountaintops! Shout it louder to Jerusalem.* 40:13 Greek
version reads *Who can know the Lord's thoughts?*
Compare Rom 11:34; 1 Cor 2:16.

STEP **11**

Patient Waiting
BIBLE READING: Isaiah 40:28-31
**We sought through prayer and medita-
tion to improve our conscious contacts
with God, praying only for knowledge of
his will for us and the power to carry that
out.**
We all want to recover as quickly as possible. It's hard to be patient as we wait for
the process to work. Sure, we realize that
we didn't get to the difficult spot we are in
overnight. We understand that we cannot
undo a lifetime of damage in just a few
moments. But still, it is a challenge to wait
patiently. Every part of the recovery process
requires time and patience. This step also
requires that we learn to wait for God.

The prophet Isaiah gave us this promise:
"But those who trust in the Lord will find
new strength. They will soar high on wings
like eagles. They will run and not grow
weary. They will walk and not faint" (Isaiah
40:31). Jeremiah said, "The Lord is good to
those who depend on him, to those who
search for him. So it is good to wait quietly
for salvation from the Lord" (Lamentations
3:25-26).

Waiting on the Lord has its rewards. We
can remain calm when it appears that we
aren't making any progress in recovery. As
we learn to trust the Lord and wait on him,
he will lift us up like wind beneath the
wings of an eagle. God gives us the
strength and stamina to bear up under the
strain so that we won't faint or collapse
under it. As we develop patient faith in
God, we will be able to endure to the end
of the race— and win. *Turn to page 1345,
John 3.*

In his eyes they count for less than
nothing—
mere emptiness and froth.

¹⁸ To whom can you compare God?
What image can you find to resemble
him?
¹⁹ Can he be compared to an idol formed in
a mold,
overlaid with gold, and decorated with
silver chains?
²⁰ Or if people are too poor for that,
they might at least choose wood that
won't decay
and a skilled craftsman
to carve an image that won't fall down!

²¹ Haven't you heard? Don't you
understand?
Are you deaf to the words of God—
the words he gave before the world
began?
Are you so ignorant?
²² God sits above the circle of the earth.
The people below seem like
grasshoppers to him!
He spreads out the heavens like a curtain
and makes his tent from them.
²³ He judges the great people of the world
and brings them all to nothing.
²⁴ They hardly get started, barely taking
root,
when he blows on them and they
wither.
The wind carries them off like chaff.

²⁵ "To whom will you compare me?
Who is my equal?" asks the Holy One.

²⁶ Look up into the heavens.
Who created all the stars?
He brings them out like an army, one after
another,
calling each by its name.
Because of his great power and
incomparable strength,
not a single one is missing.
²⁷ O Jacob, how can you say the LORD does
not see your troubles?
O Israel, how can you say God ignores
your rights?
²⁸ Have you never heard?
Have you never understood?
The LORD is the everlasting God,
the Creator of all the earth.
He never grows weak or weary.
No one can measure the depths of his
understanding.
²⁹ He gives power to the weak

and strength to the powerless.
³⁰ Even youths will become weak and tired,
and young men will fall in exhaustion.
³¹ But those who trust in the LORD will find
new strength.
They will soar high on wings like
eagles.
They will run and not grow weary.
They will walk and not faint.

CHAPTER 41
God's Help for Israel

¹ "Listen in silence before me, you lands
beyond the sea.
Bring your strongest arguments.
Come now and speak.
The court is ready for your case.

² "Who has stirred up this king from the
east,
rightly calling him to God's service?
Who gives this man victory over many
nations
and permits him to trample their kings
underfoot?
With his sword, he reduces armies to dust.
With his bow, he scatters them like
chaff before the wind.
³ He chases them away and goes on safely,
though he is walking over unfamiliar
ground.
⁴ Who has done such mighty deeds,
summoning each new generation from
the beginning of time?
It is I, the LORD, the First and the Last.
I alone am he."

⁵ The lands beyond the sea watch in fear.
Remote lands tremble and mobilize for
war.
⁶ The idol makers encourage one another,
saying to each other, "Be strong!"
⁷ The carver encourages the goldsmith,
and the molder helps at the anvil.
"Good," they say. "It's coming along
fine."
Carefully they join the parts together,
then fasten the thing in place so it
won't fall over.

⁸ "But as for you, Israel my servant,
Jacob my chosen one,
descended from Abraham my friend,
⁹ I have called you back from the ends of
the earth,
saying, 'You are my servant.'
For I have chosen you
and will not throw you away.
¹⁰ Don't be afraid, for I am with you.

Don't be discouraged, for I am your God.
I will strengthen you and help you.
I will hold you up with my victorious
right hand.

[11] "See, all your angry enemies lie there,
confused and humiliated.
Anyone who opposes you will die
and come to nothing.
[12] You will look in vain
for those who tried to conquer you.
Those who attack you
will come to nothing.
[13] For I hold you by your right hand—
I, the LORD your God.
And I say to you,
'Don't be afraid. I am here to help you.
[14] Though you are a lowly worm, O Jacob,
don't be afraid, people of Israel, for I
will help you.
I am the LORD, your Redeemer.
I am the Holy One of Israel.'
[15] You will be a new threshing instrument
with many sharp teeth.
You will tear your enemies apart,
making chaff of mountains.
[16] You will toss them into the air,
and the wind will blow them all away;
a whirlwind will scatter them.
Then you will rejoice in the LORD.
You will glory in the Holy One of Israel.

[17] "When the poor and needy search for
water and there is none,
and their tongues are parched from thirst,
then I, the LORD, will answer them.
I, the God of Israel, will never abandon
them.
[18] I will open up rivers for them on the high
plateaus.
I will give them fountains of water in
the valleys.
I will fill the desert with pools of water.
Rivers fed by springs will flow across
the parched ground.
[19] I will plant trees in the barren desert—
cedar, acacia, myrtle, olive, cypress, fir,
and pine.

[20] I am doing this so all who see this
miracle
will understand what it means—
that it is the LORD who has done this,
the Holy One of Israel who created it.

[21] "Present the case for your idols,"
says the LORD.
"Let them show what they can do,"
says the King of Israel.*
[22] "Let them try to tell us what happened
long ago
so that we may consider the evidence.
Or let them tell us what the future holds,
so we can know what's going to
happen.
[23] Yes, tell us what will occur in the days
ahead.
Then we will know you are gods.
In fact, do anything—good or bad!
Do something that will amaze and
frighten us.
[24] But no! You are less than nothing and can
do nothing at all.
Those who choose you pollute
themselves.

[25] "But I have stirred up a leader who will
approach from the north.
From the east he will call on my name.
I will give him victory over kings and
princes.
He will trample them as a potter treads
on clay.

[26] "Who told you from the beginning
that this would happen?
Who predicted this,
making you admit that he was right?
No one said a word!
[27] I was the first to tell Zion,
'Look! Help is on the way!'*
I will send Jerusalem a messenger with
good news.
[28] Not one of your idols told you this.
Not one gave any answer when
I asked.
[29] See, they are all foolish, worthless things.
All your idols are as empty as the wind.

41:21 Hebrew *the King of Jacob.* See note on 14:1.   41:27 Or *'Look! They are coming home.'*

41:11-14 God promises that he will crush our enemies. What greater enemy is there in our life right now than our addiction or compulsion? We can't destroy it by ourself, but we can with God's help. He will hold our hand and help us all the way. We may be despised by others now for our lifestyle, but God will redeem us and make us whole again.
41:17-20 God calls us to himself to receive wholeness, pictured here by water in dry places and trees growing on barren land. To receive his fullness, however, requires that we admit that we are inadequate and needy, unable to control our life without him.

CHAPTER 42
The LORD's Chosen Servant

[1] "Look at my servant, whom I strengthen.
  He is my chosen one, who pleases me.
I have put my Spirit upon him.
  He will bring justice to the nations.
[2] He will not shout
  or raise his voice in public.
[3] He will not crush the weakest reed
  or put out a flickering candle.
He will bring justice to all who have
  been wronged.
[4] He will not falter or lose heart
  until justice prevails throughout the
  earth.
Even distant lands beyond the sea will
  wait for his instruction.*"

[5] God, the LORD, created the heavens and
  stretched them out.
He created the earth and everything
  in it.
He gives breath to everyone,
  life to everyone who walks the earth.
And it is he who says,
[6] "I, the LORD, have called you to
  demonstrate my righteousness.
I will take you by the hand and guard
  you,
and I will give you to my people, Israel,
  as a symbol of my covenant with them.
And you will be a light to guide the nations.
[7]   You will open the eyes of the blind.
You will free the captives from prison,
  releasing those who sit in dark dungeons.

[8] "I am the LORD; that is my name!
  I will not give my glory to anyone else,
  nor share my praise with carved idols.
[9] Everything I prophesied has come true,
  and now I will prophesy again.
I will tell you the future before it happens."

A Song of Praise to the LORD

[10] Sing a new song to the LORD!
  Sing his praises from the ends of the
  earth!

Sing, all you who sail the seas,
  all you who live in distant coastlands.
[11] Join in the chorus, you desert towns;
  let the villages of Kedar rejoice!
Let the people of Sela sing for joy;
  shout praises from the mountaintops!
[12] Let the whole world glorify the LORD;
  let it sing his praise.
[13] The LORD will march forth like a mighty
  hero;
  he will come out like a warrior, full of
  fury.
He will shout his battle cry
  and crush all his enemies.

[14] He will say, "I have long been silent;
  yes, I have restrained myself.
But now, like a woman in labor,
  I will cry and groan and pant.
[15] I will level the mountains and hills
  and blight all their greenery.
I will turn the rivers into dry land
  and will dry up all the pools.
[16] I will lead blind Israel down a new path,
  guiding them along an unfamiliar way.
I will brighten the darkness before them
  and smooth out the road ahead
  of them.
Yes, I will indeed do these things;
  I will not forsake them.
[17] But those who trust in idols,
  who say, 'You are our gods,'
  will be turned away in shame.

Israel's Failure to Listen and See

[18] "Listen, you who are deaf!
  Look and see, you blind!
[19] Who is as blind as my own people, my
  servant?
  Who is as deaf as my messenger?
Who is as blind as my chosen people,
  the servant of the LORD?
[20] You see and recognize what is right
  but refuse to act on it.
You hear with your ears,
  but you don't really listen."

42:4 Greek version reads *And his name will be the hope of all the world.* Compare Matt 12:21.

42:1-4 This Servant song describes Jesus the Messiah and his ministry. No description could be more encouraging to us as we seek deliverance from injuries and fragile emotions. He is gentle; he will not crush us. He will encourage us and bring justice for the wrongs we have suffered. Even as children, many of us have endured abuse or wrongdoings that we did nothing to deserve. But we need to let go of the hatred and bitterness we feel because Christ will judge the people who have hurt us. We need God's help to put these events behind us so we can move on in the recovery process.
42:20-23 God encourages us to do two things: (1) We are to do what we know is right; (2) we are to learn from the past. The Israelites' flouting of God's righteous laws led to their ruin. Haven't

²¹Because he is righteous,
  the LORD has exalted his glorious law.
²²But his own people have been robbed and
    plundered,
  enslaved, imprisoned, and trapped.
They are fair game for anyone
  and have no one to protect them,
  no one to take them back home.

²³Who will hear these lessons from the past
  and see the ruin that awaits you in the
    future?
²⁴Who allowed Israel to be robbed and hurt?
  It was the LORD, against whom we
    sinned,
for the people would not walk in his path,
  nor would they obey his law.
²⁵Therefore, he poured out his fury on them
  and destroyed them in battle.
They were enveloped in flames,
  but they still refused to understand.
They were consumed by fire,
  but they did not learn their lesson.

CHAPTER 43
The Savior of Israel
¹But now, O Jacob, listen to the LORD who
    created you.
  O Israel, the one who formed you says,
"Do not be afraid, for I have ransomed
    you.
  I have called you by name; you are mine.
²When you go through deep waters,
  I will be with you.
When you go through rivers of difficulty,
  you will not drown.
When you walk through the fire of
    oppression,
  you will not be burned up;
  the flames will not consume you.
³For I am the LORD, your God,
  the Holy One of Israel, your Savior.
I gave Egypt as a ransom for your
    freedom;
  I gave Ethiopia* and Seba in your place.

43:3 Hebrew *Cush.*

⁴Others were given in exchange for you.
  I traded their lives for yours
because you are precious to me.
  You are honored, and I love you.

⁵"Do not be afraid, for I am with you.
  I will gather you and your children
    from east and west.
⁶I will say to the north and south,
  'Bring my sons and daughters back to
    Israel
  from the distant corners of the earth.
⁷Bring all who claim me as their God,
  for I have made them for my glory.
  It was I who created them.'"

⁸Bring out the people who have eyes but
    are blind,
  who have ears but are deaf.
⁹Gather the nations together!
  Assemble the peoples of the world!
Which of their idols has ever foretold
    such things?
  Which can predict what will happen
    tomorrow?
Where are the witnesses of such
    predictions?
  Who can verify that they spoke the truth?

¹⁰"But you are my witnesses, O Israel!" says
    the LORD.
  "You are my servant.
You have been chosen to know me,
    believe in me,
  and understand that I alone am God.
There is no other God—
  there never has been, and there never
    will be.
¹¹I, yes I, am the LORD,
  and there is no other Savior.
¹²First I predicted your rescue,
  then I saved you and proclaimed it to
    the world.
No foreign god has ever done this.
  You are witnesses that I am the only God,"
  says the LORD.

---

we been "robbed and plundered, enslaved, imprisoned, and trapped" by our addiction? We can become free only when we stop denying our sin and confess our addiction to God.
43:1-3 God loves us and will be there for us in times of great trouble and turmoil. As we "go through rivers of difficulty," we have a choice. We can either trust in our own abilities and drown or trust in God and be rescued. If we are honest, we will realize that our lifestyle has made our life unmanageable and that God is the only one who can redeem us.
43:9-13 There are people around us who can witness to God's power of deliverance—those who have overcome addiction or abuse. When we have doubts about the recovery process or feel like giving in to temptation, we need to find encouragement from people who have been successful in recovery. They can show us how we can overcome our dependency because their lives have been transformed by God.

¹³ "From eternity to eternity I am God.
No one can snatch anyone out of my
hand.
No one can undo what I have done."

The LORD's Promise of Victory

¹⁴ This is what the LORD says—your Redeemer,
the Holy One of Israel:

"For your sakes I will send an army
against Babylon,
forcing the Babylonians* to flee in
those ships they are so proud of.
¹⁵ I am the LORD, your Holy One,
Israel's Creator and King.
¹⁶ I am the LORD, who opened a way
through the waters,
making a dry path through the sea.
¹⁷ I called forth the mighty army of Egypt
with all its chariots and horses.
I drew them beneath the waves, and they
drowned,
their lives snuffed out like a smoldering
candlewick.
¹⁸ "But forget all that—
it is nothing compared to what I am
going to do.
¹⁹ For I am about to do something new.
See, I have already begun! Do you not
see it?
I will make a pathway through the
wilderness.
I will create rivers in the dry wasteland.
²⁰ The wild animals in the fields will thank me,
the jackals and owls, too,
for giving them water in the desert.
Yes, I will make rivers in the dry wasteland
so my chosen people can be refreshed.
²¹ I have made Israel for myself,
and they will someday honor me before
the whole world.

²² "But, dear family of Jacob, you refuse to
ask for my help.
You have grown tired of me, O Israel!
²³ You have not brought me sheep or goats
for burnt offerings.
You have not honored me with
sacrifices,
though I have not burdened and wearied
you

with requests for grain offerings and
frankincense.
²⁴ You have not brought me fragrant
calamus
or pleased me with the fat from
sacrifices.
Instead, you have burdened me with your
sins
and wearied me with your faults.

²⁵ "I—yes, I alone—will blot out your sins
for my own sake
and will never think of them again.
²⁶ Let us review the situation together,
and you can present your case to prove
your innocence.
²⁷ From the very beginning, your first
ancestor sinned against me;
all your leaders broke my laws.
²⁸ That is why I have disgraced your priests;
I have decreed complete destruction*
for Jacob
and shame for Israel.

CHAPTER 44

¹ "But now, listen to me, Jacob my servant,
Israel my chosen one.
² The LORD who made you and helps you
says:
Do not be afraid, O Jacob, my servant,
O dear Israel,* my chosen one.
³ For I will pour out water to quench your
thirst
and to irrigate your parched fields.
And I will pour out my Spirit on your
descendants,
and my blessing on your children.
⁴ They will thrive like watered grass,
like willows on a riverbank.
⁵ Some will proudly claim, 'I belong to the
LORD.'
Others will say, 'I am a descendant
of Jacob.'
Some will write the LORD's name on their
hands
and will take the name of Israel as their
own."

The Foolishness of Idols

⁶ This is what the LORD says—Israel's King
and Redeemer, the LORD of Heaven's Armies:

43:14 Or *Chaldeans*. 43:28 The Hebrew term used here refers to the complete consecration of things or people to the
LORD, either by destroying them or by giving them as an offering. 44:2 Hebrew *Jeshurun*, a term of endearment for
Israel.

44:6-8 God is our Redeemer and the Rock on whom we should build our life. He has promised to
save us from our addiction and from the sure penalty of sin—death. When we have the promise
of the all-powerful God, why look to other sources for recovery?

"I am the First and the Last;
  there is no other God.
⁷Who is like me?
  Let him step forward and prove to you
    his power.
Let him do as I have done since ancient
    times
  when I established a people and
    explained its future.
⁸Do not tremble; do not be afraid.
  Did I not proclaim my purposes for you
    long ago?
You are my witnesses—is there any other
    God?
  No! There is no other Rock—not one!"

⁹How foolish are those who manufacture
    idols.
  These prized objects are really
    worthless.
The people who worship idols don't know
    this,
  so they are all put to shame.
¹⁰Who but a fool would make his own god—
  an idol that cannot help him one bit?
¹¹All who worship idols will be disgraced
    along with all these craftsmen—mere
    humans—
  who claim they can make a god.
They may all stand together,
  but they will stand in terror and shame.

¹²The blacksmith stands at his forge to
    make a sharp tool,
  pounding and shaping it with all his
    might.
His work makes him hungry and weak.
  It makes him thirsty and faint.
¹³Then the wood-carver measures a block of
    wood
  and draws a pattern on it.
He works with chisel and plane
  and carves it into a human figure.
He gives it human beauty
  and puts it in a little shrine.
¹⁴He cuts down cedars;
  he selects the cypress and the oak;
he plants the pine in the forest
  to be nourished by the rain.
¹⁵Then he uses part of the wood to make a
    fire.

With it he warms himself and bakes his
    bread.
Then—yes, it's true—he takes the rest of it
  and makes himself a god to worship!
He makes an idol
  and bows down in front of it!
¹⁶He burns part of the tree to roast his meat
  and to keep himself warm.
He says, "Ah, that fire feels good."
¹⁷Then he takes what's left
  and makes his god: a carved idol!
He falls down in front of it,
  worshiping and praying to it.
"Rescue me!" he says.
  "You are my god!"

¹⁸Such stupidity and ignorance!
  Their eyes are closed, and they cannot
    see.
Their minds are shut, and they cannot
    think.
¹⁹The person who made the idol never stops
    to reflect,
  "Why, it's just a block of wood!
I burned half of it for heat
  and used it to bake my bread and roast
    my meat.
How can the rest of it be a god?
  Should I bow down to worship a piece
    of wood?"
²⁰The poor, deluded fool feeds on ashes.
  He trusts something that can't help him
    at all.
Yet he cannot bring himself to ask,
  "Is this idol that I'm holding in my
    hand a lie?"

Restoration for Jerusalem

²¹"Pay attention, O Jacob,
  for you are my servant, O Israel.
I, the LORD, made you,
  and I will not forget you.
²²I have swept away your sins like a cloud.
  I have scattered your offenses like the
    morning mist.
Oh, return to me,
  for I have paid the price to set you
    free."

²³Sing, O heavens, for the LORD has done
    this wondrous thing.
  Shout for joy, O depths of the earth!

44:21-28 Through Isaiah, God named Cyrus as the king who would free his people to return
from captivity. But Cyrus would not rise to power until 150 years after Isaiah's ministry! Once we
have committed our life to God, we can have confidence that he will take care of our needs and
lead us to a fulfilling life. If God could name the king who would allow Israel to rebuild Jerusalem
150 years before he came to power, God can do anything in our life to bring about recovery.

Break into song,
O mountains and forests and every tree!
For the LORD has redeemed Jacob
and is glorified in Israel.

24 This is what the LORD says—
your Redeemer and Creator:
"I am the LORD, who made all things.
I alone stretched out the heavens.
Who was with me
when I made the earth?
25 I expose the false prophets as liars
and make fools of fortune-tellers.
I cause the wise to give bad advice,
thus proving them to be fools.
26 But I carry out the predictions of my
prophets!
By them I say to Jerusalem, 'People will
live here again,'
and to the towns of Judah, 'You will
be rebuilt;
I will restore all your ruins!'
27 When I speak to the rivers and say,
'Dry up!'
they will be dry.
28 When I say of Cyrus, 'He is my shepherd,'
he will certainly do as I say.
He will command, 'Rebuild Jerusalem';
he will say, 'Restore the Temple.'"

CHAPTER 45
Cyrus, the LORD's Chosen One
1 This is what the LORD says to Cyrus, his
anointed one,
whose right hand he will empower.
Before him, mighty kings will be
paralyzed with fear.
Their fortress gates will be opened,
never to shut again.
2 This is what the LORD says:

"I will go before you, Cyrus,
and level the mountains.*
I will smash down gates of bronze
and cut through bars of iron.

3 And I will give you treasures hidden in the
darkness—
secret riches.
I will do this so you may know that I am
the LORD,
the God of Israel, the one who calls you
by name.

4 "And why have I called you for this work?
Why did I call you by name when you
did not know me?
It is for the sake of Jacob my servant,
Israel my chosen one.
5 I am the LORD;
there is no other God.
I have equipped you for battle,
though you don't even know me,
6 so all the world from east to west
will know there is no other God.
I am the LORD, and there is no other.
7   I create the light and make the
darkness.
I send good times and bad times.
I, the LORD, am the one who does these
things.

8 "Open up, O heavens,
and pour out your righteousness.
Let the earth open wide
so salvation and righteousness can
sprout up together.
I, the LORD, created them.

9 "What sorrow awaits those who argue
with their Creator.
Does a clay pot argue with its maker?
Does the clay dispute with the one who
shapes it, saying,
'Stop, you're doing it wrong!'
Does the pot exclaim,
'How clumsy can you be?'
10 How terrible it would be if a newborn
baby said to its father,
'Why was I born?'
or if it said to its mother,
'Why did you make me this way?'"

45:2 As in Dead Sea Scrolls and Greek version; Masoretic Text reads *the swellings*.

45:1-6 God was able to take a pagan king like Cyrus and use him for his purposes without Cyrus's even realizing it. God can use someone who doesn't even know him; imagine how much more he can do with us who trust in him! There are great possibilities with God. We need to have the faith to follow him.

45:9-13 The Psalms make it clear that it is acceptable to pour out our complaints and arguments to God as we try to wrestle through the problems of life. What is rebuked here is Israel's stubborn and chronic unbelief; they charged God with fumbling his control of history in raising Cyrus to power. They perceived that God was just helping another enemy. The Israelites' limited view of life did not allow them to see God's true purpose. Likewise, we may not understand why God is allowing certain things to happen, but we can trust that he is working according to his perfect plan.

[11] This is what the LORD says—
　the Holy One of Israel and your
　　Creator:
"Do you question what I do for my
　children?
Do you give me orders about the work
　of my hands?
[12] I am the one who made the earth
　and created people to live on it.
With my hands I stretched out the
　heavens.
　All the stars are at my command.
[13] I will raise up Cyrus to fulfill my righteous
　purpose,
　and I will guide his actions.
He will restore my city and free my
　captive people—
　without seeking a reward!
I, the LORD of Heaven's Armies, have
　spoken!"

Future Conversion of Gentiles
[14] This is what the LORD says:

"You will rule the Egyptians,
　the Ethiopians,* and the Sabeans.
They will come to you with all their
　merchandise,
　and it will all be yours.
They will follow you as prisoners in chains.
　They will fall to their knees in front of
　　you and say,
'God is with you, and he is the only God.
　There is no other.'"

[15] Truly, O God of Israel, our Savior,
　you work in mysterious ways.
[16] All craftsmen who make idols will be
　humiliated.
　They will all be disgraced together.
[17] But the LORD will save the people of Israel
　with eternal salvation.
Throughout everlasting ages,
　they will never again be humiliated and
　　disgraced.

[18] For the LORD is God,
　and he created the heavens and earth
　and put everything in place.
He made the world to be lived in,
　not to be a place of empty chaos.

"I am the LORD," he says,
　"and there is no other.
[19] I publicly proclaim bold promises.
　I do not whisper obscurities in some
　　dark corner.
I would not have told the people of Israel*
　to seek me
　if I could not be found.
I, the LORD, speak only what is true
　and declare only what is right.

[20] "Gather together and come,
　you fugitives from surrounding nations.
What fools they are who carry around
　their wooden idols
　and pray to gods that cannot save!
[21] Consult together, argue your case.
　Get together and decide what to say.
Who made these things known so long
　ago?
　What idol ever told you they would
　　happen?
Was it not I, the LORD?
　For there is no other God but me,
a righteous God and Savior.
　There is none but me.
[22] Let all the world look to me for salvation!
　For I am God; there is no other.
[23] I have sworn by my own name;
　I have spoken the truth,
　and I will never go back on my word:
Every knee will bend to me,
　and every tongue will declare allegiance
　　to me.*"
[24] The people will declare,
　"The LORD is the source of all my
　　righteousness and strength."
And all who were angry with him
　will come to him and be ashamed.
[25] In the LORD all the generations of Israel
　　will be justified,
　and in him they will boast.

CHAPTER 46
Babylon's False Gods
[1] Bel and Nebo, the gods of Babylon,
　bow as they are lowered to the ground.
They are being hauled away on ox carts.
　The poor beasts stagger under the
　　weight.

45:14 Hebrew *Cushites.* 45:19 Hebrew *of Jacob.* See note on 14:1. 45:23 Hebrew *will confess;* Greek version reads *will declare allegiance to God.* Compare Rom 14:11.

46:1-13 God calls us to reality and truth. People turn to many things to fill their inner needs. Anything less than God, whether ancient idols or addictions and unhealthy relationships today, will fail like an idol that cannot even hold itself on a cart. In contrast, God is the everlasting, sovereign God of history who *always* does what he says. Putting our hopes of recovery in God's hands is the only way to achieve our goal.

2 Both the idols and their owners are bowed
    down.
  The gods cannot protect the people,
and the people cannot protect the gods.
  They go off into captivity together.

3 "Listen to me, descendants of Jacob,
    all you who remain in Israel.
I have cared for you since you were born.
  Yes, I carried you before you were born.
4 I will be your God throughout your
    lifetime—
  until your hair is white with age.
I made you, and I will care for you.
  I will carry you along and save you.

5 "To whom will you compare me?
  Who is my equal?
6 Some people pour out their silver and gold
    and hire a craftsman to make a god
    from it.
  Then they bow down and worship it!
7 They carry it around on their shoulders,
    and when they set it down, it stays
    there.
  It can't even move!
And when someone prays to it, there is no
    answer.
  It can't rescue anyone from trouble.

8 "Do not forget this! Keep it in mind!
  Remember this, you guilty ones.
9 Remember the things I have done in the
    past.
  For I alone am God!
I am God, and there is none like me.
10 Only I can tell you the future
    before it even happens.
  Everything I plan will come to pass,
    for I do whatever I wish.
11 I will call a swift bird of prey from the east—
    a leader from a distant land to come
    and do my bidding.
  I have said what I would do,
    and I will do it.

12 "Listen to me, you stubborn people
  who are so far from doing right.
13 For I am ready to set things right,
  not in the distant future, but right now!
I am ready to save Jerusalem*
  and show my glory to Israel.

CHAPTER 47
Prediction of Babylon's Fall

1 "Come down, virgin daughter of Babylon,
    and sit in the dust.
  For your days of sitting on a throne
    have ended.
O daughter of Babylonia,* never again will
    you be
  the lovely princess, tender and delicate.
2 Take heavy millstones and grind flour.
  Remove your veil, and strip off your
    robe.
  Expose yourself to public view.*
3 You will be naked and burdened with
    shame.
  I will take vengeance against you
    without pity."

4 Our Redeemer, whose name is the LORD of
    Heaven's Armies,
  is the Holy One of Israel.

5 "O beautiful Babylon, sit now in darkness
    and silence.
  Never again will you be known as the
    queen of kingdoms.
6 For I was angry with my chosen people
    and punished them by letting them fall
    into your hands.
But you, Babylon, showed them no
    mercy.
  You oppressed even the elderly.
7 You said, 'I will reign forever as queen of
    the world!'
  You did not reflect on your actions
    or think about their consequences.

8 "Listen to this, you pleasure-loving
    kingdom,
  living at ease and feeling secure.
You say, 'I am the only one, and there is
    no other.
  I will never be a widow or lose my
    children.'
9 Well, both these things will come upon
    you in a moment:
  widowhood and the loss of your children.
Yes, these calamities will come upon you,
  despite all your witchcraft and magic.

10 "You felt secure in your wickedness.
  'No one sees me,' you said.

46:13 Hebrew *Zion.*   **47:1** Or *Chaldea;* also in 47:5.   **47:2** Hebrew *Bare your legs; pass through the rivers.*

47:1-15 Babylon can be compared to those who ruthlessly oppress or mistreat us. They may feel secure and think they are getting away with their evil deeds, but God has kept track of their sins and will punish them. We need not waste our time plotting revenge or hating these people. God will exact justice. We need to focus on the rest of our life, dealing with the damage that has been done.

But your 'wisdom' and 'knowledge' have
    led you astray,
  and you said, 'I am the only one, and
    there is no other.'
11 So disaster will overtake you,
  and you won't be able to charm it away.
  Calamity will fall upon you,
  and you won't be able to buy your way
    out.
  A catastrophe will strike you suddenly,
    one for which you are not prepared.

12 "Now use your magical charms!
  Use the spells you have worked at all
    these years!
  Maybe they will do you some good.
    Maybe they can make someone afraid
    of you.
13 All the advice you receive has made you
    tired.
  Where are all your astrologers,
  those stargazers who make predictions
    each month?
  Let them stand up and save you from
    what the future holds.
14 But they are like straw burning in a fire;
  they cannot save themselves from the
    flame.
  You will get no help from them at all;
    their hearth is no place to sit for
    warmth.
15 And all your friends,
    those with whom you've done business
    since childhood,
  will go their own ways,
    turning a deaf ear to your cries.

CHAPTER 48
God's Stubborn People
1 "Listen to me, O family of Jacob,
  you who are called by the name of
    Israel
  and born into the family of Judah.
  Listen, you who take oaths in the name of
    the LORD
  and call on the God of Israel.
  You don't keep your promises,
2   even though you call yourself the holy
    city
  and talk about depending on the God of
    Israel,

  whose name is the LORD of Heaven's
    Armies.
3 Long ago I told you what was going to
    happen.
  Then suddenly I took action,
  and all my predictions came true.
4 For I know how stubborn and obstinate
    you are.
  Your necks are as unbending as iron.
  Your heads are as hard as bronze.
5 That is why I told you what would
    happen;
  I told you beforehand what I was going
    to do.
  Then you could never say, 'My idols did it.
  My wooden image and metal god
    commanded it to happen!'
6 You have heard my predictions and seen
    them fulfilled,
  but you refuse to admit it.
  Now I will tell you new things,
    secrets you have not yet heard.
7 They are brand new, not things from the
    past.
  So you cannot say, 'We knew that all
    the time!'

8 "Yes, I will tell you of things that are
    entirely new,
  things you never heard of before.
  For I know so well what traitors you are.
    You have been rebels from birth.
9 Yet for my own sake and for the honor of
    my name,
  I will hold back my anger and not wipe
    you out.
10 I have refined you, but not as silver is
    refined.
  Rather, I have refined you in the
    furnace of suffering.
11 I will rescue you for my sake—
    yes, for my own sake!
  I will not let my reputation be tarnished,
    and I will not share my glory with idols!

Freedom from Babylon
12 "Listen to me, O family of Jacob,
  Israel my chosen one!
  I alone am God,
    the First and the Last.
13 It was my hand that laid the foundations
    of the earth,

48:12-17 Amidst the uncertainties and turmoils of life, we can derive comfort from knowing who
God is. He is the God of the past, who knows all of the troubles and pain we have experienced.
He is the God of the future, who knows what lies ahead for us, and he can be trusted to guide us
along the right path. He is the Creator, who has power over all his creation and sovereignty over
all history. We can surely trust a God this powerful to see us through to complete recovery.

my right hand that spread out the
heavens above.
When I call out the stars,
they all appear in order."

¹⁴ Have any of your idols ever told you this?
Come, all of you, and listen:
The LORD has chosen Cyrus as his ally.
He will use him to put an end to the
empire of Babylon
and to destroy the Babylonian* armies.

¹⁵ "I have said it: I am calling Cyrus!
I will send him on this errand and will
help him succeed.
¹⁶ Come closer, and listen to this.
From the beginning I have told you
plainly what would happen."

And now the Sovereign LORD and his
Spirit
have sent me with this message.
¹⁷ This is what the LORD says—
your Redeemer, the Holy One of Israel:
"I am the LORD your God,
who teaches you what is good for you
and leads you along the paths you
should follow.
¹⁸ Oh, that you had listened to my
commands!
Then you would have had peace
flowing like a gentle river
and righteousness rolling over you like
waves in the sea.
¹⁹ Your descendants would have been like
the sands along the seashore—
too many to count!
There would have been no need for your
destruction,
or for cutting off your family name."

²⁰ Yet even now, be free from your
captivity!
Leave Babylon and the Babylonians.*
Sing out this message!
Shout it to the ends of the earth!
The LORD has redeemed his servants,
the people of Israel.*

²¹ They were not thirsty
when he led them through the desert.
He divided the rock,
and water gushed out for them to
drink.
²² "But there is no peace for the wicked,"
says the LORD.

CHAPTER 49
The LORD's Servant Commissioned
¹ Listen to me, all you in distant lands!
Pay attention, you who are far away!
The LORD called me before my birth;
from within the womb he called me by
name.
² He made my words of judgment as sharp
as a sword.
He has hidden me in the shadow of his
hand.
I am like a sharp arrow in his quiver.

³ He said to me, "You are my servant, Israel,
and you will bring me glory."

⁴ I replied, "But my work seems so useless!
I have spent my strength for nothing
and to no purpose.
Yet I leave it all in the LORD's hand;
I will trust God for my reward."

⁵ And now the LORD speaks—
the one who formed me in my mother's
womb to be his servant,
who commissioned me to bring Israel
back to him.
The LORD has honored me,
and my God has given me strength.
⁶ He says, "You will do more than restore
the people of Israel to me.
I will make you a light to the Gentiles,
and you will bring my salvation to the
ends of the earth."

⁷ The LORD, the Redeemer
and Holy One of Israel,
says to the one who is despised and
rejected by the nations,
to the one who is the servant of rulers:

48:14 Or *Chaldean*. **48:20a** Or *the Chaldeans*. **48:20b** Hebrew *his servant, Jacob*. See note on 14:1.

48:18-22 God would bring deliverance from Babylon in spite of Judah's unworthiness, but the people of Judah would forfeit peace of mind because of their resistance to God. We can have a relationship with God and be assured of eternal peace, but we may be sacrificing the peace God wants for us on earth if we continue in our addiction. Our life can be stable if we are willing to give up our dependency and the turmoil it brings.
49:1-7 Many times it seems like our godly acts are all for nothing. Since starting recovery, we may have lost some old friends and strained some relationships, and we still struggle with our own temptations. There doesn't seem to be any good coming out of this process. But if we are honoring God, he will reward us for our faith.

"Kings will stand at attention when you
pass by.
Princes will also bow low
because of the Lord, the faithful one,
the Holy One of Israel, who has chosen
you."

Promises of Israel's Restoration

⁸This is what the Lord says:

"At just the right time, I will respond
to you.*
On the day of salvation I will help you.
I will protect you and give you to the
people
as my covenant with them.
Through you I will reestablish the land of
Israel
and assign it to its own people again.
⁹I will say to the prisoners, 'Come out in
freedom,'
and to those in darkness, 'Come into
the light.'
They will be my sheep, grazing in green
pastures
and on hills that were previously bare.
¹⁰They will neither hunger nor thirst.
The searing sun will not reach them
anymore.
For the Lord in his mercy will lead them;
he will lead them beside cool waters.
¹¹And I will make my mountains into level
paths for them.
The highways will be raised above the
valleys.
¹²See, my people will return from far
away,
from lands to the north and west,
and from as far south as Egypt.*"

¹³Sing for joy, O heavens!
Rejoice, O earth!
Burst into song, O mountains!
For the Lord has comforted his people
and will have compassion on them in
their suffering.

¹⁴Yet Jerusalem* says, "The Lord has
deserted us;
the Lord has forgotten us."

¹⁵"Never! Can a mother forget her nursing
child?
Can she feel no love for the child she
has borne?
But even if that were possible,
I would not forget you!
¹⁶See, I have written your name on the
palms of my hands.
Always in my mind is a picture of
Jerusalem's walls in ruins.
¹⁷Soon your descendants will come back,
and all who are trying to destroy you
will go away.
¹⁸Look around you and see,
for all your children will come back to
you.
As surely as I live," says the Lord,
"they will be like jewels or bridal
ornaments for you to display.

¹⁹"Even the most desolate parts of your
abandoned land
will soon be crowded with your people.
Your enemies who enslaved you
will be far away.
²⁰The generations born in exile will return
and say,
'We need more room! It's crowded
here!'
²¹Then you will think to yourself,
'Who has given me all these
descendants?
For most of my children were killed,
and the rest were carried away into
exile.
I was left here all alone.
Where did all these people come from?
Who bore these children?
Who raised them for me?'"

²²This is what the Sovereign Lord says:
"See, I will give a signal to the godless
nations.

49:8 Greek version reads *I heard you.* Compare 2 Cor 6:2. 49:12 As in Dead Sea Scrolls, which read *from the region of Aswan,* which is in southern Egypt. Masoretic Text reads *from the region of Sinim.* 49:14 Hebrew *Zion.*

49:8-12 We see here what God wants for and offers to the downtrodden through his Son, the Messiah. To those who are in spiritual and emotional bondage and depression, he offers freedom. To those who feel inner emptiness and aimlessness, he offers guidance, care, and fulfillment. To those who feel battered by life, he offers comfort. To those who are ensnared by addictions, he offers liberation.
49:13-26 The people of Judah felt abandoned by God because of the troubles they were experiencing at that time. We can be assured that even though we might feel abandoned by God because of the troubles we are going through, God will never abandon us. In spite of present appearances, God is working out his plan for us and will deliver us from our enemies.

They will carry your little sons back to
>   you in their arms;
>   they will bring your daughters on their
>   shoulders.
23 Kings and queens will serve you
>   and care for all your needs.
>   They will bow to the earth before you
>   and lick the dust from your feet.
>   Then you will know that I am the LORD.
>   Those who trust in me will never be put
>   to shame."

24 Who can snatch the plunder of war from
>   the hands of a warrior?
>   Who can demand that a tyrant* let his
>   captives go?
25 But the LORD says,
>   "The captives of warriors will be released,
>   and the plunder of tyrants will be
>   retrieved.
>   For I will fight those who fight you,
>   and I will save your children.
26 I will feed your enemies with their own
>   flesh.
>   They will be drunk with rivers of their
>   own blood.
>   All the world will know that I, the LORD,
>   am your Savior and your Redeemer,
>   the Mighty One of Israel.*"

CHAPTER 50
This is what the LORD says:

> "Was your mother sent away because
>   I divorced her?
>   Did I sell you as slaves to my creditors?
>   No, you were sold because of your sins.
>   And your mother, too, was taken
>   because of your sins.
2 Why was no one there when I came?
>   Why didn't anyone answer when I
>   called?
>   Is it because I have no power to rescue?
>   No, that is not the reason!

For I can speak to the sea and make it
>   dry up!
>   I can turn rivers into deserts covered
>   with dying fish.
3 I dress the skies in darkness,
>   covering them with clothes of
>   mourning."

The LORD's Obedient Servant
4 The Sovereign LORD has given me his
>   words of wisdom,
>   so that I know how to comfort the
>   weary.
>   Morning by morning he wakens me
>   and opens my understanding to his
>   will.
5 The Sovereign LORD has spoken to me,
>   and I have listened.
>   I have not rebelled or turned away.
6 I offered my back to those who beat me
>   and my cheeks to those who pulled out
>   my beard.
>   I did not hide my face
>   from mockery and spitting.

7 Because the Sovereign LORD helps me,
>   I will not be disgraced.
>   Therefore, I have set my face like a stone,
>   determined to do his will.
>   And I know that I will not be put to
>   shame.
8 He who gives me justice is near.
>   Who will dare to bring charges against
>   me now?
>   Where are my accusers?
>   Let them appear!
9 See, the Sovereign LORD is on my side!
>   Who will declare me guilty?
>   All my enemies will be destroyed
>   like old clothes that have been eaten by
>   moths!

10 Who among you fears the LORD
>   and obeys his servant?

49:24 As in Dead Sea Scrolls, Syriac version, and Latin Vulgate (also see 49:25); Masoretic Text reads *a righteous person.* 49:26 Hebrew *of Jacob.* See note on 14:1.

50:4-6 The Messiah is speaking here of his own determination to follow God's call to him in spite of the hardships involved. He serves as a model to us in times when we need courage to follow through and obey God. Sometimes God's program for us is difficult. It may involve receiving rebukes, suffering shame, or being misunderstood by those who do not like what we're doing. We will face opposition to the recovery process because many people don't want to lose their influence over us, or they feel threatened by our change in lifestyle. We must stand up to them and follow through with God's plan for us.

50:7-9 We are encouraged to persevere because God is close to us, defending us from our enemies. When we enter recovery, we upset the relationships in which we are entangled. Others become uncomfortable at the prospect of change and will oppose us, even tempting us to fall back into old patterns of behavior. If we stand firm in our resolve to follow God, we will triumph because "the Sovereign LORD is on [our] side!"

If you are walking in darkness,
    without a ray of light,
trust in the LORD
    and rely on your God.
[11] But watch out, you who live in your own
        light
    and warm yourselves by your own fires.
This is the reward you will receive from
        me:
    You will soon fall down in great
        torment.

CHAPTER 51
A Call to Trust the LORD

[1] "Listen to me, all who hope for
        deliverance—
    all who seek the LORD!
Consider the rock from which you were
        cut,
    the quarry from which you were mined.
[2] Yes, think about Abraham, your ancestor,
    and Sarah, who gave birth to your
        nation.
Abraham was only one man when I called
        him.
    But when I blessed him, he became a
        great nation."

[3] The LORD will comfort Israel* again
    and have pity on her ruins.
Her desert will blossom like Eden,
    her barren wilderness like the garden of
        the LORD.
Joy and gladness will be found there.
    Songs of thanksgiving will fill the air.

[4] "Listen to me, my people.
    Hear me, Israel,
for my law will be proclaimed,
    and my justice will become a light to
        the nations.
[5] My mercy and justice are coming soon.
    My salvation is on the way.
My strong arm will bring justice to the
        nations.

All distant lands will look to me
    and wait in hope for my powerful arm.
[6] Look up to the skies above,
    and gaze down on the earth below.
For the skies will disappear like smoke,
    and the earth will wear out like a piece
        of clothing.
The people of the earth will die like flies,
    but my salvation lasts forever.
    My righteous rule will never end!

[7] "Listen to me, you who know right from
        wrong,
    you who cherish my law in your hearts.
Do not be afraid of people's scorn,
    nor fear their insults.
[8] For the moth will devour them as it
        devours clothing.
    The worm will eat at them as it eats wool.
But my righteousness will last forever.
    My salvation will continue from
        generation to generation."

[9] Wake up, wake up, O LORD! Clothe
        yourself with strength!
    Flex your mighty right arm!
Rouse yourself as in the days of old
    when you slew Egypt, the dragon of the
        Nile.*
[10] Are you not the same today,
    the one who dried up the sea,
making a path of escape through the depths
    so that your people could cross over?
[11] Those who have been ransomed by the
        LORD will return.
    They will enter Jerusalem* singing,
        crowned with everlasting joy.
Sorrow and mourning will disappear,
    and they will be filled with joy and
        gladness.

[12] "I, yes I, am the one who comforts you.
    So why are you afraid of mere humans,
who wither like the grass and
        disappear?

51:3 Hebrew *Zion;* also in 51:16. 51:9 Hebrew *You slew Rahab; you pierced the dragon.* Rahab is the name of a
mythical sea monster that represents chaos in ancient literature. The name is used here as a poetic name for Egypt.
51:11 Hebrew *Zion.*

51:7-8 When we set proper boundaries, stop enabling the dysfunctions of others, and deal with
abusive relationships, we may experience others' scorn and slander. Though their rejection will
hurt, we need to see the bigger picture. These people, and eventually the entire earth, will pass
away, but God's justice, mercy, righteousness, and salvation will last forever. So we should
concentrate on pleasing God, not people.
51:12-23 God is in control of our life, yet we don't fear him as we should. Instead, we fear
people—people who don't really have any authority over us. We are tempted to retreat from
God's ways and lapse back into dysfunctional patterns, just to please others. We should strive to
please God because he has the power to bless us for seeking his will or to discipline us for
disobeying.

13 Yet you have forgotten the LORD, your Creator,
  the one who stretched out the sky like a canopy
  and laid the foundations of the earth.
Will you remain in constant dread of human oppressors?
Will you continue to fear the anger of your enemies?
Where is their fury and anger now?
  It is gone!
14 Soon all you captives will be released!
  Imprisonment, starvation, and death will not be your fate!
15 For I am the LORD your God,
  who stirs up the sea, causing its waves to roar.
My name is the LORD of Heaven's Armies.
16 And I have put my words in your mouth
  and hidden you safely in my hand.
I stretched out* the sky like a canopy
  and laid the foundations of the earth.
I am the one who says to Israel,
  'You are my people!'"

17 Wake up, wake up, O Jerusalem!
  You have drunk the cup of the LORD's fury.
You have drunk the cup of terror,
  tipping out its last drops.
18 Not one of your children is left alive
  to take your hand and guide you.
19 These two calamities have fallen on you:
  desolation and destruction, famine and war.
And who is left to sympathize with you?
  Who is left to comfort you?*
20 For your children have fainted and lie in the streets,
  helpless as antelopes caught in a net.
The LORD has poured out his fury;
  God has rebuked them.
21 But now listen to this, you afflicted ones
  who sit in a drunken stupor,
  though not from drinking wine.

22 This is what the Sovereign LORD,
  your God and Defender, says:
"See, I have taken the terrible cup from your hands.
You will drink no more of my fury.
23 Instead, I will hand that cup to your tormentors,
  those who said, 'We will trample you into the dust
  and walk on your backs.'"

CHAPTER 52
Deliverance for Jerusalem
1 Wake up, wake up, O Zion!
  Clothe yourself with strength.
Put on your beautiful clothes, O holy city of Jerusalem,
  for unclean and godless people will enter your gates no longer.
2 Rise from the dust, O Jerusalem.
  Sit in a place of honor.
Remove the chains of slavery from your neck,
  O captive daughter of Zion.
3 For this is what the LORD says:
"When I sold you into exile,
  I received no payment.
Now I can redeem you
  without having to pay for you."

4 This is what the Sovereign LORD says: "Long ago my people chose to live in Egypt. Now they are oppressed by Assyria. 5 What is this?" asks the LORD. "Why are my people enslaved again? Those who rule them shout in exultation.* My name is blasphemed all day long.* 6 But I will reveal my name to my people, and they will come to know its power. Then at last they will recognize that I am the one who speaks to them."

7 How beautiful on the mountains
  are the feet of the messenger who brings good news,
the good news of peace and salvation,
  the news that the God of Israel* reigns!

51:16 As in Syriac version (see also 51:13); Hebrew reads *planted*. 51:19 As in Dead Sea Scrolls and Greek, Latin, and Syriac versions; Masoretic Text reads *How can I comfort you?* 52:5a As in Dead Sea Scrolls; Masoretic Text reads *Those who rule them wail.* 52:5b Greek version reads *The Gentiles continually blaspheme my name because of you.* Compare Rom 2:24. 52:7 Hebrew *of Zion*.

52:1-6 We know what it feels like to be a slave—a slave to alcohol, drugs, sex, greed, or power. God promises to free us from our enslavement; he wants to remove our "chains of slavery." God is greater and more powerful than any addiction we may have. When we believe that he can free us from bondage and ask him to, he will save us.

52:7-10 God's message of salvation and deliverance is so wonderful that it deserves to be shared near and far. "Beautiful" are the feet of those who share with others the news that God reigns! Just as the message of Judah's deliverance from captivity deserved to be shared abroad, our message of salvation and recovery through Christ deserves to be shared. This is the essence of Step Twelve, which calls us to share what we have learned with others as we continue in recovery.

8 The watchmen shout and sing with joy,
 for before their very eyes
 they see the LORD returning to
 Jerusalem.*
9 Let the ruins of Jerusalem break into
 joyful song,
 for the LORD has comforted his people.
 He has redeemed Jerusalem.
10 The LORD has demonstrated his holy
 power
 before the eyes of all the nations.
 All the ends of the earth will see
 the victory of our God.

11 Get out! Get out and leave your
 captivity,
 where everything you touch is
 unclean.
 Get out of there and purify yourselves,
 you who carry home the sacred objects
 of the LORD.
12 You will not leave in a hurry,
 running for your lives.
 For the LORD will go ahead of you;
 yes, the God of Israel will protect you
 from behind.

The LORD's Suffering Servant

13 See, my servant will prosper;
 he will be highly exalted.
14 But many were amazed when they saw
 him.*
 His face was so disfigured he seemed
 hardly human,
 and from his appearance, one would
 scarcely know he was a man.
15 And he will startle* many nations.
 Kings will stand speechless in his
 presence.
 For they will see what they had not been
 told;
 they will understand what they had not
 heard about.*

CHAPTER 53

1 Who has believed our message?
 To whom has the LORD revealed his
 powerful arm?
2 My servant grew up in the LORD's presence
 like a tender green shoot,
 like a root in dry ground.
 There was nothing beautiful or majestic
 about his appearance,
 nothing to attract us to him.
3 He was despised and rejected—
 a man of sorrows, acquainted with
 deepest grief.
 We turned our backs on him and looked
 the other way.
 He was despised, and we did not care.

4 Yet it was our weaknesses he carried;
 it was our sorrows* that weighed him
 down.
 And we thought his troubles were a
 punishment from God,
 a punishment for his own sins!
5 But he was pierced for our rebellion,
 crushed for our sins.
 He was beaten so we could be whole.
 He was whipped so we could be healed.
6 All of us, like sheep, have strayed away.
 We have left God's paths to follow our
 own.
 Yet the LORD laid on him
 the sins of us all.

7 He was oppressed and treated harshly,
 yet he never said a word.
 He was led like a lamb to the slaughter.
 And as a sheep is silent before the
 shearers,
 he did not open his mouth.
8 Unjustly condemned,
 he was led away.*
 No one cared that he died without
 descendants,

52:8 Hebrew to Zion. 52:14 As in Syriac version; Hebrew reads you. 52:15a Or cleanse. 52:15b Greek version reads Those who have never been told about him will see, / and those who have never heard of him will understand. Compare Rom 15:21. 53:4 Or Yet it was our sicknesses he carried; / it was our diseases. 53:8a Greek version reads He was humiliated and received no justice. Compare Acts 8:33.

52:13–53:12 This marvelous passage describes in detail the atoning death of Jesus the Messiah, God's Suffering Servant. His death for us is the basis of salvation and our true and full recovery. Because he died for our sins, we don't have to pay for all the sins we have committed. We have to endure the consequences of whatever we have done, and we will have to make restitution, but we do not have to pay the penalty for our sins, which is eternal death (see Romans 6:23).
53:7-12 It was not easy for Jesus the Messiah to bear such abuse and shame—and it was wholly undeserved! The outcome, however, was a ministry that would change the world. This is the same pattern we can expect. When we suffer in God's will for doing what is right, we can be assured that God will use it to minister to others and will vindicate us in due time, either in this life or the next.

that his life was cut short in
midstream.*
But he was struck down
for the rebellion of my people.
⁹ He had done no wrong
and had never deceived anyone.
But he was buried like a criminal;
he was put in a rich man's grave.

¹⁰ But it was the LORD's good plan to crush
him
and cause him grief.
Yet when his life is made an offering for
sin,
he will have many descendants.
He will enjoy a long life,
and the LORD's good plan will prosper
in his hands.
¹¹ When he sees all that is accomplished by
his anguish,
he will be satisfied.
And because of his experience,
my righteous servant will make it
possible
for many to be counted righteous,
for he will bear all their sins.
¹² I will give him the honors of a victorious
soldier,
because he exposed himself
to death.
He was counted among the rebels.
He bore the sins of many and
interceded for rebels.

CHAPTER 54
Future Glory for Jerusalem
¹ "Sing, O childless woman,
you who have never given birth!
Break into loud and joyful song,
O Jerusalem,
you who have never been in labor.
For the desolate woman now has more
children
than the woman who lives with her
husband,"
says the LORD.
² "Enlarge your house; build an addition.
Spread out your home, and spare no
expense!
³ For you will soon be bursting at the seams.

Your descendants will occupy other
nations
and resettle the ruined cities.

⁴ "Fear not; you will no longer live in shame.
Don't be afraid; there is no more
disgrace for you.
You will no longer remember the shame
of your youth
and the sorrows of widowhood.
⁵ For your Creator will be your husband;
the LORD of Heaven's Armies is his name!
He is your Redeemer, the Holy One of
Israel,
the God of all the earth.
⁶ For the LORD has called you back from
your grief—
as though you were a young wife
abandoned by her husband,"
says your God.
⁷ "For a brief moment I abandoned you,
but with great compassion I will take
you back.
⁸ In a burst of anger I turned my face away
for a little while.
But with everlasting love I will have
compassion on you,"
says the LORD, your Redeemer.

⁹ "Just as I swore in the time of Noah
that I would never again let a flood
cover the earth,
so now I swear
that I will never again be angry and
punish you.
¹⁰ For the mountains may move
and the hills disappear,
but even then my faithful love for you
will remain.
My covenant of blessing will never be
broken,"
says the LORD, who has mercy on you.

¹¹ "O storm-battered city,
troubled and desolate!
I will rebuild you with precious jewels
and make your foundations from lapis
lazuli.
¹² I will make your towers of sparkling
rubies,
your gates of shining gems,
and your walls of precious stones.

53:8b Or As for his contemporaries, / who cared that his life was cut short in midstream? Greek version reads Who can
speak of his descendants? / For his life was taken from the earth. Compare Acts 8:33.

54:10 Here is a promise we can hang on to when everything seems to fall apart and nobody, not
even God, seems to care. Natural things that seem permanent, such as mountains and hills, will
not last as long as God's mercy for his people. God's promise to us of kindness and peace in the
midst of our troubles will stand forever.

¹³ I will teach all your children,
    and they will enjoy great peace.
¹⁴ You will be secure under a government
        that is just and fair.
    Your enemies will stay far away.
    You will live in peace,
        and terror will not come near.
¹⁵ If any nation comes to fight you,
        it is not because I sent them.
    Whoever attacks you will go down
        in defeat.

¹⁶ "I have created the blacksmith
    who fans the coals beneath the forge
    and makes the weapons of destruction.
        And I have created the armies that
        destroy.
¹⁷ But in that coming day
    no weapon turned against you will
        succeed.
    You will silence every voice
        raised up to accuse you.
    These benefits are enjoyed by the servants
        of the LORD;
    their vindication will come from me.
    I, the LORD, have spoken!

CHAPTER 55
Invitation to the LORD's Salvation
¹ "Is anyone thirsty?
    Come and drink—
    even if you have no money!
    Come, take your choice of wine
        or milk—
    it's all free!
² Why spend your money on food that does
        not give you strength?
    Why pay for food that does you
        no good?
    Listen to me, and you will eat what
        is good.
    You will enjoy the finest food.

³ "Come to me with your ears wide open.
    Listen, and you will find life.
    I will make an everlasting covenant with
        you.
    I will give you all the unfailing love I
        promised to David.
⁴ See how I used him to display my power
        among the peoples.
    I made him a leader among the
        nations.
⁵ You also will command nations you do
        not know,
    and peoples unknown to you will come
        running to obey,
    because I, the LORD your God,

STEP 3

Redeeming the Past
BIBLE READING: Isaiah 54:4-8
We made a decision to turn our wills and our lives over to the care of God.
Each one of us comes to God with a past. In turning our life over to him, we give him our entire self, including our past losses and shame. We hand over to him every moment of disgrace, every tear we have ever cried, every word we wish we could take back, all the broken promises, the loneliness, all the dreams that died, the dashed hopes, the broken relationships, our successes and failures—all of our yesterdays and the scars they have left in our life.

Under Old Testament law, if someone lost freedom, property, or spouse because of a disaster or a debt, the next of kin was looked to as a "redeemer." If property had been lost because of inability to pay, the redeemer would pay for it and return it to the original owner. If a woman lost her husband, the redeemer would marry her, providing her with protection and love. God tells us, "Fear not; you will no longer live in shame. Don't be afraid; there is no more disgrace for you. You will no longer remember the shame of your youth and the sorrows of widowhood. For your Creator will be your husband; the LORD of Heaven's Armies is his name! He is your Redeemer. . . . For the LORD has called you back from your grief" (Isaiah 54:4-6).

God is our Redeemer, the restorer of our losses. He is Lord of all, even of our days and our dreams in the past. When we give God the past, he can make up for all we have lost. He can rid us of the shame and fill the empty places in our heart. *Turn to page 1213, Matthew 11.*

the Holy One of Israel, have made you glorious."

⁶Seek the LORD while you can find him.
Call on him now while he is near.
⁷Let the wicked change their ways
and banish the very thought of doing wrong.
Let them turn to the LORD that he may have mercy on them.
Yes, turn to our God, for he will forgive generously.

⁸"My thoughts are nothing like your thoughts," says the LORD.
"And my ways are far beyond anything you could imagine.
⁹For just as the heavens are higher than the earth,
so my ways are higher than your ways
and my thoughts higher than your thoughts.

¹⁰"The rain and snow come down from the heavens
and stay on the ground to water the earth.
They cause the grain to grow,
producing seed for the farmer
and bread for the hungry.
¹¹It is the same with my word.
I send it out, and it always produces fruit.
It will accomplish all I want it to,
and it will prosper everywhere I send it.
¹²You will live in joy and peace.
The mountains and hills will burst into song,
and the trees of the field will clap their hands!
¹³Where once there were thorns, cypress trees will grow.
Where nettles grew, myrtles will sprout up.
These events will bring great honor to the LORD's name;
they will be an everlasting sign of his power and love."

CHAPTER 56
Blessings for All Nations
This is what the LORD says:

"Be just and fair to all.
Do what is right and good,
for I am coming soon to rescue you
and to display my righteousness among you.
²Blessed are all those
who are careful to do this.
Blessed are those who honor my Sabbath days of rest
and keep themselves from doing wrong.

³"Don't let foreigners who commit themselves to the LORD say,
'The LORD will never let me be part of his people.'
And don't let the eunuchs say,
'I'm a dried-up tree with no children and no future.'
⁴For this is what the LORD says:
I will bless those eunuchs
who keep my Sabbath days holy
and who choose to do what pleases me
and commit their lives to me.
⁵I will give them—within the walls of my house—
a memorial and a name
far greater than sons and daughters could give.
For the name I give them is an everlasting one.
It will never disappear!

⁶"I will also bless the foreigners who commit themselves to the LORD,
who serve him and love his name,
who worship him and do not desecrate the Sabbath day of rest,
and who hold fast to my covenant.
⁷I will bring them to my holy mountain of Jerusalem
and will fill them with joy in my house of prayer.
I will accept their burnt offerings and sacrifices,

55:6 We need to seek God while we still have the opportunity. If we procrastinate and make excuses long enough, we will find that without knowing it our heart has hardened. Someday our heart may be so hard that we can no longer hear God's call and respond to it. The time to repent and turn to God is now!

56:1-2 God rescues us free of charge; it is a gift. It is not something we can earn by being "good enough." While our salvation is not based on the good things we do, our deeds are an important demonstration of our faith in God. By doing what is "right and good," we are demonstrating our obedience to and respect for God. God's laws lead to a rich, full, addiction-free life. Since he created the world and us, he knows what works best for us.

because my Temple will be called a
house of prayer for all nations.
8 For the Sovereign LORD,
who brings back the outcasts of Israel,
says:
I will bring others, too,
besides my people Israel."

Sinful Leaders Condemned

9 Come, wild animals of the field!
Come, wild animals of the forest!
Come and devour my people!
10 For the leaders of my people—
the LORD's watchmen, his shepherds—
are blind and ignorant.
They are like silent watchdogs
that give no warning when danger
comes.
They love to lie around, sleeping and
dreaming.
11 Like greedy dogs, they are never
satisfied.
They are ignorant shepherds,
all following their own path
and intent on personal gain.
12 "Come," they say, "let's get some wine
and have a party.
Let's all get drunk.
Then tomorrow we'll do it again
and have an even bigger party!"

CHAPTER 57

1 Good people pass away;
the godly often die before their time.
But no one seems to care or wonder
why.
No one seems to understand
that God is protecting them from the
evil to come.
2 For those who follow godly paths
will rest in peace when they die.

Idolatrous Worship Condemned

3 "But you—come here, you witches'
children,

you offspring of adulterers and
prostitutes!
4 Whom do you mock,
making faces and sticking out your
tongues?
You children of sinners and liars!
5 You worship your idols with great passion
beneath the oaks and under every green
tree.
You sacrifice your children down in the
valleys,
among the jagged rocks in the cliffs.
6 Your gods are the smooth stones in the
valleys.
You worship them with liquid offerings
and grain offerings.
They, not I, are your inheritance.
Do you think all this makes me happy?
7 You have committed adultery on every
high mountain.
There you have worshiped idols
and have been unfaithful to me.
8 You have put pagan symbols
on your doorposts and behind your
doors.
You have left me
and climbed into bed with these
detestable gods.
You have committed yourselves to them.
You love to look at their naked bodies.
9 You have gone to Molech*
with olive oil and many perfumes,
sending your agents far and wide,
even to the world of the dead.*
10 You grew weary in your search,
but you never gave up.
Desire gave you renewed strength,
and you did not grow weary.
11 "Are you afraid of these idols?
Do they terrify you?
Is that why you have lied to me
and forgotten me and my words?
Is it because of my long silence
that you no longer fear me?

57:9a Or *to the king.*   57:9b Hebrew *to Sheol.*

56:9-12 The evil leaders of God's people will be chastised. We must be discerning of those whom
we follow. There will be those who want to give us advice and guidance but cannot be trusted
because they are intent on their own personal gain and not following God's principles. Any who
oppose what God wants should be avoided.
57:1-14 Recovery is God's desire for us, but it does not happen automatically. God judges those
who turn their backs on him and plunge headlong into sin. These people deliberately reject God
and his ways. God is not judging those who struggle with doing what is right and fail. Making
mistakes is common to all of us and should be expected from time to time because we are not
perfect. But by asking for forgiveness and help from God, we can continue toward the goal of
recovery—even after a fall.

[12] Now I will expose your so-called good
deeds.
None of them will help you.
[13] Let's see if your idols can save you
when you cry to them for help.
Why, a puff of wind can knock them
down!
If you just breathe on them, they fall
over!
But whoever trusts in me will inherit the
land
and possess my holy mountain."

God Forgives the Repentant

[14] God says, "Rebuild the road!
Clear away the rocks and stones
so my people can return from
captivity."
[15] The high and lofty one who lives in
eternity,
the Holy One, says this:
"I live in the high and holy place
with those whose spirits are contrite
and humble.
I restore the crushed spirit of the humble
and revive the courage of those with
repentant hearts.
[16] For I will not fight against you forever;
I will not always be angry.
If I were, all people would pass away—
all the souls I have made.
[17] I was angry,
so I punished these greedy people.
I withdrew from them,
but they kept going on their own
stubborn way.
[18] I have seen what they do,
but I will heal them anyway!
I will lead them.
I will comfort those who mourn,

58:1 Hebrew *Jacob*. See note on 14:1.

[19] bringing words of praise to their lips.
May they have abundant peace, both near
and far,"
says the LORD, who heals them.
[20] "But those who still reject me are like the
restless sea,
which is never still
but continually churns up mud and
dirt.
[21] There is no peace for the wicked,"
says my God.

CHAPTER 58
True and False Worship
[1] "Shout with the voice of a trumpet blast.
Shout aloud! Don't be timid.
Tell my people Israel* of their sins!
[2]   Yet they act so pious!
They come to the Temple every day
and seem delighted to learn all about
me.
They act like a righteous nation
that would never abandon the laws
of its God.
They ask me to take action on their
behalf,
pretending they want to be near me.
[3] 'We have fasted before you!' they say.
'Why aren't you impressed?
We have been very hard on ourselves,
and you don't even notice it!'

"I will tell you why!" I respond.
"It's because you are fasting to please
yourselves.
Even while you fast,
you keep oppressing your workers.
[4] What good is fasting
when you keep on fighting and
quarreling?

58:1-5 The lives of the people of Judah were full of religious activities, but their religion was just a show to impress others. They led dysfunctional lives, devoid of true obedience to God and concern for his laws. Not realizing that their own hypocrisy was at fault, they blamed God for not doing anything for them. While we may go through the motions of being religious, are we really trying to serve and honor God? Have we tried to recover from our addiction, or are we covering our dysfunctional behavior with religious acts? If we don't truly seek to live as God wants us to, he will ignore our false religious acts.
58:6-12 The path of recovery and healing includes being compassionate toward others. If we just focus on our own life and make excuses to ignore others, we will not progress very far in recovery. As we learn to help the hungry and needy, loving and serving them in Christ's name, we will find that God will bring us healing and blessing.
58:13-14 The Old Testament Sabbath regulation provided a structure within which people could regularly rest from the pressures of life, worship God, and relax with their family. We still need to set boundaries on our workaholic tendencies so we can care for ourself, our family, and our relationship with God. Such boundaries will not only help us strengthen all of these relationships but will refresh us physically and make us ready to face the work ahead of us.

This kind of fasting
will never get you anywhere with me.
⁵ You humble yourselves
by going through the motions of
penance,
bowing your heads
like reeds bending in the wind.
You dress in burlap
and cover yourselves with ashes.
Is this what you call fasting?
Do you really think this will please the
LORD?

⁶ "No, this is the kind of fasting I want:
Free those who are wrongly imprisoned;
lighten the burden of those who work
for you.
Let the oppressed go free,
and remove the chains that bind
people.
⁷ Share your food with the hungry,
and give shelter to the homeless.
Give clothes to those who need them,
and do not hide from relatives who
need your help.

⁸ "Then your salvation will come like the
dawn,
and your wounds will quickly heal.
Your godliness will lead you forward,
and the glory of the LORD will protect
you from behind.
⁹ Then when you call, the LORD will answer.
'Yes, I am here,' he will quickly reply.

"Remove the heavy yoke of oppression.
Stop pointing your finger and spreading
vicious rumors!
¹⁰ Feed the hungry,
and help those in trouble.
Then your light will shine out from the
darkness,
and the darkness around you will be as
bright as noon.
¹¹ The LORD will guide you continually,
giving you water when you are dry
and restoring your strength.
You will be like a well-watered garden,
like an ever-flowing spring.
¹² Some of you will rebuild the deserted
ruins of your cities.
Then you will be known as a rebuilder
of walls
and a restorer of homes.
¹³ "Keep the Sabbath day holy.
Don't pursue your own interests
on that day,
but enjoy the Sabbath

STEP 6

God's Abundant Pardon

BIBLE READING: Isaiah 55:1-9
We were entirely ready to have God remove all these defects of character.
People tell us to repent and stop thinking the way we do. Most of us would give anything to do this. If it were only that simple to stop our obsessive thoughts! When we are starving emotionally, it is almost impossible to stop thinking about what has fed that hunger, even when we realize it doesn't satisfy.

People don't seem to understand. They may quote a verse like, "Let the wicked change their ways and banish the very thought of doing wrong" (Isaiah 55:7). But we think, *How? My thoughts seem to be out of my control.*

God does understand. He put that verse into the larger context of dealing with the hunger within our soul. He said, "Why spend your money on food that does not give you strength? Why pay for food that does you no good? Listen to me, and you will eat what is good. You will enjoy the finest food. Come to me with your ears wide open. Listen, and you will find life. . . . Let them turn to the LORD that he may have mercy on them. Yes, turn to our God, for he will forgive generously" (Isaiah 55:2-3, 7). The word translated "generously" can be understood to mean "in progressively increasing measure each time we come."

We fight our addiction on two fronts: dealing with the hunger deep inside us and changing our thoughts of doing wrong. Neither battle is easily won; each requires our daily readiness and willingness to allow God to satisfy our hunger and help us overcome our defects of character. *Turn to page 1139, Jonah 4.*

and speak of it with delight as the
    LORD's holy day.
Honor the Sabbath in everything you do
    on that day,
    and don't follow your own desires or
      talk idly.
¹⁴ Then the LORD will be your delight.
    I will give you great honor
    and satisfy you with the inheritance I
      promised to your ancestor Jacob.
    I, the LORD, have spoken!"

CHAPTER 59
Warnings against Sin

¹ Listen! The LORD's arm is not too weak to
    save you,
    nor is his ear too deaf to hear you call.
² It's your sins that have cut you off from
    God.
    Because of your sins, he has turned away
    and will not listen anymore.
³ Your hands are the hands of murderers,
    and your fingers are filthy with sin.
    Your lips are full of lies,
    and your mouth spews corruption.

⁴ No one cares about being fair and honest.
    The people's lawsuits are based on lies.
    They conceive evil deeds
    and then give birth to sin.
⁵ They hatch deadly snakes
    and weave spiders' webs.
    Whoever eats their eggs will die;
    whoever cracks them will hatch a
      viper.
⁶ Their webs can't be made into clothing,
    and nothing they do is productive.
    All their activity is filled with sin,
    and violence is their trademark.
⁷ Their feet run to do evil,
    and they rush to commit murder.

They think only about sinning.
    Misery and destruction always follow
      them.
⁸ They don't know where to find peace
    or what it means to be just and good.
    They have mapped out crooked roads,
    and no one who follows them knows a
      moment's peace.

⁹ So there is no justice among us,
    and we know nothing about right
      living.
    We look for light but find only darkness.
    We look for bright skies but walk in gloom.
¹⁰ We grope like the blind along a wall,
    feeling our way like people without eyes.
    Even at brightest noontime,
    we stumble as though it were dark.
    Among the living,
    we are like the dead.
¹¹ We growl like hungry bears;
    we moan like mournful doves.
    We look for justice, but it never comes.
    We look for rescue, but it is far away
      from us.
¹² For our sins are piled up before God
    and testify against us.
    Yes, we know what sinners we are.
¹³ We know we have rebelled and have
    denied the LORD.
    We have turned our backs on our God.
    We know how unfair and oppressive we
      have been,
    carefully planning our deceitful lies.
¹⁴ Our courts oppose the righteous,
    and justice is nowhere to be found.
    Truth stumbles in the streets,
    and honesty has been outlawed.
¹⁵ Yes, truth is gone,
    and anyone who renounces evil is
      attacked.

59:13 We often fear dealing honestly with our sin. We are afraid that if we start opening up to the truth, we will be devastated. So we lie to cover up and hide from the truth. Before long we are fooled by our own lies. Honesty with God, with ourself, and with others is essential for growth. We can never recover in the areas where we deny that there are problems.

59:15 People are often attacked as they try to improve themselves. Friends don't want us to deal truthfully with our hang-ups because our doing so might expose their own. People may exert a great deal of influence over us, and they may not want to lose their power. The forces against us in our journey toward recovery are great because the world stands contrary to God's program. We must resist what the world says and follow God.

60:1-3 God's people are called to let their light shine to the nations. God wants to transform all of us and use us to bring his truth to others. We are reminded of Step Twelve, which says that an important part of recovery is sharing our life as living proof that recovery is possible with God's help.

60:4-22 The restoration and exaltation of Jerusalem at the end of history are described in these verses. How unbelievable this description must have seemed to the Jews of Isaiah's day, who were under the threat of Assyrian domination, and to the subsequent generations, who would be held captive in Babylonia. But God can do the seemingly impossible. He will one day restore Jerusalem, and he can restore us, too (see Ephesians 3:20).

The LORD looked and was displeased
to find there was no justice.
¹⁶ He was amazed to see that no one intervened
to help the oppressed.
So he himself stepped in to save them
with his strong arm,
and his justice sustained him.
¹⁷ He put on righteousness as his body armor
and placed the helmet of salvation on
his head.
He clothed himself with a robe of
vengeance
and wrapped himself in a cloak of
divine passion.
¹⁸ He will repay his enemies for their evil deeds.
His fury will fall on his foes.
He will pay them back even to the ends
of the earth.
¹⁹ In the west, people will respect the name
of the LORD;
in the east, they will glorify him.
For he will come like a raging flood tide
driven by the breath of the LORD.*

²⁰ "The Redeemer will come to Jerusalem
to buy back those in Israel
who have turned from their sins,"*
says the LORD.

²¹ "And this is my covenant with them,"
says the LORD. "My Spirit will not leave
them, and neither will these words I have
given you. They will be on your lips and on
the lips of your children and your children's
children forever. I, the LORD, have spoken!

CHAPTER 60
Future Glory for Jerusalem
¹ "Arise, Jerusalem! Let your light shine for
all to see.
For the glory of the LORD rises to shine
on you.
² Darkness as black as night covers all the
nations of the earth,
but the glory of the LORD rises and
appears over you.
³ All nations will come to your light;
mighty kings will come to see your
radiance.

⁴ "Look and see, for everyone is coming
home!
Your sons are coming from distant
lands;

59:19 Or *When the enemy comes like a raging flood tide, /
the Spirit of the LORD will drive him back.* 59:20 Hebrew
*The Redeemer will come to Zion / to buy back those in Jacob
/ who have turned from their sins.* Greek version reads *The
one who rescues will come on behalf of Zion, / and he will
turn Jacob away from ungodliness.* Compare Rom 11:26.

STEP 7

Clearing the Mess
BIBLE READING: Isaiah 57:12-19
**We humbly asked him to remove our
shortcomings.**
In many ways Step Seven represents a turning point in the recovery process. It forms a
bridge between the inner work of the first
six steps and the final steps, which emphasize outer work—changes in behavior. Our
shortcomings may seem to clutter our
personal road out of the past. Just because
we are working the steps doesn't mean that
our life is as it should be. Will God really
come into the mess and lead us out?

"God says, 'Rebuild the road! Clear away
the rocks and stones so my people can
return from captivity.' The high and lofty
one who lives in eternity, the Holy One, says
this: 'I live in the high and holy place with
those whose spirits are contrite and
humble. I restore the crushed spirit of the
humble and revive the courage of those
with repentant hearts. . . . I have seen what
they do, but I will heal them anyway! I will
lead them. I will comfort those who
mourn'" (Isaiah 57:14-15, 18).

God is our ultimate help in clearing the
way to a better future. He looks forward to
removing our shortcomings so we can
better avoid being tripped up. When we
come to him with humility, admitting that
we still struggle with many of our shortcomings, he refreshes us and gives us the
courage we need to continue the battle. He
isn't put off by the foolish things we do. He
sees what we do but chooses to heal us
anyway! He'll keep leading us toward recovery, one step at a time. *Turn to page 957,
Jeremiah 18.*

tyndal.es/lrbstep7

your little daughters will be carried
home.
[5] Your eyes will shine,
and your heart will thrill with joy,
for merchants from around the world will
come to you.
They will bring you the wealth of many
lands.
[6] Vast caravans of camels will converge
on you,
the camels of Midian and Ephah.
The people of Sheba will bring gold and
frankincense
and will come worshiping the LORD.
[7] The flocks of Kedar will be given to you,
and the rams of Nebaioth will be
brought for my altars.
I will accept their offerings,
and I will make my Temple glorious.

[8] "And what do I see flying like clouds to
Israel,
like doves to their nests?
[9] They are ships from the ends of the earth,
from lands that trust in me,
led by the great ships of Tarshish.
They are bringing the people of Israel
home from far away,
carrying their silver and gold.
They will honor the LORD your God,
the Holy One of Israel,
for he has filled you with splendor.

[10] "Foreigners will come to rebuild your
towns,
and their kings will serve you.
For though I have destroyed you in my
anger,
I will now have mercy on you through
my grace.
[11] Your gates will stay open day and night
to receive the wealth of many lands.
The kings of the world will be led as captives
in a victory procession.
[12] For the nations that refuse to serve you
will be destroyed.

[13] "The glory of Lebanon will be yours—
the forests of cypress, fir, and pine—
to beautify my sanctuary.
My Temple will be glorious!
[14] The descendants of your tormentors

60:16 Hebrew *of Jacob*. See note on 14:1.

will come and bow before you.
Those who despised you
will kiss your feet.
They will call you the City of the LORD,
and Zion of the Holy One of Israel.

[15] "Though you were once despised and
hated,
with no one traveling through you,
I will make you beautiful forever,
a joy to all generations.
[16] Powerful kings and mighty nations
will satisfy your every need,
as though you were a child
nursing at the breast of a queen.
You will know at last that I, the LORD,
am your Savior and your Redeemer,
the Mighty One of Israel.*
[17] I will exchange your bronze for gold,
your iron for silver,
your wood for bronze,
and your stones for iron.
I will make peace your leader
and righteousness your ruler.
[18] Violence will disappear from your land;
the desolation and destruction of war
will end.
Salvation will surround you like city walls,
and praise will be on the lips of all who
enter there.

[19] "No longer will you need the sun to shine
by day,
nor the moon to give its light by night,
for the LORD your God will be your
everlasting light,
and your God will be your glory.
[20] Your sun will never set;
your moon will not go down.
For the LORD will be your everlasting light.
Your days of mourning will come to an
end.
[21] All your people will be righteous.
They will possess their land forever,
for I will plant them there with my own
hands
in order to bring myself glory.
[22] The smallest family will become a
thousand people,
and the tiniest group will become a
mighty nation.

61:4-7 God promised rebuilding, prosperity, ministry, and honor to the people of Israel. God promises these same things, though in different forms, to all his children, Jew or Gentile. He wants to rebuild our broken life, make us spiritually prosperous, give our life significance through ministry to others, and fill us with honor through his love and grace.

At the right time, I, the LORD, will make it happen."

CHAPTER 61
Good News for the Oppressed

¹ The Spirit of the Sovereign LORD is upon me,
for the LORD has anointed me
to bring good news to the poor.
He has sent me to comfort the brokenhearted
and to proclaim that captives will be released
and prisoners will be freed.*
² He has sent me to tell those who mourn
that the time of the LORD's favor has come,*
and with it, the day of God's anger against their enemies.
³ To all who mourn in Israel,*
he will give a crown of beauty for ashes,
a joyous blessing instead of mourning,
festive praise instead of despair.
In their righteousness, they will be like great oaks
that the LORD has planted for his own glory.

⁴ They will rebuild the ancient ruins,
repairing cities destroyed long ago.
They will revive them,
though they have been deserted for many generations.
⁵ Foreigners will be your servants.
They will feed your flocks
and plow your fields
and tend your vineyards.
⁶ You will be called priests of the LORD,
ministers of our God.
You will feed on the treasures of the nations
and boast in their riches.
⁷ Instead of shame and dishonor,
you will enjoy a double share of honor.
You will possess a double portion of prosperity in your land,
and everlasting joy will be yours.

⁸ "For I, the LORD, love justice.
I hate robbery and wrongdoing.
I will faithfully reward my people for their suffering
and make an everlasting covenant with them.
⁹ Their descendants will be recognized
and honored among the nations.

61:1 Greek version reads *and the blind will see.* Compare Luke 4:18. 61:2 Or *to proclaim the acceptable year of the LORD.* 61:3 Hebrew *in Zion.*

STEP 12

Our Mission

BIBLE READING: Isaiah 61:1-3

Having had a spiritual awakening as the result of these steps, we tried to carry this message to others and to practice these principles in all our affairs.

A life set free from all addictions by the Lord is a beautiful sight to behold. When we practice these principles and share our experiences, people will see the glory of God in our life and gain hope. We know from experience the depths of suffering, affliction, and brokenness. We know the pain of being enslaved to our passions and blinded by our denial. We have endured our seasons of grieving. We can relate to those who struggle to be free. We also know that there is more to life than bondage. In Christ are healing and freedom, clarity and mercy, beauty and joy.

When Jesus came to earth he had a mission, which was expressed in these words: "The Spirit of the Sovereign LORD is upon me, for the LORD has anointed me to bring good news to the poor. He has sent me to comfort the brokenhearted and to proclaim that captives will be released and prisoners will be freed. He has sent me to tell those who mourn that the time of the LORD's favor has come. . . . To all who mourn . . . he will give a crown of beauty for ashes, a joyous blessing instead of mourning, festive praise instead of despair" (Isaiah 61:1-3).

This mission has been passed on to us. Some people talk about "preaching the gospel" but may alienate those who need the Good News the most. We are in a unique position to share our experiences, our strengths, and our hope in a way that broken people can understand and receive it. *Turn to page 1279, Mark 16.*

tyndal.es/lrbstep12

Everyone will realize that they are a people
the LORD has blessed."

10 I am overwhelmed with joy in the LORD
my God!
For he has dressed me with the clothing
of salvation
and draped me in a robe of
righteousness.
I am like a bridegroom dressed for his
wedding
or a bride with her jewels.
11 The Sovereign LORD will show his justice
to the nations of the world.
Everyone will praise him!
His righteousness will be like a garden in
early spring,
with plants springing up everywhere.

CHAPTER 62
Isaiah's Prayer for Jerusalem
1 Because I love Zion,
I will not keep still.
Because my heart yearns for Jerusalem,
I cannot remain silent.
I will not stop praying for her
until her righteousness shines like the
dawn,
and her salvation blazes like a burning
torch.
2 The nations will see your righteousness.
World leaders will be blinded by your
glory.
And you will be given a new name
by the LORD's own mouth.
3 The LORD will hold you in his hand for all
to see—
a splendid crown in the hand of God.
4 Never again will you be called "The
Forsaken City"*
or "The Desolate Land."*
Your new name will be "The City of God's
Delight"*
and "The Bride of God,"*
for the LORD delights in you

and will claim you as his bride.
5 Your children will commit themselves to
you, O Jerusalem,
just as a young man commits himself to
his bride.
Then God will rejoice over you
as a bridegroom rejoices over his bride.

6 O Jerusalem, I have posted watchmen on
your walls;
they will pray day and night,
continually.
Take no rest, all you who pray to the
LORD.
7 Give the LORD no rest until he completes
his work,
until he makes Jerusalem the pride of
the earth.
8 The LORD has sworn to Jerusalem by his
own strength:
"I will never again hand you over to
your enemies.
Never again will foreign warriors come
and take away your grain and new
wine.
9 You raised the grain, and you will eat it,
praising the LORD.
Within the courtyards of the Temple,
you yourselves will drink the wine you
have pressed."

10 Go out through the gates!
Prepare the highway for my people
to return!
Smooth out the road; pull out the
boulders;
raise a flag for all the nations to see.
11 The LORD has sent this message to every
land:
"Tell the people of Israel,*
'Look, your Savior is coming.
See, he brings his reward with him as
he comes.'"
12 They will be called "The Holy People"
and "The People Redeemed by the
LORD."

62:4a Hebrew *Azubah*, which means "forsaken." 62:4b Hebrew *Shemamah*, which means "desolate." 62:4c Hebrew
Hephzibah, which means "my delight is in her." 62:4d Hebrew *Beulah*, which means "married." 62:11 Hebrew *Tell
the daughter of Zion.*

62:1-5 God promised a glorious restoration for Jerusalem and the people in the future. The city
that had been degraded and abused by conquerors would be lifted up and honored. This is God's
desire for us, too. Whether we have been abused by parents, a spouse, friends, or strangers, or
whether our pain has been self-inflicted through our addiction, God desires to cleanse us and
restore us to health and honor. He can do this if we believe in him and ask him to save us.
62:6-7 The watchmen here were to pray to God, reminding him of his promises to Jerusalem.
They were to keep praying until God had fulfilled his word. We should not neglect continual
prayer in the recovery process. Prayer is not just a way to bring us peace of mind but a way to
bring change to us and to the world.

And Jerusalem will be known as "The
   Desirable Place"
   and "The City No Longer Forsaken."

CHAPTER 63

Judgment against the LORD's Enemies

¹ Who is this who comes from Edom,
   from the city of Bozrah,
   with his clothing stained red?
Who is this in royal robes,
   marching in his great strength?

"It is I, the LORD, announcing your
   salvation!
   It is I, the LORD, who has the power to
   save!"

² Why are your clothes so red,
   as if you have been treading out grapes?

³ "I have been treading the winepress alone;
   no one was there to help me.
In my anger I have trampled my enemies
   as if they were grapes.
In my fury I have trampled my foes.
   Their blood has stained my clothes.
⁴ For the time has come for me to avenge
   my people,
   to ransom them from their oppressors.
⁵ I was amazed to see that no one
   intervened
   to help the oppressed.
So I myself stepped in to save them with
   my strong arm,
   and my wrath sustained me.
⁶ I crushed the nations in my anger
   and made them stagger and fall to the
   ground,
   spilling their blood upon the earth."

Praise for Deliverance

⁷ I will tell of the LORD's unfailing love.
   I will praise the LORD for all he has
   done.
I will rejoice in his great goodness to
   Israel,
   which he has granted according to his
   mercy and love.
⁸ He said, "They are my very own people.
   Surely they will not betray me again."

And he became their Savior.
⁹ In all their suffering he also suffered,
   and he personally* rescued them.
In his love and mercy he redeemed them.
   He lifted them up and carried them
   through all the years.
¹⁰ But they rebelled against him
   and grieved his Holy Spirit.
So he became their enemy
   and fought against them.

¹¹ Then they remembered those days of old
   when Moses led his people out of
      Egypt.
They cried out, "Where is the one who
      brought Israel through the sea,
   with Moses as their shepherd?
Where is the one who sent his Holy Spirit
   to be among his people?
¹² Where is the one whose power was
      displayed
   when Moses lifted up his hand—
the one who divided the sea before
      them,
   making himself famous forever?
¹³ Where is the one who led them through
      the bottom of the sea?
They were like fine stallions
   racing through the desert, never
      stumbling.
¹⁴ As with cattle going down into a peaceful
      valley,
   the Spirit of the LORD gave them rest.
You led your people, LORD,
   and gained a magnificent reputation."

Prayer for Mercy and Pardon

¹⁵ LORD, look down from heaven;
   look from your holy, glorious home,
      and see us.
Where is the passion and the might
   you used to show on our behalf?
Where are your mercy and compassion
      now?
¹⁶ Surely you are still our Father!
   Even if Abraham and Jacob* would
      disown us,
LORD, you would still be our Father.
   You are our Redeemer from ages past.

63:9 Hebrew *and the angel of his presence.* 63:16 Hebrew *Israel.* See note on 14:1.

63:10-14 Isaiah recounted the history of Israel. In spite of God's deliverance of his people from
Egypt, they rebelled against him, worshiped idols, and then wondered why their lives were in
such a mess. We may be in danger of doing the same if we think that trusting God is only a stage
in recovery. After we have achieved a certain level of healing and maturity, we may stop depending on God and do things on our own. If we do, we will experience disaster. Trusting God is critical in every stage of recovery.

¹⁷LORD, why have you allowed us to turn
    from your path?
Why have you given us stubborn hearts
    so we no longer fear you?
Return and help us, for we are your servants,
    the tribes that are your special
    possession.
¹⁸How briefly your holy people possessed
    your holy place,
    and now our enemies have destroyed it.
¹⁹Sometimes it seems as though we never
    belonged to you,
    as though we had never been known as
    your people.

CHAPTER 64

¹*Oh, that you would burst from the
    heavens and come down!
How the mountains would quake in
    your presence!
²*As fire causes wood to burn
    and water to boil,
your coming would make the nations
    tremble.
Then your enemies would learn the
    reason for your fame!
³When you came down long ago,
    you did awesome deeds beyond our
    highest expectations.
    And oh, how the mountains quaked!
⁴For since the world began,
    no ear has heard
and no eye has seen a God like you,
    who works for those who wait for him!
⁵You welcome those who gladly do good,
    who follow godly ways.
But you have been very angry with us,
    for we are not godly.
We are constant sinners;
    how can people like us be saved?

⁶We are all infected and impure with sin.
    When we display our righteous deeds,
    they are nothing but filthy rags.
Like autumn leaves, we wither and fall,
    and our sins sweep us away like the
    wind.
⁷Yet no one calls on your name
    or pleads with you for mercy.
Therefore, you have turned away from us
    and turned us over* to our sins.

⁸And yet, O LORD, you are our Father.
    We are the clay, and you are the potter.
    We all are formed by your hand.
⁹Don't be so angry with us, LORD.
    Please don't remember our sins forever.
Look at us, we pray,
    and see that we are all your people.
¹⁰Your holy cities are destroyed.
    Zion is a wilderness;
    yes, Jerusalem is a desolate ruin.
¹¹The holy and beautiful Temple
    where our ancestors praised you
has been burned down,
    and all the things of beauty are destroyed.
¹²After all this, LORD, must you still refuse to
    help us?
Will you continue to be silent and
    punish us?

CHAPTER 65
Judgment and Final Salvation
The LORD says,

"I was ready to respond, but no one asked
    for help.
I was ready to be found, but no one was
    looking for me.
I said, 'Here I am, here I am!'
    to a nation that did not call on my
    name.*

64:1 In the Hebrew text this verse is included in 63:19. 64:2 Verses 64:2-12 are numbered 64:1-11 in Hebrew text.
64:7 As in Greek, Syriac, and Aramaic versions; Hebrew reads *melted us*. 65:1 Or *to a nation that did not bear my name*.

63:17-19 Turning back to God and renewing that relationship is not a push-button experience
that happens instantly. We have allowed our heart to become hardened (here Israel blamed God
for this), and it takes time to soften it again. We can begin this process, but God may not seem
near immediately. We need to move closer to him, and our relationship with him will blossom in
time. God is there; we just have trouble seeing him sometimes.
64:1-4 We see two key elements in this passage that are essential to recovery: faith and patience.
The people of Israel looked at their awesome, powerful, incomparable God. This increased their
faith. Then they patiently waited for him to bring about their deliverance. Such matters do not
happen instantly or according to our timetable. If we persevere in doing our part, God will bring
us victory in due time. If we are faithful and trust God, we will achieve our goal of recovery.
64:5 Isaiah admitted that he and his people were all sinners, and he asked how they could be
saved. The answer includes the first two steps of recovery: admitting they were powerless, that life
was unmanageable, and that only God could restore them. Of course we must go further than
this if we are to recover. We need to give our life to God and let him work in us. He can and will
deliver us from our dependency.

² All day long I opened my arms to a
rebellious people.*
But they follow their own evil paths
and their own crooked schemes.
³ All day long they insult me to my face
by worshiping idols in their sacred
gardens.
They burn incense on pagan altars.
⁴ At night they go out among the graves,
worshiping the dead.
They eat the flesh of pigs
and make stews with other forbidden
foods.
⁵ Yet they say to each other,
'Don't come too close or you will defile
me!
I am holier than you!'
These people are a stench in my
nostrils,
an acrid smell that never goes away.

⁶ "Look, my decree is written out* in front
of me:
I will not stand silent;
I will repay them in full!
Yes, I will repay them—
⁷ both for their own sins
and for those of their ancestors,"
says the LORD.
"For they also burned incense on the
mountains
and insulted me on the hills.
I will pay them back in full!

⁸ "But I will not destroy them all,"
says the LORD.
"For just as good grapes are found among
a cluster of bad ones
(and someone will say, 'Don't throw
them all away—
some of those grapes are good!'),
so I will not destroy all Israel.
For I still have true servants there.

⁹ I will preserve a remnant of the people of
Israel*
and of Judah to possess my land.
Those I choose will inherit it,
and my servants will live there.
¹⁰ The plain of Sharon will again be filled
with flocks
for my people who have searched for me,
and the valley of Achor will be a place
to pasture herds.

¹¹ "But because the rest of you have forsaken
the LORD
and have forgotten his Temple,
and because you have prepared feasts to
honor the god of Fate
and have offered mixed wine to the god
of Destiny,
¹² now I will 'destine' you for the sword.
All of you will bow down before the
executioner.
For when I called, you did not answer.
When I spoke, you did not listen.
You deliberately sinned—before my very
eyes—
and chose to do what you know I
despise."

¹³ Therefore, this is what the Sovereign LORD
says:
"My servants will eat,
but you will starve.
My servants will drink,
but you will be thirsty.
My servants will rejoice,
but you will be sad and ashamed.
¹⁴ My servants will sing for joy,
but you will cry in sorrow and despair.
¹⁵ Your name will be a curse word among my
people,
for the Sovereign LORD will destroy you
and will call his true servants by
another name.

65:1-2 Greek version reads *I was found by people who were not looking for me. / I showed myself to those who were not
asking for me. / All day long I opened my arms to them, / but they were disobedient and rebellious.* Compare Rom 10:20-21.
65:6 Or *their sins are written out;* Hebrew reads *it stands written.* 65:9 Hebrew *remnant of Jacob.* See note on 14:1.

65:3-5 Not all religious behavior is good. The Israelites had turned from the true God; they mixed
idol worship and occult practices with their worship of God. In desperation, we may feel tempted
to turn to Ouija boards, New Age spirituality, or other occult practices. Such practices promise
help, but they really only turn us away from God. To draw close to God, we must pray and study
the Bible, worship with a community of Bible-believing people, and receive encouragement from
godly friends. Following any teachings or practices contrary to what we learn from these sources
is a modern form of idol worship.
65:8-10 In the midst of national judgment, God would deal righteously with each individual,
preserving the remnant who still served him. We need not fear that God will deal with us
abusively or unfairly, basing his judgment on our family or friends. God deals with us as individuals, examining our relationship with him. This gives us hope, especially if we come from or are
presently in a dysfunctional environment.

¹⁶ All who invoke a blessing or take an oath
will do so by the God of truth.
For I will put aside my anger
and forget the evil of earlier days.

¹⁷ "Look! I am creating new heavens and a
new earth,
and no one will even think about the
old ones anymore.
¹⁸ Be glad; rejoice forever in my
creation!
And look! I will create Jerusalem as a
place of happiness.
Her people will be a source of joy.
¹⁹ I will rejoice over Jerusalem
and delight in my people.
And the sound of weeping and crying
will be heard in it no more.

²⁰ "No longer will babies die when only a
few days old.
No longer will adults die before they
have lived a full life.
No longer will people be considered old at
one hundred!
Only the cursed will die that young!
²¹ In those days people will live in the
houses they build
and eat the fruit of their own
vineyards.
²² Unlike the past, invaders will not take
their houses
and confiscate their vineyards.
For my people will live as long as trees,
and my chosen ones will have time to
enjoy their hard-won gains.
²³ They will not work in vain,
and their children will not be doomed
to misfortune.
For they are people blessed by the LORD,
and their children, too, will be
blessed.

²⁴ I will answer them before they even
call to me.
While they are still talking about their
needs,
I will go ahead and answer their
prayers!
²⁵ The wolf and the lamb will feed
together.
The lion will eat hay like a cow.
But the snakes will eat dust.
In those days no one will be hurt or
destroyed on my holy mountain.
I, the LORD, have spoken!"

CHAPTER 66

This is what the LORD says:

"Heaven is my throne,
and the earth is my footstool.
Could you build me a temple as good as
that?
Could you build me such a resting
place?
² My hands have made both heaven and
earth;
they and everything in them are
mine.*
I, the LORD, have spoken!

"I will bless those who have humble and
contrite hearts,
who tremble at my word.
³ But those who choose their own
ways—
delighting in their detestable sins—
will not have their offerings
accepted.
When such people sacrifice a bull,
it is no more acceptable than a human
sacrifice.
When they sacrifice a lamb,

66:2 As in Greek, Latin, and Syriac versions; Hebrew reads *these things are.*

65:17-25 The new heavens and new earth will be wonderful; there will be no pain, suffering, sorrow, or want. God will answer our prayers while we are still speaking them. There will be peace everywhere, even among the animals. While this level of blessing will not be achieved in this earthly lifetime, we can look forward to this in the next life if we are God's children. Recovery from our failures and sins will take away many of our pains here on earth; the coming in glory of God's Kingdom will bring us joy forever.

66:2 God will respond to us when we demonstrate these key recovery principles: the humility to acknowledge our faults, the willingness to turn from and deal with our sins (contrite heart), and a desire to do what is right no matter how difficult (tremble at God's Word). There is a double blessing when we follow these principles: We are able to overcome our addiction and share in God's Kingdom.

66:3-4 God is not fooled by our religious games. If we "play church" and have no desire to follow God but choose to go our own way, we will be judged. God's deliverance comes from honestly seeking his will and honoring and obeying him. The process of recovery will succeed when we learn to really depend on God, not just go through the motions of following him.

it's as though they had sacrificed
a dog!
When they bring an offering of grain,
they might as well offer the blood
of a pig.
When they burn frankincense,
it's as if they had blessed an idol.
⁴I will send them great trouble—
all the things they feared.
For when I called, they did not
answer.
When I spoke, they did not listen.
They deliberately sinned before my very
eyes
and chose to do what they know
I despise."

⁵Hear this message from the LORD,
all you who tremble at his words:
"Your own people hate you
and throw you out for being loyal to
my name.
'Let the LORD be honored!' they scoff.
'Be joyful in him!'
But they will be put to shame.
⁶What is all the commotion in the city?
What is that terrible noise from the
Temple?
It is the voice of the LORD
taking vengeance against his
enemies.

⁷"Before the birth pains even begin,
Jerusalem gives birth to a son.
⁸Who has ever seen anything as strange as
this?
Who ever heard of such a thing?
Has a nation ever been born in a single
day?
Has a country ever come forth in a
mere moment?
But by the time Jerusalem's* birth pains
begin,
her children will be born.
⁹Would I ever bring this nation to the
point of birth
and then not deliver it?" asks the
LORD.
"No! I would never keep this nation from
being born,"
says your God.

¹⁰"Rejoice with Jerusalem!
Be glad with her, all you who love her
and all you who mourn for her.
¹¹Drink deeply of her glory

even as an infant drinks at its mother's
comforting breasts."

¹²This is what the LORD says:
"I will give Jerusalem a river of peace and
prosperity.
The wealth of the nations will flow
to her.
Her children will be nursed at her
breasts,
carried in her arms, and held on her
lap.
¹³I will comfort you there in Jerusalem
as a mother comforts her child."

¹⁴When you see these things, your heart
will rejoice.
You will flourish like the grass!
Everyone will see the LORD's hand of
blessing on his servants—
and his anger against his enemies.
¹⁵See, the LORD is coming with fire,
and his swift chariots roar like a
whirlwind.
He will bring punishment with the
fury of his anger
and the flaming fire of his hot rebuke.
¹⁶The LORD will punish the world by fire
and by his sword.
He will judge the earth,
and many will be killed by him.

¹⁷"Those who 'consecrate' and 'purify'
themselves in a sacred garden with its idol in
the center—feasting on pork and rats and
other detestable meats—will come to a terrible end," says the LORD.

¹⁸"I can see what they are doing, and I
know what they are thinking. So I will
gather all nations and peoples together, and
they will see my glory. ¹⁹I will perform a sign
among them. And I will send those who
survive to be messengers to the nations—
to Tarshish, to the Libyans* and Lydians*
(who are famous as archers), to Tubal and
Greece,* and to all the lands beyond the sea
that have not heard of my fame or seen my
glory. There they will declare my glory to
the nations. ²⁰They will bring the remnant
of your people back from every nation.
They will bring them to my holy mountain
in Jerusalem as an offering to the LORD.
They will ride on horses, in chariots and
wagons, and on mules and camels," says the
LORD. ²¹"And I will appoint some of them to
be my priests and Levites. I, the LORD, have
spoken!

66:8 Hebrew *Zion's*. 66:19a As in some Greek manuscripts, which read *Put* [that is, *Libya*]; Hebrew reads *Pul*.
66:19b Hebrew *Lud*. 66:19c Hebrew *Javan*.

²² "As surely as my new heavens and earth
  will remain,
so will you always be my people,
  with a name that will never disappear,"
  says the LORD.
²³ "All humanity will come to worship me
  from week to week
  and from month to month.
²⁴ And as they go out, they will see

the dead bodies of those who have
  rebelled against me.
For the worms that devour them will
  never die,
  and the fire that burns them will never
  go out.
All who pass by
  will view them with utter
  horror."

66:22-24 Isaiah ends his book with a twofold promise: (1) Those who follow God will live with him forever; their names will "never disappear." (2) Those who oppose God (and his people) will suffer eternal punishment; "all who pass by will view them with utter horror." The choice is clear: We either follow God and experience healing and blessing in this life and the next, or we rebel against God and experience turmoil and pain in this life and the next.

REFLECTIONS ON ISAIAH

insights ABOUT OUR RESPONSIBILITY

We find in **Isaiah 1:2-4** that even though the people of Judah had God—the perfect parent—to lead them, they still turned against him. They were responsible for their sins and the consequences that followed. This should remind us that we often originate our own hang-ups and dependency. Even though some of our problems may be inherited from our parents, we are ultimately held accountable for our actions. Taking responsibility for our problems is an essential part of the recovery process.

The key to renewal and recovery is summed up in **Isaiah 30:12-17**. We can be like Judah, frantically turning to every source but God to try to find instant relief from our problems. Or we can admit our need for God and return to him, trusting him for deliverance. Scripture makes clear which choice will lead to recovery and which will lead to ruin. Which will we choose?

When troubles fill our life, we may be tempted to think that God has turned on us or is powerless to help us. But Isaiah made it clear in **Isaiah 50:1-2** that Judah's problems had been brought on by her own sins, not God's injustice. Most of our problems are brought on by our own sins, and those that aren't are not sent by God to abuse us. We suffer at times because we live in a world corrupted by sin. But we know that the God who controls all nature can certainly care for us if we turn to him.

In **Isaiah 54:1-8** we are told that the Israelites strayed from God and God punished them so they would see the error of their ways and return to him. Then God promised to restore them to himself and bless them. Today we may suffer from our addiction—pain that warns us of the dangers we are courting and gets us back on God's program. When we make a decision to seek recovery, we are also making a decision to follow God and turn from our old lifestyle. By doing so, we are allowing God to work in us and bless us.

In **Isaiah 59:1-14** we find that the people of Israel blamed God for failing to deliver them from their troubles. Sometimes we do the same thing. We get mad at God because he seems too weak to follow through with his promises to us. God isn't too weak, and it isn't that he can't hear us; our sins cut us off from God. If it seems that God isn't with us anymore, we should take a moral inventory to see why he seems so far away. Once we determine where we are out of God's will, we can repent and work to correct it. But until we confess those sins, we will remain cut off from God.

God doesn't tolerate inaction; not helping those who are suffering or oppressed is as bad as adding to their misery. In **Isaiah 59:16** God made it clear that his plan for us includes helping one another. We need to pray for others when they are in trouble. We may need to hold others accountable for their actions. We may also need to humbly intervene to help others deal with the problems they refuse to face.

insights ABOUT THE PERSON OF GOD

In **Isaiah 4:5-6** the prophet used the imagery of the clouds of smoke and fire to remind the people of Judah of God's protection in their desert wanderings (see Exodus 13:21–14:31). God is still there to protect us and rescue us, even though we can't see the pillars of smoke and fire. The Holy Spirit will care for us and guide us through the recovery process if we let him.

God will bless us, but his way takes time. An essential factor in the recovery process is highlighted in **Isaiah 30:18**: We may need to wait! Trying to hurry the process only leads to disaster. "Blessed are those who wait for [God's] help."

In **Isaiah 40:27-31** we find that God knows all about our troubles and understands all our pain. There is nothing he doesn't know. He knows that our recovery program takes time, and he understands when we suffer setbacks in the recovery process. We may get tired of trying to do right and want to give up and return to old habits. If we endure and "trust in the LORD," he will renew our strength so we can continue with our recovery.

We may be afraid to come to God because we think he will hold our sins against us. But in **Isaiah 43:25-28** God promises to blot out our sins when we come to him, forgetting them and cleansing us. Approaching God in humility is the only way to have the shame of our sins removed.

As we travel the path to recovery, it is comforting to know that God is with us, protecting us and bringing us out of our slavery. In **Isaiah 52:12** we are told that God goes ahead of us, showing us the way to a productive, godly life. He protects us from behind, guarding us from being attacked by our dependency or our enemies.

In **Isaiah 59:20-21** the prophet makes it clear that God desires our recovery. God gives us his Holy Spirit to empower us and the Bible, his written Word, to guide us. His desire is to change us and for us to begin a new, healthy pattern to pass on to our children and grandchildren. If we want to know how to turn back from our sins, we need to ask God to show us, and he will!

In **Isaiah 61:8-9** God shows us that he loves justice, so he himself is not going to treat us unjustly. When others have abused or mistreated us, we become afraid that everyone, even God, will treat us in the same manner. But we are assured that God will treat his people justly and reward them for their undue suffering.

When we find that we have fallen away from God, we can be encouraged to seek him again, just as Isaiah was doing on behalf of his people in **Isaiah 63:15-16**. Even if our own parents should disown us because of how far we have fallen, God will never disown us. He will welcome us back to himself and love us (see Luke 15:11-32).

In **Isaiah 63:1-6** God is pictured as a warrior returning victoriously from a battle he fought alone against the enemies of his people. Because of the troubles we encounter and the pain we bear, we sometimes wonder if God is for us or against us. As we see in these verses, God is definitely for us. He is covered with the blood of our, and his, enemies. He loves us so much that he is willing to fight single-handedly to deliver us.

When we consider our sins and failures, we often think that God must be disgusted with us and wants nothing to do with us. We see in **Isaiah 65:1-2**, however, that God stands with open arms, ready to receive us in spite of our moral failures. He welcomes those who have never sought him before, and he longs for those who have rebelled to come back to him.

Isaiah 66:7-9 shows us that God fulfills his promises, just as surely as the birth of a baby cannot be stopped once the pains have begun. When we started the recovery process, we asked God to remove our character defects and help us lead a godly life. But the initial zeal soon wore off, and we struggled and were tempted to give up. Knowing that God's promises are *always* true can give us the courage to continue in the recovery process.

insights ABOUT THE DANGERS OF IDOLATRY

In **Isaiah 44:9-20** we see the utter folly of idolatry. All man-made gods will fail us, whether alcohol, drugs, greed, power, success (workaholism), perfectionism, or false religions with their trinkets and charms. Believing that such things will deliver us is only denying reality. We need to take a moral inventory to see honestly where our trust lies. If it is in anything other than God, we should reevaluate our beliefs and seek God.

Isaiah 55:1-5 reminds us that God alone can satisfy our soul's hunger and thirst. He calls us to stop seeking our ultimate fulfillment in things that cannot satisfy—work, sex, or other obsessions. These things are like junk food; they may temporarily satisfy cravings but have no nutritional value. We spend our time chasing after this "food that does [us] no good" while we should be seeking God and "digesting" his Word, the only real nourishment for our soul.

In **Isaiah 65:11-15** the people of Israel abandoned the true God by dabbling in occult practices. They worshiped pagan gods called Fate and Destiny, hoping that these gods would be able to positively influence the future. Ironically, the suffering and judgment that the people were trying to avoid came down upon them because they sought help from these gods. God is our only reliable source of help in recovery. Any source or program that is contrary to God will leave us in worse shape than before: We will still have our dependency, and we will be further from God than we ever were.

insights ABOUT GOD'S GRACE

What encouragement we find in **Isaiah 48:1-11!** Once we have committed our life to God, we belong to him. As we commit our life to him, he is then committed to bringing spiritual blessings to us. Even our stubborn rebellion and spiritual incompetence do not keep us from God's grace. Even when we mess things up completely and deserve nothing, he will still act on behalf of his own name.

In **Isaiah 51:1-6** when the people of Judah looked to God, they could see how he had brought a whole nation out of one man—Abraham. If God could do this, he could certainly bring them joy, comfort, and deliverance. When we depend on ourself, our hopes for recovery from the complex and confusing issues that entangle us vanish. When we look to God, hope returns. To trust in anything other than God for recovery is to invite failure. Success will come from relying on God alone.

As long as we can hear God's call, it is not too late to follow him. In **Isaiah 55:7-9** we are told that no matter how great our sins, no matter how unlikely it seems that God could forgive us, God is merciful. While people may have given up on us, God hasn't. His ways are higher than our ways. Asking God for forgiveness and guidance is the first step in receiving his help. (For examples of "hopeless sinners" who received God's salvation, see Luke 19:1-10; 23:32-43; Acts 9:1-19.)

Gentiles and eunuchs were excluded from full participation in the worship ceremonies in Israel, and the Jews generally despised them. But in **Isaiah 56:3-8** we see that all are welcomed into God's family: men, women, victims of abuse, people with AIDS, alcoholics, drug abusers, murderers, etc. God loves everyone and wants the whole world to believe in him (see 1 Timothy 2:4). All who believe are welcome in his love.

In **Isaiah 57:15** God does not promise blessings only to those who can clean up their life. His blessings are given to all who are humble enough to admit their sins and weaknesses and who sincerely repent of their sins. If we are willing to do this, we will find that God's arms are open wide to accept us.

The prophet reminds us in **Isaiah 57:17-21** that God is gracious and blesses us beyond what we deserve. Even though we may have led a dysfunctional lifestyle for years, God's healing is still available to us. He still promises to comfort us and help us in the recovery process. Those who persist in their sins and reject the Lord, however, will find no peace in this life or the next.

Isaiah 60:17 is a wonderful verse for a recovery meditation. God wants to exchange all that is worthless in our life with things of value and to exchange our abusive taskmasters with situations dominated by peace and righteousness. In order to receive these blessings, we need to turn the management of our life over to God.

In **Isaiah 64:8-12** the Israelites asked God to not be angry with them but to act graciously toward them. They admitted that they were sinners and that their punishment was deserved. Now they asked God to turn away his wrath and forget their sins. In Isaiah's day there was no final provision for their request; today there is. If we put our trust in Jesus the Messiah, his blood will cleanse us from all our sins so we can spend eternity in God's presence.

insights ABOUT THE MESSIAH AND HIS KINGDOM

In **Isaiah 53:4-6** the prophet described the Messiah who would come and suffer on our behalf. Jesus Christ fulfilled Isaiah's prophecy. He came not because *some* of us needed to be saved from sin but because *all* of us have strayed from God and need salvation. Jesus suffered the punishment for the sins we committed; he completely understands what it feels like to suffer the pain of abuse. We can freely confess our anguish, anger, hatred, shame, and sorrow to Jesus, and he will comfort us.

In **Isaiah 54:11-17** we are given a vision of what lies ahead for those who trust God for forgiveness and deliverance. There will be prosperity, fairness, and justice in God's messianic kingdom. This should encourage us as we struggle with our dependency, the oppression of cruel people, or the injustices that pervade our society. No matter how rough our life gets, we have the hope of eternal security and peace with God.

In **Isaiah 61:1-3** Jesus quoted the prophecy of the Messiah's healing ministry as a description of himself (Luke 4:18-19). Jesus was sent to comfort us and to free us from our addiction. He desires to make something beautiful of the ashes of our life so that we may be filled with joy and praise him.

How much does God want to help us? The Messiah speaks in **Isaiah 61:10** and is overwhelmed with joy at the fact that God has promised future blessings for his people. God does not give to us begrudgingly, as some people we know may do. He wants to bless us! He is elated when people find salvation in him! He wants everyone to trust him and none to suffer eternal judgment (see 1 Timothy 2:4).

JEREMIAH

THE BIG PICTURE

A. JEREMIAH'S SPECIAL APPOINTMENT (1:1-19)
B. THE PROPHET DELIVERS GOD'S MESSAGES (2:1–45:5)
 1. God's Warnings to Judah (2:1–29:32)
 2. The Coming Exile and Restoration (30:1–33:26)
 3. The Fall of Jerusalem (34:1–45:5)
C. GOD'S JUDGMENT ON THE NATIONS (46:1–51:64)
D. A PAINFUL REMINDER OF PAINFUL DAYS (52:1-34)

When thinking about the future, most of us create dreams in which we are needed, loved, successful, and sought after. We certainly do not hope for deep sorrow, thankless service, and persecution, particularly at the hands of the people we care about. When God called him, Jeremiah probably had visions of people listening and responding to the messages the Lord gave him. He may have hoped that his ministry would inspire the recovery of the people of Judah. Jeremiah's hopes for success never became reality.

Jeremiah faithfully warned the Israelites of the sure punishment that would come because of their sins, but the people ignored his passionate pleas. Instead of admitting their sins and failures, they rejected, imprisoned, and abused God's prophet. No one wanted to hear what Jeremiah had to say. King Zedekiah put him into an empty cistern where the prophet sank not only into the mud but also into a mire of disdain. Virtually no one respected Jeremiah or the messages he delivered. The consequences of the people's rejecting Jeremiah and his message were great; Judah fell deeper into sin and eventually was nearly destroyed.

Like Jeremiah, we experience circumstances that are far from ideal. Many of us are suffering for our own mistakes. Jeremiah suffered innocently at the hands of selfish people. We may know how that feels, too. From a human standpoint, Jeremiah was not very successful. But in God's eyes, he was one of the most successful people in all of history. Jeremiah remained faithful despite terrible opposition. We may also experience opposition and suffering. Even so, just as he did for Jeremiah, God will fulfill his purposes for us if we are faithful to him and his program.

THE BOTTOM LINE

PURPOSE: To warn the people of Judah to turn from sin and denial, and to obey God's good plan for them. AUTHOR: The prophet Jeremiah. AUDIENCE: The people of Judah, before and during the Babylonian exile. DATE WRITTEN: The book includes oracles given throughout Jeremiah's ministry (627–586 B.C.). SETTING: The land of Judah, from the initial threats by Assyria and Egypt (627 B.C.) until after Judah's destruction by Babylon (586 B.C.). KEY VERSE: "When I discovered your words, I devoured them. They are my joy and my heart's delight, for I bear your name, O LORD God of Heaven's Armies" (15:16). KEY PEOPLE AND RELATIONSHIPS: Jeremiah with God and with the people of Judah.

RECOVERY THEMES

Faithfulness Overcomes Failure: From our human perspective, Jeremiah was a failure. But from God's point of view, Jeremiah was one of the greatest successes in the Bible. He remained faithful to God and his commands despite the powerful opposition he faced. As we move through the recovery process, we may begin to feel that our suffering has no purpose whatsoever. The obstacles may seem too big to overcome, our weaknesses too much of a liability. When we feel discouraged, we need to remember that God simply calls us to be faithful—to keep going. We don't have to be a raving success. We just need to be faithful in the long haul. God will honor our faithfulness by providing us with the strength we need for the next step.

God's Way May Be Painful: In order to avoid pain, the people of Judah refused to listen to Jeremiah's call for repentance and change in their lives. At times we may be tempted to avoid painful memories or necessary changes, but such avoidance and denial will only retard the recovery process. If we refuse to hear God's message of truth, we will create suffering even greater than the pain we are trying to avoid. We must face the pain now and allow it to lead us to inner healing and righteous living.

God Understands Our Emotions: Jeremiah has often been called the weeping prophet, but he did more than weep—he was bitter, angry, discouraged, depressed, and lonely. We have all experienced those feelings. Jeremiah even complained to God: "I sat alone because your hand was on me. . . . Your help seems as uncertain as a seasonal brook, like a spring that has gone dry" (15:17-18). God's acceptance of Jeremiah's emotions shows us that we are free to bring all of our failures and strong feelings to God. He accepts and understands us just as we are, and he is ready to heal our brokenness and pain if we are honest with him.

Hope despite Disaster: Jeremiah's warnings of God's approaching judgment are punctuated by God's promises of ultimate deliverance. Jeremiah told the people about the "new covenant" that God had for them (see 31:1-40). He said that God loved them and had a wonderful future planned for them, despite their impending doom: "'For I know the plans I have for you,' says the LORD. 'They are plans for good and not for disaster, to give you a future and a hope'" (29:11). When God confronts us with the truth about our sins, he always concludes with a message of hope. He is the God of hope and recovery.

CHAPTER 1

These are the words of Jeremiah son of Hilkiah, one of the priests from the town of Anathoth in the land of Benjamin. ²The LORD first gave messages to Jeremiah during the thirteenth year of the reign of Josiah son of Amon, king of Judah.* ³The LORD's messages continued throughout the reign of King Jehoiakim, Josiah's son, until the eleventh year of the reign of King Zedekiah, another of Josiah's sons. In August* of that eleventh year the people of Jerusalem were taken away as captives.

Jeremiah's Call and First Visions

⁴The LORD gave me this message:

⁵ "I knew you before I formed you in your
    mother's womb.
  Before you were born I set you apart
  and appointed you as my prophet to
    the nations."

⁶"O Sovereign LORD," I said, "I can't speak for you! I'm too young!"

⁷The LORD replied, "Don't say, 'I'm too young,' for you must go wherever I send you and say whatever I tell you. ⁸And don't be

---

1:2 The thirteenth year of Josiah's reign was 627 B.C. 1:3 Hebrew *In the fifth month,* of the ancient Hebrew lunar calendar. A number of events in Jeremiah can be cross-checked with dates in surviving Babylonian records and related accurately to our modern calendar. The fifth month in the eleventh year of Zedekiah's reign occurred within the months of August and September 586 B.C. Also see 52:12 and the note there.

1:1-3 Some of Jeremiah's messages were given to warn the Jews of the impending Babylonian captivity; others were given after Judah had fallen to Babylon. God often warns us of the consequences of our actions, and we would be wise to listen when he does. But we should be grateful that God still loves us and reaches out to help us, even after we have failed.
1:4-5 God probably won't call us to be a prophet like Jeremiah, but he does have a plan for each of us. If we have failed, it is our responsibility to cooperate with God now so we can return to the path he intended for us. Recovery of our life also means the recovery of God's plan for us. We need to seek out God's will and follow it. God will help and encourage us as we do.
1:11-16 God used signs to show Jeremiah that Judah would be judged for its continued idolatry. We also worship idols: Power, wealth, comfort, prestige, possessions, and position are only a few of the idols we build and protect. But our idols fail to bring us peace and satisfaction. Those who worship the true God will find complete and lasting satisfaction. No false god can deliver that.

JEREMIAH

Jeremiah was born into a priestly clan and was called to prophetic ministry when he was just a youth. In spite of his youth, Jeremiah was humble and eager to serve God. Jeremiah's ministry stretched from the thirteenth year of King Josiah's reign until after the destruction of Jerusalem.

Josiah's reign was the last high point in Judah's spiritual history, and Jeremiah was an ally in the king's reforms. After Josiah's death, Judah quickly declined spiritually, causing great sorrow to Jeremiah. During those years, Jeremiah preached against the hypocrisy and corruption of prophets, priests, and government officials alike. He also prophesied that the nation faced sure destruction because of its sins—a message that few believed. The people preferred to believe the false prophets who predicted a rosy future for Judah.

During his years of ministry, Jeremiah suffered intense persecution. He was thrown into a dungeon, beaten, put into stocks, threatened, and almost killed. Extrabiblical tradition says that he was eventually stoned to death. Jeremiah was a man of prayer and deep spirituality, and he faced his trials with courage. Despite the opposition he faced, he remained true to the messages God gave him. He confronted the Jews with their denial and called them to admit their sins and ask God for forgiveness. As God directed him, he also spoke words of comfort to a people facing disaster.

Jeremiah was always honest about how he felt. He is known as the weeping prophet. He never wept for his own suffering, but he shed many tears for his people who sinned repeatedly and would not repent. After Jerusalem was destroyed and the people exiled, Jeremiah wept for the pain and loss his people suffered. At times, Jeremiah openly and honestly complained to God about the work God had given him to do. Yet even in the midst of his "down times," Jeremiah never lost faith in God's power to judge righteously, to reward liberally, and to restore his broken and sinful people.

STRENGTHS AND ACCOMPLISHMENTS:
- Jeremiah was faithful to God's call despite the persecution he suffered.
- He showed great compassion for his people, even though they mistreated him.
- He did not hesitate to tell God exactly what he was feeling.
- He fearlessly confronted the Jews with their sins.

LESSONS FROM HIS LIFE:
- Sin is always accompanied by painful consequences.
- No matter how great our sins, God still loves us and desires recovery for us.
- God is not shocked when we openly share our feelings with him.
- True success is defined by our faithfulness to God's will for our life.

KEY VERSES:
"'For see, today I have made you strong. . . . You will stand against the whole land. . . . They will fight you, but they will fail. For I am with you, and I will take care of you. I, the LORD, have spoken!'" (Jeremiah 1:18-19).

Jeremiah's story is told primarily in the book of Jeremiah. He is also mentioned in 2 Chronicles 35–36; Ezra 1; Daniel 9; and Matthew 2; 16; 27.

---

afraid of the people, for I will be with you and will protect you. I, the LORD, have spoken!" ⁹Then the LORD reached out and touched my mouth and said,

"Look, I have put my words in your mouth!
¹⁰Today I appoint you to stand up
    against nations and kingdoms.
Some you must uproot and tear down,
    destroy and overthrow.
Others you must build up
    and plant."

¹¹Then the LORD said to me, "Look, Jeremiah! What do you see?"

And I replied, "I see a branch from an almond tree."

¹²And the LORD said, "That's right, and it means that I am watching,* and I will certainly carry out all my plans."

¹³Then the LORD spoke to me again and asked, "What do you see now?"

And I replied, "I see a pot of boiling water, spilling from the north."

1:12 The Hebrew word for "watching" *(shoqed)* sounds like the word for "almond tree" *(shaqed)*.

¹⁴"Yes," the LORD said, "for terror from the north will boil out on the people of this land. ¹⁵Listen! I am calling the armies of the kingdoms of the north to come to Jerusalem. I, the LORD, have spoken!

"They will set their thrones
    at the gates of the city.
They will attack its walls
    and all the other towns of Judah.
¹⁶I will pronounce judgment
    on my people for all their evil—
for deserting me and burning incense to
    other gods.
    Yes, they worship idols made with their
    own hands!

¹⁷"Get up and prepare for action.
    Go out and tell them everything I tell
    you to say.
Do not be afraid of them,
    or I will make you look foolish in front
    of them.
¹⁸For see, today I have made you strong
    like a fortified city that cannot be
    captured,
    like an iron pillar or a bronze wall.
You will stand against the whole
    land—
    the kings, officials, priests, and people
    of Judah.
¹⁹They will fight you, but they will fail.
    For I am with you, and I will take care
    of you.
    I, the LORD, have spoken!"

CHAPTER 2
The LORD's Case against His People

The LORD gave me another message. He said, ²"Go and shout this message to Jerusalem. This is what the LORD says:

"I remember how eager you were
    to please me
    as a young bride long ago,
how you loved me and followed me
    even through the barren wilderness.
³In those days Israel was holy to the
    LORD,
    the first of his children.*
All who harmed his people were declared
    guilty,
    and disaster fell on them.
    I, the LORD, have spoken!"

⁴Listen to the word of the LORD, people of Jacob—all you families of Israel! ⁵This is what the LORD says:

"What did your ancestors find wrong
    with me
    that led them to stray so far
    from me?
They worshiped worthless idols,
    only to become worthless themselves.
⁶They did not ask, 'Where is the LORD
    who brought us safely out of Egypt
and led us through the barren
    wilderness—
    a land of deserts and pits,
a land of drought and death,
    where no one lives or even travels?'
⁷"And when I brought you into a fruitful
    land
    to enjoy its bounty and goodness,
you defiled my land and
    corrupted the possession I had
    promised you.
⁸The priests did not ask,
    'Where is the LORD?'
Those who taught my word ignored me,
    the rulers turned against me,
and the prophets spoke in the name
    of Baal,
    wasting their time on worthless idols.

⁹Therefore, I will bring my case against
    you,"
    says the LORD.
"I will even bring charges against your
    children's children
    in the years to come.

¹⁰"Go west and look in the land
    of Cyprus*;
    go east and search through the land
    of Kedar.
Has anyone ever heard of anything
    as strange as this?
¹¹Has any nation ever traded its gods for
    new ones,
    even though they are not gods at all?
Yet my people have exchanged their
    glorious God*
    for worthless idols!
¹²The heavens are shocked at such a thing
    and shrink back in horror and dismay,"
    says the LORD.
¹³"For my people have done two evil
    things:
They have abandoned me—
    the fountain of living water.
And they have dug for themselves cracked
    cisterns
    that can hold no water at all!

2:3 Hebrew *the firstfruits of his harvest.* 2:10 Hebrew *Kittim.* 2:11 Hebrew *their glory.*

The Results of Israel's Sin

14 "Why has Israel become a slave?
      Why has he been carried away as
         plunder?
15 Strong lions have roared against him,
      and the land has been destroyed.
   The towns are now in ruins,
      and no one lives in them anymore.
16 Egyptians, marching from their cities
         of Memphis* and Tahpanhes,
      have destroyed Israel's glory and power.
17 And you have brought this upon
         yourselves
      by rebelling against the LORD your God,
   even though he was leading you on the
         way!

18 "What have you gained by your alliances
         with Egypt
      and your covenants with Assyria?
   What good to you are the streams of the
         Nile*
      or the waters of the Euphrates River?*
19 Your wickedness will bring its own
         punishment.
      Your turning from me will shame you.
   You will see what an evil, bitter thing it is
      to abandon the LORD your God and not
         to fear him.
   I, the Lord, the LORD of Heaven's
         Armies, have spoken!

20 "Long ago I broke the yoke that oppressed
         you
      and tore away the chains of your
         slavery,
   but still you said,
      'I will not serve you.'
   On every hill and under every green tree,
      you have prostituted yourselves by
         bowing down to idols.
21 But I was the one who planted you,
      choosing a vine of the purest
         stock—the very best.
   How did you grow into this corrupt
         wild vine?
22 No amount of soap or lye can make you
         clean.
      I still see the stain of your guilt.
   I, the Sovereign LORD, have spoken!

Israel, an Unfaithful Wife

23 "You say, 'That's not true!
      I haven't worshiped the images of Baal!'
   But how can you say that?
      Go and look in any valley in the land!
   Face the awful sins you have done.
      You are like a restless female camel
         desperately searching for a mate.
24 You are like a wild donkey,
      sniffing the wind at mating time.
   Who can restrain her lust?
      Those who desire her don't need to
         search,
      for she goes running to them!
25 When will you stop running?
      When will you stop panting after other
         gods?
   But you say, 'Save your breath.
      I'm in love with these foreign gods,
      and I can't stop loving them now!'

26 "Israel is like a thief
      who feels shame only when he gets
         caught.
   They, their kings, officials, priests, and
         prophets—
      all are alike in this.
27 To an image carved from a piece of wood
         they say,
      'You are my father.'
   To an idol chiseled from a block of stone
         they say,
      'You are my mother.'
   They turn their backs on me,
      but in times of trouble they cry out
         to me,
      'Come and save us!'
28 But why not call on these gods you have
         made?
      When trouble comes, let them save you
         if they can!
   For you have as many gods
      as there are towns in Judah.
29 Why do you accuse me of doing
         wrong?
      You are the ones who have rebelled,"
   says the LORD.
30 "I have punished your children,
      but they did not respond to my
         discipline.

2:16 Hebrew *Noph*. 2:18a Hebrew *of Shihor*, a branch of the Nile River. 2:18b Hebrew *the river?*

2:26-27 So often we feel guilty only if we get caught. That is why hitting bottom can be good for us, since failure helps us understand and admit our true condition. Feeling the shame, seeing our life being wasted—these show us our need for God. What can follow, if we turn to him, is the wonderful joy of knowing there is still hope for us. We can begin this process by admitting our sins to God, asking for his forgiveness, and looking to him for the help we need.

You yourselves have killed your prophets
    as a lion kills its prey.

[31] "O my people, listen to the words of the
    LORD!
  Have I been like a desert to Israel?
  Have I been to them a land of darkness?
  Why then do my people say, 'At last we
    are free from God!
  We don't need him anymore!'
[32] Does a young woman forget her jewelry,
    or a bride her wedding dress?
  Yet for years on end
    my people have forgotten me.

[33] "How you plot and scheme to win your
    lovers.
  Even an experienced prostitute could
    learn from you!
[34] Your clothing is stained with the blood
    of the innocent and the poor,
  though you didn't catch them breaking
    into your houses!
[35] And yet you say,
  'I have done nothing wrong.
    Surely God isn't angry with me!'
  But now I will punish you severely
    because you claim you have not sinned.
[36] First here, then there—
    you flit from one ally to another asking
    for help.
  But your new friends in Egypt will let you
    down,
    just as Assyria did before.
[37] In despair, you will be led into exile
    with your hands on your heads,
  for the LORD has rejected the nations you
    trust.
    They will not help you at all.

CHAPTER 3

[1] "If a man divorces a woman
    and she goes and marries someone else,
  he will not take her back again,
    for that would surely corrupt the land.
  But you have prostituted yourself with
    many lovers,

so why are you trying to come back
    to me?"
  says the LORD.
[2] "Look at the shrines on every hilltop.
  Is there any place you have not been
    defiled
    by your adultery with other gods?
  You sit like a prostitute beside the road
    waiting for a customer.
  You sit alone like a nomad in the desert.
  You have polluted the land with your
    prostitution
    and your wickedness.
[3] That's why even the spring rains have
    failed.
  For you are a brazen prostitute and
    completely shameless.
[4] Yet you say to me,
  'Father, you have been my guide since
    my youth.
[5] Surely you won't be angry forever!
  Surely you can forget about it!'
  So you talk,
    but you keep on doing all the evil you
    can."

Judah Follows Israel's Example

[6] During the reign of King Josiah, the LORD said to me, "Have you seen what fickle Israel has done? Like a wife who commits adultery, Israel has worshiped other gods on every hill and under every green tree. [7] I thought, 'After she has done all this, she will return to me.' But she did not return, and her faithless sister Judah saw this. [8] She saw* that I divorced faithless Israel because of her adultery. But that treacherous sister Judah had no fear, and now she, too, has left me and given herself to prostitution. [9] Israel treated it all so lightly—she thought nothing of committing adultery by worshiping idols made of wood and stone. So now the land has been polluted. [10] But despite all this, her faithless sister Judah has never sincerely returned to me. She has only pretended to be sorry. I, the LORD, have spoken!"

3:8 As in Dead Sea Scrolls, one Greek manuscript, and Syriac version; Masoretic Text reads *I saw.*

2:34-35 The worst result of our loss of control is the hurt we bring to the innocent. Recovery can free us of the shame we feel over the pain we have caused people who deserved better from us. Saying no to sin is difficult but liberating. We must accept God's forgiveness and make restitution for our mistakes. In God's Kingdom no one needs to wallow in remorse over sins that have already been forgiven. God forgives us when we sincerely repent and ask for forgiveness. We can expect God's judgment, however, if we continue living in denial.

3:6-9 God likens our worship of other gods to prostitution. When we worship our dependency, money, success, power, or prestige, we act like a beloved wife who runs to others to satisfy her desire for pleasure instead of remaining faithful to her loving husband. We all know that these false gods can never really satisfy. We need to turn our life over to the only true God, who will love and care for us like a faithful and loving husband.

Hope for Wayward Israel

[11]Then the LORD said to me, "Even faithless Israel is less guilty than treacherous Judah! [12]Therefore, go and give this message to Israel.* This is what the LORD says:

"O Israel, my faithless people,
    come home to me again,
for I am merciful.
    I will not be angry with you forever.
[13]Only acknowledge your guilt.
    Admit that you rebelled against the
        LORD your God
and committed adultery against him
    by worshiping idols under every green
        tree.
Confess that you refused to listen to my
    voice.
    I, the LORD, have spoken!

[14]"Return home, you wayward children,"
    says the LORD,
    "for I am your master.
I will bring you back to the land of
        Israel*—
    one from this town and two from that
        family—
    from wherever you are scattered.
[15]And I will give you shepherds after my
        own heart,
    who will guide you with knowledge and
        understanding.

[16]"And when your land is once more filled with people," says the LORD, "you will no longer wish for 'the good old days' when you possessed the Ark of the LORD's Covenant. You will not miss those days or even remember them, and there will be no need to rebuild the Ark. [17]In that day Jerusalem will be known as 'The Throne of the LORD.' All nations will come there to honor the LORD. They will no longer stubbornly follow their own evil desires. [18]In those days the people of Judah and Israel will return together from exile in the north. They will return to the land I gave your ancestors as an inheritance forever.

[19]"I thought to myself,
    'I would love to treat you as my own
        children!'
I wanted nothing more than to give you
        this beautiful land—
    the finest possession in the world.
I looked forward to your calling me
        'Father,'
    and I wanted you never to turn from
        me.
[20]But you have been unfaithful to me, you
        people of Israel!
    You have been like a faithless wife who
        leaves her husband.
    I, the LORD, have spoken."

[21]Voices are heard high on the windswept
        mountains,
    the weeping and pleading of Israel's
        people.
For they have chosen crooked paths
    and have forgotten the LORD
        their God.

[22]"My wayward children," says the LORD,
    "come back to me, and I will heal your
        wayward hearts."

"Yes, we're coming," the people reply,
    "for you are the LORD our God.
[23]Our worship of idols on the hills
    and our religious orgies on the
        mountains
    are a delusion.
Only in the LORD our God
    will Israel ever find salvation.
[24]From childhood we have watched
    as everything our ancestors worked
        for—
their flocks and herds, their sons and
        daughters—

3:12 Hebrew *toward the north.* 3:14 Hebrew *to Zion.*

3:16-17 Sometimes we stubbornly refuse to change because we are afraid we will miss the good old days, old acquaintances, even old hangouts. But when we turn our life over to God, his love will so radically change our heart that we will miss these things less and less over time. No one has ever been disappointed by turning totally to God. We may lose some of the old things and relationships, but we will gain so much more than we lost!

3:21 We may look for healing in many different places. Many people offer solutions to help us escape our guilt feelings, but many of these solutions lead only to deeper denial. The only sure way to remove guilt is to ask God to forgive our sins and believe that he will. If we don't turn to God for help, we will be left to wander on our own "crooked paths."

3:22 God's people had rebelled time after time, yet he still pleaded with them to come back to him. God never gives up on those he loves, and he will not give up on us. He will continue to seek us out. As we wander from him and try to take back control of our life, he lovingly pleads for us to return to him. We must listen to him and respond with complete obedience.

was squandered on a delusion.
²⁵ Let us now lie down in shame
  and cover ourselves with dishonor,
for we and our ancestors have sinned
  against the LORD our God.
From our childhood to this day
  we have never obeyed him."

CHAPTER 4
¹ "O Israel," says the LORD,
  "if you wanted to return to me, you
    could.
You could throw away your detestable
    idols
  and stray away no more.
² Then when you swear by my name,
    saying,
  'As surely as the LORD lives,'
you could do so
  with truth, justice, and righteousness.
Then you would be a blessing to the
    nations of the world,
  and all people would come and praise
    my name."

Coming Judgment against Judah
³ This is what the LORD says to the people of
Judah and Jerusalem:

"Plow up the hard ground of your hearts!
  Do not waste your good seed among
    thorns.
⁴ O people of Judah and Jerusalem,
  surrender your pride and power.
Change your hearts before the LORD,*
  or my anger will burn like an
    unquenchable fire
because of all your sins.

⁵ "Shout to Judah, and broadcast to
    Jerusalem!
  Tell them to sound the alarm
    throughout the land:
'Run for your lives!
  Flee to the fortified cities!'
⁶ Raise a signal flag as a warning for
    Jerusalem*:

'Flee now! Do not delay!'
For I am bringing terrible destruction
  upon you
  from the north."

⁷ A lion stalks from its den,
  a destroyer of nations.
It has left its lair and is headed your
    way.
  It's going to devastate your land!
Your towns will lie in ruins,
  with no one living in them
    anymore.
⁸ So put on clothes of mourning
  and weep with broken hearts,
for the fierce anger of the LORD
  is still upon us.

⁹ "In that day," says the LORD,
  "the king and the officials will tremble
    in fear.
The priests will be struck with horror,
  and the prophets will be appalled."

¹⁰ Then I said, "O Sovereign LORD,
  the people have been deceived by what
    you said,
for you promised peace for Jerusalem.
  But the sword is held at their throats!"

¹¹ The time is coming when the LORD will
    say
  to the people of Jerusalem,
"My dear people, a burning wind is
  blowing in from the desert,
and it's not a gentle breeze useful for
    winnowing grain.
¹² It is a roaring blast sent by me!
  Now I will pronounce your
    destruction!"

¹³ Our enemy rushes down on us like storm
    clouds!
  His chariots are like whirlwinds.
His horses are swifter than eagles.
  How terrible it will be, for we are
    doomed!
¹⁴ O Jerusalem, cleanse your heart
  that you may be saved.

4:4 Hebrew *Circumcise yourselves to the LORD, and take away the foreskins of your heart.* 4:6 Hebrew *Zion.*

4:1-2 God had always planned that his people would be living proof of his power and goodness. He wanted others to believe in him because of the blessings that Israel received through a healthy relationship with God. God also wants to use us as testimonies to his loving power. When we turn our life over to God, our increasing goodness and honesty will testify to the kind of life that is possible through God's power. What an honor for us to be used by our Creator to cause others to praise him! Our success in recovery will bring hope and encouragement to others as they struggle with their dependency.
4:14 It isn't easy to rid our mind of evil or destructive thoughts, especially if we have spent much of our life thinking this way. When we turn to God, spend time with him, and ask him to lead us,

How long will you harbor
  your evil thoughts?
[15] Your destruction has been announced
  from Dan and the hill country of
  Ephraim.

[16] "Warn the surrounding nations
  and announce this to Jerusalem:
The enemy is coming from a distant land,
  raising a battle cry against the towns of
  Judah.
[17] They surround Jerusalem like watchmen
  around a field,
  for my people have rebelled against
  me,"
  says the LORD.
[18] "Your own actions have brought this
  upon you.
  This punishment is bitter, piercing you
  to the heart!"

Jeremiah Weeps for His People

[19] My heart, my heart—I writhe in pain!
  My heart pounds within me! I cannot
  be still.
For I have heard the blast of enemy
  trumpets
  and the roar of their battle cries.
[20] Waves of destruction roll over the land,
  until it lies in complete desolation.
Suddenly my tents are destroyed;
  in a moment my shelters are crushed.
[21] How long must I see the battle flags
  and hear the trumpets of war?

[22] "My people are foolish
  and do not know me," says the LORD.
"They are stupid children
  who have no understanding.
They are clever enough at doing wrong,
  but they have no idea how to do right!"

Jeremiah's Vision of Coming Disaster

[23] I looked at the earth, and it was empty
  and formless.

4:31 Hebrew *the daughter of Zion.*

  I looked at the heavens, and there was
    no light.
[24] I looked at the mountains and hills,
  and they trembled and shook.
[25] I looked, and all the people were gone.
  All the birds of the sky had flown away.
[26] I looked, and the fertile fields had become
  a wilderness.
The towns lay in ruins,
  crushed by the LORD's fierce anger.

[27] This is what the LORD says:
"The whole land will be ruined,
  but I will not destroy it completely.
[28] The earth will mourn
  and the heavens will be draped
  in black
because of my decree against my people.
  I have made up my mind and will not
  change it."

[29] At the noise of charioteers and archers,
  the people flee in terror.
They hide in the bushes
  and run for the mountains.
All the towns have been abandoned—
  not a person remains!
[30] What are you doing,
  you who have been plundered?
Why do you dress up in beautiful
  clothing
  and put on gold jewelry?
Why do you brighten your eyes with
  mascara?
  Your primping will do you no good!
The allies who were your lovers
  despise you and seek to kill you.

[31] I hear a cry, like that of a woman
  in labor,
  the groans of a woman giving birth to
  her first child.
It is beautiful Jerusalem*
  gasping for breath and crying out,
  "Help! I'm being murdered!"

---

he will reveal his will for us and begin to reshape our thought patterns. As we continue to study and meditate on God's Word, improving our conscious contacts with our loving God, his thoughts will become our own. He will replace our evil thoughts with good and healthy ones. Developing healthy thought patterns is an essential part of the recovery process.

4:29-30 As they faced imminent destruction, the people of Israel made external changes that they hoped would bring deliverance. We sometimes do the same thing, making changes on the outside to somehow survive the next onslaught from our dependency. We try to look good on the outside to cover the terrible pain we feel inside. Covering up our sins and pain only deepens our denial. Recovery begins when we display our broken hearts to God and admit our sins. God will help us make changes on the inside. When we are concerned about what we look like to others, we can't deal with the real problems hidden beneath the surface.

CHAPTER 5

The Sins of Judah

¹ "Run up and down every street in
    Jerusalem," says the LORD.
    "Look high and low; search throughout
        the city!
If you can find even one just and honest
        person,
    I will not destroy the city.
² But even when they are under oath,
    saying, 'As surely as the LORD lives,'
    they are still telling lies!"

³ LORD, you are searching for honesty.
    You struck your people,
        but they paid no attention.
    You crushed them,
        but they refused to be corrected.
    They are determined, with faces set like
        stone;
        they have refused to repent.

⁴ Then I said, "But what can we expect from
        the poor?
    They are ignorant.
    They don't know the ways of the LORD.
    They don't understand God's laws.
⁵ So I will go and speak to their leaders.
    Surely they know the ways of the LORD
    and understand God's laws."
But the leaders, too, as one man,
    had thrown off God's yoke
    and broken his chains.
⁶ So now a lion from the forest will attack
        them;
    a wolf from the desert will pounce on
        them.
A leopard will lurk near their towns,
    tearing apart any who dare to venture
        out.
For their rebellion is great,
    and their sins are many.

⁷ "How can I pardon you?
    For even your children have turned
        from me.
They have sworn by gods that are not
        gods at all!
I fed my people until they were full.
But they thanked me by committing
        adultery
    and lining up at the brothels.

⁸ They are well-fed, lusty stallions,
    each neighing for his neighbor's wife.
⁹ Should I not punish them for this?" says
        the LORD.
    "Should I not avenge myself against
        such a nation?

¹⁰ "Go down the rows of the vineyards and
        destroy the grapevines,
    leaving a scattered few alive.
Strip the branches from the vines,
    for these people do not belong to the
        LORD.
¹¹ The people of Israel and Judah
    are full of treachery against me,"
    says the LORD.
¹² "They have lied about the LORD
    and said, 'He won't bother us!
No disasters will come upon us.
    There will be no war or famine.
¹³ God's prophets are all windbags
    who don't really speak for him.
    Let their predictions of disaster fall on
        themselves!'"

¹⁴ Therefore, this is what the LORD God of
Heaven's Armies says:

"Because the people are talking like this,
    my messages will flame out of your
        mouth
    and burn the people like kindling
        wood.
¹⁵ O Israel, I will bring a distant nation
        against you,"
    says the LORD.
"It is a mighty nation,
    an ancient nation,
a people whose language you do not
        know,
    whose speech you cannot understand.
¹⁶ Their weapons are deadly;
    their warriors are mighty.
¹⁷ They will devour the food of your
        harvest;
    they will devour your sons and
        daughters.
They will devour your flocks and herds;
    they will devour your grapes and figs.
And they will destroy your fortified
        towns,
    which you think are so safe.

5:1 It is a great honor to be called just and honest. If one person had been working at being
consistently honest and just, the course of Jerusalem's future could have been changed. We can
change history today. Our honesty can have a profound impact on the people around us and on
generations to come. Failure to deal honestly with our problems will hurt those we love now as
well as many in the future. It is up to us to take responsibility for our failures, admitting them to
God and receiving the help we need for recovery.

¹⁸"Yet even in those days I will not blot you out completely," says the LORD. ¹⁹"And when your people ask, 'Why did the LORD our God do all this to us?' you must reply, 'You rejected him and gave yourselves to foreign gods in your own land. Now you will serve foreigners in a land that is not your own.'

A Warning for God's People

²⁰"Make this announcement to Israel,*
and say this to Judah:
²¹Listen, you foolish and senseless
people,
with eyes that do not see
and ears that do not hear.
²²Have you no respect for me?
Why don't you tremble in my
presence?
I, the LORD, define the ocean's sandy
shoreline
as an everlasting boundary that the
waters cannot cross.
The waves may toss and roar,
but they can never pass the boundaries
I set.
²³But my people have stubborn and
rebellious hearts.
They have turned away and abandoned
me.
²⁴They do not say from the heart,
'Let us live in awe of the LORD
our God,
for he gives us rain each spring and fall,
assuring us of a harvest when the time
is right.'
²⁵Your wickedness has deprived you of these
wonderful blessings.
Your sin has robbed you of all these
good things.

²⁶"Among my people are wicked men
who lie in wait for victims like a hunter
hiding in a blind.
They continually set traps
to catch people.
²⁷Like a cage filled with birds,
their homes are filled with evil plots.
And now they are great and rich.
²⁸They are fat and sleek,
and there is no limit to their wicked
deeds.
They refuse to provide justice to orphans
and deny the rights of the poor.
²⁹Should I not punish them for this?" says
the LORD.
"Should I not avenge myself against
such a nation?
³⁰A horrible and shocking thing
has happened in this land—
³¹the prophets give false prophecies,
and the priests rule with an iron hand.
Worse yet, my people like it that way!
But what will you do when the end
comes?

CHAPTER 6
Jerusalem's Last Warning

¹"Run for your lives, you people of
Benjamin!
Get out of Jerusalem!
Sound the alarm in Tekoa!
Send up a signal at Beth-hakkerem!
A powerful army is coming from the
north,
coming with disaster and destruction.
²O Jerusalem,* you are my beautiful and
delicate daughter—
but I will destroy you!
³Enemies will surround you, like shepherds
camped around the city.

5:20 Hebrew *to the house of Jacob*. The names "Jacob" and "Israel" are often interchanged throughout the Old Testament, referring sometimes to the individual patriarch and sometimes to the nation. 6:2 Hebrew *Daughter of Zion*.

5:19 Everyone who rejects God will become a slave to something else. By rebelling against God's power and control, we become controlled by a destructive dependency such as drugs, alcohol, immoral sex, or other manifestations of appetites out of control. The only way to escape from these types of slavery is to allow God to take control of our life. He is the only truly kind and loving master. Trust and obedience to his will for us is always the best program for recovery.
5:21-22 A proper reverence for God and his awesome power inspires us to trust God and obey him. Such an attitude protects us from the dependencies and problems that could devour us. Disregard for God sets us up for failure as we grapple with life's difficulties with our own limited resources and understanding. Reverence for God leads to faith, obedience, honesty, and love— all important aspects of a solid recovery program.
6:1 Sometimes recovery is maintained by the one act all of us can do—run from sin! God warns us to flee temptation, to run before we have to experience the dreadful consequences of being out of control. The next time we find ourself on shaky ground, tempted by sin, perhaps we should run first, then analyze our situation later.

Each chooses a place for his troops to
devour.
[4] They shout, 'Prepare for battle!
Attack at noon!'
'No, it's too late; the day is fading,
and the evening shadows are falling.'
[5] 'Well then, let's attack at night
and destroy her palaces!'"

[6] This is what the LORD of Heaven's Armies
says:
"Cut down the trees for battering rams.
Build siege ramps against the walls
of Jerusalem.
This is the city to be punished,
for she is wicked through and through.
[7] She spouts evil like a fountain.
Her streets echo with the sounds of
violence and destruction.
I always see her sickness and sores.
[8] Listen to this warning, Jerusalem,
or I will turn from you in disgust.
Listen, or I will turn you into a heap
of ruins,
a land where no one lives."

[9] This is what the LORD of Heaven's Armies
says:
"Even the few who remain in Israel
will be picked over again,
as when a harvester checks each vine
a second time
to pick the grapes that were missed."

Judah's Constant Rebellion

[10] To whom can I give warning?
Who will listen when I speak?
Their ears are closed,
and they cannot hear.
They scorn the word of the LORD.
They don't want to listen at all.
[11] So now I am filled with the LORD's fury.
Yes, I am tired of holding it in!

"I will pour out my fury on children
playing in the streets
and on gatherings of young men,
on husbands and wives
and on those who are old and gray.
[12] Their homes will be turned over to their
enemies,

as will their fields and their wives.
For I will raise my powerful fist
against the people of this land,"
says the LORD.
[13] "From the least to the greatest,
their lives are ruled by greed.
From prophets to priests,
they are all frauds.
[14] They offer superficial treatments
for my people's mortal wound.
They give assurances of peace
when there is no peace.
[15] Are they ashamed of their disgusting
actions?
Not at all—they don't even know how
to blush!
Therefore, they will lie among the
slaughtered.
They will be brought down when I
punish them,"
says the LORD.

Judah Rejects the LORD's Way

[16] This is what the LORD says:
"Stop at the crossroads and look around.
Ask for the old, godly way, and walk
in it.
Travel its path, and you will find rest for
your souls.
But you reply, 'No, that's not the road
we want!'
[17] I posted watchmen over you who said,
'Listen for the sound of the alarm.'
But you replied,
'No! We won't pay attention!'

[18] "Therefore, listen to this, all you nations.
Take note of my people's situation.
[19] Listen, all the earth!
I will bring disaster on my people.
It is the fruit of their own schemes,
because they refuse to listen to me.
They have rejected my word.
[20] There's no use offering me sweet
frankincense from Sheba.
Keep your fragrant calamus imported
from distant lands!
I will not accept your burnt offerings.
Your sacrifices have no pleasing aroma
for me."

6:8-10 God always warns us many times before finally allowing us to experience the full consequences of our destructive behavior. He does all he can to get our attention before we have to
face his discipline and significant suffering. If we don't listen, however, we will eventually hit
bottom. Hopefully, through such experiences we discover how helpless we are without God,
turn our life over to him, and submit to his will for us. Even God's punishment is meant to lead us
back to himself. We would be wise to act before we have to deal with the terrible consequences
of chronic sin and dependency.

²¹ Therefore, this is what the LORD says:
  "I will put obstacles in my people's
    path.
Fathers and sons will both fall over them.
  Neighbors and friends will die
    together."

An Invasion from the North

²² This is what the LORD says:
  "Look! A great army coming from the
    north!
  A great nation is rising against you from
    far-off lands.
²³ They are armed with bows and spears.
  They are cruel and show no mercy.
They sound like a roaring sea
  as they ride forward on horses.
They are coming in battle formation,
  planning to destroy you, beautiful
    Jerusalem.*"

²⁴ We have heard reports about the
    enemy,
  and we wring our hands in fright.
Pangs of anguish have gripped us,
  like those of a woman in labor.
²⁵ Don't go out to the fields!
  Don't travel on the roads!
The enemy's sword is everywhere
  and terrorizes us at every turn!
²⁶ Oh, my people, dress yourselves in burlap
    and sit among the ashes.
Mourn and weep bitterly, as for the loss of
    an only son.
  For suddenly the destroying armies will
    be upon you!

²⁷ "Jeremiah, I have made you a tester of
    metals,*
  that you may determine the quality of
    my people.
²⁸ They are the worst kind of rebel,
  full of slander.
They are as hard as bronze and iron,
  and they lead others into corruption.

²⁹ The bellows fiercely fan the flames
    to burn out the corruption.
But it does not purify them,
  for the wickedness remains.
³⁰ I will label them 'Rejected Silver,'
  for I, the LORD, am discarding
    them."

CHAPTER 7
Jeremiah Speaks at the Temple

The LORD gave another message to Jeremiah. He said, ² "Go to the entrance of the LORD's Temple, and give this message to the people: 'O Judah, listen to this message from the LORD! Listen to it, all of you who worship here! ³ This is what the LORD of Heaven's Armies, the God of Israel, says:

"'Even now, if you quit your evil ways, I will let you stay in your own land. ⁴ But don't be fooled by those who promise you safety simply because the LORD's Temple is here. They chant, "The LORD's Temple is here! The LORD's Temple is here!" ⁵ But I will be merciful only if you stop your evil thoughts and deeds and start treating each other with justice; ⁶ only if you stop exploiting foreigners, orphans, and widows; only if you stop your murdering; and only if you stop harming yourselves by worshiping idols. ⁷ Then I will let you stay in this land that I gave to your ancestors to keep forever.

⁸ "'Don't be fooled into thinking that you will never suffer because the Temple is here. It's a lie! ⁹ Do you really think you can steal, murder, commit adultery, lie, and burn incense to Baal and all those other new gods of yours, ¹⁰ and then come here and stand before me in my Temple and chant, "We are safe!"—only to go right back to all those evils again? ¹¹ Don't you yourselves admit that this Temple, which bears my name, has become a den of thieves? Surely I see all the evil going on there. I, the LORD, have spoken!

6:23 Hebrew *daughter of Zion*.   **6:27** As in Greek version; Hebrew reads *a tester of my people a fortress*.

6:26 The grief from the loss of an only son is staggering. Our sorrow over our misguided life should cause us the same intensity of grief. These are words of warning; we have the opportunity today to make good choices that will lead us away from the losses we are now headed for. If we follow God's program, our life can become worthwhile again.

7:8-11 Many of God's people believed that God's presence in the Temple would protect them from enemy attack, regardless of whether or not they obeyed God's laws. But the people of Judah were not excused from obedience, and neither are we. We may claim to be exceptions to the rule: "I have special needs"; "I have a special plan"; "I understand this; others don't." This thinking, however, only supports our denial, allowing us to falsely believe that we are not accountable to God's plans, rules, and judgments. Such attitudes are destructive. God controls our world, and his plan for healthy living in his Word is the only program worth following.

[12] 'Go now to the place at Shiloh where I once put the Tabernacle that bore my name. See what I did there because of all the wickedness of my people, the Israelites. [13]While you were doing these wicked things, says the LORD, I spoke to you about it repeatedly, but you would not listen. I called out to you, but you refused to answer. [14]So just as I destroyed Shiloh, I will now destroy this Temple that bears my name, this Temple that you trust in for help, this place that I gave to you and your ancestors. [15]And I will send you out of my sight into exile, just as I did your relatives, the people of Israel.*'

Judah's Persistent Idolatry

[16]"Pray no more for these people, Jeremiah. Do not weep or pray for them, and don't beg me to help them, for I will not listen to you. [17]Don't you see what they are doing throughout the towns of Judah and in the streets of Jerusalem? [18]No wonder I am so angry! Watch how the children gather wood and the fathers build sacrificial fires. See how the women knead dough and make cakes to offer to the Queen of Heaven. And they pour out liquid offerings to their other idol gods! [19]Am I the one they are hurting?" asks the LORD. "Most of all, they hurt themselves, to their own shame."

[20]So this is what the Sovereign LORD says: "I will pour out my terrible fury on this place. Its people, animals, trees, and crops will be consumed by the unquenchable fire of my anger."

[21]This is what the LORD of Heaven's Armies, the God of Israel, says: "Take your burnt offerings and your other sacrifices and eat them yourselves! [22]When I led your ancestors out of Egypt, it was not burnt offerings and sacrifices I wanted from them. [23]This is what I told them: 'Obey me, and I will be your God, and you will be my people. Do everything as I say, and all will be well!'

[24]"But my people would not listen to me. They kept doing whatever they wanted, following the stubborn desires of their evil hearts. They went backward instead of forward. [25]From the day your ancestors left Egypt until now, I have continued to send my servants, the prophets—day in and day out. [26]But my people have not listened to me or even tried to hear. They have been stubborn and sinful—even worse than their ancestors.

[27]"Tell them all this, but do not expect them to listen. Shout out your warnings, but do not expect them to respond. [28]Say to them, 'This is the nation whose people will not obey the LORD their God and who refuse to be taught. Truth has vanished from among them; it is no longer heard on their lips. [29]Shave your head in mourning, and weep alone on the mountains. For the LORD has rejected and forsaken this generation that has provoked his fury.'

The Valley of Slaughter

[30]"The people of Judah have sinned before my very eyes," says the LORD. "They have set up their abominable idols right in the Temple that bears my name, defiling it. [31]They have built pagan shrines at Topheth, the garbage dump in the valley of Ben-Hinnom, and there they burn their sons and daughters in the fire. I have never commanded such a horrible deed; it never even crossed my mind to command such a thing! [32]So beware, for the time is coming," says the LORD, "when that garbage dump will no longer be called Topheth or the valley of Ben-Hinnom, but the Valley of Slaughter. They will bury the bodies in Topheth until there is no more room for them. [33]The bodies of my people will be food for the vultures and wild ani-

7:15 Hebrew *of Ephraim,* referring to the northern kingdom of Israel.

7:12 By examining the lives of those who have gone before us, we can see the blessings experienced by those who obeyed God and the terrible consequences suffered by those who rebelled against him. Greed, denial, and pursuit of pleasure have destroyed the lives of many of our ancestors. But if we are willing to learn from those before us, we can make the changes we need to avoid their terrible fate.

7:30-34 The depth of Judah's sin is seen in their practice of child sacrifice, a heinous act that God had clearly forbidden. How could God's people have grown so distant from his plan for them? How are we lured so far from God's plan for us? We need to take a regular moral inventory to detect the sins and denial in our own life. When we don't, one sin leads to another. As we continue to sin, we become blind to them, and our sins grow ever greater. When we take an honest moral inventory regularly, we can make the changes needed to root out our sin before it destroys us.

mals, and no one will be left to scare them away. [34]I will put an end to the happy singing and laughter in the streets of Jerusalem. The joyful voices of bridegrooms and brides will no longer be heard in the towns of Judah. The land will lie in complete desolation.

CHAPTER 8

"In that day," says the LORD, "the enemy will break open the graves of the kings and officials of Judah, and the graves of the priests, prophets, and common people of Jerusalem. [2]They will spread out their bones on the ground before the sun, moon, and stars—the gods my people have loved, served, and worshiped. Their bones will not be gathered up again or buried but will be scattered on the ground like manure. [3]And the people of this evil nation who survive will wish to die rather than live where I will send them. I, the LORD of Heaven's Armies, have spoken!

Deception by False Prophets

[4]"Jeremiah, say to the people, 'This is what the LORD says:

"'When people fall down, don't they get up again?
    When they discover they're on the wrong road, don't they turn back?
[5]Then why do these people stay on their self-destructive path?
    Why do the people of Jerusalem refuse to turn back?
They cling tightly to their lies
    and will not turn around.
[6]I listen to their conversations
    and don't hear a word of truth.
Is anyone sorry for doing wrong?
    Does anyone say, "What a terrible thing I have done"?
No! All are running down the path of sin
    as swiftly as a horse galloping into battle!

[7]Even the stork that flies across the sky
    knows the time of her migration,
as do the turtledove, the swallow, and the crane.*
    They all return at the proper time each year.
But not my people!
    They do not know the LORD's laws.

[8]"'How can you say, "We are wise because we have the word of the LORD,"
    when your teachers have twisted it by writing lies?
[9]These wise teachers will fall
    into the trap of their own foolishness,
for they have rejected the word of the LORD.
    Are they so wise after all?
[10]I will give their wives to others
    and their farms to strangers.
From the least to the greatest,
    their lives are ruled by greed.
Yes, even my prophets and priests are like that.
    They are all frauds.
[11]They offer superficial treatments
    for my people's mortal wound.
They give assurances of peace
    when there is no peace.
[12]Are they ashamed of these disgusting actions?
    Not at all—they don't even know how to blush!
Therefore, they will lie among the slaughtered.
    They will be brought down when I punish them,
    says the LORD.
[13]I will surely consume them.
    There will be no more harvests of figs and grapes.
Their fruit trees will all die.
    Whatever I gave them will soon be gone.
I, the LORD, have spoken!'

8:7 The identification of some of these birds is uncertain.

8:7 One of the reasons so many of us fall prey to addictive behaviors is that we don't follow God's principles for healthy living. Another reason is that we foolishly seek truth and meaning apart from God. Not finding it, we fill the void with whatever is most convenient. Even the animals show more wisdom than we do as they follow their God-given instincts for survival. We would be wise to follow their lead.

8:8-9 People who lead others astray will face severe judgment from God. People in recovery are often told that there are quick, easy methods for overcoming an addiction. We are also told by many that recovery requires no commitment to God. Those who claim these things are trying to sell us something. Recovery from a deep-rooted dependency or other personal problem is never fast and easy. God isn't interested in quick fixes. He is interested only in full recovery based on a strong relationship with him. Many may claim that there are other ways, but any program that excludes God and his Word should be avoided.

14 "Then the people will say,
'Why should we wait here to die?
Come, let's go to the fortified towns and
die there.
For the LORD our God has decreed our
destruction
and has given us a cup of poison to drink
because we sinned against the LORD.
15 We hoped for peace, but no peace came.
We hoped for a time of healing, but
found only terror.'

16 "The snorting of the enemies' warhorses
can be heard
all the way from the land of Dan in the
north!
The neighing of their stallions makes the
whole land tremble.
They are coming to devour the land
and everything in it—
cities and people alike.
17 I will send these enemy troops among you
like poisonous snakes you cannot
charm.
They will bite you, and you will die.
I, the LORD, have spoken!"

Jeremiah Weeps for Sinful Judah

18 My grief is beyond healing;
my heart is broken.
19 Listen to the weeping of my people;
it can be heard all across the land.
"Has the LORD abandoned Jerusalem?*"
the people ask.
"Is her King no longer there?"

"Oh, why have they provoked my anger
with their carved idols
and their worthless foreign gods?" says
the LORD.

20 "The harvest is finished,
and the summer is gone," the people cry,
"yet we are not saved!"

21 I hurt with the hurt of my people.
I mourn and am overcome with grief.
22 Is there no medicine in Gilead?
Is there no physician there?
Why is there no healing
for the wounds of my people?

CHAPTER 9

1*If only my head were a pool of water
and my eyes a fountain of tears,
I would weep day and night
for all my people who have been
slaughtered.
2*Oh, that I could go away and forget my
people
and live in a travelers' shack in the
desert.
For they are all adulterers—
a pack of treacherous liars.

Judgment for Disobedience

3 "My people bend their tongues like bows
to shoot out lies.
They refuse to stand up for the truth.
They only go from bad to worse.
They do not know me,"
says the LORD.

4 "Beware of your neighbor!
Don't even trust your brother!
For brother takes advantage of brother,
and friend slanders friend.
5 They all fool and defraud each other;
no one tells the truth.
With practiced tongues they tell lies;
they wear themselves out with all their
sinning.
6 They pile lie upon lie
and utterly refuse to acknowledge me,"
says the LORD.

7 Therefore, this is what the LORD of
Heaven's Armies says:

8:19 Hebrew *Zion?* 9:1 Verse 9:1 is numbered 8:23 in Hebrew text. 9:2 Verses 9:2-26 are numbered 9:1-25 in
Hebrew text.

8:18-19 The people of Judah had strayed far from God by worshiping idols and then complained
that God had deserted them. We often do the same thing by disobeying God. But God never
moves away from us. If we are far from God, we are the ones who have moved. Recovery comes
as we seek to rebuild our relationship with God through trust in his person and obedience to his
plan. God is eager to help all those who humbly turn to him for help.
9:7-8 The relationship between God and the people of Judah had come to a critical point. They
had ignored his warnings and continued to disobey him. God now promised destructive punishment upon them. But even their punishment was designed for their good. God would melt them
down through the Babylonian exile and reshape his people into a nation he could use. God also
uses trials to refine and test us. He may even allow us to hit bottom in order to promote our spiritual growth. We often try to escape such testing, but God uses it to remind us of how much we
need him. Unless we continue to place our life in God's hands daily, we have little chance for
recovery.

"See, I will melt them down in a crucible
  and test them like metal.
What else can I do with my people?*
8   For their tongues shoot lies like
      poisoned arrows.
They speak friendly words to their
    neighbors
    while scheming in their heart to kill
    them.
9 Should I not punish them for this?" says
    the LORD.
  "Should I not avenge myself against
    such a nation?"

10 I will weep for the mountains
    and wail for the wilderness pastures.
  For they are desolate and empty of life;
    the lowing of cattle is heard no more;
    the birds and wild animals have all fled.

11 "I will make Jerusalem into a heap of
      ruins," says the LORD.
  "It will be a place haunted by jackals.
  The towns of Judah will be ghost towns,
    with no one living in them."

12 Who is wise enough to understand all
this? Who has been instructed by the LORD
and can explain it to others? Why has the
land been so ruined that no one dares to
travel through it?

13 The LORD replies, "This has happened because my people have abandoned my instructions; they have refused to obey what I said.
14 Instead, they have stubbornly followed their
own desires and worshiped the images of
Baal, as their ancestors taught them. 15 So now,
this is what the LORD of Heaven's Armies, the
God of Israel, says: Look! I will feed them with
bitterness and give them poison to drink. 16 I
will scatter them around the world, in places
they and their ancestors never heard of, and
even there I will chase them with the sword
until I have destroyed them completely."

Weeping in Jerusalem
17 This is what the LORD of Heaven's Armies
says:
  "Consider all this, and call for the
      mourners.
    Send for the women who mourn at
      funerals.
18 Quick! Begin your weeping!
    Let the tears flow from your eyes.
19 Hear the people of Jerusalem* crying in
    despair,

9:7 Hebrew *with the daughter of my people?* Greek version
reads *with the evil daughter of my people?* 9:19 Hebrew
Zion.

HONESTY

READ JEREMIAH 9:1-9
Most of us know the pain caused by
deceit, both for the deceiver and for the
one who has been betrayed. We may be
trying to learn to trust again after living in
a situation in which we haven't been given
any reason to trust.

David cried, "Help, O LORD, for the godly
are fast disappearing! The faithful have
vanished from the earth! Neighbors lie to
each other, speaking with flattering lips
and deceitful hearts. May the LORD cut off
their flattering lips and silence their
boastful tongues. They say, 'We will lie to
our hearts' content. Our lips are our
own—who can stop us?'" (Psalm 12:1-4).

Jeremiah prophesied, "'Beware of your
neighbor! Don't even trust your brother!
For brother takes advantage of brother,
and friend slanders friend. They all fool and
defraud each other; no one tells the truth.
With practiced tongues they tell lies; they
wear themselves out with all their sinning.
They pile lie upon lie and utterly refuse to
acknowledge me,' says the LORD.
Therefore, this is what the LORD of
Heaven's Armies says: 'See, I will melt them
down in a crucible and test them like
metal'" (Jeremiah 9:4-7).

When we turn our life over to God,
learning to trust him is a process. He
understands that this will be hard. But God
is absolutely trustworthy. We should be
cautious, however, as we put our trust in
people, trusting only those who have
proven themselves trustworthy. *Turn to
page 955, Jeremiah 17.*

'We are ruined! We are completely
humiliated!
We must leave our land,
because our homes have been torn
down.'"

20 Listen, you women, to the words of the
LORD;
open your ears to what he has to say.
Teach your daughters to wail;
teach one another how to lament.
21 For death has crept in through our
windows
and has entered our mansions.
It has killed off the flower of our youth:
Children no longer play in the streets,
and young men no longer gather in the
squares.

22 This is what the LORD says:
"Bodies will be scattered across the fields
like clumps of manure,
like bundles of grain after the harvest.
No one will be left to bury them."

23 This is what the LORD says:
"Don't let the wise boast in their wisdom,
or the powerful boast in their power,
or the rich boast in their riches.
24 But those who wish to boast
should boast in this alone:
that they truly know me and understand
that I am the LORD
who demonstrates unfailing love
and who brings justice and
righteousness to the earth,
and that I delight in these things.
I, the LORD, have spoken!

25 "A time is coming," says the LORD,
"when I will punish all those who are circumcised in body but not in spirit—26 the
Egyptians, Edomites, Ammonites, Moabites,
the people who live in the desert in remote
places,* and yes, even the people of Judah.
And like all these pagan nations, the people
of Israel also have uncircumcised hearts."

9:26 Or *in the desert and clip the corners of their hair.*

CHAPTER 10
Idolatry Brings Destruction
Hear the word that the LORD speaks to you,
O Israel! 2 This is what the LORD says:

"Do not act like the other nations,
who try to read their future in the stars.
Do not be afraid of their predictions,
even though other nations are terrified
by them.
3 Their ways are futile and foolish.
They cut down a tree, and a craftsman
carves an idol.
4 They decorate it with gold and silver
and then fasten it securely with
hammer and nails
so it won't fall over.
5 Their gods are like
helpless scarecrows in a cucumber
field!
They cannot speak,
and they need to be carried because
they cannot walk.
Do not be afraid of such gods,
for they can neither harm you nor do
you any good."

6 LORD, there is no one like you!
For you are great, and your name is full
of power.
7 Who would not fear you, O King of
nations?
That title belongs to you alone!
Among all the wise people of the earth
and in all the kingdoms of the world,
there is no one like you.

8 People who worship idols are stupid and
foolish.
The things they worship are made
of wood!
9 They bring beaten sheets of silver from
Tarshish
and gold from Uphaz,
and they give these materials to skillful
craftsmen
who make their idols.

10:2-3 A horoscope—trying to read the future in the stars—is a way of seeking truth apart from
God. Instead of looking at the stars for direction in our life, we should look to the Creator of the
stars and to the Bible—his Word to us—for truth and guidance. As we seek to strengthen our relationship with God, we will discover that we have also been strengthened in recovery.
10:3-5 Trusting in anything as a substitute for God is as foolish as propping up a wooden idol
and praying to it. But we do similar foolish things. We use our dependency to "prop us up" when
we face problems that seem overwhelming. We rely on unhealthy relationships for support, or we
may enter a recovery program that excludes God. Only God can help us overcome our dependency and the underlying suffering that drives it.

Then they dress these gods in royal blue
and purple robes
made by expert tailors.
[10] But the LORD is the only true God.
He is the living God and the everlasting
King!
The whole earth trembles at his anger.
The nations cannot stand up to his wrath.

[11] Say this to those who worship other gods:
"Your so-called gods, who did not make the
heavens and earth, will vanish from the earth
and from under the heavens."*

[12] But the LORD made the earth by his power,
and he preserves it by his wisdom.
With his own understanding
he stretched out the heavens.
[13] When he speaks in the thunder,
the heavens roar with rain.
He causes the clouds to rise over the earth.
He sends the lightning with the rain
and releases the wind from his
storehouses.
[14] The whole human race is foolish and has
no knowledge!
The craftsmen are disgraced by the idols
they make,
for their carefully shaped works are a
fraud.
These idols have no breath or power.
[15] Idols are worthless; they are ridiculous
lies!
On the day of reckoning they will all be
destroyed.
[16] But the God of Israel* is no idol!
He is the Creator of everything that
exists,
including Israel, his own special possession.
The LORD of Heaven's Armies is his name!

The Coming Destruction
[17] Pack your bags and prepare to leave;
the siege is about to begin.
[18] For this is what the LORD says:
"Suddenly, I will fling out

all you who live in this land.
I will pour great troubles upon you,
and at last you will feel my anger."

[19] My wound is severe,
and my grief is great.
My sickness is incurable,
but I must bear it.
[20] My home is gone,
and no one is left to help me rebuild it.
My children have been taken away,
and I will never see them again.
[21] The shepherds of my people have lost
their senses.
They no longer seek wisdom from the
LORD.
Therefore, they fail completely,
and their flocks are scattered.
[22] Listen! Hear the terrifying roar of great
armies
as they roll down from the north.
The towns of Judah will be destroyed
and become a haunt for jackals.

Jeremiah's Prayer
[23] I know, LORD, that our lives are not our
own.
We are not able to plan our own course.
[24] So correct me, LORD, but please be gentle.
Do not correct me in anger, for I would
die.
[25] Pour out your wrath on the nations that
refuse to acknowledge you—
on the peoples that do not call upon
your name.
For they have devoured your people Israel*;
they have devoured and consumed them,
making the land a desolate wilderness.

CHAPTER 11
Judah's Broken Covenant
The LORD gave another message to Jeremiah.
He said, [2]"Remind the people of Judah and Jerusalem about the terms of my covenant with
them. [3]Say to them, 'This is what the LORD,

10:11 The original text of this verse is in Aramaic. 10:16 Hebrew *the Portion of Jacob.* See note on 5:20.
10:25 Hebrew *devoured Jacob.* See note on 5:20.

10:23-25 The prophet recognized his powerlessness and acknowledged his inability to map out
his life. This is the first step in God's program for recovery. Sadly, the people of Judah didn't share
Jeremiah's sentiments. The prophet begged God to let his people off lightly, but punishment was
the only solution for their sin and denial. It was painful for Jeremiah to watch as they experienced
the consequences of their own sins.
11:1-17 God gave his people the terms for their restoration: He asked for their obedience. We can
see from this passage that God already knew that they would refuse to repent. They had returned
to their ancestors' sins and preferred idols to the true God. We may consider God's price too high
and the reward too delayed for giving up the pleasures of our sins. If we feel this way, we will ultimately reap a harvest of suffering. Keeping the long view in mind helps us to choose God's way.

the God of Israel, says: Cursed is anyone who does not obey the terms of my covenant! [4]For I said to your ancestors when I brought them out of the iron-smelting furnace of Egypt, "If you obey me and do whatever I command you, then you will be my people, and I will be your God." [5]I said this so I could keep my promise to your ancestors to give you a land flowing with milk and honey—the land you live in today.'"

Then I replied, "Amen, LORD! May it be so."

[6]Then the LORD said, "Broadcast this message in the streets of Jerusalem. Go from town to town throughout the land and say, 'Remember the ancient covenant, and do everything it requires. [7]For I solemnly warned your ancestors when I brought them out of Egypt, "Obey me!" I have repeated this warning over and over to this day, [8]but your ancestors did not listen or even pay attention. Instead, they stubbornly followed their own evil desires. And because they refused to obey, I brought upon them all the curses described in this covenant.'"

[9]Again the LORD spoke to me and said, "I have discovered a conspiracy against me among the people of Judah and Jerusalem. [10]They have returned to the sins of their ancestors. They have refused to listen to me and are worshiping other gods. Israel and Judah have both broken the covenant I made with their ancestors. [11]Therefore, this is what the LORD says: I am going to bring calamity upon them, and they will not escape. Though they beg for mercy, I will not listen to their cries. [12]Then the people of Judah and Jerusalem will pray to their idols and burn incense before them. But the idols will not save them when disaster strikes! [13]Look now, people of Judah; you have as many gods as you have towns. You have as many altars of shame—altars for burning incense to your god Baal—as there are streets in Jerusalem.

[14]"Pray no more for these people, Jeremiah. Do not weep or pray for them, for I will not listen to them when they cry out to me in distress.

[15] "What right do my beloved people have to come to my Temple,

when they have done so many immoral things?
Can their vows and sacrifices prevent their destruction?
They actually rejoice in doing evil!
[16]I, the LORD, once called them a thriving olive tree,
beautiful to see and full of good fruit.
But now I have sent the fury of their enemies
to burn them with fire,
leaving them charred and broken.

[17]"I, the LORD of Heaven's Armies, who planted this olive tree, have ordered it destroyed. For the people of Israel and Judah have done evil, arousing my anger by burning incense to Baal."

A Plot against Jeremiah

[18]Then the LORD told me about the plots my enemies were making against me. [19]I was like a lamb being led to the slaughter. I had no idea that they were planning to kill me! "Let's destroy this man and all his words," they said. "Let's cut him down, so his name will be forgotten forever."

[20]O LORD of Heaven's Armies,
you make righteous judgments,
and you examine the deepest thoughts and secrets.
Let me see your vengeance against them,
for I have committed my cause to you.

[21]This is what the LORD says about the men of Anathoth who wanted me dead. They had said, "We will kill you if you do not stop prophesying in the LORD's name." [22]So this is what the LORD of Heaven's Armies says about them: "I will punish them! Their young men will die in battle, and their boys and girls will starve to death. [23]Not one of these plotters from Anathoth will survive, for I will bring disaster upon them when their time of punishment comes."

CHAPTER 12
Jeremiah Questions the LORD's Justice

[1]LORD, you always give me justice
when I bring a case before you.
So let me bring you this complaint:

11:5 God is waiting to do wonderful things for those who simply trust and obey him. When we reject God's program, we automatically choose the world's rules for life and the consequences that accompany them. The world will always hand us disappointment in the long run. God promises that wonderful things will be ours when we obey him.

12:1-17 It is no wonder that Jeremiah struggled deeply with his calling. He was living in the midst of Judah's sin; he could see the godless lifestyles of Judah's people, and he knew God's

Why are the wicked so prosperous?
Why are evil people so happy?
[2] You have planted them,
and they have taken root and
prospered.
Your name is on their lips,
but you are far from their hearts.
[3] But as for me, LORD, you know my
heart.
You see me and test my thoughts.
Drag these people away like sheep to be
butchered!
Set them aside to be slaughtered!

[4] How long must this land mourn?
Even the grass in the fields has
withered.
The wild animals and birds have
disappeared
because of the evil in the land.
For the people have said,
"The LORD doesn't see what's ahead
for us!"

The LORD's Reply to Jeremiah

[5] "If racing against mere men makes you
tired,
how will you race against horses?
If you stumble and fall on open ground,
what will you do in the thickets near
the Jordan?
[6] Even your brothers, members of your own
family,
have turned against you.
They plot and raise complaints against
you.
Do not trust them,
no matter how pleasantly they speak.

[7] "I have abandoned my people, my special
possession.
I have surrendered my dearest ones to
their enemies.
[8] My chosen people have roared at me like
a lion of the forest,
so I have treated them with
contempt.

12:9 Or *speckled hyenas.*

[9] My chosen people act like speckled
vultures,*
but they themselves are surrounded
by vultures.
Bring on the wild animals to pick their
corpses clean!

[10] "Many rulers have ravaged my
vineyard,
trampling down the vines
and turning all its beauty into a barren
wilderness.
[11] They have made it an empty wasteland;
I hear its mournful cry.
The whole land is desolate,
and no one even cares.
[12] On all the bare hilltops,
destroying armies can be seen.
The sword of the LORD devours
people
from one end of the nation to the
other.
No one will escape!
[13] My people have planted wheat
but are harvesting thorns.
They have worn themselves out,
but it has done them no good.
They will harvest a crop of shame
because of the fierce anger
of the LORD.

A Message for Israel's Neighbors

[14] Now this is what the LORD says: "I will uproot from their land all the evil nations reaching out for the possession I gave my people Israel. And I will uproot Judah from among them. [15] But afterward I will return and have compassion on all of them. I will bring them home to their own lands again, each nation to its own possession. [16] And if these nations truly learn the ways of my people, and if they learn to swear by my name, saying, 'As surely as the LORD lives' (just as they taught my people to swear by the name of Baal), then they will be given a place among my people. [17] But any nation who refuses to obey me will be uprooted and destroyed. I, the LORD, have spoken!"

concern about their sin. So he asked the question we often ask: Why do the wicked prosper? God answered that the wicked never prosper for long. We should not allow ourselves to be bothered by their apparent success. If we do, we are the ones who will stumble (see Psalm 73). It may be difficult to be patient, but God's truth and righteousness do prevail—always.
12:13 Often our actions produce shame, but God can turn our shameful experiences into meaningful lessons if we will submit to him. Our challenge is to take our sins and shame to God and allow him to forgive us and heal our heart. Then with renewed humility and faith, we can make significant progress toward recovery.

CHAPTER 13
Jeremiah's Linen Loincloth

This is what the LORD said to me: "Go and buy a linen loincloth and put it on, but do not wash it." ²So I bought the loincloth as the LORD directed me, and I put it on.

³Then the LORD gave me another message: ⁴"Take the linen loincloth you are wearing, and go to the Euphrates River.* Hide it there in a hole in the rocks." ⁵So I went and hid it by the Euphrates as the LORD had instructed me.

⁶A long time afterward the LORD said to me, "Go back to the Euphrates and get the loincloth I told you to hide there." ⁷So I went to the Euphrates and dug it out of the hole where I had hidden it. But now it was rotting and falling apart. The loincloth was good for nothing.

⁸Then I received this message from the LORD: ⁹"This is what the LORD says: This shows how I will rot away the pride of Judah and Jerusalem. ¹⁰These wicked people refuse to listen to me. They stubbornly follow their own desires and worship other gods. Therefore, they will become like this loincloth—good for nothing! ¹¹As a loincloth clings to a man's waist, so I created Judah and Israel to cling to me, says the LORD. They were to be my people, my pride, my glory—an honor to my name. But they would not listen to me.

¹²"So tell them, 'This is what the LORD, the God of Israel, says: May all your jars be filled with wine.' And they will reply, 'Of course! Jars are made to be filled with wine!'

¹³"Then tell them, 'No, this is what the LORD means: I will fill everyone in this land with drunkenness—from the king sitting on David's throne to the priests and the prophets, right down to the common people of Jerusalem. ¹⁴I will smash them against each other, even parents against children, says the LORD. I will not let my pity or mercy or compassion keep me from destroying them.'"

13:4 Hebrew *Perath*; also in 13:5, 6, 7.

A Warning against Pride

¹⁵Listen and pay attention!
   Do not be arrogant, for the LORD has
      spoken.
¹⁶Give glory to the LORD your God
   before it is too late.
Acknowledge him before he brings
      darkness upon you,
   causing you to stumble and fall on the
      darkening mountains.
For then, when you look for light,
   you will find only terrible darkness and
      gloom.
¹⁷And if you still refuse to listen,
   I will weep alone because of your pride.
My eyes will overflow with tears,
   because the LORD's flock will be led
      away into exile.

¹⁸Say to the king and his mother,
   "Come down from your thrones
      and sit in the dust,
for your glorious crowns
   will soon be snatched from your
      heads."
¹⁹The towns of the Negev will close their
      gates,
   and no one will be able to open them.
The people of Judah will be taken away as
      captives.
   All will be carried into exile.

²⁰Open up your eyes and see
   the armies marching down from the
      north!
Where is your flock—
   your beautiful flock—
   that he gave you to care for?
²¹What will you say when the LORD takes
      the allies you have cultivated
   and appoints them as your rulers?
Pangs of anguish will grip you,
   like those of a woman in labor!
²²You may ask yourself,
   "Why is all this happening to me?"

13:1-11 God used an object lesson to prepare Jeremiah for the devastation he would soon see. In this illustration Jeremiah represented God, and Jeremiah's linen belt represented God's people. God told Jeremiah to bury the belt and, after a long time, to dig it up again. When Jeremiah retrieved the belt, it was "rotting and falling apart." This illustrated how the people of Judah had fallen apart spiritually by going their own way. Following our selfish inclinations always leads to destruction. Following God's will leads to health and spiritual renewal.
13:15 Pride is one of the greatest barriers to the recovery process. When we hit bottom, we reach a point of emptiness in which pride loses its power over us; we become willing to comply with God's will for us. When we become proud, we should remember that pride is sin and has destroyed many people for thousands of years. Pride is not new, but we can overcome it by humbly giving control of our life to God.

It is because of your many sins!
That is why you have been stripped
and raped by invading armies.
²³ Can an Ethiopian* change the color of his
skin?
Can a leopard take away its spots?
Neither can you start doing good,
for you have always done evil.

²⁴ "I will scatter you like chaff
that is blown away by the desert winds.
²⁵ This is your allotment,
the portion I have assigned to you,"
says the LORD,
"for you have forgotten me,
putting your trust in false gods.
²⁶ I myself will strip you
and expose you to shame.
²⁷ I have seen your adultery and lust,
and your disgusting idol worship out in
the fields and on the hills.
What sorrow awaits you, Jerusalem!
How long before you are pure?"

CHAPTER 14
Judah's Terrible Drought

This message came to Jeremiah from the
LORD, explaining why he was holding back
the rain:

² "Judah wilts;
commerce at the city gates grinds to a
halt.
All the people sit on the ground in
mourning,
and a great cry rises from Jerusalem.
³ The nobles send servants to get water,
but all the wells are dry.
The servants return with empty pitchers,
confused and desperate,
covering their heads in grief.
⁴ The ground is parched
and cracked for lack of rain.
The farmers are deeply troubled;

13:23 Hebrew *a Cushite.*

they, too, cover their heads.
⁵ Even the doe abandons her newborn fawn
because there is no grass in the field.
⁶ The wild donkeys stand on the bare hills
panting like thirsty jackals.
They strain their eyes looking for grass,
but there is none to be found."

⁷ The people say, "Our wickedness has
caught up with us, LORD,
but help us for the sake of your own
reputation.
We have turned away from you
and sinned against you again and
again.
⁸ O Hope of Israel, our Savior in times of
trouble,
why are you like a stranger to us?
Why are you like a traveler passing
through the land,
stopping only for the night?
⁹ Are you also confused?
Is our champion helpless to save us?
You are right here among us, LORD.
We are known as your people.
Please don't abandon us now!"

¹⁰ So this is what the LORD says to his
people:
"You love to wander far from me
and do not restrain yourselves.
Therefore, I will no longer accept you as
my people.
Now I will remember all your
wickedness
and will punish you for your sins."

The LORD Forbids Jeremiah to Intercede

¹¹ Then the LORD said to me, "Do not pray for
these people anymore. ¹²When they fast, I
will pay no attention. When they present
their burnt offerings and grain offerings to
me, I will not accept them. Instead, I will devour them with war, famine, and disease."

13:23 We often try to change by making resolutions to do what we know is right. But change
doesn't happen overnight, and we don't have the power to do it alone. Taking action is good, but
if we try to change in our own power, we will fail. We must begin by admitting that we are
powerless to change. This is the first step toward allowing God to transform our heart and life
from the inside out. If we are willing to cooperate, God can and will make permanent changes in
our life.
14:1-10 As the people of Judah faced a terrible drought, they turned to God in desperation. How
quickly we turn to God when something goes wrong. Where yesterday's happiness found us only
vaguely aware of God's power and grace, today's pain finds us begging for his mercy. If we wait
until disaster strikes to beg for mercy, God will answer our cries, but we should realize that our
healing will come only through great suffering. It would be wiser to remain close to God even
when things are going well. Then we will know God will deliver us when we face the difficult
times.

¹³Then I said, "O Sovereign LORD, their prophets are telling them, 'All is well—no war or famine will come. The LORD will surely send you peace.'"

¹⁴Then the LORD said, "These prophets are telling lies in my name. I did not send them or tell them to speak. I did not give them any messages. They prophesy of visions and revelations they have never seen or heard. They speak foolishness made up in their own lying hearts. ¹⁵Therefore, this is what the LORD says: I will punish these lying prophets, for they have spoken in my name even though I never sent them. They say that no war or famine will come, but they themselves will die by war and famine! ¹⁶As for the people to whom they prophesy—their bodies will be thrown out into the streets of Jerusalem, victims of famine and war. There will be no one left to bury them. Husbands, wives, sons, and daughters—all will be gone. For I will pour out their own wickedness on them. ¹⁷Now, Jeremiah, say this to them:

"Night and day my eyes overflow with
    tears.
I cannot stop weeping,
for my virgin daughter—my precious
    people—
    has been struck down
    and lies mortally wounded.
¹⁸If I go out into the fields,
I see the bodies of people slaughtered
    by the enemy.
If I walk the city streets,
I see people who have died of starvation.
The prophets and priests continue with
    their work,
but they don't know what they're doing."

A Prayer for Healing

¹⁹LORD, have you completely rejected
    Judah?
Do you really hate Jerusalem?*

Why have you wounded us past all hope
    of healing?
We hoped for peace, but no peace
    came.
We hoped for a time of healing, but
    found only terror.
²⁰LORD, we confess our wickedness
    and that of our ancestors, too.
We all have sinned against you.
²¹For the sake of your reputation, LORD, do
    not abandon us.
Do not disgrace your own glorious
    throne.
Please remember us,
    and do not break your covenant
    with us.

²²Can any of the worthless foreign gods
    send us rain?
Does it fall from the sky by itself?
No, you are the one, O LORD our God!
    Only you can do such things.
So we will wait for you to help us.

CHAPTER 15
Judah's Inevitable Doom

Then the LORD said to me, "Even if Moses and Samuel stood before me pleading for these people, I wouldn't help them. Away with them! Get them out of my sight! ²And if they say to you, 'But where can we go?' tell them, 'This is what the LORD says:

"'Those who are destined for death, to
    death;
those who are destined for war, to war;
those who are destined for famine,
    to famine;
those who are destined for captivity,
    to captivity.'

³"I will send four kinds of destroyers against them," says the LORD. "I will send the sword to kill, the dogs to drag away, the vultures to devour, and the wild animals to

14:19 Hebrew *Zion?*

14:13 Many of us would go merrily on our self-destructive way if God didn't somehow intervene to stop us. We often choose to live in denial, somehow hoping that God will protect us if difficulty strikes. The sooner we accept the fact that our actions will lead to painful consequences, the sooner we will turn to God and begin to recover his plan for our life. God allows us to experience these consequences to wake us up and lead us back to himself and the healing he offers.

15:3-9 God named Manasseh as the king primarily responsible for Judah's great suffering. Manasseh had died several generations before Jeremiah's ministry began, yet his sin had infected the entire nation of Judah. The consequences of his behavior were suffered by generations of God's people. Our behavior affects not only our immediate family but also our descendants and the people who will come in contact with them. Knowing this truth should motivate us to follow God's program for our life. If we do things God's way, we will pass on peace and joy to future generations.

finish up what is left. [4]Because of the wicked things Manasseh son of Hezekiah, king of Judah, did in Jerusalem, I will make my people an object of horror to all the kingdoms of the earth.

[5] "Who will feel sorry for you, Jerusalem?
  Who will weep for you?
  Who will even bother to ask how
    you are?
[6] You have abandoned me
  and turned your back on me,"
    says the LORD.
"Therefore, I will raise my fist to destroy
    you.
  I am tired of always giving you another
    chance.
[7] I will winnow you like grain at the gates
    of your cities
  and take away the children you hold
    dear.
I will destroy my own people,
  because they refuse to change their evil
    ways.
[8] There will be more widows
  than the grains of sand on the seashore.
At noontime I will bring a destroyer
  against the mothers of young men.
I will cause anguish and terror
  to come upon them suddenly.
[9] The mother of seven grows faint and
    gasps for breath;
  her sun has gone down while it is still
    day.
She sits childless now,
  disgraced and humiliated.
And I will hand over those who are left
  to be killed by the enemy.
  I, the LORD, have spoken!"

Jeremiah's Complaint

[10] Then I said,

"What sorrow is mine, my mother.
  Oh, that I had died at birth!
  I am hated everywhere I go.
I am neither a lender who threatens to
    foreclose
  nor a borrower who refuses to pay—
    yet they all curse me."

[11] The LORD replied,

"I will take care of you, Jeremiah.
  Your enemies will ask you to plead on
    their behalf
  in times of trouble and distress.

[12] Can a man break a bar of iron from
    the north,
  or a bar of bronze?
[13] At no cost to them,
  I will hand over your wealth and
    treasures
as plunder to your enemies,
  for sin runs rampant in your land.
[14] I will tell your enemies to take you
  as captives to a foreign land.
For my anger blazes like a fire
  that will burn forever.*"

[15] Then I said,

"LORD, you know what's happening
    to me.
  Please step in and help me. Punish my
    persecutors!
Please give me time; don't let me die
    young.
  It's for your sake that I am suffering.
[16] When I discovered your words, I devoured
    them.
  They are my joy and my heart's
    delight,
for I bear your name,
  O LORD God of Heaven's Armies.
[17] I never joined the people in their merry
    feasts.
  I sat alone because your hand was
    on me.
  I was filled with indignation at their
    sins.
[18] Why then does my suffering continue?
  Why is my wound so incurable?
Your help seems as uncertain as a
    seasonal brook,
  like a spring that has gone dry."

[19] This is how the LORD responds:

"If you return to me, I will restore you
  so you can continue to serve me.
If you speak good words rather than
    worthless ones,
  you will be my spokesman.
You must influence them;
  do not let them influence you!
[20] They will fight against you like an
    attacking army,
  but I will make you as secure as a
    fortified wall of bronze.
They will not conquer you,
  for I am with you to protect and
    rescue you.
  I, the LORD, have spoken!

15:14 As in some Hebrew manuscripts (see also 17:4); most Hebrew manuscripts read *will burn against you.*

²¹Yes, I will certainly keep you safe from
   these wicked men.
   I will rescue you from their cruel
   hands."

CHAPTER 16
Jeremiah Forbidden to Marry

The LORD gave me another message. He said,
²"Do not get married or have children in this
place. ³For this is what the LORD says about
the children born here in this city and about
their mothers and fathers: ⁴They will die from
terrible diseases. No one will mourn for them
or bury them, and they will lie scattered on
the ground like manure. They will die from
war and famine, and their bodies will be food
for the vultures and wild animals."

Judah's Coming Punishment

⁵This is what the LORD says: "Do not go to funerals to mourn and show sympathy for
these people, for I have removed my protection and peace from them. I have taken away
my unfailing love and my mercy. ⁶Both the
great and the lowly will die in this land. No
one will bury them or mourn for them. Their
friends will not cut themselves in sorrow or
shave their heads in sadness. ⁷No one will
offer a meal to comfort those who mourn for
the dead—not even at the death of a mother
or father. No one will send a cup of wine to
console them.

⁸"And do not go to their feasts and parties.
Do not eat and drink with them at all. ⁹For
this is what the LORD of Heaven's Armies, the
God of Israel, says: In your own lifetime, before your very eyes, I will put an end to the
happy singing and laughter in this land. The
joyful voices of bridegrooms and brides will
no longer be heard.

¹⁰"When you tell the people all these
things, they will ask, 'Why has the LORD decreed such terrible things against us? What
have we done to deserve such treatment?
What is our sin against the LORD our God?'

¹¹"Then you will give them the LORD's reply: 'It is because your ancestors were unfaithful to me. They worshiped other gods
and served them. They abandoned me and
did not obey my word. ¹²And you are even
worse than your ancestors! You stubbornly
follow your own evil desires and refuse to listen to me. ¹³So I will throw you out of this
land and send you into a foreign land where
you and your ancestors have never been.
There you can worship idols day and night—
and I will grant you no favors!'

Hope despite the Disaster

¹⁴"But the time is coming," says the LORD,
"when people who are taking an oath will no
longer say, 'As surely as the LORD lives, who
rescued the people of Israel from the land of
Egypt.' ¹⁵Instead, they will say, 'As surely as
the LORD lives, who brought the people of Israel back to their own land from the land of
the north and from all the countries to which
he had exiled them.' For I will bring them
back to this land that I gave their ancestors.

¹⁶"But now I am sending for many fishermen who will catch them," says the LORD. "I
am sending for hunters who will hunt them
down in the mountains, hills, and caves. ¹⁷I
am watching them closely, and I see every
sin. They cannot hope to hide from me. ¹⁸I
will double their punishment for all their

16:1-13 God had worked with his people for centuries, warning them, forgiving them, and healing them; but the people had continued to ignore God and follow their own selfish ways. As a
result, God withdrew his blessings from them. God did not act out of spite; he hoped that his
children's experience in exile would lead them back to him. Painful discipline often gets our attention when everything else fails. We should learn from our painful experiences and turn to God; we
should never allow punishment to drive us away from him. His discipline is a clear sign that he
loves us and wants to have a close relationship with us.

16:8 God was telling Jeremiah not to be an enabler. The prophet was to break through the
people's denial by refusing to celebrate with them. It takes great courage to confront the denial of
those we love. They will question our choices and may even pressure us to continue our enabling
behavior. Sometimes we can help by gently showing them that they need recovery. Often,
though, a more aggressive approach may be needed. Jesus was hardly gentle when he threw the
money changers out of the Temple (see John 2:13-25)! If the situation calls for it, direct confrontation may be the best approach.

17:5-6 In recovery it is often tempting to trust someone who claims to speak for God, but here
we are reminded that God alone is worthy of our trust. Many contemporary recovery programs
assume there is no need to trust and obey God and his Word. Such programs can be dangerous,
causing us to trust people or activities that have no real power to deliver. We need to heed godly
wisdom, not one individual's distortion of it. The analogy of the stunted shrub accurately
describes what it feels like for us to live without nourishment from God.

sins, because they have defiled my land with lifeless images of their detestable gods and have filled my territory with their evil deeds."

Jeremiah's Prayer of Confidence

¹⁹ LORD, you are my strength and fortress,
    my refuge in the day of trouble!
Nations from around the world
    will come to you and say,
"Our ancestors left us a foolish heritage,
    for they worshiped worthless idols.
²⁰ Can people make their own gods?
    These are not real gods at all!"

²¹ The LORD says,
"Now I will show them my power;
    now I will show them my might.
At last they will know and understand
    that I am the LORD.

CHAPTER 17
Judah's Sin and Punishment

¹ "The sin of Judah
    is inscribed with an iron chisel—
engraved with a diamond point on their
        stony hearts
    and on the corners of their altars.
² Even their children go to worship
    at their pagan altars and Asherah poles,
beneath every green tree
    and on every high hill.
³ So I will hand over my holy mountain—
    along with all your wealth and treasures
    and your pagan shrines—
as plunder to your enemies,
    for sin runs rampant in your land.
⁴ The wonderful possession I have reserved
        for you
    will slip from your hands.
I will tell your enemies to take you
    as captives to a foreign land.
For my anger blazes like a fire
    that will burn forever."

Wisdom from the LORD

⁵ This is what the LORD says:
"Cursed are those who put their trust in
        mere humans,
    who rely on human strength
    and turn their hearts away from the
        LORD.
⁶ They are like stunted shrubs in the desert,
    with no hope for the future.
They will live in the barren wilderness,
    in an uninhabited salty land.

HOPE

READ JEREMIAH 17:1-14

We may have learned a long time ago that hoping only brings disappointment. Our hopes were dashed. The promises we believed were broken. We were left feeling like fools for ever hoping in the first place. But perhaps we were devastated because we put our hope in the wrong place.

"This is what the LORD says: 'Cursed are those who put their trust in mere humans, who rely on human strength and turn their hearts away from the LORD. They are like stunted shrubs in the desert, with no hope for the future. They will live in the barren wilderness, in an uninhabited salty land. But blessed are those who trust in the LORD and have made the LORD their hope and confidence. They are like trees planted along a riverbank, with roots that reach deep into the water. Such trees are not bothered by the heat or worried by long months of drought. Their leaves stay green, and they never stop producing fruit'" (Jeremiah 17:5-8).

Turning our life over to God means placing our hope and confidence in him instead of people, who will disappoint us. When we place *all* our hope and trust in other people, it's like expecting a tree to flourish in a barren desert. People will disappoint us and are unable to satisfy our deepest needs. Trusting God changes everything. Jesus said, "The water I give . . . becomes a fresh, bubbling spring within them, giving them eternal life" (John 4:14). When our hope is in God and our life is in his care, we are sustained when we otherwise would be devastated.
Turn to page 1007, Lamentations 3.

7 "But blessed are those who trust in the
LORD
and have made the LORD their hope and
confidence.
8 They are like trees planted along a
riverbank,
with roots that reach deep into the
water.
Such trees are not bothered by
the heat
or worried by long months of drought.
Their leaves stay green,
and they never stop producing fruit.

9 "The human heart is the most deceitful
of all things,
and desperately wicked.
Who really knows how bad it is?
10 But I, the LORD, search all hearts
and examine secret motives.
I give all people their due rewards,
according to what their actions
deserve."

Jeremiah's Trust in the LORD

11 Like a partridge that hatches eggs she has
not laid,
so are those who get their wealth by
unjust means.
At midlife they will lose their riches;
in the end, they will become poor old
fools.
12 But we worship at your throne—
eternal, high, and glorious!
13 O LORD, the hope of Israel,
all who turn away from you will be
disgraced.
They will be buried in the dust of the
earth,
for they have abandoned the LORD, the
fountain of living water.

14 O LORD, if you heal me, I will be truly
healed;
if you save me, I will be truly saved.
My praises are for you alone!
15 People scoff at me and say,
"What is this 'message from the LORD' you
talk about?
Why don't your predictions come
true?"

16 LORD, I have not abandoned my job
as a shepherd for your people.
I have not urged you to send disaster.
You have heard everything
I've said.
17 LORD, don't terrorize me!
You alone are my hope in the day of
disaster.
18 Bring shame and dismay on all who
persecute me,
but don't let me experience shame and
dismay.
Bring a day of terror on them.
Yes, bring double destruction upon
them!

Observing the Sabbath

19 This is what the LORD said to me: "Go and
stand in the gates of Jerusalem, first in the
gate where the king goes in and out, and
then in each of the other gates. 20 Say to all
the people, 'Listen to this message from the
LORD, you kings of Judah and all you people
of Judah and everyone living in Jerusalem.
21 This is what the LORD says: Listen to my
warning! Stop carrying on your trade at Jerusalem's gates on the Sabbath day. 22 Do not do
your work on the Sabbath, but make it a holy
day. I gave this command to your ancestors,
23 but they did not listen or obey. They stubbornly refused to pay attention or accept my
discipline.

17:19-27 We often lose sight of what God intended by the laws he gave us. The people of Judah
had forsaken the Sabbath day, not realizing that the day had been set aside for their benefit.
God's laws were not given to inconvenience us but to help us be all that God intends us to be. He
loves us, and his laws were given because of his love. That is why following God's program is the
only way to experience fulfillment and freedom in this life.
18:11-17 God gave the people of Judah the warnings they needed to avoid judgment, but they
would not repent and turn from their idols. They preferred their own sinful ways to God's ways.
God's ways are simple: his paths are straight; his burden is light. But we, at times, become stubborn, proud, and arrogant, choosing to do things our own way—a way that leads ultimately to
despair and pain.
18:12-15 The people of Judah were aware of their sins and even admitted them openly, yet they
stubbornly refused to change. The only recourse left to God was the destruction of Israel and the
exile of his people. His love led him to punish them in hope that they would finally respond with
repentance. We are most hopeless when we know our sins and admit them to others, yet remain
on the path toward destruction. Admission without change is meaningless. The more we know
about ourself, the greater our responsibility to change what we know needs changing.

²⁴"'But if you obey me, says the LORD, and do not carry on your trade at the gates or work on the Sabbath day, and if you keep it holy, ²⁵then kings and their officials will go in and out of these gates forever. There will always be a descendant of David sitting on the throne here in Jerusalem. Kings and their officials will always ride in and out among the people of Judah in chariots and on horses, and this city will remain forever. ²⁶And from all around Jerusalem, from the towns of Judah and Benjamin, from the western foothills* and the hill country and the Negev, the people will come with their burnt offerings and sacrifices. They will bring their grain offerings, frankincense, and thanksgiving offerings to the LORD's Temple.

²⁷"'But if you do not listen to me and refuse to keep the Sabbath holy, and if on the Sabbath day you bring loads of merchandise through the gates of Jerusalem just as on other days, then I will set fire to these gates. The fire will spread to the palaces, and no one will be able to put out the roaring flames.'"

CHAPTER 18
The Potter and the Clay

The LORD gave another message to Jeremiah. He said, ²"Go down to the potter's shop, and I will speak to you there." ³So I did as he told me and found the potter working at his wheel. ⁴But the jar he was making did not turn out as he had hoped, so he crushed it into a lump of clay again and started over.

⁵Then the LORD gave me this message: ⁶"O Israel, can I not do to you as this potter has done to his clay? As the clay is in the potter's hand, so are you in my hand. ⁷If I announce that a certain nation or kingdom is to be uprooted, torn down, and destroyed, ⁸but then that nation renounces its evil ways, I will not destroy it as I had planned. ⁹And if I announce that I will plant and build up a certain nation or kingdom, ¹⁰but then that nation turns to evil and refuses to obey me, I will not bless it as I said I would.

¹¹"Therefore, Jeremiah, go and warn all Judah and Jerusalem. Say to them, 'This is what the LORD says: I am planning disaster for you instead of good. So turn from your evil ways, each of you, and do what is right.'"

¹²But the people replied, "Don't waste your breath. We will continue to live as we want to, stubbornly following our own evil desires."

¹³So this is what the LORD says:

17:26 Hebrew *the Shephelah.*

STEP 7

Giving Up Control

BIBLE READING: Jeremiah 18:1-6
We humbly asked him to remove our shortcomings.

Giving up control may be difficult for us. When we get ready for God to remove our shortcomings, we still may want to control how he does it. We are so used to calling the shots that we'll ask for God's help as long as he does it on our terms. We may demand that the changes happen on our timetable or in the order we feel ready to give them up.

God doesn't work that way. That is why humility is such an important part of this step. God told Jeremiah to go to the potter's shop to learn a lesson. Jeremiah said, "I did as he told me and found the potter working at his wheel. But the jar he was making did not turn out as he had hoped, so he crushed it into a lump of clay and started again. Then the LORD gave me this message: . . . 'Can I not do to you as this potter has done to his clay? As the clay is in the potter's hand, so are you in my hand" (Jeremiah 18:3-6). God told Isaiah, "What sorrow awaits those who argue with their Creator. Does a clay pot ever argue with its maker? Does the clay dispute with the one who shapes it, saying, 'Stop, you're doing it wrong!' Does the pot exclaim, 'How clumsy can you be?'" (Isaiah 45:9).

When we put our life in God's hands, he will reshape us as he sees fit. It is our humility that allows us to accept the fact that he is the Creator. Our new life may be similar to the one we left behind or entirely different. God is the master craftsman. Whatever he does, we can trust that he will recreate our life beautifully, once we get out of his way! *Turn to page 1311, Luke 11.*

"Has anyone ever heard of such a thing,
   even among the pagan nations?
My virgin daughter Israel
   has done something terrible!
14 Does the snow ever disappear from the
      mountaintops of Lebanon?
   Do the cold streams flowing from those
      distant mountains ever run dry?
15 But my people are not so reliable, for they
      have deserted me;
   they burn incense to worthless idols.
They have stumbled off the ancient
      highways
   and walk in muddy paths.
16 Therefore, their land will become desolate,
   a monument to their stupidity.
All who pass by will be astonished
   and will shake their heads in
      amazement.
17 I will scatter my people before their
      enemies
   as the east wind scatters dust.
And in all their trouble I will turn my
      back on them
   and refuse to notice their distress."

A Plot against Jeremiah

18 Then the people said, "Come on, let's plot a
way to stop Jeremiah. We have plenty of
priests and wise men and prophets. We don't
need him to teach the word and give us advice and prophecies. Let's spread rumors
about him and ignore what he says."

19 LORD, hear me and help me!
   Listen to what my enemies are saying.
20 Should they repay evil for good?
   They have dug a pit to kill me,
though I pleaded for them
   and tried to protect them from your
      anger.
21 So let their children starve!
   Let them die by the sword!
Let their wives become childless widows.
   Let their old men die in a plague,
   and let their young men be killed in
      battle!
22 Let screaming be heard from their homes
   as warriors come suddenly upon them.
For they have dug a pit for me
   and have hidden traps along my path.

23 LORD, you know all about their murderous
      plots against me.
   Don't forgive their crimes and blot out
      their sins.
Let them die before you.
   Deal with them in your anger.

CHAPTER 19
Jeremiah's Shattered Jar

This is what the LORD said to me: "Go and
buy a clay jar. Then ask some of the leaders of
the people and of the priests to follow you.
2 Go out through the Gate of Broken Pots to
the garbage dump in the valley of Ben-
Hinnom, and give them this message. 3 Say to
them, 'Listen to this message from the LORD,
you kings of Judah and citizens of Jerusalem!
This is what the LORD of Heaven's Armies,
the God of Israel, says: I will bring a terrible
disaster on this place, and the ears of those
who hear about it will ring!

4 "'For Israel has forsaken me and turned
this valley into a place of wickedness. The
people burn incense to foreign gods—idols
never before acknowledged by this generation, by their ancestors, or by the kings of Judah. And they have filled this place with the
blood of innocent children. 5 They have built
pagan shrines to Baal, and there they burn
their sons as sacrifices to Baal. I have never
commanded such a horrible deed; it never
even crossed my mind to command such a
thing! 6 So beware, for the time is coming,
says the LORD, when this garbage dump will
no longer be called Topheth or the valley of
Ben-Hinnom, but the Valley of Slaughter.

7 "'For I will upset the careful plans of Judah and Jerusalem. I will allow the people to
be slaughtered by invading armies, and I will
leave their dead bodies as food for the vultures and wild animals. 8 I will reduce Jerusalem to ruins, making it a monument to their
stupidity. All who pass by will be astonished
and will gasp at the destruction they see
there. 9 I will see to it that your enemies lay
siege to the city until all the food is gone.
Then those trapped inside will eat their own
sons and daughters and friends. They will be
driven to utter despair.'

10 "As these men watch you, Jeremiah,
smash the jar you brought. 11 Then say to

19:1-15 It is hard to imagine God's people sacrificing their own children on a fiery altar. For those
who had turned away from the true God, turning to Baal and other false gods was the first step.
Making hideous sacrifices was the next step. One sin usually leads to another. When we turn to
any resource other than the true God, all kinds of problems and sins creep into our life. False
sources of help, such as alcohol or drugs, make us a prisoner to one failure after another. When
we bring our pain to God and repent, he will set us free.

them, 'This is what the LORD of Heaven's Armies says: As this jar lies shattered, so I will shatter the people of Judah and Jerusalem beyond all hope of repair. They will bury the bodies here in Topheth, the garbage dump, until there is no more room for them. ¹²This is what I will do to this place and its people, says the LORD. I will cause this city to become defiled like Topheth. ¹³Yes, all the houses in Jerusalem, including the palace of Judah's kings, will become like Topheth—all the houses where you burned incense on the rooftops to your star gods, and where liquid offerings were poured out to your idols.' "

¹⁴Then Jeremiah returned from Topheth, the garbage dump where he had delivered this message, and he stopped in front of the Temple of the LORD. He said to the people there, ¹⁵"This is what the LORD of Heaven's Armies, the God of Israel, says: 'I will bring disaster upon this city and its surrounding towns as I promised, because you have stubbornly refused to listen to me.' "

CHAPTER 20
Jeremiah and Pashhur

Now Pashhur son of Immer, the priest in charge of the Temple of the LORD, heard what Jeremiah was prophesying. ²So he arrested Jeremiah the prophet and had him whipped and put in stocks at the Benjamin Gate of the LORD's Temple.

³The next day, when Pashhur finally released him, Jeremiah said, "Pashhur, the LORD has changed your name. From now on you are to be called 'The Man Who Lives in Terror.'* ⁴For this is what the LORD says: 'I will send terror upon you and all your friends, and you will watch as they are slaughtered by the swords of the enemy. I will hand the people of Judah over to the king of Babylon. He will take them captive to Babylon or run them through with the sword. ⁵And I will let your enemies plunder Jerusalem. All the famed treasures of the city—the precious jewels and gold and silver of your kings—will be carried off to Babylon. ⁶As for you, Pashhur, you and all your household will go as captives to Babylon. There you will die and be buried, you and all your friends to

whom you prophesied that everything would be all right.' "

Jeremiah's Complaint

⁷O LORD, you misled me,
    and I allowed myself to be misled.
You are stronger than I am,
    and you overpowered me.
Now I am mocked every day;
    everyone laughs at me.
⁸When I speak, the words burst out.
    "Violence and destruction!" I shout.
So these messages from the LORD
    have made me a household joke.
⁹But if I say I'll never mention the LORD
    or speak in his name,
his word burns in my heart like a fire.
    It's like a fire in my bones!
I am worn out trying to hold it in!
    I can't do it!
¹⁰I have heard the many rumors
    about me.
    They call me "The Man Who Lives in
    Terror."
They threaten, "If you say anything, we
    will report it."
    Even my old friends are watching me,
    waiting for a fatal slip.
"He will trap himself," they say,
    "and then we will get our revenge on
    him."

¹¹But the LORD stands beside me like a great
    warrior.
    Before him my persecutors will
    stumble.
    They cannot defeat me.
They will fail and be thoroughly
    humiliated.
    Their dishonor will never be forgotten.
¹²O LORD of Heaven's Armies,
you test those who are righteous,
    and you examine the deepest thoughts
    and secrets.
Let me see your vengeance against
    them,
    for I have committed my cause to you.
¹³Sing to the LORD!
    Praise the LORD!
For though I was poor and needy,
    he rescued me from my oppressors.

20:3 Hebrew *Magor-missabib*, which means "surrounded by terror"; also in 20:10.

20:7-18 The beauty of the prophet's relationship with God lies in the freedom and honesty of their conversation. Jeremiah was free to question and lament, and he was free to praise God for his faithfulness even when hope seemed far away. God longs for such a freedom of exchange with each of us. He longs for open and honest communication with each of us.

14 Yet I curse the day I was born!
　　May no one celebrate the day of my
　　　birth.
15 I curse the messenger who told my father,
　　"Good news—you have a son!"
16 Let him be destroyed like the cities of old
　　that the LORD overthrew without mercy.
　Terrify him all day long with battle
　　　shouts,
17　　because he did not kill me at birth.
　Oh, that I had died in my mother's womb,
　　that her body had been my grave!
18 Why was I ever born?
　　My entire life has been filled
　　with trouble, sorrow, and shame.

CHAPTER 21
No Deliverance from Babylon

The LORD spoke through Jeremiah when King Zedekiah sent Pashhur son of Malkijah and Zephaniah son of Maaseiah, the priest, to speak with him. They begged Jeremiah, 2"Please speak to the LORD for us and ask him to help us. King Nebuchadnezzar* of Babylon is attacking Judah. Perhaps the LORD will be gracious and do a mighty miracle as he has done in the past. Perhaps he will force Nebuchadnezzar to withdraw his armies."

3 Jeremiah replied, "Go back to King Zedekiah and tell him, 4This is what the LORD, the God of Israel, says: I will make your weapons useless against the king of Babylon and the Babylonians* who are outside your walls attacking you. In fact, I will bring your enemies right into the heart of this city. 5I myself will fight against you with a strong hand and a powerful arm, for I am very angry. You have made me furious! 6I will send a terrible plague upon this city, and both people and animals will die. 7And after all that, says the LORD, I will hand over King Zedekiah, his staff, and everyone else in the city who survives the disease, war, and famine. I will hand them over to King Nebuchadnezzar of Babylon and to their other enemies. He will slaughter them and show them no mercy, pity, or compassion.'

8"Tell all the people, 'This is what the LORD says: Take your choice of life or death! 9Everyone who stays in Jerusalem will die from war, famine, or disease, but those who go out and surrender to the Babylonians will live. Their reward will be life! 10For I have decided to bring disaster and not good upon this city, says the LORD. It will be handed over to the king of Babylon, and he will reduce it to ashes.'

Judgment on Judah's Kings

11"Say to the royal family of Judah, 'Listen to this message from the LORD! 12This is what the LORD says to the dynasty of David:

"'Give justice each morning to the people
　　you judge!
　Help those who have been robbed;
　　rescue them from their oppressors.
Otherwise, my anger will burn like an
　　unquenchable fire
　because of all your sins.
13 I will personally fight against the people
　　in Jerusalem,
　　that mighty fortress—
　the people who boast, "No one can touch
　　us here.
　　No one can break in here."
14 And I myself will punish you for your
　　sinfulness,
　　says the LORD.
　I will light a fire in your forests
　　that will burn up everything around
　　　you.'"

CHAPTER 22
A Message for Judah's Kings

This is what the LORD said to me: "Go over and speak directly to the king of Judah. Say to him, 2'Listen to this message from the LORD, you king of Judah, sitting on David's throne. Let your attendants and your people listen, too. 3This is what the LORD says:

21:2 Hebrew *Nebuchadrezzar*, a variant spelling of Nebuchadnezzar; also in 21:7. 21:4 Or *Chaldeans*; also in 21:9.

20:14-18 In our moments of greatest despair, we may wish we were dead and regret that we were ever born as Jeremiah did. Knowing that God's power can restore us may help us cling to life at this point. We can take solace in knowing that others, including Jeremiah, have felt this way too. Despite our feelings of loss and despair, God's love is a reality. He is with us always, even when we cannot feel his presence.

21:1-14 A time comes when it is too late to avoid the painful consequences of our actions. As Nebuchadnezzar bore down on Jerusalem, King Zedekiah wanted the persecuted prophet to petition God for help. God's reply was that it was too late. Since they had failed to respond to God's numerous warnings through his prophets, they must endure incredible devastation. We would be wise to listen to the warnings we receive before it's too late.

Be fair-minded and just. Do what is right! Help those who have been robbed; rescue them from their oppressors. Quit your evil deeds! Do not mistreat foreigners, orphans, and widows. Stop murdering the innocent! ⁴If you obey me, there will always be a descendant of David sitting on the throne here in Jerusalem. The king will ride through the palace gates in chariots and on horses, with his parade of attendants and subjects. ⁵But if you refuse to pay attention to this warning, I swear by my own name, says the LORD, that this palace will become a pile of rubble.'"

A Message about the Palace

⁶Now this is what the LORD says concerning Judah's royal palace:

"I love you as much as fruitful Gilead
    and the green forests of Lebanon.
But I will turn you into a desert,
    with no one living within your walls.
⁷I will call for wreckers,
    who will bring out their tools to
        dismantle you.
They will tear out all your fine cedar
        beams
    and throw them on the fire.

⁸"People from many nations will pass by the ruins of this city and say to one another, 'Why did the LORD destroy such a great city?' ⁹And the answer will be, 'Because they violated their covenant with the LORD their God by worshiping other gods.'"

A Message about Jehoahaz

¹⁰Do not weep for the dead king or mourn his loss.
    Instead, weep for the captive king being led away!
For he will never return to see his
    native land again.

¹¹For this is what the LORD says about Jehoahaz,* who succeeded his father, King Josiah, and was taken away as a captive: "He will never return. ¹²He will die in a distant land and will never again see his own country."

A Message about Jehoiakim

¹³And the LORD says, "What sorrow awaits
        Jehoiakim,*
    who builds his palace with forced labor.*
He builds injustice into its walls,
    for he makes his neighbors work for
        nothing.
He does not pay them for their labor.
¹⁴He says, 'I will build a magnificent
        palace
    with huge rooms and many windows.
I will panel it throughout with fragrant
        cedar
    and paint it a lovely red.'
¹⁵But a beautiful cedar palace does not make
        a great king!
Your father, Josiah, also had plenty to
        eat and drink.
But he was just and right in all his
        dealings.
    That is why God blessed him.
¹⁶He gave justice and help to the poor and
        needy,
    and everything went well for him.
Isn't that what it means to know me?"
    says the LORD.
¹⁷"But you! You have eyes only for greed
        and dishonesty!
You murder the innocent,
    oppress the poor, and reign ruthlessly."

¹⁸Therefore, this is what the LORD says about Jehoiakim, son of King Josiah:

22:11 Hebrew *Shallum,* another name for Jehoahaz. 22:13a The brother and successor of the exiled Jehoahaz. See 22:18. 22:13b Hebrew *by unrighteousness.*

22:1-30 Each of us is responsible for our own actions, but leaders and teachers are held to even greater degrees of responsibility. Jeremiah confronted Judah's leaders with their sins. He called the kings to rule as David had ruled, but they refused. Instead, they encouraged their people to turn to idols. As a result, the entire nation suffered destruction. We are all leaders in some context. What do our words and actions teach our children, fellow employees, or friends? What we do and say affects others, whether we like it or not. We need to take responsibility for the sin and suffering we have caused others, whether intentionally or unintentionally, and make amends the best we can.

22:8-9 Sometimes we look at the destruction in our or someone else's life and ask, Why did God do it? Such destruction is never God's fault. Sometimes our suffering is caused by someone else's sin. Often, however, our suffering and destruction are determined by our own failures and decisions. God creates; we destroy through our rebellion, then we blame him for the results. It is important to the recovery process that we accept responsibility for what we have done to ourself and avoid blaming God or someone else for problems resulting from our own choices.

"The people will not mourn for him,
crying to one another,
'Alas, my brother! Alas, my sister!'
His subjects will not mourn for him,
crying,
'Alas, our master is dead! Alas, his
splendor is gone!'
¹⁹ He will be buried like a dead donkey—
dragged out of Jerusalem and dumped
outside the gates!
²⁰ Weep for your allies in Lebanon.
Shout for them in Bashan.
Search for them in the regions east of the
river.*
See, they are all destroyed.
Not one is left to help you.
²¹ I warned you when you were prosperous,
but you replied, 'Don't bother me.'
You have been that way since childhood—
you simply will not obey me!
²² And now the wind will blow away your
allies.
All your friends will be taken away as
captives.
Surely then you will see your
wickedness and be ashamed.
²³ It may be nice to live in a beautiful palace
paneled with wood from the cedars of
Lebanon,
but soon you will groan with pangs of
anguish—
anguish like that of a woman in labor.

A Message for Jehoiachin

²⁴ "As surely as I live," says the LORD, "I will
abandon you, Jehoiachin* son of Jehoiakim,
king of Judah. Even if you were the signet
ring on my right hand, I would pull you off.
²⁵ I will hand you over to those who seek to
kill you, those you so desperately fear—to
King Nebuchadnezzar* of Babylon and the
mighty Babylonian* army. ²⁶ I will expel you
and your mother from this land, and you
will die in a foreign country, not in your native land. ²⁷ You will never again return to the
land you yearn for.

²⁸ "Why is this man Jehoiachin like a
discarded, broken jar?
Why are he and his children to be
exiled to a foreign land?
²⁹ O earth, earth, earth!
Listen to this message from the
LORD!
³⁰ This is what the LORD says:
'Let the record show that this man
Jehoiachin was childless.
He is a failure,
for none of his children will succeed him
on the throne of David
to rule over Judah.'

CHAPTER 23
The Righteous Descendant

"What sorrow awaits the leaders of my people—the shepherds of my sheep—for they
have destroyed and scattered the very ones
they were expected to care for," says the
LORD.

²Therefore, this is what the LORD, the God
of Israel, says to these shepherds: "Instead of
caring for my flock and leading them to
safety, you have deserted them and driven
them to destruction. Now I will pour out
judgment on you for the evil you have done
to them. ³But I will gather together the remnant of my flock from the countries where I
have driven them. I will bring them back to
their own sheepfold, and they will be fruitful
and increase in number. ⁴Then I will appoint
responsible shepherds who will care for
them, and they will never be afraid again.
Not a single one will be lost or missing. I, the
LORD, have spoken!

22:20 Or *in Abarim*. 22:24 Hebrew *Coniah*, a variant spelling of Jehoiachin; also 22:28. 22:25a Hebrew
Nebuchadrezzar, a variant spelling of Nebuchadnezzar. 22:25b Or *Chaldean*.

22:21 When the people of Judah were prosperous, they didn't think they needed God and
refused to listen to his warnings. When we are progressing rapidly in the recovery process, we
may be in great danger of growing too confident in our own ability to handle our dependency.
We forget the first all-important step: "We admitted that we were powerless over our dependencies. . . ." We need to always remember that our addiction is too strong for us to handle alone.
We need God's help—even when things are going well! Those who deal with reality best are
those who plan for hard times when times are good.
23:1-4 Shepherds—the leaders of God's people—who were supposed to care for God's "sheep"
had scattered and forsaken them. Since Judah's leaders had led God's people astray, God promised to punish the leaders and gather his people "back to their own sheepfold." He vowed to
place them in the care of responsible shepherds who would love and tend them. Jesus is our good
shepherd, loving us and tending us as his flock (see John 10:1-18). If we are willing to seek out
and follow his will for our life, there is hope for us, no matter how far we may have strayed.

5 "For the time is coming,"
   says the LORD,
"when I will raise up a righteous
     descendant*
   from King David's line.
He will be a King who rules with wisdom.
   He will do what is just and right
     throughout the land.
6 And this will be his name:
   'The LORD Is Our Righteousness.'*
In that day Judah will be saved,
   and Israel will live in safety.

7 "In that day," says the LORD, "when people are taking an oath, they will no longer say, 'As surely as the LORD lives, who rescued the people of Israel from the land of Egypt.' 8 Instead, they will say, 'As surely as the LORD lives, who brought the people of Israel back to their own land from the land of the north and from all the countries to which he had exiled them.' Then they will live in their own land."

Judgment on False Prophets

9 My heart is broken because of the false
     prophets,
   and my bones tremble.
I stagger like a drunkard,
   like someone overcome by wine,
because of the holy words
   the LORD has spoken against them.
10 For the land is full of adultery,
   and it lies under a curse.
The land itself is in mourning—
   its wilderness pastures are
     dried up.
For they all do evil
   and abuse what power they have.

11 "Even the priests and prophets
     are ungodly, wicked men.
I have seen their despicable acts
   right here in my own Temple,"
   says the LORD.
12 "Therefore, the paths they take
   will become slippery.
They will be chased through the
     dark,
   and there they will fall.

For I will bring disaster upon them
   at the time fixed for their punishment.
   I, the LORD, have spoken!

13 "I saw that the prophets of Samaria were
     terribly evil,
   for they prophesied in the name of Baal
   and led my people of Israel into sin.
14 But now I see that the prophets of
     Jerusalem are even worse!
They commit adultery and love
     dishonesty.
They encourage those who are doing evil
   so that no one turns away from their
     sins.
These prophets are as wicked
   as the people of Sodom and Gomorrah
     once were."

15 Therefore, this is what the LORD of Heaven's Armies says concerning the prophets:

"I will feed them with bitterness
   and give them poison to drink.
For it is because of Jerusalem's prophets
   that wickedness has filled this land."

16 This is what the LORD of Heaven's Armies says to his people:

"Do not listen to these prophets when
     they prophesy to you,
   filling you with futile hopes.
They are making up everything they say.
   They do not speak for the LORD!
17 They keep saying to those who despise my
     word,
   'Don't worry! The LORD says you will
     have peace!'
And to those who stubbornly follow their
     own desires,
   they say, 'No harm will come your way!'
18 "Have any of these prophets been in the
     LORD's presence
   to hear what he is really saying?
Has even one of them cared enough
   to listen?
19 Look! The LORD's anger bursts out like
     a storm,
   a whirlwind that swirls down on the
     heads of the wicked.

23:5 Hebrew *a righteous branch.* 23:6 Hebrew *Yahweh Tsidqenu.*

23:5-8 The people of Judah faced a future filled with suffering, but Jeremiah gave them hope that there would be rebuilding after the destruction. Even in the darkest times, when judgment seems most severe, God reminds us that a better day is coming. How sweet these promises must have sounded to the weary prophet! As we face suffering, we can know that God desires to restore us and give us hope for the future. Perhaps our suffering will even help us admit our powerlessness and lead us to turn to God for help—the first steps in the recovery process.

²⁰The anger of the LORD will not diminish
until it has finished all he has planned.
In the days to come
you will understand all this very clearly.

²¹"I have not sent these prophets,
yet they run around claiming to speak
for me.
I have given them no message,
yet they go on prophesying.
²²If they had stood before me and listened
to me,
they would have spoken my words,
and they would have turned my people
from their evil ways and deeds.
²³Am I a God who is only close at hand?"
says the LORD.
"No, I am far away at the same time.
²⁴Can anyone hide from me in a secret place?
Am I not everywhere in all the heavens
and earth?"
says the LORD.

²⁵"I have heard these prophets say, 'Listen
to the dream I had from God last night.' And
then they proceed to tell lies in my name.
²⁶How long will this go on? If they are proph-
ets, they are prophets of deceit, inventing
everything they say. ²⁷By telling these false
dreams, they are trying to get my people to
forget me, just as their ancestors did by worshiping the idols of Baal.

²⁸"Let these false prophets tell their dreams,
but let my true messengers faithfully
proclaim my every word.
There is a difference between straw
and grain!
²⁹Does not my word burn like fire?"
says the LORD.
"Is it not like a mighty hammer
that smashes a rock to pieces?

³⁰"Therefore," says the LORD, "I am against
these prophets who steal messages from each
other and claim they are from me. ³¹I am
against these smooth-tongued prophets who
say, 'This prophecy is from the LORD!' ³²I am
against these false prophets. Their imaginary
dreams are flagrant lies that lead my people
into sin. I did not send or appoint them, and
they have no message at all for my people. I,
the LORD, have spoken!

False Prophecies and False Prophets

³³"Suppose one of the people or one of the
prophets or priests asks you, 'What prophecy
has the LORD burdened you with now?' You
must reply, 'You are the burden!* The LORD
says he will abandon you!'

³⁴"If any prophet, priest, or anyone else
says, 'I have a prophecy from the LORD,' I will
punish that person along with his entire
family. ³⁵You should keep asking each other,
'What is the LORD's answer?' or 'What is the
LORD saying?' ³⁶But stop using this phrase,
'prophecy from the LORD.' For people are using it to give authority to their own ideas,
turning upside down the words of our God,
the living God, the LORD of Heaven's Armies.

³⁷"This is what you should say to the
prophets: 'What is the LORD's answer?' or
'What is the LORD saying?' ³⁸But suppose they
respond, 'This is a prophecy from the LORD!'
Then you should say, 'This is what the LORD
says: Because you have used this phrase,
"prophecy from the LORD," even though I
warned you not to use it, ³⁹I will forget you
completely.* I will expel you from my presence, along with this city that I gave to you
and your ancestors. ⁴⁰And I will make you an
object of ridicule, and your name will be infamous throughout the ages.'"

CHAPTER 24
Good and Bad Figs
After King Nebuchadnezzar* of Babylon ex-
iled Jehoiachin* son of Jehoiakim, king of
Judah, to Babylon along with the officials of
Judah and all the craftsmen and artisans, the

23:33 As in Greek version and Latin Vulgate; Hebrew reads *What burden?* 23:39 Some Hebrew manuscripts and
Greek version read *I will surely lift you up.* 24:1a Hebrew *Nebuchadrezzar,* a variant spelling of Nebuchadnezzar.
24:1b Hebrew *Jeconiah,* a variant spelling of Jehoiachin.

23:21-22 The people of Judah still hoped to escape destruction. False prophets supported their
hopes with false predictions of deliverance, which the people accepted because it allowed them
to continue in sin without thinking of the consequences. Jeremiah, speaking for God, demanded
that they face the truth of their sins and warned them of the inevitable consequences. This infuriated the people, and they rejected Jeremiah and his message. Answering this question will often
help determine whether or not a prophet speaks for God: What is the prophet or leader getting
out of his ministry? If someone is getting rich, powerful, or famous, we should at least question
his or her legitimacy.
24:1-10 Jeremiah was given another illustration to help us understand the fate of the Jews in
captivity. The exiles who followed God were like good figs, full of nourishment. They would be

LORD gave me this vision. I saw two baskets of figs placed in front of the LORD's Temple in Jerusalem. ²One basket was filled with fresh, ripe figs, while the other was filled with bad figs that were too rotten to eat.

³Then the LORD said to me, "What do you see, Jeremiah?"

I replied, "Figs, some very good and some very bad, too rotten to eat."

⁴Then the LORD gave me this message: ⁵"This is what the LORD, the God of Israel, says: The good figs represent the exiles I sent from Judah to the land of the Babylonians.* ⁶I will watch over and care for them, and I will bring them back here again. I will build them up and not tear them down. I will plant them and not uproot them. ⁷I will give them hearts that recognize me as the LORD. They will be my people, and I will be their God, for they will return to me wholeheartedly.

⁸"But the bad figs," the LORD said, "represent King Zedekiah of Judah, his officials, all the people left in Jerusalem, and those who live in Egypt. I will treat them like bad figs, too rotten to eat. ⁹I will make them an object of horror and a symbol of evil to every nation on earth. They will be disgraced and mocked, taunted and cursed, wherever I scatter them. ¹⁰And I will send war, famine, and disease until they have vanished from the land of Israel, which I gave to them and their ancestors."

CHAPTER 25
Seventy Years of Captivity
This message for all the people of Judah came to Jeremiah from the LORD during the fourth year of Jehoiakim's reign over Judah.* This was the year when King Nebuchadnezzar* of Babylon began his reign.

²Jeremiah the prophet said to all the people in Judah and Jerusalem, ³"For the past twenty-three years—from the thirteenth year of the reign of Josiah son of Amon,* king of Judah, until now—the LORD has been giving me his messages. I have faithfully passed them on to you, but you have not listened.

⁴"Again and again the LORD has sent you his servants, the prophets, but you have not listened or even paid attention. ⁵Each time the message was this: 'Turn from the evil road you are traveling and from the evil things you are doing. Only then will I let you live in this land that the LORD gave to you and your ancestors forever. ⁶Do not provoke my anger by worshiping idols you made with your own hands. Then I will not harm you.'

⁷"But you would not listen to me," says the LORD. "You made me furious by worshiping idols you made with your own hands, bringing on yourselves all the disasters you now suffer. ⁸And now the LORD of Heaven's Armies says: Because you have not listened to me, ⁹I will gather together all the armies of the north under King Nebuchadnezzar of Babylon, whom I have appointed as my deputy. I will bring them all against this land and its people and against the surrounding nations. I will completely destroy* you and make you an object of horror and contempt and a ruin forever. ¹⁰I will take away your happy singing and laughter. The joyful voices of bridegrooms and brides will no longer be heard. Your millstones will fall silent, and the lights in your homes will go out. ¹¹This entire land will become a desolate wasteland. Israel and her neighboring lands will serve the king of Babylon for seventy years.

¹²"Then, after the seventy years of captivity are over, I will punish the king of Babylon and his people for their sins," says the LORD.

24:5 Or *Chaldeans.* **25:1a** The fourth year of Jehoiakim's reign and the accession year of Nebuchadnezzar's reign was 605 B.C. **25:1b** Hebrew *Nebuchadrezzar,* a variant spelling of Nebuchadnezzar; also in 25:9. **25:3** The thirteenth year of Josiah's reign was 627 B.C. **25:9** The Hebrew term used here refers to the complete consecration of things or people to the LORD, either by destroying them or by giving them as an offering.

---

well treated and allowed to return to their homeland. King Zedekiah and those who had led the people falsely would be like bad figs, tasteless and fit only for destruction. God made it clear that the Exile was intended to bring healing to his shattered and sin-scarred people. Our suffering works the same way. If it leads us to admit our sins and follow God's will, we will be blessed by God and experience both physical and spiritual recovery.

25:1-14 How impatient we become when the consequences of our sins last for days or weeks, much less years. The Israelites were captive under King Nebuchadnezzar for 70 years! Many of them finally learned to honor God in the midst of captivity. Since their return from Babylonian captivity, the Jews have never been known to fall into the sin of idolatry. It is important that we face the consequences of our behavior. One way we can honor God is to accept his discipline and build upon the lessons learned from the sorrow.

"I will make the country of the Babylonians* a wasteland forever. [13]I will bring upon them all the terrors I have promised in this book—all the penalties announced by Jeremiah against the nations. [14]Many nations and great kings will enslave the Babylonians, just as they enslaved my people. I will punish them in proportion to the suffering they cause my people."

The Cup of the LORD's Anger

[15]This is what the LORD, the God of Israel, said to me: "Take from my hand this cup filled to the brim with my anger, and make all the nations to whom I send you drink from it. [16]When they drink from it, they will stagger, crazed by the warfare I will send against them."

[17]So I took the cup of anger from the LORD and made all the nations drink from it—every nation to which the LORD sent me. [18]I went to Jerusalem and the other towns of Judah, and their kings and officials drank from the cup. From that day until this, they have been a desolate ruin, an object of horror, contempt, and cursing. [19]I gave the cup to Pharaoh, king of Egypt, his attendants, his officials, and all his people, [20]along with all the foreigners living in that land. I also gave it to all the kings of the land of Uz and the kings of the Philistine cities of Ashkelon, Gaza, Ekron, and what remains of Ashdod. [21]Then I gave the cup to the nations of Edom, Moab, and Ammon, [22]and the kings of Tyre and Sidon, and the kings of the regions across the sea. [23]I gave it to Dedan, Tema, and Buz, and to the people who live in distant places.* [24]I gave it to the kings of Arabia, the kings of the nomadic tribes of the desert, [25]and to the kings of Zimri, Elam, and Media. [26]And I gave it to the kings of the northern countries, far and near, one after the other—all the kingdoms of the world. And finally, the king of Babylon* himself drank from the cup of the LORD's anger.

[27]Then the LORD said to me, "Now tell them, 'This is what the LORD of Heaven's Armies, the God of Israel, says: Drink from this cup of my anger. Get drunk and vomit; fall to rise no more, for I am sending terrible wars against you.' [28]And if they refuse to accept the cup, tell them, 'The LORD of Heaven's Armies says: You have no choice but to drink from it. [29]I have begun to punish Jerusalem, the city that bears my name. Now should I let you go unpunished? No, you will not escape disaster. I will call for war against all the nations of the earth. I, the LORD of Heaven's Armies, have spoken!'

[30]"Now prophesy all these things, and say to them,

"'The LORD will roar against his own land
      from his holy dwelling in heaven.
He will shout like those who tread grapes;
      he will shout against everyone on earth.
[31]His cry of judgment will reach the ends of
            the earth,
      for the LORD will bring his case against
            all the nations.
He will judge all the people of the earth,
      slaughtering the wicked with the sword.
      I, the LORD, have spoken!'"

[32]This is what the LORD of Heaven's Armies
            says:

"Look! Disaster will fall upon nation
            after nation!
A great whirlwind of fury is rising
      from the most distant corners of the
            earth!"

[33]In that day those the LORD has slaughtered will fill the earth from one end to the other. No one will mourn for them or gather up their bodies to bury them. They will be scattered on the ground like manure.

[34]Weep and moan, you evil shepherds!
      Roll in the dust, you leaders of the
            flock!
The time of your slaughter has arrived;
      you will fall and shatter like a fragile
            vase.
[35]You will find no place to hide;
      there will be no way to escape.
[36]Listen to the frantic cries of the
            shepherds.
      The leaders of the flock are wailing in
            despair,

25:12 Or *Chaldeans.* 25:23 Or *who clip the corners of their hair.* 25:26 Hebrew *of Sheshach,* a code name for Babylon.

25:15-38 Sometimes when we are doing our best to serve God, we notice that God allows people who care nothing about him or his ways to prosper. We are reminded here that God will make all things right in his time. Sometimes God uses the ungodly for his own purposes; at other times he seems to allow the ungodly to thrive for a time. But the end result is clear. All people and all nations are subject to God, and he ultimately rewards all who sincerely seek him (see Hebrews 11:6).

for the LORD is ruining their pastures.
³⁷ Peaceful meadows will be turned into a
wasteland
by the LORD's fierce anger.
³⁸ He has left his den like a strong lion
seeking its prey,
and their land will be made desolate
by the sword* of the enemy
and the LORD's fierce anger.

CHAPTER 26
Jeremiah's Escape from Death

This message came to Jeremiah from the
LORD early in the reign of Jehoiakim son of
Josiah,* king of Judah. ²"This is what the
LORD says: Stand in the courtyard in front of
the Temple of the LORD, and make an announcement to the people who have come
there to worship from all over Judah. Give
them my entire message; include every
word. ³Perhaps they will listen and turn from
their evil ways. Then I will change my mind
about the disaster I am ready to pour out on
them because of their sins.

⁴"Say to them, 'This is what the LORD says:
If you will not listen to me and obey my
word I have given you, ⁵and if you will not
listen to my servants, the prophets—for I
sent them again and again to warn you, but
you would not listen to them—⁶then I will
destroy this Temple as I destroyed Shiloh, the
place where the Tabernacle was located. And
I will make Jerusalem an object of cursing in
every nation on earth.'"

⁷The priests, the prophets, and all the peo-
ple listened to Jeremiah as he spoke in front
of the LORD's Temple. ⁸But when Jeremiah
had finished his message, saying everything
the LORD had told him to say, the priests and
prophets and all the people at the Temple
mobbed him. "Kill him!" they shouted.
⁹"What right do you have to prophesy in the

LORD's name that this Temple will be
destroyed like Shiloh? What do you mean,
saying that Jerusalem will be destroyed and
left with no inhabitants?" And all the people
threatened him as he stood in front of the
Temple.

¹⁰When the officials of Judah heard what
was happening, they rushed over from the
palace and sat down at the New Gate of the
Temple to hold court. ¹¹The priests and
prophets presented their accusations to the
officials and the people. "This man should
die!" they said. "You have heard with your
own ears what a traitor he is, for he has
prophesied against this city."

¹²Then Jeremiah spoke to the officials and
the people in his own defense. "The LORD sent
me to prophesy against this Temple and this
city," he said. "The LORD gave me every word
that I have spoken. ¹³But if you stop your sinning and begin to obey the LORD your God, he
will change his mind about this disaster that
he has announced against you. ¹⁴As for me, I
am in your hands—do with me as you think
best. ¹⁵But if you kill me, rest assured that you
will be killing an innocent man! The responsibility for such a deed will lie on you, on this
city, and on every person living in it. For it is
absolutely true that the LORD sent me to speak
every word you have heard."

¹⁶Then the officials and the people said to
the priests and prophets, "This man does not
deserve the death sentence, for he has spoken to us in the name of the LORD our God."

¹⁷Then some of the wise old men stood
and spoke to all the people assembled there.
¹⁸They said, "Remember when Micah of
Moresheth prophesied during the reign of
King Hezekiah of Judah. He told the people
of Judah,

'This is what the LORD of Heaven's Armies
says:

25:38 As in some Hebrew manuscripts and Greek version; Masoretic Text reads *by the anger*. 26:1 The first year of
Jehoiakim's reign was 608 B.C.

26:1-24 Without question, it is most difficult to serve God when others mock, question, or entice
us to doubt. Judah's rulers tried nearly everything to silence Jeremiah; finally they threatened him
with death. Though threats can discourage, sometimes they only fuel the fire of our commitment
(see Philippians 1:12-14). As we experience God's power in recovery, we need to share the good
news. Some people might laugh at us; others may oppose us. But we should not allow this to
stop us. God's deliverance is available to all who entrust their lives to his loving direction.
26:12-15 Because of Jeremiah's faith, he was able to speak boldly for God, even when his life was
threatened. Sometimes we, like Peter, deny that we know God when we face opposition. (See
Matthew 26:69-75; Mark 14:66-72; Luke 22:54-62; John 18:15-18, 25-27.) It is easy to claim to
have faith when everything is going well. The depth of our faith is measured when we are under
pressure. We should never allow others' opinions to keep us from sharing what we know about
God and his power to deliver us from the bondage of our dependency. Someone else's life or our
own progress in recovery may depend on it!

Mount Zion will be plowed like an open field;
Jerusalem will be reduced to ruins!
A thicket will grow on the heights where the Temple now stands.'*

¹⁹But did King Hezekiah and the people kill him for saying this? No, they turned from their sins and worshiped the LORD. They begged him for mercy. Then the LORD changed his mind about the terrible disaster he had pronounced against them. So we are about to do ourselves great harm."

²⁰At this time Uriah son of Shemaiah from Kiriath-jearim was also prophesying for the LORD. And he predicted the same terrible disaster against the city and nation as Jeremiah did. ²¹When King Jehoiakim and the army officers and officials heard what he was saying, the king sent someone to kill him. But Uriah heard about the plan and escaped in fear to Egypt. ²²Then King Jehoiakim sent Elnathan son of Acbor to Egypt along with several other men to capture Uriah. ²³They took him prisoner and brought him back to King Jehoiakim. The king then killed Uriah with a sword and had him buried in an unmarked grave.

²⁴Nevertheless, Ahikam son of Shaphan stood up for Jeremiah and persuaded the court not to turn him over to the mob to be killed.

CHAPTER 27
Jeremiah Wears an Ox Yoke
This message came to Jeremiah from the LORD early in the reign of Zedekiah* son of Josiah, king of Judah.

²This is what the LORD said to me: "Make a yoke, and fasten it on your neck with leather straps. ³Then send messages to the kings of Edom, Moab, Ammon, Tyre, and Sidon through their ambassadors who have come to see King Zedekiah in Jerusalem. ⁴Give them this message for their masters: 'This is what the LORD of Heaven's Armies, the God of Is-

rael, says: ⁵With my great strength and powerful arm I made the earth and all its people and every animal. I can give these things of mine to anyone I choose. ⁶Now I will give your countries to King Nebuchadnezzar of Babylon, who is my servant. I have put everything, even the wild animals, under his control. ⁷All the nations will serve him, his son, and his grandson until his time is up. Then many nations and great kings will conquer and rule over Babylon. ⁸So you must submit to Babylon's king and serve him; put your neck under Babylon's yoke! I will punish any nation that refuses to be his slave, says the LORD. I will send war, famine, and disease upon that nation until Babylon has conquered it.

⁹" 'Do not listen to your false prophets, fortune-tellers, interpreters of dreams, mediums, and sorcerers who say, "The king of Babylon will not conquer you." ¹⁰They are all liars, and their lies will lead to your being driven out of your land. I will drive you out and send you far away to die. ¹¹But the people of any nation that submits to the king of Babylon will be allowed to stay in their own country to farm the land as usual. I, the LORD, have spoken!' "

¹²Then I repeated this same message to King Zedekiah of Judah. "If you want to live, submit to the yoke of the king of Babylon and his people. ¹³Why do you insist on dying—you and your people? Why should you choose war, famine, and disease, which the LORD will bring against every nation that refuses to submit to Babylon's king? ¹⁴Do not listen to the false prophets who keep telling you, 'The king of Babylon will not conquer you.' They are liars. ¹⁵This is what the LORD says: 'I have not sent these prophets! They are telling you lies in my name, so I will drive you from this land. You will all die—you and all these prophets, too.' "

¹⁶Then I spoke to the priests and the people and said, "This is what the LORD says: 'Do not listen to your prophets who claim that soon the gold articles taken from my Temple

26:18 Mic 3:12. 27:1 As in some Hebrew manuscripts and Syriac version (see also 27:3, 12); most Hebrew manuscripts read *Jehoiakim*.

27:1-15 Sometimes God uses the unrighteous to achieve his righteous ends. Nebuchadnezzar was not the kind of king God would normally honor, yet God used him to discipline his wayward people and lead them to repentance. God had the good of his people in mind, and he saw that his will for them was carried out. When we suffer at the hands of people who care nothing for God, we should know that God is with us through our trials. And if we are listening, we may learn some important things about ourself and our loving God during the process.
27:16-22 The people of Judah listened to the pleasant messages of the false prophets, but this only blinded them to their sins and the inevitable consequences of turning away from God. All

will be returned from Babylon. It is all a lie! [17]Do not listen to them. Surrender to the king of Babylon, and you will live. Why should this whole city be destroyed? [18]If they really are prophets and speak the LORD's messages, let them pray to the LORD of Heaven's Armies. Let them pray that the articles remaining in the LORD's Temple and in the king's palace and in the palaces of Jerusalem will not be carried away to Babylon!'

[19]"For the LORD of Heaven's Armies has spoken about the pillars in front of the Temple, the great bronze basin called the Sea, the water carts, and all the other ceremonial articles. [20]King Nebuchadnezzar of Babylon left them here when he exiled Jehoiachin* son of Jehoiakim, king of Judah, to Babylon, along with all the other nobles of Judah and Jerusalem. [21]Yes, this is what the LORD of Heaven's Armies, the God of Israel, says about the precious things still in the Temple, in the palace of Judah's king, and in Jerusalem: [22]They will all be carried away to Babylon and will stay there until I send for them,' says the LORD. 'Then I will bring them back to Jerusalem again.'"

CHAPTER 28
Jeremiah Condemns Hananiah

One day in late summer* of that same year—the fourth year of the reign of Zedekiah, king of Judah—Hananiah son of Azzur, a prophet from Gibeon, addressed me publicly in the Temple while all the priests and people listened. He said, [2]"This is what the LORD of Heaven's Armies, the God of Israel, says: 'I will remove the yoke of the king of Babylon from your necks. [3]Within two years I will bring back all the Temple treasures that King Nebuchadnezzar carried off to Babylon. [4]And I will bring back Jehoiachin* son of Jehoiakim, king of Judah, and all the other captives that were taken to Babylon. I will surely break the yoke that the king of Babylon has put on your necks. I, the LORD, have spoken!'"

[5]Jeremiah responded to Hananiah as they stood in front of all the priests and people at the Temple. [6]He said, "Amen! May your prophecies come true! I hope the LORD does everything you say. I hope he does bring back from Babylon the treasures of this Temple and all the captives. [7]But listen now to the solemn words I speak to you in the presence of all these people. [8]The ancient prophets who preceded you and me spoke against many nations, always warning of war, disaster, and disease. [9]So a prophet who predicts peace must show he is right. Only when his predictions come true can we know that he is really from the LORD."

[10]Then Hananiah the prophet took the yoke off Jeremiah's neck and broke it in pieces. [11]And Hananiah said again to the crowd that had gathered, "This is what the LORD says: 'Just as this yoke has been broken, within two years I will break the yoke of oppression from all the nations now subject to King Nebuchadnezzar of Babylon.'" With that, Jeremiah left the Temple area.

[12]Soon after this confrontation with Hananiah, the LORD gave this message to Jeremiah: [13]"Go and tell Hananiah, 'This is what the LORD says: You have broken a wooden yoke, but you have replaced it with a yoke of iron. [14]The LORD of Heaven's Armies, the God of Israel, says: I have put a yoke of iron on the necks of all these nations, forcing them into slavery under King Nebuchadnezzar of Babylon. I have put everything, even the wild animals, under his control.'"

[15]Then Jeremiah the prophet said to Hananiah, "Listen, Hananiah! The LORD has not sent you, but the people believe your lies. [16]Therefore, this is what the LORD says: 'You must die. Your life will end this very year because you have rebelled against the LORD.'"

[17]Two months later* the prophet Hananiah died.

27:20 Hebrew *Jeconiah,* a variant spelling of Jehoiachin. **28:1** Hebrew *In the fifth month,* of the ancient Hebrew lunar calendar. The fifth month in the fourth year of Zedekiah's reign occurred within the months of August and September 593 B.C. Also see note on 1:3. **28:4** Hebrew *Jeconiah,* a variant spelling of Jehoiachin. **28:17** Hebrew *In the seventh month of that same year.* See 28:1 and the note there.

---

of us are impressionable, especially when we are young or going through difficulties. It is important to build our life on a foundation of truth rather than on convenient or pleasant messages. God calls us to do some unpleasant things. He requires that each of us take an honest look at our life, admit our sins, and humbly seek to make amends with those we have hurt. Recovery is never easy; it is always painful. We must face the truth. The road of pleasant experiences will only lead to denial and destruction.

CHAPTER 29

A Letter to the Exiles

Jeremiah wrote a letter from Jerusalem to the elders, priests, prophets, and all the people who had been exiled to Babylon by King Nebuchadnezzar. ²This was after King Jehoiachin,* the queen mother, the court officials, the other officials of Judah, and all the craftsmen and artisans had been deported from Jerusalem. ³He sent the letter with Elasah son of Shaphan and Gemariah son of Hilkiah when they went to Babylon as King Zedekiah's ambassadors to Nebuchadnezzar. This is what Jeremiah's letter said:

⁴This is what the LORD of Heaven's Armies, the God of Israel, says to all the captives he has exiled to Babylon from Jerusalem: ⁵"Build homes, and plan to stay. Plant gardens, and eat the food they produce. ⁶Marry and have children. Then find spouses for them so that you may have many grandchildren. Multiply! Do not dwindle away! ⁷And work for the peace and prosperity of the city where I sent you into exile. Pray to the LORD for it, for its welfare will determine your welfare."

⁸This is what the LORD of Heaven's Armies, the God of Israel, says: "Do not let your prophets and fortune-tellers who are with you in the land of Babylon trick you. Do not listen to their dreams, ⁹because they are telling you lies in my name. I have not sent them," says the LORD.

¹⁰This is what the LORD says: "You will be in Babylon for seventy years. But then I will come and do for you all the good things I have promised, and I will bring you home again. ¹¹For I know the plans I have for you," says the LORD. "They are plans for good and not for disaster, to give you a future and a hope. ¹²In those days when you pray, I will listen. ¹³If you look for me wholeheartedly, you will find me. ¹⁴I will be found by you," says the LORD. "I will end your captivity and restore your fortunes. I will gather you out of the nations where I sent you and will bring you home again to your own land."

¹⁵You claim that the LORD has raised up prophets for you in Babylon. ¹⁶But this is what the LORD says about the king who sits on David's throne and all those still living here in Jerusalem—your relatives who were not exiled to Babylon. ¹⁷This is what the LORD of Heaven's Armies says: "I will send war, famine, and disease upon them and make them like bad figs, too rotten to eat. ¹⁸Yes, I will pursue them with war, famine, and disease, and I will scatter them around the world. In every nation where I send them, I will make them an object of damnation, horror, contempt, and mockery. ¹⁹For they refuse to listen to me, though I have spoken to them repeatedly through the prophets I sent. And you who are in exile have not listened either," says the LORD.

²⁰Therefore, listen to this message from the LORD, all you captives there in Babylon. ²¹This is what the LORD of Heaven's Armies, the God of Israel, says about your prophets—Ahab son of Kolaiah and Zedekiah son of Maaseiah—who are telling you lies in my name: "I will turn them over to Nebuchadnezzar* for execution before your eyes. ²²Their terrible fate will become proverbial, so that the Judean exiles will curse someone by saying, 'May the LORD make you like Zedekiah and Ahab, whom the king of Babylon burned alive!' ²³For these men have done terrible things among my people. They have committed adultery with their neighbors' wives and have lied in my name, saying things I did not command. I am a witness to this. I, the LORD, have spoken."

A Message for Shemaiah

²⁴The LORD sent this message to Shemaiah the Nehelamite in Babylon: ²⁵"This is what the LORD of Heaven's Armies, the God of Israel, says: You wrote a letter on your own authority to Zephaniah son of Ma-

---

29:2 Hebrew *Jeconiah,* a variant spelling of Jehoiachin.   29:21 Hebrew *Nebuchadrezzar,* a variant spelling of Nebuchadnezzar.

29:11 What comfort this verse offers! In our despair, we must remember that God has a special plan for each of us; he wants to bless us. Our challenge is to act on that knowledge. In recovery we are to pray for knowledge of God's will and the power to carry it out. Our recovery is an important part of God's will for us. We can begin the process by recognizing how helpless we are against our dependency and entrusting our life into God's powerful yet loving hands. Realizing how much God loves us gives us hope for the future.

aseiah, the priest, and you sent copies to the other priests and people in Jerusalem. You wrote to Zephaniah,

²⁶"The LORD has appointed you to replace Jehoiada as the priest in charge of the house of the LORD. You are responsible to put into stocks and neck irons any crazy man who claims to be a prophet. ²⁷So why have you done nothing to stop Jeremiah from Anathoth, who pretends to be a prophet among you? ²⁸Jeremiah sent a letter here to Babylon, predicting that our captivity will be a long one. He said, 'Build homes, and plan to stay. Plant gardens, and eat the food they produce.'"

²⁹But when Zephaniah the priest received Shemaiah's letter, he took it to Jeremiah and read it to him. ³⁰Then the LORD gave this message to Jeremiah: ³¹"Send an open letter to all the exiles in Babylon. Tell them, 'This is what the LORD says concerning Shemaiah the Nehelamite: Since he has prophesied to you when I did not send him and has tricked you into believing his lies, ³²I will punish him and his family. None of his descendants will see the good things I will do for my people, for he has incited you to rebel against me. I, the LORD, have spoken!'"

CHAPTER 30
Promises of Deliverance

The LORD gave another message to Jeremiah. He said, ²"This is what the LORD, the God of Israel, says: Write down for the record everything I have said to you, Jeremiah. ³For the time is coming when I will restore the fortunes of my people of Israel and Judah. I will bring them home to this land that I gave to their ancestors, and they will possess it again. I, the LORD, have spoken!"

⁴This is the message the LORD gave concerning Israel and Judah. ⁵This is what the LORD says:

"I hear cries of fear;
    there is terror and no peace.
⁶Now let me ask you a question:
    Do men give birth to babies?

30:7 Hebrew *Jacob*; also in 30:10b, 18. See note on 5:20.

Then why do they stand there,
    ashen-faced,
hands pressed against their sides
    like a woman in labor?
⁷In all history there has never been such a
    time of terror.
It will be a time of trouble for my
    people Israel.*
Yet in the end they will be saved!
⁸For in that day,"
    says the LORD of Heaven's Armies,
"I will break the yoke from their necks
    and snap their chains.
Foreigners will no longer be their masters.
⁹   For my people will serve the LORD their
        God
and their king descended from David—
    the king I will raise up for them.

¹⁰"So do not be afraid, Jacob, my servant;
    do not be dismayed, Israel,"
    says the LORD.
"For I will bring you home again from
    distant lands,
    and your children will return from
        their exile.
Israel will return to a life of peace and
    quiet,
    and no one will terrorize them.
¹¹For I am with you and will save you,"
    says the LORD.
"I will completely destroy the nations
    where I have scattered you,
    but I will not completely destroy you.
I will discipline you, but with justice;
    I cannot let you go unpunished."

¹²This is what the LORD says:
"Your injury is incurable—
    a terrible wound.
¹³There is no one to help you
    or to bind up your injury.
No medicine can heal you.
¹⁴All your lovers—your allies—have left you
    and do not care about you anymore.
I have wounded you cruelly,
    as though I were your enemy.
For your sins are many,
    and your guilt is great.

30:1-24 The people of Judah hungered for God's judgment to end, just as every child eagerly awaits the end of discipline. Before his wrath was fully upon them, God told his people that they would be renewed and restored. Such a promise unveils the unfailing love God has for us. His punishment is real, but it is motivated by a desire for healing and true restoration. Just like the people of Judah, we often resist God's will for us until we discover that doing things our own way leads to destruction. If we repent and follow God's will for our life, he will use our punishment as a significant step in the recovery process.

¹⁵ Why do you protest your punishment—
  this wound that has no cure?
I have had to punish you
  because your sins are many
  and your guilt is great.

¹⁶ "But all who devour you will be devoured,
  and all your enemies will be sent into
  exile.
All who plunder you will be plundered,
  and all who attack you will be
  attacked.
¹⁷ I will give you back your health
  and heal your wounds," says the LORD.
"For you are called an outcast—
  'Jerusalem* for whom no one cares.'"

¹⁸ This is what the LORD says:
"When I bring Israel home again from
  captivity
  and restore their fortunes,
Jerusalem will be rebuilt on its ruins,
  and the palace reconstructed as before.
¹⁹ There will be joy and songs of
  thanksgiving,
  and I will multiply my people, not
  diminish them;
I will honor them, not despise them.
²⁰   Their children will prosper as they did
  long ago.
I will establish them as a nation before
  me,
  and I will punish anyone who hurts
  them.
²¹ They will have their own ruler again,
  and he will come from their own
  people.
I will invite him to approach me," says
  the LORD,
  "for who would dare to come unless
  invited?
²² You will be my people,
  and I will be your God."

²³ Look! The LORD's anger bursts out like a
  storm,
  a driving wind that swirls down on the
  heads of the wicked.
²⁴ The fierce anger of the LORD will not
  diminish
  until it has finished all he has planned.

In the days to come
  you will understand all this.

CHAPTER 31
Hope for Restoration
"In that day," says the LORD, "I will be the
God of all the families of Israel, and they will
be my people. ²This is what the LORD says:

"Those who survive the coming
  destruction
  will find blessings even in the barren
  land,
  for I will give rest to the people of
  Israel."

³ Long ago the LORD said to Israel:
"I have loved you, my people, with an
  everlasting love.
With unfailing love I have drawn you
  to myself.
⁴ I will rebuild you, my virgin Israel.
  You will again be happy
  and dance merrily with your
  tambourines.
⁵ Again you will plant your vineyards on
  the mountains of Samaria
  and eat from your own gardens there.
⁶ The day will come when watchmen will
  shout
  from the hill country of Ephraim,
'Come, let us go up to Jerusalem*
  to worship the LORD our God.'"

⁷ Now this is what the LORD says:
"Sing with joy for Israel.*
  Shout for the greatest of nations!
Shout out with praise and joy:
'Save your people, O LORD,
  the remnant of Israel!'
⁸ For I will bring them from the north
  and from the distant corners of the
  earth.
I will not forget the blind and lame,
  the expectant mothers and women in
  labor.
A great company will return!
⁹ Tears of joy will stream down their
  faces,
  and I will lead them home with great
  care.

30:17 Hebrew *Zion.* 31:6 Hebrew *Zion;* also in 31:12. 31:7 Hebrew *Jacob;* also in 31:11. See note on 5:20.

31:1-40 God paints a joyful picture of recovery, with all the elements of repentance, sorrow,
forgiveness, laughter, restoration, and hope. Once again God's people would follow his plan for
them, and he would receive their worship and praise. We can experience this kind of restoration,
too. We start the process by admitting our need for God's healing power in our life. God desires
to rebuild his relationship with each of us, no matter how far we have strayed from him. He
delights in finding new ways to exhibit his love to those who belong to him.

They will walk beside quiet streams
and on smooth paths where they will
not stumble.
For I am Israel's father,
and Ephraim is my oldest child.

¹⁰ "Listen to this message from the LORD,
you nations of the world;
proclaim it in distant coastlands:
The LORD, who scattered his people,
will gather them and watch over them
as a shepherd does his flock.
¹¹ For the LORD has redeemed Israel
from those too strong for them.
¹² They will come home and sing songs of
joy on the heights of Jerusalem.
They will be radiant because of the
LORD's good gifts—
the abundant crops of grain, new wine,
and olive oil,
and the healthy flocks and herds.
Their life will be like a watered garden,
and all their sorrows will be gone.
¹³ The young women will dance for joy,
and the men—old and young—will join
in the celebration.
I will turn their mourning into joy.
I will comfort them and exchange their
sorrow for rejoicing.
¹⁴ The priests will enjoy abundance,
and my people will feast on my good
gifts.
I, the LORD, have spoken!"

Rachel's Sadness Turns to Joy

¹⁵ This is what the LORD says:

"A cry is heard in Ramah—
deep anguish and bitter weeping.
Rachel weeps for her children,
refusing to be comforted—
for her children are gone."

¹⁶ But now this is what the LORD says:
"Do not weep any longer,
for I will reward you," says the LORD.
"Your children will come back to you
from the distant land of the enemy.
¹⁷ There is hope for your future," says the
LORD.
"Your children will come again to their
own land.
¹⁸ I have heard Israel* saying,
'You disciplined me severely,
like a calf that needs training for the
yoke.
Turn me again to you and restore me,

for you alone are the LORD my God.
¹⁹ I turned away from God,
but then I was sorry.
I kicked myself for my stupidity!
I was thoroughly ashamed of all I did in
my younger days.'

²⁰ "Is not Israel still my son,
my darling child?" says the LORD.
"I often have to punish him,
but I still love him.
That's why I long for him
and surely will have mercy on him.
²¹ Set up road signs;
put up guideposts.
Mark well the path
by which you came.
Come back again, my virgin Israel;
return to your towns here.
²² How long will you wander,
my wayward daughter?
For the LORD will cause something new to
happen—
Israel will embrace her God.*"

²³ This is what the LORD of Heaven's Armies, the God of Israel, says: "When I bring them back from captivity, the people of Judah and its towns will again say, 'The LORD bless you, O righteous home, O holy mountain!' ²⁴ Townspeople and farmers and shepherds alike will live together in peace and happiness. ²⁵ For I have given rest to the weary and joy to the sorrowing."

²⁶ At this, I woke up and looked around. My sleep had been very sweet.

²⁷ "The day is coming," says the LORD, "when I will greatly increase the human population and the number of animals here in Israel and Judah. ²⁸ In the past I deliberately uprooted and tore down this nation. I overthrew it, destroyed it, and brought disaster upon it. But in the future I will just as deliberately plant it and build it up. I, the LORD, have spoken!

²⁹ "The people will no longer quote this proverb:

'The parents have eaten sour grapes,
but their children's mouths pucker at
the taste.'

³⁰ All people will die for their own sins—those who eat the sour grapes will be the ones whose mouths will pucker.

³¹ "The day is coming," says the LORD, "when I will make a new covenant with the

31:18 Hebrew *Ephraim*, referring to the northern kingdom of Israel; also in 31:20. 31:22 Hebrew *a woman will surround a man.*

people of Israel and Judah. ³²This covenant will not be like the one I made with their ancestors when I took them by the hand and brought them out of the land of Egypt. They broke that covenant, though I loved them as a husband loves his wife," says the LORD.

³³"But this is the new covenant I will make with the people of Israel after those days," says the LORD. "I will put my instructions deep within them, and I will write them on their hearts. I will be their God, and they will be my people. ³⁴And they will not need to teach their neighbors, nor will they need to teach their relatives, saying, 'You should know the LORD.' For everyone, from the least to the greatest, will know me already," says the LORD. "And I will forgive their wickedness, and I will never again remember their sins."

³⁵ It is the LORD who provides the sun to
   light the day
   and the moon and stars to light the
      night,
   and who stirs the sea into roaring
      waves.
His name is the LORD of Heaven's Armies,
   and this is what he says:
³⁶ "I am as likely to reject my people Israel
   as I am to abolish the laws of nature!"
³⁷ This is what the LORD says:
   "Just as the heavens cannot be measured
      and the foundations of the earth
         cannot be explored,
   so I will not consider casting them away
      for the evil they have done.
   I, the LORD, have spoken!

³⁸"The day is coming," says the LORD, "when all Jerusalem will be rebuilt for me, from the Tower of Hananel to the Corner Gate. ³⁹A measuring line will be stretched out

over the hill of Gareb and across to Goah. ⁴⁰And the entire area—including the graveyard and ash dump in the valley, and all the fields out to the Kidron Valley on the east as far as the Horse Gate—will be holy to the LORD. The city will never again be captured or destroyed."

CHAPTER 32
Jeremiah's Land Purchase
The following message came to Jeremiah from the LORD in the tenth year of the reign of Zedekiah,* king of Judah. This was also the eighteenth year of the reign of King Nebuchadnezzar.* ²Jerusalem was then under siege from the Babylonian army, and Jeremiah was imprisoned in the courtyard of the guard in the royal palace. ³King Zedekiah had put him there, asking why he kept giving this prophecy: "This is what the LORD says: 'I am about to hand this city over to the king of Babylon, and he will take it. ⁴King Zedekiah will be captured by the Babylonians* and taken to meet the king of Babylon face to face. ⁵He will take Zedekiah to Babylon, and I will deal with him there,' says the LORD. 'If you fight against the Babylonians, you will never succeed.'"

⁶At that time the LORD sent me a message. He said, ⁷"Your cousin Hanamel son of Shallum will come and say to you, 'Buy my field at Anathoth. By law you have the right to buy it before it is offered to anyone else.'"

⁸Then, just as the LORD had said he would, my cousin Hanamel came and visited me in the prison. He said, "Please buy my field at Anathoth in the land of Benjamin. By law you have the right to buy it before it is offered to anyone else, so buy it for yourself." Then I knew that the message I had heard was from the LORD.

32:1a The tenth year of Zedekiah's reign and the eighteenth year of Nebuchadnezzar's reign was 587 B.C.
32:1b Hebrew *Nebuchadrezzar,* a variant spelling of Nebuchadnezzar; also in 32:28. **32:4** Or *Chaldeans;* also in 32:5, 24, 25, 28, 29, 43.

32:1-5 Even though Jeremiah's prophecies were coming true, King Zedekiah still ignored his message. He and his people continued their denial. We, too, are very good at hiding from the truth. We scheme to hide our dependency and other problems from others. We even hide the truth from ourself. We cannot recover from problems that we refuse to admit. We need to face the fact that our life is out of control and we are headed for destruction. Once we have done that, we can give our sins and problems to God and allow him to deliver and restore us.
32:6-15 Jeremiah was instructed to buy land, even though the Babylonians would soon conquer Judah and their laws of ownership would no longer apply. God used Jeremiah's actions to show that there was still hope. Despite the losses they would soon experience, God would one day restore the Promised Land to his people. Jeremiah's investment in real estate would be valuable someday. We may be facing the devastating consequences of our addiction and see little hope for the future. But just as Jeremiah invested in Israel's future, God has invested in our future through the atoning death of Jesus Christ. Through him we can receive the comfort and power needed to recover from total devastation.

⁹So I bought the field at Anathoth, paying Hanamel seventeen pieces* of silver for it. ¹⁰I signed and sealed the deed of purchase before witnesses, weighed out the silver, and paid him. ¹¹Then I took the sealed deed and an unsealed copy of the deed, which contained the terms and conditions of the purchase, ¹²and I handed them to Baruch son of Neriah and grandson of Mahseiah. I did all this in the presence of my cousin Hanamel, the witnesses who had signed the deed, and all the men of Judah who were there in the courtyard of the guardhouse.

¹³Then I said to Baruch as they all listened, ¹⁴"This is what the LORD of Heaven's Armies, the God of Israel, says: 'Take both this sealed deed and the unsealed copy, and put them into a pottery jar to preserve them for a long time.' ¹⁵For this is what the LORD of Heaven's Armies, the God of Israel, says: 'Someday people will again own property here in this land and will buy and sell houses and vineyards and fields.'"

Jeremiah's Prayer

¹⁶Then after I had given the papers to Baruch, I prayed to the LORD:

¹⁷"O Sovereign LORD! You made the heavens and earth by your strong hand and powerful arm. Nothing is too hard for you! ¹⁸You show unfailing love to thousands, but you also bring the consequences of one generation's sin upon the next. You are the great and powerful God, the LORD of Heaven's Armies. ¹⁹You have all wisdom and do great and mighty miracles. You see the conduct of all people, and you give them what they deserve. ²⁰You performed miraculous signs and wonders in the land of Egypt—things still remembered to this day! And you have continued to do great miracles in Israel and all around the world. You have made your name famous to this day.

²¹"You brought Israel out of Egypt with mighty signs and wonders, with a strong hand and powerful arm, and with

overwhelming terror. ²²You gave the people of Israel this land that you had promised their ancestors long before—a land flowing with milk and honey. ²³Our ancestors came and conquered it and lived in it, but they refused to obey you or follow your word. They have not done anything you commanded. That is why you have sent this terrible disaster upon them.

²⁴"See how the siege ramps have been built against the city walls! Through war, famine, and disease, the city will be handed over to the Babylonians, who will conquer it. Everything has happened just as you said. ²⁵And yet, O Sovereign LORD, you have told me to buy the field— paying good money for it before these witnesses—even though the city will soon be handed over to the Babylonians."

A Prediction of Jerusalem's Fall

²⁶Then this message came to Jeremiah from the LORD: ²⁷"I am the LORD, the God of all the peoples of the world. Is anything too hard for me? ²⁸Therefore, this is what the LORD says: I will hand this city over to the Babylonians and to Nebuchadnezzar, king of Babylon, and he will capture it. ²⁹The Babylonians outside the walls will come in and set fire to the city. They will burn down all these houses where the people provoked my anger by burning incense to Baal on the rooftops and by pouring out liquid offerings to other gods. ³⁰Israel and Judah have done nothing but wrong since their earliest days. They have infuriated me with all their evil deeds," says the LORD. ³¹"From the time this city was built until now, it has done nothing but anger me, so I am determined to get rid of it.

³²"The sins of Israel and Judah—the sins of the people of Jerusalem, the kings, the officials, the priests, and the prophets—have stirred up my anger. ³³My people have turned their backs on me and have refused to return. Even though I diligently taught them, they would not receive instruction or obey.

32:9 Hebrew *17 shekels*, about 7 ounces or 194 grams in weight.

32:27-39 God wanted his people to accept responsibility for their sins, bad choices, and failures; their suffering in exile would force them to do this. But their story does not end with destruction and exile. God promised that he would deliver his people from captivity, restore them to their homeland, and reconcile his relationship with them. These promises must have sounded impossible to people facing warfare, famine, and disease. God began with a question to answer his people's doubt: "Is anything too hard for me?" As we face problems and dependencies that are beyond our control, there is still hope. Nothing is too hard for God!

34They have set up their abominable idols right in my own Temple, defiling it. 35They have built pagan shrines to Baal in the valley of Ben-Hinnom, and there they sacrifice their sons and daughters to Molech. I have never commanded such a horrible deed; it never even crossed my mind to command such a thing. What an incredible evil, causing Judah to sin so greatly!

A Promise of Restoration

36"Now I want to say something more about this city. You have been saying, 'It will fall to the king of Babylon through war, famine, and disease.' But this is what the LORD, the God of Israel, says: 37I will certainly bring my people back again from all the countries where I will scatter them in my fury. I will bring them back to this very city and let them live in peace and safety. 38They will be my people, and I will be their God. 39And I will give them one heart and one purpose: to worship me forever, for their own good and for the good of all their descendants. 40And I will make an everlasting covenant with them: I will never stop doing good for them. I will put a desire in their hearts to worship me, and they will never leave me. 41I will find joy doing good for them and will faithfully and wholeheartedly replant them in this land.

42"This is what the LORD says: Just as I have brought all these calamities on them, so I will do all the good I have promised them. 43Fields will again be bought and sold in this land about which you now say, 'It has been ravaged by the Babylonians, a desolate land where people and animals have all disappeared.' 44Yes, fields will once again be bought and sold—deeds signed and sealed and witnessed—in the land of Benjamin and here in Jerusalem, in the towns of Judah and in the hill country, in the foothills of Judah* and in the Negev, too. For someday I will restore prosperity to them. I, the LORD, have spoken!"

CHAPTER 33
Promises of Peace and Prosperity

While Jeremiah was still confined in the courtyard of the guard, the LORD gave him this second message: 2"This is what the LORD says—the LORD who made the earth, who formed and established it, whose name is the LORD: 3Ask me and I will tell you remarkable secrets you do not know about things to come. 4For this is what the LORD, the God of Israel, says: You have torn down the houses of this city and even the king's palace to get materials to strengthen the walls against the siege ramps and swords of the enemy. 5You expect to fight the Babylonians,* but the men of this city are already as good as dead, for I have determined to destroy them in my terrible anger. I have abandoned them because of all their wickedness.

6"Nevertheless, the time will come when I will heal Jerusalem's wounds and give it prosperity and true peace. 7I will restore the fortunes of Judah and Israel and rebuild their towns. 8I will cleanse them of their sins against me and forgive all their sins of rebellion. 9Then this city will bring me joy, glory, and honor before all the nations of the earth! The people of the world will see all the good I do for my people, and they will tremble with awe at the peace and prosperity I provide for them.

10"This is what the LORD says: You have said, 'This is a desolate land where people and animals have all disappeared.' Yet in the empty streets of Jerusalem and Judah's other towns, there will be heard once more 11the sounds of joy and laughter. The joyful voices of bridegrooms and brides will be heard again, along with the joyous songs of people bringing thanksgiving offerings to the LORD. They will sing,

'Give thanks to the LORD of Heaven's
    Armies,
  for the LORD is good.
  His faithful love endures forever!'

For I will restore the prosperity of this land to what it was in the past, says the LORD.

12"This is what the LORD of Heaven's Armies says: This land—though it is now desolate and has no people and animals— will once more have pastures where shepherds can lead their flocks. 13Once again shepherds will count their flocks in the towns of the hill country, the foothills of Ju-

32:44 Hebrew *the Shephelah.* 33:5 Or *Chaldeans.* 33:13 Hebrew *the Shephelah.*

33:1-26 When life seems like an unstable disaster, there is one thing we can count on: God is committed to us and to our recovery. He has promised to never abandon us. No matter how gray our life may be, no matter how dark the future seems, our loving and faithful God can heal us, restore our hope, and lead us toward recovery. As we trust him with our disappointments, failures, sins, and confusion, we will find him faithful to comfort, forgive, and guide us.

dah,* the Negev, the land of Benjamin, the vicinity of Jerusalem, and all the towns of Judah. I, the LORD, have spoken!

¹⁴"The day will come, says the LORD, when I will do for Israel and Judah all the good things I have promised them.

¹⁵ "In those days and at that time
   I will raise up a righteous descendant*
      from King David's line.
   He will do what is just and right
      throughout the land.
¹⁶ In that day Judah will be saved,
      and Jerusalem will live in safety.
   And this will be its name:
      'The LORD Is Our Righteousness.'*

¹⁷For this is what the LORD says: David will have a descendant sitting on the throne of Israel forever. ¹⁸And there will always be Levitical priests to offer burnt offerings and grain offerings and sacrifices to me."

¹⁹Then this message came to Jeremiah from the LORD: ²⁰"This is what the LORD says: If you can break my covenant with the day and the night so that one does not follow the other, ²¹only then will my covenant with my servant David be broken. Only then will he no longer have a descendant to reign on his throne. The same is true for my covenant with the Levitical priests who minister before me. ²²And as the stars of the sky cannot be counted and the sand on the seashore cannot be measured, so I will multiply the descendants of my servant David and the Levites who minister before me."

²³The LORD gave another message to Jeremiah. He said, ²⁴"Have you noticed what people are saying?—'The LORD chose Judah and Israel and then abandoned them!' They are sneering and saying that Israel is not worthy to be counted as a nation. ²⁵But this is what the LORD says: I would no more reject my people than I would change my laws that

govern night and day, earth and sky. ²⁶I will never abandon the descendants of Jacob or David, my servant, or change the plan that David's descendants will rule the descendants of Abraham, Isaac, and Jacob. Instead, I will restore them to their land and have mercy on them."

CHAPTER 34
A Warning for Zedekiah
King Nebuchadnezzar* of Babylon came with all the armies from the kingdoms he ruled, and he fought against Jerusalem and the towns of Judah. At that time this message came to Jeremiah from the LORD: ²"Go to King Zedekiah of Judah, and tell him, 'This is what the LORD, the God of Israel, says: I am about to hand this city over to the king of Babylon, and he will burn it down. ³You will not escape his grasp but will be captured and taken to meet the king of Babylon face to face. Then you will be exiled to Babylon.

⁴"But listen to this promise from the LORD, O Zedekiah, king of Judah. This is what the LORD says: You will not be killed in war ⁵but will die peacefully. People will burn incense in your memory, just as they did for your ancestors, the kings who preceded you. They will mourn for you, crying, "Alas, our master is dead!" This I have decreed, says the LORD.'"

⁶So Jeremiah the prophet delivered the message to King Zedekiah of Judah. ⁷At this time the Babylonian army was besieging Jerusalem, Lachish, and Azekah—the only fortified cities of Judah not yet captured.

Freedom for Hebrew Slaves
⁸This message came to Jeremiah from the LORD after King Zedekiah made a covenant with the people, proclaiming freedom for the slaves. ⁹He had ordered all the people to free their Hebrew slaves—both men and

33:15 Hebrew *a righteous branch.* 33:16 Hebrew *Yahweh Tsidqenu.* 34:1 Hebrew *Nebuchadrezzar, a variant spelling of Nebuchadnezzar.*

34:1-7 The errant Zedekiah would not be killed in war, even though his deeds had caused the sufferings of many. God was gracious and promised Zedekiah a peaceful death. We always deserve far more punishment than we actually receive. If we always received what we deserved, even the best of us would suffer terrible punishment. God deals with us by grace (see Ephesians 2:8-9), not by a strict code of justice. Such is the heart of the gospel. No matter what we have done in the past, there is still hope. If we honestly admit our sins and turn to God, he will be gracious to us and forgive us.

34:8-22 Zedekiah accepted God's grace and, in turn, extended grace to others. He called his people to free all their Hebrew slaves, one of God's requirements in the law. While the people initially obeyed Zedekiah's request, they soon returned to their disobedient ways. All the gains they had made toward healing and restoration were soon lost. Recovery is never a onetime act; it is a long-term process. If we fail to persevere in the recovery process, we may end up worse off than we were before. When God calls us to change, he calls us to change permanently.

women. No one was to keep a fellow Judean in bondage. [10]The officials and all the people had obeyed the king's command, [11]but later they changed their minds. They took back the men and women they had freed, forcing them to be slaves again.

[12]So the LORD gave them this message through Jeremiah: [13]"This is what the LORD, the God of Israel, says: I made a covenant with your ancestors long ago when I rescued them from their slavery in Egypt. [14]I told them that every Hebrew slave must be freed after serving six years. But your ancestors paid no attention to me. [15]Recently you repented and did what was right, following my command. You freed your slaves and made a solemn covenant with me in the Temple that bears my name. [16]But now you have shrugged off your oath and defiled my name by taking back the men and women you had freed, forcing them to be slaves once again.

[17]"Therefore, this is what the LORD says: Since you have not obeyed me by setting your countrymen free, I will set you free to be destroyed by war, disease, and famine. You will be an object of horror to all the nations of the earth. [18]Because you have broken the terms of our covenant, I will cut you apart just as you cut apart the calf when you walked between its halves to solemnize your vows. [19]Yes, I will cut you apart, whether you are officials of Judah or Jerusalem, court officials, priests, or common people—for you have broken your oath. [20]I will give you to your enemies, and they will kill you. Your bodies will be food for the vultures and wild animals.

[21]"I will hand over King Zedekiah of Judah and his officials to the army of the king of Babylon. And although they have left Jerusalem for a while, [22]I will call the Babylonian armies back again. They will fight against this city and will capture it and burn it down. I will see to it that all the towns of Judah are destroyed, with no one living there."

CHAPTER 35
The Faithful Recabites

This is the message the LORD gave Jeremiah when Jehoiakim son of Josiah was king of Judah: [2]"Go to the settlement where the families of the Recabites live, and invite them to the LORD's Temple. Take them into one of the inner rooms, and offer them some wine."

[3]So I went to see Jaazaniah son of Jeremiah and grandson of Habazziniah and all his brothers and sons—representing all the Recabite families. [4]I took them to the Temple, and we went into the room assigned to the sons of Hanan son of Igdaliah, a man of God. This room was located next to the one used by the Temple officials, directly above the room of Maaseiah son of Shallum, the Temple gatekeeper.

[5]I set cups and jugs of wine before them and invited them to have a drink, [6]but they refused. "No," they said, "we don't drink wine, because our ancestor Jehonadab* son of Recab gave us this command: 'You and your descendants must never drink wine. [7]And do not build houses or plant crops or vineyards, but always live in tents. If you follow these commands, you will live long, good lives in the land.' [8]So we have obeyed him in all these things. We have never had a drink of wine to this day, nor have our wives, our sons, or our daughters. [9]We haven't built houses or owned vineyards or farms or planted crops. [10]We have lived in tents and have fully obeyed all the commands of Jehonadab, our ancestor. [11]But when King Nebuchadnezzar* of Babylon attacked this country, we were afraid of the Babylonian and Syrian* armies. So we decided to move to Jerusalem. That is why we are here."

[12]Then the LORD gave this message to Jeremiah: [13]"This is what the LORD of Heaven's Armies, the God of Israel, says: Go and say to the people in Judah and Jerusalem, 'Come and learn a lesson about how to obey me. [14]The Recabites do not drink wine to this day because their ancestor Jehonadab told them not to. But I have spoken to you again and again, and you refuse to obey me. [15]Time after time I sent you prophets, who told you, "Turn from your wicked ways, and start doing things right. Stop worshiping other gods so that you might live in peace here in the land I have given to you and your ances-

---

35:6 Hebrew *Jonadab*, a variant spelling of Jehonadab; also in 35:10, 19. See 2 Kgs 10:15. **35:11a** Hebrew *Nebuchadrezzar*, a variant spelling of Nebuchadnezzar. **35:11b** Or *Chaldean and Aramean*.

35:1-19 This is a fascinating story about a family that faithfully obeyed the direction set by its ancestors, choosing to submit to a program that fostered its physical, social, and spiritual well-being. God held up this family as an example for the people of Judah. He longed for his people to obey his will just as the Recabites adhered to the instructions of their leaders. Trusting God and obeying his will for our life is the only true path to recovery.

tors." But you would not listen to me or obey me. ¹⁶The descendants of Jehonadab son of Recab have obeyed their ancestor completely, but you have refused to listen to me.'

¹⁷"Therefore, this is what the LORD God of Heaven's Armies, the God of Israel, says: 'Because you refuse to listen or answer when I call, I will send upon Judah and Jerusalem all the disasters I have threatened.'"

¹⁸Then Jeremiah turned to the Recabites and said, "This is what the LORD of Heaven's Armies, the God of Israel, says: 'You have obeyed your ancestor Jehonadab in every respect, following all his instructions.' ¹⁹Therefore, this is what the LORD of Heaven's Armies, the God of Israel, says: 'Jehonadab son of Recab will always have descendants who serve me.'"

CHAPTER 36
Baruch Reads the LORD's Messages
During the fourth year that Jehoiakim son of Josiah was king in Judah,* the LORD gave this message to Jeremiah: ²"Get a scroll, and write down all my messages against Israel, Judah, and the other nations. Begin with the first message back in the days of Josiah, and write down every message, right up to the present time. ³Perhaps the people of Judah will repent when they hear again all the terrible things I have planned for them. Then I will be able to forgive their sins and wrongdoings."

⁴So Jeremiah sent for Baruch son of Neriah, and as Jeremiah dictated all the prophecies that the LORD had given him, Baruch wrote them on a scroll. ⁵Then Jeremiah said to Baruch, "I am a prisoner here and unable to go to the Temple. ⁶So you go to the Temple on the next day of fasting, and read the messages from the LORD that I have had you write on this scroll. Read them so the people who are there from all over Judah will hear them. ⁷Perhaps even yet they will turn from their evil ways and ask the LORD's forgiveness before it is too late. For the LORD has threatened them with his terrible anger."

⁸Baruch did as Jeremiah told him and read these messages from the LORD to the people at the Temple. ⁹He did this on a day of sacred fasting held in late autumn,* during the fifth year of the reign of Jehoiakim son of Josiah. People from all over Judah had come to Jerusalem to attend the services at the Temple on that day. ¹⁰Baruch read Jeremiah's words on the scroll to all the people. He stood in front of the Temple room of Gemariah, son of Shaphan the secretary. This room was just off the upper courtyard of the Temple, near the New Gate entrance.

¹¹When Micaiah son of Gemariah and grandson of Shaphan heard the messages from the LORD, ¹²he went down to the secretary's room in the palace where the administrative officials were meeting. Elishama the secretary was there, along with Delaiah son of Shemaiah, Elnathan son of Acbor, Gemariah son of Shaphan, Zedekiah son of Hananiah, and all the other officials. ¹³When Micaiah told them about the messages Baruch was reading to the people, ¹⁴the officials sent Jehudi son of Nethaniah, grandson of Shelemiah and great-grandson of Cushi, to ask Baruch to come and read the messages to them, too. So Baruch took the scroll and went to them. ¹⁵"Sit down and read the scroll to us," the officials said, and Baruch did as they requested.

¹⁶When they heard all the messages, they looked at one another in alarm. "We must tell the king what we have heard," they said to Baruch. ¹⁷"But first, tell us how you got these messages. Did they come directly from Jeremiah?"

¹⁸So Baruch explained, "Jeremiah dictated them, and I wrote them down in ink, word for word, on this scroll."

¹⁹"You and Jeremiah should both hide," the officials told Baruch. "Don't tell anyone where you are!" ²⁰Then the officials left the scroll for safekeeping in the room of Elishama the secretary and went to tell the king what had happened.

36:1 The fourth year of Jehoiakim's reign was 605 B.C. 36:9 Hebrew *in the ninth month,* of the ancient Hebrew lunar calendar (also in 36:22). The ninth month in the fifth year of Jehoiakim's reign occurred within the months of November and December 604 B.C. Also see note on 1:3.

36:1-32 King Jehoiakim refused to listen to Jeremiah's predictions of coming destruction. He preferred the comforting lies of the false prophets to the terrifying truth of God's prophet. He tried to deny his sins and their consequences by ignoring them. He even burned the scroll on which Jeremiah had written the Lord's message. We must face the truth about our actions and circumstances if we hope to overcome them. Denial can never solve our problems; it only compounds them. Are there false prophets in our life calling us away from the truth? Are we denying our dependency? Only in admitting our dependency can we hope to deal with it.

King Jehoiakim Burns the Scroll

²¹The king sent Jehudi to get the scroll. Jehudi brought it from Elishama's room and read it to the king as all his officials stood by. ²²It was late autumn, and the king was in a winterized part of the palace, sitting in front of a fire to keep warm. ²³Each time Jehudi finished reading three or four columns, the king took a knife and cut off that section of the scroll. He then threw it into the fire, section by section, until the whole scroll was burned up. ²⁴Neither the king nor his attendants showed any signs of fear or repentance at what they heard. ²⁵Even when Elnathan, Delaiah, and Gemariah begged the king not to burn the scroll, he wouldn't listen.

²⁶Then the king commanded his son Jerahmeel, Seraiah son of Azriel, and Shelemiah son of Abdeel to arrest Baruch and Jeremiah. But the LORD had hidden them.

Jeremiah Rewrites the Scroll

²⁷After the king had burned the scroll on which Baruch had written Jeremiah's words, the LORD gave Jeremiah another message. He said, ²⁸"Get another scroll, and write everything again just as you did on the scroll King Jehoiakim burned. ²⁹Then say to the king, 'This is what the LORD says: You burned the scroll because it said the king of Babylon would destroy this land and empty it of people and animals. ³⁰Now this is what the LORD says about King Jehoiakim of Judah: He will have no heirs to sit on the throne of David. His dead body will be thrown out to lie unburied—exposed to the heat of the day and the frost of the night. ³¹I will punish him and his family and his attendants for their sins. I will pour out on them and on all the people of Jerusalem and Judah all the disasters I promised, for they would not listen to my warnings.'"

³²So Jeremiah took another scroll and dictated again to his secretary, Baruch. He wrote everything that had been on the scroll King Jehoiakim had burned in the fire. Only this time he added much more!

CHAPTER 37
Zedekiah Calls for Jeremiah

Zedekiah son of Josiah succeeded Jehoiachin* son of Jehoiakim as the king of Judah. He was appointed by King Nebuchadnezzar* of Babylon. ²But neither King Zedekiah nor his attendants nor the people who were left in the land listened to what the LORD said through Jeremiah.

³Nevertheless, King Zedekiah sent Jehucal son of Shelemiah, and Zephaniah the priest, son of Maaseiah, to ask Jeremiah, "Please pray to the LORD our God for us." ⁴Jeremiah had not yet been imprisoned, so he could come and go among the people as he pleased.

⁵At this time the army of Pharaoh Hophra* of Egypt appeared at the southern border of Judah. When the Babylonian* army heard about it, they withdrew from their siege of Jerusalem.

⁶Then the LORD gave this message to Jeremiah: ⁷"This is what the LORD, the God of Israel, says: The king of Judah sent you to ask me what is going to happen. Tell him, 'Pharaoh's army is about to return to Egypt, though he came here to help you. ⁸Then the Babylonians* will come back and capture this city and burn it to the ground.'

⁹"This is what the LORD says: Do not fool yourselves into thinking that the Babylonians are gone for good. They aren't! ¹⁰Even if you were to destroy the entire Babylonian army, leaving only a handful of wounded survivors, they would still stagger from their tents and burn this city to the ground!"

Jeremiah Is Imprisoned

¹¹When the Babylonian army left Jerusalem because of Pharaoh's approaching army, ¹²Jeremiah started to leave the city on his way to the territory of Benjamin, to claim his share of the property among his relatives there.* ¹³But as he was walking through the Benjamin Gate, a sentry arrested him and said, "You are defecting to the Babylonians!" The sentry making the arrest was Irijah son of Shelemiah, grandson of Hananiah.

¹⁴"That's not true!" Jeremiah protested. "I had no intention of doing any such thing." But Irijah wouldn't listen, and he took Jeremiah before the officials. ¹⁵They were furious with Jeremiah and had him flogged and imprisoned in the house of Jonathan the secretary. Jonathan's house had been converted into a prison. ¹⁶Jeremiah was put into a dungeon cell, where he remained for many days.

¹⁷Later King Zedekiah secretly requested that Jeremiah come to the palace, where the king asked him, "Do you have any messages from the LORD?"

37:1a Hebrew Coniah, a variant spelling of Jehoiachin. 37:1b Hebrew Nebuchadrezzar, a variant spelling of Nebuchadnezzar. 37:5a Hebrew army of Pharaoh; see 44:30. 37:5b Or Chaldean; also in 37:10, 11. 37:8 Or Chaldeans; also in 37:9, 13. 37:12 Hebrew to separate from there in the midst of the people.

"Yes, I do!" said Jeremiah. "You will be defeated by the king of Babylon."

[18]Then Jeremiah asked the king, "What crime have I committed? What have I done against you, your attendants, or the people that I should be imprisoned like this? [19]Where are your prophets now who told you the king of Babylon would not attack you or this land? [20]Listen, my lord the king, I beg you. Don't send me back to the dungeon in the house of Jonathan the secretary, for I will die there."

[21]So King Zedekiah commanded that Jeremiah not be returned to the dungeon. Instead, he was imprisoned in the courtyard of the guard in the royal palace. The king also commanded that Jeremiah be given a loaf of fresh bread every day as long as there was any left in the city. So Jeremiah was put in the palace prison.

CHAPTER 38
Jeremiah in a Cistern

Now Shephatiah son of Mattan, Gedaliah son of Pashhur, Jehucal* son of Shelemiah, and Pashhur son of Malkijah heard what Jeremiah had been telling the people. He had been saying, [2]"This is what the LORD says: 'Everyone who stays in Jerusalem will die from war, famine, or disease, but those who surrender to the Babylonians* will live. Their reward will be life. They will live!' [3]The LORD also says: 'The city of Jerusalem will certainly be handed over to the army of the king of Babylon, who will capture it.'"

[4]So these officials went to the king and said, "Sir, this man must die! That kind of talk will undermine the morale of the few fighting men we have left, as well as that of all the people. This man is a traitor!"

[5]King Zedekiah agreed. "All right," he said. "Do as you like. I can't stop you."

[6]So the officials took Jeremiah from his cell and lowered him by ropes into an empty cistern in the prison yard. It belonged to Malkijah, a member of the royal family. There was no water in the cistern, but there was a thick layer of mud at the bottom, and Jeremiah sank down into it.

[7]But Ebed-melech the Ethiopian,* an important court official, heard that Jeremiah was in the cistern. At that time the king was holding court at the Benjamin Gate, [8]so Ebed-melech rushed from the palace to speak with him. [9]"My lord the king," he said, "these men have done a very evil thing in putting Jeremiah the prophet into the cistern. He will soon die of hunger, for almost all the bread in the city is gone."

[10]So the king told Ebed-melech, "Take thirty of my men with you, and pull Jeremiah out of the cistern before he dies."

[11]So Ebed-melech took the men with him and went to a room in the palace beneath the treasury, where he found some old rags and discarded clothing. He carried these to the cistern and lowered them to Jeremiah on a rope. [12]Ebed-melech called down to Jeremiah, "Put these rags under your armpits to protect you from the ropes." Then when Jeremiah was ready, [13]they pulled him out. So Jeremiah was returned to the courtyard of the guard—the palace prison—where he remained.

Zedekiah Questions Jeremiah

[14]One day King Zedekiah sent for Jeremiah and had him brought to the third entrance of the LORD's Temple. "I want to ask you something," the king said. "And don't try to hide the truth."

[15]Jeremiah said, "If I tell you the truth, you will kill me. And if I give you advice, you won't listen to me anyway."

[16]So King Zedekiah secretly promised him, "As surely as the LORD our Creator lives, I will not kill you or hand you over to the men who want you dead."

[17]Then Jeremiah said to Zedekiah, "This is what the LORD God of Heaven's Armies, the God of Israel, says: 'If you surrender to the Babylonian officers, you and your family will live, and the city will not be burned down. [18]But if you refuse to surrender, you will not escape! This city will be handed over to the Babylonians, and they will burn it to the ground.'"

[19]"But I am afraid to surrender," the king

38:1 Hebrew *Jucal,* a variant spelling of Jehucal; see 37:3. **38:2** Or *Chaldeans;* also in 38:18, 19, 23. **38:7** Hebrew *the Cushite.*

38:14-28 Jeremiah gave Zedekiah clear direction from God, but the king was too insecure to follow the prophet's advice. We often fall into the same trap. God gives us clear direction in his Word, but we fail to act on what we know. Sometimes we are afraid of what others will think or of what God is asking; other times we simply don't want to comply, or we feel too tired to act. Seeking out God's will for us is only part of the task. We must act on our knowledge before it will become effective in our life.

said, "for the Babylonians may hand me over to the Judeans who have defected to them. And who knows what they will do to me!"

[20]Jeremiah replied, "You won't be handed over to them if you choose to obey the LORD. Your life will be spared, and all will go well for you. [21]But if you refuse to surrender, this is what the LORD has revealed to me: [22]All the women left in your palace will be brought out and given to the officers of the Babylonian army. Then the women will taunt you, saying,

'What fine friends you have!
  They have betrayed and misled you.
When your feet sank in the mud,
  they left you to your fate!'

[23]All your wives and children will be led out to the Babylonians, and you will not escape. You will be seized by the king of Babylon, and this city will be burned down."

[24]Then Zedekiah said to Jeremiah, "Don't tell anyone you told me this, or you will die! [25]My officials may hear that I spoke to you, and they may say, 'Tell us what you and the king were talking about. If you don't tell us, we will kill you.' [26]If this happens, just tell them you begged me not to send you back to Jonathan's dungeon, for fear you would die there."

[27]Sure enough, it wasn't long before the king's officials came to Jeremiah and asked him why the king had called for him. But Jeremiah followed the king's instructions, and they left without finding out the truth. No one had overheard the conversation between Jeremiah and the king. [28]And Jeremiah remained a prisoner in the courtyard of the guard until the day Jerusalem was captured.

CHAPTER 39
The Fall of Jerusalem

In January* of the ninth year of King Zedekiah's reign, King Nebuchadnezzar* of Babylon came with his entire army to besiege Jerusalem. [2]Two and a half years later, on July 18* in the eleventh year of Zedekiah's reign, a section of the city wall was broken down. [3]All the officers of the Babylonian army came in and sat in triumph at the Middle Gate: Nergal-sharezer of Samgar, and Nebosarsekim,* a chief officer, and Nergal-sharezer, the king's adviser, and all the other officers of the king of Babylon.

[4]When King Zedekiah of Judah and all the soldiers saw that the Babylonians had broken into the city, they fled. They waited for nightfall and then slipped through the gate between the two walls behind the king's garden and headed toward the Jordan Valley.*

[5]But the Babylonian* troops chased them and overtook Zedekiah on the plains of Jericho. They captured him and took him to King Nebuchadnezzar of Babylon, who was at Riblah in the land of Hamath. There the king of Babylon pronounced judgment upon Zedekiah. [6]The king of Babylon made Zedekiah watch as he slaughtered his sons at Riblah. The king of Babylon also slaughtered all the nobles of Judah. [7]Then he gouged out Zedekiah's eyes and bound him in bronze chains to lead him away to Babylon.

[8]Meanwhile, the Babylonians burned Jerusalem, including the royal palace and the houses of the people, and they tore down the walls of the city. [9]Then Nebuzaradan, the captain of the guard, took as exiles to Babylon the rest of the people who remained in the city, those who had defected to him, and everyone else who remained. [10]But Nebuzaradan allowed some of the poorest people to stay behind in the land of Judah, and he assigned them to care for the vineyards and fields.

Jeremiah Remains in Judah

[11]King Nebuchadnezzar had told Nebuzaradan, the captain of the guard, to find Jeremiah. [12]"See that he isn't hurt," he said. "Look after him well, and give him anything he wants." [13]So Nebuzaradan, the captain of the guard; Nebushazban, a chief officer; Nergal-sharezer, the king's adviser; and the other officers of Babylon's king [14]sent messengers to bring Jeremiah out of the prison.

39:1a Hebrew *in the tenth month,* of the ancient Hebrew lunar calendar. A number of events in Jeremiah can be cross-checked with dates in surviving Babylonian records and related accurately to our modern calendar. This event occurred on January 15, 588 B.C.; see 52:4a and the note there. **39:1b** Hebrew *Nebuchadrezzar,* a variant spelling of Nebuchadnezzar; also in 39:5, 11. **39:2** Hebrew *On the ninth day of the fourth month.* This day was July 18, 586 B.C.; also see note on 39:1a. **39:3** Or *Nergal-sharezer, Samgar-nebo, Sarsekim.* **39:4** Hebrew *the Arabah.* **39:5** Or *Chaldean;* similarly in 39:8.

39:1-18 Tragic scenes of murder and destruction filled Jerusalem as it fell to King Nebuchadnezzar and Jeremiah's prophecy became reality. Even when we are expecting the consequences of our sins, the resulting pain is no less difficult to bear. God doesn't enjoy our pain; he longs for us to learn from the devastation and turn to him.

They put him under the care of Gedaliah son of Ahikam and grandson of Shaphan, who took him back to his home. So Jeremiah stayed in Judah among his own people.

¹⁵The LORD had given the following message to Jeremiah while he was still in prison: ¹⁶"Say to Ebed-melech the Ethiopian,* 'This is what the LORD of Heaven's Armies, the God of Israel, says: I will do to this city everything I have threatened. I will send disaster, not prosperity. You will see its destruction, ¹⁷but I will rescue you from those you fear so much. ¹⁸Because you trusted me, I will give you your life as a reward. I will rescue you and keep you safe. I, the LORD, have spoken!'"

CHAPTER 40

The LORD gave a message to Jeremiah after Nebuzaradan, the captain of the guard, had released him at Ramah. He had found Jeremiah bound in chains among all the other captives of Jerusalem and Judah who were being sent to exile in Babylon.

²The captain of the guard called for Jeremiah and said, "The LORD your God has brought this disaster on this land, ³just as he said he would. For these people have sinned against the LORD and disobeyed him. That is why it happened. ⁴But I am going to take off your chains and let you go. If you want to come with me to Babylon, you are welcome. I will see that you are well cared for. But if you don't want to come, you may stay here. The whole land is before you—go wherever you like. ⁵If you decide to stay, then return to Gedaliah son of Ahikam and grandson of Shaphan. He has been appointed governor of Judah by the king of Babylon. Stay there with the people he rules. But it's up to you; go wherever you like."

Then Nebuzaradan, the captain of the guard, gave Jeremiah some food and money and let him go. ⁶So Jeremiah returned to Gedaliah son of Ahikam at Mizpah, and he lived in Judah with the few who were still left in the land.

Gedaliah Governs in Judah

⁷The leaders of the Judean guerrilla bands in the countryside heard that the king of Babylon had appointed Gedaliah son of Ahikam as governor over the poor people who were left behind in Judah—the men, women, and children who hadn't been exiled to Babylon. ⁸So they went to see Gedaliah at Mizpah. These included: Ishmael son of Nethaniah, Johanan and Jonathan sons of Kareah, Seraiah son of Tanhumeth, the sons of Ephai the Netophathite, Jezaniah son of the Maacathite, and all their men.

⁹Gedaliah vowed to them that the Babylonians* meant them no harm. "Don't be afraid to serve them. Live in the land and serve the king of Babylon, and all will go well for you," he promised. ¹⁰"As for me, I will stay at Mizpah to represent you before the Babylonians who come to meet with us. Settle in the towns you have taken, and live off the land. Harvest the grapes and summer fruits and olives, and store them away."

¹¹When the Judeans in Moab, Ammon, Edom, and the other nearby countries heard that the king of Babylon had left a few people in Judah and that Gedaliah was the governor, ¹²they began to return to Judah from the places to which they had fled. They stopped at Mizpah to meet with Gedaliah and then went into the Judean countryside to gather a great harvest of grapes and other crops.

A Plot against Gedaliah

¹³Soon after this, Johanan son of Kareah and the other guerrilla leaders came to Gedaliah at Mizpah. ¹⁴They said to him, "Did you know that Baalis, king of Ammon, has sent Ishmael son of Nethaniah to assassinate you?" But Gedaliah refused to believe them.

¹⁵Later Johanan had a private conference with Gedaliah and volunteered to kill Ishmael secretly. "Why should we let him come and murder you?" Johanan asked. "What will happen then to the Judeans who

---

39:16 Hebrew *the Cushite.* 40:9 Or *Chaldeans;* also in 40:10.

40:1-12 For the first time since Jeremiah's prophetic work began, we see peace and harmony in the lives of God's people. The reason was simple. They were following God's directive to serve Nebuchadnezzar. They were obeying God. There is peace both within us and among us when we seek to follow God's will for us.

40:13–43:13 When turmoil again threatened the security of the people, they chose to take matters back into their own hands. Sometimes the lessons we think we have learned must be learned all over again. When things begin to go well for us in the recovery process, we may forget our need for God and go back to doing things our way. This tendency toward self-sufficiency, however, will only lead toward a relapse. If we forget that our dependency is too strong for us and try to go it alone, there is little hope for our ultimate success.

have returned? Why should the few of us who are still left be scattered and lost?"

[16]But Gedaliah said to Johanan, "I forbid you to do any such thing, for you are lying about Ishmael."

CHAPTER 41
The Murder of Gedaliah

But in midautumn of that year,* Ishmael son of Nethaniah and grandson of Elishama, who was a member of the royal family and had been one of the king's high officials, went to Mizpah with ten men to meet Gedaliah. While they were eating together, [2]Ishmael and his ten men suddenly jumped up, drew their swords, and killed Gedaliah, whom the king of Babylon had appointed governor. [3]Ishmael also killed all the Judeans and the Babylonian* soldiers who were with Gedaliah at Mizpah.

[4]The next day, before anyone had heard about Gedaliah's murder, [5]eighty men arrived from Shechem, Shiloh, and Samaria to worship at the Temple of the LORD. They had shaved off their beards, torn their clothes, and cut themselves, and had brought along grain offerings and frankincense. [6]Ishmael left Mizpah to meet them, weeping as he went. When he reached them, he said, "Oh, come and see what has happened to Gedaliah!"

[7]But as soon as they were all inside the town, Ishmael and his men killed all but ten of them and threw their bodies into a cistern. [8]The other ten had talked Ishmael into letting them go by promising to bring him their stores of wheat, barley, olive oil, and honey that they had hidden away. [9]The cistern where Ishmael dumped the bodies of the men he murdered was the large one* dug by King Asa when he fortified Mizpah to protect himself against King Baasha of Israel. Ishmael son of Nethaniah filled it with corpses.

[10]Then Ishmael made captives of the king's daughters and the other people who had been left under Gedaliah's care in Mizpah by Nebuzaradan, the captain of the guard. Taking them with him, he started back toward the land of Ammon.

[11]But when Johanan son of Kareah and the other guerrilla leaders heard about Ishmael's crimes, [12]they took all their men and set out to stop him. They caught up with him at the large pool near Gibeon. [13]The people Ishmael had captured shouted for joy when they saw Johanan and the other guerrilla leaders. [14]And all the captives from Mizpah escaped and began to help Johanan. [15]Meanwhile, Ishmael and eight of his men escaped from Johanan into the land of Ammon.

[16]Then Johanan son of Kareah and the other guerrilla leaders took all the people they had rescued in Gibeon—the soldiers, women, children, and court officials* whom Ishmael had captured after he killed Gedaliah. [17]They took them all to the village of Geruth-kimham near Bethlehem, where they prepared to leave for Egypt. [18]They were afraid of what the Babylonians* would do when they heard that Ishmael had killed Gedaliah, the governor appointed by the Babylonian king.

CHAPTER 42
Warning to Stay in Judah

Then all the guerrilla leaders, including Johanan son of Kareah and Jezaniah* son of Hoshaiah, and all the people, from the least to the greatest, approached [2]Jeremiah the prophet. They said, "Please pray to the LORD your God for us. As you can see, we are only a tiny remnant compared to what we were before. [3]Pray that the LORD your God will show us what to do and where to go."

[4]"All right," Jeremiah replied. "I will pray to the LORD your God, as you have asked, and I will tell you everything he says. I will hide nothing from you."

[5]Then they said to Jeremiah, "May the LORD your God be a faithful witness against us if we refuse to obey whatever he tells us to do! [6]Whether we like it or not, we will obey the LORD our God to whom we are sending you with our plea. For if we obey him, everything will turn out well for us."

[7]Ten days later the LORD gave his reply to Jeremiah. [8]So he called for Johanan son of Kareah and the other guerrilla leaders, and for all the people, from the least to the greatest. [9]He said to them, "You sent me to the LORD, the God of Israel, with your request, and this is his reply: [10]'Stay here in this land. If you do, I will build you up and not tear you down; I will plant you and not uproot you. For I am sorry about all the punishment I have had to bring upon you. [11]Do not fear the king of Babylon anymore,' says the LORD. 'For I am with you and will save you and rescue you from his power. [12]I will be merciful to

---

41:1 Hebrew *in the seventh month,* of the ancient Hebrew lunar calendar. This month occurred within the months of October and November 586 B.C; also see note on 39:1a. **41:3** Or *Chaldean.* **41:9** As in Greek version; Hebrew reads *murdered because of Gedaliah was one.* **41:16** Or *eunuchs.* **41:18** Or *Chaldeans.* **42:1** Greek version reads *Azariah;* compare 43:2.

you by making him kind, so he will let you stay here in your land.'

¹³"But if you refuse to obey the LORD your God, and if you say, 'We will not stay here; ¹⁴instead, we will go to Egypt where we will be free from war, the call to arms, and hunger,' ¹⁵then hear the LORD's message to the remnant of Judah. This is what the LORD of Heaven's Armies, the God of Israel, says: 'If you are determined to go to Egypt and live there, ¹⁶the very war and famine you fear will catch up to you, and you will die there. ¹⁷That is the fate awaiting every one of you who insists on going to live in Egypt. Yes, you will die from war, famine, and disease. None of you will escape the disaster I will bring upon you there.'

¹⁸"This is what the LORD of Heaven's Armies, the God of Israel, says: 'Just as my anger and fury have been poured out on the people of Jerusalem, so they will be poured out on you when you enter Egypt. You will be an object of damnation, horror, cursing, and mockery. And you will never see your homeland again.'

¹⁹"Listen, you remnant of Judah. The LORD has told you: 'Do not go to Egypt!' Don't forget this warning I have given you today. ²⁰For you were not being honest when you sent me to pray to the LORD your God for you. You said, 'Just tell us what the LORD our God says, and we will do it!' ²¹And today I have told you exactly what he said, but you will not obey the LORD your God any better now than you have in the past. ²²So you can be sure that you will die from war, famine, and disease in Egypt, where you insist on going."

CHAPTER 43
Jeremiah Taken to Egypt

When Jeremiah had finished giving this message from the LORD their God to all the people, ²Azariah son of Hoshaiah and Johanan son of Kareah and all the other proud men said to Jeremiah, "You lie! The LORD our God hasn't forbidden us to go to Egypt! ³Baruch son of Neriah has convinced you to say this, because he wants us to stay here and

be killed by the Babylonians* or be carried off into exile."

⁴So Johanan and the other guerrilla leaders and all the people refused to obey the LORD's command to stay in Judah. ⁵Johanan and the other leaders took with them all the people who had returned from the nearby countries to which they had fled. ⁶In the crowd were men, women, and children, the king's daughters, and all those whom Nebuzaradan, the captain of the guard, had left with Gedaliah. The prophet Jeremiah and Baruch were also included. ⁷The people refused to obey the voice of the LORD and went to Egypt, going as far as the city of Tahpanhes.

⁸Then at Tahpanhes, the LORD gave another message to Jeremiah. He said, ⁹"While the people of Judah are watching, take some large rocks and bury them under the pavement stones at the entrance of Pharaoh's palace here in Tahpanhes. ¹⁰Then say to the people of Judah, 'This is what the LORD of Heaven's Armies, the God of Israel, says: I will certainly bring my servant Nebuchadnezzar,* king of Babylon, here to Egypt. I will set his throne over these stones that I have hidden. He will spread his royal canopy over them. ¹¹And when he comes, he will destroy the land of Egypt. He will bring death to those destined for death, captivity to those destined for captivity, and war to those destined for war. ¹²He will set fire to the temples of Egypt's gods; he will burn the temples and carry the idols away as plunder. He will pick clean the land of Egypt as a shepherd picks fleas from his cloak. And he himself will leave unharmed. ¹³He will break down the sacred pillars standing in the temple of the sun* in Egypt, and he will burn down the temples of Egypt's gods.'"

CHAPTER 44
Judgment for Idolatry

This is the message Jeremiah received concerning the Judeans living in northern Egypt in the cities of Migdol, Tahpanhes, and Memphis,* and in southern Egypt* as well: ²"This is what the LORD of Heaven's Armies, the God of Israel, says: You saw the calamity I brought on

---

43:3 Or *Chaldeans*. 43:10 Hebrew *Nebuchadrezzar*, a variant spelling of Nebuchadnezzar. 43:13 Or *in Heliopolis*.
44:1a Hebrew *Noph*. 44:1b Hebrew *in Pathros*.

44:1-30 Jeremiah encouraged the remnant in Egypt to learn from Judah's recent fall and to turn away from their idolatry. Their response betrayed them: "Ever since we quit burning incense to the Queen of Heaven and stopped worshiping her with liquid offerings, we have been in great trouble." Sadly, their love for God was conditional. Unless God rewarded them in the ways they expected, they would not obey him. God is worthy of our love and obedience, whether or not he gives us what we want. God can be trusted at the deepest level; his plan for our life is always best.

Jerusalem and all the towns of Judah. They now lie deserted and in ruins. ³They provoked my anger with all their wickedness. They burned incense and worshiped other gods— gods that neither they nor you nor any of your ancestors had ever even known.

⁴"Again and again I sent my servants, the prophets, to plead with them, 'Don't do these horrible things that I hate so much.' ⁵But my people would not listen or turn back from their wicked ways. They kept on burning incense to these gods. ⁶And so my fury boiled over and fell like fire on the towns of Judah and into the streets of Jerusalem, and they are still a desolate ruin today.

⁷"And now the LORD God of Heaven's Armies, the God of Israel, asks you: Why are you destroying yourselves? For not one of you will survive—not a man, woman, or child among you who has come here from Judah, not even the babies in your arms. ⁸Why provoke my anger by burning incense to the idols you have made here in Egypt? You will only destroy yourselves and make yourselves an object of cursing and mockery for all the nations of the earth. ⁹Have you forgotten the sins of your ancestors, the sins of the kings and queens of Judah, and the sins you and your wives committed in Judah and Jerusalem? ¹⁰To this very hour you have shown no remorse or reverence. No one has chosen to follow my word and the decrees I gave to you and your ancestors before you.

¹¹"Therefore, this is what the LORD of Heaven's Armies, the God of Israel, says: I am determined to destroy every one of you! ¹²I will take this remnant of Judah—those who were determined to come here and live in Egypt—and I will consume them. They will fall here in Egypt, killed by war and famine. All will die, from the least to the greatest. They will be an object of damnation, horror, cursing, and mockery. ¹³I will punish them in Egypt just as I punished them in Jerusalem, by war, famine, and disease. ¹⁴Of that remnant who fled to Egypt, hoping someday to return to Judah, there will be no survivors. Even though they long to return home, only a handful will do so."

¹⁵Then all the women present and all the men who knew that their wives had burned incense to idols—a great crowd of all the Judeans living in northern Egypt and southern Egypt*—answered Jeremiah, ¹⁶"We will not listen to your messages from the LORD! ¹⁷We will do whatever we want. We will burn

incense and pour out liquid offerings to the Queen of Heaven just as much as we like— just as we, and our ancestors, and our kings and officials have always done in the towns of Judah and in the streets of Jerusalem. For in those days we had plenty to eat, and we were well off and had no troubles! ¹⁸But ever since we quit burning incense to the Queen of Heaven and stopped worshiping her with liquid offerings, we have been in great trouble and have been dying from war and famine."

¹⁹"Besides," the women added, "do you suppose that we were burning incense and pouring out liquid offerings to the Queen of Heaven, and making cakes marked with her image, without our husbands knowing it and helping us? Of course not!"

²⁰Then Jeremiah said to all of them, men and women alike, who had given him that answer, ²¹"Do you think the LORD did not know that you and your ancestors, your kings and officials, and all the people were burning incense to idols in the towns of Judah and in the streets of Jerusalem? ²²It was because the LORD could no longer bear all the disgusting things you were doing that he made your land an object of cursing—a desolate ruin without inhabitants—as it is today. ²³All these terrible things happened to you because you have burned incense to idols and sinned against the LORD. You have refused to obey him and have not followed his instructions, his decrees, and his laws."

²⁴Then Jeremiah said to them all, including the women, "Listen to this message from the LORD, all you citizens of Judah who live in Egypt. ²⁵This is what the LORD of Heaven's Armies, the God of Israel, says: 'You and your wives have said, "We will keep our promises to burn incense and pour out liquid offerings to the Queen of Heaven," and you have proved by your actions that you meant it. So go ahead and carry out your promises and vows to her!'

²⁶"But listen to this message from the LORD, all you Judeans now living in Egypt: 'I have sworn by my great name,' says the LORD, 'that my name will no longer be spoken by any of the Judeans in the land of Egypt. None of you may invoke my name or use this oath: "As surely as the Sovereign LORD lives." ²⁷For I will watch over you to bring you disaster and not good. Everyone from Judah who is now living in Egypt will suffer war and famine until all of you are

44:15 Hebrew *in Egypt, in Pathros.*

dead. ²⁸Only a small number will escape death and return to Judah from Egypt. Then all those who came to Egypt will find out whose words are true—mine or theirs!

²⁹" 'And this is the proof I give you,' says the LORD, 'that all I have threatened will happen to you and that I will punish you here.' ³⁰This is what the LORD says: 'I will turn Pharaoh Hophra, king of Egypt, over to his enemies who want to kill him, just as I turned King Zedekiah of Judah over to King Nebuchadnezzar* of Babylon.' "

CHAPTER 45
A Message for Baruch

The prophet Jeremiah gave a message to Baruch son of Neriah in the fourth year of the reign of Jehoiakim son of Josiah,* after Baruch had written down everything Jeremiah had dictated to him. He said, ²"This is what the LORD, the God of Israel, says to you, Baruch: ³You have said, 'I am overwhelmed with trouble! Haven't I had enough pain already? And now the LORD has added more! I am worn out from sighing and can find no rest.'

⁴"Baruch, this is what the LORD says: 'I will destroy this nation that I built. I will uproot what I planted. ⁵Are you seeking great things for yourself? Don't do it! I will bring great disaster upon all these people; but I will give you your life as a reward wherever you go. I, the LORD, have spoken!' "

CHAPTER 46
Messages for the Nations

The following messages were given to Jeremiah the prophet from the LORD concerning foreign nations.

Messages about Egypt

²This message concerning Egypt was given in the fourth year of the reign of Jehoiakim son of Josiah, the king of Judah, on the occasion of the battle of Carchemish* when Pharaoh Neco, king of Egypt, and his army were defeated beside the Euphrates River by King Nebuchadnezzar* of Babylon.

³"Prepare your shields,
  and advance into battle!
⁴Harness the horses,
  and mount the stallions.
Take your positions.
  Put on your helmets.
Sharpen your spears,
  and prepare your armor.
⁵But what do I see?
  The Egyptian army flees in terror.
The bravest of its fighting men run
  without a backward glance.
They are terrorized at every turn,"
  says the LORD.
⁶"The swiftest runners cannot flee;
  the mightiest warriors cannot escape.
By the Euphrates River to the north,
  they stumble and fall.

⁷"Who is this, rising like the Nile at floodtime,
  overflowing all the land?
⁸It is the Egyptian army,
  overflowing all the land,
boasting that it will cover the earth like a flood,
  destroying cities and their people.
⁹Charge, you horses and chariots;
  attack, you mighty warriors of Egypt!
Come, all you allies from Ethiopia, Libya, and Lydia*
  who are skilled with the shield and bow!
¹⁰For this is the day of the Lord, the LORD of Heaven's Armies,
  a day of vengeance on his enemies.
The sword will devour until it is satisfied,
  yes, until it is drunk with your blood!
The Lord, the LORD of Heaven's Armies,
  will receive a sacrifice today

44:30 Hebrew *Nebuchadrezzar,* a variant spelling of Nebuchadnezzar. **45:1** The fourth year of Jehoiakim's reign was 605 B.C. **46:2a** This event occurred in 605 B.C., during the fourth year of Jehoiakim's reign (according to the calendar system in which the new year begins in the spring). **46:2b** Hebrew *Nebuchadrezzar,* a variant spelling of Nebuchadnezzar; also in 46:13, 26. **46:9** Hebrew *from Cush, Put, and Lud.*

45:1-5 As is often the case in our own life, Baruch's eyes turned toward his own comfort and security. It is rarely easy to serve others when we feel our own well-being is threatened, but God longs for us to trust him even then—especially then.

46:1–51:64 Words of judgment were pronounced on the nations that had mistreated God's chosen people. Without exception, Egypt, Philistia, Moab, Ammon, Edom, Damascus, Kedar, Hazor, Elam, and Babylon would all receive God's judgment for their wicked and ungodly practices. The wicked never prosper for long, though it may appear for a time that they do. We can rely on God's righteousness to prevail over evil. He disciplines us like a loving parent, and that discipline is always just and designed for our good.

in the north country beside the
Euphrates River.

11 "Go up to Gilead to get medicine,
 O virgin daughter of Egypt!
But your many treatments
 will bring you no healing.
12 The nations have heard of your shame.
 The earth is filled with your cries of
 despair.
Your mightiest warriors will run into each
 other
 and fall down together."

13 Then the LORD gave the prophet Jeremiah
this message about King Nebuchadnezzar's
plans to attack Egypt.

14 "Shout it out in Egypt!
 Publish it in the cities of Migdol,
 Memphis,* and Tahpanhes!
Mobilize for battle,
 for the sword will devour everyone
 around you.
15 Why have your warriors fallen?
 They cannot stand, for the LORD has
 knocked them down.
16 They stumble and fall over each other
 and say among themselves,
'Come, let's go back to our people,
 to the land of our birth.
Let's get away from the sword of the
 enemy!'
17 There they will say,
'Pharaoh, the king of Egypt, is a
 loudmouth
who missed his opportunity!'

18 "As surely as I live," says the King,
 whose name is the LORD of Heaven's
 Armies,
"one is coming against Egypt
 who is as tall as Mount Tabor,
 or as Mount Carmel by the sea!
19 Pack up! Get ready to leave for exile,
 you citizens of Egypt!
The city of Memphis will be destroyed,
 without a single inhabitant.
20 Egypt is as sleek as a beautiful heifer,
 but a horsefly from the north is on its
 way!
21 Egypt's mercenaries have become like
 fattened calves.
They, too, will turn and run,
for it is a day of great disaster for Egypt,
 a time of great punishment.
22 Egypt flees, silent as a serpent gliding
 away.

The invading army marches in;
 they come against her with axes like
 woodsmen.
23 They will cut down her people like trees,"
 says the LORD,
"for they are more numerous than
 locusts.
24 Egypt will be humiliated;
 she will be handed over to people from
 the north."

25 The LORD of Heaven's Armies, the God of
Israel, says: "I will punish Amon, the god of
Thebes,* and all the other gods of Egypt. I will
punish its rulers and Pharaoh, too, and all
who trust in him. 26 I will hand them over to
those who want them killed—to King Nebuchadnezzar of Babylon and his army. But
afterward the land will recover from the ravages of war. I, the LORD, have spoken!

27 "But do not be afraid, Jacob, my servant;
 do not be dismayed, Israel.
For I will bring you home again from
 distant lands,
and your children will return from their
 exile.
Israel* will return to a life of peace and quiet,
 and no one will terrorize them.
28 Do not be afraid, Jacob, my servant,
 for I am with you," says the LORD.
"I will completely destroy the nations to
 which I have exiled you,
but I will not completely destroy you.
I will discipline you, but with justice;
 I cannot let you go unpunished."

CHAPTER 47
A Message about Philistia
This is the LORD's message to the prophet Jeremiah concerning the Philistines of Gaza,
before it was captured by the Egyptian army.
2 This is what the LORD says:

"A flood is coming from the north
 to overflow the land.
It will destroy the land and everything
 in it—
 cities and people alike.
People will scream in terror,
 and everyone in the land will wail.
3 Hear the clatter of stallions' hooves
 and the rumble of wheels as the
 chariots rush by.
Terrified fathers run madly,
 without a backward glance at their
 helpless children.

46:14 Hebrew *Noph;* also in 46:19. 46:25 Hebrew *of No.* 46:27 Hebrew *Jacob.* See note on 5:20.

4 "The time has come for the Philistines to
be destroyed,
along with their allies from Tyre and
Sidon.
Yes, the LORD is destroying the remnant of
the Philistines,
those colonists from the island of
Crete.*
5 Gaza will be humiliated, its head shaved
bald;
Ashkelon will lie silent.
You remnant from the Mediterranean
coast,*
how long will you cut yourselves in
mourning?

6 "Now, O sword of the LORD,
when will you be at rest again?
Go back into your sheath;
rest and be still.

7 "But how can it be still
when the LORD has sent it on
a mission?
For the city of Ashkelon
and the people living along the sea
must be destroyed."

CHAPTER 48
A Message about Moab

This message was given concerning Moab.
This is what the LORD of Heaven's Armies,
the God of Israel, says:

"What sorrow awaits the city of Nebo;
it will soon lie in ruins.
The city of Kiriathaim will be humiliated
and captured;
the fortress will be humiliated and
broken down.
2 No one will ever brag about Moab again,
for in Heshbon there is a plot to destroy
her.
'Come,' they say, 'we will cut her off from
being a nation.'
The town of Madmen,* too, will be
silenced;
the sword will follow you there.
3 Listen to the cries from Horonaim,
cries of devastation and great
destruction.
4 All Moab is destroyed.
Her little ones will cry out.*
5 Her refugees weep bitterly,
climbing the slope to Luhith.

They cry out in terror,
descending the slope to Horonaim.
6 Flee for your lives!
Hide* in the wilderness!
7 Because you have trusted in your wealth
and skill,
you will be taken captive.
Your god Chemosh, with his priests and
officials,
will be hauled off to distant lands!

8 "All the towns will be destroyed,
and no one will escape—
either on the plateaus or in the valleys,
for the LORD has spoken.
9 Oh, that Moab had wings
so she could fly away,*
for her towns will be left empty,
with no one living in them.
10 Cursed are those who refuse to do the
LORD's work,
who hold back their swords from
shedding blood!

11 "From his earliest history, Moab has lived
in peace,
never going into exile.
He is like wine that has been allowed
to settle.
He has not been poured from flask to
flask,
and he is now fragrant and smooth.
12 But the time is coming soon," says the
LORD,
"when I will send men to pour him
from his jar.
They will pour him out,
then shatter the jar!
13 At last Moab will be ashamed of his idol
Chemosh,
as the people of Israel were ashamed of
their gold calf at Bethel.*

14 "You used to boast, 'We are heroes,
mighty men of war.'
15 But now Moab and his towns will be
destroyed.
His most promising youth are doomed
to slaughter,"
says the King, whose name is the LORD
of Heaven's Armies.
16 "Destruction is coming fast for Moab;
calamity threatens ominously.
17 You friends of Moab,
weep for him and cry!

47:4 Hebrew *from Caphtor.* 47:5 Hebrew *the plain.* 48:2 *Madmen* sounds like the Hebrew word for "silence"; it should not be confused with the English word *madmen.* 48:4 Greek version reads *Her cries are heard as far away as Zoar.* 48:6 Or *Hide like a wild donkey;* or *Hide like a juniper shrub;* or *Be like* [the town of] *Aroer.* The meaning of the Hebrew is uncertain. 48:9 Or *Put salt on Moab, / for she will be laid waste.* 48:13 Hebrew *ashamed when they trusted in Bethel.*

See how the strong scepter is broken,
how the beautiful staff is shattered!

¹⁸ "Come down from your glory
and sit in the dust, you people of Dibon,
for those who destroy Moab will shatter
Dibon, too.
They will tear down all your towers.
¹⁹ You people of Aroer,
stand beside the road and watch.
Shout to those who flee from Moab,
'What has happened there?'

²⁰ "And the reply comes back,
'Moab lies in ruins, disgraced;
weep and wail!
Tell it by the banks of the Arnon River:
Moab has been destroyed!'
²¹ Judgment has been poured out on the
towns of the plateau—
on Holon and Jahaz* and Mephaath,
²² on Dibon and Nebo and Beth-diblathaim,
²³ on Kiriathaim and Beth-gamul and
Beth-meon,
²⁴ on Kerioth and Bozrah—
all the towns of Moab, far and near.

²⁵ "The strength of Moab has ended.
His arm has been broken," says the
LORD.
²⁶ "Let him stagger and fall like a drunkard,
for he has rebelled against the LORD.
Moab will wallow in his own vomit,
ridiculed by all.
²⁷ Did you not ridicule the people of Israel?
Were they caught in the company of
thieves
that you should despise them as you do?

²⁸ "You people of Moab,
flee from your towns and live in the
caves.
Hide like doves that nest
in the clefts of the rocks.
²⁹ We have all heard of the pride of Moab,
for his pride is very great.
We know of his lofty pride,
his arrogance, and his haughty heart.
³⁰ I know about his insolence,"
says the LORD,
"but his boasts are empty—
as empty as his deeds.
³¹ So now I wail for Moab;
yes, I will mourn for Moab.
My heart is broken for the men
of Kir-hareseth.*

³² "You people of Sibmah, rich in vineyards,

I will weep for you even more than I
did for Jazer.
Your spreading vines once reached as far
as the Dead Sea,*
but the destroyer has stripped you bare!
He has harvested your grapes and
summer fruits.
³³ Joy and gladness are gone from fruitful
Moab.
The presses yield no wine.
No one treads the grapes with shouts of
joy.
There is shouting, yes, but not of joy.

³⁴ "Instead, their awful cries of terror can be
heard from Heshbon clear across to Elealeh
and Jahaz; from Zoar all the way to Horonaim
and Eglath-shelishiyah. Even the waters of
Nimrim are dried up now.

³⁵ "I will put an end to Moab," says the
LORD, "for the people offer sacrifices at the
pagan shrines and burn incense to their false
gods. ³⁶ My heart moans like a flute for Moab
and Kir-hareseth, for all their wealth has disappeared. ³⁷ The people shave their heads and
beards in mourning. They slash their hands
and put on clothes made of burlap. ³⁸ There is
crying and sorrow in every Moabite home
and on every street. For I have smashed Moab
like an old, unwanted jar. ³⁹ How it is shattered! Hear the wailing! See the shame of
Moab! It has become an object of ridicule, an
example of ruin to all its neighbors."
⁴⁰ This is what the LORD says:

"Look! The enemy swoops down like an
eagle,
spreading his wings over Moab.
⁴¹ Its cities will fall,
and its strongholds will be seized.
Even the mightiest warriors will be in
anguish
like a woman in labor.
⁴² Moab will no longer be a nation,
for it has boasted against the LORD.

⁴³ "Terror and traps and snares will be your
lot,
O Moab," says the LORD.
⁴⁴ "Those who flee in terror will fall into a
trap,
and those who escape the trap will step
into a snare.
I will see to it that you do not get away,
for the time of your judgment has
come,"
says the LORD.

45 "The people flee as far as Heshbon
   but are unable to go on.
For a fire comes from Heshbon,
   King Sihon's ancient home,
to devour the entire land
   with all its rebellious people.

46 "What sorrow awais you, O people of
      Moab!
   The people of the god Chemosh are
      destroyed!
Your sons and your daughters
   have been taken away as captives.
47 But I will restore the fortunes of Moab
   in days to come.
I, the LORD, have spoken!"

   This is the end of Jeremiah's prophecy
concerning Moab.

CHAPTER 49
A Message about Ammon
This message was given concerning the
Ammonites. This is what the LORD says:

   "Are there no descendants of Israel
      to inherit the land of Gad?
   Why are you, who worship Molech,*
      living in its towns?
2 In the days to come," says the LORD,
   "I will sound the battle cry against your
      city of Rabbah.
It will become a desolate heap of ruins,
   and the neighboring towns will be
      burned.
Then Israel will take back the land
   you took from her," says the LORD.

3 "Cry out, O Heshbon,
   for the town of Ai is destroyed.
Weep, O people of Rabbah!
   Put on your clothes of mourning.
Weep and wail, hiding in the hedges,
   for your god Molech, with his priests
      and officials,
   will be hauled off to distant lands.
4 You are proud of your fertile valleys,
   but they will soon be ruined.
You trusted in your wealth,
   you rebellious daughter,
   and thought no one could ever harm
      you.
5 But look! I will bring terror upon you,"
   says the Lord, the LORD of Heaven's
      Armies.
"Your neighbors will chase you from your
      land,

and no one will help your exiles as they
      flee.
6 But I will restore the fortunes of the
      Ammonites
   in days to come.
I, the LORD, have spoken."

Messages about Edom
7 This message was given concerning Edom.
This is what the LORD of Heaven's Armies
says:

   "Is there no wisdom in Teman?
      Is no one left to give wise counsel?
8 Turn and flee!
   Hide in deep caves, you people of
      Dedan!
For when I bring disaster on Edom,*
   I will punish you, too!
9 Those who harvest grapes
   always leave a few for the poor.
If thieves came at night,
   they would not take everything.
10 But I will strip bare the land of Edom,
   and there will be no place left to hide.
Its children, its brothers, and its neighbors
   will all be destroyed,
   and Edom itself will be no more.
11 But I will protect the orphans who remain
      among you.
   Your widows, too, can depend on me
      for help."

   12 And this is what the LORD says: "If the innocent must suffer, how much more must
you! You will not go unpunished! You must
drink this cup of judgment! 13 For I have
sworn by my own name," says the LORD,
"that Bozrah will become an object of horror
and a heap of ruins; it will be mocked and
cursed. All its towns and villages will be desolate forever."

14 I have heard a message from the LORD
   that an ambassador was sent to the
      nations to say,
"Form a coalition against Edom,
   and prepare for battle!"

15 The LORD says to Edom,
"I will cut you down to size among the
      nations.
   You will be despised by all.
16 You have been deceived
   by the fear you inspire in others
   and by your own pride.
You live in a rock fortress
   and control the mountain heights.

49:1 Hebrew *Malcam,* a variant spelling of Molech; also in 49:3.   49:8 Hebrew *Esau;* also in 49:10.

But even if you make your nest among the
    peaks with the eagles,
  I will bring you crashing down,"
  says the LORD.

¹⁷ "Edom will be an object of horror.
  All who pass by will be appalled
  and will gasp at the destruction they see
    there.
¹⁸ It will be like the destruction of Sodom
    and Gomorrah
  and their neighboring towns," says the
    LORD.
  "No one will live there;
  no one will inhabit it.
¹⁹ I will come like a lion from the thickets of
    the Jordan,
  leaping on the sheep in the pasture.
  I will chase Edom from its land,
  and I will appoint the leader of my
    choice.
  For who is like me, and who can
    challenge me?
  What ruler can oppose my will?"

²⁰ Listen to the LORD's plans against Edom
    and the people of Teman.
  Even the little children will be dragged off
    like sheep,
  and their homes will be destroyed.
²¹ The earth will shake with the noise of
    Edom's fall,
  and its cry of despair will be heard all
    the way to the Red Sea.*
²² Look! The enemy swoops down like an
    eagle,
  spreading his wings over Bozrah.
  Even the mightiest warriors will be in
    anguish
  like a woman in labor.

A Message about Damascus

²³ This message was given concerning Damascus. This is what the LORD says:

  "The towns of Hamath and Arpad are
    struck with fear,
  for they have heard the news of their
    destruction.
  Their hearts are troubled
  like a wild sea in a raging storm.
²⁴ Damascus has become feeble,
  and all her people turn to flee.
  Fear, anguish, and pain have gripped her
  as they grip a woman in labor.
²⁵ That famous city, a city of joy,
  will be forsaken!

²⁶ Her young men will fall in the streets and
    die.
  Her soldiers will all be killed,"
  says the LORD of Heaven's Armies.
²⁷ "And I will set fire to the walls of
    Damascus
  that will burn up the palaces of
    Ben-hadad."

A Message about Kedar and Hazor

²⁸ This message was given concerning Kedar and the kingdoms of Hazor, which were attacked by King Nebuchadnezzar* of Babylon. This is what the LORD says:

  "Advance against Kedar!
  Destroy the warriors from the East!
²⁹ Their flocks and tents will be captured,
  and their household goods and camels
    will be taken away.
  Everywhere shouts of panic will be heard:
  'We are terrorized at every turn!'
³⁰ Run for your lives," says the LORD.
  "Hide yourselves in deep caves, you
    people of Hazor,
  for King Nebuchadnezzar of Babylon has
    plotted against you
  and is preparing to destroy you.

³¹ "Go up and attack that complacent
    nation,"
  says the LORD.
  "Its people live alone in the desert
  without walls or gates.
³² Their camels and other livestock will all
    be yours.
  I will scatter to the winds these people
  who live in remote places.*
  I will bring calamity upon them
  from every direction," says the LORD.
³³ "Hazor will be inhabited by jackals,
  and it will be desolate forever.
  No one will live there;
  no one will inhabit it."

A Message about Elam

³⁴ This message concerning Elam came to the prophet Jeremiah from the LORD at the beginning of the reign of King Zedekiah of Judah. ³⁵ This is what the LORD of Heaven's Armies says:

  "I will destroy the archers of Elam—
  the best of their forces.
³⁶ I will bring enemies from all directions,
  and I will scatter the people of Elam to
    the four winds.

49:21 Hebrew *sea of reeds.* 49:28 Hebrew *Nebuchadrezzar,* a variant spelling of Nebuchadnezzar; also in 49:30.
49:32 Or *who clip the corners of their hair.*

They will be exiled to countries around
the world.
³⁷ I myself will go with Elam's enemies to
shatter it.
In my fierce anger, I will bring great
disaster
upon the people of Elam," says the
LORD.
"Their enemies will chase them with the
sword
until I have destroyed them completely.
³⁸ I will set my throne in Elam," says the
LORD,
"and I will destroy its king and officials.
³⁹ But I will restore the fortunes of Elam
in days to come.
I, the LORD, have spoken!"

CHAPTER 50
A Message about Babylon
The LORD gave Jeremiah the prophet this
message concerning Babylon and the land of
the Babylonians.* ²This is what the LORD
says:

"Tell the whole world,
and keep nothing back.
Raise a signal flag
to tell everyone that Babylon will fall!
Her images and idols* will be shattered.
Her gods Bel and Marduk will be utterly
disgraced.
³ For a nation will attack her from the
north
and bring such destruction that no one
will live there again.
Everything will be gone;
both people and animals will flee.

Hope for Israel and Judah
⁴ "In those coming days,"
says the LORD,
"the people of Israel will return home
together with the people of Judah.
They will come weeping
and seeking the LORD their God.
⁵ They will ask the way to Jerusalem*
and will start back home again.
They will bind themselves to the LORD
with an eternal covenant that will
never be forgotten.

⁶ "My people have been lost sheep.
Their shepherds have led them astray
and turned them loose in the
mountains.

They have lost their way
and can't remember how to get back to
the sheepfold.
⁷ All who found them devoured them.
Their enemies said,
'We did nothing wrong in attacking them,
for they sinned against the LORD,
their true place of rest,
and the hope of their ancestors.'

⁸ "But now, flee from Babylon!
Leave the land of the Babylonians.
Like male goats at the head of the flock,
lead my people home again.
⁹ For I am raising up an army
of great nations from the north.
They will join forces to attack Babylon,
and she will be captured.
The enemies' arrows will go straight to the
mark;
they will not miss!
¹⁰ Babylonia* will be looted
until the attackers are glutted with loot.
I, the LORD, have spoken!

Babylon's Sure Fall
¹¹ "You rejoice and are glad,
you who plundered my chosen people.
You frisk about like a calf in a meadow
and neigh like a stallion.
¹² But your homeland* will be overwhelmed
with shame and disgrace.
You will become the least of nations—
a wilderness, a dry and desolate land.
¹³ Because of the LORD's anger,
Babylon will become a deserted
wasteland.
All who pass by will be horrified
and will gasp at the destruction they see
there.

¹⁴ "Yes, prepare to attack Babylon,
all you surrounding nations.
Let your archers shoot at her; spare no
arrows.
For she has sinned against the LORD.
¹⁵ Shout war cries against her from every
side.
Look! She surrenders!
Her walls have fallen.
It is the LORD's vengeance,
so take vengeance on her.
Do to her as she has done to others!
¹⁶ Take from Babylon all those who plant
crops;
send all the harvesters away.

50:1 Or *Chaldeans;* also in 50:8, 25, 35, 45.   50:2 The Hebrew term (literally *round things*) probably alludes to dung.
50:5 Hebrew *Zion;* also in 50:28.   50:10 Or *Chaldea.*   50:12 Hebrew *your mother.*

Because of the sword of the enemy,
everyone will run away and rush back
to their own lands.

Hope for God's People

17 "The Israelites are like sheep
that have been scattered by lions.
First the king of Assyria ate them up.
Then King Nebuchadnezzar* of Babylon
cracked their bones."
18 Therefore, this is what the LORD of
Heaven's Armies,
the God of Israel, says:
"Now I will punish the king of Babylon
and his land,
just as I punished the king of Assyria.
19 And I will bring Israel home again to its
own land,
to feed in the fields of Carmel and
Bashan,
and to be satisfied once more
in the hill country of Ephraim and
Gilead.
20 In those days," says the LORD,
"no sin will be found in Israel or in
Judah,
for I will forgive the remnant I preserve.

The LORD's Judgment on Babylon

21 "Go up, my warriors, against the land of
Merathaim
and against the people of Pekod.
Pursue, kill, and completely destroy*
them,
as I have commanded you," says the
LORD.
22 "Let the battle cry be heard in the land,
a shout of great destruction.
23 Babylon, the mightiest hammer in all the
earth,
lies broken and shattered.
Babylon is desolate among the
nations!
24 Listen, Babylon, for I have set a trap for
you.
You are caught, for you have fought
against the LORD.
25 The LORD has opened his armory
and brought out weapons to vent his
fury.
The terror that falls upon the Babylonians
will be the work of the Sovereign LORD
of Heaven's Armies.
26 Yes, come against her from distant lands.
Break open her granaries.

Crush her walls and houses into heaps
of rubble.
Destroy her completely, and leave
nothing!
27 Destroy even her young bulls—
it will be terrible for them, too!
Slaughter them all!
For Babylon's day of reckoning has
come.
28 Listen to the people who have escaped
from Babylon,
as they tell in Jerusalem
how the LORD our God has taken
vengeance
against those who destroyed his
Temple.

29 "Send out a call for archers to come to
Babylon.
Surround the city so none can escape.
Do to her as she has done to others,
for she has defied the LORD, the Holy
One of Israel.
30 Her young men will fall in the streets and
die.
Her soldiers will all be killed,"
says the LORD.

31 "See, I am your enemy, you arrogant
people,"
says the Lord, the LORD of Heaven's
Armies.
"Your day of reckoning has arrived—
the day when I will punish you.
32 O land of arrogance, you will stumble and
fall,
and no one will raise you up.
For I will light a fire in the cities of
Babylon
that will burn up everything around
them."

33 This is what the LORD of Heaven's Armies
says:
"The people of Israel and Judah have been
wronged.
Their captors hold them and refuse to
let them go.
34 But the one who redeems them is strong.
His name is the LORD of Heaven's
Armies.
He will defend them
and give them rest again in Israel.
But for the people of Babylon
there will be no rest!

50:17 Hebrew *Nebuchadrezzar*, a variant spelling of Nebuchadnezzar. 50:21 The Hebrew term used here refers to the complete consecration of things or people to the LORD, either by destroying them or by giving them as an offering.

³⁵ "The sword of destruction will strike the
Babylonians,"
says the LORD.
"It will strike the people of Babylon—
her officials and wise men, too.
³⁶ The sword will strike her wise counselors,
and they will become fools.
The sword will strike her mightiest
warriors,
and panic will seize them.
³⁷ The sword will strike her horses and
chariots
and her allies from other lands,
and they will all become like women.
The sword will strike her treasures,
and they all will be plundered.
³⁸ A drought* will strike her water supply,
causing it to dry up.
And why? Because the whole land is filled
with idols,
and the people are madly in love with
them.

³⁹ "Soon Babylon will be inhabited by desert
animals and hyenas.
It will be a home for owls.
Never again will people live there;
it will lie desolate forever.
⁴⁰ I will destroy it as I* destroyed Sodom and
Gomorrah
and their neighboring towns," says the
LORD.
"No one will live there;
no one will inhabit it.

⁴¹ "Look! A great army is coming from the
north.
A great nation and many kings
are rising against you from far-off lands.
⁴² They are armed with bows and spears.
They are cruel and show no mercy.
As they ride forward on horses,
they sound like a roaring sea.
They are coming in battle formation,
planning to destroy you, Babylon.
⁴³ The king of Babylon has heard reports
about the enemy,
and he is weak with fright.
Pangs of anguish have gripped him,
like those of a woman in labor.

⁴⁴ "I will come like a lion from the thickets
of the Jordan,
leaping on the sheep in the pasture.
I will chase Babylon from its land,

and I will appoint the leader of my
choice.
For who is like me, and who can
challenge me?
What ruler can oppose my will?"

⁴⁵ Listen to the LORD's plans against Babylon
and the land of the Babylonians.
Even the little children will be dragged off
like sheep,
and their homes will be destroyed.
⁴⁶ The earth will shake with the shout,
"Babylon has been taken!"
and its cry of despair will be heard
around the world.

CHAPTER 51

¹ This is what the LORD says:
"I will stir up a destroyer against Babylon
and the people of Babylonia.*
² Foreigners will come and winnow her,
blowing her away as chaff.
They will come from every side
to rise against her in her day of trouble.
³ Don't let the archers put on their armor
or draw their bows.
Don't spare even her best soldiers!
Let her army be completely destroyed.*
⁴ They will fall dead in the land of the
Babylonians,*
slashed to death in her streets.
⁵ For the LORD of Heaven's Armies
has not abandoned Israel and Judah.
He is still their God,
even though their land was filled with
sin
against the Holy One of Israel."

⁶ Flee from Babylon! Save yourselves!
Don't get trapped in her punishment!
It is the LORD's time for vengeance;
he will repay her in full.
⁷ Babylon has been a gold cup in the LORD's
hands,
a cup that made the whole earth drunk.
The nations drank Babylon's wine,
and it drove them all mad.
⁸ But suddenly Babylon, too, has fallen.
Weep for her.
Give her medicine.
Perhaps she can yet be healed.
⁹ We would have helped her if we could,
but nothing can save her now.
Let her go; abandon her.

50:38 Or *sword*; the Hebrew words for *drought* and *sword* are very similar. 50:40 Hebrew *as God*. 51:1 Hebrew *of Leb-kamai*, a code name for Babylonia. 51:3 The Hebrew term used here refers to the complete consecration of things or people to the LORD, either by destroying them or by giving them as an offering. 51:4 Or *Chaldeans*; also in 51:54. 51:10 Hebrew *Zion*; also in 51:24.

Return now to your own land.
For her punishment reaches to the
heavens;
  it is so great it cannot be measured.
¹⁰ The LORD has vindicated us.
  Come, let us announce in Jerusalem*
  everything the LORD our God has done.

¹¹ Sharpen the arrows!
  Lift up the shields!*
For the LORD has inspired the kings of the
  Medes
    to march against Babylon and destroy
    her.
This is his vengeance against those
  who desecrated his Temple.
¹² Raise the battle flag against Babylon!
  Reinforce the guard and station the
  watchmen.
Prepare an ambush,
  for the LORD will fulfill all his plans
  against Babylon.
¹³ You are a city by a great river,
  a great center of commerce,
but your end has come.
  The thread of your life is cut.
¹⁴ The LORD of Heaven's Armies has taken
  this vow
  and has sworn to it by his own name:
"Your cities will be filled with enemies,
  like fields swarming with locusts,
  and they will shout in triumph over
  you."

A Hymn of Praise to the LORD
¹⁵ The LORD made the earth by his power,
  and he preserves it by his wisdom.
With his own understanding
  he stretched out the heavens.
¹⁶ When he speaks in the thunder,
  the heavens roar with rain.
He causes the clouds to rise over the earth.
  He sends the lightning with the rain
  and releases the wind from his
  storehouses.

¹⁷ The whole human race is foolish and has
  no knowledge!
  The craftsmen are disgraced by the idols
  they make,
for their carefully shaped works are a
  fraud.
  These idols have no breath or power.
¹⁸ Idols are worthless; they are ridiculous
  lies!

On the day of reckoning they will all be
  destroyed.
¹⁹ But the God of Israel* is no idol!
  He is the Creator of everything that
  exists,
including his people, his own special
  possession.
  The LORD of Heaven's Armies is his
  name!

Babylon's Great Punishment
²⁰ "You* are my battle-ax and sword,"
  says the LORD.
"With you I will shatter nations
  and destroy many kingdoms.
²¹ With you I will shatter armies—
  destroying the horse and rider,
  the chariot and charioteer.
²² With you I will shatter men and women,
  old people and children,
  young men and young women.
²³ With you I will shatter shepherds and
  flocks,
  farmers and oxen,
  captains and officers.

²⁴ "I will repay Babylon
  and the people of Babylonia*
for all the wrong they have done
  to my people in Jerusalem," says the
  LORD.

²⁵ "Look, O mighty mountain, destroyer of
  the earth!
  I am your enemy," says the LORD.
"I will raise my fist against you,
  to knock you down from the heights.
When I am finished,
  you will be nothing but a heap of burnt
  rubble.
²⁶ You will be desolate forever.
  Even your stones will never again be
  used for building.
You will be completely wiped out,"
  says the LORD.

²⁷ Raise a signal flag to the nations.
  Sound the battle cry!
Mobilize them all against Babylon.
  Prepare them to fight against her!
Bring out the armies of Ararat, Minni,
  and Ashkenaz.
  Appoint a commander,
  and bring a multitude of horses like
  swarming locusts!
²⁸ Bring against her the armies of the
  nations—

51:11 Greek version reads *Fill up the quivers.* 51:19 Hebrew *the Portion of Jacob.* See note on 5:20. 51:20 Possibly Cyrus, whom God used to conquer Babylon. Compare Isa 44:28; 45:1. 51:24 Or *Chaldea;* also in 51:35.

led by the kings of the Medes
and all their captains and officers.

²⁹ The earth trembles and writhes in pain,
for everything the LORD has planned
against Babylon stands unchanged.
Babylon will be left desolate without a
single inhabitant.
³⁰ Her mightiest warriors no longer fight.
They stay in their barracks, their courage
gone.
They have become like women.
The invaders have burned the houses
and broken down the city gates.
³¹ The news is passed from one runner
to the next
as the messengers hurry to tell the king
that his city has been captured.
³² All the escape routes are blocked.
The marshes have been set aflame,
and the army is in a panic.

³³ This is what the LORD of Heaven's Armies,
the God of Israel, says:
"Babylon is like wheat on a threshing floor,
about to be trampled.
In just a little while
her harvest will begin."

³⁴ "King Nebuchadnezzar* of Babylon has
eaten and crushed us
and drained us of strength.
He has swallowed us like a great monster
and filled his belly with our riches.
He has thrown us out of our own
country.
³⁵ Make Babylon suffer as she made us suffer,"
say the people of Zion.
"Make the people of Babylonia pay for
spilling our blood,"
says Jerusalem.

The LORD's Vengeance on Babylon

³⁶ This is what the LORD says to Jerusalem:

"I will be your lawyer to plead your case,
and I will avenge you.
I will dry up her river,
as well as her springs,
³⁷ and Babylon will become a heap of ruins,
haunted by jackals.
She will be an object of horror and
contempt,
a place where no one lives.
³⁸ Her people will roar together like strong
lions.
They will growl like lion cubs.

³⁹ And while they lie inflamed with all their
wine,
I will prepare a different kind of feast
for them.
I will make them drink until they fall
asleep,
and they will never wake up again,"
says the LORD.
⁴⁰ "I will bring them down
like lambs to the slaughter,
like rams and goats to be sacrificed.

⁴¹ "How Babylon* is fallen—
great Babylon, praised throughout the
earth!
Now she has become an object of horror
among the nations.
⁴² The sea has risen over Babylon;
she is covered by its crashing waves.
⁴³ Her cities now lie in ruins;
she is a dry wasteland
where no one lives or even passes by.
⁴⁴ And I will punish Bel, the god of Babylon,
and make him vomit up all he has
eaten.
The nations will no longer come and
worship him.
The wall of Babylon has fallen!

A Message for the Exiles

⁴⁵ "Come out, my people, flee from Babylon.
Save yourselves! Run from the LORD's
fierce anger.
⁴⁶ But do not panic; don't be afraid
when you hear the first rumor of
approaching forces.
For rumors will keep coming year by
year.
Violence will erupt in the land
as the leaders fight against each other.
⁴⁷ For the time is surely coming
when I will punish this great city and
all her idols.
Her whole land will be disgraced,
and her dead will lie in the streets.
⁴⁸ Then the heavens and earth will rejoice,
for out of the north will come
destroying armies
against Babylon," says the LORD.
⁴⁹ "Just as Babylon killed the people of Israel
and others throughout the world,
so must her people be killed.
⁵⁰ Get out, all you who have escaped the
sword!
Do not stand and watch—flee while
you can!

51:34 Hebrew *Nebuchadrezzar*, a variant spelling of Nebuchadnezzar. 51:41 Hebrew *Sheshach*, a code name for
Babylon.

Remember the LORD, though you are in a
    far-off land,
  and think about your home in
    Jerusalem."

51 "We are ashamed," the people say.
  "We are insulted and disgraced
because the LORD's Temple
  has been defiled by foreigners."

52 "Yes," says the LORD, "but the time is
    coming
  when I will destroy Babylon's idols.
The groans of her wounded people
  will be heard throughout the land.
53 Though Babylon reaches as high as the
    heavens
  and makes her fortifications incredibly
    strong,
I will still send enemies to plunder her.
  I, the LORD, have spoken!

Babylon's Complete Destruction

54 "Listen! Hear the cry of Babylon,
  the sound of great destruction from the
    land of the Babylonians.
55 For the LORD is destroying Babylon.
  He will silence her loud voice.
Waves of enemies pound against her;
  the noise of battle rings through the city.
56 Destroying armies come against Babylon.
  Her mighty men are captured,
  and their weapons break in their hands.
For the LORD is a God who gives just
    punishment;
  he always repays in full.
57 I will make her officials and wise men
    drunk,
  along with her captains, officers, and
    warriors.
They will fall asleep
  and never wake up again!"
says the King, whose name is
  the LORD of Heaven's Armies.

58 This is what the LORD of Heaven's Armies
says:

"The thick walls of Babylon will be leveled
    to the ground,
  and her massive gates will be burned.
The builders from many lands have
    worked in vain,
  for their work will be destroyed by fire!"

Jeremiah's Message Sent to Babylon

59 The prophet Jeremiah gave this message to
Seraiah son of Neriah and grandson of
Mahseiah, a staff officer, when Seraiah went
to Babylon with King Zedekiah of Judah.
This was during the fourth year of Zedekiah's
reign.* 60 Jeremiah had recorded on a scroll all
the terrible disasters that would soon come
upon Babylon—all the words written here.
61 He said to Seraiah, "When you get to Babylon, read aloud everything on this scroll.
62 Then say, 'LORD, you have said that you will
destroy Babylon so that neither people nor
animals will remain here. She will lie empty
and abandoned forever.' 63 When you have
finished reading the scroll, tie it to a stone
and throw it into the Euphrates River. 64 Then
say, 'In this same way Babylon and her people will sink, never again to rise, because of
the disasters I will bring upon her.'"

This is the end of Jeremiah's messages.

CHAPTER 52
The Fall of Jerusalem

Zedekiah was twenty-one years old when he
became king, and he reigned in Jerusalem
eleven years. His mother was Hamutal, the
daughter of Jeremiah from Libnah. 2 But
Zedekiah did what was evil in the LORD's
sight, just as Jehoiakim had done. 3 These
things happened because of the LORD's anger
against the people of Jerusalem and Judah,
until he finally banished them from his presence and sent them into exile.

Zedekiah rebelled against the king of Babylon. 4 So on January 15,* during the ninth
year of Zedekiah's reign, King Nebuchadnezzar* of Babylon led his entire army against
Jerusalem. They surrounded the city and built

51:59 The fourth year of Zedekiah's reign was 593 B.C. 52:4a Hebrew *on the tenth day of the tenth month,* of the
ancient Hebrew lunar calendar. A number of events in Jeremiah can be cross-checked with dates in surviving
Babylonian records and related accurately to our modern calendar. This day was January 15, 588 B.C. 52:4b Hebrew
Nebuchadrezzar, a variant spelling of Nebuchadnezzar; also in 52:12, 28, 29, 30.

52:1-34 There is perhaps no greater pain than that resulting from the memories of our sins and
the suffering we have caused others. As Jerusalem fell, the people could no longer avoid the
destructive consequences of their sin. Memories of Jerusalem's broken walls would bring their past
failures back to haunt them repeatedly. Even though we are surrounded by the devastation
caused by our poor choices and selfish actions, we can turn to God and still have hope for restoration. God loves us as no one else can and desires a relationship with us. Our sins grieve God, but
he always wants to heal and restore us.

siege ramps against its walls. [5]Jerusalem was kept under siege until the eleventh year of King Zedekiah's reign.

[6]By July 18 in the eleventh year of Zedekiah's reign,* the famine in the city had become very severe, and the last of the food was entirely gone. [7]Then a section of the city wall was broken down, and all the soldiers fled. Since the city was surrounded by the Babylonians,* they waited for nightfall. Then they slipped through the gate between the two walls behind the king's garden and headed toward the Jordan Valley.*

[8]But the Babylonian troops chased King Zedekiah and overtook him on the plains of Jericho, for his men had all deserted him and scattered. [9]They captured the king and took him to the king of Babylon at Riblah in the land of Hamath. There the king of Babylon pronounced judgment upon Zedekiah. [10]The king of Babylon made Zedekiah watch as he slaughtered his sons. He also slaughtered all the officials of Judah at Riblah. [11]Then he gouged out Zedekiah's eyes and bound him in bronze chains, and the king of Babylon led him away to Babylon. Zedekiah remained there in prison until the day of his death.

The Temple Destroyed

[12]On August 17 of that year,* which was the nineteenth year of King Nebuchadnezzar's reign, Nebuzaradan, the captain of the guard and an official of the Babylonian king, arrived in Jerusalem. [13]He burned down the Temple of the LORD, the royal palace, and all the houses of Jerusalem. He destroyed all the important buildings* in the city. [14]Then he supervised the entire Babylonian* army as they tore down the walls of Jerusalem on every side. [15]Then Nebuzaradan, the captain of the guard, took as exiles some of the poorest of the people, the rest of the people who remained in the city, the defectors who had declared their allegiance to the king of Babylon, and the rest of the craftsmen. [16]But Nebuzaradan allowed some of the poorest people to stay behind to care for the vineyards and fields.

[17]The Babylonians broke up the bronze pillars in front of the LORD's Temple, the bronze water carts, and the great bronze basin called the Sea, and they carried all the bronze away to Babylon. [18]They also took all the ash buckets, shovels, lamp snuffers, basins, dishes, and all the other bronze articles used for making sacrifices at the Temple. [19]The captain of the guard also took the small bowls, incense burners, basins, pots, lampstands, ladles, bowls used for liquid offerings, and all the other articles made of pure gold or silver.

[20]The weight of the bronze from the two pillars, the Sea with the twelve bronze oxen beneath it, and the water carts was too great to be measured. These things had been made for the LORD's Temple in the days of King Solomon. [21]Each of the pillars was 27 feet tall and 18 feet in circumference.* They were hollow, with walls 3 inches thick.* [22]The bronze capital on top of each pillar was 7½ feet* high and was decorated with a network of bronze pomegranates all the way around. [23]There were 96 pomegranates on the sides, and a total of 100 pomegranates on the network around the top.

[24]Nebuzaradan, the captain of the guard, took with him as prisoners Seraiah the high priest, Zephaniah the priest of the second rank, and the three chief gatekeepers. [25]And from among the people still hiding in the city, he took an officer who had been in charge of the Judean army; seven of the king's personal advisers; the army commander's chief secretary, who was in charge of recruitment; and sixty other citizens. [26]Nebuzaradan, the captain of the guard, took them all to the king of Babylon at Riblah. [27]And there at Riblah, in the land of Hamath, the king of Babylon had them all put to death. So the people of Judah were sent into exile from their land.

[28]The number of captives taken to Babylon in the seventh year of Nebuchadnezzar's reign* was 3,023. [29]Then in Nebuchadnezzar's eighteenth year* he took 832 more. [30]In Nebuchadnezzar's twenty-third year* he sent Nebuzaradan, the captain of the guard, who took 745 more—a total of 4,600 captives in all.

Hope for Israel's Royal Line

[31]In the thirty-seventh year of the exile of King Jehoiachin of Judah, Evil-merodach ascended to the Babylonian throne. He was kind to* Jehoiachin and released him from

52:6 Hebrew *By the ninth day of the fourth month* [in the eleventh year of Zedekiah's reign]. This day was July 18, 586 B.C.; also see note on 52:4a.   52:7a Or *the Chaldeans;* similarly in 52:8, 17.   52:7b Hebrew *the Arabah.*
52:12 Hebrew *On the tenth day of the fifth month,* of the ancient Hebrew lunar calendar. This day was August 17, 586 B.C.; also see note on 52:4a.   52:13 Or *destroyed the houses of all the important people.*   52:14 Or *Chaldean.*
52:21a Hebrew *18 cubits* [8.3 meters] *tall and 12 cubits* [5.5 meters] *in circumference.*   52:21b Hebrew *4 fingers thick* [8 centimeters].   52:22 Hebrew *5 cubits* [2.3 meters].   52:28 This exile in the seventh year of Nebuchadnezzar's reign occurred in 597 B.C.   52:29 This exile in the eighteenth year of Nebuchadnezzar's reign occurred in 586 B.C.   52:30 This exile in the twenty-third year of Nebuchadnezzar's reign occurred in 581 B.C.   52:31a Hebrew *He raised the head of.*

prison on March 31 of that year.* ³²He spoke kindly to Jehoiachin and gave him a higher place than all the other exiled kings in Babylon. ³³He supplied Jehoiachin with new clothes to replace his prison garb and al-lowed him to dine in the king's presence for the rest of his life. ³⁴So the Babylonian king gave him a regular food allowance as long as he lived. This continued until the day of his death.

52:31b Hebrew *on the twenty-fifth day of the twelfth month,* of the ancient Hebrew lunar calendar. This day was March 31, 561 B.C.; also see note on 52:4a.

REFLECTIONS ON JEREMIAH

insights ABOUT THE DANGER OF IDOLATRY

Our idols differ from the idols of the people of Judah. As we see in **Jeremiah 1:16,** their gods were hand-made, often statues of clay, wood, or precious metals. Ours may come in the form of alcohol, drugs, sex, power, or work. Whatever things may consume our time and energy and permeate our thought life have become our gods. Idolatry will destroy our relationship with God and ruin our life if we allow it to go on unchecked.

In **Jeremiah 2:13** we see that idolatry involves two grave mistakes: First, we turn away from our powerful God, the only one who can really help us. Second, we turn to idols that have no power to help us—alcohol, drugs, sex, power, or work—to deal with pain that only God can heal. We know from experience, however, that these temporary solutions only deepen our pain in the long run. God invites us to bring our problems to him and return to his loving care. He wants a relationship with us, free of the distractions of our destruc-tive addiction.

In **Jeremiah 2:24-25** the prophet compared Israel to a wild donkey at mating time, running to one male donkey after another to satisfy her lust. Israel ran after any god without much thought— she was out of control! When we reject God's power to work in our life, we will find ourself out of control. We will mind-lessly chase after old addictions that brought us so much destruction in the past. We need to recognize how helpless we are against the pull of our dependency and put our life into God's hands. Only then can we experience his power and begin the journey toward recovery.

insights ABOUT DENIAL AND HYPOCRISY

In **Jeremiah 3:9-10** we find that the people of Israel were in denial and took their sins lightly. We often do the same thing, perhaps because the consequences of our sins don't always come immediately. If nothing bad happens to us for a while, we are lulled into thinking we can get away with our destructive behavior. If the consequences struck instantly, we might take our actions more seriously. We must realize that God does not take our sins lightly. The consequences for sinful behavior will inevitably come sooner or later.

Jeremiah's audience was in denial. In **Jeremiah 5:11-13** the prophet warned them that their behavior would lead to terrible consequences, but they refused to listen. We often do the same thing. When confronted with our sinful behavior, we foolishly defend or rationalize our actions. We even project our own destruction onto others. The next time someone confronts us about our sin, we need to listen; that person may be right. We would be wise to take an inventory of our life to see whether or not it needs renewal and recovery.

In **Jeremiah 16:16–17:13** it is clear that our actions may fool others, but we can never fool God. Judg-ment came to Judah not simply because the actions of the people were grievous but also because their hearts were unrepentant. God searches our innermost parts and knows our heart. He cares about *who we* are, not just about *what we do.* Thus recovery does not begin with heroic acts on our part. It begins as we admit that we are powerless and unable to do anything on our own and turn to God with a humble and repentant heart.

insights ABOUT THE PERSON OF GOD

In **Jeremiah 1:6-8** God asked his prophet to do some difficult things. He does the same with us: He asks us to put the past behind us; he wants us to fight lust, greed, fear, hatred, and despair. But because he loves us, he never sends us into battle alone. He will always be by our side, encouraging us and showing us the way.

In **Jeremiah 3:1** God goes beyond what anyone would reasonably expect from another human to show his grace. No matter how far we wander, no matter how many false gods (our dependency, godless recovery programs, unhealthy relationships) we have worshiped, he will take us back. When we stop living in our own power, God invites us to recover through his power. No sin is so great that God's love won't forgive it.

In **Jeremiah 3:6–4:4** God feels intense emotion. He was deeply hurt by the sins of Israel and Judah, just as he is hurt by our sins. God longed for his people to return and receive forgiveness. Sin is painful to all who are touched by its perversion, yet no one grieves over sin's devastating effects more than God does. He wants us to turn to him for deliverance from the sin that is gripping our life; he wants to set us free from the painful consequences we create for ourself.

In **Jeremiah 3:19-20** God reminded his people that he wanted to be a loving father to them. Few of us understand the depth of God's fatherly love. What a wonderful God who waits patiently for the day when we turn to him and call him "Father"! To do this we have to daily allow him to be our Father by focusing on him. Since he always desires the best for us, we need to seek out his will for us and do our best to follow it. He will be with us each step of the way, giving us the strength and encouragement we need to succeed in the recovery process.

insights INTO THE PROCESS OF RECOVERY

In marriage there is a honeymoon period when we are eager to please our new spouse. In **Jeremiah 2:2-3** God remembered the time when Israel was his eager bride, happy to be faithful to him. We also have a honeymoon period in recovery when we are eager to please God and focus on him. However, disillusionment can set in when the honeymoon is over. Taking time daily to be renewed by God's love and power through prayer and Bible study, we can avoid disillusionment and relapse. Temptations will lose their power over us as we surrender our life to God's control each day.

In **Jeremiah 9:4-6** the prophet warned his audience about the power of others to lead God's people away from God. When our heart is focused on God, it won't matter what others do to us or think of us. Some people may be threatened by our recovery; others may stand to lose something. Such people may do everything they can to drag us down with slanderous lies. Even when this happens, we need to remain obedient to the truth and steadfast in our relationship with God. He will protect us if we trust in him.

Jeremiah's cry to God for help in **Jeremiah 17:14** is the cry of recovery. When we acknowledge that only God can save us and heal our hurts, we can begin our new life. Hope doesn't come from within; we don't have the power to produce it. Only God can give us hope and then provide the help we need. Only he is worthy of our praise.

insights FROM ISRAEL'S HISTORY

The prophet's message in **Jeremiah 2:1–3:5** was intended for the people of Judah. God spoke about Judah's early days as a parent might reflect on the sweeter days in the life of a troubled child. Judah had forsaken God to create her own idols (see 2:13), and God's heart had been broken. The idols in our life never bring true satisfaction. A careful inventory will reveal the things in our life that we put before God. These need to be removed before we can move forward in our relationship with God and our progress in recovery.

In **Jeremiah 2:6-8** the prophet recalls how the people of Israel soon forgot who had saved them from their bondage in Egypt. As a result, they wandered for years in the wilderness. Without God we, too, will wander in a terrible wilderness. Relapsing into our destructive, selfish ways is certain without God's help. If we refuse to acknowledge and take advantage of God's power in our life, we will find ourself in humbling situations, forced once again to acknowledge our need for God's power in our life. Why would we ever want to turn away from him?

In **Jeremiah 3:12-13** we find God's plan for change, and his plan has not changed any since that time. Change cannot take place until we admit our sins to God, openly confess that we have wandered from him, and ask for his forgiveness and restoring power. As we give our life into his hands, trusting him to help us, he will guide us through the process of recovery.

insights INTO THE VALUE OF GOD'S DISCIPLINE

Perhaps the most difficult part of discipline is allowing those we love to live with the consequences of their mistakes and bad choices. No parent enjoys the process of disciplining a child, but without it, love is incomplete. In **Jeremiah 4:5–6:30** God allows the people to suffer the consequences of their sins (see 4:18; 5:3, 19, 31; 6:18-19), yet his heart is heavy. He suffers when we suffer, and the suffering he allows us to endure is designed to lead us to repentance, healing, and recovery.

Jeremiah 8:4–10:22 is filled with predictions of God's judgment. There is nothing good left to salvage from the people of Judah. There is no truth in the mouths of God's people. The wound is incurable. The people will soon suffer terrible punishment. We may also reach a point where God allows us to reap the consequences of our sins; we may lose everything. Even if we have reached that point, we can take courage. God brings us punishment to get our attention. He disciplines us because he loves us. It is never too late for recovery. All we have to do is admit that we are powerless against our dependency and hand things over to God. He is able to rebuild our life from the ashes of destruction.

Tucked away in a long passage of judgment are the words of hope in **Jeremiah 16:14-15** that reveal God's forgiving heart. The sins of Judah would lead to punishment in exile, but God's plans for his people didn't stop there. Through their suffering, God's people were forced to recognize their sins and look to God for deliverance. God then redeemed his people from exile and led them back to the Promised Land. No matter how badly we have sinned and how terrible the consequences we have suffered, God desires to work good in our life. If we admit our sins and turn to him for help, he will be faithful to restore us to wholeness.

insights INTO THE VALUE OF GOD'S LAWS

In **Jeremiah 6:16** God promises rest for our soul if we are willing to walk in a godly way. If we spend our life rejecting God's laws, however, we only drain our resources. We end up exhausted and distant from God. The road back to God is always the right road. It allows our soul to experience the rest and serenity possible only for those who put their life in God's hands.

In **Jeremiah 17:11** we discover that ill-gotten gain will never bring satisfaction. We often try to obtain things in ways God would never allow: money through greed and extortion, or power and prestige through oppression of the poor. If we acquire our possessions and relationships through actions God forbids, we should expect to ultimately lose them. In recovery, we are called to make amends with those we have wronged. We must give up the possessions we have gained wrongly and seek to reconcile the relationships broken by our wrong actions.

An important recovery principle can be found in **Jeremiah 17:27**. When we don't obey God's command to take a day of rest, we contribute to our own destruction and lose perspective on our priorities. We need a day of rest, where we worship God and reaffirm that he is in control. One of the most important steps in recovery involves our realization of this truth. We need to reaffirm this on a regular basis. We are safe from relapse only when we allow God to take control and keep it. The more control we try to take back, the greater our danger of relapse. As we set aside time for God, we are reaffirming his importance and lordship in our life.

insights CONCERNING FALSE TEACHERS

Throughout the Bible are warnings to watch out for false prophets and false teachers. In **Jeremiah 23:9-40** the false prophets of Judah claimed that the people had nothing to fear. They said that God's presence with them in the Temple guaranteed their protection. But these prophets failed to recognize the seriousness of the people's sin. Their words only supported the people's denial. Some recovery programs offer easy methods to overcome addiction, which will only lead to denial. It is never easy to deal with the failure and pain that drive our dependencies and compulsions. God calls us to face our sins honestly and receive the forgiveness and restoration that only he can give. Anyone who teaches otherwise or who offers a program that excludes God should be shunned as a false prophet.

LAMENTATIONS

THE BIG PICTURE

A. JEREMIAH'S GRIEF EXPRESSED (1:1-22)
B. THE AGONY OF THE CONSEQUENCES (2:1-22)
C. THE PROPHET'S DEEP PAIN AND CONSOLATION (3:1-66)
D. THE PAST AND THE PRESENT IN FULL VIEW (4:1-22)
E. AN IMPASSIONED PRAYER FOR FORGIVENESS (5:1-22)

With his head bowed in humility and pain, Jeremiah penned the words of Lamentations. His heart was broken. He wept to see the great city of Jerusalem destroyed and God's people in exile. Gone were the days of obedience and prosperity. The prophet had only his memories to hold on to and a faint hope of future recovery.

Jeremiah's pain was like that of a father with an errant child. He had lived with God's people and pleaded with them to return to God. But his pleas fell on deaf ears. The prophet's tears were God's tears, for God weeps for our sin and mourns with us in our losses. Jeremiah didn't mince his words or hide his pain. He wept openly and fully. His example can help us as we grieve our own losses.

Lamentations does not provide pat answers for the suffering we experience in life. As we read, we discover that it is all right to be real, to be angry with God, to be disappointed with life, and to despair about what tomorrow holds for us. Jeremiah gained comfort as he honestly told God how he hurt. God accepted Jeremiah as he was—angry, tired, and discouraged.

Jeremiah has given us a model for expressing our pain to God. In response to his honest cries, God listened to him and comforted him. In the midst of his agony, Jeremiah found one ray of hope despite the destruction around him—God's love never ceases! As we face great losses in our life, we can also find hope as we tell God how we feel. He really does hear us, and he cares about us deeply.

THE BOTTOM LINE

PURPOSE: To lament the destruction of Jerusalem and the sins of Judah and to pray for recovery and restoration. AUTHOR: The prophet Jeremiah. AUDIENCE: The people of Judah, shortly after they were exiled to Babylon. DATE WRITTEN: Soon after the fall of Jerusalem (around 586 B.C.). SETTING: Jeremiah lamented for the exiled Jews from the ruins of Jerusalem. KEY VERSES: "Yet I still dare to hope when I remember this: The faithful love of the LORD never ends! His mercies never cease" (3:21-22). SPECIAL FEATURES: Lamentations is written in the rhythm and style of ancient Jewish funeral songs or chants. Each chapter contains an acrostic poem; each new verse opens with a successive letter of the Hebrew alphabet.

RECOVERY THEMES

The Importance of Grief: Grief is the process that helps us to recover from our losses. In it we come to terms with the past and find freedom to live in the reality of the present. It also lays the groundwork for our hope for the future. When we harden ourself to the pain involved in the grieving process, recovery cannot take place. We see that God honored Jeremiah's tears and grief. God will also honor our honesty as we share our pain with him. Then he will use our grief to bring healing for the present and hope for the future.

The Pain of Consequences: God does not always protect us from the consequences of our bad attitudes and unwise behavior. Those of us in recovery know, however, that the painful consequences we suffer can be a special gift from God. Through them we learn to take responsibility for the mistakes we have made. We learn that God can use our pain to lead us to personal and spiritual growth. As we discover that even our suffering is part of God's recovery program, we will more readily trust and obey him and do all we can to get to know him better.

The Gift of Our Emotions: Nothing is closer to the core of our beings than our emotions. If we have developed a pattern of denying or hiding our feelings, we will lose the sense of who we are before God. Jeremiah shows us that we have nothing to fear in bringing even our most raw or embarrassing emotions to God. The more honest we are about how we feel, the more completely we will become involved in our relationships with God and with others.

Forgiveness—A Way of Life: Jeremiah finished his grieving and turned to God to seek forgiveness. The book ends with a heartfelt question: "Are you angry with us still?" Behind this question is Jeremiah's humility, coupled with his hope that reconciliation and forgiveness are still possible. Jeremiah knew God's heart, so he knew that God would forgive. We can be sure that God will forgive us, too, no matter how great our sins and failures. We need to come humbly before him and place our life in his strong, gentle hands.

CHAPTER 1*
Sorrow in Jerusalem

¹Jerusalem, once so full of people,
　　is now deserted.
She who was once great among the
　　nations
now sits alone like a widow.
Once the queen of all the earth,
　　she is now a slave.

²She sobs through the night;
　　tears stream down her cheeks.
Among all her lovers,
　　there is no one left to comfort her.
All her friends have betrayed her
　　and become her enemies.

³Judah has been led away into captivity,
　　oppressed with cruel slavery.
She lives among foreign nations
　　and has no place of rest.

Her enemies have chased her down,
　　and she has nowhere to turn.

⁴The roads to Jerusalem* are in mourning,
　　for crowds no longer come to celebrate
　　　　the festivals.
The city gates are silent,
　　her priests groan,
her young women are crying—
　　how bitter is her fate!

⁵Her oppressors have become her
　　masters,
　　and her enemies prosper,
for the LORD has punished Jerusalem
　　for her many sins.
Her children have been captured
　　and taken away to distant lands.

⁶All the majesty of beautiful Jerusalem*
　　has been stripped away.

---

1 Each of the first four chapters of this book is an acrostic, laid out in the order of the Hebrew alphabet. The first word of each verse begins with a successive Hebrew letter. Chapters 1, 2, and 4 have one verse for each of the 22 Hebrew letters. Chapter 3 contains 22 stanzas of three verses each. Though chapter 5 has 22 verses, it is not an acrostic. **1:4** Hebrew *Zion;* also in 1:17. **1:6** Hebrew *of the daughter of Zion.*

1:1-11 The sins of Judah's people led to their destruction and exile. The once-prosperous nation was now "like a filthy rag." Its capital city, Jerusalem, was now silent, its beauty and majesty gone. The people felt abandoned by God. The prophet Jeremiah mourned the terrible losses. Our sins also yield devastating consequences if we allow them to continue unchecked. If we are suffering terrible losses in our life, we should assess whether or not our sins have caused them. Recovery begins as we mourn our losses and admit our sins to God. If we do this, God can rebuild our life from the ruins.

Her princes are like starving deer
   searching for pasture.
They are too weak to run
   from the pursuing enemy.

7 In the midst of her sadness and
      wandering,
   Jerusalem remembers her ancient
      splendor.
But now she has fallen to her enemy,
   and there is no one to help her.
Her enemy struck her down
   and laughed as she fell.

8 Jerusalem has sinned greatly,
   so she has been tossed away like a
      filthy rag.
All who once honored her now despise
      her,
   for they have seen her stripped naked
      and humiliated.
All she can do is groan
   and hide her face.

9 She defiled herself with immorality
   and gave no thought to her future.
Now she lies in the gutter
   with no one to lift her out.
"LORD, see my misery," she cries.
   "The enemy has triumphed."

10 The enemy has plundered her
      completely,
   taking every precious thing she owns.
She has seen foreigners violate her sacred
      Temple,
   the place the LORD had forbidden them
      to enter.

11 Her people groan as they search
      for bread.
   They have sold their treasures for food
      to stay alive.
"O LORD, look," she mourns,
   "and see how I am despised.

12 "Does it mean nothing to you, all you
      who pass by?
   Look around and see if there is any
      suffering like mine,
which the LORD brought on me
   when he erupted in fierce anger.

13 "He has sent fire from heaven that burns
      in my bones.
   He has placed a trap in my path and
      turned me back.
He has left me devastated,
   racked with sickness all day long.

14 "He wove my sins into ropes
   to hitch me to a yoke of captivity.
The Lord sapped my strength and turned
   me over to my enemies;
   I am helpless in their hands.

15 "The Lord has treated my mighty men
      with contempt.
At his command a great army has come
   to crush my young warriors.
The Lord has trampled his beloved city*
   like grapes are trampled in a winepress.

16 "For all these things I weep;
   tears flow down my cheeks.
No one is here to comfort me;
   any who might encourage me are far
      away.
My children have no future,
   for the enemy has conquered us."

17 Jerusalem reaches out for help,
   but no one comforts her.
Regarding his people Israel,*
   the LORD has said,
"Let their neighbors be their enemies!
   Let them be thrown away like a filthy
      rag!"

18 "The LORD is right," Jerusalem says,
   "for I rebelled against him.
Listen, people everywhere;
   look upon my anguish and despair,
for my sons and daughters
   have been taken captive to distant lands.

19 "I begged my allies for help,
   but they betrayed me.
My priests and leaders
   starved to death in the city,
even as they searched for food
   to save their lives.

20 "LORD, see my anguish!
   My heart is broken

1:15 Hebrew *the virgin daughter of Judah.* 1:17 Hebrew *Jacob.* The names "Jacob" and "Israel" are often interchanged throughout the Old Testament, referring sometimes to the individual patriarch and sometimes to the nation.

1:18-22 After suffering through Jerusalem's devastation and exile, many of the Jews recognized that they had sinned. Before Jerusalem's destruction, many had believed that God would protect Jerusalem and the Temple regardless of how they lived, which only supported the people's denial. The destruction of Jerusalem forced them to face reality. They had sinned, and their sins had terrible consequences. Accepting responsibility for our sins is an essential part of the recovery process.

and my soul despairs,
    for I have rebelled against you.
In the streets the sword kills,
    and at home there is only death.

21 "Others heard my groans,
    but no one turned to comfort me.
When my enemies heard about my
        troubles,
    they were happy to see what you had
        done.
Oh, bring the day you promised,
    when they will suffer as I have suffered.

22 "Look at all their evil deeds, LORD.
    Punish them,
as you have punished me
    for all my sins.
My groans are many,
    and I am sick at heart."

CHAPTER 2
God's Anger at Sin
1 The Lord in his anger
    has cast a dark shadow over beautiful
        Jerusalem.*
The fairest of Israel's cities lies in the dust,
    thrown down from the heights of
        heaven.
In his day of great anger,
    the Lord has shown no mercy even to
        his Temple.*

2 Without mercy the Lord has destroyed
    every home in Israel.*
In his anger he has broken down
    the fortress walls of beautiful
        Jerusalem.*
He has brought them to the ground,
    dishonoring the kingdom and its rulers.

3 All the strength of Israel
    vanishes beneath his fierce anger.
The Lord has withdrawn his protection
    as the enemy attacks.
He consumes the whole land of Israel
    like a raging fire.

4 He bends his bow against his people,
    as though he were their enemy.
His strength is used against them
    to kill their finest youth.

His fury is poured out like fire
    on beautiful Jerusalem.*

5 Yes, the Lord has vanquished Israel
    like an enemy.
He has destroyed her palaces
    and demolished her fortresses.
He has brought unending sorrow and
        tears
    upon beautiful Jerusalem.

6 He has broken down his Temple
    as though it were merely a garden
        shelter.
The LORD has blotted out all memory
    of the holy festivals and Sabbath days.
Kings and priests fall together
    before his fierce anger.

7 The Lord has rejected his own altar;
    he despises his own sanctuary.
He has given Jerusalem's palaces
    to her enemies.
They shout in the LORD's Temple
    as though it were a day of celebration.

8 The LORD was determined
    to destroy the walls of beautiful
        Jerusalem.
He made careful plans for their
        destruction,
    then did what he had planned.
Therefore, the ramparts and walls
    have fallen down before him.

9 Jerusalem's gates have sunk into the
        ground.
    He has smashed their locks and bars.
Her kings and princes have been exiled to
        distant lands;
    her law has ceased to exist.
Her prophets receive
    no more visions from the LORD.

10 The leaders of beautiful Jerusalem
    sit on the ground in silence.
They are clothed in burlap
    and throw dust on their heads.
The young women of Jerusalem
    hang their heads in shame.

11 I have cried until the tears no longer
        come;

2:1a Hebrew the daughter of Zion; also in 2:8, 10, 18. 2:1b Hebrew his footstool. 2:2a Hebrew Jacob; also in 2:3b. See note on 1:17. 2:2b Hebrew the daughter of Judah; also in 2:5. 2:4 Hebrew on the tent of the daughter of Zion.

2:1-18 God's anger is detailed in these verses as are the devastating consequences of his anger. God is always slow to anger and quick to forgive. The Israelites had been warned of disaster by God's prophets for centuries before their enemies finally destroyed the holy city of Jerusalem. We need to remember that God's anger is motivated by his love; it is his last resort as he seeks to get our attention. His purpose is not to destroy but to bring repentance and restoration to our life.

my heart is broken.
My spirit is poured out in agony
  as I see the desperate plight of my
  people.
Little children and tiny babies
  are fainting and dying in the
  streets.

¹² They cry out to their mothers,
  "We need food and drink!"
Their lives ebb away in the streets
  like the life of a warrior wounded in
  battle.
They gasp for life
  as they collapse in their mothers' arms.

¹³ What can I say about you?
  Who has ever seen such sorrow?
O daughter of Jerusalem,
  to what can I compare your anguish?
O virgin daughter of Zion,
  how can I comfort you?
For your wound is as deep as the sea.
  Who can heal you?

¹⁴ Your prophets have said
  so many foolish things, false to the core.
They did not save you from exile
  by pointing out your sins.
Instead, they painted false pictures,
  filling you with false hope.

¹⁵ All who pass by jeer at you.
  They scoff and insult beautiful
  Jerusalem,* saying,
"Is this the city called 'Most Beautiful in
  All the World'
  and 'Joy of All the Earth'?"

¹⁶ All your enemies mock you.
  They scoff and snarl and say,
"We have destroyed her at last!
  We have long waited for this day,
  and it is finally here!"

¹⁷ But it is the LORD who did just as he
  planned.
He has fulfilled the promises of disaster
  he made long ago.
He has destroyed Jerusalem without
  mercy.
He has caused her enemies to gloat over
  her
  and has given them power over her.

¹⁸ Cry aloud* before the Lord,
  O walls of beautiful Jerusalem!
Let your tears flow like a river
  day and night.

2:15 Hebrew *the daughter of Jerusalem.* 2:18 Hebrew
Their heart cried.

HOPE

READ LAMENTATIONS 3:1-26
Perhaps we are brokenhearted because
of bitter suffering in our family. Maybe
our once-good reputation has been ruined
and now we are ashamed. Our life has
been taken captive and destroyed before
the watchful eyes of friends and foes alike.

Jeremiah watched this happen to his
beloved nation, Israel. It's no wonder he is
known as the weeping prophet. The
people of God refused to listen to
Jeremiah's warnings, and they were taken
captive by a heathen nation as a result.
Lamentations is a record of Jeremiah's
lament over the shameful fate of God's
people. He wept, "Peace has been
stripped away, and I have forgotten what
prosperity is. I cry out, 'My splendor is
gone! Everything I had hoped for from the
LORD is lost!' The thought of my suffering
and homelessness is bitter beyond words.
I will never forget this awful time, as I
grieve over my loss. Yet I still dare to hope
when I remember this: The faithful love
of the LORD never ends! His mercies never
cease. Great is his faithfulness; his mercies
begin afresh each morning. I say to myself,
'The LORD is my inheritance; therefore, I
will hope in him!'. . . So it is good to wait
quietly for salvation from the LORD"
(Lamentations 3:17-26).

Turning our life over to God includes
giving him our pain and suffering. In our
times of grief and shame we can hope,
knowing that God will help us overcome
the problems we face. God is strong
enough to lift our burdens and loving
enough to mend our broken heart. ***Turn
to page 1099, Hosea 3.***

Give yourselves no rest;
  give your eyes no relief.

¹⁹ Rise during the night and cry out.
  Pour out your hearts like water to the
  Lord.
Lift up your hands to him in prayer,
  pleading for your children,
for in every street
  they are faint with hunger.

²⁰ "O LORD, think about this!
  Should you treat your own people this
  way?
Should mothers eat their own children,
  those they once bounced on their
  knees?
Should priests and prophets be killed
  within the Lord's Temple?

²¹ "See them lying in the streets—
  young and old,
boys and girls,
  killed by the swords of the enemy.
You have killed them in your anger,
  slaughtering them without mercy.

²² "You have invited terrors from all
  around,
  as though you were calling them to a
  day of feasting.
In the day of the LORD's anger,
  no one has escaped or survived.
The enemy has killed all the children
  whom I carried and raised."

CHAPTER 3
Hope in the LORD's Faithfulness
¹ I am the one who has seen the
  afflictions
  that come from the rod of the LORD's
  anger.
² He has led me into darkness,
  shutting out all light.
³ He has turned his hand against me
  again and again, all day long.

3:19 Or is wormwood and gall.

⁴ He has made my skin and flesh grow old.
  He has broken my bones.
⁵ He has besieged and surrounded me
  with anguish and distress.
⁶ He has buried me in a dark place,
  like those long dead.

⁷ He has walled me in, and I cannot escape.
  He has bound me in heavy chains.
⁸ And though I cry and shout,
  he has shut out my prayers.
⁹ He has blocked my way with a high stone
  wall;
  he has made my road crooked.

¹⁰ He has hidden like a bear or a lion,
  waiting to attack me.
¹¹ He has dragged me off the path and torn
  me in pieces,
  leaving me helpless and devastated.
¹² He has drawn his bow
  and made me the target for his arrows.

¹³ He shot his arrows
  deep into my heart.
¹⁴ My own people laugh at me.
  All day long they sing their mocking
  songs.
¹⁵ He has filled me with bitterness
  and given me a bitter cup of sorrow to
  drink.

¹⁶ He has made me chew on gravel.
  He has rolled me in the dust.
¹⁷ Peace has been stripped away,
  and I have forgotten what prosperity is.
¹⁸ I cry out, "My splendor is gone!
  Everything I had hoped for from the
  LORD is lost!"

¹⁹ The thought of my suffering and
  homelessness
  is bitter beyond words.*
²⁰ I will never forget this awful time,
  as I grieve over my loss.
²¹ Yet I still dare to hope
  when I remember this:

2:19-22 Jeremiah called the people to admit their helplessness and turn to God for deliverance. This is how all of us begin in recovery. Many of us can relate to the terrible losses the Jews experienced. And many of us can point to failures in our life that brought the suffering upon us. All of us, no matter what our problems, can recognize how helpless we are and then turn to God for help. As we do this, we set the process of recovery in motion.

3:1-20 The prophet's words became personal in this chapter. He was heartbroken and weary, discouraged and completely undone. He felt alone and helpless and very much afflicted by God. Jeremiah spoke frankly with God; he didn't hide his despair or anger. Expressing his feelings was an important step toward recovering his hope. Sometimes we hide our feelings from God, fearing that he will condemn us for them. God is never offended by our honest anger. Unless we speak it, we cannot deal with it and escape its destructive grip.

²² The faithful love of the LORD never ends!* His mercies never cease.
²³ Great is his faithfulness; his mercies begin afresh each morning.
²⁴ I say to myself, "The LORD is my inheritance; therefore, I will hope in him!"

²⁵ The LORD is good to those who depend on him, to those who search for him.
²⁶ So it is good to wait quietly for salvation from the LORD.
²⁷ And it is good for people to submit at an early age to the yoke of his discipline:

²⁸ Let them sit alone in silence beneath the LORD's demands.
²⁹ Let them lie face down in the dust, for there may be hope at last.
³⁰ Let them turn the other cheek to those who strike them and accept the insults of their enemies.

³¹ For no one is abandoned by the Lord forever.
³² Though he brings grief, he also shows compassion because of the greatness of his unfailing love.
³³ For he does not enjoy hurting people or causing them sorrow.

³⁴ If people crush underfoot all the prisoners of the land,
³⁵ if they deprive others of their rights in defiance of the Most High,
³⁶ if they twist justice in the courts— doesn't the Lord see all these things?

³⁷ Who can command things to happen without the Lord's permission?
³⁸ Does not the Most High send both calamity and good?

³⁹ Then why should we, mere humans, complain when we are punished for our sins?

⁴⁰ Instead, let us test and examine our ways. Let us turn back to the LORD.
⁴¹ Let us lift our hearts and hands to God in heaven and say,
⁴² "We have sinned and rebelled, and you have not forgiven us.

⁴³ "You have engulfed us with your anger, chased us down, and slaughtered us without mercy.
⁴⁴ You have hidden yourself in a cloud so our prayers cannot reach you.
⁴⁵ You have discarded us as refuse and garbage among the nations.

⁴⁶ "All our enemies have spoken out against us.
⁴⁷ We are filled with fear, for we are trapped, dèvastated, and ruined."

⁴⁸ Tears stream from my eyes because of the destruction of my people!

⁴⁹ My tears flow endlessly; they will not stop
⁵⁰ until the LORD looks down from heaven and sees.
⁵¹ My heart is breaking over the fate of all the women of Jerusalem.

⁵² My enemies, whom I have never harmed, hunted me down like a bird.
⁵³ They threw me into a pit and dropped stones on me.
⁵⁴ The water rose over my head, and I cried out, "This is the end!"

⁵⁵ But I called on your name, LORD, from deep within the pit.

3:22 As in Syriac version; Hebrew reads *of the LORD keeps us from destruction.*

3:21-26 After Jeremiah poured out his pain to God, he reflected upon God's faithfulness. What could possibly deliver him from his terrible anguish? Nothing except the mercy of a gracious and loving God. God's love is unfailing; his purposes, clear; his righteousness, unquestionable. When we come to God with our pain, we are sure to get a fair hearing. God, in his mercy and grace, will help us overcome our setbacks and gain a new perspective on life when we ask him.

3:27-39 God disciplines us because he loves us. When we are following a dangerous path, we need to be stopped. Sometimes the only way God can get our attention is by knocking us down. Though we may get angry at God for his discipline, it is an opportunity for change. We should take a moral inventory to discover the root of our problems. Then we can turn our problems and sins over to God and seek to live according to his program. As we face the pain of discipline, we would be wise to ask Jeremiah's question: "Then why should we, mere humans, complain when we are punished for our sins?"

⁵⁶ You heard me when I cried, "Listen to my
　　pleading!
　　Hear my cry for help!"
⁵⁷ Yes, you came when I called;
　　you told me, "Do not fear."

⁵⁸ Lord, you are my lawyer! Plead my case!
　　For you have redeemed my life.
⁵⁹ You have seen the wrong they have done
　　to me, LORD.
　　Be my judge, and prove me right.
⁶⁰ You have seen the vengeful plots
　　my enemies have laid against me.

⁶¹ LORD, you have heard the vile names they
　　call me.
　　You know all about the plans they have
　　made.
⁶² My enemies whisper and mutter
　　as they plot against me all day long.
⁶³ Look at them! Whether they sit or stand,
　　I am the object of their mocking songs.

⁶⁴ Pay them back, LORD,
　　for all the evil they have done.
⁶⁵ Give them hard and stubborn hearts,
　　and then let your curse fall on them!
⁶⁶ Chase them down in your anger,
　　destroying them beneath the LORD's
　　heavens.

CHAPTER 4
God's Anger Satisfied
¹ How the gold has lost its luster!
　　Even the finest gold has become dull.
The sacred gemstones
　　lie scattered in the streets!

² See how the precious children of
　　Jerusalem,*
　　worth their weight in fine gold,
are now treated like pots of clay
　　made by a common potter.

³ Even the jackals feed their young,
　　but not my people Israel.
They ignore their children's cries,
　　like ostriches in the desert.

⁴ The parched tongues of their little ones
　　stick to the roofs of their mouths in
　　thirst.

The children cry for bread,
　　but no one has any to give them.
⁵ The people who once ate the richest
　　foods
　　now beg in the streets for anything they
　　can get.
Those who once wore the finest clothes
　　now search the garbage dumps for food.

⁶ The guilt* of my people
　　is greater than that of Sodom,
where utter disaster struck in a moment
　　and no hand offered help.

⁷ Our princes once glowed with health—
　　brighter than snow, whiter than milk.
Their faces were as ruddy as rubies,
　　their appearance like fine jewels.*

⁸ But now their faces are blacker than soot.
　　No one recognizes them in the streets.
Their skin sticks to their bones;
　　it is as dry and hard as wood.

⁹ Those killed by the sword are better off
　　than those who die of hunger.
Starving, they waste away
　　for lack of food from the fields.

¹⁰ Tenderhearted women
　　have cooked their own children.
They have eaten them
　　to survive the siege.

¹¹ But now the anger of the LORD is satisfied.
　　His fierce anger has been poured out.
He started a fire in Jerusalem*
　　that burned the city to its foundations.

¹² Not a king in all the earth—
　　no one in all the world—
would have believed that an enemy
　　could march through the gates of
　　Jerusalem.

¹³ Yet it happened because of the sins of her
　　prophets
　　and the sins of her priests,
who defiled the city
　　by shedding innocent blood.

¹⁴ They wandered blindly
　　through the streets,

4:2 Hebrew *precious sons of Zion.* 4:6 Or *punishment.* 4:7 Hebrew *like lapis lazuli.* 4:11 Hebrew *in Zion.*

4:1-22 Jeremiah took a moment to reflect on the ravaged city of Jerusalem. He remembered when Jerusalem knew splendor and majesty. Now even the children were begging for bread. There was a time when no one believed that Jerusalem would be destroyed, but the holy city was now in ruins. We may think that we are safe from this kind of destruction. But if we are controlled by our sins and addictions, we are headed there fast. We need to take steps toward recovery while there is still time.

so defiled by blood
that no one dared touch them.

15 "Get away!" the people shouted
at them.
"You're defiled! Don't touch us!"
So they fled to distant lands
and wandered among foreign nations,
but none would let them stay.

16 The LORD himself has scattered them,
and he no longer helps them.
People show no respect for the priests
and no longer honor the leaders.

17 We looked in vain for our allies
to come and save us,
but we were looking to nations
that could not help us.

18 We couldn't go into the streets
without danger to our lives.
Our end was near; our days were
numbered.
We were doomed!

19 Our enemies were swifter than eagles
in flight.
If we fled to the mountains, they
found us.
If we hid in the wilderness,
they were waiting for us there.

20 Our king—the LORD's anointed, the very
life of our nation—
was caught in their snares.
We had thought that his shadow
would protect us against any nation
on earth!

21 Are you rejoicing in the land of Uz,
O people of Edom?
But you, too, must drink from the cup
of the LORD's anger.
You, too, will be stripped naked in your
drunkenness.

22 O beautiful Jerusalem,* your punishment
will end;
you will soon return from exile.
But Edom, your punishment is just
beginning;
soon your many sins will be exposed.

CHAPTER 5
Prayer for Restoration

1 LORD, remember what has happened to us.
See how we have been disgraced!
2 Our inheritance has been turned over to
strangers,
our homes to foreigners.
3 We are orphaned and fatherless.
Our mothers are widowed.
4 We have to pay for water to drink,
and even firewood is expensive.
5 Those who pursue us are at our heels;
we are exhausted but are given no rest.
6 We submitted to Egypt and Assyria
to get enough food to survive.
7 Our ancestors sinned, but they have
died—
and we are suffering the punishment
they deserved!

8 Slaves have now become our masters;
there is no one left to rescue us.
9 We hunt for food at the risk of our lives,
for violence rules the countryside.
10 The famine has blackened our skin
as though baked in an oven.
11 Our enemies rape the women in
Jerusalem*
and the young girls in all the towns of
Judah.
12 Our princes are being hanged by their
thumbs,
and our elders are treated with
contempt.
13 Young men are led away to work at
millstones,
and boys stagger under heavy loads of
wood.
14 The elders no longer sit in the city gates;
the young men no longer dance and
sing.
15 Joy has left our hearts;
our dancing has turned to mourning.
16 The garlands have* fallen from our heads.
Weep for us because we have sinned.
17 Our hearts are sick and weary,
and our eyes grow dim with tears.
18 For Jerusalem* is empty and desolate,
a place haunted by jackals.

4:22 Hebrew O daughter of Zion. 5:11 Hebrew in Zion. 5:16 Or The crown has. 5:18 Hebrew Mount Zion.

5:1-18 Jeremiah asked God to remember the suffering of his people. He listed the abuses they had endured. Notice how bold Jeremiah was in his relationship with God. When we feel upset about our situation, we often remain silent or complain under our breath. In doing so, we allow our relationship with God to grow distant. Jeremiah went directly to God with his complaints, and his relationship with God was strengthened in the process. God does hear, and he does care. We need to share our feelings and struggles with him.

19 But LORD, you remain the same forever!
  Your throne continues from generation
    to generation.
20 Why do you continue to forget us?
  Why have you abandoned us for so
    long?

21 Restore us, O LORD, and bring us back
    to you again!
  Give us back the joys we once
    had!
22 Or have you utterly rejected us?
  Are you angry with us still?

5:19-22 Jeremiah made a final and impassioned plea to God to remember and restore his broken people. And God did restore Israel after the Babylonian captivity. Under the leadership of men like Zerubbabel, Ezra, and Nehemiah, God led his people home to rebuild the holy city and the Temple. God still restores his people today. Regardless of the intensity of our pain, he is able to bring deep and abiding comfort.

EZEKIEL

THE BIG PICTURE

A. CONDEMNATION FOR JUDAH
(1:1–24:27)
   1. God's Glory in Ezekiel's Vision
      and Commission (1:1–3:27)
   2. Messages of Gloom for Israel
      (4:1–24:27)
B. CONSOLATION FOR JUDAH
(25:1–48:35)
   1. Judgment against Foreign
      Nations (25:1–32:32)
   2. Messages of Hope for Judah
      (33:1–39:29)
   3. The New Temple in
      Jerusalem (40:1–48:35)

Discouragement. Despair. Disillusionment. These are just a few of the feelings experienced by the people to whom Ezekiel ministered. The prophet Ezekiel was deported with other Jews to Babylonia about ten years before the destruction of Jerusalem. He prophesied to the Babylonian exiles during the last years of Jerusalem's survival and in the years closely following its fall. God called him to confront and then to comfort his people.

As the book of Ezekiel begins, one hope for the exiles still remained. Jerusalem was still standing; there was hope that the holy city and the Temple would yet be spared. The Jews, however, were in denial. They assumed that God's presence in the Temple would protect Jerusalem. The people failed to realize that there was no escaping the painful consequences of their sins. During this time of false hope, God called Ezekiel to proclaim that Jerusalem's destruction was certain. The people needed to realize that their sins had consequences and that they needed to repent.

The final chapters (25–48) were written after Jerusalem's destruction and are filled with hope for God's broken people. With the fall of Jerusalem (24:1-27), the predicted consequences of Israel's sins had come to pass. The people of Judah could no longer deny their sins, and they turned to God for help. God promised them future restoration and peace. Through Ezekiel's vision of dry bones coming to life, the exiled Jews received hope for a new life. God would do the impossible! He would lead his people back home and rebuild his nation from a state of total ruin.

THE BOTTOM LINE

PURPOSE: To help the exiled Jews understand how God's glory and righteousness made their present judgment necessary and their future restoration certain. AUTHOR: The prophet Ezekiel. AUDIENCE: The Jews of the Babylonian exile, before and after the fall of Jerusalem. DATE WRITTEN: The book was probably written shortly after the time period it covers (from 592 to 570 B.C.). SETTING: Ezekiel lived near the Kebar River in Babylon and ministered to the Jews in exile. KEY VERSE: "And I will give you a new heart, and I will put a new spirit in you. I will take out your stony, stubborn heart and give you a tender, responsive heart" (36:26). KEY PLACES: Jerusalem, Babylon, and Egypt. KEY PEOPLE: Ezekiel, his wife, Israel's leaders, and Nebuchadnezzar.

RECOVERY THEMES

Recovery through Confrontation: During the first part of the book of Ezekiel, the Jews were in denial. They believed that God would preserve Jerusalem regardless of how they behaved. So God's program for Judah's recovery came in the form of direct confrontation. Ezekiel confronted the Jews with the truth about their sins: their nation would be completely destroyed because of their sins. When we are in denial, direct confrontation may be the only way to get our attention. If we fail to listen to the truth, God will let us suffer the consequences. We would be wise to humbly listen to any legitimate confrontation God sends us.

Hope in Failure: Whenever we have slipped or relapsed, our dominant feeling is hopelessness. We feel that all is lost, that nothing good can happen. After the destruction of Jerusalem, God's people felt like this. Ezekiel's message of judgment had proven true. The people humbly realized that they were sinful and that their suffering was a consequence of their sins. As they saw how bleak their situation was, God sent them a message of hope and recovery. When we feel defeated because of our failures, God can bring us hope. We never intend to fail, but when we do, God is our strength and hope for recovery when we call on him.

God Is Always Available: The exiles in Babylon lived in a place that reminded them daily of their failure and shame. They felt abandoned by God. Yet God, who isn't limited by geographical boundaries, was right there with them. He met Ezekiel on foreign soil and through him spoke to his broken people. God wants to meet us no matter where we are, even when we are at our worst. And when he comes, he brings light to the darkness and hope for recovery. God is always available—even in the midst of our shame.

No Situation Is Hopeless: Many of us suffer from having been raised in a dysfunctional family. Sometimes we make bad decisions that affect our life for a long time. We probably feel a lot like the exiles in Babylon felt. They were suffering in exile because of their sins and the sins of their ancestors. They felt overwhelmed and helpless. But God entered into that hopeless situation and transformed it to bring honor and glory to his name. God hasn't changed. He still wants to come into our hopeless situation and transform us. He wants to free us from our bondage to past sins and failures.

CHAPTER 1
A Vision of Living Beings

On July 31* of my thirtieth year,* while I was with the Judean exiles beside the Kebar River in Babylon, the heavens were opened and I saw visions of God. ²This happened during the fifth year of King Jehoiachin's captivity. ³(The LORD gave this message to Ezekiel son of Buzi, a priest, beside the Kebar River in the land of the Babylonians,* and he felt the hand of the LORD take hold of him.)

⁴As I looked, I saw a great storm coming from the north, driving before it a huge cloud that flashed with lightning and shone with brilliant light. There was fire inside the cloud, and in the middle of the fire glowed something like gleaming amber.* ⁵From the center of the cloud came four living beings that looked human, ⁶except that each had four faces and four wings. ⁷Their legs were straight, and their feet had hooves like those of a calf and shone like burnished bronze. ⁸Under each of their four wings I could see human hands. So each of the four beings had four faces and four wings. ⁹The wings of each living being touched the wings of the beings be-

1:1a Hebrew *On the fifth day of the fourth month,* of the ancient Hebrew lunar calendar. A number of dates in Ezekiel can be cross-checked with dates in surviving Babylonian records and related accurately to our modern calendar. This event occurred on July 31, 593 B.C. **1:1b** Or *in the thirtieth year.* **1:3** Or *Chaldeans.* **1:4** Or *like burnished metal;* also in 1:27.

1:1-3 Ezekiel was among the people of Judah exiled to Babylon about ten years prior to Jerusalem's destruction; they had lost their homeland and their property. Yet in the early chapters of this book (1–24), the people still clung to a slim hope. Jerusalem and the Temple still stood; complete destruction had not yet fallen. So many of the people continued in their denial, believing that God would not allow their homeland to be completely destroyed. They refused to admit their sins and the sins of their ancestors. So Ezekiel's early ministry was one of confrontation. He confronted the exiles with their sins and predicted Jerusalem's destruction.

1:1-3 Having been trained as a priest, Ezekiel would have naturally associated God's presence with the Temple in Jerusalem. But he and his companions had been uprooted from their land—and from their Temple. Many wondered whether they could experience God's presence in Babylon. Through Ezekiel's visions, it became clear that God is not limited by geography. God revealed himself even in godless Babylon! God can reach us no matter where we are or what we have done. If we are willing to turn our life over to him, there is *always* hope for recovery.

EZEKIEL

Little is known of Ezekiel, the man. We know that he was a priest who faithfully obeyed God's laws and was called by God to be a prophet. He began to prophesy at age thirty, five years after he had been taken into Babylonian captivity. He settled near the Kebar River, where he prophesied to the exiles during the final years of Jerusalem's survival and in the years closely following its destruction.

The fact that Ezekiel said little about himself may indicate his humility. The prophetic work that God called him to do was certainly humbling. He was called to publicly act out God's messages for his people. On one occasion he was told to lie on his left side for 390 days to symbolize the years of Israel's sin and then on his right side for 40 days to depict the years of Judah's sin. Another time he was forbidden to mourn his wife's death to show that no one would mourn over Jerusalem after its demise.

Ezekiel's name means "God strengthens," a name appropriate to the man and his message. Ezekiel needed God's strength as he carried a message of judgment to a people who did not want to hear it. Ezekiel also carried a message of strengthening hope after Jerusalem's destruction and the loss of Israel's hope. God wanted his people to know that they could not escape the consequences of their sins. Ezekiel's message was intended to break through their denial. But God also wanted the Jews to realize that his mercy was available to those who would confess their sins and turn to him. The suffering was designed to bring his people's recovery, not their destruction.

Ezekiel's messages of confrontation and comfort are for us too. If we tend to ignore the sins in our life, we would be wise to heed these warnings. Denial only leads to suffering and destruction. If we have been broken by our failures and have turned to God for help, Ezekiel's words of comfort are meant for us as well. God can rebuild our life, no matter how broken it is. Ezekiel saw a vision in which God reassembled the scattered, dry bones of his people and brought them back to life. He can do the same in our life.

STRENGTHS AND ACCOMPLISHMENTS:
- Ezekiel was completely dedicated to God.
- He communicated God's message clearly despite opposition.
- He did not complain about the difficult tasks that God gave him.
- He was willing to be humiliated for God's cause.

LESSONS FROM HIS LIFE:
- Sin and denial lead to suffering and destruction.
- Through repentance we can receive forgiveness and restoration.
- God may call us to do difficult things to accomplish his will.
- When God calls us to speak, we must not be swayed by the opposition.

KEY VERSES:
"Then [God] added, 'Son of man, let all my words sink deep into your own heart first. Listen to them carefully for yourself. Then go to your people in exile and say to them, "This is what the Sovereign LORD says!"'" (Ezekiel 3:10-11).

Ezekiel's story is told in the book of Ezekiel.

---

side it. Each one moved straight forward in any direction without turning around.

¹⁰Each had a human face in the front, the face of a lion on the right side, the face of an ox on the left side, and the face of an eagle at the back. ¹¹Each had two pairs of outstretched wings—one pair stretched out to touch the wings of the living beings on either side of it, and the other pair covered its body. ¹²They went in whatever direction the spirit chose, and they moved straight forward in any direction without turning around.

¹³The living beings looked like bright coals of fire or brilliant torches, and lightning seemed to flash back and forth among them. ¹⁴And the living beings darted to and fro like flashes of lightning.

¹⁵As I looked at these beings, I saw four wheels touching the ground beside them, one wheel belonging to each. ¹⁶The wheels

sparkled as if made of beryl. All four wheels looked alike and were made the same; each wheel had a second wheel turning crosswise within it. [17]The beings could move in any of the four directions they faced, without turning as they moved. [18]The rims of the four wheels were tall and frightening, and they were covered with eyes all around.

[19]When the living beings moved, the wheels moved with them. When they flew upward, the wheels went up, too. [20]The spirit of the living beings was in the wheels. So wherever the spirit went, the wheels and the living beings also went. [21]When the beings moved, the wheels moved. When the beings stopped, the wheels stopped. When the beings flew upward, the wheels rose up, for the spirit of the living beings was in the wheels.

[22]Spread out above them was a surface like the sky, glittering like crystal. [23]Beneath this surface the wings of each living being stretched out to touch the others' wings, and each had two wings covering its body. [24]As they flew, their wings sounded to me like waves crashing against the shore or like the voice of the Almighty* or like the shouting of a mighty army. When they stopped, they let down their wings. [25]As they stood with wings lowered, a voice spoke from beyond the crystal surface above them.

[26]Above this surface was something that looked like a throne made of blue lapis lazuli. And on this throne high above was a figure whose appearance resembled a man. [27]From what appeared to be his waist up, he looked like gleaming amber, flickering like a fire. And from his waist down, he looked like a burning flame, shining with splendor. [28]All around him was a glowing halo, like a rainbow shining in the clouds on a rainy day. This is what the glory of the LORD looked like to me. When I saw it, I fell face down on the ground, and I heard someone's voice speaking to me.

1:24 Hebrew *Shaddai.*

CHAPTER 2
Ezekiel's Call and Commission

"Stand up, son of man," said the voice. "I want to speak with you." [2]The Spirit came into me as he spoke, and he set me on my feet. I listened carefully to his words. [3]"Son of man," he said, "I am sending you to the nation of Israel, a rebellious nation that has rebelled against me. They and their ancestors have been rebelling against me to this very day. [4]They are a stubborn and hard-hearted people. But I am sending you to say to them, 'This is what the Sovereign LORD says!' [5]And whether they listen or refuse to listen—for remember, they are rebels—at least they will know they have had a prophet among them.

[6]"Son of man, do not fear them or their words. Don't be afraid even though their threats surround you like nettles and briers and stinging scorpions. Do not be dismayed by their dark scowls, even though they are rebels. [7]You must give them my messages whether they listen or not. But they won't listen, for they are completely rebellious! [8]Son of man, listen to what I say to you. Do not join them in their rebellion. Open your mouth, and eat what I give you."

[9]Then I looked and saw a hand reaching out to me. It held a scroll, [10]which he unrolled. And I saw that both sides were covered with funeral songs, words of sorrow, and pronouncements of doom.

CHAPTER 3

The voice said to me, "Son of man, eat what I am giving you—eat this scroll! Then go and give its message to the people of Israel." [2]So I opened my mouth, and he fed me the scroll. [3]"Fill your stomach with this," he said. And when I ate it, it tasted as sweet as honey in my mouth.

[4]Then he said, "Son of man, go to the people of Israel and give them my messages. [5]I am

---

2:3-5 Why did God send a message of judgment to a group of people already in exile? At this time Jerusalem still stood, and a majority of the people still lived in Israel. Ezekiel was among a small group that had already been exiled; many of these early exiles believed their captivity would be short. Ezekiel was called to tell them that the consequences of their sins had not yet fully happened. Jerusalem was yet to be destroyed. The people needed to admit their sins and turn to God in repentance in order to fulfill God's purpose for their exile. Like the exiles, we often hold on to our denial long after we have begun to feel the destructive consequences of our actions. We must be wise and act before the full consequences of our addictions fall upon us.

3:1-3 Ezekiel was commanded to eat the scroll that contained God's words, which enabled him to perform his difficult ministry because he was sustained and directed by the words he received from God. As we face the trials of recovery, God's sustaining Word can provide us with the direction and strength we need. As we daily read and meditate on God's truths, we will discover God's power helping us to progress successfully in the recovery process.

not sending you to a foreign people whose language you cannot understand. 6No, I am not sending you to people with strange and difficult speech. If I did, they would listen! 7But the people of Israel won't listen to you any more than they listen to me! For the whole lot of them are hard-hearted and stubborn. 8But look, I have made you as obstinate and hard-hearted as they are. 9I have made your forehead as hard as the hardest rock! So don't be afraid of them or fear their angry looks, even though they are rebels."

10Then he added, "Son of man, let all my words sink deep into your own heart first. Listen to them carefully for yourself. 11Then go to your people in exile and say to them, 'This is what the Sovereign LORD says!' Do this whether they listen to you or not."

12Then the Spirit lifted me up, and I heard a loud rumbling sound behind me. (May the glory of the LORD be praised in his place!)* 13It was the sound of the wings of the living beings as they brushed against each other and the rumbling of their wheels beneath them.

14The Spirit lifted me up and took me away. I went in bitterness and turmoil, but the LORD's hold on me was strong. 15Then I came to the colony of Judean exiles in Tel-abib, beside the Kebar River. I was overwhelmed and sat among them for seven days.

A Watchman for Israel

16After seven days the LORD gave me a message. He said, 17"Son of man, I have appointed you as a watchman for Israel. Whenever you receive a message from me, warn people immediately. 18If I warn the wicked, saying, 'You are under the penalty of death,' but you fail to deliver the warning, they will die in their sins. And I will hold you responsible for their deaths. 19If you warn them and they refuse to repent and keep on sinning, they will die in their sins. But you will have saved yourself because you obeyed me.

20"If righteous people turn away from their righteous behavior and ignore the obstacles I put in their way, they will die. And if you do not warn them, they will die in their sins.

None of their righteous acts will be remembered, and I will hold you responsible for their deaths. 21But if you warn righteous people not to sin and they listen to you and do not sin, they will live, and you will have saved yourself, too."

22Then the LORD took hold of me and said, "Get up and go out into the valley, and I will speak to you there." 23So I got up and went, and there I saw the glory of the LORD, just as I had seen in my first vision by the Kebar River. And I fell face down on the ground.

24Then the Spirit came into me and set me on my feet. He spoke to me and said, "Go to your house and shut yourself in. 25There, son of man, you will be tied with ropes so you cannot go out among the people. 26And I will make your tongue stick to the roof of your mouth so that you will be speechless and unable to rebuke them, for they are rebels. 27But when I give you a message, I will loosen your tongue and let you speak. Then you will say to them, 'This is what the Sovereign LORD says!' Those who choose to listen will listen, but those who refuse will refuse, for they are rebels.

CHAPTER 4
A Sign of the Coming Siege

"And now, son of man, take a large clay brick and set it down in front of you. Then draw a map of the city of Jerusalem on it. 2Show the city under siege. Build a wall around it so no one can escape. Set up the enemy camp, and surround the city with siege ramps and battering rams. 3Then take an iron griddle and place it between you and the city. Turn toward the city and demonstrate how harsh the siege will be against Jerusalem. This will be a warning to the people of Israel.

4"Now lie on your left side and place the sins of Israel on yourself. You are to bear their sins for the number of days you lie there on your side. 5I am requiring you to bear Israel's sins for 390 days—one day for each year of their sin. 6After that, turn over and lie on your right side for 40 days—one day for each year of Judah's sin.

3:12 A possible reading for this verse is *Then the Spirit lifted me up, and as the glory of the LORD rose from its place, I heard a loud rumbling sound behind me.*

3:24 Ezekiel had just been commissioned with a gigantic ministry. He was overwhelmed by the scope of it. At this point, the Spirit entered him to empower him for the work he had to do. In recovery we are faced with major challenges. God's power in us is essential for success in performing the required tasks. As we examine our life, we should rejoice over the small miracles God has worked for us. Such things would never have happened without the Holy Spirit's intervening power.

⁷"Meanwhile, keep staring at the siege of Jerusalem. Lie there with your arm bared and prophesy her destruction. ⁸I will tie you up with ropes so you won't be able to turn from side to side until the days of your siege have been completed.

⁹"Now go and get some wheat, barley, beans, lentils, millet, and emmer wheat, and mix them together in a storage jar. Use them to make bread for yourself during the 390 days you will be lying on your side. ¹⁰Ration this out to yourself, eight ounces* of food for each day, and eat it at set times. ¹¹Then measure out a jar* of water for each day, and drink it at set times. ¹²Prepare and eat this food as you would barley cakes. While all the people are watching, bake it over a fire using dried human dung as fuel and then eat the bread." ¹³Then the LORD said, "This is how Israel will eat defiled bread in the Gentile lands to which I will banish them!"

¹⁴Then I said, "O Sovereign LORD, must I be defiled by using human dung? For I have never been defiled before. From the time I was a child until now I have never eaten any animal that died of sickness or was killed by other animals. I have never eaten any meat forbidden by the law."

¹⁵"All right," the LORD said. "You may bake your bread with cow dung instead of human dung." ¹⁶Then he told me, "Son of man, I will make food very scarce in Jerusalem. It will be weighed out with great care and eaten fearfully. The water will be rationed out drop by drop, and the people will drink it with dismay. ¹⁷Lacking food and water, people will look at one another in terror, and they will waste away under their punishment.

CHAPTER 5
A Sign of the Coming Judgment

"Son of man, take a sharp sword and use it as a razor to shave your head and beard. Use a scale to weigh the hair into three equal parts. ²Place a third of it at the center of your map of Jerusalem. After acting out the siege, burn it there. Scatter another third across your map and chop it with a sword. Scatter the last third to the wind, for I will scatter my people with the sword. ³Keep just a bit of the hair and tie it up in your robe. ⁴Then take some of these hairs out and throw them into the fire, burning them up. A fire will then spread from this remnant and destroy all of Israel.

⁵"This is what the Sovereign LORD says: This is an illustration of what will happen to Jerusalem. I placed her at the center of the nations, ⁶but she has rebelled against my regulations and decrees and has been even more wicked than the surrounding nations. She has refused to obey the regulations and decrees I gave her to follow.

⁷"Therefore, this is what the Sovereign LORD says: You people have behaved worse than your neighbors and have refused to obey my decrees and regulations. You have not even lived up to the standards of the nations around you. ⁸Therefore, I myself, the Sovereign LORD, am now your enemy. I will punish you publicly while all the nations watch. ⁹Because of your detestable idols, I will punish you like I have never punished anyone before or ever will again. ¹⁰Parents will eat their own children, and children will eat their parents. I will punish you and scatter to the winds the few who survive.

¹¹"As surely as I live, says the Sovereign LORD, I will cut you off completely. I will show you no pity at all because you have defiled my Temple with your vile images and detestable sins. ¹²A third of your people will die in the city from disease and famine. A third of them will be slaughtered by the enemy outside the city walls. And I will scatter a third to the winds, chasing them with my sword. ¹³Then

---

4:10 Hebrew *20 shekels* [228 grams].   **4:11** Hebrew ⅙ of a hin [about 1 pint or 0.6 liters].

4:9-13 Bad news is never welcome. God told Ezekiel to illustrate what it would be like for his people during the coming famine. They needed to realize that though things were already bad, the situation was going to worsen. As long as the people had any reason for hope, they would never admit their sins and trust God. Our own life may have deteriorated to an intolerable state before we were willing to admit our failures and start the rebuilding process. We must recognize our need for God and daily turn our life over to him and his power.

5:8-10 God's judgment is righteous and cannot be avoided. Its inevitability and nature were announced by Ezekiel in detail. If we refuse to repent, we also face God's judgment for our sins. It is a question of *when,* not *if.* Sin has terrible and unavoidable consequences. We cannot live a life that is out of control and hope to escape the consequences of our rebellion. God certainly loves us and wants to restore us if we confess our sins to him and ask for his forgiveness. But this does not mean we can do whatever we want to. God is just and will discipline his people when they continue to sin.

at last my anger will be spent, and I will be satisfied. And when my fury against them has subsided, all Israel will know that I, the LORD, have spoken to them in my jealous anger.

¹⁴"So I will turn you into a ruin, a mockery in the eyes of the surrounding nations and to all who pass by. ¹⁵You will become an object of mockery and taunting and horror. You will be a warning to all the nations around you. They will see what happens when the LORD punishes a nation in anger and rebukes it, says the LORD.

¹⁶"I will shower you with the deadly arrows of famine to destroy you. The famine will become more and more severe until every crumb of food is gone. ¹⁷And along with the famine, wild animals will attack you and rob you of your children. Disease and war will stalk your land, and I will bring the sword of the enemy against you. I, the LORD, have spoken!"

CHAPTER 6
Judgment against Israel's Mountains
Again a message came to me from the LORD: ²"Son of man, turn and face the mountains of Israel and prophesy against them. ³Proclaim this message from the Sovereign LORD against the mountains of Israel. This is what the Sovereign LORD says to the mountains and hills and to the ravines and valleys: I am about to bring war upon you, and I will smash your pagan shrines. ⁴All your altars will be demolished, and your places of worship will be destroyed. I will kill your people in front of your idols.* ⁵I will lay your corpses in front of your idols and scatter your bones around your altars. ⁶Wherever you live there will be desolation, and I will destroy your pagan shrines. Your altars will be demolished, your idols will be smashed, your places of worship will be torn down, and all the religious objects you

have made will be destroyed. ⁷The place will be littered with corpses, and you will know that I alone am the LORD.

⁸"But I will let a few of my people escape destruction, and they will be scattered among the nations of the world. ⁹Then when they are exiled among the nations, they will remember me. They will recognize how hurt I am by their unfaithful hearts and lustful eyes that long for their idols. Then at last they will hate themselves for all their detestable sins. ¹⁰They will know that I alone am the LORD and that I was serious when I said I would bring this calamity on them.

¹¹"This is what the Sovereign LORD says: Clap your hands in horror, and stamp your feet. Cry out because of all the detestable sins the people of Israel have committed. Now they are going to die from war and famine and disease. ¹²Disease will strike down those who are far away in exile. War will destroy those who are nearby. And anyone who survives will be killed by famine. So at last I will spend my fury on them. ¹³They will know that I am the LORD when their dead lie scattered among their idols and altars on every hill and mountain and under every green tree and every great shade tree—the places where they offered sacrifices to their idols. ¹⁴I will crush them and make their cities desolate from the wilderness in the south to Riblah* in the north. Then they will know that I am the LORD."

CHAPTER 7
The Coming of the End
Then this message came to me from the LORD: ²"Son of man, this is what the Sovereign LORD says to Israel:

"The end is here!
    Wherever you look—

6:4 The Hebrew term (literally *round things*) probably alludes to dung; also in 6:5, 6, 9, 13. 6:14 As in some Hebrew manuscripts; most Hebrew manuscripts read *Diblah*.

5:14-15 God judged the Israelites for their rebellion to show the world what happens to those who disobey him. Rebellion against God always has painful consequences. We have all seen how destructive addictions and their accompanying sins can be; many of us have firsthand experience. We would be wise to learn from the pain of others and seek God's help and forgiveness. If we don't, we may become one of God's object lessons to show others what happens to those who rebel against God.

6:8-10 God rebuked his people for their sins and assured them of coming judgment, but he did not leave them in despair. He gave them hope for recovery. God would spare a remnant who would escape destruction to eventually rebuild the nation. But in order to rebuild, it was necessary for God to first tear down. This pattern has been repeated many times in the lives of nations and individuals who have hit bottom but then found new hope as they turned to God. No matter how great our present suffering, there is always hope for the future. We can begin by viewing our pain as an important step in recovery. Then we must turn to God for the forgiveness and healing he promises.

east, west, north, or south—
   your land is finished.
3 No hope remains,
   for I will unleash my anger against you.
I will call you to account
   for all your detestable sins.
4 I will turn my eyes away and show
      no pity.
   I will repay you for all your detestable
      sins.
Then you will know that I am the LORD.

5 "This is what the Sovereign LORD says:
Disaster after disaster
   is coming your way!
6 The end has come.
   It has finally arrived.
   Your final doom is waiting!
7 O people of Israel, the day of your
      destruction is dawning.
   The time has come; the day of trouble
      is near.
Shouts of anguish will be heard on the
      mountains,
   not shouts of joy.
8 Soon I will pour out my fury on you
   and unleash my anger against you.
I will call you to account
   for all your detestable sins.
9 I will turn my eyes away and show
      no pity.
   I will repay you for all your detestable
      sins.
Then you will know that it is I, the LORD,
   who is striking the blow.

10 "The day of judgment is here;
   your destruction awaits!
The people's wickedness and pride
   have blossomed to full flower.
11 Their violence has grown into a rod
   that will beat them for their
      wickedness.

None of these proud and wicked people
   will survive.
   All their wealth and prestige will be
      swept away.
12 Yes, the time has come;
   the day is here!
Buyers should not rejoice over bargains,
   nor sellers grieve over losses,
for all of them will fall
   under my terrible anger.
13 Even if the merchants survive,
   they will never return to their business.
For what God has said applies to
      everyone—
   it will not be changed!
Not one person whose life is twisted
      by sin
   will ever recover.

The Desolation of Israel

14 "The trumpet calls Israel's army to
      mobilize,
   but no one listens,
   for my fury is against them all.
15 There is war outside the city
   and disease and famine within.
Those outside the city walls
   will be killed by enemy swords.
Those inside the city
   will die of famine and disease.
16 The survivors who escape to the
      mountains
   will moan like doves, weeping
      for their sins.
17 Their hands will hang limp,
   their knees will be weak as water.
18 They will dress themselves in burlap;
   horror and shame will cover them.
They will shave their heads
   in sorrow and remorse.

19 "They will throw their money in the
      streets,
   tossing it out like worthless trash.

7:4 "Then you will know that I am the LORD!" The people of Israel needed to learn this lesson if they hoped to recover from their punishment in exile. This is an important lesson for all of us to learn. Each of us must discover who God is and what he requires of us if we hope to succeed in the recovery process. When we give God control of our life, doing our best to obey his will, we are on the way to recovery. As we obey him, we will discover how to rebuild our life on a solid foundation.

7:5-11 Even though it can be disheartening, honest recognition of our circumstances and sins is essential before any positive steps can be taken toward recovery. Until we recognize where we are, we can never get to where we should be. The people of Israel denied their sinful past and were therefore unable to receive God's forgiveness, healing, and direction. God forced them to stop their denial with his acts of judgment. We need to admit our problems and humbly turn to God for help before we are destroyed by sin's painful consequences.

7:19 The people of Israel couldn't use their wealth to escape the coming judgment. In fact, all of their human resources proved worthless. Only God could deliver them, but since they were in

Their silver and gold won't save them
on that day of the LORD's anger.
It will neither satisfy nor feed them,
for their greed can only trip them up.
²⁰ They were proud of their beautiful jewelry
and used it to make detestable idols
and vile images.
Therefore, I will make all their wealth
disgusting to them.
²¹ I will give it as plunder to foreigners,
to the most wicked of nations,
and they will defile it.
²² I will turn my eyes from them
as these robbers invade and defile my
treasured land.

²³ "Prepare chains for my people,
for the land is bloodied by terrible crimes.
Jerusalem is filled with violence.
²⁴ I will bring the most ruthless of nations
to occupy their homes.
I will break down their proud fortresses
and defile their sanctuaries.
²⁵ Terror and trembling will overcome my
people.
They will look for peace but not find it.
²⁶ Calamity will follow calamity;
rumor will follow rumor.
They will look in vain
for a vision from the prophets.
They will receive no teaching from the
priests
and no counsel from the leaders.
²⁷ The king and the prince will stand helpless,
weeping in despair,
and the people's hands
will tremble with fear.
I will bring on them
the evil they have done to others,
and they will receive the punishment
they so richly deserve.
Then they will know that I am the LORD."

CHAPTER 8
Idolatry in the Temple

Then on September 17,* during the sixth year of King Jehoiachin's captivity, while the leaders of Judah were in my home, the Sovereign LORD took hold of me. ² I saw a figure that appeared to be a man.* From what appeared to be his waist down, he looked like a burning flame. From the waist up he looked like gleaming amber.* ³ He reached out what seemed to be a hand and took me by the hair. Then the Spirit lifted me up into the sky and transported me to Jerusalem in a vision from God. I was taken to the north gate of the inner courtyard of the Temple, where there is a large idol that has made the LORD very jealous. ⁴ Suddenly, the glory of the God of Israel was there, just as I had seen it before in the valley.

⁵ Then the LORD said to me, "Son of man, look toward the north." So I looked, and there to the north, beside the entrance to the gate near the altar, stood the idol that had made the LORD so jealous.

⁶ "Son of man," he said, "do you see what they are doing? Do you see the detestable sins the people of Israel are committing to drive me from my Temple? But come, and you will see even more detestable sins than these!" ⁷ Then he brought me to the door of the Temple courtyard, where I could see a hole in the wall. ⁸ He said to me, "Now, son of man, dig into the wall." So I dug into the wall and found a hidden doorway.

⁹ "Go in," he said, "and see the wicked and detestable sins they are committing in there!" ¹⁰ So I went in and saw the walls covered with engravings of all kinds of crawling animals and detestable creatures. I also saw the various idols* worshiped by the people of Israel. ¹¹ Seventy leaders of Israel were standing there with Jaazaniah son of Shaphan in

---

8:1 Hebrew *on the fifth [day] of the sixth month,* of the ancient Hebrew lunar calendar. This event occurred on September 17, 592 B.C.; also see note on 1:1. 8:2a As in Greek version; Hebrew reads *appeared to be fire.* 8:2b Or *like burnished metal.* 8:10 The Hebrew term (literally *round things*) probably alludes to dung.

---

denial about their sin, there was no escape from the coming judgment. When dealing with our dependencies and destructive habits, human resources alone are powerless. If we refuse to allow God to take part in the recovery process, we have no hope for success. We must avoid programs that exclude God; he is our only hope for true recovery. If we depend wholly on any other resource, we are moving toward destruction.

8:1-17 Ezekiel had a vision that revealed the religious activities of Israel's leaders. They were worshiping idols in the Temple and believed that God didn't see what they were doing or perhaps that he had deserted them. These false and dangerous misconceptions about God are still prevalent today. We believe we can actually hide our sins from God, or we believe that he is somehow looking the other way. It feeds our denial and leads to painful consequences and, ultimately, destruction. God is deeply concerned about our destructive habits and sins. The terrible fate of Israel's leaders should serve as a warning to us.

the center. Each of them held an incense burner, from which a cloud of incense rose above their heads.

¹²Then the LORD said to me, "Son of man, have you seen what the leaders of Israel are doing with their idols in dark rooms? They are saying, 'The LORD doesn't see us; he has deserted our land!'" ¹³Then the LORD added, "Come, and I will show you even more detestable sins than these!"

¹⁴He brought me to the north gate of the LORD's Temple, and some women were sitting there, weeping for the god Tammuz. ¹⁵"Have you seen this?" he asked. "But I will show you even more detestable sins than these!"

¹⁶Then he brought me into the inner courtyard of the LORD's Temple. At the entrance to the sanctuary, between the entry room and the bronze altar, there were about twenty-five men with their backs to the sanctuary of the LORD. They were facing east, bowing low to the ground, worshiping the sun!

¹⁷"Have you seen this, son of man?" he asked. "Is it nothing to the people of Judah that they commit these detestable sins, leading the whole nation into violence, thumbing their noses at me, and provoking my anger? ¹⁸Therefore, I will respond in fury. I will neither pity nor spare them. And though they cry for mercy, I will not listen."

CHAPTER 9
The Slaughter of Idolaters

Then the LORD thundered, "Bring on the men appointed to punish the city! Tell them to bring their weapons with them!" ²Six men soon appeared from the upper gate that faces north, each carrying a deadly weapon in his hand. With them was a man dressed in linen, who carried a writer's case at his side. They all went into the Temple courtyard and stood beside the bronze altar.

³Then the glory of the God of Israel rose up from between the cherubim, where it had rested, and moved to the entrance of the Temple. And the LORD called to the man dressed in linen who was carrying the writer's case. ⁴He said to him, "Walk through the streets of Jerusalem and put a mark on the foreheads of all who weep and sigh because of the detestable sins being committed in their city."

⁵Then I heard the LORD say to the other men, "Follow him through the city and kill everyone whose forehead is not marked. Show no mercy; have no pity! ⁶Kill them all—old and young, girls and women and little children. But do not touch anyone with the mark. Begin right here at the Temple." So they began by killing the seventy leaders.

⁷"Defile the Temple!" the LORD commanded. "Fill its courtyards with corpses. Go!" So they went and began killing throughout the city.

⁸While they were out killing, I was all alone. I fell face down on the ground and cried out, "O Sovereign LORD! Will your fury against Jerusalem wipe out everyone left in Israel?"

⁹Then he said to me, "The sins of the people of Israel and Judah are very, very great. The entire land is full of murder; the city is filled with injustice. They are saying, 'The LORD doesn't see it! The LORD has abandoned the land!' ¹⁰So I will not spare them or have any pity on them. I will fully repay them for all they have done."

¹¹Then the man in linen clothing, who carried the writer's case, reported back and said, "I have done as you commanded."

CHAPTER 10
The LORD's Glory Leaves the Temple

In my vision I saw what appeared to be a throne of blue lapis lazuli above the crystal surface over the heads of the cherubim. ²Then the LORD spoke to the man in linen clothing and said, "Go between the whirling wheels beneath the cherubim, and take a handful of burning coals and scatter them over the city." He did this as I watched.

³The cherubim were standing at the south end of the Temple when the man went in, and the cloud of glory filled the inner courtyard. ⁴Then the glory of the LORD rose up

---

9:1-6 In Ezekiel's day many Israelites believed they had nothing to fear because they had favored status as God's people. They thought that God's presence in the Jerusalem Temple guaranteed their safety. Here it is clear that God was not blind to their sins. He was concerned about the people's blatant disregard for his laws, and he would make sure the offenders were punished. Sin always has consequences. God will not stand by idly and allow people to rebel against him forever. We must heed his warnings and take appropriate action before it is too late.

10:1-22 In Ezekiel 8–11 we see God's glory departing from the Temple. It moved to the entrance (9:3), then to the south end of the Temple (10:3), to the east gate (10:18-19; 11:1), and finally to the mountain east of the Temple (11:23). God was leaving Jerusalem. Many Jews believed that

from above the cherubim and went over to the entrance of the Temple. The Temple was filled with this cloud of glory, and the courtyard glowed brightly with the glory of the LORD. [5]The moving wings of the cherubim sounded like the voice of God Almighty* and could be heard even in the outer courtyard.

[6]The LORD said to the man in linen clothing, "Go between the cherubim and take some burning coals from between the wheels." So the man went in and stood beside one of the wheels. [7]Then one of the cherubim reached out his hand and took some live coals from the fire burning among them. He put the coals into the hands of the man in linen clothing, and the man took them and went out. [8](All the cherubim had what looked like human hands under their wings.)

[9]I looked, and each of the four cherubim had a wheel beside him, and the wheels sparkled like beryl. [10]All four wheels looked alike and were made the same; each wheel had a second wheel turning crosswise within it. [11]The cherubim could move in any of the four directions they faced, without turning as they moved. They went straight in the direction they faced, never turning aside. [12]Both the cherubim and the wheels were covered with eyes. The cherubim had eyes all over their bodies, including their hands, their backs, and their wings. [13]I heard someone refer to the wheels as "the whirling wheels." [14]Each of the four cherubim had four faces: the first was the face of an ox,* the second was a human face, the third was the face of a lion, and the fourth was the face of an eagle.

[15]Then the cherubim rose upward. These were the same living beings I had seen beside the Kebar River. [16]When the cherubim moved, the wheels moved with them. When they lifted their wings to fly, the wheels stayed beside them. [17]When the cherubim stopped, the wheels stopped. When they flew upward, the wheels rose up, for the spirit of the living beings was in the wheels.

[18]Then the glory of the LORD moved out from the entrance of the Temple and hovered above the cherubim. [19]And as I watched, the cherubim flew with their wheels to the east gate of the LORD's Temple. And the glory of the God of Israel hovered above them.

[20]These were the same living beings I had seen beneath the God of Israel when I was by the Kebar River. I knew they were cherubim, [21]for each had four faces and four wings and what looked like human hands under their wings. [22]And their faces were just like the faces of the beings I had seen at the Kebar, and they traveled straight ahead, just as the others had.

CHAPTER 11
Judgment on Israel's Leaders

Then the Spirit lifted me and brought me to the east gateway of the LORD's Temple, where I saw twenty-five prominent men of the city. Among them were Jaazaniah son of Azzur and Pelatiah son of Benaiah, who were leaders among the people.

[2]The Spirit said to me, "Son of man, these are the men who are planning evil and giving wicked counsel in this city. [3]They say to the people, 'Is it not a good time to build houses? This city is like an iron pot. We are safe inside it like meat in a pot.*' [4]Therefore, son of man, prophesy against them loudly and clearly."

[5]Then the Spirit of the LORD came upon me, and he told me to say, "This is what the LORD says to the people of Israel: I know what you are saying, for I know every thought that comes into your minds. [6]You have murdered many in this city and filled its streets with the dead.

[7]"Therefore, this is what the Sovereign LORD says: This city is an iron pot all right, but the pieces of meat are the victims of your injustice. As for you, I will soon drag you from this pot. [8]I will bring on you the sword of war you so greatly fear, says the Sovereign LORD. [9]I will drive you out of Jerusalem and hand you over to foreigners, who will carry out my judgments against you. [10]You will be slaughtered all the way to the borders of Israel. I will execute judgment on you, and you will know that I am the LORD. [11]No, this city will not be an iron pot for you, and you will not be like meat safe inside it. I will judge you even to the borders of Israel, [12]and you will know that I am the LORD. For you have refused to obey my decrees and regulations; instead, you have copied the standards of the nations around you."

10:5 Hebrew *El-Shaddai.* 10:14 Hebrew *the face of a cherub;* compare 1:10. 11:3 Hebrew *This city is the pot, and we are the meat.*

---

they were immune to enemy attack because of God's presence among them; this made them deaf to Ezekiel's condemnation of their sin and the predicted destruction of Jerusalem. When the glory of God left the Temple, however, the people could no longer claim his divine presence to support their denial. Their sin was real, and God's judgment was near.

¹³While I was still prophesying, Pelatiah son of Benaiah suddenly died. Then I fell face down on the ground and cried out, "O Sovereign LORD, are you going to kill everyone in Israel?"

Hope for Exiled Israel

¹⁴Then this message came to me from the LORD: ¹⁵"Son of man, the people still left in Jerusalem are talking about you and your relatives and all the people of Israel who are in exile. They are saying, 'Those people are far away from the LORD, so now he has given their land to us!'

¹⁶"Therefore, tell the exiles, 'This is what the Sovereign LORD says: Although I have scattered you in the countries of the world, I will be a sanctuary to you during your time in exile. ¹⁷I, the Sovereign LORD, will gather you back from the nations where you have been scattered, and I will give you the land of Israel once again.'

¹⁸"When the people return to their homeland, they will remove every trace of their vile images and detestable idols. ¹⁹And I will give them singleness of heart and put a new spirit within them. I will take away their stony, stubborn heart and give them a tender, responsive heart,* ²⁰so they will obey my decrees and regulations. Then they will truly be my people, and I will be their God. ²¹But as for those who long for vile images and detestable idols, I will repay them fully for their sins. I, the Sovereign LORD, have spoken!"

The LORD's Glory Leaves Jerusalem

²²Then the cherubim lifted their wings and rose into the air with their wheels beside them, and the glory of the God of Israel hov-ered above them. ²³Then the glory of the LORD went up from the city and stopped above the mountain to the east.

²⁴Afterward the Spirit of God carried me back again to Babylonia,* to the people in exile there. And so ended the vision of my visit to Jerusalem. ²⁵And I told the exiles everything the LORD had shown me.

CHAPTER 12
Signs of the Coming Exile

Again a message came to me from the LORD: ²"Son of man, you live among rebels who have eyes but refuse to see. They have ears but refuse to hear. For they are a rebellious people.

³"So now, son of man, pretend you are being sent into exile. Pack the few items an exile could carry, and leave your home to go somewhere else. Do this right in front of the people so they can see you. For perhaps they will pay attention to this, even though they are such rebels. ⁴Bring your baggage outside during the day so they can watch you. Then in the evening, as they are watching, leave your house as captives do when they begin a long march to distant lands. ⁵Dig a hole through the wall while they are watching and go out through it. ⁶As they watch, lift your pack to your shoulders and walk away into the night. Cover your face so you cannot see the land you are leaving. For I have made you a sign for the people of Israel."

⁷So I did as I was told. In broad daylight I brought my pack outside, filled with the things I might carry into exile. Then in the evening while the people looked on, I dug through the wall with my hands and went out into the night with my pack on my shoulder.

11:19 Hebrew *a heart of flesh.* 11:24 Or *Chaldea.*

11:16-21 God had a purpose behind the devastation he brought upon his people. His intervention was the only thing that would penetrate their denial and motivate them to change. We are often as stubborn as the people of Israel. God may allow devastating setbacks to get our attention. As we face suffering in our life, we should be encouraged by the future God has planned for his people. God used the Exile to transform the Israelites into people who loved him. Ezekiel's prophecy can come true for us, too. As we admit our sins to God and repent, he will forgive and heal us through Jesus Christ. We, too, can become God's special people.

11:23 God's glory departed from the Temple and then from the holy city itself. God's presence in Jerusalem had been the basis for the people's hope for deliverance; its departure was a portent of the destruction to come. If we continue in our destructive ways, we will face devastating consequences. We would be wise to shed our denial through a rigorous personal inventory before it is too late. If we admit our sins to God, he will help us deal with our difficult situations and build a better future.

12:1-2 When we see the rebellion of God's people today, we tend to judge them for being spiritually blind and deaf. As we make such judgments, however, we may be like the person Jesus spoke about, who tried to remove the speck from another person's eye while having a log in his own (see Matthew 7:1-5; Luke 6:41-42). We know how easy it is to live in denial. We need to work out our own program, not others'. We have enough problems of our own.

[8]The next morning this message came to me from the LORD: [9]"Son of man, these rebels, the people of Israel, have asked you what all this means. [10]Say to them, 'This is what the Sovereign LORD says: These actions contain a message for King Zedekiah in Jerusalem* and for all the people of Israel.' [11]Explain that your actions are a sign to show what will soon happen to them, for they will be driven into exile as captives.

[12]"Even Zedekiah will leave Jerusalem at night through a hole in the wall, taking only what he can carry with him. He will cover his face, and his eyes will not see the land he is leaving. [13]Then I will throw my net over him and capture him in my snare. I will bring him to Babylon, the land of the Babylonians,* though he will never see it, and he will die there. [14]I will scatter his servants and warriors to the four winds and send the sword after them. [15]And when I scatter them among the nations, they will know that I am the LORD. [16]But I will spare a few of them from death by war, famine, or disease, so they can confess all their detestable sins to their captors. Then they will know that I am the LORD."

[17]Then this message came to me from the LORD: [18]"Son of man, tremble as you eat your food. Shake with fear as you drink your water. [19]Tell the people, 'This is what the Sovereign LORD says concerning those living in Israel and Jerusalem: They will eat their food with trembling and sip their water in despair, for their land will be stripped bare because of their violence. [20]The cities will be destroyed and the farmland made desolate. Then you will know that I am the LORD.'"

A New Proverb for Israel

[21]Again a message came to me from the LORD: [22]"Son of man, you've heard that proverb they quote in Israel: 'Time passes, and prophecies come to nothing.' [23]Tell the people, 'This is what the Sovereign LORD says: I will put an end to this proverb, and you will soon stop quoting it.' Now give them this new proverb to replace the old one: 'The time has come for every prophecy to be fulfilled!'

[24]"There will be no more false visions and flattering predictions in Israel. [25]For I am the LORD! If I say it, it will happen. There will be no more delays, you rebels of Israel. I will fulfill my threat of destruction in your own lifetime. I, the Sovereign LORD, have spoken!"

[26]Then this message came to me from the LORD: [27]"Son of man, the people of Israel are saying, 'He's talking about the distant future. His visions won't come true for a long, long time.' [28]Therefore, tell them, 'This is what the Sovereign LORD says: No more delay! I will now do everything I have threatened. I, the Sovereign LORD, have spoken!'"

CHAPTER 13
Judgment against False Prophets

Then this message came to me from the LORD: [2]"Son of man, prophesy against the false prophets of Israel who are inventing their own prophecies. Say to them, 'Listen to the word of the LORD. [3]This is what the Sovereign

12:10 Hebrew *the prince in Jerusalem;* similarly in 12:12. 12:13 Or *Chaldeans.*

12:18-20 Ezekiel demonstrated through symbolic actions the coming destruction of Jerusalem. Since negative people warn us continually that "the worst is yet to come," we usually discount their dire predictions. Ezekiel's harsh predictions, however, were God's truth, not the result of a gloomy disposition. Repeatedly he attempted to turn the people's focus from hope in Jerusalem's survival to hope in God—the only means to their ultimate deliverance. In order to escape the troubles ahead, the people had to face the truth about their sins and turn to God in repentance.
12:26-28 No matter how unlikely something might seem, if God says it will happen, it will happen. It was now time for God to follow through on his warnings of judgment. But not all of God's promises are filled with gloom. Many of his promises encourage us in our difficult circumstances. Ezekiel's messages throughout the first half of the book are concerned with judgment because the people still believed that God would protect Jerusalem whether they sinned or not. They would soon learn that God held them accountable for their actions and that their sins had consequences. The final half of this book, given to Ezekiel after Jerusalem's fall, is filled with promises of restoration and forgiveness.
13:2-3 We all face the danger of following the leadership of ungodly people. The Israelites faced terrible destruction, and only God's truth could deliver them. False prophets claimed that the people had nothing to worry about—a message the people were only too glad to believe. This gave the people an easy way out. We need to be careful that we don't fall into the same trap. If someone claims to have an easy path to recovery or if a friend assures us that we don't have a problem, we need to steer clear. God demands that we face our sins and their consequences and take responsibility for the suffering we have caused, as painful as that might be. Recovery is never easy, but we can be sure that if we obey God, he will stand by us as we take each step.

LORD says: What sorrow awaits the false prophets who are following their own imaginations and have seen nothing at all!'

⁴"O people of Israel, these prophets of yours are like jackals digging in the ruins. ⁵They have done nothing to repair the breaks in the walls around the nation. They have not helped it to stand firm in battle on the day of the LORD. ⁶Instead, they have told lies and made false predictions. They say, 'This message is from the LORD,' even though the LORD never sent them. And yet they expect him to fulfill their prophecies! ⁷Can your visions be anything but false if you claim, 'This message is from the LORD,' when I have not even spoken to you?

⁸"Therefore, this is what the Sovereign LORD says: Because what you say is false and your visions are a lie, I will stand against you, says the Sovereign LORD. ⁹I will raise my fist against all the prophets who see false visions and make lying predictions, and they will be banished from the community of Israel. I will blot their names from Israel's record books, and they will never again set foot in their own land. Then you will know that I am the Sovereign LORD.

¹⁰"This will happen because these evil prophets deceive my people by saying, 'All is peaceful' when there is no peace at all! It's as if the people have built a flimsy wall, and these prophets are trying to reinforce it by covering it with whitewash! ¹¹Tell these whitewashers that their wall will soon fall down. A heavy rainstorm will undermine it; great hailstones and mighty winds will knock it down. ¹²And when the wall falls, the people will cry out, 'What happened to your whitewash?'

¹³"Therefore, this is what the Sovereign LORD says: I will sweep away your whitewashed wall with a storm of indignation, with a great flood of anger, and with hailstones of fury. ¹⁴I will break down your wall right to its foundation, and when it falls, it will crush you. Then you will know that I am the LORD. ¹⁵At last my anger against the wall and those who covered it with whitewash will be satisfied. Then I will say to you: 'The wall and those who whitewashed it are both gone. ¹⁶They were lying prophets who claimed peace would come to Jerusalem when there was no peace. I, the Sovereign LORD, have spoken!'

Judgment against False Women Prophets

¹⁷"Now, son of man, speak out against the women who prophesy from their own imaginations. ¹⁸This is what the Sovereign LORD says: What sorrow awaits you women who are ensnaring the souls of my people, young and old alike. You tie magic charms on their wrists and furnish them with magic veils. Do you think you can trap others without bringing destruction on yourselves? ¹⁹You bring shame on me among my people for a few handfuls of barley or a piece of bread. By lying to my people who love to listen to lies, you kill those who should not die, and you promise life to those who should not live.

²⁰"This is what the Sovereign LORD says: I am against all your magic charms, which you use to ensnare my people like birds. I will tear them from your arms, setting my people free like birds set free from a cage. ²¹I will tear off the magic veils and save my people from your grasp. They will no longer be your victims. Then you will know that I am the LORD. ²²You have discouraged the righteous with your lies, but I didn't want them to be sad. And you have encouraged the wicked by promising them life, even though they continue in their sins. ²³Because of all this, you will no longer talk of seeing visions that you never saw, nor will you make predictions. For I will rescue my people from your grasp. Then you will know that I am the LORD."

CHAPTER 14
The Idolatry of Israel's Leaders

Then some of the leaders of Israel visited me, and while they were sitting with me, ²this message came to me from the LORD: ³"Son of man, these leaders have set up idols* in their

14:3 The Hebrew term (literally *round things*) probably alludes to dung; also in 14:4, 5, 6, 7.

13:10 There may be significant problems in our life, but claiming everything is all right will never solve them. In fact, such denial will only make things worse. It is unwise to proclaim peace when there is no peace. If problems exist, we need to admit them and respond with the appropriate actions. Many of us tend to look the other way, pretending everything is all right. This will only lead us deeper into slavery and eventual destruction.

14:1-5 Very often third parties are involved in the breakdown of important relationships. For example, a third party may come between a husband and wife. Our relationship with God tends to suffer similar problems, and these third parties are identified here as idols. If we hope to succeed in recovery, we must allow nothing to come between us and God. Our dependency has done that already. As we seek to overcome it, we need to be careful not to replace God with a

hearts. They have embraced things that will make them fall into sin. Why should I listen to their requests? ⁴Tell them, 'This is what the Sovereign LORD says: The people of Israel have set up idols in their hearts and fallen into sin, and then they go to a prophet asking for a message. So I, the LORD, will give them the kind of answer their great idolatry deserves. ⁵I will do this to capture the minds and hearts of all my people who have turned from me to worship their detestable idols.'

⁶"Therefore, tell the people of Israel, 'This is what the Sovereign LORD says: Repent and turn away from your idols, and stop all your detestable sins. ⁷I, the LORD, will answer all those, both Israelites and foreigners, who reject me and set up idols in their hearts and so fall into sin, and who then come to a prophet asking for my advice. ⁸I will turn against such people and make a terrible example of them, eliminating them from among my people. Then you will know that I am the LORD.

⁹"'And if a prophet is deceived into giving a message, it is because I, the LORD, have deceived that prophet. I will lift my fist against such prophets and cut them off from the community of Israel. ¹⁰False prophets and those who seek their guidance will all be punished for their sins. ¹¹In this way, the people of Israel will learn not to stray from me, polluting themselves with sin. They will be my people, and I will be their God. I, the Sovereign LORD, have spoken!'"

The Certainty of the LORD's Judgment

¹²Then this message came to me from the LORD: ¹³"Son of man, suppose the people of a country were to sin against me, and I lifted my fist to crush them, cutting off their food supply and sending a famine to destroy both people and animals. ¹⁴Even if Noah, Daniel, and Job were there, their righteousness would save no one but themselves, says the Sovereign LORD.

¹⁵"Or suppose I were to send wild animals to invade the country, kill the people, and make the land too desolate and dangerous to pass through. ¹⁶As surely as I live, says the Sovereign LORD, even if those three men were

there, they wouldn't be able to save their own sons or daughters. They alone would be saved, but the land would be made desolate.

¹⁷"Or suppose I were to bring war against the land, and I sent enemy armies to destroy both people and animals. ¹⁸As surely as I live, says the Sovereign LORD, even if those three men were there, they wouldn't be able to save their own sons or daughters. They alone would be saved.

¹⁹"Or suppose I were to pour out my fury by sending an epidemic into the land, and the disease killed people and animals alike. ²⁰As surely as I live, says the Sovereign LORD, even if Noah, Daniel, and Job were there, they wouldn't be able to save their own sons or daughters. They alone would be saved by their righteousness.

²¹"Now this is what the Sovereign LORD says: How terrible it will be when all four of these dreadful punishments fall upon Jerusalem—war, famine, wild animals, and disease—destroying all her people and animals. ²²Yet there will be survivors, and they will come here to join you as exiles in Babylon. You will see with your own eyes how wicked they are, and then you will feel better about what I have done to Jerusalem. ²³When you meet them and see their behavior, you will understand that these things are not being done to Israel without cause. I, the Sovereign LORD, have spoken!"

CHAPTER 15
Jerusalem—a Useless Vine

Then this message came to me from the LORD: ²"Son of man, how does a grapevine compare to a tree? Is a vine's wood as useful as the wood of a tree? ³Can its wood be used for making things, like pegs to hang up pots and pans? ⁴No, it can only be used for fuel, and even as fuel, it burns too quickly. ⁵Vines are useless both before and after being put into the fire!

⁶"And this is what the Sovereign LORD says: The people of Jerusalem are like grapevines growing among the trees of the forest. Since they are useless, I have thrown them on the fire to be burned. ⁷And I will see to it that if

---

recovery program or relationships with other people. Only God has the power to give us true and permanent deliverance. Everything else in our life must be shaped and directed by our relationship with him.

14:21-23 Ezekiel seems to have struggled with the impending destruction of Jerusalem. He couldn't understand how God could destroy his holy city. In these verses, God told Ezekiel that his judgments would come true, but God also assured Ezekiel that the judgments were completely just. We can trust God; his actions are always right and just. Even when we don't fully understand the circumstances we face, we can trust God to help us do the right thing.

they escape from one fire, they will fall into another. When I turn against them, you will know that I am the LORD. ⁸And I will make the land desolate because my people have been unfaithful to me. I, the Sovereign LORD, have spoken!"

CHAPTER 16
Jerusalem—an Unfaithful Wife

Then another message came to me from the LORD: ²"Son of man, confront Jerusalem with her detestable sins. ³Give her this message from the Sovereign LORD: You are nothing but a Canaanite! Your father was an Amorite and your mother a Hittite. ⁴On the day you were born, no one cared about you. Your umbilical cord was not cut, and you were never washed, rubbed with salt, and wrapped in cloth. ⁵No one had the slightest interest in you; no one pitied you or cared for you. On the day you were born, you were unwanted, dumped in a field and left to die.

⁶"But I came by and saw you there, helplessly kicking about in your own blood. As you lay there, I said, 'Live!' ⁷And I helped you to thrive like a plant in the field. You grew up and became a beautiful jewel. Your breasts became full, and your body hair grew, but you were still naked. ⁸And when I passed by again, I saw that you were old enough for love. So I wrapped my cloak around you to cover your nakedness and declared my marriage vows. I made a covenant with you, says the Sovereign LORD, and you became mine.

⁹"Then I bathed you and washed off your blood, and I rubbed fragrant oils into your skin. ¹⁰I gave you expensive clothing of fine linen and silk, beautifully embroidered, and sandals made of fine goatskin leather. ¹¹I gave you lovely jewelry, bracelets, beautiful necklaces, ¹²a ring for your nose, earrings for your ears, and a lovely crown for your head. ¹³And so you were adorned with gold and silver. Your clothes were made of fine linen and costly fabric and were beautifully embroidered. You ate the finest foods—choice flour, honey, and olive oil— and became more

beautiful than ever. You looked like a queen, and so you were! ¹⁴Your fame soon spread throughout the world because of your beauty. I dressed you in my splendor and perfected your beauty, says the Sovereign LORD.

¹⁵"But you thought your fame and beauty were your own. So you gave yourself as a prostitute to every man who came along. Your beauty was theirs for the asking. ¹⁶You used the lovely things I gave you to make shrines for idols, where you played the prostitute. Unbelievable! How could such a thing ever happen? ¹⁷You took the very jewels and gold and silver ornaments I had given you and made statues of men and worshiped them. This is adultery against me! ¹⁸You used the beautifully embroidered clothes I gave you to dress your idols. Then you used my special oil and my incense to worship them. ¹⁹Imagine it! You set before them as a sacrifice the choice flour, olive oil, and honey I had given you, says the Sovereign LORD.

²⁰"Then you took your sons and daughters—the children you had borne to me—and sacrificed them to your gods. Was your prostitution not enough? ²¹Must you also slaughter my children by sacrificing them to idols? ²²In all your years of adultery and detestable sin, you have not once remembered the days long ago when you lay naked in a field, kicking about in your own blood.

²³"What sorrow awaits you, says the Sovereign LORD. In addition to all your other wickedness, ²⁴you built a pagan shrine and put altars to idols in every town square. ²⁵On every street corner you defiled your beauty, offering your body to every passerby in an endless stream of prostitution. ²⁶Then you added lustful Egypt to your lovers, provoking my anger with your increasing promiscuity. ²⁷That is why I struck you with my fist and reduced your boundaries. I handed you over to your enemies, the Philistines, and even they were shocked by your lewd conduct. ²⁸You have prostituted yourself with the Assyrians, too. It seems you can never find enough new lovers! And after your prostitution there, you still were not satisfied. ²⁹You added to your

---

16:1-15 Ezekiel compared God's people to an unwashed, helpless baby whom God found and nurtured to become queenlike in splendor and beauty. God took unruly Israel from Egyptian slavery and strengthened it to become one of the great nations of the ancient world. God made a covenant with Israel, similar in many respects to a marriage covenant. But rather than being devoted to her husband and provider, the wife (Israel) prostituted herself to others. We face a similar trap in recovery. After we struggle through the early phases of recovery, leaning heavily on God's loving power, we tend to forget how much we owe him. It is easy to become self-satisfied and take credit for our growth, which will lead back to slavery. God is the only one who can deliver us from our dependency and set us free.

lovers by embracing Babylonia,* the land of merchants, but you still weren't satisfied.

30"What a sick heart you have, says the Sovereign LORD, to do such things as these, acting like a shameless prostitute. 31You build your pagan shrines on every street corner and your altars to idols in every square. In fact, you have been worse than a prostitute, so eager for sin that you have not even demanded payment. 32Yes, you are an adulterous wife who takes in strangers instead of her own husband. 33Prostitutes charge for their services— but not you! You give gifts to your lovers, bribing them to come and have sex with you. 34So you are the opposite of other prostitutes. You pay your lovers instead of their paying you!

Judgment on Jerusalem's Prostitution

35"Therefore, you prostitute, listen to this message from the LORD! 36This is what the Sovereign LORD says: Because you have poured out your lust and exposed yourself in prostitution to all your lovers, and because you have worshiped detestable idols,* and because you have slaughtered your children as sacrifices to your gods, 37this is what I am going to do. I will gather together all your allies—the lovers with whom you have sinned, both those you loved and those you hated— and I will strip you naked in front of them so they can stare at you. 38I will punish you for your murder and adultery. I will cover you with blood in my jealous fury. 39Then I will give you to these many nations who are your lovers, and they will destroy you. They will knock down your pagan shrines and the altars to your idols. They will strip you and take your beautiful jewels, leaving you stark naked. 40They will band together in a mob to stone you and cut you up with swords. 41They will burn your homes and punish you in front of many women. I will stop your prostitution and end your payments to your many lovers.

42"Then at last my fury against you will be spent, and my jealous anger will subside. I will be calm and will not be angry with you any-

more. 43But first, because you have not remembered your youth but have angered me by doing all these evil things, I will fully repay you for all of your sins, says the Sovereign LORD. For you have added lewd acts to all your detestable sins. 44Everyone who makes up proverbs will say of you, 'Like mother, like daughter.' 45For your mother loathed her husband and her children, and so do you. And you are exactly like your sisters, for they despised their husbands and their children. Truly your mother was a Hittite and your father an Amorite.

46"Your older sister was Samaria, who lived with her daughters in the north. Your younger sister was Sodom, who lived with her daughters in the south. 47But you have not merely sinned as they did. You quickly surpassed them in corruption. 48As surely as I live, says the Sovereign LORD, Sodom and her daughters were never as wicked as you and your daughters. 49Sodom's sins were pride, gluttony, and laziness, while the poor and needy suffered outside her door. 50She was proud and committed detestable sins, so I wiped her out, as you have seen.*

51"Even Samaria did not commit half your sins. You have done far more detestable things than your sisters ever did. They seem righteous compared to you. 52Shame on you! Your sins are so terrible that you make your sisters seem righteous, even virtuous.

53"But someday I will restore the fortunes of Sodom and Samaria, and I will restore you, too. 54Then you will be truly ashamed of everything you have done, for your sins make them feel good in comparison. 55Yes, your sisters, Sodom and Samaria, and all their people will be restored, and at that time you also will be restored. 56In your proud days you held Sodom in contempt. 57But now your greater wickedness has been exposed to all the world, and you are the one who is scorned—by Edom* and all her neighbors and by Philistia. 58This is your punishment for all your lewdness and detestable sins, says the LORD.

59"Now this is what the Sovereign LORD

16:29 Or *Chaldea.* 16:36 The Hebrew term (literally *round things*) probably alludes to dung. 16:50 As in a few Hebrew manuscripts and Greek version; Masoretic Text reads *as I have seen.* 16:57 As in many Hebrew manuscripts and Syriac version; Masoretic Text reads *Aram.*

16:59-63 Even though Israel had failed God and punishment was certain, God's promises of blessing would still be fulfilled in the end. The judgment Israel would suffer was part of the recovery. The same is true for us. As we face the consequences of our failures, we should not blame God. We must face the truth that we have failed God and others. But no matter how great our sins, we can hope for future restoration. If we listen and respond humbly to our sufferings, God will use them in our recovery process. God will never fail us if we admit our sins and seek to follow his will for our life.

says: I will give you what you deserve, for you have taken your solemn vows lightly by breaking your covenant. ⁶⁰Yet I will remember the covenant I made with you when you were young, and I will establish an everlasting covenant with you. ⁶¹Then you will remember with shame all the evil you have done. I will make your sisters, Samaria and Sodom, to be your daughters, even though they are not part of our covenant. ⁶²And I will reaffirm my covenant with you, and you will know that I am the LORD. ⁶³You will remember your sins and cover your mouth in silent shame when I forgive you of all that you have done. I, the Sovereign LORD, have spoken!"

CHAPTER 17
A Story of Two Eagles
Then this message came to me from the LORD: ²"Son of man, give this riddle, and tell this story to the people of Israel. ³Give them this message from the Sovereign LORD:

"A great eagle with broad wings and long feathers,
    covered with many-colored plumage,
    came to Lebanon.
He seized the top of a cedar tree
⁴   and plucked off its highest branch.
He carried it away to a city filled with merchants.
    He planted it in a city of traders.
⁵He also took a seedling from the land
    and planted it in fertile soil.
He placed it beside a broad river,
    where it could grow like a willow tree.
⁶It took root there and
    grew into a low, spreading vine.
Its branches turned up toward the eagle,
    and its roots grew down into the ground.
It produced strong branches
    and put out shoots.
⁷But then another great eagle came
    with broad wings and full plumage.
So the vine now sent its roots and branches
    toward him for water,

⁸even though it was already planted in good soil
    and had plenty of water
so it could grow into a splendid vine
    and produce rich leaves and luscious fruit.

⁹"So now the Sovereign LORD asks:
Will this vine grow and prosper?
    No! I will pull it up, roots and all!
I will cut off its fruit
    and let its leaves wither and die.
I will pull it up easily
    without a strong arm or a large army.
¹⁰But when the vine is transplanted,
    will it thrive?
No, it will wither away
    when the east wind blows against it.
It will die in the same good soil
    where it had grown so well."

The Riddle Explained
¹¹Then this message came to me from the LORD: ¹²"Say to these rebels of Israel: Don't you understand the meaning of this riddle of the eagles? The king of Babylon came to Jerusalem, took away her king and princes, and brought them to Babylon. ¹³He made a treaty with a member of the royal family and forced him to take an oath of loyalty. He also exiled Israel's most influential leaders, ¹⁴so Israel would not become strong again and revolt. Only by keeping her treaty with Babylon could Israel survive.

¹⁵"Nevertheless, this man of Israel's royal family rebelled against Babylon, sending ambassadors to Egypt to request a great army and many horses. Can Israel break her sworn treaties like that and get away with it? ¹⁶No! For as surely as I live, says the Sovereign LORD, the king of Israel will die in Babylon, the land of the king who put him in power and whose treaty he disregarded and broke. ¹⁷Pharaoh and all his mighty army will fail to help Israel when the king of Babylon lays siege to Jerusalem again and destroys many lives. ¹⁸For the king of Israel disregarded his treaty and broke it after swearing to obey; therefore, he will not escape.

17:1-24 This chapter reviews Judah's final years through a riddle of two eagles. It mentions the times when Jews were exiled to Babylon prior to Jerusalem's destruction and predicts the ultimate destruction of Jerusalem. The exiles who heard Ezekiel's words had been among those exiled during the events he described, but they still hoped that Jerusalem's destruction would not take place. They were still in denial about their sins and the consequences of their sins. We also often resist the truth about ourself. This is never a solution to our problems and dependency. Since God in his Word warns us about our sins, we must heed those warnings and repent. God always speaks the truth.

¹⁹"So this is what the Sovereign LORD says: As surely as I live, I will punish him for breaking my covenant and disregarding the solemn oath he made in my name. ²⁰I will throw my net over him and capture him in my snare. I will bring him to Babylon and put him on trial for this treason against me. ²¹And all his best warriors* will be killed in battle, and those who survive will be scattered to the four winds. Then you will know that I, the LORD, have spoken.

²²"This is what the Sovereign LORD says: I will take a branch from the top of a tall cedar, and I will plant it on the top of Israel's highest mountain. ²³It will become a majestic cedar, sending forth its branches and producing seed. Birds of every sort will nest in it, finding shelter in the shade of its branches. ²⁴And all the trees will know that it is I, the LORD, who cuts the tall tree down and makes the short tree grow tall. It is I who makes the green tree wither and gives the dead tree new life. I, the LORD, have spoken, and I will do what I said!"

CHAPTER 18
The Justice of a Righteous God

Then another message came to me from the LORD: ²"Why do you quote this proverb concerning the land of Israel: 'The parents have eaten sour grapes, but their children's mouths pucker at the taste'? ³As surely as I live, says the Sovereign LORD, you will not quote this proverb anymore in Israel. ⁴For all people are mine to judge—both parents and children alike. And this is my rule: The person who sins is the one who will die.

⁵"Suppose a certain man is righteous and does what is just and right. ⁶He does not feast in the mountains before Israel's idols* or worship them. He does not commit adultery or have intercourse with a woman during her menstrual period. ⁷He is a merciful creditor, not keeping the items given as security by poor debtors. He does not rob the poor but instead gives food to the hungry and provides clothes for the needy. ⁸He grants loans without interest, stays away from injustice, is honest and fair when judging others, ⁹and

faithfully obeys my decrees and regulations. Anyone who does these things is just and will surely live, says the Sovereign LORD.

¹⁰"But suppose that man has a son who grows up to be a robber or murderer and refuses to do what is right. ¹¹And that son does all the evil things his father would never do—he worships idols on the mountains, commits adultery, ¹²oppresses the poor and helpless, steals from debtors by refusing to let them redeem their security, worships idols, commits detestable sins, ¹³and lends money at excessive interest. Should such a sinful person live? No! He must die and must take full blame.

¹⁴"But suppose that sinful son, in turn, has a son who sees his father's wickedness and decides against that kind of life. ¹⁵This son refuses to worship idols on the mountains and does not commit adultery. ¹⁶He does not exploit the poor, but instead is fair to debtors and does not rob them. He gives food to the hungry and provides clothes for the needy. ¹⁷He helps the poor,* does not lend money at interest, and obeys all my regulations and decrees. Such a person will not die because of his father's sins; he will surely live. ¹⁸But the father will die for his many sins—for being cruel, robbing people, and doing what was clearly wrong among his people.

¹⁹"'What?' you ask. 'Doesn't the child pay for the parent's sins?' No! For if the child does what is just and right and keeps my decrees, that child will surely live. ²⁰The person who sins is the one who will die. The child will not be punished for the parent's sins, and the parent will not be punished for the child's sins. Righteous people will be rewarded for their own righteous behavior, and wicked people will be punished for their own wickedness. ²¹But if wicked people turn away from all their sins and begin to obey my decrees and do what is just and right, they will surely live and not die. ²²All their past sins will be forgotten, and they will live because of the righteous things they have done.

²³"Do you think that I like to see wicked

17:21 As in many Hebrew manuscripts; Masoretic Text reads *his fleeing warriors.* The meaning is uncertain. **18:6** The Hebrew term (literally *round things*) probably alludes to dung; also in 18:12, 15. **18:17** Greek version reads *He refuses to do evil.*

18:2-4 God holds us accountable for our actions. Many of us have suffered innocently at the hands of others; it is tempting to blame others for our problems and dependency. But it is never valid to blame others for the mistakes they or we have made. We cannot change the behavior of others or how they treat us, but we can forgive them and put the pain of these experiences behind us. Recovery requires that we accept responsibility for our own failures and do what we can to make amends to those we have harmed, thus breaking the chain of suffering in our family line.

people die? says the Sovereign LORD. Of course not! I want them to turn from their wicked ways and live. [24]However, if righteous people turn from their righteous behavior and start doing sinful things and act like other sinners, should they be allowed to live? No, of course not! All their righteous acts will be forgotten, and they will die for their sins.

[25]"Yet you say, 'The Lord isn't doing what's right!' Listen to me, O people of Israel. Am I the one not doing what's right, or is it you? [26]When righteous people turn from their righteous behavior and start doing sinful things, they will die for it. Yes, they will die because of their sinful deeds. [27]And if wicked people turn from their wickedness, obey the law, and do what is just and right, they will save their lives. [28]They will live because they thought it over and decided to turn from their sins. Such people will not die. [29]And yet the people of Israel keep saying, 'The Lord isn't doing what's right!' O people of Israel, it is you who are not doing what's right, not I.

[30]"Therefore, I will judge each of you, O people of Israel, according to your actions, says the Sovereign LORD. Repent, and turn from your sins. Don't let them destroy you! [31]Put all your rebellion behind you, and find yourselves a new heart and a new spirit. For why should you die, O people of Israel? [32]I don't want you to die, says the Sovereign LORD. Turn back and live!

CHAPTER 19
A Funeral Song for Israel's Kings
"Sing this funeral song for the princes of Israel:

[2]"What is your mother?
    A lioness among lions!
She lay down among the young lions
    and reared her cubs.
[3]She raised one of her cubs
    to become a strong young lion.
He learned to hunt and devour prey,
    and he became a man-eater.
[4]Then the nations heard about him,
    and he was trapped in their pit.
They led him away with hooks
    to the land of Egypt.

[5]"When the lioness saw
    that her hopes for him were gone,
she took another of her cubs
    and taught him to be a strong young
        lion.
[6]He prowled among the other lions
    and stood out among them in his
        strength.
He learned to hunt and devour prey,
    and he, too, became a man-eater.
[7]He demolished fortresses*
    and destroyed their towns and cities.
Their farms were desolated,
    and their crops were destroyed.
The land and its people trembled in fear
    when they heard him roar.
[8]Then the armies of the nations attacked
        him,
    surrounding him from every direction.
They threw a net over him
    and captured him in their pit.
[9]With hooks, they dragged him into a cage
    and brought him before the king of
        Babylon.
They held him in captivity,
    so his voice could never again be heard
        on the mountains of Israel.

[10]"Your mother was like a vine
    planted by the water's edge.
It had lush, green foliage
    because of the abundant water.
[11]Its branches became strong—
    strong enough to be a ruler's scepter.
It grew very tall,
    towering above all others.
It stood out because of its height
    and its many lush branches.
[12]But the vine was uprooted in fury
    and thrown down to the ground.
The desert wind dried up its fruit
    and tore off its strong branches,
so that it withered
    and was destroyed by fire.
[13]Now the vine is transplanted to the
        wilderness,
    where the ground is hard and dry.
[14]A fire has burst out from its branches
    and devoured its fruit.
Its remaining limbs are not
    strong enough to be a ruler's scepter.

19:7 As in Greek version; Hebrew reads *He knew widows*.

18:30-32 Some say that God is too good to damn anybody. Certainly it is true that God takes no pleasure in the death of the wicked. But he created us to be responsible individuals. God desires that each person choose him. If a person chooses not to turn from sin, the result is eternal separation from God. God wants us all to live a godly life. If we confess our sins to God, he will help us to rebuild our life, no matter how extensive the devastation.

"This is a funeral song, and it will be used in a funeral."

CHAPTER 20
The Rebellion of Israel

On August 14,* during the seventh year of King Jehoiachin's captivity, some of the leaders of Israel came to request a message from the LORD. They sat down in front of me to wait for his reply. ²Then this message came to me from the LORD: ³"Son of man, tell the leaders of Israel, 'This is what the Sovereign LORD says: How dare you come to ask me for a message? As surely as I live, says the Sovereign LORD, I will tell you nothing!'

⁴"Son of man, bring charges against them and condemn them. Make them realize how detestable the sins of their ancestors really were. ⁵Give them this message from the Sovereign LORD: When I chose Israel—when I revealed myself to the descendants of Jacob in Egypt—I took a solemn oath that I, the LORD, would be their God. ⁶I took a solemn oath that day that I would bring them out of Egypt to a land I had discovered and explored for them—a good land, a land flowing with milk and honey, the best of all lands anywhere. ⁷Then I said to them, 'Each of you, get rid of the vile images you are so obsessed with. Do not defile yourselves with the idols* of Egypt, for I am the LORD your God.'

⁸"But they rebelled against me and would not listen. They did not get rid of the vile images they were obsessed with, or forsake the idols of Egypt. Then I threatened to pour out my fury on them to satisfy my anger while they were still in Egypt. ⁹But I didn't do it, for I acted to protect the honor of my name. I would not allow shame to be brought on my name among the surrounding nations who saw me reveal myself by bringing the Israelites out of Egypt. ¹⁰So I brought them out of Egypt and led them into the wilderness. ¹¹There I gave them my decrees and regulations so they could find life by keeping them. ¹²And I gave them my Sabbath days of rest as a sign between them and me. It was to

remind them that I am the LORD, who had set them apart to be holy.

¹³"But the people of Israel rebelled against me, and they refused to obey my decrees there in the wilderness. They wouldn't obey my regulations even though obedience would have given them life. They also violated my Sabbath days. So I threatened to pour out my fury on them, and I made plans to utterly consume them in the wilderness. ¹⁴But again I held back in order to protect the honor of my name before the nations who had seen my power in bringing Israel out of Egypt. ¹⁵But I took a solemn oath against them in the wilderness. I swore I would not bring them into the land I had given them, a land flowing with milk and honey, the most beautiful place on earth. ¹⁶For they had rejected my regulations, refused to follow my decrees, and violated my Sabbath days. Their hearts were given to their idols. ¹⁷Nevertheless, I took pity on them and held back from destroying them in the wilderness.

¹⁸"Then I warned their children not to follow in their parents' footsteps, defiling themselves with their idols. ¹⁹'I am the LORD your God,' I told them. 'Follow my decrees, pay attention to my regulations, ²⁰and keep my Sabbath days holy, for they are a sign to remind you that I am the LORD your God.'

²¹"But their children, too, rebelled against me. They refused to keep my decrees and follow my regulations, even though obedience would have given them life. And they also violated my Sabbath days. So again I threatened to pour out my fury on them in the wilderness. ²²Nevertheless, I withdrew my judgment against them to protect the honor of my name before the nations that had seen my power in bringing them out of Egypt. ²³But I took a solemn oath against them in the wilderness. I swore I would scatter them among all the nations ²⁴because they did not obey my regulations. They scorned my decrees by violating my Sabbath days and longing for the idols of their ancestors. ²⁵I gave them over to worthless decrees and regulations that would not lead to life. ²⁶I let them

---

20:1 Hebrew *In the fifth month, on the tenth day,* of the ancient Hebrew lunar calendar. This day was August 14, 591 B.C.; also see note on 1:1. 20:7 The Hebrew term (literally *round things*) probably alludes to dung; also in 20:8, 16, 18, 24, 31, 39.

20:1-8 God alone defines his program for healthy living; he sets up the terms, not us. God is not a recovery gimmick. He is not a power we try to accommodate into our own recovery program. If we want to succeed in recovery, we must fit into God's plan. As the one who created us and loves us, God is uniquely qualified to lead us into the best possible future. If we try to do things our own way, however, we are only asking for trouble. The experience of the people of Judah should make these truths clear.

pollute themselves* with the very gifts I had given them, and I allowed them to give their firstborn children as offerings to their gods—so I might devastate them and remind them that I alone am the LORD.

Judgment and Restoration

27"Therefore, son of man, give the people of Israel this message from the Sovereign LORD: Your ancestors continued to blaspheme and betray me, 28for when I brought them into the land I had promised them, they offered sacrifices on every high hill and under every green tree they saw! They roused my fury as they offered up sacrifices to their gods. They brought their perfumes and incense and poured out their liquid offerings to them. 29I said to them, 'What is this high place where you are going?' (This kind of pagan shrine has been called Bamah—'high place'—ever since.)

30"Therefore, give the people of Israel this message from the Sovereign LORD: Do you plan to pollute yourselves just as your ancestors did? Do you intend to keep prostituting yourselves by worshiping vile images? 31For when you offer gifts to them and give your little children to be burned as sacrifices,* you continue to pollute yourselves with idols to this day. Should I allow you to ask for a message from me, O people of Israel? As surely as I live, says the Sovereign LORD, I will tell you nothing.

32"You say, 'We want to be like the nations all around us, who serve idols of wood and stone.' But what you have in mind will never happen. 33As surely as I live, says the Sovereign LORD, I will rule over you with an iron fist in great anger and with awesome power. 34And in anger I will reach out with my strong hand and powerful arm, and I will bring you back* from the lands where you are scattered. 35I will bring you into the wilderness of the nations, and there I will judge you face to face. 36I will judge you there just as I did your ancestors in the wilderness after bringing them out of Egypt, says the Sovereign LORD. 37I will examine you carefully and

hold you to the terms of the covenant. 38I will purge you of all those who rebel and revolt against me. I will bring them out of the countries where they are in exile, but they will never enter the land of Israel. Then you will know that I am the LORD.

39"As for you, O people of Israel, this is what the Sovereign LORD says: Go right ahead and worship your idols, but sooner or later you will obey me and will stop bringing shame on my holy name by worshiping idols. 40For on my holy mountain, the great mountain of Israel, says the Sovereign LORD, the people of Israel will someday worship me, and I will accept them. There I will require that you bring me all your offerings and choice gifts and sacrifices. 41When I bring you home from exile, you will be like a pleasing sacrifice to me. And I will display my holiness through you as all the nations watch. 42Then when I have brought you home to the land I promised with a solemn oath to give to your ancestors, you will know that I am the LORD. 43You will look back on all the ways you defiled yourselves and will hate yourselves because of the evil you have done. 44You will know that I am the LORD, O people of Israel, when I have honored my name by treating you mercifully in spite of your wickedness. I, the Sovereign LORD, have spoken!"

Judgment against the Negev

45*Then this message came to me from the LORD: 46"Son of man, turn and face the south* and speak out against it; prophesy against the brushlands of the Negev. 47Tell the southern wilderness, 'This is what the Sovereign LORD says: Hear the word of the LORD! I will set you on fire, and every tree, both green and dry, will be burned. The terrible flames will not be quenched and will scorch everything from south to north. 48And everyone in the world will see that I, the LORD, have set this fire. It will not be put out.'"

49Then I said, "O Sovereign LORD, they are saying of me, 'He only talks in riddles!'"

20:25-26 Or *I gave them worthless decrees and regulations. . . . I polluted them.* 20:31 Or *and make your little children pass through the fire.* 20:34 Greek version reads *I will welcome you.* Compare 2 Cor 6:17. 20:45 Verses 20:45-49 are numbered 21:1-5 in Hebrew text. 20:46 Hebrew *toward Teman.*

20:40-42 Ezekiel gave God's exiled people a precious promise for the future. After a period of suffering, the people would repent and experience God's cleansing; then they would be restored to the Promised Land. But of even greater significance, they would be restored to fellowship with God. Doing things God's way—admitting our sins and seeking his plan for us—is the beginning of recovery and the foundation of our hope for the future.

CHAPTER 21

The LORD's Sword of Judgment

¹*Then this message came to me from the LORD: ²"Son of man, turn and face Jerusalem and prophesy against Israel and her sanctuaries. ³Tell her, 'This is what the LORD says: I am your enemy, O Israel, and I am about to unsheath my sword to destroy your people— the righteous and the wicked alike. ⁴Yes, I will cut off both the righteous and the wicked! I will draw my sword against everyone in the land from south to north. ⁵Everyone in the world will know that I am the LORD. My sword is in my hand, and it will not return to its sheath until its work is finished.'

⁶"Son of man, groan before the people! Groan before them with bitter anguish and a broken heart. ⁷When they ask why you are groaning, tell them, 'I groan because of the terrifying news I have heard. When it comes true, the boldest heart will melt with fear; all strength will disappear. Every spirit will faint; strong knees will become as weak as water. And the Sovereign LORD says: It is coming! It's on its way!'"

⁸Then the LORD said to me, ⁹"Son of man, give the people this message from the Lord:

"A sword, a sword
   is being sharpened and polished.
¹⁰It is sharpened for terrible slaughter
   and polished to flash like lightning!
Now will you laugh?
   Those far stronger than you have fallen
      beneath its power!*
¹¹Yes, the sword is now being sharpened
   and polished;
   it is being prepared for the executioner.

¹²"Son of man, cry out and wail;
   pound your thighs in anguish,
for that sword will slaughter my people
   and their leaders—
   everyone will die!
¹³It will put them all to the test.

What chance do they have?*
   says the Sovereign LORD.

¹⁴"Son of man, prophesy to them
   and clap your hands.
Then take the sword and brandish it twice,
   even three times,
to symbolize the great massacre,
   the great massacre facing them
      on every side.
¹⁵Let their hearts melt with terror,
   for the sword glitters at every gate.
It flashes like lightning
   and is polished for slaughter!
¹⁶O sword, slash to the right,
   then slash to the left,
wherever you will,
   wherever you want.
¹⁷I, too, will clap my hands,
   and I will satisfy my fury.
I, the LORD, have spoken!"

Omens for Babylon's King

¹⁸Then this message came to me from the LORD: ¹⁹"Son of man, make a map and trace two routes on it for the sword of Babylon's king to follow. Put a signpost on the road that comes out of Babylon where the road forks into two—²⁰one road going to Ammon and its capital, Rabbah, and the other to Judah and fortified Jerusalem. ²¹The king of Babylon now stands at the fork, uncertain whether to attack Jerusalem or Rabbah. He calls his magicians to look for omens. They cast lots by shaking arrows from the quiver. They inspect the livers of animal sacrifices. ²²The omen in his right hand says, 'Jerusalem!' With battering rams his soldiers will go against the gates, shouting for the kill. They will put up siege towers and build ramps against the walls. ²³The people of Jerusalem will think it is a false omen, because of their treaty with the Babylonians. But the king of Babylon will remind the people of

21:1 Verses 21:1-32 are numbered 21:6-37 in Hebrew text.   21:10 The meaning of the Hebrew is uncertain.
21:13 The meaning of the Hebrew is uncertain.

21:3 These ominous words are addressed to the nation of Israel. God would punish the entire nation, including the few good people. Our sins always have consequences, and very often those consequences are experienced by innocent people around us. Our sins and dependency cause undeserved pain for our spouse, children, friends, co-workers, or employees. This should motivate us to seek changes in our life and make amends to those we have hurt.
21:6-7 God called Ezekiel to hold nothing back and express his anguish at Jerusalem's coming destruction as a further warning to the people that Jerusalem's destruction was certain. In contrast to the norms of our culture, uninhibited emotional expressions of this kind were normal in ancient Israel. Not only is this kind of emotional honesty good therapy for a wounded heart, it also allows others to enter into our suffering and learn from it. God's call to honesty should extend even into the realm of our emotions.

their rebellion. Then he will attack and capture them.

²⁴"Therefore, this is what the Sovereign LORD says: Again and again you remind me of your sin and your guilt. You don't even try to hide it! In everything you do, your sins are obvious for all to see. So now the time of your punishment has come!

²⁵"O you corrupt and wicked prince of Israel, your final day of reckoning is here! ²⁶This is what the Sovereign LORD says:

"Take off your jeweled crown,
    for the old order changes.
Now the lowly will be exalted,
    and the mighty will be brought down.
²⁷Destruction! Destruction!
    I will surely destroy the kingdom.
And it will not be restored until the one
        appears
    who has the right to judge it.
Then I will hand it over to him.

A Message for the Ammonites

²⁸"And now, son of man, prophesy concerning the Ammonites and their mockery. Give them this message from the Sovereign LORD:

"A sword, a sword
    is drawn for your slaughter.
It is polished to destroy,
    flashing like lightning!
²⁹Your prophets have given false visions,
    and your fortune-tellers have told lies.
The sword will fall on the necks of the
        wicked
    for whom the day of final reckoning
        has come.

³⁰"Now return the sword to its sheath,
    for in your own country,
the land of your birth,
    I will pass judgment upon you.
³¹I will pour out my fury on you
    and blow on you with the fire of my
        anger.
I will hand you over to cruel men
    who are skilled in destruction.
³²You will be fuel for the fire,

and your blood will be spilled in your
    own land.
You will be utterly wiped out,
    your memory lost to history,
    for I, the LORD, have spoken!"

CHAPTER 22
The Sins of Jerusalem

Now this message came to me from the LORD: ²"Son of man, are you ready to judge this city of murderers? Are you ready to judge this city of murderers? Publicly denounce her detestable sins, ³and give her this message from the Sovereign LORD: O city of murderers, doomed and damned—city of idols,* filthy and foul— ⁴you are guilty because of the blood you have shed. You are defiled because of the idols you have made. Your day of destruction has come! You have reached the end of your years. I will make you an object of mockery throughout the world. ⁵O infamous city, filled with confusion, you will be mocked by people far and near.

⁶"Every leader in Israel who lives within your walls is bent on murder. ⁷Fathers and mothers are treated with contempt. Foreigners are forced to pay for protection. Orphans and widows are wronged and oppressed among you. ⁸You despise my holy things and violate my Sabbath days of rest. ⁹People accuse others falsely and send them to their death. You are filled with idol worshipers and people who do obscene things. ¹⁰Men sleep with their fathers' wives and force themselves on women who are menstruating. ¹¹Within your walls live men who commit adultery with their neighbors' wives, who defile their daughters-in-law, or who rape their own sisters. ¹²There are hired murderers, loan racketeers, and extortioners everywhere. They never even think of me and my commands, says the Sovereign LORD.

¹³"But now I clap my hands in indignation over your dishonest gain and bloodshed. ¹⁴How strong and courageous will you be in my day of reckoning? I, the LORD, have spoken, and I will do what I said. ¹⁵I will scatter you among the nations and purge you of

22:3 The Hebrew term (literally *round things*) probably alludes to dung; also in 22:4.

22:2-4 In contemporary culture the reality of personal guilt is often rejected. There are programs that tell us to ignore the guilt we feel rather than deal with the sin that lies at its root. This is not to say that false guilt does not exist. Yet any therapy that denies the existence of sin and tries to find excuses rather than a permanent remedy is not in agreement with God's program. God has provided salvation from the guilt of sin through the death of his Son. There is ultimately no way for us to hide or ignore our guilt. We must choose God's remedy, which starts with the recognition of our helplessness and the confession of our sins.

your wickedness. [16]And when I have been dishonored among the nations because of you,* you will know that I am the LORD."

The LORD's Refining Furnace

[17]Then this message came to me from the LORD: [18]"Son of man, the people of Israel are the worthless slag that remains after silver is smelted. They are the dross that is left over—a useless mixture of copper, tin, iron, and lead. [19]So tell them, 'This is what the Sovereign LORD says: Because you are all worthless slag, I will bring you to my crucible in Jerusalem. [20]Just as silver, copper, iron, lead, and tin are melted down in a furnace, I will melt you down in the heat of my fury. [21]I will gather you together and blow the fire of my anger upon you, [22]and you will melt like silver in fierce heat. Then you will know that I, the LORD, have poured out my fury on you.'"

The Sins of Israel's Leaders

[23]Again a message came to me from the LORD: [24]"Son of man, give the people of Israel this message: In the day of my indignation, you will be like a polluted land, a land without rain. [25]Your princes* plot conspiracies just as lions stalk their prey. They devour innocent people, seizing treasures and extorting wealth. They make many widows in the land. [26]Your priests have violated my instructions and defiled my holy things. They make no distinction between what is holy and what is not. And they do not teach my people the difference between what is ceremonially clean and unclean. They disregard my Sabbath days so that I am dishonored among them. [27]Your leaders are like wolves who tear apart their victims. They actually destroy people's lives for money! [28]And your prophets cover up for them by announcing false visions and making lying predictions. They say, 'My message is from the Sovereign LORD,' when the LORD hasn't spoken a single word to them. [29]Even common people oppress the poor, rob the needy, and deprive foreigners of justice.

[30]"I looked for someone who might rebuild the wall of righteousness that guards the land. I searched for someone to stand in the gap in the wall so I wouldn't have to destroy the land, but I found no one. [31]So now I will pour out my fury on them, consuming them with the fire of my anger. I will heap on their heads the full penalty for all their sins. I, the Sovereign LORD, have spoken!"

CHAPTER 23

The Adultery of Two Sisters

This message came to me from the LORD: [2]"Son of man, once there were two sisters who were daughters of the same mother. [3]They became prostitutes in Egypt. Even as young girls, they allowed men to fondle their breasts. [4]The older girl was named Oholah, and her sister was Oholibah. I married them, and they bore me sons and daughters. I am speaking of Samaria and Jerusalem, for Oholah is Samaria and Oholibah is Jerusalem.

[5]"Then Oholah lusted after other lovers instead of me, and she gave her love to the Assyrian officers. [6]They were all attractive young men, captains and commanders dressed in handsome blue, charioteers driving their horses. [7]And so she prostituted herself with the most desirable men of Assyria, worshiping their idols* and defiling herself. [8]For when she left Egypt, she did not leave her spirit of prostitution behind. She was still as lewd as in her youth, when the Egyptians slept with her, fondled her breasts, and used her as a prostitute.

[9]"And so I handed her over to her Assyrian lovers, whom she desired so much. [10]They stripped her, took away her children as their slaves, and then killed her. After she received her punishment, her reputation was known to every woman in the land.

[11]"Yet even though Oholibah saw what had happened to Oholah, her sister, she followed right in her footsteps. And she was even more depraved, abandoning herself to her lust and prostitution. [12]She fawned over all the Assyrian officers—those captains and commanders in handsome uniforms, those

22:16 As in one Hebrew manuscript and Greek and Syriac versions; Masoretic Text reads *when you have been dishonored among the nations.* 22:25 As in Greek version; Hebrew reads *prophets.* 23:7 The Hebrew term (literally *round things*) probably alludes to dung; also in 23:30, 37, 39, 49.

23:1-49 Ezekiel compared the kingdoms of Judah and Israel to two adulterous sisters. Despite all the blessings God had given them, they sold themselves to idols and were unfaithful to God. God's people were guilty of spiritual harlotry. We are guilty of this same sin when we allow anything to take God's proper place in our life. This may involve an unhealthy dependency—drugs, alcohol, overwork, illicit sex—to hide from inner pain that only God can heal. It may involve using a recovery program that ignores God and leads us away from his way of life. Whatever idols we have, they must be removed if we hope to deal with our sins and rebuild a meaningful future.

charioteers driving their horses—all of them attractive young men. [13]I saw the way she was going, defiling herself just like her older sister.

[14]"Then she carried her prostitution even further. She fell in love with pictures that were painted on a wall—pictures of Babylonian* military officers, outfitted in striking red uniforms. [15]Handsome belts encircled their waists, and flowing turbans crowned their heads. They were dressed like chariot officers from the land of Babylonia.* [16]When she saw these paintings, she longed to give herself to them, so she sent messengers to Babylonia to invite them to come to her. [17]So they came and committed adultery with her, defiling her in the bed of love. After being defiled, however, she rejected them in disgust.

[18]"In the same way, I became disgusted with Oholibah and rejected her, just as I had rejected her sister, because she flaunted herself before them and gave herself to satisfy their lusts. [19]Yet she turned to even greater prostitution, remembering her youth when she was a prostitute in Egypt. [20]She lusted after lovers with genitals as large as a donkey's and emissions like those of a horse. [21]And so, Oholibah, you relived your former days as a young girl in Egypt, when you first allowed your breasts to be fondled.

The LORD's Judgment of Oholibah

[22]"Therefore, Oholibah, this is what the Sovereign LORD says: I will send your lovers against you from every direction—those very nations from which you turned away in disgust. [23]For the Babylonians will come with all the Chaldeans from Pekod and Shoa and Koa. And all the Assyrians will come with them—handsome young captains, commanders, chariot officers, and other high-ranking officers, all riding their horses. [24]They will all come against you from the north* with chariots, wagons, and a great army prepared for attack. They will take up positions on every side, surrounding you with men armed with shields and helmets. And I will hand you over to them for punishment so they can do with you as they please. [25]I will turn my jealous anger against you, and they will deal harshly with you. They will cut off your nose and ears, and any survivors will then be slaughtered by the sword. Your children will be taken away as captives, and everything that is left will be burned. [26]They will strip you of your beautiful clothes and jewels. [27]In this way, I will put a stop to the lewdness and prostitution you brought from Egypt. You will never again cast longing eyes on those things or fondly remember your time in Egypt.

[28]"For this is what the Sovereign LORD says: I will surely hand you over to your enemies, to those you loathe, those you rejected. [29]They will treat you with hatred and rob you of all you own, leaving you stark naked. The shame of your prostitution will be exposed to all the world. [30]You brought all this on yourself by prostituting yourself to other nations, defiling yourself with all their idols. [31]Because you have followed in your sister's footsteps, I will force you to drink the same cup of terror she drank.

[32]"Yes, this is what the Sovereign LORD says:

"You will drink from your sister's cup
        of terror,
    a cup that is large and deep.
It is filled to the brim
    with scorn and derision.
[33]Drunkenness and anguish will fill you,
    for your cup is filled to the brim with
        distress and desolation,
    the same cup your sister Samaria drank.
[34] You will drain that cup of terror
    to the very bottom.
Then you will smash it to pieces
    and beat your breast in anguish.
    I, the Sovereign LORD, have spoken!

[35]"And because you have forgotten me and turned your back on me, this is what the Sovereign LORD says: You must bear the consequences of all your lewdness and prostitution."

The LORD's Judgment on Both Sisters

[36]The LORD said to me, "Son of man, you must accuse Oholah and Oholibah of all their detestable sins. [37]They have committed both adultery and murder—adultery by worshiping idols and murder by burning as sacrifices the children they bore to me. [38]Furthermore, they have defiled my Temple and violated my Sabbath day! [39]On the very day that they sacrificed their children to their idols, they boldly came into my Temple to worship! They came in and defiled my house.

[40]"You sisters sent messengers to distant lands to get men. Then when they arrived, you bathed yourselves, painted your eyelids, and put on your finest jewels for them. [41]You

23:14 Or *Chaldean.* 23:15 Or *Chaldea;* also in 23:16. 23:24 As in Greek version; the meaning of the Hebrew is uncertain.

sat with them on a beautifully embroidered couch and put my incense and my special oil on a table that was spread before you. ⁴²From your room came the sound of many men carousing. They were lustful men and drunkards* from the wilderness, who put bracelets on your wrists and beautiful crowns on your heads. ⁴³Then I said, 'If they really want to have sex with old worn-out prostitutes like these, let them!' ⁴⁴And that is what they did. They had sex with Oholah and Oholibah, these shameless prostitutes. ⁴⁵But righteous people will judge these sister cities for what they really are—adulterers and murderers.

⁴⁶"Now this is what the Sovereign LORD says: Bring an army against them and hand them over to be terrorized and plundered. ⁴⁷For their enemies will stone them and kill them with swords. They will butcher their sons and daughters and burn their homes. ⁴⁸In this way, I will put an end to lewdness and idolatry in the land, and my judgment will be a warning to all women not to follow your wicked example. ⁴⁹You will be fully repaid for all your prostitution—your worship of idols. Yes, you will suffer the full penalty. Then you will know that I am the Sovereign LORD."

CHAPTER 24
The Sign of the Cooking Pot
On January 15,* during the ninth year of King Jehoiachin's captivity, this message came to me from the LORD: ²"Son of man, write down today's date, because on this very day the king of Babylon is beginning his attack against Jerusalem. ³Then give these rebels an illustration with this message from the Sovereign LORD:

"Put a pot on the fire,
    and pour in some water.
⁴Fill it with choice pieces of meat—
    the rump and the shoulder
    and all the most tender cuts.
⁵Use only the best sheep from the flock,
    and heap fuel on the fire beneath
        the pot.
    Bring the pot to a boil,

and cook the bones along with the meat.

⁶"Now this is what the Sovereign LORD says:

What sorrow awaits Jerusalem,
    the city of murderers!
She is a cooking pot
    whose corruption can't be cleaned
        out.
Take the meat out in random order,
    for no piece is better than another.
⁷For the blood of her murders
    is splashed on the rocks.
It isn't even spilled on the ground,
    where the dust could cover it!
⁸So I will splash her blood on a rock
    for all to see,
an expression of my anger
    and vengeance against her.

⁹"This is what the Sovereign LORD says:
What sorrow awaits Jerusalem,
    the city of murderers!
    I myself will pile up the fuel beneath
        her.
¹⁰Yes, heap on the wood!
    Let the fire roar to make the pot boil.
Cook the meat with many spices,
    and afterward burn the bones.
¹¹Now set the empty pot on the coals.
    Heat it red hot!
    Burn away the filth and corruption.
¹²But it's hopeless;
    the corruption can't be cleaned out.
    So throw it into the fire.
¹³Your impurity is your lewdness
    and the corruption of your idolatry.
I tried to cleanse you,
    but you refused.
So now you will remain in your filth
    until my fury against you has been
        satisfied.

¹⁴"I, the LORD, have spoken! The time has come, and I won't hold back. I will not change my mind, and I will have no pity on you. You will be judged on the basis of all your wicked actions, says the Sovereign LORD."

23:42 Or *Sabeans.* 24:1 Hebrew *On the tenth day of the tenth month,* of the ancient Hebrew lunar calendar. This event occurred on January 15, 588 B.C.; also see note on 1:1.

24:1-14 God told Ezekiel to illustrate the wickedness and destruction of Jerusalem by using a cooking pot. God had delayed his punishment for many years, giving his people ample opportunity to repent and seek forgiveness. They had failed, however, and the time of their final destruction had arrived. God gives us numerous opportunities to admit our failures and ask his forgiveness before he allows our destruction. We would be wise to listen before it is too late.

The Death of Ezekiel's Wife

¹⁵Then this message came to me from the LORD: ¹⁶"Son of man, with one blow I will take away your dearest treasure. Yet you must not show any sorrow at her death. Do not weep; let there be no tears. ¹⁷Groan silently, but let there be no wailing at her grave. Do not uncover your head or take off your sandals. Do not perform the usual rituals of mourning or accept any food brought to you by consoling friends."

¹⁸So I proclaimed this to the people the next morning, and in the evening my wife died. The next morning I did everything I had been told to do. ¹⁹Then the people asked, "What does all this mean? What are you trying to tell us?"

²⁰So I said to them, "A message came to me from the LORD, ²¹and I was told to give this message to the people of Israel. This is what the Sovereign LORD says: I will defile my Temple, the source of your security and pride, the place your heart delights in. Your sons and daughters whom you left behind in Judea will be slaughtered by the sword. ²²Then you will do as Ezekiel has done. You will not mourn in public or console yourselves by eating the food brought by friends. ²³Your heads will remain covered, and your sandals will not be taken off. You will not mourn or weep, but you will waste away because of your sins. You will groan among yourselves for all the evil you have done. ²⁴Ezekiel is an example for you; you will do just as he has done. And when that time comes, you will know that I am the Sovereign LORD."

²⁵Then the LORD said to me, "Son of man, on the day I take away their stronghold—their joy and glory, their heart's desire, their dearest treasure—I will also take away their sons and daughters. ²⁶And on that day a survivor from Jerusalem will come to you in Babylon and tell you what has happened. ²⁷And when he arrives, your voice will suddenly return so you can talk to him, and you will be a symbol for these people. Then they will know that I am the LORD."

CHAPTER 25
A Message for Ammon

Then this message came to me from the LORD: ²"Son of man, turn and face the land of Ammon and prophesy against its people. ³Give the Ammonites this message from the Sovereign LORD: Hear the word of the Sovereign LORD! Because you cheered when my Temple was defiled, mocked Israel in her desolation, and laughed at Judah as she went away into exile, ⁴I will allow nomads from the eastern deserts to overrun your country. They will set up their camps among you and pitch their tents on your land. They will harvest all your fruit and drink the milk from your livestock. ⁵And I will turn the city of Rabbah into a pasture for camels, and all the land of the Ammonites into a resting place for sheep and goats. Then you will know that I am the LORD.

⁶"This is what the Sovereign LORD says: Because you clapped and danced and cheered with glee at the destruction of my people, ⁷I will raise my fist of judgment against you. I will give you as plunder to many nations. I will cut you off from being a nation and destroy you completely. Then you will know that I am the LORD.

A Message for Moab

⁸"This is what the Sovereign LORD says: Because the people of Moab* have said that Judah is just like all the other nations, ⁹I will open up their eastern flank and wipe out their glorious frontier towns—Beth-jeshimoth, Baal-meon, and Kiriathaim. ¹⁰And I will hand Moab over to nomads from the eastern

25:8 As in Greek version; Hebrew reads *Moab and Seir.*

24:25-27 These verses conclude the long section of judgment (1:1–24:27). The exiles in Babylon would soon hear of Jerusalem's destruction, confirming the truth of all Ezekiel's words, including his condemnation of the people for their sins. Their only response could be mourning and repentance. They would have to humble themselves before God, their Judge and their Redeemer. From this point on, Ezekiel is called upon to bring a message of hope to the exiled Jews. God's judgment was not the end. First he showed his people that the foreign nations would also be judged for their sins (25–32). Then he promised the restoration of his scattered people to the land of Israel (33–39).

25:1-17 After God punished his people, he punished Israel's foreign neighbors. God's people are precious to him, so he turned his wrath upon those who had treated them badly. God is just, and his justice will prevail in the end, no matter how bad things may look now. Israel had been destroyed and the people left in hopeless exile. God began his ministry by punishing the nations that had harmed Israel earlier. Even though these nations seemed to get away with injustice, in the end they were held accountable for their sins. This should give us hope if we have been wronged, but it should also warn us to make amends now for our past failures. The consequences of past sins will always come back to haunt us and our descendants.

deserts, just as I handed over Ammon. Yes, the Ammonites will no longer be counted among the nations. [11]In the same way, I will bring my judgment down on the Moabites. Then they will know that I am the LORD.

A Message for Edom

[12]"This is what the Sovereign LORD says: The people of Edom have sinned greatly by avenging themselves against the people of Judah. [13]Therefore, says the Sovereign LORD, I will raise my fist of judgment against Edom. I will wipe out its people and animals with the sword. I will make a wasteland of everything from Teman to Dedan. [14]I will accomplish this by the hand of my people of Israel. They will carry out my vengeance with anger, and Edom will know that this vengeance is from me. I, the Sovereign LORD, have spoken!

A Message for Philistia

[15]"This is what the Sovereign LORD says: The people of Philistia have acted against Judah out of bitter revenge and long-standing contempt. [16]Therefore, this is what the Sovereign LORD says: I will raise my fist of judgment against the land of the Philistines. I will wipe out the Kerethites and utterly destroy the people who live by the sea. [17]I will execute terrible vengeance against them to punish them for what they have done. And when I have inflicted my revenge, they will know that I am the LORD."

CHAPTER 26
A Message for Tyre

On February 3, during the twelfth year of King Jehoiachin's captivity,* this message came to me from the LORD: [2]"Son of man, Tyre has rejoiced over the fall of Jerusalem, saying, 'Ha! She who was the gateway to the rich trade routes to the east has been broken, and I am the heir! Because she has been made desolate, I will become wealthy!'

[3]"Therefore, this is what the Sovereign LORD says: I am your enemy, O Tyre, and I will bring many nations against you, like the waves of the sea crashing against your shoreline. [4]They will destroy the walls of Tyre and tear down its towers. I will scrape away its soil and make it a bare rock! [5]It will be just a rock in the sea, a place for fishermen to spread their nets, for I have spoken, says the Sovereign LORD. Tyre will become the prey of many nations, [6]and its mainland villages will be destroyed by the sword. Then they will know that I am the LORD.

[7]"This is what the Sovereign LORD says: From the north I will bring King Nebuchadnezzar* of Babylon against Tyre. He is king of kings and brings his horses, chariots, charioteers, and great army. [8]First he will destroy your mainland villages. Then he will attack you by building a siege wall, constructing a ramp, and raising a roof of shields against you. [9]He will pound your walls with battering rams and demolish your towers with sledgehammers. [10]The hooves of his horses will choke the city with dust, and the noise of the charioteers and chariot wheels will shake your walls as they storm through your broken gates. [11]His horsemen will trample through every street in the city. They will butcher your people, and your strong pillars will topple.

[12]"They will plunder all your riches and merchandise and break down your walls. They will destroy your lovely homes and dump your stones and timbers and even your dust into the sea. [13]I will stop the music of your songs. No more will the sound of harps be heard among your people. [14]I will make your island a bare rock, a place for fishermen to spread their nets. You will never be rebuilt, for I, the LORD, have spoken. Yes, the Sovereign LORD has spoken!

The Effect of Tyre's Destruction

[15]"This is what the Sovereign LORD says to Tyre: The whole coastline will tremble at the sound of your fall, as the screams of the wounded echo in the continuing slaughter.

26:1 Hebrew *In the eleventh year, on the first day of the month,* of the ancient Hebrew lunar calendar year. Since an element is missing in the date formula here, scholars have reconstructed this probable reading: *In the eleventh [month of the twelfth] year, on the first day of the month.* This reading would put this message on February 3, 585 B.C.; also see note on 1:1. 26:7 Hebrew *Nebuchadrezzar,* a variant spelling of Nebuchadnezzar.

26:1-21 In the ancient world, Tyre was considered impregnable. It was surrounded by water and safe from siege. Tyre's ships could keep the city continually supplied with food and water. The people believed that no one could conquer it and that its future was secure. They were blind to the pain they had caused others. But God assures the destruction of this great city. We may think we are strong enough to withstand the power of our besetting dependency. This attitude, however, will only lead to destruction. Recovery is only possible if we give up our control to God and obey his will for our life.

16All the seaport rulers will step down from their thrones and take off their royal robes and beautiful clothing. They will sit on the ground trembling with horror at your destruction. 17Then they will wail for you, singing this funeral song:

"O famous island city,
    once ruler of the sea,
    how you have been destroyed!
Your people, with their naval power,
    once spread fear around the world.
18Now the coastlands tremble at your fall.
    The islands are dismayed as you disappear.

19"This is what the Sovereign LORD says: I will make Tyre an uninhabited ruin, like many others. I will bury you beneath the terrible waves of enemy attack. Great seas will swallow you. 20I will send you to the pit to join those who descended there long ago. Your city will lie in ruins, buried beneath the earth, like those in the pit who have entered the world of the dead. You will have no place of respect here in the land of the living. 21I will bring you to a terrible end, and you will exist no more. You will be looked for, but you will never again be found. I, the Sovereign LORD, have spoken!"

CHAPTER 27
The End of Tyre's Glory

Then this message came to me from the LORD: 2"Son of man, sing a funeral song for Tyre, 3that mighty gateway to the sea, the trading center of the world. Give Tyre this message from the Sovereign LORD:

"You boasted, O Tyre,
    'My beauty is perfect!'
4You extended your boundaries into
        the sea.
    Your builders made your beauty perfect.
5You were like a great ship
    built of the finest cypress from Senir.*
They took a cedar from Lebanon
    to make a mast for you.
6They carved your oars
    from the oaks of Bashan.
Your deck of pine from the coasts of
        Cyprus*
    was inlaid with ivory.
7Your sails were made of Egypt's finest
        linen,
    and they flew as a banner above you.
You stood beneath blue and purple
        awnings
    made bright with dyes from the coasts
        of Elishah.
8Your oarsmen came from Sidon and
        Arvad;
    your helmsmen were skilled men from
        Tyre itself.
9Wise old craftsmen from Gebal did the
        caulking.
    Ships from every land came with goods
        to barter for your trade.

10"Men from distant Persia, Lydia, and Libya* served in your great army. They hung their shields and helmets on your walls, giving you great honor. 11Men from Arvad and Helech stood on your walls. Your towers were manned by men from Gammad. Their shields hung on your walls, completing your beauty.

12"Tarshish sent merchants to buy your wares in exchange for silver, iron, tin, and lead. 13Merchants from Greece,* Tubal, and Meshech brought slaves and articles of bronze to trade with you.

14"From Beth-togarmah came riding horses, chariot horses, and mules, all in exchange for your goods. 15Merchants came to you from Dedan.* Numerous coastlands were your captive markets; they brought payment in ivory tusks and ebony wood.

16"Syria* sent merchants to buy your rich variety of goods. They traded turquoise, purple dyes, embroidery, fine linen, and jewelry of coral and rubies. 17Judah and Israel traded for your wares, offering wheat from Minnith, figs,* honey, olive oil, and balm.

18"Damascus sent merchants to buy your rich variety of goods, bringing wine from Helbon and white wool from Zahar. 19Greeks from Uzal* came to trade for your merchan-

27:5 Or *Hermon.* 27:6 Hebrew *Kittim.* 27:10 Hebrew *Paras, Lud, and Put.* 27:13 Hebrew *Javan.* 27:15 Greek version reads *Rhodes.* 27:16 Hebrew *Aram;* some manuscripts read *Edom.* 27:17 The meaning of the Hebrew is uncertain. 27:19 Hebrew *Vedan and Javan from Uzal.* The meaning of the Hebrew is uncertain.

27:3-25 Tyre congratulated itself on its beauty (27:3), military might (27:10-11), and wealth (27:12-25), but none of these could avert the disaster that would soon come. When we are gifted with intelligence, beauty, strength, or wealth, it is easy to be deceived into thinking we can overcome our dependency on our own. If we believe that, our strength is only a liability. Recovery can only begin when we realize that we can't win the fight alone. We must never let our strengths blind us to our weaknesses and lead us toward destruction.

dise. Wrought iron, cassia, and fragrant cala-mus were bartered for your wares.

20"Dedan sent merchants to trade their expensive saddle blankets with you. 21The Arabians and the princes of Kedar sent merchants to trade lambs and rams and male goats in exchange for your goods. 22The merchants of Sheba and Raamah came with all kinds of spices, jewels, and gold in exchange for your wares.

23"Haran, Canneh, Eden, Sheba, Asshur, and Kilmad came with their merchandise, too. 24They brought choice fabrics to trade—blue cloth, embroidery, and multicolored carpets rolled up and bound with cords. 25The ships of Tarshish were your ocean caravans. Your island warehouse was filled to the brim!

The Destruction of Tyre

26 "But look! Your oarsmen
      have taken you into stormy seas!
A mighty eastern gale
      has wrecked you in the heart
            of the sea!
27 Everything is lost—
      your riches and wares,
your sailors and pilots,
      your ship builders, merchants, and
            warriors.
On the day of your ruin,
      everyone on board sinks into the
            depths of the sea.
28 Your cities by the sea tremble
      as your pilots cry out in terror.
29 All the oarsmen abandon their ships;
      the sailors and pilots stand on the
            shore.
30 They cry aloud over you
      and weep bitterly.
They throw dust on their heads
      and roll in ashes.
31 They shave their heads in grief for you
      and dress themselves in burlap.

27:36 Hebrew *hiss at you.*

They weep for you with bitter anguish
      and deep mourning.
32 As they wail and mourn over you,
      they sing this sad funeral song:
'Was there ever such a city as Tyre,
      now silent at the bottom of the sea?
33 The merchandise you traded
      satisfied the desires of many nations.
Kings at the ends of the earth
      were enriched by your trade.
34 Now you are a wrecked ship,
      broken at the bottom of the sea.
All your merchandise and crew
      have gone down with you.
35 All who live along the coastlands
      are appalled at your terrible fate.
Their kings are filled with horror
      and look on with twisted faces.
36 The merchants among the nations
      shake their heads at the sight of you,*
for you have come to a horrible end
      and will exist no more.'"

CHAPTER 28
A Message for Tyre's King

Then this message came to me from the LORD: 2"Son of man, give the prince of Tyre this message from the Sovereign LORD:

"In your great pride you claim, 'I am
      a god!
I sit on a divine throne in the heart
      of the sea.'
But you are only a man and not a god,
      though you boast that you are a god.
3 You regard yourself as wiser than Daniel
      and think no secret is hidden from you.
4 With your wisdom and understanding
      you have amassed great wealth—
gold and silver for your treasuries.
5 Yes, your wisdom has made you very rich,
      and your riches have made you very
            proud.

27:26-36 Tyre had achieved success of every kind—except the kind that really mattered. The people believed that they could sufficiently handle any crisis. This city was able to stand against invaders for over two hundred years, but in the end, it was destroyed by Alexander the Great. Once again, God's Word proved true; we cannot stand against the destruction set in motion by our sins. No matter how great our successes, we are headed for destruction if our life is not in line with God's will.

28:2-10 The first lie ever told was Satan's promise to Eve, "You will be like God" (Genesis 3:5). The prince of Tyre believed that old falsehood; he pridefully claimed to be a god. If we live according to our personal program for success and pleasure, we are living the same lie. Doing things our way is evidence that we believe we are our own god. Those of us in recovery have discovered how destructive this can be. God is the only one able to see things objectively, and his plan for us is always the best. We must abdicate the throne of our life to God, the only one who can give meaning and freedom to our life.

⁶"Therefore, this is what the Sovereign
LORD says:
Because you think you are as wise as
a god,
⁷ I will now bring against you a foreign
army,
the terror of the nations.
They will draw their swords against your
marvelous wisdom
and defile your splendor!
⁸ They will bring you down to the pit,
and you will die in the heart of the sea,
pierced with many wounds.
⁹ Will you then boast, 'I am a god!'
to those who kill you?
To them you will be no god
but merely a man!
¹⁰ You will die like an outcast*
at the hands of foreigners.
I, the Sovereign LORD, have spoken!"

¹¹Then this further message came to me
from the LORD: ¹²"Son of man, sing this funeral song for the king of Tyre. Give him this
message from the Sovereign LORD:

"You were the model of perfection,
full of wisdom and exquisite in beauty.
¹³ You were in Eden,
the garden of God.
Your clothing was adorned with every
precious stone*—
red carnelian, pale-green peridot, white
moonstone,
blue-green beryl, onyx, green jasper,
blue lapis lazuli, turquoise, and
emerald—
all beautifully crafted for you
and set in the finest gold.
They were given to you
on the day you were created.
¹⁴ I ordained and anointed you
as the mighty angelic guardian.*
You had access to the holy mountain
of God
and walked among the stones of fire.

¹⁵ "You were blameless in all you did
from the day you were created
until the day evil was found in you.
¹⁶ Your rich commerce led you to violence,
and you sinned.

So I banished you in disgrace
from the mountain of God.
I expelled you, O mighty guardian,
from your place among the stones
of fire.
¹⁷ Your heart was filled with pride
because of all your beauty.
Your wisdom was corrupted
by your love of splendor.
So I threw you to the ground
and exposed you to the curious gaze
of kings.
¹⁸ You defiled your sanctuaries
with your many sins and your
dishonest trade.
So I brought fire out from within you,
and it consumed you.
I reduced you to ashes on the ground
in the sight of all who were watching.
¹⁹ All who knew you are appalled at your
fate.
You have come to a terrible end,
and you will exist no more."

A Message for Sidon

²⁰Then another message came to me from
the LORD: ²¹"Son of man, turn and face the
city of Sidon and prophesy against it. ²²Give
the people of Sidon this message from the
Sovereign LORD:

"I am your enemy, O Sidon,
and I will reveal my glory by what I do
to you.
When I bring judgment against you
and reveal my holiness among you,
everyone watching will know
that I am the LORD.
²³ I will send a plague against you,
and blood will be spilled in your streets.
The attack will come from every direction,
and your people will lie slaughtered
within your walls.
Then everyone will know
that I am the LORD.
²⁴ No longer will Israel's scornful neighbors
prick and tear at her like briers and
thorns.
For then they will know
that I am the Sovereign LORD.

28:10 Hebrew *will die the death of the uncircumcised.* 28:13 The identification of some of these gemstones is
uncertain. 28:14 Hebrew *guardian cherub;* similarly in 28:16.

28:25-26 By every human measure, the days of Israel's success were gone. The elite of Israel's
population had been in forced captivity for years. Jerusalem itself was on the verge of destruction.
But God is always in control of every situation. No matter how far a nation or a person falls, God
can pick up such a nation or individual and bring victory where defeat seemed certain.

Restoration for Israel

25"This is what the Sovereign Lord says: The people of Israel will again live in their own land, the land I gave my servant Jacob. For I will gather them from the distant lands where I have scattered them. I will reveal to the nations of the world my holiness among my people. 26They will live safely in Israel and build homes and plant vineyards. And when I punish the neighboring nations that treated them with contempt, they will know that I am the Lord their God."

CHAPTER 29
A Message for Egypt

On January 7,* during the tenth year of King Jehoiachin's captivity, this message came to me from the Lord: 2"Son of man, turn and face Egypt and prophesy against Pharaoh the king and all the people of Egypt. 3Give them this message from the Sovereign Lord:

"I am your enemy, O Pharaoh, king
    of Egypt—
  you great monster, lurking in the
    streams of the Nile.
For you have said, 'The Nile River is mine;
  I made it for myself.'
4I will put hooks in your jaws
  and drag you out on the land
    with fish sticking to your scales.
5I will leave you and all your fish
  stranded in the wilderness to die.
You will lie unburied on the open
    ground,
  for I have given you as food to the wild
    animals and birds.
6All the people of Egypt will know that I
    am the Lord,
  for to Israel you were just a staff made
    of reeds.
7When Israel leaned on you,
  you splintered and broke
    and stabbed her in the armpit.
When she put her weight on you,
  you collapsed, and her legs gave way.

8"Therefore, this is what the Sovereign Lord says: I will bring an army against you, O Egypt, and destroy both people and animals. 9The land of Egypt will become a desolate wasteland, and the Egyptians will know that I am the Lord.

"Because you said, 'The Nile River is mine; I made it,' 10I am now the enemy of both you and your river. I will make the land of Egypt a totally desolate wasteland, from Migdol to Aswan, as far south as the border of Ethiopia.* 11For forty years not a soul will pass that way, neither people nor animals. It will be completely uninhabited. 12I will make Egypt desolate, and it will be surrounded by other desolate nations. Its cities will be empty and desolate for forty years, surrounded by other ruined cities. I will scatter the Egyptians to distant lands.

13"But this is what the Sovereign Lord also says: At the end of the forty years I will bring the Egyptians home again from the nations to which they have been scattered. 14I will restore the prosperity of Egypt and bring its people back to the land of Pathros in southern Egypt from which they came. But Egypt will remain an unimportant, minor kingdom. 15It will be the lowliest of all the nations, never again great enough to rise above its neighbors.

16"Then Israel will no longer be tempted to trust in Egypt for help. Egypt's shattered condition will remind Israel of how sinful she was to trust Egypt in earlier days. Then Israel will know that I am the Sovereign Lord."

Nebuchadnezzar to Conquer Egypt

17On April 26, the first day of the new year,* during the twenty-seventh year of King Jehoiachin's captivity, this message came to me from the Lord: 18"Son of man, the army of King Nebuchadnezzar* of Babylon fought so hard against Tyre that the warriors' heads were rubbed bare and their shoulders were raw and blistered. Yet Nebuchadnezzar and

29:1 Hebrew *On the twelfth day of the tenth month,* of the ancient Hebrew lunar calendar. This event occurred on January 7, 587 B.C.; also see note on 1:1. 29:10 Hebrew *from Migdol to Syene as far as the border of Cush.* 29:17 Hebrew *On the first day of the first month,* of the ancient Hebrew lunar calendar. This event occurred on April 26, 571 B.C.; also see note on 1:1. 29:18 Hebrew *Nebuchadrezzar,* a variant spelling of Nebuchadnezzar; also in 29:19.

29:2-16 When Israel was in deep trouble, the leaders often turned in vain to Egypt for help. Egypt lacked the power to bring true and permanent deliverance. We often make a similar mistake. When we face terrible problems or pain, we may turn to strategies that provide only temporary respite or fail altogether. We may turn to alcohol, drugs, sex, or work to help us forget our pain, but we all know how destructive that can be. As we face our dependency, we may be tempted to try a humanistic recovery program that excludes God and offers only false security. Instead, we must turn to the only power able to bring true deliverance—God.

his army won no plunder to compensate them for all their work. ¹⁹Therefore, this is what the Sovereign LORD says: I will give the land of Egypt to Nebuchadnezzar, king of Babylon. He will carry off its wealth, plundering everything it has so he can pay his army. ²⁰Yes, I have given him the land of Egypt as a reward for his work, says the Sovereign LORD, because he was working for me when he destroyed Tyre.

²¹"And the day will come when I will cause the ancient glory of Israel to revive,* and then, Ezekiel, your words will be respected. Then they will know that I am the LORD."

CHAPTER 30
A Sad Day for Egypt

This is another message that came to me from the LORD: ²"Son of man, prophesy and give this message from the Sovereign LORD:

"Weep and wail
  for that day,
³for the terrible day is almost here—
  the day of the LORD!
It is a day of clouds and gloom,
  a day of despair for the nations.
⁴A sword will come against Egypt,
  and those who are slaughtered will
    cover the ground.
Its wealth will be carried away
  and its foundations destroyed.
The land of Ethiopia* will be ravished.
⁵ Ethiopia, Libya, Lydia, all Arabia,*
and all their other allies
  will be destroyed in that war.

⁶"For this is what the LORD says:
All of Egypt's allies will fall,
  and the pride of her power will end.
From Migdol to Aswan*

they will be slaughtered by the sword,
  says the Sovereign LORD.
⁷Egypt will be desolate,
  surrounded by desolate nations,
and its cities will be in ruins,
  surrounded by other ruined cities.
⁸And the people of Egypt will know that I
    am the LORD
  when I have set Egypt on fire
  and destroyed all their allies.
⁹At that time I will send swift messengers
    in ships
  to terrify the complacent Ethiopians.
Great panic will come upon them
  on that day of Egypt's certain
    destruction.
Watch for it!
  It is sure to come!

¹⁰"For this is what the Sovereign LORD says:
By the power of King Nebuchadnezzar*
    of Babylon,
  I will destroy the hordes of Egypt.
¹¹He and his armies—the most ruthless
    of all—
  will be sent to demolish the land.
They will make war against Egypt
  until slaughtered Egyptians cover the
    ground.
¹²I will dry up the Nile River
  and sell the land to wicked men.
I will destroy the land of Egypt and
    everything in it
  by the hands of foreigners.
  I, the LORD, have spoken!

¹³"This is what the Sovereign LORD says:
I will smash the idols* of Egypt
  and the images at Memphis.*
There will be no rulers left in Egypt;
  terror will sweep the land.

29:21 Hebrew *I will cause a horn to sprout for the house of Israel.* 30:4 Hebrew *Cush;* similarly in 30:9. 30:5 Hebrew *Cush, Put, Lud, all Arabia, Cub. Cub* is otherwise unknown and may be another spelling for *Lub* (Libya). 30:6 Hebrew *to Syene.* 30:10 Hebrew *Nebuchadrezzar,* a variant spelling of Nebuchadnezzar. 30:13a The Hebrew term (literally *round things*) probably alludes to dung. 30:13b Hebrew *Noph;* also in 30:16.

29:18-21 God used King Nebuchadnezzar of Babylon as an agent to achieve his sovereign will. Nebuchadnezzar disposed of people and treaties without a thought about the consequences. He even considered himself a god (see Daniel 3:1-7). It may be hard for us to accept that God would use an evil dictator as part of his plan. Sometimes God may use hostile forces to accomplish his purpose in our life. But we can be sure that if we trust in God, we will receive his best in the end. We can also be sure that the evil people he uses will ultimately be held accountable for their terrible deeds. God humbled Nebuchadnezzar and destroyed his empire, just as he will ultimately destroy our enemies.

30:2-3 In the Old Testament the day of the Lord referred to a specific time of God's intervention in the affairs of this world. When God breaks into history, judgment follows—a time of purification of his people and destruction of his enemies. Following this purging, wonderful blessings come. Although this passage refers to a specific historical event—Egypt's destruction—let us consider what it would mean for us if we faced the day of the Lord today. Would we be judged or blessed?

14 I will destroy southern Egypt,*
    set fire to Zoan,
    and bring judgment against Thebes.*
15 I will pour out my fury on Pelusium,*
    the strongest fortress of Egypt,
and I will stamp out
    the hordes of Thebes.
16 Yes, I will set fire to all Egypt!
    Pelusium will be racked with pain;
Thebes will be torn apart;
    Memphis will live in constant terror.
17 The young men of Heliopolis and
    Bubastis* will die in battle,
and the women* will be taken away
    as slaves.
18 When I come to break the proud strength
    of Egypt,
it will be a dark day for Tahpanhes,
    too.
A dark cloud will cover Tahpanhes,
    and its daughters will be led away
    as captives.
19 And so I will greatly punish Egypt,
    and they will know that I am the
    LORD.”

The Broken Arms of Pharaoh

20 On April 29,* during the eleventh year of King Jehoiachin’s captivity, this message came to me from the LORD: 21 “Son of man, I have broken the arm of Pharaoh, the king of Egypt. His arm has not been put in a cast so that it may heal. Neither has it been bound up with a splint to make it strong enough to hold a sword. 22 Therefore, this is what the Sovereign LORD says: I am the enemy of Pharaoh, the king of Egypt! I will break both of his arms—the good arm along with the broken one—and I will make his sword clatter to the ground. 23 I will scatter the Egyptians to many lands throughout the world. 24 I will strengthen the arms of Babylon’s king and put my sword in his hand. But I will break the arms of Pharaoh, king of Egypt, and he will lie there mortally wounded, groaning in pain. 25 I will strengthen the arms of the king of Babylon, while the arms of Pharaoh fall useless to his sides. And when I put my sword in the hand of Babylon’s king and he brings it against the land of Egypt, Egypt will know that I am the LORD. 26 I will scatter the Egyptians among the nations, dispersing them throughout the earth. Then they will know that I am the LORD.”

CHAPTER 31

Egypt Compared to Fallen Assyria

On June 21,* during the eleventh year of King Jehoiachin’s captivity, this message came to me from the LORD: 2 “Son of man, give this message to Pharaoh, king of Egypt, and all his hordes:

“To whom would you compare your
    greatness?
3 You are like mighty Assyria,
    which was once like a cedar of
    Lebanon,
with beautiful branches that cast deep
    forest shade
and with its top high among the clouds.
4 Deep springs watered it
    and helped it to grow tall and
    luxuriant.
The water flowed around it like a river,
    streaming to all the trees nearby.
5 This great tree towered high,
    higher than all the other trees around it.
It prospered and grew long thick branches
    because of all the water at its roots.

30:14a Hebrew *Pathros.* 30:14b Hebrew *No;* also in 30:15, 16. 30:15 Hebrew *Sin;* also in 30:16. 30:17a Hebrew *of Awen and Pi-beseth.* 30:17b Or *and her cities.* 30:20 Hebrew *On the seventh day of the first month,* of the ancient Hebrew lunar calendar. This event occurred on April 29, 587 B.C.; also see note on 1:1. 31:1 Hebrew *On the first day of the third month,* of the ancient Hebrew lunar calendar. This event occurred on June 21, 587 B.C.; also see note on 1:1.

30:21-26 God is absolutely sovereign in international affairs. And if God can work his will among hostile superpowers, how simple it must be for him to work his will in willing individuals! God wants us to succeed in recovery, and, if we submit fully to his will for us, he will accomplish just that. God is willing and able to bring about miraculous changes in this world. If we turn to him for the help he offers and obey him completely, we can be part of God’s plan for the recovery of his people and his created world.

31:2-9 In Ezekiel’s day Egypt’s pharaoh was second only to Nebuchadnezzar of Babylon in power and greatness. The pharaoh was reminded here that the great empire of Assyria, once the greatest power on earth, had already been destroyed. Pharaoh needed to learn that no one, not even a nation as powerful as Egypt, could stand against God’s ultimate plan for the world. God has created all people and things to live in close relationship with himself. Our only hope for survival and blessing is in seeking and obeying his plan for healthy living. If we refuse to take part in his program, we will face the painful consequences.

⁶The birds nested in its branches,
and in its shade all the wild animals
gave birth.
All the great nations of the world
lived in its shadow.
⁷It was strong and beautiful,
with wide-spreading branches,
for its roots went deep
into abundant water.
⁸No other cedar in the garden of God
could rival it.
No cypress had branches to equal it;
no plane tree had boughs to compare.
No tree in the garden of God
came close to it in beauty.
⁹Because I made this tree so beautiful,
and gave it such magnificent foliage,
it was the envy of all the other trees
of Eden,
the garden of God.

¹⁰"Therefore, this is what the Sovereign LORD says: Because Egypt* became proud and arrogant, and because it set itself so high above the others, with its top reaching to the clouds, ¹¹I will hand it over to a mighty nation that will destroy it as its wickedness deserves. I have already discarded it. ¹²A foreign army—the terror of the nations—has cut it down and left it fallen on the ground. Its branches are scattered across the mountains and valleys and ravines of the land. All those who lived in its shadow have gone away and left it lying there.

¹³"The birds roost on its fallen trunk,
and the wild animals lie among its
branches.
¹⁴Let the tree of no other nation
proudly exult in its own prosperity,
though it be higher than the clouds
and it be watered from the depths.
For all are doomed to die,

to go down to the depths of the earth.
They will land in the pit
along with everyone else on earth.

¹⁵"This is what the Sovereign LORD says: When Assyria went down to the grave,* I made the deep springs mourn. I stopped its rivers and dried up its abundant water. I clothed Lebanon in black and caused the trees of the field to wilt. ¹⁶I made the nations shake with fear at the sound of its fall, for I sent it down to the grave with all the others who descend to the pit. And all the other proud trees of Eden, the most beautiful and the best of Lebanon, the ones whose roots went deep into the water, took comfort to find it there with them in the depths of the earth. ¹⁷Its allies, too, were all destroyed and had passed away. They had gone down to the grave—all those nations that had lived in its shade.

¹⁸O Egypt, to which of the trees of Eden will you compare your strength and glory? You, too, will be brought down to the depths with all these other nations. You will lie there among the outcasts* who have died by the sword. This will be the fate of Pharaoh and all his hordes. I, the Sovereign LORD, have spoken!"

CHAPTER 32
A Warning for Pharaoh
On March 3,* during the twelfth year of King Jehoiachin's captivity, this message came to me from the LORD: ²"Son of man, mourn for Pharaoh, king of Egypt, and give him this message:

"You think of yourself as a strong young
lion among the nations,
but you are really just a sea monster,
heaving around in your own rivers,
stirring up mud with your feet.

31:10 Hebrew *you.* 31:15 Hebrew *to Sheol;* also in 31:16, 17. 31:18 Hebrew *among the uncircumcised.* 32:1 Hebrew *On the first day of the twelfth month,* of the ancient Hebrew lunar calendar. This event occurred on March 3, 585 B.C.; also see note on 1:1.

31:18 God's assessment of greatness was certainly different from Pharaoh's. Pharaoh thought of himself as a beautiful and sturdy tree—to be compared even with the splendor of the trees of the Garden of Eden. But as magnificent and stalwart as Pharaoh and his nation were, they would be cut down and destroyed. No one can reject God and hope to succeed for long. Pride always comes before a fall. We must learn this lesson in recovery. As soon as we begin to think we can do things our way and in our own power, we are headed for disaster.
32:2-8 It is always dangerous to think of ourself more highly than we ought to. Pharaoh thought of himself as a strong, young lion spreading fear among all who saw him. But the following verses reveal how vulnerable to capture and death he actually was. Thinking we can go it alone in recovery brings trouble. None of us is strong enough to overcome the pull of our addiction without help. If we think we can stand alone, we may reject the help and support offered by God and others. We need to be reminded continually that we are powerless over our dependency.

³Therefore, this is what the Sovereign LORD says:

I will send many people
  to catch you in my net
  and haul you out of the water.
⁴I will leave you stranded on the land
  to die.
All the birds of the heavens will land
  on you,
and the wild animals of the whole
  earth
  will gorge themselves on you.
⁵I will scatter your flesh on the hills
  and fill the valleys with your bones.
⁶I will drench the earth with your gushing
  blood
  all the way to the mountains,
  filling the ravines to the brim.
⁷When I blot you out,
  I will veil the heavens and darken
  the stars.
I will cover the sun with a cloud,
  and the moon will not give you its
  light.
⁸I will darken the bright stars overhead
  and cover your land in darkness.
I, the Sovereign LORD, have spoken!

⁹"I will disturb many hearts when I bring news of your downfall to distant nations you have never seen. ¹⁰Yes, I will shock many lands, and their kings will be terrified at your fate. They will shudder in fear for their lives as I brandish my sword before them on the day of your fall. ¹¹For this is what the Sovereign LORD says:

"The sword of the king of Babylon
  will come against you.
¹²I will destroy your hordes with the swords
  of mighty warriors—
  the terror of the nations.
They will shatter the pride of Egypt,
  and all its hordes will be destroyed.
¹³I will destroy all your flocks and herds
  that graze beside the streams.

Never again will people or animals
  muddy those waters with their feet.
¹⁴Then I will let the waters of Egypt become
  calm again,
  and they will flow as smoothly as
  olive oil,
  says the Sovereign LORD.
¹⁵And when I destroy Egypt
  and strip you of everything
  you own
  and strike down all your people,
  then you will know that I am
  the LORD.
¹⁶Yes, this is the funeral song
  they will sing for Egypt.
Let all the nations mourn.
  Let them mourn for Egypt and
  its hordes.
  I, the Sovereign LORD, have spoken!"

Egypt Falls into the Pit

¹⁷On March 17,* during the twelfth year, another message came to me from the LORD: ¹⁸"Son of man, weep for the hordes of Egypt and for the other mighty nations.* For I will send them down to the world below in company with those who descend to the pit. ¹⁹Say to them,

'O Egypt, are you lovelier than the other
  nations?
  No! So go down to the pit and lie there
  among the outcasts.*'

²⁰The Egyptians will fall with the many who have died by the sword, for the sword is drawn against them. Egypt and its hordes will be dragged away to their judgment. ²¹Down in the grave* mighty leaders will mockingly welcome Egypt and its allies, saying, 'They have come down; they lie among the outcasts, hordes slaughtered by the sword.'

²²"Assyria lies there surrounded by the graves of its army, those who were slaughtered by the sword. ²³Their graves are in the depths of the pit, and they are surrounded by

---

32:17 Hebrew *On the fifteenth day of the month,* presumably in the twelfth month of the ancient Hebrew lunar calendar (see 32:1). This would put this message at the end of King Jehoiachin's twelfth year of captivity, on March 17, 585 B.C.; also see note on 1:1. Greek version reads *On the fifteenth day of the first month,* which would put this message on April 27, 586 B.C., at the beginning of Jehoiachin's twelfth year. **32:18** The meaning of the Hebrew is uncertain. **32:19** Hebrew *the uncircumcised;* also in 32:21, 24, 25, 26, 28, 29, 30, 32. **32:21** Hebrew *in Sheol.*

32:9-10 There is something terrifying about the fall of a person or nation of great power. Pharaoh had been a figure of great domination; his authority, almost absolute. Ezekiel prophesied that when Pharaoh was judged, the world would be horrified and filled with fear. We can learn from the failure of others. People with far greater strength than ours have been destroyed by their addiction. What hope do we have of standing against ours? We must accept our powerlessness and turn for help to the only one with the power to deliver us—God himself.

their allies. They struck terror in the hearts of people everywhere, but now they have been slaughtered by the sword.

²⁴"Elam lies there surrounded by the graves of all its hordes, those who were slaughtered by the sword. They struck terror in the hearts of people everywhere, but now they have descended as outcasts to the world below. Now they lie in the pit and share the shame of those who have gone before them. ²⁵They have a resting place among the slaughtered, surrounded by the graves of all their hordes. Yes, they terrorized the nations while they lived, but now they lie in shame with others in the pit, all of them outcasts, slaughtered by the sword.

²⁶"Meshech and Tubal are there, surrounded by the graves of all their hordes. They once struck terror in the hearts of people everywhere. But now they are outcasts, all slaughtered by the sword. ²⁷They are not buried in honor like their fallen heroes, who went down to the grave* with their weapons—their shields covering their bodies* and their swords beneath their heads. Their guilt rests upon them because they brought terror to everyone while they were still alive.

²⁸"You too, Egypt, will lie crushed and broken among the outcasts, all slaughtered by the sword.

²⁹"Edom is there with its kings and princes. Mighty as they were, they also lie among those slaughtered by the sword, with the outcasts who have gone down to the pit.

³⁰"All the princes of the north and the Sidonians are there with others who have died. Once a terror, they have been put to shame. They lie there as outcasts with others who were slaughtered by the sword. They share the shame of all who have descended to the pit.

³¹"When Pharaoh and his entire army arrive, he will take comfort that he is not alone in having his hordes killed, says the Sovereign LORD. ³²Although I have caused his terror to fall upon all the living, Pharaoh and his hordes will lie there among the outcasts who were slaughtered by the sword. I, the Sovereign LORD, have spoken!"

CHAPTER 33

Ezekiel as Israel's Watchman

Once again a message came to me from the LORD: ²"Son of man, give your people this message: 'When I bring an army against a country, the people of that land choose one of their own to be a watchman. ³When the watchman sees the enemy coming, he sounds the alarm to warn the people. ⁴Then if those who hear the alarm refuse to take action, it is their own fault if they die. ⁵They heard the alarm but ignored it, so the responsibility is theirs. If they had listened to the warning, they could have saved their lives. ⁶But if the watchman sees the enemy coming and doesn't sound the alarm to warn the people, he is responsible for their captivity. They will die in their sins, but I will hold the watchman responsible for their deaths.'

⁷"Now, son of man, I am making you a watchman for the people of Israel. Therefore, listen to what I say and warn them for me. ⁸If I announce that some wicked people are sure to die and you fail to tell them to change their ways, then they will die in their sins, and I will hold you responsible for their deaths. ⁹But if you warn them to repent and they don't repent, they will die in their sins, but you will have saved yourself.

The Watchman's Message

¹⁰"Son of man, give the people of Israel this message: You are saying, 'Our sins are heavy upon us; we are wasting away! How can we survive?' ¹¹As surely as I live, says the Sovereign LORD, I take no pleasure in the death of wicked people. I only want them to turn from their wicked ways so they can live. Turn! Turn from your wickedness, O people of Israel! Why should you die?

¹²"Son of man, give your people this message: The righteous behavior of righteous people will not save them if they turn to sin, nor will the wicked behavior of wicked people destroy them if they repent and turn from their sins. ¹³When I tell righteous people that they will live, but then they sin, expecting their past righteousness to save them, then none of their righteous acts will be remembered. I will destroy them for their

---

32:27a Hebrew *to Sheol.* 32:27b The meaning of the Hebrew is uncertain.

33:2-6 The solemn responsibility of a watchman in an Old Testament town was to warn the citizens of impending danger. If the watchman was unfaithful, the result would be the tragic loss of life and property. We are watchmen for others as well. We should, as recovering people, be careful not to lead others astray or fail to warn them of the dangers of our former lifestyle.

sins. ¹⁴And suppose I tell some wicked people that they will surely die, but then they
turn from their sins and do what is just and
right. ¹⁵For instance, they might give back a
debtor's security, return what they have stolen, and obey my life-giving laws, no longer
doing what is evil. If they do this, then they
will surely live and not die. ¹⁶None of their
past sins will be brought up again, for they
have done what is just and right, and they
will surely live.

¹⁷"Your people are saying, 'The Lord isn't
doing what's right,' but it is they who are
not doing what's right. ¹⁸For again I say,
when righteous people turn away from their
righteous behavior and turn to evil, they
will die. ¹⁹But if wicked people turn from
their wickedness and do what is just and
right, they will live. ²⁰O people of Israel, you
are saying, 'The Lord isn't doing what's
right.' But I judge each of you according to
your deeds."

Explanation of Jerusalem's Fall

²¹On January 8,* during the twelfth year of
our captivity, a survivor from Jerusalem
came to me and said, "The city has fallen!"
²²The previous evening the LORD had taken
hold of me and given me back my voice. So I
was able to speak when this man arrived the
next morning.

²³Then this message came to me from the
LORD: ²⁴"Son of man, the scattered remnants
of Israel living among the ruined cities keep
saying, 'Abraham was only one man, yet he
gained possession of the entire land. We are
many; surely the land has been given to us as
a possession.' ²⁵So tell these people, 'This is
what the Sovereign LORD says: You eat meat
with blood in it, you worship idols,* and you
murder the innocent. Do you really think
the land should be yours? ²⁶Murderers! Idola-
ters! Adulterers! Should the land belong to
you?'

²⁷"Say to them, 'This is what the Sovereign
LORD says: As surely as I live, those living in
the ruins will die by the sword. And I will
send wild animals to eat those living in the
open fields. Those hiding in the forts and
caves will die of disease. ²⁸I will completely
destroy the land and demolish her pride. Her
arrogant power will come to an end. The
mountains of Israel will be so desolate that

33:21 Hebrew *On the fifth day of the tenth month,* of the
ancient Hebrew lunar calendar. This event occurred on
January 8, 585 B.C.; also see note on 1:1. 33:25 The
Hebrew term (literally *round things*) probably alludes to
dung.

STEP 9

Covering the Past

BIBLE READING: Ezekiel 33:10-16
**We made direct amends to such people
wherever possible, except when to do so
would injure them or others.**
When we walk down the wrong path in life,
we end up in bad places and experience
devastating losses. If we go far enough
down that path, we endanger our very life.
We may wonder if we have already gone
too far. Is a new way of life really possible,
even if we turn from our old ways and
make amends?

Even under the Old Testament laws,
there was hope for those who chose to turn
from sin and make amends. God spoke
through Ezekiel, saying, "Son of man, give
the people of Israel this message: You are
saying, 'Our sins are heavy upon us; we are
wasting away! How can we survive?' As
surely as I live, says the Sovereign LORD, I
take no pleasure in the death of wicked
people. I only want them to turn from their
wicked ways so they can live. Turn! Turn
from your wickedness, O people of Israel!
Why should you die? Son of man, give your
people this message: The righteous behavior of righteous people will not save them if
they turn to sin, nor will the wicked behavior of wicked people destroy them if they
repent and turn from their sins. . . . And
suppose I tell some wicked people that they
will surely die, but then they turn from their
sins and do what is just and right. For
instance, they might give back a debtor's
security, return what they have stolen, and
obey my life-giving laws, no longer doing
what is evil. If they do this, then they will
surely live and not die. None of their past
sins will be brought up again, for they have
done what is just and right, and they will
surely live" (Ezekiel 33:10-12, 14-16).

There is hope for everyone who turns
from sin and makes amends. Through
Christ our past sins can be overshadowed
by the new life ahead of us. *Turn to page
1201, Matthew 5.*

no one will even travel through them. [29]When I have completely destroyed the land because of their detestable sins, then they will know that I am the LORD.'

[30]"Son of man, your people talk about you in their houses and whisper about you at the doors. They say to each other, 'Come on, let's go hear the prophet tell us what the LORD is saying!' [31]So my people come pretending to be sincere and sit before you. They listen to your words, but they have no intention of doing what you say. Their mouths are full of lustful words, and their hearts seek only after money. [32]You are very entertaining to them, like someone who sings love songs with a beautiful voice or plays fine music on an instrument. They hear what you say, but they don't act on it! [33]But when all these terrible things happen to them—as they certainly will—then they will know a prophet has been among them."

CHAPTER 34
The Shepherds of Israel

Then this message came to me from the LORD: [2]"Son of man, prophesy against the shepherds, the leaders of Israel. Give them this message from the Sovereign LORD: What sorrow awaits you shepherds who feed yourselves instead of your flocks. Shouldn't shepherds feed their sheep? [3]You drink the milk, wear the wool, and butcher the best animals, but you let your flocks starve. [4]You have not taken care of the weak. You have not tended the sick or bound up the injured. You have not gone looking for those who have wandered away and are lost. Instead, you have ruled them with harshness and cruelty. [5]So my sheep have been scattered without a shepherd, and they are easy prey for any wild animal. [6]They have wandered through all the mountains and all the hills, across the face of the earth, yet no one has gone to search for them.

[7]"Therefore, you shepherds, hear the word of the LORD: [8]As surely as I live, says the Sovereign LORD, you abandoned my flock and left them to be attacked by every wild animal. And though you were my shepherds, you didn't search for my sheep when they were lost. You took care of yourselves and left the sheep to starve. [9]Therefore, you shepherds, hear the word of the LORD. [10]This is what the Sovereign LORD says: I now consider these shepherds my enemies, and I will hold them responsible for what has happened to my flock. I will take away their right to feed the flock, and I will stop them from feeding themselves. I will rescue my flock from their mouths; the sheep will no longer be their prey.

The Good Shepherd

[11]"For this is what the Sovereign LORD says: I myself will search and find my sheep. [12]I will be like a shepherd looking for his scattered flock. I will find my sheep and rescue them from all the places where they were scattered on that dark and cloudy day. [13]I will bring them back home to their own land of Israel from among the peoples and nations. I will feed them on the mountains of Israel and by the rivers and in all the places where people live. [14]Yes, I will give them good pastureland on the high hills of Israel. There they will lie down in pleasant places and feed in the lush pastures of the hills. [15]I myself will tend my sheep and give them a place to lie down in peace, says the Sovereign LORD. [16]I will search for my lost ones who strayed away, and I will bring them safely home again. I will bandage the injured and strengthen the weak. But I will de-

---

33:33 There is an inescapable certainty to God's pronouncements. When God's words are faithfully proclaimed, as they were by Ezekiel, the messages are confirmed when the declarations come to pass. When God says something—anything—we can be assured that his word will come to pass. God declares much of his will for us in the Scriptures. We should listen to what God says and act on it. Doing anything else will lead to painful consequences.

34:2-10 Leaders are accountable to God for their actions, and he will judge them. The more people they lead, the greater their accountability. The spiritual leaders of Israel were like evil shepherds who were cruel and could not be trusted. They took care of themselves instead of their flock. In any phase of recovery, we must be aware of our leadership responsibilities. All of us touch the lives of others in some way. Some of us may be responsible for our children; others of us may be responsible for friends. We must lead according to God's program. If we don't, we will suffer great consequences and cause suffering to many who are innocent. If we have already failed in this area, we need to work toward undoing some of the damage we have already done.

34:11-16 Even though Israel was now a conquered nation and Jerusalem had fallen, even though the people had been deported and had no real hope for the future—God had given them a promise that could be counted on: He would rescue them and bring them safely home again. No matter what our circumstances, we can be assured of God's constant care and concern for us.

stroy those who are fat and powerful. I will feed them, yes—feed them justice!

¹⁷"And as for you, my flock, this is what the Sovereign LORD says to his people: I will judge between one animal of the flock and another, separating the sheep from the goats. ¹⁸Isn't it enough for you to keep the best of the pastures for yourselves? Must you also trample down the rest? Isn't it enough for you to drink clear water for yourselves? Must you also muddy the rest with your feet? ¹⁹Why must my flock eat what you have trampled down and drink water you have fouled?

²⁰"Therefore, this is what the Sovereign LORD says: I will surely judge between the fat sheep and the scrawny sheep. ²¹For you fat sheep pushed and butted and crowded my sick and hungry flock until you scattered them to distant lands. ²²So I will rescue my flock, and they will no longer be abused. I will judge between one animal of the flock and another. ²³And I will set over them one shepherd, my servant David. He will feed them and be a shepherd to them. ²⁴And I, the LORD, will be their God, and my servant David will be a prince among my people. I, the LORD, have spoken!

The LORD's Covenant of Peace

²⁵"I will make a covenant of peace with my people and drive away the dangerous animals from the land. Then they will be able to camp safely in the wildest places and sleep in the woods without fear. ²⁶I will bless my people and their homes around my holy hill. And in the proper season I will send the showers they need. There will be showers of blessing. ²⁷The orchards and fields of my people will yield bumper crops, and everyone will live in safety. When I have broken their chains of slavery and rescued them from those who enslaved them, then they will know that I am the LORD. ²⁸They will no longer be prey for other nations, and wild animals will no longer devour them. They will live in safety, and no one will frighten them.

²⁹"And I will make their land famous for its crops, so my people will never again suffer from famines or the insults of foreign nations. ³⁰In this way, they will know that I, the LORD their God, am with them. And they will know that they, the people of Israel, are my people, says the Sovereign LORD. ³¹You are my flock, the sheep of my pasture. You are my people, and I am your God. I, the Sovereign LORD, have spoken!"

CHAPTER 35
A Message for Edom

Again a message came to me from the LORD: ²"Son of man, turn and face Mount Seir, and prophesy against its people. ³Give them this message from the Sovereign LORD:

"I am your enemy, O Mount Seir,
    and I will raise my fist against you
    to destroy you completely.
⁴I will demolish your cities
    and make you desolate.
Then you will know that I am the LORD.

⁵"Your eternal hatred for the people of Israel led you to butcher them when they were helpless, when I had already punished them for all their sins. ⁶As surely as I live, says the Sovereign LORD, since you show no distaste for blood, I will give you a bloodbath of your own. Your turn has come! ⁷I will make Mount Seir utterly desolate, killing off all who try to escape and any who return. ⁸I will fill your mountains with the dead. Your hills, your valleys, and your ravines will be filled with people slaughtered by the sword. ⁹I will make you desolate forever. Your cities will never be rebuilt. Then you will know that I am the LORD.

¹⁰"For you said, 'The lands of Israel and Judah will be ours. We will take possession of them. What do we care that the LORD is there!' ¹¹Therefore, as surely as I live, says the Sovereign LORD, I will pay back your angry deeds with my own. I will punish you for all your acts of anger, envy, and hatred. And I will make myself known to Israel* by what I do to you. ¹²Then you will know that I, the LORD, have heard every contemptuous word you spoke against the mountains of Israel. For you said, 'They are desolate; they have been given to us as food to eat!' ¹³In saying

35:11 Hebrew *to them;* Greek version reads *to you.*

34:23-24 God had promised David that someone from his family line would rule his people in peace; this descendant would be the promised Messiah. This promise was fulfilled in the person of Jesus Christ. He is the true shepherd—the Good Shepherd. We can trust him for guidance and sustenance through all situations. He promises to give us help and power to overcome the areas in our life that are drawing us toward destruction.

that, you boasted proudly against me, and I have heard it all!

¹⁴"This is what the Sovereign LORD says: The whole world will rejoice when I make you desolate. ¹⁵You rejoiced at the desolation of Israel's territory. Now I will rejoice at yours! You will be wiped out, you people of Mount Seir and all who live in Edom! Then you will know that I am the LORD.

CHAPTER 36
Restoration for Israel

"Son of man, prophesy to Israel's mountains. Give them this message: O mountains of Israel, hear the word of the LORD! ²This is what the Sovereign LORD says: Your enemies have taunted you, saying, 'Aha! Now the ancient heights belong to us!' ³Therefore, son of man, give the mountains of Israel this message from the Sovereign LORD: Your enemies have attacked you from all directions, making you the property of many nations and the object of much mocking and slander. ⁴Therefore, O mountains of Israel, hear the word of the Sovereign LORD. He speaks to the hills and mountains, ravines and valleys, and to ruined wastes and long-deserted cities that have been destroyed and mocked by the surrounding nations. ⁵This is what the Sovereign LORD says: My jealous anger burns against these nations, especially Edom, because they have shown utter contempt for me by gleefully taking my land for themselves as plunder.

⁶"Therefore, prophesy to the hills and mountains, the ravines and valleys of Israel. This is what the Sovereign LORD says: I am furious that you have suffered shame before the surrounding nations. ⁷Therefore, this is what the Sovereign LORD says: I have taken a solemn oath that those nations will soon have their own shame to endure.

⁸"But the mountains of Israel will produce heavy crops of fruit for my people—for they will be coming home again soon! ⁹See, I care about you, and I will pay attention to you. Your ground will be plowed and your crops planted. ¹⁰I will greatly increase the population of Israel, and the ruined cities will be re-built and filled with people. ¹¹I will increase not only the people, but also your animals. O mountains of Israel, I will bring people to live on you once again. I will make you even more prosperous than you were before. Then you will know that I am the LORD. ¹²I will cause my people to walk on you once again, and you will be their territory. You will never again rob them of their children.

¹³"This is what the Sovereign LORD says: The other nations taunt you, saying, 'Israel is a land that devours its own people and robs them of their children!' ¹⁴But you will never again devour your people or rob them of their children, says the Sovereign LORD. ¹⁵I will not let you hear those other nations insult you, and you will no longer be mocked by them. You will not be a land that causes its nation to fall, says the Sovereign LORD."

¹⁶Then this further message came to me from the LORD: ¹⁷"Son of man, when the people of Israel were living in their own land, they defiled it by the evil way they lived. To me their conduct was as unclean as a woman's menstrual cloth. ¹⁸They polluted the land with murder and the worship of idols,* so I poured out my fury on them. ¹⁹I scattered them to many lands to punish them for the evil way they had lived. ²⁰But when they were scattered among the nations, they brought shame on my holy name. For the nations said, 'These are the people of the LORD, but he couldn't keep them safe in his own land!' ²¹Then I was concerned for my holy name, on which my people brought shame among the nations.

²²"Therefore, give the people of Israel this message from the Sovereign LORD: I am bringing you back, but not because you deserve it. I am doing it to protect my holy name, on which you brought shame while you were scattered among the nations. ²³I will show how holy my great name is—the name on which you brought shame among the nations. And when I reveal my holiness through you before their very eyes, says the Sovereign LORD, then the nations will know that I am the LORD. ²⁴For I will gather you up from all

36:18 The Hebrew term (literally *round things*) probably alludes to dung; also in 36:25.

36:17-24 God promised the people of Israel that their nation would be restored, but not because they deserved it. God had promised to reveal himself to the world through the nation of Israel, and God's will would not be thwarted. He would deliver his people from exile and rebuild his nation to restore honor to his name. Through this nation, the Messiah would be born; he would change the face of history and transform all who give their life to him. God went to painful lengths to bring his Deliverer into the world. We must take advantage of God's gift of forgiveness and restoration through Jesus the Messiah.

the nations and bring you home again to your land.

²⁵"Then I will sprinkle clean water on you, and you will be clean. Your filth will be washed away, and you will no longer worship idols. ²⁶And I will give you a new heart, and I will put a new spirit in you. I will take out your stony, stubborn heart and give you a tender, responsive heart.* ²⁷And I will put my Spirit in you so that you will follow my decrees and be careful to obey my regulations.

²⁸"And you will live in Israel, the land I gave your ancestors long ago. You will be my people, and I will be your God. ²⁹I will cleanse you of your filthy behavior. I will give you good crops of grain, and I will send no more famines on the land. ³⁰I will give you great harvests from your fruit trees and fields, and never again will the surrounding nations be able to scoff at your land for its famines. ³¹Then you will remember your past sins and despise yourselves for all the detestable things you did. ³²But remember, says the Sovereign LORD, I am not doing this because you deserve it. O my people of Israel, you should be utterly ashamed of all you have done!

³³"This is what the Sovereign LORD says: When I cleanse you from your sins, I will repopulate your cities, and the ruins will be rebuilt. ³⁴The fields that used to lie empty and desolate in plain view of everyone will again be farmed. ³⁵And when I bring you back, people will say, 'This former wasteland is now like the Garden of Eden! The abandoned and ruined cities now have strong walls and are filled with people!' ³⁶Then the surrounding nations that survive will know that I, the LORD, have rebuilt the ruins and replanted the wasteland. For I, the LORD, have spoken, and I will do what I say.

³⁷"This is what the Sovereign LORD says: I am ready to hear Israel's prayers and to increase their numbers like a flock. ³⁸They will be as numerous as the sacred flocks that fill Jerusalem's streets at the time of her festivals. The ruined cities will be crowded with people once more, and everyone will know that I am the LORD."

CHAPTER 37
A Valley of Dry Bones

The LORD took hold of me, and I was carried away by the Spirit of the LORD to a valley filled with bones. ²He led me all around among the bones that covered the valley floor. They were scattered everywhere across the ground and were completely dried out. ³Then he asked me, "Son of man, can these bones become living people again?"

"O Sovereign LORD," I replied, "you alone know the answer to that."

⁴Then he said to me, "Speak a prophetic message to these bones and say, 'Dry bones, listen to the word of the LORD! ⁵This is what the Sovereign LORD says: Look! I am going to put breath into you and make you live again! ⁶I will put flesh and muscles on you and cover you with skin. I will put breath into you, and you will come to life. Then you will know that I am the LORD.'"

⁷So I spoke this message, just as he told me. Suddenly as I spoke, there was a rattling noise all across the valley. The bones of each body came together and attached themselves as complete skeletons. ⁸Then as I watched, muscles and flesh formed over the bones. Then skin formed to cover their bodies, but they still had no breath in them.

⁹Then he said to me, "Speak a prophetic message to the winds, son of man. Speak a

36:26 Hebrew *a heart of flesh.*

36:25-27 How can any individual please God? We have experienced how helpless we are against the destructive evils in our life, but these verses should fill us with hope. As we respond to God's gracious provision of forgiveness and restoration, God promises to give us a new obedient heart and fill us with his Spirit so that we can make right decisions that follow God's program. This new heart is his gift to those who believe in the saving work of Jesus on their behalf.

36:33 Before the nation of Israel could be rebuilt, it had to be cleansed of sin. Sin separates us from God and leads to destruction. Until the sin is dealt with, we will not experience the power that God offers us to help overcome our dependency. It is impossible to rebuild countries or lives without first dealing with the sins that are destroying them. Before we can achieve success, we must first confess our sins and accept the forgiveness and cleansing that God offers.

37:1-10 Ezekiel was shown a valley filled with dry, lifeless bones. What an illustration of powerlessness! But as the dry bones were a picture of complete helplessness and hopelessness, so God's Spirit provided new life and complete sustenance. With God, defeat became uncompromising victory. This principle applies to us as we deal with the devastation of our addiction. Alone, our failures and their terrible consequences have already been accomplished, but with God's help we can be assured of victory and new life.

prophetic message and say, 'This is what the Sovereign LORD says: Come, O breath, from the four winds! Breathe into these dead bodies so they may live again.'"

¹⁰So I spoke the message as he commanded me, and breath came into their bodies. They all came to life and stood up on their feet—a great army.

¹¹Then he said to me, "Son of man, these bones represent the people of Israel. They are saying, 'We have become old, dry bones—all hope is gone. Our nation is finished.' ¹²Therefore, prophesy to them and say, 'This is what the Sovereign LORD says: O my people, I will open your graves of exile and cause you to rise again. Then I will bring you back to the land of Israel. ¹³When this happens, O my people, you will know that I am the LORD. ¹⁴I will put my Spirit in you, and you will live again and return home to your own land. Then you will know that I, the LORD, have spoken, and I have done what I said. Yes, the LORD has spoken!'"

Reunion of Israel and Judah

¹⁵Again a message came to me from the LORD: ¹⁶"Son of man, take a piece of wood and carve on it these words: 'This represents Judah and its allied tribes.' Then take another piece and carve these words on it: 'This represents Ephraim and the northern tribes of Israel.'* ¹⁷Now hold them together in your hand as if they were one piece of wood. ¹⁸When your people ask you what your actions mean, ¹⁹say to them, 'This is what the Sovereign LORD says: I will take Ephraim and the northern tribes and join them to Judah. I will make them one piece of wood in my hand.'

²⁰"Then hold out the pieces of wood you have inscribed, so the people can see them. ²¹And give them this message from the Sovereign LORD: I will gather the people of Israel from among the nations. I will bring them home to their own land from the places where they have been scattered. ²²I will unify them into one nation on the mountains of Israel. One king will rule them all; no longer will they be divided into two nations or into

two kingdoms. ²³They will never again pollute themselves with their idols* and vile images and rebellion, for I will save them from their sinful apostasy.* I will cleanse them. Then they will truly be my people, and I will be their God.

²⁴"My servant David will be their king, and they will have only one shepherd. They will obey my regulations and be careful to keep my decrees. ²⁵They will live in the land I gave my servant Jacob, the land where their ancestors lived. They and their children and their grandchildren after them will live there forever, generation after generation. And my servant David will be their prince forever. ²⁶And I will make a covenant of peace with them, an everlasting covenant. I will give them their land and increase their numbers,* and I will put my Temple among them forever. ²⁷I will make my home among them. I will be their God, and they will be my people. ²⁸And when my Temple is among them forever, the nations will know that I am the LORD, who makes Israel holy."

CHAPTER 38
A Message for Gog

This is another message that came to me from the LORD: ²"Son of man, turn and face Gog of the land of Magog, the prince who rules over the nations of Meshech and Tubal, and prophesy against him. ³Give him this message from the Sovereign LORD: Gog, I am your enemy! ⁴I will turn you around and put hooks in your jaws to lead you out with your whole army—your horses and charioteers in full armor and a great horde armed with shields and swords. ⁵Persia, Ethiopia, and Libya* will join you, too, with all their weapons. ⁶Gomer and all its armies will also join you, along with the armies of Beth-togarmah from the distant north, and many others.

⁷"Get ready; be prepared! Keep all the armies around you mobilized, and take command of them. ⁸A long time from now you will be called into action. In the distant future you will swoop down on the land of Is-

---

37:16 Hebrew *This is Ephraim's wood, representing Joseph and all the house of Israel;* similarly in 37:19. **37:23a** The Hebrew term (literally *round things*) probably alludes to dung. **37:23b** As in many Hebrew manuscripts and Greek version; Masoretic Text reads *from all their dwelling places where they sinned.* **37:26** Hebrew reads *I will give them and increase their numbers;* Greek version lacks the entire phrase. **38:5** Hebrew *Paras, Cush, and Put.*

37:24-28 God promised that one day he would make his home among his people. This took place when God became a man in the person of Jesus Christ. As we study Jesus' life on earth, we discover who God really is. God still lives among us and in us in the person of his Spirit. Though our world is filled with sin, we can all look forward to the day when Jesus Christ, the true shepherd, will return to guide his people in righteousness and truth. We can begin God's reign in our own life today by obeying God's program for joyful and healthy living.

rael, which will be enjoying peace after recovering from war and after its people have returned from many lands to the mountains of Israel. ⁹You and all your allies—a vast and awesome army—will roll down on them like a storm and cover the land like a cloud.

¹⁰"This is what the Sovereign LORD says: At that time evil thoughts will come to your mind, and you will devise a wicked scheme. ¹¹You will say, 'Israel is an unprotected land filled with unwalled villages! I will march against her and destroy these people who live in such confidence! ¹²I will go to those formerly desolate cities that are now filled with people who have returned from exile in many nations. I will capture vast amounts of plunder, for the people are rich with livestock and other possessions now. They think the whole world revolves around them!' ¹³But Sheba and Dedan and the merchants of Tarshish will ask, 'Do you really think the armies you have gathered can rob them of silver and gold? Do you think you can drive away their livestock and seize their goods and carry off plunder?'

¹⁴"Therefore, son of man, prophesy against Gog. Give him this message from the Sovereign LORD: When my people are living in peace in their land, then you will rouse yourself.* ¹⁵You will come from your homeland in the distant north with your vast cavalry and your mighty army, ¹⁶and you will attack my people Israel, covering their land like a cloud. At that time in the distant future, I will bring you against my land as everyone watches, and my holiness will be displayed by what happens to you, Gog. Then all the nations will know that I am the LORD.

¹⁷"This is what the Sovereign LORD asks: Are you the one I was talking about long ago, when I announced through Israel's prophets that in the future I would bring you against my people? ¹⁸But this is what the Sovereign LORD says: When Gog invades the land of Israel, my fury will boil over! ¹⁹In my jealousy

and blazing anger, I promise a mighty shaking in the land of Israel on that day. ²⁰All living things—the fish in the sea, the birds of the sky, the animals of the field, the small animals that scurry along the ground, and all the people on earth—will quake in terror at my presence. Mountains will be thrown down; cliffs will crumble; walls will fall to the earth. ²¹I will summon the sword against you on all the hills of Israel, says the Sovereign LORD. Your men will turn their swords against each other. ²²I will punish you and your armies with disease and bloodshed; I will send torrential rain, hailstones, fire, and burning sulfur! ²³In this way, I will show my greatness and holiness, and I will make myself known to all the nations of the world. Then they will know that I am the LORD.

CHAPTER 39
The Slaughter of Gog's Hordes

"Son of man, prophesy against Gog. Give him this message from the Sovereign LORD: I am your enemy, O Gog, ruler of the nations of Meshech and Tubal. ²I will turn you around and drive you toward the mountains of Israel, bringing you from the distant north. ³I will knock the bow from your left hand and the arrows from your right hand, and I will leave you helpless. ⁴You and your army and your allies will all die on the mountains. I will feed you to the vultures and wild animals. ⁵You will fall in the open fields, for I have spoken, says the Sovereign LORD. ⁶And I will rain down fire on Magog and on all your allies who live safely on the coasts. Then they will know that I am the LORD.

⁷"In this way, I will make known my holy name among my people of Israel. I will not let anyone bring shame on it. And the nations, too, will know that I am the LORD, the Holy One of Israel. ⁸That day of judgment will come, says the Sovereign LORD. Everything will happen just as I have declared it.

⁹"Then the people in the towns of Israel

38:14 As in Greek version; Hebrew reads *then you will know.*

38:17-23 God declared his power in no uncertain terms. The greatest military and political powers in the world would array themselves against God and his people. But when God intervened, even the greatest enemies would be destroyed by his powerful hand. We all face powerful enemies, both internal and external, which we are powerless to stop or control. If we turn ourself over to God, however, even the most powerful enemies can be defeated. With God on our side, no enemy is too powerful, no life beyond recovery.

39:1-6 Every creature has the power to choose to either obey God or stand against him. Gog had ranged his mighty forces against God's people; he had left God and his divine will out of his thinking altogether. The destruction of Gog promised by Ezekiel reveals the consequences of choosing to stand against God and his will. As we see these terrible consequences, we should be motivated to admit our own failures and take steps to follow God's will for our life.

will go out and pick up your small and large shields, bows and arrows, javelins and spears, and they will use them for fuel. There will be enough to last them seven years! [10]They won't need to cut wood from the fields or forests, for these weapons will give them all the fuel they need. They will plunder those who planned to plunder them, and they will rob those who planned to rob them, says the Sovereign LORD.

[11]"And I will make a vast graveyard for Gog and his hordes in the Valley of the Travelers, east of the Dead Sea.* It will block the way of those who travel there, and they will change the name of the place to the Valley of Gog's Hordes. [12]It will take seven months for the people of Israel to bury the bodies and cleanse the land. [13]Everyone in Israel will help, for it will be a glorious victory for Israel when I demonstrate my glory on that day, says the Sovereign LORD.

[14]"After seven months, teams of men will be appointed to search the land for skeletons to bury, so the land will be made clean again. [15]Whenever bones are found, a marker will be set up so the burial crews will take them to be buried in the Valley of Gog's Hordes. [16](There will be a town there named Hamonah, which means 'horde.') And so the land will finally be cleansed.

[17]"And now, son of man, this is what the Sovereign LORD says: Call all the birds and wild animals. Say to them: Gather together for my great sacrificial feast. Come from far and near to the mountains of Israel, and there eat flesh and drink blood! [18]Eat the flesh of mighty men and drink the blood of princes as though they were rams, lambs, goats, and bulls—all fattened animals from Bashan! [19]Gorge yourselves with flesh until you are glutted; drink blood until you are drunk. This is the sacrificial feast I have pre-pared for you. [20]Feast at my banquet table—feast on horses and charioteers, on mighty men and all kinds of valiant warriors, says the Sovereign LORD.

[21]"In this way, I will demonstrate my glory to the nations. Everyone will see the punishment I have inflicted on them and the power of my fist when I strike. [22]And from that time on the people of Israel will know that I am the LORD their God. [23]The nations will then know why Israel was sent away to exile—it was punishment for sin, for they were unfaithful to their God. Therefore, I turned away from them and let their enemies destroy them. [24]I turned my face away and punished them because of their defilement and their sins.

Restoration for God's People

[25]"So now, this is what the Sovereign LORD says: I will end the captivity of my people*; I will have mercy on all Israel; I jealously guard my holy reputation! [26]They will accept responsibility for* their past shame and unfaithfulness after they come home to live in peace in their own land, with no one to bother them. [27]When I bring them home from the lands of their enemies, I will display my holiness among them for all the nations to see. [28]Then my people will know that I am the LORD their God, because I sent them away to exile and brought them home again. I will leave none of my people behind. [29]And I will never again turn my face from them, for I will pour out my Spirit upon the people of Israel. I, the Sovereign LORD, have spoken!"

CHAPTER 40
The New Temple Area
On April 28,* during the twenty-fifth year of our captivity—fourteen years after the fall of Jerusalem—the LORD took hold of me. [2]In a vision from God he took me to the land of

---

39:11 Hebrew *the sea.* **39:25** Hebrew *of Jacob.* **39:26** A few Hebrew manuscripts read *They will forget.* **40:1** Hebrew *At the beginning of the year, on the tenth day of the month,* of the ancient Hebrew lunar calendar. This event occurred on April 28, 573 B.C.; also see note on 1:1.

39:25-29 Without God the future of Israel was dark and hopeless. But no matter what their present suffering, they could hope in the future, knowing that God still had great things in store for them. God is a God of recovery and restoration. It is part of his plan for creation that the power of sin be broken and its destruction be reversed. God restored his people so his promise of a Savior—Jesus the Messiah—could be fulfilled. And through this Savior, we can be restored no matter how great our past sins or how terrible our present circumstances.

40:1–48:35 The final chapters of Ezekiel describe a new Temple in a new Jerusalem. Through the restoration of the Temple, we see that proper worship is being restored. In any age, God considers worship one of the most important factors of life. Life itself ought to be an expression of worship. Our hope for future restoration must involve restoring our relationship with God and worshiping him properly. Without a healthy relationship with God, permanent recovery is not possible.

40:1 God spoke to his people through Ezekiel while they were still in exile. God is never limited by where we are or what we have done. Ezekiel discovered that even under the adverse circum-

Israel and set me down on a very high mountain. From there I could see toward the south what appeared to be a city. ³As he brought me nearer, I saw a man whose face shone like bronze standing beside a gateway entrance. He was holding in his hand a linen measuring cord and a measuring rod.

⁴He said to me, "Son of man, watch and listen. Pay close attention to everything I show you. You have been brought here so I can show you many things. Then you will return to the people of Israel and tell them everything you have seen."

The East Gateway

⁵I could see a wall completely surrounding the Temple area. The man took a measuring rod that was 10½ feet* long and measured the wall, and the wall was 10½ feet* thick and 10½ feet high.

⁶Then he went over to the eastern gateway. He climbed the steps and measured the threshold of the gateway; it was 10½ feet front to back.* ⁷There were guard alcoves on each side built into the gateway passage. Each of these alcoves was 10½ feet square, with a distance between them of 8¾ feet* along the passage wall. The gateway's inner threshold, which led to the entry room at the inner end of the gateway passage, was 10½ feet front to back. ⁸He also measured the entry room of the gateway.* ⁹It was 14 feet* across, with supporting columns 3½ feet* thick. This entry room was at the inner end of the gateway structure, facing toward the Temple.

¹⁰There were three guard alcoves on each side of the gateway passage. Each had the same measurements, and the dividing walls separating them were also identical. ¹¹The man measured the gateway entrance, which was 17½ feet* wide at the opening and 22¾ feet* wide in the gateway passage. ¹²In front of each of the guard alcoves was a 21-inch* curb. The alcoves themselves were 10½ feet* on each side.

¹³Then he measured the entire width of the gateway, measuring the distance between the back walls of facing guard alcoves; this distance was 43¾ feet.* ¹⁴He measured the dividing walls all along the inside of the gateway up to the entry room of the gateway; this distance was 105 feet.* ¹⁵The full length of the gateway passage was 87½ feet* from one end to the other. ¹⁶There were recessed windows that narrowed inward through the walls of the guard alcoves and their dividing walls. There were also windows in the entry room. The surfaces of the dividing walls were decorated with carved palm trees.

The Outer Courtyard

¹⁷Then the man brought me through the gateway into the outer courtyard of the Temple. A stone pavement ran along the walls of the courtyard, and thirty rooms were built against the walls, opening onto the pavement. ¹⁸This pavement flanked the gates and extended out from the walls into the courtyard the same distance as the gateway entrance. This was the lower pavement. ¹⁹Then the man measured across the Temple's outer courtyard between the outer and inner gateways; the distance was 175 feet.*

The North Gateway

²⁰The man measured the gateway on the north just like the one on the east. ²¹Here, too, there were three guard alcoves on each side, with dividing walls and an entry room. All the measurements matched those of the east gateway. The gateway passage was 87½ feet long and 43¾ feet wide between the back walls of facing guard alcoves. ²²The windows, the entry room, and the palm tree decorations were identical to those in the east gateway. There were seven steps leading up to the gateway entrance, and the entry room was at the inner end of the gateway passage. ²³Here on the north side, just as on the east, there was

---

40:5a Hebrew *6 long cubits* [3.2 meters], *each being a cubit* [18 inches or 45 centimeters] *and a handbreadth* [3 inches or 8 centimeters] *in length*. 40:5b Hebrew *1 rod* [3.2 meters]; also in 40:5c, 7. 40:6 As in Greek version, which reads *1 rod* [3.2 meters] *deep*; Hebrew reads *1 rod deep, and 1 threshold, 1 rod deep*. 40:7 Hebrew *5 cubits* [2.7 meters]; also in 40:48. 40:8 As in many Hebrew manuscripts and Syriac version; other Hebrew manuscripts add *which faced inward toward the Temple; it was 1 rod* [10.5 feet or 3.2 meters] *deep*. ⁹*Then he measured the entry room of the gateway*. 40:9a Hebrew *8 cubits* [4.2 meters]. 40:9b Hebrew *2 cubits* [1.1 meters]. 40:11a Hebrew *10 cubits* [5.3 meters]. 40:11b Hebrew *13 cubits* [6.9 meters]. 40:12a Hebrew *1 cubit* [53 centimeters]. 40:12b Hebrew *6 cubits* [3.2 meters]. 40:13 Hebrew *25 cubits* [13.3 meters]; also in 40:21, 25, 29, 30, 33, 36. 40:14 Hebrew *60 cubits* [31.8 meters]. Greek version reads *20 cubits* [35 feet or 10.6 meters]. The meaning of the Hebrew in this verse is uncertain. 40:15 Hebrew *50 cubits* [26.5 meters]; also in 40:21, 25, 29, 33, 36. 40:19 Hebrew *100 cubits* [53 meters]; also in 40:23, 27, 47.

---

stances of exile, God was still reaching out to communicate with his people. We may feel that the terrible circumstances we face because of our foolish choices make us ineligible for God's help. We may feel that we have sinned too greatly to be forgiven by God. But, even in times of "exile," God is still reaching out to us. He desires to help us; all we need to do is admit that we need him.

another gateway leading to the Temple's inner courtyard directly opposite this outer gateway. The distance between the two gateways was 175 feet.

The South Gateway

²⁴Then the man took me around to the south gateway and measured its various parts, and they were exactly the same as in the others. ²⁵It had windows along the walls as the others did, and there was an entry room where the gateway passage opened into the outer courtyard. And like the others, the gateway passage was 87½ feet long and 43¾ feet wide between the back walls of facing guard alcoves. ²⁶This gateway also had a stairway of seven steps leading up to it, and an entry room at the inner end, and palm tree decorations along the dividing walls. ²⁷And here again, directly opposite the outer gateway, was another gateway that led into the inner courtyard. The distance between the two gateways was 175 feet.

Gateways to the Inner Courtyard

²⁸Then the man took me to the south gateway leading into the inner courtyard. He measured it, and it had the same measurements as the other gateways. ²⁹Its guard alcoves, dividing walls, and entry room were the same size as those in the others. It also had windows along its walls and in the entry room. And like the others, the gateway passage was 87½ feet long and 43¾ feet wide. ³⁰(The entry rooms of the gateways leading into the inner courtyard were 14 feet* across and 43¾ feet wide.) ³¹The entry room to the south gateway faced into the outer courtyard. It had palm tree decorations on its columns, and there were eight steps leading to its entrance.

³²Then he took me to the east gateway leading to the inner courtyard. He measured it, and it had the same measurements as the other gateways. ³³Its guard alcoves, dividing walls, and entry room were the same size as those of the others, and there were windows along the walls and in the entry room. The gateway passage measured 87½ feet long and 43¾ feet wide. ³⁴Its entry room faced into the outer courtyard. It had palm tree decorations on its columns, and there were eight steps leading to its entrance.

³⁵Then he took me around to the north gateway leading to the inner courtyard. He measured it, and it had the same measurements as the other gateways. ³⁶The guard alcoves, dividing walls, and entry room of this gateway had the same measurements as in the others and the same window arrangements. The gateway passage measured 87½ feet long and 43¾ feet wide. ³⁷Its entry room* faced into the outer courtyard, and it had palm tree decorations on the columns. There were eight steps leading to its entrance.

Rooms for Preparing Sacrifices

³⁸A door led from the entry room of one of the inner gateways into a side room, where the meat for sacrifices was washed. ³⁹On each side of this entry room were two tables, where the sacrificial animals were slaughtered for the burnt offerings, sin offerings, and guilt offerings. ⁴⁰Outside the entry room, on each side of the stairs going up to the north entrance, were two more tables. ⁴¹So there were eight tables in all—four inside and four outside—where the sacrifices were cut up and prepared. ⁴²There were also four tables of finished stone for preparation of the burnt offerings, each 31½ inches square and 21 inches high.* On these tables were placed the butchering knives and other implements for slaughtering the sacrificial animals. ⁴³There were hooks, each 3 inches* long, fastened all around the foyer walls. The sacrificial meat was laid on the tables.

Rooms for the Priests

⁴⁴Inside the inner courtyard were two rooms,* one beside the north gateway, facing south, and the other beside the south* gateway, facing north. ⁴⁵And the man said to me, "The room beside the north inner gate is for the priests who supervise the Temple maintenance. ⁴⁶The room beside the south inner gate is for the priests in charge of the altar— the descendants of Zadok—for they alone of all the Levites may approach the LORD to minister to him."

The Inner Courtyard and Temple

⁴⁷Then the man measured the inner courtyard, and it was a square, 175 feet wide and 175 feet across. The altar stood in the courtyard in front of the Temple. ⁴⁸Then he brought me to the entry room of the Temple. He measured the walls on either side of

40:30 As in 40:9, which reads 8 cubits [14 feet or 4.2 meters]; here the Hebrew reads 5 cubits [8¾ feet or 2.7 meters]. Some Hebrew manuscripts and the Greek version lack this entire verse. 40:37 As in Greek version (compare parallels at 40:26, 31, 34); Hebrew reads Its dividing wall. 40:42 Hebrew 1½ cubits [80 centimeters] long and 1½ cubits wide and 1 cubit [53 centimeters] high. 40:43 Hebrew a handbreadth [8 centimeters]. 40:44a As in Greek version; Hebrew reads rooms for singers. 40:44b As in Greek version; Hebrew reads east.

the opening to the entry room, and they were 8¾ feet thick. The entrance itself was 24½ feet wide, and the walls on each side of the entrance were an additional 5¼ feet long.* [49] The entry room was 35 feet* wide and 21 feet* deep. There were ten steps* leading up to it, with a column on each side.

CHAPTER 41

After that, the man brought me into the sanctuary of the Temple. He measured the walls on either side of its doorway,* and they were 10½ feet* thick. [2] The doorway was 17½ feet* wide, and the walls on each side of it were 8¾ feet* long. The sanctuary itself was 70 feet long and 35 feet wide.*

[3] Then he went beyond the sanctuary into the inner room. He measured the walls on either side of its entrance, and they were 3½ feet* thick. The entrance was 10½ feet wide, and the walls on each side of the entrance were 12¼ feet* long. [4] The inner room of the sanctuary was 35 feet* long and 35 feet wide. "This," he told me, "is the Most Holy Place."

[5] Then he measured the wall of the Temple, and it was 10½ feet thick. There was a row of rooms along the outside wall; each room was 7 feet* wide. [6] These side rooms were built in three levels, one above the other, with thirty rooms on each level. The supports for these side rooms rested on exterior ledges on the Temple wall; they did not extend into the wall. [7] Each level was wider than the one below it, corresponding to the narrowing of the Temple wall as it rose higher. A stairway led up from the bottom level through the middle level to the top level.

[8] I saw that the Temple was built on a terrace, which provided a foundation for the side rooms. This terrace was 10½ feet* high. [9] The outer wall of the Temple's side rooms was 8¾ feet thick. This left an open area between these side rooms [10] and the row of rooms along the outer wall of the inner courtyard. This open area was 35 feet wide, and it went all the way around the Temple. [11] Two doors opened from the side rooms into the terrace yard, which was 8¾ feet wide. One door faced north and the other south.

[12] A large building stood on the west, facing the Temple courtyard. It was 122½ feet wide and 157½ feet long, and its walls were 8¾ feet* thick. [13] Then the man measured the Temple, and it was 175 feet* long. The courtyard around the building, including its walls, was an additional 175 feet in length. [14] The inner courtyard to the east of the Temple was also 175 feet wide. [15] The building to the west, including its two walls, was also 175 feet wide.

The sanctuary, the inner room, and the entry room of the Temple [16] were all paneled with wood, as were the frames of the recessed windows. The inner walls of the Temple were paneled with wood above and below the windows. [17] The space above the door leading into the inner room, and its walls inside and out, were also paneled. [18] All the walls were decorated with carvings of cherubim, each with two faces, and there was a carving of a palm tree between each of the cherubim. [19] One face—that of a man—looked toward the palm tree on one side. The other face—that of a young lion—looked toward the palm tree on the other side. The figures were carved all along the inside of the Temple, [20] from the floor to the top of the walls, including the outer wall of the sanctuary.

[21] There were square columns at the entrance to the sanctuary, and the ones at the entrance of the Most Holy Place were similar. [22] There was an altar made of wood, 5¼ feet high and 3½ feet across.* Its corners, base, and sides were all made of wood. "This," the man told me, "is the table that stands in the LORD's presence."

[23] Both the sanctuary and the Most Holy Place had double doorways, [24] each with two swinging doors. [25] The doors leading into the sanctuary were decorated with carved cherubim and palm trees, just as on the walls. And there was a wooden roof at the front of the entry room to the Temple. [26] On both sides of the entry room were recessed windows decorated with carved palm trees. The side rooms along the outside wall also had roofs.

40:48 As in Greek version, which reads *The entrance was 14 cubits* [7.4 meters] *wide, and the walls of the entrance were 3 cubits* [1.6 meters] *on each side;* Hebrew lacks *14 cubits wide, and the walls of the entrance were.* **40:49a** Hebrew *20 cubits* [10.6 meters]. **40:49b** As in Greek version, which reads *12 cubits* [21 feet or 6.4 meters]; Hebrew reads *11 cubits* [19¼ feet or 5.8 meters]. **40:49c** As in Greek version; Hebrew reads *There were steps that were.* **41:1a** As in Greek version; the meaning of the Hebrew is uncertain. **41:1b** Hebrew *6 cubits* [3.2 meters]; also in 41:3, 5. **41:2a** Hebrew *10 cubits* [5.3 meters]. **41:2b** Hebrew *5 cubits* [2.7 meters]; also in 41:9, 11. **41:2c** Hebrew *40 cubits* [21.2 meters] *long and 20 cubits* [10.6 meters] *wide.* **41:3a** Hebrew *5 cubits* [1.1 meters]. **41:3b** Hebrew *7 cubits* [3.7 meters]. **41:4** Hebrew *20 cubits* [10.6 meters]; also in 41:4b, 10. **41:5** Hebrew *4 cubits* [2.1 meters]. **41:8** Hebrew *1 rod, 6 cubits* [3.2 meters]. **41:12** Hebrew *70 cubits* [37.1 meters] *wide and 90 cubits* [47.7 meters] *long, and its walls were 5 cubits* [2.7 meters] *thick.* **41:13** Hebrew *100 cubits* [53 meters]; also in 41:13b, 14, 15. **41:22** Hebrew *3 cubits* [1.6 meters] *high and 2 cubits* [1.1 meters] *across.*

CHAPTER 42

Rooms for the Priests

Then the man led me out of the Temple courtyard by way of the north gateway. We entered the outer courtyard and came to a group of rooms against the north wall of the inner courtyard. ²This structure, whose entrance opened toward the north, was 175 feet* long and 87½ feet* wide. ³One block of rooms overlooked the 35-foot* width of the inner courtyard. Another block of rooms looked out onto the pavement of the outer courtyard. The two blocks were built three levels high and stood across from each other. ⁴Between the two blocks of rooms ran a walkway 17½ feet* wide. It extended the entire 175 feet of the complex,* and all the doors faced north. ⁵Each of the two upper levels of rooms was narrower than the one beneath it because the upper levels had to allow space for walkways in front of them. ⁶Since there were three levels and they did not have supporting columns as in the courtyards, each of the upper levels was set back from the level beneath it. ⁷There was an outer wall that separated the rooms from the outer courtyard; it was 87½ feet long. ⁸This wall added length to the outer block of rooms, which extended for only 87½ feet, while the inner block—the rooms toward the Temple—extended for 175 feet. ⁹There was an eastern entrance from the outer courtyard to these rooms.

¹⁰On the south* side of the Temple there were two blocks of rooms just south of the inner courtyard between the Temple and the outer courtyard. These rooms were arranged just like the rooms on the north. ¹¹There was a walkway between the two blocks of rooms just like the complex on the north side of the Temple. This complex of rooms was the same length and width as the other one, and it had the same entrances and doors. The dimensions of each were identical. ¹²So there was an entrance in the wall facing the doors of the inner block of rooms, and another on the east at the end of the interior walkway.

¹³Then the man told me, "These rooms that overlook the Temple from the north and south are holy. Here the priests who offer sacrifices to the LORD will eat the most holy offerings. And because these rooms are holy, they will be used to store the sacred offerings—the grain offerings, sin offerings, and guilt offerings. ¹⁴When the priests leave the sanctuary, they must not go directly to the outer courtyard. They must first take off the clothes they wore while ministering, because these clothes are holy. They must put on other clothes before entering the parts of the building complex open to the public."

¹⁵When the man had finished measuring the inside of the Temple area, he led me out through the east gateway to measure the entire perimeter. ¹⁶He measured the east side with his measuring rod, and it was 875 feet long.* ¹⁷Then he measured the north side, and it was also 875 feet. ¹⁸The south side was also 875 feet, ¹⁹and the west side was also 875 feet. ²⁰So the area was 875 feet on each side with a wall all around it to separate what was holy from what was common.

CHAPTER 43

The LORD's Glory Returns

After this, the man brought me back around to the east gateway. ²Suddenly, the glory of the God of Israel appeared from the east. The sound of his coming was like the roar of rushing waters, and the whole landscape shone with his glory. ³This vision was just like the others I had seen, first by the Kebar River and then when he came* to destroy Jerusalem. I fell face down on the ground. ⁴And the glory of the LORD came into the Temple through the east gateway.

⁵Then the Spirit took me up and brought me into the inner courtyard, and the glory of

42:2a Hebrew *100 cubits* [53 meters]; also in 42:8.   42:2b Hebrew *50 cubits* [26.5 meters]; also in 42:7, 8.
42:3 Hebrew *20[-cubit]* [10.6-meter].   42:4a Hebrew *10 cubits* [5.3 meters].   42:4b As in Greek and Syriac versions, which read *Its length was 100 cubits* [53 meters]; Hebrew reads *and a passage 1 cubit* [21 inches or 53 centimeters] *wide.*   42:10 As in Greek version; Hebrew reads *east.*   42:16 As in 45:2 and in Greek version at 42:17, which reads *500 cubits* [265 meters]; Hebrew reads *500 rods* [5,250 feet or 1,590 meters]; similarly in 42:17, 18, 19, 20.   43:3 As in some Hebrew manuscripts and Latin Vulgate; Masoretic Text reads *I came.*

43:1-5 Ezekiel had seen the glory of God leave the Jerusalem Temple early in his prophetic career (8–11). Here he had the joy of seeing it return. As a descendant of priests, Ezekiel must have been greatly encouraged by this vision. It signaled God's renewed presence among his people and hope for their restoration. God did restore his people and then came to live among them in the person of his Son, Jesus the Messiah. Through a relationship with him today, we are assured of God's presence with us as we undergo the process of recovery. God promises us his transforming presence through his Spirit, giving us hope and courage as we face the painful process of confession and change necessary for a full recovery.

the LORD filled the Temple. [6]And I heard someone speaking to me from within the Temple, while the man who had been measuring stood beside me. [7]The LORD said to me, "Son of man, this is the place of my throne and the place where I will rest my feet. I will live here forever among the people of Israel. They and their kings will not defile my holy name any longer by their adulterous worship of other gods or by honoring the relics of their kings who have died.* [8]They put their idol altars right next to mine with only a wall between them and me. They defiled my holy name by such detestable sin, so I consumed them in my anger. [9]Now let them stop worshiping other gods and honoring the relics of their kings, and I will live among them forever.

[10]"Son of man, describe to the people of Israel the Temple I have shown you, so they will be ashamed of all their sins. Let them study its plan, [11]and they will be ashamed* of what they have done. Describe to them all the specifications of the Temple—including its entrances and exits—and everything else about it. Tell them about its decrees and laws. Write down all these specifications and decrees as they watch so they will be sure to remember and follow them. [12]And this is the basic law of the Temple: absolute holiness! The entire top of the mountain where the Temple is built is holy. Yes, this is the basic law of the Temple.

The Altar

[13]"These are the measurements of the altar*: There is a gutter all around the altar 21 inches deep and 21 inches wide,* with a curb 9 inches* wide around its edge. And this is the height* of the altar: [14]From the gutter the altar rises 3½ feet* to a lower ledge that surrounds the altar and is 21 inches* wide. From the lower ledge the altar rises 7 feet* to the upper ledge that is also 21 inches wide. [15]The top of the altar, the hearth, rises another 7 feet higher, with a horn rising up from each of the four corners. [16]The top of the altar is square, measuring 21 feet by 21 feet.* [17]The upper ledge also forms a square, measuring 24½ feet by 24½ feet,* with a 21-inch gutter and a 10½-inch curb* all around the edge. There are steps going up the east side of the altar."

[18]Then he said to me, "Son of man, this is what the Sovereign LORD says: These will be the regulations for the burning of offerings and the sprinkling of blood when the altar is built. [19]At that time, the Levitical priests of the family of Zadok, who minister before me, are to be given a young bull for a sin offering, says the Sovereign LORD. [20]You will take some of its blood and smear it on the four horns of the altar, the four corners of the upper ledge, and the curb that runs around that ledge. This will cleanse and make atonement for the altar. [21]Then take the young bull for the sin offering and burn it at the appointed place outside the Temple area.

[22]"On the second day, sacrifice as a sin offering a young male goat that has no physical defects. Then cleanse and make atonement for the altar again, just as you did with the young bull. [23]When you have finished the cleansing ceremony, offer another young bull that has no defects and a perfect ram from the flock. [24]You are to present them to the LORD, and the priests are to sprinkle salt on them and offer them as a burnt offering to the LORD.

[25]"Every day for seven days a male goat, a young bull, and a ram from the flock will be sacrificed as a sin offering. None of these animals may have physical defects of any kind. [26]Do this each day for seven days to cleanse and make atonement for the altar, thus setting it apart for holy use. [27]On the eighth day, and on each day afterward, the priests will sacrifice on the altar the burnt offerings and peace offerings of the people. Then I will accept you. I, the Sovereign LORD, have spoken!"

CHAPTER 44
The Prince, Levites, and Priests

Then the man brought me back to the east gateway in the outer wall of the Temple area, but it was closed. [2]And the LORD said to me, "This gate must remain closed; it will never again be opened. No one will ever open it and pass through, for the LORD, the God of Israel, has entered here. Therefore, it must always remain shut. [3]Only the prince himself may sit inside this gateway to feast in the LORD's presence. But he may come and go only through the entry room of the gateway."

43:7 Or *kings on their high places.* **43:11** As in Greek version; Hebrew reads *if they are ashamed.* **43:13a** Hebrew *measurements of the altar in long cubits, each being a cubit* [18 inches or 45 centimeters] *and a handbreadth* [3 inches or 8 centimeters] *in length.* **43:13b** Hebrew *a cubit* [53 centimeters] *deep and a cubit wide.* **43:13c** Hebrew *1 span* [23 centimeters]. **43:13d** As in Greek version; Hebrew reads *base.* **43:14a** Hebrew *2 cubits* [1.1 meters]. **43:14b** Hebrew *1 cubit* [53 centimeters]; also in 43:14d. **43:14c** Hebrew *4 cubits* [2.1 meters]; also in 43:15. **43:16** Hebrew *12* [cubits] [6.4 meters] *long and 12* [cubits] *wide.* **43:17a** Hebrew *14* [cubits] [7.4 meters] *long and 14* [cubits] *wide.* **43:17b** Hebrew *a gutter of 1 cubit* [53 centimeters] *and a curb of ½ a cubit* [27 centimeters].

⁴Then the man brought me through the north gateway to the front of the Temple. I looked and saw that the glory of the LORD filled the Temple of the LORD, and I fell face down on the ground.

⁵And the LORD said to me, "Son of man, take careful notice. Use your eyes and ears, and listen to everything I tell you about the regulations concerning the LORD's Temple. Take careful note of the procedures for using the Temple's entrances and exits. ⁶And give these rebels, the people of Israel, this message from the Sovereign LORD: O people of Israel, enough of your detestable sins! ⁷You have brought uncircumcised foreigners into my sanctuary—people who have no heart for God. In this way, you defiled my Temple even as you offered me my food, the fat and blood of sacrifices. In addition to all your other detestable sins, you have broken my covenant. ⁸Instead of safeguarding my sacred rituals, you have hired foreigners to take charge of my sanctuary.

⁹"So this is what the Sovereign LORD says: No foreigners, including those who live among the people of Israel, will enter my sanctuary if they have not been circumcised and have not surrendered themselves to the LORD. ¹⁰And the men of the tribe of Levi who abandoned me when Israel strayed away from me to worship idols* must bear the consequences of their unfaithfulness. ¹¹They may still be Temple guards and gatekeepers, and they may slaughter the animals brought for burnt offerings and be present to help the people. ¹²But they encouraged my people to worship idols, causing Israel to fall into deep sin. So I have taken a solemn oath that they must bear the consequences for their sins, says the Sovereign LORD. ¹³They may not approach me to minister as priests. They may not touch any of my holy things or the holy offerings, for they must bear the shame of all the detestable sins they have committed. ¹⁴They are to serve as the Temple caretakers, taking charge of the maintenance work and performing general duties.

¹⁵"However, the Levitical priests of the family of Zadok continued to minister faithfully in the Temple when Israel abandoned me for idols. These men will serve as my ministers. They will stand in my presence and offer the fat and blood of the sacrifices, says the Sovereign LORD. ¹⁶They alone will enter my sanctuary and approach my table to serve me. They will fulfill all my requirements.

¹⁷"When they enter the gateway to the inner courtyard, they must wear only linen clothing. They must wear no wool while on duty in the inner courtyard or in the Temple itself. ¹⁸They must wear linen turbans and linen undergarments. They must not wear anything that would cause them to perspire. ¹⁹When they return to the outer courtyard where the people are, they must take off the clothes they wear while ministering to me. They must leave them in the sacred rooms and put on other clothes so they do not endanger anyone by transmitting holiness to them through this clothing.

²⁰"They must neither shave their heads nor let their hair grow too long. Instead, they must trim it regularly. ²¹The priests must not drink wine before entering the inner courtyard. ²²They may choose their wives only from among the virgins of Israel or the widows of the priests. They may not marry other widows or divorced women. ²³They will teach my people the difference between what is holy and what is common, what is ceremonially clean and unclean.

²⁴"They will serve as judges to resolve any disagreements among my people. Their decisions must be based on my regulations. And the priests themselves must obey my instructions and decrees at all the sacred festivals, and see to it that the Sabbaths are set apart as holy days.

²⁵"A priest must not defile himself by being in the presence of a dead person unless it is his father, mother, child, brother, or unmarried sister. In such cases it is permitted. ²⁶Even then, he can return to his Temple duties only after being ceremonially cleansed and then waiting for seven days. ²⁷The first day he returns to work and enters the inner courtyard and the sanctuary, he must offer a sin offering for himself, says the Sovereign LORD.

44:10 The Hebrew term (literally *round things*) probably alludes to dung; also in 44:12.

44:6-7 Refusing to obey God's will always has painful consequences. God had clearly revealed his will for his people, but they had ignored the guidelines God had graciously provided. They rebelled against the plan God had laid out for them. God has clearly revealed his will for us in the Bible. It is our responsibility to follow it. Since there are consequences for failing to obey God's will, we would be wise to diligently seek God's will for our life and obey him completely. If we take these steps, God will help us.

[28]"The priests will not have any property or possession of land, for I alone am their special possession. [29]Their food will come from the gifts and sacrifices brought to the Temple by the people—the grain offerings, the sin offerings, and the guilt offerings. Whatever anyone sets apart* for the LORD will belong to the priests. [30]The first of the ripe fruits and all the gifts brought to the LORD will go to the priests. The first batch of dough must also be given to the priests so the LORD will bless your homes. [31]The priests may not eat meat from any bird or animal that dies a natural death or that dies after being attacked by another animal.

CHAPTER 45
Division of the Land

"When you divide the land among the tribes of Israel, you must set aside a section for the LORD as his holy portion. This piece of land will be 8¹/₃ miles long and 6²/₃ miles wide.* The entire area will be holy. [2]A section of this land, measuring 875 feet by 875 feet,* will be set aside for the Temple. An additional strip of land 87¹/₂ feet* wide is to be left empty all around it. [3]Within the larger sacred area, measure out a portion of land 8¹/₃ miles long and 3¹/₃ miles wide.* Within it the sanctuary of the Most Holy Place will be located. [4]This area will be holy, set aside for the priests who minister to the LORD in the sanctuary. They will use it for their homes, and my Temple will be located within it. [5]The strip of sacred land next to it, also 8¹/₃ miles long and 3¹/₃ miles wide, will be a living area for the Levites who work at the Temple. It will be their possession and a place for their towns.*

[6]"Adjacent to the larger sacred area will be a section of land 8¹/₃ miles long and 1²/₃ miles wide.* This will be set aside for a city where anyone in Israel can live.

[7]"Two special sections of land will be set apart for the prince. One section will share a border with the east side of the sacred lands and city, and the second section will share a border on the west side. Then the far eastern and western borders of the prince's lands will line up with the eastern and western boundaries of the tribal areas. [8]These sections of land will be the prince's allotment. Then my princes will no longer oppress and rob my people; they will assign the rest of the land to the people, giving an allotment to each tribe.

Rules for the Princes

[9]"For this is what the Sovereign LORD says: Enough, you princes of Israel! Stop your violence and oppression and do what is just and right. Quit robbing and cheating my people out of their land. Stop expelling them from their homes, says the Sovereign LORD. [10]Use only honest weights and scales and honest measures, both dry and liquid.* [11]The homer* will be your standard unit for measuring volume. The ephah and the bath* will each measure one-tenth of a homer. [12]The standard unit for weight will be the silver shekel.* One shekel will consist of twenty gerahs, and sixty shekels will be equal to one mina.*

Special Offerings and Celebrations

[13]"You must give this tax to the prince: one bushel of wheat or barley for every 60* you harvest, [14]one percent of your olive oil,* [15]and one sheep or goat for every 200 in your flocks in Israel. These will be the grain offerings, burnt offerings, and peace offerings that will make atonement for the people who bring them, says the Sovereign LORD. [16]All the people of Israel must join in bringing these offerings to the prince. [17]The prince will be required to provide offerings that are given at the religious festivals, the new moon celebrations, the Sabbath days, and all other similar occasions. He will provide the sin offerings, burnt offerings, grain offerings, liquid offerings, and peace offerings to purify the people of Israel, making them right with the LORD.*

[18]"This is what the Sovereign LORD says: In

44:29 The Hebrew term used here refers to the complete consecration of things or people to the LORD, either by destroying them or by giving them as an offering. 45:1 As in Greek version, which reads 25,000 [cubits] [13.3 kilometers] long and 20,000 [cubits] [10.6 kilometers] wide; Hebrew reads 25,000 [cubits] long and 10,000 [cubits] [3¹/₃ miles or 5.3 kilometers] wide. Compare 45:3, 5; 48:9. 45:2a Hebrew 500 [cubits] [265 meters] by 500 [cubits], a square. 45:2b Hebrew 50 cubits [26.5 meters]. 45:3 Hebrew 25,000 [cubits] [13.3 kilometers] long and 10,000 [cubits] [5.3 kilometers] wide; also in 45:5. 45:5 As in Greek version; Hebrew reads They will have as their possession 20 rooms. 45:6 Hebrew 25,000 [cubits] [13.3 kilometers] long and 5,000 [cubits] [2.65 kilometers] wide. 45:10 Hebrew Use honest scales, an honest ephah, and an honest bath. 45:11a The homer measures about 50 gallons or 220 liters. 45:11b The ephah is a dry measure; the bath is a liquid measure. 45:12a The shekel weighs about 0.4 ounces or 11 grams. 45:12b Elsewhere the mina is equated to 50 shekels. 45:13 Hebrew ¹/₆ of an ephah from each homer of wheat and ¹/₆ of an ephah from each homer of barley. 45:14 Hebrew the portion of oil, measured by the bath, is ¹/₁₀ of a bath from each cor, which consists of 10 baths or 1 homer, for 10 baths are equivalent to a homer. 45:17 Or to make atonement for the people of Israel.

early spring, on the first day of each new year,* sacrifice a young bull with no defects to purify the Temple. ¹⁹The priest will take blood from this sin offering and put it on the doorposts of the Temple, the four corners of the upper ledge of the altar, and the gateposts at the entrance to the inner courtyard. ²⁰Do this also on the seventh day of the new year for anyone who has sinned through error or ignorance. In this way, you will purify* the Temple.

²¹"On the fourteenth day of the first month,* you must celebrate the Passover. This festival will last for seven days. The bread you eat during that time must be made without yeast. ²²On the day of Passover the prince will provide a young bull as a sin offering for himself and the people of Israel. ²³On each of the seven days of the feast he will prepare a burnt offering to the LORD, consisting of seven young bulls and seven rams without defects. A male goat will also be given each day for a sin offering. ²⁴The prince will provide a basket of flour as a grain offering and a gallon of olive oil* with each young bull and ram.

²⁵"During the seven days of the Festival of Shelters, which occurs every year in early autumn,* the prince will provide these same sacrifices for the sin offering, the burnt offering, and the grain offering, along with the required olive oil."

CHAPTER 46

"This is what the Sovereign LORD says: The east gateway of the inner courtyard will be closed during the six workdays each week, but it will be open on Sabbath days and the days of new moon celebrations. ²The prince will enter the entry room of the gateway from the outside. Then he will stand by the gatepost while the priest offers his burnt offering and peace offering. He will bow down in worship inside the gateway passage and then go back out the way he came. The gateway will not be closed until evening. ³The common people will bow down and worship the LORD in front of this gateway on Sabbath days and the days of new moon celebrations.

⁴"Each Sabbath day the prince will present to the LORD a burnt offering of six lambs and one ram, all with no defects. ⁵He will present a grain offering of a basket of choice flour to go with the ram and whatever amount of flour he chooses to go with each lamb, and he is to offer one gallon of olive oil* for each basket of flour. ⁶At the new moon celebrations, he will bring one young bull, six lambs, and one ram, all with no defects. ⁷With the young bull he must bring a basket of choice flour for a grain offering. With the ram he must bring another basket of flour. And with each lamb he is to bring whatever amount of flour he chooses to give. With each basket of flour he must offer one gallon of olive oil.

⁸"The prince must enter the gateway through the entry room, and he must leave the same way. ⁹But when the people come in through the north gateway to worship the LORD during the religious festivals, they must leave by the south gateway. And those who entered through the south gateway must leave by the north gateway. They must never leave by the same gateway they came in, but must always use the opposite gateway. ¹⁰The prince will enter and leave with the people on these occasions.

¹¹"So at the special feasts and sacred festivals, the grain offering will be a basket of choice flour with each young bull, another basket of flour with each ram, and as much flour as the worshiper chooses to give with each lamb. Give one gallon of olive oil with each basket of flour. ¹²When the prince offers a voluntary burnt offering or peace offering

---

45:18 Hebrew *On the first day of the first month,* of the Hebrew calendar. This day in the ancient Hebrew lunar calendar occurred in March or April. **45:20** Or *will make atonement for.* **45:21** This day in the ancient Hebrew lunar calendar occurred in late March, April, or early May. **45:24** Hebrew *an ephah* [20 quarts or 22 liters] *of flour . . . and a hin* [3.8 liters] *of olive oil.* **45:25** Hebrew *the festival which begins on the fifteenth day of the seventh month* (see Lev 23:34). This day in the ancient Hebrew lunar calendar occurred in late September, October, or early November. **46:5** Hebrew *an ephah* [20 quarts or 22 liters] *of choice flour . . . a hin* [3.8 liters] *of olive oil;* similarly in 46:7, 11.

46:1-24 God gave the Israelites regulations relating to the giving of sacrifices. Sacrifices were a means of paying for the people's sins and reestablishing their relationship with God. Slaughtering animals may seem barbaric, and we may wonder why God instructed it. If we react negatively to this practice, however, it is easy for us to miss the point: God provided a way to pay for his people's sins without bringing their complete destruction. God didn't expect them to be perfect; he expected them to confess their sins and ask him for forgiveness. God expects the same from us. God has provided the ultimate sacrifice, Jesus Christ, to pay for our sins. He has provided a means for recovery if we accept this wonderful gift.

to the LORD, the east gateway to the inner courtyard will be opened for him, and he will offer his sacrifices as he does on Sabbath days. Then he will leave, and the gateway will be shut behind him.

¹³"Each morning you must sacrifice a one-year-old lamb with no defects as a burnt offering to the LORD. ¹⁴With the lamb, a grain offering must also be given to the LORD— about three quarts of flour with a third of a gallon of olive oil* to moisten the choice flour. This will be a permanent law for you. ¹⁵The lamb, the grain offering, and the olive oil must be given as a daily sacrifice every morning without fail.

¹⁶"This is what the Sovereign LORD says: If the prince gives a gift of land to one of his sons as his inheritance, it will belong to him and his descendants forever. ¹⁷But if the prince gives a gift of land from his inheritance to one of his servants, the servant may keep it only until the Year of Jubilee, which comes every fiftieth year.* At that time the land will return to the prince. But when the prince gives gifts to his sons, those gifts will be permanent. ¹⁸And the prince may never take anyone's property by force. If he gives property to his sons, it must be from his own land, for I do not want any of my people unjustly evicted from their property."

The Temple Kitchens

¹⁹In my vision, the man brought me through the entrance beside the gateway and led me to the sacred rooms assigned to the priests, which faced toward the north. He showed me a place at the extreme west end of these rooms. ²⁰He explained, "This is where the priests will cook the meat from the guilt offerings and sin offerings and bake the flour from the grain offerings into bread. They will do it here to avoid carrying the sacrifices through the outer courtyard and endangering the people by transmitting holiness to them."

²¹Then he brought me back to the outer courtyard and led me to each of its four corners. In each corner I saw an enclosure. ²²Each of these enclosures was 70 feet long and 52½ feet wide,* surrounded by walls. ²³Along the inside of these walls was a ledge of stone with fireplaces under the ledge all the way around. ²⁴The man said to me, "These are the kitchens to be used by the Temple assistants to boil the sacrifices offered by the people."

CHAPTER 47
The River of Healing

In my vision, the man brought me back to the entrance of the Temple. There I saw a stream flowing east from beneath the door of the Temple and passing to the right of the altar on its south side. ²The man brought me outside the wall through the north gateway and led me around to the eastern entrance. There I could see the water flowing out through the south side of the east gateway.

³Measuring as he went, he took me along the stream for 1,750 feet* and then led me across. The water was up to my ankles. ⁴He measured off another 1,750 feet and led me across again. This time the water was up to my knees. After another 1,750 feet, it was up to my waist. ⁵Then he measured another 1,750 feet, and the river was too deep to walk across. It was deep enough to swim in, but too deep to walk through.

⁶He asked me, "Have you been watching, son of man?" Then he led me back along the riverbank. ⁷When I returned, I was surprised by the sight of many trees growing on both sides of the river. ⁸Then he said to me, "This river flows east through the desert into the valley of the Dead Sea.* The waters of this stream will make the salty waters of the Dead Sea fresh and pure. ⁹There will be swarms of living things wherever the water of this river flows.* Fish will abound in the Dead Sea, for its waters will become fresh. Life will flourish wherever this water flows. ¹⁰Fishermen will stand along the shores of the Dead Sea. All the way from En-gedi to En-eglaim, the shores will be covered with nets drying in the sun.

46:14 Hebrew *1/6 of an ephah* [3.7 liters] *of flour with* *1/3 of a hin* [1.3 liters] *of olive oil.* **46:17** Hebrew *until the Year of Release;* see Lev 25:8-17. **46:22** Hebrew *40 [cubits]* [21.2 meters] *long and 30 [cubits]* [15.9 meters] *wide.* **47:3** Hebrew *1,000 cubits* [530 meters]; also in 47:4, 5. **47:8** Hebrew *the sea.* **47:9** As in Greek and Syriac versions; Hebrew reads *of these two rivers flow.*

47:1-12 This river of healing will flow throughout the land, giving the arid landscape vitality and life. The land was destroyed by the foolish choices of God's people, but God will restore what man has destroyed. This is our hope in the coming of Jesus the Messiah. During his first coming, Jesus made personal restoration possible for everyone through the power of his miraculous resurrection. We now look forward to his second coming, when God will restore the earth. Sin has devastated God's perfect plan for the world, but in the end, God's plan of earthly peace and prosperity will come to pass. God will restore us and our world. We can take part in God's program for recovery today by seeking his will and doing everything possible to follow it.

Fish of every kind will fill the Dead Sea, just as they fill the Mediterranean.* ¹¹But the marshes and swamps will not be purified; they will still be salty. ¹²Fruit trees of all kinds will grow along both sides of the river. The leaves of these trees will never turn brown and fall, and there will always be fruit on their branches. There will be a new crop every month, for they are watered by the river flowing from the Temple. The fruit will be for food and the leaves for healing."

Boundaries for the Land

¹³This is what the Sovereign LORD says: "Divide the land in this way for the twelve tribes of Israel: The descendants of Joseph will be given two shares of land.* ¹⁴Otherwise each tribe will receive an equal share. I took a solemn oath and swore that I would give this land to your ancestors, and it will now come to you as your possession.

¹⁵"These are the boundaries of the land: The northern border will run from the Mediterranean toward Hethlon, then on through Lebo-hamath to Zedad; ¹⁶then it will run to Berothah and Sibraim,* which are on the border between Damascus and Hamath, and finally to Hazer-hatticon, on the border of Hauran. ¹⁷So the northern border will run from the Mediterranean to Hazar-enan, on the border between Hamath to the north and Damascus to the south.

¹⁸"The eastern border starts at a point between Hauran and Damascus and runs south along the Jordan River between Israel and Gilead, past the Dead Sea* and as far south as Tamar.* This will be the eastern border.

¹⁹"The southern border will go west from Tamar to the waters of Meribah at Kadesh* and then follow the course of the Brook of Egypt to the Mediterranean. This will be the southern border.

²⁰"On the west side, the Mediterranean itself will be your border from the southern border to the point where the northern border begins, opposite Lebo-hamath.

²¹"Divide the land within these boundaries among the tribes of Israel. ²²Distribute the land as an allotment for yourselves and for the foreigners who have joined you and are raising their families among you. They will be like native-born Israelites to you and will receive an allotment among the tribes. ²³These foreigners are to be given land within the territory of the tribe with whom they now live. I, the Sovereign LORD, have spoken!

CHAPTER 48
Division of the Land

"Here is the list of the tribes of Israel and the territory each is to receive. The territory of Dan is in the extreme north. Its boundary line follows the Hethlon road to Lebo-hamath and then runs on to Hazar-enan on the border of Damascus, with Hamath to the north. Dan's territory extends all the way across the land of Israel from east to west.

²"Asher's territory lies south of Dan's and also extends from east to west. ³Naphtali's land lies south of Asher's, also extending from east to west. ⁴Then comes Manasseh south of Naphtali, and its territory also extends from east to west. ⁵South of Manasseh is Ephraim, ⁶and then Reuben, ⁷and then Judah, all of whose boundaries extend from east to west.

⁸"South of Judah is the land set aside for a special purpose. It will be 8¹/₃ miles* wide and will extend as far east and west as the tribal territories, with the Temple at the center.

⁹"The area set aside for the LORD's Temple will be 8¹/₃ miles long and 6²/₃ miles wide.* ¹⁰For the priests there will be a strip of land measuring 8¹/₃ miles long by 3¹/₃ miles wide,* with the LORD's Temple at the center. ¹¹This area is set aside for the ordained priests, the descendants of Zadok who served me faithfully and did not go astray with the people of Israel and the rest of the Levites. ¹²It will be their special portion when the land is distributed, the most sacred land of all. Next to the priests' territory will lie the land where the other Levites will live.

¹³"The land allotted to the Levites will be the same size and shape as that belonging to the priests—8¹/₃ miles long and 3¹/₃ miles wide. Together these portions of land will measure 8¹/₃ miles long by 6²/₃ miles wide.* ¹⁴None of this special land may ever be sold

47:10 Hebrew *the great sea;* also in 47:15, 17, 19, 20. **47:13** It was important to retain twelve portions of land. Since Levi had no portion, the descendants of Joseph's sons, Ephraim and Manasseh, received land as two tribes. **47:15-16** As in Greek version; Masoretic Text reads *then on through Lebo to Zedad;* ¹⁶*then it will run to Hamath, Berothah, and Sibraim.* **47:18a** Hebrew *the eastern sea.* **47:18b** As in Greek version; Hebrew reads *you will measure.* **47:19** Hebrew *waters of Meribath-kadesh.* **48:8** Hebrew *25,000 [cubits]* [13.3 kilometers]. **48:9** As in one Greek manuscript and the Greek reading in 45:1: *25,000 [cubits]* [13.3 kilometers] *long and 20,000 [cubits]* [10.6 kilometers] *wide;* Hebrew reads *25,000 [cubits] long and 10,000 [cubits]* [3¹/₂ miles or 5.3 kilometers] *wide.* Similarly in 48:13b. Compare 45:1-5; 48:10-13. **48:10** Hebrew *25,000 [cubits]* [13.3 kilometers] *long by 10,000 [cubits]* [5.3 kilometers] *wide;* also in 48:13a. **48:13** See note on 48:9.

or traded or used by others, for it belongs to the LORD; it is set apart as holy.

15"An additional strip of land 8¹/₃ miles long by 1²/₃ miles wide,* south of the sacred Temple area, will be allotted for public use—homes, pasturelands, and common lands, with a city at the center. 16The city will measure 1¹/₂ miles* on each side—north, south, east, and west. 17Open lands will surround the city for 150 yards* in every direction. 18Outside the city there will be a farming area that stretches 3¹/₃ miles to the east and 3¹/₃ miles to the west* along the border of the sacred area. This farmland will produce food for the people working in the city. 19Those who come from the various tribes to work in the city may farm it. 20This entire area—including the sacred lands and the city—is a square that measures 8¹/₃ miles* on each side.

21"The areas that remain, to the east and to the west of the sacred lands and the city, will belong to the prince. Each of these areas will be 8¹/₃ miles wide, extending in opposite directions to the eastern and western borders of Israel, with the sacred lands and the sanctuary of the Temple in the center. 22So the prince's land will include everything between the territories allotted to Judah and Benjamin, except for the areas set aside for the sacred lands and the city.

23"These are the territories allotted to the rest of the tribes. Benjamin's territory lies just south of the prince's lands, and it extends across the entire land of Israel from east to west. 24South of Benjamin's territory lies that of Simeon, also extending across the land from east to west. 25Next is the territory of Issachar with the same eastern and western boundaries.

26"Then comes the territory of Zebulun, which also extends across the land from east to west. 27The territory of Gad is just south of Zebulun with the same borders to the east and west. 28The southern border of Gad runs from Tamar to the waters of Meribah at Kadesh* and then follows the Brook of Egypt to the Mediterranean.*

29"These are the allotments that will be set aside for each tribe's exclusive possession. I, the Sovereign LORD, have spoken!

The Gates of the City

30"These will be the exits to the city: On the north wall, which is 1¹/₂ miles long, 31there will be three gates, each one named after a tribe of Israel. The first will be named for Reuben, the second for Judah, and the third for Levi. 32On the east wall, also 1¹/₂ miles long, the gates will be named for Joseph, Benjamin, and Dan. 33The south wall, also 1¹/₂ miles long, will have gates named for Simeon, Issachar, and Zebulun. 34And on the west wall, also 1¹/₂ miles long, the gates will be named for Gad, Asher, and Naphtali.

35"The distance around the entire city will be 6 miles.* And from that day the name of the city will be 'The LORD Is There.'*"

48:15 Hebrew *25,000 [cubits]* [13.3 kilometers] *long by 5,000 [cubits]* [2.65 kilometers] *wide.* 48:16 Hebrew *4,500 [cubits]* [2.4 kilometers]; also in 48:30, 32, 33, 34. 48:17 Hebrew *250 [cubits]* [133 meters]. 48:18 Hebrew *10,000 [cubits]* [5.3 kilometers] *to the east and 10,000 [cubits] to the west.* 48:20 Hebrew *25,000 [cubits]* [13.3 kilometers]; also in 48:21. 48:28a Hebrew *waters of Meribath-kadesh.* 48:28b Hebrew *the great sea.* 48:35a Hebrew *18,000 [cubits]* [9.6 kilometers]. 48:35b Hebrew *Yahweh Shammah.*

REFLECTIONS ON EZEKIEL

insights ABOUT THE PERSON OF GOD

Ezekiel 1:4-28 contains a magnificent vision of the glory of God! Many of God's people doubted whether God was even able to be there in a foreign land. Some believed that when they were defeated by Babylon, God had been defeated by the gods of Babylon. To counteract their confusion and disbelief, God revealed his glory to Ezekiel while he was in captivity in Babylon. The people of Judah needed to believe, as we do, that God could act on their behalf before they were able to entrust their recovery to him. God helped them to trust him by revealing himself in this way.

Ezekiel had been awestruck by God's glory and had fallen facedown on the ground. When we realize the depth of our helplessness and begin to understand God's limitless power, we may also fall down before him. But notice in **Ezekiel 2:1-2** that it was God's Spirit who lifted Ezekiel back to his feet. God acted for the stricken prophet and prepared him to receive his message. As we begin the recovery process, we need to recognize our helplessness and throw ourself on the mercy of God. As we give our life to God, he will lift us up and set us on the road to recovery. When we are unable to go on, God will give us the strength we need to take the next step.

insights INTO THE RESPONSIBILITIES OF RECOVERY

In **Ezekiel 2:6** the prophet was warned of the great difficulties he would face as he obeyed God. But God also made it clear that he would be with Ezekiel as the prophet trusted and obeyed him. When we seek to follow God's will in the recovery process, we can count on his protection and help. That doesn't mean things will be easy for us. In fact, sometimes things get much worse before they get better. Close friends may reject us or make fun of us. People who stand to lose something through our recovery may even try to stop us. But we don't have to be afraid. Fear incapacitates and debilitates. God's promise to Ezekiel should give us courage as we follow God's will in recovery.

For most of us confrontation is never comfortable, yet in **Ezekiel 3:7-8** the prophet was warned that his ministry would be filled with it. To accomplish God's work, Ezekiel would have to speak directly to God's people and honestly confront them with their sins. In recovery confrontation is seldom pleasant, but sometimes it is necessary. We need to remember that what we fail to deal with today often becomes a much bigger problem tomorrow.

What is our responsibility to other individuals? Do we have any obligation to others in need of recovery? Are we responsible to warn them of impending danger? People in need of recovery are often blind to the dangers they face. Some of us are in physical peril from our dependency long before we know it. We also may be in danger of damaging our relationships and the lives of the people close to us. In **Ezekiel 3:16-21** the prophet was commissioned as a watchman to warn his people of approaching danger. We should love our fellow strugglers enough to warn them before it is too late for them.

Ezekiel 33:10-16 contains a wonderful promise for recovery. Even as we suffer terrible consequences for our failures and sins, we can be sure that if we repent, God will forgive us. God does not punish us out of anger or vengeance; he punishes us because he loves us. He doesn't desire our destruction; he desires our restoration and recovery. Yet our responsibility is clear: We must repent and turn from our sins. As we do this each day, we will discover that God will help and strengthen us in the battles we face. Although we may still suffer the consequences of our past actions, our ultimate recovery is assured.

insights ABOUT DENIAL

In **Ezekiel 4:1-3** the prophet made it clear to the Jewish exiles that their troubles were not over. Many were in denial about their sins and hoped they would soon return to Jerusalem and the Temple. But Ezekiel told them that their beloved homeland would soon be destroyed. He had to help the people recognize their sins before he could help them resolve the problems. A clear understanding of our shortcomings is essential to recovery. If we know what we are fighting, we won't spend our efforts working on the wrong issues. Sometimes facing our problems is difficult and unpleasant; it certainly was painful for the exiles from Judah. But we must honestly admit them if we want to overcome them.

DANIEL

THE BIG PICTURE

A. THE CAPTURE OF INNOCENT BYSTANDERS (1:1-21)
B. GOD HUMBLES THE PROUD (2:1–7:28)
C. HOPE FOR ULTIMATE RECOVERY (8:1–12:4)
D. LIMITED ANSWERS TO LIFE'S PAINFUL QUESTIONS (12:5-13)

Innocent bystanders often get hurt by the mistakes and sins of other people. Disasters happen that can affect us for life, even though we are not responsible for the events that take place. When we suffer innocently or unfairly, we can recover from the problems we have inherited only by facing the reality of our situation.

Daniel and his friends were innocent bystanders. They suffered exile to Babylon because of Judah's prolonged disobedience to God. But they did not remain victims. With courage and faith in God, they faced the reality of their exile and lived successfully—even by Babylonian standards. Their recovery gives us insight into how to deal with the unfair circumstances in our own life.

After being taken from Jerusalem to Babylon, Daniel and his three friends were trained for service in the Babylonian government. Their captors often demanded that they do things that were contrary to God's revealed will. To protect their relationship with God, Daniel and his friends set clear boundaries for their behavior. They each followed God's program for their life, even though it conflicted with the commands of their captors. God protected these faithful young men from the foreign laws and unstable tyrants they lived under.

Daniel and his friends were exiled to Babylon for the sins of their ancestors, but they did not use that as an excuse for continued failure. Instead, they trusted God and determined to live according to his will. Because of their faith and courage, God not only repeatedly delivered them from difficult circumstances, but he also used them to prove his existence and power to others.

THE BOTTOM LINE

PURPOSE: To show how God humbles proud oppressors and vindicates those who trust him through their suffering. AUTHOR: The prophet Daniel. AUDIENCE: God's people during and after the Babylonian exile. DATE WRITTEN: The book was probably written around 535 B.C., recording events that happened between 605 and 535 B.C. SETTING: The land of Babylon after Daniel and his friends were exiled there in 605 B.C. KEY VERSE: "Those who are wise will shine as bright as the sky, and those who lead many to righteousness will shine like the stars forever" (12:3). KEY PLACES: Jerusalem, Babylon, and Susa. KEY PEOPLE AND RELATIONSHIPS: Daniel, Shadrach, Meshach, and Abednego; foreign rulers Nebuchadnezzar, Belshazzar, and Darius.

RECOVERY THEMES

Life Is Unfair: When we experience unfairness, the lives of Daniel and his three friends give us encouragement and direction. Even though he obeyed God all his life, Daniel was not protected from God's judgment on Judah. We do not have automatic protection from the unfairness of life. We will all face it at one time or another. But we do have God's assurance that he is concerned about what we are doing and will honor our faithfulness and obedience.

Not Victims Forever: Daniel was a victim. He was controlled by a powerful group of people and had no say in his future. The dynamics are similar in cases of sexual abuse or other forms of victimization. Daniel did not remain a victim, however. He knew that when he turned to God and sought to do his will, he was no longer at the mercy of selfish and unstable foreign rulers. He was in God's powerful and protecting hands. As Daniel was faithful to God and his program, God delivered Daniel from terrible situations, giving him freedom in the midst of his slavery.

God Can Do Anything: Shadrach, Meshach, and Abednego could have decided that God was unable to protect them from the fiery furnace. Daniel could have decided that God could not handle the hungry lions. These men could have decided that fudging a little on God's will for them was better than risking their lives. If they had done this, however, they would not have experienced the glorious victories God gave them. God can do anything in our life if we are willing to hand everything over to him and follow his will for us. This may mean that we have to face new conflicts with people who don't approve, but staying faithful to God's program is the only way to a lasting recovery.

Pain in Recovery: Daniel and his friends sought to live according to God's program but found that others opposed their efforts. Initially this led to great danger but ultimately to glorious victory. Shadrach, Meshach, and Abednego had to walk through a fiery furnace because they obeyed God's will for them, but only the ropes that bound them were burned. Daniel had to sleep in a den of lions because he was faithful to God, but when he left the lions' den, he was far better off than he was before. God used these trials to bring blessings to his servants and glory to himself. As we seek to do God's will, he may allow us to go through some difficult situations. God often uses such trials to bless us. We need to stick to his program, no matter what difficulties we face.

CHAPTER 1
Daniel in Nebuchadnezzar's Court

During the third year of King Jehoiakim's reign in Judah,* King Nebuchadnezzar of Babylon came to Jerusalem and besieged it. ²The Lord gave him victory over King Jehoiakim of Judah and permitted him to take some of the sacred objects from the Temple of God. So Nebuchadnezzar took them back to the land of Babylonia* and placed them in the treasure-house of his god.

³Then the king ordered Ashpenaz, his chief of staff, to bring to the palace some of the young men of Judah's royal family and other noble families, who had been brought to Babylon as captives. ⁴"Select only strong, healthy, and good-looking young men," he said. "Make sure they are well versed in every branch of learning, are gifted with knowledge and good judgment, and are suited to serve in the royal palace. Train these young men in the language and literature of Babylon.*" ⁵The king assigned them a daily ration of food and wine from his own kitchens.

1:1 This event occurred in 605 B.C., during the third year of Jehoiakim's reign (according to the calendar system in which the new year begins in the spring). 1:2 Hebrew *the land of Shinar.* 1:4 Or *of the Chaldeans.*

1:1-6 Daniel, Hananiah, Mishael, and Azariah faced troubles. Their city was conquered, and they were captured by the enemy and marched across the desert to Babylon. Life must have seemed over for the four young men. But then their fortunes changed. They were chosen to take part in a three-year training program; upon completion, some of them would become Nebuchadnezzar's advisers. No one knows what the future holds. Our current bad times may be temporary; recovery may be near. We shouldn't give up hope; God has a good plan for our life, and he will see us through.

1:7-16 When authority figures or powerful personalities try to squeeze us into their mold and get us to compromise our values, the easy thing to do is give in to their wishes. The healthy response, however, and the one that indicates progress toward recovery, is to courageously set boundaries as Daniel and his friends did by not eating food contrary to God's laws. With proper boundaries set up, we will be less tempted to compromise.

DANIEL

Daniel experienced all the forces that normally lead to discouragement and defeat, yet he stood firm in his faith and convictions. He was exiled from Judah as a youth and separated from the standards and healthy boundaries set by his family and Jewish faith. The Babylonian government chose him for service and assumed he would discard his faith and religious practices to become a Babylonian. He was even renamed Belteshazzar (meaning "Bel, protect his life"), after the chief Babylonian god Bel, to discourage Daniel's allegiance to his own God and homeland.

Daniel experienced the turmoil of transition from one culture to another, yet he recognized that God was in control. He knew that no matter what happened around him, God and his will would remain the same. Daniel knew what God expected of him and remained faithful to God's program, despite the opposition and temptations he faced. So God blessed him, and Daniel became a great success in the courts of Babylon and Persia.

Daniel's rise to power in Nebuchadnezzar's court, though a great blessing, posed many difficulties and dangers. Leaders in Babylon's government were often destroyed by the plots of power-hungry nobles; the king himself was known to dispose of his counselors on a whim. Daniel narrowly escaped destruction from both of these quarters. He trusted God to keep him safe in the dangerous world of Babylonian politics. He refused to compromise his faith in God, despite increased opposition and danger during the reign of Darius. In that world of shifting power and changing governments, Daniel held important positions for over sixty years.

As God delivered Daniel from one difficulty after another, even the kings of Babylon and Persia came to believe in God's power. Acting on his faith sometimes led Daniel into difficult situations—he was forced to spend a whole night with hungry lions because he refused to stop praying to God! God always delivered him, strengthening Daniel's faith and proving that God was in control. Daniel proved many times that doing things God's way is always best.

STRENGTHS AND ACCOMPLISHMENTS:
- Daniel refused to let the injustice he suffered affect his future.
- He had an accurate understanding of who he was as one of God's people.
- He remained faithful to God despite much opposition and many temptations.
- He handled the power given to him with humility, and he was a just leader.
- He always followed God's will for him, even when it was dangerous to do so.

LESSONS FROM HIS LIFE:
- God's help in the past can strengthen our faith for the future.
- Doing things God's way is always best.
- God's unchanging character can give us stability in our changing world.
- As we follow God's will for us, others may come to believe in God's power.
- A close, disciplined relationship with God will help us to obey God's will for us.

KEY VERSE:
"This man Daniel, whom the king named Belteshazzar, has exceptional ability and is filled with divine knowledge and understanding. He can interpret dreams, explain riddles, and solve difficult problems. Call for Daniel, and he will tell you what the writing means" (Daniel 5:12).

Daniel's story is told in the book of Daniel. He is also mentioned in Matthew 24:15.

They were to be trained for three years, and then they would enter the royal service.

⁶Daniel, Hananiah, Mishael, and Azariah were four of the young men chosen, all from the tribe of Judah. ⁷The chief of staff renamed them with these Babylonian names:

Daniel was called Belteshazzar.
Hananiah was called Shadrach.

Mishael was called Meshach.
Azariah was called Abednego.

⁸But Daniel was determined not to defile himself by eating the food and wine given to them by the king. He asked the chief of staff for permission not to eat these unacceptable foods. ⁹Now God had given the chief of staff both respect and affection for

Daniel. [10]But he responded, "I am afraid of my lord the king, who has ordered that you eat this food and wine. If you become pale and thin compared to the other youths your age, I am afraid the king will have me beheaded."

[11]Daniel spoke with the attendant who had been appointed by the chief of staff to look after Daniel, Hananiah, Mishael, and Azariah. [12]"Please test us for ten days on a diet of vegetables and water," Daniel said. [13]"At the end of the ten days, see how we look compared to the other young men who are eating the king's food. Then make your decision in light of what you see." [14]The attendant agreed to Daniel's suggestion and tested them for ten days.

[15]At the end of the ten days, Daniel and his three friends looked healthier and better nourished than the young men who had been eating the food assigned by the king. [16]So after that, the attendant fed them only vegetables instead of the food and wine provided for the others.

[17]God gave these four young men an unusual aptitude for understanding every aspect of literature and wisdom. And God gave Daniel the special ability to interpret the meanings of visions and dreams.

[18]When the training period ordered by the king was completed, the chief of staff brought all the young men to King Nebuchadnezzar. [19]The king talked with them, and no one impressed him as much as Daniel, Hananiah, Mishael, and Azariah. So they entered the royal service. [20]Whenever the king consulted them in any matter requiring wisdom and balanced judgment, he found them ten times more capable than any of the magicians and enchanters in his entire kingdom.

[21]Daniel remained in the royal service until the first year of the reign of King Cyrus.*

CHAPTER 2
Nebuchadnezzar's Dream

One night during the second year of his reign,* Nebuchadnezzar had such disturbing dreams that he couldn't sleep. [2]He called in his magicians, enchanters, sorcerers, and astrologers,* and he demanded that they tell him what he had dreamed. As they stood before the king, [3]he said, "I have had a dream that deeply troubles me, and I must know what it means."

[4]Then the astrologers answered the king in Aramaic,* "Long live the king! Tell us the dream, and we will tell you what it means."

[5]But the king said to the astrologers, "I am serious about this. If you don't tell me what my dream was and what it means, you will be torn limb from limb, and your houses will be turned into heaps of rubble! [6]But if you tell me what I dreamed and what the dream means, I will give you many wonderful gifts and honors. Just tell me the dream and what it means!"

[7]They said again, "Please, Your Majesty. Tell us the dream, and we will tell you what it means."

[8]The king replied, "I know what you are doing! You're stalling for time because you know I am serious when I say, [9]'If you don't tell me the dream, you are doomed.' So you have conspired to tell me lies, hoping I will change my mind. But tell me the dream, and then I'll know that you can tell me what it means."

[10]The astrologers replied to the king, "No one on earth can tell the king his dream! And no king, however great and powerful, has ever asked such a thing of any magician, enchanter, or astrologer! [11]The king's demand is impossible. No one except the gods can tell you your dream, and they do not live here among people."

[12]The king was furious when he heard this, and he ordered that all the wise men of Babylon be executed. [13]And because of the king's decree, men were sent to find and kill Daniel and his friends.

[14]When Arioch, the commander of the king's guard, came to kill them, Daniel handled the situation with wisdom and discretion. [15]He asked Arioch, "Why has the king issued such a harsh decree?" So Arioch told him all that had happened. [16]Daniel went at once to see the king and requested more time to tell the king what the dream meant.

[17]Then Daniel went home and told his friends Hananiah, Mishael, and Azariah what had happened. [18]He urged them to ask the God of heaven to show them his mercy by telling them the secret, so they would not be executed along with the other wise men of Babylon. [19]That night the secret was revealed to Daniel in a vision. Then Daniel praised the God of heaven. [20]He said,

"Praise the name of God forever and ever,
for he has all wisdom and power.

1:21 Cyrus began his reign (over Babylon) in 539 B.C. 2:1 The second year of Nebuchadnezzar's reign was 603 B.C. 2:2 Or *Chaldeans*; also in 2:4, 5, 10. 2:4 The original text from this point through chapter 7 is in Aramaic.

²¹He controls the course of world events;
    he removes kings and sets up other kings.
He gives wisdom to the wise
    and knowledge to the scholars.
²²He reveals deep and mysterious things
    and knows what lies hidden in
      darkness,
    though he is surrounded by light.
²³I thank and praise you, God of my
    ancestors,
    for you have given me wisdom and
      strength.
You have told me what we asked of you
    and revealed to us what the king
      demanded."

Daniel Interprets the Dream

²⁴Then Daniel went in to see Arioch, whom the king had ordered to execute the wise men of Babylon. Daniel said to him, "Don't kill the wise men. Take me to the king, and I will tell him the meaning of his dream."

²⁵Arioch quickly took Daniel to the king and said, "I have found one of the captives from Judah who will tell the king the meaning of his dream!"

²⁶The king said to Daniel (also known as Belteshazzar), "Is this true? Can you tell me what my dream was and what it means?"

²⁷Daniel replied, "There are no wise men, enchanters, magicians, or fortune-tellers who can reveal the king's secret. ²⁸But there is a God in heaven who reveals secrets, and he has shown King Nebuchadnezzar what will happen in the future. Now I will tell you your dream and the visions you saw as you lay on your bed.

²⁹"While Your Majesty was sleeping, you dreamed about coming events. He who reveals secrets has shown you what is going to happen. ³⁰And it is not because I am wiser than anyone else that I know the secret of your dream, but because God wants you to understand what was in your heart.

³¹"In your vision, Your Majesty, you saw standing before you a huge, shining statue of a man. It was a frightening sight. ³²The head of the statue was made of fine gold. Its chest and arms were silver, its belly and thighs were bronze, ³³its legs were iron, and its feet were a combination of iron and baked clay. ³⁴As you watched, a rock was cut from a mountain,* but not by human hands. It struck the feet of iron and clay, smashing them to bits. ³⁵The whole statue was crushed into small pieces of iron, clay, bronze, silver, and gold. Then the wind blew them away without a trace, like chaff on a threshing floor. But the rock that knocked the statue down became a great mountain that covered the whole earth.

³⁶"That was the dream. Now we will tell the king what it means. ³⁷Your Majesty, you are the greatest of kings. The God of heaven has given you sovereignty, power, strength, and honor. ³⁸He has made you the ruler over all the inhabited world and has put even the wild animals and birds under your control. You are the head of gold.

³⁹"But after your kingdom comes to an end, another kingdom, inferior to yours, will rise to take your place. After that kingdom has fallen, yet a third kingdom, represented by bronze, will rise to rule the world. ⁴⁰Following that kingdom, there will be a fourth one, as strong as iron. That kingdom will smash and crush all previous empires, just as iron smashes and crushes everything it strikes. ⁴¹The feet and toes you saw were a combination of iron and baked clay, showing that this kingdom will be divided. Like iron mixed with clay, it will have some of the strength of iron. ⁴²But while some parts of it will be as strong as iron, other parts will be as weak as clay. ⁴³This mixture of iron and clay also shows that these kingdoms will try to strengthen themselves by forming alliances with each other through intermarriage. But they will not hold together, just as iron and clay do not mix.

⁴⁴"During the reigns of those kings, the God of heaven will set up a kingdom that will never be destroyed or conquered. It will

---

2:34 As in Greek version (see also 2:45); Hebrew lacks *from a mountain.*

2:26-28 Daniel wisely gave God the credit for the interpretation of the dream. He could easily have told Nebuchadnezzar that *he* knew the dream, thus elevating himself above all the counselors. But he acknowledged God and his power. God works in our life, too, bringing recovery where once there was pain and despair. Have we given God the credit for our recovery, or have we told others we did it on our own? We need to follow Daniel's example and give God the credit.

2:29-45 In this vision a prominent theme of the book of Daniel is introduced: God is ultimately in control, even over seemingly unshakable human power. This passage provides the framework for interpreting all of Daniel's prophetic visions, but it also tells us that God will defeat those who are against his people. He will establish his Kingdom for those who follow his ways.

crush all these kingdoms into nothingness, and it will stand forever. ⁴⁵That is the meaning of the rock cut from the mountain, though not by human hands, that crushed to pieces the statue of iron, bronze, clay, silver, and gold. The great God was showing the king what will happen in the future. The dream is true, and its meaning is certain."

Nebuchadnezzar Rewards Daniel

⁴⁶Then King Nebuchadnezzar threw himself down before Daniel and worshiped him, and he commanded his people to offer sacrifices and burn sweet incense before him. ⁴⁷The king said to Daniel, "Truly, your God is the greatest of gods, the Lord over kings, a revealer of mysteries, for you have been able to reveal this secret."

⁴⁸Then the king appointed Daniel to a high position and gave him many valuable gifts. He made Daniel ruler over the whole province of Babylon, as well as chief over all his wise men. ⁴⁹At Daniel's request, the king appointed Shadrach, Meshach, and Abednego to be in charge of all the affairs of the province of Babylon, while Daniel remained in the king's court.

CHAPTER 3
Nebuchadnezzar's Gold Statue

King Nebuchadnezzar made a gold statue ninety feet tall and nine feet wide* and set it up on the plain of Dura in the province of Babylon. ²Then he sent messages to the high officers, officials, governors, advisers, treasurers, judges, magistrates, and all the provincial officials to come to the dedication of the statue he had set up. ³So all these officials* came and stood before the statue King Nebuchadnezzar had set up.

⁴Then a herald shouted out, "People of all races and nations and languages, listen to the king's command! ⁵When you hear the sound of the horn, flute, zither, lyre, harp, pipes, and other musical instruments,* bow to the ground to worship King Nebuchadnezzar's gold statue. ⁶Anyone who refuses to obey will immediately be thrown into a blazing furnace."

⁷So at the sound of the musical instruments,* all the people, whatever their race or nation or language, bowed to the ground and worshiped the gold statue that King Nebuchadnezzar had set up.

⁸But some of the astrologers* went to the king and informed on the Jews. ⁹They said to King Nebuchadnezzar, "Long live the king! ¹⁰You issued a decree requiring all the people to bow down and worship the gold statue when they hear the sound of the horn, flute, zither, lyre, harp, pipes, and other musical instruments. ¹¹That decree also states that those who refuse to obey must be thrown into a blazing furnace. ¹²But there are some Jews—Shadrach, Meshach, and Abednego—whom you have put in charge of the province of Babylon. They pay no attention to you, Your Majesty. They refuse to serve your gods and do not worship the gold statue you have set up."

¹³Then Nebuchadnezzar flew into a rage and ordered that Shadrach, Meshach, and Abednego be brought before him. When they were brought in, ¹⁴Nebuchadnezzar said to them, "Is it true, Shadrach, Meshach, and Abednego, that you refuse to serve my gods or to worship the gold statue I have set up? ¹⁵I will give you one more chance to bow down and worship the statue I have made when you hear the sound of the musical instruments.* But if you refuse, you will be thrown immediately into the blazing furnace. And then what god will be able to rescue you from my power?"

¹⁶Shadrach, Meshach, and Abednego replied, "O Nebuchadnezzar, we do not need to defend ourselves before you. ¹⁷If we are thrown into the blazing furnace, the God whom we serve is able to save us. He will rescue us from your power, Your Majesty. ¹⁸But even if he doesn't, we want to make it clear to you, Your Majesty, that we will never serve your gods or worship the gold statue you have set up."

3:1 Aramaic *60 cubits* [27 meters] *tall and 6 cubits* [2.7 meters] *wide.* 3:3 Aramaic *the high officers, officials, governors, advisers, treasurers, judges, magistrates, and all the provincial officials.* 3:5 The identification of some of these musical instruments is uncertain. 3:7 Aramaic *the horn, flute, zither, lyre, harp, and other musical instruments.* 3:8 Aramaic *Chaldeans.* 3:15 Aramaic *the horn, flute, zither, lyre, harp, pipes, and other musical instruments.*

3:7-15 Shadrach, Meshach, and Abednego displayed great faith and courage as they refused to bow to the statue. Nebuchadnezzar confronted them and issued an ultimatum: Either bow down or die in a blazing furnace! He reminds us of the people who bully their way through life, abusing others who won't give in to their pressure. But those people are no match for God—he will stand by us, protecting us from the various abusive personalities we encounter.

NEBUCHADNEZZAR

Nebuchadnezzar was one of the greatest conquerors in the history of the world. He dominated the people of many nations, including Judah. He possessed power, fame, wealth, and influence. At one point, he even considered himself a god. But like so many others, he lacked the one thing he needed the most—peace. His insecurities would not allow him to be at peace with himself. So how could he be at peace with others? He was unhappy with himself and hostile toward the people around him.

Nebuchadnezzar never truly discovered the peace that could have been found had he recognized his powerlessness and surrendered his life to God. Daniel and his friends were good examples of how success and peace could be found through complete dependence on God and surrender to his will. After Shadrach, Meshach, and Abednego walked out of the fiery furnace unscathed, Nebuchadnezzar realized that he had been thwarted by a higher power. He also saw that the three friends, by turning their lives over to God, had far greater power at their disposal than even he had. Despite his recognition of God's power, however, the king still remained proud.

Nebuchadnezzar continued to brag about his greatness and claimed that he alone was responsible for the great city of Babylon. He refused to recognize that all power—even his power—was granted by God. So God judged Nebuchadnezzar's pride by afflicting him with madness, and the king was forced from his throne. After a time Nebuchadnezzar turned to God and admitted his sin of pride, and God restored his sanity and rule. Nebuchadnezzar had been reminded once again that he was not ultimately in control of his world.

Sadly, it seems that Nebuchadnezzar never truly understood the nature of submission to God. He saw God act in the lives of others and even in his own life. He clearly believed in God's presence and power. Yet he could not seem to put his life into God's hands on a permanent basis. Although he may have experienced religious conviction, it seems that he never experienced spiritual conversion and lasting transformation.

**STRENGTHS AND
ACCOMPLISHMENTS:**
- Nebuchadnezzar achieved great success and accumulated astounding wealth.
- He was used by God, in spite of his pride, to accomplish God's purposes.
- He was a great leader of men.

WEAKNESSES AND MISTAKES:
- He demanded rather than earned loyalty from his subordinates.
- He wanted his people to worship him as if he were a god.
- He failed to act on his knowledge that God was ultimately in control.
- His pride kept him from submitting to God's will for his life.

LESSONS FROM HIS LIFE:
- Submitting to God's will is the first step toward receiving his power.
- If we refuse to trust God with our life, we will be plagued by fear.
- A life of peace can only be found by entrusting our life to God.
- Playing God by controlling others only leads to insecurity and hostility.
- Healing comes when we admit our sins to God and look to him for help.

KEY VERSES:
"[Nebuchadnezzar] was taking a walk on the flat roof of the royal palace in Babylon. As he looked out across the city, he said, 'Look at this great city of Babylon! By my own mighty power, I have built this beautiful city as my royal residence. . . . ' While these words were still in his mouth, a voice called down from heaven, 'O King Nebuchadnezzar, this message is for you! You are no longer ruler of this kingdom'" (Daniel 4:29-31).

Nebuchadnezzar's story is told in Daniel 1–5. He is also mentioned in 2 Kings 24–25 and 2 Chronicles 36.

The Blazing Furnace

[19]Nebuchadnezzar was so furious with Shadrach, Meshach, and Abednego that his face became distorted with rage. He commanded that the furnace be heated seven times hotter than usual. [20]Then he ordered some of the strongest men of his army to bind Shadrach, Meshach, and Abednego and throw them into the blazing furnace. [21]So they tied them up and threw them into the furnace, fully dressed in their pants, turbans, robes, and other garments. [22]And because the king, in his anger, had demanded such a hot fire in the furnace, the flames killed the soldiers as they threw the three men in. [23]So Shadrach, Meshach, and Abednego, securely tied, fell into the roaring flames.

24But suddenly, Nebuchadnezzar jumped up in amazement and exclaimed to his advisers, "Didn't we tie up three men and throw them into the furnace?"

"Yes, Your Majesty, we certainly did," they replied.

25"Look!" Nebuchadnezzar shouted. "I see four men, unbound, walking around in the fire unharmed! And the fourth looks like a god*!"

26Then Nebuchadnezzar came as close as he could to the door of the flaming furnace and shouted: "Shadrach, Meshach, and Abednego, servants of the Most High God, come out! Come here!"

So Shadrach, Meshach, and Abednego stepped out of the fire. 27Then the high officers, officials, governors, and advisers crowded around them and saw that the fire had not touched them. Not a hair on their heads was singed, and their clothing was not scorched. They didn't even smell of smoke!

28Then Nebuchadnezzar said, "Praise to the God of Shadrach, Meshach, and Abednego! He sent his angel to rescue his servants who trusted in him. They defied the king's command and were willing to die rather than serve or worship any god except their own God. 29Therefore, I make this decree: If any people, whatever their race or nation or language, speak a word against the God of Shadrach, Meshach, and Abednego, they will be torn limb from limb, and their houses will be turned into heaps of rubble. There is no other god who can rescue like this!"

30Then the king promoted Shadrach, Meshach, and Abednego to even higher positions in the province of Babylon.

CHAPTER 4
Nebuchadnezzar's Dream about a Tree

1*King Nebuchadnezzar sent this message to the people of every race and nation and language throughout the world:

"Peace and prosperity to you!

2"I want you all to know about the miraculous signs and wonders the Most High God has performed for me.

3 How great are his signs,
　　how powerful his wonders!
His kingdom will last forever,
　　his rule through all generations.

4*"I, Nebuchadnezzar, was living in my palace in comfort and prosperity. 5But one night I had a dream that frightened me; I saw visions that terrified me as I lay in my bed. 6So I issued an order calling in all the wise men of Babylon, so they could tell me what my dream meant. 7When all the magicians, enchanters, astrologers,* and fortune-tellers came in, I told them the dream, but they could not tell me what it meant. 8At last Daniel came in before me, and I told him the dream. (He was named Belteshazzar after my god, and the spirit of the holy gods is in him.)

9"I said to him, 'Belteshazzar, chief of the magicians, I know that the spirit of the holy gods is in you and that no mystery is too great for you to solve. Now tell me what my dream means.

10"'While I was lying in my bed, this is what I dreamed. I saw a large tree in the middle of the earth. 11The tree grew very tall and strong, reaching high into the heavens for all the world to see. 12It had fresh green leaves, and it was loaded with fruit for all to eat. Wild animals lived in its shade, and birds nested in its branches. All the world was fed from this tree.

13"'Then as I lay there dreaming, I saw a messenger,* a holy one, coming down from heaven. 14The messenger shouted,

"Cut down the tree and lop off its branches!

3:25 Aramaic like a son of the gods.　4:1 Verses 4:1-3 are numbered 3:31-33 in Aramaic text.　4:4 Verses 4:4-37 are numbered 4:1-34 in Aramaic text.　4:7 Or Chaldeans.　4:13 Aramaic a watcher; also in 4:23.

3:24-30 Nebuchadnezzar was amazed at what he saw and immediately worshiped the God of Shadrach, Meshach, and Abednego. If these men had not stood up to Nebuchadnezzar, he never would have seen the great power of God. The best way we can tell someone about God is to demonstrate his power in our life. This will encourage those who seek him and help in their recovery. It may even win over those who were against us at the beginning.

4:18-27 Nebuchadnezzar's dream was interpreted by Daniel (Belteshazzar) through the wisdom given by God's Spirit. The king's tragic breakdown would soon take place unless he made some drastic changes in his life. Similarly, we may be heading for a humbling experience if we continue to think we are in control of our life. Recovery is dependent on trust in God and obedience to his will for our life.

Shake off its leaves and scatter
its fruit!
Chase the wild animals from its shade
and the birds from its branches.
[15]But leave the stump and the roots in the
ground,
bound with a band of iron and
bronze
and surrounded by tender grass.
Now let him be drenched with the dew
of heaven,
and let him live with the wild
animals among the plants of the
field.
[16]For seven periods of time,
let him have the mind of a wild
animal
instead of the mind of a human.
[17]For this has been decreed by the
messengers*;
it is commanded by the holy ones,
so that everyone may know
that the Most High rules over the
kingdoms of the world.
He gives them to anyone he chooses—
even to the lowliest of people."

[18]"'Belteshazzar, that was the dream
that I, King Nebuchadnezzar, had. Now
tell me what it means, for none of the
wise men of my kingdom can do so. But
you can tell me because the spirit of the
holy gods is in you.'

Daniel Explains the Dream

[19]"Upon hearing this, Daniel (also known
as Belteshazzar) was overcome for a time,
frightened by the meaning of the dream.
Then the king said to him, 'Belteshazzar,
don't be alarmed by the dream and what
it means.'

"Belteshazzar replied, 'I wish the events
foreshadowed in this dream would
happen to your enemies, my lord, and
not to you! [20]The tree you saw was
growing very tall and strong, reaching
high into the heavens for all the world to
see. [21]It had fresh green leaves and was
loaded with fruit for all to eat. Wild
animals lived in its shade, and birds
nested in its branches. [22]That tree, Your
Majesty, is you. For you have grown
strong and great; your greatness reaches
up to heaven, and your rule to the ends
of the earth.

[23]"'Then you saw a messenger, a holy
one, coming down from heaven and

4:17 Aramaic *the watchers.*

STEP 2

Grandiose Thinking

BIBLE READING: Daniel 4:19-33

**We came to believe that a Power greater
than ourselves could restore us to sanity.**
When we are caught up in our addiction,
it's common for us to deny the truth about
our situation with grandiose thinking. We
may believe that we're above it all, a god
unto ourself, accountable to no one.

In his day, Nebuchadnezzar, king of
ancient Babylon, was the most powerful
ruler on earth. He believed he was a god
and demanded to be worshiped. Through
Daniel God said to him, "This is . . . what
the Most High has declared will happen to
[you]. You will be driven from human society, and you will live in the fields with the
wild animals . . . until you learn that the
Most High rules over the kingdoms of the
world and gives them to anyone he
chooses" (Daniel 4:24-25).

This happened just as Daniel had
predicted. At the end of the king's time in
exile, he said, "I . . . looked up to heaven.
My sanity returned, and I praised and
worshiped the Most High and honored the
one who lives forever. . . . When my sanity
returned to me, so did my honor and glory
and kingdom . . . with even greater honor
than before. Now I, Nebuchadnezzar,
praise and glorify and honor the King of
heaven. All his acts are just and true, and
he is able to humble the proud" (Daniel
4:34, 36-37).

We are not God; we are accountable to
God—a higher power. This higher power
can remedy our "madness" and restore our
life to be even better than it was before our
season of "insanity." God will do so if we
entrust our life to him. *Turn to page 1257,
Mark 5.*

saying, "Cut down the tree and destroy it. But leave the stump and the roots in the ground, bound with a band of iron and bronze and surrounded by tender grass. Let him be drenched with the dew of heaven. Let him live with the animals of the field for seven periods of time."

²⁴"'This is what the dream means, Your Majesty, and what the Most High has declared will happen to my lord the king. ²⁵You will be driven from human society, and you will live in the fields with the wild animals. You will eat grass like a cow, and you will be drenched with the dew of heaven. Seven periods of time will pass while you live this way, until you learn that the Most High rules over the kingdoms of the world and gives them to anyone he chooses. ²⁶But the stump and roots of the tree were left in the ground. This means that you will receive your kingdom back again when you have learned that heaven rules.

²⁷"'King Nebuchadnezzar, please accept my advice. Stop sinning and do what is right. Break from your wicked past and be merciful to the poor. Perhaps then you will continue to prosper.'

The Dream's Fulfillment

²⁸"But all these things did happen to King Nebuchadnezzar. ²⁹Twelve months later he was taking a walk on the flat roof of the royal palace in Babylon. ³⁰As he looked out across the city, he said, 'Look at this great city of Babylon! By my own mighty power, I have built this beautiful city as my royal residence to display my majestic splendor.'

³¹"While these words were still in his mouth, a voice called down from heaven, 'O King Nebuchadnezzar, this message is for you! You are no longer ruler of this kingdom. ³²You will be driven from human society. You will live in the fields with the wild animals, and you will eat grass like a cow. Seven periods of time

will pass while you live this way, until you learn that the Most High rules over the kingdoms of the world and gives them to anyone he chooses.'

³³"That same hour the judgment was fulfilled, and Nebuchadnezzar was driven from human society. He ate grass like a cow, and he was drenched with the dew of heaven. He lived this way until his hair was as long as eagles' feathers and his nails were like birds' claws.

Nebuchadnezzar Praises God

³⁴"After this time had passed, I, Nebuchadnezzar, looked up to heaven. My sanity returned, and I praised and worshiped the Most High and honored the one who lives forever.

His rule is everlasting,
  and his kingdom is eternal.
³⁵All the people of the earth
  are nothing compared to him.
He does as he pleases
  among the angels of heaven
  and among the people of the earth.
No one can stop him or say to him,
  'What do you mean by doing these
    things?'

³⁶"When my sanity returned to me, so did my honor and glory and kingdom. My advisers and nobles sought me out, and I was restored as head of my kingdom, with even greater honor than before.

³⁷"Now I, Nebuchadnezzar, praise and glorify and honor the King of heaven. All his acts are just and true, and he is able to humble the proud."

CHAPTER 5
The Writing on the Wall

Many years later King Belshazzar gave a great feast for 1,000 of his nobles, and he drank wine with them. ²While Belshazzar was drinking the wine, he gave orders to bring in the gold and silver cups that his predeces-

---

4:28-37 Even after a warning, Nebuchadnezzar did not change his lifestyle and give God the credit for his power. The result was seven years of humiliating insanity. But God restored Nebuchadnezzar to the throne when the king turned toward heaven for deliverance. Nebuchadnezzar praised and honored God; he didn't curse him for his many years of madness. If we experience a painful setback, God is giving us a chance to change our ways. God will remove our suffering when we have learned the lessons he wants to teach us.

5:1-6 One of the worst types of denial is that of drowning our fears and problems in compulsive behavior such as alcohol, drugs, or sex to avoid or forget. While such things may mask the fear and pain momentarily, the circumstances that led to our addiction are still there and may be getting worse. In Belshazzar's case, the "writing was on the wall"—literally! The Medo-Persian

sor,* Nebuchadnezzar, had taken from the Temple in Jerusalem. He wanted to drink from them with his nobles, his wives, and his concubines. ³So they brought these gold cups taken from the Temple, the house of God in Jerusalem, and the king and his nobles, his wives, and his concubines drank from them. ⁴While they drank from them they praised their idols made of gold, silver, bronze, iron, wood, and stone.

⁵Suddenly, they saw the fingers of a human hand writing on the plaster wall of the king's palace, near the lampstand. The king himself saw the hand as it wrote, ⁶and his face turned pale with fright. His knees knocked together in fear and his legs gave way beneath him.

⁷The king shouted for the enchanters, astrologers,* and fortune-tellers to be brought before him. He said to these wise men of Babylon, "Whoever can read this writing and tell me what it means will be dressed in purple robes of royal honor and will have a gold chain placed around his neck. He will become the third highest ruler in the kingdom!"

⁸But when all the king's wise men had come in, none of them could read the writing or tell him what it meant. ⁹So the king grew even more alarmed, and his face turned pale. His nobles, too, were shaken.

¹⁰But when the queen mother heard what was happening, she hurried to the banquet hall. She said to Belshazzar, "Long live the king! Don't be so pale and frightened. ¹¹There is a man in your kingdom who has within him the spirit of the holy gods. During Nebuchadnezzar's reign, this man was found to have insight, understanding, and wisdom like that of the gods. Your predecessor, the king—your predecessor King Nebuchadnezzar—made him chief over all the magicians, enchanters, astrologers, and fortune-tellers of Babylon. ¹²This man Daniel, whom the king named Belteshazzar, has exceptional ability and is filled with divine knowledge and understanding. He can interpret dreams, explain riddles, and solve difficult problems. Call for Daniel, and he will tell you what the writing means."

Daniel Explains the Writing

¹³So Daniel was brought in before the king. The king asked him, "Are you Daniel, one of the exiles brought from Judah by my predecessor, King Nebuchadnezzar? ¹⁴I have heard that you have the spirit of the gods within you and that you are filled with insight, understanding, and wisdom. ¹⁵My wise men and enchanters have tried to read the words on the wall and tell me their meaning, but they cannot do it. ¹⁶I am told that you can give interpretations and solve difficult problems. If you can read these words and tell me their meaning, you will be clothed in purple robes of royal honor, and you will have a gold chain placed around your neck. You will become the third highest ruler in the kingdom."

¹⁷Daniel answered the king, "Keep your gifts or give them to someone else, but I will tell you what the writing means. ¹⁸Your Majesty, the Most High God gave sovereignty, majesty, glory, and honor to your predecessor, Nebuchadnezzar. ¹⁹He made him so great that people of all races and nations and languages trembled before him in fear. He killed those he wanted to kill and spared those he wanted to spare. He honored those he wanted to honor and disgraced those he wanted to disgrace. ²⁰But when his heart and mind were puffed up with arrogance, he was brought down from his royal throne and stripped of his glory. ²¹He was driven from human society. He was given the mind of a wild animal, and he lived among the wild donkeys. He ate grass like a cow, and he was drenched with the dew of heaven, until he learned that the Most High God rules over the kingdoms of the world and appoints anyone he desires to rule over them.

²²"You are his successor,* O Belshazzar,

5:2 Aramaic *father;* also in 5:11, 13, 18. 5:7 Or *Chaldeans;* also in 5:11. 5:22 Aramaic *son.*

army had surrounded Babylon during Belshazzar's feast and would soon capture the city. We need to deal with problems when they arise and not hide behind our dependency. If we don't act right away, it may be too late to escape disaster.

5:18-31 Tragically, it is possible to wait too long to enter recovery. Belshazzar had not learned from the experiences of his predecessor Nebuchadnezzar, and his time ran out. His pride and arrogance had led him to the point where there could be no recovery; he was killed before the night was over. It doesn't have to be too late—we can find recovery when we turn to God. The time to trust God is now, while our heart is still soft enough to hear God calling. Without God, we may as well apply the writing on the wall to our own lives.

and you knew all this, yet you have not humbled yourself. [23]For you have proudly defied the Lord of heaven and have had these cups from his Temple brought before you. You and your nobles and your wives and concubines have been drinking wine from them while praising gods of silver, gold, bronze, iron, wood, and stone—gods that neither see nor hear nor know anything at all. But you have not honored the God who gives you the breath of life and controls your destiny! [24]So God has sent this hand to write this message.

[25]"This is the message that was written: MENE, MENE, TEKEL, and PARSIN. [26]This is what these words mean:

Mene means 'numbered'—God has numbered the days of your reign and has brought it to an end.
[27] Tekel means 'weighed'—you have been weighed on the balances and have not measured up.
[28] Parsin* means 'divided'—your kingdom has been divided and given to the Medes and Persians."

[29]Then at Belshazzar's command, Daniel was dressed in purple robes, a gold chain was hung around his neck, and he was proclaimed the third highest ruler in the kingdom.

[30]That very night Belshazzar, the Babylonian* king, was killed.*

[31]*And Darius the Mede took over the kingdom at the age of sixty-two.

CHAPTER 6
Daniel in the Lions' Den

[1]*Darius the Mede decided to divide the kingdom into 120 provinces, and he appointed a high officer to rule over each province. [2]The king also chose Daniel and two others as administrators to supervise the high officers and protect the king's interests. [3]Daniel soon proved himself more capable than all the other administrators and high officers. Because of Daniel's great ability, the king made plans to place him over the entire empire.

[4]Then the other administrators and high officers began searching for some fault in the way Daniel was handling government affairs, but they couldn't find anything to criticize or condemn. He was faithful, always responsible, and completely trustworthy. [5]So they concluded, "Our only chance of finding grounds for accusing Daniel will be in connection with the rules of his religion."

[6]So the administrators and high officers went to the king and said, "Long live King Darius! [7]We are all in agreement—we administrators, officials, high officers, advisers, and governors—that the king should make a law that will be strictly enforced. Give orders that for the next thirty days any person who prays to anyone, divine or human—except to you, Your Majesty—will be thrown into the den of lions. [8]And now, Your Majesty, issue and sign this law so it cannot be changed, an official law of the Medes and Persians that cannot be revoked." [9]So King Darius signed the law.

[10]But when Daniel learned that the law had been signed, he went home and knelt down as usual in his upstairs room, with its windows open toward Jerusalem. He prayed three times a day, just as he had always done, giving thanks to his God. [11]Then the officials went together to Daniel's house and found him praying and asking for God's help. [12]So they went straight to the king and reminded him about his law. "Did you not sign a law that for the next thirty days any person who prays to anyone, divine or human—except to you, Your Majesty—will be thrown into the den of lions?"

5:28 Aramaic *Peres*, the singular of *Parsin*. 5:30a Or *Chaldean*. 5:30b The Persians and Medes conquered Babylon in October 539 B.C. 5:31 Verse 5:31 is numbered 6:1 in Aramaic text. 6:1 Verses 6:1-28 are numbered 6:2-29 in Aramaic text.

6:1-4 Just because a person is healthy and balanced from an emotional and spiritual standpoint doesn't guarantee popularity or acceptance. Such wholeness, especially if it is matched with ability, can be quite intimidating to those who do not understand recovery. There will always be those who are threatened by or jealous of our progress in recovery. They may try to keep us from achieving our goals so they can feel important or powerful. When we are prepared for this, we won't be swayed by their intimidation.

6:11-17 We must always consider how our actions will affect others. The king satisfied his ego by issuing the new law but failed to realize its impact. As a result, Daniel, who was obviously close to the king, was sentenced to die. Before doing anything, it is important to evaluate the significance of a decision. Will anyone be hurt by it? Is it morally wrong? Will we regret the outcome? If any of these questions can be answered yes, we need to consider another plan of action.

"Yes," the king replied, "that decision stands; it is an official law of the Medes and Persians that cannot be revoked."

[13]Then they told the king, "That man Daniel, one of the captives from Judah, is ignoring you and your law. He still prays to his God three times a day."

[14]Hearing this, the king was deeply troubled, and he tried to think of a way to save Daniel. He spent the rest of the day looking for a way to get Daniel out of this predicament.

[15]In the evening the men went together to the king and said, "Your Majesty, you know that according to the law of the Medes and the Persians, no law that the king signs can be changed."

[16]So at last the king gave orders for Daniel to be arrested and thrown into the den of lions. The king said to him, "May your God, whom you serve so faithfully, rescue you."

[17]A stone was brought and placed over the mouth of the den. The king sealed the stone with his own royal seal and the seals of his nobles, so that no one could rescue Daniel. [18]Then the king returned to his palace and spent the night fasting. He refused his usual entertainment and couldn't sleep at all that night.

[19]Very early the next morning, the king got up and hurried out to the lions' den. [20]When he got there, he called out in anguish, "Daniel, servant of the living God! Was your God, whom you serve so faithfully, able to rescue you from the lions?"

[21]Daniel answered, "Long live the king! [22]My God sent his angel to shut the lions' mouths so that they would not hurt me, for I have been found innocent in his sight. And I have not wronged you, Your Majesty."

[23]The king was overjoyed and ordered that Daniel be lifted from the den. Not a scratch was found on him, for he had trusted in his God.

[24]Then the king gave orders to arrest the men who had maliciously accused Daniel. He had them thrown into the lions' den, along with their wives and children. The lions leaped on them and tore them apart before they even hit the floor of the den.

[25]Then King Darius sent this message to the people of every race and nation and language throughout the world:

"Peace and prosperity to you!

[26]"I decree that everyone throughout my kingdom should tremble with fear before the God of Daniel.

For he is the living God,
  and he will endure forever.
His kingdom will never be destroyed,
  and his rule will never end.
[27]He rescues and saves his people;
  he performs miraculous signs and
    wonders
  in the heavens and on earth.
He has rescued Daniel
  from the power of the lions."

[28]So Daniel prospered during the reign of Darius and the reign of Cyrus the Persian.*

CHAPTER 7
Daniel's Vision of Four Beasts

Earlier, during the first year of King Belshazzar's reign in Babylon,* Daniel had a dream and saw visions as he lay in his bed. He wrote down the dream, and this is what he saw.

[2]In my vision that night, I, Daniel, saw a great storm churning the surface of a great sea, with strong winds blowing from every direction. [3]Then four huge beasts came up out of the water, each different from the others.

6:28 Or *of Darius, that is, the reign of Cyrus the Persian.* 7:1 The first year of Belshazzar's reign (who was co-regent with his father, Nabonidus) was 556 B.C. (or perhaps as late as 553 B.C.).

6:25-27 Not only will we benefit from God's work in our life, but others will too. Darius saw the awesome power of Daniel's God and declared it to the nations; he was also relieved of the guilt he felt for sentencing Daniel to death. As we are patient in our sufferings, we may find that God is using us to reach others. Those who abuse or persecute us, whether intentionally or unintentionally, need God as much as we do. When God reveals himself to them through us, their lives can change, and they will want to tell others of the power of God.

7:1-14 This vision parallels Nebuchadnezzar's vision of the grand statue in chapter 2. Here, however, the presentation of the successive world empires is made from a godly perspective: They are "beastly" in their thirst for power and control. Their violence and pride are directly opposed to what biblical recovery is all about. We can choose to be proud and abusive, but we will suffer the same terrible fate as the fourth beast. Or we can choose to enter recovery, obeying God's will for our life. If we do, we will enjoy the glory of God's Kingdom forever.

⁴The first beast was like a lion with eagles' wings. As I watched, its wings were pulled off, and it was left standing with its two hind feet on the ground, like a human being. And it was given a human mind.

⁵Then I saw a second beast, and it looked like a bear. It was rearing up on one side, and it had three ribs in its mouth between its teeth. And I heard a voice saying to it, "Get up! Devour the flesh of many people!"

⁶Then the third of these strange beasts appeared, and it looked like a leopard. It had four bird's wings on its back, and it had four heads. Great authority was given to this beast.

⁷Then in my vision that night, I saw a fourth beast—terrifying, dreadful, and very strong. It devoured and crushed its victims with huge iron teeth and trampled their remains beneath its feet. It was different from any of the other beasts, and it had ten horns.

⁸As I was looking at the horns, suddenly another small horn appeared among them. Three of the first horns were torn out by the roots to make room for it. This little horn had eyes like human eyes and a mouth that was boasting arrogantly.

⁹ I watched as thrones were put in place
    and the Ancient One* sat down to
        judge.
His clothing was as white as snow,
    his hair like purest wool.
He sat on a fiery throne
    with wheels of blazing fire,
¹⁰ and a river of fire was pouring out,
    flowing from his presence.
Millions of angels ministered to him;
    many millions stood to attend him.
Then the court began its session,
    and the books were opened.

¹¹I continued to watch because I could hear the little horn's boastful speech. I kept watching until the fourth beast was killed and its body was destroyed by fire. ¹²The other three beasts had their authority taken from them, but they were allowed to live a while longer.*

¹³As my vision continued that night, I saw someone like a son of man* coming with the clouds of heaven. He approached the Ancient One and was led into his presence. ¹⁴He was given authority, honor, and sovereignty over all the nations of the world, so that people of every race and nation and language would obey him. His rule is eternal—it will never end. His kingdom will never be destroyed.

The Vision Is Explained

¹⁵I, Daniel, was troubled by all I had seen, and my visions terrified me. ¹⁶So I approached one of those standing beside the throne and asked him what it all meant. He explained it to me like this: ¹⁷"These four huge beasts represent four kingdoms that will arise from the earth. ¹⁸But in the end, the holy people of the Most High will be given the kingdom, and they will rule forever and ever."

¹⁹Then I wanted to know the true meaning of the fourth beast, the one so different from the others and so terrifying. It had devoured and crushed its victims with iron teeth and bronze claws, trampling their remains beneath its feet. ²⁰I also asked about the ten horns on the fourth beast's head and the little horn that came up afterward and destroyed three of the other horns. This horn had seemed greater than the others, and it had human eyes and a mouth that was boasting arrogantly. ²¹As I watched, this horn was waging war against God's holy people and was defeating them, ²²until the Ancient One—the Most High—came and judged in favor of his holy people. Then the time arrived for the holy people to take over the kingdom.

²³Then he said to me, "This fourth beast is the fourth world power that will rule the earth. It will be different from all the others. It will devour the whole world, trampling and crushing everything in its path. ²⁴Its ten horns are ten kings who will rule that empire. Then another king will arise, different from the other ten, who will subdue three of them. ²⁵He will defy the Most High and oppress the holy people of the Most High. He will try to change their sacred festivals and laws, and they will be placed under his control for a time, times, and half a time.

²⁶"But then the court will pass judgment, and all his power will be taken away and completely destroyed. ²⁷Then the sovereignty, power, and greatness of all the kingdoms under heaven will be given to the holy people of the Most High. His kingdom will last forever, and all rulers will serve and obey him."

²⁸That was the end of the vision. I, Daniel, was terrified by my thoughts and my face was pale with fear, but I kept these things to myself.

7:9 Aramaic *an Ancient of Days;* also in 7:13, 22.   7:12 Aramaic *for a season and a time.*   7:13 Or *like a Son of Man.*

CHAPTER 8
Daniel's Vision of a Ram and Goat

[1]*During the third year of King Belshazzar's reign, I, Daniel, saw another vision, following the one that had already appeared to me. [2]In this vision I was at the fortress of Susa, in the province of Elam, standing beside the Ulai River.*

[3]As I looked up, I saw a ram with two long horns standing beside the river.* One of the horns was longer than the other, even though it had grown later than the other one. [4]The ram butted everything out of his way to the west, to the north, and to the south, and no one could stand against him or help his victims. He did as he pleased and became very great.

[5]While I was watching, suddenly a male goat appeared from the west, crossing the land so swiftly that he didn't even touch the ground. This goat, which had one very large horn between its eyes, [6]headed toward the two-horned ram that I had seen standing beside the river, rushing at him in a rage. [7]The goat charged furiously at the ram and struck him, breaking off both his horns. Now the ram was helpless, and the goat knocked him down and trampled him. No one could rescue the ram from the goat's power.

[8]The goat became very powerful. But at the height of his power, his large horn was broken off. In the large horn's place grew four prominent horns pointing in the four directions of the earth. [9]Then from one of the prominent horns came a small horn whose power grew very great. It extended toward the south and the east and toward the glorious land of Israel. [10]Its power reached to the heavens, where it attacked the heavenly army, throwing some of the heavenly beings and some of the stars to the ground and trampling them. [11]It even challenged the Commander of heaven's army by canceling the daily sacrifices offered to him and by destroying his Temple. [12]The army of heaven was restrained from responding to this rebellion. So the daily sacrifice was halted, and truth was overthrown. The horn succeeded in everything it did.*

[13]Then I heard two holy ones talking to each other. One of them asked, "How long will the events of this vision last? How long will the rebellion that causes desecration stop the daily sacrifices? How long will the Temple and heaven's army be trampled on?"

[14]The other replied, "It will take 2,300 evenings and mornings; then the Temple will be made right again."

Gabriel Explains the Vision

[15]As I, Daniel, was trying to understand the meaning of this vision, someone who looked like a man stood in front of me. [16]And I heard a human voice calling out from the Ulai River, "Gabriel, tell this man the meaning of his vision."

[17]As Gabriel approached the place where I was standing, I became so terrified that I fell with my face to the ground. "Son of man," he said, "you must understand that the events you have seen in your vision relate to the time of the end."

[18]While he was speaking, I fainted and lay there with my face to the ground. But Gabriel roused me with a touch and helped me to my feet.

[19]Then he said, "I am here to tell you what will happen later in the time of wrath. What you have seen pertains to the very end of time. [20]The two-horned ram represents the kings of Media and Persia. [21]The shaggy male goat represents the king of Greece,* and the

8:1 The original text from this point through chapter 12 is in Hebrew. See note at 2:4. 8:2 Or *the Ulai Gate;* also in 8:16. 8:3 Or *the gate;* also in 8:6. 8:11-12 The meaning of the Hebrew for these verses is uncertain. 8:21 Hebrew *of Javan.*

8:5-8, 21 Although not the most prominent figure in this vision of the future, Alexander the Great, "the first king of the Greek Empire" (8:21), presents an important lesson for those in recovery. While oppressors may seem to have great power and be invincible, God is ultimately in control of their fate. There is no one in authority who has not been put there by God (see John 19:10-11). When God deems the time right, we will be delivered and our persecutors will be judged.

8:9-14, 25 This prophetic description of the domination of the Jewish people and the Jerusalem Temple by the Greek king, Antiochus IV Epiphanes, carries with it an important point for recovery. Antiochus was allowed to get away with his atrocities for a period of time, but not indefinitely. The days of his abuse were numbered (8:25), and the Temple worship would begin again (8:14). God is aware of the abuse we suffer, and he has set a limit on the amount of pain we will have to endure. In recovery we can pray to God for comfort and guidance, asking for help to get through our anguish until we are set free.

large horn between his eyes represents the first king of the Greek Empire. ²²The four prominent horns that replaced the one large horn show that the Greek Empire will break into four kingdoms, but none as great as the first.

²³"At the end of their rule, when their sin is at its height, a fierce king, a master of intrigue, will rise to power. ²⁴He will become very strong, but not by his own power. He will cause a shocking amount of destruction and succeed in everything he does. He will destroy powerful leaders and devastate the holy people. ²⁵He will be a master of deception and will become arrogant; he will destroy many without warning. He will even take on the Prince of princes in battle, but he will be broken, though not by human power.

²⁶"This vision about the 2,300 evenings and mornings* is true. But none of these things will happen for a long time, so keep this vision a secret."

²⁷Then I, Daniel, was overcome and lay sick for several days. Afterward I got up and performed my duties for the king, but I was greatly troubled by the vision and could not understand it.

CHAPTER 9
Daniel's Prayer for His People

It was the first year of the reign of Darius the Mede, the son of Ahasuerus, who became king of the Babylonians.* ²During the first year of his reign, I, Daniel, learned from reading the word of the LORD, as revealed to Jeremiah the prophet, that Jerusalem must lie desolate for seventy years.* ³So I turned to the Lord God and pleaded with him in prayer and fasting. I also wore rough burlap and sprinkled myself with ashes.

⁴I prayed to the LORD my God and confessed:

"O Lord, you are a great and awesome God! You always fulfill your covenant and keep your promises of unfailing love to those who love you and obey your commands. ⁵But we have sinned and done wrong. We have rebelled against you and scorned your commands and regulations. ⁶We have refused to listen to your servants the prophets, who spoke on your authority to our kings and princes and ancestors and to all the people of the land.

⁷"Lord, you are in the right; but as you see, our faces are covered with shame. This is true of all of us, including the people of Judah and Jerusalem and all Israel, scattered near and far, wherever you have driven us because of our disloyalty to you. ⁸O LORD, we and our kings, princes, and ancestors are covered with shame because we have sinned against you. ⁹But the Lord our God is merciful and forgiving, even though we have rebelled against him. ¹⁰We have not obeyed the LORD our God, for we have not followed the instructions he gave us through his servants the prophets. ¹¹All Israel has disobeyed your instruction and turned away, refusing to listen to your voice.

"So now the solemn curses and judgments written in the Law of Moses, the servant of God, have been poured down on us because of our sin. ¹²You have kept your word and done to us and our rulers exactly as you warned. Never has there been such a disaster as happened in Jerusalem. ¹³Every curse written against us in the Law of Moses has come true. Yet we have refused to seek mercy from the LORD our God by turning from our sins and recognizing his truth. ¹⁴Therefore, the LORD has brought

---

8:26 Hebrew *about the evenings and mornings;* compare 8:14.   9:1 Or *the Chaldeans.*   9:2 See Jer 25:11-12; 29:10.

9:1-3 Daniel makes it clear that victims of dysfunctional systems need recovery too. Because of his nation's sins, Daniel and other "innocent bystanders" had been forced into captivity. But Daniel's innocence did not stop him from fasting and pleading to God for release. We all suffer from the injustices of others. We don't enjoy being victimized. Our pain is real, and we need real healing. Crying out to God for comfort and recovery is the best thing we can do to experience healing; he hears our every cry.

9:10-14 Denial is incredibly powerful. Daniel said that the people of Israel had suffered all the curses that God had promised to send because of their disobedience. Yet even after all their suffering, the people still wouldn't follow God. Had the Israelites been honest, they could have admitted their first mistakes and turned from their sins immediately, avoiding much of the severe punishment God had prepared for them. When we first feel the harmful effects of our addiction, we need to be honest with ourself and with God and ask him to help us.

upon us the disaster he prepared. The LORD our God was right to do all of these things, for we did not obey him.

¹⁵"O Lord our God, you brought lasting honor to your name by rescuing your people from Egypt in a great display of power. But we have sinned and are full of wickedness. ¹⁶In view of all your faithful mercies, Lord, please turn your furious anger away from your city Jerusalem, your holy mountain. All the neighboring nations mock Jerusalem and your people because of our sins and the sins of our ancestors.

¹⁷"O our God, hear your servant's prayer! Listen as I plead. For your own sake, Lord, smile again on your desolate sanctuary.

¹⁸"O my God, lean down and listen to me. Open your eyes and see our despair. See how your city—the city that bears your name—lies in ruins. We make this plea, not because we deserve help, but because of your mercy.

¹⁹"O Lord, hear. O Lord, forgive. O Lord, listen and act! For your own sake, do not delay, O my God, for your people and your city bear your name."

Gabriel's Message about the Anointed One

²⁰I went on praying and confessing my sin and the sin of my people, pleading with the LORD my God for Jerusalem, his holy mountain. ²¹As I was praying, Gabriel, whom I had seen in the earlier vision, came swiftly to me at the time of the evening sacrifice. ²²He explained to me, "Daniel, I have come here to give you insight and understanding. ²³The moment you began praying, a command was given. And now I am here to tell you what it was, for you are very precious to God. Listen carefully so that you can understand the meaning of your vision.

²⁴"A period of seventy sets of seven* has been decreed for your people and your holy

city to finish their rebellion, to put an end to their sin, to atone for their guilt, to bring in everlasting righteousness, to confirm the prophetic vision, and to anoint the Most Holy Place.* ²⁵Now listen and understand! Seven sets of seven plus sixty-two sets of seven* will pass from the time the command is given to rebuild Jerusalem until a ruler—the Anointed One*—comes. Jerusalem will be rebuilt with streets and strong defenses,* despite the perilous times.

²⁶"After this period of sixty-two sets of seven,* the Anointed One will be killed, appearing to have accomplished nothing, and a ruler will arise whose armies will destroy the city and the Temple. The end will come with a flood, and war and its miseries are decreed from that time to the very end. ²⁷The ruler will make a treaty with the people for a period of one set of seven,* but after half this time, he will put an end to the sacrifices and offerings. And as a climax to all his terrible deeds,* he will set up a sacrilegious object that causes desecration,* until the fate decreed for this defiler is finally poured out on him."

CHAPTER 10
Daniel's Vision of a Messenger

In the third year of the reign of King Cyrus of Persia,* Daniel (also known as Belteshazzar) had another vision. He understood that the vision concerned events certain to happen in the future—times of war and great hardship.

²When this vision came to me, I, Daniel, had been in mourning for three whole weeks. ³All that time I had eaten no rich food. No meat or wine crossed my lips, and I used no fragrant lotions until those three weeks had passed.

⁴On April 23,* as I was standing on the bank of the great Tigris River, ⁵I looked up and saw a man dressed in linen clothing, with a belt of pure gold around his waist. ⁶His body looked like a precious gem. His

9:24a Hebrew *seventy sevens.* 9:24b Or *the Most Holy One.* 9:25a Hebrew *Seven sevens plus sixty-two sevens.* 9:25b Or *an anointed one;* similarly in 9:26. Hebrew reads *a messiah.* 9:25c Or *and a moat, or and trenches.* 9:26 Hebrew *After sixty-two sevens.* 9:27a Hebrew *for one seven.* 9:27b Hebrew *And on the wing;* the meaning of the Hebrew is uncertain. 9:27c Hebrew *an abomination of desolation.* 10:1 The third year of Cyrus's reign was 536 B.C. 10:4 Hebrew *On the twenty-fourth day of the first month,* of the ancient Hebrew lunar calendar. This date in the book of Daniel can be cross-checked with dates in surviving Persian records and can be related accurately to our modern calendar. This event occurred on April 23, 536 B.C.

9:20-27 Although Daniel was worried about his people and nation, God had a plan for their recovery. The road would not be easy, and Israel would have many years of pain ahead, but God's time to judge his enemies would come. God hasn't abandoned us in our hour of need. He is there, waiting to work his plan for our life. We are to seek and obey God, trusting in his timing for our complete recovery.

face flashed like lightning, and his eyes flamed like torches. His arms and feet shone like polished bronze, and his voice roared like a vast multitude of people.

[7]Only I, Daniel, saw this vision. The men with me saw nothing, but they were suddenly terrified and ran away to hide. [8]So I was left there all alone to see this amazing vision. My strength left me, my face grew deathly pale, and I felt very weak. [9]Then I heard the man speak, and when I heard the sound of his voice, I fainted and lay there with my face to the ground.

[10]Just then a hand touched me and lifted me, still trembling, to my hands and knees. [11]And the man said to me, "Daniel, you are very precious to God, so listen carefully to what I have to say to you. Stand up, for I have been sent to you." When he said this to me, I stood up, still trembling.

[12]Then he said, "Don't be afraid, Daniel. Since the first day you began to pray for understanding and to humble yourself before your God, your request has been heard in heaven. I have come in answer to your prayer. [13]But for twenty-one days the spirit prince* of the kingdom of Persia blocked my way. Then Michael, one of the archangels,* came to help me, and I left him there with the spirit prince of the kingdom of Persia.* [14]Now I am here to explain what will happen to your people in the future, for this vision concerns a time yet to come."

[15]While he was speaking to me, I looked down at the ground, unable to say a word. [16]Then the one who looked like a man* touched my lips, and I opened my mouth and began to speak. I said to the one standing in front of me, "I am filled with anguish because of the vision I have seen, my lord, and I am very weak. [17]How can someone like me, your servant, talk to you, my lord? My strength is gone, and I can hardly breathe."

[18]Then the one who looked like a man touched me again, and I felt my strength returning. [19]"Don't be afraid," he said, "for you are very precious to God. Peace! Be encouraged! Be strong!"

As he spoke these words to me, I suddenly felt stronger and said to him, "Please speak to me, my lord, for you have strengthened me."

[20]He replied, "Do you know why I have come? Soon I must return to fight against the spirit prince of the kingdom of Persia, and after that the spirit prince of the kingdom of Greece* will come. [21]Meanwhile, I will tell you what is written in the Book of Truth. (No one helps me against these spirit princes except Michael, your spirit prince.* [11:1]I have been standing beside Michael* to support and strengthen him since the first year of the reign of Darius the Mede.)

CHAPTER 11
Kings of the South and North

[2]"Now then, I will reveal the truth to you. Three more Persian kings will reign, to be succeeded by a fourth, far richer than the others. He will use his wealth to stir up everyone to fight against the kingdom of Greece.*

[3]"Then a mighty king will rise to power who will rule with great authority and accomplish everything he sets out to do. [4]But at the height of his power, his kingdom will be broken apart and divided into four parts. It will not be ruled by the king's descendants, nor will the kingdom hold the authority it once had. For his empire will be uprooted and given to others.

[5]"The king of the south will increase in power, but one of his own officials will become more powerful than he and will rule his kingdom with great strength.

10:13a Hebrew *the prince;* also in 10:13c, 20. 10:13b Hebrew *the chief princes.* 10:13c As in one Greek version; Hebrew reads *and I was left there with the kings of Persia.* The meaning of the Hebrew is uncertain. 10:16 As in most manuscripts of the Masoretic Text; one manuscript of the Masoretic Text and one Greek version read *Then something that looked like a human hand.* 10:20 Hebrew *of Javan.* 10:21 Hebrew *against these except Michael, your prince.* 11:1 Hebrew *him.* 11:2 Hebrew *of Javan.*

10:11, 18 Twice God assured Daniel of his great love for him. And God also loves each one of us. When we realize that the Creator of the universe finds value in us, we will understand that our identity isn't wrapped up in our job, possessions, or power. When we truly believe this, we can stop our workaholism or other addiction and begin to feel good about ourself because God loves us.
10:12-13 An important but largely overlooked aspect of recovery has to do with our prayer life and the spiritual warfare we face in the unseen realm. Those of us seeking recovery often have a difficult time praying and tend to give up easily if our prayers are not answered quickly. Satan is aware of this and uses unseen warriors to intercept God's messengers and discourage God's people (see also Ephesians 6:11-12). It may well be that God actually answers the recovering believer's prayer quickly, but the answer is delayed because of spiritual warfare. If we want answers to our prayers, we must keep praying until we get responses.

6"Some years later an alliance will be formed between the king of the north and the king of the south. The daughter of the king of the south will be given in marriage to the king of the north to secure the alliance, but she will lose her influence over him, and so will her father. She will be abandoned along with her supporters. 7But when one of her relatives* becomes king of the south, he will raise an army and enter the fortress of the king of the north and defeat him. 8When he returns to Egypt, he will carry back their idols with him, along with priceless articles of gold and silver. For some years afterward he will leave the king of the north alone.

9"Later the king of the north will invade the realm of the king of the south but will soon return to his own land. 10However, the sons of the king of the north will assemble a mighty army that will advance like a flood and carry the battle as far as the enemy's fortress.

11"Then, in a rage, the king of the south will rally against the vast forces assembled by the king of the north and will defeat them. 12After the enemy army is swept away, the king of the south will be filled with pride and will execute many thousands of his enemies. But his success will be short lived.

13"A few years later the king of the north will return with a fully equipped army far greater than before. 14At that time there will be a general uprising against the king of the south. Violent men among your own people will join them in fulfillment of this vision, but they will not succeed. 15Then the king of the north will come and lay siege to a fortified city and capture it. The best troops of the south will not be able to stand in the face of the onslaught.

16"The king of the north will march onward unopposed; none will be able to stop him. He will pause in the glorious land of Israel,* intent on destroying it. 17He will make plans to come with the might of his entire kingdom and will form an alliance with the king of the south. He will give him a daughter in marriage in order to overthrow the kingdom from within, but his plan will fail.

18"After this, he will turn his attention to the coastland and conquer many cities. But a commander from another land will put an end to his insolence and cause him to retreat in shame. 19He will take refuge in his own fortresses but will stumble and fall and be seen no more.

20"His successor will send out a tax collector to maintain the royal splendor. But after a very brief reign, he will die, though not from anger or in battle.

21"The next to come to power will be a despicable man who is not in line for royal succession. He will slip in when least expected and take over the kingdom by flattery and intrigue. 22Before him great armies will be swept away, including a covenant prince. 23With deceitful promises, he will make various alliances. He will become strong despite having only a handful of followers. 24Without warning he will enter the richest areas of the land. Then he will distribute among his followers the plunder and wealth of the rich—something his predecessors had never done. He will plot the overthrow of strongholds, but this will last for only a short while.

25"Then he will stir up his courage and raise a great army against the king of the south. The king of the south will go to battle with a mighty army, but to no avail, for there will be plots against him. 26His own household will cause his downfall. His army will be swept away, and many will be killed. 27Seeking nothing but each other's harm, these kings will plot against each other at the conference table, attempting to deceive each other. But it will make no difference, for the end will come at the appointed time.

28"The king of the north will then return home with great riches. On the way he will set himself against the people of the holy covenant, doing much damage before continuing his journey.

29"Then at the appointed time he will once again invade the south, but this time the result will be different. 30For warships from western coastlands* will scare him off, and he will withdraw and return home. But he will vent his anger against the people of the

11:7 Hebrew *a branch from her roots.* 11:16 Hebrew *the glorious land.* 11:30 Hebrew *from Kittim.*

11:12 The success of the king of the south (or the king of Egypt) would be short lived, probably as God's judgment for his pride. If there is anyone God cannot help, it is the proud person who takes the credit for all his or her success. God effects the changes within us. When we believe that we have made progress because of our own efforts, we distance ourself from God and lose ground in the recovery process. Thanking God for his work in us and giving him the credit he deserves will help us to keep depending on him.

holy covenant and reward those who forsake the covenant.

[31]"His army will take over the Temple fortress, pollute the sanctuary, put a stop to the daily sacrifices, and set up the sacrilegious object that causes desecration.* [32]He will flatter and win over those who have violated the covenant. But the people who know their God will be strong and will resist him.

[33]"Wise leaders will give instruction to many, but these teachers will die by fire and sword, or they will be jailed and robbed. [34]During these persecutions, little help will arrive, and many who join them will not be sincere. [35]And some of the wise will fall victim to persecution. In this way, they will be refined and cleansed and made pure until the time of the end, for the appointed time is still to come.

[36]"The king will do as he pleases, exalting himself and claiming to be greater than every god, even blaspheming the God of gods. He will succeed, but only until the time of wrath is completed. For what has been determined will surely take place. [37]He will have no respect for the gods of his ancestors, or for the god loved by women, or for any other god, for he will boast that he is greater than them all. [38]Instead of these, he will worship the god of fortresses—a god his ancestors never knew—and lavish on him gold, silver, precious stones, and expensive gifts. [39]Claiming this foreign god's help, he will attack the strongest fortresses. He will honor those who submit to him, appointing them to positions of authority and dividing the land among them as their reward.*

[40]"Then at the time of the end, the king of the south will attack the king of the north. The king of the north will storm out with chariots, charioteers, and a vast navy. He will invade various lands and sweep through them like a flood. [41]He will enter the glorious land of Israel,* and many nations will fall, but Moab, Edom, and the best part of Ammon will escape. [42]He will conquer many countries, and even Egypt will not escape. [43]He will gain control over the gold, silver, and treasures of Egypt, and the Libyans and Ethiopians* will be his servants.

[44]"But then news from the east and the north will alarm him, and he will set out in great anger to destroy and obliterate many. [45]He will stop between the glorious holy mountain and the sea and will pitch his royal tents. But while he is there, his time will suddenly run out, and no one will help him.

CHAPTER 12
The Time of the End

"At that time Michael, the archangel* who stands guard over your nation, will arise. Then there will be a time of anguish greater than any since nations first came into existence. But at that time every one of your people whose name is written in the book will be rescued. [2]Many of those whose bodies lie dead and buried will rise up, some to everlasting life and some to shame and everlasting disgrace. [3]Those who are wise will shine as bright as the sky, and those who lead many to righteousness will shine like the stars forever. [4]But you, Daniel, keep this prophecy a secret; seal up the book until the time of the end, when many will rush here and there, and knowledge will increase."

[5]Then I, Daniel, looked and saw two others standing on opposite banks of the river. [6]One of them asked the man dressed in linen, who was now standing above the river, "How long will it be until these shocking events are over?"

[7]The man dressed in linen, who was standing above the river, raised both his hands toward heaven and took a solemn oath by the One who lives forever, saying, "It

11:31 Hebrew *the abomination of desolation.* 11:39 Or *at a price.* 11:41 Hebrew *the glorious land.* 11:43 Hebrew *Cushites.* 12:1 Hebrew *the great prince.*

11:35 Stumbling in recovery can serve to cleanse and strengthen us. We can look at the times we stumble as a weight lifter looks at weights: If they weren't hard to lift, he wouldn't gain any muscle. At first we may stumble a lot, but as we struggle, we grow stronger. Eventually we will be able to resist greater and greater temptations where we once would have fallen. Through these spiritual workouts we gradually are transformed from weaklings into strong people.

12:1-4, 13 As we face recovery, we would probably like to believe that life will never again be as painful as it was before recovery. That, however, cannot be guaranteed. Prior to the resurrection at the end of the age, there will be a time of unparalleled suffering for God's people, and between now and then, there will be consistent tribulation for God's people (see also Acts 14:22). While we may have faith, courage, and wisdom during that time, we will never have answers to all our questions in this life. However, we have the assurance that we will live forever with God and understand everything in the end.

will go on for a time, times, and half a time. When the shattering of the holy people has finally come to an end, all these things will have happened."

⁸I heard what he said, but I did not understand what he meant. So I asked, "How will all this finally end, my lord?"

⁹But he said, "Go now, Daniel, for what I have said is kept secret and sealed until the time of the end. ¹⁰Many will be purified, cleansed, and refined by these trials. But the wicked will continue in their wickedness,

and none of them will understand. Only those who are wise will know what it means. ¹¹"From the time the daily sacrifice is stopped and the sacrilegious object that causes desecration* is set up to be worshiped, there will be 1,290 days. ¹²And blessed are those who wait and remain until the end of the 1,335 days!

¹³"As for you, go your way until the end. You will rest, and then at the end of the days, you will rise again to receive the inheritance set aside for you."

12:11 Hebrew *the abomination of desolation.*

12:10 The suffering that may have to be endured by those in recovery will, thankfully, have a very positive effect. These difficult trials will teach us lessons that will help us in the future. But for those who deny God and the truth, there will be no learning and no purification. Through openness, honesty, and self-examination we will gain recovery and become the people God wants us to be.

REFLECTIONS ON DANIEL

insights FROM DANIEL'S LIFE
When we use the talents and abilities given to us by God, others will notice. In **Daniel 1:17-21** King Nebuchadnezzar saw that Daniel and his friends had more insight than any of the king's magicians or enchanters. The wisdom of these young men is what set them apart from the other advisers and allowed them to overcome the disastrous events of the past. God supplies us with all that we need to triumph over our past.

In **Daniel 2:16-22** we are given a model for what to do when we are in trouble. Daniel needed help, so he gathered his godly friends, and they all prayed. After the prayer was answered, Daniel praised God for his blessings. Praying with others to overcome our dependency and thanking God for his help are essential to recovery. It is easy to forget that God is in control of the recovery process and think that we have defeated our addiction on our own. Thanking God for the progress he allows us to accomplish will help us maintain a proper focus on God.

In **Daniel 6:6-10** the prophet chose to ignore the king's new law and continued to worship God, who had cared for Daniel throughout his life. Fortunately, prayer doesn't earn the death penalty for most of us, but there can be drawbacks to following God. We can be laughed at, discriminated against, or beaten up by people who are threatened by our faith. No matter what oppositions we face, however, God is still worthy of our trust. Recovery depends on our worshiping him despite the consequences.

In **Daniel 6:19-23** God rescued Daniel from what seemed a sure death. The lions didn't harm

Daniel, just as the fire hadn't touched Shadrach, Meshach, and Abednego (see 3:1-30). God protects those who obey his will. He is able to save us when no one else can. Even if we are in an abusive situation with no hope of escape, God is still able to deliver us. We need to continue to trust in him.

Everyone is guilty of sinning against God, and we all need recovery from the eternal consequences of our sin—death (see Romans 6:23). In **Daniel 9:7-9** even the godly prophet Daniel admitted his sins, asked for God's mercy, and let God work in his life. These are the same steps we need to follow as we recover from our powerful dependency and its consequences. Twenty-five centuries have not changed the way God works in people's lives.

insights FROM THE LIVES OF THE THREE FRIENDS

We all face situations in which we are tempted to do things that are wrong. Sometimes there are consequences for not going along with the crowd. This fact is clearly illustrated in **Daniel 3:1-30**. The penalty for not bowing down to the king was death in a fiery furnace. When we stand for what is right and refuse to go along with the crowd, we may suffer consequences—ostracism, ridicule, or physical abuse, to name a few. But we must have the courage to do what is right and resist those who want us to step outside our established boundaries of godly behavior.

In **Daniel 3:16-23** Shadrach, Meshach, and Abednego put their faith on the line by not giving in to Nebuchadnezzar's threats. They risked their lives in order to obey what they knew to be God's will for them. To die was better than to live with the guilt and shame of disobeying God. Do we have the faith we need to stand up against our oppressors and follow God? If we do, we will be rewarded. If not, our recovery will fail.

HOSEA

THE BIG PICTURE

A. HOSEA'S MARRIAGE: A PICTURE OF GOD'S UNFAILING LOVE (1:1–3:5)
   1. Hosea's Dysfunctional Family (1:1–2:1)
   2. The Unfaithful Wife and Mother (2:2-13)
   3. The Reconciliation of Husband and Wife (2:14-23)
   4. The Recovery of the Unfaithful Wife (3:1-5)

B. HOSEA'S MESSAGES: TEACHING ABOUT GOD'S UNFAILING LOVE (4:1–14:9)
   1. God's Complaints against Israel (4:1-19)
   2. Israel's Refusal to Return to God (5:1–8:14)
   3. God Uses "Tough Love" (9:1-9)
   4. Israel's History of Rejecting God's Love (9:10–13:16)
   5. The Reconciliation of God and Israel (14:1-9)

God called Hosea to reveal through word and deed that God still loved his people and desired to restore his relationship with them. So God commanded Hosea to marry a woman who both God and Hosea knew from the start would never be faithful. As soon as Hosea and his wife's children were born, she prostituted herself again and, in time, became enslaved. In response to God's command, Hosea then redeemed his wife from slavery and restored her to the family. God intended this demonstration of unconditional love to be a symbol of his own love for the people of Israel.

The book of Hosea tells of God's stormy relationship with his people. God treated them with mercy and compassion even though they rejected him and his will for them many times. Although God was angered by the unfaithfulness of his people, he never stopped loving them or rejected them completely. Neither did he enable their sins by extending to them unqualified mercy; he allowed the people of Israel to suffer the consequences of their disobedience. He made their restoration possible through repentance and perseverance during a period of painful exile.

The story of Hosea's love for Gomer is the story of God's love for the wayward Israelites. It is also the story of God's love for us. We sometimes choose the way of disobedience that inevitably leads to suffering and exile. But as God did with Israel, he often uses the pain of exile to bring us to our senses and lead us back to him. Then we experience God's unfailing love and the healing that is possible through an intimate relationship with him.

THE BOTTOM LINE

PURPOSE: To reveal God's unending love for his sinful people and his desire to restore the relationship between himself and Israel. AUTHOR: The prophet Hosea. AUDIENCE: The people of the northern kingdom of Israel. DATE WRITTEN: Approximately 715 B.C., shortly after Hosea's ministry (755–722 B.C.). SETTING: The northern kingdom of Israel just prior to its conquest by Assyria in 722 B.C.. KEY VERSE: "Plant the good seeds of righteousness, and you will harvest a crop of love. Plow up the hard ground of your hearts, for now is the time to seek the LORD, that he may come and shower righteousness upon you" (10:12). KEY PEOPLE AND RELATIONSHIPS: Hosea, his wife Gomer, and their children.

RECOVERY THEMES

The Power of Committed Love: It is always hard to love people who don't deserve it, but these are the people who need to be loved the most. The kind of love that God pours out on us is unconditional. It has a powerful healing effect, especially when we are helplessly trapped by our dependency and feel unworthy of love. Throughout the book of Hosea we hear this message: God loves us and reaches out to us no matter how unworthy we are. Understanding this fact is foundational for our healing and recovery.

Tough Love Leads to Recovery: God will never enable us to live a destructive lifestyle. His love is tough; it is confrontational. He cares enough to stop us before we are destroyed by our decisions and activities. Sometimes God uses suffering to help us realize that our ungodly lifestyle has destructive consequences. God showed his love for his people by allowing them to suffer captivity in a foreign land. All too often our love becomes enabling instead of healing. Not so with God. He knows that it takes tough love to help us accept how powerless we are and how much we need his help in the process of recovery.

God Is Merciful: When Hosea found Gomer after she had returned to prostitution, his intent was not punishment but mercy. He wanted restoration and recovery for her. When God allowed Israel to be conquered by Assyria, it was an expression of his mercy; it was a significant part of God's program for Israel's restoration and recovery. We can be confident that as we put our life in God's hands, he will use even the pain in our life to bring healing. God is ready and willing to show mercy to all who turn to him for help.

Never "Too Far Gone" for God: Gomer was a failure; she ended up selling herself into slavery in order to survive. But Hosea did not give up on her. Likewise, Israel was a failure, turning to other gods in rebellion. But God did not give up on his people. If we have become a slave to our dependency and feel powerless to change, we can be sure that God will never give up on us. Turn to God now.

CHAPTER 1

The LORD gave this message to Hosea son of Beeri during the years when Uzziah, Jotham, Ahaz, and Hezekiah were kings of Judah, and Jeroboam son of Jehoash* was king of Israel.

Hosea's Wife and Children

²When the LORD first began speaking to Israel through Hosea, he said to him, "Go and marry a prostitute,* so that some of her children will be conceived in prostitution. This will illustrate how Israel has acted like a prostitute by turning against the LORD and worshiping other gods."

³So Hosea married Gomer, the daughter of Diblaim, and she became pregnant and gave Hosea a son. ⁴And the LORD said, "Name the child Jezreel, for I am about to punish King Jehu's dynasty to avenge the murders he committed at Jezreel. In fact, I will bring an end to Israel's independence. ⁵I will break its military power in the Jezreel Valley."

⁶Soon Gomer became pregnant again and gave birth to a daughter. And the LORD said to Hosea, "Name your daughter Lo-ruhamah—'Not loved'—for I will no longer show love to the people of Israel or forgive them. ⁷But I will show love to the people of Judah. I will free them from their enemies—not with weapons and armies or horses and charioteers, but by my power as the LORD their God."

⁸After Gomer had weaned Lo-ruhamah, she again became pregnant and gave birth to

---

1:1 Hebrew *Joash*, a variant spelling of Jehoash. 1:2 Or *a promiscuous woman.*

1:2-3 God told Hosea to marry a prostitute. Their relationship would symbolize God's relationship with the Israelites, who prostituted themselves to the false gods of their pagan neighbors. Through this analogy it is easy to see how it must hurt God when we seek other sources for recovery, whether psychics and crystals, or any recovery program that ignores God. When we are in trouble, we should turn to God, our "husband" (see 2 Corinthians 11:2). He loves us and wants to take care of us, no matter how great our past failures.

1:6 God seemed to be saying that his relationship with Israel had ended. But naming Hosea's daughter Lo-ruhamah ("not loved") showed God's tough love. In the past God had shown the Israelites mercy despite their unrepentant hearts. Now genuine love demanded that God withdraw that mercy to allow them to suffer the consequences of their actions and abandon all their false hopes. Allowing others to experience the consequences of their wrong actions is often hard to do because (1) we don't want our loved ones to suffer, and (2) we feel a sense of importance when we help them. But codependent relationships don't teach addicted people responsibility and accountability. Often the best thing to do for people who keep falling into sin is to refuse to catch them so they can learn from the painful consequences of their actions and seek recovery.

a second son. ⁹And the LORD said, "Name him Lo-ammi—'Not my people'—for Israel is not my people, and I am not their God.

¹⁰*"Yet the time will come when Israel's people will be like the sands of the seashore—too many to count! Then, at the place where they were told, 'You are not my people,' it will be said, 'You are children of the living God.' ¹¹Then the people of Judah and Israel will unite together. They will choose one leader for themselves, and they will return from exile together. What a day that will be—the day of Jezreel*—when God will again plant his people in his land.

²:¹*"In that day you will call your brothers Ammi—'My people.' And you will call your sisters Ruhamah—'The ones I love.'

CHAPTER 2
Charges against an Unfaithful Wife

² "But now bring charges against
    Israel—your mother—
  for she is no longer my wife,
    and I am no longer her husband.
  Tell her to remove the prostitute's makeup
    from her face
    and the clothing that exposes her
      breasts.
³ Otherwise, I will strip her as naked
    as she was on the day she was born.
  I will leave her to die of thirst,
    as in a dry and barren wilderness.
⁴ And I will not love her children,
    for they were conceived in prostitution.
⁵ Their mother is a shameless prostitute
    and became pregnant in a shameful
      way.
  She said, 'I'll run after other lovers
    and sell myself to them for food and
      water,
  for clothing of wool and linen,
    and for olive oil and drinks.'

⁶ "For this reason I will fence her in with
    thornbushes.
  I will block her path with a wall
    to make her lose her way.
⁷ When she runs after her lovers,

she won't be able to catch them.
  She will search for them
    but not find them.
  Then she will think,
  'I might as well return to my husband,
    for I was better off with him than I am
      now.'
⁸ She doesn't realize it was I who gave her
      everything she has—
  the grain, the new wine, the olive oil;
  I even gave her silver and gold.
    But she gave all my gifts to Baal.

⁹ "But now I will take back the ripened
    grain and new wine
  I generously provided each harvest
    season.
  I will take away the wool and linen
    clothing
  I gave her to cover her nakedness.
¹⁰ I will strip her naked in public,
    while all her lovers look on.
  No one will be able
    to rescue her from my hands.
¹¹ I will put an end to her annual festivals,
    her new moon celebrations, and her
      Sabbath days—
  all her appointed festivals.
¹² I will destroy her grapevines and fig trees,
    things she claims her lovers gave her.
  I will let them grow into tangled thickets,
    where only wild animals will eat the
      fruit.
¹³ I will punish her for all those times
    when she burned incense to her images
      of Baal,
  when she put on her earrings and jewels
    and went out to look for her lovers
  but forgot all about me,"
    says the LORD.

The LORD's Love for Unfaithful Israel

¹⁴ "But then I will win her back once again.
  I will lead her into the desert
    and speak tenderly to her there.
¹⁵ I will return her vineyards to her
    and transform the Valley of Trouble*
      into a gateway of hope.

1:10 Verses 1:10-11 are numbered 2:1-2 in Hebrew text. 1:11 *Jezreel* means "God plants." 2:1 Verses 2:1-23 are numbered 2:3-25 in Hebrew text. 2:15 Hebrew *valley of Achor.*

2:5-13 Our addictions and compulsions are like Israel's foreign gods, because in them we search for the joy and fulfillment that only God can give. God is patient with us, but if we put off recovery, he will ultimately turn us over to the shameful, painful consequences of our addiction. God will refuse to rescue us because we need to see just what our "gods" have given us. But even though we have failed, we can have hope because God loves us; we don't have to die in our sins. If we repent and turn to God for help, he will redeem us.

She will give herself to me there,
  as she did long ago when she was
  young,
  when I freed her from her captivity
  in Egypt.
[16] When that day comes," says the LORD,
  "you will call me 'my husband'
  instead of 'my master.'*
[17] O Israel, I will wipe the many names
  of Baal from your lips,
  and you will never mention them again.
[18] On that day I will make a covenant
  with all the wild animals and the birds
  of the sky
  and the animals that scurry along the
  ground
  so they will not harm you.
I will remove all weapons of war from the
  land,
  all swords and bows,
  so you can live unafraid
  in peace and safety.
[19] I will make you my wife forever,
  showing you righteousness and
  justice,
  unfailing love and compassion.
[20] I will be faithful to you and make you
  mine,
  and you will finally know me
  as the LORD.

[21] "In that day, I will answer,"
  says the LORD.
"I will answer the sky as it pleads for
  clouds.
  And the sky will answer the earth
  with rain.
[22] Then the earth will answer the thirsty
  cries
  of the grain, the grapevines, and the
  olive trees.
  And they in turn will answer,
  'Jezreel'—'God plants!'
[23] At that time I will plant a crop of Israelites
  and raise them for myself.
I will show love
  to those I called 'Not loved.'*
  And to those I called 'Not my people,'*
  I will say, 'Now you are my people.'
  And they will reply, 'You are our God!'"

CHAPTER 3
Hosea's Wife Is Redeemed
Then the LORD said to me, "Go and love your wife again, even though she* commits adultery with another lover. This will illustrate that the LORD still loves Israel, even though the people have turned to other gods and love to worship them.*"
  [2] So I bought her back for fifteen pieces of silver* and five bushels of barley and a mea-

---

2:16 Hebrew *'my baal.'* **2:23a** Hebrew *Lo-ruhamah;* see 1:6. **2:23b** Hebrew *Lo-ammi;* see 1:9. **3:1a** Or *Go and love a woman who.* **3:1b** Hebrew *love their raisin cakes.* **3:2a** Hebrew *15 [shekels] of silver,* about 6 ounces or 171 grams in weight.

2:21-22 God is in control of nature, and nature praises him. If God can control the rain and the growth of plants, he certainly can control the events of our life. Like nature, we must proclaim, "God plants," for when we seek his forgiveness for our sins, he plants in us the seeds of his love and grace. Without his help, we would still be in the parched desert of our addiction. As we share our story of deliverance, we will not only encourage others to persevere but will also find renewed strength for our own recovery.

3:1-2 Hosea was able to heal his broken family by redeeming, or buying back, his wife Gomer, which highlights his extraordinary love for her. She did not come back to him, so he went to her and paid money to buy her back. This symbolizes God's love, which is even more extraordinary. While we were still sinners, God sent his Son, Jesus, who gave his life for us (Romans 5:8). Each of us can experience the ultimate recovery by accepting Christ as our personal Savior, becoming his "bride" (see 2 Corinthians 11:2). In this relationship God offers us his constant help and companionship.

4:1-2 God wanted his people to honestly examine their lives. They had ignored the healthy boundaries set by the Ten Commandments. Their lack of commitment to God was at the root of their destructive behaviors (cursing, lying, murdering, stealing, and committing adultery). This should motivate us to take moral inventory so we can become aware of any shortcomings and correct them before we stray too far from God's laws. If we are honest in our self-examination and confession, God will give us the forgiveness and healing we need for recovery.

4:7-9 Spiritual leaders carry great responsibility. They are responsible not only for their own spiritual well-being but also for the well-being of those who follow them. If we are at the point in recovery where we are sharing the good news of God's deliverance in our life, we must be sure to stay on the right path and not lapse back into destructive patterns. Those who look to us for guidance will do as we do, not as we say. If we hope to help others stay on the road to recovery, we need to stay on the road, too.

sure of wine.* ³Then I said to her, "You must live in my house for many days and stop your prostitution. During this time, you will not have sexual relations with anyone, not even with me.*"

⁴This shows that Israel will go a long time without a king or prince, and without sacrifices, sacred pillars, priests,* or even idols! ⁵But afterward the people will return and devote themselves to the LORD their God and to David's descendant, their king.* In the last days, they will tremble in awe of the LORD and of his goodness.

CHAPTER 4
The LORD's Case against Israel

¹Hear the word of the LORD, O people
    of Israel!
The LORD has brought charges against
    you, saying:
"There is no faithfulness, no kindness,
    no knowledge of God in your land.
²You make vows and break them;
    you kill and steal and commit adultery.
There is violence everywhere—
    one murder after another.
³That is why your land is in mourning,
    and everyone is wasting away.
Even the wild animals, the birds
    of the sky,
    and the fish of the sea are disappearing.

⁴"Don't point your finger at someone else
    and try to pass the blame!
My complaint, you priests,
    is with you.*
⁵So you will stumble in broad daylight,
    and your false prophets will fall with
       you in the night.
And I will destroy Israel, your
    mother.
⁶My people are being destroyed
    because they don't know me.
Since you priests refuse to know me,
    I refuse to recognize you as my
       priests.
Since you have forgotten the laws
    of your God,
    I will forget to bless your
       children.
⁷The more priests there are,
    the more they sin against me.

3:2b As in Greek version, which reads *a homer of barley and a wineskin full of wine;* Hebrew reads *a homer* [5 bushels or 220 liters] *of barley and a lethek* [2.5 bushels or 110 liters] *of barley.* 3:3 Or *and I will live with you.* 3:4 Hebrew *ephod,* the vest worn by the priest. 3:5 Hebrew *to David their king.* 4:4 Hebrew *Your people are like those with a complaint against the priests.*

LOVE

READ HOSEA 3:1-5

If we have broken trust with a spouse, especially if we have violated our marriage vows, making amends will take time. Perhaps we have made so many false promises in the past that our spouse will need time before fully trusting our love again.

God told the prophet Hosea to marry a prostitute. His marriage was to be a living example to the nation of Israel of its infidelity toward God. It had to hurt Hosea deeply when his wife returned to her life of prostitution. Hosea said, "Then the LORD said to me, 'Go and love your wife again, even though she commits adultery with another lover. This will illustrate that the LORD still loves Israel, even though the people have turned to other gods and love to worship them.'

So I bought her back for fifteen pieces of silver and five bushels of barley and a measure of wine. Then I said to her, 'You must live in my house for many days and stop your prostitution. During this time, you will not have sexual relations with anyone, not even with me'" (Hosea 3:1-3).

Hosea needed time before he could be close to his wife again. Sometimes the best way we can make amends to our spouse is to allow time to go by. During that time we can demonstrate to them that our wrong behavior has stopped. Love and trust must come together. If our spouse feels the need for some time of separation to see if our commitment is real and trustworthy, we need to give them that time and focus on our own recovery. ***Turn to page 1105, Hosea 10.***

They have exchanged the glory
    of God
    for the shame of idols.*

8 "When the people bring their sin
    offerings, the priests get fed.
    So the priests are glad when the
    people sin!
9 'And what the priests do, the people
    also do.'
    So now I will punish both priests and
    people
    for their wicked deeds.
10 They will eat and still be hungry.
    They will play the prostitute and gain
    nothing from it,
    for they have deserted the LORD
11   to worship other gods.

"Wine has robbed my people
    of their understanding.
12 They ask a piece of wood for advice!
    They think a stick can tell them
    the future!
Longing after idols
    has made them foolish.
They have played the prostitute,
    serving other gods and deserting their
    God.
13 They offer sacrifices to idols on the
    mountaintops.
    They go up into the hills to burn
    incense
    in the pleasant shade of oaks, poplars,
    and terebinth trees.

"That is why your daughters turn to
    prostitution,
    and your daughters-in-law commit
    adultery.
14 But why should I punish them
    for their prostitution and adultery?
For your men are doing the same thing,
    sinning with whores and shrine
    prostitutes.

O foolish people! You refuse to
    understand,
    so you will be destroyed.

15 "Though you, Israel, are a prostitute,
    may Judah not be guilty of such things.
Do not join the false worship at Gilgal or
    Beth-aven,*
    and do not take oaths there in the
    LORD's name.
16 Israel is stubborn,
    like a stubborn heifer.
So should the LORD feed her
    like a lamb in a lush pasture?
17 Leave Israel* alone,
    because she is married to idolatry.
18 When the rulers of Israel finish their
    drinking,
    off they go to find some prostitutes.
    They love shame more than honor.*
19 So a mighty wind will sweep them away.
    Their sacrifices to idols will bring them
    shame.

CHAPTER 5
The Failure of Israel's Leaders

1 "Hear this, you priests.
    Pay attention, you leaders of Israel.
Listen, you members of the royal family.
    Judgment has been handed down
    against you.
For you have led the people into a snare
    by worshiping the idols at Mizpah and
    Tabor.
2 You have dug a deep pit to trap them at
    Acacia Grove.*
    But I will settle with you for what you
    have done.
3 I know what you are like, O Ephraim.
    You cannot hide yourself from me,
    O Israel.
You have left me as a prostitute leaves her
    husband;
    you are utterly defiled.

4:7 As in Syriac version and an ancient Hebrew tradition; Masoretic Text reads *I will turn their glory into shame.*
4:15 *Beth-aven* means "house of wickedness"; it is being used as another name for Bethel, which means "house of God." 4:17 Hebrew *Ephraim,* referring to the northern kingdom of Israel. 4:18 As in Greek version; the meaning of the Hebrew is uncertain. 5:2 Hebrew *at Shittim.* The meaning of the Hebrew for this sentence is uncertain.

4:15-17 The people of Judah were warned to stay away from Israel, lest they be tempted to follow in the footsteps of their unfaithful sister nation. We can heed this warning, too. Since we tend to conform to the people around us, it makes sense to stay away from those who are engaging in immoral or addictive behavior. To stay firmly on the path of recovery, we must surround ourself with people who are following God and his principles of recovery.
5:3-4 Adultery kept the people away from God. In their arrogance they refused to admit their wrongdoings and turn their lives back to God. Though our addiction may bring us temporary thrills, we can never escape its destructive consequences. Like Israel, we will stumble and fall unless we turn to God for forgiveness and healing.

⁴Your deeds won't let you return to your
   God.
      You are a prostitute through and
      through,
      and you do not know the LORD.

⁵"The arrogance of Israel testifies against
   her;
      Israel and Ephraim will stumble under
      their load of guilt.
      Judah, too, will fall with them.
⁶When they come with their flocks and
   herds
      to offer sacrifices to the LORD,
   they will not find him,
      because he has withdrawn from them.
⁷They have betrayed the honor of the
   LORD,
      bearing children that are not his.
   Now their false religion will devour them
      along with their wealth.*

⁸"Sound the alarm in Gibeah!
      Blow the trumpet in Ramah!
   Raise the battle cry in Beth-aven*!
      Lead on into battle, O warriors of
      Benjamin!
⁹One thing is certain, Israel*:
      On your day of punishment,
      you will become a heap of rubble.

¹⁰"The leaders of Judah have become like
   thieves.*
      So I will pour my anger on them like
      a waterfall.
¹¹The people of Israel will be crushed and
   broken by my judgment
      because they are determined to worship
      idols.*
¹²I will destroy Israel as a moth consumes
   wool.

I will make Judah as weak as rotten
   wood.
¹³"When Israel and Judah saw how sick
   they were,
      Israel turned to Assyria—
   to the great king there—
      but he could neither help nor cure
      them.
¹⁴I will be like a lion to Israel,
      like a strong young lion to Judah.
   I will tear them to pieces!
   I will carry them off,
      and no one will be left to rescue them.
¹⁵Then I will return to my place
      until they admit their guilt and turn
      to me.
   For as soon as trouble comes,
      they will earnestly search for me."

CHAPTER 6
A Call to Repentance
¹"Come, let us return to the LORD.
   He has torn us to pieces;
      now he will heal us.
   He has injured us;
      now he will bandage our wounds.
²In just a short time he will restore us,
      so that we may live in his presence.
³Oh, that we might know the LORD!
      Let us press on to know him.
   He will respond to us as surely as the
      arrival of dawn
      or the coming of rains in early spring."

⁴"O Israel* and Judah,
      what should I do with you?" asks the
      LORD.
   "For your love vanishes like the morning
      mist
      and disappears like dew in the
      sunlight.

5:7 The meaning of the Hebrew is uncertain. 5:8 Beth-aven means "house of wickedness"; it is being used as another name for Bethel, which means "house of God." 5:9 Hebrew Ephraim, referring to the northern kingdom of Israel; also in 5:11, 12, 13, 14. 5:10 Hebrew like those who move a boundary marker. 5:11 Or determined to follow human commands. The meaning of the Hebrew is uncertain. 6:4 Hebrew Ephraim, referring to the northern kingdom of Israel.

5:13 The people of Israel and Judah recognized their need for help, but they turned to the wrong source for recovery and paid for it with their lives. If we are honest enough in our self-examination and penetrate deeply enough, we will see that no one is able to heal our disease except God. Turning to any other source for healing would be like choosing to have a butcher rather than a doctor perform surgery on us!
6:1-3 These verses contain several of the steps to recovery. The people admitted their helplessness, viewing themselves as "torn" and "injured" (Step One). They committed their lives to God, deciding to "return to the LORD" (Step Three). They let God change them, affirming that he would "heal" them and "bandage" their wounds (Step Seven). They sought to improve their relationship with God, saying, "Oh, that we might know the LORD!" (Step Eleven). Finally, they wanted to help others by encouraging each other in the process of returning to God, "Let us press on to know him" (Step Twelve).

⁵ I sent my prophets to cut you
to pieces—
to slaughter you with my words,
with judgments as inescapable
as light.
⁶ I want you to show love,*
not offer sacrifices.
I want you to know me*
more than I want burnt offerings.
⁷ But like Adam,* you broke my covenant
and betrayed my trust.

⁸ "Gilead is a city of sinners,
tracked with footprints of blood.
⁹ Priests form bands of robbers,
waiting in ambush for their victims.
They murder travelers along the road
to Shechem
and practice every kind of sin.
¹⁰ Yes, I have seen something horrible in
Ephraim and Israel:
My people are defiled by prostituting
themselves with other gods!

¹¹ "O Judah, a harvest of punishment is also
waiting for you,
though I wanted to restore the fortunes
of my people.

CHAPTER 7
Israel's Love for Wickedness
¹ "I want to heal Israel, but its sins* are too
great.
Samaria is filled with liars.
Thieves are on the inside
and bandits on the outside!
² Its people don't realize
that I am watching them.
Their sinful deeds are all around them,
and I see them all.

³ "The people entertain the king with their
wickedness,
and the princes laugh at their lies.
⁴ They are all adulterers,
always aflame with lust.
They are like an oven that is kept hot
while the baker is kneading the dough.
⁵ On royal holidays, the princes get drunk
with wine,
carousing with those who mock them.
⁶ Their hearts are like an oven
blazing with intrigue.
Their plot smolders* through the night,
and in the morning it breaks out like a
raging fire.
⁷ Burning like an oven,
they consume their leaders.
They kill their kings one after another,
and no one cries to me for help.

⁸ "The people of Israel mingle with godless
foreigners,
making themselves as worthless as a
half-baked cake!
⁹ Worshiping foreign gods has sapped their
strength,
but they don't even know it.
Their hair is gray,
but they don't realize they're old and
weak.
¹⁰ Their arrogance testifies against them,
yet they don't return to the LORD their
God
or even try to find him.

¹¹ "The people of Israel have become like
silly, witless doves,
first calling to Egypt, then flying to
Assyria for help.
¹² But as they fly about,
I will throw my net over them

6:6a Greek version translates this Hebrew term as *to show mercy.* Compare Matt 9:13; 12:7. **6:6b** Hebrew *to know God.*
6:7 Or *But at Adam.* **7:1** Hebrew *Ephraim's,* referring to the northern kingdom of Israel; similarly in 7:8, 11.
7:6 Hebrew *Their baker sleeps.*

6:6 The way we treat other people gives us a good idea of how committed we are to God.
Worship activities can be engaged in without any sincerity, proving only that we know the rituals.
Acting kindly toward others and forgiving those who have hurt us show that we are growing spiritually and help us grow even more. Yes, God values our sincere acts of worship greatly. But if our
worship is sincere, it will always be coupled with active obedience to his will.

7:5-8 Alcohol affects our ability to perceive reality accurately and leads us to act unwisely. The
king's drunkenness led him to drink with the very people who sought his destruction. We tend to
associate with our enemies—godless people, bad habits, or harmful substances—while under the
influence. An important step toward overcoming our involvement with destructive people and
activities is to keep our mind clear and sober. We can then turn to God and seek his help as we
work to overcome the powerful temptations in our life.

7:10 Pride is a very destructive sin. It lets us assume the place of God in our own life. It tells us to
take the credit for our successes and blame others for our failures. Pride robs us of recovery
because it won't let us admit we have problems. If we really want to overcome our addiction, it is
necessary to come to God with a humble heart, admitting our weaknesses and seeking change.

and bring them down like a bird from
the sky.
I will punish them for all the evil they
do.*
¹³ "What sorrow awaits those who have
deserted me!
Let them die, for they have rebelled
against me.
I wanted to redeem them,
but they have told lies about me.
¹⁴ They do not cry out to me with sincere
hearts.
Instead, they sit on their couches and
wail.
They cut themselves,* begging foreign
gods for grain and new wine,
and they turn away from me.
¹⁵ I trained them and made them strong,
yet now they plot evil against me.
¹⁶ They look everywhere except to the
Most High.
They are as useless as a crooked bow.
Their leaders will be killed by their
enemies
because of their insolence toward me.
Then the people of Egypt
will laugh at them.

CHAPTER 8
Israel Harvests the Whirlwind
¹ "Sound the alarm!
The enemy descends like an eagle on
the people of the LORD,
for they have broken my covenant
and revolted against my law.
² Now Israel pleads with me,
'Help us, for you are our God!'
³ But it is too late.
The people of Israel have rejected what
is good,
and now their enemies will chase after
them.

⁴ The people have appointed kings without
my consent,
and princes without my approval.
By making idols for themselves from their
silver and gold,
they have brought about their own
destruction.

⁵ "O Samaria, I reject this calf—
this idol you have made.
My fury burns against you.
How long will you be incapable of
innocence?
⁶ This calf you worship, O Israel,
was crafted by your own hands!
It is not God!
Therefore, it must be smashed to bits.

⁷ "They have planted the wind
and will harvest the whirlwind.
The stalks of grain wither
and produce nothing to eat.
And even if there is any grain,
foreigners will eat it.
⁸ The people of Israel have been swallowed
up;
they lie among the nations like an old
discarded pot.
⁹ Like a wild donkey looking for a mate,
they have gone up to Assyria.
The people of Israel* have sold
themselves—
sold themselves to many lovers.
¹⁰ But though they have sold themselves to
many allies,
I will now gather them together for
judgment.
Then they will writhe
under the burden of the great king.

¹¹ "Israel has built many altars to take
away sin,
but these very altars became places
for sinning!

7:12 Hebrew *I will punish them because of what was reported against them in the assembly.* **7:14** As in Greek version;
Hebrew reads *They gather together.* **8:9** Hebrew *Ephraim,* referring to the northern kingdom of Israel; also in 8:11.

7:13 God longs to redeem us, to bring us to complete recovery. But what hinders him from
doing that? Hearts hardened by rebellion and denial. If we are to be open to God's powerful
help, we must commit ourself to following God's will. We must learn to accept reality, admitting our faults and addictions. Only when we open our heart and life to God will he be able to
help us.
8:5-6 Jeroboam feared losing control of the northern kingdom (Israel) should everyone go to
Jerusalem (in the southern kingdom) to worship God. So he made two gold calves and told his
people that these were the gods who had led them out of Egypt (1 Kings 12:28-30). God had
promised to give Jeroboam the kingdom of Israel, but Jeroboam looked to another source to
secure God's promise. This led to the destruction of Jeroboam's dynasty (1 Kings 13:33-34).
When God makes a promise, we can trust him to fulfill it in his way and in his time. Taking
matters into our own hands is always harmful and will impede the recovery process.

¹²Even though I gave them all my laws,
  they act as if those laws don't apply
    to them.
¹³The people love to offer sacrifices to me,
  feasting on the meat,
    but I do not accept their sacrifices.
I will hold my people accountable for
    their sins,
  and I will punish them.
    They will return to Egypt.
¹⁴Israel has forgotten its Maker and built
    great palaces,
  and Judah has fortified its cities.
Therefore, I will send down fire on
    their cities
  and will burn up their fortresses."

CHAPTER 9
Hosea Announces Israel's Punishment
¹O people of Israel,
  do not rejoice as other nations do.
For you have been unfaithful to
    your God,
  hiring yourselves out like prostitutes,
    worshiping other gods on every
      threshing floor.
²So now your harvests will be too small
    to feed you.
  There will be no grapes for making
    new wine.
³You may no longer stay here in the
    LORD's land.
  Instead, you will return to Egypt,
    and in Assyria you will eat food
      that is ceremonially unclean.
⁴There you will make no offerings of wine
    to the LORD.

None of your sacrifices there will please
    him.
They will be unclean, like food touched
    by a person in mourning.
  All who present such sacrifices will be
    defiled.
They may eat this food themselves,
  but they may not offer it to the LORD.
⁵What then will you do on festival days?
  How will you observe the LORD's
    festivals?
⁶Even if you escape destruction from
    Assyria,
  Egypt will conquer you, and Memphis*
    will bury you.
Nettles will take over your treasures of
    silver;
  thistles will invade your ruined homes.

⁷The time of Israel's punishment has come;
  the day of payment is here.
    Soon Israel will know this all too well.
Because of your great sin and hostility,
  you say, "The prophets are crazy
    and the inspired men are fools!"
⁸The prophet is a watchman over Israel*
    for my God,
  yet traps are laid for him wherever he
    goes.
He faces hostility even in the house of
    God.
⁹The things my people do are as depraved
    as what they did in Gibeah long ago.
  God will not forget.
    He will surely punish them for their
      sins.

¹⁰The LORD says, "O Israel, when I first
    found you,

9:6 Memphis was the capital of northern Egypt. 9:8 Hebrew *Ephraim*, referring to the northern kingdom of Israel;
also in 9:11, 13, 16.

8:12 God's laws apply to everyone, not just the people who obey them. Those who believe that
God's principles apply only to others are only harming themselves. If we drive at 90 mph in a 55
mph zone and get pulled over, it won't help to claim, "I saw the speed limit sign, but it doesn't
apply to me." God will not let us off when we refuse to obey his will revealed in the Bible. Knowing that God holds us accountable to know and obey his will should motivate us to read and
understand his Word. The Bible contains God's laws for recovery. If we refuse to obey them, we
deny reality and risk terrible consequences.
9:7 It is difficult to have the courage to change when society's values are opposed to God's.
Those who speak for the truth are considered fools; those who represent God are classed with the
insane. But when we know that God values what the world counts as foolish (1 Corinthians
1:27), it becomes easier to bear people's abuses when we follow God. To some, our recovery
program and relationship with God may seem foolish, but to us they are valuable and necessary.
10:1 The more prosperous the people of Israel became, the further they moved from God.
Unfortunately, most people think that success is measured in wealth. Even when our addiction is
killing us, we may think everything is all right if we are financially successful. But money is never
the key to a successful life; in fact, it is often a major part of the problem. Our relationship with
God is what measures true success. Living an addiction-free, godly life is infinitely better than
being rich and out of control.

it was like finding fresh grapes in the
desert.
When I saw your ancestors,
it was like seeing the first ripe figs of the
season.
But then they deserted me for Baal-peor,
giving themselves to that shameful idol.
Soon they became vile,
as vile as the god they worshiped.
[11] The glory of Israel will fly away like a bird,
for your children will not be born
or grow in the womb
or even be conceived.
[12] Even if you do have children who grow
up,
I will take them from you.
It will be a terrible day when I turn away
and leave you alone.
[13] I have watched Israel become as beautiful
as Tyre.
But now Israel will bring out her
children for slaughter.”

[14] O LORD, what should I request for your
people?
I will ask for wombs that don't give
birth
and breasts that give no milk.

[15] The LORD says, “All their wickedness
began at Gilgal;
there I began to hate them.
I will drive them from my land
because of their evil actions.
I will love them no more
because all their leaders are rebels.
[16] The people of Israel are struck down.
Their roots are dried up,
and they will bear no more fruit.
And if they give birth,
I will slaughter their beloved children.”

[17] My God will reject the people of Israel
because they will not listen or obey.
They will be wanderers,
homeless among the nations.

CHAPTER 10
The LORD's Judgment against Israel
[1] How prosperous Israel is—
a luxuriant vine loaded with fruit.
But the richer the people get,
the more pagan altars they build.
The more bountiful their harvests,
the more beautiful their sacred pillars.
[2] The hearts of the people are fickle;
they are guilty and must be punished.
The LORD will break down their altars
and smash their sacred pillars.

ACCOUNTABILITY

READ HOSEA 10:1-12
While in recovery, we learn to accept
responsibility for our actions, even when we
are powerless over our addiction. We come
to realize that all our actions yield consequences. Some of us may have deceived
ourself into thinking we can escape the
consequences of the bad choices we have
made. But with time, it becomes clear that
God has made accountability a necessary
element of healthy living.

“You will always harvest what you plant.
Those who live only to satisfy their own
sinful nature will harvest decay and death
from that sinful nature. But those who live
to please the Spirit will harvest everlasting
life from the Spirit” (Galatians 6:7-8).

The law of planting and harvesting can
also work to our benefit. God spoke
through the prophet Hosea: “Plant the
good seeds of righteousness, and you will
harvest a crop of love. Plow up the hard
ground of your hearts, for now is the time
to seek the LORD, that he may come and
shower righteousness upon you” (Hosea
10:12).

God says we *always* reap what we have
sown. Even after we have been forgiven,
we must deal with the consequences of our
actions. It may take time to finish
harvesting the negative consequences of
our past sins, but this need not discourage
us. Making a list of those we have harmed
is one step toward planting good seeds. In
time we will see a good crop begin to
grow. *Turn to page 1181, Zechariah 9.*

³ Then they will say, "We have no king
    because we didn't fear the LORD.
But even if we had a king,
    what could he do for us anyway?"
⁴ They spout empty words
    and make covenants they don't intend
        to keep.
So injustice springs up among them
    like poisonous weeds in a farmer's field.

⁵ The people of Samaria tremble in fear
    for their calf idol at Beth-aven,*
    and they mourn for it.
Though its priests rejoice over it,
    its glory will be stripped away.*
⁶ This idol will be carted away to Assyria,
    a gift to the great king there.
Ephraim will be ridiculed and Israel will
        be shamed,
    because its people have trusted in this
        idol.
⁷ Samaria and its king will be cut off;
    they will float away like driftwood on
        an ocean wave.
⁸ And the pagan shrines of Aven,* the place
        of Israel's sin, will crumble.
    Thorns and thistles will grow up around
        their altars.
They will beg the mountains, "Bury us!"
    and plead with the hills, "Fall on us!"

⁹ The LORD says, "O Israel, ever since
        Gibeah,
    there has been only sin and more sin!
You have made no progress whatsoever.
    Was it not right that the wicked men of
        Gibeah were attacked?
¹⁰ Now whenever it fits my plan,
    I will attack you, too.
I will call out the armies of the nations
    to punish you for your multiplied sins.

¹¹ "Israel* is like a trained heifer treading out
        the grain—
    an easy job she loves.
But I will put a heavy yoke on her
        tender neck.
I will force Judah to pull the plow
    and Israel* to break up the hard ground.
¹² I said, 'Plant the good seeds of
        righteousness,
    and you will harvest a crop of love.
Plow up the hard ground of your hearts,
    for now is the time to seek the LORD,
that he may come
    and shower righteousness upon you.'

¹³ "But you have cultivated wickedness
    and harvested a thriving crop of sins.
You have eaten the fruit of lies—
    trusting in your military might,
believing that great armies
    could make your nation safe.
¹⁴ Now the terrors of war
    will rise among your people.
All your fortifications will fall,
    just as when Shalman destroyed
        Beth-arbel.
Even mothers and children
    were dashed to death there.
¹⁵ You will share that fate, Bethel,
    because of your great wickedness.
When the day of judgment dawns,
    the king of Israel will be completely
        destroyed.

CHAPTER 11
The LORD's Love for Israel

¹ "When Israel was a child, I loved him,
    and I called my son out of Egypt.
² But the more I called to him,
    the farther he moved from me,*
offering sacrifices to the images of Baal
    and burning incense to idols.

10:5a *Beth-aven* means "house of wickedness"; it is being used as another name for Bethel, which means "house of God." **10:5b** Or *will be taken away into exile.* **10:8** *Aven* is a reference to Beth-aven; see 10:5a and the note there. **10:11a** Hebrew *Ephraim,* referring to the northern kingdom of Israel. **10:11b** Hebrew *Jacob.* The names "Jacob" and "Israel" are often interchanged throughout the Old Testament, referring sometimes to the individual patriarch and sometimes to the nation. **11:2** As in Greek version; Hebrew reads *the more they called to him, the farther he moved from them.*

10:8 When the addiction we have trusted fails us and we begin to experience the painful consequences, it may seem like a quick death would be better than trying to turn our life around. A quick end to our pain may be the easiest solution, but it is never the best or right way. There is always hope for a good life in the future, no matter how terrible things may seem now. We can begin by giving our life to our merciful God. He wants all of us to come to him, no matter how great our past sins.

11:1-3 Hosea here compared God's love for Israel to a father's love for his son. He paints a poignant picture of our complete dependence on God. God did everything right in raising his child, but Israel rebelled against him and sought the favor of false gods who could not offer protection from the coming destruction. We can learn from Israel's catastrophe and accept the guidance of our heavenly Father before our life is destroyed by our addiction.

³I myself taught Israel* how to walk,
    leading him along by the hand.
But he doesn't know or even care
    that it was I who took care of him.
⁴I led Israel along
    with my ropes of kindness and love.
I lifted the yoke from his neck,
    and I myself stooped to feed him.

⁵"But since my people refuse to return to me,
    they will return to Egypt
    and will be forced to serve Assyria.
⁶War will swirl through their cities;
    their enemies will crash through their
        gates.
They will destroy them,
    trapping them in their own evil plans.
⁷For my people are determined to desert me.
They call me the Most High,
    but they don't truly honor me.

⁸"Oh, how can I give you up, Israel?
    How can I let you go?
How can I destroy you like Admah
    or demolish you like Zeboiim?
My heart is torn within me,
    and my compassion overflows.
⁹No, I will not unleash my fierce anger.
    I will not completely destroy Israel,
for I am God and not a mere mortal.
    I am the Holy One living among you,
    and I will not come to destroy.
¹⁰For someday the people will follow me.
    I, the LORD, will roar like a lion.
And when I roar,
    my people will return trembling from
        the west.
¹¹Like a flock of birds, they will come from
        Egypt.
    Trembling like doves, they will return
        from Assyria.
And I will bring them home again,"
    says the LORD.

Charges against Israel and Judah

¹²*Israel surrounds me with lies and deceit,
    but Judah still obeys God
    and is faithful to the Holy One.*

CHAPTER 12

¹* The people of Israel* feed on the wind;
    they chase after the east wind all day long.

11:3 Hebrew *Ephraim,* referring to the northern kingdom of Israel; also in 11:8, 9, 12. **11:12a** Verse 11:12 is numbered 12:1 in Hebrew text. **11:12b** Or *and Judah is unruly against God, the faithful Holy One.* The meaning of the Hebrew is uncertain. **12:1a** Verses 12:1-14 are numbered 12:2-15 in Hebrew text. **12:1b** Hebrew *Ephraim,* referring to the northern kingdom of Israel; also in 12:8, 14.

STEP 5

Unending Love

BIBLE READING: Hosea 11:8-11

We admitted to God, to ourselves, and to another human being the exact nature of our wrongs.

We may be sorely aware of the deep shame, trouble, and pain we inflicted on our family when we were controlled by our addiction. We may be afraid to admit the exact nature of our wrongs because we don't understand how God could love someone who is so bad.

Hosea was a prophet to the rebellious nation of Israel. God used Hosea's life to demonstrate his unconditional love for us and his people. The Lord told Hosea to marry a prostitute. Hosea married her, loved her, and devoted himself to her. But later his wife relapsed into her old ways, broke Hosea's heart, and brought shame on their family. She fell into slavery. God then baffled Hosea by telling him, "Go and love your wife again, even though she commits adultery with another lover. This will illustrate that the LORD still loves Israel, even though the people have turned to other gods" (Hosea 3:1).

We may be asking, How could God (or anyone) still love me? But God asks, "Oh, how can I give you up . . . ? How can I let you go? How can I destroy you . . . ? My heart is torn within me, and my compassion overflows. . . . For I am God and not a mere mortal. I am the Holy One living among you, and I will not come to destroy" (Hosea 11:8-9). There is absolutely nothing we can do or confess to God that would cause him to stop loving us (see Romans 8:38-39). *Turn to page 1125, Amos 7.*

They pile up lies and violence;
    they are making an alliance with
      Assyria
    while sending olive oil to buy support
      from Egypt.
²Now the LORD is bringing charges against
    Judah.
    He is about to punish Jacob* for all his
      deceitful ways,
    and pay him back for all he has done.
³Even in the womb,
    Jacob struggled with his brother;
when he became a man,
    he even fought with God.
⁴Yes, he wrestled with the angel
    and won.
    He wept and pleaded for a blessing
      from him.
There at Bethel he met God face
    to face,
    and God spoke to him*—
⁵the LORD God of Heaven's Armies,
    the LORD is his name!
⁶So now, come back to your God.
    Act with love and justice,
    and always depend on him.

⁷But no, the people are like crafty
    merchants
    selling from dishonest scales—
    they love to cheat.
⁸Israel boasts, "I am rich!
    I've made a fortune all by myself!
No one has caught me cheating!
    My record is spotless!"

⁹"But I am the LORD your God,
    who rescued you from slavery
      in Egypt.
And I will make you live in tents again,
    as you do each year at the Festival of
      Shelters.*

¹⁰I sent my prophets to warn you
    with many visions and parables."
¹¹But the people of Gilead are worthless
    because of their idol worship.
And in Gilgal, too, they sacrifice bulls;
    their altars are lined up like the heaps
      of stone
    along the edges of a plowed field.
¹²Jacob fled to the land of Aram,
    and there he* earned a wife by tending
      sheep.
¹³Then by a prophet
    the LORD brought Jacob's descendants*
      out of Egypt;
and by that prophet
    they were protected.
¹⁴But the people of Israel
    have bitterly provoked the LORD,
so their Lord will now sentence them
    to death
    in payment for their sins.

CHAPTER 13
The LORD's Anger against Israel
¹When the tribe of Ephraim spoke,
    the people shook with fear,
    for that tribe was important in Israel.
But the people of Ephraim sinned by
      worshiping Baal
    and thus sealed their destruction.
²Now they continue to sin by making
      silver idols,
    images shaped skillfully with human
      hands.
"Sacrifice to these," they cry,
    "and kiss the calf idols!"
³Therefore, they will disappear like the
      morning mist,
    like dew in the morning sun,
like chaff blown by the wind,
    like smoke from a chimney.

12:2 *Jacob* sounds like the Hebrew word for "deceiver." 12:4 As in Greek and Syriac versions; Hebrew reads *to us.*
12:9 Hebrew *as in the days of your appointed feast.* 12:12 Hebrew *Israel.* See note on 10:11b. 12:13 Hebrew *brought Israel.* See note on 10:11b.

12:2-5 The patriarch Jacob changed from a deceiver to one who sought God's blessing. In his struggles with God he finally faced his own inadequacies and earnestly sought God's favor. Healing and growth will be found only through honest repentance and communion with God.
12:6 God asks his people to love him by loving others. We are to seek the best interests of others in a manner consistent with God's revealed will. When we are tempted to take advantage of others for personal gain, we need to ask God to help us to be just and loving. It is only with God's help that we can treat others like he wants them to be treated.
13:1-3 Israel's downfall came after it had forsaken God for false gods. Likewise, if we closely examine our life, we will find that our problems began when we replaced God with our addiction. We cannot blame God for our situation, because he lovingly cares about us and will never forsake us. We abandoned him. We can begin the recovery process by admitting our sins and dependency to God and asking him to take control of our life. He will lovingly rescue us.

⁴"I have been the L<small>ORD</small> your God
ever since I brought you out of Egypt.
You must acknowledge no God but me,
for there is no other savior.
⁵I took care of you in the wilderness,
in that dry and thirsty land.
⁶But when you had eaten and were satisfied,
you became proud and forgot me.
⁷So now I will attack you like a lion,
like a leopard that lurks along the road.
⁸Like a bear whose cubs have been taken
away,
I will tear out your heart.
I will devour you like a hungry lioness
and mangle you like a wild animal.

⁹"You are about to be destroyed, O Israel—
yes, by me, your only helper.
¹⁰Now where is* your king?
Let him save you!
Where are all the leaders of the land,
the king and the officials you
demanded of me?
¹¹In my anger I gave you kings,
and in my fury I took them away.

¹²"Ephraim's guilt has been collected,
and his sin has been stored up for
punishment.
¹³Pain has come to the people
like the pain of childbirth,
but they are like a child
who resists being born.
The moment of birth has arrived,
but they stay in the womb!

¹⁴"Should I ransom them from the grave*?
Should I redeem them from death?
O death, bring on your terrors!
O grave, bring on your plagues!*

For I will not take pity on them.
¹⁵Ephraim was the most fruitful of all his
brothers,
but the east wind—a blast from the L<small>ORD</small>—
will arise in the desert.
All their flowing springs will run dry,
and all their wells will disappear.
Every precious thing they own
will be plundered and carried away.
¹⁶* The people of Samaria
must bear the consequences of their
guilt
because they rebelled against their God.
They will be killed by an invading army,
their little ones dashed to death against
the ground,
their pregnant women ripped open by
swords."

CHAPTER 14
Healing for the Repentant

¹* Return, O Israel, to the L<small>ORD</small> your God,
for your sins have brought you down.
²Bring your confessions, and return to the
L<small>ORD</small>.
Say to him,
"Forgive all our sins and graciously
receive us,
so that we may offer you our praises.*
³Assyria cannot save us,
nor can our warhorses.
Never again will we say to the idols we
have made,
'You are our gods.'
No, in you alone
do the orphans find mercy."

⁴The L<small>ORD</small> says,
"Then I will heal you of your faithlessness;

13:10 As in Greek and Syriac versions and Latin Vulgate; Hebrew reads *I will be.* 13:14a Hebrew *Sheol;* also in 13:14b. 13:14b Greek version reads *O death, where is your punishment? / O grave* [Hades], *where is your sting?* Compare 1 Cor 15:55. 13:16 Verse 16 is numbered 14:1 in Hebrew text. 14:1 Verses 14:1-9 are numbered 14:2-10 in Hebrew text. 14:2 As in Greek and Syriac versions, which read *may repay the fruit of our lips;* Hebrew reads *may repay the bulls of our lips.* 14:8 Hebrew *Ephraim,* referring to the northern kingdom of Israel.

13:4, 13 There is no salvation except that offered by God. He offers salvation to all who will accept it (John 3:3, 16). Anyone who refuses this offer and looks to another source for salvation is like a stubborn "child who resists being born," not wanting the life being offered. Are we resisting God's offer, or have we gladly accepted the new life God has for each of us?

14:1-4 These verses contain a paradigm for recovery. The people admitted their helplessness apart from God, examined themselves, and found that they were responsible for their condition. They showed their willingness to let God change them, renounced any further dealings with gods of their own making, and committed their lives to God alone. We can follow the same steps in the recovery process, renouncing our own false gods—our addictive thoughts and behaviors—and committing our life to God and his will.

14:4-8 God's people would flourish and experience unprecedented spiritual growth as they committed their lives more deeply to him. As they allowed God to heal them, they would find that he was their source of nourishment and growth—like "refreshing dew from heaven." They would become blossoming plants that would send out roots to start new shoots. We can have the same hope today. The problems caused by our dependency can be resolved as we repent and accept God's mercy. Through him we, too, can flourish.

my love will know no bounds,
for my anger will be gone forever.
⁵ I will be to Israel
like a refreshing dew from heaven.
Israel will blossom like the lily;
it will send roots deep into the soil
like the cedars in Lebanon.
⁶ Its branches will spread out like beautiful
olive trees,
as fragrant as the cedars of Lebanon.
⁷ My people will again live under my shade.
They will flourish like grain and
blossom like grapevines.
They will be as fragrant as the wines of
Lebanon.

⁸ "O Israel,* stay away from idols!
I am the one who answers your prayers
and cares for you.
I am like a tree that is always green;
all your fruit comes from me."

⁹ Let those who are wise understand these
things.
Let those with discernment listen
carefully.
The paths of the LORD are true and right,
and righteous people live by walking
in them.
But in those paths sinners stumble and
fall.

14:9 We need God's wisdom to discern the areas of our life that need to be changed. The prophet Hosea spoke often of sin and judgment, but his message didn't end there. He always pointed the way to salvation through humble repentance. Wise people will listen and learn from the prophet's words, seeing the inherent rightness in all that God asks of them. God cares about our welfare and wants to see us healed because he loves us.

REFLECTIONS ON **HOSEA**

insights ABOUT GOD'S COMPASSION

In **Hosea 1:7–2:1** the prophet was told to name his second child Lo-ammi, which means "not my people," to illustrate that the people of Israel were no longer God's people. In essence, God was divorcing them because of their unfaithfulness. God's rejection, however, was only temporary. Lo-ammi was to be renamed Ammi, meaning "my people." The punishment and exile that were soon to arrive would someday be replaced by healing and complete restoration. That is the hope for all who are following God's path to recovery. Today's pain and suffering are here for only a season: "[God's] anger lasts only a moment, but his favor lasts a lifetime! Weeping may last through the night, but joy comes with the morning" (Psalm 30:5).

In **Hosea 10:12** God tried to break through the people's blindness by announcing his desire to restore their broken relationship with him. Earlier we saw that the people planted the wind and reaped the whirlwind (8:7). In other words, they sinned and harvested the chaotic and painful consequences. Here they were asked to plant righteousness and reap the unfailing love of God. That same offer is open to us. If we seek God and let him come into our life, he will save us from our addiction and from eternal punishment.

In **Hosea 11:8-11** we see God's anguish when his people stray from him and seek false sources of security.

Even though our dependency may have almost totally destroyed our life, we have not suffered what we deserved. God has compassion on us, his wayward people. What a wonderful God he is! He shows us mercy and provides a way to end our pain and restore our relationship with him. Recovery is possible only if we seek God and let him fill the empty places that our addiction could never fill.

insights INTO THE IMPORTANCE OF A RELATIONSHIP WITH GOD
A healthy relationship with God requires intimate knowledge of his revelations in the Bible. God desires that we have more than a mere acquaintance with the facts of his Word. In **Hosea 4:6** we find that God wants his people to know him personally. The priests of Israel were well acquainted with the laws of God, but they lived immorally because they didn't really know God. If we do not have a growing and intimate relationship with God, we will have great difficulty as we work through the recovery process.

The people of Israel started down the path to recovery, but they soon turned back. In **Hosea 6:4-5** God wondered what he should do with his wayward people. Why did they fail? Perhaps the Israelites were never really committed to following God and his will for them. Perhaps they responded only with their emotions and were soon lured away by something that seemed more attractive. The depth of our commitment to God determines whether we recover or relapse. The more committed we are to God and the more we want recovery, the better our chances are of achieving it. But if we are just going through the motions, relapse is likely.

JOEL

THE BIG PICTURE

A. A LOCUST PLAGUE: FROM CATASTROPHE TO RECOVERY (1:1–2:27)
   1. Locusts Terrify the Land (1:1-14)
   2. God Judges the Land (1:15–2:11)
   3. God Has Mercy on the Land (2:12-27)
B. THE DAY OF THE LORD: CHOOSING DENIAL OR RECOVERY (2:28–3:21)
   1. Power to Live Right: The Gift of the Spirit (2:28-29)
   2. Terror on the Earth: The Day of the Lord (2:30-31)
   3. Deliverance from Judgment: An Invitation to All (2:32)
   4. Judgment on the Earth: The Wars of God (3:1-15)
   5. Restoration of the Land: God's Kingdom (3:16-21)

Earthquakes, hurricanes, floods, tornadoes—natural catastrophes of all kinds—have a way of making us feel helpless. We can do nothing to stop them. We can only do our best to avoid them and then pick up the pieces after they have occurred. The first part of Joel's prophecy is concerned with natural disasters that would lead to great suffering for God's people—a drought of major proportions and a plague of locusts. God used these natural events to warn his people of even worse suffering in the future should they refuse to recognize their need for him.

Disasters are even more painful when they are a consequence of our own behavior. Joel realized that the natural disasters suffered by the people of Judah were God's way of getting their attention. Centuries earlier, Moses had warned that disobedience to God's plan would lead to such catastrophes (Deuteronomy 28:38-39). God sought to restore his people to a healthy relationship with himself by showing them how helpless they really were and how much they needed him. Through these natural disasters, God broke through their illusions of security and self-sufficiency, showing them how important their relationship with him was.

Many of us have suffered from "locust plagues" in our own life. Through our own actions we suffer painful consequences and are helpless to combat the powers that assail us. As we experience this helplessness, we should realize that it is not the end of our life but a wonderful opportunity for a new start! In discovering our powerlessness and recognizing our need for God, we have already begun the process of recovery.

THE BOTTOM LINE

PURPOSE: To warn God's people of impending judgment, and to urge them to admit their sins and turn back to God. AUTHOR: The prophet Joel. AUDIENCE: The people of the southern kingdom of Judah. DATE WRITTEN: The book was probably written about 800 B.C., when the high priest Jehoiada governed Judah for young King Joash (2 Kings 11; 2 Chronicles 23–24). SETTING: Jerusalem during a period of prosperity; the people had become complacent about their relationship with God. KEY VERSE: "Return to the LORD your God, for he is merciful and compassionate, slow to get angry and filled with unfailing love. He is eager to relent and not to punish" (2:13). KEY PEOPLE AND RELATIONSHIPS: Political and religious leaders, parents and children, brides and grooms, Joel and God's people.

RECOVERY THEMES

The Power of Confrontation: God's people had lost sight of their need for God and had become complacent about following the plan he had laid out for them. To break through their denial, God allowed them to suffer a series of disasters. Through their sufferings and the words of the prophet Joel, God let his people know that they needed to make some changes in their lives. God often intervenes in our life in similar ways. He allows us to suffer the consequences of our sinful behavior to awaken us from our denial and complacency. He confronts us with the painful reality of our wrong choices and actions. But we should find comfort in this, because he confronts us not to destroy us but to initiate the process of our restoration.

The Importance of Forgiveness: Joel stated that the day of accountability was coming. But with his message of warning and judgment, he also gave his listeners the grounds for hope through repentance. Repentance allows God's people to experience healing through God's forgiveness. Like the nation of Judah, each of us would love to change some of our past actions and choices. But rather than changing the past, God provides a means of resolving our past sins through forgiveness. Recovery is built on the foundation of both receiving and granting forgiveness.

God's Power Is Limitless: We can easily be overwhelmed by the power of nature when it unleashes its fury in an earthquake, volcano, or hurricane. When we look at the Pacific Northwest coastline, we marvel at how the ocean has carved out cliffs and caves. But none of these powerful acts of nature can compare to the overwhelming power of God. When we feel powerless, God invites us to come to him for help. In him we have all the power we need to overcome our problems and dependency.

God's Power within Us: Joel predicted a time when the limitless power of God would be poured out upon us through his Holy Spirit. This promise implied that God would be directly available to his people; it was fulfilled in the coming of God's Son, Jesus the Messiah, and in the pouring out of God's Spirit into each believer after Jesus ascended into heaven. This truth is of utmost importance to us in the process of recovery. God is with us. His power is within us and always available to us as we persevere in the struggle. God gives us the power we need to overcome our dependency or compulsion through the indwelling of the Holy Spirit.

CHAPTER 1

The LORD gave this message to Joel son of Pethuel.

Mourning over the Locust Plague

² Hear this, you leaders of the people.
  Listen, all who live in the land.
 In all your history,
   has anything like this happened before?
³ Tell your children about it in the years to
    come,
  and let your children tell their children.
 Pass the story down from generation to
   generation.

⁴ After the cutting locusts finished eating
   the crops,
  the swarming locusts took what was
   left!
 After them came the hopping locusts,
  and then the stripping locusts,* too!

⁵ Wake up, you drunkards, and weep!
  Wail, all you wine-drinkers!
 All the grapes are ruined,
  and all your sweet wine is gone.

⁶ A vast army of locusts* has invaded my
   land,
  a terrible army too numerous
   to count.

1:4 The precise identification of the four kinds of locusts mentioned here is uncertain. 1:6 Hebrew *A nation.*

1:2-3 The people of Joel's generation barely escaped with their lives, and Joel urged them to share with their children what they had learned. When we share the possibility of recovery with others, we need to tell the whole story so that others can see just how bad things were. We may be able to keep others from the addiction we endured by showing them the horrors and pain associated with it. And we may be able to show those who have already experienced the torture of addiction that it is never too late to enter recovery and regain a normal life.

1:4—2:11 The people needed to admit their helplessness before God could intervene on their behalf. Joel led them to do this in three areas: (1) their physical resources were depleted by the locust plague and drought (1:4-12); (2) they were spiritually destitute and could not find God through the standard method of presenting sacrifices (1:13-20); and (3) they could not rely on their own courage and self-defense because the locusts were too great a foe (2:1-11). Once we admit that we cannot save ourself, we can turn to God and ask him to mercifully rescue us from our pain.

Its teeth are like lions' teeth,
  its fangs like those of a lioness.
[7] It has destroyed my grapevines
  and ruined my fig trees,
stripping their bark and destroying it,
  leaving the branches white and bare.

[8] Weep like a bride dressed in black,
  mourning the death of her husband.
[9] For there is no grain or wine
  to offer at the Temple of the LORD.
So the priests are in mourning.
  The ministers of the LORD are weeping.
[10] The fields are ruined,
  the land is stripped bare.
The grain is destroyed,
  the grapes have shriveled,
  and the olive oil is gone.

[11] Despair, all you farmers!
  Wail, all you vine growers!
Weep, because the wheat and barley—
  all the crops of the field—are ruined.
[12] The grapevines have dried up,
  and the fig trees have withered.
The pomegranate trees, palm trees, and
  apple trees—
  all the fruit trees—have dried up.
  And the people's joy has dried up with
  them.

[13] Dress yourselves in burlap and weep, you
  priests!
  Wail, you who serve before the altar!
Come, spend the night in burlap,
  you ministers of my God.
For there is no grain or wine
  to offer at the Temple of your God.
[14] Announce a time of fasting;
  call the people together for a solemn
  meeting.
Bring the leaders
  and all the people of the land
into the Temple of the LORD your God,
  and cry out to him there.
[15] The day of the LORD is near,
  the day when destruction comes from
  the Almighty.
  How terrible that day will be!

[16] Our food disappears before our very eyes.
  No joyful celebrations are held in the
  house of our God.
[17] The seeds die in the parched ground,
  and the grain crops fail.
The barns stand empty,
  and granaries are abandoned.
[18] How the animals moan with hunger!

The herds of cattle wander about
  confused,
because they have no pasture.
  The flocks of sheep and goats bleat in
  misery.

[19] LORD, help us!
The fire has consumed the wilderness
  pastures,
  and flames have burned up all the trees.
[20] Even the wild animals cry out to you
  because the streams have dried up,
  and fire has consumed the wilderness
  pastures.

CHAPTER 2
Locusts Invade like an Army

[1] Sound the trumpet in Jerusalem*!
  Raise the alarm on my holy
  mountain!
Let everyone tremble in fear
  because the day of the LORD is upon us.
[2] It is a day of darkness and gloom,
  a day of thick clouds and deep
  blackness.
Suddenly, like dawn spreading across the
  mountains,
  a great and mighty army appears.
Nothing like it has been seen before
  or will ever be seen again.

[3] Fire burns in front of them,
  and flames follow after them.
Ahead of them the land lies
  as beautiful as the Garden of Eden.
Behind them is nothing but desolation;
  not one thing escapes.
[4] They look like horses;
  they charge forward like war-horses.*
[5] Look at them as they leap along the
  mountaintops.
  Listen to the noise they make—like the
  rumbling of chariots,
like the roar of fire sweeping across a field
  of stubble,
  or like a mighty army moving into
  battle.

[6] Fear grips all the people;
  every face grows pale with terror.
[7] The attackers march like warriors
  and scale city walls like soldiers.
Straight forward they march,
  never breaking rank.
[8] They never jostle each other;
  each moves in exactly the right
  position.

2:1 Hebrew *Zion*; also in 2:15, 23.   2:4 Or *like charioteers.*

They break through defenses
without missing a step.
⁹ They swarm over the city
and run along its walls.
They enter all the houses,
climbing like thieves through the
windows.
¹⁰ The earth quakes as they advance,
and the heavens tremble.
The sun and moon grow dark,
and the stars no longer shine.
¹¹ The LORD is at the head of the
column.
He leads them with a shout.
This is his mighty army,
and they follow his orders.
The day of the LORD is an awesome,
terrible thing.
Who can possibly survive?

A Call to Repentance

¹² That is why the LORD says,
"Turn to me now, while there is time.
Give me your hearts.
Come with fasting, weeping, and
mourning.
¹³ Don't tear your clothing in your grief,
but tear your hearts instead."
Return to the LORD your God,
for he is merciful and compassionate,
slow to get angry and filled with
unfailing love.
He is eager to relent and not punish.
¹⁴ Who knows? Perhaps he will give you a
reprieve,
sending you a blessing instead of this
curse.
Perhaps you will be able to offer grain
and wine
to the LORD your God as before.

¹⁵ Blow the ram's horn in Jerusalem!
Announce a time of fasting;
call the people together
for a solemn meeting.

2:20 Hebrew *into the eastern sea, . . . into the western sea.*

¹⁶ Gather all the people—
the elders, the children, and even the
babies.
Call the bridegroom from his quarters
and the bride from her private room.
¹⁷ Let the priests, who minister in the LORD's
presence,
stand and weep between the entry
room to the Temple and the altar.
Let them pray, "Spare your people, LORD!
Don't let your special possession
become an object of mockery.
Don't let them become a joke for
unbelieving foreigners who say,
'Has the God of Israel left them?'"

The LORD's Promise of Restoration

¹⁸ Then the LORD will pity his people
and jealously guard the honor of his
land.
¹⁹ The LORD will reply,
"Look! I am sending you grain and new
wine and olive oil,
enough to satisfy your needs.
You will no longer be an object of
mockery
among the surrounding nations.
²⁰ I will drive away these armies from the
north.
I will send them into the parched
wastelands.
Those in the front will be driven into the
Dead Sea,
and those at the rear into the
Mediterranean.*
The stench of their rotting bodies will rise
over the land."

Surely the LORD has done great things!
²¹   Don't be afraid, O land.
Be glad now and rejoice,
for the LORD has done great things.
²² Don't be afraid, you animals of the
field,
for the wilderness pastures will soon
be green.

2:12-17 God wanted the people of Judah to come to him with torn and broken hearts, admitting their guilt and helplessness, instead of responding to his judgment in the usual way (tearing their garments). The people needed to commit themselves to God, examine themselves, and let God change them. Since God is gracious and merciful (2:13), it makes sense to commit our life to him. He wants to change our pain into joy and send us a blessing.
2:18-27 If the people of Judah admitted their sins, God would take away their pain and replace it with his blessing. Likewise, when we admit our addiction and dependency and turn our life over to God, he will take away the things that torment us and replace them with his wonderful provisions. The barren, "parched wastelands" of our life will flourish. He promises that we will never have to go through the pain of our addiction again as long as we follow him.

The trees will again be filled with fruit;
  fig trees and grapevines will be loaded
    down once more.
²³ Rejoice, you people of Jerusalem!
  Rejoice in the LORD your God!
For the rain he sends demonstrates his
    faithfulness.
  Once more the autumn rains will come,
    as well as the rains of spring.
²⁴ The threshing floors will again be piled
    high with grain,
  and the presses will overflow with new
    wine and olive oil.

²⁵ The LORD says, "I will give you back what
    you lost
  to the swarming locusts, the hopping
    locusts,
the stripping locusts, and the cutting
    locusts.*
  It was I who sent this great destroying
    army against you.
²⁶ Once again you will have all the food you
    want,
  and you will praise the LORD your God,
who does these miracles for you.
  Never again will my people be
    disgraced.
²⁷ Then you will know that I am among my
    people Israel,
  that I am the LORD your God, and there
    is no other.
  Never again will my people be
    disgraced.

The LORD's Promise of His Spirit

²⁸*"Then, after doing all those things,
  I will pour out my Spirit upon all
    people.
  Your sons and daughters will prophesy.
  Your old men will dream dreams,

and your young men will see visions.
²⁹ In those days I will pour out my Spirit
  even on servants—men and women
    alike.
³⁰ And I will cause wonders in the heavens
    and on the earth—
  blood and fire and columns of smoke.
³¹ The sun will become dark,
  and the moon will turn blood red
before that great and terrible* day
    of the LORD arrives.
³² But everyone who calls on the name
    of the LORD
  will be saved,
for some on Mount Zion in Jerusalem will
    escape,
  just as the LORD has said.
These will be among the survivors
  whom the LORD has called.

CHAPTER 3
Judgment against Enemy Nations

¹*"At the time of those events," says the
    LORD,
  "when I restore the prosperity of Judah
    and Jerusalem,
² I will gather the armies of the world
  into the valley of Jehoshaphat.*
There I will judge them
  for harming my people, my special
    possession,
for scattering my people among the
    nations,
  and for dividing up my land.
³ They threw dice* to decide which
    of my people
  would be their slaves.
They traded boys to obtain prostitutes
  and sold girls for enough wine
    to get drunk.

2:25 The precise identification of the four kinds of locusts mentioned here is uncertain. 2:28 Verses 2:28-32 are numbered 3:1-5 in Hebrew text. 2:31 Greek version reads *glorious*. 3:1 Verses 3:1-21 are numbered 4:1-21 in Hebrew text. 3:2 *Jehoshaphat* means "the LORD judges." 3:3 Hebrew *They cast lots*.

2:28-29 Since this prophecy was fulfilled at Pentecost (see Acts 2), we can receive the gift of the Holy Spirit. The Holy Spirit has been changing dysfunctional lives since he was given to the world: Peter and the apostles (Acts 2), Paul (Acts 9), a demon-possessed slave girl and a prison guard (Acts 16), and others. The Spirit that Joel prophesied about, the Spirit who changed first-century lives, is available to change our life, too. We can trust the God of the Old and New Testaments to heal our broken life and help us journey toward recovery.
2:32 To call "on the name of the LORD" is to commit our life to God. When we do this, we will find deliverance. No failure in the past is too great to prevent this. No disadvantage of any kind can keep us from God's grace. When God comes to judge the world, his grace is able to keep us from all harm.
3:1-14 Those who have harmed us will not get away with their abuses. God will judge his enemies; God's enemies are those who oppress his people and ignore his power. Since they will face God's judgment on the day of the Lord, we can let go of our hatred and desire for revenge and focus on our own journey toward recovery.

⁴"What do you have against me, Tyre and Sidon and you cities of Philistia? Are you trying to take revenge on me? If you are, then watch out! I will strike swiftly and pay you back for everything you have done. ⁵You have taken my silver and gold and all my precious treasures, and have carried them off to your pagan temples. ⁶You have sold the people of Judah and Jerusalem to the Greeks,* so they could take them far from their homeland.

⁷"But I will bring them back from all the places to which you sold them, and I will pay you back for everything you have done. ⁸I will sell your sons and daughters to the people of Judah, and they will sell them to the people of Arabia,* a nation far away. I, the LORD, have spoken!"

⁹ Say to the nations far and wide:
"Get ready for war!
Call out your best warriors.
    Let all your fighting men advance for
        the attack.
¹⁰ Hammer your plowshares into swords
    and your pruning hooks into spears.
    Train even your weaklings to be
        warriors.
¹¹ Come quickly, all you nations everywhere.
    Gather together in the valley."

And now, O LORD, call out your warriors!

¹² "Let the nations be called to arms.
    Let them march to the valley of
        Jehoshaphat.
There I, the LORD, will sit
    to pronounce judgment on them all.
¹³ Swing the sickle,
    for the harvest is ripe.*
Come, tread the grapes,
    for the winepress is full.
The storage vats are overflowing
    with the wickedness of these people."

¹⁴ Thousands upon thousands are waiting in
        the valley of decision.
    There the day of the LORD will soon
        arrive.
¹⁵ The sun and moon will grow dark,
    and the stars will no longer shine.
¹⁶ The LORD's voice will roar from Zion
    and thunder from Jerusalem,
    and the heavens and the earth will
        shake.
But the LORD will be a refuge for his
        people,
    a strong fortress for the people of Israel.

Blessings for God's People

¹⁷ "Then you will know that I, the LORD your
        God,
    live in Zion, my holy mountain.
Jerusalem will be holy forever,
    and foreign armies will never conquer
        her again.
¹⁸ In that day the mountains will drip with
        sweet wine,
    and the hills will flow with milk.
Water will fill the streambeds of Judah,
    and a fountain will burst forth from the
        LORD's Temple,
    watering the arid valley of acacias.*
¹⁹ But Egypt will become a wasteland
    and Edom will become a wilderness,
because they attacked the people of Judah
    and killed innocent people in their
        land.

²⁰ "But Judah will be filled with people
        forever,
    and Jerusalem will endure through all
        generations.
²¹ I will pardon my people's crimes,
    which I have not yet pardoned;
and I, the LORD, will make my home
    in Jerusalem* with my people."

3:6 Hebrew *to the peoples of Javan.* **3:8** Hebrew *to the Sabeans.* **3:13** Greek version reads *for the harvest time has come.* Compare Mark 4:29. **3:18** Hebrew *valley of Shittim.* **3:21** Hebrew *Zion.*

3:16-21 God has planned a good future for all who trust in him. Restoration and recovery will be complete; salvation will be forever. With this hope for the future, we can find the courage we need to persevere through our problems today (Romans 8:18-21). Since the final goal of the recovery process is assured, we need not fear the hard times that may still lie ahead.

AMOS

THE BIG PICTURE

A. THINGS THAT OFFEND GOD
(1:1–2:16)
1. Inhumane Conduct between Nations (1:1–2:3)
2. Rejecting God and His Laws (2:4-5)
3. Oppressing the Poor and Helpless (2:6-8)
4. Rejecting God's Pleas to Change Behavior (2:9-16)

B. WARNINGS FROM GOD
(3:1–6:14)
1. The People Break the Covenant (3:1-15)
2. The People Refuse to Change Their Behavior (4:1-13)
3. The People Must Choose Life or Death (5:1-27)
4. Danger in Putting Confidence in the Wrong Things (6:1-14)

C. GOD'S LOVING PUNISHMENT
(7:1–9:15)
1. The Context for Punishment: Merciful Love (7:1-6)
2. The Time for Punishment: The Near Future (7:7–8:14)
3. The Extent of Punishment: The Entire Nation (9:1-6)
4. The Result of Punishment: Recovery and Restoration (9:7-15)

God is just and righteous, yet he always expresses his justice in the context of his love and compassion. He expects us to act in the same way. God's Word asks that we show mercy and understanding toward others, promoting fairness in our relationships. In Amos's day, Israel was a prosperous nation, but with their prosperity came corruption, injustice toward the poor and helpless, and religious apostasy. God had given his chosen people laws for governing human relationships, but they had refused to obey them.

God called Amos, a shepherd from Tekoa, to awaken his people from their denial and to warn them of the painful consequences that would come. Amos confronted the people of Israel with their ill treatment of the poor and oppressed, demanding that they act with justice and mercy. God gave this warning of punishment in hope that his people would change. They were reminded of their responsibilities as God's chosen people and called to evaluate their behavior honestly. Sadly, their behavior had fallen to a level even lower than that of their pagan neighbors!

God desired to show mercy to his people, but they refused to repent. So Amos's predictions for Israel's future were dark and dismal. God would allow his people to suffer through a period of destruction and exile. Despite his predictions of doom, however, Amos also spoke of the future with hope. If the people would admit their sins and ask for forgiveness, God would cleanse them and restore them completely. It is never too late to begin the recovery process. God is waiting for us to recognize how helpless we are and to call out to him for his loving help.

THE BOTTOM LINE

PURPOSE: To confront the people of Israel with their sins, calling them to confession and repentance. AUTHOR: The prophet Amos. AUDIENCE: The people of the northern kingdom of Israel. DATE WRITTEN: Between 760 and 750 B.C., when Jeroboam II was king of Israel and Uzziah was king of Judah. SETTING: The northern kingdom of Israel during a time of material prosperity and spiritual complacency. KEY VERSE: "I will bring my exiled people of Israel back from distant lands, and they will rebuild their ruined cities and live in them again. They will plant vineyards and gardens; they will eat their crops and drink their wine" (9:14). KEY PLACES: Samaria, the northern kingdom's capital, and the temple at Bethel. KEY PEOPLE AND RELATIONSHIPS: Amos and Amaziah, the priest at Bethel; the people of Israel; the Edomites.

RECOVERY THEMES

Complacency Leads to Relapse: When life is going smoothly, we need to be careful. We are ripe for falling into complacency and relapse. In Amos's day, the people of Israel were prosperous and began to think they could make it without God. This started them down a pathway toward destruction. If we are walking with the Lord when life is going well, we will recognize our need for God and his help when life becomes difficult. God is the source of power for all recovery; all success must be attributed to him. A complacent, self-sufficient attitude will only lead to a relapse.

Created for Relationships: The people in the time of Amos acted as if they were isolated individuals. They were indifferent to the pain of those around them. They exploited the weak and poor; they enslaved the helpless through extortion and heavy taxation. God has created us to live in relationship with others, not in isolation. Recovery involves recognizing our need for others and making amends to those we have wronged. God wants to help us restore our broken relationships.

God Honors Upright Hearts: Many of the people of Israel carried on the outward appearances of religion even though they had abandoned their faith in God. Sometimes we work through the recovery program in the same way. We perform to get the approval of others, but genuine internal change never takes place. We begin to hide our failures from others, pretending we are faithfully following our program. This only leads to denial. God wants us to have a genuine heart that seeks to know him better and trust him more. He doesn't care about surface appearances; he sees through our false exterior even if other people don't. God cares about the attitudes of our heart.

Recovery Begins with Helplessness: When the people of Israel went into captivity and their society was crumbling about them, their denial was broken. They knew that they needed God. The dark times of life often lead us to recovery. Our helplessness shatters our denial and awakens us from our false illusions. When our life is totally out of control and crumbling around us, our attempts to deny that we need God are futile. We can acknowledge our need and be open to God and his healing power. As we recognize our helplessness, the process of recovery can begin.

CHAPTER 1

This message was given to Amos, a shepherd from the town of Tekoa in Judah. He received this message in visions two years before the earthquake, when Uzziah was king of Judah and Jeroboam II, the son of Jehoash,* was king of Israel.

²This is what he saw and heard:

"The LORD's voice will roar from Zion
and thunder from Jerusalem!
The lush pastures of the shepherds will
dry up;
the grass on Mount Carmel will wither
and die."

God's Judgment on Israel's Neighbors

³This is what the LORD says:

"The people of Damascus have sinned
again and again,*
and I will not let them go unpunished!

They beat down my people in Gilead
as grain is threshed with iron
sledges.
⁴So I will send down fire on King Hazael's
palace,
and the fortresses of King Ben-hadad
will be destroyed.
⁵I will break down the gates of Damascus
and slaughter the people in the valley
of Aven.
I will destroy the ruler in Beth-eden,
and the people of Aram will go as
captives to Kir,"
says the LORD.

⁶This is what the LORD says:

"The people of Gaza have sinned again
and again,
and I will not let them go unpunished!
They sent whole villages into exile,
selling them as slaves to Edom.

1:1 Hebrew *Joash,* a variant spelling of Jehoash. 1:3 Hebrew *have committed three sins, even four;* also in 1:6, 9, 11, 13.

1:3–2:3 All the people on earth are accountable to God for their actions. There are certain boundaries of human behavior that God will not allow people to cross without punishment. Yet, as Jesus said, God has mercy even on the unrighteous (Matthew 5:45). God will send judgment, but only after giving all people time to repent and change their ways. God does the same thing with us. We may seem to prosper in our addiction, but this will last only a short while. If we do not admit our sins and turn our life over to God, he will leave us to the consequences of our sins.

[7] So I will send down fire on the walls of
Gaza,
and all its fortresses will be destroyed.
[8] I will slaughter the people of Ashdod
and destroy the king of Ashkelon.
Then I will turn to attack Ekron,
and the few Philistines still left will be
killed,"
says the Sovereign LORD.

[9] This is what the LORD says:

"The people of Tyre have sinned again
and again,
and I will not let them go unpunished!
They broke their treaty of brotherhood
with Israel,
selling whole villages as slaves to Edom.
[10] So I will send down fire on the walls of
Tyre,
and all its fortresses will be destroyed."

[11] This is what the LORD says:

"The people of Edom have sinned again
and again,
and I will not let them go unpunished!
They chased down their relatives, the
Israelites, with swords,
showing them no mercy.
In their rage, they slashed them
continually
and were unrelenting in their anger.
[12] So I will send down fire on Teman,
and the fortresses of Bozrah will be
destroyed."

[13] This is what the LORD says:

"The people of Ammon have sinned again
and again,
and I will not let them go unpunished!
When they attacked Gilead to extend
their borders,
they ripped open pregnant women with
their swords.
[14] So I will send down fire on the walls of
Rabbah,
and all its fortresses will be destroyed.
The battle will come upon them with shouts,
like a whirlwind in a mighty storm.

[15] And their king* and his princes will go
into exile together,"
says the LORD.

CHAPTER 2
This is what the LORD says:

"The people of Moab have sinned again
and again,*
and I will not let them go unpunished!
They desecrated the bones of Edom's king,
burning them to ashes.
[2] So I will send down fire on the land of
Moab,
and all the fortresses in Kerioth will be
destroyed.
The people will fall in the noise of battle,
as the warriors shout and the ram's
horn sounds.
[3] And I will destroy their king
and slaughter all their princes,"
says the LORD.

God's Judgment on Judah and Israel
[4] This is what the LORD says:

"The people of Judah have sinned again
and again,
and I will not let them go unpunished!
They have rejected the instruction of the
LORD,
refusing to obey his decrees.
They have been led astray by the same lies
that deceived their ancestors.
[5] So I will send down fire on Judah,
and all the fortresses of Jerusalem will
be destroyed."

[6] This is what the LORD says:

"The people of Israel have sinned again
and again,
and I will not let them go unpunished!
They sell honorable people for silver
and poor people for a pair of sandals.
[7] They trample helpless people in the dust
and shove the oppressed out of the way.
Both father and son sleep with the same
woman,
corrupting my holy name.

1:15 Hebrew *malcam*, possibly referring to their god Molech. 2:1 Hebrew *have committed three sins, even four; also
in 2:4, 6.*

2:4-8 The sins of Judah and Israel stemmed from their rejection of God's laws. They oppressed
and took advantage of the poor and perverted justice by selling people. They took bribes and
engaged in sexual sins. Obeying God's regulations would have brought them blessing, but their
evil deeds ensured their punishment. While our physical world may have changed since Bible
times, God and his laws have not. These same behaviors will still bring punishment from God. If
we have been a victim of any such sins, we can rest assured that God will judge our oppressors.

⁸ At their religious festivals,
  they lounge in clothing their debtors
    put up as security.
  In the house of their gods,*
    they drink wine bought with unjust
      fines.

⁹ "But as my people watched,
  I destroyed the Amorites,
  though they were as tall as cedars
    and as strong as oaks.
  I destroyed the fruit on their branches
    and dug out their roots.
¹⁰ It was I who rescued you from Egypt
  and led you through the desert for forty
    years,
  so you could possess the land of the
    Amorites.
¹¹ I chose some of your sons to be prophets
  and others to be Nazirites.
  Can you deny this, my people of Israel?"
    asks the LORD.
¹² "But you caused the Nazirites to sin by
    making them drink wine,
  and you commanded the prophets,
    'Shut up!'

¹³ "So I will make you groan
  like a wagon loaded down with sheaves
    of grain.
¹⁴ Your fastest runners will not get away.
  The strongest among you will become
    weak.
  Even mighty warriors will be unable to
    save themselves.
¹⁵ The archers will not stand their ground.
  The swiftest runners won't be fast enough
    to escape.
  Even those riding horses won't be able
    to save themselves.
¹⁶ On that day the most courageous of your
    fighting men
  will drop their weapons and run for
    their lives,"
  says the LORD.

2:8 Or their God. 3:9 Hebrew Ashdod.

CHAPTER 3

Listen to this message that the LORD has
spoken against you, O people of Israel—
against the entire family I rescued from
Egypt:

² "From among all the families on the earth,
  I have been intimate with you alone.
  That is why I must punish you
    for all your sins."

Witnesses against Guilty Israel

³ Can two people walk together
  without agreeing on the direction?
⁴ Does a lion ever roar in a thicket
  without first finding a victim?
  Does a young lion growl in its den
    without first catching its prey?
⁵ Does a bird ever get caught in a trap
  that has no bait?
  Does a trap spring shut
    when there's nothing to catch?
⁶ When the ram's horn blows a warning,
  shouldn't the people be alarmed?
  Does disaster come to a city
    unless the LORD has planned it?

⁷ Indeed, the Sovereign LORD never does
    anything
  until he reveals his plans to his servants
    the prophets.

⁸ The lion has roared—
  so who isn't frightened?
  The Sovereign LORD has spoken—
    so who can refuse to proclaim his
      message?
⁹ Announce this to the leaders of Philistia*
  and to the great ones of Egypt:
  "Take your seats now on the hills around
    Samaria,
  and witness the chaos and oppression
    in Israel."

¹⁰ "My people have forgotten how to do right,"
  says the LORD.

3:2 The people of Israel knew how God wanted them to act; after all, God had chosen them to
be his. They knew the laws and the consequences for disobedience, yet they flouted them and
chose to sin anyway. So God would punish them. We know the dangers and consequences of our
compulsions and addictions. If we engage in them and don't expect the consequences, we are in
denial about our destructive behaviors. The only way to avoid the consequences of our addiction
is to avoid the addictive behaviors that cause them.
3:3-8 We all receive warnings before our addiction and dysfunctional behavior overtakes us.
God's prophets had warned the people of Israel about their disobedience regularly, and they had
all seen the suffering of their ancestors. We receive regular warnings—from medical reports,
friends and family members, and the Bible. Continuing in our addiction despite the warnings is
like hearing a smoke alarm go off and waiting to be burned in the fire. We should heed the warnings we receive before it is too late.

"Their fortresses are filled with wealth
taken by theft and violence.
[11] Therefore," says the Sovereign Lord,
"an enemy is coming!
He will surround them and shatter their
defenses.
Then he will plunder all their fortresses."

[12] This is what the Lord says:

"A shepherd who tries to rescue a sheep
from a lion's mouth
will recover only two legs or a piece of
an ear.
So it will be for the Israelites in Samaria
lying on luxurious beds,
and for the people of Damascus
reclining on couches.*

[13] "Now listen to this, and announce it
throughout all Israel,*" says the Lord, the
Lord God of Heaven's Armies.

[14] "On the very day I punish Israel for its sins,
I will destroy the pagan altars at Bethel.
The horns of the altar will be cut off
and fall to the ground.
[15] And I will destroy the beautiful homes of
the wealthy—
their winter mansions and their
summer houses, too—
all their palaces filled with ivory,"
says the Lord.

CHAPTER 4
Israel's Failure to Learn
[1] Listen to me, you fat cows*
living in Samaria,
you women who oppress the poor
and crush the needy,
and who are always calling to your
husbands,
"Bring us another drink!"

[2] The Sovereign Lord has sworn this by his
holiness:
"The time will come when you will be led
away
with hooks in your noses.
Every last one of you will be dragged away
like a fish on a hook!
[3] You will be led out through the ruins of
the wall;
you will be thrown from your fortresses,*"
says the Lord.

[4] "Go ahead and offer sacrifices to the idols
at Bethel.
Keep on disobeying at Gilgal.
Offer sacrifices each morning,
and bring your tithes every three days.
[5] Present your bread made with yeast
as an offering of thanksgiving.
Then give your extra voluntary offerings
so you can brag about it everywhere!
This is the kind of thing you Israelites love
to do,"
says the Sovereign Lord.

[6] "I brought hunger to every city
and famine to every town.
But still you would not return to me,"
says the Lord.

[7] "I kept the rain from falling
when your crops needed it the most.
I sent rain on one town
but withheld it from another.
Rain fell on one field,
while another field withered away.
[8] People staggered from town to town
looking for water,
but there was never enough.
But still you would not return to me,"
says the Lord.

[9] "I struck your farms and vineyards with
blight and mildew.

3:12 The meaning of the Hebrew in this sentence is uncertain. 3:13 Hebrew *the house of Jacob.* The names "Jacob" and "Israel" are often interchanged throughout the Old Testament, referring sometimes to the individual patriarch and sometimes to the nation. 4:1 Hebrew *you cows of Bashan.* 4:3 Or *thrown out toward Harmon,* possibly a reference to Mount Hermon.

4:4-5 It is easy to find substitutes for a genuine relationship with God. One tempting substitute is religious activity. If we go to church regularly, perhaps even sing in the choir, won't that be enough? God required the Israelites to give sacrifices and tithes, but he demanded even more. An offering given because the giver is already committed to God pleases God. But if an offering is given in place of true commitment, then God regards even the offering as a sin. Our heartfelt devotion is what God really wants.
4:6-11 Modern-day parallels to these verses could be: "You've lost your job and your family left you, yet you still won't give up your alcohol and drugs." "You are empty despite all you possess, yet you still won't turn to me." "I've allowed AIDS and venereal disease to infect you, yet you continue to practice sexual sins." All the negative effects of our compulsions and addictions are signs for us to give up these detrimental pursuits and turn back to God, the giver of all that is good and perfect (James 1:17).

Locusts devoured all your fig and olive
trees.
But still you would not return to me,"
says the LORD.

[10] "I sent plagues on you
like the plagues I sent on Egypt long
ago.
I killed your young men in war
and led all your horses away.*
The stench of death filled the air!
But still you would not return to me,"
says the LORD.

[11] "I destroyed some of your cities,
as I destroyed* Sodom and Gomorrah.
Those of you who survived
were like charred sticks pulled from
a fire.
But still you would not return to me,"
says the LORD.

[12] "Therefore, I will bring upon you all the
disasters I have announced.
Prepare to meet your God in
judgment, you people of Israel!"

[13] For the LORD is the one who shaped the
mountains,
stirs up the winds, and reveals his
thoughts to mankind.
He turns the light of dawn into
darkness
and treads on the heights of the earth.
The LORD God of Heaven's Armies is his
name!

CHAPTER 5
A Call to Repentance

Listen, you people of Israel! Listen to this funeral song I am singing:

[2] "The virgin Israel has fallen,
never to rise again!
She lies abandoned on the ground,
with no one to help her up."

[3] The Sovereign LORD says:

"When a city sends a thousand men
to battle,
only a hundred will return.
When a town sends a hundred,
only ten will come back alive."

[4] Now this is what the LORD says to the family
of Israel:

"Come back to me and live!
[5] Don't worship at the pagan altars at Bethel;
don't go to the shrines at Gilgal or
Beersheba.
For the people of Gilgal will be dragged
off into exile,
and the people of Bethel will be
reduced to nothing."
[6] Come back to the LORD and live!
Otherwise, he will roar through Israel*
like a fire,
devouring you completely.
Your gods in Bethel
won't be able to quench the flames.
[7] You twist justice, making it a bitter pill
for the oppressed.
You treat the righteous like dirt.

[8] It is the LORD who created the stars,
the Pleiades and Orion.
He turns darkness into morning
and day into night.
He draws up water from the oceans
and pours it down as rain on the
land.
The LORD is his name!
[9] With blinding speed and power he
destroys the strong,
crushing all their defenses.

[10] How you hate honest judges!
How you despise people who tell the
truth!
[11] You trample the poor,
stealing their grain through taxes and
unfair rent.

4:10 Or *and slaughtered your captured horses.* 4:11 Hebrew *as when God destroyed.* 5:6 Hebrew *the house of Joseph.*

5:4-5 Israel was warned not to worship false idols, since those who do will soon face trouble.
Anything we look to for comfort other than God is a false god. We may not worship carved
images, but we turn to alcohol, drugs, work, materialism, sex, or other compulsions to hide from
our painful problems. God is there waiting to help us. He doesn't want us chasing after things
that will only lead to disappointment and death. Instead, he calls out to us, "Come back to me
and live!"
5:18-20 It is possible to fool ourself into thinking we are spiritually right with God. Amos calls
here for honest self-examination. When Jesus Christ returns, it will be a time of joy and of the
completion of recovery for those whose faith is genuine. Those of us who have not been honest
with ourselves will be lost forever (Matthew 7:21-23). Let us all take a moral inventory now.
Where do we stand with God? How can we change to be more like he wants us to be?

Therefore, though you build beautiful
stone houses,
  you will never live in them.
Though you plant lush vineyards,
  you will never drink wine from them.
¹² For I know the vast number of your sins
  and the depth of your rebellions.
You oppress good people by taking bribes
  and deprive the poor of justice in the
  courts.
¹³ So those who are smart keep their mouths
  shut,
  for it is an evil time.

¹⁴ Do what is good and run from evil
  so that you may live!
Then the LORD God of Heaven's Armies
  will be your helper,
  just as you have claimed.
¹⁵ Hate evil and love what is good;
  turn your courts into true halls of
  justice.
Perhaps even yet the LORD God of
  Heaven's Armies
  will have mercy on the remnant of his
  people.*

¹⁶ Therefore, this is what the Lord, the LORD
God of Heaven's Armies, says:

"There will be crying in all the public
  squares
  and mourning in every street.
Call for the farmers to weep with you,
  and summon professional mourners
  to wail.
¹⁷ There will be wailing in every vineyard,
  for I will destroy them all,"
  says the LORD.

Warning of Coming Judgment

¹⁸ What sorrow awaits you who say,
  "If only the day of the LORD were here!"
You have no idea what you are
  wishing for.
That day will bring darkness, not light.
¹⁹ In that day you will be like a man who
  runs from a lion—
  only to meet a bear.
Escaping from the bear, he leans his hand
  against a wall in his house—
  and he's bitten by a snake.
²⁰ Yes, the day of the LORD will be dark and
  hopeless,
  without a ray of joy or hope.

²¹ "I hate all your show and pretense—
  the hypocrisy of your religious festivals
  and solemn assemblies.

5:15 Hebrew *the remnant of Joseph.*

STEP 5

The Plumb Line

BIBLE READING: Amos 7:7-8

We admitted to God, to ourselves, and to another human being the exact nature of our wrongs.

The kinds of instruments we use to measure our life will often determine the kinds of problems we uncover. If we use faulty guidelines, we can't make accurate assessments. We may wonder why we aren't progressing in the recovery program. It may be that we need to look closely at the measuring devices we are using to uncover our problem areas.

The prophet Amos recorded this vision: "I saw the Lord standing beside a wall that had been built using a plumb line. He was using a plumb line to see if it was still straight. And the LORD said . . . 'I will test my people with this plumb line'" (Amos 7:7-8).

A plumb line is a length of string that has a weight tied to one end. When the string is held up with the weighted end hanging down, gravity ensures that the string is perfectly vertical. When held next to a building, the plumb line provides a sure measurement by which to check whether or not the structure is "in line" with the physical universe. A building in line with the plumb line will be sturdy and function well. If the building's walls are out of line, they are not straight and will eventually collapse.

The same holds true in the spiritual realm. God's Word is our spiritual plumb line. Just as we can't argue with the law of gravity, we can't change the spiritual laws revealed in the Bible. We should measure our life by the plumb line of God's Word. When things don't measure up, it is important that we admit there is a problem and start rebuilding accordingly. *Turn to page 1353, John 8.*

²² I will not accept your burnt offerings and
 grain offerings.
 I won't even notice all your choice
 peace offerings.
²³ Away with your noisy hymns of praise!
 I will not listen to the music of your harps.
²⁴ Instead, I want to see a mighty flood of
 justice,
 an endless river of righteous living.

²⁵ "Was it to me you were bringing sacrifices and offerings during the forty years in
the wilderness, Israel? ²⁶ No, you served your
pagan gods—Sakkuth your king god and
Kaiwan your star god—the images you made
for yourselves. ²⁷ So I will send you into exile,
to a land east of Damascus,* says the LORD,
whose name is the God of Heaven's Armies.

CHAPTER 6

¹ What sorrow awaits you who lounge in
 luxury in Jerusalem,*
 and you who feel secure in Samaria!
You are famous and popular in Israel,
 and people go to you for help.
² But go over to Calneh
 and see what happened there.
Then go to the great city of Hamath
 and down to the Philistine city of Gath.
You are no better than they were,
 and look at how they were destroyed.
³ You push away every thought of coming
 disaster,
 but your actions only bring the day of
 judgment closer.
⁴ How terrible for you who sprawl on ivory
 beds
 and lounge on your couches,
eating the meat of tender lambs from the
 flock
 and of choice calves fattened in the stall.

⁵ You sing trivial songs to the sound
 of the harp
 and fancy yourselves to be great
 musicians like David.
⁶ You drink wine by the bowlful
 and perfume yourselves with fragrant
 lotions.
 You care nothing about the ruin
 of your nation.*
⁷ Therefore, you will be the first to be led
 away as captives.
 Suddenly, all your parties will end.

⁸ The Sovereign LORD has sworn by his own
name, and this is what he, the LORD God of
Heaven's Armies, says:

"I despise the arrogance of Israel,*
 and I hate their fortresses.
I will give this city
 and everything in it to their enemies."

⁹ (If there are ten men left in one house, they
will all die. ¹⁰ And when a relative who is
responsible to dispose of the dead* goes into
the house to carry out the bodies, he will ask
the last survivor, "Is anyone else with you?"
When the person begins to swear, "No,
by . . . ," he will interrupt and say, "Stop!
Don't even mention the name of the LORD.")

¹¹ When the LORD gives the command,
 homes both great and small will be
 smashed to pieces.

¹² Can horses gallop over boulders?
 Can oxen be used to plow them?
But that's how foolish you are when you
 turn justice into poison
 and the sweet fruit of righteousness
 into bitterness.
¹³ And you brag about your conquest of
 Lo-debar.*

5:26-27 Greek version reads *No, you carried your pagan gods—the shrine of Molech, the star of your god Rephan, and the images you made for yourselves. So I will send you into exile, to a land east of Damascus.* Compare Acts 7:43. **6:1** Hebrew *in Zion.* **6:6** Hebrew *of Joseph.* **6:8** Hebrew *Jacob.* See note on 3:13. **6:10** Or *to burn the dead.* The meaning of the Hebrew is uncertain. **6:13a** *Lo-debar* means "nothing."

5:21-24 No amount of religious activity is going to make up for a dysfunctional lifestyle. We may fool others into believing that we are all right because we go to church three times a week or give 20 percent of our income to the church. But God will not look favorably upon our religious activities if we are not doing good to others and following his guidelines for healthy living.
6:4-7 Addiction to "the good life" can be one of the deadliest of all addictions. God has no quarrel with his people enjoying the good things he provides for them. The Israelites' problem was that they craved their enjoyments so much that they no longer cared whom they hurt in the process of getting them. Many of us are in the same situation; we get wrapped up in our pleasures and luxuries and don't care whom we step on to get them. Maybe we have ruined our family life or friendships in the pursuit of material things or our addiction. If we turn these areas over to God, he can help us recover our life and our relationships.

You boast, "Didn't we take Karnaim* by
our own strength?"

¹⁴ "O people of Israel, I am about to bring an
enemy nation against you,"
says the LORD God of Heaven's Armies.
"They will oppress you throughout your
land—
from Lebo-hamath in the north
to the Arabah Valley in the south."

CHAPTER 7
A Vision of Locusts
The Sovereign LORD showed me a vision. I saw
him preparing to send a vast swarm of locusts
over the land. This was after the king's share
had been harvested from the fields and as the
main crop was coming up. ²In my vision the
locusts ate every green plant in sight. Then I
said, "O Sovereign LORD, please forgive us or
we will not survive, for Israel* is so small."

³So the LORD relented from this plan. "I
will not do it," he said.

A Vision of Fire
⁴Then the Sovereign LORD showed me another vision. I saw him preparing to punish
his people with a great fire. The fire had
burned up the depths of the sea and was devouring the entire land. ⁵Then I said, "O Sovereign LORD, please stop or we will not
survive, for Israel is so small."

⁶Then the LORD relented from this plan,
too. "I will not do that either," said the Sovereign LORD.

A Vision of a Plumb Line
⁷Then he showed me another vision. I saw
the Lord standing beside a wall that had
been built using a plumb line. He was using a
plumb line to see if it was still straight. ⁸And
the LORD said to me, "Amos, what do you
see?"

I answered, "A plumb line."

And the Lord replied, "I will test my people
with this plumb line. I will no longer ignore
all their sins. ⁹The pagan shrines of your ancestors* will be ruined, and the temples of Israel will be destroyed; I will bring the dynasty
of King Jeroboam to a sudden end."

Amos and Amaziah
¹⁰Then Amaziah, the priest of Bethel, sent a
message to Jeroboam, king of Israel: "Amos is
hatching a plot against you right here on
your very doorstep! What he is saying is intolerable. ¹¹He is saying, 'Jeroboam will soon
be killed, and the people of Israel will be sent
away into exile.'"

¹²Then Amaziah sent orders to Amos: "Get
out of here, you prophet! Go on back to the
land of Judah, and earn your living by
prophesying there! ¹³Don't bother us with
your prophecies here in Bethel. This is the
king's sanctuary and the national place of
worship!"

¹⁴But Amos replied, "I'm not a professional
prophet, and I was never trained to be one.*
I'm just a shepherd, and I take care of sycamore-fig trees. ¹⁵But the LORD called me away
from my flock and told me, 'Go and prophesy to my people in Israel.' ¹⁶Now then, listen
to this message from the LORD:

"You say,
'Don't prophesy against Israel.
Stop preaching against my people.*'
¹⁷ But this is what the LORD says:
'Your wife will become a prostitute
in this city,
and your sons and daughters will
be killed.
Your land will be divided up,
and you yourself will die in a foreign
land.
And the people of Israel will certainly
become captives in exile,
far from their homeland.'"

6:13b *Karnaim* means "horns," a term that symbolizes strength. 7:2 Hebrew *Jacob;* also in 7:5. See note on 3:13.
7:9 Hebrew *of Isaac.* 7:14 Or *I'm not a prophet nor the son of a prophet.* 7:16 Hebrew *against the house of Isaac.*

7:7-9 God would not hold back his judgment any longer. He took a plumb line, a device used to
measure the straightness of a wall, to see just how Israel measured up to his righteous standards.
God looks at our life with a plumb line—the Bible, his word to us. On our own, when we look at
our life, it may seem straight and strong. But if we measured ourself with God's plumb line, we
would see that we are weak and sinful. Praying to God for help is the way to start the process
toward a life in line with God's standards.
7:10-17 When Amos faced opposition, he was sure of his commitment to God and boldly persevered in what he knew to be God's will. God had called him to enter new territory, and he had
done it courageously. We will face opposition in recovery, especially when we bring others the good
news of restoration. People may feel threatened by our progress and want to see us fail so they
won't feel guilty about their own lifestyle. When we are being attacked, we may feel like giving up
and giving in to others. But we must persevere, trusting God for protection and strength.

CHAPTER 8
A Vision of Ripe Fruit

Then the Sovereign LORD showed me another vision. In it I saw a basket filled with ripe fruit. [2]"What do you see, Amos?" he asked.

I replied, "A basket full of ripe fruit."

Then the LORD said, "Like this fruit, Israel is ripe for punishment! I will not delay their punishment again. [3]In that day the singing in the Temple will turn to wailing. Dead bodies will be scattered everywhere. They will be carried out of the city in silence. I, the Sovereign LORD, have spoken!"

[4]Listen to this, you who rob the poor
and trample down the needy!
[5]You can't wait for the Sabbath day to be over
and the religious festivals to end
so you can get back to cheating the helpless.
You measure out grain with dishonest measures
and cheat the buyer with dishonest scales.*
[6]And you mix the grain you sell
with chaff swept from the floor.
Then you enslave poor people
for one piece of silver or a pair of sandals.

[7]Now the LORD has sworn this oath
by his own name, the Pride of Israel*:
"I will never forget
the wicked things you have done!
[8]The earth will tremble for your deeds,
and everyone will mourn.
The ground will rise like the Nile River at floodtime;
it will heave up, then sink again.

[9]"In that day," says the Sovereign LORD,
"I will make the sun go down at noon
and darken the earth while it is still day.
[10]I will turn your celebrations into times of mourning
and your singing into weeping.
You will wear funeral clothes
and shave your heads to show your sorrow—
as if your only son had died.
How very bitter that day will be!

[11]"The time is surely coming," says the Sovereign LORD,
"when I will send a famine on the land—
not a famine of bread or water
but of hearing the words of the LORD.
[12]People will stagger from sea to sea
and wander from border to border*
searching for the word of the LORD,
but they will not find it.
[13]Beautiful girls and strong young men
will grow faint in that day,
thirsting for the LORD's word.
[14]And those who swear by the shameful idols of Samaria—
who take oaths in the name of the god of Dan
and make vows in the name of the god of Beersheba*—
they will all fall down,
never to rise again."

CHAPTER 9
A Vision of God at the Altar

Then I saw a vision of the Lord standing beside the altar. He said,

---

8:5 Hebrew *You make the ephah* [a unit for measuring grain] *small and the shekel* [a unit of weight] *great, and you deal falsely by using deceitful balances.* 8:7 Hebrew *the pride of Jacob.* See note on 3:13. 8:12 Hebrew *from north to east.* 8:14 Hebrew *the way of Beersheba.*

8:4-6 The Israelites served material wealth instead of God. They robbed the poor and were dishonest with the people. They sat through worship services but couldn't wait to cheat their helpless customers. The Israelites demonstrated the negative consequences of their addiction to material goods—dishonesty, morbid dependence on others, irresponsibility, and spiritual deadness. Serving wealth is common in our society, maybe even a way of life for some of us. But if we are devoted to money, we cannot be serving God (see Matthew 6:24). We must decide who our master will be—God, who offers eternal life and peace, or money, which can never satisfy us.

8:11-14 Why would the people not be able to find "the word of the LORD"? It wasn't because God was silent; he spoke through the prophets. The people couldn't find God's words because they looked in the wrong places. They looked for revelations from the false gods. God's people could not hear God speak to them until they admitted their sins and helplessness. They needed to seek God alone and nothing else. We, too, must stop trusting the "idols" we count on to get us through our days in order to hear the truth of God's Word. Only the hope God's Word offers us can truly satisfy.

9:1-4 It is our responsibility to commit our life to God; we cannot begin recovery unless we do. Psalm 139 speaks reassuringly of God's presence with those who seek him. Amos speaks of the

"Strike the tops of the Temple columns,
  so that the foundation will shake.
Bring down the roof
  on the heads of the people below.
I will kill with the sword those who survive.
  No one will escape!
2 "Even if they dig down to the place of the
    dead,*
  I will reach down and pull them up.
Even if they climb up into the heavens,
  I will bring them down.
3 Even if they hide at the very top of Mount
    Carmel,
  I will search them out and capture
    them.
Even if they hide at the bottom of the
    ocean,
  I will send the sea serpent after them to
    bite them.
4 Even if their enemies drive them into exile,
  I will command the sword to kill them
    there.
I am determined to bring disaster upon
    them
  and not to help them."

5 The Lord, the LORD of Heaven's Armies,
  touches the land and it melts,
  and all its people mourn.
The ground rises like the Nile River at
    floodtime,
  and then it sinks again.
6 The LORD's home reaches up to the
    heavens,
  while its foundation is on the earth.
He draws up water from the oceans
  and pours it down as rain on the land.
  The LORD is his name!

7 "Are you Israelites more important to me
  than the Ethiopians?*" asks the LORD.

"I brought Israel out of Egypt,
  but I also brought the Philistines from
    Crete*
  and led the Arameans out of Kir.

8 "I, the Sovereign LORD,
  am watching this sinful nation
    of Israel.
I will destroy it
  from the face of the earth.
But I will never completely destroy the
    family of Israel,*"
  says the LORD.
9 "For I will give the command
  and will shake Israel along with the
    other nations
as grain is shaken in a sieve,
  yet not one true kernel will be lost.
10 But all the sinners will die by the sword—
  all those who say, 'Nothing bad will
    happen to us.'

A Promise of Restoration

11 "In that day I will restore the fallen
    house* of David.
  I will repair its damaged walls.
From the ruins I will rebuild it
  and restore its former glory.
12 And Israel will possess what is left of Edom
  and all the nations I have called to be
    mine.*"
The LORD has spoken,
  and he will do these things.

13 "The time will come," says the LORD,
  "when the grain and grapes will grow
    faster
  than they can be harvested.
Then the terraced vineyards on the hills
    of Israel
  will drip with sweet wine!

9:2 Hebrew *to Sheol.* **9:7a** Hebrew *the Cushites?* **9:7b** Hebrew *Caphtor.* **9:8** Hebrew *the house of Jacob.* See note on 3:13. **9:11a** Or *kingdom;* Hebrew reads *tent.* **9:11b-12** Greek version reads *and restore its former glory, / so that the rest of humanity, including the Gentiles— / all those I have called to be mine—might seek me.* Compare Acts 15:16-17.

terrible consequences for those who refuse to commit their lives to him and continue in sin. Earthly recovery and eternal life are available to all who repent and ask God to rescue them from their past sins and mistakes.

9:10 Refusal to admit the truth can be dangerous. Outward appearances seemed to deny the truth of what Amos was saying. The nation was prosperous; enemies were weak; the military was strong; alliances were made with Egypt and other nations. Inwardly, however, the people were diseased (see Amos 6:6). Israel's spiritual sickness would lead ultimately to its destruction. The people denied the truth. Later they were destroyed and taken captive to Assyria (2 Kings 17:22-23). Denial can cost us our life and happiness. We must admit the truth to ourself and to God so we can begin recovery and enjoy the fulfillment he offers.

9:11-15 God is committed to helping his people recover. He restores what is broken and ruined, changing barren land to a place of unprecedented fruitfulness. This can only happen when we see how helpless we are without God and commit our life into his hands. The process will be painful as we grow spiritually, but the end result will be worth it.

¹⁴ I will bring my exiled people
of Israel
back from distant lands,
and they will rebuild their ruined cities
and live in them again.
They will plant vineyards and
gardens;

they will eat their crops and drink their
wine.
¹⁵ I will firmly plant them there
in their own land.
They will never again be uprooted
from the land I have given them,"
says the LORD your God.

REFLECTIONS ON AMOS

insights INTO GOD'S PERSON AND WILL

In **Amos 5:6-14** the prophet describes a life of recovery. It comes from God alone, not from anywhere else. To seek God means to admit our helplessness and commit our life to him, letting him change us. But how do we avoid the various failures mentioned in these verses? God reveals himself uniquely in the Bible; it is our infallible guide to the truth. We need to seek God's will through his Word and, with his help, live by it.

In **Amos 5:8-9** the Creator and Sustainer of the universe is described (see also 4:13; 9:6). When we seek God, we seek the all-powerful Creator of all things. He created the stars and the rest of the universe from nothing. He controls both day and night and makes it rain. He cannot be hindered or stopped by the best human efforts. When we commit our life to him, we can be sure that he is capable of helping us change.

OBADIAH

THE BIG PICTURE

A. FREEDOM THROUGH SEEING GOD'S PRINCIPLE OF JUSTICE (1:1-9)
1. Betrayal Begets Betrayal (1:1)
2. No One Can Stand against God (1:2-4)
3. Betrayers Must Lose Everything (1:5-9)

B. FREEDOM THROUGH SEEING GOD'S VIEW OF INJUSTICE (1:10-14)
1. Gloating while Others Are Hurting (1:10-12)
2. Inflicting Pain (1:13-14)

C. FREEDOM THROUGH SEEING GOD'S PLAN FOR THE FUTURE (1:15-21)

Betrayal always produces feelings of agony, and the closer our relationship with someone, the greater the pain we feel if that person betrays us. In this short book, Obadiah condemned the people of Edom for betraying their kinsmen in Judah, who were under attack by Babylonian armies. The people of Judah were descendants of Jacob, while the Edomites were descended from Jacob's twin brother, Esau. The two nations were closely related, yet over the years the Edomites treated the Israelites cruelly.

When Judah needed help to stand against the armies of Babylon, the Edomites stood by and encouraged the attackers. They cheered the enemy on! They gloated while the Babylonians sacked Jerusalem. When the Babylonians left, the Edomites entered the Holy City and helped themselves to the remaining plunder. They even captured Judeans who were trying to escape and turned them over to the Babylonians.

Obadiah reassured the hurting Judeans that justice would come. In God's timing, Edom would experience the same kind of destruction that Judah did. God promised that Judah and Israel would someday be restored, and he has been true to his word. The nation of Israel still exists, but the nation of Edom has been gone for thousands of years. When we have been betrayed and are struggling with hatred and the desire to "get even," we can leave justice in God's hands. We can rest in the knowledge that someday he will right all wrongs. Then, as we release the burden of anger and hatred to God, we can get on with the recovery process.

THE BOTTOM LINE

PURPOSE: To demonstrate how God would accomplish recovery for his people after they had been betrayed by their allies. AUTHOR: The prophet Obadiah. AUDIENCE: The people of Judah and the Edomites. DATE WRITTEN: Either shortly after Judah and Jerusalem fell to the Babylonians in 586 B.C., or perhaps much earlier when Jehoram was king of Judah in 845 B.C. SETTING: The prophet speaks alternately to the nation of Edom and to the people of Judah in Jerusalem. KEY VERSE: "Those who have been rescued will go up to Mount Zion in Jerusalem to rule over the mountains of Edom. And the LORD himself will be king!" (1:21). KEY PEOPLE AND RELATIONSHIPS: The book focuses on the relationship between the descendants of Isaac's twin sons: Jacob (the ancestor of the Judeans) and Esau (the ancestor of the Edomites).

RECOVERY THEMES

Justice Belongs to God: When we have been betrayed by someone we trusted and realize the enormity of the offense, we may become obsessed with the desire for revenge. "Justice must prevail!" might resound from our soul. Although these feelings are natural, God makes it very clear that we are not to act on them. Revenge will only bring more pain and devastation into our life. We are to confidently place the situation into God's hands and trust him to bring about true and total justice. Then we can be free from the destructive hatred that will only impede our recovery process.

The Danger of Self-Sufficiency: The Edomites were proud of their self-sufficiency and felt secure in their mountain fortress. But there is no lasting security apart from God. We need to guard our heart as we progress in recovery. Success can subtly lead us to think we can handle our dependency alone, which invariably leads to relapse and despair. As we begin to feel good about our progress in recovery, we must remember that God is the one who empowers us. We cannot stand on our own; we need God's constant help and strength.

This is the vision that the Sovereign LORD revealed to Obadiah concerning the land of Edom.

Edom's Judgment Announced

We have heard a message from the LORD
that an ambassador was sent to the
nations to say,
"Get ready, everyone!
Let's assemble our armies and attack
Edom!"

² The LORD says to Edom,
"I will cut you down to size among the
nations;
you will be greatly despised.
³ You have been deceived by your own
pride
because you live in a rock fortress
and make your home high in the
mountains.
'Who can ever reach us way up here?'
you ask boastfully.
⁴ But even if you soar as high as eagles
and build your nest among the stars,
I will bring you crashing down,"
says the LORD.

⁵ "If thieves came at night and robbed you
(what a disaster awaits you!),
they would not take everything.

Those who harvest grapes
always leave a few for the poor.
But your enemies will wipe you out
completely!
⁶ Every nook and cranny of Edom*
will be searched and looted.
Every treasure will be found and taken.

⁷ "All your allies will turn against you.
They will help to chase you from your
land.
They will promise you peace
while plotting to deceive and destroy
you.
Your trusted friends will set traps for you,
and you won't even know about it.
⁸ At that time not a single wise person
will be left in the whole land of Edom,"
says the LORD.
"For on the mountains of Edom
I will destroy everyone who has
understanding.
⁹ The mightiest warriors of Teman
will be terrified,
and everyone on the mountains
of Edom
will be cut down in the slaughter.

Reasons for Edom's Punishment
¹⁰ "Because of the violence you did
to your close relatives in Israel,*

6 Hebrew *Esau;* also in 8b, 9, 18, 19, 21. 10 Hebrew *your brother Jacob.* The names "Jacob" and "Israel" are often interchanged throughout the Old Testament, referring sometimes to the individual patriarch and sometimes to the nation.

1:3-4 Pride had distorted the Edomites' thinking. They thought they were too great and powerful for God, but God let them know that they would come "crashing down." We may think that we don't need God because of our status in society or our wealth and prestige. This pride is always destructive; whether we like it or not, we are helpless without God. If we can not admit that we need God, we have little chance of recovery. No matter how capable we are, our dependency will overwhelm us if we don't have God on our side in the battle.
1:10 The people of Edom were Israel's "close relatives." The Edomites and the Israelites were descended from Esau and Jacob, the twin sons of the patriarch Isaac. These brothers had lived in

you will be filled with shame
and destroyed forever.
[11] When they were invaded,
you stood aloof, refusing to help them.
Foreign invaders carried off their wealth
and cast lots to divide up Jerusalem,
but you acted like one of Israel's enemies.

[12] "You should not have gloated
when they exiled your relatives to
distant lands.
You should not have rejoiced
when the people of Judah suffered such
misfortune.
You should not have spoken arrogantly
in that terrible time of trouble.
[13] You should not have plundered the land
of Israel
when they were suffering such calamity.
You should not have gloated over their
destruction
when they were suffering such calamity.
You should not have seized their wealth
when they were suffering such calamity.
[14] You should not have stood at the
crossroads,
killing those who tried to escape.
You should not have captured the
survivors
and handed them over in their terrible
time of trouble.

Edom Destroyed, Israel Restored

[15] "The day is near when I, the LORD,
will judge all godless nations!
As you have done to Israel,
so it will be done to you.
All your evil deeds
will fall back on your own heads.

[16] Just as you swallowed up my people
on my holy mountain,
so you and the surrounding nations
will swallow the punishment I pour out
on you.
Yes, all you nations will drink and stagger
and disappear from history.

[17] "But Jerusalem* will become a refuge for
those who escape;
it will be a holy place.
And the people of Israel* will come back
to reclaim their inheritance.
[18] The people of Israel will be a raging fire,
and Edom a field of dry stubble.
The descendants of Joseph will be a flame
roaring across the field, devouring
everything.
There will be no survivors in Edom.
I, the LORD, have spoken!

[19] "Then my people living in the Negev
will occupy the mountains of Edom.
Those living in the foothills of Judah*
will possess the Philistine plains
and take over the fields of Ephraim and
Samaria.
And the people of Benjamin
will occupy the land of Gilead.
[20] The exiles of Israel will return to their land
and occupy the Phoenician coast as far
north as Zarephath.
The captives from Jerusalem exiled in the
north*
will return home and resettle the towns
of the Negev.
[21] Those who have been rescued* will go up
to* Mount Zion in Jerusalem
to rule over the mountains of Edom.
And the LORD himself will be king!"

17a Hebrew *Mount Zion*. **17b** Hebrew *house of Jacob;* also in 18. See note on 10. **19** Hebrew *the Shephelah*.
20 Hebrew *in Sepharad*. **21a** As in Greek and Syriac versions; Hebrew reads *Rescuers*. **21b** Or *from*.

conflict with each other; though they made a sort of reconciliation later in life, they were never able to live together for long. Through the centuries, the anger between the two families continued. Unresolved conflict always brings long-term consequences. We may be suffering for the conflicts and sins of our ancestors; we carry many of their traits and dysfunctions within us. We need to resolve such conflicts and painful issues in our own life now to avoid passing them on to future generations.

1:10-15 God held the Edomites accountable for taking advantage of their helpless relatives in Israel. People who are undergoing tribulations are precious to God; he will not tolerate those who gain from their misfortunes. God will bring justice; he says that their "evil deeds will fall back upon [their] own heads." We may have suffered unjustly in the past. If so, we can let go of our hatred or bitterness because God will see that our enemies get what they deserve. If we have taken unfair advantage of others, we need to admit our sins to God and seek to make amends. If we don't, God will not allow us to go unpunished.

1:17-21 Obadiah's words were for God's people in Israel, but they apply to all people who suffer. While we may have troubles now, God will preserve his people and bless them in the future. We will live with God as our king, while our oppressors will be destroyed. Life may be rough now, but God's promises offer us hope for our future restoration.

JONAH

THE BIG PICTURE

A. JONAH REJECTS GOD'S PROGRAM (1:1-17)
B. JONAH IS DELIVERED FROM THE CONSEQUENCES (2:1-10)
C. GOD SPARES THE PEOPLE OF NINEVEH (3:1-10)
D. THE DEBATE BETWEEN GOD AND JONAH (4:1-11)

God called Jonah to warn the people of Nineveh that they faced destruction if they refused to repent of their sins. But Jonah would rather have died than obey God's command. Jonah wanted God to destroy the wicked Assyrian capital; he didn't want the people to repent and receive God's forgiveness. So Jonah boarded a ship and headed in the opposite direction.

When Jonah chose to disobey God, he was not the only person to suffer. The life of every other person on Jonah's ship was threatened by the great storm that God sent. Terrified, the sailors sought the guilty party, and Jonah quickly suggested that he be thrown overboard. It seems he preferred death to the prospect of preaching to the godless Ninevites.

It is difficult to begin the process of forgiveness once bitterness has set in. God had to put Jonah in the belly of a great fish for three days to get his attention. In the end, Jonah finally admitted that he was helpless and asked God for deliverance. Then he grudgingly went to Nineveh to warn the people of their impending punishment. Jonah was not happy when the people responded to his message and repented, for God responded to their humility with mercy.

Even though Jonah refused to obey God, God never gave up on Jonah. Forgiving someone is never easy. God used numerous object lessons—a storm, a great fish, a large plant, a small worm, and a scorching wind—to teach Jonah about compassion and forgiveness. And in spite of Jonah's resistance to God's call, God used him to spread the good news that God desires to bring salvation to all humanity.

THE BOTTOM LINE

PURPOSE: To show that God has compassion not only for the Jews but for all peoples and nations. AUTHOR: The prophet Jonah. AUDIENCE: The people of God in Israel's northern and southern kingdoms. DATE WRITTEN: Probably around 760 B.C. SETTING: Jonah was a prophet in Israel during the time of Jeroboam II, one of the northern kingdom's most powerful kings. Jonah was sent to preach to the people of Nineveh, the capital of Assyria, the nation that would conquer the northern kingdom in 722 B.C. KEY VERSE: "I cried out to the LORD in my great trouble, and he answered me. I called to you from the land of the dead, and LORD, you heard me!" (2:2). KEY PEOPLE AND RELATIONSHIPS: Jonah, the ship's captain and crew, and the people of Nineveh.

RECOVERY THEMES

God Delivers the Powerless: None of us likes to be powerless, whether we like being in control or are accustomed to playing the victim. However, it is only when we acknowledge our powerlessness that recovery can begin. In the darkness inside the great fish, Jonah realized how helpless he was. It was there that he finally turned to God and received his help. As we recognize our helplessness, we too can receive the help God offers. Only he can redeem and deliver us from our dependency or compulsion. If we try to go it alone, we are headed for disaster.

Keeping God's Priorities: Since Jonah was a prophet of God, we might have expected him to share God's priorities. But when God told him to go to Nineveh, Jonah's response reflected his cultural heritage rather than God's values. Jonah hated the people of Nineveh just as all the people of Israel did—the Ninevites were enemies. But God had compassion on these wicked and bloodthirsty people. Jonah needed to get his priorities in line with God's. God desires the salvation of all people, regardless of their race, religion, or nationality. As we share the story of our deliverance, we need to keep this truth in mind.

God's Patience: There are many painful aspects of the recovery process. Like Jonah, we are often tempted to drag our feet. We even pout when life does not go as we would like it to. But God is patient with us, just as he was with Jonah. Rather than running *from* God and trying to avoid the pain of recovery, we need to run *to* God, who is in control and is trustworthy. He will patiently walk with us all the way, step after painful step.

Forgiveness for Everyone: Jonah was so bitter toward the people of Nineveh that he would have chosen death rather than proclaim God's good news to them. We, too, can desire revenge to the point of destroying our own life. Bitterness destroys our peace, takes away our joy, and impedes the recovery process. It is not natural to want God to forgive those who have hurt us. But God is merciful to our enemies, even as he has been merciful to us. When we experience God's forgiveness, we should respond with joy when someone else receives the same. We may even become an instrument of healing to the people who have hurt us.

CHAPTER 1
Jonah Runs from the LORD

The LORD gave this message to Jonah son of Amittai: ²"Get up and go to the great city of Nineveh. Announce my judgment against it because I have seen how wicked its people are."

³But Jonah got up and went in the opposite direction to get away from the LORD. He went down to the port of Joppa, where he found a ship leaving for Tarshish. He bought a ticket and went on board, hoping to escape from the LORD by sailing to Tarshish.

⁴But the LORD hurled a powerful wind over the sea, causing a violent storm that threatened to break the ship apart. ⁵Fearing for their lives, the desperate sailors shouted to their gods for help and threw the cargo overboard to lighten the ship.

But all this time Jonah was sound asleep down in the hold. ⁶So the captain went down after him. "How can you sleep at a time like this?" he shouted. "Get up and pray to your god! Maybe he will pay attention to us and spare our lives."

⁷Then the crew cast lots to see which of them had offended the gods and caused the

---

1:1-3 God's ways are not always our ways. God gave Jonah a message that he didn't want to hear, much less obey. It appears here that Jonah was afraid to confront this godless people with the truth about their sins. Later, however, we learn that Jonah was afraid that the Ninevites would repent and God would spare them (4:1-2). He was bitter against this bloodthirsty nation and wanted them destroyed, refusing to acknowledge that even they could receive God's forgiveness. Part of recovery includes sharing the story of deliverance with others. Are there people in our life with whom we refuse to share the Good News for fear they will repent? Harboring such bitterness will lead to our own destruction. God excludes no one from his forgiveness and restoration.

1:4-17 God created a great storm, putting the sailors in danger over which they had no control. Jonah, who was responsible for their plight, was asleep in the bottom of the boat. Often our irresponsible actions jeopardize the lives of others. Our dependency brings pain and sometimes long-term consequences into the lives of family members and friends. We, like Jonah, need to wake up from the sleep of denial, take responsibility for our failures, and do what we can to make amends to the innocent people around us.

GOD grant me the serenity
to accept the things I cannot change
the courage to change the things I can
and the wisdom to know the difference
AMEN

When people have hurt us deeply, it is easy to hate them and want vengeance. But holding tightly to hatred and bitterness can easily become a defect of character.

The bitterness we experience threatens the recovery process because it causes us to blame others for our problems. It may scare us to think of forgiving those who have hurt us. We may be afraid that releasing our hatred will require us to condone the bad things people have done to us.

Jonah felt this way. He hated the people of Nineveh for their cruelty toward Israel. God told Jonah to go to Nineveh and warn them of the destruction planned for them. Instead, he ran away by boarding a ship going the opposite direction. God caused a life-threatening storm, and Jonah ended up in the belly of a great fish. Suddenly God had Jonah's attention, and Jonah reluctantly obeyed. Jonah preached to the people of Nineveh, they changed their ways, and God put off his planned destruction. Jonah complained, "Didn't I say before I left home that you would do this, LORD? That is why I ran away. . . . You are eager to turn back from destroying people" (Jonah 4:2).

We cannot remove our bitterness on our own. And it will never be easy to accept that God wants to rescue even the people we hate. We must allow God to change our heart as we work toward forgiving those who have hurt us. This will take time. God asks only that we be willing to let him begin the work in our heart. **Turn to page 1205, Matthew 6.**

terrible storm. When they did this, the lots identified Jonah as the culprit. [8]"Why has this awful storm come down on us?" they demanded. "Who are you? What is your line of work? What country are you from? What is your nationality?"

[9]Jonah answered, "I am a Hebrew, and I worship the LORD, the God of heaven, who made the sea and the land."

[10]The sailors were terrified when they heard this, for he had already told them he was running away from the LORD. "Oh, why did you do it?" they groaned. [11]And since the storm was getting worse all the time, they asked him, "What should we do to you to stop this storm?"

[12]"Throw me into the sea," Jonah said,

"and it will become calm again. I know that this terrible storm is all my fault."

[13]Instead, the sailors rowed even harder to get the ship to the land. But the stormy sea was too violent for them, and they couldn't make it. [14]Then they cried out to the LORD, Jonah's God. "O LORD," they pleaded, "don't make us die for this man's sin. And don't hold us responsible for his death. O LORD, you have sent this storm upon him for your own good reasons."

[15]Then the sailors picked Jonah up and threw him into the raging sea, and the storm stopped at once! [16]The sailors were awestruck by the LORD's great power, and they offered him a sacrifice and vowed to serve him.

17*Now the LORD had arranged for a great fish to swallow Jonah. And Jonah was inside the fish for three days and three nights.

CHAPTER 2
Jonah's Prayer

1*Then Jonah prayed to the LORD his God from inside the fish. 2He said,

"I cried out to the LORD in my great
  trouble,
and he answered me.
I called to you from the land of the dead,*
  and LORD, you heard me!
3 You threw me into the ocean depths,
  and I sank down to the heart of
  the sea.
The mighty waters engulfed me;
  I was buried beneath your wild and
  stormy waves.
4 Then I said, 'O LORD, you have driven me
  from your presence.
Yet I will look once more toward your
  holy Temple.'
5 "I sank beneath the waves,
  and the waters closed over me.
Seaweed wrapped itself around my
  head.

6 I sank down to the very roots of the
  mountains.
I was imprisoned in the earth,
  whose gates lock shut forever.
But you, O LORD my God,
  snatched me from the jaws of death!
7 As my life was slipping away,
  I remembered the LORD.
And my earnest prayer went out to you
  in your holy Temple.
8 Those who worship false gods
  turn their backs on all God's mercies.
9 But I will offer sacrifices to you with songs
  of praise,
  and I will fulfill all my vows.
For my salvation comes from the LORD
  alone."

10 Then the LORD ordered the fish to spit Jonah out onto the beach.

CHAPTER 3
Jonah Goes to Nineveh

Then the LORD spoke to Jonah a second time: 2"Get up and go to the great city of Nineveh, and deliver the message I have given you."

3 This time Jonah obeyed the LORD's command and went to Nineveh, a city so large that it took three days to see it all.* 4On the

1:17 Verse 1:17 is numbered 2:1 in Hebrew text. 2:1 Verses 2:1-10 are numbered 2:2-11 in Hebrew text. 2:2 Hebrew *from Sheol.* 3:3 Hebrew *a great city to God, of three days' journey.*

2:1-10 It took Jonah three days inside the fish to realize that he would have to follow God's plan for his life. God had called Jonah to do something he didn't want to do. Jonah tried to do things his own way and suffered the consequences. We all have similar choices. We can do things God's way and receive his help and blessing, or we can do things our way and suffer the painful consequences. God will go a long way to rescue his wayward children and lead them back to himself. Sometimes we need to hit rock bottom to realize that God's way is the only way.

3:4-9 God's message penetrated to all levels of Ninevite society. The people immediately admitted their sins before God and dressed in sackcloth to show their sorrow. The king then took responsibility for his people and called both great and small to humble themselves before God and turn from their evil ways. When we obey God and share his transforming message with others, it brings not only deliverance for us but recovery for others as well.

3:10 God does not always use the same methods to deliver people. He saved the sailors by having Jonah willingly thrown from the boat. Here he delivered the Ninevites when Jonah unwillingly brought God's message to them and they repented. God is able to forgive and deliver even the worst of sinners. When people truly repent of their wickedness, God delivers them from judgment. God is merciful toward those who confess their sins and allow him to change them.

4:4-6 God was very patient with Jonah. Rather than condemn him for his anger or punish him for his actions, God taught Jonah another lesson. God used a fast-growing plant to protect Jonah from the scorching heat of the Mesopotamian sun. This kind act did not mean God approved of Jonah's behavior. Sometimes physical blessings from God don't necessarily equal spiritual blessings, nor do they imply the spiritual well-being of the person receiving the blessings.

4:7-9 When the plant died and the hot desert wind and sun beat fiercely against Jonah, he was miserable. He became so upset by his discomfort and the mercy God had shown the Ninevites that he wanted to die. He mistakenly thought that the world revolved around him rather than around God and his program. As long as we have a self-centered attitude like Jonah had, we will have little chance of recovery. We need to humble ourself before God and submit to his plan for us. God's plan may not be the easiest way, and it may not lead us in the direction we want to go, but we can be sure that God's way is always best in the long run.

day Jonah entered the city, he shouted to the crowds: "Forty days from now Nineveh will be destroyed!" [5]The people of Nineveh believed God's message, and from the greatest to the least, they declared a fast and put on burlap to show their sorrow.

[6]When the king of Nineveh heard what Jonah was saying, he stepped down from his throne and took off his royal robes. He dressed himself in burlap and sat on a heap of ashes. [7]Then the king and his nobles sent this decree throughout the city:

"No one, not even the animals from your herds and flocks, may eat or drink anything at all. [8]People and animals alike must wear garments of mourning, and everyone must pray earnestly to God. They must turn from their evil ways and stop all their violence. [9]Who can tell? Perhaps even yet God will change his mind and hold back his fierce anger from destroying us."

[10]When God saw what they had done and how they had put a stop to their evil ways, he changed his mind and did not carry out the destruction he had threatened.

CHAPTER 4
Jonah's Anger at the LORD's Mercy
This change of plans greatly upset Jonah, and he became very angry. [2]So he complained to the LORD about it: "Didn't I say before I left home that you would do this, LORD? That is why I ran away to Tarshish! I knew that you are a merciful and compassionate God, slow to get angry and filled with unfailing love. You are eager to turn back from destroying people. [3]Just kill me now, LORD! I'd rather be dead than alive if what I predicted will not happen."

[4]The LORD replied, "Is it right for you to be angry about this?"

[5]Then Jonah went out to the east side of the city and made a shelter to sit under as he waited to see what would happen to the city. [6]And the LORD God arranged for a leafy plant to grow there, and soon it spread its broad leaves over Jonah's head, shading him from the sun. This eased his discomfort, and Jonah was very grateful for the plant.

[7]But God also arranged for a worm! The next morning at dawn the worm ate through the stem of the plant so that it withered away. [8]And as the sun grew hot, God arranged for a scorching east wind to blow on Jonah. The sun beat down on his head until

STEP 6
Removing Deeper Hurts
BIBLE READING: Jonah 4:4-8
We were entirely ready to have God remove all these defects of character.
When we are upset, we often depend on our addiction to make us feel better. As we get rid of our addiction, we face the deeper character defects that God wants to heal. Our addiction functions as a place of "shelter" from our pain. But when that "shelter" is removed, deep anger may surface, exposing even deeper character flaws that need healing.

Jonah had a glaring defect of character: He couldn't forgive and have compassion on the people of Nineveh, whom he hated. When God decided not to destroy them, Jonah threw a temper tantrum. "The LORD replied, 'Is it right for you to be angry about this?' Then Jonah went out to the east side of the city. . . . And the LORD God arranged for a leafy plant to grow there, and soon it spread its broad leaves over Jonah's head, shading him from the sun. . . . The next morning . . . the plant . . . withered away. And as the sun grew hot, God arranged for a scorching east wind to blow on Jonah. The sun beat down on his head until he grew faint and wished to die" (Jonah 4:4-8).

God did this to show Jonah that the real problem wasn't the loss of his shelter. Hatred was the real problem. The removal of our sheltering addiction may expose deeper problems. This may spark defensive anger as God touches our deepest hurts. It is all right to let the anger out. But it is also important to let God take care of the real problem. *Turn to page 1347, John 5.*

he grew faint and wished to die. "Death is certainly better than living like this!" he exclaimed.

⁹Then God said to Jonah, "Is it right for you to be angry because the plant died?"

"Yes," Jonah retorted, "even angry enough to die!"

¹⁰Then the LORD said, "You feel sorry about the plant, though you did nothing to put it there. It came quickly and died quickly. ¹¹But Nineveh has more than 120,000 people living in spiritual darkness,* not to mention all the animals. Shouldn't I feel sorry for such a great city?"

4:11 Hebrew *people who don't know their right hand from their left.*

REFLECTIONS ON JONAH

insights FROM JONAH'S LIFE

In **Jonah 3:1-3** God once again commanded Jonah to go to Nineveh to proclaim his message. This time, deciding that it was better to obey God than to face his wrath, Jonah obeyed and preached to the people of Nineveh, whom he despised. Sometimes God calls us to do things that we would rather not do. The easy road is usually the wrong road; the right road costs us something. In the end, however, the right way always leads to recovery, blessing, and deliverance.

That which ordinarily would have been considered a great success became a source of great agitation to Jonah. In **Jonah 4:1-3** the prophet became incensed because God decided to forgive the wicked Ninevites. God often chooses to answer our prayers in ways we would never ask for but that brings a much greater good. If we hope to please God and strengthen our relationship with him, we need to commit ourself to obeying his will completely. If we do things our own way, we will face frustration and pain. Jonah needed to learn that God's way is the only good way.

In **Jonah 4:10-11** the prophet put his own desires before the needs of others. God was concerned for the spiritual well-being of the more than 120,000 Ninevites. When we are controlled by our dependency, we often put our own needs before the needs of others. We seek to salve our inner pain at the expense of causing great suffering to those who love us. When God begins to work recovery in our life, we begin to see, as Jonah finally did, just how foolish our selfish attitudes are and how we can act responsibly toward God and others.

MICAH

THE BIG PICTURE

A. THE DOWNFALL OF THE HAUGHTY (1:1–2:13)
   1. Judgment Comes to Those Who Live Disruptive Lives (1:1–2:11)
   2. Hope Comes to Those Who Live Dedicated Lives (2:12-13)

B. THE DELIVERANCE OF THE HELPLESS (3:1–5:15)
   1. Judgment Comes to Those Who Serve Themselves (3:1-12)
   2. Hope Comes from the One Who Serves Others (4:1–5:15)

C. THE DEFEAT OF THE OPPRESSORS (6:1–7:20)
   1. Judgment Comes to Those Who Give Misery to Others (6:1–7:13)
   2. Hope Comes for the One Who Gives Meaning to Others (7:14-20)

The people of Micah's day were not much different from people today. Many of them lived self-centered lives driven by greed and false pride. They spent their nights plotting against the helpless and their days taking advantage of the weak. Their spiritual lives were hypocritical, and they used religion for their personal gain. They lied to make themselves look good and deceived others to cover their corruption. The kingdoms of Israel and Judah had wandered far from God's plan for them, and they would soon suffer the painful consequences.

Centuries before, God had agreed to uniquely bless the people of Israel because of their faithfulness. The people had agreed to follow God's will, but they had never lived up to their promise. So through his prophet Micah, God took his wayward people to court. God was the prosecutor and plaintiff, Micah was the plaintiff's spokesman, Israel was the defendant, and the witnesses were heaven and earth. God could do nothing but judge them guilty as charged. The consequence would be judgment through exile. The northern kingdom of Israel fell to Assyria soon after this prophecy; the southern kingdom of Judah fell to Babylon a few centuries later.

Micah made it clear that no satisfaction can be found in this life apart from God. Only when we accept our own weaknesses and submit to his program for healthy living can we hope to escape the destructive consequences of self-centeredness. Through our repentance, God always offers us his forgiveness, compassion, and unfailing love. By admitting that we are trapped by our sins and dependency, and turning to God for help, we can have hope for the future.

THE BOTTOM LINE

PURPOSE: To warn God's people of the destructive consequences of disobedience and to offer peace to those willing to obey God's revealed will. AUTHOR: The prophet Micah. AUDIENCE: The people of God in Israel's northern and southern kingdoms. DATE WRITTEN: Sometime between 742 and 687 B.C. SETTING: Micah spoke to God's people in the northern and southern kingdoms during the period described in 2 Kings 15–20 and 2 Chronicles 26–30. KEY VERSE: "No, O people, the LORD has told you what is good, and this is what he requires of you: to do what is right, to love mercy, and to walk humbly with your God" (6:8). KEY PLACES: Samaria, Jerusalem, and Bethlehem. KEY PEOPLE AND RELATIONSHIPS: Micah and the people of Samaria and Jerusalem.

RECOVERY THEMES

The Dangers of Pretense: The people in Micah's day were extremely hypocritical. All their religious activities were designed only to make them look good to others. Honestly assessing our actions and doing away with pretense are necessary if we want to progress in recovery. Selfish motives mixed with empty displays of religious or recovery activities pervert the meaning of faith. But turning to God in our need and honestly repenting of our destructive behaviors and attitudes are genuine responses that lead to healing. Anything less will only set us up for failure and relapse.

God Delivers the Powerless: Even though God's judgment against his rebellious people was sure, he promised that a remnant would trust him and survive the trials ahead. Out of hopelessness, God can bring hope. God's ways are different from the ways of the world. To prove this to us, he often ignores what we consider significant and brings deliverance in ways we least expect. Micah makes it clear that when we acknowledge our weaknesses, God will step in to deliver us.

God Cares for the Hurting: God cares for those who are hurting and helpless. He shows tenderness to those who suffer and have been rejected. He reaches out in love and mercy to bring healing and hope. And he calls on us to do the same. As we progress in recovery, we can become instruments of God to bring healing to others. An important part of the recovery process is to share our story of healing with those who are still in bondage. As we do this, we will give hope to others and experience renewed encouragement to persevere in our own program of recovery.

CHAPTER 1

The LORD gave this message to Micah of Moresheth during the years when Jotham, Ahaz, and Hezekiah were kings of Judah. The visions he saw concerned both Samaria and Jerusalem.

Grief over Samaria and Jerusalem

² Attention! Let all the people of the world listen!
  Let the earth and everything in it hear.
The Sovereign LORD is making accusations against you;
  the Lord speaks from his holy Temple.
³ Look! The LORD is coming!
  He leaves his throne in heaven
  and tramples the heights of the earth.
⁴ The mountains melt beneath his feet
  and flow into the valleys
like wax in a fire,
  like water pouring down a hill.
⁵ And why is this happening?
  Because of the rebellion of Israel*—
  yes, the sins of the whole nation.
Who is to blame for Israel's rebellion?

Samaria, its capital city!
Where is the center of idolatry in Judah?
In Jerusalem, its capital!

⁶ "So I, the LORD, will make the city of Samaria
  a heap of ruins.
Her streets will be plowed up
  for planting vineyards.
I will roll the stones of her walls into the valley below,
  exposing her foundations.
⁷ All her carved images will be smashed.
  All her sacred treasures will be burned.
These things were bought with the money
  earned by her prostitution,
and they will now be carried away
  to pay prostitutes elsewhere."

⁸ Therefore, I will mourn and lament.
  I will walk around barefoot and naked.
I will howl like a jackal
  and moan like an owl.
⁹ For my people's wound
  is too deep to heal.

1:5 Hebrew *Jacob*; also in 1:5b. The names "Jacob" and "Israel" are often interchanged throughout the Old Testament, referring sometimes to the individual patriarch and sometimes to the nation.

1:2-7 God announced the coming of a sudden and intense judgment on his people, who had refused to trust and obey him. They had rebelled and sought help from powerless idols. God showed them how useless their idol worship was by allowing them to suffer the consequences of seeking help from sources that could not deliver. Our addiction may be an idol that we call upon to escape our pain—pain that only God can truly heal. We may make recovery fads our idols and expect them to lead us to an easy recovery. If we pursue help from idols, however, we will only be disappointed. Only God has the power to help us persevere in the process of recovery.

It has reached into Judah,
 even to the gates of Jerusalem.

[10] Don't tell our enemies in Gath*;
 don't weep at all.
You people in Beth-leaphrah,*
 roll in the dust to show your despair.
[11] You people in Shaphir,*
 go as captives into exile—naked and
 ashamed.
The people of Zaanan*
 dare not come outside their walls.
The people of Beth-ezel* mourn,
 for their house has no support.
[12] The people of Maroth* anxiously wait
 for relief,
 but only bitterness awaits them
as the LORD's judgment reaches
 even to the gates of Jerusalem.

[13] Harness your chariot horses and flee,
 you people of Lachish.*
You were the first city in Judah
 to follow Israel in her rebellion,
 and you led Jerusalem* into sin.
[14] Send farewell gifts to Moresheth-gath*;
 there is no hope of saving it.
The town of Aczib*
 has deceived the kings of Israel.
[15] O people of Mareshah,*
 I will bring a conqueror to capture
 your town.
And the leaders* of Israel
 will go to Adullam.

[16] Oh, people of Judah, shave your heads
 in sorrow,
 for the children you love will be
 snatched away.
Make yourselves as bald as a vulture,

for your little ones will be exiled to
 distant lands.

CHAPTER 2
Judgment against Wealthy Oppressors

[1] What sorrow awaits you who lie awake
 at night,
 thinking up evil plans.
You rise at dawn and hurry to carry
 them out,
 simply because you have the power
 to do so.
[2] When you want a piece of land,
 you find a way to seize it.
When you want someone's house,
 you take it by fraud and violence.
You cheat a man of his property,
 stealing his family's inheritance.

[3] But this is what the LORD says:
"I will reward your evil with evil;
 you won't be able to pull your neck out
 of the noose.
You will no longer walk around
 proudly,
 for it will be a terrible time."

[4] In that day your enemies will make fun
 of you
 by singing this song of despair about
 you:
"We are finished,
 completely ruined!
God has confiscated our land,
 taking it from us.
He has given our fields
 to those who betrayed us.*"
[5] Others will set your boundaries then,
 and the LORD's people will have no say
 in how the land is divided.

1:10a *Gath* sounds like the Hebrew term for "tell." 1:10b *Beth-leaphrah* means "house of dust." 1:11a *Shaphir* means "pleasant." 1:11b *Zaanan* sounds like the Hebrew term for "come out." 1:11c *Beth-ezel* means "adjoining house." 1:12 *Maroth* sounds like the Hebrew term for "bitter." 1:13a *Lachish* sounds like the Hebrew term for "team of horses." 1:13b Hebrew *the daughter of Zion.* 1:14a *Moresheth* sounds like the Hebrew term for "gift" or "dowry." 1:14b *Aczib* means "deception." 1:15a *Mareshah* sounds like the Hebrew term for "conqueror." 1:15b Hebrew *the glory.* 2:4 Or *to those who took us captive.*

1:12-16 If we don't repent of our dependency and sins, we cannot expect God's blessing. We should never expect to experience good times when God is dealing with the sin in our life. Without repentance, sin is contagious, and its effects are far-reaching. Even the innocent children would be exiled because of their parents' sins. We often fail to realize that our dependency may cause great suffering for future generations. We need to act now, admitting our sins and giving our life into God's gracious hands. With God's help we can overcome our addiction and set our children and grandchildren free from a painful future.

2:1-5 Many of Israel's influential people spent their time planning ways to ruin the lives of others. They sought personal wealth and power; they took people's land and homes by fraud and violence. They were blind to much of the pain they caused and unaware of the judgment ahead for them. Our addiction often drives us to make the same mistakes. As we take inventory of our life, we should think clearly about those we have hurt and seek ways to make amends. If we don't, God will defend the helpless from our selfish actions and bring judgment against us.

True and False Prophets

6 "Don't say such things,"
   the people respond.*
"Don't prophesy like that.
   Such disasters will never come our way!"

7 Should you talk that way, O family
      of Israel?*
   Will the LORD's Spirit have patience
      with such behavior?
   If you would do what is right,
      you would find my words comforting.
8 Yet to this very hour
      my people rise against me like an
         enemy!
   You steal the shirts right off the backs
      of those who trusted you,
   making them as ragged as men
      returning from battle.
9 You have evicted women from their
      pleasant homes
   and forever stripped their children of all
      that God would give them.
10 Up! Begone!
      This is no longer your land and home,
   for you have filled it with sin
      and ruined it completely.

11 Suppose a prophet full of lies would say
      to you,
   "I'll preach to you the joys of wine and
      alcohol!"
   That's just the kind of prophet you would
      like!

Hope for Restoration

12 "Someday, O Israel, I will gather you;
      I will gather the remnant who
         are left.

I will bring you together again like sheep
      in a pen,
   like a flock in its pasture.
   Yes, your land will again
      be filled with noisy crowds!
13 Your leader will break out
      and lead you out of exile,
   out through the gates of the enemy
         cities,
      back to your own land.
   Your king will lead you;
      the LORD himself will guide you."

CHAPTER 3
Judgment against Israel's Leaders

1 I said, "Listen, you leaders of Israel!
      You are supposed to know right from
         wrong,

2 but you are the very ones
      who hate good and love evil.
   You skin my people alive
      and tear the flesh from their bones.
3 Yes, you eat my people's flesh,
      strip off their skin,
      and break their bones.
   You chop them up
      like meat for the cooking pot.
4 Then you beg the LORD for help in times
         of trouble!
   Do you really expect him
      to answer?
   After all the evil you have done,
      he won't even look at you!"

5 This is what the LORD says:
   "You false prophets are leading my
         people astray!

2:6 Or *the prophets respond;* Hebrew reads *they prophesy.* 2:7 Hebrew *O house of Jacob?* See note on 1:5a.

2:12-13 Even though God warned his people of their imminent destruction, he also gave them a reason to hope for the future: Someday he would restore the nation he was about to punish. As we face the inescapable consequences of our past actions, we can still have hope for the future. Even though there may be hard times ahead, if we trust God and obey his will for our life, there is always hope for recovery. No matter how great our sins and sufferings, God can forgive and restore us.

3:1-4 Israel's leaders failed to fulfill their responsibilities before God—to defend the poor and helpless in society. In fact, they took advantage of the very people they were to protect. They could expect only punishment from God. We may have suffered innocently at the hands of our parents or other people in authority. Perhaps their sins against us are at the root of our own destructive behaviors. We can be sure that God will punish those who have wronged us. We can leave the situation in God's hands and spend our energy dealing with our own problems and dependency. If we have harmed innocent people, we must repent and make amends.

3:5-12 Some of us serve God only for what we can get out of it. When all is going well, we act piously; when things don't go our way, however, we use pressure tactics to secure personal gain. Manipulating others must stop if our recovery is to be complete. God does not always pick up the pieces of our mistakes and bad decisions. He may allow us to experience the full negative impact of our actions. Sometimes it takes such suffering to awaken us from our denial and help us realize how much we need God.

You promise peace for those who give you
food,
but you declare war on those who
refuse to feed you.
[6] Now the night will close around you,
cutting off all your visions.
Darkness will cover you,
putting an end to your predictions.
The sun will set for you prophets,
and your day will come to an end.
[7] Then you seers will be put to shame,
and you fortune-tellers will be disgraced.
And you will cover your faces
because there is no answer from God."

[8] But as for me, I am filled with power—
with the Spirit of the LORD.
I am filled with justice and strength
to boldly declare Israel's sin and
rebellion.
[9] Listen to me, you leaders of Israel!
You hate justice and twist all that is
right.
[10] You are building Jerusalem
on a foundation of murder and
corruption.
[11] You rulers make decisions based on bribes;
you priests teach God's laws only
for a price;
you prophets won't prophesy unless you
are paid.
Yet all of you claim to depend on the
LORD.
"No harm can come to us," you say,
"for the LORD is here among us."
[12] Because of you, Mount Zion will be
plowed like an open field;
Jerusalem will be reduced to ruins!
A thicket will grow on the heights
where the Temple now stands.

CHAPTER 4
The LORD's Future Reign
[1] In the last days, the mountain of the
LORD's house
will be the highest of all—
the most important place on earth.
It will be raised above the other hills,

and people from all over the world will
stream there to worship.
[2] People from many nations will come and
say,
"Come, let us go up to the mountain of
the LORD,
to the house of Jacob's God.
There he will teach us his ways,
and we will walk in his paths."
For the LORD's teaching will go out from
Zion;
his word will go out from Jerusalem.
[3] The LORD will mediate between peoples
and will settle disputes between strong
nations far away.
They will hammer their swords into
plowshares
and their spears into pruning hooks.
Nation will no longer fight against
nation,
nor train for war anymore.
[4] Everyone will live in peace and
prosperity,
enjoying their own grapevines and
fig trees,
for there will be nothing to fear.
The LORD of Heaven's Armies
has made this promise!
[5] Though the nations around us follow
their idols,
we will follow the LORD our God forever
and ever.

Israel's Return from Exile
[6] "In that coming day," says the LORD,
"I will gather together those who are
lame,
those who have been exiles,
and those whom I have filled with grief.
[7] Those who are weak will survive as a
remnant;
those who were exiles will become a
strong nation.
Then I, the LORD, will rule from
Jerusalem*
as their king forever."
[8] As for you, Jerusalem,
the citadel of God's people,*

4:7 Hebrew *Mount Zion.* 4:8 Hebrew *As for you, Migdal-eder, / the Ophel of the daughter of Zion.*

4:1-5 If everyone obeyed God, our world would be filled with peace and prosperity. Life would be meaningful and joyful. But we continue to reject God's program and insist on doing things our own way. We live for personal gratification and blind ourselves to the needs of others. As we recognize the destruction and pain we have caused by doing things our own way, it might help to reflect on how things could be if we followed God's way. God desires that we live in a world of joy and harmony. If we admit our failures and seek to live according to his will for us, there is still hope that our corner of the world can reflect God's good intentions for wellness and peace.

your royal might and power
will come back to you again.
The kingship will be restored
to my precious Jerusalem.

⁹ But why are you now screaming in terror?
Have you no king to lead you?
Have your wise people all died?
Pain has gripped you like a woman in
childbirth.
¹⁰ Writhe and groan like a woman in labor,
you people of Jerusalem,*
for now you must leave this city
to live in the open country.
You will soon be sent in exile
to distant Babylon.
But the LORD will rescue you there;
he will redeem you from the grip of
your enemies.

¹¹ Now many nations have gathered against
you.
"Let her be desecrated," they say.
"Let us see the destruction of Jerusalem.*"
¹² But they do not know the LORD's thoughts
or understand his plan.
These nations don't know
that he is gathering them together
to be beaten and trampled
like sheaves of grain on a threshing
floor.
¹³ "Rise up and crush the nations,
O Jerusalem!"*
says the LORD.
"For I will give you iron horns and bronze
hooves,
so you can trample many nations
to pieces.
You will present their stolen riches
to the LORD,
their wealth to the Lord of all the
earth."

CHAPTER 5

¹*Mobilize! Marshal your troops!
The enemy is laying siege to Jerusalem.
They will strike Israel's leader
in the face with a rod.

A Ruler from Bethlehem

²*But you, O Bethlehem Ephrathah,
are only a small village among all the
people of Judah.
Yet a ruler of Israel,
whose origins are in the distant past,
will come from you on my behalf.
³ The people of Israel will be abandoned to
their enemies
until the woman in labor gives birth.
Then at last his fellow countrymen
will return from exile to their
own land.
⁴ And he will stand to lead his flock with
the LORD's strength,
in the majesty of the name of the
LORD his God.
Then his people will live there
undisturbed,
for he will be highly honored around
the world.
⁵ And he will be the source of peace.

When the Assyrians invade our land
and break through our defenses,
we will appoint seven rulers to watch
over us,
eight princes to lead us.
⁶ They will rule Assyria with drawn
swords
and enter the gates of the land of
Nimrod.
He will rescue us from the Assyrians
when they pour over the borders to
invade our land.

4:10 Hebrew *O daughter of Zion.* **4:11** Hebrew *of Zion.* **4:13** Hebrew *"Rise up and thresh, O daughter of Zion."*
5:1 Verse 5:1 is numbered 4:14 in Hebrew text. **5:2** Verses 5:2-15 are numbered 5:1-14 in Hebrew text.

4:9-13 God's people needed to accept the consequences of their actions. God had to remove their world of false security and send them into exile in order to help them realize that they needed him. But God did this only to make them stronger and more righteous. Punishment was only a small part of his much bigger plan to restore and heal them. God works the same in our life. The pain we face now for our past sins is real, but it is only a small part of God's recovery program. In the end, God's judgments will become a source of great blessing for us if we trust God and obey his will.

5:1-5 From a place that the world considered insignificant, God would bring greatness. God made the tiny village of Bethlehem internationally famous when he chose it as the birthplace of the Messiah. God uses "insignificant" people and places to achieve great things. He can take our broken and useless life and turn it into a blessing to others if we let him. This can begin as we share how God delivered us. As others hear how God has blessed us, they will experience hope that God can do the same for them. Out of hopeless situations, God can bring hope. Out of the confusion and chaos we have created, God can rebuild a world of peace.

The Remnant Purified

7 Then the remnant left in Israel*
    will take their place among the nations.
They will be like dew sent by the LORD
    or like rain falling on the grass,
which no one can hold back
    and no one can restrain.
8 The remnant left in Israel
    will take their place among the nations.
They will be like a lion among the animals
        of the forest,
    like a strong young lion among flocks
        of sheep and goats,
pouncing and tearing as they go
    with no rescuer in sight.
9 The people of Israel will stand up
        to their foes,
    and all their enemies will be wiped out.

10 "In that day," says the LORD,
    "I will slaughter your horses
        and destroy your chariots.
11 I will tear down your walls
        and demolish your defenses.
12 I will put an end to all witchcraft,
        and there will be no more
        fortune-tellers.
13 I will destroy all your idols and sacred
        pillars,
    so you will never again worship the
        work of your own hands.
14 I will abolish your idol shrines with their
        Asherah poles
    and destroy your pagan cities.
15 I will pour out my vengeance
    on all the nations that refuse
        to obey me."

5:7 Hebrew *in Jacob;* also in 5:8. See note on 1:5a.   6:5 Hebrew *Shittim.*

CHAPTER 6
The LORD's Case against Israel
Listen to what the LORD is saying:

    "Stand up and state your case against me.
        Let the mountains and hills be called to
        witness your complaints.
2 And now, O mountains,
    listen to the LORD's complaint!
He has a case against his people.
    He will bring charges against Israel.

3 "O my people, what have I done to you?
    What have I done to make you tired
        of me?
    Answer me!
4 For I brought you out of Egypt
    and redeemed you from slavery.
I sent Moses, Aaron, and Miriam to
        help you.
5 Don't you remember, my people,
    how King Balak of Moab tried to have
        you cursed
    and how Balaam son of Beor blessed
        you instead?
And remember your journey from Acacia
        Grove* to Gilgal,
    when I, the LORD, did everything I
        could
    to teach you about my faithfulness."

6 What can we bring to the LORD?
    Should we bring him burnt
        offerings?
    Should we bow before God Most High
        with offerings of yearling calves?
7 Should we offer him thousands of rams
    and ten thousand rivers of olive oil?

5:10-15 God promised to destroy all the useless things his people had depended on for security. They relied on weapons and walled cities for protection from their enemies. They sought spiritual guidance in the occult, astrology, and idol worship. God's people would discover that their so-called strengths were only illusions; these things could never help them. We do the same thing when we turn to our dependency—drugs, alcohol, sex, work—to help us deal with our pain. Sometimes we turn to other "spiritual" remedies for our addiction, which only leads us away from the one true source of help—God. These useless resources will fail when we really need them. Only God can bring us deliverance and true healing.

6:4-5 The people of Israel had become smug and self-sufficient, forgetting that they were helpless without God's power. When we begin to succeed in recovery, it is easy to forget that God delivered us. We tend to take some of the credit and place less importance on our relationship with God. When we fail to recognize God's help in our earlier successes, we can almost count on painful relapses. God is the only one who can deliver us from bondage and sustain us in recovery.

6:6-8 When we consider who God is and who we are, we realize that there is nothing we can truly give to him—neither our possessions nor our most prized treasures—that will impress him or win his favor. God, in the final sense, does not desire our religious acts of worship unless they are accompanied by a life that pleases him. He desires that we treat others responsibly, that we demonstrate mercy toward others, and that we fully rely on him. These are important features of any godly recovery program.

Should we sacrifice our firstborn children
    to pay for our sins?

[8] No, O people, the LORD has told you what
    is good,
    and this is what he requires of you:
to do what is right, to love mercy,
    and to walk humbly with your God.

Israel's Guilt and Punishment

[9] Fear the LORD if you are wise!
    His voice calls to everyone in Jerusalem:
"The armies of destruction are coming;
    the LORD is sending them.*
[10] What shall I say about the homes of the
    wicked
    filled with treasures gained by cheating?
What about the disgusting practice
    of measuring out grain with dishonest
    measures?*
[11] How can I tolerate your merchants
    who use dishonest scales and weights?
[12] The rich among you have become
    wealthy
    through extortion and violence.
Your citizens are so used to lying
    that their tongues can no longer tell the
    truth.

[13] "Therefore, I will wound you!
    I will bring you to ruin for all your sins.
[14] You will eat but never have enough.
    Your hunger pangs and emptiness will
    remain.
And though you try to save your money,
    it will come to nothing in the end.
You will save a little,
    but I will give it to those who conquer
    you.
[15] You will plant crops
    but not harvest them.
You will press your olives
    but not get enough oil to anoint
    yourselves.
You will trample the grapes
    but get no juice to make your wine.
[16] You keep only the laws of evil King Omri;
    you follow only the example of wicked
    King Ahab!

Therefore, I will make an example of you,
    bringing you to complete ruin.
You will be treated with contempt,
    mocked by all who see you."

CHAPTER 7
Misery Turned to Hope
[1] How miserable I am!
    I feel like the fruit picker after the harvest
    who can find nothing to eat.
Not a cluster of grapes or a single early fig
    can be found to satisfy my hunger.
[2] The godly people have all disappeared;
    not one honest person is left on the
    earth.
They are all murderers,
    setting traps even for their own
    brothers.
[3] Both their hands are equally skilled at
    doing evil!
    Officials and judges alike demand
    bribes.
The people with influence get what they
    want,
    and together they scheme to twist
    justice.
[4] Even the best of them is like a brier;
    the most honest is as dangerous as a
    hedge of thorns.
But your judgment day is coming swiftly
    now.
    Your time of punishment is here, a time
    of confusion.
[5] Don't trust anyone—
    not your best friend or even your wife!
[6] For the son despises his father.
    The daughter defies her mother.
The daughter-in-law defies her
    mother-in-law.
    Your enemies are right in your own
    household!

[7] As for me, I look to the LORD for help.
    I wait confidently for God to save me,
    and my God will certainly hear me.
[8] Do not gloat over me, my enemies!
    For though I fall, I will rise again.
Though I sit in darkness,
    the LORD will be my light.

6:9 Hebrew *"Listen to the rod. / Who appointed it?"* **6:10** Hebrew *of using the short ephah?* The ephah was a unit for measuring grain.

7:1-6 When people live for personal gain and turn away from God, the results are always disastrous. Following God's program leads to a society of peace and prosperity. Following personal gratification leads to a world where business becomes unproductive and competition becomes cruel. The leaders of the government become corrupt and no one can be trusted—even members of one's own family! Instead of following our selfish inclinations, we must choose to obey God's will for our life; it will lead to peace.

⁹I will be patient as the LORD punishes me,
  for I have sinned against him.
But after that, he will take up my case
  and give me justice for all I have
    suffered from my enemies.
The LORD will bring me into the light,
  and I will see his righteousness.
¹⁰Then my enemies will see that the LORD is
    on my side.
  They will be ashamed that they taunted
    me, saying,
"So where is the LORD—
  that God of yours?"
With my own eyes I will see their
    downfall;
  they will be trampled like mud in the
    streets.

¹¹In that day, Israel, your cities will be
    rebuilt,
  and your borders will be extended.
¹²People from many lands will come and
    honor you—
  from Assyria all the way to the towns of
    Egypt,
  from Egypt all the way to the Euphrates
    River,*
  and from distant seas and mountains.
¹³But the land* will become empty and
    desolate
  because of the wickedness of those who
    live there.

The LORD's Compassion on Israel

¹⁴O LORD, protect your people with your
    shepherd's staff;
  lead your flock, your special possession.
Though they live alone in a thicket
  on the heights of Mount Carmel,*

let them graze in the fertile pastures of
    Bashan and Gilead
  as they did long ago.

¹⁵"Yes," says the LORD,
  "I will do mighty miracles for you,
like those I did when I rescued you
  from slavery in Egypt."

¹⁶All the nations of the world will stand
    amazed
  at what the LORD will do for you.
They will be embarrassed
  at their feeble power.
They will cover their mouths in silent
    awe,
  deaf to everything around them.
¹⁷Like snakes crawling from their holes,
  they will come out to meet the LORD
    our God.
They will fear him greatly,
  trembling in terror at his presence.

¹⁸Where is another God like you,
  who pardons the guilt of the remnant,
  overlooking the sins of his special
    people?
You will not stay angry with your people
    forever,
  because you delight in showing
    unfailing love.
¹⁹Once again you will have compassion on
    us.
  You will trample our sins under your
    feet
and throw them into the depths of the
    ocean!
²⁰You will show us your faithfulness and
    unfailing love
  as you promised to our ancestors
    Abraham and Jacob long ago.

7:12 Hebrew *the river.* 7:13 Or *earth.* 7:14 Or *surrounded by a fruitful land.*

7:15-20 What beautiful words of comfort! No matter how terrible our past sins, there is always hope for the future when we turn our life over to God. As we follow God's will for us, we will experience God's full pardon and be the beneficiary of his perfect compassion. He will free us from the clutches of our dependency and make us a blessing to others. We can be assured of God's promises by looking back at how he has kept his promises in the past. As we hear how God has worked in the lives of others in recovery, we can be encouraged to rely on his promise for our own healing.

REFLECTIONS ON MICAH

insights ABOUT GOD'S DISCIPLINE

The people of Israel did not face up to their sins and refused to listen to Micah's messages warning them of God's punishment, so they would face the consequences of their actions. Perhaps their suffering would lead them to repentance. In **Micah 2:6-7** God let his wayward people know that he planned to punish them because he loved them, not because he wanted vengeance. God wanted to lead his people back into a healthy relationship with himself. The painful consequences we suffer for our addictive behaviors are one way God uses to call us back into relationship with himself. Sometimes our denial is so strong that nothing short of disaster can get our attention. We can be sure that no matter how much pain we feel now, God still loves us and desires to restore us.

In **Micah 4:6-7** we see how much God cares about hurting people. He consistently shows deep tenderness to those rejected by society. God also demonstrates fatherly concern toward those he has disciplined. His very discipline is a clear sign of his love (see Hebrews 12:6-7). Although God's discipline may hurt, it helps us recognize the destructive forces in our life and is often the impetus to recovery. As we recover from the consequences of past failures, we need to remember that God hasn't forgotten us, no matter how many others have turned against us and are reluctant to forgive us.

In **Micah 7:9-14** the prophet spoke for God's people, recognizing that they had sinned and that their suffering was a part of God's plan for their restoration. The prophet was willing to face the consequences of his people's behavior, knowing that God would use their suffering to bring healing and recovery in the end. Instead of seeking to escape the pain of the well-deserved consequences of our sins, we can turn our life over to God. He will use our pain to help us grow. God is in the business of recovery. Just as he recovered his people from the exile caused by their sins, he desires to deliver us from bondage and give us lives filled with meaning and joy.

insights ABOUT GOD'S JUSTICE

The prophet made it clear in **Micah 6:10-16** that God despises those who treat others unfairly or who cheat others for personal gain (see Deuteronomy 25:13-16; Proverbs 11:1; 20:10, 23). God will bring sickness to the souls of such people, and they will experience emptiness that cannot be satisfied by the things of this world. Ultimately they will not enjoy the rewards of their labor; instead, they will suffer destruction, derision, and reproach. As we humbly accept our defects of character, we will become less prone to victimize fellow strugglers. Learning such humility is an important part of the recovery process.

NAHUM

THE BIG PICTURE

A. JUDAH'S COMFORT IN GOD'S CHARACTER (1:1-15)
1. God's Justice (1:1-3)
2. God's Sovereignty (1:4-6)
3. God's Mercy toward His People (1:7)
4. God's Judgment toward His Enemies (1:8)
5. God's Good News of Restoration and Recovery (1:9-15)

B. ASSYRIA'S FEAR AT GOD'S JUDGMENT (2:1–3:19)
1. Judgment Predicted (2:1-2)
2. Judgment Described (2:3-10)
3. Judgment Justified (2:11–3:19)

The prophet Nahum ministered in Judah during a time of great fear. Judah had barely survived attacks from the brutal Assyrians, and its sister nation, Israel, had long since been destroyed by Assyria's bloodthirsty armies. The people of Judah lived in constant fear of being overrun. Their enemy was indifferent to their suffering and well known for its cruelty and oppression.

Nahum, whose name means "comfort," was God's prophet of consolation during these troubled times. His words were meant to lift the hearts of Judah's oppressed people and to address their unspoken doubts. Nahum began by reminding the people that God is a powerful refuge for people in trouble. He told them that God would judge Judah's cruel oppressors and that Judah would someday regain significance and wholeness.

Nahum's words were also for the people of Nineveh, Assyria's capital. He predicted its imminent doom, and God's judgment came soon after the prophet spoke. The city was plundered by the Medes and Babylonians, and the Assyrian Empire soon crumbled. Nineveh's demise was a consequence of its harsh treatment of others, especially the people of God.

A century earlier, the prophet Jonah had gone to Nineveh, and the city had been spared destruction because the people had repented. But their failure to stay on the right track led to severe consequences in Nahum's day. Repentance is not a onetime thing; it is something we need to do on a regular basis. True repentance means that we act on our promises to change. Apparently the Assyrians repented only because they feared destruction, not because they sincerely desired change. We can learn from Assyria's mistakes.

THE BOTTOM LINE

PURPOSE: To prophesy the overthrow of Assyria, showing that God is all-powerful and fully able to help those who are oppressed and in trouble. AUTHOR: The prophet Nahum. AUDIENCE: The people of Judah and Nineveh. DATE WRITTEN: Sometime between 663 and 612 B.C., preceding Nineveh's fall in 612 B.C. SETTING: In Nahum's day, Assyria controlled most of the ancient Near East and had already destroyed the northern kingdom of Israel (722 B.C.). KEY VERSE: "The LORD is good, a strong refuge when trouble comes. He is close to those who trust in him" (1:7). KEY PLACE: Nineveh, the capital of Assyria. KEY PEOPLE AND RELATIONSHIPS: Nahum, the people of Judah, and the people of Nineveh.

RECOVERY THEMES

Rescued from Fear: Our fears can destroy us if we allow them to control our life. The people of Judah lived under the threat of Assryian attack for many years. Nahum comforted them by helping them turn their eyes away from their cruel enemy and toward their powerful and loving God. He called them to make God their source of strength. As we contend daily with our own powerful enemy—our dependency—we can easily be overcome by fear. We may begin to feel so helpless that we give in to the constant temptation. If we turn our eyes away from our enemy and toward God, who loves us and desires recovery for us, our fears and helplessness can be overcome. God is there to help us when we come to the end of our rope.

Recovery Occurs within Boundaries: God created us to function best when we do things his way. The people of Nineveh broke all of God's principles for godly living, and they were allowed to continue in their destructive behavior for quite some time before the consequences caught up with them. But God's inevitable judgment did come down on them. We need to live within the boundaries of God's revealed will so that our recovery can take place without delay. Rejecting God's program always leads to pain and devastation.

The Importance of Perseverance: Nahum was not the first of God's prophets to warn Nineveh of destruction. Over one hundred years earlier, Jonah had called the Ninevites to repentance. Amazingly, the Assyrians had responded to Jonah's message and were spared destruction at that time. But they failed to keep their initial promises. They did little to change their behavior and, before long, were worse off than when they started. Recovery doesn't happen all at once. It needs regular attention. And it demands action—we need to follow through on our promises to change. Without perseverance, we will end up like Nineveh—devasted beyond recognition.

CHAPTER 1

This message concerning Nineveh came as a vision to Nahum, who lived in Elkosh.

The Lord's Anger against Nineveh

² The Lord is a jealous God,
  filled with vengeance and rage.
He takes revenge on all who oppose him
  and continues to rage against his
    enemies!
³ The Lord is slow to get angry, but his
    power is great,
  and he never lets the guilty go
    unpunished.
He displays his power in the whirlwind
    and the storm.
The billowing clouds are the dust
    beneath his feet.
⁴ At his command the oceans dry up,
  and the rivers disappear.
The lush pastures of Bashan and
    Carmel fade,
  and the green forests of Lebanon
    wither.

⁵ In his presence the mountains quake,
  and the hills melt away;
the earth trembles,
  and its people are destroyed.
⁶ Who can stand before his fierce anger?
  Who can survive his burning fury?
His rage blazes forth like fire,
  and the mountains crumble to dust in
    his presence.

⁷ The Lord is good,
  a strong refuge when trouble comes.
  He is close to those who trust in him.
⁸ But he will sweep away his enemies*
  in an overwhelming flood.
He will pursue his foes
  into the darkness of night.

⁹ Why are you scheming against the Lord?
  He will destroy you with one blow;
  he won't need to strike twice!
¹⁰ His enemies, tangled like thornbushes
    and staggering like drunks,
  will be burned up like dry stubble in a
    field.

1:8 As in Greek version; Hebrew reads *sweep away her place.*

1:2-8 The people of Judah were helpless against Assyria's great power. There was no way they could have withstood an extended attack without God's help. In recovery we begin by recognizing that we can't stand against our dependency without God's help. We need a power greater than ourself to help us make the changes needed for a restored life. God is all-knowing, righteous, all-powerful, and good. He is slow to anger but has the power to take radical steps to arrest the progression of injustice and further the recovery of his people.

11 Who is this wicked counselor of yours
     who plots evil against the LORD?

12 This is what the LORD says:
   "Though the Assyrians have many allies,
     they will be destroyed and disappear.
   O my people, I have punished you
       before,
     but I will not punish you again.
13 Now I will break the yoke of bondage
       from your neck
     and tear off the chains of Assyrian
       oppression."

14 And this is what the LORD says concerning
     the Assyrians in Nineveh:
   "You will have no more children to carry
       on your name.
   I will destroy all the idols in the temples
       of your gods.
   I am preparing a grave for you
     because you are despicable!"

15 *Look! A messenger is coming over the
       mountains with good news!
   He is bringing a message of peace.
   Celebrate your festivals, O people
       of Judah,
     and fulfill all your vows,
   for your wicked enemies will never invade
       your land again.
   They will be completely destroyed!

CHAPTER 2
The Fall of Nineveh

1 *Your enemy is coming to crush you,
     Nineveh.
   Man the ramparts! Watch the roads!
   Prepare your defenses! Call out your
       forces!

2 Even though the destroyer has destroyed
     Judah,
   the LORD will restore its honor.
   Israel's vine has been stripped
     of branches,

   but he will restore its splendor.

3 Shields flash red in the sunlight!
   See the scarlet uniforms of the valiant
       troops!
   Watch as their glittering chariots move
       into position,
     with a forest of spears waving above
       them.*
4 The chariots race recklessly along the
       streets
     and rush wildly through the squares.
   They flash like firelight
     and move as swiftly as lightning.
5 The king shouts to his officers;
     they stumble in their haste,
   rushing to the walls to set up their
       defenses.
6 The river gates have been torn open!
   The palace is about to collapse!
7 Nineveh's exile has been decreed,
     and all the servant girls mourn its
       capture.
   They moan like doves
     and beat their breasts in sorrow.
8 Nineveh is like a leaking water
       reservoir!
   The people are slipping away.
   "Stop, stop!" someone shouts,
     but no one even looks back.
9 Loot the silver!
   Plunder the gold!
   There's no end to Nineveh's treasures—
     its vast, uncounted wealth.
10 Soon the city is plundered, empty, and
       ruined.
   Hearts melt and knees shake.
   The people stand aghast,
     their faces pale and trembling.

11 Where now is that great Nineveh,
     that den filled with young lions?
   It was a place where people—like lions
     and their cubs—
   walked freely and without fear.

1:15 Verse 1:15 is numbered 2:1 in Hebrew text.   2:1 Verses 2:1-13 are numbered 2:2-14 in Hebrew text.   2:3 Greek
and Syriac versions read *into position, / the horses whipped into a frenzy.*

1:15 This same language was used in Isaiah 52:7 of heralds poised on the hills of Judah shouting
the good news of Judah's liberation. The kingdom of Israel had already been destroyed by
Assyria, and Judah had lived under a continual threat of attack for many years. The conquest of
Nineveh by the Babylonians and Medes would be good news for the desperate, helpless people
of Judah. This event took place in 612 B.C.; Nahum 2:3-10 gives an account of Nineveh's defeat.
Now the people of Judah could celebrate and praise God for this message of peace. We, too,
must always praise God for the victories in our life and the peace he can bring us.
2:2 Assyria had rendered God's people powerless. However, because of God's righteousness and
his faithfulness to his people, God promised that the past honor and glory of Judah and Israel
would be restored with the defeat of God's enemies. There is always hope for recovery for those
who trust in God.

¹² The lion tore up meat for his cubs
 and strangled prey for his mate.
He filled his den with prey,
 his caverns with his plunder.

¹³ "I am your enemy!"
 says the LORD of Heaven's Armies.
"Your chariots will soon go up in smoke.
 Your young men* will be killed in
 battle.
Never again will you plunder conquered
 nations.
 The voices of your proud messengers
 will be heard no more."

CHAPTER 3
The LORD's Judgment against Nineveh

¹ What sorrow awaits Nineveh,
 the city of murder and lies!
She is crammed with wealth
 and is never without victims.
² Hear the crack of whips,
 the rumble of wheels!
Horses' hooves pound,
 and chariots clatter wildly.
³ See the flashing swords and glittering
 spears
 as the charioteers charge past!
There are countless casualties,
 heaps of bodies—
so many bodies that
 people stumble over them.
⁴ All this because Nineveh,
 the beautiful and faithless city,
mistress of deadly charms,
 enticed the nations with her beauty.
She taught them all her magic,
 enchanting people everywhere.

⁵ "I am your enemy!"
 says the LORD of Heaven's Armies.
"And now I will lift your skirts
 and show all the earth your nakedness
 and shame.
⁶ I will cover you with filth
 and show the world how vile you really
 are.
⁷ All who see you will shrink back and say,
 'Nineveh lies in ruins.

Where are the mourners?'
 Does anyone regret your destruction?"

⁸ Are you any better than the city of
 Thebes,*
 situated on the Nile River, surrounded
 by water?
She was protected by the river on all sides,
 walled in by water.
⁹ Ethiopia* and the land of Egypt
 gave unlimited assistance.
The nations of Put and Libya
 were among her allies.
¹⁰ Yet Thebes fell,
 and her people were led away as
 captives.
Her babies were dashed to death
 against the stones of the streets.
Soldiers threw dice* to get Egyptian
 officers as servants.
All their leaders were bound in chains.

¹¹ And you, Nineveh, will also stagger like a
 drunkard.
 You will hide for fear of the attacking
 enemy.
¹² All your fortresses will fall.
 They will be devoured like the ripe figs
 that fall into the mouths
 of those who shake the trees.
¹³ Your troops will be as weak
 and helpless as women.
The gates of your land will be opened
 wide to the enemy
 and set on fire and burned.
¹⁴ Get ready for the siege!
 Store up water!
 Strengthen the defenses!
Go into the pits to trample clay,
 and pack it into molds,
 making bricks to repair the walls.

¹⁵ But the fire will devour you;
 the sword will cut you down.
The enemy will consume you like locusts,
 devouring everything they see.
There will be no escape,
 even if you multiply like swarming
 locusts.

2:13 Hebrew *young lions*. 3:8 Hebrew *No-amon;* also in 3:10. 3:9 Hebrew *Cush*. 3:10 Hebrew *They cast lots*.

2:13–3:1 Nineveh's destruction was certain. God's people would be delivered, and those who
supported Assyria would be silenced forever. It is easy to become discouraged as we see injustices
all around us. We may wonder why God seems to do so little about them. Here we see that God
holds unjust people accountable and will administer justice according to his own timetable. Our
recovery process can be slowed if we worry constantly about the injustices we have suffered. God
wants us to remember that he is just and will deal with those who have hurt us. We must focus
on our own sins, repent, and follow God's perfect will for our life.

¹⁶ Your merchants have multiplied
until they outnumber the stars.
But like a swarm of locusts,
they strip the land and fly away.
¹⁷ Your guards* and officials are also like
swarming locusts
that crowd together in the hedges on a
cold day.
But like locusts that fly away when the
sun comes up,
all of them will fly away and
disappear.

¹⁸ Your shepherds are asleep, O Assyrian king;
your princes lie dead in the dust.
Your people are scattered across the
mountains
with no one to gather them together.
¹⁹ There is no healing for your wound;
your injury is fatal.
All who hear of your destruction
will clap their hands for joy.
Where can anyone be found
who has not suffered from your
continual cruelty?

3:17 Or *princes.*

HABAKKUK

THE BIG PICTURE

A. HABAKKUK'S PERPLEXITY AND DOUBT (1:1-17)
B. HABAKKUK PERCEIVES GOD'S PURPOSES (2:1-20)
C. HABAKKUK PRAISES GOD (3:1-19)

Habakkuk was troubled by the evil he saw running rampant in Judah. He brought his honest concerns to God but was not prepared for God's answer. God planned to use the cruel and violent Babylonians to punish Judah! Judah, even with all its sin, was far more righteous than Babylon. How could God support Babylon's success while bringing destruction on Judah?

Life is filled with such questions. We are familiar with injustice in our society; often the bad guys seem to win. Why does God allow it? Habakkuk's prophecy assures us that no matter what we face in life, God never changes his personality or his promises. His holy and loving character remains the same, even when everything seems to be falling apart. He will fulfill all the promises of his Word, even when the future seems to hold nothing but pain. God is powerful enough to use even the bad things in our life to bring about his good will for us and his world.

This prophecy is unique because the prophet never took the role of God's spokesman. Instead, Habakkuk recorded how God responded to his honest questions about life. God wants us to come to him with our questions and doubts. If we listen to God's reply, we, like Habakkuk, can have our heart stirred to renewed trust and hope in God. Habakkuk realized that remembering past displays of God's power would give him faith in God for future struggles. This is part of the value of sharing our stories of deliverance with others. As we remember what God has done for us in recovery, we and others will be strengthened for the conflicts yet to come.

THE BOTTOM LINE

PURPOSE: To deal with doubt by affirming that in spite of the evil in the world, God has not changed in his person or his purpose. AUTHOR: The prophet Habakkuk. AUDIENCE: The people of the southern kingdom of Judah. DATE WRITTEN: Between 612 and 589 B.C. SETTING: The kingdom of Judah, just prior to the Babylonian invasions and the destruction of Jerusalem. KEY VERSE: "Look at the proud! They trust in themselves, and their lives are crooked. But the righteous will live by their faithfulness to God" (2:4). KEY PEOPLE AND RELATIONSHIPS: Habakkuk and the Babylonians, Habakkuk and God.

RECOVERY THEMES

The Value of Doubt: We all have questions; they are part of life. We may not always find the answers, but we always have the right to ask them. Habakkuk felt free to ask such questions, even of God. We have the same freedom. When circumstances around us or within us seem unbearable, we can remember that God is in control. He does care, and he wants us to come to him with our doubts. It is often during times of doubt that we surge forward in recovery. In these times of honest confusion, we are better able to recognize our helplessness and entrust our life to God.

God Never Changes: For most of us, life is hard and filled with struggles. As we seek to overcome our problems and dependency, pondering God's faithfulness to us in the past can be a source of continual strength. The prophet Habakkuk was greatly encouraged as he remembered all that God had done for his people. Because God never changes, we can be confident that what he has done in the past, he will continue to do in the future. This is one of the reasons why sharing our recovery is so important. By telling others about what God has done for us, we give them reason to believe that he will work the same miracle for them.

God Is Our Source of Hope: Our hope must be built upon the foundation of our powerful and loving God. Because Habakkuk's hope was in God, he could patiently wait for God to bring the day of judgment against Babylon. We live—really live—by trusting God. We will make progress in recovery as we improve our relationship with him and seek his face each day. He is our strength and our place of safety. He is the basis of our hope for recovery.

CHAPTER 1

This is the message that the prophet Habakkuk received in a vision.

Habakkuk's Complaint

²How long, O LORD, must I call for help?
  But you do not listen!
"Violence is everywhere!" I cry,
  but you do not come to save.
³Must I forever see these evil deeds?
  Why must I watch all this misery?
Wherever I look,
  I see destruction and violence.
I am surrounded by people
  who love to argue and fight.
⁴The law has become paralyzed,
  and there is no justice in the
  courts.
The wicked far outnumber the
  righteous,
  so that justice has become perverted.

The LORD's Reply

⁵The LORD replied,

"Look around at the nations;
  look and be amazed!*
For I am doing something in your own
  day,
  something you wouldn't believe
  even if someone told you about it.
⁶I am raising up the Babylonians,*
  a cruel and violent people.
They will march across the world
  and conquer other lands.
⁷They are notorious for their cruelty
  and do whatever they like.
⁸Their horses are swifter than
  cheetahs*
  and fiercer than wolves at dusk.
Their charioteers charge from far
  away.
Like eagles, they swoop down to devour
  their prey.

1:5 Greek version reads *Look, you mockers; / look and be amazed and die.* Compare Acts 13:41. 1:6 Or *Chaldeans.* 1:8 Or *leopards.*

1:1-4 Habakkuk, a contemporary of the prophets Jeremiah, Daniel, and Ezekiel, was appalled at the wickedness that swirled about him like a windstorm. Lawlessness and injustice were rampant in the nation of Judah. The prophet, sensitive to the sin around him, called out to God. Today's society is not much different. We often find ourself wondering, *Will this ever end?* The rest of Habakkuk's book provides an answer to this question.

1:5-11 God's solution for Judah's sin was exile in Babylon. He would allow the Babylonians to destroy Judah and Jerusalem to teach them that ignoring his plan for them was not the way to live. It was God's way of helping his people reach bottom so they could begin the process of recovery. God often allows us to live out our dependency for just so long before he lets the consequences catch up with us. As we hit bottom, we realize that we can't make it alone. We can then turn to God and discover that his plan for us is the only way to recovery.

⁹ "On they come, all bent on violence.
  Their hordes advance like a desert wind,
  sweeping captives ahead of them like
    sand.
¹⁰ They scoff at kings and princes
  and scorn all their fortresses.
  They simply pile ramps of earth
  against their walls and capture them!
¹¹ They sweep past like the wind
  and are gone.
  But they are deeply guilty,
  for their own strength is their god."

Habakkuk's Second Complaint

¹² O LORD my God, my Holy One, you who
    are eternal—
  surely you do not plan to wipe us out?
  O LORD, our Rock, you have sent these
    Babylonians to correct us,
  to punish us for our many sins.
¹³ But you are pure and cannot stand the
    sight of evil.
  Will you wink at their treachery?
  Should you be silent while the wicked
  swallow up people more righteous than
    they?

¹⁴ Are we only fish to be caught and killed?
  Are we only sea creatures that have no
    leader?
¹⁵ Must we be strung up on their hooks
  and caught in their nets while they
  rejoice and celebrate?
¹⁶ Then they will worship their nets
  and burn incense in front of them.
  "These nets are the gods who have made
    us rich!"
  they will claim.
¹⁷ Will you let them get away with this
  forever?

Will they succeed forever in their
  heartless conquests?

CHAPTER 2

¹ I will climb up to my watchtower
  and stand at my guardpost.
  There I will wait to see what the LORD says
  and how he* will answer my complaint.

The LORD's Second Reply

² Then the LORD said to me,

  "Write my answer plainly on tablets,
  so that a runner can carry the correct
    message to others.
³ This vision is for a future time.
  It describes the end, and it will be
    fulfilled.
  If it seems slow in coming, wait patiently,
  for it will surely take place.
  It will not be delayed.

⁴ "Look at the proud!
  They trust in themselves, and their lives
  are crooked.
  But the righteous will live by their
  faithfulness to God.*
⁵ Wealth* is treacherous,
  and the arrogant are never at rest.
  They open their mouths as wide as the
    grave,*
  and like death, they are never satisfied.
  In their greed they have gathered up
    many nations
  and swallowed many peoples.

⁶ "But soon their captives will taunt them.
  They will mock them, saying,
  'What sorrow awaits you thieves!
  Now you will get what you deserve!
  You've become rich by extortion,

2:1 As in Syriac version; Hebrew reads *I.* 2:3b-4 Greek version reads *If the vision is delayed, wait patiently, / for it will surely come and not delay. / ⁴I will take no pleasure in anyone who turns away. / But the righteous person will live by my faith.* Compare Rom 1:17; Gal 3:11; Heb 10:37-38. 2:5a As in Dead Sea Scroll 1QpHab; other Hebrew manuscripts read *Wine.* 2:5b Hebrew *as Sheol.*

1:12–2:3 When faced with destruction by the Babylonians, it seemed to Habakkuk that the cure was worse than the disease. How could God allow this godless nation to destroy God's own people? It didn't seem right. Like Habakkuk, we sometimes wonder why people even more wicked than we are are allowed to prosper. But rather than turn away in confusion and resentment, we need to turn and face our own problems and dependency. God will deal with the other people when the time is right. He is ultimately in control.
2:4 Wicked people trust in themselves; they proudly try to make their own way in the world under their own power. Most of us have experienced the consequences of such an attitude. We have discovered that without God, we cannot live a healthy and meaningful life. We become enslaved to alcohol, drugs, sexual pleasure, work, or religious activities to try to fill the empty space inside us that only God can fill. God knows what is best for us; he can give our life meaning. Being righteous does not depend on doing the right things. It has to do with faith in God. We can be made righteous, no matter how terrible our past sins have been, by believing in Christ and accepting him as our personal Savior.

but how much longer can this go on?'
⁷Suddenly, your debtors will take action.
  They will turn on you and take all you
    have,
    while you stand trembling and helpless.
⁸Because you have plundered many
    nations,
  now all the survivors will plunder you.
  You committed murder throughout the
    countryside
  and filled the towns with violence.

⁹"What sorrow awaits you who build big
    houses
  with money gained dishonestly!
  You believe your wealth will buy security,
    putting your family's nest beyond the
    reach of danger.
¹⁰But by the murders you committed,
  you have shamed your name and
    forfeited your lives.
¹¹The very stones in the walls cry out
    against you,
  and the beams in the ceilings echo the
    complaint.

¹²"What sorrow awaits you who build cities
  with money gained through murder
    and corruption!
¹³Has not the LORD of Heaven's Armies
    promised
  that the wealth of nations will turn to
    ashes?
  They work so hard,
    but all in vain!
¹⁴For as the waters fill the sea,
  the earth will be filled with an
    awareness
  of the glory of the LORD.

¹⁵"What sorrow awaits you who make your
    neighbors drunk!
  You force your cup on them
  so you can gloat over their shameful
    nakedness.
¹⁶But soon it will be your turn to be
    disgraced.

Come, drink and be exposed!*
Drink from the cup of the LORD's
    judgment,
  and all your glory will be turned to
    shame.
¹⁷You cut down the forests of Lebanon.
  Now you will be cut down.
  You destroyed the wild animals,
    so now their terror will be yours.
  You committed murder throughout the
    countryside
  and filled the towns with violence.

¹⁸"What good is an idol carved by man,
  or a cast image that deceives you?
  How foolish to trust in your own
    creation—
    a god that can't even talk!
¹⁹What sorrow awaits you who say to
    wooden idols,
    'Wake up and save us!'
  To speechless stone images you say,
    'Rise up and teach us!'
  Can an idol tell you what to do?
  They may be overlaid with gold and silver,
    but they are lifeless inside.
²⁰But the LORD is in his holy Temple.
  Let all the earth be silent before him."

CHAPTER 3
Habakkuk's Prayer
This prayer was sung by the prophet Habakkuk*:

²I have heard all about you, LORD.
  I am filled with awe by your amazing
    works.
  In this time of our deep need,
    help us again as you did in years
    gone by.
  And in your anger,
    remember your mercy.

³I see God moving across the deserts from
    Edom,*
  the Holy One coming from Mount
    Paran.*

2:16 Dead Sea Scrolls and Greek and Syriac versions read *and stagger!* **3:1** Hebrew adds *according to shigionoth,* probably indicating the musical setting for the prayer. **3:3a** Hebrew *Teman.* **3:3b** Hebrew adds *selah;* also in 3:9, 13. The meaning of this Hebrew term is uncertain; it is probably a musical or literary term.

3:1-2 Habakkuk praised God, not only for answering his questions but also for the knowledge he had gained about the person of God. Habakkuk learned how much his people needed God's discipline (Hebrews 12:5-6), so he acknowledged God's righteousness in their coming judgment. Then he looked past the coming punishment to their restoration. God's punishment is always for the purpose of growth and blessing. If we recognize our need for God and follow his good plans for us, we can receive the blessings he intended for us to gain through our painful experiences. **3:3-16** Remembering the powerful acts of God in the past can give us confidence in what God can do now and in the future. During recovery, it is extremely helpful to read what God has done

His brilliant splendor fills the heavens,
and the earth is filled with his praise.
⁴His coming is as brilliant as the sunrise.
Rays of light flash from his hands,
where his awesome power is hidden.
⁵Pestilence marches before him;
plague follows close behind.
⁶When he stops, the earth shakes.
When he looks, the nations tremble.
He shatters the everlasting mountains
and levels the eternal hills.
He is the Eternal One!*
⁷I see the people of Cushan in distress,
and the nation of Midian trembling in
terror.

⁸Was it in anger, Lord, that you struck the
rivers
and parted the sea?
Were you displeased with them?
No, you were sending your chariots of
salvation!
⁹You brandished your bow
and your quiver of arrows.
You split open the earth with flowing
rivers.
¹⁰The mountains watched and trembled.
Onward swept the raging waters.
The mighty deep cried out,
lifting its hands in submission.
¹¹The sun and moon stood still in the sky
as your brilliant arrows flew
and your glittering spear flashed.

¹²You marched across the land in anger
and trampled the nations in your fury.

¹³You went out to rescue your chosen
people,
to save your anointed ones.
You crushed the heads of the wicked
and stripped their bones from head to
toe.
¹⁴With his own weapons,
you destroyed the chief of those
who rushed out like a whirlwind,
thinking Israel would be easy prey.
¹⁵You trampled the sea with your horses,
and the mighty waters piled high.

¹⁶I trembled inside when I heard this;
my lips quivered with fear.
My legs gave way beneath me,*
and I shook in terror.
I will wait quietly for the coming day
when disaster will strike the people who
invade us.
¹⁷Even though the fig trees have no
blossoms,
and there are no grapes on the vines;
even though the olive crop fails,
and the fields lie empty and barren;
even though the flocks die in the fields,
and the cattle barns are empty,
¹⁸yet I will rejoice in the Lord!
I will be joyful in the God of my
salvation!
¹⁹The Sovereign Lord is my strength!
He makes me as surefooted as a deer,*
able to tread upon the heights.

(For the choir director: This prayer is to be
accompanied by stringed instruments.)

3:6 Or *The ancient paths belong to him.* **3:16** Hebrew *Decay entered my bones.* **3:19** Or *He gives me the speed of a deer.*

in the lives of his people and be encouraged by their examples (see Romans 15:4; 1 Corinthians 10:11). God's work in our own life can also be of great help to others. As we share how God delivered us in the past, not only will others receive new hope for recovery, but we also will be encouraged by recalling what God has already done for us.
3:17-19 Habakkuk's prayer came to a climax in a beautiful affirmation of faith. Although there would be hard times ahead, Habakkuk knew that he could trust God to provide him with the strength he needed to persevere. Verse 19 provides a picture of the surefooted confidence we can have in our God. He is our strength and safety, a great assurance for all of us in recovery.

ZEPHANIAH

THE BIG PICTURE

A. PROPHECIES OF JUDGMENT AGAINST JUDAH (1:1–2:3)
   1. Judah's Moral and Spiritual Irresponsibility (1:1-13)
   2. Judah's Accountability before God (1:14-18)
   3. Judah's Opportunity for Recovery (2:1-3)
B. PROPHECIES OF JUDGMENT AGAINST THE NATIONS (2:4-15)
C. PROPHECIES OF JUDGMENT AGAINST JERUSALEM (3:1-8)
D. PROMISES OF BLESSING TO THOSE WHO TRUST IN GOD (3:9-20)

If only . . . is a haunting phrase. It implies that we have failed and that we wish we could go back and do things differently. As we work through the process of recovery, we often become sad and ashamed when we reflect on the past. We regret our irresponsible and destructive behavior and wish we could erase past mistakes. This must have been how the people of Judah felt when they heard the prophetic words of Zephaniah. *If only* they had obeyed and trusted God!

God called Zephaniah during the days of King Josiah, the last of Judah's good kings. The prophet's condemnation of Judah's idol worship and self-centered living fit well with the early part of Josiah's reign, when his purges against idolatry were just beginning. Zephaniah's prophetic support of Josiah's actions would certainly have bolstered Josiah's efforts. However, the apostasy of Judah's previous kings, Manasseh and Amon, had left deep spiritual wounds in Judah. Despite Zephaniah's ministry and Josiah's noble reforms, visible scars remained in Judah even at the end of Josiah's righteous reign.

The people of Judah were in need of major changes. They had seen the northern kingdom of Israel exiled to Assyria but assumed that the presence of God in the Jerusalem Temple would protect them from foreign invaders. They needed to be shocked out of their denial and spiritual indifference. Zephaniah warned the people that Judah would be destroyed if they didn't act right away. He also let them know that recovery was still possible. Spiritual awakening could still occur if they would admit their sins and trust God. Josiah and the people listened to Zephaniah, responded, and experienced revival and recovery.

THE BOTTOM LINE

PURPOSE: To shake the people of Judah out of their complacency and get them back on the path of recovery. AUTHOR: The prophet Zephaniah. AUDIENCE: The people of the southern kingdom of Judah. DATE WRITTEN: Sometime between 640 and 621 B.C., just prior to King Josiah's great reformation. SETTING: The kingdom of Judah during the years of King Josiah; Zephaniah's ministry may have helped to motivate the young king's reforms. KEY VERSE: "On that day you will no longer need to be ashamed, for you will no longer be rebels against me. I will remove all proud and arrogant people from among you. There will be no more haughtiness on my holy mountain" (3:11). KEY PLACE: Jerusalem. KEY PEOPLE AND RELATIONSHIPS: Zephaniah and the people of Judah.

RECOVERY THEMES

The Consequences of Irresponsibility: Many of our troubles are direct consequences of our irresponsibility. Judah was irresponsible in her covenant relationship with God. The people worshiped false gods and ignored God's laws that were intended for their own good. But Zephaniah made it clear that Judah's irresponsibility would carry heavy consequences. Encouraged by Zephaniah and led by Josiah, the people of Judah took responsibility for their sins and turned their lives over to God. As a result, they received substantial healing. When we are irresponsible in our relationships with God and with others, our situation in life will grow progressively worse. But as we learn to live responsibly, we begin to experience God's blessings.

Complacency Leads to Relapse: Prosperity and success often lead to complacency. Josiah's great-grandfather, Hezekiah, had been one of Judah's greatest kings. He had led his people back to God, and God had greatly blessed them. However, Judah's next two kings, Manasseh and Amon, led the people into complacency. With time, the complacency led to sin and its consequences. Josiah followed in the footsteps of Hezekiah and helped lead the people back to God. Often our greatest failures follow our greatest victories. In order to prevent relapses, we need to inventory our life on a regular basis. We must maintain a heart that is vulnerable and dependent on God, regardless of our successes in recovery.

Recovery Leads to Joy: The process of recovery almost always starts out painfully. Telling the truth about ourself hurts. But as we admit our failures to God, to ourself, and to others, we find the great relief and hope that God offers. Then we can look forward to the joy and celebration we will experience as God restores us to himself and to the people we love.

CHAPTER 1

The LORD gave this message to Zephaniah when Josiah son of Amon was king of Judah. Zephaniah was the son of Cushi, son of Gedaliah, son of Amariah, son of Hezekiah.

Coming Judgment against Judah

² "I will sweep away everything
    from the face of the earth," says the
    LORD.
³ "I will sweep away people and animals
    alike.
I will sweep away the birds of the sky
    and the fish in the sea.
I will reduce the wicked to heaps of
    rubble,*
and I will wipe humanity from the face
    of the earth," says the LORD.
⁴ "I will crush Judah and Jerusalem with
    my fist
and destroy every last trace of their
    Baal worship.
I will put an end to all the idolatrous priests,
    so that even the memory of them will
    disappear.

⁵ For they go up to their roofs
    and bow down to the sun, moon,
    and stars.
They claim to follow the LORD,
    but then they worship Molech,* too.
⁶ And I will destroy those who used to
    worship me
but now no longer do.
They no longer ask for the LORD's
    guidance
or seek my blessings."

⁷ Stand in silence in the presence of the
    Sovereign LORD,
for the awesome day of the LORD's
    judgment is near.
The LORD has prepared his people for a
    great slaughter
and has chosen their executioners.*
⁸ "On that day of judgment,"
    says the LORD,
"I will punish the leaders and princes
    of Judah
and all those following pagan
    customs.

1:3 The meaning of the Hebrew is uncertain. 1:5 Hebrew *Malcam*, a variant spelling of Molech; or it could possibly mean *their king.* 1:7 Hebrew *has prepared a sacrifice and sanctified his guests.*

1:4-13 Through Zephaniah, God condemned the irresponsible behavior of Judah's leaders—perhaps Manasseh and Amon, two of Judah's most wicked kings. During their reigns, the people had increasingly depended upon false gods, had ceased to worship the true God, and had built a society in which deceitful and immoral people could prosper. When we turn from the true God, society and its members begin to deteriorate. We all need God. Unless we recognize this fact, our life will continue on a downhill trend. As we recognize our powerlessness and turn to God for help, he gives us the power to live a healthy and meaningful life.

9 Yes, I will punish those who participate in
    pagan worship ceremonies,
  and those who fill their masters' houses
    with violence and deceit.

10 "On that day," says the LORD,
    "a cry of alarm will come from the
      Fish Gate
  and echo throughout the New Quarter
    of the city.*
  And a great crash will sound from the
    hills.
11 Wail in sorrow, all you who live in the
    market area,*
  for all the merchants and traders will
    be destroyed.

12 "I will search with lanterns in Jerusalem's
    darkest corners
  to punish those who sit complacent
    in their sins.
  They think the LORD will do nothing
    to them,
    either good or bad.
13 So their property will be plundered,
    their homes will be ransacked.
  They will build new homes
    but never live in them.
  They will plant vineyards
    but never drink wine from them.

14 "That terrible day of the LORD is near.
    Swiftly it comes—
  a day of bitter tears,
    a day when even strong men will
      cry out.
15 It will be a day when the LORD's anger is
    poured out—
  a day of terrible distress and
    anguish,
  a day of ruin and desolation,
    a day of darkness and gloom,
  a day of clouds and blackness,

16   a day of trumpet calls and battle
      cries.
  Down go the walled cities
    and the strongest battlements!

17 "Because you have sinned against the
    LORD,
  I will make you grope around like the
    blind.
  Your blood will be poured into
    the dust,
  and your bodies will lie rotting on the
    ground."

18 Your silver and gold will not
    save you
  on that day of the LORD's anger.
  For the whole land will be devoured
    by the fire of his jealousy.
  He will make a terrifying end
    of all the people on earth.*

CHAPTER 2
A Call to Repentance

1 Gather together—yes, gather
    together,
  you shameless nation.
2 Gather before judgment begins,
    before your time to repent is blown
      away like chaff.
  Act now, before the fierce fury of the
    LORD falls
  and the terrible day of the LORD's
    anger begins.
3 Seek the LORD, all who are humble,
    and follow his commands.
  Seek to do what is right
    and to live humbly.
  Perhaps even yet the LORD will protect
    you—
  protect you from his anger on that day
    of destruction.

1:10 Or the Second Quarter, a newer section of Jerusalem. Hebrew reads the Mishneh. 1:11 Or in the valley, a lower
section of Jerusalem. Hebrew reads the Maktesh. 1:18 Or the people living in the land.

1:14-18 The prophet warned of "that terrible day of the LORD"—a day of reckoning with God. At
that time Judah would be conquered and the people led away to Babylon as slaves. God mercifully offered his people numerous chances to repent, but there would come a time when judgment would fall. We should be aware that God will not allow us to reject his way forever. When
we do things our way, we only hurt ourself and the people we love. If we listen to the early warnings we receive and act appropriately, we need not fear a future day of reckoning.
2:1-3 The purpose of God's judgment was to encourage the people of Judah to depend on him.
The prophet called the people to repent, hoping that they would be spared the coming devastation. The people responded favorably to Zephaniah's message, and King Josiah led them in a
great reformation, which led to the last spiritual high point in Judah's history. Though the day of
reckoning did come, it was delayed for several generations. If we respond to the warnings we
receive, confessing our sins and asking God to help us, he may spare us from some of the painful
consequences we deserve.

Judgment against Philistia

⁴ Gaza and Ashkelon will be abandoned,
Ashdod and Ekron torn down.
⁵ And what sorrow awaits you Philistines*
who live along the coast and in the
land of Canaan,
for this judgment is against you, too!
The LORD will destroy you
until not one of you is left.
⁶ The Philistine coast will become a
wilderness pasture,
a place of shepherd camps
and enclosures for sheep and goats.
⁷ The remnant of the tribe of Judah will
pasture there.
They will rest at night in the
abandoned houses in Ashkelon.
For the LORD their God will visit his
people in kindness
and restore their prosperity again.

Judgment against Moab and Ammon

⁸ "I have heard the taunts of the Moabites
and the insults of the Ammonites,
mocking my people
and invading their borders.
⁹ Now, as surely as I live,"
says the LORD of Heaven's Armies, the
God of Israel,
"Moab and Ammon will be destroyed—
destroyed as completely as Sodom and
Gomorrah.
Their land will become a place of stinging
nettles,
salt pits, and eternal desolation.
The remnant of my people will plunder
them
and take their land."

¹⁰ They will receive the wages of their
pride,
for they have scoffed at the people of
the LORD of Heaven's Armies.

2:5 Hebrew *Kerethites.* 2:12 Hebrew *Cushites.*

¹¹ The LORD will terrify them
as he destroys all the gods in the land.
Then nations around the world will
worship the LORD,
each in their own land.

Judgment against Ethiopia and Assyria

¹² "You Ethiopians* will also be slaughtered
by my sword," says the LORD.

¹³ And the LORD will strike the lands of the
north with his fist,
destroying the land of Assyria.
He will make its great capital, Nineveh, a
desolate wasteland,
parched like a desert.
¹⁴ The proud city will become a pasture for
flocks and herds,
and all sorts of wild animals will settle
there.
The desert owl and screech owl will roost
on its ruined columns,
their calls echoing through the gaping
windows.
Rubble will block all the doorways,
and the cedar paneling will be exposed
to the weather.
¹⁵ This is the boisterous city,
once so secure.
"I am the greatest!" it boasted.
"No other city can compare with me!"
But now, look how it has become an utter
ruin,
a haven for wild animals.
Everyone passing by will laugh
in derision
and shake a defiant fist.

CHAPTER 3
Jerusalem's Rebellion and Redemption

¹ What sorrow awaits rebellious, polluted
Jerusalem,
the city of violence and crime!

2:4-15 Zephaniah listed the nations that had influenced Judah in its idolatrous practices. God would judge these nations, and they would lose their corrupting influence. God gives us great potential to influence others for good, but we often end up leading others in the wrong direction. Taking responsibility for those we have led astray in some way is part of our moral inventory. Maybe we have led our children astray, or perhaps friends or co-workers. Part of making amends is doing what we can to get those people back on the right track.

3:1-5 The destructive behavior of Judah's people, though influenced by other nations, was ultimately their own responsibility. They refused to admit their sins to God and rejected all his warnings and correction. We have all been influenced negatively by others, but pointing the finger at them will only slow us in the recovery process. These people are responsible to deal with their problems; we are responsible for our own. As we take responsibility for our actions, recognizing how much we need God, we will step toward recovery. If we continue to blame others for our problems, we are headed for destruction.

² No one can tell it anything;
  it refuses all correction.
It does not trust in the LORD
  or draw near to its God.
³ Its leaders are like roaring lions
  hunting for their victims.
Its judges are like ravenous wolves at
    evening time,
  who by dawn have left no trace of their
    prey.
⁴ Its prophets are arrogant liars seeking
    their own gain.
Its priests defile the Temple by
  disobeying God's instructions.
⁵ But the LORD is still there in the city,
  and he does no wrong.
Day by day he hands down justice,
  and he does not fail.
But the wicked know no shame.

⁶ "I have wiped out many nations,
  devastating their fortress walls and
    towers.
Their streets are now deserted;
  their cities lie in silent ruin.
There are no survivors—
  none at all.
⁷ I thought, 'Surely they will have reverence
    for me now!
Surely they will listen to my warnings.
Then I won't need to strike again,
  destroying their homes.'
But no, they get up early
  to continue their evil deeds.
⁸ Therefore, be patient," says the LORD.
  "Soon I will stand and accuse these evil
    nations.
For I have decided to gather the kingdoms
    of the earth
  and pour out my fiercest anger and fury
    on them.
All the earth will be devoured
  by the fire of my jealousy.

⁹ "Then I will purify the speech of all
    people,
  so that everyone can worship the LORD
    together.
¹⁰ My scattered people who live beyond the
    rivers of Ethiopia*

will come to present their offerings.
¹¹ On that day you will no longer need
    to be ashamed,
  for you will no longer be rebels against
    me.
I will remove all proud and arrogant
    people from among you.
  There will be no more haughtiness on
    my holy mountain.
¹² Those who are left will be the lowly and
    humble,
  for it is they who trust in the name
    of the LORD.
¹³ The remnant of Israel will do no wrong;
  they will never tell lies or deceive one
    another.
They will eat and sleep in safety,
  and no one will make them afraid."

¹⁴ Sing, O daughter of Zion;
  shout aloud, O Israel!
Be glad and rejoice with all your heart,
  O daughter of Jerusalem!
¹⁵ For the LORD will remove his hand
    of judgment
  and will disperse the armies of your
    enemy.
And the LORD himself, the King of Israel,
  will live among you!
At last your troubles will be over,
  and you will never again fear
    disaster.
¹⁶ On that day the announcement to
    Jerusalem will be,
  "Cheer up, Zion! Don't be afraid!
¹⁷ For the LORD your God is living among
    you.
  He is a mighty savior.
He will take delight in you with
    gladness.
  With his love, he will calm all your
    fears.*
He will rejoice over you with joyful
    songs."

¹⁸ "I will gather you who mourn for the
    appointed festivals;
  you will be disgraced no more.*
¹⁹ And I will deal severely with all who have
    oppressed you.

3:10 Hebrew *Cush.* 3:17 Or *He will be silent in his love.* Greek and Syriac versions read *He will renew you with his love.*
3:18 The meaning of the Hebrew for this verse is uncertain.

3:9-20 Zephaniah described a future age that would follow the ultimate "day of the LORD." This
will be an age of blessing marked by honest and pure worship of God. God will remove all
dysfunctions from our personalities and relationships; sorrows and burdens will no longer exist;
and the nation of Israel will finally be restored to its land of hope and security. As we journey
toward full recovery, even in a physical sense, we can rejoice in this promise.

I will save the weak and helpless
  ones;
I will bring together
  those who were chased away.
I will give glory and fame to my former
  exiles,
  wherever they have been mocked and
  shamed.

20 On that day I will gather you together
  and bring you home again.
I will give you a good name, a name of
  distinction,
  among all the nations of the earth,
  as I restore your fortunes before their very
  eyes.
  I, the LORD, have spoken!"

HAGGAI

THE BIG PICTURE

A. INTRODUCTION (1:1)
B. THE FIRST SERMON: REBUKE (1:2-15)
  1. The Prophet's Challenge to Rebuild the Temple (1:2-11)
  2. The People Respond with Action (1:12-15)
C. THE SECOND SERMON: RENEWAL (2:1-9)
D. THE THIRD SERMON: RESTORATION (2:10-19)
E. THE FOURTH SERMON: REASSURANCE (2:20-23)

Haggai was called to encourage the people of Jerusalem to return to the task of rebuilding God's house. About eighteen years had passed since Cyrus released Zerubbabel with a group of Jewish exiles to return to Jerusalem to rebuild the Temple. They had arrived filled with hope, but pressure from the local authorities and selfish decisions led them to quit. They turned instead to building their own homes. Their priorities were out of order.

Haggai's task was to arouse the people to complete the rebuilding of God's Temple. Over a six-month period, he gave four messages designed to get the people back on track. He began by telling them to stop making excuses and get back to work. He showed them how their present sufferings resulted from their failure to put God first in their lives. They needed to get their spiritual lives in shape and let their actions prove that they had done so before they could expect God's blessings. Haggai's next messages continued the encouragement by promising God's help as they continued to work.

Rebuilding the Temple was difficult; so is the task of rebuilding our life. There will always be obstacles, but we don't have to let them stop us. When we feel like quitting, we can remember Haggai's message. God is there to help and protect us each step of the way. As God's people had to reassess their spiritual lives in the rebuilding process, we need to examine our life and act to prove our inner changes. Like the people of Jerusalem, we can respond to Haggai's message and move forward in the rebuilding process.

THE BOTTOM LINE

PURPOSE: To challenge the people to complete the rebuilding of God's Temple, their community, and their lives. AUTHOR: The prophet Haggai. AUDIENCE: The people living in Jerusalem, including those who had returned from Babylonian exile. DATE WRITTEN: Between August and December, 520 B.C. SETTING: Jerusalem had been in ruins since its destruction by the Babylonians in 586 B.C. The people had started to rebuild the Temple but had failed to complete the task. KEY VERSE: "Why are you living in luxurious houses while [God's] house lies in ruins?" (1:4). KEY PLACES: Jerusalem and the Temple. KEY PEOPLE AND RELATIONSHIPS: Zerubbabel (the political leader), Jeshua (the priestly leader), and the prophets Haggai and Zechariah.

RECOVERY THEMES

God's Plan Must Come First: When we face obstacles to God's plan for us, it is easy to get sidetracked; it is tempting to follow the way of least resistance. The people of Jerusalem started rebuilding God's Temple but met with stiff opposition. Instead of trusting God and standing up to the opposition, the people quit the rebuilding project God had for them and built their own homes instead. We tend to make the same mistake. When we face an obstacle to God's program for recovery, we turn away and take the way of least resistance. We hang on to destructive habits, activities, and relationships because it is easier. We may even begin a recovery program that looks easier but excludes God. When we reject God's program for recovery, we reject his power and blessings in our life.

We Will Face Obstacles: The rebuilding process is never easy. Old friends may be threatened by the changes in our life and set out to stop us. A codependent spouse may become insecure as we begin to grow and may make things difficult for us. We might fear the pain we feel and try to escape it. Temptation will rear its ugly head time and again as we work through our program. The Jews faced numerous obstacles as they sought to rebuild the Temple. Local leaders tried to stop the work many times. The people became afraid and gave up on the task God had given them to do. With God's help and Haggai's encouragement, however, the task resumed and God's Temple was completed. God wants us to recover. He will help us overcome the obstacles if we look to him for help.

Recovery Requires Action: It is much easier to recognize a problem than it is to do something about it. God's people in Jerusalem knew the Temple needed to be rebuilt if their nation was to get back on the right track spiritually. They had set out to complete the task but had become discouraged and failed to follow through. Their failure to act over a period of years brought continued suffering upon them. Haggai called the people to act; we are called to do the same. Our recovery project must go beyond recognizing our problems. We must take active steps toward reconciliation with God, ourself, and others. As we take these steps, as painful as they may be, we will be moving toward the recovery of our life and our relationships.

CHAPTER 1
A Call to Rebuild the Temple

On August 29* of the second year of King Darius's reign, the LORD gave a message through the prophet Haggai to Zerubbabel son of Shealtiel, governor of Judah, and to Jeshua* son of Jehozadak, the high priest.

²"This is what the LORD of Heaven's Armies says: The people are saying, 'The time has not yet come to rebuild the house of the LORD.'"

³Then the LORD sent this message through the prophet Haggai: ⁴"Why are you living in luxurious houses while my house lies in ruins? ⁵This is what the LORD of Heaven's Armies says: Look at what's happening to you! ⁶You have planted much but harvest little. You eat but are not satisfied. You drink but are still thirsty. You put on clothes but cannot keep warm. Your wages disappear as though you were putting them in pockets filled with holes!

⁷"This is what the LORD of Heaven's Armies says: Look at what's happening to you! ⁸Now go up into the hills, bring down timber, and rebuild my house. Then I will take pleasure in it and be honored, says the LORD. ⁹You hoped for rich harvests, but they were poor. And when you brought your harvest home, I blew it away. Why? Because my house lies in ruins, says the LORD of Heaven's Armies, while all of you are busy building your own fine houses. ¹⁰It's because of you that the heavens withhold the dew and the earth produces no crops. ¹¹I have called for a drought on your fields and hills—a drought to wither

---

1:1a Hebrew *On the first day of the sixth month,* of the ancient Hebrew lunar calendar. A number of dates in Haggai can be cross-checked with dates in surviving Persian records and related accurately to our modern calendar. This event occurred on August 29, 520 B.C. 1:1b Hebrew *Joshua,* a variant spelling of Jeshua; also in 1:12, 14.

1:2-8 God called the people in Jerusalem to inventory their priorities. The people had returned from exile and started to rebuild the Temple, but they had stopped when they faced opposition. They chose to build beautiful homes for themselves instead of finishing God's house. Their actions had proven that they considered personal comfort more important than God. As a result, they suffered hard times. When we put God in the backseat of our life, we become enslaved to other things—alcohol, sex, work, relationships, money, pleasure, or even religious activities. We must put God back in the driver's seat. If we give God top priority in our life and seek to follow his will, no addiction is too great to overcome.

the grain and grapes and olive trees and all your other crops, a drought to starve you and your livestock and to ruin everything you have worked so hard to get."

Obedience to God's Call

[12]Then Zerubbabel son of Shealtiel, and Jeshua son of Jehozadak, the high priest, and the whole remnant of God's people began to obey the message from the LORD their God. When they heard the words of the prophet Haggai, whom the LORD their God had sent, the people feared the LORD. [13]Then Haggai, the LORD's messenger, gave the people this message from the LORD: "I am with you, says the LORD!"

[14]So the LORD sparked the enthusiasm of Zerubbabel son of Shealtiel, governor of Judah, and the enthusiasm of Jeshua son of Jehozadak, the high priest, and the enthusiasm of the whole remnant of God's people. They began to work on the house of their God, the LORD of Heaven's Armies, [15]on September 21* of the second year of King Darius's reign.

CHAPTER 2
The New Temple's Diminished Splendor

Then on October 17 of that same year,* the LORD sent another message through the prophet Haggai. [2]"Say this to Zerubbabel son of Shealtiel, governor of Judah, and to Jeshua* son of Jehozadak, the high priest, and to the remnant of God's people there in the land: [3]'Does anyone remember this house—this Temple—in its former splendor? How, in comparison, does it look to you now? It must seem like nothing at all! [4]But now the LORD says: Be strong, Zerubbabel. Be strong, Jeshua son of Jehozadak, the high priest. Be strong, all you people still left in the land. And now get to work, for I am with you, says the LORD of Heaven's Armies. [5]My Spirit remains among you, just as I promised when you came out of Egypt. So do not be afraid.'

[6]"For this is what the LORD of Heaven's Armies says: In just a little while I will again shake the heavens and the earth, the oceans and the dry land. [7]I will shake all the nations, and the treasures of all the nations will be brought to this Temple. I will fill this place with glory, says the LORD of Heaven's Armies. [8]The silver is mine, and the gold is mine, says the LORD of Heaven's Armies. [9]The future glory of this Temple will be greater than its past glory, says the LORD of Heaven's Armies. And in this place I will bring peace. I, the LORD of Heaven's Armies, have spoken!"

Blessings Promised for Obedience

[10]On December 18* of the second year of King Darius's reign, the LORD sent this message to the prophet Haggai: [11]"This is what the LORD of Heaven's Armies says. Ask the priests this question about the law: [12]If one of you is carrying some meat from a holy sacrifice in his robes and his robe happens to brush against some bread or stew, wine or olive oil, or any other kind of food, will it also become holy?'"

The priests replied, "No."

[13]Then Haggai asked, "If someone becomes ceremonially unclean by touching a

---

1:15 Hebrew *on the twenty-fourth day of the sixth month,* of the ancient Hebrew lunar calendar. This event occurred on September 21, 520 B.C.; also see note on 1:1a. **2:1** Hebrew *on the twenty-first day of the seventh month,* of the ancient Hebrew lunar calendar. This event (in the second year of Darius's reign) occurred on October 17, 520 B.C.; also see note on 1:1a. **2:2** Hebrew *Joshua,* a variant spelling of Jeshua; also in 2:4. **2:10** Hebrew *On the twenty-fourth day of the ninth month,* of the ancient Hebrew lunar calendar (similarly in 2:18). This event occurred on December 18, 520 B.C.; also see note on 1:1a.

1:13-15 There is a point in recovery when we must get beyond mere self-examination; we need to stop talking about our problems and take concrete steps to change. We are like the people in Haggai's day who already knew God's will for them—they were to rebuild God's Temple. They just needed to act on their knowledge. The Israelites finally took concrete steps to complete the task God had given them. As we take our inventory regularly, we soon become aware of the things we need to change. We know whom we have hurt and have a good idea of what we should do. When we reach this point, it is time to act! If we don't take concrete, active steps, we cannot progress in recovery.

2:3-9 The former Temple had been destroyed nearly seventy years earlier, so there were few alive who could remember it. The few elderly people who had seen Solomon's Temple were sad because the new Temple would never match the old one in splendor. God made it clear, however, that their rebuilding project would result in a temple even more glorious than the first. As we work toward recovery, the pain over what we have lost through our addiction need not distract us from building for a worthwhile future. There is always hope when we rebuild with God's help.

dead person and then touches any of these foods, will the food be defiled?"

And the priests answered, "Yes."

[14]Then Haggai responded, "That is how it is with this people and this nation, says the LORD. Everything they do and everything they offer is defiled by their sin. [15]Look at what was happening to you before you began to lay the foundation of the LORD's Temple. [16]When you hoped for a twenty-bushel crop, you harvested only ten. When you expected to draw fifty gallons from the winepress, you found only twenty. [17]I sent blight and mildew and hail to destroy everything you worked so hard to produce. Even so, you refused to return to me, says the LORD.

[18]"Think about this eighteenth day of December, the day* when the foundation of the LORD's Temple was laid. Think carefully. [19]I am giving you a promise now while the seed is still in the barn.* You have not yet harvested your grain, and your grapevines, fig trees, pomegranates, and olive trees have not yet produced their crops. But from this day onward I will bless you."

Promises for Zerubbabel

[20]On that same day, December 18,* the LORD sent this second message to Haggai: [21]"Tell Zerubbabel, the governor of Judah, that I am about to shake the heavens and the earth. [22]I will overthrow royal thrones and destroy the power of foreign kingdoms. I will overturn their chariots and riders. The horses will fall, and their riders will kill each other.

[23]"But when this happens, says the LORD of Heaven's Armies, I will honor you, Zerubbabel son of Shealtiel, my servant. I will make you like a signet ring on my finger, says the LORD, for I have chosen you. I, the LORD of Heaven's Armies, have spoken!"

2:18 Or *On this eighteenth day of December, think about the day.* **2:19** Hebrew *Is the seed yet in the barn?* **2:20** Hebrew *On the twenty-fourth day of the [ninth] month;* see note on 2:10.

2:12-13 Purity and cleanness do not rub off; impurity and dirtiness do rub off. This is true not only in a physical sense but also in a spiritual sense. That is one reason we are told to avoid people associated with our addiction, especially in our early years of recovery. They are far more likely to lead us astray than we are to influence them for good. In recovery, our associations—circumstantial and personal—must pass the test of God's approval.

ZECHARIAH

THE BIG PICTURE

At times life seems intolerable, especially for those of us who have been victims most of our life. Though we may finally escape an abusive relationship or a dysfunctional home, we are not automatically freed from the emotional grasp of the past. As a result, we feel that people are hostile or that they do not care about us. Eventually, immobilizing despair sets in. Motivation and enthusiasm for life are gone. We become emotionally crippled.

That was probably what it was like for God's people in Judah. Because of the repeated sins of their ancestors, their families had been displaced from Palestine to Assyria and Babylon. Seventy years later, at the decree of Cyrus, a remnant of Jews returned to Jerusalem under the leadership of Zerubbabel. Their first goal was to rebuild the house of God, but their initial enthusiasm was dampened by opposition from local residents. The work of rebuilding the Temple soon stopped.

To counter this hopelessness, God appointed the elderly Haggai and the young Zechariah to prophesy, encouraging the returned exiles to rebuild God's Temple in Jerusalem. Zechariah, whose name means "the Lord remembers," reminded the Jews that God had not forgotten them. Rather, he had a certain and dynamic plan for their restoration.

Hope for the future can provide great encouragement for the present. The promise of deliverance makes it possible to be renewed and to continue in the process of recovery. This book is a fascinating study of how God, through his prophets, led his hurting people from hopelessness to commitment, through self-examination and transformation to a deepening spiritual perception. It is an account of rebuilding and recovery.

THE BOTTOM LINE

PURPOSE: To encourage God's people to complete the task of rebuilding God's Temple, their society, and their lives. AUTHOR: The prophet Zechariah. AUDIENCE: The people living in Jerusalem, including those who had returned from Babylonian exile. DATE WRITTEN: Chapters 1–8 were written between 528 and 520 B.C., and chapters 9–14 were written around 480 B.C. SETTING: The people had started to rebuild God's Temple in Jerusalem but had failed to complete the task. KEY VERSE: "Come back to the place of safety, all you prisoners who still have hope! I promise this very day that I will repay two blessings for each of your troubles" (9:12). KEY PLACES: Jerusalem and the Temple. KEY PEOPLE AND RELATIONSHIPS: Zerubbabel, Jeshua the priest, and the prophets Haggai and Zechariah.

RECOVERY THEMES

Disappointment Leads to Despair: When faced with disappointment, we have a choice: We can nurture our negative feelings, or we can confront them and find solutions for them. The people of God chose to hold on to their disappointment. This led to despair. To avoid despair we must give our disappointments to God and confront those aspects of them that we can change. As we take small steps toward recovery, we will find that our feelings of despair will pass. But we cannot just wait for healing. We need to become actively involved in God's recovery program.

Hope Encourages Us Today: Zechariah's visions of the future gave hope to the people and helped them face the tasks of their present. The hope that we have of God's final healing can encourage us to endure the pain that is involved in recovery today. We won't always feel so hurt and confused. If we follow God's will for us in faith, we will experience God's healing in our life and discover the joy that only he can give.

Recovery Involves the Heart: Zechariah told the people that God did not care about their fasts and religious observances. He cared about the attitudes of their hearts. Spiritual recovery involves the attitudes of our heart; it is not just a matter of doing and saying the right things. Only as our mind and heart are changed by God does true deliverance occur. As our heart is transformed, our attitudes and actions will also be transformed. If we go through the motions of recovery without ever changing on the inside, our recovery will never last. We need to be changed from the inside out. Just as this was true for the people in Jerusalem in Zechariah's day, it is true for us today.

CHAPTER 1
A Call to Return to the LORD

In November* of the second year of King Darius's reign, the LORD gave this message to the prophet Zechariah son of Berekiah and grandson of Iddo:

²"I, the LORD, was very angry with your ancestors. ³Therefore, say to the people, 'This is what the LORD of Heaven's Armies says: Return to me, and I will return to you, says the LORD of Heaven's Armies.' ⁴Don't be like your ancestors who would not listen or pay attention when the earlier prophets said to them, 'This is what the LORD of Heaven's Armies says: Turn from your evil ways, and stop all your evil practices.'

⁵"Where are your ancestors now? They and the prophets are long dead. ⁶But everything I said through my servants the prophets happened to your ancestors, just as I said. As a result, they repented and said, 'We have received what we deserved from the LORD of Heaven's Armies. He has done what he said he would do.'"

A Man among the Myrtle Trees

⁷Three months later, on February 15,* the LORD sent another message to the prophet Zechariah son of Berekiah and grandson of Iddo.

⁸In a vision during the night, I saw a man sitting on a red horse that was standing among some myrtle trees in a small valley. Behind him were riders on red, brown, and white horses. ⁹I asked the angel who was talking with me, "My lord, what do these horses mean?"

"I will show you," the angel replied.

¹⁰The rider standing among the myrtle trees then explained, "They are the ones the LORD has sent out to patrol the earth."

¹¹Then the other riders reported to the angel of the LORD, who was standing among the myrtle trees, "We have been patrolling the earth, and the whole earth is at peace."

¹²Upon hearing this, the angel of the LORD prayed this prayer: "O LORD of Heaven's Armies, for seventy years now you have been angry with Jerusalem and the towns of Judah. How long until you again show mercy to them?" ¹³And the LORD spoke kind and comforting words to the angel who talked with me.

¹⁴Then the angel said to me, "Shout this message for all to hear: 'This is what the LORD of Heaven's Armies says: My love for Jerusa-

---

1:1 Hebrew *In the eighth month.* A number of dates in Zechariah can be cross-checked with dates in surviving Persian records and related accurately to our modern calendar. This month of the ancient Hebrew lunar calendar occurred within the months of October and November 520 B.C. 1:7 Hebrew *On the twenty-fourth day of the eleventh month, the month of Shebat, in the second year of Darius.* This event occurred on February 15, 519 B.C.; also see note on 1:1.

1:1-6 The prophet begins his message by confronting the Jews with their sins. These people had recently returned from Babylonian exile, so Zechariah reminded them that God would deal with their sins just as he had punished their ancestors with the captivity they had recently escaped. It is never safe to ignore a call to turn back to God. Hearing demands heeding! God's promises of future comfort, victory, and deliverance must not lead us to a false sense of security. Neglected spiritual opportunities are lost opportunities.

lem and Mount Zion is passionate and strong. ¹⁵But I am very angry with the other nations that are now enjoying peace and security. I was only a little angry with my people, but the nations inflicted harm on them far beyond my intentions.

¹⁶" 'Therefore, this is what the LORD says: I have returned to show mercy to Jerusalem. My Temple will be rebuilt, says the LORD of Heaven's Armies, and measurements will be taken for the reconstruction of Jerusalem.*'

¹⁷"Say this also: 'This is what the LORD of Heaven's Armies says: The towns of Israel will again overflow with prosperity, and the LORD will again comfort Zion and choose Jerusalem as his own.'"

Four Horns and Four Blacksmiths

¹⁸*Then I looked up and saw four animal horns. ¹⁹"What are these?" I asked the angel who was talking with me.

He replied, "These horns represent the nations that scattered Judah, Israel, and Jerusalem."

²⁰Then the LORD showed me four blacksmiths. ²¹"What are these men coming to do?" I asked.

The angel replied, "These four horns—these nations—scattered and humbled Judah. Now these blacksmiths have come to terrify those nations and throw them down and destroy them."

CHAPTER 2
Future Prosperity of Jerusalem

¹*When I looked again, I saw a man with a measuring line in his hand. ²"Where are you going?" I asked.

He replied, "I am going to measure Jerusalem, to see how wide and how long it is."

³Then the angel who was with me went to meet a second angel who was coming toward him. ⁴The other angel said, "Hurry, and say to that young man, 'Jerusalem will someday be so full of people and livestock that there won't be room enough for everyone! Many will live outside the city walls. ⁵Then I, myself, will be a protective wall of fire around Jerusalem, says the LORD. And I will be the glory inside the city!'"

The Exiles Are Called Home

⁶The LORD says, "Come away! Flee from Babylon in the land of the north, for I have scattered you to the four winds. ⁷Come away, people of Zion, you who are exiled in Babylon!"

⁸After a period of glory, the LORD of Heaven's Armies sent me* against the nations who plundered you. For he said, "Anyone who harms you harms my most precious possession.* ⁹I will raise my fist to crush them, and their own slaves will plunder them." Then you will know that the LORD of Heaven's Armies has sent me.

¹⁰The LORD says, "Shout and rejoice, O beautiful Jerusalem,* for I am coming to live among you. ¹¹Many nations will join themselves to the LORD on that day, and they, too, will be my people. I will live among you, and you will know that the LORD of Heaven's Armies sent me to you. ¹²The land of Judah will be the LORD's special possession in the holy land, and he will once again choose Jerusalem to be his own city. ¹³Be silent before the LORD, all humanity, for he is springing into action from his holy dwelling."

1:16 Hebrew *and the measuring line will be stretched out over Jerusalem.* 1:18 Verses 1:18-21 are numbered 2:1-4 in Hebrew text. 2:1 Verses 2:1-13 are numbered 2:5-17 in Hebrew text. 2:8a The meaning of the Hebrew is uncertain. 2:8b Hebrew *Anyone who touches you touches the pupil of his eye.* 2:10 Hebrew *O daughter of Zion.*

1:18-21 The vision of the four horns (the horn is a symbol of power) and the four blacksmiths was a vision of reflection. It pointed to the four world empires that oppressed Israel: Egypt, Assyria, Babylon, and Medo-Persia. The four blacksmiths represented the nations God used to defeat Israel's enemies. God's dejected people can find courage and hope in the fact that he will eventually overthrow the oppressive powers that dominate them.

2:1-13 The vision of the man with a measuring line concerned the reconstruction and repatriation of Israel. Many of the Jews had become comfortable in exile and were reluctant to return to Palestine. They were probably afraid they would return to a land of confusion and strife. There was no need to fear, however, for God had promised a future of prosperity and peace. For any of us who wrestle with fear in the wake of traumatic experiences, we also are given the assurance of God's special protection. If we want to escape bondage, we need to trust God and follow his plan for deliverance.

CHAPTER 3
Cleansing for the High Priest

Then the angel showed me Jeshua* the high priest standing before the angel of the LORD. The Accuser, Satan,* was there at the angel's right hand, making accusations against Jeshua. ²And the LORD said to Satan, "I, the LORD, reject your accusations, Satan. Yes, the LORD, who has chosen Jerusalem, rebukes you. This man is like a burning stick that has been snatched from the fire."

³Jeshua's clothing was filthy as he stood there before the angel. ⁴So the angel said to the others standing there, "Take off his filthy clothes." And turning to Jeshua he said, "See, I have taken away your sins, and now I am giving you these fine new clothes."

⁵Then I said, "They should also place a clean turban on his head." So they put a clean priestly turban on his head and dressed him in new clothes while the angel of the LORD stood by.

⁶Then the angel of the LORD spoke very solemnly to Jeshua and said, ⁷"This is what the LORD of Heaven's Armies says: If you follow my ways and carefully serve me, then you will be given authority over my Temple and its courtyards. I will let you walk among these others standing here.

⁸"Listen to me, O Jeshua the high priest, and all you other priests. You are symbols of things to come. Soon I am going to bring my servant, the Branch. ⁹Now look at the jewel I have set before Jeshua, a single stone with seven facets.* I will engrave an inscription on it, says the LORD of Heaven's Armies, and I will remove the sins of this land in a single day.

¹⁰"And on that day, says the LORD of Heaven's Armies, each of you will invite your neighbor to sit with you peacefully under your own grapevine and fig tree."

CHAPTER 4
A Lampstand and Two Olive Trees

Then the angel who had been talking with me returned and woke me, as though I had been asleep. ²"What do you see now?" he asked.

I answered, "I see a solid gold lampstand with a bowl of oil on top of it. Around the bowl are seven lamps, each having seven spouts with wicks. ³And I see two olive trees, one on each side of the bowl." ⁴Then I asked the angel, "What are these, my lord? What do they mean?"

⁵"Don't you know?" the angel asked.

"No, my lord," I replied.

⁶Then he said to me, "This is what the LORD says to Zerubbabel: It is not by force nor by strength, but by my Spirit, says the LORD of Heaven's Armies. ⁷Nothing, not even a mighty mountain, will stand in Zerubbabel's way; it will become a level plain before him! And when Zerubbabel sets the final stone of the Temple in place, the people will shout: 'May God bless it! May God bless it!'*"

⁸Then another message came to me from

3:1a Hebrew *Joshua*, a variant spelling of Jeshua; also in 3:3, 4, 6, 8, 9. 3:1b Hebrew *The satan*; similarly in 3:2.
3:9 Hebrew *seven eyes*. 4:7 Hebrew *'Grace, grace to it.'*

3:1-4 This vision of Jeshua the high priest teaches us much about God's mercy and forgiveness. Jeshua ben-Jehozadak, the high priest at that time, appeared here in soiled garments, symbolizing how Israel looked to God in its sinful state. Satan stood before him, "making accusations against Jeshua" for Israel's failures. We still wrestle with sin today, and Satan is always there to accuse us before God for sins that have demoralized and immobilized us. Yet God is always there to defend us when we come to him for forgiveness and cleansing.

3:5-10 God would purify Jeshua, and he would be a living illustration of the good things that would be experienced under the Messiah's rule. This is cause for real hope here. When restoration is complete, suffering people will experience God's healing. Their sorrow and isolation will be replaced by joy and true fellowship with friends and neighbors. As we experience God's powerful deliverance, we can demonstrate what happens in a life that is ruled and directed by our loving God. As we share God's deliverance with others through words and deeds, they, too, can experience his healing power.

4:1-14 The vision of two olive trees pouring oil into a bowl on a gold lampstand points to the power by which Messiah's Kingdom will be inaugurated, namely the power of the Holy Spirit (see 4:6). Zechariah should have known from Scripture what the symbols meant. Likewise, we become confused when we don't know what God's Word has promised us. In studying the Bible, we discover the truth we need to understand God's will for us and the promise of God's power to help us as we follow his truth.

4:6-10 Zerubbabel had led a contingent of Jews to Jerusalem to rebuild the Temple, but their efforts had been stopped by political opposition. They became discouraged and wondered if God was with them. Here God gave Zechariah a message of encouragement for his disheartened

the LORD: [9]"Zerubbabel is the one who laid the foundation of this Temple, and he will complete it. Then you will know that the LORD of Heaven's Armies has sent me. [10]Do not despise these small beginnings, for the LORD rejoices to see the work begin, to see the plumb line in Zerubbabel's hand."

(The seven lamps* represent the eyes of the LORD that search all around the world.)

[11]Then I asked the angel, "What are these two olive trees on each side of the lampstand, [12]and what are the two olive branches that pour out golden oil through two gold tubes?"

[13]"Don't you know?" he asked.

"No, my lord," I replied.

[14]Then he said to me, "They represent the two anointed ones* who stand in the court of the Lord of all the earth."

CHAPTER 5
A Flying Scroll
I looked up again and saw a scroll flying through the air.

[2]"What do you see?" the angel asked.

"I see a flying scroll," I replied. "It appears to be about 30 feet long and 15 feet wide.*"

[3]Then he said to me, "This scroll contains the curse that is going out over the entire land. One side of the scroll says that those who steal will be banished from the land; the other side says that those who swear falsely will be banished from the land. [4]And this is what the LORD of Heaven's Armies says: I am sending this curse into the house of every thief and into the house of everyone who swears falsely using my name. And my curse will remain in that house and completely destroy it—even its timbers and stones."

A Woman in a Basket
[5]Then the angel who was talking with me came forward and said, "Look up and see what's coming."

[6]"What is it?" I asked.

He replied, "It is a basket for measuring grain,* and it's filled with the sins* of everyone throughout the land."

[7]Then the heavy lead cover was lifted off the basket, and there was a woman sitting inside it. [8]The angel said, "The woman's name is Wickedness," and he pushed her back into the basket and closed the heavy lid again.

[9]Then I looked up and saw two women flying toward us, gliding on the wind. They had wings like a stork, and they picked up the basket and flew into the sky.

[10]"Where are they taking the basket?" I asked the angel.

[11]He replied, "To the land of Babylonia,* where they will build a temple for the basket. And when the temple is ready, they will set the basket there on its pedestal."

CHAPTER 6
Four Chariots
Then I looked up again and saw four chariots coming from between two bronze mountains. [2]The first chariot was pulled by red horses, the second by black horses, [3]the third by white horses, and the fourth by powerful dappled-gray horses. [4]"And what are these, my lord?" I asked the angel who was talking with me.

[5]The angel replied, "These are the four spirits* of heaven who stand before the Lord of all the earth. They are going out to do his work. [6]The chariot with black horses is going north, the chariot with white horses is going

---

4:10 Or The seven facets (see 3:9); Hebrew reads These seven. 4:14 Or two heavenly beings; Hebrew reads two sons of fresh oil. 5:2 Hebrew 20 cubits [9.2 meters] long and 10 cubits [4.6 meters] wide. 5:6a Hebrew an ephah [20 quarts or 22 liters]; also in 5:7, 8, 9, 10, 11. 5:6b As in Greek version; Hebrew reads the appearance. 5:11 Hebrew the land of Shinar. 6:5 Or the four winds.

---

people. They needed to remember that success was not the result of human strength or ingenuity but a fruit of the Holy Spirit's power. With this power the difficult task of rebuilding could yet be accomplished. We often become discouraged as we face the massive task of recovery, especially when we experience regular opposition from people, emotions, and temptations. But when we recognize our own powerlessness, God can step in. His power is more than sufficient for the task of recovery.

6:1-8 The vision of the four chariots was God's way of promising his righteous judgment against the Gentile nations. Famine, war, and pestilence would be his divine weapons. We who are wrestling with recovery from victimization must remember that God knows all about our suffering and will deal with those who have hurt us in his own time. We can release our hatred and desire for revenge, because vengeance belongs to God (Leviticus 19:18; Deuteronomy 32:35; Romans 12:17-19). Only when we stop blaming others for our problems can we take responsible steps toward recovery.

west,* and the chariot with dappled-gray horses is going south."

⁷The powerful horses were eager to set out to patrol the earth. And the LORD said, "Go and patrol the earth!" So they left at once on their patrol.

⁸Then the LORD summoned me and said, "Look, those who went north have vented the anger of my Spirit* there in the land of the north."

The Crowning of Jeshua

⁹Then I received another message from the LORD: ¹⁰"Heldai, Tobijah, and Jedaiah will bring gifts of silver and gold from the Jews exiled in Babylon. As soon as they arrive, meet them at the home of Josiah son of Zephaniah. ¹¹Accept their gifts, and make a crown from the silver and gold. Then put the crown on the head of Jeshua* son of Jehozadak, the high priest. ¹²Tell him, 'This is what the LORD of Heaven's Armies says: Here is the man called the Branch. He will branch out from where he is and build the Temple of the LORD. ¹³Yes, he will build the Temple of the LORD. Then he will receive royal honor and will rule as king from his throne. He will also serve as priest from his throne,* and there will be perfect harmony between his two roles.'

¹⁴"The crown will be a memorial in the Temple of the LORD to honor those who gave it—Heldai,* Tobijah, Jedaiah, and Josiah* son of Zephaniah."

¹⁵People will come from distant lands to rebuild the Temple of the LORD. And when this happens, you will know that my messages have been from the LORD of Heaven's Armies. All this will happen if you carefully obey what the LORD your God says.

CHAPTER 7
A Call to Justice and Mercy

On December 7* of the fourth year of King Darius's reign, another message came to Zechariah from the LORD. ²The people of Bethel had sent Sharezer and Regemmelech,* along with their attendants, to seek the LORD's favor. ³They were to ask this question of the prophets and the priests at the Temple of the LORD of Heaven's Armies: "Should we continue to mourn and fast each summer on the anniversary of the Temple's destruction,* as we have done for so many years?"

⁴The LORD of Heaven's Armies sent me this message in reply: ⁵"Say to all your people and your priests, 'During these seventy years of exile, when you fasted and mourned in the summer and in early autumn,* was it really for me that you were fasting? ⁶And even now in your holy festivals, aren't you eating and drinking just to please yourselves? ⁷Isn't this the same message the LORD proclaimed through the prophets in years past when Jerusalem and the towns of Judah were bustling with people, and the Negev and the foothills of Judah* were well populated?'"

6:6 Hebrew *is going after them.* 6:8 Hebrew *have given my Spirit rest.* 6:11 Hebrew *Joshua,* a variant spelling of Jeshua. 6:13 Or *There will be a priest by his throne.* 6:14a As in Syriac version (compare 6:10); Hebrew reads *Helem.* 6:14b As in Syriac version (compare 6:10); Hebrew reads *Hen.* 7:1 Hebrew *On the fourth day of the ninth month, the month of Kislev,* of the ancient Hebrew lunar calendar. This event occurred on December 7, 518 B.C.; also see note on 1:1. 7:2 Or *Bethel-sharezer had sent Regemmelech.* 7:3 Hebrew *mourn and fast in the fifth month.* The Temple had been destroyed in the fifth month of the ancient Hebrew lunar calendar (August 586 B.C.); see 2 Kgs 25:8. 7:5 Hebrew *fasted and mourned in the fifth and seventh months.* The fifth month of the ancient Hebrew lunar calendar usually occurs within the months of July and August. The seventh month usually occurs within the months of September and October; both the Day of Atonement and the Festival of Shelters were celebrated in the seventh month. 7:7 Hebrew *the Shephelah.*

6:9-15 In this climax to the visions, Zechariah was instructed to receive gifts designated for the work of rebuilding the Temple from a delegation of Jews from Babylon. From the silver and gold, he was to make a crown to set upon Jeshua's head, foreshadowing the royal priesthood that would come with the Messiah (Psalm 110:1-4; Hebrews 7:1-3). Once again, however, the obligation upon God's people was clear. God would not bless them unless they were willing to follow his will for them. The same is true for us. There is little hope for our recovery unless we recognize our need for God and seek to do things his way.

7:1-7 Two years had elapsed since Zechariah received the visions (chapters 1–6). Since then, the work on the Temple had progressed, and the people had turned back to God. The citizens of Bethel sent a delegation to Jerusalem asking if they should continue the annual mourning and fasting for the Temple's destruction, especially since the Temple was being rebuilt. God made it clear through Zechariah's answer that he was more concerned about the attitudes of their hearts than whether or not they fasted. Many of us have come to realize that true recovery, whether from addictive or abusive behaviors, codependency, or victimization, must involve deep internal change. Only as God changes our heart can real deliverance occur.

⁸Then this message came to Zechariah from the LORD: ⁹"This is what the LORD of Heaven's Armies says: Judge fairly, and show mercy and kindness to one another. ¹⁰Do not oppress widows, orphans, foreigners, and the poor. And do not scheme against each other.

¹¹"Your ancestors refused to listen to this message. They stubbornly turned away and put their fingers in their ears to keep from hearing. ¹²They made their hearts as hard as stone, so they could not hear the instructions or the messages that the LORD of Heaven's Armies had sent them by his Spirit through the earlier prophets. That is why the LORD of Heaven's Armies was so angry with them.

¹³"Since they refused to listen when I called to them, I would not listen when they called to me, says the LORD of Heaven's Armies. ¹⁴As with a whirlwind, I scattered them among the distant nations, where they lived as strangers. Their land became so desolate that no one even traveled through it. They turned their pleasant land into a desert."

CHAPTER 8
Promised Blessings for Jerusalem

Then another message came to me from the LORD of Heaven's Armies: ²"This is what the LORD of Heaven's Armies says: My love for Mount Zion is passionate and strong; I am consumed with passion for Jerusalem!

³"And now the LORD says: I am returning to Mount Zion, and I will live in Jerusalem. Then Jerusalem will be called the Faithful City; the mountain of the LORD of Heaven's Armies will be called the Holy Mountain.

⁴"This is what the LORD of Heaven's Armies says: Once again old men and women will walk Jerusalem's streets with their canes and will sit together in the city squares. ⁵And the streets of the city will be filled with boys and girls at play.

⁶"This is what the LORD of Heaven's Armies says: All this may seem impossible to you now, a small remnant of God's people. But is it impossible for me? says the LORD of Heaven's Armies.

⁷"This is what the LORD of Heaven's Armies says: You can be sure that I will rescue my people from the east and from the west. ⁸I will bring them home again to live safely in Jerusalem. They will be my people, and I will be faithful and just toward them as their God.

⁹"This is what the LORD of Heaven's Armies says: Be strong and finish the task! Ever since the laying of the foundation of the Temple of the LORD of Heaven's Armies, you have heard what the prophets have been saying about completing the building. ¹⁰Before the work on the Temple began, there were no jobs and no money to hire people or animals. No traveler was safe from the enemy, for there were enemies on all sides. I had turned everyone against each other.

¹¹"But now I will not treat the remnant of my people as I treated them before, says the LORD of Heaven's Armies. ¹²For I am planting seeds of peace and prosperity among you. The grapevines will be heavy with fruit. The earth will produce its crops, and the heavens will release the dew. Once more I will cause the remnant in Judah and Israel to inherit these blessings. ¹³Among the other nations, Judah and Israel became symbols of a cursed nation. But no longer! Now I will rescue you and make you both a symbol and a source of blessing. So don't be afraid. Be strong, and get on with rebuilding the Temple!

¹⁴"For this is what the LORD of Heaven's Armies says: I was determined to punish you when your ancestors angered me, and I did not change my mind, says the LORD of Heaven's Armies. ¹⁵But now I am determined to bless Jerusalem and the people of Judah. So don't be afraid. ¹⁶But this is what you must do: Tell the truth to each other. Render verdicts in your courts that are just and that

---

7:8-10 For the recovering exiles, the test of their faith was simple: love for others (Leviticus 19:18), especially the helpless—widows, orphans, foreigners, and the poor. The final step and ultimate proof of our recovery is our desire to help others who are suffering under the burden of their dependency. As we reach out to them to offer them the second chance that we have already received, we will discover the joy of loving others, and our own recovery will be strengthened as a result.

8:1-17 The most important way to identify true commitment to God is to see how it affects our daily life. God promised wonderful blessings when the Jews completed rebuilding his Temple. Their action in rebuilding God's house would prove their commitment to his revealed will. Recovery cannot stop with self-examination; taking moral inventory must lead to appropriate action. Obeying God proves that we trust his program to the point of shaping our life around it. This is the kind of faith we need for genuine spirituality and successful recovery.

lead to peace. [17]Don't scheme against each other. Stop your love of telling lies that you swear are the truth. I hate all these things, says the LORD."

[18]Here is another message that came to me from the LORD of Heaven's Armies. [19]"This is what the LORD of Heaven's Armies says: The traditional fasts and times of mourning you have kept in early summer, midsummer, autumn, and winter* are now ended. They will become festivals of joy and celebration for the people of Judah. So love truth and peace.

[20]"This is what the LORD of Heaven's Armies says: People from nations and cities around the world will travel to Jerusalem. [21]The people of one city will say to the people of another, 'Come with us to Jerusalem to ask the LORD to bless us. Let's worship the LORD of Heaven's Armies. I'm determined to go.' [22]Many peoples and powerful nations will come to Jerusalem to seek the LORD of Heaven's Armies and to ask for his blessing.

[23]"This is what the LORD of Heaven's Armies says: In those days ten men from different nations and languages of the world will clutch at the sleeve of one Jew. And they will say, 'Please let us walk with you, for we have heard that God is with you.'"

CHAPTER 9
Judgment against Israel's Enemies

This is the message* from the LORD against the land of Aram* and the city of Damascus, for the eyes of humanity, including all the tribes of Israel, are on the LORD.

[2]Doom is certain for Hamath,
near Damascus,

and for the cities of Tyre and Sidon,
though they are so clever.
[3]Tyre has built a strong fortress
and has made silver and gold
as plentiful as dust in the streets!
[4]But now the Lord will strip away Tyre's
possessions
and hurl its fortifications into the sea,
and it will be burned to the ground.
[5]The city of Ashkelon will see Tyre fall
and will be filled with fear.
Gaza will shake with terror,
as will Ekron, for their hopes will be
dashed.
Gaza's king will be killed,
and Ashkelon will be deserted.
[6]Foreigners will occupy the city of Ashdod.
I will destroy the pride of the
Philistines.
[7]I will grab the bloody meat from their
mouths
and snatch the detestable sacrifices
from their teeth.
Then the surviving Philistines will
worship our God
and become like a clan in Judah.*
The Philistines of Ekron will join my
people,
as the ancient Jebusites once did.
[8]I will guard my Temple
and protect it from invading armies.
I am watching closely to ensure
that no more foreign oppressors
overrun my people's land.

Zion's Coming King
[9]Rejoice, O people of Zion!*
Shout in triumph, O people of
Jerusalem!

8:19 Hebrew *in the fourth, fifth, seventh, and tenth months.* The fourth month of the ancient Hebrew lunar calendar usually occurs within the months of June and July. The fifth month usually occurs within the months of July and August. The seventh month usually occurs within the months of September and October. The tenth month usually occurs within the months of December and January. 9:1a Hebrew *An Oracle: The message.* 9:1b Hebrew *land of Hadrach.* 9:7 Hebrew *like a leader in Judah.* 9:9a Hebrew *O daughter of Zion!*

9:1-8 God declared judgment against the Gentile nations. All of Israel's neighbors would be overrun, but God would protect his land from the invading armies. This prophecy probably referred to the conquests of Alexander the Great that took place during the intertestamental period. These verses trace Alexander's campaign through Syria, Phoenicia, and Philistia (334–332 B.C.). But in Jerusalem, God would stop Alexander from destroying the Temple. This would have given hope to the Jews, who had lived for centuries with the threat of invading armies. Fear often paralyzes us. God's assurance of his presence, however, leads to courage. As we face the difficulties of recovery, God's presence gives us the courage to conquer our fears and persevere.
9:13–10:1 Recovery is a matter of committing our life to God and patiently waiting for his timely intervention. The Jews' victory over the Greek tyrants is described here in a series of metaphors. God's people are seen as instruments of conquest: the bow and arrow, and a warrior's sword. God would give his people victory over the oppressive powers that assailed them. We may feel trapped by a powerful dependency or oppressive relationship, but God can bring deliverance. Through his bountiful power, he can restore beauty and freedom to any damaged life.

Look, your king is coming to you.
  He is righteous and victorious,*
  yet he is humble, riding on a donkey—
  riding on a donkey's colt.
¹⁰ I will remove the battle chariots from Israel*
  and the warhorses from Jerusalem.
I will destroy all the weapons used in
    battle,
  and your king will bring peace to the
    nations.
His realm will stretch from sea to sea
  and from the Euphrates River* to the
    ends of the earth.*
¹¹ Because of the covenant I made with you,
    sealed with blood,
I will free your prisoners
  from death in a waterless dungeon.
¹² Come back to the place of safety,
  all you prisoners who still have hope!
I promise this very day
  that I will repay two blessings for each
    of your troubles.
¹³ Judah is my bow,
  and Israel is my arrow.
Jerusalem* is my sword,
  and like a warrior, I will brandish it
    against the Greeks.*

¹⁴ The LORD will appear above his people;
  his arrows will fly like lightning!
The Sovereign LORD will sound the ram's
    horn
  and attack like a whirlwind from the
    southern desert.
¹⁵ The LORD of Heaven's Armies will protect
    his people,
  and they will defeat their enemies by
    hurling great stones.
They will shout in battle as though drunk
    with wine.
  They will be filled with blood like
    a bowl,
  drenched with blood like the corners
    of the altar.
¹⁶ On that day the LORD their God will
    rescue his people,
  just as a shepherd rescues his sheep.
They will sparkle in his land
  like jewels in a crown.
¹⁷ How wonderful and beautiful they will be!
  The young men will thrive on
    abundant grain,
  and the young women will flourish on
    new wine.

9:9b Hebrew *and is being vindicated.* 9:10a Hebrew
Ephraim, referring to the northern kingdom of Israel;
also in 9:13. 9:10b Hebrew *the river.* 9:10c Or *the end of
the land.* 9:13a Hebrew *Zion.* 9:13b Hebrew *the sons of
Javan.*

HOPE

READ ZECHARIAH 9:9-17

We may feel as if our life is a battlefield.
We may be a prisoner in the ongoing war
between good and evil. When we turn our
life over to God, will he rescue us and keep
us safe?

Five hundred years before the birth of
Jesus, the prophet Zechariah wrote these
words: "Rejoice, O people of Zion! Shout in
triumph, O people of Jerusalem! Look, your
king is coming to you. He is righteous and
victorious, yet he is humble, riding on a
donkey—riding on a donkey's colt. [This
prophecy was fulfilled by the coming of
Jesus (see Matthew 21:4-11).] I will remove
the battle chariots from Israel and the
warhorses from Jerusalem. I will destroy all
the weapons used in battle, and your king
will bring peace to the nations. His realm
will stretch from sea to sea and from the
Euphrates River to the ends of the earth.
Because of the covenant I made with you,
sealed with blood, I will free your prisoners
from death in a waterless dungeon. Come
back to the place of safety, all you prisoners
who still have hope! I promise this very day
that I will repay two blessings for each of
your troubles" (Zechariah 9:9-12).

Jesus fulfilled part of these prophecies
when he came the first time. He delivered
us from death by shedding his own blood
to seal our pardon. When he comes again
as he promised, he will bring peace on
earth. For now, we can take refuge in Jesus.
When the war is over and Jesus is crowned
King of kings, he will repay all those who
are his, two mercies for every woe suffered
in the war! No matter how terrible the
battles we face, we can turn our life over to
God and have a sure hope for the future.
Turn to page 1199, Matthew 4.

CHAPTER 10
The LORD Will Restore His People

¹ Ask the LORD for rain in the spring,
  for he makes the storm clouds.
And he will send showers of rain
  so every field becomes a lush pasture.
² Household gods give worthless advice,
  fortune-tellers predict only lies,
and interpreters of dreams pronounce
  falsehoods that give no comfort.
So my people are wandering like lost sheep;
  they are attacked because they have
    no shepherd.

³ "My anger burns against your shepherds,
  and I will punish these leaders.*
For the LORD of Heaven's Armies has arrived
  to look after Judah, his flock.
He will make them strong and glorious,
  like a proud warhorse in battle.
⁴ From Judah will come the cornerstone,
  the tent peg,
the bow for battle,
  and all the rulers.
⁵ They will be like mighty warriors in battle,
  trampling their enemies in the mud
    under their feet.
Since the LORD is with them as they fight,
  they will overthrow even the enemy's
    horsemen.

⁶ "I will strengthen Judah and save Israel*;
  I will restore them because of my
    compassion.
It will be as though I had never rejected
    them,
  for I am the LORD their God, who will
    hear their cries.
⁷ The people of Israel* will become like
    mighty warriors,
  and their hearts will be made happy as
    if by wine.
Their children, too, will see it and be glad;
  their hearts will rejoice in the LORD.
⁸ When I whistle to them, they will come
    running,
  for I have redeemed them.
From the few who are left,
  they will grow as numerous as they
    were before.

⁹ Though I have scattered them like seeds
    among the nations,
  they will still remember me in distant
    lands.
They and their children will survive
  and return again to Israel.
¹⁰ I will bring them back from Egypt
  and gather them from Assyria.
I will resettle them in Gilead and
    Lebanon
  until there is no more room for
    them all.
¹¹ They will pass safely through the sea of
    distress,*
  for the waves of the sea will be held back,
  and the waters of the Nile will dry up.
The pride of Assyria will be crushed,
  and the rule of Egypt will end.
¹² By my power* I will make my people
    strong,
  and by my authority they will go
    wherever they wish.
  I, the LORD, have spoken!"

CHAPTER 11

¹ Open your doors, Lebanon,
  so that fire may devour your cedar
    forests.
² Weep, you cypress trees, for all the ruined
    cedars;
  the most majestic ones have fallen.
Weep, you oaks of Bashan,
  for the thick forests have been cut down.
³ Listen to the wailing of the shepherds,
  for their rich pastures are destroyed.
Hear the young lions roaring,
  for their thickets in the Jordan Valley
    are ruined.

The Good and Evil Shepherds

⁴ This is what the LORD my God says: "Go and care for the flock that is intended for slaughter. ⁵ The buyers slaughter their sheep without remorse. The sellers say, 'Praise the LORD! Now I'm rich!' Even the shepherds have no compassion for them. ⁶ Likewise, I will no longer have pity on the people of the land," says the LORD. "I will let them fall into each other's hands and into the hands of their

---

10:3 Or *these male goats.* **10:6** Hebrew *save the house of Joseph.* **10:7** Hebrew *of Ephraim.* **10:11** Or *the sea of Egypt,* referring to the Red Sea. **10:12** Hebrew *In the LORD.*

10:8-12 Like a shepherd who whistles to his flocks, God will call his people back from exile. Political restoration would not be enough, however; the Jews needed to return in faith to their God. Similarly, God has a perfect plan for each of us, and he will not rest until each one has been perfected according to his sovereign will (Romans 8:30-32). In recovery, we must seek God's will for us and do all we can to follow it. If we follow God's plan, he will help us along the way.

king. They will turn the land into a wilderness, and I will not rescue them."

[7]So I cared for the flock intended for slaughter—the flock that was oppressed. Then I took two shepherd's staffs and named one Favor and the other Union. [8]I got rid of their three evil shepherds in a single month.

But I became impatient with these sheep, and they hated me, too. [9]So I told them, "I won't be your shepherd any longer. If you die, you die. If you are killed, you are killed. And let those who remain devour each other!"

[10]Then I took my staff called Favor and cut it in two, showing that I had revoked the covenant I had made with all the nations. [11]That was the end of my covenant with them. The suffering flock was watching me, and they knew that the LORD was speaking through my actions.

[12]And I said to them, "If you like, give me my wages, whatever I am worth; but only if you want to." So they counted out for my wages thirty pieces of silver.

[13]And the LORD said to me, "Throw it to the potter*"—this magnificent sum at which they valued me! So I took the thirty coins and threw them to the potter in the Temple of the LORD.

[14]Then I took my other staff, Union, and cut it in two, showing that the bond of unity between Judah and Israel was broken.

[15]Then the LORD said to me, "Go again and play the part of a worthless shepherd. [16]This illustrates how I will give this nation a shepherd who will not care for those who are dying, nor look after the young, nor heal the injured, nor feed the healthy. Instead, this shepherd will eat the meat of the fattest sheep and tear off their hooves.

[17] "What sorrow awaits this worthless
    shepherd
    who abandons the flock!
The sword will cut his arm
    and pierce his right eye.
His arm will become useless,
    and his right eye completely blind."

CHAPTER 12
Future Deliverance for Jerusalem

This* message concerning the fate of Israel came from the LORD: "This message is from the LORD, who stretched out the heavens, laid the foundations of the earth, and formed the human spirit. [2]I will make Jerusalem like an intoxicating drink that makes the nearby nations stagger when they send their armies to besiege Jerusalem and Judah. [3]On that day I will make Jerusalem an immovable rock. All the nations will gather against it to try to move it, but they will only hurt themselves.

[4]"On that day," says the LORD, "I will cause every horse to panic and every rider to lose his nerve. I will watch over the people of Judah, but I will blind all the horses of their enemies. [5]And the clans of Judah will say to themselves, 'The people of Jerusalem have found strength in the LORD of Heaven's Armies, their God.'

[6]"On that day I will make the clans of Judah like a flame that sets a woodpile ablaze or like a burning torch among sheaves of grain. They will burn up all the neighboring nations right and left, while the people living in Jerusalem remain secure.

[7]"The LORD will give victory to the rest of Judah first, before Jerusalem, so that the people of Jerusalem and the royal line of David will not have greater honor than the rest of Judah. [8]On that day the LORD will defend the people of Jerusalem; the weakest among them will be as mighty as King David! And the royal descendants will be like God, like the angel of the LORD who goes before them! [9]For on that day I will begin to destroy all the nations that come against Jerusalem.

[10]"Then I will pour out a spirit* of grace

11:13 Syriac version reads *into the treasury;* also in 11:13b. Compare Matt 27:6-10. 12:1 Hebrew *An Oracle: This.*
12:10 Or *the Spirit.*

12:1-9 Zechariah again spoke of a time when the nations would try to oppress Israel, but this time they would not succeed. Though Israel would suffer confusion and panic, it would be encouraged by God's delivering intervention. When we who have been victimized turn to God, he will deliver us. Our oppressors cannot ultimately prevail against his limitless power.
12:10–13:1 These verses describe a national conversion in Israel, but they also outline our own spiritual conversion. Here is the secret for anyone trapped in an abusive or codependent situation with no apparent hope. First, we must recognize that we are helpless without God and depend on him to show us the areas of sin and failure in our life. Second, we need to confess our sin, repent, and seek to follow God's will. Next we must accept the free cleansing that God offers us. Because of what Jesus Christ has done on our behalf, we can be confident of God's total forgiveness of all our past sins.

and prayer on the family of David and on the people of Jerusalem. They will look on me whom they have pierced and mourn for him as for an only son. They will grieve bitterly for him as for a firstborn son who has died. ¹¹The sorrow and mourning in Jerusalem on that day will be like the great mourning for Hadad-rimmon in the valley of Megiddo.

¹²"All Israel will mourn, each clan by itself, and with the husbands separate from their wives. The clan of David will mourn alone, as will the clan of Nathan, ¹³the clan of Levi, and the clan of Shimei. ¹⁴Each of the surviving clans from Judah will mourn separately, and with the husbands separate from their wives.

CHAPTER 13
A Fountain of Cleansing
"On that day a fountain will be opened for the dynasty of David and for the people of Jerusalem, a fountain to cleanse them from all their sins and impurity.

²"And on that day," says the LORD of Heaven's Armies, "I will erase idol worship throughout the land, so that even the names of the idols will be forgotten. I will remove from the land both the false prophets and the spirit of impurity that came with them. ³If anyone continues to prophesy, his own father and mother will tell him, 'You must die, for you have prophesied lies in the name of the LORD.' And as he prophesies, his own father and mother will stab him.

⁴"On that day people will be ashamed to claim the prophetic gift. No one will pretend to be a prophet by wearing prophet's clothes. ⁵He will say, 'I'm no prophet; I'm a farmer. I began working for a farmer as a boy.' ⁶And if someone asks, 'Then what about those wounds on your chest?*' he will say, 'I was wounded at my friends' house!'

The Scattering of the Sheep
⁷ "Awake, O sword, against my shepherd, the man who is my partner,"

says the LORD of Heaven's Armies.
"Strike down the shepherd,
and the sheep will be scattered,
and I will turn against the lambs.
⁸ Two-thirds of the people in the land
will be cut off and die," says the LORD.
"But one-third will be left in the land.
⁹ I will bring that group through the fire
and make them pure.
I will refine them like silver
and purify them like gold.
They will call on my name,
and I will answer them.
I will say, 'These are my people,'
and they will say, 'The LORD is our
God.'"

CHAPTER 14
The LORD Will Rule the Earth
Watch, for the day of the LORD is coming when your possessions will be plundered right in front of you! ²I will gather all the nations to fight against Jerusalem. The city will be taken, the houses looted, and the women raped. Half the population will be taken into captivity, and the rest will be left among the ruins of the city.

³Then the LORD will go out to fight against those nations, as he has fought in times past. ⁴On that day his feet will stand on the Mount of Olives, east of Jerusalem. And the Mount of Olives will split apart, making a wide valley running from east to west. Half the mountain will move toward the north and half toward the south. ⁵You will flee through this valley, for it will reach across to Azal.* Yes, you will flee as you did from the earthquake in the days of King Uzziah of Judah. Then the LORD my God will come, and all his holy ones with him.*

⁶On that day the sources of light will no longer shine,* ⁷yet there will be continuous day! Only the LORD knows how this could happen. There will be no normal day and night, for at evening time it will still be light.

13:6 Hebrew *wounds between your hands?* 14:5a The meaning of the Hebrew is uncertain. 14:5b As in Greek version; Hebrew reads *with you.* 14:6 Hebrew *the precious ones shall diminish;* or *the precious ones and frost.* The meaning of the Hebrew is uncertain.

13:2-4 Part of God's program for Israel's recovery included getting rid of the idols and false prophets. The people had learned to depend upon teachings and objects that had no power to deliver. God would remove those sources of false hope so the people could learn to depend on him alone. We are often guilty of bowing to idols or following false prophets. Our dependency itself is an idol, since we use it to deal with pain that only God can heal. The false prophets of recovery fads and New Age spirituality can also lead us away from true dependence on God. Recovery depends upon our removing idols and false prophets from our life. God is the only one able to fulfill his promises of deliverance.

⁸On that day life-giving waters will flow out from Jerusalem, half toward the Dead Sea and half toward the Mediterranean,* flowing continuously in both summer and winter.

⁹And the LORD will be king over all the earth. On that day there will be one LORD— his name alone will be worshiped.

¹⁰All the land from Geba, north of Judah, to Rimmon, south of Jerusalem, will become one vast plain. But Jerusalem will be raised up in its original place and will be inhabited all the way from the Benjamin Gate over to the site of the old gate, then to the Corner Gate, and from the Tower of Hananel to the king's winepresses. ¹¹And Jerusalem will be filled, safe at last, never again to be cursed and destroyed.

¹²And the LORD will send a plague on all the nations that fought against Jerusalem. Their people will become like walking corpses, their flesh rotting away. Their eyes will rot in their sockets, and their tongues will rot in their mouths. ¹³On that day they will be terrified, stricken by the LORD with great panic. They will fight their neighbors hand to hand. ¹⁴Judah, too, will be fighting at Jerusalem. The wealth of all the neighboring nations will be captured—great quantities of gold and silver and fine clothing. ¹⁵This same plague will strike the horses, mules, camels, donkeys, and all the other animals in the enemy camps.

¹⁶In the end, the enemies of Jerusalem who survive the plague will go up to Jerusalem each year to worship the King, the LORD of Heaven's Armies, and to celebrate the Festival of Shelters. ¹⁷Any nation in the world that refuses to come to Jerusalem to worship the King, the LORD of Heaven's Armies, will have no rain. ¹⁸If the people of Egypt refuse to attend the festival, the LORD will punish* them with the same plague that he sends on the other nations who refuse to go. ¹⁹Egypt and the other nations will all be punished if they don't go to celebrate the Festival of Shelters.

²⁰On that day even the harness bells of the horses will be inscribed with these words: HOLY TO THE LORD. And the cooking pots in the Temple of the LORD will be as sacred as the basins used beside the altar. ²¹In fact, every cooking pot in Jerusalem and Judah will be holy to the LORD of Heaven's Armies. All who come to worship will be free to use any of these pots to boil their sacrifices. And on that day there will no longer be traders* in the Temple of the LORD of Heaven's Armies.

14:8 Hebrew *half toward the eastern sea and half toward the western sea.* **14:18** As in some Hebrew manuscripts and Greek and Syriac versions; Masoretic Text reads *will not punish.* **14:21** Hebrew *Canaanites.*

14:8-15 At last Zechariah reached the goal of his prophecy—and of all history—the messianic kingdom. The Messiah will be king over all the earth. All of earth's inhabitants will know, worship, and serve him. When the whole world runs according to God's program, life for everyone will be characterized by peace and joy. Part of the recovery process requires that we live according to God's will—today. We don't have to wait until the end of the world to put him in charge of our life. When God occupies the place of absolute authority, radical changes will take place. Our life will take on new beauty and peace as we become part of God's program of cosmic restoration.
14:16-21 When the Messiah rules, Israel will be sanctified as God's priestly nation and characterized by holiness. Nothing unclean will be allowed to defile the Temple precincts. We are reminded here that God desires his people to be holy, just as he is holy. We are made holy by accepting God's work on our behalf through Jesus Christ. Because God dwells in us through his Holy Spirit, our body becomes his temple, where nothing unclean should be allowed to enter (1 Corinthians 6:19-20). This provides a strong motivation for us to stay free of enslavement to our addiction.

REFLECTIONS ON ZECHARIAH

insights ABOUT GOD'S DISCIPLINE

In **Zechariah 7:8-14** we are reminded of how the ancestors of Zechariah's Jewish audience had stubbornly turned away from all of God's appeals to show mercy and kindness to the poor and helpless. Because they would not listen, God refused to listen to their prayers. Merely attending church or saying formal prayers to God will not lead to recovery. True emotional and spiritual healing always involves obedience to God's revealed will. We cannot do things our own way and expect God's help in our deliverance. It is only as we give our life over to God and submit to his perfect plan for us that real progress can be made in recovery.

insights INTO THE HOPE GOD OFFERS

At the very center of Israel's hope was the Messiah, whose promised coming was a source of great hope and joy. As we see in **Zechariah 9:9-10**, his credentials were his righteousness, his offer of salvation, and his humility, distinguishing him from all other earthly rulers. The one who demonstrated these credentials was, of course, Jesus of Nazareth. Clearly, God's people must place their hope for recovery not primarily in human sources but in a personal relationship with God through Jesus Christ. If we put our hope and trust in God, no problem is too great for us to overcome.

In **Zechariah 14:1-7** the prophet foresaw a time of terrible desolation, but in the midst of the horrible suffering, God would step in to deliver his people. Throughout the Scriptures we find God transforming terrible situations into amazing victories. This prophecy looks to a future time when God will do this in an ultimate sense. We all have experienced deep pain, and many of us are experiencing this even today. Sometimes we must reach a point of extreme desperation before we can understand our helplessness and realize how useless it is to go on alone. God is able to heal our deepest hurts and restore our life, no matter how terrible our past.

MALACHI

THE BIG PICTURE

When recovery involves only changes in external behavioral without internal change, there is the constant threat of relapse. This seemed to be the case with the people in Jerusalem. Under Nehemiah's leadership, the people had rebuilt the walls of the city and their lives. But when Nehemiah returned to Persia, all the excellent activities and attitudes that he had fostered in the people disappeared.

Malachi preached to a nation of backsliders—people who had relapsed. Even the spiritual leaders had fallen into old, sinful patterns. As a result, they were suffering the consequences of economic depression, poor crops, and attacks of foreign marauders. Family life had dissolved, and divorce was rampant. The people's religious lives were cold and empty.

Malachi gave a message of hope to a nation that knew repeated failure. After being restored to their homeland, the Jews had forgotten the one who had delivered them. We tend to make the same mistake. As soon as we overcome our pressing problems, we forget the one who helped us escape—God. Without a continued relationship with God, our hope of sustaining recovery is slim at best. We need to keep our eyes on God, the source and means for success in recovery.

Although Malachi presented a long list of the people's sins, woven throughout his words of judgment is a clear message of hope and forgiveness. As the final book of the Old Testament, Malachi forms a bridge with the New Testament with its promise of the coming of another prophet like Elijah (4:5-6). This promise was fulfilled in the coming of John the Baptist, who prepared the way for the Messiah—Jesus Christ. With God, there is always hope!

THE BOTTOM LINE

PURPOSE: To confront the people about getting back on track after they had relapsed into old patterns of sin. AUTHOR: The prophet Malachi. AUDIENCE: The people in Judah shortly after Nehemiah helped rebuild Jerusalem's walls. DATE WRITTEN: Sometime between 432 and 420 B.C. SETTING: After the Temple and Jerusalem's walls were rebuilt, the people began to fall back into sinful behavior. Malachi confronted God's people with their sins and called them to restore their relationship with God. KEY VERSE: "I am the LORD, and I do not change. That is why you descendants of Jacob are not already destroyed [for my mercy endures forever]" (3:6). KEY PLACES: Jerusalem and the Temple. KEY PEOPLE: Malachi and the priests.

RECOVERY THEMES

God Always Loves Us: God's love for the people of Jerusalem and to us cannot be explained. God knows the depth of our sins; he knows how weak we are, yet he still loves us. There is nothing that we can do to lose this love that we never deserved in the first place. God's love has the power to heal the broken places in our life; our failures, relapses, and defenses cannot stop God from wanting to heal us. This fact should give us hope for recovery, no matter how terrible our past sins and failures.

Forgiveness Is Foundational for Recovery: The way of forgiveness always leads us on the path back to a relationship with God. God wants us not only to receive his forgiveness, but also to be forgiving people, passing on to others what he has so freely given to us. If we can receive God's forgiveness and grant forgiveness to others, we will have laid a solid foundation for lasting recovery.

God Is Always with Us: God wants us to turn to him for healing and forgiveness. He was patient for hundreds of years with the people of Israel in spite of their sins. He is just as patient with us now. When God spoke through the prophets, he had a message of hope woven into his warnings of judgment. In Malachi, God continued this theme by promising a prophet like Elijah who would come and bring forgiveness and freedom to all people. God is with us even now to help us manage our unmanageable life. We can receive his help by trusting him and obeying his will for our life.

CHAPTER 1

This is the message* that the LORD gave to Israel through the prophet Malachi.*

The LORD's Love for Israel

²"I have always loved you," says the LORD.

But you retort, "Really? How have you loved us?"

And the LORD replies, "This is how I showed my love for you: I loved your ancestor Jacob, ³but I rejected his brother, Esau, and devastated his hill country. I turned Esau's inheritance into a desert for jackals."

⁴Esau's descendants in Edom may say, "We have been shattered, but we will rebuild the ruins."

But the LORD of Heaven's Armies replies, "They may try to rebuild, but I will demolish them again. Their country will be known as 'The Land of Wickedness,' and their people will be called 'The People with Whom the LORD Is Forever Angry.' ⁵When you see the destruction for yourselves, you will say, 'Truly, the LORD's greatness reaches far beyond Israel's borders!'"

Unworthy Sacrifices

⁶The LORD of Heaven's Armies says to the priests: "A son honors his father, and a servant respects his master. If I am your father and master, where are the honor and respect I deserve? You have shown contempt for my name!

"But you ask, 'How have we ever shown contempt for your name?'

⁷"You have shown contempt by offering defiled sacrifices on my altar.

"Then you ask, 'How have we defiled the sacrifices?*'

"You defile them by saying the altar of the LORD deserves no respect. ⁸When you give blind animals as sacrifices, isn't that wrong? And isn't it wrong to offer animals that are crippled and diseased? Try giving gifts like

---

1:1a Hebrew *An Oracle: The message.* 1:1b *Malachi* means "my messenger." 1:7 As in Greek version; Hebrew reads *defiled you?*

1:5 The Judeans had experienced many recent triumphs through God's power. God had allowed them to return to the Promised Land after years in exile. Then with God's help they overcame great obstacles and rebuilt the Temple and the city of Jerusalem. The people had many reasons to thank God and recognize his power of restoration. Despite the great triumphs they had experienced, however, they quickly returned to their sinful ways. After experiencing great victories with God's help, we can easily fall back into our old destructive patterns. We can be reminded regularly of what God has done and can do by listening to others' stories of deliverance and recovery. **1:7-14** God did not want empty words of repentance; he wanted the people to back up their words with appropriate action. If they were really sorry for their sins and honored God in their hearts, they would have brought their best offerings to him. Instead, they exposed their insincerity by bringing blemished sacrifices, keeping the best for themselves. If we don't back up our mental resolutions with actions, all our thoughts and resolutions pertaining to recovery will achieve nothing.

that to your governor, and see how pleased he is!" says the LORD of Heaven's Armies.

9"Go ahead, beg God to be merciful to you! But when you bring that kind of offering, why should he show you any favor at all?" asks the LORD of Heaven's Armies.

10"How I wish one of you would shut the Temple doors so that these worthless sacrifices could not be offered! I am not pleased with you," says the LORD of Heaven's Armies, "and I will not accept your offerings. 11But my name is honored* by people of other nations from morning till night. All around the world they offer* sweet incense and pure offerings in honor of my name. For my name is great among the nations," says the LORD of Heaven's Armies.

12"But you dishonor my name with your actions. By bringing contemptible food, you are saying it's all right to defile the Lord's table. 13You say, 'It's too hard to serve the LORD,' and you turn up your noses at my commands," says the LORD of Heaven's Armies. "Think of it! Animals that are stolen and crippled and sick are being presented as offerings! Should I accept from you such offerings as these?" asks the LORD.

14"Cursed is the cheat who promises to give a fine ram from his flock but then sacrifices a defective one to the Lord. For I am a great king," says the LORD of Heaven's Armies, "and my name is feared among the nations!

CHAPTER 2
A Warning to the Priests

"Listen, you priests—this command is for you! 2Listen to me and make up your minds to honor my name," says the LORD of Heaven's Armies, "or I will bring a terrible curse against you. I will curse even the blessings you receive. Indeed, I have already cursed them, because you have not taken my warning to heart. 3I will punish your descendants and splatter your faces with the manure from your festival sacrifices, and I will throw you on the manure pile. 4Then at last you will know it was I who sent you this warning so that my covenant with the Levites can continue," says the LORD of Heaven's Armies.

5"The purpose of my covenant with the Levites was to bring life and peace, and that is what I gave them. This required reverence from them, and they greatly revered me and stood in awe of my name. 6They passed on to the people the truth of the instructions they received from me. They did not lie or cheat; they walked with me, living good and righteous lives, and they turned many from lives of sin.

7"The words of a priest's lips should preserve knowledge of God, and people should go to him for instruction, for the priest is the messenger of the LORD of Heaven's Armies. 8But you priests have left God's paths. Your instructions have caused many to stumble into sin. You have corrupted the covenant I made with the Levites," says the LORD of Heaven's Armies. 9"So I have made you despised and humiliated in the eyes of all the people. For you have not obeyed me but have shown favoritism in the way you carry out my instructions."

A Call to Faithfulness

10Are we not all children of the same Father? Are we not all created by the same God? Then why do we betray each other, violating the covenant of our ancestors?

11Judah has been unfaithful, and a detestable thing has been done in Israel and in Jerusalem. The men of Judah have defiled the LORD's beloved sanctuary by marrying women who worship idols. 12May the LORD cut off from the nation of Israel* every last man who has done this and yet brings an offering to the LORD of Heaven's Armies.

13Here is another thing you do. You cover the LORD's altar with tears, weeping and groaning because he pays no attention to your offerings and doesn't accept them with

1:11a Or *will be honored.* 1:11b Or *will offer.* 2:12 Hebrew *from the tents of Jacob.* The names "Jacob" and "Israel" are often interchanged throughout the Old Testament, referring sometimes to the individual patriarch and sometimes to the nation.

2:1-9 Even Israel's religious leaders failed to show God proper respect. God singled these people out for special punishment because they used their influence to hurt rather than help the people under them. We are all in a position of influence at some level. Some of us are responsible for many; others of us influence only our family, spouse, or a few friends. No matter what our position, we can influence people for either good or evil. If we have led someone astray, our responsibility is to acknowledge our failure and do what we can to make amends. This may mean helping this person overcome a dependency that we led him or her to.

pleasure. [14]You cry out, "Why doesn't the LORD accept my worship?" I'll tell you why! Because the LORD witnessed the vows you and your wife made when you were young. But you have been unfaithful to her, though she remained your faithful partner, the wife of your marriage vows.

[15]Didn't the LORD make you one with your wife? In body and spirit you are his.* And what does he want? Godly children from your union. So guard your heart; remain loyal to the wife of your youth. [16]"For I hate divorce!"* says the LORD, the God of Israel. "To divorce your wife is to overwhelm her with cruelty,*" says the LORD of Heaven's Armies. "So guard your heart; do not be unfaithful to your wife."

[17]You have wearied the LORD with your words.

"How have we wearied him?" you ask.

You have wearied him by saying that all who do evil are good in the LORD's sight, and he is pleased with them. You have wearied him by asking, "Where is the God of justice?"

CHAPTER 3
The Coming Day of Judgment

"Look! I am sending my messenger, and he will prepare the way before me. Then the Lord you are seeking will suddenly come to his Temple. The messenger of the covenant, whom you look for so eagerly, is surely coming," says the LORD of Heaven's Armies.

[2]"But who will be able to endure it when he comes? Who will be able to stand and face him when he appears? For he will be like a blazing fire that refines metal, or like a strong soap that bleaches clothes. [3]He will sit like a refiner of silver, burning away the dross. He will purify the Levites, refining them like gold and silver, so that they may once again offer acceptable sacrifices to the LORD. [4]Then once more the LORD will accept the offerings brought to him by the people of Judah and Jerusalem, as he did in the past.

[5]"At that time I will put you on trial. I am eager to witness against all sorcerers and adulterers and liars. I will speak against those who cheat employees of their wages, who oppress widows and orphans, or who deprive the foreigners living among you of justice, for these people do not fear me," says the LORD of Heaven's Armies.

A Call to Repentance

[6]"I am the LORD, and I do not change. That is why you descendants of Jacob are not already destroyed. [7]Ever since the days of your ancestors, you have scorned my decrees and failed to obey them. Now return to me, and I will return to you," says the LORD of Heaven's Armies.

"But you ask, 'How can we return when we have never gone away?'

2:15 Or *Didn't the one LORD make us and preserve our life and breath?* or *Didn't the one LORD make her, both flesh and spirit?* The meaning of the Hebrew is uncertain. 2:16a Hebrew *For he hates divorcing.* 2:16b Hebrew *to cover one's garment with violence.*

2:14-16 Some of the Judeans had been disloyal to their wives and divorced them, putting these women in a situation where they had no means of supporting themselves. This practice was unethical and terribly cruel. God hates divorce. The family was his idea, and family commitments were intended to be binding. Many of us have experienced firsthand the pain of a broken marriage. For some of us, that is the pain driving our addiction. For others of us, our addiction was a primary cause of our family's dissolution. A broken family is a serious hindrance to recovery. We need strong relationships to hold us accountable and keep us on the right track. Part of recovery includes making amends to family members and rebuilding our damaged relationships.
2:17 God's standards cannot be ignored with impunity. The people had built walls of denial so thick that they considered their evil deeds to be good. If we refuse to recognize and respect God's standards, we will suffer severe consequences. Recovery is possible only if we recognize our need for God and the value of his program. As long as we fight it, we will face a steady decline leading to disaster. If we trust God and follow his will, we can be sure he will strengthen us as we work toward recovery.
3:3-4 Precious metals are refined by the searing heat of the furnace. Cleansing of filthy fabric requires the use of caustic soap. God often uses the fire of difficult times to ready us for his restoring work. He uses suffering to lead us to the first step in recovery—a recognition that we are powerless. If we recognize this fact and turn to God for help, he will deliver us from destruction and encourage us as we walk the upward path of recovery.
3:7 The denial of God's people was great. God confronted them directly with their sins, but they still refused to acknowledge them. Our addiction can lead us into denial that is equally powerful. While we refuse to admit our sins and failures there is no hope for recovery. We can receive help only after we have recognized that we have sinned. As long as we think we are all right, God cannot help us.

8"Should people cheat God? Yet you have cheated me!

"But you ask, 'What do you mean? When did we ever cheat you?'

"You have cheated me of the tithes and offerings due to me. 9You are under a curse, for your whole nation has been cheating me. 10Bring all the tithes into the storehouse so there will be enough food in my Temple. If you do," says the LORD of Heaven's Armies, "I will open the windows of heaven for you. I will pour out a blessing so great you won't have enough room to take it in! Try it! Put me to the test! 11Your crops will be abundant, for I will guard them from insects and disease.* Your grapes will not fall from the vine before they are ripe," says the LORD of Heaven's Armies. 12"Then all nations will call you blessed, for your land will be such a delight," says the LORD of Heaven's Armies.

13"You have said terrible things about me," says the LORD.

"But you say, 'What do you mean? What have we said against you?'

14"You have said, 'What's the use of serving God? What have we gained by obeying his commands or by trying to show the LORD of Heaven's Armies that we are sorry for our sins? 15From now on we will call the arrogant blessed. For those who do evil get rich, and those who dare God to punish them suffer no harm.'"

The LORD's Promise of Mercy

16Then those who feared the LORD spoke with each other, and the LORD listened to what they said. In his presence, a scroll of remembrance was written to record the names of those who feared him and always thought about the honor of his name.

17"They will be my people," says the LORD of Heaven's Armies. "On the day when I act in judgment, they will be my own special treasure. I will spare them as a father spares an obedient child. 18Then you will again see the difference between the righteous and the wicked, between those who serve God and those who do not."

CHAPTER 4
The Coming Day of Judgment

1*The LORD of Heaven's Armies says, "The day of judgment is coming, burning like a furnace. On that day the arrogant and the wicked will be burned up like straw. They will be consumed—roots, branches, and all.

2"But for you who fear my name, the Sun of Righteousness will rise with healing in his wings.* And you will go free, leaping with joy like calves let out to pasture. 3On the day when I act, you will tread upon the wicked as if they were dust under your feet," says the LORD of Heaven's Armies.

4"Remember to obey the Law of Moses, my servant—all the decrees and regulations that I gave him on Mount Sinai* for all Israel.

5"Look, I am sending you the prophet Elijah before the great and dreadful day of the LORD arrives. 6His preaching will turn the hearts of fathers to their children, and the hearts of children to their fathers. Otherwise I will come and strike the land with a curse."

3:11 Hebrew *from the devourer.* 4:1 Verses 4:1-6 are numbered 3:19-24 in Hebrew text. 4:2 Or *the sun of righteousness will rise with healing in its wings.* 4:4 Hebrew *Horeb,* another name for Sinai.

4:1 It is not a popular theme, but the Bible is filled with warnings about proud and sinful people. People who think they don't need God are doomed to destruction. We may react negatively to God's warnings because we don't really understand his heart. God warns us of destruction, hoping that we will change and experience deliverance and recovery. If we were left to our selfish ways, we would destroy not only our own life but also the lives of many of the people around us. When we hit bottom, we come to this hard realization. If we never realize this, however, we will never experience the rich and meaningful life that God wants for each of us.

4:2-6 Fear is never a pleasant subject, but healthy fear is the beginning of a proper view of God. As we recognize God's goodness and power, we learn to trust him and become willing to follow his program for healthy living. A proper view of God will lead to healing in our life. Someday the entire world will recognize God for who he is and will worship and obey him. Life in God's Kingdom will be characterized by wholeness and peace. Until that time, however, we can put God in charge of our life and experience his healing in our own corner of the world. As we grow to respect God as he deserves, we will joyfully follow his perfect plan for us.

NEW TESTAMENT

MATTHEW

THE BIG PICTURE

A. JESUS' INTRODUCTION AS THE
   PROMISED KING (1:1–4:11)
   1. His Family History (1:1-17)
   2. His Birth and Development
      (1:18–2:23)
   3. His Baptism and Temptation
      (3:1–4:11)
B. JESUS' KINGLY MINISTRY AND
   MESSAGE (4:12–20:34)
   1. Jesus' Early Ministry
      (4:12-25)
   2. Jesus' Sermon on the Mount
      (5:1–7:29)
   3. Jesus Performs Many Miracles
      (8:1–10:42)
   4. Jesus Teaches about His
      Kingdom (11:1–20:34)
C. JESUS, THE REJECTED
   REDEEMER (21:1–27:66)
   1. Jesus the King Enters
      Jerusalem (21:1-17)
   2. Jesus Teaches His Disciples
      (21:18–25:46)
   3. Jesus Is Rejected and
      Crucified (26:1–27:66)
D. JESUS, THE RESURRECTED
   SAVIOR (28:1-20)

Many Jews of Jesus' day harbored some form of "messianic hope." They were suffering at the hands of their Roman oppressors and clung to the belief that a Savior would emerge to deliver them. Based on the Old Testament promises of a delivering king, they eagerly awaited the Messiah's coming.

God wanted the world to accept Jesus as the Messiah and Savior. Through Jesus' ancestry, virgin birth, fulfillment of Old Testament prophecies, teachings, and miracles, God demonstrated who Jesus was. But during Jesus' earthly ministry, most people were unwilling to face the reality of who he was. Instead of looking to him as their long-awaited Messiah, they crucified him. And instead of finding deliverance, they remained in a state of oppression.

To deal with our problems, we may have focused our hopes on various "deliverers." Some of us are still looking to our addiction for deliverance from inner pain, a choice that only leads to greater suffering. Some of us hope for "freedom" through recovery programs that emphasize "self-actualization," but these programs only lead us away from our true Deliverer. The Gospel of Matthew makes it clear that our only hope for recovery lies in Jesus the Messiah.

Jesus deserves our trust and commitment as we seek recovery from our dependency and sins. When we rely on the power of forgiveness gained through his death and the hope for new life found in his resurrection, we have true hope for genuine recovery. But it is up to us to place our hope in God. We must let go of our selfish denial and make Jesus the king of our life. He alone is worthy of that honor and responsibility.

THE BOTTOM LINE

PURPOSE: To prove that Jesus was the promised Messiah and to show that God offers recovery to anyone through him. AUTHOR: Matthew, the apostle and former tax collector. AUDIENCE: Matthew wrote primarily for Jewish readers. DATE WRITTEN: Probably between A.D. 60 and 65. SETTING: Matthew emphasized the fulfillment of Old Testament prophecy in the person of Jesus Christ, making this Gospel the connecting link between Old and New Testaments. KEY VERSE: "Don't misunderstand why I have come. I did not come to abolish the law of Moses or the writings of the prophets. No, I came to accomplish their purpose" (5:17). KEY PEOPLE AND RELATIONSHIPS: Jesus in relationship with his ancestors, Mary and Joseph, John the Baptist, Jesus' disciples, and the Jewish and Roman leaders.

RECOVERY THEMES

The Power of the Resurrection: Sometimes we look for the power to recover within ourself. We don't want to depend on a power that is outside of us. But the power within us can be only as strong as we are, and we have already recognized that we are powerless. In the Gospels God demonstrated his power in many ways, but the ultimate example was in the resurrection of Jesus Christ. In his victory over sin and death, Jesus established his credentials as king and his power and authority over all evil. That's the kind of power we need in recovery. It is available to us when we turn our life over to him.

The Importance of Hope: Without hope we are miserable; hope is the driving force behind all recovery. If we had no hope, there would be no possibility of recovery. Understanding who Jesus is gives each of us a hope that can transcend even our deepest despair. In the Gospel of Matthew, we see and hear the message of hope that is available to everyone, not just to a select group of people. Jesus' resurrection forms the basis of our hope because in it God demonstrated his power over death.

The Dangers of Denial: Often people say that if they could just see a miracle, they would believe. But as we see in Matthew, many people denied the truth about Jesus despite the miracles he did for them. Our denial system is well entrenched. God can handle our doubts and fears, but cynicism and unbelief shut us off from his transforming power. Let us be like the disciples, who stood in awe on the Mount of Transfiguration and wondered what kind of man Jesus was. That kind of openness facilitates the recovery process.

God's Kingdom—A Model for Recovery: Jesus came to earth to inaugurate his Kingdom. His complete rule, however, will be realized only when he returns. His Kingdom will be made up of all those who, in faith, have turned their lives over to God and sought to follow him. We begin the recovery process by believing in him. But living as children of the King requires moment-by-moment acts of faith and trust. Recovery works the same way. Just as in this life we never fully enter into God's Kingdom, we never really finish recovery. We look forward to that day when we will see Jesus face to face and know that our recovery is complete—in him.

CHAPTER 1
The Ancestors of Jesus the Messiah

This is a record of the ancestors of Jesus the Messiah, a descendant of David and of Abraham*:

2 Abraham was the father of Isaac.
Isaac was the father of Jacob.
Jacob was the father of Judah and his brothers.
3 Judah was the father of Perez and Zerah (whose mother was Tamar).
Perez was the father of Hezron.
Hezron was the father of Ram.*
4 Ram was the father of Amminadab.
Amminadab was the father of Nahshon.
Nahshon was the father of Salmon.
5 Salmon was the father of Boaz (whose mother was Rahab).

Boaz was the father of Obed (whose mother was Ruth).
Obed was the father of Jesse.
6 Jesse was the father of King David.
David was the father of Solomon (whose mother was Bathsheba, the widow of Uriah).
7 Solomon was the father of Rehoboam.
Rehoboam was the father of Abijah.
Abijah was the father of Asa.*
8 Asa was the father of Jehoshaphat.
Jehoshaphat was the father of Jehoram.*
Jehoram was the father* of Uzziah.
9 Uzziah was the father of Jotham.
Jotham was the father of Ahaz.
Ahaz was the father of Hezekiah.

1:1 Greek *Jesus the Messiah, Son of David and son of Abraham.* 1:3 Greek *Aram,* a variant spelling of Ram; also in 1:4. See 1 Chr 2:9-10. 1:7 Greek *Asaph,* a variant spelling of Asa; also in 1:8. See 1 Chr 3:10. 1:8a Greek *Joram,* a variant spelling of Jehoram; also in 1:8b. See 1 Kgs 22:50 and note at 1 Chr 3:11. 1:8b Or *ancestor;* also in 1:11.

1:1-16 The family tree of Jesus, the sinless God-man, was far from perfect. Judah fathered Perez with his daughter-in-law Tamar, thinking she was a prostitute (1:3; see Genesis 38); Salmon married Rahab, a former prostitute in Jericho (1:5; see Joshua 6); and David had an adulterous affair with Uriah's wife, Bathsheba (1:6; see 2 Samuel 11). Throughout history God has used imperfect people to work his will. He was more concerned about the attitude of their heart than about the mistakes they made. God is never fooled or discouraged by people's past mistakes. This should give us hope that God can give us a productive future no matter how destructive our past has been. For a new start, we must admit our sins and commit our life to God.

JOSEPH & MARY

Trust can be rebuilt when it has been broken, but this does not happen automatically. Such a process takes work and commitment, especially when a relationship has been threatened by unfaithfulness. This was the challenge that Joseph and Mary faced.

   Months before their planned wedding, Mary became pregnant. Because Joseph knew that this was not his child, he assumed that she had been unfaithful to him. Though he was troubled by doubts and anger, he chose to break off the engagement as inconspicuously as possible. He was a man of integrity and mercy, so he did not want to hurt or embarrass Mary.

   God had other plans, however. He sent an angel to speak to Joseph and assured him that Mary's baby had been supernaturally conceived by the Holy Spirit. The child's name would be Jesus, and he would be the Savior of the world, the one who would offer spiritual recovery to all. Because Joseph believed God, his perspective changed. Mary and Joseph's mutual commitment to and trust in God served as the foundation upon which their trust in each other could be reestablished.

   Mary and Joseph humbly and joyfully entered a new life together. Joseph did all that was possible to protect Mary and the baby Jesus when he was born. He became a loving father who carefully taught his son the carpentry trade. Mary was an attentive and caring mother. This relationship demonstrates that it is possible to rebuild trust and repair love in relationships that were once very fragile.

STRENGTHS AND ACCOMPLISHMENTS:
- Joseph and Mary's relationship was founded on their commitment to God.
- They were open to God's will and willing to change their opinions.
- They obeyed God despite the embarrassment they would suffer.

WEAKNESSES AND MISTAKES:
- Joseph did not give Mary the benefit of the doubt early in her pregnancy.
- They failed to understand Jesus' need to spend time in his Father's house.

LESSONS FROM THEIR LIVES:
- Relationships should not be destroyed by unsubstantiated doubts.
- Trust can always be rebuilt if God is at the center of a relationship.
- Things are not always what they seem to be.
- Trust in God is foundational for trust between people.

KEY VERSES:
"Joseph . . . did not want to disgrace her publicly, so he decided to break the engagement quietly. As he considered this, an angel of the Lord appeared to him in a dream. 'Joseph, son of David,' the angel said, 'do not be afraid to take Mary as your wife. For the child within her was conceived by the Holy Spirit'" (Matthew 1:19-20).

The story of Joseph and Mary is told in the Gospels, notably in Matthew 1–2 and Luke 1–2. Mary is also mentioned in Acts 1:14.

---

[10] Hezekiah was the father of Manasseh.
Manasseh was the father of Amon.*
Amon was the father of Josiah.
[11] Josiah was the father of Jehoiachin* and his brothers (born at the time of the exile to Babylon).
[12] After the Babylonian exile:
Jehoiachin was the father of Shealtiel.
Shealtiel was the father of Zerubbabel.
[13] Zerubbabel was the father of Abiud.
Abiud was the father of Eliakim.
Eliakim was the father of Azor.
[14] Azor was the father of Zadok.
Zadok was the father of Akim.

Akim was the father of Eliud.
[15] Eliud was the father of Eleazar.
Eleazar was the father of Matthan.
Matthan was the father of Jacob.
[16] Jacob was the father of Joseph, the husband of Mary.
Mary gave birth to Jesus, who is called the Messiah.

[17]All those listed above include fourteen generations from Abraham to David, fourteen from David to the Babylonian exile, and fourteen from the Babylonian exile to the Messiah.

1:10 Greek *Amos*, a variant spelling of Amon; also in 1:10b. See 1 Chr 3:14. **1:11** Greek *Jeconiah*, a variant spelling of Jehoiachin; also in 1:12. See 2 Kgs 24:6 and note at 1 Chr 3:16.

The Birth of Jesus the Messiah

[18]This is how Jesus the Messiah was born. His mother, Mary, was engaged to be married to Joseph. But before the marriage took place, while she was still a virgin, she became pregnant through the power of the Holy Spirit. [19]Joseph, her fiancé, was a good man and did not want to disgrace her publicly, so he decided to break the engagement* quietly.

[20]As he considered this, an angel of the Lord appeared to him in a dream. "Joseph, son of David," the angel said, "do not be afraid to take Mary as your wife. For the child within her was conceived by the Holy Spirit. [21]And she will have a son, and you are to name him Jesus,* for he will save his people from their sins."

[22]All of this occurred to fulfill the Lord's message through his prophet:

[23] "Look! The virgin will conceive a child!
  She will give birth to a son,
and they will call him Immanuel,*
  which means 'God is with us.'"

[24]When Joseph woke up, he did as the angel of the Lord commanded and took Mary as his wife. [25]But he did not have sexual relations with her until her son was born. And Joseph named him Jesus.

CHAPTER 2
Visitors from the East

Jesus was born in Bethlehem in Judea, during the reign of King Herod. About that time some wise men* from eastern lands arrived in Jerusalem, asking, [2]"Where is the newborn king of the Jews? We saw his star as it rose,* and we have come to worship him."

[3]King Herod was deeply disturbed when he heard this, as was everyone in Jerusalem. [4]He called a meeting of the leading priests and teachers of religious law and asked, "Where is the Messiah supposed to be born?"

[5]"In Bethlehem in Judea," they said, "for this is what the prophet wrote:

[6] 'And you, O Bethlehem in the land
    of Judah,
  are not least among the ruling cities*
    of Judah,
for a ruler will come from you
  who will be the shepherd for my
    people Israel.'*"

[7]Then Herod called for a private meeting with the wise men, and he learned from them the time when the star first appeared. [8]Then he told them, "Go to Bethlehem and search carefully for the child. And when you find him, come back and tell me so that I can go and worship him, too!"

[9]After this interview the wise men went their way. And the star they had seen in the east guided them to Bethlehem. It went ahead of them and stopped over the place where the child was. [10]When they saw the star, they were filled with joy! [11]They entered the house and saw the child with his mother, Mary, and they bowed down and worshiped him. Then they opened their treasure chests and gave him gifts of gold, frankincense, and myrrh.

[12]When it was time to leave, they returned to their own country by another route, for God had warned them in a dream not to return to Herod.

The Escape to Egypt

[13]After the wise men were gone, an angel of the Lord appeared to Joseph in a dream. "Get

1:19 Greek *to divorce her.* **1:21** *Jesus* means "The LORD saves." **1:23** Isa 7:14; 8:8, 10 (Greek version). **2:1** Or *royal astrologers;* Greek reads *magi;* also in 2:7, 16. **2:2** Or *star in the east.* **2:6a** Greek *the rulers.* **2:6b** Mic 5:2; 2 Sam 5:2.

1:18-19 Joseph reacted to the implications of Mary's pregnancy by deciding to break their engagement. Although he was a man of principle and well intentioned, his choice was still short-sighted (see 1:20-23). Attitudes and decisions based on incomplete understandings are significant problems related to recovery. Patience, honesty, and perseverance in communication are crucial to preventing far-reaching mistakes such as broken relationships.

2:3-8, 12-18 King Herod was a tyrant who could charm and manipulate others to achieve his ends. Herod thought he could get information about the identity and whereabouts of the Messiah from the wise men by feigning interest in and a desire to worship him. Frequently, abusive or oppressive personalities will "play along" in the earliest stages of recovery, hoping to crush any resistance to their domination later. We need to be careful to avoid such people, as did the wise men and Joseph.

3:1-2 John the Baptist preached a centuries-old message: repentance. People could easily have dismissed his message by saying, "I've heard this before" or "I'll quit sinning tomorrow." But John presented the need for an immediate moral U-turn with fresh urgency: "The Kingdom of Heaven is near." Repentance requires honest self-examination. The sense of urgency in John's message is similar to the urgency for recovery. There is no time like the present to face reality and turn from our self-destructive behavior.

up! Flee to Egypt with the child and his mother," the angel said. "Stay there until I tell you to return, because Herod is going to search for the child to kill him."

¹⁴That night Joseph left for Egypt with the child and Mary, his mother, ¹⁵and they stayed there until Herod's death. This fulfilled what the Lord had spoken through the prophet: "I called my Son out of Egypt."*

¹⁶Herod was furious when he realized that the wise men had outwitted him. He sent soldiers to kill all the boys in and around Bethlehem who were two years old and under, based on the wise men's report of the star's first appearance. ¹⁷Herod's brutal action fulfilled what God had spoken through the prophet Jeremiah:

¹⁸ "A cry was heard in Ramah—
    weeping and great mourning.
Rachel weeps for her children,
    refusing to be comforted,
    for they are dead."*

The Return to Nazareth

¹⁹When Herod died, an angel of the Lord appeared in a dream to Joseph in Egypt. ²⁰"Get up!" the angel said. "Take the child and his mother back to the land of Israel, because those who were trying to kill the child are dead."

²¹So Joseph got up and returned to the land of Israel with Jesus and his mother. ²²But when he learned that the new ruler of Judea was Herod's son Archelaus, he was afraid to go there. Then, after being warned in a dream, he left for the region of Galilee. ²³So the family went and lived in a town called Nazareth. This fulfilled what the prophets had said: "He will be called a Nazarene."

CHAPTER 3
John the Baptist Prepares the Way

In those days John the Baptist came to the Judean wilderness and began preaching. His message was, ²"Repent of your sins and turn to God, for the Kingdom of Heaven is near.*"
³The prophet Isaiah was speaking about John when he said,

"He is a voice shouting in the wilderness,
'Prepare the way for the LORD's coming!
    Clear the road for him!'"*

⁴John's clothes were woven from coarse camel hair, and he wore a leather belt around his waist. For food he ate locusts and wild

2:15 Hos 11:1. 2:18 Jer 31:15. 3:2 Or *has come*, or *is coming soon*. 3:3 Isa 40:3 (Greek version).

DELAYED GRATIFICATION

READ MATTHEW 4:1-11
We may be searching for shortcuts to happiness. The road of life often takes us through painful places we would rather avoid. Some of us have gotten off the right track, lured away by hopes of faster and easier ways to "the good life."

Jesus faced this same temptation. He was destined to become the King of all the earth. The plan was that he would come to earth as a man, live a sinless life, die to pay for our sins, rise from the dead, and return to heaven to wait for those who would be his. Then he would return to earth to claim his people and his rightful place as King of kings. Satan offered Jesus a shortcut. "The devil . . . showed him all the kingdoms of the world and their glory. 'I will give it all to you,' he said, 'if you will kneel down and worship me.' 'Get out of here, Satan,' Jesus told him. 'For the Scriptures say, "You must worship the LORD your God and serve only him"'" (Matthew 4:8-10). If Jesus had fallen for this trick, he would have sinned and lost everything.

We need to beware of "shortcuts" that take us even one step outside of God's will. We are warned: "Resist the devil, and he will flee from you" (James 4:7). We can show this resistance by ignoring offers that are "too good to be true." There are really no quick fixes in life. The path of recovery can be long and hard, but many have gone before us and have been successful. As we stay on the path, taking one step at a time, we'll find the good things in life God has for us. *Turn to page 1203, Matthew 6.*

honey. [5]People from Jerusalem and from all of Judea and all over the Jordan Valley went out to see and hear John. [6]And when they confessed their sins, he baptized them in the Jordan River.

[7]But when he saw many Pharisees and Sadducees coming to watch him baptize,* he denounced them. "You brood of snakes!" he exclaimed. "Who warned you to flee God's coming wrath? [8]Prove by the way you live that you have repented of your sins and turned to God. [9]Don't just say to each other, 'We're safe, for we are descendants of Abraham.' That means nothing, for I tell you, God can create children of Abraham from these very stones. [10]Even now the ax of God's judgment is poised, ready to sever the roots of the trees. Yes, every tree that does not produce good fruit will be chopped down and thrown into the fire.

[11]"I baptize with* water those who repent of their sins and turn to God. But someone is coming soon who is greater than I am—so much greater that I'm not worthy even to be his slave and carry his sandals. He will baptize you with the Holy Spirit and with fire.* [12]He is ready to separate the chaff from the wheat with his winnowing fork. Then he will clean up the threshing area, gathering the wheat into his barn but burning the chaff with never-ending fire."

The Baptism of Jesus

[13]Then Jesus went from Galilee to the Jordan River to be baptized by John. [14]But John tried to talk him out of it. "I am the one who needs to be baptized by you," he said, "so why are you coming to me?"

[15]But Jesus said, "It should be done, for we must carry out all that God requires.*" So John agreed to baptize him.

[16]After his baptism, as Jesus came up out of the water, the heavens were opened* and he saw the Spirit of God descending like a dove and settling on him. [17]And a voice from heaven said, "This is my dearly loved Son, who brings me great joy."

CHAPTER 4
The Temptation of Jesus

Then Jesus was led by the Spirit into the wilderness to be tempted there by the devil. [2]For forty days and forty nights he fasted and became very hungry.

[3]During that time the devil* came and said to him, "If you are the Son of God, tell these stones to become loaves of bread."

[4]But Jesus told him, "No! The Scriptures say,

'People do not live by bread alone,
    but by every word that comes from the
       mouth of God.'* "

[5]Then the devil took him to the holy city, Jerusalem, to the highest point of the Temple, [6]and said, "If you are the Son of God, jump off! For the Scriptures say,

'He will order his angels to protect you.
And they will hold you up with
    their hands
  so you won't even hurt your foot
    on a stone.'*"

[7]Jesus responded, "The Scriptures also say, 'You must not test the LORD your God.'* "

3:7 Or *coming to be baptized.* 3:11a Or *in.* 3:11b Or *in the Holy Spirit and in fire.* 3:15 Or *for we must fulfill all righteousness.* 3:16 Some manuscripts read *opened to him.* 4:3 Greek *the tempter.* 4:4 Deut 8:3. 4:6 Ps 91:11-12. 4:7 Deut 6:16.

3:16-17 After Jesus' baptism, the Holy Spirit was seen in visible form, and the Father commended his Son. Jesus is thus shown to be in perfect harmony with his Father and the Holy Spirit. While those of us seeking recovery will never have perfect unity in our relationships, we can draw support from those who affirm us. As we study the Bible, God's love letter to the human race, we see numerous evidences of God's unlimited love for us. Knowing how much our heavenly Father loves us can help offset the lack of love and affirmation from our earthly relationships.

4:3-7 Satan did not doubt that Jesus was the Son of God. Satan appealed to real needs and possible doubts that were common to all humanity. Like us, Jesus needed food, security, protection, significance, and achievement. Had Jesus faltered in his humanity, Satan could have called into question Jesus' right to rule and his perfection as the unique God-man. Similarly, Satan and his forces will attack those of us pursuing recovery at our most vulnerable points. It is important that we be on guard against these attacks.

4:12-16 The way of recovery through Jesus Christ is open to everyone, not just the "religious." Jesus can heal anyone, regardless of past history, religious affiliation, or nationality. Jesus himself proved this by spending his early years in the cosmopolitan region of Galilee. The Jews in this area were not considered "good Jews" by those in Judea because of their contact with the many Gentiles who lived there. But Jesus showed God's love for them. And he continues to show his love to all who trust him, no matter who we are or how great our past sins.

⁸Next the devil took him to the peak of a very high mountain and showed him all the kingdoms of the world and their glory. ⁹"I will give it all to you," he said, "if you will kneel down and worship me."

¹⁰"Get out of here, Satan," Jesus told him. "For the Scriptures say,

'You must worship the LORD your God
   and serve only him.'* "

¹¹Then the devil went away, and angels came and took care of Jesus.

The Ministry of Jesus Begins

¹²When Jesus heard that John had been arrested, he left Judea and returned to Galilee. ¹³He went first to Nazareth, then left there and moved to Capernaum, beside the Sea of Galilee, in the region of Zebulun and Naphtali. ¹⁴This fulfilled what God said through the prophet Isaiah:

¹⁵ "In the land of Zebulun and of Naphtali,
   beside the sea, beyond the Jordan River,
   in Galilee where so many Gentiles live,
¹⁶ the people who sat in darkness
   have seen a great light.
And for those who lived in the land where
      death casts its shadow,
   a light has shined."*

¹⁷From then on Jesus began to preach, "Repent of your sins and turn to God, for the Kingdom of Heaven is near.*"

The First Disciples

¹⁸One day as Jesus was walking along the shore of the Sea of Galilee, he saw two brothers—Simon, also called Peter, and Andrew—throwing a net into the water, for they fished for a living. ¹⁹Jesus called out to them, "Come, follow me, and I will show you how to fish for people!" ²⁰And they left their nets at once and followed him.

²¹A little farther up the shore he saw two other brothers, James and John, sitting in a boat with their father, Zebedee, repairing their nets. And he called them to come, too. ²²They immediately followed him, leaving the boat and their father behind.

Crowds Follow Jesus

²³Jesus traveled throughout the region of Galilee, teaching in the synagogues and announcing the Good News about the Kingdom. And he healed every kind of disease

4:10 Deut 6:13. 4:15-16 Isa 9:1-2 (Greek version).
4:17 Or has come, or is coming soon.

STEP 9

Making Peace

BIBLE READING: Matthew 5:23-25

We made direct amends to such people wherever possible, except when to do so would injure them or others.

We all suffer brokenness in our life, in our relationship with God, and in our relationships with others. Brokenness tends to weigh us down and can easily lead us back into our addiction. Recovery isn't complete until all areas of brokenness are mended.

Jesus taught: "So if you are presenting a sacrifice at the altar in the Temple and you suddenly remember that someone has something against you, leave your sacrifice there at the altar. Go and be reconciled to that person. Then come and offer your sacrifice to God" (Matthew 5:23-24).

The apostle John wrote: "If someone says, 'I love God,' but hates a Christian brother or sister, that person is a liar; for if we don't love people we can see, how can we love God, whom we cannot see?" (1 John 4:20).

Much of recovery involves repairing the brokenness in our life. This requires that we make peace with God, with ourself, and with others whom we have alienated. Unresolved issues in relationships can keep us from being at peace with God and ourself. Once we go through the process of making amends, we must keep our mind and heart open to anyone we may have overlooked. God will often remind us of relationships that need attention. We should not delay going to those we have offended and seeking to repair the damage we have caused. *Turn to page 1325, Luke 19.*

and illness. [24]News about him spread as far as Syria, and people soon began bringing to him all who were sick. And whatever their sickness or disease, or if they were demon possessed or epileptic or paralyzed—he healed them all. [25]Large crowds followed him wherever he went—people from Galilee, the Ten Towns,* Jerusalem, from all over Judea, and from east of the Jordan River.

CHAPTER 5
The Sermon on the Mount
One day as he saw the crowds gathering, Jesus went up on the mountainside and sat down. His disciples gathered around him, [2]and he began to teach them.

The Beatitudes
[3]"God blesses those who are poor and realize their need for him,*
　　for the Kingdom of Heaven is theirs.
[4]God blesses those who mourn,
　　for they will be comforted.
[5]God blesses those who are humble,
　　for they will inherit the whole earth.
[6]God blesses those who hunger and thirst for justice,*
　　for they will be satisfied.
[7]God blesses those who are merciful,
　　for they will be shown mercy.
[8]God blesses those whose hearts are pure,
　　for they will see God.
[9]God blesses those who work for peace,
　　for they will be called the children of God.
[10]God blesses those who are persecuted for doing right,
　　for the Kingdom of Heaven is theirs.

[11]"God blesses you when people mock you and persecute you and lie about you and say all sorts of evil things against you because you are my followers. [12]Be happy about it! Be very glad! For a great reward awaits you in heaven. And remember, the ancient prophets were persecuted in the same way.

Teaching about Salt and Light
[13]"You are the salt of the earth. But what good is salt if it has lost its flavor? Can you make it salty again? It will be thrown out and trampled underfoot as worthless.

[14]"You are the light of the world—like a city on a hilltop that cannot be hidden. [15]No one lights a lamp and then puts it under a basket. Instead, a lamp is placed on a stand, where it gives light to everyone in the house. [16]In the same way, let your good deeds shine out for all to see, so that everyone will praise your heavenly Father.

Teaching about the Law
[17]"Don't misunderstand why I have come. I did not come to abolish the law of Moses or the writings of the prophets. No, I came to accomplish their purpose. [18]I tell you the truth, until heaven and earth disappear, not even the smallest detail of God's law will disappear until its purpose is achieved. [19]So if you ignore the least commandment and teach others to do the same, you will be called the least in the Kingdom of Heaven. But anyone who obeys God's laws and teaches them will be called great in the Kingdom of Heaven.

[20]"But I warn you—unless your righteousness is better than the righteousness of the teachers of religious law and the Pharisees, you will never enter the Kingdom of Heaven!

Teaching about Anger
[21]"You have heard that our ancestors were told, 'You must not murder. If you commit murder, you are subject to judgment.'* [22]But I say, if you are even angry with someone,* you are subject to judgment! If you call someone an idiot,* you are in danger of

---

4:25 Greek *Decapolis.* **5:3** Greek *poor in spirit.* **5:6** Or *for righteousness.* **5:21** Exod 20:13; Deut 5:17. **5:22a** Some manuscripts add *without cause.* **5:22b** Greek uses an Aramaic term of contempt: *If you say to your brother, 'Raca.'*

5:3-5 We cannot experience God-blessed recovery without true humility. Pride often stands in the way of our dealing with painful problems and a destructive dependency. If we cannot admit our problems and sins, there can be no real cure for us. When we humble ourself before God, we mourn and grieve over our mistakes and losses. As we do this, we will experience the wonderful comfort that only God can offer (see 2 Corinthians 1:3-5).

5:21-22, 27-29 Anger and lust are two dangerous pitfalls that threaten all of us in one way or another. Intense emotions and desires must be dealt with from the inside out. Those of us burning with rage, lust, or some other addictive behavior generally think we can control it. But we eventually and invariably lose control. Jesus shows how the patterns of anger and lust are serious and far too powerful for us to control alone. We can begin the path toward victory by admitting that we are powerless and looking to our powerful God for help.

being brought before the court. And if you curse someone,* you are in danger of the fires of hell.*

23"So if you are presenting a sacrifice* at the altar in the Temple and you suddenly remember that someone has something against you, 24leave your sacrifice there at the altar. Go and be reconciled to that person. Then come and offer your sacrifice to God.

25"When you are on the way to court with your adversary, settle your differences quickly. Otherwise, your accuser may hand you over to the judge, who will hand you over to an officer, and you will be thrown into prison. 26And if that happens, you surely won't be free again until you have paid the last penny.*

Teaching about Adultery

27"You have heard the commandment that says, 'You must not commit adultery.'* 28But I say, anyone who even looks at a woman with lust has already committed adultery with her in his heart. 29So if your eye—even your good eye*—causes you to lust, gouge it out and throw it away. It is better for you to lose one part of your body than for your whole body to be thrown into hell. 30And if your hand—even your stronger hand*—causes you to sin, cut it off and throw it away. It is better for you to lose one part of your body than for your whole body to be thrown into hell.

Teaching about Divorce

31"You have heard the law that says, 'A man can divorce his wife by merely giving her a written notice of divorce.'* 32But I say that a man who divorces his wife, unless she has been unfaithful, causes her to commit adultery. And anyone who marries a divorced woman also commits adultery.

Teaching about Vows

33"You have also heard that our ancestors were told, 'You must not break your vows; you must carry out the vows you make to the LORD.'* 34But I say, do not make any vows! Do not say, 'By heaven!' because heaven is God's throne. 35And do not say, 'By the earth!' because the earth is his footstool. And do not say, 'By Jerusalem!' for Jerusalem is the city of the great King. 36Do not even say, 'By my head!' for you can't turn one hair white or

FORGIVENESS

READ MATTHEW 6:9-15

Some of us become so focused on our personal failures in recovery that we don't deal with the pain we have suffered at the hands of others. Some of us, on the other hand, focus too much on the ways we have been mistreated and use these as excuses for our behavior. Either approach to past abuse leaves us with emotional baggage that will hinder our progress in recovery. Forgiving others is an important part of turning our will over to God.

Jesus taught his disciples: "Pray like this: Our Father in heaven, may your name be kept holy. May your Kingdom come soon. May your will be done on earth, as it is in heaven. Give us today the food we need, and forgive us our sins, as we have forgiven those who sin against us. And don't let us yield to temptation, but rescue us from the evil one. If you forgive those who sin against you, your heavenly Father will forgive you. But if you refuse to forgive others, your Father will not forgive your sins" (Matthew 6:9-15).

Being forgiven for the wrongs we have done to others does not excuse us from our actions or make our actions right. When we forgive others of the wrongs they have committed against us, we do not excuse what they have done. We simply recognize that we have been hurt unjustly and turn the matter over to God. This helps us face the truth about our own pain. It also rids us of any excuse to continue our compulsive behavior because of what has been done to us. ***Turn to page 1221, Matthew 15.***

5:22c Greek *if you say, 'You fool.'* 5:22d Greek *Gehenna;* also in 5:29, 30. 5:23 Greek *gift;* also in 5:24. 5:26 Greek *the last kodrantes* [i.e., quadrans]. 5:27 Exod 20:14; Deut 5:18. 5:29 Greek *your right eye.* 5:30 Greek *your right hand.* 5:31 Deut 24:1. 5:33 Num 30:2.

black. [37]Just say a simple, 'Yes, I will,' or 'No, I won't.' Anything beyond this is from the evil one.

Teaching about Revenge

[38]"You have heard the law that says the punishment must match the injury: 'An eye for an eye, and a tooth for a tooth.'* [39]But I say, do not resist an evil person! If someone slaps you on the right cheek, offer the other cheek also. [40]If you are sued in court and your shirt is taken from you, give your coat, too. [41]If a soldier demands that you carry his gear for a mile,* carry it two miles. [42]Give to those who ask, and don't turn away from those who want to borrow.

Teaching about Love for Enemies

[43]"You have heard the law that says, 'Love your neighbor'* and hate your enemy. [44]But I say, love your enemies!* Pray for those who persecute you! [45]In that way, you will be acting as true children of your Father in heaven. For he gives his sunlight to both the evil and the good, and he sends rain on the just and the unjust alike. [46]If you love only those who love you, what reward is there for that? Even corrupt tax collectors do that much. [47]If you are kind only to your friends,* how are you different from anyone else? Even pagans do that. [48]But you are to be perfect, even as your Father in heaven is perfect.

CHAPTER 6
Teaching about Giving to the Needy

"Watch out! Don't do your good deeds publicly, to be admired by others, for you will lose the reward from your Father in heaven. [2]When you give to someone in need, don't do as the hypocrites do—blowing trumpets in the synagogues and streets to call attention to their acts of charity! I tell you the truth, they have received all the reward they will ever get. [3]But when you give to someone in need, don't let your left hand know what your right hand is doing. [4]Give your gifts in private, and your Father, who sees everything, will reward you.

Teaching about Prayer and Fasting

[5]"When you pray, don't be like the hypocrites who love to pray publicly on street corners and in the synagogues where everyone can see them. I tell you the truth, that is all the reward they will ever get. [6]But when you pray, go away by yourself, shut the door behind you, and pray to your Father in private. Then your Father, who sees everything, will reward you.

[7]"When you pray, don't babble on and on as people of other religions do. They think their prayers are answered merely by repeating their words again and again. [8]Don't be like them, for your Father knows exactly what you need even before you ask him! [9]Pray like this:

Our Father in heaven,
   may your name be kept holy.
[10]May your Kingdom come soon.
May your will be done on earth,
   as it is in heaven.
[11]Give us today the food we
   need,*

5:38 Greek *the law that says: 'An eye for an eye and a tooth for a tooth.'* Exod 21:24; Lev 24:20; Deut 19:21. 5:41 Greek *milion* [4,854 feet or 1,478 meters]. 5:43 Lev 19:18. 5:44 Some manuscripts add *Bless those who curse you. Do good to those who hate you.* Compare Luke 6:27-28. 5:47 Greek *your brothers.* 6:11 Or *Give us today our food for the day;* or *Give us today our food for tomorrow.*

5:43-48 When we love our enemies, we can be sure that we are making progress in recovery. Loving our enemies doesn't mean we have to like them, but it does mean we must forgive them and desire what is best for them. If we harbor anger and bitterness toward others, we hurt only ourself; such emotions keep us from making progress in recovery. God loved us while we were still his enemies (see Romans 5:8); he loves us even though we are far from perfect. Recovery is not perfectionism; it is developing the ability to follow God and shape our decisions and actions according to his will for us.

6:5-8 Public prayer is open to many distortions and abuses. Some individuals use majestic-sounding, churchy jargon that impresses people, but not God. Others think that the key to answered prayer is repetition, thus reducing it almost to a chant or mantra. Both attitudes miss the mark because they assume prayer has more to do with technique than internal attitudes and realities. True heart-to-heart communication with God, whether private or public, is rewarded and will have a profound effect on our progress in recovery.

6:12, 14-15 True forgiveness is an essential part of any recovery program. We often have difficulty getting past our anger and bitterness toward those who have mistreated or abused us. However, asking God's forgiveness for our personal shortcomings and sins is hypocritical unless we are willing to forgive others. We forfeit forgiveness from God by denying forgiveness to others, to the detriment of our recovery program. This is not only selfish but also self-destructive.

READ MATTHEW 6:25-34

GOD grant me the serenity to accept the things I cannot change the courage to change the things I can and the wisdom to know the difference

A M E N

Living one day at a time is a discipline we all have to focus on when we are in recovery.

It is easy to slip back into worrying about tomorrow, dwelling on the "what ifs" and the "if onlys." Each day brings a host of things we cannot change; there will always be circumstances beyond our control. We must also face the reality of who we are—human beings confined within the slice of life we call today. It is tempting to deny the present, but escaping reality is part of the insanity of our addictive way of life.

Jesus said, "Can all your worries add a single moment to your life? . . . Don't worry about tomorrow, for tomorrow will bring its own worries. Today's trouble is enough for today" (Matthew 6:27, 34). The prophet Jeremiah said, "The faithful love of the LORD never ends! His mercies never cease. Great is his faithfulness; his mercies begin afresh each morning" (Lamentations 3:22-23). Since God's grace comes in daily doses, that's the best way to face life.

We need to ask ourself at every turn in life, Am I accepting this present moment, or am I pretending—trying to escape into the past or the future? Each day there is something to find joy in, and there is strength promised for the troubles of that day. The psalmist wrote, "This is the day the LORD has made. We will rejoice and be glad in it" (Psalm 118:24). We, too, can choose to find joy, strength, and sanity when we accept each day's realities. ***Turn to page 1219, Matthew 14.***

---

¹²and forgive us our sins,
  as we have forgiven those who sin
    against us.
¹³ And don't let us yield to temptation,*
  but rescue us from the evil one.*

¹⁴"If you forgive those who sin against you, your heavenly Father will forgive you. ¹⁵But if you refuse to forgive others, your Father will not forgive your sins.

¹⁶"And when you fast, don't make it obvious, as the hypocrites do, for they try to look miserable and disheveled so people will admire them for their fasting. I tell you the truth, that is the only reward they will ever get. ¹⁷But when you fast, comb your hair* and wash your face. ¹⁸Then no one will notice that you are fasting, except your Father, who knows what you do in private. And your Father, who sees everything, will reward you.

Teaching about Money and Possessions

¹⁹"Don't store up treasures here on earth, where moths eat them and rust destroys them, and where thieves break in and steal. ²⁰Store your treasures in heaven, where moths and rust cannot destroy, and thieves do not break in and steal. ²¹Wherever your treasure is, there the desires of your heart will also be.

²²"Your eye is a lamp that provides light for your body. When your eye is good, your whole body is filled with light. ²³But when your eye is bad, your whole body is filled with darkness. And if the light you think you have is actually darkness, how deep that darkness is!

²⁴"No one can serve two masters. For you will hate one and love the other; you will be devoted to one and despise the other. You cannot serve both God and money.

6:13a Or *And keep us from being tested.* 6:13b Or *from evil.* Some manuscripts add *For yours is the kingdom and the power and the glory forever. Amen.* 6:17 Greek *anoint your head.*

25"That is why I tell you not to worry about everyday life—whether you have enough food and drink, or enough clothes to wear. Isn't life more than food, and your body more than clothing? 26Look at the birds. They don't plant or harvest or store food in barns, for your heavenly Father feeds them. And aren't you far more valuable to him than they are? 27Can all your worries add a single moment to your life?

28"And why worry about your clothing? Look at the lilies of the field and how they grow. They don't work or make their clothing, 29yet Solomon in all his glory was not dressed as beautifully as they are. 30And if God cares so wonderfully for wildflowers that are here today and thrown into the fire tomorrow, he will certainly care for you. Why do you have so little faith?

31"So don't worry about these things, saying, 'What will we eat? What will we drink? What will we wear?' 32These things dominate the thoughts of unbelievers, but your heavenly Father already knows all your needs. 33Seek the Kingdom of God* above all else, and live righteously, and he will give you everything you need.

34"So don't worry about tomorrow, for tomorrow will bring its own worries. Today's trouble is enough for today.

CHAPTER 7
Do Not Judge Others
"Do not judge others, and you will not be judged. 2For you will be treated as you treat others.* The standard you use in judging is the standard by which you will be judged.*

3"And why worry about a speck in your friend's eye* when you have a log in your own? 4How can you think of saying to your friend,* 'Let me help you get rid of that speck in your eye,' when you can't see past the log in your own eye? 5Hypocrite! First get rid of the log in your own eye; then you will see well enough to deal with the speck in your friend's eye.

6"Don't waste what is holy on people who are unholy.* Don't throw your pearls to pigs! They will trample the pearls, then turn and attack you.

Effective Prayer
7"Keep on asking, and you will receive what you ask for. Keep on seeking, and you will find. Keep on knocking, and the door will be opened to you. 8For everyone who asks, receives. Everyone who seeks, finds. And to everyone who knocks, the door will be opened.

9"You parents—if your children ask for a loaf of bread, do you give them a stone instead? 10Or if they ask for a fish, do you give them a snake? Of course not! 11So if you sinful people know how to give good gifts to your children, how much more will your heavenly Father give good gifts to those who ask him.

The Golden Rule
12"Do to others whatever you would like them to do to you. This is the essence of all that is taught in the law and the prophets.

The Narrow Gate
13"You can enter God's Kingdom only through the narrow gate. The highway to

---

6:33 Some manuscripts do not include *of God.* 7:2a Or *For God will judge you as you judge others.* 7:2b Or *The measure you give will be the measure you get back.* 7:3 Greek *your brother's eye;* also in 7:5. 7:4 Greek *your brother.* 7:6 Greek *Don't give the sacred to dogs.*

7:7-11 Prayer can teach us perseverance. These three commands ("keep on asking," "keep on seeking," and "keep on knocking") are positive habits we should develop. We will persist in prayer with realistic hopes once we fully appreciate the kind of father who hears our prayers. Many of us in recovery have suffered because of dysfunctional, even abusive, parents who often gave us "stones" and "snakes." Thus, often we must completely rethink our concept of God as a father who gives good gifts to his children. As we discover God's loving character, we will be encouraged to ask him for the gift of recovery.

7:15-20 The good fruit that our life should be producing is "love, joy, peace, patience, kindness, goodness, faithfulness, gentleness, and self-control" (Galatians 5:22-23). In the throes of an addiction, however, we are without peace and totally out of control. If we take an honest moral inventory, we will admit that the fruits of our life are not those that God intends for us. Once we admit our failures, we can enter recovery and work to produce the fruit that God wants for us.

8:2-4 Jesus' healing of the leper demonstrated his ability to bring about instant physical recovery in response to faith. Jesus then directed the grateful leper to be examined immediately, calling him to display his deliverance and faith publicly. Emotional and spiritual recovery generally involves a longer process than was the leper's physical healing. Yet both timetables for recovery have the same starting and ending points. The same Jesus who healed instantly is also the originator and perfecter of the recovery process (see Hebrews 12:2).

hell* is broad, and its gate is wide for the many who choose that way. ¹⁴But the gateway to life is very narrow and the road is difficult, and only a few ever find it.

The Tree and Its Fruit

¹⁵"Beware of false prophets who come disguised as harmless sheep but are really vicious wolves. ¹⁶You can identify them by their fruit, that is, by the way they act. Can you pick grapes from thornbushes, or figs from thistles? ¹⁷A good tree produces good fruit, and a bad tree produces bad fruit. ¹⁸A good tree can't produce bad fruit, and a bad tree can't produce good fruit. ¹⁹So every tree that does not produce good fruit is chopped down and thrown into the fire. ²⁰Yes, just as you can identify a tree by its fruit, so you can identify people by their actions.

True Disciples

²¹"Not everyone who calls out to me, 'Lord! Lord!' will enter the Kingdom of Heaven. Only those who actually do the will of my Father in heaven will enter. ²²On judgment day many will say to me, 'Lord! Lord! We prophesied in your name and cast out demons in your name and performed many miracles in your name.' ²³But I will reply, 'I never knew you. Get away from me, you who break God's laws.'

Building on a Solid Foundation

²⁴"Anyone who listens to my teaching and follows it is wise, like a person who builds a house on solid rock. ²⁵Though the rain comes in torrents and the floodwaters rise and the winds beat against that house, it won't collapse because it is built on bedrock. ²⁶But anyone who hears my teaching and doesn't obey it is foolish, like a person who builds a house on sand. ²⁷When the rains and floods come and the winds beat against that house, it will collapse with a mighty crash."

²⁸When Jesus had finished saying these things, the crowds were amazed at his teaching, ²⁹for he taught with real authority—quite unlike their teachers of religious law.

CHAPTER 8
Jesus Heals a Man with Leprosy

Large crowds followed Jesus as he came down the mountainside. ²Suddenly, a man with leprosy approached him and knelt before him. "Lord," the man said, "if you are willing, you can heal me and make me clean."

7:13 Greek *The road that leads to destruction.*

STEP 4

Finger Pointing

BIBLE READING: Matthew 7:1-5

We made a searching and fearless moral inventory of ourselves.

There have probably been times when we have ignored our own sins and problems and pointed a finger at someone else. We may be out of touch with our internal affairs because we are still blaming others for our moral choices. Or perhaps we avoid self-examination by making moral inventories of the people around us.

When God asked Adam and Eve about their sin, they each pointed a finger at someone else. "'Have you eaten from the tree whose fruit I commanded you not to eat?' The man replied, 'It was the woman you gave me who gave me the fruit, and I ate it.' Then the LORD God asked the woman, 'What have you done?' 'The serpent deceived me,' she replied" (Genesis 3:11-13). It seems to be human nature to blame others as our first line of defense.

We also may avoid our own problems by evaluating and criticizing others. Jesus tells us, "And why worry about a speck in your friend's eye when you have a log in your own? . . . Hypocrite! First get rid of the log in your own eye; then you will see well enough to deal with the speck in your friend's eye" (Matthew 7:3, 5).

While doing this step, we must constantly remember that this is a season of *self*-examination. We must guard against blaming and examining the lives of others. There will be time in the future for helping others after we have taken responsibility for our own life. *Turn to page 1489, 2 Corinthians 7.*

[3]Jesus reached out and touched him. "I am willing," he said. "Be healed!" And instantly the leprosy disappeared. [4]Then Jesus said to him, "Don't tell anyone about this. Instead, go to the priest and let him examine you. Take along the offering required in the law of Moses for those who have been healed of leprosy.* This will be a public testimony that you have been cleansed."

The Faith of a Roman Officer

[5]When Jesus returned to Capernaum, a Roman officer* came and pleaded with him, [6]"Lord, my young servant* lies in bed, paralyzed and in terrible pain."

[7]Jesus said, "I will come and heal him."

[8]But the officer said, "Lord, I am not worthy to have you come into my home. Just say the word from where you are, and my servant will be healed. [9]I know this because I am under the authority of my superior officers, and I have authority over my soldiers. I only need to say, 'Go,' and they go, or 'Come,' and they come. And if I say to my slaves, 'Do this,' they do it."

[10]When Jesus heard this, he was amazed. Turning to those who were following him, he said, "I tell you the truth, I haven't seen faith like this in all Israel! [11]And I tell you this, that many Gentiles will come from all over the world—from east and west—and sit down with Abraham, Isaac, and Jacob at the feast in the Kingdom of Heaven. [12]But many Israelites—those for whom the Kingdom was prepared—will be thrown into outer darkness, where there will be weeping and gnashing of teeth."

[13]Then Jesus said to the Roman officer, "Go back home. Because you believed, it has happened." And the young servant was healed that same hour.

Jesus Heals Many People

[14]When Jesus arrived at Peter's house, Peter's mother-in-law was sick in bed with a high fever. [15]But when Jesus touched her hand, the fever left her. Then she got up and prepared a meal for him.

[16]That evening many demon-possessed people were brought to Jesus. He cast out the evil spirits with a simple command, and he healed all the sick. [17]This fulfilled the word of the Lord through the prophet Isaiah, who said,

"He took our sicknesses
and removed our diseases."*

The Cost of Following Jesus

[18]When Jesus saw the crowd around him, he instructed his disciples to cross to the other side of the lake.

[19]Then one of the teachers of religious law said to him, "Teacher, I will follow you wherever you go."

[20]But Jesus replied, "Foxes have dens to live in, and birds have nests, but the Son of Man* has no place even to lay his head."

[21]Another of his disciples said, "Lord, first let me return home and bury my father."

[22]But Jesus told him, "Follow me now. Let the spiritually dead bury their own dead.*"

Jesus Calms the Storm

[23]Then Jesus got into the boat and started across the lake with his disciples. [24]Suddenly, a fierce storm struck the lake, with waves breaking into the boat. But Jesus was sleeping. [25]The disciples went and woke him up, shouting, "Lord, save us! We're going to drown!"

[26]Jesus responded, "Why are you afraid? You have so little faith!" Then he got up and rebuked the wind and waves, and suddenly there was a great calm.

[27]The disciples were amazed. "Who is this man?" they asked. "Even the winds and waves obey him!"

8:4 See Lev 14:2-32. **8:5** Greek *a centurion;* similarly in 8:8, 13. **8:6** Or *child;* also in 8:13. **8:17** Isa 53:4. **8:20** "Son of Man" is a title Jesus used for himself. **8:22** Greek *Let the dead bury their own dead.*

8:5-13 The healing of the Roman officer's servant has much to teach all of us who are in recovery. The officer understood and humbly admitted his need, believing that Jesus could heal his young servant even from a distance. Jesus marveled because such faith was rare, even among God's chosen people, the Jews. We see here that Jesus came to bring deliverance to all people, Jew or Gentile, man or woman, rich or poor, religious or nonreligious. With God's help we can all have hope for recovery, no matter who we are or what we have done.

8:23-32 In this passage Jesus exhibited power over both the weather and the demonic realm. In both cases his disciples learned about faith in the incredible power of God. Since Jesus has the ability to calm a mighty storm and rid people of demonic influence, he can certainly empower us in the recovery process. We can experience God's power by first recognizing how powerless we are and then by giving our life to him.

Jesus Heals Two Demon-Possessed Men

²⁸When Jesus arrived on the other side of the lake, in the region of the Gadarenes,* two men who were possessed by demons met him. They lived in a cemetery and were so violent that no one could go through that area.

²⁹They began screaming at him, "Why are you interfering with us, Son of God? Have you come here to torture us before God's appointed time?"

³⁰There happened to be a large herd of pigs feeding in the distance. ³¹So the demons begged, "If you cast us out, send us into that herd of pigs."

³²"All right, go!" Jesus commanded them. So the demons came out of the men and entered the pigs, and the whole herd plunged down the steep hillside into the lake and drowned in the water.

³³The herdsmen fled to the nearby town, telling everyone what happened to the demon-possessed men. ³⁴Then the entire town came out to meet Jesus, but they begged him to go away and leave them alone.

CHAPTER 9

Jesus Heals a Paralyzed Man

Jesus climbed into a boat and went back across the lake to his own town. ²Some people brought to him a paralyzed man on a mat. Seeing their faith, Jesus said to the paralyzed man, "Be encouraged, my child! Your sins are forgiven."

³But some of the teachers of religious law said to themselves, "That's blasphemy! Does he think he's God?"

⁴Jesus knew* what they were thinking, so he asked them, "Why do you have such evil thoughts in your hearts? ⁵Is it easier to say 'Your sins are forgiven,' or 'Stand up and walk'? ⁶So I will prove to you that the Son of Man* has the authority on earth to forgive sins." Then Jesus turned to the paralyzed man and said, "Stand up, pick up your mat, and go home!"

⁷And the man jumped up and went home! ⁸Fear swept through the crowd as they saw this happen. And they praised God for sending a man with such great authority.*

Jesus Calls Matthew

⁹As Jesus was walking along, he saw a man named Matthew sitting at his tax collector's booth. "Follow me and be my disciple," Jesus said to him. So Matthew got up and followed him.

¹⁰Later, Matthew invited Jesus and his disciples to his home as dinner guests, along with many tax collectors and other disreputable sinners. ¹¹But when the Pharisees saw this, they asked his disciples, "Why does your teacher eat with such scum?*"

¹²When Jesus heard this, he said, "Healthy people don't need a doctor—sick people do." ¹³Then he added, "Now go and learn the meaning of this Scripture: 'I want you to show mercy, not offer sacrifices.'* For I have come to call not those who think they are righteous, but those who know they are sinners."

A Discussion about Fasting

¹⁴One day the disciples of John the Baptist came to Jesus and asked him, "Why don't your disciples fast* like we do and the Pharisees do?"

¹⁵Jesus replied, "Do wedding guests mourn while celebrating with the groom? Of course not. But someday the groom will be taken away from them, and then they will fast.

¹⁶"Besides, who would patch old clothing

8:28 Other manuscripts read *Gerasenes;* still others read *Gergesenes.* Compare Mark 5:1; Luke 8:26. 9:4 Some manuscripts read *saw.* 9:6 "Son of Man" is a title Jesus used for himself. 9:8 Greek *for giving such authority to human beings.* 9:11 Greek *with tax collectors and sinners?* 9:13 Hos 6:6 (Greek version). 9:14 Some manuscripts read *fast often.*

9:1-7 The Jewish religious leaders thought it blasphemous that Jesus claimed to forgive sins, but they considered it just as impossible for him to heal the paralyzed man. By doing the impossible—healing the paralytic—Jesus made it clear to his critics that he also had the power to forgive sins. Implicit in his actions was his claim to deity, because only God can forgive sins. Knowing this truth should give us the courage to turn to Jesus for help. As God's own Son, Jesus has the power to offer forgiveness and recovery to all who trust in him.

9:14-17 Using two analogies, Jesus contrasted religious ritualism that cannot save with true spiritual power that can transform a life. The unshrunk cloth and new wine represent the power for recovery that Jesus offers. The old garment and wineskins refer to the ritualistic lifestyles and outward appearances characteristic of many Jews in Jesus' day. Jesus could just as easily be speaking directly to us who need recovery today. Small, external adjustments will not bring relief from our addiction. We need the newness of full recovery in Jesus Christ.

with new cloth? For the new patch would shrink and rip away from the old cloth, leaving an even bigger tear than before.

¹⁷"And no one puts new wine into old wineskins. For the old skins would burst from the pressure, spilling the wine and ruining the skins. New wine is stored in new wineskins so that both are preserved."

Jesus Heals in Response to Faith

¹⁸As Jesus was saying this, the leader of a synagogue came and knelt before him. "My daughter has just died," he said, "but you can bring her back to life again if you just come and lay your hand on her."

¹⁹So Jesus and his disciples got up and went with him. ²⁰Just then a woman who had suffered for twelve years with constant bleeding came up behind him. She touched the fringe of his robe, ²¹for she thought, "If I can just touch his robe, I will be healed."

²²Jesus turned around, and when he saw her he said, "Daughter, be encouraged! Your faith has made you well." And the woman was healed at that moment.

²³When Jesus arrived at the official's home, he saw the noisy crowd and heard the funeral music. ²⁴"Get out!" he told them. "The girl isn't dead; she's only asleep." But the crowd laughed at him. ²⁵After the crowd was put outside, however, Jesus went in and took the girl by the hand, and she stood up! ²⁶The report of this miracle swept through the entire countryside.

Jesus Heals the Blind

²⁷After Jesus left the girl's home, two blind men followed along behind him, shouting, "Son of David, have mercy on us!"

²⁸They went right into the house where he was staying, and Jesus asked them, "Do you believe I can make you see?"

"Yes, Lord," they told him, "we do."

²⁹Then he touched their eyes and said, "Because of your faith, it will happen." ³⁰Then their eyes were opened, and they could see! Jesus sternly warned them, "Don't tell anyone about this." ³¹But instead, they went out and spread his fame all over the region.

³²When they left, a demon-possessed man who couldn't speak was brought to Jesus. ³³So Jesus cast out the demon, and then the man began to speak. The crowds were amazed. "Nothing like this has ever happened in Israel!" they exclaimed.

³⁴But the Pharisees said, "He can cast out demons because he is empowered by the prince of demons."

The Need for Workers

³⁵Jesus traveled through all the towns and villages of that area, teaching in the synagogues and announcing the Good News about the Kingdom. And he healed every kind of disease and illness. ³⁶When he saw the crowds, he had compassion on them because they were confused and helpless, like sheep without a shepherd. ³⁷He said to his disciples, "The harvest is great, but the workers are few. ³⁸So pray to the Lord who is in charge of the harvest; ask him to send more workers into his fields."

CHAPTER 10
Jesus Sends Out the Twelve Apostles

Jesus called his twelve disciples together and gave them authority to cast out evil* spirits and to heal every kind of disease and illness. ²Here are the names of the twelve apostles:

first, Simon (also called Peter),
then Andrew (Peter's brother),
James (son of Zebedee),
John (James's brother),
³ Philip,
Bartholomew,
Thomas,
Matthew (the tax collector),
James (son of Alphaeus),
Thaddaeus,*
⁴ Simon (the zealot*),
Judas Iscariot (who later betrayed him).

⁵Jesus sent out the twelve apostles with these instructions: "Don't go to the Gentiles or the Samaritans, ⁶but only to the people of

10:1 Greek *unclean.* 10:3 Other manuscripts read *Lebbaeus;* still others read *Lebbaeus who is called Thaddaeus.*
10:4 Greek *the Cananean,* an Aramaic term for Jewish nationalists.

9:18-33 More miracles prove that Jesus is the Messiah and the source of recovery for all kinds of hurting people. Jesus restored life to a dead girl and stopped a woman's chronic hemorrhage. Then he healed two blind men and a demon-possessed man who was unable to speak. Jesus showed his power to help people who were living, or even dying, under the power of personal demons. No matter what the issue, recognizing our need and turning to God in faith are the first steps to recovery.

MATTHEW & SIMON THE ZEALOT

It has been said that opposites attract; just as often, however, opposites repel. The differences between people often result in complementary relationships in which the strengths of one make up for the weaknesses of the other. But in some cases the differences lead only to continual strife. Marriage relationships are often comprised of two opposites, resulting in either great teamwork or terrible conflict.

Two of Jesus' twelve disciples, Matthew and Simon the Zealot, were opposites. Matthew was a Jew who worked for the Roman government as a tax collector. People of this occupation were known for their corruption. They grew rich by extorting excess taxes from their own oppressed people. These tax collectors were nonreligious and, needless to say, were hated and despised as traitors by their countrymen.

As indicated by his title "the Zealot," Simon, at the very least, was a religious fanatic. This term was sometimes used to label people with intense zeal for the law of Moses and Jewish religious tradition. It could also identify someone who belonged to the religious-political party known as the Zealots, which wanted to overthrow the Roman government. If Simon was a member, he would have been strongly opposed to the Roman occupation of Judea, while Matthew was an integral part of its government. Clearly, these men were opposites.

Both Matthew and Simon met Jesus and realized the emptiness and futility of their former pursuits. Both gave up what they had been to follow Christ in faith and experience new life—life that developed from the inside out. Both were transformed by the God of recovery into people who could love and accept those who were very different from themselves.

STRENGTHS AND ACCOMPLISHMENTS:
- Matthew and Simon both apparently were capable men.
- Both men were willing to recognize that they needed to change.
- Both men made Jesus the center of their life, enabling them to work with people quite different from themselves.

WEAKNESSES AND MISTAKES:
- Both had been driven by shortsighted motivations before following Jesus.
- As a tax collector, Matthew probably used his position to extort money from the poor.
- As a Zealot, Simon probably condoned the use of violence for achieving his political ends.

LESSONS FROM THEIR LIVES:
- Financial success cannot replace the need for a relationship with God.
- If Christ is at the center of a relationship, no difference is too great to overcome.
- Differences can be used to strengthen relationships and should not be used as an excuse to destroy them.

KEY VERSES:
"[The disciples] went to the upstairs room of the house where they were staying. Here are the names of those who were present: . . . Matthew, . . . Simon (the Zealot)" (Acts 1:13).

The story of the apostles Matthew and Simon the Zealot is found in the Gospels. Both men are also mentioned in Acts 1:13.

Israel—God's lost sheep. [7]Go and announce to them that the Kingdom of Heaven is near.* [8]Heal the sick, raise the dead, cure those with leprosy, and cast out demons. Give as freely as you have received!

[9]"Don't take any money in your money belts—no gold, silver, or even copper coins. [10]Don't carry a traveler's bag with a change of clothes and sandals or even a walking stick. Don't hesitate to accept hospitality, because those who work deserve to be fed.

[11]"Whenever you enter a city or village, search for a worthy person and stay in his home until you leave town. [12]When you enter the home, give it your blessing. [13]If it turns out to be a worthy home, let your blessing stand; if it is not, take back the blessing. [14]If any household or town refuses to welcome you or listen to your message, shake its dust from your feet as you leave. [15]I tell you the truth, the wicked cities of Sodom and Gomorrah will be better off than such a town on the judgment day.

[16]"Look, I am sending you out as sheep among wolves. So be as shrewd as snakes and harmless as doves. [17]But beware! For you

10:7 Or *has come,* or *is coming soon.*

will be handed over to the courts and will be flogged with whips in the synagogues. [18]You will stand trial before governors and kings because you are my followers. But this will be your opportunity to tell the rulers and other unbelievers about me.* [19]When you are arrested, don't worry about how to respond or what to say. God will give you the right words at the right time. [20]For it is not you who will be speaking—it will be the Spirit of your Father speaking through you.

[21]"A brother will betray his brother to death, a father will betray his own child, and children will rebel against their parents and cause them to be killed. [22]And all nations will hate you because you are my followers.* But everyone who endures to the end will be saved. [23]When you are persecuted in one town, flee to the next. I tell you the truth, the Son of Man* will return before you have reached all the towns of Israel.

[24]"Students* are not greater than their teacher, and slaves are not greater than their master. [25]Students are to be like their teacher, and slaves are to be like their master. And since I, the master of the household, have been called the prince of demons,* the members of my household will be called by even worse names!

[26]"But don't be afraid of those who threaten you. For the time is coming when everything that is covered will be revealed, and all that is secret will be made known to all. [27]What I tell you now in the darkness, shout abroad when daybreak comes. What I whisper in your ear, shout from the housetops for all to hear!

[28]"Don't be afraid of those who want to kill your body; they cannot touch your soul. Fear only God, who can destroy both soul and body in hell.* [29]What is the price of two sparrows—one copper coin*? But not a single sparrow can fall to the ground without your Father knowing it. [30]And the very hairs on your head are all numbered. [31]So don't be afraid; you are more valuable to God than a whole flock of sparrows.

[32]"Everyone who acknowledges me publicly here on earth, I will also acknowledge before my Father in heaven. [33]But everyone who denies me here on earth, I will also deny before my Father in heaven.

[34]"Don't imagine that I came to bring peace to the earth! I came not to bring peace, but a sword.

[35] 'I have come to set a man against his
father,
a daughter against her mother,
and a daughter-in-law against her
mother-in-law.
[36]   Your enemies will be right in your own
household!'*

[37]"If you love your father or mother more than you love me, you are not worthy of being mine; or if you love your son or daughter more than me, you are not worthy of being mine. [38]If you refuse to take up your cross and follow me, you are not worthy of being mine. [39]If you cling to your life, you will lose it; but if you give up your life for me, you will find it.

[40]"Anyone who receives you receives me, and anyone who receives me receives the Father who sent me. [41]If you receive a prophet

10:18 Or *But this will be your testimony against the rulers and other unbelievers.* 10:22 Greek *on account of my name.* 10:23 "Son of Man" is a title Jesus used for himself. 10:24 Or *Disciples.* 10:25 Greek *Beelzeboul;* other manuscripts read *Beezeboul;* Latin version reads *Beelzebub.* 10:28 Greek *Gehenna.* 10:29 Greek *one assarion* [i.e., one "as," a Roman coin equal to 1/16 of a denarius]. 10:35-36 Mic 7:6.

10:16-26 Those of us living for God and pursuing recovery may feel like sheep in the presence of wolves. But when wisdom and honesty define our behavior and relationships, we can face the inevitable misunderstandings and persecutions. Jesus suffered much at the hands of godless men, and those who are committed to him often receive similar treatment. If we persevere in following God's will for us, we will receive a great reward in heaven (see 5:11-12).

10:39 The only way to find life (and get control of it) is to submit to God through Jesus Christ. Living for self, we become a slave to material success, work, alcohol, illicit sex, or any number of other destructive behaviors. We have lost control of our life and are in trouble. By turning to Jesus, we allow him to cleanse us of our addiction and show us the way to real life—a life free of any destructive dependency. As we obey God, we will find meaning in our present life and eternal peace with God.

11:2-6 Doubt is a troubling reality for those of us in recovery. We doubt ourself, and we doubt others. Even John the Baptist doubted that Jesus was the promised Messiah, the one who would come to offer physical and spiritual healing to his people. Jesus answered John's doubts by pointing to his miraculous healings and restorations. Such an impressive résumé should also convince us that Jesus is willing and able to meet even our greatest needs for recovery and restoration.

as one who speaks for God,* you will be given the same reward as a prophet. And if you receive righteous people because of their righteousness, you will be given a reward like theirs. ⁴²And if you give even a cup of cold water to one of the least of my followers, you will surely be rewarded."

CHAPTER 11
Jesus and John the Baptist
When Jesus had finished giving these instructions to his twelve disciples, he went out to teach and preach in towns throughout the region.

²John the Baptist, who was in prison, heard about all the things the Messiah was doing. So he sent his disciples to ask Jesus, ³"Are you the Messiah we've been expecting,* or should we keep looking for someone else?"

⁴Jesus told them, "Go back to John and tell him what you have heard and seen—⁵the blind see, the lame walk, the lepers are cured, the deaf hear, the dead are raised to life, and the Good News is being preached to the poor. ⁶And tell him, 'God blesses those who do not turn away because of me.*' "

⁷As John's disciples were leaving, Jesus began talking about him to the crowds. "What kind of man did you go into the wilderness to see? Was he a weak reed, swayed by every breath of wind? ⁸Or were you expecting to see a man dressed in expensive clothes? No, people with expensive clothes live in palaces. ⁹Were you looking for a prophet? Yes, and he is more than a prophet. ¹⁰John is the man to whom the Scriptures refer when they say,

'Look, I am sending my messenger ahead of you,
and he will prepare your way before you.'*

¹¹"I tell you the truth, of all who have ever lived, none is greater than John the Baptist. Yet even the least person in the Kingdom of Heaven is greater than he is! ¹²And from the time John the Baptist began preaching until now, the Kingdom of Heaven has been forcefully advancing,* and violent people are attacking it. ¹³For before John came, all the prophets and the law of Moses looked forward to this present time. ¹⁴And if you are willing to accept what I say, he is Elijah, the one the prophets said would come.* ¹⁵Anyone

---

10:41 Greek *receive a prophet in the name of a prophet.*
11:3 Greek *Are you the one who is coming?* 11:6 Or *who are not offended by me.* 11:10 Mal 3:1. 11:12 Or *the Kingdom of Heaven has suffered from violence.* 11:14 See Mal 4:5.

STEP 3

Submission and Rest
BIBLE READING: Matthew 11:27-30
We made a decision to turn our wills and our lives over to the care of God.
When our burdens become heavy and we find that our way of life is leading us toward death, we may finally be willing to let someone else do the driving. We may have worked hard at getting our life on the right track but still feel as if we always end up on dead-end streets.

Proverbs tells us, "There is a path before each person that seems right, but it ends in death" (Proverbs 14:12). When we began our addictive behavior, we were probably seeking pleasure or looking for a way to overcome our pain. The way seemed right at first, but it wasn't long before it became clear that we were on the wrong track. By then we were unable to turn around on our own. Jesus said, "Come to me, all of you who are weary and carry heavy burdens, and I will give you rest. Take my yoke upon you. Let me teach you, because I am humble and gentle at heart, and you will find rest for your souls" (Matthew 11:28-29).

Taking on a yoke implies being united to another in order to work together. Those who are yoked together must go in the same direction; by doing so, their work is made considerably easier. When we finally decide to submit our life and our will to God's direction, our burdens will become manageable. When we let him do the driving, we will "find rest" for our soul. He knows the way and has the strength to turn us around and get us on the road toward recovery. *Turn to page 1409, Acts 17.*

with ears to hear should listen and understand!

16"To what can I compare this generation? It is like children playing a game in the public square. They complain to their friends,

17 'We played wedding songs,
and you didn't dance,
so we played funeral songs,
and you didn't mourn.'

18For John didn't spend his time eating and drinking, and you say, 'He's possessed by a demon.' 19The Son of Man,* on the other hand, feasts and drinks, and you say, 'He's a glutton and a drunkard, and a friend of tax collectors and other sinners!' But wisdom is shown to be right by its results."

Judgment for the Unbelievers

20Then Jesus began to denounce the towns where he had done so many of his miracles, because they hadn't repented of their sins and turned to God. 21"What sorrow awaits you, Korazin and Bethsaida! For if the miracles I did in you had been done in wicked Tyre and Sidon, their people would have repented of their sins long ago, clothing themselves in burlap and throwing ashes on their heads to show their remorse. 22I tell you, Tyre and Sidon will be better off on judgment day than you.

23"And you people of Capernaum, will you be honored in heaven? No, you will go down to the place of the dead.* For if the miracles I did for you had been done in wicked Sodom, it would still be here today. 24I tell you, even Sodom will be better off on judgment day than you."

Jesus' Prayer of Thanksgiving

25At that time Jesus prayed this prayer: "O Father, Lord of heaven and earth, thank you for hiding these things from those who think themselves wise and clever, and for revealing them to the childlike. 26Yes, Father, it pleased you to do it this way!

27"My Father has entrusted everything to me. No one truly knows the Son except the Father, and no one truly knows the Father except the Son and those to whom the Son chooses to reveal him."

28Then Jesus said, "Come to me, all of you who are weary and carry heavy burdens, and I will give you rest. 29Take my yoke upon you. Let me teach you, because I am humble and gentle at heart, and you will find rest for your souls. 30For my yoke is easy to bear, and the burden I give you is light."

CHAPTER 12
A Discussion about the Sabbath

At about that time Jesus was walking through some grainfields on the Sabbath. His disciples were hungry, so they began breaking off some heads of grain and eating them. 2But some Pharisees saw them do it and protested, "Look, your disciples are breaking the law by harvesting grain on the Sabbath."

3Jesus said to them, "Haven't you read in the Scriptures what David did when he and his companions were hungry? 4He went into the house of God, and he and his companions broke the law by eating the sacred loaves of bread that only the priests are allowed to eat. 5And haven't you read in the law of Moses that the priests on duty in the Temple may work on the Sabbath? 6I tell you, there is one here who is even greater than the Temple! 7But you would not have condemned my innocent disciples if you knew the meaning of this Scripture: 'I want you to show mercy, not offer sacrifices.'* 8For the Son of Man* is Lord, even over the Sabbath!"

11:19 "Son of Man" is a title Jesus used for himself. 11:23 Greek *to Hades.* 12:7 Hos 6:6 (Greek version). 12:8 "Son of Man" is a title Jesus used for himself.

11:16-19 When we are in denial, we tend to resist those who challenge our comfort zones. We find excuses not to accept the good advice of others no matter what they do or say. We become cynical and try to justify our inconsistencies. The message of recovery is too joyful and hopeful for some, or it is too realistic and direct for others. Recovery is too structured for those of us who are used to doing our own thing; it is too liberating for those of us from a legalistic background. But such perspectives are only blind excuses that keep us from facing our need for recovery.

12:1-8 God's standards were intended for our good—to mercifully meet his people's needs. But legalism abuses his laws. Following God's laws to the letter can easily violate the very reasons that God gave them in the first place. God gave the Sabbath laws to protect his people from overwork, but the Pharisees applied this law so rigidly that the Sabbath became a day of rigorous self-denial—the opposite of what God intended. The Pharisees employed God's Word for restrictive and enslaving purposes rather than for spiritual freedom and balance. In his mercy, God offers us recovery and hope instead of condemnation. If God had wanted to crush us with legalism, he would never have sent Jesus to die for us. He would have let us die in our sins.

Jesus Heals on the Sabbath

[9]Then Jesus went over to their synagogue, [10]where he noticed a man with a deformed hand. The Pharisees asked Jesus, "Does the law permit a person to work by healing on the Sabbath?" (They were hoping he would say yes, so they could bring charges against him.)

[11]And he answered, "If you had a sheep that fell into a well on the Sabbath, wouldn't you work to pull it out? Of course you would. [12]And how much more valuable is a person than a sheep! Yes, the law permits a person to do good on the Sabbath."

[13]Then he said to the man, "Hold out your hand." So the man held out his hand, and it was restored, just like the other one! [14]Then the Pharisees called a meeting to plot how to kill Jesus.

Jesus, God's Chosen Servant

[15]But Jesus knew what they were planning. So he left that area, and many people followed him. He healed all the sick among them, [16]but he warned them not to reveal who he was. [17]This fulfilled the prophecy of Isaiah concerning him:

[18] "Look at my Servant, whom I have chosen.
    He is my Beloved, who pleases me.
I will put my Spirit upon him,
    and he will proclaim justice to the
        nations.
[19] He will not fight or shout
    or raise his voice in public.
[20] He will not crush the weakest reed
    or put out a flickering candle.
    Finally he will cause justice to be
        victorious.
[21] And his name will be the hope
    of all the world."*

Jesus and the Prince of Demons

[22]Then a demon-possessed man, who was blind and couldn't speak, was brought to Jesus. He healed the man so that he could both speak and see. [23]The crowd was amazed and asked, "Could it be that Jesus is the Son of David, the Messiah?"

[24]But when the Pharisees heard about the miracle, they said, "No wonder he can cast out demons. He gets his power from Satan,* the prince of demons."

[25]Jesus knew their thoughts and replied, "Any kingdom divided by civil war is doomed. A town or family splintered by feuding will fall apart. [26]And if Satan is casting out Satan, he is divided and fighting against himself. His own kingdom will not survive. [27]And if I am empowered by Satan, what about your own exorcists? They cast out demons, too, so they will condemn you for what you have said. [28]But if I am casting out demons by the Spirit of God, then the Kingdom of God has arrived among you. [29]For who is powerful enough to enter the house of a strong man like Satan and plunder his goods? Only someone even stronger—someone who could tie him up and then plunder his house.

[30]"Anyone who isn't with me opposes me, and anyone who isn't working with me is actually working against me.

[31]"So I tell you, every sin and blasphemy can be forgiven—except blasphemy against the Holy Spirit, which will never be forgiven. [32]Anyone who speaks against the Son of Man can be forgiven, but anyone who speaks against the Holy Spirit will never be forgiven, either in this world or in the world to come.

[33]"A tree is identified by its fruit. If a tree is good, its fruit will be good. If a tree is bad, its fruit will be bad. [34]You brood of snakes! How could evil men like you speak what is good and right? For whatever is in your heart determines what you say. [35]A good person produces good things from the treasury of a good heart, and an evil person produces evil things from the treasury of an evil heart. [36]And I tell you this, you must give an

12:18-21 Isa 42:1-4 (Greek version for 42:4). 12:24 Greek Beelzeboul; also in 12:27. Other manuscripts read Beezeboul; Latin version reads Beelzebub.

12:17-21 Centuries earlier the prophet Isaiah had described the Messiah (Isaiah 42:1-4); Matthew recognized how Jesus fulfilled that prophecy. This passage offers a powerful message of hope for those of us in recovery. Jesus the Messiah is both our servant and our leader. He is strong enough to lead and judge the nations, yet tender enough to care for the weak and helpless. He is the world's hope for salvation and our hope for recovery.

12:22-32 Only God through Jesus Christ can offer us the power we need for recovery. If we look to any other source for help, our recovery will be limited at best. Secular, New Age, and even occult approaches to recovery are available. It is tragic that Christ-centered recovery is often doubted by many who need it the most, but it is even more tragic when people who find deliverance through Christ are later told that it is all a lie. God's way of recovery is the way of Jesus Christ; through him we receive the power we need for recovery and restoration.

account on judgment day for every idle word you speak. [37] The words you say will either acquit you or condemn you."

The Sign of Jonah

[38] One day some teachers of religious law and Pharisees came to Jesus and said, "Teacher, we want to show us a miraculous sign to prove your authority."

[39] But Jesus replied, "Only an evil, adulterous generation would demand a miraculous sign; but the only sign I will give them is the sign of the prophet Jonah. [40] For as Jonah was in the belly of the great fish for three days and three nights, so will the Son of Man be in the heart of the earth for three days and three nights.

[41] "The people of Nineveh will stand up against this generation on judgment day and condemn it, for they repented of their sins at the preaching of Jonah. Now someone greater than Jonah is here—but you refuse to repent. [42] The queen of Sheba* will also stand up against this generation on judgment day and condemn it, for she came from a distant land to hear the wisdom of Solomon. Now someone greater than Solomon is here—but you refuse to listen.

[43] "When an evil* spirit leaves a person, it goes into the desert, seeking rest but finding none. [44] Then it says, 'I will return to the person I came from.' So it returns and finds its former home empty, swept, and in order. [45] Then the spirit finds seven other spirits more evil than itself, and they all enter the person and live there. And so that person is worse off than before. That will be the experience of this evil generation."

The True Family of Jesus

[46] As Jesus was speaking to the crowd, his mother and brothers stood outside, asking to speak to him. [47] Someone told Jesus, "Your mother and your brothers are standing outside, and they want to speak to you."*

[48] Jesus asked, "Who is my mother? Who are my brothers?" [49] Then he pointed to his disciples and said, "Look, these are my mother and brothers. [50] Anyone who does the will of my Father in heaven is my brother and sister and mother!"

CHAPTER 13

Parable of the Farmer Scattering Seed

Later that same day Jesus left the house and sat beside the lake. [2] A large crowd soon gathered around him, so he got into a boat. Then he sat there and taught as the people stood on the shore. [3] He told many stories in the form of parables, such as this one:

"Listen! A farmer went out to plant some seeds. [4] As he scattered them across his field, some seeds fell on a footpath, and the birds came and ate them. [5] Other seeds fell on shallow soil with underlying rock. The seeds sprouted quickly because the soil was shallow. [6] But the plants soon wilted under the hot sun, and since they didn't have deep roots, they died. [7] Other seeds fell among thorns that grew up and choked out the tender plants. [8] Still other seeds fell on fertile soil, and they produced a crop that was thirty, sixty, and even a hundred times as much as had been planted! [9] Anyone with ears to hear should listen and understand."

[10] His disciples came and asked him, "Why

12:42 Greek *The queen of the south.* **12:43** Greek *unclean.* **12:47** Some manuscripts do not include verse 47. Compare Mark 3:32 and Luke 8:20.

12:43-45 Incomplete recovery can leave a person "worse off than before." To be rid of what afflicts us is only half the battle. Once we kick an addiction or dependency, there is a void in our life that was once filled with our old behavior. We must fill that emptiness with God's Spirit and godly attitudes and actions through prayer and reading God's Word. Otherwise, a new addiction or dependency can move in and cause further problems in our life.

13:1-9, 18-23 The story about the farmer and the four soils applies directly to recovery. The varied responses to the "seed" of the gospel are like the many responses to recovery. Some embrace recovery wholeheartedly, some only halfheartedly or temporarily, and some pass up the opportunity, denying they need it. Generally, various trials clarify which recovery category we fit into. If we hope to succeed in recovery and experience new life, we must allow God to prepare the soil of our heart, making it ready to receive his healing message.

13:10-17 Jesus' explanation for teaching with stories and illustrations fits well with the dynamics of recovery and denial. Those of us who respond in faith to what we already know will be given more insight as we progress in recovery. Those who do not respond properly will become more and more spiritually blind and hardened in denial. Amazingly, God continues to offer recovery even to those who have turned their back on him in denial. When we are ready to ask God what to do, he will be there with the answer (see James 1:5).

do you use parables when you talk to the people?"

[11]He replied, "You are permitted to understand the secrets* of the Kingdom of Heaven, but others are not. [12]To those who listen to my teaching, more understanding will be given, and they will have an abundance of knowledge. But for those who are not listening, even what little understanding they have will be taken away from them. [13]That is why I use these parables,

For they look, but they don't really see.
They hear, but they don't really listen
or understand.

[14]This fulfills the prophecy of Isaiah that says,

'When you hear what I say,
you will not understand.
When you see what I do,
you will not comprehend.
[15]For the hearts of these people are
hardened,
and their ears cannot hear,
and they have closed their eyes—
so their eyes cannot see,
and their ears cannot hear,
and their hearts cannot understand,
and they cannot turn to me
and let me heal them.'*

[16]"But blessed are your eyes, because they see; and your ears, because they hear. [17]I tell you the truth, many prophets and righteous people longed to see what you see, but they didn't see it. And they longed to hear what you hear, but they didn't hear it.

[18]"Now listen to the explanation of the parable about the farmer planting seeds: [19]The seed that fell on the footpath represents those who hear the message about the Kingdom and don't understand it. Then the evil one comes and snatches away the seed that was planted in their hearts. [20]The seed on the rocky soil represents those who hear the message and immediately receive it with joy. [21]But since they don't have deep roots, they don't last long. They fall away as soon as they have problems or are persecuted for

believing God's word. [22]The seed that fell among the thorns represents those who hear God's word, but all too quickly the message is crowded out by the worries of this life and the lure of wealth, so no fruit is produced. [23]The seed that fell on good soil represents those who truly hear and understand God's word and produce a harvest of thirty, sixty, or even a hundred times as much as had been planted!"

Parable of the Wheat and Weeds

[24]Here is another story Jesus told: "The Kingdom of Heaven is like a farmer who planted good seed in his field. [25]But that night as the workers slept, his enemy came and planted weeds among the wheat, then slipped away. [26]When the crop began to grow and produce grain, the weeds also grew.

[27]"The farmer's workers went to him and said, 'Sir, the field where you planted that good seed is full of weeds! Where did they come from?'

[28]"'An enemy has done this!' the farmer exclaimed.

"'Should we pull out the weeds?' they asked.

[29]"'No,' he replied, 'you'll uproot the wheat if you do. [30]Let both grow together until the harvest. Then I will tell the harvesters to sort out the weeds, tie them into bundles, and burn them, and to put the wheat in the barn.' "

Parable of the Mustard Seed

[31]Here is another illustration Jesus used: "The Kingdom of Heaven is like a mustard seed planted in a field. [32]It is the smallest of all seeds, but it becomes the largest of garden plants; it grows into a tree, and birds come and make nests in its branches."

Parable of the Yeast

[33]Jesus also used this illustration: "The Kingdom of Heaven is like the yeast a woman used in making bread. Even though she put only a little yeast in three measures of flour, it permeated every part of the dough."

13:11 Greek *the mysteries.* 13:14-15 Isa 6:9-10 (Greek version).

13:24-30, 36-43 The story about the wheat and the weeds applies to those of us considering recovery. Ultimately, there are two kinds of people in the world: Some submit to God's will and experience the restoration he offers in Jesus Christ; the others, whether they realize it or not, have submitted to the control of Satan. This stark but realistic contrast shows us that if we do not choose God, we choose Satan by default. If we have already undertaken a form of recovery but have not yet committed our life to Jesus Christ, we still have one more step to go before experiencing the victory available in God's recovery program.

[34]Jesus always used stories and illustrations like these when speaking to the crowds. In fact, he never spoke to them without using such parables. [35]This fulfilled what God had spoken through the prophet:

"I will speak to you in parables.
I will explain things hidden since the creation of the world.*"

Parable of the Wheat and Weeds Explained
[36]Then, leaving the crowds outside, Jesus went into the house. His disciples said, "Please explain to us the story of the weeds in the field."

[37]Jesus replied, "The Son of Man* is the farmer who plants the good seed. [38]The field is the world, and the good seed represents the people of the Kingdom. The weeds are the people who belong to the evil one. [39]The enemy who planted the weeds among the wheat is the devil. The harvest is the end of the world,* and the harvesters are the angels.

[40]"Just as the weeds are sorted out and burned in the fire, so it will be at the end of the world. [41]The Son of Man will send his angels, and they will remove from his Kingdom everything that causes sin and all who do evil. [42]And the angels will throw them into the fiery furnace, where there will be weeping and gnashing of teeth. [43]Then the righteous will shine like the sun in their Father's Kingdom. Anyone with ears to hear should listen and understand!

Parables of the Hidden Treasure and the Pearl
[44]"The Kingdom of Heaven is like a treasure that a man discovered hidden in a field. In his excitement, he hid it again and sold everything he owned to get enough money to buy the field.

[45]"Again, the Kingdom of Heaven is like a merchant on the lookout for choice pearls. [46]When he discovered a pearl of great value, he sold everything he owned and bought it!

Parable of the Fishing Net
[47]"Again, the Kingdom of Heaven is like a fishing net that was thrown into the water and caught fish of every kind. [48]When the net was full, they dragged it up onto the shore, sat down, and sorted the good fish into crates, but threw the bad ones away. [49]That is the way it will be at the end of the world. The angels will come and separate the wicked people from the righteous, [50]throwing the wicked into the fiery furnace, where there will be weeping and gnashing of teeth. [51]Do you understand all these things?"

"Yes," they said, "we do."

[52]Then he added, "Every teacher of religious law who becomes a disciple in the Kingdom of Heaven is like a homeowner who brings from his storeroom new gems of truth as well as old."

Jesus Rejected at Nazareth
[53]When Jesus had finished telling these stories and illustrations, he left that part of the country. [54]He returned to Nazareth, his hometown. When he taught there in the synagogue, everyone was amazed and said, "Where does he get this wisdom and the power to do miracles?" [55]Then they scoffed, "He's just the carpenter's son, and we know Mary, his mother, and his brothers—James, Joseph,* Simon, and Judas. [56]All his sisters live right here among us. Where did he learn all these things?" [57]And they were deeply offended and refused to believe in him.

Then Jesus told them, "A prophet is hon-

13:35 Some manuscripts do not include *of the world.* Ps 78:2. 13:37 "Son of Man" is a title Jesus used for himself. 13:39 Or *the age;* also in 13:40, 49. 13:55 Other manuscripts read *Joses;* still others read *John.*

13:53-58 We must always fight the preconceived notions that others have of us. We might leave our dysfunctional family or group of friends and enter a successful recovery program. When we return, we shouldn't be surprised to find that others will ignore our message of recovery, saying that we are *just* so-and-so or *just* the kid they went to school with. They won't listen to us because they are too close to who we were and cannot see who we have become through God's grace. As we share our recovery story with those who know our past, it may take time to convince them of our sincerity and our new life.

14:15-21 Jesus fed multitudes of hungry people on more than one occasion (see also 15:32-39). Jesus is not only able to do the impossible, but he is also concerned with our pressing human needs. He is committed to meeting our most basic physical needs, but how much more is he committed to meeting our emotional needs related to recovery! Jesus did not do everything himself; his disciples helped meet the people's needs. Jesus often meets our needs through human instruments. God may be working our recovery through concerned friends or others who are hurting like us. We should never refuse help from godly friends. As we have opportunities to encourage others in recovery, we can be thankful that God has chosen to use us.

GOD grant me the serenity
to accept the things I cannot change
the courage to change the things I can
and the wisdom to know the difference

AMEN

Having God deal with our defects can be frightening. We may stay trapped in destructive life patterns because we fear change.

If we wait for all our fears to go away before we take steps, we will never make significant progress in recovery. Courage isn't the absence of fear. Courage means that we take advantage of the little strength we find within ourself, that we find little ways to encourage ourself, and that we stubbornly stick to God's program for us. Courage doesn't mean being free of fear. It means finding enough strength to take the next step.

The disciples were terrified when they saw Jesus walk on water. "Then Peter called to him, 'Lord, if it's really you, tell me to come to you, walking on the water.' 'Yes, come,' Jesus said. So Peter went over the side of the boat and walked on the water toward Jesus. But when he saw the strong wind and the waves, he was terrified and began to sink. 'Save me, Lord!' he shouted. Jesus immediately reached out and grabbed him" (Matthew 14:28-31).

Peter gathered up enough courage to take one step and venture out into a new experience. When he got in over his head, he called out to Jesus and found the help he needed. We only need to summon the courage to take the next step. This doesn't mean that we won't be afraid or don't need help. It does mean that with God's help, we can make it. All we need is the courage to take just one more step. *Turn to page 1275, Mark 14.*

ored everywhere except in his own hometown and among his own family." [58]And so he did only a few miracles there because of their unbelief.

CHAPTER 14
The Death of John the Baptist
When Herod Antipas, the ruler of Galilee,* heard about Jesus, [2]he said to his advisers, "This must be John the Baptist raised from the dead! That is why he can do such miracles."

[3]For Herod had arrested and imprisoned John as a favor to his wife Herodias (the former wife of Herod's brother Philip). [4]John had been telling Herod, "It is against God's law for you to marry her." [5]Herod wanted to kill John, but he was afraid of a riot, because all the people believed John was a prophet.

[6]But at a birthday party for Herod, Herodias's daughter performed a dance that greatly pleased him, [7]so he promised with a vow to give her anything she wanted. [8]At her mother's urging, the girl said, "I want the head of John the Baptist on a tray!" [9]Then the king regretted what he had said; but because of the vow he had made in front of his guests, he issued the necessary orders. [10]So John was beheaded in the prison, [11]and his head was brought on a tray and given to the girl, who took it to her mother. [12]Later, John's disciples came for his body and buried it. Then they went and told Jesus what had happened.

Jesus Feeds Five Thousand
[13]As soon as Jesus heard the news, he left in a boat to a remote area to be alone. But the crowds heard where he was headed and followed on foot from many towns. [14]Jesus saw the huge crowd as he stepped from the boat, and he had compassion on them and healed their sick.

[15]That evening the disciples came to him

14:1 Greek *Herod the tetrarch*. Herod Antipas was a son of King Herod and was ruler over Galilee.

and said, "This is a remote place, and it's already getting late. Send the crowds away so they can go to the villages and buy food for themselves."

[16]But Jesus said, "That isn't necessary—you feed them."

[17]"But we have only five loaves of bread and two fish!" they answered.

[18]"Bring them here," he said. [19]Then he told the people to sit down on the grass. Jesus took the five loaves and two fish, looked up toward heaven, and blessed them. Then, breaking the loaves into pieces, he gave the bread to the disciples, who distributed it to the people. [20]They all ate as much as they wanted, and afterward, the disciples picked up twelve baskets of leftovers. [21]About 5,000 men were fed that day, in addition to all the women and children!

Jesus Walks on Water

[22]Immediately after this, Jesus insisted that his disciples get back into the boat and cross to the other side of the lake, while he sent the people home. [23]After sending them home, he went up into the hills by himself to pray. Night fell while he was there alone.

[24]Meanwhile, the disciples were in trouble far away from land, for a strong wind had risen, and they were fighting heavy waves. [25]About three o'clock in the morning* Jesus came toward them, walking on the water. [26]When the disciples saw him walking on the water, they were terrified. In their fear, they cried out, "It's a ghost!"

[27]But Jesus spoke to them at once. "Don't be afraid," he said. "Take courage. I am here!*"

[28]Then Peter called to him, "Lord, if it's really you, tell me to come to you, walking on the water."

[29]"Yes, come," Jesus said.

So Peter went over the side of the boat and walked on the water toward Jesus. [30]But when he saw the strong* wind and the waves, he was terrified and began to sink. "Save me, Lord!" he shouted.

[31]Jesus immediately reached out and grabbed him. "You have so little faith," Jesus said. "Why did you doubt me?"

[32]When they climbed back into the boat, the wind stopped. [33]Then the disciples worshiped him. "You really are the Son of God!" they exclaimed.

[34]After they had crossed the lake, they landed at Gennesaret. [35]When the people recognized Jesus, the news of his arrival spread quickly throughout the whole area, and soon people were bringing all their sick to be healed. [36]They begged him to let the sick touch at least the fringe of his robe, and all who touched him were healed.

CHAPTER 15
Jesus Teaches about Inner Purity

[1]Some Pharisees and teachers of religious law now arrived from Jerusalem to see Jesus. They asked him, [2]"Why do your disciples disobey our age-old tradition? For they ignore our tradition of ceremonial hand washing before they eat."

[3]Jesus replied, "And why do you, by your traditions, violate the direct commandments of God? [4]For instance, God says, 'Honor your father and mother,'* and 'Anyone who speaks disrespectfully of father or mother must be put to death.'* [5]But you say it is all right for people to say to their parents, 'Sorry, I can't help you. For I have vowed to give to God what I would have given to you.' [6]In this way, you say they don't need to honor their parents.* And so you cancel the word of God for the sake of your own tradition. [7]You hypocrites! Isaiah was right when he prophesied about you, for he wrote,

[8]'These people honor me with
their lips,
but their hearts are far from me.

14:25 Greek *In the fourth watch of the night.* 14:27 Or *The 'I AM' is here;* Greek reads *I am.* See Exod 3:14. 14:30 Some manuscripts do not include *strong.* 15:4a Exod 20:12; Deut 5:16. 15:4b Exod 21:17 (Greek version); Lev 20:9 (Greek version). 15:6 Greek *their father;* other manuscripts read *their father or their mother.*

14:22-23 Time alone to focus on our tasks and pray is necessary if we are engaged in any form of prolonged recovery program. Although we may feel we are wasting time, it is important to recharge our battery—physically, emotionally, and spiritually. If we don't, we will burn out. Since Jesus took time out to pray and recharge, we should follow his example.
15:1-20 Some people will look down on us and criticize us for our dependency and our need for recovery. They will assume a self-righteous posture because they are fulfilling all their proper "religious" obligations, while we are far from being a model church member. Jesus says that outward activities don't necessarily correspond to inner righteousness. If we do all the right things with a proud and selfish heart, we will be judged by God. If we have accepted Jesus into our heart and are humbly trying to recover, God is pleased with us, no matter what others may say.

⁹Their worship is a farce,
for they teach man-made ideas as
commands from God.'* "

¹⁰Then Jesus called to the crowd to come and hear. "Listen," he said, "and try to understand. ¹¹It's not what goes into your mouth that defiles you; you are defiled by the words that come out of your mouth."

¹²Then the disciples came to him and asked, "Do you realize you offended the Pharisees by what you just said?"

¹³Jesus replied, "Every plant not planted by my heavenly Father will be uprooted, ¹⁴so ignore them. They are blind guides leading the blind, and if one blind person guides another, they will both fall into a ditch."

¹⁵Then Peter said to Jesus, "Explain to us the parable that says people aren't defiled by what they eat."

¹⁶"Don't you understand yet?" Jesus asked. ¹⁷"Anything you eat passes through the stomach and then goes into the sewer. ¹⁸But the words you speak come from the heart—that's what defiles you. ¹⁹For from the heart come evil thoughts, murder, adultery, all sexual immorality, theft, lying, and slander. ²⁰These are what defile you. Eating with unwashed hands will never defile you."

The Faith of a Gentile Woman

²¹Then Jesus left Galilee and went north to the region of Tyre and Sidon. ²²A Gentile* woman who lived there came to him, pleading, "Have mercy on me, O Lord, Son of David! For my daughter is possessed by a demon that torments her severely."

²³But Jesus gave her no reply, not even a word. Then his disciples urged him to send her away. "Tell her to go away," they said. "She is bothering us with all her begging."

²⁴Then Jesus said to the woman, "I was sent only to help God's lost sheep—the people of Israel."

²⁵But she came and worshiped him, pleading again, "Lord, help me!"

²⁶Jesus responded, "It isn't right to take food from the children and throw it to the dogs."

²⁷She replied, "That's true, Lord, but even dogs are allowed to eat the scraps that fall beneath their masters' table."

²⁸"Dear woman," Jesus said to her, "your faith is great. Your request is granted." And her daughter was instantly healed.

15:8-9 Isa 29:13 (Greek version). 15:22 Greek Canaanite.

FAITH

READ MATTHEW 15:22-28

Sometimes the insanity of living with our own addiction or with people who are acting in bizarre ways can cause us to become desperate for help. Jesus once dealt with a woman who was driven to him out of desperation.

"A Gentile woman who lived there came to him, pleading, 'Have mercy on me, O Lord, Son of David! For my daughter is possessed by a demon that torments her severely.' But Jesus gave her no reply, not even a word. . . . Then Jesus said to the woman, 'I was sent only to help God's lost sheep—the people of Israel.' But she came and worshiped him, pleading again, 'Lord, help me!' Jesus responded, 'It isn't right to take food from the children and throw it to the dogs.' She replied, 'That's true, Lord, but even dogs are allowed to eat the scraps that fall beneath their master's table.' 'Dear woman,' Jesus said to her, 'your faith is great. Your request is granted.' And her daughter was instantly healed" (Matthew 15:22-28).

It took a lot of courage for this woman to even speak to Jesus because of the racism of their time. She was despised and ridiculed for seeking an end to her family's torment, but she didn't give up. She believed God was the only one who could help her, and she would not be deterred. Our own desperation can lead to sincere faith that can be of tremendous help to us in recovery. *Turn to page 1223, Matthew 16.*

Jesus Heals Many People

²⁹Jesus returned to the Sea of Galilee and climbed a hill and sat down. ³⁰A vast crowd brought to him people who were lame, blind, crippled, those who couldn't speak, and many others. They laid them before Jesus, and he healed them all. ³¹The crowd was amazed! Those who hadn't been able to speak were talking, the crippled were made well, the lame were walking, and the blind could see again! And they praised the God of Israel.

Jesus Feeds Four Thousand

³²Then Jesus called his disciples and told them, "I feel sorry for these people. They have been here with me for three days, and they have nothing left to eat. I don't want to send them away hungry, or they will faint along the way."

³³The disciples replied, "Where would we get enough food here in the wilderness for such a huge crowd?"

³⁴Jesus asked, "How much bread do you have?"

They replied, "Seven loaves, and a few small fish."

³⁵So Jesus told all the people to sit down on the ground. ³⁶Then he took the seven loaves and the fish, thanked God for them, and broke them into pieces. He gave them to the disciples, who distributed the food to the crowd.

³⁷They all ate as much as they wanted. Afterward, the disciples picked up seven large baskets of leftover food. ³⁸There were 4,000 men who were fed that day, in addition to all the women and children. ³⁹Then Jesus sent

the people home, and he got into a boat and crossed over to the region of Magadan.

CHAPTER 16
Leaders Demand a Miraculous Sign

One day the Pharisees and Sadducees came to test Jesus, demanding that he show them a miraculous sign from heaven to prove his authority.

²He replied, "You know the saying, 'Red sky at night means fair weather tomorrow; ³red sky in the morning means foul weather all day.' You know how to interpret the weather signs in the sky, but you don't know how to interpret the signs of the times!* ⁴Only an evil, adulterous generation would demand a miraculous sign, but the only sign I will give them is the sign of the prophet Jonah.*" Then Jesus left them and went away.

Yeast of the Pharisees and Sadducees

⁵Later, after they crossed to the other side of the lake, the disciples discovered they had forgotten to bring any bread. ⁶"Watch out!" Jesus warned them. "Beware of the yeast of the Pharisees and Sadducees."

⁷At this they began to argue with each other because they hadn't brought any bread. ⁸Jesus knew what they were saying, so he said, "You have so little faith! Why are you arguing with each other about having no bread? ⁹Don't you understand even yet? Don't you remember the 5,000 I fed with five loaves, and the baskets of leftovers you picked up? ¹⁰Or the 4,000 I fed with seven loaves, and the large baskets of leftovers you picked up? ¹¹Why can't you understand that I'm not talking about bread? So again I say,

16:2-3 Several manuscripts do not include any of the words in 16:2-3 after *He replied.* 16:4 Greek *the sign of Jonah.*

15:32-38 The feeding of the four thousand is both similar to and different from the previous feeding of the five thousand (see 14:15-21). In both cases Jesus cared about those in need; he took a small amount of food and fed a large number of people; he used the disciples to distribute the resources; and much more was left over at the end than they had in the beginning. Since the reason for concern was somewhat different, as were the location and the number of people fed, we see that Jesus tailored his resources to meet the various situations and needs. We can count on God to show similar concern and unlimited power to support us in our recovery process.
16:1-4 The Pharisees had the kind of attitude that often hinders recovery. They wanted Jesus to show them miraculous signs to prove that he was the Messiah. We make the same mistake when we expect an instant cure or supernatural intervention in our life. Looking for quick fixes to life-long problems is tantamount to seeking "a sign from heaven." It often takes a lifetime of hard work to remain victorious over our addiction. When we recognize this truth, we will be less likely to be disappointed by the difficulties of the recovery process. We will also be more aware of the small victories that God gives us along the way.
16:13-17 There are many answers to the question, Who is Jesus? but only one of them is correct. The insight that Jesus is the promised Messiah and the Son of God comes from God himself, not from any human source. Likewise, the realization that the God of the Bible is the higher power we need for recovery is a revelation from God's Word. To put our trust in any other power for recovery will only lead to disappointment and failure.

'Beware of the yeast of the Pharisees and Sadducees.' "

¹²Then at last they understood that he wasn't speaking about the yeast in bread, but about the deceptive teaching of the Pharisees and Sadducees.

Peter's Declaration about Jesus

¹³When Jesus came to the region of Caesarea Philippi, he asked his disciples, "Who do people say that the Son of Man is?"*

¹⁴"Well," they replied, "some say John the Baptist, some say Elijah, and others say Jeremiah or one of the other prophets."

¹⁵Then he asked them, "But who do you say I am?"

¹⁶Simon Peter answered, "You are the Messiah,* the Son of the living God."

¹⁷Jesus replied, "You are blessed, Simon son of John,* because my Father in heaven has revealed this to you. You did not learn this from any human being. ¹⁸Now I say to you that you are Peter (which means 'rock'),* and upon this rock I will build my church, and all the powers of hell* will not conquer it. ¹⁹And I will give you the keys of the Kingdom of Heaven. Whatever you forbid* on earth will be forbidden in heaven, and whatever you permit* on earth will be permitted in heaven."

²⁰Then he sternly warned the disciples not to tell anyone that he was the Messiah.

Jesus Predicts His Death

²¹From then on Jesus* began to tell his disciples plainly that it was necessary for him to go to Jerusalem, and that he would suffer many terrible things at the hands of the elders, the leading priests, and the teachers of religious law. He would be killed, but on the third day he would be raised from the dead.

²²But Peter took him aside and began to reprimand him* for saying such things. "Heaven forbid, Lord," he said. "This will never happen to you!"

²³Jesus turned to Peter and said, "Get away from me, Satan! You are a dangerous trap to me. You are seeing things merely from a human point of view, not from God's."

²⁴Then Jesus said to his disciples, "If any of

16:13 "Son of Man" is a title Jesus used for himself.
16:16 Or *the Christ. Messiah* (a Hebrew term) and *Christ* (a Greek term) both mean "anointed one." 16:17 Greek *Simon bar-Jonah;* see John 1:42; 21:15-17. 16:18a Greek *that you are Peter.* 16:18b Greek *and the gates of Hades.* 16:19a Or *bind,* or *lock.* 16:19b Or *loose,* or *open.* 16:21 Some manuscripts read *Jesus the Messiah.* 16:22 Or *began to correct him.*

DELAYED GRATIFICATION

READ MATTHEW 16:24-26

Some of us are addicted to chaos. We may be so used to crisis that we don't know how to enjoy the calm. Life in recovery may seem boring in comparison to our old ways. We may even miss the excitement and danger. The rewards may seem too slow in coming.

The apostle Paul said, "So let's not get tired of doing what is good. At just the right time we will reap a harvest of blessing if we don't give up" (Galatians 6:9). Weeds spring up quickly. Good crops grow more slowly and must be tended steadily, even before we can see anything sprout. It's only in time that we will enjoy the fruit.

Jesus suggested that we expand our perspective even further, with a view toward eternity. "Jesus said to his disciples, 'If any of you wants to be my follower, you must turn from your selfish ways, take up your cross, and follow me. If you try to hang on to your life, you will lose it. But if you give up your life for my sake, you will save it. And what do you benefit if you gain the whole world but lose your own soul?' " (Matthew 16:24-26).

It is God's will for us to have a rewarding and fulfilled life. It may be easier to adjust to our new way of life if we remember that denying ourself immediate pleasures will bring a harvest of rich rewards in this life and in the life to come. *Turn to page 1235, Matthew 25.*

you wants to be my follower, you must turn from your selfish ways, take up your cross, and follow me. ²⁵If you try to hang on to your life, you will lose it. But if you give up your life for my sake, you will save it. ²⁶And what do you benefit if you gain the whole world but lose your own soul?* Is anything worth more than your soul? ²⁷For the Son of Man will come with his angels in the glory of his Father and will judge all people according to their deeds. ²⁸And I tell you the truth, some standing here right now will not die before they see the Son of Man coming in his Kingdom."

CHAPTER 17
The Transfiguration
Six days later Jesus took Peter and the two brothers, James and John, and led them up a high mountain to be alone. ²As the men watched, Jesus' appearance was transformed so that his face shone like the sun, and his clothes became as white as light. ³Suddenly, Moses and Elijah appeared and began talking with Jesus.

⁴Peter exclaimed, "Lord, it's wonderful for us to be here! If you want, I'll make three shelters as memorials*—one for you, one for Moses, and one for Elijah."

⁵But even as he spoke, a bright cloud overshadowed them, and a voice from the cloud said, "This is my dearly loved Son, who brings me great joy. Listen to him." ⁶The disciples were terrified and fell face down on the ground.

⁷Then Jesus came over and touched them. "Get up," he said. "Don't be afraid." ⁸And when they looked up, Moses and Elijah were gone, and they saw only Jesus.

⁹As they went back down the mountain, Jesus commanded them, "Don't tell anyone what you have seen until the Son of Man* has been raised from the dead."

¹⁰Then his disciples asked him, "Why do the teachers of religious law insist that Elijah must return before the Messiah comes?*"

¹¹Jesus replied, "Elijah is indeed coming first to get everything ready. ¹²But I tell you, Elijah has already come, but he wasn't recognized, and they chose to abuse him. And in the same way they will also make the Son of Man suffer." ¹³Then the disciples realized he was talking about John the Baptist.

Jesus Heals a Demon-Possessed Boy
¹⁴At the foot of the mountain, a large crowd was waiting for them. A man came and knelt before Jesus and said, ¹⁵"Lord, have mercy on my son. He has seizures and suffers terribly. He often falls into the fire or into the water. ¹⁶So I brought him to your disciples, but they couldn't heal him."

¹⁷Jesus said, "You faithless and corrupt people! How long must I be with you? How long must I put up with you? Bring the boy here to me." ¹⁸Then Jesus rebuked the demon in the boy, and it left him. From that moment the boy was well.

¹⁹Afterward the disciples asked Jesus privately, "Why couldn't we cast out that demon?"

²⁰"You don't have enough faith," Jesus told them. "I tell you the truth, if you had faith even as small as a mustard seed, you could say to this mountain, 'Move from here

16:26 Or *your self?* also in 16:26b. **17:4** Greek *three tabernacles.* **17:9** "Son of Man" is a title Jesus used for himself. **17:10** Greek *that Elijah must come first?*

17:1-8 Even before Jesus' transfiguration, Jesus was the glorious Son of God. But Peter, James, and John had never seen Jesus in that way. After their experience on the Mount of Transfiguration, these disciples would never again consider Jesus as anything less than God's Son without being in full-scale denial. Through the words of Matthew and the testimony of other believers, we too are witnesses of God's glory in Jesus Christ. To deny his authority over our life is to assure the failure of any recovery program. Jesus is the only one who can transform our broken life.
17:14-21 This account of the disciples' failure to cast out a demon teaches us a crucial lesson about the role of faith in recovery. Jesus criticized the disciples for their lack of faith in God's power to heal the boy. We don't need a large amount of faith to begin the healing process in our life; we need "faith even as small as a mustard seed" to effect change. Prayer and faith in God are the tools for recovery; with these we can move mountains!
18:2-6 By calling the little children to come to him, Jesus revealed his love for each of us. He warned that terrible judgment would come upon those who harm his followers or cause them to lose faith. This is encouraging for those of us who have suffered injustices or abuse from others, especially when we were children. We don't have to carry our hate with us or waste our energy dreaming of revenge. God will judge those who have harmed us. We should focus on recovery, not on the punishment of the people who have hurt us.

to there,' and it would move. Nothing would be impossible.*"

Jesus Again Predicts His Death

²²After they gathered again in Galilee, Jesus told them, "The Son of Man is going to be betrayed into the hands of his enemies. ²³He will be killed, but on the third day he will be raised from the dead." And the disciples were filled with grief.

Payment of the Temple Tax

²⁴On their arrival in Capernaum, the collectors of the Temple tax* came to Peter and asked him, "Doesn't your teacher pay the Temple tax?"

²⁵"Yes, he does," Peter replied. Then he went into the house.

But before he had a chance to speak, Jesus asked him, "What do you think, Peter?* Do kings tax their own people or the people they have conquered?*"

²⁶"They tax the people they have conquered," Peter replied.

"Well, then," Jesus said, "the citizens are free! ²⁷However, we don't want to offend them, so go down to the lake and throw in a line. Open the mouth of the first fish you catch, and you will find a large silver coin.* Take it and pay the tax for both of us."

CHAPTER 18
The Greatest in the Kingdom

About that time the disciples came to Jesus and asked, "Who is greatest in the Kingdom of Heaven?"

²Jesus called a little child to him and put the child among them. ³Then he said, "I tell you the truth, unless you turn from your sins and become like little children, you will never get into the Kingdom of Heaven. ⁴So anyone who becomes as humble as this little child is the greatest in the Kingdom of Heaven.

⁵"And anyone who welcomes a little child like this on my behalf* is welcoming me. ⁶But if you cause one of these little ones who trusts in me to fall into sin, it would be better for you to have a large millstone tied around your neck and be drowned in the depths of the sea.

⁷"What sorrow awaits the world, because it

17:20 Some manuscripts add verse 21, *But this kind of demon won't leave except by prayer and fasting.* Compare Mark 9:29. 17:24 Greek *the two-drachma [tax];* also in 17:24b. See Exod 30:13-16; Neh 10:32-33.
17:25a Greek *Simon?* 17:25b Greek *their sons or others?*
17:27 Greek *a stater* [a Greek coin equivalent to four drachmas]. 18:5 Greek *in my name.*

STEP 8

Forgiven to Forgive

BIBLE READING: Matthew 18:23-35

We made a list of all persons we had harmed and became willing to make amends to them all.

Listing all the people we have harmed will probably trigger a natural defensiveness. With each name we write down, another mental list may begin to form—a list of the wrongs that have been done to us. How can we deal with the resentment we hold toward others so we can move toward making amends?

Jesus told this story: "A king . . . decided to bring his accounts up to date with servants who had borrowed money from him. In the process, one of his debtors was brought in who owed him millions of dollars" (Matthew 18:23-24). The man begged for forgiveness because he couldn't pay. The king "was filled with pity for him, and he released him and forgave his debt. But when the man left the king, he went to a fellow servant who owed him a few thousand dollars. He grabbed him by the throat and demanded instant payment" (18:27-28). This was reported to the king. "Then the king called in the man he had forgiven and said, 'You evil servant! I forgave you that tremendous debt because you pleaded with me. Shouldn't you have mercy on your fellow servant . . . ?' Then the angry king sent the man to prison to be tortured until he had paid his entire debt. That's what my heavenly Father will do to you if you refuse to forgive your brothers and sisters" (18:32-35).

When we look at all that God has forgiven us, it makes sense to choose to forgive others. This also frees us from the torture of festering resentment. We can't change what others have done to us, but we can write off their debts and become willing to make amends. ***Turn to page 1481, 2 Corinthians 2.***

tempts people to sin. Temptations are inevitable, but what sorrow awaits the person who does the tempting. [8]So if your hand or foot causes you to sin, cut it off and throw it away. It's better to enter eternal life with only one hand or one foot than to be thrown into eternal fire with both of your hands and feet. [9]And if your eye causes you to sin, gouge it out and throw it away. It's better to enter eternal life with only one eye than to have two eyes and be thrown into the fire of hell.*

[10]"Beware that you don't look down on any of these little ones. For I tell you that in heaven their angels are always in the presence of my heavenly Father.*

Parable of the Lost Sheep

[12]"If a man has a hundred sheep and one of them wanders away, what will he do? Won't he leave the ninety-nine others on the hills and go out to search for the one that is lost? [13]And if he finds it, I tell you the truth, he will rejoice over it more than over the ninety-nine that didn't wander away! [14]In the same way, it is not my heavenly Father's will that even one of these little ones should perish.

Correcting Another Believer

[15]"If another believer* sins against you,* go privately and point out the offense. If the other person listens and confesses it, you have won that person back. [16]But if you are unsuccessful, take one or two others with you and go back again, so that everything you say may be confirmed by two or three witnesses. [17]If the person still refuses to listen, take your case to the church. Then if he or she won't accept the church's decision, treat that person as a pagan or a corrupt tax collector.

[18]"I tell you the truth, whatever you forbid* on earth will be forbidden in heaven, and whatever you permit* on earth will be permitted in heaven.

[19]"I also tell you this: If two of you agree here on earth concerning anything you ask, my Father in heaven will do it for you. [20]For where two or three gather together as my followers,* I am there among them."

Parable of the Unforgiving Debtor

[21]Then Peter came to him and asked, "Lord, how often should I forgive someone* who sins against me? Seven times?"

[22]"No, not seven times," Jesus replied, "but seventy times seven!*

[23]"Therefore, the Kingdom of Heaven can be compared to a king who decided to bring his accounts up to date with servants who had borrowed money from him. [24]In the process, one of his debtors was brought in who owed him millions of dollars.* [25]He couldn't pay, so his master ordered that he be sold—along with his wife, his children, and everything he owned—to pay the debt.

[26]"But the man fell down before his master and begged him, 'Please, be patient with me, and I will pay it all.' [27]Then his master was filled with pity for him, and he released him and forgave his debt.

[28]"But when the man left the king, he went to a fellow servant who owed him a few thousand dollars.* He grabbed him by the throat and demanded instant payment.

[29]"His fellow servant fell down before him and begged for a little more time. 'Be patient with me, and I will pay it,' he pleaded. [30]But his creditor wouldn't wait. He had the man arrested and put in prison until the debt could be paid in full.

[31]"When some of the other servants saw this, they were very upset. They went to the king and told him everything that had happened. [32]Then the king called in the man he had forgiven and said, 'You evil servant! I forgave you that tremendous debt because you pleaded with me. [33]Shouldn't you have mercy on your fellow servant, just as I had mercy on you?' [34]Then the angry king sent the man to prison to be tortured until he had paid his entire debt.

[35]"That's what my heavenly Father will do

18:9 Greek *the Gehenna of fire.* 18:10 Some manuscripts add verse 11, *And the Son of Man came to save those who are lost.* Compare Luke 19:10. 18:15a Greek *If your brother.* 18:15b Some manuscripts do not include *against you.* 18:18a Or *bind,* or *lock.* 18:18b Or *loose,* or *open.* 18:20 Greek *gather together in my name.* 18:21 Greek *my brother.* 18:22 Or *seventy-seven times.* 18:24 Greek *10,000 talents* [375 tons or 340 metric tons of silver]. 18:28 Greek *100 denarii.* A denarius was equivalent to a laborer's full day's wage.

18:10-14 Many children and adults believe the lie that they are worthless to other people and insignificant to God. Jesus indicated that he came to save the lost, no matter how few or how "insignificant" they seemed. God the Father does not want anyone to miss the opportunity for salvation or recovery in Jesus Christ. God values each one of us, no matter how painful our past or how far we have strayed. If we admit our need for him and seek to follow his will for us, we will discover how very important we are to God and the people close to us.

to you if you refuse to forgive your brothers and sisters* from your heart."

CHAPTER 19
Discussion about Divorce and Marriage
When Jesus had finished saying these things, he left Galilee and went down to the region of Judea east of the Jordan River. ²Large crowds followed him there, and he healed their sick.

³Some Pharisees came and tried to trap him with this question: "Should a man be allowed to divorce his wife for just any reason?"

⁴"Haven't you read the Scriptures?" Jesus replied. "They record that from the beginning 'God made them male and female.'*" ⁵And he said, "'This explains why a man leaves his father and mother and is joined to his wife, and the two are united into one.'* ⁶Since they are no longer two but one, let no one split apart what God has joined together."

⁷"Then why did Moses say in the law that a man could give his wife a written notice of divorce and send her away?"* they asked.

⁸Jesus replied, "Moses permitted divorce only as a concession to your hard hearts, but it was not what God had originally intended. ⁹And I tell you this, whoever divorces his wife and marries someone else commits adultery—unless his wife has been unfaithful.*"

¹⁰Jesus' disciples then said to him, "If this is the case, it is better not to marry!"

¹¹"Not everyone can accept this statement," Jesus said. "Only those whom God helps. ¹²Some are born as eunuchs, some have been made eunuchs by others, and some choose not to marry* for the sake of the Kingdom of Heaven. Let anyone accept this who can."

Jesus Blesses the Children
¹³One day some parents brought their children to Jesus so he could lay his hands on them and pray for them. But the disciples scolded the parents for bothering him.

¹⁴But Jesus said, "Let the children come to me. Don't stop them! For the Kingdom of Heaven belongs to those who are like these children." ¹⁵And he placed his hands on their heads and blessed them before he left.

The Rich Man
¹⁶Someone came to Jesus with this question: "Teacher,* what good deed must I do to have eternal life?"

¹⁷"Why ask me about what is good?" Jesus replied. "There is only One who is good. But to answer your question—if you want to receive eternal life, keep* the commandments."

¹⁸"Which ones?" the man asked.

And Jesus replied: " 'You must not murder. You must not commit adultery. You must not steal. You must not testify falsely. ¹⁹Honor your father and mother. Love your neighbor as yourself.'* "

²⁰"I've obeyed all these commandments," the young man replied. "What else must I do?"

²¹Jesus told him, "If you want to be perfect, go and sell all your possessions and give the money to the poor, and you will have treasure in heaven. Then come, follow me."

²²But when the young man heard this, he went away sad, for he had many possessions.

²³Then Jesus said to his disciples, "I tell you the truth, it is very hard for a rich person to enter the Kingdom of Heaven. ²⁴I'll say it again—it is easier for a camel to go through the eye of a needle than for a rich person to enter the Kingdom of God!"

18:35 Greek *your brother.* **19:4** Gen 1:27; 5:2. **19:5** Gen 2:24. **19:7** See Deut 24:1. **19:9** Some manuscripts add *And anyone who marries a divorced woman commits adultery.* Compare Matt 5:32. **19:12** Greek *and some make themselves eunuchs.* **19:16** Some manuscripts read *Good Teacher.* **19:17** Some manuscripts read *continue to keep.* **19:18-19** Exod 20:12-16; Deut 5:16-20; Lev 19:18.

19:3-12 Jesus affirmed the importance of the marriage relationship. We may find it confining to be without an "escape hatch" in marriage, but God has always intended that marriage be a life-long commitment. Realizing that marriage is permanent and that a husband and wife are one through marriage should make us consider how much our sins and dependency harm our spouse. Even though divorce may end the conflict between a couple, it will not correct the attitudes or behaviors that brought about the conflict. Unless we correct the root problems in ourself, we will have the same conflicts in future relationships.

19:16-24 The rich young man was trying to work (and buy) his way to heaven. Jesus played along with this man's shortsighted attempt to claim he was perfect. But it soon became clear that the man was addicted to his material wealth and the security it bought him. His possessions had a higher priority in his life than God did. Materialism is a form of addiction or compulsion that makes it nearly impossible to be humble and trust Jesus Christ alone for salvation and recovery. As long as we believe we can buy our way out of our problems, we will never achieve lasting recovery.

²⁵The disciples were astounded. "Then who in the world can be saved?" they asked.

²⁶Jesus looked at them intently and said, "Humanly speaking, it is impossible. But with God everything is possible."

²⁷Then Peter said to him, "We've given up everything to follow you. What will we get?"

²⁸Jesus replied, "I assure you that when the world is made new* and the Son of Man* sits upon his glorious throne, you who have been my followers will also sit on twelve thrones, judging the twelve tribes of Israel. ²⁹And everyone who has given up houses or brothers or sisters or father or mother or children or property, for my sake, will receive a hundred times as much in return and will inherit eternal life. ³⁰But many who are the greatest now will be least important then, and those who seem least important now will be the greatest then.*

CHAPTER 20
Parable of the Vineyard Workers

"For the Kingdom of Heaven is like the landowner who went out early one morning to hire workers for his vineyard. ²He agreed to pay the normal daily wage* and sent them out to work.

³"At nine o'clock in the morning he was passing through the marketplace and saw some people standing around doing nothing. ⁴So he hired them, telling them he would pay them whatever was right at the end of the day. ⁵So they went to work in the vineyard. At noon and again at three o'clock he did the same thing.

⁶"At five o'clock that afternoon he was in town again and saw some more people standing around. He asked them, 'Why haven't you been working today?'

⁷"They replied, 'Because no one hired us.'

"The landowner told them, 'Then go out and join the others in my vineyard.'

⁸"That evening he told the foreman to call the workers in and pay them, beginning with the last workers first. ⁹When those hired at five o'clock were paid, each received a full day's wage. ¹⁰When those hired first came to get their pay, they assumed they would receive more. But they, too, were paid a day's wage. ¹¹When they received their pay, they protested to the owner, ¹²'Those people worked only one hour, and yet you've paid them just as much as you paid us who worked all day in the scorching heat.'

¹³"He answered one of them, 'Friend, I haven't been unfair! Didn't you agree to work all day for the usual wage? ¹⁴Take your money and go. I wanted to pay this last worker the same as you. ¹⁵Is it against the law for me to do what I want with my money? Should you be jealous because I am kind to others?'

¹⁶"So those who are last now will be first then, and those who are first will be last."

Jesus Again Predicts His Death

¹⁷As Jesus was going up to Jerusalem, he took the twelve disciples aside privately and told them what was going to happen to him. ¹⁸"Listen," he said, "we're going up to Jerusalem, where the Son of Man* will be betrayed to the leading priests and the teachers of religious law. They will sentence him to die. ¹⁹Then they will hand him over to the Romans* to be mocked, flogged with a whip, and crucified. But on the third day he will be raised from the dead."

Jesus Teaches about Serving Others

²⁰Then the mother of James and John, the sons of Zebedee, came to Jesus with her sons.

19:28a Or *in the regeneration.* 19:28b "Son of Man" is a title Jesus used for himself. 19:30 Greek *But many who are first will be last; and the last, first.* 20:2 Greek *a denarius,* the payment for a full day's labor; similarly in 20:9, 10, 13. 20:18 "Son of Man" is a title Jesus used for himself. 20:19 Greek *the Gentiles.*

19:25-26 These verses are true not only for salvation but also for recovery. Left on our own, we would fall deeper into the pit of our addiction, never gaining control over it. But with God's help, the inconceivable is possible. He can turn our life around, bringing hope and health where once despair and pain had reigned. Giving God control of our life is the only way to regain independence from our addiction and other compulsive behaviors.
20:1-16 The story about the workers and their pay speaks strongly about God's grace. No matter when we begin to follow Jesus, we receive the same amount of grace from God. That may seem unfair to some; but God in his mercy accepts all people who turn to him for salvation and recovery, no matter how early or late in life. It is never too late to begin the process of recovery!
20:20-28 The other disciples were indignant at the request for special recognition made by James's and John's mother because they, too, wanted positions of honor in God's Kingdom. This

She knelt respectfully to ask a favor. ²¹"What is your request?" he asked.

She replied, "In your Kingdom, please let my two sons sit in places of honor next to you, one on your right and the other on your left."

²²But Jesus answered by saying to them, "You don't know what you are asking! Are you able to drink from the bitter cup of suffering I am about to drink?"

"Oh yes," they replied, "we are able!"

²³Jesus told them, "You will indeed drink from my bitter cup. But I have no right to say who will sit on my right or my left. My Father has prepared those places for the ones he has chosen."

²⁴When the ten other disciples heard what James and John had asked, they were indignant. ²⁵But Jesus called them together and said, "You know that the rulers in this world lord it over their people, and officials flaunt their authority over those under them. ²⁶But among you it will be different. Whoever wants to be a leader among you must be your servant, ²⁷and whoever wants to be first among you must become your slave. ²⁸For even the Son of Man came not to be served but to serve others and to give his life as a ransom for many."

Jesus Heals Two Blind Men

²⁹As Jesus and the disciples left the town of Jericho, a large crowd followed behind. ³⁰Two blind men were sitting beside the road. When they heard that Jesus was coming that way, they began shouting, "Lord, Son of David, have mercy on us!"

³¹"Be quiet!" the crowd yelled at them.

But they only shouted louder, "Lord, Son of David, have mercy on us!"

³²When Jesus heard them, he stopped and called, "What do you want me to do for you?"

³³"Lord," they said, "we want to see!"
³⁴Jesus felt sorry for them and touched their eyes. Instantly they could see! Then they followed him.

CHAPTER 21
Jesus' Triumphant Entry

As Jesus and the disciples approached Jerusalem, they came to the town of Bethphage on the Mount of Olives. Jesus sent two of them on ahead. ²"Go into the village over there," he said. "As soon as you enter it, you will see a donkey tied there, with its colt beside it. Untie them and bring them to me. ³If anyone asks what you are doing, just say, 'The Lord needs them,' and he will immediately let you take them."

⁴This took place to fulfill the prophecy that said,

⁵ "Tell the people of Jerusalem,*
    'Look, your King is coming to you.
 He is humble, riding on a donkey—
    riding on a donkey's colt.'"*

⁶The two disciples did as Jesus commanded. ⁷They brought the donkey and the colt to him and threw their garments over the colt, and he sat on it.*

⁸Most of the crowd spread their garments on the road ahead of him, and others cut branches from the trees and spread them on the road. ⁹Jesus was in the center of the procession, and the people all around him were shouting,

"Praise God* for the Son of David!
 Blessings on the one who comes in the
    name of the LORD!
 Praise God in highest heaven!"*

¹⁰The entire city of Jerusalem was in an uproar as he entered. "Who is this?" they asked.

¹¹And the crowds replied, "It's Jesus, the prophet from Nazareth in Galilee."

Jesus Clears the Temple

¹²Jesus entered the Temple and began to drive out all the people buying and selling

---

21:5a Greek *Tell the daughter of Zion.* Isa 62:11. 21:5b Zech 9:9. 21:7 Greek *over them, and he sat on them.*
21:9a Greek *Hosanna,* an exclamation of praise that literally means "save now"; also in 21:9b, 15. 21:9b Pss 118:25-26; 148:1.

---

prideful attitude contradicted what Jesus taught and is always detrimental to recovery. Becoming great in God's sight is achieved through humbly serving others. This is also one of our goals in recovery. As we receive God's grace and restoration, we are called to carry God's message to others and to help them in the recovery process.

20:29-34 Jesus' sensitivity to the needs of two blind men in a huge crowd shows that God cares very much for individuals who hurt. Jesus healed them because they asked him to. They believed in him and did not listen to the bystanders' discouraging remarks. They persevered despite opposition and continued with their humble pleas for help. In recovery we may encounter opposition; we may need to swallow our pride and just keep going. We can be sure that even if others laugh at us or discourage us, God is listening and will help us in the recovery process.

animals for sacrifice. He knocked over the tables of the money changers and the chairs of those selling doves. [13]He said to them, "The Scriptures declare, 'My Temple will be called a house of prayer,' but you have turned it into a den of thieves!"*

[14]The blind and the lame came to him in the Temple, and he healed them. [15]The leading priests and the teachers of religious law saw these wonderful miracles and heard even the children in the Temple shouting, "Praise God for the Son of David."

But the leaders were indignant. [16]They asked Jesus, "Do you hear what these children are saying?"

"Yes," Jesus replied. "Haven't you ever read the Scriptures? For they say, 'You have taught children and infants to give you praise.'* " [17]Then he returned to Bethany, where he stayed overnight.

Jesus Curses the Fig Tree

[18]In the morning, as Jesus was returning to Jerusalem, he was hungry, [19]and he noticed a fig tree beside the road. He went over to see if there were any figs, but there were only leaves. Then he said to it, "May you never bear fruit again!" And immediately the fig tree withered up.

[20]The disciples were amazed when they saw this and asked, "How did the fig tree wither so quickly?"

[21]Then Jesus told them, "I tell you the truth, if you have faith and don't doubt, you can do things like this and much more. You can even say to this mountain, 'May you be lifted up and thrown into the sea,' and it will happen. [22]You can pray for anything, and if you have faith, you will receive it."

The Authority of Jesus Challenged

[23]When Jesus returned to the Temple and began teaching, the leading priests and elders came up to him. They demanded, "By what authority are you doing all these things? Who gave you the right?"

[24]"I'll tell you by what authority I do these things if you answer one question," Jesus replied. [25]"Did John's authority to baptize come from heaven, or was it merely human?"

They talked it over among themselves. "If we say it was from heaven, he will ask us why we didn't believe John. [26]But if we say it was merely human, we'll be mobbed because the people believe John was a prophet." [27]So they finally replied, "We don't know."

And Jesus responded, "Then I won't tell you by what authority I do these things.

Parable of the Two Sons

[28]"But what do you think about this? A man with two sons told the older boy, 'Son, go out and work in the vineyard today.' [29]The son answered, 'No, I won't go,' but later he changed his mind and went anyway. [30]Then the father told the other son, 'You go,' and he said, 'Yes, sir, I will.' But he didn't go.

[31]"Which of the two obeyed his father?"

They replied, "The first."*

Then Jesus explained his meaning: "I tell you the truth, corrupt tax collectors and prostitutes will get into the Kingdom of God before you do. [32]For John the Baptist came and showed you the right way to live, but you didn't believe him, while tax collectors and prostitutes did. And even when you saw this happening, you refused to believe him and repent of your sins.

Parable of the Evil Farmers

[33]"Now listen to another story. A certain landowner planted a vineyard, built a wall around it, dug a pit for pressing out the grape juice, and built a lookout tower. Then he

21:13 Isa 56:7; Jer 7:11. 21:16 Ps 8:2. 21:29-31 Other manuscripts read *"The second."* In still other manuscripts the first son says "Yes" but does nothing, the second son says "No" but then repents and goes, and the answer to Jesus' question is that the second son obeyed his father.

21:18-22 Jesus again commented on the power of faith. Seemingly impossible answers to prayer, including life-transforming recovery, can occur as we live by faith and grow in commitment to God. This passage does not suggest that we pray for the withering of a fig tree or the actual relocation of a mountain. It tells us, however, that incredible answers are given when we pray to God and believe that he will answer.

21:28-32 Before we began the recovery process, we were like the first son, saying no to his father's wishes. We turned our back to God and indulged our selfish desires. But later we saw where we were headed, changed our mind, and followed our Father. Although we have messed up our life, we are now obeying God. This is in sharp contrast to the son who said he would obey and then didn't. People like this may be part of the established "church" and think they are following God but are far from his ways. Our change of heart and lifestyle will gain us eternal life; their denial will earn them eternal punishment.

leased the vineyard to tenant farmers and moved to another country. [34]At the time of the grape harvest, he sent his servants to collect his share of the crop. [35]But the farmers grabbed his servants, beat one, killed one, and stoned another. [36]So the landowner sent a larger group of his servants to collect for him, but the results were the same.

[37]"Finally, the owner sent his son, thinking, 'Surely they will respect my son.'

[38]"But when the tenant farmers saw his son coming, they said to one another, 'Here comes the heir to this estate. Come on, let's kill him and get the estate for ourselves!' [39]So they grabbed him, dragged him out of the vineyard, and murdered him.

[40]"When the owner of the vineyard returns," Jesus asked, "what do you think he will do to those farmers?"

[41]The religious leaders replied, "He will put the wicked men to a horrible death and lease the vineyard to others who will give him his share of the crop after each harvest."

[42]Then Jesus asked them, "Didn't you ever read this in the Scriptures?

'The stone that the builders rejected
  has now become the cornerstone.
This is the LORD's doing,
  and it is wonderful to see.'*

[43]I tell you, the Kingdom of God will be taken away from you and given to a nation that will produce the proper fruit. [44]Anyone who stumbles over that stone will be broken to pieces, and it will crush anyone it falls on.*"

[45]When the leading priests and Pharisees heard this parable, they realized he was telling the story against them—they were the wicked farmers. [46]They wanted to arrest him, but they were afraid of the crowds, who considered Jesus to be a prophet.

CHAPTER 22
Parable of the Great Feast

Jesus also told them other parables. He said, [2]"The Kingdom of Heaven can be illustrated by the story of a king who prepared a great wedding feast for his son. [3]When the ban-

quet was ready, he sent his servants to notify those who were invited. But they all refused to come!

[4]"So he sent other servants to tell them, 'The feast has been prepared. The bulls and fattened cattle have been killed, and everything is ready. Come to the banquet!' [5]But the guests he had invited ignored them and went their own way, one to his farm, another to his business. [6]Others seized his messengers and insulted them and killed them.

[7]"The king was furious, and he sent out his army to destroy the murderers and burn their town. [8]And he said to his servants, 'The wedding feast is ready, and the guests I invited aren't worthy of the honor. [9]Now go out to the street corners and invite everyone you see.' [10]So the servants brought in everyone they could find, good and bad alike, and the banquet hall was filled with guests.

[11]"But when the king came in to meet the guests, he noticed a man who wasn't wearing the proper clothes for a wedding. [12]'Friend,' he asked, 'how is it that you are here without wedding clothes?' But the man had no reply. [13]Then the king said to his aides, 'Bind his hands and feet and throw him into the outer darkness, where there will be weeping and gnashing of teeth.'

[14]"For many are called, but few are chosen."

Taxes for Caesar

[15]Then the Pharisees met together to plot how to trap Jesus into saying something for which he could be arrested. [16]They sent some of their disciples, along with the supporters of Herod, to meet with him. "Teacher," they said, "we know how honest you are. You teach the way of God truthfully. You are impartial and don't play favorites. [17]Now tell us what you think about this: Is it right to pay taxes to Caesar or not?"

[18]But Jesus knew their evil motives. "You hypocrites!" he said. "Why are you trying to trap me? [19]Here, show me the coin used for the tax." When they handed him a Roman coin,* [20]he asked, "Whose picture and title are stamped on it?"

21:42 Ps 118:22-23. 21:44 This verse is not included in some early manuscripts. Compare Luke 20:18. 22:19 Greek a denarius.

22:1-10 When the king's servants brought everyone they could find to the wedding feast, there were good and bad people. The offer was open to anyone who wanted to come. So it is with heaven: Everyone is invited, and anyone can refuse the offer. The same principles apply to recovery. God wants everyone to lead a healthy, productive, godly life; but anyone can refuse to start the recovery process. Will we be like the first group of guests and suffer for our decision, or will we be like the second group and enjoy what God offers us?

²¹"Caesar's," they replied.

"Well, then," he said, "give to Caesar what belongs to Caesar, and give to God what belongs to God."

²²His reply amazed them, and they went away.

Discussion about Resurrection

²³That same day Jesus was approached by some Sadducees—religious leaders who say there is no resurrection from the dead. They posed this question: ²⁴"Teacher, Moses said, 'If a man dies without children, his brother should marry the widow and have a child who will carry on the brother's name.'* ²⁵Well, suppose there were seven brothers. The oldest one married and then died without children, so his brother married the widow. ²⁶But the second brother also died, and the third brother married her. This continued with all seven of them. ²⁷Last of all, the woman also died. ²⁸So tell us, whose wife will she be in the resurrection? For all seven were married to her."

²⁹Jesus replied, "Your mistake is that you don't know the Scriptures, and you don't know the power of God. ³⁰For when the dead rise, they will neither marry nor be given in marriage. In this respect they will be like the angels in heaven.

³¹"But now, as to whether there will be a resurrection of the dead—haven't you ever read about this in the Scriptures? Long after Abraham, Isaac, and Jacob had died, God said,* ³²'I am the God of Abraham, the God of Isaac, and the God of Jacob.'* So he is the God of the living, not the dead."

³³When the crowds heard him, they were astounded at his teaching.

The Most Important Commandment

³⁴But when the Pharisees heard that he had silenced the Sadducees with his reply, they met together to question him again. ³⁵One of them, an expert in religious law, tried to trap him with this question: ³⁶"Teacher, which is the most important commandment in the law of Moses?"

³⁷Jesus replied, " 'You must love the LORD your God with all your heart, all your soul, and all your mind.'* ³⁸This is the first and greatest commandment. ³⁹A second is equally important: 'Love your neighbor as yourself.'* ⁴⁰The entire law and all the demands of the prophets are based on these two commandments."

Whose Son Is the Messiah?

⁴¹Then, surrounded by the Pharisees, Jesus asked them a question: ⁴²"What do you think about the Messiah? Whose son is he?"

They replied, "He is the son of David."

⁴³Jesus responded, "Then why does David, speaking under the inspiration of the Spirit, call the Messiah 'my Lord'? For David said,

⁴⁴'The LORD said to my Lord,
　Sit in the place of honor at my
　　right hand
　until I humble your enemies beneath
　　your feet.'*

⁴⁵Since David called the Messiah 'my Lord,' how can the Messiah be his son?"

⁴⁶No one could answer him. And after that, no one dared to ask him any more questions.

CHAPTER 23
Jesus Criticizes the Religious Leaders

Then Jesus said to the crowds and to his disciples, ²"The teachers of religious law and the Pharisees are the official interpreters of the law of Moses.* ³So practice and obey whatever they tell you, but don't follow their example. For they don't practice what they

---

22:24 Deut 25:5-6. **22:31** Greek *read about this? God said.* **22:32** Exod 3:6. **22:37** Deut 6:5. **22:39** Lev 19:18.
22:44 Ps 110:1. **23:2** Greek *and the Pharisees sit in the seat of Moses.*

22:33-40 To simplify our priorities, Jesus narrowed the six hundred–plus regulations of the law of Moses into two foundational commandments: Love God with everything we are and have; love our neighbors as ourself. To do these is to obey every other law. A better two-point summary of the Twelve Steps could not be found. When we love God with our very life, we will not want to do anything to disgrace him or make him angry. Loving others should make us aware of the pain others feel when we engage in our addiction; our concern and love for them should make us think twice before causing them to suffer.

23:1-12 The Pharisees and Jewish leaders are classic examples of people who live by a double standard. They made the standards of behavior for others impossibly difficult, but they failed to keep these stipulations themselves. In spite of their shortcomings, they demanded to be called by titles fit only for God. They did not realize that true greatness begins with humility and is proven by a willingness to help others. The Pharisees' pride kept them from seeing their true need for God.

teach. [4]They crush people with unbearable religious demands and never lift a finger to ease the burden.

[5]"Everything they do is for show. On their arms they wear extra wide prayer boxes with Scripture verses inside, and they wear robes with extra long tassels.* [6]And they love to sit at the head table at banquets and in the seats of honor in the synagogues. [7]They love to receive respectful greetings as they walk in the marketplaces, and to be called 'Rabbi.'*

[8]"Don't let anyone call you 'Rabbi,' for you have only one teacher, and all of you are equal as brothers and sisters.* [9]And don't address anyone here on earth as 'Father,' for only God in heaven is your spiritual Father. [10]And don't let anyone call you 'Teacher,' for you have only one teacher, the Messiah. [11]The greatest among you must be a servant. [12]But those who exalt themselves will be humbled, and those who humble themselves will be exalted.

[13]"What sorrow awaits you teachers of religious law and you Pharisees. Hypocrites! For you shut the door of the Kingdom of Heaven in people's faces. You won't go in yourselves, and you don't let others enter either.*

[15]"What sorrow awaits you teachers of religious law and you Pharisees. Hypocrites! For you cross land and sea to make one convert, and then you turn that person into twice the child of hell* you yourselves are!

[16]"Blind guides! What sorrow awaits you! For you say that it means nothing to swear 'by God's Temple,' but that it is binding to swear 'by the gold in the Temple.' [17]Blind fools! Which is more important—the gold or the Temple that makes the gold sacred? [18]And you say that to swear 'by the altar' is not binding, but to swear 'by the gifts on the altar' is binding. [19]How blind! For which is more important—the gift on the altar or the altar that makes the gift sacred? [20]When you

swear 'by the altar,' you are swearing by it and by everything on it. [21]And when you swear 'by the Temple,' you are swearing by it and by God, who lives in it. [22]And when you swear 'by heaven,' you are swearing by the throne of God and by God, who sits on the throne.

[23]"What sorrow awaits you teachers of religious law and you Pharisees. Hypocrites! For you are careful to tithe even the tiniest income from your herb gardens,* but you ignore the more important aspects of the law—justice, mercy, and faith. You should tithe, yes, but do not neglect the more important things. [24]Blind guides! You strain your water so you won't accidentally swallow a gnat, but you swallow a camel!*

[25]"What sorrow awaits you teachers of religious law and you Pharisees. Hypocrites! For you are so careful to clean the outside of the cup and the dish, but inside you are filthy—full of greed and self-indulgence! [26]You blind Pharisee! First wash the inside of the cup and the dish,* and then the outside will become clean, too.

[27]"What sorrow awaits you teachers of religious law and you Pharisees. Hypocrites! For you are like whitewashed tombs—beautiful on the outside but filled on the inside with dead people's bones and all sorts of impurity. [28]Outwardly you look like righteous people, but inwardly your hearts are filled with hypocrisy and lawlessness.

[29]"What sorrow awaits you teachers of religious law and you Pharisees. Hypocrites! For you build tombs for the prophets your ancestors killed, and you decorate the monuments of the godly people your ancestors destroyed. [30]Then you say, 'If we had lived in the days of our ancestors, we would never have joined them in killing the prophets.' [31]But in saying that, you testify against yourselves that you are indeed the descendants of those who murdered the prophets.

23:5 Greek *They enlarge their phylacteries and lengthen their tassels.* **23:7** *Rabbi,* from Aramaic, means "master" or "teacher." **23:8** Greek *brothers.* **23:13** Some manuscripts add verse 14, *What sorrow awaits you teachers of religious law and you Pharisees. Hypocrites! You shamelessly cheat widows out of their property and then pretend to be pious by making long prayers in public. Because of this, you will be severely punished.* Compare Mark 12:40 and Luke 20:47. **23:15** Greek *of Gehenna;* also in 23:33. **23:23** Greek *tithe the mint, the dill, and the cumin.* **23:24** See Lev 11:4, 23, where gnats and camels are both forbidden as food. **23:26** Some manuscripts do not include *and the dish.*

23:13-36 Jesus gave warnings of judgment to all the spiritually blind religious leaders because of their hypocrisy. Their external rhetoric and ritualism were shams, all show with no inner reality. Such people cause others great pain and are far from recovery themselves. However, there is hope for everyone—even hypocrites! Joseph of Arimathea and Nicodemus, once numbered among the hypocrites, eventually found recovery through belief in Jesus (see John 19:38-42). If we search for Jesus, we will find him, and he will help us in the recovery process.

³²Go ahead and finish what your ancestors started. ³³Snakes! Sons of vipers! How will you escape the judgment of hell?

³⁴"Therefore, I am sending you prophets and wise men and teachers of religious law. But you will kill some by crucifixion, and you will flog others with whips in your synagogues, chasing them from city to city. ³⁵As a result, you will be held responsible for the murder of all godly people of all time—from the murder of righteous Abel to the murder of Zechariah son of Berekiah, whom you killed in the Temple between the sanctuary and the altar. ³⁶I tell you the truth, this judgment will fall on this very generation.

Jesus Grieves over Jerusalem

³⁷"O Jerusalem, Jerusalem, the city that kills the prophets and stones God's messengers! How often I have wanted to gather your children together as a hen protects her chicks beneath her wings, but you wouldn't let me. ³⁸And now, look, your house is abandoned and desolate.* ³⁹For I tell you this, you will never see me again until you say, 'Blessings on the one who comes in the name of the LORD!'* "

CHAPTER 24
Jesus Foretells the Future

As Jesus was leaving the Temple grounds, his disciples pointed out to him the various Temple buildings. ²But he responded, "Do you see all these buildings? I tell you the truth, they will be completely demolished. Not one stone will be left on top of another!"

³Later, Jesus sat on the Mount of Olives. His disciples came to him privately and said, "Tell us, when will all this happen? What sign will signal your return and the end of the world?*"

⁴Jesus told them, "Don't let anyone mislead you, ⁵for many will come in my name, claiming, 'I am the Messiah.' They will deceive many. ⁶And you will hear of wars and threats of wars, but don't panic. Yes, these things must take place, but the end won't follow immediately. ⁷Nation will go to war against nation, and kingdom against kingdom. There will be famines and earthquakes in many parts of the world. ⁸But all this is only the first of the birth pains, with more to come.

⁹"Then you will be arrested, persecuted, and killed. You will be hated all over the world because you are my followers.* ¹⁰And many will turn away from me and betray and hate each other. ¹¹And many false prophets will appear and will deceive many people. ¹²Sin will be rampant everywhere, and the love of many will grow cold. ¹³But the one who endures to the end will be saved. ¹⁴And the Good News about the Kingdom will be preached throughout the whole world, so that all nations* will hear it; and then the end will come.

¹⁵"The day is coming when you will see what Daniel the prophet spoke about—the sacrilegious object that causes desecration* standing in the Holy Place." (Reader, pay attention!) ¹⁶"Then those in Judea must flee to the hills. ¹⁷A person out on the deck of a roof must not go down into the house to pack. ¹⁸A person out in the field must not return even to get a coat. ¹⁹How terrible it will be for pregnant women and for nursing mothers in those days. ²⁰And pray that your flight will not be in winter or on the Sabbath. ²¹For there will be greater anguish than at any time

---

23:38 Some manuscripts do not include *and desolate.* 23:39 Ps 118:26. 24:3 Or *the age?* 24:9 Greek *on account of my name.* 24:14 Or *all peoples.* 24:15 Greek *the abomination of desolation.* See Dan 9:27; 11:31; 12:11.

24:2-8 Many people needing or seeking recovery are greatly discouraged by the fear that things will go on indefinitely in the same miserable, dysfunctional way they are now. As Jesus began his Olivet discourse (Matthew 24–25), he looked ahead to events surrounding his return to earth, and he promised that someday true recovery would take place (24:13). But things may get worse before they get better, which parallels the normal course for recovery. We need to hang in there until our program is complete and we are restored.

24:14 Because God loves everyone, he is delaying the world's judgment until all parts of the world have heard the message of salvation. This does not mean that everyone will accept the gospel; but every group will have had a chance to respond. As we get closer to world evangelization, we get closer to Christ's second coming. Have we accepted Jesus and his plan for salvation and recovery? If not, time is running out.

24:36-51 Jesus did not tell us when the final redemption of this evil world will come. In the same way, we may not know when our personal recovery is to be complete. All of us are still recovering, one day at a time. None of us has arrived. Not until Christ's second coming will we be relieved of daily working, watching, and recovering.

since the world began. And it will never be so great again. ²²In fact, unless that time of calamity is shortened, not a single person will survive. But it will be shortened for the sake of God's chosen ones.

²³"Then if anyone tells you, 'Look, here is the Messiah,' or 'There he is,' don't believe it. ²⁴For false messiahs and false prophets will rise up and perform great signs and wonders so as to deceive, if possible, even God's chosen ones. ²⁵See, I have warned you about this ahead of time.

²⁶"So if someone tells you, 'Look, the Messiah is out in the desert,' don't bother to go and look. Or, 'Look, he is hiding here,' don't believe it! ²⁷For as the lightning flashes in the east and shines to the west, so it will be when the Son of Man* comes. ²⁸Just as the gathering of vultures shows there is a carcass nearby, so these signs indicate that the end is near.*

²⁹"Immediately after the anguish of those days,

the sun will be darkened,
the moon will give no light,
the stars will fall from the sky,
and the powers in the heavens will be shaken.*

³⁰And then at last, the sign that the Son of Man is coming will appear in the heavens, and there will be deep mourning among all the peoples of the earth. And they will see the Son of Man coming on the clouds of heaven with power and great glory.* ³¹And he will send out his angels with the mighty blast of a trumpet, and they will gather his chosen ones from all over the world*—from the farthest ends of the earth and heaven.

³²"Now learn a lesson from the fig tree. When its branches bud and its leaves begin to sprout, you know that summer is near. ³³In the same way, when you see all these things, you can know his return is very near, right at the door. ³⁴I tell you the truth, this generation* will not pass from the scene until all these things take place. ³⁵Heaven and earth will disappear, but my words will never disappear.

³⁶"However, no one knows the day or hour when these things will happen, not even the angels in heaven or the Son himself.* Only the Father knows.

24:27 "Son of Man" is a title Jesus used for himself.
24:28 Greek *Wherever the carcass is, the vultures gather.*
24:29 See Isa 13:10; 34:4; Joel 2:10. 24:30 See Dan 7:13.
24:31 Greek *from the four winds.* 24:34 Or *this age,* or *this nation.* 24:36 Some manuscripts do not include *or the Son himself.*

PERFECTIONISM

READ MATTHEW 25:14-30
Perfectionism can paralyze us. Perhaps we have been shamed for not being exactly what others wanted us to be. Now the shadow of unrealistic expectations is cast over how we see ourself, creating unrealistic expectations for our progress.

Jesus told the story of a man who loaned three servants money to invest for him while he was away. The first two men invested and doubled the money; the third hid his money in a hole. The third servant saw the master through the eyes of fear. He "came and said, 'Master, I knew you were a harsh man, harvesting crops you didn't plant and gathering crops you didn't cultivate. I was afraid I would lose your money, so I hid it in the earth. Look, here is your money back.' But the master replied, ' . . . Why didn't you deposit my money into the bank? At least I could have gotten some interest on it'" (Matthew 25:24-27).

When we measure ourself by the expectations of others or by our own need to be perfect, we may fall so short that we may not even try to succeed. All God asks of us is that we try to do something with our abilities and resources. When we allow ourself the option of just making modest progress, we will find the courage to progress in recovery. Even the least improvement is better than not trying at all or being doomed to complete failure by our perfectionism. *Turn to page 1299, Luke 6.*

37"When the Son of Man returns, it will be like it was in Noah's day. 38In those days before the flood, the people were enjoying banquets and parties and weddings right up to the time Noah entered his boat. 39People didn't realize what was going to happen until the flood came and swept them all away. That is the way it will be when the Son of Man comes.

40"Two men will be working together in the field; one will be taken, the other left. 41Two women will be grinding flour at the mill; one will be taken, the other left.

42"So you, too, must keep watch! For you don't know what day your Lord is coming. 43Understand this: If a homeowner knew exactly when a burglar was coming, he would keep watch and not permit his house to be broken into. 44You also must be ready all the time, for the Son of Man will come when least expected.

45"A faithful, sensible servant is one to whom the master can give the responsibility of managing his other household servants and feeding them. 46If the master returns and finds that the servant has done a good job, there will be a reward. 47I tell you the truth, the master will put that servant in charge of all he owns. 48But what if the servant is evil and thinks, 'My master won't be back for a while,' 49and he begins beating the other servants, partying, and getting drunk? 50The master will return unannounced and unexpected, 51and he will cut the servant to pieces and assign him a place with the hypocrites. In that place there will be weeping and gnashing of teeth.

CHAPTER 25
Parable of the Ten Bridesmaids

"Then the Kingdom of Heaven will be like ten bridesmaids* who took their lamps and went to meet the bridegroom. 2Five of them were foolish, and five were wise. 3The five who were foolish didn't take enough olive oil for their lamps, 4but the other five were wise enough to take along extra oil. 5When the bridegroom was delayed, they all became drowsy and fell asleep.

6"At midnight they were roused by the shout, 'Look, the bridegroom is coming! Come out and meet him!'

7"All the bridesmaids got up and prepared their lamps. 8Then the five foolish ones asked the others, 'Please give us some of your oil because our lamps are going out.'

9"But the others replied, 'We don't have enough for all of us. Go to a shop and buy some for yourselves.'

10"But while they were gone to buy oil, the bridegroom came. Then those who were ready went in with him to the marriage feast, and the door was locked. 11Later, when the other five bridesmaids returned, they stood outside, calling, 'Lord! Lord! Open the door for us!'

12"But he called back, 'Believe me, I don't know you!'

13"So you, too, must keep watch! For you do not know the day or hour of my return.

Parable of the Three Servants

14"Again, the Kingdom of Heaven can be illustrated by the story of a man going on a long trip. He called together his servants and entrusted his money to them while he was gone. 15He gave five bags of silver* to one, two bags of silver to another, and one bag of silver to the last—dividing it in proportion to their abilities. He then left on his trip.

16"The servant who received the five bags of silver began to invest the money and earned five more. 17The servant with two bags of silver also went to work and earned two more. 18But the servant who received the one bag of silver dug a hole in the ground and hid the master's money.

19"After a long time their master returned from his trip and called them to give an account of how they had used his money. 20The servant to whom he had entrusted the five bags of silver came forward with five more and said, 'Master, you gave me five bags of silver to invest, and I have earned five more.'

21"The master was full of praise. 'Well done, my good and faithful servant. You

25:1 Or *virgins;* also in 25:7, 11. 25:15 Greek *talents;* also throughout the story. A talent is equal to 75 pounds or 34 kilograms.

25:1-13 The story of the ten bridesmaids reinforces the need for wise preparation and readiness for Christ's coming. Those who have not readied themselves for the return of Jesus, the heavenly bridegroom—by faith, commitment, and responsible living—will be left behind. For those of us who have suffered from a dysfunctional background, recovery is a very important part of that preparation.

have been faithful in handling this small amount, so now I will give you many more responsibilities. Let's celebrate together!*'

²²"The servant who had received the two bags of silver came forward and said, 'Master, you gave me two bags of silver to invest, and I have earned two more.'

²³"The master said, 'Well done, my good and faithful servant. You have been faithful in handling this small amount, so now I will give you many more responsibilities. Let's celebrate together!'

²⁴"Then the servant with the one bag of silver came and said, 'Master, I knew you were a harsh man, harvesting crops you didn't plant and gathering crops you didn't cultivate. ²⁵I was afraid I would lose your money, so I hid it in the earth. Look, here is your money back.'

²⁶"But the master replied, 'You wicked and lazy servant! If you knew I harvested crops I didn't plant and gathered crops I didn't cultivate, ²⁷why didn't you deposit my money in the bank? At least I could have gotten some interest on it.'

²⁸"Then he ordered, 'Take the money from this servant, and give it to the one with the ten bags of silver. ²⁹To those who use well what they are given, even more will be given, and they will have an abundance. But from those who do nothing, even what little they have will be taken away. ³⁰Now throw this useless servant into outer darkness, where there will be weeping and gnashing of teeth.'

The Final Judgment

³¹"But when the Son of Man* comes in his glory, and all the angels with him, then he will sit upon his glorious throne. ³²All the nations* will be gathered in his presence, and he will separate the people as a shepherd separates the sheep from the goats. ³³He will place the sheep at his right hand and the goats at his left.

³⁴"Then the King will say to those on his right, 'Come, you who are blessed by my Father, inherit the Kingdom prepared for you

from the creation of the world. ³⁵For I was hungry, and you fed me. I was thirsty, and you gave me a drink. I was a stranger, and you invited me into your home. ³⁶I was naked, and you gave me clothing. I was sick, and you cared for me. I was in prison, and you visited me.'

³⁷"Then these righteous ones will reply, 'Lord, when did we ever see you hungry and feed you? Or thirsty and give you something to drink? ³⁸Or a stranger and show you hospitality? Or naked and give you clothing? ³⁹When did we ever see you sick or in prison and visit you?'

⁴⁰"And the King will say, 'I tell you the truth, when you did it to one of the least of these my brothers and sisters,* you were doing it to me!'

⁴¹"Then the King will turn to those on the left and say, 'Away with you, you cursed ones, into the eternal fire prepared for the devil and his demons.* ⁴²For I was hungry, and you didn't feed me. I was thirsty, and you didn't give me a drink. ⁴³I was a stranger, and you didn't invite me into your home. I was naked, and you didn't give me clothing. I was sick and in prison, and you didn't visit me.'

⁴⁴"Then they will reply, 'Lord, when did we ever see you hungry or thirsty or a stranger or naked or sick or in prison, and not help you?'

⁴⁵"And he will answer, 'I tell you the truth, when you refused to help the least of these my brothers and sisters, you were refusing to help me.'

⁴⁶"And they will go away into eternal punishment, but the righteous will go into eternal life."

CHAPTER 26
The Plot to Kill Jesus

When Jesus had finished saying all these things, he said to his disciples, ²"As you know, Passover begins in two days, and the Son of Man* will be handed over to be crucified."

³At that same time the leading priests and elders were meeting at the residence of Caiaphas, the high priest, ⁴plotting how to

---

25:21 Greek *Enter into the joy of your master* [or *your Lord*]; also in 25:23. 25:31 "Son of Man" is a title Jesus used for himself. 25:32 Or *peoples*. 25:40 Greek *my brothers*. 25:41 Greek *his angels*. 26:2 "Son of Man" is a title Jesus used for himself.

25:31-46 Ultimately we will all be accountable to God on judgment day. We will be responsible not only for our own recovery but also for how we have helped others. The last step in recovery is to tell others about our recovery and encourage them in the recovery process. Since Jesus identifies himself with those who suffer, we should follow his example and be especially alert to the needs of others.

capture Jesus secretly and kill him. ⁵"But not during the Passover celebration," they agreed, "or the people may riot."

Jesus Anointed at Bethany

⁶Meanwhile, Jesus was in Bethany at the home of Simon, a man who had previously had leprosy. ⁷While he was eating,* a woman came in with a beautiful alabaster jar of expensive perfume and poured it over his head.

⁸The disciples were indignant when they saw this. "What a waste!" they said. ⁹"It could have been sold for a high price and the money given to the poor."

¹⁰But Jesus, aware of this, replied, "Why criticize this woman for doing such a good thing to me? ¹¹You will always have the poor among you, but you will not always have me. ¹²She has poured this perfume on me to prepare my body for burial. ¹³I tell you the truth, wherever the Good News is preached throughout the world, this woman's deed will be remembered and discussed."

Judas Agrees to Betray Jesus

¹⁴Then Judas Iscariot, one of the twelve disciples, went to the leading priests ¹⁵and asked, "How much will you pay me to betray Jesus to you?" And they gave him thirty pieces of silver. ¹⁶From that time on, Judas began looking for an opportunity to betray Jesus.

The Last Supper

¹⁷On the first day of the Festival of Unleavened Bread, the disciples came to Jesus and asked, "Where do you want us to prepare the Passover meal for you?"

¹⁸"As you go into the city," he told them, "you will see a certain man. Tell him, 'The Teacher says: My time has come, and I will eat the Passover meal with my disciples at your house.' " ¹⁹So the disciples did as Jesus told them and prepared the Passover meal there.

²⁰When it was evening, Jesus sat down at the table* with the Twelve. ²¹While they were eating, he said, "I tell you the truth, one of you will betray me."

²²Greatly distressed, each one asked in turn, "Am I the one, Lord?"

²³He replied, "One of you who has just eaten from this bowl with me will betray me. ²⁴For the Son of Man must die, as the Scriptures declared long ago. But how terrible it will be for the one who betrays him. It would be far better for that man if he had never been born!"

²⁵Judas, the one who would betray him, also asked, "Rabbi, am I the one?"

And Jesus told him, "You have said it."

²⁶As they were eating, Jesus took some bread and blessed it. Then he broke it in pieces and gave it to the disciples, saying, "Take this and eat it, for this is my body."

²⁷And he took a cup of wine and gave thanks to God for it. He gave it to them and said, "Each of you drink from it, ²⁸for this is my blood, which confirms the covenant* between God and his people. It is poured out as a sacrifice to forgive the sins of many. ²⁹Mark my words—I will not drink wine again until the day I drink it new with you in my Father's Kingdom."

³⁰Then they sang a hymn and went out to the Mount of Olives.

26:7 Or *reclining.* **26:20** Or *Jesus reclined.* **26:28** Some manuscripts read *the new covenant.*

26:6-13 This woman expressed her love for Jesus the best way she knew how. The disciples criticized her wastefulness, but Jesus commended her action. There will always be someone who thinks we are foolish for expressing our gratitude to God. But we should continue to praise him because he is the one who is working our recovery, and it gives us a chance to tell others what God has done for us. God loves our praise.

26:14-16, 20-25 Judas thought he could hide his dealings with the chief priests, but Jesus saw right through his false front. Jesus discreetly yet openly made Judas aware that he knew exactly what was going on. Judas, however, passed up an opportunity to confess his actions and restore his relationship with Jesus. When we are confronted with our sins, will we do as Judas did and deny our involvement, or will we use the chance to turn to God?

26:26-28 Through the Last Supper, Jesus communicated why he came to earth to die on the cross. His body would be broken, like the bread, so we could receive continued spiritual sustenance. His blood, represented by the wine, was the eternal payment for our sins. When we acknowledge Jesus as the Lord of our life, we become a member of his body, forgiven because of his blood. There are no restrictions based on race, sex, occupation, or past failures. All who look to Jesus are forgiven through the blood he shed on the cross.

Jesus Predicts Peter's Denial

³¹On the way, Jesus told them, "Tonight all of you will desert me. For the Scriptures say,

'God will strike* the Shepherd,
    and the sheep of the flock will be
    scattered.'

³²But after I have been raised from the dead, I will go ahead of you to Galilee and meet you there."

³³Peter declared, "Even if everyone else deserts you, I will never desert you."

³⁴Jesus replied, "I tell you the truth, Peter—this very night, before the rooster crows, you will deny three times that you even know me."

³⁵"No!" Peter insisted. "Even if I have to die with you, I will never deny you!" And all the other disciples vowed the same.

Jesus Prays in Gethsemane

³⁶Then Jesus went with them to the olive grove called Gethsemane, and he said, "Sit here while I go over there to pray." ³⁷He took Peter and Zebedee's two sons, James and John, and he became anguished and distressed. ³⁸He told them, "My soul is crushed with grief to the point of death. Stay here and keep watch with me."

³⁹He went on a little farther and bowed with his face to the ground, praying, "My Father! If it is possible, let this cup of suffering be taken away from me. Yet I want your will to be done, not mine."

⁴⁰Then he returned to the disciples and found them asleep. He said to Peter, "Couldn't you watch with me even one hour? ⁴¹Keep watch and pray, so that you will not give in to temptation. For the spirit is willing, but the body is weak!"

⁴²Then Jesus left them a second time and prayed, "My Father! If this cup cannot be taken away* unless I drink it, your will be done." ⁴³When he returned to them again, he found them sleeping, for they couldn't keep their eyes open.

⁴⁴So he went to pray a third time, saying the same things again. ⁴⁵Then he came to the disciples and said, "Go ahead and sleep. Have your rest. But look—the time has come. The Son of Man is betrayed into the hands of sinners. ⁴⁶Up, let's be going. Look, my betrayer is here!"

Jesus Is Betrayed and Arrested

⁴⁷And even as Jesus said this, Judas, one of the twelve disciples, arrived with a crowd of men armed with swords and clubs. They had been sent by the leading priests and elders of the people. ⁴⁸The traitor, Judas, had given them a prearranged signal: "You will know which one to arrest when I greet him with a kiss." ⁴⁹So Judas came straight to Jesus. "Greetings, Rabbi!" he exclaimed and gave him the kiss.

⁵⁰Jesus said, "My friend, go ahead and do what you have come for."

Then the others grabbed Jesus and arrested him. ⁵¹But one of the men with Jesus pulled out his sword and struck the high priest's slave, slashing off his ear.

⁵²"Put away your sword," Jesus told him. "Those who use the sword will die by the sword. ⁵³Don't you realize that I could ask my Father for thousands* of angels to protect us, and he would send them instantly? ⁵⁴But if I did, how would the Scriptures be fulfilled that describe what must happen now?"

⁵⁵Then Jesus said to the crowd, "Am I some dangerous revolutionary, that you come with swords and clubs to arrest me? Why didn't you arrest me in the Temple? I was there teaching every day. ⁵⁶But this is all happening to fulfill the words of the prophets as recorded in the Scriptures." At that point, all the disciples deserted him and fled.

Jesus before the Council

⁵⁷Then the people who had arrested Jesus led him to the home of Caiaphas, the high priest, where the teachers of religious law and the elders had gathered. ⁵⁸Meanwhile, Peter followed him at a distance and came to the high priest's courtyard. He went in and sat with the guards and waited to see how it would all end.

⁵⁹Inside, the leading priests and the entire high council* were trying to find witnesses

26:31 Greek *I will strike.* Zech 13:7. 26:42 Greek *If this cannot pass.* 26:53 Greek *twelve legions.* 26:59 Greek *the Sanhedrin.*

26:31-75 Like Peter, we often go through stages as we give in to our weaknesses. First we claim that we will never fail in a certain way (26:31-35). Then we do what we promised we wouldn't do (26:56, 69-74). Next we realize that we have failed miserably (26:75). From there we have two options: We can work to overcome our weakness and learn from the experience, as Peter did; or we can wallow in our sins and never grow spiritually, as Judas did (27:5).

who would lie about Jesus, so they could put him to death. [60]But even though they found many who agreed to give false witness, they could not use anyone's testimony. Finally, two men came forward [61]who declared, "This man said, 'I am able to destroy the Temple of God and rebuild it in three days.'"

[62]Then the high priest stood up and said to Jesus, "Well, aren't you going to answer these charges? What do you have to say for yourself?" [63]But Jesus remained silent. Then the high priest said to him, "I demand in the name of the living God—tell us if you are the Messiah, the Son of God."

[64]Jesus replied, "You have said it. And in the future you will see the Son of Man seated in the place of power at God's right hand* and coming on the clouds of heaven."*

[65]Then the high priest tore his clothing to show his horror and said, "Blasphemy! Why do we need other witnesses? You have all heard his blasphemy. [66]What is your verdict?"

"Guilty!" they shouted. "He deserves to die!"

[67]Then they began to spit in Jesus' face and beat him with their fists. And some slapped him, [68]jeering, "Prophesy to us, you Messiah! Who hit you that time?"

Peter Denies Jesus

[69]Meanwhile, Peter was sitting outside in the courtyard. A servant girl came over and said to him, "You were one of those with Jesus the Galilean."

[70]But Peter denied it in front of everyone. "I don't know what you're talking about," he said.

[71]Later, out by the gate, another servant girl noticed him and said to those standing around, "This man was with Jesus of Nazareth.*"

[72]Again Peter denied it, this time with an oath. "I don't even know the man," he said.

[73]A little later some of the other bystanders came over to Peter and said, "You must be one of them; we can tell by your Galilean accent."

[74]Peter swore, "A curse on me if I'm lying—I don't know the man!" And immediately the rooster crowed.

[75]Suddenly, Jesus' words flashed through Peter's mind: "Before the rooster crows, you will deny three times that you even know me." And he went away, weeping bitterly.

CHAPTER 27
Judas Hangs Himself

Very early in the morning the leading priests and the elders of the people met again to lay plans for putting Jesus to death. [2]Then they bound him, led him away, and took him to Pilate, the Roman governor.

[3]When Judas, who had betrayed him, realized that Jesus had been condemned to die, he was filled with remorse. So he took the thirty pieces of silver back to the leading priests and the elders. [4]"I have sinned," he declared, "for I have betrayed an innocent man."

"What do we care?" they retorted. "That's your problem."

[5]Then Judas threw the silver coins down in the Temple and went out and hanged himself.

[6]The leading priests picked up the coins. "It wouldn't be right to put this money in the Temple treasury," they said, "since it was payment for murder."* [7]After some discussion they finally decided to buy the potter's field, and they made it into a cemetery for foreigners. [8]That is why the field is still called the Field of Blood. [9]This fulfilled the prophecy of Jeremiah that says,

"They took* the thirty pieces of silver—
    the price at which he was valued
      by the people of Israel,
[10]and purchased the potter's field,
    as the LORD directed.*"

Jesus' Trial before Pilate

[11]Now Jesus was standing before Pilate, the Roman governor. "Are you the king of the Jews?" the governor asked him.

26:64a Greek *seated at the right hand of the power.* See Ps 110:1. **26:64b** See Dan 7:13. **26:71** Or *Jesus the Nazarene.*
27:6 Greek *since it is the price for blood.* **27:9** Or *I took.* **27:9-10** Greek *as the LORD directed me.* Zech 11:12-13; Jer 32:6-9.

27:3-8 The religious leaders refused to accept the blood money that Judas tried to return. It may have been their way of denying that they were responsible for the death of Jesus. If we are not careful, we can fall into this kind of hypocrisy and denial. Sometimes we hide behind righteous activities to conceal terrible sins. We should take moral inventory of our whole life and see which of our actions do not align with God's desires. Denying even one area of sin can jeopardize our entire recovery.
27:11-26 Pontius Pilate's handling of Jesus' trial indicates that he was a man consumed with pleasing others. Although he was convinced that Jesus was innocent and righteous (27:23-24),

Jesus replied, "You have said it."

¹²But when the leading priests and the elders made their accusations against him, Jesus remained silent. ¹³"Don't you hear all these charges they are bringing against you?" Pilate demanded. ¹⁴But Jesus made no response to any of the charges, much to the governor's surprise.

¹⁵Now it was the governor's custom each year during the Passover celebration to release one prisoner to the crowd—anyone they wanted. ¹⁶This year there was a notorious prisoner, a man named Barabbas.* ¹⁷As the crowds gathered before Pilate's house that morning, he asked them, "Which one do you want me to release to you—Barabbas, or Jesus who is called the Messiah?" ¹⁸(He knew very well that the religious leaders had arrested Jesus out of envy.)

¹⁹Just then, as Pilate was sitting on the judgment seat, his wife sent him this message: "Leave that innocent man alone. I suffered through a terrible nightmare about him last night."

²⁰Meanwhile, the leading priests and the elders persuaded the crowd to ask for Barabbas to be released and for Jesus to be put to death. ²¹So the governor asked again, "Which of these two do you want me to release to you?"

The crowd shouted back, "Barabbas!"

²²Pilate responded, "Then what should I do with Jesus who is called the Messiah?"

They shouted back, "Crucify him!"

²³"Why?" Pilate demanded. "What crime has he committed?"

But the mob roared even louder, "Crucify him!"

²⁴Pilate saw that he wasn't getting anywhere and that a riot was developing. So he sent for a bowl of water and washed his hands before the crowd, saying, "I am innocent of this man's blood. The responsibility is yours!"

²⁵And all the people yelled back, "We will take responsibility for his death—we and our children!"*

²⁶So Pilate released Barabbas to them. He ordered Jesus flogged with a lead-tipped whip, then turned him over to the Roman soldiers to be crucified.

The Soldiers Mock Jesus

²⁷Some of the governor's soldiers took Jesus into their headquarters* and called out the entire regiment. ²⁸They stripped him and put a scarlet robe on him. ²⁹They wove thorn branches into a crown and put it on his head, and they placed a reed stick in his right hand as a scepter. Then they knelt before him in mockery and taunted, "Hail! King of the Jews!" ³⁰And they spit on him and grabbed the stick and struck him on the head with it. ³¹When they were finally tired of mocking him, they took off the robe and put his own clothes on him again. Then they led him away to be crucified.

The Crucifixion

³²Along the way, they came across a man named Simon, who was from Cyrene,* and the soldiers forced him to carry Jesus' cross. ³³And they went out to a place called Golgotha (which means "Place of the Skull"). ³⁴The soldiers gave Jesus wine mixed with bitter gall, but when he had tasted it, he refused to drink it.

³⁵After they had nailed him to the cross, the soldiers gambled for his clothes by throwing dice.* ³⁶Then they sat around and kept guard as he hung there. ³⁷A sign was fastened above Jesus' head, announcing the charge against him. It read: "This is Jesus, the King of the Jews." ³⁸Two revolutionaries* were crucified with him, one on his right and one on his left.

³⁹The people passing by shouted abuse,

27:16 Some manuscripts read *Jesus Barabbas;* also in 27:17. 27:25 Greek *"His blood be on us and on our children."* 27:27 Or *into the Praetorium.* 27:32 *Cyrene* was a city in northern Africa. 27:35 Greek *by casting lots.* A few late manuscripts add *This fulfilled the word of the prophet: "They divided my garments among themselves and cast lots for my robe."* See Ps 22:18. 27:38 Or *criminals;* also in 27:44.

---

he bowed to public opinion. Pilate exemplifies someone in need of recovery who knows the right thing to do but does not have the courage to follow through and risk angering others. Since it is impossible to please everyone all the time, we must make sure that what we do is honest and pleasing to God. We should be more concerned about sinning against God than about angering other people.

27:26-54 The narrative of Jesus' crucifixion and death records one act of brutal abuse after another. Jesus was beaten, ridiculed, tortured, and killed. Thus, he can understand the feelings of those who have been abused or oppressed. Jesus can also redeem oppressors or abusers who come to faith, as did the Roman officer and other soldiers at the cross. Jesus' death and resurrection were intended to bring deliverance for everyone.

shaking their heads in mockery. [40]"Look at you now!" they yelled at him. "You said you were going to destroy the Temple and rebuild it in three days. Well then, if you are the Son of God, save yourself and come down from the cross!"

[41]The leading priests, the teachers of religious law, and the elders also mocked Jesus. [42]"He saved others," they scoffed, "but he can't save himself! So he is the King of Israel, is he? Let him come down from the cross right now, and we will believe in him! [43]He trusted God, so let God rescue him now if he wants him! For he said, 'I am the Son of God.'" [44]Even the revolutionaries who were crucified with him ridiculed him in the same way.

The Death of Jesus

[45]At noon, darkness fell across the whole land until three o'clock. [46]At about three o'clock, Jesus called out with a loud voice, "*Eli, Eli,* lema sabachthani?" which means "My God, my God, why have you abandoned me?"*

[47]Some of the bystanders misunderstood and thought he was calling for the prophet Elijah. [48]One of them ran and filled a sponge with sour wine, holding it up to him on a reed stick so he could drink. [49]But the rest said, "Wait! Let's see whether Elijah comes to save him."*

[50]Then Jesus shouted out again, and he released his spirit. [51]At that moment the curtain in the sanctuary of the Temple was torn in two, from top to bottom. The earth shook, rocks split apart, [52]and tombs opened. The bodies of many godly men and women who had died were raised from the dead. [53]They left the cemetery after Jesus' resurrection, went into the holy city of Jerusalem, and appeared to many people.

[54]The Roman officer* and the other soldiers at the crucifixion were terrified by the earthquake and all that had happened. They said, "This man truly was the Son of God!"

[55]And many women who had come from Galilee with Jesus to care for him were watching from a distance. [56]Among them were Mary Magdalene, Mary (the mother of James and Joseph), and the mother of James and John, the sons of Zebedee.

The Burial of Jesus

[57]As evening approached, Joseph, a rich man from Arimathea who had become a follower of Jesus, [58]went to Pilate and asked for Jesus' body. And Pilate issued an order to release it to him. [59]Joseph took the body and wrapped it in a long sheet of clean linen cloth. [60]He placed it in his own new tomb, which had been carved out of the rock. Then he rolled a great stone across the entrance and left. [61]Both Mary Magdalene and the other Mary were sitting across from the tomb and watching.

The Guard at the Tomb

[62]The next day, on the Sabbath,* the leading priests and Pharisees went to see Pilate. [63]They told him, "Sir, we remember what that deceiver once said while he was still alive: 'After three days I will rise from the dead.' [64]So we request that you seal the tomb until the third day. This will prevent his disciples from coming and stealing his body and then telling everyone he was raised from the dead! If that happens, we'll be worse off than we were at first."

[65]Pilate replied, "Take guards and secure it

27:46a Some manuscripts read *Eloi, Eloi.* **27:46b** Ps 22:1. **27:49** Some manuscripts add *And another took a spear and pierced his side, and out flowed water and blood.* Compare John 19:34. **27:54** Greek *The centurion.* **27:62** Or *On the next day, which is after the Preparation.*

27:57-60 Joseph of Arimathea was a secret disciple (see John 19:38) who revealed his faith at a crisis point. He was like the people who toy with recovery in a limited and private sense, but then come to the point of decision where they either have to reject their program or make a deeper commitment to it. Joseph's willingness to approach Pilate, as well as his generous burial of Jesus, indicates that he took a step of faith toward a stronger commitment to the Lord. What kind of crisis will it take to inspire us to devote our life wholeheartedly to God and his program of recovery?

27:62–28:15 The religious leaders went to a lot of trouble to be free of Jesus' message. They discredited him in front of the crowds and plotted his murder. When they caught him, they tried to come up with witnesses and had to convince Rome that Jesus should be killed. After Jesus' death, the leaders feared he would come back to life, so they sealed and guarded the tomb. Finally, they invented a story to explain the disappearance of Jesus' body. It would have been easier to accept Jesus' message and make appropriate changes in their lives and beliefs. We must not become so hardened by denial that we, like the Jewish leaders, go to great lengths to avoid accepting the lifesaving message of the gospel.

the best you can." [66]So they sealed the tomb and posted guards to protect it.

CHAPTER 28
The Resurrection

Early on Sunday morning,* as the new day was dawning, Mary Magdalene and the other Mary went out to visit the tomb.

[2]Suddenly there was a great earthquake! For an angel of the Lord came down from heaven, rolled aside the stone, and sat on it. [3]His face shone like lightning, and his clothing was as white as snow. [4]The guards shook with fear when they saw him, and they fell into a dead faint.

[5]Then the angel spoke to the women. "Don't be afraid!" he said. "I know you are looking for Jesus, who was crucified. [6]He isn't here! He is risen from the dead, just as he said would happen. Come, see where his body was lying. [7]And now, go quickly and tell his disciples that he has risen from the dead, and he is going ahead of you to Galilee. You will see him there. Remember what I have told you."

[8]The women ran quickly from the tomb. They were very frightened but also filled with great joy, and they rushed to give the disciples the angel's message. [9]And as they went, Jesus met them and greeted them. And they ran to him, grasped his feet, and worshiped him. [10]Then Jesus said to them, "Don't be afraid! Go tell my brothers to leave for Galilee, and they will see me there."

The Report of the Guard

[11]As the women were on their way, some of the guards went into the city and told the leading priests what had happened. [12]A meeting with the elders was called, and they decided to give the soldiers a large bribe. [13]They told the soldiers, "You must say, 'Jesus' disciples came during the night while we were sleeping, and they stole his body.' [14]If the governor hears about it, we'll stand up for you so you won't get in trouble." [15]So the guards accepted the bribe and said what they were told to say. Their story spread widely among the Jews, and they still tell it today.

The Great Commission

[16]Then the eleven disciples left for Galilee, going to the mountain where Jesus had told them to go. [17]When they saw him, they worshiped him—but some of them doubted! [18]Jesus came and told his disciples, "I have been given all authority in heaven and on earth. [19]Therefore, go and make disciples of all the nations,* baptizing them in the name of the Father and the Son and the Holy Spirit. [20]Teach these new disciples to obey all the commands I have given you. And be sure of this: I am with you always, even to the end of the age."

28:1 Greek *After the Sabbath, on the first day of the week.* 28:19 Or *all peoples.*

28:16-20 Some disciples adjusted to the reality of Jesus' resurrection quite readily, while others still doubted. But Jesus' resurrection was not an end in itself, nor was it for just his closest disciples. This new life through faith in the crucified and resurrected Christ is offered to all the people of the world. Those who by faith enter true spiritual recovery are baptized to show their commitment. Studying God's Word and regular instruction in the faith help those in recovery grow spiritually. Recovery is available through God's power until Jesus returns at the end of the age.

REFLECTIONS ON MATTHEW

insights ABOUT THE PERSON OF JESUS

The mention of Tamar, Rahab, Ruth, and Bathsheba in Jesus' lineage in **Matthew 1:1-16** is significant. Each of these women was almost certainly non-Jewish in ethnic background. Yet God used them along the way to prepare for the coming of the Jewish Messiah. Similarly, God often employs people from diverse and unusual backgrounds to accomplish his purposes. His grace is stronger than the presumed limitations of our past. He can use us regardless of our background.

In **Matthew 3:13-15** Jesus was baptized by John the Baptist. Jesus had no real reason to follow John's call to baptism because Jesus had never sinned and had no reason to repent. Jesus was baptized anyway because it was the right thing to do, and his actions modeled the importance of baptism to others. We who seek recovery need examples of those who do the right things for the right reasons, thus modeling a balanced life. As we proceed in the recovery process, we can become a model for others in need of recovery. Being an example for others through our words and deeds will not only help others but also encourage us to persevere in our own recovery.

In **Matthew 4:23-25** Jesus offered healing and restoration—physically, spiritually, and interpersonally. He provides recovery from the pain of abuse and dysfunctional relationships, areas that trouble an ever-increasing number of people. Such recovery is extended through faith in Jesus Christ. Through him, true recovery is open to all who believe in him. No part of our life is beyond his healing touch.

insights CONCERNING OBSTACLES TO RECOVERY

In **Matthew 1:18-25** Joseph was in a difficult predicament. His fiancée, Mary, had become pregnant, so he was considering how he could break their engagement quietly. But when Joseph was shown that the Holy Spirit was responsible for the pregnancy, he immediately changed his decision about breaking the engagement and obeyed God. He married her as the angel of the Lord commanded, despite the rumors that would surely surround their marriage. Pride can easily become an obstacle to the restoration of our damaged relationships. We should resist pride and obey God as Joseph did.

When we enter recovery, we should not mistakenly think that our faith and spiritual growth will insulate us from temptation. On the contrary, in **Matthew 4:1-2** Jesus was actually led into the wilderness by the Holy Spirit for a prolonged siege of temptation. This should serve as a fair warning that temptation may follow quickly on the heels of a spiritual high. God often uses such trials in our life to remind us of how helpless we are without him.

In **Matthew 5:10-12** we are reminded that persecution can be a real problem for us as we try to live by God's principles. Old friends may try to intimidate us into giving up on recovery. Family members may be threatened by the changes we are making and try to discourage us. We must realize that it is more important to please God than other people. As we do things God's way, we will be set free from our destructive and codependent relationships. Then we can build healthy relationships with others and continue to strengthen our all-important relationship with God.

In **Matthew 6:19-34** Jesus made it clear that living for personal gain will only lead to great anxiety. Materialism and anxiety are two enemies of recovery. They often work together to lead us away from a balanced life. We need to realize that the essence of life is not found in the possession of things and that worry about the future availability of material things is never helpful. We are powerless to change the future and must trust God to take care of us and empower us in recovery. As we entrust our life to him, we will no longer need to worry about what is around the corner.

People who refuse to admit they need recovery are usually the first to stand in the way of someone else's recovery. Instead of praising God for the miracle that Jesus performed, in **Matthew 12:9-12** the Pharisees judged Jesus for breaking the Sabbath laws. To the Pharisees, it was more important to preserve their legalistic observances than to see a man healed of his deformity. They chose to be ruled by their interpretations of the law and rejected the rule of the compassionate Messiah-King. There will be people who oppose our recovery, doing anything they can to keep us enslaved to our addiction. We should make every effort to overcome our dependency, regardless of the pressures from those around us. With God's help, no obstacle is too great to overcome.

In **Matthew 14:1-11** John the Baptist was arrested because he had condemned Herod Antipas for marrying his brother's wife, Herodias. Rather than admit his sin, Herod put John in prison, hoping to silence him. Herodias wanted John silenced too, but she was more vicious than her husband and wanted John executed. In the end, Herod was too weak to refuse his wife's request, and the prophet was beheaded. Our shame from one sin often leads us to commit greater sins. To avoid the downward spiral, we must have the courage to admit our smaller sins and problems before they grow larger. As we turn our sins and failures over to God, we can be confident that we will receive his healing help.

insights ABOUT HONESTY AND DENIAL

It is clear from **Matthew 3:5-9** that not everyone who listened to John the Baptist wanted to repent and find a new life. John saw that the Pharisees and others like them were merely going through the motions, trusting external appearances for their salvation. Similarly, some of us who claim to be in recovery are simply going through the motions, appearing to work on the addiction while not having changed our heart through repentance. If this is the case, we are headed for painful relapses. We need to begin with an honest assessment of our weaknesses and failures before we can receive God's help and forgiveness.

In **Matthew 3:7-11** John the Baptist confronted the Pharisees with their denial. These religious leaders were blind to the sins of their hearts and believed they were beyond the reach of God's judgment. Perhaps we have acted as if the consequences of our actions would never catch up with us. Our denial may have been so deep that we weren't even aware of the serious consequences we would have to face. It is only a matter of time before God will take his ax of judgment to "unproductive trees"—those who are not following him. For those of us who truly repent, God fuels our recovery with the power of his Holy Spirit. The choice is ours: Either we continue as we are and await God's judgment, or we turn from our present lifestyle and enter recovery, depending on God's Spirit to help us change.

In **Matthew 7:1-5** Jesus warned against our tendency of being critical of others. It is easy to hide from the sins and dependency ("logs") in our own life by pointing out the small failures ("specks") in the lives of others. This kind of denial destroys the relationships we need for recovery and blinds us to our own sins and their destructive consequences. To be truly helpful to others, we must first recognize sin in our own life and deal with it. After humbling ourself in this way, we will be ready to confront others about their need for recovery.

The tax collectors in Judea during Jesus' time were Jews who had sold out to the oppressive Roman government. They used their position to extort money from their own people. They were hated by the Jewish population, who considered them traitors to God and their homeland. In **Matthew 9:9-13** the Jews were surprised that Jesus would even speak to such people. Matthew, the author of this Gospel, and his friends were surprisingly open to grace and forgiveness. As dysfunctional as they were, they admitted their need and responded to Jesus with humility. On the other hand, the Pharisees clung to their self-righteous denial, not recognizing their own desperate need for recovery. It is not how we appear to others that matters; it is whether or not we are willing to let God free us from the power of sin in our life.

In **Matthew 10:14-15** we discover that denial has eternal ramifications. Those who refuse the offer of recovery in Christ are making an eternal mistake. This message may seem threatening at the moment, but it is meant to bring peace and serenity. In the end, we who have become comfortable in our ever-increasing denial will have to answer to God at the time of our final judgment.

insights ABOUT GOD'S PRIORITIES

The Beatitudes in **Matthew 5:1-12** contain much of what God desires of us as we seek to follow his will for our life. This lifestyle affirms God's perspective, priorities, and boundaries. As we look over God's program in this passage, we may wonder how anyone could live up to it. The truth is, no one can do it without God's help. Following God's program requires wisdom and grace from above. But the lifestyle found in these verses can replace our warped human outlook with God's enduring perspective.

In **Matthew 6:1-4** we see that God's priorities are very different from ours. God is more interested in our quiet service to others than our outward worldly success. Each of us has a public and a private life, but the reward systems for each are very different. While we may succeed in the world by becoming famous or wealthy, we will never receive further reward from God for our public success. If we humbly seek to help others, we will be openly rewarded by our heavenly Father. What seems private and unnoticed by other people is public, even center stage, before God.

insights INTO SHARING THE GOOD NEWS

In **Matthew 5:13-16** Jesus described what we should be like. If we have been delivered by God's power, we are witnesses to his power to save. We are to carry the light of his good news to people imprisoned in the darkness of addiction and sin. Dysfunctional behavior and warped relationships abound, in part due to our lack of healthy, Christian role models. People are desperate for seasoning and light. We can make a significant impact on individuals, relationships, and even societal structures if we let our spiritual light shine for others to see. As we experience God's deliverance, we are called to share our recovery with others. This will not only extend hope to hurting people, but it will also encourage us as we face new trials ahead.

Jesus had great compassion for those who had no protection or guidance. So in **Matthew 9:36–10:8** Jesus began training his closest disciples to help fill the need. They were to go out and use God's power to heal and encourage those needing physical or spiritual recovery. They were not expected to reach everyone, but they were to make a difference in at least one needy group. As we share our story of recovery with others, we cannot expect to reach everyone with the good news of recovery. We can, however, share the message with a few, who will also share their story with others. As we use our own recovery to encourage the recovery of others, we will start a chain reaction that will touch the lives of many.

Matthew 25:14-30 is about using our gifts wisely, and it provides needed encouragement and sobering reality to those of us in recovery. Even though this parable is about money, it can, by extension, also refer to God-given abilities. Everyone has been given various abilities by God; no one is untalented or worthless. That should encourage us. On the other hand, we are each responsible to use our abilities for God. After suffering for years as a slave to our destructive addiction, some of us may wonder if we have anything to offer. Yet even if we have nothing else, we have something to tell others. As we share our experiences of deliverance, we will give others hope for recovery. Our years of suffering may become the gift of life to someone in need.

insights ABOUT PRAYER

In **Matthew 6:9-13** Jesus gave his disciples a model prayer to follow. This prayer is more than just a model for our prayers; it is a model for our life in recovery. We are to acknowledge God in our life and honor his name. Our greatest desire should be to see his Kingdom established and his will done on earth, both in our life and in the world in general. God's daily provision for us is another petition important for recovery. We must ask for forgiveness of our sins and forgive those who have wronged us. Finally, God wants us to ask for protection from Satan's temptations we face each day. If we are praying these things and living them in our walk with God, we are truly on the path of recovery.

insights CONCERNING TRUE FAITH

In **Matthew 7:24-27** we are told that two kinds of life-building foundations are available. One foundation is as solid as rock—the foundation of faith in Jesus Christ. The other foundation is like shifting sand—the foundation of human pride and selfish endeavor. Our life might be outwardly impressive, but if it is built on the wrong foundation, difficult circumstances will soon level what we have built. Like a fragile house of cards, our life will come crashing down. How much better to build our life on the solid foundation of faith in Jesus Christ. Then when the inevitable storms of life come, we will not be destroyed.

In **Matthew 11:25-30** we are told of the importance of childlike faith. Only when we come to Jesus as little children can we find recovery and relief for our emotional pain. Many of us think we can work things out our own way. In doing this, we miss this simple truth: God alone has the power to enable us in recovery. We cannot even begin recovery until we are willing to admit how powerless we are; this is the importance of childlike faith. Children are powerless and are very aware of that fact; they entrust themselves to their parents each and every day. As we recognize how powerless we are over our dependency, we can entrust ourself to God's loving care. He has all the power we need for full recovery.

In **Matthew 14:25-33** Jesus walked on water and then enabled Peter, through faith, to do the same. Before we began the process of recovery, our life was as turbulent as a stormy sea. When we trusted God for recovery, we, like Peter, stepped out in faith into that storm-tossed sea. As long as we hold on to our faith and keep our eyes on Jesus, we will succeed over the waves of life. When we focus on the troubled waters around us and forget God's assistance, we start to sink and are overwhelmed by our dependency and character flaws. If we want to make continued progress, we need to focus on Christ.

In **Matthew 15:21-28** a Gentile woman showed great perseverance and faith, and Jesus rewarded her for it. When we seek recovery, we must truly believe that God is able to effect our recovery. We also must be prepared to persist in our program, not giving up even when there seems to be little hope for success. God will reward our efforts if we are fully committed to following his will and prove it by our actions.

MARK

THE BIG PICTURE

A. JESUS PREPARES FOR SERVICE (1:1-13)
B. JESUS SERVES THROUGH WORD AND DEED (1:14–13:37)
  1. Jesus Serves in Galilee (1:14–9:50)
  2. Jesus Serves beyond Jerusalem (10:1-45)
  3. Jesus Serves in Jerusalem (10:46–13:37)
C. JESUS SERVES THROUGH SELF-SACRIFICE (14:1–16:20)

When our life was out of control, we responded to our trials in various ways—with anger, bitterness, or rebellion. Our addiction determined our behavior and attitudes. We eventually realized that our life had become unmanageable and that we were destroying not only ourself but our loved ones, too. We needed to break the cycle, but we were powerless to do so.

The Gospel of Mark is written for people like us; it shows that Jesus is powerful and wants to help us. In this Gospel we see Jesus' power displayed again and again: He raised the dead, gave sight to the blind, restored deformed limbs, made lame people walk, cast out demons, healed incurable skin diseases, and quieted stormy waters. Although Mark is the shortest Gospel, it records more miracles than any of the others. It proves that Jesus is a powerful Savior and is more than able to help suffering people.

This Gospel also emphasizes the fact that Jesus wants to help us. Jesus spent his energy to the point of exhaustion healing those who came to him for help. By recording a rapid succession of vivid pictures of Jesus in action, the Gospel writer has shown that Jesus came to help us. This truth is driven home by Jesus' willingness to suffer a painful death to free us from our bondage to sin.

Jesus has power over the problems that bind us. He is more powerful than our dependency, problems, and weaknesses. He has the power to help us all with recovery, no matter how terrible our past experiences. All we have to do is look to him and admit that we need his help.

THE BOTTOM LINE

PURPOSE: To encourage us to continue trusting and serving God, especially through life's difficulties. AUTHOR: John Mark. AUDIENCE: The Christians in Rome. DATE WRITTEN: Probably between A.D. 55 and 65. SETTING: The Roman Empire had unified the known world, and its use of a common language made conditions ideal for the spread of the gospel in written form. KEY VERSE: "For even the Son of Man came not to be served but to serve others and to give his life as a ransom for many" (10:45). SPECIAL FEATURES: The Gospel of Mark is characterized by its fast-paced narrative. KEY PEOPLE AND RELATIONSHIPS: Jesus with his disciples, especially Peter.

RECOVERY THEMES

Jesus as the Servant: The Twelfth Step tells us that our recovery should lead us to be servants and share our story of deliverance with others. Real greatness in God's eyes is demonstrated by a willingness to serve and sacrifice for others. Jesus didn't come as a conquering king; he came as a servant. He chose to obey his Father and die for us. When personal ambition and hunger for power control our life, we live in contradiction to the principles of recovery and to God's will for our life.

The Power of God: The Gospel of Mark is filled with amazing events that display the awesome power of God in Jesus. Mark recorded more of Jesus' miracles than his sermons. He wanted us to see God's power in action. The more we are convinced that Jesus is God, the more we will see his power and his love in action in our own life. His greatest miracles are still those that involve forgiveness, healing of relationships, and the restoration of lost or wasted pasts. The same power we see in Mark's Gospel is available to us today.

Recovery Is Not the Goal: Some people are afraid of recovery because it seems all-consuming. They have a distorted image of what recovery is all about. Our goal is not recovery; our goal is spiritual and emotional growth, demonstrated by sacrificial service. That is one reason we can never claim to have recovered. Jesus set the pace for us with his example of service. His whole purpose in coming was to serve, not to be served. That principle—that we seek to give away what we have gained—is an essential part of the recovery process.

Sharing the Message: There is no such thing as a secret disciple or a private recovery. Discipleship and recovery take place within relationships. God's good news is meant to be shared. As we share the joys and struggles of our own experiences in recovery, we encourage others in recovery. The message transcends national, racial, and economic barriers, reaching out to all those who are willing to admit their powerlessness. The message of recovery is worth sharing with others.

CHAPTER 1
John the Baptist Prepares the Way

This is the Good News about Jesus the Messiah, the Son of God.* It began ²just as the prophet Isaiah had written:

"Look, I am sending my messenger ahead
　　of you,
　and he will prepare your way.*
³ He is a voice shouting in the wilderness,
　'Prepare the way for the LORD's coming!
　　Clear the road for him!'*"

⁴This messenger was John the Baptist. He was in the wilderness and preached that people should be baptized to show that they had repented of their sins and turned to God to be forgiven. ⁵All of Judea, including all the people of Jerusalem, went out to see and hear John. And when they confessed their sins, he baptized them in the Jordan River. ⁶His clothes were woven from coarse camel hair, and he wore a leather belt around his waist. For food he ate locusts and wild honey.

⁷John announced: "Someone is coming soon who is greater than I am—so much greater that I'm not even worthy to stoop down like a slave and untie the straps of his sandals. ⁸I baptize you with* water, but he will baptize you with the Holy Spirit!"

The Baptism and Temptation of Jesus

⁹One day Jesus came from Nazareth in Galilee, and John baptized him in the Jordan River. ¹⁰As Jesus came up out of the water, he saw the heavens splitting apart and the Holy Spirit descending on him* like a dove. ¹¹And a voice from heaven said, "You are my dearly loved Son, and you bring me great joy."

¹²The Spirit then compelled Jesus to go into the wilderness, ¹³where he was tempted by Satan for forty days. He was out among the wild animals, and angels took care of him.

¹⁴Later on, after John was arrested, Jesus went into Galilee, where he preached God's Good News.* ¹⁵"The time promised by God

1:1 Some manuscripts do not include *the Son of God.* 1:2 Mal 3:1. 1:3 Isa 40:3 (Greek version). 1:8 Or *in;* also in 1:8b. 1:10 Or *toward him,* or *into him.* 1:14 Some manuscripts read *the Good News of the Kingdom of God.*

1:1-13 Only belief in a Power greater than ourself can restore us to sanity. That's how John the Baptist saw Jesus—as one far greater than he was. Jesus demonstrated his great power through victory over Satan and his temptations. This should encourage us as we face our own temptations. With his help, we can stand up to anything. Under our own power, we are helpless against the power of our dependency. We can tap into God's power by making a conscious decision to turn our back on sin (1:4) and by entrusting our life to God's care.

SIMON PETER

Simon the fisherman was reckless, vacillating, and often thoughtless. We would never nickname such a person *Peter*, which means "rock." Jesus did. What greater evidence could there be that Jesus not only accepted Simon as he was but also envisioned what he would become? By the end of his life Simon's nickname, Peter, appropriately described his steadfast maturity. What an amazing transformation took place in that burly fisherman!

Most of us readily identify with Simon Peter. His intentions were usually good, but he was impetuous in speech and impulsive in action. Instead of standing in awe at the Transfiguration, he blurted out the first idea that came into his head. When Jesus revealed that his divine mission would involve a painful death, Peter rashly told Jesus to stop talking that way. At the Last Supper he brazenly objected to Jesus washing his feet. When Jesus was arrested, Peter bravely but brashly cut off the ear of the high priest's servant. Finally, at a critical point in his life, Peter denied Jesus three times. Even as Jesus was restoring Peter from this failure, Peter's attention was on John rather than on what God was doing for him.

Later in Simon's life we see what Jesus saw when he called him "Rock." Peter presided over the meeting to select a successor to Judas. At Pentecost he preached publicly about Jesus despite the opposition he knew he would face. Peter performed several miracles and was himself miraculously rescued from prison. Peter was the apostle who had the spiritual insight to proclaim the great confession at Caesarea Philippi, stating clearly that Jesus Christ is the only means to salvation.

In Simon Peter's life we see hope for our transformation and recovery. He was amazingly transformed by God, but we should remember that he was never made perfect. The apostle Paul described in Galatians 2:11-14 how Peter acted hypocritically. Despite his imperfections, however, his transformation had a profound effect on the world around him; his words, actions, and letters became a significant part of the early church's spiritual foundation.

STRENGTHS AND ACCOMPLISHMENTS:
- Simon's natural boldness was used to spread the good news of Jesus Christ.
- He was the recognized leader and spokesman for the twelve disciples.
- He was inspired to write letters to encourage believers (1 and 2 Peter).
- His natural enthusiasm was later channeled into disciplined courage.

WEAKNESSES AND MISTAKES:
- Simon often spoke and acted before he thought about the consequences.
- His temperament was mercurial; he quickly moved from professed loyalty to betrayal.
- Even after his transformation, he allowed a situation to govern his actions at least once (Galatians 2:11-14).

LESSONS FROM HIS LIFE:
- Jesus Christ has enough power to transform even the most unlikely people.
- God can transform our faults into powerful tools for use in his Kingdom.
- When people make themselves available, they can always be used by God.

KEY VERSE:
"Now I say to you that you are Peter (which means 'rock') and upon this rock I will build my church, and all the powers of hell will not conquer it" (Matthew 16:18).

There is extensive biblical material on Simon Peter in the Gospels and Acts 1–15. In Paul's letters, Peter is mentioned in 1 Corinthians 1:12; 3:22; 9:5; 15:5; and Galatians 1:18; 2:7-14. Some material about him may also be gleaned from his two letters, 1 and 2 Peter.

---

has come at last!" he announced. "The Kingdom of God is near! Repent of your sins and believe the Good News!"

The First Disciples
[16]One day as Jesus was walking along the shore of the Sea of Galilee, he saw Simon* and his brother Andrew throwing a net into the water, for they fished for a living. [17]Jesus called out to them, "Come, follow me, and I will show you how to fish for people!" [18]And they left their nets at once and followed him.

[19]A little farther up the shore Jesus saw Zebedee's sons, James and John, in a boat repairing their nets. [20]He called them at once, and they also followed him, leaving their father, Zebedee, in the boat with the hired men.

1:16 *Simon* is called "Peter" in 3:16 and thereafter.

Jesus Casts Out an Evil Spirit

[21]Jesus and his companions went to the town of Capernaum. When the Sabbath day came, he went into the synagogue and began to teach. [22]The people were amazed at his teaching, for he taught with real authority—quite unlike the teachers of religious law.

[23]Suddenly, a man in the synagogue who was possessed by an evil* spirit began shouting, [24]"Why are you interfering with us, Jesus of Nazareth? Have you come to destroy us? I know who you are—the Holy One of God!"

[25]Jesus cut him short. "Be quiet! Come out of the man," he ordered. [26]At that, the evil spirit screamed, threw the man into a convulsion, and then came out of him.

[27]Amazement gripped the audience, and they began to discuss what had happened. "What sort of new teaching is this?" they asked excitedly. "It has such authority! Even evil spirits obey his orders!" [28]The news about Jesus spread quickly throughout the entire region of Galilee.

Jesus Heals Many People

[29]After Jesus left the synagogue with James and John, they went to Simon and Andrew's home. [30]Now Simon's mother-in-law was sick in bed with a high fever. They told Jesus about her right away. [31]So he went to her bedside, took her by the hand, and helped her sit up. Then the fever left her, and she prepared a meal for them.

[32]That evening after sunset, many sick and demon-possessed people were brought to Jesus. [33]The whole town gathered at the door to watch. [34]So Jesus healed many people who were sick with various diseases, and he cast out many demons. But because the demons knew who he was, he did not allow them to speak.

Jesus Preaches in Galilee

[35]Before daybreak the next morning, Jesus got up and went out to an isolated place to pray. [36]Later Simon and the others went out to find him. [37]When they found him, they said, "Everyone is looking for you."

[38]But Jesus replied, "We must go on to other towns as well, and I will preach to them, too. That is why I came." [39]So he traveled throughout the region of Galilee, preaching in the synagogues and casting out demons.

Jesus Heals a Man with Leprosy

[40]A man with leprosy came and knelt in front of Jesus, begging to be healed. "If you are willing, you can heal me and make me clean," he said.

[41]Moved with compassion,* Jesus reached out and touched him. "I am willing," he said. "Be healed!" [42]Instantly the leprosy disappeared, and the man was healed. [43]Then Jesus sent him on his way with a stern warning: [44]"Don't tell anyone about this. Instead, go to the priest and let him examine you. Take along the offering required in the law of Moses for those who have been healed of leprosy.* This will be a public testimony that you have been cleansed."

[45]But the man went and spread the word, proclaiming to everyone what had happened. As a result, large crowds soon surrounded Jesus, and he couldn't publicly enter a town anywhere. He had to stay out in the secluded places, but people from everywhere kept coming to him.

CHAPTER 2

Jesus Heals a Paralyzed Man

When Jesus returned to Capernaum several days later, the news spread quickly that he was back home. [2]Soon the house where he

---

1:23 Greek *unclean;* also in 1:26, 27. 1:41 Some manuscripts read *Moved with anger.* 1:44 See Lev 14:2-32.

1:35-39 If Jesus, the Son of God, took time from his busy schedule to pray to his Father, how much more do we need to do so. By placing a high priority on prayer, Jesus could persevere in his ministry and keep from burning out. We who seek recovery for ourself and for others cannot get by without prayer. The busier the day ahead, the more we need to meditate on God's Word and pray for his strength and wisdom.

2:1-12 Jesus came not only to heal physical problems but also to solve the sin problem. If we do not know Jesus yet, we are paralyzed in spirit, as powerless to help ourselves as was this paralytic. If our faith is still too weak to carry us to the point of healing, the faith of "four friends" may be enough to get us there. Notice that it was not enough for Jesus to mouth the words of forgiveness; he proved his authority and intent with action. In the same way, it is not enough for us to mouth words of faith. We must take responsible action if we expect spiritual cleansing and physical healing.

was staying was so packed with visitors that there was no more room, even outside the door. While he was preaching God's word to them, [3]four men arrived carrying a paralyzed man on a mat. [4]They couldn't bring him to Jesus because of the crowd, so they dug a hole through the roof above his head. Then they lowered the man on his mat, right down in front of Jesus. [5]Seeing their faith, Jesus said to the paralyzed man, "My child, your sins are forgiven."

[6]But some of the teachers of religious law who were sitting there thought to themselves, [7]"What is he saying? This is blasphemy! Only God can forgive sins!"

[8]Jesus knew immediately what they were thinking, so he asked them, "Why do you question this in your hearts? [9]Is it easier to say to the paralyzed man 'Your sins are forgiven,' or 'Stand up, pick up your mat, and walk'? [10]So I will prove to you that the Son of Man* has the authority on earth to forgive sins." Then Jesus turned to the paralyzed man and said, [11]"Stand up, pick up your mat, and go home!"

[12]And the man jumped up, grabbed his mat, and walked out through the stunned onlookers. They were all amazed and praised God, exclaiming, "We've never seen anything like this before!"

Jesus Calls Levi (Matthew)

[13]Then Jesus went out to the lakeshore again and taught the crowds that were coming to him. [14]As he walked along, he saw Levi son of Alphaeus sitting at his tax collector's booth. "Follow me and be my disciple," Jesus said to him. So Levi got up and followed him.

[15]Later, Levi invited Jesus and his disciples to his home as dinner guests, along with many tax collectors and other disreputable sinners. (There were many people of this kind among Jesus' followers.) [16]But when the teachers of religious law who were Pharisees* saw him eating with tax collectors and other sinners, they asked his disciples, "Why does he eat with such scum?*"

[17]When Jesus heard this, he told them, "Healthy people don't need a doctor—sick people do. I have come to call not those who think they are righteous, but those who know they are sinners."

A Discussion about Fasting

[18]Once when John's disciples and the Pharisees were fasting, some people came to Jesus and asked, "Why don't your disciples fast like John's disciples and the Pharisees do?"

[19]Jesus replied, "Do wedding guests fast while celebrating with the groom? Of course not. They can't fast while the groom is with them. [20]But someday the groom will be taken away from them, and then they will fast.

[21]"Besides, who would patch old clothing with new cloth? For the new patch would shrink and rip away from the old cloth, leaving an even bigger tear than before.

[22]"And no one puts new wine into old wineskins. For the wine would burst the wineskins, and the wine and the skins would both be lost. New wine calls for new wineskins."

A Discussion about the Sabbath

[23]One Sabbath day as Jesus was walking through some grainfields, his disciples began breaking off heads of grain to eat. [24]But the Pharisees said to Jesus, "Look, why are they breaking the law by harvesting grain on the Sabbath?"

[25]Jesus said to them, "Haven't you ever read in the Scriptures what David did when he and his companions were hungry? [26]He went into the house of God (during the days when Abiathar was high priest) and broke

2:10 "Son of Man" is a title Jesus used for himself. 2:16a Greek *the scribes of the Pharisees.* 2:16b Greek *with tax collectors and sinners?*

2:13-17 Because of their reputed cheating and support of pagan Rome, tax collectors were considered notorious sinners by the Jews, especially the self-righteous religious leaders. But it was for people like this that Jesus came to bring salvation. Levi (Matthew) proved he meant business with Jesus by immediately witnessing to his friends, colleagues, and collaborators in sin. Some may question whether a person so new and immature in his faith should be telling his story to others. But the account here illustrates the truth that we are strengthened in recovery when we share our story with others, no matter the extent of our knowledge, skills, or experiences.
2:18-22 The old wineskins of Jewish religious practice were too rigid to carry the expansive, life-changing message of God's love in Jesus Christ. Religious activities are never enough unless they are coupled with genuine repentance. We must start by recognizing the sins in our life and then look to the only one who can make things right again—God in Jesus Christ. If we repent and look to him for help, he will forgive us and get us back on the right track. God will make our hard heart open and pliable like a fresh wineskin, so we can receive his gift of grace.

the law by eating the sacred loaves of bread that only the priests are allowed to eat. He also gave some to his companions."

²⁷Then Jesus said to them, "The Sabbath was made to meet the needs of people, and not people to meet the requirements of the Sabbath. ²⁸So the Son of Man is Lord, even over the Sabbath!"

CHAPTER 3
Jesus Heals on the Sabbath

Jesus went into the synagogue again and noticed a man with a deformed hand. ²Since it was the Sabbath, Jesus' enemies watched him closely. If he healed the man's hand, they planned to accuse him of working on the Sabbath.

³Jesus said to the man with the deformed hand, "Come and stand in front of everyone." ⁴Then he turned to his critics and asked, "Does the law permit good deeds on the Sabbath, or is it a day for doing evil? Is this a day to save life or to destroy it?" But they wouldn't answer him.

⁵He looked around at them angrily and was deeply saddened by their hard hearts. Then he said to the man, "Hold out your hand." So the man held out his hand, and it was restored! ⁶At once the Pharisees went away and met with the supporters of Herod to plot how to kill Jesus.

Crowds Follow Jesus

⁷Jesus went out to the lake with his disciples, and a large crowd followed him. They came from all over Galilee, Judea, ⁸Jerusalem, Idumea, from east of the Jordan River, and even from as far north as Tyre and Sidon. The news about his miracles had spread far and wide, and vast numbers of people came to see him.

⁹Jesus instructed his disciples to have a boat ready so the crowd would not crush him. ¹⁰He had healed many people that day, so all the sick people eagerly pushed forward to touch him. ¹¹And whenever those possessed by evil* spirits caught sight of him, the spirits would throw them to the ground in front of him shrieking, "You are the Son of God!" ¹²But Jesus sternly commanded the spirits not to reveal who he was.

Jesus Chooses the Twelve Apostles

¹³Afterward Jesus went up on a mountain and called out the ones he wanted to go with him. And they came to him. ¹⁴Then he appointed twelve of them and called them his apostles.* They were to accompany him, and he would send them out to preach, ¹⁵giving them authority to cast out demons. ¹⁶These are the twelve he chose:

Simon (whom he named Peter),
¹⁷ James and John (the sons of Zebedee, but Jesus nicknamed them "Sons of Thunder"*),
¹⁸ Andrew,
Philip,
Bartholomew,
Matthew,
Thomas,
James (son of Alphaeus),
Thaddaeus,
Simon (the zealot*),
¹⁹ Judas Iscariot (who later betrayed him).

Jesus and the Prince of Demons

²⁰One time Jesus entered a house, and the crowds began to gather again. Soon he and his disciples couldn't even find time to eat. ²¹When his family heard what was happening, they tried to take him away. "He's out of his mind," they said.

²²But the teachers of religious law who had

3:11 Greek *unclean;* also in 3:30. **3:14** Some manuscripts do not include *and called them his apostles.* **3:17** Greek *whom he named Boanerges, which means Sons of Thunder.* **3:18** Greek *the Cananean,* an Aramaic term for Jewish nationalists. **3:22** Greek *Beelzeboul;* other manuscripts read *Beezeboul;* Latin version reads *Beelzebub.*

3:7-19 Despite rejection by the religious establishment, Jesus enjoyed an ever-growing following, even from places he had not yet ministered in. Nearly halfway through three years of public ministry, Jesus' popularity peaked. The great demands on Jesus for service may have prompted him to appoint the twelve members of his close support group. Not even Jesus attempted to minister alone. We need to surround ourself with those who will support us and help us maintain what we have gained through recovery.

3:20-30 Although Satan causes a great deal of trouble in our world, God has power over him. Since Jesus is God, he has the power to work his will with Satan. Binding Satan's stronghold of demons and loosening his grip on our life is the solemn work of recovery. Not one of our past sins is so heinous that it cannot be forgiven, no hurt so deep that it cannot be healed. The one exception to this is blasphemy against the Holy Spirit, which is denying God's power through his Son, Jesus Christ.

JAMES & JOHN

Sons of Thunder! Why would Jesus use such a powerful description for two Galilean fishermen, James and John? We are given a glimpse of their fiery personalities when, after they were rejected by the people of a Samaritan village, James and John asked Jesus if they should call down fire from heaven to consume the village. Jesus rebuked them for their impulse to retaliate.

Jesus worked in these brothers' lives so that they became men known for their love and forgiveness, not for their anger and revenge. John, "the disciple Jesus loved," wrote powerful words on the importance of love. He had discovered that he didn't have to earn God's love but that he could freely receive it and pass it on to others.

James was the first of the twelve disciples to give his life for his faith. He was killed in Jerusalem by order of Herod Agrippa. John became an important leader in the church of Asia Minor and was later exiled to the island of Patmos, where he wrote the book of Revelation. He apparently outlived the rest of the twelve disciples.

Although the two brothers had once been ambitious for personal advancement, they became ambitious to advance the lives of others by sharing God's love with them. The brothers had discovered the important truth that when we understand and experience God's love, we are free to live and grow. And as we grow and share our discovery with others, God can use us to touch the lives of many in need of his help and healing.

STRENGTHS AND ACCOMPLISHMENTS:
- With Peter, James and John formed the inner circle of Jesus' disciples.
- Both men were important leaders in the early church.
- John was inspired to write five New Testament books (the Gospel of John; 1, 2, & 3 John; and Revelation).

WEAKNESSES AND MISTAKES:
- They apparently had a tendency to react angrily to anyone who opposed them.
- They selfishly tried to promote themselves ahead of the other disciples.

LESSONS FROM THEIR LIVES:
- It is important to experience God's love and act with love toward others.
- God can take our weaknesses and change them into strengths.

KEY VERSES:
"Then [Jesus] appointed twelve of them and called them his apostles. They were to accompany him. . . . These are the twelve he chose: . . . James and John (the sons of Zebedee, but Jesus nicknamed them 'Sons of Thunder')" (Mark 3:14-17).

The stories of James and John are told in Matthew 4:21-22; 20:20-28; Mark 1:19; 3:13-19; 9:1-9; 10:35-40; Luke 9:49-56; John 13:23-25; 19:26-27; 21:20-24; Acts 4:1-23; 8:14-25; 12:2; and Revelation 1:1-2, 9; 22:8.

---

arrived from Jerusalem said, "He's possessed by Satan,* the prince of demons. That's where he gets the power to cast out demons."

[23]Jesus called them over and responded with an illustration. "How can Satan cast out Satan?" he asked. [24]"A kingdom divided by civil war will collapse. [25]Similarly, a family splintered by feuding will fall apart. [26]And if Satan is divided and fights against himself, how can he stand? He would never survive. [27]Let me illustrate this further. Who is powerful enough to enter the house of a strong man like Satan and plunder his goods? Only someone even stronger—someone who could tie him up and then plunder his house.

[28]"I tell you the truth, all sin and blasphemy can be forgiven, [29]but anyone who blasphemes the Holy Spirit will never be forgiven. This is a sin with eternal consequences." [30]He told them this because they were saying, "He's possessed by an evil spirit."

The True Family of Jesus

[31]Then Jesus' mother and brothers came to see him. They stood outside and sent word for him to come out and talk with them. [32]There was a crowd sitting around Jesus, and someone said, "Your mother and your brothers* are outside asking for you."

[33]Jesus replied, "Who is my mother? Who are my brothers?" [34]Then he looked at those around him and said, "Look, these are my mother and brothers. [35]Anyone who does God's will is my brother and sister and mother."

3:32 Some manuscripts add *and sisters.*

CHAPTER 4
Parable of the Farmer Scattering Seed

Once again Jesus began teaching by the lakeshore. A very large crowd soon gathered around him, so he got into a boat. Then he sat in the boat while all the people remained on the shore. ²He taught them by telling many stories in the form of parables, such as this one:

³"Listen! A farmer went out to plant some seed. ⁴As he scattered it across his field, some of the seed fell on a footpath, and the birds came and ate it. ⁵Other seed fell on shallow soil with underlying rock. The seed sprouted quickly because the soil was shallow. ⁶But the plant soon wilted under the hot sun, and since it didn't have deep roots, it died. ⁷Other seed fell among thorns that grew up and choked out the tender plants so they produced no grain. ⁸Still other seeds fell on fertile soil, and they sprouted, grew, and produced a crop that was thirty, sixty, and even a hundred times as much as had been planted!" ⁹Then he said, "Anyone with ears to hear should listen and understand."

¹⁰Later, when Jesus was alone with the twelve disciples and with the others who were gathered around, they asked him what the parables meant.

¹¹He replied, "You are permitted to understand the secret* of the Kingdom of God. But I use parables for everything I say to outsiders, ¹²so that the Scriptures might be fulfilled:

'When they see what I do,
    they will learn nothing.
When they hear what I say,
    they will not understand.

Otherwise, they will turn to me
    and be forgiven.'*"

¹³Then Jesus said to them, "If you can't understand the meaning of this parable, how will you understand all the other parables? ¹⁴The farmer plants seed by taking God's word to others. ¹⁵The seed that fell on the footpath represents those who hear the message, only to have Satan come at once and take it away. ¹⁶The seed on the rocky soil represents those who hear the message and immediately receive it with joy. ¹⁷But since they don't have deep roots, they don't last long. They fall away as soon as they have problems or are persecuted for believing God's word. ¹⁸The seed that fell among the thorns represents others who hear God's word, ¹⁹but all too quickly the message is crowded out by the worries of this life, the lure of wealth, and the desire for other things, so no fruit is produced. ²⁰And the seed that fell on good soil represents those who hear and accept God's word and produce a harvest of thirty, sixty, or even a hundred times as much as had been planted!"

Parable of the Lamp

²¹Then Jesus asked them, "Would anyone light a lamp and then put it under a basket or under a bed? Of course not! A lamp is placed on a stand, where its light will shine. ²²For everything that is hidden will eventually be brought into the open, and every secret will be brought to light. ²³Anyone with ears to hear should listen and understand."

²⁴Then he added, "Pay close attention to

4:11 Greek *mystery.* 4:12 Isa 6:9-10 (Greek version).

4:1-20 Some welcome recovery, while others reject it. The mystery of this is revealed in the stories Jesus tells about the Kingdom, four of which are given in 4:1-34. God's Kingdom refers to God's hidden reign in the world that will be made visible at the return of Christ. This first story dramatizes varying responses to God's message in the hearts of his people. As we proceed with recovery and learn to seek out God's will for us, we are placing ourself under the just and loving rule of God. And we can be sure that as we plow the soil of our heart through self-examination, we will experience a fruitful and meaningful life.

4:21-25 The lamp represents the truth about Jesus. We hide that light every time we put a box over it. As we progress in recovery, it is important that we remove the boxes of guilt, bitterness, anger, shame, or denial that we hide behind. It is extremely important that we humbly share our story of pain and deliverance with others. We may need to start by taking moral inventory of our life to uncover the attitudes that keep us from sharing who we are and what God has done for us. As we discover the things that cause us to hide the light, we can give them to God and ask for his help in removing them. We must let God's truth shine from our life.

4:35-41 The disciples were awed when Jesus demonstrated his power over nature; even the wind and the waves obeyed him! Seeing this incredible display of power should strengthen our faith in God. Just as he was able to calm the stormy sea, he has the power to calm our storm-tossed life. With Jesus in our boat, we need not fear the storms of life that threaten to drown us. No storm is too violent or powerful for Jesus to calm. We should never hesitate to cry out, "Teacher, don't you care that we're going to drown?" (4:38).

what you hear. The closer you listen, the more understanding you will be given*—and you will receive even more. ²⁵To those who listen to my teaching, more understanding will be given. But for those who are not listening, even what little understanding they have will be taken away from them."

Parable of the Growing Seed

²⁶Jesus also said, "The Kingdom of God is like a farmer who scatters seed on the ground. ²⁷Night and day, while he's asleep or awake, the seed sprouts and grows, but he does not understand how it happens. ²⁸The earth produces the crops on its own. First a leaf blade pushes through, then the heads of wheat are formed, and finally the grain ripens. ²⁹And as soon as the grain is ready, the farmer comes and harvests it with a sickle, for the harvest time has come."

Parable of the Mustard Seed

³⁰Jesus said, "How can I describe the Kingdom of God? What story should I use to illustrate it? ³¹It is like a mustard seed planted in the ground. It is the smallest of all seeds, ³²but it becomes the largest of all garden plants; it grows long branches, and birds can make nests in its shade."

³³Jesus used many similar stories and illustrations to teach the people as much as they could understand. ³⁴In fact, in his public ministry he never taught without using parables; but afterward, when he was alone with his disciples, he explained everything to them.

Jesus Calms the Storm

³⁵As evening came, Jesus said to his disciples, "Let's cross to the other side of the lake." ³⁶So they took Jesus in the boat and started out, leaving the crowds behind (although other boats followed). ³⁷But soon a fierce storm came up. High waves were breaking into the boat, and it began to fill with water. ³⁸Jesus was sleeping at the back of the boat with his head on a cushion. The disciples woke him up, shouting, "Teacher, don't you care that we're going to drown?"

³⁹When Jesus woke up, he rebuked the wind and said to the waves, "Silence! Be still!" Suddenly the wind stopped, and there was a great calm. ⁴⁰Then he asked them, "Why are you afraid? Do you still have no faith?"

4:24 Or *The measure you give will be the measure you get back.*

STEP 2

Internal Bondage

BIBLE READING: Mark 5:1-13

We came to believe that a Power greater than ourselves could restore us to sanity. When we are under the influence of our addiction, its hold may seem to have supernatural force. We may give up on living and throw ourself into self-destructive behaviors with reckless abandon. People may also give up on us. They may distance themselves from us, as though we were already dead. Whether our "insanity" is self-induced or has a more sinister origin, there is power available to restore us to sanity and wholeness.

Jesus helped a man who was acting insanely. "This man lived among the burial caves and could no longer be restrained, even with a chain. Whenever he was put into chains and shackles—as he often was—he snapped the chains from his wrists and smashed the shackles. No one was strong enough to subdue him. Day and night he wandered among the burial caves and in the hills, howling and cutting himself with sharp stones" (Mark 5:3-5). Jesus went into the graveyard and assessed the situation. He dealt with the forces of darkness that were afflicting the man and restored him to sanity. He then sent him home to his friends to tell them what God had done for him.

We may have gone so far into our addiction that we have broken all restraints. We struggle to be free from the control of society and loved ones, only to discover that our bondage doesn't come from outside sources. All hope seems lost, but where there is still life, there is still hope. God can touch our insanity and restore us to sanity. *Turn to page 1305, Luke 8.*

[41]The disciples were absolutely terrified. "Who is this man?" they asked each other. "Even the wind and waves obey him!"

CHAPTER 5
Jesus Heals a Demon-Possessed Man

So they arrived at the other side of the lake, in the region of the Gerasenes.* [2]When Jesus climbed out of the boat, a man possessed by an evil* spirit came out from a cemetery to meet him. [3]This man lived among the burial caves and could no longer be restrained, even with a chain. [4]Whenever he was put into chains and shackles—as he often was— he snapped the chains from his wrists and smashed the shackles. No one was strong enough to subdue him. [5]Day and night he wandered among the burial caves and in the hills, howling and cutting himself with sharp stones.

[6]When Jesus was still some distance away, the man saw him, ran to meet him, and bowed low before him. [7]With a shriek, he screamed, "Why are you interfering with me, Jesus, Son of the Most High God? In the name of God, I beg you, don't torture me!" [8]For Jesus had already said to the spirit, "Come out of the man, you evil spirit."

[9]Then Jesus demanded, "What is your name?"

And he replied, "My name is Legion, because there are many of us inside this man." [10]Then the evil spirits begged him again and again not to send them to some distant place.

[11]There happened to be a large herd of pigs feeding on the hillside nearby. [12]"Send us into those pigs," the spirits begged. "Let us enter them."

[13]So Jesus gave them permission. The evil spirits came out of the man and entered the pigs, and the entire herd of about 2,000 pigs plunged down the steep hillside into the lake and drowned in the water.

[14]The herdsmen fled to the nearby town and the surrounding countryside, spreading the news as they ran. People rushed out to see what had happened. [15]A crowd soon gathered around Jesus, and they saw the man who had been possessed by the legion of demons. He was sitting there fully clothed and perfectly sane, and they were all afraid. [16]Then those who had seen what happened told the others about the demon-possessed man and the pigs. [17]And the crowd began pleading with Jesus to go away and leave them alone.

[18]As Jesus was getting into the boat, the man who had been demon possessed begged to go with him. [19]But Jesus said, "No, go home to your family, and tell them everything the Lord has done for you and how merciful he has been." [20]So the man started off to visit the Ten Towns* of that region and began to proclaim the great things Jesus had done for him; and everyone was amazed at what he told them.

Jesus Heals in Response to Faith

[21]Jesus got into the boat again and went back to the other side of the lake, where a large crowd gathered around him on the shore. [22]Then a leader of the local synagogue, whose name was Jairus, arrived. When he saw Jesus, he fell at his feet, [23]pleading fervently with him. "My little daughter is dying," he said. "Please come and lay your hands on her; heal her so she can live."

[24]Jesus went with him, and all the people followed, crowding around him. [25]A woman in the crowd had suffered for twelve years with constant bleeding. [26]She had suffered a

---

5:1 Other manuscripts read *Gadarenes;* still others read *Gergesenes.* See Matt 8:28; Luke 8:26. 5:2 Greek *unclean;* also in 5:8, 13. 5:20 Greek *Decapolis.*

5:21-43 Jairus was among a minority of Jewish leaders who responded positively to Jesus. Driven by love for his daughter and faith that Jesus could help her, Jairus risked the scorn of his peers by publicly seeking Jesus' help. In the end, we see that his humble faith paid off. Some of us avoid recovery because we are too ashamed to admit publicly that we have problems. But if we cannot humbly confess our sins, there is little hope for our healing. Like Jairus, we must risk the scorn of friends and enemies and admit our failures. If we do, we can be sure that Jesus will be there to help us. No problem is too great for him to solve; no wound is too deep for him to heal.

5:25-34 Sometimes we feel so ashamed of our sins that we think God's opinion of us must mirror the social ostracism or self-loathing we have experienced. Such was the case with the woman who had been bleeding for twelve years and probably lived as an outcast. This hemorrhage was likely a menstrual or uterine disorder, which would have made her ritually "unclean" (see Leviticus 15:25-27). According to Jewish law, anyone who touched her would also be rendered unclean. But instead of shrinking back from touching Jesus, she reached out in faith and was miraculously healed. We must never allow fear or shame to keep us from approaching God for forgiveness and healing. He is waiting for us to reach out and touch him.

great deal from many doctors, and over the years she had spent everything she had to pay them, but she had gotten no better. In fact, she had gotten worse. [27]She had heard about Jesus, so she came up behind him through the crowd and touched his robe. [28]For she thought to herself, "If I can just touch his robe, I will be healed." [29]Immediately the bleeding stopped, and she could feel in her body that she had been healed of her terrible condition.

[30]Jesus realized at once that healing power had gone out from him, so he turned around in the crowd and asked, "Who touched my robe?"

[31]His disciples said to him, "Look at this crowd pressing around you. How can you ask, 'Who touched me?'"

[32]But he kept on looking around to see who had done it. [33]Then the frightened woman, trembling at the realization of what had happened to her, came and fell to her knees in front of him and told him what she had done. [34]And he said to her, "Daughter, your faith has made you well. Go in peace. Your suffering is over."

[35]While he was still speaking to her, messengers arrived from the home of Jairus, the leader of the synagogue. They told him, "Your daughter is dead. There's no use troubling the Teacher now."

[36]But Jesus overheard* them and said to Jairus, "Don't be afraid. Just have faith."

[37]Then Jesus stopped the crowd and wouldn't let anyone go with him except Peter, James, and John (the brother of James). [38]When they came to the home of the synagogue leader, Jesus saw much commotion and weeping and wailing. [39]He went inside and asked, "Why all this commotion and weeping? The child isn't dead; she's only asleep."

[40]The crowd laughed at him. But he made them all leave, and he took the girl's father and mother and his three disciples into the room where the girl was lying. [41]Holding her hand, he said to her, *"Talitha koum,"* which means "Little girl, get up!" [42]And the girl, who was twelve years old, immediately stood up and walked around! They were overwhelmed and totally amazed. [43]Jesus gave them strict orders not to tell anyone what had happened, and then he told them to give her something to eat.

CHAPTER 6
Jesus Rejected at Nazareth
Jesus left that part of the country and returned with his disciples to Nazareth, his hometown. [2]The next Sabbath he began teaching in the synagogue, and many who heard him were amazed. They asked, "Where did he get all this wisdom and the power to perform such miracles?" [3]Then they scoffed, "He's just a carpenter, the son of Mary* and the brother of James, Joseph,* Judas, and Simon. And his sisters live right here among us." They were deeply offended and refused to believe in him.

[4]Then Jesus told them, "A prophet is honored everywhere except in his own hometown and among his relatives and his own family." [5]And because of their unbelief, he couldn't do any miracles among them except to place his hands on a few sick people and heal them. [6]And he was amazed at their unbelief.

Jesus Sends Out the Twelve Disciples
Then Jesus went from village to village, teaching the people. [7]And he called his twelve disciples together and began sending them out two by two, giving them authority to cast out evil* spirits. [8]He told them to take nothing for their journey except a walking stick—no food, no traveler's bag, no money.* [9]He allowed them to wear sandals but not to take a change of clothes.

[10]"Wherever you go," he said, "stay in the same house until you leave town. [11]But if any place refuses to welcome you or listen to you, shake its dust from your feet as you leave to show that you have abandoned those people to their fate."

[12]So the disciples went out, telling everyone they met to repent of their sins and turn to God. [13]And they cast out many demons

---

5:36 Or *ignored.* **6:3a** Some manuscripts read *He's just the son of the carpenter and of Mary.* **6:3b** Most manuscripts read *Joses;* see Matt 13:55. **6:7** Greek *unclean.* **6:8** Greek *no copper coins in their money belts.*

6:7-13 When we experience the joy of recovery, we naturally want to share the good news of the Messiah's coming with others. Yet we are not always well received. The disciples faced rejection as they traveled, healed people, and preached repentance and deliverance. They were paired off and told what to take, where to stay and for how long, and what to do when rejected. As we share the healing we have experienced in the recovery process, not everyone will be responsive. When ridiculed or rejected, we must press on to share our hope with the next fellow struggler we meet. Sharing our message may be the difference between life and death for someone in need.

and healed many sick people, anointing them with olive oil.

The Death of John the Baptist

[14]Herod Antipas, the king, soon heard about Jesus, because everyone was talking about him. Some were saying,* "This must be John the Baptist raised from the dead. That is why he can do such miracles." [15]Others said, "He's the prophet Elijah." Still others said, "He's a prophet like the other great prophets of the past."

[16]When Herod heard about Jesus, he said, "John, the man I beheaded, has come back from the dead."

[17]For Herod had sent soldiers to arrest and imprison John as a favor to Herodias. She had been his brother Philip's wife, but Herod had married her. [18]John had been telling Herod, "It is against God's law for you to marry your brother's wife." [19]So Herodias bore a grudge against John and wanted to kill him. But without Herod's approval she was powerless, [20]for Herod respected John; and knowing that he was a good and holy man, he protected him. Herod was greatly disturbed whenever he talked with John, but even so, he liked to listen to him.

[21]Herodias's chance finally came on Herod's birthday. He gave a party for his high government officials, army officers, and the leading citizens of Galilee. [22]Then his daughter, also named Herodias,* came in and performed a dance that greatly pleased Herod and his guests. "Ask me for anything you like," the king said to the girl, "and I will give it to you." [23]He even vowed, "I will give you whatever you ask, up to half my kingdom!"

[24]She went out and asked her mother, "What should I ask for?"

Her mother told her, "Ask for the head of John the Baptist!"

[25]So the girl hurried back to the king and told him, "I want the head of John the Baptist, right now, on a tray!"

[26]Then the king deeply regretted what he had said; but because of the vows he had made in front of his guests, he couldn't refuse her. [27]So he immediately sent an executioner to the prison to cut off John's head and bring it to him. The soldier beheaded John in the prison, [28]brought his head on a tray, and gave it to the girl, who took it to her mother. [29]When John's disciples heard what had happened, they came to get his body and buried it in a tomb.

Jesus Feeds Five Thousand

[30]The apostles returned to Jesus from their ministry tour and told him all they had done and taught. [31]Then Jesus said, "Let's go off by ourselves to a quiet place and rest awhile." He said this because there were so many people coming and going that Jesus and his apostles didn't even have time to eat.

[32]So they left by boat for a quiet place, where they could be alone. [33]But many people recognized them and saw them leaving, and people from many towns ran ahead along the shore and got there ahead of them. [34]Jesus saw the huge crowd as he stepped from the boat, and he had compassion on them because they were like sheep without a shepherd. So he began teaching them many things.

[35]Late in the afternoon his disciples came to him and said, "This is a remote place, and it's already getting late. [36]Send the crowds away so they can go to the nearby farms and villages and buy something to eat."

[37]But Jesus said, "You feed them."

"With what?" they asked. "We'd have to work for months to earn enough money* to buy food for all these people!"

6:14 Some manuscripts read *He was saying.* 6:22 Some manuscripts read *the daughter of Herodias herself.* 6:37 Greek *It would take 200 denarii.* A denarius was equivalent to a laborer's full day's wage.

6:30-32 The disciples demonstrated accountability to Jesus by reporting their activities to him. At the same time, Jesus encouraged them to take care of themselves by drawing them away for rest and solitude. To continue helping others, the disciples needed time apart for personal reflection and refreshment. Unfortunately, their time apart was delayed by the many who followed them. We must balance our life too, taking time apart to recharge our spiritual and emotional batteries. As we take time to reflect, we will learn the lessons of humility and dependence on God that are necessary for our progress in recovery.

6:45-52 We may lose sight of Jesus, but Jesus never loses sight of us. That's the lesson for people in "deep water" who appreciate his threefold miracle: (1) Jesus walked on water; (2) he calmed the storm; and (3) he saw the disciples' boat safely to shore (see John 6:21). Despite many such miracles, the disciples still had not realized how powerful Jesus was. All of us can recall some time when Jesus intervened in our life to show us how much he cares. When we begin to waver in our faith, we should recall the times when he has helped us in the past. This should give us the courage to continue in his loving care.

HEROD & FAMILY

Certain names in history immediately bring to mind images of horror, violence, greed, and cruelty. Several Herods are mentioned in the New Testament. The first, Herod the Great, was called "great" because of his ambitious and lavish building projects, including the rebuilding of the Temple in Jerusalem. His character, however, was anything but great. He was known for his cruelty, jealousy, and insatiable lust for power and wealth.

Herod was appointed king by the Romans, but many of his Jewish subjects never really accepted him as a legitimate ruler. Herod was not really of Jewish descent; he was actually an Idumean from the land south of Judea. Because of this, Herod was uneasy about any threat to his position and responded with swift cruelty to the slightest rumor of disloyalty. The Herods didn't hesitate to have even their own family members murdered if it would be to their own advantage.

Herod Antipas, Herod the Great's son, is well known for his role in killing John the Baptist. Another descendant, Herod Agrippa I, was responsible for the death of the apostle James. A grandson, Agrippa II, heard the truth of the gospel directly from the apostle Paul. In fact, each of the Herods had an encounter with a messenger from God but refused to respond to the truth.

Herod the Great's failure to respond to God's truth grew out of his greed and insecurity. As a result, Herod left his children and grandchildren a heritage of greed and cruelty. It is important that we seriously consider what heritage we are leaving our children. We can either remain in our denial and pass on our dysfunctions, or we can choose the path of recovery and build happy and meaningful futures for our children and grandchildren. There is a great deal at stake in recovery. We are fighting for more than just our own life; we are fighting for the lives of countless descendants as well.

STRENGTHS AND ACCOMPLISHMENTS:
- Herod and his family were industrious builders.
- They were extremely clever at political maneuvering.

WEAKNESSES AND MISTAKES:
- Herod and his family lusted for power and possessions.
- They didn't hesitate to destroy innocent people who stood in their way.
- They were extremely insecure and suspicious of the people around them.

LESSONS FROM THEIR LIVES:
- Having power and wealth doesn't guarantee success and happiness.
- We must carefully consider the heritage we will leave our children.
- Those who live for themselves at the expense of others will pay the price in the end.

KEY VERSE:
"Herod was furious when he realized that the wise men had outwitted him. He sent soldiers to kill all the boys in and around Bethlehem who were two years old and under" (Matthew 2:16).

Herod and members of his family are mentioned in Matthew 2:1-11; Mark 6:14-29; Luke 1:5; and Acts 4:27; 12:1-23; 13:1; and 25:13—26:32.

---

[38]"How much bread do you have?" he asked. "Go and find out."

They came back and reported, "We have five loaves of bread and two fish."

[39]Then Jesus told the disciples to have the people sit down in groups on the green grass. [40]So they sat down in groups of fifty or a hundred.

[41]Jesus took the five loaves and two fish, looked up toward heaven, and blessed them. Then, breaking the loaves into pieces, he kept giving the bread to the disciples so they could distribute it to the people. He also divided the fish for everyone to share. [42]They all ate as much as they wanted, [43]and afterward, the disciples picked up twelve baskets of leftover bread and fish. [44]A total of 5,000 men and their families were fed.*

Jesus Walks on Water

[45]Immediately after this, Jesus insisted that his disciples get back into the boat and head across the lake to Bethsaida, while he sent the people home. [46]After telling everyone good-bye, he went up into the hills by himself to pray.

[47]Late that night, the disciples were in their boat in the middle of the lake, and

6:44 Some manuscripts read *fed from the loaves.*

Jesus was alone on land. [48]He saw that they were in serious trouble, rowing hard and struggling against the wind and waves. About three o'clock in the morning* Jesus came toward them, walking on the water. He intended to go past them, [49]but when they saw him walking on the water, they cried out in terror, thinking he was a ghost. [50]They were all terrified when they saw him.

But Jesus spoke to them at once. "Don't be afraid," he said. "Take courage! I am here!*" [51]Then he climbed into the boat, and the wind stopped. They were totally amazed, [52]for they still didn't understand the significance of the miracle of the loaves. Their hearts were too hard to take it in.

[53]After they had crossed the lake, they landed at Gennesaret. They brought the boat to shore [54]and climbed out. The people recognized Jesus at once, [55]and they ran throughout the whole area, carrying sick people on mats to wherever they heard he was. [56]Wherever he went—in villages, cities, or the countryside—they brought the sick out to the marketplaces. They begged him to let the sick touch at least the fringe of his robe, and all who touched him were healed.

CHAPTER 7
Jesus Teaches about Inner Purity

One day some Pharisees and teachers of religious law arrived from Jerusalem to see Jesus. [2]They noticed that some of his disciples failed to follow the Jewish ritual of hand washing before eating. [3](The Jews, especially the Pharisees, do not eat until they have poured water over their cupped hands,* as required by their ancient traditions. [4]Similarly, they don't eat anything from the market until they immerse their hands* in water.

This is but one of many traditions they have clung to—such as their ceremonial washing of cups, pitchers, and kettles.*)

[5]So the Pharisees and teachers of religious law asked him, "Why don't your disciples follow our age-old tradition? They eat without first performing the hand-washing ceremony."

[6]Jesus replied, "You hypocrites! Isaiah was right when he prophesied about you, for he wrote,

'These people honor me with their lips,
    but their hearts are far from me.
[7]Their worship is a farce,
    for they teach man-made ideas as
        commands from God.'*

[8]For you ignore God's law and substitute your own tradition."

[9]Then he said, "You skillfully sidestep God's law in order to hold on to your own tradition. [10]For instance, Moses gave you this law from God: 'Honor your father and mother,'* and 'Anyone who speaks disrespectfully of father or mother must be put to death.'* [11]But you say it is all right for people to say to their parents, 'Sorry, I can't help you. For I have vowed to give to God what I would have given to you.'* [12]In this way, you let them disregard their needy parents. [13]And so you cancel the word of God in order to hand down your own tradition. And this is only one example among many others."

[14]Then Jesus called to the crowd to come and hear. "All of you listen," he said, "and try to understand. [15]It's not what goes into your body that defiles you; you are defiled by what comes from your heart.*"

[17]Then Jesus went into a house to get away from the crowd, and his disciples asked him

6:48 Greek *About the fourth watch of the night.* **6:50** Or *The 'I AM' is here;* Greek reads *I am.* See Exod 3:14. **7:3** Greek *have washed with the fist.* **7:4a** Some manuscripts read *sprinkle themselves.* **7:4b** Some manuscripts add *and dining couches.* **7:7** Isa 29:13 (Greek version). **7:10a** Exod 20:12; Deut 5:16. **7:10b** Exod 21:17 (Greek version); Lev 20:9 (Greek version). **7:11** Greek *'What I would have given to you is Corban' (that is, a gift).* **7:15** Some manuscripts add verse 16, *Anyone with ears to hear should listen and understand.* Compare 4:9, 23.

7:1-13 For many of the Jewish leaders, man-made tradition had begun to supersede God's revealed Word. Ritual had begun to replace a relationship with God; reputation had become more important than godliness. Jesus called this hypocrisy, and it is a dangerous form of denial. If we hide the pain we feel and the mistakes we make, we will never be able to deal with them and experience healing. Recovery can succeed only if we are willing to be honest in taking our moral inventory, using God's Word as our standard. As we seek to follow God's will for our life, we will experience his powerful help and direction.

7:14-23 Jesus explained that defilement does not come from our external behavior, but that it comes from within our heart. Most of us have tried to control our dependency by changing various aspects of our external behavior. The fact that this never worked for long is clear evidence that our real problems lie within. We should find it encouraging that God goes right to the root of our problems; he works his healing from the inside out. By recognizing our need for internal healing, we open our life to God's healing power.

what he meant by the parable he had just used. ¹⁸"Don't you understand either?" he asked. "Can't you see that the food you put into your body cannot defile you? ¹⁹Food doesn't go into your heart, but only passes through the stomach and then goes into the sewer." (By saying this, he declared that every kind of food is acceptable in God's eyes.)

²⁰And then he added, "It is what comes from inside that defiles you. ²¹For from within, out of a person's heart, come evil thoughts, sexual immorality, theft, murder, ²²adultery, greed, wickedness, deceit, lustful desires, envy, slander, pride, and foolishness. ²³All these vile things come from within; they are what defile you."

The Faith of a Gentile Woman

²⁴Then Jesus left Galilee and went north to the region of Tyre.* He didn't want anyone to know which house he was staying in, but he couldn't keep it a secret. ²⁵Right away a woman who had heard about him came and fell at his feet. Her little girl was possessed by an evil* spirit, ²⁶and she begged him to cast out the demon from her daughter.

Since she was a Gentile, born in Syrian Phoenicia, ²⁷Jesus told her, "First I should feed the children—my own family, the Jews.* It isn't right to take food from the children and throw it to the dogs."

²⁸She replied, "That's true, Lord, but even the dogs under the table are allowed to eat the scraps from the children's plates."

²⁹"Good answer!" he said. "Now go home, for the demon has left your daughter." ³⁰And when she arrived home, she found her little girl lying quietly in bed, and the demon was gone.

Jesus Heals a Deaf Man

³¹Jesus left Tyre and went up to Sidon before going back to the Sea of Galilee and the region of the Ten Towns.* ³²A deaf man with a speech impediment was brought to him, and the people begged Jesus to lay his hands on the man to heal him.

³³Jesus led him away from the crowd so they could be alone. He put his fingers into the man's ears. Then, spitting on his own fingers, he touched the man's tongue. ³⁴Looking up to heaven, he sighed and said, "*Ephphatha,*" which means, "Be opened!" ³⁵Instantly the man could hear perfectly, and his tongue was freed so he could speak plainly!

³⁶Jesus told the crowd not to tell anyone, but the more he told them not to, the more they spread the news. ³⁷They were completely amazed and said again and again, "Everything he does is wonderful. He even makes the deaf to hear and gives speech to those who cannot speak."

CHAPTER 8
Jesus Feeds Four Thousand

About this time another large crowd had gathered, and the people ran out of food again. Jesus called his disciples and told them, ²"I feel sorry for these people. They have been here with me for three days, and they have nothing left to eat. ³If I send them home hungry, they will faint along the way. For some of them have come a long distance."

⁴His disciples replied, "How are we supposed to find enough food to feed them out here in the wilderness?"

⁵Jesus asked, "How much bread do you have?"

"Seven loaves," they replied.

7:24 Some manuscripts add *and Sidon.* 7:25 Greek *unclean.* 7:27 Greek *Let the children eat first.* 7:31 Greek *Decapolis.*

7:24-30 By helping this Gentile woman, Jesus made it clear that his message of hope was for everyone, not just a privileged few. Jesus responded not only to the woman's humility and accurate self-perception but also to her great faith and perseverance. The more we trust God, the more he can do for us and through us. Conversely, a lack of faith and perseverance will prevent God from working his healing in our life and in the lives of our loved ones.
7:31-37 One key to recovery can be other people who lead us to the help we need. In this account, a group of people apparently cared enough for this deaf man to do something about his problem. They brought their friend to Jesus and begged Jesus to heal him. We may be the one God will use to give other hurting people hope and direction for recovery. As we share our story of deliverance and God's power for bringing recovery, we can give others the gift of life and health. We will not only give hope to others, but we will also experience a renewed commitment to our own recovery.
8:1-9 We sometimes feel like our prayers never get beyond the ceiling. We wonder if the hot line to God is busy and if we have been left indefinitely on hold. The truth is, God is never too busy to concern himself with the daily needs of his people. Jesus was moved by pity to feed four thousand hungry people, even though he was busy with a preaching and healing campaign. There is no need too small or request too large that God will not hear and respond to.

[6]So Jesus told all the people to sit down on the ground. Then he took the seven loaves, thanked God for them, and broke them into pieces. He gave them to his disciples, who distributed the bread to the crowd. [7]A few small fish were found, too, so Jesus also blessed these and told the disciples to distribute them.

[8]They ate as much as they wanted. Afterward, the disciples picked up seven large baskets of leftover food. [9]There were about 4,000 people in the crowd that day, and Jesus sent them home after they had eaten. [10]Immediately after this, he got into a boat with his disciples and crossed over to the region of Dalmanutha.

Pharisees Demand a Miraculous Sign

[11]When the Pharisees heard that Jesus had arrived, they came and started to argue with him. Testing him, they demanded that he show them a miraculous sign from heaven to prove his authority.

[12]When he heard this, he sighed deeply in his spirit and said, "Why do these people keep demanding a miraculous sign? I tell you the truth, I will not give this generation any such sign." [13]So he got back into the boat and left them, and he crossed to the other side of the lake.

Yeast of the Pharisees and Herod

[14]But the disciples had forgotten to bring any food. They had only one loaf of bread with them in the boat. [15]As they were crossing the lake, Jesus warned them, "Watch out! Beware of the yeast of the Pharisees and of Herod."

[16]At this they began to argue with each other because they hadn't brought any bread. [17]Jesus knew what they were saying, so he said, "Why are you arguing about having no bread? Don't you know or understand even yet? Are your hearts too hard to take it in? [18]You have eyes—can't you see? You have ears—can't you hear?'* Don't you remember anything at all? [19]When I fed the 5,000 with five loaves of bread, how many baskets of leftovers did you pick up afterward?"

"Twelve," they said.

[20]"And when I fed the 4,000 with seven loaves, how many large baskets of leftovers did you pick up?"

"Seven," they said.

[21]"Don't you understand yet?" he asked them.

Jesus Heals a Blind Man

[22]When they arrived at Bethsaida, some people brought a blind man to Jesus, and they begged him to touch the man and heal him. [23]Jesus took the blind man by the hand and led him out of the village. Then, spitting on the man's eyes, he laid his hands on him and asked, "Can you see anything now?"

[24]The man looked around. "Yes," he said, "I see people, but I can't see them very clearly. They look like trees walking around."

[25]Then Jesus placed his hands on the man's eyes again, and his eyes were opened. His sight was completely restored, and he could see everything clearly. [26]Jesus sent him away, saying, "Don't go back into the village on your way home."

Peter's Declaration about Jesus

[27]Jesus and his disciples left Galilee and went up to the villages near Caesarea Philippi. As they were walking along, he asked them, "Who do people say I am?"

[28]"Well," they replied, "some say John the Baptist, some say Elijah, and others say you are one of the other prophets."

[29]Then he asked them, "But who do you say I am?"

Peter replied, "You are the Messiah.*"

[30]But Jesus warned them not to tell anyone about him.

Jesus Predicts His Death

[31]Then Jesus began to tell them that the Son of Man* must suffer many terrible things and be rejected by the elders, the leading priests, and the teachers of religious law. He would be

---

8:18 Jer 5:21. 8:29 Or *the Christ. Messiah* (a Hebrew term) and *Christ* (a Greek term) both mean "anointed one." 8:31 "Son of Man" is a title Jesus used for himself.

8:10-21 Jesus was troubled by his disciples' lack of faith and their seeming inability to learn the basic lessons he was trying to teach them. As slow to catch on as they were, Jesus still nurtured them in faith. We may tend to progress in recovery in a series of lurches and falls. When we fail, we can recover by quickly admitting our limitations, accepting God's forgiveness, and continuing to depend on his power, day by day. God will be patient with us if we are willing to stick with his program for recovery.

8:31–9:1 When Jesus told his disciples that his ministry would lead to suffering and death, he was sharing a basic truth about life. When we are dealing with the destructive effects of sin,

killed, but three days later he would rise from the dead. ³²As he talked about this openly with his disciples, Peter took him aside and began to reprimand him for saying such things.*

³³Jesus turned around and looked at his disciples, then reprimanded Peter. "Get away from me, Satan!" he said. "You are seeing things merely from a human point of view, not from God's."

³⁴Then, calling the crowd to join his disciples, he said, "If any of you wants to be my follower, you must turn from your selfish ways, take up your cross, and follow me. ³⁵If you try to hang on to your life, you will lose it. But if you give up your life for my sake and for the sake of the Good News, you will save it. ³⁶And what do you benefit if you gain the whole world but lose your own soul?* ³⁷Is anything worth more than your soul? ³⁸If anyone is ashamed of me and my message in these adulterous and sinful days, the Son of Man will be ashamed of that person when he returns in the glory of his Father with the holy angels."

CHAPTER 9

Jesus went on to say, "I tell you the truth, some standing here right now will not die before they see the Kingdom of God arrive in great power!"

The Transfiguration

²Six days later Jesus took Peter, James, and John, and led them up a high mountain to be alone. As the men watched, Jesus' appearance was transformed, ³and his clothes became dazzling white, far whiter than any earthly bleach could ever make them. ⁴Then Elijah and Moses appeared and began talking with Jesus.

⁵Peter exclaimed, "Rabbi, it's wonderful for us to be here! Let's make three shelters as memorials*—one for you, one for Moses,

and one for Elijah." ⁶He said this because he didn't really know what else to say, for they were all terrified.

⁷Then a cloud overshadowed them, and a voice from the cloud said, "This is my dearly loved Son. Listen to him." ⁸Suddenly, when they looked around, Moses and Elijah were gone, and they saw only Jesus with them.

⁹As they went back down the mountain, he told them not to tell anyone what they had seen until the Son of Man* had risen from the dead. ¹⁰So they kept it to themselves, but they often asked each other what he meant by "rising from the dead."

¹¹Then they asked him, "Why do the teachers of religious law insist that Elijah must return before the Messiah comes?*"

¹²Jesus responded, "Elijah is indeed coming first to get everything ready. Yet why do the Scriptures say that the Son of Man must suffer greatly and be treated with utter contempt? ¹³But I tell you, Elijah has already come, and they chose to abuse him, just as the Scriptures predicted."

Jesus Heals a Demon-Possessed Boy

¹⁴When they returned to the other disciples, they saw a large crowd surrounding them, and some teachers of religious law were arguing with them. ¹⁵When the crowd saw Jesus, they were overwhelmed with awe, and they ran to greet him.

¹⁶"What is all this arguing about?" Jesus asked.

¹⁷One of the men in the crowd spoke up and said, "Teacher, I brought my son so you could heal him. He is possessed by an evil spirit that won't let him talk. ¹⁸And whenever this spirit seizes him, it throws him violently to the ground. Then he foams at the mouth and grinds his teeth and becomes rigid.* So I asked your disciples to cast out the evil spirit, but they couldn't do it."

8:32 Or *began to correct him.* 8:36 Or *your self?* also in 8:37. 9:5 Greek *three tabernacles.* 9:9 "Son of Man" is a title Jesus used for himself. 9:11 Greek *that Elijah must come first?* 9:18 Or *becomes weak.*

---

victory usually comes only after pain and tears. No cross, no resurrection. No pain, no gain. Jesus had to suffer in order to overcome the destructive power of sin in our world. Recovery from our destructive habits will also involve pain, but we should not let this discourage us. Jesus has already paid the price for our sins. If we confess our sins and accept God's forgiveness, we can be sure of victory over our addiction with God's daily help.

9:14-29 Through honest self-examination, the father of the demon-possessed boy acknowledged both belief and doubt. He believed that Jesus could restore his son to health, but he questioned whether Jesus would do so. Sometimes we feel the same way. We see how God has delivered others and believe that God can help, but we fear that he will refuse to help us. Perhaps we are afraid that God will think us unworthy of his deliverance. God never works that way. Not only is he *able* to help us, but he also *wants* to help us. We must turn to him in faith, ask for his help and forgiveness, and follow his revealed will for us. God will do the rest.

[19]Jesus said to them,* "You faithless people! How long must I be with you? How long must I put up with you? Bring the boy to me."

[20]So they brought the boy. But when the evil spirit saw Jesus, it threw the child into a violent convulsion, and he fell to the ground, writhing and foaming at the mouth.

[21]"How long has this been happening?" Jesus asked the boy's father.

He replied, "Since he was a little boy. [22]The spirit often throws him into the fire or into water, trying to kill him. Have mercy on us and help us, if you can."

[23]"What do you mean, 'If I can'?" Jesus asked. "Anything is possible if a person believes."

[24]The father instantly cried out, "I do believe, but help me overcome my unbelief!"

[25]When Jesus saw that the crowd of onlookers was growing, he rebuked the evil* spirit. "Listen, you spirit that makes this boy unable to hear and speak," he said. "I command you to come out of this child and never enter him again!"

[26]Then the spirit screamed and threw the boy into another violent convulsion and left him. The boy appeared to be dead. A murmur ran through the crowd as people said, "He's dead." [27]But Jesus took him by the hand and helped him to his feet, and he stood up.

[28]Afterward, when Jesus was alone in the house with his disciples, they asked him, "Why couldn't we cast out that evil spirit?"

[29]Jesus replied, "This kind can be cast out only by prayer.*"

Jesus Again Predicts His Death

[30]Leaving that region, they traveled through Galilee. Jesus didn't want anyone to know he was there, [31]for he wanted to spend more time with his disciples and teach them. He said to them, "The Son of Man is going to be betrayed into the hands of his enemies. He will be killed, but three days later he will rise from the dead." [32]They didn't understand what he was saying, however, and they were afraid to ask him what he meant.

The Greatest in the Kingdom

[33]After they arrived at Capernaum and settled in a house, Jesus asked his disciples, "What were you discussing out on the road?" [34]But they didn't answer, because they had been arguing about which of them was the greatest. [35]He sat down, called the twelve disciples over to him, and said, "Whoever

9:19 Or *said to his disciples.* 9:25 Greek *unclean.* 9:29 Some manuscripts read *by prayer and fasting.*

9:30-37 The argument over who would be the greatest in God's Kingdom ran counter to everything Jesus stood for. True greatness is measured by how we serve others. That service, for the disciples, included showing love for all people, even a little child. We may not be tempted to turn away from needy children, but what about the many adults who need our help? Do we turn away people who are poor, homeless, hungry, or addicted? God heals our hurts so we can help others get the healing they need, not so we can rise to a higher position in society. If we fail to help needy people, we are pushing Jesus right out of our life.

9:38-42 Cooperation and peace, not cutthroat competition, must characterize our interpersonal relationships. Jesus instructed his disciples to fully and peacefully accept others who ministered in his name. He accepted those not under his own direct authority but who were building up the Kingdom of God. So must we. If we fail to do so and cause others to lose their faith, we will suffer the painful consequences.

9:43-50 Through a series of startling statements, Jesus admonished his disciples to get rid of anything in their lives that might draw them away from God. For us, this could refer to our besetting addiction and the emotional baggage that supports it. We can identify our weaknesses by making an honest moral inventory of our life and then take action to "cut off" our offensive parts so we can begin the process of healing. It is usually wise to have the help of a support group as we follow through on such drastic measures.

10:1-12 The Pharisees were not looking for guidance when they asked Jesus about divorce; they were looking for a means to trap him. Jesus offered no grounds for divorce, with the possible exception of infidelity (see Matthew 19:9). Today many believe divorce is a good way to deal with conflict. Most of us have discovered, however, that interpersonal conflicts follow us wherever we go because they are only evidence of much deeper problems. These same problems may also drive our dependency. Marriage is not always easy; neither is recovery. But both can be of great help to each other. Marriage gives us a context of accountability and loving support to help us through recovery. Recovery gives us the program for personal growth and reestablishing our family and marriage relationships.

wants to be first must take last place and be the servant of everyone else."

³⁶Then he put a little child among them. Taking the child in his arms, he said to them, ³⁷"Anyone who welcomes a little child like this on my behalf* welcomes me, and anyone who welcomes me welcomes not only me but also my Father who sent me."

Using the Name of Jesus
³⁸John said to Jesus, "Teacher, we saw someone using your name to cast out demons, but we told him to stop because he wasn't in our group."

³⁹"Don't stop him!" Jesus said. "No one who performs a miracle in my name will soon be able to speak evil of me. ⁴⁰Anyone who is not against us is for us. ⁴¹If anyone gives you even a cup of water because you belong to the Messiah, I tell you the truth, that person will surely be rewarded.

⁴²"But if you cause one of these little ones who trusts in me to fall into sin, it would be better for you to be thrown into the sea with a large millstone hung around your neck. ⁴³If your hand causes you to sin, cut it off. It's better to enter eternal life with only one hand than to go into the unquenchable fires of hell* with two hands.* ⁴⁵If your foot causes you to sin, cut it off. It's better to enter eternal life with only one foot than to be thrown into hell with two feet.* ⁴⁷And if your eye causes you to sin, gouge it out. It's better to enter the Kingdom of God with only one eye than to have two eyes and be thrown into hell, ⁴⁸'where the maggots never die and the fire never goes out.'*

⁴⁹"For everyone will be tested with fire.* ⁵⁰Salt is good for seasoning. But if it loses its flavor, how do you make it salty again? You must have the qualities of salt among yourselves and live in peace with each other."

CHAPTER 10
Discussion about Divorce and Marriage
Then Jesus left Capernaum and went down to the region of Judea and into the area east of the Jordan River. Once again crowds gathered around him, and as usual he was teaching them.

²Some Pharisees came and tried to trap

9:37 Greek *in my name.* 9:43a Greek *Gehenna;* also in 9:45, 47. 9:43b Some manuscripts add verse 44, *'where the maggots never die and the fire never goes out.'* See 9:48. 9:45 Some manuscripts add verse 46, *'where the maggots never die and the fire never goes out.'* See 9:48. 9:48 Isa 66:24. 9:49 Greek *salted with fire;* other manuscripts add *and every sacrifice will be salted with salt.*

STEP 1

Like Little Children
BIBLE READING: Mark 10:13-16
We admitted that we were powerless over our problems—that our lives had become unmanageable.
For many of us in recovery, memories of childhood are full of the terrors associated with being powerless. If we were raised in a family that was out of control, where we were neglected, abused, or exposed to domestic violence and dysfunctional behavior, the thought of being powerless might be very frightening. We may have silently vowed never again to be as vulnerable as we were when we were children.

Jesus tells us that in order to enter the Kingdom of God we must become like little children, and this involves being powerless. He said, "I tell you the truth, anyone who doesn't receive the Kingdom of God like a child will never enter it" (Mark 10:15).

In any society, children are the most dependent members. They have no inherent power for self-protection—no means to ensure that their lives will be safe, comfortable, or fulfilling. Little children are singularly reliant on the love, care, and nurture of others for their most basic needs. They *must* cry out even though they may not know exactly what they need. They *must* trust their lives to someone who is more powerful than they, and, hopefully, they will be heard and lovingly cared for.

We, too, must admit that we are truly powerless if our life is to become healthy. This doesn't mean we have to become victims again. Admitting our powerlessness is an honest appraisal of our situation in life and a positive step toward recovery. *Turn to page 1395, Acts 9.*

him with this question: "Should a man be allowed to divorce his wife?"

³Jesus answered them with a question: "What did Moses say in the law about divorce?"

⁴"Well, he permitted it," they replied. "He said a man can give his wife a written notice of divorce and send her away."*

⁵But Jesus responded, "He wrote this commandment only as a concession to your hard hearts. ⁶But 'God made them male and female'* from the beginning of creation. ⁷This explains why a man leaves his father and mother and is joined to his wife,* ⁸and the two are united into one.'* Since they are no longer two but one, ⁹let no one split apart what God has joined together."

¹⁰Later, when he was alone with his disciples in the house, they brought up the subject again. ¹¹He told them, "Whoever divorces his wife and marries someone else commits adultery against her. ¹²And if a woman divorces her husband and marries someone else, she commits adultery."

Jesus Blesses the Children

¹³One day some parents brought their children to Jesus so he could touch and bless them. But the disciples scolded the parents for bothering him.

¹⁴When Jesus saw what was happening, he was angry with his disciples. He said to them, "Let the children come to me. Don't stop them! For the Kingdom of God belongs to those who are like these children. ¹⁵I tell you the truth, anyone who doesn't receive the Kingdom of God like a child will never enter it." ¹⁶Then he took the children in his arms and placed his hands on their heads and blessed them.

The Rich Man

¹⁷As Jesus was starting out on his way to Jerusalem, a man came running up to him, knelt down, and asked, "Good Teacher, what must I do to inherit eternal life?"

¹⁸"Why do you call me good?" Jesus asked. "Only God is truly good. ¹⁹But to answer your question, you know the commandments: 'You must not murder. You must not commit adultery. You must not steal. You must not testify falsely. You must not cheat anyone. Honor your father and mother.'*"

²⁰"Teacher," the man replied, "I've obeyed all these commandments since I was young."

²¹Looking at the man, Jesus felt genuine love for him. "There is still one thing you haven't done," he told him. "Go and sell all your possessions and give the money to the poor, and you will have treasure in heaven. Then come, follow me."

²²At this the man's face fell, and he went away sad, for he had many possessions.

²³Jesus looked around and said to his disciples, "How hard it is for the rich to enter the Kingdom of God!" ²⁴This amazed them. But Jesus said again, "Dear children, it is very hard* to enter the Kingdom of God. ²⁵In fact, it is easier for a camel to go through the eye of a needle than for a rich person to enter the Kingdom of God!"

²⁶The disciples were astounded. "Then who in the world can be saved?" they asked.

²⁷Jesus looked at them intently and said, "Humanly speaking, it is impossible. But not with God. Everything is possible with God."

²⁸Then Peter began to speak up. "We've given up everything to follow you," he said.

²⁹"Yes," Jesus replied, "and I assure you that everyone who has given up house or brothers or sisters or mother or father or children or property, for my sake and for the Good News, ³⁰will receive now in return a hundred times as many houses, brothers, sisters, mothers, children, and property— along with persecution. And in the world to come that person will have eternal life. ³¹But many who are the greatest now will be least important then, and those who seem least important now will be the greatest then.*"

10:4 See Deut 24:1. 10:6 Gen 1:27; 5:2. 10:7 Some manuscripts do not include *and is joined to his wife.* 10:7-8 Gen 2:24. 10:19 Exod 20:12-16; Deut 5:16-20. 10:24 Some manuscripts read *very hard for those who trust in riches.* 10:31 Greek *But many who are first will be last; and the last, first.*

10:23-31 Most people in Jesus' day believed that wealth was a reward from God for being good. Thus, the wealthy usually enjoyed a measure of prestige. Jesus amazed his audience by showing how very difficult it was for the rich to enter God's Kingdom. Wealthy people have a hard time recognizing their need for anything, and the only way to receive God's help is by recognizing how much we need him. The rich young man needed to see his helplessness before he could be helped. But even this problem is not too big for God; he gets the attention of even the proud and self-sufficient. Many of us have learned through painful experiences that we are helpless and need God's intervention in our life. God often lets us hit bottom so we can begin to experience his healing and forgiveness.

Jesus Again Predicts His Death

[32]They were now on the way up to Jerusalem, and Jesus was walking ahead of them. The disciples were filled with awe, and the people following behind were overwhelmed with fear. Taking the twelve disciples aside, Jesus once more began to describe everything that was about to happen to him. [33]"Listen," he said, "we're going up to Jerusalem, where the Son of Man* will be betrayed to the leading priests and the teachers of religious law. They will sentence him to die and hand him over to the Romans.* [34]They will mock him, spit on him, flog him with a whip, and kill him, but after three days he will rise again."

Jesus Teaches about Serving Others

[35]Then James and John, the sons of Zebedee, came over and spoke to him. "Teacher," they said, "we want you to do us a favor."

[36]"What is your request?" he asked.

[37]They replied, "When you sit on your glorious throne, we want to sit in places of honor next to you, one on your right and the other on your left."

[38]But Jesus said to them, "You don't know what you are asking! Are you able to drink from the bitter cup of suffering I am about to drink? Are you able to be baptized with the baptism of suffering I must be baptized with?"

[39]"Oh yes," they replied, "we are able!"

Then Jesus told them, "You will indeed drink from my bitter cup and be baptized with my baptism of suffering. [40]But I have no right to say who will sit on my right or my left. God has prepared those places for the ones he has chosen."

[41]When the ten other disciples heard what James and John had asked, they were indignant. [42]So Jesus called them together and said, "You know that the rulers in this world lord it over their people, and officials flaunt their au-thority over those under them. [43]But among you it will be different. Whoever wants to be a leader among you must be your servant, [44]and whoever wants to be first among you must be the slave of everyone else. [45]For even the Son of Man came not to be served but to serve others and to give his life as a ransom for many."

Jesus Heals Blind Bartimaeus

[46]Then they reached Jericho, and as Jesus and his disciples left town, a large crowd followed him. A blind beggar named Bartimaeus (son of Timaeus) was sitting beside the road. [47]When Bartimaeus heard that Jesus of Nazareth was nearby, he began to shout, "Jesus, Son of David, have mercy on me!"

[48]"Be quiet!" many of the people yelled at him.

But he only shouted louder, "Son of David, have mercy on me!"

[49]When Jesus heard him, he stopped and said, "Tell him to come here."

So they called the blind man. "Cheer up," they said. "Come on, he's calling you!" [50]Bartimaeus threw aside his coat, jumped up, and came to Jesus.

[51]"What do you want me to do for you?" Jesus asked.

"My Rabbi,*" the blind man said, "I want to see!"

[52]And Jesus said to him, "Go, for your faith has healed you." Instantly the man could see, and he followed Jesus down the road.*

CHAPTER 11

Jesus' Triumphant Entry

As Jesus and his disciples approached Jerusalem, they came to the towns of Bethphage and Bethany on the Mount of Olives. Jesus sent two of them on ahead. [2]"Go into that

---

10:33a "Son of Man" is a title Jesus used for himself. 10:33b Greek *the Gentiles.* 10:51 Greek uses the Hebrew term *Rabboni.* 10:52 Or *on the way.*

10:46-52 Faith brought sight to blind Bartimaeus. He persevered in faith despite the initial opposition he experienced from Jesus' followers. In Jesus' day, blindness was considered a divine curse for sin (see John 9:2), but Jesus refuted this notion by both word and deed. We sometimes face opposition in our recovery process. Sometimes those who claim to be God's people reject us and make us feel unwelcome because we are trapped by our dependency. Even when others reject us, we can be sure that Jesus will never turn us away. We should persevere like Bartimaeus did, knowing that Jesus has the power and the desire to help us overcome our besetting weaknesses.

11:1-10 As we suffer the pain of our addiction, we often look for instant relief. We wish someone would come and sweep all our problems away. The Judeans were expecting the same kind of deliverance from their Messiah. They wanted a glorious political king on a warhorse to ride into Jerusalem and sweep the Romans out of power. Instead, Jesus came riding on a lowly donkey, in peace. God does not offer instant cures; he works our recovery through a process of personal growth, from the inside out. He helps us recognize our sins and our need for help, and he gives us the strength to take the necessary steps toward recovery.

village over there," he told them. "As soon as you enter it, you will see a young donkey tied there that no one has ever ridden. Untie it and bring it here. ³If anyone asks, 'What are you doing?' just say, 'The Lord needs it and will return it soon.'"

⁴The two disciples left and found the colt standing in the street, tied outside the front door. ⁵As they were untying it, some bystanders demanded, "What are you doing, untying that colt?" ⁶They said what Jesus had told them to say, and they were permitted to take it. ⁷Then they brought the colt to Jesus and threw their garments over it, and he sat on it.

⁸Many in the crowd spread their garments on the road ahead of him, and others spread leafy branches they had cut in the fields. ⁹Jesus was in the center of the procession, and the people all around him were shouting,

"Praise God!*
　　Blessings on the one who comes in the
　　　name of the LORD!
¹⁰ Blessings on the coming Kingdom of our
　　　ancestor David!
　　Praise God in highest heaven!"*

¹¹So Jesus came to Jerusalem and went into the Temple. After looking around carefully at everything, he left because it was late in the afternoon. Then he returned to Bethany with the twelve disciples.

Jesus Curses the Fig Tree

¹²The next morning as they were leaving Bethany, Jesus was hungry. ¹³He noticed a fig tree in full leaf a little way off, so he went over to see if he could find any figs. But there were only leaves because it was too early in the season for fruit. ¹⁴Then Jesus said to the tree, "May no one ever eat your fruit again!" And the disciples heard him say it.

Jesus Clears the Temple

¹⁵When they arrived back in Jerusalem, Jesus entered the Temple and began to drive out the people buying and selling animals for sacrifices. He knocked over the tables of the money changers and the chairs of those selling doves, ¹⁶and he stopped everyone from using the Temple as a marketplace.* ¹⁷He said to them, "The Scriptures declare, 'My Temple will be called a house of prayer for all nations,' but you have turned it into a den of thieves."*

¹⁸When the leading priests and teachers of religious law heard what Jesus had done, they began planning how to kill him. But they were afraid of him because the people were so amazed at his teaching.

¹⁹That evening Jesus and the disciples left* the city.

²⁰The next morning as they passed by the fig tree he had cursed, the disciples noticed it had withered from the roots up. ²¹Peter remembered what Jesus had said to the tree on the previous day and exclaimed, "Look, Rabbi! The fig tree you cursed has withered and died!"

²²Then Jesus said to the disciples, "Have faith in God. ²³I tell you the truth, you can say to this mountain, 'May you be lifted up and thrown into the sea,' and it will happen. But you must really believe it will happen and have no doubt in your heart. ²⁴I tell you, you can pray for anything, and if you believe that you've received it, it will be yours. ²⁵But when you are praying, first forgive anyone you are holding a grudge against, so that your Father in heaven will forgive your sins, too.*"

The Authority of Jesus Challenged

²⁷Again they entered Jerusalem. As Jesus was walking through the Temple area, the lead-

11:9 Greek *Hosanna*, an exclamation of praise that literally means "save now"; also in 11:10. **11:9-10** Pss 118:25-26; 148:1. **11:16** Or *from carrying merchandise through the Temple.* **11:17** Isa 56:7; Jer 7:11. **11:19** Greek *they left;* other manuscripts read *he left.* **11:25** Some manuscripts add verse 26, *But if you refuse to forgive, your Father in heaven will not forgive your sins.* Compare Matt 6:15.

11:12-19 The barren fig tree is analogous to spiritually bankrupt people. If the fig tree did not produce fruit, as it was designed to do, then it had no real reason to exist. If the Temple did not produce true worship and prayer but only ill-gotten gain for the money changers, then the Temple had to be judged and cleansed as well. So also in recovery. If our life in recovery is not bearing the fruit of new behavior patterns, then it must be overhauled. If we only go through the motions of recovery, then our faith has no substance, and our attempts to recover are only pretenses.

11:20-25 God wants us to pray for his will to be done in our life as much as he wants us to pray for fruitfulness in his Kingdom work. It is God's will, however, to remove mountains of resistance or denial from our life. God has the power to do miracles—but not if we doubt him. The God of the Kingdom and of recovery is the God of the impossible. If we want God to work a miracle of healing in our life, we must pray and believe that he will. We need to admit our helplessness and put our life into God's hands. He will then walk with us as we face each new step in recovery.

ing priests, the teachers of religious law, and the elders came up to him. [28]They demanded, "By what authority are you doing all these things? Who gave you the right to do them?"

[29]"I'll tell you by what authority I do these things if you answer one question," Jesus replied. [30]"Did John's authority to baptize come from heaven, or was it merely human? Answer me!"

[31]They talked it over among themselves. "If we say it was from heaven, he will ask why we didn't believe John. [32]But do we dare say it was merely human?" For they were afraid of what the people would do, because everyone believed that John was a prophet. [33]So they finally replied, "We don't know."

And Jesus responded, "Then I won't tell you by what authority I do these things."

CHAPTER 12
Parable of the Evil Farmers
Then Jesus began teaching them with stories: "A man planted a vineyard. He built a wall around it, dug a pit for pressing out the grape juice, and built a lookout tower. Then he leased the vineyard to tenant farmers and moved to another country. [2]At the time of the grape harvest, he sent one of his servants to collect his share of the crop. [3]But the farmers grabbed the servant, beat him up, and sent him back empty-handed. [4]The owner then sent another servant, but they insulted him and beat him over the head. [5]The next servant he sent was killed. Others he sent were either beaten or killed, [6]until there was only one left—his son whom he loved dearly. The owner finally sent him, thinking, 'Surely they will respect my son.'

[7]"But the tenant farmers said to one another, 'Here comes the heir to this estate. Let's kill him and get the estate for ourselves!' [8]So they grabbed him and murdered him and threw his body out of the vineyard.

[9]"What do you suppose the owner of the vineyard will do?" Jesus asked. "I'll tell you—he will come and kill those farmers and lease the vineyard to others. [10]Didn't you ever read this in the Scriptures?

'The stone that the builders rejected
has now become the cornerstone.
[11]This is the LORD's doing,
and it is wonderful to see.'*"

[12]The religious leaders* wanted to arrest Jesus because they realized he was telling the story against them—they were the wicked farmers. But they were afraid of the crowd, so they left him and went away.

Taxes for Caesar
[13]Later the leaders sent some Pharisees and supporters of Herod to trap Jesus into saying something for which he could be arrested. [14]"Teacher," they said, "we know how honest you are. You are impartial and don't play favorites. You teach the way of God truthfully. Now tell us—is it right to pay taxes to Caesar or not? [15]Should we pay them, or shouldn't we?"

Jesus saw through their hypocrisy and said, "Why are you trying to trap me? Show me a Roman coin,* and I'll tell you." [16]When they handed it to him, he asked, "Whose picture and title are stamped on it?"

"Caesar's," they replied.

[17]"Well, then," Jesus said, "give to Caesar what belongs to Caesar, and give to God what belongs to God."

His reply completely amazed them.

Discussion about Resurrection
[18]Then Jesus was approached by some Sadducees—religious leaders who say there is no

12:10-11 Ps 118:22-23. 12:12 Greek *They.* 12:15 Greek *a denarius.*

12:1-12 Jesus confronted the religious leaders with their hypocrisy and denial with this story. The leaders were the wicked farmers who had rejected God, the owner of his people (who were represented by the vineyard). These leaders pretended to be in touch with God, but their actions and attitudes proved otherwise. Jesus confronted them, hoping they would listen and change. We also need to be awakened from our denial if we hope to recover. God often brings people into our life to wake us up. We must not be like the proud Pharisees. If we refuse to admit our sins, we will never receive God's help for recovery.
12:18-27 Jesus avoided another trick question, this one by the Sadducees, who did not believe in the resurrection after death. Again Jesus cleverly exposed the moral shortcomings of those who had the form of religion but denied its power. Book learning, even Scripture memory, is not enough to keep us from sin or help us recover from our dependency. We must know the living God personally and accept the help he offers as our Savior. The God of the patriarchs is not the God of philosophical speculation. He is our God, active today in our recovery. He is the God of hope and resurrection.

resurrection from the dead. They posed this question: [19]"Teacher, Moses gave us a law that if a man dies, leaving a wife without children, his brother should marry the widow and have a child who will carry on the brother's name.* [20]Well, suppose there were seven brothers. The oldest one married and then died without children. [21]So the second brother married the widow, but he also died without children. Then the third brother married her. [22]This continued with all seven of them, and still there were no children. Last of all, the woman also died. [23]So tell us, whose wife will she be in the resurrection? For all seven were married to her."

[24]Jesus replied, "Your mistake is that you don't know the Scriptures, and you don't know the power of God. [25]For when the dead rise, they will neither marry nor be given in marriage. In this respect they will be like the angels in heaven.

[26]"But now, as to whether the dead will be raised—haven't you ever read about this in the writings of Moses, in the story of the burning bush? Long after Abraham, Isaac, and Jacob had died, God said to Moses,* 'I am the God of Abraham, the God of Isaac, and the God of Jacob.'* [27]So he is the God of the living, not the dead. You have made a serious error."

The Most Important Commandment

[28]One of the teachers of religious law was standing there listening to the debate. He realized that Jesus had answered well, so he asked, "Of all the commandments, which is the most important?"

[29]Jesus replied, "The most important commandment is this: 'Listen, O Israel! The LORD our God is the one and only LORD. [30]And you must love the LORD your God with all your heart, all your soul, all your mind, and all your strength.'* [31]The second is equally important: 'Love your neighbor as yourself.'* No other commandment is greater than these."

[32]The teacher of religious law replied, "Well said, Teacher. You have spoken the truth by saying that there is only one God and no other. [33]And I know it is important to love him with all my heart and all my understanding and all my strength, and to love my neighbor as myself. This is more important than to offer all of the burnt offerings and sacrifices required in the law."

[34]Realizing how much the man understood, Jesus said to him, "You are not far from the Kingdom of God." And after that, no one dared to ask him any more questions.

Whose Son Is the Messiah?

[35]Later, as Jesus was teaching the people in the Temple, he asked, "Why do the teachers of religious law claim that the Messiah is the son of David? [36]For David himself, speaking under the inspiration of the Holy Spirit, said,

'The LORD said to my Lord,
Sit in the place of honor at my right hand
    until I humble your enemies beneath
        your feet.'*

[37]Since David himself called the Messiah 'my Lord,' how can the Messiah be his son?" The large crowd listened to him with great delight.

[38]Jesus also taught: "Beware of these teachers of religious law! For they like to parade around in flowing robes and receive respectful greetings as they walk in the marketplaces. [39]And how they love the seats of honor in the synagogues and the head table at banquets. [40]Yet they shamelessly cheat widows out of their property and then pretend to be pious by making long prayers in public. Because of this, they will be more severely punished."

The Widow's Offering

[41]Jesus sat down near the collection box in the Temple and watched as the crowds dropped in their money. Many rich people put in large amounts. [42]Then a poor widow came and dropped in two small coins.* [43]Jesus called his disciples to him and said,

12:19 See Deut 25:5-6. 12:26a Greek *in the story of the bush? God said to him.* 12:26b Exod 3:6. 12:29-30 Deut 6:4-5. 12:31 Lev 19:18. 12:36 Ps 110:1. 12:42 Greek *two lepta, which is a kodrantes* [i.e., a quadrans].

12:28-34 Many think of religion, with all its commandments, as a burdensome straitjacket, antithetical to true recovery. This may have been true, in some sense, of the Judaism in Jesus' day, and it is sometimes true today among people who claim to belong to God. Jesus wanted to correct this false understanding of true faith. He summed up the numerous Jewish laws in two simple but profound commandments: Love God totally and love others as much as we love ourself. If these two thoughts rule our heart and mind, we will be well along the path toward recovery.

"I tell you the truth, this poor widow has given more than all the others who are making contributions. [44]For they gave a tiny part of their surplus, but she, poor as she is, has given everything she had to live on."

CHAPTER 13
Jesus Foretells the Future

As Jesus was leaving the Temple that day, one of his disciples said, "Teacher, look at these magnificent buildings! Look at the impressive stones in the walls."

[2]Jesus replied, "Yes, look at these great buildings. But they will be completely demolished. Not one stone will be left on top of another!"

[3]Later, Jesus sat on the Mount of Olives across the valley from the Temple. Peter, James, John, and Andrew came to him privately and asked him, [4]"Tell us, when will all this happen? What sign will show us that these things are about to be fulfilled?"

[5]Jesus replied, "Don't let anyone mislead you, [6]for many will come in my name, claiming, 'I am the Messiah.'* They will deceive many. [7]And you will hear of wars and threats of wars, but don't panic. Yes, these things must take place, but the end won't follow immediately. [8]Nation will go to war against nation, and kingdom against kingdom. There will be earthquakes in many parts of the world, as well as famines. But this is only the first of the birth pains, with more to come.

[9]"When these things begin to happen, watch out! You will be handed over to the local councils and beaten in the synagogues. You will stand trial before governors and kings because you are my followers. But this will be your opportunity to tell them about me.* [10]For the Good News must first be preached to all nations.* [11]But when you are arrested and stand trial, don't worry in advance about what to say. Just say what God tells you at that time, for it is not you who will be speaking, but the Holy Spirit.

[12]"A brother will betray his brother to death, a father will betray his own child, and children will rebel against their parents and cause them to be killed. [13]And everyone will hate you because you are my followers.* But the one who endures to the end will be saved.

[14]"The day is coming when you will see the sacrilegious object that causes desecration* standing where he* should not be." (Reader, pay attention!) "Then those in Judea must flee to the hills. [15]A person out on the deck of a roof must not go down into the house to pack. [16]A person out in the field must not return even to get a coat. [17]How terrible it will be for pregnant women and for nursing mothers in those days. [18]And pray that your flight will not be in winter. [19]For there will be greater anguish in those days than at any time since God created the world. And it will never be so great again. [20]In fact, unless the Lord shortens that time of calamity, not a single person will survive. But for the sake of his chosen ones he has shortened those days.

[21]"Then if anyone tells you, 'Look, here is the Messiah,' or 'There he is,' don't believe it. [22]For false messiahs and false prophets will rise up and perform signs and wonders so as to deceive, if possible, even God's chosen ones. [23]Watch out! I have warned you about this ahead of time!

[24]"At that time, after the anguish of those days,

the sun will be darkened,
the moon will give no light,

13:6 Greek *claiming, 'I am.'* **13:9** Or *But this will be your testimony against them.* **13:10** Or *all peoples.* **13:13** Greek *on account of my name.* **13:14a** Greek *the abomination of desolation.* See Dan 9:27; 11:31; 12:11. **13:14b** Or *it.*

13:1-20 The Olivet discourse (13:1-37) speaks to the all-too-human preoccupation with the uncertainty of the future. The disciples worried about the future of their nation after Jesus predicted the destruction of the Temple that was then being rebuilt. We may worry about whether or not we will survive future conflicts and temptations. As we face an uncertain future, we are encouraged to live one day at a time. God makes it clear that despite our trials, we should not worry. If we entrust our life to God, his Spirit will be with us during our difficult times. Recovery is never easy, but it is always possible with God's help.

13:21-37 Jesus did not reveal when the end would come, but this should motivate us to remain alert and watchful from now until the end. As we are unsure of the future of our world, we are also uncertain about the timing and difficulties we will face in recovery. We are never completely recovered; we are always in recovery. We will experience total victory only after Jesus has returned to make us into new people. Preparation for his return must be made one day at a time. We cannot calculate the day of his return and plan to change just before he comes. Our daily preparation and actions are important keys to our spiritual health and recovery.

²⁵ the stars will fall from the sky,
and the powers in the heavens will be shaken.*

²⁶Then everyone will see the Son of Man* coming on the clouds with great power and glory.* ²⁷And he will send out his angels to gather his chosen ones from all over the world*—from the farthest ends of the earth and heaven.

²⁸"Now learn a lesson from the fig tree. When its branches bud and its leaves begin to sprout, you know that summer is near. ²⁹In the same way, when you see all these things taking place, you can know that his return is very near, right at the door. ³⁰I tell you the truth, this generation* will not pass from the scene before all these things take place. ³¹Heaven and earth will disappear, but my words will never disappear.

³²"However, no one knows the day or hour when these things will happen, not even the angels in heaven or the Son himself. Only the Father knows. ³³And since you don't know when that time will come, be on guard! Stay alert*!

³⁴"The coming of the Son of Man can be illustrated by the story of a man going on a long trip. When he left home, he gave each of his slaves instructions about the work they were to do, and he told the gatekeeper to watch for his return. ³⁵You, too, must keep watch! For you don't know when the master of the household will return—in the evening, at midnight, before dawn, or at daybreak. ³⁶Don't let him find you sleeping when he arrives without warning. ³⁷I say to you what I say to everyone: Watch for him!"

CHAPTER 14
Jesus Anointed at Bethany

It was now two days before Passover and the Festival of Unleavened Bread. The leading priests and the teachers of religious law were still looking for an opportunity to capture Jesus secretly and kill him. ²"But not during the Passover celebration," they agreed, "or the people may riot."

³Meanwhile, Jesus was in Bethany at the home of Simon, a man who had previously had leprosy. While he was eating,* a woman came in with a beautiful alabaster jar of expensive perfume made from essence of nard. She broke open the jar and poured the perfume over his head.

⁴Some of those at the table were indignant. "Why waste such expensive perfume?" they asked. ⁵"It could have been sold for a year's wages* and the money given to the poor!" So they scolded her harshly.

⁶But Jesus replied, "Leave her alone. Why criticize her for doing such a good thing to me? ⁷You will always have the poor among you, and you can help them whenever you want to. But you will not always have me. ⁸She has done what she could and has anointed my body for burial ahead of time. ⁹I tell you the truth, wherever the Good News is preached throughout the world, this woman's deed will be remembered and discussed."

Judas Agrees to Betray Jesus

¹⁰Then Judas Iscariot, one of the twelve disciples, went to the leading priests to arrange to betray Jesus to them. ¹¹They were delighted when they heard why he had come, and they promised to give him money. So he began looking for an opportunity to betray Jesus.

The Last Supper

¹²On the first day of the Festival of Unleavened Bread, when the Passover lamb is sacrificed, Jesus' disciples asked him, "Where do you want us to go to prepare the Passover meal for you?"

¹³So Jesus sent two of them into Jerusalem with these instructions: "As you go into the city, a man carrying a pitcher of water will meet you. Follow him. ¹⁴At the house he enters, say to the owner, 'The Teacher asks: Where is the guest room where I can eat the

---

13:24-25 See Isa 13:10; 34:4; Joel 2:10. **13:26a** "Son of Man" is a title Jesus used for himself. **13:26b** See Dan 7:13. **13:27** Greek *from the four winds*. **13:30** Or *this age*, or *this nation*. **13:33** Some manuscripts add *and pray*. **14:3** Or *reclining*. **14:5** Greek *for 300 denarii*. A denarius was equivalent to a laborer's full day's wage.

14:10-26 We are often shocked by Judas's betrayal of Jesus. Since Judas had spent about three years in close friendship with Jesus, we wonder what could have prompted him to act as he did. Yet if we are truly honest with ourself, we may see the same potential in our own heart. Whenever we refuse to give Jesus authority over a certain area of our life, we act like Judas. Whenever we promise to do one thing and then do another, we act like Judas. We all have betrayed God in some way or another. We should use Judas's failure as an opportunity to take a hard look at our own life. In what ways are we betraying God?

GOD grant me the serenity to accept the things I cannot change the courage to change the things I can and the wisdom to know the difference

AMEN

As we pray the serenity prayer, we learn to think in new ways. We learn to ask questions that will lead us away from our destructive past and into a productive future.

We begin to ask, What can we change in our situation? What things are beyond our control? What are our responsibilities in the situations we face? As we develop these new thought processes, we may lack confidence in our own wisdom and common sense. We may hesitate to carry out God's will if we are afraid of the criticism of the people around us.

Common sense could be defined as our ability to figure out in advance what the likely consequences of our choices and actions will be. We are told that "Getting wisdom is the wisest thing you can do! And whatever else you do, develop good judgment" (Proverbs 4:7). We can exercise our common sense by thinking about what we can do and then doing the things that we can.

A woman wanted to do something to demonstrate her love for Jesus, so she poured some expensive perfume on his head. The disciples criticized her for doing this. Jesus came to her defense with these words: "Leave her alone. Why criticize her for doing such a good thing to me? . . . She has done what she could" (Mark 14:6-8). These are words we can cling to.

God wants to renew our mind and help us develop wisdom and common sense. As we try to sort out our choices and develop common sense, people may criticize us. But we can trust that God will come to our defense, as long as we do what Scripture directs us to do. *Turn to page 1313, Luke 11.*

Passover meal with my disciples?' ¹⁵He will take you upstairs to a large room that is already set up. That is where you should prepare our meal." ¹⁶So the two disciples went into the city and found everything just as Jesus had said, and they prepared the Passover meal there.

¹⁷In the evening Jesus arrived with the Twelve. ¹⁸As they were at the table* eating, Jesus said, "I tell you the truth, one of you eating with me here will betray me."

¹⁹Greatly distressed, each one asked in turn, "Am I the one?"

²⁰He replied, "It is one of you twelve who is eating from this bowl with me. ²¹For the Son of Man* must die, as the Scriptures declared long ago. But how terrible it will be for the one who betrays him. It would be far better for that man if he had never been born!"

²²As they were eating, Jesus took some bread and blessed it. Then he broke it in pieces and gave it to the disciples, saying, "Take it, for this is my body."

²³And he took a cup of wine and gave thanks to God for it. He gave it to them, and they all drank from it. ²⁴And he said to them, "This is my blood, which confirms the covenant* between God and his people. It is poured out as a sacrifice for many. ²⁵I tell you the truth, I will not drink wine again until the day I drink it new in the Kingdom of God."

²⁶Then they sang a hymn and went out to the Mount of Olives.

14:18 Or *As they reclined.* 14:21 "Son of Man" is a title Jesus used for himself. 14:24 Some manuscripts read *the new covenant.*

Jesus Predicts Peter's Denial

[27]On the way, Jesus told them, "All of you will desert me. For the Scriptures say,

'God will strike* the Shepherd,
   and the sheep will be scattered.'

[28]But after I am raised from the dead, I will go ahead of you to Galilee and meet you there."

[29]Peter said to him, "Even if everyone else deserts you, I never will."

[30]Jesus replied, "I tell you the truth, Peter—this very night, before the rooster crows twice, you will deny three times that you even know me."

[31]"No!" Peter declared emphatically. "Even if I have to die with you, I will never deny you!" And all the others vowed the same.

Jesus Prays in Gethsemane

[32]They went to the olive grove called Gethsemane, and Jesus said, "Sit here while I go and pray." [33]He took Peter, James, and John with him, and he became deeply troubled and distressed. [34]He told them, "My soul is crushed with grief to the point of death. Stay here and keep watch with me."

[35]He went on a little farther and fell to the ground. He prayed that, if it were possible, the awful hour awaiting him might pass him by. [36]"Abba, Father,"* he cried out, "everything is possible for you. Please take this cup of suffering away from me. Yet I want your will to be done, not mine."

[37]Then he returned and found the disciples asleep. He said to Peter, "Simon, are you asleep? Couldn't you watch with me even one hour? [38]Keep watch and pray, so that you will not give in to temptation. For the spirit is willing, but the body is weak."

[39]Then Jesus left them again and prayed the same prayer as before. [40]When he returned to them again, he found them sleeping, for they couldn't keep their eyes open. And they didn't know what to say.

[41]When he returned to them the third time, he said, "Go ahead and sleep. Have your rest. But no—the time has come. The Son of Man is betrayed into the hands of sinners. [42]Up, let's be going. Look, my betrayer is here!"

Jesus Is Betrayed and Arrested

[43]And immediately, even as Jesus said this, Judas, one of the twelve disciples, arrived with a crowd of men armed with swords and clubs. They had been sent by the leading priests, the teachers of religious law, and the elders. [44]The traitor, Judas, had given them a prearranged signal: "You will know which one to arrest when I greet him with a kiss. Then you can take him away under guard." [45]As soon as they arrived, Judas walked up to Jesus. "Rabbi!" he exclaimed, and gave him the kiss.

[46]Then the others grabbed Jesus and arrested him. [47]But one of the men with Jesus pulled out his sword and struck the high priest's slave, slashing off his ear.

[48]Jesus asked them, "Am I some dangerous revolutionary, that you come with swords and clubs to arrest me? [49]Why didn't you arrest me in the Temple? I was there among you teaching every day. But these things are happening to fulfill what the Scriptures say about me."

[50]Then all his disciples deserted him and ran away. [51]One young man following behind was clothed only in a long linen shirt. When the mob tried to grab him, [52]he slipped out of his shirt and ran away naked.

14:27 Greek *I will strike.* Zech 13:7. 14:36 *Abba* is an Aramaic term for "father."

14:27-31 Peter wasn't honest with himself when he promised to stay with Jesus no matter what the cost. He still did not realize that following Jesus would lead him to the foot of the cross. When things got tough, Peter backed out of his commitment (see 14:66-71). We often do the same thing in recovery. We determine to escape the pain of our addiction and commit ourself to recovery. But we may be unaware of the hard times we must face along the way. As recovery becomes difficult and we experience opposition, we are tempted to give up and fall back into our destructive habits. We should consider the difficulties we may face before we start the journey. Then we won't be devastated when we have to face them.

14:32-42 Jesus opened his heart to Peter, James, and John: "My soul is crushed with grief to the point of death. Stay here and keep watch with me" (14:34). Jesus demonstrated qualities that are important for us in recovery: honesty, transparency, and trust. Jesus evidently needed others for support in this hour of agony shortly before his death. If Jesus needed human support to face his trials, we must need it even more. It is important that we develop a support group that will hold us accountable to our commitment to recovery. Unless we can develop and maintain meaningful human relationships, it will be nearly impossible to continue in recovery.

Jesus before the Council

[53]They took Jesus to the high priest's home where the leading priests, the elders, and the teachers of religious law had gathered. [54]Meanwhile, Peter followed him at a distance and went right into the high priest's courtyard. There he sat with the guards, warming himself by the fire.

[55]Inside, the leading priests and the entire high council* were trying to find evidence against Jesus, so they could put him to death. But they couldn't find any. [56]Many false witnesses spoke against him, but they contradicted each other. [57]Finally, some men stood up and gave this false testimony: [58]"We heard him say, 'I will destroy this Temple made with human hands, and in three days I will build another, made without human hands.'" [59]But even then they didn't get their stories straight!

[60]Then the high priest stood up before the others and asked Jesus, "Well, aren't you going to answer these charges? What do you have to say for yourself?" [61]But Jesus was silent and made no reply. Then the high priest asked him, "Are you the Messiah, the Son of the Blessed One?"

[62]Jesus said, "I AM.* And you will see the Son of Man seated in the place of power at God's right hand* and coming on the clouds of heaven.*"

[63]Then the high priest tore his clothing to show his horror and said, "Why do we need other witnesses? [64]You have all heard his blasphemy. What is your verdict?"

"Guilty!" they all cried. "He deserves to die!"

[65]Then some of them began to spit at him, and they blindfolded him and beat him with their fists. "Prophesy to us," they jeered. And the guards slapped him as they took him away.

Peter Denies Jesus

[66]Meanwhile, Peter was in the courtyard below. One of the servant girls who worked for the high priest came by [67]and noticed Peter warming himself at the fire. She looked at him closely and said, "You were one of those with Jesus of Nazareth.*"

[68]But Peter denied it. "I don't know what you're talking about," he said, and he went out into the entryway. Just then, a rooster crowed.*

[69]When the servant girl saw him standing there, she began telling the others, "This man is definitely one of them!" [70]But Peter denied it again.

A little later some of the other bystanders confronted Peter and said, "You must be one of them, because you are a Galilean."

[71]Peter swore, "A curse on me if I'm lying—I don't know this man you're talking about!" [72]And immediately the rooster crowed the second time.

Suddenly, Jesus' words flashed through Peter's mind: "Before the rooster crows twice, you will deny three times that you even know me." And he broke down and wept.

CHAPTER 15
Jesus' Trial before Pilate

Very early in the morning the leading priests, the elders, and the teachers of religious

---

14:55 Greek the Sanhedrin. 14:62a Or The 'I AM' is here; or I am the LORD. See Exod 3:14. 14:62b Greek at the right hand of the power. See Ps 110:1. 14:62c See Dan 7:13. 14:67 Or Jesus the Nazarene. 14:68 Some manuscripts do not include Just then, a rooster crowed.

14:53-65 Jesus was a victim of abuse and injustice: He was lied about, falsely accused and convicted, and physically assaulted. But instead of returning words or blows in kind, he entrusted himself to his Father's care (1 Peter 2:23). Jesus modeled the kind of trust that a person with a history of abuse might emulate. As we remember the pain of past abuses in our life, we can turn all the hurtful events and vengeful feelings over to God. We can then focus on our own problems and dependency, knowing that God will deal justly with the people who have hurt us in the past.
14:66-72 Peter apparently didn't know himself as well as he thought he did. Earlier he had claimed that he would never deny Jesus (14:29, 31); here he denied his Master three times. Peter could have profited from Jesus' earlier prediction of his denial (14:30). Instead of shrugging it off, he should have responded to Jesus' words with honest self-examination. Denying the sad truth about ourself usually leads to the loss of important opportunities to correct our character flaws. This, in turn, stops our progress in recovery and stunts our spiritual growth.
15:1-15 Pilate told Jesus' accusers that he found no guilt in Jesus, yet he handed him over for execution. The Jews' strong emotions and Pilate's desire to pacify them at all costs led to the death of an innocent man. We have a lot in common with Pilate. When we sacrifice the truth in order to please the crowd, we crucify Jesus. Our challenge in recovery is to stand firm in our faith and not succumb to cynicism, compromises, or moral laxity. When we take the first step toward relapse, we must recover our footing with courage and wisdom.

law—the entire high council*—met to discuss their next step. They bound Jesus, led him away, and took him to Pilate, the Roman governor.

²Pilate asked Jesus, "Are you the king of the Jews?"

Jesus replied, "You have said it."

³Then the leading priests kept accusing him of many crimes, ⁴and Pilate asked him, "Aren't you going to answer them? What about all these charges they are bringing against you?" ⁵But Jesus said nothing, much to Pilate's surprise.

⁶Now it was the governor's custom each year during the Passover celebration to release one prisoner—anyone the people requested. ⁷One of the prisoners at that time was Barabbas, a revolutionary who had committed murder in an uprising. ⁸The crowd went to Pilate and asked him to release a prisoner as usual.

⁹"Would you like me to release to you this 'King of the Jews'?" Pilate asked. ¹⁰(For he realized by now that the leading priests had arrested Jesus out of envy.) ¹¹But at this point the leading priests stirred up the crowd to demand the release of Barabbas instead of Jesus. ¹²Pilate asked them, "Then what should I do with this man you call the king of the Jews?"

¹³They shouted back, "Crucify him!"

¹⁴"Why?" Pilate demanded. "What crime has he committed?"

But the mob roared even louder, "Crucify him!"

¹⁵So to pacify the crowd, Pilate released Barabbas to them. He ordered Jesus flogged with a lead-tipped whip, then turned him over to the Roman soldiers to be crucified.

The Soldiers Mock Jesus

¹⁶The soldiers took Jesus into the courtyard of the governor's headquarters (called the Praetorium) and called out the entire regiment. ¹⁷They dressed him in a purple robe, and they wove thorn branches into a crown and put it on his head. ¹⁸Then they saluted him and taunted, "Hail! King of the Jews!" ¹⁹And they struck him on the head with a reed stick, spit on him, and dropped to their knees in mock worship. ²⁰When they were finally tired of mocking him, they took off the purple robe and put his own clothes on him again. Then they led him away to be crucified.

The Crucifixion

²¹A passerby named Simon, who was from Cyrene,* was coming in from the countryside just then, and the soldiers forced him to carry Jesus' cross. (Simon was the father of Alexander and Rufus.) ²²And they brought Jesus to a place called Golgotha (which means "Place of the Skull"). ²³They offered him wine drugged with myrrh, but he refused it.

²⁴Then the soldiers nailed him to the cross. They divided his clothes and threw dice* to decide who would get each piece. ²⁵It was nine o'clock in the morning when they crucified him. ²⁶A sign announced the charge against him. It read, "The King of the Jews." ²⁷Two revolutionaries* were crucified with him, one on his right and one on his left.*

²⁹The people passing by shouted abuse, shaking their heads in mockery. "Ha! Look at you now!" they yelled at him. "You said you were going to destroy the Temple and re-

---

15:1 Greek *the Sanhedrin;* also in 15:43. **15:21** *Cyrene* was a city in northern Africa. **15:24** Greek *cast lots.* See Ps 22:18. **15:27a** Or *Two criminals.* **15:27b** Some manuscripts add verse 28, *And the Scripture was fulfilled that said, "He was counted among those who were rebels."* See Isa 53:12; also compare Luke 22:37.

15:16-32 Jesus suffered verbal and physical abuse when he was spat upon, beaten, mocked, and nailed to a cross. Knowing that Jesus did all this to provide a powerful means for recovery should give us hope. No matter how terrible our past actions or how great our mistakes, Jesus has paid the penalty for our sins. Because of his suffering, we can each have a true relationship with our powerful God. As we grow in our relationship with him, we will discover that there is sufficient power available for the recovery of all who truly desire it.

15:33-41 Jesus' purpose in coming to earth was to serve others and to give his life as payment for our sins; this is a key thought in Mark's Gospel (10:45). At this excruciating moment, the Savior bore the pain and punishment for all the sins ever committed (1 Peter 2:24). This is truly good news! Although we are never good enough to gain God's favor, Jesus' sacrifice provides the eternal security necessary for complete recovery. No matter how hard we try, we can never attain recovery from sin and its effects under our own power or effort. But with God's help we can overcome even the most terrible sin, dependency, or compulsion.

build it in three days. [30]Well then, save yourself and come down from the cross!"

[31]The leading priests and teachers of religious law also mocked Jesus. "He saved others," they scoffed, "but he can't save himself! [32]Let this Messiah, this King of Israel, come down from the cross so we can see it and believe him!" Even the men who were crucified with Jesus ridiculed him.

The Death of Jesus

[33]At noon, darkness fell across the whole land until three o'clock. [34]Then at three o'clock Jesus called out with a loud voice, *"Eloi, Eloi, lema sabachthani?"* which means "My God, my God, why have you abandoned me?"*

[35]Some of the bystanders misunderstood and thought he was calling for the prophet Elijah. [36]One of them ran and filled a sponge with sour wine, holding it up to him on a reed stick so he could drink. "Wait!" he said. "Let's see whether Elijah comes to take him down!"

[37]Then Jesus uttered another loud cry and breathed his last. [38]And the curtain in the sanctuary of the Temple was torn in two, from top to bottom.

[39]When the Roman officer* who stood facing him* saw how he had died, he exclaimed, "This man truly was the Son of God!"

[40]Some women were there, watching from a distance, including Mary Magdalene, Mary (the mother of James the younger and of Joseph*), and Salome. [41]They had been followers of Jesus and had cared for him while he was in Galilee. Many other women who had come with him to Jerusalem were also there.

The Burial of Jesus

[42]This all happened on Friday, the day of preparation,* the day before the Sabbath. As evening approached, [43]Joseph of Arimathea took a risk and went to Pilate and asked for Jesus' body. (Joseph was an honored member of the high council, and he was waiting for the Kingdom of God to come.) [44]Pilate couldn't believe that Jesus was already dead, so he called for the Roman officer and asked if he had died yet. [45]The officer confirmed that Jesus was dead, so Pilate told Joseph he could have the body. [46]Joseph bought a long sheet of linen cloth. Then he took Jesus' body down from the cross, wrapped it in the

15:34 Ps 22:1. 15:39a Greek *the centurion;* similarly in 15:44, 45. 15:39b Some manuscripts add *heard his cry and.* 15:40 Greek *Joses;* also in 15:47. See Matt 27:56. 15:42 Greek *It was the day of preparation.*

STEP 12

Our Story

BIBLE READING: Mark 16:14-18

Having had a spiritual awakening as the result of these steps, we tried to carry this message to others and to practice these principles in all our affairs.

Each one of us has a valuable story to tell. We may be shy and feel awkward about speaking. We may think that what we have to share is too trivial. Is it actually going to help anyone else? We may struggle to get beyond the shame of our past experiences. But our recovery story can help others who are trapped back where we were. Are we willing to allow God to use us to help free others?

Jesus left us with this vital task: "Go into all the world and preach the Good News [of salvation from the bondage and penalty of sin] to everyone" (Mark 16:15). The apostle Paul traveled the world over telling everyone of his conversion. He ended up in chains, but his spirit was free. He presented his defense (and his own story of redemption) before kings. King Agrippa interrupted him to say, "'Do you think you can persuade me to become a Christian so quickly?' Paul replied, 'Whether quickly or not, I pray to God that both you and everyone here in this audience might become the same as I am, except for these chains'" (Acts 26:28-29).

Within each personal journey from bondage to freedom is a microcosm of the gospel. When people hear our story, even if it seems trivial, we are offering them the chance to loosen their chains and begin their own recovery. ***Turn to page 1367, John 15.***

cloth, and laid it in a tomb that had been carved out of the rock. Then he rolled a stone in front of the entrance. [47]Mary Magdalene and Mary the mother of Joseph saw where Jesus' body was laid.

CHAPTER 16
The Resurrection

Saturday evening, when the Sabbath ended, Mary Magdalene, Mary the mother of James, and Salome went out and purchased burial spices so they could anoint Jesus' body. [2]Very early on Sunday morning,* just at sunrise, they went to the tomb. [3]On the way they were asking each other, "Who will roll away the stone for us from the entrance to the tomb?" [4]But as they arrived, they looked up and saw that the stone, which was very large, had already been rolled aside.

[5]When they entered the tomb, they saw a young man clothed in a white robe sitting on the right side. The women were shocked, [6]but the angel said, "Don't be alarmed. You are looking for Jesus of Nazareth,* who was crucified. He isn't here! He is risen from the dead! Look, this is where they laid his body. [7]Now go and tell his disciples, including Peter, that Jesus is going ahead of you to Galilee. You will see him there, just as he told you before he died."

[8]The women fled from the tomb, trembling and bewildered, and they said nothing to anyone because they were too frightened.*

[*The most ancient manuscripts of Mark conclude with verse 16:8. Later manuscripts add one or both of the following endings*]

[*Shorter Ending of Mark*]

Then they briefly reported all this to Peter and his companions. Afterward Jesus himself sent them out from east to west with the sacred and unfailing message of salvation that gives eternal life. Amen.

[*Longer Ending of Mark*]

[9]After Jesus rose from the dead early on Sunday morning, the first person who saw him was Mary Magdalene, the woman from whom he had cast out seven demons. [10]She went to the disciples, who were grieving and weeping, and told them what had happened. [11]But when she told them that Jesus was alive and she had seen him, they didn't believe her.

[12]Afterward he appeared in a different form to two of his followers who were walking from Jerusalem into the country. [13]They rushed back to tell the others, but no one believed them.

[14]Still later he appeared to the eleven disciples as they were eating together. He rebuked them for their stubborn unbelief because they refused to believe those who had seen him after he had been raised from the dead.*

[15]And then he told them, "Go into all the world and preach the Good News to every-

16:2 Greek *on the first day of the week;* also in 16:9. 16:6 Or *Jesus the Nazarene.* 16:8 The most reliable early manuscripts of the Gospel of Mark end at verse 8. Other manuscripts include various endings to the Gospel. A few include both the "shorter ending" and the "longer ending." The majority of manuscripts include the "longer ending" immediately after verse 8. 16:14 Some early manuscripts add: *And they excused themselves, saying, "This age of lawlessness and unbelief is under Satan, who does not permit God's truth and power to conquer the evil [unclean] spirits. Therefore, reveal your justice now." This is what they said to Christ. And Christ replied to them, "The period of years of Satan's power has been fulfilled, but other dreadful things will happen soon. And I was handed over to death for those who have sinned, so that they may return to the truth and sin no more, and so they may inherit the spiritual, incorruptible, and righteous glory in heaven."*

16:1-7 These women were wondering how they could ever roll the great stone from the tomb entrance, when, to their amazement, they found it already gone. The tomb was empty! The women had only wanted to roll back the stone, but God had accomplished so much more: He had raised Jesus from the dead! If God can give life to a dead body, he surely can restore our life to wholeness. We must put our trust in him. There is always hope. With God, all things are possible! He specializes in rolling away burdens too great for our feeble human strength to handle. And, if we set out to do what we can in the recovery process, we will likely discover that God has already accomplished our goals—and even more!

16:9-20 Many of the disciples had a hard time believing that Jesus had risen from the dead. When they finally met the resurrected Jesus, he rebuked them for their unbelief. Then Jesus rewarded his followers as they came to believe. Faith is foundational for salvation and recovery; unbelief leads to condemnation and relapse. As we grow in our faith in Jesus, we will discover that the power of his resurrection can touch and transform our life. Then we can become a source of encouragement to others as we share how God has delivered us.

one. ¹⁶Anyone who believes and is baptized will be saved. But anyone who refuses to believe will be condemned. ¹⁷These miraculous signs will accompany those who believe: They will cast out demons in my name, and they will speak in new languages.* ¹⁸They will be able to handle snakes with safety, and if they drink anything poisonous, it won't hurt them. They will be able to place their hands on the sick, and they will be healed."

¹⁹When the Lord Jesus had finished talking with them, he was taken up into heaven and sat down in the place of honor at God's right hand. ²⁰And the disciples went everywhere and preached, and the Lord worked through them, confirming what they said by many miraculous signs.

16:17 Or *new tongues;* some manuscripts do not include *new.*

REFLECTIONS ON MARK

insights CONCERNING TRUE FAITH

In **Mark 1:16-20** Jesus called four burly fishermen to be his disciples. We are not sure how many times Jesus called Simon Peter, Andrew, James, and John to follow him. On two other occasions, a similar call went out to these four fishermen (see Luke 5:1-11; John 1:35-42). Their response to Jesus' call on any one occasion, as here, seems to have been "immediate." But it seems that they soon went back to their old occupation and way of life. So it is in recovery. Our faith in God will grow over time, at an uneven rate and with uncertain steps. Each step of faith we take requires that we drop whatever else we are doing and follow Jesus wholeheartedly.

In **Mark 10:13-22** two kinds of people are contrasted: the little children, who came to Jesus with innocent trust; and a wealthy young man, who trusted in his wealth and was unwilling to give it up to follow Jesus. The only way to enter the Kingdom of God is through childlike trust. This is also the only way we can enter recovery. As long as we think we can make it on our own, we are hopelessly entrapped by our dependency. Anyone who has tried to recover alone has discovered that it is a losing battle. We must begin by admitting that we are helpless, just like little children. Then we must put our life into God's hands and do what we can to follow his program for us. If we trust in our abilities or wealth for deliverance, we are doomed to self-inflicted destruction.

The women who followed Jesus to the cross in **Mark 15:47–16:11** were not in a position to stop the Crucifixion. But instead of running away, they stayed at the foot of the cross, watched to see where Jesus would be buried, and prepared spices to embalm his body. They were willing to do this even though the twelve disciples had run for their lives. Their resourcefulness and faithful devotion to the very end were honored by an opportunity to see the risen Jesus. As we continue in the process of recovery, we should never waste time waiting for something to happen. We need to take full advantage of the opportunities God gives us for recovery.

insights ABOUT GOD'S POWER TO SAVE

In **Mark 1:40-45** Jesus displayed his power by healing a man with leprosy. Leprosy is a progressive, contagious, and crippling skin disease. In ancient times it was often considered a form of divine retribution (see Numbers 12:9-10; 2 Chronicles 26:16-23). Since there was no cure, except by a miracle from God, a person with leprosy was socially ostracized (see Leviticus 13). Modern medicine has all but eliminated this disease, but we must consider what it must have been like. We all are "lepers," infected by the incurable disease of sin, which has made us ugly and separated us from the people we love. Yet there is hope for us. We can be restored to healthy living and fellowship by the healing touch of Jesus. First we must realize our inability to cure ourself. Then we can trust Jesus' power and love for cleansing and recovery.

In **Mark 4:26-29** Jesus used an illustration to show how God works in the recovery process. Just as seeds silently grow in the soil, God gradually and relentlessly changes us from the inside out. We have come to recognize how helpless we are against our dependency. We already know that we are powerless to change alone. We have already failed many times by trying to participate in the right activities and behaviors. We know we can't change from the outside in. Here we are given a wonderful message of hope! God changes us from the inside out! He has the power to make us into new people and will sustain us in the recovery process.

The miracle of **Mark 6:35-44** displays an important recovery principle: Our needs are never greater than God's supply. That's the lesson for people in recovery who appreciate Jesus' miraculous supply of food for more than five thousand people. The twelve disciples should have learned this lesson through Jesus' ample provision but failed to do so (6:52). They should have learned that when confronted with impossible situations, Jesus could be trusted. We also need to remember that no obstacle to recovery is too great for God. He is sufficient to meet all of our needs.

In **Mark 9:2-13** Jesus was transfigured on the mountain. In this amazing event, we are given a picture of what we can hope for in our own life. Someday we will be changed; we will be made perfect. We may be struggling with destructive dependency, in despair about our devastated life. At such times, it might help to reflect on who we will become if we entrust our life to God through Jesus Christ. God wants to begin the process of leading us toward a healthy and productive life now. When he returns in glory, he will restore us and his entire creation to perfection. With this hope in mind, let us start the process of recovery now.

insights ABOUT GOD'S PRIORITIES

God gave the Sabbath laws (Exodus 34:21) to protect his people from overwork and keep their lives in proper balance. Like all of God's laws, these laws were intended for the good of his people. When the disciples picked grain at the edge of a farmer's field in **Mark 2:23-28**, they were actually following one of the provisions God had prescribed in his law (Leviticus 19:9-10). Yet the Pharisees, with their man-made rules and false assumptions, accused Jesus of breaking the law by working on the Sabbath. Sadly, as they pretended to uphold the law, the Pharisees actually stood counter to God's intentions. Today our preconceptions about disease, sin, or God's plan can cause us to block the path of recovery for others. We must never set up roadblocks to the healing of hurting people, especially by using God's Word. It is part of God's plan that people should live healthy lives; we should do all we can to support his plan.

We find in **Mark 10:32-45** that immediately after Jesus warned his disciples of his impending suffering and death, James and John requested positions of honor and authority. They were blind to the fact that the call to follow Jesus would involve suffering and persecution. Following Jesus on the road to recovery is never easy. It demands that we swallow our pride and admit our mistakes. It calls us to give up the dependency that we have used to try to escape our inner pain. It means that we have to come out of hiding and show the world how ugly we are inside. We must humble ourself before the people we have wronged. Following Jesus is never the easiest path, but it is the only path that will lead us to restoration, joy, and fulfillment.

Jesus expressed his true feelings in **Mark 14:35-36**, as he begged his Father to remove the cup of suffering before him, but he never rebelled against God's will. He was willing to suffer and die so that all of us could experience forgiveness from sin and recovery from its painful effects. As much as we might want to escape certain unpleasant tasks in the recovery process, we must submit all such desires to God's will. God may lead us into some tough experiences, but, as painful as they may be, we can be assured that he has our best in mind. We can also be sure that he will stand with us throughout the process.

insights CONCERNING OBSTACLES TO RECOVERY

The Sabbath controversy recorded in **Mark 3:1-6** reveals two ways of dealing with anger. Anger itself is a normal human emotion; it is morally neutral. What we do with our anger is what counts. Jesus was angry at the Pharisees for making up rules about the Sabbath that stood counter to God's real intentions in the law. Jesus used his anger constructively—not to tear people down, but to heal a man's deformed hand. Jesus' enemies, in their anger, plotted to kill him. Anger expressed in selfish or harmful ways will always stand in the way of recovery.

After healing a demon-possessed man, Jesus faced opposition from the people of the nearby town in **Mark 5:1-20**. The demons left the man and entered a herd of pigs, causing them to run wildly into the lake and drown. The people of the town did not like losing their source of livelihood and felt threatened when the status quo of their world was disturbed. We may experience similar opposition when God begins to change us. Friends and family members may feel threatened by the changes and try to stop us. If we experience opposition from codependents, we should be neither surprised nor discouraged. We should simply continue trusting God to change us so we can help our friends and families.

In **Mark 14:1-9** a woman showed her devotion to Jesus by anointing him with expensive perfume (equal in value to a year's wages), as if preparing a king for burial. Her devotion was mocked by some of the disciples, but it was praised by Jesus as an example for all believers to follow. Our faith in God and commitment to recovery often receive the criticism of others. Sometimes family members have a hard time believing we are sincere. Our friends may even feel threatened by the changes they see in us. We can be sure, however, that no matter what others might say, Jesus is pleased with the steps we are taking. If we persevere, we will discover that others will someday praise our efforts, too.

insights ABOUT THE PERSON OF JESUS
In **Mark 6:1-6** Jesus visited his hometown of Nazareth, where he was looked upon as a mere man, a carpenter, Mary's boy. The people's unbelief kept Jesus from performing "mighty miracles" in Nazareth. Unfortunately for the people of Nazareth, their familiarity with Jesus bred contempt. Fortunately for us, Jesus left and went elsewhere to minister to those who would believe in his miracles and message. Our world has tried to pass Jesus off as just another man, a good teacher, or a wise prophet. Anyone who focuses on Jesus' humanity to the exclusion of his divinity makes a grave mistake. If Jesus were not the Son of God, there would be little hope for any recovery, including our own.

insights ABOUT HONESTY AND DENIAL
Herod Antipas did not like being corrected. So in **Mark 6:14-29,** when John the Baptist confronted him concerning his immoral marriage to his brother's wife, the prophet paid for it with his life. Herod denied his sin and did not like to be reminded of what he had done. But his denial only led to an even greater sin—murder. We are guilty of the same thing when we refuse to listen to warnings about our destructive behavior. We need to learn that our denial will never help things; it will only lead to greater suffering and devastation. We must act immediately and heed the warnings we receive. If we don't, we are headed for even greater trouble.

LUKE

THE BIG PICTURE

A. THE SAVIOR'S BIRTH AND PREPARATION (1:1–4:13)
B. THE SAVIOR'S MINISTRY IN WORD AND DEED (4:14–21:38)
1. Jesus' Ministry in Galilee (4:14–9:50)
2. Jesus' Ministry on the Way to Jerusalem (9:51–19:27)
3. Jesus' Ministry in Jerusalem (19:28–21:38)
C. THE SAVIOR'S DEATH AND RESURRECTION (22:1–24:53)

Luke was a physician and a historian. He presented Jesus as a man who cared greatly for suffering and downtrodden people, a man who brought healing to the hurting. In the genealogy of Jesus, Luke traced Jesus' human ancestors back to Adam, the father of the human race. Luke's stories about Jesus focused on his relationships with individual people. Jesus paid special attention to people who were often ignored in society—women, children, the poor, prostitutes, despised tax collectors, and sinners of every sort.

Jesus offered salvation, strength, and spiritual recovery to everyone he met, but his greatest concern was for the outcasts of society. Luke stressed Jesus' humanity and compassion more than any of the other Gospel writers did. His narrative made it clear that God, through his Son Jesus, reaches out in love to the unlovable of our world. Ever since Adam and Eve's first sin in the Garden of Eden, God has passionately desired and pursued the recovery of broken people. His love and concern for us are unstoppable!

As we work through the process of recovery, many of us discover just how terrible and destructive our sins have been. As the levels of denial peel away, we begin to see how sick and broken we really are. We may wonder whether there is any hope for us. How could God care for us after all we have done? In reading the Gospel of Luke, we can gain hope from the compassion God showed toward people who were a lot like us. God wants to show us how much he loves us, regardless of our past mistakes. He wants to have an active role in our recovery.

THE BOTTOM LINE

PURPOSE: To confirm the historical record of the life of Jesus Christ, whose universal message offers hope and salvation to all who turn to him. AUTHOR: Luke, the physician. AUDIENCE: Theophilus, whose name means "lover of God." DATE WRITTEN: Probably about A.D. 60. KEY VERSES: "Jesus responded, 'Salvation has come to this home today, for this man has shown himself to be a true son of Abraham. For the Son of Man came to seek and save those who are lost'" (19:9-10). SPECIAL FEATURES: Luke focused on Jesus' relationships with people, particularly those who were in need, and he placed special emphasis on the role of women. KEY PEOPLE AND RELATIONSHIPS: Jesus and his disciples, Zechariah and Elizabeth, Mary, Mary Magdalene, and John the Baptist.

RECOVERY THEMES

Jesus Loves the Outcast: Jesus paid special attention to the poor, the despised, the hurt, and the sinful. He rejected no one; he ignored no one. No one today is beyond the scope of his love or beyond his ability to help—including us. He cares for us no matter what we have done or what we have suffered. Only this kind of deep love can satisfy our deepest needs and mobilize us to recovery. When our life is most unmanageable and we are faced with our own powerlessness, we often feel that no one can understand or care. Luke shows us that God understands and cares. We can safely turn our life over to him!

The Power of the Resurrection: Paul wrote to the Philippians and told them that he longed to "experience the mighty power that raised [Jesus] from the dead" (Philippians 3:10). Like the other Gospel writers, Luke showed in detail the events surrounding the death and resurrection of Jesus. There is no greater example of God's power at work than that which can bring the dead back to life again. God specializes in demonstrating that kind of power. In recovery, we experience his power at work within us, bringing our soul and body back to life. With God, nothing is too difficult.

God's Passion for Our Recovery: God wants us to experience recovery even more than we do because he loves and cares about us. Jesus showed this by revealing his intense interest in people and relationships. He cared for his followers and friends. He was interested in all types of people—men, women, and children. His concern transcended all barriers and extended to all he met. He longed to see people whole, well, and growing in their knowledge of God. As we come to know him and share his heart, we experience his passion for our wholeness and recovery.

The Power of the Holy Spirit: Jesus lived in complete dependence on the Holy Spirit. The Holy Spirit was present at the birth of Jesus, at his baptism, in his ministry, and in his resurrection. The Holy Spirit was sent by the Father to confirm Jesus' authority. Today the Holy Spirit is given to empower us to live as God wants us to live. By faith, we can receive the Holy Spirit's presence and power within us, enabling us in the recovery process and in our spiritual growth.

CHAPTER 1
Introduction
Many people have set out to write accounts about the events that have been fulfilled among us. ²They used the eyewitness reports circulating among us from the early disciples.* ³Having carefully investigated everything from the beginning, I also have decided to write a careful account for you, most honorable Theophilus, ⁴so you can be certain of the truth of everything you were taught.

The Birth of John the Baptist Foretold
⁵When Herod was king of Judea, there was a Jewish priest named Zechariah. He was a member of the priestly order of Abijah, and his wife, Elizabeth, was also from the priestly line of Aaron. ⁶Zechariah and Elizabeth were righteous in God's eyes, careful to obey all of the Lord's commandments and regulations. ⁷They had no children because Elizabeth was unable to conceive, and they were both very old.

⁸One day Zechariah was serving God in

1:2 Greek *from those who from the beginning were servants of the word.*

1:1-4 In this preface Luke testified that the gospel of Jesus is based upon historical facts and not theories or myths. Speculative religions, secular philosophies, or political leaders do not meet the deepest needs of the human heart. History is filled with people who aspired to be gods, but only one is truly God. All the other would-be "messiahs" or gods—Alexander the Great, King Tut, Julius Caesar, Napoleon, Adolf Hitler—fell short. Jesus alone can meet our deepest needs.
1:5-7 Zechariah and Elizabeth were godly people. They were childless, and Elizabeth was well past the childbearing years. Their situation was discouraging, even depressing, as many couples in our society can testify. In their society childlessness was taken as a sign of God's curse or displeasure. But Zechariah and Elizabeth remained faithful in trusting God. This was a key to the blessings they received later on. Their faithfulness and patient perseverance are good examples for those of us in recovery.
1:16-17 John the Baptist's ministry would turn the hearts of parents to their children (Malachi 4:5-6). This need is felt by many in recovery. John the Baptist called for personal repentance and the restoration of broken family relationships. Even though the complete fulfillment of these words is still in the future, the principle has always been true. Spiritual cleansing by God is the first foundational step toward the rebuilding of hurting and broken family relationships. When God is at work, even the most resistant hearts can be softened and the most dysfunctional families restored.

LUKE

Luke wrote more of the New Testament than did any other author. He gave a detailed account of the life of Jesus in his Gospel and a description of the early church in Acts. He was a physician by profession, and his writing reveals his compassion for people. Even his efforts to write his two books were motivated by a concern to help a friend grow in faith. Consistent with this, Luke pointed his readers to the healing work and person of Jesus, the Great Physician.

Luke's concern for the spiritual health of others was matched by his compassion for their physical well-being. Throughout his books he noted the physical suffering of people and the care that those people received. He recounted many times how Jesus and his apostles brought physical and spiritual healing into hurting and broken lives. Luke also noticed how Jesus paid special attention to the helpless in society. Jesus helped not only the wealthy or religious but also the outcasts, lepers, prostitutes, and hated tax collectors. Luke's compassionate heart led him to emphasize Jesus' compassion for the rejects of society.

Luke was also noted for his commitment and loyalty to the apostle Paul as they traveled together spreading the gospel in Asia Minor and Greece. In prison, near the end of his life, Paul wrote of his appreciation for Luke. He called Luke a beloved friend, for he had stayed with Paul even when most of Paul's friends had deserted him. Luke was willing to follow God, even when it led him to share in Paul's sufferings.

Luke did not aspire to greatness or try to grab the spotlight. His goal in life was to serve and care for others. We need people like Luke in our life and should do what we can to build relationships with compassionate, godly people. Perhaps an even greater need, however, is for us to learn how we can become an instrument of healing in the lives of the people around us. Sharing what Christ has done in our life can help others and is one of the important goals of recovery.

STRENGTHS AND ACCOMPLISHMENTS:
- Luke proclaimed the merits of Jesus without promoting himself.
- He used his talents in medicine and writing to help others.
- He had great compassion for those with physical and spiritual needs.
- He was a loyal and faithful friend to the apostle Paul.
- He persevered in following God, even when he encountered tough times.

LESSONS FROM HIS LIFE:
- Our care for others should meet spiritual, emotional, and physical needs.
- Being loyal to our friends during hard times is very important.
- God's good will for us sometimes leads us through difficult times.
- If we offer our abilities to God, he will use them to do something of eternal significance.

KEY VERSES:
"Demas has deserted me because he loves the things of this life and has gone to Thessalonica. Crescens has gone to Galatia, and Titus has gone to Dalmatia. Only Luke is with me" (2 Timothy 4:10-11).

Luke included himself in the "we" sections of Acts 16–28. He is also mentioned in Luke 1:3; Acts 1:1-2; Colossians 4:14; 2 Timothy 4:11; and Philemon 1:24.

---

the Temple, for his order was on duty that week. ⁹As was the custom of the priests, he was chosen by lot to enter the sanctuary of the Lord and burn incense. ¹⁰While the incense was being burned, a great crowd stood outside, praying.

¹¹While Zechariah was in the sanctuary, an angel of the Lord appeared to him, standing to the right of the incense altar. ¹²Zechariah was shaken and overwhelmed with fear when he saw him. ¹³But the angel said, "Don't be afraid, Zechariah! God has heard your prayer. Your wife, Elizabeth, will give you a son, and you are to name him John. ¹⁴You will have great joy and gladness, and many will rejoice at his birth, ¹⁵for he will be great in the eyes of the Lord. He must never touch wine or other alcoholic drinks. He will be filled with the Holy Spirit, even before his birth.* ¹⁶And he will turn many Israelites to the Lord their God. ¹⁷He will be a man with the spirit and power of Elijah. He will prepare the people for the coming of the Lord. He will turn the hearts of the fathers to their children,* and

1:15 Or *even from birth.* 1:17 See Mal 4:5-6.

he will cause those who are rebellious to accept the wisdom of the godly."

¹⁸Zechariah said to the angel, "How can I be sure this will happen? I'm an old man now, and my wife is also well along in years."

¹⁹Then the angel said, "I am Gabriel! I stand in the very presence of God. It was he who sent me to bring you this good news! ²⁰But now, since you didn't believe what I said, you will be silent and unable to speak until the child is born. For my words will certainly be fulfilled at the proper time."

²¹Meanwhile, the people were waiting for Zechariah to come out of the sanctuary, wondering why he was taking so long. ²²When he finally did come out, he couldn't speak to them. Then they realized from his gestures and his silence that he must have seen a vision in the sanctuary.

²³When Zechariah's week of service in the Temple was over, he returned home. ²⁴Soon afterward his wife, Elizabeth, became pregnant and went into seclusion for five months. ²⁵"How kind the Lord is!" she exclaimed. "He has taken away my disgrace of having no children."

The Birth of Jesus Foretold

²⁶In the sixth month of Elizabeth's pregnancy, God sent the angel Gabriel to Nazareth, a village in Galilee, ²⁷to a virgin named Mary. She was engaged to be married to a man named Joseph, a descendant of King David. ²⁸Gabriel appeared to her and said, "Greetings, favored woman! The Lord is with you!*"

²⁹Confused and disturbed, Mary tried to think what the angel could mean. ³⁰"Don't be afraid, Mary," the angel told her, "for you have found favor with God! ³¹You will conceive and give birth to a son, and you will name him Jesus. ³²He will be very great and will be called the Son of the Most High. The Lord God will give him the throne of his ancestor David. ³³And he will reign over Israel* forever; his Kingdom will never end!"

³⁴Mary asked the angel, "But how can this happen? I am a virgin."

³⁵The angel replied, "The Holy Spirit will come upon you, and the power of the Most High will overshadow you. So the baby to be born will be holy, and he will be called the Son of God. ³⁶What's more, your relative Elizabeth has become pregnant in her old age! People used to say she was barren, but she has conceived a son and is now in her sixth month. ³⁷For the word of God will never fail.*"

³⁸Mary responded, "I am the Lord's servant. May everything you have said about me come true." And then the angel left her.

Mary Visits Elizabeth

³⁹A few days later Mary hurried to the hill country of Judea, to the town ⁴⁰where Zechariah lived. She entered the house and greeted Elizabeth. ⁴¹At the sound of Mary's greeting, Elizabeth's child leaped within her, and Elizabeth was filled with the Holy Spirit.

⁴²Elizabeth gave a glad cry and exclaimed to Mary, "God has blessed you above all women, and your child is blessed. ⁴³Why am I so honored, that the mother of my Lord should visit me? ⁴⁴When I heard your greeting, the baby in my womb jumped for joy. ⁴⁵You are blessed because you believed that the Lord would do what he said."

The Magnificat: Mary's Song of Praise

⁴⁶Mary responded,

"Oh, how my soul praises the Lord.
⁴⁷ How my spirit rejoices in God
    my Savior!
⁴⁸For he took notice of his lowly servant
    girl,
    and from now on all generations will
    call me blessed.
⁴⁹For the Mighty One is holy,
    and he has done great things
    for me.
⁵⁰He shows mercy from generation to
    generation
    to all who fear him.

1:28 Some manuscripts add *Blessed are you among women.* 1:33 Greek *over the house of Jacob.* 1:37 Some manuscripts read *For nothing is impossible with God.*

1:18-20 As godly as Zechariah was, he still did not believe the angel Gabriel's promise. From a natural frame of reference, it seemed impossible that he and Elizabeth could conceive a child in their old age. The consequence of even this short-term unbelief was substantial—Zechariah could not speak during Elizabeth's miraculous pregnancy. Unbelief can have a numbing effect on our recovery as well. Confession of faith before God and others, as Zechariah was eventually able to do (1:63-64), will help us along the path of recovery. Honestly admitting our doubts is a good place to start.

[51] His mighty arm has done tremendous
   things!
   He has scattered the proud and haughty
      ones.
[52] He has brought down princes from their
      thrones
   and exalted the humble.
[53] He has filled the hungry with good things
   and sent the rich away with empty
      hands.
[54] He has helped his servant Israel
   and remembered to be merciful.
[55] For he made this promise to our ancestors,
   to Abraham and his children forever."

[56] Mary stayed with Elizabeth about three months and then went back to her own home.

The Birth of John the Baptist

[57] When it was time for Elizabeth's baby to be born, she gave birth to a son. [58] And when her neighbors and relatives heard that the Lord had been very merciful to her, everyone rejoiced with her.

[59] When the baby was eight days old, they all came for the circumcision ceremony. They wanted to name him Zechariah, after his father. [60] But Elizabeth said, "No! His name is John!"

[61] "What?" they exclaimed. "There is no one in all your family by that name." [62] So they used gestures to ask the baby's father what he wanted to name him. [63] He motioned for a writing tablet, and to everyone's surprise he wrote, "His name is John." [64] Instantly Zechariah could speak again, and he began praising God.

[65] Awe fell upon the whole neighborhood, and the news of what had happened spread throughout the Judean hills. [66] Everyone who heard about it reflected on these events and asked, "What will this child turn out to be?" For the hand of the Lord was surely upon him in a special way.

Zechariah's Prophecy

[67] Then his father, Zechariah, was filled with the Holy Spirit and gave this prophecy:

[68] "Praise the Lord, the God of Israel,
   because he has visited and redeemed his
      people.
[69] He has sent us a mighty Savior*
   from the royal line of his servant David,
[70] just as he promised
   through his holy prophets long ago.
[71] Now we will be saved from our enemies
   and from all who hate us.
[72] He has been merciful to our ancestors
   by remembering his sacred covenant—
[73] the covenant he swore with an oath
   to our ancestor Abraham.
[74] We have been rescued from our enemies
   so we can serve God without fear,
[75] in holiness and righteousness
   for as long as we live.

[76] "And you, my little son,
   will be called the prophet of the Most
      High,
   because you will prepare the way for
      the Lord.
[77] You will tell his people how to find
      salvation
   through forgiveness of their sins.
[78] Because of God's tender mercy,
   the morning light from heaven is about
      to break upon us,*
[79] to give light to those who sit in darkness
   and in the shadow of death,
   and to guide us to the path of peace."

[80] John grew up and became strong in spirit. And he lived in the wilderness until he began his public ministry to Israel.

CHAPTER 2
The Birth of Jesus

At that time the Roman emperor, Augustus, decreed that a census should be taken throughout the Roman Empire. [2] (This was the first census taken when Quirinius was governor of Syria.) [3] All returned to their own ancestral towns to register for this census. [4] And because Joseph was a descendant of King David, he had to go to Bethlehem in Judea, David's ancient home. He traveled there from the village of Nazareth in Galilee.

1:69 Greek *has raised up a horn of salvation for us.* **1:78** Or *the Morning Light from Heaven is about to visit us.*

1:51-55 These words from Mary's song present God's priorities in stark contrast to the way our world thinks. When life seems unfair and does not turn out the way we might have chosen, it is important to realize that God's ways are not our ways. Personal fulfillment and genuine recovery do not come through human greatness and success, but through repentance and sincere humility. The most important relationships in life are not with the rich and famous but often with the lowly, the needy, and those in recovery.

[5]He took with him Mary, his fiancée, who was now obviously pregnant.

[6]And while they were there, the time came for her baby to be born. [7]She gave birth to her first child, a son. She wrapped him snugly in strips of cloth and laid him in a manger, because there was no lodging available for them.

The Shepherds and Angels

[8]That night there were shepherds staying in the fields nearby, guarding their flocks of sheep. [9]Suddenly, an angel of the Lord appeared among them, and the radiance of the Lord's glory surrounded them. They were terrified, [10]but the angel reassured them. "Don't be afraid!" he said. "I bring you good news that will bring great joy to all people. [11]The Savior—yes, the Messiah, the Lord—has been born today in Bethlehem, the city of David! [12]And you will recognize him by this sign: You will find a baby wrapped snugly in strips of cloth, lying in a manger."

[13]Suddenly, the angel was joined by a vast host of others—the armies of heaven—praising God and saying,

[14]"Glory to God in highest heaven,
and peace on earth to those with whom God is pleased."

[15]When the angels had returned to heaven, the shepherds said to each other,

2:23 Exod 13:2. 2:24 Lev 12:8.

"Let's go to Bethlehem! Let's see this thing that has happened, which the Lord has told us about."

[16]They hurried to the village and found Mary and Joseph. And there was the baby, lying in the manger. [17]After seeing him, the shepherds told everyone what had happened and what the angel had said to them about this child. [18]All who heard the shepherds' story were astonished, [19]but Mary kept all these things in her heart and thought about them often. [20]The shepherds went back to their flocks, glorifying and praising God for all they had heard and seen. It was just as the angel had told them.

Jesus Is Presented in the Temple

[21]Eight days later, when the baby was circumcised, he was named Jesus, the name given him by the angel even before he was conceived.

[22]Then it was time for their purification offering, as required by the law of Moses after the birth of a child; so his parents took him to Jerusalem to present him to the Lord. [23]The law of the Lord says, "If a woman's first child is a boy, he must be dedicated to the LORD."* [24]So they offered the sacrifice required in the law of the Lord—"either a pair of turtledoves or two young pigeons."*

2:6-7 Jesus' welcome in Bethlehem illustrates how most people respond to him today. Jesus' birthplace was hardly an idyllic place like the ones pictured on our Christmas cards. It was probably a cold, damp, dark, dirty cave with a hollowed-out feeding trough or manger. Jesus entered a world unfit for his royal presence. God's willingness to enter our world, darkened and dirtied by sin, is a reason to be thankful. We don't have to clean up our act first in order to make room for him. When Jesus comes into our life, he accepts us as we are—that's when the real housecleaning and moral inventory begin. Thankfully, he is there to help us with the process.

2:8-12 Encounters with the living God inevitably elicit fear. The angels reassured the shepherds: "Don't be afraid!" Once the shepherds realized that God accepted them and wanted to communicate with them, they were free to worship the Christ child. Jesus' coming in the flesh reassures us that our holy and almighty God is also a personal God. God is with us and for us. We need not fear the unknown future or the all-too-familiar past. When we put our faith in the living God of yesterday, today, and tomorrow, his perfect love expels all fear (see 1 John 4:18).

2:19 In recovery painful thoughts of a guilt-ridden past or an uncertain future often intrude and disrupt the present and sometimes cause us to feel depressed. Certainly these darker issues must be faced for us to break free from the patterns of the past. But Mary shows us how thoughts about God can lift our spirits and give us the courage to take the next step. She meditated on the things God was doing and wanted to do in her life. When we do the same, we take a step toward recovery and wholeness. Pondering the joy with the sorrow, the awesome with the awful, the gain with the pain will lead to emotional and spiritual healing.

2:29-32 Simeon's words reveal the universality of God's plan of salvation. It was a rare thing for a Jew to declare that the Messiah would bring deliverance to the whole world, not just the Jews. God reaches out to all people, not just one ethnic group. He gives light, life, and contentment to all who put their faith in him through Jesus Christ. God will accept any who turn to him for help, regardless of background or situation in life. He is the universal Savior. With faith in Jesus we can go through life and death "in peace," as did Simeon.

ELIZABETH & ZECHARIAH

Many loving couples who long for children are unable to have them. Often their attempts to conceive a child go on for years. As each month passes, they go through a painful progression from hope, to fear, to terrible disappointment. Through the years all their lingering hopes disappear; they are left with shattered dreams and empty resignation.

This was what it must have been like for Elizabeth and Zechariah. Their desire for children had not been fulfilled, and they concluded that they would remain childless for the rest of their lives. But suddenly life changed for them. While serving in the Jerusalem Temple, an angel visited Zechariah and announced that he and Elizabeth would have a son. He was to be called John and would become the forerunner of the Messiah.

Understandably shocked, Zechariah doubted the angel's words. Because of his unbelief, he was rendered speechless until the child's birth. When Elizabeth heard the news, she believed the angel's message and was excited about her forthcoming pregnancy. When she was six months pregnant, Elizabeth was visited by her cousin, Mary, who was pregnant with the child Jesus. Filled with the Holy Spirit, Elizabeth praised Mary's faith.

When Elizabeth's baby was born, Zechariah, who still could not speak, wrote down the name the angel had given him—John. At that point, God restored his voice. With his first joyful words, Zechariah praised God for his loving concern for them in giving them this wonderful son. God can bless the childless with children or give the helpless his powerful presence. We see from the lives of Elizabeth and Zechariah that God is intimately involved in our pain and that he desires to fill the empty places in our life.

STRENGTHS AND ACCOMPLISHMENTS:
- Zechariah and Elizabeth were known as godly people.
- Zechariah overcame his doubt and praised God for his power.
- Zechariah obeyed the angel and named his son John.
- Elizabeth commended Mary for her role as the Messiah's mother.

WEAKNESSES AND MISTAKES:
- Zechariah doubted God's ability to give them a child in their older years.

LESSONS FROM THEIR LIVES:
- God is fully aware of the painful disappointment of childless people.
- God is intimately aware of the pain of hurting people.
- All things are possible with God.
- God can use older people to make significant contributions to his plan.

KEY VERSE:
"Zechariah and Elizabeth were righteous in God's eyes, careful to obey all of the Lord's commandments and regulations" (Luke 1:6).

The story of Elizabeth and Zechariah is told in Luke 1:5-80.

The Prophecy of Simeon

²⁵At that time there was a man in Jerusalem named Simeon. He was righteous and devout and was eagerly waiting for the Messiah to come and rescue Israel. The Holy Spirit was upon him ²⁶and had revealed to him that he would not die until he had seen the Lord's Messiah. ²⁷That day the Spirit led him to the Temple. So when Mary and Joseph came to present the baby Jesus to the Lord as the law required, ²⁸Simeon was there. He took the child in his arms and praised God, saying,

²⁹"Sovereign Lord, now let your servant die in peace,
    as you have promised.
³⁰I have seen your salvation,
³¹   which you have prepared for all people.
³²He is a light to reveal God to the nations,
    and he is the glory of your people Israel!"

³³Jesus' parents were amazed at what was being said about him. ³⁴Then Simeon blessed them, and he said to Mary, the baby's mother, "This child is destined to cause many in Israel to fall, but he will be a joy to many others. He has been sent as a sign from God, but many will oppose him. ³⁵As a result, the deepest thoughts of many hearts will be revealed. And a sword will pierce your very soul."

The Prophecy of Anna

³⁶Anna, a prophet, was also there in the Temple. She was the daughter of Phanuel from the tribe of Asher, and she was very old. Her husband died when they had been married only seven years. ³⁷Then she lived as a widow to the age of eighty-four.* She never left the Temple but stayed there day and night, worshiping God with fasting and prayer. ³⁸She came along just as Simeon was talking with Mary and Joseph, and she began praising God. She talked about the child to everyone who had been waiting expectantly for God to rescue Jerusalem.

³⁹When Jesus' parents had fulfilled all the requirements of the law of the Lord, they returned home to Nazareth in Galilee. ⁴⁰There the child grew up healthy and strong. He was filled with wisdom, and God's favor was on him.

Jesus Speaks with the Teachers

⁴¹Every year Jesus' parents went to Jerusalem for the Passover festival. ⁴²When Jesus was twelve years old, they attended the festival as usual. ⁴³After the celebration was over, they started home to Nazareth, but Jesus stayed behind in Jerusalem. His parents didn't miss him at first, ⁴⁴because they assumed he was among the other travelers. But when he didn't show up that evening, they started looking for him among their relatives and friends.

⁴⁵When they couldn't find him, they went back to Jerusalem to search for him there. ⁴⁶Three days later they finally discovered him in the Temple, sitting among the religious teachers, listening to them and asking questions. ⁴⁷All who heard him were amazed at his understanding and his answers.

⁴⁸His parents didn't know what to think. "Son," his mother said to him, "why have you done this to us? Your father and I have been frantic, searching for you everywhere."

⁴⁹"But why did you need to search?" he asked. "Didn't you know that I must be in my Father's house?"* ⁵⁰But they didn't understand what he meant.

⁵¹Then he returned to Nazareth with them and was obedient to them. And his mother stored all these things in her heart.

⁵²Jesus grew in wisdom and in stature and in favor with God and all the people.

CHAPTER 3
John the Baptist Prepares the Way

It was now the fifteenth year of the reign of Tiberius, the Roman emperor. Pontius Pilate was governor over Judea; Herod Antipas was ruler* over Galilee; his brother Philip was ruler* over Iturea and Traconitis; Lysanias was ruler over Abilene. ²Annas and Caiaphas were the high priests. At this time a message from God came to John son of Zechariah, who was living in the wilderness. ³Then John went from place to place on both sides of the Jordan River, preaching that people should be baptized to show that they had repented of their sins and turned to God to be forgiven. ⁴Isaiah had spoken of John when he said,

"He is a voice shouting in the wilderness,
'Prepare the way for the LORD's coming!
  Clear the road for him!
⁵ The valleys will be filled,
  and the mountains and hills made
      level.
The curves will be straightened,
  and the rough places made smooth.
⁶ And then all people will see
  the salvation sent from God.'"*

⁷When the crowds came to John for baptism, he said, "You brood of snakes! Who

---

2:37 Or *She had been a widow for eighty-four years.* 2:49 Or *"Didn't you realize that I should be involved with my Father's affairs?"* 3:1a Greek *Herod was tetrarch.* Herod Antipas was a son of King Herod. 3:1b Greek *tetrarch;* also in 3:1c. 3:4-6 Isa 40:3-5 (Greek version).

2:36-38 Anna modeled how the power of faith can bring meaning to life for people in recovery. After many years of widowhood, Anna did not allow bitterness to set in. Instead, she found that her singleness gave her more opportunities to serve God in the Temple. She overcame adversity by drawing closer to God through prayer and fasting, and she was given the gift of prophecy. Anna accepted God's plan for her, which included a glimpse of the Messiah she had been longing for. Decades of unwanted singleness can drive many of us to find love in all the wrong places. We must trust God in that area of life as well.

3:1-6 The road to recovery can be as treacherous, fatiguing, dry, and deserted as a trek through the Judean wilderness. John knew that, so he preached a discomforting message about God's "bulldozer" preparing the way for the world's Savior. Those who were honest with themselves in their immermost heart knew that John was right. All that remained was a public confession of faith. Those of us in recovery need to take responsibility for our sinful actions, turn our life over to God, and experience God's power to "smooth out" our life.

warned you to flee God's coming wrath? [8]Prove by the way you live that you have repented of your sins and turned to God. Don't just say to each other, 'We're safe, for we are descendants of Abraham.' That means nothing, for I tell you, God can create children of Abraham from these very stones. [9]Even now the ax of God's judgment is poised, ready to sever the roots of the trees. Yes, every tree that does not produce good fruit will be chopped down and thrown into the fire."

[10]The crowds asked, "What should we do?"

[11]John replied, "If you have two shirts, give one to the poor. If you have food, share it with those who are hungry."

[12]Even corrupt tax collectors came to be baptized and asked, "Teacher, what should we do?"

[13]He replied, "Collect no more taxes than the government requires."

[14]"What should we do?" asked some soldiers.

John replied, "Don't extort money or make false accusations. And be content with your pay."

[15]Everyone was expecting the Messiah to come soon, and they were eager to know whether John might be the Messiah. [16]John answered their questions by saying, "I baptize you with* water; but someone is coming soon who is greater than I am—so much greater that I'm not even worthy to be his slave and untie the straps of his sandals. He will baptize you with the Holy Spirit and with fire.* [17]He is ready to separate the chaff from the wheat with his winnowing fork. Then he will clean up the threshing area, gathering the wheat into his barn but burn-

ing the chaff with never-ending fire." [18]John used many such warnings as he announced the Good News to the people.

[19]John also publicly criticized Herod Antipas, the ruler of Galilee,* for marrying Herodias, his brother's wife, and for many other wrongs he had done. [20]So Herod put John in prison, adding this sin to his many others.

The Baptism of Jesus

[21]One day when the crowds were being baptized, Jesus himself was baptized. As he was praying, the heavens opened, [22]and the Holy Spirit, in bodily form, descended on him like a dove. And a voice from heaven said, "You are my dearly loved Son, and you bring me great joy.*"

The Ancestors of Jesus

[23]Jesus was about thirty years old when he began his public ministry.

Jesus was known as the son of Joseph.
Joseph was the son of Heli.
[24] Heli was the son of Matthat.
Matthat was the son of Levi.
Levi was the son of Melki.
Melki was the son of Jannai.
Jannai was the son of Joseph.
[25] Joseph was the son of Mattathias.
Mattathias was the son of Amos.
Amos was the son of Nahum.
Nahum was the son of Esli.
Esli was the son of Naggai.
[26] Naggai was the son of Maath.
Maath was the son of Mattathias.
Mattathias was the son of Semein.

3:16a Or *in.* 3:16b Or *in the Holy Spirit and in fire.* 3:19 Greek *Herod the tetrarch.* 3:22 Some manuscripts read *my Son, and today I have become your Father.*

3:21-22 By settling upon him in the form of a dove, God the Holy Spirit visibly showed not only that he identified with Jesus but that God's power was with him. God the Father showed how pleased he was with his Son by speaking directly from heaven. If we are trusting Christ through recovery, we will experience God's heavenly power in us, his fatherly love for us, and his supreme identification with us. We, too, are God's "beloved children," and he loves us very much.

3:23 Even though Jesus knew from his youth what his mission on earth would be, this "son of Joseph" patiently persevered as an obscure carpenter in Nazareth until the age of thirty. He never rushed to accomplish his ambitious God-given task. He modeled for us the patience and trust in God's timing that we need as we progress through recovery. As we are faithful, God will work his healing power within us over time.

3:23-38 Jesus' genealogy is rooted in the very beginning of the human race, showing his close identification with all humanity. Jesus' genealogy is sprinkled with people known for their mistakes. Judah fathered Perez through an illicit relationship with his daughter Tamar. Salmon fathered Boaz through his marriage with Rahab, a former prostitute from Jericho. Boaz fathered Obed through his marriage with the Moabitess, Ruth. David fathered Solomon through Bathsheba, the wife of another man. Jesus is clearly "one of us." No problem in our life is "foreign" to him. By becoming flesh, God in Jesus Christ was subject to the weaknesses of humanity and even suffered death for us. Jesus truly understands the difficulties we face in recovery.

Semein was the son of Josech.
Josech was the son of Joda.
²⁷ Joda was the son of Joanan.
Joanan was the son of Rhesa.
Rhesa was the son of Zerubbabel.
Zerubbabel was the son of Shealtiel.
Shealtiel was the son of Neri.
²⁸ Neri was the son of Melki.
Melki was the son of Addi.
Addi was the son of Cosam.
Cosam was the son of Elmadam.
Elmadam was the son of Er.
²⁹ Er was the son of Joshua.
Joshua was the son of Eliezer.
Eliezer was the son of Jorim.
Jorim was the son of Matthat.
Matthat was the son of Levi.
³⁰ Levi was the son of Simeon.
Simeon was the son of Judah.
Judah was the son of Joseph.
Joseph was the son of Jonam.
Jonam was the son of Eliakim.
³¹ Eliakim was the son of Melea.
Melea was the son of Menna.
Menna was the son of Mattatha.
Mattatha was the son of Nathan.
Nathan was the son of David.
³² David was the son of Jesse.
Jesse was the son of Obed.
Obed was the son of Boaz.
Boaz was the son of Salmon.*
Salmon was the son of Nahshon.
³³ Nahshon was the son of Amminadab.
Amminadab was the son of Admin.
Admin was the son of Arni.*
Arni was the son of Hezron.
Hezron was the son of Perez.
Perez was the son of Judah.
³⁴ Judah was the son of Jacob.
Jacob was the son of Isaac.
Isaac was the son of Abraham.
Abraham was the son of Terah.
Terah was the son of Nahor.
³⁵ Nahor was the son of Serug.
Serug was the son of Reu.
Reu was the son of Peleg.
Peleg was the son of Eber.

Eber was the son of Shelah.
³⁶ Shelah was the son of Cainan.
Cainan was the son of Arphaxad.
Arphaxad was the son of Shem.
Shem was the son of Noah.
Noah was the son of Lamech.
³⁷ Lamech was the son of Methuselah.
Methuselah was the son of Enoch.
Enoch was the son of Jared.
Jared was the son of Mahalalel.
Mahalalel was the son of Kenan.
³⁸ Kenan was the son of Enosh.*
Enosh was the son of Seth.
Seth was the son of Adam.
Adam was the son of God.

CHAPTER 4
The Temptation of Jesus

Then Jesus, full of the Holy Spirit, returned from the Jordan River. He was led by the Spirit in the wilderness,* ²where he was tempted by the devil for forty days. Jesus ate nothing all that time and became very hungry.

³Then the devil said to him, "If you are the Son of God, tell this stone to become a loaf of bread."

⁴But Jesus told him, "No! The Scriptures say, 'People do not live by bread alone.'*"

⁵Then the devil took him up and revealed to him all the kingdoms of the world in a moment of time. ⁶"I will give you the glory of these kingdoms and authority over them," the devil said, "because they are mine to give to anyone I please. ⁷I will give it all to you if you will worship me."

⁸Jesus replied, "The Scriptures say,

'You must worship the LORD your God
    and serve only him.'*"

⁹Then the devil took him to Jerusalem, to the highest point of the Temple, and said, "If you are the Son of God, jump off! ¹⁰For the Scriptures say,

'He will order his angels to protect and
    guard you.

3:32 Greek *Sala*, a variant spelling of Salmon; also in 3:32b. See Ruth 4:20-21. **3:33** Some manuscripts read *Amminadab was the son of Aram. Arni* and *Aram* are alternate spellings of Ram. See 1 Chr 2:9-10. **3:38** Greek *Enos*, a variant spelling of Enosh; also in 3:38b. See Gen 5:6. **4:1** Some manuscripts read *into the wilderness*. **4:4** Deut 8:3. **4:8** Deut 6:13.

4:1-2 Alone in the Judean wastelands, Jesus was sorely tempted for forty days. Here, as in every aspect of his life, he overcame adversity by depending on the power of the Holy Spirit working through him. This same power is available for us today. Believers have immediate access to this power through God's Holy Spirit dwelling within them. This power within our heart is great enough to help us resist the most tempting sins the world, the flesh, or the Devil has to throw at us (1 John 2:16; 4:4). Even the most powerful addiction is no match for the Holy Spirit.

[11]And they will hold you up with their
hands
so you won't even hurt your foot on a
stone.'*"

[12]Jesus responded, "The Scriptures also say,
'You must not test the LORD your God.'*"
[13]When the devil had finished tempting
Jesus, he left him until the next opportunity
came.

Jesus Rejected at Nazareth

[14]Then Jesus returned to Galilee, filled with
the Holy Spirit's power. Reports about him
spread quickly through the whole region.
[15]He taught regularly in their synagogues and
was praised by everyone.
[16]When he came to the village of Nazareth,
his boyhood home, he went as usual to the
synagogue on the Sabbath and stood up to
read the Scriptures. [17]The scroll of Isaiah the
prophet was handed to him. He unrolled the
scroll and found the place where this was
written:

[18]"The Spirit of the LORD is upon me,
for he has anointed me to bring Good
News to the poor.
He has sent me to proclaim that captives
will be released,
that the blind will see,
that the oppressed will be set free,
[19] and that the time of the LORD's favor
has come.*"

[20]He rolled up the scroll, handed it back to
the attendant, and sat down. All eyes in the
synagogue looked at him intently. [21]Then he
began to speak to them. "The Scripture
you've just heard has been fulfilled this very
day!"
[22]Everyone spoke well of him and was
amazed by the gracious words that came
from his lips. "How can this be?" they asked.
"Isn't this Joseph's son?"
[23]Then he said, "You will undoubtedly
quote me this proverb: 'Physician, heal yourself'—meaning, 'Do miracles here in your
hometown like those you did in Capernaum.' [24]But I tell you the truth, no prophet
is accepted in his own hometown.
[25]"Certainly there were many needy widows in Israel in Elijah's time, when the heavens were closed for three and a half years,
and a severe famine devastated the land.
[26]Yet Elijah was not sent to any of them. He
was sent instead to a foreigner—a widow of
Zarephath in the land of Sidon. [27]And there
were many lepers in Israel in the time of the
prophet Elisha, but the only one healed was
Naaman, a Syrian."
[28]When they heard this, the people in the
synagogue were furious. [29]Jumping up, they
mobbed him and forced him to the edge of
the hill on which the town was built. They
intended to push him over the cliff, [30]but he
passed right through the crowd and went on
his way.

Jesus Casts Out a Demon

[31]Then Jesus went to Capernaum, a town in
Galilee, and taught there in the synagogue
every Sabbath day. [32]There, too, the people

4:10-11 Ps 91:11-12. **4:12** Deut 6:16. **4:18-19** Or *and to proclaim the acceptable year of the LORD.* Isa 61:1-2 (Greek
version); 58:6.

4:13 Temptation by the Devil is an ongoing reality. After unsuccessfully tempting Jesus in the
wilderness, Satan gave up, but only temporarily. He would save his best punch for later (at the
cross). Satan exhausted his most compelling temptations to no avail and left defeated. But he
continued to try to undermine Jesus' ministry, especially through the people around him (see
Luke 11:14-22). If we in recovery withstand temptation at one point, Satan will eventually try
again, either in the same area or in another. We must be on guard against Satan's repeated
attacks.
4:18-21 When Jesus claimed to fulfill the words of Isaiah 61, he was directly claiming to be
Israel's long-awaited Messiah. Isaiah beautifully characterized a major focus of the Messiah's
ministry. The Messiah would deliver those who were captives to the power of sin and spiritual
discouragement. He would give sight to the physically and spiritually blind. He would bring freedom from their oppressors to the downtrodden. A relationship with God through Jesus Christ
provides these limitless resources to all of us in recovery.
4:28-30 The response of this hard-hearted, hometown crowd in Nazareth to Jesus' remarks is an
example of what happens when denial is mixed with anger. When Jesus challenged their unbelief,
their surface appreciation of his ministry turned to outrage. They wondered how this hometown
boy could claim to be a prophet. Their attempt at mob violence showed how hysterical and resistant to the truth even religious people can be. We need to overcome the areas of denial in our life
if we want God to step in and transform us into new and healthy people. God cannot heal us
until we are willing to recognize our problems and our unbelief.

were amazed at his teaching, for he spoke with authority.

[33]Once when he was in the synagogue, a man possessed by a demon—an evil* spirit—began shouting at Jesus, [34]"Go away! Why are you interfering with us, Jesus of Nazareth? Have you come to destroy us? I know who you are—the Holy One of God!"

[35]Jesus cut him short. "Be quiet! Come out of the man," he ordered. At that, the demon threw the man to the floor as the crowd watched; then it came out of him without hurting him further.

[36]Amazed, the people exclaimed, "What authority and power this man's words possess! Even evil spirits obey him, and they flee at his command!" [37]The news about Jesus spread through every village in the entire region.

Jesus Heals Many People

[38]After leaving the synagogue that day, Jesus went to Simon's home, where he found Simon's mother-in-law very sick with a high fever. "Please heal her," everyone begged. [39]Standing at her bedside, he rebuked the fever, and it left her. And she got up at once and prepared a meal for them.

[40]As the sun went down that evening, people throughout the village brought sick family members to Jesus. No matter what their diseases were, the touch of his hand healed every one. [41]Many were possessed by demons; and the demons came out at his command, shouting, "You are the Son of God!" But because they knew he was the Messiah, he rebuked them and refused to let them speak.

Jesus Continues to Preach

[42]Early the next morning Jesus went out to an isolated place. The crowds searched everywhere for him, and when they finally found him, they begged him not to leave them. [43]But he replied, "I must preach the Good News of the Kingdom of God in other towns, too, because that is why I was sent." [44]So he continued to travel around, preaching in synagogues throughout Judea.*

CHAPTER 5
The First Disciples

One day as Jesus was preaching on the shore of the Sea of Galilee,* great crowds pressed in on him to listen to the word of God. [2]He noticed two empty boats at the water's edge, for the fishermen had left them and were washing their nets. [3]Stepping into one of the boats, Jesus asked Simon,* its owner, to push it out into the water. So he sat in the boat and taught the crowds from there.

[4]When he had finished speaking, he said to Simon, "Now go out where it is deeper, and let down your nets to catch some fish."

[5]"Master," Simon replied, "we worked hard all last night and didn't catch a thing. But if you say so, I'll let the nets down again." [6]And this time their nets were so full of fish they began to tear! [7]A shout for help brought their partners in the other boat, and soon both boats were filled with fish and on the verge of sinking.

[8]When Simon Peter realized what had happened, he fell to his knees before Jesus and said, "Oh, Lord, please leave me—I'm too much of a sinner to be around you." [9]For he was awestruck by the number of fish they had caught, as were the others with him. [10]His partners, James and John, the sons of Zebedee, were also amazed.

Jesus replied to Simon, "Don't be afraid! From now on you'll be fishing for people!" [11]And as soon as they landed, they left everything and followed Jesus.

Jesus Heals a Man with Leprosy

[12]In one of the villages, Jesus met a man with an advanced case of leprosy. When the man saw Jesus, he bowed with his face to the ground, begging to be healed. "Lord," he said, "if you are willing, you can heal me and make me clean."

[13]Jesus reached out and touched him. "I am willing," he said. "Be healed!" And instantly the leprosy disappeared. [14]Then Jesus instructed him not to tell anyone what had happened. He said, "Go to the priest and let him examine you. Take along the offering re-

4:33 Greek *unclean;* also in 4:36. 4:44 Some manuscripts read *Galilee.* 5:1 Greek *Lake Gennesaret,* another name for the Sea of Galilee. 5:3 *Simon* is called "Peter" in 6:14 and thereafter.

5:4-11 The disciples were certainly persistent in their fishing, but doing things their way just wasn't enough. As soon as they followed Jesus' advice, they experienced success. We may be struggling to attain recovery on our own. We may be diligent, hardworking, and disciplined. But if we aren't doing things God's way, no amount of hard work will bring success. Following God's will for our life will lead to healing and success. Some may think the truth found in God's Word seems crazy. But as we follow God's program obediently and seek his gracious help, we will experience his powerful deliverance.

quired in the law of Moses for those who have been healed of leprosy.* This will be a public testimony that you have been cleansed."

[15]But despite Jesus' instructions, the report of his power spread even faster, and vast crowds came to hear him preach and to be healed of their diseases. [16]But Jesus often withdrew to the wilderness for prayer.

Jesus Heals a Paralyzed Man

[17]One day while Jesus was teaching, some Pharisees and teachers of religious law were sitting nearby. (It seemed that these men showed up from every village in all Galilee and Judea, as well as from Jerusalem.) And the Lord's healing power was strongly with Jesus.

[18]Some men came carrying a paralyzed man on a sleeping mat. They tried to take him inside to Jesus, [19]but they couldn't reach him because of the crowd. So they went up to the roof and took off some tiles. Then they lowered the sick man on his mat down into the crowd, right in front of Jesus. [20]Seeing their faith, Jesus said to the man, "Young man, your sins are forgiven."

[21]But the Pharisees and teachers of religious law said to themselves, "Who does he think he is? That's blasphemy! Only God can forgive sins!"

[22]Jesus knew what they were thinking, so he asked them, "Why do you question this in your hearts? [23]Is it easier to say 'Your sins are forgiven,' or 'Stand up and walk'? [24]So I will prove to you that the Son of Man* has the authority on earth to forgive sins." Then Jesus turned to the paralyzed man and said, "Stand up, pick up your mat, and go home!"

[25]And immediately, as everyone watched, the man jumped up, picked up his mat, and went home praising God. [26]Everyone was gripped with great wonder and awe, and they praised God, exclaiming, "We have seen amazing things today!"

Jesus Calls Levi (Matthew)

[27]Later, as Jesus left the town, he saw a tax collector named Levi sitting at his tax collector's booth. "Follow me and be my disciple," Jesus said to him. [28]So Levi got up, left everything, and followed him.

[29]Later, Levi held a banquet in his home with Jesus as the guest of honor. Many of Levi's fellow tax collectors and other guests also ate with them. [30]But the Pharisees and their teachers of religious law complained bitterly to Jesus' disciples, "Why do you eat and drink with such scum?*"

[31]Jesus answered them, "Healthy people don't need a doctor—sick people do. [32]I have come to call not those who think they are righteous, but those who know they are sinners and need to repent."

A Discussion about Fasting

[33]One day some people said to Jesus, "John the Baptist's disciples fast and pray regularly, and so do the disciples of the Pharisees. Why are your disciples always eating and drinking?"

[34]Jesus responded, "Do wedding guests fast while celebrating with the groom? Of course not. [35]But someday the groom will be taken away from them, and then they will fast."

[36]Then Jesus gave them this illustration: "No one tears a piece of cloth from a new garment and uses it to patch an old garment. For then the new garment would be ruined, and the new patch wouldn't even match the old garment.

[37]"And no one puts new wine into old wineskins. For the new wine would burst the wineskins, spilling the wine and ruining the skins. [38]New wine must be stored in new wineskins. [39]But no one who drinks the old wine seems to want the new wine. 'The old is just fine,' they say."

CHAPTER 6

A Discussion about the Sabbath

One Sabbath day as Jesus was walking through some grainfields, his disciples broke off heads of grain, rubbed off the husks in their hands, and ate the grain. [2]But some Pharisees said, "Why are you breaking the law by harvesting grain on the Sabbath?"

[3]Jesus replied, "Haven't you read in the Scriptures what David did when he and his

---

5:14 See Lev 14:2-32. 5:24 "Son of Man" is a title Jesus used for himself. 5:30 Greek *with tax collectors and sinners?*

5:30-32 To receive Jesus' help and begin recovery, we must first recognize and admit how helpless we are. Jesus' greatest priority was ministering to the so-called notorious sinners (social outcasts) because they admitted their lowly, helpless position. The Pharisees were also sinners, but they denied their sins. Because of their self-righteousness and self-sufficiency, Jesus could do nothing for them. When we recognize our need for help and admit our failures to God and others, Jesus will reach out and help us.

companions were hungry? [4]He went into the house of God and broke the law by eating the sacred loaves of bread that only the priests can eat. He also gave some to his companions." [5]And Jesus added, "The Son of Man* is Lord, even over the Sabbath."

Jesus Heals on the Sabbath

[6]On another Sabbath day, a man with a deformed right hand was in the synagogue while Jesus was teaching. [7]The teachers of religious law and the Pharisees watched Jesus closely. If he healed the man's hand, they planned to accuse him of working on the Sabbath.

[8]But Jesus knew their thoughts. He said to the man with the deformed hand, "Come and stand in front of everyone." So the man came forward. [9]Then Jesus said to his critics, "I have a question for you. Does the law permit good deeds on the Sabbath, or is it a day for doing evil? Is this a day to save life or to destroy it?"

[10]He looked around at them one by one and then said to the man, "Hold out your hand." So the man held out his hand, and it was restored! [11]At this, the enemies of Jesus were wild with rage and began to discuss what to do with him.

Jesus Chooses the Twelve Apostles

[12]One day soon afterward Jesus went up on a mountain to pray, and he prayed to God all night. [13]At daybreak he called together all of his disciples and chose twelve of them to be apostles. Here are their names:

[14] Simon (whom he named Peter),
Andrew (Peter's brother),
James,
John,
Philip,
Bartholomew,

[15] Matthew,
Thomas,
James (son of Alphaeus),
Simon (who was called the zealot),
[16] Judas (son of James),
Judas Iscariot (who later betrayed him).

Crowds Follow Jesus

[17]When they came down from the mountain, the disciples stood with Jesus on a large, level area, surrounded by many of his followers and by the crowds. There were people from all over Judea and from Jerusalem and from as far north as the seacoasts of Tyre and Sidon. [18]They had come to hear him and to be healed of their diseases; and those troubled by evil* spirits were healed. [19]Everyone tried to touch him, because healing power went out from him, and he healed everyone.

The Beatitudes

[20]Then Jesus turned to his disciples and said,

"God blesses you who are poor,
for the Kingdom of God is yours.
[21] God blesses you who are hungry now,
for you will be satisfied.
God blesses you who weep now,
for in due time you will laugh.

[22]What blessings await you when people hate you and exclude you and mock you and curse you as evil because you follow the Son of Man. [23]When that happens, be happy! Yes, leap for joy! For a great reward awaits you in heaven. And remember, their ancestors treated the ancient prophets that same way.

Sorrows Foretold

[24] "What sorrow awaits you who are rich,
for you have your only happiness
now.

6:5 "Son of Man" is a title Jesus used for himself. 6:18 Greek *unclean.*

6:6-11 Jesus routinely healed people on the Sabbath. This angered his opponents, especially the Pharisees. Not everyone will be pleased with our recovery. Friends also caught in the trap of addiction may be threatened by the changes in us and become angry. People who have used our addiction to gain power over us may also be upset as they lose their ability to manipulate us. These friends may resemble the scribes and Pharisees. No matter how great the opposition to our recovery, Jesus wants us to be healed. As we trust in him and obey him, we will experience healing.

6:20-26 When Jesus spoke about Kingdom values, he was speaking about the importance of following God's priorities in life. He pronounced blessings and joy for those who follow him and hunger for God. But he pronounced sorrows on those who selfishly seek to be rich and live for the moment. By his strong words, Jesus was creating a crisis intervention of sorts. Those who put their greatest trust in money and material goods and do not realize their need for God will one day meet the great Equalizer. Those who trust in God will be rewarded.

²⁵ What sorrow awaits you who are fat and
     prosperous now,
     for a time of awful hunger awaits you.
What sorrow awaits you who laugh now,
     for your laughing will turn to mourning
     and sorrow.
²⁶ What sorrow awaits you who are praised
     by the crowds,
     for their ancestors also praised false
     prophets.

Love for Enemies

²⁷"But to you who are willing to listen, I say,
love your enemies! Do good to those who
hate you. ²⁸Bless those who curse you. Pray
for those who hurt you. ²⁹If someone slaps
you on one cheek, offer the other cheek also.
If someone demands your coat, offer your
shirt also. ³⁰Give to anyone who asks; and
when things are taken away from you, don't
try to get them back. ³¹Do to others as you
would like them to do to you.

³²"If you love only those who love you,
why should you get credit for that? Even sinners love those who love them! ³³And if you
do good only to those who do good to you,
why should you get credit? Even sinners do
that much! ³⁴And if you lend money only to
those who can repay you, why should you
get credit? Even sinners will lend to other
sinners for a full return.

³⁵"Love your enemies! Do good to them.
Lend to them without expecting to be repaid. Then your reward from heaven will be
very great, and you will truly be acting as
children of the Most High, for he is kind to
those who are unthankful and wicked. ³⁶You
must be compassionate, just as your Father is
compassionate.

Do Not Judge Others

³⁷"Do not judge others, and you will not be
judged. Do not condemn others, or it will all
come back against you. Forgive others, and
you will be forgiven. ³⁸Give, and you will
receive. Your gift will return to you in
full—pressed down, shaken together to make
room for more, running over, and poured
into your lap. The amount you give will determine the amount you get back.*"

³⁹Then Jesus gave the following illustration:
"Can one blind person lead another? Won't
they both fall into a ditch? ⁴⁰Students* are not
greater than their teacher. But the student
who is fully trained will become like the
teacher.

6:38 Or *The measure you give will be the measure you get
back.* 6:40 Or *Disciples.*

FORGIVENESS

READ LUKE 6:27-36

As we set out to mend relationships, there
may be some things that are beyond our
control. Some people may refuse to be
reconciled, even when we do our best to
make amends. This may leave us feeling
like victims. Once again we are stuck with
the pain of unresolved issues. We may be
left with negative feelings that continue to
surface. What can we do to gain control in
these situations?

Jesus said, "But to you who are willing to
listen, I say, love your enemies! Do good to
those who hate you. Bless those who curse
you. Pray for those who hurt you. . . . Love
your enemies! Do good to them. Lend to
them without expecting to be repaid. Then
your reward from heaven will be very
great, and you will truly be acting as
children of the Most High, for he is kind to
those who are unthankful and wicked"
(Luke 6:27-28, 35).

We no longer need to be controlled by
other people's dispositions and actions.
Even when we have done our best to make
amends for the wrongs we have done, the
situation may not change. And even when
we have come to terms with the wrongs
that have been done against us, our
feelings may not change. But we don't
have to be held captive by our feelings or
the feelings of others. We can choose to
forgive and act in loving ways. This will free
us from being controlled by anyone other
than God. As we choose to forgive others
and do good, our feelings will change with
time. ***Turn to page 1321, Luke 17.***

[41]"And why worry about a speck in your friend's eye* when you have a log in your own? [42]How can you think of saying, 'Friend,* let me help you get rid of that speck in your eye,' when you can't see past the log in your own eye? Hypocrite! First get rid of the log in your own eye; then you will see well enough to deal with the speck in your friend's eye.

The Tree and Its Fruit

[43]"A good tree can't produce bad fruit, and a bad tree can't produce good fruit. [44]A tree is identified by its fruit. Figs are never gathered from thornbushes, and grapes are not picked from bramble bushes. [45]A good person produces good things from the treasury of a good heart, and an evil person produces evil things from the treasury of an evil heart. What you say flows from what is in your heart.

Building on a Solid Foundation

[46]"So why do you keep calling me 'Lord, Lord!' when you don't do what I say? [47]I will show you what it's like when someone comes to me, listens to my teaching, and then follows it. [48]It is like a person building a house who digs deep and lays the foundation on solid rock. When the floodwaters rise and break against that house, it stands firm because it is well built. [49]But anyone who hears and doesn't obey is like a person who builds a house without a foundation. When the floods sweep down against that house, it will collapse into a heap of ruins."

CHAPTER 7
The Faith of a Roman Officer

When Jesus had finished saying all this to the people, he returned to Capernaum. [2]At that time the highly valued slave of a Roman officer* was sick and near death. [3]When the officer heard about Jesus, he sent some respected Jewish elders to ask him to come and heal his slave. [4]So they earnestly begged Jesus to help the man. "If anyone deserves your help, he does," they said, [5]"for he loves the Jewish people and even built a synagogue for us."

[6]So Jesus went with them. But just before they arrived at the house, the officer sent some friends to say, "Lord, don't trouble yourself by coming to my home, for I am not worthy of such an honor. [7]I am not even worthy to come and meet you. Just say the word from where you are, and my servant will be healed. [8]I know this because I am under the authority of my superior officers, and I have authority over my soldiers. I only need to say, 'Go,' and they go, or 'Come,' and they come. And if I say to my slaves, 'Do this,' they do it."

[9]When Jesus heard this, he was amazed. Turning to the crowd that was following him, he said, "I tell you, I haven't seen faith like this in all Israel!" [10]And when the officer's friends returned to his house, they found the slave completely healed.

Jesus Raises a Widow's Son

[11]Soon afterward Jesus went with his disciples to the village of Nain, and a large crowd followed him. [12]A funeral procession was coming out as he approached the village gate. The young man who had died was a widow's only son, and a large crowd from the village was with her. [13]When the Lord saw her, his heart overflowed with compassion. "Don't cry!" he said. [14]Then he walked over to the coffin and touched it, and the bearers stopped. "Young man," he said, "I tell you, get up." [15]Then the dead boy sat up and began to talk! And Jesus gave him back to his mother.

[16]Great fear swept the crowd, and they praised God, saying, "A mighty prophet has risen among us," and "God has visited his

---

6:41 Greek *your brother's eye;* also in 6:42. **6:42** Greek *Brother.* **7:2** Greek *a centurion;* similarly in 7:6.

7:1-10 The Roman officer demonstrated qualities that are key elements in receiving God's greatest blessings. The officer showed compassion to people of a lower social class and people of another race and religion. He was humble and recognized his own unworthiness despite being a man of authority. He wholeheartedly placed his faith in Jesus to heal his valued slave. Jesus marveled at such faith and answered his request. Those who have been raised in religious circles are expected to have faith but very often do not. Sometimes true faith is found in places we least expect—among the unchurched and the outcasts, who recognize their need for help and cry out to God in their helplessness. This kind of faith is necessary to the recovery process.

7:11-15 By raising the young boy from the dead, Jesus showed his compassion for people experiencing great loss. This woman had previously lost her husband, and now her only son was dead. This miracle shows us that no situation in our life is beyond the restoring power of God. Even in the midst of what seems like a dead end, God is not limited. This same power that can raise the dead can certainly bring health for the sick and freedom for the addicted.

people today." [17]And the news about Jesus spread throughout Judea and the surrounding countryside.

Jesus and John the Baptist

[18]The disciples of John the Baptist told John about everything Jesus was doing. So John called for two of his disciples, [19]and he sent them to the Lord to ask him, "Are you the Messiah we've been expecting,* or should we keep looking for someone else?"

[20]John's two disciples found Jesus and said to him, "John the Baptist sent us to ask, 'Are you the Messiah we've been expecting, or should we keep looking for someone else?'"

[21]At that very time, Jesus cured many people of their diseases, illnesses, and evil spirits, and he restored sight to many who were blind. [22]Then he told John's disciples, "Go back to John and tell him what you have seen and heard—the blind see, the lame walk, the lepers are cured, the deaf hear, the dead are raised to life, and the Good News is being preached to the poor. [23]And tell him, 'God blesses those who do not turn away because of me.*'"

[24]After John's disciples left, Jesus began talking about him to the crowds. "What kind of man did you go into the wilderness to see? Was he a weak reed, swayed by every breath of wind? [25]Or were you expecting to see a man dressed in expensive clothes? No, people who wear beautiful clothes and live in luxury are found in palaces. [26]Were you looking for a prophet? Yes, and he is more than a prophet. [27]John is the man to whom the Scriptures refer when they say,

'Look, I am sending my messenger ahead of you,
and he will prepare your way before you.'*

[28]I tell you, of all who have ever lived, none is greater than John. Yet even the least person in the Kingdom of God is greater than he is!"

[29]When they heard this, all the people—even the tax collectors—agreed that God's way was right,* for they had been baptized by John. [30]But the Pharisees and experts in religious law rejected God's plan for them, for they had refused John's baptism.

[31]"To what can I compare the people of this generation?" Jesus asked. "How can I describe them? [32]They are like children playing a game in the public square. They complain to their friends,

'We played wedding songs,
and you didn't dance,
so we played funeral songs,
and you didn't weep.'

[33]For John the Baptist didn't spend his time eating bread or drinking wine, and you say, 'He's possessed by a demon.' [34]The Son of Man,* on the other hand, feasts and drinks, and you say, 'He's a glutton and a drunkard, and a friend of tax collectors and other sinners!' [35]But wisdom is shown to be right by the lives of those who follow it.*"

Jesus Anointed by a Sinful Woman

[36]One of the Pharisees asked Jesus to have dinner with him, so Jesus went to his home and sat down to eat.* [37]When a certain immoral woman from that city heard he was eating there, she brought a beautiful alabaster jar filled with expensive perfume. [38]Then she knelt behind him at his feet, weeping. Her tears fell on his feet, and she wiped them off with her hair. Then she kept kissing his feet and putting perfume on them.

[39]When the Pharisee who had invited him saw this, he said to himself, "If this man were

7:19 Greek *Are you the one who is coming?* Also in 7:20. 7:23 Or *who are not offended by me.* 7:27 Mal 3:1. 7:29 Or *praised God for his justice.* 7:34 "Son of Man" is a title Jesus used for himself. 7:35 Or *But wisdom is justified by all her children.* 7:36 Or *and reclined.*

7:18-23 John the Baptist's experience shows that even the strongest believers will go through times of discouragement and doubt. John had been imprisoned and was facing death (Matthew 11:2). Jesus' seeming inability or unwillingness to set up his Kingdom led John to send these inquirers. Jesus deeply respected John (Luke 7:28), even with his doubts. John's questions were honestly asked in a time of acute suffering, so Jesus affirmed him and answered him accordingly. God invites us to bring our doubts to him, and he will gently move us along the path of discovery and recovery.

7:24-28 Because of his strength of character, John the Baptist did not allow himself to be squeezed into anyone else's mold. He committed himself to fulfill his God-given role as a prophet and forerunner of the Messiah. Just as he did for John, God has a purpose for each one of us. As we discover what our role in his plan is, he will reveal his will to us and bring us joy. As we obey him, he will always be with us, guiding and strengthening us along the way. Trying to be someone we were never intended to be only slows our spiritual growth and our progress in recovery.

a prophet, he would know what kind of woman is touching him. She's a sinner!"

⁴⁰Then Jesus answered his thoughts. "Simon," he said to the Pharisee, "I have something to say to you."

"Go ahead, Teacher," Simon replied.

⁴¹Then Jesus told him this story: "A man loaned money to two people—500 pieces of silver* to one and 50 pieces to the other. ⁴²But neither of them could repay him, so he kindly forgave them both, canceling their debts. Who do you suppose loved him more after that?"

⁴³Simon answered, "I suppose the one for whom he canceled the larger debt."

"That's right," Jesus said. ⁴⁴Then he turned to the woman and said to Simon, "Look at this woman kneeling here. When I entered your home, you didn't offer me water to wash the dust from my feet, but she has washed them with her tears and wiped them with her hair. ⁴⁵You didn't greet me with a kiss, but from the time I first came in, she has not stopped kissing my feet. ⁴⁶You neglected the courtesy of olive oil to anoint my head, but she has anointed my feet with rare perfume.

⁴⁷"I tell you, her sins—and they are many—have been forgiven, so she has shown me much love. But a person who is forgiven little shows only little love." ⁴⁸Then Jesus said to the woman, "Your sins are forgiven."

⁴⁹The men at the table said among themselves, "Who is this man, that he goes around forgiving sins?"

⁵⁰And Jesus said to the woman, "Your faith has saved you; go in peace."

CHAPTER 8
Women Who Followed Jesus

Soon afterward Jesus began a tour of the nearby towns and villages, preaching and announcing the Good News about the Kingdom of God. He took his twelve disciples with him, ²along with some women who had been cured of evil spirits and diseases. Among them were Mary Magdalene, from whom he had cast out seven demons; ³Joanna, the wife of Chuza, Herod's business manager; Susanna; and many others who were contributing from their own resources to support Jesus and his disciples.

Parable of the Farmer Scattering Seed

⁴One day Jesus told a story in the form of a parable to a large crowd that had gathered from many towns to hear him: ⁵"A farmer went out to plant his seed. As he scattered it across his field, some seed fell on a footpath, where it was stepped on, and the birds ate it. ⁶Other seed fell among rocks. It began to grow, but the plant soon wilted and died for lack of moisture. ⁷Other seed fell among thorns that grew up with it and choked out the tender plants. ⁸Still other seed fell on fertile soil. This seed grew and produced a crop that was a hundred times as much as had been planted!" When he had said this, he called out, "Anyone with ears to hear should listen and understand."

⁹His disciples asked him what this parable meant. ¹⁰He replied, "You are permitted to understand the secrets* of the Kingdom of God. But I use parables to teach the others so that the Scriptures might be fulfilled:

'When they look, they won't really see.
  When they hear, they won't
    understand.'*

¹¹"This is the meaning of the parable: The seed is God's word. ¹²The seeds that fell on the footpath represent those who hear the message, only to have the devil come and take it away from their hearts and prevent them from believing and being saved. ¹³The seeds on the rocky soil represent those who hear the message and receive it with joy. But since they don't have deep roots, they believe for a while, then they fall away when they face temptation. ¹⁴The seeds that fell among the thorns represent those who hear the message, but all too quickly the message is crowded out by the cares and riches and

---

7:41 Greek *500 denarii*. A denarius was equivalent to a laborer's full day's wage. 8:10a Greek *mysteries*. 8:10b Isa 6:9 (Greek version).

8:4-15 This story about the farmer and the soils emphasizes accountability and discipleship in our relationship with God. The attitudes and condition of our heart matter more than our outward profession of faith. The pressures that draw us back into addiction are well known to those of us in recovery. We face continual temptation to give in to our destructive habit, so we must be consistent and watchful in the recovery process. Taking regular moral inventory helps us avoid the problems that tend to creep into our life through the back door. As we keep our heart focused on God, he will give us a new lease on life.

pleasures of this life. And so they never grow into maturity. [15]And the seeds that fell on the good soil represent honest, good-hearted people who hear God's word, cling to it, and patiently produce a huge harvest.

Parable of the Lamp

[16]"No one lights a lamp and then covers it with a bowl or hides it under a bed. A lamp is placed on a stand, where its light can be seen by all who enter the house. [17]For all that is secret will eventually be brought into the open, and everything that is concealed will be brought to light and made known to all.

[18]"So pay attention to how you hear. To those who listen to my teaching, more understanding will be given. But for those who are not listening, even what they think they understand will be taken away from them."

The True Family of Jesus

[19]Then Jesus' mother and brothers came to see him, but they couldn't get to him because of the crowd. [20]Someone told Jesus, "Your mother and your brothers are standing outside, and they want to see you."

[21]Jesus replied, "My mother and my brothers are all those who hear God's word and obey it."

Jesus Calms the Storm

[22]One day Jesus said to his disciples, "Let's cross to the other side of the lake." So they got into a boat and started out. [23]As they sailed across, Jesus settled down for a nap. But soon a fierce storm came down on the lake. The boat was filling with water, and they were in real danger.

[24]The disciples went and woke him up, shouting, "Master, Master, we're going to drown!"

When Jesus woke up, he rebuked the wind and the raging waves. Suddenly the storm stopped and all was calm. [25]Then he asked them, "Where is your faith?"

The disciples were terrified and amazed. "Who is this man?" they asked each other. "When he gives a command, even the wind and waves obey him!"

Jesus Heals a Demon-Possessed Man

[26]So they arrived in the region of the Gerasenes,* across the lake from Galilee. [27]As Jesus was climbing out of the boat, a man who was possessed by demons came out to meet him. For a long time he had been homeless and naked, living in a cemetery outside the town.

[28]As soon as he saw Jesus, he shrieked and fell down in front of him. Then he screamed, "Why are you interfering with me, Jesus, Son of the Most High God? Please, I beg you, don't torture me!" [29]For Jesus had already commanded the evil* spirit to come out of him. This spirit had often taken control of the man. Even when he was placed under guard and put in chains and shackles, he simply broke them and rushed out into the wilderness, completely under the demon's power.

[30]Jesus demanded, "What is your name?"

"Legion," he replied, for he was filled with many demons. [31]The demons kept begging Jesus not to send them into the bottomless pit.*

[32]There happened to be a large herd of pigs feeding on the hillside nearby, and the demons begged him to let them enter into the pigs.

So Jesus gave them permission. [33]Then the demons came out of the man and entered the pigs, and the entire herd plunged down the steep hillside into the lake and drowned.

[34]When the herdsmen saw it, they fled to the nearby town and the surrounding countryside, spreading the news as they ran.

8:26 Other manuscripts read *Gadarenes;* still others read *Gergesenes;* also in 8:37. See Matt 8:28; Mark 5:1; 8:29 Greek *unclean.* 8:31 Or *the abyss,* or *the underworld.*

8:16-17 Just as lamps expose everything else to the light, so God will someday bring our thoughts out into the open. Our thoughts and habits are already known to God (see Psalm 139:1-4); someday others will know them, too. As we are open, honest, and transparent in confessing our sins, God can work his plan of recovery and healing in us.
8:26-37 The life of this demon-possessed man was a complete disaster. Desperately in need of healing, he was a physical and emotional wreck, an embarrassing social outcast. But only Jesus had, and still has, the power to break satanic bondage and bring recovery. Yet the people of the community were more concerned about their loss of a herd of pigs than they were with the healing of this helpless and broken man. Regrettably, we sometimes experience opposition to recovery. No matter what obstacles we face, however, Jesus desires to deliver us from bondage and will help us progress toward recovery.

35People rushed out to see what had happened. A crowd soon gathered around Jesus, and they saw the man who had been freed from the demons. He was sitting at Jesus' feet, fully clothed and perfectly sane, and they were all afraid. 36Then those who had seen what happened told the others how the demon-possessed man had been healed. 37And all the people in the region of the Gerasenes begged Jesus to go away and leave them alone, for a great wave of fear swept over them.

So Jesus returned to the boat and left, crossing back to the other side of the lake. 38The man who had been freed from the demons begged to go with him. But Jesus sent him home, saying, 39"No, go back to your family, and tell them everything God has done for you." So he went all through the town proclaiming the great things Jesus had done for him.

Jesus Heals in Response to Faith

40On the other side of the lake the crowds welcomed Jesus, because they had been waiting for him. 41Then a man named Jairus, a leader of the local synagogue, came and fell at Jesus' feet, pleading with him to come home with him. 42His only daughter,* who was about twelve years old, was dying.

As Jesus went with him, he was surrounded by the crowds. 43A woman in the crowd had suffered for twelve years with constant bleeding,* and she could find no cure. 44Coming up behind Jesus, she touched the fringe of his robe. Immediately, the bleeding stopped.

45"Who touched me?" Jesus asked.

Everyone denied it, and Peter said, "Master, this whole crowd is pressing up against you."

46But Jesus said, "Someone deliberately touched me, for I felt healing power go out from me." 47When the woman realized that she could not stay hidden, she began to tremble and fell to her knees in front of him. The whole crowd heard her explain why she had touched him and that she had been immediately healed. 48"Daughter," he said to her, "your faith has made you well. Go in peace."

49While he was still speaking to her, a messenger arrived from the home of Jairus, the leader of the synagogue. He told him, "Your daughter is dead. There's no use troubling the Teacher now."

50But when Jesus heard what had happened, he said to Jairus, "Don't be afraid. Just have faith, and she will be healed."

51When they arrived at the house, Jesus wouldn't let anyone go in with him except Peter, John, James, and the little girl's father and mother. 52The house was filled with people weeping and wailing, but he said, "Stop the weeping! She isn't dead; she's only asleep."

53But the crowd laughed at him because they all knew she had died. 54Then Jesus took her by the hand and said in a loud voice, "My child, get up!" 55And at that moment her life* returned, and she immediately stood up! Then Jesus told them to give her something to eat. 56Her parents were overwhelmed, but Jesus insisted that they not tell anyone what had happened.

CHAPTER 9
Jesus Sends Out the Twelve Disciples

One day Jesus called together his twelve disciples* and gave them power and authority to cast out all demons and to heal all diseases. 2Then he sent them out to tell everyone about the Kingdom of God and to heal the sick. 3"Take nothing for your journey," he instructed them. "Don't take a walking stick, a traveler's bag, food, money,* or even

8:42 Or *His only child, a daughter.* 8:43 Some manuscripts add *having spent everything she had on doctors.* 8:55 Or *her spirit.* 9:1 Greek *the Twelve;* other manuscripts read *the twelve apostles.* 9:3 Or *silver coins.*

8:43-44 Luke, with his background in medicine, noted that medical doctors had been able to do nothing for this woman's chronic illness. By faith, God's power did the impossible. As with many of Jesus' miracles, this incident shows that one who trusts in God can experience hope where previously there had been only despair. Recovery may seem beyond the scope of most doctors, but it is well within the miraclous works that God does for people who look to him in faith.

9:10-20 Once again Jesus demonstrated his desire to meet needs at various levels. In feeding the five thousand he supplied a basic need—food. Earlier Jesus had been dealing primarily with various problems that called for physical healing. Here Jesus met the intellectual and emotional needs of his disciples as well as the crowd's physical need. As God helps us toward recovery, he ultimately meets our spiritual need for a right relationship with God. Jesus the Messiah offers recovery that touches every area of our life. With his help we can take steps to live in harmony with God, the people around us, and the world.

a change of clothes. ⁴Wherever you go, stay in the same house until you leave town. ⁵And if a town refuses to welcome you, shake its dust from your feet as you leave to show that you have abandoned those people to their fate."

⁶So they began their circuit of the villages, preaching the Good News and healing the sick.

Herod's Confusion
⁷When Herod Antipas, the ruler of Galilee,* heard about everything Jesus was doing, he was puzzled. Some were saying that John the Baptist had been raised from the dead. ⁸Others thought Jesus was Elijah or one of the other prophets risen from the dead.

⁹"I beheaded John," Herod said, "so who is this man about whom I hear such stories?" And he kept trying to see him.

Jesus Feeds Five Thousand
¹⁰When the apostles returned, they told Jesus everything they had done. Then he slipped quietly away with them toward the town of Bethsaida. ¹¹But the crowds found out where he was going, and they followed him. He welcomed them and taught them about the Kingdom of God, and he healed those who were sick.

¹²Late in the afternoon the twelve disciples came to him and said, "Send the crowds away to the nearby villages and farms, so they can find food and lodging for the night. There is nothing to eat here in this remote place."

¹³But Jesus said, "You feed them."

"But we have only five loaves of bread and two fish," they answered. "Or are you expecting us to go and buy enough food for this whole crowd?" ¹⁴For there were about 5,000 men there.

Jesus replied, "Tell them to sit down in groups of about fifty each." ¹⁵So the people all sat down. ¹⁶Jesus took the five loaves and two fish, looked up toward heaven, and blessed them. Then, breaking the loaves into pieces, he kept giving the bread and fish to the disciples so they could distribute it to the people. ¹⁷They all ate as much as they wanted, and afterward, the disciples picked up twelve baskets of leftovers!

Peter's Declaration about Jesus
¹⁸One day Jesus left the crowds to pray alone. Only his disciples were with him, and he asked them, "Who do people say I am?"

9:7 Greek *Herod the tetrarch.* Herod Antipas was a son of King Herod and was ruler over Galilee.

STEP 2

Healing Faith
BIBLE READING: Luke 8:43-48
We came to believe that a Power greater than ourselves could restore us to sanity.
Faith is a key to successfully working the second step. For some of us faith comes easily. For others, especially if we have experienced betrayal, it may be more difficult. Sometimes we must exhaust all of our own resources in trying to overcome our addictive "disease" before we will risk believing in a higher Power.

When Jesus lived on earth, he was so renowned for his healing power that crowds of sick people constantly pressed in on him. One day there was "a woman in the crowd [who] had suffered for twelve years with constant bleeding, and she could find no cure. Coming up behind Jesus, she touched the fringe of his robe. Immediately, the bleeding stopped." Jesus realized that someone had deliberately touched him, because he felt healing power go out from him. When the woman confessed that she was the one who had been healed, Jesus said, "your faith has made you well. Go in peace" (Luke 8:43-44, 48).

In order to recover we must follow the example of this woman. We cannot afford to stand back, hoping for "cures," and avoid deliberate action because of our lack of faith. We may have lived with our condition for many years, spending our resources on promising "cures" without success. When we can come to believe in God, a power greater than ourself, and have the faith to take hold of our own recovery, we will find the healing power we have been looking for. *Turn to page 1319, Luke 15.*

¹⁹"Well," they replied, "some say John the Baptist, some say Elijah, and others say you are one of the other ancient prophets risen from the dead."

²⁰Then he asked them, "But who do you say I am?"

Peter replied, "You are the Messiah* sent from God!"

Jesus Predicts His Death

²¹Jesus warned his disciples not to tell anyone who he was. ²²"The Son of Man* must suffer many terrible things," he said. "He will be rejected by the elders, the leading priests, and the teachers of religious law. He will be killed, but on the third day he will be raised from the dead."

²³Then he said to the crowd, "If any of you wants to be my follower, you must turn from your selfish ways, take up your cross daily, and follow me. ²⁴If you try to hang on to your life, you will lose it. But if you give up your life for my sake, you will save it. ²⁵And what do you benefit if you gain the whole world but are yourself lost or destroyed? ²⁶If anyone is ashamed of me and my message, the Son of Man will be ashamed of that person when he returns in his glory and in the glory of the Father and the holy angels. ²⁷I tell you the truth, some standing here right now will not die before they see the Kingdom of God."

The Transfiguration

²⁸About eight days later Jesus took Peter, John, and James up on a mountain to pray. ²⁹And as he was praying, the appearance of his face was transformed, and his clothes became dazzling white. ³⁰Suddenly, two men, Moses and Elijah, appeared and began talking with Jesus. ³¹They were glorious to see. And they were speaking about his exodus from this world, which was about to be fulfilled in Jerusalem.

³²Peter and the others had fallen asleep. When they woke up, they saw Jesus' glory and the two men standing with him. ³³As Moses and Elijah were starting to leave, Peter, not even knowing what he was saying, blurted out, "Master, it's wonderful for us to be here! Let's make three shelters as memorials*—one for you, one for Moses, and one for Elijah." ³⁴But even as he was saying this, a cloud overshadowed them, and terror gripped them as the cloud covered them.

³⁵Then a voice from the cloud said, "This is my Son, my Chosen One.* Listen to him." ³⁶When the voice finished, Jesus was there alone. They didn't tell anyone at that time what they had seen.

Jesus Heals a Demon-Possessed Boy

³⁷The next day, after they had come down the mountain, a large crowd met Jesus. ³⁸A man in the crowd called out to him, "Teacher, I beg you to look at my son, my only child. ³⁹An evil spirit keeps seizing him, making him scream. It throws him into convulsions so that he foams at the mouth. It batters him and hardly ever leaves him alone. ⁴⁰I begged your disciples to cast out the spirit, but they couldn't do it."

⁴¹Jesus said, "You faithless and corrupt people! How long must I be with you and put up with you?" Then he said to the man, "Bring your son here."

⁴²As the boy came forward, the demon knocked him to the ground and threw him into a violent convulsion. But Jesus rebuked the evil* spirit and healed the boy. Then he gave him back to his father. ⁴³Awe gripped the people as they saw this majestic display of God's power.

9:20 Or *the Christ*. *Messiah* (a Hebrew term) and *Christ* (a Greek term) both mean "anointed one." 9:22 "Son of Man" is a title Jesus used for himself. 9:33 Greek *three tabernacles*. 9:35 Some manuscripts read *This is my dearly loved Son*. 9:42 Greek *unclean*.

9:23-27 In this confrontation of wills, Jesus shows the critical importance of submitting our will to God's will. Jesus has a prior claim on our life that supersedes our personal conveniences or desires. Clinging to selfish ambition and worldly desires will destroy us. Paradoxically, to "give up your life" in a relationship with God through Jesus is the only sure way of finding ultimate meaning and purpose. This teaching opposes our natural inclinations and can only be accepted by faith. But if we submit our will to God's will, we will begin to experience the meaningful life that God wants us to have.

9:28-36 While initial impressions mean a lot and many judge others based on appearances, things often are not as they seem to be. Peter relied too much on first impressions and outward appearances, so he jumped to some foolish conclusions. To Peter, these two great Old Testament prophets appeared to be on a par with Jesus. Yet God's voice and later events confirmed that Jesus was God's Son. If we are to progress in recovery, we need to stop judging on outward appearances, explore spiritual realities, and always listen to God.

Jesus Again Predicts His Death

While everyone was marveling at everything he was doing, Jesus said to his disciples, 44"Listen to me and remember what I say. The Son of Man is going to be betrayed into the hands of his enemies." 45But they didn't know what he meant. Its significance was hidden from them, so they couldn't understand it, and they were afraid to ask him about it.

The Greatest in the Kingdom

46Then his disciples began arguing about which of them was the greatest. 47But Jesus knew their thoughts, so he brought a little child to his side. 48Then he said to them, "Anyone who welcomes a little child like this on my behalf* welcomes me, and anyone who welcomes me also welcomes my Father who sent me. Whoever is the least among you is the greatest."

Using the Name of Jesus

49John said to Jesus, "Master, we saw someone using your name to cast out demons, but we told him to stop because he isn't in our group."

50But Jesus said, "Don't stop him! Anyone who is not against you is for you."

Opposition from Samaritans

51As the time drew near for him to ascend to heaven, Jesus resolutely set out for Jerusalem. 52He sent messengers ahead to a Samaritan village to prepare for his arrival. 53But the people of the village did not welcome Jesus because he was on his way to Jerusalem. 54When James and John saw this, they said to Jesus, "Lord, should we call down fire from heaven to burn them up*?" 55But Jesus turned and rebuked them.* 56So they went on to another village.

The Cost of Following Jesus

57As they were walking along, someone said to Jesus, "I will follow you wherever you go."

58But Jesus replied, "Foxes have dens to live in, and birds have nests, but the Son of Man has no place even to lay his head."

59He said to another person, "Come, follow me."

The man agreed, but he said, "Lord, first let me return home and bury my father."

60But Jesus told him, "Let the spiritually dead bury their own dead!* Your duty is to go and preach about the Kingdom of God."

61Another said, "Yes, Lord, I will follow you, but first let me say good-bye to my family."

62But Jesus told him, "Anyone who puts a hand to the plow and then looks back is not fit for the Kingdom of God."

CHAPTER 10
Jesus Sends Out His Disciples

The Lord now chose seventy-two* other disciples and sent them ahead in pairs to all the towns and places he planned to visit. 2These were his instructions to them: "The harvest is great, but the workers are few. So pray to the Lord who is in charge of the harvest; ask him to send more workers into his fields. 3Now go, and remember that I am sending you out as lambs among wolves. 4Don't take any money with you, nor a traveler's bag, nor an extra pair of sandals. And don't stop to greet anyone on the road.

5"Whenever you enter someone's home, first say, 'May God's peace be on this house.' 6If those who live there are peaceful, the blessing will stand; if they are not, the blessing will return to you. 7Don't move around from home to home. Stay in one place, eating and drinking what they provide. Don't hesitate to accept hospitality, because those who work deserve their pay.

8"If you enter a town and it welcomes you, eat whatever is set before you. 9Heal the sick, and tell them, 'The Kingdom of God is near you now.' 10But if a town refuses to welcome you, go out into its streets and say, 11"We wipe even the dust of your town from our

9:48 Greek *in my name.* 9:54 Some manuscripts add *as Elijah did.* 9:55 Some manuscripts add an expanded conclusion to verse 55 and an additional sentence in verse 56: *And he said, "You don't realize what your hearts are like.* 56*For the Son of Man has not come to destroy people's lives, but to save them."* 9:60 Greek *Let the dead bury their own dead.* 10:1 Some manuscripts read *seventy;* also in 10:17.

10:8-16 The disciples were given the ambitious task and privilege of sharing the message of the Messiah throughout the land. Their ministry would not always be well received. One who follows Jesus toward recovery will encounter similar setbacks, such as rejection and ridicule. As we share our story of deliverance with others, we may find we are not always welcome in our old stomping grounds. When we experience rejection, we should be prepared to make a timely exit, go in peace, and find a more receptive audience.

feet to show that we have abandoned you to your fate. And know this—the Kingdom of God is near!' ¹²I assure you, even wicked Sodom will be better off than such a town on judgment day.

¹³"What sorrow awaits you, Korazin and Bethsaida! For if the miracles I did in you had been done in wicked Tyre and Sidon, their people would have repented of their sins long ago, clothing themselves in burlap and throwing ashes on their heads to show their remorse. ¹⁴Yes, Tyre and Sidon will be better off on judgment day than you. ¹⁵And you people of Capernaum, will you be honored in heaven? No, you will go down to the place of the dead.*"

¹⁶Then he said to the disciples, "Anyone who accepts your message is also accepting me. And anyone who rejects you is rejecting me. And anyone who rejects me is rejecting God, who sent me."

¹⁷When the seventy-two disciples returned, they joyfully reported to him, "Lord, even the demons obey us when we use your name!"

¹⁸"Yes," he told them, "I saw Satan fall from heaven like lightning! ¹⁹Look, I have given you authority over all the power of the enemy, and you can walk among snakes and scorpions and crush them. Nothing will injure you. ²⁰But don't rejoice because evil spirits obey you; rejoice because your names are registered in heaven."

Jesus' Prayer of Thanksgiving

²¹At that same time Jesus was filled with the joy of the Holy Spirit, and he said, "O Father, Lord of heaven and earth, thank you for hiding these things from those who think themselves wise and clever, and for revealing them to the childlike. Yes, Father, it pleased you to do it this way.

²²"My Father has entrusted everything to me. No one truly knows the Son except the Father, and no one truly knows the Father except the Son and those to whom the Son chooses to reveal him."

²³Then when they were alone, he turned to the disciples and said, "Blessed are the eyes that see what you have seen. ²⁴I tell you, many prophets and kings longed to see what you see, but they didn't see it. And they longed to hear what you hear, but they didn't hear it."

The Most Important Commandment

²⁵One day an expert in religious law stood up to test Jesus by asking him this question: "Teacher, what should I do to inherit eternal life?"

²⁶Jesus replied, "What does the law of Moses say? How do you read it?"

²⁷The man answered, " 'You must love the LORD your God with all your heart, all your soul, all your strength, and all your mind.' And, 'Love your neighbor as yourself.' "*

²⁸"Right!" Jesus told him. "Do this and you will live!"

²⁹The man wanted to justify his actions, so he asked Jesus, "And who is my neighbor?"

Parable of the Good Samaritan

³⁰Jesus replied with a story: "A Jewish man was traveling from Jerusalem down to Jericho, and he was attacked by bandits. They stripped him of his clothes, beat him up, and left him half dead beside the road.

³¹"By chance a priest came along. But when he saw the man lying there, he crossed to the other side of the road and passed him by. ³²A Temple assistant* walked over and looked at him lying there, but he also passed by on the other side.

³³"Then a despised Samaritan came along,

10:15 Greek *to Hades*. 10:27 Deut 6:5; Lev 19:18. 10:32 Greek *A Levite*.

10:25-37 The story of the Good Samaritan teaches that true love for God expresses itself in caring for others' needs. In Jesus' day the Jews and Samaritans hated each other. So when the despised Samaritan proved to be the good neighbor to the wounded Jew, Jesus was showing that concern for others has no boundaries. When God has brought us healing and recovery, we become an effective instrument in reaching others with similar needs. Sharing the good news of our deliverance is a responsibility we receive from God. As we share, we will experience great joy as others gain hope for recovery. Our own faith and recovery are also strengthened as we remember what God has done on our behalf.

10:38-42 There is a difference between being spiritually committed to recovery and being preoccupied with recovery. This story about Mary and Martha illustrates the difference. Martha was so busy "doing for others" that she had no time or energy left for simply being with Jesus. In all her doing, Martha even became irritated at Mary for not being equally busy. Mary, on the other hand, took time out to listen to Jesus. Recovery must be a recovery from the heart, not just a recovery where we act compulsively to look the part.

MARY & MARTHA

As with all siblings, Mary and Martha each had unique gifts and personality. Martha was industrious and concerned about detail, while Mary, the contemplative one, treasured sitting at his feet and being a student of Jesus.

We are given a glimpse into the heart of Mary when we see her anoint Jesus with costly perfume shortly before his death. Mary's extravagant act of love and devotion was hypocritically criticized by Judas. In the process of recovery it may be necessary to take steps that others will criticize, but we must remember that the bottom line is whether or not God is pleased with our actions.

When their brother Lazarus died, the events that followed allowed both sisters to grow in their understanding of Jesus. Jesus knew that if he delayed coming to them, he wouldn't arrive until after Lazarus's death. If he had come before Lazarus died, he certainly could have healed him; but by coming later, Jesus was able to do something even more glorious—raise him from the dead!

For Mary and Martha, the delay was painful. The ultimate outcome, however, was a deeper faith and a fuller experience of the joy that comes from trusting God with the details of life. As we go through difficult times, we may not always understand what God is doing, but we will grow in strength and faith as we patiently endure. There is always hope when the God who can raise the dead is on our side.

STRENGTHS AND ACCOMPLISHMENTS:
- Both were devoted followers of Jesus.
- Martha was hardworking, efficient, and conscientious.
- Mary had a heart that was devoted to God.

WEAKNESSES AND MISTAKES:
- Martha was so worried about details that she missed spending time with Jesus.

LESSONS FROM THEIR LIVES:
- We may get so busy doing things in the recovery process—even good things—that we forget to spend time with Jesus.
- Jesus valued the contribution of these women among his followers.
- It is important to see each of our children as a unique individual.

KEY VERSES:
"Martha. . . . came to Jesus and said, 'Lord, doesn't it seem unfair to you that my sister just sits here while I do all the work? Tell her to come and help me.' But the Lord said to her, 'My dear Martha, you are worried and upset over all these details! There is only one thing worth being concerned about. Mary has discovered it, and it will not be taken away from her'" (Luke 10:40-42).

The story of Mary and Martha is found in Matthew 26:6-13; Luke 10:38-42; and John 11:1-45; 12:1-8.

---

and when he saw the man, he felt compassion for him. [34]Going over to him, the Samaritan soothed his wounds with olive oil and wine and bandaged them. Then he put the man on his own donkey and took him to an inn, where he took care of him. [35]The next day he handed the innkeeper two silver coins,* telling him, 'Take care of this man. If his bill runs higher than this, I'll pay you the next time I'm here.'

[36]"Now which of these three would you say was a neighbor to the man who was attacked by bandits?" Jesus asked.

[37]The man replied, "The one who showed him mercy."

Then Jesus said, "Yes, now go and do the same."

Jesus Visits Martha and Mary

[38]As Jesus and the disciples continued on their way to Jerusalem, they came to a certain village where a woman named Martha welcomed him into her home. [39]Her sister, Mary, sat at the Lord's feet, listening to what he taught. [40]But Martha was distracted by the big dinner she was preparing. She came to Jesus and said, "Lord, doesn't it seem unfair to you that my sister just sits here while I do all the work? Tell her to come and help me."

[41]But the Lord said to her, "My dear Martha, you are worried and upset over all these details! [42]There is only one thing worth being concerned about. Mary has discovered it, and it will not be taken away from her."

CHAPTER 11
Teaching about Prayer

Once Jesus was in a certain place praying. As he finished, one of his disciples came to

10:35 Greek *two denarii.* A denarius was equivalent to a laborer's full day's wage.

him and said, "Lord, teach us to pray, just as John taught his disciples."

²Jesus said, "This is how you should pray:*

"Father, may your name be kept holy.
    May your Kingdom come soon.
³ Give us each day the food we need,*
⁴ and forgive us our sins,
    as we forgive those who sin against us.
    And don't let us yield to temptation.*"

⁵Then, teaching them more about prayer, he used this story: "Suppose you went to a friend's house at midnight, wanting to borrow three loaves of bread. You say to him, ⁶'A friend of mine has just arrived for a visit, and I have nothing for him to eat.' ⁷And suppose he calls out from his bedroom, 'Don't bother me. The door is locked for the night, and my family and I are all in bed. I can't help you.' ⁸But I tell you this—though he won't do it for friendship's sake, if you keep knocking long enough, he will get up and give you whatever you need because of your shameless persistence.*

⁹"And so I tell you, keep on asking, and you will receive what you ask for. Keep on seeking, and you will find. Keep on knocking, and the door will be opened to you. ¹⁰For everyone who asks, receives. Everyone who seeks, finds. And to everyone who knocks, the door will be opened.

¹¹"You fathers—if your children ask* for a fish, do you give them a snake instead? ¹²Or if they ask for an egg, do you give them a scorpion? Of course not! ¹³So if you sinful people know how to give good gifts to your children, how much more will your heavenly Father give the Holy Spirit to those who ask him."

Jesus and the Prince of Demons

¹⁴One day Jesus cast out a demon from a man who couldn't speak, and when the demon was gone, the man began to speak. The crowds were amazed, ¹⁵but some of them said, "No wonder he can cast out demons. He gets his power from Satan,* the prince of demons." ¹⁶Others, trying to test Jesus, demanded that he show them a miraculous sign from heaven to prove his authority.

¹⁷He knew their thoughts, so he said, "Any kingdom divided by civil war is doomed. A family splintered by feuding will fall apart. ¹⁸You say I am empowered by Satan. But if Satan is divided and fighting against himself, how can his kingdom survive? ¹⁹And if I am empowered by Satan, what about your own exorcists? They cast out demons, too, so they will condemn you for what you have said. ²⁰But if I am casting out demons by the power of God,* then the Kingdom of God has arrived among you. ²¹For when a strong man like Satan is fully armed and guards his palace, his possessions are safe—²²until someone even stronger attacks and overpowers him, strips him of his weapons, and carries off his belongings.

²³"Anyone who isn't with me opposes me, and anyone who isn't working with me is actually working against me.

²⁴"When an evil* spirit leaves a person, it goes into the desert, searching for rest. But when it finds none, it says, 'I will return to the person I came from.' ²⁵So it returns and finds that its former home is all swept and in order. ²⁶Then the spirit finds seven other spirits more evil than itself, and they all enter

11:2 Some manuscripts add additional phrases from the Lord's Prayer as it reads in Matt 6:9-13. 11:3 Or *Give us each day our food for the day;* or *Give us each day our food for tomorrow.* 11:4 Or *And keep us from being tested.* 11:8 Or *in order to avoid shame,* or *so his reputation won't be damaged.* 11:11 Some manuscripts add *for bread, do you give them a stone? Or [if they ask].* 11:15 Greek *Beelzeboul;* also in 11:18, 19. Other manuscripts read *Beezeboul;* Latin version reads *Beelzebub.* 11:20 Greek *by the finger of God.* 11:24 Greek *unclean.*

11:2 The opening of this prayer, "Father," describes the attitude and relationship with which we are to approach God. Luke used an intimate word that a child might use in speaking to an earthly father. The equivalent in our everyday speech would be addressing God as "Daddy." Only through this kind of intimate prayer relationship with our heavenly Father can we find strength to tackle the big challenges of lifelong recovery.
11:4 God's forgiveness of us and our forgiveness of others are inextricably linked together. Jesus said that if we refuse to forgive others, God will not forgive our sins (Matthew 6:14-15). To fully experience God's forgiveness, we must be willing to forgive others. Conversely, unforgiving spirits hinder our ability to enjoy the freedom found in God's forgiveness. To harbor anger and an unforgiving spirit when God has forgiven us so much is hypocritical and a roadblock to recovery.
11:4 The honesty of this prayer recognizes our own weakness and vulnerability to temptation. The prayer of faith asks God to help us to not yield to temptation. As a model prayer, this principle is especially important when we seek victory over areas of our life where sin has gained a stronghold. The recovery process involves not only recognizing our own sins and character defects but also avoiding situations that might lead to temptation and a fall.

the person and live there. And so that person is worse off than before."

²⁷As he was speaking, a woman in the crowd called out, "God bless your mother—the womb from which you came, and the breasts that nursed you!"

²⁸Jesus replied, "But even more blessed are all who hear the word of God and put it into practice."

The Sign of Jonah

²⁹As the crowd pressed in on Jesus, he said, "This evil generation keeps asking me to show them a miraculous sign. But the only sign I will give them is the sign of Jonah. ³⁰What happened to him was a sign to the people of Nineveh that God had sent him. What happens to the Son of Man* will be a sign to these people that he was sent by God.

³¹"The queen of Sheba* will stand up against this generation on judgment day and condemn it, for she came from a distant land to hear the wisdom of Solomon. Now someone greater than Solomon is here—but you refuse to listen. ³²The people of Nineveh will also stand up against this generation on judgment day and condemn it, for they repented of their sins at the preaching of Jonah. Now someone greater than Jonah is here—but you refuse to repent.

Receiving the Light

³³"No one lights a lamp and then hides it or puts it under a basket.* Instead, a lamp is placed on a stand, where its light can be seen by all who enter the house.

³⁴"Your eye is a lamp that provides light for your body. When your eye is good, your whole body is filled with light. But when it is bad, your body is filled with darkness. ³⁵Make sure that the light you think you have is not actually darkness. ³⁶If you are filled with light, with no dark corners, then your whole life will be radiant, as though a floodlight were filling you with light."

Jesus Criticizes the Religious Leaders

³⁷As Jesus was speaking, one of the Pharisees invited him home for a meal. So he went in and took his place at the table.* ³⁸His host was amazed to see that he sat down to eat without first performing the hand-washing ceremony required by Jewish custom. ³⁹Then the Lord said to him, "You Pharisees are so

11:30 "Son of Man" is a title Jesus used for himself. 11:31 Greek *The queen of the south.* 11:33 Some manuscripts do not include *or puts it under a basket.* 11:37 Or *and reclined.*

STEP 7

Pride Born of Hurt

BIBLE READING: Luke 11:5-13

We humbly asked him to remove our shortcomings.

Our pride can keep us from asking for what we need. We may have grown up in a family where we were consistently ignored or disappointed. Perhaps our needs were seldom met. Some of us may have reacted by becoming self-sufficient. We determined never to ask anyone for help. In fact, we were going to strive to never need anyone's help ever again!

It is this type of pride, born of hurt, that will hold us back from asking God to help us deal with our shortcomings. Jesus said, "And so I tell you, keep on asking, and you will receive what you ask for. Keep on seeking, and you will find. Keep on knocking, and the door will be opened to you. For everyone who asks, receives. Everyone who seeks, finds. And to everyone who knocks, the door will be opened" (Luke 11:9-10). "You parents—if your children ask for a loaf of bread, do you give them a stone instead? Or if they ask for a fish, do you give them a snake? Of course not! So if you sinful people know how to give good gifts to your children, how much more will your heavenly Father give good gifts to those who ask him" (Matthew 7:9-11).

We must come to the place of giving up our prideful self-sufficiency; we must be willing to ask for help. And we can't ask for help just once and be done with it. We must be persistent and ask repeatedly as the needs arise. When we practice Step Seven in this way, we can be assured that our loving heavenly Father will respond by giving us good gifts and removing our shortcomings. *Turn to page 1323, Luke 18.*

careful to clean the outside of the cup and the dish, but inside you are filthy—full of greed and wickedness! ⁴⁰Fools! Didn't God make the inside as well as the outside? ⁴¹So clean the inside by giving gifts to the poor, and you will be clean all over.

⁴²"What sorrow awaits you Pharisees! For you are careful to tithe even the tiniest income from your herb gardens,* but you ignore justice and the love of God. You should tithe, yes, but do not neglect the more important things.

⁴³"What sorrow awaits you Pharisees! For you love to sit in the seats of honor in the synagogues and receive respectful greetings as you walk in the marketplaces. ⁴⁴Yes, what sorrow awaits you! For you are like hidden graves in a field. People walk over them without knowing the corruption they are stepping on."

⁴⁵"Teacher," said an expert in religious law, "you have insulted us, too, in what you just said."

⁴⁶"Yes," said Jesus, "what sorrow also awaits you experts in religious law! For you crush people with unbearable religious demands, and you never lift a finger to ease the burden. ⁴⁷What sorrow awaits you! For you build monuments for the prophets your own ancestors killed long ago. ⁴⁸But in fact, you stand as witnesses who agree with what your ancestors did. They killed the prophets, and you join in their crime by building the monuments! ⁴⁹This is what God in his wisdom said about you:* 'I will send prophets and apostles to them, but they will kill some and persecute the others.'

⁵⁰"As a result, this generation will be held responsible for the murder of all God's prophets from the creation of the world—

⁵¹from the murder of Abel to the murder of Zechariah, who was killed between the altar and the sanctuary. Yes, it will certainly be charged against this generation.

⁵²"What sorrow awaits you experts in religious law! For you remove the key to knowledge from the people. You don't enter the Kingdom yourselves, and you prevent others from entering."

⁵³As Jesus was leaving, the teachers of religious law and the Pharisees became hostile and tried to provoke him with many questions. ⁵⁴They wanted to trap him into saying something they could use against him.

CHAPTER 12
A Warning against Hypocrisy

Meanwhile, the crowds grew until thousands were milling about and stepping on each other. Jesus turned first to his disciples and warned them, "Beware of the yeast of the Pharisees—their hypocrisy. ²The time is coming when everything that is covered up will be revealed, and all that is secret will be made known to all. ³Whatever you have said in the dark will be heard in the light, and what you have whispered behind closed doors will be shouted from the housetops for all to hear!

⁴"Dear friends, don't be afraid of those who want to kill your body; they cannot do any more to you after that. ⁵But I'll tell you whom to fear. Fear God, who has the power to kill you and then throw you into hell.* Yes, he's the one to fear.

⁶"What is the price of five sparrows—two copper coins*? Yet God does not forget a single one of them. ⁷And the very hairs on your head are all numbered. So don't be afraid; you are more valuable to God than a whole flock of sparrows.

11:42 Greek *tithe the mint, the rue, and every herb.* 11:49 Greek *Therefore, the wisdom of God said.* 12:5 Greek *Gehenna.* 12:6 Greek *two assaria* [Roman coins equal to ¹/₁₆ of a denarius].

12:6-7 If God cares for even the smallest sparrow, then he cares even more for us. If he cares enough to count the hairs on our head, then he cares even more about our thoughts and feelings. Dwelling on this reality can help us when we feel depressed or lonely. The most powerful and important person in the universe cares deeply and personally about us.

12:13-21 Jesus continually emphasized the dangers of materialism. Materialism was not just a problem for the rich people Jesus encountered or for the characters in his stories. The tendency to desire more of everything is endemic to human nature. Jesus was concerned not so much with how much we possess but with how much our wealth possesses us. True freedom and contentment cannot be found in the things we own; recovery can never be bought. These gifts are freely given to us as we humbly turn to God for his gracious help.

12:22-31 True freedom and contentment are found by depending exclusively on God and obeying him. Jesus pointed out the worthlessness of spending time worrying about things God has already taken care of. Since neither animals nor plants worry about food and clothing, neither should we. As God takes care of them while they live from day to day, so also will God take care of us if we make his Kingdom our primary concern. Trusting God's supreme providential care enables people in recovery to live one day at a time.

GOD grant me the serenity
to accept the things I cannot change
the courage to change the things I can
and the wisdom to know the difference

A M E N

We often stay in relationships in which we seem powerless, for in doing so, we maintain built-in excuses for failure. We may also spend time looking down on others who are "worse" than we are, thus avoiding an examination of our own corruption. But in doing these things, we fail to take responsibility for our own life through honest self-examination.

We often protect ourself by focusing our attention on other people and their behaviors. That way we don't have to examine our own.

Jesus confronted the Pharisees, saying, "You Pharisees are so careful to clean the outside of the cup and the dish, but inside you are filthy—full of greed and wickedness!" (Luke 11:39). Can you imagine washing only the outside of a cup that is moldy on the inside and then drinking from it? Of course not! But we do this in a spiritual sense because it is hard to deal with the "dirt" inside our heart.

Changing those things in our life that we can change involves taking steps to clean the inside of our "cup," our heart. We must begin by turning our eyes away from everyone around us, including those we blame for our condition in life or those we condemn to make our wrongs seem less in comparison. Then we can get back to looking within ourself. We all contain some residue of wrongdoing. When we admit this to God, to ourself, and to others, we will experience the cleansing of humility and forgiveness. Then we will have a life that can bring refreshment to others. *Turn to page 1469, 1 Corinthians 10.*

---

[8]"I tell you the truth, everyone who acknowledges me publicly here on earth, the Son of Man* will also acknowledge in the presence of God's angels. [9]But anyone who denies me here on earth will be denied before God's angels. [10]Anyone who speaks against the Son of Man can be forgiven, but anyone who blasphemes the Holy Spirit will not be forgiven.

[11]"And when you are brought to trial in the synagogues and before rulers and authorities, don't worry about how to defend yourself or what to say, [12]for the Holy Spirit will teach you at that time what needs to be said."

Parable of the Rich Fool

[13]Then someone called from the crowd, "Teacher, please tell my brother to divide our father's estate with me."

[14]Jesus replied, "Friend, who made me a judge over you to decide such things as that?" [15]Then he said, "Beware! Guard against every kind of greed. Life is not measured by how much you own."

[16]Then he told them a story: "A rich man had a fertile farm that produced fine crops. [17]He said to himself, 'What should I do? I don't have room for all my crops.' [18]Then he said, 'I know! I'll tear down my barns and build bigger ones. Then I'll have room enough to store all my wheat and other goods. [19]And I'll sit back and say to myself, "My friend, you have enough stored away for years to come. Now take it easy! Eat, drink, and be merry!"'

[20]"But God said to him, 'You fool! You will die this very night. Then who will get everything you worked for?'

[21]"Yes, a person is a fool to store up earthly wealth but not have a rich relationship with God."

12:8 "Son of Man" is a title Jesus used for himself.

Teaching about Money and Possessions

²²Then, turning to his disciples, Jesus said, "That is why I tell you not to worry about everyday life—whether you have enough food to eat or enough clothes to wear. ²³For life is more than food, and your body more than clothing. ²⁴Look at the ravens. They don't plant or harvest or store food in barns, for God feeds them. And you are far more valuable to him than any birds! ²⁵Can all your worries add a single moment to your life? ²⁶And if worry can't accomplish a little thing like that, what's the use of worrying over bigger things?

²⁷"Look at the lilies and how they grow. They don't work or make their clothing, yet Solomon in all his glory was not dressed as beautifully as they are. ²⁸And if God cares so wonderfully for flowers that are here today and thrown into the fire tomorrow, he will certainly care for you. Why do you have so little faith?

²⁹"And don't be concerned about what to eat and what to drink. Don't worry about such things. ³⁰These things dominate the thoughts of unbelievers all over the world, but your Father already knows your needs. ³¹Seek the Kingdom of God above all else, and he will give you everything you need.

³²"So don't be afraid, little flock. For it gives your Father great happiness to give you the Kingdom.

³³"Sell your possessions and give to those in need. This will store up treasure for you in heaven! And the purses of heaven never get old or develop holes. Your treasure will be safe; no thief can steal it and no moth can destroy it. ³⁴Wherever your treasure is, there the desires of your heart will also be.

Be Ready for the Lord's Coming

³⁵"Be dressed for service and keep your lamps burning, ³⁶as though you were waiting for your master to return from the wedding feast. Then you will be ready to open the door and let him in the moment he arrives and knocks. ³⁷The servants who are ready and waiting for his return will be rewarded. I tell you the truth, he himself will seat them,

put on an apron, and serve them as they sit and eat! ³⁸He may come in the middle of the night or just before dawn.* But whenever he comes, he will reward the servants who are ready.

³⁹"Understand this: If a homeowner knew exactly when a burglar was coming, he would not permit his house to be broken into. ⁴⁰You also must be ready all the time, for the Son of Man will come when least expected."

⁴¹Peter asked, "Lord, is that illustration just for us or for everyone?"

⁴²And the Lord replied, "A faithful, sensible servant is one to whom the master can give the responsibility of managing his other household servants and feeding them. ⁴³If the master returns and finds that the servant has done a good job, there will be a reward. ⁴⁴I tell you the truth, the master will put that servant in charge of all he owns. ⁴⁵But what if the servant thinks, 'My master won't be back for a while,' and he begins beating the other servants, partying, and getting drunk? ⁴⁶The master will return unannounced and unexpected, and he will cut the servant in pieces and banish him with the unfaithful.

⁴⁷"And a servant who knows what the master wants, but isn't prepared and doesn't carry out those instructions, will be severely punished. ⁴⁸But someone who does not know, and then does something wrong, will be punished only lightly. When someone has been given much, much will be required in return; and when someone has been entrusted with much, even more will be required.

Jesus Causes Division

⁴⁹"I have come to set the world on fire, and I wish it were already burning! ⁵⁰I have a terrible baptism of suffering ahead of me, and I am under a heavy burden until it is accomplished. ⁵¹Do you think I have come to bring peace to the earth? No, I have come to divide people against each other! ⁵²From now on families will be split apart, three in favor of me, and two against—or two in favor and three against.

12:38 Greek *in the second or third watch.*

12:32-34 The heart represents all that motivates us—our thoughts, ideals, inclinations, priorities, convictions, worries, and fears. If we want genuine recovery in problem areas of our life, we must first release our heartfelt attachments to the dependency or compulsion we are struggling with. The things we value most and spend time and money pursuing—that's where our deep attachments and personal identity can be found. Our checkbook and date book are barometers of our heart condition and our progress in recovery.

53 'Father will be divided against son
  and son against father;
mother against daughter
  and daughter against mother;
and mother-in-law against
  daughter-in-law
and daughter-in-law against
  mother-in-law.'*"

54Then Jesus turned to the crowd and said, "When you see clouds beginning to form in the west, you say, 'Here comes a shower.' And you are right. 55When the south wind blows, you say, 'Today will be a scorcher.' And it is. 56You fools! You know how to interpret the weather signs of the earth and sky, but you don't know how to interpret the present times.

57"Why can't you decide for yourselves what is right? 58When you are on the way to court with your accuser, try to settle the matter before you get there. Otherwise, your accuser may drag you before the judge, who will hand you over to an officer, who will throw you into prison. 59And if that happens, you won't be free again until you have paid the very last penny.*"

CHAPTER 13
A Call to Repentance
About this time Jesus was informed that Pilate had murdered some people from Galilee as they were offering sacrifices at the Temple. 2"Do you think those Galileans were worse sinners than all the other people from Galilee?" Jesus asked. "Is that why they suffered? 3Not at all! And you will perish, too, unless you repent of your sins and turn to God. 4And what about the eighteen people who died when the tower in Siloam fell on them? Were they the worst sinners in Jerusalem? 5No, and I tell you again that unless you repent, you will perish, too."

Parable of the Barren Fig Tree
6Then Jesus told this story: "A man planted a fig tree in his garden and came again and again to see if there was any fruit on it, but he was always disappointed. 7Finally, he said

to his gardener, 'I've waited three years, and there hasn't been a single fig! Cut it down. It's just taking up space in the garden.'

8"The gardener answered, 'Sir, give it one more chance. Leave it another year, and I'll give it special attention and plenty of fertilizer. 9If we get figs next year, fine. If not, then you can cut it down.'"

Jesus Heals on the Sabbath
10One Sabbath day as Jesus was teaching in a synagogue, 11he saw a woman who had been crippled by an evil spirit. She had been bent double for eighteen years and was unable to stand up straight. 12When Jesus saw her, he called her over and said, "Dear woman, you are healed of your sickness!" 13Then he touched her, and instantly she could stand straight. How she praised God!

14But the leader in charge of the synagogue was indignant that Jesus had healed her on the Sabbath day. "There are six days of the week for working," he said to the crowd. "Come on those days to be healed, not on the Sabbath."

15But the Lord replied, "You hypocrites! Each of you works on the Sabbath day! Don't you untie your ox or your donkey from its stall on the Sabbath and lead it out for water? 16This dear woman, a daughter of Abraham, has been held in bondage by Satan for eighteen years. Isn't it right that she be released, even on the Sabbath?"

17This shamed his enemies, but all the people rejoiced at the wonderful things he did.

Parable of the Mustard Seed
18Then Jesus said, "What is the Kingdom of God like? How can I illustrate it? 19It is like a tiny mustard seed that a man planted in a garden; it grows and becomes a tree, and the birds make nests in its branches."

Parable of the Yeast
20He also asked, "What else is the Kingdom of God like? 21It is like the yeast a woman used in making bread. Even though she put only a little yeast in three measures of flour, it permeated every part of the dough."

12:53 Mic 7:6. 12:59 Greek *last lepton* [the smallest Jewish coin].

13:10-13 Jesus cared for social outcasts, emotional and physical cripples, and those in spiritual bondage. This handicapped woman was hurting in all three respects. In eighteen years she had probably tried everything to be healed, but now was resigned to her painful limitations. The power of an evil spirit had crippled her. But the power of Jesus Christ knows no limitations. Jesus healed this woman who had given up all hope for a new life. He can do the same for us by bringing us healing and deliverance.

The Narrow Door

²²Jesus went through the towns and villages, teaching as he went, always pressing on toward Jerusalem. ²³Someone asked him, "Lord, will only a few be saved?"

He replied, ²⁴"Work hard to enter the narrow door to God's Kingdom, for many will try to enter but will fail. ²⁵When the master of the house has locked the door, it will be too late. You will stand outside knocking and pleading, 'Lord, open the door for us!' But he will reply, 'I don't know you or where you come from.' ²⁶Then you will say, 'But we ate and drank with you, and you taught in our streets.' ²⁷And he will reply, 'I tell you, I don't know you or where you come from. Get away from me, all you who do evil.'

²⁸"There will be weeping and gnashing of teeth, for you will see Abraham, Isaac, Jacob, and all the prophets in the Kingdom of God, but you will be thrown out. ²⁹And people will come from all over the world—from east and west, north and south—to take their places in the Kingdom of God. ³⁰And note this: Some who seem least important now will be the greatest then, and some who are the greatest now will be least important then.*"

Jesus Grieves over Jerusalem

³¹At that time some Pharisees said to him, "Get away from here if you want to live! Herod Antipas wants to kill you!"

³²Jesus replied, "Go tell that fox that I will keep on casting out demons and healing people today and tomorrow; and the third day I will accomplish my purpose. ³³Yes, today, tomorrow, and the next day I must proceed on my way. For it wouldn't do for a prophet of God to be killed except in Jerusalem!

³⁴"O Jerusalem, Jerusalem, the city that kills the prophets and stones God's messengers! How often I have wanted to gather your children together as a hen protects her chicks beneath her wings, but you wouldn't let me. ³⁵And now, look, your house is abandoned. And you will never see me again until you say, 'Blessings on the one who comes in the name of the LORD!'*"

CHAPTER 14
Jesus Heals on the Sabbath

One Sabbath day Jesus went to eat dinner in the home of a leader of the Pharisees, and the people were watching him closely. ²There was a man there whose arms and legs were swollen.* ³Jesus asked the Pharisees and experts in religious law, "Is it permitted in the law to heal people on the Sabbath day, or not?" ⁴When they refused to answer, Jesus touched the sick man and healed him and sent him away. ⁵Then he turned to them and said, "Which of you doesn't work on the Sabbath? If your son* or your cow falls into a pit, don't you rush to get him out?" ⁶Again they could not answer.

Jesus Teaches about Humility

⁷When Jesus noticed that all who had come to the dinner were trying to sit in the seats of honor near the head of the table, he gave them this advice: ⁸"When you are invited to a wedding feast, don't sit in the seat of honor. What if someone who is more distinguished than you has also been invited? ⁹The host will come and say, 'Give this person your seat.' Then you will be embarrassed, and you will have to take whatever seat is left at the foot of the table!

¹⁰"Instead, take the lowest place at the foot of the table. Then when your host sees you, he will come and say, 'Friend, we have a better place for you!' Then you will be honored in front of all the other guests. ¹¹For those who exalt themselves will be humbled, and those who humble themselves will be exalted."

¹²Then he turned to his host. "When you put on a luncheon or a banquet," he said, "don't invite your friends, brothers, rela-

---

13:30 Greek *Some are last who will be first, and some are first who will be last.* **13:35** Ps 118:26. **14:2** Or *who had dropsy.* **14:5** Some manuscripts read *donkey.*

13:22-30 Appearances can be deceiving. But God is not fooled—he knows the real intent of our heart. We can go to church, teach Sunday school, or sing in the choir and, like the religious hypocrites of Jesus' day, still lack a real relationship with God. Being sincere, not merely religious, is crucial to recovery. God will judge religious hypocrisy, and he will honor honest attempts to obey him and know him better—no matter how many times we fail.

14:12-24 This story about the great feast illustrates one of the major themes in Luke's Gospel. God extends his saving grace and blessing to all people, including the poor and the handicapped of society, who in almost every case are ignored, even abused. Extending mercy to such people will be rewarded by God. An important step in following Jesus and in our own recovery program is our willingness to help others less fortunate than we.

tives, and rich neighbors. For they will invite you back, and that will be your only reward. [13]Instead, invite the poor, the crippled, the lame, and the blind. [14]Then at the resurrection of the righteous, God will reward you for inviting those who could not repay you."

Parable of the Great Feast

[15]Hearing this, a man sitting at the table with Jesus exclaimed, "What a blessing it will be to attend a banquet* in the Kingdom of God!"

[16]Jesus replied with this story: "A man prepared a great feast and sent out many invitations. [17]When the banquet was ready, he sent his servant to tell the guests, 'Come, the banquet is ready.' [18]But they all began making excuses. One said, 'I have just bought a field and must inspect it. Please excuse me.' [19]Another said, 'I have just bought five pairs of oxen, and I want to try them out. Please excuse me.' [20]Another said, 'I now have a wife, so I can't come.'

[21]"The servant returned and told his master what they had said. His master was furious and said, 'Go quickly into the streets and alleys of the town and invite the poor, the crippled, the blind, and the lame.' [22]After the servant had done this, he reported, 'There is still room for more.' [23]So his master said, 'Go out into the country lanes and behind the hedges and urge anyone you find to come, so that the house will be full. [24]For none of those I first invited will get even the smallest taste of my banquet.'"

The Cost of Being a Disciple

[25]A large crowd was following Jesus. He turned around and said to them, [26]"If you want to be my disciple, you must hate everyone else by comparison—your father and mother, wife and children, brothers and sisters—yes, even your own life. Otherwise, you cannot be my disciple. [27]And if you do not

14:15 Greek *to eat bread.*

carry your own cross and follow me, you cannot be my disciple.

[28]"But don't begin until you count the cost. For who would begin construction of a building without first calculating the cost to see if there is enough money to finish it? [29]Otherwise, you might complete only the foundation before running out of money, and then everyone would laugh at you. [30]They would say, 'There's the person who started that building and couldn't afford to finish it!'

[31]"Or what king would go to war against another king without first sitting down with his counselors to discuss whether his army of 10,000 could defeat the 20,000 soldiers marching against him? [32]And if he can't, he will send a delegation to discuss terms of peace while the enemy is still far away. [33]So you cannot become my disciple without giving up everything you own.

[34]"Salt is good for seasoning. But if it loses its flavor, how do you make it salty again? [35]Flavorless salt is good neither for the soil nor for the manure pile. It is thrown away. Anyone with ears to hear should listen and understand!"

CHAPTER 15
Parable of the Lost Sheep

Tax collectors and other notorious sinners often came to listen to Jesus teach. [2]This made the Pharisees and teachers of religious law complain that he was associating with such sinful people—even eating with them!

[3]So Jesus told them this story: [4]"If a man has a hundred sheep and one of them gets lost, what will he do? Won't he leave the ninety-nine others in the wilderness and go to search for the one that is lost until he finds it? [5]And when he has found it, he will joyfully carry it home on his shoulders. [6]When he arrives, he will call together his friends and neighbors, saying, 'Rejoice with

---

14:26-33 "Counting the cost" applies not only to the decision to follow Jesus, but it also speaks of our need to weigh the cost of recovery. A searching and fearless moral inventory of our life is required in both cases. If commitment to Jesus and recovery are more valuable to us than our compulsion, addiction, or dysfunctional behavior, then recovery in the fullest sense will be realized. If we cannot give up the pleasures of our sinful lifestyle, our recovery will be short-lived. We will compromise our commitment and remain enslaved to our dependency and its painful consequences.

15:3-10 The stories of the lost coin and the lost sheep show God's grace toward those who have strayed and his great joy in finding them. Though our past may be tarnished, we are extremely valuable in God's eyes, which is reflected symbolically by the coin and sheep (valuable commodities in that day). That the owner would stop everything to search for the lost sheep or coin shows how valuable we are to the one who owns us.

me because I have found my lost sheep.' [7]In the same way, there is more joy in heaven over one lost sinner who repents and returns to God than over ninety-nine others who are righteous and haven't strayed away!

Parable of the Lost Coin

[8]"Or suppose a woman has ten silver coins* and loses one. Won't she light a lamp and sweep the entire house and search carefully until she finds it? [9]And when she finds it, she will call in her friends and neighbors and say, 'Rejoice with me because I have found my lost coin.' [10]In the same way, there is joy in the presence of God's angels when even one sinner repents."

Parable of the Lost Son

[11]To illustrate the point further, Jesus told them this story: "A man had two sons. [12]The younger son told his father, 'I want my share of your estate now before you die.' So his father agreed to divide his wealth between his sons.

[13]"A few days later this younger son packed all his belongings and moved to a distant land, and there he wasted all his money in wild living. [14]About the time his money ran out, a great famine swept over the land, and he began to starve. [15]He persuaded a local farmer to hire him, and the man sent him into his fields to feed the pigs. [16]The young man became so hungry that even the pods he was feeding the pigs looked good to him. But no one gave him anything.

[17]"When he finally came to his senses, he said to himself, 'At home even the hired servants have food enough to spare, and here I am dying of hunger! [18]I will go home to my father and say, "Father, I have sinned against both heaven and you, [19]and I am no longer worthy of being called your son. Please take me on as a hired servant."'

[20]"So he returned home to his father. And while he was still a long way off, his father saw him coming. Filled with love and compassion, he ran to his son, embraced him, and kissed him. [21]His son said to him, 'Father, I have sinned against both heaven and you, and I am no longer worthy of being called your son.*'

[22]"But his father said to the servants, 'Quick! Bring the finest robe in the house and put it on him. Get a ring for his finger and sandals for his feet. [23]And kill the calf we have been fattening. We must celebrate with a feast, [24]for this son of mine was dead and has now returned to life. He was lost, but now he is found.' So the party began.

[25]"Meanwhile, the older son was in the fields working. When he returned home, he heard music and dancing in the house, [26]and he asked one of the servants what was going on. [27]'Your brother is back,' he was told, 'and your father has killed the fattened calf. We are celebrating because of his safe return.'

[28]"The older brother was angry and wouldn't go in. His father came out and begged him, [29]but he replied, 'All these years I've slaved for you and never once refused to do a single thing you told me to. And in all that time you never gave me even one young goat for a feast with my friends. [30]Yet when this son of yours comes back after

15:8 Greek *ten drachmas*. A drachma was the equivalent of a full day's wage. 15:21 Some manuscripts add *Please take me on as a hired servant.*

15:20-24 The father's great compassion for his returning son portrays God's response to a repentant sinner. Like the father in this story, God waits for the sinner to come to return to him of his own volition. Our heavenly Father does not wait for total amends or cleanup acts. (Those steps in the recovery process can wait.) The father in the story ran to his penitent son, hugged and kissed him, and threw a party—thus relieving him of all shame and guilt. In the same way, God actively seeks those of us who have strayed in our walk of faith as well as those who do not have a personal relationship with him.

15:25-30 God asks us to share his love with those who are helpless and lost and to carry the message of salvation and hope to them. The older brother's selfish attitude is shown to be sinful and self-centered. He represents the religious leadership of that time, as well as those of us who still cling to our own self-sufficiency. The father in this story demonstrates God's willingness to accept repentant sinners. God desires our restoration, whether the people around us like it or not. He also wants to use us to support, not hinder, fellow strugglers in the recovery process.

16:1-13 This story teaches the importance of using our material possessions to help bring eternal life and spiritual blessing to others. If the shrewd accountant is commended for cleverly using his talent for winning friends and influencing people, how much more the honest steward who dedicates all to God. Using material possessions and God-given talent merely for personal enjoyment, with no concern for others, is wrong. That may mean that our possessions have possessed us or that our goods have become our gods. Serving God alone will lead us to recovery.

squandering your money on prostitutes, you celebrate by killing the fattened calf!'

³¹"His father said to him, 'Look, dear son, you have always stayed by me, and everything I have is yours. ³²We had to celebrate this happy day. For your brother was dead and has come back to life! He was lost, but now he is found!'"

CHAPTER 16
Parable of the Shrewd Manager
Jesus told this story to his disciples: "There was a certain rich man who had a manager handling his affairs. One day a report came that the manager was wasting his employer's money. ²So the employer called him in and said, 'What's this I hear about you? Get your report in order, because you are going to be fired.'

³"The manager thought to himself, 'Now what? My boss has fired me. I don't have the strength to dig ditches, and I'm too proud to beg. ⁴Ah, I know how to ensure that I'll have plenty of friends who will give me a home when I am fired.'

⁵"So he invited each person who owed money to his employer to come and discuss the situation. He asked the first one, 'How much do you owe him?' ⁶The man replied, 'I owe him 800 gallons of olive oil.' So the manager told him, 'Take the bill and quickly change it to 400 gallons.*'

⁷"'And how much do you owe my employer?' he asked the next man. 'I owe him 1,000 bushels of wheat,' was the reply. 'Here,' the manager said, 'take the bill and change it to 800 bushels.*'

⁸"The rich man had to admire the dishonest rascal for being so shrewd. And it is true that the children of this world are more shrewd in dealing with the world around them than are the children of the light. ⁹Here's the lesson: Use your worldly resources to benefit others and make friends. Then, when your earthly possessions are gone, they will welcome you to an eternal home.*

¹⁰"If you are faithful in little things, you will be faithful in large ones. But if you are dishonest in little things, you won't be honest with greater responsibilities. ¹¹And if you are untrustworthy about worldly wealth, who will trust you with the true riches of heaven? ¹²And if you are not faithful with other people's things, why should you be trusted with things of your own?

16:6 Greek 100 baths . . . 50 [baths]. 16:7 Greek 100 korous . . . 80 [korous]. 16:9 Or you will be welcomed into eternal homes.

STEP 2

Restoration
BIBLE READING: Luke 15:11-24

We came to believe that a Power greater than ourselves could restore us to sanity.
In the natural progression of addiction, life degenerates. In one way or another, many of us wake up one day to realize that we are living like an animal. How true this is depends on the nature of our addiction. Some of us may be living like an animal in terms of our physical surroundings. Others of us may be a slave to our animal passions—powerful emotions that dehumanize us and others.

A young man took an early inheritance and traveled away from home. When the money was spent, the women just a memory, and the "high" long gone, he resorted to slopping pigs to earn a meager living. When he became so hungry that he eyed the pigs' slop with envy, he realized he had a problem. "When he finally came to his senses, he said to himself, 'At home even the hired servants have food enough to spare, and here I am dying of hunger! I will go home to my father. . . .' So he returned home to his father. And while he was still a long way off, his father saw him coming. Filled with love and compassion, he ran to his son, embraced him, and kissed him" (Luke 15:17-18, 20).

The fact that we are able to recognize our life as degenerate or insane proves that there is hope for a better way of life. We are reminded of times when life was good, and we long to have that goodness restored. When we turn to God, who is powerful enough to help us build something better, we will discover that his power can restore us to sanity. *Turn to page 1431, Romans 1.*

¹³"No one can serve two masters. For you will hate one and love the other; you will be devoted to one and despise the other. You cannot serve both God and money."

¹⁴The Pharisees, who dearly loved their money, heard all this and scoffed at him. ¹⁵Then he said to them, "You like to appear righteous in public, but God knows your hearts. What this world honors is detestable in the sight of God.

¹⁶"Until John the Baptist, the law of Moses and the messages of the prophets were your guides. But now the Good News of the Kingdom of God is preached, and everyone is eager to get in.* ¹⁷But that doesn't mean that the law has lost its force. It is easier for heaven and earth to disappear than for the smallest point of God's law to be overturned.

¹⁸"For example, a man who divorces his wife and marries someone else commits adultery. And anyone who marries a woman divorced from her husband commits adultery."

Parable of the Rich Man and Lazarus

¹⁹Jesus said, "There was a certain rich man who was splendidly clothed in purple and fine linen and who lived each day in luxury. ²⁰At his gate lay a poor man named Lazarus who was covered with sores. ²¹As Lazarus lay there longing for scraps from the rich man's table, the dogs would come and lick his open sores.

²²"Finally, the poor man died and was carried by the angels to be with Abraham.* The rich man also died and was buried, ²³and his soul went to the place of the dead.* There, in torment, he saw Abraham in the far distance with Lazarus at his side.

²⁴"The rich man shouted, 'Father Abraham, have some pity! Send Lazarus over here to dip the tip of his finger in water and cool my tongue. I am in anguish in these flames.'

²⁵"But Abraham said to him, 'Son, remember that during your lifetime you had everything you wanted, and Lazarus had nothing. So now he is here being comforted, and you are in anguish. ²⁶And besides, there is a great chasm separating us. No one can cross over to you from here, and no one can cross over to us from there.'

²⁷"Then the rich man said, 'Please, Father Abraham, at least send him to my father's home. ²⁸For I have five brothers, and I want him to warn them so they don't end up in this place of torment.'

²⁹"But Abraham said, 'Moses and the prophets have warned them. Your brothers can read what they wrote.'

³⁰"The rich man replied, 'No, Father Abraham! But if someone is sent to them from the dead, then they will repent of their sins and turn to God.'

³¹"But Abraham said, 'If they won't listen to Moses and the prophets, they won't be persuaded even if someone rises from the dead.'"

CHAPTER 17
Teachings about Forgiveness and Faith

One day Jesus said to his disciples, "There will always be temptations to sin, but what sorrow awaits the person who does the tempting! ²It would be better to be thrown into the sea with a millstone hung around your neck than to cause one of these little ones to fall into sin. ³So watch yourselves!

"If another believer* sins, rebuke that per-

16:16 Or *everyone is urged to enter in.* 16:22 Greek *into Abraham's bosom.* 16:23 Greek *to Hades.* 17:3 Greek *If your brother.*

16:19-31 Here we see the consequences of selfishness. Insulated by all the material comforts of life, this rich man never took inventory of his deepest needs and sins. Because he was hardhearted and selfish, refusing to feed the beggar Lazarus, he was consigned to hell. Lazarus, on the other hand, lacked basic material needs and suffered physical pain in his lifetime, but he was prepared for eternity. Death proved to be the great equalizer, effecting a reversal of fortune for these two. God wants us to have the proper attitude toward money and possessions and to use them unselfishly to help others.

17:1-4 Knowing when to forgive and when to confront is critical to the recovery process. Jesus taught that forgiveness is to be freely and frequently extended to others with no strings attached. On the other hand, the recovery process sometimes calls for tough love. If our friends are clearly acting counter to God's Word, we need to confront them for their own good. Woe to the person, however, who tempts a person in recovery. Strong drink or drugs, for example, should never be offered to people in recovery. Those who offer such temptations will pay dearly when they stand before God.

17:11-19 These ten lepers illustrate Jesus' great compassion for the hurting and his desire to make them whole. Only one of the ten lepers returned to say thanks, and that one was a Samaritan. In recovery most people will not appreciate our efforts to intervene on their behalf. Those few who are grateful are the faithful ones who get well.

son; then if there is repentance, forgive. [4]Even if that person wrongs you seven times a day and each time turns again and asks forgiveness, you must forgive."

[5]The apostles said to the Lord, "Show us how to increase our faith."

[6]The Lord answered, "If you had faith even as small as a mustard seed, you could say to this mulberry tree, 'May you be uprooted and thrown into the sea,' and it would obey you!

[7]"When a servant comes in from plowing or taking care of sheep, does his master say, 'Come in and eat with me'? [8]No, he says, 'Prepare my meal, put on your apron, and serve me while I eat. Then you can eat later.' [9]And does the master thank the servant for doing what he was told to do? Of course not. [10]In the same way, when you obey me you should say, 'We are unworthy servants who have simply done our duty.'"

Ten Healed of Leprosy

[11]As Jesus continued on toward Jerusalem, he reached the border between Galilee and Samaria. [12]As he entered a village there, ten lepers stood at a distance, [13]crying out, "Jesus, Master, have mercy on us!"

[14]He looked at them and said, "Go show yourselves to the priests."* And as they went, they were cleansed of their leprosy.

[15]One of them, when he saw that he was healed, came back to Jesus, shouting, "Praise God!" [16]He fell to the ground at Jesus' feet, thanking him for what he had done. This man was a Samaritan.

[17]Jesus asked, "Didn't I heal ten men? Where are the other nine? [18]Has no one returned to give glory to God except this foreigner?" [19]And Jesus said to the man, "Stand up and go. Your faith has healed you.*"

The Coming of the Kingdom

[20]One day the Pharisees asked Jesus, "When will the Kingdom of God come?"

Jesus replied, "The Kingdom of God can't be detected by visible signs.* [21]You won't be able to say, 'Here it is!' or 'It's over there!' For the Kingdom of God is already among you.*"

[22]Then he said to his disciples, "The time is coming when you will long to see the day when the Son of Man returns,* but you won't see it. [23]People will tell you, 'Look, there is the Son of Man,' or 'Here he is,' but

17:14 See Lev 14:2-32. 17:19 Or *Your faith has saved you.* 17:20 Or *by your speculations.* 17:21 Or *is within you,* or *is in your grasp.* 17:22 Or *long for even one day with the Son of Man.* "Son of Man" is a title Jesus used for himself.

FAITH

READ LUKE 17:1-10

How many times have we wished that we could overcome the addiction or compulsion that keeps us in bondage? We know what it is like to struggle with the effects of addiction and the craziness this brings to our life. We may feel despair and wonder if there really is any way out of the insanity of our current circumstances. Maybe our plight is impossible, at least without God's help, but faith can make even the impossible happen.

"The apostles said to the Lord, 'Show us how to increase our faith.' The Lord answered, 'If you had faith even as small as a mustard seed, you could say to this mulberry tree, "May you be uprooted and thrown into the sea," and it would obey you!'" (Luke 17:5-6). Matthew also recorded Jesus' words: "I tell you the truth, if you had faith even as small as a mustard seed, you could say to this mountain, 'Move from here to there,' and it would move. Nothing would be impossible" (Matthew 17:20).

Faith is a mysterious commodity. Jesus says that if we have faith, real faith, it only takes a small amount to make a big difference. We may be exercising faith without even realizing it. It takes faith to believe that a Power greater than ourself could restore us to sanity. It takes faith to work through the steps of a recovery program. It is comforting to know that God only needs a tiny bit of faith in order to work in powerful ways to restore our sanity. ***Turn to page 1331, Luke 22.***

don't go out and follow them. [24]For as the lightning flashes and lights up the sky from one end to the other, so it will be on the day* when the Son of Man comes. [25]But first the Son of Man must suffer terribly* and be rejected by this generation.

[26]"When the Son of Man returns, it will be like it was in Noah's day. [27]In those days, the people enjoyed banquets and parties and weddings right up to the time Noah entered his boat and the flood came and destroyed them all.

[28]"And the world will be as it was in the days of Lot. People went about their daily business—eating and drinking, buying and selling, farming and building—[29]until the morning Lot left Sodom. Then fire and burning sulfur rained down from heaven and destroyed them all. [30]Yes, it will be 'business as usual' right up to the day when the Son of Man is revealed. [31]On that day a person out on the deck of a roof must not go down into the house to pack. A person out in the field must not return home. [32]Remember what happened to Lot's wife! [33]If you cling to your life, you will lose it, and if you let your life go, you will save it. [34]That night two people will be asleep in one bed; one will be taken, the other left. [35]Two women will be grinding flour together at the mill; one will be taken, the other left.*"

[37]"Where will this happen, Lord?"* the disciples asked.

Jesus replied, "Just as the gathering of vultures shows there is a carcass nearby, so these signs indicate that the end is near."*

CHAPTER 18
Parable of the Persistent Widow

One day Jesus told his disciples a story to show that they should always pray and never give up. [2]"There was a judge in a certain city," he said, "who neither feared God nor cared about people. [3]A widow of that city came to him repeatedly, saying, 'Give me justice in this dispute with my enemy.' [4]The judge ignored her for a while, but finally he said to himself, 'I don't fear God or care about people, [5]but this woman is driving me crazy. I'm going to see that she gets justice, because she is wearing me out with her constant requests!'"

[6]Then the Lord said, "Learn a lesson from this unjust judge. [7]Even he rendered a just decision in the end. So don't you think God will surely give justice to his chosen people who cry out to him day and night? Will he keep putting them off? [8]I tell you, he will grant justice to them quickly! But when the Son of Man* returns, how many will he find on the earth who have faith?"

Parable of the Pharisee and Tax Collector

[9]Then Jesus told this story to some who had great confidence in their own righteousness and scorned everyone else: [10]"Two men went to the Temple to pray. One was a Pharisee, and the other was a despised tax collector. [11]The Pharisee stood by himself and prayed this prayer*: 'I thank you, God, that I am not a sinner like everyone else. For I don't cheat, I don't sin, and I don't commit adultery. I'm certainly not like that tax collector! [12]I fast twice a week, and I give you a tenth of my income.'

[13]"But the tax collector stood at a distance and dared not even lift his eyes to heaven as he prayed. Instead, he beat his chest in sorrow, saying, 'O God, be merciful to me, for I am a sinner.' [14]I tell you, this sinner, not the Pharisee, returned home justified before God. For those who exalt themselves will be humbled, and those who humble themselves will be exalted."

17:24 Some manuscripts do not include *on the day*. 17:25 Or *suffer many things*. 17:35 Some manuscripts add verse 36, *Two men will be working in the field; one will be taken, the other left*. Compare Matt 24:40. 17:37a Greek *"Where, Lord?"* 17:37b Greek *"Wherever the carcass is, the vultures gather."* 18:8 "Son of Man" is a title Jesus used for himself. 18:11 Some manuscripts read *stood and prayed this prayer to himself*.

18:1-8 Many of us have experienced injustice at the hands of authority figures, such as family-court judges, mean bosses, or parole officers. This story contrasts God with the unfair judge and makes the point that even if life is unfair, God is fair. If an evil judge finally answers the pleas of a persistent widow, how much more will a just God respond to those in need who pray to him in faith. When trials and challenges make life seem unfair, we can still trust God to deliver us. Seeking God in prayer requires patience and persistence, but he always answers.

18:15-17 Children trust naturally; God wants our relationship with him to be driven by that kind of simple trust. Any other kind of "faith" is inappropriate, unnatural, and ineffective. If we are unable to trust, it may help to understand the hurts in our past that make it so difficult to do this. Childlike faith is itself a gift from God that may take time for him to restore in us, especially if we have been abused (spiritually, emotionally, sexually, or physically). In recovery we are told to keep it simple; a simple faith in an almighty God is necessary for a successful recovery.

Jesus Blesses the Children

¹⁵One day some parents brought their little children to Jesus so he could touch and bless them. But when the disciples saw this, they scolded the parents for bothering him.

¹⁶Then Jesus called for the children and said to the disciples, "Let the children come to me. Don't stop them! For the Kingdom of God belongs to those who are like these children. ¹⁷I tell you the truth, anyone who doesn't receive the Kingdom of God like a child will never enter it."

The Rich Man

¹⁸Once a religious leader asked Jesus this question: "Good Teacher, what should I do to inherit eternal life?"

¹⁹"Why do you call me good?" Jesus asked him. "Only God is truly good. ²⁰But to answer your question, you know the commandments: 'You must not commit adultery. You must not murder. You must not steal. You must not testify falsely. Honor your father and mother.'*"

²¹The man replied, "I've obeyed all these commandments since I was young."

²²When Jesus heard his answer, he said, "There is still one thing you haven't done. Sell all your possessions and give the money to the poor, and you will have treasure in heaven. Then come, follow me."

²³But when the man heard this he became very sad, for he was very rich.

²⁴When Jesus saw this,* he said, "How hard it is for the rich to enter the Kingdom of God! ²⁵In fact, it is easier for a camel to go through the eye of a needle than for a rich person to enter the Kingdom of God!"

²⁶Those who heard this said, "Then who in the world can be saved?"

²⁷He replied, "What is impossible for people is possible with God."

²⁸Peter said, "We've left our homes to follow you."

²⁹"Yes," Jesus replied, "and I assure you that everyone who has given up house or wife or brothers or parents or children, for the sake of the Kingdom of God, ³⁰will be repaid many times over in this life, and will have eternal life in the world to come."

Jesus Again Predicts His Death

³¹Taking the twelve disciples aside, Jesus said, "Listen, we're going up to Jerusalem, where all the predictions of the prophets concerning the Son of Man will come true. ³²He will

18:20 Exod 20:12-16; Deut 5:16-20. 18:24 Some manuscripts read *When Jesus saw how sad the man was.*

STEP 7

A Humble Heart

BIBLE READING: Luke 18:10-14

We humbly asked him to remove our shortcomings.

After examining our life closely (as we did in Steps Four, Five, and Six), we may feel cut off from God. Considering the scope of what we have done, we may feel unworthy to ask God for anything. Maybe our sinful behaviors are despised as the lowest kind of evil by those whom we consider respectable. We may struggle with self-hatred. Our genuine remorse may cause us to wonder if we even dare approach God to ask for his help.

God welcomes us, even when we feel this way. Jesus told this story: "Two men went to the Temple to pray. One was a Pharisee, and the other was a despised tax collector. The Pharisee stood by himself and prayed this prayer: 'I thank you, God, that I am not a sinner like everyone else. For I don't cheat, I don't sin, I don't commit adultery. I'm certainly not like that tax collector! I fast twice a week, and I give you a tenth of my income.' But the tax collector stood at a distance and dared not even lift his eyes to heaven as he prayed. Instead, he beat his chest in sorrow, saying, 'O God, be merciful to me, for I am a sinner.' I tell you, this sinner, not the Pharisee, returned home justified before God. For those who exalt themselves will be humbled, and those who humble themselves will be exalted" (Luke 18:10-14).

Tax collectors were among the most despised citizens in Jewish society. Pharisees, on the other hand, commanded the highest respect. Jesus purposely chose this illustration to show that it doesn't matter where we fit in society's hierarchy. It is the humble heart that opens the door to God's forgiveness. *Turn to page 1437, Romans 3.*

be handed over to the Romans,* and he will be mocked, treated shamefully, and spit upon. [33]They will flog him with a whip and kill him, but on the third day he will rise again."

[34]But they didn't understand any of this. The significance of his words was hidden from them, and they failed to grasp what he was talking about.

Jesus Heals a Blind Beggar

[35]As Jesus approached Jericho, a blind beggar was sitting beside the road. [36]When he heard the noise of a crowd going past, he asked what was happening. [37]They told him that Jesus the Nazarene* was going by. [38]So he began shouting, "Jesus, Son of David, have mercy on me!"

[39]"Be quiet!" the people in front yelled at him.

But he only shouted louder, "Son of David, have mercy on me!"

[40]When Jesus heard him, he stopped and ordered that the man be brought to him. As the man came near, Jesus asked him, [41]"What do you want me to do for you?"

"Lord," he said, "I want to see!"

[42]And Jesus said, "All right, receive your sight! Your faith has healed you." [43]Instantly the man could see, and he followed Jesus, praising God. And all who saw it praised God, too.

CHAPTER 19
Jesus and Zacchaeus

Jesus entered Jericho and made his way through the town. [2]There was a man there named Zacchaeus. He was the chief tax collector in the region, and he had become very rich. [3]He tried to get a look at Jesus, but he was too short to see over the crowd. [4]So he ran ahead and climbed a sycamore-fig tree beside the road, for Jesus was going to pass that way.

[5]When Jesus came by, he looked up at Zacchaeus and called him by name. "Zacchaeus!" he said. "Quick, come down! I must be a guest in your home today."

[6]Zacchaeus quickly climbed down and took Jesus to his house in great excitement and joy. [7]But the people were displeased. "He has gone to be the guest of a notorious sinner," they grumbled.

[8]Meanwhile, Zacchaeus stood before the Lord and said, "I will give half my wealth to the poor, Lord, and if I have cheated people on their taxes, I will give them back four times as much!"

[9]Jesus responded, "Salvation has come to this home today, for this man has shown himself to be a true son of Abraham. [10]For the Son of Man* came to seek and save those who are lost."

Parable of the Ten Servants

[11]The crowd was listening to everything Jesus said. And because he was nearing Jerusalem, he told them a story to correct the impression that the Kingdom of God would begin right away. [12]He said, "A nobleman was called away to a distant empire to be crowned king and then return. [13]Before he left, he called together ten of his servants and divided among them ten pounds of silver,* saying, 'Invest this for me while I am gone.' [14]But his people hated him and sent a delegation after him to say, 'We do not want him to be our king.'

[15]"After he was crowned king, he returned and called in the servants to whom he had given the money. He wanted to find out what their profits were. [16]The first servant reported, 'Master, I invested your money and made ten times the original amount!'

18:32 Greek *the Gentiles.* 18:37 Or *Jesus of Nazareth.* 19:10 "Son of Man" is a title Jesus used for himself.
19:13 Greek *ten minas;* one mina was worth about three months' wages.

18:31-34 Jesus predicted the suffering he would endure on his way to the cross. While his pain and disgrace would be extreme, he was willing to accept it as a necessary part of the process toward the goal of salvation. In recovery the process of spiritual growth often involves pain and sacrifice. Reversing patterns of sinful or addictive behavior can be extremely difficult and discouraging; so it is essential that we keep our focus on the goal—recovery—which is worth the sacrifice.

19:11-27 This story teaches stewardship—accountability before God to use wisely the gifts, abilities, and possessions he has entrusted to us. Wisely using what God has given will result in generous rewards; refusing to do so will bring a stern reprimand from God. Whatever opportunities and resources God gives us—time, money, talents, or relationships—we are to use in the lives of others. After years of pain and devastation, we may wonder what we have to offer. Our story of deliverance may be all someone needs to take a step toward God and recovery. Sharing ourself with others may help save the life of a needy person.

¹⁷" 'Well done!' the king exclaimed. 'You are a good servant. You have been faithful with the little I entrusted to you, so you will be governor of ten cities as your reward.'

¹⁸"The next servant reported, 'Master, I invested your money and made five times the original amount.'

¹⁹" 'Well done!' the king said. 'You will be governor over five cities.'

²⁰"But the third servant brought back only the original amount of money and said, 'Master, I hid your money and kept it safe. ²¹I was afraid because you are a hard man to deal with, taking what isn't yours and harvesting crops you didn't plant.'

²²" 'You wicked servant!' the king roared. 'Your own words condemn you. If you knew that I'm a hard man who takes what isn't mine and harvests crops I didn't plant, ²³why didn't you deposit my money in the bank? At least I could have gotten some interest on it.'

²⁴"Then, turning to the others standing nearby, the king ordered, 'Take the money from this servant, and give it to the one who has ten pounds.'

²⁵" 'But, master,' they said, 'he already has ten pounds!'

²⁶" 'Yes,' the king replied, 'and to those who use well what they are given, even more will be given. But from those who do nothing, even what little they have will be taken away. ²⁷And as for these enemies of mine who didn't want me to be their king—bring them in and execute them right here in front of me.'"

Jesus' Triumphant Entry

²⁸After telling this story, Jesus went on toward Jerusalem, walking ahead of his disciples. ²⁹As he came to the towns of Bethphage and Bethany on the Mount of Olives, he sent two disciples ahead. ³⁰"Go into that village over there," he told them. "As you enter it, you will see a young donkey tied there that no one has ever ridden. Untie it and bring it here. ³¹If anyone asks, 'Why are you untying that colt?' just say, 'The Lord needs it.'"

³²So they went and found the colt, just as Jesus had said. ³³And sure enough, as they were untying it, the owners asked them, "Why are you untying that colt?"

³⁴And the disciples simply replied, "The Lord needs it." ³⁵So they brought the colt to Jesus and threw their garments over it for him to ride on.

³⁶As he rode along, the crowds spread out

STEP 9

From Taker to Giver

BIBLE READING: Luke 19:1-10

We made direct amends to such people wherever possible, except when to do so would injure them or others.

When we are feeding our addiction, it is easy to become consumed by our own needs. Nothing matters except getting what we crave so desperately. We may have to lie, cheat, kill, or steal; but that doesn't stop us. Within our family and community we become known as "takers," trampling over the feelings and needs of others.

Zacchaeus had the same problem. His hunger for riches drove him to betray his own people by collecting taxes for the oppressive Roman government. He was hated by his own people and considered a thief, an extortioner, and a traitor. But when Jesus reached out to him, he changed dramatically. "Meanwhile, Zacchaeus stood before the Lord and said, 'I will give half my wealth to the poor, Lord, and if I have cheated people on their taxes, I will give them back four times as much!' Jesus responded, 'Salvation has come to this home today'" (Luke 19:8-9).

Zacchaeus went beyond just paying back what he had taken. For the first time in a long time, he saw the needs of others and wanted to be a "giver." Making amends includes paying back what we have taken whenever possible. Some of us may even seize the opportunity to go further, giving more than we took. As we begin to see the needs of others and respond by choice, our self-esteem will rise. We will realize that we can give to others, instead of just being a burden. *Turn to page 1575, Philemon 1.*

their garments on the road ahead of him. [37]When he reached the place where the road started down the Mount of Olives, all of his followers began to shout and sing as they walked along, praising God for all the wonderful miracles they had seen.

[38] "Blessings on the King who comes in the name of the LORD!

Peace in heaven, and glory in highest heaven!"*

[39]But some of the Pharisees among the crowd said, "Teacher, rebuke your followers for saying things like that!"

[40]He replied, "If they kept quiet, the stones along the road would burst into cheers!"

Jesus Weeps over Jerusalem

[41]But as he came closer to Jerusalem and saw the city ahead, he began to weep. [42]"How I wish today that you of all people would understand the way to peace. But now it is too late, and peace is hidden from your eyes. [43]Before long your enemies will build ramparts against your walls and encircle you and close in on you from every side. [44]They will crush you into the ground, and your children with you. Your enemies will not leave a single stone in place, because you did not recognize it when God visited you.*"

Jesus Clears the Temple

[45]Then Jesus entered the Temple and began to drive out the people selling animals for sacrifices. [46]He said to them, "The Scriptures declare, 'My Temple will be a house of prayer,' but you have turned it into a den of thieves."*

[47]After that, he taught daily in the Temple, but the leading priests, the teachers of religious law, and the other leaders of the people began planning how to kill him. [48]But they could think of nothing, because all the people hung on every word he said.

CHAPTER 20
The Authority of Jesus Challenged

One day as Jesus was teaching the people and preaching the Good News in the Temple, the leading priests, the teachers of religious law, and the elders came up to him. [2]They demanded, "By what authority are you doing all these things? Who gave you the right?"

[3]"Let me ask you a question first," he replied. [4]"Did John's authority to baptize come from heaven, or was it merely human?"

[5]They talked it over among themselves. "If we say it was from heaven, he will ask why we didn't believe John. [6]But if we say it was merely human, the people will stone us because they are convinced John was a prophet." [7]So they finally replied that they didn't know.

[8]And Jesus responded, "Then I won't tell you by what authority I do these things."

Parable of the Evil Farmers

[9]Now Jesus turned to the people again and told them this story: "A man planted a vineyard, leased it to tenant farmers, and moved to another country to live for several years. [10]At the time of the grape harvest, he sent one of his servants to collect his share of the crop. But the farmers attacked the servant, beat him up, and sent him back empty-handed. [11]So the owner sent another servant, but they also insulted him, beat him up, and sent him away empty-handed. [12]A third man was sent, and they wounded him and chased him away.

[13]" 'What will I do?' the owner asked himself. 'I know! I'll send my cherished son. Surely they will respect him.'

[14]"But when the tenant farmers saw his son, they said to each other, 'Here comes the heir to this estate. Let's kill him and get the

---

19:38 Pss 118:26; 148:1. 19:44 Greek *did not recognize the time of your visitation,* a reference to the Messiah's coming. 19:46 Isa 56:7; Jer 7:11.

19:45-48 The people's worship had become so dysfunctional that Jesus became angry and drove the merchants out of God's Temple. Correcting this gross perversion was not appreciated and did not produce the desired change in the worshipers. Instead, the priests, religious teachers, and leaders were angry and desired vengeance. Change, even much-needed change for the better, is resisted by those in denial.

20:9-18 This story is unmistakably blunt. No one likes being confronted with their denial and blindness. The farmers rejected the messages of the servants and killed the owner's son. Jesus' audience, especially the priests and religious teachers, did the same; they didn't like the message, so they killed the messenger (Jesus). When we deny the truth, there is not much God or others can do. Sometimes the truth can penetrate our denial when someone speaks plainly but indirectly as Nathan did with David by telling him a story, which motivated David to repent of his sin (2 Samuel 12). Yet some people in denial, like the ones Jesus was speaking to, will resist to their dying day.

estate for ourselves!' ¹⁵So they dragged him out of the vineyard and murdered him.

"What do you suppose the owner of the vineyard will do to them?" Jesus asked. ¹⁶"I'll tell you—he will come and kill those farmers and lease the vineyard to others."

"How terrible that such a thing should ever happen," his listeners protested.

¹⁷Jesus looked at them and said, "Then what does this Scripture mean?

'The stone that the builders rejected
  has now become the cornerstone.'*

¹⁸Everyone who stumbles over that stone will be broken to pieces, and it will crush anyone it falls on."

¹⁹The teachers of religious law and the leading priests wanted to arrest Jesus immediately because they realized he was telling the story against them—they were the wicked farmers. But they were afraid of the people's reaction.

Taxes for Caesar

²⁰Watching for their opportunity, the leaders sent spies pretending to be honest men. They tried to get Jesus to say something that could be reported to the Roman governor so he would arrest Jesus. ²¹"Teacher," they said, "we know that you speak and teach what is right and are not influenced by what others think. You teach the way of God truthfully. ²²Now tell us—is it right for us to pay taxes to Caesar or not?"

²³He saw through their trickery and said, ²⁴"Show me a Roman coin.* Whose picture and title are stamped on it?"

"Caesar's," they replied.

²⁵"Well then," he said, "give to Caesar what belongs to Caesar, and give to God what belongs to God."

²⁶So they failed to trap him by what he said in front of the people. Instead, they were amazed by his answer, and they became silent.

Discussion about Resurrection

²⁷Then Jesus was approached by some Sadducees—religious leaders who say there is no resurrection from the dead. ²⁸They posed this question: "Teacher, Moses gave us a law that if a man dies, leaving a wife but no children, his brother should marry the widow and have a child who will carry on the brother's name.* ²⁹Well, suppose there were seven brothers. The oldest one married and then died without children. ³⁰So the second brother married the widow, but he also died. ³¹Then the third brother married her. This continued with all seven of them, who died without children. ³²Finally, the woman also died. ³³So tell us, whose wife will she be in the resurrection? For all seven were married to her!"

³⁴Jesus replied, "Marriage is for people here on earth. ³⁵But in the age to come, those worthy of being raised from the dead will neither marry nor be given in marriage. ³⁶And they will never die again. In this respect they will be like angels. They are children of God and children of the resurrection.

³⁷"But now, as to whether the dead will be raised—even Moses proved this when he wrote about the burning bush. Long after Abraham, Isaac, and Jacob had died, he referred to the Lord* as 'the God of Abraham, the God of Isaac, and the God of Jacob.'* ³⁸So he is the God of the living, not the dead, for they are all alive to him."

³⁹"Well said, Teacher!" remarked some of the teachers of religious law who were standing there. ⁴⁰And then no one dared to ask him any more questions.

Whose Son Is the Messiah?

⁴¹Then Jesus presented them with a question. "Why is it," he asked, "that the Messiah is said to be the son of David? ⁴²For David himself wrote in the book of Psalms:

'The LORD said to my Lord,
  Sit in the place of honor at my right
    hand
⁴³until I humble your enemies,
  making them a footstool under your
    feet.'*

⁴⁴Since David called the Messiah 'Lord,' how can the Messiah be his son?"

⁴⁵Then, with the crowds listening, he turned to his disciples and said, ⁴⁶"Beware of these teachers of religious law! For they like to parade around in flowing robes and love to receive respectful greetings as they walk in the marketplaces. And how they love the seats of honor in the synagogues and the head table at banquets. ⁴⁷Yet they shamelessly cheat widows out of their property and then pretend to be pious by making long prayers in public. Because of this, they will be severely punished."

20:17 Ps 118:22. 20:24 Greek *a denarius*. 20:28 See Deut 25:5-6. 20:37a Greek *when he wrote about the bush. He referred to the Lord.* 20:37b Exod 3:6. 20:42-43 Ps 110:1.

CHAPTER 21

The Widow's Offering

While Jesus was in the Temple, he watched the rich people dropping their gifts in the collection box. 2Then a poor widow came by and dropped in two small coins.*

3"I tell you the truth," Jesus said, "this poor widow has given more than all the rest of them. 4For they have given a tiny part of their surplus, but she, poor as she is, has given everything she has."

Jesus Foretells the Future

5Some of his disciples began talking about the majestic stonework of the Temple and the memorial decorations on the walls. But Jesus said, 6"The time is coming when all these things will be completely demolished. Not one stone will be left on top of another!"

7"Teacher," they asked, "when will all this happen? What sign will show us that these things are about to take place?"

8He replied, "Don't let anyone mislead you, for many will come in my name, claiming, 'I am the Messiah,'* and saying, 'The time has come!' But don't believe them. 9And when you hear of wars and insurrections, don't panic. Yes, these things must take place first, but the end won't follow immediately." 10Then he added, "Nation will go to war against nation, and kingdom against kingdom. 11There will be great earthquakes, and there will be famines and plagues in many lands, and there will be terrifying things and great miraculous signs from heaven.

12"But before all this occurs, there will be a time of great persecution. You will be dragged into synagogues and prisons, and you will stand trial before kings and governors because you are my followers. 13But this will be your opportunity to tell them about

me.* 14So don't worry in advance about how to answer the charges against you, 15for I will give you the right words and such wisdom that none of your opponents will be able to reply or refute you! 16Even those closest to you—your parents, brothers, relatives, and friends—will betray you. They will even kill some of you. 17And everyone will hate you because you are my followers.* 18But not a hair of your head will perish! 19By standing firm, you will win your souls.

20"And when you see Jerusalem surrounded by armies, then you will know that the time of its destruction has arrived. 21Then those in Judea must flee to the hills. Those in Jerusalem must get out, and those out in the country should not return to the city. 22For those will be days of God's vengeance, and the prophetic words of the Scriptures will be fulfilled. 23How terrible it will be for pregnant women and for nursing mothers in those days. For there will be disaster in the land and great anger against this people. 24They will be killed by the sword or sent away as captives to all the nations of the world. And Jerusalem will be trampled down by the Gentiles until the period of the Gentiles comes to an end.

25"And there will be strange signs in the sun, moon, and stars. And here on earth the nations will be in turmoil, perplexed by the roaring seas and strange tides. 26People will be terrified at what they see coming upon the earth, for the powers in the heavens will be shaken. 27Then everyone will see the Son of Man* coming on a cloud with power and great glory.* 28So when all these things begin to happen, stand and look up, for your salvation is near!"

29Then he gave them this illustration: "Notice the fig tree, or any other tree. 30When the

---

21:2 Greek *two lepta* [the smallest of Jewish coins]. 21:8 Greek *claiming, 'I am.'* 21:13 Or *This will be your testimony against them.* 21:17 Greek *on account of my name.* 21:27a "Son of Man" is a title Jesus used for himself. 21:27b See Dan 7:13.

21:1-4 God has a unique standard by which he measures giving and givers. With God, attitude counts more than amount, so Jesus praised this widow. A generous person is not one who gives conveniently and comfortably out of abundance. A generous person in God's eyes risks all, sacrifices cheerfully, and gives without demanding attention or expecting a reward. Whether it's our time, talents, or money, God wants us to turn everything in our life over to his care. One small step in giving may become one giant leap toward recovery.

21:16-17 What happened to Jesus leading up to the cross and what would happen to his disciples afterward illustrate an important principle in recovery. Family members and friends are not always overjoyed at our changed life. Faith in Jesus, as well as freedom from sin and addiction, often threatens the status quo. Often those closest to us become the greatest hindrances to our healing and recovery as they resist what we know is best for us. As we become aware of this, we cannot allow them to impede our progress. In time they will discover that the recovery process is good for us and for them.

leaves come out, you know without being told that summer is near. ³¹In the same way, when you see all these things taking place, you can know that the Kingdom of God is near. ³²I tell you the truth, this generation will not pass from the scene until all these things have taken place. ³³Heaven and earth will disappear, but my words will never disappear.

³⁴"Watch out! Don't let your hearts be dulled by carousing and drunkenness, and by the worries of this life. Don't let that day catch you unaware, ³⁵like a trap. For that day will come upon everyone living on the earth. ³⁶Keep alert at all times. And pray that you might be strong enough to escape these coming horrors and stand before the Son of Man."

³⁷Every day Jesus went to the Temple to teach, and each evening he returned to spend the night on the Mount of Olives. ³⁸The crowds gathered at the Temple early each morning to hear him.

CHAPTER 22
Judas Agrees to Betray Jesus
The Festival of Unleavened Bread, which is also called Passover, was approaching. ²The leading priests and teachers of religious law were plotting how to kill Jesus, but they were afraid of the people's reaction.

³Then Satan entered into Judas Iscariot, who was one of the twelve disciples, ⁴and he went to the leading priests and captains of the Temple guard to discuss the best way to betray Jesus to them. ⁵They were delighted, and they promised to give him money. ⁶So he agreed and began looking for an opportunity to betray Jesus so they could arrest him when the crowds weren't around.

The Last Supper
⁷Now the Festival of Unleavened Bread arrived, when the Passover lamb is sacrificed. ⁸Jesus sent Peter and John ahead and said, "Go and prepare the Passover meal, so we can eat it together."

⁹"Where do you want us to prepare it?" they asked him.

¹⁰He replied, "As soon as you enter Jerusalem, a man carrying a pitcher of water will meet you. Follow him. At the house he enters, ¹¹say to the owner, 'The Teacher asks: Where is the guest room where I can eat the Passover meal with my disciples?' ¹²He will take you upstairs to a large room that is already set up. That is where you should prepare our meal." ¹³They went off to the city and found everything just as Jesus had said, and they prepared the Passover meal there.

¹⁴When the time came, Jesus and the apostles sat down together at the table.* ¹⁵Jesus said, "I have been very eager to eat this Passover meal with you before my suffering begins. ¹⁶For I tell you now that I won't eat this meal again until its meaning is fulfilled in the Kingdom of God."

¹⁷Then he took a cup of wine and gave thanks to God for it. Then he said, "Take this and share it among yourselves. ¹⁸For I will not drink wine again until the Kingdom of God has come."

¹⁹He took some bread and gave thanks to God for it. Then he broke it in pieces and gave it to the disciples, saying, "This is my body, which is given for you. Do this to remember me."

²⁰After supper he took another cup of wine and said, "This cup is the new covenant between God and his people—an agreement

22:14 Or *reclined together.*

21:34-36 This charge follows a lengthy prophecy about the coming days of destruction (21:5-31), and it illustrates the biblical purpose of prophecy. Prophecy is never given simply to satisfy the curiosity of those who wonder about God's plan for the future. Prophecy is primarily a call for believers to repent, stay alert, and prepare spiritually for the coming of God's Kingdom. As we await the triumphant return of Christ, or even the recovery of sanity, God warns about the dangers of being controlled by sin. We only fool ourself if we think we have all the time in the world to get ready. If we continue to put off recovery until tomorrow, one day tomorrow will not come!

22:3-6 At the deepest level, the brokenness, the bondage, and the uncontrolled nature of our life is due to Satan. Spiritual warfare plays itself out in personal relationships—in Judas's betrayal of Jesus and in the breakup of our own relationships. Spiritual warfare undermines and destroys relational boundaries and renders our life unmanageable. (Judas would later commit suicide.) But Satan's involvement does not excuse human sin, addiction, and betrayal; we are responsible for our behavior. God is in control of every situation. Jesus' death (at the hands of Satan) was part of God's plan all along. No matter how Satan harms us, God can use Satan's evil plans to work his good for us (Romans 8:28) when we trust and obey him.

confirmed with my blood, which is poured out as a sacrifice for you.*

²¹"But here at this table, sitting among us as a friend, is the man who will betray me. ²²For it has been determined that the Son of Man* must die. But what sorrow awaits the one who betrays him." ²³The disciples began to ask each other which of them would ever do such a thing.

²⁴Then they began to argue among themselves about who would be the greatest among them. ²⁵Jesus told them, "In this world the kings and great men lord it over their people, yet they are called 'friends of the people.' ²⁶But among you it will be different. Those who are the greatest among you should take the lowest rank, and the leader should be like a servant. ²⁷Who is more important, the one who sits at the table or the one who serves? The one who sits at the table, of course. But not here! For I am among you as one who serves.

²⁸"You have stayed with me in my time of trial. ²⁹And just as my Father has granted me a Kingdom, I now grant you the right ³⁰to eat and drink at my table in my Kingdom. And you will sit on thrones, judging the twelve tribes of Israel.

Jesus Predicts Peter's Denial

³¹"Simon, Simon, Satan has asked to sift each of you like wheat. ³²But I have pleaded in prayer for you, Simon, that your faith should not fail. So when you have repented and turned to me again, strengthen your brothers."

³³Peter said, "Lord, I am ready to go to prison with you, and even to die with you."

³⁴But Jesus said, "Peter, let me tell you something. Before the rooster crows tomorrow morning, you will deny three times that you even know me."

³⁵Then Jesus asked them, "When I sent you out to preach the Good News and you did not have money, a traveler's bag, or an extra pair of sandals, did you need anything?"

"No," they replied.

³⁶"But now," he said, "take your money and a traveler's bag. And if you don't have a sword, sell your cloak and buy one! ³⁷For the time has come for this prophecy about me to be fulfilled: 'He was counted among the rebels.'* Yes, everything written about me by the prophets will come true."

³⁸"Look, Lord," they replied, "we have two swords among us."

"That's enough," he said.

Jesus Prays on the Mount of Olives

³⁹Then, accompanied by the disciples, Jesus left the upstairs room and went as usual to the Mount of Olives. ⁴⁰There he told them, "Pray that you will not give in to temptation."

⁴¹He walked away, about a stone's throw, and knelt down and prayed, ⁴²"Father, if you are willing, please take this cup of suffering away from me. Yet I want your will to be done, not mine." ⁴³Then an angel from heaven appeared and strengthened him. ⁴⁴He prayed more fervently, and he was in such ag-

---

22:19-20 Some manuscripts do not include 22:19b-20, *which is given for you . . . which is poured out as a sacrifice for you.* 22:22 "Son of Man" is a title Jesus used for himself. 22:37 Isa 53:12.

22:24-30 This upper-room discourse contrasts Jesus' humility and servant's heart with the selfish intentions of his twelve closest followers. In going to the cross, Jesus showed his disciples what it meant to be a servant-leader. The disciples' desire for a special place at God's table was not what Jesus had intended to teach them. Jesus calls us to put the needs of others before our own and serve others rather than expecting to be served. Our life should be defined and motivated by humility.
22:39-46 Jesus' prayer on the Mount of Olives reflected the awesome task before him: He was about to shoulder the sins of the world. He persevered through fear and agony of spirit and submitted to God's sovereign will. His absolute commitment to God's will is an example for us to follow. Jesus could have selfishly seized the privileges of deity and avoided the cross (see Philippians 2:6-8), but he willingly delayed the gratification of heaven's glory to accomplish the task set before him by his Father. Although our challenges in life are not of this magnitude, God enables us to persevere through the tough stages of recovery to reap the rewards that follow.
22:54-62 Peter's denial of Jesus is a classic story of recovery. Although Peter believed he could never stoop so low (22:31-34), he denied Jesus completely when the heat was on. Peter disappointed Jesus and himself, but even then, all was not lost. His experience led to genuine sorrow and healthy repentance. Peter's threefold denial was followed by a threefold affirmation and his restoration to full-fledged service (John 21:15-19). Later Peter became the leading spokesman for the early church, powerfully proclaiming the message of the risen Christ. Only through God's complete forgiveness could Peter have so effectively recovered from the depths of despair.

ony of spirit that his sweat fell to the ground like great drops of blood.*

⁴⁵At last he stood up again and returned to the disciples, only to find them asleep, exhausted from grief. ⁴⁶"Why are you sleeping?" he asked them. "Get up and pray, so that you will not give in to temptation."

Jesus Is Betrayed and Arrested

⁴⁷But even as Jesus said this, a crowd approached, led by Judas, one of the twelve disciples. Judas walked over to Jesus to greet him with a kiss. ⁴⁸But Jesus said, "Judas, would you betray the Son of Man with a kiss?"

⁴⁹When the other disciples saw what was about to happen, they exclaimed, "Lord, should we fight? We brought the swords!" ⁵⁰And one of them struck at the high priest's slave, slashing off his right ear.

⁵¹But Jesus said, "No more of this." And he touched the man's ear and healed him.

⁵²Then Jesus spoke to the leading priests, the captains of the Temple guard, and the elders who had come for him. "Am I some dangerous revolutionary," he asked, "that you come with swords and clubs to arrest me? ⁵³Why didn't you arrest me in the Temple? I was there every day. But this is your moment, the time when the power of darkness reigns."

Peter Denies Jesus

⁵⁴So they arrested him and led him to the high priest's home. And Peter followed at a distance. ⁵⁵The guards lit a fire in the middle of the courtyard and sat around it, and Peter joined them there. ⁵⁶A servant girl noticed him in the firelight and began staring at him. Finally she said, "This man was one of Jesus' followers!"

⁵⁷But Peter denied it. "Woman," he said, "I don't even know him!"

⁵⁸After a while someone else looked at him and said, "You must be one of them!"

"No, man, I'm not!" Peter retorted.

⁵⁹About an hour later someone else insisted, "This must be one of them, because he is a Galilean, too."

⁶⁰But Peter said, "Man, I don't know what you are talking about." And immediately, while he was still speaking, the rooster crowed.

⁶¹At that moment the Lord turned and looked at Peter. Suddenly, the Lord's words flashed through Peter's mind: "Before the rooster crows tomorrow morning, you will deny three times that you even know me."

22:43-44 Verses 43 and 44 are not included in the most ancient manuscripts.

FAITH

READ LUKE 22:31-34

It is easy to lose faith when we are troubled. As we are buffeted about by the storms of life, we may feel like the faith we once had has slipped away. We may begin to feel anger toward God.

Simon Peter had his ups and downs with God. On the night Simon Peter would deny him, Jesus said to him, "Simon, Simon, Satan has asked to sift each of you like wheat. But I have pleaded in prayer for you, Simon, that your faith should not fail. So when you have repented and turned to me again, strengthen your brothers" (Luke 22:31-32).

Jesus pointed out that Simon had an assailant in the spiritual realm. Jesus knew Peter would be attacked and "sifted," but he also was confident that afterward Peter would return to God. Wheat is sifted by throwing it repeatedly into the air. The kernels are separated from the chaff as the lighter chaff is carried away by the wind. All that remain are the good, solid wheat kernels.

We should not be surprised that we face times when our faith seems to disappear. We may feel as if we are being ripped open and our faith is being blown away like chaff. But we needn't worry. We will find the core of our faith again. And when we do, we will be all the better for it— and better able to encourage others, too. *Turn to page 1355, John 8.*

[62]And Peter left the courtyard, weeping bitterly.

[63]The guards in charge of Jesus began mocking and beating him. [64]They blindfolded him and said, "Prophesy to us! Who hit you that time?" [65]And they hurled all sorts of terrible insults at him.

Jesus before the Council

[66]At daybreak all the elders of the people assembled, including the leading priests and the teachers of religious law. Jesus was led before this high council,* [67]and they said, "Tell us, are you the Messiah?"

But he replied, "If I tell you, you won't believe me. [68]And if I ask you a question, you won't answer. [69]But from now on the Son of Man will be seated in the place of power at God's right hand.*"

[70]They all shouted, "So, are you claiming to be the Son of God?"

And he replied, "You say that I am."

[71]"Why do we need other witnesses?" they said. "We ourselves heard him say it."

CHAPTER 23
Jesus' Trial before Pilate

Then the entire council took Jesus to Pilate, the Roman governor. [2]They began to state their case: "This man has been leading our people astray by telling them not to pay their taxes to the Roman government and by claiming he is the Messiah, a king."

[3]So Pilate asked him, "Are you the king of the Jews?"

Jesus replied, "You have said it."

[4]Pilate turned to the leading priests and to the crowd and said, "I find nothing wrong with this man!"

[5]Then they became insistent. "But he is causing riots by his teaching wherever he goes—all over Judea, from Galilee to Jerusalem!"

[6]"Oh, is he a Galilean?" Pilate asked. [7]When they said that he was, Pilate sent him to Herod Antipas, because Galilee was under Herod's jurisdiction, and Herod happened to be in Jerusalem at the time.

[8]Herod was delighted at the opportunity to see Jesus, because he had heard about him and had been hoping for a long time to see him perform a miracle. [9]He asked Jesus question after question, but Jesus refused to answer. [10]Meanwhile, the leading priests and the teachers of religious law stood there shouting their accusations. [11]Then Herod and his soldiers began mocking and ridiculing Jesus. Finally, they put a royal robe on him and sent him back to Pilate. [12](Herod and Pilate, who had been enemies before, became friends that day.)

[13]Then Pilate called together the leading priests and other religious leaders, along with the people, [14]and he announced his verdict. "You brought this man to me, accusing him of leading a revolt. I have examined him thoroughly on this point in your presence and find him innocent. [15]Herod came to the same conclusion and sent him back to us. Nothing this man has done calls for the death penalty. [16]So I will have him flogged, and then I will release him."*

[18]Then a mighty roar rose from the crowd, and with one voice they shouted, "Kill him, and release Barabbas to us!" [19](Barabbas was in prison for taking part in an insurrection in Jerusalem against the government, and for murder.) [20]Pilate argued with them, because he wanted to release Jesus. [21]But they kept shouting, "Crucify him! Crucify him!"

[22]For the third time he demanded, "Why? What crime has he committed? I have found no reason to sentence him to death. So I will have him flogged, and then I will release him."

[23]But the mob shouted louder and louder, demanding that Jesus be crucified, and their voices prevailed. [24]So Pilate sentenced Jesus

22:66 Greek *before their Sanhedrin.* **22:69** See Ps 110:1. **23:16** Some manuscripts add verse 17, *Now it was necessary for him to release one prisoner to them during the Passover celebration.* Compare Matt 27:15; Mark 15:6; John 18:39.

23:1-5 The Jewish council attempted to manipulate Pilate's verdict about Jesus by telling half-truths, even outright lies. In denial, the subtle (and not-so-subtle) lies we tell ourself and others keep us from making progress in recovery. Lying is often used by others to knock us off track and to maintain the status quo. Often others are not even aware of their need to keep everything, including us, in place. Recovery is based on the principles of truth and honesty.

23:13-25 Pilate initially saw through all the lies of Jesus' accusers. That is an indictment of his accusers, not Jesus. Yet Pilate could not follow through on his convictions. He acquiesced to political expediency and moral compromise to save his job. In seeing Jesus as a political threat, Pilate denied him his human dignity and rights. Often the truth does come out, vindicating the innocent person, but not before a price has been paid. In the recovery process, telling the truth and doing the right thing are always crucial.

to die as they demanded. [25]As they had requested, he released Barabbas, the man in prison for insurrection and murder. But he turned Jesus over to them to do as they wished.

The Crucifixion

[26]As they led Jesus away, a man named Simon, who was from Cyrene,* happened to be coming in from the countryside. The soldiers seized him and put the cross on him and made him carry it behind Jesus. [27]A large crowd trailed behind, including many grief-stricken women. [28]But Jesus turned and said to them, "Daughters of Jerusalem, don't weep for me, but weep for yourselves and for your children. [29]For the days are coming when they will say, 'Fortunate indeed are the women who are childless, the wombs that have not borne a child and the breasts that have never nursed.' [30]People will beg the mountains, 'Fall on us,' and plead with the hills, 'Bury us.'* [31]For if these things are done when the tree is green, what will happen when it is dry?*"

[32]Two others, both criminals, were led out to be executed with him. [33]When they came to a place called The Skull,* they nailed him to the cross. And the criminals were also crucified—one on his right and one on his left. [34]Jesus said, "Father, forgive them, for they don't know what they are doing."* And the soldiers gambled for his clothes by throwing dice.*

[35]The crowd watched and the leaders scoffed. "He saved others," they said, "let him save himself if he is really God's Messiah, the Chosen One." [36]The soldiers mocked him, too, by offering him a drink of sour wine. [37]They called out to him, "If you are the King of the Jews, save yourself!" [38]A sign was fastened above him with these words: "This is the King of the Jews."

[39]One of the criminals hanging beside him scoffed, "So you're the Messiah, are you? Prove it by saving yourself—and us, too, while you're at it!"

[40]But the other criminal protested, "Don't you fear God even when you have been sentenced to die? [41]We deserve to die for our crimes, but this man hasn't done anything wrong." [42]Then he said, "Jesus, remember me when you come into your Kingdom."

[43]And Jesus replied, "I assure you, today you will be with me in paradise."

The Death of Jesus

[44]By this time it was about noon, and darkness fell across the whole land until three o'clock. [45]The light from the sun was gone. And suddenly, the curtain in the sanctuary of the Temple was torn down the middle. [46]Then Jesus shouted, "Father, I entrust my spirit into your hands!"* And with those words he breathed his last.

[47]When the Roman officer* overseeing the execution saw what had happened, he worshiped God and said, "Surely this man was innocent.*" [48]And when all the crowd that came to see the crucifixion saw what had happened, they went home in deep sorrow.* [49]But Jesus' friends, including the women who had followed him from Galilee, stood at a distance watching.

The Burial of Jesus

[50]Now there was a good and righteous man named Joseph. He was a member of the Jewish high council, [51]but he had not agreed with the decision and actions of the other religious leaders. He was from the town of Arimathea in Judea, and he was waiting for the Kingdom of God to come. [52]He went to Pilate and asked for Jesus' body. [53]Then he took the body down from the cross and wrapped it in a long sheet of linen cloth and

23:26 *Cyrene* was a city in northern Africa. **23:30** Hos 10:8. **23:31** Or *If these things are done to me, the living tree, what will happen to you, the dry tree?* **23:33** Sometimes rendered *Calvary*, which comes from the Latin word for "skull." **23:34a** This sentence is not included in many ancient manuscripts. **23:34b** Greek *by casting lots*. See Ps 22:18. **23:46** Ps 31:5. **23:47a** Greek *the centurion*. **23:47b** Or *righteous*. **23:48** Greek *went home beating their breasts*.

23:32-34 Jesus forgave those who nailed him to the cross. Here in the most unjust situation in history, unlimited forgiveness was extended. If Christ forgave in this way from the cross, no sin we've committed is too great for his forgiveness. As we accept his forgiveness, we are freed to forgive those who have sinned against us. Christ helps us release our bitterness and resentment, which only imprison us. His forgiveness empowers us to be forgiving people—forgiving ourself and those who have hurt us.

23:40-43 The piercing self-examination of the criminal crucified next to Jesus was the prelude to his salvation. His attitude stands in stark contrast to the self-sufficient bitterness and cynicism of the other criminal, who died in bondage to sin and despair. God always preserves the element of choice in the recovery process, right up to the end of life. It is not too late to begin the process!

laid it in a new tomb that had been carved out of rock. ⁵⁴This was done late on Friday afternoon, the day of preparation,* as the Sabbath was about to begin.

⁵⁵As his body was taken away, the women from Galilee followed and saw the tomb where his body was placed. ⁵⁶Then they went home and prepared spices and ointments to anoint his body. But by the time they were finished the Sabbath had begun, so they rested as required by the law.

CHAPTER 24
The Resurrection

But very early on Sunday morning* the women went to the tomb, taking the spices they had prepared. ²They found that the stone had been rolled away from the entrance. ³So they went in, but they didn't find the body of the Lord Jesus. ⁴As they stood there puzzled, two men suddenly appeared to them, clothed in dazzling robes.

⁵The women were terrified and bowed with their faces to the ground. Then the men asked, "Why are you looking among the dead for someone who is alive? ⁶He isn't here! He is risen from the dead! Remember what he told you back in Galilee, ⁷that the Son of Man* must be betrayed into the hands of sinful men and be crucified, and that he would rise again on the third day."

⁸Then they remembered that he had said this. ⁹So they rushed back from the tomb to tell his eleven disciples—and everyone else—what had happened. ¹⁰It was Mary Magdalene, Joanna, Mary the mother of James, and several other women who told the apostles what had happened. ¹¹But the story sounded like nonsense to the men, so they didn't believe it. ¹²However, Peter jumped up and ran to the tomb to look. Stooping, he peered in and saw the empty

linen wrappings; then he went home again, wondering what had happened.

The Walk to Emmaus

¹³That same day two of Jesus' followers were walking to the village of Emmaus, seven miles* from Jerusalem. ¹⁴As they walked along they were talking about everything that had happened. ¹⁵As they talked and discussed these things, Jesus himself suddenly came and began walking with them. ¹⁶But God kept them from recognizing him.

¹⁷He asked them, "What are you discussing so intently as you walk along?"

They stopped short, sadness written across their faces. ¹⁸Then one of them, Cleopas, replied, "You must be the only person in Jerusalem who hasn't heard about all the things that have happened there the last few days."

¹⁹"What things?" Jesus asked.

"The things that happened to Jesus, the man from Nazareth," they said. "He was a prophet who did powerful miracles, and he was a mighty teacher in the eyes of God and all the people. ²⁰But our leading priests and other religious leaders handed him over to be condemned to death, and they crucified him. ²¹We had hoped he was the Messiah who had come to rescue Israel. This all happened three days ago.

²²"Then some women from our group of his followers were at his tomb early this morning, and they came back with an amazing report. ²³They said his body was missing, and they had seen angels who told them Jesus is alive! ²⁴Some of our men ran out to see, and sure enough, his body was gone, just as the women had said."

²⁵Then Jesus said to them, "You foolish people! You find it so hard to believe all that the prophets wrote in the Scriptures. ²⁶Wasn't it clearly predicted that the Messiah would

---

23:54 Greek *It was the day of preparation.* **24:1** Greek *But on the first day of the week, very early in the morning.*
24:7 "Son of Man" is a title Jesus used for himself. **24:13** Greek *60 stadia* [11.1 kilometers].

24:1-12 During Jesus' arrest and trial, the disciples showed complete helplessness in dealing with the circumstances at hand. But after the Resurrection, in the book of Acts, a new Power enabled them to recover their courage and go into the world with the message of God's good news. The Resurrection is both a historical fact and an experiential power. This power is greater than death itself and can help us overcome our dependency or compulsion. The Resurrection is the very source of recovery. As we experience the power of Christ's resurrection in our life, we will enjoy victory over temptation and freedom from the bondage of our addiction.

24:13-24 The two followers on the road to Emmaus were deeply discouraged and grieved by the events of the past few days. They did not fully comprehend who Jesus was nor the kind of faith needed to recover from their pain. Through a step of faith, however, they were lifted from their grief to become people who would help change the world. By meeting and speaking with Jesus, the road from the cross to Emmaus became their path of recovery and wholeness.

have to suffer all these things before entering his glory?" ²⁷Then Jesus took them through the writings of Moses and all the prophets, explaining from all the Scriptures the things concerning himself.

²⁸By this time they were nearing Emmaus and the end of their journey. Jesus acted as if he were going on, ²⁹but they begged him, "Stay the night with us, since it is getting late." So he went home with them. ³⁰As they sat down to eat,* he took the bread and blessed it. Then he broke it and gave it to them. ³¹Suddenly, their eyes were opened, and they recognized him. And at that moment he disappeared!

³²They said to each other, "Didn't our hearts burn within us as he talked with us on the road and explained the Scriptures to us?" ³³And within the hour they were on their way back to Jerusalem. There they found the eleven disciples and the others who had gathered with them, ³⁴who said, "The Lord has really risen! He appeared to Peter.*"

Jesus Appears to the Disciples

³⁵Then the two from Emmaus told their story of how Jesus had appeared to them as they were walking along the road, and how they had recognized him as he was breaking the bread. ³⁶And just as they were telling about it, Jesus himself was suddenly standing there among them. "Peace be with you," he said. ³⁷But the whole group was startled and frightened, thinking they were seeing a ghost!

³⁸"Why are you frightened?" he asked. "Why are your hearts filled with doubt?

³⁹Look at my hands. Look at my feet. You can see that it's really me. Touch me and make sure that I am not a ghost, because ghosts don't have bodies, as you see that I do." ⁴⁰As he spoke, he showed them his hands and his feet.

⁴¹Still they stood there in disbelief, filled with joy and wonder. Then he asked them, "Do you have anything here to eat?" ⁴²They gave him a piece of broiled fish, ⁴³and he ate it as they watched.

⁴⁴Then he said, "When I was with you before, I told you that everything written about me in the law of Moses and the prophets and in the Psalms must be fulfilled." ⁴⁵Then he opened their minds to understand the Scriptures. ⁴⁶And he said, "Yes, it was written long ago that the Messiah would suffer and die and rise from the dead on the third day. ⁴⁷It was also written that this message would be proclaimed in the authority of his name to all the nations,* beginning in Jerusalem: 'There is forgiveness of sins for all who repent.' ⁴⁸You are witnesses of all these things.

⁴⁹"And now I will send the Holy Spirit, just as my Father promised. But stay here in the city until the Holy Spirit comes and fills you with power from heaven."

The Ascension

⁵⁰Then Jesus led them to Bethany, and lifting his hands to heaven, he blessed them. ⁵¹While he was blessing them, he left them and was taken up to heaven. ⁵²So they worshiped him and then returned to Jerusalem filled with great joy. ⁵³And they spent all of their time in the Temple, praising God.

24:30 Or *As they reclined.* 24:34 Greek *Simon.* 24:47 Or *all peoples.*

24:36-49 Jesus is alive and well, yet this was not immediately evident to his followers in the upper room. As they were banded together in their grief and pain, the living Christ appeared. This living Christ, the Holy Spirit, is present in us; only he can calm our fears and doubts. The task of spreading the good news of resurrection and recovery was overwhelming. Through the promised Holy Spirit (see Acts 2), Jesus gave them the peace and power to do all things through Christ. He can do the same for anyone in recovery who trusts in him.

REFLECTIONS ON LUKE

insights ABOUT THE PERSON OF JESUS

Jesus Christ is portrayed in **Luke 1:76-79** as light shining on those living in darkness. This metaphor might have reminded the original readers of a group of travelers overtaken by darkness, who were left in danger by the roadside all night. Such people, helpless to defend themselves against the attacks of robbers, would have welcomed the light of the rising sun. This is a picture of what Jesus can do for any of us who are "in darkness," helpless to defend ourself against the draw of our powerful dependency. We move from darkness into light as we receive God's gift of forgiveness and make a personal commitment to him. As we experience new hope in Jesus, we can tell fellow strugglers about the "sunrise" that is just around the corner when they accept Christ as their Savior.

Jesus, of course, did not need recovery because he was the sinless God-man. From **Luke 2:52** it is clear that from childhood to adulthood Jesus was a perfect model of balanced growth as he developed physically, intellectually, spiritually, and socially. He displayed both personal and interpersonal growth. No dimension of his growth was overemphasized, underdeveloped, or rejected. Our own life needs to be balanced in a similar way as we work through the process of recovery.

Jesus did not succumb to temptation, yet he fully experienced, in one form or another, every temptation known to humanity. The Bible clearly affirms that Jesus was vulnerable to sin because of his humanity, yet he did not sin. If Jesus would have been unable to sin because of his deity, then the temptations given by Satan in **Luke 4:3-13** would have been meaningless. If Jesus was beyond temptation, he would be unable to sympathize with our weaknesses (see Hebrews 4:15). When we experience temptation, especially from our injuries or addiction of the past, we can remember that Jesus understands.

insights ABOUT GOD'S POWER TO SAVE

In **Luke 4:33-37** Jesus displayed his ability to deliver people from demon possession. Luke and the other Gospel writers repeatedly affirmed Jesus' power in this arena. In Jesus' day, being possessed by a demon was believed to be the greatest adversity one could suffer. By his absolute control over demons, Jesus proved his sovereignty over all the adversity that this world and the world below could heap on humanity. To this day, no evil or adversity in life is too great for God's power to overcome.

The story of Zacchaeus in **Luke 19:1-10** beautifully illustrates God's acceptance and restoration of repentant sinners. After admitting his sins to God, to himself, and to others, Zacchaeus was willing to repay the people he had wronged. Making restitution to those we have harmed or cheated is crucial to repentance and recovery, unless the process of making amends will only cause further injury to people we have wronged. In such cases, it is enough to admit our wrongdoings to God, to ourself, and to another person.

Luke 19:9-10 captures the central theme of Luke's Gospel: Jesus' passion to find and restore those who are lost and alienated from God. This priority has been on the heart of God since the first sin in the Garden of Eden. Immediately after Adam and Eve sinned, God sought them out as they hid in fear. He restored fellowship with them and offered them a way of recovery from their sin (Genesis 3). The work of Jesus on the cross represents the culmination of God's plan for forgiveness, hope, and restored fellowship with God.

The cup of wine shared by Jesus and his disciples in **Luke 22:20** symbolized the blood of Jesus, which would institute the New Covenant (see Jeremiah 31:31-34). Jesus Christ was the ultimate sacrificial Lamb of God, who has taken away the sins of the world (see John 1:29). Without this provision for sin once and for all, we have no peace or serenity. Without the cup of God's salvation, we are still in sin and insecurity, and many will keep looking for salvation in a bottle. We have an open invitation to receive God's gracious forgiveness. Through Christ we can now rest secure in God's grace, which allows us to escape the guilt of our past.

insights ABOUT PRAYER

In **Luke 6:12-16** Jesus spent an entire night in prayer before choosing his twelve disciples. Despite the care he took, however, among them was Judas Iscariot, who would betray him. Jesus did not make a mistake; Judas was chosen purposely and prayerfully. Unlike Jesus, we make foolish choices no matter how careful we are. Yet we are like Jesus in that the prayerful choices we make in recovery may still result in betrayal. Even though we may still be betrayed through no fault of our own, we can take comfort from the fact that God can and will use this for good in our life.

Luke 11:5-13 emphasizes that God wants us to approach him with shameless persistence. The commands to ask, seek, and knock are all given in the present tense, emphasizing continuous, persistent action on our part. It is the persistence of the seeker, not necessarily the kindness of the giver, that gets results. To practice this quality in our prayer life and recovery program, we must first have a personal relationship with the giver of all good gifts. Through faith, we can expect that God, who is kinder than any human father, wants us to experience wholeness and will answer our prayers for recovery.

insights CONCERNING TRUE FAITH

Luke 10:21 tells us where to look for true wisdom. Many of us have spent years looking for wisdom that will help us in the recovery process. We may have begun to think it is hard, if not impossible, to come by. Often the reason we find true wisdom so elusive is that it is divinely and simply revealed to "the childlike." True wisdom does not come from the worldly wise or from ivory-tower intellectuals. God's wisdom for recovery comes from reading his Word and simply trusting him, one day at a time. People in recovery can gain a great deal by following God's leading in childlike simplicity and trust.

In **Luke 15:1-2** we see that Jesus attracted many of the outcasts of Jewish religious and social life. Perhaps this was because he was the only one who did not despise and reject them. Jesus preferred these downcast people because they were aware of their sinfulness and they approached God with humble attitudes. In contrast, the religious leaders, who were outwardly moral but inwardly proud, were not at all attracted to Jesus. To this day, religion can still hinder recovery. But an admission of powerlessness and a relationship with Jesus will help the recovery process.

The story of the lost son in **Luke 15:11-32** wonderfully illustrates the theme of Luke's Gospel (Luke 19:9-10) and the steps of recovery. Like the younger son, we have been guilty of choosing a life of pleasure. With time, however, we discovered that we had become a slave to our selfish lifestyle. Some of us never even saw how lost we were until we hit bottom. The bottom for this son was his realization that the pigs were eating better than he was. When we realize that our life is hopelessly out of control, we have made the first step toward recovery. When we are humbled by our helplessness, we are in the best situation to establish a healthy relationship with our gracious God.

In **Luke 18:40-43** Jesus miraculously healed a blind man. Jesus would not have healed this man, however, had the man not trusted in Jesus' power to do so. On the other hand, it was not simply the blind man's faith that healed him. Faith heals to the extent that it is clearly focused on the proper and powerful object of faith—God in Jesus Christ. Recovery is based not on our own power or our faith, but on our loving God, who has the power and desire to heal us. Our part is to look to him for help.

insights CONCERNING OBSTACLES TO RECOVERY

In **Luke 11:14-23** Jesus was accused of being an ally of Satan. Through Jesus' words and actions, however, it became clear that these accusations were false. Unseen powers of darkness are agents of Satan's kingdom and are behind a great deal of human bondage. When we understand this, then "riding the fence" between living for God and living for ourself is no longer an option. Our success in recovery leaves no room for neutrality or moral compromise. Not to decide for God in Jesus Christ is to decide for Satan and his world of bondage. Only through uncompromising faith in Jesus Christ can we achieve victory and lifelong recovery.

We see in **Luke 22:31-34** that Simon Peter was influenced by Satan to break his commitment to Jesus and found his life careening out of control. While it pained Peter to hear that he would betray Jesus, Jesus held out to him the hope of repentance and restoration. Jesus knows when we will betray or deny him, and he makes gracious provision for that. Though we may have been "sifted by Satan," it is never too late to turn back to Jesus. By continuing to take personal moral inventory, our relapses from recovery will become shorter in duration and fewer in number.

insights ABOUT HONESTY AND DENIAL

The Pharisee in **Luke 18:10-14** did not have an accurate self-perception. He looked upon himself as better than others; his pride hindered his ability to see himself or others as God did. He is a good example of what we are like when we are in denial. Most of us are guilty of ignoring our own dependency by pointing a hypocritical finger at others worse off than we are. Some of us have hidden behind the respectable image we hold in our community. God sees our heart and will reward us (forgive us, heal us, aid us in recovery) according to our humble faith. The tax collector, with humble and honest self-awareness, was well on his way to recovery; the Pharisee was headed for spiritual disaster.

Our true spiritual condition is evidenced not so much by our religious activities as it is by what we depend on for security. In **Luke 18:18-23** Jesus exposed a wealthy young man's dependence on his possessions. Jesus brought him face to face with a common human problem—misplaced devotion. We don't know whether or not this young man ever repented of his attachment to his belongings, but each of us is faced with the same choice. Only by renouncing our unhealthy dependency can we receive lasting spiritual treasure—a healthy, fulfilling relationship with God, ourself, and others.

JOHN

THE BIG PICTURE

A. THE GLORIOUS SOURCE OF RECOVERY IS REVEALED (1:1-18)
B. JESUS GIVES NEW LIFE (1:19-3:36)
C. SATISFYING THE LONGINGS OF THE SOUL (4:1-7:53)
D. COMING INTO THE LIGHT TO BE FREED FROM A PAINFUL PAST (8:1-9:41)
E. EMBRACING AND CELEBRATING AN ABUNDANT LIFE (10:1-12:50)
F. LOVING OTHERS AS JESUS HAS LOVED US (13:1-17:26)
G. THE CRUCIFIXION: EVERYTHING SEEMS TO FALL APART (18:1-19:42)
H. THE RESURRECTION: MIRACULOUS RECOVERY (20:1-21:25)

From the vast stretches of eternity to the confines of time—so the Son of God entered into this world. Jesus was the Creator of this world, but then he immersed himself in his creation. God became a man and willingly sacrificed himself so that all who would receive him could have forgiveness and redemption.

John used a number of images to illustrate who Jesus is and how he gives us eternal life: Jesus is the unblemished Lamb of God who is sacrificed for us; the bread of life who satisfies our spiritual hunger; the living water who satisfies our spiritual thirst; the light who guides us; the good shepherd who leads us; the true vine who gives us life; and the counselor who comforts and teaches us. Through these images, John demonstrated that Jesus can give us all we need for a new, abundant life.

John also used the miracles Jesus performed to show us Jesus' power to transform lives. This Gospel is filled with examples of the power of God in lives needing recovery. With God's help, we can drink the new wine of a changed life; take responsibility to walk away from the sins that paralyze us; recover from our sicknesses; be healed of our blindness to the truth; escape from our sinful addictions and the people who condemn us; and be raised to new life from a dead and empty existence.

John collected this series of images and miracles to help us recognize who Jesus is—the Son of God. When we accept Jesus as our Lord and Savior, we can begin to experience the new life that he offers to all who believe in him.

THE BOTTOM LINE

PURPOSE: To reveal Jesus as the Son of God and show that by faith in him we can experience true love, forgiveness, and recovery. AUTHOR: John the apostle, brother of James, called a "Son of Thunder." AUDIENCE: All people everywhere. DATE WRITTEN: Probably between A.D. 80 and 90. SETTING: After many years of reflecting on his experience as a disciple of Jesus, the apostle John recorded his unique perspective on the gospel. KEY VERSE: "These [things] are written so that you may continue to believe that Jesus is the Messiah, the Son of God, and that by believing in him you will have life" (20:31). KEY PEOPLE AND RELATIONSHIPS: Jesus with John the Baptist, the disciples, Mary, Martha, Lazarus, the religious leaders, Pilate, and Mary Magdalene.

RECOVERY THEMES

The Power of God: Each of the miracles recorded by John, six of which are not recorded in the other Gospels, clearly demonstrates God's power. Jesus healed a man born blind; he walked on water and then calmed a storm; he healed a nobleman's son without even being there; he raised Lazarus from the dead after the man had been dead for more than three days. John did not simply tell us about the life of Christ—he made the important point that Jesus is the embodiment of all of God's power. That power is promised to us when we come to him in our powerlessness and turn our life over to him.

God's Power Can Be within Us: Recovery is based on God's power at work within us. Jesus gave us several pictures of how we can have God's power. He described how the branch abides in the vine and draws life and power from the vine. He told us that he is the bread of life, and that we are to eat that bread. He said that he has water for us to drink that will quench our thirst forever. Each of these images illustrates the promise he made in the upper room: The Holy Spirit would be available to teach us, comfort us, and empower us daily. When we turn our life over to God, the Holy Spirit comes to live within us and take us step-by-step to wholeness and healing.

The Dangers of Denial: In Jesus' early ministry, large crowds followed him. But as Jesus confronted the people with the truth of their sins, the crowds gradually dwindled. Eventually, as people were unwilling to face the realities Jesus exposed in their lives, they rejected the only one who could help them. Times have changed, but the pattern of denial remains the same: We begin with some question about the truth and over time develop rigid resistance to it. Gradually our heart becomes hardened, and we no longer see the obvious truth. Just as he confronted the crowds, Jesus also confronts us with the changes we need to make. It takes courage to be open and willing to face the truth; admitting the truth is the first step toward recovery.

The Invitation to Relationship: Although each of the Gospels shows us the love of Jesus, John presented it as a central theme. In the upper room, Jesus said that the mark of following him is loving others. He prayed that we would be united in love as he and the Father are. John referred to himself in this Gospel as "the disciple Jesus loved" (21:20). In one of his later letters, John wrote that the greatest evidence of God's presence in our life is our love for others (see 1 John 4:11-12, 20-21). Central to the recovery process and to our relationship with God is our recognition of God's love for us and our willingness to value and respect others.

CHAPTER 1
Prologue: Christ, the Eternal Word

¹ In the beginning the Word already
existed.
The Word was with God,
and the Word was God.
² He existed in the beginning
with God.
³ God created everything through him,
and nothing was created except
through him.

⁴ The Word gave life to everything that was
created,*
and his life brought light to
everyone.
⁵ The light shines in the darkness,
and the darkness can never
extinguish it.*

⁶ God sent a man, John the Baptist,* ⁷ to tell about the light so that everyone might believe because of his testimony. ⁸ John himself

---

1:3-4 Or *and nothing that was created was created except through him. The Word gave life to everything.* **1:5** Or *and the darkness has not understood it.* **1:6** Greek *a man named John.*

1:1-13 The same Power that created the universe is available to create a new life from our shattered hopes. The light of life that exposes and drives away the darkness of the human race is the same light that brightens the dark corners of our world. This source of all life and true light of the world is the source of all recovery. Eternal life and true recovery are ours when we believe what God says, renounce our tendency to do things our way, and receive the one whom God sent to help us.

1:14-18 The true light of the world became a human being known to us as Jesus Christ, who was full of God's unfailing love and faithfulness. Through Jesus, who was both fully God and fully human, we can know what God is like and enjoy a relationship with him. Jesus Christ came to bring us God's unfailing love and forgiveness and to reveal God's faithfulness to us. God's forgiving grace says, "I forgive you for your wrongs; I love and accept you freely for the person you are." His faithfulness says, "I will follow through on all I have promised."

JOHN THE BAPTIST

A thunderstorm swept in from the wilderness of Judea, stirring many from their slumber, demolishing old structures and soaking the moisture-starved fields. Many were afraid of the fierce deluge, but others were thankful for the future bounty its rain would provide. In the same way, John the Baptist broke onto the scene in Judea. He challenged the power structure of the Jewish leadership and paved the way for what was to come.

From the day an angel appeared to John's father to announce his birth, it was clear that John was special, set aside for a unique purpose. John boldly preached a clear and powerful message: The Kingdom of God was coming, and people were called to turn from their sins and be baptized as a sign of their repentance.

Some were deeply moved by John's words and humbly sought to change their lives; others were hardened in their pride and arrogance. When King Herod married Herodias, his brother's wife, John did not remain silent but pointed out the king's neglect of God's law. Herodias was angered by John's words of condemnation and had him killed. She was able to stomp out the messenger but not the message. The way had been prepared; the Messiah had broken onto the scene. John had done his job.

John felt he was not worthy even to be Jesus' slave. Jesus, however, said that there was no one greater than John in the history of the human race. John did not have a self-esteem problem; he had appropriate humility. When we truly understand the greatness of Jesus, our own self-importance, pride, and self-sufficiency will be transformed into humble gratitude and a desire to please him.

STRENGTHS AND ACCOMPLISHMENTS:
- John spoke the truth no matter what the cost.
- He cared about God's opinion, not what others thought.
- He fulfilled God's will for him by preparing the way for the Messiah.
- He put God first in everything he did and said.
- He honestly expressed his feelings of confusion and doubt.

LESSONS FROM HIS LIFE:
- Standing for the truth may be costly, but it is worthwhile in the end.
- There is joy in telling others about God's Kingdom and Jesus the King.
- An accurate self-perception is a key to faithful service.

KEY VERSE:
"John replied in the words of the prophet Isaiah: 'I am a voice shouting in the wilderness, "Clear the way for the LORD's coming!"'" (John 1:23).

John's story is found in Matthew 3:1-17; 11:18-19; 14:1-12; Mark 1:1-11; 6:14-29; Luke 1:5-25, 39-45, 57-80; 3:1-22; 7:18-35; 9:7-9; John 1:6-9, 19-37. He is also mentioned in Acts 1:5, 21-22; 10:36-37; 11:16; 13:24-25; 18:25-26; 19:3-4.

---

was not the light; he was simply a witness to tell about the light. ⁹The one who is the true light, who gives light to everyone, was coming into the world.

¹⁰He came into the very world he created, but the world didn't recognize him. ¹¹He came to his own people, and even they rejected him. ¹²But to all who believed him and accepted him, he gave the right to become children of God. ¹³They are reborn—not with a physical birth resulting from human passion or plan, but a birth that comes from God.

¹⁴So the Word became human* and made his home among us. He was full of unfailing love and faithfulness.* And we have seen his glory, the glory of the Father's one and only Son.

¹⁵John testified about him when he shouted to the crowds, "This is the one I was talking about when I said, 'Someone is coming after me who is far greater than I am, for he existed long before me.'"

¹⁶From his abundance we have all received one gracious blessing after another.* ¹⁷For the law was given through Moses, but God's unfailing love and faithfulness came through Jesus Christ. ¹⁸No one has ever seen God. But the unique One, who is himself God,* is near to the Father's heart. He has revealed God to us.

1:14a Greek *became flesh.* **1:14b** Or *grace and truth;* also in 1:17. **1:16** Or *received the grace of Christ rather than the grace of the law;* Greek reads *received grace upon grace.* **1:18** Some manuscripts read *But the one and only Son.*

The Testimony of John the Baptist

[19]This was John's testimony when the Jewish leaders sent priests and Temple assistants* from Jerusalem to ask John, "Who are you?" [20]He came right out and said, "I am not the Messiah."

[21]"Well then, who are you?" they asked. "Are you Elijah?"

"No," he replied.

"Are you the Prophet we are expecting?"* "No."

[22]"Then who are you? We need an answer for those who sent us. What do you have to say about yourself?"

[23]John replied in the words of the prophet Isaiah:

"I am a voice shouting in the wilderness, 'Clear the way for the LORD's coming!'"*

[24]Then the Pharisees who had been sent [25]asked him, "If you aren't the Messiah or Elijah or the Prophet, what right do you have to baptize?"

[26]John told them, "I baptize with* water, but right here in the crowd is someone you do not recognize. [27]Though his ministry follows mine, I'm not even worthy to be his slave and untie the straps of his sandal."

[28]This encounter took place in Bethany, an area east of the Jordan River, where John was baptizing.

Jesus, the Lamb of God

[29]The next day John saw Jesus coming toward him and said, "Look! The Lamb of God who takes away the sin of the world! [30]He is the one I was talking about when I said, 'A man is coming after me who is far greater than I am, for he existed long before me.' [31]I did not recognize him as the Messiah, but I have been baptizing with water so that he might be revealed to Israel."

[32]Then John testified, "I saw the Holy Spirit descending like a dove from heaven and resting upon him. [33]I didn't know he was the one, but when God sent me to baptize with water, he told me, 'The one on whom you see the Spirit descend and rest is the one who will baptize with the Holy Spirit.' [34]I saw this happen to Jesus, so I testify that he is the Chosen One of God.*"

The First Disciples

[35]The following day John was again standing with two of his disciples. [36]As Jesus walked by, John looked at him and declared, "Look! There is the Lamb of God!" [37]When John's two disciples heard this, they followed Jesus.

[38]Jesus looked around and saw them following. "What do you want?" he asked them.

They replied, "Rabbi" (which means "Teacher"), "where are you staying?"

[39]"Come and see," he said. It was about four o'clock in the afternoon when they went with him to the place where he was staying, and they remained with him the rest of the day.

[40]Andrew, Simon Peter's brother, was one of these men who heard what John said and then followed Jesus. [41]Andrew went to find his brother, Simon, and told him, "We have found the Messiah" (which means "Christ"*).

[42]Then Andrew brought Simon to meet Jesus. Looking intently at Simon, Jesus said, "Your name is Simon, son of John—but you will be called Cephas" (which means "Peter"*).

[43]The next day Jesus decided to go to Galilee. He found Philip and said to him, "Come, follow me." [44]Philip was from Bethsaida, Andrew and Peter's hometown.

[45]Philip went to look for Nathanael and told him, "We have found the very person Moses* and the prophets wrote about! His name is Jesus, the son of Joseph from Nazareth."

[46]"Nazareth!" exclaimed Nathanael. "Can anything good come from Nazareth?"

"Come and see for yourself," Philip replied.

[47]As they approached, Jesus said, "Now

1:19 Greek *and Levites.* 1:21 Greek *Are you the Prophet?* See Deut 18:15, 18; Mal 4:5-6. 1:23 Isa 40:3. 1:26 Or *in;* also in 1:31, 33. 1:34 Some manuscripts read *the Son of God.* 1:41 *Messiah* (a Hebrew term) and *Christ* (a Greek term) both mean "anointed one." 1:42 The names *Cephas* (from Aramaic) and *Peter* (from Greek) both mean "rock." 1:45 Greek *Moses in the law.*

1:19-28 John the Baptist was an original messenger of repentance and recovery. He was not the true light or source of recovery; he merely pointed to the one who was. Likewise, those of us in recovery reflect God's light and merely point the way to recovery. We should not draw followers to ourself any more than John did. We are mere beggars telling other beggars where to find food. When we lay aside pride in our achievements and abilities as John the Baptist did, we are better able to serve Christ by showing fellow strugglers the way to recovery.

here is a genuine son of Israel—a man of complete integrity."

[48]"How do you know about me?" Nathanael asked.

Jesus replied, "I could see you under the fig tree before Philip found you."

[49]Then Nathanael exclaimed, "Rabbi, you are the Son of God—the King of Israel!"

[50]Jesus asked him, "Do you believe this just because I told you I had seen you under the fig tree? You will see greater things than this." [51]Then he said, "I tell you the truth, you will all see heaven open and the angels of God going up and down on the Son of Man, the one who is the stairway between heaven and earth.*"

CHAPTER 2
The Wedding at Cana

The next day* there was a wedding celebration in the village of Cana in Galilee. Jesus' mother was there, [2]and Jesus and his disciples were also invited to the celebration. [3]The wine supply ran out during the festivities, so Jesus' mother told him, "They have no more wine."

[4]"Dear woman, that's not our problem," Jesus replied. "My time has not yet come."

[5]But his mother told the servants, "Do whatever he tells you."

[6]Standing nearby were six stone water jars, used for Jewish ceremonial washing. Each could hold twenty to thirty gallons.* [7]Jesus told the servants, "Fill the jars with water." When the jars had been filled, [8]he said, "Now dip some out, and take it to the master of ceremonies." So the servants followed his instructions.

[9]When the master of ceremonies tasted the water that was now wine, not knowing where it had come from (though, of course, the servants knew), he called the bridegroom over. [10]"A host always serves the best wine first," he said. "Then, when everyone has had a lot to drink, he brings out the less expensive wine. But you have kept the best until now!"

[11]This miraculous sign at Cana in Galilee was the first time Jesus revealed his glory. And his disciples believed in him.

[12]After the wedding he went to Capernaum for a few days with his mother, his brothers, and his disciples.

Jesus Clears the Temple

[13]It was nearly time for the Jewish Passover celebration, so Jesus went to Jerusalem. [14]In the Temple area he saw merchants selling cattle, sheep, and doves for sacrifices; he also saw dealers at tables exchanging foreign money. [15]Jesus made a whip from some ropes and chased them all out of the Temple. He drove out the sheep and cattle, scattered the money changers' coins over the floor, and turned over their tables. [16]Then, going over to the people who sold doves, he told them, "Get these things out of here. Stop turning my Father's house into a marketplace!"

[17]Then his disciples remembered this prophecy from the Scriptures: "Passion for God's house will consume me."*

[18]But the Jewish leaders demanded, "What are you doing? If God gave you authority to do this, show us a miraculous sign to prove it."

[19]"All right," Jesus replied. "Destroy this temple, and in three days I will raise it up."

[20]"What!" they exclaimed. "It has taken forty-six years to build this Temple, and you can rebuild it in three days?" [21]But when Jesus said "this temple," he meant his own body. [22]After he was raised from the dead, his

---

1:51 Greek *going up and down on the Son of Man;* see Gen 28:10-17. "Son of Man" is a title Jesus used for himself. 2:1 Greek *On the third day;* see 1:35, 43. 2:6 Greek *2 or 3 measures* [75 to 113 liters]. 2:17 Or *"Concern for God's house will be my undoing."* Ps 69:9.

2:1-12 Jesus was at a wedding celebration with family and friends when the wine ran out. So Jesus turned the water in six stone waterpots into enough wine for the rest of the celebration. If we are in recovery, this abundance of wine would be dangerous. But one truth should be encouraging to us all: Jesus valued the celebration of people at a wedding feast. God is concerned about the seemingly mundane needs we have and has the power to meet those needs. He may call us to do some painful things in the process of recovery, but his ultimate goal for us is a life of peace and wholeness.

2:13-16 Jesus was angry at those who turned the Temple courts into a marketplace of unjust profit. The merchants forced the people to buy "approved" sacrificial animals at exorbitant prices and exchanged their currency for Temple currency at inflated rates. They abused the public trust and mocked holy worship. Anger that is measured and authorized by God's purposes is justified. Sometimes this kind of anger can play an important role in our spiritual, emotional, and physical recovery. We may need to stand up to the abusive forces in our life and make changes that will set us free from their grip. As we do, God will stand by us.

disciples remembered he had said this, and they believed both the Scriptures and what Jesus had said.

Jesus and Nicodemus

23Because of the miraculous signs Jesus did in Jerusalem at the Passover celebration, many began to trust in him. 24But Jesus didn't trust them, because he knew all about people. 25No one needed to tell him about human nature, for he knew what was in each person's heart.

CHAPTER 3

There was a man named Nicodemus, a Jewish religious leader who was a Pharisee. 2After dark one evening, he came to speak with Jesus. "Rabbi," he said, "we all know that God has sent you to teach us. Your miraculous signs are evidence that God is with you."

3Jesus replied, "I tell you the truth, unless you are born again,* you cannot see the Kingdom of God."

4"What do you mean?" exclaimed Nicodemus. "How can an old man go back into his mother's womb and be born again?"

5Jesus replied, "I assure you, no one can enter the Kingdom of God without being born of water and the Spirit.* 6Humans can reproduce only human life, but the Holy Spirit gives birth to spiritual life.* 7So don't be surprised when I say, 'You* must be born again.' 8The wind blows wherever it wants. Just as you can hear the wind but can't tell where it comes from or where it is going, so you can't explain how people are born of the Spirit."

9"How are these things possible?" Nicodemus asked.

10Jesus replied, "You are a respected Jewish teacher, and yet you don't understand these things? 11I assure you, we tell you what we know and have seen, and yet you won't believe our testimony. 12But if you don't believe me when I tell you about earthly things, how can you possibly believe if I tell you about heavenly things? 13No one has ever gone to heaven and returned. But the Son of Man* has come down from heaven. 14And as Moses lifted up the bronze snake on a pole in the wilderness, so the Son of Man must be lifted up, 15so that everyone who believes in him will have eternal life.*

16"For this is how God loved the world: He gave* his one and only Son, so that everyone who believes in him will not perish but have eternal life. 17God sent his Son into the world not to judge the world, but to save the world through him.

18"There is no judgment against anyone who believes in him. But anyone who does not believe in him has already been judged for not believing in God's one and only Son. 19And the judgment is based on this fact: God's light came into the world, but people loved the darkness more than the light, for their actions were evil. 20All who do evil hate the light and refuse to go near it for fear their sins will be exposed. 21But those who do what is right come to the light so others can see that they are doing what God wants.*"

John the Baptist Exalts Jesus

22Then Jesus and his disciples left Jerusalem and went into the Judean countryside. Jesus

---

3:3 Or *born from above;* also in 3:7. **3:5** Or *and spirit.* The Greek word for *Spirit* can also be translated *wind;* see 3:8. **3:6** Greek *what is born of the Spirit is spirit.* **3:7** The Greek word for *you* is plural; also in 3:12. **3:13** Some manuscripts add *who lives in heaven.* "Son of Man" is a title Jesus used for himself. **3:15** Or *everyone who believes will have eternal life in him.* **3:16** Or *For God loved the world so much that he gave.* **3:21** Or *can see God at work in what he is doing.*

3:1-12 Spiritual rebirth is as necessary to the recovery process as it is to entering God's Kingdom. Being born again is the beginning—a baby step in the process. The hard part comes each subsequent day as we submit our stubborn heart and will to the control of God's Spirit. True recovery is not attained by our trying harder to live a better life. As we repent, entrust our life to God, and seek to obey him, we will receive forgiveness and true recovery.

3:16-18 Faith says yes to God's loving overtures to us. God cared enough to send his own Son, Jesus Christ, to pay for our sins. True faith has nothing to do with our human efforts, social achievements, or material wealth. True faith says to God, "I'm a helpless sinner, unable to effect my own recovery. I trust your forgiveness, which you freely offer me in Jesus Christ." This faith delivers us from the ultimate consequence of our sins—eternal separation from God. It also empowers us to make changes in the present that will plant the seeds for a new life.

4:4-27 The disciples were surprised to find Jesus speaking with the woman at the well: She was a Samaritan (half Jew and half Gentile), she was a woman, and she had a questionable past. Any one of these factors would have disqualified her from speaking with a "righteous" Jewish man. Jesus broke down the traditional barriers, accepting her as she was and giving her a fresh start in life. Jesus demonstrated God's love for all who have been rejected, condemned, or shunned, which should encourage us. No matter what we have done, God offers us his unconditional acceptance in Jesus. With his powerful help, nothing can stand between us and recovery.

spent some time with them there, baptizing people.

²³At this time John the Baptist was baptizing at Aenon, near Salim, because there was plenty of water there; and people kept coming to him for baptism. ²⁴(This was before John was thrown into prison.) ²⁵A debate broke out between John's disciples and a certain Jew* over ceremonial cleansing. ²⁶So John's disciples came to him and said, "Rabbi, the man you met on the other side of the Jordan River, the one you identified as the Messiah, is also baptizing people. And everybody is going to him instead of coming to us."

²⁷John replied, "No one can receive anything unless God gives it from heaven. ²⁸You yourselves know how plainly I told you, 'I am not the Messiah. I am only here to prepare the way for him.' ²⁹It is the bridegroom who marries the bride, and the best man is simply glad to stand with him and hear his vows. Therefore, I am filled with joy at his success. ³⁰He must become greater and greater, and I must become less and less.

³¹"He has come from above and is greater than anyone else. We are of the earth, and we speak of earthly things, but he has come from heaven and is greater than anyone else.* ³²He testifies about what he has seen and heard, but how few believe what he tells them! ³³Anyone who accepts his testimony can affirm that God is true. ³⁴For he is sent by God. He speaks God's words, for God gives him the Spirit without limit. ³⁵The Father loves his Son and has put everything into his hands. ³⁶And anyone who believes in God's Son has eternal life. Anyone who doesn't obey the Son will never experience eternal life but remains under God's angry judgment."

CHAPTER 4
Jesus and the Samaritan Woman
Jesus* knew the Pharisees had heard that he was baptizing and making more disciples than John ²(though Jesus himself didn't baptize them—his disciples did). ³So he left Judea and returned to Galilee.

⁴He had to go through Samaria on the way. ⁵Eventually he came to the Samaritan village of Sychar, near the field that Jacob gave to his son Joseph. ⁶Jacob's well was there; and Jesus, tired from the long walk, sat wearily beside the well about noontime. ⁷Soon a Samaritan woman came to draw water, and Jesus said to

3:25 Some manuscripts read *some Jews.* 3:31 Some manuscripts do not include *and is greater than anyone else.* 4:1 Some manuscripts read *The Lord.*

STEP 11

Friends of the Light
BIBLE READING: John 3:18-21
We sought through prayer and meditation to improve our conscious contacts with God, praying only for knowledge of his will for us and the power to carry that out.

Sometimes we don't want to know God's will because there are areas in our life that we aren't ready to deal with yet. Recovery is a process for us. We may be ready to pray for God's will in some areas but feel uncomfortable having God's light shine into the areas that are still hidden in shame.

When talking about those who refuse to trust him with their life, Jesus said, "God's light came into the world, but people loved the darkness more than the light, for their actions were evil. . . . [They] refuse to go near it for fear their sins will be exposed." (John 3:19-20). Later, in one of his talks, Jesus said to the people, "I am the light of the world. If you follow me, you won't have to walk in darkness, because you will have the light that leads to life" (John 8:12).

Darkness is great when we are trying to hide something, but light is needed when we are trying to walk without falling. When we were hiding our shameful behavior and holding on to our addiction, the darkness seemed like our friend. Now that we are trying to walk toward recovery, we need the light to keep us from stumbling. We don't have to be afraid of God's light anymore since we have his forgiveness through Christ. He wants to safely guide us on the right path. *Turn to Step Twelve, page 917, Isaiah 61.*

her, "Please give me a drink." [8]He was alone at the time because his disciples had gone into the village to buy some food.

[9]The woman was surprised, for Jews refuse to have anything to do with Samaritans.* She said to Jesus, "You are a Jew, and I am a Samaritan woman. Why are you asking me for a drink?"

[10]Jesus replied, "If you only knew the gift God has for you and who you are speaking to, you would ask me, and I would give you living water."

[11]"But sir, you don't have a rope or a bucket," she said, "and this well is very deep. Where would you get this living water? [12]And besides, do you think you're greater than our ancestor Jacob, who gave us this well? How can you offer better water than he and his sons and his animals enjoyed?"

[13]Jesus replied, "Anyone who drinks this water will soon become thirsty again. [14]But those who drink the water I give will never be thirsty again. It becomes a fresh, bubbling spring within them, giving them eternal life."

[15]"Please, sir," the woman said, "give me this water! Then I'll never be thirsty again, and I won't have to come here to get water."

[16]"Go and get your husband," Jesus told her.

[17]"I don't have a husband," the woman replied.

Jesus said, "You're right! You don't have a husband—[18]for you have had five husbands, and you aren't even married to the man you're living with now. You certainly spoke the truth!"

[19]"Sir," the woman said, "you must be a prophet. [20]So tell me, why is it that you Jews insist that Jerusalem is the only place of worship, while we Samaritans claim it is here at Mount Gerizim,* where our ancestors worshiped?"

[21]Jesus replied, "Believe me, dear woman, the time is coming when it will no longer matter whether you worship the Father on this mountain or in Jerusalem. [22]You Samaritans know very little about the one you worship, while we Jews know all about him, for salvation comes through the Jews. [23]But the time is coming—indeed it's here now—when true worshipers will worship the Father in spirit and in truth. The Father is looking for those who will worship him that way. [24]For God is Spirit, so those who worship him must worship in spirit and in truth."

[25]The woman said, "I know the Messiah is coming—the one who is called Christ. When he comes, he will explain everything to us."

[26]Then Jesus told her, "I AM the Messiah!"*

[27]Just then his disciples came back. They were shocked to find him talking to a woman, but none of them had the nerve to ask, "What do you want with her?" or "Why are you talking to her?" [28]The woman left her water jar beside the well and ran back to the village, telling everyone, [29]"Come and see a man who told me everything I ever did! Could he possibly be the Messiah?" [30]So the people came streaming from the village to see him.

[31]Meanwhile, the disciples were urging Jesus, "Rabbi, eat something."

[32]But Jesus replied, "I have a kind of food you know nothing about."

[33]"Did someone bring him food while we were gone?" the disciples asked each other.

[34]Then Jesus explained: "My nourishment comes from doing the will of God, who sent me, and from finishing his work. [35]You know the saying, 'Four months between planting and harvest.' But I say, wake up and look around. The fields are already ripe* for harvest. [36]The harvesters are paid good wages, and the fruit they harvest is people brought to eternal life. What joy awaits both the planter and the harvester alike! [37]You know the saying, 'One plants and another harvests.' And it's true. [38]I sent you to harvest where you didn't plant; others had already

---

4:9 Some manuscripts do not include this sentence. 4:20 Greek on this mountain. 4:26 Or "The 'I AM' is here"; or "I am the LORD"; Greek reads "I am, the one speaking to you." See Exod 3:14. 4:35 Greek white.

4:39-42 The Samaritan woman put her faith in Jesus, who knew all her faults yet loved and respected her. She responded to God's gracious forgiveness by immediately telling her neighbors about the Messiah who had given her a new life. As a result, many were blessed with faith in Jesus Christ. As we experience God's powerful deliverance, it is important that we share the good news with others. It may be the difference between life and death for people we know. As we share what God has done for us, we will experience anew the great joy of victory in Christ.
4:46-53 The government official demonstrated faith in Jesus by humbly asking him to heal his son. He believed Jesus' word to be true even though he hadn't yet seen the results. Our faith is expressed in similar ways. We can begin by humbly and honestly seeking God's help. He will help us even though we may not see immediate results. The recovery process takes time. We can believe that God is working and persevere, even when the results are not immediately evident.

done the work, and now you will get to gather the harvest."

Many Samaritans Believe

³⁹Many Samaritans from the village believed in Jesus because the woman had said, "He told me everything I ever did!" ⁴⁰When they came out to see him, they begged him to stay in their village. So he stayed for two days, ⁴¹long enough for many more to hear his message and believe. ⁴²Then they said to the woman, "Now we believe, not just because of what you told us, but because we have heard him ourselves. Now we know that he is indeed the Savior of the world."

Jesus Heals an Official's Son

⁴³At the end of the two days, Jesus went on to Galilee. ⁴⁴He himself had said that a prophet is not honored in his own hometown. ⁴⁵Yet the Galileans welcomed him, for they had been in Jerusalem at the Passover celebration and had seen everything he did there.

⁴⁶As he traveled through Galilee, he came to Cana, where he had turned the water into wine. There was a government official in nearby Capernaum whose son was very sick. ⁴⁷When he heard that Jesus had come from Judea to Galilee, he went and begged Jesus to come to Capernaum to heal his son, who was about to die.

⁴⁸Jesus asked, "Will you never believe in me unless you see miraculous signs and wonders?"

⁴⁹The official pleaded, "Lord, please come now before my little boy dies."

⁵⁰Then Jesus told him, "Go back home. Your son will live!" And the man believed what Jesus said and started home.

⁵¹While the man was on his way, some of his servants met him with the news that his son was alive and well. ⁵²He asked them when the boy had begun to get better, and they replied, "Yesterday afternoon at one o'clock his fever suddenly disappeared!" ⁵³Then the father realized that that was the very time Jesus had told him, "Your son will live." And he and his entire household believed in Jesus. ⁵⁴This was the second miraculous sign Jesus did in Galilee after coming from Judea.

CHAPTER 5
Jesus Heals a Lame Man

Afterward Jesus returned to Jerusalem for one of the Jewish holy days. ²Inside the city, near the Sheep Gate, was the pool of Bethesda,*

5:2 Other manuscripts read *Beth-zatha;* still others read *Bethsaida.*

STEP 6

Discovering Hope

BIBLE READING: John 5:1-15

We were entirely ready to have God remove all these defects of character. How can we honestly say that we are entirely ready for God to remove our defects of character? If we think in terms of all or nothing, we may get stuck here because we will never feel entirely ready. It is important to keep in mind that the Twelve Steps are guiding ideals. No one can work them perfectly. Our part is to keep moving, to get as close as we can to being ready.

In Jesus' day there was a pool where people went, hoping to experience miraculous healing. "One of the men lying there had been sick for thirty-eight years. When Jesus saw him and knew he had been ill for a long time, he asked him, 'Would you like to get well?' 'I can't, sir,' the sick man said, 'for I have no one to put me into the pool when the water bubbles up. Someone else always gets there ahead of me.' Jesus told him, 'Stand up, pick up your mat, and walk!' Instantly, the man was healed! He rolled up his sleeping mat and began walking!" (John 5:5-9).

This man was so crippled that he couldn't go any farther on his own. He camped as near as he could to a place where there was hope for recovery. God met him there and brought him the rest of the way. For us, "entirely ready" may mean getting as close to the hope of healing as we can in our crippled condition. When we do, God will meet us there and take us the rest of the way. *Turn to page 1443, Romans 6.*

with five covered porches. ³Crowds of sick people—blind, lame, or paralyzed—lay on the porches.* ⁵One of the men lying there had been sick for thirty-eight years. ⁶When Jesus saw him and knew he had been ill for a long time, he asked him, "Would you like to get well?"

⁷"I can't, sir," the sick man said, "for I have no one to put me into the pool when the water bubbles up. Someone else always gets there ahead of me."

⁸Jesus told him, "Stand up, pick up your mat, and walk!"

⁹Instantly, the man was healed! He rolled up his sleeping mat and began walking! But this miracle happened on the Sabbath, ¹⁰so the Jewish leaders objected. They said to the man who was cured, "You can't work on the Sabbath! The law doesn't allow you to carry that sleeping mat!"

¹¹But he replied, "The man who healed me told me, 'Pick up your mat and walk.'"

¹²"Who said such a thing as that?" they demanded.

¹³The man didn't know, for Jesus had disappeared into the crowd. ¹⁴But afterward Jesus found him in the Temple and told him, "Now you are well; so stop sinning, or something even worse may happen to you." ¹⁵Then the man went and told the Jewish leaders that it was Jesus who had healed him.

Jesus Claims to Be the Son of God

¹⁶So the Jewish leaders began harassing* Jesus for breaking the Sabbath rules. ¹⁷But Jesus replied, "My Father is always working, and so am I." ¹⁸So the Jewish leaders tried all the harder to find a way to kill him. For he not only broke the Sabbath, he called God his Father, thereby making himself equal with God.

¹⁹So Jesus explained, "I tell you the truth, the Son can do nothing by himself. He does only what he sees the Father doing. Whatever the Father does, the Son also does. ²⁰For the Father loves the Son and shows him everything he is doing. In fact, the Father will show him how to do even greater works than healing this man. Then you will truly be astonished. ²¹For just as the Father gives life to those he raises from the dead, so the Son gives life to anyone he wants. ²²In addi-

tion, the Father judges no one. Instead, he has given the Son absolute authority to judge, ²³so that everyone will honor the Son, just as they honor the Father. Anyone who does not honor the Son is certainly not honoring the Father who sent him.

²⁴"I tell you the truth, those who listen to my message and believe in God who sent me have eternal life. They will never be condemned for their sins, but they have already passed from death into life.

²⁵"And I assure you that the time is coming, indeed it's here now, when the dead will hear my voice—the voice of the Son of God. And those who listen will live. ²⁶The Father has life in himself, and he has granted that same life-giving power to his Son. ²⁷And he has given him authority to judge everyone because he is the Son of Man.* ²⁸Don't be so surprised! Indeed, the time is coming when all the dead in their graves will hear the voice of God's Son, ²⁹and they will rise again. Those who have done good will rise to experience eternal life, and those who have continued in evil will rise to experience judgment. ³⁰I can do nothing on my own. I judge as God tells me. Therefore, my judgment is just, because I carry out the will of the one who sent me, not my own will.

Witnesses to Jesus

³¹"If I were to testify on my own behalf, my testimony would not be valid. ³²But someone else is also testifying about me, and I assure you that everything he says about me is true. ³³In fact, you sent investigators to listen to John the Baptist, and his testimony about me was true. ³⁴Of course, I have no need of human witnesses, but I say these things so you might be saved. ³⁵John was like a burning and shining lamp, and you were excited for a while about his message. ³⁶But I have a greater witness than John— my teachings and my miracles. The Father gave me these works to accomplish, and they prove that he sent me. ³⁷And the Father who sent me has testified about me himself. You have never heard his voice or seen him face to face, ³⁸and you do not have his message in your hearts, because you do not believe me—the one he sent to you.

³⁹"You search the Scriptures because you

5:3 Some manuscripts add an expanded conclusion to verse 3 and all of verse 4: *waiting for a certain movement of the water,* ⁴*for an angel of the Lord came from time to time and stirred up the water. And the first person to step in after the water was stirred was healed of whatever disease he had.* 5:16 Or *persecuting.* 5:27 "Son of Man" is a title Jesus used for himself.

5:39-40 The Jewish leaders knew the Scriptures backward and forward, yet they were spiritually dead. They missed the whole purpose of the Scriptures—to bring people into a vital relationship

think they give you eternal life. But the Scriptures point to me! [40]Yet you refuse to come to me to receive this life.

[41]"Your approval means nothing to me, [42]because I know you don't have God's love within you. [43]For I have come to you in my Father's name, and you have rejected me. Yet if others come in their own name, you gladly welcome them. [44]No wonder you can't believe! For you gladly honor each other, but you don't care about the honor that comes from the one who alone is God.*

[45]"Yet it isn't I who will accuse you before the Father. Moses will accuse you! Yes, Moses, in whom you put your hopes. [46]If you really believed Moses, you would believe me, because he wrote about me. [47]But since you don't believe what he wrote, how will you believe what I say?"

CHAPTER 6
Jesus Feeds Five Thousand
After this, Jesus crossed over to the far side of the Sea of Galilee, also known as the Sea of Tiberias. [2]A huge crowd kept following him wherever he went, because they saw his miraculous signs as he healed the sick. [3]Then Jesus climbed a hill and sat down with his disciples around him. [4](It was nearly time for the Jewish Passover celebration.) [5]Jesus soon saw a huge crowd of people coming to look for him. Turning to Philip, he asked, "Where can we buy bread to feed all these people?" [6]He was testing Philip, for he already knew what he was going to do.

[7]Philip replied, "Even if we worked for months, we wouldn't have enough money* to feed them!"

[8]Then Andrew, Simon Peter's brother, spoke up. [9]"There's a young boy here with five barley loaves and two fish. But what good is that with this huge crowd?"

[10]"Tell everyone to sit down," Jesus said. So they all sat down on the grassy slopes. (The men alone numbered about 5,000.) [11]Then Jesus took the loaves, gave thanks to God, and distributed them to the people. Afterward he did the same with the fish. And they all ate as much as they wanted. [12]After everyone was full, Jesus told his disciples, "Now gather the leftovers, so that nothing is wasted." [13]So they picked up the pieces and filled twelve baskets with scraps left by the people who had eaten from the five barley loaves.

[14]When the people saw him* do this miraculous sign, they exclaimed, "Surely, he is the Prophet we have been expecting!"* [15]When Jesus saw that they were ready to force him to be their king, he slipped away into the hills by himself.

Jesus Walks on Water
[16]That evening Jesus' disciples went down to the shore to wait for him. [17]But as darkness fell and Jesus still hadn't come back, they got into the boat and headed across the lake toward Capernaum. [18]Soon a gale swept down upon them, and the sea grew very rough. [19]They had rowed three or four miles* when suddenly they saw Jesus walking on the water toward the boat. They were terrified, [20]but he called out to them, "Don't be afraid.

5:44 Some manuscripts read *from the only One.* 6:7 Greek *Two hundred denarii would not be enough.* A denarius was equivalent to a laborer's full day's wage. 6:14a Some manuscripts read *Jesus.* 6:14b See Deut 18:15, 18; Mal 4:5-6. 6:19 Greek *25 or 30 stadia* [4.6 or 5.5 kilometers].

---

with the God of grace. Intellectual knowledge about the Bible does not bring us into a transforming relationship with God unless we act on that knowledge. Knowing about God's truth concerning recovery without applying it personally only results in failure. Real growth and recovery come through knowing God through Jesus Christ.

5:41-44 Jesus called the Pharisees to task for being more concerned about what others thought of them than about what God thought. At times during recovery it may be necessary to do things that are neither understood nor approved of by those around us. The bottom line for us is whether or not God approves of what we are doing, not what others think. As we take our moral inventory, God and his Word—not the opinions of others—are the standards for our behavior.

6:1-15 Jesus often used people as channels of his grace. In feeding 5,000 hungry men (plus women and children), Jesus used a young boy's provisions. In effecting our recovery—or others' recovery—God allows us to have a part in what he does. When we willingly dedicate our own small resources—time, talents, or possessions—to God, he can work a miracle of recovery for us and others. God can take our limited resources and multiply them beyond our wildest expectations.

6:16-21 It was a dark and stormy night on Lake Galilee. The disciples were cold, wet, and exhausted from rowing almost four miles in storm-tossed waters. They had been impatient and left safe shores without Jesus, but he came to their rescue anyway—walking on the stormy sea toward their boat! When Jesus got in the boat, he brought them safely to shore. We would be wise to stay with Jesus and his plan for us. Going off on our own will inevitably lead us into some stormy situations. When we leave Jesus behind, however, he will still rescue us if we look to him for help.

I am here!*" [21]Then they were eager to let him in the boat, and immediately they arrived at their destination!

Jesus, the Bread of Life

[22]The next day the crowd that had stayed on the far shore saw that the disciples had taken the only boat, and they realized Jesus had not gone with them. [23]Several boats from Tiberias landed near the place where the Lord had blessed the bread and the people had eaten. [24]So when the crowd saw that neither Jesus nor his disciples were there, they got into the boats and went across to Capernaum to look for him. [25]They found him on the other side of the lake and asked, "Rabbi, when did you get here?"

[26]Jesus replied, "I tell you the truth, you want to be with me because I fed you, not because you understood the miraculous signs. [27]But don't be so concerned about perishable things like food. Spend your energy seeking the eternal life that the Son of Man* can give you. For God the Father has given me the seal of his approval."

[28]They replied, "We want to perform God's works, too. What should we do?"

[29]Jesus told them, "This is the only work God wants from you: Believe in the one he has sent."

[30]They answered, "Show us a miraculous sign if you want us to believe in you. What can you do? [31]After all, our ancestors ate manna while they journeyed through the wilderness! The Scriptures say, 'Moses gave them bread from heaven to eat.'*"

[32]Jesus said, "I tell you the truth, Moses didn't give you bread from heaven. My Father did. And now he offers you the true bread from heaven. [33]The true bread of God is the one who comes down from heaven and gives life to the world."

[34]"Sir," they said, "give us that bread every day."

[35]Jesus replied, "I am the bread of life. Whoever comes to me will never be hungry again. Whoever believes in me will never be thirsty.

[36]But you haven't believed in me even though you have seen me. [37]However, those the Father has given me will come to me, and I will never reject them. [38]For I have come down from heaven to do the will of God who sent me, not to do my own will. [39]And this is the will of God, that I should not lose even one of all those he has given me, but that I should raise them up at the last day. [40]For it is my Father's will that all who see his Son and believe in him should have eternal life. I will raise them up at the last day."

[41]Then the people* began to murmur in disagreement because he had said, "I am the bread that came down from heaven." [42]They said, "Isn't this Jesus, the son of Joseph? We know his father and mother. How can he say, 'I came down from heaven'?"

[43]But Jesus replied, "Stop complaining about what I said. [44]For no one can come to me unless the Father who sent me draws them to me, and at the last day I will raise them up. [45]As it is written in the Scriptures,* 'They will all be taught by God.' Everyone who listens to the Father and learns from him comes to me. [46](Not that anyone has ever seen the Father; only I, who was sent from God, have seen him.)

[47]"I tell you the truth, anyone who believes has eternal life. [48]Yes, I am the bread of life! [49]Your ancestors ate manna in the wilderness, but they all died. [50]Anyone who eats the bread from heaven, however, will never die. [51]I am the living bread that came down from heaven. Anyone who eats this bread will live forever; and this bread, which I will offer so the world may live, is my flesh."

[52]Then the people began arguing with each other about what he meant. "How can this man give us his flesh to eat?" they asked.

[53]So Jesus said again, "I tell you the truth, unless you eat the flesh of the Son of Man and drink his blood, you cannot have eternal life within you. [54]But anyone who eats my flesh and drinks my blood has eternal life, and I will raise that person at the last day. [55]For my flesh is true food, and my blood is

6:20 Or The 'I AM' is here; Greek reads I am. See Exod 3:14. 6:27 "Son of Man" is a title Jesus used for himself. 6:31 Exod 16:4; Ps 78:24. 6:41 Greek Jewish people; also in 6:52. 6:45 Greek in the prophets. Isa 54:13.

6:32-40 After feeding more than 5,000 hungry people with five loaves of bread and two fish, Jesus explained that he himself was the bread of life. Jesus feeds the hungry with himself. His is a perfect love that never rejects us, no matter what our past sins are. He satisfies the deepest hungers of our soul and wants to help us complete our recovery. Until the end of time, Jesus will work toward the healing and recovery of all the broken people in his world. Our part is to turn to him and believe in his power to help us.

6:53-58 Jesus' words here are jarring. In saying we need to eat his flesh and drink his blood to have eternal life, Jesus offended many people, but he made some important points. Jesus' flesh

true drink. ⁵⁶Anyone who eats my flesh and drinks my blood remains in me, and I in him. ⁵⁷I live because of the living Father who sent me; in the same way, anyone who feeds on me will live because of me. ⁵⁸I am the true bread that came down from heaven. Anyone who eats this bread will not die as your ancestors did (even though they ate the manna) but will live forever."

⁵⁹He said these things while he was teaching in the synagogue in Capernaum.

Many Disciples Desert Jesus

⁶⁰Many of his disciples said, "This is very hard to understand. How can anyone accept it?"

⁶¹Jesus was aware that his disciples were complaining, so he said to them, "Does this offend you? ⁶²Then what will you think if you see the Son of Man ascend to heaven again? ⁶³The Spirit alone gives eternal life. Human effort accomplishes nothing. And the very words I have spoken to you are spirit and life. ⁶⁴But some of you do not believe me." (For Jesus knew from the beginning which ones didn't believe, and he knew who would betray him.) ⁶⁵Then he said, "That is why I said that people can't come to me unless the Father gives them to me."

⁶⁶At this point many of his disciples turned away and deserted him. ⁶⁷Then Jesus turned to the Twelve and asked, "Are you also going to leave?"

⁶⁸Simon Peter replied, "Lord, to whom would we go? You have the words that give eternal life. ⁶⁹We believe, and we know you are the Holy One of God.*"

⁷⁰Then Jesus said, "I chose the twelve of you, but one is a devil." ⁷¹He was speaking of Judas, son of Simon Iscariot, one of the Twelve, who would later betray him.

CHAPTER 7
Jesus and His Brothers

After this, Jesus traveled around Galilee. He wanted to stay out of Judea, where the Jewish leaders were plotting his death. ²But soon it was time for the Jewish Festival of Shelters, ³and Jesus' brothers said to him, "Leave here and go to Judea, where your followers can see your miracles! ⁴You can't become famous if you hide like this! If you can do such wonderful things, show yourself to the world!" ⁵For even his brothers didn't believe in him.

⁶Jesus replied, "Now is not the right time for me to go, but you can go anytime. ⁷The world can't hate you, but it does hate me because I accuse it of doing evil. ⁸You go on. I'm not going* to this festival, because my time has not yet come." ⁹After saying these things, Jesus remained in Galilee.

Jesus Teaches Openly at the Temple

¹⁰But after his brothers left for the festival, Jesus also went, though secretly, staying out

6:69 Other manuscripts read *you are the Christ, the Holy One of God;* still others read *you are the Christ, the Son of God;* and still others read *you are the Christ, the Son of the living God.* 7:8 Some manuscripts read *not yet going.*

reminds us that he was fully human so he understands our temptations and struggles. Jesus' mention of his blood anticipated his death on the cross—in our place, for our sins. To "eat" his flesh and "drink" his blood was a call to make him and his teachings our very life, not just an intellectual activity. We are to make Jesus the core of our being—emotional, spiritual, and physical. As we feed our body with food, we are to feed our soul with the spiritual reality represented by the body and blood of Christ.

6:68-69 Sales pitches for enticing products assault us daily. Publishers' sweepstakes, lottery games, television specials, political causes, religious gurus all call for our time, money, and devotion. They promise to give us what we need and desire. When all is said and done, however, we are left with Peter's question, "Lord, to whom would we go?" Jesus is the answer to our every need—including recovery. He alone can deliver us from our powerful addiction or compulsion. He alone deserves our total commitment.

7:3-10 Jesus experienced firsthand the ridicule and rejection from family that many of us in recovery have experienced. Jesus knew what was right and when to act. He resisted the timetables, agendas, and expectations that others—even his own brothers—foisted upon him. Timetables for recovery, going public, or staging a comeback will vary for each person. Premature publicity of our conversion to Christ or commitment to recovery may lead to unnecessary attacks from others or inflated pride about our personal successes. Either will stand in the way of what God is trying to accomplish in and through our life. Often it is best to remain anonymous until the time is right.

7:10-15, 25-27, 40-49 In this chapter the author polled the audience for opinions about who Jesus actually is. Some believed he was a wonderful teacher. Others thought he was a fraud or a madman. Still others conceded he might be the Messiah or at least a prophet. The religious authorities saw him as a political threat and wanted him arrested, even killed. We, too, must decide who Jesus is and what he means to us. Our decision about Jesus is very important. It will not only affect our recovery; it will have eternal consequences as well (see 8:24).

of public view. [11]The Jewish leaders tried to find him at the festival and kept asking if anyone had seen him. [12]There was a lot of grumbling about him among the crowds. Some argued, "He's a good man," but others said, "He's nothing but a fraud who deceives the people." [13]But no one had the courage to speak favorably about him in public, for they were afraid of getting in trouble with the Jewish leaders.

[14]Then, midway through the festival, Jesus went up to the Temple and began to teach. [15]The people* were surprised when they heard him. "How does he know so much when he hasn't been trained?" they asked.

[16]So Jesus told them, "My message is not my own; it comes from God who sent me. [17]Anyone who wants to do the will of God will know whether my teaching is from God or is merely my own. [18]Those who speak for themselves want glory only for themselves, but a person who seeks to honor the one who sent him speaks truth, not lies. [19]Moses gave you the law, but none of you obeys it! In fact, you are trying to kill me."

[20]The crowd replied, "You're demon possessed! Who's trying to kill you?"

[21]Jesus replied, "I did one miracle on the Sabbath, and you were amazed. [22]But you work on the Sabbath, too, when you obey Moses' law of circumcision. (Actually, this tradition of circumcision began with the patriarchs, long before the law of Moses.) [23]For if the correct time for circumcising your son falls on the Sabbath, you go ahead and do it so as not to break the law of Moses. So why should you be angry with me for healing a man on the Sabbath? [24]Look beneath the surface so you can judge correctly."

Is Jesus the Messiah?

[25]Some of the people who lived in Jerusalem started to ask each other, "Isn't this the man they are trying to kill? [26]But here he is, speaking in public, and they say nothing to him. Could our leaders possibly believe that he is the Messiah? [27]But how could he be? For we know where this man comes from. When the Messiah comes, he will simply appear; no one will know where he comes from."

[28]While Jesus was teaching in the Temple, he called out, "Yes, you know me, and you know where I come from. But I'm not here on my own. The one who sent me is true, and you don't know him. [29]But I know him because I come from him, and he sent me to you." [30]Then the leaders tried to arrest him; but no one laid a hand on him, because his time* had not yet come.

[31]Many among the crowds at the Temple believed in him. "After all," they said, "would you expect the Messiah to do more miraculous signs than this man has done?"

[32]When the Pharisees heard that the crowds were whispering such things, they and the leading priests sent Temple guards to arrest Jesus. [33]But Jesus told them, "I will be with you only a little longer. Then I will return to the one who sent me. [34]You will search for me but not find me. And you cannot go where I am going."

[35]The Jewish leaders were puzzled by this statement. "Where is he planning to go?" they asked. "Is he thinking of leaving the country and going to the Jews in other lands?* Maybe he will even teach the Greeks! [36]What does he mean when he says, 'You will search for me but not find me,' and 'You cannot go where I am going'?"

Jesus Promises Living Water

[37]On the last day, the climax of the festival, Jesus stood and shouted to the crowds, "Anyone who is thirsty may come to me! [38]Anyone who believes in me may come and drink! For the Scriptures declare, 'Rivers of living water will flow from his heart.' "* [39](When he said "living water," he was speaking of the Spirit, who would be given to everyone believing in him. But the Spirit had not yet been given,* because Jesus had not yet entered into his glory.)

7:15 Greek *Jewish people.* 7:30 Greek *his hour.* 7:35 Or *the Jews who live among the Greeks?* 7:37-38 Or *"Let anyone who is thirsty come to me and drink. 38For the Scriptures declare, 'Rivers of living water will flow from the heart of anyone who believes in me.'"* 7:39 Several early manuscripts read *But as yet there was no Spirit.* Still others read *But as yet there was no Holy Spirit.*

7:37-39 Jesus is the living water who satisfies our thirst. When we believe in him, he gives us his Spirit. The Holy Spirit becomes an inexhaustible river of living water, welling up in us and flowing through us. The indwelling and eternal Holy Spirit goes with us wherever we go and can quench even our strongest spiritual thirsts and meet our deepest needs. Having this water "on tap" is the key to resisting the temptation of alcohol, food, sex, work, a codependent relationship, or any other compulsion.

Division and Unbelief

⁴⁰When the crowds heard him say this, some of them declared, "Surely this man is the Prophet we've been expecting."* ⁴¹Others said, "He is the Messiah." Still others said, "But he can't be! Will the Messiah come from Galilee? ⁴²For the Scriptures clearly state that the Messiah will be born of the royal line of David, in Bethlehem, the village where King David was born."* ⁴³So the crowd was divided about him. ⁴⁴Some even wanted him arrested, but no one laid a hand on him.

⁴⁵When the Temple guards returned without having arrested Jesus, the leading priests and Pharisees demanded, "Why didn't you bring him in?"

⁴⁶"We have never heard anyone speak like this!" the guards responded.

⁴⁷"Have you been led astray, too?" the Pharisees mocked. ⁴⁸"Is there a single one of us rulers or Pharisees who believes in him? ⁴⁹This foolish crowd follows him, but they are ignorant of the law. God's curse is on them!"

⁵⁰Then Nicodemus, the leader who had met with Jesus earlier, spoke up. ⁵¹"Is it legal to convict a man before he is given a hearing?" he asked.

⁵²They replied, "Are you from Galilee, too? Search the Scriptures and see for yourself—no prophet ever comes* from Galilee!"

[The most ancient Greek manuscripts do not include John 7:53–8:11.]

⁵³Then the meeting broke up, and everybody went home.

CHAPTER 8
A Woman Caught in Adultery

Jesus returned to the Mount of Olives, ²but early the next morning he was back again at the Temple. A crowd soon gathered, and he sat down and taught them. ³As he was speaking, the teachers of religious law and the Pharisees brought a woman who had been caught in the act of adultery. They put her in front of the crowd.

⁴"Teacher," they said to Jesus, "this woman was caught in the act of adultery. ⁵The law of Moses says to stone her. What do you say?"

⁶They were trying to trap him into saying something they could use against him, but Jesus stooped down and wrote in the dust

7:40 See Deut 18:15, 18; Mal 4:5-6. 7:42 See Mic 5:2.
7:52 Some manuscripts read *the prophet does not come.*

STEP 5

Feelings of Shame

BIBLE READING: John 8:3-11
We admitted to God, to ourselves, and to another human being the exact nature of our wrongs.

Shame has kept many of us in hiding. The thought of admitting our sins and revealing ourself to other human beings stirs up feelings of shame and the fear of being publicly exposed.

"The teachers of religious law and the Pharisees brought a woman who had been caught in the act of adultery. They put her in front of the crowd. 'Teacher,' they said to Jesus, '. . . the law of Moses says to stone her. What do you say?' . . . Jesus stooped down and wrote in the dust with his finger. They kept demanding an answer, so he stood up again and said, 'All right, but let the one who has never sinned throw the first stone!' Then he stooped down again and wrote in the dust. When the accusers heard this, they slipped away one by one . . . until only Jesus was left in the middle of the crowd with the woman" (John 8:3-9).

Many believe that it was Jesus' writing in the dust that caused the accusers to leave. Perhaps he was listing the secret sins of the Jewish leaders. If this is true, it gives us a beautiful picture of the kind of person Jesus is—a person to whom we can safely expose our secrets. Our confessor needs to be someone who is not surprised by sin and will not be waiting to condemn us. Such a person needs to take private note of our wrongs, writing them in the soft dust, not etching them in stone and posting them in public. Since shame can be a trigger for addictive behavior, we need to be careful about whom we choose to confide in. *Turn to page 1421, Acts 26.*

with his finger. [7]They kept demanding an answer, so he stood up again and said, "All right, but let the one who has never sinned throw the first stone!" [8]Then he stooped down again and wrote in the dust.

[9]When the accusers heard this, they slipped away one by one, beginning with the oldest, until only Jesus was left in the middle of the crowd with the woman. [10]Then Jesus stood up again and said to the woman, "Where are your accusers? Didn't even one of them condemn you?"

[11]"No, Lord," she said.

And Jesus said, "Neither do I. Go and sin no more."

Jesus, the Light of the World

[12]Jesus spoke to the people once more and said, "I am the light of the world. If you follow me, you won't have to walk in darkness, because you will have the light that leads to life."

[13]The Pharisees replied, "You are making those claims about yourself! Such testimony is not valid."

[14]Jesus told them, "These claims are valid even though I make them about myself. For I know where I came from and where I am going, but you don't know this about me. [15]You judge me by human standards, but I do not judge anyone. [16]And if I did, my judgment would be correct in every respect because I am not alone. The Father* who sent me is with me. [17]Your own law says that if two people agree about something, their witness is accepted as fact.* [18]I am one witness, and my Father who sent me is the other."

[19]"Where is your father?" they asked.

Jesus answered, "Since you don't know who I am, you don't know who my Father is. If you knew me, you would also know my Fa-

ther." [20]Jesus made these statements while he was teaching in the section of the Temple known as the Treasury. But he was not arrested, because his time* had not yet come.

The Unbelieving People Warned

[21]Later Jesus said to them again, "I am going away. You will search for me but will die in your sin. You cannot come where I am going."

[22]The people* asked, "Is he planning to commit suicide? What does he mean, 'You cannot come where I am going'?"

[23]Jesus continued, "You are from below; I am from above. You belong to this world; I do not. [24]That is why I said that you will die in your sins; for unless you believe that I AM who I claim to be,* you will die in your sins."

[25]"Who are you?" they demanded.

Jesus replied, "The one I have always claimed to be.* [26]I have much to say about you and much to condemn, but I won't. For I say only what I have heard from the one who sent me, and he is completely truthful." [27]But they still didn't understand that he was talking about his Father.

[28]So Jesus said, "When you have lifted up the Son of Man on the cross, then you will understand that I AM he.* I do nothing on my own but say only what the Father taught me. [29]And the one who sent me is with me— he has not deserted me. For I always do what pleases him." [30]Then many who heard him say these things believed in him.

Jesus and Abraham

[31]Jesus said to the people who believed in him, "You are truly my disciples if you remain faithful to my teachings. [32]And you will know the truth, and the truth will set you free."

[33]"But we are descendants of Abraham," they said. "We have never been slaves to anyone. What do you mean, 'You will be set free'?"

8:16 Some manuscripts read *The One.* 8:17 See Deut 19:15. 8:20 Greek *his hour.* 8:22 Greek *Jewish people;* also in 8:31, 48, 52, 57. 8:24 Greek *unless you believe that I am.* See Exod 3:14. 8:25 Or *Why do I speak to you at all?* 8:28 Greek *When you have lifted up the Son of Man, then you will know that I am.* "Son of Man" is a title Jesus used for himself.

8:12 As the light of the world, Jesus exposes what has been hidden and guides us down the path of life and recovery. In part, to walk in the light means to be honest and vulnerable with others and to walk in fellowship with God (see 1 John 1:5-7). As we express our needs and feelings, our sins and struggles, with the people we trust, light will fall on our failures and strengths. This will give us the direction we need to make significant progress in recovery.

8:31-36 To be "set free" is to know the truth—the truth about ourself and about Jesus our liberator. The truth is this: We are a slave to sin and powerless to manage our life effectively. With God's truth as a standard for our moral inventory, we can recognize and confess our needs and struggles, our sins and addiction. As we confess these to God, to ourself, and to at least one other person, we share the truth about our life. When we turn our broken life over to God, who alone can make us whole, we are again acknowledging the truth. These different applications of the truth can combine to set us free from sinful habits, chemical dependencies, and emotional bondage.

³⁴Jesus replied, "I tell you the truth, everyone who sins is a slave of sin. ³⁵A slave is not a permanent member of the family, but a son is part of the family forever. ³⁶So if the Son sets you free, you are truly free. ³⁷Yes, I realize that you are descendants of Abraham. And yet some of you are trying to kill me because there's no room in your hearts for my message. ³⁸I am telling you what I saw when I was with my Father. But you are following the advice of your father."

³⁹"Our father is Abraham!" they declared.

"No," Jesus replied, "for if you were really the children of Abraham, you would follow his example.* ⁴⁰Instead, you are trying to kill me because I told you the truth, which I heard from God. Abraham never did such a thing. ⁴¹No, you are imitating your real father."

They replied, "We aren't illegitimate children! God himself is our true Father."

⁴²Jesus told them, "If God were your Father, you would love me, because I have come to you from God. I am not here on my own, but he sent me. ⁴³Why can't you understand what I am saying? It's because you can't even hear me! ⁴⁴For you are the children of your father the devil, and you love to do the evil things he does. He was a murderer from the beginning. He has always hated the truth, because there is no truth in him. When he lies, it is consistent with his character; for he is a liar and the father of lies. ⁴⁵So when I tell the truth, you just naturally don't believe me! ⁴⁶Which of you can truthfully accuse me of sin? And since I am telling you the truth, why don't you believe me? ⁴⁷Anyone who belongs to God listens gladly to the words of God. But you don't listen because you don't belong to God."

⁴⁸The people retorted, "You Samaritan devil! Didn't we say all along that you were possessed by a demon?"

⁴⁹"No," Jesus said, "I have no demon in me. For I honor my Father—and you dishonor me. ⁵⁰And though I have no wish to glorify myself, God is going to glorify me. He is the true judge. ⁵¹I tell you the truth, anyone who obeys my teaching will never die!"

⁵²The people said, "Now we know you are possessed by a demon. Even Abraham and the prophets died, but you say, 'Anyone who obeys my teaching will never die!' ⁵³Are you greater than our father Abraham? He died, and so did the prophets. Who do you think you are?"

8:39 Some manuscripts read *if you are really the children of Abraham, follow his example.*

HONESTY

READ JOHN 8:30-36

Living in denial is living dishonestly. How many times have we lied to ourself and others, saying, "I can stop any time I want to!" or "I have the right to choose how I live my own life!" or "My behavior doesn't affect anyone but me!" Ironically, as we asserted our freedom to live as we chose, we soon lost the freedom to choose anything other than our dependency; we became enslaved to it.

Jesus said to some people who believed in him: "You are truly my disciples if you remain faithful to my teachings. And you will know the truth, and the truth will set you free. . . . I tell you the truth, everyone who sins is a slave of sin. A slave is not a permanent member of the family, but a son is part of the family forever. So if the Son sets you free, you are truly free. . . . Why can't you understand what I am saying? It's because you can't even hear me! For you are the children of your father the devil. . . . He was a murderer from the beginning. He has always hated the truth, because there is no truth in him. When he lies, it is consistent with his character; for he is a liar and the father of lies" (John 8:31-36, 43-44).

The spiritual forces that sway our life have roots in either truth or deceit. Truth leads to freedom; deceit leads to bondage and death. Denial is a lie that keeps us in slavery. When we are a slave to our addiction, we lose the right to choose any other way of life. It is only when we break the cycle of denial, when we become brutally honest about our bondage, that there is any chance for real freedom.
Turn to page 1365, John 14.

54Jesus answered, "If I want glory for myself, it doesn't count. But it is my Father who will glorify me. You say, 'He is our God,*' 55but you don't even know him. I know him. If I said otherwise, I would be as great a liar as you! But I do know him and obey him. 56Your father Abraham rejoiced as he looked forward to my coming. He saw it and was glad."

57The people said, "You aren't even fifty years old. How can you say you have seen Abraham?*"

58Jesus answered, "I tell you the truth, before Abraham was even born, I AM!*" 59At that point they picked up stones to throw at him. But Jesus was hidden from them and left the Temple.

CHAPTER 9
Jesus Heals a Man Born Blind

As Jesus was walking along, he saw a man who had been blind from birth. 2"Rabbi," his disciples asked him, "why was this man born blind? Was it because of his own sins or his parents' sins?"

3"It was not because of his sins or his parents' sins," Jesus answered. "This happened so the power of God could be seen in him. 4We must quickly carry out the tasks assigned us by the one who sent us.* The night is coming, and then no one can work. 5But while I am here in the world, I am the light of the world."

6Then he spit on the ground, made mud with the saliva, and spread the mud over the blind man's eyes. 7He told him, "Go wash yourself in the pool of Siloam (Siloam means "sent"). So the man went and washed and came back seeing!

8His neighbors and others who knew him as a blind beggar asked each other, "Isn't this the man who used to sit and beg?" 9Some said he was, and others said, "No, he just looks like him!"

But the beggar kept saying, "Yes, I am the same one!"

10They asked, "Who healed you? What happened?"

11He told them, "The man they call Jesus made mud and spread it over my eyes and told me, 'Go to the pool of Siloam and wash yourself.' So I went and washed, and now I can see!"

12"Where is he now?" they asked.

"I don't know," he replied.

13Then they took the man who had been blind to the Pharisees, 14because it was on the Sabbath that Jesus had made the mud and healed him. 15The Pharisees asked the man all about it. So he told them, "He put the mud over my eyes, and when I washed it away, I could see!"

16Some of the Pharisees said, "This man Jesus is not from God, for he is working on the Sabbath." Others said, "But how could an ordinary sinner do such miraculous signs?" So there was a deep division of opinion among them.

17Then the Pharisees again questioned the man who had been blind and demanded, "What's your opinion about this man who healed you?"

The man replied, "I think he must be a prophet."

18The Jewish leaders still refused to believe the man had been blind and could now see, so they called in his parents. 19They asked them, "Is this your son? Was he born blind? If so, how can he now see?"

20His parents replied, "We know this is our son and that he was born blind, 21but we

8:54 Some manuscripts read *your God.* 8:57 Some manuscripts read *How can you say Abraham has seen you?* 8:58 Or *before Abraham was even born, I have always been alive;* Greek reads *before Abraham was, I am.* See Exod 3:14.
9:4 Other manuscripts read *I must quickly carry out the tasks assigned me by the one who sent me;* still others read *We must quickly carry out the tasks assigned us by the one who sent me.*

9:1-12, 35-41 Imagine being blind from birth, not being able to see the people we love and the world around us. Then imagine people insinuating that we are blind because of our personal sins or the sins of our parents! Jesus healed this man's blindness, but the real miracle occurred later when the man's spiritual blindness was healed. He saw through eyes of faith that Jesus truly was the Messiah, the Savior of the world. We, too, must recognize that God has the power and the desire to free us from habitual sins, chemical dependencies, and character flaws. Recognizing Jesus as our deliverer is the beginning of our spiritual sight.

9:13-34 The Pharisees were so blinded by their legalistic attitudes that they could not see a wonderful miracle of healing taking place right in front of them. They were more concerned about the letter of the law and the threat Jesus posed to their authority than the amazing healing. They were exposed to the power of God but chose to remain blind to the truth. Those who are teachable and humble will discover that God can heal even the most terrible affliction. Often the people we think least likely to make progress in recovery experience healing and deliverance because they are humble enough to ask God for help.

don't know how he can see or who healed him. Ask him. He is old enough to speak for himself." [22]His parents said this because they were afraid of the Jewish leaders, who had announced that anyone saying Jesus was the Messiah would be expelled from the synagogue. [23]That's why they said, "He is old enough. Ask him."

[24]So for the second time they called in the man who had been blind and told him, "God should get the glory for this,* because we know this man Jesus is a sinner."

[25]"I don't know whether he is a sinner," the man replied. "But I know this: I was blind, and now I can see!"

[26]"But what did he do?" they asked. "How did he heal you?"

[27]"Look!" the man exclaimed. "I told you once. Didn't you listen? Why do you want to hear it again? Do you want to become his disciples, too?"

[28]Then they cursed him and said, "You are his disciple, but we are disciples of Moses! [29]We know God spoke to Moses, but we don't even know where this man comes from."

[30]"Why, that's very strange!" the man replied. "He healed my eyes, and yet you don't know where he comes from? [31]We know that God doesn't listen to sinners, but he is ready to hear those who worship him and do his will. [32]Ever since the world began, no one has been able to open the eyes of someone born blind. [33]If this man were not from God, he couldn't have done it."

[34]"You were born a total sinner!" they answered. "Are you trying to teach us?" And they threw him out of the synagogue.

Spiritual Blindness
[35]When Jesus heard what had happened, he found the man and asked, "Do you believe in the Son of Man?*"

[36]The man answered, "Who is he, sir? I want to believe in him."

[37]"You have seen him," Jesus said, "and he is speaking to you!"

[38]"Yes, Lord, I believe!" the man said. And he worshiped Jesus.

[39]Then Jesus told him,* "I entered this world to render judgment—to give sight to the blind and to show those who think they see* that they are blind."

[40]Some Pharisees who were standing nearby heard him and asked, "Are you saying we're blind?"

[41]"If you were blind, you wouldn't be guilty," Jesus replied. "But you remain guilty because you claim you can see.

CHAPTER 10
The Good Shepherd and His Sheep
"I tell you the truth, anyone who sneaks over the wall of a sheepfold, rather than going through the gate, must surely be a thief and a robber! [2]But the one who enters through the gate is the shepherd of the sheep. [3]The gatekeeper opens the gate for him, and the sheep recognize his voice and come to him. He calls his own sheep by name and leads them out. [4]After he has gathered his own flock, he walks ahead of them, and they follow him because they know his voice. [5]They won't follow a stranger; they will run from him because they don't know his voice."

[6]Those who heard Jesus use this illustration didn't understand what he meant, [7]so he explained it to them: "I tell you the truth, I am the gate for the sheep. [8]All who came before me* were thieves and robbers. But the true sheep did not listen to them. [9]Yes, I am the gate. Those who come in through me will be saved.* They will come and go freely and will

9:24 Or *Give glory to God, not to Jesus;* Greek reads *Give glory to God.* 9:35 Some manuscripts read *the Son of God?* "Son of Man" is a title Jesus used for himself. 9:38-39a Some manuscripts do not include *"Yes, Lord, I believe!" the man said. And he worshiped Jesus. Then Jesus told him.* 9:39b Greek *those who see.* 10:8 Some manuscripts do not include *before me.* 10:9 Or *will find safety.*

10:1-5 The shepherd knows each of his sheep by name, and they know and respond only to his voice. In like manner, Jesus knows our personality, needs, feelings, and desires. He even knows our faults and our sins, yet he still loves us! He calls out to us and leads us in the way that is best for us. To be set free from the pain of our past, we must respond to the guiding voice of our shepherd, who knows us fully and loves us completely.

10:7-18 At night shepherds in Bible times led their flocks to lie down in a sheepfold (an area boxed in by brush or rock). The shepherd slept in the opening and literally became the gate to the sheepfold. He protected the sheep from wild animals and robbers with his own body. Jesus, our gate and good shepherd, does this for us. By sacrificing his life he has provided the means for our salvation and protection from temptations and addictions. In Christ we can find security and serenity, even when we fail. God is able to use our sins and failures to bring about our ultimate good if we trust him and obey his plan for our life.

find good pastures. ¹⁰The thief's purpose is to steal and kill and destroy. My purpose is to give them a rich and satisfying life.

¹¹"I am the good shepherd. The good shepherd sacrifices his life for the sheep. ¹²A hired hand will run when he sees a wolf coming. He will abandon the sheep because they don't belong to him and he isn't their shepherd. And so the wolf attacks them and scatters the flock. ¹³The hired hand runs away because he's working only for the money and doesn't really care about the sheep.

¹⁴"I am the good shepherd; I know my own sheep, and they know me, ¹⁵just as my Father knows me and I know the Father. So I sacrifice my life for the sheep. ¹⁶I have other sheep, too, that are not in this sheepfold. I must bring them also. They will listen to my voice, and there will be one flock with one shepherd.

¹⁷"The Father loves me because I sacrifice my life so I may take it back again. ¹⁸No one can take my life from me. I sacrifice it voluntarily. For I have the authority to lay it down when I want to and also to take it up again. For this is what my Father has commanded."

¹⁹When he said these things, the people* were again divided in their opinions about him. ²⁰Some said, "He's demon possessed and out of his mind. Why listen to a man like that?" ²¹Others said, "This doesn't sound like a man possessed by a demon! Can a demon open the eyes of the blind?"

Jesus Claims to Be the Son of God

²²It was now winter, and Jesus was in Jerusalem at the time of Hanukkah, the Festival of Dedication. ²³He was in the Temple, walking through the section known as Solomon's Colonnade. ²⁴The people surrounded him and asked, "How long are you going to keep us in suspense? If you are the Messiah, tell us plainly."

²⁵Jesus replied, "I have already told you, and you don't believe me. The proof is the work I do in my Father's name. ²⁶But you don't believe me because you are not my sheep. ²⁷My sheep listen to my voice; I know them, and they follow me. ²⁸I give them eternal life, and they will never perish. No one can snatch them away from me, ²⁹for my Father has given them to me, and he is more powerful than anyone else.* No one can snatch them from the Father's hand. ³⁰The Father and I are one."

³¹Once again the people picked up stones to kill him. ³²Jesus said, "At my Father's direction I have done many good works. For which one are you going to stone me?"

³³They replied, "We're stoning you not for any good work, but for blasphemy! You, a mere man, claim to be God."

³⁴Jesus replied, "It is written in your own Scriptures* that God said to certain leaders of the people, 'I say, you are gods!'* ³⁵And you know that the Scriptures cannot be altered. So if those people who received God's message were called 'gods,' ³⁶why do you call it blasphemy when I say, 'I am the Son of God'? After all, the Father set me apart and sent me into the world. ³⁷Don't believe me unless I carry out my Father's work. ³⁸But if I do his work, believe in the evidence of the miraculous works I have done, even if you don't believe me. Then you will know and understand that the Father is in me, and I am in the Father."

³⁹Once again they tried to arrest him, but he got away and left them. ⁴⁰He went beyond the Jordan River near the place where John was first baptizing and stayed there awhile. ⁴¹And many followed him. "John didn't perform miraculous signs," they remarked to one another, "but everything he said about

---

10:19 Greek *Jewish people;* also in 10:24, 31. **10:29** Other manuscripts read *for what my Father has given me is more powerful than anything;* still others read *for regarding that which my Father has given me, he is greater than all.* **10:34a** Greek *your own law.* **10:34b** Ps 82:6.

10:27-29 When we entrust ourself to Jesus, we can feel safe and secure. No one can take us away from him and his care, not even the Devil! Such security is sometimes hard for us to grasp emotionally, especially if we have been a victim of abuse; we may have been so emotionally damaged that life can seem very unsafe. Unsure of whom we can trust and not wanting to be hurt again, we keep everyone at a distance—even God. Recovery from abuse can occur only in a safe relationship that God offers to us in which divine love and protection are expressed.

10:30-38 Jesus said that he and the Father are one; this was a clear claim to divinity. Jesus was God in human flesh (1:14). He was one with his Father in essence, in purpose, in words, and in thoughts. All of Jesus' miracles attest to his divine authority (10:37-38), as do the Scriptures (5:39). Only a God-man could perfectly understand our human weaknesses yet command our complete trust. Only the divine miracle worker, Jesus, can effect the everyday and everlasting recovery that we need.

this man has come true." [42]And many who were there believed in Jesus.

CHAPTER 11
The Raising of Lazarus

A man named Lazarus was sick. He lived in Bethany with his sisters, Mary and Martha. [2]This is the Mary who later poured the expensive perfume on the Lord's feet and wiped them with her hair.* Her brother, Lazarus, was sick. [3]So the two sisters sent a message to Jesus telling him, "Lord, your dear friend is very sick."

[4]But when Jesus heard about it he said, "Lazarus's sickness will not end in death. No, it happened for the glory of God so that the Son of God will receive glory from this." [5]So although Jesus loved Martha, Mary, and Lazarus, [6]he stayed where he was for the next two days. [7]Finally, he said to his disciples, "Let's go back to Judea."

[8]But his disciples objected. "Rabbi," they said, "only a few days ago the people* in Judea were trying to stone you. Are you going there again?"

[9]Jesus replied, "There are twelve hours of daylight every day. During the day people can walk safely. They can see because they have the light of this world. [10]But at night there is danger of stumbling because they have no light." [11]Then he said, "Our friend Lazarus has fallen asleep, but now I will go and wake him up."

[12]The disciples said, "Lord, if he is sleeping, he will soon get better!" [13]They thought Jesus meant Lazarus was simply sleeping, but Jesus meant Lazarus had died.

[14]So he told them plainly, "Lazarus is dead. [15]And for your sakes, I'm glad I wasn't there, for now you will really believe. Come, let's go see him."

[16]Thomas, nicknamed the Twin,* said to his fellow disciples, "Let's go, too—and die with Jesus."

[17]When Jesus arrived at Bethany, he was told that Lazarus had already been in his grave for four days. [18]Bethany was only a few miles* down the road from Jerusalem, [19]and many of the people had come to console Martha and Mary in their loss. [20]When Martha got word that Jesus was coming, she went to meet him. But Mary stayed in the house. [21]Martha said to Jesus, "Lord, if only you had been here, my brother would not have died. [22]But even now I know that God will give you whatever you ask."

[23]Jesus told her, "Your brother will rise again."

[24]"Yes," Martha said, "he will rise when everyone else rises, at the last day."

[25]Jesus told her, "I am the resurrection and the life.* Anyone who believes in me will live, even after dying. [26]Everyone who lives in me and believes in me will never ever die. Do you believe this, Martha?"

[27]"Yes, Lord," she told him. "I have always believed you are the Messiah, the Son of God, the one who has come into the world from God." [28]Then she returned to Mary. She called Mary aside from the mourners and told her, "The Teacher is here and wants to see you." [29]So Mary immediately went to him.

[30]Jesus had stayed outside the village, at the place where Martha met him. [31]When the people who were at the house consoling Mary saw her leave so hastily, they assumed she was going to Lazarus's grave to weep. So they followed her there. [32]When Mary arrived and saw Jesus, she fell at his feet and said, "Lord, if only you had been here, my brother would not have died."

[33]When Jesus saw her weeping and saw the other people wailing with her, a deep anger welled up within him,* and he was deeply troubled. [34]"Where have you put him?" he asked them.

They told him, "Lord, come and see." [35]Then Jesus wept. [36]The people who were standing nearby said, "See how much he

---

11:2 This incident is recorded in chapter 12. 11:8 Greek *Jewish people;* also in 11:19, 31, 33, 36, 45, 54. 11:16 Greek *Thomas, who was called Didymus.* 11:18 Greek *was about 15 stadia* [about 2.8 kilometers]. 11:25 Some manuscripts do not include *and the life.* 11:33 Or *he was angry in his spirit.*

11:3-4 When faced with a critical illness or a hopeless situation, we have options. We can whine and look for pity, we can complain and blame God, or we can see the crisis as an opportunity to make requests of God. Mary and Martha asked Jesus to help them with their sick brother. Then they gave him the glory for the amazing miracle he did—raising their brother, Lazarus, from the dead. If we can learn to humbly ask God for help, we will make progress in recovery. If he can raise someone from the dead, he is powerful enough to help us overcome our dependency and character flaws.

loved him!" ³⁷But some said, "This man healed a blind man. Couldn't he have kept Lazarus from dying?"

³⁸Jesus was still angry as he arrived at the tomb, a cave with a stone rolled across its entrance. ³⁹"Roll the stone aside," Jesus told them.

But Martha, the dead man's sister, protested, "Lord, he has been dead for four days. The smell will be terrible."

⁴⁰Jesus responded, "Didn't I tell you that you would see God's glory if you believe?" ⁴¹So they rolled the stone aside. Then Jesus looked up to heaven and said, "Father, thank you for hearing me. ⁴²You always hear me, but I said it out loud for the sake of all these people standing here, so that they will believe you sent me." ⁴³Then Jesus shouted, "Lazarus, come out!" ⁴⁴And the dead man came out, his hands and feet bound in graveclothes, his face wrapped in a headcloth. Jesus told them, "Unwrap him and let him go!"

The Plot to Kill Jesus

⁴⁵Many of the people who were with Mary believed in Jesus when they saw this happen. ⁴⁶But some went to the Pharisees and told them what Jesus had done. ⁴⁷Then the leading priests and Pharisees called the high council* together. "What are we going to do?" they asked each other. "This man certainly performs many miraculous signs. ⁴⁸If we allow him to go on like this, soon everyone will believe in him. Then the Roman army will come and destroy both our Temple* and our nation."

⁴⁹Caiaphas, who was high priest at that time,* said, "You don't know what you're talking about! ⁵⁰You don't realize that it's better for you that one man should die for the people than for the whole nation to be destroyed."

⁵¹He did not say this on his own; as high priest at that time he was led to prophesy that Jesus would die for the entire nation. ⁵²And not only for that nation, but to bring together and unite all the children of God scattered around the world.

⁵³So from that time on, the Jewish leaders began to plot Jesus' death. ⁵⁴As a result, Jesus stopped his public ministry among the people and left Jerusalem. He went to a place near the wilderness, to the village of Ephraim, and stayed there with his disciples.

⁵⁵It was now almost time for the Jewish Passover celebration, and many people from all over the country arrived in Jerusalem several days early so they could go through the purification ceremony before Passover began. ⁵⁶They kept looking for Jesus, but as they stood around in the Temple, they said to each other, "What do you think? He won't come for Passover, will he?" ⁵⁷Meanwhile, the leading priests and Pharisees had publicly ordered that anyone seeing Jesus must report it immediately so they could arrest him.

CHAPTER 12
Jesus Anointed at Bethany

Six days before the Passover celebration began, Jesus arrived in Bethany, the home of Lazarus—the man he had raised from the dead. ²A dinner was prepared in Jesus' honor. Martha served, and Lazarus was among those who ate* with him. ³Then Mary took a twelve-ounce jar* of expensive perfume made

---

11:47 Greek *the Sanhedrin.* 11:48 Or *our position;* Greek reads *our place.* 11:49 Greek *that year;* also in 11:51. 12:2 Or *who reclined.* 12:3 Greek *took 1 litra [327 grams].*

11:37-44 Imagine being there when Jesus raised Lazarus from the dead. The man had been dead for four days, and his body had begun to smell. Suddenly he responded to Jesus' voice and walked out of the grave wrapped up like a mummy! Lazarus was alive! The one who has power over the grave has power to bring new life to us (11:25-27). Jesus Christ has set us free from the bondage of sin and death, but our "graveclothes"—destructive habits and dependencies—have got to go!

12:1-8 Mary's faith in Jesus is a testimony to us all. Scripture records that she knelt in humble faith at Jesus' feet three times: She sat at Jesus' feet listening to his every word (Luke 10:39); she fell at his feet crying and seeking comfort (John 11:32); and here she knelt to anoint his feet with expensive perfume. Jesus was first in her heart, and she surrendered herself to him. The decision to surrender all we are and have to God is a crucial step in the recovery process. When we do, God will help us with our problems.

12:12-19 The crowds hailed Jesus as the promised Messiah, but his days of popularity would be few. He had just raised Lazarus from the dead in front of many witnesses. In a few days, however, the people would do nothing as the Jewish leaders and Roman governors crowned Jesus with thorns and executed him as a pretentious "King of the Jews" (18:39–19:21). The recovery process can be like that for us—full of heated curiosity one week and hollow commitment the next. If we hope to benefit from our recovery program, our commitment must be wholehearted. A halfhearted commitment to recovery could leave us worse off than we were before we started.

JUDAS ISCARIOT

In the life of Judas we find a terrible tragedy—the tragedy of having been so close to Jesus yet never really knowing him. For Judas the bottom line was profit. He was always looking for a way to gain something for himself. In following Jesus, Judas thought he was on a sure road to political and financial success. Indeed, Judas was excited about the role he would have in the Kingdom that Jesus would set up.

Listening to Jesus talk of death and sacrifice, Judas, as well as the other disciples, couldn't see how that could be part of God's plan. In his disappointment, Judas failed to perceive that Jesus would do much more than simply challenge the political system in one corner of the world and dispose of the hated Roman oppressors. Instead, by his sacrificial death, Jesus would bring true freedom—freedom from spiritual oppression, freedom from the darkness of sin.

Judas betrayed Jesus with a kiss, turning a sign of affection and respect into a token of betrayal. Judas did feel great remorse for his actions, but his feelings of guilt never led to true repentance. In contrast to Peter, who also betrayed Jesus, Judas destroyed himself instead of turning to the mercy and forgiveness of God. For those of us in recovery, it is vital to remember that Jesus waits for us with open arms, wanting to give us the gifts of mercy and forgiveness. We can run to him in times of need because he does not condemn us—he longs to change us, heal the pain, and take away the guilt in our life.

STRENGTHS AND ACCOMPLISHMENTS:
- He was the only non-Galilean disciple.
- He was trusted enough to be made treasurer of the group.
- He recognized how wrong his betrayal of Jesus was.

WEAKNESSES AND MISTAKES:
- Judas valued material wealth over spiritual wealth.
- He was more interested in what he could get from Jesus than in who Jesus was.

LESSONS FROM HIS LIFE:
- Spiritual wealth is more valuable than material wealth.
- God always offers us what is best for us, not always what we want.
- It is easy to underestimate the value of spiritual growth when we are preoccupied with material gain.
- We cannot stop at admitting our sins; we must also turn to God for healing and forgiveness.

KEY VERSES:
"Then Satan entered into Judas Iscariot, who was one of the twelve disciples, and he went to the leading priests and captains of the Temple guard to discuss the best way to betray Jesus to them" (Luke 22:3-4).

The story of Judas Iscariot is found in the Gospels; see especially Luke 22:3-6 and John 12:4-6. He is also mentioned in Acts 1:16-19.

---

from essence of nard, and she anointed Jesus' feet with it, wiping his feet with her hair. The house was filled with the fragrance.

⁴But Judas Iscariot, the disciple who would soon betray him, said, ⁵"That perfume was worth a year's wages.* It should have been sold and the money given to the poor." ⁶Not that he cared for the poor—he was a thief, and since he was in charge of the disciples' money, he often stole some for himself.

⁷Jesus replied, "Leave her alone. She did this in preparation for my burial. ⁸You will always have the poor among you, but you will not always have me."

⁹When all the people* heard of Jesus' arrival, they flocked to see him and also to see Lazarus, the man Jesus had raised from the dead. ¹⁰Then the leading priests decided to kill Lazarus, too, ¹¹for it was because of him that many of the people had deserted them* and believed in Jesus.

Jesus' Triumphant Entry

¹²The next day, the news that Jesus was on the way to Jerusalem swept through the city. A large crowd of Passover visitors ¹³took palm branches and went down the road to meet him. They shouted,

"Praise God!*
Blessings on the one who comes in the name of the LORD!
Hail to the King of Israel!"*

12:5 Greek *worth 300 denarii.* A denarius was equivalent to a laborer's full day's wage. **12:9** Greek *Jewish people;* also in 12:11. **12:11** Or *had deserted their traditions;* Greek reads *had deserted.* **12:13a** Greek *Hosanna,* an exclamation of praise adapted from a Hebrew expression that means "save now." **12:13b** Ps 118:25-26; Zeph 3:15.

¹⁴Jesus found a young donkey and rode on it, fulfilling the prophecy that said:

¹⁵ "Don't be afraid, people of Jerusalem.*
Look, your King is coming,
riding on a donkey's colt."*

¹⁶His disciples didn't understand at the time that this was a fulfillment of prophecy. But after Jesus entered into his glory, they remembered what had happened and realized that these things had been written about him.

¹⁷Many in the crowd had seen Jesus call Lazarus from the tomb, raising him from the dead, and they were telling others* about it. ¹⁸That was the reason so many went out to meet him—because they had heard about this miraculous sign. ¹⁹Then the Pharisees said to each other, "There's nothing we can do. Look, everyone* has gone after him!"

Jesus Predicts His Death

²⁰Some Greeks who had come to Jerusalem for the Passover celebration ²¹paid a visit to Philip, who was from Bethsaida in Galilee. They said, "Sir, we want to meet Jesus." ²²Philip told Andrew about it, and they went together to ask Jesus.

²³Jesus replied, "Now the time has come for the Son of Man* to enter into his glory. ²⁴I tell you the truth, unless a kernel of wheat is planted in the soil and dies, it remains alone. But its death will produce many new kernels—a plentiful harvest of new lives. ²⁵Those who love their life in this world will lose it. Those who care nothing for their life in this world will keep it for eternity. ²⁶Anyone who wants to serve me must follow me, because my servants must be where I am. And the Father will honor anyone who serves me.

²⁷"Now my soul is deeply troubled. Should I pray, 'Father, save me from this hour'? But this is the very reason I came! ²⁸Father, bring glory to your name."

Then a voice spoke from heaven, saying, "I have already brought glory to my name, and I will do so again." ²⁹When the crowd heard the voice, some thought it was thunder, while others declared an angel had spoken to him.

³⁰Then Jesus told them, "The voice was for your benefit, not mine. ³¹The time for judging this world has come, when Satan, the ruler of this world, will be cast out. ³²And when I am lifted up from the earth, I will draw everyone to myself." ³³He said this to indicate how he was going to die.

³⁴The crowd responded, "We understood from Scripture* that the Messiah would live forever. How can you say the Son of Man will die? Just who is this Son of Man, anyway?"

³⁵Jesus replied, "My light will shine for you just a little longer. Walk in the light while you can, so the darkness will not overtake you. Those who walk in the darkness cannot see where they are going. ³⁶Put your trust in the light while there is still time; then you will become children of the light."

After saying these things, Jesus went away and was hidden from them.

The Unbelief of the People

³⁷But despite all the miraculous signs Jesus had done, most of the people still did not believe in him. ³⁸This is exactly what Isaiah the prophet had predicted:

"LORD, who has believed our message?
To whom has the LORD revealed his
powerful arm?"*

³⁹But the people couldn't believe, for as Isaiah also said,

⁴⁰ "The Lord has blinded their eyes
and hardened their hearts—
so that their eyes cannot see,
and their hearts cannot
understand,
and they cannot turn to me
and have me heal them."*

⁴¹Isaiah was referring to Jesus when he said this, because he saw the future and spoke of the Messiah's glory. ⁴²Many people did believe in him, however, including some of the

12:15a Greek *daughter of Zion.* 12:15b Zech 9:9. 12:17 Greek *were testifying.* 12:19 Greek *the world.* 12:23 "Son of Man" is a title Jesus used for himself. 12:34 Greek *from the law.* 12:38 Isa 53:1. 12:40 Isa 6:10.

12:23-25 Instead of giving a king's acceptance speech, Jesus explained why he would have to die. He said, in effect: "I must die so that I can bring new life to you. If you want this new life, then turn away from your current way of living!" This message can be hard for us to accept, just as it was for the Jews of Jesus' day. But in order to move through recovery—from addiction to freedom, from brokenness to healing, from guilt to forgiveness, or from isolation to intimacy—we must accept it. No longer can we embrace lives of escapism and denial. We must honestly embrace the painful realities in our life and patiently allow God's love to make us whole.

Jewish leaders. But they wouldn't admit it for fear that the Pharisees would expel them from the synagogue. [43]For they loved human praise more than the praise of God.

[44]Jesus shouted to the crowds, "If you trust me, you are trusting not only me, but also God who sent me. [45]For when you see me, you are seeing the one who sent me. [46]I have come as a light to shine in this dark world, so that all who put their trust in me will no longer remain in the dark. [47]I will not judge those who hear me but don't obey me, for I have come to save the world and not to judge it. [48]But all who reject me and my message will be judged on the day of judgment by the truth I have spoken. [49]I don't speak on my own authority. The Father who sent me has commanded me what to say and how to say it. [50]And I know his commands lead to eternal life; so I say whatever the Father tells me to say."

CHAPTER 13
Jesus Washes His Disciples' Feet
Before the Passover celebration, Jesus knew that his hour had come to leave this world and return to his Father. He had loved his disciples during his ministry on earth, and now he loved them to the very end.* [2]It was time for supper, and the devil had already prompted Judas,* son of Simon Iscariot, to betray Jesus. [3]Jesus knew that the Father had given him authority over everything and that he had come from God and would return to God. [4]So he got up from the table, took off his robe, wrapped a towel around his waist, [5]and poured water into a basin. Then he began to wash the disciples' feet, drying them with the towel he had around him.

[6]When Jesus came to Simon Peter, Peter said to him, "Lord, are you going to wash my feet?"

[7]Jesus replied, "You don't understand now what I am doing, but someday you will."

[8]"No," Peter protested, "you will never ever wash my feet!"

Jesus replied, "Unless I wash you, you won't belong to me."

[9]Simon Peter exclaimed, "Then wash my hands and head as well, Lord, not just my feet!"

[10]Jesus replied, "A person who has bathed all over does not need to wash, except for the feet,* to be entirely clean. And you disciples are clean, but not all of you." [11]For Jesus knew who would betray him. That is what he meant when he said, "Not all of you are clean."

[12]After washing their feet, he put on his robe again and sat down and asked, "Do you understand what I was doing? [13]You call me 'Teacher' and 'Lord,' and you are right, because that's what I am. [14]And since I, your Lord and Teacher, have washed your feet, you ought to wash each other's feet. [15]I have given you an example to follow. Do as I have done to you. [16]I tell you the truth, slaves are not greater than their master. Nor is the messenger more important than the one who sends the message. [17]Now that you know these things, God will bless you for doing them.

Jesus Predicts His Betrayal
[18]"I am not saying these things to all of you; I know the ones I have chosen. But this fulfills the Scripture that says, 'The one who eats my food has turned against me.'* [19]I tell you this beforehand, so that when it happens you will believe that I AM the Messiah.* [20]I tell you the truth, anyone who welcomes my messenger is welcoming me, and anyone

13:1 Or he showed them the full extent of his love. 13:2 Or the devil had already intended for Judas. 13:10 Some manuscripts do not include except for the feet. 13:18 Ps 41:9. 13:19 Or that the 'I AM' has come; or that I am the LORD; Greek reads that I am. See Exod 3:14.

12:42-43 Many of the Jewish leaders believed in Jesus, but their faith was rendered ineffective by fear and isolation. They were more concerned about what their peers thought of them than about what God thought. This weak faith will never take us far in recovery. If we want real progress in recovery, we need to share our belief in God with at least one other person. When we tell others about our belief and change in our life, we are inviting them to hold us accountable. Accountability for our intentions, attitudes, and actions is a necessary part of recovery. Making others a significant part of our life is crucial to the recovery process and our growth; we cannot do it alone.
13:1-7 The Son of God came not as a proud master who demanded service from others but as a humble servant who delighted in helping others. In stooping down to do the most menial job (washing his disciples' feet), Jesus showed them that true leaders serve their followers. To follow Jesus' example and serve others, we start by allowing him to serve us. As we experience his cleansing power in our life, we can serve others—sharing our story, listening to their confessions, feeling their pain, and standing by them in the tough times. As we support others in the recovery process, we will be strengthened as we continue toward recovery.

who welcomes me is welcoming the Father who sent me."

²¹Now Jesus was deeply troubled,* and he exclaimed, "I tell you the truth, one of you will betray me!"

²²The disciples looked at each other, wondering whom he could mean. ²³The disciple Jesus loved was sitting next to Jesus at the table.* ²⁴Simon Peter motioned to him to ask, "Who's he talking about?" ²⁵So that disciple leaned over to Jesus and asked, "Lord, who is it?"

²⁶Jesus responded, "It is the one to whom I give the bread I dip in the bowl." And when he had dipped it, he gave it to Judas, son of Simon Iscariot. ²⁷When Judas had eaten the bread, Satan entered into him. Then Jesus told him, "Hurry and do what you're going to do." ²⁸None of the others at the table knew what Jesus meant. ²⁹Since Judas was their treasurer, some thought Jesus was telling him to go and pay for the food or to give some money to the poor. ³⁰So Judas left at once, going out into the night.

Jesus Predicts Peter's Denial

³¹As soon as Judas left the room, Jesus said, "The time has come for the Son of Man* to enter into his glory, and God will be glorified because of him. ³²And since God receives

glory because of the Son,* he will give his own glory to the Son, and he will do so at once. ³³Dear children, I will be with you only a little longer. And as I told the Jewish leaders, you will search for me, but you can't come where I am going. ³⁴So now I am giving you a new commandment: Love each other. Just as I have loved you, you should love each other. ³⁵Your love for one another will prove to the world that you are my disciples."

³⁶Simon Peter asked, "Lord, where are you going?"

And Jesus replied, "You can't go with me now, but you will follow me later."

³⁷"But why can't I come now, Lord?" he asked. "I'm ready to die for you."

³⁸Jesus answered, "Die for me? I tell you the truth, Peter—before the rooster crows tomorrow morning, you will deny three times that you even know me.

CHAPTER 14
Jesus, the Way to the Father

"Don't let your hearts be troubled. Trust in God, and trust also in me. ²There is more than enough room in my Father's home.* If this were not so, would I have told you that I am going to prepare a place for you?* ³When everything is ready, I will come and

13:21 Greek *was troubled in his spirit.* 13:23 Greek *was reclining on Jesus' bosom.* The "disciple Jesus loved" was probably John. 13:31 "Son of Man" is a title Jesus used for himself. 13:32 Several early manuscripts do not include *And since God receives glory because of the Son.* 14:2a Or *There are many rooms in my Father's house.* 14:2b Or *If this were not so, I would have told you that I am going to prepare a place for you.* Some manuscripts read *If this were not so, I would have told you. I am going to prepare a place for you.*

13:20 One way God speaks to us is through his chosen messengers. We may experience God's love and healing through the godly people he sends into our life. This may be very difficult for us if we have been a victim of abuse. We may feel that we never want to be close to other people. But as we allow godly people into our life, we learn that they bring the healing touch of Jesus with them. As we reach out to others in Jesus' name, we in turn become his messenger. God will use us to bring his powerful deliverance into others' lives.

13:34-35 Our ability to love others (and ourself) is based on the degree to which we have received God's love (most often through other people). When we try to love others without God's love, we try to give what we don't have; we end up giving to others in hopes of receiving something in return. This kind of selfish gift never feels good to us or to the person we are trying to help. When we love one another out of the overflow of God's love, our witness and service can be effective toward recovery.

14:1-4 We receive lasting comfort by putting our trust in God. Sometimes God gives us immediate deliverance from a painful situation. More often, he walks with us as we struggle with problems that never seem to end. Our struggles may be direct consequences of our past mistakes; they may be the result of other people's failures. God allows us to experience such trying circumstances to build character in us and strengthen our faith. When we place our trust in Jesus, we receive his peace in this life and the promise of a home with him in eternity.

14:5-11 Faith in Jesus is the only way to truly know God and receive the meaningful life that God wants for each of us. Despite living with Jesus for many months, Thomas and Philip did not yet know God through his Son, Jesus. Many people know about God and Jesus Christ, but they don't know God personally. Genuine faith is personal and relational and based upon the truths about God found in Scripture. Jesus Christ is the way, the truth, and the life for anyone going through recovery. He has the power to forgive our sins, help us overcome our addiction, and give us a new life.

get you, so that you will always be with me where I am. ⁴And you know the way to where I am going."

⁵"No, we don't know, Lord," Thomas said. "We have no idea where you are going, so how can we know the way?"

⁶Jesus told him, "I am the way, the truth, and the life. No one can come to the Father except through me. ⁷If you had really known me, you would know who my Father is.* From now on, you do know him and have seen him!"

⁸Philip said, "Lord, show us the Father, and we will be satisfied."

⁹Jesus replied, "Have I been with you all this time, Philip, and yet you still don't know who I am? Anyone who has seen me has seen the Father! So why are you asking me to show him to you? ¹⁰Don't you believe that I am in the Father and the Father is in me? The words I speak are not my own, but my Father who lives in me does his work through me. ¹¹Just believe that I am in the Father and the Father is in me. Or at least believe because of the work you have seen me do.

¹²"I tell you the truth, anyone who believes in me will do the same works I have done, and even greater works, because I am going to be with the Father. ¹³You can ask for anything in my name, and I will do it, so that the Son can bring glory to the Father. ¹⁴Yes, ask me for anything in my name, and I will do it!

Jesus Promises the Holy Spirit

¹⁵"If you love me, obey* my commandments. ¹⁶And I will ask the Father, and he will give you another Advocate,* who will never leave you. ¹⁷He is the Holy Spirit, who leads into all truth. The world cannot receive him, because it isn't looking for him and doesn't recognize him. But you know him, because he lives with you now and later will be in you.* ¹⁸No, I will not abandon you as orphans—I will come to you. ¹⁹Soon the world will no longer see me, but you will see me. Since I live, you also will live. ²⁰When I am raised to life again, you will know that I am in my Father, and you are in me, and I am in you. ²¹Those who accept my commandments and obey them are the ones who love me. And because they love me, my Father will love them. And I will love them and reveal myself to each of them."

14:7 Some manuscripts read *If you have really known me, you will know who my Father is.* 14:15 Other manuscripts read *you will obey;* still others read *you should obey.* 14:16 Or *Comforter,* or *Encourager,* or *Counselor.* Greek reads *Paraclete;* also in 14:26. 14:17 Some manuscripts read *and is in you.*

LOVE

READ JOHN 14:15-26

Real love brings security into our life. For many of us, feelings of insecurity contribute to the power of our dependency. Believing that love can bring lasting security may be hard for those of us who have been abandoned. Maybe someone we loved betrayed our trust. Perhaps someone turned away from us when we betrayed theirs. It could be that someone we needed died, leaving us permanently.

Jesus promised, "No, I will not abandon you as orphans—I will come to you" (John 14:18). We may ask, How can I trust in God's love when it feels like all I've ever known is love that disappoints? Here's the difference: Jesus is the only one who entered our life through the "one way" door of death. "God showed how much he loved us by sending his one and only Son into the world so that we might have eternal life through him. This is real love—not that we loved God, but that he loved us and sent his Son as a sacrifice to take away our sins" (1 John 4:9-10). The psalmist wrote, "For he knows how weak we are; he remembers we are only dust. . . . The wind blows, and we are gone . . . But the love of the LORD remains forever with those who fear him" (Psalm 103:14-17).

God's love is unconditional and always waiting for us. Turning our life over to God involves opening the door of our heart to his love. Filling up on God's love helps us to avoid relapses. It meets us at our deepest need and overcomes our most powerful insecurities. ***Turn to page 1375, John 21.***

[22]Judas (not Judas Iscariot, but the other disciple with that name) said to him, "Lord, why are you going to reveal yourself only to us and not to the world at large?"

[23]Jesus replied, "All who love me will do what I say. My Father will love them, and we will come and make our home with each of them. [24]Anyone who doesn't love me will not obey me. And remember, my words are not my own. What I am telling you is from the Father who sent me. [25]I am telling you these things now while I am still with you. [26]But when the Father sends the Advocate as my representative—that is, the Holy Spirit—he will teach you everything and will remind you of everything I have told you.

[27]"I am leaving you with a gift—peace of mind and heart. And the peace I give is a gift the world cannot give. So don't be troubled or afraid. [28]Remember what I told you: I am going away, but I will come back to you again. If you really loved me, you would be happy that I am going to the Father, who is greater than I am. [29]I have told you these things before they happen so that when they do happen, you will believe.

[30]"I don't have much more time to talk to you, because the ruler of this world approaches. He has no power over me, [31]but I will do what the Father requires of me, so that the world will know that I love the Father. Come, let's be going.

CHAPTER 15
Jesus, the True Vine

"I am the true grapevine, and my Father is the gardener. [2]He cuts off every branch of mine that doesn't produce fruit, and he prunes the branches that do bear fruit so they will produce even more. [3]You have already been pruned and purified by the message I have given you. [4]Remain in me, and I will remain in you. For a branch cannot produce fruit if it is severed from the vine, and you cannot be fruitful unless you remain in me.

[5]"Yes, I am the vine; you are the branches. Those who remain in me, and I in them, will produce much fruit. For apart from me you can do nothing. [6]Anyone who does not remain in me is thrown away like a useless branch and withers. Such branches are gathered into a pile to be burned. [7]But if you remain in me and my words remain in you, you may ask for anything you want, and it will be granted! [8]When you produce much fruit, you are my true disciples. This brings great glory to my Father.

[9]"I have loved you even as the Father has loved me. Remain in my love. [10]When you obey my commandments, you remain in my love, just as I obey my Father's commandments and remain in his love. [11]I have told you these things so that you will be filled with my joy. Yes, your joy will overflow! [12]This is my commandment: Love each other in the same way I have loved you. [13]There is no greater love than to lay down one's life for one's friends. [14]You are my friends if you do what I command. [15]I no longer call you slaves, because a master doesn't confide in his slaves. Now you are my friends, since I have told you everything the Father told me. [16]You didn't choose me. I chose you. I appointed you to go and produce lasting fruit, so that the Father will give you whatever you ask for, using my name. [17]This is my command: Love each other.

14:27 Many of us are dealing with stress and anxiety, grief and loss; we long for peace of mind and heart. So did the early disciples—they were about to lose their best friend and their Messiah. Their souls were indeed troubled, like many of us recovering from the loss of a job, a spouse, or children, or from a chemical addiction. They were looking for something to fill the void. Yet Jesus said he was leaving them with wholesome, fulfilling peace—*shalom*—unlike worldly peace, which is merely an absence of conflict. God can bring us peace even in the midst of our troubles (see 16:33).

15:1-8 God desires that our life be like the fruitful branches of a grapevine. The only way to be fruitful is to remain connected to Jesus, the vine, and to allow God, the gardener, to prune our life to stimulate growth and fruitfulness. It is God's cultivating, weeding, and pruning in our life that brings forth spiritual fruit, character development, and progress in recovery. Just as sustenance for the desired fruit comes through the vine, so fullness of life comes through faith in Jesus Christ. We need to stay close to Jesus, the source of power and practical help for recovery.

15:15 Jesus demonstrated God's desire to be our friend, not our taskmaster. Many of us in recovery have never experienced God on such friendly, intimate terms. Rare in our experience is the authority figure who actually seeks to confide in us and befriend us, rather than lording his power over us. So we find it hard to imagine God as a friend. Jesus urges us to trust in him. By becoming our friend, God, through Jesus, empowers us and enables us to become accountable, responsible, and trustworthy.

The World's Hatred

18"If the world hates you, remember that it hated me first. 19The world would love you as one of its own if you belonged to it, but you are no longer part of the world. I chose you to come out of the world, so it hates you. 20Do you remember what I told you? 'A slave is not greater than the master.' Since they persecuted me, naturally they will persecute you. And if they had listened to me, they would listen to you. 21They will do all this to you because of me, for they have rejected the one who sent me. 22They would not be guilty if I had not come and spoken to them. But now they have no excuse for their sin. 23Anyone who hates me also hates my Father. 24If I hadn't done such miraculous signs among them that no one else could do, they would not be guilty. But as it is, they have seen everything I did, yet they still hate me and my Father. 25This fulfills what is written in their Scriptures*: 'They hated me without cause.'

26"But I will send you the Advocate*—the Spirit of truth. He will come to you from the Father and will testify all about me. 27And you must also testify about me because you have been with me from the beginning of my ministry.

CHAPTER 16

"I have told you these things so that you won't abandon your faith. 2For you will be expelled from the synagogues, and the time is coming when those who kill you will think they are doing a holy service for God. 3This is because they have never known the Father or me. 4Yes, I'm telling you these things now, so that when they happen, you will remember my warning. I didn't tell you earlier because I was going to be with you for a while longer.

The Work of the Holy Spirit

5"But now I am going away to the one who sent me, and not one of you is asking where I am going. 6Instead, you grieve because of what I've told you. 7But in fact, it is best for you that I go away, because if I don't, the Advocate* won't come. If I do go away, then I will send him to you. 8And when he comes, he will convict the world of its sin, and of God's righteousness, and of the coming judgment. 9The world's sin is that it refuses

15:25 Greek *in their law.* Pss 35:19; 69:4. **15:26** Or *Comforter,* or *Encourager,* or *Counselor.* Greek reads *Paraclete.* **16:7** Or *Comforter,* or *Encourager,* or *Counselor.* Greek reads *Paraclete.*

STEP 12

Sharing Together

BIBLE READING: John 15:5-15

Having had a spiritual awakening as the result of these steps, we tried to carry this message to others and to practice these principles in all our affairs.

Since we have worked through the Twelve Steps, we are in a special position to carry the message to others. We can recognize the warning signs of addictive/compulsive tendencies in those around us, as well as in ourself. When touching on such deep and sensitive issues, it is important to speak in the language of love, not condemnation.

The Bible tells us that if someone "is overcome by some sin, you who are godly should gently and humbly help that person back onto the right path. And be careful not to fall into the same temptation yourself. Share each other's burdens, and in this way obey the law of Christ" (Galatians 6:1-2). The command was the one Jesus taught his disciples: "So now I am giving you a new commandment: Love each other. Just as I have loved you, you should love each other" (John 13:34). "This is my commandment: Love each other in the same way I have loved you. There is no greater love than to lay down one's life for one's friends" (15:12-13).

We are not the Savior, but we can love others as he has loved us. Love goes beyond mere words. Sometimes it is spoken in silence, when we don't condemn someone who comes to us looking for help. Love doesn't just tell them what the problems are. It helps carry the weight of their burdens. We can be part of a support network to help carry our friends until they are able to take steps toward recovery on their own initiative. *Turn to page 1393, Acts 8.*

to believe in me. [10]Righteousness is available because I go to the Father, and you will see me no more. [11]Judgment will come because the ruler of this world has already been judged.

[12]"There is so much more I want to tell you, but you can't bear it now. [13]When the Spirit of truth comes, he will guide you into all truth. He will not speak on his own but will tell you what he has heard. He will tell you about the future. [14]He will bring me glory by telling you whatever he receives from me. [15]All that belongs to the Father is mine; this is why I said, 'The Spirit will tell you whatever he receives from me.'

Sadness Will Be Turned to Joy

[16]"In a little while you won't see me anymore. But a little while after that, you will see me again."

[17]Some of the disciples asked each other, "What does he mean when he says, 'In a little while you won't see me, but then you will see me,' and 'I am going to the Father'? [18]And what does he mean by 'a little while'? We don't understand."

[19]Jesus realized they wanted to ask him about it, so he said, "Are you asking yourselves what I meant? I said in a little while you won't see me, but a little while after that you will see me again. [20]I tell you the truth, you will weep and mourn over what is going to happen to me, but the world will rejoice. You will grieve, but your grief will suddenly turn to wonderful joy. [21]It will be like a woman suffering the pains of labor. When her child is born, her anguish gives way to joy because she has brought a new baby into the world. [22]So you have sorrow now, but I will see you again; then you will rejoice, and no one

can rob you of that joy. [23]At that time you won't need to ask me for anything. I tell you the truth, you will ask the Father directly, and he will grant your request because you use my name. [24]You haven't done this before. Ask, using my name, and you will receive, and you will have abundant joy.

[25]"I have spoken of these matters in figures of speech, but soon I will stop speaking figuratively and will tell you plainly all about the Father. [26]Then you will ask in my name. I'm not saying I will ask the Father on your behalf, [27]for the Father himself loves you dearly because you love me and believe that I came from God.* [28]Yes, I came from the Father into the world, and now I will leave the world and return to the Father."

[29]Then his disciples said, "At last you are speaking plainly and not figuratively. [30]Now we understand that you know everything, and there's no need to question you. From this we believe that you came from God."

[31]Jesus asked, "Do you finally believe? [32]But the time is coming—indeed it's here now—when you will be scattered, each one going his own way, leaving me alone. Yet I am not alone because the Father is with me. [33]I have told you all this so that you may have peace in me. Here on earth you will have many trials and sorrows. But take heart, because I have overcome the world."

CHAPTER 17
The Prayer of Jesus

After saying all these things, Jesus looked up to heaven and said, "Father, the hour has come. Glorify your Son so he can give glory back to you. [2]For you have given him authority over everyone. He gives eternal life to each one you have given him. [3]And this is

16:27 Some manuscripts read *from the Father.*

16:20-22 Jesus' followers certainly grieved the imminent loss of their friend and master. Losing a loved one is a painful and universal experience. We may grieve the loss of our childhood, our innocence, our spouse, or our only means of livelihood. We even grieve the loss of our addiction that we have used to numb our pain. Abuse, abandonment, or neglect by someone we trust is painful. But there is no pain so great that Jesus cannot heal it. When we find the courage to honestly face and grieve over our losses and injuries, we can discover what lies beyond grief—freedom and joy!

16:33 In this world, especially in recovery, we encounter "many trials and sorrows," many of them beyond our control. These can be endured with God's help. On the other hand, some of our suffering is self-inflicted and can be avoided. In such situations, God still offers us peace as we muster the courage to make needed changes in our life. God's forgiveness and loving acceptance can give us peace as we face all of our our trials and sorrows. God's power can lead us through recovery; he has already overcome all the obstacles that stand in our way!

17:1-26 Jesus is our high priest and intercessor (Hebrews 8:1-6). He makes God's will known to us and our heartfelt needs known to God. Jesus' words and deeds reveal God's mercy, justice, glory, truth, and his desire to establish a personal relationship with each of us. Jesus intercedes

the way to have eternal life—to know you, the only true God, and Jesus Christ, the one you sent to earth. [4]I brought glory to you here on earth by completing the work you gave me to do. [5]Now, Father, bring me into the glory we shared before the world began.

[6]"I have revealed you* to the ones you gave me from this world. They were always yours. You gave them to me, and they have kept your word. [7]Now they know that everything I have is a gift from you, [8]for I have passed on to them the message you gave me. They accepted it and know that I came from you, and they believe you sent me.

[9]"My prayer is not for the world, but for those you have given me, because they belong to you. [10]All who are mine belong to you, and you have given them to me, so they bring me glory. [11]Now I am departing from the world; they are staying in this world, but I am coming to you. Holy Father, you have given me your name;* now protect them by the power of your name so that they will be united just as we are. [12]During my time here, I protected them by the power of the name you gave me.* I guarded them so that not one was lost, except the one headed for destruction, as the Scriptures foretold.

[13]"Now I am coming to you. I told them many things while I was with them in this world so they would be filled with my joy. [14]I have given them your word. And the world hates them because they do not belong to the world, just as I do not belong to the world. [15]I'm not asking you to take them out of the world, but to keep them safe from the evil one. [16]They do not belong to this world any more than I do. [17]Make them holy by your truth; teach them your word, which is truth. [18]Just as you sent me into the world, I am sending them into the world. [19]And I give myself as a holy sacrifice for them so they can be made holy by your truth.

[20]"I am praying not only for these disciples but also for all who will ever believe in me through their message. [21]I pray that they will all be one, just as you and I are one—as you are in me, Father, and I am in you. And may they be in us so that the world will believe you sent me.

[22]"I have given them the glory you gave me, so they may be one as we are one. [23]I am in them and you are in me. May they experience such perfect unity that the world will know that you sent me and that you love them as much as you love me. [24]Father, I want these whom you have given me to be with me where I am. Then they can see all the glory you gave me because you loved me even before the world began!

[25]"O righteous Father, the world doesn't know you, but I do; and these disciples know you sent me. [26]I have revealed you to them, and I will continue to do so. Then your love for me will be in them, and I will be in them."

CHAPTER 18
Jesus Is Betrayed and Arrested

After saying these things, Jesus crossed the Kidron Valley with his disciples and entered a grove of olive trees. [2]Judas, the betrayer, knew this place, because Jesus had often gone there with his disciples. [3]The leading priests and Pharisees had given Judas a contingent of Roman soldiers and Temple guards to accompany him. Now with blazing torches, lanterns, and weapons, they arrived at the olive grove.

[4]Jesus fully realized all that was going to happen to him, so he stepped forward to meet them. "Who are you looking for?" he asked.

[5]"Jesus the Nazarene,"* they replied.

"I AM he,"* Jesus said. (Judas, who betrayed him, was standing with them.) [6]As Jesus said "I AM he," they all drew back and fell to the ground! [7]Once more he asked them, "Who are you looking for?"

And again they replied, "Jesus the Nazarene."

[8]"I told you that I AM he," Jesus said. "And since I am the one you want, let these others go." [9]He did this to fulfill his own statement: "I did not lose a single one of those you have given me."*

[10]Then Simon Peter drew a sword and

17:6 Greek *have revealed your name;* also in 17:26. **17:11** Some manuscripts read *you have given me these [disciples].* 17:12 Some manuscripts read *I protected those you gave me, by the power of your name.* **18:5a** Or *Jesus of Nazareth;* also in 18:7. **18:5b** Or *"The 'I AM' is here";* or *"I am the LORD";* Greek reads *I am;* also in 18:6, 8. See Exod 3:14. **18:9** See John 6:39 and 17:12.

with God the Father on our behalf, bringing our needs and requests continually before God. He prays that we would know his perfect joy, be protected from all evil, grow in truth and holiness, and show love toward all people. Jesus prayed this prayer for his twelve disciples as they faced his imminent death. Yet this prayer is for all of us as we follow Jesus through the process of recovery.

slashed off the right ear of Malchus, the high priest's slave. [11]But Jesus said to Peter, "Put your sword back into its sheath. Shall I not drink from the cup of suffering the Father has given me?"

Jesus at the High Priest's House

[12]So the soldiers, their commanding officer, and the Temple guards arrested Jesus and tied him up. [13]First they took him to Annas, since he was the father-in-law of Caiaphas, the high priest at that time.* [14]Caiaphas was the one who had told the other Jewish leaders, "It's better that one man should die for the people."

Peter's First Denial

[15]Simon Peter followed Jesus, as did another of the disciples. That other disciple was acquainted with the high priest, so he was allowed to enter the high priest's courtyard with Jesus. [16]Peter had to stay outside the gate. Then the disciple who knew the high priest spoke to the woman watching at the gate, and she let Peter in. [17]The woman asked Peter, "You're not one of that man's disciples, are you?"

"No," he said, "I am not."

[18]Because it was cold, the household servants and the guards had made a charcoal fire. They stood around it, warming themselves, and Peter stood with them, warming himself.

The High Priest Questions Jesus

[19]Inside, the high priest began asking Jesus about his followers and what he had been teaching them. [20]Jesus replied, "Everyone knows what I teach. I have preached regularly in the synagogues and the Temple, where the people* gather. I have not spoken in secret. [21]Why are you asking me this question? Ask those who heard me. They know what I said."

[22]Then one of the Temple guards standing nearby slapped Jesus across the face. "Is that the way to answer the high priest?" he demanded.

[23]Jesus replied, "If I said anything wrong, you must prove it. But if I'm speaking the truth, why are you beating me?"

[24]Then Annas bound Jesus and sent him to Caiaphas, the high priest.

Peter's Second and Third Denials

[25]Meanwhile, as Simon Peter was standing by the fire warming himself, they asked him again, "You're not one of his disciples, are you?"

He denied it, saying, "No, I am not."

[26]But one of the household slaves of the high priest, a relative of the man whose ear Peter had cut off, asked, "Didn't I see you out there in the olive grove with Jesus?" [27]Again Peter denied it. And immediately a rooster crowed.

Jesus' Trial before Pilate

[28]Jesus' trial before Caiaphas ended in the early hours of the morning. Then he was taken to the headquarters of the Roman governor.* His accusers didn't go inside because it would defile them, and they wouldn't be allowed to celebrate the Passover. [29]So Pilate, the governor, went out to them and asked, "What is your charge against this man?"

[30]"We wouldn't have handed him over to you if he weren't a criminal!" they retorted.

[31]"Then take him away and judge him by your own law," Pilate told them.

"Only the Romans are permitted to execute someone," the Jewish leaders replied. [32](This fulfilled Jesus' prediction about the way he would die.*)

[33]Then Pilate went back into his headquarters and called for Jesus to be brought to him.

18:13 Greek *that year.* **18:20** Greek *Jewish people;* also in 18:38. **18:28** Greek *to the Praetorium;* also in 18:33. **18:32** See John 12:32-33.

18:15-18, 25-27 Peter denied Jesus not only once but three times, despite his earlier assurances of loyalty. We have often done the same thing. We have professed our faith, only to turn around and deny Christ's lordship over crucial areas of our life. Peter meant well when he assured Jesus of his loyalty, but he still failed. Yet his relapse was not the end of the story (see 21:15-19), just as our relapses don't have to be the end of our recovery. With Jesus Christ, there is always hope for restoration.

18:28-38 Many people believe that truth is relative, as did Pilate. Modern moral relativists live without absolute guidelines for right and wrong, not realizing how destructive even the most private sins can be. Since we are all tempted at times to disregard God's guidelines for healthy living, we need to be held accountable to God's truth. We need godly people who can help us measure our attitudes and actions against the truth of God's Word. If we try to write our own rules for recovery, we are headed for painful relapses.

MARY MAGDALENE

The people who have been healed of the worst afflictions are often the most grateful for their new lease on life. Once enslaved by seven demons but freed by Jesus, Mary Magdalene became a shining example of a life filled with gratitude and loyalty to Jesus.

We know few details of Mary's life. She was apparently from Magdala in Galilee and was an early follower of Jesus. Her life was dramatically changed by Jesus when he released her from demons. She traveled with Jesus and the disciples and helped meet the practical needs of the group. During Jesus' crucifixion, when many of the disciples were not to be found, she was one of the few courageous ones to stay at the foot of the cross. She was also one of the women who wanted to make sure Jesus had a proper burial.

Some have suggested that since the twelve disciples were all men, Jesus must not have considered women very important to his ministry. But the role of Mary Magdalene and the other women who followed Jesus shows that this was definitely not the case. Jesus treated women in a manner far beyond the cultural expectation of the day, respecting them fully as persons and considering them a necessary part of his ministry.

We may identify with Mary Magdalene, either as a woman or as one who has been delivered from a life of total bondage. She was an outcast in society, a woman of ill repute. But through her desire for healing and her trusting obedience to Jesus, she became a significant person in the history of our world. Her life gives us the courage to come boldly before God, knowing that his love extends to all of us, regardless of our situation. He specializes in tough cases.

STRENGTHS AND ACCOMPLISHMENTS:
• Mary supported the work of Jesus and his disciples.
• She was present at Jesus' death.
• She was the first to see the risen Jesus.
• She was given the responsibility of telling the disciples about the Resurrection.

WEAKNESSES AND MISTAKES:
• Mary had somehow become enslaved by demonic forces.

LESSONS FROM HER LIFE:
• Those who have been forgiven much by God are often the most grateful.
• God intends women to play essential roles in his ministry.
• The forgiveness we experience can motivate us to live our life for God.

KEY VERSE:
"After Jesus rose from the dead early on Sunday morning, the first person who saw him was Mary Magdalene, the woman from whom he had cast out seven demons" (Mark 16:9).

Mary Magdalene's story is found in Matthew 27:55–28:10; Mark 15:40–16:11; Luke 8:1-3; and John 20:1-18.

"Are you the king of the Jews?" he asked him.

³⁴Jesus replied, "Is this your own question, or did others tell you about me?"

³⁵"Am I a Jew?" Pilate retorted. "Your own people and their leading priests brought you to me for trial. Why? What have you done?"

³⁶Jesus answered, "My Kingdom is not an earthly kingdom. If it were, my followers would fight to keep me from being handed over to the Jewish leaders. But my Kingdom is not of this world."

³⁷Pilate said, "So you are a king?"

Jesus responded, "You say I am a king. Actually, I was born and came into the world to testify to the truth. All who love the truth recognize that what I say is true."

³⁸"What is truth?" Pilate asked. Then he went out again to the people and told them, "He is not guilty of any crime. ³⁹But you have a custom of asking me to release one prisoner each year at Passover. Would you like me to release this 'King of the Jews'?"

⁴⁰But they shouted back, "No! Not this man. We want Barabbas!" (Barabbas was a revolutionary.)

CHAPTER 19
Jesus Sentenced to Death
Then Pilate had Jesus flogged with a lead-tipped whip. ²The soldiers wove a crown of thorns and put it on his head, and

they put a purple robe on him. ³"Hail! King of the Jews!" they mocked, as they slapped him across the face.

⁴Pilate went outside again and said to the people, "I am going to bring him out to you now, but understand clearly that I find him not guilty." ⁵Then Jesus came out wearing the crown of thorns and the purple robe. And Pilate said, "Look, here is the man!"

⁶When they saw him, the leading priests and Temple guards began shouting, "Crucify him! Crucify him!"

"Take him yourselves and crucify him," Pilate said. "I find him not guilty."

⁷The Jewish leaders replied, "By our law he ought to die because he called himself the Son of God."

⁸When Pilate heard this, he was more frightened than ever. ⁹He took Jesus back into the headquarters* again and asked him, "Where are you from?" But Jesus gave no answer. ¹⁰"Why don't you talk to me?" Pilate demanded. "Don't you realize that I have the power to release you or crucify you?"

¹¹Then Jesus said, "You would have no power over me at all unless it were given to you from above. So the one who handed me over to you has the greater sin."

¹²Then Pilate tried to release him, but the Jewish leaders shouted, "If you release this man, you are no 'friend of Caesar.'* Anyone who declares himself a king is a rebel against Caesar."

¹³When they said this, Pilate brought Jesus out to them again. Then Pilate sat down on the judgment seat on the platform that is called the Stone Pavement (in Hebrew, *Gabbatha*). ¹⁴It was now about noon on the day of preparation for the Passover. And Pilate said to the people,* "Look, here is your king!"

¹⁵"Away with him," they yelled. "Away with him! Crucify him!"

"What? Crucify your king?" Pilate asked.

"We have no king but Caesar," the leading priests shouted back.

¹⁶Then Pilate turned Jesus over to them to be crucified.

The Crucifixion

So they took Jesus away. ¹⁷Carrying the cross by himself, he went to the place called Place of the Skull (in Hebrew, *Golgotha*). ¹⁸There they nailed him to the cross. Two others were crucified with him, one on either side, with Jesus between them. ¹⁹And Pilate posted a sign on the cross that read, "Jesus of Nazareth,* the King of the Jews." ²⁰The place where Jesus was crucified was near the city, and the sign was written in Hebrew, Latin, and Greek, so that many people could read it.

²¹Then the leading priests objected and said to Pilate, "Change it from 'The King of the Jews' to 'He said, I am King of the Jews.'"

²²Pilate replied, "No, what I have written, I have written."

²³When the soldiers had crucified Jesus, they divided his clothes among the four of them. They also took his robe, but it was seamless, woven in one piece from top to bottom. ²⁴So they said, "Rather than tearing it apart, let's throw dice* for it." This fulfilled the Scripture that says, "They divided my garments among themselves and threw dice for my clothing."* So that is what they did.

²⁵Standing near the cross were Jesus' mother, and his mother's sister, Mary (the wife of Clopas), and Mary Magdalene. ²⁶When Jesus saw his mother standing there beside the disciple he loved, he said to her, "Dear woman, here is your son." ²⁷And he said to this disciple, "Here is your mother." And from then on this disciple took her into his home.

19:9 Greek *the Praetorium.* 19:12 "Friend of Caesar" is a technical term that refers to an ally of the emperor. 19:14 Greek *Jewish people;* also in 19:20. 19:19 Or *Jesus the Nazarene.* 19:24a Greek *cast lots.* 19:24b Ps 22:18.

19:4-16 The people shouting "Crucify him! Crucify him!" had hailed Jesus as their king just days before (12:12-13). Perhaps we have done a similar thing. We may have entrusted our life to God only to discover that his recovery program wasn't quite what we had in mind. We may have wanted a quick fix for our problems or an easy way out of our pain. When we realized that recovery was painful and laborious, even with God's help, we turned against him. The people in Jerusalem, even Jesus' twelve disciples, lost hope as Jesus hung on the cross. But three days later they discovered that even death gave way to God's power! The path of pain and death led to the greatest of victories—the Resurrection! The same is true in recovery.
19:28-30 What did Jesus finish? On the cross Jesus finished the work he was sent to do (17:4) and fully paid for our sins (1 Peter 3:18). In the greatest act of love in history and in fulfillment of a complicated, centuries-old system of sacrifices, he became the perfect sacrificial Lamb of God (see 1:29; Hebrews 9:11-12). The miracle of the Resurrection (20:1-9) confirmed that Jesus is the Savior who can bring salvation and forgiveness, new life, and recovery to all of us.

THOMAS

Although distrust or wavering faith is a reality for most of us, it is painful to be labeled a "doubting Thomas." We might wonder what it was like for Thomas, the disciple of Jesus who became known for his doubting. He simply did not believe that Jesus had risen from the dead. But that is not the end of his story.

Didymus was the other name given for Thomas in the Gospels; it means "twin." Like most twins, Thomas was probably compared to, often in conflict with, and forced to share with his twin sibling. This background could easily have instilled a habit of doubt or distrust into his outlook on life. In spite of this, however, Thomas became one of the inner circle of Jesus' followers and at times exhibited great courage. When Jesus went with his disciples to Bethany to raise Lazarus from the dead, they were walking into a dangerous situation. The religious leaders were actively plotting to kill Jesus. Thomas and the other disciples bravely chose to go along.

Thomas did not doubt Jesus' resurrection out of fear. He continued to meet with the followers of Jesus in the upper room. He just happened to be absent when the risen Jesus first appeared to them. Thomas wanted some kind of proof that his companions had not just been seeing things. Thomas was given the undeniable evidence that he needed when Jesus appeared a second time, permanently dispelling his doubts.

We also have undeniable evidence for the Resurrection. As we trust in Jesus as our Savior, we will experience his power to transform our life, giving us firsthand knowledge of his power. We can overcome our troubling doubts as we continue to trust God to show his power in our life. When Thomas overcame his doubts, he set out on a ministry that exhibited extraordinary faith. As we experience God's power in deliverance, we, too, can minister to others through the power of the Holy Spirit.

STRENGTHS AND ACCOMPLISHMENTS:
- Thomas was willing to give up everything to follow Jesus.
- He was a man of conviction and courage.
- He was a keen thinker and analyst of events.
- He was willing to admit his mistake.

WEAKNESSES AND MISTAKES:
- Thomas discounted the supernatural explanation of the Resurrection.
- He wanted unquestionable evidence before he was willing to believe.

LESSONS FROM HIS LIFE:
- People from difficult family backgrounds can recover by following Jesus.
- Doubt can lead to deeper faith if faced honestly.
- Undeniable evidence is not necessary to begin a life of faith.
- God's work in our life can lead to deeper faith.

KEY VERSE:
"Then Jesus told [Thomas], 'You believe because you have seen me. Blessed are those who believe without seeing me'" (John 20:29).

Thomas's story is told in several passages in the Gospels. He is also mentioned in Acts 1:14.

The Death of Jesus
[28]Jesus knew that his mission was now finished, and to fulfill Scripture he said, "I am thirsty."* [29]A jar of sour wine was sitting there, so they soaked a sponge in it, put it on a hyssop branch, and held it up to his lips. [30]When Jesus had tasted it, he said, "It is finished!" Then he bowed his head and released his spirit.

[31]It was the day of preparation, and the Jewish leaders didn't want the bodies hanging there the next day, which was the Sabbath (and a very special Sabbath, because it was the Passover). So they asked Pilate to hasten their deaths by ordering that their legs be broken. Then their bodies could be taken down. [32]So the soldiers came and broke the legs of the two men crucified with Jesus. [33]But when they came to Jesus, they saw that he was already dead, so they didn't break his legs. [34]One of the soldiers, however, pierced his side with a spear, and immediately blood and water flowed out. [35](This report is from an eyewitness giving an accurate account. He speaks the truth so that you also may continue to believe.*)

19:28 See Pss 22:15; 69:21. **19:35** Some manuscripts read *that you also may believe.*

1373

³⁶These things happened in fulfillment of the Scriptures that say, "Not one of his bones will be broken,"* ³⁷and "They will look on the one they pierced."*

The Burial of Jesus

³⁸Afterward Joseph of Arimathea, who had been a secret disciple of Jesus (because he feared the Jewish leaders), asked Pilate for permission to take down Jesus' body. When Pilate gave permission, Joseph came and took the body away. ³⁹With him came Nicodemus, the man who had come to Jesus at night. He brought about seventy-five pounds* of perfumed ointment made from myrrh and aloes. ⁴⁰Following Jewish burial custom, they wrapped Jesus' body with the spices in long sheets of linen cloth. ⁴¹The place of crucifixion was near a garden, where there was a new tomb, never used before. ⁴²And so, because it was the day of preparation for the Jewish Passover* and since the tomb was close at hand, they laid Jesus there.

CHAPTER 20
The Resurrection

Early on Sunday morning,* while it was still dark, Mary Magdalene came to the tomb and found that the stone had been rolled away from the entrance. ²She ran and found Simon Peter and the other disciple, the one whom Jesus loved. She said, "They have taken the Lord's body out of the tomb, and we don't know where they have put him!"

³Peter and the other disciple started out for the tomb. ⁴They were both running, but the other disciple outran Peter and reached the tomb first. ⁵He stooped and looked in and saw the linen wrappings lying there, but he didn't go in. ⁶Then Simon Peter arrived and went inside. He also noticed the linen wrappings lying there, ⁷while the cloth that had covered Jesus' head was folded up and lying apart from the other wrappings. ⁸Then the disciple who had reached the tomb first also went in, and he saw and believed—⁹for until then they still hadn't understood the Scriptures that said Jesus must rise from the dead. ¹⁰Then they went home.

Jesus Appears to Mary Magdalene

¹¹Mary was standing outside the tomb crying, and as she wept, she stooped and looked in. ¹²She saw two white-robed angels, one sitting at the head and the other at the foot of the place where the body of Jesus had been lying. ¹³"Dear woman, why are you crying?" the angels asked her.

"Because they have taken away my Lord," she replied, "and I don't know where they have put him."

¹⁴She turned to leave and saw someone standing there. It was Jesus, but she didn't recognize him. ¹⁵"Dear woman, why are you crying?" Jesus asked her. "Who are you looking for?"

She thought he was the gardener. "Sir," she said, "if you have taken him away, tell

19:36 Exod 12:46; Num 9:12; Ps 34:20.   19:37 Zech 12:10.   19:39 Greek *100 litras* [32.7 kilograms].   19:42 Greek *because of the Jewish day of preparation.*   20:1 Greek *On the first day of the week.*

20:11-18 Mary Magdalene modeled an essential part of the recovery process—telling others the good news. Once healed of seven demons (Mark 16:9), Mary had supported the ministry of Jesus financially (Luke 8:2-3) and was a faithful follower from early in his ministry. Her faithfulness was honored when the risen Christ appeared and spoke to her before he spoke to anyone else! After seeing the resurrected Jesus, she went immediately and told the disciples. When we realize the power that the risen Christ can bring us through the recovery process, we can show our gratitude by doing as Mary did—carrying the message to others.

20:22-23 The risen Christ did as he had promised (see 14:16-17; 15:26; 16:7) and breathed his Holy Spirit on his disciples. This life-bringing, truth-revealing, sin-convicting, comfort-giving Spirit is also a Spirit of forgiveness. Just as we receive God's forgiveness for our sins, so we are exhorted and enabled to forgive those who sin against us. If we refuse to forgive others, we will miss the blessed freedom that God offers. He wants us to experience the emotional healing that comes only from working through our anger and hurt to the point of releasing it to God. By God's Spirit, recovery from our painful past can be completed.

20:24-29 Here doubting Thomas earned his reputation. He refused to believe in Jesus' resurrection until he saw and felt the risen Christ with his own eyes and hands. In recovery we often experience doubts. We have a hard time believing that God is at work in our life when we don't see immediate changes or miraculous results. Recovery can be a painstaking process without much to show for it at first. Even when evidence of God's power is not immediate, if we persevere in faith, we will experience the peace that comes from trusting God with our present problems and the unknown future.

me where you have put him, and I will go and get him."

[16]"Mary!" Jesus said.

She turned to him and cried out, "Rabboni!" (which is Hebrew for "Teacher").

[17]"Don't cling to me," Jesus said, "for I haven't yet ascended to the Father. But go find my brothers and tell them, 'I am ascending to my Father and your Father, to my God and your God.'"

[18]Mary Magdalene found the disciples and told them, "I have seen the Lord!" Then she gave them his message.

Jesus Appears to His Disciples

[19]That Sunday evening* the disciples were meeting behind locked doors because they were afraid of the Jewish leaders. Suddenly, Jesus was standing there among them! "Peace be with you," he said. [20]As he spoke, he showed them the wounds in his hands and his side. They were filled with joy when they saw the Lord! [21]Again he said, "Peace be with you. As the Father has sent me, so I am sending you." [22]Then he breathed on them and said, "Receive the Holy Spirit. [23]If you forgive anyone's sins, they are forgiven. If you do not forgive them, they are not forgiven."

Jesus Appears to Thomas

[24]One of the twelve disciples, Thomas (nicknamed the Twin),* was not with the others when Jesus came. [25]They told him, "We have seen the Lord!"

But he replied, "I won't believe it unless I see the nail wounds in his hands, put my fingers into them, and place my hand into the wound in his side."

[26]Eight days later the disciples were together again, and this time Thomas was with them. The doors were locked; but suddenly, as before, Jesus was standing among them. "Peace be with you," he said. [27]Then he said to Thomas, "Put your finger here, and look at my hands. Put your hand into the wound in my side. Don't be faithless any longer. Believe!"

[28]"My Lord and my God!" Thomas exclaimed.

[29]Then Jesus told him, "You believe because you have seen me. Blessed are those who believe without seeing me."

Purpose of the Book

[30]The disciples saw Jesus do many other miraculous signs in addition to the ones

20:19 Greek *In the evening of that day, the first day of the week.* 20:24 Greek *Thomas, who was called Didymus.*

LOVE

READ JOHN 21:14-25

We may wonder how we can love people but still hurt them. This paradox causes shame and sometimes erects barriers between us and the ones we love. We may be afraid to say that we love them, thinking, *If I really loved them, I wouldn't let them down the way I have.*

Peter had once sworn his love for Jesus. But after Jesus was arrested, Peter protected himself by denying that he even knew Jesus. Jesus wasn't surprised, but Peter had a hard time forgiving himself. After Jesus rose from the dead, he talked with Peter: "Jesus asked Simon Peter, 'Simon son of John, do you love me more than these?' 'Yes, Lord,' Peter replied, 'you know I love you.' . . . Jesus repeated the question: 'Simon son of John, do you love me?' 'Yes, Lord,' Peter said, 'you know I love you.' . . . A third time he asked him, 'Simon son of John, do you love me?' Peter was hurt that Jesus asked the question a third time. He said, 'Lord, you know everything. You know that I love you'" (John 21:15-17).

Jesus allowed Peter to affirm his love the best he could and accepted Peter as he was. In this way Jesus reduced the shame and restored the relationship. Shame and isolation can lead us back to our addiction. For the sake of recovery, we must not let our shame cause us to avoid the people we love. It is all right if we love others imperfectly—no one is perfect. But we must keep our love relationships together until we have had time to heal. ***Turn to page 1435, Romans 3.***

recorded in this book. [31]But these are written so that you may continue to believe* that Jesus is the Messiah, the Son of God, and that by believing in him you will have life by the power of his name.

CHAPTER 21
Epilogue: Jesus Appears to Seven Disciples

Later, Jesus appeared again to the disciples beside the Sea of Galilee.* This is how it happened. [2]Several of the disciples were there—Simon Peter, Thomas (nicknamed the Twin),* Nathanael from Cana in Galilee, the sons of Zebedee, and two other disciples.

[3]Simon Peter said, "I'm going fishing."

"We'll come, too," they all said. So they went out in the boat, but they caught nothing all night.

[4]At dawn Jesus was standing on the beach, but the disciples couldn't see who he was. [5]He called out, "Fellows,* have you caught any fish?"

"No," they replied.

[6]Then he said, "Throw out your net on the right-hand side of the boat, and you'll get some!" So they did, and they couldn't haul in the net because there were so many fish in it.

[7]Then the disciple Jesus loved said to Peter, "It's the Lord!" When Simon Peter heard that it was the Lord, he put on his tunic (for he had stripped for work), jumped into the water, and headed to shore. [8]The others stayed with the boat and pulled the loaded net to the shore, for they were only about a hundred yards* from shore. [9]When they got there, they found breakfast waiting for them—fish cooking over a charcoal fire, and some bread.

[10]"Bring some of the fish you've just caught," Jesus said. [11]So Simon Peter went aboard and dragged the net to the shore. There were 153 large fish, and yet the net hadn't torn.

[12]"Now come and have some breakfast!" Jesus said. None of the disciples dared to ask him, "Who are you?" They knew it was the Lord. [13]Then Jesus served them the bread and the fish. [14]This was the third time Jesus had appeared to his disciples since he had been raised from the dead.

[15]After breakfast Jesus asked Simon Peter, "Simon son of John, do you love me more than these?*"

"Yes, Lord," Peter replied, "you know I love you."

"Then feed my lambs," Jesus told him.

[16]Jesus repeated the question: "Simon son of John, do you love me?"

"Yes, Lord," Peter said, "you know I love you."

"Then take care of my sheep," Jesus said.

[17]A third time he asked him, "Simon son of John, do you love me?"

Peter was hurt that Jesus asked the question a third time. He said, "Lord, you know everything. You know that I love you."

Jesus said, "Then feed my sheep.

[18]"I tell you the truth, when you were young, you were able to do as you liked; you dressed yourself and went wherever you wanted to go. But when you are old, you will stretch out your hands, and others* will dress you and take you where you don't want to go." [19]Jesus said this to let him know by what kind of death he would glorify God. Then Jesus told him, "Follow me."

[20]Peter turned around and saw behind them the disciple Jesus loved—the one who had leaned over to Jesus during supper and asked, "Lord, who will betray you?" [21]Peter asked Jesus, "What about him, Lord?"

20:31 Some manuscripts read *that you may believe.* 21:1 Greek *Sea of Tiberias,* another name for the Sea of Galilee. 21:2 Greek *Thomas, who was called Didymus.* 21:5 Greek *Children.* 21:8 Greek *200 cubits* [90 meters]. 21:15 Or *more than these others do?* 21:18 Some manuscripts read *and another one.*

21:1-14 Imagine what the disciples must have felt! These professional fishermen had spent an entire night fishing and hadn't caught anything. Then Jesus called to them and told them to throw the net on the other side of the boat. The disciples' first response must have been to laugh. But when they obeyed Jesus, they caught so many fish that the net began to break. As strange as it may sound, that is how the recovery process works. When we have tried everything and finally realize our helplessness, we need to follow God's instructions for healthy living. It may seem foolish at first, but as we trust God and obey his will, we learn that God's power can rebuild our life.
21:15-17 Peter had denied Jesus three times, so Jesus allowed Peter to declare his love for him three times. Each time Jesus affirmed his confidence in Peter by commissioning him to feed his flock. Later Peter fulfilled this commission when he was filled with the mighty power of the Holy Spirit at Pentecost. He became a key leader in the early church. Although we may experience failures and relapses, when we open our heart to God, he can and will restore us—even to the point where our life becomes a model of recovery to others.

²²Jesus replied, "If I want him to remain alive until I return, what is that to you? As for you, follow me." ²³So the rumor spread among the community of believers* that this disciple wouldn't die. But that isn't what Jesus said at all. He only said, "If I want him to remain alive until I return, what is that to you?"

21:23 Greek *the brothers*.

²⁴This disciple is the one who testifies to these events and has recorded them here. And we know that his account of these things is accurate.

²⁵Jesus also did many other things. If they were all written down, I suppose the whole world could not contain the books that would be written.

REFLECTIONS ON JOHN

insights FROM JESUS' WORDS AND DEEDS

Jesus was a perfect picture of God and a perfect teacher of God's truth. In **John 1:29-31** we find that he was also the perfect sacrifice—the Lamb of God. The Old Testament sacrificial system required that an unblemished lamb be slain on the altar in place of the people on at least a yearly basis. Through its death the people could be forgiven of their sins and given a fresh start. By dying on the cross, Jesus fulfilled the requirements of that sacrificial system completely and forever. He is the Lamb of God who deals with our sins, our powerlessness, and our shortcomings. He gives each of us a chance for a new start, no matter how terrible our past has been.

Those who witnessed Jesus' actions and heard his words had to choose between belief and unbelief. Our choice, like that of the Pharisees in **John 2:17-25**, is to accept or reject Jesus' claims about his mission and authority. Was he just a fascinating man who did amazing deeds? Was he just a good teacher with an interesting message? Was he a madman with delusions of grandeur? Or was Jesus actually God, who came to live among us? According to the Bible, Jesus is God, and he has the power to offer each of us a new life. The disciples discovered this truth and were transformed from rough, inexperienced men into some of the greatest leaders of their day. God has the power to transform us, too.

The paralyzed man in **John 5:1-15** had waited at the pool of Bethesda for many years, hoping to be healed. He was as hopelessly trapped by his physical handicap as we are by our dependency. He was full of excuses for why things weren't working out for him. He couldn't stand up and walk until he took responsibility for his life and put his faith in Jesus' power to heal him. After Jesus healed him, he stood up to Jesus' critics and witnessed to others about God's power to save. Recovery does not come to those who wallow in the blame game but only to those who are willing to take small steps of faith.

In **John 8:1-11** the Pharisees brought to Jesus a woman who had been caught in the act of adultery. Jewish law required that she be stoned to death (Leviticus 20:10; Deuteronomy 22:22). The Pharisees hoped to trap him by asking him to judge the situation. If Jesus said to stone her, they could have brought him before the Roman authorities. The Romans did not allow the Jews to implement their own death sentences. If Jesus had pardoned this woman, the Pharisees could have claimed he was a false prophet for ignoring God's law. Jesus wisely escaped the trap by showing the Pharisees that they had no grounds for judging since they sinned too. Then Jesus told the woman to go and sin no more. Jesus did not ignore this woman's sin, but he forgave her and gave her a new start in life. Jesus can give each of us a new life, no matter how terrible our past.

When we are ridiculed, rejected, or abused, we should look to Jesus' experiences leading to the cross. In **John 19:1-3** Jesus suffered the pain and humiliation of being whipped, mocked, crowned with thorns, and struck in the face. He was shamefully exposed on the cross yet held his head high enough to shout, "It is finished!" (19:30). Because of the shame Jesus suffered, we can hold our heads high as we look to God. We have been forgiven. Through Jesus, our sins and shames are removed, and we have been offered another chance at life.

insights FROM THE DISCIPLES' LIVES

Once Andrew had met Jesus and realized who he was, he was quick to carry the saving message to others. In **John 1:40-42** he rushed off to find his brother, Simon, whom he immediately brought to Jesus. When we experience God's power in our life, we will be just as eager to share our newfound hope with others. This is an essential part of the recovery process. As we share the good news of God's power to deliver, we will give great hope to fellow strugglers. We will also be encouraged to persevere when we remember all the great things God has done for us.

Throughout his Gospel (see **John 13:23; 19:26; 21:20**), the apostle John referred to himself as "the disciple Jesus loved." John was probably Jesus' closest friend during the years of his ministry, but John was not boasting about this. The apostle was basing his self-perception solely upon God's unconditional love for him. When we see ourself as God does—deeply loved—we will have an accurate self-image and make healthy progress toward recovery.

It is easy to fall into the trap of comparing ourself to others, as Peter did with John in **John 21:20-25**. We sometimes take solace in comparing ourself to people who are still in bondage to an addiction. Or we may look at others in recovery and become jealous of how quickly they seem to progress. Focusing on the failures and successes of others in recovery is an easy distraction from our own life and recovery. Our challenge is to make a searching inventory of our own life, not the lives of others. When we focus on our own issues, we will soon begin to make progress in recovery.

insights ABOUT OUR RELATIONSHIP WITH GOD

In **John 6:28-29** the people asked Jesus, "What should we do?" That question has plagued the human race since Adam and Eve first sinned. Many of us live by a list of shoulds and shouldn'ts in our efforts to earn God's acceptance. Some of us learned this as children, when our parents persistently pressured us to measure up to their ideals. In turn, we may do this to our own children. The good news is that we can receive God's help and forgiveness! God in Jesus Christ has taken the initiative; we simply need to repent and receive him by faith. Our growth begins as we respond to God's love for us.

As we see in **John 15:9-12**, the ability to show genuine, unconditional love to others comes from the abundant love God gives us. Conversely, unhealthy, selfish, codependent love starts with our emptiness and need for love. We may try to love others in an attempt to earn their love in return. Only when we experience and remain in God's love (shared by godly people we trust and respect) can we genuinely love ourself and others. God's joy is made complete in us when we experience his love in our life. Then we can offer his unselfish love to others out of an overflowing heart (see also 13:34-35).

insights CONCERNING THE HOLY SPIRIT

God desires a special kind of relationship with us. When Jesus ascended to the Father in heaven, he sent his Spirit to live within his followers. In **John 14:15-18** the Holy Spirit is called the Counselor. Other translations call him the Comforter or Advocate. By whatever name, he ministers God's compassion to us, brings to mind Jesus' teachings, guides us into doing justice and knowing all truth, and brings our needs before God the Father (see 14:26; 15:26; 16:5-15). Many of us in recovery feel like emotional orphans or cripples who have been abandoned or neglected. God, the Holy Spirit, will never leave us. He is with us at all times, and he has the power to help us overcome our sins and dependency.

In recovery it is crucial that we learn to depend on the Holy Spirit. In **John 15:26-27** we find that the Holy Spirit reveals the truth of God's Word, holds us accountable to other believers, and helps us conform to the image of his Son. As the "Spirit of truth," he gives wisdom to help us examine our life; he helps us see past our denial and self-deception. The Holy Spirit can guide us to an accurate perception of ourself, just like an unflattering mirror. The result will be convicting, but fulfilling—so much so that we cannot help but share the good news with others.

ACTS OF THE APOSTLES

THE BIG PICTURE

A. TO JERUSALEM: TELLING THEIR STORY AT HOME (1:1–8:40)

B. TO JUDEA AND SAMARIA: TRANSITION TO OUTSIDERS (9:1–12:25)

C. TO THE WHOLE WORLD: HOW OUTSIDERS BECOME INSIDERS (13:1–21:40)

D. JERUSALEM TO ROME: THE COST OF FOLLOWING JESUS (22:1–28:31)

What occurred during Jesus' brief earthly life was limited to a small corner of the world. Most of civilization never noticed Jesus bringing hope to a hurting and seemingly forsaken group of people. But just as Jesus predicted, the small band of disciples that met in Jerusalem following his death and resurrection turned the world upside down. Life on planet earth hasn't been the same since.

Written by Luke as a sequel to his Gospel, Acts records the history of the early believers and the church. Through the examples of these early believers, we see that the Holy Spirit has the power to change lives. We learn that God can transform our life and help us live at peace with him and with others.

The first half of this book focuses on the ministry of Peter—how he was transformed from an impulsive and unreliable, though well-intentioned, follower of Jesus to a bold and dedicated leader. The second half of the book presents us with the life and ministry of Paul. Paul and his companions faced all kinds of difficulties and opposition, but through the power of God they spread the good news about Jesus throughout the Mediterranean world.

These men should be an encouragement to us. Both made serious mistakes as younger men, but as they turned their lives over to God, they were gradually changed. Paul, who as an angry young man helped to kill the first Christian martyr, Stephen, later became a selfless and dedicated missionary. Peter, whose cockiness often prevented him from overcoming his weaknesses, became a humble and effective leader. The changes in both men demonstrate what God can do in our life, too.

THE BOTTOM LINE

PURPOSE: To trace how the Jewish Jesus movement became a worldwide movement through the impetus of the Holy Spirit. AUTHOR: Luke, the physician. AUDIENCE: Theophilus, whose name means "lover of God." DATE WRITTEN: Sometime between A.D. 63 and 70. SETTING: Acts provides a history of the events that followed the resurrection of Jesus. KEY VERSE: "But you will receive power when the Holy Spirit comes upon you. And you will be my witnesses, telling people about me everywhere—in Jerusalem, throughout Judea, in Samaria, and to the ends of the earth" (1:8). SPECIAL FEATURES: The book of Acts is a sequel to the Gospel of Luke. KEY PEOPLE: Peter, John, Stephen, Philip, Paul, Barnabas, Silas, Timothy, and Luke.

RECOVERY THEMES

The Power of the Holy Spirit: Jesus promised the disciples that after he left, the Holy Spirit would bring them power. Little did they know just what kind of power! As they learned firsthand, the Holy Spirit and his power are real. When we compare Peter in the Gospels with Peter in the book of Acts, we see that his life was changed. When we look at Saul doing his utmost to destroy the early church and then see his dedicated missionary service, we can tell that he was radically transformed by God. The power of God changed their hearts and gave them confidence to tell the truth about him. In our powerlessness, God makes his power available to us through the Holy Spirit. With his help, no problem is too great to overcome; no life is so far gone that it cannot be made new.

Commitment That Overcomes Opposition: Luke did not idealize the people of the early church. They did not have an easy task that swiftly and smoothly moved to its objective. Instead, they struggled with controversy, opposition, and discouragement. They were misunderstood by religious and irreligious people alike. But their common bond was a commitment to God at any cost. As we commit our life to God and to recovery, we can expect to face obstacles, but we can also expect to overcome any problems or opposing forces with God's power.

Living beyond Circumstances: When we read about the early Christians and how they shared what they had and took care of each other, it is easy to think that somehow they did not experience the kinds of problems we do. This was not the case. They learned how to live above their circumstances. They weren't in denial; they were more conscious of God than they were of their problems. When we focus on our problems, we lose sight of our source of power. We try to generate the power from within, only to fail and become discouraged. It does no good to deny or ignore our circumstances, but it does a world of good to trust God and turn our life and our circumstances over to him.

Sharing the Message: As Peter, John, Philip, Paul, Barnabas, and others came to faith in Jesus, they shared the Good News with others. God's healing power is good news! As we share the message of our own spiritual awakening with others in need, we share the good news of God's healing power, as did those early disciples. In so doing, we become stronger in our own recovery and stronger in our faith in God.

CHAPTER 1
The Promise of the Holy Spirit

In my first book* I told you, Theophilus, about everything Jesus began to do and teach ²until the day he was taken up to heaven after giving his chosen apostles further instructions through the Holy Spirit. ³During the forty days after he suffered and died, he appeared to the apostles from time to time, and he proved to them in many ways that he was actually alive. And he talked to them about the Kingdom of God.

⁴Once when he was eating with them, he commanded them, "Do not leave Jerusalem until the Father sends you the gift he promised, as I told you before. ⁵John baptized with* water, but in just a few days you will be baptized with the Holy Spirit."

The Ascension of Jesus

⁶So when the apostles were with Jesus, they kept asking him, "Lord, has the time come for you to free Israel and restore our kingdom?"

⁷He replied, "The Father alone has the authority to set those dates and times, and they

1:1 The reference is to the Gospel of Luke. 1:5 Or *in*; also in 1:5b.

1:1-5 This sequel to Luke's Gospel picks up where the Gospel left off. It records the activities of the apostles soon after Jesus' resurrection. Before ascending to heaven, Jesus assured his followers that the Holy Spirit he had promised to send would come upon them as they waited in Jerusalem (Luke 24:49). At the appointed time, the early Christians received the power they needed to reach the world with the good news of Jesus Christ. God offers us this same power through the Holy Spirit to overcome the barriers in our recovery process.

1:6-11 When the disciples asked Jesus about the coming of his earthly Kingdom, they yearned for the Messiah's reign of freedom and peace. But Jesus turned their eyes to the present. With the power of the Holy Spirit, they were to share the good news of salvation through Jesus Christ with others. Sometimes we do what the disciples did, looking forward to a time of complete freedom and peace, while we should be taking productive steps of action here and now. The Holy Spirit gives us the power necessary for a successful recovery. An important part of that recovery process is to share the Good News with others.

are not for you to know. [8]But you will receive power when the Holy Spirit comes upon you. And you will be my witnesses, telling people about me everywhere—in Jerusalem, throughout Judea, in Samaria, and to the ends of the earth."

[9]After saying this, he was taken up into a cloud while they were watching, and they could no longer see him. [10]As they strained to see him rising into heaven, two white-robed men suddenly stood among them. [11]"Men of Galilee," they said, "why are you standing here staring into heaven? Jesus has been taken from you into heaven, but someday he will return from heaven in the same way you saw him go!"

Matthias Replaces Judas

[12]Then the apostles returned to Jerusalem from the Mount of Olives, a distance of half a mile.* [13]When they arrived, they went to the upstairs room of the house where they were staying.

Here are the names of those who were present: Peter, John, James, Andrew, Philip, Thomas, Bartholomew, Matthew, James (son of Alphaeus), Simon (the Zealot), and Judas (son of James). [14]They all met together and were constantly united in prayer, along with Mary the mother of Jesus, several other women, and the brothers of Jesus.

[15]During this time, when about 120 believers* were together in one place, Peter stood up and addressed them. [16]"Brothers," he said, "the Scriptures had to be fulfilled concerning Judas, who guided those who arrested Jesus. This was predicted long ago by the Holy Spirit, speaking through King David. [17]Judas was one of us and shared in the ministry with us."

[18](Judas had bought a field with the money he received for his treachery. Falling headfirst there, his body split open, spilling out all his intestines. [19]The news of his death spread to all the people of Jerusalem, and they gave the place the Aramaic name *Akeldama,* which means "Field of Blood.")

[20]Peter continued, "This was written in the book of Psalms, where it says, 'Let his home become desolate, with no one living in it.' It also says, 'Let someone else take his position.'*

[21]"So now we must choose a replacement for Judas from among the men who were with us the entire time we were traveling with the Lord Jesus—[22]from the time he was baptized by John until the day he was taken from us. Whoever is chosen will join us as a witness of Jesus' resurrection."

[23]So they nominated two men: Joseph called Barsabbas (also known as Justus) and Matthias. [24]Then they all prayed, "O Lord, you know every heart. Show us which of these men you have chosen [25]as an apostle to replace Judas in this ministry, for he has deserted us and gone where he belongs." [26]Then they cast lots, and Matthias was selected to become an apostle with the other eleven.

CHAPTER 2
The Holy Spirit Comes

On the day of Pentecost* all the believers were meeting together in one place. [2]Suddenly, there was a sound from heaven like the roaring of a mighty windstorm, and it filled the house where they were sitting. [3]Then, what looked like flames or tongues of fire appeared and settled on each of them. [4]And everyone present was filled with the Holy Spirit and began speaking in other languages,* as the Holy Spirit gave them this ability.

[5]At that time there were devout Jews from every nation living in Jerusalem. [6]When they heard the loud noise, everyone came running, and they were bewildered to hear their own languages being spoken by the believers. [7]They were completely amazed. "How can this be?" they exclaimed. "These people are all from Galilee, [8]and yet we hear them speaking in our own native languages! [9]Here we are—Parthians, Medes, Elamites, people from Mesopotamia, Judea, Cappadocia, Pontus, the province of Asia, [10]Phrygia, Pamphylia, Egypt, and the areas of Libya around Cyrene,

---

1:12 Greek *a Sabbath day's journey.* 1:15 Greek *brothers.* 1:20 Pss 69:25; 109:8. 2:1 The Festival of Pentecost came 50 days after Passover (when Jesus was crucified). 2:4 Or *in other tongues.*

2:1-4 On the day of Pentecost, the disciples obeyed Jesus and waited in Jerusalem. Suddenly the Holy Spirit manifested his presence by sound (wind), sight (fire), and speech (new languages). The believers were filled with the Holy Spirit, and God's renewing power began its work of transforming them from the inside out. This marked a new era in history as God's powerful presence entered the hearts of all believers. God's powerful presence can still indwell us, transforming our life and healing our wounds. As we trust God, his Spirit empowers us in recovery.

visitors from Rome [11](both Jews and converts to Judaism), Cretans, and Arabs. And we all hear these people speaking in our own languages about the wonderful things God has done!" [12]They stood there amazed and perplexed. "What can this mean?" they asked each other.

[13]But others in the crowd ridiculed them, saying, "They're just drunk, that's all!"

Peter Preaches to the Crowd

[14]Then Peter stepped forward with the eleven other apostles and shouted to the crowd, "Listen carefully, all of you, fellow Jews and residents of Jerusalem! Make no mistake about this. [15]These people are not drunk, as some of you are assuming. Nine o'clock in the morning is much too early for that. [16]No, what you see was predicted long ago by the prophet Joel:

[17] 'In the last days,' God says,
    'I will pour out my Spirit upon all
        people.
    Your sons and daughters will prophesy.
    Your young men will see visions,
        and your old men will dream dreams.
[18] In those days I will pour out my Spirit
        even on my servants—men and women
        alike—
        and they will prophesy.
[19] And I will cause wonders in the heavens
        above
        and signs on the earth below—
        blood and fire and clouds of smoke.
[20] The sun will become dark,
        and the moon will turn blood red
        before that great and glorious day of the
        LORD arrives.
[21] But everyone who calls on the name of
        the LORD
        will be saved.'*

[22]"People of Israel, listen! God publicly endorsed Jesus the Nazarene* by doing powerful miracles, wonders, and signs through him, as you well know. [23]But God knew what would happen, and his prearranged plan was carried out when Jesus was betrayed. With the help of lawless Gentiles, you nailed him to a cross and killed him. [24]But God released him from the horrors of death and raised him back to life, for death could not keep him in its grip. [25]King David said this about him:

'I see that the LORD is always with me.
    I will not be shaken, for he is right
        beside me.
[26] No wonder my heart is glad,
        and my tongue shouts his praises!
    My body rests in hope.
[27] For you will not leave my soul among the
        dead*
        or allow your Holy One to rot in the
        grave.
[28] You have shown me the way of life,
        and you will fill me with the joy of your
        presence.'*

[29]"Dear brothers, think about this! You can be sure that the patriarch David wasn't referring to himself, for he died and was buried, and his tomb is still here among us. [30]But he was a prophet, and he knew God had promised with an oath that one of David's own descendants would sit on his throne. [31]David was looking into the future and speaking of the Messiah's resurrection. He was saying that God would not leave him among the dead or allow his body to rot in the grave.

[32]"God raised Jesus from the dead, and we are all witnesses of this. [33]Now he is exalted to the place of highest honor in heaven, at God's right hand. And the Father, as he had promised, gave him the Holy Spirit to pour out upon us, just as you see and hear today. [34]For David himself never ascended into heaven, yet he said,

'The LORD said to my Lord,
    "Sit in the place of honor at my right
        hand
[35] until I humble your enemies,
        making them a footstool under
        your feet."'*

2:17-21 Joel 2:28-32. 2:22 Or *Jesus of Nazareth.* 2:27 Greek *in Hades;* also in 2:31. 2:25-28 Ps 16:8-11 (Greek version). 2:34-35 Ps 110:1.

2:14-21 After asserting the sobriety of the believers, Peter told the crowd about the power they just witnessed. The amazing power of the Holy Spirit had been promised by the prophet Joel centuries earlier. By quoting Joel 2:28-32, Peter stressed the universal impact of the Holy Spirit; it would be given to all God's people—young and old, men and women, masters and servants. God's power is available to everyone—regardless of race, gender, or social class—who recognizes his or her helpless state and asks for God's mercy (2:21). No one with a humble heart is beyond the reach of God's power.

³⁶"So let everyone in Israel know for certain that God has made this Jesus, whom you crucified, to be both Lord and Messiah!"

³⁷Peter's words pierced their hearts, and they said to him and to the other apostles, "Brothers, what should we do?"

³⁸Peter replied, "Each of you must repent of your sins and turn to God, and be baptized in the name of Jesus Christ for the forgiveness of your sins. Then you will receive the gift of the Holy Spirit. ³⁹This promise is to you, to your children, and to those far away*—all who have been called by the Lord our God." ⁴⁰Then Peter continued preaching for a long time, strongly urging all his listeners, "Save yourselves from this crooked generation!"

⁴¹Those who believed what Peter said were baptized and added to the church that day—about 3,000 in all.

The Believers Form a Community

⁴²All the believers devoted themselves to the apostles' teaching, and to fellowship, and to sharing in meals (including the Lord's Supper*), and to prayer.

⁴³A deep sense of awe came over them all, and the apostles performed many miraculous signs and wonders. ⁴⁴And all the believers met together in one place and shared everything they had. ⁴⁵They sold their property and possessions and shared the money with those in need. ⁴⁶They worshiped together at the Temple each day, met in homes for the Lord's Supper, and shared their meals with great joy and generosity*—⁴⁷all the while praising God and enjoying the good-

will of all the people. And each day the Lord added to their fellowship those who were being saved.

CHAPTER 3
Peter Heals a Crippled Beggar

Peter and John went to the Temple one afternoon to take part in the three o'clock prayer service. ²As they approached the Temple, a man lame from birth was being carried in. Each day he was put beside the Temple gate, the one called the Beautiful Gate, so he could beg from the people going into the Temple. ³When he saw Peter and John about to enter, he asked them for some money.

⁴Peter and John looked at him intently, and Peter said, "Look at us!" ⁵The lame man looked at them eagerly, expecting some money. ⁶But Peter said, "I don't have any silver or gold for you. But I'll give you what I have. In the name of Jesus Christ the Nazarene,* get up and* walk!"

⁷Then Peter took the lame man by the right hand and helped him up. And as he did, the man's feet and ankles were instantly healed and strengthened. ⁸He jumped up, stood on his feet, and began to walk! Then, walking, leaping, and praising God, he went into the Temple with them.

⁹All the people saw him walking and heard him praising God. ¹⁰When they realized he was the lame beggar they had seen so often at the Beautiful Gate, they were absolutely astounded! ¹¹They all rushed out in amazement to Solomon's Colonnade, where the man was holding tightly to Peter and John.

2:39 Or *and to people far in the future,* or *and to the Gentiles.* 2:42 Greek *the breaking of bread;* also in 2:46.
2:46 Or *and sincere hearts.* 3:6a Or *Jesus Christ of Nazareth.* 3:6b Some manuscripts do not include *get up and.*

2:37-39 Peter's preaching led the people to examine their lives, and they readily recognized their need for salvation in Christ. Peter assured them that by turning from their sins and entrusting their lives to God, they would be forgiven and receive gift of the Holy Spirit. We can expect the same blessings if we bring our sins before God. His forgiveness will set us free from bondage to our sins of the past. The presence of his Holy Spirit will give us the power to persevere through hard times. If God is in our life, he will lead us to successful recovery.
2:42-47 Luke mentioned the activities that characterized the early Christian community. They committed themselves to spiritual growth by studying the Scriptures together, sharing together, and praying together. They helped those in need by selling their possessions and generously sharing the proceeds with them. Their faith, joy, and loving support were so contagious that many more became believers. Recovery follows the same pattern as we grow in faith—it is never done in isolation. We need people to walk with us, encouraging us when we become discouraged and holding us accountable when we stray.
3:1-11 This crippled man was truly helpless; he was a prime candidate for God's powerful help. Notice the steps in this healing. Peter established personal contact by asking the man to look at him. Then Peter told the man to get up and walk in Jesus' name. Peter helped the man up, and suddenly he was walking, leaping, and praising God! Healing can come as God touches our life through the ministry of others. As we experience healing and share our story, we can bless others by leading them to Jesus Christ.

Peter Preaches in the Temple

¹²Peter saw his opportunity and addressed the crowd. "People of Israel," he said, "what is so surprising about this? And why stare at us as though we had made this man walk by our own power or godliness? ¹³For it is the God of Abraham, Isaac, and Jacob—the God of all our ancestors—who has brought glory to his servant Jesus by doing this. This is the same Jesus whom you handed over and rejected before Pilate, despite Pilate's decision to release him. ¹⁴You rejected this holy, righteous one and instead demanded the release of a murderer. ¹⁵You killed the author of life, but God raised him from the dead. And we are witnesses of this fact!

¹⁶"Through faith in the name of Jesus, this man was healed—and you know how crippled he was before. Faith in Jesus' name has healed him before your very eyes.

¹⁷"Friends,* I realize that what you and your leaders did to Jesus was done in ignorance. ¹⁸But God was fulfilling what all the prophets had foretold about the Messiah—that he must suffer these things. ¹⁹Now repent of your sins and turn to God, so that your sins may be wiped away. ²⁰Then times of refreshment will come from the presence of the Lord, and he will again send you Jesus, your appointed Messiah. ²¹For he must remain in heaven until the time for the final restoration of all things, as God promised long ago through his holy prophets. ²²Moses said, 'The LORD your God will raise up for you a Prophet like me from among your own people. Listen carefully to everything he tells you.'* ²³Then Moses said, 'Anyone who will not listen to that Prophet will be completely cut off from God's people.'*

²⁴"Starting with Samuel, every prophet spoke about what is happening today. ²⁵You are the children of those prophets, and you are included in the covenant God promised to your ancestors. For God said to Abraham, 'Through your descendants* all the families on earth will be blessed.' ²⁶When God raised up his servant, Jesus, he sent him first to you people of Israel, to bless you by turning each of you back from your sinful ways."

CHAPTER 4

Peter and John before the Council

While Peter and John were speaking to the people, they were confronted by the priests, the captain of the Temple guard, and some of the Sadducees. ²These leaders were very disturbed that Peter and John were teaching the people that through Jesus there is a resurrection of the dead. ³They arrested them and, since it was already evening, put them in jail until morning. ⁴But many of the people who heard their message believed it, so the number of believers now totaled about 5,000 men, not counting women and children.*

⁵The next day the council of all the rulers and elders and teachers of religious law met in Jerusalem. ⁶Annas the high priest was there, along with Caiaphas, John, Alexander, and other relatives of the high priest. ⁷They brought in the two disciples and demanded, "By what power, or in whose name, have you done this?"

⁸Then Peter, filled with the Holy Spirit, said to them, "Rulers and elders of our people, ⁹are we being questioned today because we've done a good deed for a crippled man? Do you want to know how he was healed? ¹⁰Let me clearly state to all of you and to all the people of Israel that he was healed by the powerful name of Jesus Christ the Nazarene,* the man you crucified but whom God raised from the dead. ¹¹For Jesus is the one referred to in the Scriptures, where it says,

'The stone that you builders rejected
has now become the cornerstone.'*

¹²There is salvation in no one else! God has given no other name under heaven by which we must be saved."

¹³The members of the council were amazed when they saw the boldness of Peter

3:17 Greek *Brothers.* 3:22 Deut 18:15. 3:23 Deut 18:19; Lev 23:29. 3:25 Greek *your seed;* see Gen 12:3; 22:18. 4:4 Greek *5,000 adult males.* 4:10 Or *Jesus Christ of Nazareth.* 4:11 Ps 118:22.

4:10-12 Peter consistently held his listeners accountable for their actions (4:10; see 2:36; 3:12-23), but he never concluded his messages negatively. He always declared that God can do what we are powerless to do—deliver us from the destructive grip of sin. We all need the forgiveness and recovery offered only by Jesus Christ. Jesus desires complete recovery for us—spiritual, emotional, and physical—and he has the power to bring it about.
4:13-22 Peter's boldness and power took the religious leaders by surprise, and they were uncertain about how they should proceed. They commanded Peter to stop preaching and healing, but Peter refused to obey, affirming his commitment to an even higher Power. The leaders could not

and John, for they could see that they were ordinary men with no special training in the Scriptures. They also recognized them as men who had been with Jesus. ¹⁴But since they could see the man who had been healed standing right there among them, there was nothing the council could say. ¹⁵So they ordered Peter and John out of the council chamber* and conferred among themselves.

¹⁶"What should we do with these men?" they asked each other. "We can't deny that they have performed a miraculous sign, and everybody in Jerusalem knows about it. ¹⁷But to keep them from spreading their propaganda any further, we must warn them not to speak to anyone in Jesus' name again." ¹⁸So they called the apostles back in and commanded them never again to speak or teach in the name of Jesus.

¹⁹But Peter and John replied, "Do you think God wants us to obey you rather than him? ²⁰We cannot stop telling about everything we have seen and heard."

²¹The council then threatened them further, but they finally let them go because they didn't know how to punish them without starting a riot. For everyone was praising God ²²for this miraculous sign—the healing of a man who had been lame for more than forty years.

The Believers Pray for Courage

²³As soon as they were freed, Peter and John returned to the other believers and told them what the leading priests and elders had said. ²⁴When they heard the report, all the believers lifted their voices together in prayer to God: "O Sovereign Lord, Creator of heaven and earth, the sea, and everything in them—²⁵you

spoke long ago by the Holy Spirit through our ancestor David, your servant, saying,

'Why were the nations so angry?
    Why did they waste their time with
        futile plans?
²⁶The kings of the earth prepared for battle;
    the rulers gathered together
against the LORD
    and against his Messiah.'*

²⁷"In fact, this has happened here in this very city! For Herod Antipas, Pontius Pilate the governor, the Gentiles, and the people of Israel were all united against Jesus, your holy servant, whom you anointed. ²⁸But everything they did was determined beforehand according to your will. ²⁹And now, O Lord, hear their threats, and give us, your servants, great boldness in preaching your word. ³⁰Stretch out your hand with healing power; may miraculous signs and wonders be done through the name of your holy servant Jesus."

³¹After this prayer, the meeting place shook, and they were all filled with the Holy Spirit. Then they preached the word of God with boldness.

The Believers Share Their Possessions

³²All the believers were united in heart and mind. And they felt that what they owned was not their own, so they shared everything they had. ³³The apostles testified powerfully to the resurrection of the Lord Jesus, and God's great blessing was upon them all. ³⁴There were no needy people among them, because those who owned land or houses would sell them ³⁵and bring the money to the apostles to give to those in need.

4:15 Greek *the Sanhedrin.* 4:25-26 Or *his anointed one;* or *his Christ.* Ps 2:1-2.

stop the spread of Jesus' message in Jerusalem and beyond. God wants people the world over to find forgiveness and freedom, despite what government authorities might say. Once we have experienced the reality of God's power and guidance in our life, we won't want to return to our old way of life.

4:23-31 Peter and John were released by the religious leaders and returned to their support group. They dealt with their difficulties by discussing the issues, worshiping God, and praying. This resulted in a new manifestation of God's presence among them and a new boldness empowered by the Holy Spirit. We can learn from these early believers. We can find help in support groups, where our problems can safely be discussed and prayed over. As we depend on God, he gives us the power to persevere despite difficulties. When we bring our problems to God, he can turn seemingly devastating circumstances into occasions for joy.

4:32-37 The early Christians were growing spiritually by caring for each other, by meeting each other's basic needs, and by carrying the Good News to people who hadn't yet heard. Barnabas was a good example. His name was Joseph, but the apostles nicknamed him Barnabas, meaning "Son of Encouragement." He sold a field he owned to help those in need. As a part of the recovery process, we may need to give ourself a new name that reflects what we are becoming in Christ. Who knows? We might also become sons or daughters of encouragement.

[36]For instance, there was Joseph, the one the apostles nicknamed Barnabas (which means "Son of Encouragement"). He was from the tribe of Levi and came from the island of Cyprus. [37]He sold a field he owned and brought the money to the apostles.

CHAPTER 5
Ananias and Sapphira
But there was a certain man named Ananias who, with his wife, Sapphira, sold some property. [2]He brought part of the money to the apostles, claiming it was the full amount. With his wife's consent, he kept the rest.

[3]Then Peter said, "Ananias, why have you let Satan fill your heart? You lied to the Holy Spirit, and you kept some of the money for yourself. [4]The property was yours to sell or not sell, as you wished. And after selling it, the money was also yours to give away. How could you do a thing like this? You weren't lying to us but to God!"

[5]As soon as Ananias heard these words, he fell to the floor and died. Everyone who heard about it was terrified. [6]Then some young men got up, wrapped him in a sheet, and took him out and buried him.

[7]About three hours later his wife came in, not knowing what had happened. [8]Peter asked her, "Was this the price you and your husband received for your land?"

"Yes," she replied, "that was the price."

[9]And Peter said, "How could the two of you even think of conspiring to test the Spirit of the Lord like this? The young men who buried your husband are just outside the door, and they will carry you out, too."

[10]Instantly, she fell to the floor and died. When the young men came in and saw that she was dead, they carried her out and buried her beside her husband. [11]Great fear gripped the entire church and everyone else who heard what had happened.

The Apostles Heal Many
[12]The apostles were performing many miraculous signs and wonders among the people. And all the believers were meeting regularly at the Temple in the area known as Solomon's Colonnade. [13]But no one else dared to join them, even though all the people had high regard for them. [14]Yet more and more people believed and were brought to the Lord— crowds of both men and women. [15]As a result of the apostles' work, sick people were brought out into the streets on beds and mats so that Peter's shadow might fall across some of them as he went by. [16]Crowds came from the villages around Jerusalem, bringing their sick and those possessed by evil* spirits, and they were all healed.

The Apostles Meet Opposition
[17]The high priest and his officials, who were Sadducees, were filled with jealousy. [18]They arrested the apostles and put them in the public jail. [19]But an angel of the Lord came at night, opened the gates of the jail, and brought them out. Then he told them, [20]"Go

5:16 Greek *unclean.*

5:1-11 God's judgment of Ananias and Sapphira is a unique event in the history of the church but universal in its application. God does not normally punish denial and misrepresentation with immediate death. We all are guilty of denial and trying to impress others with lies and half-truths. Although the consequences may not be as serious today, lying is sinful and destructive to the recovery process. Our regular moral inventory needs to focus on our destructive tendency toward deceit and denial. Then we can take the necessary steps to root it out.

5:9-11 Peter confronted Ananias and Sapphira about their dishonesty, holding them accountable for their sins. Honest confrontation is essential for recovery today, just as it was necessary for maintaining the spiritual health of this early Christian community. Confrontation and discipline are vital in any community, whether a Christian church, a recovery group, or a family. As we are confronted with the truth about ourself, we need to humbly and honestly admit our sins and defects of character. As we do this, God will help us overcome them.

5:12-16 We may wonder how God could possibly do anything for us. We may have never seen, heard, or felt him. In the activities of the early church, we are shown the primary means that God uses to work in people's lives. He touches hurting people through the help of other hurting people. God channels his power through people like us so others can experience his power for healing and recovery. God has probably touched our life through the help of individuals or groups. As we carry the Good News to others through our words and deeds, God can use us to bring hope and healing to others.

5:17-42 This power struggle between the religious establishment and the apostles is instructive for recovery. We may have already faced opposition. People may have tried to stand in our way as we grew in our relationship with God or participated in recovery activities. They may have sought

to the Temple and give the people this message of life!"

[21]So at daybreak the apostles entered the Temple, as they were told, and immediately began teaching.

When the high priest and his officials arrived, they convened the high council*—the full assembly of the elders of Israel. Then they sent for the apostles to be brought from the jail for trial. [22]But when the Temple guards went to the jail, the men were gone. So they returned to the council and reported, [23]"The jail was securely locked, with the guards standing outside, but when we opened the gates, no one was there!"

[24]When the captain of the Temple guard and the leading priests heard this, they were perplexed, wondering where it would all end. [25]Then someone arrived with startling news: "The men you put in jail are standing in the Temple, teaching the people!"

[26]The captain went with his Temple guards and arrested the apostles, but without violence, for they were afraid the people would stone them. [27]Then they brought the apostles before the high council, where the high priest confronted them. [28]"We gave you strict orders never again to teach in this man's name!" he said. "Instead, you have filled all Jerusalem with your teaching about him, and you want to make us responsible for his death!"

[29]But Peter and the apostles replied, "We must obey God rather than any human authority. [30]The God of our ancestors raised Jesus from the dead after you killed him by hanging him on a cross.* [31]Then God put him in the place of honor at his right hand as Prince and Savior. He did this so the people of Israel would repent of their sins and be forgiven. [32]We are witnesses of these things and so is the Holy Spirit, who is given by God to those who obey him."

[33]When they heard this, the high council was furious and decided to kill them. [34]But one member, a Pharisee named Gamaliel, who was an expert in religious law and respected by all the people, stood up and ordered that the men be sent outside the council chamber for a while. [35]Then he said to his colleagues, "Men of Israel, take care what you are planning to do to these men! [36]Some time ago there was that fellow Theudas, who pretended to be someone great. About 400 others joined him, but he was killed, and all his followers went their various ways. The whole movement came to nothing. [37]After him, at the time of the census, there was Judas of Galilee. He got people to follow him, but he was killed, too, and all his followers were scattered.

[38]"So my advice is, leave these men alone. Let them go. If they are planning and doing these things merely on their own, it will soon be overthrown. [39]But if it is from God, you will not be able to overthrow them. You may even find yourselves fighting against God!"

[40]The others accepted his advice. They called in the apostles and had them flogged. Then they ordered them never again to speak in the name of Jesus, and they let them go.

[41]The apostles left the high council rejoicing that God had counted them worthy to suffer disgrace for the name of Jesus.* [42]And every day, in the Temple and from house to house, they continued to teach and preach this message: "Jesus is the Messiah."

CHAPTER 6
Seven Men Chosen to Serve
But as the believers* rapidly multiplied, there were rumblings of discontent. The Greek-speaking believers complained about the Hebrew-speaking believers, saying that their widows were being discriminated against in the daily distribution of food.

[2]So the Twelve called a meeting of all the believers. They said, "We apostles should spend our time teaching the word of God,

---

5:21 Greek *Sanhedrin;* also in 5:27, 41. 5:30 Greek *on a tree.* 5:41 Greek *for the name.* 6:1 Greek *disciples;* also in 6:2, 7.

---

to impose their will on us, hindering us from following God's will. Recovery must be centered around God and his will for us; then nothing can stop our progress. The key is to obey God rather than other people.

6:2-6 Conflict resolution is vital to recovery today, just as it was to the early church. The early believers acknowledged their limitations, set their priorities, and laid out specific tasks that would fulfill their needs. In this case they sought God's wisdom and selected seven Spirit-filled, well-respected leaders to administer the food program. No problem in recovery is insurmountable. With God's wisdom, together with a network of godly support, we can work through old dysfunctional patterns and find healthy, balanced ways to rebuild our life and meet the needs of the people around us.

not running a food program. ³And so, brothers, select seven men who are well respected and are full of the Spirit and wisdom. We will give them this responsibility. ⁴Then we apostles can spend our time in prayer and teaching the word."

⁵Everyone liked this idea, and they chose the following: Stephen (a man full of faith and the Holy Spirit), Philip, Procorus, Nicanor, Timon, Parmenas, and Nicolas of Antioch (an earlier convert to the Jewish faith). ⁶These seven were presented to the apostles, who prayed for them as they laid their hands on them.

⁷So God's message continued to spread. The number of believers greatly increased in Jerusalem, and many of the Jewish priests were converted, too.

Stephen Is Arrested

⁸Stephen, a man full of God's grace and power, performed amazing miracles and signs among the people. ⁹But one day some men from the Synagogue of Freed Slaves, as it was called, started to debate with him. They were Jews from Cyrene, Alexandria, Cilicia, and the province of Asia. ¹⁰None of them could stand against the wisdom and the Spirit with which Stephen spoke.

¹¹So they persuaded some men to lie about Stephen, saying, "We heard him blaspheme Moses, and even God." ¹²This roused the people, the elders, and the teachers of religious law. So they arrested Stephen and brought him before the high council.*

¹³The lying witnesses said, "This man is always speaking against the holy Temple and against the law of Moses. ¹⁴We have heard him say that this Jesus of Nazareth* will destroy the Temple and change the customs Moses handed down to us."

¹⁵At this point everyone in the high council stared at Stephen, because his face became as bright as an angel's.

CHAPTER 7
Stephen Addresses the Council

Then the high priest asked Stephen, "Are these accusations true?"

²This was Stephen's reply: "Brothers and fathers, listen to me. Our glorious God appeared to our ancestor Abraham in Mesopotamia before he settled in Haran.* ³God told him, 'Leave your native land and your relatives, and come into the land that I will show you.'* ⁴So Abraham left the land of the Chaldeans and lived in Haran until his father died. Then God brought him here to the land where you now live.

⁵"But God gave him no inheritance here, not even one square foot of land. God did promise, however, that eventually the whole land would belong to Abraham and his descendants—even though he had no children yet. ⁶God also told him that his descendants would live in a foreign land, where they would be oppressed as slaves for 400 years. ⁷'But I will punish the nation that enslaves them,' God said, 'and in the end they will come out and worship me here in this place.'*

⁸"God also gave Abraham the covenant of circumcision at that time. So when Abraham became the father of Isaac, he circumcised him on the eighth day. And the practice was continued when Isaac became the father of Jacob, and when Jacob became the father of the twelve patriarchs of the Israelite nation.

⁹"These patriarchs were jealous of their brother Joseph, and they sold him to be a slave in Egypt. But God was with him ¹⁰and rescued him from all his troubles. And God gave him favor before Pharaoh, king of Egypt. God also gave Joseph unusual wisdom, so that Pharaoh appointed him gover-

6:12 Greek *Sanhedrin;* also in 6:15. 6:14 Or *Jesus the Nazarene.* 7:2 *Mesopotamia* was the region now called Iraq. *Haran* was a city in what is now called Syria. 7:3 Gen 12:1. 7:5-7 Gen 12:7; 15:13-14; Exod 3:12.

6:8-15 Stephen was "a man full of God's grace and power" and performed amazing miracles among the people. The Jewish establishment falsely accused Stephen of attacking the law of Moses and the Jerusalem Temple. Stephen confronted them with their false religion and denial and called them to face the truth. We may need to do the same for our fellow strugglers. This requires God's wisdom and power. We can receive God's wisdom and power by entrusting our life to God and faithfully obeying his Word.

7:1-53 Stephen did not get defensive about or take personally the accusations of his fellow Jews. Instead, he took control of the situation and boldly defended his faith. Like Stephen, we do not need to be ashamed about our faith or recovery. When we are experiencing God's healing power in our life, we can boldly carry that message to others without apology, fear, or shame. Others may try to harm us, as they did Stephen, but that does not negate the reality of God's power in our life.

STEPHEN

Stephen was a man filled with the Holy Spirit, exhibiting God's power and love in everything he did. He was known for performing amazing miracles and helping people in need. He was called to be one of the first deacons, and it was his job to make sure that no one (especially widows) was overlooked in the distribution of food. Stephen also proclaimed the good news of Jesus with boldness and power. Even as he was stoned to death by the religious leaders, God's hand was clearly upon him.

Stephen demonstrated God's message publicly through the miracles he did in Jesus' name. Those who tried to disprove the truth about Jesus Christ were not able to stand against his wisdom and spirit. So they lied about him in order to have him arrested and brought before the council of Jewish leaders.

Stephen responded to the inquisition by telling the history of the Jewish people, beginning with Abraham, progressing through Moses, and ending with the coming of Jesus the Messiah. He concluded with a scathing attack on the religious leaders who, like many of their ancestors, resisted the essential message of God's revealed Word and the leading of the Holy Spirit.

Stephen's words angered the Jewish leaders so much that they rushed him out of the city and stoned him to death. As he stumbled under the rain of stones, Stephen called upon God to receive his spirit and to forgive the people who were killing him. Unlike Stephen, many of us hold on to grudges and past hurts and allow them to control our life. This makes complete healing and recovery impossible. If we entrust our life to God, we can live and die with joy, knowing that God will take care of the details we cannot control or change.

STRENGTHS AND ACCOMPLISHMENTS:
- Stephen really knew God, both personally and through the Scriptures.
- Because he trusted God, he was able to rise above his circumstances.
- He had a passion for God and compassion for others.
- He used his many gifts to serve the poor and helpless.

LESSONS FROM HIS LIFE:
- Serving others becomes natural when we have given our life to God.
- If we can trust God in daily life, we will be able to face death with joy.
- We can face even the most terrible circumstances if God is with us.

KEY VERSE:
"Stephen, a man full of God's grace and power, performed amazing miracles and signs among the people" (Acts 6:8).

Stephen's story is told in Acts 6–8, 11, and 22.

---

nor over all of Egypt and put him in charge of the palace.

¹¹"But a famine came upon Egypt and Canaan. There was great misery, and our ancestors ran out of food. ¹²Jacob heard that there was still grain in Egypt, so he sent his sons—our ancestors—to buy some. ¹³The second time they went, Joseph revealed his identity to his brothers,* and they were introduced to Pharaoh. ¹⁴Then Joseph sent for his father, Jacob, and all his relatives to come to Egypt, seventy-five persons in all. ¹⁵So Jacob went to Egypt. He died there, as did our ancestors. ¹⁶Their bodies were taken to Shechem and buried in the tomb Abraham had bought for a certain price from Hamor's sons in Shechem.

¹⁷"As the time drew near when God would fulfill his promise to Abraham, the number of our people in Egypt greatly increased. ¹⁸But then a new king came to the throne of Egypt who knew nothing about Joseph. ¹⁹This king exploited our people and oppressed them, forcing parents to abandon their newborn babies so they would die.

²⁰"At that time Moses was born—a beautiful child in God's eyes. His parents cared

7:13 Other manuscripts read *Joseph was recognized by his brothers.*

for him at home for three months. ²¹When they had to abandon him, Pharaoh's daughter adopted him and raised him as her own son. ²²Moses was taught all the wisdom of the Egyptians, and he was powerful in both speech and action.

²³"One day when Moses was forty years old, he decided to visit his relatives, the people of Israel. ²⁴He saw an Egyptian mistreating an Israelite. So Moses came to the man's defense and avenged him, killing the Egyptian. ²⁵Moses assumed his fellow Israelites would realize that God had sent him to rescue them, but they didn't.

²⁶"The next day he visited them again and saw two men of Israel fighting. He tried to be a peacemaker. 'Men,' he said, 'you are brothers. Why are you fighting each other?'

²⁷"But the man in the wrong pushed Moses aside. 'Who made you a ruler and judge over us?' he asked. ²⁸'Are you going to kill me as you killed that Egyptian yesterday?' ²⁹When Moses heard that, he fled the country and lived as a foreigner in the land of Midian. There his two sons were born.

³⁰"Forty years later, in the desert near Mount Sinai, an angel appeared to Moses in the flame of a burning bush. ³¹When Moses saw it, he was amazed at the sight. As he went to take a closer look, the voice of the LORD called out to him, ³²'I am the God of your ancestors—the God of Abraham, Isaac, and Jacob.' Moses shook with terror and did not dare to look.

³³"Then the LORD said to him, 'Take off your sandals, for you are standing on holy ground. ³⁴I have certainly seen the oppression of my people in Egypt. I have heard their groans and have come down to rescue them. Now go, for I am sending you back to Egypt.'*

³⁵"So God sent back the same man his people had previously rejected when they demanded, 'Who made you a ruler and judge over us?' Through the angel who appeared to him in the burning bush, God sent Moses to be their ruler and savior. ³⁶And by means of many wonders and miraculous signs, he led them out of Egypt, through the Red Sea, and through the wilderness for forty years.

³⁷"Moses himself told the people of Israel, 'God will raise up for you a Prophet like me from among your own people.'* ³⁸Moses was with our ancestors, the assembly of God's people in the wilderness, when the angel spoke to him at Mount Sinai. And there Moses received life-giving words to pass on to us.*

³⁹"But our ancestors refused to listen to Moses. They rejected him and wanted to return to Egypt. ⁴⁰They told Aaron, 'Make us some gods who can lead us, for we don't know what has become of this Moses, who brought us out of Egypt.' ⁴¹So they made an idol shaped like a calf, and they sacrificed to it and celebrated over this thing they had made. ⁴²Then God turned away from them and abandoned them to serve the stars of heaven as their gods! In the book of the prophets it is written,

'Was it to me you were bringing sacrifices
    and offerings
  during those forty years in the
    wilderness, Israel?
⁴³No, you carried your pagan gods—
  the shrine of Molech,
  the star of your god Rephan,
  and the images you made to worship
    them.
So I will send you into exile
  as far away as Babylon.'*

⁴⁴"Our ancestors carried the Tabernacle* with them through the wilderness. It was constructed according to the plan God had shown to Moses. ⁴⁵Years later, when Joshua led our ancestors in battle against the nations that God drove out of this land, the Tabernacle was taken with them into their new territory. And it stayed there until the time of King David.

⁴⁶"David found favor with God and asked for the privilege of building a permanent Temple for the God of Jacob.* ⁴⁷But it was Solomon who actually built it. ⁴⁸However,

7:31-34 Exod 3:5-10. 7:37 Deut 18:15. 7:38 Some manuscripts read to you. 7:42-43 Amos 5:25-27 (Greek version). 7:44 Greek the tent of witness. 7:46 Some manuscripts read the house of Jacob.

7:44-50 Stephen referred to the Temple to make a point that is important to us in recovery. Israel had limited God to the Temple and the institutions that surrounded the worship there. They had taken the eternal God—the Master of the universe—and had figuratively bound him inside the Temple walls. Sometimes we define God in ways we can understand and control. We shape and limit him with our theological systems, our church dogmas, our political presuppositions, and our personal experiences. God is much bigger than any concept we could ever have of him. His omnipresence and abundant grace fill the entire universe! As we more accurately understand God and his power, we will discover that he is far bigger than our problems.

the Most High doesn't live in temples made by human hands. As the prophet says,

49 'Heaven is my throne,
    and the earth is my footstool.
Could you build me a temple as good as
        that?'
    asks the LORD.
  'Could you build me such a resting place?
50   Didn't my hands make both heaven
        and earth?'*

51"You stubborn people! You are heathen* at heart and deaf to the truth. Must you forever resist the Holy Spirit? That's what your ancestors did, and so do you! 52Name one prophet your ancestors didn't persecute! They even killed the ones who predicted the coming of the Righteous One—the Messiah whom you betrayed and murdered. 53You deliberately disobeyed God's law, even though you received it from the hands of angels."

54The Jewish leaders were infuriated by Stephen's accusation, and they shook their fists at him in rage.* 55But Stephen, full of the Holy Spirit, gazed steadily into heaven and saw the glory of God, and he saw Jesus standing in the place of honor at God's right hand. 56And he told them, "Look, I see the heavens opened and the Son of Man standing in the place of honor at God's right hand!"

57Then they put their hands over their ears and began shouting. They rushed at him 58and dragged him out of the city and began to stone him. His accusers took off their coats and laid them at the feet of a young man named Saul.* 59As they stoned him, Stephen prayed, "Lord Jesus, receive my spirit." 60He fell to his knees, shouting, "Lord, don't charge them with this sin!" And with that, he died.

CHAPTER 8
Saul was one of the witnesses, and he agreed completely with the killing of Stephen.

Persecution Scatters the Believers
A great wave of persecution began that day, sweeping over the church in Jerusalem; and all the believers except the apostles were scattered through the regions of Judea and Samaria. 2(Some devout men came and buried Stephen with great mourning.) 3But Saul was going everywhere to destroy the church. He went from house to house, dragging out both men and women to throw them into prison.

Philip Preaches in Samaria
4But the believers who were scattered preached the Good News about Jesus wherever they went. 5Philip, for example, went to

7:49-50 Isa 66:1-2. 7:51 Greek *uncircumcised.* 7:54 Greek *they were grinding their teeth against him.* 7:58 Saul is later called Paul; see 13:9.

7:51-60 Stephen confronted the religious leaders about their stubborn denial. They were resisting the Holy Spirit and didn't like being rebuked. We would think that as mature adults, these leaders would have pondered Stephen's words and made some kind of honest self-assessment. But they were infuriated and set out to kill Stephen. Despite their rage, Stephen did not desire revenge or harbor a grudge. He kept his focus on Christ, forgiving the people even as they killed him. Stephen's peace and self-control are gifts of the Holy Spirit that are available to us all through faith.

8:1-3 The people who seem the most unlikely candidates for recovery are often at the top of God's list. Saul (later called Paul; see 13:9) was one such candidate. Saul witnessed Stephen's death and was one of the dreaded enemies of the fledgling Christian movement. He went from house to house, dragging believers to jail. Yet Saul's story is really a story of God's amazing grace. Saul the persecutor became Paul the apostle, one of the greatest leaders in Christian history. Many of us began the recovery process as unlikely candidates, but there is no limit to what we can become with God's powerful and gracious help.

8:1-3 God used the terrible circumstances of persecution for his glory. The believers were driven from their homes in Jerusalem, but they shared the Good News wherever they went. God often uses painful circumstances for his glory. Many of us would not be in recovery were it not for the suffering caused by our addiction. Our pain has awakened us to the opportunity to build a new life of faith. We can rebuild our broken relationships and make amends with the people we have hurt. God has used our painful circumstances to give each of us a second chance.

8:4-17 Philip had preached boldly to the Samaritans, whom the Jews considered no better than Gentiles because of the Samaritans' mixed ancestry. The Samaritans responded to the gospel message in great numbers, and many were baptized. Hearing about the successful ministry there, Peter and John joined Philip and prayed for the Samaritan believers to receive the Holy Spirit. The Good News of salvation in Christ was not just for the Jews—it was for all people, including the Samaritans. The Good News of Jesus Christ is for us, too, no matter who we are or what we have done.

the city of Samaria and told the people there about the Messiah. [6]Crowds listened intently to Philip because they were eager to hear his message and see the miraculous signs he did. [7]Many evil* spirits were cast out, screaming as they left their victims. And many who had been paralyzed or lame were healed. [8]So there was great joy in that city.

[9]A man named Simon had been a sorcerer there for many years, amazing the people of Samaria and claiming to be someone great. [10]Everyone, from the least to the greatest, often spoke of him as "the Great One—the Power of God." [11]They listened closely to him because for a long time he had astounded them with his magic.

[12]But now the people believed Philip's message of Good News concerning the Kingdom of God and the name of Jesus Christ. As a result, many men and women were baptized. [13]Then Simon himself believed and was baptized. He began following Philip wherever he went, and he was amazed by the signs and great miracles Philip performed.

[14]When the apostles in Jerusalem heard that the people of Samaria had accepted God's message, they sent Peter and John there. [15]As soon as they arrived, they prayed for these new believers to receive the Holy Spirit. [16]The Holy Spirit had not yet come upon any of them, for they had only been baptized in the name of the Lord Jesus. [17]Then Peter and John laid their hands upon these believers, and they received the Holy Spirit.

[18]When Simon saw that the Spirit was given when the apostles laid their hands on people, he offered them money to buy this power. [19]"Let me have this power, too," he exclaimed, "so that when I lay my hands on people, they will receive the Holy Spirit!"

[20]But Peter replied, "May your money be destroyed with you for thinking God's gift can be bought! [21]You can have no part in this, for your heart is not right with God. [22]Repent of your wickedness and pray to the Lord. Perhaps he will forgive your evil thoughts, [23]for I can see that you are full of bitter jealousy and are held captive by sin."

[24]"Pray to the Lord for me," Simon exclaimed, "that these terrible things you've said won't happen to me!"

[25]After testifying and preaching the word of the Lord in Samaria, Peter and John returned to Jerusalem. And they stopped in many Samaritan villages along the way to preach the Good News.

Philip and the Ethiopian Eunuch

[26]As for Philip, an angel of the Lord said to him, "Go south* down the desert road that runs from Jerusalem to Gaza." [27]So he started out, and he met the treasurer of Ethiopia, a eunuch of great authority under the Kandake, the queen of Ethiopia. The eunuch had gone to Jerusalem to worship, [28]and he was now returning. Seated in his carriage, he was reading aloud from the book of the prophet Isaiah.

[29]The Holy Spirit said to Philip, "Go over and walk along beside the carriage."

[30]Philip ran over and heard the man reading from the prophet Isaiah. Philip asked, "Do you understand what you are reading?"

[31]The man replied, "How can I, unless someone instructs me?" And he urged Philip to come up into the carriage and sit with him.

[32]The passage of Scripture he had been reading was this:

"He was led like a sheep to the slaughter.
    And as a lamb is silent before the
        shearers,
    he did not open his mouth.

8:7 Greek *unclean.* 8:26 Or *Go at noon.*

8:18-25 When Simon the sorcerer saw the ministry of Peter and John, he offered to buy the secret of their power. This showed Peter that Simon did not understand his relationship with God; he only sought God for what he might get out of the relationship. Perhaps he wanted to gain back the prestige he had lost when Philip came to town (see 8:9-13). Peter warned Simon that he needed to examine himself and repent. This problem of impure motives also applies to recovery. If we are in recovery just to look good, we are in it for the wrong reason. When we look to God for help, we are making his will our own. We succeed in recovery only as we submit completely to God's will for our life.

9:10-16 During Saul's intense self-examination, God sent Ananias to befriend him, pray for him, and restore his sight. Ananias was afraid at first because he wasn't sure that Saul had really changed. When he met with Saul, however, Ananias discovered that no one is beyond God's help. By coming to help Saul, Ananias discovered a truth that we learn in recovery. When we reach out to others and share the Good News, God not only uses us to help others, he also strengthens our own faith.

³³He was humiliated and received no justice.
Who can speak of his descendants?
For his life was taken from the earth."*

³⁴The eunuch asked Philip, "Tell me, was the prophet talking about himself or someone else?" ³⁵So beginning with this same Scripture, Philip told him the Good News about Jesus.

³⁶As they rode along, they came to some water, and the eunuch said, "Look! There's some water! Why can't I be baptized?"* ³⁸He ordered the carriage to stop, and they went down into the water, and Philip baptized him.

³⁹When they came up out of the water, the Spirit of the Lord snatched Philip away. The eunuch never saw him again but went on his way rejoicing. ⁴⁰Meanwhile, Philip found himself farther north at the town of Azotus. He preached the Good News there and in every town along the way until he came to Caesarea.

CHAPTER 9
Saul's Conversion

Meanwhile, Saul was uttering threats with every breath and was eager to kill the Lord's followers.* So he went to the high priest. ²He requested letters addressed to the synagogues in Damascus, asking for their cooperation in the arrest of any followers of the Way he found there. He wanted to bring them—both men and women—back to Jerusalem in chains.

³As he was approaching Damascus on this mission, a light from heaven suddenly shone down around him. ⁴He fell to the ground and heard a voice saying to him, "Saul! Saul! Why are you persecuting me?"

⁵"Who are you, lord?" Saul asked.

And the voice replied, "I am Jesus, the one you are persecuting! ⁶Now get up and go into the city, and you will be told what you must do."

⁷The men with Saul stood speechless, for they heard the sound of someone's voice but saw no one! ⁸Saul picked himself up off the ground, but when he opened his eyes he was blind. So his companions led him by the hand to Damascus. ⁹He remained there blind for three days and did not eat or drink.

¹⁰Now there was a believer* in Damascus named Ananias. The Lord spoke to him in a vision, calling, "Ananias!"

8:32-33 Isa 53:7-8 (Greek version). 8:36 Some manuscripts add verse 37, *"You can," Philip answered, "if you believe with all your heart." And the eunuch replied, "I believe that Jesus Christ is the Son of God."* 9:1 Greek *disciples.* 9:10 Greek *disciple;* also in 9:26, 36.

STEP 12

Listening First
BIBLE READING: Acts 8:26-40

Having had a spiritual awakening as the result of these steps, we tried to carry this message to others and to practice these principles in all our affairs.

We may be so excited about what God has done for us that we want to rush right out and tell everyone our story. Or we may be very shy and hesitate to tell people, especially if we think they are better than we are. We all have a valuable story to tell; we just need to discover the best way to communicate it.

God led the evangelist Philip to meet an influential traveler who "had gone to Jerusalem to worship, and he was now returning . . . reading aloud from the book of the prophet Isaiah. The Holy Spirit said to Philip, 'Go over and walk along beside the carriage.' Philip ran over and heard the man reading from the prophet Isaiah. Philip asked, 'Do you understand what you are reading?' The man replied, 'How can I, unless someone instructs me?' . . . So beginning with this same Scripture, Philip told him the Good News about Jesus" (Acts 8:27-31, 35).

The way Philip communicated is a model for us. He was sensitive to allow God to lead him to someone who was ready. He wasn't intimidated by the man's status and did not hesitate to tell him the Good News about Jesus. Philip began by listening carefully. He tuned into the man's need and interests and then explained their relationship to the message he was prepared to share. Whether we are zealous or shy, following this model can help us communicate our message in a way that people can understand and receive it. *Turn to page 1555, 1 Timothy 4.*

"Yes, Lord!" he replied.

[11]The Lord said, "Go over to Straight Street, to the house of Judas. When you get there, ask for a man from Tarsus named Saul. He is praying to me right now. [12]I have shown him a vision of a man named Ananias coming in and laying hands on him so he can see again."

[13]"But Lord," exclaimed Ananias, "I've heard many people talk about the terrible things this man has done to the believers* in Jerusalem! [14]And he is authorized by the leading priests to arrest everyone who calls upon your name."

[15]But the Lord said, "Go, for Saul is my chosen instrument to take my message to the Gentiles and to kings, as well as to the people of Israel. [16]And I will show him how much he must suffer for my name's sake."

[17]So Ananias went and found Saul. He laid his hands on him and said, "Brother Saul, the Lord Jesus, who appeared to you on the road, has sent me so that you might regain your sight and be filled with the Holy Spirit." [18]Instantly something like scales fell from Saul's eyes, and he regained his sight. Then he got up and was baptized. [19]Afterward he ate some food and regained his strength.

Saul in Damascus and Jerusalem

Saul stayed with the believers* in Damascus for a few days. [20]And immediately he began preaching about Jesus in the synagogues, saying, "He is indeed the Son of God!"

[21]All who heard him were amazed. "Isn't this the same man who caused such devastation among Jesus' followers in Jerusalem?" they asked. "And didn't he come here to arrest them and take them in chains to the leading priests?"

[22]Saul's preaching became more and more powerful, and the Jews in Damascus couldn't refute his proofs that Jesus was indeed the Messiah. [23]After a while some of the Jews plotted together to kill him. [24]They were watching for him day and night at the city gate so they could murder him, but Saul was told about their plot. [25]So during the night, some of the other believers* lowered him in a large basket through an opening in the city wall.

[26]When Saul arrived in Jerusalem, he tried to meet with the believers, but they were all afraid of him. They did not believe he had truly become a believer! [27]Then Barnabas brought him to the apostles and told them how Saul had seen the Lord on the way to Damascus and how the Lord had spoken to Saul. He also told them that Saul had preached boldly in the name of Jesus in Damascus.

[28]So Saul stayed with the apostles and went all around Jerusalem with them, preaching boldly in the name of the Lord. [29]He debated with some Greek-speaking Jews, but they tried to murder him. [30]When the believers* heard about this, they took him down to Caesarea and sent him away to Tarsus, his hometown.

[31]The church then had peace throughout

9:13 Greek *God's holy people;* also in 9:32, 41. 9:19 Greek *disciples;* also in 9:26, 38. 9:25 Greek *his disciples.*
9:30 Greek *brothers.*

9:20-25 Saul stayed with the Christians in Damascus for a few days and shared the Good News of salvation in Jesus Christ, demonstrating that his transformation was real. Both Jews and Christians were astounded at the changes in Saul. The Jews turned against him and plotted to kill him, but his new Christian friends helped him escape. We may also experience opposition from our old friends when we enter the recovery process. They may feel guilty about their own dependency, or they may be afraid they will lose a friend. Whatever the reason, our old friends may try to thwart our recovery. This is where our new support groups take on an essential role, protecting and guiding us through these difficult times.

9:26-30 Saul returned to Jerusalem and tried to meet with the Christian believers there. He immediately met skepticism. They couldn't believe that such a cruel enemy could have changed so quickly. In time Saul proved his sincerity and was accepted. When we enter recovery, we may meet skepticism for a while. Friends and family members may turn away. In time, however, if we continue to follow God's will for our life and seek to make amends, broken relationships will begin to heal. Our broken relationships, like our addiction, took time to develop. Recovery also will take time.

9:36-43 Peter received a call for help from grieving friends in Joppa. Dorcas, a believer who had served other widows and helped the poor, had just died, and those who loved her had sent for Peter. Implementing God's power over death (see Luke 8:41-42, 49-56), Peter prayed and brought this woman back to life. When God's power is at work within us, nothing is impossible. God's power can pull us out of our addiction, as if from death, and give us a new life in Jesus Christ.

Judea, Galilee, and Samaria, and it became stronger as the believers lived in the fear of the Lord. And with the encouragement of the Holy Spirit, it also grew in numbers.

Peter Heals Aeneas and Raises Dorcas

³²Meanwhile, Peter traveled from place to place, and he came down to visit the believers in the town of Lydda. ³³There he met a man named Aeneas, who had been paralyzed and bedridden for eight years. ³⁴Peter said to him, "Aeneas, Jesus Christ heals you! Get up, and roll up your sleeping mat!" And he was healed instantly. ³⁵Then the whole population of Lydda and Sharon saw Aeneas walking around, and they turned to the Lord.

³⁶There was a believer in Joppa named Tabitha (which in Greek is Dorcas*). She was always doing kind things for others and helping the poor. ³⁷About this time she became ill and died. Her body was washed for burial and laid in an upstairs room. ³⁸But the believers had heard that Peter was nearby at Lydda, so they sent two men to beg him, "Please come as soon as possible!"

³⁹So Peter returned with them; and as soon as he arrived, they took him to the upstairs room. The room was filled with widows who were weeping and showing him the coats and other clothes Dorcas had made for them. ⁴⁰But Peter asked them all to leave the room; then he knelt and prayed. Turning to the body he said, "Get up, Tabitha." And she opened her eyes! When she saw Peter, she sat up! ⁴¹He gave her his hand and helped her up. Then he called in the widows and all the believers, and he presented her to them alive.

⁴²The news spread through the whole town, and many believed in the Lord. ⁴³And Peter stayed a long time in Joppa, living with Simon, a tanner of hides.

CHAPTER 10
Cornelius Calls for Peter

In Caesarea there lived a Roman army officer* named Cornelius, who was a captain of the Italian Regiment. ²He was a devout, God-fearing man, as was everyone in his household. He gave generously to the poor and prayed regularly to God. ³One afternoon about three o'clock, he had a vision in which he saw an angel of God coming toward him. "Cornelius!" the angel said.

⁴Cornelius stared at him in terror. "What is it, sir?" he asked the angel.

9:36 The names *Tabitha* in Aramaic and *Dorcas* in Greek both mean "gazelle." 10:1 Greek *a centurion;* similarly in 10:22.

STEP 1

A Time to Choose

BIBLE READING: Acts 9:1-9

We admitted that we were powerless over our problems—that our lives had become unmanageable.

There are important moments in life that can change our destiny. These are often times when we are confronted with how powerless we are over the events of our life. These moments can either destroy us or forever set the course of our life in a much better direction.

Saul of Tarsus (later called Paul; see 13:9) had such a moment. After Jesus' ascension, Saul took it upon himself to rid the world of Christians. As he headed to Damascus on this mission, "a light from heaven suddenly shone down around him. He fell to the ground and heard a voice saying to him, 'Saul! Saul! Why are you persecuting me? . . . I am Jesus, the one you are persecuting! Now get up and go into the city, and you will be told what you must do.' . . . Saul picked himself up off the ground, but when he opened his eyes he was blind. So his companions led him by the hand to Damascus. He remained there blind for three days and did not eat or drink" (Acts 9:3-6, 8-9).

Saul was suddenly confronted with the fact that his life wasn't as perfect as he had thought. Self-righteousness had been his trademark. By letting go of his illusions of power, however, he became one of the most powerful men ever—the apostle Paul. When we are confronted with the knowledge that our life isn't under our control, we have a choice. We can continue in denial and self-righteousness, or we can face the fact that we have been blind to some important issues. If we become willing to be led into recovery and into a whole new way of life, we will find true power. *Turn to page 1483, 2 Corinthians 4.*

And the angel replied, "Your prayers and gifts to the poor have been received by God as an offering! [5]Now send some men to Joppa, and summon a man named Simon Peter. [6]He is staying with Simon, a tanner who lives near the seashore."

[7]As soon as the angel was gone, Cornelius called two of his household servants and a devout soldier, one of his personal attendants. [8]He told them what had happened and sent them off to Joppa.

Peter Visits Cornelius

[9]The next day as Cornelius's messengers were nearing the town, Peter went up on the flat roof to pray. It was about noon, [10]and he was hungry. But while a meal was being prepared, he fell into a trance. [11]He saw the sky open, and something like a large sheet was let down by its four corners. [12]In the sheet were all sorts of animals, reptiles, and birds. [13]Then a voice said to him, "Get up, Peter; kill and eat them."

[14]"No, Lord," Peter declared. "I have never eaten anything that our Jewish laws have declared impure and unclean.*"

[15]But the voice spoke again: "Do not call something unclean if God has made it clean." [16]The same vision was repeated three times. Then the sheet was suddenly pulled up to heaven.

[17]Peter was very perplexed. What could the vision mean? Just then the men sent by Cornelius found Simon's house. Standing outside the gate, [18]they asked if a man named Simon Peter was staying there.

[19]Meanwhile, as Peter was puzzling over the vision, the Holy Spirit said to him,

"Three men have come looking for you. [20]Get up, go downstairs, and go with them without hesitation. Don't worry, for I have sent them."

[21]So Peter went down and said, "I'm the man you are looking for. Why have you come?"

[22]They said, "We were sent by Cornelius, a Roman officer. He is a devout and God-fearing man, well respected by all the Jews. A holy angel instructed him to summon you to his house so that he can hear your message." [23]So Peter invited the men to stay for the night. The next day he went with them, accompanied by some of the brothers from Joppa.

[24]They arrived in Caesarea the following day. Cornelius was waiting for them and had called together his relatives and close friends. [25]As Peter entered his home, Cornelius fell at his feet and worshiped him. [26]But Peter pulled him up and said, "Stand up! I'm a human being just like you!" [27]So they talked together and went inside, where many others were assembled.

[28]Peter told them, "You know it is against our laws for a Jewish man to enter a Gentile home like this or to associate with you. But God has shown me that I should no longer think of anyone as impure or unclean. [29]So I came without objection as soon as I was sent for. Now tell me why you sent for me."

[30]Cornelius replied, "Four days ago I was praying in my house about this same time, three o'clock in the afternoon. Suddenly, a man in dazzling clothes was standing in front of me. [31]He told me, 'Cornelius, your prayer has been heard, and your gifts to the

10:14 Greek *anything common and unclean.*

10:9-20 God sent a special vision to Peter to reveal to him some of his hidden prejudices. Peter saw a large sheet covered with animals that according to Jewish law were unclean. At first Peter refused to have anything to do with them. But God sent the vision three times, challenging Peter's view of what was clean or unclean. God was preparing Peter to carry the Good News to the "unclean" Gentiles and to the home of Cornelius. Peter needed to realize that God accepts people of all backgrounds. This truth is important for us as well. As we share the Good News with others, we must not allow our prejudices to stand in the way of God's will. If God opens a door to share the gospel with someone, we need to step through it in faith. God will go with us as we spread his message of hope.

10:21-33 Peter didn't want to visit the home of this "unclean" Gentile. But when Peter and Cornelius met, they excitedly shared the unusual things they had just seen and heard. God had worked to remove the prejudices that would have kept them from speaking to each other. As a result, the Holy Spirit filled all the Gentiles who were in Cornelius's home. God drew people close who had once been separated by immense barriers. We may have relationships that seem broken beyond repair. Harsh emotions and the prejudices formed during our years in bondage have made communication almost impossible. As hopeless as such relationships seem, God can work to soften our defenses and enhance communication. He will do this as we entrust our life to him and seek to follow his will.

CORNELIUS & FAMILY

Recovery usually doesn't happen overnight; it is a process. When Cornelius and his family came into the spotlight in Acts 10, the process of their recovery had already begun. From a Roman religious and a military background, this army officer and his family were "God-fearing." They prayed to the God of Israel and gave generously to charity.

Cornelius's family had undoubtedly changed many of the habitual patterns and perspectives that had come from their Roman background. At this point God intervened and allowed them to proceed to a deeper understanding of God, which led to eternal life. God met them by sending the apostle Peter who came to them with the needed spiritual insight.

The scene in Cornelius's home is a model of family recovery. As Cornelius and his family came to believe in the redemptive work of Jesus, they also entered a phase of spiritual recovery augmented by the power of the Holy Spirit. This wasn't the end of their recovery process by any means. But they were well on their way because they had established healthy relationships with each other and with God.

When the family of Cornelius received the gift of the Holy Spirit, a new era of history was born. For the first time God showed that *all* people were acceptable to God through Jesus Christ—even "unclean" Gentiles. Because of his cultural prejudices, Peter had a hard time accepting this truth, but when Cornelius and his family received the Holy Spirit, Peter could no longer deny it. God desires to make the Holy Spirit's power a part of all our life. If we repent of our sins and accept God's forgiveness on the basis of the work of Jesus Christ, we can experience God's power in our life. With God's help, no problem or dependency is too great to overcome.

STRENGTHS AND ACCOMPLISHMENTS:
- Cornelius believed God to the degree that he understood him.
- He led his family to know God the best way he knew how.
- He was not satisfied with his level of maturity and sought to grow further.
- He and his family were open to change and embraced new life in Jesus Christ.

WEAKNESSES AND MISTAKES:
- Cornelius's understanding was limited, and he initially worshiped Peter.

LESSONS FROM THEIR LIVES:
- God reaches out to all those who want to know him better.
- The power of Jesus is for everyone, regardless of race or background.
- Recovery often requires guidance from others who have already been there.

KEY VERSE:
"Everyone who believes in [Jesus Christ] will have their sins forgiven through his name" (Acts 10:43).

The story of Cornelius and his family is told in Acts 10–11.

---

poor have been noticed by God! ³²Now send messengers to Joppa, and summon a man named Simon Peter. He is staying in the home of Simon, a tanner who lives near the seashore.' ³³So I sent for you at once, and it was good of you to come. Now we are all here, waiting before God to hear the message the Lord has given you."

The Gentiles Hear the Good News
³⁴Then Peter replied, "I see very clearly that God shows no favoritism. ³⁵In every nation he accepts those who fear him and do what is right. ³⁶This is the message of Good News for the people of Israel—that there is peace with God through Jesus Christ, who is Lord of all. ³⁷You know what happened throughout Judea, beginning in Galilee, after John began preaching his message of baptism. ³⁸And you know that God anointed Jesus of Nazareth with the Holy Spirit and with power. Then Jesus went around doing good and healing all who were oppressed by the devil, for God was with him.

³⁹"And we apostles are witnesses of all he did throughout Judea and in Jerusalem. They put him to death by hanging him on a cross,* ⁴⁰but God raised him to life on the

10:39 Greek *on a tree.*

third day. Then God allowed him to appear, [41]not to the general public,* but to us whom God had chosen in advance to be his witnesses. We were those who ate and drank with him after he rose from the dead. [42]And he ordered us to preach everywhere and to testify that Jesus is the one appointed by God to be the judge of all—the living and the dead. [43]He is the one all the prophets testified about, saying that everyone who believes in him will have their sins forgiven through his name."

The Gentiles Receive the Holy Spirit

[44]Even as Peter was saying these things, the Holy Spirit fell upon all who were listening to the message. [45]The Jewish believers* who came with Peter were amazed that the gift of the Holy Spirit had been poured out on the Gentiles, too. [46]For they heard them speaking in other tongues* and praising God.

Then Peter asked, [47]"Can anyone object to their being baptized, now that they have received the Holy Spirit just as we did?" [48]So he gave orders for them to be baptized in the name of Jesus Christ. Afterward Cornelius asked him to stay with them for several days.

CHAPTER 11
Peter Explains His Actions

Soon the news reached the apostles and other believers* in Judea that the Gentiles had received the word of God. [2]But when Peter arrived back in Jerusalem, the Jewish believers* criticized him. [3]"You entered the home of Gentiles* and even ate with them!" they said.

[4]Then Peter told them exactly what had happened. [5]"I was in the town of Joppa," he said, "and while I was praying, I went into a trance and saw a vision. Something like a large sheet was let down by its four corners from the sky. And it came right down to me. [6]When I looked inside the sheet, I saw all sorts of tame and wild animals, reptiles, and birds. [7]And I heard a voice say, 'Get up, Peter; kill and eat them.'

[8]"'No, Lord,' I replied. 'I have never eaten anything that our Jewish laws have declared impure or unclean.*'

[9]"But the voice from heaven spoke again: 'Do not call something unclean if God has made it clean.' [10]This happened three times before the sheet and all it contained was pulled back up to heaven.

[11]"Just then three men who had been sent from Caesarea arrived at the house where we were staying. [12]The Holy Spirit told me to go with them and not to worry that they were Gentiles. These six brothers here accompanied me, and we soon entered the home of the man who had sent for us. [13]He told us how an angel had appeared to him in his home and had told him, 'Send messengers to Joppa, and summon a man named Simon Peter. [14]He will tell you how you and everyone in your household can be saved!'

[15]"As I began to speak," Peter continued, "the Holy Spirit fell on them, just as he fell on us at the beginning. [16]Then I thought of the Lord's words when he said, 'John baptized with* water, but you will be baptized with the Holy Spirit.' [17]And since God gave these Gentiles the same gift he gave us when we believed in the Lord Jesus Christ, who was I to stand in God's way?"

[18]When the others heard this, they stopped objecting and began praising God.

10:41 Greek *the people.* 10:45 Greek *The faithful ones of the circumcision.* 10:46 Or *in other languages.* 11:1 Greek *brothers.* 11:2 Greek *those of the circumcision.* 11:3 Greek *of uncircumcised men.* 11:8 Greek *anything common or unclean.* 11:16 Or *in;* also in 11:16b.

11:1-3 Even before Peter arrived home, the Jewish believers heard that Gentiles had believed in Christ. Because of their prejudice, they did not accept what they had heard, so they immediately confronted Peter. Earlier, when faced with opposition before Christ's death (Luke 22:54-62), Peter had denied his faith. But he did not fold this time; God had made some amazing changes in him since that painful failure. Peter defended the truth that had been revealed to him without concern for the cost to himself. Sometimes we may be surprised by the changes that God has worked in our life. Recognizing how far we have already come can encourage us to persevere in the process.

11:4-18 The Jewish believers were slow to accept Gentile believers into their fellowship. They criticized an event that actually was reason for rejoicing. They had succeeded in obeying Jesus' mandate to testify about him "in Jerusalem, throughout Judea, in Samaria, and to the ends of the earth" (1:8). Numerous Samaritans had already believed in Christ (8:1-25), and now Gentiles from the ends of the earth had joined the Christian community (see also 8:26-40). We may have friends who cannot recognize our moments of triumph in recovery. They may try to discourage us as we take significant steps to follow God's will. We must not allow them to dampen our faith or discourage our progress.

They said, "We can see that God has also given the Gentiles the privilege of repenting of their sins and receiving eternal life."

The Church in Antioch of Syria

¹⁹Meanwhile, the believers who had been scattered during the persecution after Stephen's death traveled as far as Phoenicia, Cyprus, and Antioch of Syria. They preached the word of God, but only to Jews. ²⁰However, some of the believers who went to Antioch from Cyprus and Cyrene began preaching to the Gentiles* about the Lord Jesus. ²¹The power of the Lord was with them, and a large number of these Gentiles believed and turned to the Lord.

²²When the church at Jerusalem heard what had happened, they sent Barnabas to Antioch. ²³When he arrived and saw this evidence of God's blessing, he was filled with joy, and he encouraged the believers to stay true to the Lord. ²⁴Barnabas was a good man, full of the Holy Spirit and strong in faith. And many people were brought to the Lord.

²⁵Then Barnabas went on to Tarsus to look for Saul. ²⁶When he found him, he brought him back to Antioch. Both of them stayed there with the church for a full year, teaching large crowds of people. (It was at Antioch that the believers* were first called Christians.)

²⁷During this time some prophets traveled from Jerusalem to Antioch. ²⁸One of them named Agabus stood up in one of the meetings and predicted by the Spirit that a great famine was coming upon the entire Roman world. (This was fulfilled during the reign of Claudius.) ²⁹So the believers in Antioch decided to send relief to the brothers and sisters* in Judea, everyone giving as much as they could. ³⁰This they did, entrusting their gifts to Barnabas and Saul to take to the elders of the church in Jerusalem.

CHAPTER 12

James Is Killed and Peter Is Imprisoned

About that time King Herod Agrippa* began to persecute some believers in the church.

²He had the apostle James (John's brother) killed with a sword. ³When Herod saw how much this pleased the Jewish people, he also arrested Peter. (This took place during the Passover celebration.*) ⁴Then he imprisoned him, placing him under the guard of four squads of four soldiers each. Herod intended to bring Peter out for public trial after the Passover. ⁵But while Peter was in prison, the church prayed very earnestly for him.

Peter's Miraculous Escape from Prison

⁶The night before Peter was to be placed on trial, he was asleep, fastened with two chains between two soldiers. Others stood guard at the prison gate. ⁷Suddenly, there was a bright light in the cell, and an angel of the Lord stood before Peter. The angel struck him on the side to awaken him and said, "Quick! Get up!" And the chains fell off his wrists. ⁸Then the angel told him, "Get dressed and put on your sandals." And he did. "Now put on your coat and follow me," the angel ordered.

⁹So Peter left the cell, following the angel. But all the time he thought it was a vision. He didn't realize it was actually happening. ¹⁰They passed the first and second guard posts and came to the iron gate leading to the city, and this opened for them all by itself. So they passed through and started walking down the street, and then the angel suddenly left him.

¹¹Peter finally came to his senses. "It's really true!" he said. "The Lord has sent his angel and saved me from Herod and from what the Jewish leaders* had planned to do to me!"

¹²When he realized this, he went to the home of Mary, the mother of John Mark, where many were gathered for prayer. ¹³He knocked at the door in the gate, and a servant girl named Rhoda came to open it. ¹⁴When she recognized Peter's voice, she was so overjoyed that, instead of opening the door, she ran back inside and told everyone, "Peter is standing at the door!"

¹⁵"You're out of your mind!" they said.

11:20 Greek *the Hellenists* (i.e., those who speak Greek); other manuscripts read *the Greeks.* 11:26 Greek *disciples;* also in 11:29. 11:29 Greek *the brothers.* 12:1 Greek *Herod the king.* He was the nephew of Herod Antipas and a grandson of Herod the Great. 12:3 Greek *the days of unleavened bread.* 12:11 Or *the Jewish people.*

12:1-11 Peter's miraculous escape from prison shows that nothing can thwart God's plans. In response to prayer, God can always overcome the obstacles that stand in our way. He may even use supernatural means to deliver us. This does not mean we will never face difficulties in our walk with God. Even as the early church enjoyed phenomenal success, it still suffered severe trials. We will always face obstacles as we seek to live out God's plan for our life. But since God wants us to succeed in recovery, nothing can stand in the way of our success if we entrust our life to his care.

When she insisted, they decided, "It must be his angel."

[16]Meanwhile, Peter continued knocking. When they finally opened the door and saw him, they were amazed. [17]He motioned for them to quiet down and told them how the Lord had led him out of prison. "Tell James and the other brothers what happened," he said. And then he went to another place.

[18]At dawn there was a great commotion among the soldiers about what had happened to Peter. [19]Herod Agrippa ordered a thorough search for him. When he couldn't be found, Herod interrogated the guards and sentenced them to death. Afterward Herod left Judea to stay in Caesarea for a while.

The Death of Herod Agrippa

[20]Now Herod was very angry with the people of Tyre and Sidon. So they sent a delegation to make peace with him because their cities were dependent upon Herod's country for food. The delegates won the support of Blastus, Herod's personal assistant, [21]and an appointment with Herod was granted. When the day arrived, Herod put on his royal robes, sat on his throne, and made a speech to them. [22]The people gave him a great ovation, shouting, "It's the voice of a god, not of a man!"

[23]Instantly, an angel of the Lord struck Herod with a sickness, because he accepted the people's worship instead of giving the glory to God. So he was consumed with worms and died.

[24]Meanwhile, the word of God continued to spread, and there were many new believers.

[25]When Barnabas and Saul had finished their mission to Jerusalem, they returned,* taking John Mark with them.

CHAPTER 13
Barnabas and Saul Are Commissioned

Among the prophets and teachers of the church at Antioch of Syria were Barnabas, Simeon (called "the black man"*), Lucius (from Cyrene), Manaen (the childhood companion of King Herod Antipas*), and Saul. [2]One day as these men were worshiping the Lord and fasting, the Holy Spirit said, "Dedicate Barnabas and Saul for the special work to which I have called them." [3]So after more fasting and prayer, the men laid their hands on them and sent them on their way.

Paul's First Missionary Journey

[4]So Barnabas and Saul were sent out by the Holy Spirit. They went down to the seaport of Seleucia and then sailed for the island of Cyprus. [5]There, in the town of Salamis, they went to the Jewish synagogues and preached the word of God. John Mark went with them as their assistant.

[6]Afterward they traveled from town to town across the entire island until finally they reached Paphos, where they met a Jewish sorcerer, a false prophet named Bar-Jesus. [7]He had attached himself to the governor, Sergius Paulus, who was an intelligent man. The governor invited Barnabas and Saul to

12:25 Or mission, they returned to Jerusalem. Other manuscripts read mission, they returned from Jerusalem; still others read mission, they returned from Jerusalem to Antioch. **13:1a** Greek who was called Niger. **13:1b** Greek Herod the tetrarch.

12:20-24 Herod Agrippa pompously considered himself entirely self-sufficient; he saw no need for others, much less any higher Power. He enjoyed the worship he received from his people, playing the role of a god in their lives. What a contrast to the helpless way he died. Death is the great leveler of the whole human race. God will not be mocked; he will judge those who try to displace him on the throne of their life. When we give up our self-sufficiency and turn to God, our true king, we learn that his mercy and justice are sufficient for each day and for eternity.

13:1-3 However reluctant the church in Antioch may have been to lose Paul and Barnabas, they immediately submitted to the voice of the Holy Spirit. Although it meant a major change, they released and commissioned these key leaders to missionary service. Before sending them on their way, the people fasted, prayed, and laid their hands on them. In like manner, we can support one another in recovery. If God is number one in our life, we must be willing to give up our possessions, lifestyle, or codependent relationship to obey God. Although this may include personal sacrifice, it will lead us to joy and serenity.

13:13-14 John Mark left the missionary team and returned to Jerusalem. We aren't sure why he deserted the team; perhaps it was due to lack of faith, disappointment in Paul's leadership, culture shock, homesickness, or fear. His failure here may remind us of our experiences of relapse. It is encouraging to see that later John Mark was restored to fellowship with Barnabas and Paul. Barnabas took John Mark under his wing, even when Paul rejected him (15:37-39). From Paul's letters a decade later (Colossians 4:10; 2 Timothy 4:11), we know that John Mark became a faithful minister in the early church. Our failures can become opportunities to start over and to keep learning and growing.

PAUL

Saul the Pharisee (later called Paul) was exemplary in his religious fervor, and he backed up his convictions with immediate and decisive action. No one could doubt his sincerity. His number one priority was to wipe out the church of Jesus Christ—and he thought this was what God wanted him to do. He pursued the first Christians with a vengeance.

One day Jesus Christ confronted this proud religious leader on the road to Damascus. He intervened in Saul's life when Saul was driven by an angry religious fanaticism. Although God blinded Saul physically, he gave him clear spiritual insight. In one moment Saul was broken, humbled, and set on the road to recovery. He was freed from the legalistic mind-set that had controlled his life. Saul had experienced the transforming power of God.

With the same kind of commitment and intensity that he had displayed as a Pharisee, Saul, now called Paul, set out to tell the world about Jesus Christ. He endured sickness, rejection, and repeated attacks on his life to bring the message of God's forgiveness to needy people. He spoke before Jews, Greeks, and Romans. He defended his faith before kings and emperors. By the end of his life, much of the Mediterranean world had been reached with the gospel. This former Pharisee became the greatest missionary of the early church.

As we rejoice in the transformation of Paul's life, it is important to remember that this change took place because of the marvelous grace of God. Originally he was highly dysfunctional, driven by his misplaced passion. As a result of his conversion, however, he was set free from his unhealthy attitudes and behaviors. We can also experience this freeing and transforming grace of God. We can be healed and transformed, no matter how dark our past or how great our mistakes.

STRENGTHS AND ACCOMPLISHMENTS:
- Paul displayed great commitment to the causes he pursued.
- He was a brilliant spokesperson for Jesus Christ.
- He was no longer driven to self-serving achievement after his conversion.
- Paul was largely responsible for the dramatic spread of the gospel.

WEAKNESSES AND MISTAKES:
- Before his conversion, Paul sought to destroy the church of Jesus Christ.
- Before he came to believe, Paul vehemently denied the truth about Jesus.

LESSONS FROM HIS LIFE:
- Zeal and energy alone do not impress God or make a person successful.
- A person can be healed from the past and find hope for the future.
- No matter when we begin recovery, we can still make an impact on others.

KEY VERSES:
"No, dear brothers and sisters, I have not achieved it, but I focus on this one thing: Forgetting the past and looking forward to what lies ahead, I press on to reach the end of the race and receive the heavenly prize for which God, through Christ Jesus, is calling us" (Philippians 3:13-14).

Paul's story is told in Acts 7–28. Additional information can be found in the various letters he wrote. He is also mentioned in 2 Peter 3:15-16.

---

visit him, for he wanted to hear the word of God. [8]But Elymas, the sorcerer (as his name means in Greek), interfered and urged the governor to pay no attention to what Barnabas and Saul said. He was trying to keep the governor from believing.

[9]Saul, also known as Paul, was filled with the Holy Spirit, and he looked the sorcerer in the eye. [10]Then he said, "You son of the devil, full of every sort of deceit and fraud, and enemy of all that is good! Will you never stop perverting the true ways of the Lord? [11]Watch now, for the Lord has laid his hand of punishment upon you, and you will be struck blind. You will not see the sunlight for some time."

Instantly mist and darkness came over the man's eyes, and he began groping around begging for someone to take his hand and lead him.

[12]When the governor saw what had happened, he became a believer, for he was astonished at the teaching about the Lord.

Paul Preaches in Antioch of Pisidia

[13]Paul and his companions then left Paphos by ship for Pamphylia, landing at the port town of Perga. There John Mark left them and returned to Jerusalem. [14]But Paul and Barnabas traveled inland to Antioch of Pisidia.*

13:13-14 *Pamphylia* and *Pisidia* were districts in what is now Turkey.

On the Sabbath they went to the synagogue for the services. [15]After the usual readings from the books of Moses* and the prophets, those in charge of the service sent them this message: "Brothers, if you have any word of encouragement for the people, come and give it."

[16]So Paul stood, lifted his hand to quiet them, and started speaking. "Men of Israel," he said, "and you God-fearing Gentiles, listen to me.

[17]"The God of this nation of Israel chose our ancestors and made them multiply and grow strong during their stay in Egypt. Then with a powerful arm he led them out of their slavery. [18]He put up with them* through forty years of wandering in the wilderness. [19]Then he destroyed seven nations in Canaan and gave their land to Israel as an inheritance. [20]All this took about 450 years.

"After that, God gave them judges to rule until the time of Samuel the prophet. [21]Then the people begged for a king, and God gave them Saul son of Kish, a man of the tribe of Benjamin, who reigned for forty years. [22]But God removed Saul and replaced him with David, a man about whom God said, 'I have found David son of Jesse, a man after my own heart. He will do everything I want him to do.'*

[23]"And it is one of King David's descendants, Jesus, who is God's promised Savior of Israel! [24]Before he came, John the Baptist preached that all the people of Israel needed to repent of their sins and turn to God and be baptized. [25]As John was finishing his ministry he asked, 'Do you think I am the Messiah? No, I am not! But he is coming soon—and I'm not even worthy to be his slave and untie the sandals on his feet.'

[26]"Brothers—you sons of Abraham, and also you God-fearing Gentiles—this message of salvation has been sent to us! [27]The people in Jerusalem and their leaders did not recognize Jesus as the one the prophets had spoken about. Instead, they condemned him, and in doing this they fulfilled the prophets'

words that are read every Sabbath. [28]They found no legal reason to execute him, but they asked Pilate to have him killed anyway.

[29]"When they had done all that the prophecies said about him, they took him down from the cross* and placed him in a tomb. [30]But God raised him from the dead! [31]And over a period of many days he appeared to those who had gone with him from Galilee to Jerusalem. They are now his witnesses to the people of Israel.

[32]"And now we are here to bring you this Good News. The promise was made to our ancestors, [33]and God has now fulfilled it for us, their descendants, by raising Jesus. This is what the second psalm says about Jesus:

'You are my Son.
    Today I have become your Father.*'

[34]For God had promised to raise him from the dead, not leaving him to rot in the grave. He said, 'I will give you the sacred blessings I promised to David.'* [35]Another psalm explains it more fully: 'You will not allow your Holy One to rot in the grave.'* [36]This is not a reference to David, for after David had done the will of God in his own generation, he died and was buried with his ancestors, and his body decayed. [37]No, it was a reference to someone else—someone whom God raised and whose body did not decay.

[38]"Brothers, listen! We are here to proclaim that through this man Jesus there is forgiveness for your sins. [39]Everyone who believes in him is declared right with God—something the law of Moses could never do. [40]Be careful! Don't let the prophets' words apply to you. For they said,

[41]'Look, you mockers,
    be amazed and die!
For I am doing something in your own
        day,
    something you wouldn't believe
    even if someone told you about it.'*"

[42]As Paul and Barnabas left the synagogue that day, the people begged them to speak

---

13:15 Greek *from the law.* 13:18 Some manuscripts read *He cared for them;* compare Deut 1:31. 13:22 1 Sam 13:14. 13:29 Greek *from the tree.* 13:33 Or *Today I reveal you as my Son.* Ps 2:7. 13:34 Isa 55:3. 13:35 Ps 16:10. 13:38 English translations divide verses 38 and 39 in various ways. 13:41 Hab 1:5 (Greek version).

13:44–14:6 Jealousy, rejection, ridicule, revenge, physical abuse, murder plots—Paul and Barnabas experienced all that and more as they preached the Good News to others. Sometimes Paul and Barnabas stayed in a town for weeks; other times they had to run for their lives after a short stay. When we reach out to others in recovery, we may need courage to hang in there with unreceptive people who present challenges to our message. In other cases we may need to cut our losses and run. It takes wisdom from above to know how to react in any given situation.

BARNABAS & JOHN MARK

Discouragement often drains our energy, especially when we face the trials of recovery. At such times it is very helpful to spend time with people who know how to encourage. Some people know just what to do or say to remind us that life is worthwhile, even in the midst of pain and failure. They know how to inspire hope when there seems to be nothing to hope for. Barnabas, whose name means "Son of Encouragement," was just that kind of person.

Barnabas's gift of encouragement was demonstrated through his financial generosity, his leadership, his teaching of new believers at Antioch, and his acceptance of Paul when others were afraid of him and doubted his conversion. It is probably accurate to say that Barnabas changed the course of church history and even the shape of the New Testament itself by persevering in his encouragement of John Mark.

Unfortunately, John Mark bailed out of his responsibilities on the first missionary journey with Paul and Barnabas. Later Barnabas was willing to give the younger man an opportunity for recovery by including him in a second journey, but Paul wouldn't hear of it. The disagreement between Paul and Barnabas was so great that they parted company. Paul went back to Asia Minor with his new partner, Silas; Barnabas went on his own missionary journey with John Mark at his side.

With Barnabas's encouragement, Mark was faithful in his missionary ministry and soon regained Paul's respect. Later Mark would also work with the apostle Peter. He is the author of the Gospel of Mark, written to encourage others to consider faith in Jesus Christ. As was true for John Mark, failure need not be the end for us. The recovery offered by Jesus Christ gives each of us the chance for a new start. As we recover, we also have the privilege of encouraging others along the way.

STRENGTHS AND ACCOMPLISHMENTS:
- Barnabas was a gifted encourager.
- Barnabas was willing to invest in John Mark even after his failure.
- John Mark became a great minister and writer.

WEAKNESSES AND MISTAKES:
- John Mark gave up and went home during Paul's first missionary journey.

LESSONS FROM THEIR LIVES:
- As we work through the process of recovery, we need encouragers to give us perspective.
- At times we may need to make personal sacrifices to encourage others.
- Although it can lead to disappointment, encouragement can pay huge dividends.

KEY VERSES:
"Barnabas . . . wanted to take along John Mark. But Paul disagreed strongly, since John Mark had deserted them in Pamphylia and had not continued with them in their work. Their disagreement was so sharp that they separated. Barnabas took John Mark with him and sailed for Cyprus" (Acts 15:37-39).

The story of Barnabas and John Mark is told in Acts 12:25–15:39. Both are also mentioned in Colossians 4:10. Barnabas is referred to in Acts 4, 9, and 11; 1 Corinthians 9; and Galatians 2. John Mark is referred to in 2 Timothy 4; Philemon 1:24; and 1 Peter 5.

---

about these things again the next week. [43]Many Jews and devout converts to Judaism followed Paul and Barnabas, and the two men urged them to continue to rely on the grace of God.

Paul Turns to the Gentiles
[44]The following week almost the entire city turned out to hear them preach the word of the Lord. [45]But when some of the Jews saw the crowds, they were jealous; so they slandered Paul and argued against whatever he said.

[46]Then Paul and Barnabas spoke out boldly and declared, "It was necessary that we first preach the word of God to you Jews. But since you have rejected it and judged yourselves unworthy of eternal life, we will offer it to the Gentiles. [47]For the Lord gave us this command when he said,

'I have made you a light to the Gentiles,
to bring salvation to the farthest
corners of the earth.'*"

[48]When the Gentiles heard this, they were very glad and thanked the Lord for his message; and all who were chosen for

13:47 Isa 49:6.

1403

eternal life became believers. [49]So the Lord's message spread throughout that region.

[50]Then the Jews stirred up the influential religious women and the leaders of the city, and they incited a mob against Paul and Barnabas and ran them out of town. [51]So they shook the dust from their feet as a sign of rejection and went to the town of Iconium. [52]And the believers* were filled with joy and with the Holy Spirit.

CHAPTER 14
Paul and Barnabas in Iconium
The same thing happened in Iconium.* Paul and Barnabas went to the Jewish synagogue and preached with such power that a great number of both Jews and Greeks became believers. [2]Some of the Jews, however, spurned God's message and poisoned the minds of the Gentiles against Paul and Barnabas. [3]But the apostles stayed there a long time, preaching boldly about the grace of the Lord. And the Lord proved their message was true by giving them power to do miraculous signs and wonders. [4]But the people of the town were divided in their opinion about them. Some sided with the Jews, and some with the apostles.

[5]Then a mob of Gentiles and Jews, along with their leaders, decided to attack and stone them. [6]When the apostles learned of it, they fled to the region of Lycaonia—to the towns of Lystra and Derbe and the surrounding area. [7]And there they preached the Good News.

Paul and Barnabas in Lystra and Derbe
[8]While they were at Lystra, Paul and Barnabas came upon a man with crippled feet. He had been that way from birth, so he had never walked. He was sitting [9]and listening as Paul preached. Looking straight at him, Paul realized he had faith to be healed. [10]So Paul called to him in a loud voice, "Stand up!" And the man jumped to his feet and started walking.

[11]When the crowd saw what Paul had done,

they shouted in their local dialect, "These men are gods in human form!" [12]They decided that Barnabas was the Greek god Zeus and that Paul was Hermes, since he was the chief speaker. [13]Now the temple of Zeus was located just outside the town. So the priest of the temple and the crowd brought bulls and wreaths of flowers to the town gates, and they prepared to offer sacrifices to the apostles.

[14]But when the apostles Barnabas and Paul heard what was happening, they tore their clothing in dismay and ran out among the people, shouting, [15]"Friends,* why are you doing this? We are merely human beings—just like you! We have come to bring you the Good News that you should turn from these worthless things and turn to the living God, who made heaven and earth, the sea, and everything in them. [16]In the past he permitted all the nations to go their own ways, [17]but he never left them without evidence of himself and his goodness. For instance, he sends you rain and good crops and gives you food and joyful hearts." [18]But even with these words, Paul and Barnabas could scarcely restrain the people from sacrificing to them.

[19]Then some Jews arrived from Antioch and Iconium and won the crowds to their side. They stoned Paul and dragged him out of town, thinking he was dead. [20]But as the believers* gathered around him, he got up and went back into the town. The next day he left with Barnabas for Derbe.

Paul and Barnabas Return to Antioch of Syria
[21]After preaching the Good News in Derbe and making many disciples, Paul and Barnabas returned to Lystra, Iconium, and Antioch of Pisidia, [22]where they strengthened the believers. They encouraged them to continue in the faith, reminding them that we must suffer many hardships to enter the Kingdom of God. [23]Paul and Barnabas also appointed elders in every church. With prayer and fasting, they turned the elders over to the care of the Lord, in whom they had put their trust.

13:52 Greek *the disciples.* 14:1 *Iconium,* as well as *Lystra* and *Derbe* (14:6), were towns in what is now Turkey. 14:15 Greek *Men.* 14:20 Greek *disciples;* also in 14:22, 28.

14:14-20 The crowds at Lystra erroneously thought Paul and Barnabas were Greek gods. The missionaries were horrified by such sadly misplaced worship. They quickly sought to clear up the misunderstanding. Soon after this, Jews from the neighboring towns of Antioch and Iconium persuaded the crowds that Paul was a charlatan. As a result, Paul was nearly killed, but God intervened to spare his life. The people at Lystra changed their attitudes and opinions about God very quickly and on very little evidence. The result was destructive. If we persevere in our faith and commitment to God, we will enjoy long-term recovery.

[24]Then they traveled back through Pisidia to Pamphylia. [25]They preached the word in Perga, then went down to Attalia.

[26]Finally, they returned by ship to Antioch of Syria, where their journey had begun. The believers there had entrusted them to the grace of God to do the work they had now completed. [27]Upon arriving in Antioch, they called the church together and reported everything God had done through them and how he had opened the door of faith to the Gentiles, too. [28]And they stayed there with the believers for a long time.

CHAPTER 15
The Council at Jerusalem

While Paul and Barnabas were at Antioch of Syria, some men from Judea arrived and began to teach the believers*: "Unless you are circumcised as required by the law of Moses, you cannot be saved." [2]Paul and Barnabas disagreed with them, arguing vehemently. Finally, the church decided to send Paul and Barnabas to Jerusalem, accompanied by some local believers, to talk to the apostles and elders about this question. [3]The church sent the delegates to Jerusalem, and they stopped along the way in Phoenicia and Samaria to visit the believers. They told them— much to everyone's joy—that the Gentiles, too, were being converted.

[4]When they arrived in Jerusalem, Barnabas and Paul were welcomed by the whole church, including the apostles and elders. They reported everything God had done through them. [5]But then some of the believers who belonged to the sect of the Pharisees stood up and insisted, "The Gentile converts must be circumcised and required to follow the law of Moses."

[6]So the apostles and elders met together to resolve this issue. [7]At the meeting, after a long discussion, Peter stood and addressed them as follows: "Brothers, you all know that God chose me from among you some time ago to preach to the Gentiles so that they could hear the Good News and believe. [8]God knows people's hearts, and he confirmed that he accepts Gentiles by giving them the Holy Spirit, just as he did to us. [9]He made no distinction between us and them, for he cleansed their hearts through faith. [10]So why are you now challenging God by burdening the Gentile believers* with a yoke that neither we nor our ancestors were able to bear? [11]We believe that we are all saved the same way, by the undeserved grace of the Lord Jesus."

[12]Everyone listened quietly as Barnabas and Paul told about the miraculous signs and wonders God had done through them among the Gentiles.

[13]When they had finished, James stood and said, "Brothers, listen to me. [14]Peter* has told you about the time God first visited the Gentiles to take from them a people for himself. [15]And this conversion of Gentiles is exactly what the prophets predicted. As it is written:

[16]'Afterward I will return
    and restore the fallen house* of David.
I will rebuild its ruins
    and restore it,
[17]so that the rest of humanity might seek
    the LORD,
    including the Gentiles—
    all those I have called to be mine.

15:1 Greek *brothers;* also in 15:3, 23, 32, 33, 36, 40. **15:10** Greek *disciples.* **15:14** Greek *Simeon.* **15:16** Or *kingdom;* Greek reads *tent.*

15:1-5 The Jerusalem Council marked a crisis point in the history of Christianity. At the center of this crisis was the Jewish law. Jewish Christians thought Gentile Christians should be required to keep the law of Moses, including the rite of circumcision. The council's answer would affect the basis for faith, fellowship, outreach, and leadership in the church. The very gospel of grace was at stake. Is Christ's work alone sufficient for salvation? Or do we also have to follow the law of Moses? In the end, the sufficiency of Christ was defended. Self-examination and crisis intervention were essential to the health of the early church, just as they are to recovery today. Reaffirming the basis of our faith regularly and at crucial moments is important to the recovery and renewal process.

15:12-21 At this council meeting James concluded the discussion and confirmed Peter's view that Gentiles were acceptable to God through Christ without adhering to Jewish law. James defended his view using the Scriptures as his final authority for faith and practice. Gentile believers did not have to keep the Jewish law in order to be accepted in the Christian community. Just as the Jews wisely did not add unnecessary requirements for salvation in Christ, we must be careful to keep the requirements for involvement in recovery simple. God is the ultimate director of recovery. As we continue to submit to his will, he will show us what is essential.

The LORD has spoken—
18 he who made these things known so long ago.'*

19"And so my judgment is that we should not make it difficult for the Gentiles who are turning to God. 20Instead, we should write and tell them to abstain from eating food offered to idols, from sexual immorality, from eating the meat of strangled animals, and from consuming blood. 21For these laws of Moses have been preached in Jewish synagogues in every city on every Sabbath for many generations."

The Letter for Gentile Believers
22Then the apostles and elders together with the whole church in Jerusalem chose delegates, and they sent them to Antioch of Syria with Paul and Barnabas to report on this decision. The men chosen were two of the church leaders*—Judas (also called Barsabbas) and Silas. 23This is the letter they took with them:

"This letter is from the apostles and elders, your brothers in Jerusalem. It is written to the Gentile believers in Antioch, Syria, and Cilicia. Greetings!

24"We understand that some men from here have troubled you and upset you with their teaching, but we did not send them! 25So we decided, having come to complete agreement, to send you official representatives, along with our beloved Barnabas and Paul, 26who have risked their lives for the name of our Lord Jesus Christ. 27We are sending Judas and Silas to confirm what we have decided concerning your question.

28"For it seemed good to the Holy Spirit and to us to lay no greater burden on you than these few requirements: 29You must abstain from eating food offered to idols, from consuming blood or the meat of strangled animals, and from sexual immorality. If you do this, you will do well. Farewell."

30The messengers went at once to Antioch, where they called a general meeting of the believers and delivered the letter. 31And there was great joy throughout the church that day as they read this encouraging message.

32Then Judas and Silas, both being prophets, spoke at length to the believers, encouraging and strengthening their faith. 33They stayed for a while, and then the believers sent them back to the church in Jerusalem with a blessing of peace.* 35Paul and Barnabas stayed in Antioch. They and many others taught and preached the word of the Lord there.

Paul and Barnabas Separate
36After some time Paul said to Barnabas, "Let's go back and visit each city where we previously preached the word of the Lord, to see how the new believers are doing." 37Barnabas agreed and wanted to take along John Mark. 38But Paul disagreed strongly, since John Mark had deserted them in Pamphylia and had not continued with them in their work. 39Their disagreement was so sharp that they separated. Barnabas took John Mark with him and sailed for Cyprus. 40Paul chose Silas, and as he left, the believers entrusted him to the Lord's gracious care. 41Then he traveled throughout Syria and Cilicia, strengthening the churches there.

CHAPTER 16
Paul's Second Missionary Journey
Paul went first to Derbe and then to Lystra, where there was a young disciple named Timothy. His mother was a Jewish believer,

15:16-18 Amos 9:11-12 (Greek version); Isa 45:21. 15:22 Greek *were leaders among the brothers.* 15:33 Some manuscripts add verse 34, *But Silas decided to stay there.*

15:36-41 Recovery and spiritual growth are processes we never complete—a fact demonstrated in the conflict between Paul and Barnabas over John Mark. Paul could not forgive John Mark for abandoning them on the first missionary journey (see 13:13-14). This resulted in a sharp disagreement and split between Paul and Barnabas. Even as mature men of faith, Paul and Barnabas had to deal with conflict and anger. They still needed to examine their motives and make amends. We know from Paul's letters that all three later reconciled, due in part to Barnabas's willingness to take John Mark with him. Like these godly men, we are never beyond the need for recovery and restoration.

16:1-3 Paul advised Timothy to submit to the Jewish practice of circumcision, even though it wasn't necessary for his salvation—the Jerusalem Council had established that fact (see 15:12-21). Timothy voluntarily followed Paul's advice in order to remove any possible stumbling block to his communicating with a Jewish audience. As we seek to share the Good News of God's powerful deliverance, we must remove any cultural or social barriers to effective communication. In this way we can get the message out to as many people in need of recovery as possible.

but his father was a Greek. [2]Timothy was well thought of by the believers* in Lystra and Iconium, [3]so Paul wanted him to join them on their journey. In deference to the Jews of the area, he arranged for Timothy to be circumcised before they left, for everyone knew that his father was a Greek. [4]Then they went from town to town, instructing the believers to follow the decisions made by the apostles and elders in Jerusalem. [5]So the churches were strengthened in their faith and grew larger every day.

A Call from Macedonia

[6]Next Paul and Silas traveled through the area of Phrygia and Galatia, because the Holy Spirit had prevented them from preaching the word in the province of Asia at that time. [7]Then coming to the borders of Mysia, they headed north for the province of Bithynia,* but again the Spirit of Jesus did not allow them to go there. [8]So instead, they went on through Mysia to the seaport of Troas.

[9]That night Paul had a vision: A man from Macedonia in northern Greece was standing there, pleading with him, "Come over to Macedonia and help us!" [10]So we* decided to leave for Macedonia at once, having concluded that God was calling us to preach the Good News there.

Lydia of Philippi Believes in Jesus

[11]We boarded a boat at Troas and sailed straight across to the island of Samothrace, and the next day we landed at Neapolis. [12]From there we reached Philippi, a major city of that district of Macedonia and a Roman colony. And we stayed there several days.

[13]On the Sabbath we went a little way outside the city to a riverbank, where we thought people would be meeting for prayer, and we sat down to speak with some women who had gathered there. [14]One of them was Lydia from Thyatira, a merchant of expensive purple cloth, who worshiped God. As she listened to us, the Lord opened her heart, and she accepted what Paul was saying. [15]She and her household were baptized, and she asked us to be her guests. "If you agree that I am a true believer in the Lord," she said, "come and stay at my home." And she urged us until we agreed.

Paul and Silas in Prison

[16]One day as we were going down to the place of prayer, we met a slave girl who had a spirit that enabled her to tell the future. She earned a lot of money for her masters by telling fortunes. [17]She followed Paul and the rest of us, shouting, "These men are servants of the Most High God, and they have come to tell you how to be saved."

[18]This went on day after day until Paul got so exasperated that he turned and said to the demon within her, "I command you in the name of Jesus Christ to come out of her." And instantly it left her.

[19]Her masters' hopes of wealth were now shattered, so they grabbed Paul and Silas and dragged them before the authorities at the marketplace. [20]"The whole city is in an uproar because of these Jews!" they shouted to the city officials. [21]"They are teaching customs that are illegal for us Romans to practice."

[22]A mob quickly formed against Paul and Silas, and the city officials ordered them stripped and beaten with wooden rods. [23]They were severely beaten, and then they were thrown into prison. The jailer was ordered to make sure they didn't escape. [24]So the jailer put them into the inner dungeon and clamped their feet in the stocks. [25]Around midnight Paul and Silas were praying and singing hymns to God, and the

---

16:2 Greek *brothers;* also in 16:40. 16:6-7 *Phrygia, Galatia, Asia, Mysia,* and *Bithynia* were all districts in what is now Turkey. 16:10 Luke, the writer of this book, here joined Paul and accompanied him on his journey.

16:11-18 In Macedonia Paul's first converts were women. One was a businesswoman named Lydia, who sold expensive purple cloth to the wealthy. Another convert was a demon-possessed slave girl. These two females from entirely different economic and social levels in society both played key roles in the growth of the Philippian church. We are all welcome into the throne room of God through our relationship with Christ. We may be tempted to discriminate against others on the basis of gender, age, social class, employment status, marital status, or handicap. But God's power for recovery is available to everyone who believes in him.

16:25-34 Paul and Silas had been beaten and jailed. Yet they sang praises to God despite the painful circumstances they faced. God was not finished with Paul and Silas, and he delivered them from this abusive situation. In so doing he taught a clear lesson to the Philippian rulers: God can deliver and sustain us in even the most abusive circumstances. When our focus is on God and all he has done for us, our identity and inner strength will be sustained. Our inner joy and ability to praise God in the midst of persecution and hardship are signs of God's power in us and may even result in our enemies believing in God, as the jailer did.

other prisoners were listening. ²⁶Suddenly, there was a massive earthquake, and the prison was shaken to its foundations. All the doors immediately flew open, and the chains of every prisoner fell off! ²⁷The jailer woke up to see the prison doors wide open. He assumed the prisoners had escaped, so he drew his sword to kill himself. ²⁸But Paul shouted to him, "Stop! Don't kill yourself! We are all here!"

²⁹The jailer called for lights and ran to the dungeon and fell down trembling before Paul and Silas. ³⁰Then he brought them out and asked, "Sirs, what must I do to be saved?"

³¹They replied, "Believe in the Lord Jesus and you will be saved, along with everyone in your household." ³²And they shared the word of the Lord with him and with all who lived in his household. ³³Even at that hour of the night, the jailer cared for them and washed their wounds. Then he and everyone in his household were immediately baptized. ³⁴He brought them into his house and set a meal before them, and he and his entire household rejoiced because they all believed in God.

³⁵The next morning the city officials sent the police to tell the jailer, "Let those men go!" ³⁶So the jailer told Paul, "The city officials have said you and Silas are free to leave. Go in peace."

³⁷But Paul replied, "They have publicly beaten us without a trial and put us in prison—and we are Roman citizens. So now they want us to leave secretly? Certainly not! Let them come themselves to release us!"

³⁸When the police reported this, the city officials were alarmed to learn that Paul and Silas were Roman citizens. ³⁹So they came to the jail and apologized to them. Then they brought them out and begged them to leave the city. ⁴⁰When Paul and Silas left the prison, they returned to the home of Lydia. There they met with the believers and encouraged them once more. Then they left town.

CHAPTER 17
Paul Preaches in Thessalonica

Paul and Silas then traveled through the towns of Amphipolis and Apollonia and came to Thessalonica, where there was a Jewish synagogue. ²As was Paul's custom, he went to the synagogue service, and for three Sabbaths in a row he used the Scriptures to reason with the people. ³He explained the prophecies and proved that the Messiah must suffer and rise from the dead. He said, "This Jesus I'm telling you about is the Messiah." ⁴Some of the Jews who listened were persuaded and joined Paul and Silas, along with many God-fearing Greek men and quite a few prominent women.*

⁵But some of the Jews were jealous, so they gathered some troublemakers from the marketplace to form a mob and start a riot. They attacked the home of Jason, searching for Paul and Silas so they could drag them out to the crowd.* ⁶Not finding them there, they dragged out Jason and some of the other believers* instead and took them before the city council. "Paul and Silas have caused trouble all over the world," they shouted, "and now they are here disturbing our city, too. ⁷And Jason has welcomed them into his

17:4 Some manuscripts read *quite a few of the wives of the leading men.* 17:5 Or *the city council.* 17:6 Greek *brothers;* also in 17:10, 14.

17:1-9 At Thessalonica Paul interpreted Scriptures and explained prophecies to his largely Jewish audience. As a result, many Jews and Gentiles turned their lives over to God. Nevertheless, many more Jews objected to Paul's message. So they stirred up the crowds and city officials to run Paul out of town. This mixed response is similar to the response generated by the recovery movement. Just because some people do not agree with our God-centered approach to recovery doesn't mean it is wrong. We must keep God central to our program and persevere in the face of opposition, just as Paul and Silas did.

17:10-12 At Berea Paul enjoyed a most eager response from the Jewish community. The Bereans searched the Scriptures to see if Paul and Silas were really teaching the truth. How exciting when someone is eager to hear the Good News of God's plan of salvation and recovery. But no one should simply take our word alone as truth. Fortunately, we have the Scriptures to back up every claim we make about God's grace and his power to deliver.

17:22-31 In Athens Paul preached in the synagogue as he normally did upon entering a new town. But then he also shared the Good News with intellectuals and philosophers in the public square. Paul began by acknowledging their belief in an unnamed higher Power—the "Unknown God." Then he identified that higher Power as the heavenly Father, the Creator, the risen Lord, and the future Judge. Thanks to Jesus Christ, we can know God personally (see 1 John 1:1-3). We don't have to look to some unnamed or unknowable higher power for help in recovery. We can trust in a powerful, loving, and personal God.

home. They are all guilty of treason against Caesar, for they profess allegiance to another king, named Jesus."

⁸The people of the city, as well as the city council, were thrown into turmoil by these reports. ⁹So the officials forced Jason and the other believers to post bond, and then they released them.

Paul and Silas in Berea
¹⁰That very night the believers sent Paul and Silas to Berea. When they arrived there, they went to the Jewish synagogue. ¹¹And the people of Berea were more open-minded than those in Thessalonica, and they listened eagerly to Paul's message. They searched the Scriptures day after day to see if Paul and Silas were teaching the truth. ¹²As a result, many Jews believed, as did many of the prominent Greek women and men.

¹³But when some Jews in Thessalonica learned that Paul was preaching the word of God in Berea, they went there and stirred up trouble. ¹⁴The believers acted at once, sending Paul on to the coast, while Silas and Timothy remained behind. ¹⁵Those escorting Paul went with him all the way to Athens; then they returned to Berea with instructions for Silas and Timothy to hurry and join him.

Paul Preaches in Athens
¹⁶While Paul was waiting for them in Athens, he was deeply troubled by all the idols he saw everywhere in the city. ¹⁷He went to the synagogue to reason with the Jews and the God-fearing Gentiles, and he spoke daily in the public square to all who happened to be there.

¹⁸He also had a debate with some of the Epicurean and Stoic philosophers. When he told them about Jesus and his resurrection, they said, "What's this babbler trying to say with these strange ideas he's picked up?" Others said, "He seems to be preaching about some foreign gods."

¹⁹Then they took him to the high council of the city.* "Come and tell us about this new teaching," they said. ²⁰"You are saying some rather strange things, and we want to know what it's all about." ²¹(It should be explained that all the Athenians as well as the foreigners in Athens seemed to spend all their time discussing the latest ideas.)

²²So Paul, standing before the council,*

17:19 Or the most learned society of philosophers in the city. Greek reads the Areopagus. 17:22 Traditionally rendered standing in the middle of Mars Hill; Greek reads standing in the middle of the Areopagus.

STEP 3

Discovering God
BIBLE READING: Acts 17:23-28
We made a decision to turn our wills and our lives over to the care of God.
Before we can turn our life over to God, we need to have an accurate understanding of who he is. It is crucial that we entrust ourself to the God who loves us and not to the "god" of this world, who seeks only to deceive and destroy us. The apostle Paul described the deceiver this way: "Satan, who is the god of this world, has blinded the minds of those who don't believe. They are unable to see the glorious light of the Good News. They don't understand this message about the glory of Christ, who is the exact likeness of God" (2 Corinthians 4:4). Has Satan deceived us? How can we be sure that we have a true understanding of God?

When Paul addressed the men of Athens, he said, "I saw your many shrines. And one of your altars had this inscription on it: 'To an Unknown God.' This God, whom you worship without knowing, is the one I'm telling you about. . . . His purpose was for the nations to seek after God and perhaps feel their way toward him and find him—though he is not far from any one of us. For in him we live and move and exist" (Acts 17:23, 27-28).

Even though God may be unknown to us, he is near and willing to reveal himself. God has promised that "if you look for me in wholeheartedly, you will find me" (Jeremiah 29:13). Turning over our will involves accepting God as he is instead of insisting on creating him in our own image. When we seek God with an open heart and mind, we will find him. *Turn to page 1607, James 4.*

addressed them as follows: "Men of Athens, I notice that you are very religious in every way, [23]for as I was walking along I saw your many shrines. And one of your altars had this inscription on it: 'To an Unknown God.' This God, whom you worship without knowing, is the one I'm telling you about.

[24]"He is the God who made the world and everything in it. Since he is Lord of heaven and earth, he doesn't live in man-made temples, [25]and human hands can't serve his needs—for he has no needs. He himself gives life and breath to everything, and he satisfies every need. [26]From one man* he created all the nations throughout the whole earth. He decided beforehand when they should rise and fall, and he determined their boundaries.

[27]"His purpose was for the nations to seek after God and perhaps feel their way toward him and find him—though he is not far from any one of us. [28]For in him we live and move and exist. As some of your* own poets have said, 'We are his offspring.' [29]And since this is true, we shouldn't think of God as an idol designed by craftsmen from gold or silver or stone.

[30]"God overlooked people's ignorance about these things in earlier times, but now he commands everyone everywhere to repent of their sins and turn to him. [31]For he has set a day for judging the world with justice by the man he has appointed, and he proved to everyone who this is by raising him from the dead."

[32]When they heard Paul speak about the resurrection of the dead, some laughed in contempt, but others said, "We want to hear more about this later." [33]That ended Paul's discussion with them, [34]but some joined him and became believers. Among them were Dionysius, a member of the council,* a woman named Damaris, and others with them.

CHAPTER 18
Paul Meets Priscilla and Aquila in Corinth

Then Paul left Athens and went to Corinth.* [2]There he became acquainted with a Jew named Aquila, born in Pontus, who had recently arrived from Italy with his wife, Priscilla. They had left Italy when Claudius Caesar deported all Jews from Rome. [3]Paul lived and worked with them, for they were tentmakers* just as he was.

[4]Each Sabbath found Paul at the synagogue, trying to convince the Jews and Greeks alike. [5]And after Silas and Timothy came down from Macedonia, Paul spent all his time preaching the word. He testified to the Jews that Jesus was the Messiah. [6]But when they opposed and insulted him, Paul shook the dust from his clothes and said, "Your blood is upon your own heads—I am innocent. From now on I will go preach to the Gentiles."

[7]Then he left and went to the home of Titius Justus, a Gentile who worshiped God and lived next door to the synagogue. [8]Crispus, the leader of the synagogue, and everyone in his household believed in the Lord. Many others in Corinth also heard Paul, became believers, and were baptized.

[9]One night the Lord spoke to Paul in a vision and told him, "Don't be afraid! Speak out! Don't be silent! [10]For I am with you, and no one will attack and harm you, for many people in this city belong to me." [11]So Paul stayed there for the next year and a half, teaching the word of God.

[12]But when Gallio became governor of Achaia, some Jews rose up together against

---

17:26 Greek *From one;* other manuscripts read *From one blood.* 17:28 Some manuscripts read *our.* 17:34 Greek *an Areopagite.* 18:1 *Athens* and *Corinth* were major cities in Achaia, the region in the southern portion of the Greek peninsula. 18:3 Or *leatherworkers.*

18:1-9 Perhaps Paul was discouraged because his Athens ministry had resulted in very few converts. That might explain his discouragement in Corinth and account for the direct encouragement he received from God while there. We all go through hard times, especially as we pursue recovery. If we follow God's will, however, he will be there to encourage us when times get tough. God doesn't help us along to a certain point just to leave us to be destroyed.

18:24-28 Apollos was very well educated in philosophy and the Scriptures, and he was a skilled orator. Yet after hearing him speak in the synagogue, Priscilla and Aquila realized that his knowledge of Scripture was incomplete. They took him aside and explained the gospel to him more accurately, filling him in on the things he didn't yet know or understand. We may know people who seem to have it all together, yet they are missing an essential truth in their understanding of the gospel and their relationship with God. Their giftedness need not intimidate us from sharing the truth with them. We may find that they sense the need for recovery in their life and are ready to respond to our message.

PRISCILLA & AQUILA

Priscilla and Aquila were united not only in marriage but also in ministry. In writing of this godly couple, Paul and Luke never mentioned them apart from each other. Their abilities and talents were complementary; together they were able to enrich the lives of the people around them.

Priscilla and Aquila moved to Corinth, Greece, to build a new life after the Jews were commanded to leave the city of Rome. While adjusting to this change, they opened their home to the apostle Paul. He had recently experienced intense trials in his ministry and needed a place to rest and recuperate. In the home of Priscilla and Aquila, Paul found not only acceptance and love but a livelihood as well. Paul joined them in their tent-making business.

Paul rested and was greatly encouraged from his time with Priscilla and Aquila. Refreshed from his visit in this godly home, Paul responded to God's challenge and entered new territories of ministry. Aquila and Priscilla moved to Ephesus with Paul and helped him in the ministry. Their faithful friendship provided Paul with a relationship of accountability and encouragement.

When Paul left Ephesus, Aquila and Priscilla stayed and oversaw the ministry there. They became aware that a young Jew, Apollos, was speaking with great zeal but with incomplete knowledge of the truth. They patiently explained the things of God to him more accurately. Apollos soon became one of the most gifted preachers in the early church.

As a result of their perseverance in God's work, Priscilla and Aquila eventually had a church meeting in their home. Their strong relationship with God and godly example made them ideal leaders in the early church. Though they never became famous preachers or leaders themselves, they were used by God to minister to some great leaders of the early church.

STRENGTHS AND ACCOMPLISHMENTS:
- Priscilla and Aquila shared responsibilities in their marriage.
- They enjoyed a marriage built on respect and love.
- They were willing to take risks and accept new challenges.
- They opened their home to help and encourage others.

LESSONS FROM THEIR LIVES:
- A healthy marriage allows both husband and wife the opportunity to exercise their gifts.
- A godly and healthy home is always open to minister to others in need.
- Rest is often needed before and after times of stress and change.

KEY VERSES:
"Give my greetings to Priscilla and Aquila, my co-workers in the ministry of Christ Jesus. In fact, they once risked their lives for me. I am thankful to them, and so are all the Gentile churches" (Romans 16:3-4).

Priscilla and Aquila's story is told in Acts 18. Both are also mentioned in Romans 16:3; 1 Corinthians 16:19; and 2 Timothy 4:19.

Paul and brought him before the governor for judgment. [13]They accused Paul of "persuading people to worship God in ways that are contrary to our law."

[14]But just as Paul started to make his defense, Gallio turned to Paul's accusers and said, "Listen, you Jews, if this were a case involving some wrongdoing or a serious crime, I would have a reason to accept your case. [15]But since it is merely a question of words and names and your Jewish law, take care of it yourselves. I refuse to judge such matters."

[16]And he threw them out of the courtroom.

[17]The crowd* then grabbed Sosthenes, the leader of the synagogue, and beat him right there in the courtroom. But Gallio paid no attention.

Paul Returns to Antioch of Syria
[18]Paul stayed in Corinth for some time after that, then said good-bye to the brothers and sisters* and went to nearby Cenchrea. There he shaved his head according to

18:17 Greek *Everyone;* other manuscripts read *All the Greeks.* **18:18** Greek *brothers;* also in 18:27.

Jewish custom, marking the end of a vow. Then he set sail for Syria, taking Priscilla and Aquila with him.

[19]They stopped first at the port of Ephesus, where Paul left the others behind. While he was there, he went to the synagogue to reason with the Jews. [20]They asked him to stay longer, but he declined. [21]As he left, however, he said, "I will come back later,* God willing." Then he set sail from Ephesus. [22]The next stop was at the port of Caesarea. From there he went up and visited the church at Jerusalem* and then went back to Antioch.

[23]After spending some time in Antioch, Paul went back through Galatia and Phrygia, visiting and strengthening all the believers.*

Apollos Instructed at Ephesus

[24]Meanwhile, a Jew named Apollos, an eloquent speaker who knew the Scriptures well, had arrived in Ephesus from Alexandria in Egypt. [25]He had been taught the way of the Lord, and he taught others about Jesus with an enthusiastic spirit* and with accuracy. However, he knew only about John's baptism. [26]When Priscilla and Aquila heard him preaching boldly in the synagogue, they took him aside and explained the way of God even more accurately.

[27]Apollos had been thinking about going to Achaia, and the brothers and sisters in Ephesus encouraged him to go. They wrote to the believers in Achaia, asking them to welcome him. When he arrived there, he proved to be of great benefit to those who, by God's grace, had believed. [28]He refuted the Jews with powerful arguments in public debate. Using the Scriptures, he explained to them that Jesus was the Messiah.

CHAPTER 19
Paul's Third Missionary Journey

While Apollos was in Corinth, Paul traveled through the interior regions until he reached Ephesus, on the coast, where he found several believers.* [2]"Did you receive the Holy Spirit when you believed?" he asked them.

"No," they replied, "we haven't even heard that there is a Holy Spirit."

[3]"Then what baptism did you experience?" he asked.

And they replied, "The baptism of John."

[4]Paul said, "John's baptism called for repentance from sin. But John himself told the people to believe in the one who would come later, meaning Jesus."

[5]As soon as they heard this, they were baptized in the name of the Lord Jesus. [6]Then when Paul laid his hands on them, the Holy Spirit came on them, and they spoke in other tongues* and prophesied. [7]There were about twelve men in all.

Paul Ministers in Ephesus

[8]Then Paul went to the synagogue and preached boldly for the next three months, arguing persuasively about the Kingdom of God. [9]But some became stubborn, rejecting his message and publicly speaking against the Way. So Paul left the synagogue and took the believers with him. Then he held daily discussions at the lecture hall of Tyrannus. [10]This went on for the next two years, so that people throughout the province of Asia— both Jews and Greeks—heard the word of the Lord.

[11]God gave Paul the power to perform unusual miracles. [12]When handkerchiefs or aprons that had merely touched his skin were placed on sick people, they were healed of their diseases, and evil spirits were expelled.

[13]A group of Jews was traveling from town to town casting out evil spirits. They tried to use the name of the Lord Jesus in their incantation, saying, "I command you in the name of Jesus, whom Paul preaches, to come out!" [14]Seven sons of Sceva, a leading priest, were doing this. [15]But one time when they tried it, the evil spirit replied, "I know Jesus, and I know Paul, but who are you?" [16]Then the

---

18:21 Some manuscripts read *"I must by all means be at Jerusalem for the upcoming festival, but I will come back later."* 18:22 Greek *the church.* 18:23 Greek *disciples;* also in 18:27. 18:25 Or *with enthusiasm in the Spirit.* 19:1 Greek *disciples;* also in 19:9, 30. 19:6 Or *in other languages.*

19:11-20 The people of Ephesus were in bondage to their fear of the spiritual realm, and the seven sons of Sceva made their living by allaying those fears. When they were confronted by a real demon, however, these men were powerless. But the demon recognized the authority of Jesus Christ and Paul because they were representatives of God himself. When the people heard this story that proved God's sovereignty over the demonic realm, they were filled with a healthy awe of Jesus Christ and his true representatives. Like the evil spirits, our compulsions and addictions are more powerful than we are. We need God's power to work in our life because no other power can overcome our destructive habits and sustain us in recovery.

APOLLOS

Apollos was a Jewish Bible teacher and skilled orator from Alexandria. He had heard about John the Baptist's message concerning the coming Messiah. Because he had studied the Scriptures seriously, he knew John's message was true. Apollos traveled north to Ephesus, preaching the message of God's Kingdom and zealously debating the skeptics.

Priscilla and Aquila heard Apollos preach in Ephesus. They were two devoted followers of Christ who had been greatly impacted by Paul's ministry. Although they appreciated his zeal, they discerned that he had incomplete knowledge of the Scriptures. So they took him aside and more fully explained the truth about Jesus Christ, the salvation he brought, and the Holy Spirit who indwelt and empowered believers. For the first time, Apollos was able to put it all together!

With this new understanding, Apollos went to minister in the city of Corinth. His ministry was so effective that Paul had to warn the believers there to keep their eyes on Christ, rather than on Apollos or himself. Apollos continued to travel and speak throughout Greece. Paul appreciated him so much that he encouraged Titus to support Apollos as much as possible.

The story of Apollos demonstrates the tremendous value of wise counsel in our life. Unfortunately, the counsel many seek lacks true spiritual insight. Some of us stumble through life with a very limited view of the love and power available to us in Jesus Christ. The more we are exposed to truth through wise counsel, the more we will fully comprehend Christ's work on our behalf. As this occurs, we can internalize the healing nature of the gospel and become better equipped to minister to others in need.

STRENGTHS AND ACCOMPLISHMENTS:
- Apollos believed God and was committed to him.
- He used his strengths and abilities for the Kingdom of God.
- He was teachable when confronted with the truth.

WEAKNESSES AND MISTAKES:
- Initially, Apollos was operating on an incomplete understanding of the truth.

LESSONS FROM HIS LIFE:
- God's wisdom and truth are available for our personal healing.
- As we discover God's truth and experience his power, we are better able to help our fellow strugglers.
- If we are willing to act on the little we do know, God will make it possible for us to learn the full truth.

KEY VERSES:
"Meanwhile, a Jew named Apollos, an eloquent speaker who knew the Scriptures well. . . . taught others about Jesus with an enthusiastic spirit and with accuracy. However, he knew only about John's baptism. When Priscilla and Aquila heard him preaching boldly in the synagogue, they took him aside and explained the way of God even more accurately" (Acts 18:24-26).

The story of Apollos is told in Acts 18:24-28. He is also mentioned in 1 Corinthians 1:12; 3:4-6, 22; 4:1, 6; 16:12; and Titus 3:13.

---

man with the evil spirit leaped on them, overpowered them, and attacked them with such violence that they fled from the house, naked and battered.

[17]The story of what happened spread quickly all through Ephesus, to Jews and Greeks alike. A solemn fear descended on the city, and the name of the Lord Jesus was greatly honored. [18]Many who became believers confessed their sinful practices. [19]A number of them who had been practicing sorcery brought their incantation books and burned them at a public bonfire. The value of the books was several million dollars.* [20]So the message about the Lord spread widely and had a powerful effect.

[21]Afterward Paul felt compelled by the Spirit* to go over to Macedonia and Achaia before going to Jerusalem. "And after that," he said, "I must go on to Rome!" [22]He sent his two assistants, Timothy and Erastus, ahead to Macedonia while he stayed awhile longer in the province of Asia.

The Riot in Ephesus

[23]About that time, serious trouble developed in Ephesus concerning the Way. [24]It began with Demetrius, a silversmith who had a large business manufacturing silver shrines of the Greek goddess Artemis.* He kept many craftsmen busy. [25]He called

19:19 Greek *50,000 pieces of silver,* each of which was the equivalent of a day's wage. 19:21 Or *decided in his spirit.* 19:24 *Artemis* is otherwise known as Diana.

them together, along with others employed in similar trades, and addressed them as follows:

"Gentlemen, you know that our wealth comes from this business. ²⁶But as you have seen and heard, this man Paul has persuaded many people that handmade gods aren't really gods at all. And he's done this not only here in Ephesus but throughout the entire province! ²⁷Of course, I'm not just talking about the loss of public respect for our business. I'm also concerned that the temple of the great goddess Artemis will lose its influence and that Artemis—this magnificent goddess worshiped throughout the province of Asia and all around the world—will be robbed of her great prestige!"

²⁸At this their anger boiled, and they began shouting, "Great is Artemis of the Ephesians!" ²⁹Soon the whole city was filled with confusion. Everyone rushed to the amphitheater, dragging along Gaius and Aristarchus, who were Paul's traveling companions from Macedonia. ³⁰Paul wanted to go in, too, but the believers wouldn't let him. ³¹Some of the officials of the province, friends of Paul, also sent a message to him, begging him not to risk his life by entering the amphitheater.

³²Inside, the people were all shouting, some one thing and some another. Everything was in confusion. In fact, most of them didn't even know why they were there. ³³The Jews in the crowd pushed Alexander forward and told him to explain the situation. He motioned for silence and tried to speak. ³⁴But when the crowd realized he was a Jew, they started shouting again and kept it up for about two hours: "Great is Artemis of the Ephesians! Great is Artemis of the Ephesians!"

³⁵At last the mayor was able to quiet them down enough to speak. "Citizens of Ephesus," he said. "Everyone knows that Ephesus is the official guardian of the temple of the great Artemis, whose image fell down to us from heaven. ³⁶Since this is an undeniable fact, you should stay calm and not do anything rash. ³⁷You have brought these men here, but they have stolen nothing from the temple and have not spoken against our goddess.

³⁸"If Demetrius and the craftsmen have a case against them, the courts are in session and the officials can hear the case at once. Let them make formal charges. ³⁹And if there are complaints about other matters, they can be settled in a legal assembly. ⁴⁰I am afraid we are in danger of being charged with rioting by the Roman government, since there is no cause for all this commotion. And if Rome demands an explanation, we won't know what to say." ⁴¹*Then he dismissed them, and they dispersed.

CHAPTER 20
Paul Goes to Macedonia and Greece

When the uproar was over, Paul sent for the believers* and encouraged them. Then he said good-bye and left for Macedonia. ²While there, he encouraged the believers in all the towns he passed through. Then he traveled down to Greece, ³where he stayed for three months. He was preparing to sail back to Syria when he discovered a plot by some Jews against his life, so he decided to return through Macedonia.

⁴Several men were traveling with him. They were Sopater son of Pyrrhus from Berea; Aristarchus and Secundus from Thessalonica; Gaius from Derbe; Timothy; and Tychicus and Trophimus from the province of Asia. ⁵They went on ahead and waited for us at Troas. ⁶After the Passover* ended, we boarded a ship at Philippi in Macedonia and five days later joined them in Troas, where we stayed a week.

Paul's Final Visit to Troas

⁷On the first day of the week, we gathered with the local believers to share in the Lord's Supper.* Paul was preaching to them, and since he was leaving the next day, he kept

---

19:41 Some translations include verse 41 as part of verse 40. 20:1 Greek *disciples.* 20:6 Greek *the days of unleavened bread.* 20:7 Greek *to break bread.*

20:1-6 Paul did not operate as a lone ranger; he traveled with other godly men to whom he was accountable. He was responsible to and for others. He didn't just make converts; he cared for them and helped them to grow spiritually. When we share our message of hope and recovery with others, it is important to do more than just share the Good News. We need to walk through each new step in recovery with those who desire to change. Paul's entourage worked as a team for the welfare of the believers. So we also can join hands with other believers to help hurting people make progress and to receive encouragement for our own daily struggles.
20:7-12 Eutychus fell asleep while Paul was preaching and fell to his death. But Paul brought him back to life. When we know the happy outcome, this story can seem somewhat humorous—especially since we sense a kindred spirit with Eutychus. (Who among us has not fallen asleep

talking until midnight. [8]The upstairs room where we met was lighted with many flickering lamps. [9]As Paul spoke on and on, a young man named Eutychus, sitting on the windowsill, became very drowsy. Finally, he fell sound asleep and dropped three stories to his death below. [10]Paul went down, bent over him, and took him into his arms. "Don't worry," he said, "he's alive!" [11]Then they all went back upstairs, shared in the Lord's Supper,* and ate together. Paul continued talking to them until dawn, and then he left. [12]Meanwhile, the young man was taken home alive and well, and everyone was greatly relieved.

Paul Meets the Ephesian Elders

[13]Paul went by land to Assos, where he had arranged for us to join him, while we traveled by ship. [14]He joined us there, and we sailed together to Mitylene. [15]The next day we sailed past the island of Kios. The following day we crossed to the island of Samos, and* a day later we arrived at Miletus.

[16]Paul had decided to sail on past Ephesus, for he didn't want to spend any more time in the province of Asia. He was hurrying to get to Jerusalem, if possible, in time for the Festival of Pentecost. [17]But when we landed at Miletus, he sent a message to the elders of the church at Ephesus, asking them to come and meet him.

[18]When they arrived he declared, "You know that from the day I set foot in the province of Asia until now [19]I have done the Lord's work humbly and with many tears. I have endured the trials that came to me from the plots of the Jews. [20]I never shrank back from telling you what you needed to hear, either publicly or in your homes. [21]I have had one message for Jews and Greeks alike—the necessity of repenting from sin and turning to God, and of having faith in our Lord Jesus.

[22]"And now I am bound by the Spirit* to go to Jerusalem. I don't know what awaits me, [23]except that the Holy Spirit tells me in city after city that jail and suffering lie ahead. [24]But my life is worth nothing to me unless I use it for finishing the work assigned me by the Lord Jesus—the work of telling others the Good News about the wonderful grace of God.

[25]"And now I know that none of you to whom I have preached the Kingdom will ever see me again. [26]I declare today that I have been faithful. If anyone suffers eternal death, it's not my fault,* [27]for I didn't shrink from declaring all that God wants you to know.

[28]"So guard yourselves and God's people. Feed and shepherd God's flock—his church, purchased with his own blood*—over which the Holy Spirit has appointed you as elders.* [29]I know that false teachers, like vicious wolves, will come in among you after I leave, not sparing the flock. [30]Even some men from your own group will rise up and distort the truth in order to draw a following. [31]Watch out! Remember the three years I was with you—my constant watch and care over you night and day, and my many tears for you.

[32]"And now I entrust you to God and the message of his grace that is able to build you up and give you an inheritance with all those he has set apart for himself.

[33]"I have never coveted anyone's silver or gold or fine clothes. [34]You know that these hands of mine have worked to supply my own needs and even the needs of those who were with me. [35]And I have been a constant example of how you can help those in need by working hard. You should remember the words of the Lord Jesus: 'It is more blessed to give than to receive.'"

[36]When he had finished speaking, he knelt and prayed with them. [37]They all cried as they embraced and kissed him good-bye.

20:11 Greek *broke the bread.* 20:15 Some manuscripts read *and having stayed at Trogyllium.* 20:22 Or *by my spirit,* or *by an inner compulsion;* Greek reads *by the spirit.* 20:26 Greek *I am innocent of the blood of all.* 20:28a Or *with the blood of his own [Son].* 20:28b Greek *overseers.*

---

during a sermon?) Luke recounts this event to remind us that God has the power to restore the dead to new life. God works beyond our own natural laws and capabilities, doing what we would consider impossible. He can do the same for those of us who are dead in sin and gripped by addictions. We can find hope for restoration in this amazing story of resurrection.

20:22-38 As Paul met with the Ephesian elders, he told them of his plans to return to Jerusalem. Paul sensed a clear leading by the Holy Spirit and was determined to follow it. Apparently, Paul was aware that God's plan would lead him through difficult circumstances. Yet he felt compelled to do the work God assigned him. Following God's will in recovery is not easy. Sometimes it leads to loneliness and loss. Sometimes it causes conflict with our friends and family. Even though following God's will can be hard at times, it is always the best way. Paul's example encourages us to pray for clear knowledge of God's will and the power to obey it.

[38]They were sad most of all because he had said that they would never see him again. Then they escorted him down to the ship.

CHAPTER 21
Paul's Journey to Jerusalem

After saying farewell to the Ephesian elders, we sailed straight to the island of Cos. The next day we reached Rhodes and then went to Patara. [2]There we boarded a ship sailing for Phoenicia. [3]We sighted the island of Cyprus, passed it on our left, and landed at the harbor of Tyre, in Syria, where the ship was to unload its cargo.

[4]We went ashore, found the local believers,* and stayed with them a week. These believers prophesied through the Holy Spirit that Paul should not go on to Jerusalem. [5]When we returned to the ship at the end of the week, the entire congregation, including women* and children, left the city and came down to the shore with us. There we knelt, prayed, [6]and said our farewells. Then we went aboard, and they returned home.

[7]The next stop after leaving Tyre was Ptolemais, where we greeted the brothers and sisters* and stayed for one day. [8]The next day we went on to Caesarea and stayed at the home of Philip the Evangelist, one of the seven men who had been chosen to distribute food. [9]He had four unmarried daughters who had the gift of prophecy.

[10]Several days later a man named Agabus, who also had the gift of prophecy, arrived from Judea. [11]He came over, took Paul's belt, and bound his own feet and hands with it. Then he said, "The Holy Spirit declares, 'So shall the owner of this belt be bound by the Jewish leaders in Jerusalem and turned over to the Gentiles.'" [12]When we heard this, we and the local believers all begged Paul not to go on to Jerusalem.

[13]But he said, "Why all this weeping? You are breaking my heart! I am ready not only to be jailed at Jerusalem but even to die for the sake of the Lord Jesus." [14]When it was clear that we couldn't persuade him, we gave up and said, "The Lord's will be done."

Paul Arrives at Jerusalem

[15]After this we packed our things and left for Jerusalem. [16]Some believers from Caesarea accompanied us, and they took us to the home of Mnason, a man originally from Cyprus and one of the early believers. [17]When we arrived, the brothers and sisters in Jerusalem welcomed us warmly.

[18]The next day Paul went with us to meet with James, and all the elders of the Jerusalem church were present. [19]After greeting them, Paul gave a detailed account of the things God had accomplished among the Gentiles through his ministry.

[20]After hearing this, they praised God. And then they said, "You know, dear brother, how many thousands of Jews have also believed, and they all follow the law of Moses very seriously. [21]But the Jewish believers here in Jerusalem have been told that you are teaching all the Jews who live among the Gentiles to turn their backs on the laws of Moses. They've heard that you teach them not to circumcise their children or follow other Jewish customs. [22]What should we do? They will certainly hear that you have come.

[23]"Here's what we want you to do. We have four men here who have completed their vow. [24]Go with them to the Temple and join them in the purification ceremony, paying for them to have their heads ritually shaved. Then everyone will know that the rumors are all false and that you yourself observe the Jewish laws.

[25]"As for the Gentile believers, they should do what we already told them in a letter: They should abstain from eating food of-

21:4 Greek *disciples;* also in 21:16. 21:5 Or *wives.* 21:7 Greek *brothers;* also in 21:17.

21:7-9 The last recorded event involving Philip had taken place some twenty-five years earlier while he traveled to Caesarea (8:40). After that time, Philip had not only a continuing ministry but also a godly family with four daughters gifted in prophecy. Philip had instilled in them his faith in Christ and God's power for life and ministry. This indicates that Christianity, though new, had the power to transform lives on a permanent basis. Philip demonstrated the kind of perseverance and fruitfulness we can have as we work our recovery program today.

21:18-26 Paul had been accused of encouraging Jews to live a Gentile lifestyle. So James suggested that Paul participate in a special vow to show the Jews that he was still one of them. Paul's love for his brothers and sisters led him to do what he could to remove anything that might destroy the faith of a Jewish believer. Thus, Paul followed James's advice and participated in the prescribed Temple worship. Like Paul, we may need to make some personal sacrifices in order to encourage someone in the recovery process. As we learn to give up our own rights for the sake of others, we will discover the joy of serving God and his people.

fered to idols, from consuming blood or the meat of strangled animals, and from sexual immorality."

Paul Is Arrested

[26]So Paul went to the Temple the next day with the other men. They had already started the purification ritual, so he publicly announced the date when their vows would end and sacrifices would be offered for each of them.

[27]The seven days were almost ended when some Jews from the province of Asia saw Paul in the Temple and roused a mob against him. They grabbed him, [28]yelling, "Men of Israel, help us! This is the man who preaches against our people everywhere and tells everybody to disobey the Jewish laws. He speaks against the Temple—and even defiles this holy place by bringing in Gentiles.*" [29](For earlier that day they had seen him in the city with Trophimus, a Gentile from Ephesus,* and they assumed Paul had taken him into the Temple.)

[30]The whole city was rocked by these accusations, and a great riot followed. Paul was grabbed and dragged out of the Temple, and immediately the gates were closed behind him. [31]As they were trying to kill him, word reached the commander of the Roman regiment that all Jerusalem was in an uproar. [32]He immediately called out his soldiers and officers* and ran down among the crowd. When the mob saw the commander and the troops coming, they stopped beating Paul.

[33]Then the commander arrested him and ordered him bound with two chains. He asked the crowd who he was and what he had done. [34]Some shouted one thing and some another. Since he couldn't find out the truth in all the uproar and confusion, he ordered that Paul be taken to the fortress. [35]As Paul reached the stairs, the mob grew so violent the soldiers had to lift him to their shoulders to protect him. [36]And the crowd followed behind, shouting, "Kill him, kill him!"

Paul Speaks to the Crowd

[37]As Paul was about to be taken inside, he said to the commander, "May I have a word with you?"

"Do you know Greek?" the commander asked, surprised. [38]"Aren't you the Egyptian who led a rebellion some time ago and took 4,000 members of the Assassins out into the desert?"

[39]"No," Paul replied, "I am a Jew and a citizen of Tarsus in Cilicia, which is an important city. Please, let me talk to these people." [40]The commander agreed, so Paul stood on the stairs and motioned to the people to be quiet. Soon a deep silence enveloped the crowd, and he addressed them in their own language, Aramaic.*

CHAPTER 22
"Brothers and esteemed fathers," Paul said, "listen to me as I offer my defense." [2]When they heard him speaking in their own language,* the silence was even greater.

[3]Then Paul said, "I am a Jew, born in Tarsus, a city in Cilicia, and I was brought up and educated here in Jerusalem under Gamaliel. As his student, I was carefully trained in our Jewish laws and customs. I became very zealous to honor God in everything I did, just like all of you today. [4]And I persecuted the followers of the Way, hounding some to death, arresting both men and women and throwing them in prison. [5]The high priest and the whole council of elders can testify that this is so. For I received letters from them to our Jewish brothers in Damascus, authorizing me to bring the followers of the Way from there to Jerusalem, in chains, to be punished.

[6]"As I was on the road, approaching Damascus about noon, a very bright light from heaven suddenly shone down around me. [7]I fell to the ground and heard a voice saying to me, 'Saul, Saul, why are you persecuting me?'

[8]"'Who are you, lord?' I asked.

"And the voice replied, 'I am Jesus the Nazarene,* the one you are persecuting.'

21:28 Greek *Greeks.* 21:29 Greek *Trophimus, the Ephesian.* 21:32 Greek *centurions.* 21:40 Or *Hebrew.* 22:2 Greek *in Aramaic,* or *in Hebrew.* 22:8 Or *Jesus of Nazareth.*

22:1-21 In this second account of Paul's conversion (see 9:1-18), we learn one additional detail: Paul studied under the great rabbinic scholar, Gamaliel. We are reminded of Paul's rage against the believers prior to his conversion. But despite Paul's former self-sufficiency, he quickly admitted his helplessness when Christ appeared to him in a blinding light. His powerless state was so complete that others had to lead him by the hand due to his temporary blindness. Fortunately, we don't all need such a dramatic event to force us to face our powerlessness. But we must all realize that without God we cannot overcome our compulsion or addiction. When we understand this truth, we have started down the road of recovery.

⁹The people with me saw the light but didn't understand the voice speaking to me.

¹⁰"I asked, 'What should I do, Lord?'

"And the Lord told me, 'Get up and go into Damascus, and there you will be told everything you are to do.'

¹¹"I was blinded by the intense light and had to be led by the hand to Damascus by my companions. ¹²A man named Ananias lived there. He was a godly man, deeply devoted to the law, and well regarded by all the Jews of Damascus. ¹³He came and stood beside me and said, 'Brother Saul, regain your sight.' And that very moment I could see him!

¹⁴"Then he told me, 'The God of our ancestors has chosen you to know his will and to see the Righteous One and hear him speak. ¹⁵For you are to be his witness, telling everyone what you have seen and heard. ¹⁶What are you waiting for? Get up and be baptized. Have your sins washed away by calling on the name of the Lord.'

¹⁷"After I returned to Jerusalem, I was praying in the Temple and fell into a trance. ¹⁸I saw a vision of Jesus* saying to me, 'Hurry! Leave Jerusalem, for the people here won't accept your testimony about me.'

¹⁹"'But Lord,' I argued, 'they certainly know that in every synagogue I imprisoned and beat those who believed in you. ²⁰And I was in complete agreement when your witness Stephen was killed. I stood by and kept the coats they took off when they stoned him.'

²¹"But the Lord said to me, 'Go, for I will send you far away to the Gentiles!'"

²²The crowd listened until Paul said that word. Then they all began to shout, "Away with such a fellow! He isn't fit to live!" ²³They yelled, threw off their coats, and tossed handfuls of dust into the air.

Paul Reveals His Roman Citizenship

²⁴The commander brought Paul inside and ordered him lashed with whips to make him confess his crime. He wanted to find out why the crowd had become so furious. ²⁵When they tied Paul down to lash him, Paul said to the officer* standing there, "Is it legal for you to whip a Roman citizen who hasn't even been tried?"

²⁶When the officer heard this, he went to the commander and asked, "What are you doing? This man is a Roman citizen!"

²⁷So the commander went over and asked Paul, "Tell me, are you a Roman citizen?"

"Yes, I certainly am," Paul replied.

²⁸"I am, too," the commander muttered, "and it cost me plenty!"

Paul answered, "But I am a citizen by birth!"

²⁹The soldiers who were about to interrogate Paul quickly withdrew when they heard he was a Roman citizen, and the commander was frightened because he had ordered him bound and whipped.

Paul before the High Council

³⁰The next day the commander ordered the leading priests into session with the Jewish high council.* He wanted to find out what the trouble was all about, so he released Paul to have him stand before them.

CHAPTER 23

Gazing intently at the high council,* Paul began: "Brothers, I have always lived before God with a clear conscience!"

²Instantly Ananias the high priest commanded those close to Paul to slap him on the mouth. ³But Paul said to him, "God will slap you, you corrupt hypocrite!* What kind of judge are you to break the law yourself by ordering me struck like that?"

⁴Those standing near Paul said to him, "Do you dare to insult God's high priest?"

⁵"I'm sorry, brothers. I didn't realize he was the high priest," Paul replied, "for the Scriptures say, 'You must not speak evil of any of your rulers.'*"

⁶Paul realized that some members of the high council were Sadducees and some were Pharisees, so he shouted, "Brothers, I am a Pharisee, as were my ancestors! And I am on trial because my hope is in the resurrection of the dead!"

⁷This divided the council—the Pharisees against the Sadducees—⁸for the Sadducees say there is no resurrection or angels or spirits, but the Pharisees believe in all of these. ⁹So there was a great uproar. Some of the teachers of religious law who were Pharisees jumped up and began to argue forcefully. "We see nothing wrong with him," they shouted. "Perhaps a spirit or an angel spoke to him." ¹⁰As the conflict grew more violent, the commander was afraid they would tear Paul apart. So he ordered his soldiers to go

22:18 Greek *him.* 22:25 Greek *the centurion; also in 22:26.* 22:30 Greek *Sanhedrin.* 23:1 Greek *Sanhedrin; also in 23:6, 15, 20, 28.* 23:3 Greek *you whitewashed wall.* 23:5 Exod 22:28.

and rescue him by force and take him back to the fortress.

[11]That night the Lord appeared to Paul and said, "Be encouraged, Paul. Just as you have been a witness to me here in Jerusalem, you must preach the Good News in Rome as well."

The Plan to Kill Paul

[12]The next morning a group of Jews* got together and bound themselves with an oath not to eat or drink until they had killed Paul. [13]There were more than forty of them in the conspiracy. [14]They went to the leading priests and elders and told them, "We have bound ourselves with an oath to eat nothing until we have killed Paul. [15]So you and the high council should ask the commander to bring Paul back to the council again. Pretend you want to examine his case more fully. We will kill him on the way."

[16]But Paul's nephew—his sister's son—heard of their plan and went to the fortress and told Paul. [17]Paul called for one of the Roman officers* and said, "Take this young man to the commander. He has something important to tell him."

[18]So the officer did, explaining, "Paul, the prisoner, called me over and asked me to bring this young man to you because he has something to tell you."

[19]The commander took his hand, led him aside, and asked, "What is it you want to tell me?"

[20]Paul's nephew told him, "Some Jews are going to ask you to bring Paul before the high council tomorrow, pretending they want to get some more information. [21]But don't do it! There are more than forty men hiding along the way ready to ambush him. They have vowed not to eat or drink anything until they have killed him. They are ready now, just waiting for your consent."

[22]"Don't let anyone know you told me this," the commander warned the young man.

Paul Is Sent to Caesarea

[23]Then the commander called two of his officers and ordered, "Get 200 soldiers ready to leave for Caesarea at nine o'clock tonight. Also take 200 spearmen and 70 mounted troops. [24]Provide horses for Paul to ride, and get him safely to Governor Felix." [25]Then he wrote this letter to the governor:

[26]"From Claudius Lysias, to his Excellency, Governor Felix: Greetings!

[27]"This man was seized by some Jews, and they were about to kill him when I arrived with the troops. When I learned that he was a Roman citizen, I removed him to safety. [28]Then I took him to their high council to try to learn the basis of the accusations against him. [29]I soon discovered the charge was something regarding their religious law—certainly nothing worthy of imprisonment or death. [30]But when I was informed of a plot to kill him, I immediately sent him on to you. I have told his accusers to bring their charges before you."

[31]So that night, as ordered, the soldiers took Paul as far as Antipatris. [32]They returned to the fortress the next morning, while the mounted troops took him on to Caesarea. [33]When they arrived in Caesarea, they presented Paul and the letter to Governor Felix. [34]He read it and then asked Paul what province he was from. "Cilicia," Paul answered.

[35]"I will hear your case myself when your accusers arrive," the governor told him. Then the governor ordered him kept in the prison at Herod's headquarters.*

CHAPTER 24

Paul Appears before Felix

Five days later Ananias, the high priest, arrived with some of the Jewish elders and the lawyer* Tertullus, to present their case against Paul to the governor. [2]When Paul was called in, Tertullus presented the charges against Paul in the following address to the governor:

"You have provided a long period of peace for us Jews and with foresight have enacted reforms for us. [3]For all of this, Your Excellency, we are very grateful to you. [4]But I

23:12 Greek *the Jews.* 23:17 Greek *centurions;* also in 23:23. 23:35 Greek *Herod's Praetorium.* 24:1 Greek *some elders and an orator.*

23:12-35 Paul's brave, young nephew risked his life to warn his uncle of a plot against his life. With this intelligence information, the Roman commander made adjustments in his plan and moved Paul safely to Caesarea. A military escort accompanied Paul on his journey that very night, and a cover letter to Governor Felix won Paul another chance to speak for himself and for God. Thus God providentially worked through various people to move Paul one step closer to Rome. God uses people—little children and governors alike—to accomplish his divine will.

don't want to bore you, so please give me your attention for only a moment. [5]We have found this man to be a troublemaker who is constantly stirring up riots among the Jews all over the world. He is a ringleader of the cult known as the Nazarenes. [6]Furthermore, he was trying to desecrate the Temple when we arrested him.* [8]You can find out the truth of our accusations by examining him yourself." [9]Then the other Jews chimed in, declaring that everything Tertullus said was true.

[10]The governor then motioned for Paul to speak. Paul said, "I know, sir, that you have been a judge of Jewish affairs for many years, so I gladly present my defense before you. [11]You can quickly discover that I arrived in Jerusalem no more than twelve days ago to worship at the Temple. [12]My accusers never found me arguing with anyone in the Temple, nor stirring up a riot in any synagogue or on the streets of the city. [13]These men cannot prove the things they accuse me of doing.

[14]"But I admit that I follow the Way, which they call a cult. I worship the God of our ancestors, and I firmly believe the Jewish law and everything written in the prophets. [15]I have the same hope in God that these men have, that he will raise both the righteous and the unrighteous. [16]Because of this, I always try to maintain a clear conscience before God and all people.

[17]"After several years away, I returned to Jerusalem with money to aid my people and to offer sacrifices to God. [18]My accusers saw me in the Temple as I was completing a purification ceremony. There was no crowd around me and no rioting. [19]But some Jews from the province of Asia were there—and they ought to be here to bring charges if they have anything against me! [20]Ask these men here what crime the Jewish high council* found me guilty of, [21]except for the one time I shouted out, 'I am on trial before you today because I believe in the resurrection of the dead!' "

[22]At that point Felix, who was quite familiar with the Way, adjourned the hearing and said, "Wait until Lysias, the garrison commander, arrives. Then I will decide the case."

[23]He ordered an officer* to keep Paul in custody but to give him some freedom and allow his friends to visit him and take care of his needs.

[24]A few days later Felix came back with his wife, Drusilla, who was Jewish. Sending for Paul, they listened as he told them about faith in Christ Jesus. [25]As he reasoned with them about righteousness and self-control and the coming day of judgment, Felix became frightened. "Go away for now," he replied. "When it is more convenient, I'll call for you again." [26]He also hoped that Paul would bribe him, so he sent for him quite often and talked with him.

[27]After two years went by in this way, Felix was succeeded by Porcius Festus. And because Felix wanted to gain favor with the Jewish people, he left Paul in prison.

CHAPTER 25
Paul Appears before Festus

Three days after Festus arrived in Caesarea to take over his new responsibilities, he left for Jerusalem, [2]where the leading priests and other Jewish leaders met with him and made their accusations against Paul. [3]They asked Festus as a favor to transfer Paul to Jerusalem (planning to ambush and kill him on the way). [4]But Festus replied that Paul was at Caesarea and he himself would be returning there soon. [5]So he said, "Those of you in authority can return with me. If Paul has done anything wrong, you can make your accusations."

[6]About eight or ten days later Festus returned to Caesarea, and on the following day he took his seat in court and ordered that Paul be brought in. [7]When Paul arrived, the Jewish leaders from Jerusalem gathered around and made many serious accusations they couldn't prove.

[8]Paul denied the charges. "I am not guilty of any crime against the Jewish laws or the Temple or the Roman government," he said.

[9]Then Festus, wanting to please the Jews, asked him, "Are you willing to go to Jerusalem and stand trial before me there?"

24:6 Some manuscripts add an expanded conclusion to verse 6, all of verse 7, and an additional phrase in verse 8: *We would have judged him by our law, [7]but Lysias, the commander of the garrison, came and violently took him away from us, [8]commanding his accusers to come before you.* 24:20 Greek *Sanhedrin.* 24:23 Greek *a centurion.*

24:26-27 Felix made no decision on Paul's case. He probably was afraid that if he set Paul free, the Jews would rebel. Felix left Paul in prison for two years. Perhaps he hoped Paul would bribe him to buy his release. No doubt the miserable prison conditions challenged Paul to the depth of his being. By the grace of God he patiently endured his years in bondage. Paul depended on God to help him one day at a time; we can do the same.

¹⁰But Paul replied, "No! This is the official Roman court, so I ought to be tried right here. You know very well I am not guilty of harming the Jews. ¹¹If I have done something worthy of death, I don't refuse to die. But if I am innocent, no one has a right to turn me over to these men to kill me. I appeal to Caesar!"

¹²Festus conferred with his advisers and then replied, "Very well! You have appealed to Caesar, and to Caesar you will go!"

¹³A few days later King Agrippa arrived with his sister, Bernice,* to pay their respects to Festus. ¹⁴During their stay of several days, Festus discussed Paul's case with the king. "There is a prisoner here," he told him, "whose case was left for me by Felix. ¹⁵When I was in Jerusalem, the leading priests and Jewish elders pressed charges against him and asked me to condemn him. ¹⁶I pointed out to them that Roman law does not convict people without a trial. They must be given an opportunity to confront their accusers and defend themselves.

¹⁷"When his accusers came here for the trial, I didn't delay. I called the case the very next day and ordered Paul brought in. ¹⁸But the accusations made against him weren't any of the crimes I expected. ¹⁹Instead, it was something about their religion and a dead man named Jesus, who Paul insists is alive. ²⁰I was at a loss to know how to investigate these things, so I asked him whether he would be willing to stand trial on these charges in Jerusalem. ²¹But Paul appealed to have his case decided by the emperor. So I ordered that he be held in custody until I could arrange to send him to Caesar."

²²"I'd like to hear the man myself," Agrippa said.

And Festus replied, "You will—tomorrow!"

Paul Speaks to Agrippa

²³So the next day Agrippa and Bernice arrived at the auditorium with great pomp, accompanied by military officers and prominent men of the city. Festus ordered that Paul be brought in. ²⁴Then Festus said, "King Agrippa and all who are here, this is the man whose death is demanded by all the Jews, both here and in Jerusalem. ²⁵But in my opinion he has done nothing deserving death. However, since he appealed his case to the emperor, I have decided to send him to Rome.

²⁶"But what shall I write the emperor? For there is no clear charge against him. So I

25:13 Greek *Agrippa the king and Bernice arrived.*

STEP 5

Receiving Forgiveness
BIBLE READING: Acts 26:12-18
We admitted to God, to ourselves, and to another human being the exact nature of our wrongs.

As we work our recovery program, we go through a process of accepting the truth about our life and the consequences of our choices. We may feel that we have to earn forgiveness instead of just receiving it. We may find it easier to forgive others who have hurt us than to forgive ourself for the hurts we have caused.

When Jesus confronted the apostle Paul, he gave him this mission: "Now get to your feet! For I have appeared to you to appoint you as my servant and my witness. . . . Yes, I am sending you to the Gentiles to open their eyes, so they may turn from darkness to light and from the power of Satan to God. Then they will receive forgiveness for their sins and be given a place among God's people, who are set apart by faith in me" (Acts 26:16-18).

God's goal in sending his Word to us is that we may receive forgiveness. The process involves first opening our eyes to our true condition, which happens in Steps One, Two, and Four. This allows us the opportunity to repent, changing our mind so that we are in agreement with God and ready to admit our sins. God wants us to receive immediate forgiveness based on the finished work of Jesus Christ. We are not second-class citizens in the Kingdom of God. We don't have to work the rest of the Twelve Steps as a form of penance. Forgiveness awaits us right now if we will only receive it. *Turn to page 1433, Romans 2.*

have brought him before all of you, and especially you, King Agrippa, so that after we examine him, I might have something to write. ²⁷For it makes no sense to send a prisoner to the emperor without specifying the charges against him!"

CHAPTER 26

Then Agrippa said to Paul, "You may speak in your defense."

So Paul, gesturing with his hand, started his defense: ²"I am fortunate, King Agrippa, that you are the one hearing my defense today against all these accusations made by the Jewish leaders, ³for I know you are an expert on all Jewish customs and controversies. Now please listen to me patiently!

⁴"As the Jewish leaders are well aware, I was given a thorough Jewish training from my earliest childhood among my own people and in Jerusalem. ⁵If they would admit it, they know that I have been a member of the Pharisees, the strictest sect of our religion. ⁶Now I am on trial because of my hope in the fulfillment of God's promise made to our ancestors. ⁷In fact, that is why the twelve tribes of Israel zealously worship God night and day, and they share the same hope I have. Yet, Your Majesty, they accuse me for having this hope! ⁸Why does it seem incredible to any of you that God can raise the dead?

⁹"I used to believe that I ought to do everything I could to oppose the very name of Jesus the Nazarene.* ¹⁰Indeed, I did just that in Jerusalem. Authorized by the leading priests, I caused many believers* there to be sent to prison. And I cast my vote against them when they were condemned to death. ¹¹Many times I had them punished in the synagogues to get them to curse Jesus.* I was so violently opposed to them that I even chased them down in foreign cities.

¹²"One day I was on such a mission to Damascus, armed with the authority and commission of the leading priests. ¹³About noon, Your Majesty, as I was on the road, a light from heaven brighter than the sun shone down on me and my companions. ¹⁴We all fell down, and I heard a voice saying to me in Aramaic,* 'Saul, Saul, why are you persecuting me? It is useless for you to fight against my will.*'

¹⁵"'Who are you, lord?' I asked.

"And the Lord replied, 'I am Jesus, the one you are persecuting. ¹⁶Now get to your feet! For I have appeared to you to appoint you as my servant and witness. Tell people that you have seen me, and tell them what I will show you in the future. ¹⁷And I will rescue you from both your own people and the Gentiles. Yes, I am sending you to the Gentiles ¹⁸to open their eyes, so they may turn from darkness to light and from the power of Satan to God. Then they will receive forgiveness for their sins and be given a place among God's people, who are set apart by faith in me.'

¹⁹"And so, King Agrippa, I obeyed that vision from heaven. ²⁰I preached first to those in Damascus, then in Jerusalem and throughout all Judea, and also to the Gentiles, that all must repent of their sins and turn to God—and prove they have changed by the good things they do. ²¹Some Jews arrested me in the Temple for preaching this, and they tried to kill me. ²²But God has protected me right up to this present time so I can testify to everyone, from the least to the greatest. I teach nothing except what the prophets and Moses said would happen—²³that the Messiah would suffer and be the first to rise from the dead, and in this way announce God's light to Jews and Gentiles alike."

26:9 Or *Jesus of Nazarene.* 26:10 Greek *many of God's holy people.* 26:11 Greek *to blaspheme.* 26:14a Or *Hebrew.* 26:14b Greek *It is hard for you to kick against the oxgoads.*

26:1-23 This is the third account of Paul's conversion in the book of Acts (see 9:1-20; 22:1-21). Paul had become quite skilled at sharing his story with anyone who would listen. Before meeting Christ, Paul was a powerful enemy of the Christian faith and did horrible things to try and stop its growth. When Paul met Jesus in a dramatic way, it led to his painful spiritual awakening. After his conversion Paul preached to others who needed to hear the message of God's salvation. If we aren't sure how to share our story with others, it might help to follow Paul's example by telling others what happened in our life before, during, and after we experienced God's deliverance.
26:19-23 Paul assured King Agrippa that he was suffering persecution, not because he had done anything wrong but because he was preaching the faith he had once tried to destroy. Paul showed that his preaching was in agreement with the Old Testament Scriptures. The basic teaching of the Old and New Testaments is that God desires to deliver all people from the power of sin and has done so perfectly through the work of God's anointed one—the Messiah. Knowing that God desires to save us is essential to the recovery process.

²⁴Suddenly, Festus shouted, "Paul, you are insane. Too much study has made you crazy!"

²⁵But Paul replied, "I am not insane, Most Excellent Festus. What I am saying is the sober truth. ²⁶And King Agrippa knows about these things. I speak boldly, for I am sure these events are all familiar to him, for they were not done in a corner! ²⁷King Agrippa, do you believe the prophets? I know you do—"

²⁸Agrippa interrupted him. "Do you think you can persuade me to become a Christian so quickly?"*

²⁹Paul replied, "Whether quickly or not, I pray to God that both you and everyone here in this audience might become the same as I am, except for these chains."

³⁰Then the king, the governor, Bernice, and all the others stood and left. ³¹As they went out, they talked it over and agreed, "This man hasn't done anything to deserve death or imprisonment."

³²And Agrippa said to Festus, "He could have been set free if he hadn't appealed to Caesar."

CHAPTER 27
Paul Sails for Rome

When the time came, we set sail for Italy. Paul and several other prisoners were placed in the custody of a Roman officer* named Julius, a captain of the Imperial Regiment. ²Aristarchus, a Macedonian from Thessalonica, was also with us. We left on a ship whose home port was Adramyttium on the northwest coast of the province of Asia;* it was scheduled to make several stops at ports along the coast of the province.

³The next day when we docked at Sidon, Julius was very kind to Paul and let him go ashore to visit with friends so they could provide for his needs. ⁴Putting out to sea from there, we encountered strong headwinds that made it difficult to keep the ship on course, so we sailed north of Cyprus between the island and the mainland. ⁵Keeping to the open sea, we passed along the coast of Cilicia and Pamphylia, landing at Myra, in the province of Lycia. ⁶There the commanding officer found an Egyptian ship from Alexandria that was bound for Italy, and he put us on board.

⁷We had several days of slow sailing, and after great difficulty we finally neared Cnidus. But the wind was against us, so we sailed across to Crete and along the sheltered coast of the island, past the cape of Salmone. ⁸We struggled along the coast with great difficulty and finally arrived at Fair Havens, near the town of Lasea. ⁹We had lost a lot of time. The weather was becoming dangerous for sea travel because it was so late in the fall,* and Paul spoke to the ship's officers about it.

¹⁰"Men," he said, "I believe there is trouble ahead if we go on—shipwreck, loss of cargo, and danger to our lives as well." ¹¹But the officer in charge of the prisoners listened more to the ship's captain and the owner than to Paul. ¹²And since Fair Havens was an exposed harbor—a poor place to spend the winter— most of the crew wanted to go on to Phoenix, farther up the coast of Crete, and spend the winter there. Phoenix was a good harbor with only a southwest and northwest exposure.

The Storm at Sea

26:28 Or "A little more, and your arguments would make me a Christian." 27:1 Greek centurion; similarly in 27:6, 11, 31, 43. 27:2 Asia was a Roman province in what is now western Turkey. 27:9 Greek because the fast was now already gone by. This fast was associated with the Day of Atonement (Yom Kippur), which occurred in late September or early October.

26:24-29 Paul was so concerned about the salvation of other people that he had little time to worry about his own problems. Here he risked his life to share his testimony with a man who had the power to have him killed. This conversation with King Agrippa shows Paul's burning desire to soften and reclaim even the most hardened hearts. For everyone in recovery it is helpful to get our eyes off our own afflictions and focus on the needs of others. As we help others discover the way to recovery, we will be freed from our self-centeredness and strengthened in our own recovery.

27:1-15 It was God's plan that Paul go to Rome, but his journey there was hardly straightforward. After years in prison, Paul was finally put on a ship bound for Rome; he arrived there only after surviving a life-threatening storm and shipwreck. Paul had no control over the means or timing of getting to his destination. But Paul knew God wanted him in Rome and was confident he would eventually get there. We can be sure that God wants us to make progress in recovery. Yet, like Paul, we don't have complete control over the route we will take to get there. Faithfulness does not ensure a life without storms or shipwrecks. Yet God guarantees that his presence and power will be with us and that we will arrive at our ultimate destination.

[13]When a light wind began blowing from the south, the sailors thought they could make it. So they pulled up anchor and sailed close to the shore of Crete. [14]But the weather changed abruptly, and a wind of typhoon strength (called a "northeaster") burst across the island and blew us out to sea. [15]The sailors couldn't turn the ship into the wind, so they gave up and let it run before the gale.

[16]We sailed along the sheltered side of a small island named Cauda,* where with great difficulty we hoisted aboard the lifeboat being towed behind us. [17]Then the sailors bound ropes around the hull of the ship to strengthen it. They were afraid of being driven across to the sandbars of Syrtis off the African coast, so they lowered the sea anchor to slow the ship and were driven before the wind.

[18]The next day, as gale-force winds continued to batter the ship, the crew began throwing the cargo overboard. [19]The following day they even took some of the ship's gear and threw it overboard. [20]The terrible storm raged for many days, blotting out the sun and the stars, until at last all hope was gone.

[21]No one had eaten for a long time. Finally, Paul called the crew together and said, "Men, you should have listened to me in the first place and not left Crete. You would have avoided all this damage and loss. [22]But take courage! None of you will lose your lives, even though the ship will go down. [23]For last night an angel of the God to whom I belong and whom I serve stood beside me, [24]and he said, 'Don't be afraid, Paul, for you will surely stand trial before Caesar! What's more, God in his goodness has granted safety to everyone sailing with you.' [25]So take courage! For I believe God. It will be just as he said. [26]But we will be shipwrecked on an island."

The Shipwreck

[27]About midnight on the fourteenth night of the storm, as we were being driven across the Sea of Adria,* the sailors sensed land was near. [28]They dropped a weighted line and found that the water was 120 feet deep. But a little later they measured again and found it was only 90 feet deep.* [29]At this rate they were afraid we would soon be driven against the rocks along the shore, so they threw out four anchors from the back of the ship and prayed for daylight.

[30]Then the sailors tried to abandon the ship; they lowered the lifeboat as though they were going to put out anchors from the front of the ship. [31]But Paul said to the commanding officer and the soldiers, "You will all die unless the sailors stay aboard." [32]So the soldiers cut the ropes to the lifeboat and let it drift away.

[33]Just as day was dawning, Paul urged everyone to eat. "You have been so worried that you haven't touched food for two weeks," he said. [34]"Please eat something now for your own good. For not a hair of your heads will perish." [35]Then he took some bread, gave thanks to God before them all, and broke off a piece and ate it. [36]Then everyone was encouraged and began to eat—[37]all 276 of us who were on board. [38]After eating, the crew lightened the ship further by throwing the cargo of wheat overboard.

[39]When morning dawned, they didn't recognize the coastline, but they saw a bay with a beach and wondered if they could get to shore by running the ship aground. [40]So they cut off the anchors and left them in the sea. Then they lowered the rudders, raised the foresail, and headed toward shore. [41]But they hit a shoal and ran the ship aground too soon. The bow of the ship stuck fast, while the stern was repeatedly smashed by the force of the waves and began to break apart.

27:16 Some manuscripts read *Clauda*. **27:27** The *Sea of Adria* includes the central portion of the Mediterranean. **27:28** Greek *20 fathoms . . . 15 fathoms* [37 meters . . . 27 meters].

27:13-26 After two storm-tossed weeks, the sailors had given up hope, and everyone was hungry and terrified. Yet Paul urged all to believe his promise from God that they would survive. The fate of 276 people—passengers and crew—hung in the balance. Paul's courageous faith was met with assurances that he would reach Rome, yet not without hardships. Life in recovery is often like that. We are assured by faith of a positive outcome, but it is usually attained by persevering through difficult times.

27:27-42 Earlier the ship's captain and owner had ignored Paul (27:9-12), but this time they listened carefully (27:30-32). Paul assured them that even though the ship would be destroyed, all the passengers would reach land safely. The next day the ship ran aground and was destroyed by the winds and waves. But all the passengers were safe. Few of us have an awareness of the future like Paul did. But we can have the same confidence in God's power to protect us when we follow his will. We can have success in recovery by walking obediently by faith, one step at a time.

⁴²The soldiers wanted to kill the prisoners to make sure they didn't swim ashore and escape. ⁴³But the commanding officer wanted to spare Paul, so he didn't let them carry out their plan. Then he ordered all who could swim to jump overboard first and make for land. ⁴⁴The others held on to planks or debris from the broken ship.* So everyone escaped safely to shore.

CHAPTER 28
Paul on the Island of Malta

Once we were safe on shore, we learned that we were on the island of Malta. ²The people of the island were very kind to us. It was cold and rainy, so they built a fire on the shore to welcome us.

³As Paul gathered an armful of sticks and was laying them on the fire, a poisonous snake, driven out by the heat, bit him on the hand. ⁴The people of the island saw it hanging from his hand and said to each other, "A murderer, no doubt! Though he escaped the sea, justice will not permit him to live." ⁵But Paul shook off the snake into the fire and was unharmed. ⁶The people waited for him to swell up or suddenly drop dead. But when they had waited a long time and saw that he wasn't harmed, they changed their minds and decided he was a god.

⁷Near the shore where we landed was an estate belonging to Publius, the chief official of the island. He welcomed us and treated us kindly for three days. ⁸As it happened, Publius's father was ill with fever and dysentery. Paul went in and prayed for him, and laying his hands on him, he healed him. ⁹Then all the other sick people on the island came and were healed. ¹⁰As a result we were showered with honors, and when the time came to sail, people supplied us with everything we would need for the trip.

Paul Arrives at Rome

¹¹It was three months after the shipwreck that we set sail on another ship that had wintered at the island—an Alexandrian ship with the twin gods* as its figurehead. ¹²Our first stop was Syracuse,* where we stayed three days. ¹³From there we sailed across to Rhegium.* A day later a south wind began blowing, so the following day we sailed up the coast to Puteoli. ¹⁴There we found some believers,* who invited us to spend a week with them. And so we came to Rome.

¹⁵The brothers and sisters* in Rome had heard we were coming, and they came to meet us at the Forum* on the Appian Way. Others joined us at The Three Taverns.* When Paul saw them, he was encouraged and thanked God.

¹⁶When we arrived in Rome, Paul was permitted to have his own private lodging, though he was guarded by a soldier.

Paul Preaches at Rome under Guard

¹⁷Three days after Paul's arrival, he called together the local Jewish leaders. He said to them, "Brothers, I was arrested in Jerusalem and handed over to the Roman government, even though I had done nothing against our people or the customs of our ancestors. ¹⁸The Romans tried me and wanted to release me, because they found no cause for the death sentence. ¹⁹But when the Jewish leaders protested the decision, I felt it necessary to appeal to Caesar, even though I had no desire to press charges against my own people. ²⁰I asked you to come here today so we could get acquainted and so I could explain to you that I am bound with this chain because I believe that the hope of Israel—the Messiah—has already come."

²¹They replied, "We have had no letters from Judea or reports against you from anyone who has come here. ²²But we want to hear what you believe, for the only thing we know about this movement is that it is denounced everywhere."

²³So a time was set, and on that day a large number of people came to Paul's lodging. He explained and testified about the Kingdom of God and tried to persuade them about Jesus from the Scriptures. Using the law of

27:44 Or *or were helped by members of the ship's crew.* 28:11 The *twin gods* were the Roman gods Castor and Pollux. 28:12 *Syracuse* was on the island of Sicily. 28:13 *Rhegium* was on the southern tip of Italy. 28:14 Greek *brothers.* 28:15a Greek *brothers.* 28:15b *The Forum* was about 43 miles (70 kilometers) from Rome. 28:15c *The Three Taverns* was about 35 miles (57 kilometers) from Rome.

28:1-10 The ship's crew and passengers spent the winter safely on the island of Malta. If stormy seas and a shipwreck couldn't thwart God's plan for Paul, neither would the bite of a poisonous snake. Paul was bitten by a deadly snake, yet he suffered no ill effects. While Paul was deterred from reaching Rome, he helped the people around him. To Paul, even obstacles were opportunities to serve others and share his faith. As we work through the process of recovery, we too can turn our obstacles into wonderful opportunities for growth and service.

Moses and the books of the prophets, he spoke to them from morning until evening. ²⁴Some were persuaded by the things he said, but others did not believe. ²⁵And after they had argued back and forth among themselves, they left with this final word from Paul: "The Holy Spirit was right when he said to your ancestors through Isaiah the prophet,

²⁶ 'Go and say to this people:
When you hear what I say,
    you will not understand.
When you see what I do,
    you will not comprehend.
²⁷ For the hearts of these people are
    hardened,

and their ears cannot hear,
    and they have closed their eyes—
so their eyes cannot see,
    and their ears cannot hear,
    and their hearts cannot understand,
and they cannot turn to me
    and let me heal them.'*

²⁸So I want you to know that this salvation from God has also been offered to the Gentiles, and they will accept it."*

³⁰For the next two years, Paul lived in Rome at his own expense.* He welcomed all who visited him, ³¹boldly proclaiming the Kingdom of God and teaching about the Lord Jesus Christ. And no one tried to stop him.

28:26-27 Isa 6:9-10 (Greek version). 28:28 Some manuscripts add verse 29, *And when he had said these words, the Jews departed, greatly disagreeing with each other.* 28:30 Or *in his own rented quarters.*

28:30-31 Even under house arrest, Paul experienced the peace and contentment that come only by following God's will. Paul carried the message of salvation to people in need through all circumstances in his life. His life is an example to each of us, showing the importance and benefits of persisting in our relationship with God and sharing our faith. As we know God better, learn to trust in his love and power, and share this power for recovery with others, we can live each new day with serenity and courage.

REFLECTIONS ON ACTS

insights CONCERNING THE HOLY SPIRIT
In **Acts 2:5-15**, when the Holy Spirit came in power, the results were immediately apparent in the believers, especially Peter. This man, who had previously failed to live up to his commitment to Christ (Luke 22:54-62), was now confidently preaching and helping others discover this new power for living. When we experience God's power in our life, we will never be the same, nor will we be able to keep the Good News to ourself.

insights FROM THE EARLY CHRISTIAN COMMUNITY
As the Christian community grew, various problems arose. One such problem is mentioned in **Acts 6:1** concerning the distribution of food to needy widows. The conflict was apparently rooted in the cultural differences between the various church members. Most of the church members were Hebrew-speaking Palestinian Jews, but there were also Greek-speaking Jews among them who had been raised outside of Palestine. Apparently, the Greek-speaking Jews were being neglected by the Jews native to Palestine.

Relationships within the church, as well as in the recovery movement, can be stretched, even broken, if members refuse to accept each other. As we humbly recognize our own need for God's gracious forgiveness, we will have less trouble accepting others who are different from us.

insights FROM PHILIP'S LIFE

In **Acts 8:26-40** Philip was called to share the Good News with an Ethiopian eunuch. Philip is an excellent model of how we can effectively engage in this important recovery activity. He didn't rush in and start preaching. He took time to understand where the Ethiopian was concerning his faith. Then he proceeded humbly and confidently to share God's truth—that Jesus is the Messiah and that through him we can experience deliverance from sin and its power. Sharing our faith as Philip did takes time; it requires patience and sensitivity. But as we follow Philip's example, we will learn to share our faith with not only words but also with deeds.

insights FROM PAUL'S LIFE

In **Acts 9:3-9** Paul is traveling to Damascus to persecute the Christians there. As he neared his destination, he was suddenly struck down by a brilliant light from heaven. Blind and helpless, Paul was led to Damascus to await further instructions from God. For three days he ate and drank nothing. He was forced into a period of rigorous self-examination. This kind of experience is often helpful in recovery. Some of us may have been confronted suddenly and dramatically with the painful truth about our life. But whether it happened with a bang or with a whisper, we all have come face to face with our sins and character flaws. Recovery begins as we discover our helplessness; it continues with honest self-examination and continued dependence on God's power.

ROMANS

THE BIG PICTURE

A. GREETINGS AND THANKS (1:1-15)

B. THE THEME OF THE LETTER (1:16-18)

C. OUR NEED FOR RECOVERY (1:19–4:25)

D. GOD'S POWER FOR OUR DELIVERANCE (5:1–8:39)

E. QUESTIONS ABOUT ISRAEL'S RECOVERY (9:1–11:36)

F. THE BEHAVIORS OF RECOVERY (12:1–15:13)

G. CONCLUSION (15:14–16:27)

The church in Rome was a testimony to God's power. It had flourished despite the obstacles posed by the surrounding pagan culture. Yet these believers were not perfect; in fact, they had some serious problems. Though they were well established in their faith, their convictions and unity as a group were threatened by racial and cultural division.

The main topic in this letter is the gospel—the good news that salvation from sin is available through Jesus Christ. At the core of the gospel is the truth that God is bigger than the past. No matter who we are or what we have done, we can be saved by grace (undeserved favor from God) through faith (complete trust) in Christ. We can stand before God, justified—declared "not guilty." That's good news!

In Romans Paul explains four major points. First, God makes no distinction between us as individuals—we are all guilty, and we are all offered his free gift of salvation. Second, we can all be freed from sin's power through God's grace and the Holy Spirit within us. Third, we are all "in recovery" and therefore have no grounds for arrogance. And fourth, because of God's mercy we all must respect one another, despite our differences.

Many people have called this letter the greatest theological treatise ever written, but it's really a letter about how to live. It teaches us how to deal with our sinful attitudes and behaviors and tells us how to get back on the right track. Paul's letter applies directly to us, showing us how to recover from the effects of sin and dysfunction in our life.

THE BOTTOM LINE

PURPOSE: To introduce Paul to the church at Rome and summarize his message before he arrived there. AUTHOR: The apostle Paul. AUDIENCE: The church at Rome. DATE WRITTEN: A.D. 57, from Corinth, just before Paul's return to Jerusalem. SETTING: Paul wrote this letter in anticipation of a future visit to the believers in Rome. KEY VERSES: "And I am convinced that nothing can ever separate us from God's love. Neither death nor life, neither angels nor demons, neither our fears for today nor our worries about tomorrow—not even the powers of hell can separate us from God's love. . . . Nothing in all creation will ever be able to separate us from the love of God" (8:38-39). KEY PEOPLE AND RELATIONSHIPS: Paul with the believers in Rome and with Phoebe, who helped Paul in his ministry.

RECOVERY THEMES

Our Universal Need: All of us have sinned; we have all fallen short of God's glorious standard. Regardless of whether we have fallen deeply into a controlling addiction, been abused by dysfunctional family members, or escaped severe trauma—we are all in need of recovery from sin of one kind or another. Ever since Adam and Eve rebelled against God, our nature has been to disobey him; we have been addicted to ignoring God's will. We are all powerless in our sin and need God to save us.

God's Power to Deliver: Our need for recovery involves the need to be forgiven and to forgive, as well as to be cleansed from the effects of the past. Although we are powerless to help ourself and don't really deserve to be helped, God, in his great love, reaches out to us, offering to forgive us, cleanse us, and empower us to become what he wants us to be. This is truly good news! Our part is to admit our powerlessness and turn our life and will over to this powerful, loving God.

Recovery Leads to Freedom: Because God has attacked our problems at the roots—that is, he has made it possible for us to be freed from our sins—we can be free from our controlling addiction. Through God's power, our life can become manageable. Although the process is never easy, over time we can become more and more like Christ as we walk one day at a time with him. The better we know him, the more empowered we can be. By continuing to take inventory, confessing our sins, asking for his forgiveness, and seeking to make amends to those whom we have wronged, we can experience true freedom.

The Role of Faith: Much of this letter describes the importance of faith or trust in God. "It is through faith that a righteous person has life" (1:17). There is no other way to recovery; the role of faith is central. The recovery process began with faith when we turned our will and our life over to God, and each step of the way built on that first step of faith. There is no magic formula for this—it is a daily act of trusting our all-powerful God, who promises never to forsake us and to always love us no matter how unlovable we are.

CHAPTER 1
Greetings from Paul

This letter is from Paul, a slave of Christ Jesus, chosen by God to be an apostle and sent out to preach his Good News. ²God promised this Good News long ago through his prophets in the holy Scriptures. ³The Good News is about his Son. In his earthly life he was born into King David's family line, ⁴and he was shown to be* the Son of God when he was raised from the dead by the power of the Holy Spirit.* He is Jesus Christ our Lord. ⁵Through Christ, God has given us the privilege* and authority as apostles to tell Gentiles everywhere what God has done for them, so that they will believe and obey him, bringing glory to his name.

⁶And you are included among those Gentiles who have been called to belong to Jesus Christ. ⁷I am writing to all of you in Rome who are loved by God and are called to be his own holy people.

May God our Father and the Lord Jesus Christ give you grace and peace.

1:4a Or *and was designated.* 1:4b Or *by the Spirit of holiness;* or *in the new realm of the Spirit.* 1:5 Or *the grace.*

1:1 In this letter Paul introduced himself as a slave of Jesus Christ. Paul was a Roman citizen; for him to choose a life of slavery was unthinkable. But Paul purposely used this word to demonstrate his humility and dependence upon God. Paul demonstrated the type of humility we need in recovery. We make progress in recovery when we recognize how helpless we are and how much we need God. Only when we joyfully submit to God's will for our life can we begin the recovery process.

1:16-17 All of us have failed in one way or another, and we all know what shame feels like. We are ashamed of our past failures, our bad habits, or even the abuses we have suffered. Paul tells us that the Good News of Jesus Christ is God's power to deliver us from all the shameful things in our life. And it's for everyone! God has the power to deliver and transform us when we turn our life over to him. The Good News of salvation is certainly nothing to be ashamed of!

1:21-32 When we refuse to admit our powerlessness and hold on to our self-sufficiency, we follow the downward path that Paul describes here. First, we exchange worship of God for worship of things—our addiction or compulsion. Second, we exchange our worship of the living God for a willful form of sin. Third, we move beyond these forms of sin to deep denial—we believe lies and reject truth. This passage describes lives that have become totally unmanageable, the natural consequence of refusing to acknowledge God. The only way to escape such destruction is to recognize our powerlessness and turn our life over to God.

God's Good News

8Let me say first that I thank my God through Jesus Christ for all of you, because your faith in him is being talked about all over the world. 9God knows how often I pray for you. Day and night I bring you and your needs in prayer to God, whom I serve with all my heart* by spreading the Good News about his Son.

10One of the things I always pray for is the opportunity, God willing, to come at last to see you. 11For I long to visit you so I can bring you some spiritual gift that will help you grow strong in the Lord. 12When we get together, I want to encourage you in your faith, but I also want to be encouraged by yours.

13I want you to know, dear brothers and sisters,* that I planned many times to visit you, but I was prevented until now. I want to work among you and see spiritual fruit, just as I have seen among other Gentiles. 14For I have a great sense of obligation to people in both the civilized world and the rest of the world,* to the educated and uneducated alike. 15So I am eager to come to you in Rome, too, to preach the Good News.

16For I am not ashamed of this Good News about Christ. It is the power of God at work, saving everyone who believes—the Jew first and also the Gentile.* 17This Good News tells us how God makes us right in his sight. This is accomplished from start to finish by faith. As the Scriptures say, "It is through faith that a righteous person has life."*

God's Anger at Sin

18But God shows his anger from heaven against all sinful, wicked people who suppress the truth by their wickedness.* 19They know the truth about God because he has made it obvious to them. 20For ever since the world was created, people have seen the earth and sky. Through everything God made, they can clearly see his invisible qualities—his eternal power and divine nature. So they have no excuse for not knowing God.

21Yes, they knew God, but they wouldn't worship him as God or even give him thanks. And they began to think up foolish ideas of what God was like. As a result, their minds became dark and confused. 22Claiming to be wise, they instead became utter

1:9 Or *in my spirit.* 1:13 Greek *brothers.* 1:14 Greek *to Greeks and barbarians.* 1:16 Greek *also the Greek.* 1:17 Or *"The righteous will live by faith."* Hab 2:4. 1:18 Or *who, by their wickedness, prevent the truth from being known.*

STEP 2

Coming to Believe

BIBLE READING: Romans 1:18-20

We came to believe that a Power greater than ourselves could restore us to sanity. Saying that we "came to believe" suggests a process. Belief is the result of consideration, doubt, reasoning, and concluding. The ability to form beliefs is part of what it means to be made in God's image. It involves emotion and logic. It leads to action. What, then, is the process that leads us to solid belief and changes our life?

We start with our own experiences, and we see what doesn't work. Looking at the condition of our life, we realize that we don't have enough power to overcome our dependency. We try with all our might, but to no avail. When we are quiet enough to listen, we hear that still, small voice inside us saying, "There is a powerful God, and he is able and willing to help us." The apostle Paul said it this way: "They [the people who need God] know the truth about God because he has made it obvious to them" (Romans 1:19).

Recognizing our internal weaknesses is the first step toward recovery. When we look beyond ourself, we see that there are others who have struggled with an addiction and recovered. We know that they, too, were unable to heal themselves, yet they now live free of addictive behaviors. We conclude that there must be a greater Power that helped them. Since we can see the similarities between their struggles and our own, we come to believe that our powerful God can restore us to sanity. This is where many people are when they get to Step Two, and it's a good place to be on the way to recovery. *Turn to page 1589, Hebrews 11.*

fools. [23]And instead of worshiping the glorious, ever-living God, they worshiped idols made to look like mere people and birds and animals and reptiles.

[24]So God abandoned them to do whatever shameful things their hearts desired. As a result, they did vile and degrading things with each other's bodies. [25]They traded the truth about God for a lie. So they worshiped and served the things God created instead of the Creator himself, who is worthy of eternal praise! Amen. [26]That is why God abandoned them to their shameful desires. Even the women turned against the natural way to have sex and instead indulged in sex with each other. [27]And the men, instead of having normal sexual relations with women, burned with lust for each other. Men did shameful things with other men, and as a result of this sin, they suffered within themselves the penalty they deserved.

[28]Since they thought it foolish to acknowledge God, he abandoned them to their foolish thinking and let them do things that should never be done. [29]Their lives became full of every kind of wickedness, sin, greed, hate, envy, murder, quarreling, deception, malicious behavior, and gossip. [30]They are backstabbers, haters of God, insolent, proud, and boastful. They invent new ways of sinning, and they disobey their parents. [31]They refuse to understand, break their promises, are heartless, and have no mercy. [32]They know God's justice requires that those who do these things deserve to die, yet they do them anyway. Worse yet, they encourage others to do them, too.

2:9 Greek *also for the Greek;* also in 2:10.

CHAPTER 2
God's Judgment of Sin

You may think you can condemn such people, but you are just as bad, and you have no excuse! When you say they are wicked and should be punished, you are condemning yourself, for you who judge others do these very same things. [2]And we know that God, in his justice, will punish anyone who does such things. [3]Since you judge others for doing these things, why do you think you can avoid God's judgment when you do the same things? [4]Don't you see how wonderfully kind, tolerant, and patient God is with you? Does this mean nothing to you? Can't you see that his kindness is intended to turn you from your sin?

[5]But because you are stubborn and refuse to turn from your sin, you are storing up terrible punishment for yourself. For a day of anger is coming, when God's righteous judgment will be revealed. [6]He will judge everyone according to what they have done. [7]He will give eternal life to those who keep on doing good, seeking after the glory and honor and immortality that God offers. [8]But he will pour out his anger and wrath on those who live for themselves, who refuse to obey the truth and instead live lives of wickedness. [9]There will be trouble and calamity for everyone who keeps on doing what is evil—for the Jew first and also for the Gentile.* [10]But there will be glory and honor and peace from God for all who do good—for the Jew first and also for the Gentile. [11]For God does not show favoritism.

[12]When the Gentiles sin, they will be destroyed, even though they never had God's

---

2:1-4 As we see people whose lives are wicked and completely out of control, it is easy to feel superior and point a finger at them. Paul quickly corrects the tendency to do this by showing that everyone is in the same boat. We all do things that are wrong; we hide all kinds of problems, habits, and sins in the dark recesses of our life. If we often apply this passage to other people, we probably really need to apply it to ourself. Recovery begins with an honest personal inventory.

2:5-16 God is impartial. He doesn't forgive us because we are members of a special group of people. He doesn't judge us by the way we talk, walk, or dress. He judges us by whether or not we obey and believe in him. The Jews of Paul's day believed that they had special privileges from God, but here we find that God treats all people the same. If we admit our failures and seek to follow God's will for us, we are his special people. We are also on the way to recovery. Some of us have felt like an outsider all our life, having been rejected by others because of our problems or failures. God will never reject us if we confess our sins, accept his forgiveness, and humbly obey him.

2:28-29 Paul made an important point very clear in these verses: God is concerned that our heart be open and obedient to him. Our outward religious or recovery activities are important only if they reflect our love for God and others. We can always fake recovery, just as we can fake our relationship with God. If we just go through the motions and make no real commitment to God, we cannot make progress for long. But if we are filled with his Spirit and motivated by our love for God and other people, no obstacle to recovery is too great to overcome.

written law. And the Jews, who do have God's law, will be judged by that law when they fail to obey it. ¹³For merely listening to the law doesn't make us right with God. It is obeying the law that makes us right in his sight. ¹⁴Even Gentiles, who do not have God's written law, show that they know his law when they instinctively obey it, even without having heard it. ¹⁵They demonstrate that God's law is written in their hearts, for their own conscience and thoughts either accuse them or tell them they are doing right. ¹⁶And this is the message I proclaim—that the day is coming when God, through Christ Jesus, will judge everyone's secret life.

The Jews and the Law
¹⁷You who call yourselves Jews are relying on God's law, and you boast about your special relationship with him. ¹⁸You know what he wants; you know what is right because you have been taught his law. ¹⁹You are convinced that you are a guide for the blind and a light for people who are lost in darkness. ²⁰You think you can instruct the ignorant and teach children the ways of God. For you are certain that God's law gives you complete knowledge and truth.

²¹Well then, if you teach others, why don't you teach yourself? You tell others not to steal, but do you steal? ²²You say it is wrong to commit adultery, but do you commit adultery? You condemn idolatry, but do you use items stolen from pagan temples?* ²³You are so proud of knowing the law, but you dishonor God by breaking it. ²⁴No wonder the Scriptures say, "The Gentiles blaspheme the name of God because of you."*

²⁵The Jewish ceremony of circumcision has value only if you obey God's law. But if you don't obey God's law, you are no better off than an uncircumcised Gentile. ²⁶And if the Gentiles obey God's law, won't God declare them to be his own people? ²⁷In fact, uncircumcised Gentiles who keep God's law will condemn you Jews who are circumcised and possess God's law but don't obey it.

²⁸For you are not a true Jew just because you were born of Jewish parents or because you have gone through the ceremony of circumcision. ²⁹No, a true Jew is one whose heart is right with God. And true circumcision is not merely obeying the letter of the law; rather, it is a change of heart produced by the Spirit. And a person with a changed heart seeks praise* from God, not from people.

2:22 Greek *do you steal from temples?* 2:24 Isa 52:5 (Greek version). 2:29 Or *receives praise.*

STEP 5

Freedom through Confession
BIBLE READING: Romans 2:12-15
We admitted to God, to ourselves, and to another human being the exact nature of our wrongs.
All of us struggle with our conscience, trying to make peace within our own heart. We may deny what we have done, find excuses, or try to squirm out from beneath the full weight of our conduct. We may work hard to be "good," trying to counteract our wrongs. We do everything we can to even out the score. In order to put the past to rest, however, we must stop rationalizing our sins and admit the truth.

We are all born with a built-in alarm that alerts us when we do wrong. God holds everyone accountable: "They demonstrate that God's law is written in their hearts, for their own conscience and thoughts either accuse them or tell them they are doing right" (Romans 2:15).

In Step Five we set out to stop this internal struggle and admit that wrong is wrong. It is time to be honest with God and ourself about our cover-ups and the exact nature of our wrongs. We need to admit the sins we have committed and the pain we have caused others. We may have spent years constructing alibis, coming up with excuses, and trying to plea-bargain. It is time to come clean. It is time to admit what we know deep down inside to be true: "Yes, I'm guilty as charged."

There is no real freedom without confession. What a relief it is to finally give up the weight of our lies and excuses. When we confess our sins, we will find the internal peace we lost so long ago. We will also be one step closer to recovery. *Turn to page 1503, Galatians 6.*

CHAPTER 3
God Remains Faithful

Then what's the advantage of being a Jew? Is there any value in the ceremony of circumcision? [2]Yes, there are great benefits! First of all, the Jews were entrusted with the whole revelation of God.*

[3]True, some of them were unfaithful; but just because they were unfaithful, does that mean God will be unfaithful? [4]Of course not! Even if everyone else is a liar, God is true. As the Scriptures say about him,

"You will be proved right in what you say, and you will win your case in court."*

[5]"But," some might say, "our sinfulness serves a good purpose, for it helps people see how righteous God is. Isn't it unfair, then, for him to punish us?" (This is merely a human point of view.) [6]Of course not! If God were not entirely fair, how would he be qualified to judge the world? [7]"But," someone might still argue, "how can God condemn me as a sinner if my dishonesty highlights his truthfulness and brings him more glory?" [8]And some people even slander us by claiming that we say, "The more we sin, the better it is!" Those who say such things deserve to be condemned.

All People Are Sinners

[9]Well then, should we conclude that we Jews are better than others? No, not at all, for we have already shown that all people, whether Jews or Gentiles,* are under the power of sin. [10]As the Scriptures say,

"No one is righteous—
 not even one.
[11]No one is truly wise;
 no one is seeking God.
[12]All have turned away;
 all have become useless.
No one does good,
 not a single one."*
[13]"Their talk is foul, like the stench
 from an open grave.
 Their tongues are filled with lies."
"Snake venom drips from their lips."*
[14] "Their mouths are full of cursing and
 bitterness."*
[15]"They rush to commit murder.
[16] Destruction and misery always follow
 them.
[17]They don't know where to find peace."*
[18] "They have no fear of God at all."*

[19]Obviously, the law applies to those to whom it was given, for its purpose is to keep people from having excuses, and to show that the entire world is guilty before God. [20]For no one can ever be made right with God by doing what the law commands. The law simply shows us how sinful we are.

Christ Took Our Punishment

[21]But now God has shown us a way to be made right with him without keeping the requirements of the law, as was promised in the

3:2 Greek *the oracles of God.* 3:4 Ps 51:4 (Greek version). 3:9 Greek *or Greeks.* 3:10-12 Pss 14:1-3; 53:1-3 (Greek version). 3:13 Pss 5:9 (Greek version); 140:3. 3:14 Ps 10:7 (Greek version). 3:15-17 Isa 59:7-8. 3:18 Ps 36:1.

3:20 The more we know about God's laws, God's heart, and God's claim on our life, the clearer it becomes that we don't measure up. God's Old Testament laws represent his will for us; following them leads to a godly life. But none of us can follow these ideals with our own power. We must recognize our need for God's gracious forgiveness and his power on a daily basis to help us follow his program for healthy living. When we fail in our walk with God, we can remind ourself that we are powerless without him. This is the first step back into the process of recovery.

3:21-26 This portion of Scripture clearly states why Jesus died on the cross. We are all made right with God through faith in Jesus Christ. None of us are so good that we don't need God; none of us are so bad that we are beyond the reach of God's loving grace. Jesus has declared us not guilty and set us free from God's anger. Salvation is freely given, but it was expensively purchased by God!

3:27 God deals with all people on the same basis, regardless of race or social class. In our day Paul might have said that God gives the same attention to the cry of the homeless alcoholic as he does to that of the richest person in the world. No one can earn God's acceptance. All must come to recovery through faith and trust in God. This leaves us nothing to boast about; none of us can be saved by anything we do or say. But there is no reason for us to hide from God either; nothing is so bad in our life that it cannot be forgiven completely by our gracious and loving God.

4:6-8 Many of us have failed desperately; we have hurt others in ways that cannot easily be repaired. What can we do about our guilt? King David was guilty of serious sins—adultery, deceit, and murder—yet when he acknowledged his guilt, confessed his sins to God, and experienced God's forgiveness, he found joy. Each of these steps was an act of faith, but the result was joy. Each of the steps we take in recovery is also an act of faith, but as we faithfully work each step, we will also experience God's forgiveness and joy.

writings of Moses* and the prophets long ago. ²²We are made right with God by placing our faith in Jesus Christ. And this is true for everyone who believes, no matter who we are.

²³For everyone has sinned; we all fall short of God's glorious standard. ²⁴Yet God freely and graciously declares that we are righteous. He did this through Christ Jesus when he freed us from the penalty for our sins. ²⁵For God presented Jesus as the sacrifice for sin. People are made right with God when they believe that Jesus sacrificed his life, shedding his blood. This sacrifice shows that God was being fair when he held back and did not punish those who sinned in times past, ²⁶for he was looking ahead and including them in what he would do in this present time. God did this to demonstrate his righteousness, for he himself is fair and just, and he declares sinners to be right in his sight when they believe in Jesus.

²⁷Can we boast, then, that we have done anything to be accepted by God? No, because our acquittal is not based on obeying the law. It is based on faith. ²⁸So we are made right with God through faith and not by obeying the law.

²⁹After all, is God the God of the Jews only? Isn't he also the God of the Gentiles? Of course he is. ³⁰There is only one God, and he makes people right with himself only by faith, whether they are Jews or Gentiles.* ³¹Well then, if we emphasize faith, does this mean that we can forget about the law? Of course not! In fact, only when we have faith do we truly fulfill the law.

CHAPTER 4
The Faith of Abraham

Abraham was, humanly speaking, the founder of our Jewish nation. What did he discover about being made right with God? ²If his good deeds had made him acceptable to God, he would have had something to boast about. But that was not God's way. ³For the Scriptures tell us, "Abraham believed God, and God counted him as righteous because of his faith."*

⁴When people work, their wages are not a gift, but something they have earned. ⁵But people are counted as righteous, not because of their work, but because of their faith in God who forgives sinners. ⁶David also spoke of this when he described the happiness of those who are declared righteous without working for it:

3:21 Greek in the law. 3:30 Greek whether they are circumcised or uncircumcised. 4:3 Gen 15:6.

SELF-PERCEPTION

READ ROMANS 3:10-12

We may feel that we are different from other people—either much worse or much better. We may look down on ourself and continually compare ourself with "good" people. Or perhaps our addiction seems more socially acceptable than others. So we console ourself by looking down on others whose sins seem worse than ours.

"As the Scriptures say, 'No one is righteous—not even one. No one is truly wise; no one is seeking God. All have turned away; all have become useless'" (Romans 3:10-12).

The first chapter of Romans is often used to condemn sexual sins or sexual addictions. People tend to skip over the last few verses, which condemn the more "acceptable" sins such as backbiting, disobeying parents, or bragging. In the second chapter the apostle Paul speaks to people who see themselves as better than others: "You may think you can condemn such people, but you are just as bad, and you have no excuse! When you say they are wicked and should be punished, you are condemning yourself, for you who judge others do these very same things" (Romans 2:1).

Every one of us is made of the same stuff—both good and bad. We may act out in different ways, but in God's eyes we are all the same. When we focus on admitting our wrongs, it helps us remember that we are not so different from others after all. As we call on God and admit our helplessness, we can begin the steps toward healing and recovery. *Turn to page 1439, Romans 4.*

7 "Oh, what joy for those
   whose disobedience is forgiven,
   whose sins are put out of sight.
8 Yes, what joy for those
   whose record the LORD has cleared
       of sin."*

9 Now, is this blessing only for the Jews, or is it also for uncircumcised Gentiles?* Well, we have been saying that Abraham was counted as righteous by God because of his faith. 10 But how did this happen? Was he counted as righteous only after he was circumcised, or was it before he was circumcised? Clearly, God accepted Abraham before he was circumcised!

11 Circumcision was a sign that Abraham already had faith and that God had already accepted him and declared him to be righteous—even before he was circumcised. So Abraham is the spiritual father of those who have faith but have not been circumcised. They are counted as righteous because of their faith. 12 And Abraham is also the spiritual father of those who have been circumcised, but only if they have the same kind of faith Abraham had before he was circumcised.

13 Clearly, God's promise to give the whole earth to Abraham and his descendants was based not on his obedience to God's law, but on a right relationship with God that comes by faith. 14 If God's promise is only for those who obey the law, then faith is not necessary and the promise is pointless. 15 For the law al-ways brings punishment on those who try to obey it. (The only way to avoid breaking the law is to have no law to break!)

16 So the promise is received by faith. It is given as a free gift. And we are all certain to receive it, whether or not we live according to the law of Moses, if we have faith like Abraham's. For Abraham is the father of all who believe. 17 That is what the Scriptures mean when God told him, "I have made you the father of many nations."* This happened because Abraham believed in the God who brings the dead back to life and who creates new things out of nothing.

18 Even when there was no reason for hope, Abraham kept hoping—believing that he would become the father of many nations. For God had said to him, "That's how many descendants you will have!"* 19 And Abraham's faith did not weaken, even though, at about 100 years of age, he figured his body was as good as dead—and so was Sarah's womb.

20 Abraham never wavered in believing God's promise. In fact, his faith grew stronger, and in this he brought glory to God. 21 He was fully convinced that God is able to do whatever he promises. 22 And because of Abraham's faith, God counted him as righteous. 23 And when God counted him as righteous, it wasn't just for Abraham's benefit. It was recorded 24 for our benefit, too, assuring us that God will also count us as righteous if we believe in him, the one who raised Jesus our Lord from the dead. 25 He

4:7-8 Ps 32:1-2 (Greek version). 4:9 Greek *is this blessing only for the circumcised, or is it also for the uncircumcised?* 4:17 Gen 17:5. 4:18 Gen 15:5.

4:23-25 When we believe in God and the restoration he offers in Jesus Christ, an exchange takes place. We turn our unmanageable life over to God, including all our sins and guilt, and he gives us his goodness and forgiveness in return. When Jesus died on the cross, he took our sins and guilt away. When Jesus rose from the grave, God demonstrated his power to transform us and fill us with his goodness. As we follow God's program for restoration, we die to our sins and failures and experience a new and better life through God's power.

5:12-14 How can we be judged for something Adam did thousands of years ago? It doesn't seem fair. Many of us find it easy to blame others for our problems, citing our parents or even Adam and Eve as the cause of our failures and sins. Paul made it clear that Adam's sin and the sins of our ancestors are not our primary concern. Our problems may have started with the mistakes of others, but we have all solidly aligned ourselves with Adam by repeatedly making the same mistakes. We are made of the same stuff, prone to rebel against God and his ways. We will suffer the consequences for our sins if God doesn't intervene. We don't need fairness from God; we need his mercy. And that is what God provides for all who believe in him.

5:15-21 Paul had already asserted that we stand forgiven and joyful in God's grace (5:2), and here he elaborated on that reality. The essential nature of God's grace is that it rules over sin and death in our world. While Adam's sin brought sin and death, Jesus Christ has brought life through his grace for all who are willing to receive it. Our old sinful life represents the rule of death through Adam. Our life in recovery through Jesus Christ represents the rule of God's grace, kindness, and love. When we turn our life over to God, we can begin to receive the wonderful joy and forgiveness that he offers.

was handed over to die because of our sins, and he was raised to life to make us right with God.

CHAPTER 5
Faith Brings Joy

Therefore, since we have been made right in God's sight by faith, we have peace* with God because of what Jesus Christ our Lord has done for us. ²Because of our faith, Christ has brought us into this place of undeserved privilege where we now stand, and we confidently and joyfully look forward to sharing God's glory.

³We can rejoice, too, when we run into problems and trials, for we know that they help us develop endurance. ⁴And endurance develops strength of character, and character strengthens our confident hope of salvation. ⁵And this hope will not lead to disappointment. For we know how dearly God loves us, because he has given us the Holy Spirit to fill our hearts with his love.

⁶When we were utterly helpless, Christ came at just the right time and died for us sinners. ⁷Now, most people would not be willing to die for an upright person, though someone might perhaps be willing to die for a person who is especially good. ⁸But God showed his great love for us by sending Christ to die for us while we were still sinners. ⁹And since we have been made right in God's sight by the blood of Christ, he will certainly save us from God's condemnation. ¹⁰For since our friendship with God was restored by the death of his Son while we were still his enemies, we will certainly be saved through the life of his Son. ¹¹So now we can rejoice in our wonderful new relationship with God because our Lord Jesus Christ has made us friends of God.

Adam and Christ Contrasted

¹²When Adam sinned, sin entered the world. Adam's sin brought death, so death spread to everyone, for everyone sinned. ¹³Yes, people sinned even before the law was given. But it was not counted as sin because there was not yet any law to break. ¹⁴Still, everyone died—from the time of Adam to the time of Moses—even those who did not disobey an explicit commandment of God, as Adam did. Now Adam is a symbol, a representation of Christ, who was yet to come. ¹⁵But there is a great difference between Adam's sin and God's gracious gift. For the sin of this one man, Adam, brought death to many. But even greater is God's wonderful grace and his

5:1 Some manuscripts read *let us have peace.*

STEP 7

Declared "Not Guilty"

BIBLE READING: Romans 3:23-28
We humbly asked him to remove our shortcomings.

What are our shortcomings? We all realize that we have them. Is this just another way of saying that we have fallen short of our personal ideals? At some time all of us have held high ideals to define what we think our life should be like. But most of us learned early on that we couldn't measure up to them. Worse yet, we have often fallen short of the expectations of others and the standards of God. Oh, the weight of guilt we carry! Oh, the pain to think of how we have disappointed those we love! Oh, the longing for some way to be what we should be!

The apostle Paul wrote: "For everyone has sinned; we all fall short of God's glorious standard. Yet God, with undeserved kindness, declares that we are righteous. He did this through Christ Jesus when he freed us from the penalty for our sins" (Romans 3:23-24). Paul goes on to ask, "Can we boast, then, that we have done anything to be accepted by God? No, because our acquittal is not based on obeying the law. It is based on faith. So we are made right with God through faith and not by obeying the law" (3:27-28).

When God removes our sins, he does a great job! "He has removed our sins as far from us as the east is from the west" (Psalm 103:12). We can trust God to remove our shortcomings, moment by moment, if we humble ourself to obey his Word. That means having faith in Jesus Christ to make up for our weaknesses in both character and action. *Turn to page 1523, Philippians 2.*

gift of forgiveness to many through this other man, Jesus Christ. ¹⁶And the result of God's gracious gift is very different from the result of that one man's sin. For Adam's sin led to condemnation, but God's free gift leads to our being made right with God, even though we are guilty of many sins. ¹⁷For the sin of this one man, Adam, caused death to rule over many. But even greater is God's wonderful grace and his gift of righteousness, for all who receive it will live in triumph over sin and death through this one man, Jesus Christ.

¹⁸Yes, Adam's one sin brings condemnation for everyone, but Christ's one act of righteousness brings a right relationship with God and new life for everyone. ¹⁹Because one person disobeyed God, many became sinners. But because one other person obeyed God, many will be made righteous.

²⁰God's law was given so that all people could see how sinful they were. But as people sinned more and more, God's wonderful grace became more abundant. ²¹So just as sin ruled over all people and brought them to death, now God's wonderful grace rules instead, giving us right standing with God and resulting in eternal life through Jesus Christ our Lord.

CHAPTER 6
Sin's Power Is Broken

Well then, should we keep on sinning so that God can show us more and more of his wonderful grace? ²Of course not! Since we have died to sin, how can we continue to live in it? ³Or have you forgotten that when we were joined with Christ Jesus in baptism, we joined him in his death? ⁴For we died and were buried with Christ by baptism. And just as Christ was raised from the dead by the glorious power of the Father, now we also may live new lives.

⁵Since we have been united with him in his death, we will also be raised to life as he was. ⁶We know that our old sinful selves were crucified with Christ so that sin might lose its power in our lives. We are no longer slaves to sin. ⁷For when we died with Christ we were set free from the power of sin. ⁸And since we died with Christ, we know we will also live with him. ⁹We are sure of this because Christ was raised from the dead, and he will never die again. Death no longer has any power over him. ¹⁰When he died, he died once to break the power of sin. But now that he lives, he lives for the glory of God. ¹¹So you also should consider yourselves to be dead to the power of sin and alive to God through Christ Jesus.

¹²Do not let sin control the way you live;* do not give in to sinful desires. ¹³Do not let any part of your body become an instrument of evil to serve sin. Instead, give yourselves completely to God, for you were dead, but now you have new life. So use your whole body as an instrument to do what is right for the glory of God. ¹⁴Sin is no longer your mas-

---

6:12 Or *Do not let sin reign in your body, which is subject to death.*

6:1-3 If God loves to forgive, why not sin to give him added opportunities to forgive us? We may not admit it, but we act on this principle all too often. Paul's response to this excuse for sin is an emphatic *no!* Such an attitude presumes upon God's grace and is clear evidence that we are in denial. When we knowingly continue to sin, we are making light of the tremendous cost of our salvation. It is unthinkable to continue to allow sin to be our master when we have turned our life over to God.

6:12-14 As we recover from our addiction or compulsive behaviors, we may become very discouraged because the old desires still tempt us. Paul recognized that temptation would be an ongoing problem, so he gave us this warning: "Do not give in." The temptations we face are extensions of the defects of character that exist in each of us. Though we cannot overcome our sinful nature alone, we can ask God to help us. As God helps us clear the destructive patterns from our life, we can replace them with healthy patterns and desires. As we are transformed with God's help, we will overcome the powerful temptations in our life.

6:19-22 It is impossible to be neutral. We all have a master—either sin or God. Making sin our master may seem easier and fun for a while, but it will lead only to pain and destruction. When we turn our life over to God and work on recovery, we are affirming that God is our master. This is the only way we can experience restoration for our life. At first God's way may look harder than the way of sin, but in time we will discover that God's way is the only way to a joyful and meaningful life.

7:1-6 Paul used a marriage analogy to clarify his reasoning. If the person we have married dies, the laws of marriage no longer apply to us. We are not bound to the dead spouse. In the same way, when we turn our life over to God, our old bondage to sin no longer applies. We now are "married" to God, giving him a position of power and authority in our life. If we are willing to live under God's authority, we will experience the meaningful life that he wants for every one of his people.

ter, for you no longer live under the requirements of the law. Instead, you live under the freedom of God's grace.

¹⁵Well then, since God's grace has set us free from the law, does that mean we can go on sinning? Of course not! ¹⁶Don't you realize that you become the slave of whatever you choose to obey? You can be a slave to sin, which leads to death, or you can choose to obey God, which leads to righteous living. ¹⁷Thank God! Once you were slaves of sin, but now you wholeheartedly obey this teaching we have given you. ¹⁸Now you are free from your slavery to sin, and you have become slaves to righteous living.

¹⁹Because of the weakness of your human nature, I am using the illustration of slavery to help you understand all this. Previously, you let yourselves be slaves to impurity and lawlessness, which led ever deeper into sin. Now you must give yourselves to be slaves to righteous living so that you will become holy. ²⁰When you were slaves to sin, you were free from the obligation to do right. ²¹And what was the result? You are now ashamed of the things you used to do, things that end in eternal doom. ²²But now you are free from the power of sin and have become slaves of God. Now you do those things that lead to holiness and result in eternal life. ²³For the wages of sin is death, but the free gift of God is eternal life through Christ Jesus our Lord.

CHAPTER 7
No Longer Bound to the Law
Now, dear brothers and sisters*—you who are familiar with the law—don't you know that the law applies only while a person is living? ²For example, when a woman marries, the law binds her to her husband as long as he is alive. But if he dies, the laws of marriage no longer apply to her. ³So while her husband is alive, she would be committing adultery if she married another man. But if her husband dies, she is free from that law and does not commit adultery when she remarries.

⁴So, my dear brothers and sisters, this is the point: You died to the power of the law when you died with Christ. And now you are united with the one who was raised from the dead. As a result, we can produce a harvest of good deeds for God. ⁵When we were controlled by our old nature,* sinful desires were at work within us, and the law aroused these evil desires that produced a harvest of sinful

7:1 Greek *brothers;* also in 7:4. 7:5 Greek *When we were in the flesh.*

FAITH

READ ROMANS 4:1-5
Our addictive patterns are "sinful," so it is common to feel awkward about getting close to God. We may feel ineligible to receive God's love and, instead, expect his angry judgment. We might feel guilty and be afraid that God will reject us. Secretly we wish that we could have a loving relationship with God, but we are afraid we could never be good enough.

The apostle Paul has shown us that we can have the love and acceptance we desire: "For the Scriptures tell us, 'Abraham believed God, and God counted him as righteous because of his faith.' When people work, their wages are not a gift, but something they have earned. But people are counted as righteous, not because of their work, but because of their faith in God who forgives sinners. . . . And when God counted him as righteous, it wasn't just for Abraham's benefit. It was recorded for our benefit, too, assuring us that God will also count us as righteous if we believe in him, the one who raised Jesus our Lord from the dead. He was handed over to die because of our sins, and he was raised to life to make us right with God" (Romans 4:3-5, 23-25).

There are free gifts waiting for us that are essential to the recovery process: God's forgiveness, acceptance, and powerful support. God makes it clear that we have been declared "not guilty" in his court of justice if we have trusted Christ. He has promised to give us a special home in heaven with our name on it. There is no need for us to do anything but accept his free gifts. When we turn our life over to God, we gain far more than we could ever lose! *Turn to page 1445, Romans 7.*

deeds, resulting in death. [6]But now we have been released from the law, for we died to it and are no longer captive to its power. Now we can serve God, not in the old way of obeying the letter of the law, but in the new way of living in the Spirit.

God's Law Reveals Our Sin

[7]Well then, am I suggesting that the law of God is sinful? Of course not! In fact, it was the law that showed me my sin. I would never have known that coveting is wrong if the law had not said, "You must not covet."* [8]But sin used this command to arouse all kinds of covetous desires within me! If there were no law, sin would not have that power. [9]At one time I lived without understanding the law. But when I learned the command not to covet, for instance, the power of sin came to life, [10]and I died. So I discovered that the law's commands, which were supposed to bring life, brought spiritual death instead. [11]Sin took advantage of those commands and

deceived me; it used the commands to kill me. [12]But still, the law itself is holy, and its commands are holy and right and good.

[13]But how can that be? Did the law, which is good, cause my death? Of course not! Sin used what was good to bring about my condemnation to death. So we can see how terrible sin really is. It uses God's good commands for its own evil purposes.

Struggling with Sin

[14]So the trouble is not with the law, for it is spiritual and good. The trouble is with me, for I am all too human, a slave to sin. [15]I don't really understand myself, for I want to do what is right, but I don't do it. Instead, I do what I hate. [16]But if I know that what I am doing is wrong, this shows that I agree that the law is good. [17]So I am not the one doing wrong; it is sin living in me that does it.

[18]And I know that nothing good lives in me, that is, in my sinful nature.* I want to do what is right, but I can't. [19]I want to do what is

7:7 Exod 20:17; Deut 5:21. 7:18 Greek *my flesh;* also in 7:25.

7:13 Paul didn't want to leave us with the impression that God's laws are bad. They were meant to help us lead a godly life in close fellowship with him. The real problem is our inability to live up to the standard God has set. By nature we are flawed and sinful creatures. Few of us set out to become enslaved to a destructive substance or relationship, but we are overcome by our inherent tendency to sin. We can be thankful that God has made a provision for our sin through the death and resurrection of Jesus Christ. Now if we turn our life over to God, we can experience his transforming power. He will help us overcome our destructive behaviors.

7:14-17 We can all identify with the struggle Paul described. We long to do what is good, healthy, and right, but we end up doing the same old destructive things. As we take personal inventory, we admit our failures and seek to change, but then we fall right back into our destructive habits. We are not alone in this struggle—it is part of being human. We must not become discouraged. Instead, we must use our failures to inspire new moral inventory and then get on with recovery once again. In time our sins and failures will become fewer as God begins to transform us.

8:1 This is one of the great affirmations of Scripture. We will never be condemned by God for our sins, because Jesus Christ has paid the price once and for all. When we decide to turn our life over to God's care, we can be confident that we will not be condemned by him. If we have confessed our sins and accepted God's forgiveness in Christ, there is "no condemnation."

8:2-4 Once we recognize how helpless we are to fight our dependency, we must look outside ourself to God for the power we need. The life-giving Spirit that Paul mentioned here is the Holy Spirit. He was present at the creation of the world (Genesis 1–2) and is available to help us as we seek to rebuild our life. We cannot overcome our addiction or compulsion alone, but God is more than able to help us. He sent his Son and destroyed the power of sin through his death and resurrection. Now we can follow God's program for godly living through the power of the Holy Spirit within us.

8:5-6 Paul puts people in two categories—those who let themselves be controlled by their self-serving "sinful natures" and those who are controlled by the Holy Spirit. Once we have made the decision to turn our life over to God, we must consciously choose to follow his way for continued recovery daily. We need to continually reassess our progress, taking a regular moral inventory of our life.

8:9-11 Either we have the Spirit of God living in us, or we don't. How does the Spirit of God come to live within us? By our act of faith in turning our life over to God and by our acceptance of the work of Christ on our behalf. Can we feel the Spirit of God within us? Sometimes, but we can know he is there whether we feel his presence or not. God has promised to give us the Holy Spirit when we ask. We receive the same Holy Spirit who raised Jesus from the dead. God will use this same power in us to bring about our recovery.

good, but I don't. I don't want to do what is wrong, but I do it anyway. ²⁰But if I do what I don't want to do, I am not really the one doing wrong; it is sin living in me that does it.

²¹I have discovered this principle of life—that when I want to do what is right, I inevitably do what is wrong. ²²I love God's law with all my heart. ²³But there is another power* within me that is at war with my mind. This power makes me a slave to the sin that is still within me. ²⁴Oh, what a miserable person I am! Who will free me from this life that is dominated by sin and death? ²⁵Thank God! The answer is in Jesus Christ our Lord. So you see how it is: In my mind I really want to obey God's law, but because of my sinful nature I am a slave to sin.

CHAPTER 8
Life in the Spirit
So now there is no condemnation for those who belong to Christ Jesus. ²And because you belong to him, the power* of the life-giving Spirit has freed you* from the power of sin that leads to death. ³The law of Moses was unable to save us because of the weakness of our sinful nature.* So God did what the law could not do. He sent his own Son in a body like the bodies we sinners have. And in that body God declared an end to sin's control over us by giving his Son as a sacrifice for our sins. ⁴He did this so that the just requirement of the law would be fully satisfied for us, who no longer follow our sinful nature but instead follow the Spirit.

⁵Those who are dominated by the sinful nature think about sinful things, but those who are controlled by the Holy Spirit think about things that please the Spirit. ⁶So letting your sinful nature control your mind leads to death. But letting the Spirit control your mind leads to life and peace. ⁷For the sinful nature is always hostile to God. It never did obey God's laws, and it never will. ⁸That's why those who are still under the control of their sinful nature can never please God.

⁹But you are not controlled by your sinful nature. You are controlled by the Spirit if you have the Spirit of God living in you. (And remember that those who do not have the Spirit of Christ living in them do not belong to him at all.) ¹⁰And Christ lives within you, so even though your body will die because of sin, the Spirit gives you life*

7:23 Greek law; also in 7:23b. 8:2a Greek the law; also in 8:2b. 8:2b Some manuscripts read me. 8:3 Greek our flesh; similarly in 8:4, 5, 6, 7, 8, 9, 12. 8:10 Or your spirit is alive.

Repeated Forgiveness
BIBLE READING: Romans 5:3-5
We continued to take personal inventory and when we were wrong promptly admitted it.
We may grow impatient with ourself when we continue to commit the same sins over and over again. This may cause us to get discouraged, or we may be afraid that we are doomed to relapse.

Peter asked Jesus, "'Lord, how often should I forgive someone who sins against me? Seven times?' 'No, not seven times,' Jesus replied, 'but seventy times seven!'" (Matthew 18:21-22). If this is to be our attitude toward others, doesn't it make sense that we should extend the same grace to ourself? We need to be as patient with ourself as God expects us to be with others.

Paul wrote: "We can rejoice, too, when we run into problems and trials, for we know that they help us develop endurance. And endurance develops strength of character, and character strengthens our confident hope of salvation. . . . For we know how dearly God loves us, because he has given us the Holy Spirit to fill our hearts with his love" (Romans 5:3-5).

Learning to wait patiently is an important characteristic for us to develop. Each time we admit sin and accept God's forgiveness, our hope and faith have a chance to be exercised and grow stronger. We no longer have to hide in shame every time we slip. We can admit our wrongs and move on. God's love for us is reaffirmed every time we rely on it. In this way God helps us hold our head high no matter what happens. *Turn to page 1517, Ephesians 4.*

because you have been made right with God. [11]The Spirit of God, who raised Jesus from the dead, lives in you. And just as God raised Christ Jesus from the dead, he will give life to your mortal bodies by this same Spirit living within you.

[12]Therefore, dear brothers and sisters,* you have no obligation to do what your sinful nature urges you to do. [13]For if you live by its dictates, you will die. But if through the power of the Spirit you put to death the deeds of your sinful nature,* you will live. [14]For all who are led by the Spirit of God are children* of God.

[15]So you have not received a spirit that makes you fearful slaves. Instead, you received God's Spirit when he adopted you as his own children.* Now we call him, "Abba, Father."* [16]For his Spirit joins with our spirit to affirm that we are God's children. [17]And since we are his children, we are his heirs. In fact, together with Christ we are heirs of God's glory. But if we are to share his glory, we must also share his suffering.

The Future Glory

[18]Yet what we suffer now is nothing compared to the glory he will reveal to us later. [19]For all creation is waiting eagerly for that future day when God will reveal who his children really are. [20]Against its will, all creation was subjected to God's curse. But with eager hope, [21]the creation looks forward to the day when it will join God's children in glorious freedom from death and decay. [22]For we know that all creation has been groaning as in the pains of childbirth right up to the present time. [23]And we believers also groan, even though we have the Holy Spirit within us as a foretaste of future glory, for we long for our bodies to be released from sin and suffering. We, too, wait with eager hope for the day when God will give us our full rights as his adopted children,* including the new bodies he has promised us. [24]We were given this hope when we were saved. (If we already have something, we don't need to hope* for it. [25]But if we look forward to something we

don't yet have, we must wait patiently and confidently.)

[26]And the Holy Spirit helps us in our weakness. For example, we don't know what God wants us to pray for. But the Holy Spirit prays for us with groanings that cannot be expressed in words. [27]And the Father who knows all hearts knows what the Spirit is saying, for the Spirit pleads for us believers* in harmony with God's own will. [28]And we know that God causes everything to work together* for the good of those who love God and are called according to his purpose for them. [29]For God knew his people in advance, and he chose them to become like his Son, so that his Son would be the firstborn* among many brothers and sisters. [30]And having chosen them, he called them to come to him. And having called them, he gave them right standing with himself. And having given them right standing, he gave them his glory.

Nothing Can Separate Us from God's Love

[31]What shall we say about such wonderful things as these? If God is for us, who can ever be against us? [32]Since he did not spare even his own Son but gave him up for us all, won't he also give us everything else? [33]Who dares accuse us whom God has chosen for his own? No one—for God himself has given us right standing with himself. [34]Who then will condemn us? No one—for Christ Jesus died for us and was raised to life for us, and he is sitting in the place of honor at God's right hand, pleading for us.

[35]Can anything ever separate us from Christ's love? Does it mean he no longer loves us if we have trouble or calamity, or are persecuted, or hungry, or destitute, or in danger, or threatened with death? [36](As the Scriptures say, "For your sake we are killed every day; we are being slaughtered like sheep."*) [37]No, despite all these things, overwhelming victory is ours through Christ, who loved us.

[38]And I am convinced that nothing can ever separate us from God's love. Neither death nor life, neither angels nor demons,* neither our fears for today nor our worries

---

8:12 Greek *brothers;* also in 8:29. 8:13 Greek *deeds of the body.* 8:14 Greek *sons;* also in 8:19. 8:15a Greek *you received a spirit of sonship.* 8:15b *Abba* is an Aramaic term for "father." 8:23 Greek *wait anxiously for sonship.* 8:24 Some manuscripts read *wait.* 8:27 Greek *for God's holy people.* 8:28 Some manuscripts read *And we know that everything works together.* 8:29 Or *would be supreme.* 8:36 Ps 44:22. 8:38 Greek *nor rulers.*

8:31-39 Our security in life and in recovery is based on God's unshakable love for us. The love God has for us is not just an emotion but a matter of historical record. God proved his love for us by willingly sending his Son to suffer and die. So why would he hold back any lesser gift? In fact, there is nothing in the whole universe that can separate us from God's love! What more could God say or do to us to make us more secure in his love?

about tomorrow—not even the powers of hell can separate us from God's love. ³⁹No power in the sky above or in the earth below—indeed, nothing in all creation will ever be able to separate us from the love of God that is revealed in Christ Jesus our Lord.

CHAPTER 9
God's Selection of Israel
With Christ as my witness, I speak with utter truthfulness. My conscience and the Holy Spirit confirm it. ²My heart is filled with bitter sorrow and unending grief ³for my people, my Jewish brothers and sisters.* I would be willing to be forever cursed—cut off from Christ!—if that would save them. ⁴They are the people of Israel, chosen to be God's adopted children.* God revealed his glory to them. He made covenants with them and gave them his law. He gave them the privilege of worshiping him and receiving his wonderful promises. ⁵Abraham, Isaac, and Jacob are their ancestors, and Christ himself was an Israelite as far as his human nature is concerned. And he is God, the one who rules over everything and is worthy of eternal praise! Amen.*

⁶Well then, has God failed to fulfill his promise to Israel? No, for not all who are born into the nation of Israel are truly members of God's people! ⁷Being descendants of Abraham doesn't make them truly Abraham's children. For the Scriptures say, "Isaac is the son through whom your descendants will be counted,"* though Abraham had other children, too. ⁸This means that Abraham's physical descendants are not necessarily children of God. Only the children of the promise are considered to be Abraham's children. ⁹For God had promised, "I will return about this time next year, and Sarah will have a son."*

¹⁰This son was our ancestor Isaac. When he married Rebekah, she gave birth to twins.* ¹¹But before they were born, before they had done anything good or bad, she received a message from God. (This message shows that God chooses people according to his own purposes; ¹²he calls people, but not according to their good or bad works.) She was told, "Your older son will serve your younger son."* ¹³In the words of the Scriptures, "I loved Jacob, but I rejected Esau."*

9:3 Greek *my brothers.* 9:4 Greek *chosen for sonship.*
9:5 Or *May God, the one who rules over everything, be praised forever. Amen.* 9:7 Gen 21:12. 9:9 Gen 18:10, 14.
9:10 Greek *she conceived children through this one man.*
9:12 Gen 25:23. 9:13 Mal 1:2-3.

STEP 6

Removed, Not Improved
BIBLE READING: Romans 6:5-11
We were entirely ready to have God remove all these defects of character. Most of us have made numerous attempts at self-improvement. Perhaps we have consciously tried to improve our attitudes, our education, our appearance, or our habits. We may have had success in self-improvement on some level. However, when it comes to our struggles with defects of character, chances are we have experienced only deep frustration.

There is a reason for our frustration. These character defects can only be removed, never improved! The illustration given us in the Bible is that our sins and defects of character must be put to death, as Jesus was, with the hope of new life to follow. The apostle Paul wrote: "Our old sinful selves were crucified with Christ so that sin might lose its power in our lives. We are no longer slaves to sin" (Romans 6:6). "Those who belong to Christ Jesus have nailed the passions and desires of their sinful nature to his cross and crucified them there" (Galatians 5:24).

There is no Band-Aid cure for our sins and defects of character. They have been fatally wounded and must die on the cross. This process is never easy. Who goes to a crucifixion without some measure of anxiety? But when we accept this and allow God to remove our defects, we will be pleasantly surprised by the new life that awaits us. *Turn to page 1525, Philippians 3.*

[14]Are we saying, then, that God was unfair? Of course not! [15]For God said to Moses,

"I will show mercy to anyone I choose,
and I will show compassion to anyone I choose."*

[16]So it is God who decides to show mercy. We can neither choose it nor work for it.

[17]For the Scriptures say that God told Pharaoh, "I have appointed you for the very purpose of displaying my power in you and to spread my fame throughout the earth."* [18]So you see, God chooses to show mercy to some, and he chooses to harden the hearts of others so they refuse to listen.

[19]Well then, you might say, "Why does God blame people for not responding? Haven't they simply done what he makes them do?"

[20]No, don't say that. Who are you, a mere human being, to argue with God? Should the thing that was created say to the one who created it, "Why have you made me like this?" [21]When a potter makes jars out of clay, doesn't he have a right to use the same lump of clay to make one jar for decoration and another to throw garbage into? [22]In the same way, even though God has the right to show his anger and his power, he is very patient with those on whom his anger falls, who are destined for destruction. [23]He does this to make the riches of his glory shine even brighter on those to whom he shows mercy, who were prepared in advance for glory. [24]And we are among those whom he selected, both from the Jews and from the Gentiles.

[25]Concerning the Gentiles, God says in the prophecy of Hosea,

"Those who were not my people,
I will now call my people.
And I will love those
whom I did not love before."*

[26]And,

"Then, at the place where they were told,
'You are not my people,'
there they will be called
'children of the living God.'"*

[27]And concerning Israel, Isaiah the prophet cried out,

"Though the people of Israel are as
numerous as the sand of the
seashore,
only a remnant will be saved.
[28]For the LORD will carry out his sentence
upon the earth
quickly and with finality."*

[29]And Isaiah said the same thing in another place:

"If the LORD of Heaven's Armies
had not spared a few of our children,
we would have been wiped out like
Sodom,
destroyed like Gomorrah."*

Israel's Unbelief

[30]What does all this mean? Even though the Gentiles were not trying to follow God's standards, they were made right with God. And it was by faith that this took place. [31]But the people of Israel, who tried so hard to get right with God by keeping the law, never succeeded. [32]Why not? Because they were trying to get right with God by keeping the law* instead of by trusting in him. They stumbled over the great rock in their path. [33]God warned them of this in the Scriptures when he said,

---

9:15 Exod 33:19. 9:17 Exod 9:16 (Greek version). 9:25 Hos 2:23. 9:26 Greek *sons of the living God.* Hos 1:10.
9:27-28 Isa 10:22-23 (Greek version). 9:29 Isa 1:9. 9:32 Greek *by works.*

9:25-26 God specializes in loving those who are unlovely and undeserving. None of us deserve God's love, and those of us who think we do are in denial. God's love is bestowed on all who admit their need and respond to his love for them. Sometimes the most undeserving are the first to admit their need for God. No one is entirely innocent of wrongdoing; yet no sin is too great for God to forgive. Thus, desperate addicts who have confessed their sins are better off than "respectable" people who deny their need for God. Admitting that we have failed and that we need God is an essential part of the recovery process.

10:8-15 Salvation comes by trusting Jesus Christ; we can do nothing to earn it. Many of us have spent our entire life trying to earn the approval of others. Perhaps the pain we feel at our failure to achieve perfection is at the heart of our compulsive behavior. We can be thankful that God does not accept us on the basis of our performance. He accepts us because of what Christ has done on our behalf, no matter how great our sins have been. We have no reason to hide our sins from God; he wants only to relieve us of our burdens. He invites us to entrust our life to him and seek to follow his will.

"I am placing a stone in Jerusalem* that
    makes people stumble,
  a rock that makes them fall.
But anyone who trusts in him
    will never be disgraced."*

CHAPTER 10

Dear brothers and sisters,* the longing of my
heart and my prayer to God is for the people
of Israel to be saved. [2]I know what enthusiasm they have for God, but it is misdirected
zeal. [3]For they don't understand God's way
of making people right with himself. Refusing to accept God's way, they cling to their
own way of getting right with God by trying
to keep the law. [4]For Christ has already accomplished the purpose for which the law
was given.* As a result, all who believe in
him are made right with God.

Salvation Is for Everyone

[5]For Moses writes that the law's way of making a person right with God requires obedience to all of its commands.* [6]But faith's way
of getting right with God says, "Don't say in
your heart, 'Who will go up to heaven?' (to
bring Christ down to earth). [7]And don't say,
'Who will go down to the place of the dead?'
(to bring Christ back to life again)." [8]In fact,
it says,

  "The message is very close at hand;
    it is on your lips and in your heart."*

And that message is the very message about
faith that we preach: [9]If you openly declare
that Jesus is Lord and believe in your heart
that God raised him from the dead, you will
be saved. [10]For it is by believing in your heart
that you are made right with God, and it is
by openly declaring your faith that you are
saved. [11]As the Scriptures tell us, "Anyone
who trusts in him will never be disgraced."*
[12]Jew and Gentile* are the same in this respect. They have the same Lord, who gives
generously to all who call on him. [13]For "Everyone who calls on the name of the LORD
will be saved."*

[14]But how can they call on him to save
them unless they believe in him? And how
can they believe in him if they have never
heard about him? And how can they hear
about him unless someone tells them? [15]And
how will anyone go and tell them without

9:33a Greek *in Zion.* 9:33b Isa 8:14; 28:16 (Greek
version). 10:1 Greek *Brothers.* 10:4 Or *For Christ is the
end of the law.* 10:5 See Lev 18:5. 10:6-8 Deut 30:12-14.
10:11 Isa 28:16 (Greek version). 10:12 Greek *and Greek.*
10:13 Joel 2:32.

SELF-PERCEPTION

READ ROMANS 7:18-25

We may have begun to realize that we have
character flaws that are beyond our
control. Deep down inside there is a sense
of brokenness that is a constant reminder
of our humanity. Hopefully, we will get to a
place where our behavior is under control,
and we will be able to maintain sobriety.
But as long as we are in a human body, we
will have to contend with our sinful nature.

Paul said of himself, "I know that nothing
good lives in me, that is, in my sinful
nature. I want to do what is right, but I
can't. I want to do what is good, but I
don't. . . . There is another power within
me that is at war with my mind. This power
makes me a slave to the sin that is still
within me" (Romans 7:18, 23). King David
described God's tenderness toward us
because of our human condition: "The
LORD is like a father to his children, tender
and compassionate to those who fear him.
For he knows how weak we are; he
remembers we are only dust" (Psalm
103:13-15).

No matter how far we progress, our
sinful nature will always incline toward and
be susceptible to the lure of our addiction.
We can't afford to forget this or let down
our guard. Maintaining sobriety is something we will need to nurture for the rest
of our life, one day at a time. But we also
have a reason for great hope. By trusting
Christ and recognizing our helplessness
against the power of sin, we open our life
to the transforming power of God. *Turn to
page 1449, Romans 12.*

1445

being sent? That is why the Scriptures say, "How beautiful are the feet of messengers who bring good news!"*

[16]But not everyone welcomes the Good News, for Isaiah the prophet said, "LORD, who has believed our message?"* [17]So faith comes from hearing, that is, hearing the Good News about Christ. [18]But I ask, have the people of Israel actually heard the message? Yes, they have:

"The message has gone throughout the
     earth,
and the words to all the world."*

[19]But I ask, did the people of Israel really understand? Yes, they did, for even in the time of Moses, God said,

"I will rouse your jealousy through people
     who are not even a nation.
I will provoke your anger through the
     foolish Gentiles."*

[20]And later Isaiah spoke boldly for God, saying,

"I was found by people who were not
     looking for me.
I showed myself to those who were not
     asking for me."*

[21]But regarding Israel, God said,

"All day long I opened my arms to them,
     but they were disobedient and
     rebellious."*

CHAPTER 11
God's Mercy on Israel
I ask, then, has God rejected his own people, the nation of Israel? Of course not! I myself am an Israelite, a descendant of Abraham and a member of the tribe of Benjamin.

[2]No, God has not rejected his own people, whom he chose from the very beginning. Do you realize what the Scriptures say about this? Elijah the prophet complained to God about the people of Israel and said, [3]"LORD, they have killed your prophets and torn

down your altars. I am the only one left, and now they are trying to kill me, too."*

[4]And do you remember God's reply? He said, "No, I have 7,000 others who have never bowed down to Baal!"*

[5]It is the same today, for a few of the people of Israel* have remained faithful because of God's grace—his undeserved kindness in choosing them. [6]And since it is through God's kindness, then it is not by their good works. For in that case, God's grace would not be what it really is—free and undeserved.

[7]So this is the situation: Most of the people of Israel have not found the favor of God they are looking for so earnestly. A few have—the ones God has chosen—but the hearts of the rest were hardened. [8]As the Scriptures say,

"God has put them into a deep sleep.
To this day he has shut their eyes so they
     do not see,
and closed their ears so they do not
     hear."*

[9]Likewise, David said,

"Let their bountiful table become a snare,
     a trap that makes them think all is well.
Let their blessings cause them to stumble,
     and let them get what they deserve.
[10]Let their eyes go blind so they cannot see,
     and let their backs be bent forever."*

[11]Did God's people stumble and fall beyond recovery? Of course not! They were disobedient, so God made salvation available to the Gentiles. But he wanted his own people to become jealous and claim it for themselves. [12]Now if the Gentiles were enriched because the people of Israel turned down God's offer of salvation, think how much greater a blessing the world will share when they finally accept it.

[13]I am saying all this especially for you Gentiles. God has appointed me as the apostle to the Gentiles. I stress this, [14]for I want somehow to make the people of Israel jeal-

---

10:15 Isa 52:7. 10:16 Isa 53:1. 10:18 Ps 19:4. 10:19 Deut 32:21. 10:20 Isa 65:1 (Greek version). 10:21 Isa 65:2 (Greek version). 11:3 1 Kgs 19:10, 14. 11:4 1 Kgs 19:18. 11:5 Greek *for a remnant.* 11:8 Isa 29:10; Deut 29:4. 11:9-10 Ps 69:22-23 (Greek version).

11:1-10 Paul asked, "Has God rejected his own people, the nation of Israel?" The apostle answered his own question with a resounding *no!* Even though a majority of Jews had rejected Jesus' messianic claims, there was still hope for them. It is never too late to turn our life over to God and experience his healing power and grace. As long as we have breath, we can still ask for God's help and forgiveness. Even though this is true, however, an extended period of denial is always costly. We may cause great pain to others, and the longer we wait, the more difficult it will be to change. The time to seek change is now!

ous of what you Gentiles have, so I might save some of them. [15]For since their rejection meant that God offered salvation to the rest of the world, their acceptance will be even more wonderful. It will be life for those who were dead! [16]And since Abraham and the other patriarchs were holy, their descendants will also be holy—just as the entire batch of dough is holy because the portion given as an offering is holy. For if the roots of the tree are holy, the branches will be, too.

[17]But some of these branches from Abraham's tree—some of the people of Israel—have been broken off. And you Gentiles, who were branches from a wild olive tree, have been grafted in. So now you also receive the blessing God has promised Abraham and his children, sharing in the rich nourishment from the root of God's special olive tree. [18]But you must not brag about being grafted in to replace the branches that were broken off. You are just a branch, not the root.

[19]"Well," you may say, "those branches were broken off to make room for me." [20]Yes, but remember—those branches were broken off because they didn't believe in Christ, and you are there because you do believe. So don't think highly of yourself, but fear what could happen. [21]For if God did not spare the original branches, he won't* spare you either.

[22]Notice how God is both kind and severe. He is severe toward those who disobeyed, but kind to you if you continue to trust in his kindness. But if you stop trusting, you also will be cut off. [23]And if the people of Israel turn from their unbelief, they will be grafted in again, for God has the power to graft them back into the tree. [24]You, by nature, were a branch cut from a wild olive tree. So if God was willing to do something contrary to nature by grafting you into his cultivated tree, he will be far more eager to graft the original branches back into the tree where they belong.

God's Mercy Is for Everyone

[25]I want you to understand this mystery, dear brothers and sisters,* so that you will not feel proud about yourselves. Some of the people of Israel have hard hearts, but this will last only until the full number of Gentiles comes to Christ. [26]And so all Israel will be saved. As the Scriptures say,

"The one who rescues will come from
    Jerusalem,*
  and he will turn Israel* away from
    ungodliness.
[27] And this is my covenant with them,
  that I will take away their sins."*

[28]Many of the people of Israel are now enemies of the Good News, and this benefits you Gentiles. Yet they are still the people he loves because he chose their ancestors Abraham, Isaac, and Jacob. [29]For God's gifts and his call can never be withdrawn. [30]Once, you Gentiles were rebels against God, but when the people of Israel rebelled against him, God was merciful to you instead. [31]Now they are the rebels, and God's mercy has come to you so that they, too, will share* in God's mercy. [32]For God has imprisoned everyone in disobedience so he could have mercy on everyone.

[33]Oh, how great are God's riches and wisdom and knowledge! How impossible it is for us to understand his decisions and his ways!

[34] For who can know the LORD's thoughts?
  Who knows enough to give him
    advice?*
[35] And who has given him so much
  that he needs to pay it back?*

[36]For everything comes from him and exists by his power and is intended for his glory. All glory to him forever! Amen.

CHAPTER 12
A Living Sacrifice to God

And so, dear brothers and sisters,* I plead with you to give your bodies to God because of all he has done for you. Let them be a living and holy sacrifice—the kind he will find acceptable. This is truly the way to worship him.* [2]Don't copy the behavior and customs of this world, but let God transform you into

11:21 Some manuscripts read *perhaps he won't.* 11:25 Greek *brothers.* 11:26a Greek *from Zion.* 11:26b Greek *Jacob.* 11:26-27 Isa 59:20-21; 27:9 (Greek version). 11:31 Other manuscripts read *will now share;* still others read *will someday share.* 11:34 Isa 40:13 (Greek version). 11:35 See Job 41:11. 12:1a Greek *brothers.* 12:1b Or *This is your spiritual worship;* or *This is your reasonable service.*

11:33-36 After sketching out the broad contours of God's plan for us, Paul could only worship God's majesty. God's plan, wisdom, knowledge, and ways are all so far beyond ours that we have only one option: to humbly give him the praise he deserves! For those of us who recognize how limited and helpless we are, the fact that God's power and wisdom are great can be an encouragement, especially since he loves us and wants to help us.

a new person by changing the way you think. Then you will learn to know God's will for you, which is good and pleasing and perfect.

³Because of the privilege and authority* God has given me, I give each of you this warning: Don't think you are better than you really are. Be honest in your evaluation of yourselves, measuring yourselves by the faith God has given us.* ⁴Just as our bodies have many parts and each part has a special function, ⁵so it is with Christ's body. We are many parts of one body, and we all belong to each other.

⁶In his grace, God has given us different gifts for doing certain things well. So if God has given you the ability to prophesy, speak out with as much faith as God has given you. ⁷If your gift is serving others, serve them well. If you are a teacher, teach well. ⁸If your gift is to encourage others, be encouraging. If

it is giving, give generously. If God has given you leadership ability, take the responsibility seriously. And if you have a gift for showing kindness to others, do it gladly.

⁹Don't just pretend to love others. Really love them. Hate what is wrong. Hold tightly to what is good. ¹⁰Love each other with genuine affection,* and take delight in honoring each other. ¹¹Never be lazy, but work hard and serve the Lord enthusiastically.* ¹²Rejoice in our confident hope. Be patient in trouble, and keep on praying. ¹³When God's people are in need, be ready to help them. Always be eager to practice hospitality.

¹⁴Bless those who persecute you. Don't curse them; pray that God will bless them. ¹⁵Be happy with those who are happy, and weep with those who weep. ¹⁶Live in harmony with each other. Don't be too proud to enjoy the company of ordinary people. And don't think you know it all!

12:3a Or *Because of the grace;* compare 1:5. 12:3b Or *by the faith God has given you;* or *by the standard of our God-given faith.* 12:10 Greek *with brotherly love.* 12:11 Or *but serve the Lord with a zealous spirit;* or *but let the Spirit excite you as you serve the Lord.*

12:3 This verse is a call to honesty and true humility. We are to take personal inventory of our life, making an honest assessment of both our strengths and weaknesses and measuring our value by our faith. This will teach us humility as we uncover our sins and faults. It will also help us develop a grateful attitude toward God as we discover the many gifts he has given us.

12:4-8 God has an important role for each of us, even though we may wonder how he could use us significantly. Our addiction may have decimated our resources and destroyed our relationships. We may feel useless, isolated, and alone. But we are all given special gifts that are needed by others. Paul mentioned the gift of encouraging others—something we in recovery are especially suited to do. Who could better help a person devastated by addiction than someone who has already been there? Part of recovery involves sharing our story of deliverance with others. It could mean the difference between life and death for someone in need. As we reach out to encourage others, our isolation will give way to fellowship.

12:9-21 God tells us to let love govern all our attitudes and actions; this certainly applies to the process of recovery. We are called to even love our enemies. We have all been wronged by others. God's love allows us to forgive them and seek reconciliation. All of us have hurt others. Love enables us to ask for their forgiveness and seek to make amends for the trouble and pain we have caused. Often we need to make a special effort to reach out to immediate family members— parents, siblings, children, spouse. Love in action is not easy; it demands that we swallow our pride and admit our wrongs to others. As painful as love may be, however, it is the only way to experience the joy of rebuilding our relationships and progressing in recovery.

13:1-7 Our lifestyle in recovery includes the way we relate to governmental authorities. Paul pointed out that government exists because God put it there. Therefore, we need to submit to the government as we would submit to God himself. Some of us may have suffered great abuse by people in authority over us. How could God want us to submit to authorities who do not act wisely or justly? Elsewhere in Scripture we find that there is a place for civil disobedience (see Acts 4:13-22). Sometimes we need to resist the injustices that are being done against us. We can do this by communicating with trustworthy people about the abuses we have suffered. We are called to support and obey authorities that seek to uphold justice. But when they stand in direct contradiction to God's will, we need to seek the support of others and try to change the situation.

13:8-10 Progress in recovery can take place only as we learn to love others. Love is not an emotion we feel; it is an attitude and outpouring of unselfish concern for others. If we love God and the people around us, we will treat others with respect. We would never steal from or harm them in any way to satisfy our own selfish desires. As we continue to take regular personal inventory, we can use love as the standard by which we judge our behavior. Do we act with the best interests of others in mind? If we measure all our actions against God's standard of love, we will experience great progress in recovery and in our relationships.

¹⁷Never pay back evil with more evil. Do things in such a way that everyone can see you are honorable. ¹⁸Do all that you can to live in peace with everyone.

¹⁹Dear friends, never take revenge. Leave that to the righteous anger of God. For the Scriptures say,

"I will take revenge;
I will pay them back,"*
    says the LORD.

²⁰Instead,

"If your enemies are hungry, feed them.
    If they are thirsty, give them something
        to drink.
In doing this, you will heap
    burning coals of shame on their
        heads."*

²¹Don't let evil conquer you, but conquer evil by doing good.

CHAPTER 13
Respect for Authority
Everyone must submit to governing authorities. For all authority comes from God, and those in positions of authority have been placed there by God. ²So anyone who rebels against authority is rebelling against what God has instituted, and they will be punished. ³For the authorities do not strike fear in people who are doing right, but in those who are doing wrong. Would you like to live without fear of the authorities? Do what is right, and they will honor you. ⁴The authorities are God's servants, sent for your good. But if you are doing wrong, of course you should be afraid, for they have the power to punish you. They are God's servants, sent for the very purpose of punishing those who do what is wrong. ⁵So you must submit to them, not only to avoid punishment, but also to keep a clear conscience.

⁶Pay your taxes, too, for these same reasons. For government workers need to be paid. They are serving God in what they do. ⁷Give to everyone what you owe them: Pay your taxes and government fees to those who collect them, and give respect and honor to those who are in authority.

Love Fulfills God's Requirements
⁸Owe nothing to anyone—except for your obligation to love one another. If you love your neighbor, you will fulfill the requirements of God's law. ⁹For the commandments

12:19 Deut 32:35. **12:20** Prov 25:21-22.

SELF-PERCEPTION

READ ROMANS 12:1-2

How many times have we wished that we could be someone else? Perhaps one reason we act out our addiction is that we hate ourself. Self-hatred is often associated with an addictive/compulsive personality. If we don't like who we are and feel helpless to change, we can be reassured in knowing that God has the power to change us dramatically.

The apostle Paul wrote: "I plead with you to give your bodies to God because of all he has done for you. Let them be a living and holy sacrifice—the kind he will find acceptable. This is truly the way to worship him. Don't copy the behavior and customs of this world, but let God transform you into a new person by changing the way you think. Then you will learn to know God's will for you, which is good and pleasing and perfect" (Romans 12:1-2).

Paul tells us to avoid being like the world around us. If we copy the behavior and customs of this world, we will head straight toward selfish ways and destructive dependencies. Our part is to turn our will and our life over to the care of God. As we trust and obey him, he will work changes in us and make us new people. God wants to change us from the inside out. As we are changed on the inside, we will begin to evidence those changes in our external attitudes and actions.

We all have great potential for change, but we cannot do it under our own power. As we yield our life and will to God, we can depend on him to renew our mind and heart. He will help us overcome our defects of character, transforming us from the inside out. *Turn to page 1463, 1 Corinthians 6.*

say, "You must not commit adultery. You must not murder. You must not steal. You must not covet."* These—and other such commandments—are summed up in this one commandment: "Love your neighbor as yourself."* ¹⁰Love does no wrong to others, so love fulfills the requirements of God's law.

¹¹This is all the more urgent, for you know how late it is; time is running out. Wake up, for our salvation is nearer now than when we first believed. ¹²The night is almost gone; the day of salvation will soon be here. So remove your dark deeds like dirty clothes, and put on the shining armor of right living. ¹³Because we belong to the day, we must live decent lives for all to see. Don't participate in the darkness of wild parties and drunkenness, or in sexual promiscuity and immoral living, or in quarreling and jealousy. ¹⁴Instead, clothe yourself with the presence of the Lord Jesus Christ. And don't let yourself think about ways to indulge your evil desires.

CHAPTER 14
The Danger of Criticism

Accept other believers who are weak in faith, and don't argue with them about what they think is right or wrong. ²For instance, one person believes it's all right to eat anything. But another believer with a sensitive conscience will eat only vegetables. ³Those who feel free to eat anything must not look down on those who don't. And those who don't eat certain foods must not condemn those who do, for God has accepted them. ⁴Who are you to condemn someone else's servants? Their own master will judge whether they stand or fall. And with the Lord's help, they will stand and receive his approval.

⁵In the same way, some think one day is more holy than another day, while others think every day is alike. You should each be fully convinced that whichever day you choose is acceptable. ⁶Those who worship the Lord on a special day do it to honor him. Those who eat any kind of food do so to honor the Lord, since they give thanks to God before eating. And those who refuse to eat certain foods also want to please the Lord and give thanks to God. ⁷For we don't live for ourselves or die for ourselves. ⁸If we live, it's to honor the Lord. And if we die, it's to honor the Lord. So whether we live or die, we belong to the Lord. ⁹Christ died and rose again for this very purpose—to be Lord both of the living and of the dead.

¹⁰So why do you condemn another believer*? Why do you look down on another believer? Remember, we will all stand before the judgment seat of God. ¹¹For the Scriptures say,

"'As surely as I live,' says the LORD,
'every knee will bend to me,
    and every tongue will declare allegiance
    to God.*'"

¹²Yes, each of us will give a personal account to God. ¹³So let's stop condemning each other. Decide instead to live in such a way that you will not cause another believer to stumble and fall.

¹⁴I know and am convinced on the authority of the Lord Jesus that no food, in and of itself, is wrong to eat. But if someone believes it is wrong, then for that person it is wrong. ¹⁵And if another believer is distressed by what

13:9a Exod 20:13-15, 17. 13:9b Lev 19:18. 14:10 Greek *your brother;* also in 14:10b, 13, 15, 21. 14:11 Or *declare praise for God.* Isa 49:18; 45:23 (Greek version).

13:12-14 When we turn our life over to God, we are given a new identity; we become children of the light. People who live in the light are awake—their eyes are open. They are not in the darkness of denial; they have the ability to see and admit the truth about themselves. One way to make sure we are walking in the light is to take regular moral inventory. This will help us shed our evil deeds and "live decent lives for all to see."

14:1-4 We may have a tendency to judge others who are still struggling in recovery, with one foot still in the old patterns of the past. We might even be tempted to show them how "strong" we are by participating in activities that would still lead them into destructive falls. Even if we have progressed in recovery to the point that certain circumstances no longer tempt us, we still need to be sensitive to the fact that our friends may be led astray by our activities. Our love for others will lead us to avoid activities that might lead to their downfall. The more mature we are, the more responsible we will be in responding to others in loving ways.

14:10-12 Paul reminds us that we are not to take inventory for others. Many of us find it easier to point out the failures of others than to look critically and honestly at our own life. But it isn't our primary responsibility to straighten out other people's lives. We must remember that all of us will be personally accountable before God for our actions. If we spend our time pointing a finger at others, we will never clean up our own act and progress in our own recovery.

you eat, you are not acting in love if you eat it. Don't let your eating ruin someone for whom Christ died. ¹⁶Then you will not be criticized for doing something you believe is good. ¹⁷For the Kingdom of God is not a matter of what we eat or drink, but of living a life of goodness and peace and joy in the Holy Spirit. ¹⁸If you serve Christ with this attitude, you will please God, and others will approve of you, too. ¹⁹So then, let us aim for harmony in the church and try to build each other up.

²⁰Don't tear apart the work of God over what you eat. Remember, all foods are acceptable, but it is wrong to eat something if it makes another person stumble. ²¹It is better not to eat meat or drink wine or do anything else if it might cause another believer to stumble.* ²²You may believe there's nothing wrong with what you are doing, but keep it between yourself and God. Blessed are those who don't feel guilty for doing something they have decided is right. ²³But if you have doubts about whether or not you should eat something, you are sinning if you go ahead and do it. For you are not following your convictions. If you do anything you believe is not right, you are sinning.*

CHAPTER 15
Living to Please Others
We who are strong must be considerate of those who are sensitive about things like this. We must not just please ourselves. ²We should help others do what is right and build them up in the Lord. ³For even Christ didn't live to please himself. As the Scriptures say, "The insults of those who insult you, O God, have fallen on me."* ⁴Such things were written in the Scriptures long ago to teach us. And the Scriptures give us hope and encour-

agement as we wait patiently for God's promises to be fulfilled.

⁵May God, who gives this patience and encouragement, help you live in complete harmony with each other, as is fitting for followers of Christ Jesus. ⁶Then all of you can join together with one voice, giving praise and glory to God, the Father of our Lord Jesus Christ.

⁷Therefore, accept each other just as Christ has accepted you so that God will be given glory. ⁸Remember that Christ came as a servant to the Jews* to show that God is true to the promises he made to their ancestors. ⁹He also came so that the Gentiles might give glory to God for his mercies to them. That is what the psalmist meant when he wrote:

"For this, I will praise you among the Gentiles;
I will sing praises to your name."*

¹⁰And in another place it is written,

"Rejoice with his people,
you Gentiles."*

¹¹And yet again,

"Praise the LORD, all you Gentiles.
Praise him, all you people of the earth."*

¹²And in another place Isaiah said,

"The heir to David's throne* will come,
and he will rule over the Gentiles.
They will place their hope on him."*

¹³I pray that God, the source of hope, will fill you completely with joy and peace because you trust in him. Then you will overflow with confident hope through the power of the Holy Spirit.

14:21 Some manuscripts read *to stumble or be offended or be weakened.* 14:23 Some manuscripts place the text of 16:25-27 here. 15:3 Greek *who insult you have fallen on me.* Ps 69:9. 15:8 Greek *servant of circumcision.* 15:9 Ps 18:49. 15:10 Deut 32:43. 15:11 Ps 117:1. 15:12a Greek *The root of Jesse.* David was the son of Jesse. 15:12b Isa 11:10 (Greek version).

14:22-23 In the process of recovery we sometimes are tempted to do things that are not necessarily wrong but could lead us toward a fall. We know such activities are dangerous, but it is hard to turn away, especially if our friends are involved. We need to learn that when we *feel* something is wrong for us, it *is* wrong for us. If we do it anyway, we are sinning. Many activities are wrong, purely and simply. But the activities or thoughts that are not specifically sinful are the ones we need to be especially careful of. If we have any doubts about something, we shouldn't do it. We must ask God for wisdom and the power to resist it.

15:1-6 Showing consideration to others is crucial for successful recovery. Our human relationships are second in importance only to our relationship with God. If we are not at peace with others, we will be at war within ourself. And that is a perfect recipe for relapse. We need to learn to delay our personal gratification for the sake of others. This will help us form healthy relationships with the significant people in our life, a necessity for progress in any recovery program. Such relationships will help us to find balance between meeting the needs of others and finding healthy ways to meet our own needs.

Paul's Reason for Writing

[14]I am fully convinced, my dear brothers and sisters,* that you are full of goodness. You know these things so well you can teach each other all about them. [15]Even so, I have been bold enough to write about some of these points, knowing that all you need is this reminder. For by God's grace, [16]I am a special messenger from Christ Jesus to you Gentiles. I bring you the Good News so that I might present you as an acceptable offering to God, made holy by the Holy Spirit. [17]So I have reason to be enthusiastic about all Christ Jesus has done through me in my service to God. [18]Yet I dare not boast about anything except what Christ has done through me, bringing the Gentiles to God by my message and by the way I worked among them. [19]They were convinced by the power of miraculous signs and wonders and by the power of God's Spirit.* In this way, I have fully presented the Good News of Christ from Jerusalem all the way to Illyricum.*

[20]My ambition has always been to preach the Good News where the name of Christ has never been heard, rather than where a church has already been started by someone else. [21]I have been following the plan spoken of in the Scriptures, where it says,

"Those who have never been told about
        him will see,
    and those who have never heard of him
        will understand."*

[22]In fact, my visit to you has been delayed so long because I have been preaching in these places.

Paul's Travel Plans

[23]But now I have finished my work in these regions, and after all these long years of waiting, I am eager to visit you. [24]I am planning to go to Spain, and when I do, I will stop off in Rome. And after I have enjoyed your fellowship for a little while, you can provide for my journey.

[25]But before I come, I must go to Jerusalem to take a gift to the believers* there. [26]For you see, the believers in Macedonia and Achaia* have eagerly taken up an offering for the poor among the believers in Jerusalem. [27]They were glad to do this because they feel they owe a real debt to them. Since the Gentiles received the spiritual blessings of the Good News from the believers in Jerusalem, they feel the least they can do in return is to help them financially. [28]As soon as I have delivered this money and completed this good deed of theirs, I will come to see you on my way to Spain. [29]And I am sure that when I come, Christ will richly bless our time together.

[30]Dear brothers and sisters, I urge you in the name of our Lord Jesus Christ to join in my struggle by praying to God for me. Do this because of your love for me, given to you by the Holy Spirit. [31]Pray that I will be rescued from those in Judea who refuse to obey God. Pray also that the believers there will be willing to accept the donation* I am taking to Jerusalem. [32]Then, by the will of God, I will be able to come to you with a joyful heart, and we will be an encouragement to each other.

[33]And now may God, who gives us his peace, be with you all. Amen.*

CHAPTER 16
Paul Greets His Friends

I commend to you our sister Phoebe, who is a deacon in the church in Cenchrea. [2]Welcome her in the Lord as one who is worthy of honor among God's people. Help her in whatever she needs, for she has been helpful to many, and especially to me.

[3]Give my greetings to Priscilla and Aquila, my co-workers in the ministry of Christ Jesus. [4]In fact, they once risked their lives for me. I am thankful to them, and so are all the Gentile churches. [5]Also give my greetings to the church that meets in their home.

Greet my dear friend Epenetus. He was the first person from the province of Asia to become a follower of Christ. [6]Give my greetings to Mary, who has worked so hard for your benefit. [7]Greet Andronicus and Junia,* my fellow Jews,* who were in prison with me. They are highly respected among the apostles and became followers of Christ before I did. [8]Greet Ampliatus, my dear friend in the Lord. [9]Greet Urbanus, our co-worker in Christ, and my dear friend Stachys.

[10]Greet Apelles, a good man whom Christ approves. And give my greetings to the believers from the household of Aristobulus.

15:14 Greek *brothers;* also in 15:30. 15:19a Other manuscripts read *the Spirit;* still others read *the Holy Spirit.*
15:19b *Illyricum* was a region northeast of Italy. 15:21 Isa 52:15 (Greek version). 15:25 Greek *God's holy people;* also in 15:26, 31. 15:26 *Macedonia* and *Achaia* were the northern and southern regions of Greece. 15:31 Greek *ministry;* other manuscripts read *the gift.* 15:33 Some manuscripts do not include *Amen.* One very early manuscript places 16:25-27 here. 16:7a *Junia* is a feminine name. Some late manuscripts accent the word so it reads *Junias,* a masculine name; still others read *Julia* (feminine). 16:7b Or *compatriots;* also in 16:21.

[11]Greet Herodion, my fellow Jew.* Greet the Lord's people from the household of Narcissus. [12]Give my greetings to Tryphena and Tryphosa, the Lord's workers, and to dear Persis, who has worked so hard for the Lord. [13]Greet Rufus, whom the Lord picked out to be his very own; and also his dear mother, who has been a mother to me.

[14]Give my greetings to Asyncritus, Phlegon, Hermes, Patrobas, Hermas, and the brothers and sisters* who meet with them. [15]Give my greetings to Philologus, Julia, Nereus and his sister, and to Olympas and all the believers* who meet with them. [16]Greet each other with a sacred kiss. All the churches of Christ send you their greetings.

Paul's Final Instructions

[17]And now I make one more appeal, my dear brothers and sisters. Watch out for people who cause divisions and upset people's faith by teaching things contrary to what you have been taught. Stay away from them. [18]Such people are not serving Christ our Lord; they are serving their own personal interests. By smooth talk and glowing words they deceive innocent people. [19]But every-

one knows that you are obedient to the Lord. This makes me very happy. I want you to be wise in doing right and to stay innocent of any wrong. [20]The God of peace will soon crush Satan under your feet. May the grace of our Lord Jesus* be with you.

[21]Timothy, my fellow worker, sends you his greetings, as do Lucius, Jason, and Sosipater, my fellow Jews.

[22]I, Tertius, the one writing this letter for Paul, send my greetings, too, as one of the Lord's followers.

[23]Gaius says hello to you. He is my host and also serves as host to the whole church. Erastus, the city treasurer, sends you his greetings, and so does our brother Quartus.*

[25]Now all glory to God, who is able to make you strong, just as my Good News says. This message about Jesus Christ has revealed his plan for you Gentiles, a plan kept secret from the beginning of time. [26]But now as the prophets* foretold and as the eternal God has commanded, this message is made known to all Gentiles everywhere, so that they too might believe and obey him. [27]All glory to the only wise God, through Jesus Christ, forever. Amen.*

16:11 Or *compatriot.* **16:14** Greek *brothers;* also in 16:17. **16:15** Greek *all of God's holy people.* **16:20** Some manuscripts read *Lord Jesus Christ.* **16:23** Some manuscripts add verse 24, *May the grace of our Lord Jesus Christ be with you all. Amen.* Still others add this sentence after verse 27. **16:26** Greek *the prophetic writings.* **16:25-27** Various manuscripts place the doxology (shown here as 16:25-27) after 14:23 or after 15:33 or after 16:23.

REFLECTIONS ON ROMANS

insights ABOUT THE POWER OF CHRIST'S RESURRECTION

In **Romans 6:2-11** Paul examined how we can receive new life through the death and resurrection of Jesus Christ. He traced the history of Jesus' life: (1) his earthly body subjected to death; (2) his death, burial, and resurrection; (3) his resurrection body that was no longer under the power of death. Next Paul showed how our own life can be parallel to that of Jesus: (1) we begin under the mastery of sin and death; (2) we identify with Jesus' death, burial, and resurrection; (3) we receive new life, with the power to overcome sin and death. God has the power to take a life headed for destruction and set it on the road to new life.

insights ABOUT OUR HELPLESSNESS

In **Romans 3:9-10** Paul summarized his earlier discussion by concluding that "all people . . . are under the power of sin." No one is exempt—we are all fallen and dysfunctional; we are all in need of salvation and recovery. If we pretend to be healthy and without sin, we only prove that we are in denial. Recovery can begin only after we have admitted this truth. When we recognize that we are broken and helpless and turn to God, he steps in and provides the power we need for recovery.

In **Romans 5:1-11** Paul used several phrases to describe our painful condition: "we were utterly helpless" (5:6); we were "sinners" (5:6, 8-9); and we were God's "enemies" (5:10). It was precisely when we were in this condition that God decided to solve our sin problem for us. He loved us so much that he sent his Son to die on the cross to set us free from the power of sin. We cannot be any worse than the way Paul described us here, so God's love and acceptance of us can never be negated by mistakes in our past! With a Savior like that, we can confidently turn our life over to him.

In **Romans 7:18-20** Paul recognized the power of sin in his life and admitted how helpless he was against its persistence and strength. As he admitted his powerlessness, he was starting down the lifelong road toward recovery from his illusion that he could be saved by doing all the right things. When we can admit how powerless we are over our dependency, we will have made a significant step toward recovery. Only then will we be ready to accept God's help; only with God's power will we be able to overcome the temptations we face.

insights ABOUT FAITH

In **Romans 4:1-3** Paul showed how Abraham was accepted by God and declared righteous because of his faith. As we look at Abraham in the book of Genesis, we find a man who was set apart for God. Despite his mistakes, he could be considered a person who had it all together. But Abraham had to come to God the same way we do—through faith. He did nothing to deserve the special promises that God gave him. In the same way, we can do nothing to deserve the promises of forgiveness and recovery that God offers us. No social status or good deed can make us deserving of God's gracious forgiveness; yet no failure is too great an obstacle for God's restoring power. When we entrust our life to God and believe that he can help us, God gives us the power and courage to move forward one step at a time.

insights ABOUT PRAYER

Prayer is listed in **Romans 8:26-28** as one of the ways we improve our conscious contact with God. Paul assures us that the indwelling Holy Spirit is at work within us as we pray. We are not left alone to work out our problems. As we entrust our life to God, he allows the events of our life, even the painful ones, for our good. He can turn even our sins and mistakes into the means for our growth and blessing.

insights ABOUT THE BENEFITS OF SUBMISSION TO GOD

In **Romans 12:1-2** we are told to offer our life to God as a living and holy sacrifice. We are exhorted to turn our life and will over to God so he can transform us into the godly person he wants us to be. We are called to follow God's program for our life, utilizing the power he offers. As we do this, we will become an example to others of what God's transforming power can do. And as we grow, we will discover the joy and meaning that can be experienced when we offer our life to God. When we sacrifice all we are and have to God, he will return what we gave up, multiplied many times over.

1 CORINTHIANS

THE BIG PICTURE

**A. THE CHURCH IN DENIAL
(1:1–6:20)**
1. Divisions: Infighting among
   the Believers (1:1–4:21)
2. Disorders: Serving Self before
   God (5:1–6:20)

**B. THE CHURCH IN RECOVERY
(7:1–16:24)**
1. Contentment: Being Happy
   Where We Are (7:1-40)
2. Instruction: Personal Worship
   (8:1–10:33)
3. Instruction: Public Worship
   (11:1–14:40)
4. Encouragement: Christ Is
   with Us (15:1–16:24)

The Greek city of Corinth was known for its corruption, immorality, and pagan religion. Following Christ in that setting meant leaving behind many of the practices accepted by the larger culture. This presented the new believers there with all kinds of temptations and problems.

Although the Corinthian believers had received new life in Christ, they had much to learn. It would take time for them to mature in their faith. In short, their intentions were fine, but they needed further instruction about following Christ. They needed to get a handle on God's perspectives concerning right and wrong. Paul wrote this letter to help them make progress—to give them advice about how to change.

The recovery process often requires a similar struggle against the surrounding environment. Though we determine to change, the world in which we live stays much the same. We live and work with the same people, go to many of the same places, and do many of the same things—all while trying to make radical changes in our life. The feelings of loneliness that result can make us as vulnerable as the Corinthian believers once were.

Despite the difficulties we face, God understands our struggle. That is why he has given us his Word, his power, and his people; they are all available to help us take one step at a time. This letter alone contains numerous insights for recovery. Through it we can learn how to separate ourself from our old way of life and open ourself to God's new standard. The transformation may be slow or even painful, but by God's grace and our commitment, it will happen.

THE BOTTOM LINE

PURPOSE: To encourage the believers living in Corinth to resolve their problems and honor God. AUTHOR: The apostle Paul. AUDIENCE: The church at Corinth, a city in Greece. DATE WRITTEN: Around A.D. 55, near the end of Paul's three-year stay in Ephesus. SETTING: Corinth was a large cosmopolitan city that teemed with idolatry and immorality. The church in Corinth was fairly new and made up primarily of non-Jewish (Gentile) believers. KEY VERSE: "But whatever I am now, it is all because God poured out his special favor on me—and not without results. For I have worked harder than any of the other apostles; yet it was not I but God who was working through me by his grace" (15:10). KEY PEOPLE AND RELATIONSHIPS: Paul with Timothy, Chloe's household, and the Corinthian believers.

RECOVERY THEMES

Jesus Is the Center of Recovery: The believers in Corinth show us what happens when we take our eyes off Jesus Christ. Though they were followers of Christ, they identified themselves primarily with their various teachers. This caused unnecessary divisions among them and kept them from growing spiritually. While the support and advice of others are important, our Savior is Jesus Christ. He is the center of all our efforts; we must focus on him. People and recovery techniques are his tools, not ours.

Freedom with Loving Restraint: The new believers in Corinth had to make a clean break with their past. Some of these believers were quite mature and were no longer bothered by the temptations that had plagued them before. But others were not so secure. Paul therefore instructed the more mature ones not to flaunt their freedom around those who still struggled. Successful recovery or spiritual maturity doesn't give us license to be inconsiderate or insensitive to others. We can support one another by being careful how we use our freedom. We will always have this responsibility to look out for one another.

Life Is to Be Enjoyed Responsibly: The believers in Corinth lived in a very immoral, pleasure-seeking society. The standards of conduct that God had for them were quite different from what they were used to in their culture. But if those believers thought those standards seemed too restrictive, they were mistaken. Longing for "freedom" from God's laws is like longing for the "fun" of being an alcoholic. It is like wanting to be trapped in a life of addiction, compulsion, or other destructive behaviors, reasoning that turning our life over to God would keep us from having fun. On the contrary, God challenges us to live an uncompromising life because that is the way to enjoy life at its fullest. The same is true for us in recovery—we are discovering what life was meant to be!

The Invitation to Love: One of the most beautiful passages on love ever written is found in chapter 13 of this letter to the Corinthians. Paul points out that love is more than an emotion; it is selfless action. If we love, then we will act in selfless ways. When we don't feel loving or don't feel loved, 1 Corinthians 13 is a wonderful reminder of how God loves us and how we can show love to others.

CHAPTER 1
Greetings from Paul

This letter is from Paul, chosen by the will of God to be an apostle of Christ Jesus, and from our brother Sosthenes.

²I am writing to God's church in Corinth,* to you who have been called by God to be his own holy people. He made you holy by means of Christ Jesus,* just as he did for all people everywhere who call on the name of our Lord Jesus Christ, their Lord and ours.

³May God our Father and the Lord Jesus Christ give you grace and peace.

Paul Gives Thanks to God

⁴I always thank my God for you and for the gracious gifts he has given you, now that you belong to Christ Jesus. ⁵Through him, God has enriched your church in every way— with all of your eloquent words and all of your knowledge. ⁶This confirms that what I told you about Christ is true. ⁷Now you have every spiritual gift you need as you eagerly wait for the return of our Lord Jesus Christ. ⁸He will keep you strong to the end so that you will be free from all blame on the day when our Lord Jesus Christ returns. ⁹God will

1:2a *Corinth* was the capital city of Achaia, the southern region of the Greek peninsula. 1:2b Or *because you belong to Christ Jesus.*

1:2 Corinth was a giant cultural melting pot with a great diversity of ethnic groups, religions, intellectual perspectives, and moral standards. It had a reputation for being fiercely independent and decadent. Idolatry flourished; more than a dozen pagan temples at one time had employed at least a thousand religious prostitutes. The new believers in Corinth had to deal with many deep-rooted habits and attitudes as they sought to nurture their new lives in Christ. Temptations of all kinds abounded throughout the city. Corinth was not unlike our world today. The apostle Paul's advice to these early believers will touch on many of the issues we face today.
1:4-9 Although there were problems among the Corinthian believers, Paul began his letter to them on a positive note. He understood that confronting others about their failures is more effective when we approach them diplomatically. We need to gain a hearing by recognizing the good things in the lives of those we need to confront. In this way, we show that we are concerned about them and value them as people. Our intervention will be effective only when we first show that we love the people we want to help.

do this, for he is faithful to do what he says, and he has invited you into partnership with his Son, Jesus Christ our Lord.

Divisions in the Church

[10]I appeal to you, dear brothers and sisters,* by the authority of our Lord Jesus Christ, to live in harmony with each other. Let there be no divisions in the church. Rather, be of one mind, united in thought and purpose. [11]For some members of Chloe's household have told me about your quarrels, my dear brothers and sisters. [12]Some of you are saying, "I am a follower of Paul." Others are saying, "I follow Apollos," or "I follow Peter,*" or "I follow only Christ."

[13]Has Christ been divided into factions? Was I, Paul, crucified for you? Were any of you baptized in the name of Paul? Of course not! [14]I thank God that I did not baptize any of you except Crispus and Gaius, [15]for now no one can say they were baptized in my name. [16](Oh yes, I also baptized the household of Stephanas, but I don't remember baptizing anyone else.) [17]For Christ didn't send me to baptize, but to preach the Good News—and not with clever speech, for fear that the cross of Christ would lose its power.

The Wisdom of God

[18]The message of the cross is foolish to those who are headed for destruction! But we who are being saved know it is the very power of God. [19]As the Scriptures say,

"I will destroy the wisdom of
the wise
and discard the intelligence of the
intelligent."*

[20]So where does this leave the philosophers, the scholars, and the world's brilliant debaters? God has made the wisdom of this world look foolish. [21]Since God in his wisdom saw to it that the world would never know him through human wisdom, he has used our foolish preaching to save those who believe. [22]It is foolish to the Jews, who ask for signs from heaven. And it is foolish to the Greeks, who seek human wisdom. [23]So when we preach that Christ was crucified, the Jews are offended and the Gentiles say it's all nonsense.

[24]But to those called by God to salvation, both Jews and Gentiles,* Christ is the power of God and the wisdom of God. [25]This foolish plan of God is wiser than the wisest of human plans, and God's weakness is stronger than the greatest of human strength.

[26]Remember, dear brothers and sisters, that few of you were wise in the world's eyes or powerful or wealthy* when God called you. [27]Instead, God chose things the world considers foolish in order to shame those who think they are wise. And he chose things that are powerless to shame those who are powerful. [28]God chose things despised by the world,* things counted as nothing at all, and used them to bring to nothing what the world considers important. [29]As a result, no one can ever boast in the presence of God.

[30]God has united you with Christ Jesus. For our benefit God made him to be wisdom itself. Christ made us right with God; he made us pure and holy, and he freus from sin. [31]Therefore, as the Scriptures say, "If you want to boast, boast only about the LORD."*

1:10 Greek *brothers;* also in 1:11, 26. 1:12 Greek *Cephas.* 1:19 Isa 29:14. 1:24 Greek *and Greeks.* 1:26 Or *high born.* 1:28 Or *God chose those who are low born.* 1:31 Jer 9:24.

1:12 The Corinthian believers had begun to elevate various leaders to unhealthy positions in their lives. They were attributing power and wisdom to these people that no one but God could legitimately claim. This is a form of idolatry—a sin God forbids (see Exodus 20:3). All too often we give people, perhaps religious leaders or the leaders of recovery movements, positions of gods in our life. We believe everything they say and are willing to do anything they ask us to do. This is dangerous. We must remember that all people are powerless—the only one worthy of worship is Christ himself. We must measure everything we hear against the eternal truth of God's Word.
1:18-19 Some Corinthian believers followed the human wisdom of the day, which called the idea of salvation in Christ into question. It seemed too simple! How could God forgive us through what Christ did on the cross? Surely we need to do something special or know something special to be saved! Paul made it clear that we need nothing but a willing heart to receive God's power and forgiveness. We have no power or ability that can overcome the power of sin in our life. In fact, a life of self-sufficiency is ultimately self-destructive. When we turn our life over to God, we accept his way—the way of the cross. Only then can we experience God's power.

CHAPTER 2
Paul's Message of Wisdom

When I first came to you, dear brothers and sisters,* I didn't use lofty words and impressive wisdom to tell you God's secret plan.* ²For I decided that while I was with you I would forget everything except Jesus Christ, the one who was crucified. ³I came to you in weakness—timid and trembling. ⁴And my message and my preaching were very plain. Rather than using clever and persuasive speeches, I relied only on the power of the Holy Spirit. ⁵I did this so you would trust not in human wisdom but in the power of God.

⁶Yet when I am among mature believers, I do speak with words of wisdom, but not the kind of wisdom that belongs to this world or to the rulers of this world, who are soon forgotten. ⁷No, the wisdom we speak of is the mystery of God*—his plan that was previously hidden, even though he made it for our ultimate glory before the world began. ⁸But the rulers of this world have not understood it; if they had, they would not have crucified our glorious Lord. ⁹That is what the Scriptures mean when they say,

"No eye has seen, no ear has heard,
    and no mind has imagined
what God has prepared
    for those who love him."*

¹⁰But* it was to us that God revealed these things by his Spirit. For his Spirit searches out everything and shows us God's deep secrets. ¹¹No one can know a person's thoughts except that person's own spirit, and no one can know God's thoughts except God's own Spirit. ¹²And we have received God's Spirit (not the world's spirit), so we can know the wonderful things God has freely given us.

¹³When we tell you these things, we do not use words that come from human wisdom. Instead, we speak words given to us by the Spirit, using the Spirit's words to explain spiritual truths.* ¹⁴But people who aren't spiritual* can't receive these truths from God's Spirit. It all sounds foolish to them and they can't understand it, for only those who are spiritual can understand what the Spirit means. ¹⁵Those who are spiritual can evaluate all things, but they themselves cannot be evaluated by others. ¹⁶For,

"Who can know the LORD's thoughts?
    Who knows enough to teach him?"*

But we understand these things, for we have the mind of Christ.

CHAPTER 3
Paul and Apollos, Servants of Christ

Dear brothers and sisters,* when I was with you I couldn't talk to you as I would to spiritual people.* I had to talk as though you be-

---

2:1a Greek *brothers.* 2:1b Greek *God's mystery;* other manuscripts read *God's testimony.* 2:7 Greek *But we speak God's wisdom in a mystery.* 2:9 Isa 64:4. 2:10 Some manuscripts read *For.* 2:13 Or *explaining spiritual truths in spiritual language,* or *explaining spiritual truths to spiritual people.* 2:14 Or *who don't have the Spirit;* or *who have only physical life.* 2:16 Isa 40:13 (Greek version). 3:1a Greek *Brothers.* 3:1b Or *to people who have the Spirit.*

2:1-5 Many times when we seek to help others, we overwhelm them with complicated theories and instructions. Paul realized that doing this would only confuse the Corinthians, making them think that salvation was dependent on some kind of special wisdom or knowledge. So he brought them the plain, simple message of the gospel: There is nothing we can do to save ourself, for God has done everything necessary for our deliverance. As we share our story of deliverance with others, we need to keep things simple and trust the power of the Holy Spirit to work in their lives.
2:7 God has had a good plan for us from the beginning of time. If we allow him to work in our life, that plan will come about. No matter how badly we have sinned, God can still turn things around so they work out according to his will. Our part is to entrust our life to him and seek to follow his will as he reveals it to us. No matter what we have done in the past, God still chooses to love us and to work his restoration within us.
2:9-10 When our life is unmanageable and we feel as if we have lost direction, we often blame God or feel that somehow he is making things worse. Paul reminded the Corinthians that God had wonderful things planned for them, things even more wonderful than they could imagine. This message is for us, too. If we turn our life and will over to God, he can build a new life for us that is beyond our wildest dreams.
2:14-15 People who refuse to turn their life over to the care of God cannot understand God's truth or his plan. That's why recovery begins not with understanding but with a decision to follow God. Prior to that decision, God's way may seem like madness. Only when we face the fact that our life is insane can we open ourself to God and his good plan for us.
3:1-4 Part of maturing is realizing that following our own desires leads down a dead-end street. We remain "infants" as long as we try to do things our own way. Maturity occurs only as we

longed to this world or as though you were infants in Christ. [2]I had to feed you with milk, not with solid food, because you weren't ready for anything stronger. And you still aren't ready, [3]for you are still controlled by your sinful nature. You are jealous of one another and quarrel with each other. Doesn't that prove you are controlled by your sinful nature? Aren't you living like people of the world? [4]When one of you says, "I am a follower of Paul," and another says, "I follow Apollos," aren't you acting just like people of the world?

[5]After all, who is Apollos? Who is Paul? We are only God's servants through whom you believed the Good News. Each of us did the work the Lord gave us. [6]I planted the seed in your hearts, and Apollos watered it, but it was God who made it grow. [7]It's not important who does the planting, or who does the watering. What's important is that God makes the seed grow. [8]The one who plants and the one who waters work together with the same purpose. And both will be rewarded for their own hard work. [9]For we are both God's workers. And you are God's field. You are God's building.

[10]Because of God's grace to me, I have laid the foundation like an expert builder. Now others are building on it. But whoever is building on this foundation must be very careful. [11]For no one can lay any foundation other than the one we already have—Jesus Christ.

[12]Anyone who builds on that foundation may use a variety of materials—gold, silver, jewels, wood, hay, or straw. [13]But on the judgment day, fire will reveal what kind of work each builder has done. The fire will show if a person's work has any value. [14]If the work survives, that builder will receive a reward. [15]But if the work is burned up, the builder will suffer great loss. The builder will be saved, but like someone barely escaping through a wall of flames.

[16]Don't you realize that all of you together are the temple of God and that the Spirit of God lives in* you? [17]God will destroy anyone who destroys this temple. For God's temple is holy, and you are that temple.

[18]Stop deceiving yourselves. If you think you are wise by this world's standards, you need to become a fool to be truly wise. [19]For the wisdom of this world is foolishness to God. As the Scriptures say,

"He traps the wise
 in the snare of their own
  cleverness."*

[20]And again,

"The LORD knows the thoughts of the
  wise;
 he knows they are worthless."*

3:16 Or *among.* 3:19 Job 5:13. 3:20 Ps 94:11.

---

begin to follow God's will for our life. Then we will consider what God wants and what others need before we act. To do this we have to give the control of our life and will over to God. It may also mean that we have to delay self-gratification at times for the sake of others. This is not easy, but when we do it, we will experience the meaningful life that God wants for each of us.

3:5-6 As we progress in recovery, we are to reach out to others. As we tell them about our deliverance, hoping to help them turn their lives around, these verses should encourage us. Even when the message doesn't seem to be getting through, we can leave the results in God's hands. Sometimes people respond to our story immediately and enter recovery. At other times our words are only seeds that over time will grow and lead someone to be changed by God's power. Perhaps we are just one of many people God will use to change someone's life. One thing is sure: If we speak out, God will use us to change lives.

3:13-15 Many of us struggle with denial because the truth is so painful. We avoid the truth about our sins so we won't have to make difficult changes in our life. But no matter how much we hide from our mistakes, in time they will come back to haunt us. Allowing our dependency to continue unchecked will lead to painful consequences. Here we are reminded that those consequences continue into eternity. A day of reckoning will come! Have we put our life in God's hands? As we turn our life over to him, he will help us build on a solid foundation. When the day of reckoning arrives, we will still be standing.

3:18-20 It is possible for intelligence to hinder progress in recovery. As we analyze the steps we are asked to take, we may find them somewhat foolish or demeaning. The truth is, sometimes following God's plan will not make perfect sense to us. We may wonder how entrusting our life to God can change anything. We might even find that following God's will is embarrassing at times. True understanding often happens only as we take steps to obey God's program for healing. We may be better off throwing aside our need to analyze and understand so that we can experience God's healing power through simple faith and obedience.

²¹So don't boast about following a particular human leader. For everything belongs to you—²²whether Paul or Apollos or Peter,* or the world, or life and death, or the present and the future. Everything belongs to you, ²³and you belong to Christ, and Christ belongs to God.

CHAPTER 4
Paul's Relationship with the Corinthians
So look at Apollos and me as mere servants of Christ who have been put in charge of explaining God's mysteries. ²Now, a person who is put in charge as a manager must be faithful. ³As for me, it matters very little how I might be evaluated by you or by any human authority. I don't even trust my own judgment on this point. ⁴My conscience is clear, but that doesn't prove I'm right. It is the Lord himself who will examine me and decide.

⁵So don't make judgments about anyone ahead of time—before the Lord returns. For he will bring our darkest secrets to light and will reveal our private motives. Then God will give to each one whatever praise is due.

⁶Dear brothers and sisters,* I have used Apollos and myself to illustrate what I've been saying. If you pay attention to what I have quoted from the Scriptures,* you won't be proud of one of your leaders at the expense of another. ⁷For what gives you the right to make such a judgment? What do you have that God hasn't given you? And if everything you have is from God, why boast as though it were not a gift?

⁸You think you already have everything you need. You think you are already rich. You have begun to reign in God's kingdom without us! I wish you really were reigning already, for then we would be reigning with you. ⁹Instead, I sometimes think God has put us apostles on display, like prisoners of war at the end of a victor's parade, condemned to die. We have become a spectacle to the entire world—to people and angels alike.

¹⁰Our dedication to Christ makes us look like fools, but you claim to be so wise in Christ! We are weak, but you are so powerful! You are honored, but we are ridiculed. ¹¹Even now we go hungry and thirsty, and we don't have enough clothes to keep warm. We are often beaten and have no home. ¹²We work wearily with our own hands to earn our living. We bless those who curse us. We are patient with those who abuse us. ¹³We appeal gently when evil things are said about us. Yet we are treated like the world's garbage, like everybody's trash—right up to the present moment.

¹⁴I am not writing these things to shame you, but to warn you as my beloved children. ¹⁵For even if you had ten thousand others to teach you about Christ, you have only one spiritual father. For I became your father in Christ Jesus when I preached the Good News to you. ¹⁶So I urge you to imitate me.

¹⁷That's why I have sent Timothy, my beloved and faithful child in the Lord. He will remind you of how I follow Christ Jesus, just as I teach in all the churches wherever I go.

¹⁸Some of you have become arrogant, thinking I will not visit you again. ¹⁹But I will come—and soon—if the Lord lets me, and then I'll find out whether these arrogant people just give pretentious speeches or whether they really have God's power. ²⁰For the Kingdom of God is not just a lot of talk; it is living by God's power. ²¹Which do you choose? Should I come with a rod to punish you, or should I come with love and a gentle spirit?

3:22 Greek *Cephas*. **4:6a** Greek *Brothers*. **4:6b** Or *If you learn not to go beyond "what is written."*

4:6-13 How easy it is to become puffed up about our success and forget that pride leads to a fall. The Corinthian believers were very self-sufficient, looking down on Paul and his ministry among them. Their prideful attitudes led them away from Paul's teachings about Christ, a dangerous thing for anyone living in a diverse religious environment like theirs. It is just as dangerous for us to become proud about our success in recovery. We forget that it was God's power that delivered us and that we continue to need his help. If we allow pride to get a foothold in our life, we will discover that self-sufficiency leads to relapse.

4:17 Paul sent Timothy to remind the Corinthian believers of what Paul had taught them. The apostle realized that they needed someone to hold them accountable to the truth they had been taught and to encourage them to persevere in their faith. One of the best ways to protect ourself from self-sufficiency is to be accountable to others. Mentors and sponsors are there to help us remember what works in recovery. They are also there to help us learn how to develop faithfulness in our life, an essential part of our spiritual growth.

CHAPTER 5
Paul Condemns Spiritual Pride

I can hardly believe the report about the sexual immorality going on among you—something that even pagans don't do. I am told that a man in your church is living in sin with his stepmother.* ²You are so proud of yourselves, but you should be mourning in sorrow and shame. And you should remove this man from your fellowship.

³Even though I am not with you in person, I am with you in the Spirit.* And as though I were there, I have already passed judgment on this man ⁴in the name of the Lord Jesus. You must call a meeting of the church.* I will be present with you in spirit, and so will the power of our Lord Jesus. ⁵Then you must throw this man out and hand him over to Satan so that his sinful nature will be destroyed* and he himself * will be saved on the day the Lord* returns.

⁶Your boasting about this is terrible. Don't you realize that this sin is like a little yeast that spreads through the whole batch of dough? ⁷Get rid of the old "yeast" by removing this wicked person from among you. Then you will be like a fresh batch of dough made without yeast, which is what you really are. Christ, our Passover Lamb, has been sacrificed for us.* ⁸So let us celebrate the festival, not with the old bread* of wickedness and evil, but with the new bread* of sincerity and truth.

⁹When I wrote to you before, I told you not to associate with people who indulge in sexual sin. ¹⁰But I wasn't talking about unbelievers who indulge in sexual sin, or are greedy, or cheat people, or worship idols. You would have to leave this world to avoid people like that. ¹¹I meant that you are not to associate with anyone who claims to be a believer* yet indulges in sexual sin, or is greedy, or worships idols, or is abusive, or is a drunkard, or cheats people. Don't even eat with such people.

¹²It isn't my responsibility to judge outsiders, but it certainly is your responsibility to judge those inside the church who are sinning. ¹³God will judge those on the outside; but as the Scriptures say, "You must remove the evil person from among you."*

CHAPTER 6
Avoiding Lawsuits with Christians

When one of you has a dispute with another believer, how dare you file a lawsuit

---

5:1 Greek *his father's wife.* 5:3 Or *in spirit.* 5:4 Or *In the name of the Lord Jesus, you must call a meeting of the church.*
5:5a Or *so that his body will be destroyed;* Greek reads *for the destruction of the flesh.* 5:5b Greek *and the spirit.*
5:5c Other manuscripts read *the Lord Jesus;* still others read *our Lord Jesus Christ.* 5:7 Greek *has been sacrificed.*
5:8a Greek *not with old leaven.* 5:8b Greek *but with unleavened [bread].* 5:11 Greek *a brother.* 5:13 Deut 17:7.

5:1-5 We face many of the same forms of sexual immorality that the Corinthians faced. Like the believers in Corinth, we tend to put on a blindfold and tell ourself that everything is all right. Our denial of illicit sexual activity and sexual abuse, however, only builds barriers between us and others. In time we even grow distant from God. Such denial allows the problems in our churches and communities to fester until individuals and families are torn apart. We need to open our eyes to the problems around us and confront them together as a community, as Paul advised the Corinthians to do.

5:6-8 Paul called the Corinthian believers to remove the unrepentant sinner from their fellowship. If they didn't, his destructive activities would eat away at their church fellowship like a cancer. This principle is important in recovery. As we begin our program, we need to give up the relationships and activities that are likely to lead to our downfall. When Paul called the Corinthians to excommunicate this unrepentant sinner, he also instructed them to take part in wholesome activities. Likewise, when we give up our destructive activities and relationships, we must replace them with wholesome activities and godly people who will encourage us in the recovery process.

5:9-13 Paul warned his people to avoid close relationships with other believers who were in denial about their sins. But they were not to totally isolate themselves from unbelievers either. They were still to share the Good News with people who needed to hear the message. We also need to avoid close relationships with people who will drag us down and try to hinder our recovery. Yet as we experience God's power in our life, we need to share this news with others. Our story of deliverance may save the lives of others in bondage. As we share the message, not only will we be a source of hope to others, but we will also find renewed strength to continue our own recovery.

6:1-6 Taking someone to court, as painful as it may be, is often the easy way out of a conflict. Instead of working our problems out, we hand them over to an impartial judge. Dealing with conflict in such an indirect way usually leads to separation rather than reconciliation. Paul warned the Corinthian believers not to go to unbelieving judges to settle their disputes. If God's power is at work within us, we can use the wisdom and guidance of the Holy Spirit to settle our conflicts. We need to keep this in mind as we seek to make amends with those we have harmed.

and ask a secular court to decide the matter instead of taking it to other believers*! [2]Don't you realize that someday we believers will judge the world? And since you are going to judge the world, can't you decide even these little things among yourselves? [3]Don't you realize that we will judge angels? So you should surely be able to resolve ordinary disputes in this life. [4]If you have legal disputes about such matters, why go to outside judges who are not respected by the church? [5]I am saying this to shame you. Isn't there anyone in all the church who is wise enough to decide these issues? [6]But instead, one believer* sues another—right in front of unbelievers!

[7]Even to have such lawsuits with one another is a defeat for you. Why not just accept the injustice and leave it at that? Why not let yourselves be cheated? [8]Instead, you yourselves are the ones who do wrong and cheat even your fellow believers.*

[9]Don't you realize that those who do wrong will not inherit the Kingdom of God? Don't fool yourselves. Those who indulge in sexual sin, or who worship idols, or commit adultery, or are male prostitutes, or practice homosexuality, [10]or are thieves, or greedy people, or drunkards, or are abusive, or cheat people—none of these will inherit the Kingdom of God. [11]Some of you were once like that. But you were cleansed; you were made holy; you were made right with God by calling on the name of the Lord Jesus Christ and by the Spirit of our God.

Avoiding Sexual Sin

[12]You say, "I am allowed to do anything"—but not everything is good for you. And even though "I am allowed to do anything," I must not become a slave to anything. [13]You say, "Food was made for the stomach, and the stomach for food." (This is true, though someday God will do away with both of them.) But you can't say that our bodies were made for sexual immorality. They were made for the Lord, and the Lord cares about our bodies. [14]And God will raise us from the dead by his power, just as he raised our Lord from the dead.

[15]Don't you realize that your bodies are actually parts of Christ? Should a man take his body, which is part of Christ, and join it to a prostitute? Never! [16]And don't you realize that if a man joins himself to a prostitute, he becomes one body with her? For the Scriptures say, "The two are united into one."* [17]But the person who is joined to the Lord is one spirit with him.

[18]Run from sexual sin! No other sin so

6:1 Greek *God's holy people;* also in 6:2. 6:6 Greek *one brother.* 6:8 Greek *even the brothers.* 6:16 Gen 2:24.

6:18-20 Sexual sin affects us like no other sin. It isn't that it is the heaviest on some imaginary sin scale, but its effects are broad and devastating. In sexual sin, we sin not only against ourself but also against other people and against God. Our body is the dwelling place of God's Holy Spirit, and it belongs to God. This is a convincing reason for taking care of our body and seeking a new life in recovery.

7:2-5 Marriage is the God-given place for sexual expression and fulfillment. Our body doesn't belong to us; it belongs to God. But here Paul is saying that our body also belongs to our spouse. If we seek sexual fulfillment outside of marriage, we will be trapped by selfish pleasure seeking. Only in marriage can our sexuality be acted out with concern for and commitment to the other person involved. If we belong to God and to our spouse, we have the potential to act in ways to bring them great joy. Our challenge is to not seek only our personal gratification. As we keep our sexuality within the bounds of marriage, we experience the joy that comes from living faithfully with another person before God.

7:8-9 If we are single, we may feel that recovery would be easier if we had the help of a spouse. If we are married, we may think we could focus more on recovery if we were unmarried. Whether we are single or married, there are difficulties that we must deal with. When we wish we were in a different situation, we are usually wanting to avoid the responsibilities of our present situation. We should seek ways to improve the situation we are in rather than abandoning it for something else. Abandoning relationships or desperately grasping at new ones will never solve our problems.

7:10-15 Many of us have been hurt by divorce, either as participants or as children of divorced parents. Paul firmly reminded his readers of God's command to avoid divorce at all cost. Yet he recognized that there are situations in which divorce is a legitimate option. God wants us to live in harmony with one another. When we are not experiencing harmony, we need to examine our life to see where we might need to change. If, after making appropriate changes, we still face significant problems, we may need to help our spouse through a similar process. Often a marriage counselor can facilitate this process. Divorce is an option only when one of the partners refuses to remain faithful to the marriage commitment.

clearly affects the body as this one does. For sexual immorality is a sin against your own body. [19]Don't you realize that your body is the temple of the Holy Spirit, who lives in you and was given to you by God? You do not belong to yourself, [20]for God bought you with a high price. So you must honor God with your body.

CHAPTER 7
Instruction on Marriage

Now regarding the questions you asked in your letter. Yes, it is good to abstain from sexual relations.* [2]But because there is so much sexual immorality, each man should have his own wife, and each woman should have her own husband.

[3]The husband should fulfill his wife's sexual needs, and the wife should fulfill her husband's needs. [4]The wife gives authority over her body to her husband, and the husband gives authority over his body to his wife.

[5]Do not deprive each other of sexual relations, unless you both agree to refrain from sexual intimacy for a limited time so you can give yourselves more completely to prayer. Afterward, you should come together again so that Satan won't be able to tempt you because of your lack of self-control. [6]I say this as a concession, not as a command. [7]But I wish everyone were single, just as I am. Yet each person has a special gift from God, of one kind or another.

[8]So I say to those who aren't married and to widows—it's better to stay unmarried, just as I am. [9]But if they can't control themselves, they should go ahead and marry. It's better to marry than to burn with lust.

[10]But for those who are married, I have a command that comes not from me, but from the Lord.* A wife must not leave her husband. [11]But if she does leave him, let her remain single or else be reconciled to him. And the husband must not leave his wife.

[12]Now, I will speak to the rest of you, though I do not have a direct command from the Lord. If a fellow believer* has a wife who is not a believer and she is willing to continue living with him, he must not leave her. [13]And if a believing woman has a husband who is not a believer and he is willing to continue living with her, she must not leave him. [14]For the believing wife brings holiness to her marriage, and the believing husband* brings holiness to his marriage.

7:1 Or to live a celibate life; Greek reads It is good for a man not to touch a woman. 7:10 See Matt 5:32; 19:9; Mark 10:11-12; Luke 16:18. 7:12 Greek a brother. 7:14 Greek the brother.

DELAYED GRATIFICATION

READ 1 CORINTHIANS 6:1-13
Our appetites can overtake and enslave us. Perfectly good activities can get us into trouble when we fail to practice them in moderation. Or there may be times when we don't feed our appetites in balanced ways. Then we become so starved that we fall to the temptation of our addiction at the first opportunity.

This happened to Esau. One day he came home so hungry that he promised his birthright to his younger brother in exchange for a bowl of porridge. We are warned: "Make sure that no one is immoral or godless like Esau, who traded his birthright as the firstborn son for a single meal. You know that afterward, when he wanted his father's blessing, he was rejected. It was too late for repentance, even though he begged with bitter tears" (Hebrews 12:16-17). The apostle Paul wrote: "You say, 'I am allowed to do anything'—but not everything is good for you. And even though 'I am allowed to do anything,' I must not become a slave to anything" (1 Corinthians 6:12).

We need to satisfy our appetites in appropriate ways so we don't become starved and thus more susceptible to temptation. There may be some good things that have such control over us that it's best to avoid them altogether. If we allow the demands of our appetites to become overpowering, we risk losing things (or people) that we might never get back. *Turn to page 1471, 1 Corinthians 13.*

Otherwise, your children would not be holy, but now they are holy. [15](But if the husband or wife who isn't a believer insists on leaving, let them go. In such cases the believing husband or wife* is no longer bound to the other, for God has called you* to live in peace.) [16]Don't you wives realize that your husbands might be saved because of you? And don't you husbands realize that your wives might be saved because of you?

[17]Each of you should continue to live in whatever situation the Lord has placed you, and remain as you were when God first called you. This is my rule for all the churches. [18]For instance, a man who was circumcised before he became a believer should not try to reverse it. And the man who was uncircumcised when he became a believer should not be circumcised now. [19]For it makes no difference whether or not a man has been circumcised. The important thing is to keep God's commandments.

[20]Yes, each of you should remain as you were when God called you. [21]Are you a slave? Don't let that worry you—but if you get a chance to be free, take it. [22]And remember, if you were a slave when the Lord called you, you are now free in the Lord. And if you were free when the Lord called you, you are now a slave of Christ. [23]God paid a high price for you, so don't be enslaved by the world.* [24]Each of you, dear brothers and sisters,* should remain as you were when God first called you.

[25]Now regarding your question about the young women who are not yet married. I do not have a command from the Lord for them. But the Lord in his mercy has given me wisdom that can be trusted, and I will share it with you. [26]Because of the present crisis,* I think it is best to remain as you are. [27]If you have a wife, do not seek to end the marriage. If you do not have a wife, do not seek to get married. [28]But if you do get married, it is not a sin. And if a young woman gets married, it is not a sin. However, those who get married at this time will have troubles, and I am trying to spare you those problems.

[29]But let me say this, dear brothers and sisters: The time that remains is very short. So from now on, those with wives should not focus only on their marriage. [30]Those who weep or who rejoice or who buy things should not be absorbed by their weeping or their joy or their possessions. [31]Those who use the things of the world should not become attached to them. For this world as we know it will soon pass away.

[32]I want you to be free from the concerns of this life. An unmarried man can spend his time doing the Lord's work and thinking how to please him. [33]But a married man has to think about his earthly responsibilities and how to please his wife. [34]His interests are divided. In the same way, a woman who is no longer married or has never been married can be devoted to the Lord and holy in body and in spirit. But a married woman has to think about her earthly responsibilities and how to please her husband. [35]I am saying this for your benefit, not to place restrictions on you. I want you to do whatever will help you serve the Lord best, with as few distractions as possible.

[36]But if a man thinks that he's treating his fiancée improperly and will inevitably give in to his passion, let him marry her as he wishes. It is not a sin. [37]But if he has decided firmly not to marry and there is no urgency and he can control his passion, he does well not to marry. [38]So the person who marries his fiancée does well, and the person who doesn't marry does even better.

[39]A wife is bound to her husband as long as he lives. If her husband dies, she is free to marry anyone she wishes, but only if he loves the Lord.* [40]But in my opinion it would be better for her to stay single, and I think I am giving you counsel from God's Spirit when I say this.

7:15a Greek *the brother or sister.* 7:15b Some manuscripts read *us.* 7:23 Greek *don't become slaves of people.*
7:24 Greek *brothers;* also in 7:29. 7:26 Or *the pressures of life.* 7:39 Greek *but only in the Lord.*

7:20-24 The Roman world was filled with oppressed people, many of whom had been taken as children to a foreign land to serve as slaves. Some of these slaves came to believe in Christ, and, naturally, they yearned for freedom. They may have thought they could be better Christians if they were free. We may fall into the same trap. We look at others and think that different circumstances would make recovery easier for us. Instead of wishing for miracles, we can start the recovery process no matter what our situation. When we turn our will and our life over to God, we have a new power at work within us—regardless of our outward circumstances.

CHAPTER 8
Food Sacrificed to Idols

Now regarding your question about food that has been offered to idols. Yes, we know that "we all have knowledge" about this issue. But while knowledge makes us feel important, it is love that strengthens the church. ²Anyone who claims to know all the answers doesn't really know very much. ³But the person who loves God is the one whom God recognizes.*

⁴So, what about eating meat that has been offered to idols? Well, we all know that an idol is not really a god and that there is only one God. ⁵There may be so-called gods both in heaven and on earth, and some people actually worship many gods and many lords. ⁶But for us,

There is one God, the Father,
   by whom all things were created,
   and for whom we live.
And there is one Lord, Jesus Christ,
   through whom all things were created,
   and through whom we live.

⁷However, not all believers know this. Some are accustomed to thinking of idols as being real, so when they eat food that has been offered to idols, they think of it as the worship of real gods, and their weak consciences are violated. ⁸It's true that we can't win God's approval by what we eat. We don't lose anything if we don't eat it, and we don't gain anything if we do.

⁹But you must be careful so that your freedom does not cause others with a weaker conscience to stumble. ¹⁰For if others see you—with your "superior knowledge"—eating in the temple of an idol, won't they be encouraged to violate their conscience by eating food that has been offered to an idol? ¹¹So because of your superior knowledge, a weak believer* for whom Christ died will be destroyed. ¹²And when you sin against other believers* by encouraging them to do something they believe is wrong, you are sinning against Christ. ¹³So if what I eat causes another believer to sin, I will never eat meat again as long as I live—for I don't want to cause another believer to stumble.

CHAPTER 9
Paul Gives Up His Rights

Am I not as free as anyone else? Am I not an apostle? Haven't I seen Jesus our Lord with my own eyes? Isn't it because of my work that you belong to the Lord? ²Even if others think I am not an apostle, I certainly am to you. You yourselves are proof that I am the Lord's apostle.

³This is my answer to those who question my authority.* ⁴Don't we have the right to live in your homes and share your meals? ⁵Don't we have the right to bring a believing wife* with us as the other apostles and the Lord's brothers do, and as Peter* does? ⁶Or is it only Barnabas and I who have to work to support ourselves?

⁷What soldier has to pay his own expenses? What farmer plants a vineyard and doesn't have the right to eat some of its fruit? What shepherd cares for a flock of sheep and isn't allowed to drink some of the milk? ⁸Am I expressing merely a human opinion, or

---

8:3 Some manuscripts read *the person who loves has full knowledge.* 8:11 Greek *brother;* also in 8:13. 8:12 Greek *brothers.* 9:3 Greek *those who examine me.* 9:5a Greek *a sister a wife.* 9:5b Greek *Cephas.*

8:1-3 Love is a lifestyle in which all our thoughts and actions are guided by our concern for others. Most of us need recovery because we have lived for our own gratification. As we sought to escape our inner pain through the fleeting pleasures of addictive activities or substances, we became blind to the needs of the people around us. That lifestyle left our past littered with hurt people and broken relationships. A life governed by selfless love is the only path to rebuilding our broken past. Knowing that God loves us no matter what our past is the place to start recovery.
8:10-13 Our personal freedom is a precious right until it deprives someone else of his or her personal freedom. We can try to justify our actions by intellectualizing them, but love is the only principle that will guide us to make legitimate moral choices. When we love, our freedom to do certain things will not be as important as our relationships with others. We must learn to put the needs of others before our own desires. Love is to be the standard for our moral inventory and the motivation for making amends with the people we have wronged.
9:4-12 Paul modeled giving up personal freedom to show love toward others. Paul had all the rights we have, but he willingly gave them up because of his relationship with Jesus Christ and his desire to help others. We may feel that we have certain freedoms and rights, but if we desire to make progress in recovery, we may have to give up some of those rights. We may have the right to take part in certain activities or frequent certain places, but we probably know that some of these things will lead to a fall. We need to give up activities and relationships that will lead to relapse. We may also need to relinquish some of our rights to support others in recovery.

does the law say the same thing? [9]For the law of Moses says, "You must not muzzle an ox to keep it from eating as it treads out the grain."* Was God thinking only about oxen when he said this? [10]Wasn't he actually speaking to us? Yes, it was written for us, so that the one who plows and the one who threshes the grain might both expect a share of the harvest.

[11]Since we have planted spiritual seed among you, aren't we entitled to a harvest of physical food and drink? [12]If you support others who preach to you, shouldn't we have an even greater right to be supported? But we have never used this right. We would rather put up with anything than be an obstacle to the Good News about Christ.

[13]Don't you realize that those who work in the temple get their meals from the offerings brought to the temple? And those who serve at the altar get a share of the sacrificial offerings. [14]In the same way, the Lord ordered that those who preach the Good News should be supported by those who benefit from it. [15]Yet I have never used any of these rights. And I am not writing this to suggest that I want to start now. In fact, I would rather die than lose my right to boast about preaching without charge. [16]Yet preaching the Good News is not something I can boast about. I am compelled by God to do it. How terrible for me if I didn't preach the Good News!

[17]If I were doing this on my own initiative, I would deserve payment. But I have no choice, for God has given me this sacred trust. [18]What then is my pay? It is the opportunity to preach the Good News without charging anyone. That's why I never demand my rights when I preach the Good News.

[19]Even though I am a free man with no master, I have become a slave to all people to bring many to Christ. [20]When I was with the Jews, I lived like a Jew to bring the Jews to Christ. When I was with those who follow the Jewish law, I too lived under that law. Even though I am not subject to the law, I did this so I could bring to Christ those who are under the law. [21]When I am with the Gentiles who do not follow the Jewish law,* I too live apart from that law so I can bring them to Christ. But I do not ignore the law of God; I obey the law of Christ.

[22]When I am with those who are weak, I share their weakness, for I want to bring the weak to Christ. Yes, I try to find common ground with everyone, doing everything I can to save some. [23]I do everything to spread the Good News and share in its blessings.

[24]Don't you realize that in a race everyone runs, but only one person gets the prize? So run to win! [25]All athletes are disciplined in their training. They do it to win a prize that will fade away, but we do it for an eternal prize. [26]So I run with purpose in every step. I

9:9 Deut 25:4. 9:21 Greek *those without the law.*

9:15-18 Paul gave up his right to be paid for his work in the ministry, choosing instead to support himself. The point wasn't whether or not he should have been paid. He was illustrating the principle that when God has called us to do something, we may have to give up some of our rights and freedoms to accomplish it. If we hope to progress in recovery, our relationship with Jesus Christ and adherence to his program need to take the central place in our life. We may need to give up some of our possessions, activities, and codependent relationships to achieve the freedom that we long for.

9:19-23 An essential part of recovery is sharing the Good News of God's forgiveness and help. Paul shows us that if we want to communicate to others, we must first take the time to understand where they are coming from. Paul listened to his audience and found common ground with them before he helped them change. As we seek to help others, we begin by gaining their confidence. We don't need to be good at winning arguments; we need to be good at listening and showing that we care. Paul listened to the needs of people and then presented his message in a way that met their specific needs. We can do the same as we carry the message of hope to hurting people.

9:24-27 The process of recovery is a lot like training for a title bout in boxing or preparing for a marathon. These activities require a great deal of endurance and strict discipline for those who want to win. No one ever said recovery would be easy, and Paul makes it clear that growing in our relationship with God can be tough. If we want to succeed in recovery and grow spiritually, we need to focus on those goals. We need to give up the destructive activities that will slow us down and train rigorously. If we recognize that things won't be easy at the outset of our program and persevere toward our eternal prize, we will experience God's power and the freedom of recovery.

am not just shadowboxing. [27]I discipline my body like an athlete, training it to do what it should. Otherwise, I fear that after preaching to others I myself might be disqualified.

CHAPTER 10
Lessons from Israel's Idolatry

I don't want you to forget, dear brothers and sisters,* about our ancestors in the wilderness long ago. All of them were guided by a cloud that moved ahead of them, and all of them walked through the sea on dry ground. [2]In the cloud and in the sea, all of them were baptized as followers of Moses. [3]All of them ate the same spiritual food, [4]and all of them drank the same spiritual water. For they drank from the spiritual rock that traveled with them, and that rock was Christ. [5]Yet God was not pleased with most of them, and their bodies were scattered in the wilderness.

[6]These things happened as a warning to us, so that we would not crave evil things as they did, [7]or worship idols as some of them did. As the Scriptures say, "The people celebrated with feasting and drinking, and they indulged in pagan revelry."* [8]And we must not engage in sexual immorality as some of them did, causing 23,000 of them to die in one day.

[9]Nor should we put Christ* to the test, as some of them did and then died from snakebites. [10]And don't grumble as some of them did, and then were destroyed by the angel of death. [11]These things happened to them as examples for us. They were written down to warn us who live at the end of the age.

[12]If you think you are standing strong, be careful not to fall. [13]The temptations in your life are no different from what others experience. And God is faithful. He will not allow the temptation to be more than you can stand. When you are tempted, he will show you a way out so that you can endure.

[14]So, my dear friends, flee from the worship of idols. [15]You are reasonable people. Decide for yourselves if what I am saying is true. [16]When we bless the cup at the Lord's Table, aren't we sharing in the blood of Christ? And when we break the bread, aren't we sharing in the body of Christ? [17]And though we are many, we all eat from one loaf of bread, showing that we are one body. [18]Think about the people of Israel. Weren't they united by eating the sacrifices at the altar?

[19]What am I trying to say? Am I saying that food offered to idols has some significance, or that idols are real gods? [20]No, not at all. I am saying that these sacrifices are offered to demons, not to God. And I don't want you to participate with demons. [21]You cannot drink from the cup of the Lord and from the cup of demons, too. You cannot eat at the Lord's Table and at the table of demons, too. [22]What? Do we dare to rouse the Lord's jealousy? Do you think we are stronger than he is?

[23]You say, "I am allowed to do anything"*— but not everything is good for you. You say, "I am allowed to do anything"—but not everything is beneficial. [24]Don't be concerned for your own good but for the good of others.

[25]So you may eat any meat that is sold in the marketplace without raising questions of conscience. [26]For "the earth is the LORD's, and everything in it."*

[27]If someone who isn't a believer asks you home for dinner, accept the invitation if you

---

10:1 Greek *brothers.* **10:7** Exod 32:6. **10:9** Some manuscripts read *the Lord.* **10:23** Greek *All things are lawful;* also in 10:23b. **10:26** Ps 24:1.

10:1-13 Paul had just used himself as an example of the disciplined, vigilant athlete. Here he used the history of Israel to show us what not to be like. The Israelites' lack of self-discipline and vigilance against temptation led them into sin. They were overconfident, and that attitude led them to disobey God's good instructions for them. Paul held up Israel's failure as a warning to us. If we follow their example, we will suffer the same painful consequences that they did.

10:19-22 We cannot serve both Christ and the devil. We cannot be in recovery and dabble in our old lifestyle. Compromising our personal standards to please those who represent our dysfunctional past is walking on dangerous ground. If we continue in this pattern, our relationship with God will soon falter, and our recovery will be in jeopardy. Recovery requires a choice, and that choice means we have to leave some things behind.

10:23-33 Paul sought to balance his argument here, for it is easy to become too legalistic as we work through the recovery process. The balance can be found by being willing to give up any of our rights that might cause others to fall while also not forcing our standards on anyone else. This does not lead to codependency, where we seek to please others for unhealthy reasons. Paul sought to please others for the specific purpose of leading them to salvation. If our actions are governed by our love for others, we will be well on the way to developing strong relationships and overcoming the problems that drive our addiction or compulsion. God will also use us as powerful instruments to help other hurting people.

want to. Eat whatever is offered to you without raising questions of conscience. 28(But suppose someone tells you, "This meat was offered to an idol." Don't eat it, out of consideration for the conscience of the one who told you. 29It might not be a matter of conscience for you, but it is for the other person.) For why should my freedom be limited by what someone else thinks? 30If I can thank God for the food and enjoy it, why should I be condemned for eating it?

31So whether you eat or drink, or whatever you do, do it all for the glory of God. 32Don't give offense to Jews or Gentiles* or the church of God. 33I, too, try to please everyone in everything I do. I don't just do what is best for me; I do what is best for others so that many may be saved. 11:1And you should imitate me, just as I imitate Christ.

CHAPTER 11
Instructions for Public Worship
2I am so glad that you always keep me in your thoughts, and that you are following the teachings I passed on to you. 3But there is one thing I want you to know: The head of every man is Christ, the head of woman is man, and the head of Christ is God.* 4A man dishonors his head* if he covers his head while praying or prophesying. 5But a woman dishonors her head* if she prays or prophesies without a covering on her head, for this is the same as shaving her head. 6Yes, if she refuses to wear a head covering, she should cut off all her hair! But since it is shameful for a woman to have her hair cut or her head shaved, she should wear a covering.*

7A man should not wear anything on his head when worshiping, for man is made in God's image and reflects God's glory. And woman reflects man's glory. 8For the first man didn't come from woman, but the first woman came from man. 9And man was not made for woman, but woman was made for man. 10For this reason, and because the angels are watching, a woman should wear a covering on her head to show she is under authority.*

11But among the Lord's people, women are not independent of men, and men are not independent of women. 12For although the first woman came from man, every other man was born from a woman, and everything comes from God.

13Judge for yourselves. Is it right for a woman to pray to God in public without covering her head? 14Isn't it obvious that it's disgraceful for a man to have long hair? 15And isn't long hair a woman's pride and joy? For it has been given to her as a covering. 16But if anyone wants to argue about this, I simply say that we have no other custom than this, and neither do God's other churches.

Order at the Lord's Supper
17But in the following instructions, I cannot praise you. For it sounds as if more harm than good is done when you meet together. 18First, I hear that there are divisions among you when you meet as a church, and to some extent I believe it. 19But, of course, there must be divisions among you so that you who have God's approval will be recognized! 20When you meet together, you are not really interested in the Lord's Supper. 21For

10:32 Greek or Greeks. 11:3 Or to know: The source of every man is Christ, the source of woman is man, and the source of Christ is God. Or to know: Every man is responsible to Christ, a woman is responsible to her husband, and Christ is responsible to God. 11:4 Or dishonors Christ. 11:5 Or dishonors her husband. 11:6 Or should have long hair. 11:10 Greek should have an authority on her head.

11:17-22 Paul tried to solve a problem in the Corinthian church. Apparently some of the wealthier believers looked down on the poorer members and refused to share from their abundance at the communion meal. Paul made it clear that a superior attitude is extremely destructive. As we undergo recovery, we must share the process with others. There may be people in our groups whom we feel are below us, but this kind of attitude is destructive. In God's eyes, no one is better than anyone else. We are all broken by sin and need God's transforming power. Our material well-being or educational level does not make us better. When we recognize this and humbly share our failures with others, we can make progress in recovery.
11:27-30 In these verses Paul called the Corinthians to make a searching and fearless moral inventory of their lives. Some of them needed to recognize their pride and take steps to remove it. This is something we all need to do regularly; it must be a way of life for us. Spiritual growth, emotional growth, and recovery depend on our faithfulness in taking our personal inventory. Paul noted here that even physical illness can be the result of not examining our life before taking Communion. When we take the time for a regular moral inventory we will gain victory over the destructive forces in our life.

GOD grant me the serenity to accept the things I cannot change the courage to change the things I can and the wisdom to know the difference AMEN

Belief in an instant cure for addiction will put our recovery at risk; on the other hand, belief that we will someday be beyond the reach of temptation is also dangerous.

Unfortunately, temptation is a permanent part of our sinful world and of human experience. The Bible says, "The temptations in your life are no different from what others experience" (1 Corinthians 10:13). Not only is temptation all around us; it is within us as well. "Temptation comes from our own desires, which entice us and drag us away" (James 1:14). Even if we could rid ourself of all external temptations, we would still have to live with the destructive desires within our old nature.

Even Jesus Christ faced temptation, and yet he never sinned. Before he was tempted, he spent an extended period of time alone in the wilderness, and he went without food. We are usually tempted the most when we are lonely or hungry.

Facing temptation is part of accepting reality. We need to accept the fact that we will always be susceptible to temptation in our areas of weakness and predisposition. When we receive Christ as our Savior, God gives us a new nature, but it is unrealistic to believe that our old sinful nature will ever disappear. When we put away the false belief that temptation will magically disappear when we turn to God, we will be more aware and better able to avoid yielding to temptation's power. We need to prayerfully seek God's help in dealing with this reality of life. *Turn to page 1527, Philippians 4.*

some of you hurry to eat your own meal without sharing with others. As a result, some go hungry while others get drunk. ²²What? Don't you have your own homes for eating and drinking? Or do you really want to disgrace God's church and shame the poor? What am I supposed to say? Do you want me to praise you? Well, I certainly will not praise you for this!

²³For I pass on to you what I received from the Lord himself. On the night when he was betrayed, the Lord Jesus took some bread ²⁴and gave thanks to God for it. Then he broke it in pieces and said, "This is my body, which is given for you.* Do this to remember me." ²⁵In the same way, he took the cup of wine after supper, saying, "This cup is the new covenant between God and his people—an agreement confirmed with my blood. Do this to remember me as often as

you drink it." ²⁶For every time you eat this bread and drink this cup, you are announcing the Lord's death until he comes again.

²⁷So anyone who eats this bread or drinks this cup of the Lord unworthily is guilty of sinning against* the body and blood of the Lord. ²⁸That is why you should examine yourself before eating the bread and drinking the cup. ²⁹For if you eat the bread or drink the cup without honoring the body of Christ,* you are eating and drinking God's judgment upon yourself. ³⁰That is why many of you are weak and sick and some have even died.

³¹But if we would examine ourselves, we would not be judged by God in this way. ³²Yet when we are judged by the Lord, we are being disciplined so that we will not be condemned along with the world.

³³So, my dear brothers and sisters,* when

11:24 Greek *which is for you;* other manuscripts read *which is broken for you.* 11:27 Or *is responsible for.* 11:29 Greek *the body;* other manuscripts read *the Lord's body.* 11:33 Greek *brothers.*

you gather for the Lord's Supper, wait for each other. [34]If you are really hungry, eat at home so you won't bring judgment upon yourselves when you meet together. I'll give you instructions about the other matters after I arrive.

CHAPTER 12
Spiritual Gifts

Now, dear brothers and sisters,* regarding your question about the special abilities the Spirit gives us. I don't want you to misunderstand this. [2]You know that when you were still pagans, you were led astray and swept along in worshiping speechless idols. [3]So I want you to know that no one speaking by the Spirit of God will curse Jesus, and no one can say Jesus is Lord, except by the Holy Spirit.

[4]There are different kinds of spiritual gifts, but the same Spirit is the source of them all. [5]There are different kinds of service, but we serve the same Lord. [6]God works in different ways, but it is the same God who does the work in all of us.

[7]A spiritual gift is given to each of us so we can help each other. [8]To one person the Spirit gives the ability to give wise advice*; to another the same Spirit gives a message of special knowledge.* [9]The same Spirit gives great faith to another, and to someone else the one Spirit gives the gift of healing. [10]He gives one person the power to perform miracles, and another the ability to prophesy. He gives someone else the ability to discern whether a message is from the Spirit of God or from another spirit. Still another person is given the ability to speak in unknown languages,* while another is given the ability to interpret what is being said. [11]It is the one and only Spirit who distributes all these gifts. He alone decides which gift each person should have.

One Body with Many Parts

[12]The human body has many parts, but the many parts make up one whole body. So it is with the body of Christ. [13]Some of us are Jews, some are Gentiles,* some are slaves, and some are free. But we have all been baptized into one body by one Spirit, and we all share the same Spirit.*

[14]Yes, the body has many different parts, not just one part. [15]If the foot says, "I am not a part of the body because I am not a hand," that does not make it any less a part of the body. [16]And if the ear says, "I am not part of the body because I am not an eye," would that make it any less a part of the body? [17]If the whole body were an eye, how would you hear? Or if your whole body were an ear, how would you smell anything?

[18]But our bodies have many parts, and God has put each part just where he wants it. [19]How strange a body would be if it had only one part! [20]Yes, there are many parts, but only one body. [21]The eye can never say to the hand, "I don't need you." The head can't say to the feet, "I don't need you."

[22]In fact, some parts of the body that seem weakest and least important are actually the most necessary. [23]And the parts we regard as less honorable are those we clothe with the greatest care. So we carefully protect those parts that should not be seen, [24]while the more honorable parts do not require this

---

12:1 Greek *brothers.* **12:8a** Or *gives a word of wisdom.* **12:8b** Or *gives a word of knowledge.* **12:10** Or *in various tongues;* also in 12:28, 30. **12:13a** Greek *some are Greeks.* **12:13b** Greek *we were all given one Spirit to drink.*

12:4-11 God has gifted each of us in some way. No one is without talents and special abilities. When we put ourself down, we are rejecting these gifts from God rather than delighting in them. We don't need to build up our self-esteem; we just need to see more accurately who we are and how God has gifted us. Whether we have recognized it or not, being in recovery is a unique gift in itself. Having suffered through the process of failure and deliverance, we are uniquely gifted to help others struggling in similar ways. By sharing what God has done for us, we may be giving the gift of life to someone else in need.

12:12-26 When we become proud of our gifts and accomplishments, we invariably end up hurting ourself and others. God has gifted all of us in some way or another. If we do not recognize this truth, we may take credit for our progress in recovery and flaunt our success. This kind of pride causes pain to others and leads us toward a fall. When we have an accurate view of ourself, we will give God the credit for the gifts he has given us and be thankful for his help in recovery. If we cannot do this, we need to go back to Step One and once again admit how powerless we really are.

13:1-3 Paul was writing to a group of believers who had started to forget what real love is. He showed them that all their abilities, talents, and spiritual gifts amounted to nothing if they didn't love each other. Without selfless love, we have nothing. Loving relationships are also essential to the recovery process.

special care. So God has put the body together such that extra honor and care are given to those parts that have less dignity. ²⁵This makes for harmony among the members, so that all the members care for each other. ²⁶If one part suffers, all the parts suffer with it, and if one part is honored, all the parts are glad.

²⁷All of you together are Christ's body, and each of you is a part of it. ²⁸Here are some of the parts God has appointed for the church:

first are apostles,
second are prophets,
third are teachers,
then those who do miracles,
those who have the gift of healing,
those who can help others,
those who have the gift of leadership,
those who speak in unknown languages.

²⁹Are we all apostles? Are we all prophets? Are we all teachers? Do we all have the power to do miracles? ³⁰Do we all have the gift of healing? Do we all have the ability to speak in unknown languages? Do we all have the ability to interpret unknown languages? Of course not! ³¹So you should earnestly desire the most helpful gifts.

But now let me show you a way of life that is best of all.

CHAPTER 13
Love Is the Greatest

If I could speak all the languages of earth and of angels, but didn't love others, I would only be a noisy gong or a clanging cymbal. ²If I had the gift of prophecy, and if I understood all of God's secret plans and possessed all knowledge, and if I had such faith that I could move mountains, but didn't love others, I would be nothing. ³If I gave everything I have to the poor and even sacrificed my body, I could boast about it;* but if I didn't love others, I would have gained nothing.

⁴Love is patient and kind. Love is not jealous or boastful or proud ⁵or rude. It does not demand its own way. It is not irritable, and it keeps no record of being wronged. ⁶It does not rejoice about injustice but rejoices whenever the truth wins out. ⁷Love never gives up, never loses faith, is always hopeful, and endures through every circumstance.

⁸Prophecy and speaking in unknown languages* and special knowledge will become useless. But love will last forever! ⁹Now our knowledge is partial and incomplete,

13:3 Some manuscripts read *sacrificed my body to be burned.* 13:8 Or *in tongues.*

LOVE

READ 1 CORINTHIANS 13:1-7
We may have given up on love. Perhaps we have waited for love to find us, only to be disappointed. Maybe our loved ones have hurt us so badly that we needed to numb ourself from the pain. In the past our addiction helped to keep us numb, but now that we are in recovery, we have to find ways to deal with the issue of love once again.

It is God's will that we love others; without love nothing else matters (see 1 Corinthians 13:1-3). Love is more than a feeling; it is choosing to behave in loving ways. It is a fruit of the Holy Spirit, produced in our life as we yield to God. The Bible defines it this way: "Love is patient and kind. Love is not jealous or boastful or proud or rude. . . . Love never gives up, never loses faith, is always hopeful, and endures through every circumstance" (1 Corinthians 13:4-7).

This passage is a description of how God loves us. As we begin to absorb his love, we will find ourself reaching out to love again. No one loves perfectly, but we must learn how to love. We can ask God to help us love others and stop waiting for them to love us. We cannot expect to be good at loving right away; we should be patient as God's love grows within us and he teaches us how to love. When we choose to act in loving ways, the emotions will follow, and we will find that our love will be returned. ***Turn to page 1485, 2 Corinthians 5.***

and even the gift of prophecy reveals only part of the whole picture! [10]But when the time of perfection comes, these partial things will become useless.

[11]When I was a child, I spoke and thought and reasoned as a child. But when I grew up, I put away childish things. [12]Now we see things imperfectly, like puzzling reflections in a mirror, but then we will see everything with perfect clarity.* All that I know now is partial and incomplete, but then I will know everything completely, just as God now knows me completely.

[13]Three things will last forever—faith, hope, and love—and the greatest of these is love.

CHAPTER 14
Tongues and Prophecy
Let love be your highest goal! But you should also desire the special abilities the Spirit gives—especially the ability to prophesy. [2]For if you have the ability to speak in tongues,* you will be talking only to God, since people won't be able to understand you. You will be speaking by the power of the Spirit,* but it will all be mysterious. [3]But one who prophesies strengthens others, encourages them, and comforts them. [4]A person who speaks in tongues is strengthened personally, but one who speaks a word of prophecy strengthens the entire church.

[5]I wish you could all speak in tongues, but even more I wish you could all prophesy. For prophecy is greater than speaking in tongues, unless someone interprets what you are saying so that the whole church will be strengthened.

[6]Dear brothers and sisters,* if I should come to you speaking in an unknown language,* how would that help you? But if I bring you a revelation or some special knowledge or prophecy or teaching, that will be helpful.

[7]Even lifeless instruments like the flute or the harp must play the notes clearly, or no one will recognize the melody. [8]And if the bugler doesn't sound a clear call, how will the soldiers know they are being called to battle?

[9]It's the same for you. If you speak to people in words they don't understand, how will they know what you are saying? You might as well be talking into empty space.

[10]There are many different languages in the world, and every language has meaning. [11]But if I don't understand a language, I will be a foreigner to someone who speaks it, and the one who speaks it will be a foreigner to me. [12]And the same is true for you. Since you are so eager to have the special abilities the Spirit gives, seek those that will strengthen the whole church.

[13]So anyone who speaks in tongues should pray also for the ability to interpret what has been said. [14]For if I pray in tongues, my spirit is praying, but I don't understand what I am saying.

[15]Well then, what shall I do? I will pray in the spirit,* and I will also pray in words I understand. I will sing in the spirit, and I will also sing in words I understand. [16]For if you praise God only in the spirit, how can those who don't understand you praise God along with you? How can they join you in giving thanks when they don't understand what you are saying? [17]You will be giving thanks very well, but it won't strengthen the people who hear you.

[18]I thank God that I speak in tongues more than any of you. [19]But in a church meeting I would rather speak five understandable words to help others than ten thousand words in an unknown language.

[20]Dear brothers and sisters, don't be childish in your understanding of these things. Be

---

13:12 Greek *see face to face.* **14:2a** Or *in unknown languages;* also in 14:4, 5, 13, 14, 18, 22, 26, 27, 28, 39. **14:2b** Or *speaking in your spirit.* **14:6a** Greek *brothers;* also in 14:20, 26, 39. **14:6b** Or *in tongues;* also in 14:19, 23. **14:15** Or *in the Spirit;* also in 14:15b, 16.

13:11-13 Recovery and growth are never complete in this life; we are always in recovery—always growing. We are still like children, needing to mature. Only when we see God face to face will we be complete and whole. Paul shares this truth not to discourage us, but to give us hope that someday we will be made perfect. We will persevere in the process of recovery if we have *faith* in God and those around us. We need *hope* to endure and be healed from our painful problems and addiction. Most of all we need genuine *love* to conquer the barriers and bondage of our past. Faith, hope, and love are all necessary to successful recovery. Genuine love, however, is the greatest healer of all.

14:1-12 Paul returned to the subject of spiritual gifts. He warned us not to use our gifts to build ourself up or to reinforce our own sense of self-sufficiency. All spiritual gifts are just that—gifts. They are given to us by God to be used to build others up and encourage them in their spiritual growth. Using our God-given gifts for our own purposes shows that we have forgotten the one who gave the gifts in the first place—God. This kind of attitude invariably leads to failure. We will succeed as we acknowledge that we are powerless and in need of God's powerful help.

innocent as babies when it comes to evil, but be mature in understanding matters of this kind. [21]It is written in the Scriptures*:

"I will speak to my own people
    through strange languages
    and through the lips of foreigners.
But even then, they will not listen
        to me,"*
    says the LORD.

[22]So you see that speaking in tongues is a sign, not for believers, but for unbelievers. Prophecy, however, is for the benefit of believers, not unbelievers. [23]Even so, if unbelievers or people who don't understand these things come into your church meeting and hear everyone speaking in an unknown language, they will think you are crazy. [24]But if all of you are prophesying, and unbelievers or people who don't understand these things come into your meeting, they will be convicted of sin and judged by what you say. [25]As they listen, their secret thoughts will be exposed, and they will fall to their knees and worship God, declaring, "God is truly here among you."

A Call to Orderly Worship

[26]Well, my brothers and sisters, let's summarize. When you meet together, one will sing, another will teach, another will tell some special revelation God has given, one will speak in tongues, and another will interpret what is said. But everything that is done must strengthen all of you.

[27]No more than two or three should speak in tongues. They must speak one at a time, and someone must interpret what they say. [28]But if no one is present who can interpret, they must be silent in your church meeting and speak in tongues to God privately.

[29]Let two or three people prophesy, and let the others evaluate what is said. [30]But if someone is prophesying and another person

receives a revelation from the Lord, the one who is speaking must stop. [31]In this way, all who prophesy will have a turn to speak, one after the other, so that everyone will learn and be encouraged. [32]Remember that people who prophesy are in control of their spirit and can take turns. [33]For God is not a God of disorder but of peace, as in all the meetings of God's holy people.*

[34]Women should be silent during the church meetings. It is not proper for them to speak. They should be submissive, just as the law says. [35]If they have any questions, they should ask their husbands at home, for it is improper for women to speak in church meetings.*

[36]Or do you think God's word originated with you Corinthians? Are you the only ones to whom it was given? [37]If you claim to be a prophet or think you are spiritual, you should recognize that what I am saying is a command from the Lord himself. [38]But if you do not recognize this, you yourself will not be recognized.*

[39]So, my dear brothers and sisters, be eager to prophesy, and don't forbid speaking in tongues. [40]But be sure that everything is done properly and in order.

CHAPTER 15
The Resurrection of Christ

Let me now remind you, dear brothers and sisters,* of the Good News I preached to you before. You welcomed it then, and you still stand firm in it. [2]It is this Good News that saves you if you continue to believe the message I told you—unless, of course, you believed something that was never true in the first place.*

[3]I passed on to you what was most important and what had also been passed on to me. Christ died for our sins, just as the Scriptures said. [4]He was buried, and he was raised from the dead on the third day, just as the

---

14:21a Greek *in the law.* 14:21b Isa 28:11-12. 14:33 The phrase *as in all the meetings of God's holy people* could instead be joined to the beginning of 14:34. 14:35 Some manuscripts place verses 34-35 after 14:40. 14:38 Some manuscripts read *If you are ignorant of this, stay in your ignorance.* 15:1 Greek *brothers;* also in 15:31, 50, 58. 15:2 Or *unless you never believed it in the first place.*

14:26-39 Paul summarized his teachings on relationships, especially those characterized by healthy interdependence. We are to live in community with others, building them up and meeting their needs. It is important to distinguish between this kind of relationship and a codependent relationship, in which we relate to others for an ulterior motive, perhaps seeking to meet our own lack or need. Healthy interdependent relationships attempt to meet others' needs without seeking some hidden reward. When we learn to love selflessly as Paul proposed, the physical and emotional needs of everyone in our community will be met. One of the goals of recovery is restoring our broken, dysfunctional relationships, turning them into healthy, interdependent ones.

Scriptures said. [5]He was seen by Peter* and then by the Twelve. [6]After that, he was seen by more than 500 of his followers* at one time, most of whom are still alive, though some have died. [7]Then he was seen by James and later by all the apostles. [8]Last of all, as though I had been born at the wrong time, I also saw him. [9]For I am the least of all the apostles. In fact, I'm not even worthy to be called an apostle after the way I persecuted God's church.

[10]But whatever I am now, it is all because God poured out his special favor on me—and not without results. For I have worked harder than any of the other apostles; yet it was not I but God who was working through me by his grace. [11]So it makes no difference whether I preach or they preach, for we all preach the same message you have already believed.

The Resurrection of the Dead

[12]But tell me this—since we preach that Christ rose from the dead, why are some of you saying there will be no resurrection of the dead? [13]For if there is no resurrection of the dead, then Christ has not been raised either. [14]And if Christ has not been raised, then all our preaching is useless, and your faith is useless. [15]And we apostles would all be lying about God—for we have said that God raised Christ from the grave. But that can't be true if there is no resurrection of the dead. [16]And if there is no resurrection of the dead, then Christ has not been raised. [17]And if Christ has not been raised, then your faith is useless and you are still guilty of your sins.

15:5 Greek *Cephas.* 15:6 Greek *the brothers.* 15:27 Ps 8:6.

[18]In that case, all who have died believing in Christ are lost! [19]And if our hope in Christ is only for this life, we are more to be pitied than anyone in the world.

[20]But in fact, Christ has been raised from the dead. He is the first of a great harvest of all who have died.

[21]So you see, just as death came into the world through a man, now the resurrection from the dead has begun through another man. [22]Just as everyone dies because we all belong to Adam, everyone who belongs to Christ will be given new life. [23]But there is an order to this resurrection: Christ was raised as the first of the harvest; then all who belong to Christ will be raised when he comes back.

[24]After that the end will come, when he will turn the Kingdom over to God the Father, having destroyed every ruler and authority and power. [25]For Christ must reign until he humbles all his enemies beneath his feet. [26]And the last enemy to be destroyed is death. [27]For the Scriptures say, "God has put all things under his authority."* (Of course, when it says "all things are under his authority," that does not include God himself, who gave Christ his authority.) [28]Then, when all things are under his authority, the Son will put himself under God's authority, so that God, who gave his Son authority over all things, will be utterly supreme over everything everywhere.

[29]If the dead will not be raised, what point is there in people being baptized for those who are dead? Why do it unless the dead will someday rise again?

15:10 In recovery we often say something beginning with "But for the grace of God, I . . ." Such statements started with Paul as he recognized that without God's grace, he never would have achieved any of his success. We must recognize that our success in recovery is from God. When we fail to give the credit to God for what has happened in our life, we negate our progress by forgetting the lessons of its earliest steps. Notice, however, that Paul also recognized his own hard work in the process. Recovery is based on the grace of God and his desire to help us, but we still have a part in the equation: We have to work hard! Recovery takes a combination of God's power and our faithful willingness to obey him.

15:12-20 Some of the Corinthian believers had begun to question the hope of being resurrected to new life at Christ's second coming. So Paul reemphasized the importance of the resurrection and the hope it offers to all, even those who are already dead. The greatest expression of God's power was raising Jesus from the dead. If God could do that, then he has the power to do anything! If God did not raise Jesus from the grave, however, then our God is powerless, and we are lost. Paul affirmed the truth that Jesus did rise from the dead; in so doing, he also affirmed that we have access to the greatest power in the universe—God himself.

15:29-34 If death is the end of everything, then a selfish, pleasure-seeking lifestyle may be a justifiable alternative. But Paul reminds us that our hope and our recovery lead to an existence beyond the grave. It is this truth about the resurrection that motivates us to make right choices and leave behind our old way of life. If we do things God's way, we have an eternity of joy and peace to look forward to. If we do things our own way, we face an eternity of suffering.

³⁰And why should we ourselves risk our lives hour by hour? ³¹For I swear, dear brothers and sisters, that I face death daily. This is as certain as my pride in what Christ Jesus our Lord has done in you. ³²And what value was there in fighting wild beasts—those people of Ephesus*—if there will be no resurrection from the dead? And if there is no resurrection, "Let's feast and drink, for tomorrow we die!"* ³³Don't be fooled by those who say such things, for "bad company corrupts good character." ³⁴Think carefully about what is right, and stop sinning. For to your shame I say that some of you don't know God at all.

The Resurrection Body

³⁵But someone may ask, "How will the dead be raised? What kind of bodies will they have?" ³⁶What a foolish question! When you put a seed into the ground, it doesn't grow into a plant unless it dies first. ³⁷And what you put in the ground is not the plant that will grow, but only a bare seed of wheat or whatever you are planting. ³⁸Then God gives it the new body he wants it to have. A different plant grows from each kind of seed. ³⁹Similarly there are different kinds of flesh—one kind for humans, another for animals, another for birds, and another for fish.

⁴⁰There are also bodies in the heavens and bodies on the earth. The glory of the heavenly bodies is different from the glory of the earthly bodies. ⁴¹The sun has one kind of glory, while the moon and stars each have another kind. And even the stars differ from each other in their glory.

⁴²It is the same way with the resurrection of the dead. Our earthly bodies are planted in the ground when we die, but they will be raised to live forever. ⁴³Our bodies are buried in brokenness, but they will be raised in glory. They are buried in weakness, but they will be raised in strength. ⁴⁴They are buried as natural human bodies, but they will be raised as spiritual bodies. For just as there are natural bodies, there are also spiritual bodies.

⁴⁵The Scriptures tell us, "The first man, Adam, became a living person."* But the last Adam—that is, Christ—is a life-giving Spirit. ⁴⁶What comes first is the natural body, then the spiritual body comes later. ⁴⁷Adam, the first man, was made from the dust of the earth, while Christ, the second man, came from heaven. ⁴⁸Earthly people are like the earthly man, and heavenly people are like the heavenly man. ⁴⁹Just as we are now like the earthly man, we will someday be like* the heavenly man.

⁵⁰What I am saying, dear brothers and sisters, is that our physical bodies cannot inherit the Kingdom of God. These dying bodies cannot inherit what will last forever.

⁵¹But let me reveal to you a wonderful secret. We will not all die, but we will all be transformed! ⁵²It will happen in a moment, in the blink of an eye, when the last trumpet is blown. For when the trumpet sounds, those who have died will be raised to live forever. And we who are living will also be transformed. ⁵³For our dying bodies must be transformed into bodies that will never die; our mortal bodies must be transformed into immortal bodies.

⁵⁴Then, when our dying bodies have been transformed into bodies that will never die,* this Scripture will be fulfilled:

"Death is swallowed up in victory.*
⁵⁵ O death, where is your victory?
O death, where is your sting?*"

⁵⁶For sin is the sting that results in death, and the law gives sin its power. ⁵⁷But thank God! He gives us victory over sin and death through our Lord Jesus Christ.

⁵⁸So, my dear brothers and sisters, be strong and immovable. Always work enthusiastically for the Lord, for you know that nothing you do for the Lord is ever useless.

CHAPTER 16
The Collection for Jerusalem

Now regarding your question about the money being collected for God's people in Jerusalem. You should follow the same

---

15:32a Greek *fighting wild beasts in Ephesus.* 15:32b Isa 22:13. 15:45 Gen 2:7. 15:49 Some manuscripts read *let us be like.* 15:54a Some manuscripts add *and our mortal bodies have been transformed into immortal bodies.* 15:54b Isa 25:8. 15:55 Hos 13:14 (Greek version).

15:35-58 No matter how terrifying our dependency may have become, death is probably still our greatest fear. Sometimes fear of death can motivate us to seek God for help with our destructive problems. Yet our fear of death can also lead us to despair and may actually feed our dependency. Paul reminds us of a fact that can remove our fear of death: Jesus Christ has conquered death. His resurrection conquered death and the "sting" of death, which is sin. With the resurrection power of Jesus Christ at work within us, nothing we do is ever wasted. God can use even our failures and relapses to teach us something for his glory.

procedure I gave to the churches in Galatia. [2]On the first day of each week, you should each put aside a portion of the money you have earned. Don't wait until I get there and then try to collect it all at once. [3]When I come, I will write letters of recommendation for the messengers you choose to deliver your gift to Jerusalem. [4]And if it seems appropriate for me to go along, they can travel with me.

Paul's Final Instructions

[5]I am coming to visit you after I have been to Macedonia,* for I am planning to travel through Macedonia. [6]Perhaps I will stay awhile with you, possibly all winter, and then you can send me on my way to my next destination. [7]This time I don't want to make just a short visit and then go right on. I want to come and stay awhile, if the Lord will let me. [8]In the meantime, I will be staying here at Ephesus until the Festival of Pentecost. [9]There is a wide-open door for a great work here, although many oppose me.

[10]When Timothy comes, don't intimidate him. He is doing the Lord's work, just as I am. [11]Don't let anyone treat him with contempt. Send him on his way with your blessing when he returns to me. I expect him to come with the other believers.* [12]Now about our brother Apollos—I urged him to visit you with the other believers, but he was not willing to go right now. He will see you later when he has the opportunity.

[13]Be on guard. Stand firm in the faith. Be courageous.* Be strong. [14]And do everything with love.

[15]You know that Stephanas and his household were the first of the harvest of believers in Greece,* and they are spending their lives in service to God's people. I urge you, dear brothers and sisters,* [16]to submit to them and others like them who serve with such devotion. [17]I am very glad that Stephanas, Fortunatus, and Achaicus have come here. They have been providing the help you weren't here to give me. [18]They have been a wonderful encouragement to me, as they have been to you. You must show your appreciation to all who serve so well.

Paul's Final Greetings

[19]The churches here in the province of Asia* send greetings in the Lord, as do Aquila and Priscilla* and all the others who gather in their home for church meetings. [20]All the brothers and sisters here send greetings to you. Greet each other with a sacred kiss.

[21]HERE IS MY GREETING IN MY OWN HANDWRITING—PAUL.

[22]If anyone does not love the Lord, that person is cursed. Our Lord, come!*

[23]May the grace of the Lord Jesus be with you.

[24]My love to all of you in Christ Jesus.*

16:5 *Macedonia* was in the northern region of Greece. 16:11 Greek *with the brothers;* also in 16:12. 16:13 Greek *Be men.* 16:15a Greek *in Achaia,* the southern region of the Greek peninsula. 16:15b Greek *brothers;* also in 16:20. 16:19a *Asia* was a Roman province in what is now western Turkey. 16:19b Greek *Prisca.* 16:22 From Aramaic, *Marana tha.* Some manuscripts read *Maran atha, "Our Lord has come."* 16:24 Some manuscripts add *Amen.*

16:5-18 Throughout this letter Paul encouraged the Corinthians in their recovery and spiritual growth. In closing Paul revealed his love and trust in them by making personal requests. There is always a balance between caring for the hurts and needs of others and being able to ask for what we need as well. Healthy relationships are characterized by this kind of balanced give-and-take.

REFLECTIONS ON 1 CORINTHIANS

insights ABOUT OUR POWERLESSNESS AND GOD'S POWER

Through a series of illustrations in **1 Corinthians 1:26-31**, Paul pointed out that God's plan for recovery doesn't utilize our human wisdom, strength, or skill. We don't have to be famous or rich to receive God's forgiveness and power. For self-sufficient people this may be hard to accept. We want to feel worthy of our salvation or recovery. But until we can admit that we are powerless to change without God's help, we are doomed to cycles of painful failure. God's free gifts of forgiveness and the power to live a new life may appear foolish to us. But when we accept Christ as our Savior and we turn our will and our life over to him, we will discover genuine power and release from the bondage of our past.

insights INTO FINDING GOD'S WILL

Some of us may wonder how we could ever know God's will for our life. In **1 Corinthians 2:11-12** we find that we can know God's mind and heart because he has placed his Holy Spirit within us to communicate these things to us. Often the Holy Spirit uses God's Word to communicate with us. What a privilege to read God's thoughts and feelings! God's presence in us will help us know how to deal with our painful past as he helps us make an accurate personal inventory. This will lead to a healthy view of ourself and the restoration of our broken life and relationships. If we consistently follow God's direction in our life through the Holy Spirit, our recovery is assured.

insights INTO HEALTHY RELATIONSHIPS

In **1 Corinthians 6:12** Paul told the Corinthian believers to avoid involvement in activities that could likely seduce them back into their old way of life. This warning is important for us in recovery, too. Many of our old activities and relationships are not wrong in themselves, but staying involved in those things will naturally lead us toward relapses. If this is the case, these activities are not good for us or our recovery. We need to avoid anything that might stop or hinder our spiritual growth in any way.

insights ABOUT LOVE

Most of us define love as an emotion and stop there. But in **1 Corinthians 13:4-7** Paul defined love as a commitment to act a certain way toward others. We may not always be able to conjure up the emotions and feelings of love, but we can certainly choose to practice the behaviors he listed in these verses. The apostle knew that when we behave in loving ways, feelings of love soon follow. As we seek to restore our broken relationships and make amends, we will find that Paul's description of loving action is a powerful prescription for restoration and healing.

2 CORINTHIANS

THE BIG PICTURE

A. PAUL DISCUSSES HIS MOTIVES AND ACTIONS (1:1–2:13)
B. PAUL RELATES HIS MINISTRY TO THE NEW COVENANT (2:14–7:16)
C. PAUL APPEALS TO HIS READERS FOR SUPPORT (8:1–9:15)
D. PAUL DEFENDS HIS APOSTOLIC AUTHORITY (10:1–13:13)

Paul wrote this letter mainly to defend the authority of his teachings about Christ. The church at Corinth was struggling, and one of its problems was the presence of members who openly challenged Paul's authority. These challengers slandered Paul's character and questioned the message he preached. They also introduced a number of dangerous false teachings. Since the believers in Corinth had come to faith through Paul's ministry, this put the entire church at risk.

The false teachers claimed that following the Jewish laws was a requirement for salvation. To counteract this false teaching, Paul emphasized the truth that God changes us from the inside out. We cannot change ourself by changing our external behavior. As we are reconciled to God, he transforms us into entirely new people; our old self is fundamentally changed.

Of course, change is never easy when it involves our lifestyle. Old habits die hard, and positive habits have a way of falling prey to neglect. Typically the habits that die hardest are our negative or unhealthy thoughts and behavioral patterns. "Out with the old; in with the new!" sounds simple, but even as we long for an end to our bad habits, we cling to them.

Fortunately, God has done something about our helpless situation. That is why we can admit our powerlessness and come to him for help. It is essential for recovery that we turn our life over to God. Through Christ's death and resurrection, God made it possible for us to experience the changes we long for. By being reconciled to him, we can have a new life in Christ, transformed from the inside out.

THE BOTTOM LINE

PURPOSE: To explain new life in Christ while also defending Paul's authority to preach. AUTHOR: The apostle Paul. AUDIENCE: The church at Corinth, a city in Greece. DATE WRITTEN: About A.D. 55 from Macedonia. SETTING: After hearing several accusations against himself circulating in Corinth, Paul wrote to the Corinthian believers to correct their misunderstandings and help them with other problems. KEY VERSE: "Anyone who belongs to Christ has become a new person. The old life is gone; a new life has begun!" (5:17). KEY PLACES: Corinth, Macedonia, Troas, Jerusalem. KEY PEOPLE AND RELATIONSHIPS: Paul with Timothy, Titus, the Corinthian believers, and some false apostles.

RECOVERY THEMES

God's Power for Our Recovery: All of us have made resolutions about how we are going to change. The results are usually the same—we end up falling back into the same old bad habits we promised to stop. The Corinthians were apparently doing the same thing, with the same results. What they failed to grasp as they listened to the false teachers was that only God's power could enable them to make changes in their lives. Likewise, our own efforts always fall short. Instead of merely making resolutions, we need to admit our powerlessness and turn our life over to God. Then we can allow his power to change us from within.

Learning to Accept Criticism: One of Paul's purposes in writing this letter was to discipline those who needed to be corrected. Criticism usually hurts. Yet it also forces us to face our problems and helps us see what we need to change. If we are going to be successful in recovery, we must confront and solve problems, not ignore them. That means being open to criticism.

Conflict Can Inspire Growth: Interpersonal conflicts are an inevitable part of being human. They can also be so discouraging that they cause us to give in to failure. But what conflicts do to us depends on how we handle them. If we view them as opportunities for growth, as Paul urged the Corinthians to do, they can urge us into being productive. If we face them and try to solve them in loving ways, they can motivate us to make progress in recovery and recommitment to one another. If we ignore them, they can eat away at us like a cancer, destroying the work of recovery not only within us but also in others around us. Conflicts are opportunities for growth if we use them as such.

God's Strength in Our Weakness: In this letter of Paul's, he told about a particular "thorn" in his flesh (12:7). We don't know what this problem was because he didn't tell us. Some have suggested that it was a physical ailment or even a disease affecting his eyes. Whatever it was, it was debilitating and chronic, and at times, it interfered with his work. It also kept Paul humble because it forced him to depend on God. Through this hardship, Paul learned to thank God for his weakness. In each of us there will always be weaknesses holding us back and bogging us down. But our weaknesses have a purpose—to bring us to God. To what better place can our weaknesses take us?

CHAPTER 1
Greetings from Paul

This letter is from Paul, chosen by the will of God to be an apostle of Christ Jesus, and from our brother Timothy.

I am writing to God's church in Corinth and to all of his holy people throughout Greece.*

²May God our Father and the Lord Jesus Christ give you grace and peace.

God Offers Comfort to All

³All praise to God, the Father of our Lord Jesus Christ. God is our merciful Father and the source of all comfort. ⁴He comforts us in all our troubles so that we can comfort oth-ers. When they are troubled, we will be able to give them the same comfort God has given us. ⁵For the more we suffer for Christ, the more God will shower us with his comfort through Christ. ⁶Even when we are weighed down with troubles, it is for your comfort and salvation! For when we ourselves are comforted, we will certainly comfort you. Then you can patiently endure the same things we suffer. ⁷We are confident that as you share in our sufferings, you will also share in the comfort God gives us.

⁸We think you ought to know, dear brothers and sisters,* about the trouble we went through in the province of Asia. We were crushed and overwhelmed beyond our abil-

---

1:1 Greek *Achaia,* the southern region of the Greek peninsula. 1:8 Greek *brothers.*

1:1-7 Not only is God the God of peace, but he is also the God of mercy and comfort. That's good news, both when we are going through particular trials and when we are trying to recover from dysfunctional or abusive situations. Jesus Christ suffered greatly and unjustly when he went to the cross. He fully understands and identifies with our suffering, and he knows the kind of comfort we need. He is worthy of our trust and able to deliver us from our painful circumstances.
1:8-10 Paul wrote of his own recent need for comfort from God (see 1:3-7). Apparently, Paul and his missionary group had been almost killed as they ministered in the Roman province of Asia, now southwestern Turkey. Even though Paul and his companions thought the end had come, God delivered them. Many of us have experienced God's delivering power in our own life. Even when everything seems to be coming apart, God can rescue us from what appears to be sure destruction.

ity to endure, and we thought we would never live through it. ⁹In fact, we expected to die. But as a result, we stopped relying on ourselves and learned to rely only on God, who raises the dead. ¹⁰And he did rescue us from mortal danger, and he will rescue us again. We have placed our confidence in him, and he will continue to rescue us. ¹¹And you are helping us by praying for us. Then many people will give thanks because God has graciously answered so many prayers for our safety.

Paul's Change of Plans

¹²We can say with confidence and a clear conscience that we have lived with a God-given holiness* and sincerity in all our dealings. We have depended on God's grace, not on our own human wisdom. That is how we have conducted ourselves before the world, and especially toward you. ¹³Our letters have been straightforward, and there is nothing written between the lines and nothing you can't understand. I hope someday you will fully understand us, ¹⁴even if you don't understand us now. Then on the day when the Lord Jesus* returns, you will be proud of us in the same way we are proud of you.

¹⁵Since I was so sure of your understanding and trust, I wanted to give you a double blessing by visiting you twice—¹⁶first on my way to Macedonia and again when I returned from Macedonia.* Then you could send me on my way to Judea.

¹⁷You may be asking why I changed my plan. Do you think I make my plans carelessly? Do you think I am like people of the world who say "Yes" when they really mean "No"? ¹⁸As surely as God is faithful, our word to you does not waver between "Yes" and "No." ¹⁹For Jesus Christ, the Son of God, does not waver between "Yes" and "No." He is the one whom Silas,* Timothy, and I preached to you, and as God's ultimate "Yes," he always does what he says. ²⁰For all of God's promises have been fulfilled in Christ with a resounding "Yes!" And through Christ, our "Amen" (which means "Yes") ascends to God for his glory.

²¹It is God who enables us, along with you, to stand firm for Christ. He has commissioned us, ²²and he has identified us as his own by placing the Holy Spirit in our hearts as the first installment that guarantees everything he has promised us.

1:12 Some manuscripts read *honesty*. 1:14 Some manuscripts read *our Lord Jesus*. 1:16 *Macedonia* was in the northern region of Greece. 1:19 Greek *Silvanus*.

STEP 8

The Fruit of Forgiveness

BIBLE READING: 2 Corinthians 2:5-8

We made a list of all persons we had harmed and became willing to make amends to them all.

Some of the things we have done have earned us disapproval and possibly loss of love. We have found that some people love us only if they can approve of our behavior. We may have struggled with bitterness toward them because we feel as if they have been trying to punish us. If our "sins" have been made public, we may assume that we have lost the love of everyone who disapproves of our actions. This fear of rejection might deter us from reaching out to make amends.

In the young Corinthian church, a man was cut off from church fellowship when his sins were made public. After he turned around and tried to make amends, some people refused to welcome him back into the church. The apostle Paul told the believers: "The man who caused all the trouble hurt all of you more than he hurt me. Most of you opposed him, and that was punishment enough. Now, however, it is time to forgive him and comfort him. Otherwise he may be overcome by discouragement. So I urge you now to reaffirm your love for him." (2 Corinthians 2:5-8). Some people will follow this advice and reaffirm their love for you when you go to them.

There will be some people who will respond with forgiveness, comfort, acceptance, and love. This will help us overcome the grief, the bitterness, and the discouragement we may feel. Their forgiveness will help us move on with recovery. *Turn to page 1505, Galatians 6.*

²³Now I call upon God as my witness that I am telling the truth. The reason I didn't return to Corinth was to spare you from a severe rebuke. ²⁴But that does not mean we want to dominate you by telling you how to put your faith into practice. We want to work together with you so you will be full of joy, for it is by your own faith that you stand firm.

CHAPTER 2

So I decided that I would not bring you grief with another painful visit. ²For if I cause you grief, who will make me glad? Certainly not someone I have grieved. ³That is why I wrote to you as I did, so that when I do come, I won't be grieved by the very ones who ought to give me the greatest joy. Surely you all know that my joy comes from your being joyful. ⁴I wrote that letter in great anguish, with a troubled heart and many tears. I didn't want to grieve you, but I wanted to let you know how much love I have for you.

Forgiveness for the Sinner

⁵I am not overstating it when I say that the man who caused all the trouble hurt all of you more than he hurt me. ⁶Most of you opposed him, and that was punishment enough. ⁷Now, however, it is time to forgive and comfort him. Otherwise he may be overcome by discouragement. ⁸So I urge you now to reaffirm your love for him.

⁹I wrote to you as I did to test you and see if you would fully comply with my instructions. ¹⁰When you forgive this man, I forgive him, too. And when I forgive whatever needs to be forgiven, I do so with Christ's authority for your benefit, ¹¹so that Satan will not outsmart us. For we are familiar with his evil schemes.

¹²When I came to the city of Troas to preach the Good News of Christ, the Lord opened a door of opportunity for me. ¹³But I had no peace of mind because my dear brother Titus hadn't yet arrived with a report from you. So I said good-bye and went on to Macedonia to find him.

Ministers of the New Covenant

¹⁴But thank God! He has made us his captives and continues to lead us along in Christ's triumphal procession. Now he uses us to spread the knowledge of Christ everywhere, like a sweet perfume. ¹⁵Our lives are a Christ-like fragrance rising up to God. But this fragrance is perceived differently by those who are being saved and by those who are perishing. ¹⁶To those who are perishing, we are a dreadful smell of death and doom. But to those who are being saved, we are a life-giving perfume. And who is adequate for such a task as this?

1:23–2:4 For all of his strength of personality, Paul was not insensitive to the pain of his readers. The apostle knew that the strong rebuke he needed to give these people would be devastating. He truly wanted to be positive, but he concluded that there was no way to avoid honestly confronting them about their responsibilities before God and others. Sometimes we need to be comforted; sometimes we need to be confronted. When we confront others about their failures, we must make sure that we are seeking their best, just as Paul did. It is sometimes tempting to judge others in order to cover up our own shortcomings.

2:14-17 Continued recovery is based on sharing the Good News of God's deliverance. For some of us, this may seem impossible and terrifying. Paul shows us here that it is a natural outworking of God's grace in our life. As God transforms us, giving us victory over our dependency, we begin to reflect his grace in our life. The fragrance of God's transforming work will be a "life-giving perfume" to others if we are open and transparent with them. We don't have to be an eloquent speaker to share our story and the Good News of salvation. Our humble message passed along by our words and deeds may encourage someone who needs to get his or her life back on track.

3:4-5 In his letters Paul frequently comes across as a very confident person. He explained here, however, that his confidence was not so much self-confidence as it was "God-inspired" confidence. If we trust God to work in and through us, we can know with confidence that the resources are available to overcome any problems we might face. The most healthy foundation for self-esteem is the knowledge that we are made in God's image (see Genesis 1:26-27) and that we are competent because of Christ's work on our behalf.

3:6-16 Paul's contrast between the old covenant (the law of Moses) and the new covenant (salvation through Jesus Christ) is applicable to the recovery process. The glory of the law, as well as the glory of God shining on Moses' face, faded, implying that the law was not a long-term solution to the sin problem. Likewise, the many humanistic recovery programs and other means for dealing with pain and dependencies may seem "gloriously" effective in the short run, but success through them rapidly fades. The new life that God offers through an ongoing relationship with Jesus Christ is the only means to a permanent recovery.

¹⁷You see, we are not like the many hucksters* who preach for personal profit. We preach the word of God with sincerity and with Christ's authority, knowing that God is watching us.

CHAPTER 3

Are we beginning to praise ourselves again? Are we like others, who need to bring you letters of recommendation, or who ask you to write such letters on their behalf? Surely not! ²The only letter of recommendation we need is you yourselves. Your lives are a letter written in our* hearts; everyone can read it and recognize our good work among you. ³Clearly, you are a letter from Christ showing the result of our ministry among you. This "letter" is written not with pen and ink, but with the Spirit of the living God. It is carved not on tablets of stone, but on human hearts.

⁴We are confident of all this because of our great trust in God through Christ. ⁵It is not that we think we are qualified to do anything on our own. Our qualification comes from God. ⁶He has enabled us to be ministers of his new covenant. This is a covenant not of written laws, but of the Spirit. The old written covenant ends in death; but under the new covenant, the Spirit gives life.

The Glory of the New Covenant

⁷The old way,* with laws etched in stone, led to death, though it began with such glory that the people of Israel could not bear to look at Moses' face. For his face shone with the glory of God, even though the brightness was already fading away. ⁸Shouldn't we expect far greater glory under the new way, now that the Holy Spirit is giving life? ⁹If the old way, which brings condemnation, was glorious, how much more glorious is the new way, which makes us right with God! ¹⁰In fact, that first glory was not glorious at all compared with the overwhelming glory of the new way. ¹¹So if the old way, which has been replaced, was glorious, how much more glorious is the new, which remains forever!

¹²Since this new way gives us such confidence, we can be very bold. ¹³We are not like Moses, who put a veil over his face so the people of Israel would not see the glory, even though it was destined to fade away. ¹⁴But

2:17 Some manuscripts read *the rest of the hucksters.*
3:2 Some manuscripts read *your.* 3:7 Or *ministry;* also in 3:8, 9, 10, 11, 12.

STEP 1

The Paradox of Powerlessness

BIBLE READING: 2 Corinthians 4:7-10

We admitted that we were powerless over our problems—that our lives had become unmanageable.

We may be afraid to admit that we are powerless and that our life is unmanageable. If we admit that we are powerless, won't we be tempted to give up completely in the struggle against our addiction? It doesn't seem to make sense that we can admit powerlessness and still find the power to go on. This paradox will be dealt with as we go on to Steps Two and Three.

Life is full of paradoxes. The apostle Paul tells us, "This precious treasure—this light and power that now shines within us—is held in perishable containers, that is, in our weak bodies. So everyone can see that our glorious power is from God and is not our own. We are pressed on every side by troubles, but we are not crushed and broken" (2 Corinthians 4:7-8).

The picture here contrasts a precious treasure and the simple container in which the treasure is stored. The living power poured into our life from above is the treasure. Our human body, with all its flaws and weaknesses, is the perishable container. As human beings, we are imperfect.

Once we recognize the paradox of powerlessness, we can be quite relieved. We don't have to always be strong or pretend to be perfect. We can live a real life, with its daily struggles, in a human body beset with weakness and still find the power from above to keep going without being crushed and broken. *Turn to Step Two, page 651, Job 14.*

the people's minds were hardened, and to this day whenever the old covenant is being read, the same veil covers their minds so they cannot understand the truth. And this veil can be removed only by believing in Christ. [15]Yes, even today when they read Moses' writings, their hearts are covered with that veil, and they do not understand.

[16]But whenever someone turns to the Lord, the veil is taken away. [17]For the Lord is the Spirit, and wherever the Spirit of the Lord is, there is freedom. [18]So all of us who have had that veil removed can see and reflect the glory of the Lord. And the Lord—who is the Spirit—makes us more and more like him as we are changed into his glorious image.

CHAPTER 4
Treasure in Fragile Clay Jars

Therefore, since God in his mercy has given us this new way,* we never give up. [2]We reject all shameful deeds and underhanded methods. We don't try to trick anyone or distort the word of God. We tell the truth before God, and all who are honest know this.

[3]If the Good News we preach is hidden behind a veil, it is hidden only from people who are perishing. [4]Satan, who is the god of this world, has blinded the minds of those who don't believe. They are unable to see the glorious light of the Good News. They don't understand this message about the glory of Christ, who is the exact likeness of God.

[5]You see, we don't go around preaching about ourselves. We preach that Jesus Christ is Lord, and we ourselves are your servants for Jesus' sake. [6]For God, who said, "Let there be light in the darkness," has made this light shine in our hearts so we could know the glory of God that is seen in the face of Jesus Christ.

[7]We now have this light shining in our hearts, but we ourselves are like fragile clay jars containing this great treasure.* This makes it clear that our great power is from God, not from ourselves.

[8]We are pressed on every side by troubles, but we are not crushed. We are perplexed, but not driven to despair. [9]We are hunted down, but never abandoned by God. We get knocked down, but we are not destroyed. [10]Through suffering, our bodies continue to share in the death of Jesus so that the life of Jesus may also be seen in our bodies.

[11]Yes, we live under constant danger of death because we serve Jesus, so that the life

4:1 Or *ministry.* 4:7 Greek *We now have this treasure in clay jars.*

3:17-18 The glory of God is seen in the new covenant as well as the old. But rather than being reflected on the outside, as with Moses' face, the glory of the new covenant is a transformation from the inside out. This glory shines through the lives of all who trust Jesus Christ and pursue true recovery in the power of the Holy Spirit. The further we progress in our relationship with God, the more visible God's glory becomes in our life.

4:3-4 If we will not recognize the sins in our life, we are in denial and are headed for destruction. If Satan has blinded us to our sins and addiction, we cannot accept the gift of forgiveness that God offers us through a relationship with Jesus Christ. The only way to overcome the powerful effects of our sins is to admit our helplessness and entrust our life to God. He will help us take an honest inventory of our life and empower us to change. But we begin the process by shedding our denial and accepting the Good News of salvation through Jesus Christ.

4:16-18 When we entrust our life to God, two opposite and somewhat confusing processes are simultaneously at work. On the one hand, the body's physical deterioration and eventual death are inevitable, as are the distressing trials that accompany life on this earth. On the other hand, our spirit is being renewed, preparing us day-by-day for the overwhelming glory and blessing we will experience in the presence of God throughout eternity. If we trust God to help us in our troubles now, we can look beyond those troubles to the everlasting joy he has for us in eternity.

5:6-9 The fact that God is preparing a new body and a better home for us at the end of our life cannot be proven scientifically; it must be accepted by faith because God told us so (see Hebrews 11:1). Such faith always pleases God, and it helps us overcome our great fear of death—the doorway to eternal life with God (see John 14:2-3). It is important in recovery that we entrust our life to God and seek to please him. Knowing that God wants to give us something special after this life can give us confidence and motivate us to trust him now.

5:10-11 Consequences and motives are major issues in the recovery process. Consequences for selfish and destructive actions reach even beyond the boundaries of this life. All of us will have to stand before Christ and receive his piercing evaluation. For those of us who have believed in Jesus Christ for salvation, this judgment will also include the giving of rewards. Understanding that our actions and commitments have eternal consequences can help us think twice before we act and motivate us to live according to God's program.

of Jesus will be evident in our dying bodies. ¹²So we live in the face of death, but this has resulted in eternal life for you.

¹³But we continue to preach because we have the same kind of faith the psalmist had when he said, "I believed in God, so I spoke."* ¹⁴We know that God, who raised the Lord Jesus,* will also raise us with Jesus and present us to himself together with you. ¹⁵All of this is for your benefit. And as God's grace reaches more and more people, there will be great thanksgiving, and God will receive more and more glory.

¹⁶That is why we never give up. Though our bodies are dying, our spirits are* being renewed every day. ¹⁷For our present troubles are small and won't last very long. Yet they produce for us a glory that vastly outweighs them and will last forever! ¹⁸So we don't look at the troubles we can see now; rather, we fix our gaze on things that cannot be seen. For the things we see now will soon be gone, but the things we cannot see will last forever.

CHAPTER 5
New Bodies

For we know that when this earthly tent we live in is taken down (that is, when we die and leave this earthly body), we will have a house in heaven, an eternal body made for us by God himself and not by human hands. ²We grow weary in our present bodies, and we long to put on our heavenly bodies like new clothing. ³For we will put on heavenly bodies; we will not be spirits without bodies.* ⁴While we live in these earthly bodies, we groan and sigh, but it's not that we want to die and get rid of these bodies that clothe us. Rather, we want to put on our new bodies so that these dying bodies will be swallowed up by life. ⁵God himself has prepared us for this, and as a guarantee he has given us his Holy Spirit.

⁶So we are always confident, even though we know that as long as we live in these bodies we are not at home with the Lord. ⁷For we live by believing and not by seeing. ⁸Yes, we are fully confident, and we would rather be away from these earthly bodies, for then we will be at home with the Lord. ⁹So whether we are here in this body or away from this body, our goal is to please him. ¹⁰For we must all stand before Christ to be judged. We will each receive whatever we deserve for the good or evil we have done in this earthly body.

4:13 Ps 116:10. 4:14 Some manuscripts read *who raised Jesus.* 4:16 Greek *our inner being is.* 5:3 Greek *we will not be naked.*

SELF-PERCEPTION

READ 2 CORINTHIANS 5:12-21
Our addiction may be so ingrained in us that we define our identity by it. We may even begin to feel that we are predisposed to behave as we do. We may grow discouraged as we are condemned for behaviors that seem beyond our control. How can we escape our self-perception that causes us to define ourself in terms of the addiction that dominates our life?

One passage in Scripture seems to identify people by their behavior: "Those who indulge in sexual sin, or who worship idols, or commit adultery, or are male prostitutes, or practice homosexuality, or are thieves, or greedy people, or drunkards, or are abusive, or cheat people—none of these will inherit the Kingdom of God" (1 Corinthians 6:9-10). This doesn't seem fair. We feel like we will never be able to escape our addictive nature. But the passage continues: "Some of you were once like that. But you were cleansed; you were made holy; you were made right with God by calling on the name of the Lord Jesus Christ and by the Spirit of our God" (6:11). "Anyone who belongs to Christ has become a new person. The old life is gone; a new life has begun!" (2 Corinthians 5:17).

God doesn't just erase our sinful behaviors. When we identify ourself with Christ, he gives us a new identity. We will always remember what we were and realize that our sinful nature and our body may always be predisposed to a particular addiction. We may even still slip up at times, but we need no longer define ourself by our addiction. In Christ we are all the forgiven, cleansed, and holy children of God. *Turn to page 1501, Galatians 5.*

We Are God's Ambassadors

[11]Because we understand our fearful responsibility to the Lord, we work hard to persuade others. God knows we are sincere, and I hope you know this, too. [12]Are we commending ourselves to you again? No, we are giving you a reason to be proud of us,* so you can answer those who brag about having a spectacular ministry rather than having a sincere heart. [13]If it seems we are crazy, it is to bring glory to God. And if we are in our right minds, it is for your benefit. [14]Either way, Christ's love controls us.* Since we believe that Christ died for all, we also believe that we have all died to our old life.* [15]He died for everyone so that those who receive his new life will no longer live for themselves. Instead, they will live for Christ, who died and was raised for them.

[16]So we have stopped evaluating others from a human point of view. At one time we thought of Christ merely from a human point of view. How differently we know him now! [17]This means that anyone who belongs to Christ has become a new person. The old life is gone; a new life has begun!

[18]And all of this is a gift from God, who brought us back to himself through Christ. And God has given us this task of reconciling people to him. [19]For God was in Christ, reconciling the world to himself, no longer counting people's sins against them. And he gave us this wonderful message of reconciliation. [20]So we are Christ's ambassadors; God is making his appeal through us. We speak for Christ when we plead, "Come back to God!" [21]For God made Christ, who never sinned, to be the offering for our sin,* so that we could be made right with God through Christ.

CHAPTER 6

As God's partners,* we beg you not to accept this marvelous gift of God's kindness and then ignore it. [2]For God says,

"At just the right time, I heard you.
On the day of salvation, I helped you."*

Indeed, the "right time" is now. Today is the day of salvation.

Paul's Hardships

[3]We live in such a way that no one will stumble because of us, and no one will find fault with our ministry. [4]In everything we do, we show that we are true ministers of God. We patiently endure troubles and hardships and calamities of every kind. [5]We have been beaten, been put in prison, faced angry mobs, worked to exhaustion, endured sleepless nights, and gone without food. [6]We prove ourselves by our purity, our understanding, our patience, our kindness, by the Holy Spirit within us,* and by our sincere love. [7]We faithfully preach the truth. God's power is working in us. We use the weapons of righteousness in the right hand for attack and the left hand for defense. [8]We serve God whether people honor us or despise us, whether they slander us or praise us. We are honest, but they call us impostors. [9]We are

5:12 Some manuscripts read *proud of yourselves.* 5:14a Or *urges us on.* 5:14b Greek *Since one died for all, then all died.* 5:21 Or *to become sin itself.* 6:1 Or *As we work together.* 6:2 Isa 49:8 (Greek version). 6:6 Or *by our holiness of spirit.*

5:17 The new life we experience in Jesus Christ is so far-reaching and complete that we become a brand-new person through him. That does not mean that our thoughts and habits, including our compulsion or addiction, will automatically vanish. But it does mean that from God's point of view, we have been forgiven—we are a new creature in his sight. And through the power of God's Holy Spirit, we have all the power necessary for complete transformation in every area of our life.

5:18-21 One of the great needs in most recovery contexts is the reconciliation of dysfunctional or fractured relationships. At the human level, this is very difficult to do. But in the case of our broken relationship with God, he has already met us more than halfway by offering us reconciliation through Jesus Christ. God's work of reconciliation is even more profound since God committed none of the wrongs in our relationship with him. By accepting the forgiveness he offers, our relationship with God can be restored. We are also called to follow God and forgive others. If the gift of forgiveness is offered by someone else, we can humbly accept it. In this way we can begin rebuilding our relationships and making amends to the people we have wronged.

6:8-10 When we live for God and follow his program for godly living, others will react to us in one of two ways. Some honor us as genuine and support what we are trying to do; others will malign and dishonor us. If we are trying to impress others to bolster our self-esteem, we will be devastated when people react negatively. This may lead us to give up on what we have started. Paul received his self-esteem from his relationship with God and did not need to be honored by others. He knew that he could never please everyone anyway. If we live to please God, we will find that as we build healthy relationships with others we will have joy.

ignored, even though we are well known. We live close to death, but we are still alive. We have been beaten, but we have not been killed. [10]Our hearts ache, but we always have joy. We are poor, but we give spiritual riches to others. We own nothing, and yet we have everything.

[11]Oh, dear Corinthian friends! We have spoken honestly with you, and our hearts are open to you. [12]There is no lack of love on our part, but you have withheld your love from us. [13]I am asking you to respond as if you were my own children. Open your hearts to us!

The Temple of the Living God

[14]Don't team up with those who are unbelievers. How can righteousness be a partner with wickedness? How can light live with darkness? [15]What harmony can there be between Christ and the devil*? How can a believer be a partner with an unbeliever? [16]And what union can there be between God's temple and idols? For we are the temple of the living God. As God said:

"I will live in them
    and walk among them.
I will be their God,
    and they will be my people.*
[17]Therefore, come out from among
        unbelievers,
    and separate yourselves from them,
        says the LORD.

Don't touch their filthy things,
    and I will welcome you.*
[18]And I will be your Father,
    and you will be my sons and daughters,
    says the LORD Almighty.*"

CHAPTER 7

Because we have these promises, dear friends, let us cleanse ourselves from everything that can defile our body or spirit. And let us work toward complete holiness because we fear God.

[2]Please open your hearts to us. We have not done wrong to anyone, nor led anyone astray, nor taken advantage of anyone. [3]I'm not saying this to condemn you. I said before that you are in our hearts, and we live or die together with you. [4]I have the highest confidence in you, and I take great pride in you. You have greatly encouraged me and made me happy despite all our troubles.

Paul's Joy at the Church's Repentance

[5]When we arrived in Macedonia, there was no rest for us. We faced conflict from every direction, with battles on the outside and fear on the inside. [6]But God, who encourages those who are discouraged, encouraged us by the arrival of Titus. [7]His presence was a joy, but so was the news he brought of the encouragement he received from you. When he told us how much you long to see me, and how sorry you are for what happened,

---

6:15 Greek *Beliar*; various other manuscripts render this proper name of the devil as *Belian, Beliab,* or *Belial.*
6:16 Lev 26:12; Ezek 37:27. 6:17 Isa 52:11; Ezek 20:34 (Greek version). 6:18 2 Sam 7:14.

6:11-13 Paul went the extra mile to reconcile with the Corinthians. Having defended his sincerity toward them earlier (see 1:12-23), he again pledged his honest affection to his readers, challenging them to do the same for him. In recovering relationships, one party often withholds affection to childishly punish the other. This only leads to deeper alienation and loss. We may not be able to control how other people act in a broken relationship, but we can control how *we* act. We should never withhold forgiveness. Like Paul, we should extend the invitation of reconciliation to others, humbly and without reservation.

6:14-18 Since we started the recovery process, we may have struggled with our past friendships. Some old friends may be uncomfortable with us because they feel guilty about their own dependency. Others may be threatened by the changes we are making because they can no longer control us. These people may try to stop us from making progress. Very often we need to put our codependent relationships on hold for a time, sometimes even permanently. This does not mean we do not reach out to unbelievers; it only means that we do not become too close to people who could lead us away from God and the recovery he desires for us. Our primary relationships need to be with unselfish, godly people who will support our recovery.

7:5-7 For all his determined and aggressive style of ministry, Paul was definitely a man with emotions. Here he freely admitted his fears during a very difficult time. But he was greatly comforted by God through the arrival of Titus from Corinth. Titus brought news that the Corinthian believers had changed their negative attitudes toward Paul. In recovery it is important that we keep a similar balance between our personal tasks and our relationships. If we get so focused on the recovery tasks that we undervalue our relationships, our recovery is at risk. One of the most important parts of recovery is reconciliation with other people, without which long-term success is impossible.

and how loyal you are to me, I was filled with joy!

⁸I am not sorry that I sent that severe letter to you, though I was sorry at first, for I know it was painful to you for a little while. ⁹Now I am glad I sent it, not because it hurt you, but because the pain caused you to repent and change your ways. It was the kind of sorrow God wants his people to have, so you were not harmed by us in any way. ¹⁰For the kind of sorrow God wants us to experience leads us away from sin and results in salvation. There's no regret for that kind of sorrow. But worldly sorrow, which lacks repentance, results in spiritual death.

¹¹Just see what this godly sorrow produced in you! Such earnestness, such concern to clear yourselves, such indignation, such alarm, such longing to see me, such zeal, and such a readiness to punish wrong. You showed that you have done everything necessary to make things right. ¹²My purpose, then, was not to write about who did the wrong or who was wronged. I wrote to you so that in the sight of God you could see for yourselves how loyal you are to us. ¹³We have been greatly encouraged by this.

In addition to our own encouragement, we were especially delighted to see how happy Titus was about the way all of you welcomed him and set his mind* at ease. ¹⁴I had told him how proud I was of you—and you didn't disappoint me. I have always told you the truth, and now my boasting to Titus has also proved true! ¹⁵Now he cares for you more than ever when he remembers the way all of you obeyed him and welcomed him with such fear and deep respect. ¹⁶I am very happy now because I have complete confidence in you.

CHAPTER 8
A Call to Generous Giving
Now I want you to know, dear brothers and sisters,* what God in his kindness has done through the churches in Macedonia. ²They are being tested by many troubles, and they are very poor. But they are also filled with abundant joy, which has overflowed in rich generosity.

³For I can testify that they gave not only what they could afford, but far more. And they did it of their own free will. ⁴They begged us again and again for the privilege of sharing in the gift for the believers in Jerusalem.* ⁵They even did more than we had hoped, for their first action was to give themselves to the Lord and to us, just as God wanted them to do.

⁶So we have urged Titus, who encouraged your giving in the first place, to return to you and encourage you to finish this ministry of giving. ⁷Since you excel in so many ways—in your faith, your gifted speakers, your knowledge, your enthusiasm, and your love from us*—I want you to excel also in this gracious act of giving.

7:13 Greek *his spirit.* 8:1 Greek *brothers.* 8:4 Greek *for God's holy people.* 8:7 Some manuscripts read *your love for us.*

7:11-13 When we admit our sins to God and others and do what we can to follow God's will, wonderful changes take place in our life. In these verses we see that such repentance produces fruit on three fronts: (1) it purifies and revitalizes our life and emotions in a remarkable way; (2) it renews our relationship with God; and (3) it has an amazing effect for good on our relationships with other people, both those we have wronged and onlookers who are encouraged by the refreshing changes that have taken place.

7:15 For all the mistakes the Corinthians made in their relationship with Paul, they did do one thing right. They listened when Titus presented Paul's version of some earlier events that they had misinterpreted. This teachability and lack of defensiveness drew great admiration and love from both Titus and Paul. A willingness to listen and be teachable is necessary for a successful recovery. It will help us take honest moral inventory and follow God's good plan for our life.

8:9 Jesus Christ is the perfect model for graciously helping others. He became a lowly human being and died like a criminal on a cross to conquer our enemies—sin and death. He gave up his heavenly glory and willingly suffered on our behalf (see Philippians 2:6-8). Thus, besides enriching our life spiritually, Christ can also strongly identify with our pain and temptation (see Hebrews 4:15). He is available and able to help us in recovery. As we receive his help, we can then reach out helping hands to others in need.

8:10-12 It is much easier to start something than to finish it. This is especially true as we work through the recovery process. Thus, perseverance is crucial for those of us with the tendency to "run out of gas." The Corinthians had enthusiastically started a relief fund for the Jerusalem church but failed to follow through on their commitment. Paul confronted them and encouraged them to persevere in this worthy task. Recovery is no less worthy of perseverance. We need to do more than make promises and verbal commitments to recovery; we need to follow through on them as well.

8I am not commanding you to do this. But I am testing how genuine your love is by comparing it with the eagerness of the other churches.

9You know the generous grace of our Lord Jesus Christ. Though he was rich, yet for your sakes he became poor, so that by his poverty he could make you rich.

10Here is my advice: It would be good for you to finish what you started a year ago. Last year you were the first who wanted to give, and you were the first to begin doing it. 11Now you should finish what you started. Let the eagerness you showed in the beginning be matched now by your giving. Give in proportion to what you have. 12Whatever you give is acceptable if you give it eagerly. And give according to what you have, not what you don't have. 13Of course, I don't mean your giving should make life easy for others and hard for yourselves. I only mean that there should be some equality. 14Right now you have plenty and can help those who are in need. Later, they will have plenty and can share with you when you need it. In this way, things will be equal. 15As the Scriptures say,

"Those who gathered a lot had nothing
     left over,
and those who gathered only a little
     had enough."*

Titus and His Companions

16But thank God! He has given Titus the same enthusiasm for you that I have. 17Titus welcomed our request that he visit you again. In fact, he himself was very eager to go and see you. 18We are also sending another brother with Titus. All the churches praise him as a preacher of the Good News. 19He was appointed by the churches to accompany us as we take the offering to Jerusalem*—a service that glorifies the Lord and shows our eagerness to help.

20We are traveling together to guard against any criticism for the way we are handling this generous gift. 21We are careful to be honorable before the Lord, but we also want everyone else to see that we are honorable.

22We are also sending with them another of our brothers who has proven himself many times and has shown on many occasions how eager he is. He is now even more enthusiastic because of his great confidence in you. 23If anyone asks about Titus, say that he is my partner who works with me to help

8:15 Exod 16:18. 8:19 See 1 Cor 16:3-4.

STEP 4

Constructive Sorrow

BIBLE READING: 2 Corinthians 7:8-11
We made a searching and fearless moral inventory of ourselves.
We all have to deal with sorrow. We may try to stuff it down and ignore it. We may try to drown it by giving in to our addiction or avoid feeling it by intellectualizing. But sorrow doesn't go away. We need to accept the sorrow that will be a part of the inventory process.

Not all sorrow is bad for us. The apostle Paul had written a letter to the church in Corinth that made them very sad because Paul confronted them about something they were doing wrong. At first he was sorry that he had hurt them, but later he said, "Now I am glad I sent it, not because it hurt you, but because the pain caused you to repent and change your ways. It was the kind of sorrow God wants his people to have. . . . For the kind of sorrow God wants us to experience leads us away from sin and results in salvation. There's no regret for that kind of sorrow. . . . Just see what this godly sorrow produced in you! . . . You showed that you have done everything necessary to make things right" (2 Corinthians 7:9-11).

Jeremiah said, "Though [God] brings grief, he also shows compassion because of the greatness of his unfailing love. For he does not enjoy hurting people or causing them sorrow" (Lamentations 3:32-33).

The Corinthians' grief was good, it came from honest self-evaluation, not morbid self-condemnation. We can learn to accept our sorrow as a positive part of recovery, not as punishment. *Turn to page 1667, Revelation 20.*

you. And the brothers with him have been sent by the churches,* and they bring honor to Christ. [24]So show them your love, and prove to all the churches that our boasting about you is justified.

CHAPTER 9
The Collection for Christians in Jerusalem

I really don't need to write to you about this ministry of giving for the believers in Jerusalem.* [2]For I know how eager you are to help, and I have been boasting to the churches in Macedonia that you in Greece* were ready to send an offering a year ago. In fact, it was your enthusiasm that stirred up many of the Macedonian believers to begin giving.

[3]But I am sending these brothers to be sure you really are ready, as I have been telling them, and that your money is all collected. I don't want to be wrong in my boasting about you. [4]We would be embarrassed—not to mention your own embarrassment—if some Macedonian believers came with me and found that you weren't ready after all I had told them! [5]So I thought I should send these brothers ahead of me to make sure the gift you promised is ready. But I want it to be a willing gift, not one given grudgingly.

[6]Remember this—a farmer who plants only a few seeds will get a small crop. But the one who plants generously will get a generous crop. [7]You must each decide in your heart how much to give. And don't give reluctantly or in response to pressure. "For God loves a person who gives cheerfully."* [8]And God will generously provide all you need. Then you will always have everything you need and plenty left over to share with others. [9]As the Scriptures say,

"They share freely and give generously to the poor.
Their good deeds will be remembered forever."*

[10]For God is the one who provides seed for the farmer and then bread to eat. In the same way, he will provide and increase your resources and then produce a great harvest of generosity* in you.

[11]Yes, you will be enriched in every way so that you can always be generous. And when we take your gifts to those who need them, they will thank God. [12]So two good things will result from this ministry of giving—the needs of the believers in Jerusalem* will be met, and they will joyfully express their thanks to God.

[13]As a result of your ministry, they will give glory to God. For your generosity to them and to all believers will prove that you are obedient to the Good News of Christ. [14]And they will pray for you with deep affection because of the overflowing grace God has given to you. [15]Thank God for this gift* too wonderful for words!

CHAPTER 10
Paul Defends His Authority

Now I, Paul, appeal to you with the gentleness and kindness of Christ—though I realize you think I am timid in person and bold only when I write from far away. [2]Well, I am begging you now so that when I come I won't have to be bold with those who think we act from human motives.

[3]We are human, but we don't wage war as humans do. [4]We use God's mighty weapons, not worldly weapons, to knock down the strongholds of human reasoning and to destroy false arguments. [5]We destroy every proud obstacle that keeps people from knowing God. We capture their rebellious thoughts and teach them to obey Christ. [6]And after you have become fully obedient, we will punish everyone who remains disobedient.

[7]Look at the obvious facts.* Those who say they belong to Christ must recognize that we belong to Christ as much as they do. [8]I may seem to be boasting too much about the authority given to us by the Lord. But our authority builds you up; it doesn't tear you

---

8:23 Greek *are apostles of the churches.* 9:1 Greek *about the offering for God's holy people.* 9:2 Greek *in Achaia,* the southern region of the Greek peninsula. *Macedonia* was in the northern region of Greece. 9:7 See footnote on Prov 22:8. 9:9 Ps 112:9. 9:10 Greek *righteousness.* 9:12 Greek *of God's holy people.* 9:15 Greek *his gift.* 10:4 English translations divide verses 4 and 5 in various ways. 10:7 Or *You look at things only on the basis of appearance.*

9:6-9 The more spiritual seeds we plant by generously helping others, the greater will be our harvest of spiritual fruit. God never forces us to give; he wants us to give with willing hearts. God is not only interested in what we do; he is also interested in the attitudes and motives behind our actions. Some of us may feel that we don't have much to offer people in need. Our life may be in ruins; we may have gone into debt to support destructive habits. But even if we have nothing else to give, we can share our story of how God gave us a second chance. As little as this may seem to us, it may be the gift of life to someone in the throes of an addiction.

down. So I will not be ashamed of using my authority.

⁹I'm not trying to frighten you by my letters. ¹⁰For some say, "Paul's letters are demanding and forceful, but in person he is weak, and his speeches are worthless!" ¹¹Those people should realize that our actions when we arrive in person will be as forceful as what we say in our letters from far away.

¹²Oh, don't worry; we wouldn't dare say that we are as wonderful as these other men who tell you how important they are! But they are only comparing themselves with each other, using themselves as the standard of measurement. How ignorant!

¹³We will not boast about things done outside our area of authority. We will boast only about what has happened within the boundaries of the work God has given us, which includes our working with you. ¹⁴We are not reaching beyond these boundaries when we claim authority over you, as if we had never visited you. For we were the first to travel all the way to Corinth with the Good News of Christ.

¹⁵Nor do we boast and claim credit for the work someone else has done. Instead, we hope that your faith will grow so that the boundaries of our work among you will be extended. ¹⁶Then we will be able to go and preach the Good News in other places far beyond you, where no one else is working. Then there will be no question of our boasting about work done in someone else's territory. ¹⁷As the Scriptures say, "If you want to boast, boast only about the LORD."*

¹⁸When people commend themselves, it doesn't count for much. The important thing is for the Lord to commend them.

CHAPTER 11
Paul and the False Apostles

I hope you will put up with a little more of my foolishness. Please bear with me. ²For I am jealous for you with the jealousy of God himself. I promised you as a pure bride* to one husband—Christ. ³But I fear that somehow your pure and undivided devotion to Christ will be corrupted, just as Eve was deceived by the cunning ways of the serpent. ⁴You happily put up with whatever anyone tells you, even if they preach a different Jesus than the one we preach, or a different kind of Spirit than the one you received, or a different kind of gospel than the one you believed.

⁵But I don't consider myself inferior in any way to these "super apostles" who teach such things. ⁶I may be unskilled as a speaker, but I'm not lacking in knowledge. We have made this clear to you in every possible way.

⁷Was I wrong when I humbled myself and honored you by preaching God's Good News to you without expecting anything in return? ⁸I "robbed" other churches by accepting their contributions so I could serve you at no cost. ⁹And when I was with you and didn't have enough to live on, I did not become a financial burden to anyone. For the brothers who came from Macedonia brought me all that I needed. I have never been a burden to you, and I never will be. ¹⁰As surely as the truth of Christ is in me, no one in all of Greece* will ever stop me from boasting about this. ¹¹Why? Because I don't love you? God knows that I do.

¹²But I will continue doing what I have always done. This will undercut those who are looking for an opportunity to boast that their work is just like ours. ¹³These people are

10:17 Jer 9:24. 11:2 Greek *a virgin.* 11:10 Greek *Achaia,* the southern region of the Greek peninsula.

10:13-15 From a recovery perspective, it is illuminating to note that Paul had set limits on his ministry based on his understanding of God's will for him. Our recovery activities also need to be in line with God's plan. We must concentrate our limited energy on priorities that reflect God's will. Paul was sensitive to God's will for his life, and he was confident that his leadership over the Corinthian church was a part of that plan. We can be sure that recovery is part of God's plan for us. We need to learn what activities he wants us to be involved in on a daily basis. Insight concerning God's will for us is likely to come through prayer, study of the Scriptures, the help of godly friends, or the guidance from the Holy Spirit.

11:2-4 Paul was worried that the Corinthian believers would replace their faith in Jesus with a false faith. Corinth was a cosmopolitan city; numerous pagan religions and cults were practiced there. Paul also was concerned because rejecting Christ would lead to painful consequences. Believers might reject the abundant life offered by Jesus Christ for lives of ultimate disaster. We also live in a world of multiple religions; recovery programs can be found that represent most of them. But true recovery is possible only through the work of Jesus Christ and the power of the Holy Spirit. Rejecting the hope offered in Christ is rejecting the only real power available for recovery. Looking to any other power will lead to disappointment and failure.

false apostles. They are deceitful workers who disguise themselves as apostles of Christ. [14]But I am not surprised! Even Satan disguises himself as an angel of light. [15]So it is no wonder that his servants also disguise themselves as servants of righteousness. In the end they will get the punishment their wicked deeds deserve.

Paul's Many Trials

[16]Again I say, don't think that I am a fool to talk like this. But even if you do, listen to me, as you would to a foolish person, while I also boast a little. [17]Such boasting is not from the Lord, but I am acting like a fool. [18]And since others boast about their human achievements, I will, too. [19]After all, you think you are so wise, but you enjoy putting up with fools! [20]You put up with it when someone enslaves you, takes everything you have, takes advantage of you, takes control of everything, and slaps you in the face. [21]I'm ashamed to say that we've been too "weak" to do that!

But whatever they dare to boast about—I'm talking like a fool again—I dare to boast about it, too. [22]Are they Hebrews? So am I. Are they Israelites? So am I. Are they descendants of Abraham? So am I. [23]Are they servants of Christ? I know I sound like a madman, but I have served him far more! I have worked harder, been put in prison more often, been whipped times without number, and faced death again and again. [24]Five different times the Jewish leaders gave me thirty-nine lashes. [25]Three times I was beaten with rods. Once I was stoned. Three times I was shipwrecked. Once I spent a whole night and a day adrift at sea. [26]I have traveled on many long journeys. I have faced danger from rivers and from robbers. I have faced danger from my own people, the Jews, as well as from the Gentiles. I have faced danger in the cities, in the deserts, and on the seas. And I have faced danger from men who claim to be believers but are not.* [27]I have worked hard and long, enduring many sleepless nights. I have been hungry and thirsty and have often gone without food. I have shivered in the cold, without enough clothing to keep me warm.

[28]Then, besides all this, I have the daily burden of my concern for all the churches. [29]Who is weak without my feeling that weakness? Who is led astray, and I do not burn with anger?

[30]If I must boast, I would rather boast about the things that show how weak I am. [31]God, the Father of our Lord Jesus, who is worthy of eternal praise, knows I am not lying. [32]When I was in Damascus, the governor under King Aretas kept guards at the city gates to catch me. [33]I had to be lowered in a basket through a window in the city wall to escape from him.

CHAPTER 12
Paul's Vision and His Thorn in the Flesh

This boasting will do no good, but I must go on. I will reluctantly tell about visions and revelations from the Lord. [2]I* was caught up to the third heaven fourteen years ago. Whether I was in my body or out of my body, I don't know—only God knows. [3]Yes, only God knows whether I was in my body or outside my body. But I do know [4]that I was caught up* to paradise and heard things so astounding that they cannot be expressed in words, things no human is allowed to tell.

11:26 Greek *from false brothers.* 12:2 Greek *I know a man in Christ who.* 12:3-4 Greek *But I know such a man,* [4]*that he was caught up.*

11:13-15 The Corinthian believers had apparently rejected Paul's teachings in order to follow a number of false teachers who had twisted the Christian message. These false leaders were probably Judaizers who taught that salvation came through faith in Christ plus adherence to the Jewish law (see 11:22). Sometimes we are tempted to follow the same heresy. We want to earn our recovery by working hard. This approach, however, is powerless over our dependency. We need God's help. Paul made it clear in all of his letters that salvation is a free gift, paid for by the sacrificial work of Jesus Christ. Without God, we are helpless against the power of sin in our life. But with his help, we can overcome our dependency.

11:23-29 Paul demonstrated his commitment to Jesus Christ by listing the tremendous hardships he had suffered. If nothing else, such ongoing mistreatment, deprivation, and the burden of his ministry responsibility revealed his perseverance. Paul was definitely no fair-weather minister or friend. If we display the kind of commitment to recovery that Paul had for his ministry, we will receive the same kind of powerful help that Paul experienced in his service for Christ.

11:30; 12:1-10 Paul's "boasting" was not intended to make him look better than he really was. He boasted about his weakness so Christ could work through him (see 12:9). Even though the apostle told of his incredible vision of heaven (12:1-4), he quickly admitted his own weaknesses (11:30; 12:5). He recounted how he sensed God's grace even through his chronic physical

⁵That experience is worth boasting about, but I'm not going to do it. I will boast only about my weaknesses. ⁶If I wanted to boast, I would be no fool in doing so, because I would be telling the truth. But I won't do it, because I don't want anyone to give me credit beyond what they can see in my life or hear in my message, ⁷even though I have received such wonderful revelations from God. So to keep me from becoming proud, I was given a thorn in my flesh, a messenger from Satan to torment me and keep me from becoming proud.

⁸Three different times I begged the Lord to take it away. ⁹Each time he said, "My grace is all you need. My power works best in weakness." So now I am glad to boast about my weaknesses, so that the power of Christ can work through me. ¹⁰That's why I take pleasure in my weaknesses, and in the insults, hardships, persecutions, and troubles that I suffer for Christ. For when I am weak, then I am strong.

Paul's Concern for the Corinthians

¹¹You have made me act like a fool. You ought to be writing commendations for me, for I am not at all inferior to these "super apostles," even though I am nothing at all. ¹²When I was with you, I certainly gave you proof that I am an apostle. For I patiently did many signs and wonders and miracles among you. ¹³The only thing I failed to do, which I do in the other churches, was to become a financial burden to you. Please forgive me for this wrong!

¹⁴Now I am coming to you for the third time, and I will not be a burden to you. I don't want what you have—I want you. After all, children don't provide for their parents. Rather, parents provide for their children. ¹⁵I will gladly spend myself and all I have for you, even though it seems that the more I love you, the less you love me.

¹⁶Some of you admit I was not a burden to you. But others still think I was sneaky and took advantage of you by trickery. ¹⁷But how? Did any of the men I sent to you take advantage of you? ¹⁸When I urged Titus to visit you and sent our other brother with him, did Titus take advantage of you? No! For we have the same spirit and walk in each other's steps, doing things the same way.

¹⁹Perhaps you think we're saying these things just to defend ourselves. No, we tell you this as Christ's servants, and with God as our witness. Everything we do, dear friends, is to strengthen you. ²⁰For I am afraid that when I come I won't like what I find, and you won't like my response. I am afraid that I will find quarreling, jealousy, anger, selfishness, slander, gossip, arrogance, and disorderly behavior. ²¹Yes, I am afraid that when I come again, God will humble me in your presence. And I will be grieved because many of you have not given up your old sins. You have not repented of your impurity, sexual immorality, and eagerness for lustful pleasure.

CHAPTER 13
Paul's Final Advice

This is the third time I am coming to visit you (and as the Scriptures say, "The facts of every case must be established by the testimony of two or three witnesses"*). ²I have

13:1 Deut 19:15.

---

suffering and spiritual warfare (12:9-10). Paul honestly assessed his life, recognizing both his strengths and weaknesses. Then he accepted and received the power that God offers to all who look to him. Paul is a good model for us to follow. When we make an honest assessment of our life and learn to depend upon God's infinite resources, we will make significant progress in recovery.

12:19-21 Everything that Paul said to the Corinthians, both negative and positive, was intended for their good. Paul was concerned that they mature in their faith, and he did what he could to encourage their spiritual growth. The demands he made on these believers were motivated by his love and concern for them. Many of us have realized that we often communicate with others for selfish reasons. When we compliment people, we are looking for something in return rather than trying to honestly build them up. When we criticize others, we are seeking to destroy rather than correct. As we take moral inventory, we need to be aware of our tendency to use others for our own ends. As we seek to restore our damaged relationships, the apostle Paul is an excellent model to follow.

13:2-3 Paul had warned the Corinthians earlier that discipline would be forthcoming if they did not face their personal and interpersonal sins. Here he gave them an additional warning because he had been away from Corinth for longer than he had intended. He wanted to make sure that the people knew his warning was not hollow. Paul would indeed follow through forcefully and hold the Corinthian believers accountable to their commitments to God. We all need people like Paul in our life—godly people who can hold us accountable to our recovery commitments and our obedience to God.

already warned those who had been sinning when I was there on my second visit. Now I again warn them and all others, just as I did before, that next time I will not spare them.

³I will give you all the proof you want that Christ speaks through me. Christ is not weak when he deals with you; he is powerful among you. ⁴Although he was crucified in weakness, he now lives by the power of God. We, too, are weak, just as Christ was, but when we deal with you we will be alive with him and will have God's power.

⁵Examine yourselves to see if your faith is genuine. Test yourselves. Surely you know that Jesus Christ is among you*; if not, you have failed the test of genuine faith. ⁶As you test yourselves, I hope you will recognize that we have not failed the test of apostolic authority.

⁷We pray to God that you will not do what is wrong by refusing our correction. I hope we won't need to demonstrate our authority when we arrive. Do the right thing before we come—even if that makes it look like we have failed to demonstrate our authority. ⁸For we cannot oppose the truth, but must always stand for the truth. ⁹We are glad to seem weak if it helps show that you are actually strong. We pray that you will become mature.

¹⁰I am writing this to you before I come, hoping that I won't need to deal severely with you when I do come. For I want to use the authority the Lord has given me to strengthen you, not to tear you down.

Paul's Final Greetings

¹¹Dear brothers and sisters,* I close my letter with these last words: Be joyful. Grow to maturity. Encourage each other. Live in harmony and peace. Then the God of love and peace will be with you.

¹²Greet each other with a sacred kiss. ¹³All of God's people here send you their greetings.

¹⁴*May the grace of the Lord Jesus Christ, the love of God, and the fellowship of the Holy Spirit be with you all.

13:5 Or *in you.* **13:11** Greek *Brothers.* **13:14** Some English translations include verse 13 as part of verse 12, and then verse 14 becomes verse 13.

13:5-6 Paul urged the Corinthian believers to seriously examine themselves. He wanted them to assess the nature of their commitment to God by looking closely at their own lives. This is an essential part of the recovery process. We need to engage in honest self-examination if we hope to uncover the problems that tear down our relationships and drive our dependency. As we admit our failures to God, he will forgive us and help us make progress in recovery.

13:11 As Paul closed this letter to the Corinthians, he left them with some worthy challenges and goals to pursue. In essence, he admonished the people to open their minds and hearts to personal change and the healing of their relationships. Such spiritual growth and interpersonal harmony can be fueled by faith in God, the ultimate source of healing love and peace. As modern readers of this letter, we, too, can benefit by acting on Paul's wise counsel.

REFLECTIONS ON 2 CORINTHIANS

insights ABOUT PRAYER

It is essential that we learn to encourage others in recovery without giving up the balance in our own life. That is exactly what Paul was asking the Corinthians to do in **2 Corinthians 1:11** when he requested their prayers. By praying for the needs of the apostle and his companions, the Corinthian believers would be helping and strengthening them from a distance. Because of our own weaknesses, we sometimes are unable to help some of the people we care about. To maintain our own recovery, we have to keep our distance. But this does not mean that we need to forget about them. We can help them by praying that they will discover how helpless they are without God and that they will turn to him for help. God has the power to do for them what we may not be able to do through direct contact.

insights ABOUT RESTORING RELATIONSHIPS

A problem in the Corinthian church (probably the one described in **1 Corinthians 5:1-11**) was the basis for Paul's rebuke in **2 Corinthians 2:5-11.** When the troublemaker in question repented of his sin and honestly faced the consequences of his behavior, the Corinthian believers refused to forgive him. Paul pointed out how cruel it was to withhold forgiveness. The apostle explained that through their lack of forgiveness they were actually playing right into Satan's hands by discouraging the repentant party. We need to make sure that when others repent of their sins, we do our part to encourage the process of restoration and healing. Most of us have experienced the pain of being rejected, even after admitting our mistakes and trying to change. We should be the last to cause the same kind of pain to others.

insights FOR SURVIVAL DURING TOUGH TIMES

In **2 Corinthians 4:8-11** Paul reflects on the value of suffering. The hard times in life tend to either crush and disillusion or challenge and stimulate us. It is hard for us to keep going when the going gets tough. But it can be a real encouragement to know that God is with us in the midst of the trials we face, and that he can use even our weaknesses for his glory. In fact, our perseverance in recovery from our addiction may be the gift of life to other people in bondage to a powerful dependency. As they see God's work in our life, they may gain the courage to face and conquer their own addiction with God's powerful help.

In **2 Corinthians 5:1-5** Paul reminded his readers that their weak bodies would someday be replaced by glorious new ones. To many of us, the aging process is a depressing reality—one we'd like to avoid. The fact that we pay great sums of money for cosmetic surgery, hair coloring, and the like is evidence of that. But there is a comforting side to aging if we trust Jesus Christ for our salvation and recovery. Before long, we will "check in" our present physical body and receive a glorified eternal body. The Holy Spirit's presence in our life is the guarantee that we are drawing ever closer to that point.

insights ABOUT SHARING THE GOOD NEWS

We find in **2 Corinthians 6:3-4** that Paul sought to live in such a way that no one would be offended or kept away from God on his account. He was a model for other believers to look up to and follow. Some of us who have been in recovery for a while may have found it exhausting to be a model for the recovery of others. We have felt the burdens of numerous expectations. As a result, some of us may have quit trying to help others in recovery. As we grow spiritually, the responsibility to help others will always be there. The apostle Paul took this responsibility very seriously and acted out of concern for the well-being of others. Though this may be a difficult burden for some of us, it may help us to realize that being a model for others in recovery is one of the ways that God keeps us on the road toward wholeness.

insights ABOUT CONFRONTATION

Paul had apparently written a short letter between 1 and 2 Corinthians that was not included among the New Testament books. From his mention of the letter in **2 Corinthians 7:8-10**, it must have been quite sharp in tone. He admits that he had mixed feelings about sending that letter. But because of the Corinthians' positive response to his tough love, all his regrets had vanished. In recovery situations, we must realize that when we confront others, we are taking a calculated risk that might lead to either healing or alienation. When we do confront people about their problems, we must do so with humility and love, and entrust the situation to God. If we do this, God will work things out according to his perfect will.

GALATIANS

THE BIG PICTURE

A. GREETINGS (1:1-5)
B. THE PEOPLE'S REJECTION OF
   GOD'S GRACE (1:6-10)
C. PAUL'S DEFENSE OF THE
   GOSPEL OF GRACE (1:11-6:10)
   1. Confirmed by the Apostles
      (1:11-2:21)
   2. Confirmed by the People's
      Membership in God's Family
      (3:1-4:31)
   3. Confirmed by the People's
      Deliverance from Sin's Power
      (5:1-6:10)
D. CONCLUSION (6:11-18)

Paul planted the churches in Galatia during his first missionary journey in Asia Minor. But within months of Paul's ministry there, certain people began to contradict the Good News Paul had preached. These teachers claimed that non-Jewish converts to Christ had to keep the Jewish law in order to be saved. This meant that all Gentiles who sought membership in the church would have to be circumcised.

This alternative gospel was very enticing to the Galatian believers. For one thing, its proponents claimed to have the direct blessing of the apostles back in Jerusalem. Their arguments from the Old Testament seemed flawless and irrefutable. But because Paul knew how destructive this teaching could be, he wrote this letter to correct them.

Paul made it clear to the Galatians that in Christ they were truly free. They were free from the demands of the Jewish law, free from the power of sin, and free to live under God's grace. We may wonder why the Galatians would ever want to give up the freedom they had in Christ. But bondage is subtle. No one ever starts drinking with a determination to become an alcoholic. We slowly become dependent on certain behaviors, substances, or attitudes. And, in a pathetic sort of way, our bondage gives us security.

This letter to the Galatian believers challenges us to hold on to our freedom. Being controlled by alcohol or drugs means living in slavery. So does being involved in any recovery program that is based on our own abilities and strengths. We cannot escape the grip of addiction and sin alone, but as we turn our life over to God, he will graciously give us the power we need to overcome our dependency.

THE BOTTOM LINE

PURPOSE: To encourage readers to depend on Christ alone for salvation and daily strength. AUTHOR: The apostle Paul. AUDIENCE: Several churches in southern Galatia. DATE WRITTEN: Probably around A.D. 49. SETTING: The most pressing controversy in the early church was whether new non-Jewish converts needed to accept Jewish laws to be a part of the church. Paul wrote this letter to answer that question. KEY VERSE: "So Christ has truly set us free. Now make sure that you stay free, and don't get tied up again in slavery to the law" (5:1). KEY PEOPLE AND RELATIONSHIPS: Paul with the Galatian believers and with the Jerusalem apostles, as well as the false teachers.

RECOVERY THEMES

The Seduction of the Law: For some of us, following a set of rules may seem easier than working on a personal inventory, praying, meditating on Scripture, or engaging in other activities that lead to a deeper relationship with God. We would rather have someone tell us what to do. Perhaps the Galatians felt the same way. They may have said, "Just give us some rules to follow, like the Mosaic law." Just following a set of rules for recovery is never the way to success. It is impossible for us to do by ourself, and it also leads us away from our dependence on God, the only real source for success.

Recovery Leads to True Freedom: This letter was written to show us how to find true spiritual freedom. Paul's advice to the Galatians applies to us as we search for freedom from our addiction, dysfunctional family, compulsive behavior, or codependent relationship. True freedom is found as we turn our life over to God, depending not on our own self-sufficiency but on his powerful and firm intervention. Having faith in Christ is the only way we can have true freedom from sin and its consequences, and from bondage to our defects of character.

The Power of the Holy Spirit: We become believers through the work of the Holy Spirit, the personal expression of the power of God. We also are empowered in recovery by the Holy Spirit. He brings new life to us; even the faith to believe and the courage to admit our own powerlessness are gifts from him. The Holy Spirit instructs, guides, leads, and gives us power. It is he who delivers us from our bondage to evil desires and addictive patterns and creates in us love, joy, peace, and serenity.

The Necessity of Faith: Many of us have been frustrated, even discouraged to the point of giving up, by our failed efforts to change. Recovery from sin and its destructive effects, including our dependency, is only possible through trust in Jesus Christ. Turning our will and our life over to God does not miraculously and instantly transform us (though some changes may happen right away). But by placing our trust and confidence in Jesus Christ, we experience God's forgiveness and unconditional acceptance. Then his power begins to work within us to enable our continued growth and recovery.

CHAPTER 1
Greetings from Paul

This letter is from Paul, an apostle. I was not appointed by any group of people or any human authority, but by Jesus Christ himself and by God the Father, who raised Jesus from the dead.

²All the brothers and sisters* here join me in sending this letter to the churches of Galatia.

³May God the Father and our Lord Jesus Christ* give you grace and peace. ⁴Jesus gave his life for our sins, just as God our Father planned, in order to rescue us from this evil world in which we live. ⁵All glory to God forever and ever! Amen.

There Is Only One Good News

⁶I am shocked that you are turning away so soon from God, who called you to himself through the loving mercy of Christ.* You are following a different way that pretends to be the Good News ⁷but is not the Good News at all. You are being fooled by those who deliberately twist the truth concerning Christ.

⁸Let God's curse fall on anyone, including us or even an angel from heaven, who preaches a different kind of Good News than the one we preached to you. ⁹I say again what we have said before: If anyone preaches any other Good News than the one you welcomed, let that person be cursed.

¹⁰Obviously, I'm not trying to win the ap-

1:2 Greek *brothers;* also in 1:11. **1:3** Some manuscripts read *God our Father and the Lord Jesus Christ.* **1:6** Some manuscripts read *through loving mercy.*

1:1-5 In this letter Paul gave much more than the brief, customary greeting. He introduced the main themes: his God-given apostolic authority, and clear teachings about the fatherhood of God and the delivering power of Jesus Christ. God, our loving Father, had a plan to rescue us from this evil world through the death of his Son. When we turn our life over to him, God is able to help us overcome our problems and shortcomings.

1:6-10 The Galatians faced a choice between the true gospel Paul preached and the false gospel preached by his opponents. The choice we face as we look for a way to deal with our sins and failures is just as clear. We can listen to those who offer us amazing and easy recovery fads. Or we can yield to a legalistic system that manipulates us through our guilt to effect our own recovery by adhering to a set of rules. Or we can accept what God says about the power of sin and his ability to set us free if we focus on him. Only God through Jesus Christ can offer us the power we need for true recovery. No other solution to our problems and dependency will ever lead to real or permanent change.

proval of people, but of God. If pleasing people were my goal, I would not be Christ's servant.

Paul's Message Comes from Christ

[11]Dear brothers and sisters, I want you to understand that the gospel message I preach is not based on mere human reasoning. [12]I received my message from no human source, and no one taught me. Instead, I received it by direct revelation from Jesus Christ.*

[13]You know what I was like when I followed the Jewish religion—how I violently persecuted God's church. I did my best to destroy it. [14]I was far ahead of my fellow Jews in my zeal for the traditions of my ancestors.

[15]But even before I was born, God chose me and called me by his marvelous grace. Then it pleased him [16]to reveal his Son to me* so that I would proclaim the Good News about Jesus to the Gentiles.

When this happened, I did not rush out to consult with any human being.* [17]Nor did I go up to Jerusalem to consult with those who were apostles before I was. Instead, I went away into Arabia, and later I returned to the city of Damascus.

[18]Then three years later I went to Jerusalem to get to know Peter,* and I stayed with him for fifteen days. [19]The only other apostle I met at that time was James, the Lord's brother. [20]I declare before God that what I am writing to you is not a lie.

[21]After that visit I went north into the provinces of Syria and Cilicia. [22]And still the churches in Christ that are in Judea didn't know me personally. [23]All they knew was that people were saying, "The one who used to persecute us is now preaching the very faith he tried to destroy!" [24]And they praised God because of me.

CHAPTER 2
The Apostles Accept Paul

Then fourteen years later I went back to Jerusalem again, this time with Barnabas; and Titus came along, too. [2]I went there because God revealed to me that I should go. While I was there I met privately with those considered to be leaders of the church and shared with them the message I had been preaching to the Gentiles. I wanted to make sure that we were in agreement, for fear that all my efforts had been wasted and I was running the race for nothing. [3]And they supported me and did not even demand that my companion Titus be circumcised, though he was a Gentile.*

[4]Even that question came up only because of some so-called believers there—false ones, really*—who were secretly brought in. They sneaked in to spy on us and take away the freedom we have in Christ Jesus. They wanted to enslave us and force us to follow their Jewish regulations. [5]But we refused to give in to them for a single moment. We wanted to preserve the truth of the gospel message for you.

[6]And the leaders of the church had nothing to add to what I was preaching. (By the way, their reputation as great leaders made no difference to me, for God has no favorites.) [7]Instead, they saw that God had given me the responsibility of preaching the gospel to the Gentiles, just as he had given Peter the responsibility of preaching to the Jews. [8]For

1:12 Or *by the revelation of Jesus Christ.* 1:16a Or *in me.* 1:16b Greek *with flesh and blood.* 1:18 Greek *Cephas.* 2:3 Greek *a Greek.* 2:4 Greek *some false brothers.*

1:11-24 As Paul looked back on his conversion, he recalled how he had once been an extremely religious Jew. He had actively worked to defend his faith against the threat of Christianity. But by grace, God reached out and radically transformed him. Paul recognized that all his religious activities were ultimately fruitless; they could never deliver him from the power of sin. Only God could forgive his sins and give him the power to start over again. If we have tried to overcome our dependency through behavior modification or religious activities, we already know what it means to fail. But if we have entrusted our life to God and are living by his power, we know the secret of victory. God's power through Jesus Christ is the only means to lasting recovery.

2:1-10 Paul presented a clear argument against the teachings of the Judaizers. These people recognized that God's work through Jesus Christ was important, but they also believed that people were required to follow the Jewish laws to obtain salvation. For them, salvation was based on actions, not solely on God's gracious gift. Paul wanted the Galatians to realize that none of us can follow God's laws adequately on our own. Christ alone has the power to release us from sin and its destructive consequences. Most of us have already discovered how powerless we are against sin. We know that we need God's power to help us overcome our addictions and compulsions. Paul's message of grace is a source of hope for us as we trust God to help us overcome our dependency.

the same God who worked through Peter as the apostle to the Jews also worked through me as the apostle to the Gentiles.

[9]In fact, James, Peter,* and John, who were known as pillars of the church, recognized the gift God had given me, and they accepted Barnabas and me as their co-workers. They encouraged us to keep preaching to the Gentiles, while they continued their work with the Jews. [10]Their only suggestion was that we keep on helping the poor, which I have always been eager to do.

Paul Confronts Peter

[11]But when Peter came to Antioch, I had to oppose him to his face, for what he did was very wrong. [12]When he first arrived, he ate with the Gentile believers, who were not circumcised. But afterward, when some friends of James came, Peter wouldn't eat with the Gentiles anymore. He was afraid of criticism from these people who insisted on the necessity of circumcision. [13]As a result, other Jewish believers followed Peter's hypocrisy, and even Barnabas was led astray by their hypocrisy.

[14]When I saw that they were not following the truth of the gospel message, I said to Peter in front of all the others, "Since you, a Jew by birth, have discarded the Jewish laws and are living like a Gentile, why are you now trying to make these Gentiles follow the Jewish traditions?

[15]"You and I are Jews by birth, not 'sinners' like the Gentiles. [16]Yet we know that a person is made right with God by faith in Jesus Christ, not by obeying the law. And we have believed in Christ Jesus, so that we might be made right with God because of our faith in Christ, not because we have obeyed the law. For no one will ever be made right with God by obeying the law."*

[17]But suppose we seek to be made right with God through faith in Christ and then we are found guilty because we have abandoned the law. Would that mean Christ has led us into sin? Absolutely not! [18]Rather, I am a sinner if I rebuild the old system of law I already tore down. [19]For when I tried to keep the law, it condemned me. So I died to the law—I stopped trying to meet all its requirements—so that I might live for God. [20]My old self has been crucified with Christ.* It is no longer I who live, but Christ lives in me. So I live in this earthly body by trusting in the Son of God, who loved me and gave himself for me. [21]I do not treat the grace of God as meaningless. For if keeping the law could make us right with God, then there was no need for Christ to die.

CHAPTER 3
The Law and Faith in Christ
Oh, foolish Galatians! Who has cast an evil spell on you? For the meaning of Jesus Christ's death was made as clear to you as if

2:9 Greek *Cephas;* also in 2:11, 14. 2:16 Some translators hold that the quotation extends through verse 14; others through verse 16; and still others through verse 21. 2:20 Some English translations put this sentence in verse 19.

2:11-16 The apostle Peter, a Jewish Christian, knew that salvation is a free gift of grace. While in Antioch, he freely associated with the Gentile Christians, even though they had not fulfilled the Jewish law of circumcision. When other Jewish Christian leaders arrived, however, Peter stopped associating with the Gentile believers. He was influenced by his Jewish peers and began to act as if obeying the Jewish laws was necessary for salvation. Paul confronted Peter about his prejudice, and the problem was resolved. Some of us know how Peter felt when his Jewish friends arrived. As we became involved in recovery, we may have been embarrassed among our old friends. We may have succumbed to the pressure to turn from our commitment to the truth about our need for recovery. Like Peter, we can humbly assess our failures and get back on the right track.
2:20-21 Paul showed that our old lifestyle died on the cross with Jesus Christ. The Jewish Christians had to give up trying to earn salvation by following the Jewish law. Many of us have struggled with this very problem. Some of us have worked very hard to overcome our addiction but have achieved no real freedom. Paul wanted the Jewish believers to realize that they could gain nothing by trying harder. They had to give up control and allow God to heal them and empower them in battling sin. We must give up our old ways of looking for deliverance and accept God's grace—the free gift of forgiveness and healing offered by Jesus Christ.
3:1-14 Paul appealed to the clear evidence seen among the Galatians when they received the Holy Spirit upon believing in Christ. We become children of Abraham, as the Bible says, when we receive the redemption available to us through the sacrifice of Jesus Christ. The evidence of becoming Abraham's sons and daughters is not circumcision but the presence of the Holy Spirit in our life. We can be sure of the Holy Spirit's presence when we begin to change. Knowing God and being in a right relationship with him enables us to know his will and follow it. But trying to follow God's laws in our human strength will never bring us into right relationship with God.

you had seen a picture of his death on the cross. ²Let me ask you this one question: Did you receive the Holy Spirit by obeying the law of Moses? Of course not! You received the Spirit because you believed the message you heard about Christ. ³How foolish can you be? After starting your new lives in the Spirit, why are you now trying to become perfect by your own human effort? ⁴Have you experienced* so much for nothing? Surely it was not in vain, was it?

⁵I ask you again, does God give you the Holy Spirit and work miracles among you because you obey the law? Of course not! It is because you believe the message you heard about Christ.

⁶In the same way, "Abraham believed God, and God counted him as righteous because of his faith."* ⁷The real children of Abraham, then, are those who put their faith in God.

⁸What's more, the Scriptures looked forward to this time when God would declare the Gentiles to be righteous because of their faith. God proclaimed this good news to Abraham long ago when he said, "All nations will be blessed through you."* ⁹So all who put their faith in Christ share the same blessing Abraham received because of his faith.

¹⁰But those who depend on the law to make them right with God are under his curse, for the Scriptures say, "Cursed is everyone who does not observe and obey all the commands that are written in God's Book of the Law."* ¹¹So it is clear that no one can be made right with God by trying to keep the law. For the Scriptures say, "It is through faith that a righteous person has life."* ¹²This way of faith is very different from the way of law, which says, "It is through obeying the law that a person has life."*

¹³But Christ has rescued us from the curse pronounced by the law. When he was hung on the cross, he took upon himself the curse for our wrongdoing. For it is written in the Scriptures, "Cursed is everyone who is hung on a tree."* ¹⁴Through Christ Jesus, God has blessed the Gentiles with the same blessing he promised to Abraham, so that we who are believers might receive the promised* Holy Spirit through faith.

The Law and God's Promise

¹⁵Dear brothers and sisters,* here's an example from everyday life. Just as no one can set

3:4 Or *Have you suffered.* 3:6 Gen 15:6. 3:8 Gen 12:3; 18:18; 22:18. 3:10 Deut 27:26. 3:11 Hab 2:4. 3:12 Lev 18:5. 3:13 Deut 21:23 (Greek version). 3:14 Some manuscripts read *the blessing of the.* 3:15 Greek *Brothers.*

SELF-CONTROL

READ GALATIANS 5:16-23

There's a struggle going on inside of us—a fight for control. Our willpower fails us repeatedly. Where can we turn when we realize that we can't get control of our life?

The apostle Paul said: "I say, let the Holy Spirit guide your lives. Then you won't be doing what your sinful nature craves. The sinful nature wants to do evil, which is just the opposite of what the Spirit wants. And the Spirit gives us desires that are the opposite of what the sinful nature desires. These two forces are constantly fighting each other, so you are not free to carry out your good intentions. . . . But the Holy Spirit produces this kind of fruit in our lives: love, joy, peace, patience, kindness, goodness, faithfulness, gentleness, and self-control" (Galatians 5:16-17, 22-23).

Self-control is not willpower. It is not something we get by gritting our teeth and forcing ourselves to "just say no." Self-control is called a fruit. Fruit doesn't instantly pop out on the tree. As the tree grows and seasons pass, the fruit naturally develops. As we continue to follow God's guidance, taking one step at a time, our self-control will gradually grow. Our job is to stay connected to God. It is the Holy Spirit's job to produce the fruit of self-control in our life. *Turn to page 1513, Ephesians 2.*

aside or amend an irrevocable agreement, so it is in this case. ¹⁶God gave the promises to Abraham and his child.* And notice that the Scripture doesn't say "to his children,*" as if it meant many descendants. Rather, it says "to his child"—and that, of course, means Christ. ¹⁷This is what I am trying to say: The agreement God made with Abraham could not be canceled 430 years later when God gave the law to Moses. God would be breaking his promise. ¹⁸For if the inheritance could be received by keeping the law, then it would not be the result of accepting God's promise. But God graciously gave it to Abraham as a promise.

¹⁹Why, then, was the law given? It was given alongside the promise to show people their sins. But the law was designed to last only until the coming of the child who was promised. God gave his law through angels to Moses, who was the mediator between God and the people. ²⁰Now a mediator is helpful if more than one party must reach an agreement. But God, who is one, did not use a mediator when he gave his promise to Abraham.

²¹Is there a conflict, then, between God's law and God's promises?* Absolutely not! If the law could give us new life, we could be made right with God by obeying it. ²²But the Scriptures declare that we are all prisoners of sin, so we receive God's promise of freedom only by believing in Jesus Christ.

God's Children through Faith

²³Before the way of faith in Christ was available to us, we were placed under guard by the law. We were kept in protective custody, so to speak, until the way of faith was revealed.

²⁴Let me put it another way. The law was our guardian until Christ came; it protected us until we could be made right with God through faith. ²⁵And now that the way of faith has come, we no longer need the law as our guardian.

²⁶For you are all children* of God through faith in Christ Jesus. ²⁷And all who have been united with Christ in baptism have put on Christ, like putting on new clothes.* ²⁸There is no longer Jew or Gentile,* slave or free, male and female. For you are all one in Christ Jesus. ²⁹And now that you belong to Christ, you are the true children* of Abraham. You are his heirs, and God's promise to Abraham belongs to you.

CHAPTER 4

Think of it this way. If a father dies and leaves an inheritance for his young children, those

3:16a Greek *seed;* also in 3:16c, 19. See notes on Gen 12:7 and 13:15. 3:16b Greek *seeds.* 3:21 Some manuscripts read *and the promises?* 3:26 Greek *sons.* 3:27 Greek *have put on Christ.* 3:28 Greek *Jew or Greek.* 3:29 Greek *seed.*

3:15-29 God's relationship with us is not based on our keeping the law but on the promises made to Abraham to bless all humanity through his offspring, Jesus Christ. The law shows us that we are sinners deserving punishment and in need of a Savior. Following the law is not the solution to the sin problem; the law is a measuring stick that reveals the sin problem. None of us are capable of true and complete obedience. Despite our helplessness God desires to bless us when we trust in his promises, not when we perform according to his perfect standards. Knowing that God loves us enough to pay for our sins can help us be more fearless as we take our moral inventory. When we confess our sins to God, he will set us free from their destructive power.

3:26-29 When we entrust our life to God through Jesus Christ, we become his children. What an amazing truth! We are each given a place in God's family, no matter what our past sins, no matter how dysfunctional our family, no matter how deeply we have been hurt. He has a plan for each of us, and like any parent, he wants to help us succeed. Faith in Christ is all we need to enter into this privileged status. Each one of us is important to God, and he loves us enough to help us overcome our weaknesses and character flaws.

4:8-11 If we are not willing to trust and obey God, we soon become enslaved to other things. We turn to other activities or substances to help us deal with our problems. Most of us realize that this often leads to various forms of addiction. We have discovered that drugs, alcohol, sexual immorality, work, or even religious activities can never solve our problems. In fact, depending on anything other than God himself leads to even deeper problems. Only God offers us the power to be delivered from bondage to build a new life. Turning to him for help is really the only valid option we have.

4:17-20 Paul was trying to help the Galatians experience the new life that God offers through Jesus Christ. The false teachers were trying to lead the people back into bondage under the Jewish law. There was a distinct contrast between Paul's attitudes and actions and those of the false teachers. The false teachers were not concerned about the people's good; Paul was. We have all seen recovery fads that promise amazing results. These programs usually cost a lot of money and yield, at best, only temporary results. The only real means to recovery is God's power—and it's free of charge! All we have to do is accept it.

children are not much better off than slaves until they grow up, even though they actually own everything their father had. ²They have to obey their guardians until they reach whatever age their father set. ³And that's the way it was with us before Christ came. We were like children; we were slaves to the basic spiritual principles* of this world.

⁴But when the right time came, God sent his Son, born of a woman, subject to the law. ⁵God sent him to buy freedom for us who were slaves to the law, so that he could adopt us as his very own children.* ⁶And because we* are his children, God has sent the Spirit of his Son into our hearts, prompting us to call out, "Abba, Father."* ⁷Now you are no longer a slave but God's own child.* And since you are his child, God has made you his heir.

Paul's Concern for the Galatians

⁸Before you Gentiles knew God, you were slaves to so-called gods that do not even exist. ⁹So now that you know God (or should I say, now that God knows you), why do you want to go back again and become slaves once more to the weak and useless spiritual principles of this world? ¹⁰You are trying to earn favor with God by observing certain days or months or seasons or years. ¹¹I fear for you. Perhaps all my hard work with you was for nothing. ¹²Dear brothers and sisters,* I plead with you to live as I do in freedom from these things, for I have become like you Gentiles—free from those laws.

You did not mistreat me when I first preached to you. ¹³Surely you remember that I was sick when I first brought you the Good News. ¹⁴But even though my condition tempted you to reject me, you did not despise me or turn me away. No, you took me in and cared for me as though I were an angel from God or even Christ Jesus himself. ¹⁵Where is that joyful and grateful spirit you felt then? I am sure you would have taken out your own eyes and given them to me if it had been possible. ¹⁶Have I now become your enemy because I am telling you the truth?

¹⁷Those false teachers are so eager to win your favor, but their intentions are not good. They are trying to shut you off from me so that you will pay attention only to them. ¹⁸If someone is eager to do good things for you,

4:3 Or *powers;* also in 4:9. 4:5 Greek *sons;* also in 4:6. 4:6a Greek *you.* 4:6b *Abba* is an Aramaic term for "father." 4:7 Greek *son;* also in 4:7b. 4:12 Greek *brothers;* also in 4:28, 31.

STEP 5

Escaping Self-Deception

BIBLE READING: Galatians 6:7-10

We admitted to God, to ourselves, and to another human being the exact nature of our wrongs.

We may fool ourself into believing that we can simply bury our wrongs and go on without ever having to admit them. In time, we all discover that those deeds we thought were buried once and for all were actually seeds. They grow and bear fruit. Eventually we have to deal with a crop of consequences and face the fact that self-deception doesn't work to our advantage.

"You will always harvest what you plant. Those who live only to satisfy their own sinful nature will harvest decay and death from that sinful nature. But those who live to please the Spirit will harvest everlasting life from the Spirit" (Galatians 6:7-8). "If we claim we have no sin, we are only fooling ourselves and not living in the truth. But if we confess our sins to [God], he is faithful and just to forgive us our sins and to cleanse us from all wickedness" (1 John 1:8-9).

Step Five says good-bye to self-deception and hello to forgiveness and cleansing. We should note that there is cleansing from every wrong, not from "wrongdoing" in a general sense. Admitting the exact nature of our wrongs includes giving our accounts in exact and specific terms. It is only when we get specific that we will no longer be able to fool ourself about the nature of our wrongs. Since we cannot ignore God and get away with it anyway, we might as well come clean and be forgiven. *Turn to Step Six, page 33, Genesis 23.*

that's all right; but let them do it all the time, not just when I'm with you.

¹⁹Oh, my dear children! I feel as if I'm going through labor pains for you again, and they will continue until Christ is fully developed in your lives. ²⁰I wish I were with you right now so I could change my tone. But at this distance I don't know how else to help you.

Abraham's Two Children

²¹Tell me, you who want to live under the law, do you know what the law actually says? ²²The Scriptures say that Abraham had two sons, one from his slave wife and one from his freeborn wife.* ²³The son of the slave wife was born in a human attempt to bring about the fulfillment of God's promise. But the son of the freeborn wife was born as God's own fulfillment of his promise.

²⁴These two women serve as an illustration of God's two covenants. The first woman, Hagar, represents Mount Sinai where people received the law that enslaved them. ²⁵And now Jerusalem is just like Mount Sinai in Arabia,* because she and her children live in slavery to the law. ²⁶But the other woman, Sarah, represents the heavenly Jerusalem. She is the free woman, and she is our mother. ²⁷As Isaiah said,

"Rejoice, O childless woman,
  you who have never given birth!
Break into a joyful shout,
  you who have never been in labor!
For the desolate woman now has more
  children
    than the woman who lives with her
    husband!"*

²⁸And you, dear brothers and sisters, are children of the promise, just like Isaac. ²⁹But you are now being persecuted by those who want you to keep the law, just as Ishmael, the child born by human effort, persecuted Isaac, the child born by the power of the Spirit.

³⁰But what do the Scriptures say about that? "Get rid of the slave and her son, for the son of the slave woman will not share the inheritance with the free woman's son."* ³¹So, dear brothers and sisters, we are not children of the slave woman; we are children of the free woman.

CHAPTER 5
Freedom in Christ

So Christ has truly set us free. Now make sure that you stay free, and don't get tied up again in slavery to the law.

²Listen! I, Paul, tell you this: If you are counting on circumcision to make you right with God, then Christ will be of no benefit to you. ³I'll say it again. If you are trying to find favor with God by being circumcised, you must obey every regulation in the whole law of Moses. ⁴For if you are trying to make yourselves right with God by keeping the law, you have been cut off from Christ! You have fallen away from God's grace.

⁵But we who live by the Spirit eagerly wait to receive by faith the righteousness God has promised to us. ⁶For when we place our faith in Christ Jesus, there is no benefit in being circumcised or being uncircumcised. What is important is faith expressing itself in love.

⁷You were running the race so well. Who has held you back from following the truth? ⁸It certainly isn't God, for he is the one who called you to freedom. ⁹This false teaching is like a little yeast that spreads through the whole batch of dough! ¹⁰I am trusting the Lord to keep you from believing false teachings. God will judge that person, whoever he is, who has been confusing you.

4:22 See Gen 16:15; 21:2-3. **4:25** Greek *And Hagar, which is Mount Sinai in Arabia, is now like Jerusalem;* other manuscripts read *And Mount Sinai in Arabia is now like Jerusalem.* **4:27** Isa 54:1. **4:30** Gen 21:10.

5:1-12 The Galatians faced the same basic choice that all of us face. Should we choose power and freedom in Christ or slavery through useless and destructive solutions? If we make a bad choice, we risk being cut off from the deliverance available to God's people. There is no deliverance from the power of sin except through Christ and his powerful presence within us. Only his power can restore us.

5:22-24 These qualities are produced by the Holy Spirit's work in a life submitted to God. Just as a tree bears fruit by means of God's silent work in nature, we experience these fruits of the Spirit by means of God's power alone. Our part is to entrust our life to him. When the Holy Spirit begins to bear these fruits in our life, our dependency loses its power. With *joy* and *peace* we overcome the pain of our broken past. With *love, kindness, goodness, faithfulness,* and *gentleness* we restore our relationships and make amends. With *patience* we persevere through the difficult times. With *self-control* we stand against our tendency to relapse. God's Spirit can supply everything necessary for a successful recovery.

¹¹Dear brothers and sisters,* if I were still preaching that you must be circumcised—as some say I do—why am I still being persecuted? If I were no longer preaching salvation through the cross of Christ, no one would be offended. ¹²I just wish that those troublemakers who want to mutilate you by circumcision would mutilate themselves.*

¹³For you have been called to live in freedom, my brothers and sisters. But don't use your freedom to satisfy your sinful nature. Instead, use your freedom to serve one another in love. ¹⁴For the whole law can be summed up in this one command: "Love your neighbor as yourself."* ¹⁵But if you are always biting and devouring one another, watch out! Beware of destroying one another.

Living by the Spirit's Power

¹⁶So I say, let the Holy Spirit guide your lives. Then you won't be doing what your sinful nature craves. ¹⁷The sinful nature wants to do evil, which is just the opposite of what the Spirit wants. And the Spirit gives us desires that are the opposite of what the sinful nature desires. These two forces are constantly fighting each other, so you are not free to carry out your good intentions. ¹⁸But when you are directed by the Spirit, you are not under obligation to the law of Moses.

¹⁹When you follow the desires of your sinful nature, the results are very clear: sexual immorality, impurity, lustful pleasures, ²⁰idolatry, sorcery, hostility, quarreling, jealousy, outbursts of anger, selfish ambition, dissension, division, ²¹envy, drunkenness, wild parties, and other sins like these. Let me tell you again, as I have before, that anyone living that sort of life will not inherit the Kingdom of God.

²²But the Holy Spirit produces this kind of fruit in our lives: love, joy, peace, patience, kindness, goodness, faithfulness, ²³gentleness, and self-control. There is no law against these things!

²⁴Those who belong to Christ Jesus have nailed the passions and desires of their sinful nature to his cross and crucified them there. ²⁵Since we are living by the Spirit, let us follow the Spirit's leading in every part of our lives. ²⁶Let us not become conceited, or provoke one another, or be jealous of one another.

5:11 Greek *Brothers;* similarly in 5:13. **5:12** Or *castrate themselves,* or *cut themselves off from you;* Greek reads *cut themselves off.* **5:14** Lev 19:18.

STEP 8

Reaping Goodness

BIBLE READING: Galatians 6:7-10

We made a list of all persons we had harmed and became willing to make amends to them all.

While in recovery, we learn to accept responsibility for our actions, even when we are powerless over our addiction. We come to realize that all our actions yield consequences. Some of us may have fooled ourself into thinking we could escape the consequences of the things we did. But with time, it has become clear that God has made accountability a necessary element of healthy living.

"You will always harvest what you plant! Those who live only to satisfy their own sinful nature will harvest decay and death from that sinful nature. But those who live to please the Spirit will harvest everlasting life from the Spirit" (Galatians 6:7-8).

The law of sowing and reaping can also work for us. God spoke through the prophet Hosea: "Plant the good seeds of righteousness, and you will harvest a crop of love. Plow up the hard ground of your hearts, for now is the time to seek the LORD, that he may come and shower righteousness upon you" (Hosea 10:12).

God says we *always* reap what we have sown. Even after we have been forgiven, we must deal with the consequences of our actions. It may take time to finish harvesting the negative consequences from our past, but we don't have to let this discourage us. Making our list of those we have harmed is a step toward planting good seeds. In time we will see a good crop begin to grow. *Turn to Step Nine, page 49, Genesis 33.*

CHAPTER 6
We Harvest What We Plant

Dear brothers and sisters, if another believer*
is overcome by some sin, you who are godly*
should gently and humbly help that person
back onto the right path. And be careful not
to fall into the same temptation yourself.
²Share each other's burdens, and in this way
obey the law of Christ. ³If you think you are
too important to help someone, you are only
fooling yourself. You are not that important.

⁴Pay careful attention to your own work,
for then you will get the satisfaction of a job
well done, and you won't need to compare
yourself to anyone else. ⁵For we are each responsible for our own conduct.

⁶Those who are taught the word of God
should provide for their teachers, sharing all
good things with them.

⁷Don't be misled—you cannot mock the
justice of God. You will always harvest what
you plant. ⁸Those who live only to satisfy
their own sinful nature will harvest decay
and death from that sinful nature. But those
who live to please the Spirit will harvest everlasting life from the Spirit. ⁹So let's not get
tired of doing what is good. At just the right
time we will reap a harvest of blessing if we
don't give up. ¹⁰Therefore, whenever we have
the opportunity, we should do good to
everyone—especially to those in the family
of faith.

Paul's Final Advice

¹¹NOTICE WHAT LARGE LETTERS I USE AS I WRITE
THESE CLOSING WORDS IN MY OWN HANDWRITING.

¹²Those who are trying to force you to be
circumcised want to look good to others.
They don't want to be persecuted for teaching that the cross of Christ alone can save.
¹³And even those who advocate circumcision don't keep the whole law themselves.
They only want you to be circumcised so
they can boast about it and claim you as
their disciples.

¹⁴As for me, may I never boast about anything except the cross of our Lord Jesus
Christ. Because of that cross,* my interest in
this world has been crucified, and the world's
interest in me has also died. ¹⁵It doesn't matter whether we have been circumcised or not.
What counts is whether we have been transformed into a new creation. ¹⁶May God's
peace and mercy be upon all who live by this
principle; they are the new people of God.*

¹⁷From now on, don't let anyone trouble
me with these things. For I bear on my body
the scars that show I belong to Jesus.

¹⁸Dear brothers and sisters,* may the grace
of our Lord Jesus Christ be with your spirit.
Amen.

6:1a Greek *Brothers, if a man.* 6:1b Greek *spiritual.* 6:14 Or *Because of him.* 6:16 Greek *this principle, and upon the*
Israel of God. 6:18 Greek *Brothers.*

6:1-3 Paul told the Galatians to share their troubles with one another. This would bring healing
to hurting people and provide opportunities for the believers to help each other. Paul included a
special note to encourage those who might be too proud to admit their problems. An essential
part of recovery is admitting to others the exact nature of our wrongs. As we share with others,
we will discover that much of the burden of our painful past or our addictive tendency will be
lifted. With their encouragement and call to accountability, we can shed our painful past and
move on to a productive future.

6:11-18 In these closing verses Paul recapped his major arguments with an emotional appeal to
stand firm against false teachers who try to attract people away from the liberating message of
the gospel. Admitting that we are helpless to overcome our sins and accepting God's help are
responsible decisions. Rather than humiliating us, God bestows dignity and healing upon us
when we enter the process of recovery through faith in Christ. As God heals us, we can take the
Good News to others as Paul did with the Galatian believers.

REFLECTIONS ON GALATIANS

insights INTO GOD'S WILL

Very often God's will for us stands in direct opposition to our natural desires. Recovery depends on our accepting the fact that following our own selfish desires is destructive. In **Galatians 5:16-21** we find a whole list of destructive behaviors that flow out of a self-centered life. When we turn our life over to God, however, we allow his Spirit to help us control those evil desires, and God's desires become our own desires more and more. Submitting our life to God's will is the best choice we can make.

insights ABOUT CONSEQUENCES

In **Galatians 6:7-10** Paul left an important reminder for us all. We will always reap what we have sown. In other words, sins and addictions have painful consequences. For a while we might be able to fool ourself into thinking that certain activities and relationships are all right. But when the consequences catch up with us, there will be no denying the facts. We need to take this warning seriously and take steps to change now. We don't have to wait to hit bottom before we act. Using God's Word as our standard, we can take a fearless moral inventory and work toward a godly life before it's too late.

EPHESIANS

THE BIG PICTURE

A. GREETINGS (1:1-2)
B. ASSURANCE OF GOD'S PROGRAM FOR SPIRITUAL WHOLENESS (1:3–3:21)
C. ACCEPTANCE OF OUR RESPONSIBILITY FOR SPIRITUAL WHOLENESS (4:1–6:9)
D. AWARENESS OF OUR ROLE IN SPIRITUAL WARFARE (6:10-20)
E. CLOSING REMARKS (6:21-24)

The Ephesian church had been planted through Paul's influence, and for a few years he had served as its pastor. This church thrived in a city renowned as a center for the worship of the goddess Artemis (also known as Diana). While Paul was there, the Ephesian believers maintained a strong attachment to him, and when he left they openly expressed their sorrow.

How could the Ephesian church survive for the long haul in its hostile environment? They could not depend on Paul's presence forever; with God's help they would have to learn to stand on their own. Paul wrote this letter to remind the Ephesian believers to place their faith in the only solid foundation for healthy living—God.

How can we maintain our recovery in a hostile environment? None of us have the resources or strength to initiate and sustain our recovery alone. Paul asserted one important fact: We can change! But our transformation is possible only on God's terms. We can recover if we break with our former way of life and depend on God's power to help us change. While programs and supportive people are helpful, lasting recovery happens only when we recognize our need for a higher power—the God who created us and sustains our life.

Belief in God and obedience to his will are keys to a genuine, stable recovery. If we adopt an attitude of submission to God's authority and care, and our attitudes and actions reflect God's truth, we will indeed make progress. Recovery that ignores God is doomed to failure; recovery that depends on God will succeed.

THE BOTTOM LINE

PURPOSE: To strengthen the believers in Ephesus in their relationships with God and with each other. AUTHOR: The apostle Paul. AUDIENCE: The believers in Ephesus, a city in western Asia Minor, and all believers everywhere. DATE WRITTEN: Around A.D. 60, during Paul's imprisonment in Rome. SETTING: This letter was not sent to solve any particular problem. Rather, it was a somewhat personal message from Paul to some dear friends in the mother church of Asia. Paul probably intended this to be a circular letter passed from church to church for encouragement. KEY VERSE: "A final word: Be strong in the Lord and in his mighty power" (6:10). KEY PEOPLE AND RELATIONSHIPS: Paul with Tychicus, and with his close friends in the Ephesian church.

RECOVERY THEMES

God Desires Recovery for Us: God has had a plan for each of us since the beginning of time. His plan doesn't include bondage to sin or the past. He wants us to have a relationship with him so we can enjoy his love and presence. He wants us to recover even more than we do! Many of us have a distorted image of God based on painful images of authority figures in our past. This letter shows us that God is a father who has loved us from the beginning of time. He will continue to love us, no matter what we do.

The Importance of Jesus Christ: In the New Testament and especially in Ephesians, Jesus Christ is exalted as the focus of all history and as the only means for experiencing a meaningful life. Only through God's Son, Jesus Christ, can the power of sin be overcome. This letter urges us to keep Christ at the center of all we do, maintaining conscious contact with him on a daily basis.

True Recovery Leads to Wise Conduct: It is easy to think of recovery only in terms of stopping destructive behavior patterns. But it is important to see that the best way to stop destructive habits is to build constructive ones to replace them. We are able to lay aside old patterns when we consciously repent, turn our life over to God, and seek his will for us each day. As we begin to obey God's will for our life, we will find we are no longer following the path toward destruction.

Adoption into God's Family: Many of us have painful memories from the past, particularly from the experiences we had in our family. Some of us have no positive memories of family life at all. The letter to the Ephesians reminds us that when we trust God as our Savior, he adopts us into a new family. In this family, God is our perfect and loving father. Even God's family, the church, has its limitations and imperfections. But our Father is perfect, and becoming a part of his family is an all-important step in recovery.

CHAPTER 1
Greetings from Paul

This letter is from Paul, chosen by the will of God to be an apostle of Christ Jesus.

I am writing to God's holy people in Ephesus,* who are faithful followers of Christ Jesus.

²May God our Father and the Lord Jesus Christ give you grace and peace.

Spiritual Blessings

³All praise to God, the Father of our Lord Jesus Christ, who has blessed us with every spiritual blessing in the heavenly realms because we are united with Christ. ⁴Even before he made the world, God loved us and chose us in Christ to be holy and without fault in his eyes. ⁵God decided in advance to adopt us into his own family by bringing us to himself through Jesus Christ. This is what he wanted to do, and it gave him great pleasure. ⁶So we praise God for the glorious grace he has poured out on us who belong to his dear Son.* ⁷He is so rich in kindness and grace that he purchased our freedom with the blood of his Son and forgave our sins. ⁸He has showered his kindness on us, along with all wisdom and understanding.

⁹God has now revealed to us his mysterious plan regarding Christ, a plan to fulfill his own good pleasure. ¹⁰And this is the plan: At the right time he will bring everything together under the authority of Christ—everything in heaven and on earth. ¹¹Furthermore, because we are united with Christ, we have received an inheritance from God,*

1:1 The most ancient manuscripts do not include *in Ephesus.* 1:6 Greek *to us in the beloved.* 1:11 Or *we have become God's inheritance.*

1:3-6 Recovery cannot begin until we admit that our life is unmanageable and that we are powerless over our circumstances. The apostle Paul reminds us that God is sovereign over all the details of our life. God has a special plan for each of us, and that unchanging plan includes adopting us into his family. We have already realized that doing things our way leads to painful consequences. With this in mind, we can be motivated to submit to God's perfect will for our life. God wants only what is best for us. It is always God's will for us to find new life in him.

1:11-12 Some of us may wonder how we can know God's will for our life. While there are details we may never know in advance, God's Word points us in the right direction. God desires many things for all of us, and these are revealed in Scripture. God wants us to experience an intimate relationship with him through Christ. In this relationship, God will delight in us and we will praise him in return. This is an amazing truth: God wants to have a close relationship with us, no matter who we are or what we have done. Because of what God has done for us through Jesus Christ, we can praise him and share the Good News with others in need.

for he chose us in advance, and he makes everything work out according to his plan. [12]God's purpose was that we Jews who were the first to trust in Christ would bring praise and glory to God. [13]And now you Gentiles have also heard the truth, the Good News that God saves you. And when you believed in Christ, he identified you as his own* by giving you the Holy Spirit, whom he promised long ago. [14]The Spirit is God's guarantee that he will give us the inheritance he promised and that he has purchased us to be his own people. He did this so we would praise and glorify him.

Paul's Prayer for Spiritual Wisdom

[15]Ever since I first heard of your strong faith in the Lord Jesus and your love for God's people everywhere,* [16]I have not stopped thanking God for you. I pray for you constantly, [17]asking God, the glorious Father of our Lord Jesus Christ, to give you spiritual wisdom* and insight so that you might grow in your knowledge of God. [18]I pray that your hearts will be flooded with light so that you can understand the confident hope he has given to those he called—his holy people who are his rich and glorious inheritance.*

[19]I also pray that you will understand the incredible greatness of God's power for us who believe him. This is the same mighty power [20]that raised Christ from the dead and seated him in the place of honor at God's right hand in the heavenly realms. [21]Now he is far above any ruler or authority or power or leader or anything else—not only in this world but also in the world to come. [22]God has put all things under the authority of Christ and has made him head over all things for the benefit of the church. [23]And the church is his body; it is made full and complete by Christ, who fills all things everywhere with himself.

CHAPTER 2
Made Alive with Christ

Once you were dead because of your disobedience and your many sins. [2]You used to live in sin, just like the rest of the world, obeying the devil—the commander of the powers in the unseen world.* He is the spirit at work in the hearts of those who refuse to obey God. [3]All of us used to live that way, following the passionate desires and inclinations of our sinful nature. By our very nature we were subject to God's anger, just like everyone else.

[4]But God is so rich in mercy, and he loved us so much, [5]that even though we were dead because of our sins, he gave us life when he raised Christ from the dead. (It is only by God's grace that you have been saved!) [6]For he raised us from the dead along with Christ and seated us with him in the heavenly realms because we are united with Christ Jesus. [7]So God can point to us in all future ages as examples of the incredible wealth of his grace and kindness toward us, as shown in all he has done for us who are united with Christ Jesus.

[8]God saved you by his grace when you believed. And you can't take credit for this; it is a gift from God. [9]Salvation is not a reward for the good things we have done, so none of us can boast about it. [10]For we are God's masterpiece. He has created us anew in Christ Jesus, so we can do the good things he planned for us long ago.

Oneness and Peace in Christ

[11]Don't forget that you Gentiles used to be outsiders. You were called "uncircumcised heathens" by the Jews, who were proud of their circumcision, even though it affected only their bodies and not their hearts. [12]In those days you were living apart from Christ. You were excluded from citizenship among the people of Israel, and you did not know

---

1:13 Or *he put his seal on you.* 1:15 Some manuscripts read *your faithfulness to the Lord Jesus and to God's people everywhere.* 1:17 Or *to give you the Spirit of wisdom.* 1:18 Or *called, and the rich and glorious inheritance he has given to his holy people.* 2:2 Greek *obeying the commander of the power of the air.*

1:13-14 God's plan for our salvation is continued by the sealing work of the Holy Spirit. Just as an official marks a document as genuine, so the Holy Spirit's work within us guarantees our identity as God's adopted child. This is all made possible by Jesus Christ and his saving work on our behalf. It becomes a reality in our life when we place our faith in him. Our knowledge of God's love for us and the help he offers gives us reason for hope as we seek to overcome our problems and dependency. When we trust God, we become part of his powerful solution to deal with sin in our world.

2:1-10 Here Paul affirms two essential truths related to recovery: (1) we are all born with an evil nature, powerless to stand against our tendency toward sin and failure; (2) God is rich in mercy and love, and even though we are far from him and entrapped by sin, God graciously reaches out to us. God wants to forgive us and give us the power to rebuild our life. Through the work of Jesus Christ, God has already conquered the power of sin and death. When we admit that we need God's help and ask him to act on our behalf, God empowers us to overcome our problems and dependency.

the covenant promises God had made to them. You lived in this world without God and without hope. [13]But now you have been united with Christ Jesus. Once you were far away from God, but now you have been brought near to him through the blood of Christ.

[14]For Christ himself has brought peace to us. He united Jews and Gentiles into one people when, in his own body on the cross, he broke down the wall of hostility that separated us. [15]He did this by ending the system of law with its commandments and regulations. He made peace between Jews and Gentiles by creating in himself one new people from the two groups. [16]Together as one body, Christ reconciled both groups to God by means of his death on the cross, and our hostility toward each other was put to death.

[17]He brought this Good News of peace to you Gentiles who were far away from him, and peace to the Jews who were near. [18]Now all of us can come to the Father through the same Holy Spirit because of what Christ has done for us.

A Temple for the Lord

[19]So now you Gentiles are no longer strangers and foreigners. You are citizens along with all of God's holy people. You are members of God's family. [20]Together, we are his house, built on the foundation of the apostles and the prophets. And the cornerstone is Christ Jesus himself. [21]We are carefully joined together in him, becoming a holy temple for the Lord. [22]Through him you Gentiles are also being made part of this dwelling where God lives by his Spirit.

CHAPTER 3
God's Mysterious Plan Revealed

When I think of all this, I, Paul, a prisoner of Christ Jesus for the benefit of you Gentiles*. . . [2]assuming, by the way, that you know God gave me the special responsibility of extending his grace to you Gentiles. [3]As I briefly wrote earlier, God himself revealed his mysterious plan to me. [4]As you read what I have written, you will understand my insight into this plan regarding Christ. [5]God did not reveal it to previous generations, but now by his Spirit he has revealed it to his holy apostles and prophets.

[6]And this is God's plan: Both Gentiles and Jews who believe the Good News share equally in the riches inherited by God's children. Both are part of the same body, and both enjoy the promise of blessings because

---

3:1 Paul resumes this thought in verse 14: "When I think of all this, I fall to my knees and pray to the Father."

2:14-19 Through Jesus Christ, the barrier between God and his sinful creatures has been removed. But Christ's work of reconciliation does not stop there. He can also remove the obstacles that alienate us from other people. In Christ we can have peace with God and with others. Restoration of our broken relationships is a necessary part of the recovery process. Some of us may feel that our relationships could never be salvaged. But realizing that Christ can give us the power to live at peace with others gives us new hope. His power will enable us to make amends to people we have wronged. All who believe in Christ are made brothers and sisters in him.

3:1-13 In these verses one truth stands out: God accepts all of us through faith. Race, reputation, and position have no bearing on God's forgiveness. Paul wrote these words to convince the believers of their oneness in Christ. Apparently some of the Jewish believers claimed superiority because of their relationship to God in the Old Testament Scriptures. Paul refuted their view by reminding them that our relationship with God is based on our trust in Jesus Christ, not our personal history or position in society. This important truth is encouraging for us in recovery. Our addiction may have destroyed the reputation we once commanded. None of this matters to God. If we seek his forgiveness, he will accept us and help us make a new start.

3:14-21 For churches or small groups to function effectively as vehicles for recovery, they must be driven by God's dynamic and unlimited love. Paul prayed that his friends might be deeply anchored and rooted in the soil of God's love. As we learn how much God loves us, we will become confident that he is able to do far more in and through us than we could ever imagine! We can bank our recovery on this truth! We may feel that our life is hopeless and beyond recovery. But through God restoration and healing are possible. When we are grounded in God's love, recovery will follow.

4:1-6 Even though God's program for recovery is centered on his sovereign purposes and power, we have important responsibilities as well. What we believe about God is crucial, but so is the manner in which we live. For many of us, the recovery process is hindered by our faults, especially our stubborn pride that prevents us from taking searching and fearless inventory of our life. Recovery is impossible until we humbly admit that we are powerless and need God's help. As we trust God to help us, his Holy Spirit will replace our character flaws with humility, love, and patience. When God asks us to live a certain way, he provides the power we need to succeed.

they belong to Christ Jesus.* ⁷By God's grace and mighty power, I have been given the privilege of serving him by spreading this Good News.

⁸Though I am the least deserving of all God's people, he graciously gave me the privilege of telling the Gentiles about the endless treasures available to them in Christ. ⁹I was chosen to explain to everyone* this mysterious plan that God, the Creator of all things, had kept secret from the beginning.

¹⁰God's purpose in all this was to use the church to display his wisdom in its rich variety to all the unseen rulers and authorities in the heavenly places. ¹¹This was his eternal plan, which he carried out through Christ Jesus our Lord.

¹²Because of Christ and our faith in him,* we can now come boldly and confidently into God's presence. ¹³So please don't lose heart because of my trials here. I am suffering for you, so you should feel honored.

Paul's Prayer for Spiritual Growth

¹⁴When I think of all this, I fall to my knees and pray to the Father,* ¹⁵the Creator of everything in heaven and on earth.* ¹⁶I pray that from his glorious, unlimited resources he will empower you with inner strength through his Spirit. ¹⁷Then Christ will make his home in your hearts as you trust in him. Your roots will grow down into God's love and keep you strong. ¹⁸And may you have the power to understand, as all God's people should, how wide, how long, how high, and how deep his love is. ¹⁹May you experience the love of Christ, though it is too great to understand fully. Then you will be made complete with all the fullness of life and power that comes from God.

²⁰Now all glory to God, who is able, through his mighty power at work within us, to accomplish infinitely more than we might ask or think. ²¹Glory to him in the church and in Christ Jesus through all generations forever and ever! Amen.

CHAPTER 4
Unity in the Body

Therefore I, a prisoner for serving the Lord, beg you to lead a life worthy of your calling, for you have been called by God. ²Always be humble and gentle. Be patient with each

3:6 Or *because they are united with Christ Jesus.* 3:9 Some manuscripts do not include *to everyone.* 3:12 Or *Because of Christ's faithfulness.* 3:14 Some manuscripts read *the Father of our Lord Jesus Christ.* 3:15 Or *from whom every family in heaven and on earth takes its name.*

SELF-PERCEPTION

READ EPHESIANS 2:1-13

We may feel like we are not good enough to be an example for others. We may realize that we need other people but find it hard to believe that our story of deliverance could help anyone else.

The apostle Paul said, "Just as our bodies have many parts and each part has a special function, so it is with Christ's body. We are many parts of one body, and we all belong to each other" (Romans 12:4-5). "We are God's masterpiece. He has created us anew in Christ Jesus, so we can do the good things he planned for us long ago" (Ephesians 2:10).

To have a true view of where we fit in the scheme of things, we need to see that God has a purpose for our life. God created each of us with abilities and talents. He likens us to a part of a body where every part is needed for the proper working of the whole. If you isolate any one part of a body and examine it apart from its proper place among the other members, it may seem odd and useless. Only when it is connected to the body and doing its appointed job is its usefulness realized. And so it is with us.

We need to find places where our talents and abilities can be used to help others. Doing this will show that we have gained an honest understanding of who God created us to be. He loves us and wants to help each of us realize our place in the body of Christ and our unique purpose in life. *Turn to page 1515, Ephesians 4.*

other, making allowance for each other's faults because of your love. ³Make every effort to keep yourselves united in the Spirit, binding yourselves together with peace. ⁴For there is one body and one Spirit, just as you have been called to one glorious hope for the future.

⁵There is one Lord, one faith, one baptism, ⁶one God and Father of all,
who is over all, in all, and living
through all.

⁷However, he has given each one of us a special gift* through the generosity of Christ. ⁸That is why the Scriptures say,

"When he ascended to the heights,
he led a crowd of captives
and gave gifts to his people."*

⁹Notice that it says "he ascended." This clearly means that Christ also descended to our lowly world.* ¹⁰And the same one who descended is the one who ascended higher than all the heavens, so that he might fill the entire universe with himself.

¹¹Now these are the gifts Christ gave to the church: the apostles, the prophets, the evangelists, and the pastors and teachers. ¹²Their responsibility is to equip God's people to do his work and build up the church, the body of Christ. ¹³This will continue until we all come to such unity in our faith and knowledge of God's Son that we will be mature in the Lord, measuring up to the full and complete standard of Christ.

¹⁴Then we will no longer be immature like children. We won't be tossed and blown about by every wind of new teaching. We will not be influenced when people try to trick us with lies so clever they sound like the truth. ¹⁵Instead, we will speak the truth in love, growing in every way more and more like Christ, who is the head of his body, the church. ¹⁶He makes the whole body fit together perfectly. As each part does its own special work, it helps the other parts grow, so that the whole body is healthy and growing and full of love.

Living as Children of Light

¹⁷With the Lord's authority I say this: Live no longer as the Gentiles do, for they are hopelessly confused. ¹⁸Their minds are full of darkness; they wander far from the life God gives because they have closed their minds and hardened their hearts against him. ¹⁹They have no sense of shame. They live for lustful pleasure and eagerly practice every kind of impurity.

²⁰But that isn't what you learned about Christ. ²¹Since you have heard about Jesus and have learned the truth that comes from him, ²²throw off your old sinful nature and your former way of life, which is corrupted by lust and deception. ²³Instead, let the Spirit renew your thoughts and attitudes. ²⁴Put on your new nature, created to be like God—truly righteous and holy.

²⁵So stop telling lies. Let us tell our neighbors the truth, for we are all parts of the same body. ²⁶And "don't sin by letting anger control you."* Don't let the sun go down while you are still angry, ²⁷for anger gives a foothold to the devil.

²⁸If you are a thief, quit stealing. Instead, use your hands for good hard work, and then give

4:7 Greek *a grace*. 4:8 Ps 68:18. 4:9 Some manuscripts read *to the lower parts of the earth.* 4:26 Ps 4:4.

4:7-16 We have been gifted in ways that make us necessary to others. Others have been gifted in ways that make them necessary to us. Some of us have special gifts for teaching others about God. Others may have the gift of caring for hurting people. Our individual gifts are important for the emotional and spiritual growth of others. God has a purpose for each of us, so we must strive to know him better through prayer and meditation on his Word. He will show us what our gifts are and how we can use them to help others. As we share our gifts and receive the benefits of other people's gifts, we will find the body of Christ growing stronger and full of love.

4:31-32 A life of recovery is committed to knowing God better through prayer and meditation on his Word. In examining our life, we realize just how demanding God's standards for righteous living are, but since it is God's grace that helps us conform to his will, we need not despair. As we obey him, he will teach us to live without bitterness, anger, or harsh words. God is in the business of healing our relationships. When we do things his way, we are well on the way to reconciling with our alienated friends and building solid foundations for recovery.

5:1-7 In recovery we are told to follow God's example in all we do. God wants us to be like Jesus Christ—to think and act like him. We are to love our enemies. We are to avoid sexual immorality, greed, and obscene language, since they stand counter to God's character. These requirements are right in line with what is needed in recovery. We are to seek to rebuild our broken relationships, avoid destructive behaviors, admit our wrongs, and seek to make amends for the pain we have caused. As difficult as imitating Christ might sound, anything is possible with God's powerful help.

generously to others in need. ²⁹Don't use foul or abusive language. Let everything you say be good and helpful, so that your words will be an encouragement to those who hear them.

³⁰And do not bring sorrow to God's Holy Spirit by the way you live. Remember, he has identified you as his own,* guaranteeing that you will be saved on the day of redemption.

³¹Get rid of all bitterness, rage, anger, harsh words, and slander, as well as all types of evil behavior. ³²Instead, be kind to each other, tenderhearted, forgiving one another, just as God through Christ has forgiven you.

CHAPTER 5
Living in the Light
Imitate God, therefore, in everything you do, because you are his dear children. ²Live a life filled with love, following the example of Christ. He loved us* and offered himself as a sacrifice for us, a pleasing aroma to God.

³Let there be no sexual immorality, impurity, or greed among you. Such sins have no place among God's people. ⁴Obscene stories, foolish talk, and coarse jokes—these are not for you. Instead, let there be thankfulness to God. ⁵You can be sure that no immoral, impure, or greedy person will inherit the Kingdom of Christ and of God. For a greedy person is an idolater, worshiping the things of this world.

⁶Don't be fooled by those who try to excuse these sins, for the anger of God will fall on all who disobey him. ⁷Don't participate in the things these people do. ⁸For once you were full of darkness, but now you have light from the Lord. So live as people of light! ⁹For this light within you produces only what is good and right and true.

¹⁰Carefully determine what pleases the Lord. ¹¹Take no part in the worthless deeds of evil and darkness; instead, expose them. ¹²It is shameful even to talk about the things that ungodly people do in secret. ¹³But their evil intentions will be exposed when the light shines on them, ¹⁴for the light makes everything visible. This is why it is said,

"Awake, O sleeper,
 rise up from the dead,
 and Christ will give you light."

Living by the Spirit's Power
¹⁵So be careful how you live. Don't live like fools, but like those who are wise. ¹⁶Make the most of every opportunity in these evil days.

4:30 Or *has put his seal on you.* 5:2 Some manuscripts read *loved you.*

HONESTY

READ EPHESIANS 4:12-27
We may have grown up believing lies about life, about ourself, about our family. We may still experience confusion and uncertainty because we don't have a strong sense of what is really true. The lies we believe can contribute to our addictive ways, so we need to reexamine our life in the light of what is true.

The apostle Paul talked about how the people who believed in Christ were to function like a single body. Each member is to be "mature in the Lord" (Ephesians 4:13), offering the gifts he or she has to help the whole body mature. Since Jesus described himself as "the truth" (John 14:6) and we are to be filled with him, the recovery process involves becoming "truth-full." Paul continued: "Then we will no longer be immature like children. We won't be tossed and blown about by every wind of new teaching. We will not be influenced when people try to trick us with lies so clever they sound like the truth. Instead, we will speak the truth in love, growing in every way more and more like Christ" (Ephesians 4:14-15).

Recovery can be like growing up all over again. As we grow, we are to continue to aim for what is true. In the past we measured truth against whatever sounded right to us at the time. Now we can have the sure measurement of God's Word and Jesus Christ himself. From this perspective we can reevaluate our beliefs. What is true about God? What is true about me? What is right? What is wrong? ***Turn to page 1521, Philippians 1.***

¹⁷Don't act thoughtlessly, but understand what the Lord wants you to do. ¹⁸Don't be drunk with wine, because that will ruin your life. Instead, be filled with the Holy Spirit, ¹⁹singing psalms and hymns and spiritual songs among yourselves, and making music to the Lord in your hearts. ²⁰And give thanks for everything to God the Father in the name of our Lord Jesus Christ.

Spirit-Guided Relationships: Wives and Husbands

²¹And further, submit to one another out of reverence for Christ.

²²For wives, this means submit to your husbands as to the Lord. ²³For a husband is the head of his wife as Christ is the head of the church. He is the Savior of his body, the church. ²⁴As the church submits to Christ, so you wives should submit to your husbands in everything.

²⁵For husbands, this means love your wives, just as Christ loved the church. He gave up his life for her ²⁶to make her holy and clean, washed by the cleansing of God's word.* ²⁷He did this to present her to himself as a glorious church without a spot or wrinkle or any other blemish. Instead, she will be holy and without fault. ²⁸In the same way, husbands ought to love their wives as they love their own bodies. For a man who loves his wife actually shows love for himself. ²⁹No one hates his own body but feeds and cares for it, just as Christ cares for the church. ³⁰And we are members of his body.

³¹As the Scriptures say, "A man leaves his father and mother and is joined to his wife, and the two are united into one."* ³²This is a great mystery, but it is an illustration of the way Christ and the church are one. ³³So again I say, each man must love his wife as he loves himself, and the wife must respect her husband.

CHAPTER 6
Children and Parents

Children, obey your parents because you belong to the Lord,* for this is the right thing to do. ²"Honor your father and mother." This is the first commandment with a promise: ³If you honor your father and mother, "things will go well for you, and you will have a long life on the earth."*

⁴Fathers,* do not provoke your children to anger by the way you treat them. Rather, bring them up with the discipline and instruction that comes from the Lord.

5:26 Greek *washed by water with the word.* 5:31 Gen 2:24. 6:1 Or *Children, obey your parents who belong to the Lord;* some manuscripts read simply *Children, obey your parents.* 6:2-3 Exod 20:12; Deut 5:16. 6:4 Or *Parents.*

5:21-33 When our life is out of control, family tensions and conflict are common. Paul tells us that the home should be a place where love and mutual respect are shown. Husbands and wives should love each other and be sensitive to each other's needs, showing the same love Christ showed the church. The painful consequences of our addiction are felt most deeply by our family. By selfishly seeking to meet our own needs through addictive behavior, we have neglected and hurt the people it was our responsibility to love and support. Rebuilding family relationships is one of the most important tasks we face in recovery. As we admit the nature of our wrongs and seek to make amends to our loved ones, we can begin to reestablish a family atmosphere of love and mutual respect.

6:1-4 Paul directed both parents and children to show love toward one another. Children are to honor their parents. The widespread disrespect shown toward parents today leads to deep emotional scars both in parents and children. Paul also warned parents to treat their children with love and respect. Through ridicule and neglect parents can create resentment that may scar their children for life. Whether we are parents or children who have failed, we need to admit our failures and seek to make amends wherever possible.

6:10-12 While we may be firmly grounded in sound doctrine and accept our responsibility to live a godly life, we must be aware of the fierce, invisible warfare Satan wages against us. Many of our struggles with addiction could be the result of direct attacks by spiritual enemies. Since we continue to struggle with a dependency that once rendered us powerless, we need to admit our inability to manage our life. Then as we turn our life and will over to God, he will stand with us in the battle.

6:13-20 Notice that each piece of spiritual armor (except the sword) is defensive in nature. As recovering addicts, we need to improve our conscious contact with God, to know him better, and to surround ourselves with truth, righteousness, faith, and prayer. These will protect us against the assault of hostile spiritual forces. The forces arrayed against us are powerful, but the weapons God gives us are adequate for our defense. Part of that armor—the shoes—enables us to share the Good News of God's delivering power with others, giving hope to them while strengthening our own recovery.

Slaves and Masters

⁵Slaves, obey your earthly masters with deep respect and fear. Serve them sincerely as you would serve Christ. ⁶Try to please them all the time, not just when they are watching you. As slaves of Christ, do the will of God with all your heart. ⁷Work with enthusiasm, as though you were working for the Lord rather than for people. ⁸Remember that the Lord will reward each one of us for the good we do, whether we are slaves or free.

⁹Masters, treat your slaves in the same way. Don't threaten them; remember, you both have the same Master in heaven, and he has no favorites.

The Whole Armor of God

¹⁰A final word: Be strong in the Lord and in his mighty power. ¹¹Put on all of God's armor so that you will be able to stand firm against all strategies of the devil. ¹²For we* are not fighting against flesh-and-blood enemies, but against evil rulers and authorities of the unseen world, against mighty powers in this dark world, and against evil spirits in the heavenly places.

¹³Therefore, put on every piece of God's armor so you will be able to resist the enemy in the time of evil. Then after the battle you will still be standing firm. ¹⁴Stand your ground, putting on the belt of truth and the body armor of God's righteousness. ¹⁵For shoes, put on the peace that comes from the Good News so that you will be fully prepared.* ¹⁶In addition to all of these, hold up the shield of faith to stop the fiery arrows of the devil.* ¹⁷Put on salvation as your helmet, and take the sword of the Spirit, which is the word of God.

¹⁸Pray in the Spirit at all times and on every occasion. Stay alert and be persistent in your prayers for all believers everywhere.*

¹⁹And pray for me, too. Ask God to give me the right words so I can boldly explain God's mysterious plan that the Good News is for Jews and Gentiles alike.* ²⁰I am in chains now, still preaching this message as God's ambassador. So pray that I will keep on speaking boldly for him, as I should.

Final Greetings

²¹To bring you up to date, Tychicus will give you a full report about what I am doing and

6:12 Some manuscripts read *you.* 6:15 Or *For shoes, put on the readiness to preach the Good News of peace with God.* 6:16 Greek *the evil one.* 6:18 Greek *all of God's holy people.* 6:19 Greek *explain the mystery of the Good News;* some manuscripts read simply *explain the mystery.*

STEP 10

Dealing with Anger

BIBLE READING: Ephesians 4:26-27

We continued to take personal inventory and when we were wrong promptly admitted it.

Many of us have a hard time dealing with anger. Some of us have a history of rage, so we try to stifle our feelings. Others of us stuff down the feelings of anger, pretending they don't exist, because we were never allowed to express them in the past. If some of our problems stem from not knowing how to express anger properly, we may try to avoid dealing with it altogether. We may try to "put it off" and hope it goes away. Evaluating how to deal with anger appropriately is an important part of our daily inventory.

The apostle Paul said, "'Don't sin by letting anger control you.' Don't let the sun go down while you are still angry, for anger gives a foothold to the devil" (Ephesians 4:26-27). One key is to have daily time limits for handling our anger—time to find ways to express the feelings and then let them go.

Dealing with anger promptly is important because when it is left to fester, it becomes bitterness. Bitterness is anger that has been buried and given time to grow. The Bible warns us: "Get rid of all bitterness, rage, anger, harsh words, and slander, as well as all types of evil behavior. Instead, be kind to each other, tenderhearted, forgiving one another, just as God through Christ has forgiven you" (Ephesians 4:31-32).

Alcoholics Anonymous teaches that we should never allow ourselves to become too hungry, angry, lonely, or tired. We can help accomplish this by promptly dealing with our anger when it occurs. *Turn to page 1553, 1 Timothy 4.*

how I am getting along. He is a beloved brother and faithful helper in the Lord's work. [22]I have sent him to you for this very purpose—to let you know how we are doing and to encourage you.

6:23 Greek *brothers*.

[23]Peace be with you, dear brothers and sisters,* and may God the Father and the Lord Jesus Christ give you love with faithfulness. [24]May God's grace be eternally upon all who love our Lord Jesus Christ.

PHILIPPIANS

THE BIG PICTURE

A. JOY IN THE MIDST OF DIFFICULT CIRCUMSTANCES (1:1-30)
B. THE SECRET OF VICTORIOUS LIVING (2:1-30)
C. HAVING A VICTORIOUS FOCUS (3:1-21)
D. FINDING A JOYFUL FELLOWSHIP (4:1-23)

As a missionary and a traveling pastor, Paul sometimes had to depend on others for financial support. The Philippian church, which Paul planted during his second missionary journey, had supported him for ten years. They were compassionate people whose commitment to Christ and support of Christ's work were well known.

Paul wrote this letter to thank the Philippians and to challenge them to remain true to Christ and joyful in their circumstances. Wholeness of life, he reminded them, does not come from material things or pleasant circumstances. Genuine joy, meaning, and satisfaction come as we follow Christ and help others to grow spiritually.

Paul knew what he was talking about. He wrote this encouraging letter while facing a trial in Rome that, for all he knew, might lead to his execution. Paul had been both rich and poor, comfortable and in pain, healthy and sick, popular and the target of mobs. He had learned to be content, even joyful, no matter what his physical circumstances.

The letter to the Philippians has much to say to us. Our life had become unmanageable, and we had hurt people we loved. We had come to the end of our rope. Though the worst is behind us, we still must contend with day-to-day frustration, anger, and conflict. Yet despite our painful circumstances, Christ can be our joy. Recovery will probably never be pleasant, but at the same time we need to remember that we have God helping us. Because of that, we can have joy. The secret of being full of joy can be found by getting to know Christ better and making him the center of our life each day.

THE BOTTOM LINE

PURPOSE: To thank the Philippian believers for their support of Paul's ministry and to encourage them.
AUTHOR: The apostle Paul. AUDIENCE: The believers in Philippi, a city in Macedonia. DATE WRITTEN: Around A.D. 61–62. SETTING: Paul, a prisoner in Rome, wrote this warm letter to the believers at Philippi after they sent him a generous gift. KEY VERSE: "Keep putting into practice all you learned and received from me—everything you heard from me and saw me doing. Then the God of peace will be with you" (4:9).
KEY PEOPLE AND RELATIONSHIPS: Paul with Timothy, Epaphroditus, and the Philippian believers.

RECOVERY THEMES

The Importance of Humility: When we turn our life over to God, we experience the power of his Holy Spirit at work within us. He changes our life and gives us the control we once lacked. But a long time in successful recovery can make us prone to pride. We may begin to forget the source of our power and start to feel self-sufficient. The letter to the Philippians reminds us to be humble, to adopt the attitude of Christ, who, though he was God, "did not think of equality with God as something to cling to" (2:6). Recovery must always involve humility.

Recovery Leads to True Joy: Our life has been unmanageable and out of control. When we admit our power-lessness and turn our life over to God, we not only start the recovery process but also take the first steps toward finding true joy. We can have joy even during the tough times—because real joy does not come from outward circumstances but from inward strength. Joy comes from knowing Christ personally and from depending on his strength and power on a daily basis.

Recovery Requires Sacrifice: A sure sign of progress in recovery is when we begin to care about those around us who are still in bondage to their addiction. As Christ suffered and died so we might have life, we must sacrifice for others as well. It takes maturity to lay aside our own interests and agenda in order to share the message of hope and recovery with others. But such sacrifices are part of recovery. Staying self-absorbed can set us up for pride and relapse; carrying the message of recovery to others will always strengthen us.

Fighting the Real Enemies: As we struggle through the recovery process, it is common to have conflicts with other people. We are sometimes in pain, and it can be very easy to turn against the people who are causing that pain. The believers at Philippi sometimes "picked at each other." But as this letter reminds us, our battles should not be waged against one another. We need to concentrate our energy against much greater enemies—our powerful dependency and destructive pride.

CHAPTER 1
Greetings from Paul

This letter is from Paul and Timothy, slaves of Christ Jesus.

I am writing to all of God's holy people in Philippi who belong to Christ Jesus, including the elders* and deacons.

²May God our Father and the Lord Jesus Christ give you grace and peace.

1:1 Or *overseers;* or *bishops.*

Paul's Thanksgiving and Prayer

³Every time I think of you, I give thanks to my God. ⁴Whenever I pray, I make my requests for all of you with joy, ⁵for you have been my partners in spreading the Good News about Christ from the time you first heard it until now. ⁶And I am certain that God, who began the good work within you, will continue his work until it is finally

---

1:3-11 Paul told the Philippians that he had been praying for them, which would have greatly encouraged those early believers. Our spiritual awakening will lead us to feel a growing concern for people in need. As we share the message of hope with others, we should also pray for their progress as part of serving them. Our prayers for other people struggling with addiction will significantly impact their spiritual growth. As we let them know we are behind them, not only will they grow in their faith, but we will be encouraged to persevere in recovery.

1:12-14 In retrospect, Paul could see that God had allowed the events of his life, both good and bad, to help him spread the Good News. If we take an honest look at our life, we may find the same to be true. Through our painful addiction we have gained the perspective needed to share the message of hope with others. Our personal story of deliverance is an essential tool for reaching others in need of recovery. As with Paul, our painful past and God's powerful deliverance open the door to our serving God by helping others.

1:19-24 We cannot lose if we belong to God. Whether we live or die, we know we will win in the end. During times of relapse and failure we may be tempted to give up on life completely. Paul's primary motivation for persevering was his deep concern for others who still needed to hear the Good News of God's loving power. No matter how bad things are, if we trust God, he will come through for us. We will then have one more victory story to share with others. No matter how deeply we have failed or how many times we have fallen, God can still use us to save the lives of others just like us. There is always a reason to live.

finished on the day when Christ Jesus returns.

⁷So it is right that I should feel as I do about all of you, for you have a special place in my heart. You share with me the special favor of God, both in my imprisonment and in defending and confirming the truth of the Good News. ⁸God knows how much I love you and long for you with the tender compassion of Christ Jesus.

⁹I pray that your love will overflow more and more, and that you will keep on growing in knowledge and understanding. ¹⁰For I want you to understand what really matters, so that you may live pure and blameless lives until the day of Christ's return. ¹¹May you always be filled with the fruit of your salvation—the righteous character produced in your life by Jesus Christ*—for this will bring much glory and praise to God.

Paul's Joy That Christ Is Preached

¹²And I want you to know, my dear brothers and sisters,* that everything that has happened to me here has helped to spread the Good News. ¹³For everyone here, including the whole palace guard,* knows that I am in chains because of Christ. ¹⁴And because of my imprisonment, most of the believers* here have gained confidence and boldly speak God's message* without fear.

¹⁵It's true that some are preaching out of jealousy and rivalry. But others preach about Christ with pure motives. ¹⁶They preach because they love me, for they know I have been appointed to defend the Good News. ¹⁷Those others do not have pure motives as they preach about Christ. They preach with selfish ambition, not sincerely, intending to make my chains more painful to me. ¹⁸But that doesn't matter. Whether their motives are false or genuine, the message about Christ is being preached either way, so I rejoice. And I will continue to rejoice. ¹⁹For I know that as you pray for me and the Spirit of Jesus Christ helps me, this will lead to my deliverance.

Paul's Life for Christ

²⁰For I fully expect and hope that I will never be ashamed, but that I will continue to be bold for Christ, as I have been in the past. And I trust that my life will bring honor to Christ, whether I live or die. ²¹For to me,

---

1:11 Greek *with the fruit of righteousness through Jesus Christ.* 1:12 Greek *brothers.* 1:13 Greek *including all the Praetorium.* 1:14a Greek *brothers in the Lord.* 1:14b Some manuscripts read *speak the message.*

PERSEVERANCE

READ PHILIPPIANS 1:2-6
Sometimes we may feel like giving up the struggle. We try to persevere, only to fall once again. We take two steps forward but then stumble backward. We feel condemned, and we fear that even God may give up on us. At times there are so many difficulties, so many issues to work through, so many patterns in our life that have to be changed, that we begin to feel as if we are going crazy.

God acknowledges the difficulties we face, but he also promises us victory in the end. The apostle Paul wrote: "Overwhelming victory is ours through Christ, who loved us. And I am convinced that nothing can ever separate us from God's love. Neither death nor life, neither angels nor demons, neither our fears for today nor our worries about tomorrow—not even the powers of hell can separate us from God's love. . . . Nothing in all creation will ever be able to separate us from the love of God that is revealed in Christ Jesus our Lord" (Romans 8:37-39). Paul also said, "I am certain that God, who began the good work within you, will continue his work until it is finally finished on the day when Christ Jesus returns" (Philippians 1:6).

When we feel as if we are going crazy and don't think we can handle life, God is there. He is determined not to give up on us. We can rely on his persistent love. God has promised to keep working on us until we are whole. There will still be tough times, but with his help we can handle them, one day at a time. ***Turn to page 1533, Colossians 3.***

living means living for Christ, and dying is even better. ²²But if I live, I can do more fruitful work for Christ. So I really don't know which is better. ²³I'm torn between two desires: I long to go and be with Christ, which would be far better for me. ²⁴But for your sakes, it is better that I continue to live.

²⁵Knowing this, I am convinced that I will remain alive so I can continue to help all of you grow and experience the joy of your faith. ²⁶And when I come to you again, you will have even more reason to take pride in Christ Jesus because of what he is doing through me.

Live as Citizens of Heaven

²⁷Above all, you must live as citizens of heaven, conducting yourselves in a manner worthy of the Good News about Christ. Then, whether I come and see you again or only hear about you, I will know that you are standing together with one spirit and one purpose, fighting together for the faith, which is the Good News. ²⁸Don't be intimidated in any way by your enemies. This will be a sign to them that they are going to be destroyed, but that you are going to be saved, even by God himself. ²⁹For you have been given not only the privilege of trusting in Christ but also the privilege of suffering for him. ³⁰We are in this struggle together. You have seen my struggle in the past, and you know that I am still in the midst of it.

CHAPTER 2
Have the Attitude of Christ

Is there any encouragement from belonging to Christ? Any comfort from his love? Any fellowship together in the Spirit? Are your hearts tender and compassionate? ²Then make me truly happy by agreeing wholeheartedly with each other, loving one another, and working together with one mind and purpose.

³Don't be selfish; don't try to impress others. Be humble, thinking of others as better than yourselves. ⁴Don't look out only for your own interests, but take an interest in others, too.

⁵You must have the same attitude that Christ Jesus had.

⁶ Though he was God,*
he did not think of equality with God
as something to cling to.
⁷ Instead, he gave up his divine privileges*;
he took the humble position of a slave*
and was born as a human being.
When he appeared in human form,*
⁸ he humbled himself in obedience
to God
and died a criminal's death on a cross.

⁹ Therefore, God elevated him to the place
of highest honor
and gave him the name above all
other names,

2:6 Or *Being in the form of God.* 2:7a Greek *he emptied himself.* 2:7b Or *the form of a slave.* 2:7c Some English translations put this phrase in verse 8.

2:1-4 We are never an island unto ourself; we are a part of a whole, a member of Christ's body. If we are part of a loving community, when others hurt, we hurt; when we hurt, others hurt. Early in the recovery process we may need to concentrate on our own welfare. But as we grow, we have to move beyond self-centeredness and become interested in others. Part of making amends to people we have harmed is showing them that we have changed. As we love others, we will find that others will love us. As our relationships grow stronger, our addiction will lose its grip on us.

2:5-11 Jesus Christ is our ideal model for humility in obedience and service. Our thoughts, attitudes, and actions are to be patterned after Christ. His willingness to humbly obey his Father is a great example for us. As we take an honest moral inventory of our life, we must humbly admit our faults so we can begin to change our destructive patterns. If we follow Jesus Christ in humility, learning to admit our failures without hesitation, nothing will be able to stop our recovery.

2:12-18 Obedience to God's program is one of the requirements for spiritual growth. But how can we lead a clean, innocent life like he wants us to? We have already admitted that we are powerless over our addiction. God not only asks us to live a godly life, he also provides us with the power to do it. He works in us, giving us the desire and the ability to obey him. As we get to know God by reading the Bible and spending time with him in prayer, he can transform us from the inside out so we can shine brightly for him.

2:25-28 Believing in Christ is not always easy. As Epaphroditus clearly demonstrated, we need stamina to do the work and a servant's attitude to succeed in our spiritual battles. We must give ourself to the cause of Christ, putting others' needs before our personal comforts. As we carry the message of salvation and recovery to fellow strugglers despite difficulties and ridicule, we realize that when we give up our desires in order to meet the needs of others, we also leave behind the burden of our addiction. As we serve others, we build meaningful relationships and a strong foundation for permanent recovery. By helping others, we help ourself.

¹⁰that at the name of Jesus every knee
should bow,
in heaven and on earth and under the
earth,
¹¹and every tongue declare that Jesus Christ
is Lord,
to the glory of God the Father.

Shine Brightly for Christ

¹²Dear friends, you always followed my instructions when I was with you. And now that I am away, it is even more important. Work hard to show the results of your salvation, obeying God with deep reverence and fear. ¹³For God is working in you, giving you the desire and the power to do what pleases him.

¹⁴Do everything without complaining and arguing, ¹⁵so that no one can criticize you. Live clean, innocent lives as children of God, shining like bright lights in a world full of crooked and perverse people. ¹⁶Hold firmly to the word of life; then, on the day of Christ's return, I will be proud that I did not run the race in vain and that my work was not useless. ¹⁷But I will rejoice even if I lose my life, pouring it out like a liquid offering to God,* just like your faithful service is an offering to God. And I want all of you to share that joy. ¹⁸Yes, you should rejoice, and I will share your joy.

Paul Commends Timothy

¹⁹If the Lord Jesus is willing, I hope to send Timothy to you soon for a visit. Then he can cheer me up by telling me how you are getting along. ²⁰I have no one else like Timothy, who genuinely cares about your welfare. ²¹All the others care only for themselves and not for what matters to Jesus Christ. ²²But you know how Timothy has proved himself. Like a son with his father, he has served with me in preaching the Good News. ²³I hope to send him to you just as soon as I find out what is going to happen to me here. ²⁴And I have confidence from the Lord that I myself will come to see you soon.

Paul Commends Epaphroditus

²⁵Meanwhile, I thought I should send Epaphroditus back to you. He is a true brother, coworker, and fellow soldier. And he was your messenger to help me in my need. ²⁶I am sending him because he has been longing to see you, and he was very distressed that you heard he was ill. ²⁷And he certainly was ill; in

2:17 Greek *I will rejoice even if I am to be poured out as a liquid offering.*

STEP 7

Into the Open

BIBLE READING: Philippians 2:5-9
We humbly asked him to remove our shortcomings.

Because of our pride, we may hide behind defenses during the recovery process. We may hide behind our good reputation, our important position, or a delusion of our superiority. We may feel such inner shame that we go overboard to cover up with a self-righteous public identity. Those of us who have tried to protect ourself in these ways will need a dramatic change of attitude.

The apostle Paul wrote: "You must have the same attitude that Christ Jesus had. Though he was God, he did not think of equality with God as something to cling to. Instead, he gave up his divine privileges; he took the humble position of a slave and was born as a human being. When he appeared in human form, he humbled himself in obedience to God and died a criminal's death on a cross. Therefore, God elevated him to the place of highest honor and gave him the name above all other names" (Philippians 2:5-9). The author of Hebrews wrote: "We do this by keeping our eyes on Jesus, the champion who initiates and perfects our faith. Because of the joy awaiting him, he endured the cross, disregarding its shame. Now he is seated in the place of honor beside God's throne" (Hebrews 12:2).

We can ask God to change our attitudes. When he deals with our pride, we will be able to stop hiding behind our reputation. We can allow ourself to become "anonymous," each of us known as just another person struggling with addiction. When we humbly yield ourself to God in recovery, he promises us future honor and the restoration of our good name. *Turn to page 1633, 1 John 5.*

fact, he almost died. But God had mercy on him—and also on me, so that I would not have one sorrow after another.

²⁸So I am all the more anxious to send him back to you, for I know you will be glad to see him, and then I will not be so worried about you. ²⁹Welcome him in the Lord's love* and with great joy, and give him the honor that people like him deserve. ³⁰For he risked his life for the work of Christ, and he was at the point of death while doing for me what you couldn't do from far away.

CHAPTER 3
The Priceless Value of Knowing Christ

Whatever happens, my dear brothers and sisters,* rejoice in the Lord. I never get tired of telling you these things, and I do it to safeguard your faith.

²Watch out for those dogs, those people who do evil, those mutilators who say you must be circumcised to be saved. ³For we who worship by the Spirit of God* are the ones who are truly circumcised. We rely on what Christ Jesus has done for us. We put no confidence in human effort, ⁴though I could have confidence in my own effort if anyone could. Indeed, if others have reason for confidence in their own efforts, I have even more!

⁵I was circumcised when I was eight days old. I am a pure-blooded citizen of Israel and a member of the tribe of Benjamin—a real Hebrew if there ever was one! I was a member of the Pharisees, who demand the strictest obedience to the Jewish law. ⁶I was so zealous that I harshly persecuted the church. And as for righteousness, I obeyed the law without fault.

⁷I once thought these things were valuable, but now I consider them worthless because of what Christ has done. ⁸Yes, everything else is worthless when compared with the infinite value of knowing Christ Jesus my Lord. For his sake I have discarded everything else, counting it all as garbage, so that I could gain Christ ⁹and become one with him. I no longer count on my own righteousness through obeying the law; rather, I become righteous through faith in Christ.* For God's way of making us right with himself depends on faith. ¹⁰I want to know Christ and experience the mighty power that raised him from the dead. I want to suffer with him, sharing in his death, ¹¹so that one way or another I will experience the resurrection from the dead!

Pressing toward the Goal

¹²I don't mean to say that I have already achieved these things or that I have already reached perfection. But I press on to possess that perfection for which Christ Jesus first possessed me. ¹³No, dear brothers and sisters,

2:29 Greek *in the Lord.* **3:1** Greek *brothers;* also in 3:13, 17. **3:3** Some manuscripts read *worship God in spirit;* one early manuscript reads *worship in spirit.* **3:9** Or *through the faithfulness of Christ.*

3:2-3 The world is full of deceivers. We must be especially alert for those who offer recovery plans that exclude God. The false teachers Paul mentioned demanded that Gentile Christians obey the Jewish law of circumcision in order to be saved. The apostle stood against this claim, reminding the Philippians that only God through Jesus Christ could bring them deliverance. This message is for us, too. If people claim we don't need God for a successful recovery, we should walk the other way. Programs that depend on our actions will never succeed for long. Until we admit that we are powerless to help ourself, our recovery won't succeed.

3:4-11 Paul made a detailed inventory of his past behaviors—including his religious activities—and found nothing worth hanging on to. He threw out his past life and replaced it with his new life in Christ. We should engage in an honest inventory of our heritage and accomplishments as Paul did. As we compare the value of our past accomplishments to the power offered by Christ, we will find the new life God offers is the obvious choice. Our personal inventory helps us discover that the things of this world can't satisfy our eternal needs—only God can.

3:17-21 On the human level, we need to pattern our life after those who, despite difficulties, have successfully lived for Christ. Those who fail to examine themselves end up spending all their efforts living only for themselves, enslaved by destructive habits and dependencies. Full recovery, however, can be experienced by trusting Jesus Christ and following in his steps. Some of us may wonder if we will ever get beyond the pain we experience on a daily basis. But even if the pain remains throughout our life, we will be changed completely when Jesus Christ returns.

4:1-3 Since we know with certainty what our ultimate destiny is, we can confidently face the hardships of life. Paul set a good example for how to grow spiritually and encourage others in their growth. To encourage these two Christian women to reestablish a harmonious relationship, he complimented them on their previous service to God. He was assuming that they were humble enough to take criticism and change for the better. When we keep a close watch on our own life, as Paul did his, we will be better able to hold others accountable to their recovery commitment.

I have not achieved it,* but I focus on this one thing: Forgetting the past and looking forward to what lies ahead, [14]I press on to reach the end of the race and receive the heavenly prize for which God, through Christ Jesus, is calling us.

[15]Let all who are spiritually mature agree on these things. If you disagree on some point, I believe God will make it plain to you. [16]But we must hold on to the progress we have already made.

[17]Dear brothers and sisters, pattern your lives after mine, and learn from those who follow our example. [18]For I have told you often before, and I say it again with tears in my eyes, that there are many whose conduct shows they are really enemies of the cross of Christ. [19]They are headed for destruction. Their god is their appetite, they brag about shameful things, and they think only about this life here on earth. [20]But we are citizens of heaven, where the Lord Jesus Christ lives. And we are eagerly waiting for him to return as our Savior. [21]He will take our weak mortal bodies and change them into glorious bodies like his own, using the same power with which he will bring everything under his control.

CHAPTER 4

Therefore, my dear brothers and sisters,* stay true to the Lord. I love you and long to see you, dear friends, for you are my joy and the crown I receive for my work.

Words of Encouragement

[2]Now I appeal to Euodia and Syntyche. Please, because you belong to the Lord, settle your disagreement. [3]And I ask you, my true partner,* to help these two women, for they worked hard with me in telling others the Good News. They worked along with Clement and the rest of my co-workers, whose names are written in the Book of Life.

[4]Always be full of joy in the Lord. I say it again—rejoice! [5]Let everyone see that you are considerate in all you do. Remember, the Lord is coming soon.*

[6]Don't worry about anything; instead, pray about everything. Tell God what you need, and thank him for all he has done. [7]Then you will experience God's peace, which exceeds anything we can understand. His peace will guard your hearts and minds as you live in Christ Jesus.

[8]And now, dear brothers and sisters, one

3:13 Some manuscripts read *not yet achieved it.*
4:1 Greek *brothers;* also in 4:8. 4:3 Or *loyal Syzygus.*
4:5 Greek *the Lord is near.*

STEP 6

Attitudes and Actions

BIBLE READING: Philippians 3:12-14
We were entirely ready to have God remove all these defects of character. Getting "entirely ready" to have God remove "all" our defects of character sounds impossible. In reality we know that such perfection is out of human reach. This is another way of saying that we are going to do our best to work toward a lifelong goal that no one ever reaches until eternity.

The apostle Paul expressed a similar thought: "I don't mean to say that I have already achieved these things or that I have already reached perfection. But I press on to possess that perfection for which Christ Jesus first possessed me. . . . Forgetting the past and looking forward to what lies ahead, I press on to reach the end of the race and receive the heavenly prize for which God, through Christ Jesus, is calling us" (Philippians 3:12-14).

This combination of a positive attitude and energetic effort is part of the mystery of our cooperation with God. Paul said: "Work hard to show the results of your salvation, obeying God with deep reverence and fear. For God is working in you, giving you the desire and the power to do what pleases him" (Philippians 2:12-13).

We will need to practice these steps the rest of our life. We don't have to demand perfection of ourself; it is enough to keep moving ahead as best we can. We can look forward to our rewards with the hope of becoming all that God intends us to be. God will strengthen and encourage us as we do so. *Turn to Step Seven, page 915, Isaiah 57.*

final thing. Fix your thoughts on what is true, and honorable, and right, and pure, and lovely, and admirable. Think about things that are excellent and worthy of praise. [9]Keep putting into practice all you learned and received from me—everything you heard from me and saw me doing. Then the God of peace will be with you.

Paul's Thanks for Their Gifts

[10]How I praise the Lord that you are concerned about me again. I know you have always been concerned for me, but you didn't have the chance to help me. [11]Not that I was ever in need, for I have learned how to be content with whatever I have. [12]I know how to live on almost nothing or with everything. I have learned the secret of living in every situation, whether it is with a full stomach or empty, with plenty or little. [13]For I can do everything through Christ,* who gives me strength. [14]Even so, you have done well to share with me in my present difficulty.

[15]As you know, you Philippians were the only ones who gave me financial help when I first brought you the Good News and then traveled on from Macedonia. No other church did this. [16]Even when I was in Thessalonica you sent help more than once. [17]I don't say this because I want a gift from you. Rather, I want you to receive a reward for your kindness.

[18]At the moment I have all I need—and more! I am generously supplied with the gifts you sent me with Epaphroditus. They are a sweet-smelling sacrifice that is acceptable and pleasing to God. [19]And this same God who takes care of me will supply all your needs from his glorious riches, which have been given to us in Christ Jesus.

[20]Now all glory to God our Father forever and ever! Amen.

Paul's Final Greetings

[21]Give my greetings to each of God's holy people—all who belong to Christ Jesus. The brothers who are with me send you their greetings. [22]And all the rest of God's people send you greetings, too, especially those in Caesar's household.

[23]May the grace of the Lord Jesus Christ be with your spirit.*

4:13 Greek *through the one.* 4:23 Some manuscripts add *Amen.*

4:4-9 True happiness can be found in every situation of life when we recognize that God is at work and always in control. Because Christ is with us and his return is certain, we can act calmly in pain and difficulty. Peace and joy come when we focus on those things that provide lasting value to our life. The more we commit ourself to knowing God's will through prayer and study of his Word, the better prepared we are to help ourself and others in the process of recovery.

4:12-13 Some of us may wonder if we will ever experience peace again. Our battle against addiction seems endless and hard. We continually find ourself in helpless situations. When we get discouraged and recognize that recovery is too hard for us to achieve alone, we can claim these verses for renewed hope. God wants us to make progress in recovery, and he has the power to help us do it. As we entrust our life to God, we can make progress in recovery with the help of Christ, who gives us the strength we need. With God, nothing is impossible!

4:15-20 Paul's relationship with the Philippian believers was characterized by mutual respect and sharing—important qualities in any strong relationship, including our relationships in recovery. Paul was a respected Christian leader in the early church. Many in his position would have had difficulty accepting the Philippians' help and might have refused it. It is sometimes difficult to accept help from others. Perhaps we feel they really don't understand where we are coming from or are just trying to manipulate us, doing things that make them feel good about themselves. If we hope to succeed in recovery, however, we need to follow Paul's example. He joyfully received the help from the Philippian believers and, as a result, he stood firm through tough, lonely times.

GOD grant me the serenity
to accept the things I cannot change
the courage to change the things I can
and the wisdom to know the difference

AMEN

Serenity is having an inner calm in the midst of the ups and downs of life. It involves learning to be content with the things in our life that cannot be changed.

Some of us have never accepted the hurtful circumstances of our life. We may be living in denial to avoid the pain. We continue to struggle against the painful realities, to rebel against who we are or what has happened to us. Others of us have accepted the bad, even to the point of feeling that it's normal and comfortable. Therefore, we repeat the destructive cycle of behavior.

The apostle Paul wrote: "I have learned how to be content with whatever I have. I know how to live on almost nothing or with everything. I have learned the secret of living in every situation, whether it is with a full stomach or empty, with plenty or little" (Philippians 4:11-12). When Paul wrote this, he was in a Roman prison waiting to hear if he would be executed. And yet we hear no whining or complaining. Instead, he learned to accept the circumstances he could not change.

The process of recovery is a time of learning to find serenity while also accepting life as it is. Life isn't always fair. It isn't predictable or controllable. It can be wonderfully rich in some ways and terribly difficult in others. When we become willing to face the hurt in our life and consider how we have reacted to it, then our discomfort can lead us to break the destructive cycle. Then we can learn to be content with the things we cannot change. *Turn to page 1531, Colossians 1.*

COLOSSIANS

THE BIG PICTURE

A. THE POWER OF JESUS CHRIST
   (1:1–2:23)
B. CHRIST'S POWER WITHIN US
   (3:1–4:18)

Colossians is a letter about the greatness of Christ. Since their conversion, the believers in the city of Colosse had heard many theories about salvation, all of which diminished Christ in some way. Some people had faith in angels, some in rituals, and others in various religious philosophies or practices. Paul wrote to correct them all: Christ is God in the flesh and the only one sufficient to save us from sin and its destructive power.

In this letter Paul included practical advice about how the believers were to live. He called them to adhere to the truth, to live sexually pure lives, to live in peace with their friends and neighbors, and to live in dependence on God. Paul did not expect the Colossians to accomplish these things on their own. He emphasized that when we seek to do God's will, we can depend on God's help. Our actions can be energized by the greatest power in the universe—the power of God in Jesus Christ.

Recovery is easier when we lean on others, but ultimately God is the only one who can rescue us completely. We need God's power to begin the process of healing in recovery. The same power that made salvation possible makes it possible for us to recover. We can trust Christ to save us, and we can trust his power to help us with our struggles as we live each day as it comes.

THE BOTTOM LINE

PURPOSE: To show us that Christ is the only real source of power in our life. AUTHOR: The apostle Paul. AUDIENCE: The believers at Colosse, a city in Asia Minor. DATE WRITTEN: Around A.D. 60, while Paul was in prison in Rome. SETTING: Paul was writing to a church that he had never visited. It had been started by some of his converts, including a man named Epaphras. KEY VERSES: "For in Christ lives all the fullness of God in a human body. So you also are complete through your union with Christ, who is the head over every ruler and authority" (2:9-10). KEY PEOPLE AND RELATIONSHIPS: Paul with Timothy, Tychicus, Onesimus, John Mark, and Epaphras.

RECOVERY THEMES

Recovery Is a Lifelong Process: We may long for a day when we will be totally free from the bondage of our past—a day when recovery will be complete and we can go on with our life. But recovery is a lifelong process, with daily challenges to maintain contact with our powerful and loving God. From this letter to the Colossian believers, we learn that our life with Christ is not just a onetime rescue operation but a lifelong commitment.

True Recovery Involves Faith in God: One danger we face after a period of successful recovery is the tendency to forget how much we need God. It is easy to start thinking we can go it alone, depending on rules or formulas for success. Paul warned the Colossians about this danger, urging them to live in daily contact and communication with God. It is true that with maturity comes strength of character, but it is not true that we can end our need for faith in God. Self-sufficiency got us into trouble in the first place, and it can lead us to relapse as well. If we are to experience true recovery, we need to acknowledge our ongoing need for faith in God.

Jesus Is Lord of the Universe: The entire universe is being held together by the power of Jesus Christ. He is the supreme ruler and Lord of all creation. He is the reflection of the invisible God. He is eternal, preexistent, omnipotent, and equal with the Father. He is also the Lord of every successful recovery. What a privilege to depend not merely on some anonymous "higher Power," but on the highest Power of all! How incredible that he invites each of us to have a personal relationship with him!

Healthy Relationships: An important part of the recovery process involves making amends to the people we have wronged. This letter to the Colossians gives us practical guidance in this area. Paul calls us to live according to the principles of selfless love and to mutually respect all the people in our life. If we treat others in ways that build them up, our relationships will grow stronger and support us in the recovery process.

CHAPTER 1
Greetings from Paul
This letter is from Paul, chosen by the will of God to be an apostle of Christ Jesus, and from our brother Timothy.

²We are writing to God's holy people in the city of Colosse, who are faithful brothers and sisters* in Christ.

May God our Father give you grace and peace.

Paul's Thanksgiving and Prayer
³We always pray for you, and we give thanks to God, the Father of our Lord Jesus Christ. ⁴For we have heard of your faith in Christ Jesus and your love for all of God's people, ⁵which come from your confident hope of what God has reserved for you in heaven. You have had this expectation ever since you first heard the truth of the Good News.

⁶This same Good News that came to you is going out all over the world. It is bearing fruit everywhere by changing lives, just as it changed your lives from the day you first heard and understood the truth about God's wonderful grace.

⁷You learned about the Good News from Epaphras, our beloved co-worker. He is Christ's faithful servant, and he is helping us on your behalf.* ⁸He has told us about the love for others that the Holy Spirit has given you.

⁹So we have not stopped praying for you since we first heard about you. We ask God

1:2 Greek *faithful brothers.* 1:7 Or *he is ministering on your behalf;* some manuscripts read *he is ministering on our behalf.*

1:11-14 As always, Paul was careful to point out that our strength and power come not from ourself but from God. Only God's "glorious" power at work within us can strengthen us and give us "endurance and patience" for recovery. We have already admitted that we are powerless over our dependency. By recognizing that God has the power to restore us, we can begin to think more positively about recovery.

1:15-17 These verses describe God in Jesus Christ, our higher power. As the Creator of our world, he has the means to rebuild our life, no matter how broken it is. In fact, the entire universe would dissolve if he stopped holding it together. Even people who seem to have things under control could not exist a moment longer if it weren't for the power of God extended on their behalf. We all need God and his power, whether we admit it or not. God is our infinite power source, and he can provide all the power we need to pursue recovery.

GOD grant me the serenity
to accept the things I cannot change
the courage to change the things I can
and the wisdom to know the difference

AMEN

Many of us in recovery are learning to think and act in new ways. We may find it hard to recognize true wisdom, even when it's staring us in the face.

We may need some guidelines to help us identify wisdom in our thoughts and choices. According to the Bible, there are two aspects of wisdom: the spiritual and the practical. Spiritual wisdom gives insight into the true nature of things. Paul said: "We ask God to give you complete knowledge of his will and to give you spiritual wisdom and understanding. Then . . . you will grow as you learn to know God better and better" (Colossians 1:9-10). Special wisdom is also sometimes given "that your hearts will be flooded with light so that you can understand the confident hope he has given to those he called" (Ephesians 1:18).

Godly wisdom can be evaluated by its qualities. The Bible tells us that God's wisdom is "first of all pure. It is also peace loving, gentle at all times, and willing to yield to others. It is full of mercy and good deeds. It shows no favoritism and is always sincere" (James 3:17).

On the practical level, our wisdom can be judged by whether or not our actions conform to God's instructions. God's instructions were given to us because they naturally lead to healthy living. Following them, we can find the wisdom we need to walk toward wholeness. This can be one of the standards we use in our continuing daily inventory. *Turn to page 1563, 2 Timothy 4.*

---

to give you complete knowledge of his will and to give you spiritual wisdom and understanding. [10]Then the way you live will always honor and please the Lord, and your lives will produce every kind of good fruit. All the while, you will grow as you learn to know God better and better.

[11]We also pray that you will be strengthened with all his glorious power so you will have all the endurance and patience you need. May you be filled with joy,* [12]always thanking the Father. He has enabled you to share in the inheritance that belongs to his people, who live in the light. [13]For he has rescued us from the kingdom of darkness and transferred us into the Kingdom of his dear Son, [14]who purchased our freedom* and forgave our sins.

Christ Is Supreme

[15]Christ is the visible image of the invisible God.
> He existed before anything was created and is supreme over all creation,*
[16]for through him God created everything
> in the heavenly realms and on earth.
> He made the things we can see and the things we can't see—
> such as thrones, kingdoms, rulers, and authorities in the unseen world.
> Everything was created through him and for him.
[17]He existed before anything else, and he holds all creation together.

1:11 Or *all the patience and endurance you need with joy.* 1:14 Some manuscripts add *with his blood.* 1:15 Or *He is the firstborn of all creation.*

¹⁸ Christ is also the head of the church,
    which is his body.
He is the beginning,
    supreme over all who rise from the dead.*
    So he is first in everything.
¹⁹ For God in all his fullness
    was pleased to live in Christ,
²⁰ and through him God reconciled
    everything to himself.
He made peace with everything in heaven
    and on earth
    by means of Christ's blood on the cross.

²¹This includes you who were once far away from God. You were his enemies, separated from him by your evil thoughts and actions. ²²Yet now he has reconciled you to himself through the death of Christ in his physical body. As a result, he has brought you into his own presence, and you are holy and blameless as you stand before him without a single fault.

²³But you must continue to believe this truth and stand firmly in it. Don't drift away from the assurance you received when you heard the Good News. The Good News has been preached all over the world, and I, Paul, have been appointed as God's servant to proclaim it.

Paul's Work for the Church

²⁴I am glad when I suffer for you in my body, for I am participating in the sufferings of Christ that continue for his body, the church. ²⁵God has given me the responsibility of serving his church by proclaiming his entire message to you. ²⁶This message was kept secret for centuries and generations past, but now it has been revealed to God's people. ²⁷For God wanted them to know that the riches and glory of Christ are for you Gentiles, too. And this is the secret: Christ lives in you. This gives you assurance of sharing his glory.

²⁸So we tell others about Christ, warning everyone and teaching everyone with all the wisdom God has given us. We want to present them to God, perfect* in their relationship to Christ. ²⁹That's why I work and struggle so hard, depending on Christ's mighty power that works within me.

CHAPTER 2

I want you to know how much I have agonized for you and for the church at Laodicea, and for many other believers who have never met me personally. ²I want them to be encouraged and knit together by strong ties of love. I want them to have complete confidence that they understand God's mysterious plan, which is Christ himself. ³In him lie hidden all the treasures of wisdom and knowledge.

⁴I am telling you this so no one will deceive you with well-crafted arguments. ⁵For though I am far away from you, my heart is with you. And I rejoice that you are living as you should and that your faith in Christ is strong.

Freedom from Rules and New Life in Christ

⁶And now, just as you accepted Christ Jesus as your Lord, you must continue to follow him. ⁷Let your roots grow down into him, and let

---

1:18 Or *the firstborn from the dead.* 1:28 Or *mature.*

1:20-23 When our life is unmanageable and out of control, we are God's enemies, and our thoughts and actions separate us from him. But God through Christ's death on the cross reaches out to make us his friends. When we turn our life and our will over to him, he brings us into the very presence of God and makes us blameless before God!

1:28-29 An essential part of rebuilding our life is to carry the message of our recovery in Jesus Christ to others. We were far away from God, yet he provided not only the solution to our problem but also the power to change. That is news worth sharing! We may be afraid to do this at first, but the power available for our recovery is also available to help us share our story.

2:6-7 The same faith that we exercised when we turned our life over to God must continue daily as we walk with and obey him. Paul urges us to improve our conscious contact with God so that his power will be at work within us, filling us with joy and thanksgiving. Without God's power nourishing us, we are at the mercy of our destructive habits and dependency.

2:9-10 When we tried to change through our own efforts, we realized just how powerless we were. It was then that we realized the truth found in Paul's statement—that everything we need is found not in ourself, or even in other people, but in Jesus Christ. A recovery that is not built on the person and power of Jesus Christ will always be incomplete.

2:11-15 The power of Christ is able to restore us to sanity and help us overcome our destructive patterns from the past. Since he has authority over every other power, including the power of evil in our life, Jesus can set us free. Our freedom is not just from the physical bondage of the past but also from the spiritual bondage of our old sinful nature. In Christ we can experience the life of peace, joy, and victory that God intends for us.

your lives be built on him. Then your faith will grow strong in the truth you were taught, and you will overflow with thankfulness.

8Don't let anyone capture you with empty philosophies and high-sounding nonsense that come from human thinking and from the spiritual powers* of this world, rather than from Christ. 9For in Christ lives all the fullness of God in a human body.* 10So you also are complete through your union with Christ, who is the head over every ruler and authority.

11When you came to Christ, you were "circumcised," but not by a physical procedure. Christ performed a spiritual circumcision—the cutting away of your sinful nature.* 12For you were buried with Christ when you were baptized. And with him you were raised to new life because you trusted the mighty power of God, who raised Christ from the dead.

13You were dead because of your sins and because your sinful nature was not yet cut away. Then God made you alive with Christ, for he forgave all our sins. 14He canceled the record of the charges against us and took it away by nailing it to the cross. 15In this way, he disarmed* the spiritual rulers and authorities. He shamed them publicly by his victory over them on the cross.

16So don't let anyone condemn you for what you eat or drink, or for not celebrating certain holy days or new moon ceremonies or Sabbaths. 17For these rules are only shadows of the reality yet to come. And Christ himself is that reality. 18Don't let anyone condemn you by insisting on pious self-denial or the worship of angels,* saying they have had visions about these things. Their sinful minds have made them proud, 19and they are not connected to Christ, the head of the body. For he holds the whole body together with its joints and ligaments, and it grows as God nourishes it.

20You have died with Christ, and he has set you free from the spiritual powers of this world. So why do you keep on following the rules of the world, such as, 21"Don't handle! Don't taste! Don't touch!"? 22Such rules are mere human teachings about things that deteriorate as we use them. 23These rules may seem wise because they require strong devotion, pious self-denial, and severe bodily discipline. But they provide no help in conquering a person's evil desires.

2:8 Or the spiritual principles; also in 2:20. 2:9 Or in him dwells all the completeness of the Godhead bodily.
2:11 Greek the cutting away of the body of the flesh.
2:15 Or he stripped off. 2:18 Or or worshiping with angels.

SELF-PROTECTION

READ COLOSSIANS 3:1-4

The world doesn't get any better just because we are in recovery! We still have to pay our bills, deal with people, and face the stressful changes that recovery can bring. There are pressures beyond our control that will tend to make us anxious or wear us down if we aren't careful to protect ourself from the world's onslaught.

The apostle Paul gave us a strategy to help guard against the troubles of daily life. He wrote: "Think about the things of heaven, not the things of earth" (Colossians 3:2). The apostle also wrote: "Don't worry about anything; instead, pray about everything. Tell God what you need, and thank him for all he has done. Then you will experience God's peace, which exceeds anything we can understand. His peace will guard your hearts and minds as you live in Christ Jesus" (Philippians 4:6-7).

The idea of God guarding us from the evil we face in life is comforting. God's peace is promised only if we routinely turn every worry and need over to him and develop a grateful attitude. When we turn our worries over to God's care, we will discover his protection and experience the inner peace that passes all understanding.

Turn to page 1545, 2 Thessalonians 3.

CHAPTER 3
Living the New Life

Since you have been raised to new life with Christ, set your sights on the realities of heaven, where Christ sits in the place of honor at God's right hand. [2]Think about the things of heaven, not the things of earth. [3]For you died to this life, and your real life is hidden with Christ in God. [4]And when Christ, who is your* life, is revealed to the whole world, you will share in all his glory.

[5]So put to death the sinful, earthly things lurking within you. Have nothing to do with sexual immorality, impurity, lust, and evil desires. Don't be greedy, for a greedy person is an idolater, worshiping the things of this world. [6]Because of these sins, the anger of God is coming.* [7]You used to do these things when your life was still part of this world. [8]But now is the time to get rid of anger, rage, malicious behavior, slander, and dirty language. [9]Don't lie to each other, for you have stripped off your old sinful nature and all its wicked deeds. [10]Put on your new nature, and be renewed as you learn to know your Creator and become like him. [11]In this new life, it doesn't matter if you are a Jew or a Gentile,* circumcised or uncircumcised, barbaric, uncivilized,* slave, or free. Christ is all that matters, and he lives in all of us.

[12]Since God chose you to be the holy people he loves, you must clothe yourselves with tenderhearted mercy, kindness, humility, gentleness, and patience. [13]Make allowance for each other's faults, and forgive anyone who offends you. Remember, the Lord forgave you, so you must forgive others. [14]Above all, clothe yourselves with love, which binds us all together in perfect harmony. [15]And let the peace that comes from Christ rule in your hearts. For as members of one body you are called to live in peace. And always be thankful.

[16]Let the message about Christ, in all its richness, fill your lives. Teach and counsel each other with all the wisdom he gives. Sing psalms and hymns and spiritual songs to God with thankful hearts. [17]And whatever you do or say, do it as a representative of the Lord Jesus, giving thanks through him to God the Father.

Instructions for Christian Households

[18]Wives, submit to your husbands, as is fitting for those who belong to the Lord.

[19]Husbands, love your wives and never treat them harshly.

[20]Children, always obey your parents, for this pleases the Lord. [21]Fathers, do not aggravate your children, or they will become discouraged.

[22]Slaves, obey your earthly masters in everything you do. Try to please them all the time, not just when they are watching you.

3:4 Some manuscripts read *our*. **3:6** Some manuscripts read *is coming on all who disobey him*. **3:11a** Greek *a Greek*. **3:11b** Greek *Barbarian, Scythian*.

2:20-23 There are many recovery programs with strict rules to follow. Perhaps we have chosen the programs with the most rules to try to break free from our bondage. "We just need to try harder," we tell ourself. But Paul tells us that we won't find success in our own strength or rules, which lead us away from the only adequate power source—God. He is the only one with the power to transform us and help us conquer evil and rebuild our life.

3:1-3 Paul isn't urging us to deny the harsh realities of life; he is simply reminding us of where our focus should be. When our eyes are on Christ, we see this life from a different perspective. We realize that there is hope, even when everything seems dark and hopeless. As we look with an eternal perspective, the struggles of recovery don't disappear; rather, they are seen in the proper light. They no longer have the terrifying power that they once did. When we keep our eyes on Christ and his promises for recovery, no obstacle is too great for us to overcome.

3:9-11 To make progress in recovery it is essential that we take a personal inventory and then make amends to the people we have hurt. This involves shedding our denial and being honest about our failures. As we recognize our character flaws and seek to change with God's help, we begin to live a new kind of life. This new kind of life with God at the center involves taking an honest personal inventory regularly. Although we will never reach perfection in this life, by noting our progress, we affirm the new life that God is creating within us through Jesus Christ.

3:12-13 Paul urges us to maintain our relationships with other people. Our addiction has probably destroyed or severely strained all our important relationships, and we have a lot of work to do on this front. We need to make amends where necessary, seek forgiveness from those we have hurt, and forgive those who have hurt us. Obviously, there are some situations where we cannot, or should not, directly involve the people we have harmed. In such cases Paul urges caution, telling us to be gentle and not to hold grudges. As we seek to make amends, our actions are to be governed by the principle of selfless love.

Serve them sincerely because of your reverent fear of the Lord. [23]Work willingly at whatever you do, as though you were working for the Lord rather than for people. [24]Remember that the Lord will give you an inheritance as your reward, and that the Master you are serving is Christ.* [25]But if you do what is wrong, you will be paid back for the wrong you have done. For God has no favorites.

CHAPTER 4

Masters, be just and fair to your slaves. Remember that you also have a Master—in heaven.

An Encouragement for Prayer

[2]Devote yourselves to prayer with an alert mind and a thankful heart. [3]Pray for us, too, that God will give us many opportunities to speak about his mysterious plan concerning Christ. That is why I am here in chains. [4]Pray that I will proclaim this message as clearly as I should.

[5]Live wisely among those who are not believers, and make the most of every opportunity. [6]Let your conversation be gracious and attractive* so that you will have the right response for everyone.

Paul's Final Instructions and Greetings

[7]Tychicus will give you a full report about how I am getting along. He is a beloved brother and faithful helper who serves with me in the Lord's work. [8]I have sent him to you for this very purpose—to let you know how we are doing and to encourage you. [9]I am also sending Onesimus, a faithful and beloved brother, one of your own people. He and Tychicus will tell you everything that's happening here.

[10]Aristarchus, who is in prison with me, sends you his greetings, and so does Mark, Barnabas's cousin. As you were instructed before, make Mark welcome if he comes your way. [11]Jesus (the one we call Justus) also sends his greetings. These are the only Jewish believers among my co-workers; they are working with me here for the Kingdom of God. And what a comfort they have been!

[12]Epaphras, a member of your own fellowship and a servant of Christ Jesus, sends you his greetings. He always prays earnestly for you, asking God to make you strong and perfect, fully confident that you are following the whole will of God. [13]I can assure you that he prays hard for you and also for the believers in Laodicea and Hierapolis.

[14]Luke, the beloved doctor, sends his greetings, and so does Demas. [15]Please give my greetings to our brothers and sisters* at Laodicea, and to Nympha and the church that meets in her house.

[16]After you have read this letter, pass it on to the church at Laodicea so they can read it, too. And you should read the letter I wrote to them.

[17]And say to Archippus, "Be sure to carry out the ministry the Lord gave you."

[18]HERE IS MY GREETING IN MY OWN HANDWRITING—PAUL.

Remember my chains.

May God's grace be with you.

3:24 Or *and serve Christ as your Master.* **4:6** Greek *and seasoned with salt.* **4:15** Greek *brothers.*

4:2-3 Paul encouraged the Colossian believers to devote themselves to prayer. This is good advice for us, too. As we pray, we acknowledge our need for God and are reminded to keep our eyes on him. As we make prayer a daily priority, we are to thank God for his help, and we become increasingly aware of his activity in our life. When we are feeling weak, we can still come to God in prayer, and he will empower us to "keep at it." As we turn to God in prayer, we embrace the power sufficient to meet all our needs in recovery.

1 THESSALONIANS

THE BIG PICTURE

Paul and his companions Silas and Timothy first traveled to Thessalonica on their second missionary journey (see Acts 17:1-4). Many people there who had worshiped idols turned their lives over to God, and for this Paul commended them. The believers in Thessalonica had turned from depending on material things and empty rituals to serving the living and true God.

Their new lives of faith were not easy, though. Many of their friends and relatives opposed their faith. Despite the positive changes God had made in them, some people harassed and mocked them. This same persecution forced Paul and his companions to leave Thessalonica. After he left, Paul became concerned about the new believers who had remained there. Were they grounded enough in their new faith in God? Would they relapse into old patterns of belief and practice? Paul sent Timothy to check on them, and, encouraged by Timothy's report, Paul sent them this letter of encouragement.

When we meet with opposition in recovery, we can identify with Paul and the believers at Thessalonica. Friends and family members may not understand our faith; old habits may be a source of pressure, pushing us from within to return to our old ways. But we can be encouraged by the progress we have already made. God's power is at work within us. We don't have to quit just because we face opposition.

THE BOTTOM LINE

PURPOSE: To commend the believers in Thessalonica for their trust in God, to encourage them to continue trusting, and to reassure them that Christ would return. AUTHOR: The apostle Paul. AUDIENCE: The believers in Thessalonica, a city in Macedonia. DATE WRITTEN: About A.D. 50–51, during Paul's second missionary journey. SETTING: The church in Thessalonica was only two or three years old when Paul wrote this letter. The believers there needed to mature spiritually, and they needed help in understanding what to expect at the return of Christ. KEY VERSE: "For you are all children of the light and of the day; we don't belong to darkness and night" (5:5). KEY PEOPLE AND RELATIONSHIPS: Paul with the believers at Thessalonica and with Timothy.

RECOVERY THEMES

God Is Our Source of Hope: If we have placed our trust in Christ to save us from sin, we will live with him forever—we have eternal life. But we can hope in more than just life beyond the grave; we can also hope in what God brings to our life in the present. The power that raised Jesus Christ from the dead is nothing less than the power of God—the God to whom we have entrusted our life. With this kind of power available to us, there is always hope!

Recovery Is a Way of Life: Paul challenged the Thessalonians to live at all times in humble anticipation of Christ's coming—to live each day as if it were important. In a similar way, we need to live one day at a time, realizing that we will never complete the recovery process in this life. We need to live responsibly, working and living in dependence on God at all times. We are always in recovery; when we become complacent and forget that fact, we set ourself up for relapse.

Commitment That Overcomes Obstacles: We are all flawed human beings with numerous limitations and problems. Because of this, we will always face obstacles to our continued recovery. Living in this world means we need to stand firm in our commitment to recovery, knowing that the Holy Spirit empowers us with God's strength. Although God's power is available to all of us, God will not do the work of recovery for us. To make progress, we must ask for his help and commit ourself to the task.

CHAPTER 1
Greetings from Paul
This letter is from Paul, Silas,* and Timothy.

We are writing to the church in Thessalonica, to you who belong to God the Father and the Lord Jesus Christ.

May God give you grace and peace.

The Faith of the Thessalonian Believers
²We always thank God for all of you and pray for you constantly. ³As we pray to our God and Father about you, we think of your faithful work, your loving deeds, and the enduring hope you have because of our Lord Jesus Christ.

⁴We know, dear brothers and sisters,* that God loves you and has chosen you to be his own people. ⁵For when we brought you the Good News, it was not only with words but also with power, for the Holy Spirit gave you full assurance* that what we said was true. And you know of our concern for you from the way we lived when we were with you. ⁶So you received the message with joy from the Holy Spirit in spite of the severe suffering it brought you. In this way, you imitated both us and the Lord. ⁷As a result, you have become an example to all the believers in Greece—throughout both Macedonia and Achaia.*

⁸And now the word of the Lord is ringing out from you to people everywhere, even beyond Macedonia and Achaia, for wherever we go we find people telling us about your faith in God. We don't need to tell them about it, ⁹for they keep talking about the

1:1 Greek *Silvanus*, the Greek form of the name. 1:4 Greek *brothers*. 1:5 Or *with the power of the Holy Spirit, so you can have full assurance.* 1:7 *Macedonia* and *Achaia* were the northern and southern regions of Greece.

1:2-3 Paul is thankful for the Thessalonian believers and their love for each other, their faithful work, and their hope in Christ's return. The triad of faith, love, and hope summarizes the Christian life (see 1 Corinthians 13:13). *Faith* in an all-powerful God is demonstrated by living one day at a time. *Love* is shown as principles of truth are demonstrated through sacrificial service to others. *Hope* carries us through the hard times as we depend on God.

1:4-6 The Thessalonians had been restored to productive roles in God's Kingdom and had gained freedom from bondage to idols because they believed in Jesus Christ and experienced his transforming power in their lives. This same power—our higher Power—makes all the difference between a doomed do-it-yourself recovery and true, God-centered recovery. When we recognize our powerlessness and entrust our life to God, we allow God's infinite resources to work on our behalf.

1:7-9 The Thessalonian believers had experienced spiritual awakening through belief in Jesus Christ. As they imitated his ways, despite the persecution it brought them, they became examples that led many in the surrounding area to experience the salvation offered by God. An essential part of recovery is sharing the good news of God's powerful deliverance with others—a natural outflow of our salvation experience. As God delivers us from our dependency, we can give hope to others by sharing our story. We will not only inspire hope in others, but we will also be personally encouraged as we recall all that God has done for us.

wonderful welcome you gave us and how you turned away from idols to serve the living and true God. ¹⁰And they speak of how you are looking forward to the coming of God's Son from heaven—Jesus, whom God raised from the dead. He is the one who has rescued us from the terrors of the coming judgment.

CHAPTER 2
Paul Remembers His Visit

You yourselves know, dear brothers and sisters,* that our visit to you was not a failure. ²You know how badly we had been treated at Philippi just before we came to you and how much we suffered there. Yet our God gave us the courage to declare his Good News to you boldly, in spite of great opposition. ³So you can see we were not preaching with any deceit or impure motives or trickery.

⁴For we speak as messengers approved by God to be entrusted with the Good News. Our purpose is to please God, not people. He alone examines the motives of our hearts. ⁵Never once did we try to win you with flattery, as you well know. And God is our witness that we were not pretending to be your friends just to get your money! ⁶As for human praise, we have never sought it from you or anyone else.

⁷As apostles of Christ we certainly had a right to make some demands of you, but instead we were like children* among you. Or we were like a mother feeding and caring for her own children. ⁸We loved you so much that we shared with you not only God's Good News but our own lives, too.

⁹Don't you remember, dear brothers and sisters, how hard we worked among you? Night and day we toiled to earn a living so that we would not be a burden to any of you as we preached God's Good News to you.

¹⁰You yourselves are our witnesses—and so is God—that we were devout and honest and faultless toward all of you believers. ¹¹And you know that we treated each of you as a father treats his own children. ¹²We pleaded with you, encouraged you, and urged you to live your lives in a way that God would consider worthy. For he called you to share in his Kingdom and glory.

¹³Therefore, we never stop thanking God that when you received his message from us, you didn't think of our words as mere human ideas. You accepted what we said as the very word of God—which, of course, it is. And this word continues to work in you who believe.

¹⁴And then, dear brothers and sisters, you suffered persecution from your own countrymen. In this way, you imitated the believers in God's churches in Judea who, because of their belief in Christ Jesus, suffered from their own people, the Jews. ¹⁵For some of the Jews killed the prophets, and some even killed the Lord Jesus. Now they have persecuted us, too. They fail to please God and work against all humanity ¹⁶as they try to keep us from preaching the Good News of salvation to the Gentiles. By doing this, they continue to pile up their sins. But the anger of God has caught up with them at last.

Timothy's Good Report about the Church

¹⁷Dear brothers and sisters, after we were separated from you for a little while (though our hearts never left you), we tried very hard to come back because of our intense longing to see you again. ¹⁸We wanted very much to come to you, and I, Paul, tried again and again, but Satan prevented us. ¹⁹After all, what gives us hope and joy, and what will be our proud reward and crown as we stand

2:1 Greek *brothers*; also in 2:9, 14, 17. 2:7 Some manuscripts read *we were gentle*.

2:3-12 Paul did not minister in Thessalonica for personal gain. Yet to discredit Paul, his enemies charged him with that very thing. The apostle recalled his ministry among them, showing that he had gained nothing from it. Paul's work among the Thessalonians had been motivated by his sincere love and empathy. In recovery we are to carry the message of hope to others. But before getting involved in others' lives, we need to examine our motives. Are we helping other people for personal gain or because we are sincerely concerned about them? We should make this question an integral part of our personal moral inventory.

2:19-20 Paul had discovered the message of hope in the gospel of Jesus Christ. As he grew in faith, he joyfully shared it with others. Paul's ministry helped not only the Thessalonians, but it also helped Paul. As he saw the Thessalonians grow spiritually, he experienced incredible joy in his own life. Just as their sorrow had been his sorrow, their victory became his victory. The Thessalonians became Paul's "reward and crown" and "pride and joy." The common bond that we share with others in Christ can be a source of great joy and encouragement as we continue in recovery.

before our Lord Jesus when he returns? It is you! [20]Yes, you are our pride and joy.

CHAPTER 3

Finally, when we could stand it no longer, we decided to stay alone in Athens, [2]and we sent Timothy to visit you. He is our brother and God's co-worker* in proclaiming the Good News of Christ. We sent him to strengthen you, to encourage you in your faith, [3]and to keep you from being shaken by the troubles you were going through. But you know that we are destined for such troubles. [4]Even while we were with you, we warned you that troubles would soon come—and they did, as you well know. [5]That is why, when I could bear it no longer, I sent Timothy to find out whether your faith was still strong. I was afraid that the tempter had gotten the best of you and that our work had been useless.

[6]But now Timothy has just returned, bringing us good news about your faith and love. He reports that you always remember our visit with joy and that you want to see us as much as we want to see you. [7]So we have been greatly encouraged in the midst of our troubles and suffering, dear brothers and sisters,* because you have remained strong in your faith. [8]It gives us new life to know that you are standing firm in the Lord.

[9]How we thank God for you! Because of you we have great joy as we enter God's pres-ence. [10]Night and day we pray earnestly for you, asking God to let us see you again to fill the gaps in your faith.

[11]May God our Father and our Lord Jesus bring us to you very soon. [12]And may the Lord make your love for one another and for all people grow and overflow, just as our love for you overflows. [13]May he, as a result, make your hearts strong, blameless, and holy as you stand before God our Father when our Lord Jesus comes again with all his holy peo-ple. Amen.

CHAPTER 4
Live to Please God

Finally, dear brothers and sisters,* we urge you in the name of the Lord Jesus to live in a way that pleases God, as we have taught you. You live this way already, and we encourage you to do so even more. [2]For you remember what we taught you by the authority of the Lord Jesus.

[3]God's will is for you to be holy, so stay away from all sexual sin. [4]Then each of you will control his own body* and live in holi-ness and honor—[5]not in lustful passion like the pagans who do not know God and his ways. [6]Never harm or cheat a fellow believer in this matter by violating his wife,* for the Lord avenges all such sins, as we have sol-emnly warned you before. [7]God has called us to live holy lives, not impure lives. [8]There-

---

3:2 Other manuscripts read *and God's servant;* still others read *and a co-worker,* or *and a servant and co-worker for God,* or *and God's servant and our co-worker.*   **3:7** Greek *brothers.*   **4:1** Greek *brothers;* also in 4:10, 13.   **4:4** Or *will know how to take a wife for himself;* or *will learn to live with his own wife;* Greek reads *will know how to possess his own vessel.*
4:6 Greek *Never harm or cheat a brother in this matter.*

3:2-4 Paul made it clear that troubles are to be expected in life, even a life of recovery in Christ. When we trust God, we cannot expect everything to go smoothly. God never promised to miracu-lously remove our dependency, though he may do so on rare occasions. God stands with us as we face our problems, giving us strength to confront each new challenge. Realizing that we will always have troubles in this life can help us to survive the hard times in the recovery process. As we face the struggles inherent to all humans, we can count on God's presence with us.
3:6-8 Timothy returned with good news from Thessalonica. The spiritual well-being of the Thessalonians was a great encouragement to Paul, and it helped him make it through his own tough times. Our relationships with others in recovery can be an essential source of mutual help. When we are down, the successes of others can lift us up. When we are up, our joy can lift others out of their despair. As we share our life with one another, we will build each other up and provide the needed encouragement for successful recovery.
3:11-13 Paul concluded this portion of his letter with a short prayer for the Thessalonian believers. Paul prayed that these spiritually transformed people would continue to mature in their love for God. He requested that their new love for God would "grow and overflow" to others. Paul's prayer for these believers can be a model for us as we seek to encourage others in recovery. We can continually lift others to God in prayer and then rejoice as we see God transforming their lives.
4:3-8 The Bible paints a clear picture of what God wants us to be like. Here we are given charac-teristics we will exemplify if we are following God's will. Passages like this can serve as a measuring stick for us as we take our personal inventory. If we don't measure up to God's standards, we must admit our failures to him and allow him to change us. As we entrust our life to him, we will begin to see the positive characteristics growing in our life.

fore, anyone who refuses to live by these rules is not disobeying human teaching but is rejecting God, who gives his Holy Spirit to you.

⁹But we don't need to write to you about the importance of loving each other,* for God himself has taught you to love one another. ¹⁰Indeed, you already show your love for all the believers* throughout Macedonia. Even so, dear brothers and sisters, we urge you to love them even more.

¹¹Make it your goal to live a quiet life, minding your own business and working with your hands, just as we instructed you before. ¹²Then people who are not believers will respect the way you live, and you will not need to depend on others.

The Hope of the Resurrection

¹³And now, dear brothers and sisters, we want you to know what will happen to the believers who have died* so you will not grieve like people who have no hope. ¹⁴For since we believe that Jesus died and was raised to life again, we also believe that when Jesus returns, God will bring back with him the believers who have died.

¹⁵We tell you this directly from the Lord: We who are still living when the Lord returns will not meet him ahead of those who have died.* ¹⁶For the Lord himself will come down from heaven with a commanding shout, with the voice of the archangel, and with the trumpet call of God. First, the believers who have died* will rise from their graves. ¹⁷Then, together with them, we who are still alive and remain on the earth will be caught up in the clouds to meet the Lord in the air. Then we will be with the Lord for-

ever. ¹⁸So encourage each other with these words.

CHAPTER 5

Now concerning how and when all this will happen, dear brothers and sisters,* we don't really need to write you. ²For you know quite well that the day of the Lord's return will come unexpectedly, like a thief in the night. ³When people are saying, "Everything is peaceful and secure," then disaster will fall on them as suddenly as a pregnant woman's labor pains begin. And there will be no escape.

⁴But you aren't in the dark about these things, dear brothers and sisters, and you won't be surprised when the day of the Lord comes like a thief.* ⁵For you are all children of the light and of the day; we don't belong to darkness and night. ⁶So be on your guard, not asleep like the others. Stay alert and be clearheaded. ⁷Night is the time when people sleep and drinkers get drunk. ⁸But let us who live in the light be clearheaded, protected by the armor of faith and love, and wearing as our helmet the confidence of our salvation.

⁹For God chose to save us through our Lord Jesus Christ, not to pour out his anger on us. ¹⁰Christ died for us so that, whether we are dead or alive when he returns, we can live with him forever. ¹¹So encourage each other and build each other up, just as you are already doing.

Paul's Final Advice

¹²Dear brothers and sisters, honor those who are your leaders in the Lord's work. They work hard among you and give you

---

4:9 Greek *about brotherly love.* 4:10 Greek *the brothers.* 4:13 Greek *those who have fallen asleep;* also in 4:14. 4:15 Greek *those who have fallen asleep.* 4:16 Greek *the dead in Christ.* 5:1 Greek *brothers;* also in 5:4, 12, 14, 25, 26, 27. 5:4 Some manuscripts read *comes upon you as if you were thieves.*

4:13-18 Apparently the Thessalonian believers were afraid that believers who died before Jesus returned would lose the opportunity of sharing in Christ's glorious reign. Paul explained that dead Christians would be raised and share in the fellowship and reign of Jesus in God's Kingdom. We all have this hope in our future as well. All believers can be sure that they will have a special part to play when Christ returns. It doesn't matter whether we are dead or alive; God's plan includes us.
5:1-11 Paul warns us that God will hold all people accountable for their attitudes and actions. This day of the Lord will come unexpectedly, so we need to stay alert and ready at all times. This is especially important for those of us who procrastinate, thinking we can start recovery anytime. God wants us to act immediately to receive his forgiveness and power to help us change. Those of us who belong to God will give evidence of our faith by acting in ways that testify to God's work in our life. If we entrust our life to God and seek to follow his will, we have nothing to fear. If we continue to do things our own way, rejecting God's plan of salvation, this day of accountability will be our day of doom.

spiritual guidance. [13]Show them great respect and wholehearted love because of their work. And live peacefully with each other.

[14]Brothers and sisters, we urge you to warn those who are lazy. Encourage those who are timid. Take tender care of those who are weak. Be patient with everyone.

[15]See that no one pays back evil for evil, but always try to do good to each other and to all people.

[16]Always be joyful. [17]Never stop praying. [18]Be thankful in all circumstances, for this is God's will for you who belong to Christ Jesus.

[19]Do not stifle the Holy Spirit. [20]Do not scoff at prophecies, [21]but test everything that is said. Hold on to what is good. [22]Stay away from every kind of evil.

Paul's Final Greetings

[23]Now may the God of peace make you holy in every way, and may your whole spirit and soul and body be kept blameless until our Lord Jesus Christ comes again. [24]God will make this happen, for he who calls you is faithful.

[25]Dear brothers and sisters, pray for us.

[26]Greet all the brothers and sisters with a sacred kiss.

[27]I command you in the name of the Lord to read this letter to all the brothers and sisters.

[28]May the grace of our Lord Jesus Christ be with you.

5:14-28 Paul leaves us with his final good advice. If we follow these instructions with God's help, we will be well on our way in the recovery process. We are called to minister to others, a part of recovery that gives hope to others and reinforces our own success. Paul tells us to rebuild our relationships by repaying the wrongs of others with kindness. We are called to live a joyful life, always prayerful, continually seeking God's will. We are reminded of the gift of the Holy Spirit, God's continual helping presence in our life. God gives us what we need to succeed in recovery. Our part is to participate in the good plan he has set out for us.

2 THESSALONIANS

THE BIG PICTURE

A. GREETINGS (1:1-2)

B. COMMENDATIONS IN THE MIDST OF PERSECUTION (1:3-12)

C. CORRECTION CONCERNING THE DAY OF THE LORD (2:1-17)

D. ENCOURAGEMENT FOR PRAYER AND A DISCIPLINED LIFE (3:1-15)

E. CONCLUDING REMARKS (3:16-18)

The messages we receive are not always the messages that were sent. Paul's first letter to the Thessalonians had made an impact on its readers, but it wasn't the impact the apostle intended. Paul had affirmed that Jesus would return soon. In response, some of the people assumed that they should stop everything and wait for Christ to return. Some even stopped working, expecting that they would no longer need food and other supplies.

Not every believer in Thessalonica thought that way; many continued to act responsibly even as they anticipated Christ's return. But this only added to the tension among church members. The diligent ones felt pressure to pick up the slack left by the others. The lazy ones claimed they were living a life of true faith. After hearing about this problem, Paul sent the Thessalonians this second letter.

Though Paul wrote to correct his audience's misunderstanding, he commended them for their faithfulness to God. He was confident, because of their commitment to doing God's will, that God would help them resolve this issue. Paul's message was simple. He urged them to be content with their situation and disciplined about fulfilling their responsibilities.

Second Thessalonians is a good reminder for us in recovery. While we have turned our life over to God and look forward to the day when all our problems will be behind us, we have to live here and now. Being in recovery does not mean we can neglect our family, work, or friends. Continuing with the responsibilities God has given us helps us get our life back to normal. Recovery involves taking on our responsibilities, not laying them aside.

THE BOTTOM LINE

PURPOSE: To encourage the Thessalonian believers to fulfill their day-to-day responsibilities while anticipating Christ's return. AUTHOR: The apostle Paul. AUDIENCE: The church at Thessalonica, a city in Macedonia. DATE WRITTEN: About A.D. 51–52, during Paul's second missionary journey; shortly after he had written 1 Thessalonians. SETTING: Some of these young believers had misunderstood Paul's first letter; they thought that Christ was to return at any moment, and they used that assumption as an excuse for being lazy and disruptive while waiting for Christ to return. KEY VERSE: "May the Lord lead your hearts into a full understanding and expression of the love of God and the patient endurance that comes from Christ" (3:5). KEY PEOPLE AND RELATIONSHIPS: Paul with Silas, Timothy, and the believers at Thessalonica.

RECOVERY THEMES

God Is the Source of Our Hope: Sometimes we take our eyes off God and focus too much on recovery. We tell ourself that if we only keep up our resolve, all will be well. But when we place our hope in anything other than God, we set ourself up for relapse. Part of the reason we are in recovery is that we recognized that our life had become unmanageable and that we needed God's help. If we depend on resolve alone, we will eventually get so tired of our burdens that we will want to quit. But if we depend on God, he will provide us with the strength and joy we need to persevere.

The Importance of Perseverance: Some of the believers in Thessalonica were sitting back and waiting for the return of Christ. Their lazy, indifferent attitude toward the concerns of everyday life kept them from living responsibly. They soon became a burden to others. Entrusting our life to God does not give us license to just sit around. We must continue to put forth effort, trusting God to sustain us and bring about the desired result of recovery. Our dependence on God is a partnership with him; he doesn't become our slave. Expecting him to do all the work leads to relapse and will alienate the people who have to pick up after us.

God's Reassuring Power and Presence: We live in a time when evil seems to be on the increase, as it was in Thessalonica. From the New Testament we know that until Christ returns, evil will continue to increase. But we don't need to be surprised or afraid; God is sovereign over the earth, no matter how evil our world becomes. As we consciously work on our relationship with God and continue to turn our life and will over to him, he promises to guard us from evil. We can have victory over the evil in our life by remaining faithful to God and obeying him.

CHAPTER 1
Greetings from Paul

This letter is from Paul, Silas,* and Timothy.

We are writing to the church in Thessalonica, to you who belong to God our Father and the Lord Jesus Christ.

²May God our Father* and the Lord Jesus Christ give you grace and peace.

Encouragement during Persecution

³Dear brothers and sisters,* we can't help but thank God for you, because your faith is flourishing and your love for one another is growing. ⁴We proudly tell God's other churches about your endurance and faithfulness in all the persecutions and hardships you are suffering. ⁵And God will use this persecution to show his justice and to make you worthy of his Kingdom, for which you are suffering. ⁶In his justice he will pay back those who persecute you.

⁷And God will provide rest for you who are being persecuted and also for us when the Lord Jesus appears from heaven. He will come with his mighty angels, ⁸in flaming fire, bringing judgment on those who don't

1:1 Greek *Silvanus,* the Greek form of the name. 1:2 Some manuscripts read *God the Father.* 1:3 Greek *Brothers.*

1:3-5 Paul rejoiced that the Thessalonians were maturing in their faith. Their hardships were an important impetus to their spiritual growth. Paul reminds us that hardships are learning opportunities. Most of us would not be in recovery except for the pain caused by our dependency. Just as God used hardships to inspire growth among the Thessalonians, he does the same with us. Painful situations force us to admit that we cannot make it without God. When we realize that we are powerless, we can begin to rebuild our life on the only sure foundation—Jesus Christ.

1:5-8 We often look upon difficulty as something to avoid at all costs. We run from painful situations, however, only to be trapped by other serious problems. Sometimes the desire to escape pain is the foundation for our destructive addiction and compulsion. As we learn to face painful circumstances with God's help, we will be freed from the addictive habit we once used as an escape. Hardships can become an impetus for spiritual growth, not a cause for failure and relapse.

1:9-10 Everlasting destruction refers not to complete annihilation but to eternal separation from God's healing presence and glorious power. The Thessalonians escaped such a terrible fate by committing their lives to God. We have the same opportunity—beginning the process of faith that leads to emotional, physical, and spiritual recovery.

2:3-10 Paul warned the Thessalonians of an evil power at work in the world. These new believers had experienced the work of this oppressor during their years as idol worshipers. We experience that same evil power at work in our addiction, compulsion, or other dysfunctional behavior. We can rejoice that when Jesus Christ returns, he will completely overcome the evil powers in this world. And if we entrust our life to him now, he will begin his delivering work in our life right away.

know God and on those who refuse to obey the Good News of our Lord Jesus. [9]They will be punished with eternal destruction, forever separated from the Lord and from his glorious power. [10]When he comes on that day, he will receive glory from his holy people—praise from all who believe. And this includes you, for you believed what we told you about him.

[11]So we keep on praying for you, asking our God to enable you to live a life worthy of his call. May he give you the power to accomplish all the good things your faith prompts you to do. [12]Then the name of our Lord Jesus will be honored because of the way you live, and you will be honored along with him. This is all made possible because of the grace of our God and Lord, Jesus Christ.*

CHAPTER 2

Events prior to the Lord's Second Coming

Now, dear brothers and sisters,* let us clarify some things about the coming of our Lord Jesus Christ and how we will be gathered to meet him. [2]Don't be so easily shaken or alarmed by those who say that the day of the Lord has already begun. Don't believe them, even if they claim to have had a spiritual vision, a revelation, or a letter supposedly from us. [3]Don't be fooled by what they say. For that day will not come until there is a great rebellion against God and the man of lawlessness* is revealed—the one who brings destruction.* [4]He will exalt himself and defy everything that people call god and every object of worship. He will even sit in the temple of God, claiming that he himself is God.

[5]Don't you remember that I told you about all this when I was with you? [6]And you know what is holding him back, for he can be revealed only when his time comes. [7]For this lawlessness is already at work secretly, and it will remain secret until the one who is holding it back steps out of the way. [8]Then the man of lawlessness will be revealed, but the Lord Jesus will kill him with the breath of his mouth and destroy him by the splendor of his coming.

[9]This man will come to do the work of Satan with counterfeit power and signs and miracles. [10]He will use every kind of evil deception to fool those on their way to destruction, because they refuse to love and accept

SELF-PROTECTION

READ 2 THESSALONIANS 3:1-8

Many of us know what it is like to be a burden to others. It is a common side effect of being controlled by an addiction or compulsive behavior. Sometimes our behavior has made us lose our job. As a result, we have found ourself in financial need. This humiliation can affect our family in many ways. We may have caused our loved ones great stress and shame because we haven't provided for their needs.

The apostle Paul taught us to follow this standard: "For you know that you ought to imitate us. We were not idle when we were with you. We never accepted food from anyone without paying for it. We worked hard day and night" (2 Thessalonians 3:7-8). "Make it your goal to live a quiet life, minding your own business and working with your hands. . . . Then, people . . . will respect the way you live, and you will not need to depend on others" (1 Thessalonians 4:11-12).

It is important for us to think about how our irresponsibility has affected others. Much pain may have been caused by our failure to provide for our family's needs. We need to reflect on how this failure has caused us to lose their respect and trust. The shame of not facing this aspect of our life can be terribly discouraging. Once we face this and become willing to make amends, our sense of self-respect will improve significantly. This step will help us get rid of some of our daily stresses, freeing us to proceed further with recovery. ***Turn to page 1587, Hebrews 10.***

1:12 Or *of our God and our Lord Jesus Christ.* 2:1 Greek *brothers;* also in 2:13, 15. 2:3a Some manuscripts read *the man of sin.* 2:3b Greek *the son of destruction.*

the truth that would save them. [11]So God will cause them to be greatly deceived, and they will believe these lies. [12]Then they will be condemned for enjoying evil rather than believing the truth.

Believers Should Stand Firm

[13]As for us, we can't help but thank God for you, dear brothers and sisters loved by the Lord. We are always thankful that God chose you to be among the first* to experience salvation—a salvation that came through the Spirit who makes you holy and through your belief in the truth. [14]He called you to salvation when we told you the Good News; now you can share in the glory of our Lord Jesus Christ.

[15]With all these things in mind, dear brothers and sisters, stand firm and keep a strong grip on the teaching we passed on to you both in person and by letter.

[16]Now may our Lord Jesus Christ himself and God our Father, who loved us and by his grace gave us eternal comfort and a wonderful hope, [17]comfort you and strengthen you in every good thing you do and say.

CHAPTER 3
Paul's Request for Prayer

Finally, dear brothers and sisters,* we ask you to pray for us. Pray that the Lord's message will spread rapidly and be honored wherever it goes, just as when it came to you. [2]Pray, too, that we will be rescued from wicked and evil people, for not everyone is a believer. [3]But the Lord is faithful; he will strengthen you and guard you from the evil one.* [4]And we are confident in the Lord that you are doing and will continue to do the things we commanded you. [5]May the Lord lead your hearts into a full understanding and expression of the love of God and the patient endurance that comes from Christ.

An Exhortation to Proper Living

[6]And now, dear brothers and sisters, we give you this command in the name of our Lord Jesus Christ: Stay away from all believers* who live idle lives and don't follow the tradition they received* from us. [7]For you know that you ought to imitate us. We were not idle when we were with you. [8]We never accepted food from anyone without paying for it. We worked hard day and night so we would not be a burden to any of you. [9]We certainly had the right to ask you to feed us, but we wanted to give you an example to follow. [10]Even while we were with you, we gave you this command: "Those unwilling to work will not get to eat."

[11]Yet we hear that some of you are living idle lives, refusing to work and meddling in other people's business. [12]We command such people and urge them in the name of the

---

2:13 Some manuscripts read *chose you from the very beginning.* 3:1 Greek *brothers;* also in 3:6, 13. 3:3 Or *from evil.* 3:6a Greek *from every brother.* 3:6b Some manuscripts read *you received.*

2:15-16 Paul praised the Thessalonians for their exemplary faith and encouraged them to stand firm and keep a strong grip on the truths they had been taught. We must do the same if we hope to make progress in recovery. If we cannot face the truth about our own life, we cannot even begin the process. We need to recognize that we are powerless and that we need God's help to survive and grow spiritually. Recognizing this truth is a foundational step toward recovery.

3:1-2 Paul drew his readers into his life and ministry by asking them to pray for him. He didn't set himself above them but shared how he needed their prayers, just as he needed God's power for continued safety. Paul shows us how his own survival was tied to the spiritual growth of others. As the Thessalonians prayed for Paul, they shared in his life—his struggles and his victories. As Paul experienced deliverance, they rejoiced and were strengthened by God's clear answers to their prayers. Our relationships in recovery yield mutual encouragement in similar ways.

3:6-10 Apparently many of the Thessalonian believers had stopped working in anticipation of Christ's return. Their false understandings had led them to live irresponsibly. So Paul told these believers to get back to work. If they refused to work, they would have to face the consequence—they shouldn't eat. Since God has promised to help us in recovery, we might be tempted to think we can sit idly by and watch it happen. This is not the case. We need to participate in the plan God has for us. If we don't take the necessary steps of faith, we will have to face the consequence—failed recovery.

3:11-13 Some Thessalonians had begun to meddle in other people's business. This practice is extremely destructive to the process of recovery. Not only does it breed discouragement among the people being bothered, but it also keeps us from examining our own life as we should. Instead of taking inventory of our own life, we focus on the lives of others. Paul exhorted the Thessalonians to set things straight and to live in the power of God. If they didn't, their gossiping lifestyle would cause them to shrink away from their own recovery, while also discouraging others.

Lord Jesus Christ to settle down and work to earn their own living. [13]As for the rest of you, dear brothers and sisters, never get tired of doing good.

[14]Take note of those who refuse to obey what we say in this letter. Stay away from them so they will be ashamed. [15]Don't think of them as enemies, but warn them as you would a brother or sister.*

3:15 Greek *as a brother.*

Paul's Final Greetings

[16]Now may the Lord of peace himself give you his peace at all times and in every situation. The Lord be with you all.

[17]HERE IS MY GREETING IN MY OWN HANDWRITING—PAUL. I DO THIS IN ALL MY LETTERS TO PROVE THEY ARE FROM ME.

[18]May the grace of our Lord Jesus Christ be with you all.

1 TIMOTHY

THE BIG PICTURE

A. A CALL TO SOUND DOCTRINE (1:1-20)

B. A CALL TO ORDER AMONG THE BELIEVERS (2:1–4:16)

C. A CALL TO PROPER RELATIONSHIPS (5:1–6:2)

D. A CALL TO SPIRITUAL DISCERNMENT (6:3-21)

Paul and Timothy had a special relationship. Timothy came to faith in Christ as a result of Paul's ministry, and he quickly joined the apostle's traveling team. As they traveled and ministered together, the two became as close as father and son. As Timothy matured in his faith, Paul sent him to lead the church in Ephesus. As a young minister, Timothy faced many challenges and problems. Paul wrote this letter to counsel and encourage his young protégé.

Although this letter is personal in nature, Paul included in it a wealth of advice about how to deal with problems in the church. He also painted a clear picture of what the Christian church should be like. Every church, for example, should have sound spiritual teaching, faithful worship, strong leadership, dedication to God's Word, and caring ministries. These characteristics are what make a church community a place of redemption and healing.

Recovery is a long-term process. In the search for wholeness we need a safe, nurturing environment in which we can set things straight and build a new life for ourself. Professional counselors or recovery groups are limited in this respect. We need to find a more permanent context for our long-term care and support.

The ideal context for this kind of help is a healthy church community. Not all churches, however, qualify for this distinction. An ideal church provides loving accountability, like the church described in this letter. A church should be a hospital for the hurting, a place where old wounds can heal and lives can be rebuilt. We all need a healthy church family to help us in the long-term process of recovery.

THE BOTTOM LINE

PURPOSE: To encourage Timothy, a young minister of the gospel, at a time when he was facing difficult circumstances. AUTHOR: The apostle Paul. AUDIENCE: Timothy. DATE WRITTEN: Around A.D. 64, just before Paul was imprisoned in Rome. SETTING: Timothy was one of Paul's closest friends. Paul had sent him to help the church at Ephesus and was now writing to offer him practical advice on issues Timothy was facing. KEY VERSE: "Cling to your faith in Christ, and keep your conscience clear" (1:19). KEY PEOPLE AND RELATIONSHIPS: Paul with Timothy.

RECOVERY THEMES

The Truth Brings Healing: Paul urged Timothy to preserve the Christian faith and to speak only the truth. Timothy was opposing false teachers who were trying to undermine his work. The only weapons he had were the truth about Christ and a godly lifestyle that backed up everything he taught. Paul knew that only the truth about God in Jesus Christ could bring healing and recovery to broken people, and he wanted Timothy to be convinced of that as well. It is still true: Only Jesus Christ offers us true freedom. Our job is to defend and share the message of God's healing power through belief in Christ. We can do this by speaking the truth about God's power and by backing up our words with our transformed life.

The Importance of Discipline: Paul urged Timothy to discipline himself. Self-discipline does not negate our need for God's power, just as God's gracious help does not negate our need for self-discipline. Both are necessary in a successful recovery program. We need to stay in good spiritual and emotional condition in order to receive the powerful help that God offers us. We must continue to take personal inventory and right the wrongs we uncover. We also must involve ourself in activities that increase our conscious contact with God. These disciplines will encourage our spiritual growth and keep us on track in recovery.

God Works through People: An important part of recovery involves our relationships with other people. Paul gave Timothy specific instructions on how to relate to the people in his church. Paul's advice relates to our relationships as well, especially as we carry the message of hope to others. Caring for each other demonstrates God's power at work within us and also reminds us of how we were cared for when we entered recovery.

Taking Inventory Leads to Wise Conduct: Recovery always takes place in the context of relationships. So taking our personal inventory in the recovery process must lead us to make improvements in how we relate to others. We may not be in a position of leadership, but we are always an example to others. When we are taking inventory on a regular basis, everyone wins: We do because we grow; others do because they are encouraged. A successful recovery will lead to the healing of our broken relationships.

CHAPTER 1
Greetings from Paul

This letter is from Paul, an apostle of Christ Jesus, appointed by the command of God our Savior and Christ Jesus, who gives us hope.

²I am writing to Timothy, my true son in the faith.

May God the Father and Christ Jesus our Lord give you grace, mercy, and peace.

Warnings against False Teachings

³When I left for Macedonia, I urged you to stay there in Ephesus and stop those whose teaching is contrary to the truth. ⁴Don't let them waste their time in endless discussion of myths and spiritual pedigrees. These things only lead to meaningless speculations,* which don't help people live a life of faith in God.*

⁵The purpose of my instruction is that all believers would be filled with love that comes from a pure heart, a clear conscience, and genuine faith. ⁶But some people have missed this whole point. They have turned away from these things and spend their time in meaningless discussions. ⁷They want to be known as teachers of the law of Moses, but they don't know what they are talking about, even though they speak so confidently.

⁸We know that the law is good when used correctly. ⁹For the law was not intended for people who do what is right. It is for people who are lawless and rebellious, who are ungodly and sinful, who consider nothing sacred and defile what is holy, who kill their father or mother or commit other murders. ¹⁰The law is for people who are sexually immoral, or who practice homosexuality, or are

1:4a Greek *in myths and endless genealogies, which cause speculation.* 1:4b Greek *a stewardship of God in faith.*

1:3-7 Apparently false teachers in Ephesus were claiming that certain knowledge and activities were necessary for salvation. Their teachings were dividing the believers, and some of them claimed to have special knowledge. This also led the believers away from the essentials of the faith and the only way to salvation—faith in Jesus Christ. Many today claim to have solutions for recovery, and many of their programs assume we can accomplish recovery without God's help. We must heed Paul's exhortation and steer clear of people who teach such things. Only God has the power to deliver us.

TIMOTHY

When we have found a good friend, we have found a treasure. This is especially true as we struggle through the stages of recovery. We need people who are faithful and willing to persevere with us through the hard times. We need the love and acceptance that only true friends can offer. The friendship between young Timothy and the apostle Paul brought significant support and encouragement to both men.

Paul described Timothy as a faithful brother with a solid reputation. Timothy was devoted to Paul and shared many of the triumphant victories in Paul's ministry. But Timothy didn't stay around only when things were going well. He persevered with Paul during the difficult times of imprisonment, torture, and mockery. Their years of shared ministry grew into a lifelong friendship.

Paul referred to Timothy with admiration in many of his letters. He called him "my beloved and faithful child in the Lord" (1 Corinthians 4:17) and "my fellow worker" (Romans 16:21). In his letter to the Philippians, Paul referred to Timothy with the highest praise and said that he had been "like a son" to him (Philippians 2:22). In his letters to Timothy, Paul expressed great affection for him. Paul's personal involvement in Timothy's ministry was evident when Paul reminded him "to fan into flames the spiritual gift God gave you when I laid my hands on you" (2 Timothy 1:6).

Timothy was never known as a charismatic or strong leader. He was apparently somewhat timid and afraid to confront his people, especially the older men. But he was faithful and persevered in his ministry despite his fears and trials. Paul supported Timothy in his ministry, realizing that God had called this young man into special service for him. Despite his weaknesses, Timothy was used by God to build the church and to encourage his more charismatic co-worker, Paul.

Recovery requires that we allow people into our life for both support and accountability. We need to ask God for "Timothys"— people who have integrity, who can be trusted, and who will stand by us through anything. When we find our Timothys, we will be better equipped to face the trials of recovery.

STRENGTHS AND ACCOMPLISHMENTS:
- Timothy had an excellent reputation for his faithfulness.
- He was a special friend to the apostle Paul.
- He stood by Paul even in the most difficult circumstances.
- He was a faithful minister of the gospel.

WEAKNESSES AND MISTAKES:
- Timothy struggled with his youth and timidity.
- He had stomach problems, possibly related to anxiety.

LESSONS FROM HIS LIFE:
- Our fears and inadequacies need not stop us from serving God.
- Good friendships are extremely valuable, especially in recovery.

KEY VERSES:
"Finally, when we could stand it no longer, we decided to stay alone in Athens, and we sent Timothy to visit you. He is our brother and God's co-worker in proclaiming the Good News of Christ. We sent him to strengthen you, to encourage you in your faith, and to keep you from being shaken by the troubles you were going through" (1 Thessalonians 3:1-3).

Timothy is first named in Acts 16:1-5 and is mentioned at various other points in the book. He is the recipient of Paul's letters 1 and 2 Timothy. He is also mentioned in Romans 16:21; 1 Corinthians 4:17; 16:10-11; 2 Corinthians 1:1, 19; Philippians 1:1; 2:19-23; Colossians 1:1; 1 Thessalonians 1:1-10; 3:2-6; Philemon 1:1; and Hebrews 13:23.

---

slave traders,* liars, promise breakers, or who do anything else that contradicts the wholesome teaching [11]that comes from the glorious Good News entrusted to me by our blessed God.

1:10 Or *kidnappers*.

Paul's Gratitude for God's Mercy

[12]I thank Christ Jesus our Lord, who has given me strength to do his work. He considered me trustworthy and appointed me to serve him, [13]even though I used to

blaspheme the name of Christ. In my insolence, I persecuted his people. But God had mercy on me because I did it in ignorance and unbelief. [14]Oh, how generous and gracious our Lord was! He filled me with the faith and love that come from Christ Jesus.

[15]This is a trustworthy saying, and everyone should accept it: "Christ Jesus came into the world to save sinners"—and I am the worst of them all. [16]But God had mercy on me so that Christ Jesus could use me as a prime example of his great patience with even the worst sinners. Then others will realize that they, too, can believe in him and receive eternal life. [17]All honor and glory to God forever and ever! He is the eternal King, the unseen one who never dies; he alone is God. Amen.

Timothy's Responsibility

[18]Timothy, my son, here are my instructions for you, based on the prophetic words spoken about you earlier. May they help you fight well in the Lord's battles. [19]Cling to your faith in Christ, and keep your conscience clear. For some people have deliberately violated their consciences; as a result, their faith has been shipwrecked. [20]Hymenaeus and Alexander are two examples. I threw them out and handed them over to Satan so they might learn not to blaspheme God.

2:9 Or to pray in modest apparel.

CHAPTER 2
Instructions about Worship

I urge you, first of all, to pray for all people. Ask God to help them; intercede on their behalf, and give thanks for them. [2]Pray this way for kings and all who are in authority so that we can live peaceful and quiet lives marked by godliness and dignity. [3]This is good and pleases God our Savior, [4]who wants everyone to be saved and to understand the truth. [5]For,

There is one God and one Mediator who can reconcile God and humanity—the man Christ Jesus. [6]He gave his life to purchase freedom for everyone.

This is the message God gave to the world at just the right time. [7]And I have been chosen as a preacher and apostle to teach the Gentiles this message about faith and truth. I'm not exaggerating— just telling the truth.

[8]In every place of worship, I want men to pray with holy hands lifted up to God, free from anger and controversy.

[9]And I want women to be modest in their appearance.* They should wear decent and appropriate clothing and not draw attention to themselves by the way they fix their hair or by wearing gold or pearls or expensive clothes. [10]For women who claim to be devoted to God should make themselves attractive by the good things they do.

[11]Women should learn quietly and sub-

1:18-20 Paul commanded Timothy to fight God's battles well. In one sense this continued his earlier thoughts about upholding God's truth against false teachers. Yet the real battle was not in the realm of ideas; it involved acting in ways that reflected a close relationship with God. Paul told Timothy to cling to his faith and keep his conscience clear. He was to live in ways that showed God's power. Our beliefs are important, too, but we must go beyond *thinking* the right things to *doing* the right things. That is where God's real battles are won. Our commitment to recovery is evidenced when we take the necessary steps, some of them painful, and live out our relationship with God, showing others the comfort and deliverance that can be found in him.

2:1-2 Here Paul shows why prayer is essential for establishing a peaceful context for spiritual growth. Through prayer, both public and private, order and peace are promoted and strengthened. Prayer involves thanksgiving for God's blessings and intercession for others. It is one of the assets we often overlook as we work our program. We can easily become so focused on our own activities that we forget to turn to God for help. Prayer improves our conscious contact with God. Regular prayer also reminds us that we are helpless without God's continual and powerful help.

2:3-5 That God wants everyone to be saved is encouraging news. No matter how hopeless our life may seem, how bad we have been, or how badly others have treated us, God wants us to come to him. The truth is that all of us are separated from God by sin until we give our life to Christ, the one who bridges the gulf between man and God. God gives us power for recovery when we confess our powerlessness and ask Jesus for forgiveness, salvation, and assistance.

3:1-7 Paul described the prospective leader as someone who has self-control, spiritual maturity, and strong management of his own family. The home is the most reliable proving ground for potential leaders. It is also the place where we can give evidence of our progress in recovery. Since our family members have probably been hurt by our dependency, it is essential that we make amends to them. Sometimes it is hardest to restore our closest relationships. But successful recovery always involves the people in our family and leads to the restoration of broken family relationships.

missively. [12]I do not let women teach men or have authority over them.* Let them listen quietly. [13]For God made Adam first, and afterward he made Eve. [14]And it was not Adam who was deceived by Satan. The woman was deceived, and sin was the result. [15]But women will be saved through childbearing,* assuming they continue to live in faith, love, holiness, and modesty.

CHAPTER 3
Leaders in the Church

This is a trustworthy saying: "If someone aspires to be an elder,* he desires an honorable position." [2]So an elder must be a man whose life is above reproach. He must be faithful to his wife.* He must exercise self-control, live wisely, and have a good reputation. He must enjoy having guests in his home, and he must be able to teach. [3]He must not be a heavy drinker* or be violent. He must be gentle, not quarrelsome, and not love money. [4]He must manage his own family well, having children who respect and obey him. [5]For if a man cannot manage his own household, how can he take care of God's church?

[6]An elder must not be a new believer, because he might become proud, and the devil would cause him to fall.* [7]Also, people outside the church must speak well of him so that he will not be disgraced and fall into the devil's trap.

[8]In the same way, deacons must be well respected and have integrity. They must not be heavy drinkers or dishonest with money. [9]They must be committed to the mystery of the faith now revealed and must live with a clear conscience. [10]Before they are appointed as deacons, let them be closely examined. If they pass the test, then let them serve as deacons.

[11]In the same way, their wives* must be respected and must not slander others. They must exercise self-control and be faithful in everything they do.

[12]A deacon must be faithful to his wife, and he must manage his children and household well. [13]Those who do well as deacons will be rewarded with respect from others

2:12 Or teach men or usurp their authority. 2:15 Or will be saved by accepting their role as mothers, or will be saved by the birth of the Child. 3:1 Or an overseer, or a bishop; also in 3:2, 6. 3:2 Or must have only one wife, or must be married only once; Greek reads must be the husband of one wife; also in 3:12. 3:3 Greek must not drink too much wine; similarly in 3:8. 3:6 Or he might fall into the same judgment as the devil. 3:11 Or the women deacons. The Greek word can be translated women or wives.

STEP 10

Spiritual Exercises
BIBLE READING: 1 Timothy 4:7-8
We continued to take personal inventory and when we were wrong promptly admitted it.
It is amazing what human beings can achieve through consistent disciplined effort. How many times have we watched seasoned gymnasts or other athletes and marveled at the ease with which they performed? We realize that they developed those abilities through rigorous training, which is what sets the true athletes apart from the spectators. Continuing our regular personal inventory requires similar self-discipline.

Paul wrote to Timothy: "Train yourself to be godly. Physical training is good, but training for godliness is much better" (1 Timothy 4:7-8). The word translated "training" referred specifically to the disciplined training done by gymnasts in Paul's day.

Spiritual strength and agility come only through practice. We need to develop our spiritual muscles through consistent effort and daily discipline. Continuing to take our personal inventory is one of the disciplines we need to develop. Like the athlete, we can motivate ourself to continue in disciplined routines by looking forward to our reward. This kind of discipline promises "benefits in this life and in the life to come" (1 Timothy 4:8). Results won't happen overnight. But as we continue practicing these disciplines each day, we will eventually reap the benefits. *Turn to page 1561, 2 Timothy 2.*

and will have increased confidence in their faith in Christ Jesus.

The Truths of Our Faith

[14] I am writing these things to you now, even though I hope to be with you soon, [15] so that if I am delayed, you will know how people must conduct themselves in the household of God. This is the church of the living God, which is the pillar and foundation of the truth.

[16] Without question, this is the great mystery of our faith*:

Christ* was revealed in a human body
    and vindicated by the Spirit.*
He was seen by angels
    and announced to the nations.

He was believed in throughout the world
    and taken to heaven in glory.

CHAPTER 4
Warnings against False Teachers

Now the Holy Spirit tells us clearly that in the last times some will turn away from the true faith; they will follow deceptive spirits and teachings that come from demons. [2] These people are hypocrites and liars, and their consciences are dead.*

[3] They will say it is wrong to be married and wrong to eat certain foods. But God created those foods to be eaten with thanks by faithful people who know the truth. [4] Since everything God created is good, we should not reject any of it but receive it with thanks.

3:16a Or *of godliness.* 3:16b Greek *He who;* other manuscripts read *God.* 3:16c Or *in his spirit.* 4:2 Greek *are seared.*

3:16 Paul had been reminding the Thessalonian believers that the way to godly living is never easy. We all know this. We have already recognized that we cannot do it alone. Even with God's powerful help, each step of confession and healing can be painful. Yet Jesus Christ has paid the debt for our sins and failures. He has paved the way for our recovery and will stand beside us each step of the way. As difficult as the recovery process may be, Jesus Christ can give us the power to start over. He already has been resurrected to a new life; he now offers us the same.

4:1-5 One of the errors Paul warned Timothy about was religiously motivated self-denial. What is wrong with this? Isn't it self-indulgence that gets most of us in trouble in the first place? Paul pointed out that the pleasures offered by God should be enjoyed with thanksgiving and not rejected in the name of spirituality. Some recovery leaders have called their followers to give up all forms of pleasure to purge their lives of the tendency toward addiction. If we have tried this, however, we know that deprivation leads to a deeper hunger and an eventual relapse. God has given us many legitimate earthly pleasures. When we learn how to replace our enslaving dependency with wholesome activities, we will be less tempted to escape life through our addiction.

4:7-10 Paul warned Timothy not to argue about insignificant issues and tells him to focus on training himself for spiritual fitness. In recovery it is easy to get sidetracked by new ideas and solutions to our problems or the strengths and weaknesses of certain programs over others. We can keep spiritually fit only by taking regular moral inventory, admitting our failures, and seeking to make amends to those we have wronged. We can make progress in recovery only if we are willing to take the first steps and train hard.

4:11-16 Timothy is admonished to share the Good News of new life in Christ through word and deed. We sometimes forget that the most effective way to share our story of deliverance is to live it. Nothing we say can witness as powerfully to God's power as the changes people can see in us and in our actions. Some people will always question the legitimacy of what we say, but no one can question the evidence of a transformed life. When we entrust our life to God, we can experience the transforming power promised through Jesus Christ. Allowing God to change us is the best way to help others enter the path of recovery.

5:1-2 Paul reminded Timothy to treat all people, young and old, with respect. He reminds us of the importance of healthy relationships in the Christian community. Sound doctrine, proper worship, and godly leadership are all important, but unless we treat people with love and respect, the church will never be a place where people in recovery can grow. The courtesy and affection requested by Paul will make the Christian community a place where healing can take place and lives can be rebuilt.

5:3-10 Paul made it clear that the Christian community was to show special attention to their widows. Paul's directions here reflect God's concern for the helpless and rejected in society. This is encouraging to us because we all know what it feels like to be helpless and rejected. But God wants us to be included among his people; there is a place for everyone in his church. No matter who we are or what we have done, we are accepted on the basis of our faith in Jesus Christ. God reaches out to us, as helpless and rejected as we may be, and calls each one of us to be part of his family.

⁵For we know it is made acceptable* by the word of God and prayer.

A Good Servant of Christ Jesus

⁶If you explain these things to the brothers and sisters,* Timothy, you will be a worthy servant of Christ Jesus, one who is nourished by the message of faith and the good teaching you have followed. ⁷Do not waste time arguing over godless ideas and old wives' tales. Instead, train yourself to be godly. ⁸"Physical training is good, but training for godliness is much better, promising benefits in this life and in the life to come." ⁹This is a trustworthy saying, and everyone should accept it. ¹⁰This is why we work hard and continue to struggle,* for our hope is in the living God, who is the Savior of all people and particularly of all believers.

¹¹Teach these things and insist that everyone learn them. ¹²Don't let anyone think less of you because you are young. Be an example to all believers in what you say, in the way you live, in your love, your faith, and your purity. ¹³Until I get there, focus on reading the Scriptures to the church, encouraging the believers, and teaching them.

¹⁴Do not neglect the spiritual gift you received through the prophecy spoken over you when the elders of the church laid their hands on you. ¹⁵Give your complete attention to these matters. Throw yourself into your tasks so that everyone will see your progress. ¹⁶Keep a close watch on how you live and on your teaching. Stay true to what is right for the sake of your own salvation and the salvation of those who hear you.

CHAPTER 5
Advice about Widows, Elders, and Slaves

Never speak harshly to an older man,* but appeal to him respectfully as you would to your own father. Talk to younger men as you would to your own brothers. ²Treat older women as you would your mother, and treat younger women with all purity as you would your own sisters.

³Take care of* any widow who has no one else to care for her. ⁴But if she has children or grandchildren, their first responsibility is to show godliness at home and repay their parents by taking care of them. This is something that pleases God.

⁵Now a true widow, a woman who is truly alone in this world, has placed her hope in

4:5 Or *made holy.* 4:6 Greek *brothers.* 4:10 Some manuscripts read *continue to suffer.* 5:1 Or *an elder.* 5:3 Or *Honor.*

STEP 12

Talking the Walk

BIBLE READING: 1 Timothy 4:14-16

Having had a spiritual awakening as the result of these steps, we tried to carry this message to others and to practice these principles in all our affairs.

When we realize everything we have gained by following the Twelve Steps, it will be natural to want to share this life-giving message with others. If we think back to the time before we entered recovery, we will probably recall that we didn't respond very well to "preaching." Yet we also realize that there are people in our life who could be helped by our message. That is why we need to communicate our story, but do it with sensitivity.

The apostle Paul taught Timothy that to get the gospel message across, he was not only to teach others but also be an example by putting his beliefs into practice. Paul said: "Give your complete attention to these matters. Throw yourself into your tasks so that everyone will see your progress. Keep a close watch on how you live and on your teaching. Stay true to what is right for the sake of your own salvation and the salvation of those who hear you" (1 Timothy 4:15-16). When we practice the principles of the Twelve Steps, others will be watching and notice the changes. This will open the doors for us to share our story.

Every addict is a precious lost soul whom God loves and wants to rescue. "If someone among you wanders away from the truth . . . whoever brings the sinner back will save that person from death and bring about the forgiveness of many sins" (James 5:19-20). *Turn to page 1571, Titus 3.*

God. She prays night and day, asking God for his help. 6But the widow who lives only for pleasure is spiritually dead even while she lives. 7Give these instructions to the church so that no one will be open to criticism.

8But those who won't care for their relatives, especially those in their own household, have denied the true faith. Such people are worse than unbelievers.

9A widow who is put on the list for support must be a woman who is at least sixty years old and was faithful to her husband.* 10She must be well respected by everyone because of the good she has done. Has she brought up her children well? Has she been kind to strangers and served other believers humbly?* Has she helped those who are in trouble? Has she always been ready to do good?

11The younger widows should not be on the list, because their physical desires will overpower their devotion to Christ and they will want to remarry. 12Then they would be guilty of breaking their previous pledge. 13And if they are on the list, they will learn to be lazy and will spend their time gossiping from house to house, meddling in other people's business and talking about things they shouldn't. 14So I advise these younger widows to marry again, have children, and take care of their own homes. Then the enemy will not be able to say anything against them. 15For I am afraid that some of them have already gone astray and now follow Satan.

16If a woman who is a believer has relatives who are widows, she must take care of them and not put the responsibility on the church. Then the church can care for the widows who are truly alone.

17Elders who do their work well should be respected and paid well,* especially those who work hard at both preaching and teaching. 18For the Scripture says, "You must not muzzle an ox to keep it from eating as it treads out the grain." And in another place, "Those who work deserve their pay!"*

19Do not listen to an accusation against an elder unless it is confirmed by two or three witnesses. 20Those who sin should be reprimanded in front of the whole church; this will serve as a strong warning to others.

21I solemnly command you in the presence of God and Christ Jesus and the highest angels to obey these instructions without taking sides or showing favoritism to anyone.

22Never be in a hurry about appointing a church leader.* Do not share in the sins of others. Keep yourself pure.

23Don't drink only water. You ought to drink a little wine for the sake of your stomach because you are sick so often.

24Remember, the sins of some people are obvious, leading them to certain judgment. But there are others whose sins will not be revealed until later. 25In the same way, the good deeds of some people are obvious. And the good deeds done in secret will someday come to light.

CHAPTER 6

All slaves should show full respect for their masters so they will not bring shame on the name of God and his teaching. 2If the masters are believers, that is no excuse for being disrespectful. Those slaves should work all the harder because their efforts are helping other believers* who are well loved.

False Teaching and True Riches

Teach these things, Timothy, and encourage everyone to obey them. 3Some people may

---

5:9 Greek *was the wife of one husband.* **5:10** Greek *and washed the feet of God's holy people?* **5:17** Greek *should be worthy of double honor.* **5:18** Deut 25:4; Luke 10:7. **5:22** Greek *about the laying on of hands.* **6:2** Greek *brothers.*

5:19-20 Paul called Timothy to confront his fellow church leaders who were living sinful lives. By confronting them about their failures, Timothy would save them from the consequences that continued disobedience would bring them on judgment day. This advice to confront wrongdoers is a call to tough love. Sometimes we must do the same for the people we love. As we notice the growing power of people's addictive behaviors, we can say something before they hit bottom. In so doing, we will give them the opportunity to admit their helplessness and receive God's transforming help.

6:3-5 Paul warned Timothy about those who spread false teachings among the believers. The apostle wanted to protect the message of free salvation offered by Jesus Christ from the distorting lies of money-hungry charlatans. Paul's advice is valuable for us in recovery. Recovery through any power other than God's through Jesus Christ is false. Only God can deliver us from our sins and weaknesses. Anyone claiming to have another solution to our problems likely has something to gain from the program being offered. Only God's solution through Jesus Christ can heal our deepest wounds, and the power he offers is free of charge.

contradict our teaching, but these are the wholesome teachings of the Lord Jesus Christ. These teachings promote a godly life. ⁴Anyone who teaches something different is arrogant and lacks understanding. Such a person has an unhealthy desire to quibble over the meaning of words. This stirs up arguments ending in jealousy, division, slander, and evil suspicions. ⁵These people always cause trouble. Their minds are corrupt, and they have turned their backs on the truth. To them, a show of godliness is just a way to become wealthy.

⁶Yet true godliness with contentment is itself great wealth. ⁷After all, we brought nothing with us when we came into the world, and we can't take anything with us when we leave it. ⁸So if we have enough food and clothing, let us be content.

⁹But people who long to be rich fall into temptation and are trapped by many foolish and harmful desires that plunge them into ruin and destruction. ¹⁰For the love of money is the root of all kinds of evil. And some people, craving money, have wandered from the true faith and pierced themselves with many sorrows.

Paul's Final Instructions
¹¹But you, Timothy, are a man of God; so run from all these evil things. Pursue righteousness and a godly life, along with faith, love, perseverance, and gentleness. ¹²Fight the good fight for the true faith. Hold tightly to the eternal life to which God has called you, which you have declared so well before many witnesses. ¹³And I charge you before God, who gives life to all, and before Christ Jesus, who gave a good testimony before Pontius Pilate, ¹⁴that you obey this command without wavering. Then no one can find fault with you from now until our Lord Jesus Christ comes again. ¹⁵For,

At just the right time Christ will be revealed from heaven by the blessed and only almighty God, the King of all kings and Lord of all lords. ¹⁶He alone can never die, and he lives in light so brilliant that no human can approach him. No human eye has ever seen him, nor ever will. All honor and power to him forever! Amen.

¹⁷Teach those who are rich in this world not to be proud and not to trust in their money, which is so unreliable. Their trust should be in God, who richly gives us all we need for our enjoyment. ¹⁸Tell them to use their money to do good. They should be rich in good works and generous to those in need, always being ready to share with others. ¹⁹By doing this they will be storing up their treasure as a good foundation for the future so that they may experience true life.

²⁰Timothy, guard what God has entrusted to you. Avoid godless, foolish discussions with those who oppose you with their so-called knowledge. ²¹Some people have wandered from the faith by following such foolishness.

May God's grace be with you all.

6:17-19 Paul warned Timothy about the pitfall of trusting in money. Some of us may have already experienced the emptiness of such misplaced trust. We may have thought that wealth could buy solutions to all our problems. We now know, however, that money cannot deliver us from the power of our dependency. Whether we are rich or poor, the pull of our addiction can be overcome only when we admit our helplessness and turn to God for help. The only way to a successful life in God's eyes is to pursue godliness. By taking steps of faith in God we can experience his help in the recovery process and renewed life.

REFLECTIONS ON 1 TIMOTHY

insights ABOUT GOD'S LAW

In **1 Timothy 1:8-11** Paul pointed out that God's law is intended to convict us of our sins and lead us to admit our helplessness and receive his forgiveness. It is not primarily a set of rules for us to live by. It is true that recovery involves acknowledging that there are healthy boundaries for our actions. But recovery will never be successful by observing the Old Testament law, which is beyond our ability to keep (see Acts 15:10). Attempting to do so will lead to frustration and guilt, which will stymie rather than encourage us in recovery. We need to use the law as a means for discovering how helpless we are. Then we can entrust our life to God and trust him to help us take each new step in recovery.

insights ABOUT GOD'S TRANSFORMING POWER

In **1 Timothy 1:12-17** Paul recounted how he had once done everything he could to stop the growth of the early Christian community. But God mercifully intervened in Paul's life, transforming him into one of the most dynamic leaders of the early Christian church. As he shared his story, his previous status as an enemy made his message all the more powerful. The amazing changes in his life testified to God's transforming power. Some of us may feel that we will never be able to impact the lives of others. We may feel that we are so terrible that we are beyond the point of recovery. But God can change us no matter who we are or what we have done. As we share our story of deliverance, others will receive hope as they see what God has done in our life.

2 TIMOTHY

When a loved one is about to die, we strain to hear any whispered words of blessing or advice, knowing they will be the last. When an important person is at death's door, people crowd around for words of enduring wisdom. In this letter Paul wrote his final words of blessing, advice, and comfort. It is Paul's deathbed communication to Timothy, his son in the faith.

As he wrote this letter, Paul was awaiting his execution in a Roman prison. He expected the end to come soon, so he penned these words of advice and encouragement to his young protégé in Ephesus. He wanted to make sure that Timothy had all the tools he needed to be an effective minister of the gospel.

Paul told Timothy to develop his relationship with God and to serve God faithfully. Paul knew that Timothy would face many problems as a church leader, so he encouraged Timothy to persevere. He challenged the young minister to be faithful to his duties, to use the gifts God had given him, to hold on to the truth of God's Word, to teach others, and to be willing to suffer for the sake of Christ.

Paul had made mistakes in the past, but that didn't disqualify him from helping Timothy. Neither do our mistakes disqualify us from reaching out to others. God gives each of us something to share from our experiences in life. Paul had much to pass on to Timothy. Through our recovery, God has given us important insights from which others can benefit. Sharing those insights with others is an important part of our own journey toward wholeness.

THE BOTTOM LINE

PURPOSE: To encourage a faithful but discouraged Timothy in continuing to do God's work. AUTHOR: The apostle Paul. AUDIENCE: Timothy, a young minister of the gospel. DATE WRITTEN: Sometime between A.D. 66 and 67, shortly before Paul's death during the reign of Emperor Nero. SETTING: When Paul wrote this letter, he was in prison; only his friend Luke was with him. This is a very personal letter, showing Paul's vulnerability and loneliness as he faced death. It also reveals his inner strength as he continued, even in his desperate situation, to encourage young Timothy. KEY VERSE: "Run from anything that stimulates youthful lusts. Instead, pursue righteous living, faithfulness, love and peace. Enjoy the companionship of those who call on the Lord with pure hearts" (2:22). KEY PEOPLE AND RELATIONSHIPS: Paul, with Timothy, Luke, and Mark.

RECOVERY THEMES

God's Way Can Be Difficult: We don't like giving up destructive behaviors because it is painful, and the changes required for recovery are often especially painful. Some of us would rather suffer in a known situation than risk moving into the unknown world of recovery. As it was for Timothy, so it is with us: Our growth involves some pain, but we can be confident that the sacrifices we make will be ultimately worthwhile. Knowing that there will be hard times in recovery can help us face them and persevere in the healing process.

The Importance of Faithfulness: We can count on opposition as we pursue recovery, but that is not all bad. Opposition can clue us in to the fact that important changes are taking place in our life. Not everyone likes to see us change, even if those changes are good and healthy. Some people may be afraid that they are losing an old friend. Others may begin to feel guilty about their own dependency and try to stop our progress. We don't have to figure out why people want to stand in our way; our job is to be faithful to our program of recovery and spiritual growth. Paul was faithful to God, and he called Timothy to follow his example. God calls each of us to do the same.

The Power of God's Word: One of the primary sources of strength and guidance for us in recovery is God's Word. Paul challenged Timothy to know what God's Word says and means (2:15). He described how God's Word helps us as it teaches us what is true, makes us realize what is wrong in our life, points us in the right direction, and helps us do what is right (3:16). Our praying and thinking are to focus on God's Word, for it equips us to live as God wants us to live.

CHAPTER 1
Greetings from Paul

This letter is from Paul, chosen by the will of God to be an apostle of Christ Jesus. I have been sent out to tell others about the life he has promised through faith in Christ Jesus.

²I am writing to Timothy, my dear son.

May God the Father and Christ Jesus our Lord give you grace, mercy, and peace.

Encouragement to Be Faithful

³Timothy, I thank God for you—the God I serve with a clear conscience, just as my ancestors did. Night and day I constantly remember you in my prayers. ⁴I long to see you again, for I remember your tears as we parted. And I will be filled with joy when we are together again.

⁵I remember your genuine faith, for you

1:5 We all learn from our parents and pass on the lessons we learn—good or bad—to our children. We blame our parents for our defects of character and weep because we have passed those same defects on to our children. But we can stop the cycle of passing destructive traits from one generation to the next by turning our life over to God. Timothy's mother and grandmother were models of faith and passed their faith on to Timothy. As we obey God, we will model a transformed life to our children. As they see the power of our vibrant faith in God, they will be likely to follow in our steps. Like Timothy's mother and grandmother, we will be able to rejoice in our godly children.

1:7-14 Timothy did not have all the character traits normally expected of a leader. He may have been fearful and timid at times, but Paul said that God gives "power, love, and self-discipline." Paul told Timothy not to let his weakness stop him from ministering to others. His success was not based on his ability, skill, or courage; it was based on the Holy Spirit's power working in him. In recovery we don't have the inherent strength, courage, and self-discipline needed to overcome our dependency. Through God's power, however, we can succeed in recovery.

1:15-18 Paul was in prison when he wrote this letter; he had been deserted by most of his friends and followers. His friend Onesiphorus, however, stood with Paul even though it was risky. Onesiphorus teaches us how to show loyalty and love to someone in need. Like Paul, we may have been abandoned by our friends as we entered recovery. We may also know how Paul must have felt toward his loyal friend. We may have an Onesiphorus in our life, too. Realizing how essential these people are to our recovery encourages us to take every opportunity to be a loyal friend to others. This is part of sharing the message of hope with others and helping them toward recovery.

2:1-2 Paul didn't tell Timothy just to be strong; he told him to be strong in Christ Jesus. The apostle knew that Timothy could never succeed in his ministry by depending on his own strength. He needed the only power sufficient for godly living—God. The truth that God gives us the power to live a transformed life is good news, and we need to pass it on to others! That is what recovery is all about. As each of us hears about and experiences God's power, we pass the word on to others. In this way others receive God's gracious help, and we discover the joy of helping others and growing in our faith.

share the faith that first filled your grandmother Lois and your mother, Eunice. And I know that same faith continues strong in you. ⁶This is why I remind you to fan into flames the spiritual gift God gave you when I laid my hands on you. ⁷For God has not given us a spirit of fear and timidity, but of power, love, and self-discipline.

⁸So never be ashamed to tell others about our Lord. And don't be ashamed of me, either, even though I'm in prison for him. With the strength God gives you, be ready to suffer with me for the sake of the Good News. ⁹For God saved us and called us to live a holy life. He did this, not because we deserved it, but because that was his plan from before the beginning of time—to show us his grace through Christ Jesus. ¹⁰And now he has made all of this plain to us by the appearing of Christ Jesus, our Savior. He broke the power of death and illuminated the way to life and immortality through the Good News. ¹¹And God chose me to be a preacher, an apostle, and a teacher of this Good News.

¹²That is why I am suffering here in prison. But I am not ashamed of it, for I know the one in whom I trust, and I am sure that he is able to guard what I have entrusted to him* until the day of his return.

¹³Hold on to the pattern of wholesome teaching you learned from me—a pattern shaped by the faith and love that you have in Christ Jesus. ¹⁴Through the power of the Holy Spirit who lives within us, carefully guard the precious truth that has been entrusted to you.

¹⁵As you know, everyone from the province of Asia has deserted me—even Phygelus and Hermogenes.

¹⁶May the Lord show special kindness to Onesiphorus and all his family because he often visited and encouraged me. He was never ashamed of me because I was in chains. ¹⁷When he came to Rome, he searched everywhere until he found me. ¹⁸May the Lord show him special kindness on the day of Christ's return. And you know very well how helpful he was in Ephesus.

CHAPTER 2
A Good Soldier of Christ Jesus
Timothy, my dear son, be strong through the grace that God gives you in Christ Jesus. ²You have heard me teach things that have been confirmed by many reliable witnesses. Now teach these truths to other trustworthy

1:12 Or *what has been entrusted to me.*

STEP **10**

Perseverance
BIBLE READING: 2 Timothy 2:1-8
We continued to take personal inventory and when we were wrong promptly admitted it.
Recovery is a lifelong process. There will be times when we grow weary and want to throw in the towel. We will experience pain, fear, and a host of other emotions. We will win some battles but lose others in the war to achieve wholeness. We may get discouraged at times when we can't see any progress, even though we have been working hard. But if we persevere through it all, we can maintain the ground we have gained.

The apostle Paul used three illustrations to teach about perseverance. He wrote to Timothy: "Endure suffering along with me, as a good soldier of Christ Jesus. Soldiers don't get tied up in the affairs of civilian life, for then they cannot please the officer who enlisted them. And athletes cannot win the prize unless they follow the rules. And hardworking farmers should be the first to enjoy the fruit of their labor. Think about what I am saying. The Lord will help you understand all these things" (2 Timothy 2:3-7).

Like a soldier, we are in a war that we can win only if we fight to the end. Like an athlete, we must train for a new way of life and follow the steps of recovery to the finish line. Like a farmer, we must do our work in every season and then wait patiently until we see growth. If we stop working our program before reaching the goal, we may lose everything we have fought, trained, and worked hard for. ***Turn to page 1601, James 1.***

people who will be able to pass them on to others.

³Endure suffering along with me, as a good soldier of Christ Jesus. ⁴Soldiers don't get tied up in the affairs of civilian life, for then they cannot please the officer who enlisted them. ⁵And athletes cannot win the prize unless they follow the rules. ⁶And hardworking farmers should be the first to enjoy the fruit of their labor. ⁷Think about what I am saying. The Lord will help you understand all these things.

⁸Always remember that Jesus Christ, a descendant of King David, was raised from the dead. This is the Good News I preach. ⁹And because I preach this Good News, I am suffering and have been chained like a criminal. But the word of God cannot be chained. ¹⁰So I am willing to endure anything if it will bring salvation and eternal glory in Christ Jesus to those God has chosen.

¹¹This is a trustworthy saying:

If we die with him,
    we will also live with him.
¹²If we endure hardship,
    we will reign with him.
If we deny him,
    he will deny us.
¹³If we are unfaithful,
    he remains faithful,
    for he cannot deny who he is.

¹⁴Remind everyone about these things, and command them in God's presence to stop fighting over words. Such arguments are useless, and they can ruin those who hear them.

An Approved Worker

¹⁵Work hard so you can present yourself to God and receive his approval. Be a good worker, one who does not need to be ashamed and who correctly explains the word of truth. ¹⁶Avoid worthless, foolish talk that only leads to more godless behavior. ¹⁷This kind of talk spreads like cancer,* as in the case of Hymenaeus and Philetus. ¹⁸They have left the path of truth, claiming that the resurrection of the dead has already occurred; in this way, they have turned some people away from the faith.

¹⁹But God's truth stands firm like a foundation stone with this inscription: "The LORD knows those who are his,"* and "All who belong to the LORD must turn away from evil."*

²⁰In a wealthy home some utensils are made of gold and silver, and some are made of wood and clay. The expensive utensils are used for special occasions, and the cheap ones are for everyday use. ²¹If you keep yourself pure, you will be a special utensil for honorable use. Your life will be clean, and you will be ready for the Master to use you for every good work.

²²Run from anything that stimulates youthful lusts. Instead, pursue righteous living, faithfulness, love, and peace. Enjoy the

2:17 Greek *gangrene.* 2:19a Num 16:5. 2:19b See Isa 52:11.

2:3-7 Recovery and spiritual growth are never easy. Progress requires that we follow principles of disciplined faith on a daily basis. Like soldiers we need to put aside the obstacles to our spiritual growth—our dependency, our pursuit of pleasure, our denial. Like athletes we need to follow the rules for healthy living—God's will for our life. Like farmers we need to work hard—persevering through the tough times. If we follow these examples, God will work in our life and help us win life's hard battles. He will reward us with understanding and a rich harvest of blessings.

2:15 Paul told Timothy to work hard to receive God's approval by diligently studying God's Word to discover God's will for him in both attitude and action. We cannot know God's will unless we know what the Bible says. Since recovery is dependent upon our following God's will, we need to study his Word to discover how God wants us to live. This will enable us to follow his instructions for rebuilding our broken life.

2:22 Paul's advice to Timothy is appropriate for us too. We need to run from the places and situations that are likely to tempt us. We should avoid spending time with people who will lead us to relapses. Instead, we should be with people who will encourage us and support our progress in recovery and spiritual growth. If we don't have friends or activities that support our recovery, we need to seek out and get involved in a community of godly and supportive people.

3:1-9 These verses describe people we should not imitate. Sadly, under the influence of our addiction, however, many of us fit this description. We lived selfishly, with little thought for the other people in our life. Many of us may be suffering the consequences for our actions right now, feeling alone, lost, and abandoned. Paul made it clear that these attitudes and actions have severe consequences as most of us have already discovered. By continuing to take inventory of our attitudes and actions, we can uncover our destructive character traits and ask God to transform us. With the help God offers through Jesus Christ, we can become new people.

GOD grant me the serenity
to accept the things I cannot change
the courage to change the things I can
and the wisdom to know the difference

AMEN

We cannot change our past, yet it is hard to accept the truth about it. It is hard to face the things that others have done to us and all the mistakes we have made.

In recovery we all struggle to move out of a difficult past and into a healthier future. Our energy can easily be misspent trying to rewrite the past—a hopeless task. In the recovery process we need to honestly evaluate our life, including everything in the past, and then concentrate our energy on rebuilding a new life.

Jesus said, "You will know the truth, and the truth will set you free" (John 8:32). The path to freedom always leads to the truth, even the truth about the past. The apostle Paul once wrote to young Timothy: "Alexander the coppersmith did me much harm, but the Lord will judge him for what he has done" (2 Timothy 4:14). Paul stated the truth about someone who had hurt him but leaves the matter in God's hands. We, too, need to honestly accept the things that have been done to us and then let them go, leaving them in God's hands.

Elsewhere Paul examined his past, honestly reviewing his earthly accomplishments, his wrongs, his mistakes, his family, his gains, and his losses. It was from this broad perspective that he could write these words: "I don't mean to say that I have already achieved these things or that I have already reached perfection. But I press on to possess that perfection for which Christ Jesus first possessed me" (Philippians 3:12). When we face the truth about our past, we can finally let it go. Then we can journey into a healthier future. *Turn to page 1569, Titus 2.*

---

companionship of those who call on the Lord with pure hearts.

²³Again I say, don't get involved in foolish, ignorant arguments that only start fights. ²⁴A servant of the Lord must not quarrel but must be kind to everyone, be able to teach, and be patient with difficult people. ²⁵Gently instruct those who oppose the truth. Perhaps God will change those people's hearts, and they will learn the truth. ²⁶Then they will come to their senses and escape from the devil's trap. For they have been held captive by him to do whatever he wants.

CHAPTER 3
The Dangers of the Last Days

You should know this, Timothy, that in the last days there will be very difficult times. ²For people will love only themselves and

their money. They will be boastful and proud, scoffing at God, disobedient to their parents, and ungrateful. They will consider nothing sacred. ³They will be unloving and unforgiving; they will slander others and have no self-control. They will be cruel and hate what is good. ⁴They will betray their friends, be reckless, be puffed up with pride, and love pleasure rather than God. ⁵They will act religious, but they will reject the power that could make them godly. Stay away from people like that!

⁶They are the kind who work their way into people's homes and win the confidence of* vulnerable women who are burdened with the guilt of sin and controlled by various desires. ⁷(Such women are forever following new teachings, but they are never able to understand the truth.) ⁸These teachers

3:6 Greek *and take captive.*

oppose the truth just as Jannes and Jambres opposed Moses. They have depraved minds and a counterfeit faith. [9]But they won't get away with this for long. Someday everyone will recognize what fools they are, just as with Jannes and Jambres.

Paul's Charge to Timothy

[10]But you, Timothy, certainly know what I teach, and how I live, and what my purpose in life is. You know my faith, my patience, my love, and my endurance. [11]You know how much persecution and suffering I have endured. You know all about how I was persecuted in Antioch, Iconium, and Lystra—but the Lord rescued me from all of it. [12]Yes, and everyone who wants to live a godly life in Christ Jesus will suffer persecution. [13]But evil people and impostors will flourish. They will deceive others and will themselves be deceived.

[14]But you must remain faithful to the things you have been taught. You know they are true, for you know you can trust those who taught you. [15]You have been taught the holy Scriptures from childhood, and they have given you the wisdom to receive the salvation that comes by trusting in Christ Jesus. [16]All Scripture is inspired by God and is useful to teach us what is true and to make us realize what is wrong in our lives. It corrects us when we are wrong and teaches us to do what is right. [17]God uses it to prepare and equip his people to do every good work.

CHAPTER 4

I solemnly urge you in the presence of God and Christ Jesus, who will someday judge the living and the dead when he comes to set up his Kingdom: [2]Preach the word of God. Be prepared, whether the time is favorable or not. Patiently correct, rebuke, and encourage your people with good teaching.

[3]For a time is coming when people will no longer listen to sound and wholesome teaching. They will follow their own desires and will look for teachers who will tell them whatever their itching ears want to hear. [4]They will reject the truth and chase after myths.

[5]But you should keep a clear mind in every situation. Don't be afraid of suffering for the Lord. Work at telling others the Good News, and fully carry out the ministry God has given you.

[6]As for me, my life has already been poured out as an offering to God. The time of my death is near. [7]I have fought the good fight, I have finished the race, and I have remained faithful. [8]And now the prize awaits me—the crown of righteousness, which the Lord, the righteous Judge, will give me on the day of his return. And the prize is not just for me but for all who eagerly look forward to his appearing.

Paul's Final Words

[9]Timothy, please come as soon as you can. [10]Demas has deserted me because he loves the

---

3:14-17 Paul reminded Timothy of the wonderful resource that God has left us—the Bible. It is the ultimate guide to help us realize what is wrong in our life. It is the only accurate measuring tool available to help us make an honest moral inventory. It reveals God's program for healthy living and shows us how to relate properly and unselfishly to God and to other people. God's Word offers more than just good advice. It promises God's powerful help to all who turn to him with a humble heart. Our recovery will benefit when we take the time to understand it and apply it to our life.

4:1-5 Paul strongly encouraged Timothy to share the Good News of Jesus Christ with others. This is an integral part of Christian living. The good news of recovery in Christ is also something to be shared. In fact, strong and permanent recovery is impossible unless we make sharing our story an integral part of our life. By sharing what God has done for us we can offer new life to other needy people and be encouraged to persevere in our own recovery. We will build strong relationships with others as we walk through recovery with them. This will lead to the healthy community life necessary to support our recovery on a permanent basis.

4:6-8 Paul left his young protégé with these reflections to encourage him as he struggled to live a godly life. Paul had fought hard to live for God and had suffered greatly for the sake of the gospel. Now he could look forward to the wonderful reward he would receive in God's presence. Giving Timothy an eternal perspective would help him approach the tough times with the hope of future blessings. We are given this same hope. It is not easy to walk the path of recovery and spiritual growth. We will experience painful times as we recognize our desperate need for God. We will experience rejection as we seek to share our hope with others. But God rewards our faithfulness and perseverance with eternal peace and joy.

things of this life and has gone to Thessalonica. Crescens has gone to Galatia, and Titus has gone to Dalmatia. ¹¹Only Luke is with me. Bring Mark with you when you come, for he will be helpful to me in my ministry. ¹²I sent Tychicus to Ephesus. ¹³When you come, be sure to bring the coat I left with Carpus at Troas. Also bring my books, and especially my papers.*

¹⁴Alexander the coppersmith did me much harm, but the Lord will judge him for what he has done. ¹⁵Be careful of him, for he fought against everything we said.

¹⁶The first time I was brought before the judge, no one came with me. Everyone abandoned me. May it not be counted against them. ¹⁷But the Lord stood with me and gave me strength so that I might preach the Good News in its entirety for all the Gentiles to hear. And he rescued me from certain death.* ¹⁸Yes, and the Lord will deliver me from every evil attack and will bring me safely into his heavenly Kingdom. All glory to God forever and ever! Amen.

Paul's Final Greetings

¹⁹Give my greetings to Priscilla and Aquila and those living in the household of Onesiphorus. ²⁰Erastus stayed at Corinth, and I left Trophimus sick at Miletus.

²¹Do your best to get here before winter. Eubulus sends you greetings, and so do Pudens, Linus, Claudia, and all the brothers and sisters.*

²²May the Lord be with your spirit. And may his grace be with all of you.

4:13 Greek *especially the parchments.* **4:17** Greek *from the mouth of a lion.* **4:21** Greek *brothers.*

4:11 Mark had forsaken Paul and Barnabas during their first missionary journey (see Acts 13:13), so Paul did not allow his participation in the second journey, resulting in the separation of Paul and Barnabas (Acts 15:36-41). Though Mark had failed miserably earlier, it is clear in this passage that his relationship with Paul had been fully restored. Mark's recovery from a past mistake can encourage all who have failed and wondered whether recovery was even possible. Mark wrote the Gospel of Mark, which has touched the lives of millions over the past twenty centuries. No matter how great our failures in the past, God can use us in amazing ways if we entrust our life—failures and all—to him.

4:16-18 Paul recalled his loneliness during his first Roman imprisonment. He remembered how God had stayed with him even after all his human companions had forsaken him. Only God could strengthen him and bring him deliverance when he was a helpless prisoner. Some of us know what it is like to be forsaken by our friends. Under the influence of our addiction we may have destroyed healthy family relationships. And when we entered recovery, the friends who supported our addiction soon left us. We don't have to face the dark days of recovery alone; God is always with us. As we grow in our faith, God will provide the healthy relationships we need to support our progress.

TITUS

THE BIG PICTURE

A. THREATS TO THE TRUTH ABOUT GOD'S GRACE (1:1-16)
B. SOUND TEACHINGS WITH RESPECT TO GOD'S GRACE (2:1–3:11)
  1. Applying God's Truth to Various Age-Groups (2:1-10)
  2. God's Grace As a Motivation for Godly Living (2:11–3:8)
  3. Applying God's Truth to the Problem of Legalism (3:9-11)
C. FINAL PERSONAL REMARKS (3:12-15)

Paul wrote this letter to Titus, a young pastor on the island of Crete. Titus faced two primary problems in his church. On the one hand, some claimed that immoral living was all right because God's grace was sufficient for forgiveness. On the other hand, there were those who claimed that acceptance by God came through obeying God's laws. Paul encouraged Titus to confront both groups for undermining God's gracious gift of forgiveness in Christ.

Paul solved Titus's dual problem by reminding him of the importance of God's grace. When we discover the amazing grace that God has bestowed on us, we will feel an incredible sense of gratitude. This will motivate us to delight in obeying God's will for our life, not to live immorally because our forgiveness is guaranteed. God is not a harsh taskmaster whose favor depends on our slavish obedience to his rules. He is a gracious Father who offers us a relationship with him, both now and throughout eternity. We can live a godly life out of gratitude to God because he loves and forgives us.

The fact that God is gracious and forgiving is essential to recovery. We already know that we are powerless against sin and our dependency. We have all failed many times over. We don't need to be afraid to admit our sins and failures to our gracious God. He will forgive us and help us start over again. Because God is gracious, we can continue our honest self-examination without fear. God will never write us off for our failures and mistakes. God accepts us just as we are.

THE BOTTOM LINE

PURPOSE: To encourage Titus to be faithful in applying the grace of God to various circumstances. AUTHOR: The apostle Paul. AUDIENCE: Titus, a pastor on the island of Crete. DATE WRITTEN: Between Paul's first and second Roman imprisonments (A.D. 63–66). SETTING: Titus pastored the believers on the island of Crete, a place well known for its immorality. Also, a group of Jewish legalists had made inroads into the church. Titus thus had to deal with both immorality and legalism. KEY VERSES: "For the grace of God has been revealed, bringing salvation to all people. And we are instructed to turn from godless living and sinful pleasures. We should live in this evil world with wisdom, righteousness, and devotion to God" (2:11-12). KEY PEOPLE AND RELATIONSHIPS: Paul with Titus.

RECOVERY THEMES

The Blessings of God's Grace: Salvation through Jesus Christ is good news! This is especially true because God offers it to us freely even though we do not deserve it. This Good News goes beyond God's offer to pay for our sins; God also seeks to transform us so that we can live day by day with the reality of his power inside us. We don't need to be afraid as we come before God, regardless of our sinful past or our failures. Our relationship with God is not based on our success at following his laws. It is based on his gracious provision for the forgiveness of our sins—Jesus Christ. As we entrust our life to God, he forgives us and empowers us to live according to his perfect will.

The Importance of Accountability: We can never make much progress in recovery when we are isolated from others. Developing healthy relationships goes right along with turning our life over to God. On our own, we are helpless against the power of our dependency. God often uses other people to give us the help and encouragement we need to persevere. Paul urged Titus to be accountable to others. By depending on others, he was able to stand firm and reflect God's love and power in his life. Relationships that hold us accountable can give us the courage to do as Titus did.

Recovery Requires Sacrifice: When we enter into recovery, we also enter into new relationships. As we see in this letter, there is an order to all our relationships. Everyone's role is important, and if we are going to be faithful to our role, we must make sacrifices for others. Recovery, like salvation, can begin with a selfish motive. We tend to focus on our own problems and needs. But a healthy recovery moves beyond this self-focus to reach out to others. Each of us has something to share. We must make the sacrifices necessary to be helpful to others in need of recovery.

CHAPTER 1
Greetings from Paul

This letter is from Paul, a slave of God and an apostle of Jesus Christ. I have been sent to proclaim faith to* those God has chosen and to teach them to know the truth that shows them how to live godly lives. ²This truth gives them confidence that they have eternal life, which God—who does not lie—promised them before the world began. ³And now at just the right time he has revealed this message, which we announce to everyone. It is by the command of God our Savior that I have been entrusted with this work for him.

⁴I am writing to Titus, my true son in the faith that we share.

May God the Father and Christ Jesus our Savior give you grace and peace.

Titus's Work in Crete

⁵I left you on the island of Crete so you could complete our work there and appoint elders in each town as I instructed you. ⁶An elder must live a blameless life. He must be faithful

1:1 Or *to strengthen the faith of.*

1:4-5 Paul had planted churches on the island of Crete, and Titus was to finish Paul's work. He was to strengthen the believers and appoint leaders. Paul recognized that Titus could not do everything alone. He probably also recognized that having a single leader is never ideal. Organizations that revolve around one person are likely to reflect the flaws of their leader. A leadership group provides balance. If church or recovery leaders try to control everything without sharing the responsibilities and power with others, we should wonder whether they are there to help other people or themselves. We need to steer clear of this kind of situation.

1:6-9 These character traits for church leaders make no mention of social standing, financial resources, or professional accomplishments. Church leaders must be good spouses and parents; they need to have good reputations; they need to be humble, patient, self-controlled, hospitable, sensible, and fair. No one can buy these character traits; no one can demand them. We get them only by entrusting our life to God and seeking his will. God can help these character traits grow in our life, regardless of our circumstances. Whether we are a respected millionaire or a homeless addict, God can transform us into someone worthy of being a church leader.

1:10-14 Paul encouraged Titus to confront both the Cretans, who abused God's grace by living in sin, and the Jewish legalists, who denied God's grace by requiring believers to do good works to earn salvation. Paul's primary concern was with the legalists, since they undermined a life of grace with their rules and traditions (see Mark 7:1-8). Legalism makes obedience to rules and traditions more important than our personal and transforming relationship with God. It falsely assumes that we can be good under our own power. In recovery we recognize our powerlessness. We cannot change without God's power, so we need to trust him to help us. Paul was defending two of the basic tenets of recovery: our powerlessness and God's sufficiency.

READ TITUS 2:11-14

GOD grant me the serenity
to accept the things I cannot change
the courage to change the things I can
and the wisdom to know the difference

AMEN

No matter how terrible our past has been, we can make changes for the better in our mind, body, and spirit.

Some of us may have come to the conclusion that we just can't change. But if we are willing to place our life in God's hands, there is always hope for positive change and a bright future. The apostle Paul wrote: "Now may the God of peace make you holy in every way, and may your whole spirit and soul and body be kept blameless until our Lord Jesus Christ comes again. God will make this happen, for he who calls you is faithful" (1 Thessalonians 5:23-24).

"For the grace of God has been revealed, bringing salvation to all people. And we are instructed to turn from godless living and sinful pleasures. We should live in this evil world with wisdom, righteousness, and devotion to God, while we look forward with hope to that wonderful day when the glory of our great God and Savior, Jesus Christ, will be revealed. He gave his life to free us from every kind of sin, to cleanse us, and to make us his very own people, totally committed to doing good deeds" (Titus 2:11-14).

God has promised us a wonderful future! In the present, he can keep us from constantly falling into sin if we call on him. Our willingness to let go of the things we cannot change in our past will free us to make positive changes for a healthy future. *Turn to page 1669, Revelation 21.*

---

to his wife,* and his children must be believers who don't have a reputation for being wild or rebellious. ⁷An elder* is a manager of God's household, so he must live a blameless life. He must not be arrogant or quick-tempered; he must not be a heavy drinker,* violent, or dishonest with money.

⁸Rather, he must enjoy having guests in his home, and he must love what is good. He must live wisely and be just. He must live a devout and disciplined life. ⁹He must have a strong belief in the trustworthy message he was taught; then he will be able to encourage others with wholesome teaching and show those who oppose it where they are wrong.

¹⁰For there are many rebellious people who engage in useless talk and deceive others. This is especially true of those who insist on circumcision for salvation. ¹¹They must be si-

lenced, because they are turning whole families away from the truth by their false teaching. And they do it only for money. ¹²Even one of their own men, a prophet from Crete, has said about them, "The people of Crete are all liars, cruel animals, and lazy gluttons."* ¹³This is true. So reprimand them sternly to make them strong in the faith. ¹⁴They must stop listening to Jewish myths and the commands of people who have turned away from the truth.

¹⁵Everything is pure to those whose hearts are pure. But nothing is pure to those who are corrupt and unbelieving, because their minds and consciences are corrupted. ¹⁶Such people claim they know God, but they deny him by the way they live. They are detestable and disobedient, worthless for doing anything good.

1:6 Or *must have only one wife,* or *must be married only once;* Greek reads *must be the husband of one wife.* **1:7a** Or *An overseer,* or *A bishop.* **1:7b** Greek *must not drink too much wine.* **1:12** This quotation is from Epimenides of Knossos.

CHAPTER 2
Promote Right Teaching

As for you, Titus, promote the kind of living that reflects wholesome teaching. [2]Teach the older men to exercise self-control, to be worthy of respect, and to live wisely. They must have sound faith and be filled with love and patience.

[3]Similarly, teach the older women to live in a way that honors God. They must not slander others or be heavy drinkers.* Instead, they should teach others what is good. [4]These older women must train the younger women to love their husbands and their children, [5]to live wisely and be pure, to work in their homes,* to do good, and to be submissive to their husbands. Then they will not bring shame on the word of God.

[6]In the same way, encourage the young men to live wisely. [7]And you yourself must be an example to them by doing good works of every kind. Let everything you do reflect the integrity and seriousness of your teaching. [8]Teach the truth so that your teaching can't be criticized. Then those who oppose us will be ashamed and have nothing bad to say about us.

[9]Slaves must always obey their masters and do their best to please them. They must not talk back [10]or steal, but must show themselves to be entirely trustworthy and good. Then they will make the teaching about God our Savior attractive in every way.

[11]For the grace of God has been revealed, bringing salvation to all people. [12]And we are instructed to turn from godless living and sinful pleasures. We should live in this evil world with wisdom, righteousness, and devotion to God, [13]while we look forward with hope to that wonderful day when the glory of our great God and Savior, Jesus Christ, will be revealed. [14]He gave his life to free us from

2:3 Greek *be enslaved to much wine.* 2:5 Some manuscripts read *to care for their homes.*

2:1-5 Paul called on older men and women to take a special role in the Christian community—to be role models, teaching others by the way they lived. Many of us have experienced the importance of having a godly mentor to encourage us. The most helpful recovery groups have a healthy mix of people, with sponsors who provide encouragement through their words and their actions. As we grow spiritually and progress in recovery, we can become a healthy role model to others in need of recovery. As they see our transformed life and hear our story of deliverance through Christ, they will be encouraged to take the steps necessary to restore their lives.

2:6 Paul told Titus to encourage the young people in his church to "live wisely." Young people are often blind to the consequences of certain activities. They tend to act first and think later. Many of us were very shortsighted when we became involved in our addiction. We probably started out innocently enough, using alcohol or other addictive substances socially. We didn't think through the possible consequences before we took the first dangerous steps toward addiction. Now we are reaping the painful consequences of our unwise choices. If we think before we act and conform our actions to God's will, we will build a meaningful future.

2:11-15 When we realize how much God loves us and that he provides the power for us to live a godly life, we are motivated to entrust our life to him and seek his will. The proper response to God's grace is right conduct. The Bible never considered guilt and fear appropriate motivations for righteousness. We obey God because he loves us and desires to help us succeed. Seeing God as accepting, gracious, and compassionate instead of harsh, condemning, and punitive is critical for our spiritual growth. We don't need to fear God because of our sins. He still loves us and will help us rebuild our life when we admit our failures to him. This can give us hope as we work through recovery.

3:3 We, too, were "foolish and disobedient" and became a slave to our dependency; we were filled with resentment, envy, and hate. But God delivered us from this through his Son, Jesus Christ. Our broken life is the back backdrop against which the bright jewels of God's mercy and gracious salvation are displayed. None of us deserves God's mercy and grace. He loves us simply because he chooses to, more in spite of us than because we deserve it. This truth makes it easier to admit our powerlessness and commit our life to God. No matter how terrible our past, God is willing to forgive and transform us.

3:4-8 Notice the terms that describe God's grace: "kindness and love" (3:4) and "mercy" (3:5). We are justified by God's grace, declared "righteous" in God's eyes by virtue of belonging to Christ. This takes us off the performance treadmill, relieving us of the need to measure up to God's standards. Some of us have spent our life trying to measure up. We bear the guilt of failing to fulfill the unrealistic ideals of our parents, teachers, or bosses. The resulting anger and pain have helped to drive our addiction. But God accepts us just as we are. He doesn't expect us to be perfect; he knows we cannot do it alone. When he calls us to holy living, he also provides the power and direction we need to build a new life.

every kind of sin, to cleanse us, and to make us his very own people, totally committed to doing good deeds.

¹⁵You must teach these things and encourage the believers to do them. You have the authority to correct them when necessary, so don't let anyone disregard what you say.

CHAPTER 3
Do What Is Good

Remind the believers to submit to the government and its officers. They should be obedient, always ready to do what is good. ²They must not slander anyone and must avoid quarreling. Instead, they should be gentle and show true humility to everyone.

³Once we, too, were foolish and disobedient. We were misled and became slaves to many lusts and pleasures. Our lives were full of evil and envy, and we hated each other. ⁴But—

> When God our Savior revealed his kindness and love, ⁵he saved us, not because of the righteous things we had done, but because of his mercy. He washed away our sins, giving us a new birth and new life through the Holy Spirit.* ⁶He generously poured out the Spirit upon us through Jesus Christ our Savior. ⁷Because of his grace he declared us righteous and gave us confidence that we will inherit eternal life.

⁸This is a trustworthy saying, and I want you to insist on these teachings so that all who trust in God will devote themselves to doing good. These teachings are good and beneficial for everyone.

⁹Do not get involved in foolish discussions about spiritual pedigrees* or in quarrels and fights about obedience to Jewish laws. These things are useless and a waste of time. ¹⁰If people are causing divisions among you, give a first and second warning. After that, have nothing more to do with them. ¹¹For people like that have turned away from the truth, and their own sins condemn them.

Paul's Final Remarks and Greetings

¹²I am planning to send either Artemas or Tychicus to you. As soon as one of them arrives, do your best to meet me at Nicopolis, for I have decided to stay there for the winter. ¹³Do everything you can to help Zenas the lawyer and Apollos with their trip. See

3:5 Greek *He saved us through the washing of regeneration and renewing of the Holy Spirit.* 3:9 Or *spiritual genealogies.*

STEP 12

Never Forget

BIBLE READING: Titus 3:1-5

Having had a spiritual awakening as the result of these steps, we tried to carry this message to others and to practice these principles in all our affairs.

As we get further along in recovery, the memory of how bad our life really was may begin to fade. Do we vividly remember what we once were? Can we humbly recall the dark emotions that filled our soul? Do we have true compassion and genuine sympathy for those to whom we try to carry the message?

When we take the message of recovery to others, we must never forget where we came from and how we got where we are. Paul told Titus: "Once we, too, were foolish and disobedient. We were misled and became slaves to many lusts and pleasures. . . . But—'When God our Savior revealed his kindness and love, he saved us, not because of the righteous things we had done, but because of his mercy. He washed away our sins, giving us a new birth and new life through the Holy Spirit'" (Titus 3:3-5).

As we share our message, let us never forget the following truths: We were once a slave, just as others are today. Our heart was filled with the confusion and painful emotions that others still feel. We were saved because of the love and kindness of God, not because we were good enough. We must also remember that we can stay free because God is with us, upholding us every step of the way. *Turn to page 1617, 1 Peter 4.*

that they are given everything they need. [14]Our people must learn to do good by meeting the urgent needs of others; then they will not be unproductive.

[15]Everybody here sends greetings. Please give my greetings to the believers—all who love us.

May God's grace be with you all.

PHILEMON

THE BIG PICTURE

A. GREETINGS (1:1-3)
B. PAUL COMMENDS PHILEMON (1:4-7)
C. PAUL REQUESTS CONSIDERATION FOR ONESIMUS (1:8-21)
D. CONCLUDING REMARKS (1:22-25)

There were millions of slaves in the Roman Empire; Onesimus was one of them. He was owned by a kind Christian leader named Philemon. Out of desperation, Onesimus stole from his master and ran away. But as so often happens, his attempt at a solution only added to his problem. According to the law, a runaway slave could be branded on the forehead or even executed.

Onesimus hid in Rome, and while there he met Paul. Through the apostle's influence, Onesimus came to believe in Jesus Christ. Paul, himself a prisoner at the time, wrote to his friend Philemon to tell him of Onesimus's conversion. The apostle begged Philemon to forgive Onesimus and welcome him home as a "beloved brother." We do not know how Philemon responded, but it seems reasonable to assume that he forgave Onesimus.

We all know what it's like to be a slave. We have been enslaved to an addictive substance, to other people, to compulsive behavior, and even to the injuries of our past. Slavery of any kind takes away our dignity and humanity, turning us into a mere tool in the hands of our master. We know the utter powerlessness we felt in that condition.

Paul's letter to Philemon reminds us that God still loves us. God cares for us, just as he cared for Onesimus, no matter what we have done in the past. God can step into the middle of our unmanageable life and bring us real hope for the future. As long as we do our part—facing our powerlessness, turning our life over to God, confessing our sins, and seeking to make amends—we can count on a life of freedom.

THE BOTTOM LINE

PURPOSE: To convince Philemon, a slave owner, to forgive a slave for running away. AUTHOR: The apostle Paul. AUDIENCE: Philemon, a believer in the early church. DATE WRITTEN: About A.D. 60, during Paul's imprisonment in Rome. SETTING: Slavery was common in the Roman Empire, even among the new believers. Paul did not speak directly against slavery, but he did take a radical step by calling the slave Onesimus "a beloved brother" (1:16). KEY VERSE: "Onesimus [whose name means 'useful'] hasn't been of much use to you in the past, but now he is very useful to both of us" (1:11). KEY PEOPLE AND RELATIONSHIPS: Paul with Onesimus and Philemon.

RECOVERY THEMES

God Cares for the Dispossessed: Onesimus was one of the rejects of his society. As a slave, he had no worth apart from what he was able to do for his master. When he intensified his problems by stealing and running away, his value was diminished even further—he was worthless. But to God he was highly valued; no one is ever worthless in the eyes of God. God's values are different from ours: he cares deeply about all people who have been broken and dispossessed. No matter what we have done in the past, he calls us to himself and offers us recovery and hope.

The Necessity of Forgiveness: Anyone in the Roman Empire would have expected Onesimus to be condemned to death for what he had done. But from God's perspective, Onesimus was deemed worthy of forgiveness because of his relationship with Jesus Christ. The foundation of the change in Onesimus's life was the forgiveness he would receive from God. And the foundation of his continued relationship with Philemon was the forgiveness he received from his master. The forgiveness granted by God and by others is what makes recovery possible. We can rejoice that when we entrust our life to God, he forgives us and transforms our life. Then he helps us make amends to the people we have harmed, paving the way for our forgiveness and restoration.

Greetings from Paul

This letter is from Paul, a prisoner for preaching the Good News about Christ Jesus, and from our brother Timothy.

I am writing to Philemon, our beloved co-worker, ²and to our sister Apphia, and to our fellow soldier Archippus, and to the church that meets in your* house.

³May God our Father and the Lord Jesus Christ give you grace and peace.

Paul's Thanksgiving and Prayer

⁴I always thank my God when I pray for you, Philemon, ⁵because I keep hearing about your faith in the Lord Jesus and your love for all of God's people. ⁶And I am praying that you will put into action the generosity that comes from your faith as you understand and experience all the good things we have in Christ. ⁷Your love has given me much joy and comfort, my brother, for your

2 Throughout this letter, *you* and *your* are singular except in verses 3, 22, and 25.

1:3-9 Before bringing up the problem of the runaway Onesimus, Paul established his lines of communication with Philemon. The apostle showed an appreciation for Philemon and a real concern for his family. Paul's example can help us in recovery. Sometimes we must confront others about their dependency or deal with another touchy problem. As we face confrontation, we need to make sure we value the people involved and take the time to establish strong lines of communication. If we jump in too soon, they may feel that we are just trying to hurt them. If we prove our love beforehand, however, they will be more receptive to what we say.

1:10-13 Onesimus had been reconciled to God and had experienced God's forgiveness. But the fact that God had forgiven him did not exempt him from the consequences of his earlier actions. He still had to return to Philemon to make amends for his wrongs. Restitution is one of the hardest parts of recovery. Our actions have painful consequences; they hurt other people. Even after we have been reconciled to God, we still need to make amends to the people we have wronged. We can be sure that God will stand with us in the process. Onesimus returned to his master bearing Paul's letter. There is no record of the outcome of Onesimus's return, but it is unlikely that this letter would have survived had Philemon not taken Paul's advice to forgive Onesimus.

1:14-17 Both Onesimus and Philemon had a responsibility. Onesimus had to do what he could to make amends to Philemon; Philemon was responsible to accept the overtures of the repentant Onesimus. Old resentments had to be set aside, and Philemon was called upon to forgive and accept his repentant new brother in Christ. If we have wronged others, we need to take clear steps toward making amends. It is equally important, however, that we forgive someone who humbly seeks to make amends to us. Bearing grudges against others is destructive to the people we turn away; it also fills us with unresolved bitterness, hindering our progress in recovery.

1:18-21 With the phrase "charge it to me," Paul was asking Philemon to charge Onesimus's debt against Paul's account. Philemon was to welcome Onesimus back into his household as if Paul was the one returning. Paul intervened to arrest the progression of resentment and brokenness in this relationship. This is a beautiful illustration of what God does for us through Jesus Christ. God charges all our sins and failures to the account of Jesus Christ, who has paid the price through his death on the cross. Then God joyfully receives us into his family, just as he would welcome his own Son (see 2 Corinthians 5:21).

kindness has often refreshed the hearts of God's people.

Paul's Appeal for Onesimus

[8]That is why I am boldly asking a favor of you. I could demand it in the name of Christ because it is the right thing for you to do. [9]But because of our love, I prefer simply to ask you. Consider this as a request from me—Paul, an old man and now also a prisoner for the sake of Christ Jesus.*

[10]I appeal to you to show kindness to my child, Onesimus. I became his father in the faith while here in prison. [11]Onesimus* hasn't been of much use to you in the past, but now he is very useful to both of us. [12]I am sending him back to you, and with him comes my own heart.

[13]I wanted to keep him here with me while I am in these chains for preaching the Good News, and he would have helped me on your behalf. [14]But I didn't want to do anything without your consent. I wanted you to help because you were willing, not because you were forced. [15]It seems you lost Onesimus for a little while so that you could have him back forever. [16]He is no longer like a slave to you. He is more than a slave, for he is a beloved brother, especially to me. Now he will mean much more to you, both as a man and as a brother in the Lord.

[17]So if you consider me your partner, welcome him as you would welcome me. [18]If he has wronged you in any way or owes you anything, charge it to me. [19]I, PAUL, WRITE THIS WITH MY OWN HAND: I WILL REPAY IT. AND I WON'T MENTION THAT YOU OWE ME YOUR VERY SOUL!

[20]Yes, my brother, please do me this favor* for the Lord's sake. Give me this encouragement in Christ.

[21]I am confident as I write this letter that you will do what I ask and even more! [22]One more thing—please prepare a guest room for me, for I am hoping that God will answer your prayers and let me return to you soon.

Paul's Final Greetings

[23]Epaphras, my fellow prisoner in Christ Jesus, sends you his greetings. [24]So do Mark, Aristarchus, Demas, and Luke, my co-workers.

[25]May the grace of the Lord Jesus Christ be with your spirit.

9 Or *a prisoner of Christ Jesus.* **11** *Onesimus* means "useful." **20** Greek *onaimen,* a play on the name Onesimus.

STEP 9

Unfinished Business

BIBLE READING: Philemon 1:13-16

We made direct amends to such people wherever possible, except when to do so would injure them or others.

Sometimes we need to complete unfinished business before we can move forward toward new opportunities in life. Some of us may have left trails of broken laws and relationships—things we need to address before moving on.

Our new life does not excuse us from past obligations. While the apostle Paul was in prison, he led a runaway slave named Onesimus to a new life in Christ. Then Paul sent him back to his master, even though Onesimus faced possible death for his offense. Since his previous master was a friend of Paul's and a Christian brother, they hoped that Onesimus would be forgiven.

Onesimus carried a letter from Paul to his master, which read: "I wanted to keep [Onesimus] here with me. . . . But I didn't want to do anything without your consent. . . . It seems you lost Onesimus for a little while so that you could have him back forever. He is no longer like a slave to you. He is more than a slave, for he is a beloved brother. . . . If he has wronged you in any way or owes you anything, charge it to me" (Philemon 1:13-16, 18).

Before we can move ahead to a new future, we must face the unfinished business of the past. This includes offering to pay back what we owe, coming clean before the law, and going back to the people from whom we ran away. We can't assume forgiveness from people, although we can hope for it. In some cases we may be surprised to find pardon and release from the bondage of our past. *Turn to page 1613, 1 Peter 2.*

HEBREWS

THE BIG PICTURE

A. THE SUPERIORITY OF JESUS AS OUR POWER FOR RECOVERY (1:1–10:18)
 1. He Is More Powerful Than the Angels (1:1–2:18)
 2. He Is Greater Than Moses and Joshua (3:1–4:13)
 3. He Surpasses Everything in the Old Covenant Priesthood (4:14–7:28)
 4. His New Covenant Is Superior (8:1–10:18)
B. THE FREEING POWER OF FAITH AND HUMILITY (10:19–13:25)
 1. Faith Needed in Hard Times (10:19-39)
 2. Faith Seen in Old Testament Times (11:1-40)
 3. Faithfulness and the Loving Discipline of God (12:1-29)
 4. Faithfulness and the Trustworthy Foundation of Christ (13:1-25)

All of us have felt the tug of old habits or our former lifestyle. We have known the frustration it creates as we long for the familiar, even if it is destructive. Perhaps at times the challenge of recovery seems too hard for us. Our old life beckons, tempting us with familiar sources of comfort.

Many of the Jewish Christians of the first century thought about returning to the Jewish faith. Some of Jesus' teachings didn't seem to line up with the teachings of the Jewish rabbis. Was Jesus really the Messiah? Did following him mean they had to give up their old, familiar forms of worship? Would it be wrong to go back to their old beliefs and traditions? Did it make sense to follow this "new way" when it led to harsh persecution?

The writer of Hebrews dealt with the doubts of Jewish believers by showing how salvation in Jesus Christ is clearly superior to the way of the Jewish law. The Jewish readers are told to hold on to their new faith, to encourage each other, and to look forward to Jesus the Messiah's return. They are warned of the consequences of rejecting the salvation offered by God through Christ and reminded of the blessings promised to those who trust him.

Entering recovery requires that we entrust our life to God through Jesus Christ and follow his ways. From time to time we will almost certainly feel tempted to return to our former lifestyle. But God is the only one who can empower us in recovery. When we give our life to him, we take the leap of faith necessary to begin the process of recovery.

THE BOTTOM LINE

PURPOSE: To demonstrate the wisdom of following Christ and the foolishness of looking elsewhere for salvation. AUTHOR: The author is unknown; but Paul, Luke, Barnabas, Apollos, Silas, Philip, Priscilla, and others have been suggested as possibilities. AUDIENCE: Jewish believers. DATE WRITTEN: Probably shortly before the destruction of the Jerusalem Temple in A.D. 70. SETTING: Hebrews was written to encourage Jewish believers who were being severely persecuted. They needed to be reassured that Jesus was who he claimed to be—the Son of God and the promised Messiah. KEY VERSE: "The Son radiates God's own glory and expresses the very character of God" (1:3). KEY PEOPLE AND RELATIONSHIPS: Jesus Christ, along with many men and women of faith.

RECOVERY THEMES

The Primacy of Jesus Christ: The book of Hebrews describes Jesus as God. It explains that Jesus is the ultimate power and authority in the universe, superior to any and every other leader in history. He is the full and complete revelation of God to us. And Jesus is the one who can forgive our sins. Christ is the center of our hope and trust, and for that reason he is our only real hope for recovery.

God Delivers the Powerless: Because Jesus was the perfect sacrifice, he fulfilled all that the Old Testament sacrifices represented—he was the means of God's complete forgiveness of our sins. That means every sin can be forgiven completely—past, present, and future. Through Christ, God did for us what we could not do. Jesus removed the barrier of sin between us and God so we could have access to God's very presence. Christ's complete sacrifice removed the guilt that accompanied our sins. Through his sacrificial death and powerful resurrection, he has delivered the powerless!

The Necessity of Faith: Faith is "the confidence that what we hope for will actually happen; it gives us assurance about things we cannot see" (11:1). Recovery is based on faith—our confident trust that God will help us do what we are powerless to do. As we place our trust in God, he will transform us with his power. He has promised this to all who believe.

The Importance of Perseverance: It is one thing to know that recovery is a lifelong process; it is another to persevere when obstacles and problems block our way. The first readers of the book of Hebrews experienced incredible persecution for their faith. But the writer assured them that they would be able to endure it if they did not give up or turn back. We need to pray for the strength to endure, because perseverance is essential to any successful recovery.

CHAPTER 1
Jesus Christ Is God's Son

Long ago God spoke many times and in many ways to our ancestors through the prophets. ²And now in these final days, he has spoken to us through his Son. God promised everything to the Son as an inheritance, and through the Son he created the universe. ³The Son radiates God's own glory and expresses the very character of God, and he sustains everything by the mighty power of his command. When he had cleansed us from our sins, he sat down in the place of honor at the right hand of the majestic God in heaven. ⁴This shows that the Son is far greater than the angels, just as the name God gave him is greater than their names.

The Son Is Greater Than the Angels
⁵For God never said to any angel what he said to Jesus:

"You are my Son.
　Today I have become your Father.*"

God also said,

"I will be his Father,
　and he will be my Son."*

⁶And when he brought his supreme* Son into the world, God said,*

1:5a Or *Today I reveal you as my Son.* Ps 2:7. 1:5b 2 Sam 7:14. 1:6a Or *firstborn.* 1:6b Or *when he again brings his supreme Son [or firstborn Son] into the world, God will say.*

1:1-2 Jesus Christ, the Son of God, is God's final and most perfect revelation. Yet God the Son shaped the original creation as well. As "the Alpha and the Omega—the beginning and the end" (Revelation 1:8), he is the only Power capable of the re-creation and transformation we seek in recovery. As the heir of all the treasures of heaven and earth, Jesus Christ stands ready and able to help those who come to him with empty hands, acknowledging their needs and problems.
1:3 There is a vast difference between the divine infinite Being (God) and limited human beings. The only way a person can come to understand something of God's glory and power is to get to know Jesus Christ by faith. Christ is simultaneously both an incredibly powerful expression of God's person and the one who lovingly entered sinful human existence to redeem and renew needy souls. When we acknowledge how powerless we are to save ourself, we can then come to the only power who can accomplish what we cannot—God in Jesus Christ.
1:4-6 The Jews greatly esteemed angels as servants of God, largely because of their role in the Old Testament. But as glorious as angels are, there is still no comparison between the angels and Jesus Christ. Christ is clearly superior in his person and in his works; he also has a unique relationship with the heavenly Father as his Son (see Psalm 2:7; 2 Samuel 7:14). It is into this wonderful Father-child relationship that he draws us (Hebrews 2:11). Through Jesus we have access to the Father who loves us and cares for our every need tenderly and with infinite wisdom (see Galatians 4:6; Ephesians 2:18). This is good news indeed!

"Let all of God's angels worship him."*

[7] Regarding the angels, he says,

"He sends his angels like the winds,
his servants like flames of fire."*

[8] But to the Son he says,

"Your throne, O God, endures forever and
ever.
You rule with a scepter of justice.
[9] You love justice and hate evil.
Therefore, O God, your God has
anointed you,
pouring out the oil of joy on you more
than on anyone else."*

[10] He also says to the Son,

"In the beginning, Lord, you laid the
foundation of the earth
and made the heavens with your hands.
[11] They will perish, but you remain forever.
They will wear out like old clothing.
[12] You will fold them up like a cloak
and discard them like old clothing.
But you are always the same;
you will live forever."*

[13] And God never said to any of the angels,

"Sit in the place of honor at my right
hand
until I humble your enemies,
making them a footstool under your
feet."*

[14] Therefore, angels are only servants—spirits
sent to care for people who will inherit salvation.

CHAPTER 2
A Warning against Drifting Away

So we must listen very carefully to the truth
we have heard, or we may drift away from it.
[2] For the message God delivered through angels has always stood firm, and every violation of the law and every act of disobedience
was punished. [3] So what makes us think we
can escape if we ignore this great salvation
that was first announced by the Lord Jesus
himself and then delivered to us by those
who heard him speak? [4] And God confirmed
the message by giving signs and wonders
and various miracles and gifts of the Holy
Spirit whenever he chose.

Jesus, the Man

[5] And furthermore, it is not angels who will
control the future world we are talking
about. [6] For in one place the Scriptures say,

"What are mere mortals that you should
think about them,
or a son of man* that you should care
for him?
[7] Yet you made them only a little lower
than the angels
and crowned them with glory and
honor.*
[8] You gave them authority over all things."*

Now when it says "all things," it means
nothing is left out. But we have not yet seen
all things put under their authority. [9] What
we do see is Jesus, who was given a position
"a little lower than the angels"; and because
he suffered death for us, he is now "crowned

1:6c Deut 32:43. 1:7 Ps 104:4 (Greek version). 1:8-9 Ps 45:6-7. 1:10-12 Ps 102:25-27. 1:13 Ps 110:1. 2:6 Or *the Son of Man.* 2:7 Some manuscripts add *You gave them charge of everything you made.* 2:6-8 Ps 8:4-6 (Greek version).

2:1-3 This is the first of many "warning" passages in Hebrews. By it, the author sought to alert
the Jewish readers to the subtle danger of drifting back into their former lifestyle in Judaism. In
recovery, too, there is always the danger of falling back into old ways. This passage makes clear
the consequences of our decisions: There will be either just punishment for ignoring the opportunity Christ offers for recovery, or wonderful salvation by trusting God and receiving his special
favor and transforming power.
2:5-8 The writer of Hebrews used Psalm 8:4-6 most likely because of its reference to the "Son of
Man." In Psalm 8 itself it is not obvious that these verses are messianic (referring to Christ); they
seem to refer to humanity's status: "lower than the angels," yet having "authority over all things."
The writer of Hebrews adds a new twist by applying these verses to Christ. As the Son of Man,
Christ was lower than the angels for a time, but now is exalted to a position of authority over all
things. He went before us and now gives us hope for our future. No matter how difficult things
are for us now, our eternal destiny is to rule in heaven with Christ if we believe in him.
2:8-14 Believers who are in recovery are on the way to an eternity with God, moving through
difficult territory where Christ has already been. It was God's great love and grace that led Jesus to
his death; by his death salvation was made available to all. It is also God's grace that leads us
through suffering in recovery. Often it is only through the refining fire of suffering that we achieve
balance and true holiness. When we suffer, we can be sure that Jesus is with us, that he went
before us, and that God will use our pain for his purposes.

with glory and honor." Yes, by God's grace, Jesus tasted death for everyone. [10]God, for whom and through whom everything was made, chose to bring many children into glory. And it was only right that he should make Jesus, through his suffering, a perfect leader, fit to bring them into their salvation.

[11]So now Jesus and the ones he makes holy have the same Father. That is why Jesus is not ashamed to call them his brothers and sisters.* [12]For he said to God,

"I will proclaim your name to my brothers and sisters.
I will praise you among your assembled people."*

[13]He also said,

"I will put my trust in him,"
that is, "I and the children God has given me."*

[14]Because God's children are human beings—made of flesh and blood—the Son also became flesh and blood. For only as a human being could he die, and only by dying could he break the power of the devil, who had* the power of death. [15]Only in this way could he set free all who have lived their lives as slaves to the fear of dying.

[16]We also know that the Son did not come to help angels; he came to help the descendants of Abraham. [17]Therefore, it was neces-sary for him to be made in every respect like us, his brothers and sisters,* so that he could be our merciful and faithful High Priest before God. Then he could offer a sacrifice that would take away the sins of the people. [18]Since he himself has gone through suffering and testing, he is able to help us when we are being tested.

CHAPTER 3
Jesus Is Greater Than Moses

And so, dear brothers and sisters who belong to God and* are partners with those called to heaven, think carefully about this Jesus whom we declare to be God's messenger* and High Priest. [2]For he was faithful to God, who appointed him, just as Moses served faithfully when he was entrusted with God's entire* house.

[3]But Jesus deserves far more glory than Moses, just as a person who builds a house deserves more praise than the house itself. [4]For every house has a builder, but the one who built everything is God.

[5]Moses was certainly faithful in God's house as a servant. His work was an illustra-tion of the truths God would reveal later. [6]But Christ, as the Son, is in charge of God's entire house. And we are God's house, if we keep our courage and remain confident in our hope in Christ.*

[7]That is why the Holy Spirit says,

2:11 Greek brothers; also in 2:12. 2:12 Ps 22:22. 2:13 Isa 8:17-18. 2:14 Or has. 2:17 Greek like the brothers.
3:1a Greek And so, holy brothers who. 3:1b Greek God's apostle. 3:2 Some manuscripts do not include entire.
3:6 Some manuscripts add faithful to the end.

2:17-18 When we are depressed or struggling in recovery, we may feel that nobody cares about us or understands what we are going through. No person has ever gone to greater lengths to identify with us than Jesus Christ; though he was limitless God, he subjected himself to all our human limitations. He lived in our world as a human being and suffered as we do—therefore he understands our pain and suffering from personal experience. He has been where we are, and he is both eager and able to help us.

3:1 The writer of Hebrews reminded his readers that they were God's special people, set apart, chosen for heaven. Periodically in our recovery work we need to remember who we are and where we are headed. Before we began recovery, our past controlled our present. Now in recovery, because of the faith we exercise, our future sets the direction and tone of our life. As often as we need to, we can affirm who we are in Christ and the glorious destiny that awaits us.

3:2-6 Christ's superiority to Moses was underlined by comparing the positions held by each. Christ was like a builder of a fine house (as Creator), while Moses was like the house itself or even a servant in that house. God may use many means to help us in recovery: therapists, recovery groups, pastors, sponsors, books, meetings, tapes, journaling, prayer. But God lovingly controls the reconstruction of our life. In that knowledge we can find comfort, confidence, and joy.

3:7–4:13 In this second and more extended "warning" (see note on 2:1-3), readers are cautioned to avoid the mistake made by the Israelites who received the law at Mount Sinai. In spite of all their spiritual privileges and visual awareness of God's awesome power, they still refused to exer-cise faith and enter the Promised Land that God graciously offered. Many of us have made a simi-lar mistake upon entering recovery. Either we don't persevere, or we don't anchor our recovery in Christ, the only true source of healing. All of Scripture, including the book of Hebrews, is geared toward helping us put our full trust in God as he is revealed in Jesus Christ.

"Today when you hear his voice,
8   don't harden your hearts
as Israel did when they rebelled,
    when they tested me in the wilderness.
⁹There your ancestors tested and tried my
    patience,
    even though they saw my miracles
        for forty years.
¹⁰So I was angry with them, and I said,
'Their hearts always turn away from me.
    They refuse to do what I tell them.'
¹¹So in my anger I took an oath:
'They will never enter my place
    of rest.'"*

¹²Be careful then, dear brothers and sisters.*
Make sure that your own hearts are not evil
and unbelieving, turning you away from
the living God. ¹³You must warn each other
every day, while it is still "today," so that
none of you will be deceived by sin and
hardened against God. ¹⁴For if we are faithful to the end, trusting God just as firmly as
when we first believed, we will share in all
that belongs to Christ. ¹⁵Remember what it
says:

"Today when you hear his voice,
    don't harden your hearts
    as Israel did when they rebelled."*

¹⁶And who was it who rebelled against
God, even though they heard his voice?
Wasn't it the people Moses led out of Egypt?
¹⁷And who made God angry for forty
years? Wasn't it the people who sinned,
whose corpses lay in the wilderness? ¹⁸And to
whom was God speaking when he took an
oath that they would never enter his rest?
Wasn't it the people who disobeyed him?
¹⁹So we see that because of their unbelief
they were not able to enter his rest.

CHAPTER 4
Promised Rest for God's People
God's promise of entering his rest still
stands, so we ought to tremble with fear that
some of you might fail to experience it. ²For
this good news—that God has prepared this
rest—has been announced to us just as it was
to them. But it did them no good because
they didn't share the faith of those who listened to God.* ³For only we who believe can
enter his rest. As for the others, God said,

"In my anger I took an oath:
'They will never enter my place
    of rest.'"*

even though this rest has been ready since he
made the world. ⁴We know it is ready because of the place in the Scriptures where it
mentions the seventh day: "On the seventh
day God rested from all his work."* ⁵But in
the other passage God said, "They will never
enter my place of rest."*

⁶So God's rest is there for people to enter,
but those who first heard this good news
failed to enter because they disobeyed God.
⁷So God set another time for entering his
rest, and that time is today. God announced
this through David much later in the words
already quoted:

"Today when you hear his voice,
    don't harden your hearts."*

⁸Now if Joshua had succeeded in giving
them this rest, God would not have spoken
about another day of rest still to come. ⁹So
there is a special rest* still waiting for the
people of God. ¹⁰For all who have entered
into God's rest have rested from their labors,
just as God did after creating the world. ¹¹So
let us do our best to enter that rest. But if we
disobey God, as the people of Israel did, we
will fall.

3:7-11 Ps 95:7-11. 3:12 Greek *brothers*. 3:15 Ps 95:7-8. 4:2 Some manuscripts read *they didn't combine what they
heard with faith*. 4:3 Ps 95:11. 4:4 Gen 2:2. 4:5 Ps 95:11. 4:7 Ps 95:7-8. 4:9 Or *a Sabbath rest*.

4:1-3 God is always ready, willing, and able to fulfill his promises of freedom and rest. Only one
thing stops him—our unbelief or lack of faith. God wants us to receive wonderful blessings and
freedom from our dependency, but these can only be received by faith. Just as the Jews of Moses'
day didn't believe what God told them, sometimes we allow the difficulties of the present to cause
us to doubt God's promises. Recovery is hard, painful work at times. When the going seems the
hardest, we must consciously fix our mind on God's promises. Faith in Christ, not in our own
efforts, is the only way to true recovery.
4:4-11 Though God is by no means presently inactive, he, in a very real sense, entered his "rest"
at the end of the Creation (see Genesis 2:1-3). The writer understood David's renewed offer of rest
in Psalm 95 to mean that the special rest was not secured when Joshua and Israel entered the
Promised Land. Therefore, God's offer of rest, which certainly includes the goals of recovery (peace
with God, self, and others; healthy relationships; the ability to cope with life) remains available to
those who pursue it with faith and perseverance.

¹²For the word of God is alive and powerful. It is sharper than the sharpest two-edged sword, cutting between soul and spirit, between joint and marrow. It exposes our innermost thoughts and desires. ¹³Nothing in all creation is hidden from God. Everything is naked and exposed before his eyes, and he is the one to whom we are accountable.

Christ Is Our High Priest

¹⁴So then, since we have a great High Priest who has entered heaven, Jesus the Son of God, let us hold firmly to what we believe. ¹⁵This High Priest of ours understands our weaknesses, for he faced all of the same testings we do, yet he did not sin. ¹⁶So let us come boldly to the throne of our gracious God. There we will receive his mercy, and we will find grace to help us when we need it most.

CHAPTER 5

Every high priest is a man chosen to represent other people in their dealings with God. He presents their gifts to God and offers sacrifices for their sins. ²And he is able to deal gently with ignorant and wayward people because he himself is subject to the same weaknesses. ³That is why he must offer sacrifices for his own sins as well as theirs.

⁴And no one can become a high priest simply because he wants such an honor. He must be called by God for this work, just as Aaron was. ⁵That is why Christ did not honor himself by assuming he could become High Priest. No, he was chosen by God, who said to him,

"You are my Son.
Today I have become your Father.*"

⁶And in another passage God said to him,

"You are a priest forever in the order of Melchizedek."*

⁷While Jesus was here on earth, he offered prayers and pleadings, with a loud cry and tears, to the one who could rescue him from death. And God heard his prayers because of his deep reverence for God. ⁸Even though Jesus was God's Son, he learned obedience from the things he suffered. ⁹In this way, God qualified him as a perfect High Priest, and he became the source of eternal salvation for all those who obey him. ¹⁰And God designated him to be a High Priest in the order of Melchizedek.

A Call to Spiritual Growth

¹¹There is much more we would like to say about this, but it is difficult to explain, especially since you are spiritually dull and don't seem to listen. ¹²You have been believers so long now that you ought to be teaching others. Instead, you need someone to teach you again the basic things about God's word.* You are like babies who need milk and cannot eat solid food. ¹³For someone who lives on milk is still an infant and doesn't know how to do what is right. ¹⁴Solid food is for those who are mature, who through training have the skill to recognize the difference between right and wrong.

5:5 Or *Today I reveal you as my Son.* Ps 2:7.   5:6 Ps 110:4.   5:12 Or *about the oracles of God.*

4:12-13 During hard times our faith tends to dwindle; we may grow angry and harden our heart to the truth about ourself. The antidote to this problem is the living Word of God, which has power to penetrate even the deepest denial. This is good news for those of us struggling to overcome a dysfunctional lifestyle and having a tendency to distort reality. God knows everything about us, even the things we try to hide from ourself. We can count on him, through his Word, to expose the problems and needs we will face in recovery.

5:4-10 Like any high priest, Jesus Christ had to be chosen for his role. But Christ was a different priest from the Jewish priests descended from Aaron. Jesus is the final (and eternal) High Priest in the line of Melchizedek (see 7:1-21; Psalm 110:4). To prepare for that unique calling, Jesus, the perfect High Priest (see Hebrews 13:8), had to go through a painful growing and learning process (see Luke 2:52) that culminated in his death on the cross. His success in that process lends us great hope as we pursue recovery. He is the one who goes before us and has prepared the way, and he is with us in every step we take.

5:11-13 The writer interrupted his discussion of Melchizedek to warn the people about the spiritual dynamics underlying their immaturity in Christ. Having adequate time to grow and change was not the problem. But the people (like many of us today) continued to manifest childlike behavior instead of growing to spiritual adulthood. Sometimes in recovery it takes a long time to see any progress. But this passage suggests that growth is the norm, even though it is often slow. If we don't see any progress in our recovery over time, we should seek to find out why.

5:14 Spiritual growth, eventual maturity, and balance can happen only through application—acting on what we know to be true. As we meditate on God's Word, we will do the right things;

CHAPTER 6

So let us stop going over the basic teachings about Christ again and again. Let us go on instead and become mature in our understanding. Surely we don't need to start again with the fundamental importance of repenting from evil deeds* and placing our faith in God. ²You don't need further instruction about baptisms, the laying on of hands, the resurrection of the dead, and eternal judgment. ³And so, God willing, we will move forward to further understanding.

⁴For it is impossible to bring back to repentance those who were once enlightened—those who have experienced the good things of heaven and shared in the Holy Spirit, ⁵who have tasted the goodness of the word of God and the power of the age to come—⁶and who then turn away from God. It is impossible to bring such people back to repentance; by rejecting the Son of God, they themselves are nailing him to the cross once again and holding him up to public shame.

⁷When the ground soaks up the falling rain and bears a good crop for the farmer, it has God's blessing. ⁸But if a field bears thorns and thistles, it is useless. The farmer will soon condemn that field and burn it.

⁹Dear friends, even though we are talking this way, we really don't believe it applies to you. We are confident that you are meant for better things, things that come with salvation. ¹⁰For God is not unjust. He will not forget how hard you have worked for him and how you have shown your love to him by caring for other believers,* as you still do. ¹¹Our great desire is that you will keep on loving others as long as life lasts, in order to make certain that what you hope for will come true. ¹²Then you will not become spiritually dull and indifferent. Instead, you will follow the example of those who are going to inherit God's promises because of their faith and endurance.

God's Promises Bring Hope

¹³For example, there was God's promise to Abraham. Since there was no one greater to swear by, God took an oath in his own name, saying:

¹⁴ "I will certainly bless you,
and I will multiply your descendants
beyond number."*

¹⁵Then Abraham waited patiently, and he received what God had promised.

¹⁶Now when people take an oath, they call on someone greater than themselves to hold them to it. And without any question that oath is binding. ¹⁷God also bound himself with an oath, so that those who received the promise could be perfectly sure that he would never change his mind. ¹⁸So God has given both his promise and his oath. These two things are unchangeable because it is impossible for God to lie. Therefore, we who have fled to him for refuge can have great confidence as we hold to the hope that lies before us. ¹⁹This hope is a strong and

6:1 Greek *from dead works.* 6:10 Greek *for God's holy people.* 6:14 Gen 22:17.

---

the more we do what is right, the more it becomes second nature to us. Like an athlete, we need to discipline our body, training it to do what it should through making right choices, which leads to spiritual and emotional maturity.

6:4-8 This section refers either to believers who turned from their salvation or to unbelievers who came close to salvation but then turned away. Either way, the agricultural analogy brings out the truth that if there is real spiritual life, there will be some evidence of it. In recovery, let us look for and cherish any and all signs of growth, even if they are small—green shoots where before there was dry, barren ground. If we are seeking wholeness through faith in Christ, we can be assured that there will, in good time, be fruit.

6:9-12 In confronting his readers regarding their spiritual lethargy (see 5:11-14), the writer's words were strong and direct, though here he still chose to be positive and think the best about them. He knew from the past how hard they had worked. But he also faced the reality of their immaturity and challenged them to persevere in spiritual growth and recovery with patient faith. In our recovery we sometimes need to be corrected and challenged. This passage gives us an example of how to confront when necessary and yet be open to correction from the people who love us.

6:13-20 Abraham, the father of the Jewish nation, exemplified patient faith. After waiting for many years, he finally received his promised son, Isaac, the first of many descendants (see Genesis 12:1-3; 22:16-18). Abraham's persevering faith (see 11:8-19) was anchored in God's promises, which were based on God's unchanging nature. Like Abraham, we can trust God's promises and find absolute security in the resurrected Christ, who is our High Priest and who connects us with the living God.

trustworthy anchor for our souls. It leads us through the curtain into God's inner sanctuary. [20]Jesus has already gone in there for us. He has become our eternal High Priest in the order of Melchizedek.

CHAPTER 7
Melchizedek Is Greater Than Abraham

This Melchizedek was king of the city of Salem and also a priest of God Most High. When Abraham was returning home after winning a great battle against the kings, Melchizedek met him and blessed him. [2]Then Abraham took a tenth of all he had captured in battle and gave it to Melchizedek. The name Melchizedek means "king of justice," and king of Salem means "king of peace." [3]There is no record of his father or mother or any of his ancestors—no beginning or end to his life. He remains a priest forever, resembling the Son of God.

[4]Consider then how great this Melchizedek was. Even Abraham, the great patriarch of Israel, recognized this by giving him a tenth of what he had taken in battle. [5]Now the law of Moses required that the priests, who are descendants of Levi, must collect a tithe from the rest of the people of Israel,* who are also descendants of Abraham. [6]But Melchizedek, who was not a descendant of Levi, collected a tenth from Abraham. And Melchizedek placed a blessing upon Abraham, the one who had already received the promises of God. [7]And without question, the person who has the power to give a blessing is greater than the one who is blessed.

[8]The priests who collect tithes are men who die, so Melchizedek is greater than they are, because we are told that he lives on. [9]In addition, we might even say that these Levites—the ones who collect the tithe—paid a tithe to Melchizedek when their ancestor Abraham paid a tithe to him. [10]For although Levi wasn't born yet, the seed from which he came was in Abraham's body when Melchizedek collected the tithe from him.

[11]So if the priesthood of Levi, on which the law was based, could have achieved the perfection God intended, why did God need to establish a different priesthood, with a priest in the order of Melchizedek instead of the order of Levi and Aaron?*

[12]And if the priesthood is changed, the law must also be changed to permit it. [13]For the priest we are talking about belongs to a different tribe, whose members have never served at the altar as priests. [14]What I mean is, our Lord came from the tribe of Judah, and Moses never mentioned priests coming from that tribe.

Jesus Is like Melchizedek

[15]This change has been made very clear since a different priest, who is like Melchizedek, has appeared. [16]Jesus became a priest, not by meeting the physical requirement of belonging to the tribe of Levi, but by the power of a life that cannot be destroyed. [17]And the psalmist pointed this out when he prophesied,

"You are a priest forever in the order of Melchizedek."*

[18]Yes, the old requirement about the priesthood was set aside because it was weak and useless. [19]For the law never made anything

7:5 Greek *from their brothers.* 7:11 Greek *the order of Aaron?* 7:17 Ps 110:4.

7:1-3 The discussion returned to Melchizedek (see 5:6-10). These ideas may have been too deep for the original readers to fully understand in their state of spiritual infancy, but the writer thought it was crucial that they try to understand. Aspects of Melchizedek's life (see Genesis 14:18-20) were amazingly parallel to events in the life of Christ. This was to emphasize that Christ truly did qualify as a priest in the line of Melchizedek (see 6:20) and thus as our perpetual anchor for recovery and reconciliation.
7:4-10 Abraham recognized Melchizedek as greater than himself, and thus he was obviously greater than any of Abraham's descendants, including Levi and the priests who descended from him. The priesthood Christ came from—the priesthood of Melchizedek—is actually older (implying more stability) than that of Aaron. Such stability can be a great comfort to a person in the turmoil of recovery. Our life may seem to fall apart and circumstances may constantly change, but Christ, our perfect High Priest, will never change.
7:11-19 The new priesthood of Christ was desperately needed because the Levitical priesthood and the Mosaic law were incapable of producing true spiritual maturity. A better priesthood, a better law, and a better hope for living in a growing relationship with God were necessary. Christ's qualification as High Priest came not because of tribal descent but because of his resurrection to new life. The Mosaic law could not make people right with God. Only Christ could do that. In our recovery, Jesus will work his lasting changes in our life.

perfect. But now we have confidence in a better hope, through which we draw near to God.

20This new system was established with a solemn oath. Aaron's descendants became priests without such an oath, 21but there was an oath regarding Jesus. For God said to him,

"The LORD has taken an oath and will not break his vow:
'You are a priest forever.'"*

22Because of this oath, Jesus is the one who guarantees this better covenant with God.

23There were many priests under the old system, for death prevented them from remaining in office. 24But because Jesus lives forever, his priesthood lasts forever. 25Therefore he is able, once and forever, to save* those who come to God through him. He lives forever to intercede with God on their behalf.

26He is the kind of high priest we need because he is holy and blameless, unstained by sin. He has been set apart from sinners and has been given the highest place of honor in heaven.* 27Unlike those other high priests, he does not need to offer sacrifices every day. They did this for their own sins first and then for the sins of the people. But Jesus did this once for all when he offered himself as the sacrifice for the people's sins. 28The law appointed high priests who were limited by human weakness. But after the law was given, God appointed his Son with an oath, and his Son has been made the perfect High Priest forever.

CHAPTER 8
Christ Is Our High Priest
Here is the main point: We have a High Priest who sat down in the place of honor beside the throne of the majestic God in heaven. 2There he ministers in the heavenly Tabernacle,* the true place of worship that was built by the Lord and not by human hands.

3And since every high priest is required to offer gifts and sacrifices, our High Priest must make an offering, too. 4If he were here on earth, he would not even be a priest, since there already are priests who offer the gifts required by the law. 5They serve in a system of worship that is only a copy, a shadow of the real one in heaven. For when Moses was getting ready to build the Tabernacle, God gave him this warning: "Be sure that you make everything according to the pattern I have shown you here on the mountain."*

6But now Jesus, our High Priest, has been given a ministry that is far superior to the old priesthood, for he is the one who mediates for us a far better covenant with God, based on better promises.

7If the first covenant had been faultless, there would have been no need for a second covenant to replace it. 8But when God found fault with the people, he said:

"The day is coming, says the LORD,
    when I will make a new covenant
    with the people of Israel and Judah.
9This covenant will not be like the one
    I made with their ancestors
when I took them by the hand
    and led them out of the land of Egypt.
They did not remain faithful to my
    covenant,
    so I turned my back on them, says
    the LORD.
10But this is the new covenant I will make
    with the people of Israel on that day,*
    says the LORD:

7:21 Ps 110:4. 7:25 Or is able to save completely. 7:26 Or has been exalted higher than the heavens. 8:2 Or tent; also in 8:5. 8:5 Exod 25:40; 26:30. 8:10 Greek after those days.

7:20-26 God's unchanging oath regarding Christ's priesthood stated prophetically in Psalm 110:4 meant that Christ's priesthood was forever and was related to a better and final covenant. This permanence means that Christ will see our recovery through to the end, that he is always available to help, and that he is always our perfect model for godly living.
8:1-6 Christ, our High Priest, sits at the highest place of honor in heaven—God's right hand. This is the true place of worship, built by God, not by human hands like the Tabernacle, which was only a copy of the real worship place in heaven. Through Christ's death and resurrection the limited, earthly priesthood gave way to the perfect, heavenly priesthood. This heavenly priesthood is far superior: It is based on better promises and guarantees the needed resources for recovery.
8:7-13 Six centuries before Christ died on the cross to provide a new way for us to relate to God (see Luke 22:20), the prophet Jeremiah predicted that a "new covenant," totally unlike the Old Testament law, was needed to breach the separation between God and humans (see Jeremiah 31:31-34). Thus, rather than turning back to the old legalistic ways of Judaism, the readers should have been aware that God's old program had been on its way out for a long time. They were looking for recovery in the wrong place. There is only one way to experience recovery and reconciliation—through faith in Jesus Christ.

I will put my laws in their minds,
   and I will write them on their hearts.
I will be their God,
   and they will be my people.
[11] And they will not need to teach their
      neighbors,
   nor will they need to teach their
      relatives,*
   saying, 'You should know the LORD.'
For everyone, from the least to the
      greatest,
   will know me already.
[12] And I will forgive their wickedness,
   and I will never again remember their
      sins."*

[13]When God speaks of a "new" covenant, it means he has made the first one obsolete. It is now out of date and will soon disappear.

CHAPTER 9
Old Rules about Worship

That first covenant between God and Israel had regulations for worship and a place of worship here on earth. [2]There were two rooms in that Tabernacle.* In the first room were a lampstand, a table, and sacred loaves of bread on the table. This room was called the Holy Place. [3]Then there was a curtain, and behind the curtain was the second room* called the Most Holy Place. [4]In that room were a gold incense altar and a wooden chest called the Ark of the Covenant, which was covered with gold on all sides. Inside the Ark were a gold jar containing manna, Aaron's staff that sprouted leaves, and the stone tablets of the covenant. [5]Above the Ark were the cherubim of divine glory, whose wings stretched out over the Ark's cover, the place of atonement. But we cannot explain these things in detail now.

[6]When these things were all in place, the priests regularly entered the first room* as they performed their religious duties. [7]But only the high priest ever entered the Most Holy Place, and only once a year. And he always offered blood for his own sins and for the sins the people had committed in ignorance. [8]By these regulations the Holy Spirit revealed that the entrance to the Most Holy Place was not freely open as long as the Tabernacle* and the system it represented were still in use.

[9]This is an illustration pointing to the present time. For the gifts and sacrifices that the priests offer are not able to cleanse the consciences of the people who bring them. [10]For that old system deals only with food and drink and various cleansing ceremonies—physical regulations that were in effect only until a better system could be established.

Christ Is the Perfect Sacrifice

[11]So Christ has now become the High Priest over all the good things that have come.* He has entered that greater, more perfect Tabernacle in heaven, which was not made by human hands and is not part of this created world. [12]With his own blood—not the blood of goats and calves—he entered the Most Holy Place once for all time and secured our redemption forever.

[13]Under the old system, the blood of goats and bulls and the ashes of a heifer could cleanse people's bodies from ceremonial impurity. [14]Just think how much more the

8:11 Greek *their brother.* 8:8-12 Jer 31:31-34. 9:2 Or *tent;* also in 9:11, 21. 9:3 Greek *second tent.* 9:6 Greek *first tent.*
9:8 Or *the first room;* Greek reads *the first tent.* 9:11 Some manuscripts read *that are about to come.*

8:10-13 The new covenant established by God through Jesus Christ is exciting. God would write his laws on his people's hearts, giving them a new desire to obey him. They would have a special, close relationship with God and new fellowship with other believers. God would forgive their past sins and character defects. In Christ, we can receive spiritual and emotional healing and have all the help necessary for a successful recovery.

9:1-10 The regulations for worship in the Old Testament were striking and powerfully symbolized the painful consequences of sin. But the old sacrificial system was effective on a short-term basis and was not a permanent solution to the sin problem. It could not produce immediate personal access to God or a clear conscience. These regulations sufficed until God's final and complete revelation arrived in the person of Jesus Christ. Again we see that for those of us in need of recovery and spiritual transformation, Christ is the only viable option. Only through him can God effect permanent changes in our life.

9:11-15 There was absolutely no comparison between the ongoing sacrifices of the earthly Temple in Jerusalem and the sacrifice provided by Christ, our great High Priest and mediator. Christ accomplished what the Old Testament sacrificial system never could—once and for all, he completed redemption. Trusting the work that Christ did is the only way to have complete forgiveness, a clear conscience, and eternal life. Now when we put our faith in Christ, we are free to joyfully know and serve God.

blood of Christ will purify our consciences from sinful deeds* so that we can worship the living God. For by the power of the eternal Spirit, Christ offered himself to God as a perfect sacrifice for our sins. [15]That is why he is the one who mediates a new covenant between God and people, so that all who are called can receive the eternal inheritance God has promised them. For Christ died to set them free from the penalty of the sins they had committed under that first covenant.

[16]Now when someone leaves a will,* it is necessary to prove that the person who made it is dead.* [17]The will goes into effect only after the person's death. While the person who made it is still alive, the will cannot be put into effect.

[18]That is why even the first covenant was put into effect with the blood of an animal. [19]For after Moses had read each of God's commandments to all the people, he took the blood of calves and goats,* along with water, and sprinkled both the book of God's law and all the people, using hyssop branches and scarlet wool. [20]Then he said, "This blood confirms the covenant God has made with you."* [21]And in the same way, he sprinkled blood on the Tabernacle and on everything used for worship. [22]In fact, according to the law of Moses, nearly everything was purified with blood. For without the shedding of blood, there is no forgiveness.

[23]That is why the Tabernacle and everything in it, which were copies of things in heaven, had to be purified by the blood of animals. But the real things in heaven had to be purified with far better sacrifices than the blood of animals.

[24]For Christ did not enter into a holy place made with human hands, which was only a copy of the true one in heaven. He entered into heaven itself to appear now before God on our behalf. [25]And he did not enter heaven to offer himself again and again, like the high priest here on earth who enters the Most Holy Place year after year with the blood of an animal. [26]If that had been necessary, Christ would have had to die again and again, ever since the world began. But now, once for all time, he has appeared at the end of the age* to remove sin by his own death as a sacrifice.

9:14 Greek *from dead works.* 9:16a Or *covenant;* also in 9:17. 9:16b Or *Now when someone makes a covenant, it is necessary to ratify it with the death of a sacrifice.* 9:19 Some manuscripts do not include *and goats.* 9:20 Exod 24:8. 9:26 Greek *the ages.*

SELF-PROTECTION

READ HEBREWS 10:23-34

Recovery is not a battle anyone wins alone. We help each other to think and live in new ways. Alone, we are vulnerable to temptation; together, we form a shield of protection for one another.

The apostle Paul wrote: "Hold up the shield of faith to stop the fiery arrows of the devil" (Ephesians 6:16). Faith here refers to trusting in Christ for salvation. In general terms it also means being steadfast in our convictions. This can apply to our convictions about God's wisdom in the Bible or our confidence in the Twelve Steps. The shield of faith was likened to the shields carried by Roman soldiers, which covered the entire body. To advance in battle, a group of soldiers would assemble together, making a wall of shields for protection as they moved forward.

In like manner, we are told to stick together. The writer of Hebrews wrote: "Let us not neglect our meeting together, as some people do, but encourage one another" (Hebrews 10:25). We are to take our place in a fellowship of people that provides us with the mutual protection we need to stand firm in recovery.

We need to assemble with others who share the common beliefs helpful in recovery. Our encouragement of one another, our shared faith in God and his Word, and the principles of the Twelve Steps will be a form of strength and protection as we advance in the recovery process. *Turn to page 1591, Hebrews 12.*

²⁷And just as each person is destined to die once and after that comes judgment, ²⁸so also Christ was offered once for all time as a sacrifice to take away the sins of many people. He will come again, not to deal with our sins, but to bring salvation to all who are eagerly waiting for him.

CHAPTER 10
Christ's Sacrifice Once for All

The old system under the law of Moses was only a shadow, a dim preview of the good things to come, not the good things themselves. The sacrifices under that system were repeated again and again, year after year, but they were never able to provide perfect cleansing for those who came to worship. ²If they could have provided perfect cleansing, the sacrifices would have stopped, for the worshipers would have been purified once for all time, and their feelings of guilt would have disappeared.

³But instead, those sacrifices actually reminded them of their sins year after year. ⁴For it is not possible for the blood of bulls and goats to take away sins. ⁵That is why, when Christ* came into the world, he said to God,

"You did not want animal sacrifices or sin offerings.

10:5 Greek *he*; also in 10:8. 10:5-7 Ps 40:6-8 (Greek version).

But you have given me a body to offer.
⁶ You were not pleased with burnt offerings or other offerings for sin.
⁷ Then I said, 'Look, I have come to do your will, O God—
as is written about me in the Scriptures.'"*

⁸First, Christ said, "You did not want animal sacrifices or sin offerings or burnt offerings or other offerings for sin, nor were you pleased with them" (though they are required by the law of Moses). ⁹Then he said, "Look, I have come to do your will." He cancels the first covenant in order to put the second into effect. ¹⁰For God's will was for us to be made holy by the sacrifice of the body of Jesus Christ, once for all time.

¹¹Under the old covenant, the priest stands and ministers before the altar day after day, offering the same sacrifices again and again, which can never take away sins. ¹²But our High Priest offered himself to God as a single sacrifice for sins, good for all time. Then he sat down in the place of honor at God's right hand. ¹³There he waits until his enemies are humbled and made a footstool under his feet. ¹⁴For by that one offering he forever made perfect those who are being made holy.

9:27-28 Hope for the future must be based on our facing the reality of the past and present. Death (and the following judgment) is the ultimate reality of this life; even Jesus Christ, in his humanity, died! But because of his resurrection he is able to offer salvation and spare believers from the fear of judgment. This blend of reality and hope through faith can calm our fearful heart as we struggle with recovery issues. We can face any sin, any character defect, any hurt, knowing that Christ's sacrifice is completely sufficient to offer cleansing and new life.

10:3-10 As this section on the superiority of the new covenant (8:1–10:18) ends, the writer asserts that the ineffective repetition of old covenant sacrifices has now been replaced by Christ's coming and offering himself once and for all in accord with God's will. To not pursue recovery by faith in Christ is to openly reject the superior nature of God's will for history and for individual human lives. If we reject God's offer of salvation and transformation through Jesus Christ, we are rejecting the only means available to sustain us in permanent recovery.

10:19-25 This climactic section of Hebrews (10:19–13:25) begins with a summary of the argument for Christ's superiority, then shifts its emphasis to the transformed attitudes. Since Christ is the final redemptive sacrifice and great High Priest, we can enjoy the full privileges he has secured for us: personal access to God through Christ without an elaborate system, full assurance of our faith and salvation, hope for the future, and encouragement from other people of faith. Through Christ and a community of believers we can receive everything necessary for successful recovery.

10:24-25 Sometimes in recovery we may pull away from healthy relationships or fall into codependent or negative situations that undermine our recovery. These verses remind us that relationships with other believers are crucial to our spiritual growth; godly people can encourage us and hold us accountable. No one can stand alone for long in the recovery process. If we run from healthy relationships, we are running straight toward a painful relapse.

10:26-39 This "warning" summarizes the only way to a wholehearted pursuit of emotional and spiritual healing. First we can find release by repenting of sinful patterns and receiving forgiveness. Then we can take positive steps by strengthening our healthy behavioral patterns and attitudes, particularly our faith in God.

¹⁵And the Holy Spirit also testifies that this is so. For he says,

¹⁶ "This is the new covenant I will make
with my people on that day,* says the
LORD:
I will put my laws in their hearts,
and I will write them on their
minds."*

¹⁷Then he says,

"I will never again remember
their sins and lawless deeds."*

¹⁸And when sins have been forgiven, there is no need to offer any more sacrifices.

A Call to Persevere

¹⁹And so, dear brothers and sisters,* we can boldly enter heaven's Most Holy Place because of the blood of Jesus. ²⁰By his death,* Jesus opened a new and life-giving way through the curtain into the Most Holy Place. ²¹And since we have a great High Priest who rules over God's house, ²²let us go right into the presence of God with sincere hearts fully trusting him. For our guilty consciences have been sprinkled with Christ's blood to make us clean, and our bodies have been washed with pure water.

²³Let us hold tightly without wavering to the hope we affirm, for God can be trusted to keep his promise. ²⁴Let us think of ways to motivate one another to acts of love and good works. ²⁵And let us not neglect our meeting together, as some people do, but encourage one another, especially now that the day of his return is drawing near.

²⁶Dear friends, if we deliberately continue sinning after we have received knowledge of the truth, there is no longer any sacrifice that will cover these sins. ²⁷There is only the terrible expectation of God's judgment and the raging fire that will consume his enemies. ²⁸For anyone who refused to obey the law of Moses was put to death without mercy on the testimony of two or three witnesses. ²⁹Just think how much worse the punishment will be for those who have trampled on the Son of God, and have treated the blood of the covenant, which made us holy, as if it were common and unholy, and have insulted and disdained the Holy Spirit who brings God's mercy to us. ³⁰For we know the one who said,

10:16a Greek *after those days.* **10:16b** Jer 31:33a.
10:17 Jer 31:34b. **10:19** Greek *brothers.* **10:20** Greek
Through his flesh.

STEP 2

Hope in Faith

BIBLE READING: Hebrews 11:1-10

We came to believe that a Power greater than ourselves could restore us to sanity.
Step Two is often referred to as "the hope step." In coming to believe that a Power greater than ourself can restore us to sanity, we will remember what it was like to live sanely and have the faith to hope that sanity can return.

"Faith is the confidence that what we hope for will actually happen; it gives us assurance about things we cannot see" (Hebrews 11:1). How can we be confident that something we want is going to happen, especially if all of our hopes have been dashed? How can we risk believing that the life we hope for is waiting for us around the bend?

The Bible tells us that the key is in the nature of the higher Power we look to. We are told that "anyone who wants to come to him must believe that God exists and that he rewards those who sincerely seek him" (Hebrews 11:6). If we see God as one who is reaching out to help us, we will be more eager to look for him. If our faith has not matured to that point yet, we can ask for help. One man came to Jesus asking him to help his young son who was afflicted by a demon. He said to Jesus, "'Have mercy on us and help us, if you can.' 'What do you mean, "If I can"?' Jesus asked. 'Anything is possible if a person believes.' The father instantly cried out, 'I do believe, but help me overcome my unbelief!'" (Mark 9:22-24). We can start by asking God to help us have more faith. Then we can ask him for the courage to hope for a better future. *Turn to Step Three, page 203, Numbers 23.*

"I will take revenge.
I will pay them back."*

He also said,

"The LORD will judge his own people."*

[31]It is a terrible thing to fall into the hands of the living God.

[32]Think back on those early days when you first learned about Christ.* Remember how you remained faithful even though it meant terrible suffering. [33]Sometimes you were exposed to public ridicule and beaten, and sometimes you helped others who were suffering the same things. [34]You suffered along with those who were thrown into jail, and when all you owned was taken from you, you accepted it with joy. You knew there were better things waiting for you that will last forever.

[35]So do not throw away this confident trust in the Lord. Remember the great reward it brings you! [36]Patient endurance is what you need now, so that you will continue to do God's will. Then you will receive all that he has promised.

[37] "For in just a little while,
the Coming One will come and not delay.
[38] And my righteous ones will live by faith.*
But I will take no pleasure in anyone who turns away."*

[39]But we are not like those who turn away from God to their own destruction. We are the faithful ones, whose souls will be saved.

CHAPTER 11
Great Examples of Faith

Faith is the confidence that what we hope for will actually happen; it gives us assurance about things we cannot see. [2]Through their faith, the people in days of old earned a good reputation.

[3]By faith we understand that the entire universe was formed at God's command, that what we now see did not come from anything that can be seen.

[4]It was by faith that Abel brought a more acceptable offering to God than Cain did. Abel's offering gave evidence that he was a righteous man, and God showed his approval of his gifts. Although Abel is long dead, he still speaks to us by his example of faith.

[5]It was by faith that Enoch was taken up to heaven without dying—"he disappeared, because God took him."* For before he was taken up, he was known as a person who pleased God. [6]And it is impossible to please God without faith. Anyone who wants to come to him must believe that God exists and that he rewards those who sincerely seek him.

[7]It was by faith that Noah built a large boat to save his family from the flood. He obeyed God, who warned him about things that had never happened before. By his faith Noah condemned the rest of the world, and he received the righteousness that comes by faith.

[8]It was by faith that Abraham obeyed when God called him to leave home and go to another land that God would give him as his inheritance. He went without knowing where he was going. [9]And even when he reached the land God promised him, he lived there by faith—for he was like a foreigner, living in tents. And so did Isaac and Jacob, who inherited the same promise. [10]Abraham was confidently looking forward to a city with eternal foundations, a city designed and built by God.

10:30a Deut 32:35. 10:30b Deut 32:36. 10:32 Greek *when you were first enlightened.* 10:38 Or *my righteous ones will live by their faithfulness;* Greek reads *my righteous one will live by faith.* 10:37-38 Hab 2:3-4. 11:5 Gen 5:24.

11:5-7 Enoch was unique (along with Elijah; see 2 Kings 2) in that he did not die (11:5; see Genesis 5:21-24). Noah also played a unique role with the ark, the Flood, and earth's new beginning (see Genesis 6–9). These two biblical characters illustrate the utter necessity of having faith and being right in God's sight. As we trust and depend on God for each aspect of the recovery process, we can be confident that such trust pleases God and will be rewarded with his powerful help.

11:8-19 Abraham fathered the Jewish nation and repeatedly lived by faith as he encountered circumstances that seemed to undermine the fulfillment of God's promises. Sometimes in recovery it seems like forever before we see any changes. At such times we can remind ourself that people of God who are most famous for their faith had to persevere without seeing visible results. We can trust that God will come through for us, even when the struggle seems to go on forever. Abraham had to wait most of his lifetime to see God's promises even partially fulfilled.

11:20-31 The writer demonstrates that many people between the life of Abraham and Israel's entrance into the Promised Land exhibited exemplary faith. God accomplishes his purposes because of the faith of his people. As we trust him with every aspect of our life and recovery, he will accomplish the healing that is surely his will for us. If we trust in God, nothing is impossible!

¹¹It was by faith that even Sarah was able to have a child, though she was barren and was too old. She believed* that God would keep his promise. ¹²And so a whole nation came from this one man who was as good as dead—a nation with so many people that, like the stars in the sky and the sand on the seashore, there is no way to count them.

¹³All these people died still believing what God had promised them. They did not receive what was promised, but they saw it all from a distance and welcomed it. They agreed that they were foreigners and nomads here on earth. ¹⁴Obviously people who say such things are looking forward to a country they can call their own. ¹⁵If they had longed for the country they came from, they could have gone back. ¹⁶But they were looking for a better place, a heavenly homeland. That is why God is not ashamed to be called their God, for he has prepared a city for them.

¹⁷It was by faith that Abraham offered Isaac as a sacrifice when God was testing him. Abraham, who had received God's promises, was ready to sacrifice his only son, Isaac, ¹⁸even though God had told him, "Isaac is the son through whom your descendants will be counted."* ¹⁹Abraham reasoned that if Isaac died, God was able to bring him back to life again. And in a sense, Abraham did receive his son back from the dead.

²⁰It was by faith that Isaac promised blessings for the future to his sons, Jacob and Esau.

²¹It was by faith that Jacob, when he was old and dying, blessed each of Joseph's sons and bowed in worship as he leaned on his staff.

²²It was by faith that Joseph, when he was about to die, said confidently that the people of Israel would leave Egypt. He even commanded them to take his bones with them when they left.

²³It was by faith that Moses' parents hid him for three months when he was born. They saw that God had given them an unusual child, and they were not afraid to disobey the king's command.

²⁴It was by faith that Moses, when he grew up, refused to be called the son of Pharaoh's daughter. ²⁵He chose to share the oppression of God's people instead of enjoying the fleeting pleasures of sin. ²⁶He thought it was better to suffer for the sake of Christ than to own the treasures of Egypt, for he was

11:11 Or *It was by faith that he [Abraham] was able to have a child, even though Sarah was barren and he was too old. He believed.* **11:18** Gen 21:12.

FAITH

READ HEBREWS 12:1-4

Our addiction interferes with our ability to win in the race of life. Many of us feel like a loser who has just dropped out of the race. Faith in God can give us the motivation to run the race, with a real chance at winning life's rewards.

Hebrews 11 has been called the "Hall of Faith." It mentions a long list of people whose lives were used by God because of their faith. The next chapter begins this way: "Since we are surrounded by such a huge crowd of witnesses to the life of faith, let us strip off every weight that slows us down, especially the sin that so easily trips us up. And let us run with endurance the race God has set before us" (Hebrews 12:1).

This illustration referred to the ancient Olympic games. In Bible times men wore flowing robes. Before an event, the athletes would strip off their robes and lay them aside to run without encumbrance. If someone tried to compete in his robe, he would get tangled up, losing both the race and the prize.

It is God's will for us to win the race of life. The robe of our recurring sins needs to be laid aside. There will be pain from the exertion, but we are told to pace ourself and bear the pain with patience. And remember, others who have run the same race and finished well are cheering us on!
Turn to page 1593, Hebrews 12.

looking ahead to his great reward. [27]It was by faith that Moses left the land of Egypt, not fearing the king's anger. He kept right on going because he kept his eyes on the one who is invisible. [28]It was by faith that Moses commanded the people of Israel to keep the Passover and to sprinkle blood on the doorposts so that the angel of death would not kill their firstborn sons.

[29]It was by faith that the people of Israel went right through the Red Sea as though they were on dry ground. But when the Egyptians tried to follow, they were all drowned.

[30]It was by faith that the people of Israel marched around Jericho for seven days, and the walls came crashing down.

[31]It was by faith that Rahab the prostitute was not destroyed with the people in her city who refused to obey God. For she had given a friendly welcome to the spies.

[32]How much more do I need to say? It would take too long to recount the stories of the faith of Gideon, Barak, Samson, Jephthah, David, Samuel, and all the prophets. [33]By faith these people overthrew kingdoms, ruled with justice, and received what God had promised them. They shut the mouths of lions, [34]quenched the flames of fire, and escaped death by the edge of the sword. Their weakness was turned to strength. They became strong in battle and put whole armies to flight. [35]Women received their loved ones back again from death.

But others were tortured, refusing to turn from God in order to be set free. They placed their hope in a better life after the resurrec-tion. [36]Some were jeered at, and their backs were cut open with whips. Others were chained in prisons. [37]Some died by stoning, some were sawed in half,* and others were killed with the sword. Some went about wearing skins of sheep and goats, destitute and oppressed and mistreated. [38]They were too good for this world, wandering over deserts and mountains, hiding in caves and holes in the ground.

[39]All these people earned a good reputation because of their faith, yet none of them received all that God had promised. [40]For God had something better in mind for us, so that they would not reach perfection without us.

CHAPTER 12
God's Discipline Proves His Love

Therefore, since we are surrounded by such a huge crowd of witnesses to the life of faith, let us strip off every weight that slows us down, especially the sin that so easily trips us up. And let us run with endurance the race God has set before us. [2]We do this by keeping our eyes on Jesus, the champion who initiates and perfects our faith.* Because of the joy* awaiting him, he endured the cross, disregarding its shame. Now he is seated in the place of honor beside God's throne. [3]Think of all the hostility he endured from sinful people;* then you won't become weary and give up. [4]After all, you have not yet given your lives in your struggle against sin.

[5]And have you forgotten the encouraging words God spoke to you as his children?* He said,

11:37 Some manuscripts add *some were tested.* 12:2a Or *Jesus, the originator and perfecter of our faith.* 12:2b Or *Instead of the joy.* 12:3 Some manuscripts read *Think of how people hurt themselves by opposing him.* 12:5a Greek *sons;* also in 12:7, 8.

11:32-39 The writer continues the list of Old Testament people who demonstrated powerful faith and received God's approval. Clearly, even in Old Testament times faith was not just a strict obedience to Mosaic law; it was heartfelt trust in a personal God. The readers would know that many before them had faced difficult times and persevered by faith. When we feel our faith faltering, it is good to remember others who have gone before us. We can turn both to the Bible and to other Christians in recovery for real-life testimonies of how God works powerfully through faith.

12:14-29 This is the last of the "warnings" throughout Hebrews (see 2:1-4; 3:7–4:13; 5:11–6:12; 10:26-39). In effect, the writer was confronting his readers about their apparent defection from Christ to Judaism and the Mosaic law. After exhorting the readers not to squander God's grace, the writer considers the serious consequences of rejecting faith in Christ and the recovery he offers. Our choices have eternal consequences! If we reject Christ, we also reject the only means for eternal salvation and recovery from our destructive dependency.

12:15 When we deal with difficult circumstances or face painful recovery issues, we may grow angry or bitter. Sometimes we don't perceive our own bitterness taking root; we need others to point it out to us. The feelings are understandable, especially if we have been victimized; allowing ourself to feel them can be a first step in recovery. But we need to forgive and to release the injustices and hurts to God in order to experience his overwhelming forgiveness (see Matthew 18:21-35). When we hang on to our bitterness, we not only hinder our own healing but also hurt others along the way.

"My child,* don't make light of the
LORD's discipline,
and don't give up when he corrects
you.
⁶For the LORD disciplines those he loves,
and he punishes each one he accepts as
his child."*

⁷As you endure this divine discipline, remember that God is treating you as his own children. Who ever heard of a child who is never disciplined by its father? ⁸If God doesn't discipline you as he does all of his children, it means that you are illegitimate and are not really his children at all. ⁹Since we respected our earthly fathers who disciplined us, shouldn't we submit even more to the discipline of the Father of our spirits, and live forever?*

¹⁰For our earthly fathers disciplined us for a few years, doing the best they knew how. But God's discipline is always good for us, so that we might share in his holiness. ¹¹No discipline is enjoyable while it is happening—it's painful! But afterward there will be a peaceful harvest of right living for those who are trained in this way.

¹²So take a new grip with your tired hands and strengthen your weak knees. ¹³Mark out a straight path for your feet so that those who are weak and lame will not fall but become strong.

A Call to Listen to God

¹⁴Work at living in peace with everyone, and work at living a holy life, for those who are not holy will not see the Lord. ¹⁵Look after each other so that none of you fails to receive the grace of God. Watch out that no poisonous root of bitterness grows up to trouble you, corrupting many. ¹⁶Make sure that no one is immoral or godless like Esau, who traded his birthright as the firstborn son for a single meal. ¹⁷You know that afterward, when he wanted his father's blessing, he was rejected. It was too late for repentance, even though he begged with bitter tears.

¹⁸You have not come to a physical mountain,* to a place of flaming fire, darkness, gloom, and whirlwind, as the Israelites did at Mount Sinai. ¹⁹For they heard an awesome trumpet blast and a voice so terrible that they begged God to stop speaking. ²⁰They staggered back under God's command: "If

12:5b Greek *son;* also in 12:6, 7. **12:5-6** Prov 3:11-12 (Greek version). **12:9** Or *and really live?* **12:18** Greek *to something that can be touched.*

FAITH

READ HEBREWS 12:5-11
Some phases of our recovery may be very painful. We may feel that we are being punished for our failures. We may assume that bad things are happening to us because we are bad. And we may even begin to believe that God doesn't love us.

It may hurt when God disciplines us, but this in itself displays his love for us. The Bible says: "'My child, don't make light of the LORD's discipline. . . . For the LORD disciplines those he loves, and he punishes each one he accepts as his child.' As you endure this divine discipline, remember that God is treating you as his own children. Who ever heard of a child who was never disciplined by its father? . . . God's discipline is always good for us, so that we might share in his holiness. No discipline is enjoyable while it is happening—it's painful! But afterward there will be a peaceful harvest of right living for those who are trained in this way" (Hebrews 12:5-7, 10-11).

Recovery is a time of correction, a time of facing problems and character flaws and changing incorrect beliefs. There may be seasons when we do have to pay for our past. God will use these times to redirect our life toward something better. His correction isn't arbitrary or abusive, but it is still painful. Knowing that God's discipline demonstrates his love for us can be comforting in the midst of our pain. It helps to remember that his love will allow only that which is for our ultimate good.
Turn to page 1605, James 3.

even an animal touches the mountain, it must be stoned to death."* ²¹Moses himself was so frightened at the sight that he said, "I am terrified and trembling."*

²²No, you have come to Mount Zion, to the city of the living God, the heavenly Jerusalem, and to countless thousands of angels in a joyful gathering. ²³You have come to the assembly of God's firstborn children, whose names are written in heaven. You have come to God himself, who is the judge over all things. You have come to the spirits of the righteous ones in heaven who have now been made perfect. ²⁴You have come to Jesus, the one who mediates the new covenant between God and people, and to the sprinkled blood, which speaks of forgiveness instead of crying out for vengeance like the blood of Abel.

²⁵Be careful that you do not refuse to listen to the One who is speaking. For if the people of Israel did not escape when they refused to listen to Moses, the earthly messenger, we will certainly not escape if we reject the One who speaks to us from heaven! ²⁶When God spoke from Mount Sinai his voice shook the earth, but now he makes another promise: "Once again I will shake not only the earth but the heavens also."* ²⁷This means that all of creation will be shaken and removed, so that only unshakable things will remain.

²⁸Since we are receiving a Kingdom that is unshakable, let us be thankful and please God by worshiping him with holy fear and awe. ²⁹For our God is a devouring fire.

CHAPTER 13
Concluding Words

Keep on loving each other as brothers and sisters.* ²Don't forget to show hospitality to strangers, for some who have done this have entertained angels without realizing it! ³Remember those in prison, as if you were there yourself. Remember also those being mistreated, as if you felt their pain in your own bodies.

⁴Give honor to marriage, and remain faithful to one another in marriage. God will surely judge people who are immoral and those who commit adultery.

⁵Don't love money; be satisfied with what you have. For God has said,

"I will never fail you.
I will never abandon you."*

⁶So we can say with confidence,

"The LORD is my helper,
so I will have no fear.
What can mere people do to me?"*

⁷Remember your leaders who taught you the word of God. Think of all the good that has come from their lives, and follow the example of their faith.

⁸Jesus Christ is the same yesterday, today, and forever. ⁹So do not be attracted by strange, new ideas. Your strength comes from God's grace, not from rules about food, which don't help those who follow them.

¹⁰We have an altar from which the priests in the Tabernacle* have no right to eat. ¹¹Un-

12:20 Exod 19:13. 12:21 Deut 9:19. 12:26 Hag 2:6. 13:1 Greek *Continue in brotherly love.* 13:5 Deut 31:6, 8. 13:6 Ps 118:6. 13:10 Or *tent.*

12:22-24 There is a wonderful reward waiting for those who, by faith in Christ, have endured in the recovery process. The references to Mount Zion, Jerusalem, angels, the firstborn, God, mediation, and blood were intended to show that the new covenant and Christ offer the very things that the readers mistakenly sought by returning to Judaism. Again we see that full spiritual recovery is available only through faith in Jesus Christ.

13:1-6 The writer lists practical commands for faithfulness in service to others—to strangers, prisoners, those who are suffering, and to our spouse. We are also warned about the love of money. Perhaps the readers were seriously struggling in these areas, even as many professing believers struggle today. Many of us with a dysfunctional background struggle to determine which behaviors and attitudes are acceptable; God's clear standards can guide us. We can be confident that God's presence and power are available to help us practice right living.

13:7, 17 Many of us in recovery may have difficulty dealing with authority figures. Apparently the readers of Hebrews, in returning to Judaism, were ignoring their spiritual leaders. So the writer admonished his readers to imitate the faith and lifestyle of their leaders and to obey them and not cause them sorrow. In our recovery work, let us remember the importance of leaders in our life, especially those who model godliness and are concerned about our spiritual growth.

13:8, 15-16 Even if our human leaders were to fail or be abusive, Jesus Christ is totally consistent and trustworthy. He will always be there for us, no matter what. As that kind of God and friend, Christ deserves to receive the new covenant equivalent of old covenant sacrifices: (1) praise for who he is and what he has done; (2) good works of service; and (3) sharing with others in need

der the old system, the high priest brought the blood of animals into the Holy Place as a sacrifice for sin, and the bodies of the animals were burned outside the camp. [12]So also Jesus suffered and died outside the city gates to make his people holy by means of his own blood. [13]So let us go out to him, outside the camp, and bear the disgrace he bore. [14]For this world is not our permanent home; we are looking forward to a home yet to come.

[15]Therefore, let us offer through Jesus a continual sacrifice of praise to God, proclaiming our allegiance to his name. [16]And don't forget to do good and to share with those in need. These are the sacrifices that please God.

[17]Obey your spiritual leaders, and do what they say. Their work is to watch over your souls, and they are accountable to God. Give them reason to do this with joy and not with sorrow. That would certainly not be for your benefit.

[18]Pray for us, for our conscience is clear and we want to live honorably in everything we do. [19]And especially pray that I will be able to come back to you soon.

[20]Now may the God of peace—
who brought up from the dead our
Lord Jesus,
the great Shepherd of the sheep,
and ratified an eternal covenant with
his blood—
[21]may he equip you with all you need
for doing his will.
May he produce in you,*
through the power of Jesus Christ,
every good thing that is pleasing
to him.
All glory to him forever and ever!
Amen.

[22]I urge you, dear brothers and sisters,* to pay attention to what I have written in this brief exhortation.

[23]I want you to know that our brother Timothy has been released from jail. If he comes here soon, I will bring him with me to see you.

[24]Greet all your leaders and all the believers there.* The believers from Italy send you their greetings.

[25]May God's grace be with you all.

13:21 Some manuscripts read *in us.* **13:22** Greek *brothers.* **13:24** Greek *all of God's holy people.*

(see 13:2-3). These activities all support an essential step in our ongoing recovery—telling others what God has done in our life and reaching out to people in need.

13:20-25 The letter to the Hebrews concludes with a double benediction. The first is a summary prayer, asking for the power of Christ's resurrection to enable the readers to do God's will and please him. Unlike some human fathers, God the Father readily helps his children to succeed by equipping them to do his will. This leads beautifully to the final concept of the letter—grace. God will provide us with what we need to overcome our dependency, according to his grace and mercy.

REFLECTIONS ON HEBREWS

insights ABOUT THE PERSON OF CHRIST

Hebrews 1:7-13 quotes from several messianic psalms, showing that even though angels are powerful spirits, Christ's power and glory are far greater because of: Christ's clear right to rule as messianic King; his power over Creation and the final re-creation when it occurs; and his current status of honor beside the Father. Christ can provide all the resources necessary for our recovery when we entrust our life to his greatness and his loving plan for us.

It would be terrifying to admit our failures to a perfect God if Jesus wasn't our High Priest. But we see in **Hebrews 4:14–5:3** that Jesus became a man and is able to deal gently with our weaknesses because he understands our problems. Unlike the human priests, Jesus Christ, the ultimate High Priest, has already been glorified in heaven. He suffered the same temptations we do, but did not sin; yet he became the sacrifice for the sins of the world. That combination of glory and understanding beckons us to pray confidently and continually for God's grace and mercy. The first steps in recovery involve admitting powerlessness over our problems, acknowledging that only God can restore us, and turning our will and life over to God. **Hebrews 4:14-16** gives us the scriptural confidence that as we work those steps, God can and will give us the mercy and grace we need.

insights ABOUT ANGELS

Although Jesus is far superior to the angels, in **Hebrews 1:14** we are also told that angels are involved in helping God's people. Angels are God's servants who constantly serve and protect those who have already entered the process of recovery through faith in Christ. We may also interpret this verse to mean that God's "guardian angels" are somehow watching over all those who will yet receive salvation by faith.

insights ABOUT GOD'S TRANSFORMING POWER

In **Hebrews 2:4** the power of God to confirm the message of salvation through "signs and wonders" is tremendously impressive. In the apostles' generation (see 2 Corinthians 12:12), which was drawing to a close, miracles were more the rule in the newborn church than the exception. Though miraculous healings and immediate transformations may still happen today, it seems more likely that recovery is often a long process, even for committed believers with great faith. Nevertheless, the signs and wonders God demonstrated in the past remind us that he still works just as powerfully, though perhaps in different ways. The "gifts of the Holy Spirit" God assigns to us may have more to do with perseverance or a new ability to resist temptation, but they are no less miraculous than an immediate healing by God.

insights ABOUT ACCOUNTABILITY AND RESPONSIBILITY

Most of **Hebrews 3:7-13** is a paraphrase of Psalm 95:7-11. The writer was reminding his Jewish audience of the mistakes their ancestors had made, recalling how they had been unfaithful to God and had suffered the painful consequences. The writer used past events to show his readers that they would be held accountable to live out their faith in whatever context God placed them. Most recovery programs incorporate this kind of accountability through such things as attending meetings and working with sponsors. These verses underline the importance of such measures, especially obeying the living God, to whom we are most accountable.

In **Hebrews 3:14-19** the writer confirms the need to act immediately as well as the necessity to accept full responsibility for wrong actions. The urgency to act immediately is underlined here by the emphasis on "today" in Psalm 95:7. The importance of taking responsibility becomes clear as we see that the Israelites truly had no one to blame but themselves for their sojourn in the wilderness. Acting immediately and taking responsibility for our life are both crucial aspects of the recovery process.

insights ABOUT TRUE FAITH

In **Hebrews 11:1-3, 39-40** we find that faith blends our trust in the dependability of God working in the unseen spiritual realm and our reliance upon the evidence of God's past actions in the real world. Those who want a vibrant spiritual life must live by such faith (11:2). Amazingly, by trusting and obeying God, we can still make a place for ourself in the "Hall of Faith." The day of induction is still in the future! Seeking approval from other people is a constant battle for some of us in recovery. We need to remember that we cannot please everyone. We will make progress only when we stop trying to please others and put our trust in God, following his will for our life.

Hebrews 12:1-3 shows us that many "witnesses," including some very unlikely candidates, have already "won" the race of faith along the rocky road of recovery. The author of Hebrews advises us to strip off our weights and sins that hinder us—chemical dependencies, immoral sex, unbalanced work habits, even false religious activities—and focus on Christ every step of the way, knowing that Jesus suffered a shameful death for us and emerged victorious (see 4:14-15). Such perseverance in faith can help us face the reality of delayed gratification and prevent burnout in recovery.

insights ABOUT GOD'S DISCIPLINE

We are reminded in **Hebrews 12:5-10** that true discipline is a form of loving correction, not hateful destruction. Many of us have suffered painful consequences because of our dependency. We may have become angry and wondered why God allowed us to suffer so deeply. Often, painful consequences are used by God for discipline. But God does not allow us to suffer because he wants revenge or he wants to destroy us. He allows us to suffer because he loves us. Sometimes harsh discipline is the only way to break through our denial and get us into recovery. As we look back, we can realize that our most painful days led to our first steps in recovery. Through the pain we realized how powerless we were and turned to God for help. By allowing us to suffer, God was leading us into a vital relationship with himself.

JAMES

THE BIG PICTURE

A. WISDOM: THE FOUNDA-
   TION OF RECOVERY (1:1-27)
B. FAITH: THE SUBSTANCE OF
   RECOVERY (2:1-26)
C. SELF-CONTROL: SETTING
   BOUNDARIES IN RECOVERY
   (3:1-18)
D. HUMILITY: THE ATTITUDE OF
   RECOVERY (4:1-17)
E. GIVING OF OURSELF: THE
   EVIDENCE OF RECOVERY
   (5:1-20)

When we think of hypocrisy, we tend to think of those who overtly live inconsistent lives, people who live in constant denial. Yet in one way or another we are all hypocrites at times. This is true in the church community as well as in our recovery group. We have all said that we believe in something, only to prove by our actions that we really don't!

James—the half brother of Jesus and one of the leaders of the Jerusalem church—wrote bluntly against hypocrisy. He recognized that being human means that we tend to hear God's Word without putting it into practice. His goal was simple: to get his audience, and all believers, to face their denial and start acting on what they claim to believe.

James challenged his readers to be full of wisdom, faith, forgiveness, self-control, and generosity to others. He encouraged them to not rely on mind games or tricks but to simply do what God asked them to do. If their progress started anywhere, it started with an admission that they were responsible to obey God. Only then could they conquer denial and forge ahead with the activities and attitudes that reflected God's will.

It is easy to buy into a recovery program in principle but never take the steps necessary for progress. James reminds us that just saying we believe God can help us is not enough. We need to show our faith and commitment by taking actual steps of faith. If we don't take active steps toward recovery, we will never move forward in the process.

THE BOTTOM LINE

PURPOSE: To show God's people how to live. AUTHOR: James, the half brother of Jesus. AUDIENCE: Probably primarily the Jewish believers living in Gentile communities outside of Palestine. DATE WRITTEN: This short letter was probably written between A.D. 44 and A.D. 49, before the Jerusalem Council held in A.D. 50 (Acts 15:1-35). SETTING: James wrote to the persecuted believers who were once part of the church in Jerusalem. He wanted to encourage them to live out their faith in everyday life. KEY VERSE: "Confess your sins to each other and pray for each other so that you may be healed" (5:16). KEY PEOPLE AND RELATIONSHIPS: James with his audience.

RECOVERY THEMES

The Importance of Action: If faith can be alive, it can also be dead. Dead faith is belief that does not prove itself in action. It claims to be something when it is not. Turning our life over to God always involves action. If we simply say that we have entrusted our life to God but do not make amends to others or confess our wrongs, then we are only fooling ourself. Effective recovery involves following through on our profession of faith and good intentions.

Gaining Strength from Hard Trials: Strength of character comes from patiently facing life's problems. Since most of us try to avoid our problems, how can we develop strength of character? We can learn to welcome trials and problems as opportunities to pray for wisdom, to ask God to give us patience, and to learn to depend on him. When we turn to God in times of trial, he can teach us the lessons we need to grow spiritually and make progress in recovery.

True Recovery Leads to Wise Speech: One of the hardest things for us to control is our tongue (1:26). James gives us very practical advice about how to handle our tongue. We are to ask God for wisdom, be slow to speak, and listen more than we talk. Since our speech is a reflection of what is in our heart, we can check our speech for clues to our inner strengths and weaknesses. As we take our personal inventory and confess our sins to God, he will begin to change us inside. Only then will we find our inner change reflected in our words.

CHAPTER 1

Greetings from James

This letter is from James, a slave of God and of the Lord Jesus Christ.

I am writing to the "twelve tribes"—Jewish believers scattered abroad.

Greetings!

Faith and Endurance

[2] Dear brothers and sisters,* when troubles of any kind come your way, consider it an opportunity for great joy. [3] For you know that when your faith is tested, your endurance has a chance to grow. [4] So let it grow, for when your endurance is fully developed, you will be perfect and complete, needing nothing.

[5] If you need wisdom, ask our generous God, and he will give it to you. He will not rebuke you for asking. [6] But when you ask him, be sure that your faith is in God alone. Do not waver, for a person with divided loyalty is as unsettled as a wave of the sea that is blown and tossed by the wind. [7] Such people should not expect to receive anything from the Lord. [8] Their loyalty is divided between God and the world, and they are unstable in everything they do.

[9] Believers who are* poor have something

1:2 Greek *brothers;* also in 1:16, 19. 1:9 Greek *The brother who is.*

1:2-4 Difficulties and temptations are facts of life for everyone, particularly those of us with a background of addiction, abuse, or other dysfunction. We may be tempted to return to our destructive behaviors. As we face difficult times, though, our attitude can make all the difference. James tells us to be happy as we face difficulties and temptations. This is hardly a natural reaction to a painful situation. Seeing our trials as building blocks to God's work in our life, however, may help us change our negative attitude toward tough times. We can have joy during these trials because through them we learn patience, an essential ingredient for successful recovery.

1:5 How many times have we scolded ourself for making unwise decisions? All of us have made wrong choices that have led us into trouble, ultimately affecting our relationship with God and with others. When we ask God for wisdom, he is more than willing to give it. Since God is the source of all wisdom, we can make fewer unwise decisions by turning to him for guidance. In recovery we are told to improve our conscious contact with God so we can better know his will for us. This can be achieved by studying God's Word and praying regularly.

1:19-20 Who or what is in control of our life? Is it God? Is it other people? Is it a controlling dependency or compulsion or an overpowering emotion? The issue of control is vital to our spiritual growth and recovery. For some of us, the emotion of anger is overpowering. James advises us to listen before we speak, to have self-control, and to be patient, not letting anger control our actions in any situation. We may be angry over our past as well as over current events. To control our anger, we need to give our life over to God. Even when we feel out of control, he can help us maintain our composure. He can give us the strength and wisdom to think and listen before we speak or act.

to boast about, for God has honored them. ¹⁰And those who are rich should boast that God has humbled them. They will fade away like a little flower in the field. ¹¹The hot sun rises and the grass withers; the little flower droops and falls, and its beauty fades away. In the same way, the rich will fade away with all of their achievements.

¹²God blesses those who patiently endure testing and temptation. Afterward they will receive the crown of life that God has promised to those who love him. ¹³And remember, when you are being tempted, do not say, "God is tempting me." God is never tempted to do wrong,* and he never tempts anyone else. ¹⁴Temptation comes from our own desires, which entice us and drag us away. ¹⁵These desires give birth to sinful actions. And when sin is allowed to grow, it gives birth to death.

¹⁶So don't be misled, my dear brothers and sisters. ¹⁷Whatever is good and perfect is a gift coming down to us from God our Father, who created all the lights in the heavens.* He never changes or casts a shifting shadow.* ¹⁸He chose to give birth to us by giving us his true word. And we, out of all creation, became his prized possession.*

Listening and Doing

¹⁹Understand this, my dear brothers and sisters: You must all be quick to listen, slow to speak, and slow to get angry. ²⁰Human anger* does not produce the righteousness* God desires. ²¹So get rid of all the filth and evil in your lives, and humbly accept the word God has planted in your hearts, for it has the power to save your souls.

²²But don't just listen to God's word. You must do what it says. Otherwise, you are only fooling yourselves. ²³For if you listen to the word and don't obey, it is like glancing at your face in a mirror. ²⁴You see yourself, walk away, and forget what you look like. ²⁵But if you look carefully into the perfect law that sets you free, and if you do what it says and don't forget what you heard, then God will bless you for doing it.

²⁶If you claim to be religious but don't control your tongue, you are fooling yourself, and your religion is worthless. ²⁷Pure and genuine religion in the sight of God the Father means caring for orphans and widows in their distress and refusing to let the world corrupt you.

1:13 Or *God should not be put to a test by evil people.*
1:17a Greek *from above, from the Father of lights.*
1:17b Some manuscripts read *He never changes, as a shifting shadow does.* 1:18 Greek *we became a kind of firstfruit of his creatures.* 1:20a Greek *A man's anger.*
1:20b Or *the justice.*

STEP 10

Looking in the Mirror

BIBLE READING: James 1:21-25

We continued to take personal inventory and when we were wrong promptly admitted it.

How many times do we look in the mirror each day? Suppose we looked in the mirror and found that we had mustard smeared around our mouth. Wouldn't we immediately wash our face and clean up the problem? In the same way, we need to routinely look at ourself in our "spiritual mirror," the Bible. Then if anything is wrong, we can take the proper steps to fix it.

James uses a similar illustration to show how God's Word should be like a spiritual mirror in our life. He said: "But don't just listen to God's word. You must do what it says. Otherwise, you are only fooling yourselves. For if you listen to the word and don't obey, it is like glancing at your face in a mirror. You see yourself, walk away, and forget what you look like. But if you look carefully into the perfect law that sets you free, and if you do what it says and don't forget what you heard, then God will bless you for doing it" (James 1:22-25).

This illustration supports the sensibleness of making a routine personal inventory. As we examine our life, we need to respond with immediate action if something has changed since we last looked. If we put off taking care of a problem, it may soon slip our mind. Just as we would think it foolish to go all day knowing there is mustard on our face, it is not logical to notice a problem that could lead to a fall and not correct it promptly. *Turn to page 1629, 1 John 1.*

CHAPTER 2
A Warning against Prejudice

My dear brothers and sisters,* how can you claim to have faith in our glorious Lord Jesus Christ if you favor some people over others?

[2]For example, suppose someone comes into your meeting* dressed in fancy clothes and expensive jewelry, and another comes in who is poor and dressed in dirty clothes. [3]If you give special attention and a good seat to the rich person, but you say to the poor one, "You can stand over there, or else sit on the floor"—well, [4]doesn't this discrimination show that your judgments are guided by evil motives?

[5]Listen to me, dear brothers and sisters. Hasn't God chosen the poor in this world to be rich in faith? Aren't they the ones who will inherit the Kingdom he promised to those who love him? [6]But you dishonor the poor! Isn't it the rich who oppress you and drag you into court? [7]Aren't they the ones who slander Jesus Christ, whose noble name* you bear?

[8]Yes indeed, it is good when you obey the royal law as found in the Scriptures: "Love your neighbor as yourself."* [9]But if you favor some people over others, you are committing a sin. You are guilty of breaking the law.

[10]For the person who keeps all of the laws except one is as guilty as a person who has broken all of God's laws. [11]For the same God who said, "You must not commit adultery," also said, "You must not murder."* So if you murder someone but do not commit adultery, you have still broken the law.

[12]So whatever you say or whatever you do, remember that you will be judged by the law that sets you free. [13]There will be no mercy for those who have not shown mercy to others. But if you have been merciful, God will be merciful when he judges you.

Faith without Good Deeds Is Dead

[14]What good is it, dear brothers and sisters, if you say you have faith but don't show it by your actions? Can that kind of faith save anyone? [15]Suppose you see a brother or sister who has no food or clothing, [16]and you say, "Good-bye and have a good day; stay warm and eat well"—but then you don't give that person any food or clothing. What good does that do?

[17]So you see, faith by itself isn't enough. Unless it produces good deeds, it is dead and useless.

[18]Now someone may argue, "Some people have faith; others have good deeds." But I say, "How can you show me your faith if you don't have good deeds? I will show you my faith by my good deeds."

[19]You say you have faith, for you believe that there is one God.* Good for you! Even the demons believe this, and they tremble in terror. [20]How foolish! Can't you see that faith without good deeds is useless?

[21]Don't you remember that our ancestor Abraham was shown to be right with God by his actions when he offered his son Isaac on the altar? [22]You see, his faith and his actions worked together. His actions made his

---

2:1 Greek *brothers;* also in 2:5, 14. 2:2 Greek *your synagogue.* 2:7 Greek *slander the noble name.* 2:8 Lev 19:18.
2:11 Exod 20:13-14; Deut 5:17-18. 2:19 Some manuscripts read *that God is one;* see Deut 6:4.

2:1-9 Since participation in recovery may lead to rejection by others, the process can be painful. Old friends may reject us for trying to escape our bondage. Sometimes a Christian community or society at large may reject us, treating us like unworthy outcasts because of their prejudice. We all need acceptance. Jesus intended for the Christian community to graciously accept and love people whether they are wealthy and influential or poor and homeless. We need to welcome outcasts who are honestly struggling with their problems. Jesus calls us to treat others just as we want them to treat us (see Matthew 7:12).

2:14-26 Faith, the cornerstone of recovery, needs to be accompanied by action. Some of us may have found it easy to admit we needed God's help, but when called upon to actively prove our faith, we refused. We all have made commitments that we failed to back up with our actions. James left us this powerful reminder: "Faith by itself isn't enough. Unless it produces good deeds, it is dead and useless" (2:17). If we believe in the principles of recovery but refuse to act upon them, we are not in recovery. If we believe God can help us but refuse to obey his will, we prove that our faith is dead. True faith in God expresses itself in committed actions; our actions need to back up our words if we want to succeed in recovery.

3:1-2 James was deeply aware of the destructive power of words. We all are guilty of offending others by our words or actions. When we offend someone, we need to ask forgiveness and make amends for the wrongs we have committed. This is an essential part of the recovery process. Sometimes a quiet change of behavior can be the most effective way to make amends. By treating others with respect, we can slowly rebuild the trust we have destroyed. As we follow God's program for healthy living, we can learn to encourage, instead of offend, others with our words and deeds.

JAMES & JUDE

It is difficult to live up to the high standards set by older brothers and sisters. It can be equally difficult, and sometimes more painful, to live down the embarrassing reputation of an older sibling. James and Jude had to deal with both challenges. Their older half brother, Jesus, was both perfect and embarrassing.

It is probable that Mary, their mother, had always told James and Jude that Jesus was unique. But it is doubtful that they had any idea just how special Jesus was. One thing is certain: Jesus must have been a hard act to follow. It must have been difficult for James, Jude, and the rest of their siblings to feel close to their wonderful, though different, big half brother. The situation probably became even worse after their father, Joseph, died. As the oldest child, Jesus probably had to take on the role of substitute dad.

After Jesus' public ministry began, James and Jude took a stand-back-and-watch attitude. One day Jesus would do great miracles and be acclaimed as a hero. The next he would present a convicting message and offend the powerful religious and political authorities. He claimed to be not only the promised Messiah, but also God himself! At this point, James and Jude probably thought that their half brother had gone off the deep end. In the end, Jesus was sentenced to death.

James and Jude had lost their father, Joseph, when they were young. Now they had lost their famous, though embarrassing, older sibling. Could the family recover? The resurrection of Jesus brought the resounding answer: *yes!* After Jesus rose from the dead, he overcame the doubts of his younger half brothers who later became leaders in the early church. Their relationships with Jesus had been restored. Both brothers are remembered for the books in the Bible they wrote.

The transforming power of Christ's resurrection is still available to us today. As we read of the painful trial and death of Jesus, we see God's loving sacrifice on our behalf. As we claim his resurrection and experience its power in our life, we discover that the power that transformed James and Jude can transform us, too.

STRENGTHS AND ACCOMPLISHMENTS:
- James and Jude apparently wanted to understand and know Jesus.
- Both grew beyond the relational problems that surely existed in their family.
- Both became effective leaders and writers.

WEAKNESSES AND MISTAKES:
- James and Jude did not really understand Jesus until after his resurrection.
- They became disillusioned with Jesus' claims when he faced opposition.

LESSONS FROM THEIR LIVES:
- Finding our own identity when following gifted siblings can be painful.
- Even the confused and disillusioned can regain trust and hope.
- Recovery offers hope for restoring broken relationships.

KEY VERSE:
[Jesus said,] "Anyone who does the will of my Father in heaven is my brother and sister and mother!" (Matthew 12:50).

James and Jude are named or alluded to in the Gospels and Acts 1:14. James is mentioned in Acts 15; 21; Galatians 2; the book of James; and Jude 1:1. Jude's name is found in Jude 1:1.

---

faith complete. ²³And so it happened just as the Scriptures say: "Abraham believed God, and God counted him as righteous because of his faith."* He was even called the friend of God.* ²⁴So you see, we are shown to be right with God by what we do, not by faith alone.

²⁵Rahab the prostitute is another example. She was shown to be right with God by her actions when she hid those messengers and sent them safely away by a different road. ²⁶Just as the body is dead without breath,* so also faith is dead without good works.

CHAPTER 3
Controlling the Tongue
Dear brothers and sisters,* not many of you should become teachers in the church, for we who teach will be judged more strictly.

2:23a Gen 15:6. 2:23b See Isa 41:8. 2:26 Or *without spirit.* 3:1 Greek *brothers;* also in 3:10.

²Indeed, we all make many mistakes. For if we could control our tongues, we would be perfect and could also control ourselves in every other way.

³We can make a large horse go wherever we want by means of a small bit in its mouth. ⁴And a small rudder makes a huge ship turn wherever the pilot chooses to go, even though the winds are strong. ⁵In the same way, the tongue is a small thing that makes grand speeches.

But a tiny spark can set a great forest on fire. ⁶And among all the parts of the body, the tongue is a flame of fire. It is a whole world of wickedness, corrupting your entire body. It can set your whole life on fire, for it is set on fire by hell itself.*

⁷People can tame all kinds of animals, birds, reptiles, and fish, ⁸but no one can tame the tongue. It is restless and evil, full of deadly poison. ⁹Sometimes it praises our Lord and Father, and sometimes it curses those who have been made in the image of God. ¹⁰And so blessing and cursing come pouring out of the same mouth. Surely, my brothers and sisters, this is not right! ¹¹Does a spring of water bubble out with both fresh water and bitter water? ¹²Does a fig tree produce olives, or a grapevine produce figs? No, and you can't draw fresh water from a salty spring.*

True Wisdom Comes from God

¹³If you are wise and understand God's ways, prove it by living an honorable life, doing good works with the humility that comes from wisdom. ¹⁴But if you are bitterly jealous and there is selfish ambition in your heart, don't cover up the truth with boasting and lying. ¹⁵For jealousy and selfishness are not God's kind of wisdom. Such things are earthly, unspiritual, and demonic. ¹⁶For wherever there is jealousy and selfish ambi-

3:6 Or *for it will burn in hell* (Greek *Gehenna*). 3:12 Greek *from salt.*

3:3-12 The tongue is difficult to control, but what it does is extremely important. Like a rudder that steers a ship or a bit that directs a horse, our tongue does much to control and shape our life. Our speech may have destroyed our relationships, which caused us great pain. Our tongue may be out of control, enslaved to our destructive dependency. If this is so, our recovery must include yielding our tongue to God's control. Even when we feel powerless to control our destructive words, God can still tame our tongue. As he transforms our heart, our words will soon begin to reflect this change. God can then use our words to heal our relationships and encourage others in the recovery process.

3:13-18 Wisdom is essential to recovery. It must, however, be godly wisdom, not earthly wisdom. Earthly wisdom leads to selfishness and pride, invariably causing confusion and strife. True wisdom is based on the knowledge of God. It brings peace and leads to selfless living and faith that works; it never distinguishes between groups of people but treats everyone with respect and love. Godly wisdom allows us to admit our failures and rebuild our life from the ashes of defeat. It frees us from our destructive dependency; it helps us live for others and builds relationships that will support our recovery.

4:1-4 A right relationship with God is essential to the recovery process. Most of us would like to receive the freedom God offers, but we generally make mistakes that hold us back: (1) We try to gain our freedom by working hard. We forget to ask God for help and thus never receive the life that God wants to give us; (2) if we do ask God for help, we ask with wrong motives. We ask for his blessings to satisfy our personal pleasure, ignoring the fact that seeking friendship with the world makes us God's enemies. God wants to give us abundant lives so we can tell others about him. We experience the freedom God offers by drawing close to and asking for his guidance and help.

4:6-10 Most of us have a hard time modeling submission and humility—qualities that are essential to the recovery process because they show dependence on God and a willingness to be guided by him. Satan's pride—and our adoption of it—opposes God's program for healthy and godly living. As many of us know from experience, the way of pride and selfishness only leads to confusion and strife. True contentment comes only when we submit our life to God and his program. As we admit our failures and humbly seek to do God's will, we will draw closer to God. As we draw close to God, the grip of our dependency will weaken, and he will lift us up to rebuild our life.

4:11-12 Many Christian communities are rendered ineffective because of self-righteous criticism. People become critical of anyone who doesn't measure up to their ideals of perfection. Some of us may have experienced this kind of destructive criticism as our addiction became public. Perhaps we even left a church community for that very reason. Sadly, some of us are also guilty of criticizing others. We may look down on people who make slower progress than we do in the recovery process. We must maintain healthy humility. No one is perfect except God; only he is in a position to judge others (see Romans 14:10-12). We need to focus on our own faults, including our tendency to criticize others. If we don't, our recovery is at risk.

tion, there you will find disorder and evil of every kind.

¹⁷But the wisdom from above is first of all pure. It is also peace loving, gentle at all times, and willing to yield to others. It is full of mercy and the fruit of good deeds. It shows no favoritism and is always sincere. ¹⁸And those who are peacemakers will plant seeds of peace and reap a harvest of righteousness.*

CHAPTER 4

Drawing Close to God

What is causing the quarrels and fights among you? Don't they come from the evil desires at war within you? ²You want what you don't have, so you scheme and kill to get it. You are jealous of what others have, but you can't get it, so you fight and wage war to take it away from them. Yet you don't have what you want because you don't ask God for it. ³And even when you ask, you don't get it because your motives are all wrong—you want only what will give you pleasure.

⁴You adulterers!* Don't you realize that friendship with the world makes you an enemy of God? I say it again: If you want to be a friend of the world, you make yourself an enemy of God. ⁵Do you think the Scriptures have no meaning? They say that God is passionate that the spirit he has placed within us should be faithful to him. * ⁶And he gives grace generously. As the Scriptures say,

"God opposes the proud
    but gives grace to the humble."*

⁷So humble yourselves before God. Resist the devil, and he will flee from you. ⁸Come close to God, and God will come close to you. Wash your hands, you sinners; purify your hearts, for your loyalty is divided between God and the world. ⁹Let there be tears for what you have done. Let there be sorrow and deep grief. Let there be sadness instead of laughter, and gloom instead of joy. ¹⁰Humble yourselves before the Lord, and he will lift you up in honor.

Warning against Judging Others

¹¹Don't speak evil against each other, dear brothers and sisters.* If you criticize and judge each other, then you are criticizing and judging God's law. But your job is to

3:18 Or *of good things,* or *of justice.* 4:4 Greek *You adulteresses!* 4:5 Or *They say that the spirit God has placed within us is filled with envy;* or *They say that the Holy Spirit, whom God has placed within us, opposes our envy.* 4:6 Prov 3:34 (Greek version). 4:11 Greek *brothers.*

WISDOM

READ JAMES 3:13-18
When we get caught up in catering to our addiction, it is almost like we are two different people—as if there are two of us tied up together. The Bible recognizes this dual nature in each of us. One part yearns for good, and the other part is drawn toward corrupt desires and animal passions. The Bible describes a kind of "worldly" wisdom that justifies destructive behavior and leads to disorder, instability, and confusion.

We need to beware of this type of wisdom, which is characterized by jealousy and selfishness. James wrote: "For jealousy and selfishness are not God's kind of wisdom. Such things are earthly, unspiritual, and demonic. For wherever there is jealousy and selfish ambition, there you will find disorder and evil of every kind" (James 3:15-16).

This kind of thinking causes us to focus on what others are and have. It makes us envy others so much that we are always dissatisfied. It is easy to become so consumed by our own desires that we become inconsiderate of others, often hurting the people we love. This type of wisdom is inspired by the Devil and will lead to our ultimate destruction, since Satan's "purpose is to steal and kill and destroy" (John 10:10).

If our thoughts are still dominated by jealousy and selfishness, we need to ask God to replace our earthly wisdom with his godly wisdom. We can trust him to change our mind and our life. ***Turn to page 1611, 1 Peter 1.***

obey the law, not to judge whether it applies to you. [12]God alone, who gave the law, is the Judge. He alone has the power to save or to destroy. So what right do you have to judge your neighbor?

Warning about Self-Confidence

[13]Look here, you who say, "Today or tomorrow we are going to a certain town and will stay there a year. We will do business there and make a profit." [14]How do you know what your life will be like tomorrow? Your life is like the morning fog—it's here a little while, then it's gone. [15]What you ought to say is, "If the Lord wants us to, we will live and do this or that." [16]Otherwise you are boasting about your own pretentious plans, and all such boasting is evil.

[17]Remember, it is sin to know what you ought to do and then not do it.

CHAPTER 5
Warning to the Rich

Look here, you rich people: Weep and groan with anguish because of all the terrible troubles ahead of you. [2]Your wealth is rotting away, and your fine clothes are moth-eaten rags. [3]Your gold and silver are corroded. The very wealth you were counting on will eat away your flesh like fire. This corroded treasure you have hoarded will testify against you on the day of judgment. [4]For listen! Hear the cries of the field workers whom you have cheated of their pay. The cries of those who harvest your fields have reached the ears of the LORD of Heaven's Armies.

[5]You have spent your years on earth in luxury, satisfying your every desire. You have fattened yourselves for the day of slaughter. [6]You have condemned and killed innocent people,* who do not resist you.*

Patience and Endurance

[7]Dear brothers and sisters,* be patient as you wait for the Lord's return. Consider the farmers who patiently wait for the rains in the fall and in the spring. They eagerly look for the valuable harvest to ripen. [8]You, too, must be patient. Take courage, for the coming of the Lord is near.

[9]Don't grumble about each other, brothers and sisters, or you will be judged. For look—the Judge is standing at the door!

[10]For examples of patience in suffering, dear brothers and sisters, look at the prophets who spoke in the name of the Lord. [11]We give great honor to those who endure under suffering. For instance, you know about Job, a man of great endurance. You can see how the Lord was kind to him at the end, for the Lord is full of tenderness and mercy.

[12]But most of all, my brothers and sisters, never take an oath, by heaven or earth or anything else. Just say a simple yes or no, so that you will not sin and be condemned.

The Power of Prayer

[13]Are any of you suffering hardships? You should pray. Are any of you happy? You

5:6a Or *killed the Righteous One.* 5:6b Or *Don't they resist you?* or *Doesn't God oppose you?* or *Aren't they now accusing you before God?* 5:7 Greek *brothers;* also in 5:9, 10, 12, 19.

5:1-5 Some of us may wonder why we have to give up our pursuit of pleasure. Often people living for wealth and pleasure seem to be happier than we are. James reminded his audience that a selfish lifestyle inevitably leads to painful consequences. Some of us have already experienced the pain and emptiness brought on by selfish pleasures. A selfish lifestyle never yields lasting joy and peace; it always leads to some kind of bondage. When we make God's will our own and follow his program, we experience freedom and become a blessing to others.
5:7-11 We have all probably asked ourself this question: Why are these terrible things happening to me? This question might become especially urgent after we have entered the recovery process. We may recognize that God used our sufferings to get us started in our program, but why does he allow suffering to continue? Recovery is a painful, lifelong process. Just as our addiction didn't appear overnight, recovery will also take time. We need to learn patience as we take small steps forward, planting the seeds that will yield a harvest of healing and restoration. God will nurture the seeds we have planted, transforming our life from the inside.
5:13-15 Since God has the power to heal us spiritually, emotionally, and physically, prayer is one of the most powerful tools available to us in recovery. When we pray to God, we call upon that power and display our faith that he can help us. Prayer is essential in the process of putting our broken life into God's caring and capable hands. He is more than able to help us and guide us to blessings and peace. When our life seems out of control and we are in despair, we can begin the healing process by bringing our problems to God. He is listening, and he has the power to rebuild even the most shattered life.

should sing praises. ¹⁴Are any of you sick? You should call for the elders of the church to come and pray over you, anointing you with oil in the name of the Lord. ¹⁵Such a prayer offered in faith will heal the sick, and the Lord will make you well. And if you have committed any sins, you will be forgiven.

¹⁶Confess your sins to each other and pray for each other so that you may be healed. The earnest prayer of a righteous person has great power and produces wonderful results. ¹⁷Elijah was as human as we are, and yet when he prayed earnestly that no rain would fall, none fell for three and a half years! ¹⁸Then, when he prayed again, the sky sent down rain and the earth began to yield its crops.

Restore Wandering Believers

¹⁹My dear brothers and sisters, if someone among you wanders away from the truth and is brought back, ²⁰you can be sure that whoever brings the sinner back from wandering will save that person from death and bring about the forgiveness of many sins.

STEP 3

Single-Minded Devotion

BIBLE READING: James 4:7-10

We made a decision to turn our will and our life over to the care of God.

We may have already chosen to follow God, letting him define the overall direction of our life. Even so, many of us still try to keep parts of our heart hidden from God. We have devoted these parts of ourself to gratifying our addiction, to doing things that are contrary to the will of God. This sets us up for living a double life, which can fill us with guilt, shame, and instability.

Even those of us who have given our heart to God face new temptations and decisions every day. James was addressing believers when he wrote: "So humble yourselves before God. Resist the devil, and he will flee from you. Come close to God, and God will come close to you" (James 4:7-8).

If we choose to live a double life, we may begin to doubt whether God hears us at all. As James wrote: "A person with divided loyalty is as unsettled as a wave of the sea that is blown and tossed by the wind. Such people should not expect to receive anything from the Lord. Their loyalty is divided between God and the world, and they are unstable in everything they do" (James 1:6-8).

When we resist the devil at every turn and draw close to God, he will draw close to us. When we open the hidden portions of our heart and begin to make choices in favor of recovery, we will soon grow confident that God desires to help us. *Turn to Step Four, page 9, Genesis 3.*

REFLECTIONS ON JAMES

insights ABOUT TRUE FAITH

We see in James 1:6-8 that all truly wise decisions are rooted in a vital faith in God. Faith "is the confident assurance that what we hope for is going to happen. It is the evidence of things we cannot yet see" (Hebrews 11:1). God wants us to make progress in recovery. When we ask God to help us make wise decisions, we can do so without any trace of doubt, fully believing that whatever we ask for in faith will be granted. God will supply the wisdom we need to make the right decisions for successful recovery.

insights ABOUT HONEST CONFESSION

As we try to make an honest personal inventory, some of us may have nothing to measure our attitudes or actions against. We may never have had any good role models to follow. In James 1:22-25 we are reminded that God's Word functions like a mirror in our life. As we read it, we are given a clear picture of what God wants us to be like. It shows us where we don't measure up to God's standards and provides a measuring stick for our personal inventory. But James also warns us not to stop after that inventory. We should not look into God's Word only to walk away and forget what we saw there. To make real progress in recovery we need to enlist God's help and take concrete steps to live according to God's Word.

Admitting our faults to God and to a trustworthy person is an essential step in the recovery process. When we share our faults with others, we give them the opportunity to uphold us in prayer. James reminds us in James 5:16-20 that confession is an important part of our personal prayer life. God invites us to confess our sins and failures to him through prayer. When we bring our sins and defects of character before God, he starts the healing process in us. Prayer is never a waste of time; it yields amazing results! God responds powerfully when we display our faith by sharing our problems with him.

1 PETER

THE BIG PICTURE

A. SUFFERING IS A VALUABLE PART OF LIFE (1:1-25)
B. LIVING HONESTLY AS WE WORK AT RELATIONSHIPS (2:1-10)
C. HOW TO LIVE WELL IN A DIFFICULT WORLD (2:11–4:6)
D. THE HOPE OF ULTIMATE RESTORATION (4:7–5:14)

Peter's audience was made up of hurting people. They were suffering persecution from unbelievers in the form of rejection and, in many cases, outright physical abuse. The price they paid for their beliefs included everything from broken relationships to physical pain and rejection.

Peter wrote to encourage them. The wonderful part of his message lay in the perspective he offered his audience. In response to their cries of anguish he did not say, "There must be something wrong with you" or "Pray harder and your problems will go away." Neither did he flippantly promise them an easy road ahead. Instead, he gave them this hope: They belonged to God, and he would never fail them. These words offer the same hope to us.

Most of us would agree that suffering is one of the most difficult parts of life to accept, much less understand. Though we wish we were exempt or cushioned from life's harsh blows, pain is a reality. All of us suffer, and suffering is part of recovery. We must accept the fact that we will hurt from time to time.

God equips us to live at peace in the midst of tough times. We obtain God's powerful help when we hold fast to Christ and live according to his will. This does not mean that our troubles will vanish because we believe in God. Rather, it means that God will surround us with his love when problems seem overwhelming. The way out of the storm is to take comfort in God's presence and persevere through it. As we do, God will use the trials to bring about our growth.

THE BOTTOM LINE

PURPOSE: To show us how to live well in a shattered and hopeless world. AUTHOR: The apostle Peter. AUDIENCE: Jewish Christians who were suffering persecution for their faith. DATE WRITTEN: Around A.D. 64, just prior to Nero's persecutions of the early Christians. SETTING: This letter was written when Peter and other Christians were being tortured and martyred for their faith. The believers faced opposition from both Jewish and secular authorities. KEY VERSE: "For you are free, yet you are God's slaves, so don't use your freedom as an excuse to do evil" (2:16). KEY PEOPLE AND RELATIONSHIPS: Peter with Silas and with John Mark.

RECOVERY THEMES

God's Way Can Be Painful: Part of the reason we may be afraid of recovery is that we know the changes God asks us to make will be painful. There was pain in our old way of life, but we usually found ways to escape it. When we enter the recovery process, we also decide to face our pain head-on. Turning our life over to God, taking moral inventory, making amends, and allowing God to remove our defects are all painful steps. But because they are part of God's plan, they will also lead to joy and wholeness.

Nothing Is Hopeless with God: As we struggle in recovery, we may begin to feel helpless. We might be tempted to throw up our hands and say, "What's the use?" But *feeling* helpless is different from *being* helpless. We are never really helpless, for with God, help is close at hand. We are not without hope, for God is the source of all hope. When we struggle with despair, this letter reminds us to turn our life over to God and totally depend on his power. God will never leave us to face our trials alone.

The Importance of Relationships: Accepting Jesus Christ as our Savior makes us part of God's family. We enter into a community that has Jesus Christ as its founder and leader. Everyone in this community is related; no one stands alone. All healing and recovery take place in the context of relationships with others. Peter teaches us how to manage those relationships: with loyalty, care, and humility, praying that we will become what God wants us to be.

CHAPTER 1
Greetings from Peter

This letter is from Peter, an apostle of Jesus Christ.

I am writing to God's chosen people who are living as foreigners in the provinces of Pontus, Galatia, Cappadocia, Asia, and Bithynia.* ²God the Father knew you and chose you long ago, and his Spirit has made you holy. As a result, you have obeyed him and have been cleansed by the blood of Jesus Christ.

May God give you more and more grace and peace.

The Hope of Eternal Life

³All praise to God, the Father of our Lord Jesus Christ. It is by his great mercy that we have been born again, because God raised Jesus Christ from the dead. Now we live with great expectation, ⁴and we have a priceless inheritance—an inheritance that is kept in heaven for you, pure and undefiled, beyond the reach of change and decay. ⁵And through

---

1:1 *Pontus, Galatia, Cappadocia, Asia,* and *Bithynia* were Roman provinces in what is now Turkey.

1:7 The refiner would heat the gold in the fire in order to separate the worthless and impure dross from the precious and beautiful gold. The dross would be skimmed off until the refiner could see his image in the liquid gold. God uses the fiery trials and tribulations in our life to purify and beautify our faith so that one day he will see clearly his image in us. This truth offers great comfort to those of us who struggle to make sense of a past marked by suffering. We can be confident that God will separate something priceless from the dross of our experiences.

1:8-9 Turning our will and our life over to God is a critical step in the recovery process. During our most painful trials, we may fail to see God with us. Yet Peter suggests that, strange as it may seem at the time, surrendering to God in difficult times can be a joyful experience. If we trust that God will use our trials to further the process of healing in our life, even the tough times can become times of celebration.

1:10-13 The good news of God's forgiveness in Christ flows from a plan that took God centuries to complete. Now that it is complete, we can count on God's continuing kindness as we trust in him until Jesus returns. We don't have to wonder if we are being tricked into believing something that isn't true. Centuries of history and numerous promises stand behind the revelation of God through Jesus Christ. As we turn our life and will over to him, we can be sure that his power is sufficient for a successful recovery.

1:17-20 It is impossible for us to earn God's favor and acceptance. Many people misunderstand Peter's counsel to reverently fear God; they think it means that God is looking to catch us in sin to punish us, so we should be afraid of him. Actually, if we perceive God and ourself correctly, we see that God knows we can't measure up on our own. He accepts our limitations, forgives our sins, seeks to help us learn from our mistakes, and helps us progress toward a more godly life.

your faith, God is protecting you by his power until you receive this salvation, which is ready to be revealed on the last day for all to see.

⁶So be truly glad.* There is wonderful joy ahead, even though you must endure many trials for a little while. ⁷These trials will show that your faith is genuine. It is being tested as fire tests and purifies gold—though your faith is far more precious than mere gold. So when your faith remains strong through many trials, it will bring you much praise and glory and honor on the day when Jesus Christ is revealed to the whole world.

⁸You love him even though you have never seen him. Though you do not see him now, you trust him; and you rejoice with a glorious, inexpressible joy. ⁹The reward for trusting him will be the salvation of your souls.

¹⁰This salvation was something even the prophets wanted to know more about when they prophesied about this gracious salvation prepared for you. ¹¹They wondered what time or situation the Spirit of Christ within them was talking about when he told them in advance about Christ's suffering and his great glory afterward.

¹²They were told that their messages were not for themselves, but for you. And now this Good News has been announced to you by those who preached in the power of the Holy Spirit sent from heaven. It is all so wonderful that even the angels are eagerly watching these things happen.

A Call to Holy Living

¹³So prepare your minds for action and exercise self-control. Put all your hope in the gracious salvation that will come to you when Jesus Christ is revealed to the world. ¹⁴So you must live as God's obedient children. Don't slip back into your old ways of living to satisfy your own desires. You didn't know any better then. ¹⁵But now you must be holy in everything you do, just as God who chose you is holy. ¹⁶For the Scriptures say, "You must be holy because I am holy."*

¹⁷And remember that the heavenly Father to whom you pray has no favorites. He will judge or reward you according to what you do. So you must live in reverent fear of him during your time here as "temporary residents." ¹⁸For you know that God paid a ransom to save you from the empty life you inherited from your ancestors. And it was not paid with mere gold or silver, which lose

1:6 Or *So you are truly glad.*   1:16 Lev 11:44-45; 19:2; 20:7.

HOPE

READ 1 PETER 1:3-7
Life is rough. We must constantly struggle against the sin inherent in our mortal body. We live with the realities of pain, sickness, and death. We live in a world that is constantly decaying. Even if we turn our life over to God, what is there to look forward to?

Peter tells us: "Now we live with great expectation, and we have a priceless inheritance—an inheritance that is kept in heaven for you. . . . And through your faith, God is protecting you by his power until you receive this salvation, which is ready to be revealed on the last day for all to see. So be truly glad. There is wonderful joy ahead, even though you have to endure many trials for a little while" (1 Peter 1:3-6).

Paul offers this encouragement: "Since we are his children, we are his heirs. In fact, together with Christ we are heirs of God's glory. But if we are to share his glory, we must also share his suffering. Yet what we suffer now is nothing compared to the glory he will reveal to us later. For all creation is waiting eagerly for that future day when God will reveal who his children really are" (Romans 8:17-19). These promises are for us! *Turn to page 1615, 1 Peter 3.*

their value. [19]It was the precious blood of Christ, the sinless, spotless Lamb of God. [20]God chose him as your ransom long before the world began, but now in these last days he has been revealed for your sake.

[21]Through Christ you have come to trust in God. And you have placed your faith and hope in God because he raised Christ from the dead and gave him great glory.

[22]You were cleansed from your sins when you obeyed the truth, so now you must show sincere love to each other as brothers and sisters.* Love each other deeply with all your heart.*

[23]For you have been born again, but not to a life that will quickly end. Your new life will last forever because it comes from the eternal, living word of God. [24]As the Scriptures say,

"People are like grass;
    their beauty is like a flower in
        the field.
The grass withers and the flower fades.
[25]   But the word of the Lord remains
        forever."*

And that word is the Good News that was preached to you.

CHAPTER 2

So get rid of all evil behavior. Be done with all deceit, hypocrisy, jealousy, and all unkind speech. [2]Like newborn babies, you must crave pure spiritual milk so that you will grow into a full experience of salvation. Cry out for this nourishment, [3]now that you have had a taste of the Lord's kindness.

Living Stones for God's House

[4]You are coming to Christ, who is the living cornerstone of God's temple. He was rejected by people, but he was chosen by God for great honor.

[5]And you are living stones that God is building into his spiritual temple. What's more, you are his holy priests.* Through the mediation of Jesus Christ, you offer spiritual sacrifices that please God. [6]As the Scriptures say,

"I am placing a cornerstone in Jerusalem,*
    chosen for great honor,
and anyone who trusts in him
    will never be disgraced."*

[7]Yes, you who trust him recognize the honor God has given him.* But for those who reject him,

"The stone that the builders rejected
    has now become the cornerstone."*

[8]And,

"He is the stone that makes people
        stumble,
    the rock that makes them fall."*

They stumble because they do not obey God's word, and so they meet the fate that was planned for them.

[9]But you are not like that, for you are a chosen people. You are royal priests,* a holy

---

1:22a Greek *must have brotherly love.* 1:22b Some manuscripts read *with a pure heart.* 1:24-25 Isa 40:6-8. 2:5 Greek *holy priesthood.* 2:6a Greek *in Zion.* 2:6b Isa 28:16 (Greek version). 2:7a Or *Yes, for you who believe, there is honor.* 2:7b Ps 118:22. 2:8 Isa 8:14. 2:9 Greek *a royal priesthood.*

2:2-3 Here Peter pinpointed an insight for helping us resist sin: We can live a godly life because we have tasted of God's kindness. To the extent that we experience God's love (which often comes through our relationships with other people), we won't want to sin because we will see that it isn't good for us, and it grieves God's Spirit. This puts the focus in recovery work not on improving outward behavior (which is more the result) but on seeking to please God and experience more of his kindness. We can come to him with all our needs, and he will fill our heart with the love we crave.

2:9-10 The Christian's true identity is no longer that of a sinner but that of a holy saint. We are no longer a slave, but a chosen priest of the King. We have been called out of the darkness of our dependency to receive God's healing love so we can share it with others who are hurting.

2:11 Sin is alluring because there is pleasure in it. Many of us have struggled with the temptation to escape the painful realities of life by turning to the "pleasures" of alcohol, drugs, food, sex, work, money, or even religious activity. Yet sooner or later we realized that these pleasures, when used wrongly, fought against the well-being of our soul. By seeing ourself as a "foreigner" on earth with our real home in heaven, we can learn to delay gratification, which leads to wisdom—and recovery.

2:15 The testimony of a changed life is a far better witness of God's grace than a lecture is. When hurting people who haven't yet started in recovery see how God has brought us through our challenges to a place of increased growth and contentment, they may want to know what God can do for them.

nation, God's very own possession. As a result, you can show others the goodness of God, for he called you out of the darkness into his wonderful light.

[10] "Once you had no identity as a people;
now you are God's people.
Once you received no mercy;
now you have received God's mercy."*

[11]Dear friends, I warn you as "temporary residents and foreigners" to keep away from worldly desires that wage war against your very souls. [12]Be careful to live properly among your unbelieving neighbors. Then even if they accuse you of doing wrong, they will see your honorable behavior, and they will give honor to God when he judges the world.*

Respecting People in Authority
[13]For the Lord's sake, submit to all human authority—whether the king as head of state, [14]or the officials he has appointed. For the king has sent them to punish those who do wrong and to honor those who do right.

[15]It is God's will that your honorable lives should silence those ignorant people who make foolish accusations against you. [16]For you are free, yet you are God's slaves, so don't use your freedom as an excuse to do evil. [17]Respect everyone, and love the family of believers.* Fear God, and respect the king.

Slaves
[18]You who are slaves must submit to your masters with all respect.* Do what they tell you—not only if they are kind and reasonable, but even if they are cruel. [19]For God is pleased when, conscious of his will, you patiently endure unjust treatment. [20]Of course, you get no credit for being patient if you are beaten for doing wrong. But if you suffer for doing good and endure it patiently, God is pleased with you.

[21]For God called you to do good, even if it means suffering, just as Christ suffered* for you. He is your example, and you must follow in his steps.

[22]He never sinned,
nor ever deceived anyone.*
[23]He did not retaliate when he was insulted,
nor threaten revenge when he suffered.
He left his case in the hands of God,

2:10 Hos 1:6, 9; 2:23. 2:12 Or *on the day of visitation.*
2:17 Greek *love the brotherhood.* 2:18 Or *because you fear God;* Greek reads *in all fear.* 2:21 Some manuscripts read *died.* 2:22 Isa 53:9.

A Servant's Heart
BIBLE READING: 1 Peter 2:18-25
We made direct amends to such people wherever possible, except when to do so would injure them or others.
At this point in recovery, most of us have experienced some major changes in our attitudes. At one time, we were so consumed by our addiction that we thought only of ourself, failing to show any consideration for others. This step focuses on the interests and needs of others.

The apostle Paul taught: "Don't be selfish; don't try to impress others. Be humble, thinking of others as better than yourselves. Don't look out only for your own interests, but take an interest in others, too" (Philippians 2:3-4). Whether we make amends directly to others or choose not to because of the injury it would cause, we should be concerned with protecting others from pain and suffering.

There may be situations in which we will suffer if we go back to make amends. This is part of the work of recovery, and the potential pain should not deter us. The apostle Peter wrote: "If you suffer for doing good and endure it patiently, God is pleased with you. . . . Christ suffered for you. He is your example, and you must follow in his steps. He never sinned, nor ever deceived anyone. He did not retaliate when he was insulted, nor threaten revenge when he suffered. He left his case in the hands of God, who always judges fairly" (1 Peter 2:20-23).

This step can be very difficult as we face the painful consequences of past actions. During this time we need to turn our life over to God, who always judges justly. *Turn to Step Ten, page 45, Genesis 31.*

who always judges fairly.
²⁴ He personally carried our sins
     in his body on the cross
so that we can be dead to sin
     and live for what is right.
By his wounds
     you are healed.
²⁵ Once you were like sheep
     who wandered away.
But now you have turned to your Shepherd,
     the Guardian of your souls.

CHAPTER 3
Wives

In the same way, you wives must accept the authority of your husbands. Then, even if some refuse to obey the Good News, your godly lives will speak to them without any words. They will be won over ²by observing your pure and reverent lives.

³Don't be concerned about the outward beauty of fancy hairstyles, expensive jewelry, or beautiful clothes. ⁴You should clothe yourselves instead with the beauty that comes from within, the unfading beauty of a gentle and quiet spirit, which is so precious to God. ⁵This is how the holy women of old made themselves beautiful. They put their trust in God and accepted the authority of their husbands. ⁶For instance, Sarah obeyed her husband, Abraham, and called him her master. You are her daughters when you do what is right without fear of what your husbands might do.

3:8 Greek *Show brotherly love.* 3:10-12 Ps 34:12-16.

Husbands

⁷In the same way, you husbands must give honor to your wives. Treat your wife with understanding as you live together. She may be weaker than you are, but she is your equal partner in God's gift of new life. Treat her as you should so your prayers will not be hindered.

All Christians

⁸Finally, all of you should be of one mind. Sympathize with each other. Love each other as brothers and sisters.* Be tenderhearted, and keep a humble attitude. ⁹Don't repay evil for evil. Don't retaliate with insults when people insult you. Instead, pay them back with a blessing. That is what God has called you to do, and he will grant you his blessing. ¹⁰For the Scriptures say,

"If you want to enjoy life
     and see many happy days,
keep your tongue from speaking evil
     and your lips from telling lies.
¹¹ Turn away from evil and do good.
     Search for peace, and work to
          maintain it.
¹² The eyes of the LORD watch over those
          who do right,
     and his ears are open to their prayers.
But the LORD turns his face
     against those who do evil."*

Suffering for Doing Good

¹³Now, who will want to harm you if you are eager to do good? ¹⁴But even if you suffer for

---

2:23-24 Not only does Jesus show us how to deal with suffering, but he also suffered for us. He received the ultimate punishment for our sins so we wouldn't have to. Instead of facing terrible punishment, we can receive his mercy. He desires to set us free from bondage and heal us from the devastating effects of our sins.

3:1-7 God's design for marriage is for the wife to respect her husband and the husband to be sensitive and loving toward his wife. Husband and wife are to receive through each other the blessings of God's loving grace and guiding truth. This sounds wonderful, but, as anyone who is married knows, it can be hard and painful! It requires being vulnerable, resolving conflicts, and being confronted with the truth even when it hurts. Working through such difficulties is part of God's plan for helping us mature.

3:8-11 The Christian community is to be like a healthy, loving family. Some of us who come from a dysfunctional family may not know what this means, but Peter spelled it out: people share their hurts and find sympathy; they humbly express their needs and receive loving care; they forgive one another rather than plot revenge; they pray for each other; they are careful not to say things that will unnecessarily hurt others; they can be honest about who they are; they seek to do good for one another; and they try to live in peace by resolving conflicts with each other. These same qualities are ideal for helping us with the recovery process.

3:13-17 We all know what it feels like to be hurt by someone we are trying to help, or to have someone falsely accuse us of wrongdoing. It is not uncommon in recovery for people to misunderstand us and resist the changes we are trying to make. The challenge in such situations is to be patient and maintain quiet trust in God's promises. If we persevere in doing what is right, God will reward us.

doing what is right, God will reward you for it. So don't worry or be afraid of their threats. [15]Instead, you must worship Christ as Lord of your life. And if someone asks about your hope as a believer, always be ready to explain it. [16]But do this in a gentle and respectful way.* Keep your conscience clear. Then if people speak against you, they will be ashamed when they see what a good life you live because you belong to Christ. [17]Remember, it is better to suffer for doing good, if that is what God wants, than to suffer for doing wrong!

[18]Christ suffered* for our sins once for all time. He never sinned, but he died for sinners to bring you safely home to God. He suffered physical death, but he was raised to life in the Spirit.*

[19]So he went and preached to the spirits in prison—[20]those who disobeyed God long ago when God waited patiently while Noah was building his boat. Only eight people were saved from drowning in that terrible flood.* [21]And that water is a picture of baptism, which now saves you, not by removing dirt from your body, but as a response to God from* a clean conscience. It is effective because of the resurrection of Jesus Christ.

[22]Now Christ has gone to heaven. He is seated in the place of honor next to God, and all the angels and authorities and powers accept his authority.

CHAPTER 4
Living for God
So then, since Christ suffered physical pain, you must arm yourselves with the same attitude he had, and be ready to suffer, too. For if you have suffered physically for Christ, you have finished with sin.* [2]You won't spend the rest of your lives chasing your own desires, but you will be anxious to do the will of God. [3]You have had enough in the past of the evil things that godless people enjoy—their immorality and lust, their feasting and drunkenness and wild parties, and their terrible worship of idols.

[4]Of course, your former friends are surprised when you no longer plunge into the flood of wild and destructive things they do. So they slander you. [5]But remember that they will have to face God, who stands ready to judge everyone, both the living and the dead. [6]That is why the Good News was preached to

3:16 Some English translations put this sentence in verse 15. 3:18a Some manuscripts read *died.* 3:18b Or *in spirit.* 3:20 Greek *saved through water.* 3:21 Or *as an appeal to God for.* 4:1 Or *For the one* [or *One*] *who has suffered physically has finished with sin.*

HONESTY

READ 1 PETER 3:10-17
Lying can become a way of life. We may even have lied to ourself, pretending we don't have any problems with lying. We may have learned to cover up our problems by becoming excellent liars. But when we choose to face reality, we will see the unhappiness caused by our lies and how they have hurt us and our loved ones. Only when we stop lying can God begin to bring blessing and change into our life.

Think about these verses: "Does anyone want to live a life that is long and prosperous? Then keep your tongue from speaking evil and your lips from telling lies!" (Psalm 34:12-13). "If you want to enjoy life and see many happy days, keep your tongue from speaking evil and your lips from telling lies." (1 Peter 3:10). "Don't lie to each other, for you have stripped off your old sinful nature and all its wicked deeds. Put on your new nature, and be renewed as you learn to know your Creator and become like him" (Colossians 3:9-10).

There are great benefits to honesty. What other virtue is accompanied by such promises? Telling the truth is vital to recovery. Since lying may be second nature to us, it may be difficult to change. Part of any successful recovery involves guarding our lips and our thoughts from lies that will hurt us and others. Since lying may have been a lifelong way of coping, we must accept that learning to tell the truth may involve hard work. *Turn to page 1623, 2 Peter 1.*

those who are now dead*—so although they were destined to die like all people,* they now live forever with God in the Spirit.*

⁷The end of the world is coming soon. Therefore, be earnest and disciplined in your prayers. ⁸Most important of all, continue to show deep love for each other, for love covers a multitude of sins. ⁹Cheerfully share your home with those who need a meal or a place to stay.

¹⁰God has given each of you a gift from his great variety of spiritual gifts. Use them well to serve one another. ¹¹Do you have the gift of speaking? Then speak as though God himself were speaking through you. Do you have the gift of helping others? Do it with all the strength and energy that God supplies. Then everything you do will bring glory to God through Jesus Christ. All glory and power to him forever and ever! Amen.

Suffering for Being a Christian

¹²Dear friends, don't be surprised at the fiery trials you are going through, as if something strange were happening to you. ¹³Instead, be very glad—for these trials make you partners with Christ in his suffering, so that you will have the wonderful joy of seeing his glory when it is revealed to all the world.

¹⁴If you are insulted because you bear the name of Christ, you will be blessed, for the glorious Spirit of God* rests upon you.* ¹⁵If

---

4:6a Greek *preached even to the dead.* **4:6b** Or *so although people had judged them worthy of death.* **4:6c** Or *in spirit.* **4:14a** Or *for the glory of God, which is his Spirit.* **4:14b** Some manuscripts add *On their part he is blasphemed, but on your part he is glorified.*

4:8 Real love for others requires that we face our own sinfulness and consider the well-being of those we have wronged in the past. In many cases this means humbly and sincerely asking the people we have offended for forgiveness; sometimes we may need to take the further step of making amends.

4:10-11 Unfortunately, many of us don't realize that God has given each of us special and unique abilities. Discovering these is a part of recovery. It is a process of learning to esteem ourself and receive respect and encouragement from God and from other people. Then we can pass on God's blessings to others, relying on his strength to enable us to use the gifts he has given us.

4:12-13 Peter returned to a central theme of his letter: We should not only expect to experience trials, but we should also rejoice in them. Through our difficult circumstances we receive opportunities to share in Christ's sufferings as well as in his glory. This theme offers great hope for those of us in recovery, because it affirms that our suffering has a purpose. Through it, God will draw us close and transform us into the person he intended us to be.

4:14-16 We need wisdom to know the difference between suffering because of our own sins and suffering for doing what is right. If we ask for wisdom, God will grant it (see James 1:5). When we suffer because of our own sins, we naturally feel ashamed; it is then we need divine courage to change. When we are persecuted for our Christian conduct or godly character, we can rejoice in that suffering; in this case, we need divine serenity to help us accept the things we cannot change.

5:1-4 Several qualities are necessary for a Christian leader: the willingness to care for others, a desire to serve others, and the ability to lead by example rather than force. We may have grown up surrounded by leaders who embodied none of these principles, and now we are in a position of leadership at work, at church, or in our family. How do we avoid following the negative models that have influenced us? Jesus has provided the best example for us to follow. To become the type of person God wants us to be, we must submit to Christ's leadership and allow his grace, peace, and wisdom to flow through us.

5:7 God cares about our troubles. He watches over us and is continually concerned about our welfare! If we truly believed this, we would turn our worries over to him. However, many of us find it hard to trust God so completely. Because of our past, we may have trouble believing that anyone is that concerned about us. We may have found that if we didn't worry about our problems, no one would. One way to increase our level of trust in God is to find a friend further along in recovery and Christian maturity with whom we can learn to trust. As we are able to share our concerns with caring people, we can consciously remind ourself that God's concern is like our friends'—only much wider and deeper.

5:8-9 Satan is ultimately responsible for the evil that happens to us. Whether he tempts us to relapse in recovery or kicks us when we are already down, Satan is lurking and prowling about. We are commanded to be careful and stand firm against Satan. We are not alone; others are suffering like we are and fighting the same battles. Meeting with others in recovery will help us see that victory over addiction is attainable and that we are not alone in the battle.

5:10-11 God's promise to us when we fall down or are suffering is that he will restore us, set us in a good and secure place, and use the difficulties we have been through to make us stronger than ever! It is this hope that gives us the courage to persevere in our journey of recovery.

you suffer, however, it must not be for murder, stealing, making trouble, or prying into other people's affairs. ¹⁶But it is no shame to suffer for being a Christian. Praise God for the privilege of being called by his name! ¹⁷For the time has come for judgment, and it must begin with God's household. And if judgment begins with us, what terrible fate awaits those who have never obeyed God's Good News? ¹⁸And also,

"If the righteous are barely saved,
    what will happen to godless sinners?"*

¹⁹So if you are suffering in a manner that pleases God, keep on doing what is right, and trust your lives to the God who created you, for he will never fail you.

CHAPTER 5
Advice for Elders and Young Men
And now, a word to you who are elders in the churches. I, too, am an elder and a witness to the sufferings of Christ. And I, too, will share in his glory when it is revealed to the whole world. As a fellow elder, I appeal to you: ²Care for the flock that God has entrusted to you. Watch over it willingly, not grudgingly—not for what you will get out of it, but because you are eager to serve God. ³Don't lord it over the people assigned to your care, but lead them by your own good example. ⁴And when the Great Shepherd appears, you will receive a crown of never-ending glory and honor.

⁵In the same way, you who are younger must accept the authority of the elders. And all of you, dress yourselves in humility as you relate to one another, for

"God opposes the proud
    but gives grace to the humble."*

⁶So humble yourselves under the mighty power of God, and at the right time he will lift you up in honor. ⁷Give all your worries and cares to God, for he cares about you.

⁸Stay alert! Watch out for your great enemy, the devil. He prowls around like a roaring lion, looking for someone to devour. ⁹Stand firm against him, and be strong in your faith. Remember that your family of believers* all over the world is going through the same kind of suffering you are.

¹⁰In his kindness God called you to share in his eternal glory by means of Christ Jesus. So after you have suffered a little while, he will restore, support, and strengthen you,

4:18 Prov 11:31 (Greek version). 5:5 Prov 3:34 (Greek version). 5:9 Greek *your brotherhood.*

STEP 12

The Narrow Road
BIBLE READING: 1 Peter 4:1-4
Having had a spiritual awakening as the result of these steps, we tried to carry this message to others and to practice these principles in all our affairs.
We probably came into recovery because we'd had enough! We'd had enough of the pain, the lies, and the destruction that resulted from our addictive behavior. One day at a time, we learned the principles on the road to recovery. Now we are at a place we weren't sure we could ever reach—Step Twelve. Now we are encouraged to share the message with others— even though not everyone will welcome it.

Peter pointed out: "You have had enough in the past of the evil things that godless people enjoy—their immorality and lust, their feasting and drunkenness and wild parties. . . . Of course, your former friends are surprised when you no longer plunge into the flood of wild and destructive things they do. So they slander you" (1 Peter 4:3-4).

Jesus said: "You can enter God's Kingdom only through the narrow gate. The highway to hell is broad, and its gate is wide for the many who choose that way. But the gateway to life is very narrow and the road is difficult, and only a few ever find it" (Matthew 7:13-14).

Our message won't be accepted by the masses. The people on the "highway to hell" won't eagerly restrict themselves to the clearly defined steps on the road to recovery. But for those who do listen, our story could be the difference between life and death for them. *End of the Twelve Step Reading Program.*

and he will place you on a firm foundation. ¹¹All power to him forever! Amen.

Peter's Final Greetings

¹²I have written and sent this short letter to you with the help of Silas,* whom I commend to you as a faithful brother. My purpose in writing is to encourage you and assure you that what you are experiencing is truly part of God's grace for you. Stand firm in this grace.

¹³Your sister church here in Babylon* sends you greetings, and so does my son Mark. ¹⁴Greet each other with a kiss of love.*

Peace be with all of you who are in Christ.

5:12 Greek *Silvanus.* 5:13 Greek *The elect one in Babylon.* Babylon was probably symbolic for Rome.

REFLECTIONS ON 1 PETER

insights ABOUT THE PERSON OF GOD

As the apostle greeted his friends in **1 Peter 1:1-2**, he reminded them of how they were related to the triune God: They were chosen by God the Father, cleansed by the blood of Jesus Christ, and renewed by the Holy Spirit, who was at work in their hearts. On the basis of God's work in our life, we can be confident that he will bless us richly and grant us increasing freedom from anxiety and fear. Becoming free from anxiety is a process that continues as we trust him (1:8).

In **1 Peter 1:3-6** the apostle praised our Father God for the free gift of his loving grace. All who receive God's gift become his children and belong together in his family and have a "priceless inheritance." All who trust in him share the hope of eternal life with God. This hope gives us the strength to persevere in recovery with joy, despite the difficult and painful circumstances we face.

1 Peter 2:4-6 leaves us with two wonderful promises upon which we can build our life and recovery: We are acceptable to God because of Jesus, and God will never disappoint us if we trust in him. With these truths as our foundation, we can live to please God. As we join other believers in Christ's Spirit of love, together we can create a place where others feel safe and included.

insights ABOUT THE DANGER OF RELAPSE

In **1 Peter 1:14-17** the apostle warned his readers about the temptation to give up on their faith. Peter knew how it felt to slip back into old ways. Once he boldly proclaimed that he was willing to die in Jesus' defense. A few hours later he denied knowing Jesus just to save his reputation (see Matthew 26:31-35, 69-75). The only way to keep from slipping back into sinful and unhealthy patterns is to maintain a conscious and sober awareness of our identity: We are children of a holy God. Like children, we are weak and dependent, but the Father we depend on is strong, loving, just, and perfect.

insights ABOUT OUR NEW LIFE IN CHRIST

In **1 Peter 1:23-25** the apostle contrasts the new life we have in Christ with the natural life our parents gave us. Even the most positive legacy from our natural parents will fade and decay, for from them we inherited the dysfunctions of a sinful human race. But the life God gives us increases in beauty and lasts forever. God's promises to save us will never fail.

In **1 Peter 2:1** the apostle tells us to avoid five destructive behaviors: hanging on to hatred and malicious behavior; pretending to be good when there is unacknowledged sin in our heart; not being honest about our feelings and behavior; being jealous of others instead of making the best of our own situation; and talking about people behind their backs instead of directly to them. Peter knew that doing these things would hurt us and hinder the growth of loving and intimate relationships. We must examine our heart and continue to work toward the recovery goals of forgiveness, honesty, contentment, and openness.

In **1 Peter 4:1-5** we are called to follow Christ's example, resisting the sinful pleasures that come our way and focusing instead on living according to God's will. The sins Peter listed here can exert incredible power over us when they become the central focus of our life. To break free of an addictive lifestyle, we have to cut ourself off from past practices and sometimes even from past relationships. To "just say no" alone won't set us free. We also need to say yes to God and redirect our energy to our recovery activities and, eventually, to the recovery of others.

insights ABOUT PERSEVERING THROUGH TRIALS

In **1 Peter 2:21-23** it is clear that persevering through difficulty and pain is the God-ordained path to maturity. God does not ask us to endure anything that he did not endure himself in Christ. Like us, Jesus felt temptations to give in to sinful pleasures, to lie his way out of dilemmas, to return insult for insult, and to seek revenge. Like Jesus, we can respond to injustice with faith that entrusts matters into God's hands, knowing that ultimately he will bring about justice.

In **1 Peter 4:19** we are encouraged to keep doing what is right, even if we are suffering. We may have been persecuted by old friends who want us to return to our old lifestyle. Perhaps family members are afraid of the changes we are making and are hindering our progress. As we face these trials we can trust that God will be faithful to us and remember that he can use even our painful experiences for our good. God wants us to continue in recovery. So if we are suffering for our work in recovery, we need to keep on doing what we know to be right. No matter what obstacles may be placed in our way, God will never desert us, once we have entrusted our life to him.

2 PETER

THE BIG PICTURE

A. A WORD OF BLESSING (1:1-2)
B. GOD HAS EVERYTHING WE NEED (1:3-21)
C. THE PERIL WITHIN: BEWARE! (2:1-22)
D. HOPE FOR TOMORROW; PURPOSE FOR TODAY (3:1-18)

Peter's audience had a problem. False teachers were moving into church fellowships and promoting wrong ideas about God. In many of these early churches a majority of the people were uneducated. They were easily swayed by the eloquence of traveling false teachers who intentionally deceived the people, using lies and half-truths to manipulate the believers for the teachers' own ends.

The apostle Peter sent warnings to his readers: Watch out for false teachers; remember that they will have to give account for their errors; recognize false teachers by their deeds; and remember the price they will pay for misleading people. Peter wanted his readers to experience the life-changing power of God in their lives, and that would mean avoiding man-made substitutes. How could Peter's audience follow Christ if they believed all kinds of false teachings about him?

The challenge Peter left them went beyond a mere warning, however. He included a plan of action: "May God give you more and more grace and peace as you grow in your knowledge of God and Jesus our Lord. By his divine power, God has given us everything we need for living a godly life " (1:2-3).

Why do the pains, disappointments, and sins of life bring us down? Why do we hurt those we love the most? Perhaps we will never learn the answers to those questions. But 2 Peter does tell us how to change: Get to know God. The God of the universe has made himself available to us on a personal level. As we get to know him, he will help us overcome our shortcomings and replace them with self-control, kindness, love, forgiveness, perseverance, patience, and peace.

THE BOTTOM LINE

PURPOSE: To help his readers keep their focus on God's grace and truth. AUTHOR: The apostle Peter. AUDIENCE: All believers everywhere. DATE WRITTEN: Around A.D. 66–67, a few years after 1 Peter was written. SETTING: Peter was probably writing from Rome, giving encouragement and warning to people he did not expect to see again. He wanted them to watch out for false teachings and to be faithful to God and one another. KEY VERSE: "By his divine power, God has given us everything we need for living a godly life. We have received all of this by coming to know him, the one who called us to himself by means of his marvelous glory and excellence" (1:3). KEY PEOPLE AND RELATIONSHIPS: Peter with Paul and with the church at large.

RECOVERY THEMES

True Recovery Involves Surrender to God: In recovery, some people say that we have the power to heal ourself. That false idea is fed by our own wishful thinking. We wish we had the power within ourself to overcome our problems. This idea also assumes that recovery is a simple process. But for recovery to be successful, it must involve our entire self—our heart, our mind, our spirit, and our will—being handed over to God's rule. Recovery is never an easy and painless process. It demands complete commitment and surrender to God. But if we are willing to entrust our life to God, we will discover the joy and peace that God intends for each of us.

God Is Our Help and Hope: Peter wrote to people who were facing severe opposition. The Roman emperor Nero had begun heavy persecution of Christians, and many would soon face death at his hands. At the same time, false ideas about God threatened their new faith. Peter helped them face these assaults on their faith by reminding them to keep their eyes on God, the only reliable source of help and hope. As we focus on God, we will find new hope no matter what circumstances we face. Then, as we persevere through tough times, our behavior will show that God is working powerfully in our life.

The Importance of Perseverance: God does not require that we suddenly become perfect. He knows we will slip and fall at times. But, as Peter warned his audience, we must be careful not to get tangled up in our sins to the point of becoming enslaved again. This only adds to our burden of guilt and makes the recovery process much more difficult. Making progress depends on perseverance. With God's help we can get up and get back on track as soon as possible, no matter what our circumstances. When we confess our sins to God and accept his free gift of forgiveness, we will grow closer to God, who loves us and promises to be with us. God helps us to persevere through the tough times and experience his joy in the process.

CHAPTER 1
Greetings from Peter

This letter is from Simon* Peter, a slave and apostle of Jesus Christ.

I am writing to you who share the same precious faith we have. This faith was given to you because of the justice and fairness* of Jesus Christ, our God and Savior.

²May God give you more and more grace and peace as you grow in your knowledge of God and Jesus our Lord.

Growing in Faith

³By his divine power, God has given us everything we need for living a godly life. We have

received all of this by coming to know him, the one who called us to himself by means of his marvelous glory and excellence. ⁴And because of his glory and excellence, he has given us great and precious promises. These are the promises that enable you to share his divine nature and escape the world's corruption caused by human desires.

⁵In view of all this, make every effort to respond to God's promises. Supplement your faith with a generous provision of moral excellence, and moral excellence with knowledge, ⁶and knowledge with self-control, and self-control with patient endurance, and patient endurance with godliness, ⁷and godli-

1:1a Greek *Simeon.* **1:1b** Or *to you in the righteousness.*

1:1-2 Peter greeted his readers by reminding them of the gift of forgiveness and new life they had received through faith in Jesus Christ. It is a gift because no one can claim to be worthy of the salvation God offers through Christ (see Ephesians 2:8-9). Truly God is good! Experiencing God's kindness and peace depends on knowing him. Sometimes we expect peace to come before we make healthy choices, but Peter reminds us that grace and peace come when we concentrate on getting to know God. We can take concrete steps to improve our conscious contact with God through prayer and meditation on his Word.

1:3-4 One of the most comforting by-products of faith is the simple awareness that we possess everything we need to live a full and meaningful life. How do we experience this provision? By participating in God's nature through faith and by growing through practice into all that he has designed us to be. The past is part of who we are, the future is securely in God's hands, and today is filled with opportunities to grow in our understanding of love, forgiveness, truth, and grace! Just as parents provide for their children's needs, so God supplies all that we need, including the ability to rise above our circumstances and temptations.

2:1-12 Here we are reminded of the consequences of rejecting God's program and leading others away from the truth. Perhaps this describes the way we were before entering recovery. Thankfully, God has provided us with the help we need to start again and rebuild our life according to his will. The consequences of the self-centered pursuit of pleasure and power are terrible. It is good to be reminded every so often of what we have been delivered from—"sudden destruction."

ness with brotherly affection, and brotherly affection with love for everyone.

⁸The more you grow like this, the more productive and useful you will be in your knowledge of our Lord Jesus Christ. ⁹But those who fail to develop in this way are shortsighted or blind, forgetting that they have been cleansed from their old sins.

¹⁰So, dear brothers and sisters,* work hard to prove that you really are among those God has called and chosen. Do these things, and you will never fall away. ¹¹Then God will give you a grand entrance into the eternal Kingdom of our Lord and Savior Jesus Christ.

Paying Attention to Scripture

¹²Therefore, I will always remind you about these things—even though you already know them and are standing firm in the truth you have been taught. ¹³And it is only right that I should keep on reminding you as long as I live.* ¹⁴For our Lord Jesus Christ has shown me that I must soon leave this earthly life,* ¹⁵so I will work hard to make sure you always remember these things after I am gone.

¹⁶For we were not making up clever stories when we told you about the powerful coming of our Lord Jesus Christ. We saw his majestic splendor with our own eyes ¹⁷when he received honor and glory from God the Father. The voice from the majestic glory of God said to him, "This is my dearly loved Son, who brings me great joy."* ¹⁸We ourselves heard that voice from heaven when we were with him on the holy mountain.

¹⁹Because of that experience, we have even greater confidence in the message proclaimed by the prophets. You must pay close attention to what they wrote, for their words are like a lamp shining in a dark place—until the Day dawns, and Christ the Morning Star shines* in your hearts. ²⁰Above all, you must realize that no prophecy in Scripture ever came from the prophet's own understanding,* ²¹or from human initiative. No, those prophets were moved by the Holy Spirit, and they spoke from God.

CHAPTER 2
The Danger of False Teachers

But there were also false prophets in Israel, just as there will be false teachers among you. They will cleverly teach destructive heresies

1:10 Greek brothers. 1:13 Greek as long as I am in this tent [or tabernacle]. 1:14 Greek I must soon put off my tent [or tabernacle]. 1:17 Matt 17:5; Mark 9:7; Luke 9:35. 1:19 Or rises. 1:20 Or is a matter of one's own interpretation.

SELF-CONTROL

READ 2 PETER 1:2-9

We would love to have self-control! But trying to find it within ourself can become as much of an obsession as our primary addiction. The more we try to get a hold on it, the more elusive it seems.

According to Peter, self-control is one step in the middle of a larger progression: "May God give you more and more grace and peace as you grow in your knowledge of God and Jesus our Lord. By his divine power, God has given us everything we need for living a godly life. We have received all of this by coming to know him, the one who called us to himself by means of his marvelous glory and excellence. And because of his glory and excellence, he has given us great and precious promises. These are the promises that enable you to share his divine nature and escape the world's corruption caused by human desires. In view of all this, make every effort to respond to God's promises. Supplement your faith with a generous provision of moral excellence, and moral excellence with knowledge, and knowledge with self-control, and self-control with patient endurance, and patient endurance with godliness, and godliness with brotherly affection, and brotherly affection with love for everyone" (2 Peter 1:2-7).

Self-control is something that comes as we grow closer to God. As we take one step at a time, one day at a time, God will give us his own character, including self-control. *Turn to page 1631, 1 John 2.*

and even deny the Master who bought them. In this way, they will bring sudden destruction on themselves. ²Many will follow their evil teaching and shameful immorality. And because of these teachers, the way of truth will be slandered. ³In their greed they will make up clever lies to get hold of your money. But God condemned them long ago, and their destruction will not be delayed.

⁴For God did not spare even the angels who sinned. He threw them into hell,* in gloomy pits of darkness,* where they are being held until the day of judgment. ⁵And God did not spare the ancient world—except for Noah and the seven others in his family. Noah warned the world of God's righteous judgment. So God protected Noah when he destroyed the world of ungodly people with a vast flood. ⁶Later, God condemned the cities of Sodom and Gomorrah and turned them into heaps of ashes. He made them an example of what will happen to ungodly people. ⁷But God also rescued Lot out of Sodom because he was a righteous man who was sick of the shameful immorality of the wicked people around him. ⁸Yes, Lot was a righteous man who was tormented in his soul by the wickedness he saw and heard day after day. ⁹So you see, the Lord knows how to rescue godly people from their trials, even while keeping the wicked under punishment until the day of final judgment. ¹⁰He is especially hard on those who follow their own twisted sexual desire, and who despise authority.

These people are proud and arrogant, daring even to scoff at supernatural beings* without so much as trembling. ¹¹But the angels, who are far greater in power and strength, do not dare to bring from the Lord* a charge of blasphemy against those supernatural beings.

¹²These false teachers are like unthinking animals, creatures of instinct, born to be caught and destroyed. They scoff at things they do not understand, and like animals, they will be destroyed. ¹³Their destruction is their reward for the harm they have done.

They love to indulge in evil pleasures in broad daylight. They are a disgrace and a stain among you. They delight in deception* even as they eat with you in your fellowship meals. ¹⁴They commit adultery with their eyes, and their desire for sin is never satisfied. They lure unstable people into sin, and they are well trained in greed. They live under God's curse. ¹⁵They have wandered off the right road and followed the footsteps of Balaam son of Beor,* who loved to earn money by doing wrong. ¹⁶But Balaam was stopped from his mad course when his donkey rebuked him with a human voice.

¹⁷These people are as useless as dried-up springs or as mist blown away by the wind. They are doomed to blackest darkness. ¹⁸They brag about themselves with empty, foolish boasting. With an appeal to twisted sexual desires, they lure back into sin those who have barely escaped from a lifestyle of deception. ¹⁹They promise freedom, but they themselves are slaves of sin and corruption. For you are a slave to whatever controls you. ²⁰And when people escape from the wickedness of the world by knowing our Lord and Savior Jesus Christ and then get tangled up and enslaved by sin again, they are worse off than before. ²¹It would be better if they had never known the way to righteousness than to know it and then reject the command they were given to live a holy life. ²²They prove the truth of this proverb: "A dog returns to its vomit."* And another says, "A washed pig returns to the mud."

CHAPTER 3
The Day of the Lord Is Coming

This is my second letter to you, dear friends, and in both of them I have tried to stimulate your wholesome thinking and refresh your memory. ²I want you to remember what the holy prophets said long ago and what our Lord and Savior commanded through your apostles.

2:4a Greek *Tartarus*. 2:4b Some manuscripts read *in chains of gloom*. 2:10 Greek *at glorious ones*, which are probably evil angels. 2:11 Other manuscripts read *to the Lord*; still others do not include this phrase at all. 2:13 Some manuscripts read *in fellowship meals*. 2:15 Some manuscripts read *Bosor*. 2:22 Prov 26:11.

2:13-22 An important part of recovery is setting appropriate boundaries. People who do not have our best interests at heart abound, even in the Christian community. Peter emphasized the need for discernment. Apparently, the church in Peter's day was plagued by those who once professed faith in Christ but then "added to" the simple truth of the gospel. They advocated "freedom," but that freedom was really only a license to become enslaved to sin once again. Setting healthy boundaries for behavior involves knowing God's truth and allowing neither the false teachings of others nor our own sinful inclinations to lead us astray.

[3]Most importantly, I want to remind you that in the last days scoffers will come, mocking the truth and following their own desires. [4]They will say, "What happened to the promise that Jesus is coming again? From before the times of our ancestors, everything has remained the same since the world was first created."

[5]They deliberately forget that God made the heavens long ago by the word of his command, and he brought the earth out from the water and surrounded it with water. [6]Then he used the water to destroy the ancient world with a mighty flood. [7]And by the same word, the present heavens and earth have been stored up for fire. They are being kept for the day of judgment, when ungodly people will be destroyed.

[8]But you must not forget this one thing, dear friends: A day is like a thousand years to the Lord, and a thousand years is like a day. [9]The Lord isn't really being slow about his promise, as some people think. No, he is being patient for your sake. He does not want anyone to be destroyed, but wants everyone to repent. [10]But the day of the Lord will come as unexpectedly as a thief. Then the heavens will pass away with a terrible noise, and the very elements themselves will disappear in fire, and the earth and everything on it will be found to deserve judgment.*

[11]Since everything around us is going to be destroyed like this, what holy and godly lives you should live, [12]looking forward to the day of God and hurrying it along. On that day, he will set the heavens on fire, and the elements will melt away in the flames. [13]But we are looking forward to the new heavens and new earth he has promised, a world filled with God's righteousness.

[14]And so, dear friends, while you are waiting for these things to happen, make every effort to be found living peaceful lives that are pure and blameless in his sight.

[15]And remember, our Lord's patience gives people time to be saved. This is what our beloved brother Paul also wrote to you with the wisdom God gave him—[16]speaking of these things in all of his letters. Some of his comments are hard to understand, and those who are ignorant and unstable have twisted his letters to mean something quite different, just as they do with other parts of Scripture. And this will result in their destruction.

Peter's Final Words

[17]You already know these things, dear friends. So be on guard; then you will not be carried away by the errors of these wicked people and lose your own secure footing. [18]Rather, you must grow in the grace and knowledge of our Lord and Savior Jesus Christ.

All glory to him, both now and forever! Amen.

3:10 Other manuscripts read *will be burned up;* still others read *will be found destroyed.*

3:3-9 It is difficult to wait on God, particularly when he seems so slow in bringing about our healing. Why doesn't God return for us now? Why does he allow further suffering and frustration? The answer is simple yet profoundly full of love: God is patient! He wants all to come to him and discover the only true way of salvation and life. As we wait, we can trust that it is always for a good purpose.

3:10-16 We live in a world that encourages and rewards our active lifestyle. We are doers and fixers, arrangers and controllers. We seek to bolster our sense of self-esteem by the things we do. When Christ returns, however, who we *are* will be far more important than what we *do.* Peter reminds us that as we wait for this day, we are called to be God's people. It is good to take time to ask, Am I enjoying the privilege of being? In all my doing, have I lost sight of what's important—the kind of person I am, and the person I am becoming?

REFLECTIONS ON 2 PETER

insights ABOUT OUR ROLE IN RECOVERY

When we entrust our life to God, we might wonder if there is any part for us to play. In **2 Peter 1:5-11** we are reminded that God expects us to do our part in the recovery process. As we actively seek change in our life, we will share in God's nature and receive the ability to think new thoughts and formulate new behavior patterns. "Work hard to prove that you really are among those God has called and chosen," Peter urges. "Do these things, and you will never fall away. Then God will give you a grand entrance into the eternal Kingdom of our Lord and Savior Jesus Christ."

It is easy to remember the painful moments of life—the disappointments and the people who disappointed us. It is sometimes harder to remember the many blessings we receive in small ways each day. In **2 Peter 1:12-18** the apostle reminded his readers that they could overcome the pain of past trials by focusing on God: his power and his coming again, his splendor and his majesty. Peter wanted to etch the truth of God's amazing love into their minds. We must work through our painful memories (they do not disappear on their own!), but as we do, we can also reflect on God's majesty and amazing love. As we recall the good things God has done, the painful memories will begin to fade.

insights ABOUT GOD'S TRUTH

God's truth is dependable; our human perspective often is not. In **2 Peter 1:19-21** the apostle made this distinction clear. God's truth is not weak or questionable; it is not a theory waiting to be proven false. God's truth is certain and can be counted on. In recovery a central question is, Are we ready to believe what God says? Or do we prefer the perspective of fallible people, the messages ingrained in our minds from past events, the doubts instilled by friends not yet in recovery? As we take God's Word to heart, we come to understand more and more of the truth—about God, about ourself, and about our future in Christ.

1 JOHN

THE BIG PICTURE

A. INTRODUCTION (1:1–2:2)
B. RECOVERY FROM FALSE THINKING: OBEDIENCE (2:3-27)
C. RECOVERY FROM FALSE THINKING: THE WORK OF CHRIST (2:28–4:6)
D. RECOVERY FROM FALSE THINKING: THE GIFTS OF GOD (4:7–5:5)
E. CONCLUSION: ASSURANCE OF SPIRITUAL RECOVERY (5:6-21)

False spiritual teachers were a big problem in the early church. Because there was no New Testament that new believers could refer to, many churches fell prey to pretenders who taught their own ideas and advanced themselves as leaders. John wrote this letter to set the record straight on some important issues, particularly concerning the identity of Jesus Christ.

Because John's letter was about the basics of faith in Christ, it helped his readers take inventory of their faith. It helped them answer the question, Are we true believers? John told them that they could tell by looking at their actions: Loving one another was evidence of God's presence in their lives. But if they bickered and fought all the time, or were selfish and did not look out for one another, they were revealing that they, in fact, did not know God.

That did not mean they had to be perfect. John also recognized that believing involved admitting our sins and seeking God's forgiveness. Depending on God for cleansing from sin and freedom from guilt through admitting our wrongs against others and making amends was also important in getting to know God.

God's recovery program requires us to make amends because this is essential to successful recovery. John's letter challenges us to treat others with respect and dignity as we grow spiritually. People transformed by Christ will show it in how they treat others. In a similar way, we will progress in recovery only as far as we right the wrongs we have committed against others. It takes humility and commitment to live at peace with others, but it is a price worth paying as we seek God's blessings.

THE BOTTOM LINE

PURPOSE: To set boundaries on the content of faith and to give believers assurance of their salvation. AUTHOR: The apostle John. AUDIENCE: Circulated through an unnamed group of early churches. DATE WRITTEN: Probably between A.D. 85 and 96. SETTING: John was the only surviving apostle when he wrote this circular letter. He was living in Ephesus, supervising the churches of Asia Minor. KEY VERSE: "I have written this to you who believe in the name of the Son of God, so that you may know you have eternal life" (5:13). KEY PEOPLE AND RELATIONSHIPS: John, with the believers to whom he wrote.

RECOVERY THEMES

God Desires Our Recovery: One of the ways God cares for us is by listening to us. When Satan (called the "accuser" in Revelation 12:10) plants thoughts of hopelessness in our mind and tells us that we have gone too far for God to forgive us, John urges us not to give up hope. Jesus Christ, our advocate, has already paid the penalty for any and every sin we have done or could do. We do not need to shy away from asking Christ to plead our case; he has already won it.

The Invitation to Love: One of the evidences of salvation in a person's life is love for others—shown in action, not just words. An important part of recovery is being willing to extend God's love to others as God has shown his love toward us. He loved us while we were in the middle of insanity—we did not have to clean up our act to get him to love us. Through us he wants to love others in the midst of their insanity, using us to carry the message of God's love and forgiveness to them. God loves us enough to free us from bondage and use us to show his love toward others in need of recovery.

The Importance of Boundaries: The false teachers whom John corrected said that the people could throw off all moral restraints because what they did "in the body" did not matter. Those who listened to that message were becoming indifferent to sin and returning to old, sinful habits. They were relapsing into immorality and thinking it was all right. John pointed out that there are boundaries around what we believe and that Jesus Christ is the focus. Anything that leads us away from Christ is outside the boundaries. Staying focused on Christ is the most essential part of our spiritual growth and the only means for successful recovery.

CHAPTER 1
Introduction

We proclaim to you the one who existed from the beginning,* whom we have heard and seen. We saw him with our own eyes and touched him with our own hands. He is the Word of life. ²This one who is life itself was revealed to us, and we have seen him. And now we testify and proclaim to you that he is the one who is eternal life. He was with the Father, and then he was revealed to us. ³We proclaim to you what we ourselves have actually seen and heard so that you may have fellowship with us. And our fellowship is with the Father and with his Son, Jesus Christ. ⁴We are writing these things so that you may fully share our joy.*

Living in the Light

⁵This is the message we heard from Jesus* and now declare to you: God is light, and there is no darkness in him at all. ⁶So we are lying if we say we have fellowship with God but go on living in spiritual darkness; we are not practicing the truth. ⁷But if we are living in the light, as God is in the light, then we have

1:1 Greek *What was from the beginning.* 1:4 Or *so that our joy may be complete;* some manuscripts read *your joy.* 1:5 Greek *from him.*

1:1-4 John wrote to assure those who doubted the value of their faith in God. He showed that faith in Christ is intellectually, socially, and emotionally satisfying. Spiritual recovery takes place only where there is a healthy balance among the intellectual, social, and emotional aspects of life, all centered on genuine faith in God. Dealing with our shortcomings and making amends where possible means facing all our shortcomings—in all areas of our life.

1:5-7 There is a strong contrast between the light in the Christian life and the darkness in a life controlled by sin. If we live in sin while claiming to be a Christian, we are lying and will never successfully navigate the recovery process. Honest, accurate self-examination and personal inventory of our spiritual state are crucial. Choosing to live in the light—continually acknowledging our flaws as the light reveals them—results in a cleansed conscience and fulfilling relationships.

2:3-6 How can we be sure that we belong to Christ? Our assurance is validated by our continuing desire to obey God's will for us. Those who claim to be saved but continually disobey God are liars. We cannot make progress in recovery unless we are willing to submit to God's program for godly living. That means continuing our personal inventory, promptly admitting our wrongs to others, and confessing our sins to God. As we learn to love God more and more, our actions will show it.

2:7-11 Another distinctive mark of our faith is loving others. Hatred toward others is a sure sign that recovery has not yet begun. Light and darkness cannot exist in the same heart. The absence of love will keep us in the dark and prove a severe hindrance to progress in recovery. Love is never weak or compromising; it is the evidence of emotional strength. The love God gives us provides the energy to approach those we have harmed and to make amends when possible.

fellowship with each other, and the blood of Jesus, his Son, cleanses us from all sin.

⁸If we claim we have no sin, we are only fooling ourselves and not living in the truth. ⁹But if we confess our sins to him, he is faithful and just to forgive us our sins and to cleanse us from all wickedness. ¹⁰If we claim we have not sinned, we are calling God a liar and showing that his word has no place in our hearts.

CHAPTER 2

My dear children, I am writing this to you so that you will not sin. But if anyone does sin, we have an advocate who pleads our case before the Father. He is Jesus Christ, the one who is truly righteous. ²He himself is the sacrifice that atones for our sins—and not only our sins but the sins of all the world.

³And we can be sure that we know him if we obey his commandments. ⁴If someone claims, "I know God," but doesn't obey God's commandments, that person is a liar and is not living in the truth. ⁵But those who obey God's word truly show how completely they love him. That is how we know we are living in him. ⁶Those who say they live in God should live their lives as Jesus did.

A New Commandment

⁷Dear friends, I am not writing a new commandment for you; rather it is an old one you have had from the very beginning. This old commandment—to love one another—is the same message you heard before. ⁸Yet it is also new. Jesus lived the truth of this commandment, and you also are living it. For the darkness is disappearing, and the true light is already shining.

⁹If anyone claims, "I am living in the light," but hates a fellow believer,* that person is still living in darkness. ¹⁰Anyone who loves a fellow believer* is living in the light and does not cause others to stumble. ¹¹But anyone who hates a fellow believer is still living and walking in darkness. Such a person does not know the way to go, having been blinded by the darkness.

¹²I am writing to you who are God's children
because your sins have been forgiven through Jesus.*
¹³I am writing to you who are mature in the faith*

2:9 Greek *hates his brother;* also in 2:11. 2:10 Greek *loves his brother.* 2:12 Greek *through his name.* 2:13 Or *to you fathers;* also in 2:14.

STEP 10

Recurrent Sins

BIBLE READING: 1 John 1:8-10

We continued to take personal inventory and when we were wrong promptly admitted it.

We may feel awkward about bringing our recurrent sins before God. We may be embarrassed by the number of times we have had to deal with the same issues—issues that stubbornly refuse to be washed away. We may imagine that God is collecting a long list of repeated offenses to be used against us.

The apostle John wrote: "If we claim we have no sin, we are only fooling ourselves and not living in the truth. But if we confess our sins to him, he is faithful and just to forgive us our sins and to cleanse us from all wickedness. If we claim we have not sinned, we are calling God a liar and showing that his word has no place in our hearts" (1 John 1:8-10).

To confess means to agree with God that what he declares to be wrong really is wrong. This means we need to recognize our wrongs when they occur. John says that God will forgive us and cleanse us of *every* wrong. Each time we confess a sin it is washed away. Our life is like a slate that has been wiped clean. Our sins are not recorded on some celestial list; they are gone forever! Even when we make the same mistakes over and over again, God keeps forgiving us if we are truly repentant. Some areas of our life need more cleaning than others! God doesn't get angry when we come back to him repeatedly. There is no need to feel awkward. God wants us to come to him every time we sin. *Turn to Step Eleven, page 419, 2 Samuel 22.*

because you know Christ, who existed
from the beginning.
I am writing to you who are young in the
faith
because you have won your battle with
the evil one.
[14] I have written to you who are God's
children
because you know the Father.
I have written to you who are mature in
the faith
because you know Christ, who existed
from the beginning.
I have written to you who are young in
the faith
because you are strong.
God's word lives in your hearts,
and you have won your battle with the
evil one.

Do Not Love This World

[15] Do not love this world nor the things it offers you, for when you love the world, you do not have the love of the Father in you. [16] For the world offers only a craving for physical pleasure, a craving for everything we see, and pride in our achievements and possessions. These are not from the Father, but are from this world. [17] And this world is fading away, along with everything that people crave. But anyone who does what pleases God will live forever.

Warning about Antichrists

[18] Dear children, the last hour is here. You have heard that the Antichrist is coming, and already many such antichrists have appeared. From this we know that the last hour has come. [19] These people left our churches, but they never really belonged with us; otherwise they would have stayed with us. When they left, it proved that they did not belong with us.

[20] But you are not like that, for the Holy One has given you his Spirit,* and all of you know the truth. [21] So I am writing to you not because you don't know the truth but because you know the difference between truth and lies. [22] And who is a liar? Anyone who says that Jesus is not the Christ.* Anyone who denies the Father and the Son is an antichrist.* [23] Anyone who denies the Son doesn't have the Father, either. But anyone who acknowledges the Son has the Father also.

[24] So you must remain faithful to what you have been taught from the beginning. If you do, you will remain in fellowship with the Son and with the Father. [25] And in this fellowship we enjoy the eternal life he promised us.

[26] I am writing these things to warn you about those who want to lead you astray. [27] But you have received the Holy Spirit,* and he lives within you, so you don't need anyone to teach you what is true. For the Spirit*

2:20 Greek *But you have an anointing from the Holy One.* **2:22a** Or *not the Messiah.* **2:22b** Or *the antichrist.* **2:27a** Greek *the anointing from him.* **2:27b** Greek *the anointing.*

2:24-27 Belief in Jesus as the Son of God and reliance upon the Holy Spirit within us will guard us against being deceived by false doctrines. The quest for new, sophisticated solutions to the consequences of sin and despair only leads to new kinds of enslavement to cultic religions, substance abuse, or codependency. Historical Christianity gives us the only perspective of ourself and the world that leads to true freedom from the enslavement of sin because only the Christian faith asserts that Jesus took upon himself the penalty for our sins.

2:28–3:3 Many of us struggle with shame. John tells us that as we live in Christ, trusting him for forgiveness and walking with him consistently, we will have no reason to be ashamed when Christ returns. We can rest assured that we are loved and acceptable because God himself has made us his children. As his children, we long to be with him and to be like him. The ultimate step in recovery is for this longing to be fulfilled. In the meantime, the knowledge that Jesus is coming again provides powerful motivation to live a godly life and to know God better through prayer and meditation on his Word.

3:4-9 As we take moral inventory of our life, let's face the essence of sin honestly: It is breaking God's law, doing things our own way rather than God's way. Once we commit our life to God, he gives us a new nature that is no longer comfortable with sin. We still sin, but we no longer make it a practice. We know that Jesus gave his life on the cross for our sins, so now we desire to please him because we have a new nature. Whereas before—in our sins, codependency, and/or addiction—we continued with little sense of wrongdoing, now we know better. In recovery we constantly affirm that we have God's power to break old patterns.

3:10-20 Using Cain and Abel as examples, John underscored the importance of love. Having true love means being willing to make sacrifices for the ones we love. In recovery the best way to express our love for God is to be willing to make amends for the wrongs we have done to others. Our actions toward others, not just our words, will reveal what's in our heart.

teaches you everything you need to know, and what he teaches is true—it is not a lie. So just as he has taught you, remain in fellowship with Christ.

Living as Children of God

²⁸And now, dear children, remain in fellowship with Christ so that when he returns, you will be full of courage and not shrink back from him in shame.

²⁹Since we know that Christ is righteous, we also know that all who do what is right are God's children.

CHAPTER 3

See how very much our Father loves us, for he calls us his children, and that is what we are! But the people who belong to this world don't recognize that we are God's children because they don't know him. ²Dear friends, we are already God's children, but he has not yet shown us what we will be like when Christ appears. But we do know that we will be like him, for we will see him as he really is. ³And all who have this eager expectation will keep themselves pure, just as he is pure.

⁴Everyone who sins is breaking God's law, for all sin is contrary to the law of God. ⁵And you know that Jesus came to take away our sins, and there is no sin in him. ⁶Anyone who continues to live in him will not sin. But anyone who keeps on sinning does not know him or understand who he is.

⁷Dear children, don't let anyone deceive you about this: When people do what is right, it shows that they are righteous, even as Christ is righteous. ⁸But when people keep on sinning, it shows that they belong to the devil, who has been sinning since the beginning. But the Son of God came to destroy the works of the devil. ⁹Those who have been born into God's family do not make a practice of sinning, because God's life* is in them. So they can't keep on sinning, because they are children of God. ¹⁰So now we can tell who are children of God and who are children of the devil. Anyone who does not live righteously and does not love other believers* does not belong to God.

Love One Another

¹¹This is the message you have heard from the beginning: We should love one another. ¹²We must not be like Cain, who belonged to the evil one and killed his brother. And why did he kill him? Because Cain had been

3:9 Greek *because his seed.* 3:10 Greek *does not love his brother.*

FORGIVENESS

READ 1 JOHN 2:1-6

At times we may feel as if we are the worst sinner on earth. We just seem to keep doing the same bad things over and over. We feel guilty! Can God just wink at our sins and pretend that everything is all right? How can he repeatedly forgive us for committing the same wrongs?

The apostle John said: "My dear children, I am writing this to you so that you will not sin. But if anyone does sin, we have an advocate who pleads our case before the Father. He is Jesus Christ, the one who is truly righteous. He himself is the sacrifice that atones for our sins—and not only our sins but the sins of all the world" (1 John 2:1-2).

God takes sin very seriously. As a righteous judge, he can't just ignore sin and act as if it doesn't matter. But he forgives us completely and repeatedly. The words used here are legal terms. Jesus is our advocate, our defense attorney in a court of law, who intercedes for us, the law-breakers. But he is not only the defense attorney; he is also "the sacrifice that atones for our sins." This means that Jesus' death has been accepted by the court as admissible payment for all of our sins. We are all guilty. The sentence is death! But our sentence has already been paid by Jesus. When we bring our sins to Jesus, he goes back to the judge, his Father, on our behalf, reminding him that our sentence has already been paid. ***Turn to page 1645, Jude 1.***

doing what was evil, and his brother had been doing what was righteous. [13]So don't be surprised, dear brothers and sisters,* if the world hates you.

[14]If we love our brothers and sisters who are believers,* it proves that we have passed from death to life. But a person who has no love is still dead. [15]Anyone who hates another brother or sister* is really a murderer at heart. And you know that murderers don't have eternal life within them.

[16]We know what real love is because Jesus gave up his life for us. So we also ought to give up our lives for our brothers and sisters. [17]If someone has enough money to live well and sees a brother or sister* in need but shows no compassion—how can God's love be in that person?

[18]Dear children, let's not merely say that we love each other; let us show the truth by our actions. [19]Our actions will show that we belong to the truth, so we will be confident when we stand before God. [20]Even if we feel guilty, God is greater than our feelings, and he knows everything.

[21]Dear friends, if we don't feel guilty, we can come to God with bold confidence. [22]And we will receive from him whatever we ask because we obey him and do the things that please him.

[23]And this is his commandment: We must believe in the name of his Son, Jesus Christ, and love one another, just as he commanded us. [24]Those who obey God's commandments remain in fellowship with him, and he with

them. And we know he lives in us because the Spirit he gave us lives in us.

CHAPTER 4
Discerning False Prophets

Dear friends, do not believe everyone who claims to speak by the Spirit. You must test them to see if the spirit they have comes from God. For there are many false prophets in the world. [2]This is how we know if they have the Spirit of God: If a person claiming to be a prophet* acknowledges that Jesus Christ came in a real body, that person has the Spirit of God. [3]But if someone claims to be a prophet and does not acknowledge the truth about Jesus, that person is not from God. Such a person has the spirit of the Antichrist, which you heard is coming into the world and indeed is already here.

[4]But you belong to God, my dear children. You have already won a victory over those people, because the Spirit who lives in you is greater than the spirit who lives in the world. [5]Those people belong to this world, so they speak from the world's viewpoint, and the world listens to them. [6]But we belong to God, and those who know God listen to us. If they do not belong to God, they do not listen to us. That is how we know if someone has the Spirit of truth or the spirit of deception.

Loving One Another

[7]Dear friends, let us continue to love one another, for love comes from God. Anyone

---

3:13 Greek *brothers*. 3:14 Greek *the brothers;* similarly in 3:16. 3:15 Greek *hates his brother*. 3:17 Greek *sees his brother*. 4:2 Greek *If a spirit;* similarly in 4:3.

4:1-6 No religious system can be true if it denies that Jesus was God in a human body. A clear view of who Jesus is will help us develop a relationship with God; through prayer and studying his Word we can know what his will is and how to accomplish it in our life. Even if other people don't understand or accept our new way of life, as we walk with God, we can know that he who lives in our heart is stronger than our past and our present struggles with sin.

4:7-12 Recovery depends upon God's gifts, and the most important among them is the provision of a Savior. The Father loves us enough to have sent his Son to save us. As we grow to be more like him, we also grow in our ability to love others with sacrificial love. Many of us feel the recovery process would be greatly expedited if only we could see God. But God is usually seen only through his people when they love one another. That is why it is so important for us to restore relationships with the people we have harmed. That is also why we need the fellowship of believers—because we desperately need the love they offer.

4:16–5:3 John spoke again about the importance of love. True Christianity is characterized by loving relationships in which there is no fear. Experiencing such relationships—first with God, then with other believers—is at the heart of recovery. We can trust God wholly, without fear, because the punishment for our sins has already taken place (through Christ). Where love reigns, we can be open and vulnerable with fellow believers, trusting that our honesty will not be used to hurt us. Mature Christian love delights in helping others. It creates an environment in which we can develop accountability and a new sense of responsibility toward ourself and others.

who loves is a child of God and knows God. ⁸But anyone who does not love does not know God, for God is love.

⁹God showed how much he loved us by sending his one and only Son into the world so that we might have eternal life through him. ¹⁰This is real love—not that we loved God, but that he loved us and sent his Son as a sacrifice to take away our sins.

¹¹Dear friends, since God loved us that much, we surely ought to love each other. ¹²No one has ever seen God. But if we love each other, God lives in us, and his love is brought to full expression in us.

¹³And God has given us his Spirit as proof that we live in him and he in us. ¹⁴Furthermore, we have seen with our own eyes and now testify that the Father sent his Son to be the Savior of the world. ¹⁵All who declare that Jesus is the Son of God have God living in them, and they live in God. ¹⁶We know how much God loves us, and we have put our trust in his love.

God is love, and all who live in love live in God, and God lives in them. ¹⁷And as we live in God, our love grows more perfect. So we will not be afraid on the day of judgment, but we can face him with confidence because we live like Jesus here in this world.

¹⁸Such love has no fear, because perfect love expels all fear. If we are afraid, it is for fear of punishment, and this shows that we have not fully experienced his perfect love. ¹⁹We love each other* because he loved us first.

²⁰If someone says, "I love God," but hates a fellow believer,* that person is a liar; for if we don't love people we can see, how can we love God, whom we cannot see? ²¹And he has given us this command: Those who love God must also love their fellow believers.*

CHAPTER 5
Faith in the Son of God

Everyone who believes that Jesus is the Christ* has become a child of God. And everyone who loves the Father loves his children, too. ²We know we love God's children if we love God and obey his commandments. ³Loving God means keeping his commandments, and his commandments are not burdensome. ⁴For every child of God defeats this evil world, and we achieve this victory through our faith. ⁵And who can win

4:19 Greek *We love*. Other manuscripts read *We love God*; still others read *We love him*. 4:20 Greek *hates his brother*. 4:21 Greek *The one who loves God must also love his brother*. 5:1 Or *the Messiah*.

STEP 7

Eyes of Love

BIBLE READING: 1 John 5:11-15

We humbly asked him to remove our shortcomings.

Most of us probably aren't used to getting the things we ask for. How can we have confidence that God will hear our prayers? How do we know he will answer when we ask him to remove our shortcomings?

The apostle Paul wrote: "Even before he made the world, God loved us and chose us in Christ to be holy and without fault in his eyes" (Ephesians 1:4). God's primary goal is to make us holy—that is, to form his character in us. Looking through the eyes of love, he already sees us as we will be when his work is done. Then he works out his goals for us in the arena of everyday life. The Bible tells us: "God's discipline is always good for us, so that we might share in his holiness" (Hebrews 12:10). Our holiness—the removal of our shortcomings—is God's will for each of us. The apostle John wrote: "We are confident that he hears us whenever we ask for anything that pleases him. And since we know he hears us when we make our requests, we also know that he will give us what we ask for" (1 John 5:14-15).

It is clearly God's will to have our sinful shortcomings removed. And he has promised to give us anything we ask for in line with his will. Therefore, we can have full confidence that God will remove our shortcomings in his time. *Turn to Step Eight, page 107, Exodus 22.*

this battle against the world? Only those who believe that Jesus is the Son of God.

⁶And Jesus Christ was revealed as God's Son by his baptism in water and by shedding his blood on the cross*—not by water only, but by water and blood. And the Spirit, who is truth, confirms it with his testimony. ⁷So we have these three witnesses*—⁸the Spirit, the water, and the blood—and all three agree. ⁹Since we believe human testimony, surely we can believe the greater testimony that comes from God. And God has testified about his Son. ¹⁰All who believe in the Son of God know in their hearts that this testimony is true. Those who don't believe this are actually calling God a liar because they don't believe what God has testified about his Son.

¹¹And this is what God has testified: He has given us eternal life, and this life is in his Son. ¹²Whoever has the Son has life; whoever does not have God's Son does not have life.

Conclusion

¹³I have written this to you who believe in the name of the Son of God, so that you may know you have eternal life. ¹⁴And we are confident that he hears us whenever we ask for anything that pleases him. ¹⁵And since we know he hears us when we make our requests, we also know that he will give us what we ask for.

¹⁶If you see a fellow believer* sinning in a way that does not lead to death, you should pray, and God will give that person life. But there is a sin that leads to death, and I am not saying you should pray for those who commit it. ¹⁷All wicked actions are sin, but not every sin leads to death.

¹⁸We know that God's children do not make a practice of sinning, for God's Son holds them securely, and the evil one cannot touch them. ¹⁹We know that we are children of God and that the world around us is under the control of the evil one.

²⁰And we know that the Son of God has come, and he has given us understanding so that we can know the true God.* And now we live in fellowship with the true God because we live in fellowship with his Son, Jesus Christ. He is the only true God, and he is eternal life.

²¹Dear children, keep away from anything that might take God's place in your hearts.*

5:6 Greek *This is he who came by water and blood.* 5:7 A few very late manuscripts add *in heaven—the Father, the Word, and the Holy Spirit, and these three are one. And we have three witnesses on earth.* 5:16 Greek *a brother.* 5:20 Greek *the one who is true.* 5:21 Greek *keep yourselves from idols.*

5:6-13 How can we who are committed to recovery know that we are actually achieving it in a way that pleases God? Scripture tells us that we can look for certain evidence: Belief that Jesus is the Son of God and commitment to obey him are two sources of assurance. Another is the witness of the Holy Spirit, who points to Christ in our life. God gives us a sense of rightness as we maintain contact with him through prayer and study of his Word and as we obey his revealed will.

5:16-19 Another evidence of spiritual recovery is godly discernment—the spiritual capacity to know right from wrong. This power of discernment is lost in codependent relationships; regaining it is at the heart of the recovery process. Until we see ourself as God sees us, our moral inventory will be flawed and self-excusing.

5:20-21 John concludes his letter by reminding us who the true God is and warning us not to let anything take God's place in our heart. He cautions against entertaining any false ideas about God. We can know the true God through his Son, Jesus Christ. Recovery involves eliminating all wrong ideas about God, any material substitutes for him, and all controlling sins. Recovery means putting God in his rightful place as the absolute Lord of our life. Someone has said, "Only Jesus Christ is able to control a person's life without destroying it." In a restored relationship with God, the submission of our life and will to his control is the way back to sanity.

REFLECTIONS ON 1 JOHN

insights ABOUT CONFESSION AND FORGIVENESS

Accurate personal inventory normally leads to an awareness of sin. We are assured in **1 John 1:8-10** that if we confess our sins, we will experience the forgiveness and cleansing God has provided through the blood shed by his Son, Jesus Christ. The lesson is simple: Confession must precede cleansing. Confession should be followed by a willingness to change and make amends where possible.

In most recovery situations, whether the need is for cleansing from sin or for deliverance from the trauma of abuse or codependence, honest self-evaluation will lead to an admission of powerlessness. We see in **1 John 2:1-2** that we can turn to the greatest resource and advocate of all— Jesus Christ. Because he received the full force of God's anger against sin, we in recovery need not live in fear of God's anger for our past transgressions. Trusting that Christ suffered for our sins, we can now come to the Father freely, with complete trust that we will be accepted unconditionally.

insights ABOUT THE DANGER OF WORLDLY VALUES

In **1 John 2:15-17** we are reminded that the more we are wrapped up in this world and its attractions, the harder it will be to establish spiritual goals for our life. If we feed our desires with what the world offers, we starve ourself spiritually. The best way to avoid entanglement with worldly values is to "feed" our spirits by seeking God through prayer and meditation on his Word. Then we will discover his will and his help in redirecting our life.

insights ABOUT THE IMPORTANCE OF RIGHT BELIEFS

In **1 John 2:18-23** we learn that an important aspect of recovery is commitment to right beliefs. As we rely on the Holy Spirit to know the truth, we are able to recognize the spirit of antichrist. The critical doctrinal issue for John was that of the deity of Jesus Christ. One cannot genuinely profess belief in God while denying his Son. Full spiritual recovery cannot take place unless we recognize Jesus as the Son of God and the higher power who can restore us to sane living.

We are told in **1 John 5:4-5** that if we believe in Jesus and live by faith, we are equipped to triumph over the negative influences of our hostile world. For those of us who trust Christ with our life, recovery is not only possible but certain. Neither addictive behaviors nor abusive people can dominate where God has promised the power to overcome.

insights ABOUT ASSURANCE IN SALVATION AND RECOVERY

In **1 John 4:13-15** we are told that assurance of salvation comes from believing that Jesus is the Son of God, because that ability to believe is proof that God himself, through the Holy Spirit, is living in us. Confession of who Christ is is both the evidence and the expression of a genuine faith. It is more than intellectual belief; believing that Christ is the Son of God and Savior of the world leads us to confession of sin and commitment to live for God. We do this as we take responsibility for our life and deal with our past failures and broken relationships.

In **1 John 5:14-15** we see that another encouraging sign of true recovery is answered prayer. It is gratifying to know that when we pray according to the will of God, he has promised to hear and to answer us. Our greatest resources for recovery are the Word of God, by which we learn God's will, and prayer, through which we talk to God and present our needs to him.

2 JOHN

Recovery is a fragile process. Without vigilance and encouragement from others, we live with the prospect of relapse. In the face of this, we need help from others who have courage and sensitivity toward our situation. Harsh "reprogramming" will not help us, but neither will friends who flatter us with falsely positive words. Diligence together with faithful support is what we need.

This letter is a highly personal one that deals with the kinds of issues that are addressed more broadly in 1 John. The tone is warm and pastoral. John wrote this letter with a twofold purpose: to commend and to encourage "the chosen lady," his addressee. She had already demonstrated her faithfulness to God; she did not need to be corrected. But John did not want her to trip over the obstacles ahead that might threaten her continued service to God.

In balancing commendation and encouragement, John proves to be a wise counselor and a splendid example to all of us in recovery. We need to recognize and affirm each other's past successes. At the same time, we must be willing to point out the hazards ahead when we see them, sharing our hard-won wisdom as warnings for the unwary. Pointing out the obstacles ahead and encouraging one another to be careful are the loving things to do. Thus, this letter underscores the critical importance of carrying the message of recovery to others.

THE BOTTOM LINE

PURPOSE: To commend the chosen lady and to encourage her to continue teaching others about Christ. AUTHOR: The apostle John. AUDIENCE: "The chosen lady" and her children. DATE WRITTEN: Probably written before 1 John, sometime near A.D. 90. SETTING: The woman to whom John wrote was probably involved in one of the churches that John oversaw, although it is uncertain whether the "chosen lady" was an individual; John may have been writing to a local church. KEY VERSE: "If anyone comes to your meeting and does not teach the truth about Christ, don't invite that person into your home or give any kind of encouragement" (1:10). KEY PEOPLE AND RELATIONSHIPS: John, with the chosen lady and her children.

RECOVERY THEMES

The Importance of Boundaries: John urged this special lady to be careful about those whom she let into her life. Like David, who in Psalm 101 vowed not to allow deceitful people to stay in his house, she was not to allow false teachers into her home. In fact, she was not to encourage them in any way. Sometimes we think that out of fairness we need to listen to everyone, but there are dangers in this attitude. We must carefully set limits on whom we listen to if we are to protect ourself in recovery and in our spiritual growth.

The Challenge to Love: Loving one another is the most basic act of obedience to God. It is also an important ingredient in recovery. As we recover, we may tend to focus inward or become self-centered. Loving others will not only please God, but it will go a long way toward healing our relationships.

Greetings

This letter is from John, the elder.*

I am writing to the chosen lady and to her children,* whom I love in the truth—as does everyone else who knows the truth—²because the truth lives in us and will be with us forever.

³Grace, mercy, and peace, which come from God the Father and from Jesus Christ—the Son of the Father—will continue to be with us who live in truth and love.

Live in the Truth

⁴How happy I was to meet some of your children and find them living according to the truth, just as the Father commanded.

⁵I am writing to remind you, dear friends,* that we should love one another. This is not a new commandment, but one we have had from the beginning. ⁶Love means doing what God has commanded us, and he has commanded us to love one another, just as you heard from the beginning.

⁷I say this because many deceivers have gone out into the world. They deny that Jesus Christ came* in a real body. Such a person is a deceiver and an antichrist. ⁸Watch out that you do not lose what we* have worked so hard to achieve. Be diligent so that you receive your full reward. ⁹Anyone who wanders away from this teaching has no relationship with God. But anyone who remains in the teaching of Christ has a relationship with both the Father and the Son.

¹⁰If anyone comes to your meeting and does not teach the truth about Christ, don't invite that person into your home or give any kind of encouragement. ¹¹Anyone who encourages such people becomes a partner in their evil work.

Conclusion

¹²I have much more to say to you, but I don't want to do it with paper and ink. For I hope to visit you soon and talk with you face to face. Then our joy will be complete.

¹³Greetings from the children of your sister,* chosen by God.

1a Greek *From the elder.* 1b Or *the church God has chosen and its members.* 5 Greek *I urge you, lady.* 7 Or *will come.* 8 Some manuscripts read *you.* 13 Or *from the members of your sister church.*

1:4-6 Note the wise approach John used here: First he commended this woman and her children for their faithfulness; then he exhorted them to act according to Christian love; finally he followed his exhortation with an explanation. There is a sequential pattern for helping others: encouragement, exhortation, and explanation. Even though we are teaching truths established by the authority of God's Word, sharing the Good News must still be done in ways that will communicate to people. An initial commendation will edify and build rapport; exhortation will communicate the truth or confront a problem; and an explanation will establish the truth and build relationships.

1:7-9 Clear boundaries for belief and practice are essential for spiritual growth and effective recovery. Many of us have been deceived and pulled into unhealthy relationships, damaging habits, or false religions. People may even have tried to convince us that such things would lead to recovery. We need to be aware of the subtle lies and distortions of truth some people use to deceive us. The best way to avoid being deceived is to anchor our faith in God's Word and seek his will for us through prayer. Faith in God through Jesus Christ is the only viable means for successful recovery.

1:10-11 With heresy on the rise, John warned believers not to allow those with suspect doctrinal views to infiltrate the Christian community. He did not want new believers who had made a good beginning in the Christian faith to be led astray. We also need godly people in our life—people like John—who can warn us about false teachings and dangerous activities. If we don't have relationships that hold us accountable, we need to develop them. All of us are susceptible to being deceived and led astray. Building healthy relationships with wise and godly people is vital to any successful recovery program.

3 JOHN

THE BIG PICTURE

A. SALUTATION (1:1)
B. GAIUS: A CASE FOR COMMENDATION (1:2-8)
C. DIOTREPHES: A CASE FOR CONFRONTATION (1:9-10)
D. DEMETRIUS: A CASE FOR CONGRATULATION (1:11-12)
E. CONCLUDING REMARKS (1:13-15)

We know little about Gaius except that he was generous and hospitable and highly regarded by the apostle John. Apparently, Gaius took it upon himself to provide free room and board for traveling pastors and missionaries. In a day when most preachers had to travel from town to town with no regular means of support, the service Gaius provided was greatly needed. John wrote this letter to commend him and to warn him to watch out for a self-important spiritual teacher named Diotrephes. John challenged Gaius not to be influenced by Diotrephes's bad example and to warn others about him, too.

Aside from his warning about Diotrephes, John was primarily concerned with encouraging his friend Gaius. This reminds us that the simple act of including others in our life and sharing ourself with them is especially pleasing to God. One of the reasons God places people in our life is so we can support and encourage them. As we reach out to help others, we will discover that we, too, are blessed and strengthened in a special way.

Hospitality doesn't have to be complicated. It can mean setting an extra place at the table, offering a ride, giving a hug or a handshake, or speaking a word of greeting. We all need a little support sometimes; it is part of the process of recovery to open up and support one another as we face our struggles. How affirming it is to be shown some hospitality or to be invited into someone else's life. Hospitality can be such a simple act; yet it is a potent way to show love, appreciation, and support, and each of us has some of it to share.

THE BOTTOM LINE

PURPOSE: To commend Gaius for his hospitality and to encourage him in his faithfulness. AUTHOR: The apostle John. AUDIENCE: Gaius, a prominent believer, perhaps from Derbe in Asia Minor. DATE WRITTEN: Around A.D. 90. SETTING: Like 1 and 2 John, 3 John was probably written from Ephesus and circulated among the churches in Asia Minor. KEY VERSE: "Dear friend, don't let this bad example influence you. Follow only what is good. Remember that those who do good prove that they are God's children, and those who do evil prove that they do not know God" (1:11). KEY PEOPLE AND RELATIONSHIPS: John with Gaius, with Diotrephes, and with Demetrius.

RECOVERY THEMES

Pride Leads to Relapse: Diotrephes refused to humble himself before others and decided that he alone would be the boss. His arrogant attitude disqualified him from the leadership role he coveted. One of the vices we face in recovery is pride. As we experience success, it is all too easy to feel as if we have arrived. We begin to think we are self-sufficient and superior to others. A word to the wise: Pride and self-sufficiency often lead to relapse.

The Importance of Helping Others: In contrast to Diotrephes, Gaius and Demetrius were commended for their faithful service to others. They had generously shared with others, both in hospitality and in their teaching of the truth, without complaint. In their own ways they were carrying the message of God's transforming power to people who were still in bondage. John did not take them for granted; he commended them for their service. Today they live on as godly examples for each of us to follow.

Greetings

This letter is from John, the elder.*

I am writing to Gaius, my dear friend, whom I love in the truth.

²Dear friend, I hope all is well with you and that you are as healthy in body as you are strong in spirit. ³Some of the traveling teachers* recently returned and made me very happy by telling me about your faithfulness and that you are living according to the truth. ⁴I could have no greater joy than to hear that my children are following the truth.

Caring for the Lord's Workers

⁵Dear friend, you are being faithful to God when you care for the traveling teachers who pass through, even though they are strangers to you. ⁶They have told the church here of your loving friendship. Please continue providing for such teachers in a manner that pleases God. ⁷For they are traveling for the Lord,* and they accept nothing from people who are not believers.* ⁸So we ourselves should support them so that we can be their partners as they teach the truth.

⁹I wrote to the church about this, but Diotrephes, who loves to be the leader, refuses to have anything to do with us. ¹⁰When I come, I will report some of the things he is doing and the evil accusations he is making against us. Not only does he refuse to welcome the traveling teachers, he also tells others not to help them. And when they do help, he puts them out of the church.

1 Greek *From the elder.* 3 Greek *the brothers;* also in verses 5 and 10. 7a Greek *They went out on behalf of the Name.* 7b Greek *from Gentiles.*

1:1-4 Recovery is a process that involves our total being. Spiritual difficulties are often intimately tied to personal problems or physical disorders, and resolving these problems may be key to restoring both spiritual and physical health. Conversely, neglecting our spiritual needs may contribute to our physical and emotional problems. As we make honest and fearless inventory of our life, we need to examine how our unhealthy spiritual condition contributes to our physical problems.

1:5-8 John commended Gaius for his hospitality toward the Christian teachers who periodically passed through town. Hospitality is a special gift and often overlooked. Some of us may feel that we're not good at sharing our faith with others and wonder if there is any way we can encourage others in recovery. Hospitality is one way to show others what God has done for us. By quietly serving others in our home, we show them that we have become new people. They may wonder how it happened, which would open a natural opportunity for us to share our faith in God. Opening our home to others may also give needy people a place to relax and explore the truth about themselves.

1:9-11 Confrontation is a necessary part of the recovery process, but it scares many of us. Here John dealt with an individual who was hurting people in the Christian community. He warned Gaius and his fellow believers about Diotrephes and told them not to let his bad example influence them. We may know people who are trying to stop our recovery. We may need to confront them, which may be difficult and painful. We need to be honest with other people and break free of them if they are trying to make us reject God's will for our life. God wants us to make progress in recovery; he will help us deal wisely with the people who stand in our way.

1:11-12 Having a good role model is an important part of effective recovery. John urged Gaius to follow good examples and to avoid imitating anyone who was doing evil. This means that we should put relationships that lead us back into our dependency on hold for a while and build relationships with people who model a godly lifestyle and will encourage us in recovery. Since God desires our success in recovery, he will help us build healthy relationships in our life.

[11]Dear friend, don't let this bad example influence you. Follow only what is good. Remember that those who do good prove that they are God's children, and those who do evil prove that they do not know God.*

[12]Everyone speaks highly of Demetrius, as does the truth itself. We ourselves can say the same for him, and you know we speak the truth.

Conclusion

[13]I have much more to say to you, but I don't want to write it with pen and ink. [14]For I hope to see you soon, and then we will talk face to face.

[15]*Peace be with you.

Your friends here send you their greetings. Please give my personal greetings to each of our friends there.

11 Greek *they have not seen God.* **15** Some English translations combine verses 14 and 15 into verse 14.

JUDE

THE BIG PICTURE

A. A CAUTION TO BELIEVERS
(1:1-16)

B. A CHALLENGE TO BELIEVERS
(1:17-25)

Jude wrote this letter to young believers who had left their old life behind to follow Christ. They had made spiritual and moral commitments to do what God wanted them to do. But some false teachers claimed that believers could live however they wanted because God had already paid for their sins. Consequently, many new believers were tempted to go back to their old destructive lifestyle.

Jude urged his readers to stand up for the truth and not fall back into their old way of life. He explained that the false teachers were wrong; it did matter how they lived, and their actions did have consequences. They could not go back to their old, sinful ways without paying a terrible price.

Pressures to return to our addiction surround us, but perhaps at no time are they more difficult to resist than when they come from other people. There will always be people who make us feel like giving up on recovery. Some try to get us to give in just a little. "Just take one drink," they say. Others discourage us by their contempt for us or lack of hope that we will ever change.

It pays to recognize and stand up for God's truth. Our addiction is like a hungry lion, devouring whatever it touches. God has gone to great lengths to help us and wants us to succeed even more than we do. When we trust him fully and faithfully obey his will for our life, we will experience the freedom from bondage that he wants for us.

THE BOTTOM LINE

PURPOSE: To warn believers of the dangers of false teachings about God. AUTHOR: Jude, the brother of James and half brother of Jesus. AUDIENCE: All believers everywhere. DATE WRITTEN: Probably around A.D. 65–70. SETTING: From the beginning the church had been threatened by false teachers. Jude wrote this letter to caution all believers not to accept just any teaching about God but to defend the truth they had received from the apostles. KEY VERSES: "But you, dear friends, must build each other up in your most holy faith, pray in the power of the Holy Spirit, and await the mercy of our Lord Jesus Christ, who will bring you eternal life" (1:20-21). KEY PEOPLE AND RELATIONSHIPS: Jude with his audience.

RECOVERY THEMES

The Importance of Action: This letter is a call to action, a call to "defend the faith" (1:3). Recovery is an active, not a passive, process. Once we are over the crises that led us into recovery, there is always the temptation to sit back and relax. But actively repenting and confessing our sins, taking regular inventory, making amends, and asking God to remove our defects of character are all part of the recovery process. We need to persevere in the process of recovery, always taking action toward wholeness.

Carrying the Message to Others: Because following Jesus is not a solitary activity, Jude urged his audience to intervene in one another's lives. He told them to be merciful and gently confront others, keeping them from falling prey to destructive beliefs and activities. Recovery always involves us with other people. We cannot become stabilized in recovery unless we make carrying the message of hope to others an integral part of our life. We will discover that as we share our story of deliverance, we will gain new strength to persevere in our own struggle.

Greetings from Jude

This letter is from Jude, a slave of Jesus Christ and a brother of James.

I am writing to all who have been called by God the Father, who loves you and keeps you safe in the care of Jesus Christ.*

²May God give you more and more mercy, peace, and love.

The Danger of False Teachers

³Dear friends, I had been eagerly planning to write to you about the salvation we all share. But now I find that I must write about something else, urging you to defend the faith that God has entrusted once for all time to his holy people. ⁴I say this because some ungodly people have wormed their way into your churches, saying that God's marvelous grace allows us to live immoral lives. The condemnation of such people was recorded long ago, for they have denied our only Master and Lord, Jesus Christ.

⁵So I want to remind you, though you already know these things, that Jesus* first rescued the nation of Israel from Egypt, but later he destroyed those who did not remain faithful. ⁶And I remind you of the angels who did not stay within the limits of authority God gave them but left the place where they belonged. God has kept them securely chained in prisons of darkness, waiting for the great day of judgment. ⁷And don't forget Sodom and Gomorrah and their neighboring towns, which were filled with immorality and every kind of sexual perversion. Those cities were destroyed by fire and serve as a warning of the eternal fire of God's judgment.

1 Or *keeps you for Jesus Christ.* 5 Other manuscripts read *[the] Lord,* or *God,* or *God Christ.*

1:3-7 Problems don't usually attack us head-on; they often come when we least expect them. Sometimes we are completely unaware of the dangers that certain people, ideas, or activities pose to us. Jude warned his readers about people who would try to lead them away from true faith in Jesus Christ by claiming that God's grace set them free to do whatever they wanted. Our society often proclaims a similar message: Boundaries to behavior are limiting and destructive. Most of us have discovered firsthand, however, that this teaching leads to painful bondage. We should take Jude's warning seriously. We should avoid people and activities that could lead us back into slavery. The only road to freedom is God's program for healthy living.

1:14-16 Jude reminded his readers that the false teachers among them would suffer terrible consequences for their selfish and sinful lifestyle. We may be tempted to follow our old friends back into the "pleasures" of our old sinful habits. Jude's warning can help us turn away from any such temptations. If we take part in destructive activities, we will be enslaved and then destroyed. If we plant seeds of righteousness by following God's will, we will receive God's blessings and help. True freedom can be found only through a vibrant relationship with God.

1:17-23 God's Word is reliable and true. It warns us about people who might try to hinder our spiritual growth. When we learn to expect such people, we can prepare to stand firm against the temptations they offer us. By learning to recognize our weaknesses and walk humbly, depending on the Holy Spirit's guidance, we can shun the things that tear us down. When we encourage others in recovery, the story we tell must be clear and consistent with our lifestyle. We can share God's message of hope by showing others the kind of selfless love that God has already shown to us. We cannot live this way under our own power; we can do it only by receiving the power God offers through his Holy Spirit.

8In the same way, these people—who claim authority from their dreams—live immoral lives, defy authority, and scoff at supernatural beings.* 9But even Michael, one of the mightiest of the angels,* did not dare accuse the devil of blasphemy, but simply said, "The Lord rebuke you!" (This took place when Michael was arguing with the devil about Moses' body.) 10But these people scoff at things they do not understand. Like unthinking animals, they do whatever their instincts tell them, and so they bring about their own destruction. 11What sorrow awaits them! For they follow in the footsteps of Cain, who killed his brother. Like Balaam, they deceive people for money. And like Korah, they perish in their rebellion.

12When these people eat with you in your fellowship meals commemorating the Lord's love, they are like dangerous reefs that can shipwreck you.* They are like shameless shepherds who care only for themselves. They are like clouds blowing over the land without giving any rain. They are like trees in autumn that are doubly dead, for they bear no fruit and have been pulled up by the roots. 13They are like wild waves of the sea, churning up the foam of their shameful deeds. They are like wandering stars, doomed forever to blackest darkness.

14Enoch, who lived in the seventh generation after Adam, prophesied about these people. He said, "Listen! The Lord is coming with countless thousands of his holy ones 15to execute judgment on the people of the world. He will convict every person of all the ungodly things they have done and for all the insults that ungodly sinners have spoken against him."*

16These people are grumblers and complainers, living only to satisfy their desires. They brag loudly about themselves, and they flatter others to get what they want.

A Call to Remain Faithful

17But you, my dear friends, must remember what the apostles of our Lord Jesus Christ predicted. 18They told you that in the last times there would be scoffers whose purpose in life is to satisfy their ungodly desires. 19These people are the ones who are creating divisions among you. They follow their

8 Greek *at glorious ones*, which are probably evil angels. 9 Greek *Michael, the archangel*. 12 Or *they are contaminants among you;* or *they are stains*. 14-15 The quotation comes from intertestamental literature: Enoch 1:9.

ACCOUNTABILITY

READ JUDE 1:20-23
As we grapple with our addiction we are likely to avoid honest communication with others about our problems. It is important, however, that we return to the relationships that will help us face the truth. Paul spoke of the value of honesty: "So stop telling lies. Let us tell our neighbors the truth, for we are all parts of the same body" (Ephesians 4:25). Jude, the half brother of Jesus, reminded his readers that they were to deal honestly and directly with those who were doing wrong: "Show mercy to those whose faith is wavering. . . . Show mercy to still others, but do so with great caution, hating the sins that contaminate their lives" (Jude 1:22-23).

Jesus even gave specific instructions for dealing with people who have done wrong but persist in denying it: "If another believer sins against you, go privately and point out the offense. If the other person listens and confesses it, you have won that person back. But if you are unsuccessful, take one or two others with you and go back again, so that everything you say may be confirmed by two or three witnesses. If the person still refuses to listen, take your case to the church. Then if he or she won't accept the church's decision, treat that person as a pagan or a corrupt tax collector" (Matthew 18:15-17).

Accountability and honesty in our relationships are essential to successful recovery. When we make ourself accountable to others, the caring influence of godly friends can help keep us on the right track. They can provide us with an objective perspective, helping us to admit the truth. We often become isolated as a result of our shame or fear that we will be rejected if we ever reveal who we really are. Admitting our wrongs to trustworthy people helps break down the isolation.
Turn to page 1653, Revelation 3.

natural instincts because they do not have God's Spirit in them.

20But you, dear friends, must build each other up in your most holy faith, pray in the power of the Holy Spirit,* 21and await the mercy of our Lord Jesus Christ, who will bring you eternal life. In this way, you will keep yourselves safe in God's love.

22And you must show mercy to* those whose faith is wavering. 23Rescue others by snatching them from the flames of judgment. Show mercy to still others,* but do so with great caution, hating the sins that contaminate their lives.*

A Prayer of Praise

24Now all glory to God, who is able to keep you from falling away and will bring you with great joy into his glorious presence without a single fault. 25All glory to him who alone is God, our Savior through Jesus Christ our Lord. All glory, majesty, power, and authority are his before all time, and in the present, and beyond all time! Amen.

20 Greek *pray in the Holy Spirit.* **22** Some manuscripts read *must reprove.* **22-23a** Some manuscripts have only two categories of people: (1) those whose faith is wavering and therefore need to be snatched from the flames of judgment, and (2) those who need to be shown mercy. **23b** Greek *with fear, hating even the clothing stained by the flesh.*

REVELATION

THE BIG PICTURE

A. JOHN'S PAIN AND GOD'S GLORY (1:1-20)

B. THE NEED FOR RECOVERY AMONG THE CHURCHES (2:1–3:22)

C. GOD'S GLORIOUS POWER—HOPE FOR RECOVERY (4:1–5:14)

D. GOD'S WRATH TOWARD UNBELIEF AND DENIAL (6:1–16:21)

E. BABYLON'S GRAND APPEARANCE AND FIERCE JUDGMENT (17:1–18:24)

F. CHRIST'S VICTORY, RULE, AND FINAL JUDGMENT (19:1–20:15)

G. THE NEW HEAVENS AND NEW EARTH (21:1–22:21)

From beginning to end, the book of Revelation is about struggle. In its opening chapters are John's seven dictated letters from the resurrected Christ to seven churches. Each church had its own struggles, but some had deeper problems than others. In each letter Jesus urged his people to cling to him and do what they knew to be right. The ones who listened he called overcomers.

The rest of the book contains the story of another dramatic struggle: God's plan to rid the world of sin and its destructive consequences. John describes when Jesus will return in glory to conquer Satan and restore his broken world, vindicating God's people and judging the wicked. All people will get their dues when Christ returns. Believers will receive eternal joy; unbelievers, unending separation from God. In the end, God will rebuild what has been broken by sin. He will introduce a new heaven and a new earth.

The book of Revelation ends with Christ as victor over all. All that he said will come true; all that he taught will be proven right; all who followed him will be vindicated; and all who rejected him will be judged. God will have his way. He wants nothing more than to have us stand beside him as victors! We face struggles in recovery; God knows that. Through this book he urges us to not give up but to believe in him and to overcome. As he renews our broken world, he will make our broken life new and perfect as well.

THE BOTTOM LINE

PURPOSE: To give hope to believers and warn them not to compromise their loyalty to God. AUTHOR: The apostle John. AUDIENCE: Seven churches in Asia Minor. DATE WRITTEN: Probably about A.D. 95, during the Roman emperor Domitian's persecution of Christians. SETTING: John, who was in exile on the island of Patmos, wrote to the seven churches to urge them to devote themselves to Christ. KEY VERSE: "Look! I stand at the door and knock. If you hear my voice and open the door, I will come in, and we will share a meal together as friends" (3:20). KEY PLACES: Patmos, seven cities in Asia Minor, Babylon, and the New Jerusalem. KEY PEOPLE: John, the risen Christ, and members of the churches of Asia Minor.

RECOVERY THEMES

God Is Over All: God is sovereign. He is greater than any other power in the universe—including our dependency. Nothing can compare to him. When we look at the abuse we may have suffered as children or at the pain we may have caused others, we may feel powerless to change things or make amends. But John wrote this book to assure us that though evil may seem to win today's battles, God is all-powerful and will assert his power for his people. Ultimately all things will be made new in Christ. As we submit our life to God, he will begin the process of renewal right away.

God Is the Source of Our Hope: We may feel helpless and about to give up all hope. But the book of Revelation reveals to us the ultimate source of hope—Jesus Christ. He is coming again and will deal with the problems of our sin-tattered world, restoring what is broken and dealing with the injustices around us. Life is never hopeless, regardless of what has happened to us or what we have done. We can focus on God's love, grace, and forgiveness. He has made our restoration possible through Christ, and he will return to complete his task of universal renewal. If we are looking to Christ, we can claim our hope despite the difficult circumstances we may face.

The Pain of Consequences: Something in every one of us cries out for justice. When evil and injustice prosper, we may become angry and think that people ultimately get away with their selfish and wicked deeds. But in reality God will judge all wicked actions. Those who openly defy him will face awful consequences in the end. Those who turn to him for forgiveness need not fear the future day of judgment. Judgment is an awful thing, but the pain of sin's consequences can motivate us to turn our life over to God and obediently follow his plan.

Justice Belongs to God: Being in recovery does not release us from our sense of justice. As we deal with the wrongs we have done, we may feel that others are not dealing with theirs and that we have legitimate grudges to harbor. While these feelings are natural, they are not godly and endanger our recovery. The book of Revelation makes it clear that justice belongs to God; he alone has the right to avenge the wrongs of others. What's more, he alone has the power to change their lives. Anger and bitterness make recovery more difficult than it already is. Part of giving our life and our will over to God is releasing the bitterness we feel toward others.

CHAPTER 1
Prologue

This is a revelation from* Jesus Christ, which God gave him to show his servants the events that must soon* take place. He sent an angel to present this revelation to his servant John, ²who faithfully reported everything he saw. This is his report of the word of God and the testimony of Jesus Christ.

³God blesses the one who reads the words of this prophecy to the church, and he blesses all who listen to its message and obey what it says, for the time is near.

John's Greeting to the Seven Churches

⁴This letter is from John to the seven churches in the province of Asia.*

Grace and peace to you from the one who is, who always was, and who is still to come; from the sevenfold Spirit* before his throne; ⁵and from Jesus Christ. He is the faithful witness to these things, the first to rise from the dead, and the ruler of all the kings of the world.

All glory to him who loves us and has freed us from our sins by shedding his blood for us. ⁶He has made us a Kingdom of priests

---

1:1a Or *of.* **1:1b** Or *suddenly,* or *quickly.* **1:4a** *Asia* was a Roman province in what is now western Turkey. **1:4b** Greek *the seven spirits.*

1:1-2 The book of Revelation describes what will happen in the future. It looks forward to the time of Christ's return, when our new life in Christ will be perfected. It also tells about the hard battle God will fight to restore our world from the destructive consequences of sin. Many of this book's symbols are difficult to interpret, but one message comes through clearly: No matter how bad things are right now, God has a solution! Jesus Christ will return to re-create our broken and polluted world. He will give us a new body and a healed heart. God has already started his healing in us through our relationship with Christ; he will complete this task when he returns to rule. **1:4-6** The powerful work of Jesus Christ is the only valid foundation for recovery. Christ shed his redemptive blood on the cross to free us from bondage to sin, past abuse, destructive habits, compulsions, and addictions. God loved us enough to send his Son to die on our behalf. But, praise God, Jesus rose from the dead, conquering death forever! Through him we can rise to new life. No matter who we are or what we have done, God has solutions for our problems. Through Christ, we have been made citizens of his eternal Kingdom (see Philippians 3:20); therefore we can look forward to an eternity of joy and being in God's presence.

for God his Father. All glory and power to him forever and ever! Amen.

⁷Look! He comes with the clouds of heaven.
And everyone will see him—
even those who pierced him.
And all the nations of the world
will mourn for him.
Yes! Amen!

⁸"I am the Alpha and the Omega—the beginning and the end,"* says the Lord God. "I am the one who is, who always was, and who is still to come—the Almighty One."

Vision of the Son of Man

⁹I, John, am your brother and your partner in suffering and in God's Kingdom and in the patient endurance to which Jesus calls us. I was exiled to the island of Patmos for preaching the word of God and for my testimony about Jesus. ¹⁰It was the Lord's Day, and I was worshiping in the Spirit.* Suddenly, I heard behind me a loud voice like a trumpet blast. ¹¹It said, "Write in a book* everything you see, and send it to the seven churches in the cities of Ephesus, Smyrna, Pergamum, Thyatira, Sardis, Philadelphia, and Laodicea."

¹²When I turned to see who was speaking to me, I saw seven gold lampstands. ¹³And standing in the middle of the lampstands was someone like the Son of Man.* He was wearing a long robe with a gold sash across his chest. ¹⁴His head and his hair were white like wool, as white as snow. And his eyes were like flames of fire. ¹⁵His feet were like polished bronze refined in a furnace, and his voice thundered like mighty ocean waves. ¹⁶He held seven stars in his right hand, and a sharp two-edged sword came from his mouth. And his face was like the sun in all its brilliance.

¹⁷When I saw him, I fell at his feet as if I were dead. But he laid his right hand on me and said, "Don't be afraid! I am the First and the Last. ¹⁸I am the living one. I died, but look—I am alive forever and ever! And I hold the keys of death and the grave.*

¹⁹"Write down what you have seen—both the things that are now happening and the things that will happen.* ²⁰This is the meaning of the mystery of the seven stars you saw in my right hand and the seven gold lampstands: The seven stars are the angels* of the seven churches, and the seven lampstands are the seven churches.

CHAPTER 2
The Message to the Church in Ephesus
"Write this letter to the angel* of the church in Ephesus. This is the message from the one who holds the seven stars in his right hand, the one who walks among the seven gold lampstands:

²"I know all the things you do. I have seen your hard work and your patient endurance. I know you don't tolerate evil people. You have examined the claims of those who say they are apostles but are not. You have discovered they are liars. ³You have patiently suffered for me without quitting.

1:8 Greek *I am the Alpha and the Omega,* referring to the first and last letters of the Greek alphabet. 1:10 Or *in spirit.* 1:11 Or *on a scroll.* 1:13 Or *like a son of man.* See Dan 7:13. "Son of Man" is a title Jesus used for himself. 1:18 Greek *and Hades.* 1:19 Or *what you have seen and what they mean—the things that have already begun to happen.* 1:20 Or *the messengers.* 2:1 Or *the messenger;* also in 2:8, 12, 18.

1:7-8 The future coming of Jesus Christ will be desperately painful for those who refuse to believe and follow him. The terrifying consequences of their denial will be eternal judgment (see 20:11-15). On the other hand, if we pursue recovery by faith in Christ, we can rejoice in the new life his return will bring. God is "the beginning and the end" of all things. We can have hope because God is in control of our past, present, and future.
1:9-11 John suffered a great deal for Christ and persevered through it all. All the pain and exile had not embittered him toward God; the apostle still worshiped God faithfully. John was worshiping when he received the visions recorded in this book. It is easy to become discouraged as we work our program. Some people may reject us because we are trying to change or because we have problems. We know what it's like to be looked down upon. John's example provides encouragement to persevere despite the difficulties we face. If we give up now, we face sure disaster in the future. If we stick with recovery, God will help us to build a new life.
2:1-7 Christ addressed the church in Ephesus first. It was the largest congregation and probably responsible for planting the other churches (see Acts 19:1, 10). John began on a positive note by commending the Ephesian believers for their perseverance through hardship. Then he confronted the more painful realities and challenged his readers to repent and rekindle their love, which had waned. Confrontations are best made in the context of love. We need to begin our conversations by building others up and showing that we care. After laying the groundwork lovingly, we can better communicate the more painful messages.

4"But I have this complaint against you. You don't love me or each other as you did at first!* 5Look how far you have fallen! Turn back to me and do the works you did at first. If you don't repent, I will come and remove your lampstand from its place among the churches. 6But this is in your favor: You hate the evil deeds of the Nicolaitans, just as I do.

7"Anyone with ears to hear must listen to the Spirit and understand what he is saying to the churches. To everyone who is victorious I will give fruit from the tree of life in the paradise of God.

The Message to the Church in Smyrna

8"Write this letter to the angel of the church in Smyrna. This is the message from the one who is the First and the Last, who was dead but is now alive:

9"I know about your suffering and your poverty—but you are rich! I know the blasphemy of those opposing you. They say they are Jews, but they are not, because their synagogue belongs to Satan. 10Don't be afraid of what you are about to suffer. The devil will throw some of you into prison to test you. You will suffer for ten days. But if you remain faithful even when facing death, I will give you the crown of life.

11"Anyone with ears to hear must listen to the Spirit and understand what he is saying to the churches. Whoever is victorious will not be harmed by the second death.

2:4 Greek *You have lost your first love.*

The Message to the Church in Pergamum

12"Write this letter to the angel of the church in Pergamum. This is the message from the one with the sharp two-edged sword:

13"I know that you live in the city where Satan has his throne, yet you have remained loyal to me. You refused to deny me even when Antipas, my faithful witness, was martyred among you there in Satan's city.

14"But I have a few complaints against you. You tolerate some among you whose teaching is like that of Balaam, who showed Balak how to trip up the people of Israel. He taught them to sin by eating food offered to idols and by committing sexual sin. 15In a similar way, you have some Nicolaitans among you who follow the same teaching. 16Repent of your sin, or I will come to you suddenly and fight against them with the sword of my mouth.

17"Anyone with ears to hear must listen to the Spirit and understand what he is saying to the churches. To everyone who is victorious I will give some of the manna that has been hidden away in heaven. And I will give to each one a white stone, and on the stone will be engraved a new name that no one understands except the one who receives it.

The Message to the Church in Thyatira

18"Write this letter to the angel of the church in Thyatira. This is the message from the Son of God, whose eyes are like flames of fire, whose feet are like polished bronze:

2:8-11 The church in Smyrna was the closest of the other six to Ephesus, and it was experiencing similar hardships. This small Christian community was suffering from unrelenting oppression by Satan and his evil spiritual forces. John's vision reminded the believers that their perseverance through dangerous times would be rewarded with the crown of life for their faithfulness. We too are called to persevere through the tough times. As we entrust our life to God and obey him, he will slowly transform us. At Christ's return, we will receive a new body and a cleansed heart—a completely new life!

2:12-17 The church in Pergamum had remained intensely loyal to Jesus Christ through a satanic onslaught. But some in the church had given in to sexual misconduct. Such relational and spiritual dysfunctions threatened to undermine, or at least neutralize, the testimony of this Christian community. Sometimes great victories in recovery can be neutralized by small mistakes. We need to be consistent in our walk with God, making sure that all areas of our life are yielded to his control. Ignoring even the smallest sin or bad habit could lead to our undoing.

2:18-29 The church in Thyatira was commended for its acts of faith, love, and patience, and it was encouraged to persevere in doing them. But a serious spiritual cancer was growing in their midst—a self-styled prophetess named Jezebel was encouraging a profligate lifestyle. God punished this woman harshly to show how much he wanted to protect his people from her evil influence. This gives us some idea of how dangerous it is to have relationships with people who might lead us astray. We need to choose our relationships carefully. Dysfunctional relationships may lead us away from God and quickly destroy our progress in recovery.

[19]"I know all the things you do. I have seen your love, your faith, your service, and your patient endurance. And I can see your constant improvement in all these things. [20]"But I have this complaint against you. You are permitting that woman—that Jezebel who calls herself a prophet—to lead my servants astray. She teaches them to commit sexual sin and to eat food offered to idols. [21]I gave her time to repent, but she does not want to turn away from her immorality.

[22]"Therefore, I will throw her on a bed of suffering,* and those who commit adultery with her will suffer greatly unless they repent and turn away from her evil deeds. [23]I will strike her children dead. Then all the churches will know that I am the one who searches out the thoughts and intentions of every person. And I will give to each of you whatever you deserve.

[24]"But I also have a message for the rest of you in Thyatira who have not followed this false teaching ('deeper truths,' as they call them—depths of Satan, actually). I will ask nothing more of you [25]except that you hold tightly to what you have until I come. [26]To all who are victorious, who obey me to the very end,

> To them I will give authority over all
>   the nations.
> [27]They will rule the nations with an iron
>   rod
> and smash them like clay pots.*

[28]They will have the same authority I received from my Father, and I will also give them the morning star!

[29]"Anyone with ears to hear must listen to the Spirit and understand what he is saying to the churches.

CHAPTER 3
The Message to the Church in Sardis

"Write this letter to the angel* of the church in Sardis. This is the message from the one who has the sevenfold Spirit* of God and the seven stars:

"I know all the things you do, and that you have a reputation for being alive—but you are dead. [2]Wake up! Strengthen what little remains, for even what is left is almost dead. I find that your actions do not meet the requirements of my God. [3]Go back to what you heard and believed at first; hold to it firmly. Repent and turn to me again. If you don't wake up, I will come to you suddenly, as unexpected as a thief.

[4]"Yet there are some in the church in Sardis who have not soiled their clothes with evil. They will walk with me in white, for they are worthy. [5]All who are victorious will be clothed in white. I will never erase their names from the Book of Life, but I will announce before my Father and his angels that they are mine.

[6]"Anyone with ears to hear must listen to the Spirit and understand what he is saying to the churches.

The Message to the Church in Philadelphia

[7]"Write this letter to the angel of the church in Philadelphia.

> This is the message from the one who is
>   holy and true,
>   the one who has the key of David.
> What he opens, no one can close;

2:22 Greek *a bed.* 2:26-27 Ps 2:8-9 (Greek version). 3:1a Or *the messenger;* also in 3:7, 14. 3:1b Greek *the seven spirits.*

3:1-6 The believers in Sardis were, for the most part, just going through the motions of being spiritual. They were warned to make immediate changes or they would suffer painful consequences. Fortunately, some believers in Sardis stood firm in their faith, and they would be rewarded accordingly. With God's help, it is possible to stand firm even when everyone around us is falling away. We don't have to follow the crowd or be a victim of our environment; we can follow God instead. As we do, he will bless us and write our name in the Book of Life.
3:7-13 The church in Philadelphia was not strong, but it had remained obedient to God and stood firm against satanic oppression. So Christ promised this church protection from the greatest time of tribulation that would ever come upon the whole world. He encouraged them to persevere, promising that they would live forever with Christ in his new Jerusalem. This promise has been greatly delayed, but that doesn't make it any less secure (see 21:1–22:21). We have this same hope if we entrust our life to God through faith in Jesus Christ. Though the years of recovery may seem long, our hope in God's eternal deliverance is just as certain.

and what he closes, no one can open:*

8"I know all the things you do, and I have opened a door for you that no one can close. You have little strength, yet you obeyed my word and did not deny me. 9Look, I will force those who belong to Satan's synagogue—those liars who say they are Jews but are not—to come and bow down at your feet. They will acknowledge that you are the ones I love.

10"Because you have obeyed my command to persevere, I will protect you from the great time of testing that will come upon the whole world to test those who belong to this world. 11I am coming soon.* Hold on to what you have, so that no one will take away your crown. 12All who are victorious will become pillars in the Temple of my God, and they will never have to leave it. And I will write on them the name of my God, and they will be citizens in the city of my God—the new Jerusalem that comes down from heaven from my God. And I will also write on them my new name.

13"Anyone with ears to hear must listen to the Spirit and understand what he is saying to the churches.

The Message to the Church in Laodicea

14"Write this letter to the angel of the church in Laodicea. This is the message from the one who is the Amen—the faithful and true witness, the beginning* of God's new creation:

15"I know all the things you do, that you are neither hot nor cold. I wish that you were one or the other! 16But since you are like lukewarm water, neither hot nor cold, I will spit you out of my mouth! 17You say, 'I am rich. I have everything I want. I don't need a thing!' And you don't realize that you are wretched and miserable and poor and blind and naked. 18So I advise you to buy gold from me—gold that has been purified by fire. Then you will be rich. Also buy white garments from me so you will not be shamed by your nakedness, and ointment for your eyes so you will be able to see. 19I correct and discipline everyone I love. So be diligent and turn from your indifference.

20"Look! I stand at the door and knock. If you hear my voice and open the door, I

3:7 Isa 22:22. **3:11** Or *suddenly,* or *quickly.* **3:14** Or *the ruler,* or *the source.*

3:14-21 The believers in Laodicea were engaged in full-blown denial. Though they portrayed themselves as being self-sustaining and having no needs, Christ saw their situation differently. To him they were spiritually blind and destitute. But, worst of all, they were spiritually indifferent—lukewarm. Sometimes after making progress in recovery we grow indifferent to our new lifestyle. We forget how desperate we were before entering recovery and that God is the one who set us free. We begin to long for things that will lead us back into bondage. We can avoid that long slide backward by taking honest moral inventory and getting back on track.

4:1-3 The apostle John saw this spectacular scene in God's heavenly throne room (4:1–5:14) while he was a prisoner on the island of Patmos. We may also be living in bondage, feeling hopelessly entrapped and distant from help or deliverance. But like John, we can draw close to God even when the world around us is dark and foreboding. John's vision of heaven gave him the hope he needed to face the lonely days ahead. And the record the apostle left us can give us hope during hard times, too. Even when we are alone and helpless, God is still with us, and we can draw near to him. God's grace and power are never limited by the circumstances we are in.

4:4-8 Two principles from this passage can encourage us as we work toward recovery: (1) The fact that the twenty-four elders represent the people of God shows that believers are honored significantly by God in heaven; (2) the diverse appearances of the four living beings implies that God wants all of us to be unique, utilizing our special characteristics for his glory. God values us because he created us; each of us has unique gifts to use in his service and for his glory. These truths can encourage us as we deal with the problems and pressures of the recovery process.

4:8-11 God is worthy of our continuous praise. Even the great spiritual beings in heaven fervently praised God. As we make God a daily focus in our life and offer him our gratitude and praise, we will discover new freedom from our problems and dependency. Our painful circumstances will begin to fade away in the light of his glorious love and power. God is greater and more powerful than anything we have to face. We can entrust our life to him, follow his will, and then praise him for the amazing things he will do in our life.

will come in, and we will share a meal together as friends. ²¹Those who are victorious will sit with me on my throne, just as I was victorious and sat with my Father on his throne.

²²"Anyone with ears to hear must listen to the Spirit and understand what he is saying to the churches."

CHAPTER 4
Worship in Heaven

Then as I looked, I saw a door standing open in heaven, and the same voice I had heard before spoke to me like a trumpet blast. The voice said, "Come up here, and I will show you what must happen after this." ²And instantly I was in the Spirit,* and I saw a throne in heaven and someone sitting on it. ³The one sitting on the throne was as brilliant as gemstones—like jasper and carnelian. And the glow of an emerald circled his throne like a rainbow. ⁴Twenty-four thrones surrounded him, and twenty-four elders sat on them. They were all clothed in white and had gold crowns on their heads. ⁵From the throne came flashes of lightning and the rumble of thunder. And in front of the throne were seven torches with burning flames. This is the sevenfold Spirit* of God. ⁶In front of the throne was a shiny sea of glass, sparkling like crystal.

In the center and around the throne were four living beings, each covered with eyes, front and back. ⁷The first of these living beings was like a lion; the second was like an ox; the third had a human face; and the fourth was like an eagle in flight. ⁸Each of these living beings had six wings, and their wings were covered all over with eyes, inside and out. Day after day and night after night they keep on saying,

"Holy, holy, holy is the Lord God, the
  Almighty—
 the one who always was, who is, and
  who is still to come."

⁹Whenever the living beings give glory and honor and thanks to the one sitting on the throne (the one who lives forever and ever), ¹⁰the twenty-four elders fall down and worship the one sitting on the throne (the one who lives forever and ever). And they lay their crowns before the throne and say,

¹¹"You are worthy, O Lord our God,
 to receive glory and honor and
  power.

4:2 Or *in spirit.* 4:5 Greek *They are the seven spirits.*

LOVE

READ REVELATION 3:14-22
We may feel like love just doesn't seem to work for us. We may wonder if we are doing something wrong. Perhaps we have problems loving because we are disconnected from the source of true love.

The apostle John wrote: "Dear friends, let us continue to love one another, for love comes from God. . . . But anyone who does not love does not know God, for God is love" (1 John 4:7-8).

Jesus said: "I am giving you a new commandment: Love each other. Just as I have loved you, you should love each other" (John 13:34). Trying to love without first receiving God's love is like trying to water something with a hose that's disconnected from the faucet. When we receive God's unconditional love, we can begin to love ourself. We are then told to love others as we love ourself and as Jesus has loved us. There is a boundless reservoir of love available to us; but without receiving the love of God in Christ, we will quickly run dry.

Jesus is waiting for us to open our heart and receive his love. He said: "Look! I stand at the door and knock. If you hear my voice and open the door, I will come in, and we will share a meal together as friends" (Revelation 3:20). Love is waiting. We receive it when we open up to the love God offers us. *Turn to page 1671, Revelation 22.*

For you created all things,
and they exist because you created what
you pleased."

CHAPTER 5
The Lamb Opens the Scroll

Then I saw a scroll* in the right hand of the
one who was sitting on the throne. There
was writing on the inside and the outside of
the scroll, and it was sealed with seven seals.
²And I saw a strong angel, who shouted with
a loud voice: "Who is worthy to break the
seals on this scroll and open it?" ³But no one
in heaven or on earth or under the earth was
able to open the scroll and read it.

⁴Then I began to weep bitterly because no
one was found worthy to open the scroll and
read it. ⁵But one of the twenty-four elders
said to me, "Stop weeping! Look, the Lion of
the tribe of Judah, the heir to David's
throne,* has won the victory. He is worthy to
open the scroll and its seven seals."

⁶Then I saw a Lamb that looked as if it had
been slaughtered, but it was now standing
between the throne and the four living beings and among the twenty-four elders. He
had seven horns and seven eyes, which represent the sevenfold Spirit* of God that is
sent out into every part of the earth. ⁷He
stepped forward and took the scroll from the
right hand of the one sitting on the throne.
⁸And when he took the scroll, the four living
beings and the twenty-four elders fell down
before the Lamb. Each one had a harp, and
they held gold bowls filled with incense,
which are the prayers of God's people. ⁹And
they sang a new song with these words:

"You are worthy to take the scroll
and break its seals and open it.
For you were slaughtered, and
your blood has ransomed people
for God
from every tribe and language and
people and nation.
¹⁰ And you have caused them to become
a Kingdom of priests for our God.
And they will reign* on the earth."

¹¹Then I looked again, and I heard the
voices of thousands and millions of angels
around the throne and of the living beings
and the elders. ¹²And they sang in a mighty
chorus:

"Worthy is the Lamb who was
slaughtered—
to receive power and riches
and wisdom and strength
and honor and glory and blessing."

¹³And then I heard every creature in
heaven and on earth and under the earth
and in the sea. They sang:

"Blessing and honor and glory and power
belong to the one sitting on the throne
and to the Lamb forever and ever."

¹⁴And the four living beings said, "Amen!"
And the twenty-four elders fell down and
worshiped the Lamb.

5:1 Or *book;* also in 5:2, 3, 4, 5, 7, 8, 9. **5:5** Greek *the root of David.* See Isa 11:10. **5:6** Greek *which are the seven spirits.*
5:10 Some manuscripts read *they are reigning.*

5:1-7 Many of us know the tremendous pain of not being able to live up to our perfectionistic
goals. Expecting absolute perfection in this life is unrealistic. In heaven, however, perfection will
be the norm. Even there, though, initially there was no one worthy to open the scroll of revelation and judgment. The Lamb—Jesus Christ—is the only one worthy to open the scroll. He is
perfect and has conquered sin and death through his death and resurrection. Because of him,
we can overcome our sins and dependency. Christ will open the scroll, beginning the process of
recovery for our broken and sinful world. If we entrust our life to him, he will begin the same
process of restoration in our life. Someday, by God's grace and power, we will be made perfect.
5:9-10 By shedding his blood on the cross, Jesus Christ, the Lamb, made salvation possible for all.
But God does far more than deliver us from our sins and dependency. He promises to make us
part of his team for restoring and maintaining his world. We will be members of God's kingdom
of priests. As soon as we entrust our life to God and seek to follow his will, we can begin our
priestly duties. This involves sharing our story of deliverance and calling others to faith in Jesus
Christ—the only power available for true recovery.
5:11-14 In these final verses of John's description of the heavenly throne room, praise for the
divine Lamb spills over from heaven to the rest of the created realm. No matter how much unbelief and sin dominate the earthly scene today, a time will come when all will honor God. Such
praise will necessarily include the admission of guilt, responsibility, and unbelieving denial by
many (see Philippians 2:9-11). We don't have to wait until Christ returns to acknowledge his lordship in our life. We can do it today and begin to enjoy the immediate benefits of a vital relationship with God through Jesus Christ.

CHAPTER 6

The Lamb Breaks the First Six Seals

As I watched, the Lamb broke the first of the seven seals on the scroll.* Then I heard one of the four living beings say with a voice like thunder, "Come!" ²I looked up and saw a white horse standing there. Its rider carried a bow, and a crown was placed on his head. He rode out to win many battles and gain the victory.

³When the Lamb broke the second seal, I heard the second living being say, "Come!" ⁴Then another horse appeared, a red one. Its rider was given a mighty sword and the authority to take peace from the earth. And there was war and slaughter everywhere.

⁵When the Lamb broke the third seal, I heard the third living being say, "Come!" I looked up and saw a black horse, and its rider was holding a pair of scales in his hand. ⁶And I heard a voice from among the four living beings say, "A loaf of wheat bread or three loaves of barley will cost a day's pay.* And don't waste* the olive oil and wine."

⁷When the Lamb broke the fourth seal, I heard the fourth living being say, "Come!" ⁸I looked up and saw a horse whose color was pale green. Its rider was named Death, and his companion was the Grave.* These two were given authority over one-fourth of the earth, to kill with the sword and famine and disease* and wild animals.

⁹When the Lamb broke the fifth seal, I saw under the altar the souls of all who had been martyred for the word of God and for being faithful in their testimony. ¹⁰They shouted to the Lord and said, "O Sovereign Lord, holy and true, how long before you judge the people who belong to this world and avenge our blood for what they have done to us?" ¹¹Then a white robe was given to each of them. And they were told to rest a little longer until the full number of their brothers and sisters*—their fellow servants of Jesus who were to be martyred—had joined them.

¹²I watched as the Lamb broke the sixth seal, and there was a great earthquake. The sun became as dark as black cloth, and the moon became as red as blood. ¹³Then the stars of the sky fell to the earth like green figs falling from a tree shaken by a strong wind. ¹⁴The sky was rolled up like a scroll, and all of the mountains and islands were moved from their places.

¹⁵Then everyone—the kings of the earth, the rulers, the generals, the wealthy, the powerful, and every slave and free person—all hid themselves in the caves and among the rocks of the mountains. ¹⁶And they cried to the mountains and the rocks, "Fall on us and hide us from the face of the one who sits on the throne and from the wrath of the Lamb. ¹⁷For the great day of their wrath has come, and who is able to survive?"

6:1 Or book. 6:6a Greek A choinix [1 quart or 1 liter] of wheat for a denarius, and 3 choinix of barley for a denarius. A denarius was equivalent to a laborer's full day's wage. 6:6b Or harm. 6:8a Greek was Hades. 6:8b Greek death. 6:11 Greek their brothers.

6:1-8 Jesus Christ, the Lamb, begins opening the scroll (see 5:1), setting in motion the events leading to God's victory over sin and death. War, famine, and disease will be rampant during the period of the first four seals. The first steps toward God's cosmic restoration lead through painful times. Millions of people will die as God deals with the sin that dominates our world. God often leads us through periods of pain as we suffer the consequences of our behavior, but he does so for our ultimate good. Even though he allows us to suffer for a time, he plans for our restoration and recovery. Sometimes the trials brought on by our dependency are the only way God can teach us how helpless we are and how much we need him.

6:9-11 The opening of the fifth seal reveals those who have died in God's service; they are waiting for God to avenge their unjust deaths. God tells them that they will have to wait because still other martyrs will join them. Many of us have suffered abuse in the past. Perhaps the abuse we suffered is at the root of our present problems and dependency. We may desire revenge against people who have wronged us. Maybe we blame others for our addiction. Like the martyrs of Revelation, we must let God avenge the wrongs done to us. When we release our bitterness and forgive our abusers, we will make progress in recovery. Ultimately we are responsible for our addiction, whatever other factors may be involved.

6:12-17 The opening of the sixth seal is followed by a huge earthquake and amazing phenomena in the sky. Those who don't believe in Christ will want to die, mistakenly thinking they can escape God's terrible judgment. Sadly, their hearts are so hard that though they recognize God, they will not repent and turn to him in faith (see 9:20-21) and they will be destroyed. Continuing in denial about our destructive dependency or compulsion will lead to a similar end. If we refuse to recognize God's rule in our life, we will inevitably head toward deeper bondage and ultimate destruction. God wants to give us a meaningful and joyful life, but to receive this gift we need to accept his program for godly living.

CHAPTER 7
God's People Will Be Preserved

Then I saw four angels standing at the four corners of the earth, holding back the four winds so they did not blow on the earth or the sea, or even on any tree. ²And I saw another angel coming up from the east, carrying the seal of the living God. And he shouted to those four angels, who had been given power to harm land and sea, ³"Wait! Don't harm the land or the sea or the trees until we have placed the seal of God on the foreheads of his servants."

⁴And I heard how many were marked with the seal of God—144,000 were sealed from all the tribes of Israel:

⁵ from Judah	12,000
from Reuben	12,000
from Gad	12,000
⁶ from Asher	12,000
from Naphtali	12,000
from Manasseh	12,000
⁷ from Simeon	12,000
from Levi	12,000
from Issachar	12,000
⁸ from Zebulun	12,000
from Joseph	12,000
from Benjamin	12,000

Praise from the Great Crowd

⁹After this I saw a vast crowd, too great to count, from every nation and tribe and people and language, standing in front of the throne and before the Lamb. They were clothed in white robes and held palm branches in their hands. ¹⁰And they were shouting with a great roar,

"Salvation comes from our God who sits
on the throne
and from the Lamb!"

¹¹And all the angels were standing around the throne and around the elders and the four living beings. And they fell before the throne with their faces to the ground and worshiped God. ¹²They sang,

"Amen! Blessing and glory and wisdom
and thanksgiving and honor
and power and strength belong to our God
forever and ever! Amen."

¹³Then one of the twenty-four elders asked me, "Who are these who are clothed in white? Where did they come from?"

¹⁴And I said to him, "Sir, you are the one who knows."

Then he said to me, "These are the ones who died in* the great tribulation.* They have washed their robes in the blood of the Lamb and made them white.

¹⁵ "That is why they stand in front of God's
throne
and serve him day and night in his
Temple.
And he who sits on the throne
will give them shelter.
¹⁶ They will never again be hungry or thirsty;
they will never be scorched by the heat
of the sun.
¹⁷ For the Lamb on the throne*
will be their Shepherd.
He will lead them to springs of life-giving
water.
And God will wipe every tear from their
eyes."

7:14a Greek *who came out of.* 7:14b Or *the great suffering.* 7:17 Greek *on the center of the throne.*

7:1-3 As difficult as things will be during the period of the seals, God will protect those who belong to him. They will be "sealed" with God's sign of ownership and protection. Perhaps this seal is similar to the seal of the Holy Spirit now present in the lives of all who believe in Jesus Christ (see Ephesians 1:13-14; 4:30). This seal signifies an eternal relationship with God. We can begin our eternal relationship with God right now if we accept God's loving forgiveness through Jesus Christ and submit our life to his will.

7:9-14 This vast multitude from all races and nations is the harvest Christ envisioned from his great commission (see Matthew 28:19). They are truly thankful and worshipful toward God, greatly appreciating the salvation and recovery he has promised. The white garments they wear speak not only of the purity of their lifestyle but also of their redemption through the blood of Christ. By entering recovery, admitting our sins and failures, accepting God's forgiveness through Jesus Christ, and obeying God we can join this joyful throng of people who have been saved by God's wonderful grace.

7:15-17 This majestic passage describes the heavenly relationship between Christ and his people. They will serve him constantly, and he will always protect them. All their other needs will be met by Christ, the Lamb, who is also the Shepherd. In such a close and secure relationship, all the tears of painful oppression, loss, and misunderstanding will be wiped away. What wonderful hope these verses offer! By trusting in Jesus Christ, we can hope for a future filled with joy and peace.

CHAPTER 8
The Lamb Breaks the Seventh Seal
When the Lamb broke the seventh seal on the scroll,* there was silence throughout heaven for about half an hour. ²I saw the seven angels who stand before God, and they were given seven trumpets.

³Then another angel with a gold incense burner came and stood at the altar. And a great amount of incense was given to him to mix with the prayers of God's people as an offering on the gold altar before the throne. ⁴The smoke of the incense, mixed with the prayers of God's holy people, ascended up to God from the altar where the angel had poured them out. ⁵Then the angel filled the incense burner with fire from the altar and threw it down upon the earth; and thunder crashed, lightning flashed, and there was a terrible earthquake.

The First Four Trumpets
⁶Then the seven angels with the seven trumpets prepared to blow their mighty blasts.

⁷The first angel blew his trumpet, and hail and fire mixed with blood were thrown down on the earth. One-third of the earth was set on fire, one-third of the trees were burned, and all the green grass was burned.

⁸Then the second angel blew his trumpet, and a great mountain of fire was thrown into the sea. One-third of the water in the sea became blood, ⁹one-third of all things living in the sea died, and one-third of all the ships on the sea were destroyed.

¹⁰Then the third angel blew his trumpet, and a great star fell from the sky, burning like a torch. It fell on one-third of the rivers and on the springs of water. ¹¹The name of the star was Bitterness.* It made one-third of the water bitter, and many people died from drinking the bitter water.

¹²Then the fourth angel blew his trumpet, and one-third of the sun was struck, and one-third of the moon, and one-third of the stars, and they became dark. And one-third of the day was dark, and also one-third of the night.

¹³Then I looked, and I heard a single eagle crying loudly as it flew through the air, "Terror, terror, terror to all who belong to this world because of what will happen when the last three angels blow their trumpets."

CHAPTER 9
The Fifth Trumpet Brings the First Terror
Then the fifth angel blew his trumpet, and I saw a star that had fallen to earth from the sky, and he was given the key to the shaft of the bottomless pit.* ²When he opened it, smoke poured out as though from a huge furnace, and the sunlight and air turned dark from the smoke.

³Then locusts came from the smoke and descended on the earth, and they were given power to sting like scorpions. ⁴They were told not to harm the grass or plants or trees, but only the people who did not have the seal of God on their foreheads. ⁵They were told not to kill them but to torture them for five months with pain like the pain of a scorpion sting. ⁶In those days people will seek death but will not find it. They will long to die, but death will flee from them!

8:1 Or *book*. 8:11 Greek *Wormwood*. 9:1 Or *the abyss*, or *the underworld*; also in 9:11.

8:1-2 The opening of the seventh seal on the scroll of judgment brings a short period of silence throughout heaven, offering people the chance to prepare for the incredibly difficult time ahead. Sometimes in recovery we get these "silence before the storm" experiences. Things may be good at the moment, but we sense that difficult times lie ahead. We can use these quiet times to get ready for what is to come by continuing with our honest personal inventory and giving our life—problems and all—to God. If God is with us, no future trial or testing will be too great to overcome.
8:6-13 At the blowing of the first four trumpets, the people of our dysfunctional and sinful world will suffer the terrible consequences for their sins and the sins of their ancestors. There is a day of reckoning for all who reject God. Many of us have experienced similar days of reckoning in our own life. Our attitudes and actions led to periods of great suffering. When we shed our denial and confess our sins, however, Jesus Christ will deliver us from our powerful dependency and help us escape these terrible judgments.
9:1-4 As the fifth trumpet blows, a locust plague will be unleashed. Unlike regular locusts, however, these creatures will attack people, not plants. God will not allow these creatures to harm everyone—just those not protected by God's seal. As we seek recovery with God's help, we can be secure knowing that God is able and willing to protect us. He may allow hard times into our life to help us grow. If we continue to trust and obey him, he won't allow us to be destroyed by sin and its terrible consequences.

[7]The locusts looked like horses prepared for battle. They had what looked like gold crowns on their heads, and their faces looked like human faces. [8]They had hair like women's hair and teeth like the teeth of a lion. [9]They wore armor made of iron, and their wings roared like an army of chariots rushing into battle. [10]They had tails that stung like scorpions, and for five months they had the power to torment people. [11]Their king is the angel from the bottomless pit; his name in Hebrew is *Abaddon,* and in Greek, *Apollyon*—the Destroyer.

[12]The first terror is past, but look, two more terrors are coming!

The Sixth Trumpet Brings the Second Terror

[13]Then the sixth angel blew his trumpet, and I heard a voice speaking from the four horns of the gold altar that stands in the presence of God. [14]And the voice said to the sixth angel who held the trumpet, "Release the four angels who are bound at the great Euphrates River." [15]Then the four angels who had been prepared for this hour and day and month and year were turned loose to kill one-third of all the people on earth. [16]I heard the size of their army, which was 200 million mounted troops.

[17]And in my vision, I saw the horses and the riders sitting on them. The riders wore armor that was fiery red and dark blue and yellow. The horses had heads like lions, and fire and smoke and burning sulfur billowed from their mouths. [18]One-third of all the people on earth were killed by these three plagues—by the fire and smoke and burning sulfur that came from the mouths of the horses. [19]Their power was in their mouths and in

their tails. For their tails had heads like snakes, with the power to injure people.

[20]But the people who did not die in these plagues still refused to repent of their evil deeds and turn to God. They continued to worship demons and idols made of gold, silver, bronze, stone, and wood—idols that can neither see nor hear nor walk! [21]And they did not repent of their murders or their witchcraft or their sexual immorality or their thefts.

CHAPTER 10
The Angel and the Small Scroll

Then I saw another mighty angel coming down from heaven, surrounded by a cloud, with a rainbow over his head. His face shone like the sun, and his feet were like pillars of fire. [2]And in his hand was a small scroll* that had been opened. He stood with his right foot on the sea and his left foot on the land. [3]And he gave a great shout like the roar of a lion. And when he shouted, the seven thunders answered.

[4]When the seven thunders spoke, I was about to write. But I heard a voice from heaven saying, "Keep secret* what the seven thunders said, and do not write it down."

[5]Then the angel I saw standing on the sea and on the land raised his right hand toward heaven. [6]He swore an oath in the name of the one who lives forever and ever, who created the heavens and everything in them, the earth and everything in it, and the sea and everything in it. He said, "There will be no more delay. [7]When the seventh angel blows his trumpet, God's mysterious plan will be fulfilled. It will happen just as he announced it to his servants the prophets."

[8]Then the voice from heaven spoke to me

10:2 Or *book;* also in 10:8, 9, 10. 10:4 Greek *Seal up.*

9:13-21 As the sixth trumpet blows, a demonically led army will slaughter one-third of the remaining population of the world (see 6:8). Certainly circumstances would seem completely hopeless to most inhabitants of the earth at this point. They could either humble themselves and begin recovery by faith, or sink into depressed denial. Sadly, only a few will accept God's gracious offer of forgiveness at that late stage. We have a similar choice before us today as we face the destructive, painful consequences of our sins. We can either give up and fall into deeper bondage, or we can recognize how helpless we are and receive God's gift of deliverance and recovery. The choice is ours!

10:1-4 As the mighty angel from heaven shouts out the contents of the additional scroll, John assumes that he is to record it. But God prevents him from doing so. This episode reminds us that along with honesty, we need God-directed discretion. In recovery we are told to make amends to those we have wronged, except when doing so would injure them or others. Sometimes we need to refrain and be discreet because telling our whole story or seeking restoration might damage someone else. God can help us use discretion, but the guiding principle is love. We need to do what is best for others, not just what is best for ourself.

10:8-10 John was told to eat the scroll, much as the prophet Ezekiel had been instructed to do (see Ezekiel 2:8; 3:1-3). The scroll would be sweet in his mouth but bitter in his stomach. God's

again: "Go and take the open scroll from the hand of the angel who is standing on the sea and on the land."

⁹So I went to the angel and told him to give me the small scroll. "Yes, take it and eat it," he said. "It will be sweet as honey in your mouth, but it will turn sour in your stomach!" ¹⁰So I took the small scroll from the hand of the angel, and I ate it! It was sweet in my mouth, but when I swallowed it, it turned sour in my stomach.

¹¹Then I was told, "You must prophesy again about many peoples, nations, languages, and kings."

CHAPTER 11
The Two Witnesses

Then I was given a measuring stick, and I was told, "Go and measure the Temple of God and the altar, and count the number of worshipers. ²But do not measure the outer courtyard, for it has been turned over to the nations. They will trample the holy city for 42 months. ³And I will give power to my two witnesses, and they will be clothed in burlap and will prophesy during those 1,260 days."

⁴These two prophets are the two olive trees and the two lampstands that stand before the Lord of all the earth. ⁵If anyone tries to harm them, fire flashes from their mouths and consumes their enemies. This is how anyone who tries to harm them must die. ⁶They have power to shut the sky so that no rain will fall for as long as they prophesy. And they have the power to turn the rivers and oceans into blood, and to strike the earth with every kind of plague as often as they wish.

⁷When they complete their testimony, the beast that comes up out of the bottomless pit* will declare war against them, and he will conquer them and kill them. ⁸And their bodies will lie in the main street of Jerusalem,* the city that is figuratively called "Sodom" and "Egypt," the city where their Lord was crucified. ⁹And for three and a half days, all peoples, tribes, languages, and nations will stare at their bodies. No one will be allowed to bury them. ¹⁰All the people who belong to this world will gloat over them and give presents to each other to celebrate the death of the two prophets who had tormented them.

¹¹But after three and a half days, God breathed life into them, and they stood up! Terror struck all who were staring at them. ¹²Then a loud voice from heaven called to the two prophets, "Come up here!" And they rose to heaven in a cloud as their enemies watched.

¹³At the same time there was a terrible earthquake that destroyed a tenth of the city. Seven thousand people died in that earthquake, and everyone else was terrified and gave glory to the God of heaven.

¹⁴The second terror is past, but look, the third terror is coming quickly.

The Seventh Trumpet Brings the Third Terror

¹⁵Then the seventh angel blew his trumpet, and there were loud voices shouting in heaven:

"The world has now become the Kingdom
    of our Lord and of his Christ,*
    and he will reign forever and ever."

11:7 Or *the abyss*, or *the underworld*. 11:8 Greek *the great city*. 11:15 Or *his Messiah*.

Word can sometimes work that way. It contains a sweet message of deliverance for all who repent, but it also calls us to account for our sinful actions. If we abide by the wise boundaries that God has set for us, his Word is filled with promises of joy and peace. If, on the other hand, we choose to reject God's program, his Word will be filled with predictions of eternal judgment.

11:1-13 These two witnesses serve as God's prophets. During their 1,260-day ministry, they will be empowered and protected by God. They will then be killed by the beast from the pit. God's two prophets are treated even more despicably than Christ, who was at least given a decent burial (see Matthew 27:57-61). In three and a half days, however, God will raise them from the dead, showing that even death cannot thwart his plans. No obstacle is so great that God has to abandon his plan for the world and its people. We can be confident that God wants us to experience effective recovery. So if we trust him and follow his plan, no obstacle will be too great for us to overcome.

11:15-18 The sounding of the seventh trumpet accompanies a proclamation of God's control over his Kingdom. Many among the nations of the earth have been angry with God without just cause, but now God's righteous anger will be released. Those who have committed themselves to God will be rewarded, while those who have turned their backs on him will be judged. The same principle holds true for us. If we reject God and his plan for us, we will have to face his terrible anger. If we commit our life to God, he will lovingly heal us.

[16] The twenty-four elders sitting on their thrones before God fell with their faces to the ground and worshiped him. [17] And they said,

"We give thanks to you, Lord God, the Almighty,
> the one who is and who always was,
for now you have assumed your great power
> and have begun to reign.
[18] The nations were filled with wrath,
> but now the time of your wrath has come.
It is time to judge the dead
> and reward your servants the prophets,
> as well as your holy people,
and all who fear your name,
> from the least to the greatest.
It is time to destroy
> all who have caused destruction on the earth."

[19] Then, in heaven, the Temple of God was opened and the Ark of his covenant could be seen inside the Temple. Lightning flashed, thunder crashed and roared, and there was an earthquake and a terrible hailstorm.

CHAPTER 12
The Woman and the Dragon

Then I witnessed in heaven an event of great significance. I saw a woman clothed with the sun, with the moon beneath her feet, and a crown of twelve stars on her head. [2] She was pregnant, and she cried out because of her labor pains and the agony of giving birth.

[3] Then I witnessed in heaven another significant event. I saw a large red dragon with seven heads and ten horns, with seven crowns on his heads. [4] His tail swept away one-third of the stars in the sky, and he threw them to the earth. He stood in front of the woman as she was about to give birth, ready to devour her baby as soon as it was born.

[5] She gave birth to a son who was to rule all nations with an iron rod. And her child was snatched away from the dragon and was caught up to God and to his throne. [6] And the woman fled into the wilderness, where God had prepared a place to care for her for 1,260 days.

[7] Then there was war in heaven. Michael and his angels fought against the dragon and his angels. [8] And the dragon lost the battle, and he and his angels were forced out of heaven. [9] This great dragon—the ancient serpent called the devil, or Satan, the one deceiving the whole world—was thrown down to the earth with all his angels.

[10] Then I heard a loud voice shouting across the heavens,

"It has come at last—
> salvation and power
and the Kingdom of our God,
> and the authority of his Christ.*
For the accuser of our brothers and sisters*
> has been thrown down to earth—
the one who accuses them
> before our God day and night.
[11] And they have defeated him by the blood of the Lamb
> and by their testimony.
And they did not love their lives so much
> that they were afraid to die.
[12] Therefore, rejoice, O heavens!
> And you who live in the heavens, rejoice!
But terror will come on the earth and the sea,
> for the devil has come down to you in great anger,
> knowing that he has little time."

[13] When the dragon realized that he had been thrown down to the earth, he pursued the woman who had given birth to the male child. [14] But she was given two wings like those of a great eagle so she could fly to the place prepared for her in the wilderness. There she would be cared for and protected from the dragon* for a time, times, and half a time.

[15] Then the dragon tried to drown the woman with a flood of water that flowed from his mouth. [16] But the earth helped her

12:10a Or *his Messiah.* 12:10b Greek *brothers.* 12:14 Greek *the serpent;* also in 12:15. See 12:9.

12:1-14 The birth of Christ and Satan's opposition to it are graphically depicted here. Jesus the Messiah was born into this world to implement God's plan for its restoration. Satan had planted sin into God's good creation by tempting Adam and Eve. Since Jesus was born to reverse the effects of that sin, Satan did all he could to destroy the infant Savior. Thankfully, Satan failed and the future ruler of the world completed his earthly mission. As much as Satan tries to thwart God's plan for the world's recovery, he will not be able to. Our personal recovery is an important part of God's plan for cosmic recovery. If we entrust our life to God and obey him, he will certainly complete the task of recovery in our life.

by opening its mouth and swallowing the river that gushed out from the mouth of the dragon. ¹⁷And the dragon was angry at the woman and declared war against the rest of her children—all who keep God's commandments and maintain their testimony for Jesus.

¹⁸Then the dragon took his stand* on the shore beside the sea.

CHAPTER 13
The Beast out of the Sea

Then I saw a beast rising up out of the sea. It had seven heads and ten horns, with ten crowns on its horns. And written on each head were names that blasphemed God. ²This beast looked like a leopard, but it had the feet of a bear and the mouth of a lion! And the dragon gave the beast his own power and throne and great authority.

³I saw that one of the heads of the beast seemed wounded beyond recovery—but the fatal wound was healed! The whole world marveled at this miracle and gave allegiance to the beast. ⁴They worshiped the dragon for giving the beast such power, and they also worshiped the beast. "Who is as great as the beast?" they exclaimed. "Who is able to fight against him?"

⁵Then the beast was allowed to speak great blasphemies against God. And he was given authority to do whatever he wanted for forty-two months. ⁶And he spoke terrible words of blasphemy against God, slandering his name and his dwelling—that is, those who dwell in heaven.* ⁷And the beast was allowed to wage war against God's holy people and to conquer them. And he was given au-

thority to rule over every tribe and people and language and nation. ⁸And all the people who belong to this world worshiped the beast. They are the ones whose names were not written in the Book of Life that belongs to the Lamb who was slaughtered before the world was made.*

⁹ Anyone with ears to hear
should listen and understand.
¹⁰ Anyone who is destined for prison
will be taken to prison.
Anyone destined to die by the sword
will die by the sword.

This means that God's holy people must endure persecution patiently and remain faithful.

The Beast out of the Earth

¹¹Then I saw another beast come up out of the earth. He had two horns like those of a lamb, but he spoke with the voice of a dragon. ¹²He exercised all the authority of the first beast. And he required all the earth and its people to worship the first beast, whose fatal wound had been healed. ¹³He did astounding miracles, even making fire flash down to earth from the sky while everyone was watching. ¹⁴And with all the miracles he was allowed to perform on behalf of the first beast, he deceived all the people who belong to this world. He ordered the people to make a great statue of the first beast, who was fatally wounded and then came back to life. ¹⁵He was then permitted to give life to this statue so that it could speak. Then the statue of the beast commanded that anyone refusing to worship it must die.

12:18 Greek *Then he took his stand;* some manuscripts read *Then I took my stand.* Some translations put this entire sentence into 13:1. 13:6 Some manuscripts read *and his dwelling and all who dwell in heaven.* 13:8 Or *not written in the Book of Life before the world was made—the Book that belongs to the Lamb who was slaughtered.*

13:1-10 These are some of Satan's primary representatives. For a time, God will allow them free rein in the world as they battle all who trust Christ. Ever since Jesus Christ walked this earth, Satan has sought to lead people away from the delivering power God offers. These creatures are an intensified form of the spirit of antichrist already active in our world. We will face opposition as we seek recovery from addiction and its power. Satan doesn't want us to succeed at recovery; he only wants to destroy us. Despite the power Satan wields in our world, he cannot remove us from God's loving care. When we trust in God to help us and obey him, our recovery is assured. Satan and his henchmen will be powerless.

13:11-18 Another creature representing Satan rises from the earth. It looks like a lamb, Satan's attempt to copy the appearance of Christ, the Lamb (see 5:6). This creature's miracles copy the amazing deeds that were performed by God's two witnesses (see 11:5-6). Satan is trying to deceive people into thinking this lamb represents the true God. He is trying to sell a counterfeit in order to lead people away from the true deliverer—Jesus Christ. Satan uses this same strategy today. Numerous recovery plans claim to offer deliverance, but only God can truly deliver. If we seek help from any other source, Satan has succeeded in leading us away from the only real Power that can save us. We need to be on guard against the counterfeit solutions that Satan puts before us.

¹⁶He required everyone—small and great, rich and poor, free and slave—to be given a mark on the right hand or on the forehead. ¹⁷And no one could buy or sell anything without that mark, which was either the name of the beast or the number representing his name. ¹⁸Wisdom is needed here. Let the one with understanding solve the meaning of the number of the beast, for it is the number of a man.* His number is 666.*

CHAPTER 14
The Lamb and the 144,000
Then I saw the Lamb standing on Mount Zion, and with him were 144,000 who had his name and his Father's name written on their foreheads. ²And I heard a sound from heaven like the roar of mighty ocean waves or the rolling of loud thunder. It was like the sound of many harpists playing together.

³This great choir sang a wonderful new song in front of the throne of God and before the four living beings and the twenty-four elders. No one could learn this song except the 144,000 who had been redeemed from the earth. ⁴They have kept themselves as pure as virgins,* following the Lamb wherever he goes. They have been purchased from among the people on the earth as a special offering* to God and to the Lamb. ⁵They have told no lies; they are without blame.

The Three Angels
⁶And I saw another angel flying through the sky, carrying the eternal Good News to proclaim to the people who belong to this world—to every nation, tribe, language, and people. ⁷"Fear God," he shouted. "Give glory to him. For the time has come when he will sit as judge. Worship him who made the heavens, the earth, the sea, and all the springs of water."

⁸Then another angel followed him through the sky, shouting, "Babylon is fallen—that great city is fallen—because she made all the nations of the world drink the wine of her passionate immorality."

⁹Then a third angel followed them, shouting, "Anyone who worships the beast and his statue or who accepts his mark on the forehead or on the hand ¹⁰must drink the wine of God's anger. It has been poured full strength into God's cup of wrath. And they will be tormented with fire and burning sulfur in the presence of the holy angels and the Lamb. ¹¹The smoke of their torment will rise forever and ever, and they will have no relief day or night, for they have worshiped the beast and his statue and have accepted the mark of his name."

¹²This means that God's holy people must endure persecution patiently, obeying his commands and maintaining their faith in Jesus.

¹³And I heard a voice from heaven saying, "Write this down: Blessed are those who die in the Lord from now on. Yes, says the Spirit, they are blessed indeed, for they will rest from their hard work; for their good deeds follow them!"

The Harvest of the Earth
¹⁴Then I saw a white cloud, and seated on the cloud was someone like the Son of Man.* He had a gold crown on his head and a sharp sickle in his hand.

¹⁵Then another angel came from the Temple and shouted to the one sitting on the cloud, "Swing the sickle, for the time of harvest has come; the crop on earth is ripe." ¹⁶So the one sitting on the cloud swung his sickle over the earth, and the whole earth was harvested.

¹⁷After that, another angel came from the Temple in heaven, and he also had a sharp sickle. ¹⁸Then another angel, who had power to destroy with fire, came from the altar. He shouted to the angel with the sharp sickle, "Swing your sickle now to gather the clusters of grapes from the vines of the earth, for they are ripe for judgment." ¹⁹So the angel swung his sickle over the earth and loaded the grapes into the great winepress of God's wrath. ²⁰The grapes were trampled in the winepress outside the city, and blood flowed from the winepress in a stream about 180 miles* long and as high as a horse's bridle.

13:18a Or *of humanity.* **13:18b** Some manuscripts read *616.* **14:4a** Greek *They are virgins who have not defiled themselves with women.* **14:4b** Greek *as firstfruits.* **14:14** Or *like a son of man.* See Dan 7:13. "Son of Man" is a title Jesus used for himself. **14:20** Greek *1,600 stadia* [300 kilometers].

14:1-20 In these verses we see some of the blessings enjoyed by those who trust in Christ; then we see the terrible consequences of rejecting him. The deliverance that God offers us through Jesus Christ is good news. We are called to rejoice in God's infinite rule, praising him for his greatness. If we refuse to acknowledge God's rule and do things our own way, we are headed toward complete destruction. But when we persevere in our faith in Jesus Christ, God will reward us with eternal rest.

CHAPTER 15
The Song of Moses and of the Lamb

Then I saw in heaven another marvelous event of great significance. Seven angels were holding the seven last plagues, which would bring God's wrath to completion. [2]I saw before me what seemed to be a glass sea mixed with fire. And on it stood all the people who had been victorious over the beast and his statue and the number representing his name. They were all holding harps that God had given them. [3]And they were singing the song of Moses, the servant of God, and the song of the Lamb:

"Great and marvelous are your works,
O Lord God, the Almighty.
Just and true are your ways,
O King of the nations.*
[4]Who will not fear you, Lord,
and glorify your name?
For you alone are holy.
All nations will come and worship before you,
for your righteous deeds have been revealed."

The Seven Bowls of the Seven Plagues

[5]Then I looked and saw that the Temple in heaven, God's Tabernacle, was thrown wide open. [6]The seven angels who were holding the seven plagues came out of the Temple. They were clothed in spotless white linen* with gold sashes across their chests. [7]Then one of the four living beings handed each of the seven angels a gold bowl filled with the wrath of God, who lives forever and ever. [8]The Temple was filled with smoke from God's glory and power. No one could enter the Temple until the seven angels had completed pouring out the seven plagues.

CHAPTER 16

Then I heard a mighty voice from the Temple say to the seven angels, "Go your ways and pour out on the earth the seven bowls containing God's wrath."

[2]So the first angel left the Temple and poured out his bowl on the earth, and horrible, malignant sores broke out on everyone who had the mark of the beast and who worshiped his statue.

[3]Then the second angel poured out his bowl on the sea, and it became like the blood of a corpse. And everything in the sea died.

[4]Then the third angel poured out his bowl on the rivers and springs, and they became blood. [5]And I heard the angel who had authority over all water saying,

"You are just, O Holy One, who is and who always was,
because you have sent these judgments.
[6] Since they shed the blood
of your holy people and your prophets,
you have given them blood to drink.
It is their just reward."

[7]And I heard a voice from the altar,* saying,

"Yes, O Lord God, the Almighty,
your judgments are true and just."

[8]Then the fourth angel poured out his bowl on the sun, causing it to scorch everyone with its fire. [9]Everyone was burned by this blast of heat, and they cursed the name of God, who had control over all these plagues. They did not repent of their sins and turn to God and give him glory.

[10]Then the fifth angel poured out his bowl on the throne of the beast, and his kingdom was plunged into darkness. His subjects ground their teeth* in anguish, [11]and they cursed the God of heaven for their pains and sores. But they did not repent of their evil deeds and turn to God.

[12]Then the sixth angel poured out his bowl on the great Euphrates River, and it dried up so that the kings from the east could march their armies toward the west without hindrance. [13]And I saw three evil* spirits that looked like frogs leap from the mouths of the dragon, the beast, and the false prophet.

15:3 Some manuscripts read *King of the ages.* 15:6 Other manuscripts read *white stone;* still others read *white [garments] made of linen.* 16:7 Greek *I heard the altar.* 16:10 Greek *gnawed their tongues.* 16:13 Greek *unclean.*

15:1–16:21 The seven angels with the bowls of God's judgment are portrayed in these chapters. God's wrath against the unbelieving world will be complete (see 6:17; 11:18) when the angels pour out their bowls of plagues over the earth. The day of reckoning will surely arrive, even though those in denial live as though things will continue forever just as they are. We cannot live forever in bondage to sin or a powerful addiction. There will be a day when we have to face the truth about our life. We have the choice to submit our life to God and his good plan before the bottom drops out from under us.

[14]They are demonic spirits who work miracles and go out to all the rulers of the world to gather them for battle against the Lord on that great judgment day of God the Almighty.

[15]"Look, I will come as unexpectedly as a thief! Blessed are all who are watching for me, who keep their clothing ready so they will not have to walk around naked and ashamed."

[16]And the demonic spirits gathered all the rulers and their armies to a place with the Hebrew name *Armageddon.**

[17]Then the seventh angel poured out his bowl into the air. And a mighty shout came from the throne in the Temple, saying, "It is finished!" [18]Then the thunder crashed and rolled, and lightning flashed. And a great earthquake struck—the worst since people were placed on the earth. [19]The great city of Babylon split into three sections, and the cities of many nations fell into heaps of rubble. So God remembered all of Babylon's sins, and he made her drink the cup that was filled with the wine of his fierce wrath. [20]And every island disappeared, and all the mountains were leveled. [21]There was a terrible hailstorm, and hailstones weighing as much as seventy-five pounds* fell from the sky onto the people below. They cursed God because of the terrible plague of the hailstorm.

CHAPTER 17
The Great Prostitute

One of the seven angels who had poured out the seven bowls came over and spoke to me. "Come with me," he said, "and I will show you the judgment that is going to come on the great prostitute, who rules over many waters. [2]The kings of the world have committed adultery with her, and the people who belong to this world have been made drunk by the wine of her immorality."

[3]So the angel took me in the Spirit* into the wilderness. There I saw a woman sitting on a scarlet beast that had seven heads and ten horns, and blasphemies against God

were written all over it. [4]The woman wore purple and scarlet clothing and beautiful jewelry made of gold and precious gems and pearls. In her hand she held a gold goblet full of obscenities and the impurities of her immorality. [5]A mysterious name was written on her forehead: "Babylon the Great, Mother of All Prostitutes and Obscenities in the World." [6]I could see that she was drunk—drunk with the blood of God's holy people who were witnesses for Jesus. I stared at her in complete amazement.

[7]"Why are you so amazed?" the angel asked. "I will tell you the mystery of this woman and of the beast with seven heads and ten horns on which she sits. [8]The beast you saw was once alive but isn't now. And yet he will soon come up out of the bottomless pit* and go to eternal destruction. And the people who belong to this world, whose names were not written in the Book of Life before the world was made, will be amazed at the reappearance of this beast who had died.

[9]"This calls for a mind with understanding: The seven heads of the beast represent the seven hills where the woman rules. They also represent seven kings. [10]Five kings have already fallen, the sixth now reigns, and the seventh is yet to come, but his reign will be brief.

[11]"The scarlet beast that was, but is no longer, is the eighth king. He is like the other seven, and he, too, is headed for destruction. [12]The ten horns of the beast are ten kings who have not yet risen to power. They will be appointed to their kingdoms for one brief moment to reign with the beast. [13]They will all agree to give him their power and authority. [14]Together they will go to war against the Lamb, but the Lamb will defeat them because he is Lord of all lords and King of all kings. And his called and chosen and faithful ones will be with him."

[15]Then the angel said to me, "The waters where the prostitute is ruling represent masses of people of every nation and language. [16]The scarlet beast and his ten horns all hate the prostitute. They will strip her na-

16:16 Or *Harmagedon.* 16:21 Greek *1 talent* [34 kilograms]. 17:3 Or *in spirit.* 17:8 Or *the abyss,* or *the underworld.*

17:1–19:5 Just as the previous chapters portray God's judgment of those who refuse to believe in Christ, these chapters foretell God's conquest over Satan's henchmen. Even Satan's power will be overthrown by God when the time is right. The Devil's representatives will be called to account for the suffering they imposed on God's people. God's team will always win out in the end. To be on the winning side, we need to admit our need for God and trust him to deliver us from the power of sin. That way we won't weep when the evil powers in this world are destroyed; we will rejoice.

ked, eat her flesh, and burn her remains with fire. [17]For God has put a plan into their minds, a plan that will carry out his purposes. They will agree to give their authority to the scarlet beast, and so the words of God will be fulfilled. [18]And this woman you saw in your vision represents the great city that rules over the kings of the world."

CHAPTER 18
The Fall of Babylon

After all this I saw another angel come down from heaven with great authority, and the earth grew bright with his splendor. [2]He gave a mighty shout:

"Babylon is fallen—that great city is
      fallen!
   She has become a home for demons.
She is a hideout for every foul* spirit,
   a hideout for every foul vulture
   and every foul and dreadful animal.*
[3]For all the nations have fallen*
   because of the wine of her passionate
      immorality.
The kings of the world
   have committed adultery with her.
Because of her desires for extravagant
      luxury,
   the merchants of the world have
      grown rich."

[4]Then I heard another voice calling from heaven,

"Come away from her, my people.
   Do not take part in her sins,
   or you will be punished with her.
[5]For her sins are piled as high as heaven,
   and God remembers her evil deeds.
[6]Do to her as she has done to others.
   Double her penalty* for all her evil
      deeds.
She brewed a cup of terror for others,
   so brew twice as much* for her.
[7]She glorified herself and lived in
      luxury,
   so match it now with torment and
      sorrow.
She boasted in her heart,
   'I am queen on my throne.
I am no helpless widow,
   and I have no reason to mourn.'
[8]Therefore, these plagues will overtake her
      in a single day—
   death and mourning and famine.

She will be completely consumed by fire,
   for the Lord God who judges her is
      mighty."

[9]And the kings of the world who committed adultery with her and enjoyed her great luxury will mourn for her as they see the smoke rising from her charred remains. [10]They will stand at a distance, terrified by her great torment. They will cry out,

"How terrible, how terrible for you,
   O Babylon, you great city!
In a single moment
   God's judgment came on you."

[11]The merchants of the world will weep and mourn for her, for there is no one left to buy their goods. [12]She bought great quantities of gold, silver, jewels, and pearls; fine linen, purple, silk, and scarlet cloth; things made of fragrant thyine wood, ivory goods, and objects made of expensive wood; and bronze, iron, and marble. [13]She also bought cinnamon, spice, incense, myrrh, frankincense, wine, olive oil, fine flour, wheat, cattle, sheep, horses, wagons, and bodies— that is, human slaves.

[14]"The fancy things you loved so much
   are gone," they cry.
"All your luxuries and splendor
   are gone forever,
   never to be yours again."

[15]The merchants who became wealthy by selling her these things will stand at a distance, terrified by her great torment. They will weep and cry out,

[16]"How terrible, how terrible for that great
      city!
   She was clothed in finest purple and
      scarlet linens,
   decked out with gold and precious
      stones and pearls!
[17]In a single moment
   all the wealth of the city is gone!"

And all the captains of the merchant ships and their passengers and sailors and crews will stand at a distance. [18]They will cry out as they watch the smoke ascend, and they will say, "Where is there another city as great as this?" [19]And they will weep and throw dust on their heads to show their grief. And they will cry out,

18:2a Greek *unclean;* also in each of the two following phrases. 18:2b Some manuscripts condense the last two lines to read *a hideout for every foul [unclean] and dreadful vulture.* 18:3 Some manuscripts read *have drunk.* 18:6a Or *Give her an equal penalty.* 18:6b Or *brew just as much.*

"How terrible, how terrible for that great
city!
The shipowners became wealthy
by transporting her great wealth on the
seas.
In a single moment it is all gone."

20 Rejoice over her fate, O heaven
and people of God and apostles and
prophets!
For at last God has judged her
for your sakes.

21 Then a mighty angel picked up a boulder
the size of a huge millstone. He threw it into
the ocean and shouted,

"Just like this, the great city Babylon
will be thrown down with violence
and will never be found again.
22 The sound of harps, singers, flutes, and
trumpets
will never be heard in you again.
No craftsmen and no trades
will ever be found in you again.
The sound of the mill
will never be heard in you again.
23 The light of a lamp
will never shine in you again.
The happy voices of brides and grooms
will never be heard in you again.
For your merchants were the greatest in
the world,
and you deceived the nations with your
sorceries.
24 In your* streets flowed the blood of the
prophets and of God's holy people
and the blood of people slaughtered all
over the world."

CHAPTER 19
Songs of Victory in Heaven
After this, I heard what sounded like a vast
crowd in heaven shouting,

"Praise the LORD!*
Salvation and glory and power belong
to our God.
2 His judgments are true and just.
He has punished the great prostitute
who corrupted the earth with her
immorality.
He has avenged the murder of his
servants."

3 And again their voices rang out:

"Praise the LORD!
The smoke from that city ascends
forever and ever!"

4 Then the twenty-four elders and the four
living beings fell down and worshiped God,
who was sitting on the throne. They cried
out, "Amen! Praise the LORD!"
5 And from the throne came a voice that
said,

"Praise our God,
all his servants,
all who fear him,
from the least to the greatest."

6 Then I heard again what sounded like the
shout of a vast crowd or the roar of mighty
ocean waves or the crash of loud thunder:

"Praise the LORD!
For the Lord our God,* the Almighty,
reigns.
7 Let us be glad and rejoice,
and let us give honor to him.
For the time has come for the wedding
feast of the Lamb,
and his bride has prepared herself.
8 She has been given the finest of pure
white linen to wear."
For the fine linen represents the good
deeds of God's holy people.

9 And the angel said to me, "Write this:
Blessed are those who are invited to the wedding feast of the Lamb." And he added,
"These are true words that come from God."
10 Then I fell down at his feet to worship
him, but he said, "No, don't worship me. I
am a servant of God, just like you and your
brothers and sisters* who testify about their
faith in Jesus. Worship only God. For the essence of prophecy is to give a clear witness
for Jesus.*"

18:24 Greek her. 19:1 Greek Hallelujah; also in 19:3, 4, 6. Hallelujah is the transliteration of a Hebrew term that
means "Praise the LORD." 19:6 Some manuscripts read the Lord God. 19:10a Greek brothers. 19:10b Or is the message
confirmed by Jesus.

19:6–20:10 Here we see a glimpse of Christ, the conquering King. He will return to deliver all
those who believe in him. Though great human armies led by Satan and his representatives will
gather to resist, there will be no contest. Jesus Christ will ride to an overwhelming victory. As
Christ triumphs over Satan and his armies, he will vindicate our individual battles against sin and
addiction. What a glorious day that will be! All our efforts to overcome our dependency will be
supported by Christ's final conquest over sin and evil. Satan and his helpers will be bound forever!

The Rider on the White Horse

¹¹Then I saw heaven opened, and a white horse was standing there. Its rider was named Faithful and True, for he judges fairly and wages a righteous war. ¹²His eyes were like flames of fire, and on his head were many crowns. A name was written on him that no one understood except himself. ¹³He wore a robe dipped in blood, and his title was the Word of God. ¹⁴The armies of heaven, dressed in the finest of pure white linen, followed him on white horses. ¹⁵From his mouth came a sharp sword to strike down the nations. He will rule them with an iron rod. He will release the fierce wrath of God, the Almighty, like juice flowing from a winepress. ¹⁶On his robe at his thigh* was written this title: King of all kings and Lord of all lords.

¹⁷Then I saw an angel standing in the sun, shouting to the vultures flying high in the sky: "Come! Gather together for the great banquet God has prepared. ¹⁸Come and eat the flesh of kings, generals, and strong warriors; of horses and their riders; and of all humanity, both free and slave, small and great."

¹⁹Then I saw the beast and the kings of the world and their armies gathered together to fight against the one sitting on the horse and his army. ²⁰And the beast was captured, and with him the false prophet who did mighty miracles on behalf of the beast—miracles that deceived all who had accepted the mark of the beast and who worshiped his statue. Both the beast and his false prophet were thrown alive into the fiery lake of burning sulfur. ²¹Their entire army was killed by the sharp sword that came from the mouth of the one riding the white horse. And the vultures all gorged themselves on the dead bodies.

CHAPTER 20
The Thousand Years

Then I saw an angel coming down from heaven with the key to the bottomless pit* and a heavy chain in his hand. ²He seized the dragon—that old serpent, who is the devil, Satan—and bound him in chains for a thousand years. ³The angel threw him into the bottomless pit, which he then shut and locked so Satan could not deceive the nations anymore until the thousand years were finished. Afterward he must be released for a little while.

⁴Then I saw thrones, and the people sitting on them had been given the authority to

19:16 Or *On his robe and thigh.* 20:1 Or *the abyss,* or *the underworld;* also in 20:3.

STEP 4

God's Mercy

BIBLE READING: Revelation 20:11-15

We made a searching and fearless moral inventory of ourselves.

We may wish we could avoid taking moral inventory; it's normal to want to hide from personal examination. But in our heart we probably sense that a day will come when we will have to face the truth about ourself and our life.

The Bible tells us there is a day coming when an inventory will be made of every life. No one will be able to hide. In John's vision he saw "a great white throne and the one sitting on it. The earth and sky fled from his presence, but they found no place to hide. I saw the dead, both great and small, standing before God's throne. And the books were opened, including the Book of Life. And the dead were judged according to what they had done, as recorded in the books. . . . And anyone whose name was not found recorded in the Book of Life was thrown into the lake of fire" (Revelation 20:11-12, 15).

It is best to do our own earthly moral inventory now so we can be ready for the one to come. Anyone whose name is in the Book of Life will be saved, including all whose sins have been atoned for by the death of Jesus. Those who refuse God's offer of mercy are left to be judged on the basis of their own deeds recorded in "the books." No one will pass that test! Perhaps now is a good time to make sure that our name is in the right book. Knowing that our sins are covered with God's forgiveness can help us examine our life fearlessly and honestly. *Turn to Step Five, page 59, Genesis 38.*

judge. And I saw the souls of those who had been beheaded for their testimony about Jesus and for proclaiming the word of God. They had not worshiped the beast or his statue, nor accepted his mark on their foreheads or their hands. They all came to life again, and they reigned with Christ for a thousand years.

⁵This is the first resurrection. (The rest of the dead did not come back to life until the thousand years had ended.) ⁶Blessed and holy are those who share in the first resurrection. For them the second death holds no power, but they will be priests of God and of Christ and will reign with him a thousand years.

The Defeat of Satan

⁷When the thousand years come to an end, Satan will be let out of his prison. ⁸He will go out to deceive the nations—called Gog and Magog—in every corner of the earth. He will gather them together for battle—a mighty army, as numberless as sand along the seashore. ⁹And I saw them as they went up on the broad plain of the earth and surrounded God's people and the beloved city. But fire from heaven came down on the attacking armies and consumed them.

¹⁰Then the devil, who had deceived them,

20:13 Greek *and Hades;* also in 20:14.

was thrown into the fiery lake of burning sulfur, joining the beast and the false prophet. There they will be tormented day and night forever and ever.

The Final Judgment

¹¹And I saw a great white throne and the one sitting on it. The earth and sky fled from his presence, but they found no place to hide. ¹²I saw the dead, both great and small, standing before God's throne. And the books were opened, including the Book of Life. And the dead were judged according to what they had done, as recorded in the books. ¹³The sea gave up its dead, and death and the grave* gave up their dead. And all were judged according to their deeds. ¹⁴Then death and the grave were thrown into the lake of fire. This lake of fire is the second death. ¹⁵And anyone whose name was not found recorded in the Book of Life was thrown into the lake of fire.

CHAPTER 21
The New Jerusalem

Then I saw a new heaven and a new earth, for the old heaven and the old earth had disappeared. And the sea was also gone. ²And I saw the holy city, the new Jerusalem, coming

20:11-15 At the climactic "white throne" judgment, those who reject God will face eternal consequences. Believers in Christ, however, will be shown amazing grace. Most of us expect our judgment to be based upon whether or not we are guilty. At this judgment, though, everyone is guilty. The people who have believed in Christ will be forgiven. Those who have chosen to go their own way are headed to a place of eternal torment. No matter who we are or how terrible our past, we can have our name written in the Book of Life. We cannot earn a place in that book; we can only receive it as a gift. By admitting our failures, entrusting our life to God in Jesus Christ, and building a new life according to God's will, we become a member of God's family.

21:1-7 What hope this scene gives us! Ever since the first sin in the Garden of Eden, God has been working to restore his earth to its original perfection. He even sent his Son to suffer and die to overcome the power of sin and death and to begin the process of healing in those who love him. It is God's will to make old things new; he will make a new heaven and a new earth for his people! By following his will for our life, we become part of God's plan of restoration. He will free our soul from its bondage to sin. We can receive him into our life today and begin this restoration process without delay.

21:7-8 At the conclusion of these wonderful promises of restoration, we are reminded that some will mourn at Christ's return. Those who have rejected God by their selfish and ungodly living will be thrown into the lake of fire. If we remain enslaved to our dependency, we are headed for that terrible end. Rejecting God's offer of healing will lead to an eternity of suffering—the second death. But we can choose to stop being controlled by ungodly people and destructive substances and put our life into God's hands. Only he has the power to deliver us from the power of sin and addiction. If we rely on him, he can restore our life and make us part of his plan for restoring his created world.

21:10-27 The new Jerusalem is portrayed as the radiant bride of the Lamb (see 21:2). The eternal city has twelve gates, representing the twelve tribes of Israel (see 7:4-8), and twelve foundation stones, representing the twelve apostles of Christ. Thus, the city—the bride—represents the people of God. We as the community of faith are members of the church—the bride of Christ. What a wonderful picture of grace! No matter how many mistakes we have made in the past, God forgives us through Christ, and we are brought into intimate relationship with God. We can begin this healing relationship with God today by giving our life to him.

GOD grant me the serenity to accept the things I cannot change the courage to change the things I can and the wisdom to know the difference AMEN

Removing our defects may seem to be an overwhelming task, despite the fact that God has promised to do the work. Perhaps if we could just catch a glimpse of life beyond recovery, our hope would be revived. The apostle Paul wrote: "And I am certain that God, who began the good work within you, will continue his work until it is finally finished on that day when Christ Jesus returns" (Philippians 1:6).

As we think about making changes in our life, we may find ourself dwelling on the defects in our character.

The apostle John wrote: "I heard a loud shout from the throne, saying, 'Look, God's home is now among his people! He will live with them, and they will be his people. God himself will be with them. He will wipe every tear from their eyes, and there will be no more death or sorrow or crying or pain. All these things are gone forever.' And the one sitting on the throne said, 'Look, I am making everything new!' And then he said to me, 'Write this down, for what I tell you is trustworthy and true.' And he also said, 'It is finished! I am the Alpha and the Omega—the Beginning and the End. To all who are thirsty I will give freely from the springs of the water of life'" (Revelation 21:3-6).

There is hope for all of us, no matter how terrible our past or the problems we face today. Someday all our defects will be gone; all things will be made new; the thirst of our soul will be quenched by the Water of Life. ***End of the Serenity Prayer reading plan.***

---

down from God out of heaven like a bride beautifully dressed for her husband.

³I heard a loud shout from the throne, saying, "Look, God's home is now among his people! He will live with them, and they will be his people. God himself will be with them.* ⁴He will wipe every tear from their eyes, and there will be no more death or sorrow or crying or pain. All these things are gone forever."

⁵And the one sitting on the throne said, "Look, I am making everything new!" And then he said to me, "Write this down, for what I tell you is trustworthy and true." ⁶And he also said, "It is finished! I am the Alpha and the Omega—the Beginning and the End. To all who are thirsty I will give freely from the springs of the water of life. ⁷All who are victorious will inherit all these blessings, and I will be their God, and they will be my children.

⁸"But cowards, unbelievers, the corrupt, murderers, the immoral, those who practice witchcraft, idol worshipers, and all liars— their fate is in the fiery lake of burning sulfur. This is the second death."

⁹Then one of the seven angels who held the seven bowls containing the seven last plagues came and said to me, "Come with me! I will show you the bride, the wife of the Lamb."

¹⁰So he took me in the Spirit* to a great, high mountain, and he showed me the holy city, Jerusalem, descending out of heaven from God. ¹¹It shone with the glory of God and sparkled like a precious stone—like jasper as clear as crystal. ¹²The city wall was broad and high, with twelve gates guarded by twelve angels. And the names of the twelve tribes of Israel were written on the gates. ¹³There were three gates on each side— east, north, south, and west. ¹⁴The wall of the

21:3 Some manuscripts read *God himself will be with them, their God.* 21:10 Or *in spirit.*

city had twelve foundation stones, and on them were written the names of the twelve apostles of the Lamb.

[15]The angel who talked to me held in his hand a gold measuring stick to measure the city, its gates, and its wall. [16]When he measured it, he found it was a square, as wide as it was long. In fact, its length and width and height were each 1,400 miles.* [17]Then he measured the walls and found them to be 216 feet thick* (according to the human standard used by the angel).

[18]The wall was made of jasper, and the city was pure gold, as clear as glass. [19]The wall of the city was built on foundation stones inlaid with twelve precious stones:* the first was jasper, the second sapphire, the third agate, the fourth emerald, [20]the fifth onyx, the sixth carnelian, the seventh chrysolite, the eighth beryl, the ninth topaz, the tenth chrysoprase, the eleventh jacinth, the twelfth amethyst.

[21]The twelve gates were made of pearls— each gate from a single pearl! And the main street was pure gold, as clear as glass.

[22]I saw no temple in the city, for the Lord God Almighty and the Lamb are its temple. [23]And the city has no need of sun or moon, for the glory of God illuminates the city, and the Lamb is its light. [24]The nations will walk in its light, and the kings of the world will enter the city in all their glory. [25]Its gates will never be closed at the end of day because there is no night there. [26]And all the nations will bring their glory and honor into the city. [27]Nothing evil* will be allowed to enter, nor anyone who practices shameful idolatry and dishonesty—but only those whose names are written in the Lamb's Book of Life.

CHAPTER 22

Then the angel showed me a river with the water of life, clear as crystal, flowing from the throne of God and of the Lamb. [2]It flowed down the center of the main street. On each side of the river grew a tree of life, bearing twelve crops of fruit,* with a fresh crop each month. The leaves were used for medicine to heal the nations.

[3]No longer will there be a curse upon anything. For the throne of God and of the Lamb will be there, and his servants will worship him. [4]And they will see his face, and his name will be written on their foreheads. [5]And there will be no night there—no need for lamps or sun—for the Lord God will shine on them. And they will reign forever and ever.

[6]Then the angel said to me, "Everything you have heard and seen is trustworthy and true. The Lord God, who inspires his prophets,* has sent his angel to tell his servants what will happen soon.*"

Jesus Is Coming

[7]"Look, I am coming soon! Blessed are those who obey the words of prophecy written in this book.*"

[8]I, John, am the one who heard and saw all these things. And when I heard and saw them, I fell down to worship at the feet of the angel who showed them to me. [9]But he said, "No, don't worship me. I am a servant of God, just like you and your brothers the prophets, as well as all who obey what is written in this book. Worship only God!"

21:16 Greek *12,000 stadia* [2,220 kilometers]. 21:17 Greek *144 cubits* [65 meters]. 21:19 The identification of some of these gemstones is uncertain. 21:27 Or *ceremonially unclean.* 22:2 Or *twelve kinds of fruit.* 22:6a Or *The Lord, the God of the spirits of the prophets.* 22:6b Or *suddenly,* or *quickly;* also in 22:7, 12, 20. 22:7 Or *scroll;* also in 22:9, 10, 18, 19.

22:1-5 The book of Revelation climaxes here, portraying the eternal state as a new and better Garden of Eden. God will re-create his broken creation. God's healing power will be easily accessible and intimate, and face-to-face relationships with God will be the norm. God's presence will bring light to everything, making cruelty and deception impossibilities in his new world. What can only be a dream in our present sinful world will then be eternal reality. What a source of hope this picture is for us! No matter how bad our life may be now, there is hope for the future. If we accept the wonderful offer of salvation that God holds out to us through Jesus Christ, we will someday be a part of that blessed world.

22:20-21 It is unhealthy to harbor unrealistic dreams about a future that will never come about. But it is very healthy for us to anchor our new life and recovery in the certainty of Christ's return. By trusting Christ with our future, we can better deal with our past and live a more productive present. Like the apostle John, we can pray for Christ to return soon, because we know for certain that he will come. This will not only give us hope to persevere during tough times; it will deepen our personal relationship with him. As we trust in him and possess the hope of meeting him face to face, we will grow closer to him. Then Christ's unconditional acceptance and unlimited power will continually undergird us in recovery.

¹⁰Then he instructed me, "Do not seal up the prophetic words in this book, for the time is near. ¹¹Let the one who is doing harm continue to do harm; let the one who is vile continue to be vile; let the one who is righteous continue to live righteously; let the one who is holy continue to be holy."

¹²"Look, I am coming soon, bringing my reward with me to repay all people according to their deeds. ¹³I am the Alpha and the Omega, the First and the Last, the Beginning and the End."

¹⁴Blessed are those who wash their robes. They will be permitted to enter through the gates of the city and eat the fruit from the tree of life. ¹⁵Outside the city are the dogs—the sorcerers, the sexually immoral, the murderers, the idol worshipers, and all who love to live a lie.

¹⁶"I, Jesus, have sent my angel to give you this message for the churches. I am both the source of David and the heir to his throne.* I am the bright morning star."

¹⁷The Spirit and the bride say, "Come." Let anyone who hears this say, "Come." Let anyone who is thirsty come. Let anyone who desires drink freely from the water of life. ¹⁸And I solemnly declare to everyone who hears the words of prophecy written in this book: If anyone adds anything to what is written here, God will add to that person the plagues described in this book. ¹⁹And if anyone removes any of the words from this book of prophecy, God will remove that person's share in the tree of life and in the holy city that are described in this book.

²⁰He who is the faithful witness to all these things says, "Yes, I am coming soon!"

Amen! Come, Lord Jesus!

²¹May the grace of the Lord Jesus be with God's holy people.*

22:16 Greek I am the root and offspring of David.
22:21 Other manuscripts read be with all; still others read be with all of God's holy people. Some manuscripts add Amen.

FORGIVENESS

READ REVELATION 22:1-5

We all suffer from brokenness in our life, in our relationship with God, and in our relationships with others. Brokenness tends to weigh us down and can easily lead us back into our addiction. Recovery isn't complete until all the areas of brokenness are healed.

God's ultimate plan for us and our world involves our complete healing. In Revelation the apostle John saw a vision of a new heaven and new earth where this ultimate healing will take place: "Then the angel showed me a river with the water of life, clear as crystal, flowing from the throne of God and of the Lamb. . . . On each side of the river grew a tree of life. . . . The leaves were used for medicine to heal the nations" (Revelation 22:1-2).

Although we know that God will heal all things when he returns to rule, we still need to work toward healing the brokenness right now. Jesus taught: "So if you are presenting a sacrifice at the altar in the Temple and you suddenly remember that someone has something against you, leave your sacrifice there at the altar. Go and be reconciled to that person. Then come and offer your sacrifice to God" (Matthew 5:23-24).

Giving and receiving forgiveness is an essential part of our present healing. This requires that we make peace—with God, within ourself, and with others whom we have alienated. Once we go through the process of making amends, we must keep our mind and heart open to anyone we may have overlooked. God will often remind us of relationships that need attention. When these come to mind, we should stop everything and go to those we have offended and seek to repair the damage. *End of the Recovery Principle reading plan.*

The Serenity Prayer

God, grant me the serenity to accept the things I cannot change,

the courage to change the things I can,

and the wisdom to know the difference.

Living one day at a time, enjoying one moment at a time,

accepting hardship as the pathway to peace.

Taking, as Christ did, this sinful world as it is,

not as I would have it.

Trusting that He will make all things right

if I surrender to His will.

That I may be reasonably happy in this life

and supremely happy with Him forever in the next.

Amen

LIFE RECOVERY TOPICAL INDEX

This index locates the notes, profiles, devotionals, and recovery themes related to key issues in recovery. Page numbers are provided to make it easy to find all the features listed. Related issues are named in parentheses to make an expanded study on any topic a simple task. For additional information, see the other specialized indexes that follow this topical index: Index to Recovery Profiles, Index to Twelve Step Devotionals, Index to Recovery Principle Devotionals, Index to Serenity Prayer Devotionals, Index to Recovery Reflections.

CRITICISM (*see also* Blame, Communication)

DECEPTION

DECISIONS (*see* Choices)

DELAYED GRATIFICATION (*see also* Patience, Self-Control)

DELIVERANCE (*see* Salvation)

DENIAL (*see also* Blame, Honesty, Truth)

PROFILES

TWELVE STEP DEVOTIONALS

RECOVERY PRINCIPLE DEVOTIONALS

SERENITY PRAYER DEVOTIONAL

RECOVERY THEMES IN . . .

DEPENDENCIES (*see also* Drinking)

NOTES

TWELVE STEP DEVOTIONALS

RECOVERY PRINCIPLE DEVOTIONAL

SERENITY PRAYER DEVOTIONAL

DEPRESSION (*see* Discouragement)

DESCENDANTS (*see* Inheritance)

DESPAIR (*see* Discouragement)

DILIGENCE (*see* Perseverance)

DISCIPLINE (*see also* Consequences, Self-Discipline)

NOTES

DISCOURAGEMENT (*see also* Rejection, Sadness)

DIVORCE (*see* Marriage)

DOUBT (*see also* Faith)

DRINKING (*see also* Dependencies)

DRUG ABUSE (*see* Dependencies)

DYSFUNCTIONAL FAMILY (*see* Family, Inheritance)

FAITHFULNESS (*see also* Commitments, Marriage)

FALL (*see* Relapse, Sin)

FALSE GODS (*see* Idolatry)

FALSE TEACHINGS (*see* Deception)

FAMILY (*see also* Inheritance, Marriage, Parenting)

FAVORITISM (*see* Partiality)

FEAR (*see also* Worry)

NOTES

FELLOWSHIP (*see also* Accountability, Mentors)

NOTES

FORGIVENESS (*see also* Repentance, Restoration)

FREEDOM (*see also* Choices, Bondage)

PROFILES

TWELVE STEP DEVOTIONALS

RECOVERY PRINCIPLE DEVOTIONALS

SERENITY PRAYER DEVOTIONALS

RECOVERY THEMES IN . . .

FRIENDSHIP (*see also* Mentors, Peer Pressure)

NOTES

PROFILES

FUN (see Enjoyment)

GIVING (see Service)

GOD'S POWER

NOTES

GOD'S SUFFICIENCY (see God's Power)

GOD'S WILL (see also Guidance)

NOTES

GOD'S WORD (see also Guidance, Wisdom)

NOTES

GOSSIP (*see also* Communication, Lying)

GRACE (*see also* Legalism)

GRATITUDE (*see also* Praise)

GREED (*see also* Materialism)

GRIEF (*see* Sadness)

GUIDANCE (*see also* God's Will, Holy Spirit, Mentors)

GUILT (*see also* Forgiveness, Repentance)

HOMOSEXUALITY (*see* Sexuality)

HONESTY (*see also* Lying, Truth)

HOPE

HOPELESSNESS

INSECURITY (*see* Fear)

INTEGRITY (*see* Honesty)

INVENTORY (*see also* Repentance)

NOTES

JEALOUSY

NOTES

JOY (*see also* Enjoyment, Happiness)

NOTES

JUDGMENT (see also Consequences)

JUSTICE (see Fairness)

KINDNESS

RECOVERY PRINCIPLE DEVOTIONAL

RECOVERY THEMES IN . . .

LAZINESS (see Procrastination)

LEGALISM (see also Freedom, Grace)

LIES (see Lying)

LONELINESS

LOVE

MIRACLES (*see also* God's Power)

OBEDIENCE (*see also* Surrender)

OBSTACLES (*see also* Trials)

PROFILES

TWELVE STEP DEVOTIONALS

RECOVERY PRINCIPLE DEVOTIONAL

RECOVERY THEMES IN . . .

PERSISTENCE (*see* Perseverance)

POWERLESSNESS (*see also* Hopelessness)

NOTES

PROFILES

TWELVE STEP DEVOTIONALS

PRAISE (*see also* Celebration, Gratitude, Worship)

PRAYER (*see also* Praise, Worship)

PREJUDICE (*see* Partiality)

PRIDE (*see also* Humility, Self-Sufficiency)

PROCRASTINATION (*see also* Rationalization)

PROMISES (*see also* Commitments)

PUNISHMENT (*see* Consequences, Judgment)

RATIONALIZATION (*see also* Procrastination)

NOTES

RECONCILIATION (*see also* Relationships,
  Restoration)

NOTES

REDEMPTION (*see also* Salvation)

NOTES

REJECTION (*see also* Discouragement)

NOTES

REST (see also Peace, Serenity)

RESTITUTION

RESTORATION (see also Forgiveness, Reconciliation)

PROFILES

TWELVE STEP DEVOTIONALS

RECOVERY PRINCIPLE DEVOTIONAL

RECOVERY THEMES IN . . .

REVENGE (*see also* Anger, Hatred)

NOTES

PROFILE

RECOVERY PRINCIPLE DEVOTIONAL

RECOVERY THEMES IN . . .

SADNESS (*see also* Discouragement, Rejection)

NOTES

PROFILES

TWELVE STEP DEVOTIONALS

RECOVERY PRINCIPLE DEVOTIONAL

RECOVERY THEMES IN . . .

UNITY (*see* Fellowship, Reconciliation)

VICTIMIZATION (*see* Abuse, Incest, Oppression)

VOWS (*see* Promises)

WAITING (*see* Patience, Perseverance)

WHOLENESS (*see also* Healing, Peace)

WISDOM (*see also* Truth)

WITNESSING (*see also* Communication)

INDEX TO RECOVERY PROFILES

INDEX TO TWELVE STEP DEVOTIONALS

INDEX TO RECOVERY PRINCIPLE DEVOTIONALS

INDEX TO SERENITY PRAYER DEVOTIONALS

INDEX TO RECOVERY REFLECTIONS

CONTRIBUTORS

Executive Editors
David A. Stoop
Stephen F. Arterburn

Associate Editors
A. Boyd Luter
Connie Neal

Managing Editor
Mark R. Norton

Editorial Staff
Derrick Blanchette
Meg Diehl
Diane Eble
Betsy Elliott
Adam Graber
Dietrich Gruen
Lucille Leonard
Phyllis LePeau
Daryl Lucas
Judith Morse
Kathy Olson
Jan Pigott
Leanne Rolland
Jeremy Taylor
Ramona Tucker
Sally van der Graaff
Esther Waldrop
Karen Walker
Wightman Weese

Print Buyer
Timothy Bensen

Graphic Designer
Timothy R. Botts

Writers
Donald E. Anderson
Shelly M. Chapin
R. Tony Cothren
Shelly O. Cunningham
Barry C. Davis
Harold Dollar
Joseph M. Espinoza
Thomas J. Finley
William J. Gaultiere
Ronald N. Glass
Daniel M. Hahn
Eric Hoey
Mark W. Hoffman
John C. Hutchison
Tommy A. Jarrett
Stephen M. Johnson
G. Ted Martinez
Kathy McReynolds
V. Eric Nachtrieb
Connie Neal
Stephen L. Newman
T. Ken Oberholtzer
Scott B. Rae
Richard O. Rigsby
Jane E. Rodgers
Walter B. Russell
Richard F. Travis